America's Top-Rated Cities: A Statistical Handbook

Volume 1

2019
Twenty-sixth Edition

America's
Top-Rated Cities:
A Statistical Handbook

Volume 1: Southern Region

A UNIVERSAL REFERENCE BOOK

Grey House
Publishing

Cover image – Atlanta, Georgia

PRESIDENT: Richard Gottlieb
PUBLISHER: Leslie Mackenzie
EDITORIAL DIRECTOR: Laura Mars
SENIOR EDITOR: David Garoogian

RESEARCHER & WRITER: Jael Bridgemahon
PRODUCTION MANAGER: Kristen Hayes
MARKETING DIRECTOR: Jessica Moody

A Universal Reference Book
Grey House Publishing, Inc.
4919 Route 22
Amenia, NY 12501
518.789.8700 • Fax 845.373.6390
www.greyhouse.com
books@greyhouse.com

Twenty-sixth Edition
Printed in Canada

Publisher's Cataloging-in-Publication Data
(Prepared by The Donohue Group, Inc.)

America's top-rated cities. Vol. I, Southern region : a statistical handbook. — 1992-

    v. : ill. ; cm.
    Annual, 1995-
    Irregular, 1992-1993
    ISSN: 1082-7102

1. Cities and towns--Ratings--Southern States--Statistics--Periodicals. 2. Cities and towns--Southern States--Statistics--Periodicals. 3. Social indicators--Southern States--Periodicals. 4. Quality of life--Southern States--Statistics--Periodicals. 5. Southern States--Social conditions--Statistics--Periodicals. I. Title: America's top rated cities. II. Title: Southern region

HT123.5.S6 A44
307.76/0973/05   95644648

4-Volume Set	ISBN: 978-1-64265-079-2
Volume 1	**ISBN: 978-1-64265-080-8**
Volume 2	ISBN: 978-1-64265-081-5
Volume 3	ISBN: 978-1-64265-082-2
Volume 4	ISBN: 978-1-64265-083-9

Athens, Georgia

Atlanta, Georgia

Austin, Texas

Baton Rouge, Louisiana

Cape Coral, Florida

Clarksville, Tennessee

Charleston, South Carolina

College Station, Texas

Columbia, South Carolina

Dallas, Texas

El Paso, Texas

Fort Worth, Texas

Gainesville, Florida

Houston, Texas

Huntsville, Alabama

Jacksonville, Florida

Savannah, Georgia

Tallahassee, Florida

Tampa, Florida

Tyler, Texas

Appendices

Introduction

This twenty-sixth edition of *America's Top-Rated Cities* is a concise, statistical, 4-volume work identifying America's top-rated cities with estimated populations of approximately 100,000 or more. It profiles 100 cities that have received high marks for business and living from prominent sources such as *Forbes, Fortune, U.S. News & World Report, The Brookings Institution, U.S. Conference of Mayors, The Wall Street Journal,* and *CNNMoney.*

Each volume covers a different region of the country—Southern, Western, Central and Eastern—and includes a detailed Table of Contents, City Chapters, Appendices, and Maps. Each city chapter incorporates information from hundreds of resources to create the following major sections:

- **Background**—lively narrative of significant, up-to-date news for both businesses and residents. These combine historical facts with current developments, "known-for" annual events, and climate data.
- **Rankings**—fun-to-read, bulleted survey results from over 250 books, magazines, and online articles, ranging from general (Great Places to Live), to specific (Friendliest Cities), and everything in between.
- **Statistical Tables**—126 tables and detailed topics that offer an unparalleled view of each city's Business and Living Environments. They are carefully organized with data that is easy to read and understand.
- **Appendices**—five in all, appearing at the end of each volume. These range from listings of Metropolitan Statistical Areas to Comparative Statistics for all 100 cities.

This new edition of *America's Top-Rated Cities* includes cities that not only surveyed well, but ranked highest using our unique weighting system. We looked at violent crime, property crime, population growth, median household income, housing affordability, poverty, educational attainment, and unemployment. You'll find that a number of American cities remain "top-rated" despite less-than-stellar numbers. New York, Los Angeles, and Miami remain world-class cities despite challenges faced by many large urban centers. A final consideration is location—we strive to include as many states in the country as possible.

Part of this year's city criteria is that it be the "primary" city in a given metropolitan area. For example, if the metro area is Raleigh-Cary, NC, we would consider Raleigh, not Cary. This allows for a more equitable core city comparison. In general, the core city of a metro area is defined as having substantial influence on neighboring cities.

New to this edition are: Evansville, IN; Tyler, TX; and Visalia, CA.

Praise for previous editions:

> *"...[ATRC] has...proven its worth to a wide audience...from businesspeople and corporations planning to launch, relocate, or expand their operations to market researchers, real estate professionals, urban planners, job-seekers, students...interested in...reliable, attractively presented statistical information about larger U.S. cities."*
> —ARBA

> *"...For individuals or businesses looking to relocate, this resource conveniently reports rankings from more than 300 sources for the top 100 US cities. Recommended..."*
> —Choice

> *"...While patrons are becoming increasingly comfortable locating statistical data online, there is still something to be said for the ease associated with such a compendium of otherwise scattered data. A well-organized and appropriate update...*
> —Library Journal

BACKGROUND

Each city begins with an informative Background that combines history with current events. These narratives often reflect changes that have occurred during the past year, and touch on the city's environment, politics, employment, cultural offerings, and climate, and include interesting trivia. For example: Peregrine Falcons were rehabilitated and released into the wild from Boise City's World Center for Birds of Prey; Gainesville is home to a 6,800 square-foot living Butterfly Rainforest; Grand Rapids was the first city to introduce fluoride into its drinking water in 1945; and Thomas Alva Edison discovered the phonograph and the light bulb in the city whose name was changed in 1954 from Raritan Township to Edison in his honor.

RANKINGS

This section has rankings from a possible 263 books, articles, and reports. For easy reference, these Rankings are categorized into 16 topics including Business/Finance, Dating/Romance, and Health/Fitness.

The Rankings are presented in an easy-to-read, bulleted format and include results from both annual surveys and one-shot studies. **Fastest-Growing Economies . . . Best Drivers . . . Most Well-Read . . . Most Wired . . . Healthiest for Women . . . Best for Minority Entrepreneurs . . . Safest . . . Best to Retire . . . Most Polite . . . Best for Moviemakers . . . Most Frugal . . . Best for Bikes . . . Most Cultured . . . Least Stressful . . . Best for Families . . . Most Romantic . . . Most Charitable . . . Most Attractive . . . Best for Telecommuters . . . Best for Singles . . . Nerdiest . . . Fittest . . . Best for Dogs . . . Most Tattooed . . . Best for Wheelchair Users**, and more.

Sources for these Rankings include both well-known magazines and other media, including *Forbes, Fortune, USA Today, Condé Nast Traveler, Gallup, Kiplinger's Personal Finance, Men's Journal,* and *Travel + Leisure,* as well as *Asthma & Allergy Foundation of America, American Lung Association, League of American Bicyclists, The Advocate, National Civic League, National Alliance to End Homelessness, MovieMaker Magazine, National Insurance Crime Bureau, Center for Digital Government, National Association of Home Builders,* and the *Milken Institute.*

Rankings cover a variety of geographic areas; see Appendix B for full geographic definitions.

STATISTICAL TABLES

Each city chapter includes a possible 126 tables and detailed topics—69 in BUSINESS and 57 in LIVING. Over 95% of statistical data has been updated. In addition to more detailed data on individual income tax rates, the Health Risk section now includes four tables: Health Risk Factors; Health Screening and Vaccination Rates; Disability Status; and Acute and Chronic Health Conditions. New subcategories include shingles vaccination and high blood pressure rates. The table on Disability Status is brand new and includes the following subcategories: adults who reported being deaf or blind; adults who reported having difficulty doing errands alone; adults who reported difficulty dressing or bathing; adults who reported having serious difficulty concentrating/remembering/making decisions; adults who reported having serious difficulty walking or climbing stairs; and adults who reported being limited in their usual daily activities due to arthritis.

Business Environment includes hard facts and figures on 10 major categories, including City Finances, Demographics, Income, Economy, Employment, and Taxes. *Living Environment* includes 11 major categories, such as Cost of Living, Housing, Health, Education, Safety, Recreation, and Climate.

To compile the Statistical Tables, editors have again turned to a wide range of sources, some well known, such as the *U.S. Census Bureau, U.S. Environmental Protection Agency, Bureau of Labor Statistics, Centers for Disease Control and Prevention,* and the *Federal Bureau of Investigation*, plus others like *The Council for Community and Economic Research, Texas Transportation Institute,* and *Federation of Tax Administrators.*

APPENDICES: Data for all cities appear in all volumes.
- **Appendix A**—*Comparative Statistics*
- **Appendix B**—*Metropolitan Area Definitions*
- **Appendix C**—*Government Type and County*
- **Appendix D**—*Chambers of Commerce and Economic Development Organizations*
- **Appendix E**—*State Departments of Labor and Employment*

Material provided by public and private agencies and organizations was supplemented by original research, numerous library sources and Internet sites. *America's Top-Rated Cities, 2019,* is designed for a wide range of readers: private individuals considering relocating a residence or business; professionals considering expanding their businesses or changing careers; corporations considering relocating, opening up additional offices or creating new divisions; government agencies; general and market researchers; real estate consultants; human resource personnel; urban planners; investors; and urban government students.

Customers who purchase the four-volume set receive free online access to *America's Top-Rated Cities* allowing them to download city reports and sort and rank by 50-plus data points.

AMERICA'S TOP-RATED CITIES

CBSA: Core Based Statistical Area

STATE
- Top Rated City
- East Region
- Central Region
- West Region
- South Region

©Larry Mandelin 2018

AMERICA'S TOP-RATED CITIES

CBSA: Core Based Statistical Area

STATE

○ Top Rated City

Southern Region

©Larry Mandelin 2019

Seattle
Seattle-Tacoma-Bellevue, WA

WASHINGTON

Portland
Portland-Vancouver-Hillsboro, OR-WA

Salem
Salem, OR

Eugene
Eugene, OR

OREGON

MONTANA

Billings, MT

Billings

NORTH DAKOTA

SOUTH DAKOTA

Boise City
Boise City-Nampa, ID

IDAHO

WYOMING

NEBRASKA

Reno, NV

CALIFORNIA

Santa Rosa, CA

Santa Rosa

Reno

NEVADA

Salt Lake City
Salt Lake City, UT

Provo
Provo-Orem, UT

Fort Collins
Fort Collins-Loveland, CO

Greeley, CO

Greeley
Boulder

Boulder, CO

Denver
Denver-Aurora-Lakewood, CO

Colorado Springs
Colorado Springs, CO

KS

San Francisco
San Francisco-Oakland-Hayward, CA

San Jose
San Jose-Sunnyvale-Santa Clara, CA

UTAH

COLORADO

Visalia
Visalia-Porterville, CA

Las Vegas-Henderson-Paradise, NV

Las Vegas

ARIZONA

Los Angeles
Los Angeles-Long Beach-Anaheim, CA

Albuquerque
Albuquerque, NM

TEXAS

San Diego
San Diego-Carlsbad, CA

Phoenix
Phoenix-Mesa-Scottsdale, AZ

NEW MEXICO

Las Cruces
Las Cruces, NM

ALASKA

Anchorage, AK

Anchorage

Urban Honolulu, HI

Honolulu

HAWAII

AMERICA'S TOP-RATED CITIES

CBSA: Core Based Statistical Area
STATE
○ Top Rated City
Western Region

©Larry Mandelin 2019

N
W E
S

AMERICA'S TOP- RATED CITIES

CBSA: Core Based Statistical Area
STATE
○ Top Rated City
Central Region

AMERICA'S TOP-RATED CITIES

CBSA: Core Based Statistical Area
STATE
○ Top Rated City
Eastern Region

MAINE

VT   NH

NEW YORK   **Manchester**
Manchester-Nashua, NH ○

Boston-Cambridge-Newton,
MA-NH

○ **Boston**

Albany ○
Albany-Schenectady-Troy, NY

MA

○ **Providence**
CT   RI   Providence-Warwick, RI-MA

MICHIGAN

Allentown-Bethlehem-Easton,
PA-NJ

New York

Allentown
○

Edison
○   New York-Newark-Jersey City,
NY-NJ-PA

PENNSYLVANIA

OHIO   **Pittsburgh**
○
Pittsburgh, PA

Philadelphia
○
NJ   Philadelphia-Camden-Wilmington,
PA-NJ-DE-MD

Columbus
○
Columbus, OH

DE
MD

INDIANA

WV

Washington
○
Washington-Arlington-Alexandria, DC-VA-MD-WV

IL

Richmond
○
Virginia Beach-Norfolk-Newport News, VA-NC

Louisville/Jefferson
County, KY-IN   **Lexington**   **Roanoke**
○   ○   ○

VA

Virginia Beach
○

Richmond, VA

Louisville   Lexington-Fayette, KY   Roanoke, VA   Durham-Chapel Hill, NC

Greensboro   **Durham**
○   ○
Winston-Salem ○   ○ **Raleigh**

KENTUCKY   Winston-Salem, NC   Raleigh, NC

Greensboro-High Point, NC

Fayetteville
○

TENNESSEE   NC   **Charlotte**   **Wilmington**
○
Fayetteville, NC   ○
Charlotte-   Wilmington, NC
Concord-
Gastonia, NC-SC

S.CAROLINA

MS   ALABAMA   GEORGIA

©Larry Mandelin 2019

Athens, Georgia

Background

Athens, home to the University of Georgia, retains its old charms while cultivating new ideas. Antebellum homes that grace the city still stand because Gen. William Tecumseh Sherman's March to the Sea took a route that left this northeast Georgia town intact (while burning Atlanta, about 60 miles to the southwest). The Athens Music History Walking Tour, available through the local convention and visitors' bureau, stops at Weaver D's soul food restaurant with the slogan, "Automatic for the People," that went national as the name of locally-grown REM's 1992 album. The college music scene that spawned the B-52s and the Indigo Girls in the 1970s and 1980s, continues to support a thriving music industry.

Present-day Athens started as a small settlement where an old Cherokee trail crossed the Oconee River. In 1785 the state's General Assembly chartered the university, which established a campus here in 1801. Three years later, the school held its first graduation ceremony. The city was named for the ancient Greece's center of learning.

Undoubtedly the major influence in the city and surrounding Clarke County, the University of Georgia is also the area's largest employer. The comprehensive land grant and sea-grant institution offers all levels of degree programs in numerous disciplines. Other educational institutions in Athens are the Navy Supply School, Athens Technical College, and branches of Piedmont College and Old Dominion University.

Other major employers are focused on health care, government, and manufacturing. They include Athens Regional Medical Center and St. Mary's Health Care System, which have enlarged their facilities and specialized in areas including oncology, pediatrics and heart disease. Manufacturing is a major employment sector.

The city's official government merged with its home county in 1991, creating the Unified Government of Athens-Clark County.

With its shops, boutiques and restaurants, Athens offers plenty to do. The Georgia State Museum of Art, Museum of Natural History, and the State Botanical Garden here are affiliated with the university. The restored 1910 Morton Theater once hosted Cab Calloway, Duke Ellington, and Louis Armstrong, and now hosts dramatic and musical performances. Undoubtedly the strong presence of young people in Athens has contributed to its burgeoning artistic scene. The city center is home to bars, galleries, cafes, and music venues that cater to the city's creative climate. The annual AthFest in June, hosts 120 bands to support local education. The city's charms, attractive to all ages, have not gone unnoticed by the media. Athens has been named one of the best places for small business, the best college town for retirees, and the best place to recapture your youth. The city also has a lively bicycle culture, and hosts several annual bicycle races.

The climate is mild, with average temperatures about 20 degrees warmer than the U.S. average. Snowfall is next to nothing, but precipitation is at its highest from January-March. Spring is lovely, with three to four inches of rain, sunshine up to 70 percent of the time starting in April, and temperatures averaging in the 70s.

Rankings

Business/Finance Rankings

- Metro areas with the largest gap in income between rich and poor residents were identified by 24/7 Wall Street using the U.S. Census Bureau's 2013 American Community Survey. The Athens metro area placed #14 among metro areas with the widest wealth gap between rich and poor. *247wallst.com, "20 Cities with the Widest Gap between the Rich and Poor," July 8, 2015*

- The Athens metro area appeared on the Milken Institute "2018 Best Performing Cities" list. Rank: #8 out of 201 small metro areas. Criteria: job growth; wage and salary growth; high-tech output growth. *Milken Institute, "Best-Performing Cities 2018," January 24, 2019*

- *Forbes* ranked 200 smaller metro areas (population under 265,400) to determine the nation's "Best Small Places for Business and Careers." The Athens metro area was ranked #6. Criteria: costs (business and living); job growth (past and projected); income growth; quality of life; educational attainment (college and high school); projected economic growth; cultural and recreational opportunities; net migration patterns; number of highly ranked colleges. *Forbes, "The Best Small Cities for Business and Careers 2018," October, 24 2018*

Safety Rankings

- The National Insurance Crime Bureau ranked 382 metro areas in the U.S. in terms of per capita rates of vehicle theft. The Athens metro area ranked #231 (#1 = highest rate). Criteria: number of vehicle theft offenses per 100,000 inhabitants in 2017. *National Insurance Crime Bureau, "Hot Spots 2017," July 12, 2018*

Seniors/Retirement Rankings

- From its Best Cities for Successful Aging indexes, the Milken Institute generated rankings for metropolitan areas, weighing data in nine categories—health care, wellness, living arrangements, transportation and convenience, financial characteristics, education, employment, community engagement, and overall livability. The Athens metro area was ranked #62 overall in the small metro area category. *Milken Institute, "Best Cities for Successful Aging, 2017" March 14, 2017*

- Athens made the 2018 *Forbes* list of "25 Best Places to Retire." Criteria, focused on a high-quality retirement living an affordable price, include: housing/living costs compared to the national average and state taxes; weather and air quality; crime rates; vibrant economy and low unemployment; doctor availability; bikability; walkability; healthy living and volunteering. *Forbes.com, "The Best Places to Retire in 2018," April 23, 2018*

- Athens was identified as one of the most popular places to retire by *Topretirements.com*. The list reflects the 100 cities that visitors to the website are most interested in for retirement, based on the number of times a city's review was viewed on the website. *Topretirements.com, "100 Most Popular Places to Retire for 2017," July 27, 2017*

Business Environment

CITY FINANCES

City Government Finances

Component	2016 ($000)	2016 ($ per capita)
Total Revenues	243,786	1,967
Total Expenditures	251,255	2,028
Debt Outstanding	288,072	2,325
Cash and Securities[1]	424,265	3,424

Note: (1) Cash and security holdings of a government at the close of its fiscal year, including those of its dependent agencies, utilities, and liquor stores.
Source: U.S. Census Bureau, State & Local Government Finances 2016

City Government Revenue by Source

Source	2016 ($000)	2016 ($ per capita)	2016 (%)
General Revenue			
From Federal Government	10,115	82	4.1
From State Government	3,328	27	1.4
From Local Governments	53,142	429	21.8
Taxes			
Property	52,012	420	21.3
Sales and Gross Receipts	21,363	172	8.8
Personal Income	0	0	0.0
Corporate Income	0	0	0.0
Motor Vehicle License	0	0	0.0
Other Taxes	4,349	35	1.8
Current Charges	75,581	610	31.0
Liquor Store	0	0	0.0
Utility	18,689	151	7.7
Employee Retirement	-1,506	-12	-0.6

Source: U.S. Census Bureau, State & Local Government Finances 2016

City Government Expenditures by Function

Function	2016 ($000)	2016 ($ per capita)	2016 (%)
General Direct Expenditures			
Air Transportation	2,055	16	0.8
Corrections	21,007	169	8.4
Education	0	0	0.0
Employment Security Administration	0	0	0.0
Financial Administration	7,914	63	3.1
Fire Protection	14,687	118	5.8
General Public Buildings	6,389	51	2.5
Governmental Administration, Other	14,119	113	5.6
Health	2,041	16	0.8
Highways	13,032	105	5.2
Hospitals	0	0	0.0
Housing and Community Development	0	0	0.0
Interest on General Debt	17,633	142	7.0
Judicial and Legal	12,836	103	5.1
Libraries	6,201	50	2.5
Parking	0	0	0.0
Parks and Recreation	9,734	78	3.9
Police Protection	27,160	219	10.8
Public Welfare	670	5	0.3
Sewerage	13,801	111	5.5
Solid Waste Management	7,541	60	3.0
Veterans' Services	0	0	0.0
Liquor Store	0	0	0.0
Utility	21,389	172	8.5
Employee Retirement	11,399	92	4.5

Source: U.S. Census Bureau, State & Local Government Finances 2016

DEMOGRAPHICS

Population Growth

Area	1990 Census	2000 Census	2010 Census	2017* Estimate	Population Growth (%)	
					1990-2017	2010-2017
City	86,561	100,266	115,452	122,292	41.3	5.9
MSA[1]	136,025	166,079	192,541	202,780	49.1	5.3
U.S.	248,709,873	281,421,906	308,745,538	321,004,407	29.1	4.0

Note: (1) Figures cover the Athens-Clarke County, GA Metropolitan Statistical Area—see Appendix B for areas included; (*) 2013-2017 5-year estimated population
Source: U.S. Census Bureau, 1990 Census, Census 2000, Census 2010, 2013-2017 American Community Survey 5-Year Estimates

Household Size

Area	Persons in Household (%)							Average Household Size
	One	Two	Three	Four	Five	Six	Seven or More	
City	35.0	34.8	14.2	10.3	3.5	1.5	0.7	2.40
MSA[1]	29.6	35.3	15.4	12.1	4.9	1.8	0.7	2.60
U.S.	27.7	33.8	15.7	13.0	6.0	2.3	1.4	2.60

Note: (1) Figures cover the Athens-Clarke County, GA Metropolitan Statistical Area—see Appendix B for areas included
Source: U.S. Census Bureau, 2013-2017 American Community Survey 5-Year Estimates

Race

Area	White Alone[2] (%)	Black Alone[2] (%)	Asian Alone[2] (%)	AIAN[3] Alone[2] (%)	NHOPI[4] Alone[2] (%)	Other Race Alone[2] (%)	Two or More Races (%)
City	63.2	27.5	4.3	0.1	0.0	2.6	2.2
MSA[1]	72.0	20.1	3.6	0.1	0.0	2.1	2.0
U.S.	73.0	12.7	5.4	0.8	0.2	4.8	3.1

Note: (1) Figures cover the Athens-Clarke County, GA Metropolitan Statistical Area—see Appendix B for areas included; (2) Alone is defined as not being in combination with one or more other races; (3) American Indian and Alaska Native; (4) Native Hawaiian and Other Pacific Islander
Source: U.S. Census Bureau, 2013-2017 American Community Survey 5-Year Estimates

Hispanic or Latino Origin

Area	Total (%)	Mexican (%)	Puerto Rican (%)	Cuban (%)	Other (%)
City	10.7	6.9	0.9	0.3	2.7
MSA[1]	8.3	5.2	0.7	0.2	2.2
U.S.	17.6	11.1	1.7	0.7	4.1

Note: Persons of Hispanic or Latino origin can be of any race; (1) Figures cover the Athens-Clarke County, GA Metropolitan Statistical Area—see Appendix B for areas included
Source: U.S. Census Bureau, 2013-2017 American Community Survey 5-Year Estimates

Segregation

Type	Segregation Indices[1]				Percent Change		
	1990	2000	2010	2010 Rank[2]	1990-2000	1990-2010	2000-2010
Black/White	n/a	n/a	n/a	n/a	n/a	n/a	n/a
Asian/White	n/a	n/a	n/a	n/a	n/a	n/a	n/a
Hispanic/White	n/a	n/a	n/a	n/a	n/a	n/a	n/a

Note: All figures cover the Metropolitan Statistical Area—see Appendix B for areas included; Figures are based on an analysis of 1990, 2000, and 2010 Census Decennial Census tract data by William H. Frey, Brookings Institution and the University of Michigan Social Science Data Analysis Network. In this analysis all racial groups (whites, blacks, and asians) are non-Hispanic members of those races. Hispanics are shown as a separate category; (1) Segregation Indices are Dissimilarity Indices that measure the degree to which the minority group is distributed differently than whites across census tracts. They range from 0 (complete integration) to 100 (complete segregation) where the value indicates the percentage of the minority group that needs to move to be distributed exactly like whites; (2) Ranges from 1 (most segregated) to 102 (least segregated); n/a not available.
Source: www.CensusScope.org

Ancestry

Area	German	Irish	English	American	Italian	Polish	French[2]	Scottish	Dutch
City	8.8	8.5	9.0	5.5	3.2	1.6	1.7	2.9	0.9
MSA[1]	8.6	9.3	10.0	9.4	2.9	1.4	1.7	2.9	1.0
U.S.	14.1	10.1	7.5	6.6	5.3	2.9	2.5	1.7	1.3

Note: Figures are the percentage of the total population reporting a particular ancestry. The nine most commonly reported ancestries in the U.S. are shown. Figures include multiple ancestries (e.g. if a person reported being Irish and Italian, they were included in both columns); (1) Figures cover the Athens-Clarke County, GA Metropolitan Statistical Area—see Appendix B for areas included; (2) Excludes Basque
Source: U.S. Census Bureau, 2013-2017 American Community Survey 5-Year Estimates

Foreign-Born Population

Area	Any Foreign Country	Asia	Mexico	Europe	Carribean	Central America[2]	South America	Africa	Canada
City	10.4	3.3	3.3	1.0	0.3	1.0	0.7	0.5	0.2
MSA[1]	8.1	2.7	2.4	0.9	0.2	0.9	0.5	0.4	0.2
U.S.	13.4	4.1	3.6	1.5	1.3	1.0	0.9	0.6	0.3

Note: (1) Figures cover the Athens-Clarke County, GA Metropolitan Statistical Area—see Appendix B for areas included; (2) Excludes Mexico.
Source: U.S. Census Bureau, 2013-2017 American Community Survey 5-Year Estimates

Marital Status

Area	Never Married	Now Married[2]	Separated	Widowed	Divorced
City	55.5	30.9	1.6	3.8	8.1
MSA[1]	43.3	40.9	1.7	5.0	9.1
U.S.	33.1	48.2	2.0	5.8	10.9

Note: Figures are percentages and cover the population 15 years of age and older; (1) Figures cover the Athens-Clarke County, GA Metropolitan Statistical Area—see Appendix B for areas included; (2) Excludes separated
Source: U.S. Census Bureau, 2013-2017 American Community Survey 5-Year Estimates

Disability by Age

Area	All Ages	Under 18 Years Old	18 to 64 Years Old	65 Years and Over
City	10.5	3.6	9.1	33.7
MSA[1]	11.9	4.4	10.1	34.8
U.S.	12.6	4.2	10.3	35.5

Note: Figures show percent of the civilian noninstitutionalized population that reported having a disability. Disability status is determined from six types of difficulty: vision, hearing, cognitive, ambulatory, self-care, and independent living. For children under 5 years old, hearing and vision difficulty are used to determine disability status. For children between the ages of 5 and 14, disability status is determined from hearing, vision, cognitive, ambulatory, and self-care difficulties. For people aged 15 years and older, they are considered to have a disability if they have difficulty with any one of the six difficulty types; Note: (1) Figures cover the Athens-Clarke County, GA Metropolitan Statistical Area—see Appendix B for areas included
Source: U.S. Census Bureau, 2013-2017 American Community Survey 5-Year Estimates

Age

Area	Under Age 5	Age 5–19	Age 20–34	Age 35–44	Age 45–54	Age 55–64	Age 65–74	Age 75–84	Age 85+	Median Age
City	5.5	20.9	35.2	11.0	8.8	8.8	5.8	2.7	1.3	27.2
MSA[1]	5.5	21.0	27.5	12.1	11.1	10.6	7.4	3.3	1.4	31.8
U.S.	6.2	19.5	20.7	12.7	13.4	12.7	8.6	4.4	1.9	37.8

Note: (1) Figures cover the Athens-Clarke County, GA Metropolitan Statistical Area—see Appendix B for areas included
Source: U.S. Census Bureau, 2013-2017 American Community Survey 5-Year Estimates

Gender

Area	Males	Females	Males per 100 Females
City	58,197	64,095	90.8
MSA[1]	98,156	104,624	93.8
U.S.	158,018,753	162,985,654	97.0

Note: (1) Figures cover the Athens-Clarke County, GA Metropolitan Statistical Area—see Appendix B for areas included
Source: U.S. Census Bureau, 2013-2017 American Community Survey 5-Year Estimates

Religious Groups by Family

Area	Catholic	Baptist	Non-Den.	Methodist[2]	Lutheran	LDS[3]	Pente-costal	Presby-terian[4]	Muslim[5]	Judaism
MSA[1]	4.4	16.3	2.3	8.4	0.4	0.8	2.8	2.0	0.4	0.2
U.S.	19.1	9.3	4.0	4.0	2.3	2.0	1.9	1.6	0.8	0.7

Note: Figures are the number of adherents as a percentage of the total population; (1) Figures cover the Athens-Clarke County, GA Metropolitan Statistical Area—see Appendix B for areas included; (2) Methodist/Pietist; (3) Latter Day Saints; (4) Reformed; (5) Figures are estimates
Source: Association of Statisticians of American Religious Bodies, 2010 U.S. Religion Census: Religious Congregations & Membership Study

Religious Groups by Tradition

Area	Catholic	Evangelical Protestant	Mainline Protestant	Other Tradition	Black Protestant	Orthodox
MSA[1]	4.4	21.1	9.8	1.7	2.5	0.1
U.S.	19.1	16.2	7.3	4.3	1.6	0.3

Note: Figures are the number of adherents as a percentage of the total population; (1) Figures cover the Athens-Clarke County, GA Metropolitan Statistical Area—see Appendix B for areas included
Source: Association of Statisticians of American Religious Bodies, 2010 U.S. Religion Census: Religious Congregations & Membership Study

ECONOMY

Gross Metropolitan Product

Area	2016	2017	2018	2019	Rank[2]
MSA[1]	8.8	9.3	9.7	10.1	218

Note: Figures are in billions of dollars; (1) Figures cover the Athens-Clarke County, GA Metropolitan Statistical Area—see Appendix B for areas included; (2) Rank is based on 2017 data and ranges from 1 to 381
Source: U.S. Conference of Mayors, U.S. Metro Economies: Economic Growth & Full Employment, June 2018

Economic Growth

Area	2017-2018 (%)	2019-2020 (%)	2021-2022 (%)
MSA[1]	2.6	1.7	1.1

Note: Figures are real gross metropolitan product (GMP) growth rates and represent average annual percent change; (1) Figures cover the Athens-Clarke County, GA Metropolitan Statistical Area—see Appendix B for areas included
Source: U.S. Conference of Mayors, U.S. Metro Economies: Economic Growth & Full Employment, June 2018

Metropolitan Area Exports

Area	2012	2013	2014	2015	2016	2017	Rank[2]
MSA[1]	229.7	286.0	320.8	327.4	332.1	297.7	253

Note: Figures are in millions of dollars; (1) Figures cover the Athens-Clarke County, GA Metropolitan Statistical Area—see Appendix B for areas included; (2) Rank is based on 2017 data and ranges from 1 to 387
Source: U.S. Department of Commerce, International Trade Administration, Office of Trade and Economic Analysis, Industry and Analysis, Exports by Metropolitan Area, extracted March 25, 2019

Building Permits

Area	Single-Family			Multi-Family			Total		
	2016	2017	Pct. Chg.	2016	2017	Pct. Chg.	2016	2017	Pct. Chg.
City	115	189	64.3	4	176	4,300.0	119	365	206.7
MSA[1]	523	581	11.1	61	190	211.5	584	771	32.0
U.S.	750,800	820,000	9.2	455,800	462,000	1.4	1,206,600	1,282,000	6.2

Note: (1) Figures cover the Athens-Clarke County, GA Metropolitan Statistical Area—see Appendix B for areas included; Figures represent new, privately-owned housing units authorized (unadjusted data); All permit data are based on estimates with imputation
Source: U.S. Census Bureau, Manufacturing, Mining, and Construction Statistics, Building Permits, 2016, 2017

Bankruptcy Filings

Area	Business Filings			Nonbusiness Filings		
	2017	2018	% Chg.	2017	2018	% Chg.
Clarke County	5	8	60.0	368	345	-6.3
U.S.	23,157	22,232	-4.0	765,863	751,186	-1.9

Note: Business filings include Chapter 7, Chapter 11, Chapter 12, and Chapter 13; Nonbusiness filings include Chapter 7, Chapter 11, and Chapter 13
Source: Administrative Office of the U.S. Courts, Business and Nonbusiness Bankruptcy, County Cases Commenced by Chapter of the Bankruptcy Code, During the 12-Month Period Ending December 31, 2017 and Business and Nonbusiness Bankruptcy, County Cases Commenced by Chapter of the Bankruptcy Code, During the 12-Month Period Ending December 31, 2018

Housing Vacancy Rates

Area	Gross Vacancy Rate[2] (%)			Year-Round Vacancy Rate[3] (%)			Rental Vacancy Rate[4] (%)			Homeowner Vacancy Rate[5] (%)		
	2016	2017	2018	2016	2017	2018	2016	2017	2018	2016	2017	2018
MSA[1]	n/a	n/a	n/a	n/a	n/a	n/a	n/a	n/a	n/a	n/a	n/a	n/a
U.S.	12.8	12.7	12.3	9.9	9.9	9.7	6.9	7.2	6.9	1.7	1.6	1.5

Note: (1) Figures cover the Athens-Clarke County, GA Metropolitan Statistical Area—see Appendix B for areas included; (2) The percentage of the total housing inventory that is vacant; (3) The percentage of the housing inventory (excluding seasonal units) that is year-round vacant; (4) The percentage of rental inventory that is vacant for rent; (5) The percentage of homeowner inventory that is vacant for sale; n/a not available
Source: U.S. Census Bureau, Housing Vacancies and Homeownership Annual Statistics: 2016, 2017, 2018

INCOME

Income

Area	Per Capita ($)	Median Household ($)	Average Household ($)
City	21,111	34,258	53,394
MSA[1]	24,581	42,418	63,569
U.S.	31,177	57,652	81,283

Note: (1) Figures cover the Athens-Clarke County, GA Metropolitan Statistical Area—see Appendix B for areas included
Source: U.S. Census Bureau, 2013-2017 American Community Survey 5-Year Estimates

Household Income Distribution

Area	Percent of Households Earning							
	Under $15,000	$15,000 -$24,999	$25,000 -$34,999	$35,000 -$49,999	$50,000 -$74,999	$75,000 -$99,999	$100,000 -$149,999	$150,000 and up
City	24.6	14.6	11.5	13.4	13.2	8.1	9.0	5.6
MSA[1]	18.9	13.0	10.8	13.8	15.1	9.5	11.2	7.7
U.S.	11.6	9.8	9.5	13.0	17.7	12.3	14.1	12.1

Note: (1) Figures cover the Athens-Clarke County, GA Metropolitan Statistical Area—see Appendix B for areas included
Source: U.S. Census Bureau, 2013-2017 American Community Survey 5-Year Estimates

Poverty Rate

Area	All Ages	Under 18 Years Old	18 to 64 Years Old	65 Years and Over
City	34.4	39.8	36.4	10.8
MSA[1]	25.4	29.4	27.1	9.2
U.S.	14.6	20.3	13.7	9.3

Note: Figures are percentage of people whose income during the past 12 months was below the poverty level; (1) Figures cover the Athens-Clarke County, GA Metropolitan Statistical Area—see Appendix B for areas included
Source: U.S. Census Bureau, 2013-2017 American Community Survey 5-Year Estimates

EMPLOYMENT

Labor Force and Employment

Area	Civilian Labor Force			Workers Employed		
	Dec. 2017	Dec. 2018	% Chg.	Dec. 2017	Dec. 2018	% Chg.
City	60,911	62,570	2.7	58,343	60,290	3.3
MSA[1]	100,971	103,672	2.7	96,987	100,137	3.2
U.S.	159,880,000	162,510,000	1.6	153,602,000	156,481,000	1.9

Note: Data is not seasonally adjusted and covers workers 16 years of age and older; (1) Figures cover the Athens-Clarke County, GA Metropolitan Statistical Area—see Appendix B for areas included
Source: Bureau of Labor Statistics, Local Area Unemployment Statistics

Unemployment Rate

Area	2018											
	Jan.	Feb.	Mar.	Apr.	May	Jun.	Jul.	Aug.	Sep.	Oct.	Nov.	Dec.
City	4.3	4.5	4.0	3.6	3.4	4.5	4.1	3.7	3.2	3.6	3.2	3.6
MSA[1]	4.0	4.1	3.8	3.4	3.2	4.1	3.7	3.5	3.0	3.4	3.0	3.4
U.S.	4.5	4.4	4.1	3.7	3.6	4.2	4.1	3.9	3.6	3.5	3.5	3.7

Note: Data is not seasonally adjusted and covers workers 16 years of age and older; (1) Figures cover the Athens-Clarke County, GA Metropolitan Statistical Area—see Appendix B for areas included
Source: Bureau of Labor Statistics, Local Area Unemployment Statistics

Average Wages

Occupation	$/Hr.	Occupation	$/Hr.
Accountants and Auditors	33.50	Maids and Housekeeping Cleaners	10.20
Automotive Mechanics	21.70	Maintenance and Repair Workers	16.90
Bookkeepers	16.60	Marketing Managers	72.40
Carpenters	20.40	Nuclear Medicine Technologists	n/a
Cashiers	9.90	Nurses, Licensed Practical	21.10
Clerks, General Office	14.20	Nurses, Registered	32.40
Clerks, Receptionists/Information	12.90	Nursing Assistants	12.60
Clerks, Shipping/Receiving	16.90	Packers and Packagers, Hand	10.90
Computer Programmers	37.20	Physical Therapists	43.60
Computer Systems Analysts	33.90	Postal Service Mail Carriers	24.40
Computer User Support Specialists	21.50	Real Estate Brokers	n/a
Cooks, Restaurant	11.90	Retail Salespersons	11.80
Dentists	64.70	Sales Reps., Exc. Tech./Scientific	30.80
Electrical Engineers	n/a	Sales Reps., Tech./Scientific	26.20
Electricians	23.00	Secretaries, Exc. Legal/Med./Exec.	16.50
Financial Managers	61.00	Security Guards	n/a
First-Line Supervisors/Managers, Sales	20.60	Surgeons	n/a
Food Preparation Workers	10.40	Teacher Assistants*	9.20
General and Operations Managers	49.10	Teachers, Elementary School*	25.70
Hairdressers/Cosmetologists	12.10	Teachers, Secondary School*	27.20
Internists, General	n/a	Telemarketers	9.90
Janitors and Cleaners	11.90	Truck Drivers, Heavy/Tractor-Trailer	24.70
Landscaping/Groundskeeping Workers	15.20	Truck Drivers, Light/Delivery Svcs.	19.70
Lawyers	43.10	Waiters and Waitresses	10.60

Note: Wage data covers the Athens-Clarke County, GA Metropolitan Statistical Area—see Appendix B for areas included; (*) Hourly wages for elementary/secondary school teachers and teacher assistants were calculated by the editors from annual wage data based on a 40 hour work week; n/a not available.
Source: Bureau of Labor Statistics, Metro Area Occupational Employment & Wage Estimates, May 2018

Employment by Occupation

Occupation Classification	City (%)	MSA[1] (%)	U.S. (%)
Management, Business, Science, and Arts	40.6	40.9	37.4
Natural Resources, Construction, and Maintenance	5.7	7.2	8.9
Production, Transportation, and Material Moving	12.5	13.4	12.2
Sales and Office	19.8	20.1	23.5
Service	21.3	18.4	18.0

Note: Figures cover employed civilians 16 years of age and older; (1) Figures cover the Athens-Clarke County, GA Metropolitan Statistical Area—see Appendix B for areas included
Source: U.S. Census Bureau, 2013-2017 American Community Survey 5-Year Estimates

Employment by Industry

Sector	MSA[1]		U.S.
	Number of Employees	Percent of Total	Percent of Total
Construction, Mining, and Logging	n/a	n/a	5.3
Education and Health Services	n/a	n/a	15.9
Financial Activities	n/a	n/a	5.7
Government	29,700	29.8	15.1
Information	n/a	n/a	1.9
Leisure and Hospitality	11,300	11.3	10.7
Manufacturing	n/a	n/a	8.5
Other Services	n/a	n/a	3.9
Professional and Business Services	9,300	9.3	14.1
Retail Trade	11,000	11.0	10.8
Transportation, Warehousing, and Utilities	n/a	n/a	4.2
Wholesale Trade	n/a	n/a	3.9

Note: Figures are non-farm employment as of December 2018. Figures are not seasonally adjusted and include workers 16 years of age and older; (1) Figures cover the Athens-Clarke County, GA Metropolitan Statistical Area—see Appendix B for areas included; n/a not available
Source: Bureau of Labor Statistics, Current Employment Statistics, Employment, Hours, and Earnings

Occupations with Greatest Projected Employment Growth: 2018 – 2020

Occupation[1]	2018 Employment	2020 Projected Employment	Numeric Employment Change	Percent Employment Change
Combined Food Preparation and Serving Workers, Including Fast Food	115,500	124,220	8,720	7.5
Laborers and Freight, Stock, and Material Movers, Hand	119,650	127,750	8,100	6.8
General and Operations Managers	96,530	101,830	5,300	5.5
Waiters and Waitresses	81,500	86,240	4,740	5.8
Construction Laborers	40,040	44,600	4,560	11.4
Customer Service Representatives	103,570	107,780	4,210	4.1
Retail Salespersons	141,820	146,020	4,200	3.0
Heavy and Tractor-Trailer Truck Drivers	58,780	62,290	3,510	6.0
Janitors and Cleaners, Except Maids and Housekeeping Cleaners	56,440	59,660	3,220	5.7
Office Clerks, General	88,900	91,910	3,010	3.4

Note: Projections cover Georgia; (1) Sorted by numeric employment change
Source: www.projectionscentral.com, State Occupational Projections, 2018–2020 Short-Term Projections

Fastest Growing Occupations: 2018 – 2020

Occupation[1]	2018 Employment	2020 Projected Employment	Numeric Employment Change	Percent Employment Change
Helpers—Pipelayers, Plumbers, Pipefitters, and Steamfitters	2,220	2,640	420	18.9
Helpers—Brickmasons, Blockmasons, Stonemasons, and Tile and Marble Setters	270	320	50	18.5
Mechanical Door Repairers	490	580	90	18.4
Structural Iron and Steel Workers	1,410	1,660	250	17.7
Elevator Installers and Repairers	1,190	1,400	210	17.6
Costume Attendants	290	340	50	17.2
Helpers—Electricians	4,070	4,760	690	17.0
Glaziers	1,130	1,320	190	16.8
Fence Erectors	550	640	90	16.4
Cement Masons and Concrete Finishers	3,190	3,710	520	16.3

Note: Projections cover Georgia; (1) Sorted by percent employment change and excludes occupations with numeric employment change less than 50
Source: www.projectionscentral.com, State Occupational Projections, 2018–2020 Short-Term Projections

TAXES

State Corporate Income Tax Rates

State	Tax Rate (%)	Income Brackets ($)	Num. of Brackets	Financial Institution Tax Rate (%)[a]	Federal Income Tax Ded.
Georgia	5.75	Flat rate	1	5.75	No

Note: Tax rates as of January 1, 2019; (a) Rates listed are the corporate income tax rate applied to financial institutions or excise taxes based on income. Some states have other taxes based upon the value of deposits or shares.
Source: Federation of Tax Administrators, Range of State Corporate Income Tax Rates, January 1, 2019

State Individual Income Tax Rates

State	Tax Rate (%)	Income Brackets ($)	Personal Exemptions ($)			Standard Ded. ($)	
			Single	Married	Depend.	Single	Married
Georgia	1.0 - 5.75	750 - 7,001 (i)	2,700	7,400	3,000	4,600	6,000

Note: Tax rates as of January 1, 2019; Local- and county-level taxes are not included; n/a not applicable; Federal income tax is not deductible on state income tax returns; (i) The Georgia income brackets reported are for single individuals. For married couples filing jointly, the same tax rates apply to income brackets ranging from $1,000, to $10,000.
Source: Federation of Tax Administrators, State Individual Income Tax Rates, January 1, 2019

Various State Sales and Excise Tax Rates

State	State Sales Tax (%)	Gasoline[1] (¢/gal.)	Cigarette[2] ($/pack)	Spirits[3] ($/gal.)	Wine[4] ($/gal.)	Beer[5] ($/gal.)	Recreational Marijuana (%)
Georgia	4	35.28	0.37	3.79 (f)	1.51 (l)	0.48 (q)(r)	Not legal

Note: All tax rates as of January 1, 2019; (1) The American Petroleum Institute has developed a methodology for determining the average tax rate on a gallon of fuel. Rates may include any of the following: excise taxes, environmental fees, storage tank fees, other fees or taxes, general sales tax, and local taxes. In states where gasoline is subject to the general sales tax, or where the fuel tax is based on the average sale price, the average rate determined by API is sensitive to changes in the price of gasoline. States that fully or partially apply general sales taxes to gasoline: CA, CO, GA, IL, IN, MI, NY; (2) The federal excise tax of $1.0066 per pack and local taxes are not included; (3) Rates are those applicable to off-premise sales of 40% alcohol by volume (a.b.v.) distilled spirits in 750ml containers. Local excise taxes are excluded; (4) Rates are those applicable to off-premise sales of 11% a.b.v. non-carbonated wine in 750ml containers; (5) Rates are those applicable to off-premise sales of 4.7% a.b.v. beer in 12 ounce containers; (f) Different rates also applicable according to alcohol content, place of production, size of container, or place purchased (on- or off-premise or onboard airlines); (l) Different rates also applicable to alcohol content, place of production, size of container, place purchased (on- or off-premise or on board airlines) or type of wine (carbonated, vermouth, etc.); (q) Different rates also applicable according to alcohol content, place of production, size of container, or place purchased (on- or off-premise or onboard airlines); (r) Includes statewide local rate in Alabama ($0.52) and Georgia ($0.53).
Source: Tax Foundation, 2019 Facts & Figures: How Does Your State Compare?

State Business Tax Climate Index Rankings

State	Overall Rank	Corporate Tax Rank	Individual Income Tax Rank	Sales Tax Rank	Unemployment Insurance Tax Rank	Property Tax Rank
Georgia	33	8	38	29	38	24

Note: The index is a measure of how each state's tax laws affect economic performance. The lower the rank, the more favorable a state's tax system is for business. States without a given tax are given a ranking of 1. The scores/rankings for the District of Columbia do not affect other states. The 2019 index represents the tax climate as of July 1, 2018.
Source: Tax Foundation, State Business Tax Climate Index 2019

COMMERCIAL UTILITIES

Typical Monthly Electric Bills

Area	Commercial Service ($/month)		Industrial Service ($/month)	
	1,500 kWh	40 kW demand 14,000 kWh	1,000 kW demand 200,000 kWh	50,000 kW demand 32,500,000 kWh
City	n/a	n/a	n/a	n/a
Average[1]	203	1,619	25,886	2,540,077

Note: Figures are based on annualized rates; (1) Average based on 187 utilities surveyed; n/a not available
Source: Edison Electric Institute, Typical Bills and Average Rates Report, Summer 2018

TRANSPORTATION

Means of Transportation to Work

Area	Car/Truck/Van		Public Transportation			Bicycle	Walked	Other Means	Worked at Home
	Drove Alone	Car-pooled	Bus	Subway	Railroad				
City	74.5	10.3	4.5	0.1	0.0	1.3	3.9	1.2	4.2
MSA[1]	78.4	9.8	2.8	0.0	0.0	0.8	2.6	1.1	4.4
U.S.	76.4	9.2	2.5	1.9	0.6	0.6	2.7	1.3	4.7

Note: Figures are percentages and cover workers 16 years of age and older; (1) Figures cover the Athens-Clarke County, GA Metropolitan Statistical Area—see Appendix B for areas included
Source: U.S. Census Bureau, 2013-2017 American Community Survey 5-Year Estimates

Travel Time to Work

Area	Less Than 10 Minutes	10 to 19 Minutes	20 to 29 Minutes	30 to 44 Minutes	45 to 59 Minutes	60 to 89 Minutes	90 Minutes or More
City	16.1	48.8	16.9	9.3	3.9	3.2	1.9
MSA[1]	13.4	41.4	21.2	13.5	4.8	3.5	2.1
U.S.	12.7	28.9	20.9	20.5	8.1	6.2	2.7

Note: Note: Figures are percentages and include workers 16 years old and over; (1) Figures cover the Athens-Clarke County, GA Metropolitan Statistical Area—see Appendix B for areas included
Source: U.S. Census Bureau, 2013-2017 American Community Survey 5-Year Estimates

Freeway Travel Time Index

Area	1985	1990	1995	2000	2005	2010	2014
Urban Area Rank[1,2]	n/a	n/a	n/a	n/a	n/a	n/a	n/a
Urban Area Index[1]	n/a	n/a	n/a	n/a	n/a	n/a	n/a
Average Index[3]	1.09	1.11	1.14	1.17	1.20	1.19	1.20

Note: Freeway Travel Time Index—the ratio of travel time in the peak period to the travel time at free-flow conditions. For example, a value of 1.30 indicates a 20-minute free-flow trip takes 26 minutes in the peak (20 minutes x 1.30 = 26 minutes); (1) Data for the Athens-Clarke County, GA urban area was not available; (2) Rank is based on 101 urban areas (#1 = highest travel time index); (3) Average of 101 urban areas
Source: Texas Transportation Institute, 2015 Urban Mobility Scorecard, August 2015

Freeway Commuter Stress Index

Area	1985	1990	1995	2000	2005	2010	2014
Urban Area Rank[1,2]	n/a	n/a	n/a	n/a	n/a	n/a	n/a
Urban Area Index[1]	n/a	n/a	n/a	n/a	n/a	n/a	n/a
Average Index[3]	1.13	1.16	1.19	1.22	1.25	1.24	1.25

Note: The Freeway Commuter Stress Index is the same as the Freeway Travel Time Index (see table above) except that it includes only the travel in the peak directions during the peak periods; the TTI includes travel in all directions during the peak period. Thus, the CSI is more indicative of the work trip experienced by each commuter on a daily basis; (1) Data for the Athens-Clarke County, GA urban area was not available; (2) Rank is based on 101 urban areas (#1 = highest travel time index); (3) Average of 101 urban areas
Source: Texas Transportation Institute, 2015 Urban Mobility Scorecard, August 2015

Public Transportation

Agency Name / Mode of Transportation	Vehicles Operated in Maximum Service[1]	Annual Unlinked Passenger Trips[2] (in thous.)	Annual Passenger Miles[3] (in thous.)
Athens Transit System			
Bus (directly operated)	22	1,553.3	5,598.0
Demand Response (directly operated)	3	6.8	35.7

Note: (1) The number of revenue vehicles operated by the given mode and type of service to meet the annual maximum service requirement. This is the revenue vehicle count during the peak season of the year; on the week and day that maximum service is provided. Vehicles operated in maximum service (VOMS) exclude atypical days and one-time special events; (2) The number of passengers who boarded public transportation vehicles. Passengers are counted each time they board a vehicle no matter how many vehicles they use to travel from their origin to their destination. (3) The sum of the distances ridden by all passengers during the entire fiscal year.
Source: Federal Transit Administration, National Transit Database, 2017

Air Transportation

Airport Name and Code / Type of Service	Passenger Airlines[1]	Passenger Enplanements	Freight Carriers[2]	Freight (lbs)
Athens Municipal (AHN)				
Domestic service (U.S. carriers - 2018)	5	1,108	0	0
International service (U.S. carriers - 2017)	0	0	0	0

Note: (1) Includes all U.S.-based major, minor and commuter airlines that carried at least one passenger during the year; (2) Includes all U.S.-based airlines and freight carriers that transported at least one pound of freight during the year.
Source: Bureau of Transportation Statistics, The Intermodal Transportation Database, Air Carriers: T-100 Domestic Market (U.S. Carriers), 2018; Bureau of Transportation Statistics, The Intermodal Transportation Database, Air Carriers: T-100 International Market (U.S. Carriers), 2017

Other Transportation Statistics

Major Highways:	CR-82 connecting to I-85 (18 miles)
Amtrak Service:	No
Major Waterways/Ports:	None

Source: Amtrak.com; Google Maps

BUSINESSES

Major Business Headquarters

Company Name	Industry	Rankings	
		Fortune[1]	Forbes[2]
No companies listed	-	-	-

Note: (1) Companies that produce a 10-K are ranked 1 to 500 based on 2017 revenue; (2) All private companies with at least $2 billion in annual revenue through the end of their most current fiscal year are ranked 1 to 229; companies listed are headquartered in the city; dashes indicate no ranking
Source: Fortune, "Fortune 500," June 2018; Forbes, "America's Largest Private Companies," 2018 Rankings

Fast-Growing Businesses

According to *Inc.*, Athens is home to one of America's 500 fastest-growing private companies: **Seller Labs** (#148). Criteria: must be an independent, privately-held, for-profit, U.S. corporation, proprietorship or partnership as of December 31, 2017; revenues must be at least $100,000 in 2014 and $2 million in 2017; must have four-year operating/sales history. Holding companies, regulated banks, and utilities were excluded. *Inc., "America's 500 Fastest-Growing Private Companies," 2018*

According to Deloitte, Athens is home to one of North America's 500 fastest-growing high-technology companies: **Seller Labs** (#51). Companies are ranked by percentage growth in revenue over a four-year period. Criteria for inclusion: company must be headquartered within North America; must own proprietary intellectual property or technology that is sold to customers in products that contributes to a significant portion of the company's operating revenue; must have been in business for a minumum of four years with 2014 operating revenues of at least $50,000 USD/CD and 2017 operating revenues of at least $5 million USD/CD. *Deloitte, 2018 Technology Fast 500*[TM]

Minority- and Women-Owned Businesses

Group	All Firms		Firms with Paid Employees			
	Firms	Sales ($000)	Firms	Sales ($000)	Employees	Payroll ($000)
AIAN[1]	49	(s)	0	(s)	0 - 19	(s)
Asian	312	177,716	126	163,331	590	13,621
Black	2,197	43,604	41	(s)	20 - 99	(s)
Hispanic	384	43,246	30	(s)	100 - 249	(s)
NHOPI[2]	n/a	n/a	n/a	n/a	n/a	n/a
Women	3,465	(s)	366	(s)	2,500 - 4,999	(s)
All Firms	9,397	9,208,939	2,241	8,914,892	41,671	1,478,632

Note: Figures cover firms located in the city; minority- and women-owned business are defined as firms in which the corresponding group own 51% or more of the stock or equity of the company; (1) American Indian and Alaska Native; (2) Native Hawaiian and Other Pacific Islander; (s) estimates are suppressed when publication standards are not met; n/a not available
Source: U.S. Census Bureau, 2012 Economic Census, Survey of Business Owners

**HOTELS &
CONVENTION
CENTERS**

Hotels, Motels and Vacation Rentals

Area	5 Star		4 Star		3 Star		2 Star		1 Star		Not Rated	
	Num.	Pct.[3]	Num.	Pct.[3]	Num.	Pct.[3]	Num.	Pct.[3]	Num.	Pct.[3]	Num.	Pct.[3]
City[1]	0	0.0	2	1.0	17	8.7	65	33.2	1	0.5	111	56.6
Total[2]	286	0.4	5,236	7.1	16,715	22.6	10,259	13.9	293	0.4	41,056	55.6

Note: (1) Figures cover Athens and vicinity; (2) Figures cover all 100 cities in this book; (3) Percentage of hotels which have a given star rating; Star ratings are determined by expedia.com and offer an indication of the general quality of a particular hotel.
Source: www.expedia.com, April 3, 2019

Major Convention Centers

Name	Overall Space (sq. ft.)	Exhibit Space (sq. ft.)	Meeting Space (sq. ft.)	Meeting Rooms
The Classic Center	104,540	56,000	n/a	35

Note: Table includes convention centers located in the Athens-Clarke County, GA metro area; n/a not available
Source: Original research

Living Environment

COST OF LIVING

Cost of Living Index

Composite Index	Groceries	Housing	Utilities	Trans-portation	Health Care	Misc. Goods/ Services
n/a	n/a	n/a	n/a	n/a	n/a	n/a

Note: The Cost of Living Index measures regional differences in the cost of consumer goods and services, excluding taxes and non-consumer expenditures, for professional and managerial households in the top income quintile. It is based on more than 50,000 prices covering almost 60 different items for which prices are collected three times a year by chambers of commerce, economic development organizations or university applied economic centers in each participating urban area. The numbers shown should be read as a percentage above or below the national average of 100. For example, a value of 115.4 in the groceries column indicates that grocery prices are 15.4% higher than the national average. Small differences in the index numbers should not be interpreted as significant; n/a not available.
Source: The Council for Community and Economic Research, ACCRA Cost of Living Index, 2018

Grocery Prices

Area[1]	T-Bone Steak ($/pound)	Frying Chicken ($/pound)	Whole Milk ($/half gal.)	Eggs ($/dozen)	Orange Juice ($/64 oz.)	Coffee ($/11.5 oz.)
City[2]	n/a	n/a	n/a	n/a	n/a	n/a
Avg.	11.35	1.42	1.94	1.81	3.52	4.35
Min.	7.45	0.92	0.80	0.75	2.72	3.06
Max.	15.05	2.76	4.18	4.00	5.36	8.20

Note: (1) Values for the local area are compared with the average, minimum and maximum values for all 291 areas in the Cost of Living Index; (2) Figures cover the Athens GA urban area; n/a not available; **T-Bone Steak** (price per pound); **Frying Chicken** (price per pound, whole fryer); **Whole Milk** (half gallon carton); **Eggs** (price per dozen, Grade A, large); **Orange Juice** (64 oz. Tropicana or Florida Natural); **Coffee** (11.5 oz. can, vacuum-packed, Maxwell House, Hills Bros, or Folgers).
Source: The Council for Community and Economic Research, ACCRA Cost of Living Index, 2018

Housing and Utility Costs

Area[1]	New Home Price ($)	Apartment Rent ($/month)	All Electric ($/month)	Part Electric ($/month)	Other Energy ($/month)	Telephone ($/month)
City[2]	n/a	n/a	n/a	n/a	n/a	n/a
Avg.	347,000	1,087	165.93	100.16	67.73	178.70
Min.	200,468	500	93.58	25.64	26.78	163.10
Max.	1,901,222	4,888	388.65	246.86	332.81	197.70

Note: (1) Values for the local area are compared with the average, minimum and maximum values for all 291 areas in the Cost of Living Index; (2) Figures cover the Athens GA urban area; n/a not available; **New Home Price** (2,400 sf living area, 8,000 sf lot, in urban area with full utilities); **Apartment Rent** (950 sf 2 bedroom/1.5 or 2 bath, unfurnished, excluding all utilities except water); **All Electric** (average monthly cost for an all-electric home); **Part Electric** (average monthly cost for a part-electric home); **Other Energy** (average monthly cost for natural gas, fuel oil, coal, wood, and any other forms of energy except electricity); **Telephone** (price includes the base monthly rate plus taxes and fees for three lines of mobile phone service).
Source: The Council for Community and Economic Research, ACCRA Cost of Living Index, 2018

Health Care, Transportation, and Other Costs

Area[1]	Doctor ($/visit)	Dentist ($/visit)	Optometrist ($/visit)	Gasoline ($/gallon)	Beauty Salon ($/visit)	Men's Shirt ($)
City[2]	n/a	n/a	n/a	n/a	n/a	n/a
Avg.	110.71	95.11	103.74	2.61	37.48	32.03
Min.	33.60	62.55	54.63	1.89	17.00	11.44
Max.	195.97	153.93	225.79	3.59	71.88	58.64

Note: (1) Values for the local area are compared with the average, minimum and maximum values for all 291 areas in the Cost of Living Index; (2) Figures cover the Athens GA urban area; n/a not available; **Doctor** (general practitioners routine exam of an established patient); **Dentist** (adult teeth cleaning and periodic oral examination); **Optometrist** (full vision eye exam for established adult patient); **Gasoline** (one gallon regular unleaded, national brand, including all taxes, cash price at self-service pump if available); **Beauty Salon** (woman's shampoo, trim, and blow-dry); **Men's Shirt** (cotton/polyester dress shirt, pinpoint weave, long sleeves).
Source: The Council for Community and Economic Research, ACCRA Cost of Living Index, 2018

HOUSING

House Price Index (HPI)

Area	National Ranking[2]	Quarterly Change (%)	One-Year Change (%)	Five-Year Change (%)
MSA[1]	150	-2.93	5.58	36.35
U.S.[3]	–	1.12	5.73	32.81

Note: The HPI is a weighted repeat sales index. It measures average price changes in repeat sales or refinancings on the same properties. This information is obtained by reviewing repeat mortgage transactions on single-family properties whose mortgages have been purchased or securitized by Fannie Mae or Freddie Mac in January 1975; (1) Figures cover the Athens-Clarke County, GA Metropolitan Statistical Area—see Appendix B for areas included; (2) Rankings are based on annual percentage change for all metro areas containing at least 15,000 transactions over the last 10 years and ranges from 1 to 245; (3) figures based on a weighted average of Census Division estimates using a seasonally adjusted, purchase-only index; all figures are for the period ending December 31, 2018
Source: Federal Housing Finance Agency, House Price Index, February 26, 2019

Median Single-Family Home Prices

Area	2016	2017	2018[p]	Percent Change 2017 to 2018
MSA[1]	n/a	n/a	n/a	n/a
U.S. Average	235.5	248.8	261.6	5.1

Note: Figures are median sales prices of existing single-family homes in thousands of dollars; (p) preliminary; n/a not available; (1) Figures cover the Athens-Clarke County, GA Metropolitan Statistical Area—see Appendix B for areas included
Source: National Association of Realtors, Median Sales Price of Existing Single-Family Homes for Metropolitan Areas, 4th Quarter 2018

Qualifying Income Based on Median Sales Price of Existing Single-Family Homes

Area	With 5% Down ($)	With 10% Down ($)	With 20% Down ($)
MSA[1]	n/a	n/a	n/a
U.S. Average	62,954	59,640	53,013

Note: Figures are preliminary; Qualifying income is based on a mortgage rate of 4.9%. Monthly principal and interest payment is limited to 25% of income; n/a not available; (1) Figures cover the Athens-Clarke County, GA Metropolitan Statistical Area—see Appendix B for areas included
Source: National Association of Realtors, Qualifying Income Based on Median Sales Price of Existing Single-Family Homes for Metropolitan Areas, 4th Quarter 2018

Median Apartment Condo-Coop Home Prices

Area	2016	2017	2018[p]	Percent Change 2017 to 2018
MSA[1]	n/a	n/a	n/a	n/a
U.S. Average	220.7	234.3	241.0	2.9

Note: Figures are median sales prices of existing apartment condo-coop homes in thousands of dollars; (p) preliminary; n/a not available; (1) Figures cover the Athens-Clarke County, GA Metropolitan Statistical Area—see Appendix B for areas included
Source: National Association of Realtors, Median Sales Price of Existing Apartment Condo-Coop Homes for Metropolitan Areas, 4th Quarter 2018

Home Value Distribution

Area	Under $50,000	$50,000 -$99,999	$100,000 -$149,999	$150,000 -$199,999	$200,000 -$299,999	$300,000 -$499,999	$500,000 -$999,999	$1,000,000 or more
City	7.4	18.0	22.2	20.6	16.9	10.8	3.8	0.4
MSA[1]	9.8	16.0	18.9	17.1	19.3	13.6	4.6	0.7
U.S.	8.3	13.9	14.7	14.6	18.7	17.3	9.7	2.7

Note: Figures are percentages and cover owner-occupied housing units; (1) Figures cover the Athens-Clarke County, GA Metropolitan Statistical Area—see Appendix B for areas included
Source: U.S. Census Bureau, 2013-2017 American Community Survey 5-Year Estimates

Homeownership Rate

Area	2010 (%)	2011 (%)	2012 (%)	2013 (%)	2014 (%)	2015 (%)	2016 (%)	2017 (%)	2018 (%)
MSA[1]	n/a	n/a	n/a	n/a	n/a	n/a	n/a	n/a	n/a
U.S.	66.9	66.1	65.4	65.1	64.5	63.7	63.4	63.9	64.4

Note: (1) Figures cover the Athens-Clarke County, GA Metropolitan Statistical Area—see Appendix B for areas included; n/a not available
Source: U.S. Census Bureau, Housing Vacancies and Homeownership Annual Statistics: 2010-2018

Year Housing Structure Built

Area	2010 or Later	2000 -2009	1990 -1999	1980 -1989	1970 -1979	1960 -1969	1950 -1959	1940 -1949	Before 1940	Median Year
City	2.5	17.3	19.7	16.0	18.0	12.0	6.9	2.6	4.9	1983
MSA[1]	2.9	19.2	20.6	16.9	17.4	9.9	5.9	2.3	5.0	1986
U.S.	3.2	14.5	14.0	13.6	15.5	10.8	10.5	5.1	12.9	1977

Note: Figures are percentages except for Median Year; Note: (1) Figures cover the Athens-Clarke County, GA Metropolitan Statistical Area—see Appendix B for areas included
Source: U.S. Census Bureau, 2013-2017 American Community Survey 5-Year Estimates

Gross Monthly Rent

Area	Under $500	$500 -$999	$1,000 -$1,499	$1,500 -$1,999	$2,000 -$2,499	$2,500 -$2,999	$3,000 and up	Median ($)
City	8.8	61.9	22.1	5.4	1.4	0.1	0.2	815
MSA[1]	9.2	62.3	21.5	5.1	1.3	0.3	0.2	813
U.S.	10.5	41.1	28.7	11.7	4.5	1.8	1.7	982

Note: Figures are percentages except for Median; Gross rent is the contract rent plus the estimated average monthly cost of utilities (electricity, gas, and water and sewer) and fuels (oil, coal, kerosene, wood, etc.) if these are paid by the renter (or paid for the renter by someone else); (1) Figures cover the Athens-Clarke County, GA Metropolitan Statistical Area—see Appendix B for areas included
Source: U.S. Census Bureau, 2013-2017 American Community Survey 5-Year Estimates

HEALTH

Health Risk Factors

Category	MSA[1] (%)	U.S. (%)
Adults aged 18–64 who have any kind of health care coverage	n/a	87.3
Adults who reported being in good or better health	n/a	82.4
Adults who have been told they have high blood cholesterol	n/a	33.0
Adults who have been told they have high blood pressure	n/a	32.3
Adults who are current smokers	n/a	17.1
Adults who currently use E-cigarettes	n/a	4.6
Adults who currently use chewing tobacco, snuff, or snus	n/a	4.0
Adults who are heavy drinkers[2]	n/a	6.3
Adults who are binge drinkers[3]	n/a	17.4
Adults who are overweight (BMI 25.0 - 29.9)	n/a	35.3
Adults who are obese (BMI 30.0 - 99.8)	n/a	31.3
Adults who participated in any physical activities in the past month	n/a	74.4
Adults who always or nearly always wears a seat belt	n/a	94.3

Note: n/a not available; (1) Figures cover the Athens-Clarke County, GA Metropolitan Statistical Area—see Appendix B for areas included; (2) Heavy drinkers are classified as adult men having more than 14 drinks per week and adult women having more than 7 drinks per week; (3) Binge drinkers are classified as males having five or more drinks on one occasion or females having four or more drinks on one occasion
Source: Centers for Disease Control and Prevention, Behavioral Risk Factor Surveillance System, SMART: Selected Metropolitan Area Risk Trends, 2017

Acute and Chronic Health Conditions

Category	MSA[1] (%)	U.S. (%)
Adults who have ever been told they had a heart attack	n/a	4.2
Adults who have ever been told they have angina or coronary heart disease	n/a	3.9
Adults who have ever been told they had a stroke	n/a	3.0
Adults who have ever been told they have asthma	n/a	14.2
Adults who have ever been told they have arthritis	n/a	24.9
Adults who have ever been told they have diabetes[2]	n/a	10.5
Adults who have ever been told they had skin cancer	n/a	6.2
Adults who have ever been told they had any other types of cancer	n/a	7.1
Adults who have ever been told they have COPD	n/a	6.5
Adults who have ever been told they have kidney disease	n/a	3.0
Adults who have ever been told they have a form of depression	n/a	20.5

Note: n/a not available; (1) Figures cover the Athens-Clarke County, GA Metropolitan Statistical Area—see Appendix B for areas included; (2) Figures do not include pregnancy-related, borderline, or pre-diabetes
Source: Centers for Disease Control and Prevention, Behaviorial Risk Factor Surveillance System, SMART: Selected Metropolitan Area Risk Trends, 2017

Health Screening and Vaccination Rates

Category	MSA[1] (%)	U.S. (%)
Adults aged 65+ who have had flu shot within the past year	n/a	60.7
Adults aged 65+ who have ever had a pneumonia vaccination	n/a	75.4
Adults who have ever been tested for HIV	n/a	36.1
Adults who have ever had the shingles or zoster vaccine?	n/a	28.9
Adults who have had their blood cholesterol checked within the last five years	n/a	85.9

Note: n/a not available; (1) Figures cover the Athens-Clarke County, GA Metropolitan Statistical Area—see Appendix B for areas included.
Source: Centers for Disease Control and Prevention, Behaviorial Risk Factor Surveillance System, SMART: Selected Metropolitan Area Risk Trends, 2017

Disability Status

Category	MSA[1] (%)	U.S. (%)
Adults who reported being deaf	n/a	6.7
Are you blind or have serious difficulty seeing, even when wearing glasses?	n/a	4.5
Are you limited in any way in any of your usual activities due of arthritis?	n/a	12.9
Do you have difficulty doing errands alone?	n/a	6.8
Do you have difficulty dressing or bathing?	n/a	3.6
Do you have serious difficulty concentrating/remembering/making decisions?	n/a	10.7
Do you have serious difficulty walking or climbing stairs?	n/a	13.6

Note: n/a not available; (1) Figures cover the Athens-Clarke County, GA Metropolitan Statistical Area—see Appendix B for areas included.
Source: Centers for Disease Control and Prevention, Behaviorial Risk Factor Surveillance System, SMART: Selected Metropolitan Area Risk Trends, 2017

Mortality Rates for the Top 10 Causes of Death in the U.S.

ICD-10[a] Sub-Chapter	ICD-10[a] Code	Age-Adjusted Mortality Rate[1] per 100,000 population	
		County[2]	U.S.
Malignant neoplasms	C00-C97	141.9	155.5
Ischaemic heart diseases	I20-I25	54.0	94.8
Other forms of heart disease	I30-I51	95.8	52.9
Chronic lower respiratory diseases	J40-J47	43.4	41.0
Cerebrovascular diseases	I60-I69	50.1	37.5
Other degenerative diseases of the nervous system	G30-G31	57.3	35.0
Other external causes of accidental injury	W00-X59	24.4	33.7
Organic, including symptomatic, mental disorders	F01-F09	39.8	31.0
Hypertensive diseases	I10-I15	27.7	21.9
Diabetes mellitus	E10-E14	16.4	21.2

Note: (a) ICD-10 = International Classification of Diseases 10th Revision; (1) Mortality rates are a three year average covering 2015-2017; (2) Figures cover Clarke County.
Source: Centers for Disease Control and Prevention, National Center for Health Statistics. Underlying Cause of Death 1999-2017 on CDC WONDER Online Database

Mortality Rates for Selected Causes of Death

ICD-10[a] Sub-Chapter	ICD-10[a] Code	Age-Adjusted Mortality Rate[1] per 100,000 population	
		County[2]	U.S.
Assault	X85-Y09	Unreliable	5.9
Diseases of the liver	K70-K76	16.9	14.1
Human immunodeficiency virus (HIV) disease	B20-B24	Suppressed	1.8
Influenza and pneumonia	J09-J18	9.9	14.3
Intentional self-harm	X60-X84	14.3	13.6
Malnutrition	E40-E46	Unreliable	1.6
Obesity and other hyperalimentation	E65-E68	Suppressed	2.1
Renal failure	N17-N19	22.4	13.0
Transport accidents	V01-V99	10.6	12.4
Viral hepatitis	B15-B19	Suppressed	1.6

Note: (a) ICD-10 = International Classification of Diseases 10th Revision; (1) Mortality rates are a three year average covering 2015-2017; (2) Figures cover Clarke County; Data are suppressed when the data meet the criteria for confidentiality constraints; Mortality rates are flagged as unreliable when the rate would be calculated with a numerator of 20 or less.
Source: Centers for Disease Control and Prevention, National Center for Health Statistics. Underlying Cause of Death 1999-2017 on CDC WONDER Online Database

Health Insurance Coverage

Area	With Health Insurance	With Private Health Insurance	With Public Health Insurance	Without Health Insurance	Population Under Age 18 Without Health Insurance
City	85.3	67.7	26.3	14.7	8.3
MSA[1]	86.7	69.0	27.8	13.3	6.9
U.S.	89.5	67.2	33.8	10.5	5.7

Note: Figures are percentages that cover the civilian noninstitutionalized population; (1) Figures cover the Athens-Clarke County, GA Metropolitan Statistical Area—see Appendix B for areas included
Source: U.S. Census Bureau, 2013-2017 American Community Survey 5-Year Estimates

Number of Medical Professionals

Area	MDs[3]	DOs[3,4]	Dentists	Podiatrists	Chiropractors	Optometrists
County[1] (number)	363	16	69	6	29	21
County[1] (rate[2])	290.4	12.8	54.3	4.7	22.8	16.5
U.S. (rate[2])	279.3	23.0	68.4	6.0	27.1	16.2

Note: Data as of 2017 unless noted; (1) Data covers Clarke County; (2) Rate per 100,000 population; (3) Data as of 2016 and includes all active, non-federal physicians; (4) Doctor of Osteopathic Medicine
Source: U.S. Department of Health and Human Services, Health Resources and Services Administration, Bureau of Health Professions, Area Resource File (ARF) 2017-2018

EDUCATION

Public School District Statistics

District Name	Schls	Pupils	Pupil/ Teacher Ratio	Minority Pupils[1] (%)	Free Lunch Eligible[2] (%)	IEP[3] (%)
Clarke County	22	13,447	12.4	79.4	92.1	13.1

Note: Table includes school districts with 2,000 or more students; (1) Percentage of students that are not non-Hispanic white; (2) Percentage of students that are eligible for the free lunch program; (3) Percentage of students that have an Individualized Education Program.
Source: U.S. Department of Education, National Center for Education Statistics, Common Core of Data, Local Education Agency (School District) Universe Survey: School Year 2016-2017; U.S. Department of Education, National Center for Education Statistics, Common Core of Data, Public Elementary/Secondary School Universe Survey: School Year 2016-2017

Highest Level of Education

Area	Less than H.S.	H.S. Diploma	Some College, No Deg.	Associate Degree	Bachelor's Degree	Master's Degree	Prof. School Degree	Doctorate Degree
City	13.4	21.0	17.7	6.6	20.7	12.3	2.6	5.7
MSA[1]	13.3	25.1	18.1	7.1	18.4	10.9	2.7	4.5
U.S.	12.7	27.3	20.8	8.3	19.1	8.4	2.0	1.4

Note: Figures cover persons age 25 and over; (1) Figures cover the Athens-Clarke County, GA Metropolitan Statistical Area—see Appendix B for areas included
Source: U.S. Census Bureau, 2013-2017 American Community Survey 5-Year Estimates

Educational Attainment by Race

Area	High School Graduate or Higher (%)					Bachelor's Degree or Higher (%)				
	Total	White	Black	Asian	Hisp.[2]	Total	White	Black	Asian	Hisp.[2]
City	86.6	90.3	80.0	94.0	49.6	41.3	52.1	15.6	79.3	13.4
MSA[1]	86.7	89.5	78.4	91.6	50.3	36.4	41.3	15.1	72.5	14.4
U.S.	87.3	89.3	84.9	86.5	66.7	30.9	32.2	20.6	52.7	15.2

Note: Figures shown cover persons 25 years old and over; (1) Figures cover the Athens-Clarke County, GA Metropolitan Statistical Area—see Appendix B for areas included; (2) People of Hispanic origin can be of any race
Source: U.S. Census Bureau, 2013-2017 American Community Survey 5-Year Estimates

School Enrollment by Grade and Control

Area	Preschool (%)		Kindergarten (%)		Grades 1 - 4 (%)		Grades 5 - 8 (%)		Grades 9 - 12 (%)	
	Public	Private	Public	Private	Public	Private	Public	Private	Public	Private
City	64.7	35.3	90.6	9.4	89.7	10.3	89.9	10.1	84.5	15.5
MSA[1]	64.6	35.4	90.8	9.2	89.1	10.9	86.9	13.1	84.3	15.7
U.S.	58.8	41.2	87.7	12.3	89.7	10.3	89.6	10.4	90.3	9.7

Note: Figures shown cover persons 3 years old and over; (1) Figures cover the Athens-Clarke County, GA Metropolitan Statistical Area—see Appendix B for areas included
Source: U.S. Census Bureau, 2013-2017 American Community Survey 5-Year Estimates

Average Salaries of Public School Classroom Teachers

Area	2016		2017		Change from 2016 to 2017	
	Dollars	Rank[1]	Dollars	Rank[1]	Percent	Rank[2]
Georgia	54,190	23	55,532	23	2.5	15
U.S. Average	58,479	–	59,660	–	2.0	–

Note: (1) Rank ranges from 1 to 51 where 1 indicates highest salary; (2) Rank ranges from 1 to 51 where 1 indicates highest percent change.
Source: National Education Association, Rankings & Estimates: Rankings of the States 2017 and Estimates of School Statistics 2018

Higher Education

Four-Year Colleges			Two-Year Colleges			Medical Schools[1]	Law Schools[2]	Voc/ Tech[3]
Public	Private Non-profit	Private For-profit	Public	Private Non-profit	Private For-profit			
1	0	0	1	0	0	0	1	1

Note: Figures cover institutions located within the city limits and include main campuses only; (1) includes schools accredited by the Liaison Committee on Medical Education and the American Osteopathic Association's Commission on Osteopathic College Accreditation; (2) includes ABA-accredited schools, schools with provisional ABA accreditation, and state accredited schools; (3) includes all schools with programs that are less than 2 years.
Source: National Center for Education Statistics, Integrated Postsecondary Education System (IPEDS), 2017-18; Wikipedia, List of Medical Schools in the United States, accessed April 3, 2019; Wikipedia, List of Law Schools in the United States, accessed April 3, 2019

According to *U.S. News & World Report*, the Athens-Clarke County, GA metro area is home to one of the best national universities in the U.S.: **University of Georgia** (#46 tie). The indicators used to capture academic quality fall into a number of categories: assessment by administrators at peer institutions; retention of students; faculty resources; student selectivity; financial resources; alumni giving; high school counselor ratings of colleges; and graduation rate. *U.S. News & World Report, "America's Best Colleges 2019"*

According to *U.S. News & World Report*, the Athens-Clarke County, GA metro area is home to one of the top 100 law schools in the U.S.: **University of Georgia** (#27 tie). The rankings are based on a weighted average of 12 measures of quality: peer assessment score; assessment score by lawyers/judges; median LSAT scores; median undergrad GPA; acceptance rate; employment rates for graduates; placement success; bar passage rate; faculty resources; expenditures per student; student/faculty ratio; and library resources. *U.S. News & World Report, "America's Best Graduate Schools, Law, 2020"*

According to *U.S. News & World Report*, the Athens-Clarke County, GA metro area is home to one of the top 75 business schools in the U.S.: **University of Georgia (Terry)** (#37). The rankings are based on a weighted average of the following nine measures: quality assessment; peer assessment; recruiter assessment; placement success; mean starting salary and bonus; student selectivity; mean GMAT and GRE scores; mean undergraduate GPA; and acceptance rate. *U.S. News & World Report, "America's Best Graduate Schools, Business, 2020"*

PRESIDENTIAL ELECTION

2016 Presidential Election Results

Area	Clinton	Trump	Johnson	Stein	Other
Clarke County	65.1	28.0	4.4	0.7	1.8
U.S.	48.0	45.9	3.3	1.1	1.7

Note: Results are percentages and may not add to 100% due to rounding
Source: Dave Leip's Atlas of U.S. Presidential Elections

EMPLOYERS

Major Employers

Company Name	Industry
Athens Regional Health Care	Healthcare
Athens-Clarke County	Government
Baldor	Industrial motors
Burton+Burton	Balloons & gifts
Carrier Transicold	Truck refrigeration units
Caterpillar	Excavators
Certainteed	Fiberglass insulation
Clarke County School District	Education
DialAmerica	Telemarketing
McCann	Aerospace products
Merial	Animal health products
Noramco	Medical grade products
Pilgrim's	Food processing
Power Partners	Transformers, chillers, solar panels
Skaps	Non-woven plastics
St. Mary's Healthcare	Healthcare
University of Georgia	Higher education

Note: Companies shown are located within the Athens-Clarke County, GA Metropolitan Statistical Area.
Source: Hoovers.com; Wikipedia

PUBLIC SAFETY

Crime Rate

Area	All Crimes	Violent Crimes				Property Crimes		
		Murder	Rape[3]	Robbery	Aggrav. Assault	Burglary	Larceny -Theft	Motor Vehicle Theft
City	3,562.0	4.8	45.6	98.5	266.6	546.8	2,415.5	184.1
Suburbs[1]	1,855.9	1.2	18.1	14.5	111.2	289.0	1,349.3	72.5
Metro[2]	2,882.3	3.4	34.7	65.0	204.7	444.1	1,990.8	139.7
U.S.	2,756.1	5.3	41.7	98.0	248.9	430.4	1,694.4	237.4

Note: Figures are crimes per 100,000 population; (1) All areas within the metro area that are located outside the city limits; (2) Figures cover the Athens-Clarke County, GA Metropolitan Statistical Area—see Appendix B for areas included; (3) The city and U.S. figures shown were reported using the revised Uniform Crime Reporting (UCR) definition of rape. The suburban and metro area figures shown are an aggregate total of the data submitted using both the revised and legacy UCR definitions.
Source: FBI Uniform Crime Reports, 2017

Hate Crimes

Area	Number of Quarters Reported	Number of Incidents per Bias Motivation					
		Race/Ethnicity/ Ancestry	Religion	Sexual Orientation	Disability	Gender	Gender Identity
City	3	0	0	0	0	0	0
U.S.	4	4,131	1,564	1,130	116	46	119

Source: Federal Bureau of Investigation, Hate Crime Statistics 2017

Identity Theft Consumer Reports

Area	Reports	Reports per 100,000 Population	Rank[2]
MSA[1]	247	120	76
U.S.	444,602	135	-

Note: (1) Figures cover the Athens-Clarke County, GA Metropolitan Statistical Area—see Appendix B for areas included; (2) Rank ranges from 1 to 389 where 1 indicates greatest number of identity theft reports per 100,000 population
Source: Federal Trade Commission, Consumer Sentinel Network Data Book for January–December 2018

Fraud and Other Consumer Reports

Area	Reports	Reports per 100,000 Population	Rank[2]
MSA[1]	901	439	270
U.S.	2,552,917	776	-

Note: (1) Figures cover the Athens-Clarke County, GA Metropolitan Statistical Area—see Appendix B for areas included; (2) Rank ranges from 1 to 389 where 1 indicates greatest number of fraud and other consumer reports per 100,000 population
Source: Federal Trade Commission, Consumer Sentinel Network Data Book for January–December 2018

SPORTS

Professional Sports Teams

Team Name	League	Year Established

No teams are located in the metro area
Source: Wikipedia, Major Professional Sports Teams of the United States and Canada, April 5, 2019

CLIMATE

Average and Extreme Temperatures

Temperature	Jan	Feb	Mar	Apr	May	Jun	Jul	Aug	Sep	Oct	Nov	Dec	Yr.
Extreme High (°F)	79	80	85	93	95	101	105	102	98	95	84	77	105
Average High (°F)	52	56	64	73	80	86	88	88	82	73	63	54	72
Average Temp. (°F)	43	46	53	62	70	77	79	79	73	63	53	45	62
Average Low (°F)	33	36	42	51	59	66	70	69	64	52	42	35	52
Extreme Low (°F)	-8	5	10	26	37	46	53	55	36	28	3	0	-8

Note: Figures cover the years 1945-1990
Source: National Climatic Data Center, International Station Meteorological Climate Summary, 9/96

Average Precipitation/Snowfall/Humidity

Precip./Humidity	Jan	Feb	Mar	Apr	May	Jun	Jul	Aug	Sep	Oct	Nov	Dec	Yr.
Avg. Precip. (in.)	4.7	4.6	5.7	4.3	4.0	3.5	5.1	3.6	3.4	2.8	3.8	4.2	49.8
Avg. Snowfall (in.)	1	1	Tr	Tr	0	0	0	0	0	0	Tr	Tr	2
Avg. Rel. Hum. 7am (%)	79	77	78	78	82	83	88	89	88	84	81	79	82
Avg. Rel. Hum. 4pm (%)	56	50	48	45	49	52	57	56	56	51	52	55	52

Note: Figures cover the years 1945-1990; Tr = Trace amounts (<0.05 in. of rain; <0.5 in. of snow)
Source: National Climatic Data Center, International Station Meteorological Climate Summary, 9/96

Weather Conditions

Temperature			Daytime Sky			Precipitation		
10°F & below	32°F & below	90°F & above	Clear	Partly cloudy	Cloudy	0.01 inch or more precip.	0.1 inch or more snow/ice	Thunder-storms
1	49	38	98	147	120	116	3	48

Note: Figures are average number of days per year and cover the years 1945-1990
Source: National Climatic Data Center, International Station Meteorological Climate Summary, 9/96

HAZARDOUS WASTE

Superfund Sites

The Athens-Clarke County, GA metro area has no sites on the EPA's Superfund Final National Priorities List. There are a total of 1,390 Superfund sites with a status of proposed or final on the list in the U.S. *U.S. Environmental Protection Agency, National Priorities List, April 5, 2019*

**AIR & WATER
QUALITY**

Air Quality Trends: Ozone

	1990	1995	2000	2005	2010	2012	2014	2015	2016	2017
MSA[1]	n/a	n/a	n/a	n/a	n/a	n/a	n/a	n/a	n/a	n/a
U.S.	0.088	0.089	0.082	0.080	0.073	0.075	0.067	0.068	0.069	0.068

Note: (1) Data covers the Athens-Clarke County, GA Metropolitan Statistical Area—see Appendix B for areas included; n/a not available. The values shown are the composite ozone concentration averages among trend sites based on the highest fourth daily maximum 8-hour concentration in parts per million. These trends are based on sites having an adequate record of monitoring data during the trend period. Data from exceptional events are included.
Source: U.S. Environmental Protection Agency, Air Quality Monitoring Information, "Air Quality Trends by City, 1990-2017"

Air Quality Index

Area	Percent of Days when Air Quality was...[2]					AQI Statistics[2]	
	Good	Moderate	Unhealthy for Sensitive Groups	Unhealthy	Very Unhealthy	Maximum	Median
MSA[1]	87.2	12.8	0.0	0.0	0.0	97	38

Note: (1) Data covers the Athens-Clarke County, GA Metropolitan Statistical Area—see Appendix B for areas included; (2) Based on 360 days with AQI data in 2017. Air Quality Index (AQI) is an index for reporting daily air quality. EPA calculates the AQI for five major air pollutants regulated by the Clean Air Act: ground-level ozone, particle pollution (aka particulate matter), carbon monoxide, sulfur dioxide, and nitrogen dioxide. The AQI runs from 0 to 500. The higher the AQI value, the greater the level of air pollution and the greater the health concern. There are six AQI categories: "Good" AQI is between 0 and 50. Air quality is considered satisfactory; "Moderate" AQI is between 51 and 100. Air quality is acceptable; "Unhealthy for Sensitive Groups" When AQI values are between 101 and 150, members of sensitive groups may experience health effects; "Unhealthy" When AQI values are between 151 and 200 everyone may begin to experience health effects; "Very Unhealthy" AQI values between 201 and 300 trigger a health alert; "Hazardous" AQI values over 300 trigger warnings of emergency conditions (not shown).
Source: U.S. Environmental Protection Agency, Air Quality Index Report, 2017

Air Quality Index Pollutants

Area	Percent of Days when AQI Pollutant was...[2]					
	Carbon Monoxide	Nitrogen Dioxide	Ozone	Sulfur Dioxide	Particulate Matter 2.5	Particulate Matter 10
MSA[1]	0.0	0.0	52.2	0.0	47.8	0.0

Note: (1) Data covers the Athens-Clarke County, GA Metropolitan Statistical Area—see Appendix B for areas included; (2) Based on 360 days with AQI data in 2017. The Air Quality Index (AQI) is an index for reporting daily air quality. EPA calculates the AQI for five major air pollutants regulated by the Clean Air Act: ground-level ozone, particle pollution (also known as particulate matter), carbon monoxide, sulfur dioxide, and nitrogen dioxide. The AQI runs from 0 to 500. The higher the AQI value, the greater the level of air pollution and the greater the health concern.
Source: U.S. Environmental Protection Agency, Air Quality Index Report, 2017

Maximum Air Pollutant Concentrations: Particulate Matter, Ozone, CO and Lead

	Particulate Matter 10 (ug/m^3)	Particulate Matter 2.5 Wtd AM (ug/m^3)	Particulate Matter 2.5 24-Hr (ug/m^3)	Ozone (ppm)	Carbon Monoxide (ppm)	Lead (ug/m^3)
MSA[1] Level	n/a	7.8	16	0.063	n/a	n/a
NAAQS[2]	150	15	35	0.075	9	0.15
Met NAAQS[2]	n/a	Yes	Yes	Yes	n/a	n/a

Note: (1) Data covers the Athens-Clarke County, GA Metropolitan Statistical Area—see Appendix B for areas included; Data from exceptional events are included; (2) National Ambient Air Quality Standards; ppm = parts per million; ug/m^3 = micrograms per cubic meter; n/a not available.
Concentrations: Particulate Matter 10 (coarse particulate)—highest second maximum 24-hour concentration; Particulate Matter 2.5 Wtd AM (fine particulate)—highest weighted annual mean concentration; Particulate Matter 2.5 24-Hour (fine particulate)—highest 98th percentile 24-hour concentration; Ozone—highest fourth daily maximum 8-hour concentration; Carbon Monoxide—highest second maximum non-overlapping 8-hour concentration; Lead—maximum running 3-month average
Source: U.S. Environmental Protection Agency, Air Quality Monitoring Information, "Air Quality Statistics by City, 2017"

Maximum Air Pollutant Concentrations: Nitrogen Dioxide and Sulfur Dioxide

	Nitrogen Dioxide AM (ppb)	Nitrogen Dioxide 1-Hr (ppb)	Sulfur Dioxide AM (ppb)	Sulfur Dioxide 1-Hr (ppb)	Sulfur Dioxide 24-Hr (ppb)
MSA[1] Level	n/a	n/a	n/a	n/a	n/a
NAAQS[2]	53	100	30	75	140
Met NAAQS[2]	n/a	n/a	n/a	n/a	n/a

Note: (1) Data covers the Athens-Clarke County, GA Metropolitan Statistical Area—see Appendix B for areas included; Data from exceptional events are included; (2) National Ambient Air Quality Standards; ppm = parts per million; ug/m³ = micrograms per cubic meter; n/a not available.
Concentrations: Nitrogen Dioxide AM—highest arithmetic mean concentration; Nitrogen Dioxide 1-Hr—highest 98th percentile 1-hour daily maximum concentration; Sulfur Dioxide AM—highest annual mean concentration; Sulfur Dioxide 1-Hr—highest 99th percentile 1-hour daily maximum concentration; Sulfur Dioxide 24-Hr—highest second maximum 24-hour concentration
Source: U.S. Environmental Protection Agency, Air Quality Monitoring Information, "Air Quality Statistics by City, 2017"

Drinking Water

Water System Name	Pop. Served	Primary Water Source Type	Violations[1]	
			Health Based	Monitoring/ Reporting
Athens-Clarke Co. Water System	120,266	Surface	0	0

Note: (1) Based on violation data from January 1, 2018 to December 31, 2018
Source: U.S. Environmental Protection Agency, Office of Ground Water and Drinking Water, Safe Drinking Water Information System (based on data extracted April 5, 2019)

Atlanta, Georgia

Background

Atlanta was born of a rough-and-tumble past, first as a natural outgrowth of a thriving railroad network in the 1840s, and second as a resilient go-getter that proudly rose again above the rubble of the Civil War.

Blanketed over the rolling hills of the Piedmont Plateau, at the foot of the Blue Ridge Mountains, Georgia's capital stands 1,000 feet above sea level. Atlanta is located in the northwest corner of Georgia where the terrain is rolling to hilly, and slopes downward to the east, west, and south.

Atlanta proper begins at the "terminus," or zero mile mark, of the now defunct Western and Atlantic Railroad Line. However its metropolitan area comprises 28 counties that include Fulton, DeKalb, Clayton and Gwinnet, among others. Population-wise, Atlanta is the largest city in the southeast United States, and has been growing at a steady rate for the last decade. Within the city itself, Atlanta's has a diversified economy that allows for employment in a variety of sectors such as manufacturing, retail, and government. The city hosts many of the nation's Fortune 500 company headquarters, including CNN, as well as the nation's Centers for Disease Control and Prevention (CDC).

These accomplishments are the result of an involved city government that seeks to work closely with its business community, due in part to a change in the city charter in 1974, when greater administrative powers were vested in the mayoral office, and the city inaugurated its first black mayor.

While schools in the city remain predominantly black and schools in its suburbs predominantly white, Atlanta boasts a racially progressive climate. The Martin Luther King, Jr. Historic Site and Preservation District is located in the Sweet Auburn neighborhood, which includes King's birth home and the Ebenezer Baptist Church, where both he and his father preached. The city's consortium of black colleges that includes Morehouse College and the Interdenominational Theological Center testifies to the city's appreciation for a people who have always been one-third of Atlanta's population. Atlanta has become a major regional center for film and television production in recent years, with Tyler Perry Studios, TurnerStudios and EVE/ScreenGems Studio in the city.

Indeed, King is one of Atlanta's two Nobel Peace Prize winners. The second, former President Jimmy Carter, famously of Plains, Georgia, also brings his name to Atlanta via the Carter Center. Devoted to human rights, the center is operated with neighboring Emory University, and sits adjacent to the Jimmy Carter Library and Museum on a hill overlooking the city. Habitat for Humanity, also founded by Carter, is headquartered in Atlanta.

Hartsfield-Jackson Atlanta International Airport, the world's busiest passenger airport, underwent significant expansion in recent years. MARTA, the city's public transport system, is the nation's 9th largest and transports on average 500,000 passengers daily on a 48-mile, 38-station rapid rail system with connections to hundreds of bus routes.

The Appalachian chain of mountains, the Gulf of Mexico, and the Atlantic Ocean influence Atlanta's climate. Temperatures are moderate to hot throughout the year, but extended periods of heat are unusual and the city rarely reaches 100-degrees. Atlanta winters are mild with a few, short-lived cold spells. Summers can be humid.

Rankings

General Rankings

- *Insider* listed 33 places in the U.S. that were a must see vacation destination. Whether it is the great beaches, exploring a new city or experiencing the great outdoors, according to the website thisisinsider.com Atlanta is a place to visit in 2018. *Insider, "33 Trips Everyone Should Take in the U.S. in 2018,"November 27, 2017*

- Atlanta appeared on *Business Insider's* list of the "13 Hottest American Cities for 2016." Criteria: job and population growth; demographics; affordability; livability; residents' health and welfare; technological innovation; sustainability; burgeoning art and food scenes. *www.businessinsider.com, "The Thirteen Hottest American Cities for 2016," December 4, 2015*

- The Atlanta metro area was identified as one of America's fastest-growing areas in terms of population and business growth by *MagnifyMoney*. The area ranked #32 out of 35. The 100 most populous metro areas in the U.S. were evaluated on their change from 2011-2016 in the following categories: people and housing; workforce and employment opportunities; growing industry. *www.businessinsider.com, "The 35 Cities in the US with the Biggest Influx of People, the Most Work Opportunities, and the Hottest Business Growth," August 12, 2018*

- The human resources consulting firm Mercer ranked 231 major cities worldwide in terms of overall quality of life. Atlanta ranked #64. Criteria: political, social, economic, and socio-cultural factors; medical and health considerations; schools and education; public services and transportation; recreation; consumer goods; housing; and natural environment. *Mercer, "Mercer 2019 Quality of Living Survey," March 13, 2019*

Business/Finance Rankings

- According to *Business Insider*, the Atlanta metro area is where startup growth is on the rise. Based on the 2017 Kauffman Index of Growth Entrepreneurship, which measured in-depth national entrepreneurial trends in 40 metro areas, it ranked #5 in highest startup growth. *www.businessinsider.com, "The 21 U.S. Cities with the Highest Startup Growth," October 21, 2017*

- The personal finance site NerdWallet analyzed 183 American metropolitan areas with populations over 250,000 and more than 15,000 businesses to rank where entrepreneurs find the most success. Criteria included area economy, annual income, housing cost, unemployment rate, and the success rate of area businesses. Atlanta ranked #86. *www.nerdwallet.com, "Best Places to Start a Business," April 27, 2015*

- Recognizing the sizeable percentage of American workers who are self-employed, NerdWallet editors assessed the country's cities according to percentage of freelancers, median rental costs, cell phone plans/taxes, and healthcare affordability and access. By these criteria, Atlanta placed #4 among the best cities for independent workers. *www.nerdwallet.com, "Best Places for Freelance Workers," August 30, 2016*

- Based on metro area social media reviews, the employment opinion group Glassdoor surveyed 50 of the largest U.S. metro areas and equally weighed cost of living, hiring opportunity, and job satisfaction to compose a list of "25 Best Cities for Jobs." Median pay and home value, in-demand jobs and number of current job openings was also factored in. The Atlanta metro area was ranked #19 in overall job satisfaction. *www.glassdoor.com, "Best Cities for Jobs," October 16, 2018*

- In a survey of economic confidence in the nation's 50 largest metropolitan areas conducted January–December 2014, the Atlanta metro area placed #21, according to Gallup's 2014 Economic Confidence Index. *Gallup, "San Jose and San Francisco Lead in Economic Confidence," March 19, 2015*

- Using data from the Council for Community and Economic Research's 2014 cost of living index, NerdWallet ranked the 100 most affordable cities in America. Median income was compared with cost of living to find truly affordable places. Atlanta ranked #76. *NerdWallet.com, "America's Most Affordable Places," May 18, 2015*

- NerdWallet.com identified the 10 most promising cities for job seekers of the nation's 100 largest cities. Atlanta was ranked #6. Criteria: job availability; annual salary; workforce growth; affordability. *NerdWallet.com, "Best Cities for Job Seekers in 2017," December 19, 2016*

- The Brookings Institution ranked the nation's largest cities based on income inequality. Atlanta was ranked #1 (#1 = greatest inequality). Criteria: the "95/20 ratio," a figure representing the income at which a household earns more than 95 percent of all other households, divided by the income at which a household earns more than only 20 percent of all other households. *Brookings Institution, "Household Income Inequality, Largest Cities of 97 Large U.S. Metro Areas, 2014-2016," February 5, 2018*

- The Brookings Institution ranked the 100 largest metro areas in the U.S. based on income inequality. Atlanta was ranked #26 (#1 = greatest inequality). Criteria: the "95/20 ratio," a figure representing the income at which a household earns more than 95 percent of all other households, divided by the income at which a household earns more than only 20 percent of all other households. *Brookings Institution, "Household Income Inequality, 100 Largest U.S. Metro Areas, 2014-2016," February 5, 2018*

- *Forbes* ranked the 100 largest metro areas in the U.S. in terms of the "Best Cities for Young Professionals." The Atlanta metro area ranked #21 out of 25. (Large metro areas were divided into metro divisions.) Criteria: median rent of a two-bedroom apartment; job growth and unemployment rate; median salary of college graduates with 5 or less years of work experience; networking opportunities; social outlook; percentage of population 25 years of age and older with college degrees. *Forbes.com, "America's 25 Best Cities for Young Professionals in 2017," May 22, 2017*

- Payscale.com ranked the 32 largest metro areas in terms of wage growth. The Atlanta metro area ranked #12. Criteria: private-sector wage growth between the 4th quarter of 2017 and the 4th quarter of 2018. *PayScale, "Wage Trends by Metro Area-4th Quarter," January 8, 2019*

- The Atlanta metro area was identified as one of the most debt-ridden places in America by the finance site Credit.com. The metro area was ranked #7. Criteria: residents' average credit card debt as well as median income. *Credit.com, "25 Cities With the Most Credit Card Debt," February 28, 2018*

- Atlanta was identified as one of America's most frugal metro areas by *Coupons.com*. The city ranked #8 out of 25. Criteria: digital coupon usage. *Coupons.com, "America's Most Frugal Cities of 2017," March 22, 2018*

- Atlanta was cited as one of America's top metros for new and expanded facility projects in 2018. The area ranked #3 in the large metro area category (population over 1 million). *Site Selection, "Top Metros of 2018," March 2019*

- Atlanta was identified as one of the happiest cities to work in by CareerBliss.com, an online community for career advancement. The city ranked #3 out of 10. Criteria: an employee's relationship with his or her boss and co-workers; daily tasks; general work environment; compensation; opportunities for advancement; company culture and job reputation; and resources. *Businesswire.com, "CareerBliss Happiest Cities to Work 2019," February 12, 2019*

- The Atlanta metro area appeared on the Milken Institute "2018 Best Performing Cities" list. Rank: #17 out of 200 large metro areas. Criteria: job growth; wage and salary growth; high-tech output growth. *Milken Institute, "Best-Performing Cities 2018," January 24, 2019*

- *Forbes* ranked the 200 most populous metro areas to determine the nation's "Best Places for Business and Careers." The Atlanta metro area was ranked #11. Criteria: costs (business and living); job growth (past and projected); income growth; quality of life; educational attainment (college and high school); projected economic growth; cultural and recreational opportunities; net migration patterns; number of highly ranked colleges. *Forbes, "The Best Places for Business and Careers 2018: Seattle Leads the Way," October 24, 2018*

- Mercer Human Resources Consulting ranked 209 cities worldwide in terms of cost-of-living. Atlanta ranked #95 (the lower the ranking, the higher the cost-of-living). The survey measured the comparative cost of over 200 items (such as housing, food, clothing, household goods, transportation, and entertainment) in each location. *Mercer, "2018 Cost of Living Survey," June 26, 2018*

Children/Family Rankings

- Atlanta was selected as one of the most playful cities in the U.S. by KaBOOM! The organization's Playful City USA initiative honors cities and towns across the nation that have made their communities more playable. Criteria: pledging to integrate play as a solution to challenges in their communities; making it easy for children to get active and balanced play; creating more family-friendly and innovative communities as a result. *KaBOOM! National Campaign for Play, "2017 Playful City USA Communities"*

Culture/Performing Arts Rankings

- Atlanta was selected as one of the twenty best large U.S. cities for moviemakers. Of cities with a population over 400,000, the city was ranked #2. Criteria: film community and culture; access to equipment and facilities; film activity in 2018; number of film schools; tax incentives. ease of movement and traffic. *MovieMaker Magazine, "Best Places to Live and Work as a Moviemaker: 2019," January 16, 2019*

- Atlanta was selected as one of "America's Favorite Cities." The city ranked #9 in the "Culture" category. Respondents to an online survey were asked to rate 38 top urban destinations in the U.S. from a visitor's perspective. Criteria: theater scene and community; number of bookstores; live music; and sense of history. *Travelandleisure.com, "These Are America's 20 Most Cultured Cities," October 2016*

- Atlanta was selected as one of "America's Favorite Cities." The city ranked #13 in the "Culture: Music Scene " category. Respondents to an online survey were asked to rate 38 top urban destinations in the U.S. from a visitor's perspective. *Travelandleisure.com, "From the Honkytonk Capital to Jazz's Birthplace: America's Best Music Scenes," October 2016*

Dating/Romance Rankings

- Atlanta took the #8 spot on NerdWallet's list of best cities for singles wanting to date, based on the availability of singles; "date-friendliness," as determined by a city's walkability and the number of bars and restaurants per thousand residents; and the affordability of dating in terms of the cost of movie tickets, pizza, and wine for two. *www.nerdwallet.com, "Best Cities for Singles," February 2, 2015*

- Atlanta was selected as one of the nation's most romantic cities with 100,000 or more residents by Amazon.com. The city ranked #9 of 20. Criteria: per capita sales of romance novels, relationship books, romantic comedy movies, romantic music, and sexual wellness products. *Amazon.com, "Top 20 Most Romantic Cities in the U.S.," February 1, 2017*

Education Rankings

- Personal finance website *WalletHub* analyzed the 150 largest U.S. metropolitan statistical areas to determine where the most educated Americans are choosing to settle. Criteria: education quality and attainment gap; education levels; percentage of workers with degrees; public school quality rankings; quality and size of each metro area's universities. Atlanta was ranked #23 (#1 = most educated city). *www.WalletHub.com, "2018's Most and Least Educated Cities in America, " July 24, 2018*

- Atlanta was selected as one of America's most literate cities. The city ranked #4 out of the 82 largest U.S. cities. Criteria: number of booksellers; library resources; Internet resources; educational attainment; periodical publishing resources; newspaper circulation. *Central Connecticut State University, "America's Most Literate Cities, 2016," March 31, 2017*

Environmental Rankings

- The U.S. Environmental Protection Agency (EPA) released a list of U.S. metropolitan areas with the most ENERGY STAR certified buildings in 2017. The Atlanta metro area was ranked #4 out of 25. *U.S. Environmental Protection Agency, "2018 Energy Star Top Cities," April 11, 2018*

- Atlanta was highlighted as one of the 25 most ozone-polluted metro areas in the U.S. during 2014 through 2016. The area ranked #23. *American Lung Association, State of the Air 2018*

- Atlanta was highlighted as one of the 25 metro areas most polluted by year-round particle pollution (Annual PM 2.5) in the U.S. during 2014 through 2016. The area ranked #22. *American Lung Association, State of the Air 2018*

Food/Drink Rankings

- *Men's Health* ranked 100 major U.S. cities in terms of alcohol intoxication. Atlanta ranked #84 (#1 = most sober).Criteria: binge drinking; alcohol-related traffic accidents, arrests, and fatalities. *Men's Health, "America's Drunkest Cities," March 9, 2015*

Health/Fitness Rankings

- For each of the 100 largest cities in the United States, the American College of Sports Medicine's American Fitness Index evaluated infrastructure, community assets, and policies that encourage healthy and fit lifestyles, including preventive health behaviors, levels of chronic disease conditions, health care access, and community resources and policies that support physical activity. Atlanta ranked #20 for "community fitness." *www.americanfitnessindex.org, "ACSM American Fitness Index Health and Community Fitness Status of the 100 Largest U.S. Cities," May 2018*

- The Atlanta metro area was identified as one of the worst cities for bed bugs in America by pest control company Orkin. The area ranked #9 out of 50 based on the number of bed bug treatments Orkin performed from December 2017 to November 2018. *Orkin, "Baltimore Remains Front Runner, Atlanta and Philadelphia Break Into Top 10," January 14, 2019*

- Atlanta was identified as a "2018 Spring Allergy Capital." The area ranked #76 out of 100. Three groups of factors were used to identify the most challenging cities for people with allergies during the spring season: annual pollen levels; medicine utilization; access to board-certified allergists. *Asthma and Allergy Foundation of America, "Spring Allergy Capitals 2018"*

- Atlanta was identified as a "2018 Fall Allergy Capital." The area ranked #76 out of 100. Three groups of factors were used to identify the most challenging cities for people with allergies during the fall season: annual pollen levels; medicine utilization; access to board-certified allergists. *Asthma and Allergy Foundation of America, "Fall Allergy Capitals 2018"*

- Atlanta was identified as a "2018 Asthma Capital." The area ranked #55 out of the nation's 100 largest metropolitan areas. Criteria: estimated prevalence; self-reported prevalence; crude death rate for asthma; annual pollen score; annual air quality; public smoking laws; number of board-certified asthma specialists; school inhaler access laws; rescue medication use; controller medication use; ER visits for asthma; uninsured rate; poverty rate. *Asthma and Allergy Foundation of America, "Asthma Capitals 2018: The Most Challenging Places to Live With Asthma"*

- *Men's Health* ranked 100 major U.S. cities in terms of the best cities for men. Atlanta ranked #38. Criteria: health; fitness; quality of life. *Men's Health, "The Best & Worst Cities for Men Who Want to Be Fit and Happy," January 1, 2016*

- The Atlanta metro area ranked #81 out of 189 in The Gallup-Healthways Well-Being Index. Criteria: purpose; social well being; financial health; community and physical health. Results are based on telephone interviews with adults, aged 18 and older, living in metropolitan areas in the 50 U.S. states and the District of Columbia. *Gallup-Healthways, "State of American Well-Being, 2017 Community Well-Being Rankings" March 2018*

Real Estate Rankings

- FitSmallBusiness looked at 50 of the largest metropolitan areas in the U.S. to determine which metro was the best to start a real estate business. Data was compiled from such sources as: Zillow, Trulia, U.S. Census Bureau, and the Bureau of Labor Statistics. Criteria: location; inventory; annual wages; median sales price of homes; days on the market; median price cut percentage; and other factors that would influence real estate professional growth. The Atlanta metro area ranked #23. *fitsmallbusiness.com, "The Best Cities to Become a Real Estate Agent in 2018," January 30, 2018*

- *WalletHub* compared the most populated U.S. cities, as well as at least two of the most populated cities in each state, for a total of 179, to determine which had the best markets for real estate agents. Atlanta ranked #30 where demand was high and pay was the best. Criteria: sales per agent; annual median wage for real-estate agents; monthly average starting salary for real estate agents; real estate job density and competition; unemployment rate; housing-market health index; and other relevant metrics. *www.WalletHub.com, "2018's Best Places to Be a Real Estate Agent," April 25, 2018*

- According to Penske Truck Rental, the Atlanta metro area was named the #1 moving destination in 2018, based on one-way consumer truck rental reservations made through Penske's website, rental locations, and reservations call center. *blog.gopenske.com, "Penske Truck Rental's 2018 Top Moving Destinations," January 16, 2019*

- The Atlanta metro area was identified as one of the top 20 housing markets to invest in for 2019 by *Forbes*. Criteria: strong job and population growth; stable local economy; anticipated home price appreciation; and other factors. *Forbes.com, "The Best Markets for Real Estate Investments In 2019," January 7, 2019*

- Atlanta was ranked #128 out of 237 metro areas in terms of housing affordability in 2018 by the National Association of Home Builders (#1 = most affordable). Criteria: the share of homes sold in that area affordable to a family earning the local median income, based on standard mortgage underwriting criteria. *National Association of Home Builders®, NAHB-Wells Fargo Housing Opportunity Index, 4th Quarter 2018*

Safety Rankings

- Allstate ranked the 200 largest cities in America in terms of driver safety. Atlanta ranked #186. Criteria: internal property damage claims over a two-year period from January 2015 to December 2016. The report helps increase the importance of safety awareness behind the wheel. *Allstate, "Allstate America's Best Drivers Report, 2018" August 28, 2018*

- Atlanta was identified as one of the most dangerous cities in America by NeighborhoodScout. The city ranked #80 out of 100. Criteria: number of violent crimes per 1,000 residents. The editors only considered cities with 25,000 or more residents. *NeighborhoodScout.com, "Top 100 Most Dangerous Cities in the U.S. 2019" January 2, 2019*

- The National Insurance Crime Bureau ranked 382 metro areas in the U.S. in terms of per capita rates of vehicle theft. The Atlanta metro area ranked #67 (#1 = highest rate). Criteria: number of vehicle theft offenses per 100,000 inhabitants in 2017. *National Insurance Crime Bureau, "Hot Spots 2017," July 12, 2018*

Seniors/Retirement Rankings

- From its Best Cities for Successful Aging indexes, the Milken Institute generated rankings for metropolitan areas, weighing data in nine categories—health care, wellness, living arrangements, transportation and convenience, financial characteristics, education, employment, community engagement, and overall livability. The Atlanta metro area was ranked #62 overall in the large metro area category. *Milken Institute, "Best Cities for Successful Aging, 2017" March 14, 2017*

Sports/Recreation Rankings

- Atlanta was selected as one of "America's Most Miserable Sports Cities" by *Forbes*. The city was ranked #5. Criteria: postseason losses/misery; years since last title; and number of teams lost to relocation. Contenders were limited to cities with at least 75 cumulative pro seasons of NFL, NBA, NHL, MLS and MLB play. *Forbes, "America's Most Miserable Sports Cities 2016," April 20, 2016*

- Atlanta was chosen as one of America's best cities for bicycling. The city ranked #42 out of 50. Criteria: cycling infrastructure that is safe and friendly for all ages; energy and bike culture. The editors only considered cities with populations of 100,000 or more. *Bicycling, "The 50 Best Bike Cities in America," October 10, 2018*

Transportation Rankings

- NerdWallet surveyed average annual car insurance premiums in 125 U.S. cities to identify the least expensive U.S. cities in which to insure a car. Locations with no-fault insurance laws was a strong determinant. Atlanta came in at #26 for the most expensive rates. *www.nerdwallet.com, "Best Cities for Cheap Car Insurance," February 3, 2014*

Women/Minorities Rankings

- Atlanta was selected as one of "America's Favorite Cities." The city ranked #5 in the "Type of Trip: Gay-friendly Vacation" category. Respondents to an online survey were asked to rate 38 top urban destinations in the United States from visitor's perspective. Criteria: gay-friendly. *Travel + Leisure, "America's Favorite Cities 2015"*

- Atlanta was selected as one of the gayest cities in America by *The Advocate*. The city ranked #6 out of 25. Criteria, among many: Trans Pride parades/festivals; gay rugby teams; lesbian bars; LGBT centers; theater screenings of "Moonlight"; LGBT-inclusive nondiscrimination ordinances; and gay bowling teams. *The Advocate, "Queerest Cities in America 2017" January 12, 2017*

- Personal finance website *WalletHub* compared more than 180 U.S. cities—including the 150 most populated U.S. cities, plus at least two of the most populated cities in each state—across two key dimensions, "Hispanic Business-Friendliness" and "Hispanic Purchasing Power", to arrive at the most favorable conditions for Hispanic entrepreneurs. Atlanta was ranked #49 out of 182. Criteria includes: share of Hispanic-Owned Businesses; Hispanic entrepreneurship rate to median annual income of Hispanics; Small Business-Friendliness score; cost of living; and number of Hispanics with at least a bachelor's degree. *WalletHub.com, "2018's Best Cities for Hispanic Entrepreneurs," April 26, 2018*

Miscellaneous Rankings

- *MoveHub* ranked the coolest cities, appealing to young people, using its U.S. Hipster Index and Atlanta came out as #8. Criteria: number of thrift stores; density of tattoo parlors, vegan stores and microbreweries; and amount of rent increase. *www.thisisinsider.com, "The 20 Most Hipster Cities in the US-and Why You Should Consider Moving to One," April 10, 2018*

- In its roundup of St. Patrick's Day parades "Gayot" listed the best festivals and parades of all things Irish. The festivities in Atlanta as among the best. *www.gayot.com, "Best St. Patrick's Day Parades," March 17, 2018*

- The watchdog site Charity Navigator conducts an annual study of charities in the nation's major markets both to analyze statistical differences in their financial, accountability, and transparency practices and to track year-to-year variations in individual philanthropic communities. Charity Navigator's analysis demonstrated that the financial, accountability and transparency behaviors of America's largest charities can be influenced by the metropolitan market within which the charity operates. The Atlanta metro area was ranked #18 among the 30 metro markets in the rating category of Overall Score. *www.charitynavigator.org, "2017 Metro Market Study," May 1, 2017*

- *WalletHub* compared the 150 most populated U.S. cities to determine their operating efficiency. A "Quality of Services" score was constructed for each city and then divided by the total budget per capita to reveal which were managed the best. Atlanta ranked #137. Criteria: financial stability; economy; education; safety; health; infrastructure and pollution. *www.WalletHub.com, "2018's Best- & Worst-Run Cities in America," July 9, 2018*

- Atlanta appeared on *Travel + Leisure's* list of America's cities with the least attractive people. Criteria: cities were selected by readers in their annual America's Favorite Cities survey. The city ranked #8 out of 10. *Travel + Leisure, "America's Most and Least Attractive People," September 2, 2016*

- The National Alliance to End Homelessness listed the 25 most populous metro areas with the highest rate of homelessness. The Atlanta metro area had a high rate of homelessness. Criteria: number of homeless people per 10,000 population in 2016. *National Alliance to End Homelessness, "Homelessness in the 25 Most Populous U.S. Metro Areas," September 1, 2017*

Business Environment

CITY FINANCES

City Government Finances

Component	2016 ($000)	2016 ($ per capita)
Total Revenues	2,114,350	4,558
Total Expenditures	2,234,500	4,817
Debt Outstanding	8,143,539	17,555
Cash and Securities[1]	5,406,101	11,654

Note: (1) Cash and security holdings of a government at the close of its fiscal year, including those of its dependent agencies, utilities, and liquor stores.
Source: U.S. Census Bureau, State & Local Government Finances 2016

City Government Revenue by Source

Source	2016 ($000)	2016 ($ per capita)	2016 (%)
General Revenue			
From Federal Government	46,651	101	2.2
From State Government	11,332	24	0.5
From Local Governments	246,491	531	11.7
Taxes			
Property	353,792	763	16.7
Sales and Gross Receipts	166,293	358	7.9
Personal Income	0	0	0.0
Corporate Income	0	0	0.0
Motor Vehicle License	0	0	0.0
Other Taxes	79,963	172	3.8
Current Charges	849,650	1,832	40.2
Liquor Store	0	0	0.0
Utility	267,814	577	12.7
Employee Retirement	35,100	76	1.7

Source: U.S. Census Bureau, State & Local Government Finances 2016

City Government Expenditures by Function

Function	2016 ($000)	2016 ($ per capita)	2016 (%)
General Direct Expenditures			
Air Transportation	497,398	1,072	22.3
Corrections	33,281	71	1.5
Education	0	0	0.0
Employment Security Administration	0	0	0.0
Financial Administration	47,561	102	2.1
Fire Protection	83,883	180	3.8
General Public Buildings	18,055	38	0.8
Governmental Administration, Other	53,543	115	2.4
Health	902	1	0.0
Highways	91,172	196	4.1
Hospitals	0	0	0.0
Housing and Community Development	0	0	0.0
Interest on General Debt	189,611	408	8.5
Judicial and Legal	29,375	63	1.3
Libraries	0	0	0.0
Parking	0	0	0.0
Parks and Recreation	50,342	108	2.3
Police Protection	184,108	396	8.2
Public Welfare	0	0	0.0
Sewerage	89,982	194	4.0
Solid Waste Management	62,149	134	2.8
Veterans' Services	0	0	0.0
Liquor Store	0	0	0.0
Utility	259,149	558	11.6
Employee Retirement	275,618	594	12.3

Source: U.S. Census Bureau, State & Local Government Finances 2016

DEMOGRAPHICS

Population Growth

Area	1990 Census	2000 Census	2010 Census	2017* Estimate	Population Growth (%) 1990-2017	Population Growth (%) 2010-2017
City	394,092	416,474	420,003	465,230	18.1	10.8
MSA[1]	3,069,411	4,247,981	5,268,860	5,700,990	85.7	8.2
U.S.	248,709,873	281,421,906	308,745,538	321,004,407	29.1	4.0

Note: (1) Figures cover the Atlanta-Sandy Springs-Roswell, GA Metropolitan Statistical Area—see Appendix B for areas included; (*) 2013-2017 5-year estimated population
Source: U.S. Census Bureau, 1990 Census, Census 2000, Census 2010, 2013-2017 American Community Survey 5-Year Estimates

Household Size

Area	Persons in Household (%) One	Two	Three	Four	Five	Six	Seven or More	Average Household Size
City	47.4	29.7	10.5	7.4	3.2	1.1	0.7	2.20
MSA[1]	26.6	31.4	17.1	14.4	6.6	2.5	1.4	2.80
U.S.	27.7	33.8	15.7	13.0	6.0	2.3	1.4	2.60

Note: (1) Figures cover the Atlanta-Sandy Springs-Roswell, GA Metropolitan Statistical Area—see Appendix B for areas included
Source: U.S. Census Bureau, 2013-2017 American Community Survey 5-Year Estimates

Race

Area	White Alone[2] (%)	Black Alone[2] (%)	Asian Alone[2] (%)	AIAN[3] Alone[2] (%)	NHOPI[4] Alone[2] (%)	Other Race Alone[2] (%)	Two or More Races (%)
City	40.1	52.3	4.0	0.3	0.0	1.0	2.3
MSA[1]	54.6	33.7	5.6	0.3	0.0	3.2	2.5
U.S.	73.0	12.7	5.4	0.8	0.2	4.8	3.1

Note: (1) Figures cover the Atlanta-Sandy Springs-Roswell, GA Metropolitan Statistical Area—see Appendix B for areas included; (2) Alone is defined as not being in combination with one or more other races; (3) American Indian and Alaska Native; (4) Native Hawaiian and Other Pacific Islander
Source: U.S. Census Bureau, 2013-2017 American Community Survey 5-Year Estimates

Hispanic or Latino Origin

Area	Total (%)	Mexican (%)	Puerto Rican (%)	Cuban (%)	Other (%)
City	4.6	2.3	0.7	0.3	1.3
MSA[1]	10.5	5.8	1.0	0.4	3.4
U.S.	17.6	11.1	1.7	0.7	4.1

Note: Persons of Hispanic or Latino origin can be of any race; (1) Figures cover the Atlanta-Sandy Springs-Roswell, GA Metropolitan Statistical Area—see Appendix B for areas included
Source: U.S. Census Bureau, 2013-2017 American Community Survey 5-Year Estimates

Segregation

Type	Segregation Indices[1] 1990	2000	2010	2010 Rank[2]	Percent Change 1990-2000	1990-2010	2000-2010
Black/White	66.3	64.3	59.0	41	-2.0	-7.2	-5.3
Asian/White	42.5	46.9	48.5	10	4.4	6.0	1.5
Hispanic/White	35.3	51.6	49.5	27	16.3	14.1	-2.1

Note: All figures cover the Metropolitan Statistical Area—see Appendix B for areas included; Figures are based on an analysis of 1990, 2000, and 2010 Census Decennial Census tract data by William H. Frey, Brookings Institution and the University of Michigan Social Science Data Analysis Network. In this analysis all racial groups (whites, blacks, and asians) are non-Hispanic members of those races. Hispanics are shown as a separate category; (1) Segregation Indices are Dissimilarity Indices that measure the degree to which the minority group is distributed differently than whites across census tracts. They range from 0 (complete integration) to 100 (complete segregation) where the value indicates the percentage of the minority group that needs to move to be distributed exactly like whites; (2) Ranges from 1 (most segregated) to 102 (least segregated); n/a not available.
Source: www.CensusScope.org

Ancestry

Area	German	Irish	English	American	Italian	Polish	French[2]	Scottish	Dutch
City	5.8	5.3	7.0	6.0	2.3	1.3	1.6	1.7	0.5
MSA[1]	6.9	7.1	7.3	9.5	2.5	1.3	1.4	1.8	0.7
U.S.	14.1	10.1	7.5	6.6	5.3	2.9	2.5	1.7	1.3

Note: Figures are the percentage of the total population reporting a particular ancestry. The nine most commonly reported ancestries in the U.S. are shown. Figures include multiple ancestries (e.g. if a person reported being Irish and Italian, they were included in both columns); (1) Figures cover the Atlanta-Sandy Springs-Roswell, GA Metropolitan Statistical Area—see Appendix B for areas included; (2) Excludes Basque
Source: U.S. Census Bureau, 2013-2017 American Community Survey 5-Year Estimates

Foreign-Born Population

Area	Percent of Population Born in								
	Any Foreign Country	Asia	Mexico	Europe	Carribean	Central America[2]	South America	Africa	Canada
City	6.9	2.7	0.9	1.1	0.6	0.2	0.4	0.6	0.2
MSA[1]	13.6	4.3	2.8	1.2	1.4	1.1	1.0	1.5	0.2
U.S.	13.4	4.1	3.6	1.5	1.3	1.0	0.9	0.6	0.3

Note: (1) Figures cover the Atlanta-Sandy Springs-Roswell, GA Metropolitan Statistical Area—see Appendix B for areas included; (2) Excludes Mexico.
Source: U.S. Census Bureau, 2013-2017 American Community Survey 5-Year Estimates

Marital Status

Area	Never Married	Now Married[2]	Separated	Widowed	Divorced
City	54.3	27.1	2.0	5.7	10.9
MSA[1]	35.0	47.4	2.1	4.6	11.0
U.S.	33.1	48.2	2.0	5.8	10.9

Note: Figures are percentages and cover the population 15 years of age and older; (1) Figures cover the Atlanta-Sandy Springs-Roswell, GA Metropolitan Statistical Area—see Appendix B for areas included; (2) Excludes separated
Source: U.S. Census Bureau, 2013-2017 American Community Survey 5-Year Estimates

Disability by Age

Area	All Ages	Under 18 Years Old	18 to 64 Years Old	65 Years and Over
City	12.1	4.2	9.9	38.9
MSA[1]	10.1	3.4	8.7	33.9
U.S.	12.6	4.2	10.3	35.5

Note: Figures show percent of the civilian noninstitutionalized population that reported having a disability. Disability status is determined from six types of difficulty: vision, hearing, cognitive, ambulatory, self-care, and independent living. For children under 5 years old, hearing and vision difficulty are used to determine disability status. For children between the ages of 5 and 14, disability status is determined from hearing, vision, cognitive, ambulatory, and self-care difficulties. For people aged 15 years and older, they are considered to have a disability if they have difficulty with any one of the six difficulty types; Note: (1) Figures cover the Atlanta-Sandy Springs-Roswell, GA Metropolitan Statistical Area—see Appendix B for areas included
Source: U.S. Census Bureau, 2013-2017 American Community Survey 5-Year Estimates

Age

Area	Percent of Population									Median Age
	Under Age 5	Age 5–19	Age 20–34	Age 35–44	Age 45–54	Age 55–64	Age 65–74	Age 75–84	Age 85+	
City	5.8	16.8	30.1	14.2	12.2	9.6	6.8	3.2	1.3	33.5
MSA[1]	6.5	21.4	20.6	14.4	14.5	11.4	7.1	3.0	1.1	36.1
U.S.	6.2	19.5	20.7	12.7	13.4	12.7	8.6	4.4	1.9	37.8

Note: (1) Figures cover the Atlanta-Sandy Springs-Roswell, GA Metropolitan Statistical Area—see Appendix B for areas included
Source: U.S. Census Bureau, 2013-2017 American Community Survey 5-Year Estimates

Gender

Area	Males	Females	Males per 100 Females
City	228,038	237,192	96.1
MSA[1]	2,759,925	2,941,065	93.8
U.S.	158,018,753	162,985,654	97.0

Note: (1) Figures cover the Atlanta-Sandy Springs-Roswell, GA Metropolitan Statistical Area—see Appendix B for areas included
Source: U.S. Census Bureau, 2013-2017 American Community Survey 5-Year Estimates

Religious Groups by Family

Area	Catholic	Baptist	Non-Den.	Methodist[2]	Lutheran	LDS[3]	Pentecostal	Presbyterian[4]	Muslim[5]	Judaism
MSA[1]	7.5	17.5	6.9	7.9	0.5	0.8	2.6	1.8	0.8	0.6
U.S.	19.1	9.3	4.0	4.0	2.3	2.0	1.9	1.6	0.8	0.7

Note: Figures are the number of adherents as a percentage of the total population; (1) Figures cover the Atlanta-Sandy Springs-Roswell, GA Metropolitan Statistical Area—see Appendix B for areas included; (2) Methodist/Pietist; (3) Latter Day Saints; (4) Reformed; (5) Figures are estimates
Source: Association of Statisticians of American Religious Bodies, 2010 U.S. Religion Census: Religious Congregations & Membership Study

Religious Groups by Tradition

Area	Catholic	Evangelical Protestant	Mainline Protestant	Other Tradition	Black Protestant	Orthodox
MSA[1]	7.5	26.1	9.8	2.9	3.2	0.3
U.S.	19.1	16.2	7.3	4.3	1.6	0.3

Note: Figures are the number of adherents as a percentage of the total population; (1) Figures cover the Atlanta-Sandy Springs-Roswell, GA Metropolitan Statistical Area—see Appendix B for areas included
Source: Association of Statisticians of American Religious Bodies, 2010 U.S. Religion Census: Religious Congregations & Membership Study

ECONOMY

Gross Metropolitan Product

Area	2016	2017	2018	2019	Rank[2]
MSA[1]	368.8	384.3	402.8	425.7	10

Note: Figures are in billions of dollars; (1) Figures cover the Atlanta-Sandy Springs-Roswell, GA Metropolitan Statistical Area—see Appendix B for areas included; (2) Rank is based on 2017 data and ranges from 1 to 381
Source: U.S. Conference of Mayors, U.S. Metro Economies: Economic Growth & Full Employment, June 2018

Economic Growth

Area	2017-2018 (%)	2019-2020 (%)	2021-2022 (%)
MSA[1]	2.8	2.8	2.0

Note: Figures are real gross metropolitan product (GMP) growth rates and represent average annual percent change; (1) Figures cover the Atlanta-Sandy Springs-Roswell, GA Metropolitan Statistical Area—see Appendix B for areas included
Source: U.S. Conference of Mayors, U.S. Metro Economies: Economic Growth & Full Employment, June 2018

Metropolitan Area Exports

Area	2012	2013	2014	2015	2016	2017	Rank[2]
MSA[1]	18,169.1	18,827.9	19,870.3	19,163.9	20,480.1	21,748.0	14

Note: Figures are in millions of dollars; (1) Figures cover the Atlanta-Sandy Springs-Roswell, GA Metropolitan Statistical Area—see Appendix B for areas included; (2) Rank is based on 2017 data and ranges from 1 to 387
Source: U.S. Department of Commerce, International Trade Administration, Office of Trade and Economic Analysis, Industry and Analysis, Exports by Metropolitan Area, extracted March 25, 2019

Building Permits

Area	Single-Family			Multi-Family			Total		
	2016	2017	Pct. Chg.	2016	2017	Pct. Chg.	2016	2017	Pct. Chg.
City	855	922	7.8	7,176	4,179	-41.8	8,031	5,101	-36.5
MSA[1]	23,100	24,973	8.1	13,257	8,859	-33.2	36,357	33,832	-6.9
U.S.	750,800	820,000	9.2	455,800	462,000	1.4	1,206,600	1,282,000	6.2

Note: (1) Figures cover the Atlanta-Sandy Springs-Roswell, GA Metropolitan Statistical Area—see Appendix B for areas included; Figures represent new, privately-owned housing units authorized (unadjusted data); All permit data are based on estimates with imputation
Source: U.S. Census Bureau, Manufacturing, Mining, and Construction Statistics, Building Permits, 2016, 2017

Bankruptcy Filings

Area	Business Filings			Nonbusiness Filings		
	2017	2018	% Chg.	2017	2018	% Chg.
Fulton County	108	165	52.8	4,600	4,465	-2.9
U.S.	23,157	22,232	-4.0	765,863	751,186	-1.9

Note: Business filings include Chapter 7, Chapter 11, Chapter 12, and Chapter 13; Nonbusiness filings include Chapter 7, Chapter 11, and Chapter 13
Source: Administrative Office of the U.S. Courts, Business and Nonbusiness Bankruptcy, County Cases Commenced by Chapter of the Bankruptcy Code, During the 12-Month Period Ending December 31, 2017 and Business and Nonbusiness Bankruptcy, County Cases Commenced by Chapter of the Bankruptcy Code, During the 12-Month Period Ending December 31, 2018

Housing Vacancy Rates

Area	Gross Vacancy Rate[2] (%)			Year-Round Vacancy Rate[3] (%)			Rental Vacancy Rate[4] (%)			Homeowner Vacancy Rate[5] (%)		
	2016	2017	2018	2016	2017	2018	2016	2017	2018	2016	2017	2018
MSA[1]	9.7	8.9	7.8	9.4	8.4	7.4	6.2	7.0	6.6	1.6	1.0	1.1
U.S.	12.8	12.7	12.3	9.9	9.9	9.7	6.9	7.2	6.9	1.7	1.6	1.5

Note: (1) Figures cover the Atlanta-Sandy Springs-Roswell, GA Metropolitan Statistical Area—see Appendix B for areas included; (2) The percentage of the total housing inventory that is vacant; (3) The percentage of the housing inventory (excluding seasonal units) that is year-round vacant; (4) The percentage of rental inventory that is vacant for rent; (5) The percentage of homeowner inventory that is vacant for sale
Source: U.S. Census Bureau, Housing Vacancies and Homeownership Annual Statistics: 2016, 2017, 2018

INCOME

Income

Area	Per Capita ($)	Median Household ($)	Average Household ($)
City	40,595	51,701	92,186
MSA[1]	31,784	61,733	85,937
U.S.	31,177	57,652	81,283

Note: (1) Figures cover the Atlanta-Sandy Springs-Roswell, GA Metropolitan Statistical Area—see Appendix B for areas included
Source: U.S. Census Bureau, 2013-2017 American Community Survey 5-Year Estimates

Household Income Distribution

Area	Percent of Households Earning							
	Under $15,000	$15,000 -$24,999	$25,000 -$34,999	$35,000 -$49,999	$50,000 -$74,999	$75,000 -$99,999	$100,000 -$149,999	$150,000 and up
City	17.0	10.6	9.1	11.8	15.1	9.6	11.5	15.3
MSA[1]	9.8	8.6	9.1	13.1	18.3	12.8	14.9	13.4
U.S.	11.6	9.8	9.5	13.0	17.7	12.3	14.1	12.1

Note: (1) Figures cover the Atlanta-Sandy Springs-Roswell, GA Metropolitan Statistical Area—see Appendix B for areas included
Source: U.S. Census Bureau, 2013-2017 American Community Survey 5-Year Estimates

Poverty Rate

Area	All Ages	Under 18 Years Old	18 to 64 Years Old	65 Years and Over
City	22.4	35.7	19.8	15.0
MSA[1]	13.9	20.1	12.4	8.9
U.S.	14.6	20.3	13.7	9.3

Note: Figures are percentage of people whose income during the past 12 months was below the poverty level; (1) Figures cover the Atlanta-Sandy Springs-Roswell, GA Metropolitan Statistical Area—see Appendix B for areas included
Source: U.S. Census Bureau, 2013-2017 American Community Survey 5-Year Estimates

EMPLOYMENT

Labor Force and Employment

Area	Civilian Labor Force			Workers Employed		
	Dec. 2017	Dec. 2018	% Chg.	Dec. 2017	Dec. 2018	% Chg.
City	252,504	255,674	1.3	240,597	245,200	1.9
MSA[1]	3,056,722	3,097,603	1.3	2,931,140	2,986,890	1.9
U.S.	159,880,000	162,510,000	1.6	153,602,000	156,481,000	1.9

Note: Data is not seasonally adjusted and covers workers 16 years of age and older; (1) Figures cover the Atlanta-Sandy Springs-Roswell, GA Metropolitan Statistical Area—see Appendix B for areas included
Source: Bureau of Labor Statistics, Local Area Unemployment Statistics

Unemployment Rate

Area	2018											
	Jan.	Feb.	Mar.	Apr.	May	Jun.	Jul.	Aug.	Sep.	Oct.	Nov.	Dec.
City	5.0	4.9	4.5	4.0	3.9	4.5	4.3	4.1	3.5	3.8	3.6	4.1
MSA[1]	4.3	4.3	4.0	3.6	3.4	4.0	3.8	3.6	3.1	3.4	3.2	3.6
U.S.	4.5	4.4	4.1	3.7	3.6	4.2	4.1	3.9	3.6	3.5	3.5	3.7

Note: Data is not seasonally adjusted and covers workers 16 years of age and older; (1) Figures cover the Atlanta-Sandy Springs-Roswell, GA Metropolitan Statistical Area—see Appendix B for areas included
Source: Bureau of Labor Statistics, Local Area Unemployment Statistics

Average Wages

Occupation	$/Hr.	Occupation	$/Hr.
Accountants and Auditors	37.70	Maids and Housekeeping Cleaners	10.30
Automotive Mechanics	21.20	Maintenance and Repair Workers	18.70
Bookkeepers	20.40	Marketing Managers	70.30
Carpenters	23.90	Nuclear Medicine Technologists	38.10
Cashiers	10.20	Nurses, Licensed Practical	21.20
Clerks, General Office	15.40	Nurses, Registered	35.20
Clerks, Receptionists/Information	14.00	Nursing Assistants	13.40
Clerks, Shipping/Receiving	16.70	Packers and Packagers, Hand	11.80
Computer Programmers	46.20	Physical Therapists	41.00
Computer Systems Analysts	44.90	Postal Service Mail Carriers	24.60
Computer User Support Specialists	26.30	Real Estate Brokers	28.00
Cooks, Restaurant	12.00	Retail Salespersons	12.70
Dentists	78.40	Sales Reps., Exc. Tech./Scientific	31.60
Electrical Engineers	42.70	Sales Reps., Tech./Scientific	37.50
Electricians	25.70	Secretaries, Exc. Legal/Med./Exec.	17.40
Financial Managers	74.00	Security Guards	13.80
First-Line Supervisors/Managers, Sales	22.70	Surgeons	126.80
Food Preparation Workers	10.60	Teacher Assistants*	11.20
General and Operations Managers	59.00	Teachers, Elementary School*	27.50
Hairdressers/Cosmetologists	13.30	Teachers, Secondary School*	28.30
Internists, General	49.80	Telemarketers	12.10
Janitors and Cleaners	12.00	Truck Drivers, Heavy/Tractor-Trailer	21.20
Landscaping/Groundskeeping Workers	14.30	Truck Drivers, Light/Delivery Svcs.	18.40
Lawyers	65.80	Waiters and Waitresses	9.80

Note: Wage data covers the Atlanta-Sandy Springs-Roswell, GA Metropolitan Statistical Area—see Appendix B for areas included; (*) Hourly wages for elementary/secondary school teachers and teacher assistants were calculated by the editors from annual wage data based on a 40 hour work week; n/a not available.
Source: Bureau of Labor Statistics, Metro Area Occupational Employment & Wage Estimates, May 2018

Employment by Occupation

Occupation Classification	City (%)	MSA[1] (%)	U.S. (%)
Management, Business, Science, and Arts	52.1	40.4	37.4
Natural Resources, Construction, and Maintenance	3.0	7.9	8.9
Production, Transportation, and Material Moving	7.1	11.1	12.2
Sales and Office	22.9	25.0	23.5
Service	14.9	15.6	18.0

Note: Figures cover employed civilians 16 years of age and older; (1) Figures cover the Atlanta-Sandy Springs-Roswell, GA Metropolitan Statistical Area—see Appendix B for areas included
Source: U.S. Census Bureau, 2013-2017 American Community Survey 5-Year Estimates

Employment by Industry

Sector	MSA[1]		U.S.
	Number of Employees	Percent of Total	Percent of Total
Construction	129,900	4.6	4.8
Education and Health Services	361,200	12.7	15.9
Financial Activities	175,500	6.2	5.7
Government	339,000	12.0	15.1
Information	97,500	3.4	1.9
Leisure and Hospitality	301,300	10.6	10.7
Manufacturing	172,900	6.1	8.5
Mining and Logging	1,600	0.1	0.5
Other Services	96,800	3.4	3.9
Professional and Business Services	539,300	19.0	14.1
Retail Trade	300,900	10.6	10.8
Transportation, Warehousing, and Utilities	164,000	5.8	4.2
Wholesale Trade	155,400	5.5	3.9

Note: Figures are non-farm employment as of December 2018. Figures are not seasonally adjusted and include workers 16 years of age and older; (1) Figures cover the Atlanta-Sandy Springs-Roswell, GA Metropolitan Statistical Area—see Appendix B for areas included
Source: Bureau of Labor Statistics, Current Employment Statistics, Employment, Hours, and Earnings

Occupations with Greatest Projected Employment Growth: 2018 – 2020

Occupation[1]	2018 Employment	2020 Projected Employment	Numeric Employment Change	Percent Employment Change
Combined Food Preparation and Serving Workers, Including Fast Food	115,500	124,220	8,720	7.5
Laborers and Freight, Stock, and Material Movers, Hand	119,650	127,750	8,100	6.8
General and Operations Managers	96,530	101,830	5,300	5.5
Waiters and Waitresses	81,500	86,240	4,740	5.8
Construction Laborers	40,040	44,600	4,560	11.4
Customer Service Representatives	103,570	107,780	4,210	4.1
Retail Salespersons	141,820	146,020	4,200	3.0
Heavy and Tractor-Trailer Truck Drivers	58,780	62,290	3,510	6.0
Janitors and Cleaners, Except Maids and Housekeeping Cleaners	56,440	59,660	3,220	5.7
Office Clerks, General	88,900	91,910	3,010	3.4

Note: Projections cover Georgia; (1) Sorted by numeric employment change
Source: www.projectionscentral.com, State Occupational Projections, 2018–2020 Short-Term Projections

Fastest Growing Occupations: 2018 – 2020

Occupation[1]	2018 Employment	2020 Projected Employment	Numeric Employment Change	Percent Employment Change
Helpers—Pipelayers, Plumbers, Pipefitters, and Steamfitters	2,220	2,640	420	18.9
Helpers—Brickmasons, Blockmasons, Stonemasons, and Tile and Marble Setters	270	320	50	18.5
Mechanical Door Repairers	490	580	90	18.4
Structural Iron and Steel Workers	1,410	1,660	250	17.7
Elevator Installers and Repairers	1,190	1,400	210	17.6
Costume Attendants	290	340	50	17.2
Helpers—Electricians	4,070	4,760	690	17.0
Glaziers	1,130	1,320	190	16.8
Fence Erectors	550	640	90	16.4
Cement Masons and Concrete Finishers	3,190	3,710	520	16.3

Note: Projections cover Georgia; (1) Sorted by percent employment change and excludes occupations with numeric employment change less than 50
Source: www.projectionscentral.com, State Occupational Projections, 2018–2020 Short-Term Projections

TAXES

State Corporate Income Tax Rates

State	Tax Rate (%)	Income Brackets ($)	Num. of Brackets	Financial Institution Tax Rate (%)[a]	Federal Income Tax Ded.
Georgia	5.75	Flat rate	1	5.75	No

Note: Tax rates as of January 1, 2019; (a) Rates listed are the corporate income tax rate applied to financial institutions or excise taxes based on income. Some states have other taxes based upon the value of deposits or shares.
Source: Federation of Tax Administrators, Range of State Corporate Income Tax Rates, January 1, 2019

State Individual Income Tax Rates

State	Tax Rate (%)	Income Brackets ($)	Personal Exemptions ($)			Standard Ded. ($)	
			Single	Married	Depend.	Single	Married
Georgia	1.0 - 5.75	750 - 7,001 (i)	2,700	7,400	3,000	4,600	6,000

Note: Tax rates as of January 1, 2019; Local- and county-level taxes are not included; n/a not applicable; Federal income tax is not deductible on state income tax returns; (i) The Georgia income brackets reported are for single individuals. For married couples filing jointly, the same tax rates apply to income brackets ranging from $1,000, to $10,000.
Source: Federation of Tax Administrators, State Individual Income Tax Rates, January 1, 2019

Various State Sales and Excise Tax Rates

State	State Sales Tax (%)	Gasoline[1] (¢/gal.)	Cigarette[2] ($/pack)	Spirits[3] ($/gal.)	Wine[4] ($/gal.)	Beer[5] ($/gal.)	Recreational Marijuana (%)
Georgia	4	35.28	0.37	3.79 (f)	1.51 (l)	0.48 (q)(r)	Not legal

Note: All tax rates as of January 1, 2019; (1) The American Petroleum Institute has developed a methodology for determining the average tax rate on a gallon of fuel. Rates may include any of the following: excise taxes, environmental fees, storage tank fees, other fees or taxes, general sales tax, and local taxes. In states where gasoline is subject to the general sales tax, or where the fuel tax is based on the average sale price, the average rate determined by API is sensitive to changes in the price of gasoline. States that fully or partially apply general sales taxes to gasoline: CA, CO, GA, IL, IN, MI, NY; (2) The federal excise tax of $1.0066 per pack and local taxes are not included; (3) Rates are those applicable to off-premise sales of 40% alcohol by volume (a.b.v.) distilled spirits in 750ml containers. Local excise taxes are excluded; (4) Rates are those applicable to off-premise sales of 11% a.b.v. non-carbonated wine in 750ml containers; (5) Rates are those applicable to off-premise sales of 4.7% a.b.v. beer in 12 ounce containers; (f) Different rates also applicable according to alcohol content, place of production, size of container, or place purchased (on- or off-premise or onboard airlines); (l) Different rates also applicable to alcohol content, place of production, size of container, place purchased (on- or off-premise or on board airlines) or type of wine (carbonated, vermouth, etc.); (q) Different rates also applicable according to alcohol content, place of production, size of container, or place purchased (on- or off-premise or onboard airlines); (r) Includes statewide local rate in Alabama ($0.52) and Georgia ($0.53).
Source: Tax Foundation, 2019 Facts & Figures: How Does Your State Compare?

State Business Tax Climate Index Rankings

State	Overall Rank	Corporate Tax Rank	Individual Income Tax Rank	Sales Tax Rank	Unemployment Insurance Tax Rank	Property Tax Rank
Georgia	33	8	38	29	38	24

Note: The index is a measure of how each state's tax laws affect economic performance. The lower the rank, the more favorable a state's tax system is for business. States without a given tax are given a ranking of 1. The scores/rankings for the District of Columbia do not affect other states. The 2019 index represents the tax climate as of July 1, 2018.
Source: Tax Foundation, State Business Tax Climate Index 2019

COMMERCIAL REAL ESTATE

Office Market

Market Area	Inventory (sq. ft.)	Vacancy Rate (%)	Under Construction (sq. ft.)	YTD Net Absorption (sq. ft.)	Total Average Asking Rent ($/sq. ft./year)
Atlanta	147,498,301	17.3	3,957,702	-41,870	27.86
National	4,905,867,938	13.1	83,553,714	45,846,470	28.46

Source: Newmark Grubb Knight Frank, National Office Market Report, 4th Quarter 2018

Industrial/Warehouse/R&D Market

Market Area	Inventory (sq. ft.)	Vacancy Rate (%)	Under Construction (sq. ft.)	YTD Net Absorption (sq. ft.)	Total Average Asking Rent ($/sq. ft./year)
Atlanta	603,752,177	6.8	20,776,956	19,639,897	5.37
National	14,796,839,085	5.0	262,662,294	238,014,726	7.16

Source: Newmark Grubb Knight Frank, National Industrial Market Report, 4th Quarter 2018

COMMERCIAL UTILITIES

Typical Monthly Electric Bills

Area	Commercial Service ($/month)		Industrial Service ($/month)	
	1,500 kWh	40 kW demand 14,000 kWh	1,000 kW demand 200,000 kWh	50,000 kW demand 32,500,000 kWh
City	258	1,598	31,467	2,254,556
Average[1]	203	1,619	25,886	2,540,077

Note: Figures are based on annualized rates; (1) Average based on 187 utilities surveyed
Source: Edison Electric Institute, Typical Bills and Average Rates Report, Summer 2018

TRANSPORTATION

Means of Transportation to Work

Area	Car/Truck/Van Drove Alone	Car-pooled	Public Transportation Bus	Subway	Railroad	Bicycle	Walked	Other Means	Worked at Home
City	68.7	6.9	6.8	3.1	0.2	0.9	4.4	1.5	7.6
MSA[1]	77.6	9.8	2.1	0.8	0.1	0.2	1.3	1.5	6.5
U.S.	76.4	9.2	2.5	1.9	0.6	0.6	2.7	1.3	4.7

Note: Figures are percentages and cover workers 16 years of age and older; (1) Figures cover the Atlanta-Sandy Springs-Roswell, GA Metropolitan Statistical Area—see Appendix B for areas included
Source: U.S. Census Bureau, 2013-2017 American Community Survey 5-Year Estimates

Travel Time to Work

Area	Less Than 10 Minutes	10 to 19 Minutes	20 to 29 Minutes	30 to 44 Minutes	45 to 59 Minutes	60 to 89 Minutes	90 Minutes or More
City	7.2	29.6	27.8	20.5	7.2	4.9	2.8
MSA[1]	7.3	22.8	20.0	24.4	12.2	9.9	3.5
U.S.	12.7	28.9	20.9	20.5	8.1	6.2	2.7

Note: Note: Figures are percentages and include workers 16 years old and over; (1) Figures cover the Atlanta-Sandy Springs-Roswell, GA Metropolitan Statistical Area—see Appendix B for areas included
Source: U.S. Census Bureau, 2013-2017 American Community Survey 5-Year Estimates

Freeway Travel Time Index

Area	1985	1990	1995	2000	2005	2010	2014
Urban Area Rank[1,2]	24	21	13	19	21	25	25
Urban Area Index[1]	1.11	1.15	1.22	1.24	1.26	1.23	1.24
Average Index[3]	1.09	1.11	1.14	1.17	1.20	1.19	1.20

Note: Freeway Travel Time Index—the ratio of travel time in the peak period to the travel time at free-flow conditions. For example, a value of 1.30 indicates a 20-minute free-flow trip takes 26 minutes in the peak (20 minutes x 1.30 = 26 minutes); (1) Covers the Atlanta GA urban area; (2) Rank is based on 101 urban areas (#1 = highest travel time index); (3) Average of 101 urban areas
Source: Texas Transportation Institute, 2015 Urban Mobility Scorecard, August 2015

Freeway Commuter Stress Index

Area	1985	1990	1995	2000	2005	2010	2014
Urban Area Rank[1,2]	24	22	13	16	18	22	23
Urban Area Index[1]	1.18	1.22	1.29	1.32	1.33	1.31	1.32
Average Index[3]	1.13	1.16	1.19	1.22	1.25	1.24	1.25

Note: The Freeway Commuter Stress Index is the same as the Freeway Travel Time Index (see table above) except that it includes only the travel in the peak directions during the peak periods; the TTI includes travel in all directions during the peak period. Thus, the CSI is more indicative of the work trip experienced by each commuter on a daily basis; (1) Covers the Atlanta GA urban area; (2) Rank is based on 101 urban areas (#1 = highest travel time index); (3) Average of 101 urban areas
Source: Texas Transportation Institute, 2015 Urban Mobility Scorecard, August 2015

Public Transportation

Agency Name / Mode of Transportation	Vehicles Operated in Maximum Service[1]	Annual Unlinked Passenger Trips[2] (in thous.)	Annual Passenger Miles[3] (in thous.)
Metropolitan Atlanta Rapid Transit Authority (MARTA)			
Bus (directly operated)	466	57,460.3	251,234.9
Demand Response (purchased transportation)	169	687.5	9,343.8
Heavy Rail (directly operated)	210	68,280.9	468,811.4

Note: (1) The number of revenue vehicles operated by the given mode and type of service to meet the annual maximum service requirement. This is the revenue vehicle count during the peak season of the year; on the week and day that maximum service is provided. Vehicles operated in maximum service (VOMS) exclude atypical days and one-time special events; (2) The number of passengers who boarded public transportation vehicles. Passengers are counted each time they board a vehicle no matter how many vehicles they use to travel from their origin to their destination. (3) The sum of the distances ridden by all passengers during the entire fiscal year.
Source: Federal Transit Administration, National Transit Database, 2017

Air Transportation

Airport Name and Code / Type of Service	Passenger Airlines[1]	Passenger Enplanements	Freight Carriers[2]	Freight (lbs)
Hartsfield-Jackson Atlanta International Airport (ATL)				
Domestic service (U.S. carriers - 2018)	33	45,727,607	18	283,687,830
International service (U.S. carriers - 2017)	9	4,915,201	8	84,061,641

Note: (1) Includes all U.S.-based major, minor and commuter airlines that carried at least one passenger during the year; (2) Includes all U.S.-based airlines and freight carriers that transported at least one pound of freight during the year.
Source: Bureau of Transportation Statistics, The Intermodal Transportation Database, Air Carriers: T-100 Domestic Market (U.S. Carriers), 2018; Bureau of Transportation Statistics, The Intermodal Transportation Database, Air Carriers: T-100 International Market (U.S. Carriers), 2017

Other Transportation Statistics

Major Highways:	I-20; I-75; I-85
Amtrak Service:	Yes
Major Waterways/Ports:	None

Source: Amtrak.com; Google Maps

BUSINESSES

Major Business Headquarters

Company Name	Industry	Rankings	
		Fortune[1]	Forbes[2]
Coca-Cola	Beverages	87	-
Cox Enterprises	Media	-	15
Delta Air Lines	Airlines	75	-
First Data	Financial Data Services	254	-
Genuine Parts	Wholesalers: Diversified	177	-
HD Supply Holdings	Wholesalers: Diversified	430	-
Holder Construction	Construction	-	126
Home Depot	Specialty Retailers: Other	23	-
Intercontinental Exchange	Securities	477	-
Newell Brands	Home Equipment, Furnishings	196	-
PulteGroup	Homebuilders	341	-
RaceTrac Petroleum	Convenience Stores & Gas Stations	-	39
Southern	Utilities: Gas and Electric	126	-
SunTrust Banks	Commercial Banks	303	-
UPS	Mail, Package, and Freight	44	-
Veritiv	Wholesalers: Diversified	346	-

Note: (1) Companies that produce a 10-K are ranked 1 to 500 based on 2017 revenue; (2) All private companies with at least $2 billion in annual revenue through the end of their most current fiscal year are ranked 1 to 229; companies listed are headquartered in the city; dashes indicate no ranking
Source: Fortune, "Fortune 500," June 2018; Forbes, "America's Largest Private Companies," 2018 Rankings

Fast-Growing Businesses

According to *Inc.*, Atlanta is home to 14 of America's 500 fastest-growing private companies: **HealPros** (#90); **Thought Logic Consulting** (#93); **Recleim** (#101); **QASymphony** (#230); **IT**

Works Recruitment (#250); **Private Label Extensions** (#278); **Springbot** (#301); **PeachCap** (#320); **Birdsey Construction Management** (#326); **Ally Commerce** (#338); **IBOX Global** (#357); **Aspirent** (#361); **Crisp Video Group** (#432); **Gather** (#442). Criteria: must be an independent, privately-held, for-profit, U.S. corporation, proprietorship or partnership as of December 31, 2017; revenues must be at least $100,000 in 2014 and $2 million in 2017; must have four-year operating/sales history. Holding companies, regulated banks, and utilities were excluded. *Inc., "America's 500 Fastest-Growing Private Companies," 2018*

According to *Fortune*, Atlanta is home to two of the 100 fastest-growing companies in the world: **Marine Products** (#73); **Gray Television** (#93). Companies were ranked by their revenue growth rate; their EPS growth rate; and their three-year annualized total return to investors for the period ending June 30, 2018. Criteria for inclusion: a company, foreign or domestic, must trade on a major U.S. stock exchange; must file quarterly reports with the SEC; must have a minimum market capitalization of $250 million; must have a stock price of at least $5 on June 30, 2018; must have been trading continuously since June 30, 2015; must have revenue and net income for the four quarters ended on or before April 30, 2018, of at least $50 million and $10 million, respectively; and must have posted a compound annual growth in revenue and earnings per share of at least 15% annually over the three years ending on or before April 30, 2018. Real estate investment trusts, limited-liability companies, limited parterships, business development companies, closed-end investment firms, companies about to be acquired, and companies that lost money in the quarter ending April 30, 2018 were excluded. *Fortune, "100 Fastest-Growing Companies," 2018*

According to *Initiative for a Competitive Inner City (ICIC)*, Atlanta is home to one of America's 100 fastest-growing "inner city" companies: **Caduceus Healthcare** (#15). Criteria for inclusion: company must be headquartered in or have 51 percent or more of its physical operations in an economically distressed urban area; must be an independent, for-profit corporation, partnership or proprietorship; must have 10 or more employees and have a five-year sales history that includes sales of at least $200,000 in the base year and at least $1 million in the current year with no decrease in sales over the two most recent years. Companies were ranked overall by revenue growth over the five-year period between 2013 and 2017. *Initiative for a Competitive Inner City (ICIC), "Inner City 100 Companies," 2018*

According to Deloitte, Atlanta is home to 14 of North America's 500 fastest-growing high-technology companies: **QASymphony** (#67); **Springbot** (#83); **MacStadium** (#182); **CallRail** (#183); **Kabbage** (#209); **Sharecare** (#213); **SalesLoft** (#216); **Phobio** (#221); **PureCars** (#234); **Urjanet** (#271); **QGenda** (#302); **Parkmobile** (#382); **Wahoo Fitness** (#412); **ClickDimensions** (#422). Companies are ranked by percentage growth in revenue over a four-year period. Criteria for inclusion: company must be headquartered within North America; must own proprietary intellectual property or technology that is sold to customers in products that contributes to a significant portion of the company's operating revenue; must have been in business for a minumum of four years with 2014 operating revenues of at least $50,000 USD/CD and 2017 operating revenues of at least $5 million USD/CD. *Deloitte, 2018 Technology Fast 500*™

Minority Business Opportunity

Atlanta is home to three companies which are on the *Black Enterprise* Industrial/Service list (100 largest companies based on gross sales): **H. J. Russell & Co.** (#20); **Jackmont Hospitality** (#24); **B & S Electric Supply Co.** (#57). Criteria: operational in previous calendar year; at least 51% black-owned and manufactures/owns the product it sells or provides industrial or consumer services. Brokerages, real estate firms and firms that provide professional services are not eligible. *Black Enterprise, B.E. 100s, 2018*

Atlanta is home to one company which is on the *Black Enterprise* Auto Dealer list (45 largest dealers based on gross sales): **The Baran Co.** (#18). Criteria: company must be operational in previous calendar year and be at least 51% black-owned. *Black Enterprise, B.E. 100s, 2018*

Atlanta is home to one company which is on the *Black Enterprise* Bank list (15 largest banks based on total assets, capital, deposits and loans, including mortgage-backed securities for the calendar year): **Citizens Bancshares Corp. (Citzens Trust Bank)** (#4). Only commercial banks or savings and loans that are classified by the Federal Reserve as black institutions and have been fully operational for the previous calendar year were considered. *Black Enterprise, B.E. 100s, 2018*

Atlanta is home to three companies which are on the *Hispanic Business* 500 list (500 largest U.S. Hispanic-owned companies based on revenue): **Precision 2000** (#293); **Caduceus Healthcare** (#406); **GSB Architects** (#468). Companies included must show at least 51 percent ownership by Hispanic U.S. citizens, and must maintain headquarters in one of the 50 states or Washington, D.C. *Hispanic Business, "Hispanic Business 500," June 20, 2013*

Minority- and Women-Owned Businesses

Group	All Firms		Firms with Paid Employees			
	Firms	Sales ($000)	Firms	Sales ($000)	Employees	Payroll ($000)
AIAN[1]	447	17,570	34	6,892	61	2,031
Asian	2,708	1,912,091	1,198	1,793,100	9,858	264,816
Black	25,457	1,478,681	1,110	1,022,746	8,749	302,904
Hispanic	1,865	887,510	207	810,240	3,557	97,876
NHOPI[2]	n/a	n/a	n/a	n/a	n/a	n/a
Women	28,172	3,824,959	2,886	3,231,346	19,400	786,560
All Firms	64,593	124,166,628	13,871	121,884,769	393,117	25,192,620

Note: Figures cover firms located in the city; minority- and women-owned business are defined as firms in which the corresponding group own 51% or more of the stock or equity of the company; (1) American Indian and Alaska Native; (2) Native Hawaiian and Other Pacific Islander; n/a not available
Source: U.S. Census Bureau, 2012 Economic Census, Survey of Business Owners

HOTELS & CONVENTION CENTERS

Hotels, Motels and Vacation Rentals

Area	5 Star		4 Star		3 Star		2 Star		1 Star		Not Rated	
	Num.	Pct.[3]	Num.	Pct.[3]	Num.	Pct.[3]	Num.	Pct.[3]	Num.	Pct.[3]	Num.	Pct.[3]
City[1]	5	0.3	61	3.4	216	12.0	234	13.0	14	0.8	1,272	70.6
Total[2]	286	0.4	5,236	7.1	16,715	22.6	10,259	13.9	293	0.4	41,056	55.6

Note: (1) Figures cover Atlanta and vicinity; (2) Figures cover all 100 cities in this book; (3) Percentage of hotels which have a given star rating; Star ratings are determined by expedia.com and offer an indication of the general quality of a particular hotel.
Source: www.expedia.com, April 3, 2019

Major Convention Centers

Name	Overall Space (sq. ft.)	Exhibit Space (sq. ft.)	Meeting Space (sq. ft.)	Meeting Rooms
AmericasMart Atlanta	n/a	441,000	n/a	38
Cobb Galleria Centre	320,000	144,000	20,000	20
Georgia International Convention Center	n/a	150,000	16,000	n/a
Georgia World Congress Center	3,900,000	1,400,000	n/a	106

Note: Table includes convention centers located in the Atlanta-Sandy Springs-Roswell, GA metro area; n/a not available
Source: Original research

Living Environment

COST OF LIVING

Cost of Living Index

Composite Index	Groceries	Housing	Utilities	Trans-portation	Health Care	Misc. Goods/ Services
102.0	99.6	106.6	87.1	99.8	108.9	102.6

Note: The Cost of Living Index measures regional differences in the cost of consumer goods and services, excluding taxes and non-consumer expenditures, for professional and managerial households in the top income quintile. It is based on more than 50,000 prices covering almost 60 different items for which prices are collected three times a year by chambers of commerce, economic development organizations or university applied economic centers in each participating urban area. The numbers shown should be read as a percentage above or below the national average of 100. For example, a value of 115.4 in the groceries column indicates that grocery prices are 15.4% higher than the national average. Small differences in the index numbers should not be interpreted as significant; Figures cover the Atlanta GA urban area.
Source: The Council for Community and Economic Research, ACCRA Cost of Living Index, 2018

Grocery Prices

Area[1]	T-Bone Steak ($/pound)	Frying Chicken ($/pound)	Whole Milk ($/half gal.)	Eggs ($/dozen)	Orange Juice ($/64 oz.)	Coffee ($/11.5 oz.)
City[2]	12.21	1.39	1.90	1.98	3.50	4.77
Avg.	11.35	1.42	1.94	1.81	3.52	4.35
Min.	7.45	0.92	0.80	0.75	2.72	3.06
Max.	15.05	2.76	4.18	4.00	5.36	8.20

Note: (1) Values for the local area are compared with the average, minimum and maximum values for all 291 areas in the Cost of Living Index; (2) Figures cover the Atlanta GA urban area; T-Bone Steak (price per pound); Frying Chicken (price per pound, whole fryer); Whole Milk (half gallon carton); Eggs (price per dozen, Grade A, large); Orange Juice (64 oz. Tropicana or Florida Natural); Coffee (11.5 oz. can, vacuum-packed, Maxwell House, Hills Bros, or Folgers).
Source: The Council for Community and Economic Research, ACCRA Cost of Living Index, 2018

Housing and Utility Costs

Area[1]	New Home Price ($)	Apartment Rent ($/month)	All Electric ($/month)	Part Electric ($/month)	Other Energy ($/month)	Telephone ($/month)
City[2]	348,121	1,334	-	91.36	36.83	179.50
Avg.	347,000	1,087	165.93	100.16	67.73	178.70
Min.	200,468	500	93.58	25.64	26.78	163.10
Max.	1,901,222	4,888	388.65	246.86	332.81	197.70

Note: (1) Values for the local area are compared with the average, minimum and maximum values for all 291 areas in the Cost of Living Index; (2) Figures cover the Atlanta GA urban area; New Home Price (2,400 sf living area, 8,000 sf lot, in urban area with full utilities); Apartment Rent (950 sf 2 bedroom/1.5 or 2 bath, unfurnished, excluding all utilities except water); All Electric (average monthly cost for an all-electric home); Part Electric (average monthly cost for a part-electric home); Other Energy (average monthly cost for natural gas, fuel oil, coal, wood, and any other forms of energy except electricity); Telephone (price includes the base monthly rate plus taxes and fees for three lines of mobile phone service).
Source: The Council for Community and Economic Research, ACCRA Cost of Living Index, 2018

Health Care, Transportation, and Other Costs

Area[1]	Doctor ($/visit)	Dentist ($/visit)	Optometrist ($/visit)	Gasoline ($/gallon)	Beauty Salon ($/visit)	Men's Shirt ($)
City[2]	110.08	120.36	103.60	2.64	44.77	28.68
Avg.	110.71	95.11	103.74	2.61	37.48	32.03
Min.	33.60	62.55	54.63	1.89	17.00	11.44
Max.	195.97	153.93	225.79	3.59	71.88	58.64

Note: (1) Values for the local area are compared with the average, minimum and maximum values for all 291 areas in the Cost of Living Index; (2) Figures cover the Atlanta GA urban area; Doctor (general practitioners routine exam of an established patient); Dentist (adult teeth cleaning and periodic oral examination); Optometrist (full vision eye exam for established adult patient); Gasoline (one gallon regular unleaded, national brand, including all taxes, cash price at self-service pump if available); Beauty Salon (woman's shampoo, trim, and blow-dry); Men's Shirt (cotton/polyester dress shirt, pinpoint weave, long sleeves).
Source: The Council for Community and Economic Research, ACCRA Cost of Living Index, 2018

HOUSING

House Price Index (HPI)

Area	National Ranking[2]	Quarterly Change (%)	One-Year Change (%)	Five-Year Change (%)
MSA[1]	35	0.03	9.25	49.09
U.S.[3]	—	1.12	5.73	32.81

Note: The HPI is a weighted repeat sales index. It measures average price changes in repeat sales or refinancings on the same properties. This information is obtained by reviewing repeat mortgage transactions on single-family properties whose mortgages have been purchased or securitized by Fannie Mae or Freddie Mac in January 1975; (1) Figures cover the Atlanta-Sandy Springs-Roswell, GA Metropolitan Statistical Area—see Appendix B for areas included; (2) Rankings are based on annual percentage change for all metro areas containing at least 15,000 transactions over the last 10 years and ranges from 1 to 245; (3) figures based on a weighted average of Census Division estimates using a seasonally adjusted, purchase-only index; all figures are for the period ending December 31, 2018
Source: Federal Housing Finance Agency, House Price Index, February 26, 2019

Median Single-Family Home Prices

Area	2016	2017	2018p	Percent Change 2017 to 2018
MSA[1]	184.5	198.5	219.9	10.8
U.S. Average	235.5	248.8	261.6	5.1

Note: Figures are median sales prices of existing single-family homes in thousands of dollars; (p) preliminary; (1) Figures cover the Atlanta-Sandy Springs-Roswell, GA Metropolitan Statistical Area—see Appendix B for areas included
Source: National Association of Realtors, Median Sales Price of Existing Single-Family Homes for Metropolitan Areas, 4th Quarter 2018

Qualifying Income Based on Median Sales Price of Existing Single-Family Homes

Area	With 5% Down ($)	With 10% Down ($)	With 20% Down ($)
MSA[1]	52,812	50,032	44,473
U.S. Average	62,954	59,640	53,013

Note: Figures are preliminary; Qualifying income is based on a mortgage rate of 4.9%. Monthly principal and interest payment is limited to 25% of income; (1) Figures cover the Atlanta-Sandy Springs-Roswell, GA Metropolitan Statistical Area—see Appendix B for areas included
Source: National Association of Realtors, Qualifying Income Based on Median Sales Price of Existing Single-Family Homes for Metropolitan Areas, 4th Quarter 2018

Median Apartment Condo-Coop Home Prices

Area	2016	2017	2018p	Percent Change 2017 to 2018
MSA[1]	167.3	181.6	195.9	7.9
U.S. Average	220.7	234.3	241.0	2.9

Note: Figures are median sales prices of existing apartment condo-coop homes in thousands of dollars; (p) preliminary; (1) Figures cover the Atlanta-Sandy Springs-Roswell, GA Metropolitan Statistical Area—see Appendix B for areas included
Source: National Association of Realtors, Median Sales Price of Existing Apartment Condo-Coop Homes for Metropolitan Areas, 4th Quarter 2018

Home Value Distribution

Area	Under $50,000	$50,000 -$99,999	$100,000 -$149,999	$150,000 -$199,999	$200,000 -$299,999	$300,000 -$499,999	$500,000 -$999,999	$1,000,000 or more
City	7.4	13.6	10.8	11.3	15.9	16.9	16.5	7.6
MSA[1]	5.6	13.7	17.6	17.7	19.8	16.9	7.3	1.5
U.S.	8.3	13.9	14.7	14.6	18.7	17.3	9.7	2.7

Note: Figures are percentages and cover owner-occupied housing units; (1) Figures cover the Atlanta-Sandy Springs-Roswell, GA Metropolitan Statistical Area—see Appendix B for areas included
Source: U.S. Census Bureau, 2013-2017 American Community Survey 5-Year Estimates

Homeownership Rate

Area	2010 (%)	2011 (%)	2012 (%)	2013 (%)	2014 (%)	2015 (%)	2016 (%)	2017 (%)	2018 (%)
MSA[1]	67.2	65.8	62.1	61.6	61.6	61.7	61.5	62.4	64.0
U.S.	66.9	66.1	65.4	65.1	64.5	63.7	63.4	63.9	64.4

Note: (1) Figures cover the Atlanta-Sandy Springs-Roswell, GA Metropolitan Statistical Area—see Appendix B for areas included
Source: U.S. Census Bureau, Housing Vacancies and Homeownership Annual Statistics: 2010-2018

Year Housing Structure Built

Area	2010 or Later	2000 -2009	1990 -1999	1980 -1989	1970 -1979	1960 -1969	1950 -1959	1940 -1949	Before 1940	Median Year
City	4.7	23.5	10.6	7.8	8.7	13.6	11.5	6.3	13.2	1976
MSA[1]	3.3	25.7	22.3	17.9	12.9	7.9	4.9	2.0	3.1	1991
U.S.	3.2	14.5	14.0	13.6	15.5	10.8	10.5	5.1	12.9	1977

Note: Figures are percentages except for Median Year; Note: (1) Figures cover the Atlanta-Sandy Springs-Roswell, GA Metropolitan Statistical Area—see Appendix B for areas included
Source: U.S. Census Bureau, 2013-2017 American Community Survey 5-Year Estimates

Gross Monthly Rent

Area	Under $500	$500 -$999	$1,000 -$1,499	$1,500 -$1,999	$2,000 -$2,499	$2,500 -$2,999	$3,000 and up	Median ($)
City	11.9	35.1	34.0	13.6	3.4	1.1	1.0	1,037
MSA[1]	5.1	39.5	40.8	11.0	2.4	0.7	0.6	1,053
U.S.	10.5	41.1	28.7	11.7	4.5	1.8	1.7	982

Note: Figures are percentages except for Median; Gross rent is the contract rent plus the estimated average monthly cost of utilities (electricity, gas, and water and sewer) and fuels (oil, coal, kerosene, wood, etc.) if these are paid by the renter (or paid for the renter by someone else); (1) Figures cover the Atlanta-Sandy Springs-Roswell, GA Metropolitan Statistical Area—see Appendix B for areas included
Source: U.S. Census Bureau, 2013-2017 American Community Survey 5-Year Estimates

HEALTH

Health Risk Factors

Category	MSA[1] (%)	U.S. (%)
Adults aged 18–64 who have any kind of health care coverage	80.9	87.3
Adults who reported being in good or better health	84.0	82.4
Adults who have been told they have high blood cholesterol	29.2	33.0
Adults who have been told they have high blood pressure	30.8	32.3
Adults who are current smokers	14.9	17.1
Adults who currently use E-cigarettes	4.5	4.6
Adults who currently use chewing tobacco, snuff, or snus	3.7	4.0
Adults who are heavy drinkers[2]	5.3	6.3
Adults who are binge drinkers[3]	13.6	17.4
Adults who are overweight (BMI 25.0 - 29.9)	33.6	35.3
Adults who are obese (BMI 30.0 - 99.8)	29.9	31.3
Adults who participated in any physical activities in the past month	72.3	74.4
Adults who always or nearly always wears a seat belt	96.0	94.3

Note: (1) Figures cover the Atlanta-Sandy Springs-Roswell, GA Metropolitan Statistical Area—see Appendix B for areas included; (2) Heavy drinkers are classified as adult men having more than 14 drinks per week and adult women having more than 7 drinks per week; (3) Binge drinkers are classified as males having five or more drinks on one occasion or females having four or more drinks on one occasion
Source: Centers for Disease Control and Prevention, Behavioral Risk Factor Surveillance System, SMART: Selected Metropolitan Area Risk Trends, 2017

Acute and Chronic Health Conditions

Category	MSA[1] (%)	U.S. (%)
Adults who have ever been told they had a heart attack	3.0	4.2
Adults who have ever been told they have angina or coronary heart disease	2.8	3.9
Adults who have ever been told they had a stroke	3.2	3.0
Adults who have ever been told they have asthma	12.3	14.2
Adults who have ever been told they have arthritis	19.2	24.9
Adults who have ever been told they have diabetes[2]	10.4	10.5
Adults who have ever been told they had skin cancer	4.7	6.2
Adults who have ever been told they had any other types of cancer	5.4	7.1
Adults who have ever been told they have COPD	5.2	6.5
Adults who have ever been told they have kidney disease	2.5	3.0
Adults who have ever been told they have a form of depression	15.5	20.5

Note: (1) Figures cover the Atlanta-Sandy Springs-Roswell, GA Metropolitan Statistical Area—see Appendix B for areas included; (2) Figures do not include pregnancy-related, borderline, or pre-diabetes
Source: Centers for Disease Control and Prevention, Behavioral Risk Factor Surveillance System, SMART: Selected Metropolitan Area Risk Trends, 2017

Health Screening and Vaccination Rates

Category	MSA[1] (%)	U.S. (%)
Adults aged 65+ who have had flu shot within the past year	63.3	60.7
Adults aged 65+ who have ever had a pneumonia vaccination	72.8	75.4
Adults who have ever been tested for HIV	48.8	36.1
Adults who have ever had the shingles or zoster vaccine?	26.0	28.9
Adults who have had their blood cholesterol checked within the last five years	90.3	85.9

Note: n/a not available; (1) Figures cover the Atlanta-Sandy Springs-Roswell, GA Metropolitan Statistical Area—see Appendix B for areas included.
Source: Centers for Disease Control and Prevention, Behaviorial Risk Factor Surveillance System, SMART: Selected Metropolitan Area Risk Trends, 2017

Disability Status

Category	MSA[1] (%)	U.S. (%)
Adults who reported being deaf	5.4	6.7
Are you blind or have serious difficulty seeing, even when wearing glasses?	4.4	4.5
Are you limited in any way in any of your usual activities due of arthritis?	9.6	12.9
Do you have difficulty doing errands alone?	5.2	6.8
Do you have difficulty dressing or bathing?	2.7	3.6
Do you have serious difficulty concentrating/remembering/making decisions?	10.3	10.7
Do you have serious difficulty walking or climbing stairs?	12.0	13.6

Note: (1) Figures cover the Atlanta-Sandy Springs-Roswell, GA Metropolitan Statistical Area—see Appendix B for areas included.
Source: Centers for Disease Control and Prevention, Behaviorial Risk Factor Surveillance System, SMART: Selected Metropolitan Area Risk Trends, 2017

Mortality Rates for the Top 10 Causes of Death in the U.S.

ICD-10[a] Sub-Chapter	ICD-10[a] Code	Age-Adjusted Mortality Rate[1] per 100,000 population	
		County[2]	U.S.
Malignant neoplasms	C00-C97	146.7	155.5
Ischaemic heart diseases	I20-I25	54.3	94.8
Other forms of heart disease	I30-I51	60.0	52.9
Chronic lower respiratory diseases	J40-J47	27.0	41.0
Cerebrovascular diseases	I60-I69	40.3	37.5
Other degenerative diseases of the nervous system	G30-G31	47.5	35.0
Other external causes of accidental injury	W00-X59	30.0	33.7
Organic, including symptomatic, mental disorders	F01-F09	24.8	31.0
Hypertensive diseases	I10-I15	42.2	21.9
Diabetes mellitus	E10-E14	18.2	21.2

Note: (a) ICD-10 = International Classification of Diseases 10th Revision; (1) Mortality rates are a three year average covering 2015-2017; (2) Figures cover Fulton County.
Source: Centers for Disease Control and Prevention, National Center for Health Statistics. Underlying Cause of Death 1999-2017 on CDC WONDER Online Database

Mortality Rates for Selected Causes of Death

ICD-10[a] Sub-Chapter	ICD-10[a] Code	Age-Adjusted Mortality Rate[1] per 100,000 population	
		County[2]	U.S.
Assault	X85-Y09	12.1	5.9
Diseases of the liver	K70-K76	10.4	14.1
Human immunodeficiency virus (HIV) disease	B20-B24	7.0	1.8
Influenza and pneumonia	J09-J18	10.3	14.3
Intentional self-harm	X60-X84	10.2	13.6
Malnutrition	E40-E46	3.2	1.6
Obesity and other hyperalimentation	E65-E68	1.4	2.1
Renal failure	N17-N19	17.9	13.0
Transport accidents	V01-V99	10.6	12.4
Viral hepatitis	B15-B19	1.4	1.6

Note: (a) ICD-10 = International Classification of Diseases 10th Revision; (1) Mortality rates are a three year average covering 2015-2017; (2) Figures cover Fulton County; Data are suppressed when the data meet the criteria for confidentiality constraints; Mortality rates are flagged as unreliable when the rate would be calculated with a numerator of 20 or less.
Source: Centers for Disease Control and Prevention, National Center for Health Statistics. Underlying Cause of Death 1999-2017 on CDC WONDER Online Database

Health Insurance Coverage

Area	With Health Insurance	With Private Health Insurance	With Public Health Insurance	Without Health Insurance	Population Under Age 18 Without Health Insurance
City	87.2	66.5	28.8	12.8	5.5
MSA[1]	85.7	68.0	26.3	14.3	7.8
U.S.	89.5	67.2	33.8	10.5	5.7

Note: Figures are percentages that cover the civilian noninstitutionalized population; (1) Figures cover the Atlanta-Sandy Springs-Roswell, GA Metropolitan Statistical Area—see Appendix B for areas included
Source: U.S. Census Bureau, 2013-2017 American Community Survey 5-Year Estimates

Number of Medical Professionals

Area	MDs[3]	DOs[3,4]	Dentists	Podiatrists	Chiropractors	Optometrists
County[1] (number)	5,131	123	737	51	550	166
County[1] (rate[2])	501.0	12.0	70.8	4.9	52.8	15.9
U.S. (rate[2])	279.3	23.0	68.4	6.0	27.1	16.2

Note: Data as of 2017 unless noted; (1) Data covers Fulton County; (2) Rate per 100,000 population; (3) Data as of 2016 and includes all active, non-federal physicians; (4) Doctor of Osteopathic Medicine
Source: U.S. Department of Health and Human Services, Health Resources and Services Administration, Bureau of Health Professions, Area Resource File (ARF) 2017-2018

Best Hospitals

According to *U.S. News,* the Atlanta-Sandy Springs-Roswell, GA metro area is home to two of the best hospitals in the U.S.: **Emory University Hospital** (4 adult specialties); **Shepherd Center** (1 adult specialty). The hospitals listed were nationally ranked in at least one of 16 adult or 10 pediatric specialties. Only 170 hospitals nationwide were nationally ranked in one or more adult or pediatric specialty. Twenty hospitals in the U.S. made the Honor Roll. The Best Hospitals Honor Roll takes both the national rankings and the procedure and condition ratings into account. Hospitals received points if they were nationally ranked in one of the 16 adult specialties—the higher they ranked, the more points they got—and how many ratings of "high performing" they earned in the nine procedures and conditions. *U.S. News Online, "America's Best Hospitals 2018-19"*

According to *U.S. News,* the Atlanta-Sandy Springs-Roswell, GA metro area is home to one of the best children's hospitals in the U.S.: **Children's Healthcare of Atlanta** (10 pediatric specialties). The hospital listed was highly ranked in at least one of 10 pediatric specialties. Eighty-six children's hospitals in the U.S. were nationally ranked in at least one specialty. Hospitals received points for being ranked in a specialty, and the 10 hospitals with the most points across the 10 specialties make up the Honor Roll. *U.S. News Online, "America's Best Children's Hospitals 2018-19"*

EDUCATION

Public School District Statistics

District Name	Schls	Pupils	Pupil/ Teacher Ratio	Minority Pupils[1] (%)	Free Lunch Eligible[2] (%)	IEP[3] (%)
Atlanta Public Schools	89	51,927	13.4	84.8	75.6	10.3
Fulton County	107	96,122	15.0	71.0	43.5	10.2
State Charter Schls - GA Cyber Acad	1	14,319	39.9	50.5	50.3	12.7

Note: Table includes school districts with 2,000 or more students; (1) Percentage of students that are not non-Hispanic white; (2) Percentage of students that are eligible for the free lunch program; (3) Percentage of students that have an Individualized Education Program.
Source: U.S. Department of Education, National Center for Education Statistics, Common Core of Data, Local Education Agency (School District) Universe Survey: School Year 2016-2017; U.S. Department of Education, National Center for Education Statistics, Common Core of Data, Public Elementary/Secondary School Universe Survey: School Year 2016-2017

Highest Level of Education

Area	Less than H.S.	H.S. Diploma	Some College, No Deg.	Associate Degree	Bachelor's Degree	Master's Degree	Prof. School Degree	Doctorate Degree
City	10.1	19.4	16.8	5.0	27.3	14.1	5.1	2.2
MSA[1]	11.1	24.3	20.2	7.3	23.3	9.9	2.4	1.4
U.S.	12.7	27.3	20.8	8.3	19.1	8.4	2.0	1.4

Note: Figures cover persons age 25 and over; (1) Figures cover the Atlanta-Sandy Springs-Roswell, GA Metropolitan Statistical Area—see Appendix B for areas included
Source: U.S. Census Bureau, 2013-2017 American Community Survey 5-Year Estimates

Educational Attainment by Race

Area	High School Graduate or Higher (%)					Bachelor's Degree or Higher (%)				
	Total	White	Black	Asian	Hisp.[2]	Total	White	Black	Asian	Hisp.[2]
City	89.9	97.2	83.1	96.9	79.4	48.7	75.7	22.9	83.8	43.1
MSA[1]	88.9	90.2	89.5	86.7	63.1	37.0	40.8	28.7	55.4	18.6
U.S.	87.3	89.3	84.9	86.5	66.7	30.9	32.2	20.6	52.7	15.2

Note: Figures shown cover persons 25 years old and over; (1) Figures cover the Atlanta-Sandy Springs-Roswell, GA Metropolitan Statistical Area—see Appendix B for areas included; (2) People of Hispanic origin can be of any race
Source: U.S. Census Bureau, 2013-2017 American Community Survey 5-Year Estimates

School Enrollment by Grade and Control

Area	Preschool (%)		Kindergarten (%)		Grades 1 - 4 (%)		Grades 5 - 8 (%)		Grades 9 - 12 (%)	
	Public	Private	Public	Private	Public	Private	Public	Private	Public	Private
City	53.8	46.2	83.7	16.3	85.5	14.5	81.1	18.9	78.3	21.7
MSA[1]	57.3	42.7	86.3	13.7	90.7	9.3	89.8	10.2	89.8	10.2
U.S.	58.8	41.2	87.7	12.3	89.7	10.3	89.6	10.4	90.3	9.7

Note: Figures shown cover persons 3 years old and over; (1) Figures cover the Atlanta-Sandy Springs-Roswell, GA Metropolitan Statistical Area—see Appendix B for areas included
Source: U.S. Census Bureau, 2013-2017 American Community Survey 5-Year Estimates

Average Salaries of Public School Classroom Teachers

Area	2016		2017		Change from 2016 to 2017	
	Dollars	Rank[1]	Dollars	Rank[1]	Percent	Rank[2]
Georgia	54,190	23	55,532	23	2.5	15
U.S. Average	58,479	–	59,660	–	2.0	–

Note: (1) Rank ranges from 1 to 51 where 1 indicates highest salary; (2) Rank ranges from 1 to 51 where 1 indicates highest percent change.
Source: National Education Association, Rankings & Estimates: Rankings of the States 2017 and Estimates of School Statistics 2018

Higher Education

Four-Year Colleges			Two-Year Colleges			Medical Schools[1]	Law Schools[2]	Voc/ Tech[3]
Public	Private Non-profit	Private For-profit	Public	Private Non-profit	Private For-profit			
3	11	7	3	0	5	2	3	7

Note: Figures cover institutions located within the city limits and include main campuses only; (1) includes schools accredited by the Liaison Committee on Medical Education and the American Osteopathic Association's Commission on Osteopathic College Accreditation; (2) includes ABA-accredited schools, schools with provisional ABA accreditation, and state accredited schools; (3) includes all schools with programs that are less than 2 years.
Source: National Center for Education Statistics, Integrated Postsecondary Education System (IPEDS), 2017-18; Wikipedia, List of Medical Schools in the United States, accessed April 3, 2019; Wikipedia, List of Law Schools in the United States, accessed April 3, 2019

According to *U.S. News & World Report*, the Atlanta-Sandy Springs-Roswell, GA metro area is home to three of the best national universities in the U.S.: **Emory University** (#21); **Georgia Institute of Technology** (#35 tie); **Georgia State University** (#187 tie). The indicators used to capture academic quality fall into a number of categories: assessment by administrators at peer institutions; retention of students; faculty resources; student selectivity; financial resources; alumni giving; high school counselor ratings of colleges; and graduation rate. *U.S. News & World Report, "America's Best Colleges 2019"*

According to *U.S. News & World Report*, the Atlanta-Sandy Springs-Roswell, GA metro area is home to three of the best liberal arts colleges in the U.S.: **Agnes Scott College** (#51 tie); **Spelman College** (#51 tie); **Morehouse College** (#143 tie). The indicators used to capture academic quality fall into a number of categories: assessment by administrators at peer institutions; retention of students; faculty resources; student selectivity; financial resources; alumni giving; high school counselor ratings of colleges; and graduation rate. *U.S. News & World Report, "America's Best Colleges 2019"*

According to *U.S. News & World Report,* the Atlanta-Sandy Springs-Roswell, GA metro area is home to two of the top 100 law schools in the U.S.: **Emory University** (#26); **Georgia State University** (#67 tie). The rankings are based on a weighted average of 12 measures of quality: peer assessment score; assessment score by lawyers/judges; median LSAT scores; median undergrad GPA; acceptance rate; employment rates for graduates; placement success; bar passage rate; faculty resources; expenditures per student; student/faculty ratio; and library resources. *U.S. News & World Report, "America's Best Graduate Schools, Law, 2020"*

According to *U.S. News & World Report,* the Atlanta-Sandy Springs-Roswell, GA metro area is home to one of the top 75 medical schools for research in the U.S.: **Emory University** (#24 tie). The rankings are based on a weighted average of 11 measures of quality: quality assessment; peer assessment score; assessment score by residency directors; research activity; total research activity; average research activity per faculty member; student selectivity; median MCAT total score; median undergraduate GPA; acceptance rate; and faculty resources. *U.S. News & World Report, "America's Best Graduate Schools, Medical, 2020"*

According to *U.S. News & World Report,* the Atlanta-Sandy Springs-Roswell, GA metro area is home to two of the top 75 business schools in the U.S.: **Emory University (Goizueta)** (#21 tie); **Georgia Institute of Technology (Scheller)** (#29 tie). The rankings are based on a weighted average of the following nine measures: quality assessment; peer assessment; recruiter assessment; placement success; mean starting salary and bonus; student selectivity; mean GMAT and GRE scores; mean undergraduate GPA; and acceptance rate. *U.S. News & World Report, "America's Best Graduate Schools, Business, 2020"*

PRESIDENTIAL ELECTION

2016 Presidential Election Results

Area	Clinton	Trump	Johnson	Stein	Other
Fulton County	67.7	26.8	3.6	0.1	1.8
U.S.	48.0	45.9	3.3	1.1	1.7

Note: Results are percentages and may not add to 100% due to rounding
Source: Dave Leip's Atlas of U.S. Presidential Elections

EMPLOYERS

Major Employers

Company Name	Industry
Apartments.com	Apartment locating service
Aquilex Holdings	Facilities support services
AT&T	Engineering services
Children's Healthcare of Atlanta	Healthcare
Clayton County Board of Education	Public elementary & secondary schools
County of Gwinnett	County commissioner
Delta Air Lines	Air transportation, scheduled
Georgia Department of Behavioral Health	Administration of public health programs
Georgia Department of Human Resoures	Administration of public health programs
Georgia Department of Transportation	Regulation, administration of transportation
IBM	Engineering services
Internal Revenue Service	Taxation department, government
Lockheed Martin Aeronautical Company	Aircraft
NCR Corporation	Calculating and accounting equipment
Northide Hospital	Healthcare
Progressive Logistics Services	Labor organizations
Robert Half International	Employment agencies
Saint Joseph's Hospital	Healthcare
The Coca-Cola Company	Bottled and canned soft drinks
The Fulton-Dekalb Hospital Authority	General medical & surgical hospitals
The Home Depot	Hardware stores
U.S. Army	U.S. military
WellStar Kennestone Hospital	General medical & surgical hospitals
World Travel Partners Group	Travel agencies

Note: Companies shown are located within the Atlanta-Sandy Springs-Roswell, GA Metropolitan Statistical Area.
Source: Hoovers.com; Wikipedia

Best Companies to Work For

Alston & Bird; Children's Healthcare of Atlanta; Delta Air Lines, headquartered in Atlanta, are among "The 100 Best Companies to Work For." To pick the best companies, *Fortune* partnered with the Great Place to Work Institute. Two-thirds of a company's score is based on the results of the Institute's Trust Index survey, which is sent to a random sample of employees from each company. The questions related to attitudes about management's credibility, job satisfaction, and camaraderie. The other third of the scoring is based on the company's responses to the Institute's Culture Audit, which includes detailed questions about pay and benefit programs, and a series of open-ended questions about hiring practices, internal communication, training, recognition programs, and diversity efforts. Any company that is at least five years old with more than 1,000 U.S. employees is eligible. *Fortune, "The 100 Best Companies to Work For," 2019*

Children's Healthcare of Atlanta; Turner, headquartered in Atlanta, are among the "100 Best Companies for Working Mothers." Criteria: paid time off and leaves; workforce profile; benefits; women's issues and advancement; flexible work; company culture and work life programs. *Working Mother, "100 Best Companies 2018"*

Children's Healthcare of Atlanta; Southern Co, headquartered in Atlanta, are among the "100 Best Places to Work in IT." To qualify, companies had to be U.S.-based organizations or be non-U.S.- based employers that met the following criteria: have a minimum of 300 total employees at a U.S. headquarters and a minimum of 30 IT employees in the U.S., with at least 50% of their IT employees based in the U.S. The best places to work were selected based on compensation, benefits, work/life balance, employee morale, and satisfaction with training and development programs. In addition, *Computerworld* looked at retention efforts, programs for recognizing and rewarding outstanding performances, and benefits such as flextime, elder care and child care, and reimbursement for college tuition and the cost of pursuing technology certifications. *Computerworld, "100 Best Places to Work in IT 2018"*

PUBLIC SAFETY

Crime Rate

Area	All Crimes	Violent Crimes				Property Crimes		
		Murder	Rape[3]	Robbery	Aggrav. Assault	Burglary	Larceny -Theft	Motor Vehicle Theft
City	5,712.1	16.4	58.6	293.6	567.2	704.3	3,387.2	685.0
Suburbs[1]	3,012.4	5.9	23.2	99.6	188.4	459.6	1,963.5	272.3
Metro[2]	3,233.3	6.7	26.1	115.4	219.4	479.7	2,080.0	306.0
U.S.	2,756.1	5.3	41.7	98.0	248.9	430.4	1,694.4	237.4

Note: Figures are crimes per 100,000 population; (1) All areas within the metro area that are located outside the city limits; (2) Figures cover the Atlanta-Sandy Springs-Roswell, GA Metropolitan Statistical Area—see Appendix B for areas included; (3) The city and U.S. figures shown were reported using the revised Uniform Crime Reporting (UCR) definition of rape. The suburban and metro area figures shown are an aggregate total of the data submitted using both the revised and legacy UCR definitions.
Source: FBI Uniform Crime Reports, 2017

Hate Crimes

Area	Number of Quarters Reported	Number of Incidents per Bias Motivation					
		Race/Ethnicity/ Ancestry	Religion	Sexual Orientation	Disability	Gender	Gender Identity
City	4	0	1	2	0	0	0
U.S.	4	4,131	1,564	1,130	116	46	119

Source: Federal Bureau of Investigation, Hate Crime Statistics 2017

Identity Theft Consumer Reports

Area	Reports	Reports per 100,000 Population	Rank[2]
MSA[1]	16,902	292	3
U.S.	444,602	135	-

Note: (1) Figures cover the Atlanta-Sandy Springs-Roswell, GA Metropolitan Statistical Area—see Appendix B for areas included; (2) Rank ranges from 1 to 389 where 1 indicates greatest number of identity theft reports per 100,000 population
Source: Federal Trade Commission, Consumer Sentinel Network Data Book for January–December 2018

Fraud and Other Consumer Reports

Area	Reports	Reports per 100,000 Population	Rank[2]
MSA[1]	47,707	824	5
U.S.	2,552,917	776	-

Note: (1) Figures cover the Atlanta-Sandy Springs-Roswell, GA Metropolitan Statistical Area—see Appendix B for areas included; (2) Rank ranges from 1 to 389 where 1 indicates greatest number of fraud and other consumer reports per 100,000 population
Source: Federal Trade Commission, Consumer Sentinel Network Data Book for January–December 2018

SPORTS

Professional Sports Teams

Team Name	League	Year Established
Atlanta Braves	Major League Baseball (MLB)	1966
Atlanta Falcons	National Football League (NFL)	1966
Atlanta Hawks	National Basketball Association (NBA)	1968
Atlanta United FC	Major League Soccer (MLS)	2017

Note: Includes teams located in the Atlanta-Sandy Springs-Roswell, GA Metropolitan Statistical Area.
Source: Wikipedia, Major Professional Sports Teams of the United States and Canada, April 5, 2019

CLIMATE

Average and Extreme Temperatures

Temperature	Jan	Feb	Mar	Apr	May	Jun	Jul	Aug	Sep	Oct	Nov	Dec	Yr.
Extreme High (°F)	79	80	85	93	95	101	105	102	98	95	84	77	105
Average High (°F)	52	56	64	73	80	86	88	88	82	73	63	54	72
Average Temp. (°F)	43	46	53	62	70	77	79	79	73	63	53	45	62
Average Low (°F)	33	36	42	51	59	66	70	69	64	52	42	35	52
Extreme Low (°F)	-8	5	10	26	37	46	53	55	36	28	3	0	-8

Note: Figures cover the years 1945-1990
Source: National Climatic Data Center, International Station Meteorological Climate Summary, 9/96

Average Precipitation/Snowfall/Humidity

Precip./Humidity	Jan	Feb	Mar	Apr	May	Jun	Jul	Aug	Sep	Oct	Nov	Dec	Yr.
Avg. Precip. (in.)	4.7	4.6	5.7	4.3	4.0	3.5	5.1	3.6	3.4	2.8	3.8	4.2	49.8
Avg. Snowfall (in.)	1	1	Tr	Tr	0	0	0	0	0	0	Tr	Tr	2
Avg. Rel. Hum. 7am (%)	79	77	78	78	82	83	88	89	88	84	81	79	82
Avg. Rel. Hum. 4pm (%)	56	50	48	45	49	52	57	56	56	51	52	55	52

Note: Figures cover the years 1945-1990; Tr = Trace amounts (<0.05 in. of rain; <0.5 in. of snow)
Source: National Climatic Data Center, International Station Meteorological Climate Summary, 9/96

Weather Conditions

Temperature			Daytime Sky			Precipitation		
10°F & below	32°F & below	90°F & above	Clear	Partly cloudy	Cloudy	0.01 inch or more precip.	0.1 inch or more snow/ice	Thunder-storms
1	49	38	98	147	120	116	3	48

Note: Figures are average number of days per year and cover the years 1945-1990
Source: National Climatic Data Center, International Station Meteorological Climate Summary, 9/96

HAZARDOUS WASTE

Superfund Sites

The Atlanta-Sandy Springs-Roswell, GA metro area has no sites on the EPA's Superfund Final National Priorities List. There are a total of 1,390 Superfund sites with a status of proposed or final on the list in the U.S. *U.S. Environmental Protection Agency, National Priorities List, April 5, 2019*

AIR & WATER QUALITY

Air Quality Trends: Ozone

	1990	1995	2000	2005	2010	2012	2014	2015	2016	2017
MSA[1]	0.104	0.103	0.101	0.087	0.076	0.079	0.072	0.070	0.073	0.068
U.S.	0.088	0.089	0.082	0.080	0.073	0.075	0.067	0.068	0.069	0.068

Note: (1) Data covers the Atlanta-Sandy Springs-Roswell, GA Metropolitan Statistical Area—see Appendix B for areas included. The values shown are the composite ozone concentration averages among trend sites based on the highest fourth daily maximum 8-hour concentration in parts per million. These trends are based on sites having an adequate record of monitoring data during the trend period. Data from exceptional events are included.
Source: U.S. Environmental Protection Agency, Air Quality Monitoring Information, "Air Quality Trends by City, 1990-2017"

Air Quality Index

| Area | Percent of Days when Air Quality was...[2] | | | | | AQI Statistics[2] | |
	Good	Moderate	Unhealthy for Sensitive Groups	Unhealthy	Very Unhealthy	Maximum	Median
MSA[1]	47.7	49.3	3.0	0.0	0.0	150	51

Note: (1) Data covers the Atlanta-Sandy Springs-Roswell, GA Metropolitan Statistical Area—see Appendix B for areas included; (2) Based on 365 days with AQI data in 2017. Air Quality Index (AQI) is an index for reporting daily air quality. EPA calculates the AQI for five major air pollutants regulated by the Clean Air Act: ground-level ozone, particle pollution (aka particulate matter), carbon monoxide, sulfur dioxide, and nitrogen dioxide. The AQI runs from 0 to 500. The higher the AQI value, the greater the level of air pollution and the greater the health concern. There are six AQI categories: "Good" AQI is between 0 and 50. Air quality is considered satisfactory; "Moderate" AQI is between 51 and 100. Air quality is acceptable; "Unhealthy for Sensitive Groups" When AQI values are between 101 and 150, members of sensitive groups may experience health effects; "Unhealthy" When AQI values are between 151 and 200 everyone may begin to experience health effects; "Very Unhealthy" AQI values between 201 and 300 trigger a health alert; "Hazardous" AQI values over 300 trigger warnings of emergency conditions (not shown).
Source: U.S. Environmental Protection Agency, Air Quality Index Report, 2017

Air Quality Index Pollutants

| Area | Percent of Days when AQI Pollutant was...[2] | | | | | |
	Carbon Monoxide	Nitrogen Dioxide	Ozone	Sulfur Dioxide	Particulate Matter 2.5	Particulate Matter 10
MSA[1]	0.0	4.4	44.4	0.0	51.2	0.0

Note: (1) Data covers the Atlanta-Sandy Springs-Roswell, GA Metropolitan Statistical Area—see Appendix B for areas included; (2) Based on 365 days with AQI data in 2017. The Air Quality Index (AQI) is an index for reporting daily air quality. EPA calculates the AQI for five major air pollutants regulated by the Clean Air Act: ground-level ozone, particle pollution (also known as particulate matter), carbon monoxide, sulfur dioxide, and nitrogen dioxide. The AQI runs from 0 to 500. The higher the AQI value, the greater the level of air pollution and the greater the health concern.
Source: U.S. Environmental Protection Agency, Air Quality Index Report, 2017

Maximum Air Pollutant Concentrations: Particulate Matter, Ozone, CO and Lead

	Particulate Matter 10 (ug/m^3)	Particulate Matter 2.5 Wtd AM (ug/m^3)	Particulate Matter 2.5 24-Hr (ug/m^3)	Ozone (ppm)	Carbon Monoxide (ppm)	Lead (ug/m^3)
MSA[1] Level	41	10.4	23	0.074	2	n/a
NAAQS[2]	150	15	35	0.075	9	0.15
Met NAAQS[2]	Yes	Yes	Yes	Yes	Yes	n/a

Note: (1) Data covers the Atlanta-Sandy Springs-Roswell, GA Metropolitan Statistical Area—see Appendix B for areas included; Data from exceptional events are included; (2) National Ambient Air Quality Standards; ppm = parts per million; ug/m^3 = micrograms per cubic meter; n/a not available.
Concentrations: Particulate Matter 10 (coarse particulate)—highest second maximum 24-hour concentration; Particulate Matter 2.5 Wtd AM (fine particulate)—highest weighted annual mean concentration; Particulate Matter 2.5 24-Hour (fine particulate)—highest 98th percentile 24-hour concentration; Ozone—highest fourth daily maximum 8-hour concentration; Carbon Monoxide—highest second maximum non-overlapping 8-hour concentration; Lead—maximum running 3-month average
Source: U.S. Environmental Protection Agency, Air Quality Monitoring Information, "Air Quality Statistics by City, 2017"

Maximum Air Pollutant Concentrations: Nitrogen Dioxide and Sulfur Dioxide

	Nitrogen Dioxide AM (ppb)	Nitrogen Dioxide 1-Hr (ppb)	Sulfur Dioxide AM (ppb)	Sulfur Dioxide 1-Hr (ppb)	Sulfur Dioxide 24-Hr (ppb)
MSA[1] Level	18	53	n/a	7	n/a
NAAQS[2]	53	100	30	75	140
Met NAAQS[2]	Yes	Yes	n/a	Yes	n/a

Note: (1) Data covers the Atlanta-Sandy Springs-Roswell, GA Metropolitan Statistical Area—see Appendix B for areas included; Data from exceptional events are included; (2) National Ambient Air Quality Standards; ppm = parts per million; ug/m^3 = micrograms per cubic meter; n/a not available.
Concentrations: Nitrogen Dioxide AM—highest arithmetic mean concentration; Nitrogen Dioxide 1-Hr—highest 98th percentile 1-hour daily maximum concentration; Sulfur Dioxide AM—highest annual mean concentration; Sulfur Dioxide 1-Hr—highest 99th percentile 1-hour daily maximum concentration; Sulfur Dioxide 24-Hr—highest second maximum 24-hour concentration
Source: U.S. Environmental Protection Agency, Air Quality Monitoring Information, "Air Quality Statistics by City, 2017"

Drinking Water

Water System Name	Pop. Served	Primary Water Source Type	Violations[1]	
			Health Based	Monitoring/ Reporting
Atlanta	650,000	Surface	1	0

Note: (1) Based on violation data from January 1, 2018 to December 31, 2018
Source: U.S. Environmental Protection Agency, Office of Ground Water and Drinking Water, Safe Drinking Water Information System (based on data extracted April 5, 2019)

Austin, Texas

Background

Starting out in 1730 as a peaceful Spanish mission on the north bank of the Colorado River in south-central Texas, Austin soon engaged in an imbroglio of territorial wars, beginning when the "Father of Texas," Stephen F. Austin, annexed the territory from Mexico in 1833 as his own. Later, the Republic of Texas named the territory Austin in honor of the colonizer, and conferred upon it state capital status. Challenges to this decision ensued, ranging from an invasion by the Mexican government to reclaim its land, to Sam Houston's call that the capital ought to move from Austin to Houston.

During peaceful times, however, Austin has been called the "City of the Violet Crown." Coined by the short story writer, William Sydney Porter, or O. Henry, the name refers to the purple mist that circles the surrounding hills of the Colorado River Valley.

This city of technological innovation is home to a strong computer and electronics industry. Austin offers hundreds of free wireless spots, including its city parks, and its technology focus has traditionally drawn numerous high-tech companies. Samsung Electronics' major computer chip plant was built in Austin in the late 1990s with expansions and a new, huge facility, since. Along with this technology growth came increased traffic, especially on Interstate 35, the main highway linking the U.S. and Mexico. A new 89-mile bypass has helped to relieve some of the traffic difficulties long associated with I-35, after which Facebook opened a sales and operations facility in the city.

In addition to its traditional business community, Austin is home to the main campus of the University of Texas. The university provides Austin with diverse lifestyles; today there is a solid mix of white-collar workers, students, professors, blue-collar workers, musicians and artists, and members of the booming tech industry who all call themselves Austinites.

The influx of young people centered on university life has contributed to the city's growth as a thriving live music scene. It is so important to the city that its local government maintains the Austin Music Commission to promote the local music industry.

A notable industry conference takes place here each spring. The South by Southwest Conference (SXSW) showcases more than 2,000 performers at 90+ venues throughout the city. The growing film and interactive industries have been added to the conference in recent years.

The civic-minded city operates from a new city hall, which is also home to a public plaza facing Town Lake. One of the town's cultural hubs, the Long Center for the Performing Arts, underwent a major renovation in the last decade.

It is most likely Austinites' pride in their creative and independent culture that has spawned a movement to keep the city from too much corporate development. The slogan "Keep Austin Weird" was adopted by the Austin Independent Business Alliance as a way to promote local and alternative business.

Austin's skyline is no longer dominated by the Texas State Capitol and the University of Texas. Many new high-rise towers have been constructed in recent years, including The Austonian, with more high-rise projects under construction in Austin's downtown.

Austin consistently gets high marks in best city surveys. The city sits at a desirable location along the Colorado River, and many recreational activities center on the water. For instance, Austin boasts three spring-fed swimming pools enjoyed by its residents, as well as the Lance Armstrong Crosstown Bikeway. The city has more than 100 miles of bike paths.

The climate of Austin is subtropical with hot summers. Winters are mild, with below-freezing temperatures occurring on an average of 25 days a year. Cold spells are short, seldom lasting more than two days. Daytime temperatures in summer are hot, while summer nights are usually pleasant.

Rankings

General Rankings

- *US News & World Report* conducted a survey of more than 2,000 people and analyzed the 125 largest metropolitan areas to determine what matters the most when selecting the next place to live. Austin ranked #1 out of the top 25 as having the best combination of desirable factors. Criteria: cost of living; quality of education; job market, crime rates; and other factors. *realestate.usnews.com, "The 25 Best Places to Live in the U.S. in 2018," April 10, 2018*

- *Insider* listed 33 places in the U.S. that were a must see vacation destination. Whether it is the great beaches, exploring a new city or experiencing the great outdoors, according to the website thisisinsider.com Austin is a place to visit in 2018. *Insider, "33 Trips Everyone Should Take in the U.S. in 2018," November 27, 2017*

- Austin appeared on *Business Insider's* list of the "13 Hottest American Cities for 2016." Criteria: job and population growth; demographics; affordability; livability; residents' health and welfare; technological innovation; sustainability; burgeoning art and food scenes. *www.businessinsider.com, "The Thirteen Hottest American Cities for 2016," December 4, 2015*

- The Austin metro area was identified as one of America's fastest-growing areas in terms of population and business growth by *MagnifyMoney.* The area ranked #1 out of 35. The 100 most populous metro areas in the U.S. were evaluated on their change from 2011-2016 in the following categories: people and housing; workforce and employment opportunities; growing industry. *www.businessinsider.com, "The 35 Cities in the US with the Biggest Influx of People, the Most Work Opportunities, and the Hottest Business Growth," August 12, 2018*

- The Austin metro area was identified as one of America's fastest-growing areas in terms of population and economy by *Forbes.* The area ranked #8 out of 25. The 100 most populous metro areas in the U.S. were evaluated on the following criteria: estimated population growth; employment; economic output; wages; home values. *Forbes, "America's Fastest-Growing Cities 2018," February 28, 2018*

- Austin was identified as one of America's fastest-growing cities in terms of population growth by CNNMoney.com. The area ranked #4 out of 10. Criteria: population growth between July 2015 and July 2016; cities and towns with populations of 50,000. *CNNMoney, "10 Fastest-Growing Cities," June 2, 2017*

- Austin was selected as one of the best places to live in America by *Outside Magazine.* Criteria included great access to trails and public lands, great for children, delicious food and drink, and welcoming to people of all backgrounds. Three decades of coverage was combined with the expertise of an advisory council to pick the finalists. *Outside Magazine, "The 25 Best Towns of 2017," July 2017*

- The U.S. Conference of Mayors and Waste Management, Inc. sponsor the City Livability Awards Program, which recognize mayors for exemplary leadership in developing and implementing specific programs that improve the quality of life in America's cities. Austin received an Outstanding Achievement Award in the large cities category. *U.S. Conference of Mayors, "2018 City Livability Awards"*

- Austin appeared on *Travel + Leisure's* list of the fifteen best cities in the United States. The city was ranked #13. Criteria: sights/landmarks; culture/arts; cuisine; people/friendliness; shopping; and value. *Travel + Leisure, "The World's Best Awards 2018" July 10, 2018*

Business/Finance Rankings

- According to *Business Insider,* the Austin metro area is where startup growth is on the rise. Based on the 2017 Kauffman Index of Growth Entrepreneurship, which measured in-depth national entrepreneurial trends in 40 metro areas, it ranked #2 in highest startup growth. *www.businessinsider.com, "The 21 U.S. Cities with the Highest Startup Growth," October 21, 2017*

- The personal finance site NerdWallet analyzed 183 American metropolitan areas with populations over 250,000 and more than 15,000 businesses to rank where entrepreneurs find the most success. Criteria included area economy, annual income, housing cost, unemployment rate, and the success rate of area businesses. Austin ranked #89. *www.nerdwallet.com, "Best Places to Start a Business," April 27, 2015*

- Austin was the #15-ranked city for savers, according to a study by the finance site GOBankingRates, which considered the prospects for people trying to save money. Criteria: average monthly cost of grocery items; median home listing price; median rent; median income; unemployment rate; gas prices; and sales tax in the nation's 60 largest cities. *www.gobankingrates.com, "Best Cities for Saving Money," June 22, 2018*

- Austin was ranked #15 among the nation's 60 largest cities for most difficult conditions for savers, according to a study by the finance site GOBankingRates. Criteria: average monthly cost of grocery items; median home listing price; median rent; median income; unemployment rate; gas prices; and sales tax. *www.gobankingrates.com, "Worst Cities for Saving Money," June 22, 2018*

- Recognizing the sizeable percentage of American workers who are self-employed, NerdWallet editors assessed the country's cities according to percentage of freelancers, median rental costs, cell phone plans/taxes, and healthcare affordability and access. By these criteria, Austin placed #1 among the best cities for independent workers. *www.nerdwallet.com, "Best Places for Freelance Workers," August 30, 2016*

- 24/7 Wall Street used Brookings Institution research on 50 advanced industries to identify the proportion of workers in the nation's largest metropolitan areas that were employed in jobs requiring knowledge in the science, technology, engineering, or math (STEM) fields and where there was heavy investment in research and development (R&D). The Austin metro area was #9. *247wallst.com, "15 Cities with the Most High-Tech Jobs," February 23, 2017*

- In a survey of economic confidence in the nation's 50 largest metropolitan areas conducted January–December 2014, the Austin metro area placed #9, according to Gallup's 2014 Economic Confidence Index. *Gallup, "San Jose and San Francisco Lead in Economic Confidence," March 19, 2015*

- Using data from the Council for Community and Economic Research's 2014 cost of living index, NerdWallet ranked the 100 most affordable cities in America. Median income was compared with cost of living to find truly affordable places. Austin ranked #17. *NerdWallet.com, "America's Most Affordable Places," May 18, 2015*

- NerdWallet.com identified the 10 most promising cities for job seekers of the nation's 100 largest cities. Austin was ranked #1. Criteria: job availability; annual salary; workforce growth; affordability. *NerdWallet.com, "Best Cities for Job Seekers in 2017," December 19, 2016*

- The Brookings Institution ranked the nation's largest cities based on income inequality. Austin was ranked #47 (#1 = greatest inequality). Criteria: the "95/20 ratio," a figure representing the income at which a household earns more than 95 percent of all other households, divided by the income at which a household earns more than only 20 percent of all other households. *Brookings Institution, "Household Income Inequality, Largest Cities of 97 Large U.S. Metro Areas, 2014-2016," February 5, 2018*

- The Brookings Institution ranked the 100 largest metro areas in the U.S. based on income inequality. Austin was ranked #37 (#1 = greatest inequality). Criteria: the "95/20 ratio," a figure representing the income at which a household earns more than 95 percent of all other households, divided by the income at which a household earns more than only 20 percent of all other households. *Brookings Institution, "Household Income Inequality, 100 Largest U.S. Metro Areas, 2014-2016," February 5, 2018*

- *Forbes* ranked the 100 largest metro areas in the U.S. in terms of the "Best Cities for Young Professionals." The Austin metro area ranked #2 out of 25. (Large metro areas were divided into metro divisions.) Criteria: median rent of a two-bedroom apartment; job growth and unemployment rate; median salary of college graduates with 5 or less years of work experience; networking opportunities; social outlook; percentage of population 25 years of age and older with college degrees. *Forbes.com, "America's 25 Best Cities for Young Professionals in 2017," May 22, 2017*

- Payscale.com ranked the 32 largest metro areas in terms of wage growth. The Austin metro area ranked #20. Criteria: private-sector wage growth between the 4th quarter of 2017 and the 4th quarter of 2018. *PayScale, "Wage Trends by Metro Area-4th Quarter," January 8, 2019*

- The Austin metro area was identified as one of the most affordable metropolitan areas in America by *Forbes*. The area ranked #19 out of 20 based on the National Association of Home Builders/Wells Fargo Housing Affordability Index and Sperling's Best Places' cost-of-living index. *Forbes.com, "America's Most Affordable Cities in 2015," March 12, 2015*

- Austin was identified as one of the happiest cities to work in by CareerBliss.com, an online community for career advancement. The city ranked #10 out of 10. Criteria: an employee's relationship with his or her boss and co-workers; daily tasks; general work environment; compensation; opportunities for advancement; company culture and job reputation; and resources. *Businesswire.com, "CareerBliss Happiest Cities to Work 2019," February 12, 2019*

- The Austin metro area appeared on the Milken Institute "2018 Best Performing Cities" list. Rank: #3 out of 200 large metro areas. Criteria: job growth; wage and salary growth; high-tech output growth. *Milken Institute, "Best-Performing Cities 2018," January 24, 2019*

- *Forbes* ranked the 200 most populous metro areas to determine the nation's "Best Places for Business and Careers." The Austin metro area was ranked #8. Criteria: costs (business and living); job growth (past and projected); income growth; quality of life; educational attainment (college and high school); projected economic growth; cultural and recreational opportunities; net migration patterns; number of highly ranked colleges. *Forbes, "The Best Places for Business and Careers 2018: Seattle Leads the Way," October 24, 2018*

Children/Family Rankings

- *Forbes* analyzed data on the 100 largest metropolitan areas in the United States to compile its 2016 ranking of the best cities for raising a family. The Austin metro area was ranked #14. Criteria: median income; childcare costs; percent of population under 18; commuting delays; crime rate; percentage of families owning homes; education quality (mainly test scores). Overall cost of living and housing affordability was also unofficially considered. *Forbes, "America's Best Cities for Raising a Family 2016," August 30, 2016*

Culture/Performing Arts Rankings

- Austin was selected as one of the twenty best large U.S. cities for moviemakers. Of cities with a population over 400,000, the city was ranked #8. Criteria: film community and culture; access to equipment and facilities; film activity in 2018; number of film schools; tax incentives. ease of movement and traffic. *MovieMaker Magazine, "Best Places to Live and Work as a Moviemaker: 2019," January 16, 2019*

- Austin was selected as one of "America's Favorite Cities." The city ranked #2 in the "Culture: Concerts " category. Respondents to an online survey were asked to rate 38 top urban destinations in the U.S. from a visitor's perspective. Criteria: number and quality of concerts. *Travelandleisure.com, "America's Favorite Cities," October 11, 2015*

- Austin was selected as one of "America's Favorite Cities." The city ranked #2 in the "Culture: Music Scene " category. Respondents to an online survey were asked to rate 38 top urban destinations in the U.S. from a visitor's perspective. *Travelandleisure.com, "From the Honkytonk Capital to Jazz's Birthplace: America's Best Music Scenes," October 2016*

Dating/Romance Rankings

- *Apartment List* conducted its annual survey of renters to compile a list of cities that have the best opportunities for dating. More than 9,000 respondents, from February 2018 through the end of December 2018, rated their current city or neighborhood for opportunities to date and make friends. Austin ranked #1 out of 66 where single residents were very satisfied or somewhat satisfied, making it among the ten best metros for dating opportunities. Other criteria analyzed included gender and education levels of renters. *Apartment List, "The Best & Worst Cities for Dating 2019," February 8, 2019*

- Austin was selected as one of the best cities for post grads by *Rent.com*. The city ranked #6 of 10. Criteria: millennial population; jobs per capita; unemployment rate; median rent; number of bars and restaurants; access to nightlife and entertainment. *Rent.com, "Top 10 Best Cities for Post Grads," April 3, 2015*

Education Rankings

- Personal finance website *WalletHub* analyzed the 150 largest U.S. metropolitan statistical areas to determine where the most educated Americans are choosing to settle. Criteria: education quality and attainment gap; education levels; percentage of workers with degrees; public school quality rankings; quality and size of each metro area's universities. Austin was ranked #8 (#1 = most educated city). *www.WalletHub.com, "2018's Most and Least Educated Cities in America, " July 24, 2018*

- Austin was selected as one of the most well-read cities in America by Amazon.com. The city ranked #5 among the top 20. Cities with populations greater than 500,000 were evaluated based on per capita sales of books, magazines and newspapers (both print and Kindle format). *Amazon.com, "The 20 Most Well-Read Cities in America," May 24, 2016*

- Austin was selected as one of America's most literate cities. The city ranked #17 out of the 82 largest U.S. cities. Criteria: number of booksellers; library resources; Internet resources; educational attainment; periodical publishing resources; newspaper circulation. *Central Connecticut State University, "America's Most Literate Cities, 2016," March 31, 2017*

Environmental Rankings

- Sperling's BestPlaces assessed the 50 largest metropolitan areas of the United States for the likelihood of dangerously extreme weather events or earthquakes. In general the Southeast and South-Central regions have the highest risk of weather extremes and earthquakes, while the Pacific Northwest enjoys the lowest risk. Of the most risky metropolitan areas, the Austin metro area was ranked #2. *www.bestplaces.net, "Avoid Natural Disasters: BestPlaces Reveals The Top 10 Safest Places to Live," October 25, 2017*

- The U.S. Environmental Protection Agency (EPA) released a list of U.S. metropolitan areas with the most ENERGY STAR certified buildings in 2017. The Austin metro area was ranked #17 out of 25. *U.S. Environmental Protection Agency, "2018 Energy Star Top Cities," April 11, 2018*

- The U.S. Conference of Mayors and Walmart Stores sponsor the Mayors' Climate Protection Awards Program which recognize mayors for outstanding and innovative practices that mayors are taking to increase energy efficiency in their cities, reduce carbon emissions and expand renewable energy. Austin received First Place Honors in the large city category. *U.S. Conference of Mayors, "2018 Mayors' Climate Protection Awards Program," June 8, 2018*

- Austin was highlighted as one of the top 90 cleanest metro areas for short-term particle pollution (24-hour PM 2.5) in the U.S. during 2014 through 2016. Monitors in these cities reported no days with unhealthful PM 2.5 levels. *American Lung Association, State of the Air 2018*

Food/Drink Rankings

- The U.S. Chamber of Commerce Foundation conducted an in-depth study on local food truck regulations, surveyed 288 food truck owners, and ranked 20 major American cities based on how friendly they are for operating a food truck. The compiled index assessed the following: procedures for obtaining permits and licenses; complying with restrictions; and financial obligations associated with operating a food truck. Austin ranked #7 overall (1 being the best) for ease in operating a food truck. *www.foodtrucknation.us, "Food Truck Nation," March 20, 2018*

- According to Fodor's Travel, Austin placed among the 14 best U.S. cities for food-truck cuisine. *www.fodors.com, "America's Best Food Truck Cities," August 23, 2016*

- *Men's Health* ranked 100 major U.S. cities in terms of alcohol intoxication. Austin ranked #5 (#1 = most sober).Criteria: binge drinking; alcohol-related traffic accidents, arrests, and fatalities. *Men's Health, "America's Drunkest Cities," March 9, 2015*

- Austin was identified as one of the cities in America most likely to order vegetarian menu options by GrubHub.com, the nation's largest food ordering service. The city ranked #8 out of 10. Criteria: percentage of vegetarian restaurants. *GrubHub.com, "Top U.S. Cities for Vegans and Vegetarians," November 17, 2015*

Health/Fitness Rankings

- For each of the 100 largest cities in the United States, the American College of Sports Medicine's American Fitness Index evaluated infrastructure, community assets, and policies that encourage healthy and fit lifestyles, including preventive health behaviors, levels of chronic disease conditions, health care access, and community resources and policies that support physical activity. Austin ranked #42 for "community fitness." *www.americanfitnessindex.org, "ACSM American Fitness Index Health and Community Fitness Status of the 100 Largest U.S. Cities," May 2018*

- Austin was identified as a "2018 Spring Allergy Capital." The area ranked #49 out of 100. Three groups of factors were used to identify the most challenging cities for people with allergies during the spring season: annual pollen levels; medicine utilization; access to board-certified allergists. *Asthma and Allergy Foundation of America, "Spring Allergy Capitals 2018"*

- Austin was identified as a "2018 Fall Allergy Capital." The area ranked #42 out of 100. Three groups of factors were used to identify the most challenging cities for people with allergies during the fall season: annual pollen levels; medicine utilization; access to board-certified allergists. *Asthma and Allergy Foundation of America, "Fall Allergy Capitals 2018"*

- Austin was identified as a "2018 Asthma Capital." The area ranked #79 out of the nation's 100 largest metropolitan areas. Criteria: estimated prevalence; self-reported prevalence; crude death rate for asthma; annual pollen score; annual air quality; public smoking laws; number of board-certified asthma specialists; school inhaler access laws; rescue medication use; controller medication use; ER visits for asthma; uninsured rate; poverty rate. *Asthma and Allergy Foundation of America, "Asthma Capitals 2018: The Most Challenging Places to Live With Asthma"*

- *Men's Health* ranked 100 major U.S. cities in terms of the best cities for men. Austin ranked #7. Criteria: health; fitness; quality of life. *Men's Health, "The Best & Worst Cities for Men Who Want to Be Fit and Happy," January 1, 2016*

- The Austin metro area ranked #49 out of 189 in The Gallup-Healthways Well-Being Index. Criteria: purpose; social well being; financial health; community and physical health. Results are based on telephone interviews with adults, aged 18 and older, living in metropolitan areas in the 50 U.S. states and the District of Columbia. *Gallup-Healthways, "State of American Well-Being, 2017 Community Well-Being Rankings" March 2018*

Pet Rankings

- Austin was selected as the best city for dogs in America by *Dog Fancy*. Criteria: dog-friendly open spaces and dog parks; events celebrating dogs and their owners; vet-to-dog ratios; abundant pet supply and other services; municipal laws that support and protect all pets. *Dog Fancy, "DogTown USA 2014," July 16, 2014*

Real Estate Rankings

- FitSmallBusiness looked at 50 of the largest metropolitan areas in the U.S. to determine which metro was the best to start a real estate business. Data was compiled from such sources as: Zillow, Trulia, U.S. Census Bureau, and the Bureau of Labor Statistics. Criteria: location; inventory; annual wages; median sales price of homes; days on the market; median price cut percentage; and other factors that would influence real estate professional growth. The Austin metro area ranked #13. *fitsmallbusiness.com, "The Best Cities to Become a Real Estate Agent in 2018," January 30, 2018*

- *WalletHub* compared the most populated U.S. cities, as well as at least two of the most populated cities in each state, for a total of 179, to determine which had the best markets for real estate agents. Austin ranked #27 where demand was high and pay was the best. Criteria: sales per agent; annual median wage for real-estate agents; monthly average starting salary for real estate agents; real estate job density and competition; unemployment rate; housing-market health index; and other relevant metrics. *www.WalletHub.com, "2018's Best Places to Be a Real Estate Agent," April 25, 2018*

- According to Penske Truck Rental, the Austin metro area was named the #9 moving destination in 2018, based on one-way consumer truck rental reservations made through Penske's website, rental locations, and reservations call center. *blog.gopenske.com, "Penske Truck Rental's 2018 Top Moving Destinations," January 16, 2019*

- Austin was ranked #160 out of 237 metro areas in terms of housing affordability in 2018 by the National Association of Home Builders (#1 = most affordable). Criteria: the share of homes sold in that area affordable to a family earning the local median income, based on standard mortgage underwriting criteria. *National Association of Home Builders®, NAHB-Wells Fargo Housing Opportunity Index, 4th Quarter 2018*

Safety Rankings

- Allstate ranked the 200 largest cities in America in terms of driver safety. Austin ranked #159. Criteria: internal property damage claims over a two-year period from January 2015 to December 2016. The report helps increase the importance of safety awareness behind the wheel. *Allstate, "Allstate America's Best Drivers Report, 2018" August 28, 2018*

- The National Insurance Crime Bureau ranked 382 metro areas in the U.S. in terms of per capita rates of vehicle theft. The Austin metro area ranked #187 (#1 = highest rate). Criteria: number of vehicle theft offenses per 100,000 inhabitants in 2017. *National Insurance Crime Bureau, "Hot Spots 2017," July 12, 2018*

Seniors/Retirement Rankings

- From its Best Cities for Successful Aging indexes, the Milken Institute generated rankings for metropolitan areas, weighing data in nine categories—health care, wellness, living arrangements, transportation and convenience, financial characteristics, education, employment, community engagement, and overall livability. The Austin metro area was ranked #6 overall in the large metro area category. *Milken Institute, "Best Cities for Successful Aging, 2017" March 14, 2017*

- Austin was identified as one of the most popular places to retire by *Topretirements.com*. The list reflects the 100 cities that visitors to the website are most interested in for retirement, based on the number of times a city's review was viewed on the website. *Topretirements.com, "100 Most Popular Places to Retire for 2017," July 27, 2017*

Sports/Recreation Rankings

- Austin was chosen as one of America's best cities for bicycling. The city ranked #13 out of 50. Criteria: cycling infrastructure that is safe and friendly for all ages; energy and bike culture. The editors only considered cities with populations of 100,000 or more. *Bicycling, "The 50 Best Bike Cities in America," October 10, 2018*

Women/Minorities Rankings

- For its trip ideas, *Travel + Leisure* listed the best cities in the US for a memorable and fun girls' trip. Whether it is for a special occasion or just to get away, Austin is sure to have something for everyone. *Travel + Leisure, "America's Best Cities for Getting Away With the Girls," March 18, 2019*

- The *Houston Chronicle* listed the Austin metro area as #2 in top places for young Latinos to live in the U.S. Research was largely based on housing and occupational data from the largest metropolitan areas performed by *Forbes* and NBC Universo. Criteria: percentage of 18-34 year-olds; Latino college grad rates; and diversity. *blog.chron.com, "The 15 Best Big Cities for Latino Millenials," January 26, 2016*

- *Women's Health*, together with the site Yelp, identified the 15 "Wellthiest" spots in the U.S. Austin appeared among the top for happiest, healthiest, outdoorsiest and Zen-iest. *Women's Health, "The 15 Wellthiest Cities in the U.S." July 5, 2017*

- Personal finance website *WalletHub* compared more than 180 U.S. cities—including the 150 most populated U.S. cities, plus at least two of the most populated cities in each state—across two key dimensions, "Hispanic Business-Friendliness" and "Hispanic Purchasing Power", to arrive at the most favorable conditions for Hispanic entrepreneurs. Austin was ranked #20 out of 182. Criteria includes: share of Hispanic-Owned Businesses; Hispanic entrepreneurship rate to median annual income of Hispanics; Small Business-Friendliness score; cost of living; and number of Hispanics with at least a bachelor's degree. *WalletHub.com, "2018's Best Cities for Hispanic Entrepreneurs," April 26, 2018*

Miscellaneous Rankings

- *WalletHub* compared the 150 most populated U.S. cities to determine their operating efficiency. A "Quality of Services" score was constructed for each city and then divided by the total budget per capita to reveal which were managed the best. Austin ranked #73. Criteria: financial stability; economy; education; safety; health; infrastructure and pollution. *www.WalletHub.com, "2018's Best- & Worst-Run Cities in America," July 9, 2018*

Business Environment

CITY FINANCES

City Government Finances

Component	2016 ($000)	2016 ($ per capita)
Total Revenues	3,569,225	3,830
Total Expenditures	3,684,408	3,954
Debt Outstanding	6,452,607	6,925
Cash and Securities[1]	5,800,812	6,225

Note: (1) Cash and security holdings of a government at the close of its fiscal year, including those of its dependent agencies, utilities, and liquor stores.
Source: U.S. Census Bureau, State & Local Government Finances 2016

City Government Revenue by Source

Source	2016 ($000)	2016 ($ per capita)	2016 (%)
General Revenue			
From Federal Government	60,258	65	1.7
From State Government	21,050	23	0.6
From Local Governments	14,313	15	0.4
Taxes			
Property	474,704	509	13.3
Sales and Gross Receipts	335,045	360	9.4
Personal Income	0	0	0.0
Corporate Income	0	0	0.0
Motor Vehicle License	0	0	0.0
Other Taxes	39,802	43	1.1
Current Charges	762,293	818	21.4
Liquor Store	0	0	0.0
Utility	1,608,381	1,726	45.1
Employee Retirement	89,764	96	2.5

Source: U.S. Census Bureau, State & Local Government Finances 2016

City Government Expenditures by Function

Function	2016 ($000)	2016 ($ per capita)	2016 (%)
General Direct Expenditures			
Air Transportation	138,270	148	3.8
Corrections	0	0	0.0
Education	0	0	0.0
Employment Security Administration	0	0	0.0
Financial Administration	37,162	39	1.0
Fire Protection	156,426	167	4.2
General Public Buildings	0	0	0.0
Governmental Administration, Other	47,548	51	1.3
Health	140,823	151	3.8
Highways	165,949	178	4.5
Hospitals	0	0	0.0
Housing and Community Development	64,865	69	1.8
Interest on General Debt	89,763	96	2.4
Judicial and Legal	35,341	37	1.0
Libraries	71,499	76	1.9
Parking	220	< 1	< 0.1
Parks and Recreation	162,678	174	4.4
Police Protection	323,735	347	8.8
Public Welfare	0	0	0.0
Sewerage	153,817	165	4.2
Solid Waste Management	104,407	112	2.8
Veterans' Services	0	0	0.0
Liquor Store	0	0	0.0
Utility	1,525,827	1,637	41.4
Employee Retirement	253,231	271	6.9

Source: U.S. Census Bureau, State & Local Government Finances 2016

DEMOGRAPHICS

Population Growth

Area	1990 Census	2000 Census	2010 Census	2017* Estimate	Population Growth (%) 1990-2017	2010-2017
City	499,053	656,562	790,390	916,906	83.7	16.0
MSA[1]	846,217	1,249,763	1,716,289	2,000,590	136.4	16.6
U.S.	248,709,873	281,421,906	308,745,538	321,004,407	29.1	4.0

Note: (1) Figures cover the Austin-Round Rock, TX Metropolitan Statistical Area—see Appendix B for areas included; (*) 2013-2017 5-year estimated population
Source: U.S. Census Bureau, 1990 Census, Census 2000, Census 2010, 2013-2017 American Community Survey 5-Year Estimates

Household Size

Area	Persons in Household (%) One	Two	Three	Four	Five	Six	Seven or More	Average Household Size
City	34.3	32.9	14.3	11.2	4.5	1.7	1.0	2.50
MSA[1]	27.9	33.3	15.6	13.8	5.9	2.1	1.4	2.70
U.S.	27.7	33.8	15.7	13.0	6.0	2.3	1.4	2.60

Note: (1) Figures cover the Austin-Round Rock, TX Metropolitan Statistical Area—see Appendix B for areas included
Source: U.S. Census Bureau, 2013-2017 American Community Survey 5-Year Estimates

Race

Area	White Alone[2] (%)	Black Alone[2] (%)	Asian Alone[2] (%)	AIAN[3] Alone[2] (%)	NHOPI[4] Alone[2] (%)	Other Race Alone[2] (%)	Two or More Races (%)
City	75.0	7.6	7.0	0.5	0.1	6.7	3.1
MSA[1]	77.7	7.3	5.5	0.4	0.1	5.8	3.3
U.S.	73.0	12.7	5.4	0.8	0.2	4.8	3.1

Note: (1) Figures cover the Austin-Round Rock, TX Metropolitan Statistical Area—see Appendix B for areas included; (2) Alone is defined as not being in combination with one or more other races; (3) American Indian and Alaska Native; (4) Native Hawaiian and Other Pacific Islander
Source: U.S. Census Bureau, 2013-2017 American Community Survey 5-Year Estimates

Hispanic or Latino Origin

Area	Total (%)	Mexican (%)	Puerto Rican (%)	Cuban (%)	Other (%)
City	34.5	28.3	0.8	0.6	4.8
MSA[1]	32.2	26.9	0.8	0.5	4.0
U.S.	17.6	11.1	1.7	0.7	4.1

Note: Persons of Hispanic or Latino origin can be of any race; (1) Figures cover the Austin-Round Rock, TX Metropolitan Statistical Area—see Appendix B for areas included
Source: U.S. Census Bureau, 2013-2017 American Community Survey 5-Year Estimates

Segregation

Type	Segregation Indices[1] 1990	2000	2010	2010 Rank[2]	Percent Change 1990-2000	1990-2010	2000-2010
Black/White	54.1	52.1	50.1	70	-1.9	-4.0	-2.1
Asian/White	39.4	42.3	41.2	49	2.9	1.8	-1.2
Hispanic/White	41.7	45.6	43.2	51	3.9	1.5	-2.4

Note: All figures cover the Metropolitan Statistical Area—see Appendix B for areas included; Figures are based on an analysis of 1990, 2000, and 2010 Census Decennial Census tract data by William H. Frey, Brookings Institution and the University of Michigan Social Science Data Analysis Network. In this analysis all racial groups (whites, blacks, and asians) are non-Hispanic members of those races. Hispanics are shown as a separate category; (1) Segregation Indices are Dissimilarity Indices that measure the degree to which the minority group is distributed differently than whites across census tracts. They range from 0 (complete integration) to 100 (complete segregation) where the value indicates the percentage of the minority group that needs to be distributed exactly like whites; (2) Ranges from 1 (most segregated) to 102 (least segregated); n/a not available.
Source: www.CensusScope.org

Ancestry

Area	German	Irish	English	American	Italian	Polish	French[2]	Scottish	Dutch
City	11.2	7.3	7.6	3.3	2.9	1.7	2.3	2.0	0.8
MSA[1]	13.0	7.7	8.1	4.1	2.8	1.6	2.5	2.1	0.9
U.S.	14.1	10.1	7.5	6.6	5.3	2.9	2.5	1.7	1.3

Note: Figures are the percentage of the total population reporting a particular ancestry. The nine most commonly reported ancestries in the U.S. are shown. Figures include multiple ancestries (e.g. if a person reported being Irish and Italian, they were included in both columns); (1) Figures cover the Austin-Round Rock, TX Metropolitan Statistical Area—see Appendix B for areas included; (2) Excludes Basque
Source: U.S. Census Bureau, 2013-2017 American Community Survey 5-Year Estimates

Foreign-Born Population

Area	Percent of Population Born in								
	Any Foreign Country	Asia	Mexico	Europe	Carribean	Central America[2]	South America	Africa	Canada
City	18.4	5.4	8.1	1.2	0.5	1.6	0.6	0.6	0.3
MSA[1]	14.9	4.2	6.8	1.0	0.4	1.1	0.5	0.6	0.2
U.S.	13.4	4.1	3.6	1.5	1.3	1.0	0.9	0.6	0.3

Note: (1) Figures cover the Austin-Round Rock, TX Metropolitan Statistical Area—see Appendix B for areas included; (2) Excludes Mexico.
Source: U.S. Census Bureau, 2013-2017 American Community Survey 5-Year Estimates

Marital Status

Area	Never Married	Now Married[2]	Separated	Widowed	Divorced
City	43.5	40.3	1.9	3.1	11.1
MSA[1]	36.2	47.4	1.8	3.7	10.9
U.S.	33.1	48.2	2.0	5.8	10.9

Note: Figures are percentages and cover the population 15 years of age and older; (1) Figures cover the Austin-Round Rock, TX Metropolitan Statistical Area—see Appendix B for areas included; (2) Excludes separated
Source: U.S. Census Bureau, 2013-2017 American Community Survey 5-Year Estimates

Disability by Age

Area	All Ages	Under 18 Years Old	18 to 64 Years Old	65 Years and Over
City	8.7	3.8	7.3	32.9
MSA[1]	9.2	3.7	7.7	32.6
U.S.	12.6	4.2	10.3	35.5

Note: Figures show percent of the civilian noninstitutionalized population that reported having a disability. Disability status is determined from six types of difficulty: vision, hearing, cognitive, ambulatory, self-care, and independent living. For children under 5 years old, hearing and vision difficulty are used to determine disability status. For children between the ages of 5 and 14, disability status is determined from hearing, vision, cognitive, ambulatory, and self-care difficulties. For people aged 15 years and older, they are considered to have a disability if they have difficulty with any one of the six difficulty types; Note: (1) Figures cover the Austin-Round Rock, TX Metropolitan Statistical Area—see Appendix B for areas included
Source: U.S. Census Bureau, 2013-2017 American Community Survey 5-Year Estimates

Age

Area	Percent of Population									Median Age
	Under Age 5	Age 5–19	Age 20–34	Age 35–44	Age 45–54	Age 55–64	Age 65–74	Age 75–84	Age 85+	
City	6.7	17.3	30.3	15.7	12.0	9.6	5.2	2.2	1.0	32.7
MSA[1]	6.6	20.1	24.6	15.4	12.9	10.5	6.2	2.6	1.0	34.2
U.S.	6.2	19.5	20.7	12.7	13.4	12.7	8.6	4.4	1.9	37.8

Note: (1) Figures cover the Austin-Round Rock, TX Metropolitan Statistical Area—see Appendix B for areas included
Source: U.S. Census Bureau, 2013-2017 American Community Survey 5-Year Estimates

Gender

Area	Males	Females	Males per 100 Females
City	463,869	453,037	102.4
MSA[1]	1,001,806	998,784	100.3
U.S.	158,018,753	162,985,654	97.0

Note: (1) Figures cover the Austin-Round Rock, TX Metropolitan Statistical Area—see Appendix B for areas included
Source: U.S. Census Bureau, 2013-2017 American Community Survey 5-Year Estimates

Religious Groups by Family

Area	Catholic	Baptist	Non-Den.	Methodist[2]	Lutheran	LDS[3]	Pente-costal	Presby-terian[4]	Muslim[5]	Judaism
MSA[1]	16.0	10.3	4.5	3.6	2.0	1.2	0.8	1.1	1.2	0.3
U.S.	19.1	9.3	4.0	4.0	2.3	2.0	1.9	1.6	0.8	0.7

Note: Figures are the number of adherents as a percentage of the total population; (1) Figures cover the Austin-Round Rock, TX Metropolitan Statistical Area—see Appendix B for areas included; (2) Methodist/Pietist; (3) Latter Day Saints; (4) Reformed; (5) Figures are estimates
Source: Association of Statisticians of American Religious Bodies, 2010 U.S. Religion Census: Religious Congregations & Membership Study

Religious Groups by Tradition

Area	Catholic	Evangelical Protestant	Mainline Protestant	Other Tradition	Black Protestant	Orthodox
MSA[1]	16.0	16.1	6.3	3.9	1.4	0.1
U.S.	19.1	16.2	7.3	4.3	1.6	0.3

Note: Figures are the number of adherents as a percentage of the total population; (1) Figures cover the Austin-Round Rock, TX Metropolitan Statistical Area—see Appendix B for areas included
Source: Association of Statisticians of American Religious Bodies, 2010 U.S. Religion Census: Religious Congregations & Membership Study

ECONOMY

Gross Metropolitan Product

Area	2016	2017	2018	2019	Rank[2]
MSA[1]	133.7	142.9	153.3	162.8	26

Note: Figures are in billions of dollars; (1) Figures cover the Austin-Round Rock, TX Metropolitan Statistical Area—see Appendix B for areas included; (2) Rank is based on 2017 data and ranges from 1 to 381
Source: U.S. Conference of Mayors, U.S. Metro Economies: Economic Growth & Full Employment, June 2018

Economic Growth

Area	2017-2018 (%)	2019-2020 (%)	2021-2022 (%)
MSA[1]	4.9	3.4	2.9

Note: Figures are real gross metropolitan product (GMP) growth rates and represent average annual percent change; (1) Figures cover the Austin-Round Rock, TX Metropolitan Statistical Area—see Appendix B for areas included
Source: U.S. Conference of Mayors, U.S. Metro Economies: Economic Growth & Full Employment, June 2018

Metropolitan Area Exports

Area	2012	2013	2014	2015	2016	2017	Rank[2]
MSA[1]	8,976.6	8,870.8	9,400.0	10,094.5	10,682.7	12,451.5	27

Note: Figures are in millions of dollars; (1) Figures cover the Austin-Round Rock, TX Metropolitan Statistical Area—see Appendix B for areas included; (2) Rank is based on 2017 data and ranges from 1 to 387
Source: U.S. Department of Commerce, International Trade Administration, Office of Trade and Economic Analysis, Industry and Analysis, Exports by Metropolitan Area, extracted March 25, 2019

Building Permits

Area	Single-Family			Multi-Family			Total		
	2016	2017	Pct. Chg.	2016	2017	Pct. Chg.	2016	2017	Pct. Chg.
City	3,705	4,440	19.8	5,198	7,139	37.3	8,903	11,579	30.1
MSA[1]	13,327	16,119	20.9	8,534	10,581	24.0	21,861	26,700	22.1
U.S.	750,800	820,000	9.2	455,800	462,000	1.4	1,206,600	1,282,000	6.2

Note: (1) Figures cover the Austin-Round Rock, TX Metropolitan Statistical Area—see Appendix B for areas included; Figures represent new, privately-owned housing units authorized (unadjusted data); All permit data are based on estimates with imputation
Source: U.S. Census Bureau, Manufacturing, Mining, and Construction Statistics, Building Permits, 2016, 2017

Bankruptcy Filings

Area	Business Filings			Nonbusiness Filings		
	2017	2018	% Chg.	2017	2018	% Chg.
Travis County	122	96	-21.3	714	717	0.4
U.S.	23,157	22,232	-4.0	765,863	751,186	-1.9

Note: Business filings include Chapter 7, Chapter 11, Chapter 12, and Chapter 13; Nonbusiness filings include Chapter 7, Chapter 11, and Chapter 13
Source: Administrative Office of the U.S. Courts, Business and Nonbusiness Bankruptcy, County Cases Commenced by Chapter of the Bankruptcy Code, During the 12-Month Period Ending December 31, 2017 and Business and Nonbusiness Bankruptcy, County Cases Commenced by Chapter of the Bankruptcy Code, During the 12-Month Period Ending December 31, 2018

Housing Vacancy Rates

Area	Gross Vacancy Rate[2] (%)			Year-Round Vacancy Rate[3] (%)			Rental Vacancy Rate[4] (%)			Homeowner Vacancy Rate[5] (%)		
	2016	2017	2018	2016	2017	2018	2016	2017	2018	2016	2017	2018
MSA[1]	8.2	10.4	9.7	7.6	9.3	8.7	5.5	6.1	7.0	1.0	2.0	1.2
U.S.	12.8	12.7	12.3	9.9	9.9	9.7	6.9	7.2	6.9	1.7	1.6	1.5

Note: (1) Figures cover the Austin-Round Rock, TX Metropolitan Statistical Area—see Appendix B for areas included; (2) The percentage of the total housing inventory that is vacant; (3) The percentage of the housing inventory (excluding seasonal units) that is year-round vacant; (4) The percentage of rental inventory that is vacant for rent; (5) The percentage of homeowner inventory that is vacant for sale
Source: U.S. Census Bureau, Housing Vacancies and Homeownership Annual Statistics: 2016, 2017, 2018

INCOME

Income

Area	Per Capita ($)	Median Household ($)	Average Household ($)
City	37,888	63,717	91,811
MSA[1]	35,949	69,717	94,724
U.S.	31,177	57,652	81,283

Note: (1) Figures cover the Austin-Round Rock, TX Metropolitan Statistical Area—see Appendix B for areas included
Source: U.S. Census Bureau, 2013-2017 American Community Survey 5-Year Estimates

Household Income Distribution

Area	Percent of Households Earning							
	Under $15,000	$15,000 -$24,999	$25,000 -$34,999	$35,000 -$49,999	$50,000 -$74,999	$75,000 -$99,999	$100,000 -$149,999	$150,000 and up
City	9.9	7.7	8.6	12.9	18.3	12.2	15.1	15.3
MSA[1]	8.3	7.2	7.9	12.2	18.1	13.4	16.9	16.0
U.S.	11.6	9.8	9.5	13.0	17.7	12.3	14.1	12.1

Note: (1) Figures cover the Austin-Round Rock, TX Metropolitan Statistical Area—see Appendix B for areas included
Source: U.S. Census Bureau, 2013-2017 American Community Survey 5-Year Estimates

Poverty Rate

Area	All Ages	Under 18 Years Old	18 to 64 Years Old	65 Years and Over
City	15.4	21.4	14.3	9.7
MSA[1]	12.3	15.6	11.8	7.4
U.S.	14.6	20.3	13.7	9.3

Note: Figures are percentage of people whose income during the past 12 months was below the poverty level; (1) Figures cover the Austin-Round Rock, TX Metropolitan Statistical Area—see Appendix B for areas included
Source: U.S. Census Bureau, 2013-2017 American Community Survey 5-Year Estimates

EMPLOYMENT

Labor Force and Employment

Area	Civilian Labor Force			Workers Employed		
	Dec. 2017	Dec. 2018	% Chg.	Dec. 2017	Dec. 2018	% Chg.
City	578,582	599,854	3.7	564,005	584,814	3.7
MSA[1]	1,164,240	1,207,936	3.8	1,133,101	1,174,961	3.7
U.S.	159,880,000	162,510,000	1.6	153,602,000	156,481,000	1.9

Note: Data is not seasonally adjusted and covers workers 16 years of age and older; (1) Figures cover the Austin-Round Rock, TX Metropolitan Statistical Area—see Appendix B for areas included
Source: Bureau of Labor Statistics, Local Area Unemployment Statistics

Unemployment Rate

Area	2018											
	Jan.	Feb.	Mar.	Apr.	May	Jun.	Jul.	Aug.	Sep.	Oct.	Nov.	Dec.
City	2.8	2.8	2.9	2.6	2.6	2.9	2.8	2.8	2.7	2.5	2.5	2.5
MSA[1]	3.0	3.0	3.1	2.8	2.8	3.2	3.1	3.0	2.9	2.7	2.7	2.7
U.S.	4.5	4.4	4.1	3.7	3.6	4.2	4.1	3.9	3.6	3.5	3.5	3.7

Note: Data is not seasonally adjusted and covers workers 16 years of age and older; (1) Figures cover the Austin-Round Rock, TX Metropolitan Statistical Area—see Appendix B for areas included
Source: Bureau of Labor Statistics, Local Area Unemployment Statistics

Average Wages

Occupation	$/Hr.	Occupation	$/Hr.
Accountants and Auditors	35.50	Maids and Housekeeping Cleaners	10.60
Automotive Mechanics	27.40	Maintenance and Repair Workers	18.20
Bookkeepers	20.60	Marketing Managers	67.10
Carpenters	19.10	Nuclear Medicine Technologists	37.50
Cashiers	11.30	Nurses, Licensed Practical	22.40
Clerks, General Office	19.20	Nurses, Registered	33.80
Clerks, Receptionists/Information	14.10	Nursing Assistants	13.70
Clerks, Shipping/Receiving	15.60	Packers and Packagers, Hand	12.90
Computer Programmers	41.00	Physical Therapists	43.20
Computer Systems Analysts	43.90	Postal Service Mail Carriers	24.50
Computer User Support Specialists	24.50	Real Estate Brokers	n/a
Cooks, Restaurant	13.00	Retail Salespersons	13.30
Dentists	70.40	Sales Reps., Exc. Tech./Scientific	30.70
Electrical Engineers	54.40	Sales Reps., Tech./Scientific	61.20
Electricians	26.10	Secretaries, Exc. Legal/Med./Exec.	17.80
Financial Managers	69.30	Security Guards	15.00
First-Line Supervisors/Managers, Sales	21.70	Surgeons	106.20
Food Preparation Workers	12.60	Teacher Assistants*	12.40
General and Operations Managers	59.80	Teachers, Elementary School*	28.30
Hairdressers/Cosmetologists	14.60	Teachers, Secondary School*	27.90
Internists, General	73.00	Telemarketers	19.90
Janitors and Cleaners	12.80	Truck Drivers, Heavy/Tractor-Trailer	19.40
Landscaping/Groundskeeping Workers	14.40	Truck Drivers, Light/Delivery Svcs.	19.90
Lawyers	60.60	Waiters and Waitresses	12.90

Note: Wage data covers the Austin-Round Rock, TX Metropolitan Statistical Area—see Appendix B for areas included; (*) Hourly wages for elementary/secondary school teachers and teacher assistants were calculated by the editors from annual wage data based on a 40 hour work week; n/a not available.
Source: Bureau of Labor Statistics, Metro Area Occupational Employment & Wage Estimates, May 2018

Employment by Occupation

Occupation Classification	City (%)	MSA[1] (%)	U.S. (%)
Management, Business, Science, and Arts	47.8	45.2	37.4
Natural Resources, Construction, and Maintenance	7.8	8.4	8.9
Production, Transportation, and Material Moving	6.4	7.4	12.2
Sales and Office	21.9	23.3	23.5
Service	16.1	15.7	18.0

Note: Figures cover employed civilians 16 years of age and older; (1) Figures cover the Austin-Round Rock, TX Metropolitan Statistical Area—see Appendix B for areas included
Source: U.S. Census Bureau, 2013-2017 American Community Survey 5-Year Estimates

Employment by Industry

Sector	MSA[1]		U.S.
	Number of Employees	Percent of Total	Percent of Total
Construction, Mining, and Logging	63,400	5.9	5.3
Education and Health Services	126,900	11.7	15.9
Financial Activities	63,600	5.9	5.7
Government	182,700	16.9	15.1
Information	34,300	3.2	1.9
Leisure and Hospitality	128,700	11.9	10.7
Manufacturing	61,600	5.7	8.5
Other Services	45,100	4.2	3.9
Professional and Business Services	188,000	17.4	14.1
Retail Trade	112,200	10.4	10.8
Transportation, Warehousing, and Utilities	22,800	2.1	4.2
Wholesale Trade	52,700	4.9	3.9

Note: Figures are non-farm employment as of December 2018. Figures are not seasonally adjusted and include workers 16 years of age and older; (1) Figures cover the Austin-Round Rock, TX Metropolitan Statistical Area—see Appendix B for areas included
Source: Bureau of Labor Statistics, Current Employment Statistics, Employment, Hours, and Earnings

Occupations with Greatest Projected Employment Growth: 2018 – 2020

Occupation[1]	2018 Employment	2020 Projected Employment	Numeric Employment Change	Percent Employment Change
Combined Food Preparation and Serving Workers, Including Fast Food	351,780	372,090	20,310	5.8
Personal Care Aides	218,310	235,470	17,160	7.9
Heavy and Tractor-Trailer Truck Drivers	204,870	216,310	11,440	5.6
Laborers and Freight, Stock, and Material Movers, Hand	194,220	204,060	9,840	5.1
Waiters and Waitresses	236,020	245,790	9,770	4.1
Office Clerks, General	393,740	403,270	9,530	2.4
Customer Service Representatives	268,380	277,460	9,080	3.4
General and Operations Managers	182,190	190,620	8,430	4.6
Retail Salespersons	392,620	400,900	8,280	2.1
Construction Laborers	143,270	150,820	7,550	5.3

Note: Projections cover Texas; (1) Sorted by numeric employment change
Source: www.projectionscentral.com, State Occupational Projections, 2018–2020 Short-Term Projections

Fastest Growing Occupations: 2018 – 2020

Occupation[1]	2018 Employment	2020 Projected Employment	Numeric Employment Change	Percent Employment Change
Wind Turbine Service Technicians	1,810	2,190	380	21.0
Religious Workers, All Other	5,690	6,330	640	11.2
Fundraisers	8,830	9,670	840	9.5
Statisticians	1,870	2,040	170	9.1
Public Relations and Fundraising Managers	6,570	7,160	590	9.0
Home Health Aides	74,390	80,920	6,530	8.8
Community and Social Service Specialists, All Other	4,520	4,890	370	8.2
Personal Care Aides	218,310	235,470	17,160	7.9
Operations Research Analysts	10,920	11,760	840	7.7
Software Developers, Applications	65,190	70,140	4,950	7.6

Note: Projections cover Texas; (1) Sorted by percent employment change and excludes occupations with numeric employment change less than 50
Source: www.projectionscentral.com, State Occupational Projections, 2018–2020 Short-Term Projections

TAXES

State Corporate Income Tax Rates

State	Tax Rate (%)	Income Brackets ($)	Num. of Brackets	Financial Institution Tax Rate (%)[a]	Federal Income Tax Ded.
Texas	(w)	—	—	(w)	No

Note: Tax rates as of January 1, 2019; (a) Rates listed are the corporate income tax rate applied to financial institutions or excise taxes based on income. Some states have other taxes based upon the value of deposits or shares; (w) Texas imposes a Franchise Tax, otherwise known as margin tax, imposed on entities with more than $1,130,000 total revenues at rate of 0.75%, or 0.375% for entities primarily engaged in retail or wholesale trade, on lesser of 70% of total revenues or 100% of gross receipts after deductions for either compensation or cost of goods sold.
Source: Federation of Tax Administrators, Range of State Corporate Income Tax Rates, January 1, 2019

State Individual Income Tax Rates

State	Tax Rate (%)	Income Brackets ($)	Personal Exemptions ($)			Standard Ded. ($)	
			Single	Married	Depend.	Single	Married
Texas			— No state income tax —				

Note: Tax rates as of January 1, 2019; Local- and county-level taxes are not included; n/a not applicable;

Source: Federation of Tax Administrators, State Individual Income Tax Rates, January 1, 2019

Various State Sales and Excise Tax Rates

State	State Sales Tax (%)	Gasoline[1] (¢/gal.)	Cigarette[2] ($/pack)	Spirits[3] ($/gal.)	Wine[4] ($/gal.)	Beer[5] ($/gal.)	Recreational Marijuana (%)
Texas	6.25	20	1.41	2.40 (f)	0.20 (l)	0.20 (q)	Not legal

Note: All tax rates as of January 1, 2019; (1) The American Petroleum Institute has developed a methodology for determining the average tax rate on a gallon of fuel. Rates may include any of the following: excise taxes, environmental fees, storage tank fees, other fees or taxes, general sales tax, and local taxes. In states where gasoline is subject to the general sales tax, or where the fuel tax is based on the average sale price, the average rate determined by API is sensitive to changes in the price of gasoline. States that fully or partially apply general sales taxes to gasoline: CA, CO, GA, IL, IN, MI, NY; (2) The federal excise tax of $1.0066 per pack and local taxes are not included; (3) Rates are those applicable to off-premise sales of 40% alcohol by volume (a.b.v.) distilled spirits in 750ml containers. Local excise taxes are excluded; (4) Rates are those applicable to off-premise sales of 11% a.b.v. non-carbonated wine in 750ml containers; (5) Rates are those applicable to off-premise sales of 4.7% a.b.v. beer in 12 ounce containers; (f) Different rates also applicable according to alcohol content, place of production, size of container, or place purchased (on- or off-premise or onboard airlines); (l) Different rates also applicable to alcohol content, place of production, size of container, place purchased (on- or off-premise or on board airlines) or type of wine (carbonated, vermouth, etc.); (q) Different rates also applicable according to alcohol content, place of production, size of container, or place purchased (on- or off-premise or onboard airlines).
Source: Tax Foundation, 2019 Facts & Figures: How Does Your State Compare?

State Business Tax Climate Index Rankings

State	Overall Rank	Corporate Tax Rank	Individual Income Tax Rank	Sales Tax Rank	Unemployment Insurance Tax Rank	Property Tax Rank
Texas	15	49	6	37	18	37

Note: The index is a measure of how each state's tax laws affect economic performance. The lower the rank, the more favorable a state's tax system is for business. States without a given tax are given a ranking of 1. The scores/rankings for the District of Columbia do not affect other states. The 2019 index represents the tax climate as of July 1, 2018.
Source: Tax Foundation, State Business Tax Climate Index 2019

COMMERCIAL REAL ESTATE

Office Market

Market Area	Inventory (sq. ft.)	Vacancy Rate (%)	Under Construction (sq. ft.)	YTD Net Absorption (sq. ft.)	Total Average Asking Rent ($/sq. ft./year)
Austin	64,851,756	9.8	968,106	167,506	35.20
National	4,905,867,938	13.1	83,553,714	45,846,470	28.46

Source: Newmark Grubb Knight Frank, National Office Market Report, 4th Quarter 2018

Industrial/Warehouse/R&D Market

Market Area	Inventory (sq. ft.)	Vacancy Rate (%)	Under Construction (sq. ft.)	YTD Net Absorption (sq. ft.)	Total Average Asking Rent ($/sq. ft./year)
Austin	89,854,022	6.5	2,103,064	2,101,420	10.19
National	14,796,839,085	5.0	262,662,294	238,014,726	7.16

Source: Newmark Grubb Knight Frank, National Industrial Market Report, 4th Quarter 2018

COMMERCIAL UTILITIES

Typical Monthly Electric Bills

Area	General Service, Light ($/month)		General Service, Heavy ($/month)	
	40 kW demand 5,000 kWh	100 kW demand 10,000 kWh	500 kW demand 100,000 kWh	1,500 kW demand 500,000 kWh
City	818	1,858	12,767	48,847

Note: Figures are based on rates in effect January 1, 2018
Source: Memphis Light, Gas and Water, 2018 Utility Bill Comparisons for Selected U.S. Cities

TRANSPORTATION

Means of Transportation to Work

Area	Car/Truck/Van Drove Alone	Car-pooled	Public Transportation Bus	Subway	Railroad	Bicycle	Walked	Other Means	Worked at Home
City	73.8	9.5	3.7	0.1	0.1	1.3	2.3	1.3	7.9
MSA[1]	76.6	9.6	2.1	0.0	0.1	0.8	1.7	1.2	7.8
U.S.	76.4	9.2	2.5	1.9	0.6	0.6	2.7	1.3	4.7

Note: Figures are percentages and cover workers 16 years of age and older; (1) Figures cover the Austin-Round Rock, TX Metropolitan Statistical Area—see Appendix B for areas included
Source: U.S. Census Bureau, 2013-2017 American Community Survey 5-Year Estimates

Travel Time to Work

Area	Less Than 10 Minutes	10 to 19 Minutes	20 to 29 Minutes	30 to 44 Minutes	45 to 59 Minutes	60 to 89 Minutes	90 Minutes or More
City	9.6	33.0	24.2	21.4	6.6	3.7	1.5
MSA[1]	9.8	28.0	22.2	22.7	9.6	5.8	1.9
U.S.	12.7	28.9	20.9	20.5	8.1	6.2	2.7

Note: Note: Figures are percentages and include workers 16 years old and over; (1) Figures cover the Austin-Round Rock, TX Metropolitan Statistical Area—see Appendix B for areas included
Source: U.S. Census Bureau, 2013-2017 American Community Survey 5-Year Estimates

Freeway Travel Time Index

Area	1985	1990	1995	2000	2005	2010	2014
Urban Area Rank[1,2]	20	21	23	15	12	12	10
Urban Area Index[1]	1.12	1.15	1.19	1.26	1.31	1.29	1.33
Average Index[3]	1.09	1.11	1.14	1.17	1.20	1.19	1.20

Note: Freeway Travel Time Index—the ratio of travel time in the peak period to the travel time at free-flow conditions. For example, a value of 1.30 indicates a 20-minute free-flow trip takes 26 minutes in the peak (20 minutes x 1.30 = 26 minutes); (1) Covers the Austin TX urban area; (2) Rank is based on 101 urban areas (#1 = highest travel time index); (3) Average of 101 urban areas
Source: Texas Transportation Institute, 2015 Urban Mobility Scorecard, August 2015

Freeway Commuter Stress Index

Area	1985	1990	1995	2000	2005	2010	2014
Urban Area Rank[1,2]	18	17	11	8	7	9	7
Urban Area Index[1]	1.22	1.25	1.30	1.37	1.43	1.40	1.44
Average Index[3]	1.13	1.16	1.19	1.22	1.25	1.24	1.25

Note: The Freeway Commuter Stress Index is the same as the Freeway Travel Time Index (see table above) except that it includes only the travel in the peak directions during the peak periods; the TTI includes travel in all directions during the peak period. Thus, the CSI is more indicative of the work trip experienced by each commuter on a daily basis; (1) Covers the Austin TX urban area; (2) Rank is based on 101 urban areas (#1 = highest travel time index); (3) Average of 101 urban areas
Source: Texas Transportation Institute, 2015 Urban Mobility Scorecard, August 2015

Public Transportation

Agency Name / Mode of Transportation	Vehicles Operated in Maximum Service[1]	Annual Unlinked Passenger Trips[2] (in thous.)	Annual Passenger Miles[3] (in thous.)
Capital Metropolitan Transportation Authority (CMTA)			
Bus (purchased transportation)	314	27,297.1	115,795.8
Commuter Bus (purchased transportation)	35	527.4	7,701.9
Demand Response (purchased transportation)	162	670.7	5,548.1
Hybrid Rail (purchased transportation)	4	824.7	13,035.0
Vanpool (purchased transportation)	236	459.6	16,720.9

Note: (1) The number of revenue vehicles operated by the given mode and type of service to meet the annual maximum service requirement. This is the revenue vehicle count during the peak season of the year; on the week and day that maximum service is provided. Vehicles operated in maximum service (VOMS) exclude atypical days and one-time special events; (2) The number of passengers who boarded public transportation vehicles. Passengers are counted each time they board a vehicle no matter how many vehicles they use to travel from their origin to their destination. (3) The sum of the distances ridden by all passengers during the entire fiscal year.
Source: Federal Transit Administration, National Transit Database, 2017

Air Transportation

Airport Name and Code / Type of Service	Passenger Airlines[1]	Passenger Enplanements	Freight Carriers[2]	Freight (lbs)
Austin-Bergstrom International (AUS)				
Domestic service (U.S. carriers - 2018)	28	7,506,197	13	73,664,975
International service (U.S. carriers - 2017)	7	43,888	3	10,795,777

Note: (1) Includes all U.S.-based major, minor and commuter airlines that carried at least one passenger during the year; (2) Includes all U.S.-based airlines and freight carriers that transported at least one pound of freight during the year.
Source: Bureau of Transportation Statistics, The Intermodal Transportation Database, Air Carriers: T-100 Domestic Market (U.S. Carriers), 2018; Bureau of Transportation Statistics, The Intermodal Transportation Database, Air Carriers: T-100 International Market (U.S. Carriers), 2017

Other Transportation Statistics

Major Highways:	I-35
Amtrak Service:	Yes
Major Waterways/Ports:	None

Source: Amtrak.com; Google Maps

BUSINESSES

Major Business Headquarters

Company Name	Industry	Rankings	
		Fortune[1]	Forbes[2]
No companies listed	-	-	-

Note: (1) Companies that produce a 10-K are ranked 1 to 500 based on 2017 revenue; (2) All private companies with at least $2 billion in annual revenue through the end of their most current fiscal year are ranked 1 to 229; companies listed are headquartered in the city; dashes indicate no ranking
Source: Fortune, "Fortune 500," June 2018; Forbes, "America's Largest Private Companies," 2018 Rankings

Fast-Growing Businesses

According to *Inc.*, Austin is home to nine of America's 500 fastest-growing private companies: **Favor** (#138); **Student Loan Hero** (#140); **Wells Solar** (#207); **Axzon** (#233); **Maggie Louise Confections** (#287); **MediaSmack** (#299); **Texas Beauty Labs** (#358); **HookBang** (#390); **Simple Booth** (#414). Criteria: must be an independent, privately-held, for-profit, U.S. corporation, proprietorship or partnership as of December 31, 2017; revenues must be at least $100,000 in 2014 and $2 million in 2017; must have four-year operating/sales history. Holding companies, regulated banks, and utilities were excluded. *Inc., "America's 500 Fastest-Growing Private Companies," 2018*

According to *Fortune*, Austin is home to one of the 100 fastest-growing companies in the world: **Cirrus Logic** (#78). Companies were ranked by their revenue growth rate; their EPS growth rate; and their three-year annualized total return to investors for the period ending June 30, 2018. Criteria for inclusion: a company, foreign or domestic, must trade on a major U.S. stock exchange; must file quarterly reports with the SEC; must have a minimum market capitalization of $250 million; must have a stock price of at least $5 on June 30, 2018; must have been trading continuously since June 30, 2015; must have revenue and net income for the four quarters ended on or before April 30, 2018, of at least $50 million and $10 million, respectively; and must have posted a compound annual growth in revenue and earnings per share of at least 15% annually over the three years ending on or before April 30, 2018. Real estate investment trusts, limited-liability companies, limited parterships, business development companies, closed-end investment firms, companies about to be acquired, and companies that lost money in the quarter ending April 30, 2018 were excluded. *Fortune, "100 Fastest-Growing Companies," 2018*

According to Deloitte, Austin is home to four of North America's 500 fastest-growing high-technology companies: **Apollo Endosurgery** (#104); **Digital Turbine** (#296); **SailPoint** (#446); **Q2 Holdings** (#496). Companies are ranked by percentage growth in revenue over a four-year period. Criteria for inclusion: company must be headquartered within North America; must own proprietary intellectual property or technology that is sold to customers in products that contributes to a significant portion of the company's operating revenue; must have been in business for a minumum of four years with 2014 operating revenues of at least $50,000 USD/CD and 2017 operating revenues of at least $5 million USD/CD. *Deloitte, 2018 Technology Fast 500™*

Minority Business Opportunity

Austin is home to two companies which are on the *Black Enterprise* Auto Dealer list (45 largest dealers based on gross sales): **Barnett Auto Group** (#28); **JMC Auto Group** (#30). Criteria: company must be operational in previous calendar year and be at least 51% black-owned. *Black Enterprise, B.E. 100s, 2018*

Austin is home to one company which is on the *Black Enterprise* Private Equity list (10 largest private equity firms based on capital under management): **Vista Equity Partners** (#1). Criteria: company must be operational in previous calendar year and be at least 51% black-owned. *Black Enterprise, B.E. 100s, 2018*

Austin is home to two companies which are on the *Hispanic Business* 500 list (500 largest U.S. Hispanic-owned companies based on revenue): **Venta Financial Group** (#187); **Tramex Travel** (#233). Companies included must show at least 51 percent ownership by Hispanic U.S. citizens, and must maintain headquarters in one of the 50 states or Washington, D.C. *Hispanic Business, "Hispanic Business 500," June 20, 2013*

Minority- and Women-Owned Businesses

Group	All Firms		Firms with Paid Employees			
	Firms	Sales ($000)	Firms	Sales ($000)	Employees	Payroll ($000)
AIAN[1]	1,051	133,278	31	79,479	296	18,940
Asian	6,586	2,621,646	1,885	2,380,538	15,452	543,456
Black	3,542	394,310	247	303,024	3,916	101,082
Hispanic	18,261	1,887,923	1,440	1,286,372	10,825	369,192
NHOPI[2]	126	15,634	26	13,341	135	2,678
Women	34,253	5,161,708	3,984	4,207,425	36,075	1,139,983
All Firms	96,048	156,390,131	20,194	152,442,612	470,742	24,046,652

Note: Figures cover firms located in the city; minority- and women-owned business are defined as firms in which the corresponding group own 51% or more of the stock or equity of the company; (1) American Indian and Alaska Native; (2) Native Hawaiian and Other Pacific Islander
Source: U.S. Census Bureau, 2012 Economic Census, Survey of Business Owners

HOTELS & CONVENTION CENTERS

Hotels, Motels and Vacation Rentals

Area	5 Star		4 Star		3 Star		2 Star		1 Star		Not Rated	
	Num.	Pct.[3]	Num.	Pct.[3]	Num.	Pct.[3]	Num.	Pct.[3]	Num.	Pct.[3]	Num.	Pct.[3]
City[1]	7	0.4	124	6.9	333	18.6	155	8.7	2	0.1	1,166	65.2
Total[2]	286	0.4	5,236	7.1	16,715	22.6	10,259	13.9	293	0.4	41,056	55.6

Note: (1) Figures cover Austin and vicinity; (2) Figures cover all 100 cities in this book; (3) Percentage of hotels which have a given star rating; Star ratings are determined by expedia.com and offer an indication of the general quality of a particular hotel.
Source: www.expedia.com, April 3, 2019

Major Convention Centers

Name	Overall Space (sq. ft.)	Exhibit Space (sq. ft.)	Meeting Space (sq. ft.)	Meeting Rooms
Austin Convention Center	881,400	246,097	37,170	54

Note: Table includes convention centers located in the Austin-Round Rock, TX metro area
Source: Original research

Living Environment

COST OF LIVING

Cost of Living Index

Composite Index	Groceries	Housing	Utilities	Trans-portation	Health Care	Misc. Goods/Services
98.6	88.8	101.0	96.6	90.9	104.0	102.2

Note: The Cost of Living Index measures regional differences in the cost of consumer goods and services, excluding taxes and non-consumer expenditures, for professional and managerial households in the top income quintile. It is based on more than 50,000 prices covering almost 60 different items for which prices are collected three times a year by chambers of commerce, economic development organizations or university applied economic centers in each participating urban area. The numbers shown should be read as a percentage above or below the national average of 100. For example, a value of 115.4 in the groceries column indicates that grocery prices are 15.4% higher than the national average. Small differences in the index numbers should not be interpreted as significant; Figures cover the Austin TX urban area.
Source: The Council for Community and Economic Research, ACCRA Cost of Living Index, 2018

Grocery Prices

Area[1]	T-Bone Steak ($/pound)	Frying Chicken ($/pound)	Whole Milk ($/half gal.)	Eggs ($/dozen)	Orange Juice ($/64 oz.)	Coffee ($/11.5 oz.)
City[2]	9.85	1.15	1.52	1.70	3.09	3.84
Avg.	11.35	1.42	1.94	1.81	3.52	4.35
Min.	7.45	0.92	0.80	0.75	2.72	3.06
Max.	15.05	2.76	4.18	4.00	5.36	8.20

Note: (1) Values for the local area are compared with the average, minimum and maximum values for all 291 areas in the Cost of Living Index; (2) Figures cover the Austin TX urban area; **T-Bone Steak** (price per pound); **Frying Chicken** (price per pound, whole fryer); **Whole Milk** (half gallon carton); **Eggs** (price per dozen, Grade A, large); **Orange Juice** (64 oz. Tropicana or Florida Natural); **Coffee** (11.5 oz. can, vacuum-packed, Maxwell House, Hills Bros, or Folgers).
Source: The Council for Community and Economic Research, ACCRA Cost of Living Index, 2018

Housing and Utility Costs

Area[1]	New Home Price ($)	Apartment Rent ($/month)	All Electric ($/month)	Part Electric ($/month)	Other Energy ($/month)	Telephone ($/month)
City[2]	312,376	1,377	-	106.13	50.37	179.90
Avg.	347,000	1,087	165.93	100.16	67.73	178.70
Min.	200,468	500	93.58	25.64	26.78	163.10
Max.	1,901,222	4,888	388.65	246.86	332.81	197.70

Note: (1) Values for the local area are compared with the average, minimum and maximum values for all 291 areas in the Cost of Living Index; (2) Figures cover the Austin TX urban area; **New Home Price** (2,400 sf living area, 8,000 sf lot, in urban area with full utilities); **Apartment Rent** (950 sf 2 bedroom/1.5 or 2 bath, unfurnished, excluding all utilities except water); **All Electric** (average monthly cost for an all-electric home); **Part Electric** (average monthly cost for a part-electric home); **Other Energy** (average monthly cost for natural gas, fuel oil, coal, wood, and any other forms of energy except electricity); **Telephone** (price includes the base monthly rate plus taxes and fees for three lines of mobile phone service).
Source: The Council for Community and Economic Research, ACCRA Cost of Living Index, 2018

Health Care, Transportation, and Other Costs

Area[1]	Doctor ($/visit)	Dentist ($/visit)	Optometrist ($/visit)	Gasoline ($/gallon)	Beauty Salon ($/visit)	Men's Shirt ($)
City[2]	104.33	108.31	112.50	2.45	47.08	31.68
Avg.	110.71	95.11	103.74	2.61	37.48	32.03
Min.	33.60	62.55	54.63	1.89	17.00	11.44
Max.	195.97	153.93	225.79	3.59	71.88	58.64

Note: (1) Values for the local area are compared with the average, minimum and maximum values for all 291 areas in the Cost of Living Index; (2) Figures cover the Austin TX urban area; **Doctor** (general practitioners routine exam of an established patient); **Dentist** (adult teeth cleaning and periodic oral examination); **Optometrist** (full vision eye exam for established adult patient); **Gasoline** (one gallon regular unleaded, national brand, including all taxes, cash price at self-service pump if available); **Beauty Salon** (woman's shampoo, trim, and blow-dry); **Men's Shirt** (cotton/polyester dress shirt, pinpoint weave, long sleeves).
Source: The Council for Community and Economic Research, ACCRA Cost of Living Index, 2018

HOUSING

House Price Index (HPI)

Area	National Ranking[2]	Quarterly Change (%)	One-Year Change (%)	Five-Year Change (%)
MSA[1]	137	-0.29	5.91	49.36
U.S.[3]	–	1.12	5.73	32.81

Note: The HPI is a weighted repeat sales index. It measures average price changes in repeat sales or refinancings on the same properties. This information is obtained by reviewing repeat mortgage transactions on single-family properties whose mortgages have been purchased or securitized by Fannie Mae or Freddie Mac in January 1975; (1) Figures cover the Austin-Round Rock, TX Metropolitan Statistical Area—see Appendix B for areas included; (2) Rankings are based on annual percentage change for all metro areas containing at least 15,000 transactions over the last 10 years and ranges from 1 to 245; (3) figures based on a weighted average of Census Division estimates using a seasonally adjusted, purchase-only index; all figures are for the period ending December 31, 2018
Source: Federal Housing Finance Agency, House Price Index, February 26, 2019

Median Single-Family Home Prices

Area	2016	2017	2018p	Percent Change 2017 to 2018
MSA[1]	284.0	295.8	315.9	6.8
U.S. Average	235.5	248.8	261.6	5.1

Note: Figures are median sales prices of existing single-family homes in thousands of dollars; (p) preliminary; (1) Figures cover the Austin-Round Rock, TX Metropolitan Statistical Area—see Appendix B for areas included
Source: National Association of Realtors, Median Sales Price of Existing Single-Family Homes for Metropolitan Areas, 4th Quarter 2018

Qualifying Income Based on Median Sales Price of Existing Single-Family Homes

Area	With 5% Down ($)	With 10% Down ($)	With 20% Down ($)
MSA[1]	75,857	71,865	63,880
U.S. Average	62,954	59,640	53,013

Note: Figures are preliminary; Qualifying income is based on a mortgage rate of 4.9%. Monthly principal and interest payment is limited to 25% of income; (1) Figures cover the Austin-Round Rock, TX Metropolitan Statistical Area—see Appendix B for areas included
Source: National Association of Realtors, Qualifying Income Based on Median Sales Price of Existing Single-Family Homes for Metropolitan Areas, 4th Quarter 2018

Median Apartment Condo-Coop Home Prices

Area	2016	2017	2018p	Percent Change 2017 to 2018
MSA[1]	228.0	241.8	260.5	7.7
U.S. Average	220.7	234.3	241.0	2.9

Note: Figures are median sales prices of existing apartment condo-coop homes in thousands of dollars; (p) preliminary; (1) Figures cover the Austin-Round Rock, TX Metropolitan Statistical Area—see Appendix B for areas included
Source: National Association of Realtors, Median Sales Price of Existing Apartment Condo-Coop Homes for Metropolitan Areas, 4th Quarter 2018

Home Value Distribution

Area	Under $50,000	$50,000 -$99,999	$100,000 -$149,999	$150,000 -$199,999	$200,000 -$299,999	$300,000 -$499,999	$500,000 -$999,999	$1,000,000 or more
City	3.1	3.5	8.2	13.3	24.9	28.3	15.4	3.2
MSA[1]	4.3	5.4	11.5	16.6	26.0	23.1	10.6	2.5
U.S.	8.3	13.9	14.7	14.6	18.7	17.3	9.7	2.7

Note: Figures are percentages and cover owner-occupied housing units; (1) Figures cover the Austin-Round Rock, TX Metropolitan Statistical Area—see Appendix B for areas included
Source: U.S. Census Bureau, 2013-2017 American Community Survey 5-Year Estimates

Homeownership Rate

Area	2010 (%)	2011 (%)	2012 (%)	2013 (%)	2014 (%)	2015 (%)	2016 (%)	2017 (%)	2018 (%)
MSA[1]	65.8	58.4	60.1	59.6	61.1	57.5	56.5	55.6	56.1
U.S.	66.9	66.1	65.4	65.1	64.5	63.7	63.4	63.9	64.4

Note: (1) Figures cover the Austin-Round Rock, TX Metropolitan Statistical Area—see Appendix B for areas included
Source: U.S. Census Bureau, Housing Vacancies and Homeownership Annual Statistics: 2010-2018

Year Housing Structure Built

Area	2010 or Later	2000 -2009	1990 -1999	1980 -1989	1970 -1979	1960 -1969	1950 -1959	1940 -1949	Before 1940	Median Year
City	7.5	19.6	16.4	20.4	17.3	7.9	5.3	2.7	2.9	1987
MSA[1]	9.9	27.4	19.4	17.6	12.5	5.2	3.6	2.0	2.4	1993
U.S.	3.2	14.5	14.0	13.6	15.5	10.8	10.5	5.1	12.9	1977

Note: Figures are percentages except for Median Year; Note: (1) Figures cover the Austin-Round Rock, TX Metropolitan Statistical Area—see Appendix B for areas included
Source: U.S. Census Bureau, 2013-2017 American Community Survey 5-Year Estimates

Gross Monthly Rent

Area	Under $500	$500 -$999	$1,000 -$1,499	$1,500 -$1,999	$2,000 -$2,499	$2,500 -$2,999	$3,000 and up	Median ($)
City	3.4	29.2	42.9	17.3	4.9	1.2	1.2	1,165
MSA[1]	3.6	30.5	41.8	17.3	4.6	1.2	1.1	1,155
U.S.	10.5	41.1	28.7	11.7	4.5	1.8	1.7	982

Note: Figures are percentages except for Median; Gross rent is the contract rent plus the estimated average monthly cost of utilities (electricity, gas, and water and sewer) and fuels (oil, coal, kerosene, wood, etc.) if these are paid by the renter (or paid for the renter by someone else); (1) Figures cover the Austin-Round Rock, TX Metropolitan Statistical Area—see Appendix B for areas included
Source: U.S. Census Bureau, 2013-2017 American Community Survey 5-Year Estimates

HEALTH

Health Risk Factors

Category	MSA[1] (%)	U.S. (%)
Adults aged 18–64 who have any kind of health care coverage	78.4	87.3
Adults who reported being in good or better health	85.0	82.4
Adults who have been told they have high blood cholesterol	32.2	33.0
Adults who have been told they have high blood pressure	26.5	32.3
Adults who are current smokers	12.5	17.1
Adults who currently use E-cigarettes	4.8	4.6
Adults who currently use chewing tobacco, snuff, or snus	4.2	4.0
Adults who are heavy drinkers[2]	8.4	6.3
Adults who are binge drinkers[3]	22.9	17.4
Adults who are overweight (BMI 25.0 - 29.9)	32.8	35.3
Adults who are obese (BMI 30.0 - 99.8)	29.3	31.3
Adults who participated in any physical activities in the past month	75.2	74.4
Adults who always or nearly always wears a seat belt	98.3	94.3

Note: (1) Figures cover the Austin-Round Rock, TX Metropolitan Statistical Area—see Appendix B for areas included; (2) Heavy drinkers are classified as adult men having more than 14 drinks per week and adult women having more than 7 drinks per week; (3) Binge drinkers are classified as males having five or more drinks on one occasion or females having four or more drinks on one occasion
Source: Centers for Disease Control and Prevention, Behaviorial Risk Factor Surveillance System, SMART: Selected Metropolitan Area Risk Trends, 2017

Acute and Chronic Health Conditions

Category	MSA[1] (%)	U.S. (%)
Adults who have ever been told they had a heart attack	2.0	4.2
Adults who have ever been told they have angina or coronary heart disease	2.5	3.9
Adults who have ever been told they had a stroke	2.6	3.0
Adults who have ever been told they have asthma	11.3	14.2
Adults who have ever been told they have arthritis	17.4	24.9
Adults who have ever been told they have diabetes[2]	9.6	10.5
Adults who have ever been told they had skin cancer	4.8	6.2
Adults who have ever been told they had any other types of cancer	5.6	7.1
Adults who have ever been told they have COPD	3.1	6.5
Adults who have ever been told they have kidney disease	2.4	3.0
Adults who have ever been told they have a form of depression	16.7	20.5

Note: (1) Figures cover the Austin-Round Rock, TX Metropolitan Statistical Area—see Appendix B for areas included; (2) Figures do not include pregnancy-related, borderline, or pre-diabetes
Source: Centers for Disease Control and Prevention, Behaviorial Risk Factor Surveillance System, SMART: Selected Metropolitan Area Risk Trends, 2017

Health Screening and Vaccination Rates

Category	MSA[1] (%)	U.S. (%)
Adults aged 65+ who have had flu shot within the past year	63.4	60.7
Adults aged 65+ who have ever had a pneumonia vaccination	74.2	75.4
Adults who have ever been tested for HIV	46.3	36.1
Adults who have ever had the shingles or zoster vaccine?	29.3	28.9
Adults who have had their blood cholesterol checked within the last five years	86.9	85.9

Note: n/a not available; (1) Figures cover the Austin-Round Rock, TX Metropolitan Statistical Area—see Appendix B for areas included.
Source: Centers for Disease Control and Prevention, Behaviorial Risk Factor Surveillance System, SMART: Selected Metropolitan Area Risk Trends, 2017

Disability Status

Category	MSA[1] (%)	U.S. (%)
Adults who reported being deaf	5.2	6.7
Are you blind or have serious difficulty seeing, even when wearing glasses?	3.6	4.5
Are you limited in any way in any of your usual activities due of arthritis?	10.1	12.9
Do you have difficulty doing errands alone?	5.3	6.8
Do you have difficulty dressing or bathing?	2.4	3.6
Do you have serious difficulty concentrating/remembering/making decisions?	9.8	10.7
Do you have serious difficulty walking or climbing stairs?	9.5	13.6

Note: (1) Figures cover the Austin-Round Rock, TX Metropolitan Statistical Area—see Appendix B for areas included.
Source: Centers for Disease Control and Prevention, Behaviorial Risk Factor Surveillance System, SMART: Selected Metropolitan Area Risk Trends, 2017

Mortality Rates for the Top 10 Causes of Death in the U.S.

ICD-10[a] Sub-Chapter	ICD-10[a] Code	Age-Adjusted Mortality Rate[1] per 100,000 population	
		County[2]	U.S.
Malignant neoplasms	C00-C97	125.2	155.5
Ischaemic heart diseases	I20-I25	65.9	94.8
Other forms of heart disease	I30-I51	35.0	52.9
Chronic lower respiratory diseases	J40-J47	25.6	41.0
Cerebrovascular diseases	I60-I69	36.4	37.5
Other degenerative diseases of the nervous system	G30-G31	41.5	35.0
Other external causes of accidental injury	W00-X59	32.7	33.7
Organic, including symptomatic, mental disorders	F01-F09	39.9	31.0
Hypertensive diseases	I10-I15	17.9	21.9
Diabetes mellitus	E10-E14	14.9	21.2

Note: (a) ICD-10 = International Classification of Diseases 10th Revision; (1) Mortality rates are a three year average covering 2015-2017; (2) Figures cover Travis County.
Source: Centers for Disease Control and Prevention, National Center for Health Statistics. Underlying Cause of Death 1999-2017 on CDC WONDER Online Database

Mortality Rates for Selected Causes of Death

ICD-10[a] Sub-Chapter	ICD-10[a] Code	Age-Adjusted Mortality Rate[1] per 100,000 population	
		County[2]	U.S.
Assault	X85-Y09	3.1	5.9
Diseases of the liver	K70-K76	14.4	14.1
Human immunodeficiency virus (HIV) disease	B20-B24	1.2	1.8
Influenza and pneumonia	J09-J18	9.3	14.3
Intentional self-harm	X60-X84	12.5	13.6
Malnutrition	E40-E46	2.5	1.6
Obesity and other hyperalimentation	E65-E68	1.4	2.1
Renal failure	N17-N19	11.5	13.0
Transport accidents	V01-V99	10.4	12.4
Viral hepatitis	B15-B19	1.3	1.6

Note: (a) ICD-10 = International Classification of Diseases 10th Revision; (1) Mortality rates are a three year average covering 2015-2017; (2) Figures cover Travis County; Data are suppressed when the data meet the criteria for confidentiality constraints; Mortality rates are flagged as unreliable when the rate would be calculated with a numerator of 20 or less.
Source: Centers for Disease Control and Prevention, National Center for Health Statistics. Underlying Cause of Death 1999-2017 on CDC WONDER Online Database

Health Insurance Coverage

Area	With Health Insurance	With Private Health Insurance	With Public Health Insurance	Without Health Insurance	Population Under Age 18 Without Health Insurance
City	84.7	70.7	20.8	15.3	9.2
MSA[1]	86.3	73.2	21.6	13.7	8.6
U.S.	89.5	67.2	33.8	10.5	5.7

Note: Figures are percentages that cover the civilian noninstitutionalized population; (1) Figures cover the Austin-Round Rock, TX Metropolitan Statistical Area—see Appendix B for areas included
Source: U.S. Census Bureau, 2013-2017 American Community Survey 5-Year Estimates

Number of Medical Professionals

Area	MDs[3]	DOs[3,4]	Dentists	Podiatrists	Chiropractors	Optometrists
County[1] (number)	3,758	246	846	55	406	198
County[1] (rate[2])	312.0	20.4	69.0	4.5	33.1	16.1
U.S. (rate[2])	279.3	23.0	68.4	6.0	27.1	16.2

Note: Data as of 2017 unless noted; (1) Data covers Travis County; (2) Rate per 100,000 population; (3) Data as of 2016 and includes all active, non-federal physicians; (4) Doctor of Osteopathic Medicine
Source: U.S. Department of Health and Human Services, Health Resources and Services Administration, Bureau of Health Professions, Area Resource File (ARF) 2017-2018

EDUCATION

Public School District Statistics

District Name	Schls	Pupils	Pupil/ Teacher Ratio	Minority Pupils[1] (%)	Free Lunch Eligible[2] (%)	IEP[3] (%)
Austin ISD	130	83,067	14.3	72.6	48.0	10.6
Eanes ISD	11	8,134	13.6	30.3	1.7	8.5
Harmony Science Academy (Austin)	6	3,971	16.0	84.9	50.2	6.2
Kipp Austin Public Schools Inc	10	4,990	15.2	97.4	76.3	8.1
Lake Travis ISD	9	9,825	16.9	31.5	9.3	7.7

Note: Table includes school districts with 2,000 or more students; (1) Percentage of students that are not non-Hispanic white; (2) Percentage of students that are eligible for the free lunch program; (3) Percentage of students that have an Individualized Education Program.
Source: U.S. Department of Education, National Center for Education Statistics, Common Core of Data, Local Education Agency (School District) Universe Survey: School Year 2016-2017; U.S. Department of Education, National Center for Education Statistics, Common Core of Data, Public Elementary/Secondary School Universe Survey: School Year 2016-2017

Best High Schools

According to *U.S. News*, Austin is home to eight of the best high schools in the U.S.: **Liberal Arts and Science Academy (LASA)** (#16); **Chaparral Star Academy** (#23); **KIPP Austin Collegiate** (#53); **Richards School for Young Women Leaders** (#117); **Westlake High School** (#213); **Westwood High School** (#221); **Vandegrift High School** (#339); **Harmony School of Excellence** (#374). More than 20,000 public, magnet and charter schools were ranked based on their performance on state assessments and how well they prepare students for college. Schools with the highest unrounded College Readiness Index values were numerically ranked from 1 to 500 and were classified as gold medal winners. *U.S. News & World Report, "Best High Schools 2018"*

Highest Level of Education

Area	Less than H.S.	H.S. Diploma	Some College, No Deg.	Associate Degree	Bachelor's Degree	Master's Degree	Prof. School Degree	Doctorate Degree
City	11.5	16.3	18.1	5.2	30.8	12.7	3.1	2.4
MSA[1]	10.7	19.2	20.7	6.4	27.8	11.0	2.4	1.8
U.S.	12.7	27.3	20.8	8.3	19.1	8.4	2.0	1.4

Note: Figures cover persons age 25 and over; (1) Figures cover the Austin-Round Rock, TX Metropolitan Statistical Area—see Appendix B for areas included
Source: U.S. Census Bureau, 2013-2017 American Community Survey 5-Year Estimates

Educational Attainment by Race

Area	High School Graduate or Higher (%)					Bachelor's Degree or Higher (%)				
	Total	White	Black	Asian	Hisp.[2]	Total	White	Black	Asian	Hisp.[2]
City	88.5	90.0	89.1	92.9	70.2	49.0	52.0	24.7	73.5	23.8
MSA[1]	89.3	90.5	90.1	92.2	72.0	42.9	44.6	27.9	68.9	21.3
U.S.	87.3	89.3	84.9	86.5	66.7	30.9	32.2	20.6	52.7	15.2

Note: Figures shown cover persons 25 years old and over; (1) Figures cover the Austin-Round Rock, TX Metropolitan Statistical Area—see Appendix B for areas included; (2) People of Hispanic origin can be of any race
Source: U.S. Census Bureau, 2013-2017 American Community Survey 5-Year Estimates

School Enrollment by Grade and Control

Area	Preschool (%)		Kindergarten (%)		Grades 1 - 4 (%)		Grades 5 - 8 (%)		Grades 9 - 12 (%)	
	Public	Private	Public	Private	Public	Private	Public	Private	Public	Private
City	48.6	51.4	87.5	12.5	89.5	10.5	89.5	10.5	91.6	8.4
MSA[1]	50.5	49.5	88.7	11.3	91.0	9.0	91.2	8.8	93.3	6.7
U.S.	58.8	41.2	87.7	12.3	89.7	10.3	89.6	10.4	90.3	9.7

Note: Figures shown cover persons 3 years old and over; (1) Figures cover the Austin-Round Rock, TX Metropolitan Statistical Area—see Appendix B for areas included
Source: U.S. Census Bureau, 2013-2017 American Community Survey 5-Year Estimates

Average Salaries of Public School Classroom Teachers

Area	2016		2017		Change from 2016 to 2017	
	Dollars	Rank[1]	Dollars	Rank[1]	Percent	Rank[2]
Texas	51,890	28	52,575	28	1.3	29
U.S. Average	58,479	–	59,660	–	2.0	–

Note: (1) Rank ranges from 1 to 51 where 1 indicates highest salary; (2) Rank ranges from 1 to 51 where 1 indicates highest percent change.
Source: National Education Association, Rankings & Estimates: Rankings of the States 2017 and Estimates of School Statistics 2018

Higher Education

Four-Year Colleges			Two-Year Colleges			Medical Schools[1]	Law Schools[2]	Voc/ Tech[3]
Public	Private Non-profit	Private For-profit	Public	Private Non-profit	Private For-profit			
1	6	7	1	0	4	1	1	9

Note: Figures cover institutions located within the city limits and include main campuses only; (1) includes schools accredited by the Liaison Committee on Medical Education and the American Osteopathic Association's Commission on Osteopathic College Accreditation; (2) includes ABA-accredited schools, schools with provisional ABA accreditation, and state accredited schools; (3) includes all schools with programs that are less than 2 years.
Source: National Center for Education Statistics, Integrated Postsecondary Education System (IPEDS), 2017-18; Wikipedia, List of Medical Schools in the United States, accessed April 3, 2019; Wikipedia, List of Law Schools in the United States, accessed April 3, 2019

According to *U.S. News & World Report*, the Austin-Round Rock, TX metro area is home to one of the best national universities in the U.S.: **University of Texas—Austin** (#49 tie). The indicators used to capture academic quality fall into a number of categories: assessment by administrators at peer institutions; retention of students; faculty resources; student selectivity; financial resources; alumni giving; high school counselor ratings of colleges; and graduation rate. *U.S. News & World Report, "America's Best Colleges 2019"*

According to *U.S. News & World Report*, the Austin-Round Rock, TX metro area is home to one of the best liberal arts colleges in the U.S.: **Southwestern University** (#90 tie). The indicators used to capture academic quality fall into a number of categories: assessment by administrators at peer institutions; retention of students; faculty resources; student selectivity; financial resources; alumni giving; high school counselor ratings of colleges; and graduation rate. *U.S. News & World Report, "America's Best Colleges 2019"*

According to *U.S. News & World Report*, the Austin-Round Rock, TX metro area is home to one of the top 100 law schools in the U.S.: **University of Texas—Austin** (#16). The rankings are based on a weighted average of 12 measures of quality: peer assessment score; assessment score by lawyers/judges; median LSAT scores; median undergrad GPA; acceptance rate; employment rates for graduates; placement success; bar passage rate; faculty resources; expenditures per student; student/faculty ratio; and library resources. *U.S. News & World Report, "America's Best Graduate Schools, Law, 2020"*

According to *U.S. News & World Report,* the Austin-Round Rock, TX metro area is home to one of the top 75 business schools in the U.S.: **University of Texas—Austin (McCombs)** (#19 tie). The rankings are based on a weighted average of the following nine measures: quality assessment; peer assessment; recruiter assessment; placement success; mean starting salary and bonus; student selectivity; mean GMAT and GRE scores; mean undergraduate GPA; and acceptance rate. *U.S. News & World Report, "America's Best Graduate Schools, Business, 2020"*

PRESIDENTIAL ELECTION

2016 Presidential Election Results

Area	Clinton	Trump	Johnson	Stein	Other
Travis County	65.8	27.1	4.7	1.6	0.8
U.S.	48.0	45.9	3.3	1.1	1.7

Note: Results are percentages and may not add to 100% due to rounding
Source: Dave Leip's Atlas of U.S. Presidential Elections

EMPLOYERS

Major Employers

Company Name	Industry
Accenture	Management consulting & software development center
Apple	Computer maker's tech & admin support center
Applied Materials	Semiconductor manufacturing equip, mfg
AT&T	Telecommunications
Austin Community College	Higher education, public
Austin School Independent District	Public education
City of Austin	Government
Dell	Computer technology solutions & equipment mfg./sales
Federal Government	Government
Flextronics	Contract electronics mfg. & integrated supply chain svcs
Hays Consolidated ISD	Public education
IBM	Computer systems, hardware, software, & chip R&D
Keller Williams Realty	Residential real estate
Leander Independent School District	Public education
National Instruments	Virtual instrumentation software & hardware mfg
NXP Semiconductors	Semiconductor chip design & mfg.
Pflugerville Independent School District	Public education
Round Rock Independent School District	Public education
Samsung Austin Semiconductor	Semiconductor chip mfg., R&D
Seton Healthcare Family	Healthcare
St. David's Healthcare Partnership	Healthcare
State of Texas	State government
Texas State University-San Marcos	Higher education, public
Travis County	Government
U.S. Internal Revenue Service	Government, regional call & processing center
University of Texas at Austin	Higher education, public
Whole Foods Market	Grocery stores

Note: Companies shown are located within the Austin-Round Rock, TX Metropolitan Statistical Area.
Source: Hoovers.com; Wikipedia

Best Companies to Work For

Kendra Scott, headquartered in Austin, is among the "Top Companies for Executive Women." The 2019 National Association for Female Executives (NAFE) Top Companies for Executive Women application included more than 200 questions on female representation at all levels, but especially the corporate officer and profit-and-loss leadership ranks. The application tracked how many employees have access to programs and policies that promote the advancement of women, and how many employees take advantage of them. The application also examined how companies train managers to help women advance, and how managers are held accountable for the advancement of female employees they oversee. *National Association for Female Executives, "2019 NAFE Top 70 Companies for Executive Women"*

PUBLIC SAFETY

Crime Rate

Area	All Crimes	Violent Crimes				Property Crimes		
		Murder	Rape[3]	Robbery	Aggrav. Assault	Burglary	Larceny -Theft	Motor Vehicle Theft
City	3,604.4	2.6	85.8	101.5	224.9	450.6	2,525.0	213.9
Suburbs[1]	1,839.9	2.4	44.7	28.9	138.1	262.4	1,263.5	100.0
Metro[2]	2,650.7	2.5	63.6	62.3	178.0	348.9	1,843.2	152.3
U.S.	2,756.1	5.3	41.7	98.0	248.9	430.4	1,694.4	237.4

Note: Figures are crimes per 100,000 population; (1) All areas within the metro area that are located outside the city limits; (2) Figures cover the Austin-Round Rock, TX Metropolitan Statistical Area—see Appendix B for areas included; (3) The city and U.S. figures shown were reported using the revised Uniform Crime Reporting (UCR) definition of rape. The suburban and metro area figures shown are an aggregate total of the data submitted using both the revised and legacy UCR definitions.
Source: FBI Uniform Crime Reports, 2017

Hate Crimes

Area	Number of Quarters Reported	Number of Incidents per Bias Motivation					
		Race/Ethnicity/ Ancestry	Religion	Sexual Orientation	Disability	Gender	Gender Identity
City	4	10	3	4	0	0	1
U.S.	4	4,131	1,564	1,130	116	46	119

Source: Federal Bureau of Investigation, Hate Crime Statistics 2017

Identity Theft Consumer Reports

Area	Reports	Reports per 100,000 Population	Rank[2]
MSA[1]	2,827	137	48
U.S.	444,602	135	-

Note: (1) Figures cover the Austin-Round Rock, TX Metropolitan Statistical Area—see Appendix B for areas included; (2) Rank ranges from 1 to 389 where 1 indicates greatest number of identity theft reports per 100,000 population
Source: Federal Trade Commission, Consumer Sentinel Network Data Book for January–December 2018

Fraud and Other Consumer Reports

Area	Reports	Reports per 100,000 Population	Rank[2]
MSA[1]	11,958	582	69
U.S.	2,552,917	776	-

Note: (1) Figures cover the Austin-Round Rock, TX Metropolitan Statistical Area—see Appendix B for areas included; (2) Rank ranges from 1 to 389 where 1 indicates greatest number of fraud and other consumer reports per 100,000 population
Source: Federal Trade Commission, Consumer Sentinel Network Data Book for January–December 2018

SPORTS

Professional Sports Teams

Team Name	League	Year Established
Austin FC	Major League Soccer (MLS)	2021

Note: Includes teams located in the Austin-Round Rock, TX Metropolitan Statistical Area.
Source: Wikipedia, Major Professional Sports Teams of the United States and Canada, April 5, 2019

CLIMATE

Average and Extreme Temperatures

Temperature	Jan	Feb	Mar	Apr	May	Jun	Jul	Aug	Sep	Oct	Nov	Dec	Yr.
Extreme High (°F)	90	97	98	98	100	105	109	106	104	98	91	90	109
Average High (°F)	60	64	72	79	85	91	95	96	90	81	70	63	79
Average Temp. (°F)	50	53	61	69	75	82	85	85	80	70	60	52	69
Average Low (°F)	39	43	50	58	65	72	74	74	69	59	49	41	58
Extreme Low (°F)	-2	7	18	35	43	53	64	61	47	32	20	4	-2

Note: Figures cover the years 1948-1990
Source: National Climatic Data Center, International Station Meteorological Climate Summary, 9/96

Average Precipitation/Snowfall/Humidity

Precip./Humidity	Jan	Feb	Mar	Apr	May	Jun	Jul	Aug	Sep	Oct	Nov	Dec	Yr.
Avg. Precip. (in.)	1.6	2.3	1.8	2.9	4.3	3.5	1.9	1.9	3.3	3.5	2.1	1.9	31.1
Avg. Snowfall (in.)	1	Tr	Tr	0	0	0	0	0	0	0	Tr	Tr	1
Avg. Rel. Hum. 6am (%)	79	80	79	83	88	89	88	87	86	84	81	79	84
Avg. Rel. Hum. 3pm (%)	53	51	47	50	53	49	43	42	47	47	49	51	48

Note: Figures cover the years 1948-1990; Tr = Trace amounts (<0.05 in. of rain; <0.5 in. of snow)
Source: National Climatic Data Center, International Station Meteorological Climate Summary, 9/96

Weather Conditions

Temperature			Daytime Sky			Precipitation		
10°F & below	32°F & below	90°F & above	Clear	Partly cloudy	Cloudy	0.01 inch or more precip.	0.1 inch or more snow/ice	Thunder-storms
< 1	20	111	105	148	112	83	1	41

Note: Figures are average number of days per year and cover the years 1948-1990
Source: National Climatic Data Center, International Station Meteorological Climate Summary, 9/96

HAZARDOUS WASTE

Superfund Sites

The Austin-Round Rock, TX metro area has no sites on the EPA's Superfund Final National Priorities List. There are a total of 1,390 Superfund sites with a status of proposed or final on the list in the U.S. *U.S. Environmental Protection Agency, National Priorities List, April 5, 2019*

AIR & WATER QUALITY

Air Quality Trends: Ozone

	1990	1995	2000	2005	2010	2012	2014	2015	2016	2017
MSA[1]	0.088	0.089	0.088	0.082	0.074	0.074	0.062	0.073	0.064	0.070
U.S.	0.088	0.089	0.082	0.080	0.073	0.075	0.067	0.068	0.069	0.068

Note: (1) Data covers the Austin-Round Rock, TX Metropolitan Statistical Area—see Appendix B for areas included. The values shown are the composite ozone concentration averages among trend sites based on the highest fourth daily maximum 8-hour concentration in parts per million. These trends are based on sites having an adequate record of monitoring data during the trend period. Data from exceptional events are included.
Source: U.S. Environmental Protection Agency, Air Quality Monitoring Information, "Air Quality Trends by City, 1990-2017"

Air Quality Index

Area	Percent of Days when Air Quality was...[2]					AQI Statistics[2]	
	Good	Moderate	Unhealthy for Sensitive Groups	Unhealthy	Very Unhealthy	Maximum	Median
MSA[1]	71.8	27.1	1.1	0.0	0.0	130	43

Note: (1) Data covers the Austin-Round Rock, TX Metropolitan Statistical Area—see Appendix B for areas included; (2) Based on 365 days with AQI data in 2017. Air Quality Index (AQI) is an index for reporting daily air quality. EPA calculates the AQI for five major air pollutants regulated by the Clean Air Act: ground-level ozone, particle pollution (aka particulate matter), carbon monoxide, sulfur dioxide, and nitrogen dioxide. The AQI runs from 0 to 500. The higher the AQI value, the greater the level of air pollution and the greater the health concern. There are six AQI categories: "Good" AQI is between 0 and 50. Air quality is considered satisfactory; "Moderate" AQI is between 51 and 100. Air quality is acceptable; "Unhealthy for Sensitive Groups" When AQI values are between 101 and 150, members of sensitive groups may experience health effects; "Unhealthy" When AQI values are between 151 and 200 everyone may begin to experience health effects; "Very Unhealthy" AQI values between 201 and 300 trigger a health alert; "Hazardous" AQI values over 300 trigger warnings of emergency conditions (not shown).
Source: U.S. Environmental Protection Agency, Air Quality Index Report, 2017

Air Quality Index Pollutants

Area	Percent of Days when AQI Pollutant was...[2]					
	Carbon Monoxide	Nitrogen Dioxide	Ozone	Sulfur Dioxide	Particulate Matter 2.5	Particulate Matter 10
MSA[1]	0.0	4.9	51.0	0.0	44.1	0.0

Note: (1) Data covers the Austin-Round Rock, TX Metropolitan Statistical Area—see Appendix B for areas included; (2) Based on 365 days with AQI data in 2017. The Air Quality Index (AQI) is an index for reporting daily air quality. EPA calculates the AQI for five major air pollutants regulated by the Clean Air Act: ground-level ozone, particle pollution (also known as particulate matter), carbon monoxide, sulfur dioxide, and nitrogen dioxide. The AQI runs from 0 to 500. The higher the AQI value, the greater the level of air pollution and the greater the health concern.
Source: U.S. Environmental Protection Agency, Air Quality Index Report, 2017

Maximum Air Pollutant Concentrations: Particulate Matter, Ozone, CO and Lead

	Particulate Matter 10 (ug/m³)	Particulate Matter 2.5 Wtd AM (ug/m³)	Particulate Matter 2.5 24-Hr (ug/m³)	Ozone (ppm)	Carbon Monoxide (ppm)	Lead (ug/m³)
MSA[1] Level	39	10	25	0.07	1	n/a
NAAQS[2]	150	15	35	0.075	9	0.15
Met NAAQS[2]	Yes	Yes	Yes	Yes	Yes	n/a

Note: (1) Data covers the Austin-Round Rock, TX Metropolitan Statistical Area—see Appendix B for areas included; Data from exceptional events are included; (2) National Ambient Air Quality Standards; ppm = parts per million; ug/m³ = micrograms per cubic meter; n/a not available.
Concentrations: Particulate Matter 10 (coarse particulate)—highest second maximum 24-hour concentration; Particulate Matter 2.5 Wtd AM (fine particulate)—highest weighted annual mean concentration; Particulate Matter 2.5 24-Hour (fine particulate)—highest 98th percentile 24-hour concentration; Ozone—highest fourth daily maximum 8-hour concentration; Carbon Monoxide—highest second maximum non-overlapping 8-hour concentration; Lead—maximum running 3-month average
Source: U.S. Environmental Protection Agency, Air Quality Monitoring Information, "Air Quality Statistics by City, 2017"

Maximum Air Pollutant Concentrations: Nitrogen Dioxide and Sulfur Dioxide

	Nitrogen Dioxide AM (ppb)	Nitrogen Dioxide 1-Hr (ppb)	Sulfur Dioxide AM (ppb)	Sulfur Dioxide 1-Hr (ppb)	Sulfur Dioxide 24-Hr (ppb)
MSA[1] Level	13	47	n/a	4	n/a
NAAQS[2]	53	100	30	75	140
Met NAAQS[2]	Yes	Yes	n/a	Yes	n/a

Note: (1) Data covers the Austin-Round Rock, TX Metropolitan Statistical Area—see Appendix B for areas included; Data from exceptional events are included; (2) National Ambient Air Quality Standards; ppm = parts per million; ug/m³ = micrograms per cubic meter; n/a not available.
Concentrations: Nitrogen Dioxide AM—highest arithmetic mean concentration; Nitrogen Dioxide 1-Hr—highest 98th percentile 1-hour daily maximum concentration; Sulfur Dioxide AM—highest annual mean concentration; Sulfur Dioxide 1-Hr—highest 99th percentile 1-hour daily maximum concentration; Sulfur Dioxide 24-Hr—highest second maximum 24-hour concentration
Source: U.S. Environmental Protection Agency, Air Quality Monitoring Information, "Air Quality Statistics by City, 2017"

Drinking Water

Water System Name	Pop. Served	Primary Water Source Type	Violations[1]	
			Health Based	Monitoring/ Reporting
Austin Water & Wastewater	981,783	Surface	0	4

Note: (1) Based on violation data from January 1, 2018 to December 31, 2018
Source: U.S. Environmental Protection Agency, Office of Ground Water and Drinking Water, Safe Drinking Water Information System (based on data extracted April 5, 2019)

Baton Rouge, Louisiana

Background

Baton Rouge, the capital of Louisiana, stretches along the Istrouma Bluff on the east bank of the Mississippi River, and is the key industrial city in the area, at the center of an immense industrial and shipping complex. The seat of government for East Baton Rouge Parish, the city's greater metropolitan area, includes Baton Rouge itself, Baker, and Zachary. The metropolitan area is the second-largest in the state, next to New Orleans.

Originally the site of an Indian village, and an important trade center since 1699 when a French expedition first explored the area, Baton Rouge was incorporated in 1817 and made the state capital in 1882.

Baton Rouge, or "Red Stick," is so-named because of a distinctive boundary marker between the Oumas and Bayagoula tribes. The pole was used in earlier times as a point of reference by the many missionaries, traders, and settlers who traveled this way on the Mississippi River.

The historical complexity of Baton Rouge is hinted at by the various elements that appear on the official city flag, which is laid out on a field of crimson, and features, of course, the red, white, and blue of the United States. The flag also displays the fleur-de-lis of France, the Castile of Spain, and the union jack of Great Britain. This portrait, though, only begins to do justice to Baton Rouge's rich history. The city has lived under seven distinct governments in its 300-year development from trading post to modern metropolis: French, English, Spanish, West Floridian, Louisiana, Confederate, and American.

The state capitol building in Baton Rouge is one of America's most notable buildings. Completed in 1932, the 34-story building is located on the old campus of Louisiana State University, and surrounded by 27 acres of landscaped grounds. Ten miles of walks and drives are bordered by a collection of trees, flowering shrubs, bulbs, and flower beds, which are tended to yield maximal color in every season. From the capitol's observation tower, one can see for 30 miles in every direction. Louisiana's legendary Governor and Senator Huey P. Long, under whose administration the building was constructed, was assassinated in a corridor here in 1935 and is buried in the front grounds. A 12-foot bronze statue by Charles Keck memorializes The Kingfish, as Long was nicknamed.

Although the effects of the 2005 Katrina and Rita hurricanes were obviously felt in Baton Rouge, the city was not damaged as profoundly as was New Orleans. One of the most substantial effects was that Baton Rouge became, overnight, the largest city in Louisiana, as population temporarily surged by more than 200,000 as it accepted persons displaced by the hurricanes. In the wake of Katrina, much of the economic activity once centered in New Orleans transferred to Baton Rouge. As the city continued to meet the challenges presented by the unprecedented storms, a more prosperous Baton Rouge emerged.

As many cities in the country have enlarged their convention centers, so has Baton Rouge. The city's Riverside Centroplex Convention Center underwent major expansion, adding 100,000 square feet of convention space, 20,000 square feet of state-of-the-art meeting space and a ballroom. Although the center was used as an emergency resource in the post-Katrina period, it is now operating for its original purpose.

The film industry in Louisiana had increased dramatically in the last decade. The Baton Rouge Film Commission reported that the industry brings into the local economy more than $90 million annually. The city's increasing visual arts scene includes the Shaw Center for the Arts, the Louisiana Arts and Science Museum and the Baton Rouge Gallery. In addition to the city's strong performing arts and music scenes, the annual Mardi Gras festivals are among the city's most popular events.

Louisiana State University, a traditional leader among the nation's institutions, is located here, as are Southern University and A&M College, the largest predominantly African-American institution in the nation.

Baton Rouge has a humid, subtropical climate with mild winters and humid summers, moderate to heavy rainfall and the possibility of damaging winds and tornadoes yearlong. The city was affected by the August 2016 Louisiana floods.

Rankings

General Rankings

- In their sixth annual survey, Livability.com looked at data for more than 1,000 U.S. cities to determine the rankings for Livability's "Top 100 Best Places to Live" in 2019. Baton Rouge ranked #69. Criteria: median home value capped at $250,000; affordable living; vibrant economy; education, demographics, health care options. transportation & infrastructure; abundant lifestyle amenities. *Livability.com, "Top 100 Best Places to Live 2019" March 2019*

Business/Finance Rankings

- The personal finance site NerdWallet analyzed 183 American metropolitan areas with populations over 250,000 and more than 15,000 businesses to rank where entrepreneurs find the most success. Criteria included area economy, annual income, housing cost, unemployment rate, and the success rate of area businesses. Baton Rouge ranked #13. *www.nerdwallet.com, "Best Places to Start a Business," April 27, 2015*

- NerdWallet.com identified the 10 most promising cities for job seekers of the nation's 100 largest cities. Baton Rouge was ranked #81. Criteria: job availability; annual salary; workforce growth; affordability. *NerdWallet.com, "Best Cities for Job Seekers in 2017," December 19, 2016*

- The Brookings Institution ranked the nation's largest cities based on income inequality. Baton Rouge was ranked #9 (#1 = greatest inequality). Criteria: the "95/20 ratio," a figure representing the income at which a household earns more than 95 percent of all other households, divided by the income at which a household earns more than only 20 percent of all other households. *Brookings Institution, "Household Income Inequality, Largest Cities of 97 Large U.S. Metro Areas, 2014-2016," February 5, 2018*

- The Brookings Institution ranked the 100 largest metro areas in the U.S. based on income inequality. Baton Rouge was ranked #13 (#1 = greatest inequality). Criteria: the "95/20 ratio," a figure representing the income at which a household earns more than 95 percent of all other households, divided by the income at which a household earns more than only 20 percent of all other households. *Brookings Institution, "Household Income Inequality, 100 Largest U.S. Metro Areas, 2014-2016," February 5, 2018*

- The Baton Rouge metro area appeared on the Milken Institute "2018 Best Performing Cities" list. Rank: #145 out of 200 large metro areas. Criteria: job growth; wage and salary growth; high-tech output growth. *Milken Institute, "Best-Performing Cities 2018," January 24, 2019*

- *Forbes* ranked the 200 most populous metro areas to determine the nation's "Best Places for Business and Careers." The Baton Rouge metro area was ranked #156. Criteria: costs (business and living); job growth (past and projected); income growth; quality of life; educational attainment (college and high school); projected economic growth; cultural and recreational opportunities; net migration patterns; number of highly ranked colleges. *Forbes, "The Best Places for Business and Careers 2018: Seattle Leads the Way," October 24, 2018*

Children/Family Rankings

- Baton Rouge was selected as one of the most playful cities in the U.S. by KaBOOM! The organization's Playful City USA initiative honors cities and towns across the nation that have made their communities more playable. Criteria: pledging to integrate play as a solution to challenges in their communities; making it easy for children to get active and balanced play; creating more family-friendly and innovative communities as a result. *KaBOOM! National Campaign for Play, "2017 Playful City USA Communities"*

Dating/Romance Rankings

- Baton Rouge was ranked #1 out of 25 cities that stood out for inspiring romance and attracting diners on the website OpenTable.com. Criteria: percentage of people who dined out on Valentine's Day in 2018; percentage of romantic restaurants as rated by OpenTable diner reviews; and percentage of tables seated for two. *OpenTable, "25 Most Romantic Cities in America for 2019," February 7, 2019*

Education Rankings

- Personal finance website *WalletHub* analyzed the 150 largest U.S. metropolitan statistical areas to determine where the most educated Americans are choosing to settle. Criteria: education quality and attainment gap; education levels; percentage of workers with degrees; public school quality rankings; quality and size of each metro area's universities. Baton Rouge was ranked #110 (#1 = most educated city). *www.WalletHub.com, "2018's Most and Least Educated Cities in America," July 24, 2018*

Health/Fitness Rankings

- Analysts who tracked obesity rates in 100 of the nation's most populous areas found that the Baton Rouge metro area was one of the ten communities where residents were most likely to be obese, defined as a BMI score of 30 or above. *www.gallup.com, "Colorado Springs Residents Least Likely to Be Obese," May 28, 2015*

- For each of the 100 largest cities in the United States, the American College of Sports Medicine's American Fitness Index evaluated infrastructure, community assets, and policies that encourage healthy and fit lifestyles, including preventive health behaviors, levels of chronic disease conditions, health care access, and community resources and policies that support physical activity. Baton Rouge ranked #67 for "community fitness." *www.americanfitnessindex.org, "ACSM American Fitness Index Health and Community Fitness Status of the 100 Largest U.S. Cities," May 2018*

- Baton Rouge was identified as a "2018 Spring Allergy Capital." The area ranked #12 out of 100. Three groups of factors were used to identify the most challenging cities for people with allergies during the spring season: annual pollen levels; medicine utilization; access to board-certified allergists. *Asthma and Allergy Foundation of America, "Spring Allergy Capitals 2018"*

- Baton Rouge was identified as a "2018 Fall Allergy Capital." The area ranked #13 out of 100. Three groups of factors were used to identify the most challenging cities for people with allergies during the fall season: annual pollen levels; medicine utilization; access to board-certified allergists. *Asthma and Allergy Foundation of America, "Fall Allergy Capitals 2018"*

- Baton Rouge was identified as a "2018 Asthma Capital." The area ranked #89 out of the nation's 100 largest metropolitan areas. Criteria: estimated prevalence; self-reported prevalence; crude death rate for asthma; annual pollen score; annual air quality; public smoking laws; number of board-certified asthma specialists; school inhaler access laws; rescue medication use; controller medication use; ER visits for asthma; uninsured rate; poverty rate. *Asthma and Allergy Foundation of America, "Asthma Capitals 2018: The Most Challenging Places to Live With Asthma"*

- *Men's Health* ranked 100 major U.S. cities in terms of the best cities for men. Baton Rouge ranked #84. Criteria: health; fitness; quality of life. *Men's Health, "The Best & Worst Cities for Men Who Want to Be Fit and Happy," January 1, 2016*

- The Baton Rouge metro area ranked #160 out of 189 in The Gallup-Healthways Well-Being Index. Criteria: purpose; social well being; financial health; community and physical health. Results are based on telephone interviews with adults, aged 18 and older, living in metropolitan areas in the 50 U.S. states and the District of Columbia. *Gallup-Healthways, "State of American Well-Being, 2017 Community Well-Being Rankings" March 2018*

Real Estate Rankings

- *WalletHub* compared the most populated U.S. cities, as well as at least two of the most populated cities in each state, for a total of 179, to determine which had the best markets for real estate agents. Baton Rouge ranked #142 where demand was high and pay was the best. Criteria: sales per agent; annual median wage for real-estate agents; monthly average starting salary for real estate agents; real estate job density and competition; unemployment rate; housing-market health index; and other relevant metrics. *www.WalletHub.com, "2018's Best Places to Be a Real Estate Agent," April 25, 2018*

Safety Rankings

- Allstate ranked the 200 largest cities in America in terms of driver safety. Baton Rouge ranked #185. Criteria: internal property damage claims over a two-year period from January 2015 to December 2016. The report helps increase the importance of safety awareness behind the wheel. *Allstate, "Allstate America's Best Drivers Report, 2018" August 28, 2018*

- Baton Rouge was identified as one of the most dangerous cities in America by NeighborhoodScout. The city ranked #68 out of 100. Criteria: number of violent crimes per 1,000 residents. The editors only considered cities with 25,000 or more residents. *NeighborhoodScout.com, "Top 100 Most Dangerous Cities in the U.S. 2019" January 2, 2019*

- The National Insurance Crime Bureau ranked 382 metro areas in the U.S. in terms of per capita rates of vehicle theft. The Baton Rouge metro area ranked #82 (#1 = highest rate). Criteria: number of vehicle theft offenses per 100,000 inhabitants in 2017. *National Insurance Crime Bureau, "Hot Spots 2017," July 12, 2018*

Seniors/Retirement Rankings

- From its Best Cities for Successful Aging indexes, the Milken Institute generated rankings for metropolitan areas, weighing data in nine categories—health care, wellness, living arrangements, transportation and convenience, financial characteristics, education, employment, community engagement, and overall livability. The Baton Rouge metro area was ranked #66 overall in the large metro area category. *Milken Institute, "Best Cities for Successful Aging, 2017" March 14, 2017*

Transportation Rankings

- NerdWallet surveyed average annual car insurance premiums in 125 U.S. cities to identify the least expensive U.S. cities in which to insure a car. Locations with no-fault insurance laws was a strong determinant. Baton Rouge came in at #5 for the most expensive rates. *www.nerdwallet.com, "Best Cities for Cheap Car Insurance," February 3, 2014*

Women/Minorities Rankings

- *24/7 Wall St.* compared median earnings over a 12-month period for men and women who worked full-time, year-round, and employment composition by sector to identify the worst-paying cities for women. Of the largest 100 U.S. metropolitan areas, Baton Rouge was ranked #2 in pay disparity. *24/7 Wall St., "The Best (and Worst) Paying Cities for Women," March 27, 2017*

- Personal finance website *WalletHub* compared more than 180 U.S. cities—including the 150 most populated U.S. cities, plus at least two of the most populated cities in each state—across two key dimensions, "Hispanic Business-Friendliness" and "Hispanic Purchasing Power", to arrive at the most favorable conditions for Hispanic entrepreneurs. Baton Rouge was ranked #72 out of 182. Criteria includes: share of Hispanic-Owned Businesses; Hispanic entrepreneurship rate to median annual income of Hispanics; Small Business-Friendliness score; cost of living; and number of Hispanics with at least a bachelor's degree. *WalletHub.com, "2018's Best Cities for Hispanic Entrepreneurs," April 26, 2018*

Miscellaneous Rankings

- Baton Rouge was selected as a 2018 Digital Cities Survey winner. The city ranked #7 in the mid-sized city (125,000 to 249,999 population) category. The survey examined and assessed how city governments are utilizing technology to improve transparency, enhance cybersecurity, and solve social challenges. Survey questions focused on ten characteristics: engaged, mobile, open, secure, staffed/supported, efficient, connected, resilient, best practices, and use of innovation. *Center for Digital Government, "2018 Digital Cities Survey," November 2, 2018*

- *WalletHub* compared the 150 most populated U.S. cities to determine their operating efficiency. A "Quality of Services" score was constructed for each city and then divided by the total budget per capita to reveal which were managed the best. Baton Rouge ranked #77. Criteria: financial stability; economy; education; safety; health; infrastructure and pollution. *www.WalletHub.com, "2018's Best- & Worst-Run Cities in America," July 9, 2018*

Business Environment

CITY FINANCES

City Government Finances

Component	2016 ($000)	2016 ($ per capita)
Total Revenues	991,715	4,338
Total Expenditures	1,223,997	5,355
Debt Outstanding	1,437,260	6,288
Cash and Securities[1]	2,816,133	12,320

Note: (1) Cash and security holdings of a government at the close of its fiscal year, including those of its dependent agencies, utilities, and liquor stores.
Source: U.S. Census Bureau, State & Local Government Finances 2016

City Government Revenue by Source

Source	2016 ($000)	2016 ($ per capita)	2016 (%)
General Revenue			
From Federal Government	65,055	285	6.6
From State Government	50,687	222	5.1
From Local Governments	0	0	0.0
Taxes			
Property	201,715	882	20.3
Sales and Gross Receipts	334,955	1,465	33.8
Personal Income	0	0	0.0
Corporate Income	0	0	0.0
Motor Vehicle License	0	0	0.0
Other Taxes	4,985	22	0.5
Current Charges	301,194	1,318	30.4
Liquor Store	0	0	0.0
Utility	5,022	22	0.5
Employee Retirement	10,761	47	1.1

Source: U.S. Census Bureau, State & Local Government Finances 2016

City Government Expenditures by Function

Function	2016 ($000)	2016 ($ per capita)	2016 (%)
General Direct Expenditures			
Air Transportation	24,410	106	2.0
Corrections	57,056	249	4.7
Education	11,246	49	0.9
Employment Security Administration	0	0	0.0
Financial Administration	26,752	117	2.2
Fire Protection	84,962	371	6.9
General Public Buildings	10,050	44	0.8
Governmental Administration, Other	17,696	77	1.4
Health	46,993	205	3.8
Highways	41,694	182	3.4
Hospitals	91,553	400	7.5
Housing and Community Development	63,299	276	5.2
Interest on General Debt	78,588	343	6.4
Judicial and Legal	45,087	197	3.7
Libraries	39,687	173	3.2
Parking	656	2	0.1
Parks and Recreation	13,280	58	1.1
Police Protection	147,075	643	12.0
Public Welfare	5,373	23	0.4
Sewerage	196,776	860	16.1
Solid Waste Management	38,600	168	3.2
Veterans' Services	0	0	0.0
Liquor Store	0	0	0.0
Utility	35,176	153	2.9
Employee Retirement	78,530	343	6.4

Source: U.S. Census Bureau, State & Local Government Finances 2016

DEMOGRAPHICS

Population Growth

Area	1990 Census	2000 Census	2010 Census	2017* Estimate	Population Growth (%) 1990-2017	2010-2017
City	223,299	227,818	229,493	227,549	1.9	-0.8
MSA[1]	623,853	705,973	802,484	828,741	32.8	3.3
U.S.	248,709,873	281,421,906	308,745,538	321,004,407	29.1	4.0

Note: (1) Figures cover the Baton Rouge, LA Metropolitan Statistical Area—see Appendix B for areas included; (*) 2013-2017 5-year estimated population
Source: U.S. Census Bureau, 1990 Census, Census 2000, Census 2010, 2013-2017 American Community Survey 5-Year Estimates

Household Size

Area	One	Two	Three	Four	Five	Six	Seven or More	Average Household Size
City	36.4	33.0	15.0	8.6	4.2	1.8	1.0	2.50
MSA[1]	28.1	34.0	17.0	12.1	5.8	1.9	1.1	2.70
U.S.	27.7	33.8	15.7	13.0	6.0	2.3	1.4	2.60

Note: (1) Figures cover the Baton Rouge, LA Metropolitan Statistical Area—see Appendix B for areas included
Source: U.S. Census Bureau, 2013-2017 American Community Survey 5-Year Estimates

Race

Area	White Alone[2] (%)	Black Alone[2] (%)	Asian Alone[2] (%)	AIAN[3] Alone[2] (%)	NHOPI[4] Alone[2] (%)	Other Race Alone[2] (%)	Two or More Races (%)
City	38.6	54.8	3.6	0.3	0.0	1.3	1.3
MSA[1]	59.6	35.4	2.1	0.2	0.0	1.0	1.7
U.S.	73.0	12.7	5.4	0.8	0.2	4.8	3.1

Note: (1) Figures cover the Baton Rouge, LA Metropolitan Statistical Area—see Appendix B for areas included; (2) Alone is defined as not being in combination with one or more other races; (3) American Indian and Alaska Native; (4) Native Hawaiian and Other Pacific Islander
Source: U.S. Census Bureau, 2013-2017 American Community Survey 5-Year Estimates

Hispanic or Latino Origin

Area	Total (%)	Mexican (%)	Puerto Rican (%)	Cuban (%)	Other (%)
City	3.4	1.2	0.2	0.2	1.8
MSA[1]	3.8	1.7	0.3	0.1	1.6
U.S.	17.6	11.1	1.7	0.7	4.1

Note: Persons of Hispanic or Latino origin can be of any race; (1) Figures cover the Baton Rouge, LA Metropolitan Statistical Area—see Appendix B for areas included
Source: U.S. Census Bureau, 2013-2017 American Community Survey 5-Year Estimates

Segregation

Type	1990	2000	2010	2010 Rank[2]	1990-2000	1990-2010	2000-2010
Black/White	59.6	60.2	57.5	45	0.7	-2.1	-2.7
Asian/White	52.7	54.3	50.8	5	1.6	-1.9	-3.5
Hispanic/White	26.0	30.3	32.7	88	4.4	6.8	2.4

Note: All figures cover the Metropolitan Statistical Area—see Appendix B for areas included; Figures are based on an analysis of 1990, 2000, and 2010 Census Decennial Census tract data by William H. Frey, Brookings Institution and the University of Michigan Social Science Data Analysis Network. In this analysis all racial groups (whites, blacks, and asians) are non-Hispanic members of those races. Hispanics are shown as a separate category; (1) Segregation Indices are Dissimilarity Indices that measure the degree to which the minority group is distributed differently than whites across census tracts. They range from 0 (complete integration) to 100 (complete segregation) where the value indicates the percentage of the minority group that needs to move to be distributed exactly like whites; (2) Ranges from 1 (most segregated) to 102 (least segregated); n/a not available.
Source: www.CensusScope.org

Ancestry

Area	German	Irish	English	American	Italian	Polish	French[2]	Scottish	Dutch
City	5.5	5.1	5.2	6.2	3.1	0.6	7.3	1.2	0.3
MSA[1]	7.3	7.4	5.6	7.7	4.9	0.6	13.2	1.2	0.4
U.S.	14.1	10.1	7.5	6.6	5.3	2.9	2.5	1.7	1.3

Note: Figures are the percentage of the total population reporting a particular ancestry. The nine most commonly reported ancestries in the U.S. are shown. Figures include multiple ancestries (e.g. if a person reported being Irish and Italian, they were included in both columns); (1) Figures cover the Baton Rouge, LA Metropolitan Statistical Area—see Appendix B for areas included; (2) Excludes Basque
Source: U.S. Census Bureau, 2013-2017 American Community Survey 5-Year Estimates

Foreign-Born Population

Area	Percent of Population Born in								
	Any Foreign Country	Asia	Mexico	Europe	Carribean	Central America[2]	South America	Africa	Canada
City	5.5	3.0	0.6	0.4	0.2	0.7	0.3	0.3	0.1
MSA[1]	3.9	1.6	0.7	0.3	0.2	0.6	0.2	0.2	0.1
U.S.	13.4	4.1	3.6	1.5	1.3	1.0	0.9	0.6	0.3

Note: (1) Figures cover the Baton Rouge, LA Metropolitan Statistical Area—see Appendix B for areas included; (2) Excludes Mexico.
Source: U.S. Census Bureau, 2013-2017 American Community Survey 5-Year Estimates

Marital Status

Area	Never Married	Now Married[2]	Separated	Widowed	Divorced
City	48.7	30.6	2.5	6.8	11.3
MSA[1]	36.5	43.5	2.2	6.2	11.7
U.S.	33.1	48.2	2.0	5.8	10.9

Note: Figures are percentages and cover the population 15 years of age and older; (1) Figures cover the Baton Rouge, LA Metropolitan Statistical Area—see Appendix B for areas included; (2) Excludes separated
Source: U.S. Census Bureau, 2013-2017 American Community Survey 5-Year Estimates

Disability by Age

Area	All Ages	Under 18 Years Old	18 to 64 Years Old	65 Years and Over
City	16.1	8.2	13.2	43.9
MSA[1]	14.1	5.7	12.1	39.8
U.S.	12.6	4.2	10.3	35.5

Note: Figures show percent of the civilian noninstitutionalized population that reported having a disability. Disability status is determined from six types of difficulty: vision, hearing, cognitive, ambulatory, self-care, and independent living. For children under 5 years old, hearing and vision difficulty are used to determine disability status. For children between the ages of 5 and 14, disability status is determined from hearing, vision, cognitive, ambulatory, and self-care difficulties. For people aged 15 years and older, they are considered to have a disability if they have difficulty with any one of the six difficulty types; Note: (1) Figures cover the Baton Rouge, LA Metropolitan Statistical Area—see Appendix B for areas included
Source: U.S. Census Bureau, 2013-2017 American Community Survey 5-Year Estimates

Age

Area	Percent of Population									Median Age
	Under Age 5	Age 5–19	Age 20–34	Age 35–44	Age 45–54	Age 55–64	Age 65–74	Age 75–84	Age 85+	
City	6.6	19.1	29.7	10.2	10.4	11.0	7.4	3.8	1.7	31.1
MSA[1]	6.6	20.3	23.3	12.5	12.6	12.0	7.8	3.6	1.3	34.9
U.S.	6.2	19.5	20.7	12.7	13.4	12.7	8.6	4.4	1.9	37.8

Note: (1) Figures cover the Baton Rouge, LA Metropolitan Statistical Area—see Appendix B for areas included
Source: U.S. Census Bureau, 2013-2017 American Community Survey 5-Year Estimates

Gender

Area	Males	Females	Males per 100 Females
City	108,014	119,535	90.4
MSA[1]	406,015	422,726	96.0
U.S.	158,018,753	162,985,654	97.0

Note: (1) Figures cover the Baton Rouge, LA Metropolitan Statistical Area—see Appendix B for areas included
Source: U.S. Census Bureau, 2013-2017 American Community Survey 5-Year Estimates

Religious Groups by Family

Area	Catholic	Baptist	Non-Den.	Methodist[2]	Lutheran	LDS[3]	Pente-costal	Presby-terian[4]	Muslim[5]	Judaism
MSA[1]	22.6	18.2	9.6	4.6	0.3	0.8	1.1	0.6	0.2	0.1
U.S.	19.1	9.3	4.0	4.0	2.3	2.0	1.9	1.6	0.8	0.7

Note: Figures are the number of adherents as a percentage of the total population; (1) Figures cover the Baton Rouge, LA Metropolitan Statistical Area—see Appendix B for areas included; (2) Methodist/Pietist; (3) Latter Day Saints; (4) Reformed; (5) Figures are estimates
Source: Association of Statisticians of American Religious Bodies, 2010 U.S. Religion Census: Religious Congregations & Membership Study

Religious Groups by Tradition

Area	Catholic	Evangelical Protestant	Mainline Protestant	Other Tradition	Black Protestant	Orthodox
MSA[1]	22.6	24.9	5.7	1.6	5.2	0.1
U.S.	19.1	16.2	7.3	4.3	1.6	0.3

Note: Figures are the number of adherents as a percentage of the total population; (1) Figures cover the Baton Rouge, LA Metropolitan Statistical Area—see Appendix B for areas included
Source: Association of Statisticians of American Religious Bodies, 2010 U.S. Religion Census: Religious Congregations & Membership Study

ECONOMY

Gross Metropolitan Product

Area	2016	2017	2018	2019	Rank[2]
MSA[1]	52.0	53.7	56.3	59.2	59

Note: Figures are in billions of dollars; (1) Figures cover the Baton Rouge, LA Metropolitan Statistical Area—see Appendix B for areas included; (2) Rank is based on 2017 data and ranges from 1 to 381
Source: U.S. Conference of Mayors, U.S. Metro Economies: Economic Growth & Full Employment, June 2018

Economic Growth

Area	2017-2018 (%)	2019-2020 (%)	2021-2022 (%)
MSA[1]	1.9	2.8	2.6

Note: Figures are real gross metropolitan product (GMP) growth rates and represent average annual percent change; (1) Figures cover the Baton Rouge, LA Metropolitan Statistical Area—see Appendix B for areas included
Source: U.S. Conference of Mayors, U.S. Metro Economies: Economic Growth & Full Employment, June 2018

Metropolitan Area Exports

Area	2012	2013	2014	2015	2016	2017	Rank[2]
MSA[1]	5,820.2	6,261.5	7,528.3	6,505.4	6,580.5	8,830.3	40

Note: Figures are in millions of dollars; (1) Figures cover the Baton Rouge, LA Metropolitan Statistical Area—see Appendix B for areas included; (2) Rank is based on 2017 data and ranges from 1 to 387
Source: U.S. Department of Commerce, International Trade Administration, Office of Trade and Economic Analysis, Industry and Analysis, Exports by Metropolitan Area, extracted March 25, 2019

Building Permits

Area	Single-Family			Multi-Family			Total		
	2016	2017	Pct. Chg.	2016	2017	Pct. Chg.	2016	2017	Pct. Chg.
City	284	253	-10.9	0	0	0.0	284	253	-10.9
MSA[1]	3,402	3,586	5.4	24	53	120.8	3,426	3,639	6.2
U.S.	750,800	820,000	9.2	455,800	462,000	1.4	1,206,600	1,282,000	6.2

Note: (1) Figures cover the Baton Rouge, LA Metropolitan Statistical Area—see Appendix B for areas included; Figures represent new, privately-owned housing units authorized (unadjusted data); All permit data are based on estimates with imputation
Source: U.S. Census Bureau, Manufacturing, Mining, and Construction Statistics, Building Permits, 2016, 2017

Bankruptcy Filings

Area	Business Filings			Nonbusiness Filings		
	2017	2018	% Chg.	2017	2018	% Chg.
East Baton Rouge Parish	21	18	-14.3	616	756	22.7
U.S.	23,157	22,232	-4.0	765,863	751,186	-1.9

Note: Business filings include Chapter 7, Chapter 11, Chapter 12, and Chapter 13; Nonbusiness filings include Chapter 7, Chapter 11, and Chapter 13
Source: Administrative Office of the U.S. Courts, Business and Nonbusiness Bankruptcy, County Cases Commenced by Chapter of the Bankruptcy Code, During the 12-Month Period Ending December 31, 2017 and Business and Nonbusiness Bankruptcy, County Cases Commenced by Chapter of the Bankruptcy Code, During the 12-Month Period Ending December 31, 2018

Housing Vacancy Rates

Area	Gross Vacancy Rate[2] (%)			Year-Round Vacancy Rate[3] (%)			Rental Vacancy Rate[4] (%)			Homeowner Vacancy Rate[5] (%)		
	2016	2017	2018	2016	2017	2018	2016	2017	2018	2016	2017	2018
MSA[1]	12.3	13.6	13.0	12.0	13.0	11.8	7.4	8.7	7.6	1.5	1.0	1.4
U.S.	12.8	12.7	12.3	9.9	9.9	9.7	6.9	7.2	6.9	1.7	1.6	1.5

Note: (1) Figures cover the Baton Rouge, LA Metropolitan Statistical Area—see Appendix B for areas included; (2) The percentage of the total housing inventory that is vacant; (3) The percentage of the housing inventory (excluding seasonal units) that is year-round vacant; (4) The percentage of rental inventory that is vacant for rent; (5) The percentage of homeowner inventory that is vacant for sale
Source: U.S. Census Bureau, Housing Vacancies and Homeownership Annual Statistics: 2016, 2017, 2018

INCOME

Income

Area	Per Capita ($)	Median Household ($)	Average Household ($)
City	25,876	40,948	63,669
MSA[1]	28,962	55,329	75,819
U.S.	31,177	57,652	81,283

Note: (1) Figures cover the Baton Rouge, LA Metropolitan Statistical Area—see Appendix B for areas included
Source: U.S. Census Bureau, 2013-2017 American Community Survey 5-Year Estimates

Household Income Distribution

Area	Percent of Households Earning							
	Under $15,000	$15,000 -$24,999	$25,000 -$34,999	$35,000 -$49,999	$50,000 -$74,999	$75,000 -$99,999	$100,000 -$149,999	$150,000 and up
City	20.3	13.1	11.5	13.7	15.0	8.3	9.9	8.3
MSA[1]	13.6	10.3	9.2	12.7	16.8	11.7	14.9	10.7
U.S.	11.6	9.8	9.5	13.0	17.7	12.3	14.1	12.1

Note: (1) Figures cover the Baton Rouge, LA Metropolitan Statistical Area—see Appendix B for areas included
Source: U.S. Census Bureau, 2013-2017 American Community Survey 5-Year Estimates

Poverty Rate

Area	All Ages	Under 18 Years Old	18 to 64 Years Old	65 Years and Over
City	26.0	34.6	25.9	12.6
MSA[1]	16.9	22.6	16.0	10.5
U.S.	14.6	20.3	13.7	9.3

Note: Figures are percentage of people whose income during the past 12 months was below the poverty level; (1) Figures cover the Baton Rouge, LA Metropolitan Statistical Area—see Appendix B for areas included
Source: U.S. Census Bureau, 2013-2017 American Community Survey 5-Year Estimates

EMPLOYMENT

Labor Force and Employment

Area	Civilian Labor Force			Workers Employed		
	Dec. 2017	Dec. 2018	% Chg.	Dec. 2017	Dec. 2018	% Chg.
City	114,467	114,228	-0.2	110,218	109,416	-0.7
MSA[1]	418,468	416,996	-0.4	403,814	400,928	-0.7
U.S.	159,880,000	162,510,000	1.6	153,602,000	156,481,000	1.9

Note: Data is not seasonally adjusted and covers workers 16 years of age and older; (1) Figures cover the Baton Rouge, LA Metropolitan Statistical Area—see Appendix B for areas included
Source: Bureau of Labor Statistics, Local Area Unemployment Statistics

Unemployment Rate

Area	2018											
	Jan.	Feb.	Mar.	Apr.	May	Jun.	Jul.	Aug.	Sep.	Oct.	Nov.	Dec.
City	4.2	3.8	4.1	4.1	4.6	6.0	5.9	5.6	4.9	4.6	4.3	4.2
MSA[1]	3.9	3.5	3.8	3.8	4.2	5.4	5.3	5.0	4.5	4.2	4.0	3.9
U.S.	4.5	4.4	4.1	3.7	3.6	4.2	4.1	3.9	3.6	3.5	3.5	3.7

Note: Data is not seasonally adjusted and covers workers 16 years of age and older; (1) Figures cover the Baton Rouge, LA Metropolitan Statistical Area—see Appendix B for areas included
Source: Bureau of Labor Statistics, Local Area Unemployment Statistics

Average Wages

Occupation	$/Hr.	Occupation	$/Hr.
Accountants and Auditors	31.50	Maids and Housekeeping Cleaners	9.70
Automotive Mechanics	19.90	Maintenance and Repair Workers	18.70
Bookkeepers	18.60	Marketing Managers	54.00
Carpenters	22.80	Nuclear Medicine Technologists	31.00
Cashiers	9.50	Nurses, Licensed Practical	18.50
Clerks, General Office	12.60	Nurses, Registered	29.10
Clerks, Receptionists/Information	12.10	Nursing Assistants	11.50
Clerks, Shipping/Receiving	18.40	Packers and Packagers, Hand	11.80
Computer Programmers	34.60	Physical Therapists	40.80
Computer Systems Analysts	36.80	Postal Service Mail Carriers	24.20
Computer User Support Specialists	23.40	Real Estate Brokers	n/a
Cooks, Restaurant	11.80	Retail Salespersons	11.70
Dentists	86.10	Sales Reps., Exc. Tech./Scientific	28.80
Electrical Engineers	45.40	Sales Reps., Tech./Scientific	41.10
Electricians	25.40	Secretaries, Exc. Legal/Med./Exec.	15.70
Financial Managers	52.40	Security Guards	13.80
First-Line Supervisors/Managers, Sales	18.50	Surgeons	n/a
Food Preparation Workers	9.10	Teacher Assistants*	10.40
General and Operations Managers	59.30	Teachers, Elementary School*	23.90
Hairdressers/Cosmetologists	12.30	Teachers, Secondary School*	25.60
Internists, General	n/a	Telemarketers	n/a
Janitors and Cleaners	10.40	Truck Drivers, Heavy/Tractor-Trailer	20.70
Landscaping/Groundskeeping Workers	13.10	Truck Drivers, Light/Delivery Svcs.	15.40
Lawyers	49.20	Waiters and Waitresses	9.00

Note: Wage data covers the Baton Rouge, LA Metropolitan Statistical Area—see Appendix B for areas included; (*) Hourly wages for elementary/secondary school teachers and teacher assistants were calculated by the editors from annual wage data based on a 40 hour work week; n/a not available.
Source: Bureau of Labor Statistics, Metro Area Occupational Employment & Wage Estimates, May 2018

Employment by Occupation

Occupation Classification	City (%)	MSA[1] (%)	U.S. (%)
Management, Business, Science, and Arts	35.1	35.4	37.4
Natural Resources, Construction, and Maintenance	8.6	10.6	8.9
Production, Transportation, and Material Moving	10.5	11.8	12.2
Sales and Office	24.4	24.1	23.5
Service	21.4	18.1	18.0

Note: Figures cover employed civilians 16 years of age and older; (1) Figures cover the Baton Rouge, LA Metropolitan Statistical Area—see Appendix B for areas included
Source: U.S. Census Bureau, 2013-2017 American Community Survey 5-Year Estimates

Employment by Industry

| Sector | MSA[1] | | U.S. |
	Number of Employees	Percent of Total	Percent of Total
Construction	53,800	13.1	4.8
Education and Health Services	52,600	12.8	15.9
Financial Activities	18,800	4.6	5.7
Government	76,200	18.5	15.1
Information	5,000	1.2	1.9
Leisure and Hospitality	39,600	9.6	10.7
Manufacturing	29,800	7.2	8.5
Mining and Logging	900	0.2	0.5
Other Services	16,600	4.0	3.9
Professional and Business Services	46,900	11.4	14.1
Retail Trade	42,300	10.3	10.8
Transportation, Warehousing, and Utilities	15,300	3.7	4.2
Wholesale Trade	13,600	3.3	3.9

Note: Figures are non-farm employment as of December 2018. Figures are not seasonally adjusted and include workers 16 years of age and older; (1) Figures cover the Baton Rouge, LA Metropolitan Statistical Area—see Appendix B for areas included
Source: Bureau of Labor Statistics, Current Employment Statistics, Employment, Hours, and Earnings

Occupations with Greatest Projected Employment Growth: 2017 – 2019

Occupation[1]	2017 Employment	2019 Projected Employment	Numeric Employment Change	Percent Employment Change
Personal Care Aides	35,390	37,200	1,810	5.1
Registered Nurses	46,590	48,090	1,500	3.2
Laborers and Freight, Stock, and Material Movers, Hand	45,490	46,520	1,030	2.2
Retail Salespersons	61,790	62,820	1,030	1.7
Carpenters	18,290	19,290	1,000	5.5
Combined Food Preparation and Serving Workers, Including Fast Food	28,720	29,660	940	3.3
Construction Laborers	21,630	22,560	930	4.3
Food Preparation Workers	32,990	33,790	800	2.4
Cashiers	70,980	71,670	690	1.0
Waiters and Waitresses	38,340	38,990	650	1.7

Note: Projections cover Louisiana; (1) Sorted by numeric employment change
Source: www.projectionscentral.com, State Occupational Projections, 2017–2019 Short-Term Projections

Fastest Growing Occupations: 2017 – 2019

Occupation[1]	2017 Employment	2019 Projected Employment	Numeric Employment Change	Percent Employment Change
Web Developers	550	600	50	8.0
Operations Research Analysts	1,090	1,170	80	7.5
Structural Iron and Steel Workers	3,020	3,230	210	7.1
Millwrights	1,310	1,400	90	6.9
Veterinary Technologists and Technicians	1,120	1,190	70	6.8
Commercial Divers	850	900	50	6.4
Home Health Aides	8,530	9,060	530	6.2
Physical Therapist Assistants	1,480	1,570	90	6.0
Personal Financial Advisors	1,550	1,640	90	5.8
Software Developers, Applications	1,430	1,510	80	5.7

Note: Projections cover Louisiana; (1) Sorted by percent employment change and excludes occupations with numeric employment change less than 50
Source: www.projectionscentral.com, State Occupational Projections, 2017–2019 Short-Term Projections

TAXES

State Corporate Income Tax Rates

State	Tax Rate (%)	Income Brackets ($)	Num. of Brackets	Financial Institution Tax Rate (%)[a]	Federal Income Tax Ded.
Louisiana	4.0 - 8.0	25,000 - 200,001	5	4.0 - 8.0	Yes

Note: Tax rates as of January 1, 2019; (a) Rates listed are the corporate income tax rate applied to financial institutions or excise taxes based on income. Some states have other taxes based upon the value of deposits or shares.
Source: Federation of Tax Administrators, Range of State Corporate Income Tax Rates, January 1, 2019

State Individual Income Tax Rates

State	Tax Rate (%)	Income Brackets ($)	Personal Exemptions ($)			Standard Ded. ($)	
			Single	Married	Depend.	Single	Married
Louisiana	2.0 - 6.0	12,500 - 50,001 (b)	4,500	9,000 (k)	1,000	(k)	(k)

Note: Tax rates as of January 1, 2019; Local- and county-level taxes are not included; n/a not applicable; Federal income tax is deductible on state income tax returns; (b) For joint returns, taxes are twice the tax on half the couple's income; (k) The amounts reported for Louisiana are a combined personal exemption-standard deduction.
Source: Federation of Tax Administrators, State Individual Income Tax Rates, January 1, 2019

Various State Sales and Excise Tax Rates

State	State Sales Tax (%)	Gasoline[1] (¢/gal.)	Cigarette[2] ($/pack)	Spirits[3] ($/gal.)	Wine[4] ($/gal.)	Beer[5] ($/gal.)	Recreational Marijuana (%)
Louisiana	5	20.01	1.08	3.03 (f)	0.76 (l)	0.4	Not legal

Note: All tax rates as of January 1, 2019; (1) The American Petroleum Institute has developed a methodology for determining the average tax rate on a gallon of fuel. Rates may include any of the following: excise taxes, environmental fees, storage tank fees, other fees or taxes, general sales tax, and local taxes. In states where gasoline is subject to the general sales tax, or where the fuel tax is based on the average sale price, the average rate determined by API is sensitive to changes in the price of gasoline. States that fully or partially apply general sales taxes to gasoline: CA, CO, GA, IL, IN, MI, NY; (2) The federal excise tax of $1.0066 per pack and local taxes are not included; (3) Rates are those applicable to off-premise sales of 40% alcohol by volume (a.b.v.) distilled spirits in 750ml containers. Local excise taxes are excluded; (4) Rates are those applicable to off-premise sales of 11% a.b.v. non-carbonated wine in 750ml containers; (5) Rates are those applicable to off-premise sales of 4.7% a.b.v. beer in 12 ounce containers; (f) Different rates also applicable according to alcohol content, place of production, size of container, or place purchased (on- or off-premise or onboard airlines); (l) Different rates also applicable to alcohol content, place of production, size of container, place purchased (on- or off-premise or on board airlines) or type of wine (carbonated, vermouth, etc.).
Source: Tax Foundation, 2019 Facts & Figures: How Does Your State Compare?

State Business Tax Climate Index Rankings

State	Overall Rank	Corporate Tax Rank	Individual Income Tax Rank	Sales Tax Rank	Unemployment Insurance Tax Rank	Property Tax Rank
Louisiana	44	36	32	50	4	32

Note: The index is a measure of how each state's tax laws affect economic performance. The lower the rank, the more favorable a state's tax system is for business. States without a given tax are given a ranking of 1. The scores/rankings for the District of Columbia do not affect other states. The 2019 index represents the tax climate as of July 1, 2018.
Source: Tax Foundation, State Business Tax Climate Index 2019

COMMERCIAL UTILITIES

Typical Monthly Electric Bills

Area	Commercial Service ($/month)		Industrial Service ($/month)	
	1,500 kWh	40 kW demand 14,000 kWh	1,000 kW demand 200,000 kWh	50,000 kW demand 32,500,000 kWh
City	168	1,044	16,215	1,638,321
Average[1]	203	1,619	25,886	2,540,077

Note: Figures are based on annualized rates; (1) Average based on 187 utilities surveyed
Source: Edison Electric Institute, Typical Bills and Average Rates Report, Summer 2018

TRANSPORTATION

Means of Transportation to Work

| Area | Car/Truck/Van | | Public Transportation | | | Bicycle | Walked | Other Means | Worked at Home |
	Drove Alone	Car-pooled	Bus	Subway	Railroad				
City	79.4	10.2	2.8	0.0	0.0	0.6	3.0	0.9	2.9
MSA[1]	84.7	8.9	0.9	0.0	0.0	0.3	1.4	0.9	2.8
U.S.	76.4	9.2	2.5	1.9	0.6	0.6	2.7	1.3	4.7

Note: Figures are percentages and cover workers 16 years of age and older; (1) Figures cover the Baton Rouge, LA Metropolitan Statistical Area—see Appendix B for areas included
Source: U.S. Census Bureau, 2013-2017 American Community Survey 5-Year Estimates

Travel Time to Work

Area	Less Than 10 Minutes	10 to 19 Minutes	20 to 29 Minutes	30 to 44 Minutes	45 to 59 Minutes	60 to 89 Minutes	90 Minutes or More
City	11.0	37.7	28.2	14.8	3.6	3.2	1.4
MSA[1]	9.9	27.5	22.9	22.1	9.3	6.1	2.2
U.S.	12.7	28.9	20.9	20.5	8.1	6.2	2.7

Note: Note: Figures are percentages and include workers 16 years old and over; (1) Figures cover the Baton Rouge, LA Metropolitan Statistical Area—see Appendix B for areas included
Source: U.S. Census Bureau, 2013-2017 American Community Survey 5-Year Estimates

Freeway Travel Time Index

Area	1985	1990	1995	2000	2005	2010	2014
Urban Area Rank[1,2]	39	46	59	57	51	33	32
Urban Area Index[1]	1.08	1.10	1.12	1.15	1.17	1.21	1.22
Average Index[3]	1.09	1.11	1.14	1.17	1.20	1.19	1.20

Note: Freeway Travel Time Index—the ratio of travel time in the peak period to the travel time at free-flow conditions. For example, a value of 1.30 indicates a 20-minute free-flow trip takes 26 minutes in the peak (20 minutes x 1.30 = 26 minutes); (1) Covers the Baton Rouge LA urban area; (2) Rank is based on 101 urban areas (#1 = highest travel time index); (3) Average of 101 urban areas
Source: Texas Transportation Institute, 2015 Urban Mobility Scorecard, August 2015

Freeway Commuter Stress Index

Area	1985	1990	1995	2000	2005	2010	2014
Urban Area Rank[1,2]	48	51	61	63	53	40	38
Urban Area Index[1]	1.10	1.12	1.14	1.17	1.20	1.23	1.25
Average Index[3]	1.13	1.16	1.19	1.22	1.25	1.24	1.25

Note: The Freeway Commuter Stress Index is the same as the Freeway Travel Time Index (see table above) except that it includes only the travel in the peak directions during the peak periods; the TTI includes travel in all directions during the peak period. Thus, the CSI is more indicative of the work trip experienced by each commuter on a daily basis; (1) Covers the Baton Rouge LA urban area; (2) Rank is based on 101 urban areas (#1 = highest travel time index); (3) Average of 101 urban areas
Source: Texas Transportation Institute, 2015 Urban Mobility Scorecard, August 2015

Public Transportation

Agency Name / Mode of Transportation	Vehicles Operated in Maximum Service[1]	Annual Unlinked Passenger Trips[2] (in thous.)	Annual Passenger Miles[3] (in thous.)
Capital Area Transit System (CATS)			
Bus (directly operated)	56	3,728.4	14,675.6
Demand Response (purchased transportation)	18	84.3	981.6

Note: (1) The number of revenue vehicles operated by the given mode and type of service to meet the annual maximum service requirement. This is the revenue vehicle count during the peak season of the year; on the week and day that maximum service is provided. Vehicles operated in maximum service (VOMS) exclude atypical days and one-time special events; (2) The number of passengers who boarded public transportation vehicles. Passengers are counted each time they board a vehicle no matter how many vehicles they use to travel from their origin to their destination. (3) The sum of the distances ridden by all passengers during the entire fiscal year.
Source: Federal Transit Administration, National Transit Database, 2017

Air Transportation

Airport Name and Code / Type of Service	Passenger Airlines[1]	Passenger Enplanements	Freight Carriers[2]	Freight (lbs)
Baton Rouge Metropolitan (BTR)				
Domestic service (U.S. carriers - 2018)	21	389,782	7	57,882
International service (U.S. carriers - 2017)	0	0	0	0

Note: (1) Includes all U.S.-based major, minor and commuter airlines that carried at least one passenger during the year; (2) Includes all U.S.-based airlines and freight carriers that transported at least one pound of freight during the year.
Source: Bureau of Transportation Statistics, The Intermodal Transportation Database, Air Carriers: T-100 Domestic Market (U.S. Carriers), 2018; Bureau of Transportation Statistics, The Intermodal Transportation Database, Air Carriers: T-100 International Market (U.S. Carriers), 2017

Other Transportation Statistics

Major Highways:	I-10; I-12
Amtrak Service:	Bus connection
Major Waterways/Ports:	Mississippi River

Source: Amtrak.com; Google Maps

BUSINESSES

Major Business Headquarters

Company Name	Industry	Fortune[1]	Forbes[2]
Turner Industries Group	Construction	-	188

Note: (1) Companies that produce a 10-K are ranked 1 to 500 based on 2017 revenue; (2) All private companies with at least $2 billion in annual revenue through the end of their most current fiscal year are ranked 1 to 229; companies listed are headquartered in the city; dashes indicate no ranking
Source: Fortune, "Fortune 500," June 2018; Forbes, "America's Largest Private Companies," 2018 Rankings

Minority- and Women-Owned Businesses

Group	All Firms Firms	All Firms Sales ($000)	Firms with Paid Employees Firms	Sales ($000)	Employees	Payroll ($000)
AIAN[1]	91	(s)	20	(s)	500 - 999	(s)
Asian	1,243	346,680	405	311,558	2,554	67,003
Black	10,482	324,934	302	180,892	3,333	67,555
Hispanic	688	162,099	101	141,249	815	17,423
NHOPI[2]	n/a	n/a	n/a	n/a	n/a	n/a
Women	10,518	1,476,014	860	1,268,195	8,955	263,626
All Firms	25,952	42,372,391	6,120	41,421,713	130,095	5,800,581

Note: Figures cover firms located in the city; minority- and women-owned business are defined as firms in which the corresponding group own 51% or more of the stock or equity of the company; (1) American Indian and Alaska Native; (2) Native Hawaiian and Other Pacific Islander; (s) estimates are suppressed when publication standards are not met; n/a not available
Source: U.S. Census Bureau, 2012 Economic Census, Survey of Business Owners

HOTELS & CONVENTION CENTERS

Hotels, Motels and Vacation Rentals

Area	5 Star Num.	5 Star Pct.[3]	4 Star Num.	4 Star Pct.[3]	3 Star Num.	3 Star Pct.[3]	2 Star Num.	2 Star Pct.[3]	1 Star Num.	1 Star Pct.[3]	Not Rated Num.	Not Rated Pct.[3]
City[1]	0	0.0	4	2.1	46	24.5	85	45.2	2	1.1	51	27.1
Total[2]	286	0.4	5,236	7.1	16,715	22.6	10,259	13.9	293	0.4	41,056	55.6

Note: (1) Figures cover Baton Rouge and vicinity; (2) Figures cover all 100 cities in this book; (3) Percentage of hotels which have a given star rating; Star ratings are determined by expedia.com and offer an indication of the general quality of a particular hotel.
Source: www.expedia.com, April 3, 2019

Major Convention Centers

Name	Overall Space (sq. ft.)	Exhibit Space (sq. ft.)	Meeting Space (sq. ft.)	Meeting Rooms
Raising Cane's River Center	200,000	100,000	23,996	17

Note: Table includes convention centers located in the Baton Rouge, LA metro area
Source: Original research

Living Environment

COST OF LIVING

Cost of Living Index

Composite Index	Groceries	Housing	Utilities	Trans- portation	Health Care	Misc. Goods/ Services
100.3	106.6	92.9	87.4	103.1	110.3	105.5

Note: The Cost of Living Index measures regional differences in the cost of consumer goods and services, excluding taxes and non-consumer expenditures, for professional and managerial households in the top income quintile. It is based on more than 50,000 prices covering almost 60 different items for which prices are collected three times a year by chambers of commerce, economic development organizations or university applied economic centers in each participating urban area. The numbers shown should be read as a percentage above or below the national average of 100. For example, a value of 115.4 in the groceries column indicates that grocery prices are 15.4% higher than the national average. Small differences in the index numbers should not be interpreted as significant; Figures cover the Baton Rouge LA urban area.
Source: The Council for Community and Economic Research, ACCRA Cost of Living Index, 2018

Grocery Prices

Area[1]	T-Bone Steak ($/pound)	Frying Chicken ($/pound)	Whole Milk ($/half gal.)	Eggs ($/dozen)	Orange Juice ($/64 oz.)	Coffee ($/11.5 oz.)
City[2]	12.45	1.33	2.54	2.12	3.91	4.21
Avg.	11.35	1.42	1.94	1.81	3.52	4.35
Min.	7.45	0.92	0.80	0.75	2.72	3.06
Max.	15.05	2.76	4.18	4.00	5.36	8.20

Note: (1) Values for the local area are compared with the average, minimum and maximum values for all 291 areas in the Cost of Living Index; (2) Figures cover the Baton Rouge LA urban area; T-Bone Steak (price per pound); Frying Chicken (price per pound, whole fryer); Whole Milk (half gallon carton); Eggs (price per dozen, Grade A, large); Orange Juice (64 oz. Tropicana or Florida Natural); Coffee (11.5 oz. can, vacuum-packed, Maxwell House, Hills Bros, or Folgers).
Source: The Council for Community and Economic Research, ACCRA Cost of Living Index, 2018

Housing and Utility Costs

Area[1]	New Home Price ($)	Apartment Rent ($/month)	All Electric ($/month)	Part Electric ($/month)	Other Energy ($/month)	Telephone ($/month)
City[2]	314,060	1,029	133.63	-	-	173.60
Avg.	347,000	1,087	165.93	100.16	67.73	178.70
Min.	200,468	500	93.58	25.64	26.78	163.10
Max.	1,901,222	4,888	388.65	246.86	332.81	197.70

Note: (1) Values for the local area are compared with the average, minimum and maximum values for all 291 areas in the Cost of Living Index; (2) Figures cover the Baton Rouge LA urban area; New Home Price (2,400 sf living area, 8,000 sf lot, in urban area with full utilities); Apartment Rent (950 sf 2 bedroom/1.5 or 2 bath, unfurnished, excluding all utilities except water); All Electric (average monthly cost for an all-electric home); Part Electric (average monthly cost for a part-electric home); Other Energy (average monthly cost for natural gas, fuel oil, coal, wood, and any other forms of energy except electricity); Telephone (price includes the base monthly rate plus taxes and fees for three lines of mobile phone service).
Source: The Council for Community and Economic Research, ACCRA Cost of Living Index, 2018

Health Care, Transportation, and Other Costs

Area[1]	Doctor ($/visit)	Dentist ($/visit)	Optometrist ($/visit)	Gasoline ($/gallon)	Beauty Salon ($/visit)	Men's Shirt ($)
City[2]	121.03	113.42	118.72	2.43	46.67	44.42
Avg.	110.71	95.11	103.74	2.61	37.48	32.03
Min.	33.60	62.55	54.63	1.89	17.00	11.44
Max.	195.97	153.93	225.79	3.59	71.88	58.64

Note: (1) Values for the local area are compared with the average, minimum and maximum values for all 291 areas in the Cost of Living Index; (2) Figures cover the Baton Rouge LA urban area; Doctor (general practitioners routine exam of an established patient); Dentist (adult teeth cleaning and periodic oral examination); Optometrist (full vision eye exam for established adult patient); Gasoline (one gallon regular unleaded, national brand, including all taxes, cash price at self-service pump if available); Beauty Salon (woman's shampoo, trim, and blow-dry); Men's Shirt (cotton/polyester dress shirt, pinpoint weave, long sleeves).
Source: The Council for Community and Economic Research, ACCRA Cost of Living Index, 2018

HOUSING

House Price Index (HPI)

Area	National Ranking[2]	Quarterly Change (%)	One-Year Change (%)	Five-Year Change (%)
MSA[1]	216	-0.30	2.56	19.32
U.S.[3]	–	1.12	5.73	32.81

Note: The HPI is a weighted repeat sales index. It measures average price changes in repeat sales or refinancings on the same properties. This information is obtained by reviewing repeat mortgage transactions on single-family properties whose mortgages have been purchased or securitized by Fannie Mae or Freddie Mac in January 1975; (1) Figures cover the Baton Rouge, LA Metropolitan Statistical Area—see Appendix B for areas included; (2) Rankings are based on annual percentage change for all metro areas containing at least 15,000 transactions over the last 10 years and ranges from 1 to 245; (3) figures based on a weighted average of Census Division estimates using a seasonally adjusted, purchase-only index; all figures are for the period ending December 31, 2018
Source: Federal Housing Finance Agency, House Price Index, February 26, 2019

Median Single-Family Home Prices

Area	2016	2017	2018p	Percent Change 2017 to 2018
MSA[1]	184.0	198.6	210.6	6.0
U.S. Average	235.5	248.8	261.6	5.1

Note: Figures are median sales prices of existing single-family homes in thousands of dollars; (p) preliminary; (1) Figures cover the Baton Rouge, LA Metropolitan Statistical Area—see Appendix B for areas included
Source: National Association of Realtors, Median Sales Price of Existing Single-Family Homes for Metropolitan Areas, 4th Quarter 2018

Qualifying Income Based on Median Sales Price of Existing Single-Family Homes

Area	With 5% Down ($)	With 10% Down ($)	With 20% Down ($)
MSA[1]	51,614	48,898	43,464
U.S. Average	62,954	59,640	53,013

Note: Figures are preliminary; Qualifying income is based on a mortgage rate of 4.9%. Monthly principal and interest payment is limited to 25% of income; (1) Figures cover the Baton Rouge, LA Metropolitan Statistical Area—see Appendix B for areas included
Source: National Association of Realtors, Qualifying Income Based on Median Sales Price of Existing Single-Family Homes for Metropolitan Areas, 4th Quarter 2018

Median Apartment Condo-Coop Home Prices

Area	2016	2017	2018p	Percent Change 2017 to 2018
MSA[1]	n/a	n/a	n/a	n/a
U.S. Average	220.7	234.3	241.0	2.9

Note: Figures are median sales prices of existing apartment condo-coop homes in thousands of dollars; (p) preliminary; n/a not available; (1) Figures cover the Baton Rouge, LA Metropolitan Statistical Area—see Appendix B for areas included
Source: National Association of Realtors, Median Sales Price of Existing Apartment Condo-Coop Homes for Metropolitan Areas, 4th Quarter 2018

Home Value Distribution

Area	Under $50,000	$50,000 -$99,999	$100,000 -$149,999	$150,000 -$199,999	$200,000 -$299,999	$300,000 -$499,999	$500,000 -$999,999	$1,000,000 or more
City	7.0	19.1	17.9	19.1	18.9	12.0	4.7	1.3
MSA[1]	10.2	13.7	16.9	20.9	21.6	12.2	3.6	0.9
U.S.	8.3	13.9	14.7	14.6	18.7	17.3	9.7	2.7

Note: Figures are percentages and cover owner-occupied housing units; (1) Figures cover the Baton Rouge, LA Metropolitan Statistical Area—see Appendix B for areas included
Source: U.S. Census Bureau, 2013-2017 American Community Survey 5-Year Estimates

Homeownership Rate

Area	2010 (%)	2011 (%)	2012 (%)	2013 (%)	2014 (%)	2015 (%)	2016 (%)	2017 (%)	2018 (%)
MSA[1]	70.3	72.0	71.4	66.6	64.8	64.2	64.8	66.9	66.6
U.S.	66.9	66.1	65.4	65.1	64.5	63.7	63.4	63.9	64.4

Note: (1) Figures cover the Baton Rouge, LA Metropolitan Statistical Area—see Appendix B for areas included
Source: U.S. Census Bureau, Housing Vacancies and Homeownership Annual Statistics: 2010-2018

Year Housing Structure Built

Area	2010 or Later	2000 -2009	1990 -1999	1980 -1989	1970 -1979	1960 -1969	1950 -1959	1940 -1949	Before 1940	Median Year
City	3.4	10.3	9.2	13.6	21.5	18.0	12.6	6.0	5.4	1974
MSA[1]	5.9	21.9	14.9	15.3	17.4	10.8	7.3	2.9	3.7	1985
U.S.	3.2	14.5	14.0	13.6	15.5	10.8	10.5	5.1	12.9	1977

Note: Figures are percentages except for Median Year; Note: (1) Figures cover the Baton Rouge, LA Metropolitan Statistical Area—see Appendix B for areas included
Source: U.S. Census Bureau, 2013-2017 American Community Survey 5-Year Estimates

Gross Monthly Rent

Area	Under $500	$500 -$999	$1,000 -$1,499	$1,500 -$1,999	$2,000 -$2,499	$2,500 -$2,999	$3,000 and up	Median ($)
City	10.6	59.8	21.0	5.4	2.1	0.8	0.3	827
MSA[1]	10.1	54.9	25.2	6.9	2.1	0.5	0.3	873
U.S.	10.5	41.1	28.7	11.7	4.5	1.8	1.7	982

Note: Figures are percentages except for Median; Gross rent is the contract rent plus the estimated average monthly cost of utilities (electricity, gas, and water and sewer) and fuels (oil, coal, kerosene, wood, etc.) if these are paid by the renter (or paid for the renter by someone else); (1) Figures cover the Baton Rouge, LA Metropolitan Statistical Area—see Appendix B for areas included
Source: U.S. Census Bureau, 2013-2017 American Community Survey 5-Year Estimates

HEALTH

Health Risk Factors

Category	MSA[1] (%)	U.S. (%)
Adults aged 18–64 who have any kind of health care coverage	86.7	87.3
Adults who reported being in good or better health	80.3	82.4
Adults who have been told they have high blood cholesterol	36.4	33.0
Adults who have been told they have high blood pressure	36.6	32.3
Adults who are current smokers	21.7	17.1
Adults who currently use E-cigarettes	4.2	4.6
Adults who currently use chewing tobacco, snuff, or snus	5.9	4.0
Adults who are heavy drinkers[2]	7.0	6.3
Adults who are binge drinkers[3]	20.5	17.4
Adults who are overweight (BMI 25.0 - 29.9)	34.5	35.3
Adults who are obese (BMI 30.0 - 99.8)	33.0	31.3
Adults who participated in any physical activities in the past month	67.7	74.4
Adults who always or nearly always wears a seat belt	94.6	94.3

Note: (1) Figures cover the Baton Rouge, LA Metropolitan Statistical Area—see Appendix B for areas included; (2) Heavy drinkers are classified as adult men having more than 14 drinks per week and adult women having more than 7 drinks per week; (3) Binge drinkers are classified as males having five or more drinks on one occasion or females having four or more drinks on one occasion
Source: Centers for Disease Control and Prevention, Behaviorial Risk Factor Surveillance System, SMART: Selected Metropolitan Area Risk Trends, 2017

Acute and Chronic Health Conditions

Category	MSA[1] (%)	U.S. (%)
Adults who have ever been told they had a heart attack	4.8	4.2
Adults who have ever been told they have angina or coronary heart disease	4.6	3.9
Adults who have ever been told they had a stroke	4.6	3.0
Adults who have ever been told they have asthma	16.1	14.2
Adults who have ever been told they have arthritis	24.2	24.9
Adults who have ever been told they have diabetes[2]	11.2	10.5
Adults who have ever been told they had skin cancer	3.8	6.2
Adults who have ever been told they had any other types of cancer	6.9	7.1
Adults who have ever been told they have COPD	7.1	6.5
Adults who have ever been told they have kidney disease	2.6	3.0
Adults who have ever been told they have a form of depression	19.4	20.5

Note: (1) Figures cover the Baton Rouge, LA Metropolitan Statistical Area—see Appendix B for areas included; (2) Figures do not include pregnancy-related, borderline, or pre-diabetes
Source: Centers for Disease Control and Prevention, Behaviorial Risk Factor Surveillance System, SMART: Selected Metropolitan Area Risk Trends, 2017

Health Screening and Vaccination Rates

Category	MSA[1] (%)	U.S. (%)
Adults aged 65+ who have had flu shot within the past year	58.3	60.7
Adults aged 65+ who have ever had a pneumonia vaccination	81.4	75.4
Adults who have ever been tested for HIV	42.6	36.1
Adults who have ever had the shingles or zoster vaccine?	23.2	28.9
Adults who have had their blood cholesterol checked within the last five years	86.7	85.9

Note: n/a not available; (1) Figures cover the Baton Rouge, LA Metropolitan Statistical Area—see Appendix B for areas included.
Source: Centers for Disease Control and Prevention, Behaviorial Risk Factor Surveillance System, SMART: Selected Metropolitan Area Risk Trends, 2017

Disability Status

Category	MSA[1] (%)	U.S. (%)
Adults who reported being deaf	6.1	6.7
Are you blind or have serious difficulty seeing, even when wearing glasses?	7.3	4.5
Are you limited in any way in any of your usual activities due of arthritis?	13.2	12.9
Do you have difficulty doing errands alone?	7.2	6.8
Do you have difficulty dressing or bathing?	4.8	3.6
Do you have serious difficulty concentrating/remembering/making decisions?	11.2	10.7
Do you have serious difficulty walking or climbing stairs?	15.1	13.6

Note: (1) Figures cover the Baton Rouge, LA Metropolitan Statistical Area—see Appendix B for areas included.
Source: Centers for Disease Control and Prevention, Behaviorial Risk Factor Surveillance System, SMART: Selected Metropolitan Area Risk Trends, 2017

Mortality Rates for the Top 10 Causes of Death in the U.S.

ICD-10[a] Sub-Chapter	ICD-10[a] Code	Age-Adjusted Mortality Rate[1] per 100,000 population	
		County[2]	U.S.
Malignant neoplasms	C00-C97	163.2	155.5
Ischaemic heart diseases	I20-I25	102.8	94.8
Other forms of heart disease	I30-I51	104.2	52.9
Chronic lower respiratory diseases	J40-J47	33.6	41.0
Cerebrovascular diseases	I60-I69	46.7	37.5
Other degenerative diseases of the nervous system	G30-G31	58.5	35.0
Other external causes of accidental injury	W00-X59	39.2	33.7
Organic, including symptomatic, mental disorders	F01-F09	23.7	31.0
Hypertensive diseases	I10-I15	4.2	21.9
Diabetes mellitus	E10-E14	5.7	21.2

Note: (a) ICD-10 = International Classification of Diseases 10th Revision; (1) Mortality rates are a three year average covering 2015-2017; (2) Figures cover East Baton Rouge Parish.
Source: Centers for Disease Control and Prevention, National Center for Health Statistics. Underlying Cause of Death 1999-2017 on CDC WONDER Online Database

Mortality Rates for Selected Causes of Death

ICD-10[a] Sub-Chapter	ICD-10[a] Code	Age-Adjusted Mortality Rate[1] per 100,000 population	
		County[2]	U.S.
Assault	X85-Y09	20.0	5.9
Diseases of the liver	K70-K76	13.5	14.1
Human immunodeficiency virus (HIV) disease	B20-B24	10.0	1.8
Influenza and pneumonia	J09-J18	13.6	14.3
Intentional self-harm	X60-X84	11.2	13.6
Malnutrition	E40-E46	4.5	1.6
Obesity and other hyperalimentation	E65-E68	Unreliable	2.1
Renal failure	N17-N19	28.3	13.0
Transport accidents	V01-V99	15.7	12.4
Viral hepatitis	B15-B19	1.6	1.6

Note: (a) ICD-10 = International Classification of Diseases 10th Revision; (1) Mortality rates are a three year average covering 2015-2017; (2) Figures cover East Baton Rouge Parish; Data are suppressed when the data meet the criteria for confidentiality constraints; Mortality rates are flagged as unreliable when the rate would be calculated with a numerator of 20 or less.
Source: Centers for Disease Control and Prevention, National Center for Health Statistics. Underlying Cause of Death 1999-2017 on CDC WONDER Online Database

Health Insurance Coverage

Area	With Health Insurance	With Private Health Insurance	With Public Health Insurance	Without Health Insurance	Population Under Age 18 Without Health Insurance
City	87.2	60.3	36.0	12.8	3.1
MSA[1]	89.3	67.2	31.7	10.7	3.3
U.S.	89.5	67.2	33.8	10.5	5.7

Note: Figures are percentages that cover the civilian noninstitutionalized population; (1) Figures cover the Baton Rouge, LA Metropolitan Statistical Area—see Appendix B for areas included
Source: U.S. Census Bureau, 2013-2017 American Community Survey 5-Year Estimates

Number of Medical Professionals

Area	MDs[3]	DOs[3,4]	Dentists	Podiatrists	Chiropractors	Optometrists
County[1] (number)	1,688	32	325	18	50	60
County[1] (rate[2])	377.0	7.1	72.8	4.0	11.2	13.4
U.S. (rate[2])	279.3	23.0	68.4	6.0	27.1	16.2

Note: Data as of 2017 unless noted; (1) Data covers East Baton Rouge Parish; (2) Rate per 100,000 population; (3) Data as of 2016 and includes all active, non-federal physicians; (4) Doctor of Osteopathic Medicine
Source: U.S. Department of Health and Human Services, Health Resources and Services Administration, Bureau of Health Professions, Area Resource File (ARF) 2017-2018

EDUCATION

Public School District Statistics

District Name	Schls	Pupils	Pupil/ Teacher Ratio	Minority Pupils[1] (%)	Free Lunch Eligible[2] (%)	IEP[3] (%)
East Baton Rouge Parish	83	40,579	10.6	89.4	77.9	9.8
Louisiana Connections Academy	1	2,275	24.9	30.2	49.5	9.3

Note: Table includes school districts with 2,000 or more students; (1) Percentage of students that are not non-Hispanic white; (2) Percentage of students that are eligible for the free lunch program; (3) Percentage of students that have an Individualized Education Program.
Source: U.S. Department of Education, National Center for Education Statistics, Common Core of Data, Local Education Agency (School District) Universe Survey: School Year 2016-2017; U.S. Department of Education, National Center for Education Statistics, Common Core of Data, Public Elementary/Secondary School Universe Survey: School Year 2016-2017

Highest Level of Education

Area	Less than H.S.	H.S. Diploma	Some College, No Deg.	Associate Degree	Bachelor's Degree	Master's Degree	Prof. School Degree	Doctorate Degree
City	12.1	27.8	22.8	5.0	19.0	8.3	2.5	2.5
MSA[1]	12.6	32.3	21.6	5.9	18.0	6.5	1.8	1.4
U.S.	12.7	27.3	20.8	8.3	19.1	8.4	2.0	1.4

Note: Figures cover persons age 25 and over; (1) Figures cover the Baton Rouge, LA Metropolitan Statistical Area—see Appendix B for areas included
Source: U.S. Census Bureau, 2013-2017 American Community Survey 5-Year Estimates

Educational Attainment by Race

Area	High School Graduate or Higher (%)					Bachelor's Degree or Higher (%)				
	Total	White	Black	Asian	Hisp.[2]	Total	White	Black	Asian	Hisp.[2]
City	87.9	95.6	82.0	84.1	82.4	32.4	52.7	14.9	50.3	24.3
MSA[1]	87.4	90.6	82.0	85.2	71.5	27.6	31.9	18.3	52.4	18.3
U.S.	87.3	89.3	84.9	86.5	66.7	30.9	32.2	20.6	52.7	15.2

Note: Figures shown cover persons 25 years old and over; (1) Figures cover the Baton Rouge, LA Metropolitan Statistical Area—see Appendix B for areas included; (2) People of Hispanic origin can be of any race
Source: U.S. Census Bureau, 2013-2017 American Community Survey 5-Year Estimates

School Enrollment by Grade and Control

Area	Preschool (%)		Kindergarten (%)		Grades 1 - 4 (%)		Grades 5 - 8 (%)		Grades 9 - 12 (%)	
	Public	Private	Public	Private	Public	Private	Public	Private	Public	Private
City	63.8	36.2	72.1	27.9	79.4	20.6	79.6	20.4	81.1	18.9
MSA[1]	56.1	43.9	73.4	26.6	81.2	18.8	80.7	19.3	81.1	18.9
U.S.	58.8	41.2	87.7	12.3	89.7	10.3	89.6	10.4	90.3	9.7

Note: Figures shown cover persons 3 years old and over; (1) Figures cover the Baton Rouge, LA Metropolitan Statistical Area—see Appendix B for areas included
Source: U.S. Census Bureau, 2013-2017 American Community Survey 5-Year Estimates

Average Salaries of Public School Classroom Teachers

Area	2016		2017		Change from 2016 to 2017	
	Dollars	Rank[1]	Dollars	Rank[1]	Percent	Rank[2]
Louisiana	49,745	34	50,000	37	0.5	40
U.S. Average	58,479	–	59,660	–	2.0	–

Note: (1) Rank ranges from 1 to 51 where 1 indicates highest salary; (2) Rank ranges from 1 to 51 where 1 indicates highest percent change.
Source: National Education Association, Rankings & Estimates: Rankings of the States 2017 and Estimates of School Statistics 2018

Higher Education

Four-Year Colleges			Two-Year Colleges			Medical Schools[1]	Law Schools[2]	Voc/ Tech[3]
Public	Private Non-profit	Private For-profit	Public	Private Non-profit	Private For-profit			
3	1	1	2	2	7	0	2	9

Note: Figures cover institutions located within the city limits and include main campuses only; (1) includes schools accredited by the Liaison Committee on Medical Education and the American Osteopathic Association's Commission on Osteopathic College Accreditation; (2) includes ABA-accredited schools, schools with provisional ABA accreditation, and state accredited schools; (3) includes all schools with programs that are less than 2 years.
Source: National Center for Education Statistics, Integrated Postsecondary Education System (IPEDS), 2017-18; Wikipedia, List of Medical Schools in the United States, accessed April 3, 2019; Wikipedia, List of Law Schools in the United States, accessed April 3, 2019

According to *U.S. News & World Report,* the Baton Rouge, LA metro area is home to one of the best national universities in the U.S.: **Louisiana State University—Baton Rouge** (#140 tie). The indicators used to capture academic quality fall into a number of categories: assessment by administrators at peer institutions; retention of students; faculty resources; student selectivity; financial resources; alumni giving; high school counselor ratings of colleges; and graduation rate. *U.S. News & World Report, "America's Best Colleges 2019"*

According to *U.S. News & World Report,* the Baton Rouge, LA metro area is home to one of the top 100 law schools in the U.S.: **Louisiana State University—Baton Rouge (Hebert)** (#100 tie). The rankings are based on a weighted average of 12 measures of quality: peer assessment score; assessment score by lawyers/judges; median LSAT scores; median undergrad GPA; acceptance rate; employment rates for graduates; placement success; bar passage rate; faculty resources; expenditures per student; student/faculty ratio; and library resources. *U.S. News & World Report, "America's Best Graduate Schools, Law, 2020"*

According to *U.S. News & World Report,* the Baton Rouge, LA metro area is home to one of the top 75 business schools in the U.S.: **Louisiana State University—Baton Rouge (Ourso)** (#69 tie). The rankings are based on a weighted average of the following nine measures: quality assessment; peer assessment; recruiter assessment; placement success; mean starting salary and bonus; student selectivity; mean GMAT and GRE scores; mean undergraduate GPA; and acceptance rate. *U.S. News & World Report, "America's Best Graduate Schools, Business, 2020"*

PRESIDENTIAL ELECTION

2016 Presidential Election Results

Area	Clinton	Trump	Johnson	Stein	Other
East Baton Rouge Parish	52.3	43.1	2.5	0.8	1.2
U.S.	48.0	45.9	3.3	1.1	1.7

Note: Results are percentages and may not add to 100% due to rounding
Source: Dave Leip's Atlas of U.S. Presidential Elections

EMPLOYERS

Major Employers

Company Name	Industry
Baton Rouge General Medical Center	General medical & surgical hospitals
CB&I	Engineering, procurement and construction
City of Baton Rouge-E Baton Rouge Parish	City/county government
East Baton Rouge Parish Public Schools	Public elementary & secondary schools
ExxonMobil Chemical-Baton Rouge Refinery	Petroleum refining
Louisiana State University	Public coeducational university
Our Lady of the Lake Regional Medical Ctr	General medical & surgical hospitals
Performance Contractors	Industrial construction and pipe fabrication
State of Louisiana	State government
Turner Industries	Heavy industrial construction and maintenance

Note: Companies shown are located within the Baton Rouge, LA Metropolitan Statistical Area.
Source: Hoovers.com; Wikipedia

PUBLIC SAFETY

Crime Rate

Area	All Crimes	Violent Crimes				Property Crimes		
		Murder	Rape[3]	Robbery	Aggrav. Assault	Burglary	Larceny-Theft	Motor Vehicle Theft
City	6,620.8	38.3	44.0	381.7	562.9	1,418.6	3,739.6	435.8
Suburbs[1]	3,686.9	8.7	23.1	56.5	279.3	597.7	2,583.9	137.7
Metro[2]	4,484.3	16.7	28.8	144.9	356.4	820.8	2,898.0	218.7
U.S.	2,756.1	5.3	41.7	98.0	248.9	430.4	1,694.4	237.4

Note: Figures are crimes per 100,000 population; (1) All areas within the metro area that are located outside the city limits; (2) Figures cover the Baton Rouge, LA Metropolitan Statistical Area—see Appendix B for areas included; (3) The city and U.S. figures shown were reported using the revised Uniform Crime Reporting (UCR) definition of rape. The suburban and metro area figures shown are an aggregate total of the data submitted using both the revised and legacy UCR definitions.
Source: FBI Uniform Crime Reports, 2017

Hate Crimes

Area	Number of Quarters Reported	Number of Incidents per Bias Motivation					
		Race/Ethnicity/Ancestry	Religion	Sexual Orientation	Disability	Gender	Gender Identity
City	2	0	0	0	0	0	0
U.S.	4	4,131	1,564	1,130	116	46	119

Source: Federal Bureau of Investigation, Hate Crime Statistics 2017

Identity Theft Consumer Reports

Area	Reports	Reports per 100,000 Population	Rank[2]
MSA[1]	961	115	87
U.S.	444,602	135	-

Note: (1) Figures cover the Baton Rouge, LA Metropolitan Statistical Area—see Appendix B for areas included; (2) Rank ranges from 1 to 389 where 1 indicates greatest number of identity theft reports per 100,000 population
Source: Federal Trade Commission, Consumer Sentinel Network Data Book for January–December 2018

Fraud and Other Consumer Reports

Area	Reports	Reports per 100,000 Population	Rank[2]
MSA[1]	4,096	490	198
U.S.	2,552,917	776	-

Note: (1) Figures cover the Baton Rouge, LA Metropolitan Statistical Area—see Appendix B for areas included; (2) Rank ranges from 1 to 389 where 1 indicates greatest number of fraud and other consumer reports per 100,000 population
Source: Federal Trade Commission, Consumer Sentinel Network Data Book for January–December 2018

SPORTS

Professional Sports Teams

Team Name	League	Year Established
No teams are located in the metro area		

Source: Wikipedia, Major Professional Sports Teams of the United States and Canada, April 5, 2019

CLIMATE

Average and Extreme Temperatures

Temperature	Jan	Feb	Mar	Apr	May	Jun	Jul	Aug	Sep	Oct	Nov	Dec	Yr.
Extreme High (°F)	82	85	91	92	98	103	101	102	99	94	87	85	103
Average High (°F)	61	65	71	79	85	90	91	91	87	80	70	64	78
Average Temp. (°F)	51	54	61	68	75	81	82	82	78	69	59	53	68
Average Low (°F)	41	44	50	57	64	70	73	72	68	57	48	43	57
Extreme Low (°F)	9	13	20	32	44	53	58	59	43	30	21	8	8

Note: Figures cover the years 1948-1995
Source: National Climatic Data Center, International Station Meteorological Climate Summary, 9/96

Average Precipitation/Snowfall/Humidity

Precip./Humidity	Jan	Feb	Mar	Apr	May	Jun	Jul	Aug	Sep	Oct	Nov	Dec	Yr.
Avg. Precip. (in.)	4.9	5.1	4.8	5.5	5.0	4.4	6.6	5.4	4.1	3.1	4.2	5.3	58.5
Avg. Snowfall (in.)	Tr	Tr	Tr	0	0	0	0	0	0	0	Tr	Tr	Tr
Avg. Rel. Hum. 6am (%)	85	85	86	89	91	91	92	93	91	89	88	86	89
Avg. Rel. Hum. 3pm (%)	59	55	52	52	54	57	62	61	59	51	53	57	56

Note: Figures cover the years 1948-1995; Tr = Trace amounts (<0.05 in. of rain; <0.5 in. of snow)
Source: National Climatic Data Center, International Station Meteorological Climate Summary, 9/96

Weather Conditions

Temperature			Daytime Sky			Precipitation		
10°F & below	32°F & below	90°F & above	Clear	Partly cloudy	Cloudy	0.01 inch or more precip.	0.1 inch or more snow/ice	Thunder-storms
< 1	21	86	99	150	116	113	< 1	73

Note: Figures are average number of days per year and cover the years 1948-1995
Source: National Climatic Data Center, International Station Meteorological Climate Summary, 9/96

HAZARDOUS WASTE

Superfund Sites

The Baton Rouge, LA metro area is home to three sites on the EPA's Superfund National Priorities List: **Combustion, Inc.** (final); **Devil's Swamp Lake** (proposed); **Petro-Processors of Louisiana, Inc.** (final). There are a total of 1,390 Superfund sites with a status of proposed or final on the list in the U.S. *U.S. Environmental Protection Agency, National Priorities List, April 5, 2019*

AIR & WATER QUALITY

Air Quality Trends: Ozone

	1990	1995	2000	2005	2010	2012	2014	2015	2016	2017
MSA[1]	0.105	0.091	0.090	0.090	0.075	0.074	0.071	0.069	0.066	0.069
U.S.	0.088	0.089	0.082	0.080	0.073	0.075	0.067	0.068	0.069	0.068

Note: (1) Data covers the Baton Rouge, LA Metropolitan Statistical Area—see Appendix B for areas included. The values shown are the composite ozone concentration averages among trend sites based on the highest fourth daily maximum 8-hour concentration in parts per million. These trends are based on sites having an adequate record of monitoring data during the trend period. Data from exceptional events are included.
Source: U.S. Environmental Protection Agency, Air Quality Monitoring Information, "Air Quality Trends by City, 1990-2017"

Air Quality Index

Area	Percent of Days when Air Quality was...[2]					AQI Statistics[2]	
	Good	Moderate	Unhealthy for Sensitive Groups	Unhealthy	Very Unhealthy	Maximum	Median
MSA[1]	62.5	35.3	2.2	0.0	0.0	140	46

Note: (1) Data covers the Baton Rouge, LA Metropolitan Statistical Area—see Appendix B for areas included; (2) Based on 365 days with AQI data in 2017. Air Quality Index (AQI) is an index for reporting daily air quality. EPA calculates the AQI for five major air pollutants regulated by the Clean Air Act: ground-level ozone, particle pollution (aka particulate matter), carbon monoxide, sulfur dioxide, and nitrogen dioxide. The AQI runs from 0 to 500. The higher the AQI value, the greater the level of air pollution and the greater the health concern. There are six AQI categories: "Good" AQI is between 0 and 50. Air quality is considered satisfactory; "Moderate" AQI is between 51 and 100. Air quality is acceptable; "Unhealthy for Sensitive Groups" When AQI values are between 101 and 150, members of sensitive groups may experience health effects; "Unhealthy" When AQI values are between 151 and 200 everyone may begin to experience health effects; "Very Unhealthy" AQI values between 201 and 300 trigger a health alert; "Hazardous" AQI values over 300 trigger warnings of emergency conditions (not shown).
Source: U.S. Environmental Protection Agency, Air Quality Index Report, 2017

Air Quality Index Pollutants

Area	Percent of Days when AQI Pollutant was...[2]					
	Carbon Monoxide	Nitrogen Dioxide	Ozone	Sulfur Dioxide	Particulate Matter 2.5	Particulate Matter 10
MSA[1]	0.0	0.5	38.4	2.7	58.4	0.0

Note: (1) Data covers the Baton Rouge, LA Metropolitan Statistical Area—see Appendix B for areas included; (2) Based on 365 days with AQI data in 2017. The Air Quality Index (AQI) is an index for reporting daily air quality. EPA calculates the AQI for five major air pollutants regulated by the Clean Air Act: ground-level ozone, particle pollution (also known as particulate matter), carbon monoxide, sulfur dioxide, and nitrogen dioxide. The AQI runs from 0 to 500. The higher the AQI value, the greater the level of air pollution and the greater the health concern.
Source: U.S. Environmental Protection Agency, Air Quality Index Report, 2017

Maximum Air Pollutant Concentrations: Particulate Matter, Ozone, CO and Lead

	Particulate Matter 10 (ug/m^3)	Particulate Matter 2.5 Wtd AM (ug/m^3)	Particulate Matter 2.5 24-Hr (ug/m^3)	Ozone (ppm)	Carbon Monoxide (ppm)	Lead (ug/m^3)
MSA[1] Level	71	9.1	19	0.073	1	0
NAAQS[2]	150	15	35	0.075	9	0.15
Met NAAQS[2]	Yes	Yes	Yes	Yes	Yes	Yes

Note: (1) Data covers the Baton Rouge, LA Metropolitan Statistical Area—see Appendix B for areas included; Data from exceptional events are included; (2) National Ambient Air Quality Standards; ppm = parts per million; ug/m^3 = micrograms per cubic meter; n/a not available.
Concentrations: Particulate Matter 10 (coarse particulate)—highest second maximum 24-hour concentration; Particulate Matter 2.5 Wtd AM (fine particulate)—highest weighted annual mean concentration; Particulate Matter 2.5 24-Hour (fine particulate)—highest 98th percentile 24-hour concentration; Ozone—highest fourth daily maximum 8-hour concentration; Carbon Monoxide—highest second maximum non-overlapping 8-hour concentration; Lead—maximum running 3-month average
Source: U.S. Environmental Protection Agency, Air Quality Monitoring Information, "Air Quality Statistics by City, 2017"

Maximum Air Pollutant Concentrations: Nitrogen Dioxide and Sulfur Dioxide

	Nitrogen Dioxide AM (ppb)	Nitrogen Dioxide 1-Hr (ppb)	Sulfur Dioxide AM (ppb)	Sulfur Dioxide 1-Hr (ppb)	Sulfur Dioxide 24-Hr (ppb)
MSA[1] Level	10	46	n/a	29	n/a
NAAQS[2]	53	100	30	75	140
Met NAAQS[2]	Yes	Yes	n/a	Yes	n/a

Note: (1) Data covers the Baton Rouge, LA Metropolitan Statistical Area—see Appendix B for areas included; Data from exceptional events are included; (2) National Ambient Air Quality Standards; ppm = parts per million; ug/m^3 = micrograms per cubic meter; n/a not available.
Concentrations: Nitrogen Dioxide AM—highest arithmetic mean concentration; Nitrogen Dioxide 1-Hr—highest 98th percentile 1-hour daily maximum concentration; Sulfur Dioxide AM—highest annual mean concentration; Sulfur Dioxide 1-Hr—highest 99th percentile 1-hour daily maximum concentration; Sulfur Dioxide 24-Hr—highest second maximum 24-hour concentration
Source: U.S. Environmental Protection Agency, Air Quality Monitoring Information, "Air Quality Statistics by City, 2017"

Drinking Water

Water System Name	Pop. Served	Primary Water Source Type	Violations[1]	
			Health Based	Monitoring/ Reporting
Baton Rouge Water Company	527,067	Ground	0	0

Note: (1) Based on violation data from January 1, 2018 to December 31, 2018
Source: U.S. Environmental Protection Agency, Office of Ground Water and Drinking Water, Safe Drinking Water Information System (based on data extracted April 5, 2019)

Cape Coral, Florida

Background

Tucked along Florida's Gulf Coast 71 miles south of Sarasota, Cape Coral is a mid-twentieth century community grown from a development launched in 1957. Today, at 115 square miles, it is Florida's third-largest city by land mass and the most populous city between Tampa and Miami. To the east across the Caloosahatchie River lies Fort Myers, and to the west across Pine Island and Pine Island sound lie the fabled barrier islands of Captiva and Sanibel.

Baltimore brothers Leonard and Jack Rosen purchased the former Redfish Point for $678,000 in 1957 and renamed the property Cape Coral. By June of the following year "the Cape," as it is known, was receiving its first residents. The city incorporated in 1970 when its population reached 11,470.

Despite the city's relative youth, this self-named "Waterfront Wonderland" has developed an interest in its roots. It fosters a Cape Coral Historical Museum that is housed in the original snack bar from the local country club, and one of its oldest historical documents is the Cape's 1961 phone book.

Four hundred precious miles of salt water and fresh water canals slice through the city, providing water access to abundant recreational boaters and numerous opportunities for waterfront living.

Following the economic downturn in 2008, Cape Coral has rebounded, named a "most improved" housing market in a National Association of Builders report. The Army Reserve purchased a 15-acre Cape Coral site for use as an Army Reserve Training Center for local reservists.

Industry-wise, Cape Coral has Foreign Trade Zones in two of its three industrial parks, the 92.5 acre North Cape Industrial Park—home to light manufacturers, service industry and warehouses—and the Mid Cape Commerce Park which, at 143.37 acres, is comprised of service industries and warehouses.

A VA Clinic was recently built by the U.S. Dept. of Veteran's Affairs at the Hancock Creek Commerce Park and Indian Oaks Trade Centre. It provides a full range of services ranging from mental health and diagnostic radiology to urology and a full complement of imaging services such as CT scans and nuclear medicine. It is the centerpiece of a Veterans Investment Zone initiative designed to draw office, medical parks, assisted living facilities and the like.

Today the U.S. Bureau of Labor Statistics tracks Cape Coral's success in conjunction with that of nearby Fort Myers, and the region boasts trade, transportation and utilities as its largest economic sector. Essentially, this is a retirement and tourism destination.

Significant recreational opportunities are available in the area, and include the Four Mile Cove Ecological Preserve with its nature trail, picnic area, and warm weather kayak rentals. The Cape Coral Yacht Club, located where the city first began, includes a fishing pier, beach, and community pool. The 18-hole public Coral Oaks Golf Course (replete with pro shop and pub), the Northwest Softball Complex, the William Bill Austen Youth Center Eagle Skate Park, the Strausser BMX Sports Complex, and even the Pelican Sport Soccer Complex show the city's diverse recreational opportunities.

To the east of Cape Coral—on the other side of Fort Myers—is both the Florida Gulf Coast University and Southwest Florida International Airport.

Cape Coral's climate borders on perfect, with an average 335 days per year of sunshine (albeit hot and humid ones in summer time). Annual rainfall is 53.37 inches, with the most rain coming in summer. The city dries out from October into May.

Rankings

General Rankings

- The Cape Coral metro area was identified as one of America's fastest-growing areas in terms of population and economy by *Forbes*. The area ranked #9 out of 25. The 100 most populous metro areas in the U.S. were evaluated on the following criteria: estimated population growth; employment; economic output; wages; home values. *Forbes, "America's Fastest-Growing Cities 2018," February 28, 2018*

Business/Finance Rankings

- The personal finance site NerdWallet analyzed 183 American metropolitan areas with populations over 250,000 and more than 15,000 businesses to rank where entrepreneurs find the most success. Criteria included area economy, annual income, housing cost, unemployment rate, and the success rate of area businesses. Cape Coral ranked #123. *www.nerdwallet.com, "Best Places to Start a Business," April 27, 2015*

- The Brookings Institution ranked the nation's largest cities based on income inequality. Cape Coral was ranked #93 (#1 = greatest inequality). Criteria: the "95/20 ratio," a figure representing the income at which a household earns more than 95 percent of all other households, divided by the income at which a household earns more than only 20 percent of all other households. *Brookings Institution, "Household Income Inequality, Largest Cities of 97 Large U.S. Metro Areas, 2014-2016," February 5, 2018*

- The Brookings Institution ranked the 100 largest metro areas in the U.S. based on income inequality. Cape Coral was ranked #73 (#1 = greatest inequality). Criteria: the "95/20 ratio," a figure representing the income at which a household earns more than 95 percent of all other households, divided by the income at which a household earns more than only 20 percent of all other households. *Brookings Institution, "Household Income Inequality, 100 Largest U.S. Metro Areas, 2014-2016," February 5, 2018*

- The Cape Coral metro area appeared on the Milken Institute "2018 Best Performing Cities" list. Rank: #46 out of 200 large metro areas. Criteria: job growth; wage and salary growth; high-tech output growth. *Milken Institute, "Best-Performing Cities 2018," January 24, 2019*

- *Forbes* ranked the 200 most populous metro areas to determine the nation's "Best Places for Business and Careers." The Cape Coral metro area was ranked #75. Criteria: costs (business and living); job growth (past and projected); income growth; quality of life; educational attainment (college and high school); projected economic growth; cultural and recreational opportunities; net migration patterns; number of highly ranked colleges. *Forbes, "The Best Places for Business and Careers 2018: Seattle Leads the Way," October 24, 2018*

Education Rankings

- Personal finance website *WalletHub* analyzed the 150 largest U.S. metropolitan statistical areas to determine where the most educated Americans are choosing to settle. Criteria: education quality and attainment gap; education levels; percentage of workers with degrees; public school quality rankings; quality and size of each metro area's universities. Cape Coral was ranked #113 (#1 = most educated city). *www.WalletHub.com, "2018's Most and Least Educated Cities in America," July 24, 2018*

Environmental Rankings

- Cape Coral was highlighted as one of the top 25 cleanest metro areas for year-round particle pollution (Annual PM 2.5) in the U.S. during 2014 through 2016. The area ranked #11. *American Lung Association, State of the Air 2018*

- Cape Coral was highlighted as one of the top 90 cleanest metro areas for short-term particle pollution (24-hour PM 2.5) in the U.S. during 2014 through 2016. Monitors in these cities reported no days with unhealthful PM 2.5 levels. *American Lung Association, State of the Air 2018*

Health/Fitness Rankings

- Cape Coral was identified as a "2018 Spring Allergy Capital." The area ranked #44 out of 100. Three groups of factors were used to identify the most challenging cities for people with allergies during the spring season: annual pollen levels; medicine utilization; access to board-certified allergists. *Asthma and Allergy Foundation of America, "Spring Allergy Capitals 2018"*

- Cape Coral was identified as a "2018 Fall Allergy Capital." The area ranked #50 out of 100. Three groups of factors were used to identify the most challenging cities for people with allergies during the fall season: annual pollen levels; medicine utilization; access to board-certified allergists. *Asthma and Allergy Foundation of America, "Fall Allergy Capitals 2018"*

- Cape Coral was identified as a "2018 Asthma Capital." The area ranked #98 out of the nation's 100 largest metropolitan areas. Criteria: estimated prevalence; self-reported prevalence; crude death rate for asthma; annual pollen score; annual air quality; public smoking laws; number of board-certified asthma specialists; school inhaler access laws; rescue medication use; controller medication use; ER visits for asthma; uninsured rate; poverty rate. *Asthma and Allergy Foundation of America, "Asthma Capitals 2018: The Most Challenging Places to Live With Asthma"*

- The Cape Coral metro area ranked #22 out of 189 in The Gallup-Healthways Well-Being Index. Criteria: purpose; social well being; financial health; community and physical health. Results are based on telephone interviews with adults, aged 18 and older, living in metropolitan areas in the 50 U.S. states and the District of Columbia. *Gallup-Healthways, "State of American Well-Being, 2017 Community Well-Being Rankings" March 2018*

Real Estate Rankings

- *WalletHub* compared the most populated U.S. cities, as well as at least two of the most populated cities in each state, for a total of 179, to determine which had the best markets for real estate agents. Cape Coral ranked #95 where demand was high and pay was the best. Criteria: sales per agent; annual median wage for real-estate agents; monthly average starting salary for real estate agents; real estate job density and competition; unemployment rate; housing-market health index; and other relevant metrics. *www.WalletHub.com, "2018's Best Places to Be a Real Estate Agent," April 25, 2018*

- Cape Coral was ranked #144 out of 237 metro areas in terms of housing affordability in 2018 by the National Association of Home Builders (#1 = most affordable). Criteria: the share of homes sold in that area affordable to a family earning the local median income, based on standard mortgage underwriting criteria. *National Association of Home Builders®, NAHB-Wells Fargo Housing Opportunity Index, 4th Quarter 2018*

Safety Rankings

- Allstate ranked the 200 largest cities in America in terms of driver safety. Cape Coral ranked #8. Criteria: internal property damage claims over a two-year period from January 2015 to December 2016. The report helps increase the importance of safety awareness behind the wheel. *Allstate, "Allstate America's Best Drivers Report, 2018" August 28, 2018*

- The National Insurance Crime Bureau ranked 382 metro areas in the U.S. in terms of per capita rates of vehicle theft. The Cape Coral metro area ranked #234 (#1 = highest rate). Criteria: number of vehicle theft offenses per 100,000 inhabitants in 2017. *National Insurance Crime Bureau, "Hot Spots 2017," July 12, 2018*

Seniors/Retirement Rankings

▪ From its Best Cities for Successful Aging indexes, the Milken Institute generated rankings for metropolitan areas, weighing data in nine categories—health care, wellness, living arrangements, transportation and convenience, financial characteristics, education, employment, community engagement, and overall livability. The Cape Coral metro area was ranked #93 overall in the large metro area category. *Milken Institute, "Best Cities for Successful Aging, 2017" March 14, 2017*

Women/Minorities Rankings

▪ Personal finance website *WalletHub* compared more than 180 U.S. cities—including the 150 most populated U.S. cities, plus at least two of the most populated cities in each state—across two key dimensions, "Hispanic Business-Friendliness" and "Hispanic Purchasing Power", to arrive at the most favorable conditions for Hispanic entrepreneurs. Cape Coral was ranked #44 out of 182. Criteria includes: share of Hispanic-Owned Businesses; Hispanic entrepreneurship rate to median annual income of Hispanics; Small Business-Friendliness score; cost of living; and number of Hispanics with at least a bachelor's degree. *WalletHub.com, "2018's Best Cities for Hispanic Entrepreneurs," April 26, 2018*

Miscellaneous Rankings

▪ Cape Coral was selected as a 2018 Digital Cities Survey winner. The city ranked #2 in the mid-sized city (125,000 to 249,999 population) category. The survey examined and assessed how city governments are utilizing technology to improve transparency, enhance cybersecurity, and solve social challenges. Survey questions focused on ten characteristics: engaged, mobile, open, secure, staffed/supported, efficient, connected, resilient, best practices, and use of innovation. *Center for Digital Government, "2018 Digital Cities Survey," November 2, 2018*

Business Environment

CITY FINANCES

City Government Finances

Component	2016 ($000)	2016 ($ per capita)
Total Revenues	316,839	1,808
Total Expenditures	343,054	1,958
Debt Outstanding	852,032	4,862
Cash and Securities[1]	454,468	2,594

Note: (1) Cash and security holdings of a government at the close of its fiscal year, including those of its dependent agencies, utilities, and liquor stores.
Source: U.S. Census Bureau, State & Local Government Finances 2016

City Government Revenue by Source

Source	2016 ($000)	2016 ($ per capita)	2016 (%)
General Revenue			
From Federal Government	6,254	36	2.0
From State Government	41,737	238	13.2
From Local Governments	982	6	0.3
Taxes			
Property	78,346	447	24.7
Sales and Gross Receipts	22,357	128	7.1
Personal Income	0	0	0.0
Corporate Income	0	0	0.0
Motor Vehicle License	0	0	0.0
Other Taxes	12,134	69	3.8
Current Charges	51,487	294	16.3
Liquor Store	0	0	0.0
Utility	27,448	157	8.7
Employee Retirement	9,195	52	2.9

Source: U.S. Census Bureau, State & Local Government Finances 2016

City Government Expenditures by Function

Function	2016 ($000)	2016 ($ per capita)	2016 (%)
General Direct Expenditures			
Air Transportation	0	0	0.0
Corrections	0	0	0.0
Education	22,944	130	6.7
Employment Security Administration	0	0	0.0
Financial Administration	19,724	112	5.7
Fire Protection	26,613	151	7.8
General Public Buildings	0	0	0.0
Governmental Administration, Other	3,485	19	1.0
Health	0	0	0.0
Highways	16,307	93	4.8
Hospitals	0	0	0.0
Housing and Community Development	1,152	6	0.3
Interest on General Debt	10,342	59	3.0
Judicial and Legal	991	5	0.3
Libraries	0	0	0.0
Parking	23	< 1	< 0.1
Parks and Recreation	17,758	101	5.2
Police Protection	32,250	184	9.4
Public Welfare	0	0	0.0
Sewerage	24,234	138	7.1
Solid Waste Management	0	0	0.0
Veterans' Services	0	0	0.0
Liquor Store	0	0	0.0
Utility	86,840	495	25.3
Employee Retirement	15,086	86	4.4

Source: U.S. Census Bureau, State & Local Government Finances 2016

DEMOGRAPHICS

Population Growth

Area	1990 Census	2000 Census	2010 Census	2017* Estimate	Population Growth (%) 1990-2017	2010-2017
City	75,507	102,286	154,305	173,679	130.0	12.6
MSA[1]	335,113	440,888	618,754	700,165	108.9	13.2
U.S.	248,709,873	281,421,906	308,745,538	321,004,407	29.1	4.0

Note: (1) Figures cover the Cape Coral-Fort Myers, FL Metropolitan Statistical Area—see Appendix B for areas included; (*) 2013-2017 5-year estimated population
Source: U.S. Census Bureau, 1990 Census, Census 2000, Census 2010, 2013-2017 American Community Survey 5-Year Estimates

Household Size

Area	One	Two	Three	Four	Five	Six	Seven or More	Average Household Size
City	23.3	42.7	15.1	11.4	5.6	1.5	0.4	2.80
MSA[1]	28.0	44.4	12.0	8.8	4.3	1.7	0.9	2.60
U.S.	27.7	33.8	15.7	13.0	6.0	2.3	1.4	2.60

Note: (1) Figures cover the Cape Coral-Fort Myers, FL Metropolitan Statistical Area—see Appendix B for areas included
Source: U.S. Census Bureau, 2013-2017 American Community Survey 5-Year Estimates

Race

Area	White Alone[2] (%)	Black Alone[2] (%)	Asian Alone[2] (%)	AIAN[3] Alone[2] (%)	NHOPI[4] Alone[2] (%)	Other Race Alone[2] (%)	Two or More Races (%)
City	90.1	4.4	1.6	0.3	0.0	2.2	1.5
MSA[1]	84.7	8.7	1.6	0.2	0.1	3.0	1.8
U.S.	73.0	12.7	5.4	0.8	0.2	4.8	3.1

Note: (1) Figures cover the Cape Coral-Fort Myers, FL Metropolitan Statistical Area—see Appendix B for areas included; (2) Alone is defined as not being in combination with one or more other races; (3) American Indian and Alaska Native; (4) Native Hawaiian and Other Pacific Islander
Source: U.S. Census Bureau, 2013-2017 American Community Survey 5-Year Estimates

Hispanic or Latino Origin

Area	Total (%)	Mexican (%)	Puerto Rican (%)	Cuban (%)	Other (%)
City	20.2	2.0	5.1	6.3	6.8
MSA[1]	20.2	5.8	4.3	3.9	6.2
U.S.	17.6	11.1	1.7	0.7	4.1

Note: Persons of Hispanic or Latino origin can be of any race; (1) Figures cover the Cape Coral-Fort Myers, FL Metropolitan Statistical Area—see Appendix B for areas included
Source: U.S. Census Bureau, 2013-2017 American Community Survey 5-Year Estimates

Segregation

Type	Segregation Indices[1] 1990	2000	2010	2010 Rank[2]	Percent Change 1990-2000	1990-2010	2000-2010
Black/White	76.8	69.4	61.6	35	-7.5	-15.3	-7.8
Asian/White	23.3	28.5	25.3	96	5.3	2.0	-3.3
Hispanic/White	36.1	40.8	40.2	63	4.7	4.1	-0.6

Note: All figures cover the Metropolitan Statistical Area—see Appendix B for areas included; Figures are based on an analysis of 1990, 2000, and 2010 Census Decennial Census tract data by William H. Frey, Brookings Institution and the University of Michigan Social Science Data Analysis Network. In this analysis all racial groups (whites, blacks, and asians) are non-Hispanic members of those races. Hispanics are shown as a separate category; (1) Segregation Indices are Dissimilarity Indices that measure the degree to which the minority group is distributed differently than whites across census tracts. They range from 0 (complete integration) to 100 (complete segregation) where the value indicates the percentage of the minority group that needs to move to be distributed exactly like whites; (2) Ranges from 1 (most segregated) to 102 (least segregated); n/a not available.
Source: www.CensusScope.org

Ancestry

Area	German	Irish	English	American	Italian	Polish	French[2]	Scottish	Dutch
City	15.1	11.6	7.8	14.7	9.8	3.7	2.9	1.9	1.3
MSA[1]	14.3	11.0	8.5	14.1	7.5	3.3	2.8	1.9	1.4
U.S.	14.1	10.1	7.5	6.6	5.3	2.9	2.5	1.7	1.3

Note: Figures are the percentage of the total population reporting a particular ancestry. The nine most commonly reported ancestries in the U.S. are shown. Figures include multiple ancestries (e.g. if a person reported being Irish and Italian, they were included in both columns); (1) Figures cover the Cape Coral-Fort Myers, FL Metropolitan Statistical Area—see Appendix B for areas included; (2) Excludes Basque
Source: U.S. Census Bureau, 2013-2017 American Community Survey 5-Year Estimates

Foreign-Born Population

Area	Percent of Population Born in								
	Any Foreign Country	Asia	Mexico	Europe	Carribean	Central America[2]	South America	Africa	Canada
City	14.7	1.3	0.7	2.5	5.6	1.3	2.6	0.1	0.6
MSA[1]	16.1	1.2	2.5	2.2	5.2	1.9	1.9	0.2	1.0
U.S.	13.4	4.1	3.6	1.5	1.3	1.0	0.9	0.6	0.3

Note: (1) Figures cover the Cape Coral-Fort Myers, FL Metropolitan Statistical Area—see Appendix B for areas included; (2) Excludes Mexico.
Source: U.S. Census Bureau, 2013-2017 American Community Survey 5-Year Estimates

Marital Status

Area	Never Married	Now Married[2]	Separated	Widowed	Divorced
City	24.6	51.5	2.2	7.8	13.9
MSA[1]	26.1	50.8	1.9	8.2	13.0
U.S.	33.1	48.2	2.0	5.8	10.9

Note: Figures are percentages and cover the population 15 years of age and older; (1) Figures cover the Cape Coral-Fort Myers, FL Metropolitan Statistical Area—see Appendix B for areas included; (2) Excludes separated
Source: U.S. Census Bureau, 2013-2017 American Community Survey 5-Year Estimates

Disability by Age

Area	All Ages	Under 18 Years Old	18 to 64 Years Old	65 Years and Over
City	12.8	2.8	9.8	30.2
MSA[1]	13.8	3.9	9.9	28.6
U.S.	12.6	4.2	10.3	35.5

Note: Figures show percent of the civilian noninstitutionalized population that reported having a disability. Disability status is determined from six types of difficulty: vision, hearing, cognitive, ambulatory, self-care, and independent living. For children under 5 years old, hearing and vision difficulty are used to determine disability status. For children between the ages of 5 and 14, disability status is determined from hearing, vision, cognitive, ambulatory, and self-care difficulties. For people aged 15 years and older, they are considered to have a disability if they have difficulty with any one of the six difficulty types; Note: (1) Figures cover the Cape Coral-Fort Myers, FL Metropolitan Statistical Area—see Appendix B for areas included
Source: U.S. Census Bureau, 2013-2017 American Community Survey 5-Year Estimates

Age

Area	Percent of Population									Median Age
	Under Age 5	Age 5–19	Age 20–34	Age 35–44	Age 45–54	Age 55–64	Age 65–74	Age 75–84	Age 85+	
City	4.5	17.5	15.1	11.5	14.7	14.9	12.8	6.1	3.0	45.9
MSA[1]	4.8	15.5	15.9	10.5	12.3	14.0	15.2	8.6	3.2	47.8
U.S.	6.2	19.5	20.7	12.7	13.4	12.7	8.6	4.4	1.9	37.8

Note: (1) Figures cover the Cape Coral-Fort Myers, FL Metropolitan Statistical Area—see Appendix B for areas included
Source: U.S. Census Bureau, 2013-2017 American Community Survey 5-Year Estimates

Gender

Area	Males	Females	Males per 100 Females
City	84,138	89,541	94.0
MSA[1]	342,731	357,434	95.9
U.S.	158,018,753	162,985,654	97.0

Note: (1) Figures cover the Cape Coral-Fort Myers, FL Metropolitan Statistical Area—see Appendix B for areas included
Source: U.S. Census Bureau, 2013-2017 American Community Survey 5-Year Estimates

Religious Groups by Family

Area	Catholic	Baptist	Non-Den.	Methodist[2]	Lutheran	LDS[3]	Pente-costal	Presby-terian[4]	Muslim[5]	Judaism
MSA[1]	16.2	5.0	3.0	2.5	1.2	0.5	4.4	1.4	0.9	0.2
U.S.	19.1	9.3	4.0	4.0	2.3	2.0	1.9	1.6	0.8	0.7

Note: Figures are the number of adherents as a percentage of the total population; (1) Figures cover the Cape Coral-Fort Myers, FL Metropolitan Statistical Area—see Appendix B for areas included; (2) Methodist/Pietist; (3) Latter Day Saints; (4) Reformed; (5) Figures are estimates
Source: Association of Statisticians of American Religious Bodies, 2010 U.S. Religion Census: Religious Congregations & Membership Study

Religious Groups by Tradition

Area	Catholic	Evangelical Protestant	Mainline Protestant	Other Tradition	Black Protestant	Orthodox
MSA[1]	16.2	14.3	4.6	2.0	0.3	0.2
U.S.	19.1	16.2	7.3	4.3	1.6	0.3

Note: Figures are the number of adherents as a percentage of the total population; (1) Figures cover the Cape Coral-Fort Myers, FL Metropolitan Statistical Area—see Appendix B for areas included
Source: Association of Statisticians of American Religious Bodies, 2010 U.S. Religion Census: Religious Congregations & Membership Study

ECONOMY

Gross Metropolitan Product

Area	2016	2017	2018	2019	Rank[2]
MSA[1]	27.4	28.7	30.2	32.3	94

Note: Figures are in billions of dollars; (1) Figures cover the Cape Coral-Fort Myers, FL Metropolitan Statistical Area—see Appendix B for areas included; (2) Rank is based on 2017 data and ranges from 1 to 381
Source: U.S. Conference of Mayors, U.S. Metro Economies: Economic Growth & Full Employment, June 2018

Economic Growth

Area	2017-2018 (%)	2019-2020 (%)	2021-2022 (%)
MSA[1]	3.5	4.0	2.9

Note: Figures are real gross metropolitan product (GMP) growth rates and represent average annual percent change; (1) Figures cover the Cape Coral-Fort Myers, FL Metropolitan Statistical Area—see Appendix B for areas included
Source: U.S. Conference of Mayors, U.S. Metro Economies: Economic Growth & Full Employment, June 2018

Metropolitan Area Exports

Area	2012	2013	2014	2015	2016	2017	Rank[2]
MSA[1]	509.8	442.6	496.6	487.3	540.3	592.3	193

Note: Figures are in millions of dollars; (1) Figures cover the Cape Coral-Fort Myers, FL Metropolitan Statistical Area—see Appendix B for areas included; (2) Rank is based on 2017 data and ranges from 1 to 387
Source: U.S. Department of Commerce, International Trade Administration, Office of Trade and Economic Analysis, Industry and Analysis, Exports by Metropolitan Area, extracted March 25, 2019

Building Permits

Area	Single-Family			Multi-Family			Total		
	2016	2017	Pct. Chg.	2016	2017	Pct. Chg.	2016	2017	Pct. Chg.
City	1,443	1,842	27.7	144	708	391.7	1,587	2,550	60.7
MSA[1]	4,092	4,841	18.3	1,325	2,113	59.5	5,417	6,954	28.4
U.S.	750,800	820,000	9.2	455,800	462,000	1.4	1,206,600	1,282,000	6.2

Note: (1) Figures cover the Cape Coral-Fort Myers, FL Metropolitan Statistical Area—see Appendix B for areas included; Figures represent new, privately-owned housing units authorized (unadjusted data); All permit data are based on estimates with imputation
Source: U.S. Census Bureau, Manufacturing, Mining, and Construction Statistics, Building Permits, 2016, 2017

Bankruptcy Filings

Area	Business Filings			Nonbusiness Filings		
	2017	2018	% Chg.	2017	2018	% Chg.
Lee County	80	63	-21.3	1,130	1,106	-2.1
U.S.	23,157	22,232	-4.0	765,863	751,186	-1.9

Note: Business filings include Chapter 7, Chapter 11, Chapter 12, and Chapter 13; Nonbusiness filings include Chapter 7, Chapter 11, and Chapter 13
Source: Administrative Office of the U.S. Courts, Business and Nonbusiness Bankruptcy, County Cases Commenced by Chapter of the Bankruptcy Code, During the 12-Month Period Ending December 31, 2017 and Business and Nonbusiness Bankruptcy, County Cases Commenced by Chapter of the Bankruptcy Code, During the 12-Month Period Ending December 31, 2018

Housing Vacancy Rates

Area	Gross Vacancy Rate[2] (%)			Year-Round Vacancy Rate[3] (%)			Rental Vacancy Rate[4] (%)			Homeowner Vacancy Rate[5] (%)		
	2016	2017	2018	2016	2017	2018	2016	2017	2018	2016	2017	2018
MSA[1]	38.5	39.1	41.5	17.8	20.2	16.6	5.8	4.3	5.8	3.0	2.9	3.0
U.S.	12.8	12.7	12.3	9.9	9.9	9.7	6.9	7.2	6.9	1.7	1.6	1.5

Note: (1) Figures cover the Cape Coral-Fort Myers, FL Metropolitan Statistical Area—see Appendix B for areas included; (2) The percentage of the total housing inventory that is vacant; (3) The percentage of the housing inventory (excluding seasonal units) that is year-round vacant; (4) The percentage of rental inventory that is vacant for rent; (5) The percentage of homeowner inventory that is vacant for sale
Source: U.S. Census Bureau, Housing Vacancies and Homeownership Annual Statistics: 2016, 2017, 2018

INCOME

Income

Area	Per Capita ($)	Median Household ($)	Average Household ($)
City	26,446	53,653	68,090
MSA[1]	30,233	52,052	74,000
U.S.	31,177	57,652	81,283

Note: (1) Figures cover the Cape Coral-Fort Myers, FL Metropolitan Statistical Area—see Appendix B for areas included
Source: U.S. Census Bureau, 2013-2017 American Community Survey 5-Year Estimates

Household Income Distribution

Area	Percent of Households Earning							
	Under $15,000	$15,000 -$24,999	$25,000 -$34,999	$35,000 -$49,999	$50,000 -$74,999	$75,000 -$99,999	$100,000 -$149,999	$150,000 and up
City	9.9	9.4	10.8	14.7	22.7	13.4	12.1	6.9
MSA[1]	11.1	10.3	11.4	14.7	20.0	12.0	11.6	8.9
U.S.	11.6	9.8	9.5	13.0	17.7	12.3	14.1	12.1

Note: (1) Figures cover the Cape Coral-Fort Myers, FL Metropolitan Statistical Area—see Appendix B for areas included
Source: U.S. Census Bureau, 2013-2017 American Community Survey 5-Year Estimates

Poverty Rate

Area	All Ages	Under 18 Years Old	18 to 64 Years Old	65 Years and Over
City	12.7	17.0	12.8	8.7
MSA[1]	14.9	24.9	15.0	7.8
U.S.	14.6	20.3	13.7	9.3

Note: Figures are percentage of people whose income during the past 12 months was below the poverty level; (1) Figures cover the Cape Coral-Fort Myers, FL Metropolitan Statistical Area—see Appendix B for areas included
Source: U.S. Census Bureau, 2013-2017 American Community Survey 5-Year Estimates

EMPLOYMENT

Labor Force and Employment

Area	Civilian Labor Force			Workers Employed		
	Dec. 2017	Dec. 2018	% Chg.	Dec. 2017	Dec. 2018	% Chg.
City	87,362	89,615	2.6	84,383	86,784	2.8
MSA[1]	334,489	343,149	2.6	323,111	332,304	2.8
U.S.	159,880,000	162,510,000	1.6	153,602,000	156,481,000	1.9

Note: Data is not seasonally adjusted and covers workers 16 years of age and older; (1) Figures cover the Cape Coral-Fort Myers, FL Metropolitan Statistical Area—see Appendix B for areas included
Source: Bureau of Labor Statistics, Local Area Unemployment Statistics

Unemployment Rate

Area	2018											
	Jan.	Feb.	Mar.	Apr.	May	Jun.	Jul.	Aug.	Sep.	Oct.	Nov.	Dec.
City	3.9	3.5	3.5	3.1	3.1	3.7	3.8	3.6	2.9	3.0	3.0	3.2
MSA[1]	3.8	3.5	3.4	3.2	3.2	3.8	3.8	3.7	2.9	2.9	2.9	3.2
U.S.	4.5	4.4	4.1	3.7	3.6	4.2	4.1	3.9	3.6	3.5	3.5	3.7

Note: Data is not seasonally adjusted and covers workers 16 years of age and older; (1) Figures cover the Cape Coral-Fort Myers, FL Metropolitan Statistical Area—see Appendix B for areas included
Source: Bureau of Labor Statistics, Local Area Unemployment Statistics

Average Wages

Occupation	$/Hr.	Occupation	$/Hr.
Accountants and Auditors	29.20	Maids and Housekeeping Cleaners	11.50
Automotive Mechanics	19.00	Maintenance and Repair Workers	17.60
Bookkeepers	18.60	Marketing Managers	55.60
Carpenters	19.00	Nuclear Medicine Technologists	34.80
Cashiers	11.00	Nurses, Licensed Practical	20.80
Clerks, General Office	15.50	Nurses, Registered	32.30
Clerks, Receptionists/Information	14.30	Nursing Assistants	14.10
Clerks, Shipping/Receiving	15.70	Packers and Packagers, Hand	11.00
Computer Programmers	33.50	Physical Therapists	44.30
Computer Systems Analysts	35.00	Postal Service Mail Carriers	24.30
Computer User Support Specialists	21.70	Real Estate Brokers	39.50
Cooks, Restaurant	13.70	Retail Salespersons	12.50
Dentists	77.20	Sales Reps., Exc. Tech./Scientific	32.40
Electrical Engineers	44.40	Sales Reps., Tech./Scientific	52.20
Electricians	23.80	Secretaries, Exc. Legal/Med./Exec.	17.10
Financial Managers	51.90	Security Guards	13.10
First-Line Supervisors/Managers, Sales	22.80	Surgeons	104.50
Food Preparation Workers	11.80	Teacher Assistants*	14.20
General and Operations Managers	49.60	Teachers, Elementary School*	30.60
Hairdressers/Cosmetologists	12.80	Teachers, Secondary School*	31.10
Internists, General	n/a	Telemarketers	13.70
Janitors and Cleaners	12.60	Truck Drivers, Heavy/Tractor-Trailer	18.90
Landscaping/Groundskeeping Workers	13.10	Truck Drivers, Light/Delivery Svcs.	15.80
Lawyers	57.70	Waiters and Waitresses	11.20

Note: Wage data covers the Cape Coral-Fort Myers, FL Metropolitan Statistical Area—see Appendix B for areas included; (*) Hourly wages for elementary/secondary school teachers and teacher assistants were calculated by the editors from annual wage data based on a 40 hour work week; n/a not available.
Source: Bureau of Labor Statistics, Metro Area Occupational Employment & Wage Estimates, May 2018

Employment by Occupation

Occupation Classification	City (%)	MSA[1] (%)	U.S. (%)
Management, Business, Science, and Arts	29.4	30.4	37.4
Natural Resources, Construction, and Maintenance	11.0	11.8	8.9
Production, Transportation, and Material Moving	8.5	8.3	12.2
Sales and Office	30.5	27.7	23.5
Service	20.6	21.7	18.0

Note: Figures cover employed civilians 16 years of age and older; (1) Figures cover the Cape Coral-Fort Myers, FL Metropolitan Statistical Area—see Appendix B for areas included
Source: U.S. Census Bureau, 2013-2017 American Community Survey 5-Year Estimates

Employment by Industry

Sector	MSA[1]		U.S.
	Number of Employees	Percent of Total	Percent of Total
Construction, Mining, and Logging	32,300	11.5	5.3
Education and Health Services	31,100	11.1	15.9
Financial Activities	13,600	4.8	5.7
Government	43,600	15.5	15.1
Information	2,800	1.0	1.9
Leisure and Hospitality	43,700	15.6	10.7
Manufacturing	6,400	2.3	8.5
Other Services	11,700	4.2	3.9
Professional and Business Services	38,900	13.8	14.1
Retail Trade	43,800	15.6	10.8
Transportation, Warehousing, and Utilities	5,600	2.0	4.2
Wholesale Trade	7,500	2.7	3.9

Note: Figures are non-farm employment as of December 2018. Figures are not seasonally adjusted and include workers 16 years of age and older; (1) Figures cover the Cape Coral-Fort Myers, FL Metropolitan Statistical Area—see Appendix B for areas included
Source: Bureau of Labor Statistics, Current Employment Statistics, Employment, Hours, and Earnings

Occupations with Greatest Projected Employment Growth: 2018 – 2020

Occupation[1]	2018 Employment	2020 Projected Employment	Numeric Employment Change	Percent Employment Change
Interviewers, Except Eligibility and Loan	11,890	33,270	21,380	179.8
Combined Food Preparation and Serving Workers, Including Fast Food	242,590	256,470	13,880	5.7
Waiters and Waitresses	230,640	240,320	9,680	4.2
Registered Nurses	193,200	202,070	8,870	4.6
Customer Service Representatives	245,420	253,780	8,360	3.4
Laborers and Freight, Stock, and Material Movers, Hand	135,600	143,640	8,040	5.9
Construction Laborers	89,390	97,130	7,740	8.7
Landscaping and Groundskeeping Workers	116,440	123,040	6,600	5.7
Carpenters	72,550	78,990	6,440	8.9
Janitors and Cleaners, Except Maids and Housekeeping Cleaners	133,890	140,000	6,110	4.6

Note: Projections cover Florida; (1) Sorted by numeric employment change
Source: www.projectionscentral.com, State Occupational Projections, 2018–2020 Short-Term Projections

Fastest Growing Occupations: 2018 – 2020

Occupation[1]	2018 Employment	2020 Projected Employment	Numeric Employment Change	Percent Employment Change
Interviewers, Except Eligibility and Loan	11,890	33,270	21,380	179.8
Solar Photovoltaic Installers	1,100	1,330	230	20.9
Terrazzo Workers and Finishers	390	450	60	15.4
Helpers—Roofers	1,490	1,720	230	15.4
Helpers—Brickmasons, Blockmasons, Stonemasons, and Tile and Marble Setters	1,280	1,470	190	14.8
Helpers—Painters, Paperhangers, Plasterers, and Stucco Masons	570	650	80	14.0
Reinforcing Iron and Rebar Workers	1,100	1,250	150	13.6
Insulation Workers, Floor, Ceiling, and Wall	2,550	2,880	330	12.9
Structural Iron and Steel Workers	5,210	5,880	670	12.9
Cement Masons and Concrete Finishers	13,490	15,210	1,720	12.8

Note: Projections cover Florida; (1) Sorted by percent employment change and excludes occupations with numeric employment change less than 50
Source: www.projectionscentral.com, State Occupational Projections, 2018–2020 Short-Term Projections

TAXES

State Corporate Income Tax Rates

State	Tax Rate (%)	Income Brackets ($)	Num. of Brackets	Financial Institution Tax Rate (%)[a]	Federal Income Tax Ded.
Florida	5.5 (e)	Flat rate	1	5.5 (e)	No

Note: Tax rates as of January 1, 2019; (a) Rates listed are the corporate income tax rate applied to financial institutions or excise taxes based on income. Some states have other taxes based upon the value of deposits or shares; (e) The Florida tax rate may be adjusted downward if certain revenue targets are met.
Source: Federation of Tax Administrators, Range of State Corporate Income Tax Rates, January 1, 2019

State Individual Income Tax Rates

State	Tax Rate (%)	Income Brackets ($)	Personal Exemptions ($) Single	Married	Depend.	Standard Ded. ($) Single	Married
Florida			– No state income tax –				

Note: Tax rates as of January 1, 2019; Local- and county-level taxes are not included; n/a not applicable;

Source: Federation of Tax Administrators, State Individual Income Tax Rates, January 1, 2019

Various State Sales and Excise Tax Rates

State	State Sales Tax (%)	Gasoline[1] (¢/gal.)	Cigarette[2] ($/pack)	Spirits[3] ($/gal.)	Wine[4] ($/gal.)	Beer[5] ($/gal.)	Recreational Marijuana (%)
Florida	6	41.99	1.339	6.50 (f)	2.25 (l)	0.48 (q)	Not legal

Note: All tax rates as of January 1, 2019; (1) The American Petroleum Institute has developed a methodology for determining the average tax rate on a gallon of fuel. Rates may include any of the following: excise taxes, environmental fees, storage tank fees, other fees or taxes, general sales tax, and local taxes. In states where gasoline is subject to the general sales tax, or where the fuel tax is based on the average sale price, the average rate determined by API is sensitive to changes in the price of gasoline. States that fully or partially apply general sales taxes to gasoline: CA, CO, GA, IL, IN, MI, NY; (2) The federal excise tax of $1.0066 per pack and local taxes are not included; (3) Rates are those applicable to off-premise sales of 40% alcohol by volume (a.b.v.) distilled spirits in 750ml containers. Local excise taxes are excluded; (4) Rates are those applicable to off-premise sales of 11% a.b.v. non-carbonated wine in 750ml containers; (5) Rates are those applicable to off-premise sales of 4.7% a.b.v. beer in 12 ounce containers; (f) Different rates also applicable according to alcohol content, place of production, size of container, or place purchased (on- or off-premise or onboard airlines); (l) Different rates also applicable to alcohol content, place of production, size of container, place purchased (on- or off-premise or on board airlines) or type of wine (carbonated, vermouth, etc.); (q) Different rates also applicable according to alcohol content, place of production, size of container, or place purchased (on- or off-premise or onboard airlines).
Source: Tax Foundation, 2019 Facts & Figures: How Does Your State Compare?

State Business Tax Climate Index Rankings

State	Overall Rank	Corporate Tax Rank	Individual Income Tax Rank	Sales Tax Rank	Unemployment Insurance Tax Rank	Property Tax Rank
Florida	4	6	1	22	2	11

Note: The index is a measure of how each state's tax laws affect economic performance. The lower the rank, the more favorable a state's tax system is for business. States without a given tax are given a ranking of 1. The scores/rankings for the District of Columbia do not affect other states. The 2019 index represents the tax climate as of July 1, 2018.
Source: Tax Foundation, State Business Tax Climate Index 2019

COMMERCIAL UTILITIES

Typical Monthly Electric Bills

Area	Commercial Service ($/month) 1,500 kWh	40 kW demand 14,000 kWh	Industrial Service ($/month) 1,000 kW demand 200,000 kWh	50,000 kW demand 32,500,000 kWh
City	n/a	n/a	n/a	n/a
Average[1]	203	1,619	25,886	2,540,077

Note: Figures are based on annualized rates; (1) Average based on 187 utilities surveyed; n/a not available
Source: Edison Electric Institute, Typical Bills and Average Rates Report, Summer 2018

TRANSPORTATION

Means of Transportation to Work

Area	Car/Truck/Van		Public Transportation			Bicycle	Walked	Other Means	Worked at Home
	Drove Alone	Car-pooled	Bus	Subway	Railroad				
City	82.9	9.3	0.1	0.0	0.0	0.1	0.7	1.3	5.5
MSA[1]	79.9	9.7	0.8	0.0	0.0	0.6	1.0	2.3	5.6
U.S.	76.4	9.2	2.5	1.9	0.6	0.6	2.7	1.3	4.7

Note: Figures are percentages and cover workers 16 years of age and older; (1) Figures cover the Cape Coral-Fort Myers, FL Metropolitan Statistical Area—see Appendix B for areas included
Source: U.S. Census Bureau, 2013-2017 American Community Survey 5-Year Estimates

Travel Time to Work

Area	Less Than 10 Minutes	10 to 19 Minutes	20 to 29 Minutes	30 to 44 Minutes	45 to 59 Minutes	60 to 89 Minutes	90 Minutes or More
City	7.4	24.5	23.9	27.5	9.6	4.9	2.2
MSA[1]	8.6	26.3	22.5	26.1	9.7	4.6	2.2
U.S.	12.7	28.9	20.9	20.5	8.1	6.2	2.7

Note: Note: Figures are percentages and include workers 16 years old and over; (1) Figures cover the Cape Coral-Fort Myers, FL Metropolitan Statistical Area—see Appendix B for areas included
Source: U.S. Census Bureau, 2013-2017 American Community Survey 5-Year Estimates

Freeway Travel Time Index

Area	1985	1990	1995	2000	2005	2010	2014
Urban Area Rank[1,2]	48	46	47	46	39	39	54
Urban Area Index[1]	1.07	1.10	1.13	1.16	1.19	1.19	1.17
Average Index[3]	1.09	1.11	1.14	1.17	1.20	1.19	1.20

Note: Freeway Travel Time Index—the ratio of travel time in the peak period to the travel time at free-flow conditions. For example, a value of 1.30 indicates a 20-minute free-flow trip takes 26 minutes in the peak (20 minutes x 1.30 = 26 minutes); (1) Covers the Cape Coral FL urban area; (2) Rank is based on 101 urban areas (#1 = highest travel time index); (3) Average of 101 urban areas
Source: Texas Transportation Institute, 2015 Urban Mobility Scorecard, August 2015

Freeway Commuter Stress Index

Area	1985	1990	1995	2000	2005	2010	2014
Urban Area Rank[1,2]	66	59	61	63	53	53	71
Urban Area Index[1]	1.07	1.11	1.14	1.17	1.20	1.20	1.18
Average Index[3]	1.13	1.16	1.19	1.22	1.25	1.24	1.25

Note: The Freeway Commuter Stress Index is the same as the Freeway Travel Time Index (see table above) except that it includes only the travel in the peak directions during the peak periods; the TTI includes travel in all directions during the peak period. Thus, the CSI is more indicative of the work trip experienced by each commuter on a daily basis; (1) Covers the Cape Coral FL urban area; (2) Rank is based on 101 urban areas (#1 = highest travel time index); (3) Average of 101 urban areas
Source: Texas Transportation Institute, 2015 Urban Mobility Scorecard, August 2015

Public Transportation

Agency Name / Mode of Transportation	Vehicles Operated in Maximum Service[1]	Annual Unlinked Passenger Trips[2] (in thous.)	Annual Passenger Miles[3] (in thous.)
Lee County Transit (LeeTran)			
Bus (directly operated)	49	3,126.8	16,512.9
Demand Response (directly operated)	41	119.6	1,256.9
Vanpool (purchased transportation)	19	53.3	1,717.5

Note: (1) The number of revenue vehicles operated by the given mode and type of service to meet the annual maximum service requirement. This is the revenue vehicle count during the peak season of the year; on the week and day that maximum service is provided. Vehicles operated in maximum service (VOMS) exclude atypical days and one-time special events; (2) The number of passengers who boarded public transportation vehicles. Passengers are counted each time they board a vehicle no matter how many vehicles they use to travel from their origin to their destination. (3) The sum of the distances ridden by all passengers during the entire fiscal year.
Source: Federal Transit Administration, National Transit Database, 2017

Air Transportation

Airport Name and Code / Type of Service	Passenger Airlines[1]	Passenger Enplanements	Freight Carriers[2]	Freight (lbs)
Southwest Florida International Airport (RSW)				
Domestic service (U.S. carriers - 2018)	26	4,425,591	13	11,834,996
International service (U.S. carriers - 2017)	4	1,114	1	30,016

Note: (1) Includes all U.S.-based major, minor and commuter airlines that carried at least one passenger during the year; (2) Includes all U.S.-based airlines and freight carriers that transported at least one pound of freight during the year.
Source: Bureau of Transportation Statistics, The Intermodal Transportation Database, Air Carriers: T-100 Domestic Market (U.S. Carriers), 2018; Bureau of Transportation Statistics, The Intermodal Transportation Database, Air Carriers: T-100 International Market (U.S. Carriers), 2017

Other Transportation Statistics

Major Highways:	I-75
Amtrak Service:	Bus service only (station is located in Ft. Myers)
Major Waterways/Ports:	Gulf of Mexico; Caloosahatchee River

Source: Amtrak.com; Google Maps

Major Business Headquarters

Company Name	Industry	Fortune[1]	Forbes[2]
No companies listed	-	-	-

Note: (1) Companies that produce a 10-K are ranked 1 to 500 based on 2017 revenue; (2) All private companies with at least $2 billion in annual revenue through the end of their most current fiscal year are ranked 1 to 229; companies listed are headquartered in the city; dashes indicate no ranking
Source: Fortune, "Fortune 500," June 2018; Forbes, "America's Largest Private Companies," 2018 Rankings

Minority- and Women-Owned Businesses

Group	All Firms		Firms with Paid Employees			
	Firms	Sales ($000)	Firms	Sales ($000)	Employees	Payroll ($000)
AIAN[1]	93	(s)	1	(s)	0 - 19	(s)
Asian	565	(s)	84	(s)	250 - 499	(s)
Black	649	35,282	97	(s)	100 - 249	(s)
Hispanic	4,495	269,553	213	(s)	500 - 999	(s)
NHOPI[2]	n/a	n/a	n/a	n/a	n/a	n/a
Women	6,394	352,587	575	239,759	2,680	60,551
All Firms	18,281	4,150,947	3,058	3,649,902	21,853	687,812

Note: Figures cover firms located in the city; minority- and women-owned business are defined as firms in which the corresponding group own 51% or more of the stock or equity of the company; (1) American Indian and Alaska Native; (2) Native Hawaiian and Other Pacific Islander; (s) estimates are suppressed when publication standards are not met; n/a not available
Source: U.S. Census Bureau, 2012 Economic Census, Survey of Business Owners

Hotels, Motels and Vacation Rentals

Area	5 Star		4 Star		3 Star		2 Star		1 Star		Not Rated	
	Num.	Pct.[3]	Num.	Pct.[3]	Num.	Pct.[3]	Num.	Pct.[3]	Num.	Pct.[3]	Num.	Pct.[3]
City[1]	0	0.0	57	5.6	91	9.0	31	3.1	0	0.0	832	82.3
Total[2]	286	0.4	5,236	7.1	16,715	22.6	10,259	13.9	293	0.4	41,056	55.6

Note: (1) Figures cover Cape Coral and vicinity; (2) Figures cover all 100 cities in this book; (3) Percentage of hotels which have a given star rating; Star ratings are determined by expedia.com and offer an indication of the general quality of a particular hotel.
Source: www.expedia.com, April 3, 2019

Major Convention Centers

Name	Overall Space (sq. ft.)	Exhibit Space (sq. ft.)	Meeting Space (sq. ft.)	Meeting Rooms
Harborside Events Center (Fort Myers)	n/a	42,000	n/a	n/a

Note: Table includes convention centers located in the Cape Coral-Fort Myers, FL metro area; n/a not available
Source: Original research

Living Environment

COST OF LIVING

Cost of Living Index

Composite Index	Groceries	Housing	Utilities	Trans-portation	Health Care	Misc. Goods/ Services
95.3	105.0	86.1	100.0	114.1	102.5	92.2

Note: The Cost of Living Index measures regional differences in the cost of consumer goods and services, excluding taxes and non-consumer expenditures, for professional and managerial households in the top income quintile. It is based on more than 50,000 prices covering almost 60 different items for which prices are collected three times a year by chambers of commerce, economic development organizations or university applied economic centers in each participating urban area. The numbers shown should be read as a percentage above or below the national average of 100. For example, a value of 115.4 in the groceries column indicates that grocery prices are 15.4% higher than the national average. Small differences in the index numbers should not be interpreted as significant; Figures cover the Cape Coral-Fort Myers FL urban area.
Source: The Council for Community and Economic Research, ACCRA Cost of Living Index, 2018

Grocery Prices

Area[1]	T-Bone Steak ($/pound)	Frying Chicken ($/pound)	Whole Milk ($/half gal.)	Eggs ($/dozen)	Orange Juice ($/64 oz.)	Coffee ($/11.5 oz.)
City[2]	11.05	1.43	2.33	2.10	3.54	3.54
Avg.	11.35	1.42	1.94	1.81	3.52	4.35
Min.	7.45	0.92	0.80	0.75	2.72	3.06
Max.	15.05	2.76	4.18	4.00	5.36	8.20

Note: (1) Values for the local area are compared with the average, minimum and maximum values for all 291 areas in the Cost of Living Index; (2) Figures cover the Cape Coral-Fort Myers FL urban area; T-Bone Steak (price per pound); Frying Chicken (price per pound, whole fryer); Whole Milk (half gallon carton); Eggs (price per dozen, Grade A, large); Orange Juice (64 oz. Tropicana or Florida Natural); Coffee (11.5 oz. can, vacuum-packed, Maxwell House, Hills Bros, or Folgers).
Source: The Council for Community and Economic Research, ACCRA Cost of Living Index, 2018

Housing and Utility Costs

Area[1]	New Home Price ($)	Apartment Rent ($/month)	All Electric ($/month)	Part Electric ($/month)	Other Energy ($/month)	Telephone ($/month)
City[2]	301,867	935	165.32	-	-	181.80
Avg.	347,000	1,087	165.93	100.16	67.73	178.70
Min.	200,468	500	93.58	25.64	26.78	163.10
Max.	1,901,222	4,888	388.65	246.86	332.81	197.70

Note: (1) Values for the local area are compared with the average, minimum and maximum values for all 291 areas in the Cost of Living Index; (2) Figures cover the Cape Coral-Fort Myers FL urban area; New Home Price (2,400 sf living area, 8,000 sf lot, in urban area with full utilities); Apartment Rent (950 sf 2 bedroom/1.5 or 2 bath, unfurnished, excluding all utilities except water); All Electric (average monthly cost for an all-electric home); Part Electric (average monthly cost for a part-electric home); Other Energy (average monthly cost for natural gas, fuel oil, coal, wood, and any other forms of energy except electricity); Telephone (price includes the base monthly rate plus taxes and fees for three lines of mobile phone service).
Source: The Council for Community and Economic Research, ACCRA Cost of Living Index, 2018

Health Care, Transportation, and Other Costs

Area[1]	Doctor ($/visit)	Dentist ($/visit)	Optometrist ($/visit)	Gasoline ($/gallon)	Beauty Salon ($/visit)	Men's Shirt ($)
City[2]	115.00	99.50	64.66	2.60	26.00	25.49
Avg.	110.71	95.11	103.74	2.61	37.48	32.03
Min.	33.60	62.55	54.63	1.89	17.00	11.44
Max.	195.97	153.93	225.79	3.59	71.88	58.64

Note: (1) Values for the local area are compared with the average, minimum and maximum values for all 291 areas in the Cost of Living Index; (2) Figures cover the Cape Coral-Fort Myers FL urban area; Doctor (general practitioners routine exam of an established patient); Dentist (adult teeth cleaning and periodic oral examination); Optometrist (full vision eye exam for established adult patient); Gasoline (one gallon regular unleaded, national brand, including all taxes, cash price at self-service pump if available); Beauty Salon (woman's shampoo, trim, and blow-dry); Men's Shirt (cotton/polyester dress shirt, pinpoint weave, long sleeves).
Source: The Council for Community and Economic Research, ACCRA Cost of Living Index, 2018

HOUSING

House Price Index (HPI)

Area	National Ranking[2]	Quarterly Change (%)	One-Year Change (%)	Five-Year Change (%)
MSA[1]	176	-0.07	4.64	51.21
U.S.[3]	–	1.12	5.73	32.81

Note: The HPI is a weighted repeat sales index. It measures average price changes in repeat sales or refinancings on the same properties. This information is obtained by reviewing repeat mortgage transactions on single-family properties whose mortgages have been purchased or securitized by Fannie Mae or Freddie Mac in January 1975; (1) Figures cover the Cape Coral-Fort Myers, FL Metropolitan Statistical Area—see Appendix B for areas included; (2) Rankings are based on annual percentage change for all metro areas containing at least 15,000 transactions over the last 10 years and ranges from 1 to 245; (3) figures based on a weighted average of Census Division estimates using a seasonally adjusted, purchase-only index; all figures are for the period ending December 31, 2018
Source: Federal Housing Finance Agency, House Price Index, February 26, 2019

Median Single-Family Home Prices

Area	2016	2017	2018P	Percent Change 2017 to 2018
MSA[1]	227.4	243.5	251.0	3.1
U.S. Average	235.5	248.8	261.6	5.1

Note: Figures are median sales prices of existing single-family homes in thousands of dollars; (p) preliminary; (1) Figures cover the Cape Coral-Fort Myers, FL Metropolitan Statistical Area—see Appendix B for areas included
Source: National Association of Realtors, Median Sales Price of Existing Single-Family Homes for Metropolitan Areas, 4th Quarter 2018

Qualifying Income Based on Median Sales Price of Existing Single-Family Homes

Area	With 5% Down ($)	With 10% Down ($)	With 20% Down ($)
MSA[1]	61,072	57,857	51,429
U.S. Average	62,954	59,640	53,013

Note: Figures are preliminary; Qualifying income is based on a mortgage rate of 4.9%. Monthly principal and interest payment is limited to 25% of income; (1) Figures cover the Cape Coral-Fort Myers, FL Metropolitan Statistical Area—see Appendix B for areas included
Source: National Association of Realtors, Qualifying Income Based on Median Sales Price of Existing Single-Family Homes for Metropolitan Areas, 4th Quarter 2018

Median Apartment Condo-Coop Home Prices

Area	2016	2017	2018P	Percent Change 2017 to 2018
MSA[1]	181.0	185.0	192.0	3.8
U.S. Average	220.7	234.3	241.0	2.9

Note: Figures are median sales prices of existing apartment condo-coop homes in thousands of dollars; (p) preliminary; (1) Figures cover the Cape Coral-Fort Myers, FL Metropolitan Statistical Area—see Appendix B for areas included
Source: National Association of Realtors, Median Sales Price of Existing Apartment Condo-Coop Homes for Metropolitan Areas, 4th Quarter 2018

Home Value Distribution

Area	Under $50,000	$50,000 -$99,999	$100,000 -$149,999	$150,000 -$199,999	$200,000 -$299,999	$300,000 -$499,999	$500,000 -$999,999	$1,000,000 or more
City	2.3	8.4	18.8	21.8	26.6	16.6	4.8	0.9
MSA[1]	8.7	13.6	14.6	15.6	20.6	16.9	7.6	2.4
U.S.	8.3	13.9	14.7	14.6	18.7	17.3	9.7	2.7

Note: Figures are percentages and cover owner-occupied housing units; (1) Figures cover the Cape Coral-Fort Myers, FL Metropolitan Statistical Area—see Appendix B for areas included
Source: U.S. Census Bureau, 2013-2017 American Community Survey 5-Year Estimates

Homeownership Rate

Area	2010 (%)	2011 (%)	2012 (%)	2013 (%)	2014 (%)	2015 (%)	2016 (%)	2017 (%)	2018 (%)
MSA[1]	n/a	n/a	n/a	n/a	n/a	62.9	66.5	65.5	75.1
U.S.	66.9	66.1	65.4	65.1	64.5	63.7	63.4	63.9	64.4

Note: (1) Figures cover the Cape Coral-Fort Myers, FL Metropolitan Statistical Area—see Appendix B for areas included
Source: U.S. Census Bureau, Housing Vacancies and Homeownership Annual Statistics: 2010-2018

Year Housing Structure Built

Area	2010 or Later	2000 -2009	1990 -1999	1980 -1989	1970 -1979	1960 -1969	1950 -1959	1940 -1949	Before 1940	Median Year
City	2.0	39.3	17.0	23.4	12.2	5.0	0.7	0.2	0.2	1995
MSA[1]	3.0	32.8	17.7	21.9	15.3	5.6	2.6	0.5	0.7	1992
U.S.	3.2	14.5	14.0	13.6	15.5	10.8	10.5	5.1	12.9	1977

Note: Figures are percentages except for Median Year; Note: (1) Figures cover the Cape Coral-Fort Myers, FL Metropolitan Statistical Area—see Appendix B for areas included
Source: U.S. Census Bureau, 2013-2017 American Community Survey 5-Year Estimates

Gross Monthly Rent

Area	Under $500	$500 -$999	$1,000 -$1,499	$1,500 -$1,999	$2,000 -$2,499	$2,500 -$2,999	$3,000 and up	Median ($)
City	1.2	31.5	49.7	12.5	3.5	0.8	0.8	1,136
MSA[1]	4.4	42.0	38.2	9.4	3.2	1.2	1.7	1,035
U.S.	10.5	41.1	28.7	11.7	4.5	1.8	1.7	982

Note: Figures are percentages except for Median; Gross rent is the contract rent plus the estimated average monthly cost of utilities (electricity, gas, and water and sewer) and fuels (oil, coal, kerosene, wood, etc.) if these are paid by the renter (or paid for the renter by someone else); (1) Figures cover the Cape Coral-Fort Myers, FL Metropolitan Statistical Area—see Appendix B for areas included
Source: U.S. Census Bureau, 2013-2017 American Community Survey 5-Year Estimates

HEALTH

Health Risk Factors

Category	MSA[1] (%)	U.S. (%)
Adults aged 18–64 who have any kind of health care coverage	n/a	87.3
Adults who reported being in good or better health	n/a	82.4
Adults who have been told they have high blood cholesterol	n/a	33.0
Adults who have been told they have high blood pressure	n/a	32.3
Adults who are current smokers	n/a	17.1
Adults who currently use E-cigarettes	n/a	4.6
Adults who currently use chewing tobacco, snuff, or snus	n/a	4.0
Adults who are heavy drinkers[2]	n/a	6.3
Adults who are binge drinkers[3]	n/a	17.4
Adults who are overweight (BMI 25.0 - 29.9)	n/a	35.3
Adults who are obese (BMI 30.0 - 99.8)	n/a	31.3
Adults who participated in any physical activities in the past month	n/a	74.4
Adults who always or nearly always wears a seat belt	n/a	94.3

Note: n/a not available; (1) Figures cover the Cape Coral-Fort Myers, FL Metropolitan Statistical Area—see Appendix B for areas included; (2) Heavy drinkers are classified as adult men having more than 14 drinks per week and adult women having more than 7 drinks per week; (3) Binge drinkers are classified as males having five or more drinks on one occasion or females having four or more drinks on one occasion
Source: Centers for Disease Control and Prevention, Behaviorial Risk Factor Surveillance System, SMART: Selected Metropolitan Area Risk Trends, 2017

Acute and Chronic Health Conditions

Category	MSA[1] (%)	U.S. (%)
Adults who have ever been told they had a heart attack	n/a	4.2
Adults who have ever been told they have angina or coronary heart disease	n/a	3.9
Adults who have ever been told they had a stroke	n/a	3.0
Adults who have ever been told they have asthma	n/a	14.2
Adults who have ever been told they have arthritis	n/a	24.9
Adults who have ever been told they have diabetes[2]	n/a	10.5
Adults who have ever been told they had skin cancer	n/a	6.2
Adults who have ever been told they had any other types of cancer	n/a	7.1
Adults who have ever been told they have COPD	n/a	6.5
Adults who have ever been told they have kidney disease	n/a	3.0
Adults who have ever been told they have a form of depression	n/a	20.5

Note: n/a not available; (1) Figures cover the Cape Coral-Fort Myers, FL Metropolitan Statistical Area—see Appendix B for areas included; (2) Figures do not include pregnancy-related, borderline, or pre-diabetes
Source: Centers for Disease Control and Prevention, Behaviorial Risk Factor Surveillance System, SMART: Selected Metropolitan Area Risk Trends, 2017

Health Screening and Vaccination Rates

Category	MSA[1] (%)	U.S. (%)
Adults aged 65+ who have had flu shot within the past year	n/a	60.7
Adults aged 65+ who have ever had a pneumonia vaccination	n/a	75.4
Adults who have ever been tested for HIV	n/a	36.1
Adults who have ever had the shingles or zoster vaccine?	n/a	28.9
Adults who have had their blood cholesterol checked within the last five years	n/a	85.9

Note: n/a not available; (1) Figures cover the Cape Coral-Fort Myers, FL Metropolitan Statistical Area—see Appendix B for areas included.
Source: Centers for Disease Control and Prevention, Behaviorial Risk Factor Surveillance System, SMART: Selected Metropolitan Area Risk Trends, 2017

Disability Status

Category	MSA[1] (%)	U.S. (%)
Adults who reported being deaf	n/a	6.7
Are you blind or have serious difficulty seeing, even when wearing glasses?	n/a	4.5
Are you limited in any way in any of your usual activities due of arthritis?	n/a	12.9
Do you have difficulty doing errands alone?	n/a	6.8
Do you have difficulty dressing or bathing?	n/a	3.6
Do you have serious difficulty concentrating/remembering/making decisions?	n/a	10.7
Do you have serious difficulty walking or climbing stairs?	n/a	13.6

Note: n/a not available; (1) Figures cover the Cape Coral-Fort Myers, FL Metropolitan Statistical Area—see Appendix B for areas included.
Source: Centers for Disease Control and Prevention, Behaviorial Risk Factor Surveillance System, SMART: Selected Metropolitan Area Risk Trends, 2017

Mortality Rates for the Top 10 Causes of Death in the U.S.

ICD-10[a] Sub-Chapter	ICD-10[a] Code	Age-Adjusted Mortality Rate[1] per 100,000 population	
		County[2]	U.S.
Malignant neoplasms	C00-C97	131.1	155.5
Ischaemic heart diseases	I20-I25	80.6	94.8
Other forms of heart disease	I30-I51	19.6	52.9
Chronic lower respiratory diseases	J40-J47	32.4	41.0
Cerebrovascular diseases	I60-I69	25.2	37.5
Other degenerative diseases of the nervous system	G30-G31	33.9	35.0
Other external causes of accidental injury	W00-X59	45.7	33.7
Organic, including symptomatic, mental disorders	F01-F09	8.0	31.0
Hypertensive diseases	I10-I15	29.7	21.9
Diabetes mellitus	E10-E14	16.7	21.2

Note: (a) ICD-10 = International Classification of Diseases 10th Revision; (1) Mortality rates are a three year average covering 2015-2017; (2) Figures cover Lee County.
Source: Centers for Disease Control and Prevention, National Center for Health Statistics. Underlying Cause of Death 1999-2017 on CDC WONDER Online Database

Mortality Rates for Selected Causes of Death

ICD-10[a] Sub-Chapter	ICD-10[a] Code	Age-Adjusted Mortality Rate[1] per 100,000 population	
		County[2]	U.S.
Assault	X85-Y09	7.0	5.9
Diseases of the liver	K70-K76	15.6	14.1
Human immunodeficiency virus (HIV) disease	B20-B24	1.3	1.8
Influenza and pneumonia	J09-J18	5.3	14.3
Intentional self-harm	X60-X84	14.7	13.6
Malnutrition	E40-E46	0.5	1.6
Obesity and other hyperalimentation	E65-E68	1.8	2.1
Renal failure	N17-N19	3.6	13.0
Transport accidents	V01-V99	16.2	12.4
Viral hepatitis	B15-B19	1.4	1.6

Note: (a) ICD-10 = International Classification of Diseases 10th Revision; (1) Mortality rates are a three year average covering 2015-2017; (2) Figures cover Lee County; Data are suppressed when the data meet the criteria for confidentiality constraints; Mortality rates are flagged as unreliable when the rate would be calculated with a numerator of 20 or less.
Source: Centers for Disease Control and Prevention, National Center for Health Statistics. Underlying Cause of Death 1999-2017 on CDC WONDER Online Database

Health Insurance Coverage

Area	With Health Insurance	With Private Health Insurance	With Public Health Insurance	Without Health Insurance	Population Under Age 18 Without Health Insurance
City	85.5	63.1	36.7	14.5	9.2
MSA[1]	84.4	60.2	42.7	15.6	10.2
U.S.	89.5	67.2	33.8	10.5	5.7

Note: Figures are percentages that cover the civilian noninstitutionalized population; (1) Figures cover the Cape Coral-Fort Myers, FL Metropolitan Statistical Area—see Appendix B for areas included
Source: U.S. Census Bureau, 2013-2017 American Community Survey 5-Year Estimates

Number of Medical Professionals

Area	MDs[3]	DOs[3,4]	Dentists	Podiatrists	Chiropractors	Optometrists
County[1] (number)	1,336	209	360	59	198	94
County[1] (rate[2])	184.9	28.9	48.7	8.0	26.8	12.7
U.S. (rate[2])	279.3	23.0	68.4	6.0	27.1	16.2

Note: Data as of 2017 unless noted; (1) Data covers Lee County; (2) Rate per 100,000 population; (3) Data as of 2016 and includes all active, non-federal physicians; (4) Doctor of Osteopathic Medicine
Source: U.S. Department of Health and Human Services, Health Resources and Services Administration, Bureau of Health Professions, Area Resource File (ARF) 2017-2018

EDUCATION

Public School District Statistics

District Name	Schls	Pupils	Pupil/ Teacher Ratio	Minority Pupils[1] (%)	Free Lunch Eligible[2] (%)	IEP[3] (%)
School District of Lee County	125	92,686	16.1	59.0	49.2	12.6

Note: Table includes school districts with 2,000 or more students; (1) Percentage of students that are not non-Hispanic white; (2) Percentage of students that are eligible for the free lunch program; (3) Percentage of students that have an Individualized Education Program.
Source: U.S. Department of Education, National Center for Education Statistics, Common Core of Data, Local Education Agency (School District) Universe Survey: School Year 2016-2017; U.S. Department of Education, National Center for Education Statistics, Common Core of Data, Public Elementary/Secondary School Universe Survey: School Year 2016-2017

Highest Level of Education

Area	Less than H.S.	H.S. Diploma	Some College, No Deg.	Associate Degree	Bachelor's Degree	Master's Degree	Prof. School Degree	Doctorate Degree
City	9.0	35.8	22.2	10.5	15.1	5.4	1.2	0.7
MSA[1]	12.7	30.9	20.4	8.9	17.1	6.9	2.1	1.1
U.S.	12.7	27.3	20.8	8.3	19.1	8.4	2.0	1.4

Note: Figures cover persons age 25 and over; (1) Figures cover the Cape Coral-Fort Myers, FL Metropolitan Statistical Area—see Appendix B for areas included
Source: U.S. Census Bureau, 2013-2017 American Community Survey 5-Year Estimates

Educational Attainment by Race

Area	High School Graduate or Higher (%)					Bachelor's Degree or Higher (%)				
	Total	White	Black	Asian	Hisp.[2]	Total	White	Black	Asian	Hisp.[2]
City	91.0	91.4	90.3	88.1	81.3	22.5	23.0	17.4	12.7	19.0
MSA[1]	87.3	89.0	76.1	89.3	66.2	27.2	28.5	15.6	37.5	13.9
U.S.	87.3	89.3	84.9	86.5	66.7	30.9	32.2	20.6	52.7	15.2

Note: Figures shown cover persons 25 years old and over; (1) Figures cover the Cape Coral-Fort Myers, FL Metropolitan Statistical Area—see Appendix B for areas included; (2) People of Hispanic origin can be of any race
Source: U.S. Census Bureau, 2013-2017 American Community Survey 5-Year Estimates

School Enrollment by Grade and Control

Area	Preschool (%)		Kindergarten (%)		Grades 1 - 4 (%)		Grades 5 - 8 (%)		Grades 9 - 12 (%)	
	Public	Private	Public	Private	Public	Private	Public	Private	Public	Private
City	71.9	28.1	94.4	5.6	94.8	5.2	93.7	6.3	95.0	5.0
MSA[1]	67.6	32.4	92.3	7.7	93.2	6.8	91.8	8.2	92.9	7.1
U.S.	58.8	41.2	87.7	12.3	89.7	10.3	89.6	10.4	90.3	9.7

Note: Figures shown cover persons 3 years old and over; (1) Figures cover the Cape Coral-Fort Myers, FL Metropolitan Statistical Area—see Appendix B for areas included
Source: U.S. Census Bureau, 2013-2017 American Community Survey 5-Year Estimates

Average Salaries of Public School Classroom Teachers

Area	2016		2017		Change from 2016 to 2017	
	Dollars	Rank[1]	Dollars	Rank[1]	Percent	Rank[2]
Florida	46,612	46	47,267	45	1.4	26
U.S. Average	58,479	–	59,660	–	2.0	–

Note: (1) Rank ranges from 1 to 51 where 1 indicates highest salary; (2) Rank ranges from 1 to 51 where 1 indicates highest percent change.
Source: National Education Association, Rankings & Estimates: Rankings of the States 2017 and Estimates of School Statistics 2018

Higher Education

Four-Year Colleges			Two-Year Colleges			Medical Schools[1]	Law Schools[2]	Voc/ Tech[3]
Public	Private Non-profit	Private For-profit	Public	Private Non-profit	Private For-profit			
0	0	0	0	0	0	0	0	1

Note: Figures cover institutions located within the city limits and include main campuses only; (1) includes schools accredited by the Liaison Committee on Medical Education and the American Osteopathic Association's Commission on Osteopathic College Accreditation; (2) includes ABA-accredited schools, schools with provisional ABA accreditation, and state accredited schools; (3) includes all schools with programs that are less than 2 years.
Source: National Center for Education Statistics, Integrated Postsecondary Education System (IPEDS), 2017-18; Wikipedia, List of Medical Schools in the United States, accessed April 3, 2019; Wikipedia, List of Law Schools in the United States, accessed April 3, 2019

PRESIDENTIAL ELECTION

2016 Presidential Election Results

Area	Clinton	Trump	Johnson	Stein	Other
Lee County	37.9	58.1	2.1	0.6	1.2
U.S.	48.0	45.9	3.3	1.1	1.7

Note: Results are percentages and may not add to 100% due to rounding
Source: Dave Leip's Atlas of U.S. Presidential Elections

EMPLOYERS

Major Employers

Company Name	Industry
Arthrex	Medical device manufacturer
Charlotte County School District	Education
Charlotte Regional Medical Center	Healthcare
Chico's Fas	Retail
City of Cape Coral	Government
Collier County Administration	Government
Collier County Public Schools	Education
Florida Gulf Coast University	Education
Home Depot	Retail
Lee County School District	Education
Lee County Sherriff's Office	Government
Lee Memorial Health System	Healthcare
NCH Naples Hospitals	Healthcare
Palm Automotive	Auto sales
Publix Supermarkets	Retail grocery
St. Joseph Preferred Healthcare Inc	Healthcare
U.S. Sugar	Manufacturing
United States Postal Service	U.S. postal service
Wal-Mart Stores	Retail
Winn-Dixie	Grocery stores

Note: Companies shown are located within the Cape Coral-Fort Myers, FL Metropolitan Statistical Area.
Source: Hoovers.com; Wikipedia

PUBLIC SAFETY

Crime Rate

Area	All Crimes	Violent Crimes				Property Crimes		
		Murder	Rape[3]	Robbery	Aggrav. Assault	Burglary	Larceny -Theft	Motor Vehicle Theft
City	1,694.1	1.6	8.7	22.2	94.9	309.2	1,165.2	92.2
Suburbs[1]	1,869.4	7.5	41.7	89.5	230.4	308.6	1,050.9	140.7
Metro[2]	1,825.9	6.1	33.5	72.8	196.8	308.8	1,079.2	128.7
U.S.	2,756.1	5.3	41.7	98.0	248.9	430.4	1,694.4	237.4

Note: Figures are crimes per 100,000 population; (1) All areas within the metro area that are located outside the city limits; (2) Figures cover the Cape Coral-Fort Myers, FL Metropolitan Statistical Area—see Appendix B for areas included; (3) The city and U.S. figures shown were reported using the revised Uniform Crime Reporting (UCR) definition of rape. The suburban and metro area figures shown are an aggregate total of the data submitted using both the revised and legacy UCR definitions.
Source: FBI Uniform Crime Reports, 2017

Hate Crimes

Area	Number of Quarters Reported	Number of Incidents per Bias Motivation					
		Race/Ethnicity/ Ancestry	Religion	Sexual Orientation	Disability	Gender	Gender Identity
City	4	0	0	0	0	0	0
U.S.	4	4,131	1,564	1,130	116	46	119

Source: Federal Bureau of Investigation, Hate Crime Statistics 2017

Identity Theft Consumer Reports

Area	Reports	Reports per 100,000 Population	Rank[2]
MSA[1]	883	122	73
U.S.	444,602	135	-

Note: (1) Figures cover the Cape Coral-Fort Myers, FL Metropolitan Statistical Area—see Appendix B for areas included; (2) Rank ranges from 1 to 389 where 1 indicates greatest number of identity theft reports per 100,000 population
Source: Federal Trade Commission, Consumer Sentinel Network Data Book for January–December 2018

Fraud and Other Consumer Reports

Area	Reports	Reports per 100,000 Population	Rank[2]
MSA[1]	4,768	660	35
U.S.	2,552,917	776	-

Note: (1) Figures cover the Cape Coral-Fort Myers, FL Metropolitan Statistical Area—see Appendix B for areas included; (2) Rank ranges from 1 to 389 where 1 indicates greatest number of fraud and other consumer reports per 100,000 population
Source: Federal Trade Commission, Consumer Sentinel Network Data Book for January–December 2018

SPORTS

Professional Sports Teams

Team Name	League	Year Established

No teams are located in the metro area
Source: Wikipedia, Major Professional Sports Teams of the United States and Canada, April 5, 2019

CLIMATE

Average and Extreme Temperatures

Temperature	Jan	Feb	Mar	Apr	May	Jun	Jul	Aug	Sep	Oct	Nov	Dec	Yr.
Extreme High (°F)	88	91	93	96	99	103	98	98	96	95	95	90	103
Average High (°F)	75	76	80	85	89	91	91	92	90	86	80	76	84
Average Temp. (°F)	65	65	70	74	79	82	83	83	82	77	71	66	75
Average Low (°F)	54	54	59	62	68	73	74	75	74	68	61	55	65
Extreme Low (°F)	28	32	33	39	52	60	66	67	64	48	34	26	26

Note: Figures cover the years 1948-1995
Source: National Climatic Data Center, International Station Meteorological Climate Summary, 9/96

Average Precipitation/Snowfall/Humidity

Precip./Humidity	Jan	Feb	Mar	Apr	May	Jun	Jul	Aug	Sep	Oct	Nov	Dec	Yr.
Avg. Precip. (in.)	2.0	2.2	2.6	1.7	3.6	9.3	8.9	8.9	8.2	3.5	1.4	1.5	53.9
Avg. Snowfall (in.)	0	0	0	0	0	0	0	0	0	0	0	0	0
Avg. Rel. Hum. 7am (%)	90	89	89	88	87	89	90	91	92	90	90	90	90
Avg. Rel. Hum. 4pm (%)	56	54	52	50	53	64	68	67	66	59	58	57	59

Note: Figures cover the years 1948-1995; Tr = Trace amounts (<0.05 in. of rain; <0.5 in. of snow)
Source: National Climatic Data Center, International Station Meteorological Climate Summary, 9/96

Weather Conditions

Temperature			Daytime Sky			Precipitation		
32°F & below	45°F & below	90°F & above	Clear	Partly cloudy	Cloudy	0.01 inch or more precip.	0.1 inch or more snow/ice	Thunder-storms
1	18	115	93	220	52	110	0	92

Note: Figures are average number of days per year and cover the years 1948-1995
Source: National Climatic Data Center, International Station Meteorological Climate Summary, 9/96

HAZARDOUS WASTE

Superfund Sites

The Cape Coral-Fort Myers, FL metro area has no sites on the EPA's Superfund Final National Priorities List. There are a total of 1,390 Superfund sites with a status of proposed or final on the list in the U.S. *U.S. Environmental Protection Agency, National Priorities List, April 5, 2019*

AIR & WATER QUALITY

Air Quality Trends: Ozone

	1990	1995	2000	2005	2010	2012	2014	2015	2016	2017
MSA[1]	n/a	n/a	n/a	n/a	n/a	n/a	n/a	n/a	n/a	n/a
U.S.	0.088	0.089	0.082	0.080	0.073	0.075	0.067	0.068	0.069	0.068

Note: (1) Data covers the Cape Coral-Fort Myers, FL Metropolitan Statistical Area—see Appendix B for areas included; n/a not available. The values shown are the composite ozone concentration averages among trend sites based on the highest fourth daily maximum 8-hour concentration in parts per million. These trends are based on sites having an adequate record of monitoring data during the trend period. Data from exceptional events are included.
Source: U.S. Environmental Protection Agency, Air Quality Monitoring Information, "Air Quality Trends by City, 1990-2017"

Air Quality Index

Area	Percent of Days when Air Quality was...[2]					AQI Statistics[2]	
	Good	Moderate	Unhealthy for Sensitive Groups	Unhealthy	Very Unhealthy	Maximum	Median
MSA[1]	89.5	10.5	0.0	0.0	0.0	90	37

Note: (1) Data covers the Cape Coral-Fort Myers, FL Metropolitan Statistical Area—see Appendix B for areas included; (2) Based on 363 days with AQI data in 2017. Air Quality Index (AQI) is an index for reporting daily air quality. EPA calculates the AQI for five major air pollutants regulated by the Clean Air Act: ground-level ozone, particle pollution (aka particulate matter), carbon monoxide, sulfur dioxide, and nitrogen dioxide. The AQI runs from 0 to 500. The higher the AQI value, the greater the level of air pollution and the greater the health concern. There are six AQI categories: "Good" AQI is between 0 and 50. Air quality is considered satisfactory; "Moderate" AQI is between 51 and 100. Air quality is acceptable; "Unhealthy for Sensitive Groups" When AQI values are between 101 and 150, members of sensitive groups may experience health effects; "Unhealthy" When AQI values are between 151 and 200 everyone may begin to experience health effects; "Very Unhealthy" AQI values between 201 and 300 trigger a health alert; "Hazardous" AQI values over 300 trigger warnings of emergency conditions (not shown).
Source: U.S. Environmental Protection Agency, Air Quality Index Report, 2017

Air Quality Index Pollutants

Area	Percent of Days when AQI Pollutant was...[2]					
	Carbon Monoxide	Nitrogen Dioxide	Ozone	Sulfur Dioxide	Particulate Matter 2.5	Particulate Matter 10
MSA[1]	0.0	0.0	74.1	0.0	24.8	1.1

Note: (1) Data covers the Cape Coral-Fort Myers, FL Metropolitan Statistical Area—see Appendix B for areas included; (2) Based on 363 days with AQI data in 2017. The Air Quality Index (AQI) is an index for reporting daily air quality. EPA calculates the AQI for five major air pollutants regulated by the Clean Air Act: ground-level ozone, particle pollution (also known as particulate matter), carbon monoxide, sulfur dioxide, and nitrogen dioxide. The AQI runs from 0 to 500. The higher the AQI value, the greater the level of air pollution and the greater the health concern.
Source: U.S. Environmental Protection Agency, Air Quality Index Report, 2017

Maximum Air Pollutant Concentrations: Particulate Matter, Ozone, CO and Lead

	Particulate Matter 10 (ug/m³)	Particulate Matter 2.5 Wtd AM (ug/m³)	Particulate Matter 2.5 24-Hr (ug/m³)	Ozone (ppm)	Carbon Monoxide (ppm)	Lead (ug/m³)
MSA[1] Level	51	n/a	n/a	0.065	n/a	n/a
NAAQS[2]	150	15	35	0.075	9	0.15
Met NAAQS[2]	Yes	n/a	n/a	Yes	n/a	n/a

Note: (1) Data covers the Cape Coral-Fort Myers, FL Metropolitan Statistical Area—see Appendix B for areas included; Data from exceptional events are included; (2) National Ambient Air Quality Standards; ppm = parts per million; ug/m³ = micrograms per cubic meter; n/a not available.
Concentrations: Particulate Matter 10 (coarse particulate)—highest second maximum 24-hour concentration; Particulate Matter 2.5 Wtd AM (fine particulate)—highest weighted annual mean concentration; Particulate Matter 2.5 24-Hour (fine particulate)—highest 98th percentile 24-hour concentration; Ozone—highest fourth daily maximum 8-hour concentration; Carbon Monoxide—highest second maximum non-overlapping 8-hour concentration; Lead—maximum running 3-month average
Source: U.S. Environmental Protection Agency, Air Quality Monitoring Information, "Air Quality Statistics by City, 2017"

Maximum Air Pollutant Concentrations: Nitrogen Dioxide and Sulfur Dioxide

	Nitrogen Dioxide AM (ppb)	Nitrogen Dioxide 1-Hr (ppb)	Sulfur Dioxide AM (ppb)	Sulfur Dioxide 1-Hr (ppb)	Sulfur Dioxide 24-Hr (ppb)
MSA[1] Level	n/a	n/a	n/a	n/a	n/a
NAAQS[2]	53	100	30	75	140
Met NAAQS[2]	n/a	n/a	n/a	n/a	n/a

Note: (1) Data covers the Cape Coral-Fort Myers, FL Metropolitan Statistical Area—see Appendix B for areas included; Data from exceptional events are included; (2) National Ambient Air Quality Standards; ppm = parts per million; ug/m³ = micrograms per cubic meter; n/a not available.
Concentrations: Nitrogen Dioxide AM—highest arithmetic mean concentration; Nitrogen Dioxide 1-Hr—highest 98th percentile 1-hour daily maximum concentration; Sulfur Dioxide AM—highest annual mean concentration; Sulfur Dioxide 1-Hr—highest 99th percentile 1-hour daily maximum concentration; Sulfur Dioxide 24-Hr—highest second maximum 24-hour concentration
Source: U.S. Environmental Protection Agency, Air Quality Monitoring Information, "Air Quality Statistics by City, 2017"

Drinking Water

Water System Name	Pop. Served	Primary Water Source Type	Violations[1]	
			Health Based	Monitoring/ Reporting
City of Cape Coral	142,683	Ground	0	0

Note: (1) Based on violation data from January 1, 2018 to December 31, 2018
Source: U.S. Environmental Protection Agency, Office of Ground Water and Drinking Water, Safe Drinking Water Information System (based on data extracted April 5, 2019)

Charleston, South Carolina

Background

Charleston is located on the state's Atlantic coastline, 110 miles southeast of Columbia and 100 miles north of Savannah, Georgia. The city, named for King Charles II of England, is the county seat of Charleston County. Charleston is located on a bay at the end of a peninsula between the Ashley and Cooper rivers. The terrain is low-lying and coastal with nearby islands and inlets.

In 1670, English colonists established a nearby settlement, and subsequently moved to Charleston's present site. Charleston became an early trading center for rice, indigo, cotton and other goods. As the plantation economy grew, Charleston became a slave-trading center. In 1861, the Confederacy fired the cannon shot that launched the Civil War from the city's Battery, aimed at the Union's Fort Sumter in Charleston Harbor. Charleston was under siege during the Civil War, and experienced many difficulties during Reconstruction. Manufacturing industries including textiles and ironwork became important in the nineteenth century.

Charleston is part of a commercial and cultural center and southern transportation hub whose port is among the nation's busiest shipping facilities. Charleston's other economic sectors include manufacturing, health care, business and professional services, defense activity, retail and wholesale trade, tourism, education and construction.

Charleston is a popular tourist area, based on its scenery, history and recreation. The city's center is well known for its historic neighborhoods with distinctive early southern architecture and ambiance. As one of the first American cities in the early twentieth century to actively encourage historic restoration and preservation, Charleston has undertaken numerous revitalization initiatives, including the Charleston Place Hotel and retail complex, and Waterfront Park.

In 2000, the Confederate submarine the *HL Hunley*, which sank in 1864, was raised, and brought to a conservation laboratory at the old Charleston Naval Base. Author Patricia Cornwell has taken a great interest in the project, and is involved in the creation of a museum to house the submarine. Also, an International Museum of African American History, will sit across from Liberty Square.

Charleston is a center for health care and medical research. SPAWAR (US Navy Space and Naval Warfare Systems Command) is the area's largest single employer followed by the Medical University of South Carolina. Other area educational institutions include The College of Charleston, The Citadel Military College, Trident Technical College, Charleston Southern University, and a campus of Johnson and Wales University.

The Charleston area has numerous parks, including one with a skateboard center, and public waterfront areas. Coastal recreation activities such as boating, swimming, fishing and beaches are popular, as are golf and other land sports.

The Charleston Museum is the nation's oldest, founded in 1773. There are also several former plantations in the area. Other attractions include the South Carolina Aquarium, the American Military Museum, the Drayton Hall Plantation Museum, the Gibbes Museum of Art, the Karpeles Manuscript Museum and the North Charleston Convention Center and Performing Arts Center. Cultural organizations include the Spoleto Festival and the annual Charleston International Film Festival, CIFF.

In 2015, 21-year-old Dylann Roof entered Charleston's historic Emanuel African Methodist Episcopal Church and opened fire, killing nine people. Senior pastor Clementa Pinckney, who also served as a state senator, was among those killed during the attack, which garnered national attention, and sparked a debate on historical racism, Confederate symbolism in Southern states, and gun violence. A month after the attack, the Confederate battle flag was removed from the South Carolina State House. A memorial service on the campus of the College of Charleston was attended by President Barack Obama, Michelle Obama, Vice President Joe Biden, Jill Biden, and Speaker of the House John Boehner.

The nearby Atlantic Ocean moderates the climate, especially in winter, and keeps summer a bit cooler than expected. Expect Indian summers in fall, and a possible hurricane, while spring sharply turns from the cold winds of March to lovely May. Severe storms are possible.

Rankings

General Rankings

- For its "Best for Vets: Places to Live 2019" rankings, *Military Times* evaluated 599 cities (83 large, 234 medium, 282 small) and compared the locations across three broad categories: veteran and military culture/services; economic indicators; and livability factors such as health, crime, traffic, and school quality. Charleston ranked #24 out of the top 50, in the medium-sized city category (populations of 100,000-249,999). Data points more specific to veterans and the military weighed more heavily than the rest. *rebootcamp.militarytimes.com, "Military Times Best Places to Live 2019," September 10, 2018*

- *Insider* listed 33 places in the U.S. that were a must see vacation destination. Whether it is the great beaches, exploring a new city or experiencing the great outdoors, according to the website thisisinsider.com Charleston is a place to visit in 2018. *Insider, "33 Trips Everyone Should Take in the U.S. in 2018,"November 27, 2017*

- The Charleston metro area was identified as one of America's fastest-growing areas in terms of population and business growth by *MagnifyMoney*. The area ranked #4 out of 35. The 100 most populous metro areas in the U.S. were evaluated on their change from 2011-2016 in the following categories: people and housing; workforce and employment opportunities; growing industry. *www.businessinsider.com, "The 35 Cities in the US with the Biggest Influx of People, the Most Work Opportunities, and the Hottest Business Growth," August 12, 2018*

- Charleston was selected as one of the best places to live in America by *Outside Magazine*. Criteria included great access to trails and public lands, great for children, delicious food and drink, and welcoming to people of all backgrounds. Three decades of coverage was combined with the expertise of an advisory council to pick the finalists. *Outside Magazine, "The 25 Best Towns of 2017," July 2017*

- Charleston appeared on *Travel + Leisure's* list of the fifteen best cities in the United States. The city was ranked #1. Criteria: sights/landmarks; culture/arts; cuisine; people/friendliness; shopping; and value. *Travel + Leisure, "The World's Best Awards 2018" July 10, 2018*

- Based on more than 425,000 responses, *Condé Nast Traveler* ranked its readers' favorite cities in the U.S. The list was broken into cities over 1 million and cities under 1 million. Charleston ranked #1 in the small city category. *Condé Nast Traveler, Readers' Choice Awards 2018, "Best Small Cities in the U.S." October 9, 2018*

Business/Finance Rankings

- The personal finance site NerdWallet analyzed 183 American metropolitan areas with populations over 250,000 and more than 15,000 businesses to rank where entrepreneurs find the most success. Criteria included area economy, annual income, housing cost, unemployment rate, and the success rate of area businesses. Charleston ranked #129. *www.nerdwallet.com, "Best Places to Start a Business," April 27, 2015*

- The Brookings Institution ranked the nation's largest cities based on income inequality. Charleston was ranked #11 (#1 = greatest inequality). Criteria: the "95/20 ratio," a figure representing the income at which a household earns more than 95 percent of all other households, divided by the income at which a household earns more than only 20 percent of all other households. *Brookings Institution, "Household Income Inequality, Largest Cities of 97 Large U.S. Metro Areas, 2014-2016," February 5, 2018*

- The Brookings Institution ranked the 100 largest metro areas in the U.S. based on income inequality. Charleston was ranked #27 (#1 = greatest inequality). Criteria: the "95/20 ratio," a figure representing the income at which a household earns more than 95 percent of all other households, divided by the income at which a household earns more than only 20 percent of all other households. *Brookings Institution, "Household Income Inequality, 100 Largest U.S. Metro Areas, 2014-2016," February 5, 2018*

- The Charleston metro area appeared on the Milken Institute "2018 Best Performing Cities" list. Rank: #16 out of 200 large metro areas. Criteria: job growth; wage and salary growth; high-tech output growth. *Milken Institute, "Best-Performing Cities 2018," January 24, 2019*

- *Forbes* ranked the 200 most populous metro areas to determine the nation's "Best Places for Business and Careers." The Charleston metro area was ranked #29. Criteria: costs (business and living); job growth (past and projected); income growth; quality of life; educational attainment (college and high school); projected economic growth; cultural and recreational opportunities; net migration patterns; number of highly ranked colleges. *Forbes, "The Best Places for Business and Careers 2018: Seattle Leads the Way," October 24, 2018*

Culture/Performing Arts Rankings

- Charleston was selected as one of "America's Favorite Cities." The city ranked #17 in the "Culture" category. Respondents to an online survey were asked to rate 38 top urban destinations in the U.S. from a visitor's perspective. Criteria: theater scene and community; number of bookstores; live music; and sense of history. *Travelandleisure.com, "These Are America's 20 Most Cultured Cities," October 2016*

- Charleston was selected as one of "America's Favorite Cities." The city ranked #3 in the "Culture: Historical Sites " category. Respondents to an online survey were asked to rate 38 top urban destinations in the U.S. from a visitor's perspective. *Travelandleisure.com, "America's Favorite Cities," October 11, 2015*

- Charleston was selected as one of "America's Favorite Cities." The city ranked #5 in the "Architecture " category. Respondents to an online survey were asked to rate their favorite place (population over 100,000) in over 65 categories. *Travelandleisure.com, "America's Favorite Cities for Architecture 2016," March 2, 2017*

Education Rankings

- Personal finance website *WalletHub* analyzed the 150 largest U.S. metropolitan statistical areas to determine where the most educated Americans are choosing to settle. Criteria: education quality and attainment gap; education levels; percentage of workers with degrees; public school quality rankings; quality and size of each metro area's universities. Charleston was ranked #52 (#1 = most educated city). *www.WalletHub.com, "2018's Most and Least Educated Cities in America, " July 24, 2018*

Environmental Rankings

- The U.S. Environmental Protection Agency (EPA) released a list of mid-size U.S. metropolitan areas with the most ENERGY STAR certified buildings in 2017. The Charleston metro area was ranked #9 out of 10. *U.S. Environmental Protection Agency, "2018 Energy Star Top Cities," April 11, 2018*

- Charleston was highlighted as one of the cleanest metro areas for ozone air pollution in the U.S. during 2014 through 2016. The list represents cities with no monitored ozone air pollution in unhealthful ranges. *American Lung Association, State of the Air 2018*

Health/Fitness Rankings

- Trulia analyzed the 100 largest U.S. metro areas to identify the nation's best cities for weight loss, based on the percentage of adults who bike or walk to work, sporting goods stores, grocery stores, access to outdoor activities, weight-loss centers, gyms, and average space reserved for parks. Charleston ranked #6. *Trulia.com, "Where to Live to Get in Shape in the New Year," January 4, 2018*

- Charleston was identified as a "2018 Spring Allergy Capital." The area ranked #37 out of 100. Three groups of factors were used to identify the most challenging cities for people with allergies during the spring season: annual pollen levels; medicine utilization; access to board-certified allergists. *Asthma and Allergy Foundation of America, "Spring Allergy Capitals 2018"*

- Charleston was identified as a "2018 Fall Allergy Capital." The area ranked #36 out of 100. Three groups of factors were used to identify the most challenging cities for people with allergies during the fall season: annual pollen levels; medicine utilization; access to board-certified allergists. *Asthma and Allergy Foundation of America, "Fall Allergy Capitals 2018"*

- Charleston was identified as a "2018 Asthma Capital." The area ranked #46 out of the nation's 100 largest metropolitan areas. Criteria: estimated prevalence; self-reported prevalence; crude death rate for asthma; annual pollen score; annual air quality; public smoking laws; number of board-certified asthma specialists; school inhaler access laws; rescue medication use; controller medication use; ER visits for asthma; uninsured rate; poverty rate. *Asthma and Allergy Foundation of America, "Asthma Capitals 2018: The Most Challenging Places to Live With Asthma"*

- The Charleston metro area ranked #33 out of 189 in The Gallup-Healthways Well-Being Index. Criteria: purpose; social well being; financial health; community and physical health. Results are based on telephone interviews with adults, aged 18 and older, living in metropolitan areas in the 50 U.S. states and the District of Columbia. *Gallup-Healthways, "State of American Well-Being, 2017 Community Well-Being Rankings" March 2018*

Pet Rankings

- Charleston was selected as one of the best cities for dogs in America by *Dog Fancy*. Criteria: dog-friendly open spaces and dog parks; events celebrating dogs and their owners; vet-to-dog ratios; abundant pet supply and other services; municipal laws that support and protect all pets. *Dog Fancy, "DogTown USA 2014," July 16, 2014*

Real Estate Rankings

- *WalletHub* compared the most populated U.S. cities, as well as at least two of the most populated cities in each state, for a total of 179, to determine which had the best markets for real estate agents. Charleston ranked #65 where demand was high and pay was the best. Criteria: sales per agent; annual median wage for real-estate agents; monthly average starting salary for real estate agents; real estate job density and competition; unemployment rate; housing-market health index; and other relevant metrics. *www.WalletHub.com, "2018's Best Places to Be a Real Estate Agent," April 25, 2018*

- Charleston was ranked #147 out of 237 metro areas in terms of housing affordability in 2018 by the National Association of Home Builders (#1 = most affordable). Criteria: the share of homes sold in that area affordable to a family earning the local median income, based on standard mortgage underwriting criteria. *National Association of Home Builders®, NAHB-Wells Fargo Housing Opportunity Index, 4th Quarter 2018*

Safety Rankings

- Allstate ranked the 200 largest cities in America in terms of driver safety. Charleston ranked #105. Criteria: internal property damage claims over a two-year period from January 2015 to December 2016. The report helps increase the importance of safety awareness behind the wheel. *Allstate, "Allstate America's Best Drivers Report, 2018" August 28, 2018*

- The National Insurance Crime Bureau ranked 382 metro areas in the U.S. in terms of per capita rates of vehicle theft. The Charleston metro area ranked #74 (#1 = highest rate). Criteria: number of vehicle theft offenses per 100,000 inhabitants in 2017. *National Insurance Crime Bureau, "Hot Spots 2017," July 12, 2018*

Seniors/Retirement Rankings

- Charleston made *Southern Living's* list of charming and unique southern places to retire or dream of retiring to. The favorite places focused on the following: presence of unique amenities; opportunities to volunteer; low cost of living; continued learning opportunities; stable housing market; access to medical care; availability of part-time work; and ease of travel. *Southern Living, "Best Places to Retire in the South, 2018"*

- From its Best Cities for Successful Aging indexes, the Milken Institute generated rankings for metropolitan areas, weighing data in nine categories—health care, wellness, living arrangements, transportation and convenience, financial characteristics, education, employment, community engagement, and overall livability. The Charleston metro area was ranked #39 overall in the large metro area category. *Milken Institute, "Best Cities for Successful Aging, 2017" March 14, 2017*

- Charleston was identified as one of the most popular places to retire by *Topretirements.com.* The list reflects the 100 cities that visitors to the website are most interested in for retirement, based on the number of times a city's review was viewed on the website. *Topretirements.com, "100 Most Popular Places to Retire for 2017," July 27, 2017*

Women/Minorities Rankings

- For its trip ideas, *Travel + Leisure* listed the best cities in the US for a memorable and fun girls' trip. Whether it is for a special occasion or just to get away, Charleston is sure to have something for everyone. *Travel + Leisure, "America's Best Cities for Getting Away With the Girls," March 18, 2019*

- Personal finance website *WalletHub* compared more than 180 U.S. cities—including the 150 most populated U.S. cities, plus at least two of the most populated cities in each state—across two key dimensions, "Hispanic Business-Friendliness" and "Hispanic Purchasing Power", to arrive at the most favorable conditions for Hispanic entrepreneurs. Charleston was ranked #90 out of 182. Criteria includes: share of Hispanic-Owned Businesses; Hispanic entrepreneurship rate to median annual income of Hispanics; Small Business-Friendliness score; cost of living; and number of Hispanics with at least a bachelor's degree. *WalletHub.com, "2018's Best Cities for Hispanic Entrepreneurs," April 26, 2018*

Miscellaneous Rankings

- Based on the advice of plugged-in travel influencers and experts, Charleston appeared on a *Forbes* list of 14 U.S. cities that should be on anyone's travel wish list. Whether it be quirky things to see and do or civic revitalization, these places are emerging as must-see destinations. *Forbes, "Where To Go Next: 14 Best Places to Travel in the US in 2019," December 6, 2018*

- In *Condé Nast Traveler* magazine's 2017 Readers' Choice Survey, Charleston made the top ten list of friendliest American cities. *www.cntraveler.com, "The Friendliest Cities in the U.S.," August 16, 2017*

- *WalletHub* compared the 150 most populated U.S. cities to determine their operating efficiency. A "Quality of Services" score was constructed for each city and then divided by the total budget per capita to reveal which were managed the best. Charleston ranked #46. Criteria: financial stability; economy; education; safety; health; infrastructure and pollution. *www.WalletHub.com, "2018's Best- & Worst-Run Cities in America," July 9, 2018*

- Charleston was selected as one of the 20 memorable places in the world during Thanksgiving by *Fodor's Travel.* Criteria: attractions; history; events. *Fodors.com, "Where to Go for Thanksgiving 2016," November 4, 2016*

- Charleston appeared on *Travel + Leisure's* list of America's cities with the most attractive people. Criteria: cities were selected by readers in their annual America's Favorite Cities survey. The city ranked #7 out of 10. *Travel + Leisure, "America's Most and Least Attractive People," September 2, 2016*

- Charleston was selected as one of America's best-mannered cities. The area ranked #1. The general public determined the winners by casting votes online. *The Charleston School of Protocol and Etiquette, "2014 Most Mannerly City in America Contest," February 3, 2015*

Business Environment

CITY FINANCES

City Government Finances

Component	2016 ($000)	2016 ($ per capita)
Total Revenues	357,778	2,698
Total Expenditures	286,710	2,162
Debt Outstanding	171,674	1,295
Cash and Securities[1]	259,144	1,954

Note: (1) Cash and security holdings of a government at the close of its fiscal year, including those of its dependent agencies, utilities, and liquor stores.
Source: U.S. Census Bureau, State & Local Government Finances 2016

City Government Revenue by Source

Source	2016 ($000)	2016 ($ per capita)	2016 (%)
General Revenue			
From Federal Government	6,758	51	1.9
From State Government	5,267	40	1.5
From Local Governments	0	0	0.0
Taxes			
Property	72,067	543	20.1
Sales and Gross Receipts	45,783	345	12.8
Personal Income	0	0	0.0
Corporate Income	0	0	0.0
Motor Vehicle License	0	0	0.0
Other Taxes	48,785	368	13.6
Current Charges	39,488	298	11.0
Liquor Store	0	0	0.0
Utility	116,836	881	32.7
Employee Retirement	0	0	0.0

Source: U.S. Census Bureau, State & Local Government Finances 2016

City Government Expenditures by Function

Function	2016 ($000)	2016 ($ per capita)	2016 (%)
General Direct Expenditures			
Air Transportation	0	0	0.0
Corrections	0	0	0.0
Education	0	0	0.0
Employment Security Administration	0	0	0.0
Financial Administration	8,606	64	3.0
Fire Protection	26,967	203	9.4
General Public Buildings	139	1	0.0
Governmental Administration, Other	4,364	32	1.5
Health	0	0	0.0
Highways	7,628	57	2.7
Hospitals	0	0	0.0
Housing and Community Development	3,764	28	1.3
Interest on General Debt	3,904	29	1.4
Judicial and Legal	2,318	17	0.8
Libraries	0	0	0.0
Parking	11,047	83	3.9
Parks and Recreation	16,168	121	5.6
Police Protection	45,715	344	15.9
Public Welfare	518	3	0.2
Sewerage	3,099	23	1.1
Solid Waste Management	5,812	43	2.0
Veterans' Services	0	0	0.0
Liquor Store	0	0	0.0
Utility	117,863	888	41.1
Employee Retirement	0	0	0.0

Source: U.S. Census Bureau, State & Local Government Finances 2016

DEMOGRAPHICS

Population Growth

Area	1990 Census	2000 Census	2010 Census	2017* Estimate	Population Growth (%) 1990-2017	Population Growth (%) 2010-2017
City	96,102	96,650	120,083	131,204	36.5	9.3
MSA[1]	506,875	549,033	664,607	744,195	46.8	12.0
U.S.	248,709,873	281,421,906	308,745,538	321,004,407	29.1	4.0

Note: (1) Figures cover the Charleston-North Charleston, SC Metropolitan Statistical Area—see Appendix B for areas included; (*) 2013-2017 5-year estimated population
Source: U.S. Census Bureau, 1990 Census, Census 2000, Census 2010, 2013-2017 American Community Survey 5-Year Estimates

Household Size

Area	Persons in Household (%) One	Two	Three	Four	Five	Six	Seven or More	Average Household Size
City	35.2	37.2	14.5	9.2	2.8	0.7	0.3	2.30
MSA[1]	28.9	35.4	16.9	11.8	4.6	1.5	0.8	2.60
U.S.	27.7	33.8	15.7	13.0	6.0	2.3	1.4	2.60

Note: (1) Figures cover the Charleston-North Charleston, SC Metropolitan Statistical Area—see Appendix B for areas included
Source: U.S. Census Bureau, 2013-2017 American Community Survey 5-Year Estimates

Race

Area	White Alone[2] (%)	Black Alone[2] (%)	Asian Alone[2] (%)	AIAN[3] Alone[2] (%)	NHOPI[4] Alone[2] (%)	Other Race Alone[2] (%)	Two or More Races (%)
City	74.4	21.9	1.6	0.1	0.0	0.3	1.6
MSA[1]	67.6	26.3	1.7	0.3	0.0	1.4	2.5
U.S.	73.0	12.7	5.4	0.8	0.2	4.8	3.1

Note: (1) Figures cover the Charleston-North Charleston, SC Metropolitan Statistical Area—see Appendix B for areas included; (2) Alone is defined as not being in combination with one or more other races; (3) American Indian and Alaska Native; (4) Native Hawaiian and Other Pacific Islander
Source: U.S. Census Bureau, 2013-2017 American Community Survey 5-Year Estimates

Hispanic or Latino Origin

Area	Total (%)	Mexican (%)	Puerto Rican (%)	Cuban (%)	Other (%)
City	2.9	1.3	0.4	0.2	0.9
MSA[1]	5.4	2.8	0.8	0.1	1.6
U.S.	17.6	11.1	1.7	0.7	4.1

Note: Persons of Hispanic or Latino origin can be of any race; (1) Figures cover the Charleston-North Charleston, SC Metropolitan Statistical Area—see Appendix B for areas included
Source: U.S. Census Bureau, 2013-2017 American Community Survey 5-Year Estimates

Segregation

Type	Segregation Indices[1] 1990	2000	2010	2010 Rank[2]	Percent Change 1990-2000	1990-2010	2000-2010
Black/White	47.4	44.2	41.5	88	-3.2	-5.9	-2.7
Asian/White	34.4	34.2	33.4	84	-0.3	-1.1	-0.8
Hispanic/White	26.6	32.2	39.8	66	5.6	13.2	7.6

Note: All figures cover the Metropolitan Statistical Area—see Appendix B for areas included; Figures are based on an analysis of 1990, 2000, and 2010 Census Decennial Census tract data by William H. Frey, Brookings Institution and the University of Michigan Social Science Data Analysis Network. In this analysis all racial groups (whites, blacks, and asians) are non-Hispanic members of those races. Hispanics are shown as a separate category; (1) Segregation Indices are Dissimilarity Indices that measure the degree to which the minority group is distributed differently than whites across census tracts. They range from 0 (complete integration) to 100 (complete segregation) where the value indicates the percentage of the minority group that needs to move to be distributed exactly like whites; (2) Ranges from 1 (most segregated) to 102 (least segregated); n/a not available.
Source: www.CensusScope.org

Ancestry

Area	German	Irish	English	American	Italian	Polish	French[2]	Scottish	Dutch
City	10.9	11.0	10.8	19.9	3.9	1.8	2.3	3.1	0.6
MSA[1]	10.6	10.6	8.6	12.9	3.5	1.8	2.3	2.5	0.8
U.S.	14.1	10.1	7.5	6.6	5.3	2.9	2.5	1.7	1.3

Note: Figures are the percentage of the total population reporting a particular ancestry. The nine most commonly reported ancestries in the U.S. are shown. Figures include multiple ancestries (e.g. if a person reported being Irish and Italian, they were included in both columns); (1) Figures cover the Charleston-North Charleston, SC Metropolitan Statistical Area—see Appendix B for areas included; (2) Excludes Basque
Source: U.S. Census Bureau, 2013-2017 American Community Survey 5-Year Estimates

Foreign-Born Population

Area	Percent of Population Born in								
	Any Foreign Country	Asia	Mexico	Europe	Carribean	Central America[2]	South America	Africa	Canada
City	4.1	1.4	0.4	1.2	0.2	0.2	0.1	0.3	0.2
MSA[1]	5.0	1.3	1.1	1.0	0.3	0.4	0.5	0.2	0.2
U.S.	13.4	4.1	3.6	1.5	1.3	1.0	0.9	0.6	0.3

Note: (1) Figures cover the Charleston-North Charleston, SC Metropolitan Statistical Area—see Appendix B for areas included; (2) Excludes Mexico.
Source: U.S. Census Bureau, 2013-2017 American Community Survey 5-Year Estimates

Marital Status

Area	Never Married	Now Married[2]	Separated	Widowed	Divorced
City	41.6	40.5	1.8	5.0	11.2
MSA[1]	33.9	46.5	2.7	5.6	11.3
U.S.	33.1	48.2	2.0	5.8	10.9

Note: Figures are percentages and cover the population 15 years of age and older; (1) Figures cover the Charleston-North Charleston, SC Metropolitan Statistical Area—see Appendix B for areas included; (2) Excludes separated
Source: U.S. Census Bureau, 2013-2017 American Community Survey 5-Year Estimates

Disability by Age

Area	All Ages	Under 18 Years Old	18 to 64 Years Old	65 Years and Over
City	9.6	3.0	7.6	28.4
MSA[1]	12.0	4.1	9.9	34.7
U.S.	12.6	4.2	10.3	35.5

Note: Figures show percent of the civilian noninstitutionalized population that reported having a disability. Disability status is determined from six types of difficulty: vision, hearing, cognitive, ambulatory, self-care, and independent living. For children under 5 years old, hearing and vision difficulty are used to determine disability status. For children between the ages of 5 and 14, disability status is determined from hearing, vision, cognitive, ambulatory, and self-care difficulties. For people aged 15 years and older, they are considered to have a disability if they have difficulty with any one of the six difficulty types; Note: (1) Figures cover the Charleston-North Charleston, SC Metropolitan Statistical Area—see Appendix B for areas included
Source: U.S. Census Bureau, 2013-2017 American Community Survey 5-Year Estimates

Age

Area	Percent of Population									Median Age
	Under Age 5	Age 5–19	Age 20–34	Age 35–44	Age 45–54	Age 55–64	Age 65–74	Age 75–84	Age 85+	
City	5.9	15.4	29.8	12.2	10.7	12.2	8.6	3.4	1.9	34.4
MSA[1]	6.2	18.6	22.7	12.9	13.2	12.6	8.7	3.6	1.5	36.6
U.S.	6.2	19.5	20.7	12.7	13.4	12.7	8.6	4.4	1.9	37.8

Note: (1) Figures cover the Charleston-North Charleston, SC Metropolitan Statistical Area—see Appendix B for areas included
Source: U.S. Census Bureau, 2013-2017 American Community Survey 5-Year Estimates

Gender

Area	Males	Females	Males per 100 Females
City	62,890	68,314	92.1
MSA[1]	363,546	380,649	95.5
U.S.	158,018,753	162,985,654	97.0

Note: (1) Figures cover the Charleston-North Charleston, SC Metropolitan Statistical Area—see Appendix B for areas included
Source: U.S. Census Bureau, 2013-2017 American Community Survey 5-Year Estimates

Religious Groups by Family

Area	Catholic	Baptist	Non-Den.	Methodist[2]	Lutheran	LDS[3]	Pente-costal	Presby-terian[4]	Muslim[5]	Judaism
MSA[1]	6.2	12.4	7.1	10.0	1.1	1.0	2.0	2.4	0.2	0.3
U.S.	19.1	9.3	4.0	4.0	2.3	2.0	1.9	1.6	0.8	0.7

Note: Figures are the number of adherents as a percentage of the total population; (1) Figures cover the Charleston-North Charleston, SC Metropolitan Statistical Area—see Appendix B for areas included; (2) Methodist/Pietist; (3) Latter Day Saints; (4) Reformed; (5) Figures are estimates
Source: Association of Statisticians of American Religious Bodies, 2010 U.S. Religion Census: Religious Congregations & Membership Study

Religious Groups by Tradition

Area	Catholic	Evangelical Protestant	Mainline Protestant	Other Tradition	Black Protestant	Orthodox
MSA[1]	6.2	19.7	11.2	1.9	7.3	0.1
U.S.	19.1	16.2	7.3	4.3	1.6	0.3

Note: Figures are the number of adherents as a percentage of the total population; (1) Figures cover the Charleston-North Charleston, SC Metropolitan Statistical Area—see Appendix B for areas included
Source: Association of Statisticians of American Religious Bodies, 2010 U.S. Religion Census: Religious Congregations & Membership Study

ECONOMY

Gross Metropolitan Product

Area	2016	2017	2018	2019	Rank[2]
MSA[1]	39.0	40.7	42.6	45.2	73

Note: Figures are in billions of dollars; (1) Figures cover the Charleston-North Charleston, SC Metropolitan Statistical Area—see Appendix B for areas included; (2) Rank is based on 2017 data and ranges from 1 to 381
Source: U.S. Conference of Mayors, U.S. Metro Economies: Economic Growth & Full Employment, June 2018

Economic Growth

Area	2017-2018 (%)	2019-2020 (%)	2021-2022 (%)
MSA[1]	3.0	3.2	2.3

Note: Figures are real gross metropolitan product (GMP) growth rates and represent average annual percent change; (1) Figures cover the Charleston-North Charleston, SC Metropolitan Statistical Area—see Appendix B for areas included
Source: U.S. Conference of Mayors, U.S. Metro Economies: Economic Growth & Full Employment, June 2018

Metropolitan Area Exports

Area	2012	2013	2014	2015	2016	2017	Rank[2]
MSA[1]	2,429.8	3,464.3	5,866.7	6,457.5	9,508.1	8,845.2	39

Note: Figures are in millions of dollars; (1) Figures cover the Charleston-North Charleston, SC Metropolitan Statistical Area—see Appendix B for areas included; (2) Rank is based on 2017 data and ranges from 1 to 387
Source: U.S. Department of Commerce, International Trade Administration, Office of Trade and Economic Analysis, Industry and Analysis, Exports by Metropolitan Area, extracted March 25, 2019

Building Permits

Area	Single-Family			Multi-Family			Total		
	2016	2017	Pct. Chg.	2016	2017	Pct. Chg.	2016	2017	Pct. Chg.
City	692	766	10.7	350	303	-13.4	1,042	1,069	2.6
MSA[1]	4,787	4,726	-1.3	2,187	2,541	16.2	6,974	7,267	4.2
U.S.	750,800	820,000	9.2	455,800	462,000	1.4	1,206,600	1,282,000	6.2

Note: (1) Figures cover the Charleston-North Charleston, SC Metropolitan Statistical Area—see Appendix B for areas included; Figures represent new, privately-owned housing units authorized (unadjusted data); All permit data are based on estimates with imputation
Source: U.S. Census Bureau, Manufacturing, Mining, and Construction Statistics, Building Permits, 2016, 2017

Bankruptcy Filings

Area	Business Filings			Nonbusiness Filings		
	2017	2018	% Chg.	2017	2018	% Chg.
Charleston County	11	13	18.2	386	379	-1.8
U.S.	23,157	22,232	-4.0	765,863	751,186	-1.9

Note: Business filings include Chapter 7, Chapter 11, Chapter 12, and Chapter 13; Nonbusiness filings include Chapter 7, Chapter 11, and Chapter 13
Source: Administrative Office of the U.S. Courts, Business and Nonbusiness Bankruptcy, County Cases Commenced by Chapter of the Bankruptcy Code, During the 12-Month Period Ending December 31, 2017 and Business and Nonbusiness Bankruptcy, County Cases Commenced by Chapter of the Bankruptcy Code, During the 12-Month Period Ending December 31, 2018

Housing Vacancy Rates

Area	Gross Vacancy Rate[2] (%)			Year-Round Vacancy Rate[3] (%)			Rental Vacancy Rate[4] (%)			Homeowner Vacancy Rate[5] (%)		
	2016	2017	2018	2016	2017	2018	2016	2017	2018	2016	2017	2018
MSA[1]	14.8	16.5	16.0	13.6	16.1	14.5	12.2	17.9	17.0	2.4	1.6	3.4
U.S.	12.8	12.7	12.3	9.9	9.9	9.7	6.9	7.2	6.9	1.7	1.6	1.5

Note: (1) Figures cover the Charleston-North Charleston, SC Metropolitan Statistical Area—see Appendix B for areas included; (2) The percentage of the total housing inventory that is vacant; (3) The percentage of the housing inventory (excluding seasonal units) that is year-round vacant; (4) The percentage of rental inventory that is vacant for rent; (5) The percentage of homeowner inventory that is vacant for sale
Source: U.S. Census Bureau, Housing Vacancies and Homeownership Annual Statistics: 2016, 2017, 2018

INCOME

Income

Area	Per Capita ($)	Median Household ($)	Average Household ($)
City	38,126	61,367	88,467
MSA[1]	31,542	57,666	79,452
U.S.	31,177	57,652	81,283

Note: (1) Figures cover the Charleston-North Charleston, SC Metropolitan Statistical Area—see Appendix B for areas included
Source: U.S. Census Bureau, 2013-2017 American Community Survey 5-Year Estimates

Household Income Distribution

Area	Percent of Households Earning							
	Under $15,000	$15,000 -$24,999	$25,000 -$34,999	$35,000 -$49,999	$50,000 -$74,999	$75,000 -$99,999	$100,000 -$149,999	$150,000 and up
City	12.7	8.5	7.9	12.5	16.5	12.1	15.6	14.2
MSA[1]	11.5	9.1	9.5	13.0	18.8	12.9	14.3	10.9
U.S.	11.6	9.8	9.5	13.0	17.7	12.3	14.1	12.1

Note: (1) Figures cover the Charleston-North Charleston, SC Metropolitan Statistical Area—see Appendix B for areas included
Source: U.S. Census Bureau, 2013-2017 American Community Survey 5-Year Estimates

Poverty Rate

Area	All Ages	Under 18 Years Old	18 to 64 Years Old	65 Years and Over
City	14.6	16.5	15.7	6.9
MSA[1]	13.9	20.1	12.9	8.6
U.S.	14.6	20.3	13.7	9.3

Note: Figures are percentage of people whose income during the past 12 months was below the poverty level; (1) Figures cover the Charleston-North Charleston, SC Metropolitan Statistical Area—see Appendix B for areas included
Source: U.S. Census Bureau, 2013-2017 American Community Survey 5-Year Estimates

EMPLOYMENT

Labor Force and Employment

Area	Civilian Labor Force			Workers Employed		
	Dec. 2017	Dec. 2018	% Chg.	Dec. 2017	Dec. 2018	% Chg.
City	72,422	73,601	1.6	70,111	71,740	2.3
MSA[1]	373,329	379,429	1.6	360,371	368,841	2.4
U.S.	159,880,000	162,510,000	1.6	153,602,000	156,481,000	1.9

Note: Data is not seasonally adjusted and covers workers 16 years of age and older; (1) Figures cover the Charleston-North Charleston, SC Metropolitan Statistical Area—see Appendix B for areas included
Source: Bureau of Labor Statistics, Local Area Unemployment Statistics

Unemployment Rate

Area	2018											
	Jan.	Feb.	Mar.	Apr.	May	Jun.	Jul.	Aug.	Sep.	Oct.	Nov.	Dec.
City	3.9	3.5	3.1	2.1	2.2	2.9	2.8	2.9	2.6	2.6	2.4	2.5
MSA[1]	4.2	3.9	3.5	2.3	2.4	3.1	3.0	3.1	2.8	2.8	2.6	2.8
U.S.	4.5	4.4	4.1	3.7	3.6	4.2	4.1	3.9	3.6	3.5	3.5	3.7

Note: Data is not seasonally adjusted and covers workers 16 years of age and older; (1) Figures cover the Charleston-North Charleston, SC Metropolitan Statistical Area—see Appendix B for areas included
Source: Bureau of Labor Statistics, Local Area Unemployment Statistics

Average Wages

Occupation	$/Hr.	Occupation	$/Hr.
Accountants and Auditors	28.00	Maids and Housekeeping Cleaners	10.60
Automotive Mechanics	20.70	Maintenance and Repair Workers	18.80
Bookkeepers	17.50	Marketing Managers	54.80
Carpenters	25.70	Nuclear Medicine Technologists	36.40
Cashiers	10.10	Nurses, Licensed Practical	20.80
Clerks, General Office	12.50	Nurses, Registered	36.40
Clerks, Receptionists/Information	14.00	Nursing Assistants	13.80
Clerks, Shipping/Receiving	19.50	Packers and Packagers, Hand	11.10
Computer Programmers	36.60	Physical Therapists	39.20
Computer Systems Analysts	38.60	Postal Service Mail Carriers	24.80
Computer User Support Specialists	24.50	Real Estate Brokers	28.60
Cooks, Restaurant	12.00	Retail Salespersons	13.00
Dentists	56.30	Sales Reps., Exc. Tech./Scientific	33.70
Electrical Engineers	44.10	Sales Reps., Tech./Scientific	34.50
Electricians	20.20	Secretaries, Exc. Legal/Med./Exec.	17.50
Financial Managers	55.00	Security Guards	16.50
First-Line Supervisors/Managers, Sales	20.70	Surgeons	n/a
Food Preparation Workers	12.30	Teacher Assistants*	10.40
General and Operations Managers	51.20	Teachers, Elementary School*	23.50
Hairdressers/Cosmetologists	11.50	Teachers, Secondary School*	24.70
Internists, General	119.50	Telemarketers	9.80
Janitors and Cleaners	10.70	Truck Drivers, Heavy/Tractor-Trailer	22.70
Landscaping/Groundskeeping Workers	13.40	Truck Drivers, Light/Delivery Svcs.	16.40
Lawyers	38.00	Waiters and Waitresses	9.50

Note: Wage data covers the Charleston-North Charleston, SC Metropolitan Statistical Area—see Appendix B for areas included; (*) Hourly wages for elementary/secondary school teachers and teacher assistants were calculated by the editors from annual wage data based on a 40 hour work week; n/a not available.
Source: Bureau of Labor Statistics, Metro Area Occupational Employment & Wage Estimates, May 2018

Employment by Occupation

Occupation Classification	City (%)	MSA[1] (%)	U.S. (%)
Management, Business, Science, and Arts	46.6	38.4	37.4
Natural Resources, Construction, and Maintenance	5.5	8.8	8.9
Production, Transportation, and Material Moving	6.6	10.6	12.2
Sales and Office	22.2	23.8	23.5
Service	19.1	18.4	18.0

Note: Figures cover employed civilians 16 years of age and older; (1) Figures cover the Charleston-North Charleston, SC Metropolitan Statistical Area—see Appendix B for areas included
Source: U.S. Census Bureau, 2013-2017 American Community Survey 5-Year Estimates

Employment by Industry

Sector	MSA[1]		U.S.
	Number of Employees	Percent of Total	Percent of Total
Construction, Mining, and Logging	22,400	6.0	5.3
Education and Health Services	42,500	11.4	15.9
Financial Activities	16,100	4.3	5.7
Government	66,600	17.9	15.1
Information	6,500	1.7	1.9
Leisure and Hospitality	48,200	13.0	10.7
Manufacturing	27,600	7.4	8.5
Other Services	14,300	3.8	3.9
Professional and Business Services	57,300	15.4	14.1
Retail Trade	44,900	12.1	10.8
Transportation, Warehousing, and Utilities	15,800	4.2	4.2
Wholesale Trade	9,700	2.6	3.9

Note: Figures are non-farm employment as of December 2018. Figures are not seasonally adjusted and include workers 16 years of age and older; (1) Figures cover the Charleston-North Charleston, SC Metropolitan Statistical Area—see Appendix B for areas included
Source: Bureau of Labor Statistics, Current Employment Statistics, Employment, Hours, and Earnings

Occupations with Greatest Projected Employment Growth: 2018 – 2020

Occupation[1]	2018 Employment	2020 Projected Employment	Numeric Employment Change	Percent Employment Change
Laborers and Freight, Stock, and Material Movers, Hand	53,710	56,190	2,480	4.6
Retail Salespersons	72,070	74,520	2,450	3.4
Combined Food Preparation and Serving Workers, Including Fast Food	53,740	55,880	2,140	4.0
Heavy and Tractor-Trailer Truck Drivers	30,660	32,120	1,460	4.8
General and Operations Managers	35,170	36,440	1,270	3.6
Customer Service Representatives	50,040	51,310	1,270	2.5
Maintenance and Repair Workers, General	28,580	29,710	1,130	4.0
Cashiers	64,600	65,720	1,120	1.7
Team Assemblers	46,990	48,080	1,090	2.3
First-Line Supervisors of Retail Sales Workers	29,570	30,600	1,030	3.5

Note: Projections cover South Carolina; (1) Sorted by numeric employment change
Source: www.projectionscentral.com, State Occupational Projections, 2018–2020 Short-Term Projections

Fastest Growing Occupations: 2018 – 2020

Occupation[1]	2018 Employment	2020 Projected Employment	Numeric Employment Change	Percent Employment Change
Operations Research Analysts	1,000	1,090	90	9.0
Producers and Directors	900	970	70	7.8
Ushers, Lobby Attendants, and Ticket Takers	1,530	1,650	120	7.8
Fiberglass Laminators and Fabricators	780	840	60	7.7
Software Developers, Applications	3,920	4,210	290	7.4
Audio and Video Equipment Technicians	700	750	50	7.1
Molders, Shapers, and Casters, Except Metal and Plastic	710	760	50	7.0
Appraisers and Assessors of Real Estate	1,170	1,250	80	6.8
Industrial Engineers	7,250	7,740	490	6.8
Home Health Aides	10,890	11,630	740	6.8

Note: Projections cover South Carolina; (1) Sorted by percent employment change and excludes occupations with numeric employment change less than 50
Source: www.projectionscentral.com, State Occupational Projections, 2018–2020 Short-Term Projections

TAXES

State Corporate Income Tax Rates

State	Tax Rate (%)	Income Brackets ($)	Num. of Brackets	Financial Institution Tax Rate (%)[a]	Federal Income Tax Ded.
South Carolina	5.0	Flat rate	1	4.5 (v)	No

Note: Tax rates as of January 1, 2019; (a) Rates listed are the corporate income tax rate applied to financial institutions or excise taxes based on income. Some states have other taxes based upon the value of deposits or shares; (v) South Carolina taxes savings and loans at a 6% rate.
Source: Federation of Tax Administrators, Range of State Corporate Income Tax Rates, January 1, 2019

State Individual Income Tax Rates

State	Tax Rate (%)	Income Brackets ($)	Personal Exemptions ($) Single	Married	Depend.	Standard Ded. ($) Single	Married
South Carolina (a)	0.0 - 7.0	3,030 - 15,160	(d)	(d)	(d)	12,200	24,400 (d)

Note: Tax rates as of January 1, 2019; Local- and county-level taxes are not included; n/a not applicable; Federal income tax is not deductible on state income tax returns; (a) 19 states have statutory provision for automatically adjusting to the rate of inflation the dollar values of the income tax brackets, standard deductions, and/or personal exemptions. Michigan indexes the personal exemption only. Oregon does not index the income brackets for $125,000 and over; (d) These states use the personal exemption/standard deduction amounts provided in the federal Internal Revenue Code. Note, the Tax Cut and Reform Act of 2017 has eliminated personal exemptions from the IRC. CO, ID, NM, ND, SC, and DC have adoptedthe new exemptions and standard deduction amounts. MN conforms to a previous IRC year, while ME adopts the higher standard deduction but retains the exemption amounts.
Source: Federation of Tax Administrators, State Individual Income Tax Rates, January 1, 2019

Various State Sales and Excise Tax Rates

State	State Sales Tax (%)	Gasoline[1] (¢/gal.)	Cigarette[2] ($/pack)	Spirits[3] ($/gal.)	Wine[4] ($/gal.)	Beer[5] ($/gal.)	Recreational Marijuana (%)
South Carolina	6	20.75	0.57	5.42 (i)	1.08 (l)	0.77	Not legal

Note: All tax rates as of January 1, 2019; (1) The American Petroleum Institute has developed a methodology for determining the average tax rate on a gallon of fuel. Rates may include any of the following: excise taxes, environmental fees, storage tank fees, other fees or taxes, general sales tax, and local taxes. In states where gasoline is subject to the general sales tax, or where the fuel tax is based on the average sale price, the average rate determined by API is sensitive to changes in the price of gasoline. States that fully or partially apply general sales taxes to gasoline: CA, CO, GA, IL, IN, MI, NY; (2) The federal excise tax of $1.0066 per pack and local taxes are not included; (3) Rates are those applicable to off-premise sales of 40% alcohol by volume (a.b.v.) distilled spirits in 750ml containers. Local excise taxes are excluded; (4) Rates are those applicable to off-premise sales of 11% a.b.v. non-carbonated wine in 750ml containers; (5) Rates are those applicable to off-premise sales of 4.7% a.b.v. beer in 12 ounce containers; (i) Includes case fees and/or bottle fees which may vary with size of container; (l) Different rates also applicable to alcohol content, place of production, size of container, place purchased (on- or off-premise or on board airlines) or type of wine (carbonated, vermouth, etc.).
Source: Tax Foundation, 2019 Facts & Figures: How Does Your State Compare?

State Business Tax Climate Index Rankings

State	Overall Rank	Corporate Tax Rank	Individual Income Tax Rank	Sales Tax Rank	Unemployment Insurance Tax Rank	Property Tax Rank
South Carolina	35	19	34	34	27	27

Note: The index is a measure of how each state's tax laws affect economic performance. The lower the rank, the more favorable a state's tax system is for business. States without a given tax are given a ranking of 1. The scores/rankings for the District of Columbia do not affect other states. The 2019 index represents the tax climate as of July 1, 2018.
Source: Tax Foundation, State Business Tax Climate Index 2019

COMMERCIAL REAL ESTATE

Office Market

Market Area	Inventory (sq. ft.)	Vacancy Rate (%)	Under Construction (sq. ft.)	YTD Net Absorption (sq. ft.)	Total Average Asking Rent ($/sq. ft./year)
Charleston	14,233,699	7.6	263,650	122,478	24.11
National	4,905,867,938	13.1	83,553,714	45,846,470	28.46

Source: Newmark Grubb Knight Frank, National Office Market Report, 4th Quarter 2018

Industrial/Warehouse/R&D Market

Market Area	Inventory (sq. ft.)	Vacancy Rate (%)	Under Construction (sq. ft.)	YTD Net Absorption (sq. ft.)	Total Average Asking Rent ($/sq. ft./year)
Charleston	379,476,867	6.1	6,082,358	6,501,345	4.59
National	14,796,839,085	5.0	262,662,294	238,014,726	7.16

Source: Newmark Grubb Knight Frank, National Industrial Market Report, 4th Quarter 2018

COMMERCIAL UTILITIES

Typical Monthly Electric Bills

Area	Commercial Service ($/month)		Industrial Service ($/month)	
	1,500 kWh	40 kW demand 14,000 kWh	1,000 kW demand 200,000 kWh	50,000 kW demand 32,500,000 kWh
City	226	1,843	27,059	2,400,600
Average[1]	203	1,619	25,886	2,540,077

Note: Figures are based on annualized rates; (1) Average based on 187 utilities surveyed
Source: Edison Electric Institute, Typical Bills and Average Rates Report, Summer 2018

TRANSPORTATION

Means of Transportation to Work

Area	Car/Truck/Van		Public Transportation			Bicycle	Walked	Other Means	Worked at Home
	Drove Alone	Car-pooled	Bus	Subway	Railroad				
City	76.6	6.0	1.2	0.0	0.0	2.9	5.4	1.5	6.4
MSA[1]	81.1	8.3	1.1	0.0	0.0	0.8	2.5	1.1	5.2
U.S.	76.4	9.2	2.5	1.9	0.6	0.6	2.7	1.3	4.7

Note: Figures are percentages and cover workers 16 years of age and older; (1) Figures cover the Charleston-North Charleston, SC Metropolitan Statistical Area—see Appendix B for areas included
Source: U.S. Census Bureau, 2013-2017 American Community Survey 5-Year Estimates

Travel Time to Work

Area	Less Than 10 Minutes	10 to 19 Minutes	20 to 29 Minutes	30 to 44 Minutes	45 to 59 Minutes	60 to 89 Minutes	90 Minutes or More
City	12.4	33.3	25.2	21.0	5.3	1.8	1.2
MSA[1]	9.9	27.0	24.4	25.0	8.2	4.1	1.5
U.S.	12.7	28.9	20.9	20.5	8.1	6.2	2.7

Note: Note: Figures are percentages and include workers 16 years old and over; (1) Figures cover the Charleston-North Charleston, SC Metropolitan Statistical Area—see Appendix B for areas included
Source: U.S. Census Bureau, 2013-2017 American Community Survey 5-Year Estimates

Freeway Travel Time Index

Area	1985	1990	1995	2000	2005	2010	2014
Urban Area Rank[1,2]	26	25	26	28	32	25	29
Urban Area Index[1]	1.10	1.14	1.18	1.20	1.22	1.23	1.23
Average Index[3]	1.09	1.11	1.14	1.17	1.20	1.19	1.20

Note: Freeway Travel Time Index—the ratio of travel time in the peak period to the travel time at free-flow conditions. For example, a value of 1.30 indicates a 20-minute free-flow trip takes 26 minutes in the peak (20 minutes x 1.30 = 26 minutes); (1) Covers the Charleston-North Charleston SC urban area; (2) Rank is based on 101 urban areas (#1 = highest travel time index); (3) Average of 101 urban areas
Source: Texas Transportation Institute, 2015 Urban Mobility Scorecard, August 2015

Freeway Commuter Stress Index

Area	1985	1990	1995	2000	2005	2010	2014
Urban Area Rank[1,2]	33	36	33	36	38	33	33
Urban Area Index[1]	1.14	1.17	1.22	1.24	1.26	1.27	1.27
Average Index[3]	1.13	1.16	1.19	1.22	1.25	1.24	1.25

Note: The Freeway Commuter Stress Index is the same as the Freeway Travel Time Index (see table above) except that it includes only the travel in the peak directions during the peak periods; the TTI includes travel in all directions during the peak period. Thus, the CSI is more indicative of the work trip experienced by each commuter on a daily basis; (1) Covers the Charleston-North Charleston SC urban area; (2) Rank is based on 101 urban areas (#1 = highest travel time index); (3) Average of 101 urban areas
Source: Texas Transportation Institute, 2015 Urban Mobility Scorecard, August 2015

Public Transportation

Agency Name / Mode of Transportation	Vehicles Operated in Maximum Service[1]	Annual Unlinked Passenger Trips[2] (in thous.)	Annual Passenger Miles[3] (in thous.)
Charleston Area Regional Transportation (CARTA)			
Bus (purchased transportation)	49	3,388.8	15,791.6
Commuter Bus (purchased transportation)	8	203.3	3,063.3
Demand Response (purchased transportation)	20	71.3	639.0

Note: (1) The number of revenue vehicles operated by the given mode and type of service to meet the annual maximum service requirement. This is the revenue vehicle count during the peak season of the year; on the week and day that maximum service is provided. Vehicles operated in maximum service (VOMS) exclude atypical days and one-time special events; (2) The number of passengers who boarded public transportation vehicles. Passengers are counted each time they board a vehicle no matter how many vehicles they use to travel from their origin to their destination. (3) The sum of the distances ridden by all passengers during the entire fiscal year.
Source: Federal Transit Administration, National Transit Database, 2017

Air Transportation

Airport Name and Code / Type of Service	Passenger Airlines[1]	Passenger Enplanements	Freight Carriers[2]	Freight (lbs)
Charleston International Airport (CHS)				
Domestic service (U.S. carriers - 2018)	31	2,191,480	16	24,597,441
International service (U.S. carriers - 2017)	5	253	6	4,152,176

Note: (1) Includes all U.S.-based major, minor and commuter airlines that carried at least one passenger during the year; (2) Includes all U.S.-based airlines and freight carriers that transported at least one pound of freight during the year.
Source: Bureau of Transportation Statistics, The Intermodal Transportation Database, Air Carriers: T-100 Domestic Market (U.S. Carriers), 2018; Bureau of Transportation Statistics, The Intermodal Transportation Database, Air Carriers: T-100 International Market (U.S. Carriers), 2017

Other Transportation Statistics

Major Highways:	I-26; I-95
Amtrak Service:	Yes (station is located in North Charleston)
Major Waterways/Ports:	Atlantic Ocean

Source: Amtrak.com; Google Maps

BUSINESSES

Major Business Headquarters

Company Name	Industry	Rankings	
		Fortune[1]	Forbes[2]
No companies listed	-	-	-

Note: (1) Companies that produce a 10-K are ranked 1 to 500 based on 2017 revenue; (2) All private companies with at least $2 billion in annual revenue through the end of their most current fiscal year are ranked 1 to 229; companies listed are headquartered in the city; dashes indicate no ranking
Source: Fortune, "Fortune 500," June 2018; Forbes, "America's Largest Private Companies," 2018 Rankings

Fast-Growing Businesses

According to *Inc.*, Charleston is home to one of America's 500 fastest-growing private companies: **Gotcha Media Holdings** (#249). Criteria: must be an independent, privately-held, for-profit, U.S. corporation, proprietorship or partnership as of December 31, 2017; revenues must be at least $100,000 in 2014 and $2 million in 2017; must have four-year operating/sales history. Holding companies, regulated banks, and utilities were excluded. *Inc., "America's 500 Fastest-Growing Private Companies," 2018*

Minority- and Women-Owned Businesses

Group	All Firms		Firms with Paid Employees			
	Firms	Sales ($000)	Firms	Sales ($000)	Employees	Payroll ($000)
AIAN[1]	n/a	n/a	n/a	n/a	n/a	n/a
Asian	361	198,793	121	187,638	1,821	21,452
Black	1,495	91,265	119	62,792	698	20,404
Hispanic	352	54,889	25	44,654	133	3,398
NHOPI[2]	n/a	n/a	n/a	n/a	n/a	n/a
Women	5,609	676,439	649	555,321	4,499	139,485
All Firms	16,050	11,709,550	3,786	11,075,572	68,309	2,478,699

Note: Figures cover firms located in the city; minority- and women-owned business are defined as firms in which the corresponding group own 51% or more of the stock or equity of the company; (1) American Indian and Alaska Native; (2) Native Hawaiian and Other Pacific Islander; n/a not available
Source: U.S. Census Bureau, 2012 Economic Census, Survey of Business Owners

HOTELS & CONVENTION CENTERS

Hotels, Motels and Vacation Rentals

Area	5 Star		4 Star		3 Star		2 Star		1 Star		Not Rated	
	Num.	Pct.[3]	Num.	Pct.[3]	Num.	Pct.[3]	Num.	Pct.[3]	Num.	Pct.[3]	Num.	Pct.[3]
City[1]	5	0.2	121	4.8	624	24.6	86	3.4	2	0.1	1,695	66.9
Total[2]	286	0.4	5,236	7.1	16,715	22.6	10,259	13.9	293	0.4	41,056	55.6

Note: (1) Figures cover Charleston and vicinity; (2) Figures cover all 100 cities in this book; (3) Percentage of hotels which have a given star rating; Star ratings are determined by expedia.com and offer an indication of the general quality of a particular hotel.
Source: www.expedia.com, April 3, 2019

The Charleston-North Charleston, SC metro area is home to three of the best city hotels in the continental U.S. according to *Travel & Leisure*: **French Quarter Inn**; **Spectator Hotel**; **Planters Inn**. Magazine readers were surveyed and asked to rate hotels on the following criteria: rooms/facilities; location; service; food; and value. The list includes the top 15 city hotels in the continental U.S. *Travel & Leisure, "The World's Best Awards 2018"*

The Charleston-North Charleston, SC metro area is home to one of the best hotels in the world according to *Condé Nast Traveler*: **The Dewberry**. The selections are based on editors' picks. The list includes the top 13 hotels in the U.S. *Condé Nast Traveler, "The 78 Best Hotels in the World: The Gold List 2019"*

Major Convention Centers

Name	Overall Space (sq. ft.)	Exhibit Space (sq. ft.)	Meeting Space (sq. ft.)	Meeting Rooms
Charleston Area Convention Center Complex	n/a	76,960	n/a	n/a

Note: Table includes convention centers located in the Charleston-North Charleston, SC metro area; n/a not available
Source: Original research

Living Environment

COST OF LIVING

Cost of Living Index

Composite Index	Groceries	Housing	Utilities	Trans-portation	Health Care	Misc. Goods/ Services
100.8	95.2	94.8	127.1	90.0	106.3	103.5

Note: The Cost of Living Index measures regional differences in the cost of consumer goods and services, excluding taxes and non-consumer expenditures, for professional and managerial households in the top income quintile. It is based on more than 50,000 prices covering almost 60 different items for which prices are collected three times a year by chambers of commerce, economic development organizations or university applied economic centers in each participating urban area. The numbers shown should be read as a percentage above or below the national average of 100. For example, a value of 115.4 in the groceries column indicates that grocery prices are 15.4% higher than the national average. Small differences in the index numbers should not be interpreted as significant; Figures cover the Charleston-N Charleston SC urban area.
Source: The Council for Community and Economic Research, ACCRA Cost of Living Index, 2018

Grocery Prices

Area[1]	T-Bone Steak ($/pound)	Frying Chicken ($/pound)	Whole Milk ($/half gal.)	Eggs ($/dozen)	Orange Juice ($/64 oz.)	Coffee ($/11.5 oz.)
City[2]	9.60	1.16	1.81	1.97	3.37	3.40
Avg.	11.35	1.42	1.94	1.81	3.52	4.35
Min.	7.45	0.92	0.80	0.75	2.72	3.06
Max.	15.05	2.76	4.18	4.00	5.36	8.20

Note: (1) Values for the local area are compared with the average, minimum and maximum values for all 291 areas in the Cost of Living Index; (2) Figures cover the Charleston-N Charleston SC urban area; T-Bone Steak (price per pound); Frying Chicken (price per pound, whole fryer); Whole Milk (half gallon carton); Eggs (price per dozen, Grade A, large); Orange Juice (64 oz. Tropicana or Florida Natural); Coffee (11.5 oz. can, vacuum-packed, Maxwell House, Hills Bros, or Folgers).
Source: The Council for Community and Economic Research, ACCRA Cost of Living Index, 2018

Housing and Utility Costs

Area[1]	New Home Price ($)	Apartment Rent ($/month)	All Electric ($/month)	Part Electric ($/month)	Other Energy ($/month)	Telephone ($/month)
City[2]	288,601	1,339	246.79	-	-	181.60
Avg.	347,000	1,087	165.93	100.16	67.73	178.70
Min.	200,468	500	93.58	25.64	26.78	163.10
Max.	1,901,222	4,888	388.65	246.86	332.81	197.70

Note: (1) Values for the local area are compared with the average, minimum and maximum values for all 291 areas in the Cost of Living Index; (2) Figures cover the Charleston-N Charleston SC urban area; New Home Price (2,400 sf living area, 8,000 sf lot, in urban area with full utilities); Apartment Rent (950 sf 2 bedroom/1.5 or 2 bath, unfurnished, excluding all utilities except water); All Electric (average monthly cost for an all-electric home); Part Electric (average monthly cost for a part-electric home); Other Energy (average monthly cost for natural gas, fuel oil, coal, wood, and any other forms of energy except electricity); Telephone (price includes the base monthly rate plus taxes and fees for three lines of mobile phone service).
Source: The Council for Community and Economic Research, ACCRA Cost of Living Index, 2018

Health Care, Transportation, and Other Costs

Area[1]	Doctor ($/visit)	Dentist ($/visit)	Optometrist ($/visit)	Gasoline ($/gallon)	Beauty Salon ($/visit)	Men's Shirt ($)
City[2]	120.07	105.09	97.71	2.41	43.22	25.96
Avg.	110.71	95.11	103.74	2.61	37.48	32.03
Min.	33.60	62.55	54.63	1.89	17.00	11.44
Max.	195.97	153.93	225.79	3.59	71.88	58.64

Note: (1) Values for the local area are compared with the average, minimum and maximum values for all 291 areas in the Cost of Living Index; (2) Figures cover the Charleston-N Charleston SC urban area; Doctor (general practitioners routine exam of an established patient); Dentist (adult teeth cleaning and periodic oral examination); Optometrist (full vision eye exam for established adult patient); Gasoline (one gallon regular unleaded, national brand, including all taxes, cash price at self-service pump if available); Beauty Salon (woman's shampoo, trim, and blow-dry); Men's Shirt (cotton/polyester dress shirt, pinpoint weave, long sleeves).
Source: The Council for Community and Economic Research, ACCRA Cost of Living Index, 2018

HOUSING

House Price Index (HPI)

Area	National Ranking[2]	Quarterly Change (%)	One-Year Change (%)	Five-Year Change (%)
MSA[1]	165	1.03	4.98	48.51
U.S.[3]	–	1.12	5.73	32.81

Note: The HPI is a weighted repeat sales index. It measures average price changes in repeat sales or refinancings on the same properties. This information is obtained by reviewing repeat mortgage transactions on single-family properties whose mortgages have been purchased or securitized by Fannie Mae or Freddie Mac in January 1975; (1) Figures cover the Charleston-North Charleston, SC Metropolitan Statistical Area—see Appendix B for areas included; (2) Rankings are based on annual percentage change for all metro areas containing at least 15,000 transactions over the last 10 years and ranges from 1 to 245; (3) figures based on a weighted average of Census Division estimates using a seasonally adjusted, purchase-only index; all figures are for the period ending December 31, 2018
Source: Federal Housing Finance Agency, House Price Index, February 26, 2019

Median Single-Family Home Prices

Area	2016	2017	2018p	Percent Change 2017 to 2018
MSA[1]	252.2	268.8	283.0	5.3
U.S. Average	235.5	248.8	261.6	5.1

Note: Figures are median sales prices of existing single-family homes in thousands of dollars; (p) preliminary; (1) Figures cover the Charleston-North Charleston, SC Metropolitan Statistical Area—see Appendix B for areas included
Source: National Association of Realtors, Median Sales Price of Existing Single-Family Homes for Metropolitan Areas, 4th Quarter 2018

Qualifying Income Based on Median Sales Price of Existing Single-Family Homes

Area	With 5% Down ($)	With 10% Down ($)	With 20% Down ($)
MSA[1]	68,159	64,572	57,397
U.S. Average	62,954	59,640	53,013

Note: Figures are preliminary; Qualifying income is based on a mortgage rate of 4.9%. Monthly principal and interest payment is limited to 25% of income; (1) Figures cover the Charleston-North Charleston, SC Metropolitan Statistical Area—see Appendix B for areas included
Source: National Association of Realtors, Qualifying Income Based on Median Sales Price of Existing Single-Family Homes for Metropolitan Areas, 4th Quarter 2018

Median Apartment Condo-Coop Home Prices

Area	2016	2017	2018p	Percent Change 2017 to 2018
MSA[1]	n/a	n/a	n/a	n/a
U.S. Average	220.7	234.3	241.0	2.9

Note: Figures are median sales prices of existing apartment condo-coop homes in thousands of dollars; (p) preliminary; n/a not available; (1) Figures cover the Charleston-North Charleston, SC Metropolitan Statistical Area—see Appendix B for areas included
Source: National Association of Realtors, Median Sales Price of Existing Apartment Condo-Coop Homes for Metropolitan Areas, 4th Quarter 2018

Home Value Distribution

Area	Under $50,000	$50,000 -$99,999	$100,000 -$149,999	$150,000 -$199,999	$200,000 -$299,999	$300,000 -$499,999	$500,000 -$999,999	$1,000,000 or more
City	2.1	3.3	6.0	14.6	27.5	25.5	14.7	6.3
MSA[1]	7.4	9.3	14.3	17.2	21.3	17.8	9.4	3.4
U.S.	8.3	13.9	14.7	14.6	18.7	17.3	9.7	2.7

Note: Figures are percentages and cover owner-occupied housing units; (1) Figures cover the Charleston-North Charleston, SC Metropolitan Statistical Area—see Appendix B for areas included
Source: U.S. Census Bureau, 2013-2017 American Community Survey 5-Year Estimates

Homeownership Rate

Area	2010 (%)	2011 (%)	2012 (%)	2013 (%)	2014 (%)	2015 (%)	2016 (%)	2017 (%)	2018 (%)
MSA[1]	n/a	n/a	n/a	n/a	n/a	65.8	62.1	67.7	68.8
U.S.	66.9	66.1	65.4	65.1	64.5	63.7	63.4	63.9	64.4

Note: (1) Figures cover the Charleston-North Charleston, SC Metropolitan Statistical Area—see Appendix B for areas included
Source: U.S. Census Bureau, Housing Vacancies and Homeownership Annual Statistics: 2010-2018

Year Housing Structure Built

Area	2010 or Later	2000 -2009	1990 -1999	1980 -1989	1970 -1979	1960 -1969	1950 -1959	1940 -1949	Before 1940	Median Year
City	7.1	22.3	12.5	14.1	12.3	8.6	6.5	4.6	12.0	1984
MSA[1]	7.0	23.7	16.5	17.4	14.5	8.9	5.4	2.8	3.8	1988
U.S.	3.2	14.5	14.0	13.6	15.5	10.8	10.5	5.1	12.9	1977

Note: Figures are percentages except for Median Year; Note: (1) Figures cover the Charleston-North Charleston, SC Metropolitan Statistical Area—see Appendix B for areas included
Source: U.S. Census Bureau, 2013-2017 American Community Survey 5-Year Estimates

Gross Monthly Rent

Area	Under $500	$500 -$999	$1,000 -$1,499	$1,500 -$1,999	$2,000 -$2,499	$2,500 -$2,999	$3,000 and up	Median ($)
City	7.4	31.5	37.5	16.2	4.0	1.6	1.8	1,135
MSA[1]	6.7	38.2	37.1	12.2	3.2	1.3	1.2	1,054
U.S.	10.5	41.1	28.7	11.7	4.5	1.8	1.7	982

Note: Figures are percentages except for Median; Gross rent is the contract rent plus the estimated average monthly cost of utilities (electricity, gas, and water and sewer) and fuels (oil, coal, kerosene, wood, etc.) if these are paid by the renter (or paid for the renter by someone else); (1) Figures cover the Charleston-North Charleston, SC Metropolitan Statistical Area—see Appendix B for areas included
Source: U.S. Census Bureau, 2013-2017 American Community Survey 5-Year Estimates

HEALTH

Health Risk Factors

Category	MSA[1] (%)	U.S. (%)
Adults aged 18–64 who have any kind of health care coverage	82.3	87.3
Adults who reported being in good or better health	83.9	82.4
Adults who have been told they have high blood cholesterol	33.8	33.0
Adults who have been told they have high blood pressure	33.1	32.3
Adults who are current smokers	18.9	17.1
Adults who currently use E-cigarettes	4.3	4.6
Adults who currently use chewing tobacco, snuff, or snus	3.4	4.0
Adults who are heavy drinkers[2]	10.4	6.3
Adults who are binge drinkers[3]	22.6	17.4
Adults who are overweight (BMI 25.0 - 29.9)	34.9	35.3
Adults who are obese (BMI 30.0 - 99.8)	32.1	31.3
Adults who participated in any physical activities in the past month	75.5	74.4
Adults who always or nearly always wears a seat belt	95.4	94.3

Note: (1) Figures cover the Charleston-North Charleston, SC Metropolitan Statistical Area—see Appendix B for areas included; (2) Heavy drinkers are classified as adult men having more than 14 drinks per week and adult women having more than 7 drinks per week; (3) Binge drinkers are classified as males having five or more drinks on one occasion or females having four or more drinks on one occasion
Source: Centers for Disease Control and Prevention, Behaviorial Risk Factor Surveillance System, SMART: Selected Metropolitan Area Risk Trends, 2017

Acute and Chronic Health Conditions

Category	MSA[1] (%)	U.S. (%)
Adults who have ever been told they had a heart attack	3.4	4.2
Adults who have ever been told they have angina or coronary heart disease	3.9	3.9
Adults who have ever been told they had a stroke	3.1	3.0
Adults who have ever been told they have asthma	15.7	14.2
Adults who have ever been told they have arthritis	24.7	24.9
Adults who have ever been told they have diabetes[2]	12.7	10.5
Adults who have ever been told they had skin cancer	7.4	6.2
Adults who have ever been told they had any other types of cancer	7.5	7.1
Adults who have ever been told they have COPD	6.0	6.5
Adults who have ever been told they have kidney disease	2.5	3.0
Adults who have ever been told they have a form of depression	22.5	20.5

Note: (1) Figures cover the Charleston-North Charleston, SC Metropolitan Statistical Area—see Appendix B for areas included; (2) Figures do not include pregnancy-related, borderline, or pre-diabetes
Source: Centers for Disease Control and Prevention, Behaviorial Risk Factor Surveillance System, SMART: Selected Metropolitan Area Risk Trends, 2017

Health Screening and Vaccination Rates

Category	MSA[1] (%)	U.S. (%)
Adults aged 65+ who have had flu shot within the past year	63.9	60.7
Adults aged 65+ who have ever had a pneumonia vaccination	77.0	75.4
Adults who have ever been tested for HIV	44.7	36.1
Adults who have ever had the shingles or zoster vaccine?	26.4	28.9
Adults who have had their blood cholesterol checked within the last five years	86.0	85.9

Note: n/a not available; (1) Figures cover the Charleston-North Charleston, SC Metropolitan Statistical Area—see Appendix B for areas included.
Source: Centers for Disease Control and Prevention, Behaviorial Risk Factor Surveillance System, SMART: Selected Metropolitan Area Risk Trends, 2017

Disability Status

Category	MSA[1] (%)	U.S. (%)
Adults who reported being deaf	4.9	6.7
Are you blind or have serious difficulty seeing, even when wearing glasses?	3.5	4.5
Are you limited in any way in any of your usual activities due of arthritis?	10.8	12.9
Do you have difficulty doing errands alone?	5.9	6.8
Do you have difficulty dressing or bathing?	4.1	3.6
Do you have serious difficulty concentrating/remembering/making decisions?	13.0	10.7
Do you have serious difficulty walking or climbing stairs?	13.0	13.6

Note: (1) Figures cover the Charleston-North Charleston, SC Metropolitan Statistical Area—see Appendix B for areas included.
Source: Centers for Disease Control and Prevention, Behaviorial Risk Factor Surveillance System, SMART: Selected Metropolitan Area Risk Trends, 2017

Mortality Rates for the Top 10 Causes of Death in the U.S.

ICD-10[a] Sub-Chapter	ICD-10[a] Code	Age-Adjusted Mortality Rate[1] per 100,000 population	
		County[2]	U.S.
Malignant neoplasms	C00-C97	157.8	155.5
Ischaemic heart diseases	I20-I25	77.0	94.8
Other forms of heart disease	I30-I51	51.5	52.9
Chronic lower respiratory diseases	J40-J47	36.0	41.0
Cerebrovascular diseases	I60-I69	40.3	37.5
Other degenerative diseases of the nervous system	G30-G31	53.9	35.0
Other external causes of accidental injury	W00-X59	31.6	33.7
Organic, including symptomatic, mental disorders	F01-F09	31.4	31.0
Hypertensive diseases	I10-I15	14.5	21.9
Diabetes mellitus	E10-E14	20.0	21.2

Note: (a) ICD-10 = International Classification of Diseases 10th Revision; (1) Mortality rates are a three year average covering 2015-2017; (2) Figures cover Charleston County.
Source: Centers for Disease Control and Prevention, National Center for Health Statistics. Underlying Cause of Death 1999-2017 on CDC WONDER Online Database

Mortality Rates for Selected Causes of Death

ICD-10[a] Sub-Chapter	ICD-10[a] Code	Age-Adjusted Mortality Rate[1] per 100,000 population	
		County[2]	U.S.
Assault	X85-Y09	12.5	5.9
Diseases of the liver	K70-K76	15.3	14.1
Human immunodeficiency virus (HIV) disease	B20-B24	3.4	1.8
Influenza and pneumonia	J09-J18	9.1	14.3
Intentional self-harm	X60-X84	13.1	13.6
Malnutrition	E40-E46	3.2	1.6
Obesity and other hyperalimentation	E65-E68	Unreliable	2.1
Renal failure	N17-N19	13.0	13.0
Transport accidents	V01-V99	15.4	12.4
Viral hepatitis	B15-B19	1.3	1.6

Note: (a) ICD-10 = International Classification of Diseases 10th Revision; (1) Mortality rates are a three year average covering 2015-2017; (2) Figures cover Charleston County; Data are suppressed when the data meet the criteria for confidentiality constraints; Mortality rates are flagged as unreliable when the rate would be calculated with a numerator of 20 or less.
Source: Centers for Disease Control and Prevention, National Center for Health Statistics. Underlying Cause of Death 1999-2017 on CDC WONDER Online Database

Health Insurance Coverage

Area	With Health Insurance	With Private Health Insurance	With Public Health Insurance	Without Health Insurance	Population Under Age 18 Without Health Insurance
City	90.5	76.9	25.3	9.5	4.4
MSA[1]	88.1	69.7	30.9	11.9	5.5
U.S.	89.5	67.2	33.8	10.5	5.7

Note: Figures are percentages that cover the civilian noninstitutionalized population; (1) Figures cover the Charleston-North Charleston, SC Metropolitan Statistical Area—see Appendix B for areas included
Source: U.S. Census Bureau, 2013-2017 American Community Survey 5-Year Estimates

Number of Medical Professionals

Area	MDs[3]	DOs[3,4]	Dentists	Podiatrists	Chiropractors	Optometrists
County[1] (number)	3,145	121	422	19	185	85
County[1] (rate[2])	793.1	30.5	105.1	4.7	46.1	21.2
U.S. (rate[2])	279.3	23.0	68.4	6.0	27.1	16.2

Note: Data as of 2017 unless noted; (1) Data covers Charleston County; (2) Rate per 100,000 population; (3) Data as of 2016 and includes all active, non-federal physicians; (4) Doctor of Osteopathic Medicine
Source: U.S. Department of Health and Human Services, Health Resources and Services Administration, Bureau of Health Professions, Area Resource File (ARF) 2017-2018

Best Hospitals

According to *U.S. News,* the Charleston-North Charleston, SC metro area is home to two of the best hospitals in the U.S.: **Bon Secours St. Francis Hospital** (1 adult specialty); **MUSC Health-University Medical Center** (5 adult specialties and 6 pediatric specialties). The hospitals listed were nationally ranked in at least one of 16 adult or 10 pediatric specialties. Only 170 hospitals nationwide were nationally ranked in one or more adult or pediatric specialty. Twenty hospitals in the U.S. made the Honor Roll. The Best Hospitals Honor Roll takes both the national rankings and the procedure and condition ratings into account. Hospitals received points if they were nationally ranked in one of the 16 adult specialties—the higher they ranked, the more points they got—and how many ratings of "high performing" they earned in the nine procedures and conditions. *U.S. News Online, "America's Best Hospitals 2018-19"*

According to *U.S. News,* the Charleston-North Charleston, SC metro area is home to one of the best children's hospitals in the U.S.: **MUSC Health-Children's Hospital** (6 pediatric specialties). The hospital listed was highly ranked in at least one of 10 pediatric specialties. Eighty-six children's hospitals in the U.S. were nationally ranked in at least one specialty. Hospitals received points for being ranked in a specialty, and the 10 hospitals with the most points across the 10 specialties make up the Honor Roll. *U.S. News Online, "America's Best Children's Hospitals 2018-19"*

EDUCATION

Public School District Statistics

District Name	Schls	Pupils	Pupil/ Teacher Ratio	Minority Pupils[1] (%)	Free Lunch Eligible[2] (%)	IEP[3] (%)
Charleston 01	82	48,551	14.8	52.3	54.4	9.8

Note: Table includes school districts with 2,000 or more students; (1) Percentage of students that are not non-Hispanic white; (2) Percentage of students that are eligible for the free lunch program; (3) Percentage of students that have an Individualized Education Program.
Source: U.S. Department of Education, National Center for Education Statistics, Common Core of Data, Local Education Agency (School District) Universe Survey: School Year 2016-2017; U.S. Department of Education, National Center for Education Statistics, Common Core of Data, Public Elementary/Secondary School Universe Survey: School Year 2016-2017

Highest Level of Education

Area	Less than H.S.	H.S. Diploma	Some College, No Deg.	Associate Degree	Bachelor's Degree	Master's Degree	Prof. School Degree	Doctorate Degree
City	5.7	17.8	17.3	7.8	32.3	12.3	4.6	2.3
MSA[1]	9.9	25.6	21.1	9.3	21.9	8.5	2.3	1.4
U.S.	12.7	27.3	20.8	8.3	19.1	8.4	2.0	1.4

Note: Figures cover persons age 25 and over; (1) Figures cover the Charleston-North Charleston, SC Metropolitan Statistical Area—see Appendix B for areas included
Source: U.S. Census Bureau, 2013-2017 American Community Survey 5-Year Estimates

Educational Attainment by Race

Area	High School Graduate or Higher (%)					Bachelor's Degree or Higher (%)				
	Total	White	Black	Asian	Hisp.[2]	Total	White	Black	Asian	Hisp.[2]
City	94.3	97.2	84.0	92.3	91.6	51.4	60.0	19.6	73.1	39.7
MSA[1]	90.1	93.0	83.5	86.6	69.5	34.1	40.8	15.6	47.1	20.4
U.S.	87.3	89.3	84.9	86.5	66.7	30.9	32.2	20.6	52.7	15.2

Note: Figures shown cover persons 25 years old and over; (1) Figures cover the Charleston-North Charleston, SC Metropolitan Statistical Area—see Appendix B for areas included; (2) People of Hispanic origin can be of any race
Source: U.S. Census Bureau, 2013-2017 American Community Survey 5-Year Estimates

School Enrollment by Grade and Control

Area	Preschool (%)		Kindergarten (%)		Grades 1 - 4 (%)		Grades 5 - 8 (%)		Grades 9 - 12 (%)	
	Public	Private	Public	Private	Public	Private	Public	Private	Public	Private
City	44.5	55.5	81.1	18.9	82.6	17.4	76.7	23.3	81.3	18.7
MSA[1]	51.0	49.0	85.6	14.4	90.2	9.8	88.8	11.2	89.6	10.4
U.S.	58.8	41.2	87.7	12.3	89.7	10.3	89.6	10.4	90.3	9.7

Note: Figures shown cover persons 3 years old and over; (1) Figures cover the Charleston-North Charleston, SC Metropolitan Statistical Area—see Appendix B for areas included
Source: U.S. Census Bureau, 2013-2017 American Community Survey 5-Year Estimates

Average Salaries of Public School Classroom Teachers

Area	2016		2017		Change from 2016 to 2017	
	Dollars	Rank[1]	Dollars	Rank[1]	Percent	Rank[2]
South Carolina	48,769	37	50,000	38	2.5	14
U.S. Average	58,479	–	59,660	–	2.0	–

Note: (1) Rank ranges from 1 to 51 where 1 indicates highest salary; (2) Rank ranges from 1 to 51 where 1 indicates highest percent change.
Source: National Education Association, Rankings & Estimates: Rankings of the States 2017 and Estimates of School Statistics 2018

Higher Education

Four-Year Colleges			Two-Year Colleges			Medical Schools[1]	Law Schools[2]	Voc/ Tech[3]
Public	Private Non-profit	Private For-profit	Public	Private Non-profit	Private For-profit			
3	1	2	1	0	1	1	1	2

Note: Figures cover institutions located within the city limits and include main campuses only; (1) includes schools accredited by the Liaison Committee on Medical Education and the American Osteopathic Association's Commission on Osteopathic College Accreditation; (2) includes ABA-accredited schools, schools with provisional ABA accreditation, and state accredited schools; (3) includes all schools with programs that are less than 2 years.
Source: National Center for Education Statistics, Integrated Postsecondary Education System (IPEDS), 2017-18; Wikipedia, List of Medical Schools in the United States, accessed April 3, 2019; Wikipedia, List of Law Schools in the United States, accessed April 3, 2019

According to *U.S. News & World Report*, the Charleston-North Charleston, SC metro area is home to one of the top 75 medical schools for research in the U.S.: **Medical University of South Carolina** (#60 tie). The rankings are based on a weighted average of 11 measures of quality: quality assessment; peer assessment score; assessment score by residency directors; research activity; total research activity; average research activity per faculty member; student selectivity; median MCAT total score; median undergraduate GPA; acceptance rate; and faculty resources.
U.S. News & World Report, "America's Best Graduate Schools, Medical, 2020"

PRESIDENTIAL ELECTION

2016 Presidential Election Results

Area	Clinton	Trump	Johnson	Stein	Other
Charleston County	50.6	42.8	4.1	1.0	1.5
U.S.	48.0	45.9	3.3	1.1	1.7

Note: Results are percentages and may not add to 100% due to rounding
Source: Dave Leip's Atlas of U.S. Presidential Elections

EMPLOYERS

Major Employers

Company Name	Industry
Bi-Lo Stores	Grocery stores
Boeing South Carolina	Commercial aircraft
Charleston County Government	County government
Charleston County School District	Public elementary & secondary schools
City of Charleston	Municipal government
College of Charleston	Higher education
Evening Post Publishing Co.	Newspapers, publishing & printing
Force Protection	Mine-protected vehicle manufacturing
JEM Restaurant Group	Restaurants/hospitality
Joint Base Charleston	U.S. military
Medical University of South Carolina	State's teaching hospital, medical higher education
Piggly Wiggly Carolina Co	Grocery stores
Roper St. Francis Healthcare	Private hospital system
SAIC	Advanced security
Trident Health System	Hospital system
U.S. Postal Service	Federal mail delivery service
Verizon Wireless Call Center	Call center
Wal-Mart Stores	Retail merchandising

Note: Companies shown are located within the Charleston-North Charleston, SC Metropolitan Statistical Area.
Source: Hoovers.com; Wikipedia

PUBLIC SAFETY

Crime Rate

Area	All Crimes	Violent Crimes				Property Crimes		
		Murder	Rape[3]	Robbery	Aggrav. Assault	Burglary	Larceny -Theft	Motor Vehicle Theft
City	2,581.0	4.4	36.5	73.1	169.5	291.6	1,784.5	221.4
Suburbs[1]	n/a	9.0	39.4	88.9	302.1	n/a	2,028.9	272.8
Metro[2]	n/a	8.2	38.9	86.2	278.8	n/a	1,985.9	263.7
U.S.	2,756.1	5.3	41.7	98.0	248.9	430.4	1,694.4	237.4

Note: Figures are crimes per 100,000 population; (1) All areas within the metro area that are located outside the city limits; (2) Figures cover the Charleston-North Charleston, SC Metropolitan Statistical Area—see Appendix B for areas included; (3) The city and U.S. figures shown were reported using the revised Uniform Crime Reporting (UCR) definition of rape. The suburban and metro area figures shown are an aggregate total of the data submitted using both the revised and legacy UCR definitions.
Source: FBI Uniform Crime Reports, 2017

Hate Crimes

Area	Number of Quarters Reported	Number of Incidents per Bias Motivation					
		Race/Ethnicity/ Ancestry	Religion	Sexual Orientation	Disability	Gender	Gender Identity
City	4	1	0	0	0	0	0
U.S.	4	4,131	1,564	1,130	116	46	119

Source: Federal Bureau of Investigation, Hate Crime Statistics 2017

Identity Theft Consumer Reports

Area	Reports	Reports per 100,000 Population	Rank[2]
MSA[1]	1,038	136	49
U.S.	444,602	135	-

Note: (1) Figures cover the Charleston-North Charleston, SC Metropolitan Statistical Area—see Appendix B for areas included; (2) Rank ranges from 1 to 389 where 1 indicates greatest number of identity theft reports per 100,000 population
Source: Federal Trade Commission, Consumer Sentinel Network Data Book for January–December 2018

SPORTS

CLIMATE

HAZARDOUS WASTE

Fraud and Other Consumer Reports

Area	Reports	Reports per 100,000 Population	Rank[2]
MSA[1]	4,345	571	81
U.S.	2,552,917	776	-

Note: (1) Figures cover the Charleston-North Charleston, SC Metropolitan Statistical Area—see Appendix B for areas included; (2) Rank ranges from 1 to 389 where 1 indicates greatest number of fraud and other consumer reports per 100,000 population
Source: Federal Trade Commission, Consumer Sentinel Network Data Book for January–December 2018

Professional Sports Teams

Team Name	League	Year Established
No teams are located in the metro area		

Source: Wikipedia, Major Professional Sports Teams of the United States and Canada, April 5, 2019

Average and Extreme Temperatures

Temperature	Jan	Feb	Mar	Apr	May	Jun	Jul	Aug	Sep	Oct	Nov	Dec	Yr.
Extreme High (°F)	83	87	90	94	98	101	104	102	97	94	88	83	104
Average High (°F)	59	62	68	76	83	88	90	89	85	77	69	61	76
Average Temp. (°F)	49	51	57	65	73	78	81	81	76	67	58	51	66
Average Low (°F)	38	40	46	53	62	69	72	72	67	56	46	39	55
Extreme Low (°F)	6	12	15	30	36	50	58	56	42	27	15	8	6

Note: Figures cover the years 1945-1995
Source: National Climatic Data Center, International Station Meteorological Climate Summary, 9/96

Average Precipitation/Snowfall/Humidity

Precip./Humidity	Jan	Feb	Mar	Apr	May	Jun	Jul	Aug	Sep	Oct	Nov	Dec	Yr.
Avg. Precip. (in.)	3.5	3.1	4.4	2.8	4.1	6.0	7.2	6.9	5.6	3.1	2.5	3.1	52.1
Avg. Snowfall (in.)	Tr	Tr	Tr	0	0	0	0	0	0	0	Tr	Tr	1
Avg. Rel. Hum. 7am (%)	83	81	83	84	85	86	88	90	91	89	86	83	86
Avg. Rel. Hum. 4pm (%)	55	52	51	51	56	62	66	66	65	58	56	55	58

Note: Figures cover the years 1945-1995; Tr = Trace amounts (<0.05 in. of rain; <0.5 in. of snow)
Source: National Climatic Data Center, International Station Meteorological Climate Summary, 9/96

Weather Conditions

Temperature			Daytime Sky			Precipitation		
10°F & below	32°F & below	90°F & above	Clear	Partly cloudy	Cloudy	0.01 inch or more precip.	0.1 inch or more snow/ice	Thunder-storms
< 1	33	53	89	162	114	114	1	59

Note: Figures are average number of days per year and cover the years 1945-1995
Source: National Climatic Data Center, International Station Meteorological Climate Summary, 9/96

Superfund Sites

The Charleston-North Charleston, SC metro area is home to two sites on the EPA's Superfund National Priorities List: **Koppers Co., Inc. (Charleston Plant)** (final); **Macalloy Corporation** (final). There are a total of 1,390 Superfund sites with a status of proposed or final on the list in the U.S. *U.S. Environmental Protection Agency, National Priorities List, April 5, 2019*

**AIR & WATER
QUALITY**

Air Quality Trends: Ozone

	1990	1995	2000	2005	2010	2012	2014	2015	2016	2017
MSA[1]	0.068	0.071	0.078	0.073	0.067	0.063	0.060	0.054	0.058	0.062
U.S.	0.088	0.089	0.082	0.080	0.073	0.075	0.067	0.068	0.069	0.068

Note: (1) Data covers the Charleston-North Charleston, SC Metropolitan Statistical Area—see Appendix B for areas included. The values shown are the composite ozone concentration averages among trend sites based on the highest fourth daily maximum 8-hour concentration in parts per million. These trends are based on sites having an adequate record of monitoring data during the trend period. Data from exceptional events are included.
Source: U.S. Environmental Protection Agency, Air Quality Monitoring Information, "Air Quality Trends by City, 1990-2017"

Air Quality Index

Area	Percent of Days when Air Quality was...[2]					AQI Statistics[2]	
	Good	Moderate	Unhealthy for Sensitive Groups	Unhealthy	Very Unhealthy	Maximum	Median
MSA[1]	83.7	16.1	0.3	0.0	0.0	101	40

Note: (1) Data covers the Charleston-North Charleston, SC Metropolitan Statistical Area—see Appendix B for areas included; (2) Based on 361 days with AQI data in 2017. Air Quality Index (AQI) is an index for reporting daily air quality. EPA calculates the AQI for five major air pollutants regulated by the Clean Air Act: ground-level ozone, particle pollution (aka particulate matter), carbon monoxide, sulfur dioxide, and nitrogen dioxide. The AQI runs from 0 to 500. The higher the AQI value, the greater the level of air pollution and the greater the health concern. There are six AQI categories: "Good" AQI is between 0 and 50. Air quality is considered satisfactory; "Moderate" AQI is between 51 and 100. Air quality is acceptable; "Unhealthy for Sensitive Groups" When AQI values are between 101 and 150, members of sensitive groups may experience health effects; "Unhealthy" When AQI values are between 151 and 200 everyone may begin to experience health effects; "Very Unhealthy" AQI values between 201 and 300 trigger a health alert; "Hazardous" AQI values over 300 trigger warnings of emergency conditions (not shown).
Source: U.S. Environmental Protection Agency, Air Quality Index Report, 2017

Air Quality Index Pollutants

Area	Percent of Days when AQI Pollutant was...[2]					
	Carbon Monoxide	Nitrogen Dioxide	Ozone	Sulfur Dioxide	Particulate Matter 2.5	Particulate Matter 10
MSA[1]	0.0	1.1	56.2	0.0	42.1	0.6

Note: (1) Data covers the Charleston-North Charleston, SC Metropolitan Statistical Area—see Appendix B for areas included; (2) Based on 361 days with AQI data in 2017. The Air Quality Index (AQI) is an index for reporting daily air quality. EPA calculates the AQI for five major air pollutants regulated by the Clean Air Act: ground-level ozone, particle pollution (also known as particulate matter), carbon monoxide, sulfur dioxide, and nitrogen dioxide. The AQI runs from 0 to 500. The higher the AQI value, the greater the level of air pollution and the greater the health concern.
Source: U.S. Environmental Protection Agency, Air Quality Index Report, 2017

Maximum Air Pollutant Concentrations: Particulate Matter, Ozone, CO and Lead

	Particulate Matter 10 (ug/m^3)	Particulate Matter 2.5 Wtd AM (ug/m^3)	Particulate Matter 2.5 24-Hr (ug/m^3)	Ozone (ppm)	Carbon Monoxide (ppm)	Lead (ug/m^3)
MSA[1] Level	29	n/a	n/a	0.064	n/a	n/a
NAAQS[2]	150	15	35	0.075	9	0.15
Met NAAQS[2]	Yes	n/a	n/a	Yes	n/a	n/a

Note: (1) Data covers the Charleston-North Charleston, SC Metropolitan Statistical Area—see Appendix B for areas included; Data from exceptional events are included; (2) National Ambient Air Quality Standards; ppm = parts per million; ug/m^3 = micrograms per cubic meter; n/a not available.
Concentrations: Particulate Matter 10 (coarse particulate)—highest second maximum 24-hour concentration; Particulate Matter 2.5 Wtd AM (fine particulate)—highest weighted annual mean concentration; Particulate Matter 2.5 24-Hour (fine particulate)—highest 98th percentile 24-hour concentration; Ozone—highest fourth daily maximum 8-hour concentration; Carbon Monoxide—highest second maximum non-overlapping 8-hour concentration; Lead—maximum running 3-month average
Source: U.S. Environmental Protection Agency, Air Quality Monitoring Information, "Air Quality Statistics by City, 2017"

Maximum Air Pollutant Concentrations: Nitrogen Dioxide and Sulfur Dioxide

	Nitrogen Dioxide AM (ppb)	Nitrogen Dioxide 1-Hr (ppb)	Sulfur Dioxide AM (ppb)	Sulfur Dioxide 1-Hr (ppb)	Sulfur Dioxide 24-Hr (ppb)
MSA[1] Level	1	n/a	n/a	5	n/a
NAAQS[2]	53	100	30	75	140
Met NAAQS[2]	Yes	n/a	n/a	Yes	n/a

Note: (1) Data covers the Charleston-North Charleston, SC Metropolitan Statistical Area—see Appendix B for areas included; Data from exceptional events are included; (2) National Ambient Air Quality Standards; ppm = parts per million; ug/m^3 = micrograms per cubic meter; n/a not available.
Concentrations: Nitrogen Dioxide AM—highest arithmetic mean concentration; Nitrogen Dioxide 1-Hr—highest 98th percentile 1-hour daily maximum concentration; Sulfur Dioxide AM—highest annual mean concentration; Sulfur Dioxide 1-Hr—highest 99th percentile 1-hour daily maximum concentration; Sulfur Dioxide 24-Hr—highest second maximum 24-hour concentration
Source: U.S. Environmental Protection Agency, Air Quality Monitoring Information, "Air Quality Statistics by City, 2017"

Drinking Water

Water System Name	Pop. Served	Primary Water Source Type	Violations[1] Health Based	Violations[1] Monitoring/ Reporting
Charleston Water System	234,333	Surface	0	0

Note: (1) Based on violation data from January 1, 2018 to December 31, 2018
Source: U.S. Environmental Protection Agency, Office of Ground Water and Drinking Water, Safe Drinking Water Information System (based on data extracted April 5, 2019)

Clarksville, Tennessee

Background

Located just south of the Kentucky border and 47 miles north of Nashville, Clarksville is Tennessee's fifth-largest town and has seen significant growth in recent years. Named for Gen. George Rogers Clark, a decorated veteran of the Indian and Revolutionary Wars, the city was founded in 1784, and became incorporated by the state of Tennessee when it joined the union in 1796.

Located near the confluence of Red and Cumberland rivers, Clarksville was the site of three Confederate forts that the Union defeated in 1862. Fort Defiance transferred hands and became known as a place where fleeing or freed slaves could find refuge—and jobs. In the 1980s the well-preserved fort passed from the private hands of a local judge to the city itself, and in 2011 an interpretive center and walking trails were unveiled at what is now called Fort Defiance Civil War Park and Interpretive Center. The site features walking trails as well as the 1,500+ square foot center.

Clarksville is home to the 105,000-acre Fort Campbell, established as Camp Campbell in 1942, with nearly two-thirds of its land mass in Tennessee and the rest—including the post office—located in Kentucky. It is home to the world's only air assault division, known as the Screaming Eagles. Two special ops command units, a combat support hospital, and far more make this home to the U.S. Army's most-deployed contingency forces and the its fifth-largest military population. With more than 4,000 civilian jobs, it's the area's largest employer with services on the post ranging from bowling to the commissary to the Fort Campbell Credit Union, as well as medical services and child care.

Austin Peay State University's main campus is in Clarksville, another of the city's major employers, and named for a local son who became governor. The four-year public master's-level university saw its enrollment climb steadily throughout the last twenty years. Austin Peay also operates a center at Fort Campbell with fifteen associate, bachelor and master's level programs.

In 2012, Hemlock Semiconductor Corp, a subsidiary of Dow Corning, opened a $1.2 billion plant in the city, and the state funded a new educational center at APSU to train workers.

A 146-acre Liberty Park and Marina redevelopment project was completed in 2012, replete with pavilions, sports fields, picnic shelters, a dog park, and a ten-acre pond with a boardwalk and fishing piers. The Wilma Rudolph Pavilion and Great lawn is named for the great Olympic runner, Clarksville's native daughter. Another recent development came when the city created an Indoor Aquatic Center with an inflatable dome that allows for water sports in winter.

On the cultural side of Clarksville's quality of life, the popular Clarksville Downtown Market—with produce and arts and crafts—is a poplar summer event.

Clarksville is also home to the state's second largest general museum, called the Customs House Museum and Cultural Center, which has seen a recent facelift. Model trains, a gallery devoted to sports champions, and even a bubble cave are all part of the experience.

The climate in Clarksville means hot summers but relatively moderate winters with average lows reaching 25 degrees in January. Precipitation stays fairly steady year round, getting no higher than 5.39 in March and bottoming out at 3.27 inches in October.

Rankings

General Rankings

- For its "Best for Vets: Places to Live 2019" rankings, *Military Times* evaluated 599 cities (83 large, 234 medium, 282 small) and compared the locations across three broad categories: veteran and military culture/services; economic indicators; and livability factors such as health, crime, traffic, and school quality. Clarksville ranked #12 out of the top 50, in the medium-sized city category (populations of 100,000-249,999). Data points more specific to veterans and the military weighed more heavily than the rest. *rebootcamp.militarytimes.com, "Military Times Best Places to Live 2019," September 10, 2018*

- The U.S. Conference of Mayors and Waste Management, Inc. sponsor the City Livability Awards Program, which recognize mayors for exemplary leadership in developing and implementing specific programs that improve the quality of life in America's cities. Clarksville received an Honorable Mention Citation in the large cities category. *U.S. Conference of Mayors, "2018 City Livability Awards"*

Business/Finance Rankings

- The personal finance site NerdWallet analyzed 183 American metropolitan areas with populations over 250,000 and more than 15,000 businesses to rank where entrepreneurs find the most success. Criteria included area economy, annual income, housing cost, unemployment rate, and the success rate of area businesses. Clarksville ranked #171. *www.nerdwallet.com, "Best Places to Start a Business," April 27, 2015*

- The Clarksville metro area appeared on the Milken Institute "2018 Best Performing Cities" list. Rank: #178 out of 200 large metro areas. Criteria: job growth; wage and salary growth; high-tech output growth. *Milken Institute, "Best-Performing Cities 2018," January 24, 2019*

- *Forbes* ranked the 200 most populous metro areas to determine the nation's "Best Places for Business and Careers." The Clarksville metro area was ranked #148. Criteria: costs (business and living); job growth (past and projected); income growth; quality of life; educational attainment (college and high school); projected economic growth; cultural and recreational opportunities; net migration patterns; number of highly ranked colleges. *Forbes, "The Best Places for Business and Careers 2018: Seattle Leads the Way," October 24, 2018*

Environmental Rankings

- Clarksville was highlighted as one of the top 90 cleanest metro areas for short-term particle pollution (24-hour PM 2.5) in the U.S. during 2014 through 2016. Monitors in these cities reported no days with unhealthful PM 2.5 levels. *American Lung Association, State of the Air 2018*

Health/Fitness Rankings

- The Clarksville metro area ranked #40 out of 189 in The Gallup-Healthways Well-Being Index. Criteria: purpose; social well being; financial health; community and physical health. Results are based on telephone interviews with adults, aged 18 and older, living in metropolitan areas in the 50 U.S. states and the District of Columbia. *Gallup-Healthways, "State of American Well-Being, 2017 Community Well-Being Rankings" March 2018*

Safety Rankings

- Allstate ranked the 200 largest cities in America in terms of driver safety. Clarksville ranked #59. Criteria: internal property damage claims over a two-year period from January 2015 to December 2016. The report helps increase the importance of safety awareness behind the wheel. *Allstate, "Allstate America's Best Drivers Report, 2018" August 28, 2018*

- The National Insurance Crime Bureau ranked 382 metro areas in the U.S. in terms of per capita rates of vehicle theft. The Clarksville metro area ranked #224 (#1 = highest rate). Criteria: number of vehicle theft offenses per 100,000 inhabitants in 2017. *National Insurance Crime Bureau, "Hot Spots 2017," July 12, 2018*

Seniors/Retirement Rankings

- From its Best Cities for Successful Aging indexes, the Milken Institute generated rankings for metropolitan areas, weighing data in nine categories—health care, wellness, living arrangements, transportation and convenience, financial characteristics, education, employment, community engagement, and overall livability. The Clarksville metro area was ranked #185 overall in the small metro area category. *Milken Institute, "Best Cities for Successful Aging, 2017" March 14, 2017*

Business Environment

CITY FINANCES

City Government Finances

Component	2016 ($000)	2016 ($ per capita)
Total Revenues	397,186	2,663
Total Expenditures	412,405	2,765
Debt Outstanding	718,236	4,815
Cash and Securities[1]	394,581	2,645

Note: (1) Cash and security holdings of a government at the close of its fiscal year, including those of its dependent agencies, utilities, and liquor stores.
Source: U.S. Census Bureau, State & Local Government Finances 2016

City Government Revenue by Source

Source	2016 ($000)	2016 ($ per capita)	2016 (%)
General Revenue			
From Federal Government	5,267	35	1.3
From State Government	11,784	79	3.0
From Local Governments	16,047	108	4.0
Taxes			
Property	32,690	219	8.2
Sales and Gross Receipts	8,249	55	2.1
Personal Income	0	0	0.0
Corporate Income	0	0	0.0
Motor Vehicle License	0	0	0.0
Other Taxes	1,642	11	0.4
Current Charges	55,516	372	14.0
Liquor Store	0	0	0.0
Utility	243,646	1,633	61.3
Employee Retirement	0	0	0.0

Source: U.S. Census Bureau, State & Local Government Finances 2016

City Government Expenditures by Function

Function	2016 ($000)	2016 ($ per capita)	2016 (%)
General Direct Expenditures			
Air Transportation	0	0	0.0
Corrections	0	0	0.0
Education	0	0	0.0
Employment Security Administration	0	0	0.0
Financial Administration	1,688	11	0.4
Fire Protection	15,938	106	3.9
General Public Buildings	685	4	0.2
Governmental Administration, Other	1,753	11	0.4
Health	0	0	0.0
Highways	13,443	90	3.3
Hospitals	0	0	0.0
Housing and Community Development	0	0	0.0
Interest on General Debt	2,493	16	0.6
Judicial and Legal	875	5	0.2
Libraries	0	0	0.0
Parking	299	2	0.1
Parks and Recreation	7,724	51	1.9
Police Protection	27,978	187	6.8
Public Welfare	0	0	0.0
Sewerage	72,321	484	17.5
Solid Waste Management	0	0	0.0
Veterans' Services	0	0	0.0
Liquor Store	0	0	0.0
Utility	247,142	1,656	59.9
Employee Retirement	0	0	0.0

Source: U.S. Census Bureau, State & Local Government Finances 2016

DEMOGRAPHICS

Population Growth

Area	1990 Census	2000 Census	2010 Census	2017* Estimate	Population Growth (%) 1990-2017	Population Growth (%) 2010-2017
City	78,569	103,455	132,929	147,771	88.1	11.2
MSA[1]	189,277	232,000	273,949	278,844	47.3	1.8
U.S.	248,709,873	281,421,906	308,745,538	321,004,407	29.1	4.0

Note: (1) Figures cover the Clarksville, TN-KY Metropolitan Statistical Area—see Appendix B for areas included; (*) 2013-2017 5-year estimated population
Source: U.S. Census Bureau, 1990 Census, Census 2000, Census 2010, 2013-2017 American Community Survey 5-Year Estimates

Household Size

Area	Persons in Household (%) One	Two	Three	Four	Five	Six	Seven or More	Average Household Size
City	23.5	32.8	19.6	14.4	6.2	2.1	1.4	2.70
MSA[1]	23.8	33.3	18.4	14.3	6.4	2.5	1.3	2.70
U.S.	27.7	33.8	15.7	13.0	6.0	2.3	1.4	2.60

Note: (1) Figures cover the Clarksville, TN-KY Metropolitan Statistical Area—see Appendix B for areas included
Source: U.S. Census Bureau, 2013-2017 American Community Survey 5-Year Estimates

Race

Area	White Alone[2] (%)	Black Alone[2] (%)	Asian Alone[2] (%)	AIAN[3] Alone[2] (%)	NHOPI[4] Alone[2] (%)	Other Race Alone[2] (%)	Two or More Races (%)
City	66.6	23.4	2.3	0.7	0.5	1.6	4.9
MSA[1]	72.4	19.4	1.9	0.6	0.4	1.2	4.1
U.S.	73.0	12.7	5.4	0.8	0.2	4.8	3.1

Note: (1) Figures cover the Clarksville, TN-KY Metropolitan Statistical Area—see Appendix B for areas included; (2) Alone is defined as not being in combination with one or more other races; (3) American Indian and Alaska Native; (4) Native Hawaiian and Other Pacific Islander
Source: U.S. Census Bureau, 2013-2017 American Community Survey 5-Year Estimates

Hispanic or Latino Origin

Area	Total (%)	Mexican (%)	Puerto Rican (%)	Cuban (%)	Other (%)
City	11.3	5.1	3.6	0.3	2.3
MSA[1]	8.7	4.3	2.4	0.3	1.7
U.S.	17.6	11.1	1.7	0.7	4.1

Note: Persons of Hispanic or Latino origin can be of any race; (1) Figures cover the Clarksville, TN-KY Metropolitan Statistical Area—see Appendix B for areas included
Source: U.S. Census Bureau, 2013-2017 American Community Survey 5-Year Estimates

Segregation

Type	Segregation Indices[1] 1990	2000	2010	2010 Rank[2]	Percent Change 1990-2000	1990-2010	2000-2010
Black/White	n/a	n/a	n/a	n/a	n/a	n/a	n/a
Asian/White	n/a	n/a	n/a	n/a	n/a	n/a	n/a
Hispanic/White	n/a	n/a	n/a	n/a	n/a	n/a	n/a

Note: All figures cover the Metropolitan Statistical Area—see Appendix B for areas included; Figures are based on an analysis of 1990, 2000, and 2010 Census Decennial Census tract data by William H. Frey, Brookings Institution and the University of Michigan Social Science Data Analysis Network. In this analysis all racial groups (whites, blacks, and asians) are non-Hispanic members of those races. Hispanics are shown as a separate category; (1) Segregation Indices are Dissimilarity Indices that measure the degree to which the minority group is distributed differently than whites across census tracts. They range from 0 (complete integration) to 100 (complete segregation) where the value indicates the percentage of the minority group that needs to move to be distributed exactly like whites; (2) Ranges from 1 (most segregated) to 102 (least segregated); n/a not available.
Source: www.CensusScope.org

Ancestry

Area	German	Irish	English	American	Italian	Polish	French[2]	Scottish	Dutch
City	11.8	9.3	5.5	9.2	3.0	2.0	1.9	1.5	1.0
MSA[1]	11.2	9.7	6.8	11.3	2.8	1.6	1.7	1.6	1.0
U.S.	14.1	10.1	7.5	6.6	5.3	2.9	2.5	1.7	1.3

Note: Figures are the percentage of the total population reporting a particular ancestry. The nine most commonly reported ancestries in the U.S. are shown. Figures include multiple ancestries (e.g. if a person reported being Irish and Italian, they were included in both columns); (1) Figures cover the Clarksville, TN-KY Metropolitan Statistical Area—see Appendix B for areas included; (2) Excludes Basque
Source: U.S. Census Bureau, 2013-2017 American Community Survey 5-Year Estimates

Foreign-Born Population

Area	Any Foreign Country	Asia	Mexico	Europe	Carribean	Central America[2]	South America	Africa	Canada
City	5.5	1.6	1.3	1.0	0.4	0.3	0.5	0.3	0.1
MSA[1]	4.2	1.4	0.9	0.7	0.3	0.3	0.3	0.3	0.1
U.S.	13.4	4.1	3.6	1.5	1.3	1.0	0.9	0.6	0.3

Note: (1) Figures cover the Clarksville, TN-KY Metropolitan Statistical Area—see Appendix B for areas included; (2) Excludes Mexico.
Source: U.S. Census Bureau, 2013-2017 American Community Survey 5-Year Estimates

Marital Status

Area	Never Married	Now Married[2]	Separated	Widowed	Divorced
City	28.8	52.1	2.7	4.1	12.3
MSA[1]	27.9	52.7	2.4	5.0	12.0
U.S.	33.1	48.2	2.0	5.8	10.9

Note: Figures are percentages and cover the population 15 years of age and older; (1) Figures cover the Clarksville, TN-KY Metropolitan Statistical Area—see Appendix B for areas included; (2) Excludes separated
Source: U.S. Census Bureau, 2013-2017 American Community Survey 5-Year Estimates

Disability by Age

Area	All Ages	Under 18 Years Old	18 to 64 Years Old	65 Years and Over
City	14.7	4.7	15.5	43.8
MSA[1]	15.2	4.9	15.3	42.4
U.S.	12.6	4.2	10.3	35.5

Note: Figures show percent of the civilian noninstitutionalized population that reported having a disability. Disability status is determined from six types of difficulty: vision, hearing, cognitive, ambulatory, self-care, and independent living. For children under 5 years old, hearing and vision difficulty are used to determine disability status. For children between the ages of 5 and 14, disability status is determined from hearing, vision, cognitive, ambulatory, and self-care difficulties. For people aged 15 years and older, they are considered to have a disability if they have difficulty with any one of the six difficulty types; Note: (1) Figures cover the Clarksville, TN-KY Metropolitan Statistical Area—see Appendix B for areas included
Source: U.S. Census Bureau, 2013-2017 American Community Survey 5-Year Estimates

Age

Area	Under Age 5	Age 5–19	Age 20–34	Age 35–44	Age 45–54	Age 55–64	Age 65–74	Age 75–84	Age 85+	Median Age
City	9.2	20.5	31.0	12.7	10.3	8.2	5.0	2.4	0.6	29.4
MSA[1]	8.7	20.8	27.8	12.5	10.9	9.3	6.0	3.1	1.0	30.5
U.S.	6.2	19.5	20.7	12.7	13.4	12.7	8.6	4.4	1.9	37.8

Note: (1) Figures cover the Clarksville, TN-KY Metropolitan Statistical Area—see Appendix B for areas included
Source: U.S. Census Bureau, 2013-2017 American Community Survey 5-Year Estimates

Gender

Area	Males	Females	Males per 100 Females
City	73,898	73,873	100.0
MSA[1]	141,675	137,169	103.3
U.S.	158,018,753	162,985,654	97.0

Note: (1) Figures cover the Clarksville, TN-KY Metropolitan Statistical Area—see Appendix B for areas included
Source: U.S. Census Bureau, 2013-2017 American Community Survey 5-Year Estimates

Religious Groups by Family

Area	Catholic	Baptist	Non-Den.	Methodist[2]	Lutheran	LDS[3]	Pente-costal	Presby-terian[4]	Muslim[5]	Judaism
MSA[1]	4.1	30.9	2.3	6.2	0.6	1.5	1.8	1.1	0.1	<0.1
U.S.	19.1	9.3	4.0	4.0	2.3	2.0	1.9	1.6	0.8	0.7

Note: Figures are the number of adherents as a percentage of the total population; (1) Figures cover the Clarksville, TN-KY Metropolitan Statistical Area—see Appendix B for areas included; (2) Methodist/Pietist; (3) Latter Day Saints; (4) Reformed; (5) Figures are estimates
Source: Association of Statisticians of American Religious Bodies, 2010 U.S. Religion Census: Religious Congregations & Membership Study

Religious Groups by Tradition

Area	Catholic	Evangelical Protestant	Mainline Protestant	Other Tradition	Black Protestant	Orthodox
MSA[1]	4.1	35.4	7.3	1.7	2.4	<0.1
U.S.	19.1	16.2	7.3	4.3	1.6	0.3

Note: Figures are the number of adherents as a percentage of the total population; (1) Figures cover the Clarksville, TN-KY Metropolitan Statistical Area—see Appendix B for areas included
Source: Association of Statisticians of American Religious Bodies, 2010 U.S. Religion Census: Religious Congregations & Membership Study

ECONOMY

Gross Metropolitan Product

Area	2016	2017	2018	2019	Rank[2]
MSA[1]	10.7	10.9	11.5	12.1	194

Note: Figures are in billions of dollars; (1) Figures cover the Clarksville, TN-KY Metropolitan Statistical Area—see Appendix B for areas included; (2) Rank is based on 2017 data and ranges from 1 to 381
Source: U.S. Conference of Mayors, U.S. Metro Economies: Economic Growth & Full Employment, June 2018

Economic Growth

Area	2017-2018 (%)	2019-2020 (%)	2021-2022 (%)
MSA[1]	1.7	2.4	1.4

Note: Figures are real gross metropolitan product (GMP) growth rates and represent average annual percent change; (1) Figures cover the Clarksville, TN-KY Metropolitan Statistical Area—see Appendix B for areas included
Source: U.S. Conference of Mayors, U.S. Metro Economies: Economic Growth & Full Employment, June 2018

Metropolitan Area Exports

Area	2012	2013	2014	2015	2016	2017	Rank[2]
MSA[1]	326.3	315.9	323.7	296.5	376.1	360.2	235

Note: Figures are in millions of dollars; (1) Figures cover the Clarksville, TN-KY Metropolitan Statistical Area—see Appendix B for areas included; (2) Rank is based on 2017 data and ranges from 1 to 387
Source: U.S. Department of Commerce, International Trade Administration, Office of Trade and Economic Analysis, Industry and Analysis, Exports by Metropolitan Area, extracted March 25, 2019

Building Permits

Area	Single-Family			Multi-Family			Total		
	2016	2017	Pct. Chg.	2016	2017	Pct. Chg.	2016	2017	Pct. Chg.
City	788	806	2.3	256	227	-11.3	1,044	1,033	-1.1
MSA[1]	1,316	1,558	18.4	363	255	-29.8	1,679	1,813	8.0
U.S.	750,800	820,000	9.2	455,800	462,000	1.4	1,206,600	1,282,000	6.2

Note: (1) Figures cover the Clarksville, TN-KY Metropolitan Statistical Area—see Appendix B for areas included; Figures represent new, privately-owned housing units authorized (unadjusted data); All permit data are based on estimates with imputation
Source: U.S. Census Bureau, Manufacturing, Mining, and Construction Statistics, Building Permits, 2016, 2017

Bankruptcy Filings

Area	Business Filings			Nonbusiness Filings		
	2017	2018	% Chg.	2017	2018	% Chg.
Montgomery County	7	11	57.1	858	845	-1.5
U.S.	23,157	22,232	-4.0	765,863	751,186	-1.9

Note: Business filings include Chapter 7, Chapter 11, Chapter 12, and Chapter 13; Nonbusiness filings include Chapter 7, Chapter 11, and Chapter 13
Source: Administrative Office of the U.S. Courts, Business and Nonbusiness Bankruptcy, County Cases Commenced by Chapter of the Bankruptcy Code, During the 12-Month Period Ending December 31, 2017 and Business and Nonbusiness Bankruptcy, County Cases Commenced by Chapter of the Bankruptcy Code, During the 12-Month Period Ending December 31, 2018

Housing Vacancy Rates

Area	Gross Vacancy Rate[2] (%)			Year-Round Vacancy Rate[3] (%)			Rental Vacancy Rate[4] (%)			Homeowner Vacancy Rate[5] (%)		
	2016	2017	2018	2016	2017	2018	2016	2017	2018	2016	2017	2018
MSA[1]	n/a	n/a	n/a	n/a	n/a	n/a	n/a	n/a	n/a	n/a	n/a	n/a
U.S.	12.8	12.7	12.3	9.9	9.9	9.7	6.9	7.2	6.9	1.7	1.6	1.5

Note: (1) Figures cover the Clarksville, TN-KY Metropolitan Statistical Area—see Appendix B for areas included; (2) The percentage of the total housing inventory that is vacant; (3) The percentage of the housing inventory (excluding seasonal units) that is year-round vacant; (4) The percentage of rental inventory that is vacant for rent; (5) The percentage of homeowner inventory that is vacant for sale; n/a not available
Source: U.S. Census Bureau, Housing Vacancies and Homeownership Annual Statistics: 2016, 2017, 2018

INCOME

Income

Area	Per Capita ($)	Median Household ($)	Average Household ($)
City	23,377	51,164	61,610
MSA[1]	24,006	50,369	63,127
U.S.	31,177	57,652	81,283

Note: (1) Figures cover the Clarksville, TN-KY Metropolitan Statistical Area—see Appendix B for areas included
Source: U.S. Census Bureau, 2013-2017 American Community Survey 5-Year Estimates

Household Income Distribution

Area	Percent of Households Earning							
	Under $15,000	$15,000 -$24,999	$25,000 -$34,999	$35,000 -$49,999	$50,000 -$74,999	$75,000 -$99,999	$100,000 -$149,999	$150,000 and up
City	11.7	9.2	11.2	16.4	23.3	13.8	10.1	4.4
MSA[1]	12.5	9.8	10.9	16.4	21.4	12.9	10.7	5.5
U.S.	11.6	9.8	9.5	13.0	17.7	12.3	14.1	12.1

Note: (1) Figures cover the Clarksville, TN-KY Metropolitan Statistical Area—see Appendix B for areas included
Source: U.S. Census Bureau, 2013-2017 American Community Survey 5-Year Estimates

Poverty Rate

Area	All Ages	Under 18 Years Old	18 to 64 Years Old	65 Years and Over
City	15.3	19.6	14.3	8.3
MSA[1]	15.6	20.4	14.5	9.5
U.S.	14.6	20.3	13.7	9.3

Note: Figures are percentage of people whose income during the past 12 months was below the poverty level; (1) Figures cover the Clarksville, TN-KY Metropolitan Statistical Area—see Appendix B for areas included
Source: U.S. Census Bureau, 2013-2017 American Community Survey 5-Year Estimates

EMPLOYMENT

Labor Force and Employment

Area	Civilian Labor Force			Workers Employed		
	Dec. 2017	Dec. 2018	% Chg.	Dec. 2017	Dec. 2018	% Chg.
City	59,588	61,309	2.9	57,442	59,226	3.1
MSA[1]	110,843	114,018	2.9	106,720	109,983	3.1
U.S.	159,880,000	162,510,000	1.6	153,602,000	156,481,000	1.9

Note: Data is not seasonally adjusted and covers workers 16 years of age and older; (1) Figures cover the Clarksville, TN-KY Metropolitan Statistical Area—see Appendix B for areas included
Source: Bureau of Labor Statistics, Local Area Unemployment Statistics

Unemployment Rate

Area	2018											
	Jan.	Feb.	Mar.	Apr.	May	Jun.	Jul.	Aug.	Sep.	Oct.	Nov.	Dec.
City	4.3	4.0	3.9	3.3	3.5	4.9	5.0	4.6	4.4	4.3	3.8	3.4
MSA[1]	4.3	4.3	4.1	3.5	3.7	5.1	5.1	4.6	4.5	4.4	3.8	3.5
U.S.	4.5	4.4	4.1	3.7	3.6	4.2	4.1	3.9	3.6	3.5	3.5	3.7

Note: Data is not seasonally adjusted and covers workers 16 years of age and older; (1) Figures cover the Clarksville, TN-KY Metropolitan Statistical Area—see Appendix B for areas included
Source: Bureau of Labor Statistics, Local Area Unemployment Statistics

Average Wages

Occupation	$/Hr.	Occupation	$/Hr.
Accountants and Auditors	27.70	Maids and Housekeeping Cleaners	10.60
Automotive Mechanics	20.20	Maintenance and Repair Workers	20.40
Bookkeepers	17.60	Marketing Managers	n/a
Carpenters	19.00	Nuclear Medicine Technologists	n/a
Cashiers	9.80	Nurses, Licensed Practical	19.50
Clerks, General Office	15.80	Nurses, Registered	29.70
Clerks, Receptionists/Information	11.70	Nursing Assistants	13.90
Clerks, Shipping/Receiving	17.40	Packers and Packagers, Hand	11.30
Computer Programmers	36.70	Physical Therapists	38.70
Computer Systems Analysts	30.00	Postal Service Mail Carriers	24.30
Computer User Support Specialists	23.30	Real Estate Brokers	n/a
Cooks, Restaurant	10.80	Retail Salespersons	12.70
Dentists	102.30	Sales Reps., Exc. Tech./Scientific	29.90
Electrical Engineers	43.60	Sales Reps., Tech./Scientific	32.20
Electricians	25.10	Secretaries, Exc. Legal/Med./Exec.	15.40
Financial Managers	47.50	Security Guards	16.60
First-Line Supervisors/Managers, Sales	19.90	Surgeons	n/a
Food Preparation Workers	9.70	Teacher Assistants*	12.70
General and Operations Managers	39.30	Teachers, Elementary School*	29.70
Hairdressers/Cosmetologists	12.50	Teachers, Secondary School*	27.90
Internists, General	n/a	Telemarketers	n/a
Janitors and Cleaners	12.10	Truck Drivers, Heavy/Tractor-Trailer	17.90
Landscaping/Groundskeeping Workers	13.50	Truck Drivers, Light/Delivery Svcs.	16.10
Lawyers	35.50	Waiters and Waitresses	11.00

Note: Wage data covers the Clarksville, TN-KY Metropolitan Statistical Area—see Appendix B for areas included; (*) Hourly wages for elementary/secondary school teachers and teacher assistants were calculated by the editors from annual wage data based on a 40 hour work week; n/a not available.
Source: Bureau of Labor Statistics, Metro Area Occupational Employment & Wage Estimates, May 2018

Employment by Occupation

Occupation Classification	City (%)	MSA[1] (%)	U.S. (%)
Management, Business, Science, and Arts	31.0	31.4	37.4
Natural Resources, Construction, and Maintenance	9.6	9.6	8.9
Production, Transportation, and Material Moving	15.8	17.0	12.2
Sales and Office	24.1	23.6	23.5
Service	19.5	18.4	18.0

Note: Figures cover employed civilians 16 years of age and older; (1) Figures cover the Clarksville, TN-KY Metropolitan Statistical Area—see Appendix B for areas included
Source: U.S. Census Bureau, 2013-2017 American Community Survey 5-Year Estimates

Employment by Industry

Sector	MSA[1]		U.S.
	Number of Employees	Percent of Total	Percent of Total
Construction, Mining, and Logging	3,300	3.5	5.3
Education and Health Services	12,100	12.8	15.9
Financial Activities	3,200	3.4	5.7
Government	19,300	20.5	15.1
Information	1,100	1.2	1.9
Leisure and Hospitality	11,500	12.2	10.7
Manufacturing	13,200	14.0	8.5
Other Services	3,100	3.3	3.9
Professional and Business Services	9,300	9.9	14.1
Retail Trade	12,900	13.7	10.8
Transportation, Warehousing, and Utilities	2,600	2.8	4.2
Wholesale Trade	n/a	n/a	3.9

Note: Figures are non-farm employment as of December 2018. Figures are not seasonally adjusted and include workers 16 years of age and older; (1) Figures cover the Clarksville, TN-KY Metropolitan Statistical Area—see Appendix B for areas included; n/a not available
Source: Bureau of Labor Statistics, Current Employment Statistics, Employment, Hours, and Earnings

Occupations with Greatest Projected Employment Growth: 2018 – 2020

Occupation[1]	2018 Employment	2020 Projected Employment	Numeric Employment Change	Percent Employment Change
Combined Food Preparation and Serving Workers, Including Fast Food	78,410	82,150	3,740	4.8
Registered Nurses	59,710	61,550	1,840	3.1
Waiters and Waitresses	54,060	55,870	1,810	3.3
General and Operations Managers	47,640	49,430	1,790	3.8
Laborers and Freight, Stock, and Material Movers, Hand	99,140	100,740	1,600	1.6
Customer Service Representatives	61,220	62,780	1,560	2.5
Janitors and Cleaners, Except Maids and Housekeeping Cleaners	43,260	44,680	1,420	3.3
Stock Clerks and Order Fillers	54,500	55,920	1,420	2.6
Security Guards	24,930	26,160	1,230	4.9
Maintenance and Repair Workers, General	32,360	33,580	1,220	3.8

Note: Projections cover Tennessee; (1) Sorted by numeric employment change
Source: www.projectionscentral.com, State Occupational Projections, 2018–2020 Short-Term Projections

Fastest Growing Occupations: 2018 – 2020

Occupation[1]	2018 Employment	2020 Projected Employment	Numeric Employment Change	Percent Employment Change
Dietetic Technicians	720	810	90	12.5
Operations Research Analysts	1,910	2,080	170	8.9
Fiberglass Laminators and Fabricators	570	620	50	8.8
Software Developers, Applications	6,520	7,080	560	8.6
Home Health Aides	6,680	7,240	560	8.4
Helpers—Brickmasons, Blockmasons, Stonemasons, and Tile and Marble Setters	740	800	60	8.1
Real Estate Brokers	1,130	1,220	90	8.0
Statisticians	650	700	50	7.7
Physician Assistants	1,650	1,770	120	7.3
Brokerage Clerks	1,100	1,180	80	7.3

Note: Projections cover Tennessee; (1) Sorted by percent employment change and excludes occupations with numeric employment change less than 50
Source: www.projectionscentral.com, State Occupational Projections, 2018–2020 Short-Term Projections

TAXES

State Corporate Income Tax Rates

State	Tax Rate (%)	Income Brackets ($)	Num. of Brackets	Financial Institution Tax Rate (%)[a]	Federal Income Tax Ded.
Tennessee	6.5	Flat rate	1	6.5	No

Note: Tax rates as of January 1, 2019; (a) Rates listed are the corporate income tax rate applied to financial institutions or excise taxes based on income. Some states have other taxes based upon the value of deposits or shares.
Source: Federation of Tax Administrators, Range of State Corporate Income Tax Rates, January 1, 2019

State Individual Income Tax Rates

State	Tax Rate (%)	Income Brackets ($)	Personal Exemptions ($)			Standard Ded. ($)	
			Single	Married	Depend.	Single	Married
Tennessee		– State income tax of 2% on dividends and interest income only (x) –					

Note: Tax rates as of January 1, 2019; Local- and county-level taxes are not included; n/a not applicable; Federal income tax is not deductible on state income tax returns; (x) Tennessee Hall Tax Rate on Dividends and Interest is being phased out, 1% reduction each year
Source: Federation of Tax Administrators, State Individual Income Tax Rates, January 1, 2019

Various State Sales and Excise Tax Rates

State	State Sales Tax (%)	Gasoline[1] (¢/gal.)	Cigarette[2] ($/pack)	Spirits[3] ($/gal.)	Wine[4] ($/gal.)	Beer[5] ($/gal.)	Recreational Marijuana (%)
Tennessee	7	26.4	0.62	4.46 (i)	1.27 (o)	1.29 (u)	Not legal

Note: All tax rates as of January 1, 2019; (1) The American Petroleum Institute has developed a methodology for determining the average tax rate on a gallon of fuel. Rates may include any of the following: excise taxes, environmental fees, storage tank fees, other fees or taxes, general sales tax, and local taxes. In states where gasoline is subject to the general sales tax, or where the fuel tax is based on the average sale price, the average rate determined by API is sensitive to changes in the price of gasoline. States that fully or partially apply general sales taxes to gasoline: CA, CO, GA, IL, IN, MI, NY; (2) The federal excise tax of $1.0066 per pack and local taxes are not included; (3) Rates are those applicable to off-premise sales of 40% alcohol by volume (a.b.v.) distilled spirits in 750ml containers. Local excise taxes are excluded; (4) Rates are those applicable to off-premise sales of 11% a.b.v. non-carbonated wine in 750ml containers; (5) Rates are those applicable to off-premise sales of 4.7% a.b.v. beer in 12 ounce containers; (i) Includes case fees and/or bottle fees which may vary with size of container; (o) Includes case fees and/or bottle fees which may vary with size of container; (u) Includes the wholesale tax rate in Kentucky (10%) and Tennessee (17%), converted into a gallonage excise tax rate.
Source: Tax Foundation, 2019 Facts & Figures: How Does Your State Compare?

State Business Tax Climate Index Rankings

State	Overall Rank	Corporate Tax Rank	Individual Income Tax Rank	Sales Tax Rank	Unemployment Insurance Tax Rank	Property Tax Rank
Tennessee	16	24	8	46	22	29

Note: The index is a measure of how each state's tax laws affect economic performance. The lower the rank, the more favorable a state's tax system is for business. States without a given tax are given a ranking of 1. The scores/rankings for the District of Columbia do not affect other states. The 2019 index represents the tax climate as of July 1, 2018.
Source: Tax Foundation, State Business Tax Climate Index 2019

COMMERCIAL UTILITIES

Typical Monthly Electric Bills

Area	Commercial Service ($/month)		Industrial Service ($/month)	
	1,500 kWh	40 kW demand 14,000 kWh	1,000 kW demand 200,000 kWh	50,000 kW demand 32,500,000 kWh
City	n/a	n/a	n/a	n/a
Average[1]	203	1,619	25,886	2,540,077

Note: Figures are based on annualized rates; (1) Average based on 187 utilities surveyed; n/a not available
Source: Edison Electric Institute, Typical Bills and Average Rates Report, Summer 2018

TRANSPORTATION

Means of Transportation to Work

Area	Car/Truck/Van		Public Transportation			Bicycle	Walked	Other Means	Worked at Home
	Drove Alone	Car-pooled	Bus	Subway	Railroad				
City	86.8	6.6	1.1	0.0	0.0	0.1	1.6	1.4	2.4
MSA[1]	84.5	7.3	0.8	0.0	0.0	0.1	3.4	1.5	2.4
U.S.	76.4	9.2	2.5	1.9	0.6	0.6	2.7	1.3	4.7

Note: Figures are percentages and cover workers 16 years of age and older; (1) Figures cover the Clarksville, TN-KY Metropolitan Statistical Area—see Appendix B for areas included
Source: U.S. Census Bureau, 2013-2017 American Community Survey 5-Year Estimates

Travel Time to Work

Area	Less Than 10 Minutes	10 to 19 Minutes	20 to 29 Minutes	30 to 44 Minutes	45 to 59 Minutes	60 to 89 Minutes	90 Minutes or More
City	11.7	34.3	25.2	16.5	5.0	6.1	1.2
MSA[1]	15.6	32.5	21.8	17.2	5.8	5.5	1.5
U.S.	12.7	28.9	20.9	20.5	8.1	6.2	2.7

Note: Note: Figures are percentages and include workers 16 years old and over; (1) Figures cover the Clarksville, TN-KY Metropolitan Statistical Area—see Appendix B for areas included
Source: U.S. Census Bureau, 2013-2017 American Community Survey 5-Year Estimates

Freeway Travel Time Index

Area	1985	1990	1995	2000	2005	2010	2014
Urban Area Rank[1,2]	n/a	n/a	n/a	n/a	n/a	n/a	n/a
Urban Area Index[1]	n/a	n/a	n/a	n/a	n/a	n/a	n/a
Average Index[3]	1.09	1.11	1.14	1.17	1.20	1.19	1.20

Note: Freeway Travel Time Index—the ratio of travel time in the peak period to the travel time at free-flow conditions. For example, a value of 1.30 indicates a 20-minute free-flow trip takes 26 minutes in the peak (20 minutes x 1.30 = 26 minutes); (1) Data for the Clarksville, TN-KY urban area was not available; (2) Rank is based on 101 urban areas (#1 = highest travel time index); (3) Average of 101 urban areas
Source: Texas Transportation Institute, 2015 Urban Mobility Scorecard, August 2015

Freeway Commuter Stress Index

Area	1985	1990	1995	2000	2005	2010	2014
Urban Area Rank[1,2]	n/a	n/a	n/a	n/a	n/a	n/a	n/a
Urban Area Index[1]	n/a	n/a	n/a	n/a	n/a	n/a	n/a
Average Index[3]	1.13	1.16	1.19	1.22	1.25	1.24	1.25

Note: The Freeway Commuter Stress Index is the same as the Freeway Travel Time Index (see table above) except that it includes only the travel in the peak directions during the peak periods; the TTI includes travel in all directions during the peak period. Thus, the CSI is more indicative of the work trip experienced by each commuter on a daily basis; (1) Data for the Clarksville, TN-KY urban area was not available; (2) Rank is based on 101 urban areas (#1 = highest travel time index); (3) Average of 101 urban areas
Source: Texas Transportation Institute, 2015 Urban Mobility Scorecard, August 2015

Public Transportation

Agency Name / Mode of Transportation	Vehicles Operated in Maximum Service[1]	Annual Unlinked Passenger Trips[2] (in thous.)	Annual Passenger Miles[3] (in thous.)
Clarksville Transit System (CTS)			
Bus (directly operated)	16	683.1	n/a
Demand Response (directly operated)	10	31.9	n/a

Note: (1) The number of revenue vehicles operated by the given mode and type of service to meet the annual maximum service requirement. This is the revenue vehicle count during the peak season of the year; on the week and day that maximum service is provided. Vehicles operated in maximum service (VOMS) exclude atypical days and one-time special events; (2) The number of passengers who boarded public transportation vehicles. Passengers are counted each time they board a vehicle no matter how many vehicles they use to travel from their origin to their destination. (3) The sum of the distances ridden by all passengers during the entire fiscal year.
Source: Federal Transit Administration, National Transit Database, 2017

Air Transportation

Airport Name and Code / Type of Service	Passenger Airlines[1]	Passenger Enplanements	Freight Carriers[2]	Freight (lbs)
Outlaw Field (CKV)				
Domestic service (U.S. carriers - 2018)	0	0	0	0
International service (U.S. carriers - 2017)	0	0	0	0

Note: (1) Includes all U.S.-based major, minor and commuter airlines that carried at least one passenger during the year; (2) Includes all U.S.-based airlines and freight carriers that transported at least one pound of freight during the year.
Source: Bureau of Transportation Statistics, The Intermodal Transportation Database, Air Carriers: T-100 Domestic Market (U.S. Carriers), 2018; Bureau of Transportation Statistics, The Intermodal Transportation Database, Air Carriers: T-100 International Market (U.S. Carriers), 2017

Other Transportation Statistics

Major Highways:	I-24; SR-79; SR-41A
Amtrak Service:	No
Major Waterways/Ports:	Cumberland River

Source: Amtrak.com; Google Maps

BUSINESSES

Major Business Headquarters

Company Name	Industry	Rankings Fortune[1]	Forbes[2]
No companies listed	-	-	-

Note: (1) Companies that produce a 10-K are ranked 1 to 500 based on 2017 revenue; (2) All private companies with at least $2 billion in annual revenue through the end of their most current fiscal year are ranked 1 to 229; companies listed are headquartered in the city; dashes indicate no ranking
Source: Fortune, "Fortune 500," June 2018; Forbes, "America's Largest Private Companies," 2018 Rankings

Minority- and Women-Owned Businesses

Group	All Firms		Firms with Paid Employees			
	Firms	Sales ($000)	Firms	Sales ($000)	Employees	Payroll ($000)
AIAN[1]	47	2,417	1	(s)	0 - 19	(s)
Asian	363	87,399	120	71,457	527	10,137
Black	1,094	(s)	111	(s)	250 - 499	(s)
Hispanic	408	58,958	62	48,699	804	13,552
NHOPI[2]	n/a	n/a	n/a	n/a	n/a	n/a
Women	3,350	488,227	405	431,525	3,767	80,001
All Firms	8,100	6,713,023	1,824	6,435,545	34,870	1,089,233

Note: Figures cover firms located in the city; minority- and women-owned business are defined as firms in which the corresponding group own 51% or more of the stock or equity of the company; (1) American Indian and Alaska Native; (2) Native Hawaiian and Other Pacific Islander; (s) estimates are suppressed when publication standards are not met; n/a not available
Source: U.S. Census Bureau, 2012 Economic Census, Survey of Business Owners

HOTELS & CONVENTION CENTERS

Hotels, Motels and Vacation Rentals

Area	5 Star		4 Star		3 Star		2 Star		1 Star		Not Rated	
	Num.	Pct.[3]	Num.	Pct.[3]	Num.	Pct.[3]	Num.	Pct.[3]	Num.	Pct.[3]	Num.	Pct.[3]
City[1]	0	0.0	2	1.9	8	7.6	44	41.9	1	1.0	50	47.6
Total[2]	286	0.4	5,236	7.1	16,715	22.6	10,259	13.9	293	0.4	41,056	55.6

Note: (1) Figures cover Clarksville and vicinity; (2) Figures cover all 100 cities in this book; (3) Percentage of hotels which have a given star rating; Star ratings are determined by expedia.com and offer an indication of the general quality of a particular hotel.
Source: www.expedia.com, April 3, 2019

Major Convention Centers

Name	Overall Space (sq. ft.)	Exhibit Space (sq. ft.)	Meeting Space (sq. ft.)	Meeting Rooms

There are no major convention centers located in the metro area
Source: Original research

Living Environment

COST OF LIVING

Cost of Living Index

Composite Index	Groceries	Housing	Utilities	Trans-portation	Health Care	Misc. Goods/ Services
n/a	n/a	n/a	n/a	n/a	n/a	n/a

Note: The Cost of Living Index measures regional differences in the cost of consumer goods and services, excluding taxes and non-consumer expenditures, for professional and managerial households in the top income quintile. It is based on more than 50,000 prices covering almost 60 different items for which prices are collected three times a year by chambers of commerce, economic development organizations or university applied economic centers in each participating urban area. The numbers shown should be read as a percentage above or below the national average of 100. For example, a value of 115.4 in the groceries column indicates that grocery prices are 15.4% higher than the national average. Small differences in the index numbers should not be interpreted as significant; n/a not available.
Source: The Council for Community and Economic Research, ACCRA Cost of Living Index, 2018

Grocery Prices

Area[1]	T-Bone Steak ($/pound)	Frying Chicken ($/pound)	Whole Milk ($/half gal.)	Eggs ($/dozen)	Orange Juice ($/64 oz.)	Coffee ($/11.5 oz.)
City[2]	n/a	n/a	n/a	n/a	n/a	n/a
Avg.	11.35	1.42	1.94	1.81	3.52	4.35
Min.	7.45	0.92	0.80	0.75	2.72	3.06
Max.	15.05	2.76	4.18	4.00	5.36	8.20

Note: (1) Values for the local area are compared with the average, minimum and maximum values for all 291 areas in the Cost of Living Index; (2) Figures cover the Clarksville TN urban area; n/a not available; **T-Bone Steak** (price per pound); **Frying Chicken** (price per pound, whole fryer); **Whole Milk** (half gallon carton); **Eggs** (price per dozen, Grade A, large); **Orange Juice** (64 oz. Tropicana or Florida Natural); **Coffee** (11.5 oz. can, vacuum-packed, Maxwell House, Hills Bros, or Folgers).
Source: The Council for Community and Economic Research, ACCRA Cost of Living Index, 2018

Housing and Utility Costs

Area[1]	New Home Price ($)	Apartment Rent ($/month)	All Electric ($/month)	Part Electric ($/month)	Other Energy ($/month)	Telephone ($/month)
City[2]	n/a	n/a	n/a	n/a	n/a	n/a
Avg.	347,000	1,087	165.93	100.16	67.73	178.70
Min.	200,468	500	93.58	25.64	26.78	163.10
Max.	1,901,222	4,888	388.65	246.86	332.81	197.70

Note: (1) Values for the local area are compared with the average, minimum and maximum values for all 291 areas in the Cost of Living Index; (2) Figures cover the Clarksville TN urban area; n/a not available; **New Home Price** (2,400 sf living area, 8,000 sf lot, in urban area with full utilities); **Apartment Rent** (950 sf 2 bedroom/1.5 or 2 bath, unfurnished, excluding all utilities except water); **All Electric** (average monthly cost for an all-electric home); **Part Electric** (average monthly cost for a part-electric home); **Other Energy** (average monthly cost for natural gas, fuel oil, coal, wood, and any other forms of energy except electricity); **Telephone** (price includes the base monthly rate plus taxes and fees for three lines of mobile phone service).
Source: The Council for Community and Economic Research, ACCRA Cost of Living Index, 2018

Health Care, Transportation, and Other Costs

Area[1]	Doctor ($/visit)	Dentist ($/visit)	Optometrist ($/visit)	Gasoline ($/gallon)	Beauty Salon ($/visit)	Men's Shirt ($)
City[2]	n/a	n/a	n/a	n/a	n/a	n/a
Avg.	110.71	95.11	103.74	2.61	37.48	32.03
Min.	33.60	62.55	54.63	1.89	17.00	11.44
Max.	195.97	153.93	225.79	3.59	71.88	58.64

Note: (1) Values for the local area are compared with the average, minimum and maximum values for all 291 areas in the Cost of Living Index; (2) Figures cover the Clarksville TN urban area; n/a not available; **Doctor** (general practitioners routine exam of an established patient); **Dentist** (adult teeth cleaning and periodic oral examination); **Optometrist** (full vision eye exam for established adult patient); **Gasoline** (one gallon regular unleaded, national brand, including all taxes, cash price at self-service pump if available); **Beauty Salon** (woman's shampoo, trim, and blow-dry); **Men's Shirt** (cotton/polyester dress shirt, pinpoint weave, long sleeves).
Source: The Council for Community and Economic Research, ACCRA Cost of Living Index, 2018

HOUSING

House Price Index (HPI)

Area	National Ranking[2]	Quarterly Change (%)	One-Year Change (%)	Five-Year Change (%)
MSA[1]	(a)	n/a	10.44	22.32
U.S.[3]	–	1.12	5.73	32.81

Note: The HPI is a weighted repeat sales index. It measures average price changes in repeat sales or refinancings on the same properties. This information is obtained by reviewing repeat mortgage transactions on single-family properties whose mortgages have been purchased or securitized by Fannie Mae or Freddie Mac in January 1975; (1) Figures cover the Clarksville, TN-KY Metropolitan Statistical Area—see Appendix B for areas included; (2) Rankings are based on annual percentage change for all metro areas containing at least 15,000 transactions over the last 10 years and ranges from 1 to 245; (3) figures based on a weighted average of Census Division estimates using a seasonally adjusted, purchase-only index; all figures are for the period ending December 31, 2018; n/a not available; (a) Not ranked because of increased index variability due to smaller sample size
Source: Federal Housing Finance Agency, House Price Index, February 26, 2019

Median Single-Family Home Prices

Area	2016	2017	2018[p]	Percent Change 2017 to 2018
MSA[1]	n/a	n/a	n/a	n/a
U.S. Average	235.5	248.8	261.6	5.1

Note: Figures are median sales prices of existing single-family homes in thousands of dollars; (p) preliminary; n/a not available; (1) Figures cover the Clarksville, TN-KY Metropolitan Statistical Area—see Appendix B for areas included
Source: National Association of Realtors, Median Sales Price of Existing Single-Family Homes for Metropolitan Areas, 4th Quarter 2018

Qualifying Income Based on Median Sales Price of Existing Single-Family Homes

Area	With 5% Down ($)	With 10% Down ($)	With 20% Down ($)
MSA[1]	n/a	n/a	n/a
U.S. Average	62,954	59,640	53,013

Note: Figures are preliminary; Qualifying income is based on a mortgage rate of 4.9%. Monthly principal and interest payment is limited to 25% of income; n/a not available; (1) Figures cover the Clarksville, TN-KY Metropolitan Statistical Area—see Appendix B for areas included
Source: National Association of Realtors, Qualifying Income Based on Median Sales Price of Existing Single-Family Homes for Metropolitan Areas, 4th Quarter 2018

Median Apartment Condo-Coop Home Prices

Area	2016	2017	2018[p]	Percent Change 2017 to 2018
MSA[1]	n/a	n/a	n/a	n/a
U.S. Average	220.7	234.3	241.0	2.9

Note: Figures are median sales prices of existing apartment condo-coop homes in thousands of dollars; (p) preliminary; n/a not available; (1) Figures cover the Clarksville, TN-KY Metropolitan Statistical Area—see Appendix B for areas included
Source: National Association of Realtors, Median Sales Price of Existing Apartment Condo-Coop Homes for Metropolitan Areas, 4th Quarter 2018

Home Value Distribution

Area	Under $50,000	$50,000 -$99,999	$100,000 -$149,999	$150,000 -$199,999	$200,000 -$299,999	$300,000 -$499,999	$500,000 -$999,999	$1,000,000 or more
City	5.3	18.7	29.9	25.7	15.3	4.3	0.5	0.3
MSA[1]	7.6	20.3	24.9	21.7	16.6	7.0	1.5	0.4
U.S.	8.3	13.9	14.7	14.6	18.7	17.3	9.7	2.7

Note: Figures are percentages and cover owner-occupied housing units; (1) Figures cover the Clarksville, TN-KY Metropolitan Statistical Area—see Appendix B for areas included
Source: U.S. Census Bureau, 2013-2017 American Community Survey 5-Year Estimates

Homeownership Rate

Area	2010 (%)	2011 (%)	2012 (%)	2013 (%)	2014 (%)	2015 (%)	2016 (%)	2017 (%)	2018 (%)
MSA[1]	n/a	n/a	n/a	n/a	n/a	n/a	n/a	n/a	n/a
U.S.	66.9	66.1	65.4	65.1	64.5	63.7	63.4	63.9	64.4

Note: (1) Figures cover the Clarksville, TN-KY Metropolitan Statistical Area—see Appendix B for areas included; n/a not available
Source: U.S. Census Bureau, Housing Vacancies and Homeownership Annual Statistics: 2010-2018

Year Housing Structure Built

Area	2010 or Later	2000 -2009	1990 -1999	1980 -1989	1970 -1979	1960 -1969	1950 -1959	1940 -1949	Before 1940	Median Year
City	11.0	24.6	21.2	12.0	12.5	9.2	5.0	2.1	2.3	1993
MSA[1]	8.6	21.9	20.2	11.3	15.5	10.4	6.0	2.5	3.6	1990
U.S.	3.2	14.5	14.0	13.6	15.5	10.8	10.5	5.1	12.9	1977

Note: Figures are percentages except for Median Year; Note: (1) Figures cover the Clarksville, TN-KY Metropolitan Statistical Area—see Appendix B for areas included
Source: U.S. Census Bureau, 2013-2017 American Community Survey 5-Year Estimates

Gross Monthly Rent

Area	Under $500	$500 -$999	$1,000 -$1,499	$1,500 -$1,999	$2,000 -$2,499	$2,500 -$2,999	$3,000 and up	Median ($)
City	6.2	51.2	34.3	6.5	1.7	0.1	0.1	930
MSA[1]	9.7	52.5	30.2	6.1	1.1	0.2	0.1	878
U.S.	10.5	41.1	28.7	11.7	4.5	1.8	1.7	982

Note: Figures are percentages except for Median; Gross rent is the contract rent plus the estimated average monthly cost of utilities (electricity, gas, and water and sewer) and fuels (oil, coal, kerosene, wood, etc.) if these are paid by the renter (or paid for the renter by someone else); (1) Figures cover the Clarksville, TN-KY Metropolitan Statistical Area—see Appendix B for areas included
Source: U.S. Census Bureau, 2013-2017 American Community Survey 5-Year Estimates

HEALTH

Health Risk Factors

Category	MSA[1] (%)	U.S. (%)
Adults aged 18–64 who have any kind of health care coverage	n/a	87.3
Adults who reported being in good or better health	n/a	82.4
Adults who have been told they have high blood cholesterol	n/a	33.0
Adults who have been told they have high blood pressure	n/a	32.3
Adults who are current smokers	n/a	17.1
Adults who currently use E-cigarettes	n/a	4.6
Adults who currently use chewing tobacco, snuff, or snus	n/a	4.0
Adults who are heavy drinkers[2]	n/a	6.3
Adults who are binge drinkers[3]	n/a	17.4
Adults who are overweight (BMI 25.0 - 29.9)	n/a	35.3
Adults who are obese (BMI 30.0 - 99.8)	n/a	31.3
Adults who participated in any physical activities in the past month	n/a	74.4
Adults who always or nearly always wears a seat belt	n/a	94.3

Note: n/a not available; (1) Figures cover the Clarksville, TN-KY Metropolitan Statistical Area—see Appendix B for areas included; (2) Heavy drinkers are classified as adult men having more than 14 drinks per week and adult women having more than 7 drinks per week; (3) Binge drinkers are classified as males having five or more drinks on one occasion or females having four or more drinks on one occasion
Source: Centers for Disease Control and Prevention, Behaviorial Risk Factor Surveillance System, SMART: Selected Metropolitan Area Risk Trends, 2017

Acute and Chronic Health Conditions

Category	MSA[1] (%)	U.S. (%)
Adults who have ever been told they had a heart attack	n/a	4.2
Adults who have ever been told they have angina or coronary heart disease	n/a	3.9
Adults who have ever been told they had a stroke	n/a	3.0
Adults who have ever been told they have asthma	n/a	14.2
Adults who have ever been told they have arthritis	n/a	24.9
Adults who have ever been told they have diabetes[2]	n/a	10.5
Adults who have ever been told they had skin cancer	n/a	6.2
Adults who have ever been told they had any other types of cancer	n/a	7.1
Adults who have ever been told they have COPD	n/a	6.5
Adults who have ever been told they have kidney disease	n/a	3.0
Adults who have ever been told they have a form of depression	n/a	20.5

Note: n/a not available; (1) Figures cover the Clarksville, TN-KY Metropolitan Statistical Area—see Appendix B for areas included; (2) Figures do not include pregnancy-related, borderline, or pre-diabetes
Source: Centers for Disease Control and Prevention, Behaviorial Risk Factor Surveillance System, SMART: Selected Metropolitan Area Risk Trends, 2017

Health Screening and Vaccination Rates

Category	MSA[1] (%)	U.S. (%)
Adults aged 65+ who have had flu shot within the past year	n/a	60.7
Adults aged 65+ who have ever had a pneumonia vaccination	n/a	75.4
Adults who have ever been tested for HIV	n/a	36.1
Adults who have ever had the shingles or zoster vaccine?	n/a	28.9
Adults who have had their blood cholesterol checked within the last five years	n/a	85.9

Note: n/a not available; (1) Figures cover the Clarksville, TN-KY Metropolitan Statistical Area—see Appendix B for areas included.
Source: Centers for Disease Control and Prevention, Behaviorial Risk Factor Surveillance System, SMART: Selected Metropolitan Area Risk Trends, 2017

Disability Status

Category	MSA[1] (%)	U.S. (%)
Adults who reported being deaf	n/a	6.7
Are you blind or have serious difficulty seeing, even when wearing glasses?	n/a	4.5
Are you limited in any way in any of your usual activities due of arthritis?	n/a	12.9
Do you have difficulty doing errands alone?	n/a	6.8
Do you have difficulty dressing or bathing?	n/a	3.6
Do you have serious difficulty concentrating/remembering/making decisions?	n/a	10.7
Do you have serious difficulty walking or climbing stairs?	n/a	13.6

Note: n/a not available; (1) Figures cover the Clarksville, TN-KY Metropolitan Statistical Area—see Appendix B for areas included.
Source: Centers for Disease Control and Prevention, Behaviorial Risk Factor Surveillance System, SMART: Selected Metropolitan Area Risk Trends, 2017

Mortality Rates for the Top 10 Causes of Death in the U.S.

ICD-10[a] Sub-Chapter	ICD-10[a] Code	Age-Adjusted Mortality Rate[1] per 100,000 population	
		County[2]	U.S.
Malignant neoplasms	C00-C97	178.5	155.5
Ischaemic heart diseases	I20-I25	118.1	94.8
Other forms of heart disease	I30-I51	45.0	52.9
Chronic lower respiratory diseases	J40-J47	78.6	41.0
Cerebrovascular diseases	I60-I69	53.0	37.5
Other degenerative diseases of the nervous system	G30-G31	46.2	35.0
Other external causes of accidental injury	W00-X59	42.5	33.7
Organic, including symptomatic, mental disorders	F01-F09	35.3	31.0
Hypertensive diseases	I10-I15	26.5	21.9
Diabetes mellitus	E10-E14	29.7	21.2

Note: (a) ICD-10 = International Classification of Diseases 10th Revision; (1) Mortality rates are a three year average covering 2015-2017; (2) Figures cover Montgomery County.
Source: Centers for Disease Control and Prevention, National Center for Health Statistics. Underlying Cause of Death 1999-2017 on CDC WONDER Online Database

Mortality Rates for Selected Causes of Death

ICD-10[a] Sub-Chapter	ICD-10[a] Code	Age-Adjusted Mortality Rate[1] per 100,000 population	
		County[2]	U.S.
Assault	X85-Y09	7.4	5.9
Diseases of the liver	K70-K76	17.3	14.1
Human immunodeficiency virus (HIV) disease	B20-B24	Suppressed	1.8
Influenza and pneumonia	J09-J18	14.7	14.3
Intentional self-harm	X60-X84	20.1	13.6
Malnutrition	E40-E46	Suppressed	1.6
Obesity and other hyperalimentation	E65-E68	5.2	2.1
Renal failure	N17-N19	10.1	13.0
Transport accidents	V01-V99	14.9	12.4
Viral hepatitis	B15-B19	Suppressed	1.6

Note: (a) ICD-10 = International Classification of Diseases 10th Revision; (1) Mortality rates are a three year average covering 2015-2017; (2) Figures cover Montgomery County; Data are suppressed when the data meet the criteria for confidentiality constraints; Mortality rates are flagged as unreliable when the rate would be calculated with a numerator of 20 or less.
Source: Centers for Disease Control and Prevention, National Center for Health Statistics. Underlying Cause of Death 1999-2017 on CDC WONDER Online Database

Health Insurance Coverage

Area	With Health Insurance	With Private Health Insurance	With Public Health Insurance	Without Health Insurance	Population Under Age 18 Without Health Insurance
City	90.4	72.6	30.5	9.6	3.5
MSA[1]	90.1	69.3	33.8	9.9	5.6
U.S.	89.5	67.2	33.8	10.5	5.7

Note: Figures are percentages that cover the civilian noninstitutionalized population; (1) Figures cover the Clarksville, TN-KY Metropolitan Statistical Area—see Appendix B for areas included
Source: U.S. Census Bureau, 2013-2017 American Community Survey 5-Year Estimates

Number of Medical Professionals

Area	MDs[3]	DOs[3,4]	Dentists	Podiatrists	Chiropractors	Optometrists
County[1] (number)	199	35	90	5	31	26
County[1] (rate[2])	102.2	18.0	45.0	2.5	15.5	13.0
U.S. (rate[2])	279.3	23.0	68.4	6.0	27.1	16.2

Note: Data as of 2017 unless noted; (1) Data covers Montgomery County; (2) Rate per 100,000 population; (3) Data as of 2016 and includes all active, non-federal physicians; (4) Doctor of Osteopathic Medicine
Source: U.S. Department of Health and Human Services, Health Resources and Services Administration, Bureau of Health Professions, Area Resource File (ARF) 2017-2018

EDUCATION

Public School District Statistics

District Name	Schls	Pupils	Pupil/ Teacher Ratio	Minority Pupils[1] (%)	Free Lunch Eligible[2] (%)	IEP[3] (%)
Montgomery County	39	33,541	16.1	45.5	n/a	13.6

Note: Table includes school districts with 2,000 or more students; (1) Percentage of students that are not non-Hispanic white; (2) Percentage of students that are eligible for the free lunch program; (3) Percentage of students that have an Individualized Education Program.
Source: U.S. Department of Education, National Center for Education Statistics, Common Core of Data, Local Education Agency (School District) Universe Survey: School Year 2016-2017; U.S. Department of Education, National Center for Education Statistics, Common Core of Data, Public Elementary/Secondary School Universe Survey: School Year 2016-2017

Highest Level of Education

Area	Less than H.S.	H.S. Diploma	Some College, No Deg.	Associate Degree	Bachelor's Degree	Master's Degree	Prof. School Degree	Doctorate Degree
City	7.9	28.2	28.8	9.6	17.7	6.3	0.7	0.7
MSA[1]	10.1	30.4	26.8	9.3	15.4	6.3	1.0	0.7
U.S.	12.7	27.3	20.8	8.3	19.1	8.4	2.0	1.4

Note: Figures cover persons age 25 and over; (1) Figures cover the Clarksville, TN-KY Metropolitan Statistical Area—see Appendix B for areas included
Source: U.S. Census Bureau, 2013-2017 American Community Survey 5-Year Estimates

Educational Attainment by Race

Area	High School Graduate or Higher (%)					Bachelor's Degree or Higher (%)				
	Total	White	Black	Asian	Hisp.[2]	Total	White	Black	Asian	Hisp.[2]
City	92.1	92.6	91.6	81.2	86.4	25.5	26.7	21.4	27.6	16.9
MSA[1]	89.9	90.3	89.1	79.7	85.3	23.4	24.1	19.4	32.8	16.3
U.S.	87.3	89.3	84.9	86.5	66.7	30.9	32.2	20.6	52.7	15.2

Note: Figures shown cover persons 25 years old and over; (1) Figures cover the Clarksville, TN-KY Metropolitan Statistical Area—see Appendix B for areas included; (2) People of Hispanic origin can be of any race
Source: U.S. Census Bureau, 2013-2017 American Community Survey 5-Year Estimates

School Enrollment by Grade and Control

Area	Preschool (%)		Kindergarten (%)		Grades 1 - 4 (%)		Grades 5 - 8 (%)		Grades 9 - 12 (%)	
	Public	Private	Public	Private	Public	Private	Public	Private	Public	Private
City	63.0	37.0	95.1	4.9	94.1	5.9	96.0	4.0	94.9	5.1
MSA[1]	69.0	31.0	94.3	5.7	91.3	8.7	92.1	7.9	91.6	8.4
U.S.	58.8	41.2	87.7	12.3	89.7	10.3	89.6	10.4	90.3	9.7

Note: Figures shown cover persons 3 years old and over; (1) Figures cover the Clarksville, TN-KY Metropolitan Statistical Area—see Appendix B for areas included
Source: U.S. Census Bureau, 2013-2017 American Community Survey 5-Year Estimates

Average Salaries of Public School Classroom Teachers

Area	2016		2017		Change from 2016 to 2017	
	Dollars	Rank[1]	Dollars	Rank[1]	Percent	Rank[2]
Tennessee	48,817	36	50,099	36	2.6	12
U.S. Average	58,479	–	59,660	–	2.0	–

Note: (1) Rank ranges from 1 to 51 where 1 indicates highest salary; (2) Rank ranges from 1 to 51 where 1 indicates highest percent change.
Source: National Education Association, Rankings & Estimates: Rankings of the States 2017 and Estimates of School Statistics 2018

Higher Education

Four-Year Colleges			Two-Year Colleges			Medical Schools[1]	Law Schools[2]	Voc/ Tech[3]
Public	Private Non-profit	Private For-profit	Public	Private Non-profit	Private For-profit			
1	0	1	0	0	2	0	0	2

Note: Figures cover institutions located within the city limits and include main campuses only; (1) includes schools accredited by the Liaison Committee on Medical Education and the American Osteopathic Association's Commission on Osteopathic College Accreditation; (2) includes ABA-accredited schools, schools with provisional ABA accreditation, and state accredited schools; (3) includes all schools with programs that are less than 2 years.
Source: National Center for Education Statistics, Integrated Postsecondary Education System (IPEDS), 2017-18; Wikipedia, List of Medical Schools in the United States, accessed April 3, 2019; Wikipedia, List of Law Schools in the United States, accessed April 3, 2019

PRESIDENTIAL ELECTION

2016 Presidential Election Results

Area	Clinton	Trump	Johnson	Stein	Other
Montgomery County	37.7	56.1	4.1	0.9	1.2
U.S.	48.0	45.9	3.3	1.1	1.7

Note: Results are percentages and may not add to 100% due to rounding
Source: Dave Leip's Atlas of U.S. Presidential Elections

EMPLOYERS

Major Employers

Company Name	Industry
Agero	Call center
Akebono	Hubs, rotors
AT&T	Engineering services
Austin Peay State University	University
Bridgestone Metalpha U.S.A.	Steel tire cords & tire cord fabrics
City of Clarksville	Government
Clarksville-Montgomery School System	Education
Gateway Medical Center	General medical & surgical hospitals
Jennie Stuart Medical Center	General medical & surgical hospitals
Jostens	Yearbooks & commercial printing
Montgomery County Government	Government
Trane Company	Heating & air conditioners
Trigg County Board of Education	Elementary & secondary schools
U.S. Army	U.S. military
U.S. Army	General medical & surgical hospitals
Wal-Mart Stores	Department stores, discount

Note: Companies shown are located within the Clarksville, TN-KY Metropolitan Statistical Area.
Source: Hoovers.com; Wikipedia

PUBLIC SAFETY

Crime Rate

Area	All Crimes	Violent Crimes				Property Crimes		
		Murder	Rape[3]	Robbery	Aggrav. Assault	Burglary	Larceny -Theft	Motor Vehicle Theft
City	3,501.1	9.1	52.2	82.8	479.5	484.7	2,235.6	157.2
Suburbs[1]	2,159.1	0.8	31.5	36.8	112.6	490.2	1,352.8	134.4
Metro[2]	2,877.1	5.2	42.6	61.4	308.9	487.3	1,825.1	146.6
U.S.	2,756.1	5.3	41.7	98.0	248.9	430.4	1,694.4	237.4

Note: Figures are crimes per 100,000 population; (1) All areas within the metro area that are located outside the city limits; (2) Figures cover the Clarksville, TN-KY Metropolitan Statistical Area—see Appendix B for areas included; (3) The city and U.S. figures shown were reported using the revised Uniform Crime Reporting (UCR) definition of rape. The suburban and metro area figures shown are an aggregate total of the data submitted using both the revised and legacy UCR definitions.
Source: FBI Uniform Crime Reports, 2017

Hate Crimes

Area	Number of Quarters Reported	Number of Incidents per Bias Motivation					
		Race/Ethnicity/ Ancestry	Religion	Sexual Orientation	Disability	Gender	Gender Identity
City	4	2	0	2	0	0	0
U.S.	4	4,131	1,564	1,130	116	46	119

Source: Federal Bureau of Investigation, Hate Crime Statistics 2017

Identity Theft Consumer Reports

Area	Reports	Reports per 100,000 Population	Rank[2]
MSA[1]	222	79	230
U.S.	444,602	135	-

Note: (1) Figures cover the Clarksville, TN-KY Metropolitan Statistical Area—see Appendix B for areas included; (2) Rank ranges from 1 to 389 where 1 indicates greatest number of identity theft reports per 100,000 population
Source: Federal Trade Commission, Consumer Sentinel Network Data Book for January–December 2018

Fraud and Other Consumer Reports

Area	Reports	Reports per 100,000 Population	Rank[2]
MSA[1]	1,564	554	100
U.S.	2,552,917	776	-

Note: (1) Figures cover the Clarksville, TN-KY Metropolitan Statistical Area—see Appendix B for areas included; (2) Rank ranges from 1 to 389 where 1 indicates greatest number of fraud and other consumer reports per 100,000 population
Source: Federal Trade Commission, Consumer Sentinel Network Data Book for January–December 2018

SPORTS

Professional Sports Teams

Team Name	League	Year Established
No teams are located in the metro area
Source: Wikipedia, Major Professional Sports Teams of the United States and Canada, April 5, 2019

CLIMATE

Average and Extreme Temperatures

Temperature	Jan	Feb	Mar	Apr	May	Jun	Jul	Aug	Sep	Oct	Nov	Dec	Yr.
Extreme High (°F)	78	84	86	91	95	106	107	104	105	94	84	79	107
Average High (°F)	47	51	60	71	79	87	90	89	83	72	60	50	70
Average Temp. (°F)	38	41	50	60	68	76	80	79	72	61	49	41	60
Average Low (°F)	28	31	39	48	57	65	69	68	61	48	39	31	49
Extreme Low (°F)	-17	-13	2	23	34	42	54	49	36	26	-1	-10	-17

Note: Figures cover the years 1948-1990
Source: National Climatic Data Center, International Station Meteorological Climate Summary, 9/96

Average Precipitation/Snowfall/Humidity

Precip./Humidity	Jan	Feb	Mar	Apr	May	Jun	Jul	Aug	Sep	Oct	Nov	Dec	Yr.
Avg. Precip. (in.)	4.4	4.2	5.0	4.1	4.6	3.7	3.8	3.3	3.2	2.6	3.9	4.6	47.4
Avg. Snowfall (in.)	4	3	1	Tr	0	0	0	0	0	Tr	1	1	11
Avg. Rel. Hum. 6am (%)	81	81	80	81	86	86	88	90	90	87	83	82	85
Avg. Rel. Hum. 3pm (%)	61	57	51	48	52	52	54	53	52	49	55	59	54

Note: Figures cover the years 1948-1990; Tr = Trace amounts (<0.05 in. of rain; <0.5 in. of snow)
Source: National Climatic Data Center, International Station Meteorological Climate Summary, 9/96

Weather Conditions

Temperature			Daytime Sky			Precipitation		
10°F & below	32°F & below	90°F & above	Clear	Partly cloudy	Cloudy	0.01 inch or more precip.	0.1 inch or more snow/ice	Thunder-storms
5	76	51	98	135	132	119	8	54

Note: Figures are average number of days per year and cover the years 1948-1990
Source: National Climatic Data Center, International Station Meteorological Climate Summary, 9/96

HAZARDOUS WASTE

Superfund Sites

The Clarksville, TN-KY metro area has no sites on the EPA's Superfund Final National Priorities List. There are a total of 1,390 Superfund sites with a status of proposed or final on the list in the U.S. *U.S. Environmental Protection Agency, National Priorities List, April 5, 2019*

AIR & WATER QUALITY

Air Quality Trends: Ozone

	1990	1995	2000	2005	2010	2012	2014	2015	2016	2017
MSA[1]	n/a	n/a	n/a	n/a	n/a	n/a	n/a	n/a	n/a	n/a
U.S.	0.088	0.089	0.082	0.080	0.073	0.075	0.067	0.068	0.069	0.068

Note: (1) Data covers the Clarksville, TN-KY Metropolitan Statistical Area—see Appendix B for areas included; n/a not available. The values shown are the composite ozone concentration averages among trend sites based on the highest fourth daily maximum 8-hour concentration in parts per million. These trends are based on sites having an adequate record of monitoring data during the trend period. Data from exceptional events are included.
Source: U.S. Environmental Protection Agency, Air Quality Monitoring Information, "Air Quality Trends by City, 1990-2017"

Air Quality Index

Area	Percent of Days when Air Quality was...[2]					AQI Statistics[2]	
	Good	Moderate	Unhealthy for Sensitive Groups	Unhealthy	Very Unhealthy	Maximum	Median
MSA[1]	82.0	18.0	0.0	0.0	0.0	87	42

Note: (1) Data covers the Clarksville, TN-KY Metropolitan Statistical Area—see Appendix B for areas included; (2) Based on 362 days with AQI data in 2017. Air Quality Index (AQI) is an index for reporting daily air quality. EPA calculates the AQI for five major air pollutants regulated by the Clean Air Act: ground-level ozone, particle pollution (aka particulate matter), carbon monoxide, sulfur dioxide, and nitrogen dioxide. The AQI runs from 0 to 500. The higher the AQI value, the greater the level of air pollution and the greater the health concern. There are six AQI categories: "Good" AQI is between 0 and 50. Air quality is considered satisfactory; "Moderate" AQI is between 51 and 100. Air quality is acceptable; "Unhealthy for Sensitive Groups" When AQI values are between 101 and 150, members of sensitive groups may experience health effects; "Unhealthy" When AQI values are between 151 and 200 everyone may begin to experience health effects; "Very Unhealthy" AQI values between 201 and 300 trigger a health alert; "Hazardous" AQI values over 300 trigger warnings of emergency conditions (not shown).
Source: U.S. Environmental Protection Agency, Air Quality Index Report, 2017

Air Quality Index Pollutants

Area	Percent of Days when AQI Pollutant was...[2]					
	Carbon Monoxide	Nitrogen Dioxide	Ozone	Sulfur Dioxide	Particulate Matter 2.5	Particulate Matter 10
MSA[1]	0.0	0.0	63.0	0.0	37.0	0.0

Note: (1) Data covers the Clarksville, TN-KY Metropolitan Statistical Area—see Appendix B for areas included; (2) Based on 362 days with AQI data in 2017. The Air Quality Index (AQI) is an index for reporting daily air quality. EPA calculates the AQI for five major air pollutants regulated by the Clean Air Act: ground-level ozone, particle pollution (also known as particulate matter), carbon monoxide, sulfur dioxide, and nitrogen dioxide. The AQI runs from 0 to 500. The higher the AQI value, the greater the level of air pollution and the greater the health concern.
Source: U.S. Environmental Protection Agency, Air Quality Index Report, 2017

Maximum Air Pollutant Concentrations: Particulate Matter, Ozone, CO and Lead

	Particulate Matter 10 (ug/m^3)	Particulate Matter 2.5 Wtd AM (ug/m^3)	Particulate Matter 2.5 24-Hr (ug/m^3)	Ozone (ppm)	Carbon Monoxide (ppm)	Lead (ug/m^3)
MSA[1] Level	n/a	8.2	17	0.062	n/a	n/a
NAAQS[2]	150	15	35	0.075	9	0.15
Met NAAQS[2]	n/a	Yes	Yes	Yes	n/a	n/a

Note: (1) Data covers the Clarksville, TN-KY Metropolitan Statistical Area—see Appendix B for areas included; Data from exceptional events are included; (2) National Ambient Air Quality Standards; ppm = parts per million; ug/m^3 = micrograms per cubic meter; n/a not available.
Concentrations: Particulate Matter 10 (coarse particulate)—highest second maximum 24-hour concentration; Particulate Matter 2.5 Wtd AM (fine particulate)—highest weighted annual mean concentration; Particulate Matter 2.5 24-Hour (fine particulate)—highest 98th percentile 24-hour concentration; Ozone—highest fourth daily maximum 8-hour concentration; Carbon Monoxide—highest second maximum non-overlapping 8-hour concentration; Lead—maximum running 3-month average
Source: U.S. Environmental Protection Agency, Air Quality Monitoring Information, "Air Quality Statistics by City, 2017"

Maximum Air Pollutant Concentrations: Nitrogen Dioxide and Sulfur Dioxide

	Nitrogen Dioxide AM (ppb)	Nitrogen Dioxide 1-Hr (ppb)	Sulfur Dioxide AM (ppb)	Sulfur Dioxide 1-Hr (ppb)	Sulfur Dioxide 24-Hr (ppb)
MSA[1] Level	n/a	n/a	n/a	n/a	n/a
NAAQS[2]	53	100	30	75	140
Met NAAQS[2]	n/a	n/a	n/a	n/a	n/a

Note: (1) Data covers the Clarksville, TN-KY Metropolitan Statistical Area—see Appendix B for areas included; Data from exceptional events are included; (2) National Ambient Air Quality Standards; ppm = parts per million; ug/m^3 = micrograms per cubic meter; n/a not available.
Concentrations: Nitrogen Dioxide AM—highest arithmetic mean concentration; Nitrogen Dioxide 1-Hr—highest 98th percentile 1-hour daily maximum concentration; Sulfur Dioxide AM—highest annual mean concentration; Sulfur Dioxide 1-Hr—highest 99th percentile 1-hour daily maximum concentration; Sulfur Dioxide 24-Hr—highest second maximum 24-hour concentration
Source: U.S. Environmental Protection Agency, Air Quality Monitoring Information, "Air Quality Statistics by City, 2017"

Drinking Water

Water System Name	Pop. Served	Primary Water Source Type	Violations[1]	
			Health Based	Monitoring/ Reporting
Clarksville Water Department	206,500	Surface	0	0

Note: (1) Based on violation data from January 1, 2018 to December 31, 2018
Source: U.S. Environmental Protection Agency, Office of Ground Water and Drinking Water, Safe Drinking Water Information System (based on data extracted April 5, 2019)

College Station, Texas

Background

College Station is located 367 feet above sea level in the center of the Texas Triangle within Brazos County, and shares a border with the city of Bryan to the northwest. Named the most educated city in Texas, College Station was built alongside the prestigious Texas A&M University during the nation's centennial in 1876. The city's origins date back to 1860, when Houston and Texas Central Railway began to build through the region during the height of railroad expansion in the mid-1800s. Though this railway no longer exists, College Station's location and the university make it important to the state.

Although College Station has always been upheld by Texas A&M, the city was not incorporated until 1938. In 1942, the so-called "Father of College Station," Mayor Ernest Langford, gave the community its own, unique identity over his 26-year run. During Langford's first term, the city also adopted a council-manager system of government.

College Station is comprised of three major districts. Northgate, Wolf Pen Creek District, and Wellborn District combine to create a bustling city populated by students, professors, and their families. The city's population is young, mostly comprised of college-age individuals.

The economy of the city largely relies on the university itself, with many of its employees doing double time both attending the school and working in the city's shops or restaurants. Unemployment was among the lowest in Texas in recent years; however, underemployment continues to be an issue among the overqualified college students. Post Oak Mall provides much of the business within College Station, being the first to have opened in the area and the largest mall in Brazos Valley. Over 75 percent of retail sales in the Brazos Valley are within this mall.

The largest employer of the city is Texas A&M University. Previously known as the Agricultural and Mechanical College of Texas, TAMU is known for its triple designation as a Land-, Sea-, and Space-Grant institution, housing ongoing research projects funded by the likes of NASA, the National Institutes of Health, and the National Science Foundation.

The city's nightlife and entertainment attract its young crowd to events such as the four-day Northgate Music Festival and the live music at Church Street BBQ and Hurricane Harry's. The Texas country music scene thrives here, with many notable musicians getting their starts at these smaller stages. Among them are Robert Earl Keen, Grammy-award winner Lyle Lovett, and Roger Creager.

Alongside these celebrities are important landmarks and areas within College Station, as well. These include Church Street, made famous by the Lyle Lovett/Robert Earl Keen duet "The Front Porch Song," and the George Bush Presidential Library, which was dedicated in 1997 in honor of President George H.W. Bush. The population and popularity of this relatively small city continues to grow every year, with predictions of the population doubling by the year 2030.

With the climate sitting comfortably in the subtropical and temperate zone, College Station enjoys mild winters with its low-temperature period lasting less than two months. Snow and ice during that time are very rare, while in turn the summers are hot. During these summers, occasional rain showers are the only variation in weather. The city's average temperature is 69 degrees with annual rainfall averaging 39 inches.

Rankings

General Rankings

- In their sixth annual survey, Livability.com looked at data for more than 1,000 U.S. cities to determine the rankings for Livability's "Top 100 Best Places to Live" in 2019. College Station ranked #79. Criteria: median home value capped at $250,000; affordable living; vibrant economy; education, demographics, health care options. transportation & infrastructure; abundant lifestyle amenities. *Livability.com, "Top 100 Best Places to Live 2019" March 2019*

Business/Finance Rankings

- Metro areas with the largest gap in income between rich and poor residents were identified by 24/7 Wall Street using the U.S. Census Bureau's 2013 American Community Survey. The College Station metro area placed #6 among metro areas with the widest wealth gap between rich and poor. *247wallst.com, "20 Cities with the Widest Gap between the Rich and Poor," July 8, 2015*

- The College Station metro area appeared on the Milken Institute "2018 Best Performing Cities" list. Rank: #22 out of 201 small metro areas. Criteria: job growth; wage and salary growth; high-tech output growth. *Milken Institute, "Best-Performing Cities 2018," January 24, 2019*

- *Forbes* ranked 200 smaller metro areas (population under 265,400) to determine the nation's "Best Small Places for Business and Careers." The College Station metro area was ranked #3. Criteria: costs (business and living); job growth (past and projected); income growth; quality of life; educational attainment (college and high school); projected economic growth; cultural and recreational opportunities; net migration patterns; number of highly ranked colleges. *Forbes, "The Best Small Cities for Business and Careers 2018," October, 24 2018*

Real Estate Rankings

- College Station was ranked #146 out of 237 metro areas in terms of housing affordability in 2018 by the National Association of Home Builders (#1 = most affordable). Criteria: the share of homes sold in that area affordable to a family earning the local median income, based on standard mortgage underwriting criteria. *National Association of Home Builders®, NAHB-Wells Fargo Housing Opportunity Index, 4th Quarter 2018*

Safety Rankings

- The National Insurance Crime Bureau ranked 382 metro areas in the U.S. in terms of per capita rates of vehicle theft. The College Station metro area ranked #272 (#1 = highest rate). Criteria: number of vehicle theft offenses per 100,000 inhabitants in 2017. *National Insurance Crime Bureau, "Hot Spots 2017," July 12, 2018*

Seniors/Retirement Rankings

- From its Best Cities for Successful Aging indexes, the Milken Institute generated rankings for metropolitan areas, weighing data in nine categories—health care, wellness, living arrangements, transportation and convenience, financial characteristics, education, employment, community engagement, and overall livability. The College Station metro area was ranked #28 overall in the small metro area category. *Milken Institute, "Best Cities for Successful Aging, 2017" March 14, 2017*

Business Environment

CITY FINANCES

City Government Finances

Component	2016 ($000)	2016 ($ per capita)
Total Revenues	225,920	2,094
Total Expenditures	188,883	1,751
Debt Outstanding	260,646	2,416
Cash and Securities[1]	160,475	1,487

Note: (1) Cash and security holdings of a government at the close of its fiscal year, including those of its dependent agencies, utilities, and liquor stores.
Source: U.S. Census Bureau, State & Local Government Finances 2016

City Government Revenue by Source

Source	2016 ($000)	2016 ($ per capita)	2016 (%)
General Revenue			
From Federal Government	2,188	20	1.0
From State Government	1,048	10	0.5
From Local Governments	88	1	0.0
Taxes			
Property	29,849	277	13.2
Sales and Gross Receipts	34,679	321	15.4
Personal Income	0	0	0.0
Corporate Income	0	0	0.0
Motor Vehicle License	0	0	0.0
Other Taxes	1,466	14	0.6
Current Charges	31,439	291	13.9
Liquor Store	0	0	0.0
Utility	115,865	1,074	51.3
Employee Retirement	0	0	0.0

Source: U.S. Census Bureau, State & Local Government Finances 2016

City Government Expenditures by Function

Function	2016 ($000)	2016 ($ per capita)	2016 (%)
General Direct Expenditures			
Air Transportation	0	0	0.0
Corrections	0	0	0.0
Education	0	0	0.0
Employment Security Administration	0	0	0.0
Financial Administration	2,530	23	1.3
Fire Protection	11,566	107	6.1
General Public Buildings	1,706	15	0.9
Governmental Administration, Other	8,180	75	4.3
Health	0	0	0.0
Highways	11,358	105	6.0
Hospitals	0	0	0.0
Housing and Community Development	967	9	0.5
Interest on General Debt	1,792	16	0.9
Judicial and Legal	1,894	17	1.0
Libraries	1,139	10	0.6
Parking	706	6	0.4
Parks and Recreation	9,359	86	5.0
Police Protection	14,197	131	7.5
Public Welfare	0	0	0.0
Sewerage	10,279	95	5.4
Solid Waste Management	7,793	72	4.1
Veterans' Services	0	0	0.0
Liquor Store	0	0	0.0
Utility	97,954	907	51.9
Employee Retirement	0	0	0.0

Source: U.S. Census Bureau, State & Local Government Finances 2016

DEMOGRAPHICS

Population Growth

Area	1990 Census	2000 Census	2010 Census	2017* Estimate	Population Growth (%) 1990-2017	Population Growth (%) 2010-2017
City	53,318	67,890	93,857	107,445	101.5	14.5
MSA[1]	150,998	184,885	228,660	248,554	64.6	8.7
U.S.	248,709,873	281,421,906	308,745,538	321,004,407	29.1	4.0

Note: (1) Figures cover the College Station-Bryan, TX Metropolitan Statistical Area—see Appendix B for areas included; (*) 2013-2017 5-year estimated population
Source: U.S. Census Bureau, 1990 Census, Census 2000, Census 2010, 2013-2017 American Community Survey 5-Year Estimates

Household Size

Area	Persons in Household (%) One	Two	Three	Four	Five	Six	Seven or More	Average Household Size
City	29.1	34.2	16.2	14.8	3.6	1.6	0.6	2.50
MSA[1]	27.4	34.0	16.3	13.6	5.2	2.3	1.2	2.60
U.S.	27.7	33.8	15.7	13.0	6.0	2.3	1.4	2.60

Note: (1) Figures cover the College Station-Bryan, TX Metropolitan Statistical Area—see Appendix B for areas included
Source: U.S. Census Bureau, 2013-2017 American Community Survey 5-Year Estimates

Race

Area	White Alone[2] (%)	Black Alone[2] (%)	Asian Alone[2] (%)	AIAN[3] Alone[2] (%)	NHOPI[4] Alone[2] (%)	Other Race Alone[2] (%)	Two or More Races (%)
City	77.5	8.1	9.8	0.3	0.0	1.7	2.5
MSA[1]	75.2	11.2	5.2	0.4	0.0	5.0	2.9
U.S.	73.0	12.7	5.4	0.8	0.2	4.8	3.1

Note: (1) Figures cover the College Station-Bryan, TX Metropolitan Statistical Area—see Appendix B for areas included; (2) Alone is defined as not being in combination with one or more other races; (3) American Indian and Alaska Native; (4) Native Hawaiian and Other Pacific Islander
Source: U.S. Census Bureau, 2013-2017 American Community Survey 5-Year Estimates

Hispanic or Latino Origin

Area	Total (%)	Mexican (%)	Puerto Rican (%)	Cuban (%)	Other (%)
City	14.8	11.0	0.4	0.4	3.1
MSA[1]	24.4	21.0	0.2	0.2	3.0
U.S.	17.6	11.1	1.7	0.7	4.1

Note: Persons of Hispanic or Latino origin can be of any race; (1) Figures cover the College Station-Bryan, TX Metropolitan Statistical Area—see Appendix B for areas included
Source: U.S. Census Bureau, 2013-2017 American Community Survey 5-Year Estimates

Segregation

Type	Segregation Indices[1] 1990	2000	2010	2010 Rank[2]	Percent Change 1990-2000	1990-2010	2000-2010
Black/White	n/a	n/a	n/a	n/a	n/a	n/a	n/a
Asian/White	n/a	n/a	n/a	n/a	n/a	n/a	n/a
Hispanic/White	n/a	n/a	n/a	n/a	n/a	n/a	n/a

Note: All figures cover the Metropolitan Statistical Area—see Appendix B for areas included; Figures are based on an analysis of 1990, 2000, and 2010 Census Decennial Census tract data by William H. Frey, Brookings Institution and the University of Michigan Social Science Data Analysis Network. In this analysis all racial groups (whites, blacks, and asians) are non-Hispanic members of those races. Hispanics are shown as a separate category; (1) Segregation Indices are Dissimilarity Indices that measure the degree to which the minority group is distributed differently than whites across census tracts. They range from 0 (complete integration) to 100 (complete segregation) where the value indicates the percentage of the minority group that needs to move to be distributed exactly like whites; (2) Ranges from 1 (most segregated) to 102 (least segregated); n/a not available.
Source: www.CensusScope.org

Ancestry

Area	German	Irish	English	American	Italian	Polish	French[2]	Scottish	Dutch
City	17.8	9.4	8.9	3.6	3.5	2.7	3.5	2.8	0.8
MSA[1]	14.9	8.7	7.5	4.2	2.8	2.1	2.7	2.2	0.7
U.S.	14.1	10.1	7.5	6.6	5.3	2.9	2.5	1.7	1.3

Note: Figures are the percentage of the total population reporting a particular ancestry. The nine most commonly reported ancestries in the U.S. are shown. Figures include multiple ancestries (e.g. if a person reported being Irish and Italian, they were included in both columns); (1) Figures cover the College Station-Bryan, TX Metropolitan Statistical Area—see Appendix B for areas included; (2) Excludes Basque
Source: U.S. Census Bureau, 2013-2017 American Community Survey 5-Year Estimates

Foreign-Born Population

Area	Percent of Population Born in								
	Any Foreign Country	Asia	Mexico	Europe	Carribean	Central America[2]	South America	Africa	Canada
City	12.8	7.4	1.8	1.0	0.1	0.6	1.0	0.7	0.3
MSA[1]	12.4	4.0	5.7	0.7	0.1	0.6	0.5	0.5	0.2
U.S.	13.4	4.1	3.6	1.5	1.3	1.0	0.9	0.6	0.3

Note: (1) Figures cover the College Station-Bryan, TX Metropolitan Statistical Area—see Appendix B for areas included; (2) Excludes Mexico.
Source: U.S. Census Bureau, 2013-2017 American Community Survey 5-Year Estimates

Marital Status

Area	Never Married	Now Married[2]	Separated	Widowed	Divorced
City	61.1	30.8	0.9	2.1	5.1
MSA[1]	46.5	39.4	2.1	4.1	8.0
U.S.	33.1	48.2	2.0	5.8	10.9

Note: Figures are percentages and cover the population 15 years of age and older; (1) Figures cover the College Station-Bryan, TX Metropolitan Statistical Area—see Appendix B for areas included; (2) Excludes separated
Source: U.S. Census Bureau, 2013-2017 American Community Survey 5-Year Estimates

Disability by Age

Area	All Ages	Under 18 Years Old	18 to 64 Years Old	65 Years and Over
City	6.0	3.2	4.6	31.5
MSA[1]	9.4	3.9	7.1	38.2
U.S.	12.6	4.2	10.3	35.5

Note: Figures show percent of the civilian noninstitutionalized population that reported having a disability. Disability status is determined from six types of difficulty: vision, hearing, cognitive, ambulatory, self-care, and independent living. For children under 5 years old, hearing and vision difficulty are used to determine disability status. For children between the ages of 5 and 14, disability status is determined from hearing, vision, cognitive, ambulatory, and self-care difficulties. For people aged 15 years and older, they are considered to have a disability if they have difficulty with any one of the six difficulty types; Note: (1) Figures cover the College Station-Bryan, TX Metropolitan Statistical Area—see Appendix B for areas included
Source: U.S. Census Bureau, 2013-2017 American Community Survey 5-Year Estimates

Age

Area	Percent of Population									Median Age
	Under Age 5	Age 5–19	Age 20–34	Age 35–44	Age 45–54	Age 55–64	Age 65–74	Age 75–84	Age 85+	
City	5.3	22.7	44.7	8.7	6.9	5.8	3.7	1.6	0.7	22.7
MSA[1]	6.2	20.9	33.8	10.5	9.7	8.9	5.8	2.8	1.3	27.2
U.S.	6.2	19.5	20.7	12.7	13.4	12.7	8.6	4.4	1.9	37.8

Note: (1) Figures cover the College Station-Bryan, TX Metropolitan Statistical Area—see Appendix B for areas included
Source: U.S. Census Bureau, 2013-2017 American Community Survey 5-Year Estimates

Gender

Area	Males	Females	Males per 100 Females
City	54,425	53,020	102.6
MSA[1]	125,550	123,004	102.1
U.S.	158,018,753	162,985,654	97.0

Note: (1) Figures cover the College Station-Bryan, TX Metropolitan Statistical Area—see Appendix B for areas included
Source: U.S. Census Bureau, 2013-2017 American Community Survey 5-Year Estimates

Religious Groups by Family

Area	Catholic	Baptist	Non-Den.	Methodist[2]	Lutheran	LDS[3]	Pente-costal	Presby-terian[4]	Muslim[5]	Judaism
MSA[1]	11.7	15.7	4.0	4.8	1.5	1.2	0.7	0.9	1.1	0.1
U.S.	19.1	9.3	4.0	4.0	2.3	2.0	1.9	1.6	0.8	0.7

Note: Figures are the number of adherents as a percentage of the total population; (1) Figures cover the College Station-Bryan, TX Metropolitan Statistical Area—see Appendix B for areas included; (2) Methodist/Pietist; (3) Latter Day Saints; (4) Reformed; (5) Figures are estimates
Source: Association of Statisticians of American Religious Bodies, 2010 U.S. Religion Census: Religious Congregations & Membership Study

Religious Groups by Tradition

Area	Catholic	Evangelical Protestant	Mainline Protestant	Other Tradition	Black Protestant	Orthodox
MSA[1]	11.7	20.7	6.6	2.6	1.0	<0.1
U.S.	19.1	16.2	7.3	4.3	1.6	0.3

Note: Figures are the number of adherents as a percentage of the total population; (1) Figures cover the College Station-Bryan, TX Metropolitan Statistical Area—see Appendix B for areas included
Source: Association of Statisticians of American Religious Bodies, 2010 U.S. Religion Census: Religious Congregations & Membership Study

ECONOMY

Gross Metropolitan Product

Area	2016	2017	2018	2019	Rank[2]
MSA[1]	9.4	10.1	10.9	11.6	206

Note: Figures are in billions of dollars; (1) Figures cover the College Station-Bryan, TX Metropolitan Statistical Area—see Appendix B for areas included; (2) Rank is based on 2017 data and ranges from 1 to 381
Source: U.S. Conference of Mayors, U.S. Metro Economies: Economic Growth & Full Employment, June 2018

Economic Growth

Area	2017-2018 (%)	2019-2020 (%)	2021-2022 (%)
MSA[1]	4.9	2.8	2.1

Note: Figures are real gross metropolitan product (GMP) growth rates and represent average annual percent change; (1) Figures cover the College Station-Bryan, TX Metropolitan Statistical Area—see Appendix B for areas included
Source: U.S. Conference of Mayors, U.S. Metro Economies: Economic Growth & Full Employment, June 2018

Metropolitan Area Exports

Area	2012	2013	2014	2015	2016	2017	Rank[2]
MSA[1]	103.6	108.7	129.7	122.5	113.2	145.4	319

Note: Figures are in millions of dollars; (1) Figures cover the College Station-Bryan, TX Metropolitan Statistical Area—see Appendix B for areas included; (2) Rank is based on 2017 data and ranges from 1 to 387
Source: U.S. Department of Commerce, International Trade Administration, Office of Trade and Economic Analysis, Industry and Analysis, Exports by Metropolitan Area, extracted March 25, 2019

Building Permits

Area	Single-Family			Multi-Family			Total		
	2016	2017	Pct. Chg.	2016	2017	Pct. Chg.	2016	2017	Pct. Chg.
City	735	594	-19.2	1,165	1,319	13.2	1,900	1,913	0.7
MSA[1]	1,218	1,155	-5.2	1,642	1,928	17.4	2,860	3,083	7.8
U.S.	750,800	820,000	9.2	455,800	462,000	1.4	1,206,600	1,282,000	6.2

Note: (1) Figures cover the College Station-Bryan, TX Metropolitan Statistical Area—see Appendix B for areas included; Figures represent new, privately-owned housing units authorized (unadjusted data); All permit data are based on estimates with imputation
Source: U.S. Census Bureau, Manufacturing, Mining, and Construction Statistics, Building Permits, 2016, 2017

Bankruptcy Filings

Area	Business Filings			Nonbusiness Filings		
	2017	2018	% Chg.	2017	2018	% Chg.
Brazos County	6	12	100.0	68	71	4.4
U.S.	23,157	22,232	-4.0	765,863	751,186	-1.9

Note: Business filings include Chapter 7, Chapter 11, Chapter 12, and Chapter 13; Nonbusiness filings include Chapter 7, Chapter 11, and Chapter 13
Source: Administrative Office of the U.S. Courts, Business and Nonbusiness Bankruptcy, County Cases Commenced by Chapter of the Bankruptcy Code, During the 12-Month Period Ending December 31, 2017 and Business and Nonbusiness Bankruptcy, County Cases Commenced by Chapter of the Bankruptcy Code, During the 12-Month Period Ending December 31, 2018

Housing Vacancy Rates

Area	Gross Vacancy Rate[2] (%)			Year-Round Vacancy Rate[3] (%)			Rental Vacancy Rate[4] (%)			Homeowner Vacancy Rate[5] (%)		
	2016	2017	2018	2016	2017	2018	2016	2017	2018	2016	2017	2018
MSA[1]	n/a	n/a	n/a	n/a	n/a	n/a	n/a	n/a	n/a	n/a	n/a	n/a
U.S.	12.8	12.7	12.3	9.9	9.9	9.7	6.9	7.2	6.9	1.7	1.6	1.5

Note: (1) Figures cover the College Station-Bryan, TX Metropolitan Statistical Area—see Appendix B for areas included; (2) The percentage of the total housing inventory that is vacant; (3) The percentage of the housing inventory (excluding seasonal units) that is year-round vacant; (4) The percentage of rental inventory that is vacant for rent; (5) The percentage of homeowner inventory that is vacant for sale; n/a not available
Source: U.S. Census Bureau, Housing Vacancies and Homeownership Annual Statistics: 2016, 2017, 2018

INCOME

Income

Area	Per Capita ($)	Median Household ($)	Average Household ($)
City	24,640	39,430	66,254
MSA[1]	25,328	45,078	66,928
U.S.	31,177	57,652	81,283

Note: (1) Figures cover the College Station-Bryan, TX Metropolitan Statistical Area—see Appendix B for areas included
Source: U.S. Census Bureau, 2013-2017 American Community Survey 5-Year Estimates

Household Income Distribution

Area	Percent of Households Earning							
	Under $15,000	$15,000 -$24,999	$25,000 -$34,999	$35,000 -$49,999	$50,000 -$74,999	$75,000 -$99,999	$100,000 -$149,999	$150,000 and up
City	23.6	12.7	9.6	11.7	12.5	9.5	11.8	8.6
MSA[1]	17.9	11.5	10.4	13.5	15.9	11.1	11.4	8.2
U.S.	11.6	9.8	9.5	13.0	17.7	12.3	14.1	12.1

Note: (1) Figures cover the College Station-Bryan, TX Metropolitan Statistical Area—see Appendix B for areas included
Source: U.S. Census Bureau, 2013-2017 American Community Survey 5-Year Estimates

Poverty Rate

Area	All Ages	Under 18 Years Old	18 to 64 Years Old	65 Years and Over
City	31.8	17.5	37.5	7.0
MSA[1]	24.4	23.1	27.1	9.5
U.S.	14.6	20.3	13.7	9.3

Note: Figures are percentage of people whose income during the past 12 months was below the poverty level; (1) Figures cover the College Station-Bryan, TX Metropolitan Statistical Area—see Appendix B for areas included
Source: U.S. Census Bureau, 2013-2017 American Community Survey 5-Year Estimates

EMPLOYMENT

Labor Force and Employment

Area	Civilian Labor Force			Workers Employed		
	Dec. 2017	Dec. 2018	% Chg.	Dec. 2017	Dec. 2018	% Chg.
City	59,536	60,885	2.3	58,011	59,187	2.0
MSA[1]	131,772	134,501	2.1	128,210	130,738	2.0
U.S.	159,880,000	162,510,000	1.6	153,602,000	156,481,000	1.9

Note: Data is not seasonally adjusted and covers workers 16 years of age and older; (1) Figures cover the College Station-Bryan, TX Metropolitan Statistical Area—see Appendix B for areas included
Source: Bureau of Labor Statistics, Local Area Unemployment Statistics

Unemployment Rate

Area	2018											
	Jan.	Feb.	Mar.	Apr.	May	Jun.	Jul.	Aug.	Sep.	Oct.	Nov.	Dec.
City	2.9	2.9	2.8	2.5	2.6	3.5	3.3	3.3	2.9	2.7	2.6	2.8
MSA[1]	3.1	3.0	3.0	2.7	2.8	3.5	3.3	3.3	2.9	2.7	2.7	2.8
U.S.	4.5	4.4	4.1	3.7	3.6	4.2	4.1	3.9	3.6	3.5	3.5	3.7

Note: Data is not seasonally adjusted and covers workers 16 years of age and older; (1) Figures cover the College Station-Bryan, TX Metropolitan Statistical Area—see Appendix B for areas included
Source: Bureau of Labor Statistics, Local Area Unemployment Statistics

Average Wages

Occupation	$/Hr.	Occupation	$/Hr.
Accountants and Auditors	27.80	Maids and Housekeeping Cleaners	11.50
Automotive Mechanics	23.30	Maintenance and Repair Workers	16.20
Bookkeepers	16.30	Marketing Managers	73.30
Carpenters	15.10	Nuclear Medicine Technologists	n/a
Cashiers	10.60	Nurses, Licensed Practical	21.60
Clerks, General Office	17.20	Nurses, Registered	33.00
Clerks, Receptionists/Information	13.00	Nursing Assistants	12.90
Clerks, Shipping/Receiving	15.10	Packers and Packagers, Hand	9.30
Computer Programmers	45.60	Physical Therapists	39.30
Computer Systems Analysts	33.10	Postal Service Mail Carriers	24.70
Computer User Support Specialists	20.90	Real Estate Brokers	n/a
Cooks, Restaurant	10.60	Retail Salespersons	13.40
Dentists	102.80	Sales Reps., Exc. Tech./Scientific	33.50
Electrical Engineers	39.70	Sales Reps., Tech./Scientific	44.70
Electricians	21.20	Secretaries, Exc. Legal/Med./Exec.	15.80
Financial Managers	57.20	Security Guards	15.50
First-Line Supervisors/Managers, Sales	22.80	Surgeons	n/a
Food Preparation Workers	10.20	Teacher Assistants*	10.00
General and Operations Managers	47.40	Teachers, Elementary School*	23.30
Hairdressers/Cosmetologists	11.90	Teachers, Secondary School*	23.60
Internists, General	n/a	Telemarketers	n/a
Janitors and Cleaners	12.60	Truck Drivers, Heavy/Tractor-Trailer	21.00
Landscaping/Groundskeeping Workers	13.10	Truck Drivers, Light/Delivery Svcs.	15.70
Lawyers	43.50	Waiters and Waitresses	9.30

Note: Wage data covers the College Station-Bryan, TX Metropolitan Statistical Area—see Appendix B for areas included; (*) Hourly wages for elementary/secondary school teachers and teacher assistants were calculated by the editors from annual wage data based on a 40 hour work week; n/a not available.
Source: Bureau of Labor Statistics, Metro Area Occupational Employment & Wage Estimates, May 2018

Employment by Occupation

Occupation Classification	City (%)	MSA[1] (%)	U.S. (%)
Management, Business, Science, and Arts	48.2	39.4	37.4
Natural Resources, Construction, and Maintenance	4.7	9.7	8.9
Production, Transportation, and Material Moving	6.7	10.4	12.2
Sales and Office	23.4	22.5	23.5
Service	17.1	18.0	18.0

Note: Figures cover employed civilians 16 years of age and older; (1) Figures cover the College Station-Bryan, TX Metropolitan Statistical Area—see Appendix B for areas included
Source: U.S. Census Bureau, 2013-2017 American Community Survey 5-Year Estimates

Employment by Industry

| Sector | MSA[1] | | U.S. |
	Number of Employees	Percent of Total	Percent of Total
Construction, Mining, and Logging	7,900	6.4	5.3
Education and Health Services	12,600	10.2	15.9
Financial Activities	4,100	3.3	5.7
Government	43,900	35.7	15.1
Information	1,300	1.1	1.9
Leisure and Hospitality	17,300	14.1	10.7
Manufacturing	5,700	4.6	8.5
Other Services	3,500	2.8	3.9
Professional and Business Services	9,500	7.7	14.1
Retail Trade	12,600	10.2	10.8
Transportation, Warehousing, and Utilities	1,900	1.5	4.2
Wholesale Trade	2,800	2.3	3.9

Note: Figures are non-farm employment as of December 2018. Figures are not seasonally adjusted and include workers 16 years of age and older; (1) Figures cover the College Station-Bryan, TX Metropolitan Statistical Area—see Appendix B for areas included
Source: Bureau of Labor Statistics, Current Employment Statistics, Employment, Hours, and Earnings

Occupations with Greatest Projected Employment Growth: 2018 – 2020

Occupation[1]	2018 Employment	2020 Projected Employment	Numeric Employment Change	Percent Employment Change
Combined Food Preparation and Serving Workers, Including Fast Food	351,780	372,090	20,310	5.8
Personal Care Aides	218,310	235,470	17,160	7.9
Heavy and Tractor-Trailer Truck Drivers	204,870	216,310	11,440	5.6
Laborers and Freight, Stock, and Material Movers, Hand	194,220	204,060	9,840	5.1
Waiters and Waitresses	236,020	245,790	9,770	4.1
Office Clerks, General	393,740	403,270	9,530	2.4
Customer Service Representatives	268,380	277,460	9,080	3.4
General and Operations Managers	182,190	190,620	8,430	4.6
Retail Salespersons	392,620	400,900	8,280	2.1
Construction Laborers	143,270	150,820	7,550	5.3

Note: Projections cover Texas; (1) Sorted by numeric employment change
Source: www.projectionscentral.com, State Occupational Projections, 2018–2020 Short-Term Projections

Fastest Growing Occupations: 2018 – 2020

Occupation[1]	2018 Employment	2020 Projected Employment	Numeric Employment Change	Percent Employment Change
Wind Turbine Service Technicians	1,810	2,190	380	21.0
Religious Workers, All Other	5,690	6,330	640	11.2
Fundraisers	8,830	9,670	840	9.5
Statisticians	1,870	2,040	170	9.1
Public Relations and Fundraising Managers	6,570	7,160	590	9.0
Home Health Aides	74,390	80,920	6,530	8.8
Community and Social Service Specialists, All Other	4,520	4,890	370	8.2
Personal Care Aides	218,310	235,470	17,160	7.9
Operations Research Analysts	10,920	11,760	840	7.7
Software Developers, Applications	65,190	70,140	4,950	7.6

Note: Projections cover Texas; (1) Sorted by percent employment change and excludes occupations with numeric employment change less than 50
Source: www.projectionscentral.com, State Occupational Projections, 2018–2020 Short-Term Projections

TAXES

State Corporate Income Tax Rates

State	Tax Rate (%)	Income Brackets ($)	Num. of Brackets	Financial Institution Tax Rate (%)[a]	Federal Income Tax Ded.
Texas	(w)	–	–	(w)	No

Note: Tax rates as of January 1, 2019; (a) Rates listed are the corporate income tax rate applied to financial institutions or excise taxes based on income. Some states have other taxes based upon the value of deposits or shares; (w) Texas imposes a Franchise Tax, otherwise known as margin tax, imposed on entities with more than $1,130,000 total revenues at rate of 0.75%, or 0.375% for entities primarily engaged in retail or wholesale trade, on lesser of 70% of total revenues or 100% of gross receipts after deductions for either compensation or cost of goods sold.
Source: Federation of Tax Administrators, Range of State Corporate Income Tax Rates, January 1, 2019

State Individual Income Tax Rates

State	Tax Rate (%)	Income Brackets ($)	Personal Exemptions ($) Single	Married	Depend.	Standard Ded. ($) Single	Married
Texas				– No state income tax –			

Note: Tax rates as of January 1, 2019; Local- and county-level taxes are not included; n/a not applicable;

Source: Federation of Tax Administrators, State Individual Income Tax Rates, January 1, 2019

Various State Sales and Excise Tax Rates

State	State Sales Tax (%)	Gasoline[1] (¢/gal.)	Cigarette[2] ($/pack)	Spirits[3] ($/gal.)	Wine[4] ($/gal.)	Beer[5] ($/gal.)	Recreational Marijuana (%)
Texas	6.25	20	1.41	2.40 (f)	0.20 (l)	0.20 (q)	Not legal

Note: All tax rates as of January 1, 2019; (1) The American Petroleum Institute has developed a methodology for determining the average tax rate on a gallon of fuel. Rates may include any of the following: excise taxes, environmental fees, storage tank fees, other fees or taxes, general sales tax, and local taxes. In states where gasoline is subject to the general sales tax, or where the fuel tax is based on the average sale price, the average rate determined by API is sensitive to changes in the price of gasoline. States that fully or partially apply general sales taxes to gasoline: CA, CO, GA, IL, IN, MI, NY; (2) The federal excise tax of $1.0066 per pack and local taxes are not included; (3) Rates are those applicable to off-premise sales of 40% alcohol by volume (a.b.v.) distilled spirits in 750ml containers. Local excise taxes are excluded; (4) Rates are those applicable to off-premise sales of 11% a.b.v. non-carbonated wine in 750ml containers; (5) Rates are those applicable to off-premise sales of 4.7% a.b.v. beer in 12 ounce containers; (f) Different rates also applicable according to alcohol content, place of production, size of container, or place purchased (on- or off-premise or onboard airlines); (l) Different rates also applicable to alcohol content, place of production, size of container, place purchased (on- or off-premise or on board airlines) or type of wine (carbonated, vermouth, etc.); (q) Different rates also applicable according to alcohol content, place of production, size of container, or place purchased (on- or off-premise or onboard airlines).
Source: Tax Foundation, 2019 Facts & Figures: How Does Your State Compare?

State Business Tax Climate Index Rankings

State	Overall Rank	Corporate Tax Rank	Individual Income Tax Rank	Sales Tax Rank	Unemployment Insurance Tax Rank	Property Tax Rank
Texas	15	49	6	37	18	37

Note: The index is a measure of how each state's tax laws affect economic performance. The lower the rank, the more favorable a state's tax system is for business. States without a given tax are given a ranking of 1. The scores/rankings for the District of Columbia do not affect other states. The 2019 index represents the tax climate as of July 1, 2018.
Source: Tax Foundation, State Business Tax Climate Index 2019

COMMERCIAL UTILITIES

Typical Monthly Electric Bills

Area	Commercial Service ($/month) 1,500 kWh	40 kW demand 14,000 kWh	Industrial Service ($/month) 1,000 kW demand 200,000 kWh	50,000 kW demand 32,500,000 kWh
City	n/a	n/a	n/a	n/a
Average[1]	203	1,619	25,886	2,540,077

Note: Figures are based on annualized rates; (1) Average based on 187 utilities surveyed; n/a not available
Source: Edison Electric Institute, Typical Bills and Average Rates Report, Summer 2018

TRANSPORTATION

Means of Transportation to Work

Area	Car/Truck/Van		Public Transportation			Bicycle	Walked	Other Means	Worked at Home
	Drove Alone	Car-pooled	Bus	Subway	Railroad				
City	77.7	9.0	3.4	0.0	0.0	2.4	3.2	1.0	3.2
MSA[1]	78.1	11.5	2.1	0.0	0.0	1.6	2.4	1.0	3.3
U.S.	76.4	9.2	2.5	1.9	0.6	0.6	2.7	1.3	4.7

Note: Figures are percentages and cover workers 16 years of age and older; (1) Figures cover the College Station-Bryan, TX Metropolitan Statistical Area—see Appendix B for areas included
Source: U.S. Census Bureau, 2013-2017 American Community Survey 5-Year Estimates

Travel Time to Work

Area	Less Than 10 Minutes	10 to 19 Minutes	20 to 29 Minutes	30 to 44 Minutes	45 to 59 Minutes	60 to 89 Minutes	90 Minutes or More
City	18.5	54.6	18.2	5.8	0.7	1.3	1.0
MSA[1]	18.4	46.5	18.9	10.3	2.4	2.0	1.4
U.S.	12.7	28.9	20.9	20.5	8.1	6.2	2.7

Note: Note: Figures are percentages and include workers 16 years old and over; (1) Figures cover the College Station-Bryan, TX Metropolitan Statistical Area—see Appendix B for areas included
Source: U.S. Census Bureau, 2013-2017 American Community Survey 5-Year Estimates

Freeway Travel Time Index

Area	1985	1990	1995	2000	2005	2010	2014
Urban Area Rank[1,2]	n/a	n/a	n/a	n/a	n/a	n/a	n/a
Urban Area Index[1]	n/a	n/a	n/a	n/a	n/a	n/a	n/a
Average Index[3]	1.09	1.11	1.14	1.17	1.20	1.19	1.20

Note: Freeway Travel Time Index—the ratio of travel time in the peak period to the travel time at free-flow conditions. For example, a value of 1.30 indicates a 20-minute free-flow trip takes 26 minutes in the peak (20 minutes x 1.30 = 26 minutes); (1) Data for the College Station-Bryan, TX urban area was not available; (2) Rank is based on 101 urban areas (#1 = highest travel time index); (3) Average of 101 urban areas
Source: Texas Transportation Institute, 2015 Urban Mobility Scorecard, August 2015

Freeway Commuter Stress Index

Area	1985	1990	1995	2000	2005	2010	2014
Urban Area Rank[1,2]	n/a	n/a	n/a	n/a	n/a	n/a	n/a
Urban Area Index[1]	n/a	n/a	n/a	n/a	n/a	n/a	n/a
Average Index[3]	1.13	1.16	1.19	1.22	1.25	1.24	1.25

Note: The Freeway Commuter Stress Index is the same as the Freeway Travel Time Index (see table above) except that it includes only the travel in the peak directions during the peak periods; the TTI includes travel in all directions during the peak period. Thus, the CSI is more indicative of the work trip experienced by each commuter on a daily basis; (1) Data for the College Station-Bryan, TX urban area was not available; (2) Rank is based on 101 urban areas (#1 = highest travel time index); (3) Average of 101 urban areas
Source: Texas Transportation Institute, 2015 Urban Mobility Scorecard, August 2015

Public Transportation

Agency Name / Mode of Transportation	Vehicles Operated in Maximum Service[1]	Annual Unlinked Passenger Trips[2] (in thous.)	Annual Passenger Miles[3] (in thous.)
Brazos Transit District			
Bus (directly operated)	27	407.2	2,602.2
Demand Response (directly operated)	48	63.7	985.6

Note: (1) The number of revenue vehicles operated by the given mode and type of service to meet the annual maximum service requirement. This is the revenue vehicle count during the peak season of the year; on the week and day that maximum service is provided. Vehicles operated in maximum service (VOMS) exclude atypical days and one-time special events; (2) The number of passengers who boarded public transportation vehicles. Passengers are counted each time they board a vehicle no matter how many vehicles they use to travel from their origin to their destination. (3) The sum of the distances ridden by all passengers during the entire fiscal year.
Source: Federal Transit Administration, National Transit Database, 2017

Air Transportation

Airport Name and Code / Type of Service	Passenger Airlines[1]	Passenger Enplanements	Freight Carriers[2]	Freight (lbs)
Easterwood Airport (CLL)				
Domestic service (U.S. carriers - 2018)	17	79,129	3	157,154
International service (U.S. carriers - 2017)	0	0	0	0

Note: (1) Includes all U.S.-based major, minor and commuter airlines that carried at least one passenger during the year; (2) Includes all U.S.-based airlines and freight carriers that transported at least one pound of freight during the year.
Source: Bureau of Transportation Statistics, The Intermodal Transportation Database, Air Carriers: T-100 Domestic Market (U.S. Carriers), 2018; Bureau of Transportation Statistics, The Intermodal Transportation Database, Air Carriers: T-100 International Market (U.S. Carriers), 2017

Other Transportation Statistics

Major Highways:	CR-6; CR-30
Amtrak Service:	Bus connection (Bryan, TX)
Major Waterways/Ports:	None

Source: Amtrak.com; Google Maps

BUSINESSES

Major Business Headquarters

Company Name	Industry	Rankings Fortune[1]	Forbes[2]
No companies listed	-	-	-

Note: (1) Companies that produce a 10-K are ranked 1 to 500 based on 2017 revenue; (2) All private companies with at least $2 billion in annual revenue through the end of their most current fiscal year are ranked 1 to 229; companies listed are headquartered in the city; dashes indicate no ranking
Source: Fortune, "Fortune 500," June 2018; Forbes, "America's Largest Private Companies," 2018 Rankings

Minority- and Women-Owned Businesses

Group	All Firms Firms	Sales ($000)	Firms with Paid Employees Firms	Sales ($000)	Employees	Payroll ($000)
AIAN[1]	n/a	n/a	n/a	n/a	n/a	n/a
Asian	357	241,599	160	227,294	1,492	20,628
Black	395	86,251	6	71,780	95	6,513
Hispanic	642	(s)	106	(s)	1,000 - 2,499	(s)
NHOPI[2]	n/a	n/a	n/a	n/a	n/a	n/a
Women	1,943	438,013	282	375,193	3,759	82,855
All Firms	5,973	3,734,442	1,466	3,493,076	24,926	646,242

Note: Figures cover firms located in the city; minority- and women-owned business are defined as firms in which the corresponding group own 51% or more of the stock or equity of the company; (1) American Indian and Alaska Native; (2) Native Hawaiian and Other Pacific Islander; (s) estimates are suppressed when publication standards are not met; n/a not available
Source: U.S. Census Bureau, 2012 Economic Census, Survey of Business Owners

HOTELS & CONVENTION CENTERS

Hotels, Motels and Vacation Rentals

Area	5 Star Num.	Pct.[3]	4 Star Num.	Pct.[3]	3 Star Num.	Pct.[3]	2 Star Num.	Pct.[3]	1 Star Num.	Pct.[3]	Not Rated Num.	Pct.[3]
City[1]	0	0.0	4	1.8	32	14.7	61	28.0	1	0.5	120	55.0
Total[2]	286	0.4	5,236	7.1	16,715	22.6	10,259	13.9	293	0.4	41,056	55.6

Note: (1) Figures cover College Station and vicinity; (2) Figures cover all 100 cities in this book; (3) Percentage of hotels which have a given star rating; Star ratings are determined by expedia.com and offer an indication of the general quality of a particular hotel.
Source: www.expedia.com, April 3, 2019

Major Convention Centers

Name	Overall Space (sq. ft.)	Exhibit Space (sq. ft.)	Meeting Space (sq. ft.)	Meeting Rooms
Brazos County Expo	281,000	29,000	n/a	5
The Brazos Center	39,000	n/a	n/a	n/a

Note: Table includes convention centers located in the College Station-Bryan, TX metro area; n/a not available
Source: Original research

Living Environment

COST OF LIVING

Cost of Living Index

Composite Index	Groceries	Housing	Utilities	Trans-portation	Health Care	Misc. Goods/ Services
n/a	n/a	n/a	n/a	n/a	n/a	n/a

Note: The Cost of Living Index measures regional differences in the cost of consumer goods and services, excluding taxes and non-consumer expenditures, for professional and managerial households in the top income quintile. It is based on more than 50,000 prices covering almost 60 different items for which prices are collected three times a year by chambers of commerce, economic development organizations or university applied economic centers in each participating urban area. The numbers shown should be read as a percentage above or below the national average of 100. For example, a value of 115.4 in the groceries column indicates that grocery prices are 15.4% higher than the national average. Small differences in the index numbers should not be interpreted as significant; n/a not available.
Source: The Council for Community and Economic Research, ACCRA Cost of Living Index, 2018

Grocery Prices

Area[1]	T-Bone Steak ($/pound)	Frying Chicken ($/pound)	Whole Milk ($/half gal.)	Eggs ($/dozen)	Orange Juice ($/64 oz.)	Coffee ($/11.5 oz.)
City[2]	n/a	n/a	n/a	n/a	n/a	n/a
Avg.	11.35	1.42	1.94	1.81	3.52	4.35
Min.	7.45	0.92	0.80	0.75	2.72	3.06
Max.	15.05	2.76	4.18	4.00	5.36	8.20

*Note: (1) Values for the local area are compared with the average, minimum and maximum values for all 291 areas in the Cost of Living Index; (2) Figures cover the College Station TX urban area; n/a not available; **T-Bone Steak** (price per pound); **Frying Chicken** (price per pound, whole fryer); **Whole Milk** (half gallon carton); **Eggs** (price per dozen, Grade A, large); **Orange Juice** (64 oz. Tropicana or Florida Natural); **Coffee** (11.5 oz. can, vacuum-packed, Maxwell House, Hills Bros, or Folgers).*
Source: The Council for Community and Economic Research, ACCRA Cost of Living Index, 2018

Housing and Utility Costs

Area[1]	New Home Price ($)	Apartment Rent ($/month)	All Electric ($/month)	Part Electric ($/month)	Other Energy ($/month)	Telephone ($/month)
City[2]	n/a	n/a	n/a	n/a	n/a	n/a
Avg.	347,000	1,087	165.93	100.16	67.73	178.70
Min.	200,468	500	93.58	25.64	26.78	163.10
Max.	1,901,222	4,888	388.65	246.86	332.81	197.70

*Note: (1) Values for the local area are compared with the average, minimum and maximum values for all 291 areas in the Cost of Living Index; (2) Figures cover the College Station TX urban area; n/a not available; **New Home Price** (2,400 sf living area, 8,000 sf lot, in urban area with full utilities); **Apartment Rent** (950 sf 2 bedroom/1.5 or 2 bath, unfurnished, excluding all utilities except water); **All Electric** (average monthly cost for an all-electric home); **Part Electric** (average monthly cost for a part-electric home); **Other Energy** (average monthly cost for natural gas, fuel oil, coal, wood, and any other forms of energy except electricity); **Telephone** (price includes the base monthly rate plus taxes and fees for three lines of mobile phone service).*
Source: The Council for Community and Economic Research, ACCRA Cost of Living Index, 2018

Health Care, Transportation, and Other Costs

Area[1]	Doctor ($/visit)	Dentist ($/visit)	Optometrist ($/visit)	Gasoline ($/gallon)	Beauty Salon ($/visit)	Men's Shirt ($)
City[2]	n/a	n/a	n/a	n/a	n/a	n/a
Avg.	110.71	95.11	103.74	2.61	37.48	32.03
Min.	33.60	62.55	54.63	1.89	17.00	11.44
Max.	195.97	153.93	225.79	3.59	71.88	58.64

*Note: (1) Values for the local area are compared with the average, minimum and maximum values for all 291 areas in the Cost of Living Index; (2) Figures cover the College Station TX urban area; n/a not available; **Doctor** (general practitioners routine exam of an established patient); **Dentist** (adult teeth cleaning and periodic oral examination); **Optometrist** (full vision eye exam for established adult patient); **Gasoline** (one gallon regular unleaded, national brand, including all taxes, cash price at self-service pump if available); **Beauty Salon** (woman's shampoo, trim, and blow-dry); **Men's Shirt** (cotton/polyester dress shirt, pinpoint weave, long sleeves).*
Source: The Council for Community and Economic Research, ACCRA Cost of Living Index, 2018

HOUSING

House Price Index (HPI)

Area	National Ranking[2]	Quarterly Change (%)	One-Year Change (%)	Five-Year Change (%)
MSA[1]	(a)	n/a	7.27	42.28
U.S.[3]	–	1.12	5.73	32.81

Note: The HPI is a weighted repeat sales index. It measures average price changes in repeat sales or refinancings on the same properties. This information is obtained by reviewing repeat mortgage transactions on single-family properties whose mortgages have been purchased or securitized by Fannie Mae or Freddie Mac in January 1975; (1) Figures cover the College Station-Bryan, TX Metropolitan Statistical Area—see Appendix B for areas included; (2) Rankings are based on annual percentage change for all metro areas containing at least 15,000 transactions over the last 10 years and ranges from 1 to 245; (3) figures based on a weighted average of Census Division estimates using a seasonally adjusted, purchase-only index; all figures are for the period ending December 31, 2018; n/a not available; (a) Not ranked because of increased index variability due to smaller sample size
Source: Federal Housing Finance Agency, House Price Index, February 26, 2019

Median Single-Family Home Prices

Area	2016	2017	2018p	Percent Change 2017 to 2018
MSA[1]	n/a	n/a	n/a	n/a
U.S. Average	235.5	248.8	261.6	5.1

Note: Figures are median sales prices of existing single-family homes in thousands of dollars; (p) preliminary; n/a not available; (1) Figures cover the College Station-Bryan, TX Metropolitan Statistical Area—see Appendix B for areas included
Source: National Association of Realtors, Median Sales Price of Existing Single-Family Homes for Metropolitan Areas, 4th Quarter 2018

Qualifying Income Based on Median Sales Price of Existing Single-Family Homes

Area	With 5% Down ($)	With 10% Down ($)	With 20% Down ($)
MSA[1]	n/a	n/a	n/a
U.S. Average	62,954	59,640	53,013

Note: Figures are preliminary; Qualifying income is based on a mortgage rate of 4.9%. Monthly principal and interest payment is limited to 25% of income; n/a not available; (1) Figures cover the College Station-Bryan, TX Metropolitan Statistical Area—see Appendix B for areas included
Source: National Association of Realtors, Qualifying Income Based on Median Sales Price of Existing Single-Family Homes for Metropolitan Areas, 4th Quarter 2018

Median Apartment Condo-Coop Home Prices

Area	2016	2017	2018p	Percent Change 2017 to 2018
MSA[1]	n/a	n/a	n/a	n/a
U.S. Average	220.7	234.3	241.0	2.9

Note: Figures are median sales prices of existing apartment condo-coop homes in thousands of dollars; (p) preliminary; n/a not available; (1) Figures cover the College Station-Bryan, TX Metropolitan Statistical Area—see Appendix B for areas included
Source: National Association of Realtors, Median Sales Price of Existing Apartment Condo-Coop Homes for Metropolitan Areas, 4th Quarter 2018

Home Value Distribution

Area	Under $50,000	$50,000 -$99,999	$100,000 -$149,999	$150,000 -$199,999	$200,000 -$299,999	$300,000 -$499,999	$500,000 -$999,999	$1,000,000 or more
City	3.0	2.9	13.6	28.5	30.1	17.8	3.6	0.5
MSA[1]	12.1	16.5	17.3	19.2	18.7	11.6	3.8	0.7
U.S.	8.3	13.9	14.7	14.6	18.7	17.3	9.7	2.7

Note: Figures are percentages and cover owner-occupied housing units; (1) Figures cover the College Station-Bryan, TX Metropolitan Statistical Area—see Appendix B for areas included
Source: U.S. Census Bureau, 2013-2017 American Community Survey 5-Year Estimates

Homeownership Rate

Area	2010 (%)	2011 (%)	2012 (%)	2013 (%)	2014 (%)	2015 (%)	2016 (%)	2017 (%)	2018 (%)
MSA[1]	n/a	n/a	n/a	n/a	n/a	n/a	n/a	n/a	n/a
U.S.	66.9	66.1	65.4	65.1	64.5	63.7	63.4	63.9	64.4

Note: (1) Figures cover the College Station-Bryan, TX Metropolitan Statistical Area—see Appendix B for areas included; n/a not available
Source: U.S. Census Bureau, Housing Vacancies and Homeownership Annual Statistics: 2010-2018

Year Housing Structure Built

Area	2010 or Later	2000 -2009	1990 -1999	1980 -1989	1970 -1979	1960 -1969	1950 -1959	1940 -1949	Before 1940	Median Year
City	10.2	25.9	19.5	18.1	17.9	4.3	2.1	0.9	1.0	1993
MSA[1]	8.4	21.9	18.1	17.9	16.8	6.1	5.4	2.4	3.0	1989
U.S.	3.2	14.5	14.0	13.6	15.5	10.8	10.5	5.1	12.9	1977

Note: Figures are percentages except for Median Year; Note: (1) Figures cover the College Station-Bryan, TX Metropolitan Statistical Area—see Appendix B for areas included
Source: U.S. Census Bureau, 2013-2017 American Community Survey 5-Year Estimates

Gross Monthly Rent

Area	Under $500	$500 -$999	$1,000 -$1,499	$1,500 -$1,999	$2,000 -$2,499	$2,500 -$2,999	$3,000 and up	Median ($)
City	2.2	54.7	25.4	12.1	4.7	0.6	0.2	940
MSA[1]	5.7	57.7	22.9	9.6	3.4	0.5	0.2	885
U.S.	10.5	41.1	28.7	11.7	4.5	1.8	1.7	982

Note: Figures are percentages except for Median; Gross rent is the contract rent plus the estimated average monthly cost of utilities (electricity, gas, and water and sewer) and fuels (oil, coal, kerosene, wood, etc.) if these are paid by the renter (or paid for the renter by someone else); (1) Figures cover the College Station-Bryan, TX Metropolitan Statistical Area—see Appendix B for areas included
Source: U.S. Census Bureau, 2013-2017 American Community Survey 5-Year Estimates

HEALTH

Health Risk Factors

Category	MSA[1] (%)	U.S. (%)
Adults aged 18–64 who have any kind of health care coverage	83.7	87.3
Adults who reported being in good or better health	91.7	82.4
Adults who have been told they have high blood cholesterol	31.2	33.0
Adults who have been told they have high blood pressure	26.1	32.3
Adults who are current smokers	n/a	17.1
Adults who currently use E-cigarettes	n/a	4.6
Adults who currently use chewing tobacco, snuff, or snus	7.6	4.0
Adults who are heavy drinkers[2]	n/a	6.3
Adults who are binge drinkers[3]	24.2	17.4
Adults who are overweight (BMI 25.0 - 29.9)	34.5	35.3
Adults who are obese (BMI 30.0 - 99.8)	30.8	31.3
Adults who participated in any physical activities in the past month	80.2	74.4
Adults who always or nearly always wears a seat belt	92.1	94.3

Note: n/a not available; (1) Figures cover the College Station-Bryan, TX Metropolitan Statistical Area—see Appendix B for areas included; (2) Heavy drinkers are classified as adult men having more than 14 drinks per week and adult women having more than 7 drinks per week; (3) Binge drinkers are classified as males having five or more drinks on one occasion or females having four or more drinks on one occasion
Source: Centers for Disease Control and Prevention, Behavioral Risk Factor Surveillance System, SMART: Selected Metropolitan Area Risk Trends, 2017

Acute and Chronic Health Conditions

Category	MSA[1] (%)	U.S. (%)
Adults who have ever been told they had a heart attack	n/a	4.2
Adults who have ever been told they have angina or coronary heart disease	1.6	3.9
Adults who have ever been told they had a stroke	n/a	3.0
Adults who have ever been told they have asthma	15.9	14.2
Adults who have ever been told they have arthritis	19.1	24.9
Adults who have ever been told they have diabetes[2]	7.5	10.5
Adults who have ever been told they had skin cancer	n/a	6.2
Adults who have ever been told they had any other types of cancer	7.7	7.1
Adults who have ever been told they have COPD	n/a	6.5
Adults who have ever been told they have kidney disease	n/a	3.0
Adults who have ever been told they have a form of depression	13.4	20.5

Note: n/a not available; (1) Figures cover the College Station-Bryan, TX Metropolitan Statistical Area—see Appendix B for areas included; (2) Figures do not include pregnancy-related, borderline, or pre-diabetes
Source: Centers for Disease Control and Prevention, Behaviorial Risk Factor Surveillance System, SMART: Selected Metropolitan Area Risk Trends, 2017

Health Screening and Vaccination Rates

Category	MSA[1] (%)	U.S. (%)
Adults aged 65+ who have had flu shot within the past year	70.7	60.7
Adults aged 65+ who have ever had a pneumonia vaccination	89.7	75.4
Adults who have ever been tested for HIV	33.6	36.1
Adults who have ever had the shingles or zoster vaccine?	33.8	28.9
Adults who have had their blood cholesterol checked within the last five years	77.5	85.9

Note: n/a not available; (1) Figures cover the College Station-Bryan, TX Metropolitan Statistical Area—see Appendix B for areas included.
Source: Centers for Disease Control and Prevention, Behaviorial Risk Factor Surveillance System, SMART: Selected Metropolitan Area Risk Trends, 2017

Disability Status

Category	MSA[1] (%)	U.S. (%)
Adults who reported being deaf	n/a	6.7
Are you blind or have serious difficulty seeing, even when wearing glasses?	n/a	4.5
Are you limited in any way in any of your usual activities due of arthritis?	12.5	12.9
Do you have difficulty doing errands alone?	n/a	6.8
Do you have difficulty dressing or bathing?	n/a	3.6
Do you have serious difficulty concentrating/remembering/making decisions?	n/a	10.7
Do you have serious difficulty walking or climbing stairs?	10.0	13.6

Note: n/a not available; (1) Figures cover the College Station-Bryan, TX Metropolitan Statistical Area—see Appendix B for areas included.
Source: Centers for Disease Control and Prevention, Behaviorial Risk Factor Surveillance System, SMART: Selected Metropolitan Area Risk Trends, 2017

Mortality Rates for the Top 10 Causes of Death in the U.S.

ICD-10[a] Sub-Chapter	ICD-10[a] Code	Age-Adjusted Mortality Rate[1] per 100,000 population	
		County[2]	U.S.
Malignant neoplasms	C00-C97	130.5	155.5
Ischaemic heart diseases	I20-I25	76.9	94.8
Other forms of heart disease	I30-I51	60.2	52.9
Chronic lower respiratory diseases	J40-J47	34.1	41.0
Cerebrovascular diseases	I60-I69	37.8	37.5
Other degenerative diseases of the nervous system	G30-G31	45.3	35.0
Other external causes of accidental injury	W00-X59	14.2	33.7
Organic, including symptomatic, mental disorders	F01-F09	29.1	31.0
Hypertensive diseases	I10-I15	20.9	21.9
Diabetes mellitus	E10-E14	18.3	21.2

Note: (a) ICD-10 = International Classification of Diseases 10th Revision; (1) Mortality rates are a three year average covering 2015-2017; (2) Figures cover Brazos County.
Source: Centers for Disease Control and Prevention, National Center for Health Statistics. Underlying Cause of Death 1999-2017 on CDC WONDER Online Database

Mortality Rates for Selected Causes of Death

ICD-10[a] Sub-Chapter	ICD-10[a] Code	Age-Adjusted Mortality Rate[1] per 100,000 population	
		County[2]	U.S.
Assault	X85-Y09	Unreliable	5.9
Diseases of the liver	K70-K76	11.3	14.1
Human immunodeficiency virus (HIV) disease	B20-B24	Suppressed	1.8
Influenza and pneumonia	J09-J18	7.2	14.3
Intentional self-harm	X60-X84	9.9	13.6
Malnutrition	E40-E46	Suppressed	1.6
Obesity and other hyperalimentation	E65-E68	Suppressed	2.1
Renal failure	N17-N19	12.5	13.0
Transport accidents	V01-V99	13.0	12.4
Viral hepatitis	B15-B19	Suppressed	1.6

Note: (a) ICD-10 = International Classification of Diseases 10th Revision; (1) Mortality rates are a three year average covering 2015-2017; (2) Figures cover Brazos County; Data are suppressed when the data meet the criteria for confidentiality constraints; Mortality rates are flagged as unreliable when the rate would be calculated with a numerator of 20 or less.
Source: Centers for Disease Control and Prevention, National Center for Health Statistics. Underlying Cause of Death 1999-2017 on CDC WONDER Online Database

Health Insurance Coverage

Area	With Health Insurance	With Private Health Insurance	With Public Health Insurance	Without Health Insurance	Population Under Age 18 Without Health Insurance
City	90.9	83.7	13.4	9.1	5.3
MSA[1]	85.7	71.9	22.5	14.3	9.6
U.S.	89.5	67.2	33.8	10.5	5.7

Note: Figures are percentages that cover the civilian noninstitutionalized population; (1) Figures cover the College Station-Bryan, TX Metropolitan Statistical Area—see Appendix B for areas included
Source: U.S. Census Bureau, 2013-2017 American Community Survey 5-Year Estimates

Number of Medical Professionals

Area	MDs[3]	DOs[3,4]	Dentists	Podiatrists	Chiropractors	Optometrists
County[1] (number)	562	44	113	7	37	32
County[1] (rate[2])	256.0	20.0	50.7	3.1	16.6	14.4
U.S. (rate[2])	279.3	23.0	68.4	6.0	27.1	16.2

Note: Data as of 2017 unless noted; (1) Data covers Brazos County; (2) Rate per 100,000 population; (3) Data as of 2016 and includes all active, non-federal physicians; (4) Doctor of Osteopathic Medicine
Source: U.S. Department of Health and Human Services, Health Resources and Services Administration, Bureau of Health Professions, Area Resource File (ARF) 2017-2018

EDUCATION

Public School District Statistics

District Name	Schls	Pupils	Pupil/ Teacher Ratio	Minority Pupils[1] (%)	Free Lunch Eligible[2] (%)	IEP[3] (%)
College Station ISD	19	13,188	14.7	46.2	29.2	8.5

Note: Table includes school districts with 2,000 or more students; (1) Percentage of students that are not non-Hispanic white; (2) Percentage of students that are eligible for the free lunch program; (3) Percentage of students that have an Individualized Education Program.
Source: U.S. Department of Education, National Center for Education Statistics, Common Core of Data, Local Education Agency (School District) Universe Survey: School Year 2016-2017; U.S. Department of Education, National Center for Education Statistics, Common Core of Data, Public Elementary/Secondary School Universe Survey: School Year 2016-2017

Highest Level of Education

Area	Less than H.S.	H.S. Diploma	Some College, No Deg.	Associate Degree	Bachelor's Degree	Master's Degree	Prof. School Degree	Doctorate Degree
City	6.1	12.6	19.0	6.5	28.5	15.4	2.7	9.1
MSA[1]	14.8	23.2	20.6	6.1	19.4	9.1	2.0	4.7
U.S.	12.7	27.3	20.8	8.3	19.1	8.4	2.0	1.4

Note: Figures cover persons age 25 and over; (1) Figures cover the College Station-Bryan, TX Metropolitan Statistical Area—see Appendix B for areas included
Source: U.S. Census Bureau, 2013-2017 American Community Survey 5-Year Estimates

Educational Attainment by Race

Area	High School Graduate or Higher (%)					Bachelor's Degree or Higher (%)				
	Total	White	Black	Asian	Hisp.[2]	Total	White	Black	Asian	Hisp.[2]
City	93.9	94.9	87.0	96.3	80.3	55.8	56.5	24.8	80.5	45.9
MSA[1]	85.2	87.8	82.0	92.1	60.1	35.3	38.2	13.2	76.6	15.8
U.S.	87.3	89.3	84.9	86.5	66.7	30.9	32.2	20.6	52.7	15.2

Note: Figures shown cover persons 25 years old and over; (1) Figures cover the College Station-Bryan, TX Metropolitan Statistical Area—see Appendix B for areas included; (2) People of Hispanic origin can be of any race
Source: U.S. Census Bureau, 2013-2017 American Community Survey 5-Year Estimates

School Enrollment by Grade and Control

Area	Preschool (%)		Kindergarten (%)		Grades 1 - 4 (%)		Grades 5 - 8 (%)		Grades 9 - 12 (%)	
	Public	Private	Public	Private	Public	Private	Public	Private	Public	Private
City	44.2	55.8	86.9	13.1	87.0	13.0	93.4	6.6	91.9	8.1
MSA[1]	62.2	37.8	85.8	14.2	88.9	11.1	90.5	9.5	93.0	7.0
U.S.	58.8	41.2	87.7	12.3	89.7	10.3	89.6	10.4	90.3	9.7

Note: Figures shown cover persons 3 years old and over; (1) Figures cover the College Station-Bryan, TX Metropolitan Statistical Area—see Appendix B for areas included
Source: U.S. Census Bureau, 2013-2017 American Community Survey 5-Year Estimates

Average Salaries of Public School Classroom Teachers

Area	2016		2017		Change from 2016 to 2017	
	Dollars	Rank[1]	Dollars	Rank[1]	Percent	Rank[2]
Texas	51,890	28	52,575	28	1.3	29
U.S. Average	58,479	–	59,660	–	2.0	–

Note: (1) Rank ranges from 1 to 51 where 1 indicates highest salary; (2) Rank ranges from 1 to 51 where 1 indicates highest percent change.
Source: National Education Association, Rankings & Estimates: Rankings of the States 2017 and Estimates of School Statistics 2018

Higher Education

Four-Year Colleges			Two-Year Colleges			Medical Schools[1]	Law Schools[2]	Voc/ Tech[3]
Public	Private Non-profit	Private For-profit	Public	Private Non-profit	Private For-profit			
1	0	0	0	0	0	1	0	0

Note: Figures cover institutions located within the city limits and include main campuses only; (1) includes schools accredited by the Liaison Committee on Medical Education and the American Osteopathic Association's Commission on Osteopathic College Accreditation; (2) includes ABA-accredited schools, schools with provisional ABA accreditation, and state accredited schools; (3) includes all schools with programs that are less than 2 years.
Source: National Center for Education Statistics, Integrated Postsecondary Education System (IPEDS), 2017-18; Wikipedia, List of Medical Schools in the United States, accessed April 3, 2019; Wikipedia, List of Law Schools in the United States, accessed April 3, 2019

According to *U.S. News & World Report,* the College Station-Bryan, TX metro area is home to one of the best national universities in the U.S.: **Texas A&M University—College Station** (#66 tie). The indicators used to capture academic quality fall into a number of categories: assessment by administrators at peer institutions; retention of students; faculty resources; student selectivity; financial resources; alumni giving; high school counselor ratings of colleges; and graduation rate. *U.S. News & World Report, "America's Best Colleges 2019"*

According to *U.S. News & World Report,* the College Station-Bryan, TX metro area is home to one of the top 75 business schools in the U.S.: **Texas A&M University—College Station (Mays)** (#40 tie). The rankings are based on a weighted average of the following nine measures: quality assessment; peer assessment; recruiter assessment; placement success; mean starting salary and bonus; student selectivity; mean GMAT and GRE scores; mean undergraduate GPA; and acceptance rate. *U.S. News & World Report, "America's Best Graduate Schools, Business, 2020"*

PRESIDENTIAL ELECTION

2016 Presidential Election Results

Area	Clinton	Trump	Johnson	Stein	Other
Brazos County	34.4	57.6	5.7	0.8	1.5
U.S.	48.0	45.9	3.3	1.1	1.7

Note: Results are percentages and may not add to 100% due to rounding
Source: Dave Leip's Atlas of U.S. Presidential Elections

EMPLOYERS

Major Employers

Company Name	Industry
Bryan Independent School District	Education
City of Bryan	Government
City of College Station	Government
College Station Independent School District	Education
H-E-B Grocery	Grocery stores
New Alenco Windows	Fabricated metal products
Reynolds and Reynolds/Rentsys	Computer hardware/software
Sanderson Farms	Poultry processing
St. Joseph Regional Health Center	Health services
Texas A&M University System	Education
Wal-Mart Stores	Retail

Note: Companies shown are located within the College Station-Bryan, TX Metropolitan Statistical Area.
Source: Hoovers.com; Wikipedia

PUBLIC SAFETY

Crime Rate

Area	All Crimes	Violent Crimes				Property Crimes		
		Murder	Rape[3]	Robbery	Aggrav. Assault	Burglary	Larceny -Theft	Motor Vehicle Theft
City	2,196.7	0.9	45.9	42.5	110.1	260.1	1,635.8	101.4
Suburbs[1]	2,595.9	4.9	58.4	55.6	235.7	424.8	1,694.9	121.7
Metro[2]	2,418.2	3.1	52.9	49.8	179.8	351.5	1,668.6	112.7
U.S.	2,756.1	5.3	41.7	98.0	248.9	430.4	1,694.4	237.4

Note: Figures are crimes per 100,000 population; (1) All areas within the metro area that are located outside the city limits; (2) Figures cover the College Station-Bryan, TX Metropolitan Statistical Area—see Appendix B for areas included; (3) The city and U.S. figures shown were reported using the revised Uniform Crime Reporting (UCR) definition of rape. The suburban and metro area figures shown are an aggregate total of the data submitted using both the revised and legacy UCR definitions.
Source: FBI Uniform Crime Reports, 2017

Hate Crimes

Area	Number of Quarters Reported	Number of Incidents per Bias Motivation					
		Race/Ethnicity/ Ancestry	Religion	Sexual Orientation	Disability	Gender	Gender Identity
City	4	0	0	0	0	0	0
U.S.	4	4,131	1,564	1,130	116	46	119

Source: Federal Bureau of Investigation, Hate Crime Statistics 2017

Identity Theft Consumer Reports

Area	Reports	Reports per 100,000 Population	Rank[2]
MSA[1]	206	81	224
U.S.	444,602	135	-

Note: (1) Figures cover the College Station-Bryan, TX Metropolitan Statistical Area—see Appendix B for areas included; (2) Rank ranges from 1 to 389 where 1 indicates greatest number of identity theft reports per 100,000 population
Source: Federal Trade Commission, Consumer Sentinel Network Data Book for January–December 2018

Fraud and Other Consumer Reports

Area	Reports	Reports per 100,000 Population	Rank[2]
MSA[1]	902	354	355
U.S.	2,552,917	776	-

Note: (1) Figures cover the College Station-Bryan, TX Metropolitan Statistical Area—see Appendix B for areas included; (2) Rank ranges from 1 to 389 where 1 indicates greatest number of fraud and other consumer reports per 100,000 population
Source: Federal Trade Commission, Consumer Sentinel Network Data Book for January–December 2018

SPORTS

Professional Sports Teams

Team Name	League	Year Established
No teams are located in the metro area		

Source: Wikipedia, Major Professional Sports Teams of the United States and Canada, April 5, 2019

CLIMATE

Average and Extreme Temperatures

Temperature	Jan	Feb	Mar	Apr	May	Jun	Jul	Aug	Sep	Oct	Nov	Dec	Yr.
Extreme High (°F)	90	97	98	98	100	105	109	106	104	98	91	90	109
Average High (°F)	60	64	72	79	85	91	95	96	90	81	70	63	79
Average Temp. (°F)	50	53	61	69	75	82	85	85	80	70	60	52	69
Average Low (°F)	39	43	50	58	65	72	74	74	69	59	49	41	58
Extreme Low (°F)	-2	7	18	35	43	53	64	61	47	32	20	4	-2

Note: Figures cover the years 1948-1990
Source: National Climatic Data Center, International Station Meteorological Climate Summary, 9/96

Average Precipitation/Snowfall/Humidity

Precip./Humidity	Jan	Feb	Mar	Apr	May	Jun	Jul	Aug	Sep	Oct	Nov	Dec	Yr.
Avg. Precip. (in.)	1.6	2.3	1.8	2.9	4.3	3.5	1.9	1.9	3.3	3.5	2.1	1.9	31.1
Avg. Snowfall (in.)	1	Tr	Tr	0	0	0	0	0	0	0	Tr	Tr	1
Avg. Rel. Hum. 6am (%)	79	80	79	83	88	89	88	87	86	84	81	79	84
Avg. Rel. Hum. 3pm (%)	53	51	47	50	53	49	43	42	47	47	49	51	48

Note: Figures cover the years 1948-1990; Tr = Trace amounts (<0.05 in. of rain; <0.5 in. of snow)
Source: National Climatic Data Center, International Station Meteorological Climate Summary, 9/96

Weather Conditions

	Temperature			Daytime Sky			Precipitation	
10°F & below	32°F & below	90°F & above	Clear	Partly cloudy	Cloudy	0.01 inch or more precip.	0.1 inch or more snow/ice	Thunder-storms
< 1	20	111	105	148	112	83	1	41

Note: Figures are average number of days per year and cover the years 1948-1990
Source: National Climatic Data Center, International Station Meteorological Climate Summary, 9/96

HAZARDOUS WASTE

Superfund Sites

The College Station-Bryan, TX metro area has no sites on the EPA's Superfund Final National Priorities List. There are a total of 1,390 Superfund sites with a status of proposed or final on the list in the U.S. *U.S. Environmental Protection Agency, National Priorities List, April 5, 2019*

AIR & WATER QUALITY

Air Quality Trends: Ozone

	1990	1995	2000	2005	2010	2012	2014	2015	2016	2017
MSA[1]	n/a	n/a	n/a	n/a	n/a	n/a	n/a	n/a	n/a	n/a
U.S.	0.088	0.089	0.082	0.080	0.073	0.075	0.067	0.068	0.069	0.068

Note: (1) Data covers the College Station-Bryan, TX Metropolitan Statistical Area—see Appendix B for areas included; n/a not available. The values shown are the composite ozone concentration averages among trend sites based on the highest fourth daily maximum 8-hour concentration in parts per million. These trends are based on sites having an adequate record of monitoring data during the trend period. Data from exceptional events are included.
Source: U.S. Environmental Protection Agency, Air Quality Monitoring Information, "Air Quality Trends by City, 1990-2017"

Air Quality Index

Area	Percent of Days when Air Quality was...[2]					AQI Statistics[2]	
	Good	Moderate	Unhealthy for Sensitive Groups	Unhealthy	Very Unhealthy	Maximum	Median
MSA[1]	100.0	0.0	0.0	0.0	0.0	23	0

Note: (1) Data covers the College Station-Bryan, TX Metropolitan Statistical Area—see Appendix B for areas included; (2) Based on 365 days with AQI data in 2017. Air Quality Index (AQI) is an index for reporting daily air quality. EPA calculates the AQI for five major air pollutants regulated by the Clean Air Act: ground-level ozone, particle pollution (aka particulate matter), carbon monoxide, sulfur dioxide, and nitrogen dioxide. The AQI runs from 0 to 500. The higher the AQI value, the greater the level of air pollution and the greater the health concern. There are six AQI categories: "Good" AQI is between 0 and 50. Air quality is considered satisfactory; "Moderate" AQI is between 51 and 100. Air quality is acceptable; "Unhealthy for Sensitive Groups" When AQI values are between 101 and 150, members of sensitive groups may experience health effects; "Unhealthy" When AQI values are between 151 and 200 everyone may begin to experience health effects; "Very Unhealthy" AQI values between 201 and 300 trigger a health alert; "Hazardous" AQI values over 300 trigger warnings of emergency conditions (not shown).
Source: U.S. Environmental Protection Agency, Air Quality Index Report, 2017

Air Quality Index Pollutants

Area	Carbon Monoxide	Nitrogen Dioxide	Ozone	Sulfur Dioxide	Particulate Matter 2.5	Particulate Matter 10
	Percent of Days when AQI Pollutant was...[2]					
MSA[1]	0.0	0.0	0.0	100.0	0.0	0.0

Note: (1) Data covers the College Station-Bryan, TX Metropolitan Statistical Area—see Appendix B for areas included; (2) Based on 365 days with AQI data in 2017. The Air Quality Index (AQI) is an index for reporting daily air quality. EPA calculates the AQI for five major air pollutants regulated by the Clean Air Act: ground-level ozone, particle pollution (also known as particulate matter), carbon monoxide, sulfur dioxide, and nitrogen dioxide. The AQI runs from 0 to 500. The higher the AQI value, the greater the level of air pollution and the greater the health concern.
Source: U.S. Environmental Protection Agency, Air Quality Index Report, 2017

Maximum Air Pollutant Concentrations: Particulate Matter, Ozone, CO and Lead

	Particulate Matter 10 (ug/m³)	Particulate Matter 2.5 Wtd AM (ug/m³)	Particulate Matter 2.5 24-Hr (ug/m³)	Ozone (ppm)	Carbon Monoxide (ppm)	Lead (ug/m³)
MSA[1] Level	n/a	n/a	n/a	n/a	n/a	n/a
NAAQS[2]	150	15	35	0.075	9	0.15
Met NAAQS[2]	n/a	n/a	n/a	n/a	n/a	n/a

Note: (1) Data covers the College Station-Bryan, TX Metropolitan Statistical Area—see Appendix B for areas included; Data from exceptional events are included; (2) National Ambient Air Quality Standards; ppm = parts per million; ug/m³ = micrograms per cubic meter; n/a not available.
Concentrations: Particulate Matter 10 (coarse particulate)—highest second maximum 24-hour concentration; Particulate Matter 2.5 Wtd AM (fine particulate)—highest weighted annual mean concentration; Particulate Matter 2.5 24-Hour (fine particulate)—highest 98th percentile 24-hour concentration; Ozone—highest fourth daily maximum 8-hour concentration; Carbon Monoxide—highest second maximum non-overlapping 8-hour concentration; Lead—maximum running 3-month average
Source: U.S. Environmental Protection Agency, Air Quality Monitoring Information, "Air Quality Statistics by City, 2017"

Maximum Air Pollutant Concentrations: Nitrogen Dioxide and Sulfur Dioxide

	Nitrogen Dioxide AM (ppb)	Nitrogen Dioxide 1-Hr (ppb)	Sulfur Dioxide AM (ppb)	Sulfur Dioxide 1-Hr (ppb)	Sulfur Dioxide 24-Hr (ppb)
MSA[1] Level	n/a	n/a	n/a	13	n/a
NAAQS[2]	53	100	30	75	140
Met NAAQS[2]	n/a	n/a	n/a	Yes	n/a

Note: (1) Data covers the College Station-Bryan, TX Metropolitan Statistical Area—see Appendix B for areas included; Data from exceptional events are included; (2) National Ambient Air Quality Standards; ppm = parts per million; ug/m³ = micrograms per cubic meter; n/a not available.
Concentrations: Nitrogen Dioxide AM—highest arithmetic mean concentration; Nitrogen Dioxide 1-Hr—highest 98th percentile 1-hour daily maximum concentration; Sulfur Dioxide AM—highest annual mean concentration; Sulfur Dioxide 1-Hr—highest 99th percentile 1-hour daily maximum concentration; Sulfur Dioxide 24-Hr—highest second maximum 24-hour concentration
Source: U.S. Environmental Protection Agency, Air Quality Monitoring Information, "Air Quality Statistics by City, 2017"

Drinking Water

Water System Name	Pop. Served	Primary Water Source Type	Health Based	Monitoring/ Reporting
			Violations[1]	
City of College Station	91,428	Ground	0	0

Note: (1) Based on violation data from January 1, 2018 to December 31, 2018
Source: U.S. Environmental Protection Agency, Office of Ground Water and Drinking Water, Safe Drinking Water Information System (based on data extracted April 5, 2019)

Columbia, South Carolina

Background

Located on the Congaree River, Columbia is South Carolina's capital and largest city, and the seat of Richland County. It is a center for local and state government, and an important financial, insurance, and medical center.

The region has been a trade center since a trading post opened south of the present-day city in 1718. In 1786, Columbia was chosen as the new state's capital due to its location in the center of South Carolina, a compromise between residents on the coast and those living further inland.

The nation's second planned city, Columbia was originally 400 acres along the river. The main thoroughfares were designed 150 feet wide and other streets were also wider than most. Much of this spacious layout survives, lending an expansive feel to the city. Columbia was chartered as a town in 1805. Its first mayor—or "intendent"—John Taylor, later served in the state general assembly, in the U.S. Congress, and as governor of the state. Columbia was staunchly Confederate during the Civil War, attacked in 1865 by General Sherman's troops and set ablaze by both Union attackers and Confederate evacuees. After the war and Reconstruction, Columbia was revitalized as the state's industrial and farm products hub.

Today, a brisk renewal continues in Columbia's formerly moribund downtown thanks to the state's first Business Improvement District. The City Center Partnership, Inc., manages the district and works to bring businesses and residents into the area, via, among other things, the free ZeRover shuttle. The area's Central Business District has seen record office space occupancy.

Columbia is home to the University of South Carolina, a major employer alongside BlueCross BlueShield of SC. The USC/Columbia Technology Incubator companies generated more than $30 million in gross revenue in recent years. The university has also created the 500-acre Innovista Research District to provide office and lab space to tech and innovation businesses and startups. The health care industry is also significant. The Medical University of South Carolina and the area's largest employer, Palmetto Health, merged their medical practices in 2016 under the banner of Palmetto Health-USC Medical Group. The city's two venerable Providence Hospitals—operated by the Sisters of Charity since 1938—were recently acquired by LifePoint Health, a Tennessee-based for-profit company that operates health care facilities in 22 states.

Other large employers include Fort Jackson, the U.S. Army's largest initial entry training installation (and also home to Fort Jackson National Cemetery), and the United Parcel Service, which operates a freight service center in West Columbia. Colonial Life & Accident Insurance is also based in Columbia.

Columbia is the cultural center for the area, known as South Carolina's Midlands. The Columbia Museum of Art, with its collection of Renaissance and Baroque art, is a major regional museum. The performing arts are onstage year-round at the Koger Center for the Arts at USC. The city's Town Theatre, nearing 100, is the country's oldest community theatre in continuous use. The South Carolina State Museum "Windows to New Worlds" includes a planetarium, observatory and 4-D theater. Major historic architecture in Columbia includes the City Hall, designed by President Ulysses S. Grant's federal architect, Alfred Bult Mullet, and the Lutheran Survey Print Building.

In addition to USC, Columbia's other institutions of higher learning are Lutheran Theological Seminary, Columbia College, Benedict College, Allen University, and Columbia International University.

In March, 2015, Bree Newsome was arrested when she scaled the South Carolina State House flag pole to remove its Confederate battle flag, motivated, she said, by the Charleston Massacre. Her action garnered national news coverage, and over $60,000 was raised for her bail within hours of her arrest. Though the flag was raised again minutes after Newsome's climb, it was permanently removed in July of that year.

Located about 150 miles southeast of the Appalachian Mountains, Columbia has a relatively temperate climate. Summers are long and often hot and humid with frequent thunderstorms, thanks to the Bermuda high-pressure force. Winters are mild with little snow, while spring is changeable and can include infrequent tornadoes or hail. Fall is considered the most pleasant season.

Rankings

General Rankings

- For its "Best for Vets: Places to Live 2019" rankings, *Military Times* evaluated 599 cities (83 large, 234 medium, 282 small) and compared the locations across three broad categories: veteran and military culture/services; economic indicators; and livability factors such as health, crime, traffic, and school quality. Columbia ranked #39 out of the top 50, in the medium-sized city category (populations of 100,000-249,999). Data points more specific to veterans and the military weighed more heavily than the rest. *rebootcamp.militarytimes.com, "Military Times Best Places to Live 2019," September 10, 2018*

Business/Finance Rankings

- The personal finance site NerdWallet analyzed 183 American metropolitan areas with populations over 250,000 and more than 15,000 businesses to rank where entrepreneurs find the most success. Criteria included area economy, annual income, housing cost, unemployment rate, and the success rate of area businesses. Columbia ranked #142. *www.nerdwallet.com, "Best Places to Start a Business," April 27, 2015*

- The Brookings Institution ranked the nation's largest cities based on income inequality. Columbia was ranked #38 (#1 = greatest inequality). Criteria: the "95/20 ratio," a figure representing the income at which a household earns more than 95 percent of all other households, divided by the income at which a household earns more than only 20 percent of all other households. *Brookings Institution, "Household Income Inequality, Largest Cities of 97 Large U.S. Metro Areas, 2014-2016," February 5, 2018*

- The Brookings Institution ranked the 100 largest metro areas in the U.S. based on income inequality. Columbia was ranked #63 (#1 = greatest inequality). Criteria: the "95/20 ratio," a figure representing the income at which a household earns more than 95 percent of all other households, divided by the income at which a household earns more than only 20 percent of all other households. *Brookings Institution, "Household Income Inequality, 100 Largest U.S. Metro Areas, 2014-2016," February 5, 2018*

- The Columbia metro area appeared on the Milken Institute "2018 Best Performing Cities" list. Rank: #111 out of 200 large metro areas. Criteria: job growth; wage and salary growth; high-tech output growth. *Milken Institute, "Best-Performing Cities 2018," January 24, 2019*

- *Forbes* ranked the 200 most populous metro areas to determine the nation's "Best Places for Business and Careers." The Columbia metro area was ranked #93. Criteria: costs (business and living); job growth (past and projected); income growth; quality of life; educational attainment (college and high school); projected economic growth; cultural and recreational opportunities; net migration patterns; number of highly ranked colleges. *Forbes, "The Best Places for Business and Careers 2018: Seattle Leads the Way," October 24, 2018*

Children/Family Rankings

- Columbia was selected as one of the most playful cities in the U.S. by KaBOOM! The organization's Playful City USA initiative honors cities and towns across the nation that have made their communities more playable. Criteria: pledging to integrate play as a solution to challenges in their communities; making it easy for children to get active and balanced play; creating more family-friendly and innovative communities as a result. *KaBOOM! National Campaign for Play, "2017 Playful City USA Communities"*

Dating/Romance Rankings

- Columbia was selected as one of the nation's most romantic cities with 100,000 or more residents by Amazon.com. The city ranked #11 of 20. Criteria: per capita sales of romance novels, relationship books, romantic comedy movies, romantic music, and sexual wellness products. *Amazon.com, "Top 20 Most Romantic Cities in the U.S.," February 1, 2017*

Education Rankings

- Personal finance website *WalletHub* analyzed the 150 largest U.S. metropolitan statistical areas to determine where the most educated Americans are choosing to settle. Criteria: education quality and attainment gap; education levels; percentage of workers with degrees; public school quality rankings; quality and size of each metro area's universities. Columbia was ranked #69 (#1 = most educated city). *www.WalletHub.com, "2018's Most and Least Educated Cities in America, " July 24, 2018*

Food/Drink Rankings

- *Men's Health* ranked 100 major U.S. cities in terms of alcohol intoxication. Columbia ranked #13 (#1 = most sober).Criteria: binge drinking; alcohol-related traffic accidents, arrests, and fatalities. *Men's Health, "America's Drunkest Cities," March 9, 2015*

Health/Fitness Rankings

- Columbia was identified as a "2018 Spring Allergy Capital." The area ranked #19 out of 100. Three groups of factors were used to identify the most challenging cities for people with allergies during the spring season: annual pollen levels; medicine utilization; access to board-certified allergists. *Asthma and Allergy Foundation of America, "Spring Allergy Capitals 2018"*

- Columbia was identified as a "2018 Fall Allergy Capital." The area ranked #28 out of 100. Three groups of factors were used to identify the most challenging cities for people with allergies during the fall season: annual pollen levels; medicine utilization; access to board-certified allergists. *Asthma and Allergy Foundation of America, "Fall Allergy Capitals 2018"*

- Columbia was identified as a "2018 Asthma Capital." The area ranked #62 out of the nation's 100 largest metropolitan areas. Criteria: estimated prevalence; self-reported prevalence; crude death rate for asthma; annual pollen score; annual air quality; public smoking laws; number of board-certified asthma specialists; school inhaler access laws; rescue medication use; controller medication use; ER visits for asthma; uninsured rate; poverty rate. *Asthma and Allergy Foundation of America, "Asthma Capitals 2018: The Most Challenging Places to Live With Asthma"*

- *Men's Health* ranked 100 major U.S. cities in terms of the best cities for men. Columbia ranked #74. Criteria: health; fitness; quality of life. *Men's Health, "The Best & Worst Cities for Men Who Want to Be Fit and Happy," January 1, 2016*

- The Columbia metro area ranked #166 out of 189 in The Gallup-Healthways Well-Being Index. Criteria: purpose; social well being; financial health; community and physical health. Results are based on telephone interviews with adults, aged 18 and older, living in metropolitan areas in the 50 U.S. states and the District of Columbia. *Gallup-Healthways, "State of American Well-Being, 2017 Community Well-Being Rankings" March 2018*

Real Estate Rankings

- *WalletHub* compared the most populated U.S. cities, as well as at least two of the most populated cities in each state, for a total of 179, to determine which had the best markets for real estate agents. Columbia ranked #168 where demand was high and pay was the best. Criteria: sales per agent; annual median wage for real-estate agents; monthly average starting salary for real estate agents; real estate job density and competition; unemployment rate; housing-market health index; and other relevant metrics. *www.WalletHub.com, "2018's Best Places to Be a Real Estate Agent,"April 25, 2018*

- The Columbia metro area was identified as one of nine best housing markets to invest in. Criteria: single-family rental home investing in the first quarter of 2017 based on first-year returns. The area ranked #3. *The Business Insider, "Here are the 9 Best U.S. Housing Markets for Investment," May 11, 2017*

- Columbia was ranked #62 out of 237 metro areas in terms of housing affordability in 2018 by the National Association of Home Builders (#1 = most affordable). Criteria: the share of homes sold in that area affordable to a family earning the local median income, based on standard mortgage underwriting criteria. *National Association of Home Builders®, NAHB-Wells Fargo Housing Opportunity Index, 4th Quarter 2018*

- The nation's largest metro areas were analyzed in terms of the percentage of households entering some stage of foreclosure in 2018. The Columbia metro area ranked #7 out of 10 (#1 = highest foreclosure rate). *ATTOM Data Solutions, "2018 Year-End U.S. Foreclosure Market Report™," January 17, 2019*

Safety Rankings

- Allstate ranked the 200 largest cities in America in terms of driver safety. Columbia ranked #166. Criteria: internal property damage claims over a two-year period from January 2015 to December 2016. The report helps increase the importance of safety awareness behind the wheel. *Allstate, "Allstate America's Best Drivers Report, 2018" August 28, 2018*

- The National Insurance Crime Bureau ranked 382 metro areas in the U.S. in terms of per capita rates of vehicle theft. The Columbia metro area ranked #29 (#1 = highest rate). Criteria: number of vehicle theft offenses per 100,000 inhabitants in 2017. *National Insurance Crime Bureau, "Hot Spots 2017," July 12, 2018*

Seniors/Retirement Rankings

- From its Best Cities for Successful Aging indexes, the Milken Institute generated rankings for metropolitan areas, weighing data in nine categories—health care, wellness, living arrangements, transportation and convenience, financial characteristics, education, employment, community engagement, and overall livability. The Columbia metro area was ranked #54 overall in the large metro area category. *Milken Institute, "Best Cities for Successful Aging, 2017" March 14, 2017*

Women/Minorities Rankings

- Personal finance website *WalletHub* compared more than 180 U.S. cities—including the 150 most populated U.S. cities, plus at least two of the most populated cities in each state—across two key dimensions, "Hispanic Business-Friendliness" and "Hispanic Purchasing Power", to arrive at the most favorable conditions for Hispanic entrepreneurs. Columbia was ranked #141 out of 182. Criteria includes: share of Hispanic-Owned Businesses; Hispanic entrepreneurship rate to median annual income of Hispanics; Small Business-Friendliness score; cost of living; and number of Hispanics with at least a bachelor's degree. *WalletHub.com, "2018's Best Cities for Hispanic Entrepreneurs," April 26, 2018*

Miscellaneous Rankings

- *WalletHub* compared the 150 most populated U.S. cities to determine their operating efficiency. A "Quality of Services" score was constructed for each city and then divided by the total budget per capita to reveal which were managed the best. Columbia ranked #67. Criteria: financial stability; economy; education; safety; health; infrastructure and pollution. *www.WalletHub.com, "2018's Best- & Worst-Run Cities in America," July 9, 2018*

Business Environment

CITY FINANCES

City Government Finances

Component	2016 ($000)	2016 ($ per capita)
Total Revenues	319,590	2,389
Total Expenditures	366,044	2,736
Debt Outstanding	592,059	4,425
Cash and Securities[1]	199,849	1,494

Note: (1) Cash and security holdings of a government at the close of its fiscal year, including those of its dependent agencies, utilities, and liquor stores.
Source: U.S. Census Bureau, State & Local Government Finances 2016

City Government Revenue by Source

Source	2016 ($000)	2016 ($ per capita)	2016 (%)
General Revenue			
From Federal Government	9,009	67	2.8
From State Government	2,132	16	0.7
From Local Governments	22,985	172	7.2
Taxes			
Property	51,006	381	16.0
Sales and Gross Receipts	13,399	100	4.2
Personal Income	0	0	0.0
Corporate Income	0	0	0.0
Motor Vehicle License	0	0	0.0
Other Taxes	39,008	292	12.2
Current Charges	72,079	539	22.6
Liquor Store	0	0	0.0
Utility	80,454	601	25.2
Employee Retirement	0	0	0.0

Source: U.S. Census Bureau, State & Local Government Finances 2016

City Government Expenditures by Function

Function	2016 ($000)	2016 ($ per capita)	2016 (%)
General Direct Expenditures			
Air Transportation	0	0	0.0
Corrections	0	0	0.0
Education	0	0	0.0
Employment Security Administration	0	0	0.0
Financial Administration	4,366	32	1.2
Fire Protection	42,428	317	11.6
General Public Buildings	6,708	50	1.8
Governmental Administration, Other	5,764	43	1.6
Health	4,962	37	1.4
Highways	19,054	142	5.2
Hospitals	0	0	0.0
Housing and Community Development	7,071	52	1.9
Interest on General Debt	4,340	32	1.2
Judicial and Legal	4,568	34	1.2
Libraries	0	0	0.0
Parking	4,852	36	1.3
Parks and Recreation	41,262	308	11.3
Police Protection	39,772	297	10.9
Public Welfare	907	6	0.2
Sewerage	56,838	424	15.5
Solid Waste Management	11,145	83	3.0
Veterans' Services	0	0	0.0
Liquor Store	0	0	0.0
Utility	82,314	615	22.5
Employee Retirement	0	0	0.0

Source: U.S. Census Bureau, State & Local Government Finances 2016

DEMOGRAPHICS

Population Growth

Area	1990 Census	2000 Census	2010 Census	2017* Estimate	Population Growth (%) 1990-2017	Population Growth (%) 2010-2017
City	115,475	116,278	129,272	132,236	14.5	2.3
MSA[1]	548,325	647,158	767,598	808,377	47.4	5.3
U.S.	248,709,873	281,421,906	308,745,538	321,004,407	29.1	4.0

Note: (1) Figures cover the Columbia, SC Metropolitan Statistical Area—see Appendix B for areas included;
(*) 2013-2017 5-year estimated population
Source: U.S. Census Bureau, 1990 Census, Census 2000, Census 2010, 2013-2017 American Community
Survey 5-Year Estimates

Household Size

Area	Persons in Household (%) One	Two	Three	Four	Five	Six	Seven or More	Average Household Size
City	40.3	32.8	13.0	8.6	4.1	0.6	0.5	2.20
MSA[1]	29.4	34.4	16.1	12.3	5.3	1.6	0.9	2.50
U.S.	27.7	33.8	15.7	13.0	6.0	2.3	1.4	2.60

Note: (1) Figures cover the Columbia, SC Metropolitan Statistical Area—see Appendix B for areas included
Source: U.S. Census Bureau, 2013-2017 American Community Survey 5-Year Estimates

Race

Area	White Alone[2] (%)	Black Alone[2] (%)	Asian Alone[2] (%)	AIAN[3] Alone[2] (%)	NHOPI[4] Alone[2] (%)	Other Race Alone[2] (%)	Two or More Races (%)
City	52.3	40.9	2.6	0.1	0.2	1.2	2.6
MSA[1]	60.2	33.3	2.0	0.2	0.1	1.7	2.6
U.S.	73.0	12.7	5.4	0.8	0.2	4.8	3.1

Note: (1) Figures cover the Columbia, SC Metropolitan Statistical Area—see Appendix B for areas included;
(2) Alone is defined as not being in combination with one or more other races; (3) American Indian and Alaska
Native; (4) Native Hawaiian and Other Pacific Islander
Source: U.S. Census Bureau, 2013-2017 American Community Survey 5-Year Estimates

Hispanic or Latino Origin

Area	Total (%)	Mexican (%)	Puerto Rican (%)	Cuban (%)	Other (%)
City	5.8	2.5	1.3	0.3	1.6
MSA[1]	5.4	2.8	1.0	0.2	1.4
U.S.	17.6	11.1	1.7	0.7	4.1

Note: Persons of Hispanic or Latino origin can be of any race; (1) Figures cover the Columbia, SC
Metropolitan Statistical Area—see Appendix B for areas included
Source: U.S. Census Bureau, 2013-2017 American Community Survey 5-Year Estimates

Segregation

Type	Segregation Indices[1] 1990	2000	2010	2010 Rank[2]	Percent Change 1990-2000	1990-2010	2000-2010
Black/White	50.4	48.1	48.8	74	-2.3	-1.6	0.7
Asian/White	43.9	43.8	41.9	46	-0.1	-2.0	-1.9
Hispanic/White	37.7	34.9	34.9	82	-2.8	-2.8	0.0

Note: All figures cover the Metropolitan Statistical Area—see Appendix B for areas included; Figures are based
on an analysis of 1990, 2000, and 2010 Census Decennial Census tract data by William H. Frey, Brookings
Institution and the University of Michigan Social Science Data Analysis Network. In this analysis all racial
groups (whites, blacks, and asians) are non-Hispanic members of those races. Hispanics are shown as a
separate category; (1) Segregation Indices are Dissimilarity Indices that measure the degree to which the
minority group is distributed differently than whites across census tracts. They range from 0 (complete
integration) to 100 (complete segregation) where the value indicates the percentage of the minority group that
needs to move to be distributed exactly like whites; (2) Ranges from 1 (most segregated) to 102 (least
segregated); n/a not available.
Source: www.CensusScope.org

Ancestry

Area	German	Irish	English	American	Italian	Polish	French[2]	Scottish	Dutch
City	9.4	7.8	8.8	6.1	2.8	1.4	2.0	2.4	0.7
MSA[1]	10.8	8.0	8.0	9.1	2.4	1.2	1.7	2.0	0.8
U.S.	14.1	10.1	7.5	6.6	5.3	2.9	2.5	1.7	1.3

Note: Figures are the percentage of the total population reporting a particular ancestry. The nine most commonly reported ancestries in the U.S. are shown. Figures include multiple ancestries (e.g. if a person reported being Irish and Italian, they were included in both columns); (1) Figures cover the Columbia, SC Metropolitan Statistical Area—see Appendix B for areas included; (2) Excludes Basque
Source: U.S. Census Bureau, 2013-2017 American Community Survey 5-Year Estimates

Foreign-Born Population

Area	Percent of Population Born in								
	Any Foreign Country	Asia	Mexico	Europe	Carribean	Central America[2]	South America	Africa	Canada
City	5.6	2.3	0.9	0.9	0.2	0.3	0.5	0.4	0.1
MSA[1]	5.1	1.6	1.2	0.8	0.2	0.5	0.2	0.4	0.1
U.S.	13.4	4.1	3.6	1.5	1.3	1.0	0.9	0.6	0.3

Note: (1) Figures cover the Columbia, SC Metropolitan Statistical Area—see Appendix B for areas included; (2) Excludes Mexico.
Source: U.S. Census Bureau, 2013-2017 American Community Survey 5-Year Estimates

Marital Status

Area	Never Married	Now Married[2]	Separated	Widowed	Divorced
City	56.0	27.9	3.0	4.3	8.8
MSA[1]	36.2	44.2	3.1	5.8	10.7
U.S.	33.1	48.2	2.0	5.8	10.9

Note: Figures are percentages and cover the population 15 years of age and older; (1) Figures cover the Columbia, SC Metropolitan Statistical Area—see Appendix B for areas included; (2) Excludes separated
Source: U.S. Census Bureau, 2013-2017 American Community Survey 5-Year Estimates

Disability by Age

Area	All Ages	Under 18 Years Old	18 to 64 Years Old	65 Years and Over
City	11.7	3.5	10.0	36.6
MSA[1]	13.4	3.8	11.8	36.7
U.S.	12.6	4.2	10.3	35.5

Note: Figures show percent of the civilian noninstitutionalized population that reported having a disability. Disability status is determined from six types of difficulty: vision, hearing, cognitive, ambulatory, self-care, and independent living. For children under 5 years old, hearing and vision difficulty are used to determine disability status. For children between the ages of 5 and 14, disability status is determined from hearing, vision, cognitive, ambulatory, and self-care difficulties. For people aged 15 years and older, they are considered to have a disability if they have difficulty with any one of the six difficulty types; Note: (1) Figures cover the Columbia, SC Metropolitan Statistical Area—see Appendix B for areas included
Source: U.S. Census Bureau, 2013-2017 American Community Survey 5-Year Estimates

Age

Area	Percent of Population									Median Age
	Under Age 5	Age 5–19	Age 20–34	Age 35–44	Age 45–54	Age 55–64	Age 65–74	Age 75–84	Age 85+	
City	5.1	23.0	32.3	10.5	10.0	9.4	5.8	2.8	1.2	28.3
MSA[1]	5.9	20.4	21.9	12.5	13.1	12.5	8.4	3.8	1.4	36.3
U.S.	6.2	19.5	20.7	12.7	13.4	12.7	8.6	4.4	1.9	37.8

Note: (1) Figures cover the Columbia, SC Metropolitan Statistical Area—see Appendix B for areas included
Source: U.S. Census Bureau, 2013-2017 American Community Survey 5-Year Estimates

Gender

Area	Males	Females	Males per 100 Females
City	67,861	64,375	105.4
MSA[1]	392,671	415,706	94.5
U.S.	158,018,753	162,985,654	97.0

Note: (1) Figures cover the Columbia, SC Metropolitan Statistical Area—see Appendix B for areas included
Source: U.S. Census Bureau, 2013-2017 American Community Survey 5-Year Estimates

Religious Groups by Family

Area	Catholic	Baptist	Non-Den.	Methodist[2]	Lutheran	LDS[3]	Pente-costal	Presby-terian[4]	Muslim[5]	Judaism
MSA[1]	3.1	18.1	5.2	9.4	3.4	1.1	2.7	3.3	0.1	0.2
U.S.	19.1	9.3	4.0	4.0	2.3	2.0	1.9	1.6	0.8	0.7

Note: Figures are the number of adherents as a percentage of the total population; (1) Figures cover the Columbia, SC Metropolitan Statistical Area—see Appendix B for areas included; (2) Methodist/Pietist; (3) Latter Day Saints; (4) Reformed; (5) Figures are estimates
Source: Association of Statisticians of American Religious Bodies, 2010 U.S. Religion Census: Religious Congregations & Membership Study

Religious Groups by Tradition

Area	Catholic	Evangelical Protestant	Mainline Protestant	Other Tradition	Black Protestant	Orthodox
MSA[1]	3.1	25.6	13.5	2.1	5.5	0.1
U.S.	19.1	16.2	7.3	4.3	1.6	0.3

Note: Figures are the number of adherents as a percentage of the total population; (1) Figures cover the Columbia, SC Metropolitan Statistical Area—see Appendix B for areas included
Source: Association of Statisticians of American Religious Bodies, 2010 U.S. Religion Census: Religious Congregations & Membership Study

ECONOMY

Gross Metropolitan Product

Area	2016	2017	2018	2019	Rank[2]
MSA[1]	40.3	41.6	43.2	45.6	71

Note: Figures are in billions of dollars; (1) Figures cover the Columbia, SC Metropolitan Statistical Area—see Appendix B for areas included; (2) Rank is based on 2017 data and ranges from 1 to 381
Source: U.S. Conference of Mayors, U.S. Metro Economies: Economic Growth & Full Employment, June 2018

Economic Growth

Area	2017-2018 (%)	2019-2020 (%)	2021-2022 (%)
MSA[1]	2.1	2.8	2.0

Note: Figures are real gross metropolitan product (GMP) growth rates and represent average annual percent change; (1) Figures cover the Columbia, SC Metropolitan Statistical Area—see Appendix B for areas included
Source: U.S. Conference of Mayors, U.S. Metro Economies: Economic Growth & Full Employment, June 2018

Metropolitan Area Exports

Area	2012	2013	2014	2015	2016	2017	Rank[2]
MSA[1]	1,543.6	1,681.3	2,007.9	2,011.8	2,007.7	2,123.9	95

Note: Figures are in millions of dollars; (1) Figures cover the Columbia, SC Metropolitan Statistical Area—see Appendix B for areas included; (2) Rank is based on 2017 data and ranges from 1 to 387
Source: U.S. Department of Commerce, International Trade Administration, Office of Trade and Economic Analysis, Industry and Analysis, Exports by Metropolitan Area, extracted March 25, 2019

Building Permits

Area	Single-Family			Multi-Family			Total		
	2016	2017	Pct. Chg.	2016	2017	Pct. Chg.	2016	2017	Pct. Chg.
City	251	341	35.9	0	8	–	251	349	39.0
MSA[1]	3,916	4,072	4.0	711	557	-21.7	4,627	4,629	0.0
U.S.	750,800	820,000	9.2	455,800	462,000	1.4	1,206,600	1,282,000	6.2

Note: (1) Figures cover the Columbia, SC Metropolitan Statistical Area—see Appendix B for areas included; Figures represent new, privately-owned housing units authorized (unadjusted data); All permit data are based on estimates with imputation
Source: U.S. Census Bureau, Manufacturing, Mining, and Construction Statistics, Building Permits, 2016, 2017

Bankruptcy Filings

Area	Business Filings			Nonbusiness Filings		
	2017	2018	% Chg.	2017	2018	% Chg.
Richland County	12	9	-25.0	712	751	5.5
U.S.	23,157	22,232	-4.0	765,863	751,186	-1.9

Note: Business filings include Chapter 7, Chapter 11, Chapter 12, and Chapter 13; Nonbusiness filings include Chapter 7, Chapter 11, and Chapter 13
Source: Administrative Office of the U.S. Courts, Business and Nonbusiness Bankruptcy, County Cases Commenced by Chapter of the Bankruptcy Code, During the 12-Month Period Ending December 31, 2017 and Business and Nonbusiness Bankruptcy, County Cases Commenced by Chapter of the Bankruptcy Code, During the 12-Month Period Ending December 31, 2018

Housing Vacancy Rates

Area	Gross Vacancy Rate[2] (%)			Year-Round Vacancy Rate[3] (%)			Rental Vacancy Rate[4] (%)			Homeowner Vacancy Rate[5] (%)		
	2016	2017	2018	2016	2017	2018	2016	2017	2018	2016	2017	2018
MSA[1]	10.2	11.0	8.9	10.1	10.7	8.8	5.2	6.3	9.4	0.9	2.4	1.9
U.S.	12.8	12.7	12.3	9.9	9.9	9.7	6.9	7.2	6.9	1.7	1.6	1.5

Note: (1) Figures cover the Columbia, SC Metropolitan Statistical Area—see Appendix B for areas included; (2) The percentage of the total housing inventory that is vacant; (3) The percentage of the housing inventory (excluding seasonal units) that is year-round vacant; (4) The percentage of rental inventory that is vacant for rent; (5) The percentage of homeowner inventory that is vacant for sale
Source: U.S. Census Bureau, Housing Vacancies and Homeownership Annual Statistics: 2016, 2017, 2018

INCOME

Income

Area	Per Capita ($)	Median Household ($)	Average Household ($)
City	27,730	43,650	69,516
MSA[1]	27,694	52,728	69,810
U.S.	31,177	57,652	81,283

Note: (1) Figures cover the Columbia, SC Metropolitan Statistical Area—see Appendix B for areas included
Source: U.S. Census Bureau, 2013-2017 American Community Survey 5-Year Estimates

Household Income Distribution

Area	Percent of Households Earning							
	Under $15,000	$15,000 -$24,999	$25,000 -$34,999	$35,000 -$49,999	$50,000 -$74,999	$75,000 -$99,999	$100,000 -$149,999	$150,000 and up
City	19.0	10.9	11.3	13.2	16.6	10.1	9.4	9.6
MSA[1]	12.8	9.9	10.8	13.8	19.1	13.0	12.6	7.8
U.S.	11.6	9.8	9.5	13.0	17.7	12.3	14.1	12.1

Note: (1) Figures cover the Columbia, SC Metropolitan Statistical Area—see Appendix B for areas included
Source: U.S. Census Bureau, 2013-2017 American Community Survey 5-Year Estimates

Poverty Rate

Area	All Ages	Under 18 Years Old	18 to 64 Years Old	65 Years and Over
City	22.3	28.3	22.1	13.7
MSA[1]	15.6	21.3	15.0	8.5
U.S.	14.6	20.3	13.7	9.3

Note: Figures are percentage of people whose income during the past 12 months was below the poverty level; (1) Figures cover the Columbia, SC Metropolitan Statistical Area—see Appendix B for areas included
Source: U.S. Census Bureau, 2013-2017 American Community Survey 5-Year Estimates

EMPLOYMENT

Labor Force and Employment

Area	Civilian Labor Force			Workers Employed		
	Dec. 2017	Dec. 2018	% Chg.	Dec. 2017	Dec. 2018	% Chg.
City	59,440	59,882	0.7	56,706	57,719	1.8
MSA[1]	398,003	400,750	0.7	381,547	388,371	1.8
U.S.	159,880,000	162,510,000	1.6	153,602,000	156,481,000	1.9

Note: Data is not seasonally adjusted and covers workers 16 years of age and older; (1) Figures cover the Columbia, SC Metropolitan Statistical Area—see Appendix B for areas included
Source: Bureau of Labor Statistics, Local Area Unemployment Statistics

Unemployment Rate

Area	2018											
	Jan.	Feb.	Mar.	Apr.	May	Jun.	Jul.	Aug.	Sep.	Oct.	Nov.	Dec.
City	5.4	4.7	4.5	3.1	3.2	4.3	4.2	4.3	3.7	3.6	3.4	3.6
MSA[1]	4.9	4.4	3.9	2.7	2.8	3.5	3.4	3.6	3.2	3.2	3.0	3.1
U.S.	4.5	4.4	4.1	3.7	3.6	4.2	4.1	3.9	3.6	3.5	3.5	3.7

Note: Data is not seasonally adjusted and covers workers 16 years of age and older; (1) Figures cover the Columbia, SC Metropolitan Statistical Area—see Appendix B for areas included
Source: Bureau of Labor Statistics, Local Area Unemployment Statistics

Average Wages

Occupation	$/Hr.	Occupation	$/Hr.
Accountants and Auditors	28.90	Maids and Housekeeping Cleaners	9.80
Automotive Mechanics	20.10	Maintenance and Repair Workers	17.20
Bookkeepers	18.40	Marketing Managers	52.60
Carpenters	21.50	Nuclear Medicine Technologists	32.40
Cashiers	9.80	Nurses, Licensed Practical	20.80
Clerks, General Office	13.20	Nurses, Registered	30.50
Clerks, Receptionists/Information	13.00	Nursing Assistants	12.60
Clerks, Shipping/Receiving	14.70	Packers and Packagers, Hand	10.60
Computer Programmers	39.70	Physical Therapists	43.00
Computer Systems Analysts	35.40	Postal Service Mail Carriers	24.70
Computer User Support Specialists	22.40	Real Estate Brokers	31.90
Cooks, Restaurant	11.20	Retail Salespersons	13.00
Dentists	88.20	Sales Reps., Exc. Tech./Scientific	32.50
Electrical Engineers	44.10	Sales Reps., Tech./Scientific	35.20
Electricians	22.30	Secretaries, Exc. Legal/Med./Exec.	17.40
Financial Managers	64.80	Security Guards	16.90
First-Line Supervisors/Managers, Sales	19.70	Surgeons	n/a
Food Preparation Workers	10.90	Teacher Assistants*	11.40
General and Operations Managers	50.20	Teachers, Elementary School*	24.50
Hairdressers/Cosmetologists	15.20	Teachers, Secondary School*	25.30
Internists, General	n/a	Telemarketers	n/a
Janitors and Cleaners	12.10	Truck Drivers, Heavy/Tractor-Trailer	20.80
Landscaping/Groundskeeping Workers	12.80	Truck Drivers, Light/Delivery Svcs.	16.20
Lawyers	57.30	Waiters and Waitresses	9.60

Note: Wage data covers the Columbia, SC Metropolitan Statistical Area—see Appendix B for areas included; (*) Hourly wages for elementary/secondary school teachers and teacher assistants were calculated by the editors from annual wage data based on a 40 hour work week; n/a not available.
Source: Bureau of Labor Statistics, Metro Area Occupational Employment & Wage Estimates, May 2018

Employment by Occupation

Occupation Classification	City (%)	MSA[1] (%)	U.S. (%)
Management, Business, Science, and Arts	41.5	36.9	37.4
Natural Resources, Construction, and Maintenance	4.6	8.2	8.9
Production, Transportation, and Material Moving	8.9	11.9	12.2
Sales and Office	24.8	25.8	23.5
Service	20.2	17.2	18.0

Note: Figures cover employed civilians 16 years of age and older; (1) Figures cover the Columbia, SC Metropolitan Statistical Area—see Appendix B for areas included
Source: U.S. Census Bureau, 2013-2017 American Community Survey 5-Year Estimates

Employment by Industry

Sector	MSA[1]		U.S.
	Number of Employees	Percent of Total	Percent of Total
Construction, Mining, and Logging	17,900	4.4	5.3
Education and Health Services	47,400	11.7	15.9
Financial Activities	30,500	7.5	5.7
Government	86,800	21.4	15.1
Information	5,500	1.4	1.9
Leisure and Hospitality	40,100	9.9	10.7
Manufacturing	30,100	7.4	8.5
Other Services	16,400	4.0	3.9
Professional and Business Services	53,400	13.2	14.1
Retail Trade	44,200	10.9	10.8
Transportation, Warehousing, and Utilities	18,000	4.4	4.2
Wholesale Trade	15,000	3.7	3.9

Note: Figures are non-farm employment as of December 2018. Figures are not seasonally adjusted and include workers 16 years of age and older; (1) Figures cover the Columbia, SC Metropolitan Statistical Area—see Appendix B for areas included
Source: Bureau of Labor Statistics, Current Employment Statistics, Employment, Hours, and Earnings

Occupations with Greatest Projected Employment Growth: 2018 – 2020

Occupation[1]	2018 Employment	2020 Projected Employment	Numeric Employment Change	Percent Employment Change
Laborers and Freight, Stock, and Material Movers, Hand	53,710	56,190	2,480	4.6
Retail Salespersons	72,070	74,520	2,450	3.4
Combined Food Preparation and Serving Workers, Including Fast Food	53,740	55,880	2,140	4.0
Heavy and Tractor-Trailer Truck Drivers	30,660	32,120	1,460	4.8
General and Operations Managers	35,170	36,440	1,270	3.6
Customer Service Representatives	50,040	51,310	1,270	2.5
Maintenance and Repair Workers, General	28,580	29,710	1,130	4.0
Cashiers	64,600	65,720	1,120	1.7
Team Assemblers	46,990	48,080	1,090	2.3
First-Line Supervisors of Retail Sales Workers	29,570	30,600	1,030	3.5

Note: Projections cover South Carolina; (1) Sorted by numeric employment change
Source: www.projectionscentral.com, State Occupational Projections, 2018–2020 Short-Term Projections

Fastest Growing Occupations: 2018 – 2020

Occupation[1]	2018 Employment	2020 Projected Employment	Numeric Employment Change	Percent Employment Change
Operations Research Analysts	1,000	1,090	90	9.0
Producers and Directors	900	970	70	7.8
Ushers, Lobby Attendants, and Ticket Takers	1,530	1,650	120	7.8
Fiberglass Laminators and Fabricators	780	840	60	7.7
Software Developers, Applications	3,920	4,210	290	7.4
Audio and Video Equipment Technicians	700	750	50	7.1
Molders, Shapers, and Casters, Except Metal and Plastic	710	760	50	7.0
Appraisers and Assessors of Real Estate	1,170	1,250	80	6.8
Industrial Engineers	7,250	7,740	490	6.8
Home Health Aides	10,890	11,630	740	6.8

Note: Projections cover South Carolina; (1) Sorted by percent employment change and excludes occupations with numeric employment change less than 50
Source: www.projectionscentral.com, State Occupational Projections, 2018–2020 Short-Term Projections

TAXES

State Corporate Income Tax Rates

State	Tax Rate (%)	Income Brackets ($)	Num. of Brackets	Financial Institution Tax Rate (%)[a]	Federal Income Tax Ded.
South Carolina	5.0	Flat rate	1	4.5 (v)	No

Note: Tax rates as of January 1, 2019; (a) Rates listed are the corporate income tax rate applied to financial institutions or excise taxes based on income. Some states have other taxes based upon the value of deposits or shares; (v) South Carolina taxes savings and loans at a 6% rate.
Source: Federation of Tax Administrators, Range of State Corporate Income Tax Rates, January 1, 2019

State Individual Income Tax Rates

State	Tax Rate (%)	Income Brackets ($)	Personal Exemptions ($)			Standard Ded. ($)	
			Single	Married	Depend.	Single	Married
South Carolina (a)	0.0 - 7.0	3,030 - 15,160	(d)	(d)	(d)	12,200	24,400 (d)

Note: Tax rates as of January 1, 2019; Local- and county-level taxes are not included; n/a not applicable; Federal income tax is not deductible on state income tax returns; (a) 19 states have statutory provision for automatically adjusting to the rate of inflation the dollar values of the income tax brackets, standard deductions, and/or personal exemptions. Michigan indexes the personal exemption only. Oregon does not index the income brackets for $125,000 and over; (d) These states use the personal exemption/standard deduction amounts provided in the federal Internal Revenue Code. Note, the Tax Cut and Reform Act of 2017 has eliminated personal exemptions from the IRC. CO, ID, NM, ND, SC, and DC have adoptedthe new exemptions and standard deduction amounts. MN conforms to a previous IRC year, while ME adopts the higher standard deduction but retains the exemption amounts.
Source: Federation of Tax Administrators, State Individual Income Tax Rates, January 1, 2019

Various State Sales and Excise Tax Rates

State	State Sales Tax (%)	Gasoline[1] (¢/gal.)	Cigarette[2] ($/pack)	Spirits[3] ($/gal.)	Wine[4] ($/gal.)	Beer[5] ($/gal.)	Recreational Marijuana (%)
South Carolina	6	20.75	0.57	5.42 (i)	1.08 (l)	0.77	Not legal

Note: All tax rates as of January 1, 2019; (1) The American Petroleum Institute has developed a methodology for determining the average tax rate on a gallon of fuel. Rates may include any of the following: excise taxes, environmental fees, storage tank fees, other fees or taxes, general sales tax, and local taxes. In states where gasoline is subject to the general sales tax, or where the fuel tax is based on the average sale price, the average rate determined by API is sensitive to changes in the price of gasoline. States that fully or partially apply general sales taxes to gasoline: CA, CO, GA, IL, IN, MI, NY; (2) The federal excise tax of $1.0066 per pack and local taxes are not included; (3) Rates are those applicable to off-premise sales of 40% alcohol by volume (a.b.v.) distilled spirits in 750ml containers. Local excise taxes are excluded; (4) Rates are those applicable to off-premise sales of 11% a.b.v. non-carbonated wine in 750ml containers; (5) Rates are those applicable to off-premise sales of 4.7% a.b.v. beer in 12 ounce containers; (i) Includes case fees and/or bottle fees which may vary with size of container; (l) Different rates also applicable to alcohol content, place of production, size of container, place purchased (on- or off-premise or on board airlines) or type of wine (carbonated, vermouth, etc.).
Source: Tax Foundation, 2019 Facts & Figures: How Does Your State Compare?

State Business Tax Climate Index Rankings

State	Overall Rank	Corporate Tax Rank	Individual Income Tax Rank	Sales Tax Rank	Unemployment Insurance Tax Rank	Property Tax Rank
South Carolina	35	19	34	34	27	27

Note: The index is a measure of how each state's tax laws affect economic performance. The lower the rank, the more favorable a state's tax system is for business. States without a given tax are given a ranking of 1. The scores/rankings for the District of Columbia do not affect other states. The 2019 index represents the tax climate as of July 1, 2018.
Source: Tax Foundation, State Business Tax Climate Index 2019

COMMERCIAL REAL ESTATE

Office Market

Market Area	Inventory (sq. ft.)	Vacancy Rate (%)	Under Construction (sq. ft.)	YTD Net Absorption (sq. ft.)	Total Average Asking Rent ($/sq. ft./year)
Columbia	16,353,206	8.5	0	151,358	17.55
National	4,905,867,938	13.1	83,553,714	45,846,470	28.46

Source: Newmark Grubb Knight Frank, National Office Market Report, 4th Quarter 2018

Industrial/Warehouse/R&D Market

Market Area	Inventory (sq. ft.)	Vacancy Rate (%)	Under Construction (sq. ft.)	YTD Net Absorption (sq. ft.)	Total Average Asking Rent ($/sq. ft./year)
Columbia	58,906,140	6.7	863,056	1,669,238	4.05
National	14,796,839,085	5.0	262,662,294	238,014,726	7.16

Source: Newmark Grubb Knight Frank, National Industrial Market Report, 4th Quarter 2018

COMMERCIAL UTILITIES

Typical Monthly Electric Bills

Area	Commercial Service ($/month)		Industrial Service ($/month)	
	1,500 kWh	40 kW demand 14,000 kWh	1,000 kW demand 200,000 kWh	50,000 kW demand 32,500,000 kWh
City	n/a	n/a	n/a	n/a
Average[1]	203	1,619	25,886	2,540,077

Note: Figures are based on annualized rates; (1) Average based on 187 utilities surveyed; n/a not available
Source: Edison Electric Institute, Typical Bills and Average Rates Report, Summer 2018

TRANSPORTATION

Means of Transportation to Work

Area	Car/Truck/Van		Public Transportation			Bicycle	Walked	Other Means	Worked at Home
	Drove Alone	Car-pooled	Bus	Subway	Railroad				
City	64.3	5.9	1.6	0.0	0.0	0.5	22.2	2.1	3.4
MSA[1]	81.0	8.3	0.6	0.0	0.0	0.1	4.5	2.1	3.4
U.S.	76.4	9.2	2.5	1.9	0.6	0.6	2.7	1.3	4.7

Note: Figures are percentages and cover workers 16 years of age and older; (1) Figures cover the Columbia, SC Metropolitan Statistical Area—see Appendix B for areas included
Source: U.S. Census Bureau, 2013-2017 American Community Survey 5-Year Estimates

Travel Time to Work

Area	Less Than 10 Minutes	10 to 19 Minutes	20 to 29 Minutes	30 to 44 Minutes	45 to 59 Minutes	60 to 89 Minutes	90 Minutes or More
City	32.9	36.9	16.2	9.7	1.6	1.7	1.0
MSA[1]	13.3	29.6	24.1	21.5	6.5	3.2	1.7
U.S.	12.7	28.9	20.9	20.5	8.1	6.2	2.7

Note: Note: Figures are percentages and include workers 16 years old and over; (1) Figures cover the Columbia, SC Metropolitan Statistical Area—see Appendix B for areas included
Source: U.S. Census Bureau, 2013-2017 American Community Survey 5-Year Estimates

Freeway Travel Time Index

Area	1985	1990	1995	2000	2005	2010	2014
Urban Area Rank[1,2]	64	76	84	77	77	72	76
Urban Area Index[1]	1.05	1.07	1.08	1.12	1.14	1.15	1.15
Average Index[3]	1.09	1.11	1.14	1.17	1.20	1.19	1.20

Note: Freeway Travel Time Index—the ratio of travel time in the peak period to the travel time at free-flow conditions. For example, a value of 1.30 indicates a 20-minute free-flow trip takes 26 minutes in the peak (20 minutes x 1.30 = 26 minutes); (1) Covers the Columbia SC urban area; (2) Rank is based on 101 urban areas (#1 = highest travel time index); (3) Average of 101 urban areas
Source: Texas Transportation Institute, 2015 Urban Mobility Scorecard, August 2015

Freeway Commuter Stress Index

Area	1985	1990	1995	2000	2005	2010	2014
Urban Area Rank[1,2]	66	75	81	81	76	65	71
Urban Area Index[1]	1.07	1.09	1.11	1.14	1.17	1.18	1.18
Average Index[3]	1.13	1.16	1.19	1.22	1.25	1.24	1.25

Note: The Freeway Commuter Stress Index is the same as the Freeway Travel Time Index (see table above) except that it includes only the travel in the peak directions during the peak periods; the TTI includes travel in all directions during the peak period. Thus, the CSI is more indicative of the work trip experienced by each commuter on a daily basis; (1) Covers the Columbia SC urban area; (2) Rank is based on 101 urban areas (#1 = highest travel time index); (3) Average of 101 urban areas
Source: Texas Transportation Institute, 2015 Urban Mobility Scorecard, August 2015

Public Transportation

Agency Name / Mode of Transportation	Vehicles Operated in Maximum Service[1]	Annual Unlinked Passenger Trips[2] (in thous.)	Annual Passenger Miles[3] (in thous.)
Central Midlands Regional Transit Authority			
Bus (purchased transportation)	38	2,432.5	6,221.0
Demand Response (purchased transportation)	16	64.0	827.1

Note: (1) The number of revenue vehicles operated by the given mode and type of service to meet the annual maximum service requirement. This is the revenue vehicle count during the peak season of the year; on the week and day that maximum service is provided. Vehicles operated in maximum service (VOMS) exclude atypical days and one-time special events; (2) The number of passengers who boarded public transportation vehicles. Passengers are counted each time they board a vehicle no matter how many vehicles they use to travel from their origin to their destination. (3) The sum of the distances ridden by all passengers during the entire fiscal year.
Source: Federal Transit Administration, National Transit Database, 2017

Air Transportation

Airport Name and Code / Type of Service	Passenger Airlines[1]	Passenger Enplanements	Freight Carriers[2]	Freight (lbs)
Columbia Metropolitan (CAE)				
Domestic service (U.S. carriers - 2018)	24	566,284	19	60,962,274
International service (U.S. carriers - 2017)	1	25	3	176,610

Note: (1) Includes all U.S.-based major, minor and commuter airlines that carried at least one passenger during the year; (2) Includes all U.S.-based airlines and freight carriers that transported at least one pound of freight during the year.
Source: Bureau of Transportation Statistics, The Intermodal Transportation Database, Air Carriers: T-100 Domestic Market (U.S. Carriers), 2018; Bureau of Transportation Statistics, The Intermodal Transportation Database, Air Carriers: T-100 International Market (U.S. Carriers), 2017

Other Transportation Statistics

Major Highways:	I-20; I-26; I-77
Amtrak Service:	Yes
Major Waterways/Ports:	Congaree River

Source: Amtrak.com; Google Maps

BUSINESSES

Major Business Headquarters

Company Name	Industry	Rankings	
		Fortune[1]	Forbes[2]
No companies listed	-	-	-

Note: (1) Companies that produce a 10-K are ranked 1 to 500 based on 2017 revenue; (2) All private companies with at least $2 billion in annual revenue through the end of their most current fiscal year are ranked 1 to 229; companies listed are headquartered in the city; dashes indicate no ranking
Source: Fortune, "Fortune 500," June 2018; Forbes, "America's Largest Private Companies," 2018 Rankings

Fast-Growing Businesses

According to *Inc.*, Columbia is home to one of America's 500 fastest-growing private companies: **Parrish and Partners** (#114). Criteria: must be an independent, privately-held, for-profit, U.S. corporation, proprietorship or partnership as of December 31, 2017; revenues must be at least $100,000 in 2014 and $2 million in 2017; must have four-year operating/sales history. Holding companies, regulated banks, and utilities were excluded. *Inc., "America's 500 Fastest-Growing Private Companies," 2018*

Minority- and Women-Owned Businesses

Group	All Firms		Firms with Paid Employees			
	Firms	Sales ($000)	Firms	Sales ($000)	Employees	Payroll ($000)
AIAN[1]	70	(s)	9	(s)	20 - 99	(s)
Asian	382	177,332	193	164,800	1,931	29,035
Black	3,492	361,854	146	243,376	1,716	38,108
Hispanic	247	(s)	41	(s)	250 - 499	(s)
NHOPI[2]	n/a	n/a	n/a	n/a	n/a	n/a
Women	4,676	507,240	568	404,347	4,093	134,856
All Firms	13,080	23,539,431	3,671	22,970,665	90,529	3,952,475

Note: Figures cover firms located in the city; minority- and women-owned business are defined as firms in which the corresponding group own 51% or more of the stock or equity of the company; (1) American Indian and Alaska Native; (2) Native Hawaiian and Other Pacific Islander; (s) estimates are suppressed when publication standards are not met; n/a not available
Source: U.S. Census Bureau, 2012 Economic Census, Survey of Business Owners

**HOTELS &
CONVENTION
CENTERS**

Hotels, Motels and Vacation Rentals

Area	5 Star		4 Star		3 Star		2 Star		1 Star		Not Rated	
	Num.	Pct.[3]	Num.	Pct.[3]	Num.	Pct.[3]	Num.	Pct.[3]	Num.	Pct.[3]	Num.	Pct.[3]
City[1]	0	0.0	0	0.0	35	15.1	89	38.4	3	1.3	105	45.3
Total[2]	286	0.4	5,236	7.1	16,715	22.6	10,259	13.9	293	0.4	41,056	55.6

Note: (1) Figures cover Columbia and vicinity; (2) Figures cover all 100 cities in this book; (3) Percentage of hotels which have a given star rating; Star ratings are determined by expedia.com and offer an indication of the general quality of a particular hotel.
Source: www.expedia.com, April 3, 2019

Major Convention Centers

Name	Overall Space (sq. ft.)	Exhibit Space (sq. ft.)	Meeting Space (sq. ft.)	Meeting Rooms
Columbia Convention Center	142,500	24,700	n/a	n/a

Note: Table includes convention centers located in the Columbia, SC metro area; n/a not available
Source: Original research

Living Environment

COST OF LIVING

Cost of Living Index

Composite Index	Groceries	Housing	Utilities	Trans-portation	Health Care	Misc. Goods/ Services
97.4	109.2	77.0	124.1	91.8	91.4	105.3

Note: The Cost of Living Index measures regional differences in the cost of consumer goods and services, excluding taxes and non-consumer expenditures, for professional and managerial households in the top income quintile. It is based on more than 50,000 prices covering almost 60 different items for which prices are collected three times a year by chambers of commerce, economic development organizations or university applied economic centers in each participating urban area. The numbers shown should be read as a percentage above or below the national average of 100. For example, a value of 115.4 in the groceries column indicates that grocery prices are 15.4% higher than the national average. Small differences in the index numbers should not be interpreted as significant; Figures cover the Columbia SC urban area.
Source: The Council for Community and Economic Research, ACCRA Cost of Living Index, 2018

Grocery Prices

Area[1]	T-Bone Steak ($/pound)	Frying Chicken ($/pound)	Whole Milk ($/half gal.)	Eggs ($/dozen)	Orange Juice ($/64 oz.)	Coffee ($/11.5 oz.)
City[2]	12.27	1.30	1.88	2.02	3.92	4.70
Avg.	11.35	1.42	1.94	1.81	3.52	4.35
Min.	7.45	0.92	0.80	0.75	2.72	3.06
Max.	15.05	2.76	4.18	4.00	5.36	8.20

Note: (1) Values for the local area are compared with the average, minimum and maximum values for all 291 areas in the Cost of Living Index; (2) Figures cover the Columbia SC urban area; T-Bone Steak (price per pound); Frying Chicken (price per pound, whole fryer); Whole Milk (half gallon carton); Eggs (price per dozen, Grade A, large); Orange Juice (64 oz. Tropicana or Florida Natural); Coffee (11.5 oz. can, vacuum-packed, Maxwell House, Hills Bros, or Folgers).
Source: The Council for Community and Economic Research, ACCRA Cost of Living Index, 2018

Housing and Utility Costs

Area[1]	New Home Price ($)	Apartment Rent ($/month)	All Electric ($/month)	Part Electric ($/month)	Other Energy ($/month)	Telephone ($/month)
City[2]	254,119	938	-	122.61	116.25	180.10
Avg.	347,000	1,087	165.93	100.16	67.73	178.70
Min.	200,468	500	93.58	25.64	26.78	163.10
Max.	1,901,222	4,888	388.65	246.86	332.81	197.70

Note: (1) Values for the local area are compared with the average, minimum and maximum values for all 291 areas in the Cost of Living Index; (2) Figures cover the Columbia SC urban area; New Home Price (2,400 sf living area, 8,000 sf lot, in urban area with full utilities); Apartment Rent (950 sf 2 bedroom/1.5 or 2 bath, unfurnished, excluding all utilities except water); All Electric (average monthly cost for an all-electric home); Part Electric (average monthly cost for a part-electric home); Other Energy (average monthly cost for natural gas, fuel oil, coal, wood, and any other forms of energy except electricity); Telephone (price includes the base monthly rate plus taxes and fees for three lines of mobile phone service).
Source: The Council for Community and Economic Research, ACCRA Cost of Living Index, 2018

Health Care, Transportation, and Other Costs

Area[1]	Doctor ($/visit)	Dentist ($/visit)	Optometrist ($/visit)	Gasoline ($/gallon)	Beauty Salon ($/visit)	Men's Shirt ($)
City[2]	105.22	90.00	90.67	2.41	48.47	31.56
Avg.	110.71	95.11	103.74	2.61	37.48	32.03
Min.	33.60	62.55	54.63	1.89	17.00	11.44
Max.	195.97	153.93	225.79	3.59	71.88	58.64

Note: (1) Values for the local area are compared with the average, minimum and maximum values for all 291 areas in the Cost of Living Index; (2) Figures cover the Columbia SC urban area; Doctor (general practitioners routine exam of an established patient); Dentist (adult teeth cleaning and periodic oral examination); Optometrist (full vision eye exam for established adult patient); Gasoline (one gallon regular unleaded, national brand, including all taxes, cash price at self-service pump if available); Beauty Salon (woman's shampoo, trim, and blow-dry); Men's Shirt (cotton/polyester dress shirt, pinpoint weave, long sleeves).
Source: The Council for Community and Economic Research, ACCRA Cost of Living Index, 2018

HOUSING

House Price Index (HPI)

Area	National Ranking[2]	Quarterly Change (%)	One-Year Change (%)	Five-Year Change (%)
MSA[1]	147	1.65	5.62	22.45
U.S.[3]	–	1.12	5.73	32.81

Note: The HPI is a weighted repeat sales index. It measures average price changes in repeat sales or refinancings on the same properties. This information is obtained by reviewing repeat mortgage transactions on single-family properties whose mortgages have been purchased or securitized by Fannie Mae or Freddie Mac in January 1975; (1) Figures cover the Columbia, SC Metropolitan Statistical Area—see Appendix B for areas included; (2) Rankings are based on annual percentage change for all metro areas containing at least 15,000 transactions over the last 10 years and ranges from 1 to 245; (3) figures based on a weighted average of Census Division estimates using a seasonally adjusted, purchase-only index; all figures are for the period ending December 31, 2018
Source: Federal Housing Finance Agency, House Price Index, February 26, 2019

Median Single-Family Home Prices

Area	2016	2017	2018p	Percent Change 2017 to 2018
MSA[1]	161.8	162.3	171.6	5.7
U.S. Average	235.5	248.8	261.6	5.1

Note: Figures are median sales prices of existing single-family homes in thousands of dollars; (p) preliminary; (1) Figures cover the Columbia, SC Metropolitan Statistical Area—see Appendix B for areas included
Source: National Association of Realtors, Median Sales Price of Existing Single-Family Homes for Metropolitan Areas, 4th Quarter 2018

Qualifying Income Based on Median Sales Price of Existing Single-Family Homes

Area	With 5% Down ($)	With 10% Down ($)	With 20% Down ($)
MSA[1]	42,205	39,984	35,541
U.S. Average	62,954	59,640	53,013

Note: Figures are preliminary; Qualifying income is based on a mortgage rate of 4.9%. Monthly principal and interest payment is limited to 25% of income; (1) Figures cover the Columbia, SC Metropolitan Statistical Area—see Appendix B for areas included
Source: National Association of Realtors, Qualifying Income Based on Median Sales Price of Existing Single-Family Homes for Metropolitan Areas, 4th Quarter 2018

Median Apartment Condo-Coop Home Prices

Area	2016	2017	2018p	Percent Change 2017 to 2018
MSA[1]	n/a	n/a	n/a	n/a
U.S. Average	220.7	234.3	241.0	2.9

Note: Figures are median sales prices of existing apartment condo-coop homes in thousands of dollars; (p) preliminary; n/a not available; (1) Figures cover the Columbia, SC Metropolitan Statistical Area—see Appendix B for areas included
Source: National Association of Realtors, Median Sales Price of Existing Apartment Condo-Coop Homes for Metropolitan Areas, 4th Quarter 2018

Home Value Distribution

Area	Under $50,000	$50,000 -$99,999	$100,000 -$149,999	$150,000 -$199,999	$200,000 -$299,999	$300,000 -$499,999	$500,000 -$999,999	$1,000,000 or more
City	5.3	17.1	21.2	14.9	15.4	15.1	9.8	1.3
MSA[1]	10.1	17.9	23.9	18.0	16.2	9.5	3.6	0.7
U.S.	8.3	13.9	14.7	14.6	18.7	17.3	9.7	2.7

Note: Figures are percentages and cover owner-occupied housing units; (1) Figures cover the Columbia, SC Metropolitan Statistical Area—see Appendix B for areas included
Source: U.S. Census Bureau, 2013-2017 American Community Survey 5-Year Estimates

Homeownership Rate

Area	2010 (%)	2011 (%)	2012 (%)	2013 (%)	2014 (%)	2015 (%)	2016 (%)	2017 (%)	2018 (%)
MSA[1]	74.1	69.0	65.6	68.9	69.5	66.1	63.9	70.7	69.3
U.S.	66.9	66.1	65.4	65.1	64.5	63.7	63.4	63.9	64.4

Note: (1) Figures cover the Columbia, SC Metropolitan Statistical Area—see Appendix B for areas included
Source: U.S. Census Bureau, Housing Vacancies and Homeownership Annual Statistics: 2010-2018

Year Housing Structure Built

Area	2010 or Later	2000 -2009	1990 -1999	1980 -1989	1970 -1979	1960 -1969	1950 -1959	1940 -1949	Before 1940	Median Year
City	4.2	16.2	11.1	9.5	10.5	13.0	14.4	10.0	11.0	1971
MSA[1]	5.3	20.5	18.5	14.9	16.1	10.3	7.4	3.1	3.8	1986
U.S.	3.2	14.5	14.0	13.6	15.5	10.8	10.5	5.1	12.9	1977

Note: Figures are percentages except for Median Year; Note: (1) Figures cover the Columbia, SC Metropolitan Statistical Area—see Appendix B for areas included
Source: U.S. Census Bureau, 2013-2017 American Community Survey 5-Year Estimates

Gross Monthly Rent

Area	Under $500	$500 -$999	$1,000 -$1,499	$1,500 -$1,999	$2,000 -$2,499	$2,500 -$2,999	$3,000 and up	Median ($)
City	12.0	54.5	26.3	5.6	1.3	0.0	0.3	878
MSA[1]	8.6	55.5	27.8	6.1	1.4	0.3	0.3	889
U.S.	10.5	41.1	28.7	11.7	4.5	1.8	1.7	982

Note: Figures are percentages except for Median; Gross rent is the contract rent plus the estimated average monthly cost of utilities (electricity, gas, and water and sewer) and fuels (oil, coal, kerosene, wood, etc.) if these are paid by the renter (or paid for the renter by someone else); (1) Figures cover the Columbia, SC Metropolitan Statistical Area—see Appendix B for areas included
Source: U.S. Census Bureau, 2013-2017 American Community Survey 5-Year Estimates

HEALTH

Health Risk Factors

Category	MSA[1] (%)	U.S. (%)
Adults aged 18–64 who have any kind of health care coverage	85.6	87.3
Adults who reported being in good or better health	82.3	82.4
Adults who have been told they have high blood cholesterol	33.3	33.0
Adults who have been told they have high blood pressure	38.1	32.3
Adults who are current smokers	16.9	17.1
Adults who currently use E-cigarettes	4.6	4.6
Adults who currently use chewing tobacco, snuff, or snus	2.8	4.0
Adults who are heavy drinkers[2]	8.7	6.3
Adults who are binge drinkers[3]	17.2	17.4
Adults who are overweight (BMI 25.0 - 29.9)	34.7	35.3
Adults who are obese (BMI 30.0 - 99.8)	35.7	31.3
Adults who participated in any physical activities in the past month	73.1	74.4
Adults who always or nearly always wears a seat belt	95.8	94.3

Note: (1) Figures cover the Columbia, SC Metropolitan Statistical Area—see Appendix B for areas included; (2) Heavy drinkers are classified as adult men having more than 14 drinks per week and adult women having more than 7 drinks per week; (3) Binge drinkers are classified as males having five or more drinks on one occasion or females having four or more drinks on one occasion
Source: Centers for Disease Control and Prevention, Behaviorial Risk Factor Surveillance System, SMART: Selected Metropolitan Area Risk Trends, 2017

Acute and Chronic Health Conditions

Category	MSA[1] (%)	U.S. (%)
Adults who have ever been told they had a heart attack	3.8	4.2
Adults who have ever been told they have angina or coronary heart disease	3.8	3.9
Adults who have ever been told they had a stroke	3.1	3.0
Adults who have ever been told they have asthma	15.2	14.2
Adults who have ever been told they have arthritis	25.6	24.9
Adults who have ever been told they have diabetes[2]	12.4	10.5
Adults who have ever been told they had skin cancer	5.6	6.2
Adults who have ever been told they had any other types of cancer	6.7	7.1
Adults who have ever been told they have COPD	7.1	6.5
Adults who have ever been told they have kidney disease	2.4	3.0
Adults who have ever been told they have a form of depression	20.0	20.5

Note: (1) Figures cover the Columbia, SC Metropolitan Statistical Area—see Appendix B for areas included; (2) Figures do not include pregnancy-related, borderline, or pre-diabetes
Source: Centers for Disease Control and Prevention, Behaviorial Risk Factor Surveillance System, SMART: Selected Metropolitan Area Risk Trends, 2017

Health Screening and Vaccination Rates

Category	MSA[1] (%)	U.S. (%)
Adults aged 65+ who have had flu shot within the past year	65.0	60.7
Adults aged 65+ who have ever had a pneumonia vaccination	78.0	75.4
Adults who have ever been tested for HIV	43.6	36.1
Adults who have ever had the shingles or zoster vaccine?	26.0	28.9
Adults who have had their blood cholesterol checked within the last five years	89.1	85.9

Note: n/a not available; (1) Figures cover the Columbia, SC Metropolitan Statistical Area—see Appendix B for areas included.
Source: Centers for Disease Control and Prevention, Behaviorial Risk Factor Surveillance System, SMART: Selected Metropolitan Area Risk Trends, 2017

Disability Status

Category	MSA[1] (%)	U.S. (%)
Adults who reported being deaf	5.5	6.7
Are you blind or have serious difficulty seeing, even when wearing glasses?	4.2	4.5
Are you limited in any way in any of your usual activities due of arthritis?	12.8	12.9
Do you have difficulty doing errands alone?	5.0	6.8
Do you have difficulty dressing or bathing?	3.2	3.6
Do you have serious difficulty concentrating/remembering/making decisions?	10.0	10.7
Do you have serious difficulty walking or climbing stairs?	14.5	13.6

Note: (1) Figures cover the Columbia, SC Metropolitan Statistical Area—see Appendix B for areas included.
Source: Centers for Disease Control and Prevention, Behaviorial Risk Factor Surveillance System, SMART: Selected Metropolitan Area Risk Trends, 2017

Mortality Rates for the Top 10 Causes of Death in the U.S.

ICD-10[a] Sub-Chapter	ICD-10[a] Code	Age-Adjusted Mortality Rate[1] per 100,000 population	
		County[2]	U.S.
Malignant neoplasms	C00-C97	166.3	155.5
Ischaemic heart diseases	I20-I25	94.5	94.8
Other forms of heart disease	I30-I51	54.3	52.9
Chronic lower respiratory diseases	J40-J47	31.2	41.0
Cerebrovascular diseases	I60-I69	41.3	37.5
Other degenerative diseases of the nervous system	G30-G31	46.4	35.0
Other external causes of accidental injury	W00-X59	33.0	33.7
Organic, including symptomatic, mental disorders	F01-F09	38.9	31.0
Hypertensive diseases	I10-I15	30.9	21.9
Diabetes mellitus	E10-E14	26.4	21.1

Note: (a) ICD-10 = International Classification of Diseases 10th Revision; (1) Mortality rates are a three year average covering 2015-2017; (2) Figures cover Richland County.
Source: Centers for Disease Control and Prevention, National Center for Health Statistics. Underlying Cause of Death 1999-2017 on CDC WONDER Online Database

Mortality Rates for Selected Causes of Death

ICD-10[a] Sub-Chapter	ICD-10[a] Code	Age-Adjusted Mortality Rate[1] per 100,000 population	
		County[2]	U.S.
Assault	X85-Y09	10.1	5.9
Diseases of the liver	K70-K76	13.2	14.1
Human immunodeficiency virus (HIV) disease	B20-B24	4.5	1.8
Influenza and pneumonia	J09-J18	10.2	14.3
Intentional self-harm	X60-X84	13.7	13.6
Malnutrition	E40-E46	3.7	1.6
Obesity and other hyperalimentation	E65-E68	1.6	2.1
Renal failure	N17-N19	15.3	13.0
Transport accidents	V01-V99	14.5	12.4
Viral hepatitis	B15-B19	2.1	1.6

Note: (a) ICD-10 = International Classification of Diseases 10th Revision; (1) Mortality rates are a three year average covering 2015-2017; (2) Figures cover Richland County; Data are suppressed when the data meet the criteria for confidentiality constraints; Mortality rates are flagged as unreliable when the rate would be calculated with a numerator of 20 or less.
Source: Centers for Disease Control and Prevention, National Center for Health Statistics. Underlying Cause of Death 1999-2017 on CDC WONDER Online Database

Health Insurance Coverage

Area	With Health Insurance	With Private Health Insurance	With Public Health Insurance	Without Health Insurance	Population Under Age 18 Without Health Insurance
City	89.5	70.9	28.7	10.5	2.5
MSA[1]	89.2	69.6	32.5	10.8	4.3
U.S.	89.5	67.2	33.8	10.5	5.7

Note: Figures are percentages that cover the civilian noninstitutionalized population; (1) Figures cover the Columbia, SC Metropolitan Statistical Area—see Appendix B for areas included
Source: U.S. Census Bureau, 2013-2017 American Community Survey 5-Year Estimates

Number of Medical Professionals

Area	MDs[3]	DOs[3,4]	Dentists	Podiatrists	Chiropractors	Optometrists
County[1] (number)	1,459	67	359	25	99	78
County[1] (rate[2])	356.6	16.4	87.2	6.1	24.1	19.0
U.S. (rate[2])	279.3	23.0	68.4	6.0	27.1	16.2

Note: Data as of 2017 unless noted; (1) Data covers Richland County; (2) Rate per 100,000 population; (3) Data as of 2016 and includes all active, non-federal physicians; (4) Doctor of Osteopathic Medicine
Source: U.S. Department of Health and Human Services, Health Resources and Services Administration, Bureau of Health Professions, Area Resource File (ARF) 2017-2018

EDUCATION

Public School District Statistics

District Name	Schls	Pupils	Pupil/ Teacher Ratio	Minority Pupils[1] (%)	Free Lunch Eligible[2] (%)	IEP[3] (%)
Richland 01	48	23,886	12.6	81.4	100.0	14.6
Richland 02	32	27,802	14.7	76.5	41.3	12.7
SC Public Charter School District	35	21,540	20.4	32.7	34.4	10.7

Note: Table includes school districts with 2,000 or more students; (1) Percentage of students that are not non-Hispanic white; (2) Percentage of students that are eligible for the free lunch program; (3) Percentage of students that have an Individualized Education Program.
Source: U.S. Department of Education, National Center for Education Statistics, Common Core of Data, Local Education Agency (School District) Universe Survey: School Year 2016-2017; U.S. Department of Education, National Center for Education Statistics, Common Core of Data, Public Elementary/Secondary School Universe Survey: School Year 2016-2017

Highest Level of Education

Area	Less than H.S.	H.S. Diploma	Some College, No Deg.	Associate Degree	Bachelor's Degree	Master's Degree	Prof. School Degree	Doctorate Degree
City	11.8	19.7	19.4	6.7	23.6	12.6	3.9	2.3
MSA[1]	11.0	27.0	21.5	8.6	19.8	9.0	1.8	1.3
U.S.	12.7	27.3	20.8	8.3	19.1	8.4	2.0	1.4

Note: Figures cover persons age 25 and over; (1) Figures cover the Columbia, SC Metropolitan Statistical Area—see Appendix B for areas included
Source: U.S. Census Bureau, 2013-2017 American Community Survey 5-Year Estimates

Educational Attainment by Race

Area	High School Graduate or Higher (%)					Bachelor's Degree or Higher (%)				
	Total	White	Black	Asian	Hisp.[2]	Total	White	Black	Asian	Hisp.[2]
City	88.2	94.5	81.6	91.5	73.4	42.3	61.0	19.3	76.1	31.3
MSA[1]	89.0	91.3	86.4	87.0	63.9	31.9	36.9	22.0	52.0	17.5
U.S.	87.3	89.3	84.9	86.5	66.7	30.9	32.2	20.6	52.7	15.2

Note: Figures shown cover persons 25 years old and over; (1) Figures cover the Columbia, SC Metropolitan Statistical Area—see Appendix B for areas included; (2) People of Hispanic origin can be of any race
Source: U.S. Census Bureau, 2013-2017 American Community Survey 5-Year Estimates

School Enrollment by Grade and Control

Area	Preschool (%)		Kindergarten (%)		Grades 1 - 4 (%)		Grades 5 - 8 (%)		Grades 9 - 12 (%)	
	Public	Private	Public	Private	Public	Private	Public	Private	Public	Private
City	49.6	50.4	76.3	23.7	89.0	11.0	86.2	13.8	89.6	10.4
MSA[1]	54.9	45.1	86.1	13.9	91.9	8.1	92.6	7.4	92.1	7.9
U.S.	58.8	41.2	87.7	12.3	89.7	10.3	89.6	10.4	90.3	9.7

Note: Figures shown cover persons 3 years old and over; (1) Figures cover the Columbia, SC Metropolitan Statistical Area—see Appendix B for areas included
Source: U.S. Census Bureau, 2013-2017 American Community Survey 5-Year Estimates

Average Salaries of Public School Classroom Teachers

Area	2016		2017		Change from 2016 to 2017	
	Dollars	Rank[1]	Dollars	Rank[1]	Percent	Rank[2]
South Carolina	48,769	37	50,000	38	2.5	14
U.S. Average	58,479	–	59,660	–	2.0	–

Note: (1) Rank ranges from 1 to 51 where 1 indicates highest salary; (2) Rank ranges from 1 to 51 where 1 indicates highest percent change.
Source: National Education Association, Rankings & Estimates: Rankings of the States 2017 and Estimates of School Statistics 2018

Higher Education

Four-Year Colleges			Two-Year Colleges			Medical Schools[1]	Law Schools[2]	Voc/ Tech[3]
Public	Private Non-profit	Private For-profit	Public	Private Non-profit	Private For-profit			
1	5	2	0	0	3	1	1	6

Note: Figures cover institutions located within the city limits and include main campuses only; (1) includes schools accredited by the Liaison Committee on Medical Education and the American Osteopathic Association's Commission on Osteopathic College Accreditation; (2) includes ABA-accredited schools, schools with provisional ABA accreditation, and state accredited schools; (3) includes all schools with programs that are less than 2 years.
Source: National Center for Education Statistics, Integrated Postsecondary Education System (IPEDS), 2017-18; Wikipedia, List of Medical Schools in the United States, accessed April 3, 2019; Wikipedia, List of Law Schools in the United States, accessed April 3, 2019

According to *U.S. News & World Report*, the Columbia, SC metro area is home to one of the best national universities in the U.S.: **University of South Carolina** (#106 tie). The indicators used to capture academic quality fall into a number of categories: assessment by administrators at peer institutions; retention of students; faculty resources; student selectivity; financial resources; alumni giving; high school counselor ratings of colleges; and graduation rate. *U.S. News & World Report*, *"America's Best Colleges 2019"*

According to *U.S. News & World Report*, the Columbia, SC metro area is home to one of the top 100 law schools in the U.S.: **University of South Carolina** (#91 tie). The rankings are based on a weighted average of 12 measures of quality: peer assessment score; assessment score by lawyers/judges; median LSAT scores; median undergrad GPA; acceptance rate; employment rates for graduates; placement success; bar passage rate; faculty resources; expenditures per student; student/faculty ratio; and library resources. *U.S. News & World Report*, *"America's Best Graduate Schools, Law, 2020"*

According to *U.S. News & World Report*, the Columbia, SC metro area is home to one of the top 75 business schools in the U.S.: **University of South Carolina (Moore)** (#74 tie). The rankings are based on a weighted average of the following nine measures: quality assessment; peer assessment; recruiter assessment; placement success; mean starting salary and bonus; student selectivity; mean GMAT and GRE scores; mean undergraduate GPA; and acceptance rate. *U.S. News & World Report*, *"America's Best Graduate Schools, Business, 2020"*

PRESIDENTIAL ELECTION

2016 Presidential Election Results

Area	Clinton	Trump	Johnson	Stein	Other
Richland County	64.0	31.1	2.3	0.8	1.7
U.S.	48.0	45.9	3.3	1.1	1.7

Note: Results are percentages and may not add to 100% due to rounding
Source: Dave Leip's Atlas of U.S. Presidential Elections

EMPLOYERS

Major Employers

Company Name	Industry
AnMed Health	Healthcare
Baldor Electric Co	Utilities
Ben Arnold Beverage Co	Beverages
Berkeley County School Dist	Education
BlueCross BlueShield of SC	Finance, insurance and real estate
BMW Manufacturing Co	Manufacturing
Bon Secours St Francis Hosp	Healthcare
Charleston AIR Force Base	U.S. military
City of Columbia	Government
Clemson University Research	Healthcare
Continental Tire North America	Wholesaling/manufacturing
Corrections Dept.	Government
Crescent Moon Diving	Professional, scientific, technical
Fluor Enterprises Inc	Engineering services
Greenville Memorial Hospital	Healthcare
Lexington Medical Ctr	Healthcare
Mc Leod Health	Healthcare
Medical University of SC	Healthcare/university
Palmetto Health	Health care & social assistance
Piggly Wiggly	Grocery stores
Pilgrim's Pride Corp	Poultry processing
Richland County	Government
Richland School District 1 & 2	Education
Robert Bosch	Manufacturing
Shaw Air Force Base	U.S. military
Sonoco Plastics Inc	Manufacturing
Spartanburg Regional Healthcre	Healthcare
University of South Carolina	Education
Women's Imaging Center	Healthcare

Note: Companies shown are located within the Columbia, SC Metropolitan Statistical Area.
Source: Hoovers.com; Wikipedia

Best Companies to Work For

Palmetto Health, headquartered in Columbia, is among the "100 Best Places to Work in IT." To qualify, companies had to be U.S.-based organizations or be non-U.S.- based employers that met the following criteria: have a minimum of 300 total employees at a U.S. headquarters and a minimum of 30 IT employees in the U.S., with at least 50% of their IT employees based in the U.S. The best places to work were selected based on compensation, benefits, work/life balance, employee morale, and satisfaction with training and development programs. In addition, *Computerworld* looked at retention efforts, programs for recognizing and rewarding outstanding performances, and benefits such as flextime, elder care and child care, and reimbursement for college tuition and the cost of pursuing technology certifications. *Computerworld, "100 Best Places to Work in IT 2018"*

PUBLIC SAFETY

Crime Rate

Area	All Crimes	Violent Crimes				Property Crimes		
		Murder	Rape[3]	Robbery	Aggrav. Assault	Burglary	Larceny -Theft	Motor Vehicle Theft
City	6,020.4	7.4	48.9	202.3	475.7	706.9	3,993.1	586.1
Suburbs[1]	n/a	7.1	44.2	77.4	396.0	560.6	n/a	380.8
Metro[2]	n/a	7.1	45.0	97.8	409.0	584.4	n/a	414.4
U.S.	2,756.1	5.3	41.7	98.0	248.9	430.4	1,694.4	237.4

Note: Figures are crimes per 100,000 population; (1) All areas within the metro area that are located outside the city limits; (2) Figures cover the Columbia, SC Metropolitan Statistical Area—see Appendix B for areas included; (3) The city and U.S. figures shown were reported using the revised Uniform Crime Reporting (UCR) definition of rape. The suburban and metro area figures shown are an aggregate total of the data submitted using both the revised and legacy UCR definitions.
Source: FBI Uniform Crime Reports, 2017

Hate Crimes

Area	Number of Quarters Reported	Number of Incidents per Bias Motivation					
		Race/Ethnicity/ Ancestry	Religion	Sexual Orientation	Disability	Gender	Gender Identity
City	4	0	0	0	0	0	0
U.S.	4	4,131	1,564	1,130	116	46	119

Source: Federal Bureau of Investigation, Hate Crime Statistics 2017

Identity Theft Consumer Reports

Area	Reports	Reports per 100,000 Population	Rank[2]
MSA[1]	1,497	183	17
U.S.	444,602	135	-

Note: (1) Figures cover the Columbia, SC Metropolitan Statistical Area—see Appendix B for areas included; (2) Rank ranges from 1 to 389 where 1 indicates greatest number of identity theft reports per 100,000 population
Source: Federal Trade Commission, Consumer Sentinel Network Data Book for January–December 2018

Fraud and Other Consumer Reports

Area	Reports	Reports per 100,000 Population	Rank[2]
MSA[1]	6,255	765	8
U.S.	2,552,917	776	-

Note: (1) Figures cover the Columbia, SC Metropolitan Statistical Area—see Appendix B for areas included; (2) Rank ranges from 1 to 389 where 1 indicates greatest number of fraud and other consumer reports per 100,000 population
Source: Federal Trade Commission, Consumer Sentinel Network Data Book for January–December 2018

SPORTS

Professional Sports Teams

Team Name	League	Year Established
No teams are located in the metro area		

Source: Wikipedia, Major Professional Sports Teams of the United States and Canada, April 5, 2019

CLIMATE

Average and Extreme Temperatures

Temperature	Jan	Feb	Mar	Apr	May	Jun	Jul	Aug	Sep	Oct	Nov	Dec	Yr.
Extreme High (°F)	84	84	91	94	101	107	107	107	101	101	90	83	107
Average High (°F)	56	60	67	77	84	90	92	91	85	77	67	59	75
Average Temp. (°F)	45	48	55	64	72	78	82	80	75	64	54	47	64
Average Low (°F)	33	35	42	50	59	66	70	69	64	51	41	35	51
Extreme Low (°F)	-1	5	4	26	34	44	54	53	40	23	12	4	-1

Note: Figures cover the years 1948-1990
Source: National Climatic Data Center, International Station Meteorological Climate Summary, 9/96

Average Precipitation/Snowfall/Humidity

Precip./Humidity	Jan	Feb	Mar	Apr	May	Jun	Jul	Aug	Sep	Oct	Nov	Dec	Yr.
Avg. Precip. (in.)	4.0	4.0	4.7	3.4	3.6	4.2	5.5	5.9	4.0	2.9	2.7	3.4	48.3
Avg. Snowfall (in.)	1	1	Tr	0	0	0	0	0	0	0	Tr	Tr	2
Avg. Rel. Hum. 7am (%)	83	83	84	82	84	85	88	91	91	90	88	84	86
Avg. Rel. Hum. 4pm (%)	51	47	44	41	46	50	54	56	54	49	48	51	49

Note: Figures cover the years 1948-1990; Tr = Trace amounts (<0.05 in. of rain; <0.5 in. of snow)
Source: National Climatic Data Center, International Station Meteorological Climate Summary, 9/96

Weather Conditions

Temperature			Daytime Sky			Precipitation		
10°F & below	32°F & below	90°F & above	Clear	Partly cloudy	Cloudy	0.01 inch or more precip.	0.1 inch or more snow/ice	Thunder-storms
< 1	58	77	97	149	119	110	1	53

Note: Figures are average number of days per year and cover the years 1948-1990
Source: National Climatic Data Center, International Station Meteorological Climate Summary, 9/96

**HAZARDOUS
WASTE**

Superfund Sites

The Columbia, SC metro area is home to five sites on the EPA's Superfund National Priorities List: **Lexington County Landfill Area** (final); **Palmetto Wood Preserving** (final); **Scrdi Bluff Road** (final); **Scrdi Dixiana** (final); **Townsend Saw Chain Co.** (final). There are a total of 1,390 Superfund sites with a status of proposed or final on the list in the U.S. *U.S. Environmental Protection Agency, National Priorities List, April 5, 2019*

**AIR & WATER
QUALITY**

Air Quality Trends: Ozone

	1990	1995	2000	2005	2010	2012	2014	2015	2016	2017
MSA[1]	0.093	0.079	0.096	0.082	0.070	0.065	0.056	0.056	0.065	0.059
U.S.	0.088	0.089	0.082	0.080	0.073	0.075	0.067	0.068	0.069	0.068

Note: (1) Data covers the Columbia, SC Metropolitan Statistical Area—see Appendix B for areas included. The values shown are the composite ozone concentration averages among trend sites based on the highest fourth daily maximum 8-hour concentration in parts per million. These trends are based on sites having an adequate record of monitoring data during the trend period. Data from exceptional events are included.
Source: U.S. Environmental Protection Agency, Air Quality Monitoring Information, "Air Quality Trends by City, 1990-2017"

Air Quality Index

Area	Percent of Days when Air Quality was...[2]					AQI Statistics[2]	
	Good	Moderate	Unhealthy for Sensitive Groups	Unhealthy	Very Unhealthy	Maximum	Median
MSA[1]	74.0	25.5	0.5	0.0	0.0	113	44

Note: (1) Data covers the Columbia, SC Metropolitan Statistical Area—see Appendix B for areas included; (2) Based on 365 days with AQI data in 2017. Air Quality Index (AQI) is an index for reporting daily air quality. EPA calculates the AQI for five major air pollutants regulated by the Clean Air Act: ground-level ozone, particle pollution (aka particulate matter), carbon monoxide, sulfur dioxide, and nitrogen dioxide. The AQI runs from 0 to 500. The higher the AQI value, the greater the level of air pollution and the greater the health concern. There are six AQI categories: "Good" AQI is between 0 and 50. Air quality is considered satisfactory; "Moderate" AQI is between 51 and 100. Air quality is acceptable; "Unhealthy for Sensitive Groups" When AQI values are between 101 and 150, members of sensitive groups may experience health effects; "Unhealthy" When AQI values are between 151 and 200 everyone may begin to experience health effects; "Very Unhealthy" AQI values between 201 and 300 trigger a health alert; "Hazardous" AQI values over 300 trigger warnings of emergency conditions (not shown).
Source: U.S. Environmental Protection Agency, Air Quality Index Report, 2017

Air Quality Index Pollutants

Area	Percent of Days when AQI Pollutant was...[2]					
	Carbon Monoxide	Nitrogen Dioxide	Ozone	Sulfur Dioxide	Particulate Matter 2.5	Particulate Matter 10
MSA[1]	0.0	0.0	61.4	0.0	38.4	0.3

Note: (1) Data covers the Columbia, SC Metropolitan Statistical Area—see Appendix B for areas included; (2) Based on 365 days with AQI data in 2017. The Air Quality Index (AQI) is an index for reporting daily air quality. EPA calculates the AQI for five major air pollutants regulated by the Clean Air Act: ground-level ozone, particle pollution (also known as particulate matter), carbon monoxide, sulfur dioxide, and nitrogen dioxide. The AQI runs from 0 to 500. The higher the AQI value, the greater the level of air pollution and the greater the health concern.
Source: U.S. Environmental Protection Agency, Air Quality Index Report, 2017

Maximum Air Pollutant Concentrations: Particulate Matter, Ozone, CO and Lead

	Particulate Matter 10 (ug/m³)	Particulate Matter 2.5 Wtd AM (ug/m³)	Particulate Matter 2.5 24-Hr (ug/m³)	Ozone (ppm)	Carbon Monoxide (ppm)	Lead (ug/m³)
MSA[1] Level	32	8.1	18	0.06	1	0
NAAQS[2]	150	15	35	0.075	9	0.15
Met NAAQS[2]	Yes	Yes	Yes	Yes	Yes	Yes

Note: (1) Data covers the Columbia, SC Metropolitan Statistical Area—see Appendix B for areas included; Data from exceptional events are included; (2) National Ambient Air Quality Standards; ppm = parts per million; ug/m³ = micrograms per cubic meter; n/a not available.
Concentrations: Particulate Matter 10 (coarse particulate)—highest second maximum 24-hour concentration; Particulate Matter 2.5 Wtd AM (fine particulate)—highest weighted annual mean concentration; Particulate Matter 2.5 24-Hour (fine particulate)—highest 98th percentile 24-hour concentration; Ozone—highest fourth daily maximum 8-hour concentration; Carbon Monoxide—highest second maximum non-overlapping 8-hour concentration; Lead—maximum running 3-month average
Source: U.S. Environmental Protection Agency, Air Quality Monitoring Information, "Air Quality Statistics by City, 2017"

Maximum Air Pollutant Concentrations: Nitrogen Dioxide and Sulfur Dioxide

	Nitrogen Dioxide AM (ppb)	Nitrogen Dioxide 1-Hr (ppb)	Sulfur Dioxide AM (ppb)	Sulfur Dioxide 1-Hr (ppb)	Sulfur Dioxide 24-Hr (ppb)
MSA[1] Level	4	37	n/a	3	n/a
NAAQS[2]	53	100	30	75	140
Met NAAQS[2]	Yes	Yes	n/a	Yes	n/a

Note: (1) Data covers the Columbia, SC Metropolitan Statistical Area—see Appendix B for areas included; Data from exceptional events are included; (2) National Ambient Air Quality Standards; ppm = parts per million; ug/m³ = micrograms per cubic meter; n/a not available.
Concentrations: Nitrogen Dioxide AM—highest arithmetic mean concentration; Nitrogen Dioxide 1-Hr—highest 98th percentile 1-hour daily maximum concentration; Sulfur Dioxide AM—highest annual mean concentration; Sulfur Dioxide 1-Hr—highest 99th percentile 1-hour daily maximum concentration; Sulfur Dioxide 24-Hr—highest second maximum 24-hour concentration
Source: U.S. Environmental Protection Agency, Air Quality Monitoring Information, "Air Quality Statistics by City, 2017"

Drinking Water

Water System Name	Pop. Served	Primary Water Source Type	Violations[1] Health Based	Violations[1] Monitoring/ Reporting
City of Columbia	304,257	Surface	0	0

Note: (1) Based on violation data from January 1, 2018 to December 31, 2018
Source: U.S. Environmental Protection Agency, Office of Ground Water and Drinking Water, Safe Drinking Water Information System (based on data extracted April 5, 2019)

Dallas, Texas

Background

Dallas is one of those cities that offer everything. Founded in 1841 by Tennessee lawyer and trader, John Neely Bryan, Dallas has come to symbolize in modern times all that is big, exciting, and affluent. The city itself is in the top ten worldwide among cities with the most billionaires. When combined with those billionaires who live in Dallas's neighboring city of Fort Worth, the area has one of the greatest concentrations of billionaires in the world.

Originally one of the largest markets for cotton in the U.S., Dallas moved on to become one of the largest markets for oil in the country. In the 1930s, oil was struck on the eastern fields of Texas. As a result, oil companies were founded and millions, then billions, were made, creating the face we now associate with Dallas and the state of Texas.

Today, oil still plays a dominant role in the Dallas economy. Outside of Alaska, Texas holds most of the U.S. oil reserves. For that reason, many oil companies choose to headquarter in the silver skyscrapers of Dallas.

In addition to employment opportunities in the oil industry, the Dallas branch of the Federal Reserve Bank, and a host of other banks and investment firms clustering around the Federal Reserve hub employ thousands. Other opportunities are offered in the aircraft, advertising, motion picture, and publishing industries.

Major employers in the Dallas area include American Airlines (Dallas-Fort Worth Airport); Lockheed Martin (in nearby Fort Worth); University of North Texas in Denton; Parkland Memorial Hospital; and Baylor University Medical Center. Vought Aircraft Industries, a major supplier of aircraft components to Boeing, Sikorsky and other aircraft manufacturers, continues to expand its local operations. The city is sometimes referred to as Texas's "Silicon Prairie" because of a high concentration of telecommunications companies.

The Dallas Convention Center, with more than two million square feet of space, is the largest convention center in Texas with more than 1 million square feet of exhibit area, including nearly 800,000 square feet of same level, contiguous prime exhibit space with more than 3.8 million people attending more than 3,600 conventions and spending more than $4.2 billion annually.

Dallas also has a significant cultural presence: many independent theater groups are sponsored by Southern Methodist University; Museum of Art houses an excellent collection of modern art, especially American paintings; Winspear Opera House and three other venues comprise the AT&T Performing Arts Center; Dallas Opera has showcased Maria Callas, Joan Sutherland, and Monserrat Caballe; Winspear Opera House, Wyly Theatre, Nasher Sculpture Center, and Meyerson Symphony Center make Dallas the only city in the world with four buildings within one contiguous block that are designed by Pritzker Architecture Prize winners. The city also contains many historical districts such as the Swiss Avenue District, and elegant buildings such as the City Hall Building designed by I.M. Pei. A notable city event is the State Fair of Texas, which has been held annually at Fair Park since 1886. A massive event for the state, the fair brings an estimated $350 million to the city's economy annually.

The area's high concentration of wealth undoubtedly contributes to Dallas's wide array of shopping centers and high-end boutiques. Downtown Dallas is home to many cafes, restaurants and clubs. The city's centrally located "Arts District" is appropriately named for the independent theaters and art galleries located in the neighborhood. While northern districts of the city and the central downtown have seen much urban revival in the last 30 years, neighborhoods south of downtown have not experienced the same growth.

Colleges and universities in the Dallas area include Southern Methodist University, University of Dallas, and University of Texas at Dallas. In 2006, University of North Texas opened a branch in the southern part of the city, in part, to help accelerate development south of downtown Dallas. The city maintains 21,000 acres of park land, with over 400 parks.

The climate of Dallas is generally temperate. Occasional periods of extreme cold are short-lived, and extremely high temperatures that sometimes occur in summer usually do not last for extended periods.

Rankings

General Rankings

- *US News & World Report* conducted a survey of more than 2,000 people and analyzed the 125 largest metropolitan areas to determine what matters the most when selecting the next place to live. Dallas ranked #18 out of the top 25 as having the best combination of desirable factors. Criteria: cost of living; quality of education; job market, crime rates; and other factors. *realestate.usnews.com, "The 25 Best Places to Live in the U.S. in 2018," April 10, 2018*

- The Dallas metro area was identified as one of America's fastest-growing areas in terms of population and business growth by *MagnifyMoney*. The area ranked #7 out of 35. The 100 most populous metro areas in the U.S. were evaluated on their change from 2011-2016 in the following categories: people and housing; workforce and employment opportunities; growing industry. *www.businessinsider.com, "The 35 Cities in the US with the Biggest Influx of People, the Most Work Opportunities, and the Hottest Business Growth," August 12, 2018*

- The Dallas metro area was identified as one of America's fastest-growing areas in terms of population and economy by *Forbes*. The area ranked #3 out of 25. The 100 most populous metro areas in the U.S. were evaluated on the following criteria: estimated population growth; employment; economic output; wages; home values. *Forbes, "America's Fastest-Growing Cities 2018," February 28, 2018*

- Dallas was identified as one of America's fastest-growing cities in terms of population growth by CNNMoney.com. The area ranked #8 out of 10. Criteria: population growth between July 2015 and July 2016; cities and towns with populations of 50,000. *CNNMoney, "10 Fastest-Growing Cities," June 2, 2017*

- The human resources consulting firm Mercer ranked 231 major cities worldwide in terms of overall quality of life. Dallas ranked #63. Criteria: political, social, economic, and socio-cultural factors; medical and health considerations; schools and education; public services and transportation; recreation; consumer goods; housing; and natural environment. *Mercer, "Mercer 2019 Quality of Living Survey," March 13, 2019*

Business/Finance Rankings

- According to *Business Insider*, the Dallas metro area is where startup growth is on the rise. Based on the 2017 Kauffman Index of Growth Entrepreneurship, which measured in-depth national entrepreneurial trends in 40 metro areas, it ranked #11 in highest startup growth. *www.businessinsider.com, "The 21 U.S. Cities with the Highest Startup Growth," October 21, 2017*

- The personal finance site NerdWallet analyzed 183 American metropolitan areas with populations over 250,000 and more than 15,000 businesses to rank where entrepreneurs find the most success. Criteria included area economy, annual income, housing cost, unemployment rate, and the success rate of area businesses. Dallas ranked #117. *www.nerdwallet.com, "Best Places to Start a Business," April 27, 2015*

- Recognizing the sizeable percentage of American workers who are self-employed, NerdWallet editors assessed the country's cities according to percentage of freelancers, median rental costs, cell phone plans/taxes, and healthcare affordability and access. By these criteria, Dallas placed #3 among the best cities for independent workers. *www.nerdwallet.com, "Best Places for Freelance Workers," August 30, 2016*

- USAA and Hiring Our Heroes worked with Sperlings's BestPlaces and the Institute for Veterans and Military Families at Syracuse University to rank major metropolitan areas where military-skills-related employment is strongest. Criteria for *mid-career* veterans included veteran wage growth; recent job growth; stability; and accessible health resources. Metro areas with a higher than national average crime or unemployment rate were excluded. At #9, the Dallas metro area made the top ten. *www.usaa.com, "2015 Best Places for Veterans"*

- In a survey of economic confidence in the nation's 50 largest metropolitan areas conducted January–December 2014, the Dallas metro area placed #14, according to Gallup's 2014 Economic Confidence Index. *Gallup, "San Jose and San Francisco Lead in Economic Confidence," March 19, 2015*

- NerdWallet.com identified the 10 most promising cities for job seekers of the nation's 100 largest cities. Dallas was ranked #19. Criteria: job availability; annual salary; workforce growth; affordability. *NerdWallet.com, "Best Cities for Job Seekers in 2017," December 19, 2016*

- The Brookings Institution ranked the nation's largest cities based on income inequality. Dallas was ranked #33 (#1 = greatest inequality). Criteria: the "95/20 ratio," a figure representing the income at which a household earns more than 95 percent of all other households, divided by the income at which a household earns more than only 20 percent of all other households. *Brookings Institution, "Household Income Inequality, Largest Cities of 97 Large U.S. Metro Areas, 2014-2016," February 5, 2018*

- The Brookings Institution ranked the 100 largest metro areas in the U.S. based on income inequality. Dallas was ranked #60 (#1 = greatest inequality). Criteria: the "95/20 ratio," a figure representing the income at which a household earns more than 95 percent of all other households, divided by the income at which a household earns more than only 20 percent of all other households. *Brookings Institution, "Household Income Inequality, 100 Largest U.S. Metro Areas, 2014-2016," February 5, 2018*

- *Forbes* ranked the 100 largest metro areas in the U.S. in terms of the "Best Cities for Young Professionals." The Dallas metro area ranked #5 out of 25. (Large metro areas were divided into metro divisions.) Criteria: median rent of a two-bedroom apartment; job growth and unemployment rate; median salary of college graduates with 5 or less years of work experience; networking opportunities; social outlook; percentage of population 25 years of age and older with college degrees. *Forbes.com, "America's 25 Best Cities for Young Professionals in 2017," May 22, 2017*

- Payscale.com ranked the 32 largest metro areas in terms of wage growth. The Dallas metro area ranked #24. Criteria: private-sector wage growth between the 4th quarter of 2017 and the 4th quarter of 2018. *PayScale, "Wage Trends by Metro Area-4th Quarter," January 8, 2019*

- The Dallas metro area was identified as one of the most debt-ridden places in America by the finance site Credit.com. The metro area was ranked #2. Criteria: residents' average credit card debt as well as median income. *Credit.com, "25 Cities With the Most Credit Card Debt," February 28, 2018*

- Dallas was identified as one of America's most frugal metro areas by *Coupons.com*. The city ranked #2 out of 25. Criteria: digital coupon usage. *Coupons.com, "America's Most Frugal Cities of 2017," March 22, 2018*

- Dallas was cited as one of America's top metros for new and expanded facility projects in 2018. The area ranked #2 in the large metro area category (population over 1 million). *Site Selection, "Top Metros of 2018," March 2019*

- The Dallas metro area appeared on the Milken Institute "2018 Best Performing Cities" list. Rank: #5 out of 200 large metro areas. Criteria: job growth; wage and salary growth; high-tech output growth. *Milken Institute, "Best-Performing Cities 2018," January 24, 2019*

- *Forbes* ranked the 200 most populous metro areas to determine the nation's "Best Places for Business and Careers." The Dallas metro area was ranked #6. Criteria: costs (business and living); job growth (past and projected); income growth; quality of life; educational attainment (college and high school); projected economic growth; cultural and recreational opportunities; net migration patterns; number of highly ranked colleges. *Forbes, "The Best Places for Business and Careers 2018: Seattle Leads the Way," October 24, 2018*

- Mercer Human Resources Consulting ranked 209 cities worldwide in terms of cost-of-living. Dallas ranked #85 (the lower the ranking, the higher the cost-of-living). The survey measured the comparative cost of over 200 items (such as housing, food, clothing, household goods, transportation, and entertainment) in each location. *Mercer, "2018 Cost of Living Survey," June 26, 2018*

Culture/Performing Arts Rankings

- Dallas was selected as one of the twenty best large U.S. cities for moviemakers. Of cities with a population over 400,000, the city was ranked #17. Criteria: film community and culture; access to equipment and facilities; film activity in 2018; number of film schools; tax incentives. ease of movement and traffic. *MovieMaker Magazine, "Best Places to Live and Work as a Moviemaker: 2019," January 16, 2019*

- Dallas was selected as one of "America's Favorite Cities." The city ranked #18 in the "Culture" category. Respondents to an online survey were asked to rate 38 top urban destinations in the U.S. from a visitor's perspective. Criteria: theater scene and community; number of bookstores; live music; and sense of history. *Travelandleisure.com, "These Are America's 20 Most Cultured Cities," October 2016*

- Dallas was selected as one of "America's Favorite Cities." The city ranked #25 in the "Culture: Music Scene " category. Respondents to an online survey were asked to rate 38 top urban destinations in the U.S. from a visitor's perspective. *Travelandleisure.com, "From the Honkytonk Capital to Jazz's Birthplace: America's Best Music Scenes," October 2016*

Education Rankings

- Personal finance website *WalletHub* analyzed the 150 largest U.S. metropolitan statistical areas to determine where the most educated Americans are choosing to settle. Criteria: education quality and attainment gap; education levels; percentage of workers with degrees; public school quality rankings; quality and size of each metro area's universities. Dallas was ranked #77 (#1 = most educated city). *www.WalletHub.com, "2018's Most and Least Educated Cities in America," July 24, 2018*

- Dallas was selected as one of the most well-read cities in America by Amazon.com. The city ranked #19 among the top 20. Cities with populations greater than 500,000 were evaluated based on per capita sales of books, magazines and newspapers (both print and Kindle format). *Amazon.com, "The 20 Most Well-Read Cities in America," May 24, 2016*

- Dallas was selected as one of America's most literate cities. The city ranked #42 out of the 82 largest U.S. cities. Criteria: number of booksellers; library resources; Internet resources; educational attainment; periodical publishing resources; newspaper circulation. *Central Connecticut State University, "America's Most Literate Cities, 2016," March 31, 2017*

Environmental Rankings

- Sperling's BestPlaces assessed the 50 largest metropolitan areas of the United States for the likelihood of dangerously extreme weather events or earthquakes. In general the Southeast and South-Central regions have the highest risk of weather extremes and earthquakes, while the Pacific Northwest enjoys the lowest risk. Of the most risky metropolitan areas, the Dallas metro area was ranked #4. *www.bestplaces.net, "Avoid Natural Disasters: BestPlaces Reveals The Top 10 Safest Places to Live," October 25, 2017*

- The U.S. Environmental Protection Agency (EPA) released a list of U.S. metropolitan areas with the most ENERGY STAR certified buildings in 2017. The Dallas metro area was ranked #3 out of 25. *U.S. Environmental Protection Agency, "2018 Energy Star Top Cities," April 11, 2018*

- Dallas was highlighted as one of the 25 most ozone-polluted metro areas in the U.S. during 2014 through 2016. The area ranked #16. *American Lung Association, State of the Air 2018*

- Dallas was highlighted as one of the top 90 cleanest metro areas for short-term particle pollution (24-hour PM 2.5) in the U.S. during 2014 through 2016. Monitors in these cities reported no days with unhealthful PM 2.5 levels. *American Lung Association, State of the Air 2018*

Food/Drink Rankings

- *Men's Health* ranked 100 major U.S. cities in terms of alcohol intoxication. Dallas ranked #77 (#1 = most sober).Criteria: binge drinking; alcohol-related traffic accidents, arrests, and fatalities. *Men's Health, "America's Drunkest Cities," March 9, 2015*

- Globe Life Park was selected as one of PETA's "Top 10 Vegan-Friendly Ballparks" for 2018. The park ranked #2. *People for the Ethical Treatment of Animals, "Top 10 Vegan-Friendly Ballparks, " June 4, 2018*

Health/Fitness Rankings

- For each of the 100 largest cities in the United States, the American College of Sports Medicine's American Fitness Index evaluated infrastructure, community assets, and policies that encourage healthy and fit lifestyles, including preventive health behaviors, levels of chronic disease conditions, health care access, and community resources and policies that support physical activity. Dallas ranked #31 for "community fitness." *www.americanfitnessindex.org, "ACSM American Fitness Index Health and Community Fitness Status of the 100 Largest U.S. Cities," May 2018*

- The Dallas metro area was identified as one of the worst cities for bed bugs in America by pest control company Orkin. The area ranked #15 out of 50 based on the number of bed bug treatments Orkin performed from December 2017 to November 2018. *Orkin, "Baltimore Remains Front Runner, Atlanta and Philadelphia Break Into Top 10," January 14, 2019*

- Dallas was identified as a "2018 Spring Allergy Capital." The area ranked #31 out of 100. Three groups of factors were used to identify the most challenging cities for people with allergies during the spring season: annual pollen levels; medicine utilization; access to board-certified allergists. *Asthma and Allergy Foundation of America, "Spring Allergy Capitals 2018"*

- Dallas was identified as a "2018 Fall Allergy Capital." The area ranked #25 out of 100. Three groups of factors were used to identify the most challenging cities for people with allergies during the fall season: annual pollen levels; medicine utilization; access to board-certified allergists. *Asthma and Allergy Foundation of America, "Fall Allergy Capitals 2018"*

- Dallas was identified as a "2018 Asthma Capital." The area ranked #77 out of the nation's 100 largest metropolitan areas. Criteria: estimated prevalence; self-reported prevalence; crude death rate for asthma; annual pollen score; annual air quality; public smoking laws; number of board-certified asthma specialists; school inhaler access laws; rescue medication use; controller medication use; ER visits for asthma; uninsured rate; poverty rate. *Asthma and Allergy Foundation of America, "Asthma Capitals 2018: The Most Challenging Places to Live With Asthma"*

- *Men's Health* ranked 100 major U.S. cities in terms of the best cities for men. Dallas ranked #47. Criteria: health; fitness; quality of life. *Men's Health, "The Best & Worst Cities for Men Who Want to Be Fit and Happy," January 1, 2016*

- The Dallas metro area ranked #47 out of 189 in The Gallup-Healthways Well-Being Index. Criteria: purpose; social well being; financial health; community and physical health. Results are based on telephone interviews with adults, aged 18 and older, living in metropolitan areas in the 50 U.S. states and the District of Columbia. *Gallup-Healthways, "State of American Well-Being, 2017 Community Well-Being Rankings" March 2018*

Real Estate Rankings

- FitSmallBusiness looked at 50 of the largest metropolitan areas in the U.S. to determine which metro was the best to start a real estate business. Data was compiled from such sources as: Zillow, Trulia, U.S. Census Bureau, and the Bureau of Labor Statistics. Criteria: location; inventory; annual wages; median sales price of homes; days on the market; median price cut percentage; and other factors that would influence real estate professional growth. The Dallas metro area ranked #19. *fitsmallbusiness.com, "The Best Cities to Become a Real Estate Agent in 2018," January 30, 2018*

- *WalletHub* compared the most populated U.S. cities, as well as at least two of the most populated cities in each state, for a total of 179, to determine which had the best markets for real estate agents. Dallas ranked #52 where demand was high and pay was the best. Criteria: sales per agent; annual median wage for real-estate agents; monthly average starting salary for real estate agents; real estate job density and competition; unemployment rate; housing-market health index; and other relevant metrics. *www.WalletHub.com, "2018's Best Places to Be a Real Estate Agent," April 25, 2018*

- The Dallas metro area was identified as one of the nations's 20 hottest housing markets in 2019. Criteria: listing views as an indicator of demand and median days on the market as an indicator of supply. The area ranked #11. *Realtor.com, "January Top 20 Hottest Housing Markets," February 11, 2019*

- Dallas was ranked #182 out of 237 metro areas in terms of housing affordability in 2018 by the National Association of Home Builders (#1 = most affordable). Criteria: the share of homes sold in that area affordable to a family earning the local median income, based on standard mortgage underwriting criteria. *National Association of Home Builders®, NAHB-Wells Fargo Housing Opportunity Index, 4th Quarter 2018*

Safety Rankings

- Allstate ranked the 200 largest cities in America in terms of driver safety. Dallas ranked #178. Criteria: internal property damage claims over a two-year period from January 2015 to December 2016. The report helps increase the importance of safety awareness behind the wheel. *Allstate, "Allstate America's Best Drivers Report, 2018" August 28, 2018*

- The National Insurance Crime Bureau ranked 382 metro areas in the U.S. in terms of per capita rates of vehicle theft. The Dallas metro area ranked #88 (#1 = highest rate). Criteria: number of vehicle theft offenses per 100,000 inhabitants in 2017. *National Insurance Crime Bureau, "Hot Spots 2017," July 12, 2018*

Seniors/Retirement Rankings

- For *U.S. News & World Report's* Best Places rankings, the editors sought out affordable cities where retirees spend the least on housing and can live on $100 a day while still having access to amenities they need, such as health care, utilities, transportation and food. Dallas was among the ten cities that best satisfied their criteria. *money.usnews.com, "10 Best Places to Retire on $100 a Day," October 13, 2015*

- From its Best Cities for Successful Aging indexes, the Milken Institute generated rankings for metropolitan areas, weighing data in nine categories—health care, wellness, living arrangements, transportation and convenience, financial characteristics, education, employment, community engagement, and overall livability. The Dallas metro area was ranked #25 overall in the large metro area category. *Milken Institute, "Best Cities for Successful Aging, 2017" March 14, 2017*

Women/Minorities Rankings

- The *Houston Chronicle* listed the Dallas metro area as #7 in top places for young Latinos to live in the U.S. Research was largely based on housing and occupational data from the largest metropolitan areas performed by *Forbes* and NBC Universo. Criteria: percentage of 18-34 year-olds; Latino college grad rates; and diversity. *blog.chron.com, "The 15 Best Big Cities for Latino Millenials," January 26, 2016*

- Personal finance website *WalletHub* compared more than 180 U.S. cities—including the 150 most populated U.S. cities, plus at least two of the most populated cities in each state—across two key dimensions, "Hispanic Business-Friendliness" and "Hispanic Purchasing Power", to arrive at the most favorable conditions for Hispanic entrepreneurs. Dallas was ranked #31 out of 182. Criteria includes: share of Hispanic-Owned Businesses; Hispanic entrepreneurship rate to median annual income of Hispanics; Small Business-Friendliness score; cost of living; and number of Hispanics with at least a bachelor's degree. *WalletHub.com, "2018's Best Cities for Hispanic Entrepreneurs," April 26, 2018*

Miscellaneous Rankings

- Dallas was selected as a 2018 Digital Cities Survey winner. The city ranked #10 in the large city (500,000 or more population) category. The survey examined and assessed how city governments are utilizing technology to improve transparency, enhance cybersecurity, and solve social challenges. Survey questions focused on ten characteristics: engaged, mobile, open, secure, staffed/supported, efficient, connected, resilient, best practices, and use of innovation. *Center for Digital Government, "2018 Digital Cities Survey," November 2, 2018*

- The watchdog site Charity Navigator conducts an annual study of charities in the nation's major markets both to analyze statistical differences in their financial, accountability, and transparency practices and to track year-to-year variations in individual philanthropic communities. Charity Navigator's analysis demonstrated that the financial, accountability and transparency behaviors of America's largest charities can be influenced by the metropolitan market within which the charity operates. The Dallas metro area was ranked #5 among the 30 metro markets in the rating category of Overall Score. *www.charitynavigator.org, "2017 Metro Market Study," May 1, 2017*

- The real estate site Zillow has compiled the 2016 Trick-or-Treat Index, which used its own Home Value Index and Walk Score along with population density, age of residents, and local crime stats to determine that Dallas ranked #11 for "getting the best candy in the least amount of time." Zillow also zeroes in on the best neighborhoods in its top 20 cities. *www.zillow.com, "20 Best Cities for Trick or Treating in 2017," October 13, 2017*

- *WalletHub* compared the 150 most populated U.S. cities to determine their operating efficiency. A "Quality of Services" score was constructed for each city and then divided by the total budget per capita to reveal which were managed the best. Dallas ranked #95. Criteria: financial stability; economy; education; safety; health; infrastructure and pollution. *www.WalletHub.com, "2018's Best- & Worst-Run Cities in America," July 9, 2018*

- The National Alliance to End Homelessness listed the 25 most populous metro areas with the highest rate of homelessness. The Dallas metro area had a high rate of homelessness. Criteria: number of homeless people per 10,000 population in 2016. *National Alliance to End Homelessness, "Homelessness in the 25 Most Populous U.S. Metro Areas," September 1, 2017*

Business Environment

CITY FINANCES

City Government Finances

Component	2016 ($000)	2016 ($ per capita)
Total Revenues	3,104,595	2,388
Total Expenditures	3,938,361	3,029
Debt Outstanding	10,750,662	8,269
Cash and Securities[1]	10,850,855	8,346

Note: (1) Cash and security holdings of a government at the close of its fiscal year, including those of its dependent agencies, utilities, and liquor stores.
Source: U.S. Census Bureau, State & Local Government Finances 2016

City Government Revenue by Source

Source	2016 ($000)	2016 ($ per capita)	2016 (%)
General Revenue			
From Federal Government	47,214	36	1.5
From State Government	67,621	52	2.2
From Local Governments	8,529	7	0.3
Taxes			
Property	766,680	590	24.7
Sales and Gross Receipts	441,356	339	14.2
Personal Income	0	0	0.0
Corporate Income	0	0	0.0
Motor Vehicle License	0	0	0.0
Other Taxes	46,823	36	1.5
Current Charges	1,416,992	1,090	45.6
Liquor Store	0	0	0.0
Utility	344,488	265	11.1
Employee Retirement	-188,174	-145	-6.1

Source: U.S. Census Bureau, State & Local Government Finances 2016

City Government Expenditures by Function

Function	2016 ($000)	2016 ($ per capita)	2016 (%)
General Direct Expenditures			
Air Transportation	1,067,300	820	27.1
Corrections	1,252	1	0.0
Education	0	0	0.0
Employment Security Administration	0	0	0.0
Financial Administration	34,395	26	0.9
Fire Protection	204,334	157	5.2
General Public Buildings	29,087	22	0.7
Governmental Administration, Other	19,735	15	0.5
Health	14,435	11	0.4
Highways	176,517	135	4.5
Hospitals	0	0	0.0
Housing and Community Development	50,281	38	1.3
Interest on General Debt	399,558	307	10.1
Judicial and Legal	29,438	22	0.7
Libraries	31,903	24	0.8
Parking	122	< 1	< 0.1
Parks and Recreation	171,525	131	4.4
Police Protection	387,960	298	9.9
Public Welfare	6,903	5	0.2
Sewerage	247,878	190	6.3
Solid Waste Management	71,208	54	1.8
Veterans' Services	0	0	0.0
Liquor Store	0	0	0.0
Utility	360,313	277	9.1
Employee Retirement	472,829	363	12.0

Source: U.S. Census Bureau, State & Local Government Finances 2016

DEMOGRAPHICS

Population Growth

Area	1990 Census	2000 Census	2010 Census	2017* Estimate	Population Growth (%)	
					1990-2017	2010-2017
City	1,006,971	1,188,580	1,197,816	1,300,122	29.1	8.5
MSA[1]	3,989,294	5,161,544	6,371,773	7,104,415	78.1	11.5
U.S.	248,709,873	281,421,906	308,745,538	321,004,407	29.1	4.0

Note: (1) Figures cover the Dallas-Fort Worth-Arlington, TX Metropolitan Statistical Area—see Appendix B for areas included; (*) 2013-2017 5-year estimated population
Source: U.S. Census Bureau, 1990 Census, Census 2000, Census 2010, 2013-2017 American Community Survey 5-Year Estimates

Household Size

Area	Persons in Household (%)							Average Household Size
	One	Two	Three	Four	Five	Six	Seven or More	
City	34.4	29.1	14.4	11.3	6.4	2.6	1.8	2.60
MSA[1]	24.8	30.9	16.8	15.2	7.5	3.0	1.8	2.80
U.S.	27.7	33.8	15.7	13.0	6.0	2.3	1.4	2.60

Note: (1) Figures cover the Dallas-Fort Worth-Arlington, TX Metropolitan Statistical Area—see Appendix B for areas included
Source: U.S. Census Bureau, 2013-2017 American Community Survey 5-Year Estimates

Race

Area	White Alone[2] (%)	Black Alone[2] (%)	Asian Alone[2] (%)	AIAN[3] Alone[2] (%)	NHOPI[4] Alone[2] (%)	Other Race Alone[2] (%)	Two or More Races (%)
City	61.8	24.3	3.4	0.3	0.0	7.7	2.6
MSA[1]	69.4	15.4	6.3	0.4	0.1	5.4	2.9
U.S.	73.0	12.7	5.4	0.8	0.2	4.8	3.1

Note: (1) Figures cover the Dallas-Fort Worth-Arlington, TX Metropolitan Statistical Area—see Appendix B for areas included; (2) Alone is defined as not being in combination with one or more other races; (3) American Indian and Alaska Native; (4) Native Hawaiian and Other Pacific Islander
Source: U.S. Census Bureau, 2013-2017 American Community Survey 5-Year Estimates

Hispanic or Latino Origin

Area	Total (%)	Mexican (%)	Puerto Rican (%)	Cuban (%)	Other (%)
City	41.7	36.0	0.5	0.3	4.9
MSA[1]	28.4	23.8	0.7	0.2	3.7
U.S.	17.6	11.1	1.7	0.7	4.1

Note: Persons of Hispanic or Latino origin can be of any race; (1) Figures cover the Dallas-Fort Worth-Arlington, TX Metropolitan Statistical Area—see Appendix B for areas included
Source: U.S. Census Bureau, 2013-2017 American Community Survey 5-Year Estimates

Segregation

Type	Segregation Indices[1]				Percent Change		
	1990	2000	2010	2010 Rank[2]	1990-2000	1990-2010	2000-2010
Black/White	62.8	59.8	56.6	48	-3.1	-6.2	-3.2
Asian/White	41.8	45.6	46.6	19	3.8	4.8	1.0
Hispanic/White	48.8	52.3	50.3	24	3.5	1.5	-2.0

Note: All figures cover the Metropolitan Statistical Area—see Appendix B for areas included; Figures are based on an analysis of 1990, 2000, and 2010 Census Decennial Census tract data by William H. Frey, Brookings Institution and the University of Michigan Social Science Data Analysis Network. In this analysis all racial groups (whites, blacks, and asians) are non-Hispanic members of those races. Hispanics are shown as a separate category; (1) Segregation Indices are Dissimilarity Indices that measure the degree to which the minority group is distributed differently than whites across census tracts. They range from 0 (complete integration) to 100 (complete segregation) where the value indicates the percentage of the minority group that needs to move to be distributed exactly like whites; (2) Ranges from 1 (most segregated) to 102 (least segregated); n/a not available.
Source: www.CensusScope.org

Ancestry

Area	German	Irish	English	American	Italian	Polish	French[2]	Scottish	Dutch
City	5.6	4.1	4.8	3.2	1.4	0.8	1.3	1.2	0.5
MSA[1]	9.5	7.3	7.1	6.5	2.1	1.1	1.8	1.7	0.9
U.S.	14.1	10.1	7.5	6.6	5.3	2.9	2.5	1.7	1.3

Note: Figures are the percentage of the total population reporting a particular ancestry. The nine most commonly reported ancestries in the U.S. are shown. Figures include multiple ancestries (e.g. if a person reported being Irish and Italian, they were included in both columns); (1) Figures cover the Dallas-Fort Worth-Arlington, TX Metropolitan Statistical Area—see Appendix B for areas included; (2) Excludes Basque
Source: U.S. Census Bureau, 2013-2017 American Community Survey 5-Year Estimates

Foreign-Born Population

Area	Percent of Population Born in								
	Any Foreign Country	Asia	Mexico	Europe	Carribean	Central America[2]	South America	Africa	Canada
City	24.4	2.9	15.8	0.7	0.4	2.4	0.5	1.6	0.2
MSA[1]	18.1	4.9	8.7	0.8	0.3	1.4	0.5	1.3	0.2
U.S.	13.4	4.1	3.6	1.5	1.3	1.0	0.9	0.6	0.3

Note: (1) Figures cover the Dallas-Fort Worth-Arlington, TX Metropolitan Statistical Area—see Appendix B for areas included; (2) Excludes Mexico.
Source: U.S. Census Bureau, 2013-2017 American Community Survey 5-Year Estimates

Marital Status

Area	Never Married	Now Married[2]	Separated	Widowed	Divorced
City	41.1	40.0	3.4	4.6	10.9
MSA[1]	32.0	50.5	2.3	4.5	10.8
U.S.	33.1	48.2	2.0	5.8	10.9

Note: Figures are percentages and cover the population 15 years of age and older; (1) Figures cover the Dallas-Fort Worth-Arlington, TX Metropolitan Statistical Area—see Appendix B for areas included; (2) Excludes separated
Source: U.S. Census Bureau, 2013-2017 American Community Survey 5-Year Estimates

Disability by Age

Area	All Ages	Under 18 Years Old	18 to 64 Years Old	65 Years and Over
City	9.6	3.1	8.2	36.0
MSA[1]	9.6	3.4	8.1	34.9
U.S.	12.6	4.2	10.3	35.5

Note: Figures show percent of the civilian noninstitutionalized population that reported having a disability. Disability status is determined from six types of difficulty: vision, hearing, cognitive, ambulatory, self-care, and independent living. For children under 5 years old, hearing and vision difficulty are used to determine disability status. For children between the ages of 5 and 14, disability status is determined from hearing, vision, cognitive, ambulatory, and self-care difficulties. For people aged 15 years and older, they are considered to have a disability if they have difficulty with any one of the six difficulty types; Note: (1) Figures cover the Dallas-Fort Worth-Arlington, TX Metropolitan Statistical Area—see Appendix B for areas included
Source: U.S. Census Bureau, 2013-2017 American Community Survey 5-Year Estimates

Age

Area	Percent of Population									Median Age
	Under Age 5	Age 5–19	Age 20–34	Age 35–44	Age 45–54	Age 55–64	Age 65–74	Age 75–84	Age 85+	
City	7.8	20.0	26.3	13.9	12.0	10.3	5.8	2.8	1.2	32.5
MSA[1]	7.1	22.1	21.3	14.3	13.7	11.0	6.5	3.0	1.1	34.6
U.S.	6.2	19.5	20.7	12.7	13.4	12.7	8.6	4.4	1.9	37.8

Note: (1) Figures cover the Dallas-Fort Worth-Arlington, TX Metropolitan Statistical Area—see Appendix B for areas included
Source: U.S. Census Bureau, 2013-2017 American Community Survey 5-Year Estimates

Gender

Area	Males	Females	Males per 100 Females
City	644,344	655,778	98.3
MSA[1]	3,493,829	3,610,586	96.8
U.S.	158,018,753	162,985,654	97.0

Note: (1) Figures cover the Dallas-Fort Worth-Arlington, TX Metropolitan Statistical Area—see Appendix B for areas included
Source: U.S. Census Bureau, 2013-2017 American Community Survey 5-Year Estimates

Religious Groups by Family

Area	Catholic	Baptist	Non-Den.	Methodist[2]	Lutheran	LDS[3]	Pentecostal	Presbyterian[4]	Muslim[5]	Judaism
MSA[1]	13.3	18.7	7.8	5.3	0.8	1.2	2.2	1.0	2.4	0.4
U.S.	19.1	9.3	4.0	4.0	2.3	2.0	1.9	1.6	0.8	0.7

Note: Figures are the number of adherents as a percentage of the total population; (1) Figures cover the Dallas-Fort Worth-Arlington, TX Metropolitan Statistical Area—see Appendix B for areas included; (2) Methodist/Pietist; (3) Latter Day Saints; (4) Reformed; (5) Figures are estimates
Source: Association of Statisticians of American Religious Bodies, 2010 U.S. Religion Census: Religious Congregations & Membership Study

Religious Groups by Tradition

Area	Catholic	Evangelical Protestant	Mainline Protestant	Other Tradition	Black Protestant	Orthodox
MSA[1]	13.3	28.3	7.0	4.8	1.8	0.2
U.S.	19.1	16.2	7.3	4.3	1.6	0.3

Note: Figures are the number of adherents as a percentage of the total population; (1) Figures cover the Dallas-Fort Worth-Arlington, TX Metropolitan Statistical Area—see Appendix B for areas included
Source: Association of Statisticians of American Religious Bodies, 2010 U.S. Religion Census: Religious Congregations & Membership Study

ECONOMY

Gross Metropolitan Product

Area	2016	2017	2018	2019	Rank[2]
MSA[1]	506.8	541.1	579.3	613.4	4

Note: Figures are in billions of dollars; (1) Figures cover the Dallas-Fort Worth-Arlington, TX Metropolitan Statistical Area—see Appendix B for areas included; (2) Rank is based on 2017 data and ranges from 1 to 381
Source: U.S. Conference of Mayors, U.S. Metro Economies: Economic Growth & Full Employment, June 2018

Economic Growth

Area	2017-2018 (%)	2019-2020 (%)	2021-2022 (%)
MSA[1]	4.6	3.1	2.3

Note: Figures are real gross metropolitan product (GMP) growth rates and represent average annual percent change; (1) Figures cover the Dallas-Fort Worth-Arlington, TX Metropolitan Statistical Area—see Appendix B for areas included
Source: U.S. Conference of Mayors, U.S. Metro Economies: Economic Growth & Full Employment, June 2018

Metropolitan Area Exports

Area	2012	2013	2014	2015	2016	2017	Rank[2]
MSA[1]	27,820.9	27,596.0	28,669.4	27,372.9	27,187.8	30,269.1	9

Note: Figures are in millions of dollars; (1) Figures cover the Dallas-Fort Worth-Arlington, TX Metropolitan Statistical Area—see Appendix B for areas included; (2) Rank is based on 2017 data and ranges from 1 to 387
Source: U.S. Department of Commerce, International Trade Administration, Office of Trade and Economic Analysis, Industry and Analysis, Exports by Metropolitan Area, extracted March 25, 2019

Building Permits

Area	Single-Family			Multi-Family			Total		
	2016	2017	Pct. Chg.	2016	2017	Pct. Chg.	2016	2017	Pct. Chg.
City	1,640	2,100	28.0	8,697	5,151	-40.8	10,337	7,251	-29.9
MSA[1]	29,703	34,604	16.5	26,097	27,920	7.0	55,800	62,524	12.1
U.S.	750,800	820,000	9.2	455,800	462,000	1.4	1,206,600	1,282,000	6.2

Note: (1) Figures cover the Dallas-Fort Worth-Arlington, TX Metropolitan Statistical Area—see Appendix B for areas included; Figures represent new, privately-owned housing units authorized (unadjusted data); All permit data are based on estimates with imputation
Source: U.S. Census Bureau, Manufacturing, Mining, and Construction Statistics, Building Permits, 2016, 2017

Bankruptcy Filings

Area	Business Filings			Nonbusiness Filings		
	2017	2018	% Chg.	2017	2018	% Chg.
Dallas County	306	437	42.8	3,997	3,520	-11.9
U.S.	23,157	22,232	-4.0	765,863	751,186	-1.9

Note: Business filings include Chapter 7, Chapter 11, Chapter 12, and Chapter 13; Nonbusiness filings include Chapter 7, Chapter 11, and Chapter 13
Source: Administrative Office of the U.S. Courts, Business and Nonbusiness Bankruptcy, County Cases Commenced by Chapter of the Bankruptcy Code, During the 12-Month Period Ending December 31, 2017 and Business and Nonbusiness Bankruptcy, County Cases Commenced by Chapter of the Bankruptcy Code, During the 12-Month Period Ending December 31, 2018

Housing Vacancy Rates

Area	Gross Vacancy Rate[2] (%)			Year-Round Vacancy Rate[3] (%)			Rental Vacancy Rate[4] (%)			Homeowner Vacancy Rate[5] (%)		
	2016	2017	2018	2016	2017	2018	2016	2017	2018	2016	2017	2018
MSA[1]	7.9	7.8	7.8	7.7	7.6	7.6	6.8	7.1	7.4	1.4	0.8	1.4
U.S.	12.8	12.7	12.3	9.9	9.9	9.7	6.9	7.2	6.9	1.7	1.6	1.5

Note: (1) Figures cover the Dallas-Fort Worth-Arlington, TX Metropolitan Statistical Area—see Appendix B for areas included; (2) The percentage of the total housing inventory that is vacant; (3) The percentage of the housing inventory (excluding seasonal units) that is year-round vacant; (4) The percentage of rental inventory that is vacant for rent; (5) The percentage of homeowner inventory that is vacant for sale
Source: U.S. Census Bureau, Housing Vacancies and Homeownership Annual Statistics: 2016, 2017, 2018

INCOME

Income

Area	Per Capita ($)	Median Household ($)	Average Household ($)
City	31,260	47,285	78,925
MSA[1]	32,463	63,870	89,486
U.S.	31,177	57,652	81,283

Note: (1) Figures cover the Dallas-Fort Worth-Arlington, TX Metropolitan Statistical Area—see Appendix B for areas included
Source: U.S. Census Bureau, 2013-2017 American Community Survey 5-Year Estimates

Household Income Distribution

Area	Percent of Households Earning							
	Under $15,000	$15,000 -$24,999	$25,000 -$34,999	$35,000 -$49,999	$50,000 -$74,999	$75,000 -$99,999	$100,000 -$149,999	$150,000 and up
City	13.8	12.0	11.5	14.9	17.2	9.6	9.7	11.4
MSA[1]	8.9	8.3	9.0	12.7	18.2	12.6	15.6	14.6
U.S.	11.6	9.8	9.5	13.0	17.7	12.3	14.1	12.1

Note: (1) Figures cover the Dallas-Fort Worth-Arlington, TX Metropolitan Statistical Area—see Appendix B for areas included
Source: U.S. Census Bureau, 2013-2017 American Community Survey 5-Year Estimates

Poverty Rate

Area	All Ages	Under 18 Years Old	18 to 64 Years Old	65 Years and Over
City	21.8	34.2	18.1	14.1
MSA[1]	13.3	19.2	11.7	8.4
U.S.	14.6	20.3	13.7	9.3

Note: Figures are percentage of people whose income during the past 12 months was below the poverty level; (1) Figures cover the Dallas-Fort Worth-Arlington, TX Metropolitan Statistical Area—see Appendix B for areas included
Source: U.S. Census Bureau, 2013-2017 American Community Survey 5-Year Estimates

EMPLOYMENT

Labor Force and Employment

Area	Civilian Labor Force			Workers Employed		
	Dec. 2017	Dec. 2018	% Chg.	Dec. 2017	Dec. 2018	% Chg.
City	685,232	710,627	3.7	662,456	686,384	3.6
MD[1]	2,585,893	2,682,088	3.7	2,504,449	2,594,961	3.6
U.S.	159,880,000	162,510,000	1.6	153,602,000	156,481,000	1.9

Note: Data is not seasonally adjusted and covers workers 16 years of age and older; (1) Figures cover the Dallas-Plano-Irving, TX Metropolitan Division—see Appendix B for areas included
Source: Bureau of Labor Statistics, Local Area Unemployment Statistics

Unemployment Rate

Area	2018											
	Jan.	Feb.	Mar.	Apr.	May	Jun.	Jul.	Aug.	Sep.	Oct.	Nov.	Dec.
City	3.8	3.9	3.8	3.5	3.5	3.9	3.8	3.7	3.6	3.4	3.3	3.4
MD[1]	3.6	3.7	3.7	3.4	3.4	3.8	3.6	3.6	3.4	3.2	3.2	3.2
U.S.	4.5	4.4	4.1	3.7	3.6	4.2	4.1	3.9	3.6	3.5	3.5	3.7

Note: Data is not seasonally adjusted and covers workers 16 years of age and older; (1) Figures cover the Dallas-Plano-Irving, TX Metropolitan Division—see Appendix B for areas included
Source: Bureau of Labor Statistics, Local Area Unemployment Statistics

Average Wages

Occupation	$/Hr.	Occupation	$/Hr.
Accountants and Auditors	39.60	Maids and Housekeeping Cleaners	11.00
Automotive Mechanics	20.70	Maintenance and Repair Workers	20.40
Bookkeepers	21.20	Marketing Managers	67.10
Carpenters	19.00	Nuclear Medicine Technologists	39.20
Cashiers	10.70	Nurses, Licensed Practical	24.40
Clerks, General Office	17.50	Nurses, Registered	35.70
Clerks, Receptionists/Information	13.80	Nursing Assistants	13.40
Clerks, Shipping/Receiving	16.00	Packers and Packagers, Hand	12.50
Computer Programmers	47.00	Physical Therapists	46.00
Computer Systems Analysts	45.80	Postal Service Mail Carriers	25.20
Computer User Support Specialists	24.90	Real Estate Brokers	39.90
Cooks, Restaurant	12.30	Retail Salespersons	12.80
Dentists	91.50	Sales Reps., Exc. Tech./Scientific	33.80
Electrical Engineers	50.40	Sales Reps., Tech./Scientific	43.50
Electricians	22.70	Secretaries, Exc. Legal/Med./Exec.	18.40
Financial Managers	76.80	Security Guards	14.50
First-Line Supervisors/Managers, Sales	23.10	Surgeons	109.70
Food Preparation Workers	11.10	Teacher Assistants*	11.40
General and Operations Managers	63.80	Teachers, Elementary School*	28.60
Hairdressers/Cosmetologists	11.70	Teachers, Secondary School*	29.40
Internists, General	59.70	Telemarketers	15.70
Janitors and Cleaners	12.70	Truck Drivers, Heavy/Tractor-Trailer	23.00
Landscaping/Groundskeeping Workers	13.80	Truck Drivers, Light/Delivery Svcs.	19.30
Lawyers	77.30	Waiters and Waitresses	11.00

Note: Wage data covers the Dallas-Fort Worth-Arlington, TX Metropolitan Statistical Area—see Appendix B for areas included; (*) Hourly wages for elementary/secondary school teachers and teacher assistants were calculated by the editors from annual wage data based on a 40 hour work week; n/a not available.
Source: Bureau of Labor Statistics, Metro Area Occupational Employment & Wage Estimates, May 2018

Employment by Occupation

Occupation Classification	City (%)	MSA[1] (%)	U.S. (%)
Management, Business, Science, and Arts	33.8	38.7	37.4
Natural Resources, Construction, and Maintenance	12.0	9.4	8.9
Production, Transportation, and Material Moving	11.9	11.6	12.2
Sales and Office	23.5	24.6	23.5
Service	18.7	15.7	18.0

Note: Figures cover employed civilians 16 years of age and older; (1) Figures cover the Dallas-Fort Worth-Arlington, TX Metropolitan Statistical Area—see Appendix B for areas included
Source: U.S. Census Bureau, 2013-2017 American Community Survey 5-Year Estimates

Employment by Industry

Sector	MD[1]		U.S.
	Number of Employees	Percent of Total	Percent of Total
Construction, Mining, and Logging	149,900	5.6	5.3
Education and Health Services	318,900	11.9	15.9
Financial Activities	242,400	9.0	5.7
Government	307,400	11.5	15.1
Information	71,400	2.7	1.9
Leisure and Hospitality	270,900	10.1	10.7
Manufacturing	182,300	6.8	8.5
Other Services	85,700	3.2	3.9
Professional and Business Services	507,500	18.9	14.1
Retail Trade	266,700	10.0	10.8
Transportation, Warehousing, and Utilities	126,200	4.7	4.2
Wholesale Trade	150,400	5.6	3.9

Note: Figures are non-farm employment as of December 2018. Figures are not seasonally adjusted and include workers 16 years of age and older; (1) Figures cover the Dallas-Plano-Irving, TX Metropolitan Division—see Appendix B for areas included
Source: Bureau of Labor Statistics, Current Employment Statistics, Employment, Hours, and Earnings

Occupations with Greatest Projected Employment Growth: 2018 – 2020

Occupation[1]	2018 Employment	2020 Projected Employment	Numeric Employment Change	Percent Employment Change
Combined Food Preparation and Serving Workers, Including Fast Food	351,780	372,090	20,310	5.8
Personal Care Aides	218,310	235,470	17,160	7.9
Heavy and Tractor-Trailer Truck Drivers	204,870	216,310	11,440	5.6
Laborers and Freight, Stock, and Material Movers, Hand	194,220	204,060	9,840	5.1
Waiters and Waitresses	236,020	245,790	9,770	4.1
Office Clerks, General	393,740	403,270	9,530	2.4
Customer Service Representatives	268,380	277,460	9,080	3.4
General and Operations Managers	182,190	190,620	8,430	4.6
Retail Salespersons	392,620	400,900	8,280	2.1
Construction Laborers	143,270	150,820	7,550	5.3

Note: Projections cover Texas; (1) Sorted by numeric employment change
Source: www.projectionscentral.com, State Occupational Projections, 2018–2020 Short-Term Projections

Fastest Growing Occupations: 2018 – 2020

Occupation[1]	2018 Employment	2020 Projected Employment	Numeric Employment Change	Percent Employment Change
Wind Turbine Service Technicians	1,810	2,190	380	21.0
Religious Workers, All Other	5,690	6,330	640	11.2
Fundraisers	8,830	9,670	840	9.5
Statisticians	1,870	2,040	170	9.1
Public Relations and Fundraising Managers	6,570	7,160	590	9.0
Home Health Aides	74,390	80,920	6,530	8.8
Community and Social Service Specialists, All Other	4,520	4,890	370	8.2
Personal Care Aides	218,310	235,470	17,160	7.9
Operations Research Analysts	10,920	11,760	840	7.7
Software Developers, Applications	65,190	70,140	4,950	7.6

Note: Projections cover Texas; (1) Sorted by percent employment change and excludes occupations with numeric employment change less than 50
Source: www.projectionscentral.com, State Occupational Projections, 2018–2020 Short-Term Projections

TAXES

State Corporate Income Tax Rates

State	Tax Rate (%)	Income Brackets ($)	Num. of Brackets	Financial Institution Tax Rate (%)[a]	Federal Income Tax Ded.
Texas	(w)	–	–	(w)	No

Note: Tax rates as of January 1, 2019; (a) Rates listed are the corporate income tax rate applied to financial institutions or excise taxes based on income. Some states have other taxes based upon the value of deposits or shares; (w) Texas imposes a Franchise Tax, otherwise known as margin tax, imposed on entities with more than $1,130,000 total revenues at rate of 0.75%, or 0.375% for entities primarily engaged in retail or wholesale trade, on lesser of 70% of total revenues or 100% of gross receipts after deductions for either compensation or cost of goods sold.
Source: Federation of Tax Administrators, Range of State Corporate Income Tax Rates, January 1, 2019

State Individual Income Tax Rates

State	Tax Rate (%)	Income Brackets ($)	Personal Exemptions ($) Single	Married	Depend.	Standard Ded. ($) Single	Married
Texas			– No state income tax –				

Note: Tax rates as of January 1, 2019; Local- and county-level taxes are not included; n/a not applicable;

Source: Federation of Tax Administrators, State Individual Income Tax Rates, January 1, 2019

Various State Sales and Excise Tax Rates

State	State Sales Tax (%)	Gasoline[1] (¢/gal.)	Cigarette[2] ($/pack)	Spirits[3] ($/gal.)	Wine[4] ($/gal.)	Beer[5] ($/gal.)	Recreational Marijuana (%)
Texas	6.25	20	1.41	2.40 (f)	0.20 (l)	0.20 (q)	Not legal

Note: All tax rates as of January 1, 2019; (1) The American Petroleum Institute has developed a methodology for determining the average tax rate on a gallon of fuel. Rates may include any of the following: excise taxes, environmental fees, storage tank fees, other fees or taxes, general sales tax, and local taxes. In states where gasoline is subject to the general sales tax, or where the fuel tax is based on the average sale price, the average rate determined by API is sensitive to changes in the price of gasoline. States that fully or partially apply general sales taxes to gasoline: CA, CO, GA, IL, IN, MI, NY; (2) The federal excise tax of $1.0066 per pack and local taxes are not included; (3) Rates are those applicable to off-premise sales of 40% alcohol by volume (a.b.v.) distilled spirits in 750ml containers. Local excise taxes are excluded; (4) Rates are those applicable to off-premise sales of 11% a.b.v. non-carbonated wine in 750ml containers; (5) Rates are those applicable to off-premise sales of 4.7% a.b.v. beer in 12 ounce containers; (f) Different rates also applicable according to alcohol content, place of production, size of container, or place purchased (on- or off-premise or onboard airlines); (l) Different rates also applicable to alcohol content, place of production, size of container, place purchased (on- or off-premise or on board airlines) or type of wine (carbonated, vermouth, etc.); (q) Different rates also applicable according to alcohol content, place of production, size of container, or place purchased (on- or off-premise or onboard airlines).
Source: Tax Foundation, 2019 Facts & Figures: How Does Your State Compare?

State Business Tax Climate Index Rankings

State	Overall Rank	Corporate Tax Rank	Individual Income Tax Rank	Sales Tax Rank	Unemployment Insurance Tax Rank	Property Tax Rank
Texas	15	49	6	37	18	37

Note: The index is a measure of how each state's tax laws affect economic performance. The lower the rank, the more favorable a state's tax system is for business. States without a given tax are given a ranking of 1. The scores/rankings for the District of Columbia do not affect other states. The 2019 index represents the tax climate as of July 1, 2018.
Source: Tax Foundation, State Business Tax Climate Index 2019

COMMERCIAL REAL ESTATE

Office Market

Market Area	Inventory (sq. ft.)	Vacancy Rate (%)	Under Construction (sq. ft.)	YTD Net Absorption (sq. ft.)	Total Average Asking Rent ($/sq. ft./year)
Dallas-Fort Worth	258,387,379	19.4	2,048,642	1,738,944	25.65
National	4,905,867,938	13.1	83,553,714	45,846,470	28.46

Source: Newmark Grubb Knight Frank, National Office Market Report, 4th Quarter 2018

Industrial/Warehouse/R&D Market

Market Area	Inventory (sq. ft.)	Vacancy Rate (%)	Under Construction (sq. ft.)	YTD Net Absorption (sq. ft.)	Total Average Asking Rent ($/sq. ft./year)
Dallas-Ft. Worth	862,312,979	6.1	25,171,564	19,395,062	5.82
National	14,796,839,085	5.0	262,662,294	238,014,726	7.16

Source: Newmark Grubb Knight Frank, National Industrial Market Report, 4th Quarter 2018

COMMERCIAL UTILITIES

Typical Monthly Electric Bills

Area	Commercial Service ($/month)		Industrial Service ($/month)	
	1,500 kWh	40 kW demand 14,000 kWh	1,000 kW demand 200,000 kWh	50,000 kW demand 32,500,000 kWh
City	n/a	n/a	n/a	n/a
Average[1]	203	1,619	25,886	2,540,077

Note: Figures are based on annualized rates; (1) Average based on 187 utilities surveyed; n/a not available
Source: Edison Electric Institute, Typical Bills and Average Rates Report, Summer 2018

TRANSPORTATION

Means of Transportation to Work

Area	Car/Truck/Van		Public Transportation			Bicycle	Walked	Other Means	Worked at Home
	Drove Alone	Car-pooled	Bus	Subway	Railroad				
City	76.2	11.3	3.3	0.5	0.3	0.2	1.9	1.6	4.6
MSA[1]	80.7	9.8	0.9	0.2	0.3	0.2	1.3	1.4	5.2
U.S.	76.4	9.2	2.5	1.9	0.6	0.6	2.7	1.3	4.7

Note: Figures are percentages and cover workers 16 years of age and older; (1) Figures cover the Dallas-Fort Worth-Arlington, TX Metropolitan Statistical Area—see Appendix B for areas included
Source: U.S. Census Bureau, 2013-2017 American Community Survey 5-Year Estimates

Travel Time to Work

Area	Less Than 10 Minutes	10 to 19 Minutes	20 to 29 Minutes	30 to 44 Minutes	45 to 59 Minutes	60 to 89 Minutes	90 Minutes or More
City	8.6	26.8	22.9	26.0	8.1	5.5	2.0
MSA[1]	9.1	25.4	21.1	25.1	10.5	6.7	2.0
U.S.	12.7	28.9	20.9	20.5	8.1	6.2	2.7

Note: Note: Figures are percentages and include workers 16 years old and over; (1) Figures cover the Dallas-Fort Worth-Arlington, TX Metropolitan Statistical Area—see Appendix B for areas included
Source: U.S. Census Bureau, 2013-2017 American Community Survey 5-Year Estimates

Freeway Travel Time Index

Area	1985	1990	1995	2000	2005	2010	2014
Urban Area Rank[1,2]	6	9	10	19	21	22	19
Urban Area Index[1]	1.19	1.20	1.23	1.24	1.26	1.24	1.27
Average Index[3]	1.09	1.11	1.14	1.17	1.20	1.19	1.20

Note: Freeway Travel Time Index—the ratio of travel time in the peak period to the travel time at free-flow conditions. For example, a value of 1.30 indicates a 20-minute free-flow trip takes 26 minutes in the peak (20 minutes x 1.30 = 26 minutes); (1) Covers the Dallas-Fort Worth-Arlington TX urban area; (2) Rank is based on 101 urban areas (#1 = highest travel time index); (3) Average of 101 urban areas
Source: Texas Transportation Institute, 2015 Urban Mobility Scorecard, August 2015

Freeway Commuter Stress Index

Area	1985	1990	1995	2000	2005	2010	2014
Urban Area Rank[1,2]	12	15	13	20	22	25	20
Urban Area Index[1]	1.25	1.26	1.29	1.30	1.32	1.30	1.33
Average Index[3]	1.13	1.16	1.19	1.22	1.25	1.24	1.25

Note: The Freeway Commuter Stress Index is the same as the Freeway Travel Time Index (see table above) except that it includes only the travel in the peak directions during the peak periods; the TTI includes travel in all directions during the peak period. Thus, the CSI is more indicative of the work trip experienced by each commuter on a daily basis; (1) Covers the Dallas-Fort Worth-Arlington TX urban area; (2) Rank is based on 101 urban areas (#1 = highest travel time index); (3) Average of 101 urban areas
Source: Texas Transportation Institute, 2015 Urban Mobility Scorecard, August 2015

Public Transportation

Agency Name / Mode of Transportation	Vehicles Operated in Maximum Service[1]	Annual Unlinked Passenger Trips[2] (in thous.)	Annual Passenger Miles[3] (in thous.)
Dallas Area Rapid Transit Authority (DART)			
Bus (directly operated)	537	31,951.2	117,278.6
Commuter Rail (purchased transportation)	23	2,098.0	41,313.6
Demand Response (purchased transportation)	91	339.5	4,076.2
Demand Response Taxi (purchased transportation)	125	529.8	7,259.6
Light Rail (directly operated)	106	29,993.8	243,220.2
Streetcar Rail (directly operated)	2	155.9	243.8
Vanpool (purchased transportation)	177	514.9	19,495.8

Note: (1) The number of revenue vehicles operated by the given mode and type of service to meet the annual maximum service requirement. This is the revenue vehicle count during the peak season of the year; on the week and day that maximum service is provided. Vehicles operated in maximum service (VOMS) exclude atypical days and one-time special events; (2) The number of passengers who boarded public transportation vehicles. Passengers are counted each time they board a vehicle no matter how many vehicles they use to travel from their origin to their destination. (3) The sum of the distances ridden by all passengers during the entire fiscal year.
Source: Federal Transit Administration, National Transit Database, 2017

Air Transportation

Airport Name and Code / Type of Service	Passenger Airlines[1]	Passenger Enplanements	Freight Carriers[2]	Freight (lbs)
Dallas-Fort Worth International (DFW)				
Domestic service (U.S. carriers - 2018)	28	28,657,171	17	522,519,846
International service (U.S. carriers - 2017)	8	3,187,180	8	75,180,954
Dallas Love Field (DAL)				
Domestic service (U.S. carriers - 2018)	22	7,817,533	6	13,253,063
International service (U.S. carriers - 2017)	7	5,497	2	32,694

Note: (1) Includes all U.S.-based major, minor and commuter airlines that carried at least one passenger during the year; (2) Includes all U.S.-based airlines and freight carriers that transported at least one pound of freight during the year.
Source: Bureau of Transportation Statistics, The Intermodal Transportation Database, Air Carriers: T-100 Domestic Market (U.S. Carriers), 2018; Bureau of Transportation Statistics, The Intermodal Transportation Database, Air Carriers: T-100 International Market (U.S. Carriers), 2017

Other Transportation Statistics

Major Highways:	I-20; I-30; I-35E; I-45
Amtrak Service:	Yes
Major Waterways/Ports:	None

Source: Amtrak.com; Google Maps

BUSINESSES

Major Business Headquarters

Company Name	Industry	Rankings	
		Fortune[1]	Forbes[2]
AT&T	Telecommunications	9	-
Austin Industries	Construction	-	222
Builders FirstSource	Building Materials, Glass	400	-
Dean Foods	Food Consumer Products	362	-
DexYP	Business Services & Supplies	-	199
Energy Transfer Equity	Pipelines	64	-
Freeman	Business Services & Supplies	-	177
HollyFrontier	Petroleum Refining	206	-
Hunt Consolidated/Hunt Oil	Oil & Gas Operations	-	133
Neiman Marcus Group	Retailing	-	84
Sammons Enterprises	Multicompany	-	71
Southwest Airlines	Airlines	142	-
Tenet Healthcare	Health Care: Medical Facilities	147	-
Texas Instruments	Semiconductors & Other Electronic Parts	192	-
Vistra Energy	Energy	499	-

Note: (1) Companies that produce a 10-K are ranked 1 to 500 based on 2017 revenue; (2) All private companies with at least $2 billion in annual revenue through the end of their most current fiscal year are ranked 1 to 229; companies listed are headquartered in the city; dashes indicate no ranking
Source: Fortune, "Fortune 500," June 2018; Forbes, "America's Largest Private Companies," 2018 Rankings

Fast-Growing Businesses

According to *Inc.*, Dallas is home to four of America's 500 fastest-growing private companies: **Case Energy Partners** (#78); **Acuity Surgical** (#201); **Access Physicians** (#243); **TBX** (#348). Criteria: must be an independent, privately-held, for-profit, U.S. corporation, proprietorship or partnership as of December 31, 2017; revenues must be at least $100,000 in 2014 and $2 million in 2017; must have four-year operating/sales history. Holding companies, regulated banks, and utilities were excluded. *Inc., "America's 500 Fastest-Growing Private Companies," 2018*

According to *Fortune*, Dallas is home to one of the 100 fastest-growing companies in the world: **Builders FirstSource** (#22). Companies were ranked by their revenue growth rate; their EPS growth rate; and their three-year annualized total return to investors for the period ending June 30, 2018. Criteria for inclusion: a company, foreign or domestic, must trade on a major U.S. stock exchange; must file quarterly reports with the SEC; must have a minimum market capitalization of $250 million; must have a stock price of at least $5 on June 30, 2018; must have been trading continuously since June 30, 2015; must have revenue and net income for the four quarters ended on or before April 30, 2018, of at least $50 million and $10 million, respectively; and must have posted a compound annual growth in revenue and earnings per share of at least 15% annually over the three years ending on or before April 30, 2018. Real estate investment trusts, limited-liability companies, limited parterships, business development companies, closed-end investment firms, companies about to be acquired, and companies that lost money in the quarter ending April 30, 2018 were excluded. *Fortune, "100 Fastest-Growing Companies," 2018*

According to *Initiative for a Competitive Inner City (ICIC)*, Dallas is home to five of America's 100 fastest-growing "inner city" companies: **DHD Films** (#14); **Ascension Coffee** (#24); **Peticolas Brewing Company** (#44); **Greenville Avenue Pizza Company** (#53); **Sentry Technical Services** (#87). Criteria for inclusion: company must be headquartered in or have 51 percent or more of its physical operations in an economically distressed urban area; must be an independent, for-profit corporation, partnership or proprietorship; must have 10 or more employees and have a five-year sales history that includes sales of at least $200,000 in the base year and at least $1 million in the current year with no decrease in sales over the two most recent years. Companies were ranked overall by revenue growth over the five-year period between 2013 and 2017. *Initiative for a Competitive Inner City (ICIC), "Inner City 100 Companies," 2018*

Minority Business Opportunity

Dallas is home to two companies which are on the *Black Enterprise* Industrial/Service list (100 largest companies based on gross sales): **Parrish Restaurants Ltd** (#53); **On-Target Supplies & Logistics Ltd** (#64). Criteria: operational in previous calendar year; at least 51% black-owned and manufactures/owns the product it sells or provides industrial or consumer services. Brokerages, real estate firms and firms that provide professional services are not eligible. *Black Enterprise, B.E. 100s, 2018*

Dallas is home to eight companies which are on the *Hispanic Business* 500 list (500 largest U.S. Hispanic-owned companies based on revenue): **Sun Holdings** (#21); **Pinnacle Technical Resources** (#33); **Gilbert May** (#113); **Aguirre Roden** (#175); **ROC Construction** (#271); **Alman Electric** (#285); **Pursuit of Excellence HR** (#330); **Carrco Painting Contractor** (#341). Companies included must show at least 51 percent ownership by Hispanic U.S. citizens, and must maintain headquarters in one of the 50 states or Washington, D.C. *Hispanic Business, "Hispanic Business 500," June 20, 2013*

Minority- and Women-Owned Businesses

Group	All Firms		Firms with Paid Employees			
	Firms	Sales ($000)	Firms	Sales ($000)	Employees	Payroll ($000)
AIAN[1]	1,274	135,286	92	(s)	1,000 - 2,499	(s)
Asian	8,053	4,950,526	2,891	4,637,596	27,050	776,335
Black	24,659	1,262,682	820	841,208	7,928	205,343
Hispanic	32,822	3,549,208	1,985	2,503,595	20,278	868,599
NHOPI[2]	120	(s)	9	(s)	20 - 99	(s)
Women	52,798	10,485,652	4,618	9,017,975	50,688	1,902,625
All Firms	142,658	197,859,242	27,067	190,320,769	715,836	38,365,454

Note: Figures cover firms located in the city; minority- and women-owned business are defined as firms in which the corresponding group own 51% or more of the stock or equity of the company; (1) American Indian and Alaska Native; (2) Native Hawaiian and Other Pacific Islander; (s) estimates are suppressed when publication standards are not met
Source: U.S. Census Bureau, 2012 Economic Census, Survey of Business Owners

HOTELS & CONVENTION CENTERS

Hotels, Motels and Vacation Rentals

Area	5 Star		4 Star		3 Star		2 Star		1 Star		Not Rated	
	Num.	Pct.[3]	Num.	Pct.[3]	Num.	Pct.[3]	Num.	Pct.[3]	Num.	Pct.[3]	Num.	Pct.[3]
City[1]	4	0.3	86	6.0	281	19.7	346	24.3	9	0.6	697	49.0
Total[2]	286	0.4	5,236	7.1	16,715	22.6	10,259	13.9	293	0.4	41,056	55.6

Note: (1) Figures cover Dallas and vicinity; (2) Figures cover all 100 cities in this book; (3) Percentage of hotels which have a given star rating; Star ratings are determined by expedia.com and offer an indication of the general quality of a particular hotel.
Source: www.expedia.com, April 3, 2019

Major Convention Centers

Name	Overall Space (sq. ft.)	Exhibit Space (sq. ft.)	Meeting Space (sq. ft.)	Meeting Rooms
Dallas Convention Center	2,000,000	929,726	n/a	96
Fort Worth Convention Center	n/a	253,226	58,849	41
Frisco Conference Center	90,000	n/a	n/a	14

Note: Table includes convention centers located in the Dallas-Fort Worth-Arlington, TX metro area; n/a not available
Source: Original research

Living Environment

COST OF LIVING

Cost of Living Index

Composite Index	Groceries	Housing	Utilities	Trans-portation	Health Care	Misc. Goods/Services
105.6	107.0	106.7	105.8	98.1	105.2	106.0

Note: The Cost of Living Index measures regional differences in the cost of consumer goods and services, excluding taxes and non-consumer expenditures, for professional and managerial households in the top income quintile. It is based on more than 50,000 prices covering almost 60 different items for which prices are collected three times a year by chambers of commerce, economic development organizations or university applied economic centers in each participating urban area. The numbers shown should be read as a percentage above or below the national average of 100. For example, a value of 115.4 in the groceries column indicates that grocery prices are 15.4% higher than the national average. Small differences in the index numbers should not be interpreted as significant; Figures cover the Dallas TX urban area.
Source: The Council for Community and Economic Research, ACCRA Cost of Living Index, 2018

Grocery Prices

Area[1]	T-Bone Steak ($/pound)	Frying Chicken ($/pound)	Whole Milk ($/half gal.)	Eggs ($/dozen)	Orange Juice ($/64 oz.)	Coffee ($/11.5 oz.)
City[2]	10.82	1.63	2.62	1.87	3.77	5.29
Avg.	11.35	1.42	1.94	1.81	3.52	4.35
Min.	7.45	0.92	0.80	0.75	2.72	3.06
Max.	15.05	2.76	4.18	4.00	5.36	8.20

*Note: (1) Values for the local area are compared with the average, minimum and maximum values for all 291 areas in the Cost of Living Index; (2) Figures cover the Dallas TX urban area; **T-Bone Steak** (price per pound); **Frying Chicken** (price per pound, whole fryer); **Whole Milk** (half gallon carton); **Eggs** (price per dozen, Grade A, large); **Orange Juice** (64 oz. Tropicana or Florida Natural); **Coffee** (11.5 oz. can, vacuum-packed, Maxwell House, Hills Bros, or Folgers).*
Source: The Council for Community and Economic Research, ACCRA Cost of Living Index, 2018

Housing and Utility Costs

Area[1]	New Home Price ($)	Apartment Rent ($/month)	All Electric ($/month)	Part Electric ($/month)	Other Energy ($/month)	Telephone ($/month)
City[2]	327,946	1,440	-	126.07	58.11	179.90
Avg.	347,000	1,087	165.93	100.16	67.73	178.70
Min.	200,468	500	93.58	25.64	26.78	163.10
Max.	1,901,222	4,888	388.65	246.86	332.81	197.70

*Note: (1) Values for the local area are compared with the average, minimum and maximum values for all 291 areas in the Cost of Living Index; (2) Figures cover the Dallas TX urban area; **New Home Price** (2,400 sf living area, 8,000 sf lot, in urban area with full utilities); **Apartment Rent** (950 sf 2 bedroom/1.5 or 2 bath, unfurnished, excluding all utilities except water); **All Electric** (average monthly cost for an all-electric home); **Part Electric** (average monthly cost for a part-electric home); **Other Energy** (average monthly cost for natural gas, fuel oil, coal, wood, and any other forms of energy except electricity); **Telephone** (price includes the base monthly rate plus taxes and fees for three lines of mobile phone service).*
Source: The Council for Community and Economic Research, ACCRA Cost of Living Index, 2018

Health Care, Transportation, and Other Costs

Area[1]	Doctor ($/visit)	Dentist ($/visit)	Optometrist ($/visit)	Gasoline ($/gallon)	Beauty Salon ($/visit)	Men's Shirt ($)
City[2]	110.28	101.77	103.33	2.38	46.95	36.69
Avg.	110.71	95.11	103.74	2.61	37.48	32.03
Min.	33.60	62.55	54.63	1.89	17.00	11.44
Max.	195.97	153.93	225.79	3.59	71.88	58.64

*Note: (1) Values for the local area are compared with the average, minimum and maximum values for all 291 areas in the Cost of Living Index; (2) Figures cover the Dallas TX urban area; **Doctor** (general practitioners routine exam of an established patient); **Dentist** (adult teeth cleaning and periodic oral examination); **Optometrist** (full vision eye exam for established adult patient); **Gasoline** (one gallon regular unleaded, national brand, including all taxes, cash price at self-service pump if available); **Beauty Salon** (woman's shampoo, trim, and blow-dry); **Men's Shirt** (cotton/polyester dress shirt, pinpoint weave, long sleeves).*
Source: The Council for Community and Economic Research, ACCRA Cost of Living Index, 2018

HOUSING

House Price Index (HPI)

Area	National Ranking[2]	Quarterly Change (%)	One-Year Change (%)	Five-Year Change (%)
MD[1]	106	0.13	6.58	56.33
U.S.[3]	–	1.12	5.73	32.81

Note: The HPI is a weighted repeat sales index. It measures average price changes in repeat sales or refinancings on the same properties. This information is obtained by reviewing repeat mortgage transactions on single-family properties whose mortgages have been purchased or securitized by Fannie Mae or Freddie Mac in January 1975; (1) Figures cover the Dallas-Plano-Irving, TX Metropolitan Division—see Appendix B for areas included; (2) Rankings are based on annual percentage change for all metro areas containing at least 15,000 transactions over the last 10 years and ranges from 1 to 245; (3) figures based on a weighted average of Census Division estimates using a seasonally adjusted, purchase-only index; all figures are for the period ending December 31, 2018
Source: Federal Housing Finance Agency, House Price Index, February 26, 2019

Median Single-Family Home Prices

Area	2016	2017	2018[p]	Percent Change 2017 to 2018
MSA[1]	227.1	247.4	260.0	5.1
U.S. Average	235.5	248.8	261.6	5.1

Note: Figures are median sales prices of existing single-family homes in thousands of dollars; (p) preliminary; (1) Figures cover the Dallas-Fort Worth-Arlington, TX Metropolitan Statistical Area—see Appendix B for areas included
Source: National Association of Realtors, Median Sales Price of Existing Single-Family Homes for Metropolitan Areas, 4th Quarter 2018

Qualifying Income Based on Median Sales Price of Existing Single-Family Homes

Area	With 5% Down ($)	With 10% Down ($)	With 20% Down ($)
MSA[1]	62,294	59,015	52,458
U.S. Average	62,954	59,640	53,013

Note: Figures are preliminary; Qualifying income is based on a mortgage rate of 4.9%. Monthly principal and interest payment is limited to 25% of income; (1) Figures cover the Dallas-Fort Worth-Arlington, TX Metropolitan Statistical Area—see Appendix B for areas included
Source: National Association of Realtors, Qualifying Income Based on Median Sales Price of Existing Single-Family Homes for Metropolitan Areas, 4th Quarter 2018

Median Apartment Condo-Coop Home Prices

Area	2016	2017	2018[p]	Percent Change 2017 to 2018
MSA[1]	167.7	185.7	191.2	3.0
U.S. Average	220.7	234.3	241.0	2.9

Note: Figures are median sales prices of existing apartment condo-coop homes in thousands of dollars; (p) preliminary; (1) Figures cover the Dallas-Fort Worth-Arlington, TX Metropolitan Statistical Area—see Appendix B for areas included
Source: National Association of Realtors, Median Sales Price of Existing Apartment Condo-Coop Homes for Metropolitan Areas, 4th Quarter 2018

Home Value Distribution

Area	Under $50,000	$50,000 -$99,999	$100,000 -$149,999	$150,000 -$199,999	$200,000 -$299,999	$300,000 -$499,999	$500,000 -$999,999	$1,000,000 or more
City	8.7	24.8	15.6	9.0	12.4	15.6	10.2	3.7
MSA[1]	5.9	15.6	18.6	17.2	19.7	15.7	5.8	1.6
U.S.	8.3	13.9	14.7	14.6	18.7	17.3	9.7	2.7

Note: Figures are percentages and cover owner-occupied housing units; (1) Figures cover the Dallas-Fort Worth-Arlington, TX Metropolitan Statistical Area—see Appendix B for areas included
Source: U.S. Census Bureau, 2013-2017 American Community Survey 5-Year Estimates

Homeownership Rate

Area	2010 (%)	2011 (%)	2012 (%)	2013 (%)	2014 (%)	2015 (%)	2016 (%)	2017 (%)	2018 (%)
MSA[1]	63.8	62.6	61.8	59.9	57.7	57.8	59.7	61.8	62.0
U.S.	66.9	66.1	65.4	65.1	64.5	63.7	63.4	63.9	64.4

Note: (1) Figures cover the Dallas-Fort Worth-Arlington, TX Metropolitan Statistical Area—see Appendix B for areas included
Source: U.S. Census Bureau, Housing Vacancies and Homeownership Annual Statistics: 2010-2018

Year Housing Structure Built

Area	2010 or Later	2000 -2009	1990 -1999	1980 -1989	1970 -1979	1960 -1969	1950 -1959	1940 -1949	Before 1940	Median Year
City	4.2	11.3	10.1	18.0	17.7	13.8	13.8	5.6	5.6	1976
MSA[1]	6.1	21.6	16.7	18.8	14.5	9.0	7.6	2.8	2.9	1987
U.S.	3.2	14.5	14.0	13.6	15.5	10.8	10.5	5.1	12.9	1977

Note: Figures are percentages except for Median Year; Note: (1) Figures cover the Dallas-Fort Worth-Arlington, TX Metropolitan Statistical Area—see Appendix B for areas included
Source: U.S. Census Bureau, 2013-2017 American Community Survey 5-Year Estimates

Gross Monthly Rent

Area	Under $500	$500 -$999	$1,000 -$1,499	$1,500 -$1,999	$2,000 -$2,499	$2,500 -$2,999	$3,000 and up	Median ($)
City	5.4	51.6	29.7	8.5	2.7	1.1	0.8	937
MSA[1]	4.2	43.9	35.4	11.8	3.0	1.0	0.8	1,022
U.S.	10.5	41.1	28.7	11.7	4.5	1.8	1.7	982

Note: Figures are percentages except for Median; Gross rent is the contract rent plus the estimated average monthly cost of utilities (electricity, gas, and water and sewer) and fuels (oil, coal, kerosene, wood, etc.) if these are paid by the renter (or paid for the renter by someone else); (1) Figures cover the Dallas-Fort Worth-Arlington, TX Metropolitan Statistical Area—see Appendix B for areas included
Source: U.S. Census Bureau, 2013-2017 American Community Survey 5-Year Estimates

HEALTH

Health Risk Factors

Category	MD[1] (%)	U.S. (%)
Adults aged 18–64 who have any kind of health care coverage	80.1	87.3
Adults who reported being in good or better health	83.9	82.4
Adults who have been told they have high blood cholesterol	30.9	33.0
Adults who have been told they have high blood pressure	31.0	32.3
Adults who are current smokers	13.1	17.1
Adults who currently use E-cigarettes	3.1	4.6
Adults who currently use chewing tobacco, snuff, or snus	2.5	4.0
Adults who are heavy drinkers[2]	7.6	6.3
Adults who are binge drinkers[3]	16.9	17.4
Adults who are overweight (BMI 25.0 - 29.9)	37.2	35.3
Adults who are obese (BMI 30.0 - 99.8)	28.4	31.3
Adults who participated in any physical activities in the past month	71.2	74.4
Adults who always or nearly always wears a seat belt	96.3	94.3

Note: (1) Figures cover the Dallas-Plano-Irving, TX Metropolitan Division—see Appendix B for areas included; (2) Heavy drinkers are classified as adult men having more than 14 drinks per week and adult women having more than 7 drinks per week; (3) Binge drinkers are classified as males having five or more drinks on one occasion or females having four or more drinks on one occasion
Source: Centers for Disease Control and Prevention, Behaviorial Risk Factor Surveillance System, SMART: Selected Metropolitan Area Risk Trends, 2017

Acute and Chronic Health Conditions

Category	MD[1] (%)	U.S. (%)
Adults who have ever been told they had a heart attack	n/a	4.2
Adults who have ever been told they have angina or coronary heart disease	n/a	3.9
Adults who have ever been told they had a stroke	n/a	3.0
Adults who have ever been told they have asthma	13.7	14.2
Adults who have ever been told they have arthritis	17.7	24.9
Adults who have ever been told they have diabetes[2]	10.8	10.5
Adults who have ever been told they had skin cancer	5.7	6.2
Adults who have ever been told they had any other types of cancer	3.9	7.1
Adults who have ever been told they have COPD	2.8	6.5
Adults who have ever been told they have kidney disease	n/a	3.0
Adults who have ever been told they have a form of depression	14.2	20.5

Note: n/a not available; (1) Figures cover the Dallas-Plano-Irving, TX Metropolitan Division—see Appendix B for areas included; (2) Figures do not include pregnancy-related, borderline, or pre-diabetes
Source: Centers for Disease Control and Prevention, Behaviorial Risk Factor Surveillance System, SMART: Selected Metropolitan Area Risk Trends, 2017

Health Screening and Vaccination Rates

Category	MD[1] (%)	U.S. (%)
Adults aged 65+ who have had flu shot within the past year	53.7	60.7
Adults aged 65+ who have ever had a pneumonia vaccination	78.1	75.4
Adults who have ever been tested for HIV	42.6	36.1
Adults who have ever had the shingles or zoster vaccine?	29.0	28.9
Adults who have had their blood cholesterol checked within the last five years	86.9	85.9

Note: n/a not available; (1) Figures cover the Dallas-Plano-Irving, TX Metropolitan Division—see Appendix B for areas included.
Source: Centers for Disease Control and Prevention, Behaviorial Risk Factor Surveillance System, SMART: Selected Metropolitan Area Risk Trends, 2017

Disability Status

Category	MD[1] (%)	U.S. (%)
Adults who reported being deaf	n/a	6.7
Are you blind or have serious difficulty seeing, even when wearing glasses?	4.4	4.5
Are you limited in any way in any of your usual activities due of arthritis?	10.1	12.9
Do you have difficulty doing errands alone?	7.1	6.8
Do you have difficulty dressing or bathing?	n/a	3.6
Do you have serious difficulty concentrating/remembering/making decisions?	7.2	10.7
Do you have serious difficulty walking or climbing stairs?	11.7	13.6

Note: n/a not available; (1) Figures cover the Dallas-Plano-Irving, TX Metropolitan Division—see Appendix B for areas included.
Source: Centers for Disease Control and Prevention, Behaviorial Risk Factor Surveillance System, SMART: Selected Metropolitan Area Risk Trends, 2017

Mortality Rates for the Top 10 Causes of Death in the U.S.

ICD-10[a] Sub-Chapter	ICD-10[a] Code	Age-Adjusted Mortality Rate[1] per 100,000 population	
		County[2]	U.S.
Malignant neoplasms	C00-C97	151.9	155.5
Ischaemic heart diseases	I20-I25	87.3	94.8
Other forms of heart disease	I30-I51	51.0	52.9
Chronic lower respiratory diseases	J40-J47	35.9	41.0
Cerebrovascular diseases	I60-I69	50.4	37.5
Other degenerative diseases of the nervous system	G30-G31	50.0	35.0
Other external causes of accidental injury	W00-X59	24.6	33.7
Organic, including symptomatic, mental disorders	F01-F09	26.8	31.0
Hypertensive diseases	I10-I15	30.2	21.9
Diabetes mellitus	E10-E14	18.4	21.2

Note: (a) ICD-10 = International Classification of Diseases 10th Revision; (1) Mortality rates are a three year average covering 2015-2017; (2) Figures cover Dallas County.
Source: Centers for Disease Control and Prevention, National Center for Health Statistics. Underlying Cause of Death 1999-2017 on CDC WONDER Online Database

Mortality Rates for Selected Causes of Death

ICD-10[a] Sub-Chapter	ICD-10[a] Code	Age-Adjusted Mortality Rate[1] per 100,000 population	
		County[2]	U.S.
Assault	X85-Y09	7.8	5.9
Diseases of the liver	K70-K76	14.5	14.1
Human immunodeficiency virus (HIV) disease	B20-B24	3.5	1.8
Influenza and pneumonia	J09-J18	11.8	14.3
Intentional self-harm	X60-X84	10.9	13.6
Malnutrition	E40-E46	1.8	1.6
Obesity and other hyperalimentation	E65-E68	2.0	2.1
Renal failure	N17-N19	18.6	13.0
Transport accidents	V01-V99	12.3	12.4
Viral hepatitis	B15-B19	1.8	1.6

Note: (a) ICD-10 = International Classification of Diseases 10th Revision; (1) Mortality rates are a three year average covering 2015-2017; (2) Figures cover Dallas County; Data are suppressed when the data meet the criteria for confidentiality constraints; Mortality rates are flagged as unreliable when the rate would be calculated with a numerator of 20 or less.
Source: Centers for Disease Control and Prevention, National Center for Health Statistics. Underlying Cause of Death 1999-2017 on CDC WONDER Online Database

Health Insurance Coverage

Area	With Health Insurance	With Private Health Insurance	With Public Health Insurance	Without Health Insurance	Population Under Age 18 Without Health Insurance
City	75.1	49.6	31.2	24.9	14.6
MSA[1]	82.6	64.7	25.3	17.4	11.0
U.S.	89.5	67.2	33.8	10.5	5.7

Note: Figures are percentages that cover the civilian noninstitutionalized population; (1) Figures cover the Dallas-Fort Worth-Arlington, TX Metropolitan Statistical Area—see Appendix B for areas included
Source: U.S. Census Bureau, 2013-2017 American Community Survey 5-Year Estimates

Number of Medical Professionals

Area	MDs[3]	DOs[3,4]	Dentists	Podiatrists	Chiropractors	Optometrists
County[1] (number)	8,435	534	2,150	109	924	343
County[1] (rate[2])	326.0	20.6	82.1	4.2	35.3	13.1
U.S. (rate[2])	279.3	23.0	68.4	6.0	27.1	16.2

Note: Data as of 2017 unless noted; (1) Data covers Dallas County; (2) Rate per 100,000 population; (3) Data as of 2016 and includes all active, non-federal physicians; (4) Doctor of Osteopathic Medicine
Source: U.S. Department of Health and Human Services, Health Resources and Services Administration, Bureau of Health Professions, Area Resource File (ARF) 2017-2018

Best Hospitals

According to *U.S. News,* the Dallas-Plano-Irving, TX metro area is home to four of the best hospitals in the U.S.: **Baylor Scott and White The Heart Hospital Plano** (1 adult specialty); **Baylor University Medical Center** (2 adult specialties); **Medical City Dallas** (1 adult specialty); **UT Southwestern Medical Center** (7 adult specialties). The hospitals listed were nationally ranked in at least one of 16 adult or 10 pediatric specialties. Only 170 hospitals nationwide were nationally ranked in one or more adult or pediatric specialty. Twenty hospitals in the U.S. made the Honor Roll. The Best Hospitals Honor Roll takes both the national rankings and the procedure and condition ratings into account. Hospitals received points if they were nationally ranked in one of the 16 adult specialties—the higher they ranked, the more points they got—and how many ratings of "high performing" they earned in the nine procedures and conditions. *U.S. News Online, "America's Best Hospitals 2018-19"*

According to *U.S. News,* the Dallas-Plano-Irving, TX metro area is home to two of the best children's hospitals in the U.S.: **Children's Medical Center Dallas** (10 pediatric specialties); **Texas Scottish Rite Hospital for Children** (1 pediatric specialty). The hospitals listed were highly ranked in at least one of 10 pediatric specialties. Eighty-six children's hospitals in the U.S. were nationally ranked in at least one specialty. Hospitals received points for being ranked in a specialty, and the 10 hospitals with the most points across the 10 specialties make up the Honor Roll. *U.S. News Online, "America's Best Children's Hospitals 2018-19"*

EDUCATION

Public School District Statistics

District Name	Schls	Pupils	Pupil/ Teacher Ratio	Minority Pupils[1] (%)	Free Lunch Eligible[2] (%)	IEP[3] (%)
A W Brown-Fellowship Leadership	2	2,278	40.7	99.8	68.7	4.8
Dallas ISD	240	157,886	15.0	94.9	86.0	7.5
Highland Park ISD	7	7,044	15.0	14.3	n/a	8.2
Texans Can Academies	13	5,271	20.5	97.3	79.4	7.8
Trinity Basin Preparatory	1	2,778	17.2	99.4	79.8	7.7
Uplift Education	34	15,768	15.8	95.8	63.8	6.7

Note: Table includes school districts with 2,000 or more students; (1) Percentage of students that are not non-Hispanic white; (2) Percentage of students that are eligible for the free lunch program; (3) Percentage of students that have an Individualized Education Program.
Source: U.S. Department of Education, National Center for Education Statistics, Common Core of Data, Local Education Agency (School District) Universe Survey: School Year 2016-2017; U.S. Department of Education, National Center for Education Statistics, Common Core of Data, Public Elementary/Secondary School Universe Survey: School Year 2016-2017

Best High Schools

According to *U.S. News,* Dallas is home to 11 of the best high schools in the U.S.: **The School for the Talented and Gifted (TAG)** (#11); **Science and Engineering Magnet School (SEM)** (#13); **Irma Lerma Rangel Young Women's Leadership School** (#129); **Booker T. Washington**

SPVA (#133); **Uplift Williams Preparatory High School** (#146); **Highland Park High School** (#170); **Judge Barefoot Sanders Law Magnet** (#198); **Uplift Peak Preparatory High School** (#208); **School of Health Professions** (#389); **School of Business and Management** (#390); **Rosie Sorrells Education and Social Services High School** (#434). More than 20,000 public, magnet and charter schools were ranked based on their performance on state assessments and how well they prepare students for college. Schools with the highest unrounded College Readiness Index values were numerically ranked from 1 to 500 and were classified as gold medal winners. *U.S. News & World Report, "Best High Schools 2018"*

Highest Level of Education

Area	Less than H.S.	H.S. Diploma	Some College, No Deg.	Associate Degree	Bachelor's Degree	Master's Degree	Prof. School Degree	Doctorate Degree
City	24.1	21.4	18.3	4.5	19.9	7.9	2.8	1.1
MSA[1]	15.2	22.4	21.9	6.8	22.2	8.7	1.8	1.1
U.S.	12.7	27.3	20.8	8.3	19.1	8.4	2.0	1.4

Note: Figures cover persons age 25 and over; (1) Figures cover the Dallas-Fort Worth-Arlington, TX Metropolitan Statistical Area—see Appendix B for areas included
Source: U.S. Census Bureau, 2013-2017 American Community Survey 5-Year Estimates

Educational Attainment by Race

Area	High School Graduate or Higher (%)					Bachelor's Degree or Higher (%)				
	Total	White	Black	Asian	Hisp.[2]	Total	White	Black	Asian	Hisp.[2]
City	75.9	74.1	85.1	84.3	47.9	31.6	37.6	17.4	62.9	9.1
MSA[1]	84.8	85.3	89.9	88.2	57.6	33.7	34.6	25.6	60.1	12.5
U.S.	87.3	89.3	84.9	86.5	66.7	30.9	32.2	20.6	52.7	15.2

Note: Figures shown cover persons 25 years old and over; (1) Figures cover the Dallas-Fort Worth-Arlington, TX Metropolitan Statistical Area—see Appendix B for areas included; (2) People of Hispanic origin can be of any race
Source: U.S. Census Bureau, 2013-2017 American Community Survey 5-Year Estimates

School Enrollment by Grade and Control

Area	Preschool (%)		Kindergarten (%)		Grades 1 - 4 (%)		Grades 5 - 8 (%)		Grades 9 - 12 (%)	
	Public	Private	Public	Private	Public	Private	Public	Private	Public	Private
City	69.0	31.0	90.0	10.0	91.3	8.7	91.1	8.9	91.4	8.6
MSA[1]	58.3	41.7	89.7	10.3	92.6	7.4	92.1	7.9	92.2	7.8
U.S.	58.8	41.2	87.7	12.3	89.7	10.3	89.6	10.4	90.3	9.7

Note: Figures shown cover persons 3 years old and over; (1) Figures cover the Dallas-Fort Worth-Arlington, TX Metropolitan Statistical Area—see Appendix B for areas included
Source: U.S. Census Bureau, 2013-2017 American Community Survey 5-Year Estimates

Average Salaries of Public School Classroom Teachers

Area	2016		2017		Change from 2016 to 2017	
	Dollars	Rank[1]	Dollars	Rank[1]	Percent	Rank[2]
Texas	51,890	28	52,575	28	1.3	29
U.S. Average	58,479	–	59,660	–	2.0	–

Note: (1) Rank ranges from 1 to 51 where 1 indicates highest salary; (2) Rank ranges from 1 to 51 where 1 indicates highest percent change.
Source: National Education Association, Rankings & Estimates: Rankings of the States 2017 and Estimates of School Statistics 2018

Higher Education

Four-Year Colleges			Two-Year Colleges			Medical Schools[1]	Law Schools[2]	Voc/ Tech[3]
Public	Private Non-profit	Private For-profit	Public	Private Non-profit	Private For-profit			
2	9	3	3	1	6	1	2	10

Note: Figures cover institutions located within the city limits and include main campuses only; (1) includes schools accredited by the Liaison Committee on Medical Education and the American Osteopathic Association's Commission on Osteopathic College Accreditation; (2) includes ABA-accredited schools, schools with provisional ABA accreditation, and state accredited schools; (3) includes all schools with programs that are less than 2 years.
Source: National Center for Education Statistics, Integrated Postsecondary Education System (IPEDS), 2017-18; Wikipedia, List of Medical Schools in the United States, accessed April 3, 2019; Wikipedia, List of Law Schools in the United States, accessed April 3, 2019

According to *U.S. News & World Report*, the Dallas-Plano-Irving, TX metro division is home to three of the best national universities in the U.S.: **Southern Methodist University** (#59 tie); **University of Texas—Dallas** (#129 tie); **Dallas Baptist University** (#221 tie). The indicators used to capture academic quality fall into a number of categories: assessment by administrators at peer institutions; retention of students; faculty resources; student selectivity; financial resources; alumni giving; high school counselor ratings of colleges; and graduation rate. *U.S. News & World Report, "America's Best Colleges 2019"*

According to *U.S. News & World Report*, the Dallas-Plano-Irving, TX metro division is home to one of the top 100 law schools in the U.S.: **Southern Methodist University (Dedman)** (#52 tie). The rankings are based on a weighted average of 12 measures of quality: peer assessment score; assessment score by lawyers/judges; median LSAT scores; median undergrad GPA; acceptance rate; employment rates for graduates; placement success; bar passage rate; faculty resources; expenditures per student; student/faculty ratio; and library resources. *U.S. News & World Report, "America's Best Graduate Schools, Law, 2020"*

According to *U.S. News & World Report*, the Dallas-Plano-Irving, TX metro division is home to one of the top 75 medical schools for research in the U.S.: **University of Texas Southwestern Medical Center** (#26). The rankings are based on a weighted average of 11 measures of quality: quality assessment; peer assessment score; assessment score by residency directors; research activity; total research activity; average research activity per faculty member; student selectivity; median MCAT total score; median undergraduate GPA; acceptance rate; and faculty resources. *U.S. News & World Report, "America's Best Graduate Schools, Medical, 2020"*

According to *U.S. News & World Report*, the Dallas-Plano-Irving, TX metro division is home to two of the top 75 business schools in the U.S.: **University of Texas—Dallas** (#38 tie); **Southern Methodist University (Cox)** (#43 tie). The rankings are based on a weighted average of the following nine measures: quality assessment; peer assessment; recruiter assessment; placement success; mean starting salary and bonus; student selectivity; mean GMAT and GRE scores; mean undergraduate GPA; and acceptance rate. *U.S. News & World Report, "America's Best Graduate Schools, Business, 2020"*

PRESIDENTIAL ELECTION

2016 Presidential Election Results

Area	Clinton	Trump	Johnson	Stein	Other
Dallas County	60.2	34.3	3.1	0.8	1.5
U.S.	48.0	45.9	3.3	1.1	1.7

Note: Results are percentages and may not add to 100% due to rounding
Source: Dave Leip's Atlas of U.S. Presidential Elections

EMPLOYERS

Major Employers

Company Name	Industry
AMR Corporation	Air transportation, scheduled
Associates First Capital Corporation	Mortgage bankers
Baylor University Medical Center	General medical & surgical hospitals
Children's Medical Center Dallas	Specialty hospitals, except psychiatric
Combat Support Associates	Engineering services
County of Dallas	County government
Dallas County Hospital District	General medical & surgical hospitals
Fort Worth Independent School District	Public elementary & secondary schools
Housewares Holding Company	Toasters, electric: household
HP Enterprise Services	Computer integrated systems design
J.C. Penney Company	Department stores
JCP Publications Corp.	Department stores
L-3 Communications Corporation	Business economic service
Odyssey HealthCare	Home health care services
Romano's Macaroni Grill	Italian restaurant
SFG Management	Milk processing (pasteurizing, homogenizing, bottling)
Texas Instruments Incorporated	Semiconductors & related devices
University of North Texas	Colleges & universities
University of Texas SW Medical Center	Accident & health insurance
Verizon Business Global	Telephone communication, except radio

Note: Companies shown are located within the Dallas-Fort Worth-Arlington, TX Metropolitan Statistical Area.
Source: Hoovers.com; Wikipedia

Best Companies to Work For

Encompass Health Home Health & Hospice; Ryan, headquartered in Dallas, are among "The 100 Best Companies to Work For." To pick the best companies, *Fortune* partnered with the Great Place to Work Institute. Two-thirds of a company's score is based on the results of the Institute's Trust Index survey, which is sent to a random sample of employees from each company. The questions related to attitudes about management's credibility, job satisfaction, and camaraderie. The other third of the scoring is based on the company's responses to the Institute's Culture Audit, which includes detailed questions about pay and benefit programs, and a series of open-ended questions about hiring practices, internal communication, training, recognition programs, and diversity efforts. Any company that is at least five years old with more than 1,000 U.S. employees is eligible. *Fortune, "The 100 Best Companies to Work For," 2019*

Texas Instruments, headquartered in Dallas, is among the "100 Best Companies for Working Mothers." Criteria: paid time off and leaves; workforce profile; benefits; women's issues and advancement; flexible work; company culture and work life programs. *Working Mother, "100 Best Companies 2018"*

Axxess; Pariveda Solutions, headquartered in Dallas, are among the "100 Best Places to Work in IT." To qualify, companies had to be U.S.-based organizations or be non-U.S.- based employers that met the following criteria: have a minimum of 300 total employees at a U.S. headquarters and a minimum of 30 IT employees in the U.S., with at least 50% of their IT employees based in the U.S. The best places to work were selected based on compensation, benefits, work/life balance, employee morale, and satisfaction with training and development programs. In addition, *Computerworld* looked at retention efforts, programs for recognizing and rewarding outstanding performances, and benefits such as flextime, elder care and child care, and reimbursement for college tuition and the cost of pursuing technology certifications. *Computerworld, "100 Best Places to Work in IT 2018"*

JCPenney; Texas Instruments, headquartered in Dallas, are among the "Top Companies for Executive Women." The 2019 National Association for Female Executives (NAFE) Top Companies for Executive Women application included more than 200 questions on female representation at all levels, but especially the corporate officer and profit-and-loss leadership ranks. The application tracked how many employees have access to programs and policies that promote the advancement of women, and how many employees take advantage of them. The application also examined how companies train managers to help women advance, and how managers are held accountable for the advancement of female employees they oversee. *National Association for Female Executives, "2019 NAFE Top 70 Companies for Executive Women"*

PUBLIC SAFETY

Crime Rate

Area	All Crimes	Violent Crimes				Property Crimes		
		Murder	Rape[3]	Robbery	Aggrav. Assault	Burglary	Larceny -Theft	Motor Vehicle Theft
City	3,959.7	12.5	62.1	327.0	373.1	737.7	1,856.3	591.2
Suburbs[1]	n/a	3.5	44.1	74.6	157.1	n/a	1,628.0	206.1
Metro[2]	n/a	5.2	47.3	120.5	196.4	n/a	1,669.5	276.0
U.S.	2,756.1	5.3	41.7	98.0	248.9	430.4	1,694.4	237.4

Note: Figures are crimes per 100,000 population; (1) All areas within the metro area that are located outside the city limits; (2) Figures cover the Dallas-Plano-Irving, TX Metropolitan Division—see Appendix B for areas included; (3) The city and U.S. figures shown were reported using the revised Uniform Crime Reporting (UCR) definition of rape. The suburban and metro area figures shown are an aggregate total of the data submitted using both the revised and legacy UCR definitions.
Source: FBI Uniform Crime Reports, 2017

Hate Crimes

Area	Number of Quarters Reported	Number of Incidents per Bias Motivation					
		Race/Ethnicity/ Ancestry	Religion	Sexual Orientation	Disability	Gender	Gender Identity
City	4	2	0	12	0	0	0
U.S.	4	4,131	1,564	1,130	116	46	119

Source: Federal Bureau of Investigation, Hate Crime Statistics 2017

Identity Theft Consumer Reports

Area	Reports	Reports per 100,000 Population	Rank[2]
MSA[1]	16,342	226	8
U.S.	444,602	135	-

Note: (1) Figures cover the Dallas-Fort Worth-Arlington, TX Metropolitan Statistical Area—see Appendix B for areas included; (2) Rank ranges from 1 to 389 where 1 indicates greatest number of identity theft reports per 100,000 population
Source: Federal Trade Commission, Consumer Sentinel Network Data Book for January–December 2018

Fraud and Other Consumer Reports

Area	Reports	Reports per 100,000 Population	Rank[2]
MSA[1]	45,901	635	42
U.S.	2,552,917	776	-

Note: (1) Figures cover the Dallas-Fort Worth-Arlington, TX Metropolitan Statistical Area—see Appendix B for areas included; (2) Rank ranges from 1 to 389 where 1 indicates greatest number of fraud and other consumer reports per 100,000 population
Source: Federal Trade Commission, Consumer Sentinel Network Data Book for January–December 2018

SPORTS

Professional Sports Teams

Team Name	League	Year Established
Dallas Cowboys	National Football League (NFL)	1960
Dallas Mavericks	National Basketball Association (NBA)	1980
Dallas Stars	National Hockey League (NHL)	1993
FC Dallas	Major League Soccer (MLS)	1996
Texas Rangers	Major League Baseball (MLB)	1972

Note: Includes teams located in the Dallas-Fort Worth-Arlington, TX Metropolitan Statistical Area.
Source: Wikipedia, Major Professional Sports Teams of the United States and Canada, April 5, 2019

CLIMATE

Average and Extreme Temperatures

Temperature	Jan	Feb	Mar	Apr	May	Jun	Jul	Aug	Sep	Oct	Nov	Dec	Yr.
Extreme High (°F)	85	90	100	100	101	112	111	109	107	101	91	87	112
Average High (°F)	55	60	68	76	84	92	96	96	89	79	67	58	77
Average Temp. (°F)	45	50	57	66	74	82	86	86	79	68	56	48	67
Average Low (°F)	35	39	47	56	64	72	76	75	68	57	46	38	56
Extreme Low (°F)	-2	9	12	30	39	53	58	58	42	24	16	0	-2

Note: Figures cover the years 1945-1993
Source: National Climatic Data Center, International Station Meteorological Climate Summary, 9/96

Average Precipitation/Snowfall/Humidity

Precip./Humidity	Jan	Feb	Mar	Apr	May	Jun	Jul	Aug	Sep	Oct	Nov	Dec	Yr.
Avg. Precip. (in.)	1.9	2.3	2.6	3.8	4.9	3.4	2.1	2.3	2.9	3.3	2.3	2.1	33.9
Avg. Snowfall (in.)	1	1	Tr	Tr	0	0	0	0	0	Tr	Tr	Tr	3
Avg. Rel. Hum. 6am (%)	78	77	75	77	82	81	77	76	80	79	78	77	78
Avg. Rel. Hum. 3pm (%)	53	51	47	49	51	48	43	41	46	46	48	51	48

Note: Figures cover the years 1945-1993; Tr = Trace amounts (<0.05 in. of rain; <0.5 in. of snow)
Source: National Climatic Data Center, International Station Meteorological Climate Summary, 9/96

Weather Conditions

Temperature			Daytime Sky			Precipitation		
10°F & below	32°F & below	90°F & above	Clear	Partly cloudy	Cloudy	0.01 inch or more precip.	0.1 inch or more snow/ice	Thunderstorms
1	34	102	108	160	97	78	2	49

Note: Figures are average number of days per year and cover the years 1945-1993
Source: National Climatic Data Center, International Station Meteorological Climate Summary, 9/96

**HAZARDOUS
WASTE**

Superfund Sites

The Dallas-Plano-Irving, TX metro division is home to four sites on the EPA's Superfund National Priorities List: **Delfasco Forge** (final); **Lane Plating Works, Inc** (final); **RSR Corporation** (final); **Van Der Horst USA Corporation** (final). There are a total of 1,390 Superfund sites with a status of proposed or final on the list in the U.S. *U.S. Environmental Protection Agency, National Priorities List, April 5, 2019*

**AIR & WATER
QUALITY**

Air Quality Trends: Ozone

	1990	1995	2000	2005	2010	2012	2014	2015	2016	2017
MSA[1]	0.095	0.105	0.096	0.097	0.080	0.080	0.076	0.077	0.070	0.073
U.S.	0.088	0.089	0.082	0.080	0.073	0.075	0.067	0.068	0.069	0.068

Note: (1) Data covers the Dallas-Fort Worth-Arlington, TX Metropolitan Statistical Area—see Appendix B for areas included. The values shown are the composite ozone concentration averages among trend sites based on the highest fourth daily maximum 8-hour concentration in parts per million. These trends are based on sites having an adequate record of monitoring data during the trend period. Data from exceptional events are included.
Source: U.S. Environmental Protection Agency, Air Quality Monitoring Information, "Air Quality Trends by City, 1990-2017"

Air Quality Index

Area	Percent of Days when Air Quality was...[2]					AQI Statistics[2]	
	Good	Moderate	Unhealthy for Sensitive Groups	Unhealthy	Very Unhealthy	Maximum	Median
MSA[1]	52.6	40.8	6.6	0.0	0.0	147	50

Note: (1) Data covers the Dallas-Fort Worth-Arlington, TX Metropolitan Statistical Area—see Appendix B for areas included; (2) Based on 365 days with AQI data in 2017. Air Quality Index (AQI) is an index for reporting daily air quality. EPA calculates the AQI for five major air pollutants regulated by the Clean Air Act: ground-level ozone, particle pollution (aka particulate matter), carbon monoxide, sulfur dioxide, and nitrogen dioxide. The AQI runs from 0 to 500. The higher the AQI value, the greater the level of air pollution and the greater the health concern. There are six AQI categories: "Good" AQI is between 0 and 50. Air quality is considered satisfactory; "Moderate" AQI is between 51 and 100. Air quality is acceptable; "Unhealthy for Sensitive Groups" When AQI values are between 101 and 150, members of sensitive groups may experience health effects; "Unhealthy" When AQI values are between 151 and 200 everyone may begin to experience health effects; "Very Unhealthy" AQI values between 201 and 300 trigger a health alert; "Hazardous" AQI values over 300 trigger warnings of emergency conditions (not shown).
Source: U.S. Environmental Protection Agency, Air Quality Index Report, 2017

Air Quality Index Pollutants

Area	Percent of Days when AQI Pollutant was...[2]					
	Carbon Monoxide	Nitrogen Dioxide	Ozone	Sulfur Dioxide	Particulate Matter 2.5	Particulate Matter 10
MSA[1]	0.0	4.1	57.3	0.0	38.6	0.0

Note: (1) Data covers the Dallas-Fort Worth-Arlington, TX Metropolitan Statistical Area—see Appendix B for areas included; (2) Based on 365 days with AQI data in 2017. The Air Quality Index (AQI) is an index for reporting daily air quality. EPA calculates the AQI for five major air pollutants regulated by the Clean Air Act: ground-level ozone, particle pollution (also known as particulate matter), carbon monoxide, sulfur dioxide, and nitrogen dioxide. The AQI runs from 0 to 500. The higher the AQI value, the greater the level of air pollution and the greater the health concern.
Source: U.S. Environmental Protection Agency, Air Quality Index Report, 2017

Maximum Air Pollutant Concentrations: Particulate Matter, Ozone, CO and Lead

	Particulate Matter 10 (ug/m³)	Particulate Matter 2.5 Wtd AM (ug/m³)	Particulate Matter 2.5 24-Hr (ug/m³)	Ozone (ppm)	Carbon Monoxide (ppm)	Lead (ug/m³)
MSA[1] Level	38	9	18	0.077	1	0.17
NAAQS[2]	150	15	35	0.075	9	0.15
Met NAAQS[2]	Yes	Yes	Yes	No	Yes	No

Note: (1) Data covers the Dallas-Fort Worth-Arlington, TX Metropolitan Statistical Area—see Appendix B for areas included; Data from exceptional events are included; (2) National Ambient Air Quality Standards; ppm = parts per million; ug/m³ = micrograms per cubic meter; n/a not available.
Concentrations: Particulate Matter 10 (coarse particulate)—highest second maximum 24-hour concentration; Particulate Matter 2.5 Wtd AM (fine particulate)—highest weighted annual mean concentration; Particulate Matter 2.5 24-Hour (fine particulate)—highest 98th percentile 24-hour concentration; Ozone—highest fourth daily maximum 8-hour concentration; Carbon Monoxide—highest second maximum non-overlapping 8-hour concentration; Lead—maximum running 3-month average
Source: U.S. Environmental Protection Agency, Air Quality Monitoring Information, "Air Quality Statistics by City, 2017"

Maximum Air Pollutant Concentrations: Nitrogen Dioxide and Sulfur Dioxide

	Nitrogen Dioxide AM (ppb)	Nitrogen Dioxide 1-Hr (ppb)	Sulfur Dioxide AM (ppb)	Sulfur Dioxide 1-Hr (ppb)	Sulfur Dioxide 24-Hr (ppb)
MSA[1] Level	12	45	n/a	7	n/a
NAAQS[2]	53	100	30	75	140
Met NAAQS[2]	Yes	Yes	n/a	Yes	n/a

Note: (1) Data covers the Dallas-Fort Worth-Arlington, TX Metropolitan Statistical Area—see Appendix B for areas included; Data from exceptional events are included; (2) National Ambient Air Quality Standards; ppm = parts per million; ug/m³ = micrograms per cubic meter; n/a not available.
Concentrations: Nitrogen Dioxide AM—highest arithmetic mean concentration; Nitrogen Dioxide 1-Hr—highest 98th percentile 1-hour daily maximum concentration; Sulfur Dioxide AM—highest annual mean concentration; Sulfur Dioxide 1-Hr—highest 99th percentile 1-hour daily maximum concentration; Sulfur Dioxide 24-Hr—highest second maximum 24-hour concentration
Source: U.S. Environmental Protection Agency, Air Quality Monitoring Information, "Air Quality Statistics by City, 2017"

Drinking Water

Water System Name	Pop. Served	Primary Water Source Type	Violations[1] Health Based	Violations[1] Monitoring/ Reporting
Dallas Water Utility	1,197,816	Surface	0	0

Note: (1) Based on violation data from January 1, 2018 to December 31, 2018
Source: U.S. Environmental Protection Agency, Office of Ground Water and Drinking Water, Safe Drinking Water Information System (based on data extracted April 5, 2019)

El Paso, Texas

Background

El Paso is so named because it sits in a spectacular pass through the Franklin Mountains, at an average elevation of 3,700 feet and in direct view of peaks that rise to 7,200 feet. El Paso is the fourth-largest city in Texas. It lies just south of New Mexico on the Rio Grande and just north of Juarez, Mexico.

The early Spanish explorer Alvar Nunez Cabeza de Vaca (circa 1530) probably passed through this area, but the city was named in 1598 by Juan de Onante, who dubbed it El Paso del Rio del Norte, or The Pass at the River of the North. It was also Onante who declared the area Spanish, on the authority of King Philip II, but a mission was not established until 1649. For some time, El Paso del Norte was the seat of government for northern Mexico, but settlement in and around the present-day city was sparse for many years.

This changed considerably by 1807, when Zebulon A. Pike, a United States Army officer, was interned in El Paso after being convicted of trespassing on Spanish territory. He found the area pleasant and well tended, with many irrigated fields and vineyards and a thriving trade in brandy and wine. In spite of Pike's stay there, though, El Paso remained for many years a largely Mexican region, escaping most of the military action connected to the Texas Revolution.

In the wake of the Mexican War (1846-1848) and in response to the California gold rush in 1849, El Paso emerged as a significant way station on the road west. A federal garrison, Fort Bliss, was established there in 1849, and was briefly occupied by Confederate sympathizers in 1862. Federal forces quickly reoccupied the fort, however, and the area was firmly controlled by Union armies. El Paso was incorporated in 1873, and after 1881, growth accelerated considerably with the building of rail links through the city, giving rise to ironworks, mills, and breweries.

During the Mexican Revolution (1911), El Paso was an important and disputed city, with Pancho Villa himself a frequent visitor, and many of his followers residents of the town. Mexico's national history, in fact, continued to affect El Paso until 1967 when, by way of settling a historic border dispute, 437 acres of the city was ceded to Mexico. Much of the disputed area on both sides of the border was made into parkland. The U.S. National Parks Service maintains the Chamizal Park on the U.S. side and it plays host to a variety of community events during the year including the Chamizal Film Festival and the summer concert series, Music Under the Stars.

One of the major points of entry to the U.S. from Mexico, El Paso is a vitally important international city and a burgeoning center of rail, road, and air transportation. During the 1990s, the city's economy shifted more toward a service-oriented economy and away from a manufacturing base.

Transportation services and tourism are growing segments of the economy. Government and military are also sources of employment, with Ft. Bliss being the largest Air Defense Artillery Training Center in the world. The city hosts the University of Texas at El Paso, and a community college. Cultural amenities include the Tigua Indian Cultural Center, a Wilderness Park Museum, the El Paso Zoo, museums, a symphony orchestra, a ballet company, and many theaters. The city's "Wild West" qualities have long made it a popular destination for musicians-many of whom have recorded albums at El Paso's Sonic Ranch recording studio.

El Paso's revitalized downtown has increased the city's aesthetic appeal. It includes an open-air mall and "lifestyle center" in the city's central area, Doubletree by Hilton Hotel, and renovations of several historic downtown buildings.

El Paso is home to the world's largest inland desalination plant, designed to produce 27.5 million gallons of fresh water daily making it a critical component of the region's water portfolio.

The weather in El Paso is of the mountain-desert type, with very little precipitation. Summers are hot, humidity is low and winters are mild. However, temperatures in the flat Rio Grande Valley nearby are notably cooler at night year-round. There is plenty of sunshine and clear skies generally more than 200 days of the year.

Rankings

General Rankings

- For its "Best for Vets: Places to Live 2019" rankings, *Military Times* evaluated 599 cities (83 large, 234 medium, 282 small) and compared the locations across three broad categories: veteran and military culture/services; economic indicators; and livability factors such as health, crime, traffic, and school quality. El Paso ranked #20 out of the top 25, in the large city category (populations of more than 250,000). Data points more specific to veterans and the military weighed more heavily than the rest. *rebootcamp.militarytimes.com, "Military Times Best Places to Live 2019," September 10, 2018*

- The El Paso metro area was identified as one of America's fastest-growing areas in terms of population and business growth by *MagnifyMoney*. The area ranked #24 out of 35. The 100 most populous metro areas in the U.S. were evaluated on their change from 2011-2016 in the following categories: people and housing; workforce and employment opportunities; growing industry. *www.businessinsider.com, "The 35 Cities in the US with the Biggest Influx of People, the Most Work Opportunities, and the Hottest Business Growth," August 12, 2018*

- El Paso was selected as an "All-America City" by the National Civic League. The All-America City Award recognizes civic excellence and in 2018 honored 10 communities that best exemplify the spirit of grassroots citizen involvement and cross-sector collaborative problem solving. This year's focus was on community efforts to inspire equity and inclusion among community members to collectively tackle pressing and complex issues. *National Civic League, 2018 All-America City Awards, June 24, 2018*

Business/Finance Rankings

- The personal finance site NerdWallet analyzed 183 American metropolitan areas with populations over 250,000 and more than 15,000 businesses to rank where entrepreneurs find the most success. Criteria included area economy, annual income, housing cost, unemployment rate, and the success rate of area businesses. El Paso ranked #169. *www.nerdwallet.com, "Best Places to Start a Business," April 27, 2015*

- El Paso was the #10-ranked city for savers, according to a study by the finance site GOBankingRates, which considered the prospects for people trying to save money. Criteria: average monthly cost of grocery items; median home listing price; median rent; median income; unemployment rate; gas prices; and sales tax in the nation's 60 largest cities. *www.gobankingrates.com, "Best Cities for Saving Money," June 22, 2018*

- El Paso was ranked #10 among the nation's 60 largest cities for most difficult conditions for savers, according to a study by the finance site GOBankingRates. Criteria: average monthly cost of grocery items; median home listing price; median rent; median income; unemployment rate; gas prices; and sales tax. *www.gobankingrates.com, "Worst Cities for Saving Money," June 22, 2018*

- Using data from the Council for Community and Economic Research's 2014 cost of living index, NerdWallet ranked the 100 most affordable cities in America. Median income was compared with cost of living to find truly affordable places. El Paso ranked #98. *NerdWallet.com, "America's Most Affordable Places," May 18, 2015*

- NerdWallet.com identified the 10 most promising cities for job seekers of the nation's 100 largest cities. El Paso was ranked #58. Criteria: job availability; annual salary; workforce growth; affordability. *NerdWallet.com, "Best Cities for Job Seekers in 2017," December 19, 2016*

- The Brookings Institution ranked the nation's largest cities based on income inequality. El Paso was ranked #59 (#1 = greatest inequality). Criteria: the "95/20 ratio," a figure representing the income at which a household earns more than 95 percent of all other households, divided by the income at which a household earns more than only 20 percent of all other households. *Brookings Institution, "Household Income Inequality, Largest Cities of 97 Large U.S. Metro Areas, 2014-2016," February 5, 2018*

- The Brookings Institution ranked the 100 largest metro areas in the U.S. based on income inequality. El Paso was ranked #39 (#1 = greatest inequality). Criteria: the "95/20 ratio," a figure representing the income at which a household earns more than 95 percent of all other households, divided by the income at which a household earns more than only 20 percent of all other households. *Brookings Institution, "Household Income Inequality, 100 Largest U.S. Metro Areas, 2014-2016," February 5, 2018*

- The El Paso metro area appeared on the Milken Institute "2018 Best Performing Cities" list. Rank: #113 out of 200 large metro areas. Criteria: job growth; wage and salary growth; high-tech output growth. *Milken Institute, "Best-Performing Cities 2018," January 24, 2019*

- *Forbes* ranked the 200 most populous metro areas to determine the nation's "Best Places for Business and Careers." The El Paso metro area was ranked #170. Criteria: costs (business and living); job growth (past and projected); income growth; quality of life; educational attainment (college and high school); projected economic growth; cultural and recreational opportunities; net migration patterns; number of highly ranked colleges. *Forbes, "The Best Places for Business and Careers 2018: Seattle Leads the Way," October 24, 2018*

Education Rankings

- Personal finance website *WalletHub* analyzed the 150 largest U.S. metropolitan statistical areas to determine where the most educated Americans are choosing to settle. Criteria: education quality and attainment gap; education levels; percentage of workers with degrees; public school quality rankings; quality and size of each metro area's universities. El Paso was ranked #138 (#1 = most educated city). *www.WalletHub.com, "2018's Most and Least Educated Cities in America," July 24, 2018*

- El Paso was selected as one of America's most literate cities. The city ranked #80 out of the 82 largest U.S. cities. Criteria: number of booksellers; library resources; Internet resources; educational attainment; periodical publishing resources; newspaper circulation. *Central Connecticut State University, "America's Most Literate Cities, 2016," March 31, 2017*

Food/Drink Rankings

- *Men's Health* ranked 100 major U.S. cities in terms of alcohol intoxication. El Paso ranked #24 (#1 = most sober).Criteria: binge drinking; alcohol-related traffic accidents, arrests, and fatalities. *Men's Health, "America's Drunkest Cities," March 9, 2015*

Health/Fitness Rankings

- The Gallup-Healthways Well-Being Index tracks Americans' optimism about their communities and satisfaction with the metro areas in which they live. At least 300 adult residents in each of 186 U.S. metropolitan areas were asked whether they liked what they did each day and were motivated to achieve their goals. The El Paso metro area placed among the top five in the percentage of residents who feeling of purpose was high. *www.gallup.com, "2017 Community Well-Being Rankings," March 2018*

- For each of the 100 largest cities in the United States, the American College of Sports Medicine's American Fitness Index evaluated infrastructure, community assets, and policies that encourage healthy and fit lifestyles, including preventive health behaviors, levels of chronic disease conditions, health care access, and community resources and policies that support physical activity. El Paso ranked #79 for "community fitness." *www.americanfitnessindex.org, "ACSM American Fitness Index Health and Community Fitness Status of the 100 Largest U.S. Cities," May 2018*

- El Paso was identified as a "2018 Spring Allergy Capital." The area ranked #13 out of 100. Three groups of factors were used to identify the most challenging cities for people with allergies during the spring season: annual pollen levels; medicine utilization; access to board-certified allergists. *Asthma and Allergy Foundation of America, "Spring Allergy Capitals 2018"*

- El Paso was identified as a "2018 Fall Allergy Capital." The area ranked #11 out of 100. Three groups of factors were used to identify the most challenging cities for people with allergies during the fall season: annual pollen levels; medicine utilization; access to board-certified allergists. *Asthma and Allergy Foundation of America, "Fall Allergy Capitals 2018"*

- El Paso was identified as a "2018 Asthma Capital." The area ranked #94 out of the nation's 100 largest metropolitan areas. Criteria: estimated prevalence; self-reported prevalence; crude death rate for asthma; annual pollen score; annual air quality; public smoking laws; number of board-certified asthma specialists; school inhaler access laws; rescue medication use; controller medication use; ER visits for asthma; uninsured rate; poverty rate. *Asthma and Allergy Foundation of America, "Asthma Capitals 2018: The Most Challenging Places to Live With Asthma"*

- *Men's Health* ranked 100 major U.S. cities in terms of the best cities for men. El Paso ranked #58. Criteria: health; fitness; quality of life. *Men's Health, "The Best & Worst Cities for Men Who Want to Be Fit and Happy," January 1, 2016*

- The El Paso metro area ranked #15 out of 189 in The Gallup-Healthways Well-Being Index. Criteria: purpose; social well being; financial health; community and physical health. Results are based on telephone interviews with adults, aged 18 and older, living in metropolitan areas in the 50 U.S. states and the District of Columbia. *Gallup-Healthways, "State of American Well-Being, 2017 Community Well-Being Rankings" March 2018*

Real Estate Rankings

- *WalletHub* compared the most populated U.S. cities, as well as at least two of the most populated cities in each state, for a total of 179, to determine which had the best markets for real estate agents. El Paso ranked #141 where demand was high and pay was the best. Criteria: sales per agent; annual median wage for real-estate agents; monthly average starting salary for real estate agents; real estate job density and competition; unemployment rate; housing-market health index; and other relevant metrics. *www.WalletHub.com, "2018's Best Places to Be a Real Estate Agent," April 25, 2018*

- Despite the national slowdown trend, the El Paso metro area appeared on Realtor.com's list of hot housing markets to watch in 2019. The area ranked #3. Criteria: existing homes inventory and price; new home construction; median household incomes; local economy/population trends. *Realtor.com®, "The 10 Surprising Housing Markets Poised to Rule in 2019," January 2, 2019*

- El Paso was ranked #145 out of 237 metro areas in terms of housing affordability in 2018 by the National Association of Home Builders (#1 = most affordable). Criteria: the share of homes sold in that area affordable to a family earning the local median income, based on standard mortgage underwriting criteria. *National Association of Home Builders®, NAHB-Wells Fargo Housing Opportunity Index, 4th Quarter 2018*

Safety Rankings

- Allstate ranked the 200 largest cities in America in terms of driver safety. El Paso ranked #47. Criteria: internal property damage claims over a two-year period from January 2015 to December 2016. The report helps increase the importance of safety awareness behind the wheel. *Allstate, "Allstate America's Best Drivers Report, 2018" August 28, 2018*

- The National Insurance Crime Bureau ranked 382 metro areas in the U.S. in terms of per capita rates of vehicle theft. The El Paso metro area ranked #171 (#1 = highest rate). Criteria: number of vehicle theft offenses per 100,000 inhabitants in 2017. *National Insurance Crime Bureau, "Hot Spots 2017," July 12, 2018*

Seniors/Retirement Rankings

- From its Best Cities for Successful Aging indexes, the Milken Institute generated rankings for metropolitan areas, weighing data in nine categories—health care, wellness, living arrangements, transportation and convenience, financial characteristics, education, employment, community engagement, and overall livability. The El Paso metro area was ranked #80 overall in the large metro area category. *Milken Institute, "Best Cities for Successful Aging, 2017" March 14, 2017*

Women/Minorities Rankings

- The *Houston Chronicle* listed the El Paso metro area as #14 in top places for young Latinos to live in the U.S. Research was largely based on housing and occupational data from the largest metropolitan areas performed by *Forbes* and NBC Universo. Criteria: percentage of 18-34 year-olds; Latino college grad rates; and diversity. *blog.chron.com, "The 15 Best Big Cities for Latino Millenials," January 26, 2016*

- Personal finance website *WalletHub* compared more than 180 U.S. cities—including the 150 most populated U.S. cities, plus at least two of the most populated cities in each state—across two key dimensions, "Hispanic Business-Friendliness" and "Hispanic Purchasing Power", to arrive at the most favorable conditions for Hispanic entrepreneurs. El Paso was ranked #19 out of 182. Criteria includes: share of Hispanic-Owned Businesses; Hispanic entrepreneurship rate to median annual income of Hispanics; Small Business-Friendliness score; cost of living; and number of Hispanics with at least a bachelor's degree. *WalletHub.com, "2018's Best Cities for Hispanic Entrepreneurs," April 26, 2018*

Miscellaneous Rankings

- The real estate site Zillow has compiled the 2016 Trick-or-Treat Index, which used its own Home Value Index and Walk Score along with population density, age of residents, and local crime stats to determine that El Paso ranked #16 for "getting the best candy in the least amount of time." Zillow also zeroes in on the best neighborhoods in its top 20 cities. *www.zillow.com, "20 Best Cities for Trick or Treating in 2017," October 13, 2017*

- *WalletHub* compared the 150 most populated U.S. cities to determine their operating efficiency. A "Quality of Services" score was constructed for each city and then divided by the total budget per capita to reveal which were managed the best. El Paso ranked #40. Criteria: financial stability; economy; education; safety; health; infrastructure and pollution. *www.WalletHub.com, "2018's Best- & Worst-Run Cities in America," July 9, 2018*

Business Environment

CITY FINANCES

City Government Finances

Component	2016 ($000)	2016 ($ per capita)
Total Revenues	977,205	1,435
Total Expenditures	1,116,240	1,639
Debt Outstanding	1,825,527	2,680
Cash and Securities[1]	2,347,169	3,446

Note: (1) Cash and security holdings of a government at the close of its fiscal year, including those of its dependent agencies, utilities, and liquor stores.
Source: U.S. Census Bureau, State & Local Government Finances 2016

City Government Revenue by Source

Source	2016 ($000)	2016 ($ per capita)	2016 (%)
General Revenue			
From Federal Government	56,961	84	5.8
From State Government	25,745	38	2.6
From Local Governments	2,693	4	0.3
Taxes			
Property	227,241	334	23.3
Sales and Gross Receipts	190,119	279	19.5
Personal Income	0	0	0.0
Corporate Income	0	0	0.0
Motor Vehicle License	0	0	0.0
Other Taxes	13,032	19	1.3
Current Charges	264,443	388	27.1
Liquor Store	0	0	0.0
Utility	135,810	199	13.9
Employee Retirement	28,668	42	2.9

Source: U.S. Census Bureau, State & Local Government Finances 2016

City Government Expenditures by Function

Function	2016 ($000)	2016 ($ per capita)	2016 (%)
General Direct Expenditures			
Air Transportation	87,087	127	7.8
Corrections	0	0	0.0
Education	0	0	0.0
Employment Security Administration	0	0	0.0
Financial Administration	7,091	10	0.6
Fire Protection	96,495	141	8.6
General Public Buildings	21,723	31	1.9
Governmental Administration, Other	11,146	16	1.0
Health	19,271	28	1.7
Highways	28,226	41	2.5
Hospitals	0	0	0.0
Housing and Community Development	14,880	21	1.3
Interest on General Debt	64,725	95	5.8
Judicial and Legal	7,653	11	0.7
Libraries	10,004	14	0.9
Parking	0	0	0.0
Parks and Recreation	62,286	91	5.6
Police Protection	129,964	190	11.6
Public Welfare	541	< 1	< 0.1
Sewerage	93,054	136	8.3
Solid Waste Management	47,237	69	4.2
Veterans' Services	0	0	0.0
Liquor Store	0	0	0.0
Utility	254,742	374	22.8
Employee Retirement	123,778	181	11.1

Source: U.S. Census Bureau, State & Local Government Finances 2016

DEMOGRAPHICS

Population Growth

Area	1990 Census	2000 Census	2010 Census	2017* Estimate	Population Growth (%)	
					1990-2017	2010-2017
City	515,541	563,662	649,121	678,266	31.6	4.5
MSA[1]	591,610	679,622	800,647	838,527	41.7	4.7
U.S.	248,709,873	281,421,906	308,745,538	321,004,407	29.1	4.0

Note: (1) Figures cover the El Paso, TX Metropolitan Statistical Area—see Appendix B for areas included; (*) 2013-2017 5-year estimated population
Source: U.S. Census Bureau, 1990 Census, Census 2000, Census 2010, 2013-2017 American Community Survey 5-Year Estimates

Household Size

Area	Persons in Household (%)							Average Household Size
	One	Two	Three	Four	Five	Six	Seven or More	
City	24.3	28.1	18.4	16.1	8.3	3.3	1.5	3.00
MSA[1]	22.6	27.5	18.5	16.7	9.2	3.6	1.9	3.10
U.S.	27.7	33.8	15.7	13.0	6.0	2.3	1.4	2.60

Note: (1) Figures cover the El Paso, TX Metropolitan Statistical Area—see Appendix B for areas included
Source: U.S. Census Bureau, 2013-2017 American Community Survey 5-Year Estimates

Race

Area	White Alone[2] (%)	Black Alone[2] (%)	Asian Alone[2] (%)	AIAN[3] Alone[2] (%)	NHOPI[4] Alone[2] (%)	Other Race Alone[2] (%)	Two or More Races (%)
City	82.0	3.8	1.3	0.6	0.1	9.8	2.4
MSA[1]	81.1	3.4	1.1	0.7	0.1	11.2	2.3
U.S.	73.0	12.7	5.4	0.8	0.2	4.8	3.1

Note: (1) Figures cover the El Paso, TX Metropolitan Statistical Area—see Appendix B for areas included; (2) Alone is defined as not being in combination with one or more other races; (3) American Indian and Alaska Native; (4) Native Hawaiian and Other Pacific Islander
Source: U.S. Census Bureau, 2013-2017 American Community Survey 5-Year Estimates

Hispanic or Latino Origin

Area	Total (%)	Mexican (%)	Puerto Rican (%)	Cuban (%)	Other (%)
City	80.8	76.4	1.1	0.1	3.1
MSA[1]	82.2	78.0	1.1	0.1	3.0
U.S.	17.6	11.1	1.7	0.7	4.1

Note: Persons of Hispanic or Latino origin can be of any race; (1) Figures cover the El Paso, TX Metropolitan Statistical Area—see Appendix B for areas included
Source: U.S. Census Bureau, 2013-2017 American Community Survey 5-Year Estimates

Segregation

Type	Segregation Indices[1]				Percent Change		
	1990	2000	2010	2010 Rank[2]	1990-2000	1990-2010	2000-2010
Black/White	37.5	36.2	30.7	100	-1.3	-6.8	-5.5
Asian/White	23.8	21.9	22.2	100	-1.9	-1.7	0.2
Hispanic/White	49.7	45.2	43.3	50	-4.5	-6.5	-1.9

Note: All figures cover the Metropolitan Statistical Area—see Appendix B for areas included; Figures are based on an analysis of 1990, 2000, and 2010 Census Decennial Census tract data by William H. Frey, Brookings Institution and the University of Michigan Social Science Data Analysis Network. In this analysis all racial groups (whites, blacks, and asians) are non-Hispanic members of those races. Hispanics are shown as a separate category; (1) Segregation Indices are Dissimilarity Indices that measure the degree to which the minority group is distributed differently than whites across census tracts. They range from 0 (complete integration) to 100 (complete segregation) where the value indicates the percentage of the minority group that needs to move to be distributed exactly like whites; (2) Ranges from 1 (most segregated) to 102 (least segregated); n/a not available.
Source: www.CensusScope.org

Ancestry

Area	German	Irish	English	American	Italian	Polish	French[2]	Scottish	Dutch
City	3.6	2.3	1.6	2.9	1.2	0.4	0.7	0.4	0.3
MSA[1]	3.4	2.2	1.5	2.7	1.1	0.4	0.6	0.4	0.3
U.S.	14.1	10.1	7.5	6.6	5.3	2.9	2.5	1.7	1.3

Note: Figures are the percentage of the total population reporting a particular ancestry. The nine most commonly reported ancestries in the U.S. are shown. Figures include multiple ancestries (e.g. if a person reported being Irish and Italian, they were included in both columns); (1) Figures cover the El Paso, TX Metropolitan Statistical Area—see Appendix B for areas included; (2) Excludes Basque
Source: U.S. Census Bureau, 2013-2017 American Community Survey 5-Year Estimates

Foreign-Born Population

Area	Percent of Population Born in								
	Any Foreign Country	Asia	Mexico	Europe	Carribean	Central America[2]	South America	Africa	Canada
City	24.5	1.1	21.8	0.6	0.2	0.3	0.3	0.2	0.0
MSA[1]	25.5	1.0	23.1	0.5	0.2	0.3	0.2	0.2	0.0
U.S.	13.4	4.1	3.6	1.5	1.3	1.0	0.9	0.6	0.3

Note: (1) Figures cover the El Paso, TX Metropolitan Statistical Area—see Appendix B for areas included; (2) Excludes Mexico.
Source: U.S. Census Bureau, 2013-2017 American Community Survey 5-Year Estimates

Marital Status

Area	Never Married	Now Married[2]	Separated	Widowed	Divorced
City	33.9	45.7	3.4	5.9	11.1
MSA[1]	34.5	46.1	3.4	5.5	10.5
U.S.	33.1	48.2	2.0	5.8	10.9

Note: Figures are percentages and cover the population 15 years of age and older; (1) Figures cover the El Paso, TX Metropolitan Statistical Area—see Appendix B for areas included; (2) Excludes separated
Source: U.S. Census Bureau, 2013-2017 American Community Survey 5-Year Estimates

Disability by Age

Area	All Ages	Under 18 Years Old	18 to 64 Years Old	65 Years and Over
City	13.7	4.4	11.5	45.0
MSA[1]	13.9	5.0	12.0	46.3
U.S.	12.6	4.2	10.3	35.5

Note: Figures show percent of the civilian noninstitutionalized population that reported having a disability. Disability status is determined from six types of difficulty: vision, hearing, cognitive, ambulatory, self-care, and independent living. For children under 5 years old, hearing and vision difficulty are used to determine disability status. For children between the ages of 5 and 14, disability status is determined from hearing, vision, cognitive, ambulatory, and self-care difficulties. For people aged 15 years and older, they are considered to have a disability if they have difficulty with any one of the six difficulty types; Note: (1) Figures cover the El Paso, TX Metropolitan Statistical Area—see Appendix B for areas included
Source: U.S. Census Bureau, 2013-2017 American Community Survey 5-Year Estimates

Age

Area	Percent of Population									Median Age
	Under Age 5	Age 5–19	Age 20–34	Age 35–44	Age 45–54	Age 55–64	Age 65–74	Age 75–84	Age 85+	
City	7.6	22.5	22.7	12.5	12.0	10.5	6.7	3.9	1.6	32.8
MSA[1]	7.9	23.3	23.0	12.6	11.7	10.2	6.3	3.6	1.4	31.9
U.S.	6.2	19.5	20.7	12.7	13.4	12.7	8.6	4.4	1.9	37.8

Note: (1) Figures cover the El Paso, TX Metropolitan Statistical Area—see Appendix B for areas included
Source: U.S. Census Bureau, 2013-2017 American Community Survey 5-Year Estimates

Gender

Area	Males	Females	Males per 100 Females
City	330,360	347,906	95.0
MSA[1]	411,040	427,487	96.2
U.S.	158,018,753	162,985,654	97.0

Note: (1) Figures cover the El Paso, TX Metropolitan Statistical Area—see Appendix B for areas included
Source: U.S. Census Bureau, 2013-2017 American Community Survey 5-Year Estimates

Religious Groups by Family

Area	Catholic	Baptist	Non-Den.	Methodist[2]	Lutheran	LDS[3]	Pentecostal	Presbyterian[4]	Muslim[5]	Judaism
MSA[1]	43.2	3.8	5.0	0.9	0.3	1.6	1.4	0.2	0.1	0.2
U.S.	19.1	9.3	4.0	4.0	2.3	2.0	1.9	1.6	0.8	0.7

Note: Figures are the number of adherents as a percentage of the total population; (1) Figures cover the El Paso, TX Metropolitan Statistical Area—see Appendix B for areas included; (2) Methodist/Pietist; (3) Latter Day Saints; (4) Reformed; (5) Figures are estimates
Source: Association of Statisticians of American Religious Bodies, 2010 U.S. Religion Census: Religious Congregations & Membership Study

Religious Groups by Tradition

Area	Catholic	Evangelical Protestant	Mainline Protestant	Other Tradition	Black Protestant	Orthodox
MSA[1]	43.2	10.9	1.3	2.1	0.2	0.1
U.S.	19.1	16.2	7.3	4.3	1.6	0.3

Note: Figures are the number of adherents as a percentage of the total population; (1) Figures cover the El Paso, TX Metropolitan Statistical Area—see Appendix B for areas included
Source: Association of Statisticians of American Religious Bodies, 2010 U.S. Religion Census: Religious Congregations & Membership Study

ECONOMY

Gross Metropolitan Product

Area	2016	2017	2018	2019	Rank[2]
MSA[1]	28.4	29.8	31.3	32.7	89

Note: Figures are in billions of dollars; (1) Figures cover the El Paso, TX Metropolitan Statistical Area—see Appendix B for areas included; (2) Rank is based on 2017 data and ranges from 1 to 381
Source: U.S. Conference of Mayors, U.S. Metro Economies: Economic Growth & Full Employment, June 2018

Economic Growth

Area	2017-2018 (%)	2019-2020 (%)	2021-2022 (%)
MSA[1]	3.5	2.0	1.5

Note: Figures are real gross metropolitan product (GMP) growth rates and represent average annual percent change; (1) Figures cover the El Paso, TX Metropolitan Statistical Area—see Appendix B for areas included
Source: U.S. Conference of Mayors, U.S. Metro Economies: Economic Growth & Full Employment, June 2018

Metropolitan Area Exports

Area	2012	2013	2014	2015	2016	2017	Rank[2]
MSA[1]	12,796.9	14,359.7	20,079.3	24,560.9	26,452.8	25,814.1	12

Note: Figures are in millions of dollars; (1) Figures cover the El Paso, TX Metropolitan Statistical Area—see Appendix B for areas included; (2) Rank is based on 2017 data and ranges from 1 to 387
Source: U.S. Department of Commerce, International Trade Administration, Office of Trade and Economic Analysis, Industry and Analysis, Exports by Metropolitan Area, extracted March 25, 2019

Building Permits

Area	Single-Family			Multi-Family			Total		
	2016	2017	Pct. Chg.	2016	2017	Pct. Chg.	2016	2017	Pct. Chg.
City	2,014	2,020	0.3	829	897	8.2	2,843	2,917	2.6
MSA[1]	2,219	2,373	6.9	835	904	8.3	3,054	3,277	7.3
U.S.	750,800	820,000	9.2	455,800	462,000	1.4	1,206,600	1,282,000	6.2

Note: (1) Figures cover the El Paso, TX Metropolitan Statistical Area—see Appendix B for areas included; Figures represent new, privately-owned housing units authorized (unadjusted data); All permit data are based on estimates with imputation
Source: U.S. Census Bureau, Manufacturing, Mining, and Construction Statistics, Building Permits, 2016, 2017

Bankruptcy Filings

Area	Business Filings			Nonbusiness Filings		
	2017	2018	% Chg.	2017	2018	% Chg.
El Paso County	49	56	14.3	2,108	2,133	1.2
U.S.	23,157	22,232	-4.0	765,863	751,186	-1.9

Note: Business filings include Chapter 7, Chapter 11, Chapter 12, and Chapter 13; Nonbusiness filings include Chapter 7, Chapter 11, and Chapter 13
Source: Administrative Office of the U.S. Courts, Business and Nonbusiness Bankruptcy, County Cases Commenced by Chapter of the Bankruptcy Code, During the 12-Month Period Ending December 31, 2017 and Business and Nonbusiness Bankruptcy, County Cases Commenced by Chapter of the Bankruptcy Code, During the 12-Month Period Ending December 31, 2018

Housing Vacancy Rates

Area	Gross Vacancy Rate[2] (%)			Year-Round Vacancy Rate[3] (%)			Rental Vacancy Rate[4] (%)			Homeowner Vacancy Rate[5] (%)		
	2016	2017	2018	2016	2017	2018	2016	2017	2018	2016	2017	2018
MSA[1]	n/a	n/a	n/a	n/a	n/a	n/a	n/a	n/a	n/a	n/a	n/a	n/a
U.S.	12.8	12.7	12.3	9.9	9.9	9.7	6.9	7.2	6.9	1.7	1.6	1.5

Note: (1) Figures cover the El Paso, TX Metropolitan Statistical Area—see Appendix B for areas included; (2) The percentage of the total housing inventory that is vacant; (3) The percentage of the housing inventory (excluding seasonal units) that is year-round vacant; (4) The percentage of rental inventory that is vacant for rent; (5) The percentage of homeowner inventory that is vacant for sale; n/a not available
Source: U.S. Census Bureau, Housing Vacancies and Homeownership Annual Statistics: 2016, 2017, 2018

INCOME

Income

Area	Per Capita ($)	Median Household ($)	Average Household ($)
City	21,120	44,431	60,383
MSA[1]	19,917	43,170	58,772
U.S.	31,177	57,652	81,283

Note: (1) Figures cover the El Paso, TX Metropolitan Statistical Area—see Appendix B for areas included
Source: U.S. Census Bureau, 2013-2017 American Community Survey 5-Year Estimates

Household Income Distribution

Area	Percent of Households Earning							
	Under $15,000	$15,000 -$24,999	$25,000 -$34,999	$35,000 -$49,999	$50,000 -$74,999	$75,000 -$99,999	$100,000 -$149,999	$150,000 and up
City	15.6	12.5	11.8	15.4	18.2	10.4	10.2	5.9
MSA[1]	15.9	12.8	12.1	15.9	17.9	10.2	9.8	5.3
U.S.	11.6	9.8	9.5	13.0	17.7	12.3	14.1	12.1

Note: (1) Figures cover the El Paso, TX Metropolitan Statistical Area—see Appendix B for areas included
Source: U.S. Census Bureau, 2013-2017 American Community Survey 5-Year Estimates

Poverty Rate

Area	All Ages	Under 18 Years Old	18 to 64 Years Old	65 Years and Over
City	20.3	28.5	17.0	18.4
MSA[1]	21.8	30.3	18.1	19.7
U.S.	14.6	20.3	13.7	9.3

Note: Figures are percentage of people whose income during the past 12 months was below the poverty level; (1) Figures cover the El Paso, TX Metropolitan Statistical Area—see Appendix B for areas included
Source: U.S. Census Bureau, 2013-2017 American Community Survey 5-Year Estimates

EMPLOYMENT

Labor Force and Employment

Area	Civilian Labor Force			Workers Employed		
	Dec. 2017	Dec. 2018	% Chg.	Dec. 2017	Dec. 2018	% Chg.
City	297,041	303,631	2.2	285,407	291,848	2.3
MSA[1]	355,795	363,598	2.2	341,342	349,017	2.2
U.S.	159,880,000	162,510,000	1.6	153,602,000	156,481,000	1.9

Note: Data is not seasonally adjusted and covers workers 16 years of age and older; (1) Figures cover the El Paso, TX Metropolitan Statistical Area—see Appendix B for areas included
Source: Bureau of Labor Statistics, Local Area Unemployment Statistics

Unemployment Rate

Area	2018											
	Jan.	Feb.	Mar.	Apr.	May	Jun.	Jul.	Aug.	Sep.	Oct.	Nov.	Dec.
City	4.4	4.4	4.4	4.0	4.0	4.5	4.3	4.2	4.1	3.8	3.8	3.9
MSA[1]	4.6	4.5	4.5	4.2	4.1	4.7	4.4	4.4	4.2	3.9	3.9	4.0
U.S.	4.5	4.4	4.1	3.7	3.6	4.2	4.1	3.9	3.6	3.5	3.5	3.7

Note: Data is not seasonally adjusted and covers workers 16 years of age and older; (1) Figures cover the El Paso, TX Metropolitan Statistical Area—see Appendix B for areas included
Source: Bureau of Labor Statistics, Local Area Unemployment Statistics

Average Wages

Occupation	$/Hr.	Occupation	$/Hr.
Accountants and Auditors	30.00	Maids and Housekeeping Cleaners	9.40
Automotive Mechanics	16.20	Maintenance and Repair Workers	14.60
Bookkeepers	16.60	Marketing Managers	58.30
Carpenters	15.20	Nuclear Medicine Technologists	37.30
Cashiers	9.80	Nurses, Licensed Practical	22.80
Clerks, General Office	14.70	Nurses, Registered	33.90
Clerks, Receptionists/Information	10.90	Nursing Assistants	12.20
Clerks, Shipping/Receiving	13.80	Packers and Packagers, Hand	12.10
Computer Programmers	38.80	Physical Therapists	44.10
Computer Systems Analysts	39.70	Postal Service Mail Carriers	24.40
Computer User Support Specialists	18.50	Real Estate Brokers	n/a
Cooks, Restaurant	10.10	Retail Salespersons	12.70
Dentists	81.30	Sales Reps., Exc. Tech./Scientific	21.80
Electrical Engineers	38.60	Sales Reps., Tech./Scientific	54.20
Electricians	19.00	Secretaries, Exc. Legal/Med./Exec.	14.00
Financial Managers	52.70	Security Guards	12.90
First-Line Supervisors/Managers, Sales	20.70	Surgeons	n/a
Food Preparation Workers	10.00	Teacher Assistants*	12.80
General and Operations Managers	49.90	Teachers, Elementary School*	30.80
Hairdressers/Cosmetologists	10.70	Teachers, Secondary School*	31.40
Internists, General	n/a	Telemarketers	8.90
Janitors and Cleaners	10.90	Truck Drivers, Heavy/Tractor-Trailer	21.80
Landscaping/Groundskeeping Workers	11.10	Truck Drivers, Light/Delivery Svcs.	14.70
Lawyers	57.40	Waiters and Waitresses	10.10

Note: Wage data covers the El Paso, TX Metropolitan Statistical Area—see Appendix B for areas included;
(*) Hourly wages for elementary/secondary school teachers and teacher assistants were calculated by the editors from annual wage data based on a 40 hour work week; n/a not available.
Source: Bureau of Labor Statistics, Metro Area Occupational Employment & Wage Estimates, May 2018

Employment by Occupation

Occupation Classification	City (%)	MSA[1] (%)	U.S. (%)
Management, Business, Science, and Arts	32.1	30.1	37.4
Natural Resources, Construction, and Maintenance	7.9	9.1	8.9
Production, Transportation, and Material Moving	11.7	12.9	12.2
Sales and Office	27.3	26.9	23.5
Service	20.9	21.0	18.0

Note: Figures cover employed civilians 16 years of age and older; (1) Figures cover the El Paso, TX Metropolitan Statistical Area—see Appendix B for areas included
Source: U.S. Census Bureau, 2013-2017 American Community Survey 5-Year Estimates

Employment by Industry

Sector	MSA[1]		U.S.
	Number of Employees	Percent of Total	Percent of Total
Construction, Mining, and Logging	16,500	5.1	5.3
Education and Health Services	46,900	14.6	15.9
Financial Activities	12,700	3.9	5.7
Government	73,500	22.9	15.1
Information	4,600	1.4	1.9
Leisure and Hospitality	36,100	11.2	10.7
Manufacturing	16,500	5.1	8.5
Other Services	9,000	2.8	3.9
Professional and Business Services	35,700	11.1	14.1
Retail Trade	40,900	12.7	10.8
Transportation, Warehousing, and Utilities	16,900	5.3	4.2
Wholesale Trade	12,300	3.8	3.9

Note: Figures are non-farm employment as of December 2018. Figures are not seasonally adjusted and include workers 16 years of age and older; (1) Figures cover the El Paso, TX Metropolitan Statistical Area—see Appendix B for areas included
Source: Bureau of Labor Statistics, Current Employment Statistics, Employment, Hours, and Earnings

Occupations with Greatest Projected Employment Growth: 2018 – 2020

Occupation[1]	2018 Employment	2020 Projected Employment	Numeric Employment Change	Percent Employment Change
Combined Food Preparation and Serving Workers, Including Fast Food	351,780	372,090	20,310	5.8
Personal Care Aides	218,310	235,470	17,160	7.9
Heavy and Tractor-Trailer Truck Drivers	204,870	216,310	11,440	5.6
Laborers and Freight, Stock, and Material Movers, Hand	194,220	204,060	9,840	5.1
Waiters and Waitresses	236,020	245,790	9,770	4.1
Office Clerks, General	393,740	403,270	9,530	2.4
Customer Service Representatives	268,380	277,460	9,080	3.4
General and Operations Managers	182,190	190,620	8,430	4.6
Retail Salespersons	392,620	400,900	8,280	2.1
Construction Laborers	143,270	150,820	7,550	5.3

Note: Projections cover Texas; (1) Sorted by numeric employment change
Source: www.projectionscentral.com, State Occupational Projections, 2018–2020 Short-Term Projections

Fastest Growing Occupations: 2018 – 2020

Occupation[1]	2018 Employment	2020 Projected Employment	Numeric Employment Change	Percent Employment Change
Wind Turbine Service Technicians	1,810	2,190	380	21.0
Religious Workers, All Other	5,690	6,330	640	11.2
Fundraisers	8,830	9,670	840	9.5
Statisticians	1,870	2,040	170	9.1
Public Relations and Fundraising Managers	6,570	7,160	590	9.0
Home Health Aides	74,390	80,920	6,530	8.8
Community and Social Service Specialists, All Other	4,520	4,890	370	8.2
Personal Care Aides	218,310	235,470	17,160	7.9
Operations Research Analysts	10,920	11,760	840	7.7
Software Developers, Applications	65,190	70,140	4,950	7.6

Note: Projections cover Texas; (1) Sorted by percent employment change and excludes occupations with numeric employment change less than 50
Source: www.projectionscentral.com, State Occupational Projections, 2018–2020 Short-Term Projections

TAXES

State Corporate Income Tax Rates

State	Tax Rate (%)	Income Brackets ($)	Num. of Brackets	Financial Institution Tax Rate (%)[a]	Federal Income Tax Ded.
Texas	(w)	–	–	(w)	No

Note: Tax rates as of January 1, 2019; (a) Rates listed are the corporate income tax rate applied to financial institutions or excise taxes based on income. Some states have other taxes based upon the value of deposits or shares; (w) Texas imposes a Franchise Tax, otherwise known as margin tax, imposed on entities with more than $1,130,000 total revenues at rate of 0.75%, or 0.375% for entities primarily engaged in retail or wholesale trade, on lesser of 70% of total revenues or 100% of gross receipts after deductions for either compensation or cost of goods sold.
Source: Federation of Tax Administrators, Range of State Corporate Income Tax Rates, January 1, 2019

State Individual Income Tax Rates

State	Tax Rate (%)	Income Brackets ($)	Personal Exemptions ($)			Standard Ded. ($)	
			Single	Married	Depend.	Single	Married
Texas			– No state income tax –				

Note: Tax rates as of January 1, 2019; Local- and county-level taxes are not included; n/a not applicable;

Source: Federation of Tax Administrators, State Individual Income Tax Rates, January 1, 2019

Various State Sales and Excise Tax Rates

State	State Sales Tax (%)	Gasoline[1] (¢/gal.)	Cigarette[2] ($/pack)	Spirits[3] ($/gal.)	Wine[4] ($/gal.)	Beer[5] ($/gal.)	Recreational Marijuana (%)
Texas	6.25	20	1.41	2.40 (f)	0.20 (l)	0.20 (q)	Not legal

Note: All tax rates as of January 1, 2019; (1) The American Petroleum Institute has developed a methodology for determining the average tax rate on a gallon of fuel. Rates may include any of the following: excise taxes, environmental fees, storage tank fees, other fees or taxes, general sales tax, and local taxes. In states where gasoline is subject to the general sales tax, or where the fuel tax is based on the average sale price, the average rate determined by API is sensitive to changes in the price of gasoline. States that fully or partially apply general sales taxes to gasoline: CA, CO, GA, IL, IN, MI, NY; (2) The federal excise tax of $1.0066 per pack and local taxes are not included; (3) Rates are those applicable to off-premise sales of 40% alcohol by volume (a.b.v.) distilled spirits in 750ml containers. Local excise taxes are excluded; (4) Rates are those applicable to off-premise sales of 11% a.b.v. non-carbonated wine in 750ml containers; (5) Rates are those applicable to off-premise sales of 4.7% a.b.v. beer in 12 ounce containers; (f) Different rates also applicable according to alcohol content, place of production, size of container, or place purchased (on- or off-premise or onboard airlines); (l) Different rates also applicable to alcohol content, place of production, size of container, place purchased (on- or off-premise or on board airlines) or type of wine (carbonated, vermouth, etc.); (q) Different rates also applicable according to alcohol content, place of production, size of container, or place purchased (on- or off-premise or onboard airlines).
Source: Tax Foundation, 2019 Facts & Figures: How Does Your State Compare?

State Business Tax Climate Index Rankings

State	Overall Rank	Corporate Tax Rank	Individual Income Tax Rank	Sales Tax Rank	Unemployment Insurance Tax Rank	Property Tax Rank
Texas	15	49	6	37	18	37

Note: The index is a measure of how each state's tax laws affect economic performance. The lower the rank, the more favorable a state's tax system is for business. States without a given tax are given a ranking of 1. The scores/rankings for the District of Columbia do not affect other states. The 2019 index represents the tax climate as of July 1, 2018.
Source: Tax Foundation, State Business Tax Climate Index 2019

COMMERCIAL UTILITIES

Typical Monthly Electric Bills

Area	Commercial Service ($/month)		Industrial Service ($/month)	
	1,500 kWh	40 kW demand 14,000 kWh	1,000 kW demand 200,000 kWh	50,000 kW demand 32,500,000 kWh
City	185	1,317	24,698	1,586,802
Average[1]	203	1,619	25,886	2,540,077

Note: Figures are based on annualized rates; (1) Average based on 187 utilities surveyed
Source: Edison Electric Institute, Typical Bills and Average Rates Report, Summer 2018

TRANSPORTATION

Means of Transportation to Work

Area	Car/Truck/Van		Public Transportation			Bicycle	Walked	Other Means	Worked at Home
	Drove Alone	Car-pooled	Bus	Subway	Railroad				
City	80.3	11.1	1.7	0.0	0.0	0.2	1.6	1.9	3.2
MSA[1]	79.7	11.0	1.5	0.0	0.0	0.2	2.0	2.1	3.5
U.S.	76.4	9.2	2.5	1.9	0.6	0.6	2.7	1.3	4.7

Note: Figures are percentages and cover workers 16 years of age and older; (1) Figures cover the El Paso, TX Metropolitan Statistical Area—see Appendix B for areas included
Source: U.S. Census Bureau, 2013-2017 American Community Survey 5-Year Estimates

Travel Time to Work

Area	Less Than 10 Minutes	10 to 19 Minutes	20 to 29 Minutes	30 to 44 Minutes	45 to 59 Minutes	60 to 89 Minutes	90 Minutes or More
City	9.4	35.2	27.6	20.0	4.0	2.3	1.6
MSA[1]	10.3	33.0	26.6	21.2	4.7	2.5	1.7
U.S.	12.7	28.9	20.9	20.5	8.1	6.2	2.7

Note: Note: Figures are percentages and include workers 16 years old and over; (1) Figures cover the El Paso, TX Metropolitan Statistical Area—see Appendix B for areas included
Source: U.S. Census Bureau, 2013-2017 American Community Survey 5-Year Estimates

Freeway Travel Time Index

Area	1985	1990	1995	2000	2005	2010	2014
Urban Area Rank[1,2]	64	56	47	46	42	48	65
Urban Area Index[1]	1.05	1.09	1.13	1.16	1.18	1.17	1.16
Average Index[3]	1.09	1.11	1.14	1.17	1.20	1.19	1.20

Note: Freeway Travel Time Index—the ratio of travel time in the peak period to the travel time at free-flow conditions. For example, a value of 1.30 indicates a 20-minute free-flow trip takes 26 minutes in the peak (20 minutes x 1.30 = 26 minutes); (1) Covers the El Paso TX-NM urban area; (2) Rank is based on 101 urban areas (#1 = highest travel time index); (3) Average of 101 urban areas
Source: Texas Transportation Institute, 2015 Urban Mobility Scorecard, August 2015

Freeway Commuter Stress Index

Area	1985	1990	1995	2000	2005	2010	2014
Urban Area Rank[1,2]	53	45	43	40	41	45	49
Urban Area Index[1]	1.09	1.14	1.18	1.21	1.23	1.22	1.22
Average Index[3]	1.13	1.16	1.19	1.22	1.25	1.24	1.25

Note: The Freeway Commuter Stress Index is the same as the Freeway Travel Time Index (see table above) except that it includes only the travel in the peak directions during the peak periods; the TTI includes travel in all directions during the peak period. Thus, the CSI is more indicative of the work trip experienced by each commuter on a daily basis; (1) Covers the El Paso TX-NM urban area; (2) Rank is based on 101 urban areas (#1 = highest travel time index); (3) Average of 101 urban areas
Source: Texas Transportation Institute, 2015 Urban Mobility Scorecard, August 2015

Public Transportation

Agency Name / Mode of Transportation	Vehicles Operated in Maximum Service[1]	Annual Unlinked Passenger Trips[2] (in thous.)	Annual Passenger Miles[3] (in thous.)
Mass Transit Department-City of El Paso (Sun Metro)			
Bus (directly operated)	140	13,047.4	70,290.5
Demand Response (purchased transportation)	62	318.8	3,038.1

Note: (1) The number of revenue vehicles operated by the given mode and type of service to meet the annual maximum service requirement. This is the revenue vehicle count during the peak season of the year; on the week and day that maximum service is provided. Vehicles operated in maximum service (VOMS) exclude atypical days and one-time special events; (2) The number of passengers who boarded public transportation vehicles. Passengers are counted each time they board a vehicle no matter how many vehicles they use to travel from their origin to their destination. (3) The sum of the distances ridden by all passengers during the entire fiscal year.
Source: Federal Transit Administration, National Transit Database, 2017

Air Transportation

Airport Name and Code / Type of Service	Passenger Airlines[1]	Passenger Enplanements	Freight Carriers[2]	Freight (lbs)
El Paso International (ELP)				
Domestic service (U.S. carriers - 2018)	22	1,594,104	19	101,938,150
International service (U.S. carriers - 2017)	4	18,201	5	1,543,349

Note: (1) Includes all U.S.-based major, minor and commuter airlines that carried at least one passenger during the year; (2) Includes all U.S.-based airlines and freight carriers that transported at least one pound of freight during the year.
Source: Bureau of Transportation Statistics, The Intermodal Transportation Database, Air Carriers: T-100 Domestic Market (U.S. Carriers), 2018; Bureau of Transportation Statistics, The Intermodal Transportation Database, Air Carriers: T-100 International Market (U.S. Carriers), 2017

Other Transportation Statistics

Major Highways:	I-10
Amtrak Service:	Yes
Major Waterways/Ports:	Rio Grande

Source: Amtrak.com; Google Maps

BUSINESSES

Major Business Headquarters

Company Name	Industry	Rankings	
		Fortune[1]	Forbes[2]
No companies listed	-	-	-

Note: (1) Companies that produce a 10-K are ranked 1 to 500 based on 2017 revenue; (2) All private companies with at least $2 billion in annual revenue through the end of their most current fiscal year are ranked 1 to 229; companies listed are headquartered in the city; dashes indicate no ranking
Source: Fortune, "Fortune 500," June 2018; Forbes, "America's Largest Private Companies," 2018 Rankings

Minority Business Opportunity

El Paso is home to 28 companies which are on the *Hispanic Business* 500 list (500 largest U.S. Hispanic-owned companies based on revenue): **Fred Loya Insurance** (#19); **Bravo Southwest LP** (#71); **R. M. Personnel** (#155); **Integrated Human Capital/Santana Group** (#157); **dmDickason Personnel Services** (#195); **JACO General Contractors** (#254); **Miratek Corp.** (#275); **Thrifty Car Sales** (#312); **LGA Trucking** (#339); **Mike Garcia Merchant Security** (#354); **Aztec Contractors** (#402); **MFH Environmental Corp.** (#416); **Milvian Solutions** (#426); **Five Star Automatic Fire Protection** (#431); **American Packaging and Supply Co.** (#436); **Cesar-Scott** (#437); **El Paso Sanitation Systems** (#449); **Dynatec Scientific Laboratories** (#451); **H.G. Arias & Associates LP** (#462); **Servpro of West El Paso** (#464); **DataXport.Net** (#472); **Arrow Discount Automotive** (#474); **Accurate Collision Center** (#479); **ASEO** (#480); **Paul Meza CPA Firm** (#483); **The Saucedo Co.** (#487); **ENCON International** (#494); **Kuzzy Industrial Supplier** (#498). Companies included must show at least 51 percent ownership by Hispanic U.S. citizens, and must maintain headquarters in one of the 50 states or Washington, D.C. *Hispanic Business, "Hispanic Business 500," June 20, 2013*

Minority- and Women-Owned Businesses

Group	All Firms		Firms with Paid Employees			
	Firms	Sales ($000)	Firms	Sales ($000)	Employees	Payroll ($000)
AIAN[1]	520	21,011	5	11,663	171	2,901
Asian	1,288	740,598	511	688,883	7,726	144,969
Black	961	173,704	147	153,588	1,471	52,237
Hispanic	41,167	5,817,696	4,567	4,552,926	44,302	1,048,560
NHOPI[2]	89	(s)	8	(s)	20 - 99	(s)
Women	21,872	1,628,643	1,404	1,157,850	14,863	288,029
All Firms	55,697	48,992,324	9,202	47,010,411	200,188	5,765,449

Note: Figures cover firms located in the city; minority- and women-owned business are defined as firms in which the corresponding group own 51% or more of the stock or equity of the company; (1) American Indian and Alaska Native; (2) Native Hawaiian and Other Pacific Islander; (s) estimates are suppressed when publication standards are not met
Source: U.S. Census Bureau, 2012 Economic Census, Survey of Business Owners

**HOTELS &
CONVENTION
CENTERS**

Hotels, Motels and Vacation Rentals

Area	5 Star		4 Star		3 Star		2 Star		1 Star		Not Rated	
	Num.	Pct.[3]	Num.	Pct.[3]	Num.	Pct.[3]	Num.	Pct.[3]	Num.	Pct.[3]	Num.	Pct.[3]
City[1]	0	0.0	0	0.0	26	20.0	60	46.2	0	0.0	44	33.8
Total[2]	286	0.4	5,236	7.1	16,715	22.6	10,259	13.9	293	0.4	41,056	55.6

Note: (1) Figures cover El Paso and vicinity; (2) Figures cover all 100 cities in this book; (3) Percentage of hotels which have a given star rating; Star ratings are determined by expedia.com and offer an indication of the general quality of a particular hotel.
Source: www.expedia.com, April 3, 2019

Major Convention Centers

Name	Overall Space (sq. ft.)	Exhibit Space (sq. ft.)	Meeting Space (sq. ft.)	Meeting Rooms
Judson F. Williams Convention Center	n/a	80,000	14,900	17

Note: Table includes convention centers located in the El Paso, TX metro area; n/a not available
Source: Original research

Living Environment

COST OF LIVING

Cost of Living Index

Composite Index	Groceries	Housing	Utilities	Trans-portation	Health Care	Misc. Goods/ Services
n/a	n/a	n/a	n/a	n/a	n/a	n/a

Note: The Cost of Living Index measures regional differences in the cost of consumer goods and services, excluding taxes and non-consumer expenditures, for professional and managerial households in the top income quintile. It is based on more than 50,000 prices covering almost 60 different items for which prices are collected three times a year by chambers of commerce, economic development organizations or university applied economic centers in each participating urban area. The numbers shown should be read as a percentage above or below the national average of 100. For example, a value of 115.4 in the groceries column indicates that grocery prices are 15.4% higher than the national average. Small differences in the index numbers should not be interpreted as significant; n/a not available.
Source: The Council for Community and Economic Research, ACCRA Cost of Living Index, 2018

Grocery Prices

Area[1]	T-Bone Steak ($/pound)	Frying Chicken ($/pound)	Whole Milk ($/half gal.)	Eggs ($/dozen)	Orange Juice ($/64 oz.)	Coffee ($/11.5 oz.)
City[2]	n/a	n/a	n/a	n/a	n/a	n/a
Avg.	11.35	1.42	1.94	1.81	3.52	4.35
Min.	7.45	0.92	0.80	0.75	2.72	3.06
Max.	15.05	2.76	4.18	4.00	5.36	8.20

Note: (1) Values for the local area are compared with the average, minimum and maximum values for all 291 areas in the Cost of Living Index; (2) Figures cover the El Paso TX urban area; n/a not available; **T-Bone Steak** (price per pound); **Frying Chicken** (price per pound, whole fryer); **Whole Milk** (half gallon carton); **Eggs** (price per dozen, Grade A, large); **Orange Juice** (64 oz. Tropicana or Florida Natural); **Coffee** (11.5 oz. can, vacuum-packed, Maxwell House, Hills Bros, or Folgers).
Source: The Council for Community and Economic Research, ACCRA Cost of Living Index, 2018

Housing and Utility Costs

Area[1]	New Home Price ($)	Apartment Rent ($/month)	All Electric ($/month)	Part Electric ($/month)	Other Energy ($/month)	Telephone ($/month)
City[2]	n/a	n/a	n/a	n/a	n/a	n/a
Avg.	347,000	1,087	165.93	100.16	67.73	178.70
Min.	200,468	500	93.58	25.64	26.78	163.10
Max.	1,901,222	4,888	388.65	246.86	332.81	197.70

Note: (1) Values for the local area are compared with the average, minimum and maximum values for all 291 areas in the Cost of Living Index; (2) Figures cover the El Paso TX urban area; n/a not available; **New Home Price** (2,400 sf living area, 8,000 sf lot, in urban area with full utilities); **Apartment Rent** (950 sf 2 bedroom/1.5 or 2 bath, unfurnished, excluding all utilities except water); **All Electric** (average monthly cost for an all-electric home); **Part Electric** (average monthly cost for a part-electric home); **Other Energy** (average monthly cost for natural gas, fuel oil, coal, wood, and any other forms of energy except electricity); **Telephone** (price includes the base monthly rate plus taxes and fees for three lines of mobile phone service).
Source: The Council for Community and Economic Research, ACCRA Cost of Living Index, 2018

Health Care, Transportation, and Other Costs

Area[1]	Doctor ($/visit)	Dentist ($/visit)	Optometrist ($/visit)	Gasoline ($/gallon)	Beauty Salon ($/visit)	Men's Shirt ($)
City[2]	n/a	n/a	n/a	n/a	n/a	n/a
Avg.	110.71	95.11	103.74	2.61	37.48	32.03
Min.	33.60	62.55	54.63	1.89	17.00	11.44
Max.	195.97	153.93	225.79	3.59	71.88	58.64

Note: (1) Values for the local area are compared with the average, minimum and maximum values for all 291 areas in the Cost of Living Index; (2) Figures cover the El Paso TX urban area; n/a not available; **Doctor** (general practitioners routine exam of an established patient); **Dentist** (adult teeth cleaning and periodic oral examination); **Optometrist** (full vision eye exam for established adult patient); **Gasoline** (one gallon regular unleaded, national brand, including all taxes, cash price at self-service pump if available); **Beauty Salon** (woman's shampoo, trim, and blow-dry); **Men's Shirt** (cotton/polyester dress shirt, pinpoint weave, long sleeves).
Source: The Council for Community and Economic Research, ACCRA Cost of Living Index, 2018

HOUSING

House Price Index (HPI)

Area	National Ranking[2]	Quarterly Change (%)	One-Year Change (%)	Five-Year Change (%)
MSA[1]	240	-1.59	0.41	9.71
U.S.[3]	–	1.12	5.73	32.81

Note: The HPI is a weighted repeat sales index. It measures average price changes in repeat sales or refinancings on the same properties. This information is obtained by reviewing repeat mortgage transactions on single-family properties whose mortgages have been purchased or securitized by Fannie Mae or Freddie Mac in January 1975; (1) Figures cover the El Paso, TX Metropolitan Statistical Area—see Appendix B for areas included; (2) Rankings are based on annual percentage change for all metro areas containing at least 15,000 transactions over the last 10 years and ranges from 1 to 245; (3) figures based on a weighted average of Census Division estimates using a seasonally adjusted, purchase-only index; all figures are for the period ending December 31, 2018
Source: Federal Housing Finance Agency, House Price Index, February 26, 2019

Median Single-Family Home Prices

Area	2016	2017	2018p	Percent Change 2017 to 2018
MSA[1]	148.5	151.5	155.8	2.8
U.S. Average	235.5	248.8	261.6	5.1

Note: Figures are median sales prices of existing single-family homes in thousands of dollars; (p) preliminary; (1) Figures cover the El Paso, TX Metropolitan Statistical Area—see Appendix B for areas included
Source: National Association of Realtors, Median Sales Price of Existing Single-Family Homes for Metropolitan Areas, 4th Quarter 2018

Qualifying Income Based on Median Sales Price of Existing Single-Family Homes

Area	With 5% Down ($)	With 10% Down ($)	With 20% Down ($)
MSA[1]	38,588	36,557	32,495
U.S. Average	62,954	59,640	53,013

Note: Figures are preliminary; Qualifying income is based on a mortgage rate of 4.9%. Monthly principal and interest payment is limited to 25% of income; (1) Figures cover the El Paso, TX Metropolitan Statistical Area—see Appendix B for areas included
Source: National Association of Realtors, Qualifying Income Based on Median Sales Price of Existing Single-Family Homes for Metropolitan Areas, 4th Quarter 2018

Median Apartment Condo-Coop Home Prices

Area	2016	2017	2018p	Percent Change 2017 to 2018
MSA[1]	n/a	n/a	n/a	n/a
U.S. Average	220.7	234.3	241.0	2.9

Note: Figures are median sales prices of existing apartment condo-coop homes in thousands of dollars; (p) preliminary; n/a not available; (1) Figures cover the El Paso, TX Metropolitan Statistical Area—see Appendix B for areas included
Source: National Association of Realtors, Median Sales Price of Existing Apartment Condo-Coop Homes for Metropolitan Areas, 4th Quarter 2018

Home Value Distribution

Area	Under $50,000	$50,000 -$99,999	$100,000 -$149,999	$150,000 -$199,999	$200,000 -$299,999	$300,000 -$499,999	$500,000 -$999,999	$1,000,000 or more
City	5.9	27.6	33.0	16.8	10.8	4.4	1.2	0.2
MSA[1]	8.9	28.9	31.5	15.6	9.8	4.0	1.1	0.2
U.S.	8.3	13.9	14.7	14.6	18.7	17.3	9.7	2.7

Note: Figures are percentages and cover owner-occupied housing units; (1) Figures cover the El Paso, TX Metropolitan Statistical Area—see Appendix B for areas included
Source: U.S. Census Bureau, 2013-2017 American Community Survey 5-Year Estimates

Homeownership Rate

Area	2010 (%)	2011 (%)	2012 (%)	2013 (%)	2014 (%)	2015 (%)	2016 (%)	2017 (%)	2018 (%)
MSA[1]	n/a	n/a	n/a	n/a	n/a	n/a	n/a	n/a	n/a
U.S.	66.9	66.1	65.4	65.1	64.5	63.7	63.4	63.9	64.4

Note: (1) Figures cover the El Paso, TX Metropolitan Statistical Area—see Appendix B for areas included; n/a not available
Source: U.S. Census Bureau, Housing Vacancies and Homeownership Annual Statistics: 2010-2018

Year Housing Structure Built

Area	2010 or Later	2000 -2009	1990 -1999	1980 -1989	1970 -1979	1960 -1969	1950 -1959	1940 -1949	Before 1940	Median Year
City	7.3	16.0	13.5	13.8	16.8	12.0	11.9	4.3	4.5	1980
MSA[1]	8.0	17.5	14.7	14.4	16.2	10.8	10.6	3.8	4.1	1983
U.S.	3.2	14.5	14.0	13.6	15.5	10.8	10.5	5.1	12.9	1977

Note: Figures are percentages except for Median Year; Note: (1) Figures cover the El Paso, TX Metropolitan Statistical Area—see Appendix B for areas included
Source: U.S. Census Bureau, 2013-2017 American Community Survey 5-Year Estimates

Gross Monthly Rent

Area	Under $500	$500 -$999	$1,000 -$1,499	$1,500 -$1,999	$2,000 -$2,499	$2,500 -$2,999	$3,000 and up	Median ($)
City	19.6	53.6	22.4	3.2	0.8	0.3	0.2	792
MSA[1]	19.6	53.2	22.5	3.5	0.8	0.2	0.2	789
U.S.	10.5	41.1	28.7	11.7	4.5	1.8	1.7	982

Note: Figures are percentages except for Median; Gross rent is the contract rent plus the estimated average monthly cost of utilities (electricity, gas, and water and sewer) and fuels (oil, coal, kerosene, wood, etc.) if these are paid by the renter (or paid for the renter by someone else); (1) Figures cover the El Paso, TX Metropolitan Statistical Area—see Appendix B for areas included
Source: U.S. Census Bureau, 2013-2017 American Community Survey 5-Year Estimates

HEALTH

Health Risk Factors

Category	MSA[1] (%)	U.S. (%)
Adults aged 18–64 who have any kind of health care coverage	65.5	87.3
Adults who reported being in good or better health	74.5	82.4
Adults who have been told they have high blood cholesterol	23.7	33.0
Adults who have been told they have high blood pressure	26.9	32.3
Adults who are current smokers	10.9	17.1
Adults who currently use E-cigarettes	n/a	4.6
Adults who currently use chewing tobacco, snuff, or snus	1.4	4.0
Adults who are heavy drinkers[2]	n/a	6.3
Adults who are binge drinkers[3]	19.2	17.4
Adults who are overweight (BMI 25.0 - 29.9)	33.8	35.3
Adults who are obese (BMI 30.0 - 99.8)	34.7	31.3
Adults who participated in any physical activities in the past month	74.5	74.4
Adults who always or nearly always wears a seat belt	97.5	94.3

Note: n/a not available; (1) Figures cover the El Paso, TX Metropolitan Statistical Area—see Appendix B for areas included; (2) Heavy drinkers are classified as adult men having more than 14 drinks per week and adult women having more than 7 drinks per week; (3) Binge drinkers are classified as males having five or more drinks on one occasion or females having four or more drinks on one occasion
Source: Centers for Disease Control and Prevention, Behaviorial Risk Factor Surveillance System, SMART: Selected Metropolitan Area Risk Trends, 2017

Acute and Chronic Health Conditions

Category	MSA[1] (%)	U.S. (%)
Adults who have ever been told they had a heart attack	n/a	4.2
Adults who have ever been told they have angina or coronary heart disease	2.6	3.9
Adults who have ever been told they had a stroke	n/a	3.0
Adults who have ever been told they have asthma	10.9	14.2
Adults who have ever been told they have arthritis	18.1	24.9
Adults who have ever been told they have diabetes[2]	14.6	10.5
Adults who have ever been told they had skin cancer	n/a	6.2
Adults who have ever been told they had any other types of cancer	n/a	7.1
Adults who have ever been told they have COPD	n/a	6.5
Adults who have ever been told they have kidney disease	n/a	3.0
Adults who have ever been told they have a form of depression	15.8	20.5

Note: n/a not available; (1) Figures cover the El Paso, TX Metropolitan Statistical Area—see Appendix B for areas included; (2) Figures do not include pregnancy-related, borderline, or pre-diabetes
Source: Centers for Disease Control and Prevention, Behaviorial Risk Factor Surveillance System, SMART: Selected Metropolitan Area Risk Trends, 2017

Health Screening and Vaccination Rates

Category	MSA[1] (%)	U.S. (%)
Adults aged 65+ who have had flu shot within the past year	61.6	60.7
Adults aged 65+ who have ever had a pneumonia vaccination	68.5	75.4
Adults who have ever been tested for HIV	39.2	36.1
Adults who have ever had the shingles or zoster vaccine?	16.8	28.9
Adults who have had their blood cholesterol checked within the last five years	88.8	85.9

Note: n/a not available; (1) Figures cover the El Paso, TX Metropolitan Statistical Area—see Appendix B for areas included.
Source: Centers for Disease Control and Prevention, Behaviorial Risk Factor Surveillance System, SMART: Selected Metropolitan Area Risk Trends, 2017

Disability Status

Category	MSA[1] (%)	U.S. (%)
Adults who reported being deaf	3.7	6.7
Are you blind or have serious difficulty seeing, even when wearing glasses?	6.4	4.5
Are you limited in any way in any of your usual activities due of arthritis?	8.2	12.9
Do you have difficulty doing errands alone?	5.9	6.8
Do you have difficulty dressing or bathing?	4.0	3.6
Do you have serious difficulty concentrating/remembering/making decisions?	11.1	10.7
Do you have serious difficulty walking or climbing stairs?	13.4	13.6

Note: (1) Figures cover the El Paso, TX Metropolitan Statistical Area—see Appendix B for areas included.
Source: Centers for Disease Control and Prevention, Behaviorial Risk Factor Surveillance System, SMART: Selected Metropolitan Area Risk Trends, 2017

Mortality Rates for the Top 10 Causes of Death in the U.S.

ICD-10[a] Sub-Chapter	ICD-10[a] Code	Age-Adjusted Mortality Rate[1] per 100,000 population	
		County[2]	U.S.
Malignant neoplasms	C00-C97	133.6	155.5
Ischaemic heart diseases	I20-I25	77.0	94.8
Other forms of heart disease	I30-I51	33.1	52.9
Chronic lower respiratory diseases	J40-J47	28.7	41.0
Cerebrovascular diseases	I60-I69	33.9	37.5
Other degenerative diseases of the nervous system	G30-G31	44.7	35.0
Other external causes of accidental injury	W00-X59	21.5	33.7
Organic, including symptomatic, mental disorders	F01-F09	21.6	31.0
Hypertensive diseases	I10-I15	36.2	21.9
Diabetes mellitus	E10-E14	32.3	21.2

Note: (a) ICD-10 = International Classification of Diseases 10th Revision; (1) Mortality rates are a three year average covering 2015-2017; (2) Figures cover El Paso County.
Source: Centers for Disease Control and Prevention, National Center for Health Statistics. Underlying Cause of Death 1999-2017 on CDC WONDER Online Database

Mortality Rates for Selected Causes of Death

ICD-10[a] Sub-Chapter	ICD-10[a] Code	Age-Adjusted Mortality Rate[1] per 100,000 population	
		County[2]	U.S.
Assault	X85-Y09	3.1	5.9
Diseases of the liver	K70-K76	28.3	14.1
Human immunodeficiency virus (HIV) disease	B20-B24	2.2	1.8
Influenza and pneumonia	J09-J18	7.4	14.3
Intentional self-harm	X60-X84	9.5	13.6
Malnutrition	E40-E46	1.8	1.6
Obesity and other hyperalimentation	E65-E68	1.1	2.1
Renal failure	N17-N19	14.4	13.0
Transport accidents	V01-V99	11.6	12.4
Viral hepatitis	B15-B19	2.8	1.6

Note: (a) ICD-10 = International Classification of Diseases 10th Revision; (1) Mortality rates are a three year average covering 2015-2017; (2) Figures cover El Paso County; Data are suppressed when the data meet the criteria for confidentiality constraints; Mortality rates are flagged as unreliable when the rate would be calculated with a numerator of 20 or less.
Source: Centers for Disease Control and Prevention, National Center for Health Statistics. Underlying Cause of Death 1999-2017 on CDC WONDER Online Database

Health Insurance Coverage

Area	With Health Insurance	With Private Health Insurance	With Public Health Insurance	Without Health Insurance	Population Under Age 18 Without Health Insurance
City	79.3	52.7	33.5	20.7	9.7
MSA[1]	77.7	50.1	33.9	22.3	10.6
U.S.	89.5	67.2	33.8	10.5	5.7

Note: Figures are percentages that cover the civilian noninstitutionalized population; (1) Figures cover the El Paso, TX Metropolitan Statistical Area—see Appendix B for areas included
Source: U.S. Census Bureau, 2013-2017 American Community Survey 5-Year Estimates

Number of Medical Professionals

Area	MDs[3]	DOs[3,4]	Dentists	Podiatrists	Chiropractors	Optometrists
County[1] (number)	1,564	129	373	32	73	78
County[1] (rate[2])	186.8	15.4	44.4	3.8	8.7	9.3
U.S. (rate[2])	279.3	23.0	68.4	6.0	27.1	16.2

Note: Data as of 2017 unless noted; (1) Data covers El Paso County; (2) Rate per 100,000 population; (3) Data as of 2016 and includes all active, non-federal physicians; (4) Doctor of Osteopathic Medicine
Source: U.S. Department of Health and Human Services, Health Resources and Services Administration, Bureau of Health Professions, Area Resource File (ARF) 2017-2018

EDUCATION

Public School District Statistics

District Name	Schls	Pupils	Pupil/ Teacher Ratio	Minority Pupils[1] (%)	Free Lunch Eligible[2] (%)	IEP[3] (%)
Canutillo ISD	10	6,064	15.6	95.9	59.4	9.3
Clint ISD	14	11,511	17.0	96.5	84.1	7.4
El Paso ISD	93	59,424	14.9	90.5	65.7	10.5
Socorro ISD	49	45,927	17.7	96.4	59.4	8.9
Ysleta ISD	61	41,536	15.3	96.3	71.4	12.2

Note: Table includes school districts with 2,000 or more students; (1) Percentage of students that are not non-Hispanic white; (2) Percentage of students that are eligible for the free lunch program; (3) Percentage of students that have an Individualized Education Program.
Source: U.S. Department of Education, National Center for Education Statistics, Common Core of Data, Local Education Agency (School District) Universe Survey: School Year 2016-2017; U.S. Department of Education, National Center for Education Statistics, Common Core of Data, Public Elementary/Secondary School Universe Survey: School Year 2016-2017

Best High Schools

According to *U.S. News*, El Paso is home to one of the best high schools in the U.S.: **Harmony Science Academy (El Paso)** (#214). More than 20,000 public, magnet and charter schools were ranked based on their performance on state assessments and how well they prepare students for college. Schools with the highest unrounded College Readiness Index values were numerically ranked from 1 to 500 and were classified as gold medal winners. *U.S. News & World Report, "Best High Schools 2018"*

Highest Level of Education

Area	Less than H.S.	H.S. Diploma	Some College, No Deg.	Associate Degree	Bachelor's Degree	Master's Degree	Prof. School Degree	Doctorate Degree
City	21.0	23.6	23.6	7.7	16.3	5.8	1.2	0.7
MSA[1]	23.3	24.1	23.1	7.5	15.1	5.2	1.1	0.6
U.S.	12.7	27.3	20.8	8.3	19.1	8.4	2.0	1.4

Note: Figures cover persons age 25 and over; (1) Figures cover the El Paso, TX Metropolitan Statistical Area—see Appendix B for areas included
Source: U.S. Census Bureau, 2013-2017 American Community Survey 5-Year Estimates

Educational Attainment by Race

Area	High School Graduate or Higher (%)					Bachelor's Degree or Higher (%)				
	Total	White	Black	Asian	Hisp.[2]	Total	White	Black	Asian	Hisp.[2]
City	79.0	79.2	94.1	91.3	74.6	24.1	24.1	27.5	49.4	20.0
MSA[1]	76.7	77.3	94.0	91.7	72.2	22.1	22.3	27.8	48.6	18.1
U.S.	87.3	89.3	84.9	86.5	66.7	30.9	32.2	20.6	52.7	15.2

Note: Figures shown cover persons 25 years old and over; (1) Figures cover the El Paso, TX Metropolitan Statistical Area—see Appendix B for areas included; (2) People of Hispanic origin can be of any race
Source: U.S. Census Bureau, 2013-2017 American Community Survey 5-Year Estimates

School Enrollment by Grade and Control

Area	Preschool (%)		Kindergarten (%)		Grades 1 - 4 (%)		Grades 5 - 8 (%)		Grades 9 - 12 (%)	
	Public	Private	Public	Private	Public	Private	Public	Private	Public	Private
City	79.0	21.0	92.4	7.6	95.2	4.8	94.1	5.9	96.0	4.0
MSA[1]	82.2	17.8	93.2	6.8	95.7	4.3	94.5	5.5	96.4	3.6
U.S.	58.8	41.2	87.7	12.3	89.7	10.3	89.6	10.4	90.3	9.7

Note: Figures shown cover persons 3 years old and over; (1) Figures cover the El Paso, TX Metropolitan Statistical Area—see Appendix B for areas included
Source: U.S. Census Bureau, 2013-2017 American Community Survey 5-Year Estimates

Average Salaries of Public School Classroom Teachers

Area	2016		2017		Change from 2016 to 2017	
	Dollars	Rank[1]	Dollars	Rank[1]	Percent	Rank[2]
Texas	51,890	28	52,575	28	1.3	29
U.S. Average	58,479	–	59,660	–	2.0	–

Note: (1) Rank ranges from 1 to 51 where 1 indicates highest salary; (2) Rank ranges from 1 to 51 where 1 indicates highest percent change.
Source: National Education Association, Rankings & Estimates: Rankings of the States 2017 and Estimates of School Statistics 2018

Higher Education

Four-Year Colleges			Two-Year Colleges			Medical Schools[1]	Law Schools[2]	Voc/Tech[3]
Public	Private Non-profit	Private For-profit	Public	Private Non-profit	Private For-profit			
1	0	1	1	0	7	1	0	4

Note: Figures cover institutions located within the city limits and include main campuses only; (1) includes schools accredited by the Liaison Committee on Medical Education and the American Osteopathic Association's Commission on Osteopathic College Accreditation; (2) includes ABA-accredited schools, schools with provisional ABA accreditation, and state accredited schools; (3) includes all schools with programs that are less than 2 years.
Source: National Center for Education Statistics, Integrated Postsecondary Education System (IPEDS), 2017-18; Wikipedia, List of Medical Schools in the United States, accessed April 3, 2019; Wikipedia, List of Law Schools in the United States, accessed April 3, 2019

PRESIDENTIAL ELECTION

2016 Presidential Election Results

Area	Clinton	Trump	Johnson	Stein	Other
El Paso County	68.5	25.7	3.5	1.4	0.9
U.S.	48.0	45.9	3.3	1.1	1.7

Note: Results are percentages and may not add to 100% due to rounding
Source: Dave Leip's Atlas of U.S. Presidential Elections

EMPLOYERS

Major Employers

Company Name	Industry
Alorica	Inbound customer service
Automatic Data Processing	Contact center - private
Coca-Cola Enterprises	Bottling & distributing
Datamark	Data processing & related service
Del Sol Medical Center	Health care - private
Dish Network	Technical support center
El Paso Electric Corporation	Electric utilities
GC Services	Inbound customer service
Las Palmas Medical Center	Health care - private
Redcats USA	Inbound customer service
RM Personnel	Employment services
T&T Staff Management	Employment services
Texas Tech University Health Sci Ctr	Higher education & health care
Union Pacific Railroad Co.	Transportation
University Medical Center	Health care - public
Visiting Nurse Association of El Paso	Health care & social assistance
West Customer Management Group	Inbound customer service
Western Refining	Corporate headquarters petro chemical refinery

Note: Companies shown are located within the El Paso, TX Metropolitan Statistical Area.
Source: Hoovers.com; Wikipedia

PUBLIC SAFETY

Crime Rate

Area	All Crimes	Violent Crimes				Property Crimes		
		Murder	Rape[3]	Robbery	Aggrav. Assault	Burglary	Larceny -Theft	Motor Vehicle Theft
City	2,197.7	2.8	53.9	58.1	264.1	188.3	1,514.4	116.2
Suburbs[1]	1,369.9	1.3	44.2	20.2	192.5	193.8	855.4	62.5
Metro[2]	2,042.9	2.5	52.1	51.0	250.7	189.4	1,391.1	106.1
U.S.	2,756.1	5.3	41.7	98.0	248.9	430.4	1,694.4	237.4

Note: Figures are crimes per 100,000 population; (1) All areas within the metro area that are located outside the city limits; (2) Figures cover the El Paso, TX Metropolitan Statistical Area—see Appendix B for areas included; (3) The city and U.S. figures shown were reported using the revised Uniform Crime Reporting (UCR) definition of rape. The suburban and metro area figures shown are an aggregate total of the data submitted using both the revised and legacy UCR definitions.
Source: FBI Uniform Crime Reports, 2017

Hate Crimes

Area	Number of Quarters Reported	Number of Incidents per Bias Motivation					
		Race/Ethnicity/ Ancestry	Religion	Sexual Orientation	Disability	Gender	Gender Identity
City	4	4	0	0	0	0	0
U.S.	4	4,131	1,564	1,130	116	46	119

Source: Federal Bureau of Investigation, Hate Crime Statistics 2017

Identity Theft Consumer Reports

Area	Reports	Reports per 100,000 Population	Rank[2]
MSA[1]	919	109	102
U.S.	444,602	135	-

Note: (1) Figures cover the El Paso, TX Metropolitan Statistical Area—see Appendix B for areas included; (2) Rank ranges from 1 to 389 where 1 indicates greatest number of identity theft reports per 100,000 population
Source: Federal Trade Commission, Consumer Sentinel Network Data Book for January–December 2018

Fraud and Other Consumer Reports

Area	Reports	Reports per 100,000 Population	Rank[2]
MSA[1]	3,258	387	328
U.S.	2,552,917	776	-

*Note: (1) Figures cover the El Paso, TX Metropolitan Statistical Area—see Appendix B for areas included;
(2) Rank ranges from 1 to 389 where 1 indicates greatest number of fraud and other consumer reports per
100,000 population
Source: Federal Trade Commission, Consumer Sentinel Network Data Book for January–December 2018*

SPORTS

Professional Sports Teams

Team Name	League	Year Established

No teams are located in the metro area
Source: Wikipedia, Major Professional Sports Teams of the United States and Canada, April 5, 2019

CLIMATE

Average and Extreme Temperatures

Temperature	Jan	Feb	Mar	Apr	May	Jun	Jul	Aug	Sep	Oct	Nov	Dec	Yr.
Extreme High (°F)	80	83	89	98	104	114	112	108	104	96	87	80	114
Average High (°F)	57	63	70	79	87	96	95	93	88	79	66	58	78
Average Temp. (°F)	44	49	56	64	73	81	83	81	75	65	52	45	64
Average Low (°F)	31	35	41	49	58	66	70	68	62	50	38	32	50
Extreme Low (°F)	-8	8	14	23	31	46	57	56	42	25	1	5	-8

*Note: Figures cover the years 1948-1995
Source: National Climatic Data Center, International Station Meteorological Climate Summary, 9/96*

Average Precipitation/Snowfall/Humidity

Precip./Humidity	Jan	Feb	Mar	Apr	May	Jun	Jul	Aug	Sep	Oct	Nov	Dec	Yr.
Avg. Precip. (in.)	0.4	0.4	0.3	0.2	0.3	0.7	1.6	1.5	1.4	0.7	0.3	0.6	8.6
Avg. Snowfall (in.)	1	1	Tr	Tr	0	0	0	0	0	Tr	1	2	6
Avg. Rel. Hum. 6am (%)	68	60	50	43	44	46	63	69	72	66	63	68	59
Avg. Rel. Hum. 3pm (%)	34	27	21	17	17	17	28	30	32	29	30	36	26

*Note: Figures cover the years 1948-1995; Tr = Trace amounts (<0.05 in. of rain; <0.5 in. of snow)
Source: National Climatic Data Center, International Station Meteorological Climate Summary, 9/96*

Weather Conditions

Temperature			Daytime Sky			Precipitation		
10°F & below	32°F & below	90°F & above	Clear	Partly cloudy	Cloudy	0.01 inch or more precip.	0.1 inch or more snow/ice	Thunder-storms
1	59	106	147	164	54	49	3	35

*Note: Figures are average number of days per year and cover the years 1948-1995
Source: National Climatic Data Center, International Station Meteorological Climate Summary, 9/96*

**HAZARDOUS
WASTE**

Superfund Sites

The El Paso, TX metro area has no sites on the EPA's Superfund Final National Priorities List.
There are a total of 1,390 Superfund sites with a status of proposed or final on the list in the U.S.
U.S. Environmental Protection Agency, National Priorities List, April 5, 2019

**AIR & WATER
QUALITY**

Air Quality Trends: Ozone

	1990	1995	2000	2005	2010	2012	2014	2015	2016	2017
MSA[1]	0.080	0.078	0.082	0.075	0.072	0.072	0.068	0.070	0.068	0.073
U.S.	0.088	0.089	0.082	0.080	0.073	0.075	0.067	0.068	0.069	0.068

Note: (1) Data covers the El Paso, TX Metropolitan Statistical Area—see Appendix B for areas included. The values shown are the composite ozone concentration averages among trend sites based on the highest fourth daily maximum 8-hour concentration in parts per million. These trends are based on sites having an adequate record of monitoring data during the trend period. Data from exceptional events are included.
Source: U.S. Environmental Protection Agency, Air Quality Monitoring Information, "Air Quality Trends by City, 1990-2017"

Air Quality Index

Area	Percent of Days when Air Quality was...[2]					AQI Statistics[2]	
	Good	Moderate	Unhealthy for Sensitive Groups	Unhealthy	Very Unhealthy	Maximum	Median
MSA[1]	46.6	47.1	5.8	0.5	0.0	159	51

Note: (1) Data covers the El Paso, TX Metropolitan Statistical Area—see Appendix B for areas included; (2) Based on 365 days with AQI data in 2017. Air Quality Index (AQI) is an index for reporting daily air quality. EPA calculates the AQI for five major air pollutants regulated by the Clean Air Act: ground-level ozone, particle pollution (aka particulate matter), carbon monoxide, sulfur dioxide, and nitrogen dioxide. The AQI runs from 0 to 500. The higher the AQI value, the greater the level of air pollution and the greater the health concern. There are six AQI categories: "Good" AQI is between 0 and 50. Air quality is considered satisfactory; "Moderate" AQI is between 51 and 100. Air quality is acceptable; "Unhealthy for Sensitive Groups" When AQI values are between 101 and 150, members of sensitive groups may experience health effects; "Unhealthy" When AQI values are between 151 and 200 everyone may begin to experience health effects; "Very Unhealthy" AQI values between 201 and 300 trigger a health alert; "Hazardous" AQI values over 300 trigger warnings of emergency conditions (not shown).
Source: U.S. Environmental Protection Agency, Air Quality Index Report, 2017

Air Quality Index Pollutants

Area	Percent of Days when AQI Pollutant was...[2]					
	Carbon Monoxide	Nitrogen Dioxide	Ozone	Sulfur Dioxide	Particulate Matter 2.5	Particulate Matter 10
MSA[1]	0.0	7.4	56.7	0.0	35.3	0.5

Note: (1) Data covers the El Paso, TX Metropolitan Statistical Area—see Appendix B for areas included; (2) Based on 365 days with AQI data in 2017. The Air Quality Index (AQI) is an index for reporting daily air quality. EPA calculates the AQI for five major air pollutants regulated by the Clean Air Act: ground-level ozone, particle pollution (also known as particulate matter), carbon monoxide, sulfur dioxide, and nitrogen dioxide. The AQI runs from 0 to 500. The higher the AQI value, the greater the level of air pollution and the greater the health concern.
Source: U.S. Environmental Protection Agency, Air Quality Index Report, 2017

Maximum Air Pollutant Concentrations: Particulate Matter, Ozone, CO and Lead

	Particulate Matter 10 (ug/m^3)	Particulate Matter 2.5 Wtd AM (ug/m^3)	Particulate Matter 2.5 24-Hr (ug/m^3)	Ozone (ppm)	Carbon Monoxide (ppm)	Lead (ug/m^3)
MSA[1] Level	104	9	24	0.075	5	0.02
NAAQS[2]	150	15	35	0.075	9	0.15
Met NAAQS[2]	Yes	Yes	Yes	Yes	Yes	Yes

Note: (1) Data covers the El Paso, TX Metropolitan Statistical Area—see Appendix B for areas included; Data from exceptional events are included; (2) National Ambient Air Quality Standards; ppm = parts per million; ug/m^3 = micrograms per cubic meter; n/a not available.
Concentrations: Particulate Matter 10 (coarse particulate)—highest second maximum 24-hour concentration; Particulate Matter 2.5 Wtd AM (fine particulate)—highest weighted annual mean concentration; Particulate Matter 2.5 24-Hour (fine particulate)—highest 98th percentile 24-hour concentration; Ozone—highest fourth daily maximum 8-hour concentration; Carbon Monoxide—highest second maximum non-overlapping 8-hour concentration; Lead—maximum running 3-month average
Source: U.S. Environmental Protection Agency, Air Quality Monitoring Information, "Air Quality Statistics by City, 2017"

Maximum Air Pollutant Concentrations: Nitrogen Dioxide and Sulfur Dioxide

	Nitrogen Dioxide AM (ppb)	Nitrogen Dioxide 1-Hr (ppb)	Sulfur Dioxide AM (ppb)	Sulfur Dioxide 1-Hr (ppb)	Sulfur Dioxide 24-Hr (ppb)
MSA[1] Level	10	58	n/a	5	n/a
NAAQS[2]	53	100	30	75	140
Met NAAQS[2]	Yes	Yes	n/a	Yes	n/a

Note: (1) Data covers the El Paso, TX Metropolitan Statistical Area—see Appendix B for areas included; Data from exceptional events are included; (2) National Ambient Air Quality Standards; ppm = parts per million; ug/m³ = micrograms per cubic meter; n/a not available.
Concentrations: Nitrogen Dioxide AM—highest arithmetic mean concentration; Nitrogen Dioxide 1-Hr—highest 98th percentile 1-hour daily maximum concentration; Sulfur Dioxide AM—highest annual mean concentration; Sulfur Dioxide 1-Hr—highest 99th percentile 1-hour daily maximum concentration; Sulfur Dioxide 24-Hr—highest second maximum 24-hour concentration
Source: U.S. Environmental Protection Agency, Air Quality Monitoring Information, "Air Quality Statistics by City, 2017"

Drinking Water

Water System Name	Pop. Served	Primary Water Source Type	Violations[1] Health Based	Violations[1] Monitoring/ Reporting
El Paso Water Utilities	672,538	Surface	0	0

Note: (1) Based on violation data from January 1, 2018 to December 31, 2018
Source: U.S. Environmental Protection Agency, Office of Ground Water and Drinking Water, Safe Drinking Water Information System (based on data extracted April 5, 2019)

Fort Worth, Texas

Background

Fort Worth lies in north central Texas near the headwaters of the Trinity River. Despite its modern skyscrapers, multiple freeways, shopping malls, and extensive industry, the city is known for its easygoing, Western atmosphere.

The area has seen many travelers. Nomadic Native Americans of the plains rode through on horses bred from those brought by Spanish explorers. The 1840s saw American-Anglos settle in the region. On June 6, 1849, Major Ripley A. Arnold and his U.S. Cavalry troop established an outpost on the Trinity River to protect settlers moving westward. The fort was named for General William J. Worth, Commander of the U.S. Army's Texas department. When the fort was abandoned in 1853, settlers moved in and converted the vacant barracks into trading establishments and homes, stealing the county seat from Birdville (an act made legal in the 1860 election).

In the 1860s, Fort Worth, which was close to the Chisholm Trail, became an oasis for cowboys traveling to and from Kansas. Although the town's growth virtually stopped during the Civil War, Fort Worth was incorporated as a city in 1873. In a race against time, the final 26 miles of the Texas & Pacific Line were completed and Fort Worth survived to be a part of the West Texas oil boom in 1917.

Real prosperity followed at the end of World War II, when the city became a center for a number of military installations. Aviation is the city's principal source of economic growth. The city's leading industries include the manufacture of aircraft, automobiles, machinery, and containers, as well as food processing and brewing. Emerging economic sectors in the 21st century include semiconductor manufacturing, and communications equipment manufacturing and distribution.

Since it first began testing DNA samples in 2003, the DNA Identity Laboratory at the University of North Texas Health Science Center has made over 100 matches, helping to solve missing-persons cases and close criminal cases. The university is also home to the national Osteopathic Research Center, the only academic DNA Lab qualified to work with the FBI, the Texas Center for Health Disparities and the Health Institutes of Texas. Other colleges in Fort Worth include Texas Christian University, Southwestern Baptist Seminary, and Texas Wesleyan University.

Fort Worth's most comprehensive mixed-use project at Walsh Ranch was completed in 2017 with space for residential, commercial, office and retail. The 7,275-acre planned community is named after the original owners of the property, F. Howard and Mary D. Walsh, who were well-known ranchers, philanthropists and civic leaders. Walsh Ranch has room for 50,000 Fort Worth residents.

The Omni Fort Worth Hotel was host to the 2011 AFC champion Pittsburgh Steelers during Super Bowl XLV.

The city's 3,600-acre Greer Island Nature Center and Refuge just celebrated its 55th year.

Winter temperatures and rainfall are both modified by the northeast-northwest mountain barrier, which prevents shallow cold air masses from crossing over from the west. Summer temperatures vary with cloud and shower activity, but are generally mild. Summer precipitation is largely from local thunderstorms and varies from year to year. Damaging rains are infrequent. Hurricanes have produced heavy rainfall, but are usually not accompanied by destructive winds.

Rankings

General Rankings

- For its "Best for Vets: Places to Live 2019" rankings, *Military Times* evaluated 599 cities (83 large, 234 medium, 282 small) and compared the locations across three broad categories: veteran and military culture/services; economic indicators; and livability factors such as health, crime, traffic, and school quality. Fort Worth ranked #22 out of the top 25, in the large city category (populations of more than 250,000). Data points more specific to veterans and the military weighed more heavily than the rest. *rebootcamp.militarytimes.com, "Military Times Best Places to Live 2019," September 10, 2018*

- *US News & World Report* conducted a survey of more than 2,000 people and analyzed the 125 largest metropolitan areas to determine what matters the most when selecting the next place to live. Dallas ranked #18 out of the top 25 as having the best combination of desirable factors. Criteria: cost of living; quality of education; job market, crime rates; and other factors. *realestate.usnews.com, "The 25 Best Places to Live in the U.S. in 2018," April 10, 2018*

- The Dallas metro area was identified as one of America's fastest-growing areas in terms of population and business growth by *MagnifyMoney*. The area ranked #7 out of 35. The 100 most populous metro areas in the U.S. were evaluated on their change from 2011-2016 in the following categories: people and housing; workforce and employment opportunities; growing industry. *www.businessinsider.com, "The 35 Cities in the US with the Biggest Influx of People, the Most Work Opportunities, and the Hottest Business Growth," August 12, 2018*

- The Fort Worth metro area was identified as one of America's fastest-growing areas in terms of population and economy by *Forbes*. The area ranked #5 out of 25. The 100 most populous metro areas in the U.S. were evaluated on the following criteria: estimated population growth; employment; economic output; wages; home values. *Forbes, "America's Fastest-Growing Cities 2018," February 28, 2018*

- Fort Worth was identified as one of America's fastest-growing cities in terms of population growth by CNNMoney.com. The area ranked #9 out of 10. Criteria: population growth between July 2015 and July 2016; cities and towns with populations of 50,000. *CNNMoney, "10 Fastest-Growing Cities," June 2, 2017*

- In its eighth annual survey, *Travel + Leisure* readers nominated their favorite small cities and towns in America—those with 100,000 or fewer residents—voting on numerous attractive features in categories including culture, food and drink, quality of life, style, and people. After 50,000 votes, Fort Worth was ranked #18 among the proposed favorites. *www.travelandleisure.com, "America's Favorite Cities," October 20, 2017*

- The U.S. Conference of Mayors and Waste Management, Inc. sponsor the City Livability Awards Program, which recognize mayors for exemplary leadership in developing and implementing specific programs that improve the quality of life in America's cities. Fort Worth received an Outstanding Achievement Award in the large cities category. *U.S. Conference of Mayors, "2018 City Livability Awards"*

- In their sixth annual survey, Livability.com looked at data for more than 1,000 U.S. cities to determine the rankings for Livability's "Top 100 Best Places to Live" in 2019. Fort Worth ranked #88. Criteria: median home value capped at $250,000; affordable living; vibrant economy; education, demographics, health care options. transportation & infrastructure; abundant lifestyle amenities. *Livability.com, "Top 100 Best Places to Live 2019" March 2019*

Business/Finance Rankings

- According to *Business Insider*, the Dallas metro area is where startup growth is on the rise. Based on the 2017 Kauffman Index of Growth Entrepreneurship, which measured in-depth national entrepreneurial trends in 40 metro areas, it ranked #11 in highest startup growth. *www.businessinsider.com, "The 21 U.S. Cities with the Highest Startup Growth," October 21, 2017*

- The personal finance site NerdWallet analyzed 183 American metropolitan areas with populations over 250,000 and more than 15,000 businesses to rank where entrepreneurs find the most success. Criteria included area economy, annual income, housing cost, unemployment rate, and the success rate of area businesses. Fort Worth ranked #117. *www.nerdwallet.com, "Best Places to Start a Business," April 27, 2015*

- Fort Worth was the #8-ranked city for savers, according to a study by the finance site GOBankingRates, which considered the prospects for people trying to save money. Criteria: average monthly cost of grocery items; median home listing price; median rent; median income; unemployment rate; gas prices; and sales tax in the nation's 60 largest cities. *www.gobankingrates.com, "Best Cities for Saving Money," June 22, 2018*

- Fort Worth was ranked #8 among the nation's 60 largest cities for most difficult conditions for savers, according to a study by the finance site GOBankingRates. Criteria: average monthly cost of grocery items; median home listing price; median rent; median income; unemployment rate; gas prices; and sales tax. *www.gobankingrates.com, "Worst Cities for Saving Money," June 22, 2018*

- Recognizing the sizeable percentage of American workers who are self-employed, NerdWallet editors assessed the country's cities according to percentage of freelancers, median rental costs, cell phone plans/taxes, and healthcare affordability and access. By these criteria, Fort Worth placed #8 among the best cities for independent workers. *www.nerdwallet.com, "Best Places for Freelance Workers," August 30, 2016*

- USAA and Hiring Our Heroes worked with Sperlings's BestPlaces and the Institute for Veterans and Military Families at Syracuse University to rank major metropolitan areas where military-skills-related employment is strongest. Criteria for *mid-career* veterans included veteran wage growth; recent job growth; stability; and accessible health resources. Metro areas with a higher than national average crime or unemployment rate were excluded. At #9, the Dallas metro area made the top ten. *www.usaa.com, "2015 Best Places for Veterans"*

- In a survey of economic confidence in the nation's 50 largest metropolitan areas conducted January–December 2014, the Dallas metro area placed #14, according to Gallup's 2014 Economic Confidence Index. *Gallup, "San Jose and San Francisco Lead in Economic Confidence," March 19, 2015*

- Using data from the Council for Community and Economic Research's 2014 cost of living index, NerdWallet ranked the 100 most affordable cities in America. Median income was compared with cost of living to find truly affordable places. Fort Worth ranked #39. *NerdWallet.com, "America's Most Affordable Places," May 18, 2015*

- NerdWallet.com identified the 10 most promising cities for job seekers of the nation's 100 largest cities. Fort Worth was ranked #20. Criteria: job availability; annual salary; workforce growth; affordability. *NerdWallet.com, "Best Cities for Job Seekers in 2017," December 19, 2016*

- The Brookings Institution ranked the 100 largest metro areas in the U.S. based on income inequality. Dallas was ranked #60 (#1 = greatest inequality). Criteria: the "95/20 ratio," a figure representing the income at which a household earns more than 95 percent of all other households, divided by the income at which a household earns more than only 20 percent of all other households. *Brookings Institution, "Household Income Inequality, 100 Largest U.S. Metro Areas, 2014-2016," February 5, 2018*

- *Forbes* ranked the 100 largest metro areas in the U.S. in terms of the "Best Cities for Young Professionals." The Dallas metro area ranked #5 out of 25. (Large metro areas were divided into metro divisions.) Criteria: median rent of a two-bedroom apartment; job growth and unemployment rate; median salary of college graduates with 5 or less years of work experience; networking opportunities; social outlook; percentage of population 25 years of age and older with college degrees. *Forbes.com, "America's 25 Best Cities for Young Professionals in 2017," May 22, 2017*

- Payscale.com ranked the 32 largest metro areas in terms of wage growth. The Dallas metro area ranked #24. Criteria: private-sector wage growth between the 4th quarter of 2017 and the 4th quarter of 2018. *PayScale, "Wage Trends by Metro Area-4th Quarter," January 8, 2019*

- The Dallas metro area was identified as one of the most debt-ridden places in America by the finance site Credit.com. The metro area was ranked #2. Criteria: residents' average credit card debt as well as median income. *Credit.com, "25 Cities With the Most Credit Card Debt," February 28, 2018*

- Dallas was identified as one of America's most frugal metro areas by *Coupons.com*. The city ranked #2 out of 25. Criteria: digital coupon usage. *Coupons.com, "America's Most Frugal Cities of 2017," March 22, 2018*

- Fort Worth was cited as one of America's top metros for new and expanded facility projects in 2018. The area ranked #2 in the large metro area category (population over 1 million). *Site Selection, "Top Metros of 2018," March 2019*

- Fort Worth was identified as one of the unhappiest cities to work in by CareerBliss.com, an online community for career advancement. The city ranked #2 out of 5. Criteria: an employee's relationship with his or her boss and co-workers; general work environment; compensation; opportunities for advancement; company culture and job reputation; and resources. *Businesswire.com, "CareerBliss Unhappiest Cities to Work 2019," February 12, 2019*

- The Fort Worth metro area appeared on the Milken Institute "2018 Best Performing Cities" list. Rank: #70 out of 200 large metro areas. Criteria: job growth; wage and salary growth; high-tech output growth. *Milken Institute, "Best-Performing Cities 2018," January 24, 2019*

- *Forbes* ranked the 200 most populous metro areas to determine the nation's "Best Places for Business and Careers." The Fort Worth metro area was ranked #36. Criteria: costs (business and living); job growth (past and projected); income growth; quality of life; educational attainment (college and high school); projected economic growth; cultural and recreational opportunities; net migration patterns; number of highly ranked colleges. *Forbes, "The Best Places for Business and Careers 2018: Seattle Leads the Way," October 24, 2018*

Culture/Performing Arts Rankings

- Fort Worth was selected as one of "America's Favorite Cities." The city ranked #15 in the "Architecture" category. Respondents to an online survey were asked to rate their favorite place (population over 100,000) in over 65 categories. *Travelandleisure.com, "America's Favorite Cities for Architecture 2016," March 2, 2017*

Education Rankings

- Personal finance website *WalletHub* analyzed the 150 largest U.S. metropolitan statistical areas to determine where the most educated Americans are choosing to settle. Criteria: education quality and attainment gap; education levels; percentage of workers with degrees; public school quality rankings; quality and size of each metro area's universities. Fort Worth was ranked #77 (#1 = most educated city). *www.WalletHub.com, "2018's Most and Least Educated Cities in America," July 24, 2018*

- Fort Worth was selected as one of America's most literate cities. The city ranked #64 out of the 82 largest U.S. cities. Criteria: number of booksellers; library resources; Internet resources; educational attainment; periodical publishing resources; newspaper circulation. *Central Connecticut State University, "America's Most Literate Cities, 2016," March 31, 2017*

Environmental Rankings

- Sperling's BestPlaces assessed the 50 largest metropolitan areas of the United States for the likelihood of dangerously extreme weather events or earthquakes. In general the Southeast and South-Central regions have the highest risk of weather extremes and earthquakes, while the Pacific Northwest enjoys the lowest risk. Of the most risky metropolitan areas, the Fort Worth metro area was ranked #4. *www.bestplaces.net, "Avoid Natural Disasters: BestPlaces Reveals The Top 10 Safest Places to Live," October 25, 2017*

- The U.S. Environmental Protection Agency (EPA) released a list of U.S. metropolitan areas with the most ENERGY STAR certified buildings in 2017. The Dallas metro area was ranked #3 out of 25. *U.S. Environmental Protection Agency, "2018 Energy Star Top Cities," April 11, 2018*

- Fort Worth was highlighted as one of the 25 most ozone-polluted metro areas in the U.S. during 2014 through 2016. The area ranked #16. *American Lung Association, State of the Air 2018*

- Fort Worth was highlighted as one of the top 90 cleanest metro areas for short-term particle pollution (24-hour PM 2.5) in the U.S. during 2014 through 2016. Monitors in these cities reported no days with unhealthful PM 2.5 levels. *American Lung Association, State of the Air 2018*

Food/Drink Rankings

- *Men's Health* ranked 100 major U.S. cities in terms of alcohol intoxication. Fort Worth ranked #55 (#1 = most sober).Criteria: binge drinking; alcohol-related traffic accidents, arrests, and fatalities. *Men's Health, "America's Drunkest Cities," March 9, 2015*

- Globe Life Park was selected as one of PETA's "Top 10 Vegan-Friendly Ballparks" for 2018. The park ranked #2. *People for the Ethical Treatment of Animals, "Top 10 Vegan-Friendly Ballparks," June 4, 2018*

Health/Fitness Rankings

- For each of the 100 largest cities in the United States, the American College of Sports Medicine's American Fitness Index evaluated infrastructure, community assets, and policies that encourage healthy and fit lifestyles, including preventive health behaviors, levels of chronic disease conditions, health care access, and community resources and policies that support physical activity. Fort Worth ranked #56 for "community fitness." *www.americanfitnessindex.org, "ACSM American Fitness Index Health and Community Fitness Status of the 100 Largest U.S. Cities," May 2018*

- The Dallas metro area was identified as one of the worst cities for bed bugs in America by pest control company Orkin. The area ranked #15 out of 50 based on the number of bed bug treatments Orkin performed from December 2017 to November 2018. *Orkin, "Baltimore Remains Front Runner, Atlanta and Philadelphia Break Into Top 10," January 14, 2019*

- Dallas was identified as a "2018 Spring Allergy Capital." The area ranked #31 out of 100. Three groups of factors were used to identify the most challenging cities for people with allergies during the spring season: annual pollen levels; medicine utilization; access to board-certified allergists. *Asthma and Allergy Foundation of America, "Spring Allergy Capitals 2018"*

- Dallas was identified as a "2018 Fall Allergy Capital." The area ranked #25 out of 100. Three groups of factors were used to identify the most challenging cities for people with allergies during the fall season: annual pollen levels; medicine utilization; access to board-certified allergists. *Asthma and Allergy Foundation of America, "Fall Allergy Capitals 2018"*

- Dallas was identified as a "2018 Asthma Capital." The area ranked #77 out of the nation's 100 largest metropolitan areas. Criteria: estimated prevalence; self-reported prevalence; crude death rate for asthma; annual pollen score; annual air quality; public smoking laws; number of board-certified asthma specialists; school inhaler access laws; rescue medication use; controller medication use; ER visits for asthma; uninsured rate; poverty rate. *Asthma and Allergy Foundation of America, "Asthma Capitals 2018: The Most Challenging Places to Live With Asthma"*

- *Men's Health* ranked 100 major U.S. cities in terms of the best cities for men. Fort Worth ranked #49. Criteria: health; fitness; quality of life. *Men's Health, "The Best & Worst Cities for Men Who Want to Be Fit and Happy," January 1, 2016*

- The Dallas metro area ranked #47 out of 189 in The Gallup-Healthways Well-Being Index. Criteria: purpose; social well being; financial health; community and physical health. Results are based on telephone interviews with adults, aged 18 and older, living in metropolitan areas in the 50 U.S. states and the District of Columbia. *Gallup-Healthways, "State of American Well-Being, 2017 Community Well-Being Rankings" March 2018*

Real Estate Rankings

- FitSmallBusiness looked at 50 of the largest metropolitan areas in the U.S. to determine which metro was the best to start a real estate business. Data was compiled from such sources as: Zillow, Trulia, U.S. Census Bureau, and the Bureau of Labor Statistics. Criteria: location; inventory; annual wages; median sales price of homes; days on the market; median price cut percentage; and other factors that would influence real estate professional growth. The Dallas metro area ranked #19. *fitsmallbusiness.com, "The Best Cities to Become a Real Estate Agent in 2018," January 30, 2018*

- *WalletHub* compared the most populated U.S. cities, as well as at least two of the most populated cities in each state, for a total of 179, to determine which had the best markets for real estate agents. Fort Worth ranked #98 where demand was high and pay was the best. Criteria: sales per agent; annual median wage for real-estate agents; monthly average starting salary for real estate agents; real estate job density and competition; unemployment rate; housing-market health index; and other relevant metrics. *www.WalletHub.com, "2018's Best Places to Be a Real Estate Agent," April 25, 2018*

- The Fort Worth metro area was identified as one of the nations's 20 hottest housing markets in 2019. Criteria: listing views as an indicator of demand and median days on the market as an indicator of supply. The area ranked #11. *Realtor.com, "January Top 20 Hottest Housing Markets," February 11, 2019*

- The Fort Worth metro area was identified as one of the top 20 housing markets to invest in for 2019 by *Forbes*. Criteria: strong job and population growth; stable local economy; anticipated home price appreciation; and other factors. *Forbes.com, "The Best Markets for Real Estate Investments In 2019," January 7, 2019*

- Fort Worth was ranked #157 out of 237 metro areas in terms of housing affordability in 2018 by the National Association of Home Builders (#1 = most affordable). Criteria: the share of homes sold in that area affordable to a family earning the local median income, based on standard mortgage underwriting criteria. *National Association of Home Builders®, NAHB-Wells Fargo Housing Opportunity Index, 4th Quarter 2018*

Safety Rankings

- Allstate ranked the 200 largest cities in America in terms of driver safety. Fort Worth ranked #139. Criteria: internal property damage claims over a two-year period from January 2015 to December 2016. The report helps increase the importance of safety awareness behind the wheel. *Allstate, "Allstate America's Best Drivers Report, 2018" August 28, 2018*

- The National Insurance Crime Bureau ranked 382 metro areas in the U.S. in terms of per capita rates of vehicle theft. The Fort Worth metro area ranked #88 (#1 = highest rate). Criteria: number of vehicle theft offenses per 100,000 inhabitants in 2017. *National Insurance Crime Bureau, "Hot Spots 2017," July 12, 2018*

Seniors/Retirement Rankings

- From its Best Cities for Successful Aging indexes, the Milken Institute generated rankings for metropolitan areas, weighing data in nine categories—health care, wellness, living arrangements, transportation and convenience, financial characteristics, education, employment, community engagement, and overall livability. The Dallas metro area was ranked #25 overall in the large metro area category. *Milken Institute, "Best Cities for Successful Aging, 2017" March 14, 2017*

Women/Minorities Rankings

- The *Houston Chronicle* listed the Dallas metro area as #7 in top places for young Latinos to live in the U.S. Research was largely based on housing and occupational data from the largest metropolitan areas performed by *Forbes* and NBC Universo. Criteria: percentage of 18-34 year-olds; Latino college grad rates; and diversity. *blog.chron.com, "The 15 Best Big Cities for Latino Millenials," January 26, 2016*

- Personal finance website *WalletHub* compared more than 180 U.S. cities—including the 150 most populated U.S. cities, plus at least two of the most populated cities in each state—across two key dimensions, "Hispanic Business-Friendliness" and "Hispanic Purchasing Power", to arrive at the most favorable conditions for Hispanic entrepreneurs. Fort Worth was ranked #18 out of 182. Criteria includes: share of Hispanic-Owned Businesses; Hispanic entrepreneurship rate to median annual income of Hispanics; Small Business-Friendliness score; cost of living; and number of Hispanics with at least a bachelor's degree. *WalletHub.com, "2018's Best Cities for Hispanic Entrepreneurs," April 26, 2018*

Miscellaneous Rankings

- The watchdog site Charity Navigator conducts an annual study of charities in the nation's major markets both to analyze statistical differences in their financial, accountability, and transparency practices and to track year-to-year variations in individual philanthropic communities. Charity Navigator's analysis demonstrated that the financial, accountability and transparency behaviors of America's largest charities can be influenced by the metropolitan market within which the charity operates. The Dallas metro area was ranked #5 among the 30 metro markets in the rating category of Overall Score. *www.charitynavigator.org, "2017 Metro Market Study," May 1, 2017*

- *WalletHub* compared the 150 most populated U.S. cities to determine their operating efficiency. A "Quality of Services" score was constructed for each city and then divided by the total budget per capita to reveal which were managed the best. Fort Worth ranked #45. Criteria: financial stability; economy; education; safety; health; infrastructure and pollution. *www.WalletHub.com, "2018's Best- & Worst-Run Cities in America," July 9, 2018*

- Fort Worth was selected as one of "America's Friendliest Cities." The city ranked #9 in the "Friendliest" category. Respondents to an online survey were asked to rate 38 top urban destinations in the United States as to general friendliness, as well as manners, politeness and warm disposition. *Travel + Leisure, "America's Friendliest Cities," October 20, 2017*

- The National Alliance to End Homelessness listed the 25 most populous metro areas with the highest rate of homelessness. The Dallas metro area had a high rate of homelessness. Criteria: number of homeless people per 10,000 population in 2016. *National Alliance to End Homelessness, "Homelessness in the 25 Most Populous U.S. Metro Areas," September 1, 2017*

Business Environment

CITY FINANCES

City Government Finances

Component	2016 ($000)	2016 ($ per capita)
Total Revenues	1,495,618	1,795
Total Expenditures	1,594,692	1,914
Debt Outstanding	1,678,773	2,015
Cash and Securities[1]	3,867,557	4,641

Note: (1) Cash and security holdings of a government at the close of its fiscal year, including those of its dependent agencies, utilities, and liquor stores.
Source: U.S. Census Bureau, State & Local Government Finances 2016

City Government Revenue by Source

Source	2016 ($000)	2016 ($ per capita)	2016 (%)
General Revenue			
From Federal Government	30,969	37	2.1
From State Government	69,130	83	4.6
From Local Governments	416	0	0.0
Taxes			
Property	419,631	504	28.1
Sales and Gross Receipts	288,088	346	19.3
Personal Income	0	0	0.0
Corporate Income	0	0	0.0
Motor Vehicle License	0	0	0.0
Other Taxes	22,076	26	1.5
Current Charges	294,817	354	19.7
Liquor Store	0	0	0.0
Utility	219,790	264	14.7
Employee Retirement	19,426	23	1.3

Source: U.S. Census Bureau, State & Local Government Finances 2016

City Government Expenditures by Function

Function	2016 ($000)	2016 ($ per capita)	2016 (%)
General Direct Expenditures			
Air Transportation	29,068	34	1.8
Corrections	0	0	0.0
Education	0	0	0.0
Employment Security Administration	0	0	0.0
Financial Administration	11,038	13	0.7
Fire Protection	126,387	151	7.9
General Public Buildings	6,500	7	0.4
Governmental Administration, Other	26,428	31	1.7
Health	11,713	14	0.7
Highways	134,454	161	8.4
Hospitals	0	0	0.0
Housing and Community Development	19,272	23	1.2
Interest on General Debt	67,519	81	4.2
Judicial and Legal	22,613	27	1.4
Libraries	19,540	23	1.2
Parking	3,463	4	0.2
Parks and Recreation	85,393	102	5.4
Police Protection	265,845	319	16.7
Public Welfare	0	0	0.0
Sewerage	200,928	241	12.6
Solid Waste Management	49,193	59	3.1
Veterans' Services	0	0	0.0
Liquor Store	0	0	0.0
Utility	214,842	257	13.5
Employee Retirement	152,299	182	9.6

Source: U.S. Census Bureau, State & Local Government Finances 2016

DEMOGRAPHICS

Population Growth

Area	1990 Census	2000 Census	2010 Census	2017* Estimate	Population Growth (%) 1990-2017	2010-2017
City	448,311	534,694	741,206	835,129	86.3	12.7
MSA[1]	3,989,294	5,161,544	6,371,773	7,104,415	78.1	11.5
U.S.	248,709,873	281,421,906	308,745,538	321,004,407	29.1	4.0

Note: (1) Figures cover the Dallas-Fort Worth-Arlington, TX Metropolitan Statistical Area—see Appendix B for areas included; (*) 2013-2017 5-year estimated population
Source: U.S. Census Bureau, 1990 Census, Census 2000, Census 2010, 2013-2017 American Community Survey 5-Year Estimates

Household Size

Area	One	Two	Three	Four	Five	Six	Seven or More	Average Household Size
City	26.5	28.8	16.0	14.9	8.1	3.4	2.3	2.90
MSA[1]	24.8	30.9	16.8	15.2	7.5	3.0	1.8	2.80
U.S.	27.7	33.8	15.7	13.0	6.0	2.3	1.4	2.60

Note: (1) Figures cover the Dallas-Fort Worth-Arlington, TX Metropolitan Statistical Area—see Appendix B for areas included
Source: U.S. Census Bureau, 2013-2017 American Community Survey 5-Year Estimates

Race

Area	White Alone[2] (%)	Black Alone[2] (%)	Asian Alone[2] (%)	AIAN[3] Alone[2] (%)	NHOPI[4] Alone[2] (%)	Other Race Alone[2] (%)	Two or More Races (%)
City	64.4	18.8	3.9	0.4	0.1	9.1	3.4
MSA[1]	69.4	15.4	6.3	0.4	0.1	5.4	2.9
U.S.	73.0	12.7	5.4	0.8	0.2	4.8	3.1

Note: (1) Figures cover the Dallas-Fort Worth-Arlington, TX Metropolitan Statistical Area—see Appendix B for areas included; (2) Alone is defined as not being in combination with one or more other races; (3) American Indian and Alaska Native; (4) Native Hawaiian and Other Pacific Islander
Source: U.S. Census Bureau, 2013-2017 American Community Survey 5-Year Estimates

Hispanic or Latino Origin

Area	Total (%)	Mexican (%)	Puerto Rican (%)	Cuban (%)	Other (%)
City	34.8	30.8	1.0	0.2	2.8
MSA[1]	28.4	23.8	0.7	0.2	3.7
U.S.	17.6	11.1	1.7	0.7	4.1

Note: Persons of Hispanic or Latino origin can be of any race; (1) Figures cover the Dallas-Fort Worth-Arlington, TX Metropolitan Statistical Area—see Appendix B for areas included
Source: U.S. Census Bureau, 2013-2017 American Community Survey 5-Year Estimates

Segregation

Type	1990	2000	2010	2010 Rank[2]	1990-2000	1990-2010	2000-2010
Black/White	62.8	59.8	56.6	48	-3.1	-6.2	-3.2
Asian/White	41.8	45.6	46.6	19	3.8	4.8	1.0
Hispanic/White	48.8	52.3	50.3	24	3.5	1.5	-2.0

Note: All figures cover the Metropolitan Statistical Area—see Appendix B for areas included; Figures are based on an analysis of 1990, 2000, and 2010 Census Decennial Census tract data by William H. Frey, Brookings Institution and the University of Michigan Social Science Data Analysis Network. In this analysis all racial groups (whites, blacks, and asians) are non-Hispanic members of those races. Hispanics are shown as a separate category; (1) Segregation Indices are Dissimilarity Indices that measure the degree to which the minority group is distributed differently than whites across census tracts. They range from 0 (complete integration) to 100 (complete segregation) where the value indicates the percentage of the minority group that needs to move to be distributed exactly like whites; (2) Ranges from 1 (most segregated) to 102 (least segregated); n/a not available.
Source: www.CensusScope.org

Ancestry

Area	German	Irish	English	American	Italian	Polish	French[2]	Scottish	Dutch
City	8.4	6.8	6.0	5.2	1.9	1.0	1.8	1.5	0.7
MSA[1]	9.5	7.3	7.1	6.5	2.1	1.1	1.8	1.7	0.9
U.S.	14.1	10.1	7.5	6.6	5.3	2.9	2.5	1.7	1.3

Note: Figures are the percentage of the total population reporting a particular ancestry. The nine most commonly reported ancestries in the U.S. are shown. Figures include multiple ancestries (e.g. if a person reported being Irish and Italian, they were included in both columns); (1) Figures cover the Dallas-Fort Worth-Arlington, TX Metropolitan Statistical Area—see Appendix B for areas included; (2) Excludes Basque
Source: U.S. Census Bureau, 2013-2017 American Community Survey 5-Year Estimates

Foreign-Born Population

Area	Percent of Population Born in								
	Any Foreign Country	Asia	Mexico	Europe	Carribean	Central America[2]	South America	Africa	Canada
City	16.9	3.1	10.3	0.7	0.3	0.8	0.4	1.0	0.2
MSA[1]	18.1	4.9	8.7	0.8	0.3	1.4	0.5	1.3	0.2
U.S.	13.4	4.1	3.6	1.5	1.3	1.0	0.9	0.6	0.3

Note: (1) Figures cover the Dallas-Fort Worth-Arlington, TX Metropolitan Statistical Area—see Appendix B for areas included; (2) Excludes Mexico.
Source: U.S. Census Bureau, 2013-2017 American Community Survey 5-Year Estimates

Marital Status

Area	Never Married	Now Married[2]	Separated	Widowed	Divorced
City	34.9	45.9	2.5	4.6	12.1
MSA[1]	32.0	50.5	2.3	4.5	10.8
U.S.	33.1	48.2	2.0	5.8	10.9

Note: Figures are percentages and cover the population 15 years of age and older; (1) Figures cover the Dallas-Fort Worth-Arlington, TX Metropolitan Statistical Area—see Appendix B for areas included; (2) Excludes separated
Source: U.S. Census Bureau, 2013-2017 American Community Survey 5-Year Estimates

Disability by Age

Area	All Ages	Under 18 Years Old	18 to 64 Years Old	65 Years and Over
City	10.5	3.6	9.7	37.5
MSA[1]	9.6	3.4	8.1	34.9
U.S.	12.6	4.2	10.3	35.5

Note: Figures show percent of the civilian noninstitutionalized population that reported having a disability. Disability status is determined from six types of difficulty: vision, hearing, cognitive, ambulatory, self-care, and independent living. For children under 5 years old, hearing and vision difficulty are used to determine disability status. For children between the ages of 5 and 14, disability status is determined from hearing, vision, cognitive, ambulatory, and self-care difficulties. For people aged 15 years and older, they are considered to have a disability if they have difficulty with any one of the six difficulty types; Note: (1) Figures cover the Dallas-Fort Worth-Arlington, TX Metropolitan Statistical Area—see Appendix B for areas included
Source: U.S. Census Bureau, 2013-2017 American Community Survey 5-Year Estimates

Age

Area	Percent of Population									Median Age
	Under Age 5	Age 5–19	Age 20–34	Age 35–44	Age 45–54	Age 55–64	Age 65–74	Age 75–84	Age 85+	
City	8.1	23.0	23.5	14.0	12.4	9.8	5.6	2.6	1.1	32.2
MSA[1]	7.1	22.1	21.3	14.3	13.7	11.0	6.5	3.0	1.1	34.6
U.S.	6.2	19.5	20.7	12.7	13.4	12.7	8.6	4.4	1.9	37.8

Note: (1) Figures cover the Dallas-Fort Worth-Arlington, TX Metropolitan Statistical Area—see Appendix B for areas included
Source: U.S. Census Bureau, 2013-2017 American Community Survey 5-Year Estimates

Gender

Area	Males	Females	Males per 100 Females
City	408,803	426,326	95.9
MSA[1]	3,493,829	3,610,586	96.8
U.S.	158,018,753	162,985,654	97.0

Note: (1) Figures cover the Dallas-Fort Worth-Arlington, TX Metropolitan Statistical Area—see Appendix B for areas included
Source: U.S. Census Bureau, 2013-2017 American Community Survey 5-Year Estimates

Religious Groups by Family

Area	Catholic	Baptist	Non-Den.	Methodist[2]	Lutheran	LDS[3]	Pente-costal	Presby-terian[4]	Muslim[5]	Judaism
MSA[1]	13.3	18.7	7.8	5.3	0.8	1.2	2.2	1.0	2.4	0.4
U.S.	19.1	9.3	4.0	4.0	2.3	2.0	1.9	1.6	0.8	0.7

Note: Figures are the number of adherents as a percentage of the total population; (1) Figures cover the Dallas-Fort Worth-Arlington, TX Metropolitan Statistical Area—see Appendix B for areas included; (2) Methodist/Pietist; (3) Latter Day Saints; (4) Reformed; (5) Figures are estimates
Source: Association of Statisticians of American Religious Bodies, 2010 U.S. Religion Census: Religious Congregations & Membership Study

Religious Groups by Tradition

Area	Catholic	Evangelical Protestant	Mainline Protestant	Other Tradition	Black Protestant	Orthodox
MSA[1]	13.3	28.3	7.0	4.8	1.8	0.2
U.S.	19.1	16.2	7.3	4.3	1.6	0.3

Note: Figures are the number of adherents as a percentage of the total population; (1) Figures cover the Dallas-Fort Worth-Arlington, TX Metropolitan Statistical Area—see Appendix B for areas included
Source: Association of Statisticians of American Religious Bodies, 2010 U.S. Religion Census: Religious Congregations & Membership Study

ECONOMY

Gross Metropolitan Product

Area	2016	2017	2018	2019	Rank[2]
MSA[1]	506.8	541.1	579.3	613.4	4

Note: Figures are in billions of dollars; (1) Figures cover the Dallas-Fort Worth-Arlington, TX Metropolitan Statistical Area—see Appendix B for areas included; (2) Rank is based on 2017 data and ranges from 1 to 381
Source: U.S. Conference of Mayors, U.S. Metro Economies: Economic Growth & Full Employment, June 2018

Economic Growth

Area	2017-2018 (%)	2019-2020 (%)	2021-2022 (%)
MSA[1]	4.6	3.1	2.3

Note: Figures are real gross metropolitan product (GMP) growth rates and represent average annual percent change; (1) Figures cover the Dallas-Fort Worth-Arlington, TX Metropolitan Statistical Area—see Appendix B for areas included
Source: U.S. Conference of Mayors, U.S. Metro Economies: Economic Growth & Full Employment, June 2018

Metropolitan Area Exports

Area	2012	2013	2014	2015	2016	2017	Rank[2]
MSA[1]	27,820.9	27,596.0	28,669.4	27,372.9	27,187.8	30,269.1	9

Note: Figures are in millions of dollars; (1) Figures cover the Dallas-Fort Worth-Arlington, TX Metropolitan Statistical Area—see Appendix B for areas included; (2) Rank is based on 2017 data and ranges from 1 to 387
Source: U.S. Department of Commerce, International Trade Administration, Office of Trade and Economic Analysis, Industry and Analysis, Exports by Metropolitan Area, extracted March 25, 2019

Building Permits

Area	Single-Family			Multi-Family			Total		
	2016	2017	Pct. Chg.	2016	2017	Pct. Chg.	2016	2017	Pct. Chg.
City	3,459	5,042	45.8	3,949	3,814	-3.4	7,408	8,856	19.5
MSA[1]	29,703	34,604	16.5	26,097	27,920	7.0	55,800	62,524	12.1
U.S.	750,800	820,000	9.2	455,800	462,000	1.4	1,206,600	1,282,000	6.2

Note: (1) Figures cover the Dallas-Fort Worth-Arlington, TX Metropolitan Statistical Area—see Appendix B for areas included; Figures represent new, privately-owned housing units authorized (unadjusted data); All permit data are based on estimates with imputation
Source: U.S. Census Bureau, Manufacturing, Mining, and Construction Statistics, Building Permits, 2016, 2017

Bankruptcy Filings

Area	Business Filings			Nonbusiness Filings		
	2017	2018	% Chg.	2017	2018	% Chg.
Tarrant County	204	190	-6.9	3,983	4,009	0.7
U.S.	23,157	22,232	-4.0	765,863	751,186	-1.9

Note: Business filings include Chapter 7, Chapter 11, Chapter 12, and Chapter 13; Nonbusiness filings include Chapter 7, Chapter 11, and Chapter 13
Source: Administrative Office of the U.S. Courts, Business and Nonbusiness Bankruptcy, County Cases Commenced by Chapter of the Bankruptcy Code, During the 12-Month Period Ending December 31, 2017 and Business and Nonbusiness Bankruptcy, County Cases Commenced by Chapter of the Bankruptcy Code, During the 12-Month Period Ending December 31, 2018

Housing Vacancy Rates

Area	Gross Vacancy Rate[2] (%)			Year-Round Vacancy Rate[3] (%)			Rental Vacancy Rate[4] (%)			Homeowner Vacancy Rate[5] (%)		
	2016	2017	2018	2016	2017	2018	2016	2017	2018	2016	2017	2018
MSA[1]	7.9	7.8	7.8	7.7	7.6	7.6	6.8	7.1	7.4	1.4	0.8	1.4
U.S.	12.8	12.7	12.3	9.9	9.9	9.7	6.9	7.2	6.9	1.7	1.6	1.5

Note: (1) Figures cover the Dallas-Fort Worth-Arlington, TX Metropolitan Statistical Area—see Appendix B for areas included; (2) The percentage of the total housing inventory that is vacant; (3) The percentage of the housing inventory (excluding seasonal units) that is year-round vacant; (4) The percentage of rental inventory that is vacant for rent; (5) The percentage of homeowner inventory that is vacant for sale
Source: U.S. Census Bureau, Housing Vacancies and Homeownership Annual Statistics: 2016, 2017, 2018

INCOME

Income

Area	Per Capita ($)	Median Household ($)	Average Household ($)
City	27,191	57,309	76,309
MSA[1]	32,463	63,870	89,486
U.S.	31,177	57,652	81,283

Note: (1) Figures cover the Dallas-Fort Worth-Arlington, TX Metropolitan Statistical Area—see Appendix B for areas included
Source: U.S. Census Bureau, 2013-2017 American Community Survey 5-Year Estimates

Household Income Distribution

Area	Percent of Households Earning							
	Under $15,000	$15,000 -$24,999	$25,000 -$34,999	$35,000 -$49,999	$50,000 -$74,999	$75,000 -$99,999	$100,000 -$149,999	$150,000 and up
City	11.7	9.2	9.7	12.7	19.0	13.2	14.5	9.9
MSA[1]	8.9	8.3	9.0	12.7	18.2	12.6	15.6	14.6
U.S.	11.6	9.8	9.5	13.0	17.7	12.3	14.1	12.1

Note: (1) Figures cover the Dallas-Fort Worth-Arlington, TX Metropolitan Statistical Area—see Appendix B for areas included
Source: U.S. Census Bureau, 2013-2017 American Community Survey 5-Year Estimates

Poverty Rate

Area	All Ages	Under 18 Years Old	18 to 64 Years Old	65 Years and Over
City	16.9	23.4	14.7	11.1
MSA[1]	13.3	19.2	11.7	8.4
U.S.	14.6	20.3	13.7	9.3

Note: Figures are percentage of people whose income during the past 12 months was below the poverty level; (1) Figures cover the Dallas-Fort Worth-Arlington, TX Metropolitan Statistical Area—see Appendix B for areas included
Source: U.S. Census Bureau, 2013-2017 American Community Survey 5-Year Estimates

EMPLOYMENT

Labor Force and Employment

Area	Civilian Labor Force			Workers Employed		
	Dec. 2017	Dec. 2018	% Chg.	Dec. 2017	Dec. 2018	% Chg.
City	416,976	430,412	3.2	403,226	415,732	3.1
MD[1]	1,241,227	1,280,488	3.2	1,201,876	1,238,690	3.1
U.S.	159,880,000	162,510,000	1.6	153,602,000	156,481,000	1.9

Note: Data is not seasonally adjusted and covers workers 16 years of age and older; (1) Figures cover the Fort Worth-Arlington, TX Metropolitan Division—see Appendix B for areas included
Source: Bureau of Labor Statistics, Local Area Unemployment Statistics

Unemployment Rate

Area	2018											
	Jan.	Feb.	Mar.	Apr.	May	Jun.	Jul.	Aug.	Sep.	Oct.	Nov.	Dec.
City	3.8	3.8	3.9	3.5	3.5	4.0	3.9	3.8	3.5	3.3	3.3	3.4
MD[1]	3.6	3.6	3.7	3.3	3.4	3.8	3.7	3.6	3.4	3.2	3.2	3.3
U.S.	4.5	4.4	4.1	3.7	3.6	4.2	4.1	3.9	3.6	3.5	3.5	3.7

Note: Data is not seasonally adjusted and covers workers 16 years of age and older; (1) Figures cover the Fort Worth-Arlington, TX Metropolitan Division—see Appendix B for areas included
Source: Bureau of Labor Statistics, Local Area Unemployment Statistics

Average Wages

Occupation	$/Hr.	Occupation	$/Hr.
Accountants and Auditors	39.60	Maids and Housekeeping Cleaners	11.00
Automotive Mechanics	20.70	Maintenance and Repair Workers	20.40
Bookkeepers	21.20	Marketing Managers	67.10
Carpenters	19.00	Nuclear Medicine Technologists	39.20
Cashiers	10.70	Nurses, Licensed Practical	24.40
Clerks, General Office	17.50	Nurses, Registered	35.70
Clerks, Receptionists/Information	13.80	Nursing Assistants	13.40
Clerks, Shipping/Receiving	16.00	Packers and Packagers, Hand	12.50
Computer Programmers	47.00	Physical Therapists	46.00
Computer Systems Analysts	45.80	Postal Service Mail Carriers	25.20
Computer User Support Specialists	24.90	Real Estate Brokers	39.90
Cooks, Restaurant	12.30	Retail Salespersons	12.80
Dentists	91.50	Sales Reps., Exc. Tech./Scientific	33.80
Electrical Engineers	50.40	Sales Reps., Tech./Scientific	43.50
Electricians	22.70	Secretaries, Exc. Legal/Med./Exec.	18.40
Financial Managers	76.80	Security Guards	14.50
First-Line Supervisors/Managers, Sales	23.10	Surgeons	109.70
Food Preparation Workers	11.10	Teacher Assistants*	11.40
General and Operations Managers	63.80	Teachers, Elementary School*	28.60
Hairdressers/Cosmetologists	11.70	Teachers, Secondary School*	29.40
Internists, General	59.70	Telemarketers	15.70
Janitors and Cleaners	12.70	Truck Drivers, Heavy/Tractor-Trailer	23.00
Landscaping/Groundskeeping Workers	13.80	Truck Drivers, Light/Delivery Svcs.	19.30
Lawyers	77.30	Waiters and Waitresses	11.00

Note: Wage data covers the Dallas-Fort Worth-Arlington, TX Metropolitan Statistical Area—see Appendix B for areas included; (*) Hourly wages for elementary/secondary school teachers and teacher assistants were calculated by the editors from annual wage data based on a 40 hour work week; n/a not available.
Source: Bureau of Labor Statistics, Metro Area Occupational Employment & Wage Estimates, May 2018

Employment by Occupation

Occupation Classification	City (%)	MSA[1] (%)	U.S. (%)
Management, Business, Science, and Arts	34.9	38.7	37.4
Natural Resources, Construction, and Maintenance	10.3	9.4	8.9
Production, Transportation, and Material Moving	14.0	11.6	12.2
Sales and Office	23.7	24.6	23.5
Service	17.2	15.7	18.0

Note: Figures cover employed civilians 16 years of age and older; (1) Figures cover the Dallas-Fort Worth-Arlington, TX Metropolitan Statistical Area—see Appendix B for areas included
Source: U.S. Census Bureau, 2013-2017 American Community Survey 5-Year Estimates

Employment by Industry

| Sector | MD[1] | | U.S. |
	Number of Employees	Percent of Total	Percent of Total
Construction, Mining, and Logging	75,600	7.0	5.3
Education and Health Services	139,000	12.9	15.9
Financial Activities	62,600	5.8	5.7
Government	140,400	13.0	15.1
Information	11,100	1.0	1.9
Leisure and Hospitality	122,800	11.4	10.7
Manufacturing	101,700	9.4	8.5
Other Services	38,300	3.5	3.9
Professional and Business Services	114,900	10.6	14.1
Retail Trade	125,600	11.6	10.8
Transportation, Warehousing, and Utilities	92,900	8.6	4.2
Wholesale Trade	54,600	5.1	3.9

Note: Figures are non-farm employment as of December 2018. Figures are not seasonally adjusted and include workers 16 years of age and older; (1) Figures cover the Fort Worth-Arlington, TX Metropolitan Division—see Appendix B for areas included
Source: Bureau of Labor Statistics, Current Employment Statistics, Employment, Hours, and Earnings

Occupations with Greatest Projected Employment Growth: 2018 – 2020

Occupation[1]	2018 Employment	2020 Projected Employment	Numeric Employment Change	Percent Employment Change
Combined Food Preparation and Serving Workers, Including Fast Food	351,780	372,090	20,310	5.8
Personal Care Aides	218,310	235,470	17,160	7.9
Heavy and Tractor-Trailer Truck Drivers	204,870	216,310	11,440	5.6
Laborers and Freight, Stock, and Material Movers, Hand	194,220	204,060	9,840	5.1
Waiters and Waitresses	236,020	245,790	9,770	4.1
Office Clerks, General	393,740	403,270	9,530	2.4
Customer Service Representatives	268,380	277,460	9,080	3.4
General and Operations Managers	182,190	190,620	8,430	4.6
Retail Salespersons	392,620	400,900	8,280	2.1
Construction Laborers	143,270	150,820	7,550	5.3

Note: Projections cover Texas; (1) Sorted by numeric employment change
Source: www.projectionscentral.com, State Occupational Projections, 2018–2020 Short-Term Projections

Fastest Growing Occupations: 2018 – 2020

Occupation[1]	2018 Employment	2020 Projected Employment	Numeric Employment Change	Percent Employment Change
Wind Turbine Service Technicians	1,810	2,190	380	21.0
Religious Workers, All Other	5,690	6,330	640	11.2
Fundraisers	8,830	9,670	840	9.5
Statisticians	1,870	2,040	170	9.1
Public Relations and Fundraising Managers	6,570	7,160	590	9.0
Home Health Aides	74,390	80,920	6,530	8.8
Community and Social Service Specialists, All Other	4,520	4,890	370	8.2
Personal Care Aides	218,310	235,470	17,160	7.9
Operations Research Analysts	10,920	11,760	840	7.7
Software Developers, Applications	65,190	70,140	4,950	7.6

Note: Projections cover Texas; (1) Sorted by percent employment change and excludes occupations with numeric employment change less than 50
Source: www.projectionscentral.com, State Occupational Projections, 2018–2020 Short-Term Projections

TAXES

State Corporate Income Tax Rates

State	Tax Rate (%)	Income Brackets ($)	Num. of Brackets	Financial Institution Tax Rate (%)[a]	Federal Income Tax Ded.
Texas	(w)	–	–	(w)	No

Note: Tax rates as of January 1, 2019; (a) Rates listed are the corporate income tax rate applied to financial institutions or excise taxes based on income. Some states have other taxes based upon the value of deposits or shares; (w) Texas imposes a Franchise Tax, otherwise known as margin tax, imposed on entities with more than $1,130,000 total revenues at rate of 0.75%, or 0.375% for entities primarily engaged in retail or wholesale trade, on lesser of 70% of total revenues or 100% of gross receipts after deductions for either compensation or cost of goods sold.
Source: Federation of Tax Administrators, Range of State Corporate Income Tax Rates, January 1, 2019

State Individual Income Tax Rates

State	Tax Rate (%)	Income Brackets ($)	Personal Exemptions ($)			Standard Ded. ($)	
			Single	Married	Depend.	Single	Married
Texas					– No state income tax –		

Note: Tax rates as of January 1, 2019; Local- and county-level taxes are not included; n/a not applicable;

Source: Federation of Tax Administrators, State Individual Income Tax Rates, January 1, 2019

Various State Sales and Excise Tax Rates

State	State Sales Tax (%)	Gasoline[1] (¢/gal.)	Cigarette[2] ($/pack)	Spirits[3] ($/gal.)	Wine[4] ($/gal.)	Beer[5] ($/gal.)	Recreational Marijuana (%)
Texas	6.25	20	1.41	2.40 (f)	0.20 (l)	0.20 (q)	Not legal

Note: All tax rates as of January 1, 2019; (1) The American Petroleum Institute has developed a methodology for determining the average tax rate on a gallon of fuel. Rates may include any of the following: excise taxes, environmental fees, storage tank fees, other fees or taxes, general sales tax, and local taxes. In states where gasoline is subject to the general sales tax, or where the fuel tax is based on the average sale price, the average rate determined by API is sensitive to changes in the price of gasoline. States that fully or partially apply general sales taxes to gasoline: CA, CO, GA, IL, IN, MI, NY; (2) The federal excise tax of $1.0066 per pack and local taxes are not included; (3) Rates are those applicable to off-premise sales of 40% alcohol by volume (a.b.v.) distilled spirits in 750ml containers. Local excise taxes are excluded; (4) Rates are those applicable to off-premise sales of 11% a.b.v. non-carbonated wine in 750ml containers; (5) Rates are those applicable to off-premise sales of 4.7% a.b.v. beer in 12 ounce containers; (f) Different rates also applicable according to alcohol content, place of production, size of container, or place purchased (on- or off-premise or onboard airlines); (l) Different rates also applicable to alcohol content, place of production, size of container, place purchased (on- or off-premise or on board airlines) or type of wine (carbonated, vermouth, etc.); (q) Different rates also applicable according to alcohol content, place of production, size of container, or place purchased (on- or off-premise or onboard airlines).
Source: Tax Foundation, 2019 Facts & Figures: How Does Your State Compare?

State Business Tax Climate Index Rankings

State	Overall Rank	Corporate Tax Rank	Individual Income Tax Rank	Sales Tax Rank	Unemployment Insurance Tax Rank	Property Tax Rank
Texas	15	49	6	37	18	37

Note: The index is a measure of how each state's tax laws affect economic performance. The lower the rank, the more favorable a state's tax system is for business. States without a given tax are given a ranking of 1. The scores/rankings for the District of Columbia do not affect other states. The 2019 index represents the tax climate as of July 1, 2018.
Source: Tax Foundation, State Business Tax Climate Index 2019

COMMERCIAL REAL ESTATE

Office Market

Market Area	Inventory (sq. ft.)	Vacancy Rate (%)	Under Construction (sq. ft.)	YTD Net Absorption (sq. ft.)	Total Average Asking Rent ($/sq. ft./year)
Dallas-Fort Worth	258,387,379	19.4	2,048,642	1,738,944	25.65
National	4,905,867,938	13.1	83,553,714	45,846,470	28.46

Source: Newmark Grubb Knight Frank, National Office Market Report, 4th Quarter 2018

Industrial/Warehouse/R&D Market

Market Area	Inventory (sq. ft.)	Vacancy Rate (%)	Under Construction (sq. ft.)	YTD Net Absorption (sq. ft.)	Total Average Asking Rent ($/sq. ft./year)
Dallas-Ft. Worth	862,312,979	6.1	25,171,564	19,395,062	5.82
National	14,796,839,085	5.0	262,662,294	238,014,726	7.16

Source: Newmark Grubb Knight Frank, National Industrial Market Report, 4th Quarter 2018

COMMERCIAL UTILITIES

Typical Monthly Electric Bills

Area	Commercial Service ($/month)		Industrial Service ($/month)	
	1,500 kWh	40 kW demand 14,000 kWh	1,000 kW demand 200,000 kWh	50,000 kW demand 32,500,000 kWh
City	n/a	n/a	n/a	n/a
Average[1]	203	1,619	25,886	2,540,077

Note: Figures are based on annualized rates; (1) Average based on 187 utilities surveyed; n/a not available
Source: Edison Electric Institute, Typical Bills and Average Rates Report, Summer 2018

TRANSPORTATION

Means of Transportation to Work

Area	Car/Truck/Van		Public Transportation			Bicycle	Walked	Other Means	Worked at Home
	Drove Alone	Car-pooled	Bus	Subway	Railroad				
City	81.5	11.4	0.6	0.0	0.2	0.2	1.3	1.2	3.6
MSA[1]	80.7	9.8	0.9	0.2	0.3	0.2	1.3	1.4	5.2
U.S.	76.4	9.2	2.5	1.9	0.6	0.6	2.7	1.3	4.7

Note: Figures are percentages and cover workers 16 years of age and older; (1) Figures cover the Dallas-Fort Worth-Arlington, TX Metropolitan Statistical Area—see Appendix B for areas included
Source: U.S. Census Bureau, 2013-2017 American Community Survey 5-Year Estimates

Travel Time to Work

Area	Less Than 10 Minutes	10 to 19 Minutes	20 to 29 Minutes	30 to 44 Minutes	45 to 59 Minutes	60 to 89 Minutes	90 Minutes or More
City	8.9	28.2	22.3	23.3	9.0	6.3	2.0
MSA[1]	9.1	25.4	21.1	25.1	10.5	6.7	2.0
U.S.	12.7	28.9	20.9	20.5	8.1	6.2	2.7

Note: Note: Figures are percentages and include workers 16 years old and over; (1) Figures cover the Dallas-Fort Worth-Arlington, TX Metropolitan Statistical Area—see Appendix B for areas included
Source: U.S. Census Bureau, 2013-2017 American Community Survey 5-Year Estimates

Freeway Travel Time Index

Area	1985	1990	1995	2000	2005	2010	2014
Urban Area Rank[1,2]	6	9	10	19	21	22	19
Urban Area Index[1]	1.19	1.20	1.23	1.24	1.26	1.24	1.27
Average Index[3]	1.09	1.11	1.14	1.17	1.20	1.19	1.20

Note: Freeway Travel Time Index—the ratio of travel time in the peak period to the travel time at free-flow conditions. For example, a value of 1.30 indicates a 20-minute free-flow trip takes 26 minutes in the peak (20 minutes x 1.30 = 26 minutes); (1) Covers the Dallas-Fort Worth-Arlington TX urban area; (2) Rank is based on 101 urban areas (#1 = highest travel time index); (3) Average of 101 urban areas
Source: Texas Transportation Institute, 2015 Urban Mobility Scorecard, August 2015

Freeway Commuter Stress Index

Area	1985	1990	1995	2000	2005	2010	2014
Urban Area Rank[1,2]	12	15	13	20	22	25	20
Urban Area Index[1]	1.25	1.26	1.29	1.30	1.32	1.30	1.33
Average Index[3]	1.13	1.16	1.19	1.22	1.25	1.24	1.25

Note: The Freeway Commuter Stress Index is the same as the Freeway Travel Time Index (see table above) except that it includes only the travel in the peak directions during the peak periods; the TTI includes travel in all directions during the peak period. Thus, the CSI is more indicative of the work trip experienced by each commuter on a daily basis; (1) Covers the Dallas-Fort Worth-Arlington TX urban area; (2) Rank is based on 101 urban areas (#1 = highest travel time index); (3) Average of 101 urban areas
Source: Texas Transportation Institute, 2015 Urban Mobility Scorecard, August 2015

Public Transportation

Agency Name / Mode of Transportation	Vehicles Operated in Maximum Service[1]	Annual Unlinked Passenger Trips[2] (in thous.)	Annual Passenger Miles[3] (in thous.)
Fort Worth Transportation Authority (The T)			
Bus (directly operated)	123	6,469.2	19,660.8
Bus (purchased transportation)	4	65.0	196.9
Demand Response (directly operated)	35	150.7	1,631.0
Demand Response (purchased transportation)	47	229.5	2,192.9

Note: (1) The number of revenue vehicles operated by the given mode and type of service to meet the annual maximum service requirement. This is the revenue vehicle count during the peak season of the year; on the week and day that maximum service is provided. Vehicles operated in maximum service (VOMS) exclude atypical days and one-time special events; (2) The number of passengers who boarded public transportation vehicles. Passengers are counted each time they board a vehicle no matter how many vehicles they use to travel from their origin to their destination. (3) The sum of the distances ridden by all passengers during the entire fiscal year.
Source: Federal Transit Administration, National Transit Database, 2017

Air Transportation

Airport Name and Code / Type of Service	Passenger Airlines[1]	Passenger Enplanements	Freight Carriers[2]	Freight (lbs)
Dallas-Fort Worth International (DFW)				
Domestic service (U.S. carriers - 2018)	28	28,657,171	17	522,519,846
International service (U.S. carriers - 2017)	8	3,187,180	8	75,180,954
Dallas Love Field (DAL)				
Domestic service (U.S. carriers - 2018)	22	7,817,533	6	13,253,063
International service (U.S. carriers - 2017)	7	5,497	2	32,694

Note: (1) Includes all U.S.-based major, minor and commuter airlines that carried at least one passenger during the year; (2) Includes all U.S.-based airlines and freight carriers that transported at least one pound of freight during the year.
Source: Bureau of Transportation Statistics, The Intermodal Transportation Database, Air Carriers: T-100 Domestic Market (U.S. Carriers), 2018; Bureau of Transportation Statistics, The Intermodal Transportation Database, Air Carriers: T-100 International Market (U.S. Carriers), 2017

Other Transportation Statistics

Major Highways:	I-20; I-35W; I-30
Amtrak Service:	Yes
Major Waterways/Ports:	None

Source: Amtrak.com; Google Maps

BUSINESSES

Major Business Headquarters

Company Name	Industry	Rankings Fortune[1]	Forbes[2]
American Airlines Group	Airlines	71	-
Ben E Keith	Food, Drink & Tobacco	-	119
D.R. Horton	Homebuilders	211	-

Note: (1) Companies that produce a 10-K are ranked 1 to 500 based on 2017 revenue; (2) All private companies with at least $2 billion in annual revenue through the end of their most current fiscal year are ranked 1 to 229; companies listed are headquartered in the city; dashes indicate no ranking
Source: Fortune, "Fortune 500," June 2018; Forbes, "America's Largest Private Companies," 2018 Rankings

Fast-Growing Businesses

According to *Inc.*, Fort Worth is home to four of America's 500 fastest-growing private companies: **Case Energy Partners** (#78); **Acuity Surgical** (#201); **Access Physicians** (#243); **TBX** (#348). Criteria: must be an independent, privately-held, for-profit, U.S. corporation, proprietorship or partnership as of December 31, 2017; revenues must be at least $100,000 in 2014 and $2 million in 2017; must have four-year operating/sales history. Holding companies, regulated banks, and utilities were excluded. *Inc., "America's 500 Fastest-Growing Private Companies," 2018*

According to *Initiative for a Competitive Inner City (ICIC)*, Fort Worth is home to one of America's 100 fastest-growing "inner city" companies: **Construction Cost Management** (#20). Criteria for inclusion: company must be headquartered in or have 51 percent or more of its physical operations in an economically distressed urban area; must be an independent, for-profit corporation, partnership or proprietorship; must have 10 or more employees and have a five-year sales history that includes sales of at least $200,000 in the base year and at least $1 million in the current year with no decrease in sales over the two most recent years. Companies were ranked overall by revenue growth over the five-year period between 2013 and 2017. *Initiative for a Competitive Inner City (ICIC), "Inner City 100 Companies," 2018*

According to Deloitte, Fort Worth is home to one of North America's 500 fastest-growing high-technology companies: **Koddi** (#135). Companies are ranked by percentage growth in revenue over a four-year period. Criteria for inclusion: company must be headquartered within North America; must own proprietary intellectual property or technology that is sold to customers in products that contributes to a significant portion of the company's operating revenue; must have been in business for a minumum of four years with 2014 operating revenues of at least $50,000 USD/CD and 2017 operating revenues of at least $5 million USD/CD. *Deloitte, 2018 Technology Fast 500*™

Minority Business Opportunity

Fort Worth is home to four companies which are on the *Hispanic Business* 500 list (500 largest U.S. Hispanic-owned companies based on revenue): **Thos. S. Byrne Ltd.** (#32); **Elite Staffing Services** (#320); **Ponce Contractors** (#405); **Open Integration Consulting** (#481). Companies included must show at least 51 percent ownership by Hispanic U.S. citizens, and must maintain headquarters in one of the 50 states or Washington, D.C. *Hispanic Business, "Hispanic Business 500," June 20, 2013*

Minority- and Women-Owned Businesses

Group	All Firms		Firms with Paid Employees			
	Firms	Sales ($000)	Firms	Sales ($000)	Employees	Payroll ($000)
AIAN[1]	716	(s)	54	(s)	250 - 499	(s)
Asian	4,835	1,223,859	1,060	1,058,035	8,146	190,901
Black	12,594	348,943	286	157,995	1,074	38,604
Hispanic	16,208	1,169,826	703	765,186	6,750	215,208
NHOPI[2]	76	991	0	0	0	0
Women	29,425	5,485,838	1,943	4,935,042	15,136	559,923
All Firms	71,545	103,753,814	10,711	99,965,646	345,483	16,388,965

Note: Figures cover firms located in the city; minority- and women-owned business are defined as firms in which the corresponding group own 51% or more of the stock or equity of the company; (1) American Indian and Alaska Native; (2) Native Hawaiian and Other Pacific Islander; (s) estimates are suppressed when publication standards are not met
Source: U.S. Census Bureau, 2012 Economic Census, Survey of Business Owners

HOTELS & CONVENTION CENTERS

Hotels, Motels and Vacation Rentals

Area	5 Star		4 Star		3 Star		2 Star		1 Star		Not Rated	
	Num.	Pct.[3]	Num.	Pct.[3]	Num.	Pct.[3]	Num.	Pct.[3]	Num.	Pct.[3]	Num.	Pct.[3]
City[1]	0	0.0	9	3.2	50	17.9	117	41.9	5	1.8	98	35.1
Total[2]	286	0.4	5,236	7.1	16,715	22.6	10,259	13.9	293	0.4	41,056	55.6

Note: (1) Figures cover Fort Worth and vicinity; (2) Figures cover all 100 cities in this book; (3) Percentage of hotels which have a given star rating; Star ratings are determined by expedia.com and offer an indication of the general quality of a particular hotel.
Source: www.expedia.com, April 3, 2019

Major Convention Centers

Name	Overall Space (sq. ft.)	Exhibit Space (sq. ft.)	Meeting Space (sq. ft.)	Meeting Rooms
Dallas Convention Center	2,000,000	929,726	n/a	96
Fort Worth Convention Center	n/a	253,226	58,849	41
Frisco Conference Center	90,000	n/a	n/a	14

Note: Table includes convention centers located in the Dallas-Fort Worth-Arlington, TX metro area; n/a not available
Source: Original research

Living Environment

COST OF LIVING

Cost of Living Index

Composite Index	Groceries	Housing	Utilities	Trans-portation	Health Care	Misc. Goods/ Services
98.1	94.7	89.8	105.2	103.2	104.5	102.5

Note: The Cost of Living Index measures regional differences in the cost of consumer goods and services, excluding taxes and non-consumer expenditures, for professional and managerial households in the top income quintile. It is based on more than 50,000 prices covering almost 60 different items for which prices are collected three times a year by chambers of commerce, economic development organizations or university applied economic centers in each participating urban area. The numbers shown should be read as a percentage above or below the national average of 100. For example, a value of 115.4 in the groceries column indicates that grocery prices are 15.4% higher than the national average. Small differences in the index numbers should not be interpreted as significant; Figures cover the Fort Worth TX urban area.
Source: The Council for Community and Economic Research, ACCRA Cost of Living Index, 2018

Grocery Prices

Area[1]	T-Bone Steak ($/pound)	Frying Chicken ($/pound)	Whole Milk ($/half gal.)	Eggs ($/dozen)	Orange Juice ($/64 oz.)	Coffee ($/11.5 oz.)
City[2]	11.55	1.50	1.53	1.29	3.27	4.07
Avg.	11.35	1.42	1.94	1.81	3.52	4.35
Min.	7.45	0.92	0.80	0.75	2.72	3.06
Max.	15.05	2.76	4.18	4.00	5.36	8.20

Note: (1) Values for the local area are compared with the average, minimum and maximum values for all 291 areas in the Cost of Living Index; (2) Figures cover the Fort Worth TX urban area; T-Bone Steak (price per pound); Frying Chicken (price per pound, whole fryer); Whole Milk (half gallon carton); Eggs (price per dozen, Grade A, large); Orange Juice (64 oz. Tropicana or Florida Natural); Coffee (11.5 oz. can, vacuum-packed, Maxwell House, Hills Bros, or Folgers).
Source: The Council for Community and Economic Research, ACCRA Cost of Living Index, 2018

Housing and Utility Costs

Area[1]	New Home Price ($)	Apartment Rent ($/month)	All Electric ($/month)	Part Electric ($/month)	Other Energy ($/month)	Telephone ($/month)
City[2]	275,461	1,243	-	125.46	57.39	179.10
Avg.	347,000	1,087	165.93	100.16	67.73	178.70
Min.	200,468	500	93.58	25.64	26.78	163.10
Max.	1,901,222	4,888	388.65	246.86	332.81	197.70

Note: (1) Values for the local area are compared with the average, minimum and maximum values for all 291 areas in the Cost of Living Index; (2) Figures cover the Fort Worth TX urban area; New Home Price (2,400 sf living area, 8,000 sf lot, in urban area with full utilities); Apartment Rent (950 sf 2 bedroom/1.5 or 2 bath, unfurnished, excluding all utilities except water); All Electric (average monthly cost for an all-electric home); Part Electric (average monthly cost for a part-electric home); Other Energy (average monthly cost for natural gas, fuel oil, coal, wood, and any other forms of energy except electricity); Telephone (price includes the base monthly rate plus taxes and fees for three lines of mobile phone service).
Source: The Council for Community and Economic Research, ACCRA Cost of Living Index, 2018

Health Care, Transportation, and Other Costs

Area[1]	Doctor ($/visit)	Dentist ($/visit)	Optometrist ($/visit)	Gasoline ($/gallon)	Beauty Salon ($/visit)	Men's Shirt ($)
City[2]	118.48	97.67	97.68	2.51	54.22	47.17
Avg.	110.71	95.11	103.74	2.61	37.48	32.03
Min.	33.60	62.55	54.63	1.89	17.00	11.44
Max.	195.97	153.93	225.79	3.59	71.88	58.64

Note: (1) Values for the local area are compared with the average, minimum and maximum values for all 291 areas in the Cost of Living Index; (2) Figures cover the Fort Worth TX urban area; Doctor (general practitioners routine exam of an established patient); Dentist (adult teeth cleaning and periodic oral examination); Optometrist (full vision eye exam for established adult patient); Gasoline (one gallon regular unleaded, national brand, including all taxes, cash price at self-service pump if available); Beauty Salon (woman's shampoo, trim, and blow-dry); Men's Shirt (cotton/polyester dress shirt, pinpoint weave, long sleeves).
Source: The Council for Community and Economic Research, ACCRA Cost of Living Index, 2018

HOUSING

House Price Index (HPI)

Area	National Ranking[2]	Quarterly Change (%)	One-Year Change (%)	Five-Year Change (%)
MD[1]	41	1.15	9.03	53.26
U.S.[3]	–	1.12	5.73	32.81

Note: The HPI is a weighted repeat sales index. It measures average price changes in repeat sales or refinancings on the same properties. This information is obtained by reviewing repeat mortgage transactions on single-family properties whose mortgages have been purchased or securitized by Fannie Mae or Freddie Mac in January 1975; (1) Figures cover the Fort Worth-Arlington, TX Metropolitan Division—see Appendix B for areas included; (2) Rankings are based on annual percentage change for all metro areas containing at least 15,000 transactions over the last 10 years and ranges from 1 to 245; (3) figures based on a weighted average of Census Division estimates using a seasonally adjusted, purchase-only index; all figures are for the period ending December 31, 2018
Source: Federal Housing Finance Agency, House Price Index, February 26, 2019

Median Single-Family Home Prices

Area	2016	2017	2018[p]	Percent Change 2017 to 2018
MSA[1]	227.1	247.4	260.0	5.1
U.S. Average	235.5	248.8	261.6	5.1

Note: Figures are median sales prices of existing single-family homes in thousands of dollars; (p) preliminary; (1) Figures cover the Dallas-Fort Worth-Arlington, TX Metropolitan Statistical Area—see Appendix B for areas included
Source: National Association of Realtors, Median Sales Price of Existing Single-Family Homes for Metropolitan Areas, 4th Quarter 2018

Qualifying Income Based on Median Sales Price of Existing Single-Family Homes

Area	With 5% Down ($)	With 10% Down ($)	With 20% Down ($)
MSA[1]	62,294	59,015	52,458
U.S. Average	62,954	59,640	53,013

Note: Figures are preliminary; Qualifying income is based on a mortgage rate of 4.9%. Monthly principal and interest payment is limited to 25% of income; (1) Figures cover the Dallas-Fort Worth-Arlington, TX Metropolitan Statistical Area—see Appendix B for areas included
Source: National Association of Realtors, Qualifying Income Based on Median Sales Price of Existing Single-Family Homes for Metropolitan Areas, 4th Quarter 2018

Median Apartment Condo-Coop Home Prices

Area	2016	2017	2018[p]	Percent Change 2017 to 2018
MSA[1]	167.7	185.7	191.2	3.0
U.S. Average	220.7	234.3	241.0	2.9

Note: Figures are median sales prices of existing apartment condo-coop homes in thousands of dollars; (p) preliminary; (1) Figures cover the Dallas-Fort Worth-Arlington, TX Metropolitan Statistical Area—see Appendix B for areas included
Source: National Association of Realtors, Median Sales Price of Existing Apartment Condo-Coop Homes for Metropolitan Areas, 4th Quarter 2018

Home Value Distribution

Area	Under $50,000	$50,000 -$99,999	$100,000 -$149,999	$150,000 -$199,999	$200,000 -$299,999	$300,000 -$499,999	$500,000 -$999,999	$1,000,000 or more
City	8.1	23.0	22.7	18.8	15.4	8.3	2.9	0.8
MSA[1]	5.9	15.6	18.6	17.2	19.7	15.7	5.8	1.6
U.S.	8.3	13.9	14.7	14.6	18.7	17.3	9.7	2.7

Note: Figures are percentages and cover owner-occupied housing units; (1) Figures cover the Dallas-Fort Worth-Arlington, TX Metropolitan Statistical Area—see Appendix B for areas included
Source: U.S. Census Bureau, 2013-2017 American Community Survey 5-Year Estimates

Homeownership Rate

Area	2010 (%)	2011 (%)	2012 (%)	2013 (%)	2014 (%)	2015 (%)	2016 (%)	2017 (%)	2018 (%)
MSA[1]	63.8	62.6	61.8	59.9	57.7	57.8	59.7	61.8	62.0
U.S.	66.9	66.1	65.4	65.1	64.5	63.7	63.4	63.9	64.4

Note: (1) Figures cover the Dallas-Fort Worth-Arlington, TX Metropolitan Statistical Area—see Appendix B for areas included
Source: U.S. Census Bureau, Housing Vacancies and Homeownership Annual Statistics: 2010-2018

Year Housing Structure Built

Area	2010 or Later	2000 -2009	1990 -1999	1980 -1989	1970 -1979	1960 -1969	1950 -1959	1940 -1949	Before 1940	Median Year
City	6.6	26.4	11.6	13.0	10.4	8.5	11.5	5.4	6.5	1986
MSA[1]	6.1	21.6	16.7	18.8	14.5	9.0	7.6	2.8	2.9	1987
U.S.	3.2	14.5	14.0	13.6	15.5	10.8	10.5	5.1	12.9	1977

Note: Figures are percentages except for Median Year; Note: (1) Figures cover the Dallas-Fort Worth-Arlington, TX Metropolitan Statistical Area—see Appendix B for areas included
Source: U.S. Census Bureau, 2013-2017 American Community Survey 5-Year Estimates

Gross Monthly Rent

Area	Under $500	$500 -$999	$1,000 -$1,499	$1,500 -$1,999	$2,000 -$2,499	$2,500 -$2,999	$3,000 and up	Median ($)
City	5.8	48.0	31.8	10.7	2.3	0.9	0.5	967
MSA[1]	4.2	43.9	35.4	11.8	3.0	1.0	0.8	1,022
U.S.	10.5	41.1	28.7	11.7	4.5	1.8	1.7	982

Note: Figures are percentages except for Median; Gross rent is the contract rent plus the estimated average monthly cost of utilities (electricity, gas, and water and sewer) and fuels (oil, coal, kerosene, wood, etc.) if these are paid by the renter (or paid for the renter by someone else); (1) Figures cover the Dallas-Fort Worth-Arlington, TX Metropolitan Statistical Area—see Appendix B for areas included
Source: U.S. Census Bureau, 2013-2017 American Community Survey 5-Year Estimates

HEALTH

Health Risk Factors

Category	MD[1] (%)	U.S. (%)
Adults aged 18–64 who have any kind of health care coverage	77.1	87.3
Adults who reported being in good or better health	77.7	82.4
Adults who have been told they have high blood cholesterol	34.3	33.0
Adults who have been told they have high blood pressure	34.6	32.3
Adults who are current smokers	15.8	17.1
Adults who currently use E-cigarettes	5.0	4.6
Adults who currently use chewing tobacco, snuff, or snus	3.9	4.0
Adults who are heavy drinkers[2]	6.3	6.3
Adults who are binge drinkers[3]	16.7	17.4
Adults who are overweight (BMI 25.0 - 29.9)	34.0	35.3
Adults who are obese (BMI 30.0 - 99.8)	36.7	31.3
Adults who participated in any physical activities in the past month	68.8	74.4
Adults who always or nearly always wears a seat belt	97.0	94.3

Note: (1) Figures cover the Fort Worth-Arlington, TX Metropolitan Division—see Appendix B for areas included; (2) Heavy drinkers are classified as adult men having more than 14 drinks per week and adult women having more than 7 drinks per week; (3) Binge drinkers are classified as males having five or more drinks on one occasion or females having four or more drinks on one occasion
Source: Centers for Disease Control and Prevention, Behaviorial Risk Factor Surveillance System, SMART: Selected Metropolitan Area Risk Trends, 2017

Acute and Chronic Health Conditions

Category	MD[1] (%)	U.S. (%)
Adults who have ever been told they had a heart attack	4.3	4.2
Adults who have ever been told they have angina or coronary heart disease	4.3	3.9
Adults who have ever been told they had a stroke	n/a	3.0
Adults who have ever been told they have asthma	14.1	14.2
Adults who have ever been told they have arthritis	20.8	24.9
Adults who have ever been told they have diabetes[2]	9.7	10.5
Adults who have ever been told they had skin cancer	6.3	6.2
Adults who have ever been told they had any other types of cancer	4.3	7.1
Adults who have ever been told they have COPD	6.0	6.5
Adults who have ever been told they have kidney disease	3.3	3.0
Adults who have ever been told they have a form of depression	17.6	20.5

Note: n/a not available; (1) Figures cover the Fort Worth-Arlington, TX Metropolitan Division—see Appendix B for areas included; (2) Figures do not include pregnancy-related, borderline, or pre-diabetes
Source: Centers for Disease Control and Prevention, Behaviorial Risk Factor Surveillance System, SMART: Selected Metropolitan Area Risk Trends, 2017

Health Screening and Vaccination Rates

Category	MD[1] (%)	U.S. (%)
Adults aged 65+ who have had flu shot within the past year	62.1	60.7
Adults aged 65+ who have ever had a pneumonia vaccination	76.8	75.4
Adults who have ever been tested for HIV	42.1	36.1
Adults who have ever had the shingles or zoster vaccine?	24.1	28.9
Adults who have had their blood cholesterol checked within the last five years	89.6	85.9

Note: n/a not available; (1) Figures cover the Fort Worth-Arlington, TX Metropolitan Division—see Appendix B for areas included.
Source: Centers for Disease Control and Prevention, Behaviorial Risk Factor Surveillance System, SMART: Selected Metropolitan Area Risk Trends, 2017

Disability Status

Category	MD[1] (%)	U.S. (%)
Adults who reported being deaf	5.8	6.7
Are you blind or have serious difficulty seeing, even when wearing glasses?	5.5	4.5
Are you limited in any way in any of your usual activities due of arthritis?	9.8	12.9
Do you have difficulty doing errands alone?	6.8	6.8
Do you have difficulty dressing or bathing?	3.9	3.6
Do you have serious difficulty concentrating/remembering/making decisions?	10.1	10.7
Do you have serious difficulty walking or climbing stairs?	13.1	13.6

Note: (1) Figures cover the Fort Worth-Arlington, TX Metropolitan Division—see Appendix B for areas included.
Source: Centers for Disease Control and Prevention, Behaviorial Risk Factor Surveillance System, SMART: Selected Metropolitan Area Risk Trends, 2017

Mortality Rates for the Top 10 Causes of Death in the U.S.

ICD-10[a] Sub-Chapter	ICD-10[a] Code	Age-Adjusted Mortality Rate[1] per 100,000 population	
		County[2]	U.S.
Malignant neoplasms	C00-C97	151.7	155.5
Ischaemic heart diseases	I20-I25	82.1	94.8
Other forms of heart disease	I30-I51	47.4	52.9
Chronic lower respiratory diseases	J40-J47	42.9	41.0
Cerebrovascular diseases	I60-I69	46.1	37.5
Other degenerative diseases of the nervous system	G30-G31	54.6	35.0
Other external causes of accidental injury	W00-X59	20.5	33.7
Organic, including symptomatic, mental disorders	F01-F09	31.5	31.0
Hypertensive diseases	I10-I15	34.1	21.9
Diabetes mellitus	E10-E14	22.3	21.2

Note: (a) ICD-10 = International Classification of Diseases 10th Revision; (1) Mortality rates are a three year average covering 2015-2017; (2) Figures cover Tarrant County.
Source: Centers for Disease Control and Prevention, National Center for Health Statistics. Underlying Cause of Death 1999-2017 on CDC WONDER Online Database

Mortality Rates for Selected Causes of Death

ICD-10[a] Sub-Chapter	ICD-10[a] Code	Age-Adjusted Mortality Rate[1] per 100,000 population	
		County[2]	U.S.
Assault	X85-Y09	5.6	5.9
Diseases of the liver	K70-K76	15.0	14.1
Human immunodeficiency virus (HIV) disease	B20-B24	1.5	1.8
Influenza and pneumonia	J09-J18	11.6	14.3
Intentional self-harm	X60-X84	12.4	13.6
Malnutrition	E40-E46	3.6	1.6
Obesity and other hyperalimentation	E65-E68	1.3	2.1
Renal failure	N17-N19	15.3	13.0
Transport accidents	V01-V99	10.9	12.4
Viral hepatitis	B15-B19	1.8	1.6

Note: (a) ICD-10 = International Classification of Diseases 10th Revision; (1) Mortality rates are a three year average covering 2015-2017; (2) Figures cover Tarrant County; Data are suppressed when the data meet the criteria for confidentiality constraints; Mortality rates are flagged as unreliable when the rate would be calculated with a numerator of 20 or less.
Source: Centers for Disease Control and Prevention, National Center for Health Statistics. Underlying Cause of Death 1999-2017 on CDC WONDER Online Database

Health Insurance Coverage

Area	With Health Insurance	With Private Health Insurance	With Public Health Insurance	Without Health Insurance	Population Under Age 18 Without Health Insurance
City	80.7	59.4	27.9	19.3	11.4
MSA[1]	82.6	64.7	25.3	17.4	11.0
U.S.	89.5	67.2	33.8	10.5	5.7

Note: Figures are percentages that cover the civilian noninstitutionalized population; (1) Figures cover the Dallas-Fort Worth-Arlington, TX Metropolitan Statistical Area—see Appendix B for areas included
Source: U.S. Census Bureau, 2013-2017 American Community Survey 5-Year Estimates

Number of Medical Professionals

Area	MDs[3]	DOs[3,4]	Dentists	Podiatrists	Chiropractors	Optometrists
County[1] (number)	3,599	756	1,186	84	517	312
County[1] (rate[2])	178.0	37.4	57.7	4.1	25.2	15.2
U.S. (rate[2])	279.3	23.0	68.4	6.0	27.1	16.2

Note: Data as of 2017 unless noted; (1) Data covers Tarrant County; (2) Rate per 100,000 population; (3) Data as of 2016 and includes all active, non-federal physicians; (4) Doctor of Osteopathic Medicine
Source: U.S. Department of Health and Human Services, Health Resources and Services Administration, Bureau of Health Professions, Area Resource File (ARF) 2017-2018

Best Hospitals

According to *U.S. News,* the Fort Worth-Arlington, TX metro area is home to one of the best children's hospitals in the U.S.: **Cook Children's Medical Center** (5 pediatric specialties). The hospital listed was highly ranked in at least one of 10 pediatric specialties. Eighty-six children's hospitals in the U.S. were nationally ranked in at least one specialty. Hospitals received points for being ranked in a specialty, and the 10 hospitals with the most points across the 10 specialties make up the Honor Roll. *U.S. News Online, "America's Best Children's Hospitals 2018-19"*

EDUCATION

Public School District Statistics

District Name	Schls	Pupils	Pupil/ Teacher Ratio	Minority Pupils[1] (%)	Free Lunch Eligible[2] (%)	IEP[3] (%)
Castleberry ISD	8	4,003	16.4	81.1	72.3	7.8
Eagle Mt-Saginaw ISD	27	19,653	16.2	56.6	34.7	8.8
Fort Worth ISD	145	87,428	15.4	88.9	69.8	8.1

Note: Table includes school districts with 2,000 or more students; (1) Percentage of students that are not non-Hispanic white; (2) Percentage of students that are eligible for the free lunch program; (3) Percentage of students that have an Individualized Education Program.
Source: U.S. Department of Education, National Center for Education Statistics, Common Core of Data, Local Education Agency (School District) Universe Survey: School Year 2016-2017; U.S. Department of Education, National Center for Education Statistics, Common Core of Data, Public Elementary/Secondary School Universe Survey: School Year 2016-2017

Highest Level of Education

Area	Less than H.S.	H.S. Diploma	Some College, No Deg.	Associate Degree	Bachelor's Degree	Master's Degree	Prof. School Degree	Doctorate Degree
City	18.5	24.8	21.6	6.7	19.0	7.0	1.3	1.0
MSA[1]	15.2	22.4	21.9	6.8	22.2	8.7	1.8	1.1
U.S.	12.7	27.3	20.8	8.3	19.1	8.4	2.0	1.4

Note: Figures cover persons age 25 and over; (1) Figures cover the Dallas-Fort Worth-Arlington, TX Metropolitan Statistical Area—see Appendix B for areas included
Source: U.S. Census Bureau, 2013-2017 American Community Survey 5-Year Estimates

Educational Attainment by Race

Area	High School Graduate or Higher (%)					Bachelor's Degree or Higher (%)				
	Total	White	Black	Asian	Hisp.[2]	Total	White	Black	Asian	Hisp.[2]
City	81.5	83.8	86.8	81.0	56.9	28.3	32.5	19.7	41.4	10.8
MSA[1]	84.8	85.3	89.9	88.2	57.6	33.7	34.6	25.6	60.1	12.5
U.S.	87.3	89.3	84.9	86.5	66.7	30.9	32.2	20.6	52.7	15.2

Note: Figures shown cover persons 25 years old and over; (1) Figures cover the Dallas-Fort Worth-Arlington, TX Metropolitan Statistical Area—see Appendix B for areas included; (2) People of Hispanic origin can be of any race
Source: U.S. Census Bureau, 2013-2017 American Community Survey 5-Year Estimates

School Enrollment by Grade and Control

Area	Preschool (%)		Kindergarten (%)		Grades 1 - 4 (%)		Grades 5 - 8 (%)		Grades 9 - 12 (%)	
	Public	Private	Public	Private	Public	Private	Public	Private	Public	Private
City	65.8	34.2	89.7	10.3	93.3	6.7	90.5	9.5	92.1	7.9
MSA[1]	58.3	41.7	89.7	10.3	92.6	7.4	92.1	7.9	92.2	7.8
U.S.	58.8	41.2	87.7	12.3	89.7	10.3	89.6	10.4	90.3	9.7

Note: Figures shown cover persons 3 years old and over; (1) Figures cover the Dallas-Fort Worth-Arlington, TX Metropolitan Statistical Area—see Appendix B for areas included
Source: U.S. Census Bureau, 2013-2017 American Community Survey 5-Year Estimates

Average Salaries of Public School Classroom Teachers

Area	2016		2017		Change from 2016 to 2017	
	Dollars	Rank[1]	Dollars	Rank[1]	Percent	Rank[2]
Texas	51,890	28	52,575	28	1.3	29
U.S. Average	58,479	–	59,660	–	2.0	–

Note: (1) Rank ranges from 1 to 51 where 1 indicates highest salary; (2) Rank ranges from 1 to 51 where 1 indicates highest percent change.
Source: National Education Association, Rankings & Estimates: Rankings of the States 2017 and Estimates of School Statistics 2018

Higher Education

Four-Year Colleges			Two-Year Colleges			Medical Schools[1]	Law Schools[2]	Voc/ Tech[3]
Public	Private Non-profit	Private For-profit	Public	Private Non-profit	Private For-profit			
1	4	1	1	0	2	2	1	2

Note: Figures cover institutions located within the city limits and include main campuses only; (1) includes schools accredited by the Liaison Committee on Medical Education and the American Osteopathic Association's Commission on Osteopathic College Accreditation; (2) includes ABA-accredited schools, schools with provisional ABA accreditation, and state accredited schools; (3) includes all schools with programs that are less than 2 years.
Source: National Center for Education Statistics, Integrated Postsecondary Education System (IPEDS), 2017-18; Wikipedia, List of Medical Schools in the United States, accessed April 3, 2019; Wikipedia, List of Law Schools in the United States, accessed April 3, 2019

According to *U.S. News & World Report*, the Fort Worth-Arlington, TX metro division is home to two of the best national universities in the U.S.: **Texas Christian University** (#80 tie); **University of Texas—Arlington** (#221 tie). The indicators used to capture academic quality fall into a number of categories: assessment by administrators at peer institutions; retention of students; faculty resources; student selectivity; financial resources; alumni giving; high school counselor ratings of colleges; and graduation rate. *U.S. News & World Report, "America's Best Colleges 2019"*

According to *U.S. News & World Report*, the Fort Worth-Arlington, TX metro division is home to one of the top 100 law schools in the U.S.: **Texas A&M University** (#83 tie). The rankings are based on a weighted average of 12 measures of quality: peer assessment score; assessment score by lawyers/judges; median LSAT scores; median undergrad GPA; acceptance rate; employment rates for graduates; placement success; bar passage rate; faculty resources; expenditures per student; student/faculty ratio; and library resources. *U.S. News & World Report, "America's Best Graduate Schools, Law, 2020"*

According to *U.S. News & World Report*, the Fort Worth-Arlington, TX metro division is home to one of the top 75 business schools in the U.S.: **Texas Christian University (Neeley)** (#61 tie). The rankings are based on a weighted average of the following nine measures: quality assessment; peer assessment; recruiter assessment; placement success; mean starting salary and bonus; student selectivity; mean GMAT and GRE scores; mean undergraduate GPA; and acceptance rate. *U.S. News & World Report, "America's Best Graduate Schools, Business, 2020"*

PRESIDENTIAL ELECTION

2016 Presidential Election Results

Area	Clinton	Trump	Johnson	Stein	Other
Tarrant County	43.1	51.7	3.6	0.8	0.7
U.S.	48.0	45.9	3.3	1.1	1.7

Note: Results are percentages and may not add to 100% due to rounding
Source: Dave Leip's Atlas of U.S. Presidential Elections

EMPLOYERS

Major Employers

Company Name	Industry
AMR Corporation	Air transportation, scheduled
Associates First Capital Corporation	Mortgage bankers
Baylor University Medical Center	General medical & surgical hospitals
Children's Medical Center Dallas	Specialty hospitals, except psychiatric
Combat Support Associates	Engineering services
County of Dallas	County government
Dallas County Hospital District	General medical & surgical hospitals
Fort Worth Independent School District	Public elementary & secondary schools
Housewares Holding Company	Toasters, electric: household
HP Enterprise Services	Computer integrated systems design
J.C. Penney Company	Department stores
JCP Publications Corp.	Department stores
L-3 Communications Corporation	Business economic service
Odyssey HealthCare	Home health care services
Romano's Macaroni Grill	Italian restaurant
SFG Management	Milk processing (pasteurizing, homogenizing, bottling)
Texas Instruments Incorporated	Semiconductors & related devices
University of North Texas	Colleges & universities
University of Texas SW Medical Center	Accident & health insurance
Verizon Business Global	Telephone communication, except radio

Note: Companies shown are located within the Dallas-Fort Worth-Arlington, TX Metropolitan Statistical Area.
Source: Hoovers.com; Wikipedia

PUBLIC SAFETY

Crime Rate

Area	All Crimes	Violent Crimes				Property Crimes		
		Murder	Rape[3]	Robbery	Aggrav. Assault	Burglary	Larceny -Theft	Motor Vehicle Theft
City	3,775.5	8.0	65.2	147.3	339.7	586.0	2,319.4	309.9
Suburbs[1]	n/a	4.8	44.9	116.9	177.1	n/a	1,582.1	271.5
Metro[2]	n/a	5.2	47.3	120.5	196.4	n/a	1,669.5	276.0
U.S.	2,756.1	5.3	41.7	98.0	248.9	430.4	1,694.4	237.4

Note: Figures are crimes per 100,000 population; (1) All areas within the metro area that are located outside the city limits; (2) Figures cover the Fort Worth-Arlington, TX Metropolitan Division—see Appendix B for areas included; (3) The city and U.S. figures shown were reported using the revised Uniform Crime Reporting (UCR) definition of rape. The suburban and metro area figures shown are an aggregate total of the data submitted using both the revised and legacy UCR definitions.
Source: FBI Uniform Crime Reports, 2017

Hate Crimes

Area	Number of Quarters Reported	Number of Incidents per Bias Motivation					
		Race/Ethnicity/ Ancestry	Religion	Sexual Orientation	Disability	Gender	Gender Identity
City	4	7	2	4	0	0	0
U.S.	4	4,131	1,564	1,130	116	46	119

Source: Federal Bureau of Investigation, Hate Crime Statistics 2017

Identity Theft Consumer Reports

Area	Reports	Reports per 100,000 Population	Rank[2]
MSA[1]	16,342	226	8
U.S.	444,602	135	-

Note: (1) Figures cover the Dallas-Fort Worth-Arlington, TX Metropolitan Statistical Area—see Appendix B for areas included; (2) Rank ranges from 1 to 389 where 1 indicates greatest number of identity theft reports per 100,000 population
Source: Federal Trade Commission, Consumer Sentinel Network Data Book for January–December 2018

Fraud and Other Consumer Reports

Area	Reports	Reports per 100,000 Population	Rank[2]
MSA[1]	45,901	635	42
U.S.	2,552,917	776	-

Note: (1) Figures cover the Dallas-Fort Worth-Arlington, TX Metropolitan Statistical Area—see Appendix B for areas included; (2) Rank ranges from 1 to 389 where 1 indicates greatest number of fraud and other consumer reports per 100,000 population
Source: Federal Trade Commission, Consumer Sentinel Network Data Book for January–December 2018

SPORTS

Professional Sports Teams

Team Name	League	Year Established
Dallas Cowboys	National Football League (NFL)	1960
Dallas Mavericks	National Basketball Association (NBA)	1980
Dallas Stars	National Hockey League (NHL)	1993
FC Dallas	Major League Soccer (MLS)	1996
Texas Rangers	Major League Baseball (MLB)	1972

Note: Includes teams located in the Dallas-Fort Worth-Arlington, TX Metropolitan Statistical Area.
Source: Wikipedia, Major Professional Sports Teams of the United States and Canada, April 5, 2019

CLIMATE

Average and Extreme Temperatures

Temperature	Jan	Feb	Mar	Apr	May	Jun	Jul	Aug	Sep	Oct	Nov	Dec	Yr.
Extreme High (°F)	88	88	96	98	103	113	110	108	107	106	89	90	113
Average High (°F)	54	59	67	76	83	92	96	96	88	79	67	58	76
Average Temp. (°F)	44	49	57	66	73	81	85	85	78	68	56	47	66
Average Low (°F)	33	38	45	54	63	71	75	74	67	56	45	37	55
Extreme Low (°F)	4	6	11	29	41	51	59	56	43	29	19	-1	-1

Note: Figures cover the years 1953-1990
Source: National Climatic Data Center, International Station Meteorological Climate Summary, 9/96

Average Precipitation/Snowfall/Humidity

Precip./Humidity	Jan	Feb	Mar	Apr	May	Jun	Jul	Aug	Sep	Oct	Nov	Dec	Yr.
Avg. Precip. (in.)	1.8	2.2	2.6	3.7	4.9	2.8	2.1	1.9	3.0	3.3	2.1	1.7	32.3
Avg. Snowfall (in.)	1	1	Tr	0	0	0	0	0	0	0	Tr	Tr	3
Avg. Rel. Hum. 6am (%)	79	79	79	81	86	85	80	79	83	82	80	79	81
Avg. Rel. Hum. 3pm (%)	52	51	48	50	53	47	42	41	46	47	49	51	48

Note: Figures cover the years 1953-1990; Tr = Trace amounts (<0.05 in. of rain; <0.5 in. of snow)
Source: National Climatic Data Center, International Station Meteorological Climate Summary, 9/96

Weather Conditions

Temperature			Daytime Sky			Precipitation		
10°F & below	32°F & below	90°F & above	Clear	Partly cloudy	Cloudy	0.01 inch or more precip.	0.1 inch or more snow/ice	Thunder-storms
1	40	100	123	136	106	79	3	47

Note: Figures are average number of days per year and cover the years 1953-1990
Source: National Climatic Data Center, International Station Meteorological Climate Summary, 9/96

**HAZARDOUS
WASTE**

Superfund Sites

The Fort Worth-Arlington, TX metro division is home to three sites on the EPA's Superfund National Priorities List: **Air Force Plant #4 (General Dynamics)** (final); **Circle Court Ground Water Plume** (final); **Sandy Beach Road Ground Water Plume** (final). There are a total of 1,390 Superfund sites with a status of proposed or final on the list in the U.S. *U.S. Environmental Protection Agency, National Priorities List, April 5, 2019*

**AIR & WATER
QUALITY**

Air Quality Trends: Ozone

	1990	1995	2000	2005	2010	2012	2014	2015	2016	2017
MSA[1]	0.095	0.105	0.096	0.097	0.080	0.080	0.076	0.077	0.070	0.073
U.S.	0.088	0.089	0.082	0.080	0.073	0.075	0.067	0.068	0.069	0.068

Note: (1) Data covers the Dallas-Fort Worth-Arlington, TX Metropolitan Statistical Area—see Appendix B for areas included. The values shown are the composite ozone concentration averages among trend sites based on the highest fourth daily maximum 8-hour concentration in parts per million. These trends are based on sites having an adequate record of monitoring data during the trend period. Data from exceptional events are included.
Source: U.S. Environmental Protection Agency, Air Quality Monitoring Information, "Air Quality Trends by City, 1990-2017"

Air Quality Index

Area	Percent of Days when Air Quality was...[2]					AQI Statistics[2]	
	Good	Moderate	Unhealthy for Sensitive Groups	Unhealthy	Very Unhealthy	Maximum	Median
MSA[1]	52.6	40.8	6.6	0.0	0.0	147	50

Note: (1) Data covers the Dallas-Fort Worth-Arlington, TX Metropolitan Statistical Area—see Appendix B for areas included; (2) Based on 365 days with AQI data in 2017. Air Quality Index (AQI) is an index for reporting daily air quality. EPA calculates the AQI for five major air pollutants regulated by the Clean Air Act: ground-level ozone, particle pollution (aka particulate matter), carbon monoxide, sulfur dioxide, and nitrogen dioxide. The AQI runs from 0 to 500. The higher the AQI value, the greater the level of air pollution and the greater the health concern. There are six AQI categories: "Good" AQI is between 0 and 50. Air quality is considered satisfactory; "Moderate" AQI is between 51 and 100. Air quality is acceptable; "Unhealthy for Sensitive Groups" When AQI values are between 101 and 150, members of sensitive groups may experience health effects; "Unhealthy" When AQI values are between 151 and 200 everyone may begin to experience health effects; "Very Unhealthy" AQI values between 201 and 300 trigger a health alert; "Hazardous" AQI values over 300 trigger warnings of emergency conditions (not shown).
Source: U.S. Environmental Protection Agency, Air Quality Index Report, 2017

Air Quality Index Pollutants

Area	Percent of Days when AQI Pollutant was...[2]					
	Carbon Monoxide	Nitrogen Dioxide	Ozone	Sulfur Dioxide	Particulate Matter 2.5	Particulate Matter 10
MSA[1]	0.0	4.1	57.3	0.0	38.6	0.0

Note: (1) Data covers the Dallas-Fort Worth-Arlington, TX Metropolitan Statistical Area—see Appendix B for areas included; (2) Based on 365 days with AQI data in 2017. The Air Quality Index (AQI) is an index for reporting daily air quality. EPA calculates the AQI for five major air pollutants regulated by the Clean Air Act: ground-level ozone, particle pollution (also known as particulate matter), carbon monoxide, sulfur dioxide, and nitrogen dioxide. The AQI runs from 0 to 500. The higher the AQI value, the greater the level of air pollution and the greater the health concern.
Source: U.S. Environmental Protection Agency, Air Quality Index Report, 2017

Maximum Air Pollutant Concentrations: Particulate Matter, Ozone, CO and Lead

	Particulate Matter 10 (ug/m³)	Particulate Matter 2.5 Wtd AM (ug/m³)	Particulate Matter 2.5 24-Hr (ug/m³)	Ozone (ppm)	Carbon Monoxide (ppm)	Lead (ug/m³)
MSA[1] Level	38	9	18	0.077	1	0.17
NAAQS[2]	150	15	35	0.075	9	0.15
Met NAAQS[2]	Yes	Yes	Yes	No	Yes	No

Note: (1) Data covers the Dallas-Fort Worth-Arlington, TX Metropolitan Statistical Area—see Appendix B for areas included; Data from exceptional events are included; (2) National Ambient Air Quality Standards; ppm = parts per million; ug/m³ = micrograms per cubic meter; n/a not available.
Concentrations: Particulate Matter 10 (coarse particulate)—highest second maximum 24-hour concentration; Particulate Matter 2.5 Wtd AM (fine particulate)—highest weighted annual mean concentration; Particulate Matter 2.5 24-Hour (fine particulate)—highest 98th percentile 24-hour concentration; Ozone—highest fourth daily maximum 8-hour concentration; Carbon Monoxide—highest second maximum non-overlapping 8-hour concentration; Lead—maximum running 3-month average
Source: U.S. Environmental Protection Agency, Air Quality Monitoring Information, "Air Quality Statistics by City, 2017"

Maximum Air Pollutant Concentrations: Nitrogen Dioxide and Sulfur Dioxide

	Nitrogen Dioxide AM (ppb)	Nitrogen Dioxide 1-Hr (ppb)	Sulfur Dioxide AM (ppb)	Sulfur Dioxide 1-Hr (ppb)	Sulfur Dioxide 24-Hr (ppb)
MSA[1] Level	12	45	n/a	7	n/a
NAAQS[2]	53	100	30	75	140
Met NAAQS[2]	Yes	Yes	n/a	Yes	n/a

Note: (1) Data covers the Dallas-Fort Worth-Arlington, TX Metropolitan Statistical Area—see Appendix B for areas included; Data from exceptional events are included; (2) National Ambient Air Quality Standards; ppm = parts per million; ug/m³ = micrograms per cubic meter; n/a not available.
Concentrations: Nitrogen Dioxide AM—highest arithmetic mean concentration; Nitrogen Dioxide 1-Hr—highest 98th percentile 1-hour daily maximum concentration; Sulfur Dioxide AM—highest annual mean concentration; Sulfur Dioxide 1-Hr—highest 99th percentile 1-hour daily maximum concentration; Sulfur Dioxide 24-Hr—highest second maximum 24-hour concentration
Source: U.S. Environmental Protection Agency, Air Quality Monitoring Information, "Air Quality Statistics by City, 2017"

Drinking Water

Water System Name	Pop. Served	Primary Water Source Type	Violations[1] Health Based	Violations[1] Monitoring/ Reporting
City of Fort Worth	806,380	Surface	0	0

Note: (1) Based on violation data from January 1, 2018 to December 31, 2018
Source: U.S. Environmental Protection Agency, Office of Ground Water and Drinking Water, Safe Drinking Water Information System (based on data extracted April 5, 2019)

Gainesville, Florida

Background

Gainesville is the cultural and educational hub of North Florida, located partway between the Atlantic Ocean and Gulf of Mexico. Alachua County's largest city has grown with a population drawn to its subtropical locale and its largest employer, the colossal University of Florida (UF). Innovation is the name of the game when it comes to the region's push for businesses emerging from the university's numerous research centers. In addition, Gainesville is only a short drive to rural Florida habitat. Ten miles south are the bison, alligators, and 270 bird species found at Paynes Prairie Preserve. Plus, North Florida has the world's largest concentration of freshwater springs.

Originally a Timucuan Indian village, present-day Gainesville was part of a Spanish land grant by 1817. The United States annexed Florida in 1825, and just over a quarter-century later came plans for the Florida Railroad. In 1853, the local citizenry opted to create a new county seat along the railroad line, and Gainesville was founded and named for Seminole Indian War General Edmund P. Gaines. After the Civil War, a Union veteran established a successful cotton shipping station here, and in 1906 UF was founded. Through the years, fire and development has destroyed many of Gainesville's early buildings; those few that remain include the Hippodrome State Theatre which was once the local Federal Building.

Emerging from the University of Florida (the nation's fifth largest university), are projects from dozens of research centers and institutes. An early success was Gatorade, invented in 1965 to hydrate the Gator football team. Alternative energy research draws accolades, and the city proper became the nation's first to implement a solar feed-in tariff, which means consumers who invest in the appropriate technology can sell their electricity back to the utility. The university's Sid Martin Biotechnology Incubator was ranked "World's Best University Biotechnology Incubator" by an international study conducted by the Sweden-based research group UBI in 2013. The university's annual economic impact is nearly $9 billion, and state-wide its activities are estimated to generate more than 107,000 jobs.

In addition to the biotechnology incubator, the city is also home to the Florida Innovation Hub, the first building of the 40-acre Innovation Square package situated as a bridge between the campus and Gainesville's downtown. Eventually, over five million square feet of space will be filled with residences, retail, hotels and open space. The Hub is a 48,000 square-foot facility that incubates start-up companies that emerge from university research. Its Office of Technology Licensing aids the push to grow new business. Also at the square: the UF Innovation Academy, an undergraduate program focusing on entrepreneurial-minded students.

A long list of rankings lauds Gainesville's quality of life for young people and retirees. As with many college towns, there's a happening music scene. Tom Petty and the Heartbreakers emerged from Gainesville. Cultural resources include the Florida Museum of Natural History, founded in 1891, fueled by donations from interested professors. In addition to its central museum and collections, it operates the Randell Research Center (a significant Calusa Indian archaeological and ancient ecological site in Lee County northwest of Fort Myers) and the McGuire Center for Lepidoptera and Biodiversity that boasts one of the world's largest butterfly and moth collections. Public exhibitions include the 6,800 square-foot living Butterfly Rainforest.

In addition, UF's Harn Museum of Art exhibits traveling shows and collections of photography and Ancient American, Asian, African, modern and contemporary art. Also in the city are the Hippodrome State Theatre, showcasing cinema and traveling theater, and the Curtis M. Phillips Center for Performing Arts. Gainesville is also known for "Gainesville Green," a potent strain of marijuana.

Famously humid, Gainesville's subtropical climate means freezes are not unheard of in winter, with December through February average highs in the 50s. June through August is notably wet, averaging more than six inches of rain the first two months of summer and eight inches in August. Equally notable, Gainesville's inland location tends to mitigate the threat of hurricanes that face Florida's coasts. Temperatures often climb into the 90s from April to October.

Rankings

General Rankings

- In their sixth annual survey, Livability.com looked at data for more than 1,000 U.S. cities to determine the rankings for Livability's "Top 100 Best Places to Live" in 2019. Gainesville ranked #92. Criteria: median home value capped at $250,000; affordable living; vibrant economy; education, demographics, health care options. transportation & infrastructure; abundant lifestyle amenities. *Livability.com, "Top 100 Best Places to Live 2019" March 2019*

Business/Finance Rankings

- The personal finance site NerdWallet analyzed 183 American metropolitan areas with populations over 250,000 and more than 15,000 businesses to rank where entrepreneurs find the most success. Criteria included area economy, annual income, housing cost, unemployment rate, and the success rate of area businesses. Gainesville ranked #102. *www.nerdwallet.com, "Best Places to Start a Business," April 27, 2015*

- Metro areas with the largest gap in income between rich and poor residents were identified by 24/7 Wall Street using the U.S. Census Bureau's 2013 American Community Survey. The Gainesville metro area placed #4 among metro areas with the widest wealth gap between rich and poor. *247wallst.com, "20 Cities with the Widest Gap between the Rich and Poor," July 8, 2015*

- The Gainesville metro area appeared on the Milken Institute "2018 Best Performing Cities" list. Rank: #96 out of 200 large metro areas. Criteria: job growth; wage and salary growth; high-tech output growth. *Milken Institute, "Best-Performing Cities 2018," January 24, 2019*

- *Forbes* ranked the 200 most populous metro areas to determine the nation's "Best Places for Business and Careers." The Gainesville metro area was ranked #67. Criteria: costs (business and living); job growth (past and projected); income growth; quality of life; educational attainment (college and high school); projected economic growth; cultural and recreational opportunities; net migration patterns; number of highly ranked colleges. *Forbes, "The Best Places for Business and Careers 2018: Seattle Leads the Way," October 24, 2018*

Dating/Romance Rankings

- Gainesville was selected as one of the nation's most romantic cities with 100,000 or more residents by Amazon.com. The city ranked #13 of 20. Criteria: per capita sales of romance novels, relationship books, romantic comedy movies, romantic music, and sexual wellness products. *Amazon.com, "Top 20 Most Romantic Cities in the U.S.," February 1, 2017*

Environmental Rankings

- Gainesville was highlighted as one of the top 90 cleanest metro areas for short-term particle pollution (24-hour PM 2.5) in the U.S. during 2014 through 2016. Monitors in these cities reported no days with unhealthful PM 2.5 levels. *American Lung Association, State of the Air 2018*

Health/Fitness Rankings

- The Gainesville metro area ranked #108 out of 189 in The Gallup-Healthways Well-Being Index. Criteria: purpose; social well being; financial health; community and physical health. Results are based on telephone interviews with adults, aged 18 and older, living in metropolitan areas in the 50 U.S. states and the District of Columbia. *Gallup-Healthways, "State of American Well-Being, 2017 Community Well-Being Rankings" March 2018*

Real Estate Rankings

- Gainesville was ranked #67 out of 237 metro areas in terms of housing affordability in 2018 by the National Association of Home Builders (#1 = most affordable). Criteria: the share of homes sold in that area affordable to a family earning the local median income, based on standard mortgage underwriting criteria. *National Association of Home Builders®, NAHB-Wells Fargo Housing Opportunity Index, 4th Quarter 2018*

Safety Rankings

- The National Insurance Crime Bureau ranked 382 metro areas in the U.S. in terms of per capita rates of vehicle theft. The Gainesville metro area ranked #183 (#1 = highest rate). Criteria: number of vehicle theft offenses per 100,000 inhabitants in 2017. *National Insurance Crime Bureau, "Hot Spots 2017," July 12, 2018*

Seniors/Retirement Rankings

- Gainesville made *Southern Living's* list of charming and unique southern places to retire or dream of retiring to. The favorite places focused on the following: presence of unique amenities; opportunities to volunteer; low cost of living; continued learning opportunities; stable housing market; access to medical care; availability of part-time work; and ease of travel. *Southern Living, "Best Places to Retire in the South, 2018"*

- From its Best Cities for Successful Aging indexes, the Milken Institute generated rankings for metropolitan areas, weighing data in nine categories—health care, wellness, living arrangements, transportation and convenience, financial characteristics, education, employment, community engagement, and overall livability. The Gainesville metro area was ranked #13 overall in the small metro area category. *Milken Institute, "Best Cities for Successful Aging, 2017" March 14, 2017*

- Gainesville was identified as one of the most popular places to retire by *Topretirements.com.* The list reflects the 100 cities that visitors to the website are most interested in for retirement, based on the number of times a city's review was viewed on the website. *Topretirements.com, "100 Most Popular Places to Retire for 2017," July 27, 2017*

Sports/Recreation Rankings

- Gainesville was chosen as one of America's best cities for bicycling. The city ranked #23 out of 50. Criteria: cycling infrastructure that is safe and friendly for all ages; energy and bike culture. The editors only considered cities with populations of 100,000 or more. *Bicycling, "The 50 Best Bike Cities in America," October 10, 2018*

Business Environment

CITY FINANCES

City Government Finances

Component	2016 ($000)	2016 ($ per capita)
Total Revenues	607,015	4,665
Total Expenditures	652,298	5,013
Debt Outstanding	1,113,641	8,558
Cash and Securities[1]	625,110	4,804

Note: (1) Cash and security holdings of a government at the close of its fiscal year, including those of its dependent agencies, utilities, and liquor stores.
Source: U.S. Census Bureau, State & Local Government Finances 2016

City Government Revenue by Source

Source	2016 ($000)	2016 ($ per capita)	2016 (%)
General Revenue			
From Federal Government	12,634	97	2.1
From State Government	20,155	155	3.3
From Local Governments	7,555	58	1.2
Taxes			
Property	28,526	219	4.7
Sales and Gross Receipts	26,302	202	4.3
Personal Income	0	0	0.0
Corporate Income	0	0	0.0
Motor Vehicle License	0	0	0.0
Other Taxes	6,601	51	1.1
Current Charges	80,549	619	13.3
Liquor Store	0	0	0.0
Utility	394,199	3,029	64.9
Employee Retirement	6,867	53	1.1

Source: U.S. Census Bureau, State & Local Government Finances 2016

City Government Expenditures by Function

Function	2016 ($000)	2016 ($ per capita)	2016 (%)
General Direct Expenditures			
Air Transportation	327	2	0.1
Corrections	0	0	0.0
Education	0	0	0.0
Employment Security Administration	0	0	0.0
Financial Administration	4,432	34	0.7
Fire Protection	18,326	140	2.8
General Public Buildings	0	0	0.0
Governmental Administration, Other	4,695	36	0.7
Health	350	2	0.1
Highways	19,920	153	3.1
Hospitals	0	0	0.0
Housing and Community Development	20,895	160	3.2
Interest on General Debt	7,133	54	1.1
Judicial and Legal	1,601	12	0.2
Libraries	0	0	0.0
Parking	589	4	0.1
Parks and Recreation	11,898	91	1.8
Police Protection	38,976	299	6.0
Public Welfare	827	6	0.1
Sewerage	33,124	254	5.1
Solid Waste Management	8,478	65	1.3
Veterans' Services	0	0	0.0
Liquor Store	0	0	0.0
Utility	430,007	3,304	65.9
Employee Retirement	17,603	135	2.7

Source: U.S. Census Bureau, State & Local Government Finances 2016

DEMOGRAPHICS

Population Growth

Area	1990 Census	2000 Census	2010 Census	2017* Estimate	Population Growth (%)	
					1990-2017	2010-2017
City	90,519	95,447	124,354	129,394	42.9	4.1
MSA[1]	191,263	232,392	264,275	277,056	44.9	4.8
U.S.	248,709,873	281,421,906	308,745,538	321,004,407	29.1	4.0

Note: (1) Figures cover the Gainesville, FL Metropolitan Statistical Area—see Appendix B for areas included;
(*) 2013-2017 5-year estimated population
Source: U.S. Census Bureau, 1990 Census, Census 2000, Census 2010, 2013-2017 American Community Survey 5-Year Estimates

Household Size

Area	Persons in Household (%)							Average Household Size
	One	Two	Three	Four	Five	Six	Seven or More	
City	42.1	33.1	13.7	7.5	2.4	1.0	0.2	2.30
MSA[1]	34.5	35.1	14.6	10.1	3.4	1.8	0.5	2.50
U.S.	27.7	33.8	15.7	13.0	6.0	2.3	1.4	2.60

Note: (1) Figures cover the Gainesville, FL Metropolitan Statistical Area—see Appendix B for areas included
Source: U.S. Census Bureau, 2013-2017 American Community Survey 5-Year Estimates

Race

Area	White Alone[2] (%)	Black Alone[2] (%)	Asian Alone[2] (%)	AIAN[3] Alone[2] (%)	NHOPI[4] Alone[2] (%)	Other Race Alone[2] (%)	Two or More Races (%)
City	66.0	22.0	6.9	0.3	0.1	0.9	3.8
MSA[1]	70.9	19.3	5.5	0.3	0.1	0.8	3.1
U.S.	73.0	12.7	5.4	0.8	0.2	4.8	3.1

Note: (1) Figures cover the Gainesville, FL Metropolitan Statistical Area—see Appendix B for areas included;
(2) Alone is defined as not being in combination with one or more other races; (3) American Indian and Alaska Native; (4) Native Hawaiian and Other Pacific Islander
Source: U.S. Census Bureau, 2013-2017 American Community Survey 5-Year Estimates

Hispanic or Latino Origin

Area	Total (%)	Mexican (%)	Puerto Rican (%)	Cuban (%)	Other (%)
City	10.7	1.3	3.1	2.4	4.0
MSA[1]	9.0	1.5	2.5	1.8	3.2
U.S.	17.6	11.1	1.7	0.7	4.1

Note: Persons of Hispanic or Latino origin can be of any race; (1) Figures cover the Gainesville, FL Metropolitan Statistical Area—see Appendix B for areas included
Source: U.S. Census Bureau, 2013-2017 American Community Survey 5-Year Estimates

Segregation

Type	Segregation Indices[1]				Percent Change		
	1990	2000	2010	2010 Rank[2]	1990-2000	1990-2010	2000-2010
Black/White	n/a	n/a	n/a	n/a	n/a	n/a	n/a
Asian/White	n/a	n/a	n/a	n/a	n/a	n/a	n/a
Hispanic/White	n/a	n/a	n/a	n/a	n/a	n/a	n/a

Note: All figures cover the Metropolitan Statistical Area—see Appendix B for areas included; Figures are based on an analysis of 1990, 2000, and 2010 Census Decennial Census tract data by William H. Frey, Brookings Institution and the University of Michigan Social Science Data Analysis Network. In this analysis all racial groups (whites, blacks, and asians) are non-Hispanic members of those races. Hispanics are shown as a separate category; (1) Segregation Indices are Dissimilarity Indices that measure the degree to which the minority group is distributed differently than whites across census tracts. They range from 0 (complete integration) to 100 (complete segregation) where the value indicates the percentage of the minority group that needs to move to be distributed exactly like whites; (2) Ranges from 1 (most segregated) to 102 (least segregated); n/a not available.
Source: www.CensusScope.org

Ancestry

Area	German	Irish	English	American	Italian	Polish	French[2]	Scottish	Dutch
City	11.3	10.4	8.2	4.0	6.2	2.8	2.7	2.4	1.3
MSA[1]	11.8	10.8	9.0	5.2	5.2	2.6	2.6	2.3	1.2
U.S.	14.1	10.1	7.5	6.6	5.3	2.9	2.5	1.7	1.3

Note: Figures are the percentage of the total population reporting a particular ancestry. The nine most commonly reported ancestries in the U.S. are shown. Figures include multiple ancestries (e.g. if a person reported being Irish and Italian, they were included in both columns); (1) Figures cover the Gainesville, FL Metropolitan Statistical Area—see Appendix B for areas included; (2) Excludes Basque
Source: U.S. Census Bureau, 2013-2017 American Community Survey 5-Year Estimates

Foreign-Born Population

Area	Any Foreign Country	Asia	Mexico	Europe	Carribean	Central America[2]	South America	Africa	Canada
City	11.1	4.8	0.4	1.4	1.4	0.3	2.0	0.6	0.2
MSA[1]	9.5	4.0	0.4	1.3	1.4	0.3	1.4	0.4	0.3
U.S.	13.4	4.1	3.6	1.5	1.3	1.0	0.9	0.6	0.3

Note: (1) Figures cover the Gainesville, FL Metropolitan Statistical Area—see Appendix B for areas included; (2) Excludes Mexico.
Source: U.S. Census Bureau, 2013-2017 American Community Survey 5-Year Estimates

Marital Status

Area	Never Married	Now Married[2]	Separated	Widowed	Divorced
City	61.0	24.9	1.7	3.7	8.7
MSA[1]	45.5	37.6	1.6	4.8	10.4
U.S.	33.1	48.2	2.0	5.8	10.9

Note: Figures are percentages and cover the population 15 years of age and older; (1) Figures cover the Gainesville, FL Metropolitan Statistical Area—see Appendix B for areas included; (2) Excludes separated
Source: U.S. Census Bureau, 2013-2017 American Community Survey 5-Year Estimates

Disability by Age

Area	All Ages	Under 18 Years Old	18 to 64 Years Old	65 Years and Over
City	10.0	2.9	8.0	36.1
MSA[1]	11.2	3.5	8.6	35.6
U.S.	12.6	4.2	10.3	35.5

Note: Figures show percent of the civilian noninstitutionalized population that reported having a disability. Disability status is determined from six types of difficulty: vision, hearing, cognitive, ambulatory, self-care, and independent living. For children under 5 years old, hearing and vision difficulty are used to determine disability status. For children between the ages of 5 and 14, disability status is determined from hearing, vision, cognitive, ambulatory, and self-care difficulties. For people aged 15 years and older, they are considered to have a disability if they have difficulty with any one of the six difficulty types; Note: (1) Figures cover the Gainesville, FL Metropolitan Statistical Area—see Appendix B for areas included
Source: U.S. Census Bureau, 2013-2017 American Community Survey 5-Year Estimates

Age

Area	Under Age 5	Age 5–19	Age 20–34	Age 35–44	Age 45–54	Age 55–64	Age 65–74	Age 75–84	Age 85+	Median Age
City	3.8	18.8	42.0	8.7	8.1	9.0	5.6	2.7	1.5	26.0
MSA[1]	5.4	18.4	30.6	10.5	10.5	11.4	7.9	3.6	1.8	31.7
U.S.	6.2	19.5	20.7	12.7	13.4	12.7	8.6	4.4	1.9	37.8

Note: (1) Figures cover the Gainesville, FL Metropolitan Statistical Area—see Appendix B for areas included
Source: U.S. Census Bureau, 2013-2017 American Community Survey 5-Year Estimates

Gender

Area	Males	Females	Males per 100 Females
City	62,173	67,221	92.5
MSA[1]	134,695	142,361	94.6
U.S.	158,018,753	162,985,654	97.0

Note: (1) Figures cover the Gainesville, FL Metropolitan Statistical Area—see Appendix B for areas included
Source: U.S. Census Bureau, 2013-2017 American Community Survey 5-Year Estimates

Religious Groups by Family

Area	Catholic	Baptist	Non-Den.	Methodist[2]	Lutheran	LDS[3]	Pente-costal	Presby-terian[4]	Muslim[5]	Judaism
MSA[1]	7.6	12.3	4.3	6.4	0.5	1.0	3.5	1.1	1.1	0.4
U.S.	19.1	9.3	4.0	4.0	2.3	2.0	1.9	1.6	0.8	0.7

Note: Figures are the number of adherents as a percentage of the total population; (1) Figures cover the Gainesville, FL Metropolitan Statistical Area—see Appendix B for areas included; (2) Methodist/Pietist; (3) Latter Day Saints; (4) Reformed; (5) Figures are estimates
Source: Association of Statisticians of American Religious Bodies, 2010 U.S. Religion Census: Religious Congregations & Membership Study

Religious Groups by Tradition

Area	Catholic	Evangelical Protestant	Mainline Protestant	Other Tradition	Black Protestant	Orthodox
MSA[1]	7.6	20.4	7.0	4.2	2.2	0.1
U.S.	19.1	16.2	7.3	4.3	1.6	0.3

Note: Figures are the number of adherents as a percentage of the total population; (1) Figures cover the Gainesville, FL Metropolitan Statistical Area—see Appendix B for areas included
Source: Association of Statisticians of American Religious Bodies, 2010 U.S. Religion Census: Religious Congregations & Membership Study

ECONOMY

Gross Metropolitan Product

Area	2016	2017	2018	2019	Rank[2]
MSA[1]	12.5	13.1	13.8	14.5	177

Note: Figures are in billions of dollars; (1) Figures cover the Gainesville, FL Metropolitan Statistical Area—see Appendix B for areas included; (2) Rank is based on 2017 data and ranges from 1 to 381
Source: U.S. Conference of Mayors, U.S. Metro Economies: Economic Growth & Full Employment, June 2018

Economic Growth

Area	2017-2018 (%)	2019-2020 (%)	2021-2022 (%)
MSA[1]	3.1	2.5	1.8

Note: Figures are real gross metropolitan product (GMP) growth rates and represent average annual percent change; (1) Figures cover the Gainesville, FL Metropolitan Statistical Area—see Appendix B for areas included
Source: U.S. Conference of Mayors, U.S. Metro Economies: Economic Growth & Full Employment, June 2018

Metropolitan Area Exports

Area	2012	2013	2014	2015	2016	2017	Rank[2]
MSA[1]	348.6	295.0	304.3	291.6	277.3	292.1	255

Note: Figures are in millions of dollars; (1) Figures cover the Gainesville, FL Metropolitan Statistical Area—see Appendix B for areas included; (2) Rank is based on 2017 data and ranges from 1 to 387
Source: U.S. Department of Commerce, International Trade Administration, Office of Trade and Economic Analysis, Industry and Analysis, Exports by Metropolitan Area, extracted March 25, 2019

Building Permits

Area	Single-Family			Multi-Family			Total		
	2016	2017	Pct. Chg.	2016	2017	Pct. Chg.	2016	2017	Pct. Chg.
City	76	118	55.3	247	1,200	385.8	323	1,318	308.0
MSA[1]	609	684	12.3	501	1,585	216.4	1,110	2,269	104.4
U.S.	750,800	820,000	9.2	455,800	462,000	1.4	1,206,600	1,282,000	6.2

Note: (1) Figures cover the Gainesville, FL Metropolitan Statistical Area—see Appendix B for areas included; Figures represent new, privately-owned housing units authorized (unadjusted data); All permit data are based on estimates with imputation
Source: U.S. Census Bureau, Manufacturing, Mining, and Construction Statistics, Building Permits, 2016, 2017

Bankruptcy Filings

Area	Business Filings			Nonbusiness Filings		
	2017	2018	% Chg.	2017	2018	% Chg.
Alachua County	13	15	15.4	238	274	15.1
U.S.	23,157	22,232	-4.0	765,863	751,186	-1.9

Note: Business filings include Chapter 7, Chapter 11, Chapter 12, and Chapter 13; Nonbusiness filings include Chapter 7, Chapter 11, and Chapter 13
Source: Administrative Office of the U.S. Courts, Business and Nonbusiness Bankruptcy, County Cases Commenced by Chapter of the Bankruptcy Code, During the 12-Month Period Ending December 31, 2017 and Business and Nonbusiness Bankruptcy, County Cases Commenced by Chapter of the Bankruptcy Code, During the 12-Month Period Ending December 31, 2018

Housing Vacancy Rates

Area	Gross Vacancy Rate[2] (%)			Year-Round Vacancy Rate[3] (%)			Rental Vacancy Rate[4] (%)			Homeowner Vacancy Rate[5] (%)		
	2016	2017	2018	2016	2017	2018	2016	2017	2018	2016	2017	2018
MSA[1]	n/a	n/a	n/a	n/a	n/a	n/a	n/a	n/a	n/a	n/a	n/a	n/a
U.S.	12.8	12.7	12.3	9.9	9.9	9.7	6.9	7.2	6.9	1.7	1.6	1.5

Note: (1) Figures cover the Gainesville, FL Metropolitan Statistical Area—see Appendix B for areas included; (2) The percentage of the total housing inventory that is vacant; (3) The percentage of the housing inventory (excluding seasonal units) that is year-round vacant; (4) The percentage of rental inventory that is vacant for rent; (5) The percentage of homeowner inventory that is vacant for sale; n/a not available
Source: U.S. Census Bureau, Housing Vacancies and Homeownership Annual Statistics: 2016, 2017, 2018

INCOME

Income

Area	Per Capita ($)	Median Household ($)	Average Household ($)
City	21,111	34,004	51,019
MSA[1]	26,103	45,323	65,637
U.S.	31,177	57,652	81,283

Note: (1) Figures cover the Gainesville, FL Metropolitan Statistical Area—see Appendix B for areas included
Source: U.S. Census Bureau, 2013-2017 American Community Survey 5-Year Estimates

Household Income Distribution

Area	Percent of Households Earning							
	Under $15,000	$15,000 -$24,999	$25,000 -$34,999	$35,000 -$49,999	$50,000 -$74,999	$75,000 -$99,999	$100,000 -$149,999	$150,000 and up
City	25.7	14.1	11.2	12.2	15.8	9.0	7.6	4.5
MSA[1]	18.4	11.9	10.5	12.8	17.1	10.5	10.4	8.6
U.S.	11.6	9.8	9.5	13.0	17.7	12.3	14.1	12.1

Note: (1) Figures cover the Gainesville, FL Metropolitan Statistical Area—see Appendix B for areas included
Source: U.S. Census Bureau, 2013-2017 American Community Survey 5-Year Estimates

Poverty Rate

Area	All Ages	Under 18 Years Old	18 to 64 Years Old	65 Years and Over
City	33.6	27.2	37.9	10.0
MSA[1]	23.1	22.8	26.2	8.7
U.S.	14.6	20.3	13.7	9.3

Note: Figures are percentage of people whose income during the past 12 months was below the poverty level; (1) Figures cover the Gainesville, FL Metropolitan Statistical Area—see Appendix B for areas included
Source: U.S. Census Bureau, 2013-2017 American Community Survey 5-Year Estimates

EMPLOYMENT

Labor Force and Employment

Area	Civilian Labor Force			Workers Employed		
	Dec. 2017	Dec. 2018	% Chg.	Dec. 2017	Dec. 2018	% Chg.
City	67,232	68,434	1.8	64,845	66,131	2.0
MSA[1]	142,110	144,576	1.7	137,447	140,175	2.0
U.S.	159,880,000	162,510,000	1.6	153,602,000	156,481,000	1.9

Note: Data is not seasonally adjusted and covers workers 16 years of age and older; (1) Figures cover the Gainesville, FL Metropolitan Statistical Area—see Appendix B for areas included
Source: Bureau of Labor Statistics, Local Area Unemployment Statistics

Unemployment Rate

Area	2018											
	Jan.	Feb.	Mar.	Apr.	May	Jun.	Jul.	Aug.	Sep.	Oct.	Nov.	Dec.
City	4.3	3.8	3.8	3.4	3.3	4.2	4.1	3.7	2.9	3.0	3.0	3.4
MSA[1]	3.9	3.4	3.4	3.1	3.0	3.7	3.6	3.4	2.7	2.8	2.8	3.0
U.S.	4.5	4.4	4.1	3.7	3.6	4.2	4.1	3.9	3.6	3.5	3.5	3.7

Note: Data is not seasonally adjusted and covers workers 16 years of age and older; (1) Figures cover the
Gainesville, FL Metropolitan Statistical Area—see Appendix B for areas included
Source: Bureau of Labor Statistics, Local Area Unemployment Statistics

Average Wages

Occupation	$/Hr.	Occupation	$/Hr.
Accountants and Auditors	29.60	Maids and Housekeeping Cleaners	11.20
Automotive Mechanics	18.10	Maintenance and Repair Workers	17.20
Bookkeepers	19.50	Marketing Managers	63.90
Carpenters	19.00	Nuclear Medicine Technologists	n/a
Cashiers	10.30	Nurses, Licensed Practical	24.80
Clerks, General Office	15.20	Nurses, Registered	33.00
Clerks, Receptionists/Information	13.40	Nursing Assistants	13.00
Clerks, Shipping/Receiving	15.90	Packers and Packagers, Hand	11.10
Computer Programmers	29.60	Physical Therapists	40.60
Computer Systems Analysts	36.20	Postal Service Mail Carriers	24.70
Computer User Support Specialists	21.70	Real Estate Brokers	23.20
Cooks, Restaurant	12.50	Retail Salespersons	12.20
Dentists	76.20	Sales Reps., Exc. Tech./Scientific	29.60
Electrical Engineers	45.30	Sales Reps., Tech./Scientific	38.20
Electricians	18.20	Secretaries, Exc. Legal/Med./Exec.	15.70
Financial Managers	60.60	Security Guards	12.60
First-Line Supervisors/Managers, Sales	21.40	Surgeons	n/a
Food Preparation Workers	10.90	Teacher Assistants*	11.30
General and Operations Managers	46.90	Teachers, Elementary School*	20.30
Hairdressers/Cosmetologists	14.70	Teachers, Secondary School*	21.50
Internists, General	n/a	Telemarketers	12.50
Janitors and Cleaners	12.40	Truck Drivers, Heavy/Tractor-Trailer	16.50
Landscaping/Groundskeeping Workers	13.00	Truck Drivers, Light/Delivery Svcs.	17.00
Lawyers	50.30	Waiters and Waitresses	11.70

Note: Wage data covers the Gainesville, FL Metropolitan Statistical Area—see Appendix B for areas included;
(*) Hourly wages for elementary/secondary school teachers and teacher assistants were calculated by the
editors from annual wage data based on a 40 hour work week; n/a not available.
Source: Bureau of Labor Statistics, Metro Area Occupational Employment & Wage Estimates, May 2018

Employment by Occupation

Occupation Classification	City (%)	MSA[1] (%)	U.S. (%)
Management, Business, Science, and Arts	45.0	45.0	37.4
Natural Resources, Construction, and Maintenance	4.0	5.7	8.9
Production, Transportation, and Material Moving	5.7	6.5	12.2
Sales and Office	24.3	23.4	23.5
Service	21.0	19.3	18.0

Note: Figures cover employed civilians 16 years of age and older; (1) Figures cover the Gainesville, FL
Metropolitan Statistical Area—see Appendix B for areas included
Source: U.S. Census Bureau, 2013-2017 American Community Survey 5-Year Estimates

Employment by Industry

Sector	MSA[1]		U.S.
	Number of Employees	Percent of Total	Percent of Total
Construction, Mining, and Logging	6,000	4.0	5.3
Education and Health Services	26,700	18.0	15.9
Financial Activities	6,700	4.5	5.7
Government	44,500	30.0	15.1
Information	1,600	1.1	1.9
Leisure and Hospitality	16,000	10.8	10.7
Manufacturing	4,600	3.1	8.5
Other Services	4,400	3.0	3.9
Professional and Business Services	14,900	10.0	14.1
Retail Trade	15,900	10.7	10.8
Transportation, Warehousing, and Utilities	3,700	2.5	4.2
Wholesale Trade	3,300	2.2	3.9

Note: Figures are non-farm employment as of December 2018. Figures are not seasonally adjusted and include workers 16 years of age and older; (1) Figures cover the Gainesville, FL Metropolitan Statistical Area—see Appendix B for areas included
Source: Bureau of Labor Statistics, Current Employment Statistics, Employment, Hours, and Earnings

Occupations with Greatest Projected Employment Growth: 2018 – 2020

Occupation[1]	2018 Employment	2020 Projected Employment	Numeric Employment Change	Percent Employment Change
Interviewers, Except Eligibility and Loan	11,890	33,270	21,380	179.8
Combined Food Preparation and Serving Workers, Including Fast Food	242,590	256,470	13,880	5.7
Waiters and Waitresses	230,640	240,320	9,680	4.2
Registered Nurses	193,200	202,070	8,870	4.6
Customer Service Representatives	245,420	253,780	8,360	3.4
Laborers and Freight, Stock, and Material Movers, Hand	135,600	143,640	8,040	5.9
Construction Laborers	89,390	97,130	7,740	8.7
Landscaping and Groundskeeping Workers	116,440	123,040	6,600	5.7
Carpenters	72,550	78,990	6,440	8.9
Janitors and Cleaners, Except Maids and Housekeeping Cleaners	133,890	140,000	6,110	4.6

Note: Projections cover Florida; (1) Sorted by numeric employment change
Source: www.projectionscentral.com, State Occupational Projections, 2018–2020 Short-Term Projections

Fastest Growing Occupations: 2018 – 2020

Occupation[1]	2018 Employment	2020 Projected Employment	Numeric Employment Change	Percent Employment Change
Interviewers, Except Eligibility and Loan	11,890	33,270	21,380	179.8
Solar Photovoltaic Installers	1,100	1,330	230	20.9
Terrazzo Workers and Finishers	390	450	60	15.4
Helpers—Roofers	1,490	1,720	230	15.4
Helpers—Brickmasons, Blockmasons, Stonemasons, and Tile and Marble Setters	1,280	1,470	190	14.8
Helpers—Painters, Paperhangers, Plasterers, and Stucco Masons	570	650	80	14.0
Reinforcing Iron and Rebar Workers	1,100	1,250	150	13.6
Insulation Workers, Floor, Ceiling, and Wall	2,550	2,880	330	12.9
Structural Iron and Steel Workers	5,210	5,880	670	12.9
Cement Masons and Concrete Finishers	13,490	15,210	1,720	12.8

Note: Projections cover Florida; (1) Sorted by percent employment change and excludes occupations with numeric employment change less than 50
Source: www.projectionscentral.com, State Occupational Projections, 2018–2020 Short-Term Projections

TAXES

State Corporate Income Tax Rates

State	Tax Rate (%)	Income Brackets ($)	Num. of Brackets	Financial Institution Tax Rate (%)[a]	Federal Income Tax Ded.
Florida	5.5 (e)	Flat rate	1	5.5 (e)	No

Note: Tax rates as of January 1, 2019; (a) Rates listed are the corporate income tax rate applied to financial institutions or excise taxes based on income. Some states have other taxes based upon the value of deposits or shares; (e) The Florida tax rate may be adjusted downward if certain revenue targets are met.
Source: Federation of Tax Administrators, Range of State Corporate Income Tax Rates, January 1, 2019

State Individual Income Tax Rates

State	Tax Rate (%)	Income Brackets ($)	Personal Exemptions ($) Single	Married	Depend.	Standard Ded. ($) Single	Married
Florida			– No state income tax –				

Note: Tax rates as of January 1, 2019; Local- and county-level taxes are not included; n/a not applicable;

Source: Federation of Tax Administrators, State Individual Income Tax Rates, January 1, 2019

Various State Sales and Excise Tax Rates

State	State Sales Tax (%)	Gasoline[1] (¢/gal.)	Cigarette[2] ($/pack)	Spirits[3] ($/gal.)	Wine[4] ($/gal.)	Beer[5] ($/gal.)	Recreational Marijuana (%)
Florida	6	41.99	1.339	6.50 (f)	2.25 (l)	0.48 (q)	Not legal

Note: All tax rates as of January 1, 2019; (1) The American Petroleum Institute has developed a methodology for determining the average tax rate on a gallon of fuel. Rates may include any of the following: excise taxes, environmental fees, storage tank fees, other fees or taxes, general sales tax, and local taxes. In states where gasoline is subject to the general sales tax, or where the fuel tax is based on the average sale price, the average rate determined by API is sensitive to changes in the price of gasoline. States that fully or partially apply general sales taxes to gasoline: CA, CO, GA, IL, IN, MI, NY; (2) The federal excise tax of $1.0066 per pack and local taxes are not included; (3) Rates are those applicable to off-premise sales of 40% alcohol by volume (a.b.v.) distilled spirits in 750ml containers. Local excise taxes are excluded; (4) Rates are those applicable to off-premise sales of 11% a.b.v. non-carbonated wine in 750ml containers; (5) Rates are those applicable to off-premise sales of 4.7% a.b.v. beer in 12 ounce containers; (f) Different rates also applicable according to alcohol content, place of production, size of container, or place purchased (on- or off-premise or onboard airlines); (l) Different rates also applicable to alcohol content, place of production, size of container, place purchased (on- or off-premise or on board airlines) or type of wine (carbonated, vermouth, etc.); (q) Different rates also applicable according to alcohol content, place of production, size of container, or place purchased (on- or off-premise or onboard airlines).
Source: Tax Foundation, 2019 Facts & Figures: How Does Your State Compare?

State Business Tax Climate Index Rankings

State	Overall Rank	Corporate Tax Rank	Individual Income Tax Rank	Sales Tax Rank	Unemployment Insurance Tax Rank	Property Tax Rank
Florida	4	6	1	22	2	11

Note: The index is a measure of how each state's tax laws affect economic performance. The lower the rank, the more favorable a state's tax system is for business. States without a given tax are given a ranking of 1. The scores/rankings for the District of Columbia do not affect other states. The 2019 index represents the tax climate as of July 1, 2018.
Source: Tax Foundation, State Business Tax Climate Index 2019

COMMERCIAL UTILITIES

Typical Monthly Electric Bills

Area	Commercial Service ($/month) 1,500 kWh	40 kW demand 14,000 kWh	Industrial Service ($/month) 1,000 kW demand 200,000 kWh	50,000 kW demand 32,500,000 kWh
City	n/a	n/a	n/a	n/a
Average[1]	203	1,619	25,886	2,540,077

Note: Figures are based on annualized rates; (1) Average based on 187 utilities surveyed; n/a not available
Source: Edison Electric Institute, Typical Bills and Average Rates Report, Summer 2018

TRANSPORTATION

Means of Transportation to Work

Area	Car/Truck/Van		Public Transportation			Bicycle	Walked	Other Means	Worked at Home
	Drove Alone	Car-pooled	Bus	Subway	Railroad				
City	68.0	7.0	7.3	0.0	0.0	4.8	5.8	2.7	4.2
MSA[1]	74.7	9.2	3.9	0.0	0.0	2.5	3.2	1.9	4.5
U.S.	76.4	9.2	2.5	1.9	0.6	0.6	2.7	1.3	4.7

Note: Figures are percentages and cover workers 16 years of age and older; (1) Figures cover the Gainesville, FL Metropolitan Statistical Area—see Appendix B for areas included
Source: U.S. Census Bureau, 2013-2017 American Community Survey 5-Year Estimates

Travel Time to Work

Area	Less Than 10 Minutes	10 to 19 Minutes	20 to 29 Minutes	30 to 44 Minutes	45 to 59 Minutes	60 to 89 Minutes	90 Minutes or More
City	14.8	51.3	20.2	9.4	2.0	1.4	1.0
MSA[1]	10.6	39.0	25.3	16.4	4.8	2.5	1.4
U.S.	12.7	28.9	20.9	20.5	8.1	6.2	2.7

Note: Note: Figures are percentages and include workers 16 years old and over; (1) Figures cover the Gainesville, FL Metropolitan Statistical Area—see Appendix B for areas included
Source: U.S. Census Bureau, 2013-2017 American Community Survey 5-Year Estimates

Freeway Travel Time Index

Area	1985	1990	1995	2000	2005	2010	2014
Urban Area Rank[1,2]	n/a	n/a	n/a	n/a	n/a	n/a	n/a
Urban Area Index[1]	n/a	n/a	n/a	n/a	n/a	n/a	n/a
Average Index[3]	1.09	1.11	1.14	1.17	1.20	1.19	1.20

Note: Freeway Travel Time Index—the ratio of travel time in the peak period to the travel time at free-flow conditions. For example, a value of 1.30 indicates a 20-minute free-flow trip takes 26 minutes in the peak (20 minutes x 1.30 = 26 minutes); (1) Data for the Gainesville, FL urban area was not available; (2) Rank is based on 101 urban areas (#1 = highest travel time index); (3) Average of 101 urban areas
Source: Texas Transportation Institute, 2015 Urban Mobility Scorecard, August 2015

Freeway Commuter Stress Index

Area	1985	1990	1995	2000	2005	2010	2014
Urban Area Rank[1,2]	n/a	n/a	n/a	n/a	n/a	n/a	n/a
Urban Area Index[1]	n/a	n/a	n/a	n/a	n/a	n/a	n/a
Average Index[3]	1.13	1.16	1.19	1.22	1.25	1.24	1.25

Note: The Freeway Commuter Stress Index is the same as the Freeway Travel Time Index (see table above) except that it includes only the travel in the peak directions during the peak periods; the TTI includes travel in all directions during the peak period. Thus, the CSI is more indicative of the work trip experienced by each commuter on a daily basis; (1) Data for the Gainesville, FL urban area was not available; (2) Rank is based on 101 urban areas (#1 = highest travel time index); (3) Average of 101 urban areas
Source: Texas Transportation Institute, 2015 Urban Mobility Scorecard, August 2015

Public Transportation

Agency Name / Mode of Transportation	Vehicles Operated in Maximum Service[1]	Annual Unlinked Passenger Trips[2] (in thous.)	Annual Passenger Miles[3] (in thous.)
Gainesville Regional Transit System (RTS)			
Bus (directly operated)	111	9,415.1	24,816.0
Demand Response (purchased transportation)	35	55.9	511.5
Vanpool (purchased transportation)	12	42.4	1,877.0

Note: (1) The number of revenue vehicles operated by the given mode and type of service to meet the annual maximum service requirement. This is the revenue vehicle count during the peak season of the year; on the week and day that maximum service is provided. Vehicles operated in maximum service (VOMS) exclude atypical days and one-time special events; (2) The number of passengers who boarded public transportation vehicles. Passengers are counted each time they board a vehicle no matter how many vehicles they use to travel from their origin to their destination. (3) The sum of the distances ridden by all passengers during the entire fiscal year.
Source: Federal Transit Administration, National Transit Database, 2017

Air Transportation

Airport Name and Code / Type of Service	Passenger Airlines[1]	Passenger Enplanements	Freight Carriers[2]	Freight (lbs)
Gainesville Regional Airport (GNV)				
Domestic service (U.S. carriers - 2018)	18	233,735	4	9,587
International service (U.S. carriers - 2017)	0	0	0	0

Note: (1) Includes all U.S.-based major, minor and commuter airlines that carried at least one passenger during the year; (2) Includes all U.S.-based airlines and freight carriers that transported at least one pound of freight during the year.
Source: Bureau of Transportation Statistics, The Intermodal Transportation Database, Air Carriers: T-100 Domestic Market (U.S. Carriers), 2018; Bureau of Transportation Statistics, The Intermodal Transportation Database, Air Carriers: T-100 International Market (U.S. Carriers), 2017

Other Transportation Statistics

Major Highways:	I-75
Amtrak Service:	Yes (train station is located in Waldo, FL)
Major Waterways/Ports:	None

Source: Amtrak.com; Google Maps

BUSINESSES

Major Business Headquarters

Company Name	Industry	Rankings	
		Fortune[1]	Forbes[2]
No companies listed	-	-	-

Note: (1) Companies that produce a 10-K are ranked 1 to 500 based on 2017 revenue; (2) All private companies with at least $2 billion in annual revenue through the end of their most current fiscal year are ranked 1 to 229; companies listed are headquartered in the city; dashes indicate no ranking
Source: Fortune, "Fortune 500," June 2018; Forbes, "America's Largest Private Companies," 2018 Rankings

Fast-Growing Businesses

According to *Inc.*, Gainesville is home to one of America's 500 fastest-growing private companies: **ITProTV** (#424). Criteria: must be an independent, privately-held, for-profit, U.S. corporation, proprietorship or partnership as of December 31, 2017; revenues must be at least $100,000 in 2014 and $2 million in 2017; must have four-year operating/sales history. Holding companies, regulated banks, and utilities were excluded. *Inc., "America's 500 Fastest-Growing Private Companies," 2018*

Minority- and Women-Owned Businesses

Group	All Firms		Firms with Paid Employees			
	Firms	Sales ($000)	Firms	Sales ($000)	Employees	Payroll ($000)
AIAN[1]	91	(s)	11	(s)	20 - 99	(s)
Asian	731	173,743	301	146,359	1,284	24,353
Black	1,377	29,781	25	13,937	219	4,355
Hispanic	628	46,678	113	32,930	270	6,360
NHOPI[2]	n/a	n/a	n/a	n/a	n/a	n/a
Women	3,408	284,998	481	241,456	2,578	56,746
All Firms	9,764	9,414,881	3,032	9,181,243	56,534	1,843,079

Note: Figures cover firms located in the city; minority- and women-owned business are defined as firms in which the corresponding group own 51% or more of the stock or equity of the company; (1) American Indian and Alaska Native; (2) Native Hawaiian and Other Pacific Islander; (s) estimates are suppressed when publication standards are not met; n/a not available
Source: U.S. Census Bureau, 2012 Economic Census, Survey of Business Owners

**HOTELS &
CONVENTION
CENTERS**

Hotels, Motels and Vacation Rentals

Area	5 Star		4 Star		3 Star		2 Star		1 Star		Not Rated	
	Num.	Pct.[3]	Num.	Pct.[3]	Num.	Pct.[3]	Num.	Pct.[3]	Num.	Pct.[3]	Num.	Pct.[3]
City[1]	0	0.0	2	1.0	23	11.9	64	33.0	5	2.6	100	51.5
Total[2]	286	0.4	5,236	7.1	16,715	22.6	10,259	13.9	293	0.4	41,056	55.6

Note: (1) Figures cover Gainesville and vicinity; (2) Figures cover all 100 cities in this book; (3) Percentage of hotels which have a given star rating; Star ratings are determined by expedia.com and offer an indication of the general quality of a particular hotel.
Source: www.expedia.com, April 3, 2019

Major Convention Centers

Name	Overall Space (sq. ft.)	Exhibit Space (sq. ft.)	Meeting Space (sq. ft.)	Meeting Rooms

There are no major convention centers located in the metro area
Source: Original research

Living Environment

COST OF LIVING

Cost of Living Index

Composite Index	Groceries	Housing	Utilities	Trans-portation	Health Care	Misc. Goods/ Services
n/a	n/a	n/a	n/a	n/a	n/a	n/a

Note: The Cost of Living Index measures regional differences in the cost of consumer goods and services, excluding taxes and non-consumer expenditures, for professional and managerial households in the top income quintile. It is based on more than 50,000 prices covering almost 60 different items for which prices are collected three times a year by chambers of commerce, economic development organizations or university applied economic centers in each participating urban area. The numbers shown should be read as a percentage above or below the national average of 100. For example, a value of 115.4 in the groceries column indicates that grocery prices are 15.4% higher than the national average. Small differences in the index numbers should not be interpreted as significant; n/a not available.
Source: The Council for Community and Economic Research, ACCRA Cost of Living Index, 2018

Grocery Prices

Area[1]	T-Bone Steak ($/pound)	Frying Chicken ($/pound)	Whole Milk ($/half gal.)	Eggs ($/dozen)	Orange Juice ($/64 oz.)	Coffee ($/11.5 oz.)
City[2]	n/a	n/a	n/a	n/a	n/a	n/a
Avg.	11.35	1.42	1.94	1.81	3.52	4.35
Min.	7.45	0.92	0.80	0.75	2.72	3.06
Max.	15.05	2.76	4.18	4.00	5.36	8.20

Note: (1) Values for the local area are compared with the average, minimum and maximum values for all 291 areas in the Cost of Living Index; (2) Figures cover the Gainesville FL urban area; n/a not available; **T-Bone Steak** (price per pound); **Frying Chicken** (price per pound, whole fryer); **Whole Milk** (half gallon carton); **Eggs** (price per dozen, Grade A, large); **Orange Juice** (64 oz. Tropicana or Florida Natural); **Coffee** (11.5 oz. can, vacuum-packed, Maxwell House, Hills Bros, or Folgers).
Source: The Council for Community and Economic Research, ACCRA Cost of Living Index, 2018

Housing and Utility Costs

Area[1]	New Home Price ($)	Apartment Rent ($/month)	All Electric ($/month)	Part Electric ($/month)	Other Energy ($/month)	Telephone ($/month)
City[2]	n/a	n/a	n/a	n/a	n/a	n/a
Avg.	347,000	1,087	165.93	100.16	67.73	178.70
Min.	200,468	500	93.58	25.64	26.78	163.10
Max.	1,901,222	4,888	388.65	246.86	332.81	197.70

Note: (1) Values for the local area are compared with the average, minimum and maximum values for all 291 areas in the Cost of Living Index; (2) Figures cover the Gainesville FL urban area; n/a not available; **New Home Price** (2,400 sf living area, 8,000 sf lot, in urban area with full utilities); **Apartment Rent** (950 sf 2 bedroom/1.5 or 2 bath, unfurnished, excluding all utilities except water); **All Electric** (average monthly cost for an all-electric home); **Part Electric** (average monthly cost for a part-electric home); **Other Energy** (average monthly cost for natural gas, fuel oil, coal, wood, and any other forms of energy except electricity); **Telephone** (price includes the base monthly rate plus taxes and fees for three lines of mobile phone service).
Source: The Council for Community and Economic Research, ACCRA Cost of Living Index, 2018

Health Care, Transportation, and Other Costs

Area[1]	Doctor ($/visit)	Dentist ($/visit)	Optometrist ($/visit)	Gasoline ($/gallon)	Beauty Salon ($/visit)	Men's Shirt ($)
City[2]	n/a	n/a	n/a	n/a	n/a	n/a
Avg.	110.71	95.11	103.74	2.61	37.48	32.03
Min.	33.60	62.55	54.63	1.89	17.00	11.44
Max.	195.97	153.93	225.79	3.59	71.88	58.64

Note: (1) Values for the local area are compared with the average, minimum and maximum values for all 291 areas in the Cost of Living Index; (2) Figures cover the Gainesville FL urban area; n/a not available; **Doctor** (general practitioners routine exam of an established patient); **Dentist** (adult teeth cleaning and periodic oral examination); **Optometrist** (full vision eye exam for established adult patient); **Gasoline** (one gallon regular unleaded, national brand, including all taxes, cash price at self-service pump if available); **Beauty Salon** (woman's shampoo, trim, and blow-dry); **Men's Shirt** (cotton/polyester dress shirt, pinpoint weave, long sleeves).
Source: The Council for Community and Economic Research, ACCRA Cost of Living Index, 2018

HOUSING

House Price Index (HPI)

Area	National Ranking[2]	Quarterly Change (%)	One-Year Change (%)	Five-Year Change (%)
MSA[1]	(a)	n/a	3.51	36.42
U.S.[3]	–	1.12	5.73	32.81

Note: The HPI is a weighted repeat sales index. It measures average price changes in repeat sales or refinancings on the same properties. This information is obtained by reviewing repeat mortgage transactions on single-family properties whose mortgages have been purchased or securitized by Fannie Mae or Freddie Mac in January 1975; (1) Figures cover the Gainesville, FL Metropolitan Statistical Area—see Appendix B for areas included; (2) Rankings are based on annual percentage change for all metro areas containing at least 15,000 transactions over the last 10 years and ranges from 1 to 245; (3) figures based on a weighted average of Census Division estimates using a seasonally adjusted, purchase-only index; all figures are for the period ending December 31, 2018; n/a not available; (a) Not ranked because of increased index variability due to smaller sample size
Source: Federal Housing Finance Agency, House Price Index, February 26, 2019

Median Single-Family Home Prices

Area	2016	2017	2018[p]	Percent Change 2017 to 2018
MSA[1]	195.0	210.0	230.0	9.5
U.S. Average	235.5	248.8	261.6	5.1

Note: Figures are median sales prices of existing single-family homes in thousands of dollars; (p) preliminary; (1) Figures cover the Gainesville, FL Metropolitan Statistical Area—see Appendix B for areas included
Source: National Association of Realtors, Median Sales Price of Existing Single-Family Homes for Metropolitan Areas, 4th Quarter 2018

Qualifying Income Based on Median Sales Price of Existing Single-Family Homes

Area	With 5% Down ($)	With 10% Down ($)	With 20% Down ($)
MSA[1]	56,942	53,945	47,951
U.S. Average	62,954	59,640	53,013

Note: Figures are preliminary; Qualifying income is based on a mortgage rate of 4.9%. Monthly principal and interest payment is limited to 25% of income; (1) Figures cover the Gainesville, FL Metropolitan Statistical Area—see Appendix B for areas included
Source: National Association of Realtors, Qualifying Income Based on Median Sales Price of Existing Single-Family Homes for Metropolitan Areas, 4th Quarter 2018

Median Apartment Condo-Coop Home Prices

Area	2016	2017	2018[p]	Percent Change 2017 to 2018
MSA[1]	n/a	n/a	n/a	n/a
U.S. Average	220.7	234.3	241.0	2.9

Note: Figures are median sales prices of existing apartment condo-coop homes in thousands of dollars; (p) preliminary; n/a not available; (1) Figures cover the Gainesville, FL Metropolitan Statistical Area—see Appendix B for areas included
Source: National Association of Realtors, Median Sales Price of Existing Apartment Condo-Coop Homes for Metropolitan Areas, 4th Quarter 2018

Home Value Distribution

Area	Under $50,000	$50,000 -$99,999	$100,000 -$149,999	$150,000 -$199,999	$200,000 -$299,999	$300,000 -$499,999	$500,000 -$999,999	$1,000,000 or more
City	6.6	21.7	22.8	20.6	18.2	7.9	1.9	0.2
MSA[1]	7.6	19.4	17.9	18.3	20.3	12.0	4.1	0.4
U.S.	8.3	13.9	14.7	14.6	18.7	17.3	9.7	2.7

Note: Figures are percentages and cover owner-occupied housing units; (1) Figures cover the Gainesville, FL Metropolitan Statistical Area—see Appendix B for areas included
Source: U.S. Census Bureau, 2013-2017 American Community Survey 5-Year Estimates

Homeownership Rate

Area	2010 (%)	2011 (%)	2012 (%)	2013 (%)	2014 (%)	2015 (%)	2016 (%)	2017 (%)	2018 (%)
MSA[1]	n/a	n/a	n/a	n/a	n/a	n/a	n/a	n/a	n/a
U.S.	66.9	66.1	65.4	65.1	64.5	63.7	63.4	63.9	64.4

Note: (1) Figures cover the Gainesville, FL Metropolitan Statistical Area—see Appendix B for areas included; n/a not available
Source: U.S. Census Bureau, Housing Vacancies and Homeownership Annual Statistics: 2010-2018

Year Housing Structure Built

Area	2010 or Later	2000 -2009	1990 -1999	1980 -1989	1970 -1979	1960 -1969	1950 -1959	1940 -1949	Before 1940	Median Year
City	2.5	13.8	15.6	19.9	21.1	12.3	9.2	3.0	2.6	1981
MSA[1]	3.0	18.4	19.7	20.5	18.4	8.6	6.6	2.1	2.5	1986
U.S.	3.2	14.5	14.0	13.6	15.5	10.8	10.5	5.1	12.9	1977

Note: Figures are percentages except for Median Year; Note: (1) Figures cover the Gainesville, FL Metropolitan Statistical Area—see Appendix B for areas included
Source: U.S. Census Bureau, 2013-2017 American Community Survey 5-Year Estimates

Gross Monthly Rent

Area	Under $500	$500 -$999	$1,000 -$1,499	$1,500 -$1,999	$2,000 -$2,499	$2,500 -$2,999	$3,000 and up	Median ($)
City	7.5	56.6	27.2	6.4	1.4	0.5	0.4	886
MSA[1]	7.8	52.5	29.7	7.2	1.5	0.8	0.5	912
U.S.	10.5	41.1	28.7	11.7	4.5	1.8	1.7	982

Note: Figures are percentages except for Median; Gross rent is the contract rent plus the estimated average monthly cost of utilities (electricity, gas, and water and sewer) and fuels (oil, coal, kerosene, wood, etc.) if these are paid by the renter (or paid for the renter by someone else); (1) Figures cover the Gainesville, FL Metropolitan Statistical Area—see Appendix B for areas included
Source: U.S. Census Bureau, 2013-2017 American Community Survey 5-Year Estimates

HEALTH

Health Risk Factors

Category	MSA[1] (%)	U.S. (%)
Adults aged 18–64 who have any kind of health care coverage	82.6	87.3
Adults who reported being in good or better health	88.2	82.4
Adults who have been told they have high blood cholesterol	29.5	33.0
Adults who have been told they have high blood pressure	31.8	32.3
Adults who are current smokers	13.0	17.1
Adults who currently use E-cigarettes	n/a	4.6
Adults who currently use chewing tobacco, snuff, or snus	5.8	4.0
Adults who are heavy drinkers[2]	6.9	6.3
Adults who are binge drinkers[3]	15.1	17.4
Adults who are overweight (BMI 25.0 - 29.9)	27.4	35.3
Adults who are obese (BMI 30.0 - 99.8)	30.8	31.3
Adults who participated in any physical activities in the past month	75.4	74.4
Adults who always or nearly always wears a seat belt	94.1	94.3

Note: n/a not available; (1) Figures cover the Gainesville, FL Metropolitan Statistical Area—see Appendix B for areas included; (2) Heavy drinkers are classified as adult men having more than 14 drinks per week and adult women having more than 7 drinks per week; (3) Binge drinkers are classified as males having five or more drinks on one occasion or females having four or more drinks on one occasion
Source: Centers for Disease Control and Prevention, Behaviorial Risk Factor Surveillance System, SMART: Selected Metropolitan Area Risk Trends, 2017

Acute and Chronic Health Conditions

Category	MSA[1] (%)	U.S. (%)
Adults who have ever been told they had a heart attack	n/a	4.2
Adults who have ever been told they have angina or coronary heart disease	4.0	3.9
Adults who have ever been told they had a stroke	n/a	3.0
Adults who have ever been told they have asthma	12.1	14.2
Adults who have ever been told they have arthritis	19.1	24.9
Adults who have ever been told they have diabetes[2]	11.8	10.5
Adults who have ever been told they had skin cancer	8.2	6.2
Adults who have ever been told they had any other types of cancer	3.9	7.1
Adults who have ever been told they have COPD	3.9	6.5
Adults who have ever been told they have kidney disease	n/a	3.0
Adults who have ever been told they have a form of depression	21.0	20.5

Note: n/a not available; (1) Figures cover the Gainesville, FL Metropolitan Statistical Area—see Appendix B for areas included; (2) Figures do not include pregnancy-related, borderline, or pre-diabetes
Source: Centers for Disease Control and Prevention, Behaviorial Risk Factor Surveillance System, SMART: Selected Metropolitan Area Risk Trends, 2017

Health Screening and Vaccination Rates

Category	MSA[1] (%)	U.S. (%)
Adults aged 65+ who have had flu shot within the past year	62.7	60.7
Adults aged 65+ who have ever had a pneumonia vaccination	70.2	75.4
Adults who have ever been tested for HIV	40.3	36.1
Adults who have ever had the shingles or zoster vaccine?	30.2	28.9
Adults who have had their blood cholesterol checked within the last five years	82.9	85.9

Note: n/a not available; (1) Figures cover the Gainesville, FL Metropolitan Statistical Area—see Appendix B for areas included.
Source: Centers for Disease Control and Prevention, Behaviorial Risk Factor Surveillance System, SMART: Selected Metropolitan Area Risk Trends, 2017

Disability Status

Category	MSA[1] (%)	U.S. (%)
Adults who reported being deaf	4.3	6.7
Are you blind or have serious difficulty seeing, even when wearing glasses?	n/a	4.5
Are you limited in any way in any of your usual activities due of arthritis?	9.8	12.9
Do you have difficulty doing errands alone?	4.6	6.8
Do you have difficulty dressing or bathing?	2.7	3.6
Do you have serious difficulty concentrating/remembering/making decisions?	10.2	10.7
Do you have serious difficulty walking or climbing stairs?	11.3	13.6

Note: n/a not available; (1) Figures cover the Gainesville, FL Metropolitan Statistical Area—see Appendix B for areas included.
Source: Centers for Disease Control and Prevention, Behaviorial Risk Factor Surveillance System, SMART: Selected Metropolitan Area Risk Trends, 2017

Mortality Rates for the Top 10 Causes of Death in the U.S.

ICD-10[a] Sub-Chapter	ICD-10[a] Code	County[2]	U.S.
Malignant neoplasms	C00-C97	166.6	155.5
Ischaemic heart diseases	I20-I25	70.0	94.8
Other forms of heart disease	I30-I51	40.3	52.9
Chronic lower respiratory diseases	J40-J47	34.9	41.0
Cerebrovascular diseases	I60-I69	38.0	37.5
Other degenerative diseases of the nervous system	G30-G31	23.8	35.0
Other external causes of accidental injury	W00-X59	34.2	33.7
Organic, including symptomatic, mental disorders	F01-F09	57.0	31.0
Hypertensive diseases	I10-I15	17.6	21.9
Diabetes mellitus	E10-E14	22.7	21.2

(Age-Adjusted Mortality Rate[1] per 100,000 population)
Note: (a) ICD-10 = International Classification of Diseases 10th Revision; (1) Mortality rates are a three year average covering 2015-2017; (2) Figures cover Alachua County.
Source: Centers for Disease Control and Prevention, National Center for Health Statistics. Underlying Cause of Death 1999-2017 on CDC WONDER Online Database

Mortality Rates for Selected Causes of Death

ICD-10[a] Sub-Chapter	ICD-10[a] Code	County[2]	U.S.
Assault	X85-Y09	3.5	5.9
Diseases of the liver	K70-K76	15.7	14.1
Human immunodeficiency virus (HIV) disease	B20-B24	4.2	1.8
Influenza and pneumonia	J09-J18	7.8	14.3
Intentional self-harm	X60-X84	12.8	13.6
Malnutrition	E40-E46	Suppressed	1.6
Obesity and other hyperalimentation	E65-E68	3.6	2.1
Renal failure	N17-N19	10.3	13.0
Transport accidents	V01-V99	12.4	12.4
Viral hepatitis	B15-B19	Unreliable	1.6

(Age-Adjusted Mortality Rate[1] per 100,000 population)
Note: (a) ICD-10 = International Classification of Diseases 10th Revision; (1) Mortality rates are a three year average covering 2015-2017; (2) Figures cover Alachua County; Data are suppressed when the data meet the criteria for confidentiality constraints; Mortality rates are flagged as unreliable when the rate would be calculated with a numerator of 20 or less.
Source: Centers for Disease Control and Prevention, National Center for Health Statistics. Underlying Cause of Death 1999-2017 on CDC WONDER Online Database

Health Insurance Coverage

Area	With Health Insurance	With Private Health Insurance	With Public Health Insurance	Without Health Insurance	Population Under Age 18 Without Health Insurance
City	89.0	74.8	22.0	11.0	3.0
MSA[1]	88.9	71.7	27.6	11.1	5.6
U.S.	89.5	67.2	33.8	10.5	5.7

Note: Figures are percentages that cover the civilian noninstitutionalized population; (1) Figures cover the Gainesville, FL Metropolitan Statistical Area—see Appendix B for areas included
Source: U.S. Census Bureau, 2013-2017 American Community Survey 5-Year Estimates

Number of Medical Professionals

Area	MDs[3]	DOs[3,4]	Dentists	Podiatrists	Chiropractors	Optometrists
County[1] (number)	2,392	69	455	10	70	47
County[1] (rate[2])	904.9	26.1	170.4	3.7	26.2	17.6
U.S. (rate[2])	279.3	23.0	68.4	6.0	27.1	16.2

Note: Data as of 2017 unless noted; (1) Data covers Alachua County; (2) Rate per 100,000 population; (3) Data as of 2016 and includes all active, non-federal physicians; (4) Doctor of Osteopathic Medicine
Source: U.S. Department of Health and Human Services, Health Resources and Services Administration, Bureau of Health Professions, Area Resource File (ARF) 2017-2018

Best Hospitals

According to *U.S. News*, the Gainesville, FL metro area is home to one of the best hospitals in the U.S.: **UF Health Shands Hospital** (6 adult specialties and 6 pediatric specialties). The hospital listed was nationally ranked in at least one of 16 adult or 10 pediatric specialties. Only 170 hospitals nationwide were nationally ranked in one or more adult or pediatric specialty. Twenty hospitals in the U.S. made the Honor Roll. The Best Hospitals Honor Roll takes both the national rankings and the procedure and condition ratings into account. Hospitals received points if they were nationally ranked in one of the 16 adult specialties—the higher they ranked, the more points they got—and how many ratings of "high performing" they earned in the nine procedures and conditions. *U.S. News Online, "America's Best Hospitals 2018-19"*

According to *U.S. News*, the Gainesville, FL metro area is home to one of the best children's hospitals in the U.S.: **UF Health Shands Children's Hospital** (6 pediatric specialties). The hospital listed was highly ranked in at least one of 10 pediatric specialties. Eighty-six children's hospitals in the U.S. were nationally ranked in at least one specialty. Hospitals received points for being ranked in a specialty, and the 10 hospitals with the most points across the 10 specialties make up the Honor Roll. *U.S. News Online, "America's Best Children's Hospitals 2018-19"*

EDUCATION

Public School District Statistics

District Name	Schls	Pupils	Pupil/ Teacher Ratio	Minority Pupils[1] (%)	Free Lunch Eligible[2] (%)	IEP[3] (%)
Alachua County Public Schools	67	29,475	19.6	56.7	46.1	12.9

Note: Table includes school districts with 2,000 or more students; (1) Percentage of students that are not non-Hispanic white; (2) Percentage of students that are eligible for the free lunch program; (3) Percentage of students that have an Individualized Education Program.
Source: U.S. Department of Education, National Center for Education Statistics, Common Core of Data, Local Education Agency (School District) Universe Survey: School Year 2016-2017; U.S. Department of Education, National Center for Education Statistics, Common Core of Data, Public Elementary/Secondary School Universe Survey: School Year 2016-2017

Highest Level of Education

Area	Less than H.S.	H.S. Diploma	Some College, No Deg.	Associate Degree	Bachelor's Degree	Master's Degree	Prof. School Degree	Doctorate Degree
City	8.5	21.2	17.6	9.6	21.5	13.0	3.8	4.8
MSA[1]	8.4	23.4	18.5	10.3	20.2	10.7	4.0	4.4
U.S.	12.7	27.3	20.8	8.3	19.1	8.4	2.0	1.4

Note: Figures cover persons age 25 and over; (1) Figures cover the Gainesville, FL Metropolitan Statistical Area—see Appendix B for areas included
Source: U.S. Census Bureau, 2013-2017 American Community Survey 5-Year Estimates

Educational Attainment by Race

Area	High School Graduate or Higher (%)					Bachelor's Degree or Higher (%)				
	Total	White	Black	Asian	Hisp.[2]	Total	White	Black	Asian	Hisp.[2]
City	91.5	94.3	83.7	93.0	91.5	43.1	49.9	18.1	67.6	45.0
MSA[1]	91.6	93.3	84.3	94.1	88.3	39.4	42.0	19.0	72.2	38.0
U.S.	87.3	89.3	84.9	86.5	66.7	30.9	32.2	20.6	52.7	15.2

Note: Figures shown cover persons 25 years old and over; (1) Figures cover the Gainesville, FL Metropolitan Statistical Area—see Appendix B for areas included; (2) People of Hispanic origin can be of any race
Source: U.S. Census Bureau, 2013-2017 American Community Survey 5-Year Estimates

School Enrollment by Grade and Control

Area	Preschool (%)		Kindergarten (%)		Grades 1 - 4 (%)		Grades 5 - 8 (%)		Grades 9 - 12 (%)	
	Public	Private	Public	Private	Public	Private	Public	Private	Public	Private
City	51.5	48.5	79.0	21.0	85.7	14.3	83.2	16.8	89.6	10.4
MSA[1]	49.8	50.2	82.5	17.5	87.4	12.6	82.8	17.2	90.6	9.4
U.S.	58.8	41.2	87.7	12.3	89.7	10.3	89.6	10.4	90.3	9.7

Note: Figures shown cover persons 3 years old and over; (1) Figures cover the Gainesville, FL Metropolitan Statistical Area—see Appendix B for areas included
Source: U.S. Census Bureau, 2013-2017 American Community Survey 5-Year Estimates

Average Salaries of Public School Classroom Teachers

Area	2016		2017		Change from 2016 to 2017	
	Dollars	Rank[1]	Dollars	Rank[1]	Percent	Rank[2]
Florida	46,612	46	47,267	45	1.4	26
U.S. Average	58,479	–	59,660	–	2.0	–

Note: (1) Rank ranges from 1 to 51 where 1 indicates highest salary; (2) Rank ranges from 1 to 51 where 1 indicates highest percent change.
Source: National Education Association, Rankings & Estimates: Rankings of the States 2017 and Estimates of School Statistics 2018

Higher Education

Four-Year Colleges			Two-Year Colleges			Medical Schools[1]	Law Schools[2]	Voc/ Tech[3]
Public	Private Non-profit	Private For-profit	Public	Private Non-profit	Private For-profit			
3	3	0	0	1	0	1	1	2

Note: Figures cover institutions located within the city limits and include main campuses only; (1) includes schools accredited by the Liaison Committee on Medical Education and the American Osteopathic Association's Commission on Osteopathic College Accreditation; (2) includes ABA-accredited schools, schools with provisional ABA accreditation, and state accredited schools; (3) includes all schools with programs that are less than 2 years.
Source: National Center for Education Statistics, Integrated Postsecondary Education System (IPEDS), 2017-18; Wikipedia, List of Medical Schools in the United States, accessed April 3, 2019; Wikipedia, List of Law Schools in the United States, accessed April 3, 2019

According to *U.S. News & World Report,* the Gainesville, FL metro area is home to one of the best national universities in the U.S.: **University of Florida** (#35 tie). The indicators used to capture academic quality fall into a number of categories: assessment by administrators at peer institutions; retention of students; faculty resources; student selectivity; financial resources; alumni giving; high school counselor ratings of colleges; and graduation rate. *U.S. News & World Report, "America's Best Colleges 2019"*

According to *U.S. News & World Report,* the Gainesville, FL metro area is home to one of the top 100 law schools in the U.S.: **University of Florida (Levin)** (#31 tie). The rankings are based on a weighted average of 12 measures of quality: peer assessment score; assessment score by lawyers/judges; median LSAT scores; median undergrad GPA; acceptance rate; employment rates for graduates; placement success; bar passage rate; faculty resources; expenditures per student; student/faculty ratio; and library resources. *U.S. News & World Report, "America's Best Graduate Schools, Law, 2020"*

According to *U.S. News & World Report,* the Gainesville, FL metro area is home to one of the top 75 medical schools for research in the U.S.: **University of Florida** (#43 tie). The rankings are based on a weighted average of 11 measures of quality: quality assessment; peer assessment score; assessment score by residency directors; research activity; total research activity; average research activity per faculty member; student selectivity; median MCAT total score; median undergraduate GPA; acceptance rate; and faculty resources. *U.S. News & World Report, "America's Best Graduate Schools, Medical, 2020"*

According to *U.S. News & World Report,* the Gainesville, FL metro area is home to one of the top 75 business schools in the U.S.: **University of Florida (Warrington)** (#25). The rankings are based on a weighted average of the following nine measures: quality assessment; peer assessment; recruiter assessment; placement success; mean starting salary and bonus; student selectivity; mean GMAT and GRE scores; mean undergraduate GPA; and acceptance rate. *U.S. News & World Report,* "America's Best Graduate Schools, Business, 2020"

PRESIDENTIAL ELECTION

2016 Presidential Election Results

Area	Clinton	Trump	Johnson	Stein	Other
Alachua County	58.3	36.0	3.1	1.2	1.4
U.S.	48.0	45.9	3.3	1.1	1.7

Note: Results are percentages and may not add to 100% due to rounding
Source: Dave Leip's Atlas of U.S. Presidential Elections

EMPLOYERS

Major Employers

Company Name	Industry
Alachua County	Government
Alachua County School Board	Education
City of Gainesville	Government
Dollar General Distribution Center	Retail
Gator Dining Services	Food services
Nationwide Insurance Company	Insurance
North Florida Regional Medical Center	Healthcare
Publix Supermarkets	Retail grocery
RTI Surgical	Medical manufacturing
Santa Fe College	Education
UF Health	Healthcare
University of Florida	Education
Veterans Affairs Medical Center	Healthcare
Wal-Mart Distribution Center	Retail
Wal-Mart Stores	Retail

Note: Companies shown are located within the Gainesville, FL Metropolitan Statistical Area.
Source: Hoovers.com; Wikipedia

PUBLIC SAFETY

Crime Rate

Area	All Crimes	Violent Crimes				Property Crimes		
		Murder	Rape[3]	Robbery	Aggrav. Assault	Burglary	Larceny -Theft	Motor Vehicle Theft
City	4,315.5	3.0	123.5	132.6	457.9	376.6	2,948.6	273.4
Suburbs[1]	2,291.7	3.3	56.8	80.5	338.6	439.6	1,260.7	112.2
Metro[2]	3,236.9	3.2	87.9	104.8	394.3	410.2	2,049.0	187.5
U.S.	2,756.1	5.3	41.7	98.0	248.9	430.4	1,694.4	237.4

Note: Figures are crimes per 100,000 population; (1) All areas within the metro area that are located outside the city limits; (2) Figures cover the Gainesville, FL Metropolitan Statistical Area—see Appendix B for areas included; (3) The city and U.S. figures shown were reported using the revised Uniform Crime Reporting (UCR) definition of rape. The suburban and metro area figures shown are an aggregate total of the data submitted using both the revised and legacy UCR definitions.
Source: FBI Uniform Crime Reports, 2017

Hate Crimes

Area	Number of Quarters Reported	Number of Incidents per Bias Motivation					
		Race/Ethnicity/ Ancestry	Religion	Sexual Orientation	Disability	Gender	Gender Identity
City	4	0	1	0	0	0	0
U.S.	4	4,131	1,564	1,130	116	46	119

Source: Federal Bureau of Investigation, Hate Crime Statistics 2017

Identity Theft Consumer Reports

Area	Reports	Reports per 100,000 Population	Rank[2]
MSA[1]	373	133	54
U.S.	444,602	135	-

Note: (1) Figures cover the Gainesville, FL Metropolitan Statistical Area—see Appendix B for areas included; (2) Rank ranges from 1 to 389 where 1 indicates greatest number of identity theft reports per 100,000 population
Source: Federal Trade Commission, Consumer Sentinel Network Data Book for January–December 2018

Fraud and Other Consumer Reports

Area	Reports	Reports per 100,000 Population	Rank[2]
MSA[1]	2,101	748	13
U.S.	2,552,917	776	-

Note: (1) Figures cover the Gainesville, FL Metropolitan Statistical Area—see Appendix B for areas included; (2) Rank ranges from 1 to 389 where 1 indicates greatest number of fraud and other consumer reports per 100,000 population
Source: Federal Trade Commission, Consumer Sentinel Network Data Book for January–December 2018

SPORTS

Professional Sports Teams

Team Name	League	Year Established

No teams are located in the metro area
Source: Wikipedia, Major Professional Sports Teams of the United States and Canada, April 5, 2019

CLIMATE

Average and Extreme Temperatures

Temperature	Jan	Feb	Mar	Apr	May	Jun	Jul	Aug	Sep	Oct	Nov	Dec	Yr.
Extreme High (°F)	83	85	90	95	98	102	99	99	95	92	88	85	102
Average High (°F)	66	68	74	81	86	89	90	90	87	81	74	68	79
Average Temp. (°F)	55	57	63	69	75	79	81	81	78	71	63	56	69
Average Low (°F)	43	45	50	56	63	69	71	71	69	60	51	44	58
Extreme Low (°F)	10	19	28	35	42	50	62	62	48	33	28	13	10

Note: Figures cover the years 1962-1995
Source: National Climatic Data Center, International Station Meteorological Climate Summary, 9/96

Average Precipitation/Snowfall/Humidity

Precip./Humidity	Jan	Feb	Mar	Apr	May	Jun	Jul	Aug	Sep	Oct	Nov	Dec	Yr.
Avg. Precip. (in.)	3.7	4.0	3.9	2.3	3.3	6.9	6.5	7.7	5.1	2.8	2.2	2.6	50.9
Avg. Snowfall (in.)	0	Tr	0	0	0	0	0	0	0	0	0	Tr	Tr
Avg. Rel. Hum. 7am (%)	90	90	92	92	91	93	94	96	96	94	94	92	93
Avg. Rel. Hum. 4pm (%)	60	55	52	50	51	61	67	67	67	63	63	61	60

Note: Figures cover the years 1962-1995; Tr = Trace amounts (<0.05 in. of rain; <0.5 in. of snow)
Source: National Climatic Data Center, International Station Meteorological Climate Summary, 9/96

Weather Conditions

Temperature			Daytime Sky			Precipitation		
32°F & below	45°F & below	90°F & above	Clear	Partly cloudy	Cloudy	0.01 inch or more precip.	0.1 inch or more snow/ice	Thunder-storms
16	73	77	88	196	81	119	0	78

Note: Figures are average number of days per year and cover the years 1962-1995
Source: National Climatic Data Center, International Station Meteorological Climate Summary, 9/96

HAZARDOUS WASTE

Superfund Sites

The Gainesville, FL metro area is home to one site on the EPA's Superfund National Priorities List: **Cabot/Koppers** (final). There are a total of 1,390 Superfund sites with a status of proposed or final on the list in the U.S. *U.S. Environmental Protection Agency, National Priorities List, April 5, 2019*

**AIR & WATER
QUALITY**

Air Quality Trends: Ozone

	1990	1995	2000	2005	2010	2012	2014	2015	2016	2017
MSA[1]	n/a	n/a	n/a	n/a	n/a	n/a	n/a	n/a	n/a	n/a
U.S.	0.088	0.089	0.082	0.080	0.073	0.075	0.067	0.068	0.069	0.068

Note: (1) Data covers the Gainesville, FL Metropolitan Statistical Area—see Appendix B for areas included; n/a not available. The values shown are the composite ozone concentration averages among trend sites based on the highest fourth daily maximum 8-hour concentration in parts per million. These trends are based on sites having an adequate record of monitoring data during the trend period. Data from exceptional events are included.
Source: U.S. Environmental Protection Agency, Air Quality Monitoring Information, "Air Quality Trends by City, 1990-2017"

Air Quality Index

Area	Percent of Days when Air Quality was...[2]					AQI Statistics[2]	
	Good	Moderate	Unhealthy for Sensitive Groups	Unhealthy	Very Unhealthy	Maximum	Median
MSA[1]	89.0	11.0	0.0	0.0	0.0	92	37

Note: (1) Data covers the Gainesville, FL Metropolitan Statistical Area—see Appendix B for areas included; (2) Based on 355 days with AQI data in 2017. Air Quality Index (AQI) is an index for reporting daily air quality. EPA calculates the AQI for five major air pollutants regulated by the Clean Air Act: ground-level ozone, particle pollution (aka particulate matter), carbon monoxide, sulfur dioxide, and nitrogen dioxide. The AQI runs from 0 to 500. The higher the AQI value, the greater the level of air pollution and the greater the health concern. There are six AQI categories: "Good" AQI is between 0 and 50. Air quality is considered satisfactory; "Moderate" AQI is between 51 and 100. Air quality is acceptable; "Unhealthy for Sensitive Groups" When AQI values are between 101 and 150, members of sensitive groups may experience health effects; "Unhealthy" When AQI values are between 151 and 200 everyone may begin to experience health effects; "Very Unhealthy" AQI values between 201 and 300 trigger a health alert; "Hazardous" AQI values over 300 trigger warnings of emergency conditions (not shown).
Source: U.S. Environmental Protection Agency, Air Quality Index Report, 2017

Air Quality Index Pollutants

Area	Percent of Days when AQI Pollutant was...[2]					
	Carbon Monoxide	Nitrogen Dioxide	Ozone	Sulfur Dioxide	Particulate Matter 2.5	Particulate Matter 10
MSA[1]	0.0	0.0	61.4	0.0	38.6	0.0

Note: (1) Data covers the Gainesville, FL Metropolitan Statistical Area—see Appendix B for areas included; (2) Based on 355 days with AQI data in 2017. The Air Quality Index (AQI) is an index for reporting daily air quality. EPA calculates the AQI for five major air pollutants regulated by the Clean Air Act: ground-level ozone, particle pollution (also known as particulate matter), carbon monoxide, sulfur dioxide, and nitrogen dioxide. The AQI runs from 0 to 500. The higher the AQI value, the greater the level of air pollution and the greater the health concern.
Source: U.S. Environmental Protection Agency, Air Quality Index Report, 2017

Maximum Air Pollutant Concentrations: Particulate Matter, Ozone, CO and Lead

	Particulate Matter 10 (ug/m^3)	Particulate Matter 2.5 Wtd AM (ug/m^3)	Particulate Matter 2.5 24-Hr (ug/m^3)	Ozone (ppm)	Carbon Monoxide (ppm)	Lead (ug/m^3)
MSA[1] Level	n/a	6.7	17	0.063	n/a	n/a
NAAQS[2]	150	15	35	0.075	9	0.15
Met NAAQS[2]	n/a	Yes	Yes	Yes	n/a	n/a

Note: (1) Data covers the Gainesville, FL Metropolitan Statistical Area—see Appendix B for areas included; Data from exceptional events are included; (2) National Ambient Air Quality Standards; ppm = parts per million; ug/m³ = micrograms per cubic meter; n/a not available.
Concentrations: Particulate Matter 10 (coarse particulate)—highest second maximum 24-hour concentration; Particulate Matter 2.5 Wtd AM (fine particulate)—highest weighted annual mean concentration; Particulate Matter 2.5 24-Hour (fine particulate)—highest 98th percentile 24-hour concentration; Ozone—highest fourth daily maximum 8-hour concentration; Carbon Monoxide—highest second maximum non-overlapping 8-hour concentration; Lead—maximum running 3-month average
Source: U.S. Environmental Protection Agency, Air Quality Monitoring Information, "Air Quality Statistics by City, 2017"

Maximum Air Pollutant Concentrations: Nitrogen Dioxide and Sulfur Dioxide

	Nitrogen Dioxide AM (ppb)	Nitrogen Dioxide 1-Hr (ppb)	Sulfur Dioxide AM (ppb)	Sulfur Dioxide 1-Hr (ppb)	Sulfur Dioxide 24-Hr (ppb)
MSA[1] Level	n/a	n/a	n/a	n/a	n/a
NAAQS[2]	53	100	30	75	140
Met NAAQS[2]	n/a	n/a	n/a	n/a	n/a

Note: (1) Data covers the Gainesville, FL Metropolitan Statistical Area—see Appendix B for areas included; Data from exceptional events are included; (2) National Ambient Air Quality Standards; ppm = parts per million; ug/m^3 = micrograms per cubic meter; n/a not available.
Concentrations: Nitrogen Dioxide AM—highest arithmetic mean concentration; Nitrogen Dioxide 1-Hr—highest 98th percentile 1-hour daily maximum concentration; Sulfur Dioxide AM—highest annual mean concentration; Sulfur Dioxide 1-Hr—highest 99th percentile 1-hour daily maximum concentration; Sulfur Dioxide 24-Hr—highest second maximum 24-hour concentration
Source: U.S. Environmental Protection Agency, Air Quality Monitoring Information, "Air Quality Statistics by City, 2017"

Drinking Water

Water System Name	Pop. Served	Primary Water Source Type	Violations[1] Health Based	Violations[1] Monitoring/ Reporting
GRU - Murphree WTP	190,600	Ground	0	0

Note: (1) Based on violation data from January 1, 2018 to December 31, 2018
Source: U.S. Environmental Protection Agency, Office of Ground Water and Drinking Water, Safe Drinking Water Information System (based on data extracted April 5, 2019)

Houston, Texas

Background

In 1836, brothers John K. and Augustus C. Allen bought a 6,642-acre tract of marshy, mosquito-infested land 56 miles north of the Gulf of Mexico and named it Houston, after the hero of San Jacinto. From that moment on, Houston has experienced continued growth.

By the end of its first year in the Republic of Texas, Houston claimed 1,500 residents, one theater, and interestingly, no churches. The first churches came three years later. By the end of its second year, Houston saw its first steamship, establishing its position as one of the top-ranking ports in the country.

Certainly, Houston owes much to the Houston ship channel, the "golden strip" on which oil refineries, chemical plants, cement factories, and grain elevators conduct their bustling economic activity. The diversity of these industries is a testament to Houston's economy in general.

Tonnage through the Port of Houston has grown to the point of being number one in the nation for foreign tonnage. The port is important to the cruise industry as well, and the Norwegian Cruise Line sails out of Houston.

As Texas' biggest city, Houston has also enjoyed manufacturing expansion in its diversified economy. The city is home to the second largest number of Fortune 500 companies, second only to New York City.

Houston is also one of the major scientific research areas in the world. The presence of the Johnson Space Center has spawned a number of related industries in medical and technological research. The Texas Medical Center oversees a network of 45 medical institutions, including St. Luke's Episcopal Hospital, the Texas Children's Hospital, and the Methodist Hospital. As a city whose reputation rests upon advanced research, Houston is also devoted to education and the arts. Rice University, for example, whose admission standards rank as one of the highest in the nation, is located in Houston, as are Dominican College and the University of St. Thomas.

Today, this relatively young city is home to a diverse range of ethnicities, including Mexican-American, Nigerian, American-Indian and Pakistani.

Houston also is patron to the Museum of Fine Arts, the Contemporary Arts Museum, and the Houston Ballet and Grand Opera. A host of smaller cultural institutions, such as the Gilbert and Sullivan Society, the Virtuoso Quartet, and the Houston Harpsichord Society enliven the scene. Two privately funded museums, the Holocaust Museum Houston and the Houston Museum of Natural Science, are historical and educational attractions, and baseball's Minute Maid Park sits in the city's downtown.

Houstonians are eagerly embracing continued revitalization. This urban comeback has resulted in a virtual explosion of dining and entertainment options in the heart of the city. The opening of the Bayou Place, Houston's largest entertainment complex, has especially generated excitement, providing a variety of restaurants and entertainment options in one facility. A highly active urban park sits on 12 acres in front of the George R. Brown Convention Center. Reliant Stadium in downtown Houston and home to the NFL's Houston Texans, hosted Superbowl XXXVIII in 2004 and LI in 2017, and WrestleMania XXV in 2009. Major league baseball team Houston Astros won the 2017 World Series. In fact, the city has sports teams for every major professional league except the National Hockey League.

Located in the flat coastal plains, Houston's climate is predominantly marine. The terrain includes many small streams and bayous which, together with the nearness to Galveston Bay, favor the development of fog. Temperatures are moderated by the influence of winds from the Gulf of Mexico, which is 50 miles away. Mild winters are the norm, as is abundant rainfall. Polar air penetrates the area frequently enough to provide variability in the weather.

In August 2017, Hurricane Harvey caused severe flooding in the Houston area, with some regions receiving over 50 inches of rain. Damage from the hurricane is estimated at $125 billion. It is considered one of the worst natural disasters in the history of the United States, with a death toll of more than 70. In 2018, Houston City Council forgave the large water bills thousands of households faced in the aftermath of Hurricane Harvey.

Rankings

General Rankings

- The Houston metro area was identified as one of America's fastest-growing areas in terms of population and business growth by *MagnifyMoney*. The area ranked #11 out of 35. The 100 most populous metro areas in the U.S. were evaluated on their change from 2011-2016 in the following categories: people and housing; workforce and employment opportunities; growing industry. *www.businessinsider.com*, *"The 35 Cities in the US with the Biggest Influx of People, the Most Work Opportunities, and the Hottest Business Growth,"* August 12, 2018

- Houston was identified as one of America's fastest-growing cities in terms of population growth by CNNMoney.com. The area ranked #2 out of 10. Criteria: population growth between July 2015 and July 2016; cities and towns with populations of 50,000. *CNNMoney*, *"10 Fastest-Growing Cities,"* June 2, 2017

- The human resources consulting firm Mercer ranked 231 major cities worldwide in terms of overall quality of life. Houston ranked #66. Criteria: political, social, economic, and socio-cultural factors; medical and health considerations; schools and education; public services and transportation; recreation; consumer goods; housing; and natural environment. *Mercer*, *"Mercer 2019 Quality of Living Survey,"* March 13, 2019

Business/Finance Rankings

- According to *Business Insider*, the Houston metro area is where startup growth is on the rise. Based on the 2017 Kauffman Index of Growth Entrepreneurship, which measured in-depth national entrepreneurial trends in 40 metro areas, it ranked #19 in highest startup growth. *www.businessinsider.com*, *"The 21 U.S. Cities with the Highest Startup Growth,"* October 21, 2017

- The personal finance site NerdWallet analyzed 183 American metropolitan areas with populations over 250,000 and more than 15,000 businesses to rank where entrepreneurs find the most success. Criteria included area economy, annual income, housing cost, unemployment rate, and the success rate of area businesses. Houston ranked #80. *www.nerdwallet.com*, *"Best Places to Start a Business,"* April 27, 2015

- Recognizing the sizeable percentage of American workers who are self-employed, NerdWallet editors assessed the country's cities according to percentage of freelancers, median rental costs, cell phone plans/taxes, and healthcare affordability and access. By these criteria, Houston placed #15 among the best cities for independent workers. *www.nerdwallet.com*, *"Best Places for Freelance Workers,"* August 30, 2016

- USAA and Hiring Our Heroes worked with Sperlings's BestPlaces and the Institute for Veterans and Military Families at Syracuse University to rank major metropolitan areas where military-skills-related employment is strongest. Criteria for *mid-career* veterans included veteran wage growth; recent job growth; stability; and accessible health resources. Metro areas with a higher than national average crime or unemployment rate were excluded. At #3, the Houston metro area made the top ten. *www.usaa.com*, *"2015 Best Places for Veterans"*

- 24/7 Wall Street used Brookings Institution research on 50 advanced industries to identify the proportion of workers in the nation's largest metropolitan areas that were employed in jobs requiring knowledge in the science, technology, engineering, or math (STEM) fields and where there was heavy investment in research and development (R&D). The Houston metro area was #13. *247wallst.com*, *"15 Cities with the Most High-Tech Jobs,"* February 23, 2017

- In a survey of economic confidence in the nation's 50 largest metropolitan areas conducted January–December 2014, the Houston metro area placed #10, according to Gallup's 2014 Economic Confidence Index. *Gallup*, *"San Jose and San Francisco Lead in Economic Confidence,"* March 19, 2015

- Using data from the Council for Community and Economic Research's 2014 cost of living index, NerdWallet ranked the 100 most affordable cities in America. Median income was compared with cost of living to find truly affordable places. Houston ranked #100. *NerdWallet.com*, *"America's Most Affordable Places,"* May 18, 2015

- NerdWallet.com identified the 10 most promising cities for job seekers of the nation's 100 largest cities. Houston was ranked #43. Criteria: job availability; annual salary; workforce growth; affordability. *NerdWallet.com, "Best Cities for Job Seekers in 2017," December 19, 2016*

- The Brookings Institution ranked the nation's largest cities based on income inequality. Houston was ranked #25 (#1 = greatest inequality). Criteria: the "95/20 ratio," a figure representing the income at which a household earns more than 95 percent of all other households, divided by the income at which a household earns more than only 20 percent of all other households. *Brookings Institution, "Household Income Inequality, Largest Cities of 97 Large U.S. Metro Areas, 2014-2016," February 5, 2018*

- The Brookings Institution ranked the 100 largest metro areas in the U.S. based on income inequality. Houston was ranked #8 (#1 = greatest inequality). Criteria: the "95/20 ratio," a figure representing the income at which a household earns more than 95 percent of all other households, divided by the income at which a household earns more than only 20 percent of all other households. *Brookings Institution, "Household Income Inequality, 100 Largest U.S. Metro Areas, 2014-2016," February 5, 2018*

- Payscale.com ranked the 32 largest metro areas in terms of wage growth. The Houston metro area ranked #24. Criteria: private-sector wage growth between the 4th quarter of 2017 and the 4th quarter of 2018. *PayScale, "Wage Trends by Metro Area-4th Quarter," January 8, 2019*

- The Houston metro area was identified as one of the most debt-ridden places in America by the finance site Credit.com. The metro area was ranked #4. Criteria: residents' average credit card debt as well as median income. *Credit.com, "25 Cities With the Most Credit Card Debt," February 28, 2018*

- Houston was identified as one of America's most frugal metro areas by *Coupons.com*. The city ranked #19 out of 25. Criteria: digital coupon usage. *Coupons.com, "America's Most Frugal Cities of 2017," March 22, 2018*

- Houston was cited as one of America's top metros for new and expanded facility projects in 2018. The area ranked #4 in the large metro area category (population over 1 million). *Site Selection, "Top Metros of 2018," March 2019*

- The Houston metro area appeared on the Milken Institute "2018 Best Performing Cities" list. Rank: #119 out of 200 large metro areas. Criteria: job growth; wage and salary growth; high-tech output growth. *Milken Institute, "Best-Performing Cities 2018," January 24, 2019*

- *Forbes* ranked the 200 most populous metro areas to determine the nation's "Best Places for Business and Careers." The Houston metro area was ranked #38. Criteria: costs (business and living); job growth (past and projected); income growth; quality of life; educational attainment (college and high school); projected economic growth; cultural and recreational opportunities; net migration patterns; number of highly ranked colleges. *Forbes, "The Best Places for Business and Careers 2018: Seattle Leads the Way," October 24, 2018*

- Mercer Human Resources Consulting ranked 209 cities worldwide in terms of cost-of-living. Houston ranked #86 (the lower the ranking, the higher the cost-of-living). The survey measured the comparative cost of over 200 items (such as housing, food, clothing, household goods, transportation, and entertainment) in each location. *Mercer, "2018 Cost of Living Survey," June 26, 2018*

Culture/Performing Arts Rankings

- Houston was selected as one of the twenty best large U.S. cities for moviemakers. Of cities with a population over 400,000, the city was ranked #19. Criteria: film community and culture; access to equipment and facilities; film activity in 2018; number of film schools; tax incentives. ease of movement and traffic. *MovieMaker Magazine, "Best Places to Live and Work as a Moviemaker: 2019," January 16, 2019*

- Houston was selected as one of "America's Favorite Cities." The city ranked #3 in the "Culture" category. Respondents to an online survey were asked to rate 38 top urban destinations in the U.S. from a visitor's perspective. Criteria: theater scene and community; number of bookstores; live music; and sense of history. *Travelandleisure.com, "These Are America's 20 Most Cultured Cities," October 2016*

- Houston was selected as one of "America's Favorite Cities." The city ranked #2 in the "Culture: Galleries " category. Respondents to an online survey were asked to rate 38 top urban destinations in the U.S. from a visitor's perspective. Criteria: number and quality of galleries. *Travelandleisure.com, "America's Favorite Cities," October 11, 2015*

- Houston was selected as one of "America's Favorite Cities." The city ranked #5 in the "Culture: Art Scene " category. Respondents to an online survey were asked to rate 38 top urban destinations in the U.S. from a visitor's perspective. Criteria: number and quality of art events. *Travelandleisure.com, "America's Favorite Cities," October 11, 2015*

- Houston was selected as one of "America's Favorite Cities." The city ranked #5 in the "Culture: Concerts " category. Respondents to an online survey were asked to rate 38 top urban destinations in the U.S. from a visitor's perspective. Criteria: number and quality of concerts. *Travelandleisure.com, "America's Favorite Cities," October 11, 2015*

- Houston was selected as one of "America's Favorite Cities." The city ranked #10 in the "Culture: Music Scene " category. Respondents to an online survey were asked to rate 38 top urban destinations in the U.S. from a visitor's perspective. *Travelandleisure.com, "From the Honkytonk Capital to Jazz's Birthplace: America's Best Music Scenes," October 2016*

- Houston was selected as one of "America's Favorite Cities." The city ranked #3 in the "Culture: Theater " category. Respondents to an online survey were asked to rate 38 top urban destinations in the U.S. from a visitor's perspective. Criteria: number and quality of theater offerings. *Travelandleisure.com, "America's Favorite Cities," October 11, 2015*

Education Rankings

- Personal finance website *WalletHub* analyzed the 150 largest U.S. metropolitan statistical areas to determine where the most educated Americans are choosing to settle. Criteria: education quality and attainment gap; education levels; percentage of workers with degrees; public school quality rankings; quality and size of each metro area's universities. Houston was ranked #92 (#1 = most educated city). *www.WalletHub.com, "2018's Most and Least Educated Cities in America," July 24, 2018*

- Houston was selected as one of the most well-read cities in America by Amazon.com. The city ranked #15 among the top 20. Cities with populations greater than 500,000 were evaluated based on per capita sales of books, magazines and newspapers (both print and Kindle format). *Amazon.com, "The 20 Most Well-Read Cities in America," May 24, 2016*

- Houston was selected as one of America's most literate cities. The city ranked #70 out of the 82 largest U.S. cities. Criteria: number of booksellers; library resources; Internet resources; educational attainment; periodical publishing resources; newspaper circulation. *Central Connecticut State University, "America's Most Literate Cities, 2016," March 31, 2017*

Environmental Rankings

- Sperling's BestPlaces assessed the 50 largest metropolitan areas of the United States for the likelihood of dangerously extreme weather events or earthquakes. In general the Southeast and South-Central regions have the highest risk of weather extremes and earthquakes, while the Pacific Northwest enjoys the lowest risk. Of the most risky metropolitan areas, the Houston metro area was ranked #5. *www.bestplaces.net, "Avoid Natural Disasters: BestPlaces Reveals The Top 10 Safest Places to Live," October 25, 2017*

- The U.S. Environmental Protection Agency (EPA) released a list of U.S. metropolitan areas with the most ENERGY STAR certified buildings in 2017. The Houston metro area was ranked #10 out of 25. *U.S. Environmental Protection Agency, "2018 Energy Star Top Cities," April 11, 2018*

- Houston was highlighted as one of the 25 most ozone-polluted metro areas in the U.S. during 2014 through 2016. The area ranked #11. *American Lung Association, State of the Air 2018*

- Houston was highlighted as one of the 25 metro areas most polluted by year-round particle pollution (Annual PM 2.5) in the U.S. during 2014 through 2016. The area ranked #15. *American Lung Association, State of the Air 2018*

Food/Drink Rankings

- The U.S. Chamber of Commerce Foundation conducted an in-depth study on local food truck regulations, surveyed 288 food truck owners, and ranked 20 major American cities based on how friendly they are for operating a food truck. The compiled index assessed the following: procedures for obtaining permits and licenses; complying with restrictions; and financial obligations associated with operating a food truck. Houston ranked #6 overall (1 being the best) for ease in operating a food truck. *www.foodtrucknation.us, "Food Truck Nation," March 20, 2018*

- *Men's Health* ranked 100 major U.S. cities in terms of alcohol intoxication. Houston ranked #47 (#1 = most sober).Criteria: binge drinking; alcohol-related traffic accidents, arrests, and fatalities. *Men's Health, "America's Drunkest Cities," March 9, 2015*

Health/Fitness Rankings

- For each of the 100 largest cities in the United States, the American College of Sports Medicine's American Fitness Index evaluated infrastructure, community assets, and policies that encourage healthy and fit lifestyles, including preventive health behaviors, levels of chronic disease conditions, health care access, and community resources and policies that support physical activity. Houston ranked #60 for "community fitness." *www.americanfitnessindex.org, "ACSM American Fitness Index Health and Community Fitness Status of the 100 Largest U.S. Cities," May 2018*

- The Houston metro area was identified as one of the worst cities for bed bugs in America by pest control company Orkin. The area ranked #26 out of 50 based on the number of bed bug treatments Orkin performed from December 2017 to November 2018. *Orkin, "Baltimore Remains Front Runner, Atlanta and Philadelphia Break Into Top 10," January 14, 2019*

- Houston was identified as a "2018 Spring Allergy Capital." The area ranked #59 out of 100. Three groups of factors were used to identify the most challenging cities for people with allergies during the spring season: annual pollen levels; medicine utilization; access to board-certified allergists. *Asthma and Allergy Foundation of America, "Spring Allergy Capitals 2018"*

- Houston was identified as a "2018 Fall Allergy Capital." The area ranked #51 out of 100. Three groups of factors were used to identify the most challenging cities for people with allergies during the fall season: annual pollen levels; medicine utilization; access to board-certified allergists. *Asthma and Allergy Foundation of America, "Fall Allergy Capitals 2018"*

- Houston was identified as a "2018 Asthma Capital." The area ranked #99 out of the nation's 100 largest metropolitan areas. Criteria: estimated prevalence; self-reported prevalence; crude death rate for asthma; annual pollen score; annual air quality; public smoking laws; number of board-certified asthma specialists; school inhaler access laws; rescue medication use; controller medication use; ER visits for asthma; uninsured rate; poverty rate. *Asthma and Allergy Foundation of America, "Asthma Capitals 2018: The Most Challenging Places to Live With Asthma"*

- *Men's Health* ranked 100 major U.S. cities in terms of the best cities for men. Houston ranked #53. Criteria: health; fitness; quality of life. *Men's Health, "The Best & Worst Cities for Men Who Want to Be Fit and Happy," January 1, 2016*

- The Houston metro area ranked #57 out of 189 in The Gallup-Healthways Well-Being Index. Criteria: purpose; social well being; financial health; community and physical health. Results are based on telephone interviews with adults, aged 18 and older, living in metropolitan areas in the 50 U.S. states and the District of Columbia. *Gallup-Healthways, "State of American Well-Being, 2017 Community Well-Being Rankings" March 2018*

Real Estate Rankings

- FitSmallBusiness looked at 50 of the largest metropolitan areas in the U.S. to determine which metro was the best to start a real estate business. Data was compiled from such sources as: Zillow, Trulia, U.S. Census Bureau, and the Bureau of Labor Statistics. Criteria: location; inventory; annual wages; median sales price of homes; days on the market; median price cut percentage; and other factors that would influence real estate professional growth. The Houston metro area ranked #38. *fitsmallbusiness.com, "The Best Cities to Become a Real Estate Agent in 2018," January 30, 2018*

- *WalletHub* compared the most populated U.S. cities, as well as at least two of the most populated cities in each state, for a total of 179, to determine which had the best markets for real estate agents. Houston ranked #150 where demand was high and pay was the best. Criteria: sales per agent; annual median wage for real-estate agents; monthly average starting salary for real estate agents; real estate job density and competition; unemployment rate; housing-market health index; and other relevant metrics. *www.WalletHub.com, "2018's Best Places to Be a Real Estate Agent," April 25, 2018*

- According to Penske Truck Rental, the Houston metro area was named the #6 moving destination in 2018, based on one-way consumer truck rental reservations made through Penske's website, rental locations, and reservations call center. *blog.gopenske.com, "Penske Truck Rental's 2018 Top Moving Destinations," January 16, 2019*

- Houston was ranked #151 out of 237 metro areas in terms of housing affordability in 2018 by the National Association of Home Builders (#1 = most affordable). Criteria: the share of homes sold in that area affordable to a family earning the local median income, based on standard mortgage underwriting criteria. *National Association of Home Builders®, NAHB-Wells Fargo Housing Opportunity Index, 4th Quarter 2018*

Safety Rankings

- To identify the most dangerous cities in America, 24/7 Wall Street focused on violent crime categories—murder, rape, robbery, and aggravated assault—and property crime as reported in the FBI's 2017 annual Uniform Crime Report. Criteria also included median income from American Community Survey and unemployment figures from Bureau of Labor Statistics. For cities with populations over 100,000, Houston was ranked #22. *247wallst.com, "25 Most Dangerous Cities in America" October 17, 2018*

- Allstate ranked the 200 largest cities in America in terms of driver safety. Houston ranked #164. Criteria: internal property damage claims over a two-year period from January 2015 to December 2016. The report helps increase the importance of safety awareness behind the wheel. *Allstate, "Allstate America's Best Drivers Report, 2018" August 28, 2018*

- Houston was identified as one of the most dangerous cities in America by NeighborhoodScout. The city ranked #53 out of 100. Criteria: number of violent crimes per 1,000 residents. The editors only considered cities with 25,000 or more residents. *NeighborhoodScout.com, "Top 100 Most Dangerous Cities in the U.S. 2019" January 2, 2019*

- The National Insurance Crime Bureau ranked 382 metro areas in the U.S. in terms of per capita rates of vehicle theft. The Houston metro area ranked #60 (#1 = highest rate). Criteria: number of vehicle theft offenses per 100,000 inhabitants in 2017. *National Insurance Crime Bureau, "Hot Spots 2017," July 12, 2018*

Seniors/Retirement Rankings

- From its Best Cities for Successful Aging indexes, the Milken Institute generated rankings for metropolitan areas, weighing data in nine categories—health care, wellness, living arrangements, transportation and convenience, financial characteristics, education, employment, community engagement, and overall livability. The Houston metro area was ranked #35 overall in the large metro area category. *Milken Institute, "Best Cities for Successful Aging, 2017" March 14, 2017*

Sports/Recreation Rankings

- Houston was selected as one of "America's Most Miserable Sports Cities" by *Forbes*. The city was ranked #9. Criteria: postseason losses/misery; years since last title; and number of teams lost to relocation. Contenders were limited to cities with at least 75 cumulative pro seasons of NFL, NBA, NHL, MLS and MLB play. *Forbes, "America's Most Miserable Sports Cities 2016," April 20, 2016*

Transportation Rankings

- NerdWallet surveyed average annual car insurance premiums in 125 U.S. cities to identify the least expensive U.S. cities in which to insure a car. Locations with no-fault insurance laws was a strong determinant. Houston came in at #28 for the most expensive rates. *www.nerdwallet.com, "Best Cities for Cheap Car Insurance," February 3, 2014*

- Houston was identified as one of the most congested metro areas in the U.S. The area ranked #8 out of 10. Criteria: yearly delay per auto commuter in hours. *Texas A&M Transportation Institute, "2015 Urban Mobility Scorecard," August 2015*

Women/Minorities Rankings

- The *Houston Chronicle* listed the Houston metro area as #11 in top places for young Latinos to live in the U.S. Research was largely based on housing and occupational data from the largest metropolitan areas performed by *Forbes* and NBC Universo. Criteria: percentage of 18-34 year-olds; Latino college grad rates; and diversity. *blog.chron.com, "The 15 Best Big Cities for Latino Millenials," January 26, 2016*

- Personal finance website *WalletHub* compared more than 180 U.S. cities—including the 150 most populated U.S. cities, plus at least two of the most populated cities in each state—across two key dimensions, "Hispanic Business-Friendliness" and "Hispanic Purchasing Power", to arrive at the most favorable conditions for Hispanic entrepreneurs. Houston was ranked #29 out of 182. Criteria includes: share of Hispanic-Owned Businesses; Hispanic entrepreneurship rate to median annual income of Hispanics; Small Business-Friendliness score; cost of living; and number of Hispanics with at least a bachelor's degree. *WalletHub.com, "2018's Best Cities for Hispanic Entrepreneurs," April 26, 2018*

Miscellaneous Rankings

- The watchdog site Charity Navigator conducts an annual study of charities in the nation's major markets both to analyze statistical differences in their financial, accountability, and transparency practices and to track year-to-year variations in individual philanthropic communities. Charity Navigator's analysis demonstrated that the financial, accountability and transparency behaviors of America's largest charities can be influenced by the metropolitan market within which the charity operates. The Houston metro area was ranked #2 among the 30 metro markets in the rating category of Overall Score. *www.charitynavigator.org, "2017 Metro Market Study," May 1, 2017*

- *WalletHub* compared the 150 most populated U.S. cities to determine their operating efficiency. A "Quality of Services" score was constructed for each city and then divided by the total budget per capita to reveal which were managed the best. Houston ranked #76. Criteria: financial stability; economy; education; safety; health; infrastructure and pollution. *www.WalletHub.com, "2018's Best- & Worst-Run Cities in America," July 9, 2018*

- Houston appeared on *Travel + Leisure's* list of America's cities with the most attractive people. Criteria: cities were selected by readers in their annual America's Favorite Cities survey. The city ranked #9 out of 10. *Travel + Leisure, "America's Most and Least Attractive People," September 2, 2016*

- The National Alliance to End Homelessness listed the 25 most populous metro areas with the highest rate of homelessness. The Houston metro area had a high rate of homelessness. Criteria: number of homeless people per 10,000 population in 2016. *National Alliance to End Homelessness, "Homelessness in the 25 Most Populous U.S. Metro Areas," September 1, 2017*

Business Environment

CITY FINANCES

City Government Finances

Component	2016 ($000)	2016 ($ per capita)
Total Revenues	4,905,830	2,136
Total Expenditures	5,079,571	2,212
Debt Outstanding	14,055,468	6,121
Cash and Securities[1]	13,821,504	6,019

Note: (1) Cash and security holdings of a government at the close of its fiscal year, including those of its dependent agencies, utilities, and liquor stores.
Source: U.S. Census Bureau, State & Local Government Finances 2016

City Government Revenue by Source

Source	2016 ($000)	2016 ($ per capita)	2016 (%)
General Revenue			
From Federal Government	97,172	42	2.0
From State Government	124,019	54	2.5
From Local Governments	90,189	39	1.8
Taxes			
Property	1,347,425	587	27.5
Sales and Gross Receipts	922,856	402	18.8
Personal Income	0	0	0.0
Corporate Income	0	0	0.0
Motor Vehicle License	0	0	0.0
Other Taxes	152,545	66	3.1
Current Charges	1,266,988	552	25.8
Liquor Store	0	0	0.0
Utility	523,162	228	10.7
Employee Retirement	-69,087	-30	-1.4

Source: U.S. Census Bureau, State & Local Government Finances 2016

City Government Expenditures by Function

Function	2016 ($000)	2016 ($ per capita)	2016 (%)
General Direct Expenditures			
Air Transportation	392,771	171	7.7
Corrections	0	0	0.0
Education	0	0	0.0
Employment Security Administration	0	0	0.0
Financial Administration	47,302	20	0.9
Fire Protection	413,016	179	8.1
General Public Buildings	41,996	18	0.8
Governmental Administration, Other	261,168	113	5.1
Health	114,621	49	2.3
Highways	207,394	90	4.1
Hospitals	0	0	0.0
Housing and Community Development	56,570	24	1.1
Interest on General Debt	662,174	288	13.0
Judicial and Legal	53,297	23	1.0
Libraries	48,729	21	1.0
Parking	11,487	5	0.2
Parks and Recreation	98,440	42	1.9
Police Protection	682,613	297	13.4
Public Welfare	0	0	0.0
Sewerage	564,496	245	11.1
Solid Waste Management	61,665	26	1.2
Veterans' Services	0	0	0.0
Liquor Store	0	0	0.0
Utility	434,914	189	8.6
Employee Retirement	620,067	270	12.2

Source: U.S. Census Bureau, State & Local Government Finances 2016

DEMOGRAPHICS

Population Growth

Area	1990 Census	2000 Census	2010 Census	2017* Estimate	Population Growth (%) 1990-2017	2010-2017
City	1,697,610	1,953,631	2,099,451	2,267,336	33.6	8.0
MSA[1]	3,767,335	4,715,407	5,946,800	6,636,208	76.2	11.6
U.S.	248,709,873	281,421,906	308,745,538	321,004,407	29.1	4.0

Note: (1) Figures cover the Houston-The Woodlands-Sugar Land, TX Metropolitan Statistical Area—see Appendix B for areas included; (*) 2013-2017 5-year estimated population
Source: U.S. Census Bureau, 1990 Census, Census 2000, Census 2010, 2013-2017 American Community Survey 5-Year Estimates

Household Size

Area	One	Two	Three	Four	Five	Six	Seven or More	Average Household Size
City	32.2	29.0	15.3	12.1	6.8	2.8	1.9	2.70
MSA[1]	24.2	29.7	17.1	15.5	8.2	3.2	2.0	2.90
U.S.	27.7	33.8	15.7	13.0	6.0	2.3	1.4	2.60

Note: (1) Figures cover the Houston-The Woodlands-Sugar Land, TX Metropolitan Statistical Area—see Appendix B for areas included
Source: U.S. Census Bureau, 2013-2017 American Community Survey 5-Year Estimates

Race

Area	White Alone[2] (%)	Black Alone[2] (%)	Asian Alone[2] (%)	AIAN[3] Alone[2] (%)	NHOPI[4] Alone[2] (%)	Other Race Alone[2] (%)	Two or More Races (%)
City	58.5	22.9	6.7	0.3	0.1	9.5	2.0
MSA[1]	65.7	17.2	7.5	0.4	0.1	6.8	2.3
U.S.	73.0	12.7	5.4	0.8	0.2	4.8	3.1

Note: (1) Figures cover the Houston-The Woodlands-Sugar Land, TX Metropolitan Statistical Area—see Appendix B for areas included; (2) Alone is defined as not being in combination with one or more other races; (3) American Indian and Alaska Native; (4) Native Hawaiian and Other Pacific Islander
Source: U.S. Census Bureau, 2013-2017 American Community Survey 5-Year Estimates

Hispanic or Latino Origin

Area	Total (%)	Mexican (%)	Puerto Rican (%)	Cuban (%)	Other (%)
City	44.5	32.3	0.5	0.7	10.8
MSA[1]	36.7	27.8	0.6	0.5	7.7
U.S.	17.6	11.1	1.7	0.7	4.1

Note: Persons of Hispanic or Latino origin can be of any race; (1) Figures cover the Houston-The Woodlands-Sugar Land, TX Metropolitan Statistical Area—see Appendix B for areas included
Source: U.S. Census Bureau, 2013-2017 American Community Survey 5-Year Estimates

Segregation

Type	Segregation Indices[1] 1990	2000	2010	2010 Rank[2]	Percent Change 1990-2000	1990-2010	2000-2010
Black/White	65.5	65.7	61.4	36	0.1	-4.1	-4.2
Asian/White	48.0	51.4	50.4	7	3.4	2.4	-1.0
Hispanic/White	47.8	53.4	52.5	18	5.6	4.7	-0.9

Note: All figures cover the Metropolitan Statistical Area—see Appendix B for areas included; Figures are based on an analysis of 1990, 2000, and 2010 Census Decennial Census tract data by William H. Frey, Brookings Institution and the University of Michigan Social Science Data Analysis Network. In this analysis all racial groups (whites, blacks, and asians) are non-Hispanic members of those races. Hispanics are shown as a separate category; (1) Segregation Indices are Dissimilarity Indices that measure the degree to which the minority group is distributed differently than whites across census tracts. They range from 0 (complete integration) to 100 (complete segregation) where the value indicates the percentage of the minority group that needs to move to be distributed exactly like whites; (2) Ranges from 1 (most segregated) to 102 (least segregated); n/a not available.
Source: www.CensusScope.org

Ancestry

Area	German	Irish	English	American	Italian	Polish	French[2]	Scottish	Dutch
City	5.0	3.7	3.9	4.0	1.5	0.9	1.6	0.9	0.4
MSA[1]	8.3	5.7	5.4	4.5	2.1	1.2	2.2	1.2	0.6
U.S.	14.1	10.1	7.5	6.6	5.3	2.9	2.5	1.7	1.3

Note: Figures are the percentage of the total population reporting a particular ancestry. The nine most commonly reported ancestries in the U.S. are shown. Figures include multiple ancestries (e.g. if a person reported being Irish and Italian, they were included in both columns); (1) Figures cover the Houston-The Woodlands-Sugar Land, TX Metropolitan Statistical Area—see Appendix B for areas included; (2) Excludes Basque
Source: U.S. Census Bureau, 2013-2017 American Community Survey 5-Year Estimates

Foreign-Born Population

Area	Percent of Population Born in								
	Any Foreign Country	Asia	Mexico	Europe	Carribean	Central America[2]	South America	Africa	Canada
City	29.2	5.9	12.2	1.2	0.9	5.9	1.1	1.7	0.2
MSA[1]	23.2	5.8	9.4	1.1	0.7	3.5	1.2	1.2	0.3
U.S.	13.4	4.1	3.6	1.5	1.3	1.0	0.9	0.6	0.3

Note: (1) Figures cover the Houston-The Woodlands-Sugar Land, TX Metropolitan Statistical Area—see Appendix B for areas included; (2) Excludes Mexico.
Source: U.S. Census Bureau, 2013-2017 American Community Survey 5-Year Estimates

Marital Status

Area	Never Married	Now Married[2]	Separated	Widowed	Divorced
City	40.5	41.6	3.2	4.7	10.0
MSA[1]	33.3	50.1	2.5	4.5	9.6
U.S.	33.1	48.2	2.0	5.8	10.9

Note: Figures are percentages and cover the population 15 years of age and older; (1) Figures cover the Houston-The Woodlands-Sugar Land, TX Metropolitan Statistical Area—see Appendix B for areas included; (2) Excludes separated
Source: U.S. Census Bureau, 2013-2017 American Community Survey 5-Year Estimates

Disability by Age

Area	All Ages	Under 18 Years Old	18 to 64 Years Old	65 Years and Over
City	9.6	3.3	7.8	36.8
MSA[1]	9.5	3.4	8.0	35.7
U.S.	12.6	4.2	10.3	35.5

Note: Figures show percent of the civilian noninstitutionalized population that reported having a disability. Disability status is determined from six types of difficulty: vision, hearing, cognitive, ambulatory, self-care, and independent living. For children under 5 years old, hearing and vision difficulty are used to determine disability status. For children between the ages of 5 and 14, disability status is determined from hearing, vision, cognitive, ambulatory, and self-care difficulties. For people aged 15 years and older, they are considered to have a disability if they have difficulty with any one of the six difficulty types; Note: (1) Figures cover the Houston-The Woodlands-Sugar Land, TX Metropolitan Statistical Area—see Appendix B for areas included
Source: U.S. Census Bureau, 2013-2017 American Community Survey 5-Year Estimates

Age

Area	Percent of Population									Median Age
	Under Age 5	Age 5–19	Age 20–34	Age 35–44	Age 45–54	Age 55–64	Age 65–74	Age 75–84	Age 85+	
City	7.8	19.8	26.0	14.0	12.0	10.3	6.0	2.9	1.2	32.9
MSA[1]	7.5	22.0	21.9	14.2	13.1	11.1	6.4	2.8	1.0	34.0
U.S.	6.2	19.5	20.7	12.7	13.4	12.7	8.6	4.4	1.9	37.8

Note: (1) Figures cover the Houston-The Woodlands-Sugar Land, TX Metropolitan Statistical Area—see Appendix B for areas included
Source: U.S. Census Bureau, 2013-2017 American Community Survey 5-Year Estimates

Gender

Area	Males	Females	Males per 100 Females
City	1,135,634	1,131,702	100.3
MSA[1]	3,297,364	3,338,844	98.8
U.S.	158,018,753	162,985,654	97.0

Note: (1) Figures cover the Houston-The Woodlands-Sugar Land, TX Metropolitan Statistical Area—see Appendix B for areas included
Source: U.S. Census Bureau, 2013-2017 American Community Survey 5-Year Estimates

Religious Groups by Family

Area	Catholic	Baptist	Non-Den.	Methodist[2]	Lutheran	LDS[3]	Pente-costal	Presby-terian[4]	Muslim[5]	Judaism
MSA[1]	17.1	16.0	7.3	4.9	1.1	1.1	1.5	0.9	2.7	0.4
U.S.	19.1	9.3	4.0	4.0	2.3	2.0	1.9	1.6	0.8	0.7

Note: Figures are the number of adherents as a percentage of the total population; (1) Figures cover the Houston-The Woodlands-Sugar Land, TX Metropolitan Statistical Area—see Appendix B for areas included; (2) Methodist/Pietist; (3) Latter Day Saints; (4) Reformed; (5) Figures are estimates
Source: Association of Statisticians of American Religious Bodies, 2010 U.S. Religion Census: Religious Congregations & Membership Study

Religious Groups by Tradition

Area	Catholic	Evangelical Protestant	Mainline Protestant	Other Tradition	Black Protestant	Orthodox
MSA[1]	17.1	24.9	6.7	4.9	1.3	0.2
U.S.	19.1	16.2	7.3	4.3	1.6	0.3

Note: Figures are the number of adherents as a percentage of the total population; (1) Figures cover the Houston-The Woodlands-Sugar Land, TX Metropolitan Statistical Area—see Appendix B for areas included
Source: Association of Statisticians of American Religious Bodies, 2010 U.S. Religion Census: Religious Congregations & Membership Study

ECONOMY

Gross Metropolitan Product

Area	2016	2017	2018	2019	Rank[2]
MSA[1]	474.1	500.8	544.6	580.0	7

Note: Figures are in billions of dollars; (1) Figures cover the Houston-The Woodlands-Sugar Land, TX Metropolitan Statistical Area—see Appendix B for areas included; (2) Rank is based on 2017 data and ranges from 1 to 381
Source: U.S. Conference of Mayors, U.S. Metro Economies: Economic Growth & Full Employment, June 2018

Economic Growth

Area	2017-2018 (%)	2019-2020 (%)	2021-2022 (%)
MSA[1]	3.6	4.1	2.8

Note: Figures are real gross metropolitan product (GMP) growth rates and represent average annual percent change; (1) Figures cover the Houston-The Woodlands-Sugar Land, TX Metropolitan Statistical Area—see Appendix B for areas included
Source: U.S. Conference of Mayors, U.S. Metro Economies: Economic Growth & Full Employment, June 2018

Metropolitan Area Exports

Area	2012	2013	2014	2015	2016	2017	Rank[2]
MSA[1]	110,297.8	114,962.6	118,966.0	97,054.3	84,105.5	95,760.3	1

Note: Figures are in millions of dollars; (1) Figures cover the Houston-The Woodlands-Sugar Land, TX Metropolitan Statistical Area—see Appendix B for areas included; (2) Rank is based on 2017 data and ranges from 1 to 387
Source: U.S. Department of Commerce, International Trade Administration, Office of Trade and Economic Analysis, Industry and Analysis, Exports by Metropolitan Area, extracted March 25, 2019

Building Permits

Area	Single-Family			Multi-Family			Total		
	2016	2017	Pct. Chg.	2016	2017	Pct. Chg.	2016	2017	Pct. Chg.
City	4,169	5,326	27.8	5,329	4,346	-18.4	9,498	9,672	1.8
MSA[1]	35,367	36,348	2.8	9,365	6,047	-35.4	44,732	42,395	-5.2
U.S.	750,800	820,000	9.2	455,800	462,000	1.4	1,206,600	1,282,000	6.2

Note: (1) Figures cover the Houston-The Woodlands-Sugar Land, TX Metropolitan Statistical Area—see Appendix B for areas included; Figures represent new, privately-owned housing units authorized (unadjusted data); All permit data are based on estimates with imputation
Source: U.S. Census Bureau, Manufacturing, Mining, and Construction Statistics, Building Permits, 2016, 2017

Bankruptcy Filings

Area	Business Filings			Nonbusiness Filings		
	2017	2018	% Chg.	2017	2018	% Chg.
Harris County	447	485	8.5	4,681	4,756	1.6
U.S.	23,157	22,232	-4.0	765,863	751,186	-1.9

Note: Business filings include Chapter 7, Chapter 11, Chapter 12, and Chapter 13; Nonbusiness filings include Chapter 7, Chapter 11, and Chapter 13
Source: Administrative Office of the U.S. Courts, Business and Nonbusiness Bankruptcy, County Cases Commenced by Chapter of the Bankruptcy Code, During the 12-Month Period Ending December 31, 2017 and Business and Nonbusiness Bankruptcy, County Cases Commenced by Chapter of the Bankruptcy Code, During the 12-Month Period Ending December 31, 2018

Housing Vacancy Rates

Area	Gross Vacancy Rate[2] (%)			Year-Round Vacancy Rate[3] (%)			Rental Vacancy Rate[4] (%)			Homeowner Vacancy Rate[5] (%)		
	2016	2017	2018	2016	2017	2018	2016	2017	2018	2016	2017	2018
MSA[1]	8.6	9.3	8.8	8.0	8.9	8.2	9.3	9.9	8.8	1.8	1.5	2.0
U.S.	12.8	12.7	12.3	9.9	9.9	9.7	6.9	7.2	6.9	1.7	1.6	1.5

Note: (1) Figures cover the Houston-The Woodlands-Sugar Land, TX Metropolitan Statistical Area—see Appendix B for areas included; (2) The percentage of the total housing inventory that is vacant; (3) The percentage of the housing inventory (excluding seasonal units) that is year-round vacant; (4) The percentage of rental inventory that is vacant for rent; (5) The percentage of homeowner inventory that is vacant for sale
Source: U.S. Census Bureau, Housing Vacancies and Homeownership Annual Statistics: 2016, 2017, 2018

INCOME

Income

Area	Per Capita ($)	Median Household ($)	Average Household ($)
City	30,547	49,399	79,344
MSA[1]	32,308	62,922	91,350
U.S.	31,177	57,652	81,283

Note: (1) Figures cover the Houston-The Woodlands-Sugar Land, TX Metropolitan Statistical Area—see Appendix B for areas included
Source: U.S. Census Bureau, 2013-2017 American Community Survey 5-Year Estimates

Household Income Distribution

Area	Percent of Households Earning							
	Under $15,000	$15,000 -$24,999	$25,000 -$34,999	$35,000 -$49,999	$50,000 -$74,999	$75,000 -$99,999	$100,000 -$149,999	$150,000 and up
City	13.5	12.2	11.0	13.7	16.7	9.7	10.9	12.2
MSA[1]	9.7	9.1	9.1	12.2	17.2	11.8	15.1	15.7
U.S.	11.6	9.8	9.5	13.0	17.7	12.3	14.1	12.1

Note: (1) Figures cover the Houston-The Woodlands-Sugar Land, TX Metropolitan Statistical Area—see Appendix B for areas included
Source: U.S. Census Bureau, 2013-2017 American Community Survey 5-Year Estimates

Poverty Rate

Area	All Ages	Under 18 Years Old	18 to 64 Years Old	65 Years and Over
City	21.2	33.3	17.6	13.8
MSA[1]	14.8	21.5	12.7	10.0
U.S.	14.6	20.3	13.7	9.3

Note: Figures are percentage of people whose income during the past 12 months was below the poverty level; (1) Figures cover the Houston-The Woodlands-Sugar Land, TX Metropolitan Statistical Area—see Appendix B for areas included
Source: U.S. Census Bureau, 2013-2017 American Community Survey 5-Year Estimates

EMPLOYMENT

Labor Force and Employment

Area	Civilian Labor Force			Workers Employed		
	Dec. 2017	Dec. 2018	% Chg.	Dec. 2017	Dec. 2018	% Chg.
City	1,155,275	1,193,791	3.3	1,107,177	1,148,266	3.7
MSA[1]	3,343,410	3,453,216	3.3	3,199,215	3,317,794	3.7
U.S.	159,880,000	162,510,000	1.6	153,602,000	156,481,000	1.9

Note: Data is not seasonally adjusted and covers workers 16 years of age and older; (1) Figures cover the Houston-The Woodlands-Sugar Land, TX Metropolitan Statistical Area—see Appendix B for areas included
Source: Bureau of Labor Statistics, Local Area Unemployment Statistics

Unemployment Rate

Area	2018											
	Jan.	Feb.	Mar.	Apr.	May	Jun.	Jul.	Aug.	Sep.	Oct.	Nov.	Dec.
City	4.6	4.6	4.5	4.2	4.1	4.5	4.3	4.2	4.1	3.7	3.7	3.8
MSA[1]	4.8	4.7	4.6	4.2	4.2	4.6	4.4	4.3	4.1	3.8	3.8	3.9
U.S.	4.5	4.4	4.1	3.7	3.6	4.2	4.1	3.9	3.6	3.5	3.5	3.7

Note: Data is not seasonally adjusted and covers workers 16 years of age and older; (1) Figures cover the Houston-The Woodlands-Sugar Land, TX Metropolitan Statistical Area—see Appendix B for areas included
Source: Bureau of Labor Statistics, Local Area Unemployment Statistics

Average Wages

Occupation	$/Hr.	Occupation	$/Hr.
Accountants and Auditors	41.40	Maids and Housekeeping Cleaners	10.20
Automotive Mechanics	21.10	Maintenance and Repair Workers	19.00
Bookkeepers	20.60	Marketing Managers	79.90
Carpenters	20.60	Nuclear Medicine Technologists	39.40
Cashiers	10.50	Nurses, Licensed Practical	23.40
Clerks, General Office	18.80	Nurses, Registered	38.50
Clerks, Receptionists/Information	13.20	Nursing Assistants	13.70
Clerks, Shipping/Receiving	16.50	Packers and Packagers, Hand	11.40
Computer Programmers	43.80	Physical Therapists	44.70
Computer Systems Analysts	53.10	Postal Service Mail Carriers	24.80
Computer User Support Specialists	29.00	Real Estate Brokers	50.00
Cooks, Restaurant	12.70	Retail Salespersons	12.40
Dentists	93.10	Sales Reps., Exc. Tech./Scientific	37.50
Electrical Engineers	52.10	Sales Reps., Tech./Scientific	46.00
Electricians	27.20	Secretaries, Exc. Legal/Med./Exec.	18.10
Financial Managers	75.50	Security Guards	14.40
First-Line Supervisors/Managers, Sales	21.80	Surgeons	117.10
Food Preparation Workers	11.50	Teacher Assistants*	10.90
General and Operations Managers	67.20	Teachers, Elementary School*	28.10
Hairdressers/Cosmetologists	12.80	Teachers, Secondary School*	29.20
Internists, General	81.30	Telemarketers	13.00
Janitors and Cleaners	11.40	Truck Drivers, Heavy/Tractor-Trailer	21.80
Landscaping/Groundskeeping Workers	14.00	Truck Drivers, Light/Delivery Svcs.	18.40
Lawyers	84.30	Waiters and Waitresses	12.60

Note: Wage data covers the Houston-The Woodlands-Sugar Land, TX Metropolitan Statistical Area—see Appendix B for areas included; (*) Hourly wages for elementary/secondary school teachers and teacher assistants were calculated by the editors from annual wage data based on a 40 hour work week; n/a not available.
Source: Bureau of Labor Statistics, Metro Area Occupational Employment & Wage Estimates, May 2018

Employment by Occupation

Occupation Classification	City (%)	MSA[1] (%)	U.S. (%)
Management, Business, Science, and Arts	35.0	37.8	37.4
Natural Resources, Construction, and Maintenance	11.9	10.9	8.9
Production, Transportation, and Material Moving	12.3	12.1	12.2
Sales and Office	21.5	22.8	23.5
Service	19.2	16.5	18.0

Note: Figures cover employed civilians 16 years of age and older; (1) Figures cover the Houston-The Woodlands-Sugar Land, TX Metropolitan Statistical Area—see Appendix B for areas included
Source: U.S. Census Bureau, 2013-2017 American Community Survey 5-Year Estimates

Employment by Industry

Sector	MSA[1] Number of Employees	MSA[1] Percent of Total	U.S. Percent of Total
Construction	222,900	7.1	4.8
Education and Health Services	398,600	12.7	15.9
Financial Activities	164,100	5.2	5.7
Government	422,100	13.5	15.1
Information	31,800	1.0	1.9
Leisure and Hospitality	323,500	10.3	10.7
Manufacturing	235,800	7.5	8.5
Mining and Logging	81,000	2.6	0.5
Other Services	112,700	3.6	3.9
Professional and Business Services	500,500	16.0	14.1
Retail Trade	314,600	10.0	10.8
Transportation, Warehousing, and Utilities	157,500	5.0	4.2
Wholesale Trade	172,600	5.5	3.9

Note: Figures are non-farm employment as of December 2018. Figures are not seasonally adjusted and include workers 16 years of age and older; (1) Figures cover the Houston-The Woodlands-Sugar Land, TX Metropolitan Statistical Area—see Appendix B for areas included
Source: Bureau of Labor Statistics, Current Employment Statistics, Employment, Hours, and Earnings

Occupations with Greatest Projected Employment Growth: 2018 – 2020

Occupation[1]	2018 Employment	2020 Projected Employment	Numeric Employment Change	Percent Employment Change
Combined Food Preparation and Serving Workers, Including Fast Food	351,780	372,090	20,310	5.8
Personal Care Aides	218,310	235,470	17,160	7.9
Heavy and Tractor-Trailer Truck Drivers	204,870	216,310	11,440	5.6
Laborers and Freight, Stock, and Material Movers, Hand	194,220	204,060	9,840	5.1
Waiters and Waitresses	236,020	245,790	9,770	4.1
Office Clerks, General	393,740	403,270	9,530	2.4
Customer Service Representatives	268,380	277,460	9,080	3.4
General and Operations Managers	182,190	190,620	8,430	4.6
Retail Salespersons	392,620	400,900	8,280	2.1
Construction Laborers	143,270	150,820	7,550	5.3

Note: Projections cover Texas; (1) Sorted by numeric employment change
Source: www.projectionscentral.com, State Occupational Projections, 2018–2020 Short-Term Projections

Fastest Growing Occupations: 2018 – 2020

Occupation[1]	2018 Employment	2020 Projected Employment	Numeric Employment Change	Percent Employment Change
Wind Turbine Service Technicians	1,810	2,190	380	21.0
Religious Workers, All Other	5,690	6,330	640	11.2
Fundraisers	8,830	9,670	840	9.5
Statisticians	1,870	2,040	170	9.1
Public Relations and Fundraising Managers	6,570	7,160	590	9.0
Home Health Aides	74,390	80,920	6,530	8.8
Community and Social Service Specialists, All Other	4,520	4,890	370	8.2
Personal Care Aides	218,310	235,470	17,160	7.9
Operations Research Analysts	10,920	11,760	840	7.7
Software Developers, Applications	65,190	70,140	4,950	7.6

Note: Projections cover Texas; (1) Sorted by percent employment change and excludes occupations with numeric employment change less than 50
Source: www.projectionscentral.com, State Occupational Projections, 2018–2020 Short-Term Projections

TAXES

State Corporate Income Tax Rates

State	Tax Rate (%)	Income Brackets ($)	Num. of Brackets	Financial Institution Tax Rate (%)[a]	Federal Income Tax Ded.
Texas	(w)	–	–	(w)	No

Note: Tax rates as of January 1, 2019; (a) Rates listed are the corporate income tax rate applied to financial institutions or excise taxes based on income. Some states have other taxes based upon the value of deposits or shares; (w) Texas imposes a Franchise Tax, otherwise known as margin tax, imposed on entities with more than $1,130,000 total revenues at rate of 0.75%, or 0.375% for entities primarily engaged in retail or wholesale trade, on lesser of 70% of total revenues or 100% of gross receipts after deductions for either compensation or cost of goods sold.
Source: Federation of Tax Administrators, Range of State Corporate Income Tax Rates, January 1, 2019

State Individual Income Tax Rates

State	Tax Rate (%)	Income Brackets ($)	Personal Exemptions ($)			Standard Ded. ($)	
			Single	Married	Depend.	Single	Married
Texas					– No state income tax –		

Note: Tax rates as of January 1, 2019; Local- and county-level taxes are not included; n/a not applicable;
Source: Federation of Tax Administrators, State Individual Income Tax Rates, January 1, 2019

Various State Sales and Excise Tax Rates

State	State Sales Tax (%)	Gasoline[1] (¢/gal.)	Cigarette[2] ($/pack)	Spirits[3] ($/gal.)	Wine[4] ($/gal.)	Beer[5] ($/gal.)	Recreational Marijuana (%)
Texas	6.25	20	1.41	2.40 (f)	0.20 (l)	0.20 (q)	Not legal

Note: All tax rates as of January 1, 2019; (1) The American Petroleum Institute has developed a methodology for determining the average tax rate on a gallon of fuel. Rates may include any of the following: excise taxes, environmental fees, storage tank fees, other fees or taxes, general sales tax, and local taxes. In states where gasoline is subject to the general sales tax, or where the fuel tax is based on the average sale price, the average rate determined by API is sensitive to changes in the price of gasoline. States that fully or partially apply general sales taxes to gasoline: CA, CO, GA, IL, IN, MI, NY; (2) The federal excise tax of $1.0066 per pack and local taxes are not included; (3) Rates are those applicable to off-premise sales of 40% alcohol by volume (a.b.v.) distilled spirits in 750ml containers. Local excise taxes are excluded; (4) Rates are those applicable to off-premise sales of 11% a.b.v. non-carbonated wine in 750ml containers; (5) Rates are those applicable to off-premise sales of 4.7% a.b.v. beer in 12 ounce containers; (f) Different rates also applicable according to alcohol content, place of production, size of container, or place purchased (on- or off-premise or onboard airlines); (l) Different rates also applicable to alcohol content, place of production, size of container, place purchased (on- or off-premise or on board airlines) or type of wine (carbonated, vermouth, etc.); (q) Different rates also applicable according to alcohol content, place of production, size of container, or place purchased (on- or off-premise or onboard airlines).
Source: Tax Foundation, 2019 Facts & Figures: How Does Your State Compare?

State Business Tax Climate Index Rankings

State	Overall Rank	Corporate Tax Rank	Individual Income Tax Rank	Sales Tax Rank	Unemployment Insurance Tax Rank	Property Tax Rank
Texas	15	49	6	37	18	37

Note: The index is a measure of how each state's tax laws affect economic performance. The lower the rank, the more favorable a state's tax system is for business. States without a given tax are given a ranking of 1. The scores/rankings for the District of Columbia do not affect other states. The 2019 index represents the tax climate as of July 1, 2018.
Source: Tax Foundation, State Business Tax Climate Index 2019

COMMERCIAL REAL ESTATE

Office Market

Market Area	Inventory (sq. ft.)	Vacancy Rate (%)	Under Construction (sq. ft.)	YTD Net Absorption (sq. ft.)	Total Average Asking Rent ($/sq. ft./year)
Houston	233,393,626	21.0	2,667,002	666,129	29.05
National	4,905,867,938	13.1	83,553,714	45,846,470	28.46

Source: Newmark Grubb Knight Frank, National Office Market Report, 4th Quarter 2018

Industrial/Warehouse/R&D Market

Market Area	Inventory (sq. ft.)	Vacancy Rate (%)	Under Construction (sq. ft.)	YTD Net Absorption (sq. ft.)	Total Average Asking Rent ($/sq. ft./year)
Houston	527,774,580	5.2	11,402,844	8,675,380	6.99
National	14,796,839,085	5.0	262,662,294	238,014,726	7.16

Source: Newmark Grubb Knight Frank, National Industrial Market Report, 4th Quarter 2018

COMMERCIAL UTILITIES

Typical Monthly Electric Bills

Area	Commercial Service ($/month)		Industrial Service ($/month)	
	1,500 kWh	40 kW demand 14,000 kWh	1,000 kW demand 200,000 kWh	50,000 kW demand 32,500,000 kWh
City	n/a	n/a	n/a	n/a
Average[1]	203	1,619	25,886	2,540,077

Note: Figures are based on annualized rates; (1) Average based on 187 utilities surveyed; n/a not available
Source: Edison Electric Institute, Typical Bills and Average Rates Report, Summer 2018

TRANSPORTATION

Means of Transportation to Work

Area	Car/Truck/Van		Public Transportation			Bicycle	Walked	Other Means	Worked at Home
	Drove Alone	Car-pooled	Bus	Subway	Railroad				
City	76.6	11.3	3.7	0.1	0.1	0.5	2.1	2.0	3.6
MSA[1]	80.4	10.4	2.1	0.0	0.0	0.3	1.4	1.4	3.9
U.S.	76.4	9.2	2.5	1.9	0.6	0.6	2.7	1.3	4.7

Note: Figures are percentages and cover workers 16 years of age and older; (1) Figures cover the Houston-The Woodlands-Sugar Land, TX Metropolitan Statistical Area—see Appendix B for areas included
Source: U.S. Census Bureau, 2013-2017 American Community Survey 5-Year Estimates

Travel Time to Work

Area	Less Than 10 Minutes	10 to 19 Minutes	20 to 29 Minutes	30 to 44 Minutes	45 to 59 Minutes	60 to 89 Minutes	90 Minutes or More
City	7.9	26.3	22.5	27.0	8.4	6.1	1.7
MSA[1]	8.0	23.9	19.6	25.9	11.5	8.7	2.4
U.S.	12.7	28.9	20.9	20.5	8.1	6.2	2.7

Note: Note: Figures are percentages and include workers 16 years old and over; (1) Figures cover the Houston-The Woodlands-Sugar Land, TX Metropolitan Statistical Area—see Appendix B for areas included
Source: U.S. Census Bureau, 2013-2017 American Community Survey 5-Year Estimates

Freeway Travel Time Index

Area	1985	1990	1995	2000	2005	2010	2014
Urban Area Rank[1,2]	3	5	13	22	17	14	10
Urban Area Index[1]	1.25	1.22	1.22	1.23	1.28	1.28	1.33
Average Index[3]	1.09	1.11	1.14	1.17	1.20	1.19	1.20

Note: Freeway Travel Time Index—the ratio of travel time in the peak period to the travel time at free-flow conditions. For example, a value of 1.30 indicates a 20-minute free-flow trip takes 26 minutes in the peak (20 minutes x 1.30 = 26 minutes); (1) Covers the Houston TX urban area; (2) Rank is based on 101 urban areas (#1 = highest travel time index); (3) Average of 101 urban areas
Source: Texas Transportation Institute, 2015 Urban Mobility Scorecard, August 2015

Freeway Commuter Stress Index

Area	1985	1990	1995	2000	2005	2010	2014
Urban Area Rank[1,2]	4	12	18	23	16	17	12
Urban Area Index[1]	1.30	1.27	1.28	1.29	1.34	1.34	1.39
Average Index[3]	1.13	1.16	1.19	1.22	1.25	1.24	1.25

Note: The Freeway Commuter Stress Index is the same as the Freeway Travel Time Index (see table above) except that it includes only the travel in the peak directions during the peak periods; the TTI includes travel in all directions during the peak period. Thus, the CSI is more indicative of the work trip experienced by each commuter on a daily basis; (1) Covers the Houston TX urban area; (2) Rank is based on 101 urban areas (#1 = highest travel time index); (3) Average of 101 urban areas
Source: Texas Transportation Institute, 2015 Urban Mobility Scorecard, August 2015

Public Transportation

Agency Name / Mode of Transportation	Vehicles Operated in Maximum Service[1]	Annual Unlinked Passenger Trips[2] (in thous.)	Annual Passenger Miles[3] (in thous.)
Metropolitan Transit Authority of Harris County (METRO)			
Bus (directly operated)	591	48,997.2	250,226.3
Bus (purchased transportation)	101	9,053.6	35,347.7
Commuter Bus (directly operated)	246	6,071.1	112,867.9
Commuter Bus (purchased transportation)	64	1,811.6	36,304.3
Demand Response (purchased transportation)	327	1,669.7	18,532.7
Demand Response Taxi (purchased transportation)	134	244.6	2,607.0
Light Rail (directly operated)	54	18,319.4	51,261.2
Vanpool (purchased transportation)	604	1,961.9	59,209.8

Note: (1) The number of revenue vehicles operated by the given mode and type of service to meet the annual maximum service requirement. This is the revenue vehicle count during the peak season of the year; on the week and day that maximum service is provided. Vehicles operated in maximum service (VOMS) exclude atypical days and one-time special events; (2) The number of passengers who boarded public transportation vehicles. Passengers are counted each time they board a vehicle no matter how many vehicles they use to travel from their origin to their destination. (3) The sum of the distances ridden by all passengers during the entire fiscal year.
Source: Federal Transit Administration, National Transit Database, 2017

Air Transportation

Airport Name and Code / Type of Service	Passenger Airlines[1]	Passenger Enplanements	Freight Carriers[2]	Freight (lbs)
George Bush Intercontinental (IAH)				
Domestic service (U.S. carriers - 2018)	24	15,910,217	15	231,699,194
International service (U.S. carriers - 2017)	12	3,608,097	9	56,827,110
William P. Hobby (HOU)				
Domestic service (U.S. carriers - 2018)	24	6,528,718	7	12,978,784
International service (U.S. carriers - 2017)	4	450,940	1	13,461

Note: (1) Includes all U.S.-based major, minor and commuter airlines that carried at least one passenger during the year; (2) Includes all U.S.-based airlines and freight carriers that transported at least one pound of freight during the year.
Source: Bureau of Transportation Statistics, The Intermodal Transportation Database, Air Carriers: T-100 Domestic Market (U.S. Carriers), 2018; Bureau of Transportation Statistics, The Intermodal Transportation Database, Air Carriers: T-100 International Market (U.S. Carriers), 2017

Other Transportation Statistics

Major Highways:	I-10; I-45
Amtrak Service:	Yes
Major Waterways/Ports:	Gulf of Mexico; Port of Houston

Source: Amtrak.com; Google Maps

BUSINESSES

Major Business Headquarters

Company Name	Industry	Rankings	
		Fortune[1]	Forbes[2]
Apache	Mining, Crude-Oil Production	438	-
BMC Software	IT Software & Services	-	224
Calpine	Energy	336	-
CenterPoint Energy	Utilities: Gas and Electric	308	-
Cheniere Energy	Energy	489	-
ConocoPhillips	Mining, Crude-Oil Production	95	-
EOG Resources	Mining, Crude-Oil Production	270	-
Enterprise Products Partners	Pipelines	105	-
Fertitta Entertainment	Hotels, Restaurants & Leisure	-	110
Group 1 Automotive	Automotive Retailing, Services	273	-
Gulf States Toyota	Consumer Durables	-	37
Halliburton	Oil and Gas Equipment, Services	146	-
Kinder Morgan	Pipelines	218	-
National Oilwell Varco	Oil and Gas Equipment, Services	388	-
Occidental Petroleum	Mining, Crude-Oil Production	220	-
Phillips 66	Petroleum Refining	28	-
Plains GP Holdings	Pipelines	115	-
Quanta Services	Engineering, Construction	316	-
Republic National Distributing Co.	Food, Drink & Tobacco	-	52
Sysco	Wholesalers: Food and Grocery	54	-
Targa Resources	Pipelines	334	-
Tauber Oil	Oil & Gas Operations	-	211
Waste Management	Waste Management	202	-
Westlake Chemical	Chemicals	352	-

Note: (1) Companies that produce a 10-K are ranked 1 to 500 based on 2017 revenue; (2) All private companies with at least $2 billion in annual revenue through the end of their most current fiscal year are ranked 1 to 229; companies listed are headquartered in the city; dashes indicate no ranking
Source: Fortune, "Fortune 500," June 2018; Forbes, "America's Largest Private Companies," 2018 Rankings

Fast-Growing Businesses

According to *Inc.*, Houston is home to six of America's 500 fastest-growing private companies: **Karya Property Management** (#145); **Rebellion Photonics** (#161); **SIA Solutions** (#173); **Discount Power Texas** (#341); **FireDisc Cookers** (#374); **Christensen Building Group** (#395). Criteria: must be an independent, privately-held, for-profit, U.S. corporation, proprietorship or partnership as of December 31, 2017; revenues must be at least $100,000 in 2014 and $2 million in 2017; must have four-year operating/sales history. Holding companies, regulated banks, and utilities were excluded. *Inc., "America's 500 Fastest-Growing Private Companies," 2018*

According to *Initiative for a Competitive Inner City (ICIC)*, Houston is home to four of America's 100 fastest-growing "inner city" companies: **J3 Resources** (#47); **UYL Color** (#66); **Langrand** (#68); **Gulfgate Animal Hospital** (#98). Criteria for inclusion: company must be headquartered in or have 51 percent or more of its physical operations in an economically distressed urban area; must be an independent, for-profit corporation, partnership or proprietorship; must have 10 or more employees and have a five-year sales history that includes sales of at least $200,000 in the base year and at least $1 million in the current year with no decrease in sales over the two most recent years. Companies were ranked overall by revenue growth over the five-year period between 2013 and 2017. *Initiative for a Competitive Inner City (ICIC), "Inner City 100 Companies," 2018*

According to Deloitte, Houston is home to two of North America's 500 fastest-growing high-technology companies: **Onit** (#264); **symplr** (#330). Companies are ranked by percentage growth in revenue over a four-year period. Criteria for inclusion: company must be headquartered within North America; must own proprietary intellectual property or technology that is sold to customers in products that contributes to a significant portion of the company's operating revenue; must have been in business for a minumum of four years with 2014 operating revenues of at least $50,000 USD/CD and 2017 operating revenues of at least $5 million USD/CD. *Deloitte, 2018 Technology Fast 500*[TM]

Minority Business Opportunity

Houston is home to two companies which are on the *Black Enterprise* Industrial/Service list (100 largest companies based on gross sales): **The Lewis Group** (#35); **ChaseSource** (#86). Criteria: operational in previous calendar year; at least 51% black-owned and manufactures/owns the product it sells or provides industrial or consumer services. Brokerages, real estate firms and firms that provide professional services are not eligible. *Black Enterprise, B.E. 100s, 2018*

Houston is home to one company which is on the *Black Enterprise* Auto Dealer list (45 largest dealers based on gross sales): **J. Davis Automotive Group** (#21). Criteria: company must be operational in previous calendar year and be at least 51% black-owned. *Black Enterprise, B.E. 100s, 2018*

Houston is home to one company which is on the *Black Enterprise* Bank list (15 largest banks based on total assets, capital, deposits and loans, including mortgage-backed securities for the calendar year): **Unity National Bank** (#13). Only commercial banks or savings and loans that are classified by the Federal Reserve as black institutions and have been fully operational for the previous calendar year were considered. *Black Enterprise, B.E. 100s, 2018*

Houston is home to one company which is on the *Black Enterprise* Asset Manager list (10 largest asset management firms based on assets under management): **Smith, Graham & Co. Investment Advisors** (#5). Criteria: company must have been operational in previous calendar year and be at least 51% black-owned. *Black Enterprise, B.E. 100s, 2018*

Houston is home to 17 companies which are on the *Hispanic Business* 500 list (500 largest U.S. Hispanic-owned companies based on revenue): **G&A Partners** (#16); **Petro Amigos Supply** (#20); **The Plaza Group** (#29); **MEI Technologies (MEIT)** (#53); **Tejas Office Products** (#134); **Lopez Negrete Communications** (#167); **Reytec Construction Resources** (#173); **MCA Communications** (#177); **Today's Business Solutions** (#194); **Tube America** (#273); **Traf-Tex** (#310); **Nino Properties** (#401); **Navarro Insurance Group** (#458); **Translation Source** (#460); **Transfinance Corp.** (#465); **Perches Land Services** (#475); **CapWest Companies** (#490). Companies included must show at least 51 percent ownership by Hispanic U.S. citizens, and must maintain headquarters in one of the 50 states or Washington, D.C. *Hispanic Business, "Hispanic Business 500," June 20, 2013*

Minority- and Women-Owned Businesses

Group	All Firms		Firms with Paid Employees			
	Firms	Sales ($000)	Firms	Sales ($000)	Employees	Payroll ($000)
AIAN[1]	2,184	679,118	232	622,739	4,166	89,083
Asian	28,467	17,121,417	8,905	16,100,040	72,190	2,087,445
Black	49,739	2,578,797	1,985	1,723,227	27,332	564,544
Hispanic	77,416	13,513,339	5,131	11,103,088	68,497	2,049,322
NHOPI[2]	251	(s)	39	(s)	250 - 499	(s)
Women	102,813	18,621,717	9,363	16,165,298	108,818	4,151,382
All Firms	260,347	852,213,744	49,541	841,435,044	1,485,205	92,556,172

Note: Figures cover firms located in the city; minority- and women-owned business are defined as firms in which the corresponding group own 51% or more of the stock or equity of the company; (1) American Indian and Alaska Native; (2) Native Hawaiian and Other Pacific Islander; (s) estimates are suppressed when publication standards are not met
Source: U.S. Census Bureau, 2012 Economic Census, Survey of Business Owners

HOTELS & CONVENTION CENTERS

Hotels, Motels and Vacation Rentals

Area	5 Star		4 Star		3 Star		2 Star		1 Star		Not Rated	
	Num.	Pct.[3]	Num.	Pct.[3]	Num.	Pct.[3]	Num.	Pct.[3]	Num.	Pct.[3]	Num.	Pct.[3]
City[1]	5	0.3	87	5.8	298	19.8	483	32.1	4	0.3	627	41.7
Total[2]	286	0.4	5,236	7.1	16,715	22.6	10,259	13.9	293	0.4	41,056	55.6

Note: (1) Figures cover Houston and vicinity; (2) Figures cover all 100 cities in this book; (3) Percentage of hotels which have a given star rating; Star ratings are determined by expedia.com and offer an indication of the general quality of a particular hotel.
Source: www.expedia.com, April 3, 2019

Major Convention Centers

Name	Overall Space (sq. ft.)	Exhibit Space (sq. ft.)	Meeting Space (sq. ft.)	Meeting Rooms
George R. Brown Convention Center	1,200,000	862,000	185,000	100
Reliant Center	1,400,000	706,000	n/a	n/a

Note: Table includes convention centers located in the Houston-The Woodlands-Sugar Land, TX metro area; n/a not available
Source: Original research

Living Environment

COST OF LIVING

Cost of Living Index

Composite Index	Groceries	Housing	Utilities	Trans- portation	Health Care	Misc. Goods/ Services
96.3	85.7	97.3	109.9	98.6	93.3	95.9

Note: The Cost of Living Index measures regional differences in the cost of consumer goods and services, excluding taxes and non-consumer expenditures, for professional and managerial households in the top income quintile. It is based on more than 50,000 prices covering almost 60 different items for which prices are collected three times a year by chambers of commerce, economic development organizations or university applied economic centers in each participating urban area. The numbers shown should be read as a percentage above or below the national average of 100. For example, a value of 115.4 in the groceries column indicates that grocery prices are 15.4% higher than the national average. Small differences in the index numbers should not be interpreted as significant; Figures cover the Houston TX urban area.
Source: The Council for Community and Economic Research, ACCRA Cost of Living Index, 2018

Grocery Prices

Area[1]	T-Bone Steak ($/pound)	Frying Chicken ($/pound)	Whole Milk ($/half gal.)	Eggs ($/dozen)	Orange Juice ($/64 oz.)	Coffee ($/11.5 oz.)
City[2]	10.31	1.15	1.18	1.58	3.29	3.51
Avg.	11.35	1.42	1.94	1.81	3.52	4.35
Min.	7.45	0.92	0.80	0.75	2.72	3.06
Max.	15.05	2.76	4.18	4.00	5.36	8.20

Note: (1) Values for the local area are compared with the average, minimum and maximum values for all 291 areas in the Cost of Living Index; (2) Figures cover the Houston TX urban area; **T-Bone Steak** (price per pound); **Frying Chicken** (price per pound, whole fryer); **Whole Milk** (half gallon carton); **Eggs** (price per dozen, Grade A, large); **Orange Juice** (64 oz. Tropicana or Florida Natural); **Coffee** (11.5 oz. can, vacuum-packed, Maxwell House, Hills Bros, or Folgers).
Source: The Council for Community and Economic Research, ACCRA Cost of Living Index, 2018

Housing and Utility Costs

Area[1]	New Home Price ($)	Apartment Rent ($/month)	All Electric ($/month)	Part Electric ($/month)	Other Energy ($/month)	Telephone ($/month)
City[2]	315,436	1,249	-	157.46	40.04	178.40
Avg.	347,000	1,087	165.93	100.16	67.73	178.70
Min.	200,468	500	93.58	25.64	26.78	163.10
Max.	1,901,222	4,888	388.65	246.86	332.81	197.70

Note: (1) Values for the local area are compared with the average, minimum and maximum values for all 291 areas in the Cost of Living Index; (2) Figures cover the Houston TX urban area; **New Home Price** (2,400 sf living area, 8,000 sf lot, in urban area with full utilities); **Apartment Rent** (950 sf 2 bedroom/1.5 or 2 bath, unfurnished, excluding all utilities except water); **All Electric** (average monthly cost for an all-electric home); **Part Electric** (average monthly cost for a part-electric home); **Other Energy** (average monthly cost for natural gas, fuel oil, coal, wood, and any other forms of energy except electricity); **Telephone** (price includes the base monthly rate plus taxes and fees for three lines of mobile phone service).
Source: The Council for Community and Economic Research, ACCRA Cost of Living Index, 2018

Health Care, Transportation, and Other Costs

Area[1]	Doctor ($/visit)	Dentist ($/visit)	Optometrist ($/visit)	Gasoline ($/gallon)	Beauty Salon ($/visit)	Men's Shirt ($)
City[2]	84.62	97.84	108.89	2.40	52.70	31.93
Avg.	110.71	95.11	103.74	2.61	37.48	32.03
Min.	33.60	62.55	54.63	1.89	17.00	11.44
Max.	195.97	153.93	225.79	3.59	71.88	58.64

Note: (1) Values for the local area are compared with the average, minimum and maximum values for all 291 areas in the Cost of Living Index; (2) Figures cover the Houston TX urban area; **Doctor** (general practitioners routine exam of an established patient); **Dentist** (adult teeth cleaning and periodic oral examination); **Optometrist** (full vision eye exam for established adult patient); **Gasoline** (one gallon regular unleaded, national brand, including all taxes, cash price at self-service pump if available); **Beauty Salon** (woman's shampoo, trim, and blow-dry); **Men's Shirt** (cotton/polyester dress shirt, pinpoint weave, long sleeves).
Source: The Council for Community and Economic Research, ACCRA Cost of Living Index, 2018

HOUSING

House Price Index (HPI)

Area	National Ranking[2]	Quarterly Change (%)	One-Year Change (%)	Five-Year Change (%)
MSA[1]	161	-0.13	5.13	36.79
U.S.[3]	—	1.12	5.73	32.81

Note: The HPI is a weighted repeat sales index. It measures average price changes in repeat sales or refinancings on the same properties. This information is obtained by reviewing repeat mortgage transactions on single-family properties whose mortgages have been purchased or securitized by Fannie Mae or Freddie Mac in January 1975; (1) Figures cover the Houston-The Woodlands-Sugar Land, TX Metropolitan Statistical Area—see Appendix B for areas included; (2) Rankings are based on annual percentage change for all metro areas containing at least 15,000 transactions over the last 10 years and ranges from 1 to 245; (3) figures based on a weighted average of Census Division estimates using a seasonally adjusted, purchase-only index; all figures are for the period ending December 31, 2018
Source: Federal Housing Finance Agency, House Price Index, February 26, 2019

Median Single-Family Home Prices

Area	2016	2017	2018[p]	Percent Change 2017 to 2018
MSA[1]	217.4	231.1	238.8	3.3
U.S. Average	235.5	248.8	261.6	5.1

Note: Figures are median sales prices of existing single-family homes in thousands of dollars; (p) preliminary; (1) Figures cover the Houston-The Woodlands-Sugar Land, TX Metropolitan Statistical Area—see Appendix B for areas included
Source: National Association of Realtors, Median Sales Price of Existing Single-Family Homes for Metropolitan Areas, 4th Quarter 2018

Qualifying Income Based on Median Sales Price of Existing Single-Family Homes

Area	With 5% Down ($)	With 10% Down ($)	With 20% Down ($)
MSA[1]	58,139	55,079	48,959
U.S. Average	62,954	59,640	53,013

Note: Figures are preliminary; Qualifying income is based on a mortgage rate of 4.9%. Monthly principal and interest payment is limited to 25% of income; (1) Figures cover the Houston-The Woodlands-Sugar Land, TX Metropolitan Statistical Area—see Appendix B for areas included
Source: National Association of Realtors, Qualifying Income Based on Median Sales Price of Existing Single-Family Homes for Metropolitan Areas, 4th Quarter 2018

Median Apartment Condo-Coop Home Prices

Area	2016	2017	2018[p]	Percent Change 2017 to 2018
MSA[1]	150.8	160.3	166.6	3.9
U.S. Average	220.7	234.3	241.0	2.9

Note: Figures are median sales prices of existing apartment condo-coop homes in thousands of dollars; (p) preliminary; (1) Figures cover the Houston-The Woodlands-Sugar Land, TX Metropolitan Statistical Area—see Appendix B for areas included
Source: National Association of Realtors, Median Sales Price of Existing Apartment Condo-Coop Homes for Metropolitan Areas, 4th Quarter 2018

Home Value Distribution

Area	Under $50,000	$50,000 -$99,999	$100,000 -$149,999	$150,000 -$199,999	$200,000 -$299,999	$300,000 -$499,999	$500,000 -$999,999	$1,000,000 or more
City	7.3	24.1	18.9	11.6	12.7	14.0	8.5	2.9
MSA[1]	6.5	16.7	19.9	17.2	18.3	13.6	5.9	1.9
U.S.	8.3	13.9	14.7	14.6	18.7	17.3	9.7	2.7

Note: Figures are percentages and cover owner-occupied housing units; (1) Figures cover the Houston-The Woodlands-Sugar Land, TX Metropolitan Statistical Area—see Appendix B for areas included
Source: U.S. Census Bureau, 2013-2017 American Community Survey 5-Year Estimates

Homeownership Rate

Area	2010 (%)	2011 (%)	2012 (%)	2013 (%)	2014 (%)	2015 (%)	2016 (%)	2017 (%)	2018 (%)
MSA[1]	61.4	61.3	62.1	60.5	60.4	60.3	59.0	58.9	60.1
U.S.	66.9	66.1	65.4	65.1	64.5	63.7	63.4	63.9	64.4

Note: (1) Figures cover the Houston-The Woodlands-Sugar Land, TX Metropolitan Statistical Area—see Appendix B for areas included
Source: U.S. Census Bureau, Housing Vacancies and Homeownership Annual Statistics: 2010-2018

Year Housing Structure Built

Area	2010 or Later	2000 -2009	1990 -1999	1980 -1989	1970 -1979	1960 -1969	1950 -1959	1940 -1949	Before 1940	Median Year
City	4.9	14.4	9.9	14.2	22.5	14.2	10.8	4.6	4.4	1977
MSA[1]	7.6	23.1	14.7	15.8	18.2	8.9	6.5	2.7	2.5	1987
U.S.	3.2	14.5	14.0	13.6	15.5	10.8	10.5	5.1	12.9	1977

Note: Figures are percentages except for Median Year; Note: (1) Figures cover the Houston-The Woodlands-Sugar Land, TX Metropolitan Statistical Area—see Appendix B for areas included
Source: U.S. Census Bureau, 2013-2017 American Community Survey 5-Year Estimates

Gross Monthly Rent

Area	Under $500	$500 -$999	$1,000 -$1,499	$1,500 -$1,999	$2,000 -$2,499	$2,500 -$2,999	$3,000 and up	Median ($)
City	4.7	51.9	28.5	10.1	2.7	1.1	1.1	940
MSA[1]	4.7	45.9	32.4	11.8	3.0	1.1	1.1	995
U.S.	10.5	41.1	28.7	11.7	4.5	1.8	1.7	982

Note: Figures are percentages except for Median; Gross rent is the contract rent plus the estimated average monthly cost of utilities (electricity, gas, and water and sewer) and fuels (oil, coal, kerosene, wood, etc.) if these are paid by the renter (or paid for the renter by someone else); (1) Figures cover the Houston-The Woodlands-Sugar Land, TX Metropolitan Statistical Area—see Appendix B for areas included
Source: U.S. Census Bureau, 2013-2017 American Community Survey 5-Year Estimates

HEALTH

Health Risk Factors

Category	MSA[1] (%)	U.S. (%)
Adults aged 18–64 who have any kind of health care coverage	66.8	87.3
Adults who reported being in good or better health	79.0	82.4
Adults who have been told they have high blood cholesterol	36.1	33.0
Adults who have been told they have high blood pressure	31.4	32.3
Adults who are current smokers	15.1	17.1
Adults who currently use E-cigarettes	3.3	4.6
Adults who currently use chewing tobacco, snuff, or snus	4.2	4.0
Adults who are heavy drinkers[2]	6.7	6.3
Adults who are binge drinkers[3]	18.8	17.4
Adults who are overweight (BMI 25.0 - 29.9)	42.7	35.3
Adults who are obese (BMI 30.0 - 99.8)	31.0	31.3
Adults who participated in any physical activities in the past month	70.6	74.4
Adults who always or nearly always wears a seat belt	95.8	94.3

Note: (1) Figures cover the Houston-The Woodlands-Sugar Land, TX Metropolitan Statistical Area—see Appendix B for areas included; (2) Heavy drinkers are classified as adult men having more than 14 drinks per week and adult women having more than 7 drinks per week; (3) Binge drinkers are classified as males having five or more drinks on one occasion or females having four or more drinks on one occasion
Source: Centers for Disease Control and Prevention, Behavioral Risk Factor Surveillance System, SMART: Selected Metropolitan Area Risk Trends, 2017

Acute and Chronic Health Conditions

Category	MSA[1] (%)	U.S. (%)
Adults who have ever been told they had a heart attack	3.3	4.2
Adults who have ever been told they have angina or coronary heart disease	3.5	3.9
Adults who have ever been told they had a stroke	3.7	3.0
Adults who have ever been told they have asthma	10.7	14.2
Adults who have ever been told they have arthritis	24.0	24.9
Adults who have ever been told they have diabetes[2]	10.0	10.5
Adults who have ever been told they had skin cancer	3.9	6.2
Adults who have ever been told they had any other types of cancer	4.9	7.1
Adults who have ever been told they have COPD	4.0	6.5
Adults who have ever been told they have kidney disease	2.5	3.0
Adults who have ever been told they have a form of depression	16.1	20.5

Note: (1) Figures cover the Houston-The Woodlands-Sugar Land, TX Metropolitan Statistical Area—see Appendix B for areas included; (2) Figures do not include pregnancy-related, borderline, or pre-diabetes
Source: Centers for Disease Control and Prevention, Behaviorial Risk Factor Surveillance System, SMART: Selected Metropolitan Area Risk Trends, 2017

Health Screening and Vaccination Rates

Category	MSA[1] (%)	U.S. (%)
Adults aged 65+ who have had flu shot within the past year	63.2	60.7
Adults aged 65+ who have ever had a pneumonia vaccination	72.4	75.4
Adults who have ever been tested for HIV	45.5	36.1
Adults who have ever had the shingles or zoster vaccine?	23.0	28.9
Adults who have had their blood cholesterol checked within the last five years	86.2	85.9

Note: n/a not available; (1) Figures cover the Houston-The Woodlands-Sugar Land, TX Metropolitan Statistical Area—see Appendix B for areas included.
Source: Centers for Disease Control and Prevention, Behaviorial Risk Factor Surveillance System, SMART: Selected Metropolitan Area Risk Trends, 2017

Disability Status

Category	MSA[1] (%)	U.S. (%)
Adults who reported being deaf	4.8	6.7
Are you blind or have serious difficulty seeing, even when wearing glasses?	5.2	4.5
Are you limited in any way in any of your usual activities due of arthritis?	13.3	12.9
Do you have difficulty doing errands alone?	8.1	6.8
Do you have difficulty dressing or bathing?	4.7	3.6
Do you have serious difficulty concentrating/remembering/making decisions?	12.1	10.7
Do you have serious difficulty walking or climbing stairs?	12.4	13.6

Note: (1) Figures cover the Houston-The Woodlands-Sugar Land, TX Metropolitan Statistical Area—see Appendix B for areas included.
Source: Centers for Disease Control and Prevention, Behaviorial Risk Factor Surveillance System, SMART: Selected Metropolitan Area Risk Trends, 2017

Mortality Rates for the Top 10 Causes of Death in the U.S.

ICD-10[a] Sub-Chapter	ICD-10[a] Code	Age-Adjusted Mortality Rate[1] per 100,000 population	
		County[2]	U.S.
Malignant neoplasms	C00-C97	143.5	155.5
Ischaemic heart diseases	I20-I25	88.7	94.8
Other forms of heart disease	I30-I51	53.6	52.9
Chronic lower respiratory diseases	J40-J47	28.7	41.0
Cerebrovascular diseases	I60-I69	41.5	37.5
Other degenerative diseases of the nervous system	G30-G31	38.1	35.0
Other external causes of accidental injury	W00-X59	26.7	33.7
Organic, including symptomatic, mental disorders	F01-F09	23.8	31.0
Hypertensive diseases	I10-I15	24.0	21.9
Diabetes mellitus	E10-E14	19.8	21.2

Note: (a) ICD-10 = International Classification of Diseases 10th Revision; (1) Mortality rates are a three year average covering 2015-2017; (2) Figures cover Harris County.
Source: Centers for Disease Control and Prevention, National Center for Health Statistics. Underlying Cause of Death 1999-2017 on CDC WONDER Online Database

Mortality Rates for Selected Causes of Death

ICD-10[a] Sub-Chapter	ICD-10[a] Code	Age-Adjusted Mortality Rate[1] per 100,000 population	
		County[2]	U.S.
Assault	X85-Y09	9.1	5.9
Diseases of the liver	K70-K76	14.3	14.1
Human immunodeficiency virus (HIV) disease	B20-B24	4.3	1.8
Influenza and pneumonia	J09-J18	12.7	14.3
Intentional self-harm	X60-X84	10.7	13.6
Malnutrition	E40-E46	2.6	1.6
Obesity and other hyperalimentation	E65-E68	1.7	2.1
Renal failure	N17-N19	18.3	13.0
Transport accidents	V01-V99	11.9	12.4
Viral hepatitis	B15-B19	1.7	1.6

Note: (a) ICD-10 = International Classification of Diseases 10th Revision; (1) Mortality rates are a three year average covering 2015-2017; (2) Figures cover Harris County; Data are suppressed when the data meet the criteria for confidentiality constraints; Mortality rates are flagged as unreliable when the rate would be calculated with a numerator of 20 or less.
Source: Centers for Disease Control and Prevention, National Center for Health Statistics. Underlying Cause of Death 1999-2017 on CDC WONDER Online Database

Health Insurance Coverage

Area	With Health Insurance	With Private Health Insurance	With Public Health Insurance	Without Health Insurance	Population Under Age 18 Without Health Insurance
City	75.9	50.5	31.2	24.1	12.9
MSA[1]	81.1	61.4	26.4	18.9	11.0
U.S.	89.5	67.2	33.8	10.5	5.7

Note: Figures are percentages that cover the civilian noninstitutionalized population; (1) Figures cover the Houston-The Woodlands-Sugar Land, TX Metropolitan Statistical Area—see Appendix B for areas included
Source: U.S. Census Bureau, 2013-2017 American Community Survey 5-Year Estimates

Number of Medical Professionals

Area	MDs[3]	DOs[3,4]	Dentists	Podiatrists	Chiropractors	Optometrists
County[1] (number)	14,819	542	3,140	222	1,014	902
County[1] (rate[2])	321.0	11.7	67.5	4.8	21.8	19.4
U.S. (rate[2])	279.3	23.0	68.4	6.0	27.1	16.2

Note: Data as of 2017 unless noted; (1) Data covers Harris County; (2) Rate per 100,000 population; (3) Data as of 2016 and includes all active, non-federal physicians; (4) Doctor of Osteopathic Medicine
Source: U.S. Department of Health and Human Services, Health Resources and Services Administration, Bureau of Health Professions, Area Resource File (ARF) 2017-2018

Best Hospitals

According to *U.S. News,* the Houston-The Woodlands-Sugar Land, TX metro area is home to six of the best hospitals in the U.S.: **Baylor St. Luke's Medical Center** (3 adult specialties); **Houston Methodist Hospital** (8 adult specialties); **Memorial Hermann-Texas Medical Center** (3 adult specialties and 2 pediatric specialties); **Menninger Clinic** (1 adult specialty); **TIRR Memorial Hermann** (1 adult specialty); **University of Texas MD Anderson Cancer Center** (2 adult specialties and 1 pediatric specialty). The hospitals listed were nationally ranked in at least one of 16 adult or 10 pediatric specialties. Only 170 hospitals nationwide were nationally ranked in one or more adult or pediatric specialty. Twenty hospitals in the U.S. made the Honor Roll. The Best Hospitals Honor Roll takes both the national rankings and the procedure and condition ratings into account. Hospitals received points if they were nationally ranked in one of the 16 adult specialties—the higher they ranked, the more points they got—and how many ratings of "high performing" they earned in the nine procedures and conditions. *U.S. News Online, "America's Best Hospitals 2018-19"*

According to *U.S. News,* the Houston-The Woodlands-Sugar Land, TX metro area is home to three of the best children's hospitals in the U.S.: **Children's Cancer Hospital-University of Texas M.D. Anderson Cancer Center** (1 pediatric specialty); **Children's Memorial Hermann Hospital** (2 pediatric specialties); **Texas Children's Hospital** (Honor Roll/10 pediatric specialties). The hospitals listed were highly ranked in at least one of 10 pediatric specialties. Eighty-six children's hospitals in the U.S. were nationally ranked in at least one specialty. Hospitals received points for being ranked in a specialty, and the 10 hospitals with the most points across the 10 specialties make up the Honor Roll. *U.S. News Online, "America's Best Children's Hospitals 2018-19"*

EDUCATION

Public School District Statistics

District Name	Schls	Pupils	Pupil/ Teacher Ratio	Minority Pupils[1] (%)	Free Lunch Eligible[2] (%)	IEP[3] (%)
Aldine ISD	79	69,768	15.0	97.8	77.2	7.2
Alief ISD	46	46,376	13.7	95.9	75.2	7.3
Cypress-Fairbanks ISD	87	114,868	16.5	74.3	42.0	7.8
Galena Park ISD	24	22,784	16.3	95.1	72.3	8.6
Harmony School of Excellence	7	4,417	16.3	87.4	44.8	6.3
Harmony School of Science-Houston	5	3,396	17.3	81.2	35.8	5.5
Harmony Science Academy	6	3,424	16.3	93.6	62.9	6.4
Harmony Science Academy (El Paso)	5	3,300	16.2	90.9	56.5	8.9
Houston Gateway Academy Inc	4	2,218	19.0	99.3	n/a	2.8
Houston ISD	287	216,106	18.7	91.2	70.9	7.2
Kipp Inc Charter	25	13,347	20.4	99.3	81.4	6.1
Sheldon ISD	13	8,884	16.1	93.5	69.2	7.4
Spring Branch ISD	49	35,079	15.6	73.4	53.0	7.3
Spring ISD	41	36,698	17.1	91.1	60.2	8.0
Yes Prep Public Schools Inc	12	10,258	14.9	98.8	76.2	5.8

Note: Table includes school districts with 2,000 or more students; (1) Percentage of students that are not non-Hispanic white; (2) Percentage of students that are eligible for the free lunch program; (3) Percentage of students that have an Individualized Education Program.
Source: U.S. Department of Education, National Center for Education Statistics, Common Core of Data, Local Education Agency (School District) Universe Survey: School Year 2016-2017; U.S. Department of Education, National Center for Education Statistics, Common Core of Data, Public Elementary/Secondary School Universe Survey: School Year 2016-2017

Best High Schools

According to *U.S. News,* Houston is home to 23 of the best high schools in the U.S.: **Carnegie Vanguard High School** (#15); **DeBakey High School for Health Professions** (#38); **Eastwood Academy** (#56); **Challenge Early College High School** (#91); **YES Prep North Forest** (#94); **YES Prep - East End** (#97); **YES Prep - Southwest** (#106); **YES Prep - Gulfton** (#118); **YES Prep - West** (#123); **YES Prep - Southeast** (#131); **Clear Horizons Early College High School** (#151); **YES Prep - Brays Oaks** (#194); **The High School for the Performing and Visual Arts** (#232); **KIPP Generations Collegiate** (#233); **YES Prep - North Central** (#234); **Victory Early College High School** (#272); **North Houston Early College High School** (#311); **East Early College High School** (#315); **Alief Early College High School** (#351); **Energized for STEM Academy West High School** (#372); **Kerr High School** (#405); **KIPP Houston High School** (#451); **Memorial High School** (#479). More than 20,000 public, magnet and charter schools were ranked based on their performance on state assessments and how well they prepare students for college. Schools with the highest unrounded College Readiness Index values were numerically ranked from 1 to 500 and were classified as gold medal winners. *U.S. News & World Report, "Best High Schools 2018"*

Highest Level of Education

Area	Less than H.S.	H.S. Diploma	Some College, No Deg.	Associate Degree	Bachelor's Degree	Master's Degree	Prof. School Degree	Doctorate Degree
City	22.1	22.8	18.3	5.1	19.3	8.3	2.5	1.6
MSA[1]	17.2	23.3	21.0	6.7	20.4	8.1	2.0	1.4
U.S.	12.7	27.3	20.8	8.3	19.1	8.4	2.0	1.4

Note: Figures cover persons age 25 and over; (1) Figures cover the Houston-The Woodlands-Sugar Land, TX Metropolitan Statistical Area—see Appendix B for areas included
Source: U.S. Census Bureau, 2013-2017 American Community Survey 5-Year Estimates

Educational Attainment by Race

Area	High School Graduate or Higher (%)					Bachelor's Degree or Higher (%)				
	Total	White	Black	Asian	Hisp.[2]	Total	White	Black	Asian	Hisp.[2]
City	77.9	76.5	87.5	86.7	56.2	31.7	35.6	21.6	58.3	12.0
MSA[1]	82.8	82.8	89.8	87.5	61.7	31.9	32.3	26.3	57.1	13.7
U.S.	87.3	89.3	84.9	86.5	66.7	30.9	32.2	20.6	52.7	15.2

Note: Figures shown cover persons 25 years old and over; (1) Figures cover the Houston-The Woodlands-Sugar Land, TX Metropolitan Statistical Area—see Appendix B for areas included; (2) People of Hispanic origin can be of any race
Source: U.S. Census Bureau, 2013-2017 American Community Survey 5-Year Estimates

School Enrollment by Grade and Control

Area	Preschool (%)		Kindergarten (%)		Grades 1 - 4 (%)		Grades 5 - 8 (%)		Grades 9 - 12 (%)	
	Public	Private	Public	Private	Public	Private	Public	Private	Public	Private
City	68.4	31.6	90.8	9.2	93.2	6.8	92.4	7.6	93.0	7.0
MSA[1]	59.8	40.2	90.0	10.0	92.8	7.2	93.1	6.9	93.4	6.6
U.S.	58.8	41.2	87.7	12.3	89.7	10.3	89.6	10.4	90.3	9.7

Note: Figures shown cover persons 3 years old and over; (1) Figures cover the Houston-The Woodlands-Sugar Land, TX Metropolitan Statistical Area—see Appendix B for areas included
Source: U.S. Census Bureau, 2013-2017 American Community Survey 5-Year Estimates

Average Salaries of Public School Classroom Teachers

Area	2016		2017		Change from 2016 to 2017	
	Dollars	Rank[1]	Dollars	Rank[1]	Percent	Rank[2]
Texas	51,890	28	52,575	28	1.3	29
U.S. Average	58,479	–	59,660	–	2.0	–

Note: (1) Rank ranges from 1 to 51 where 1 indicates highest salary; (2) Rank ranges from 1 to 51 where 1 indicates highest percent change.
Source: National Education Association, Rankings & Estimates: Rankings of the States 2017 and Estimates of School Statistics 2018

Higher Education

Four-Year Colleges			Two-Year Colleges			Medical Schools[1]	Law Schools[2]	Voc/ Tech[3]
Public	Private Non-profit	Private For-profit	Public	Private Non-profit	Private For-profit			
6	8	7	1	2	16	2	3	20

Note: Figures cover institutions located within the city limits and include main campuses only; (1) includes schools accredited by the Liaison Committee on Medical Education and the American Osteopathic Association's Commission on Osteopathic College Accreditation; (2) includes ABA-accredited schools, schools with provisional ABA accreditation, and state accredited schools; (3) includes all schools with programs that are less than 2 years.
Source: National Center for Education Statistics, Integrated Postsecondary Education System (IPEDS), 2017-18; Wikipedia, List of Medical Schools in the United States, accessed April 3, 2019; Wikipedia, List of Law Schools in the United States, accessed April 3, 2019

According to U.S. News & World Report, the Houston-The Woodlands-Sugar Land, TX metro area is home to two of the best national universities in the U.S.: **Rice University** (#16 tie); **University of Houston** (#171 tie). The indicators used to capture academic quality fall into a number of categories: assessment by administrators at peer institutions; retention of students; faculty resources; student selectivity; financial resources; alumni giving; high school counselor ratings of colleges; and graduation rate. U.S. News & World Report, "America's Best Colleges 2019"

According to U.S. News & World Report, the Houston-The Woodlands-Sugar Land, TX metro area is home to one of the top 100 law schools in the U.S.: **University of Houston** (#59 tie). The rankings are based on a weighted average of 12 measures of quality: peer assessment score; assessment score by lawyers/judges; median LSAT scores; median undergrad GPA; acceptance rate; employment rates for graduates; placement success; bar passage rate; faculty resources; expenditures per student; student/faculty ratio; and library resources. U.S. News & World Report, "America's Best Graduate Schools, Law, 2020"

According to U.S. News & World Report, the Houston-The Woodlands-Sugar Land, TX metro area is home to three of the top 75 medical schools for research in the U.S.: **Baylor College of Medicine** (#22); **University of Texas Health Science Center—Houston (McGovern)** (#52 tie); **University of Texas Medical Branch—Galveston** (#70 tie). The rankings are based on a weighted average of 11 measures of quality: quality assessment; peer assessment score; assessment score by residency directors; research activity; total research activity; average research activity per faculty member; student selectivity; median MCAT total score; median undergraduate GPA;

acceptance rate; and faculty resources. *U.S. News & World Report, "America's Best Graduate Schools, Medical, 2020"*

According to *U.S. News & World Report,* the Houston-The Woodlands-Sugar Land, TX metro area is home to one of the top 75 business schools in the U.S.: **Rice University (Jones)** (#26 tie). The rankings are based on a weighted average of the following nine measures: quality assessment; peer assessment; recruiter assessment; placement success; mean starting salary and bonus; student selectivity; mean GMAT and GRE scores; mean undergraduate GPA; and acceptance rate. *U.S. News & World Report, "America's Best Graduate Schools, Business, 2020"*

PRESIDENTIAL ELECTION

2016 Presidential Election Results

Area	Clinton	Trump	Johnson	Stein	Other
Harris County	54.0	41.6	3.0	0.9	0.5
U.S.	48.0	45.9	3.3	1.1	1.7

Note: Results are percentages and may not add to 100% due to rounding
Source: Dave Leip's Atlas of U.S. Presidential Elections

EMPLOYERS

Major Employers

Company Name	Industry
Christus Health Gulf Coast	Management consulting services
Conoco Phillips	Petroleum refining
Continental Airlines	Air transportation, scheduled
Dibellos Dynamic Orthotics & Prosthetics	Surgical appliances & supplies
El Paso E&P Company	Petroleum refining
F Charles Brunicardi MD	Accounting, auditing, & bookkeeping
Grey Wolf	Drilling oil & gas wells
Kellogg Brown &Root	Industrial plant construction
Mustang Engineers and Constructors	Construction management consultant
Philip Industrial Services	Environmental consultant
Philips Petroleum Company	Oil & gas exploration services
Quaker State Corp	Lubricating oils & greases
St. Lukes Episcopal Health System	General medical & surgical hospitals
Texas Childrens Hospital	Specialty hospitals, except psychiatric
The Methodist Hospital	General medical & surgical hospitals
Tracer Industries	Plumbing
U.S. Dept of Veteran Affairs	Administration of veterans' affairs
Univ of Texas Medical Branch at Galveston	Accident & health insurance
University of Houston System	University
University of Texas System	General medical & surgical hospitals
Veterans Health Administration	Administration of veterans' affairs

Note: Companies shown are located within the Houston-The Woodlands-Sugar Land, TX Metropolitan Statistical Area.
Source: Hoovers.com; Wikipedia

Best Companies to Work For

Camden Property Trust; David Weekley Homes, headquartered in Houston, are among "The 100 Best Companies to Work For." To pick the best companies, *Fortune* partnered with the Great Place to Work Institute. Two-thirds of a company's score is based on the results of the Institute's Trust Index survey, which is sent to a random sample of employees from each company. The questions related to attitudes about management's credibility, job satisfaction, and camaraderie. The other third of the scoring is based on the company's responses to the Institute's Culture Audit, which includes detailed questions about pay and benefit programs, and a series of open-ended questions about hiring practices, internal communication, training, recognition programs, and diversity efforts. Any company that is at least five years old with more than 1,000 U.S. employees is eligible. *Fortune, "The 100 Best Companies to Work For," 2019*

PUBLIC SAFETY

Crime Rate

Area	All Crimes	Violent Crimes				Property Crimes		
		Murder	Rape[3]	Robbery	Aggrav. Assault	Burglary	Larceny -Theft	Motor Vehicle Theft
City	5,223.6	11.5	58.4	418.0	607.3	731.7	2,900.8	495.9
Suburbs[1]	n/a	3.7	34.8	96.5	201.5	n/a	1,432.2	n/a
Metro[2]	n/a	6.4	42.8	205.2	338.8	n/a	1,928.8	n/a
U.S.	2,756.1	5.3	41.7	98.0	248.9	430.4	1,694.4	237.4

Note: Figures are crimes per 100,000 population; (1) All areas within the metro area that are located outside the city limits; (2) Figures cover the Houston-The Woodlands-Sugar Land, TX Metropolitan Statistical Area—see Appendix B for areas included; (3) The city and U.S. figures shown were reported using the revised Uniform Crime Reporting (UCR) definition of rape. The suburban and metro area figures shown are an aggregate total of the data submitted using both the revised and legacy UCR definitions.
Source: FBI Uniform Crime Reports, 2017

Hate Crimes

Area	Number of Quarters Reported	Number of Incidents per Bias Motivation					
		Race/Ethnicity/ Ancestry	Religion	Sexual Orientation	Disability	Gender	Gender Identity
City	4	2	3	1	0	0	2
U.S.	4	4,131	1,564	1,130	116	46	119

Source: Federal Bureau of Investigation, Hate Crime Statistics 2017

Identity Theft Consumer Reports

Area	Reports	Reports per 100,000 Population	Rank[2]
MSA[1]	13,300	196	11
U.S.	444,602	135	-

Note: (1) Figures cover the Houston-The Woodlands-Sugar Land, TX Metropolitan Statistical Area—see Appendix B for areas included; (2) Rank ranges from 1 to 389 where 1 indicates greatest number of identity theft reports per 100,000 population
Source: Federal Trade Commission, Consumer Sentinel Network Data Book for January–December 2018

Fraud and Other Consumer Reports

Area	Reports	Reports per 100,000 Population	Rank[2]
MSA[1]	36,812	544	116
U.S.	2,552,917	776	-

Note: (1) Figures cover the Houston-The Woodlands-Sugar Land, TX Metropolitan Statistical Area—see Appendix B for areas included; (2) Rank ranges from 1 to 389 where 1 indicates greatest number of fraud and other consumer reports per 100,000 population
Source: Federal Trade Commission, Consumer Sentinel Network Data Book for January–December 2018

SPORTS

Professional Sports Teams

Team Name	League	Year Established
Houston Astros	Major League Baseball (MLB)	1962
Houston Dynamo	Major League Soccer (MLS)	2006
Houston Rockets	National Basketball Association (NBA)	1971
Houston Texans	National Football League (NFL)	2002

Note: Includes teams located in the Houston-The Woodlands-Sugar Land, TX Metropolitan Statistical Area.
Source: Wikipedia, Major Professional Sports Teams of the United States and Canada, April 5, 2019

CLIMATE

Average and Extreme Temperatures

Temperature	Jan	Feb	Mar	Apr	May	Jun	Jul	Aug	Sep	Oct	Nov	Dec	Yr.
Extreme High (°F)	84	91	91	95	97	103	104	107	102	94	89	83	107
Average High (°F)	61	65	73	79	85	91	93	93	89	81	72	65	79
Average Temp. (°F)	51	54	62	69	75	81	83	83	79	70	61	54	69
Average Low (°F)	41	43	51	58	65	71	73	73	68	58	50	43	58
Extreme Low (°F)	12	20	22	31	44	52	62	62	48	32	19	7	7

Note: Figures cover the years 1969-1990
Source: National Climatic Data Center, International Station Meteorological Climate Summary, 9/96

Average Precipitation/Snowfall/Humidity

Precip./Humidity	Jan	Feb	Mar	Apr	May	Jun	Jul	Aug	Sep	Oct	Nov	Dec	Yr.
Avg. Precip. (in.)	3.3	2.7	3.3	3.3	5.6	4.9	3.7	3.7	4.8	4.7	3.7	3.3	46.9
Avg. Snowfall (in.)	Tr	Tr	0	0	0	0	0	0	0	0	Tr	Tr	Tr
Avg. Rel. Hum. 6am (%)	85	86	87	89	91	92	93	93	93	91	89	86	90
Avg. Rel. Hum. 3pm (%)	58	55	54	54	57	56	55	55	57	53	55	57	55

Note: Figures cover the years 1969-1990; Tr = Trace amounts (<0.05 in. of rain; <0.5 in. of snow)
Source: National Climatic Data Center, International Station Meteorological Climate Summary, 9/96

Weather Conditions

Temperature			Daytime Sky			Precipitation		
32°F & below	45°F & below	90°F & above	Clear	Partly cloudy	Cloudy	0.01 inch or more precip.	0.1 inch or more snow/ice	Thunder-storms
21	87	96	83	167	115	101	1	62

Note: Figures are average number of days per year and cover the years 1969-1990
Source: National Climatic Data Center, International Station Meteorological Climate Summary, 9/96

HAZARDOUS WASTE

Superfund Sites

The Houston-The Woodlands-Sugar Land, TX metro area is home to 21 sites on the EPA's Superfund National Priorities List: **Conroe Creosoting Co.** (final); **Crystal Chemical Co.** (final); **French, Ltd.** (final); **Geneva Industries/Fuhrmann Energy** (final); **Gulfco Marine Maintenance** (final); **Highlands Acid Pit** (final); **Jones Road Ground Water Plume** (final); **Malone Service Co - Swan Lake Plant** (final); **Many Diversified Interests, Inc.** (final); **Motco, Inc.** (final); **North Cavalcade Street** (final); **Patrick Bayou** (final); **Petro-Chemical Systems, Inc. (Turtle Bayou)** (final); **San Jacinto River Waste Pits** (final); **Sheridan Disposal Services** (final); **Sikes Disposal Pits** (final); **Sol Lynn/Industrial Transformers** (final); **South Cavalcade Street** (final); **Tex-Tin Corp.** (final); **United Creosoting Co.** (final); **Us Oil Recovery** (final). There are a total of 1,390 Superfund sites with a status of proposed or final on the list in the U.S. *U.S. Environmental Protection Agency, National Priorities List, April 5, 2019*

AIR & WATER QUALITY

Air Quality Trends: Ozone

	1990	1995	2000	2005	2010	2012	2014	2015	2016	2017
MSA[1]	0.119	0.114	0.102	0.087	0.079	0.080	0.064	0.083	0.066	0.070
U.S.	0.088	0.089	0.082	0.080	0.073	0.075	0.067	0.068	0.069	0.068

Note: (1) Data covers the Houston-The Woodlands-Sugar Land, TX Metropolitan Statistical Area—see Appendix B for areas included. The values shown are the composite ozone concentration averages among trend sites based on the highest fourth daily maximum 8-hour concentration in parts per million. These trends are based on sites having an adequate record of monitoring data during the trend period. Data from exceptional events are included.
Source: U.S. Environmental Protection Agency, Air Quality Monitoring Information, "Air Quality Trends by City, 1990-2017"

Air Quality Index

Area	Percent of Days when Air Quality was...[2]					AQI Statistics[2]	
	Good	Moderate	Unhealthy for Sensitive Groups	Unhealthy	Very Unhealthy	Maximum	Median
MSA[1]	50.4	42.7	6.0	0.8	0.0	177	50

Note: (1) Data covers the Houston-The Woodlands-Sugar Land, TX Metropolitan Statistical Area—see Appendix B for areas included; (2) Based on 365 days with AQI data in 2017. Air Quality Index (AQI) is an index for reporting daily air quality. EPA calculates the AQI for five major air pollutants regulated by the Clean Air Act: ground-level ozone, particle pollution (aka particulate matter), carbon monoxide, sulfur dioxide, and nitrogen dioxide. The AQI runs from 0 to 500. The higher the AQI value, the greater the level of air pollution and the greater the health concern. There are six AQI categories: "Good" AQI is between 0 and 50. Air quality is considered satisfactory; "Moderate" AQI is between 51 and 100. Air quality is acceptable; "Unhealthy for Sensitive Groups" When AQI values are between 101 and 150, members of sensitive groups may experience health effects; "Unhealthy" When AQI values are between 151 and 200 everyone may begin to experience health effects; "Very Unhealthy" AQI values between 201 and 300 trigger a health alert; "Hazardous" AQI values over 300 trigger warnings of emergency conditions (not shown).
Source: U.S. Environmental Protection Agency, Air Quality Index Report, 2017

Air Quality Index Pollutants

Area	Percent of Days when AQI Pollutant was...[2]					
	Carbon Monoxide	Nitrogen Dioxide	Ozone	Sulfur Dioxide	Particulate Matter 2.5	Particulate Matter 10
MSA[1]	0.0	5.2	48.8	0.0	45.8	0.3

Note: (1) Data covers the Houston-The Woodlands-Sugar Land, TX Metropolitan Statistical Area—see Appendix B for areas included; (2) Based on 365 days with AQI data in 2017. The Air Quality Index (AQI) is an index for reporting daily air quality. EPA calculates the AQI for five major air pollutants regulated by the Clean Air Act: ground-level ozone, particle pollution (also known as particulate matter), carbon monoxide, sulfur dioxide, and nitrogen dioxide. The AQI runs from 0 to 500. The higher the AQI value, the greater the level of air pollution and the greater the health concern.
Source: U.S. Environmental Protection Agency, Air Quality Index Report, 2017

Maximum Air Pollutant Concentrations: Particulate Matter, Ozone, CO and Lead

	Particulate Matter 10 (ug/m^3)	Particulate Matter 2.5 Wtd AM (ug/m^3)	Particulate Matter 2.5 24-Hr (ug/m^3)	Ozone (ppm)	Carbon Monoxide (ppm)	Lead (ug/m^3)
MSA[1] Level	80	10.1	24	0.079	2	n/a
NAAQS[2]	150	15	35	0.075	9	0.15
Met NAAQS[2]	Yes	Yes	Yes	No	Yes	n/a

Note: (1) Data covers the Houston-The Woodlands-Sugar Land, TX Metropolitan Statistical Area—see Appendix B for areas included; Data from exceptional events are included; (2) National Ambient Air Quality Standards; ppm = parts per million; ug/m³ = micrograms per cubic meter; n/a not available.
Concentrations: Particulate Matter 10 (coarse particulate)—highest second maximum 24-hour concentration; Particulate Matter 2.5 Wtd AM (fine particulate)—highest weighted annual mean concentration; Particulate Matter 2.5 24-Hour (fine particulate)—highest 98th percentile 24-hour concentration; Ozone—highest fourth daily maximum 8-hour concentration; Carbon Monoxide—highest second maximum non-overlapping 8-hour concentration; Lead—maximum running 3-month average
Source: U.S. Environmental Protection Agency, Air Quality Monitoring Information, "Air Quality Statistics by City, 2017"

Maximum Air Pollutant Concentrations: Nitrogen Dioxide and Sulfur Dioxide

	Nitrogen Dioxide AM (ppb)	Nitrogen Dioxide 1-Hr (ppb)	Sulfur Dioxide AM (ppb)	Sulfur Dioxide 1-Hr (ppb)	Sulfur Dioxide 24-Hr (ppb)
MSA[1] Level	14	52	n/a	19	n/a
NAAQS[2]	53	100	30	75	140
Met NAAQS[2]	Yes	Yes	n/a	Yes	n/a

Note: (1) Data covers the Houston-The Woodlands-Sugar Land, TX Metropolitan Statistical Area—see Appendix B for areas included; Data from exceptional events are included; (2) National Ambient Air Quality Standards; ppm = parts per million; ug/m³ = micrograms per cubic meter; n/a not available.
Concentrations: Nitrogen Dioxide AM—highest arithmetic mean concentration; Nitrogen Dioxide 1-Hr—highest 98th percentile 1-hour daily maximum concentration; Sulfur Dioxide AM—highest annual mean concentration; Sulfur Dioxide 1-Hr—highest 99th percentile 1-hour daily maximum concentration; Sulfur Dioxide 24-Hr—highest second maximum 24-hour concentration
Source: U.S. Environmental Protection Agency, Air Quality Monitoring Information, "Air Quality Statistics by City, 2017"

Drinking Water

Water System Name	Pop. Served	Primary Water Source Type	Violations[1]	
			Health Based	Monitoring/ Reporting
City of Houston	2,319,603	Surface	0	0

Note: (1) Based on violation data from January 1, 2018 to December 31, 2018
Source: U.S. Environmental Protection Agency, Office of Ground Water and Drinking Water, Safe Drinking Water Information System (based on data extracted April 5, 2019)

Huntsville, Alabama

Background

The seat of Madison County, Huntsville is richly evocative of the antebellum Deep South. It is also a uniquely cosmopolitan town that remains one of the South's fastest growing, with the highest per capita income in the Southeast.

Huntsville is the seat of Madison County, named for President James Madison. Originally home to Cherokee and Chickasaw Indians, Huntsville was rich in forests and game animals. The town is named for John Hunt, a Virginia Revolutionary War veteran who built a cabin in 1805 on today's corner of Bank Street and Oak Avenue.

The fertility of the valley attracted both smaller farmers and wealthy plantation investors. Leroy Pope, having donated land to the municipality, wanted to rename it Twickenham, after a London suburb home to his kin, poet Alexander Pope, but resentment against all things British, prevented it.

Huntsville was the largest town in the Alabama Territory by 1819, the year Alabama received statehood. It was the site of the state's first constitutional convention and, briefly, the capital. It quickly became a hub for processing corn, tobacco, and cotton, which became its economic mainstay. In 1852, the Memphis and Charleston Railway was completed, and planters, merchants, and shippers transformed Huntsville into a main commercial southern city.

Because many wealthy residents had remained loyal to the Union at the outset of the Civil War, the town was largely undamaged by occupying forces and, as a result, Huntsville boasts one of the largest collections of antebellum houses in the South. Walking tours of the Twickenham historic district offer the 1819 Weeden House Museum and the 1860 Huntsville Depot Museum. Restored nineteenth-century cabins and farm buildings are displayed at the mountaintop Burritt Museum and Park.

Huntsville's U.S. Space and Rocket Center, the state's largest tourist attraction, showcases space technology and houses Space Camp, opportunities for children and adults that promote science, engineering, aviation and exploration. The Huntsville Botanical Garden features year-long floral and aquatic gardens, and the Huntsville Museum of Art features both contemporary and classical exhibits.

The city's modern Von Braun Center hosts national and international trade shows, local sports teams, concerts and theater. The city has an outstanding symphony orchestra.

More than 25 biotechnology firms are in the city due to the Huntsville Biotech Initiative. The HudsonAlpha Institute for Biotechnology is the centerpiece of the Cummings Research Park Biotech Campus, and contributes genomics and genetics work to the Encyclopedia of DNA Elements (ENCODE). The University of Alabama in Huntsville's (UAH) doctoral program in biotechnology supports HudsonAlpha and the emerging biotechnology economy in Huntsville.

Huntsville's institutions of higher learning include a campus of the University of Alabama, Oakwood College, and Alabama A&M University in nearby Normal, Alabama.

Redstone Arsenal, home to U.S. Army Aviation and Missile Command, propelled Huntsville into a high-tech hub, and is a strategic research site for rocketry, aviation, and related programs. In 1950, German rocket scientists, most notably the famous Wernher von Braun developed rockets for the U.S. Army here. The Redstone complex developed the rocket that launched America's first satellite into space, and rockets that put astronauts into space and landed them on the moon.

Huntsville enjoys a mild, temperate climate. Only four to five weeks during the middle of winter see temperatures below freezing. Huntsville has now gone about 15 years without significant snowfall. Rainfall is fairly abundant.

Rankings

General Rankings

- *US News & World Report* conducted a survey of more than 2,000 people and analyzed the 125 largest metropolitan areas to determine what matters the most when selecting the next place to live. Huntsville ranked #7 out of the top 25 as having the best combination of desirable factors. Criteria: cost of living; quality of education; job market, crime rates; and other factors. *realestate.usnews.com, "The 25 Best Places to Live in the U.S. in 2018," April 10, 2018*

- In their sixth annual survey, Livability.com looked at data for more than 1,000 U.S. cities to determine the rankings for Livability's "Top 100 Best Places to Live" in 2019. Huntsville ranked #40. Criteria: median home value capped at $250,000; affordable living; vibrant economy; education, demographics, health care options. transportation & infrastructure; abundant lifestyle amenities. *Livability.com, "Top 100 Best Places to Live 2019" March 2019*

Business/Finance Rankings

- The personal finance site NerdWallet analyzed 183 American metropolitan areas with populations over 250,000 and more than 15,000 businesses to rank where entrepreneurs find the most success. Criteria included area economy, annual income, housing cost, unemployment rate, and the success rate of area businesses. Huntsville ranked #83. *www.nerdwallet.com, "Best Places to Start a Business," April 27, 2015*

- Using data from the Council for Community and Economic Research's 2014 cost of living index, NerdWallet ranked the 100 most affordable cities in America. Median income was compared with cost of living to find truly affordable places. Huntsville ranked #41. *NerdWallet.com, "America's Most Affordable Places," May 18, 2015*

- The Huntsville metro area appeared on the Milken Institute "2018 Best Performing Cities" list. Rank: #59 out of 200 large metro areas. Criteria: job growth; wage and salary growth; high-tech output growth. *Milken Institute, "Best-Performing Cities 2018," January 24, 2019*

- *Forbes* ranked the 200 most populous metro areas to determine the nation's "Best Places for Business and Careers." The Huntsville metro area was ranked #107. Criteria: costs (business and living); job growth (past and projected); income growth; quality of life; educational attainment (college and high school); projected economic growth; cultural and recreational opportunities; net migration patterns; number of highly ranked colleges. *Forbes, "The Best Places for Business and Careers 2018: Seattle Leads the Way," October 24, 2018*

Education Rankings

- Personal finance website *WalletHub* analyzed the 150 largest U.S. metropolitan statistical areas to determine where the most educated Americans are choosing to settle. Criteria: education quality and attainment gap; education levels; percentage of workers with degrees; public school quality rankings; quality and size of each metro area's universities. Huntsville was ranked #25 (#1 = most educated city). *www.WalletHub.com, "2018's Most and Least Educated Cities in America," July 24, 2018*

Health/Fitness Rankings

- The Huntsville metro area ranked #113 out of 189 in The Gallup-Healthways Well-Being Index. Criteria: purpose; social well being; financial health; community and physical health. Results are based on telephone interviews with adults, aged 18 and older, living in metropolitan areas in the 50 U.S. states and the District of Columbia. *Gallup-Healthways, "State of American Well-Being, 2017 Community Well-Being Rankings" March 2018*

Real Estate Rankings

- *WalletHub* compared the most populated U.S. cities, as well as at least two of the most populated cities in each state, for a total of 179, to determine which had the best markets for real estate agents. Huntsville ranked #86 where demand was high and pay was the best. Criteria: sales per agent; annual median wage for real-estate agents; monthly average starting salary for real estate agents; real estate job density and competition; unemployment rate; housing-market health index; and other relevant metrics. *www.WalletHub.com, "2018's Best Places to Be a Real Estate Agent," April 25, 2018*

- The Huntsville metro area was identified as one of the 20 best housing markets in the U.S. in 2018. The area ranked #8 out of 178 markets. Criteria: year-over-year change of median sales price of existing single-family homes between the 4th quarter of 2017 and the 4th quarter of 2018. *National Association of Realtors®, Median Sales Price of Existing Single-Family Homes for Metropolitan Areas, 4th Quarter 2018*

Safety Rankings

- Allstate ranked the 200 largest cities in America in terms of driver safety. Huntsville ranked #4. Criteria: internal property damage claims over a two-year period from January 2015 to December 2016. The report helps increase the importance of safety awareness behind the wheel. *Allstate, "Allstate America's Best Drivers Report, 2018" August 28, 2018*

- Huntsville was identified as one of the most dangerous cities in America by NeighborhoodScout. The city ranked #97 out of 100. Criteria: number of violent crimes per 1,000 residents. The editors only considered cities with 25,000 or more residents. *NeighborhoodScout.com, "Top 100 Most Dangerous Cities in the U.S. 2019" January 2, 2019*

- The National Insurance Crime Bureau ranked 382 metro areas in the U.S. in terms of per capita rates of vehicle theft. The Huntsville metro area ranked #135 (#1 = highest rate). Criteria: number of vehicle theft offenses per 100,000 inhabitants in 2017. *National Insurance Crime Bureau, "Hot Spots 2017," July 12, 2018*

Seniors/Retirement Rankings

- From its Best Cities for Successful Aging indexes, the Milken Institute generated rankings for metropolitan areas, weighing data in nine categories—health care, wellness, living arrangements, transportation and convenience, financial characteristics, education, employment, community engagement, and overall livability. The Huntsville metro area was ranked #207 overall in the small metro area category. *Milken Institute, "Best Cities for Successful Aging, 2017" March 14, 2017*

Women/Minorities Rankings

- Personal finance website *WalletHub* compared more than 180 U.S. cities—including the 150 most populated U.S. cities, plus at least two of the most populated cities in each state—across two key dimensions, "Hispanic Business-Friendliness" and "Hispanic Purchasing Power", to arrive at the most favorable conditions for Hispanic entrepreneurs. Huntsville was ranked #125 out of 182. Criteria includes: share of Hispanic-Owned Businesses; Hispanic entrepreneurship rate to median annual income of Hispanics; Small Business-Friendliness score; cost of living; and number of Hispanics with at least a bachelor's degree. *WalletHub.com, "2018's Best Cities for Hispanic Entrepreneurs," April 26, 2018*

Miscellaneous Rankings

- *MoveHub* ranked the coolest cities, appealing to young people, using its U.S. Hipster Index and Huntsville came out as #16. Criteria: number of thrift stores; density of tattoo parlors, vegan stores and microbreweries; and amount of rent increase. *www.thisisinsider.com, "The 20 Most Hipster Cities in the US-and Why You Should Consider Moving to One," April 10, 2018*

Business Environment

CITY FINANCES

City Government Finances

Component	2016 ($000)	2016 ($ per capita)
Total Revenues	993,899	5,215
Total Expenditures	966,242	5,070
Debt Outstanding	965,195	5,064
Cash and Securities[1]	463,800	2,434

Note: (1) Cash and security holdings of a government at the close of its fiscal year, including those of its dependent agencies, utilities, and liquor stores.
Source: U.S. Census Bureau, State & Local Government Finances 2016

City Government Revenue by Source

Source	2016 ($000)	2016 ($ per capita)	2016 (%)
General Revenue			
From Federal Government	2,664	14	0.3
From State Government	37,005	194	3.7
From Local Governments	0	0	0.0
Taxes			
Property	54,748	287	5.5
Sales and Gross Receipts	213,495	1,120	21.5
Personal Income	0	0	0.0
Corporate Income	0	0	0.0
Motor Vehicle License	0	0	0.0
Other Taxes	23,680	124	2.4
Current Charges	66,176	347	6.7
Liquor Store	0	0	0.0
Utility	574,358	3,014	57.8
Employee Retirement	0	0	0.0

Source: U.S. Census Bureau, State & Local Government Finances 2016

City Government Expenditures by Function

Function	2016 ($000)	2016 ($ per capita)	2016 (%)
General Direct Expenditures			
Air Transportation	0	0	0.0
Corrections	0	0	0.0
Education	0	0	0.0
Employment Security Administration	0	0	0.0
Financial Administration	10,054	52	1.0
Fire Protection	33,756	177	3.5
General Public Buildings	0	0	0.0
Governmental Administration, Other	10,154	53	1.1
Health	1,888	9	0.2
Highways	21,696	113	2.2
Hospitals	0	0	0.0
Housing and Community Development	5,953	31	0.6
Interest on General Debt	30,751	161	3.2
Judicial and Legal	5,045	26	0.5
Libraries	5,832	30	0.6
Parking	1,650	8	0.2
Parks and Recreation	24,364	127	2.5
Police Protection	43,881	230	4.5
Public Welfare	0	0	0.0
Sewerage	24,609	129	2.5
Solid Waste Management	0	0	0.0
Veterans' Services	0	0	0.0
Liquor Store	0	0	0.0
Utility	548,973	2,880	56.8
Employee Retirement	0	0	0.0

Source: U.S. Census Bureau, State & Local Government Finances 2016

DEMOGRAPHICS

Population Growth

Area	1990 Census	2000 Census	2010 Census	2017* Estimate	Population Growth (%) 1990-2017	Population Growth (%) 2010-2017
City	161,842	158,216	180,105	190,501	17.7	5.8
MSA[1]	293,047	342,376	417,593	444,908	51.8	6.5
U.S.	248,709,873	281,421,906	308,745,538	321,004,407	29.1	4.0

Note: (1) Figures cover the Huntsville, AL Metropolitan Statistical Area—see Appendix B for areas included; (*) 2013-2017 5-year estimated population
Source: U.S. Census Bureau, 1990 Census, Census 2000, Census 2010, 2013-2017 American Community Survey 5-Year Estimates

Household Size

Area	Persons in Household (%) One	Two	Three	Four	Five	Six	Seven or More	Average Household Size
City	36.4	33.4	14.0	10.0	4.2	1.3	0.7	2.30
MSA[1]	29.7	34.3	16.0	12.6	5.1	1.6	0.7	2.50
U.S.	27.7	33.8	15.7	13.0	6.0	2.3	1.4	2.60

Note: (1) Figures cover the Huntsville, AL Metropolitan Statistical Area—see Appendix B for areas included
Source: U.S. Census Bureau, 2013-2017 American Community Survey 5-Year Estimates

Race

Area	White Alone[2] (%)	Black Alone[2] (%)	Asian Alone[2] (%)	AIAN[3] Alone[2] (%)	NHOPI[4] Alone[2] (%)	Other Race Alone[2] (%)	Two or More Races (%)
City	62.3	30.8	2.6	0.3	0.1	1.3	2.5
MSA[1]	71.2	21.9	2.3	0.7	0.1	1.1	2.8
U.S.	73.0	12.7	5.4	0.8	0.2	4.8	3.1

Note: (1) Figures cover the Huntsville, AL Metropolitan Statistical Area—see Appendix B for areas included; (2) Alone is defined as not being in combination with one or more other races; (3) American Indian and Alaska Native; (4) Native Hawaiian and Other Pacific Islander
Source: U.S. Census Bureau, 2013-2017 American Community Survey 5-Year Estimates

Hispanic or Latino Origin

Area	Total (%)	Mexican (%)	Puerto Rican (%)	Cuban (%)	Other (%)
City	5.5	3.5	0.6	0.1	1.2
MSA[1]	5.0	3.1	0.7	0.2	1.0
U.S.	17.6	11.1	1.7	0.7	4.1

Note: Persons of Hispanic or Latino origin can be of any race; (1) Figures cover the Huntsville, AL Metropolitan Statistical Area—see Appendix B for areas included
Source: U.S. Census Bureau, 2013-2017 American Community Survey 5-Year Estimates

Segregation

Type	Segregation Indices[1] 1990	2000	2010	2010 Rank[2]	Percent Change 1990-2000	1990-2010	2000-2010
Black/White	n/a	n/a	n/a	n/a	n/a	n/a	n/a
Asian/White	n/a	n/a	n/a	n/a	n/a	n/a	n/a
Hispanic/White	n/a	n/a	n/a	n/a	n/a	n/a	n/a

Note: All figures cover the Metropolitan Statistical Area—see Appendix B for areas included; Figures are based on an analysis of 1990, 2000, and 2010 Census Decennial Census tract data by William H. Frey, Brookings Institution and the University of Michigan Social Science Data Analysis Network. In this analysis all racial groups (whites, blacks, and asians) are non-Hispanic members of those races. Hispanics are shown as a separate category; (1) Segregation Indices are Dissimilarity Indices that measure the degree to which the minority group is distributed differently than whites across census tracts. They range from 0 (complete integration) to 100 (complete segregation) where the value indicates the percentage of the minority group that needs to move to be distributed exactly like whites; (2) Ranges from 1 (most segregated) to 102 (least segregated); n/a not available.
Source: www.CensusScope.org

Ancestry

Area	German	Irish	English	American	Italian	Polish	French[2]	Scottish	Dutch
City	9.4	8.7	9.5	10.1	2.7	0.9	1.8	2.2	1.0
MSA[1]	9.8	9.7	10.0	11.6	2.2	1.0	1.9	2.2	0.9
U.S.	14.1	10.1	7.5	6.6	5.3	2.9	2.5	1.7	1.3

Note: Figures are the percentage of the total population reporting a particular ancestry. The nine most commonly reported ancestries in the U.S. are shown. Figures include multiple ancestries (e.g. if a person reported being Irish and Italian, they were included in both columns); (1) Figures cover the Huntsville, AL Metropolitan Statistical Area—see Appendix B for areas included; (2) Excludes Basque
Source: U.S. Census Bureau, 2013-2017 American Community Survey 5-Year Estimates

Foreign-Born Population

Area	Percent of Population Born in								
	Any Foreign Country	Asia	Mexico	Europe	Carribean	Central America[2]	South America	Africa	Canada
City	6.6	2.3	1.6	0.8	0.5	0.6	0.2	0.5	0.1
MSA[1]	5.2	1.9	1.2	0.7	0.3	0.4	0.1	0.3	0.1
U.S.	13.4	4.1	3.6	1.5	1.3	1.0	0.9	0.6	0.3

Note: (1) Figures cover the Huntsville, AL Metropolitan Statistical Area—see Appendix B for areas included; (2) Excludes Mexico.
Source: U.S. Census Bureau, 2013-2017 American Community Survey 5-Year Estimates

Marital Status

Area	Never Married	Now Married[2]	Separated	Widowed	Divorced
City	34.8	43.9	2.2	6.0	13.1
MSA[1]	30.1	50.3	1.9	5.8	11.9
U.S.	33.1	48.2	2.0	5.8	10.9

Note: Figures are percentages and cover the population 15 years of age and older; (1) Figures cover the Huntsville, AL Metropolitan Statistical Area—see Appendix B for areas included; (2) Excludes separated
Source: U.S. Census Bureau, 2013-2017 American Community Survey 5-Year Estimates

Disability by Age

Area	All Ages	Under 18 Years Old	18 to 64 Years Old	65 Years and Over
City	13.2	4.4	10.9	35.4
MSA[1]	13.4	4.8	11.0	38.1
U.S.	12.6	4.2	10.3	35.5

Note: Figures show percent of the civilian noninstitutionalized population that reported having a disability. Disability status is determined from six types of difficulty: vision, hearing, cognitive, ambulatory, self-care, and independent living. For children under 5 years old, hearing and vision difficulty are used to determine disability status. For children between the ages of 5 and 14, disability status is determined from hearing, vision, cognitive, ambulatory, and self-care difficulties. For people aged 15 years and older, they are considered to have a disability if they have difficulty with any one of the six difficulty types; Note: (1) Figures cover the Huntsville, AL Metropolitan Statistical Area—see Appendix B for areas included
Source: U.S. Census Bureau, 2013-2017 American Community Survey 5-Year Estimates

Age

Area	Percent of Population									Median Age
	Under Age 5	Age 5–19	Age 20–34	Age 35–44	Age 45–54	Age 55–64	Age 65–74	Age 75–84	Age 85+	
City	6.6	17.7	23.4	11.5	13.0	12.7	8.3	5.0	1.9	36.9
MSA[1]	5.8	19.3	20.4	12.5	15.0	12.9	8.2	4.4	1.5	38.4
U.S.	6.2	19.5	20.7	12.7	13.4	12.7	8.6	4.4	1.9	37.8

Note: (1) Figures cover the Huntsville, AL Metropolitan Statistical Area—see Appendix B for areas included
Source: U.S. Census Bureau, 2013-2017 American Community Survey 5-Year Estimates

Gender

Area	Males	Females	Males per 100 Females
City	92,044	98,457	93.5
MSA[1]	218,457	226,451	96.5
U.S.	158,018,753	162,985,654	97.0

Note: (1) Figures cover the Huntsville, AL Metropolitan Statistical Area—see Appendix B for areas included
Source: U.S. Census Bureau, 2013-2017 American Community Survey 5-Year Estimates

Religious Groups by Family

Area	Catholic	Baptist	Non-Den.	Methodist[2]	Lutheran	LDS[3]	Pente-costal	Presby-terian[4]	Muslim[5]	Judaism
MSA[1]	4.0	27.6	3.2	7.5	0.7	1.2	1.2	1.7	0.2	0.2
U.S.	19.1	9.3	4.0	4.0	2.3	2.0	1.9	1.6	0.8	0.7

Note: Figures are the number of adherents as a percentage of the total population; (1) Figures cover the Huntsville, AL Metropolitan Statistical Area—see Appendix B for areas included; (2) Methodist/Pietist; (3) Latter Day Saints; (4) Reformed; (5) Figures are estimates
Source: Association of Statisticians of American Religious Bodies, 2010 U.S. Religion Census: Religious Congregations & Membership Study

Religious Groups by Tradition

Area	Catholic	Evangelical Protestant	Mainline Protestant	Other Tradition	Black Protestant	Orthodox
MSA[1]	4.0	33.3	9.7	1.9	1.8	0.1
U.S.	19.1	16.2	7.3	4.3	1.6	0.3

Note: Figures are the number of adherents as a percentage of the total population; (1) Figures cover the Huntsville, AL Metropolitan Statistical Area—see Appendix B for areas included
Source: Association of Statisticians of American Religious Bodies, 2010 U.S. Religion Census: Religious Congregations & Membership Study

ECONOMY

Gross Metropolitan Product

Area	2016	2017	2018	2019	Rank[2]
MSA[1]	24.8	25.9	27.2	28.7	104

Note: Figures are in billions of dollars; (1) Figures cover the Huntsville, AL Metropolitan Statistical Area—see Appendix B for areas included; (2) Rank is based on 2017 data and ranges from 1 to 381
Source: U.S. Conference of Mayors, U.S. Metro Economies: Economic Growth & Full Employment, June 2018

Economic Growth

Area	2017-2018 (%)	2019-2020 (%)	2021-2022 (%)
MSA[1]	3.6	2.7	2.9

Note: Figures are real gross metropolitan product (GMP) growth rates and represent average annual percent change; (1) Figures cover the Huntsville, AL Metropolitan Statistical Area—see Appendix B for areas included
Source: U.S. Conference of Mayors, U.S. Metro Economies: Economic Growth & Full Employment, June 2018

Metropolitan Area Exports

Area	2012	2013	2014	2015	2016	2017	Rank[2]
MSA[1]	1,491.5	1,518.7	1,440.4	1,344.7	1,827.3	1,889.2	105

Note: Figures are in millions of dollars; (1) Figures cover the Huntsville, AL Metropolitan Statistical Area—see Appendix B for areas included; (2) Rank is based on 2017 data and ranges from 1 to 387
Source: U.S. Department of Commerce, International Trade Administration, Office of Trade and Economic Analysis, Industry and Analysis, Exports by Metropolitan Area, extracted March 25, 2019

Building Permits

Area	Single-Family			Multi-Family			Total		
	2016	2017	Pct. Chg.	2016	2017	Pct. Chg.	2016	2017	Pct. Chg.
City	1,091	1,144	4.9	672	380	-43.5	1,763	1,524	-13.6
MSA[1]	2,320	2,577	11.1	672	382	-43.2	2,992	2,959	-1.1
U.S.	750,800	820,000	9.2	455,800	462,000	1.4	1,206,600	1,282,000	6.2

Note: (1) Figures cover the Huntsville, AL Metropolitan Statistical Area—see Appendix B for areas included; Figures represent new, privately-owned housing units authorized (unadjusted data); All permit data are based on estimates with imputation
Source: U.S. Census Bureau, Manufacturing, Mining, and Construction Statistics, Building Permits, 2016, 2017

Bankruptcy Filings

Area	Business Filings			Nonbusiness Filings		
	2017	2018	% Chg.	2017	2018	% Chg.
Madison County	21	35	66.7	1,432	1,410	-1.5
U.S.	23,157	22,232	-4.0	765,863	751,186	-1.9

Note: Business filings include Chapter 7, Chapter 11, Chapter 12, and Chapter 13; Nonbusiness filings include Chapter 7, Chapter 11, and Chapter 13
Source: Administrative Office of the U.S. Courts, Business and Nonbusiness Bankruptcy, County Cases Commenced by Chapter of the Bankruptcy Code, During the 12-Month Period Ending December 31, 2017 and Business and Nonbusiness Bankruptcy, County Cases Commenced by Chapter of the Bankruptcy Code, During the 12-Month Period Ending December 31, 2018

Housing Vacancy Rates

Area	Gross Vacancy Rate[2] (%)			Year-Round Vacancy Rate[3] (%)			Rental Vacancy Rate[4] (%)			Homeowner Vacancy Rate[5] (%)		
	2016	2017	2018	2016	2017	2018	2016	2017	2018	2016	2017	2018
MSA[1]	n/a	n/a	n/a	n/a	n/a	n/a	n/a	n/a	n/a	n/a	n/a	n/a
U.S.	12.8	12.7	12.3	9.9	9.9	9.7	6.9	7.2	6.9	1.7	1.6	1.5

Note: (1) Figures cover the Huntsville, AL Metropolitan Statistical Area—see Appendix B for areas included; (2) The percentage of the total housing inventory that is vacant; (3) The percentage of the housing inventory (excluding seasonal units) that is year-round vacant; (4) The percentage of rental inventory that is vacant for rent; (5) The percentage of homeowner inventory that is vacant for sale; n/a not available
Source: U.S. Census Bureau, Housing Vacancies and Homeownership Annual Statistics: 2016, 2017, 2018

INCOME

Income

Area	Per Capita ($)	Median Household ($)	Average Household ($)
City	33,070	51,926	75,789
MSA[1]	32,676	59,583	80,893
U.S.	31,177	57,652	81,283

Note: (1) Figures cover the Huntsville, AL Metropolitan Statistical Area—see Appendix B for areas included
Source: U.S. Census Bureau, 2013-2017 American Community Survey 5-Year Estimates

Household Income Distribution

Area	Percent of Households Earning							
	Under $15,000	$15,000 -$24,999	$25,000 -$34,999	$35,000 -$49,999	$50,000 -$74,999	$75,000 -$99,999	$100,000 -$149,999	$150,000 and up
City	14.9	11.2	9.9	12.3	16.1	10.2	14.0	11.3
MSA[1]	11.7	9.6	9.4	12.0	16.8	12.1	15.8	12.6
U.S.	11.6	9.8	9.5	13.0	17.7	12.3	14.1	12.1

Note: (1) Figures cover the Huntsville, AL Metropolitan Statistical Area—see Appendix B for areas included
Source: U.S. Census Bureau, 2013-2017 American Community Survey 5-Year Estimates

Poverty Rate

Area	All Ages	Under 18 Years Old	18 to 64 Years Old	65 Years and Over
City	18.3	28.7	17.2	8.1
MSA[1]	13.9	20.0	12.9	8.5
U.S.	14.6	20.3	13.7	9.3

Note: Figures are percentage of people whose income during the past 12 months was below the poverty level; (1) Figures cover the Huntsville, AL Metropolitan Statistical Area—see Appendix B for areas included
Source: U.S. Census Bureau, 2013-2017 American Community Survey 5-Year Estimates

EMPLOYMENT

Labor Force and Employment

Area	Civilian Labor Force			Workers Employed		
	Dec. 2017	Dec. 2018	% Chg.	Dec. 2017	Dec. 2018	% Chg.
City	94,181	98,508	4.6	91,263	95,413	4.5
MSA[1]	216,297	226,125	4.5	209,920	219,378	4.5
U.S.	159,880,000	162,510,000	1.6	153,602,000	156,481,000	1.9

Note: Data is not seasonally adjusted and covers workers 16 years of age and older; (1) Figures cover the Huntsville, AL Metropolitan Statistical Area—see Appendix B for areas included
Source: Bureau of Labor Statistics, Local Area Unemployment Statistics

Unemployment Rate

Area	2018											
	Jan.	Feb.	Mar.	Apr.	May	Jun.	Jul.	Aug.	Sep.	Oct.	Nov.	Dec.
City	3.8	3.9	3.6	3.2	3.5	4.6	4.2	3.8	3.6	3.6	3.1	3.1
MSA[1]	3.6	3.7	3.4	3.0	3.3	4.4	3.9	3.6	3.4	3.4	2.9	3.0
U.S.	4.5	4.4	4.1	3.7	3.6	4.2	4.1	3.9	3.6	3.5	3.5	3.7

Note: Data is not seasonally adjusted and covers workers 16 years of age and older; (1) Figures cover the Huntsville, AL Metropolitan Statistical Area—see Appendix B for areas included
Source: Bureau of Labor Statistics, Local Area Unemployment Statistics

Average Wages

Occupation	$/Hr.	Occupation	$/Hr.
Accountants and Auditors	35.90	Maids and Housekeeping Cleaners	9.50
Automotive Mechanics	19.60	Maintenance and Repair Workers	20.60
Bookkeepers	19.10	Marketing Managers	68.60
Carpenters	19.40	Nuclear Medicine Technologists	26.00
Cashiers	10.60	Nurses, Licensed Practical	19.00
Clerks, General Office	12.30	Nurses, Registered	27.50
Clerks, Receptionists/Information	12.60	Nursing Assistants	12.30
Clerks, Shipping/Receiving	15.70	Packers and Packagers, Hand	12.80
Computer Programmers	46.40	Physical Therapists	43.20
Computer Systems Analysts	44.90	Postal Service Mail Carriers	24.60
Computer User Support Specialists	21.30	Real Estate Brokers	n/a
Cooks, Restaurant	11.70	Retail Salespersons	13.10
Dentists	n/a	Sales Reps., Exc. Tech./Scientific	27.50
Electrical Engineers	49.80	Sales Reps., Tech./Scientific	43.40
Electricians	22.90	Secretaries, Exc. Legal/Med./Exec.	18.10
Financial Managers	62.60	Security Guards	14.30
First-Line Supervisors/Managers, Sales	20.30	Surgeons	129.00
Food Preparation Workers	10.20	Teacher Assistants*	11.70
General and Operations Managers	66.10	Teachers, Elementary School*	24.40
Hairdressers/Cosmetologists	11.70	Teachers, Secondary School*	25.60
Internists, General	n/a	Telemarketers	11.40
Janitors and Cleaners	11.90	Truck Drivers, Heavy/Tractor-Trailer	19.30
Landscaping/Groundskeeping Workers	13.10	Truck Drivers, Light/Delivery Svcs.	15.70
Lawyers	62.10	Waiters and Waitresses	8.90

Note: Wage data covers the Huntsville, AL Metropolitan Statistical Area—see Appendix B for areas included; (*) Hourly wages for elementary/secondary school teachers and teacher assistants were calculated by the editors from annual wage data based on a 40 hour work week; n/a not available.
Source: Bureau of Labor Statistics, Metro Area Occupational Employment & Wage Estimates, May 2018

Employment by Occupation

Occupation Classification	City (%)	MSA[1] (%)	U.S. (%)
Management, Business, Science, and Arts	45.2	44.4	37.4
Natural Resources, Construction, and Maintenance	5.7	7.3	8.9
Production, Transportation, and Material Moving	10.0	11.5	12.2
Sales and Office	22.2	21.6	23.5
Service	16.8	15.3	18.0

Note: Figures cover employed civilians 16 years of age and older; (1) Figures cover the Huntsville, AL Metropolitan Statistical Area—see Appendix B for areas included
Source: U.S. Census Bureau, 2013-2017 American Community Survey 5-Year Estimates

Employment by Industry

| Sector | MSA[1] | | U.S. |
	Number of Employees	Percent of Total	Percent of Total
Construction, Mining, and Logging	9,300	3.9	5.3
Education and Health Services	21,900	9.1	15.9
Financial Activities	6,900	2.9	5.7
Government	51,500	21.4	15.1
Information	2,600	1.1	1.9
Leisure and Hospitality	22,100	9.2	10.7
Manufacturing	25,700	10.7	8.5
Other Services	8,000	3.3	3.9
Professional and Business Services	57,700	24.0	14.1
Retail Trade	25,800	10.7	10.8
Transportation, Warehousing, and Utilities	3,300	1.4	4.2
Wholesale Trade	6,100	2.5	3.9

Note: Figures are non-farm employment as of December 2018. Figures are not seasonally adjusted and include workers 16 years of age and older; (1) Figures cover the Huntsville, AL Metropolitan Statistical Area—see Appendix B for areas included
Source: Bureau of Labor Statistics, Current Employment Statistics, Employment, Hours, and Earnings

Occupations with Greatest Projected Employment Growth: 2018 – 2020

Occupation[1]	2018 Employment	2020 Projected Employment	Numeric Employment Change	Percent Employment Change
Combined Food Preparation and Serving Workers, Including Fast Food	50,700	53,000	2,300	4.5
Registered Nurses	51,340	52,670	1,330	2.6
Helpers—Production Workers	17,180	18,310	1,130	6.6
Janitors and Cleaners, Except Maids and Housekeeping Cleaners	35,340	36,430	1,090	3.1
Laborers and Freight, Stock, and Material Movers, Hand	43,780	44,870	1,090	2.5
Waiters and Waitresses	33,380	34,270	890	2.7
Personal Care Aides	16,240	16,990	750	4.6
General and Operations Managers	28,360	29,100	740	2.6
Customer Service Representatives	32,150	32,800	650	2.0
Heavy and Tractor-Trailer Truck Drivers	36,720	37,360	640	1.7

Note: Projections cover Alabama; (1) Sorted by numeric employment change
Source: www.projectionscentral.com, State Occupational Projections, 2018–2020 Short-Term Projections

Fastest Growing Occupations: 2018 – 2020

Occupation[1]	2018 Employment	2020 Projected Employment	Numeric Employment Change	Percent Employment Change
Information Security Analysts	1,010	1,090	80	7.9
Software Developers, Applications	5,920	6,340	420	7.1
Operations Research Analysts	730	780	50	6.8
Helpers—Production Workers	17,180	18,310	1,130	6.6
Fiberglass Laminators and Fabricators	790	840	50	6.3
Veterinary Technologists and Technicians	1,010	1,070	60	5.9
Veterinary Assistants and Laboratory Animal Caretakers	1,040	1,100	60	5.8
Tire Builders	2,270	2,400	130	5.7
Home Health Aides	5,720	6,040	320	5.6
Paralegals and Legal Assistants	2,930	3,090	160	5.5

Note: Projections cover Alabama; (1) Sorted by percent employment change and excludes occupations with numeric employment change less than 50
Source: www.projectionscentral.com, State Occupational Projections, 2018–2020 Short-Term Projections

TAXES

State Corporate Income Tax Rates

State	Tax Rate (%)	Income Brackets ($)	Num. of Brackets	Financial Institution Tax Rate (%)[a]	Federal Income Tax Ded.
Alabama	6.5	Flat rate	1	6.5	Yes

Note: Tax rates as of January 1, 2019; (a) Rates listed are the corporate income tax rate applied to financial institutions or excise taxes based on income. Some states have other taxes based upon the value of deposits or shares.
Source: Federation of Tax Administrators, Range of State Corporate Income Tax Rates, January 1, 2019

State Individual Income Tax Rates

State	Tax Rate (%)	Income Brackets ($)	Personal Exemptions ($)			Standard Ded. ($)	
			Single	Married	Depend.	Single	Married
Alabama	2.0 - 5.0	500 - 3,001 (b)	1,500	3,000	500 (e)	2,500	7,500 (y)

Note: Tax rates as of January 1, 2019; Local- and county-level taxes are not included; n/a not applicable; Federal income tax is deductible on state income tax returns; (b) For joint returns, taxes are twice the tax on half the couple's income; (e) In Alabama, the per-dependent exemption is $1,000 for taxpayers with state AGI of $20,000 or less, $500 with AGI from $20,001 to $100,000, and $300 with AGI over $100,000; (y) Alabama standard deduction is phased out for incomes over $23,000. Rhode Island exemptions & standard deductions phased out for incomes over $203,850; Wisconsin standard deduciton phases out for income over $15,660.
Source: Federation of Tax Administrators, State Individual Income Tax Rates, January 1, 2019

Various State Sales and Excise Tax Rates

State	State Sales Tax (%)	Gasoline[1] (¢/gal.)	Cigarette[2] ($/pack)	Spirits[3] ($/gal.)	Wine[4] ($/gal.)	Beer[5] ($/gal.)	Recreational Marijuana (%)
Alabama	4	21.09	0.675	18.27 (g)	1.70 (l)	0.53 (r)	Not legal

Note: All tax rates as of January 1, 2019; (1) The American Petroleum Institute has developed a methodology for determining the average tax rate on a gallon of fuel. Rates may include any of the following: excise taxes, environmental fees, storage tank fees, other fees or taxes, general sales tax, and local taxes. In states where gasoline is subject to the general sales tax, or where the fuel tax is based on the average sale price, the average rate determined by API is sensitive to changes in the price of gasoline. States that fully or partially apply general sales taxes to gasoline: CA, CO, GA, IL, IN, MI, NY; (2) The federal excise tax of $1.0066 per pack and local taxes are not included; (3) Rates are those applicable to off-premise sales of 40% alcohol by volume (a.b.v.) distilled spirits in 750ml containers. Local excise taxes are excluded; (4) Rates are those applicable to off-premise sales of 11% a.b.v. non-carbonated wine in 750ml containers; (5) Rates are those applicable to off-premise sales of 4.7% a.b.v. beer in 12 ounce containers; (g) Control states, where the government controls all sales. Products can be subject to ad valorem mark-up as well as excise taxes; (l) Different rates also applicable to alcohol content, place of production, size of container, place purchased (on- or off-premise or on board airlines) or type of wine (carbonated, vermouth, etc.); (r) Includes statewide local rate in Alabama ($0.52) and Georgia ($0.53).
Source: Tax Foundation, 2019 Facts & Figures: How Does Your State Compare?

State Business Tax Climate Index Rankings

State	Overall Rank	Corporate Tax Rank	Individual Income Tax Rank	Sales Tax Rank	Unemployment Insurance Tax Rank	Property Tax Rank
Alabama	39	20	30	48	12	15

Note: The index is a measure of how each state's tax laws affect economic performance. The lower the rank, the more favorable a state's tax system is for business. States without a given tax are given a ranking of 1. The scores/rankings for the District of Columbia do not affect other states. The 2019 index represents the tax climate as of July 1, 2018.
Source: Tax Foundation, State Business Tax Climate Index 2019

COMMERCIAL UTILITIES

Typical Monthly Electric Bills

Area	General Service, Light ($/month)		General Service, Heavy ($/month)	
	40 kW demand 5,000 kWh	100 kW demand 10,000 kWh	500 kW demand 100,000 kWh	1,500 kW demand 500,000 kWh
City	529	1,679	11,968	48,818

Note: Figures are based on rates in effect January 1, 2018
Source: Memphis Light, Gas and Water, 2018 Utility Bill Comparisons for Selected U.S. Cities

TRANSPORTATION

Means of Transportation to Work

Area	Car/Truck/Van		Public Transportation			Bicycle	Walked	Other Means	Worked at Home
	Drove Alone	Car-pooled	Bus	Subway	Railroad				
City	86.7	6.8	0.3	0.0	0.0	0.3	1.2	1.5	3.1
MSA[1]	87.9	6.6	0.2	0.0	0.0	0.1	0.8	1.2	3.3
U.S.	76.4	9.2	2.5	1.9	0.6	0.6	2.7	1.3	4.7

Note: Figures are percentages and cover workers 16 years of age and older; (1) Figures cover the Huntsville, AL Metropolitan Statistical Area—see Appendix B for areas included
Source: U.S. Census Bureau, 2013-2017 American Community Survey 5-Year Estimates

Travel Time to Work

Area	Less Than 10 Minutes	10 to 19 Minutes	20 to 29 Minutes	30 to 44 Minutes	45 to 59 Minutes	60 to 89 Minutes	90 Minutes or More
City	13.5	42.4	26.4	14.0	1.9	0.8	1.1
MSA[1]	10.5	32.6	28.4	21.0	5.0	1.5	1.1
U.S.	12.7	28.9	20.9	20.5	8.1	6.2	2.7

Note: Note: Figures are percentages and include workers 16 years old and over; (1) Figures cover the Huntsville, AL Metropolitan Statistical Area—see Appendix B for areas included
Source: U.S. Census Bureau, 2013-2017 American Community Survey 5-Year Estimates

Freeway Travel Time Index

Area	1985	1990	1995	2000	2005	2010	2014
Urban Area Rank[1,2]	n/a	n/a	n/a	n/a	n/a	n/a	n/a
Urban Area Index[1]	n/a	n/a	n/a	n/a	n/a	n/a	n/a
Average Index[3]	1.09	1.11	1.14	1.17	1.20	1.19	1.20

Note: Freeway Travel Time Index—the ratio of travel time in the peak period to the travel time at free-flow conditions. For example, a value of 1.30 indicates a 20-minute free-flow trip takes 26 minutes in the peak (20 minutes x 1.30 = 26 minutes); (1) Data for the Huntsville, AL urban area was not available; (2) Rank is based on 101 urban areas (#1 = highest travel time index); (3) Average of 101 urban areas
Source: Texas Transportation Institute, 2015 Urban Mobility Scorecard, August 2015

Freeway Commuter Stress Index

Area	1985	1990	1995	2000	2005	2010	2014
Urban Area Rank[1,2]	n/a	n/a	n/a	n/a	n/a	n/a	n/a
Urban Area Index[1]	n/a	n/a	n/a	n/a	n/a	n/a	n/a
Average Index[3]	1.13	1.16	1.19	1.22	1.25	1.24	1.25

Note: The Freeway Commuter Stress Index is the same as the Freeway Travel Time Index (see table above) except that it includes only the travel in the peak directions during the peak periods; the TTI includes travel in all directions during the peak period. Thus, the CSI is more indicative of the work trip experienced by each commuter on a daily basis; (1) Data for the Huntsville, AL urban area was not available; (2) Rank is based on 101 urban areas (#1 = highest travel time index); (3) Average of 101 urban areas
Source: Texas Transportation Institute, 2015 Urban Mobility Scorecard, August 2015

Public Transportation

Agency Name / Mode of Transportation	Vehicles Operated in Maximum Service[1]	Annual Unlinked Passenger Trips[2] (in thous.)	Annual Passenger Miles[3] (in thous.)
City of Huntsville - Public Transportation Division			
Bus (directly operated)	13	620.8	3,364.3
Demand Response (directly operated)	19	94.2	550.4

Note: (1) The number of revenue vehicles operated by the given mode and type of service to meet the annual maximum service requirement. This is the revenue vehicle count during the peak season of the year; on the week and day that maximum service is provided. Vehicles operated in maximum service (VOMS) exclude atypical days and one-time special events; (2) The number of passengers who boarded public transportation vehicles. Passengers are counted each time they board a vehicle no matter how many vehicles they use to travel from their origin to their destination. (3) The sum of the distances ridden by all passengers during the entire fiscal year.
Source: Federal Transit Administration, National Transit Database, 2017

Air Transportation

Airport Name and Code / Type of Service	Passenger Airlines[1]	Passenger Enplanements	Freight Carriers[2]	Freight (lbs)
Huntsville International (HSV)				
Domestic service (U.S. carriers - 2018)	14	580,481	10	33,213,646
International service (U.S. carriers - 2017)	1	4	4	67,328,584

Note: (1) Includes all U.S.-based major, minor and commuter airlines that carried at least one passenger during the year; (2) Includes all U.S.-based airlines and freight carriers that transported at least one pound of freight during the year.
Source: Bureau of Transportation Statistics, The Intermodal Transportation Database, Air Carriers: T-100 Domestic Market (U.S. Carriers), 2018; Bureau of Transportation Statistics, The Intermodal Transportation Database, Air Carriers: T-100 International Market (U.S. Carriers), 2017

Other Transportation Statistics

Major Highways:	I-65
Amtrak Service:	No
Major Waterways/Ports:	Near the Tennessee River (12 miles)

Source: Amtrak.com; Google Maps

BUSINESSES

Major Business Headquarters

Company Name	Industry	Rankings	
		Fortune[1]	Forbes[2]
No companies listed	-	-	-

Note: (1) Companies that produce a 10-K are ranked 1 to 500 based on 2017 revenue; (2) All private companies with at least $2 billion in annual revenue through the end of their most current fiscal year are ranked 1 to 229; companies listed are headquartered in the city; dashes indicate no ranking
Source: Fortune, "Fortune 500," June 2018; Forbes, "America's Largest Private Companies," 2018 Rankings

Fast-Growing Businesses

According to *Inc.*, Huntsville is home to one of America's 500 fastest-growing private companies: **Cintel** (#252). Criteria: must be an independent, privately-held, for-profit, U.S. corporation, proprietorship or partnership as of December 31, 2017; revenues must be at least $100,000 in 2014 and $2 million in 2017; must have four-year operating/sales history. Holding companies, regulated banks, and utilities were excluded. *Inc., "America's 500 Fastest-Growing Private Companies," 2018*

Minority Business Opportunity

Huntsville is home to one company which is on the *Black Enterprise* Auto Dealer list (45 largest dealers based on gross sales): **Lexus of Huntsville** (#43). Criteria: company must be operational in previous calendar year and be at least 51% black-owned. *Black Enterprise, B.E. 100s, 2018*

Huntsville is home to two companies which are on the *Hispanic Business* 500 list (500 largest U.S. Hispanic-owned companies based on revenue): **COLSA Corp.** (#37); **SEI Group** (#236). Companies included must show at least 51 percent ownership by Hispanic U.S. citizens, and must maintain headquarters in one of the 50 states or Washington, D.C. *Hispanic Business, "Hispanic Business 500," June 20, 2013*

Minority- and Women-Owned Businesses

Group	All Firms		Firms with Paid Employees			
	Firms	Sales ($000)	Firms	Sales ($000)	Employees	Payroll ($000)
AIAN[1]	150	107,063	36	103,430	727	43,728
Asian	713	1,014,889	306	1,000,780	4,473	204,785
Black	3,258	337,175	145	294,349	2,131	118,783
Hispanic	374	304,509	60	292,415	1,485	102,797
NHOPI[2]	n/a	n/a	n/a	n/a	n/a	n/a
Women	6,565	1,506,039	932	1,382,804	9,890	442,114
All Firms	16,838	28,687,132	4,741	28,168,342	112,231	5,492,793

Note: Figures cover firms located in the city; minority- and women-owned business are defined as firms in which the corresponding group own 51% or more of the stock or equity of the company; (1) American Indian and Alaska Native; (2) Native Hawaiian and Other Pacific Islander; n/a not available
Source: U.S. Census Bureau, 2012 Economic Census, Survey of Business Owners

**HOTELS &
CONVENTION
CENTERS**

Hotels, Motels and Vacation Rentals

Area	5 Star		4 Star		3 Star		2 Star		1 Star		Not Rated	
	Num.	Pct.[3]	Num.	Pct.[3]	Num.	Pct.[3]	Num.	Pct.[3]	Num.	Pct.[3]	Num.	Pct.[3]
City[1]	0	0.0	1	0.5	23	11.7	71	36.0	2	1.0	100	50.8
Total[2]	286	0.4	5,236	7.1	16,715	22.6	10,259	13.9	293	0.4	41,056	55.6

Note: (1) Figures cover Huntsville and vicinity; (2) Figures cover all 100 cities in this book; (3) Percentage of hotels which have a given star rating; Star ratings are determined by expedia.com and offer an indication of the general quality of a particular hotel.
Source: www.expedia.com, April 3, 2019

Major Convention Centers

Name	Overall Space (sq. ft.)	Exhibit Space (sq. ft.)	Meeting Space (sq. ft.)	Meeting Rooms
Von Braun Center	n/a	n/a	170,000	n/a

Note: Table includes convention centers located in the Huntsville, AL metro area; n/a not available
Source: Original research

Living Environment

COST OF LIVING

Cost of Living Index

Composite Index	Groceries	Housing	Utilities	Trans-portation	Health Care	Misc. Goods/Services
93.6	93.4	74.2	96.3	93.1	100.6	108.6

Note: The Cost of Living Index measures regional differences in the cost of consumer goods and services, excluding taxes and non-consumer expenditures, for professional and managerial households in the top income quintile. It is based on more than 50,000 prices covering almost 60 different items for which prices are collected three times a year by chambers of commerce, economic development organizations or university applied economic centers in each participating urban area. The numbers shown should be read as a percentage above or below the national average of 100. For example, a value of 115.4 in the groceries column indicates that grocery prices are 15.4% higher than the national average. Small differences in the index numbers should not be interpreted as significant; Figures cover the Huntsville AL urban area.
Source: The Council for Community and Economic Research, ACCRA Cost of Living Index, 2018

Grocery Prices

Area[1]	T-Bone Steak ($/pound)	Frying Chicken ($/pound)	Whole Milk ($/half gal.)	Eggs ($/dozen)	Orange Juice ($/64 oz.)	Coffee ($/11.5 oz.)
City[2]	11.92	1.42	1.73	1.17	3.30	4.03
Avg.	11.35	1.42	1.94	1.81	3.52	4.35
Min.	7.45	0.92	0.80	0.75	2.72	3.06
Max.	15.05	2.76	4.18	4.00	5.36	8.20

Note: (1) Values for the local area are compared with the average, minimum and maximum values for all 291 areas in the Cost of Living Index; (2) Figures cover the Huntsville AL urban area; T-Bone Steak (price per pound); Frying Chicken (price per pound, whole fryer); Whole Milk (half gallon carton); Eggs (price per dozen, Grade A, large); Orange Juice (64 oz. Tropicana or Florida Natural); Coffee (11.5 oz. can, vacuum-packed, Maxwell House, Hills Bros, or Folgers).
Source: The Council for Community and Economic Research, ACCRA Cost of Living Index, 2018

Housing and Utility Costs

Area[1]	New Home Price ($)	Apartment Rent ($/month)	All Electric ($/month)	Part Electric ($/month)	Other Energy ($/month)	Telephone ($/month)
City[2]	237,350	985	158.50	-	-	175.80
Avg.	347,000	1,087	165.93	100.16	67.73	178.70
Min.	200,468	500	93.58	25.64	26.78	163.10
Max.	1,901,222	4,888	388.65	246.86	332.81	197.70

Note: (1) Values for the local area are compared with the average, minimum and maximum values for all 291 areas in the Cost of Living Index; (2) Figures cover the Huntsville AL urban area; New Home Price (2,400 sf living area, 8,000 sf lot, in urban area with full utilities); Apartment Rent (950 sf 2 bedroom/1.5 or 2 bath, unfurnished, excluding all utilities except water); All Electric (average monthly cost for an all-electric home); Part Electric (average monthly cost for a part-electric home); Other Energy (average monthly cost for natural gas, fuel oil, coal, wood, and any other forms of energy except electricity); Telephone (price includes the base monthly rate plus taxes and fees for three lines of mobile phone service).
Source: The Council for Community and Economic Research, ACCRA Cost of Living Index, 2018

Health Care, Transportation, and Other Costs

Area[1]	Doctor ($/visit)	Dentist ($/visit)	Optometrist ($/visit)	Gasoline ($/gallon)	Beauty Salon ($/visit)	Men's Shirt ($)
City[2]	107.26	96.19	125.87	2.43	41.42	44.35
Avg.	110.71	95.11	103.74	2.61	37.48	32.03
Min.	33.60	62.55	54.63	1.89	17.00	11.44
Max.	195.97	153.93	225.79	3.59	71.88	58.64

Note: (1) Values for the local area are compared with the average, minimum and maximum values for all 291 areas in the Cost of Living Index; (2) Figures cover the Huntsville AL urban area; Doctor (general practitioners routine exam of an established patient); Dentist (adult teeth cleaning and periodic oral examination); Optometrist (full vision eye exam for established adult patient); Gasoline (one gallon regular unleaded, national brand, including all taxes, cash price at self-service pump if available); Beauty Salon (woman's shampoo, trim, and blow-dry); Men's Shirt (cotton/polyester dress shirt, pinpoint weave, long sleeves).
Source: The Council for Community and Economic Research, ACCRA Cost of Living Index, 2018

HOUSING

House Price Index (HPI)

Area	National Ranking[2]	Quarterly Change (%)	One-Year Change (%)	Five-Year Change (%)
MSA[1]	157	0.82	5.28	16.19
U.S.[3]	—	1.12	5.73	32.81

Note: The HPI is a weighted repeat sales index. It measures average price changes in repeat sales or refinancings on the same properties. This information is obtained by reviewing repeat mortgage transactions on single-family properties whose mortgages have been purchased or securitized by Fannie Mae or Freddie Mac in January 1975; (1) Figures cover the Huntsville, AL Metropolitan Statistical Area—see Appendix B for areas included; (2) Rankings are based on annual percentage change for all metro areas containing at least 15,000 transactions over the last 10 years and ranges from 1 to 245; (3) figures based on a weighted average of Census Division estimates using a seasonally adjusted, purchase-only index; all figures are for the period ending December 31, 2018
Source: Federal Housing Finance Agency, House Price Index, February 26, 2019

Median Single-Family Home Prices

Area	2016	2017	2018[p]	Percent Change 2017 to 2018
MSA[1]	184.3	189.8	205.4	8.2
U.S. Average	235.5	248.8	261.6	5.1

Note: Figures are median sales prices of existing single-family homes in thousands of dollars; (p) preliminary; (1) Figures cover the Huntsville, AL Metropolitan Statistical Area—see Appendix B for areas included
Source: National Association of Realtors, Median Sales Price of Existing Single-Family Homes for Metropolitan Areas, 4th Quarter 2018

Qualifying Income Based on Median Sales Price of Existing Single-Family Homes

Area	With 5% Down ($)	With 10% Down ($)	With 20% Down ($)
MSA[1]	53,471	50,657	45,029
U.S. Average	62,954	59,640	53,013

Note: Figures are preliminary; Qualifying income is based on a mortgage rate of 4.9%. Monthly principal and interest payment is limited to 25% of income; (1) Figures cover the Huntsville, AL Metropolitan Statistical Area—see Appendix B for areas included
Source: National Association of Realtors, Qualifying Income Based on Median Sales Price of Existing Single-Family Homes for Metropolitan Areas, 4th Quarter 2018

Median Apartment Condo-Coop Home Prices

Area	2016	2017	2018[p]	Percent Change 2017 to 2018
MSA[1]	n/a	n/a	n/a	n/a
U.S. Average	220.7	234.3	241.0	2.9

Note: Figures are median sales prices of existing apartment condo-coop homes in thousands of dollars; (p) preliminary; n/a not available; (1) Figures cover the Huntsville, AL Metropolitan Statistical Area—see Appendix B for areas included
Source: National Association of Realtors, Median Sales Price of Existing Apartment Condo-Coop Homes for Metropolitan Areas, 4th Quarter 2018

Home Value Distribution

Area	Under $50,000	$50,000 -$99,999	$100,000 -$149,999	$150,000 -$199,999	$200,000 -$299,999	$300,000 -$499,999	$500,000 -$999,999	$1,000,000 or more
City	5.8	19.8	16.8	16.4	22.0	14.1	4.1	1.1
MSA[1]	7.7	15.8	19.2	17.9	22.1	13.5	3.3	0.7
U.S.	8.3	13.9	14.7	14.6	18.7	17.3	9.7	2.7

Note: Figures are percentages and cover owner-occupied housing units; (1) Figures cover the Huntsville, AL Metropolitan Statistical Area—see Appendix B for areas included
Source: U.S. Census Bureau, 2013-2017 American Community Survey 5-Year Estimates

Homeownership Rate

Area	2010 (%)	2011 (%)	2012 (%)	2013 (%)	2014 (%)	2015 (%)	2016 (%)	2017 (%)	2018 (%)
MSA[1]	n/a	n/a	n/a	n/a	n/a	n/a	n/a	n/a	n/a
U.S.	66.9	66.1	65.4	65.1	64.5	63.7	63.4	63.9	64.4

Note: (1) Figures cover the Huntsville, AL Metropolitan Statistical Area—see Appendix B for areas included; n/a not available
Source: U.S. Census Bureau, Housing Vacancies and Homeownership Annual Statistics: 2010-2018

Year Housing Structure Built

Area	2010 or Later	2000 -2009	1990 -1999	1980 -1989	1970 -1979	1960 -1969	1950 -1959	1940 -1949	Before 1940	Median Year
City	7.8	14.2	11.3	14.4	15.1	20.8	10.6	2.8	2.9	1978
MSA[1]	7.2	20.9	19.1	15.6	12.5	13.4	6.8	2.1	2.5	1988
U.S.	3.2	14.5	14.0	13.6	15.5	10.8	10.5	5.1	12.9	1977

Note: Figures are percentages except for Median Year; Note: (1) Figures cover the Huntsville, AL Metropolitan Statistical Area—see Appendix B for areas included
Source: U.S. Census Bureau, 2013-2017 American Community Survey 5-Year Estimates

Gross Monthly Rent

Area	Under $500	$500 -$999	$1,000 -$1,499	$1,500 -$1,999	$2,000 -$2,499	$2,500 -$2,999	$3,000 and up	Median ($)
City	14.6	61.9	20.2	2.2	0.5	0.3	0.3	773
MSA[1]	14.1	60.8	20.8	3.0	0.8	0.3	0.2	779
U.S.	10.5	41.1	28.7	11.7	4.5	1.8	1.7	982

Note: Figures are percentages except for Median; Gross rent is the contract rent plus the estimated average monthly cost of utilities (electricity, gas, and water and sewer) and fuels (oil, coal, kerosene, wood, etc.) if these are paid by the renter (or paid for the renter by someone else); (1) Figures cover the Huntsville, AL Metropolitan Statistical Area—see Appendix B for areas included
Source: U.S. Census Bureau, 2013-2017 American Community Survey 5-Year Estimates

HEALTH

Health Risk Factors

Category	MSA[1] (%)	U.S. (%)
Adults aged 18–64 who have any kind of health care coverage	n/a	87.3
Adults who reported being in good or better health	n/a	82.4
Adults who have been told they have high blood cholesterol	n/a	33.0
Adults who have been told they have high blood pressure	n/a	32.3
Adults who are current smokers	n/a	17.1
Adults who currently use E-cigarettes	n/a	4.6
Adults who currently use chewing tobacco, snuff, or snus	n/a	4.0
Adults who are heavy drinkers[2]	n/a	6.3
Adults who are binge drinkers[3]	n/a	17.4
Adults who are overweight (BMI 25.0 - 29.9)	n/a	35.3
Adults who are obese (BMI 30.0 - 99.8)	n/a	31.3
Adults who participated in any physical activities in the past month	n/a	74.4
Adults who always or nearly always wears a seat belt	n/a	94.3

Note: n/a not available; (1) Figures cover the Huntsville, AL Metropolitan Statistical Area—see Appendix B for areas included; (2) Heavy drinkers are classified as adult men having more than 14 drinks per week and adult women having more than 7 drinks per week; (3) Binge drinkers are classified as males having five or more drinks on one occasion or females having four or more drinks on one occasion
Source: Centers for Disease Control and Prevention, Behavioral Risk Factor Surveillance System, SMART: Selected Metropolitan Area Risk Trends, 2017

Acute and Chronic Health Conditions

Category	MSA[1] (%)	U.S. (%)
Adults who have ever been told they had a heart attack	n/a	4.2
Adults who have ever been told they have angina or coronary heart disease	n/a	3.9
Adults who have ever been told they had a stroke	n/a	3.0
Adults who have ever been told they have asthma	n/a	14.2
Adults who have ever been told they have arthritis	n/a	24.9
Adults who have ever been told they have diabetes[2]	n/a	10.5
Adults who have ever been told they had skin cancer	n/a	6.2
Adults who have ever been told they had any other types of cancer	n/a	7.1
Adults who have ever been told they have COPD	n/a	6.5
Adults who have ever been told they have kidney disease	n/a	3.0
Adults who have ever been told they have a form of depression	n/a	20.5

Note: n/a not available; (1) Figures cover the Huntsville, AL Metropolitan Statistical Area—see Appendix B for areas included; (2) Figures do not include pregnancy-related, borderline, or pre-diabetes
Source: Centers for Disease Control and Prevention, Behavioral Risk Factor Surveillance System, SMART: Selected Metropolitan Area Risk Trends, 2017

Health Screening and Vaccination Rates

Category	MSA[1] (%)	U.S. (%)
Adults aged 65+ who have had flu shot within the past year	n/a	60.7
Adults aged 65+ who have ever had a pneumonia vaccination	n/a	75.4
Adults who have ever been tested for HIV	n/a	36.1
Adults who have ever had the shingles or zoster vaccine?	n/a	28.9
Adults who have had their blood cholesterol checked within the last five years	n/a	85.9

Note: n/a not available; (1) Figures cover the Huntsville, AL Metropolitan Statistical Area—see Appendix B for areas included.
Source: Centers for Disease Control and Prevention, Behaviorial Risk Factor Surveillance System, SMART: Selected Metropolitan Area Risk Trends, 2017

Disability Status

Category	MSA[1] (%)	U.S. (%)
Adults who reported being deaf	n/a	6.7
Are you blind or have serious difficulty seeing, even when wearing glasses?	n/a	4.5
Are you limited in any way in any of your usual activities due of arthritis?	n/a	12.9
Do you have difficulty doing errands alone?	n/a	6.8
Do you have difficulty dressing or bathing?	n/a	3.6
Do you have serious difficulty concentrating/remembering/making decisions?	n/a	10.7
Do you have serious difficulty walking or climbing stairs?	n/a	13.6

Note: n/a not available; (1) Figures cover the Huntsville, AL Metropolitan Statistical Area—see Appendix B for areas included.
Source: Centers for Disease Control and Prevention, Behaviorial Risk Factor Surveillance System, SMART: Selected Metropolitan Area Risk Trends, 2017

Mortality Rates for the Top 10 Causes of Death in the U.S.

ICD-10[a] Sub-Chapter	ICD-10[a] Code	Age-Adjusted Mortality Rate[1] per 100,000 population	
		County[2]	U.S.
Malignant neoplasms	C00-C97	155.1	155.5
Ischaemic heart diseases	I20-I25	49.3	94.8
Other forms of heart disease	I30-I51	117.0	52.9
Chronic lower respiratory diseases	J40-J47	47.0	41.0
Cerebrovascular diseases	I60-I69	44.0	37.5
Other degenerative diseases of the nervous system	G30-G31	51.3	35.0
Other external causes of accidental injury	W00-X59	27.7	33.7
Organic, including symptomatic, mental disorders	F01-F09	36.3	31.0
Hypertensive diseases	I10-I15	25.7	21.9
Diabetes mellitus	E10-E14	17.8	21.2

Note: (a) ICD-10 = International Classification of Diseases 10th Revision; (1) Mortality rates are a three year average covering 2015-2017; (2) Figures cover Madison County.
Source: Centers for Disease Control and Prevention, National Center for Health Statistics. Underlying Cause of Death 1999-2017 on CDC WONDER Online Database

Mortality Rates for Selected Causes of Death

ICD-10[a] Sub-Chapter	ICD-10[a] Code	Age-Adjusted Mortality Rate[1] per 100,000 population	
		County[2]	U.S.
Assault	X85-Y09	7.5	5.9
Diseases of the liver	K70-K76	14.6	14.1
Human immunodeficiency virus (HIV) disease	B20-B24	Suppressed	1.8
Influenza and pneumonia	J09-J18	15.5	14.3
Intentional self-harm	X60-X84	17.4	13.6
Malnutrition	E40-E46	2.9	1.6
Obesity and other hyperalimentation	E65-E68	Suppressed	2.1
Renal failure	N17-N19	18.5	13.0
Transport accidents	V01-V99	13.3	12.4
Viral hepatitis	B15-B19	1.8	1.6

Note: (a) ICD-10 = International Classification of Diseases 10th Revision; (1) Mortality rates are a three year average covering 2015-2017; (2) Figures cover Madison County; Data are suppressed when the data meet the criteria for confidentiality constraints; Mortality rates are flagged as unreliable when the rate would be calculated with a numerator of 20 or less.
Source: Centers for Disease Control and Prevention, National Center for Health Statistics. Underlying Cause of Death 1999-2017 on CDC WONDER Online Database

Health Insurance Coverage

Area	With Health Insurance	With Private Health Insurance	With Public Health Insurance	Without Health Insurance	Population Under Age 18 Without Health Insurance
City	88.9	71.7	31.7	11.1	3.9
MSA[1]	90.0	74.8	29.1	10.0	3.4
U.S.	89.5	67.2	33.8	10.5	5.7

Note: Figures are percentages that cover the civilian noninstitutionalized population; (1) Figures cover the Huntsville, AL Metropolitan Statistical Area—see Appendix B for areas included
Source: U.S. Census Bureau, 2013-2017 American Community Survey 5-Year Estimates

Number of Medical Professionals

Area	MDs[3]	DOs[3,4]	Dentists	Podiatrists	Chiropractors	Optometrists
County[1] (number)	990	48	201	14	82	65
County[1] (rate[2])	277.8	13.5	55.7	3.9	22.7	18.0
U.S. (rate[2])	279.3	23.0	68.4	6.0	27.1	16.2

Note: Data as of 2017 unless noted; (1) Data covers Madison County; (2) Rate per 100,000 population; (3) Data as of 2016 and includes all active, non-federal physicians; (4) Doctor of Osteopathic Medicine
Source: U.S. Department of Health and Human Services, Health Resources and Services Administration, Bureau of Health Professions, Area Resource File (ARF) 2017-2018

EDUCATION

Public School District Statistics

District Name	Schls	Pupils	Pupil/ Teacher Ratio	Minority Pupils[1] (%)	Free Lunch Eligible[2] (%)	IEP[3] (%)
Huntsville City	41	24,026	16.5	60.8	41.0	8.3
Madison County	29	19,352	18.3	34.5	29.4	7.6

Note: Table includes school districts with 2,000 or more students; (1) Percentage of students that are not non-Hispanic white; (2) Percentage of students that are eligible for the free lunch program; (3) Percentage of students that have an Individualized Education Program.
Source: U.S. Department of Education, National Center for Education Statistics, Common Core of Data, Local Education Agency (School District) Universe Survey: School Year 2016-2017; U.S. Department of Education, National Center for Education Statistics, Common Core of Data, Public Elementary/Secondary School Universe Survey: School Year 2016-2017

Highest Level of Education

Area	Less than H.S.	H.S. Diploma	Some College, No Deg.	Associate Degree	Bachelor's Degree	Master's Degree	Prof. School Degree	Doctorate Degree
City	10.0	19.3	20.9	8.2	25.6	12.4	1.6	2.0
MSA[1]	10.7	23.1	20.8	8.2	23.4	10.9	1.4	1.5
U.S.	12.7	27.3	20.8	8.3	19.1	8.4	2.0	1.4

Note: Figures cover persons age 25 and over; (1) Figures cover the Huntsville, AL Metropolitan Statistical Area—see Appendix B for areas included
Source: U.S. Census Bureau, 2013-2017 American Community Survey 5-Year Estimates

Educational Attainment by Race

Area	High School Graduate or Higher (%)					Bachelor's Degree or Higher (%)				
	Total	White	Black	Asian	Hisp.[2]	Total	White	Black	Asian	Hisp.[2]
City	90.0	93.0	83.2	91.5	58.3	41.6	48.0	24.7	58.3	16.7
MSA[1]	89.3	90.6	85.4	92.9	64.5	37.3	39.3	27.9	57.7	22.7
U.S.	87.3	89.3	84.9	86.5	66.7	30.9	32.2	20.6	52.7	15.2

Note: Figures shown cover persons 25 years old and over; (1) Figures cover the Huntsville, AL Metropolitan Statistical Area—see Appendix B for areas included; (2) People of Hispanic origin can be of any race
Source: U.S. Census Bureau, 2013-2017 American Community Survey 5-Year Estimates

School Enrollment by Grade and Control

Area	Preschool (%)		Kindergarten (%)		Grades 1 - 4 (%)		Grades 5 - 8 (%)		Grades 9 - 12 (%)	
	Public	Private	Public	Private	Public	Private	Public	Private	Public	Private
City	51.9	48.1	82.3	17.7	83.8	16.2	83.9	16.1	87.2	12.8
MSA[1]	50.3	49.7	87.3	12.7	85.5	14.5	85.8	14.2	87.5	12.5
U.S.	58.8	41.2	87.7	12.3	89.7	10.3	89.6	10.4	90.3	9.7

Note: Figures shown cover persons 3 years old and over; (1) Figures cover the Huntsville, AL Metropolitan Statistical Area—see Appendix B for areas included
Source: U.S. Census Bureau, 2013-2017 American Community Survey 5-Year Estimates

Average Salaries of Public School Classroom Teachers

Area	2016		2017		Change from 2016 to 2017	
	Dollars	Rank[1]	Dollars	Rank[1]	Percent	Rank[2]
Alabama	48,518	38	50,391	35	3.9	3
U.S. Average	58,479	–	59,660	–	2.0	–

Note: (1) Rank ranges from 1 to 51 where 1 indicates highest salary; (2) Rank ranges from 1 to 51 where 1 indicates highest percent change.
Source: National Education Association, Rankings & Estimates: Rankings of the States 2017 and Estimates of School Statistics 2018

Higher Education

Four-Year Colleges			Two-Year Colleges			Medical Schools[1]	Law Schools[2]	Voc/ Tech[3]
Public	Private Non-profit	Private For-profit	Public	Private Non-profit	Private For-profit			
1	2	1	1	0	0	0	0	2

Note: Figures cover institutions located within the city limits and include main campuses only; (1) includes schools accredited by the Liaison Committee on Medical Education and the American Osteopathic Association's Commission on Osteopathic College Accreditation; (2) includes ABA-accredited schools, schools with provisional ABA accreditation, and state accredited schools; (3) includes all schools with programs that are less than 2 years.
Source: National Center for Education Statistics, Integrated Postsecondary Education System (IPEDS), 2017-18; Wikipedia, List of Medical Schools in the United States, accessed April 3, 2019; Wikipedia, List of Law Schools in the United States, accessed April 3, 2019

PRESIDENTIAL ELECTION

2016 Presidential Election Results

Area	Clinton	Trump	Johnson	Stein	Other
Madison County	38.4	54.8	4.1	0.8	1.9
U.S.	48.0	45.9	3.3	1.1	1.7

Note: Results are percentages and may not add to 100% due to rounding
Source: Dave Leip's Atlas of U.S. Presidential Elections

EMPLOYERS

Major Employers

Company Name	Industry
Avocent Corporation	Computer peripheral equip
City of Huntsville	Mayor's office
City of Huntsville	Town council
COLSA Corporation	Commercial research laboratory
County of Madison	County government
Dynetics	Engineering laboratory/except testing
General Dynamics C4 Systems	Defense systems equipment
Healthcare Auth - City of Huntsville	General government
Intergraph Process & Bldg Solutions	Systems software development
Qualitest Products	Drugs & drug proprietaries
Science Applications Int'l Corporation	Computer processing services/commercial research lab
Teledyne Brown Engineering	Energy research
The Boeing Company	Aircraft/guided missiles/space vehicles
U.S. Army	U.S. military
United States Department of the Army	Army

Note: Companies shown are located within the Huntsville, AL Metropolitan Statistical Area.
Source: Hoovers.com; Wikipedia

PUBLIC SAFETY

Crime Rate

Area	All Crimes	Violent Crimes				Property Crimes		
		Murder	Rape[3]	Robbery	Aggrav. Assault	Burglary	Larceny -Theft	Motor Vehicle Theft
City	5,635.0	11.3	88.1	184.5	621.0	731.7	3,462.6	535.9
Suburbs[1]	2,220.1	4.2	32.4	31.2	227.3	432.2	1,337.1	155.6
Metro[2]	3,685.7	7.3	56.3	97.0	396.3	560.7	2,249.3	318.9
U.S.	2,756.1	5.3	41.7	98.0	248.9	430.4	1,694.4	237.4

Note: Figures are crimes per 100,000 population; (1) All areas within the metro area that are located outside the city limits; (2) Figures cover the Huntsville, AL Metropolitan Statistical Area—see Appendix B for areas included; (3) The city and U.S. figures shown were reported using the revised Uniform Crime Reporting (UCR) definition of rape. The suburban and metro area figures shown are an aggregate total of the data submitted using both the revised and legacy UCR definitions.
Source: FBI Uniform Crime Reports, 2017

Hate Crimes

Area	Number of Quarters Reported	Number of Incidents per Bias Motivation					
		Race/Ethnicity/ Ancestry	Religion	Sexual Orientation	Disability	Gender	Gender Identity
City	n/a	n/a	n/a	n/a	n/a	n/a	n/a
U.S.	4	4,131	1,564	1,130	116	46	119

Note: n/a not available.
Source: Federal Bureau of Investigation, Hate Crime Statistics 2017

Identity Theft Consumer Reports

Area	Reports	Reports per 100,000 Population	Rank[2]
MSA[1]	481	107	107
U.S.	444,602	135	-

Note: (1) Figures cover the Huntsville, AL Metropolitan Statistical Area—see Appendix B for areas included; (2) Rank ranges from 1 to 389 where 1 indicates greatest number of identity theft reports per 100,000 population
Source: Federal Trade Commission, Consumer Sentinel Network Data Book for January–December 2018

Fraud and Other Consumer Reports

Area	Reports	Reports per 100,000 Population	Rank[2]
MSA[1]	2,623	583	67
U.S.	2,552,917	776	-

Note: (1) Figures cover the Huntsville, AL Metropolitan Statistical Area—see Appendix B for areas included; (2) Rank ranges from 1 to 389 where 1 indicates greatest number of fraud and other consumer reports per 100,000 population
Source: Federal Trade Commission, Consumer Sentinel Network Data Book for January–December 2018

SPORTS

Professional Sports Teams

Team Name	League	Year Established
No teams are located in the metro area		

Source: Wikipedia, Major Professional Sports Teams of the United States and Canada, April 5, 2019

CLIMATE

Average and Extreme Temperatures

Temperature	Jan	Feb	Mar	Apr	May	Jun	Jul	Aug	Sep	Oct	Nov	Dec	Yr.
Extreme High (°F)	76	82	88	92	96	101	104	103	101	91	84	77	104
Average High (°F)	49	54	63	73	80	87	90	89	83	73	62	52	71
Average Temp. (°F)	39	44	52	61	69	76	80	79	73	62	51	43	61
Average Low (°F)	30	33	41	49	58	65	69	68	62	50	40	33	50
Extreme Low (°F)	-11	5	6	26	36	45	53	52	37	28	15	-3	-11

Note: Figures cover the years 1958-1995
Source: National Climatic Data Center, International Station Meteorological Climate Summary, 9/96

Average Precipitation/Snowfall/Humidity

Precip./Humidity	Jan	Feb	Mar	Apr	May	Jun	Jul	Aug	Sep	Oct	Nov	Dec	Yr.
Avg. Precip. (in.)	5.0	5.0	6.6	4.8	5.1	4.3	4.6	3.5	4.1	3.3	4.7	5.7	56.8
Avg. Snowfall (in.)	2	1	1	Tr	0	0	0	0	0	Tr	Tr	1	4
Avg. Rel. Hum. 7am (%)	82	81	79	78	79	81	84	86	85	86	84	81	82
Avg. Rel. Hum. 4pm (%)	60	56	51	46	51	53	56	55	54	51	55	60	54

Note: Figures cover the years 1958-1995; Tr = Trace amounts (<0.05 in. of rain; <0.5 in. of snow)
Source: National Climatic Data Center, International Station Meteorological Climate Summary, 9/96

Weather Conditions

Temperature			Daytime Sky			Precipitation		
10°F & below	32°F & below	90°F & above	Clear	Partly cloudy	Cloudy	0.01 inch or more precip.	0.1 inch or more snow/ice	Thunder-storms
2	66	49	70	118	177	116	2	54

Note: Figures are average number of days per year and cover the years 1958-1995
Source: National Climatic Data Center, International Station Meteorological Climate Summary, 9/96

HAZARDOUS WASTE

Superfund Sites

The Huntsville, AL metro area is home to two sites on the EPA's Superfund National Priorities List: **Triana/Tennessee River** (final); **Usarmy/Nasa Redstone Arsenal** (final). There are a total of 1,390 Superfund sites with a status of proposed or final on the list in the U.S. *U.S. Environmental Protection Agency, National Priorities List, April 5, 2019*

AIR & WATER QUALITY

Air Quality Trends: Ozone

	1990	1995	2000	2005	2010	2012	2014	2015	2016	2017
MSA[1]	0.079	0.080	0.088	0.075	0.071	0.076	0.064	0.063	0.066	0.063
U.S.	0.088	0.089	0.082	0.080	0.073	0.075	0.067	0.068	0.069	0.068

Note: (1) Data covers the Huntsville, AL Metropolitan Statistical Area—see Appendix B for areas included. The values shown are the composite ozone concentration averages among trend sites based on the highest fourth daily maximum 8-hour concentration in parts per million. These trends are based on sites having an adequate record of monitoring data during the trend period. Data from exceptional events are included.
Source: U.S. Environmental Protection Agency, Air Quality Monitoring Information, "Air Quality Trends by City, 1990-2017"

Air Quality Index

Area	Percent of Days when Air Quality was...[2]					AQI Statistics[2]	
	Good	Moderate	Unhealthy for Sensitive Groups	Unhealthy	Very Unhealthy	Maximum	Median
MSA[1]	89.9	10.1	0.0	0.0	0.0	100	39

Note: (1) Data covers the Huntsville, AL Metropolitan Statistical Area—see Appendix B for areas included; (2) Based on 336 days with AQI data in 2017. Air Quality Index (AQI) is an index for reporting daily air quality. EPA calculates the AQI for five major air pollutants regulated by the Clean Air Act: ground-level ozone, particle pollution (aka particulate matter), carbon monoxide, sulfur dioxide, and nitrogen dioxide. The AQI runs from 0 to 500. The higher the AQI value, the greater the level of air pollution and the greater the health concern. There are six AQI categories: "Good" AQI is between 0 and 50. Air quality is considered satisfactory; "Moderate" AQI is between 51 and 100. Air quality is acceptable; "Unhealthy for Sensitive Groups" When AQI values are between 101 and 150, members of sensitive groups may experience health effects; "Unhealthy" When AQI values are between 151 and 200 everyone may begin to experience health effects; "Very Unhealthy" AQI values between 201 and 300 trigger a health alert; "Hazardous" AQI values over 300 trigger warnings of emergency conditions (not shown).
Source: U.S. Environmental Protection Agency, Air Quality Index Report, 2017

Air Quality Index Pollutants

Area	Percent of Days when AQI Pollutant was...[2]					
	Carbon Monoxide	Nitrogen Dioxide	Ozone	Sulfur Dioxide	Particulate Matter 2.5	Particulate Matter 10
MSA[1]	0.0	0.0	68.5	0.0	15.5	16.1

Note: (1) Data covers the Huntsville, AL Metropolitan Statistical Area—see Appendix B for areas included; (2) Based on 336 days with AQI data in 2017. The Air Quality Index (AQI) is an index for reporting daily air quality. EPA calculates the AQI for five major air pollutants regulated by the Clean Air Act: ground-level ozone, particle pollution (also known as particulate matter), carbon monoxide, sulfur dioxide, and nitrogen dioxide. The AQI runs from 0 to 500. The higher the AQI value, the greater the level of air pollution and the greater the health concern.
Source: U.S. Environmental Protection Agency, Air Quality Index Report, 2017

Maximum Air Pollutant Concentrations: Particulate Matter, Ozone, CO and Lead

	Particulate Matter 10 (ug/m³)	Particulate Matter 2.5 Wtd AM (ug/m³)	Particulate Matter 2.5 24-Hr (ug/m³)	Ozone (ppm)	Carbon Monoxide (ppm)	Lead (ug/m³)
MSA[1] Level	27	7.5	17	0.063	n/a	n/a
NAAQS[2]	150	15	35	0.075	9	0.15
Met NAAQS[2]	Yes	Yes	Yes	Yes	n/a	n/a

Note: (1) Data covers the Huntsville, AL Metropolitan Statistical Area—see Appendix B for areas included; Data from exceptional events are included; (2) National Ambient Air Quality Standards; ppm = parts per million; ug/m³ = micrograms per cubic meter; n/a not available.
Concentrations: Particulate Matter 10 (coarse particulate)—highest second maximum 24-hour concentration; Particulate Matter 2.5 Wtd AM (fine particulate)—highest weighted annual mean concentration; Particulate Matter 2.5 24-Hour (fine particulate)—highest 98th percentile 24-hour concentration; Ozone—highest fourth daily maximum 8-hour concentration; Carbon Monoxide—highest second maximum non-overlapping 8-hour concentration; Lead—maximum running 3-month average
Source: U.S. Environmental Protection Agency, Air Quality Monitoring Information, "Air Quality Statistics by City, 2017"

Maximum Air Pollutant Concentrations: Nitrogen Dioxide and Sulfur Dioxide

	Nitrogen Dioxide AM (ppb)	Nitrogen Dioxide 1-Hr (ppb)	Sulfur Dioxide AM (ppb)	Sulfur Dioxide 1-Hr (ppb)	Sulfur Dioxide 24-Hr (ppb)
MSA[1] Level	n/a	n/a	n/a	n/a	n/a
NAAQS[2]	53	100	30	75	140
Met NAAQS[2]	n/a	n/a	n/a	n/a	n/a

Note: (1) Data covers the Huntsville, AL Metropolitan Statistical Area—see Appendix B for areas included; Data from exceptional events are included; (2) National Ambient Air Quality Standards; ppm = parts per million; ug/m³ = micrograms per cubic meter; n/a not available.
Concentrations: Nitrogen Dioxide AM—highest arithmetic mean concentration; Nitrogen Dioxide 1-Hr—highest 98th percentile 1-hour daily maximum concentration; Sulfur Dioxide AM—highest annual mean concentration; Sulfur Dioxide 1-Hr—highest 99th percentile 1-hour daily maximum concentration; Sulfur Dioxide 24-Hr—highest second maximum 24-hour concentration
Source: U.S. Environmental Protection Agency, Air Quality Monitoring Information, "Air Quality Statistics by City, 2017"

Drinking Water

Water System Name	Pop. Served	Primary Water Source Type	Violations[1]	
			Health Based	Monitoring/ Reporting
Huntsville Utilities	219,168	Surface	0	0

Note: (1) Based on violation data from January 1, 2018 to December 31, 2018
Source: U.S. Environmental Protection Agency, Office of Ground Water and Drinking Water, Safe Drinking Water Information System (based on data extracted April 5, 2019)

Jacksonville, Florida

Background

Modern day Jacksonville is largely a product of the reconstruction that occurred during the 1940s after a fire razed 147 city blocks a few decades earlier. Lying under the modern structures, however, is a history that dates back earlier than the settlement of Plymouth by the Pilgrims.

Located in the northeast part of Florida on the St. John's River, Jacksonville, the largest city in land area in the contiguous United States, was settled by English, Spanish, and French explorers from the sixteenth through the eighteenth centuries. Sites commemorating their presence include: Fort Caroline National Monument, marking the French settlement led by René de Goulaine Laudonnière in 1564; Spanish Pond one-quarter of a mile east of Fort Caroline, where Spanish forces led by Pedro Menendez captured the Fort; and Fort George Island, from which General James Oglethorpe led English attacks against the Spanish during the eighteenth century.

Jacksonville was attractive to these early settlers because of its easy access to the Atlantic Ocean, which meant a favorable port. Today, Jacksonville remains a military and civilian deep-water port. The city is home to Naval Station Mayport, Naval Air Station Jacksonville, the U.S. Marine Corps Bount Island command, and the Port of Jacksonville, Florida's third largest seaport. Jacksonville's military bases and the nearby Naval Submarine Base Kings Bay form the third largest military presence in the United States.

Jacksonville is the financial hub of Florida, and many business and financial companies are headquartered in the city. As with much of Florida, tourism is important to Jacksonville, particularly tourism related to golf.

Jacksonville voters approved The Better Jacksonville Plan in 2000, which authorized a half-penny sales tax that generated revenue for major improvement city projects, environmental protection and economic development.

On the cultural front, Jacksonville boasts a range of options, including the Children's Museum, the Jacksonville Symphony Orchestra, the Gator Bowl, and beach facilities. In 2005, the city hosted Super Bowl XXXIX at the former Alltel Stadium (now Jacksonville Municipal Stadium), home of the NFL's Jacksonville Jaguars. The city also boasts the largest urban park system in the United States, providing services at more than 337 locations on more than 80,000 acres located throughout the city. The Jacksonville Jazz Festival, held every April, is the second-largest jazz festival in the nation. The city is home to several theaters, including Little Theatre, which, operating since 1919, is one of the oldest operating community theaters in the nation.

Jacksonville has more than 80,000 acres of parkland throughout the city, and is renowned for its outdoor recreational facilities. The city's most recent park, The Jacksonville Arboretum and Gardens, was opened in the fall of 2008.

Summers are long, warm, and relatively humid. Winters are generally mild, although periodic invasions of cold northern air bring the temperature down. Temperatures along the beaches rarely rise above 90 degrees. Summer coastal thunderstorms usually occur before noon, and move inland in the afternoons. The greatest rainfall, as localized thundershowers, occurs during the summer months. Although the area is in the hurricane belt, this section of the coast has been very fortunate in escaping hurricane-force winds. However, in October 2016, Hurricane Matthew caused major flooding and damage to the city, Jacksonville Beach, Atlantic Beach and Neptune Beach. In September 2017, Hurricane Irma caused record breaking floods in Jacksonville not seen since 1846.

Rankings

General Rankings

- For its "Best for Vets: Places to Live 2019" rankings, *Military Times* evaluated 599 cities (83 large, 234 medium, 282 small) and compared the locations across three broad categories: veteran and military culture/services; economic indicators; and livability factors such as health, crime, traffic, and school quality. Jacksonville ranked #10 out of the top 25, in the large city category (populations of more than 250,000). Data points more specific to veterans and the military weighed more heavily than the rest. *rebootcamp.militarytimes.com, "Military Times Best Places to Live 2019," September 10, 2018*

- *Insider* listed 33 places in the U.S. that were a must see vacation destination. Whether it is the great beaches, exploring a new city or experiencing the great outdoors, according to the website thisisinsider.com Jacksonville is a place to visit in 2018. *Insider, "33 Trips Everyone Should Take in the U.S. in 2018,"November 27, 2017*

- The Jacksonville metro area was identified as one of America's fastest-growing areas in terms of population and economy by *Forbes*. The area ranked #16 out of 25. The 100 most populous metro areas in the U.S. were evaluated on the following criteria: estimated population growth; employment; economic output; wages; home values. *Forbes, "America's Fastest-Growing Cities 2018," February 28, 2018*

- In their sixth annual survey, Livability.com looked at data for more than 1,000 U.S. cities to determine the rankings for Livability's "Top 100 Best Places to Live" in 2019. Jacksonville ranked #94. Criteria: median home value capped at $250,000; affordable living; vibrant economy; education, demographics, health care options. transportation & infrastructure; abundant lifestyle amenities. *Livability.com, "Top 100 Best Places to Live 2019" March 2019*

Business/Finance Rankings

- The personal finance site NerdWallet analyzed 183 American metropolitan areas with populations over 250,000 and more than 15,000 businesses to rank where entrepreneurs find the most success. Criteria included area economy, annual income, housing cost, unemployment rate, and the success rate of area businesses. Jacksonville ranked #106. *www.nerdwallet.com, "Best Places to Start a Business," April 27, 2015*

- Jacksonville was the #14-ranked city for savers, according to a study by the finance site GOBankingRates, which considered the prospects for people trying to save money. Criteria: average monthly cost of grocery items; median home listing price; median rent; median income; unemployment rate; gas prices; and sales tax in the nation's 60 largest cities. *www.gobankingrates.com, "Best Cities for Saving Money," June 22, 2018*

- Jacksonville was ranked #14 among the nation's 60 largest cities for most difficult conditions for savers, according to a study by the finance site GOBankingRates. Criteria: average monthly cost of grocery items; median home listing price; median rent; median income; unemployment rate; gas prices; and sales tax. *www.gobankingrates.com, "Worst Cities for Saving Money," June 22, 2018*

- In a survey of economic confidence in the nation's 50 largest metropolitan areas conducted January–December 2014, the Jacksonville metro area placed #40, according to Gallup's 2014 Economic Confidence Index. *Gallup, "San Jose and San Francisco Lead in Economic Confidence," March 19, 2015*

- Using data from the Council for Community and Economic Research's 2014 cost of living index, NerdWallet ranked the 100 most affordable cities in America. Median income was compared with cost of living to find truly affordable places. Jacksonville ranked #79. *NerdWallet.com, "America's Most Affordable Places," May 18, 2015*

- NerdWallet.com identified the 10 most promising cities for job seekers of the nation's 100 largest cities. Jacksonville was ranked #72. Criteria: job availability; annual salary; workforce growth; affordability. *NerdWallet.com, "Best Cities for Job Seekers in 2017," December 19, 2016*

- The Brookings Institution ranked the nation's largest cities based on income inequality. Jacksonville was ranked #91 (#1 = greatest inequality). Criteria: the "95/20 ratio," a figure representing the income at which a household earns more than 95 percent of all other households, divided by the income at which a household earns more than only 20 percent of all other households. *Brookings Institution, "Household Income Inequality, Largest Cities of 97 Large U.S. Metro Areas, 2014-2016," February 5, 2018*

- The Brookings Institution ranked the 100 largest metro areas in the U.S. based on income inequality. Jacksonville was ranked #77 (#1 = greatest inequality). Criteria: the "95/20 ratio," a figure representing the income at which a household earns more than 95 percent of all other households, divided by the income at which a household earns more than only 20 percent of all other households. *Brookings Institution, "Household Income Inequality, 100 Largest U.S. Metro Areas, 2014-2016," February 5, 2018*

- The Jacksonville metro area appeared on the Milken Institute "2018 Best Performing Cities" list. Rank: #26 out of 200 large metro areas. Criteria: job growth; wage and salary growth; high-tech output growth. *Milken Institute, "Best-Performing Cities 2018," January 24, 2019*

- *Forbes* ranked the 200 most populous metro areas to determine the nation's "Best Places for Business and Careers." The Jacksonville metro area was ranked #14. Criteria: costs (business and living); job growth (past and projected); income growth; quality of life; educational attainment (college and high school); projected economic growth; cultural and recreational opportunities; net migration patterns; number of highly ranked colleges. *Forbes, "The Best Places for Business and Careers 2018: Seattle Leads the Way," October 24, 2018*

Dating/Romance Rankings

- Jacksonville was ranked #10 out of 25 cities that stood out for inspiring romance and attracting diners on the website OpenTable.com. Criteria: percentage of people who dined out on Valentine's Day in 2018; percentage of romantic restaurants as rated by OpenTable diner reviews; and percentage of tables seated for two. *OpenTable, "25 Most Romantic Cities in America for 2019," February 7, 2019*

Education Rankings

- Personal finance website *WalletHub* analyzed the 150 largest U.S. metropolitan statistical areas to determine where the most educated Americans are choosing to settle. Criteria: education quality and attainment gap; education levels; percentage of workers with degrees; public school quality rankings; quality and size of each metro area's universities. Jacksonville was ranked #75 (#1 = most educated city). *www.WalletHub.com, "2018's Most and Least Educated Cities in America," July 24, 2018*

- Jacksonville was selected as one of America's most literate cities. The city ranked #55 out of the 82 largest U.S. cities. Criteria: number of booksellers; library resources; Internet resources; educational attainment; periodical publishing resources; newspaper circulation. *Central Connecticut State University, "America's Most Literate Cities, 2016," March 31, 2017*

Food/Drink Rankings

- *Men's Health* ranked 100 major U.S. cities in terms of alcohol intoxication. Jacksonville ranked #33 (#1 = most sober).Criteria: binge drinking; alcohol-related traffic accidents, arrests, and fatalities. *Men's Health, "America's Drunkest Cities," March 9, 2015*

Health/Fitness Rankings

- For each of the 100 largest cities in the United States, the American College of Sports Medicine's American Fitness Index evaluated infrastructure, community assets, and policies that encourage healthy and fit lifestyles, including preventive health behaviors, levels of chronic disease conditions, health care access, and community resources and policies that support physical activity. Jacksonville ranked #64 for "community fitness." *www.americanfitnessindex.org, "ACSM American Fitness Index Health and Community Fitness Status of the 100 Largest U.S. Cities," May 2018*

- Jacksonville was identified as a "2018 Spring Allergy Capital." The area ranked #51 out of 100. Three groups of factors were used to identify the most challenging cities for people with allergies during the spring season: annual pollen levels; medicine utilization; access to board-certified allergists. *Asthma and Allergy Foundation of America, "Spring Allergy Capitals 2018"*

- Jacksonville was identified as a "2018 Fall Allergy Capital." The area ranked #52 out of 100. Three groups of factors were used to identify the most challenging cities for people with allergies during the fall season: annual pollen levels; medicine utilization; access to board-certified allergists. *Asthma and Allergy Foundation of America, "Fall Allergy Capitals 2018"*

- Jacksonville was identified as a "2018 Asthma Capital." The area ranked #68 out of the nation's 100 largest metropolitan areas. Criteria: estimated prevalence; self-reported prevalence; crude death rate for asthma; annual pollen score; annual air quality; public smoking laws; number of board-certified asthma specialists; school inhaler access laws; rescue medication use; controller medication use; ER visits for asthma; uninsured rate; poverty rate. *Asthma and Allergy Foundation of America, "Asthma Capitals 2018: The Most Challenging Places to Live With Asthma"*

- *Men's Health* ranked 100 major U.S. cities in terms of the best cities for men. Jacksonville ranked #78. Criteria: health; fitness; quality of life. *Men's Health, "The Best & Worst Cities for Men Who Want to Be Fit and Happy," January 1, 2016*

- The Jacksonville metro area ranked #66 out of 189 in The Gallup-Healthways Well-Being Index. Criteria: purpose; social well being; financial health; community and physical health. Results are based on telephone interviews with adults, aged 18 and older, living in metropolitan areas in the 50 U.S. states and the District of Columbia. *Gallup-Healthways, "State of American Well-Being, 2017 Community Well-Being Rankings" March 2018*

Real Estate Rankings

- FitSmallBusiness looked at 50 of the largest metropolitan areas in the U.S. to determine which metro was the best to start a real estate business. Data was compiled from such sources as: Zillow, Trulia, U.S. Census Bureau, and the Bureau of Labor Statistics. Criteria: location; inventory; annual wages; median sales price of homes; days on the market; median price cut percentage; and other factors that would influence real estate professional growth. The Jacksonville metro area ranked #42. *fitsmallbusiness.com, "The Best Cities to Become a Real Estate Agent in 2018," January 30, 2018*

- *WalletHub* compared the most populated U.S. cities, as well as at least two of the most populated cities in each state, for a total of 179, to determine which had the best markets for real estate agents. Jacksonville ranked #91 where demand was high and pay was the best. Criteria: sales per agent; annual median wage for real-estate agents; monthly average starting salary for real estate agents; real estate job density and competition; unemployment rate; housing-market health index; and other relevant metrics. *www.WalletHub.com, "2018's Best Places to Be a Real Estate Agent," April 25, 2018*

- The Jacksonville metro area was identified as one of the top 20 housing markets to invest in for 2019 by *Forbes*. Criteria: strong job and population growth; stable local economy; anticipated home price appreciation; and other factors. *Forbes.com, "The Best Markets for Real Estate Investments In 2019," January 7, 2019*

- Jacksonville was ranked #131 out of 237 metro areas in terms of housing affordability in 2018 by the National Association of Home Builders (#1 = most affordable). Criteria: the share of homes sold in that area affordable to a family earning the local median income, based on standard mortgage underwriting criteria. *National Association of Home Builders®, NAHB-Wells Fargo Housing Opportunity Index, 4th Quarter 2018*

- The nation's largest metro areas were analyzed in terms of the percentage of households entering some stage of foreclosure in 2018. The Jacksonville metro area ranked #10 out of 10 (#1 = highest foreclosure rate). *ATTOM Data Solutions, "2018 Year-End U.S. Foreclosure Market Report™," January 17, 2019*

Safety Rankings

- Allstate ranked the 200 largest cities in America in terms of driver safety. Jacksonville ranked #50. Criteria: internal property damage claims over a two-year period from January 2015 to December 2016. The report helps increase the importance of safety awareness behind the wheel. *Allstate, "Allstate America's Best Drivers Report, 2018" August 28, 2018*

- The National Insurance Crime Bureau ranked 382 metro areas in the U.S. in terms of per capita rates of vehicle theft. The Jacksonville metro area ranked #124 (#1 = highest rate). Criteria: number of vehicle theft offenses per 100,000 inhabitants in 2017. *National Insurance Crime Bureau, "Hot Spots 2017," July 12, 2018*

Seniors/Retirement Rankings

- For *U.S. News & World Report's* Best Places rankings, the editors sought out affordable cities where retirees spend the least on housing and can live on $100 a day while still having access to amenities they need, such as health care, utilities, transportation and food. Jacksonville was among the ten cities that best satisfied their criteria. *money.usnews.com, "10 Best Places to Retire on $100 a Day," October 13, 2015*

- From its Best Cities for Successful Aging indexes, the Milken Institute generated rankings for metropolitan areas, weighing data in nine categories—health care, wellness, living arrangements, transportation and convenience, financial characteristics, education, employment, community engagement, and overall livability. The Jacksonville metro area was ranked #63 overall in the large metro area category. *Milken Institute, "Best Cities for Successful Aging, 2017" March 14, 2017*

- Jacksonville made the 2018 *Forbes* list of "25 Best Places to Retire." Criteria, focused on a high-quality retirement living an affordable price, include: housing/living costs compared to the national average and state taxes; weather and air quality; crime rates; vibrant economy and low unemployment; doctor availability; bikability; walkability; healthy living and volunteering. *Forbes.com, "The Best Places to Retire in 2018," April 23, 2018*

- Jacksonville was identified as one of the most popular places to retire by *Topretirements.com*. The list reflects the 100 cities that visitors to the website are most interested in for retirement, based on the number of times a city's review was viewed on the website. *Topretirements.com, "100 Most Popular Places to Retire for 2017," July 27, 2017*

Women/Minorities Rankings

- Personal finance website *WalletHub* compared more than 180 U.S. cities—including the 150 most populated U.S. cities, plus at least two of the most populated cities in each state—across two key dimensions, "Hispanic Business-Friendliness" and "Hispanic Purchasing Power", to arrive at the most favorable conditions for Hispanic entrepreneurs. Jacksonville was ranked #42 out of 182. Criteria includes: share of Hispanic-Owned Businesses; Hispanic entrepreneurship rate to median annual income of Hispanics; Small Business-Friendliness score; cost of living; and number of Hispanics with at least a bachelor's degree. *WalletHub.com, "2018's Best Cities for Hispanic Entrepreneurs," April 26, 2018*

Miscellaneous Rankings

- *WalletHub* compared the 150 most populated U.S. cities to determine their operating efficiency. A "Quality of Services" score was constructed for each city and then divided by the total budget per capita to reveal which were managed the best. Jacksonville ranked #92. Criteria: financial stability; economy; education; safety; health; infrastructure and pollution. *www.WalletHub.com, "2018's Best- & Worst-Run Cities in America," July 9, 2018*

Business Environment

CITY FINANCES

City Government Finances

Component	2016 ($000)	2016 ($ per capita)
Total Revenues	3,937,086	4,536
Total Expenditures	3,747,906	4,318
Debt Outstanding	8,910,060	10,265
Cash and Securities[1]	5,083,560	5,856

Note: (1) Cash and security holdings of a government at the close of its fiscal year, including those of its dependent agencies, utilities, and liquor stores.
Source: U.S. Census Bureau, State & Local Government Finances 2016

City Government Revenue by Source

Source	2016 ($000)	2016 ($ per capita)	2016 (%)
General Revenue			
From Federal Government	97,435	112	2.5
From State Government	265,100	305	6.7
From Local Governments	237,914	274	6.0
Taxes			
Property	527,755	608	13.4
Sales and Gross Receipts	320,940	370	8.2
Personal Income	0	0	0.0
Corporate Income	0	0	0.0
Motor Vehicle License	0	0	0.0
Other Taxes	108,872	125	2.8
Current Charges	578,182	666	14.7
Liquor Store	0	0	0.0
Utility	1,529,936	1,763	38.9
Employee Retirement	-39,474	-45	-1.0

Source: U.S. Census Bureau, State & Local Government Finances 2016

City Government Expenditures by Function

Function	2016 ($000)	2016 ($ per capita)	2016 (%)
General Direct Expenditures			
Air Transportation	44,914	51	1.2
Corrections	54,328	62	1.4
Education	0	0	0.0
Employment Security Administration	0	0	0.0
Financial Administration	78,223	90	2.1
Fire Protection	146,064	168	3.9
General Public Buildings	17	< 1	< 0.1
Governmental Administration, Other	21,954	25	0.6
Health	82,235	94	2.2
Highways	33,739	38	0.9
Hospitals	41,108	47	1.1
Housing and Community Development	18,892	21	0.5
Interest on General Debt	107,457	123	2.9
Judicial and Legal	32,369	37	0.9
Libraries	31,548	36	0.8
Parking	3,496	4	0.1
Parks and Recreation	103,121	118	2.8
Police Protection	349,742	402	9.3
Public Welfare	12,458	14	0.3
Sewerage	89,869	103	2.4
Solid Waste Management	67,462	77	1.8
Veterans' Services	0	0	0.0
Liquor Store	0	0	0.0
Utility	1,734,504	1,998	46.3
Employee Retirement	332,388	382	8.9

Source: U.S. Census Bureau, State & Local Government Finances 2016

DEMOGRAPHICS

Population Growth

Area	1990 Census	2000 Census	2010 Census	2017* Estimate	Population Growth (%)	
					1990-2017	2010-2017
City	635,221	735,617	821,784	867,313	36.5	5.5
MSA[1]	925,213	1,122,750	1,345,596	1,447,884	56.5	7.6
U.S.	248,709,873	281,421,906	308,745,538	321,004,407	29.1	4.0

Note: (1) Figures cover the Jacksonville, FL Metropolitan Statistical Area—see Appendix B for areas included; (*) 2013-2017 5-year estimated population
Source: U.S. Census Bureau, 1990 Census, Census 2000, Census 2010, 2013-2017 American Community Survey 5-Year Estimates

Household Size

Area	Persons in Household (%)							Average Household Size
	One	Two	Three	Four	Five	Six	Seven or More	
City	30.2	34.0	16.4	11.6	5.0	1.8	0.9	2.60
MSA[1]	27.3	35.7	16.3	12.6	5.3	2.0	0.8	2.60
U.S.	27.7	33.8	15.7	13.0	6.0	2.3	1.4	2.60

Note: (1) Figures cover the Jacksonville, FL Metropolitan Statistical Area—see Appendix B for areas included
Source: U.S. Census Bureau, 2013-2017 American Community Survey 5-Year Estimates

Race

Area	White Alone[2] (%)	Black Alone[2] (%)	Asian Alone[2] (%)	AIAN[3] Alone[2] (%)	NHOPI[4] Alone[2] (%)	Other Race Alone[2] (%)	Two or More Races (%)
City	59.2	31.0	4.8	0.2	0.1	1.5	3.3
MSA[1]	70.0	21.5	3.8	0.2	0.1	1.3	3.1
U.S.	73.0	12.7	5.4	0.8	0.2	4.8	3.1

Note: (1) Figures cover the Jacksonville, FL Metropolitan Statistical Area—see Appendix B for areas included; (2) Alone is defined as not being in combination with one or more other races; (3) American Indian and Alaska Native; (4) Native Hawaiian and Other Pacific Islander
Source: U.S. Census Bureau, 2013-2017 American Community Survey 5-Year Estimates

Hispanic or Latino Origin

Area	Total (%)	Mexican (%)	Puerto Rican (%)	Cuban (%)	Other (%)
City	9.1	1.9	2.9	1.1	3.2
MSA[1]	8.2	1.8	2.7	1.0	2.7
U.S.	17.6	11.1	1.7	0.7	4.1

Note: Persons of Hispanic or Latino origin can be of any race; (1) Figures cover the Jacksonville, FL Metropolitan Statistical Area—see Appendix B for areas included
Source: U.S. Census Bureau, 2013-2017 American Community Survey 5-Year Estimates

Segregation

Type	Segregation Indices[1]				Percent Change		
	1990	2000	2010	2010 Rank[2]	1990-2000	1990-2010	2000-2010
Black/White	57.5	53.9	53.1	59	-3.6	-4.4	-0.8
Asian/White	34.2	37.0	37.5	71	2.8	3.2	0.4
Hispanic/White	22.1	26.6	27.6	98	4.6	5.5	1.0

Note: All figures cover the Metropolitan Statistical Area—see Appendix B for areas included; Figures are based on an analysis of 1990, 2000, and 2010 Census Decennial Census tract data by William H. Frey, Brookings Institution and the University of Michigan Social Science Data Analysis Network. In this analysis all racial groups (whites, blacks, and asians) are non-Hispanic members of those races. Hispanics are shown as a separate category; (1) Segregation Indices are Dissimilarity Indices that measure the degree to which the minority group is distributed differently than whites across census tracts. They range from 0 (complete integration) to 100 (complete segregation) where the value indicates the percentage of the minority group that needs to move to be distributed exactly like whites; (2) Ranges from 1 (most segregated) to 102 (least segregated); n/a not available.
Source: www.CensusScope.org

Ancestry

Area	German	Irish	English	American	Italian	Polish	French[2]	Scottish	Dutch
City	8.9	8.5	6.7	5.7	4.0	1.6	1.7	1.7	0.9
MSA[1]	10.7	10.0	8.4	7.9	4.8	2.0	2.3	2.1	1.0
U.S.	14.1	10.1	7.5	6.6	5.3	2.9	2.5	1.7	1.3

Note: Figures are the percentage of the total population reporting a particular ancestry. The nine most commonly reported ancestries in the U.S. are shown. Figures include multiple ancestries (e.g. if a person reported being Irish and Italian, they were included in both columns); (1) Figures cover the Jacksonville, FL Metropolitan Statistical Area—see Appendix B for areas included; (2) Excludes Basque
Source: U.S. Census Bureau, 2013-2017 American Community Survey 5-Year Estimates

Foreign-Born Population

Area	Any Foreign Country	Asia	Mexico	Europe	Carribean	Central America[2]	South America	Africa	Canada
City	10.6	4.1	0.6	1.7	1.7	0.6	1.1	0.5	0.2
MSA[1]	8.8	3.2	0.5	1.6	1.4	0.5	0.9	0.4	0.2
U.S.	13.4	4.1	3.6	1.5	1.3	1.0	0.9	0.6	0.3

Note: (1) Figures cover the Jacksonville, FL Metropolitan Statistical Area—see Appendix B for areas included; (2) Excludes Mexico.
Source: U.S. Census Bureau, 2013-2017 American Community Survey 5-Year Estimates

Marital Status

Area	Never Married	Now Married[2]	Separated	Widowed	Divorced
City	34.6	43.1	2.6	5.9	13.8
MSA[1]	30.9	48.0	2.2	5.9	13.0
U.S.	33.1	48.2	2.0	5.8	10.9

Note: Figures are percentages and cover the population 15 years of age and older; (1) Figures cover the Jacksonville, FL Metropolitan Statistical Area—see Appendix B for areas included; (2) Excludes separated
Source: U.S. Census Bureau, 2013-2017 American Community Survey 5-Year Estimates

Disability by Age

Area	All Ages	Under 18 Years Old	18 to 64 Years Old	65 Years and Over
City	13.6	4.9	11.8	38.7
MSA[1]	13.3	4.7	11.3	35.9
U.S.	12.6	4.2	10.3	35.5

Note: Figures show percent of the civilian noninstitutionalized population that reported having a disability. Disability status is determined from six types of difficulty: vision, hearing, cognitive, ambulatory, self-care, and independent living. For children under 5 years old, hearing and vision difficulty are used to determine disability status. For children between the ages of 5 and 14, disability status is determined from hearing, vision, cognitive, ambulatory, and self-care difficulties. For people aged 15 years and older, they are considered to have a disability if they have difficulty with any one of the six difficulty types; Note: (1) Figures cover the Jacksonville, FL Metropolitan Statistical Area—see Appendix B for areas included
Source: U.S. Census Bureau, 2013-2017 American Community Survey 5-Year Estimates

Age

Area	Under Age 5	Age 5–19	Age 20–34	Age 35–44	Age 45–54	Age 55–64	Age 65–74	Age 75–84	Age 85+	Median Age
City	6.9	18.5	23.4	12.7	13.3	12.3	7.7	3.4	1.6	35.8
MSA[1]	6.2	18.8	20.9	12.7	13.8	13.1	8.9	4.0	1.7	38.1
U.S.	6.2	19.5	20.7	12.7	13.4	12.7	8.6	4.4	1.9	37.8

Note: (1) Figures cover the Jacksonville, FL Metropolitan Statistical Area—see Appendix B for areas included
Source: U.S. Census Bureau, 2013-2017 American Community Survey 5-Year Estimates

Gender

Area	Males	Females	Males per 100 Females
City	419,756	447,557	93.8
MSA[1]	705,474	742,410	95.0
U.S.	158,018,753	162,985,654	97.0

Note: (1) Figures cover the Jacksonville, FL Metropolitan Statistical Area—see Appendix B for areas included
Source: U.S. Census Bureau, 2013-2017 American Community Survey 5-Year Estimates

Religious Groups by Family

Area	Catholic	Baptist	Non-Den.	Methodist[2]	Lutheran	LDS[3]	Pente-costal	Presby-terian[4]	Muslim[5]	Judaism
MSA[1]	9.9	18.5	7.8	4.5	0.7	1.1	1.9	1.6	0.6	0.4
U.S.	19.1	9.3	4.0	4.0	2.3	2.0	1.9	1.6	0.8	0.7

Note: Figures are the number of adherents as a percentage of the total population; (1) Figures cover the Jacksonville, FL Metropolitan Statistical Area—see Appendix B for areas included; (2) Methodist/Pietist; (3) Latter Day Saints; (4) Reformed; (5) Figures are estimates
Source: Association of Statisticians of American Religious Bodies, 2010 U.S. Religion Census: Religious Congregations & Membership Study

Religious Groups by Tradition

Area	Catholic	Evangelical Protestant	Mainline Protestant	Other Tradition	Black Protestant	Orthodox
MSA[1]	9.9	27.1	5.7	2.9	4.2	0.3
U.S.	19.1	16.2	7.3	4.3	1.6	0.3

Note: Figures are the number of adherents as a percentage of the total population; (1) Figures cover the Jacksonville, FL Metropolitan Statistical Area—see Appendix B for areas included
Source: Association of Statisticians of American Religious Bodies, 2010 U.S. Religion Census: Religious Congregations & Membership Study

ECONOMY

Gross Metropolitan Product

Area	2016	2017	2018	2019	Rank[2]
MSA[1]	71.7	75.0	79.0	83.7	47

Note: Figures are in billions of dollars; (1) Figures cover the Jacksonville, FL Metropolitan Statistical Area—see Appendix B for areas included; (2) Rank is based on 2017 data and ranges from 1 to 381
Source: U.S. Conference of Mayors, U.S. Metro Economies: Economic Growth & Full Employment, June 2018

Economic Growth

Area	2017-2018 (%)	2019-2020 (%)	2021-2022 (%)
MSA[1]	3.6	3.0	2.3

Note: Figures are real gross metropolitan product (GMP) growth rates and represent average annual percent change; (1) Figures cover the Jacksonville, FL Metropolitan Statistical Area—see Appendix B for areas included
Source: U.S. Conference of Mayors, U.S. Metro Economies: Economic Growth & Full Employment, June 2018

Metropolitan Area Exports

Area	2012	2013	2014	2015	2016	2017	Rank[2]
MSA[1]	2,595.0	2,467.8	2,473.7	2,564.4	2,159.0	2,141.7	94

Note: Figures are in millions of dollars; (1) Figures cover the Jacksonville, FL Metropolitan Statistical Area—see Appendix B for areas included; (2) Rank is based on 2017 data and ranges from 1 to 387
Source: U.S. Department of Commerce, International Trade Administration, Office of Trade and Economic Analysis, Industry and Analysis, Exports by Metropolitan Area, extracted March 25, 2019

Building Permits

Area	Single-Family			Multi-Family			Total		
	2016	2017	Pct. Chg.	2016	2017	Pct. Chg.	2016	2017	Pct. Chg.
City	2,678	3,005	12.2	2,839	2,874	1.2	5,517	5,879	6.6
MSA[1]	8,597	9,833	14.4	3,171	3,126	-1.4	11,768	12,959	10.1
U.S.	750,800	820,000	9.2	455,800	462,000	1.4	1,206,600	1,282,000	6.2

Note: (1) Figures cover the Jacksonville, FL Metropolitan Statistical Area—see Appendix B for areas included; Figures represent new, privately-owned housing units authorized (unadjusted data); All permit data are based on estimates with imputation
Source: U.S. Census Bureau, Manufacturing, Mining, and Construction Statistics, Building Permits, 2016, 2017

Bankruptcy Filings

Area	Business Filings			Nonbusiness Filings		
	2017	2018	% Chg.	2017	2018	% Chg.
Duval County	94	102	8.5	2,169	2,226	2.6
U.S.	23,157	22,232	-4.0	765,863	751,186	-1.9

Note: Business filings include Chapter 7, Chapter 11, Chapter 12, and Chapter 13; Nonbusiness filings include Chapter 7, Chapter 11, and Chapter 13
Source: Administrative Office of the U.S. Courts, Business and Nonbusiness Bankruptcy, County Cases Commenced by Chapter of the Bankruptcy Code, During the 12-Month Period Ending December 31, 2017 and Business and Nonbusiness Bankruptcy, County Cases Commenced by Chapter of the Bankruptcy Code, During the 12-Month Period Ending December 31, 2018

Housing Vacancy Rates

Area	Gross Vacancy Rate[2] (%)			Year-Round Vacancy Rate[3] (%)			Rental Vacancy Rate[4] (%)			Homeowner Vacancy Rate[5] (%)		
	2016	2017	2018	2016	2017	2018	2016	2017	2018	2016	2017	2018
MSA[1]	14.5	12.5	10.1	14.0	12.0	9.3	8.3	8.5	5.6	1.6	1.5	1.3
U.S.	12.8	12.7	12.3	9.9	9.9	9.7	6.9	7.2	6.9	1.7	1.6	1.5

Note: (1) Figures cover the Jacksonville, FL Metropolitan Statistical Area—see Appendix B for areas included; (2) The percentage of the total housing inventory that is vacant; (3) The percentage of the housing inventory (excluding seasonal units) that is year-round vacant; (4) The percentage of rental inventory that is vacant for rent; (5) The percentage of homeowner inventory that is vacant for sale
Source: U.S. Census Bureau, Housing Vacancies and Homeownership Annual Statistics: 2016, 2017, 2018

INCOME

Income

Area	Per Capita ($)	Median Household ($)	Average Household ($)
City	27,486	50,555	68,733
MSA[1]	30,451	56,449	77,552
U.S.	31,177	57,652	81,283

Note: (1) Figures cover the Jacksonville, FL Metropolitan Statistical Area—see Appendix B for areas included
Source: U.S. Census Bureau, 2013-2017 American Community Survey 5-Year Estimates

Household Income Distribution

Area	Percent of Households Earning							
	Under $15,000	$15,000 -$24,999	$25,000 -$34,999	$35,000 -$49,999	$50,000 -$74,999	$75,000 -$99,999	$100,000 -$149,999	$150,000 and up
City	12.9	10.0	11.3	15.2	18.9	12.5	11.6	7.6
MSA[1]	11.0	9.0	10.4	14.1	18.8	12.9	13.5	10.4
U.S.	11.6	9.8	9.5	13.0	17.7	12.3	14.1	12.1

Note: (1) Figures cover the Jacksonville, FL Metropolitan Statistical Area—see Appendix B for areas included
Source: U.S. Census Bureau, 2013-2017 American Community Survey 5-Year Estimates

Poverty Rate

Area	All Ages	Under 18 Years Old	18 to 64 Years Old	65 Years and Over
City	16.4	24.8	14.5	10.8
MSA[1]	13.9	19.9	13.0	8.7
U.S.	14.6	20.3	13.7	9.3

Note: Figures are percentage of people whose income during the past 12 months was below the poverty level; (1) Figures cover the Jacksonville, FL Metropolitan Statistical Area—see Appendix B for areas included
Source: U.S. Census Bureau, 2013-2017 American Community Survey 5-Year Estimates

EMPLOYMENT

Labor Force and Employment

Area	Civilian Labor Force			Workers Employed		
	Dec. 2017	Dec. 2018	% Chg.	Dec. 2017	Dec. 2018	% Chg.
City	457,717	464,256	1.4	441,382	449,181	1.8
MSA[1]	764,461	775,809	1.5	738,808	751,739	1.8
U.S.	159,880,000	162,510,000	1.6	153,602,000	156,481,000	1.9

Note: Data is not seasonally adjusted and covers workers 16 years of age and older; (1) Figures cover the Jacksonville, FL Metropolitan Statistical Area—see Appendix B for areas included
Source: Bureau of Labor Statistics, Local Area Unemployment Statistics

Unemployment Rate

Area	2018											
	Jan.	Feb.	Mar.	Apr.	May	Jun.	Jul.	Aug.	Sep.	Oct.	Nov.	Dec.
City	4.1	3.7	3.7	3.4	3.4	4.0	4.2	3.8	3.0	3.0	3.0	3.2
MSA[1]	3.9	3.5	3.5	3.2	3.1	3.7	3.8	3.5	2.8	2.9	2.9	3.1
U.S.	4.5	4.4	4.1	3.7	3.6	4.2	4.1	3.9	3.6	3.5	3.5	3.7

Note: Data is not seasonally adjusted and covers workers 16 years of age and older; (1) Figures cover the Jacksonville, FL Metropolitan Statistical Area—see Appendix B for areas included
Source: Bureau of Labor Statistics, Local Area Unemployment Statistics

Average Wages

Occupation	$/Hr.	Occupation	$/Hr.
Accountants and Auditors	32.40	Maids and Housekeeping Cleaners	11.10
Automotive Mechanics	18.60	Maintenance and Repair Workers	18.30
Bookkeepers	19.80	Marketing Managers	56.20
Carpenters	19.10	Nuclear Medicine Technologists	35.00
Cashiers	10.40	Nurses, Licensed Practical	21.20
Clerks, General Office	16.40	Nurses, Registered	30.10
Clerks, Receptionists/Information	13.60	Nursing Assistants	12.70
Clerks, Shipping/Receiving	16.50	Packers and Packagers, Hand	11.00
Computer Programmers	39.40	Physical Therapists	39.30
Computer Systems Analysts	39.80	Postal Service Mail Carriers	25.40
Computer User Support Specialists	24.80	Real Estate Brokers	22.80
Cooks, Restaurant	12.50	Retail Salespersons	12.50
Dentists	82.60	Sales Reps., Exc. Tech./Scientific	31.70
Electrical Engineers	41.00	Sales Reps., Tech./Scientific	36.10
Electricians	21.50	Secretaries, Exc. Legal/Med./Exec.	17.00
Financial Managers	67.40	Security Guards	12.00
First-Line Supervisors/Managers, Sales	21.10	Surgeons	n/a
Food Preparation Workers	11.40	Teacher Assistants*	12.10
General and Operations Managers	56.00	Teachers, Elementary School*	28.60
Hairdressers/Cosmetologists	18.30	Teachers, Secondary School*	29.10
Internists, General	n/a	Telemarketers	11.70
Janitors and Cleaners	12.90	Truck Drivers, Heavy/Tractor-Trailer	22.60
Landscaping/Groundskeeping Workers	12.90	Truck Drivers, Light/Delivery Svcs.	18.70
Lawyers	57.80	Waiters and Waitresses	12.20

Note: Wage data covers the Jacksonville, FL Metropolitan Statistical Area—see Appendix B for areas included; (*) Hourly wages for elementary/secondary school teachers and teacher assistants were calculated by the editors from annual wage data based on a 40 hour work week; n/a not available.
Source: Bureau of Labor Statistics, Metro Area Occupational Employment & Wage Estimates, May 2018

Employment by Occupation

Occupation Classification	City (%)	MSA[1] (%)	U.S. (%)
Management, Business, Science, and Arts	35.8	37.4	37.4
Natural Resources, Construction, and Maintenance	8.0	8.2	8.9
Production, Transportation, and Material Moving	10.5	10.0	12.2
Sales and Office	27.3	26.5	23.5
Service	18.4	17.9	18.0

Note: Figures cover employed civilians 16 years of age and older; (1) Figures cover the Jacksonville, FL Metropolitan Statistical Area—see Appendix B for areas included
Source: U.S. Census Bureau, 2013-2017 American Community Survey 5-Year Estimates

Employment by Industry

Sector	MSA[1]		U.S.
	Number of Employees	Percent of Total	Percent of Total
Construction	45,000	6.2	4.8
Education and Health Services	109,400	15.2	15.9
Financial Activities	66,600	9.2	5.7
Government	79,400	11.0	15.1
Information	9,400	1.3	1.9
Leisure and Hospitality	87,100	12.1	10.7
Manufacturing	31,900	4.4	8.5
Mining and Logging	400	0.1	0.5
Other Services	27,000	3.7	3.9
Professional and Business Services	109,000	15.1	14.1
Retail Trade	89,500	12.4	10.8
Transportation, Warehousing, and Utilities	39,400	5.5	4.2
Wholesale Trade	26,100	3.6	3.9

Note: Figures are non-farm employment as of December 2018. Figures are not seasonally adjusted and include workers 16 years of age and older; (1) Figures cover the Jacksonville, FL Metropolitan Statistical Area—see Appendix B for areas included
Source: Bureau of Labor Statistics, Current Employment Statistics, Employment, Hours, and Earnings

Occupations with Greatest Projected Employment Growth: 2018 – 2020

Occupation[1]	2018 Employment	2020 Projected Employment	Numeric Employment Change	Percent Employment Change
Interviewers, Except Eligibility and Loan	11,890	33,270	21,380	179.8
Combined Food Preparation and Serving Workers, Including Fast Food	242,590	256,470	13,880	5.7
Waiters and Waitresses	230,640	240,320	9,680	4.2
Registered Nurses	193,200	202,070	8,870	4.6
Customer Service Representatives	245,420	253,780	8,360	3.4
Laborers and Freight, Stock, and Material Movers, Hand	135,600	143,640	8,040	5.9
Construction Laborers	89,390	97,130	7,740	8.7
Landscaping and Groundskeeping Workers	116,440	123,040	6,600	5.7
Carpenters	72,550	78,990	6,440	8.9
Janitors and Cleaners, Except Maids and Housekeeping Cleaners	133,890	140,000	6,110	4.6

Note: Projections cover Florida; (1) Sorted by numeric employment change
Source: www.projectionscentral.com, State Occupational Projections, 2018–2020 Short-Term Projections

Fastest Growing Occupations: 2018 – 2020

Occupation[1]	2018 Employment	2020 Projected Employment	Numeric Employment Change	Percent Employment Change
Interviewers, Except Eligibility and Loan	11,890	33,270	21,380	179.8
Solar Photovoltaic Installers	1,100	1,330	230	20.9
Terrazzo Workers and Finishers	390	450	60	15.4
Helpers—Roofers	1,490	1,720	230	15.4
Helpers—Brickmasons, Blockmasons, Stonemasons, and Tile and Marble Setters	1,280	1,470	190	14.8
Helpers—Painters, Paperhangers, Plasterers, and Stucco Masons	570	650	80	14.0
Reinforcing Iron and Rebar Workers	1,100	1,250	150	13.6
Insulation Workers, Floor, Ceiling, and Wall	2,550	2,880	330	12.9
Structural Iron and Steel Workers	5,210	5,880	670	12.9
Cement Masons and Concrete Finishers	13,490	15,210	1,720	12.8

Note: Projections cover Florida; (1) Sorted by percent employment change and excludes occupations with numeric employment change less than 50
Source: www.projectionscentral.com, State Occupational Projections, 2018–2020 Short-Term Projections

TAXES

State Corporate Income Tax Rates

State	Tax Rate (%)	Income Brackets ($)	Num. of Brackets	Financial Institution Tax Rate (%)[a]	Federal Income Tax Ded.
Florida	5.5 (e)	Flat rate	1	5.5 (e)	No

Note: Tax rates as of January 1, 2019; (a) Rates listed are the corporate income tax rate applied to financial institutions or excise taxes based on income. Some states have other taxes based upon the value of deposits or shares; (e) The Florida tax rate may be adjusted downward if certain revenue targets are met.
Source: Federation of Tax Administrators, Range of State Corporate Income Tax Rates, January 1, 2019

State Individual Income Tax Rates

State	Tax Rate (%)	Income Brackets ($)	Personal Exemptions ($)			Standard Ded. ($)	
			Single	Married	Depend.	Single	Married
Florida					– No state income tax –		

Note: Tax rates as of January 1, 2019; Local- and county-level taxes are not included; n/a not applicable;

Source: Federation of Tax Administrators, State Individual Income Tax Rates, January 1, 2019

Various State Sales and Excise Tax Rates

State	State Sales Tax (%)	Gasoline[1] (¢/gal.)	Cigarette[2] ($/pack)	Spirits[3] ($/gal.)	Wine[4] ($/gal.)	Beer[5] ($/gal.)	Recreational Marijuana (%)
Florida	6	41.99	1.339	6.50 (f)	2.25 (l)	0.48 (q)	Not legal

Note: All tax rates as of January 1, 2019; (1) The American Petroleum Institute has developed a methodology for determining the average tax rate on a gallon of fuel. Rates may include any of the following: excise taxes, environmental fees, storage tank fees, other fees or taxes, general sales tax, and local taxes. In states where gasoline is subject to the general sales tax, or where the fuel tax is based on the average sale price, the average rate determined by API is sensitive to changes in the price of gasoline. States that fully or partially apply general sales taxes to gasoline: CA, CO, GA, IL, IN, MI, NY; (2) The federal excise tax of $1.0066 per pack and local taxes are not included; (3) Rates are those applicable to off-premise sales of 40% alcohol by volume (a.b.v.) distilled spirits in 750ml containers. Local excise taxes are excluded; (4) Rates are those applicable to off-premise sales of 11% a.b.v. non-carbonated wine in 750ml containers; (5) Rates are those applicable to off-premise sales of 4.7% a.b.v. beer in 12 ounce containers; (f) Different rates also applicable according to alcohol content, place of production, size of container, or place purchased (on- or off-premise or onboard airlines); (l) Different rates also applicable to alcohol content, place of production, size of container, place purchased (on- or off-premise or on board airlines) or type of wine (carbonated, vermouth, etc.); (q) Different rates also applicable according to alcohol content, place of production, size of container, or place purchased (on- or off-premise or onboard airlines).
Source: Tax Foundation, 2019 Facts & Figures: How Does Your State Compare?

State Business Tax Climate Index Rankings

State	Overall Rank	Corporate Tax Rank	Individual Income Tax Rank	Sales Tax Rank	Unemployment Insurance Tax Rank	Property Tax Rank
Florida	4	6	1	22	2	11

Note: The index is a measure of how each state's tax laws affect economic performance. The lower the rank, the more favorable a state's tax system is for business. States without a given tax are given a ranking of 1. The scores/rankings for the District of Columbia do not affect other states. The 2019 index represents the tax climate as of July 1, 2018.
Source: Tax Foundation, State Business Tax Climate Index 2019

COMMERCIAL REAL ESTATE

Office Market

Market Area	Inventory (sq. ft.)	Vacancy Rate (%)	Under Construction (sq. ft.)	YTD Net Absorption (sq. ft.)	Total Average Asking Rent ($/sq. ft./year)
Jacksonville	32,402,077	11.4	156,744	-320,223	19.57
National	4,905,867,938	13.1	83,553,714	45,846,470	28.46

Source: Newmark Grubb Knight Frank, National Office Market Report, 4th Quarter 2018

Industrial/Warehouse/R&D Market

Market Area	Inventory (sq. ft.)	Vacancy Rate (%)	Under Construction (sq. ft.)	YTD Net Absorption (sq. ft.)	Total Average Asking Rent ($/sq. ft./year)
Jacksonville	126,544,922	2.8	5,035,759	1,613,284	5.18
National	14,796,839,085	5.0	262,662,294	238,014,726	7.16

Source: Newmark Grubb Knight Frank, National Industrial Market Report, 4th Quarter 2018

COMMERCIAL UTILITIES

Typical Monthly Electric Bills

Area	General Service, Light ($/month)		General Service, Heavy ($/month)	
	40 kW demand 5,000 kWh	100 kW demand 10,000 kWh	500 kW demand 100,000 kWh	1,500 kW demand 500,000 kWh
City	606	1,498	13,307	57,260

Note: Figures are based on rates in effect January 1, 2018
Source: Memphis Light, Gas and Water, 2018 Utility Bill Comparisons for Selected U.S. Cities

TRANSPORTATION

Means of Transportation to Work

Area	Car/Truck/Van		Public Transportation			Bicycle	Walked	Other Means	Worked at Home
	Drove Alone	Car-pooled	Bus	Subway	Railroad				
City	80.3	9.6	2.0	0.0	0.0	0.5	1.8	1.4	4.5
MSA[1]	81.0	8.9	1.3	0.0	0.0	0.5	1.5	1.5	5.3
U.S.	76.4	9.2	2.5	1.9	0.6	0.6	2.7	1.3	4.7

Note: Figures are percentages and cover workers 16 years of age and older; (1) Figures cover the Jacksonville, FL Metropolitan Statistical Area—see Appendix B for areas included
Source: U.S. Census Bureau, 2013-2017 American Community Survey 5-Year Estimates

Travel Time to Work

Area	Less Than 10 Minutes	10 to 19 Minutes	20 to 29 Minutes	30 to 44 Minutes	45 to 59 Minutes	60 to 89 Minutes	90 Minutes or More
City	8.9	28.2	28.8	23.9	5.8	2.7	1.7
MSA[1]	9.3	25.7	25.4	24.8	8.6	4.3	1.9
U.S.	12.7	28.9	20.9	20.5	8.1	6.2	2.7

Note: Note: Figures are percentages and include workers 16 years old and over; (1) Figures cover the Jacksonville, FL Metropolitan Statistical Area—see Appendix B for areas included
Source: U.S. Census Bureau, 2013-2017 American Community Survey 5-Year Estimates

Freeway Travel Time Index

Area	1985	1990	1995	2000	2005	2010	2014
Urban Area Rank[1,2]	39	34	41	38	36	42	46
Urban Area Index[1]	1.08	1.12	1.14	1.17	1.20	1.18	1.18
Average Index[3]	1.09	1.11	1.14	1.17	1.20	1.19	1.20

Note: Freeway Travel Time Index—the ratio of travel time in the peak period to the travel time at free-flow conditions. For example, a value of 1.30 indicates a 20-minute free-flow trip takes 26 minutes in the peak (20 minutes x 1.30 = 26 minutes); (1) Covers the Jacksonville FL urban area; (2) Rank is based on 101 urban areas (#1 = highest travel time index); (3) Average of 101 urban areas
Source: Texas Transportation Institute, 2015 Urban Mobility Scorecard, August 2015

Freeway Commuter Stress Index

Area	1985	1990	1995	2000	2005	2010	2014
Urban Area Rank[1,2]	48	47	50	51	44	58	61
Urban Area Index[1]	1.10	1.13	1.16	1.19	1.22	1.19	1.19
Average Index[3]	1.13	1.16	1.19	1.22	1.25	1.24	1.25

Note: The Freeway Commuter Stress Index is the same as the Freeway Travel Time Index (see table above) except that it includes only the travel in the peak directions during the peak periods; the TTI includes travel in all directions during the peak period. Thus, the CSI is more indicative of the work trip experienced by each commuter on a daily basis; (1) Covers the Jacksonville FL urban area; (2) Rank is based on 101 urban areas (#1 = highest travel time index); (3) Average of 101 urban areas
Source: Texas Transportation Institute, 2015 Urban Mobility Scorecard, August 2015

Public Transportation

Agency Name / Mode of Transportation	Vehicles Operated in Maximum Service[1]	Annual Unlinked Passenger Trips[2] (in thous.)	Annual Passenger Miles[3] (in thous.)
Jacksonville Transportation Authority (JTA)			
Bus (directly operated)	153	10,794.8	64,694.2
Demand Response (purchased transportation)	89	368.6	4,396.2
Ferryboat (purchased transportation)	1	442.0	198.9
Monorail and Automated Guideway (directly operated)	5	1,053.6	748.1

Note: (1) The number of revenue vehicles operated by the given mode and type of service to meet the annual maximum service requirement. This is the revenue vehicle count during the peak season of the year; on the week and day that maximum service is provided. Vehicles operated in maximum service (VOMS) exclude atypical days and one-time special events; (2) The number of passengers who boarded public transportation vehicles. Passengers are counted each time they board a vehicle no matter how many vehicles they use to travel from their origin to their destination. (3) The sum of the distances ridden by all passengers during the entire fiscal year.
Source: Federal Transit Administration, National Transit Database, 2017

Air Transportation

Airport Name and Code / Type of Service	Passenger Airlines[1]	Passenger Enplanements	Freight Carriers[2]	Freight (lbs)
Jacksonville International (JAX)				
Domestic service (U.S. carriers - 2018)	31	3,118,835	10	81,512,647
International service (U.S. carriers - 2017)	4	768	0	0

Note: (1) Includes all U.S.-based major, minor and commuter airlines that carried at least one passenger during the year; (2) Includes all U.S.-based airlines and freight carriers that transported at least one pound of freight during the year.
Source: Bureau of Transportation Statistics, The Intermodal Transportation Database, Air Carriers: T-100 Domestic Market (U.S. Carriers), 2018; Bureau of Transportation Statistics, The Intermodal Transportation Database, Air Carriers: T-100 International Market (U.S. Carriers), 2017

Other Transportation Statistics

Major Highways:	I-10; I-95
Amtrak Service:	Yes
Major Waterways/Ports:	St. Johns River

Source: Amtrak.com; Google Maps

BUSINESSES

Major Business Headquarters

Company Name	Industry	Rankings Fortune[1]	Rankings Forbes[2]
CSX	Railroads	265	-
Fidelity National Financial	Insurance: Property and Casualty (Stock)	302	-
Fidelity National Information Svcs	Financial Data Services	326	-
Southeastern Grocer	Food Markets	-	35

Note: (1) Companies that produce a 10-K are ranked 1 to 500 based on 2017 revenue; (2) All private companies with at least $2 billion in annual revenue through the end of their most current fiscal year are ranked 1 to 229; companies listed are headquartered in the city; dashes indicate no ranking
Source: Fortune, "Fortune 500," June 2018; Forbes, "America's Largest Private Companies," 2018 Rankings

Fast-Growing Businesses

According to *Inc.*, Jacksonville is home to two of America's 500 fastest-growing private companies: **Live Oak Contracting** (#34); **Natural Force** (#431). Criteria: must be an independent, privately-held, for-profit, U.S. corporation, proprietorship or partnership as of December 31, 2017; revenues must be at least $100,000 in 2014 and $2 million in 2017; must have four-year operating/sales history. Holding companies, regulated banks, and utilities were excluded.
Inc., "America's 500 Fastest-Growing Private Companies," 2018

Minority Business Opportunity

Jacksonville is home to one company which is on the *Black Enterprise* Industrial/Service list (100 largest companies based on gross sales): **Raven Transport Co.** (#44). Criteria: operational in previous calendar year; at least 51% black-owned and manufactures/owns the product it sells or provides industrial or consumer services. Brokerages, real estate firms and firms that provide professional services are not eligible. *Black Enterprise, B.E. 100s, 2018*

Jacksonville is home to one company which is on the *Hispanic Business* 500 list (500 largest U.S. Hispanic-owned companies based on revenue): **Information and Computing Services** (#209). Companies included must show at least 51 percent ownership by Hispanic U.S. citizens, and must maintain headquarters in one of the 50 states or Washington, D.C. *Hispanic Business, "Hispanic Business 500," June 20, 2013*

Minority- and Women-Owned Businesses

Group	All Firms		Firms with Paid Employees			
	Firms	Sales ($000)	Firms	Sales ($000)	Employees	Payroll ($000)
AIAN[1]	527	(s)	52	(s)	1,000 - 2,499	(s)
Asian	4,460	943,211	1,191	820,008	7,226	197,858
Black	17,939	580,334	648	315,498	4,127	95,641
Hispanic	5,030	1,223,856	644	1,103,230	8,337	282,348
NHOPI[2]	78	28,037	13	27,486	67	4,042
Women	28,749	2,839,305	2,979	2,393,722	19,574	623,320
All Firms	70,192	124,233,951	16,342	122,429,627	437,619	21,663,014

Note: Figures cover firms located in the city; minority- and women-owned business are defined as firms in which the corresponding group own 51% or more of the stock or equity of the company; (1) American Indian and Alaska Native; (2) Native Hawaiian and Other Pacific Islander; (s) estimates are suppressed when publication standards are not met
Source: U.S. Census Bureau, 2012 Economic Census, Survey of Business Owners

HOTELS & CONVENTION CENTERS

Hotels, Motels and Vacation Rentals

Area	5 Star		4 Star		3 Star		2 Star		1 Star		Not Rated	
	Num.	Pct.[3]	Num.	Pct.[3]	Num.	Pct.[3]	Num.	Pct.[3]	Num.	Pct.[3]	Num.	Pct.[3]
City[1]	3	0.3	49	4.8	228	22.4	112	11.0	5	0.5	620	61.0
Total[2]	286	0.4	5,236	7.1	16,715	22.6	10,259	13.9	293	0.4	41,056	55.6

Note: (1) Figures cover Jacksonville and vicinity; (2) Figures cover all 100 cities in this book; (3) Percentage of hotels which have a given star rating; Star ratings are determined by expedia.com and offer an indication of the general quality of a particular hotel.
Source: www.expedia.com, April 3, 2019

Major Convention Centers

Name	Overall Space (sq. ft.)	Exhibit Space (sq. ft.)	Meeting Space (sq. ft.)	Meeting Rooms
Prime F. Osborn III Convention Center	296,000	100,000	48,000	22

Note: Table includes convention centers located in the Jacksonville, FL metro area
Source: Original research

Living Environment

COST OF LIVING

Cost of Living Index

Composite Index	Groceries	Housing	Utilities	Trans-portation	Health Care	Misc. Goods/ Services
92.0	98.2	86.4	97.4	87.4	82.9	95.2

Note: The Cost of Living Index measures regional differences in the cost of consumer goods and services, excluding taxes and non-consumer expenditures, for professional and managerial households in the top income quintile. It is based on more than 50,000 prices covering almost 60 different items for which prices are collected three times a year by chambers of commerce, economic development organizations or university applied economic centers in each participating urban area. The numbers shown should be read as a percentage above or below the national average of 100. For example, a value of 115.4 in the groceries column indicates that grocery prices are 15.4% higher than the national average. Small differences in the index numbers should not be interpreted as significant; Figures cover the Jacksonville FL urban area.
Source: The Council for Community and Economic Research, ACCRA Cost of Living Index, 2018

Grocery Prices

Area[1]	T-Bone Steak ($/pound)	Frying Chicken ($/pound)	Whole Milk ($/half gal.)	Eggs ($/dozen)	Orange Juice ($/64 oz.)	Coffee ($/11.5 oz.)
City[2]	11.17	1.39	2.42	2.21	3.27	3.86
Avg.	11.35	1.42	1.94	1.81	3.52	4.35
Min.	7.45	0.92	0.80	0.75	2.72	3.06
Max.	15.05	2.76	4.18	4.00	5.36	8.20

*Note: (1) Values for the local area are compared with the average, minimum and maximum values for all 291 areas in the Cost of Living Index; (2) Figures cover the Jacksonville FL urban area; **T-Bone Steak** (price per pound); **Frying Chicken** (price per pound, whole fryer); **Whole Milk** (half gallon carton); **Eggs** (price per dozen, Grade A, large); **Orange Juice** (64 oz. Tropicana or Florida Natural); **Coffee** (11.5 oz. can, vacuum-packed, Maxwell House, Hills Bros, or Folgers).*
Source: The Council for Community and Economic Research, ACCRA Cost of Living Index, 2018

Housing and Utility Costs

Area[1]	New Home Price ($)	Apartment Rent ($/month)	All Electric ($/month)	Part Electric ($/month)	Other Energy ($/month)	Telephone ($/month)
City[2]	262,790	1,244	156.94	-	-	182.70
Avg.	347,000	1,087	165.93	100.16	67.73	178.70
Min.	200,468	500	93.58	25.64	26.78	163.10
Max.	1,901,222	4,888	388.65	246.86	332.81	197.70

*Note: (1) Values for the local area are compared with the average, minimum and maximum values for all 291 areas in the Cost of Living Index; (2) Figures cover the Jacksonville FL urban area; **New Home Price** (2,400 sf living area, 8,000 sf lot, in urban area with full utilities); **Apartment Rent** (950 sf 2 bedroom/1.5 or 2 bath, unfurnished, excluding all utilities except water); **All Electric** (average monthly cost for an all-electric home); **Part Electric** (average monthly cost for a part-electric home); **Other Energy** (average monthly cost for natural gas, fuel oil, coal, wood, and any other forms of energy except electricity); **Telephone** (price includes the base monthly rate plus taxes and fees for three lines of mobile phone service).*
Source: The Council for Community and Economic Research, ACCRA Cost of Living Index, 2018

Health Care, Transportation, and Other Costs

Area[1]	Doctor ($/visit)	Dentist ($/visit)	Optometrist ($/visit)	Gasoline ($/gallon)	Beauty Salon ($/visit)	Men's Shirt ($)
City[2]	62.89	89.40	65.58	2.51	52.72	24.03
Avg.	110.71	95.11	103.74	2.61	37.48	32.03
Min.	33.60	62.55	54.63	1.89	17.00	11.44
Max.	195.97	153.93	225.79	3.59	71.88	58.64

*Note: (1) Values for the local area are compared with the average, minimum and maximum values for all 291 areas in the Cost of Living Index; (2) Figures cover the Jacksonville FL urban area; **Doctor** (general practitioners routine exam of an established patient); **Dentist** (adult teeth cleaning and periodic oral examination); **Optometrist** (full vision eye exam for established adult patient); **Gasoline** (one gallon regular unleaded, national brand, including all taxes, cash price at self-service pump if available); **Beauty Salon** (woman's shampoo, trim, and blow-dry); **Men's Shirt** (cotton/polyester dress shirt, pinpoint weave, long sleeves).*
Source: The Council for Community and Economic Research, ACCRA Cost of Living Index, 2018

HOUSING

House Price Index (HPI)

Area	National Ranking[2]	Quarterly Change (%)	One-Year Change (%)	Five-Year Change (%)
MSA[1]	100	0.05	6.78	47.34
U.S.[3]	—	1.12	5.73	32.81

Note: The HPI is a weighted repeat sales index. It measures average price changes in repeat sales or refinancings on the same properties. This information is obtained by reviewing repeat mortgage transactions on single-family properties whose mortgages have been purchased or securitized by Fannie Mae or Freddie Mac in January 1975; (1) Figures cover the Jacksonville, FL Metropolitan Statistical Area—see Appendix B for areas included; (2) Rankings are based on annual percentage change for all metro areas containing at least 15,000 transactions over the last 10 years and ranges from 1 to 245; (3) figures based on a weighted average of Census Division estimates using a seasonally adjusted, purchase-only index; all figures are for the period ending December 31, 2018
Source: Federal Housing Finance Agency, House Price Index, February 26, 2019

Median Single-Family Home Prices

Area	2016	2017	2018[p]	Percent Change 2017 to 2018
MSA[1]	211.0	228.9	247.0	7.9
U.S. Average	235.5	248.8	261.6	5.1

Note: Figures are median sales prices of existing single-family homes in thousands of dollars; (p) preliminary; (1) Figures cover the Jacksonville, FL Metropolitan Statistical Area—see Appendix B for areas included
Source: National Association of Realtors, Median Sales Price of Existing Single-Family Homes for Metropolitan Areas, 4th Quarter 2018

Qualifying Income Based on Median Sales Price of Existing Single-Family Homes

Area	With 5% Down ($)	With 10% Down ($)	With 20% Down ($)
MSA[1]	60,339	57,163	50,811
U.S. Average	62,954	59,640	53,013

Note: Figures are preliminary; Qualifying income is based on a mortgage rate of 4.9%. Monthly principal and interest payment is limited to 25% of income; (1) Figures cover the Jacksonville, FL Metropolitan Statistical Area—see Appendix B for areas included
Source: National Association of Realtors, Qualifying Income Based on Median Sales Price of Existing Single-Family Homes for Metropolitan Areas, 4th Quarter 2018

Median Apartment Condo-Coop Home Prices

Area	2016	2017	2018[p]	Percent Change 2017 to 2018
MSA[1]	138.0	152.0	162.0	6.6
U.S. Average	220.7	234.3	241.0	2.9

Note: Figures are median sales prices of existing apartment condo-coop homes in thousands of dollars; (p) preliminary; (1) Figures cover the Jacksonville, FL Metropolitan Statistical Area—see Appendix B for areas included
Source: National Association of Realtors, Median Sales Price of Existing Apartment Condo-Coop Homes for Metropolitan Areas, 4th Quarter 2018

Home Value Distribution

Area	Under $50,000	$50,000 -$99,999	$100,000 -$149,999	$150,000 -$199,999	$200,000 -$299,999	$300,000 -$499,999	$500,000 -$999,999	$1,000,000 or more
City	9.4	20.2	20.4	18.0	18.9	9.1	3.1	1.0
MSA[1]	7.4	16.0	17.3	16.9	21.2	14.2	5.4	1.6
U.S.	8.3	13.9	14.7	14.6	18.7	17.3	9.7	2.7

Note: Figures are percentages and cover owner-occupied housing units; (1) Figures cover the Jacksonville, FL Metropolitan Statistical Area—see Appendix B for areas included
Source: U.S. Census Bureau, 2013-2017 American Community Survey 5-Year Estimates

Homeownership Rate

Area	2010 (%)	2011 (%)	2012 (%)	2013 (%)	2014 (%)	2015 (%)	2016 (%)	2017 (%)	2018 (%)
MSA[1]	70.0	68.0	66.6	69.9	65.3	62.5	61.8	65.2	61.4
U.S.	66.9	66.1	65.4	65.1	64.5	63.7	63.4	63.9	64.4

Note: (1) Figures cover the Jacksonville, FL Metropolitan Statistical Area—see Appendix B for areas included
Source: U.S. Census Bureau, Housing Vacancies and Homeownership Annual Statistics: 2010-2018

Year Housing Structure Built

Area	2010 or Later	2000 -2009	1990 -1999	1980 -1989	1970 -1979	1960 -1969	1950 -1959	1940 -1949	Before 1940	Median Year
City	3.9	19.7	15.1	15.8	13.1	10.7	11.3	5.1	5.3	1983
MSA[1]	5.2	23.5	16.7	17.3	12.8	8.6	8.2	3.6	4.1	1987
U.S.	3.2	14.5	14.0	13.6	15.5	10.8	10.5	5.1	12.9	1977

Note: Figures are percentages except for Median Year; Note: (1) Figures cover the Jacksonville, FL Metropolitan Statistical Area—see Appendix B for areas included
Source: U.S. Census Bureau, 2013-2017 American Community Survey 5-Year Estimates

Gross Monthly Rent

Area	Under $500	$500 -$999	$1,000 -$1,499	$1,500 -$1,999	$2,000 -$2,499	$2,500 -$2,999	$3,000 and up	Median ($)
City	7.0	44.9	37.6	8.2	1.6	0.4	0.3	984
MSA[1]	6.1	42.2	37.7	10.5	2.4	0.6	0.5	1,019
U.S.	10.5	41.1	28.7	11.7	4.5	1.8	1.7	982

Note: Figures are percentages except for Median; Gross rent is the contract rent plus the estimated average monthly cost of utilities (electricity, gas, and water and sewer) and fuels (oil, coal, kerosene, wood, etc.) if these are paid by the renter (or paid for the renter by someone else); (1) Figures cover the Jacksonville, FL Metropolitan Statistical Area—see Appendix B for areas included
Source: U.S. Census Bureau, 2013-2017 American Community Survey 5-Year Estimates

HEALTH

Health Risk Factors

Category	MSA[1] (%)	U.S. (%)
Adults aged 18–64 who have any kind of health care coverage	85.9	87.3
Adults who reported being in good or better health	78.0	82.4
Adults who have been told they have high blood cholesterol	34.1	33.0
Adults who have been told they have high blood pressure	36.1	32.3
Adults who are current smokers	18.4	17.1
Adults who currently use E-cigarettes	3.6	4.6
Adults who currently use chewing tobacco, snuff, or snus	3.4	4.0
Adults who are heavy drinkers[2]	6.6	6.3
Adults who are binge drinkers[3]	17.3	17.4
Adults who are overweight (BMI 25.0 - 29.9)	33.5	35.3
Adults who are obese (BMI 30.0 - 99.8)	33.2	31.3
Adults who participated in any physical activities in the past month	70.3	74.4
Adults who always or nearly always wears a seat belt	95.3	94.3

Note: (1) Figures cover the Jacksonville, FL Metropolitan Statistical Area—see Appendix B for areas included; (2) Heavy drinkers are classified as adult men having more than 14 drinks per week and adult women having more than 7 drinks per week; (3) Binge drinkers are classified as males having five or more drinks on one occasion or females having four or more drinks on one occasion
Source: Centers for Disease Control and Prevention, Behaviorial Risk Factor Surveillance System, SMART: Selected Metropolitan Area Risk Trends, 2017

Acute and Chronic Health Conditions

Category	MSA[1] (%)	U.S. (%)
Adults who have ever been told they had a heart attack	3.9	4.2
Adults who have ever been told they have angina or coronary heart disease	5.5	3.9
Adults who have ever been told they had a stroke	2.9	3.0
Adults who have ever been told they have asthma	16.2	14.2
Adults who have ever been told they have arthritis	27.7	24.9
Adults who have ever been told they have diabetes[2]	12.7	10.5
Adults who have ever been told they had skin cancer	8.8	6.2
Adults who have ever been told they had any other types of cancer	7.4	7.1
Adults who have ever been told they have COPD	11.3	6.5
Adults who have ever been told they have kidney disease	3.5	3.0
Adults who have ever been told they have a form of depression	22.5	20.5

Note: (1) Figures cover the Jacksonville, FL Metropolitan Statistical Area—see Appendix B for areas included; (2) Figures do not include pregnancy-related, borderline, or pre-diabetes
Source: Centers for Disease Control and Prevention, Behaviorial Risk Factor Surveillance System, SMART: Selected Metropolitan Area Risk Trends, 2017

Health Screening and Vaccination Rates

Category	MSA[1] (%)	U.S. (%)
Adults aged 65+ who have had flu shot within the past year	65.3	60.7
Adults aged 65+ who have ever had a pneumonia vaccination	74.1	75.4
Adults who have ever been tested for HIV	54.7	36.1
Adults who have ever had the shingles or zoster vaccine?	29.6	28.9
Adults who have had their blood cholesterol checked within the last five years	89.4	85.9

Note: n/a not available; (1) Figures cover the Jacksonville, FL Metropolitan Statistical Area—see Appendix B for areas included.
Source: Centers for Disease Control and Prevention, Behaviorial Risk Factor Surveillance System, SMART: Selected Metropolitan Area Risk Trends, 2017

Disability Status

Category	MSA[1] (%)	U.S. (%)
Adults who reported being deaf	7.1	6.7
Are you blind or have serious difficulty seeing, even when wearing glasses?	5.5	4.5
Are you limited in any way in any of your usual activities due of arthritis?	14.1	12.9
Do you have difficulty doing errands alone?	9.9	6.8
Do you have difficulty dressing or bathing?	4.1	3.6
Do you have serious difficulty concentrating/remembering/making decisions?	14.6	10.7
Do you have serious difficulty walking or climbing stairs?	17.2	13.6

Note: (1) Figures cover the Jacksonville, FL Metropolitan Statistical Area—see Appendix B for areas included.
Source: Centers for Disease Control and Prevention, Behaviorial Risk Factor Surveillance System, SMART: Selected Metropolitan Area Risk Trends, 2017

Mortality Rates for the Top 10 Causes of Death in the U.S.

ICD-10[a] Sub-Chapter	ICD-10[a] Code	Age-Adjusted Mortality Rate[1] per 100,000 population	
		County[2]	U.S.
Malignant neoplasms	C00-C97	170.3	155.5
Ischaemic heart diseases	I20-I25	97.4	94.8
Other forms of heart disease	I30-I51	48.3	52.9
Chronic lower respiratory diseases	J40-J47	44.5	41.0
Cerebrovascular diseases	I60-I69	46.0	37.5
Other degenerative diseases of the nervous system	G30-G31	27.3	35.0
Other external causes of accidental injury	W00-X59	54.1	33.7
Organic, including symptomatic, mental disorders	F01-F09	46.5	31.0
Hypertensive diseases	I10-I15	30.2	21.9
Diabetes mellitus	E10-E14	24.5	21.2

Note: (a) ICD-10 = International Classification of Diseases 10th Revision; (1) Mortality rates are a three year average covering 2015-2017; (2) Figures cover Duval County.
Source: Centers for Disease Control and Prevention, National Center for Health Statistics. Underlying Cause of Death 1999-2017 on CDC WONDER Online Database

Mortality Rates for Selected Causes of Death

ICD-10[a] Sub-Chapter	ICD-10[a] Code	Age-Adjusted Mortality Rate[1] per 100,000 population	
		County[2]	U.S.
Assault	X85-Y09	13.0	5.9
Diseases of the liver	K70-K76	16.8	14.1
Human immunodeficiency virus (HIV) disease	B20-B24	5.9	1.8
Influenza and pneumonia	J09-J18	15.5	14.3
Intentional self-harm	X60-X84	15.7	13.6
Malnutrition	E40-E46	2.7	1.6
Obesity and other hyperalimentation	E65-E68	2.0	2.1
Renal failure	N17-N19	12.7	13.0
Transport accidents	V01-V99	15.8	12.4
Viral hepatitis	B15-B19	2.6	1.6

Note: (a) ICD-10 = International Classification of Diseases 10th Revision; (1) Mortality rates are a three year average covering 2015-2017; (2) Figures cover Duval County; Data are suppressed when the data meet the criteria for confidentiality constraints; Mortality rates are flagged as unreliable when the rate would be calculated with a numerator of 20 or less.
Source: Centers for Disease Control and Prevention, National Center for Health Statistics. Underlying Cause of Death 1999-2017 on CDC WONDER Online Database

Health Insurance Coverage

Area	With Health Insurance	With Private Health Insurance	With Public Health Insurance	Without Health Insurance	Population Under Age 18 Without Health Insurance
City	87.0	64.0	33.6	13.0	7.0
MSA[1]	88.1	67.8	32.3	11.9	6.8
U.S.	89.5	67.2	33.8	10.5	5.7

Note: Figures are percentages that cover the civilian noninstitutionalized population; (1) Figures cover the Jacksonville, FL Metropolitan Statistical Area—see Appendix B for areas included
Source: U.S. Census Bureau, 2013-2017 American Community Survey 5-Year Estimates

Number of Medical Professionals

Area	MDs[3]	DOs[3,4]	Dentists	Podiatrists	Chiropractors	Optometrists
County[1] (number)	3,239	213	764	80	220	149
County[1] (rate[2])	349.6	23.0	81.5	8.5	23.5	15.9
U.S. (rate[2])	279.3	23.0	68.4	6.0	27.1	16.2

Note: Data as of 2017 unless noted; (1) Data covers Duval County; (2) Rate per 100,000 population; (3) Data as of 2016 and includes all active, non-federal physicians; (4) Doctor of Osteopathic Medicine
Source: U.S. Department of Health and Human Services, Health Resources and Services Administration, Bureau of Health Professions, Area Resource File (ARF) 2017-2018

Best Hospitals

According to *U.S. News,* the Jacksonville, FL metro area is home to two of the best hospitals in the U.S.: **Flagler Hospital** (1 adult specialty); **Mayo Clinic Jacksonville** (6 adult specialties). The hospitals listed were nationally ranked in at least one of 16 adult or 10 pediatric specialties. Only 170 hospitals nationwide were nationally ranked in one or more adult or pediatric specialty. Twenty hospitals in the U.S. made the Honor Roll. The Best Hospitals Honor Roll takes both the national rankings and the procedure and condition ratings into account. Hospitals received points if they were nationally ranked in one of the 16 adult specialties—the higher they ranked, the more points they got—and how many ratings of "high performing" they earned in the nine procedures and conditions. *U.S. News Online, "America's Best Hospitals 2018-19"*

According to *U.S. News,* the Jacksonville, FL metro area is home to one of the best children's hospitals in the U.S.: **Wolfson Children's Hospital** (2 pediatric specialties). The hospital listed was highly ranked in at least one of 10 pediatric specialties. Eighty-six children's hospitals in the U.S. were nationally ranked in at least one specialty. Hospitals received points for being ranked in a specialty, and the 10 hospitals with the most points across the 10 specialties make up the Honor Roll. *U.S. News Online, "America's Best Children's Hospitals 2018-19"*

EDUCATION

Public School District Statistics

District Name	Schls	Pupils	Pupil/ Teacher Ratio	Minority Pupils[1] (%)	Free Lunch Eligible[2] (%)	IEP[3] (%)
Duval County Public Schools	209	129,479	17.8	64.8	50.3	13.9

Note: Table includes school districts with 2,000 or more students; (1) Percentage of students that are not non-Hispanic white; (2) Percentage of students that are eligible for the free lunch program; (3) Percentage of students that have an Individualized Education Program.
Source: U.S. Department of Education, National Center for Education Statistics, Common Core of Data, Local Education Agency (School District) Universe Survey: School Year 2016-2017; U.S. Department of Education, National Center for Education Statistics, Common Core of Data, Public Elementary/Secondary School Universe Survey: School Year 2016-2017

Best High Schools

According to *U.S. News,* Jacksonville is home to four of the best high schools in the U.S.: **Stanton College Preparatory School** (#28); **Paxon School/Advanced Studies** (#120); **Darnell Cookman Middle/High School** (#190); **Douglas Anderson School of the Arts** (#226). More than 20,000 public, magnet and charter schools were ranked based on their performance on state assessments and how well they prepare students for college. Schools with the highest unrounded College Readiness Index values were numerically ranked from 1 to 500 and were classified as gold medal winners. *U.S. News & World Report, "Best High Schools 2018"*

Highest Level of Education

Area	Less than H.S.	H.S. Diploma	Some College, No Deg.	Associate Degree	Bachelor's Degree	Master's Degree	Prof. School Degree	Doctorate Degree
City	11.0	28.4	22.9	10.1	18.8	6.3	1.6	0.7
MSA[1]	9.6	27.8	22.7	10.0	20.0	7.2	1.8	0.9
U.S.	12.7	27.3	20.8	8.3	19.1	8.4	2.0	1.4

Note: Figures cover persons age 25 and over; (1) Figures cover the Jacksonville, FL Metropolitan Statistical Area—see Appendix B for areas included
Source: U.S. Census Bureau, 2013-2017 American Community Survey 5-Year Estimates

Educational Attainment by Race

Area	High School Graduate or Higher (%)					Bachelor's Degree or Higher (%)				
	Total	White	Black	Asian	Hisp.[2]	Total	White	Black	Asian	Hisp.[2]
City	89.0	90.7	86.2	84.9	82.5	27.5	30.4	17.7	46.2	24.0
MSA[1]	90.4	91.9	86.4	86.8	84.4	29.9	32.1	18.2	48.7	26.6
U.S.	87.3	89.3	84.9	86.5	66.7	30.9	32.2	20.6	52.7	15.2

Note: Figures shown cover persons 25 years old and over; (1) Figures cover the Jacksonville, FL Metropolitan Statistical Area—see Appendix B for areas included; (2) People of Hispanic origin can be of any race
Source: U.S. Census Bureau, 2013-2017 American Community Survey 5-Year Estimates

School Enrollment by Grade and Control

Area	Preschool (%)		Kindergarten (%)		Grades 1 - 4 (%)		Grades 5 - 8 (%)		Grades 9 - 12 (%)	
	Public	Private	Public	Private	Public	Private	Public	Private	Public	Private
City	58.4	41.6	83.3	16.7	83.6	16.4	81.7	18.3	83.4	16.6
MSA[1]	53.9	46.1	84.9	15.1	86.0	14.0	84.3	15.7	86.1	13.9
U.S.	58.8	41.2	87.7	12.3	89.7	10.3	89.6	10.4	90.3	9.7

Note: Figures shown cover persons 3 years old and over; (1) Figures cover the Jacksonville, FL Metropolitan Statistical Area—see Appendix B for areas included
Source: U.S. Census Bureau, 2013-2017 American Community Survey 5-Year Estimates

Average Salaries of Public School Classroom Teachers

Area	2016		2017		Change from 2016 to 2017	
	Dollars	Rank[1]	Dollars	Rank[1]	Percent	Rank[2]
Florida	46,612	46	47,267	45	1.4	26
U.S. Average	58,479	–	59,660	–	2.0	–

Note: (1) Rank ranges from 1 to 51 where 1 indicates highest salary; (2) Rank ranges from 1 to 51 where 1 indicates highest percent change.
Source: National Education Association, Rankings & Estimates: Rankings of the States 2017 and Estimates of School Statistics 2018

Higher Education

Four-Year Colleges			Two-Year Colleges			Medical Schools[1]	Law Schools[2]	Voc/ Tech[3]
Public	Private Non-profit	Private For-profit	Public	Private Non-profit	Private For-profit			
2	3	2	0	1	3	0	1	10

Note: Figures cover institutions located within the city limits and include main campuses only; (1) includes schools accredited by the Liaison Committee on Medical Education and the American Osteopathic Association's Commission on Osteopathic College Accreditation; (2) includes ABA-accredited schools, schools with provisional ABA accreditation, and state accredited schools; (3) includes all schools with programs that are less than 2 years.
Source: National Center for Education Statistics, Integrated Postsecondary Education System (IPEDS), 2017-18; Wikipedia, List of Medical Schools in the United States, accessed April 3, 2019; Wikipedia, List of Law Schools in the United States, accessed April 3, 2019

PRESIDENTIAL ELECTION

2016 Presidential Election Results

Area	Clinton	Trump	Johnson	Stein	Other
Duval County	47.1	48.5	2.6	0.7	1.1
U.S.	48.0	45.9	3.3	1.1	1.7

Note: Results are percentages and may not add to 100% due to rounding
Source: Dave Leip's Atlas of U.S. Presidential Elections

EMPLOYERS

Major Employers

Company Name	Industry
Bank of America, Merrill Lynch	Financial services
Baptist Health	Healthcare
Citi	Financial services
Fleet Readiness Center SE	Aviation & aerospace
Florida Blue	Financial services
Mayo Clinic	Healthcare
Mayo Clinic	Information technology
St. Vincent's Medical Center - Riverside	Healthcare
UF Health	Healthcare

Note: Companies shown are located within the Jacksonville, FL Metropolitan Statistical Area.
Source: Hoovers.com; Wikipedia

PUBLIC SAFETY

Crime Rate

Area	All Crimes	Violent Crimes				Property Crimes		
		Murder	Rape[3]	Robbery	Aggrav. Assault	Burglary	Larceny -Theft	Motor Vehicle Theft
City	4,158.0	12.2	60.1	153.8	405.2	631.1	2,568.6	326.9
Suburbs[1]	1,941.0	2.3	30.5	36.7	191.1	329.9	1,239.0	111.7
Metro[2]	3,258.4	8.2	48.1	106.3	318.3	508.9	2,029.1	239.6
U.S.	2,756.1	5.3	41.7	98.0	248.9	430.4	1,694.4	237.4

Note: Figures are crimes per 100,000 population; (1) All areas within the metro area that are located outside the city limits; (2) Figures cover the Jacksonville, FL Metropolitan Statistical Area—see Appendix B for areas included; (3) The city and U.S. figures shown were reported using the revised Uniform Crime Reporting (UCR) definition of rape. The suburban and metro area figures shown are an aggregate total of the data submitted using both the revised and legacy UCR definitions.
Source: FBI Uniform Crime Reports, 2017

Hate Crimes

Area	Number of Quarters Reported	Number of Incidents per Bias Motivation					
		Race/Ethnicity/ Ancestry	Religion	Sexual Orientation	Disability	Gender	Gender Identity
City	4	3	2	1	0	0	0
U.S.	4	4,131	1,564	1,130	116	46	119

Source: Federal Bureau of Investigation, Hate Crime Statistics 2017

Identity Theft Consumer Reports

Area	Reports	Reports per 100,000 Population	Rank[2]
MSA[1]	2,204	149	34
U.S.	444,602	135	-

Note: (1) Figures cover the Jacksonville, FL Metropolitan Statistical Area—see Appendix B for areas included; (2) Rank ranges from 1 to 389 where 1 indicates greatest number of identity theft reports per 100,000 population
Source: Federal Trade Commission, Consumer Sentinel Network Data Book for January–December 2018

Fraud and Other Consumer Reports

Area	Reports	Reports per 100,000 Population	Rank[2]
MSA[1]	12,502	846	3
U.S.	2,552,917	776	-

Note: (1) Figures cover the Jacksonville, FL Metropolitan Statistical Area—see Appendix B for areas included; (2) Rank ranges from 1 to 389 where 1 indicates greatest number of fraud and other consumer reports per 100,000 population
Source: Federal Trade Commission, Consumer Sentinel Network Data Book for January–December 2018

SPORTS

Professional Sports Teams

Team Name	League	Year Established
Jacksonville Jaguars	National Football League (NFL)	1995

Note: Includes teams located in the Jacksonville, FL Metropolitan Statistical Area.
Source: Wikipedia, Major Professional Sports Teams of the United States and Canada, April 5, 2019

CLIMATE

Average and Extreme Temperatures

Temperature	Jan	Feb	Mar	Apr	May	Jun	Jul	Aug	Sep	Oct	Nov	Dec	Yr.
Extreme High (°F)	84	88	91	95	100	103	103	102	98	96	88	84	103
Average High (°F)	65	68	74	80	86	90	92	91	87	80	73	67	79
Average Temp. (°F)	54	57	62	69	75	80	83	82	79	71	62	56	69
Average Low (°F)	43	45	51	57	64	70	73	73	70	61	51	44	58
Extreme Low (°F)	7	22	23	34	45	47	61	63	48	36	21	11	7

Note: Figures cover the years 1948-1990
Source: National Climatic Data Center, International Station Meteorological Climate Summary, 9/96

Average Precipitation/Snowfall/Humidity

Precip./Humidity	Jan	Feb	Mar	Apr	May	Jun	Jul	Aug	Sep	Oct	Nov	Dec	Yr.
Avg. Precip. (in.)	3.0	3.7	3.8	3.0	3.6	5.3	6.2	7.4	7.8	3.7	2.0	2.6	52.0
Avg. Snowfall (in.)	Tr	Tr	Tr	0	0	0	0	0	0	0	0	Tr	0
Avg. Rel. Hum. 7am (%)	86	86	87	86	86	88	89	91	92	91	89	88	88
Avg. Rel. Hum. 4pm (%)	56	53	'50	49	54	61	64	65	66	62	58	58	58

Note: Figures cover the years 1948-1990; Tr = Trace amounts (<0.05 in. of rain; <0.5 in. of snow)
Source: National Climatic Data Center, International Station Meteorological Climate Summary, 9/96

Weather Conditions

Temperature			Daytime Sky			Precipitation		
10°F & below	32°F & below	90°F & above	Clear	Partly cloudy	Cloudy	0.01 inch or more precip.	0.1 inch or more snow/ice	Thunder-storms
< 1	16	83	86	181	98	114	1	65

Note: Figures are average number of days per year and cover the years 1948-1990
Source: National Climatic Data Center, International Station Meteorological Climate Summary, 9/96

HAZARDOUS WASTE

Superfund Sites

The Jacksonville, FL metro area is home to five sites on the EPA's Superfund National Priorities List: **Fairfax Saint Wood Treaters** (final); **Jacksonville Naval Air Station** (final); **Kerr-Mcgee Chemical Corp - Jacksonville** (final); **Pickettville Road Landfill** (final); **Usn Air Station Cecil Field** (final). There are a total of 1,390 Superfund sites with a status of proposed or final on the list in the U.S. *U.S. Environmental Protection Agency, National Priorities List, April 5, 2019*

AIR & WATER QUALITY

Air Quality Trends: Ozone

	1990	1995	2000	2005	2010	2012	2014	2015	2016	2017
MSA[1]	0.080	0.068	0.072	0.076	0.068	0.059	0.062	0.060	0.057	0.059
U.S.	0.088	0.089	0.082	0.080	0.073	0.075	0.067	0.068	0.069	0.068

Note: (1) Data covers the Jacksonville, FL Metropolitan Statistical Area—see Appendix B for areas included. The values shown are the composite ozone concentration averages among trend sites based on the highest fourth daily maximum 8-hour concentration in parts per million. These trends are based on sites having an adequate record of monitoring data during the trend period. Data from exceptional events are included. Source: U.S. Environmental Protection Agency, Air Quality Monitoring Information, "Air Quality Trends by City, 1990-2017"

Air Quality Index

Area	Percent of Days when Air Quality was...[2]					AQI Statistics[2]	
	Good	Moderate	Unhealthy for Sensitive Groups	Unhealthy	Very Unhealthy	Maximum	Median
MSA[1]	74.2	25.5	0.3	0.0	0.0	101	42

Note: (1) Data covers the Jacksonville, FL Metropolitan Statistical Area—see Appendix B for areas included; (2) Based on 365 days with AQI data in 2017. Air Quality Index (AQI) is an index for reporting daily air quality. EPA calculates the AQI for five major air pollutants regulated by the Clean Air Act: ground-level ozone, particle pollution (aka particulate matter), carbon monoxide, sulfur dioxide, and nitrogen dioxide. The AQI runs from 0 to 500. The higher the AQI value, the greater the level of air pollution and the greater the health concern. There are six AQI categories: "Good" AQI is between 0 and 50. Air quality is considered satisfactory; "Moderate" AQI is between 51 and 100. Air quality is acceptable; "Unhealthy for Sensitive Groups" When AQI values are between 101 and 150, members of sensitive groups may experience health effects; "Unhealthy" When AQI values are between 151 and 200 everyone may begin to experience health effects; "Very Unhealthy" AQI values between 201 and 300 trigger a health alert; "Hazardous" AQI values over 300 trigger warnings of emergency conditions (not shown).
Source: U.S. Environmental Protection Agency, Air Quality Index Report, 2017

Air Quality Index Pollutants

Area	Percent of Days when AQI Pollutant was...[2]					
	Carbon Monoxide	Nitrogen Dioxide	Ozone	Sulfur Dioxide	Particulate Matter 2.5	Particulate Matter 10
MSA[1]	0.3	0.8	51.8	1.9	45.2	0.0

Note: (1) Data covers the Jacksonville, FL Metropolitan Statistical Area—see Appendix B for areas included; (2) Based on 365 days with AQI data in 2017. The Air Quality Index (AQI) is an index for reporting daily air quality. EPA calculates the AQI for five major air pollutants regulated by the Clean Air Act: ground-level ozone, particle pollution (also known as particulate matter), carbon monoxide, sulfur dioxide, and nitrogen dioxide. The AQI runs from 0 to 500. The higher the AQI value, the greater the level of air pollution and the greater the health concern.
Source: U.S. Environmental Protection Agency, Air Quality Index Report, 2017

Maximum Air Pollutant Concentrations: Particulate Matter, Ozone, CO and Lead

	Particulate Matter 10 (ug/m^3)	Particulate Matter 2.5 Wtd AM (ug/m^3)	Particulate Matter 2.5 24-Hr (ug/m^3)	Ozone (ppm)	Carbon Monoxide (ppm)	Lead (ug/m^3)
MSA[1] Level	51	n/a	n/a	0.062	1	n/a
NAAQS[2]	150	15	35	0.075	9	0.15
Met NAAQS[2]	Yes	n/a	n/a	Yes	Yes	n/a

Note: (1) Data covers the Jacksonville, FL Metropolitan Statistical Area—see Appendix B for areas included; Data from exceptional events are included; (2) National Ambient Air Quality Standards; ppm = parts per million; ug/m^3 = micrograms per cubic meter; n/a not available.
Concentrations: Particulate Matter 10 (coarse particulate)—highest second maximum 24-hour concentration; Particulate Matter 2.5 Wtd AM (fine particulate)—highest weighted annual mean concentration; Particulate Matter 2.5 24-Hour (fine particulate)—highest 98th percentile 24-hour concentration; Ozone—highest fourth daily maximum 8-hour concentration; Carbon Monoxide—highest second maximum non-overlapping 8-hour concentration; Lead—maximum running 3-month average
Source: U.S. Environmental Protection Agency, Air Quality Monitoring Information, "Air Quality Statistics by City, 2017"

Maximum Air Pollutant Concentrations: Nitrogen Dioxide and Sulfur Dioxide

	Nitrogen Dioxide AM (ppb)	Nitrogen Dioxide 1-Hr (ppb)	Sulfur Dioxide AM (ppb)	Sulfur Dioxide 1-Hr (ppb)	Sulfur Dioxide 24-Hr (ppb)
MSA[1] Level	11	35	n/a	32	n/a
NAAQS[2]	53	100	30	75	140
Met NAAQS[2]	Yes	Yes	n/a	Yes	n/a

Note: (1) Data covers the Jacksonville, FL Metropolitan Statistical Area—see Appendix B for areas included; Data from exceptional events are included; (2) National Ambient Air Quality Standards; ppm = parts per million; ug/m^3 = micrograms per cubic meter; n/a not available.
Concentrations: Nitrogen Dioxide AM—highest arithmetic mean concentration; Nitrogen Dioxide 1-Hr—highest 98th percentile 1-hour daily maximum concentration; Sulfur Dioxide AM—highest annual mean concentration; Sulfur Dioxide 1-Hr—highest 99th percentile 1-hour daily maximum concentration; Sulfur Dioxide 24-Hr—highest second maximum 24-hour concentration
Source: U.S. Environmental Protection Agency, Air Quality Monitoring Information, "Air Quality Statistics by City, 2017"

Drinking Water

Water System Name	Pop. Served	Primary Water Source Type	Violations[1]	
			Health Based	Monitoring/ Reporting
JEA Major Grid	739,834	Ground	0	1

Note: (1) Based on violation data from January 1, 2018 to December 31, 2018
Source: U.S. Environmental Protection Agency, Office of Ground Water and Drinking Water, Safe Drinking Water Information System (based on data extracted April 5, 2019)

Lafayette, Louisiana

Background

Lafayette's cultural origins originated far north of the city, to Nova Scotia, Canada. In 1755, the British governor, Charles Lawrence, expelled the entire population of Canadians known as the Acadians, whose roots were French and Catholic, when they refused to pledge loyalty to the British crown. Many lost their lives in their quest for a new home, as they settled all along the eastern seaboard of the United States. A large majority of Acadians settled in southern Louisiana, in the area surrounding New Orleans.

Prior to the Acadian expulsion, southern Louisiana had remained fairly unsettled. The first known inhabitants were the Attakapas, a much-feared and brutal tribe of Native Americans. A sparse population of French trappers, traders, and ranchers occupied the region until the Spanish occupation of 1766. The 1789 French Revolution brought teams of French immigrants fleeing the brutal conditions at home. In 1803, the French sold the Louisiana territory to the United States—a transaction known as the Louisiana Purchase.

The most important early event for Lafayette was the donation of land by an Acadian named Jean Mouton, to the Catholic Church. The population began to grow in the parish then known as St. John the Evangelist of Vermillion. Lafayette's original name was Vermillionville, but it was renamed in 1884 in honor of the French Marquis de Lafayette, a Frenchman who fought under General George Washington in the American Revolution. Lafayette has been credited with bringing some of the ideals of the American Revolution to the French, partly precipitating the French Revolution. By his death, Lafayette had visited all 24 of the United States, and was an American citizen.

The word "cajun," is derived from the early Acadian settlers. In French, "Les Acadians" became "le Cadiens," which later became just "'Cadien." The French pronunciation was difficult for non-French Americans to say, so Cadien became Cajun. A primary characteristic of the Acadian/Cajun culture is what's known as "joie de vivre"—joy of living. The Cajun reputation is one of hard work and hard play, full of passion that can turn on a dime. Their greatest contribution to the fabric of America has been their food and their music—both are decidedly spicy.

Geographically, Lafayette is about 40 miles north of the Gulf of Mexico, and 100 miles west of New Orleans. The city is often referred to as the center of Cajun culture not because of its geography, but because of the strong Cajun influence in everyday life. Celebration is a major part of the Cajun culture, and this is reflected in Lafayette's many festivals and cultural traditions. The most famous of dozens of annual festivals is Mari Gras. The Festival International de Louisiana celebrates the French-speaking heritage of much of the population. Festival Acadians celebrates everything that is uniquely Cajun.

While Lafayette is known for its oil and natural gas industries, with over 600 oil-related businesses in Lafayette Parish alone, jobs in healthcare are not far behind. Education is also a big industry in Lafayette, home of the University of Louisiana's Ragin' Cajuns. UL started out as a small agricultural college with about 100 students, and today, over 17,000 students roam the 1,300-acre campus. It is the second largest public university in the state. The university's main focus is hands-on research—dubbed "research for a reason"—meaning that all students are given the opportunity to have a meaningful impact in their area of study. The University of Louisiana is considered among the top universities in computer science, engineering and nursing.

Lafayette's climate is humid and subtropical. It is typical of areas along the Gulf of Mexico with hot, humid summers and mild winters.

Rankings

Business/Finance Rankings

- The personal finance site NerdWallet analyzed 183 American metropolitan areas with populations over 250,000 and more than 15,000 businesses to rank where entrepreneurs find the most success. Criteria included area economy, annual income, housing cost, unemployment rate, and the success rate of area businesses. Lafayette ranked #108. *www.nerdwallet.com, "Best Places to Start a Business," April 27, 2015*

- According to data by the Bureau of Economic Analysis (BEA) and the Bureau of Labor Statistics (BLS), the Lafayette metro area has the fastest-shrinking GDP (gross domestic product) and negative employment trends, at #5. *247wallst.com, "Cities With the Fastest Growing (and Shrinking) Economies," September 26, 2016*

- Using data from the Council for Community and Economic Research's 2014 cost of living index, NerdWallet ranked the 100 most affordable cities in America. Median income was compared with cost of living to find truly affordable places. Lafayette ranked #73. *NerdWallet.com, "America's Most Affordable Places," May 18, 2015*

- The Lafayette metro area appeared on the Milken Institute "2018 Best Performing Cities" list. Rank: #196 out of 200 large metro areas. Criteria: job growth; wage and salary growth; high-tech output growth. *Milken Institute, "Best-Performing Cities 2018," January 24, 2019*

- *Forbes* ranked the 200 most populous metro areas to determine the nation's "Best Places for Business and Careers." The Lafayette metro area was ranked #189. Criteria: costs (business and living); job growth (past and projected); income growth; quality of life; educational attainment (college and high school); projected economic growth; cultural and recreational opportunities; net migration patterns; number of highly ranked colleges. *Forbes, "The Best Places for Business and Careers 2018: Seattle Leads the Way," October 24, 2018*

Education Rankings

- Personal finance website *WalletHub* analyzed the 150 largest U.S. metropolitan statistical areas to determine where the most educated Americans are choosing to settle. Criteria: education quality and attainment gap; education levels; percentage of workers with degrees; public school quality rankings; quality and size of each metro area's universities. Lafayette was ranked #136 (#1 = most educated city). *www.WalletHub.com, "2018's Most and Least Educated Cities in America," July 24, 2018*

Environmental Rankings

- Lafayette was highlighted as one of the cleanest metro areas for ozone air pollution in the U.S. during 2014 through 2016. The list represents cities with no monitored ozone air pollution in unhealthful ranges. *American Lung Association, State of the Air 2018*

- Lafayette was highlighted as one of the top 90 cleanest metro areas for short-term particle pollution (24-hour PM 2.5) in the U.S. during 2014 through 2016. Monitors in these cities reported no days with unhealthful PM 2.5 levels. *American Lung Association, State of the Air 2018*

Health/Fitness Rankings

- The Lafayette metro area ranked #152 out of 189 in The Gallup-Healthways Well-Being Index. Criteria: purpose; social well being; financial health; community and physical health. Results are based on telephone interviews with adults, aged 18 and older, living in metropolitan areas in the 50 U.S. states and the District of Columbia. *Gallup-Healthways, "State of American Well-Being, 2017 Community Well-Being Rankings" March 2018*

Safety Rankings

- The National Insurance Crime Bureau ranked 382 metro areas in the U.S. in terms of per capita rates of vehicle theft. The Lafayette metro area ranked #240 (#1 = highest rate). Criteria: number of vehicle theft offenses per 100,000 inhabitants in 2017. *National Insurance Crime Bureau, "Hot Spots 2017," July 12, 2018*

Seniors/Retirement Rankings

- From its Best Cities for Successful Aging indexes, the Milken Institute generated rankings for metropolitan areas, weighing data in nine categories—health care, wellness, living arrangements, transportation and convenience, financial characteristics, education, employment, community engagement, and overall livability. The Lafayette metro area was ranked #85 overall in the small metro area category. *Milken Institute, "Best Cities for Successful Aging, 2017" March 14, 2017*

Business Environment

CITY FINANCES

City Government Finances

Component	2016 ($000)	2016 ($ per capita)
Total Revenues	676,655	5,301
Total Expenditures	635,964	4,982
Debt Outstanding	995,022	7,794
Cash and Securities[1]	877,241	6,872

Note: (1) Cash and security holdings of a government at the close of its fiscal year, including those of its dependent agencies, utilities, and liquor stores.
Source: U.S. Census Bureau, State & Local Government Finances 2016

City Government Revenue by Source

Source	2016 ($000)	2016 ($ per capita)	2016 (%)
General Revenue			
From Federal Government	23,369	183	3.5
From State Government	10,993	86	1.6
From Local Governments	1,723	13	0.3
Taxes			
Property	120,989	948	17.9
Sales and Gross Receipts	138,294	1,083	20.4
Personal Income	0	0	0.0
Corporate Income	0	0	0.0
Motor Vehicle License	6	0	0.0
Other Taxes	5,762	45	0.9
Current Charges	100,956	791	14.9
Liquor Store	0	0	0.0
Utility	255,500	2,001	37.8
Employee Retirement	0	0	0.0

Source: U.S. Census Bureau, State & Local Government Finances 2016

City Government Expenditures by Function

Function	2016 ($000)	2016 ($ per capita)	2016 (%)
General Direct Expenditures			
Air Transportation	19,379	151	3.0
Corrections	5,272	41	0.8
Education	0	0	0.0
Employment Security Administration	0	0	0.0
Financial Administration	9,837	77	1.5
Fire Protection	23,284	182	3.7
General Public Buildings	5,973	46	0.9
Governmental Administration, Other	8,691	68	1.4
Health	3,537	27	0.6
Highways	40,667	318	6.4
Hospitals	0	0	0.0
Housing and Community Development	19,556	153	3.1
Interest on General Debt	16,161	126	2.5
Judicial and Legal	18,114	141	2.8
Libraries	11,734	91	1.8
Parking	743	5	0.1
Parks and Recreation	30,342	237	4.8
Police Protection	91,345	715	14.4
Public Welfare	1,078	8	0.2
Sewerage	24,824	194	3.9
Solid Waste Management	13,532	106	2.1
Veterans' Services	0	0	0.0
Liquor Store	0	0	0.0
Utility	244,177	1,912	38.4
Employee Retirement	0	0	0.0

Source: U.S. Census Bureau, State & Local Government Finances 2016

DEMOGRAPHICS

Population Growth

Area	1990 Census	2000 Census	2010 Census	2017* Estimate	Population Growth (%) 1990-2017	Population Growth (%) 2010-2017
City	104,735	110,257	120,623	126,476	20.8	4.9
MSA[1]	208,740	239,086	273,738	487,633	133.6	78.1
U.S.	248,709,873	281,421,906	308,745,538	321,004,407	29.1	4.0

Note: (1) Figures cover the Lafayette, LA Metropolitan Statistical Area—see Appendix B for areas included; (*) 2013-2017 5-year estimated population
Source: U.S. Census Bureau, 1990 Census, Census 2000, Census 2010, 2013-2017 American Community Survey 5-Year Estimates

Household Size

Area	Persons in Household (%) One	Two	Three	Four	Five	Six	Seven or More	Average Household Size
City	33.9	35.1	14.6	10.0	4.3	1.3	0.8	2.50
MSA[1]	27.2	33.6	17.4	12.8	5.9	2.1	1.0	2.70
U.S.	27.7	33.8	15.7	13.0	6.0	2.3	1.4	2.60

Note: (1) Figures cover the Lafayette, LA Metropolitan Statistical Area—see Appendix B for areas included
Source: U.S. Census Bureau, 2013-2017 American Community Survey 5-Year Estimates

Race

Area	White Alone[2] (%)	Black Alone[2] (%)	Asian Alone[2] (%)	AIAN[3] Alone[2] (%)	NHOPI[4] Alone[2] (%)	Other Race Alone[2] (%)	Two or More Races (%)
City	63.5	31.7	2.1	0.2	0.0	0.6	1.9
MSA[1]	70.7	24.6	1.7	0.2	0.0	0.9	2.0
U.S.	73.0	12.7	5.4	0.8	0.2	4.8	3.1

Note: (1) Figures cover the Lafayette, LA Metropolitan Statistical Area—see Appendix B for areas included; (2) Alone is defined as not being in combination with one or more other races; (3) American Indian and Alaska Native; (4) Native Hawaiian and Other Pacific Islander
Source: U.S. Census Bureau, 2013-2017 American Community Survey 5-Year Estimates

Hispanic or Latino Origin

Area	Total (%)	Mexican (%)	Puerto Rican (%)	Cuban (%)	Other (%)
City	4.1	1.9	0.4	0.2	1.6
MSA[1]	3.9	2.2	0.3	0.1	1.2
U.S.	17.6	11.1	1.7	0.7	4.1

Note: Persons of Hispanic or Latino origin can be of any race; (1) Figures cover the Lafayette, LA Metropolitan Statistical Area—see Appendix B for areas included
Source: U.S. Census Bureau, 2013-2017 American Community Survey 5-Year Estimates

Segregation

Type	Segregation Indices[1] 1990	2000	2010	2010 Rank[2]	Percent Change 1990-2000	1990-2010	2000-2010
Black/White	n/a	n/a	n/a	n/a	n/a	n/a	n/a
Asian/White	n/a	n/a	n/a	n/a	n/a	n/a	n/a
Hispanic/White	n/a	n/a	n/a	n/a	n/a	n/a	n/a

Note: All figures cover the Metropolitan Statistical Area—see Appendix B for areas included; Figures are based on an analysis of 1990, 2000, and 2010 Census Decennial Census tract data by William H. Frey, Brookings Institution and the University of Michigan Social Science Data Analysis Network. In this analysis all racial groups (whites, blacks, and asians) are non-Hispanic members of those races. Hispanics are shown as a separate category; (1) Segregation Indices are Dissimilarity Indices that measure the degree to which the minority group is distributed differently than whites across census tracts. They range from 0 (complete integration) to 100 (complete segregation) where the value indicates the percentage of the minority group that needs to move to be distributed exactly like whites; (2) Ranges from 1 (most segregated) to 102 (least segregated); n/a not available.
Source: www.CensusScope.org

Ancestry

Area	German	Irish	English	American	Italian	Polish	French[2]	Scottish	Dutch
City	7.5	5.6	6.4	7.1	3.6	0.5	19.8	0.9	0.6
MSA[1]	6.9	4.5	4.2	10.7	2.7	0.5	20.5	0.7	0.3
U.S.	14.1	10.1	7.5	6.6	5.3	2.9	2.5	1.7	1.3

Note: Figures are the percentage of the total population reporting a particular ancestry. The nine most commonly reported ancestries in the U.S. are shown. Figures include multiple ancestries (e.g. if a person reported being Irish and Italian, they were included in both columns); (1) Figures cover the Lafayette, LA Metropolitan Statistical Area—see Appendix B for areas included; (2) Excludes Basque
Source: U.S. Census Bureau, 2013-2017 American Community Survey 5-Year Estimates

Foreign-Born Population

Area	Percent of Population Born in								
	Any Foreign Country	Asia	Mexico	Europe	Carribean	Central America[2]	South America	Africa	Canada
City	4.9	1.8	0.9	0.7	0.3	0.5	0.1	0.3	0.2
MSA[1]	3.3	1.1	0.9	0.3	0.1	0.5	0.1	0.2	0.1
U.S.	13.4	4.1	3.6	1.5	1.3	1.0	0.9	0.6	0.3

Note: (1) Figures cover the Lafayette, LA Metropolitan Statistical Area—see Appendix B for areas included; (2) Excludes Mexico.
Source: U.S. Census Bureau, 2013-2017 American Community Survey 5-Year Estimates

Marital Status

Area	Never Married	Now Married[2]	Separated	Widowed	Divorced
City	43.3	37.9	2.2	5.6	11.0
MSA[1]	34.8	45.4	2.3	5.9	11.5
U.S.	33.1	48.2	2.0	5.8	10.9

Note: Figures are percentages and cover the population 15 years of age and older; (1) Figures cover the Lafayette, LA Metropolitan Statistical Area—see Appendix B for areas included; (2) Excludes separated
Source: U.S. Census Bureau, 2013-2017 American Community Survey 5-Year Estimates

Disability by Age

Area	All Ages	Under 18 Years Old	18 to 64 Years Old	65 Years and Over
City	12.0	3.1	10.6	34.6
MSA[1]	14.1	4.5	12.8	40.3
U.S.	12.6	4.2	10.3	35.5

Note: Figures show percent of the civilian noninstitutionalized population that reported having a disability. Disability status is determined from six types of difficulty: vision, hearing, cognitive, ambulatory, self-care, and independent living. For children under 5 years old, hearing and vision difficulty are used to determine disability status. For children between the ages of 5 and 14, disability status is determined from hearing, vision, cognitive, ambulatory, and self-care difficulties. For people aged 15 years and older, they are considered to have a disability if they have difficulty with any one of the six difficulty types; Note: (1) Figures cover the Lafayette, LA Metropolitan Statistical Area—see Appendix B for areas included
Source: U.S. Census Bureau, 2013-2017 American Community Survey 5-Year Estimates

Age

Area	Percent of Population									Median Age
	Under Age 5	Age 5–19	Age 20–34	Age 35–44	Age 45–54	Age 55–64	Age 65–74	Age 75–84	Age 85+	
City	5.6	19.0	25.9	11.0	12.5	12.9	7.4	4.1	1.6	34.7
MSA[1]	7.0	20.3	21.9	12.4	12.9	12.5	7.5	3.8	1.5	35.4
U.S.	6.2	19.5	20.7	12.7	13.4	12.7	8.6	4.4	1.9	37.8

Note: (1) Figures cover the Lafayette, LA Metropolitan Statistical Area—see Appendix B for areas included
Source: U.S. Census Bureau, 2013-2017 American Community Survey 5-Year Estimates

Gender

Area	Males	Females	Males per 100 Females
City	61,985	64,491	96.1
MSA[1]	238,051	249,582	95.4
U.S.	158,018,753	162,985,654	97.0

Note: (1) Figures cover the Lafayette, LA Metropolitan Statistical Area—see Appendix B for areas included
Source: U.S. Census Bureau, 2013-2017 American Community Survey 5-Year Estimates

Religious Groups by Family

Area	Catholic	Baptist	Non-Den.	Methodist[2]	Lutheran	LDS[3]	Pentecostal	Presbyterian[4]	Muslim[5]	Judaism
MSA[1]	47.0	14.8	4.0	2.6	0.2	0.4	2.9	0.2	0.1	0.1
U.S.	19.1	9.3	4.0	4.0	2.3	2.0	1.9	1.6	0.8	0.7

Note: Figures are the number of adherents as a percentage of the total population; (1) Figures cover the Lafayette, LA Metropolitan Statistical Area—see Appendix B for areas included; (2) Methodist/Pietist; (3) Latter Day Saints; (4) Reformed; (5) Figures are estimates
Source: Association of Statisticians of American Religious Bodies, 2010 U.S. Religion Census: Religious Congregations & Membership Study

Religious Groups by Tradition

Area	Catholic	Evangelical Protestant	Mainline Protestant	Other Tradition	Black Protestant	Orthodox
MSA[1]	47.0	12.8	3.2	0.8	9.3	0.1
U.S.	19.1	16.2	7.3	4.3	1.6	0.3

Note: Figures are the number of adherents as a percentage of the total population; (1) Figures cover the Lafayette, LA Metropolitan Statistical Area—see Appendix B for areas included
Source: Association of Statisticians of American Religious Bodies, 2010 U.S. Religion Census: Religious Congregations & Membership Study

ECONOMY

Gross Metropolitan Product

Area	2016	2017	2018	2019	Rank[2]
MSA[1]	20.9	21.6	23.0	24.3	117

Note: Figures are in billions of dollars; (1) Figures cover the Lafayette, LA Metropolitan Statistical Area—see Appendix B for areas included; (2) Rank is based on 2017 data and ranges from 1 to 381
Source: U.S. Conference of Mayors, U.S. Metro Economies: Economic Growth & Full Employment, June 2018

Economic Growth

Area	2017-2018 (%)	2019-2020 (%)	2021-2022 (%)
MSA[1]	0.8	3.4	2.6

Note: Figures are real gross metropolitan product (GMP) growth rates and represent average annual percent change; (1) Figures cover the Lafayette, LA Metropolitan Statistical Area—see Appendix B for areas included
Source: U.S. Conference of Mayors, U.S. Metro Economies: Economic Growth & Full Employment, June 2018

Metropolitan Area Exports

Area	2012	2013	2014	2015	2016	2017	Rank[2]
MSA[1]	726.0	1,261.8	1,532.7	1,165.2	1,335.2	954.8	162

Note: Figures are in millions of dollars; (1) Figures cover the Lafayette, LA Metropolitan Statistical Area—see Appendix B for areas included; (2) Rank is based on 2017 data and ranges from 1 to 387
Source: U.S. Department of Commerce, International Trade Administration, Office of Trade and Economic Analysis, Industry and Analysis, Exports by Metropolitan Area, extracted March 25, 2019

Building Permits

Area	Single-Family			Multi-Family			Total		
	2016	2017	Pct. Chg.	2016	2017	Pct. Chg.	2016	2017	Pct. Chg.
City	n/a	n/a	n/a	n/a	n/a	n/a	n/a	n/a	n/a
MSA[1]	1,518	1,746	15.0	180	25	-86.1	1,698	1,771	4.3
U.S.	750,800	820,000	9.2	455,800	462,000	1.4	1,206,600	1,282,000	6.2

Note: (1) Figures cover the Lafayette, LA Metropolitan Statistical Area—see Appendix B for areas included; Figures represent new, privately-owned housing units authorized (unadjusted data); All permit data are based on estimates with imputation
Source: U.S. Census Bureau, Manufacturing, Mining, and Construction Statistics, Building Permits, 2016, 2017

Bankruptcy Filings

Area	Business Filings			Nonbusiness Filings		
	2017	2018	% Chg.	2017	2018	% Chg.
Lafayette Parish	61	32	-47.5	561	589	5.0
U.S.	23,157	22,232	-4.0	765,863	751,186	-1.9

Note: Business filings include Chapter 7, Chapter 11, Chapter 12, and Chapter 13; Nonbusiness filings include Chapter 7, Chapter 11, and Chapter 13
Source: Administrative Office of the U.S. Courts, Business and Nonbusiness Bankruptcy, County Cases Commenced by Chapter of the Bankruptcy Code, During the 12-Month Period Ending December 31, 2017 and Business and Nonbusiness Bankruptcy, County Cases Commenced by Chapter of the Bankruptcy Code, During the 12-Month Period Ending December 31, 2018

Housing Vacancy Rates

Area	Gross Vacancy Rate[2] (%)			Year-Round Vacancy Rate[3] (%)			Rental Vacancy Rate[4] (%)			Homeowner Vacancy Rate[5] (%)		
	2016	2017	2018	2016	2017	2018	2016	2017	2018	2016	2017	2018
MSA[1]	n/a	n/a	n/a	n/a	n/a	n/a	n/a	n/a	n/a	n/a	n/a	n/a
U.S.	12.8	12.7	12.3	9.9	9.9	9.7	6.9	7.2	6.9	1.7	1.6	1.5

Note: (1) Figures cover the Lafayette, LA Metropolitan Statistical Area—see Appendix B for areas included; (2) The percentage of the total housing inventory that is vacant; (3) The percentage of the housing inventory (excluding seasonal units) that is year-round vacant; (4) The percentage of rental inventory that is vacant for rent; (5) The percentage of homeowner inventory that is vacant for sale; n/a not available
Source: U.S. Census Bureau, Housing Vacancies and Homeownership Annual Statistics: 2016, 2017, 2018

INCOME

Income

Area	Per Capita ($)	Median Household ($)	Average Household ($)
City	30,988	48,533	74,381
MSA[1]	26,768	49,514	69,156
U.S.	31,177	57,652	81,283

Note: (1) Figures cover the Lafayette, LA Metropolitan Statistical Area—see Appendix B for areas included
Source: U.S. Census Bureau, 2013-2017 American Community Survey 5-Year Estimates

Household Income Distribution

Area	Percent of Households Earning							
	Under $15,000	$15,000 -$24,999	$25,000 -$34,999	$35,000 -$49,999	$50,000 -$74,999	$75,000 -$99,999	$100,000 -$149,999	$150,000 and up
City	15.9	12.0	10.7	12.6	16.2	9.6	11.3	11.7
MSA[1]	14.7	12.0	10.5	13.2	16.7	11.1	13.1	8.7
U.S.	11.6	9.8	9.5	13.0	17.7	12.3	14.1	12.1

Note: (1) Figures cover the Lafayette, LA Metropolitan Statistical Area—see Appendix B for areas included
Source: U.S. Census Bureau, 2013-2017 American Community Survey 5-Year Estimates

Poverty Rate

Area	All Ages	Under 18 Years Old	18 to 64 Years Old	65 Years and Over
City	19.1	26.1	18.3	11.5
MSA[1]	18.1	24.7	16.3	14.0
U.S.	14.6	20.3	13.7	9.3

Note: Figures are percentage of people whose income during the past 12 months was below the poverty level; (1) Figures cover the Lafayette, LA Metropolitan Statistical Area—see Appendix B for areas included
Source: U.S. Census Bureau, 2013-2017 American Community Survey 5-Year Estimates

EMPLOYMENT

Labor Force and Employment

Area	Civilian Labor Force			Workers Employed		
	Dec. 2017	Dec. 2018	% Chg.	Dec. 2017	Dec. 2018	% Chg.
City	59,801	59,450	-0.6	57,509	57,050	-0.8
MSA[1]	210,893	209,429	-0.7	201,965	200,424	-0.8
U.S.	159,880,000	162,510,000	1.6	153,602,000	156,481,000	1.9

Note: Data is not seasonally adjusted and covers workers 16 years of age and older; (1) Figures cover the Lafayette, LA Metropolitan Statistical Area—see Appendix B for areas included
Source: Bureau of Labor Statistics, Local Area Unemployment Statistics

Unemployment Rate

Area	2018											
	Jan.	Feb.	Mar.	Apr.	May	Jun.	Jul.	Aug.	Sep.	Oct.	Nov.	Dec.
City	4.3	3.9	4.3	4.3	4.6	5.8	5.6	5.3	4.8	4.4	4.3	4.0
MSA[1]	4.6	4.3	4.6	4.5	4.9	6.1	5.9	5.5	5.0	4.7	4.5	4.3
U.S.	4.5	4.4	4.1	3.7	3.6	4.2	4.1	3.9	3.6	3.5	3.5	3.7

Note: Data is not seasonally adjusted and covers workers 16 years of age and older; (1) Figures cover the Lafayette, LA Metropolitan Statistical Area—see Appendix B for areas included
Source: Bureau of Labor Statistics, Local Area Unemployment Statistics

Average Wages

Occupation	$/Hr.	Occupation	$/Hr.
Accountants and Auditors	32.00	Maids and Housekeeping Cleaners	9.30
Automotive Mechanics	18.30	Maintenance and Repair Workers	17.20
Bookkeepers	17.80	Marketing Managers	44.00
Carpenters	19.80	Nuclear Medicine Technologists	33.00
Cashiers	9.50	Nurses, Licensed Practical	19.00
Clerks, General Office	12.30	Nurses, Registered	30.30
Clerks, Receptionists/Information	11.80	Nursing Assistants	10.00
Clerks, Shipping/Receiving	16.00	Packers and Packagers, Hand	11.50
Computer Programmers	38.90	Physical Therapists	39.90
Computer Systems Analysts	27.20	Postal Service Mail Carriers	24.70
Computer User Support Specialists	20.40	Real Estate Brokers	24.00
Cooks, Restaurant	11.70	Retail Salespersons	12.70
Dentists	52.50	Sales Reps., Exc. Tech./Scientific	28.30
Electrical Engineers	38.80	Sales Reps., Tech./Scientific	28.60
Electricians	22.50	Secretaries, Exc. Legal/Med./Exec.	14.20
Financial Managers	48.80	Security Guards	11.60
First-Line Supervisors/Managers, Sales	18.20	Surgeons	n/a
Food Preparation Workers	9.00	Teacher Assistants*	11.20
General and Operations Managers	52.50	Teachers, Elementary School*	23.20
Hairdressers/Cosmetologists	10.10	Teachers, Secondary School*	24.40
Internists, General	n/a	Telemarketers	n/a
Janitors and Cleaners	10.30	Truck Drivers, Heavy/Tractor-Trailer	19.00
Landscaping/Groundskeeping Workers	11.90	Truck Drivers, Light/Delivery Svcs.	13.70
Lawyers	44.70	Waiters and Waitresses	8.80

Note: Wage data covers the Lafayette, LA Metropolitan Statistical Area—see Appendix B for areas included; (*) Hourly wages for elementary/secondary school teachers and teacher assistants were calculated by the editors from annual wage data based on a 40 hour work week; n/a not available.
Source: Bureau of Labor Statistics, Metro Area Occupational Employment & Wage Estimates, May 2018

Employment by Occupation

Occupation Classification	City (%)	MSA[1] (%)	U.S. (%)
Management, Business, Science, and Arts	36.2	31.4	37.4
Natural Resources, Construction, and Maintenance	8.1	13.0	8.9
Production, Transportation, and Material Moving	9.5	12.7	12.2
Sales and Office	24.6	24.4	23.5
Service	21.5	18.4	18.0

Note: Figures cover employed civilians 16 years of age and older; (1) Figures cover the Lafayette, LA Metropolitan Statistical Area—see Appendix B for areas included
Source: U.S. Census Bureau, 2013-2017 American Community Survey 5-Year Estimates

Employment by Industry

Sector	MSA[1]		U.S.
	Number of Employees	Percent of Total	Percent of Total
Construction	9,700	4.7	4.8
Education and Health Services	32,500	15.9	15.9
Financial Activities	11,000	5.4	5.7
Government	27,500	13.4	15.1
Information	2,400	1.2	1.9
Leisure and Hospitality	22,000	10.7	10.7
Manufacturing	15,700	7.7	8.5
Mining and Logging	12,900	6.3	0.5
Other Services	7,100	3.5	3.9
Professional and Business Services	21,700	10.6	14.1
Retail Trade	27,500	13.4	10.8
Transportation, Warehousing, and Utilities	6,100	3.0	4.2
Wholesale Trade	8,900	4.3	3.9

Note: Figures are non-farm employment as of December 2018. Figures are not seasonally adjusted and include workers 16 years of age and older; (1) Figures cover the Lafayette, LA Metropolitan Statistical Area—see Appendix B for areas included
Source: Bureau of Labor Statistics, Current Employment Statistics, Employment, Hours, and Earnings

Occupations with Greatest Projected Employment Growth: 2017 – 2019

Occupation[1]	2017 Employment	2019 Projected Employment	Numeric Employment Change	Percent Employment Change
Personal Care Aides	35,390	37,200	1,810	5.1
Registered Nurses	46,590	48,090	1,500	3.2
Laborers and Freight, Stock, and Material Movers, Hand	45,490	46,520	1,030	2.2
Retail Salespersons	61,790	62,820	1,030	1.7
Carpenters	18,290	19,290	1,000	5.5
Combined Food Preparation and Serving Workers, Including Fast Food	28,720	29,660	940	3.3
Construction Laborers	21,630	22,560	930	4.3
Food Preparation Workers	32,990	33,790	800	2.4
Cashiers	70,980	71,670	690	1.0
Waiters and Waitresses	38,340	38,990	650	1.7

Note: Projections cover Louisiana; (1) Sorted by numeric employment change
Source: www.projectionscentral.com, State Occupational Projections, 2017–2019 Short-Term Projections

Fastest Growing Occupations: 2017 – 2019

Occupation[1]	2017 Employment	2019 Projected Employment	Numeric Employment Change	Percent Employment Change
Web Developers	550	600	50	8.0
Operations Research Analysts	1,090	1,170	80	7.5
Structural Iron and Steel Workers	3,020	3,230	210	7.1
Millwrights	1,310	1,400	90	6.9
Veterinary Technologists and Technicians	1,120	1,190	70	6.8
Commercial Divers	850	900	50	6.4
Home Health Aides	8,530	9,060	530	6.2
Physical Therapist Assistants	1,480	1,570	90	6.0
Personal Financial Advisors	1,550	1,640	90	5.8
Software Developers, Applications	1,430	1,510	80	5.7

Note: Projections cover Louisiana; (1) Sorted by percent employment change and excludes occupations with numeric employment change less than 50
Source: www.projectionscentral.com, State Occupational Projections, 2017–2019 Short-Term Projections

TAXES

State Corporate Income Tax Rates

State	Tax Rate (%)	Income Brackets ($)	Num. of Brackets	Financial Institution Tax Rate (%)[a]	Federal Income Tax Ded.
Louisiana	4.0 - 8.0	25,000 - 200,001	5	4.0 - 8.0	Yes

Note: Tax rates as of January 1, 2019; (a) Rates listed are the corporate income tax rate applied to financial institutions or excise taxes based on income. Some states have other taxes based upon the value of deposits or shares.
Source: Federation of Tax Administrators, Range of State Corporate Income Tax Rates, January 1, 2019

State Individual Income Tax Rates

State	Tax Rate (%)	Income Brackets ($)	Personal Exemptions ($)			Standard Ded. ($)	
			Single	Married	Depend.	Single	Married
Louisiana	2.0 - 6.0	12,500 - 50,001 (b)	4,500	9,000 (k)	1,000	(k)	(k)

Note: Tax rates as of January 1, 2019; Local- and county-level taxes are not included; n/a not applicable; Federal income tax is deductible on state income tax returns; (b) For joint returns, taxes are twice the tax on half the couple's income; (k) The amounts reported for Louisiana are a combined personal exemption-standard deduction.
Source: Federation of Tax Administrators, State Individual Income Tax Rates, January 1, 2019

Various State Sales and Excise Tax Rates

State	State Sales Tax (%)	Gasoline[1] (¢/gal.)	Cigarette[2] ($/pack)	Spirits[3] ($/gal.)	Wine[4] ($/gal.)	Beer[5] ($/gal.)	Recreational Marijuana (%)
Louisiana	5	20.01	1.08	3.03 (f)	0.76 (l)	0.4	Not legal

Note: All tax rates as of January 1, 2019; (1) The American Petroleum Institute has developed a methodology for determining the average tax rate on a gallon of fuel. Rates may include any of the following: excise taxes, environmental fees, storage tank fees, other fees or taxes, general sales tax, and local taxes. In states where gasoline is subject to the general sales tax, or where the fuel tax is based on the average sale price, the average rate determined by API is sensitive to changes in the price of gasoline. States that fully or partially apply general sales taxes to gasoline: CA, CO, GA, IL, IN, MI, NY; (2) The federal excise tax of $1.0066 per pack and local taxes are not included; (3) Rates are those applicable to off-premise sales of 40% alcohol by volume (a.b.v.) distilled spirits in 750ml containers. Local excise taxes are excluded; (4) Rates are those applicable to off-premise sales of 11% a.b.v. non-carbonated wine in 750ml containers; (5) Rates are those applicable to off-premise sales of 4.7% a.b.v. beer in 12 ounce containers; (f) Different rates also applicable according to alcohol content, place of production, size of container, or place purchased (on- or off-premise or onboard airlines); (l) Different rates also applicable to alcohol content, place of production, size of container, place purchased (on- or off-premise or on board airlines) or type of wine (carbonated, vermouth, etc.).
Source: Tax Foundation, 2019 Facts & Figures: How Does Your State Compare?

State Business Tax Climate Index Rankings

State	Overall Rank	Corporate Tax Rank	Individual Income Tax Rank	Sales Tax Rank	Unemployment Insurance Tax Rank	Property Tax Rank
Louisiana	44	36	32	50	4	32

Note: The index is a measure of how each state's tax laws affect economic performance. The lower the rank, the more favorable a state's tax system is for business. States without a given tax are given a ranking of 1. The scores/rankings for the District of Columbia do not affect other states. The 2019 index represents the tax climate as of July 1, 2018.
Source: Tax Foundation, State Business Tax Climate Index 2019

COMMERCIAL UTILITIES

Typical Monthly Electric Bills

Area	Commercial Service ($/month)		Industrial Service ($/month)	
	1,500 kWh	40 kW demand 14,000 kWh	1,000 kW demand 200,000 kWh	50,000 kW demand 32,500,000 kWh
City	188	1,464	15,884	1,994,941
Average[1]	203	1,619	25,886	2,540,077

Note: Figures are based on annualized rates; (1) Average based on 187 utilities surveyed
Source: Edison Electric Institute, Typical Bills and Average Rates Report, Summer 2018

TRANSPORTATION

Means of Transportation to Work

Area	Car/Truck/Van		Public Transportation			Bicycle	Walked	Other Means	Worked at Home
	Drove Alone	Car-pooled	Bus	Subway	Railroad				
City	82.1	9.4	1.0	0.0	0.0	1.1	2.3	1.0	3.2
MSA[1]	83.2	9.9	0.5	0.0	0.0	0.4	2.0	1.4	2.6
U.S.	76.4	9.2	2.5	1.9	0.6	0.6	2.7	1.3	4.7

Note: Figures are percentages and cover workers 16 years of age and older; (1) Figures cover the Lafayette, LA Metropolitan Statistical Area—see Appendix B for areas included
Source: U.S. Census Bureau, 2013-2017 American Community Survey 5-Year Estimates

Travel Time to Work

Area	Less Than 10 Minutes	10 to 19 Minutes	20 to 29 Minutes	30 to 44 Minutes	45 to 59 Minutes	60 to 89 Minutes	90 Minutes or More
City	16.4	43.2	19.9	12.0	2.1	2.9	3.5
MSA[1]	16.1	32.8	20.0	18.2	4.8	3.5	4.5
U.S.	12.7	28.9	20.9	20.5	8.1	6.2	2.7

Note: Note: Figures are percentages and include workers 16 years old and over; (1) Figures cover the Lafayette, LA Metropolitan Statistical Area—see Appendix B for areas included
Source: U.S. Census Bureau, 2013-2017 American Community Survey 5-Year Estimates

Freeway Travel Time Index

Area	1985	1990	1995	2000	2005	2010	2014
Urban Area Rank[1,2]	n/a	n/a	n/a	n/a	n/a	n/a	n/a
Urban Area Index[1]	n/a	n/a	n/a	n/a	n/a	n/a	n/a
Average Index[3]	1.09	1.11	1.14	1.17	1.20	1.19	1.20

Note: Freeway Travel Time Index—the ratio of travel time in the peak period to the travel time at free-flow conditions. For example, a value of 1.30 indicates a 20-minute free-flow trip takes 26 minutes in the peak (20 minutes x 1.30 = 26 minutes); (1) Data for the Lafayette, LA urban area was not available; (2) Rank is based on 101 urban areas (#1 = highest travel time index); (3) Average of 101 urban areas
Source: Texas Transportation Institute, 2015 Urban Mobility Scorecard, August 2015

Freeway Commuter Stress Index

Area	1985	1990	1995	2000	2005	2010	2014
Urban Area Rank[1,2]	n/a	n/a	n/a	n/a	n/a	n/a	n/a
Urban Area Index[1]	n/a	n/a	n/a	n/a	n/a	n/a	n/a
Average Index[3]	1.13	1.16	1.19	1.22	1.25	1.24	1.25

Note: The Freeway Commuter Stress Index is the same as the Freeway Travel Time Index (see table above) except that it includes only the travel in the peak directions during the peak periods; the TTI includes travel in all directions during the peak period. Thus, the CSI is more indicative of the work trip experienced by each commuter on a daily basis; (1) Data for the Lafayette, LA urban area was not available; (2) Rank is based on 101 urban areas (#1 = highest travel time index); (3) Average of 101 urban areas
Source: Texas Transportation Institute, 2015 Urban Mobility Scorecard, August 2015

Public Transportation

Agency Name / Mode of Transportation	Vehicles Operated in Maximum Service[1]	Annual Unlinked Passenger Trips[2] (in thous.)	Annual Passenger Miles[3] (in thous.)
Lafayette Transit System			
Bus (directly operated)	13	1,546.2	8,115.3
Demand Response (purchased transportation)	6	33.8	385.9

Note: (1) The number of revenue vehicles operated by the given mode and type of service to meet the annual maximum service requirement. This is the revenue vehicle count during the peak season of the year; on the week and day that maximum service is provided. Vehicles operated in maximum service (VOMS) exclude atypical days and one-time special events; (2) The number of passengers who boarded public transportation vehicles. Passengers are counted each time they board a vehicle no matter how many vehicles they use to travel from their origin to their destination. (3) The sum of the distances ridden by all passengers during the entire fiscal year.
Source: Federal Transit Administration, National Transit Database, 2017

Air Transportation

Airport Name and Code / Type of Service	Passenger Airlines[1]	Passenger Enplanements	Freight Carriers[2]	Freight (lbs)
Lafayette Regional Airport (LFT)				
Domestic service (U.S. carriers - 2018)	13	223,456	5	8,418,424
International service (U.S. carriers - 2017)	1	168	1	1,985

Note: (1) Includes all U.S.-based major, minor and commuter airlines that carried at least one passenger during the year; (2) Includes all U.S.-based airlines and freight carriers that transported at least one pound of freight during the year.
Source: Bureau of Transportation Statistics, The Intermodal Transportation Database, Air Carriers: T-100 Domestic Market (U.S. Carriers), 2018; Bureau of Transportation Statistics, The Intermodal Transportation Database, Air Carriers: T-100 International Market (U.S. Carriers), 2017

Other Transportation Statistics

Major Highways:	I-10
Amtrak Service:	Yes
Major Waterways/Ports:	Gulf of Mexico (40 miles)

Source: Amtrak.com; Google Maps

BUSINESSES

Major Business Headquarters

Company Name	Industry	Rankings Fortune[1]	Rankings Forbes[2]
No companies listed	-	-	-

Note: (1) Companies that produce a 10-K are ranked 1 to 500 based on 2017 revenue; (2) All private companies with at least $2 billion in annual revenue through the end of their most current fiscal year are ranked 1 to 229; companies listed are headquartered in the city; dashes indicate no ranking
Source: Fortune, "Fortune 500," June 2018; Forbes, "America's Largest Private Companies," 2018 Rankings

Minority- and Women-Owned Businesses

Group	All Firms Firms	All Firms Sales ($000)	Firms with Paid Employees Firms	Firms with Paid Employees Sales ($000)	Firms with Paid Employees Employees	Firms with Paid Employees Payroll ($000)
AIAN[1]	93	(s)	5	(s)	0 - 19	(s)
Asian	425	121,376	139	107,589	1,677	25,651
Black	2,878	109,668	140	(s)	1,000 - 2,499	(s)
Hispanic	287	297,341	43	280,452	837	48,524
NHOPI[2]	n/a	n/a	n/a	n/a	n/a	n/a
Women	5,987	1,496,121	793	1,358,697	9,108	364,346
All Firms	17,238	17,932,041	4,853	17,278,380	94,120	3,788,935

Note: Figures cover firms located in the city; minority- and women-owned business are defined as firms in which the corresponding group own 51% or more of the stock or equity of the company; (1) American Indian and Alaska Native; (2) Native Hawaiian and Other Pacific Islander; (s) estimates are suppressed when publication standards are not met; n/a not available
Source: U.S. Census Bureau, 2012 Economic Census, Survey of Business Owners

HOTELS & CONVENTION CENTERS

Hotels, Motels and Vacation Rentals

Area	5 Star Num.	5 Star Pct.[3]	4 Star Num.	4 Star Pct.[3]	3 Star Num.	3 Star Pct.[3]	2 Star Num.	2 Star Pct.[3]	1 Star Num.	1 Star Pct.[3]	Not Rated Num.	Not Rated Pct.[3]
City[1]	0	0.0	1	0.6	28	17.3	79	48.8	1	0.6	53	32.7
Total[2]	286	0.4	5,236	7.1	16,715	22.6	10,259	13.9	293	0.4	41,056	55.6

Note: (1) Figures cover Lafayette and vicinity; (2) Figures cover all 100 cities in this book; (3) Percentage of hotels which have a given star rating; Star ratings are determined by expedia.com and offer an indication of the general quality of a particular hotel.
Source: www.expedia.com, April 3, 2019

Major Convention Centers

Name	Overall Space (sq. ft.)	Exhibit Space (sq. ft.)	Meeting Space (sq. ft.)	Meeting Rooms
Cajundome and Convention Center	72,000	37,300	20,000	n/a

Note: Table includes convention centers located in the Lafayette, LA metro area; n/a not available
Source: Original research

Living Environment

COST OF LIVING

Cost of Living Index

Composite Index	Groceries	Housing	Utilities	Trans-portation	Health Care	Misc. Goods/ Services
90.1	99.4	78.7	88.2	103.6	87.8	93.4

Note: The Cost of Living Index measures regional differences in the cost of consumer goods and services, excluding taxes and non-consumer expenditures, for professional and managerial households in the top income quintile. It is based on more than 50,000 prices covering almost 60 different items for which prices are collected three times a year by chambers of commerce, economic development organizations or university applied economic centers in each participating urban area. The numbers shown should be read as a percentage above or below the national average of 100. For example, a value of 115.4 in the groceries column indicates that grocery prices are 15.4% higher than the national average. Small differences in the index numbers should not be interpreted as significant; Figures cover the Lafayette LA urban area.
Source: The Council for Community and Economic Research, ACCRA Cost of Living Index, 2018

Grocery Prices

Area[1]	T-Bone Steak ($/pound)	Frying Chicken ($/pound)	Whole Milk ($/half gal.)	Eggs ($/dozen)	Orange Juice ($/64 oz.)	Coffee ($/11.5 oz.)
City[2]	12.83	1.28	2.42	1.80	3.47	3.85
Avg.	11.35	1.42	1.94	1.81	3.52	4.35
Min.	7.45	0.92	0.80	0.75	2.72	3.06
Max.	15.05	2.76	4.18	4.00	5.36	8.20

Note: (1) Values for the local area are compared with the average, minimum and maximum values for all 291 areas in the Cost of Living Index; (2) Figures cover the Lafayette LA urban area; **T-Bone Steak** (price per pound); **Frying Chicken** (price per pound, whole fryer); **Whole Milk** (half gallon carton); **Eggs** (price per dozen, Grade A, large); **Orange Juice** (64 oz. Tropicana or Florida Natural); **Coffee** (11.5 oz. can, vacuum-packed, Maxwell House, Hills Bros, or Folgers).
Source: The Council for Community and Economic Research, ACCRA Cost of Living Index, 2018

Housing and Utility Costs

Area[1]	New Home Price ($)	Apartment Rent ($/month)	All Electric ($/month)	Part Electric ($/month)	Other Energy ($/month)	Telephone ($/month)
City[2]	269,749	856	-	85.05	49.43	175.40
Avg.	347,000	1,087	165.93	100.16	67.73	178.70
Min.	200,468	500	93.58	25.64	26.78	163.10
Max.	1,901,222	4,888	388.65	246.86	332.81	197.70

Note: (1) Values for the local area are compared with the average, minimum and maximum values for all 291 areas in the Cost of Living Index; (2) Figures cover the Lafayette LA urban area; **New Home Price** (2,400 sf living area, 8,000 sf lot, in urban area with full utilities); **Apartment Rent** (950 sf 2 bedroom/1.5 or 2 bath, unfurnished, excluding all utilities except water); **All Electric** (average monthly cost for an all-electric home); **Part Electric** (average monthly cost for a part-electric home); **Other Energy** (average monthly cost for natural gas, fuel oil, coal, wood, and any other forms of energy except electricity); **Telephone** (price includes the base monthly rate plus taxes and fees for three lines of mobile phone service).
Source: The Council for Community and Economic Research, ACCRA Cost of Living Index, 2018

Health Care, Transportation, and Other Costs

Area[1]	Doctor ($/visit)	Dentist ($/visit)	Optometrist ($/visit)	Gasoline ($/gallon)	Beauty Salon ($/visit)	Men's Shirt ($)
City[2]	87.50	81.13	69.86	2.30	36.27	23.78
Avg.	110.71	95.11	103.74	2.61	37.48	32.03
Min.	33.60	62.55	54.63	1.89	17.00	11.44
Max.	195.97	153.93	225.79	3.59	71.88	58.64

Note: (1) Values for the local area are compared with the average, minimum and maximum values for all 291 areas in the Cost of Living Index; (2) Figures cover the Lafayette LA urban area; **Doctor** (general practitioners routine exam of an established patient); **Dentist** (adult teeth cleaning and periodic oral examination); **Optometrist** (full vision eye exam for established adult patient); **Gasoline** (one gallon regular unleaded, national brand, including all taxes, cash price at self-service pump if available); **Beauty Salon** (woman's shampoo, trim, and blow-dry); **Men's Shirt** (cotton/polyester dress shirt, pinpoint weave, long sleeves).
Source: The Council for Community and Economic Research, ACCRA Cost of Living Index, 2018

HOUSING

House Price Index (HPI)

Area	National Ranking[2]	Quarterly Change (%)	One-Year Change (%)	Five-Year Change (%)
MSA[1]	241	-0.23	-0.36	9.63
U.S.[3]	–	1.12	5.73	32.81

Note: The HPI is a weighted repeat sales index. It measures average price changes in repeat sales or refinancings on the same properties. This information is obtained by reviewing repeat mortgage transactions on single-family properties whose mortgages have been purchased or securitized by Fannie Mae or Freddie Mac in January 1975; (1) Figures cover the Lafayette, LA Metropolitan Statistical Area—see Appendix B for areas included; (2) Rankings are based on annual percentage change for all metro areas containing at least 15,000 transactions over the last 10 years and ranges from 1 to 245; (3) figures based on a weighted average of Census Division estimates using a seasonally adjusted, purchase-only index; all figures are for the period ending December 31, 2018
Source: Federal Housing Finance Agency, House Price Index, February 26, 2019

Median Single-Family Home Prices

Area	2016	2017	2018p	Percent Change 2017 to 2018
MSA[1]	n/a	n/a	n/a	n/a
U.S. Average	235.5	248.8	261.6	5.1

Note: Figures are median sales prices of existing single-family homes in thousands of dollars; (p) preliminary; n/a not available; (1) Figures cover the Lafayette, LA Metropolitan Statistical Area—see Appendix B for areas included
Source: National Association of Realtors, Median Sales Price of Existing Single-Family Homes for Metropolitan Areas, 4th Quarter 2018

Qualifying Income Based on Median Sales Price of Existing Single-Family Homes

Area	With 5% Down ($)	With 10% Down ($)	With 20% Down ($)
MSA[1]	n/a	n/a	n/a
U.S. Average	62,954	59,640	53,013

Note: Figures are preliminary; Qualifying income is based on a mortgage rate of 4.9%. Monthly principal and interest payment is limited to 25% of income; n/a not available; (1) Figures cover the Lafayette, LA Metropolitan Statistical Area—see Appendix B for areas included
Source: National Association of Realtors, Qualifying Income Based on Median Sales Price of Existing Single-Family Homes for Metropolitan Areas, 4th Quarter 2018

Median Apartment Condo-Coop Home Prices

Area	2016	2017	2018p	Percent Change 2017 to 2018
MSA[1]	n/a	n/a	n/a	n/a
U.S. Average	220.7	234.3	241.0	2.9

Note: Figures are median sales prices of existing apartment condo-coop homes in thousands of dollars; (p) preliminary; n/a not available; (1) Figures cover the Lafayette, LA Metropolitan Statistical Area—see Appendix B for areas included
Source: National Association of Realtors, Median Sales Price of Existing Apartment Condo-Coop Homes for Metropolitan Areas, 4th Quarter 2018

Home Value Distribution

Area	Under $50,000	$50,000 -$99,999	$100,000 -$149,999	$150,000 -$199,999	$200,000 -$299,999	$300,000 -$499,999	$500,000 -$999,999	$1,000,000 or more
City	7.0	10.0	17.0	22.7	21.9	14.6	5.3	1.5
MSA[1]	17.0	18.6	16.4	18.3	17.1	8.9	3.1	0.6
U.S.	8.3	13.9	14.7	14.6	18.7	17.3	9.7	2.7

Note: Figures are percentages and cover owner-occupied housing units; (1) Figures cover the Lafayette, LA Metropolitan Statistical Area—see Appendix B for areas included
Source: U.S. Census Bureau, 2013-2017 American Community Survey 5-Year Estimates

Homeownership Rate

Area	2010 (%)	2011 (%)	2012 (%)	2013 (%)	2014 (%)	2015 (%)	2016 (%)	2017 (%)	2018 (%)
MSA[1]	n/a	n/a	n/a	n/a	n/a	n/a	n/a	n/a	n/a
U.S.	66.9	66.1	65.4	65.1	64.5	63.7	63.4	63.9	64.4

Note: (1) Figures cover the Lafayette, LA Metropolitan Statistical Area—see Appendix B for areas included; n/a not available
Source: U.S. Census Bureau, Housing Vacancies and Homeownership Annual Statistics: 2010-2018

Year Housing Structure Built

Area	2010 or Later	2000 -2009	1990 -1999	1980 -1989	1970 -1979	1960 -1969	1950 -1959	1940 -1949	Before 1940	Median Year
City	4.4	13.9	9.5	18.4	21.7	13.8	10.6	4.6	3.2	1978
MSA[1]	6.6	17.7	13.1	15.6	16.9	10.5	9.5	4.5	5.7	1982
U.S.	3.2	14.5	14.0	13.6	15.5	10.8	10.5	5.1	12.9	1977

Note: Figures are percentages except for Median Year; Note: (1) Figures cover the Lafayette, LA Metropolitan Statistical Area—see Appendix B for areas included
Source: U.S. Census Bureau, 2013-2017 American Community Survey 5-Year Estimates

Gross Monthly Rent

Area	Under $500	$500 -$999	$1,000 -$1,499	$1,500 -$1,999	$2,000 -$2,499	$2,500 -$2,999	$3,000 and up	Median ($)
City	11.3	57.3	23.7	5.4	2.0	0.2	0.1	853
MSA[1]	17.9	59.0	17.8	4.0	1.1	0.1	0.1	769
U.S.	10.5	41.1	28.7	11.7	4.5	1.8	1.7	982

Note: Figures are percentages except for Median; Gross rent is the contract rent plus the estimated average monthly cost of utilities (electricity, gas, and water and sewer) and fuels (oil, coal, kerosene, wood, etc.) if these are paid by the renter (or paid for the renter by someone else); (1) Figures cover the Lafayette, LA Metropolitan Statistical Area—see Appendix B for areas included
Source: U.S. Census Bureau, 2013-2017 American Community Survey 5-Year Estimates

HEALTH

Health Risk Factors

Category	MSA[1] (%)	U.S. (%)
Adults aged 18–64 who have any kind of health care coverage	n/a	87.3
Adults who reported being in good or better health	n/a	82.4
Adults who have been told they have high blood cholesterol	n/a	33.0
Adults who have been told they have high blood pressure	n/a	32.3
Adults who are current smokers	n/a	17.1
Adults who currently use E-cigarettes	n/a	4.6
Adults who currently use chewing tobacco, snuff, or snus	n/a	4.0
Adults who are heavy drinkers[2]	n/a	6.3
Adults who are binge drinkers[3]	n/a	17.4
Adults who are overweight (BMI 25.0 - 29.9)	n/a	35.3
Adults who are obese (BMI 30.0 - 99.8)	n/a	31.3
Adults who participated in any physical activities in the past month	n/a	74.4
Adults who always or nearly always wears a seat belt	n/a	94.3

Note: n/a not available; (1) Figures cover the Lafayette, LA Metropolitan Statistical Area—see Appendix B for areas included; (2) Heavy drinkers are classified as adult men having more than 14 drinks per week and adult women having more than 7 drinks per week; (3) Binge drinkers are classified as males having five or more drinks on one occasion or females having four or more drinks on one occasion
Source: Centers for Disease Control and Prevention, Behaviorial Risk Factor Surveillance System, SMART: Selected Metropolitan Area Risk Trends, 2017

Acute and Chronic Health Conditions

Category	MSA[1] (%)	U.S. (%)
Adults who have ever been told they had a heart attack	n/a	4.2
Adults who have ever been told they have angina or coronary heart disease	n/a	3.9
Adults who have ever been told they had a stroke	n/a	3.0
Adults who have ever been told they have asthma	n/a	14.2
Adults who have ever been told they have arthritis	n/a	24.9
Adults who have ever been told they have diabetes[2]	n/a	10.5
Adults who have ever been told they had skin cancer	n/a	6.2
Adults who have ever been told they had any other types of cancer	n/a	7.1
Adults who have ever been told they have COPD	n/a	6.5
Adults who have ever been told they have kidney disease	n/a	3.0
Adults who have ever been told they have a form of depression	n/a	20.5

Note: n/a not available; (1) Figures cover the Lafayette, LA Metropolitan Statistical Area—see Appendix B for areas included; (2) Figures do not include pregnancy-related, borderline, or pre-diabetes
Source: Centers for Disease Control and Prevention, Behaviorial Risk Factor Surveillance System, SMART: Selected Metropolitan Area Risk Trends, 2017

Health Screening and Vaccination Rates

Category	MSA[1] (%)	U.S. (%)
Adults aged 65+ who have had flu shot within the past year	n/a	60.7
Adults aged 65+ who have ever had a pneumonia vaccination	n/a	75.4
Adults who have ever been tested for HIV	n/a	36.1
Adults who have ever had the shingles or zoster vaccine?	n/a	28.9
Adults who have had their blood cholesterol checked within the last five years	n/a	85.9

Note: n/a not available; (1) Figures cover the Lafayette, LA Metropolitan Statistical Area—see Appendix B for areas included.
Source: Centers for Disease Control and Prevention, Behaviorial Risk Factor Surveillance System, SMART: Selected Metropolitan Area Risk Trends, 2017

Disability Status

Category	MSA[1] (%)	U.S. (%)
Adults who reported being deaf	n/a	6.7
Are you blind or have serious difficulty seeing, even when wearing glasses?	n/a	4.5
Are you limited in any way in any of your usual activities due of arthritis?	n/a	12.9
Do you have difficulty doing errands alone?	n/a	6.8
Do you have difficulty dressing or bathing?	n/a	3.6
Do you have serious difficulty concentrating/remembering/making decisions?	n/a	10.7
Do you have serious difficulty walking or climbing stairs?	n/a	13.6

Note: n/a not available; (1) Figures cover the Lafayette, LA Metropolitan Statistical Area—see Appendix B for areas included.
Source: Centers for Disease Control and Prevention, Behaviorial Risk Factor Surveillance System, SMART: Selected Metropolitan Area Risk Trends, 2017

Mortality Rates for the Top 10 Causes of Death in the U.S.

ICD-10[a] Sub-Chapter	ICD-10[a] Code	Age-Adjusted Mortality Rate[1] per 100,000 population	
		County[2]	U.S.
Malignant neoplasms	C00-C97	169.1	155.5
Ischaemic heart diseases	I20-I25	98.1	94.8
Other forms of heart disease	I30-I51	59.7	52.9
Chronic lower respiratory diseases	J40-J47	38.1	41.0
Cerebrovascular diseases	I60-I69	39.4	37.5
Other degenerative diseases of the nervous system	G30-G31	61.5	35.0
Other external causes of accidental injury	W00-X59	28.9	33.7
Organic, including symptomatic, mental disorders	F01-F09	9.8	31.0
Hypertensive diseases	I10-I15	38.0	21.9
Diabetes mellitus	E10-E14	24.8	21.2

Note: (a) ICD-10 = International Classification of Diseases 10th Revision; (1) Mortality rates are a three year average covering 2015-2017; (2) Figures cover Lafayette Parish.
Source: Centers for Disease Control and Prevention, National Center for Health Statistics. Underlying Cause of Death 1999-2017 on CDC WONDER Online Database

Mortality Rates for Selected Causes of Death

ICD-10[a] Sub-Chapter	ICD-10[a] Code	Age-Adjusted Mortality Rate[1] per 100,000 population	
		County[2]	U.S.
Assault	X85-Y09	9.5	5.9
Diseases of the liver	K70-K76	10.8	14.1
Human immunodeficiency virus (HIV) disease	B20-B24	Unreliable	1.8
Influenza and pneumonia	J09-J18	9.3	14.3
Intentional self-harm	X60-X84	15.3	13.6
Malnutrition	E40-E46	Unreliable	1.6
Obesity and other hyperalimentation	E65-E68	7.0	2.1
Renal failure	N17-N19	17.2	13.0
Transport accidents	V01-V99	12.1	12.4
Viral hepatitis	B15-B19	Suppressed	1.6

Note: (a) ICD-10 = International Classification of Diseases 10th Revision; (1) Mortality rates are a three year average covering 2015-2017; (2) Figures cover Lafayette Parish; Data are suppressed when the data meet the criteria for confidentiality constraints; Mortality rates are flagged as unreliable when the rate would be calculated with a numerator of 20 or less.
Source: Centers for Disease Control and Prevention, National Center for Health Statistics. Underlying Cause of Death 1999-2017 on CDC WONDER Online Database

Health Insurance Coverage

Area	With Health Insurance	With Private Health Insurance	With Public Health Insurance	Without Health Insurance	Population Under Age 18 Without Health Insurance
City	87.0	66.3	30.6	13.0	4.9
MSA[1]	87.2	63.1	34.2	12.8	4.3
U.S.	89.5	67.2	33.8	10.5	5.7

Note: Figures are percentages that cover the civilian noninstitutionalized population; (1) Figures cover the Lafayette, LA Metropolitan Statistical Area—see Appendix B for areas included
Source: U.S. Census Bureau, 2013-2017 American Community Survey 5-Year Estimates

Number of Medical Professionals

Area	MDs[3]	DOs[3,4]	Dentists	Podiatrists	Chiropractors	Optometrists
County[1] (number)	862	17	159	9	75	33
County[1] (rate[2])	356.6	7.0	65.6	3.7	30.9	13.6
U.S. (rate[2])	279.3	23.0	68.4	6.0	27.1	16.2

Note: Data as of 2017 unless noted; (1) Data covers Lafayette Parish; (2) Rate per 100,000 population; (3) Data as of 2016 and includes all active, non-federal physicians; (4) Doctor of Osteopathic Medicine
Source: U.S. Department of Health and Human Services, Health Resources and Services Administration, Bureau of Health Professions, Area Resource File (ARF) 2017-2018

EDUCATION

Public School District Statistics

District Name	Schls	Pupils	Pupil/ Teacher Ratio	Minority Pupils[1] (%)	Free Lunch Eligible[2] (%)	IEP[3] (%)
Lafayette Parish	42	30,015	17.8	53.4	61.2	8.4

Note: Table includes school districts with 2,000 or more students; (1) Percentage of students that are not non-Hispanic white; (2) Percentage of students that are eligible for the free lunch program; (3) Percentage of students that have an Individualized Education Program.
Source: U.S. Department of Education, National Center for Education Statistics, Common Core of Data, Local Education Agency (School District) Universe Survey: School Year 2016-2017; U.S. Department of Education, National Center for Education Statistics, Common Core of Data, Public Elementary/Secondary School Universe Survey: School Year 2016-2017

Highest Level of Education

Area	Less than H.S.	H.S. Diploma	Some College, No Deg.	Associate Degree	Bachelor's Degree	Master's Degree	Prof. School Degree	Doctorate Degree
City	13.3	25.3	20.9	4.5	24.1	7.7	2.7	1.6
MSA[1]	17.6	35.5	19.2	5.6	15.6	4.6	1.2	0.7
U.S.	12.7	27.3	20.8	8.3	19.1	8.4	2.0	1.4

Note: Figures cover persons age 25 and over; (1) Figures cover the Lafayette, LA Metropolitan Statistical Area—see Appendix B for areas included
Source: U.S. Census Bureau, 2013-2017 American Community Survey 5-Year Estimates

Educational Attainment by Race

Area	High School Graduate or Higher (%)					Bachelor's Degree or Higher (%)				
	Total	White	Black	Asian	Hisp.[2]	Total	White	Black	Asian	Hisp.[2]
City	86.7	92.2	73.6	88.8	51.9	36.0	45.0	14.1	44.2	22.6
MSA[1]	82.4	86.1	72.4	65.7	64.5	22.1	25.4	11.2	26.2	14.7
U.S.	87.3	89.3	84.9	86.5	66.7	30.9	32.2	20.6	52.7	15.2

Note: Figures shown cover persons 25 years old and over; (1) Figures cover the Lafayette, LA Metropolitan Statistical Area—see Appendix B for areas included; (2) People of Hispanic origin can be of any race
Source: U.S. Census Bureau, 2013-2017 American Community Survey 5-Year Estimates

School Enrollment by Grade and Control

Area	Preschool (%)		Kindergarten (%)		Grades 1 - 4 (%)		Grades 5 - 8 (%)		Grades 9 - 12 (%)	
	Public	Private	Public	Private	Public	Private	Public	Private	Public	Private
City	60.0	40.0	78.9	21.1	81.2	18.8	74.7	25.3	76.4	23.6
MSA[1]	66.0	34.0	78.4	21.6	79.8	20.2	77.4	22.6	79.2	20.8
U.S.	58.8	41.2	87.7	12.3	89.7	10.3	89.6	10.4	90.3	9.7

Note: Figures shown cover persons 3 years old and over; (1) Figures cover the Lafayette, LA Metropolitan Statistical Area—see Appendix B for areas included
Source: U.S. Census Bureau, 2013-2017 American Community Survey 5-Year Estimates

Average Salaries of Public School Classroom Teachers

Area	2016		2017		Change from 2016 to 2017	
	Dollars	Rank[1]	Dollars	Rank[1]	Percent	Rank[2]
Louisiana	49,745	34	50,000	37	0.5	40
U.S. Average	58,479	–	59,660	–	2.0	–

Note: (1) Rank ranges from 1 to 51 where 1 indicates highest salary; (2) Rank ranges from 1 to 51 where 1 indicates highest percent change.
Source: National Education Association, Rankings & Estimates: Rankings of the States 2017 and Estimates of School Statistics 2018

Higher Education

Four-Year Colleges			Two-Year Colleges			Medical Schools[1]	Law Schools[2]	Voc/ Tech[3]
Public	Private Non-profit	Private For-profit	Public	Private Non-profit	Private For-profit			
1	0	0	1	2	1	0	0	6

Note: Figures cover institutions located within the city limits and include main campuses only; (1) includes schools accredited by the Liaison Committee on Medical Education and the American Osteopathic Association's Commission on Osteopathic College Accreditation; (2) includes ABA-accredited schools, schools with provisional ABA accreditation, and state accredited schools; (3) includes all schools with programs that are less than 2 years.
Source: National Center for Education Statistics, Integrated Postsecondary Education System (IPEDS), 2017-18; Wikipedia, List of Medical Schools in the United States, accessed April 3, 2019; Wikipedia, List of Law Schools in the United States, accessed April 3, 2019

PRESIDENTIAL ELECTION

2016 Presidential Election Results

Area	Clinton	Trump	Johnson	Stein	Other
Lafayette Parish	31.0	64.6	2.7	0.8	0.9
U.S.	48.0	45.9	3.3	1.1	1.7

Note: Results are percentages and may not add to 100% due to rounding
Source: Dave Leip's Atlas of U.S. Presidential Elections

EMPLOYERS

Major Employers

Company Name	Industry
Acadian Companies	Health care
American Legion Hospital	Health care
AT&T Wireless	Telecommunications
Baker Hughes	Oil field service
Cal Dive Intl Inc	Diving instruction
Cameron Valves & Measurement	Valves, manufacturers
Cheveron USA Production Co.	Oil & gas
Fieldwood Energy	Oil & gas
Frank's Casing Crew & Rental	Oil field service
Halliburton Energy SVC	Oil field service
Lafayette General Medical Ctr	Health care
LHC Group Inc	Health care
McDonald's of Acadiana	Services
Offshore Energy Inc	Oil field service
Opelousas Health Systems	Health care
Our Lady of Lourdes Regional Medical Ctr	Health care
Petroleum Helicopters	Transportation
Quality Construction & Production	General contractors
Regional Medical Center-Acadiana	Health care
Schlumberger	Oil field service
Stuller Inc	Jewelry-manufacturers
Superior Energy Svc	Oil field service
Wal-Mart Stores	Retail
Walmart Distribution Center	Distribution centers
Weatherford	Oil field service

Note: Companies shown are located within the Lafayette, LA Metropolitan Statistical Area.
Source: Hoovers.com; Wikipedia

PUBLIC SAFETY

Crime Rate

Area	All Crimes	Violent Crimes				Property Crimes		
		Murder	Rape[3]	Robbery	Aggrav. Assault	Burglary	Larceny -Theft	Motor Vehicle Theft
City	5,116.1	17.1	16.3	136.0	390.9	785.6	3,539.5	230.8
Suburbs[1]	n/a	6.0	26.9	51.0	313.1	647.1	n/a	n/a
Metro[2]	n/a	8.9	24.1	73.2	333.4	683.2	n/a	n/a
U.S.	2,756.1	5.3	41.7	98.0	248.9	430.4	1,694.4	237.4

Note: Figures are crimes per 100,000 population; (1) All areas within the metro area that are located outside the city limits; (2) Figures cover the Lafayette, LA Metropolitan Statistical Area—see Appendix B for areas included; (3) The city and U.S. figures shown were reported using the revised Uniform Crime Reporting (UCR) definition of rape. The suburban and metro area figures shown are an aggregate total of the data submitted using both the revised and legacy UCR definitions.
Source: FBI Uniform Crime Reports, 2017

Hate Crimes

Area	Number of Quarters Reported	Number of Incidents per Bias Motivation					
		Race/Ethnicity/ Ancestry	Religion	Sexual Orientation	Disability	Gender	Gender Identity
City	2	0	0	0	0	0	0
U.S.	4	4,131	1,564	1,130	116	46	119

Source: Federal Bureau of Investigation, Hate Crime Statistics 2017

Identity Theft Consumer Reports

Area	Reports	Reports per 100,000 Population	Rank[2]
MSA[1]	435	88	180
U.S.	444,602	135	-

Note: (1) Figures cover the Lafayette, LA Metropolitan Statistical Area—see Appendix B for areas included; (2) Rank ranges from 1 to 389 where 1 indicates greatest number of identity theft reports per 100,000 population
Source: Federal Trade Commission, Consumer Sentinel Network Data Book for January–December 2018

Fraud and Other Consumer Reports

Area	Reports	Reports per 100,000 Population	Rank[2]
MSA[1]	1,989	405	313
U.S.	2,552,917	776	-

Note: (1) Figures cover the Lafayette, LA Metropolitan Statistical Area—see Appendix B for areas included; (2) Rank ranges from 1 to 389 where 1 indicates greatest number of fraud and other consumer reports per 100,000 population
Source: Federal Trade Commission, Consumer Sentinel Network Data Book for January–December 2018

SPORTS

Professional Sports Teams

Team Name	League	Year Established
No teams are located in the metro area		

Source: Wikipedia, Major Professional Sports Teams of the United States and Canada, April 5, 2019

CLIMATE

Average and Extreme Temperatures

Temperature	Jan	Feb	Mar	Apr	May	Jun	Jul	Aug	Sep	Oct	Nov	Dec	Yr.
Extreme High (°F)	82	85	91	92	98	103	101	102	99	94	87	85	103
Average High (°F)	61	65	71	79	85	90	91	91	87	80	70	64	78
Average Temp. (°F)	51	54	61	68	75	81	82	82	78	69	59	53	68
Average Low (°F)	41	44	50	57	64	70	73	72	68	57	48	43	57
Extreme Low (°F)	9	13	20	32	44	53	58	59	43	30	21	8	8

Note: Figures cover the years 1948-1995
Source: National Climatic Data Center, International Station Meteorological Climate Summary, 9/96

Average Precipitation/Snowfall/Humidity

Precip./Humidity	Jan	Feb	Mar	Apr	May	Jun	Jul	Aug	Sep	Oct	Nov	Dec	Yr.
Avg. Precip. (in.)	4.9	5.1	4.8	5.5	5.0	4.4	6.6	5.4	4.1	3.1	4.2	5.3	58.5
Avg. Snowfall (in.)	Tr	Tr	Tr	0	0	0	0	0	0	0	Tr	Tr	Tr
Avg. Rel. Hum. 6am (%)	85	85	86	89	91	91	92	93	91	89	88	86	89
Avg. Rel. Hum. 3pm (%)	59	55	52	52	54	57	62	61	59	51	53	57	56

Note: Figures cover the years 1948-1995; Tr = Trace amounts (<0.05 in. of rain; <0.5 in. of snow)
Source: National Climatic Data Center, International Station Meteorological Climate Summary, 9/96

Weather Conditions

Temperature			Daytime Sky			Precipitation		
10°F & below	32°F & below	90°F & above	Clear	Partly cloudy	Cloudy	0.01 inch or more precip.	0.1 inch or more snow/ice	Thunder-storms
< 1	21	86	99	150	116	113	< 1	73

Note: Figures are average number of days per year and cover the years 1948-1995
Source: National Climatic Data Center, International Station Meteorological Climate Summary, 9/96

HAZARDOUS WASTE

Superfund Sites

The Lafayette, LA metro area is home to one site on the EPA's Superfund National Priorities List: **Evr-Wood Treating/Evangeline Refining Company** (final). There are a total of 1,390 Superfund sites with a status of proposed or final on the list in the U.S. *U.S. Environmental Protection Agency, National Priorities List, April 5, 2019*

AIR & WATER QUALITY

Air Quality Trends: Ozone

	1990	1995	2000	2005	2010	2012	2014	2015	2016	2017
MSA[1]	n/a	n/a	n/a	n/a	n/a	n/a	n/a	n/a	n/a	n/a
U.S.	0.088	0.089	0.082	0.080	0.073	0.075	0.067	0.067	0.068	0.068

Note: (1) Data covers the Lafayette, LA Metropolitan Statistical Area—see Appendix B for areas included; n/a not available. The values shown are the composite ozone concentration averages among trend sites based on the highest fourth daily maximum 8-hour concentration in parts per million. These trends are based on sites having an adequate record of monitoring data during the trend period. Data from exceptional events are included.
Source: U.S. Environmental Protection Agency, Air Quality Monitoring Information, "Air Quality Trends by City, 1990-2017"

Air Quality Index

Area	Percent of Days when Air Quality was...[2]					AQI Statistics[2]	
	Good	Moderate	Unhealthy for Sensitive Groups	Unhealthy	Very Unhealthy	Maximum	Median
MSA[1]	71.8	27.9	0.3	0.0	0.0	105	42

Note: (1) Data covers the Lafayette, LA Metropolitan Statistical Area—see Appendix B for areas included; (2) Based on 365 days with AQI data in 2017. Air Quality Index (AQI) is an index for reporting daily air quality. EPA calculates the AQI for five major air pollutants regulated by the Clean Air Act: ground-level ozone, particle pollution (aka particulate matter), carbon monoxide, sulfur dioxide, and nitrogen dioxide. The AQI runs from 0 to 500. The higher the AQI value, the greater the level of air pollution and the greater the health concern. There are six AQI categories: "Good" AQI is between 0 and 50. Air quality is considered satisfactory; "Moderate" AQI is between 51 and 100. Air quality is acceptable; "Unhealthy for Sensitive Groups" When AQI values are between 101 and 150, members of sensitive groups may experience health effects; "Unhealthy" When AQI values are between 151 and 200 everyone may begin to experience health effects; "Very Unhealthy" AQI values between 201 and 300 trigger a health alert; "Hazardous" AQI values over 300 trigger warnings of emergency conditions (not shown).
Source: U.S. Environmental Protection Agency, Air Quality Index Report, 2017

Air Quality Index Pollutants

Area	Percent of Days when AQI Pollutant was...[2]					
	Carbon Monoxide	Nitrogen Dioxide	Ozone	Sulfur Dioxide	Particulate Matter 2.5	Particulate Matter 10
MSA[1]	0.0	0.0	65.8	0.0	34.2	0.0

Note: (1) Data covers the Lafayette, LA Metropolitan Statistical Area—see Appendix B for areas included; (2) Based on 365 days with AQI data in 2017. The Air Quality Index (AQI) is an index for reporting daily air quality. EPA calculates the AQI for five major air pollutants regulated by the Clean Air Act: ground-level ozone, particle pollution (also known as particulate matter), carbon monoxide, sulfur dioxide, and nitrogen dioxide. The AQI runs from 0 to 500. The higher the AQI value, the greater the level of air pollution and the greater the health concern.
Source: U.S. Environmental Protection Agency, Air Quality Index Report, 2017

Maximum Air Pollutant Concentrations: Particulate Matter, Ozone, CO and Lead

	Particulate Matter 10 (ug/m^3)	Particulate Matter 2.5 Wtd AM (ug/m^3)	Particulate Matter 2.5 24-Hr (ug/m^3)	Ozone (ppm)	Carbon Monoxide (ppm)	Lead (ug/m^3)
MSA[1] Level	69	8	21	0.064	n/a	n/a
NAAQS[2]	150	15	35	0.075	9	0.15
Met NAAQS[2]	Yes	Yes	Yes	Yes	n/a	n/a

Note: (1) Data covers the Lafayette, LA Metropolitan Statistical Area—see Appendix B for areas included; Data from exceptional events are included; (2) National Ambient Air Quality Standards; ppm = parts per million; ug/m^3 = micrograms per cubic meter; n/a not available.
Concentrations: Particulate Matter 10 (coarse particulate)—highest second maximum 24-hour concentration; Particulate Matter 2.5 Wtd AM (fine particulate)—highest weighted annual mean concentration; Particulate Matter 2.5 24-Hour (fine particulate)—highest 98th percentile 24-hour concentration; Ozone—highest fourth daily maximum 8-hour concentration; Carbon Monoxide—highest second maximum non-overlapping 8-hour concentration; Lead—maximum running 3-month average
Source: U.S. Environmental Protection Agency, Air Quality Monitoring Information, "Air Quality Statistics by City, 2017"

Maximum Air Pollutant Concentrations: Nitrogen Dioxide and Sulfur Dioxide

	Nitrogen Dioxide AM (ppb)	Nitrogen Dioxide 1-Hr (ppb)	Sulfur Dioxide AM (ppb)	Sulfur Dioxide 1-Hr (ppb)	Sulfur Dioxide 24-Hr (ppb)
MSA[1] Level	n/a	n/a	n/a	n/a	n/a
NAAQS[2]	53	100	30	75	140
Met NAAQS[2]	n/a	n/a	n/a	n/a	n/a

Note: (1) Data covers the Lafayette, LA Metropolitan Statistical Area—see Appendix B for areas included; Data from exceptional events are included; (2) National Ambient Air Quality Standards; ppm = parts per million; ug/m^3 = micrograms per cubic meter; n/a not available.
Concentrations: Nitrogen Dioxide AM—highest arithmetic mean concentration; Nitrogen Dioxide 1-Hr—highest 98th percentile 1-hour daily maximum concentration; Sulfur Dioxide AM—highest annual mean concentration; Sulfur Dioxide 1-Hr—highest 99th percentile 1-hour daily maximum concentration; Sulfur Dioxide 24-Hr—highest second maximum 24-hour concentration
Source: U.S. Environmental Protection Agency, Air Quality Monitoring Information, "Air Quality Statistics by City, 2017"

Drinking Water

Water System Name	Pop. Served	Primary Water Source Type	Violations[1]	
			Health Based	Monitoring/ Reporting
Lafayette Utilities Water System	198,975	Ground	0	0

Note: (1) Based on violation data from January 1, 2018 to December 31, 2018
Source: U.S. Environmental Protection Agency, Office of Ground Water and Drinking Water, Safe Drinking Water Information System (based on data extracted April 5, 2019)

McAllen, Texas

Background

The largest city in Hidalgo County, Texas, McAllen is located near the tip of southern Texas, across the Rio Grande from Reynosa, Mexico, a location that has been the key to its commercial transformation. The city grew while agriculture and petroleum were its economic mainstays, but since the North American Free Trade Agreement in 1994, international trade, health care, government administration, and tourism have become its economic engines. Tourism in McAllen has fueled the highest retail spending per capita in Texas.

In 1904 John McAllen, together with his son, James, and other partners, established a town site eight miles north of the county seat, Hidalgo. In 1907, two miles to the east, William Briggs, O. Jones, and John Closner founded a settlement called East McAllen, while the original town came to be called West McAllen. By 1911 East McAllen had a thousand residents and West McAllen had withered, and the larger town incorporated as the city of McAllen.

John McAllen experimented with growing sugarcane, cotton, alfalfa, broom corn, citrus fruits, grapes, and figs. Eventually farming, mostly by Anglo interests and dependent on the railroad and irrigation systems, displaced ranching as the primary economic activity. By the 1920s the city had some 6,000 residents.

From 1926 McAllen was linked to Reynosa by bridge. The McAllen-Hidalgo-Reynosa International Bridge proved crucial to McAllen after oil was discovered near Reynosa in the late 1940s. The bridge became the second-most-important port of entry into Mexico. Tourism and retail businesses flourished, bolstered by the cheap labor supply.

McAllen's population grew sporadically over the next several decades. In the 1970s and 1980s, however, the population boomed, owing to the *maquiladora* economy (in which U.S. companies, taking advantage of low Mexican labor costs, ship components of manufactured goods across the border to be assembled and shipped back). The McAllen Foreign-Trade Zone (FTZ), created in 1973, was the first inland U.S. foreign trade zone; there is also an FTZ site at McAllen-Miller International Airport. Anzalduas International Bridge opened in 2009 and, today the city is more than three-quarters Hispanic. Thanks to international trade, cross-border commerce, and its concentration of major health-care facilities, McAllen is the U.S. city ranked highest for long-term job growth, according to the U.S. Bureau of Labor Statistics.

South Texas College was founded in 1993. Three of its five campuses are in McAllen, including the Technical Campus. Edinburg-based University of Texas–Pan American has a branch in McAllen.

McAllen's cultural institutions include Quinta Mazatlan, a Spanish Revival Style hacienda built in 1935 and now a sanctuary known for its environmental stewardship programs. Quinta Mazatlan is one of nine Rio Grande Valley preserves administered by the World Birding Center. The oldest stand of native forest in the area is preserved in the McAllen Botanical Garden. Nearby nature preserves include the Edinburg Scenic Wetlands, Santa Ana National Wildlife Refuge, and Bentsen State Park.

McAllen has several notable museums: the International Museum of Art & Science, the Museum of South Texas History, and the McAllen Heritage Center. The Valley Symphony Orchestra and Chorale and two VSO-affiliated youth orchestras perform in McAllen and at the University of Texas–Pan American. An arts scene is coalescing, thanks to the city's Creative Arts Incubator, which sponsors a public art program, studio space for artists and performers, a monthly Artwalk, and a music series. Notable among the region's yearly festivals are the February Borderfest, at Hidalgo, and the mid-March Rio Grande Valley Livestock Show, in Mercedes. Plus, the city boasts the 18.5-acre McAllen Convention Center complex.

The Rio Grande Valley Vipers won the National Basketball Association Development League championship in 2010 and again in 2013. Like the Vipers, the Rio Grande Valley Flash indoor soccer team plays at State Farm Arena in Hidalgo. The Edinburg Roadrunners play at Edinburg Baseball Stadium, which they share with the McAllen Thunder baseball team.

The "City of Palms," as McAllen has been known since the 1940s, has sunshine and a warm climate year-round.

Rankings

General Rankings

- The McAllen metro area was identified as one of America's fastest-growing areas in terms of population and business growth by *MagnifyMoney*. The area ranked #10 out of 35. The 100 most populous metro areas in the U.S. were evaluated on their change from 2011-2016 in the following categories: people and housing; workforce and employment opportunities; growing industry. *www.businessinsider.com, "The 35 Cities in the US with the Biggest Influx of People, the Most Work Opportunities, and the Hottest Business Growth," August 12, 2018*

- The McAllen metro area was identified as one of America's fastest-growing areas in terms of population and economy by *Forbes*. The area ranked #22 out of 25. The 100 most populous metro areas in the U.S. were evaluated on the following criteria: estimated population growth; employment; economic output; wages; home values. *Forbes, "America's Fastest-Growing Cities 2018," February 28, 2018*

Business/Finance Rankings

- The personal finance site NerdWallet analyzed 183 American metropolitan areas with populations over 250,000 and more than 15,000 businesses to rank where entrepreneurs find the most success. Criteria included area economy, annual income, housing cost, unemployment rate, and the success rate of area businesses. McAllen ranked #177. *www.nerdwallet.com, "Best Places to Start a Business," April 27, 2015*

- Using data from the Council for Community and Economic Research's 2014 cost of living index, NerdWallet ranked the 100 most affordable cities in America. Median income was compared with cost of living to find truly affordable places. McAllen ranked #56. *NerdWallet.com, "America's Most Affordable Places," May 18, 2015*

- The Brookings Institution ranked the nation's largest cities based on income inequality. McAllen was ranked #45 (#1 = greatest inequality). Criteria: the "95/20 ratio," a figure representing the income at which a household earns more than 95 percent of all other households, divided by the income at which a household earns more than only 20 percent of all other households. *Brookings Institution, "Household Income Inequality, Largest Cities of 97 Large U.S. Metro Areas, 2014-2016," February 5, 2018*

- The Brookings Institution ranked the 100 largest metro areas in the U.S. based on income inequality. McAllen was ranked #11 (#1 = greatest inequality). Criteria: the "95/20 ratio," a figure representing the income at which a household earns more than 95 percent of all other households, divided by the income at which a household earns more than only 20 percent of all other households. *Brookings Institution, "Household Income Inequality, 100 Largest U.S. Metro Areas, 2014-2016," February 5, 2018*

- The McAllen metro area was identified as one of the most affordable metropolitan areas in America by *Forbes*. The area ranked #17 out of 20 based on the National Association of Home Builders/Wells Fargo Housing Affordability Index and Sperling's Best Places' cost-of-living index. *Forbes.com, "America's Most Affordable Cities in 2015," March 12, 2015*

- For its annual survey of the "10 Cheapest U.S. Cities to Live In," Kiplinger applied Cost of Living Index statistics developed by the Council for Community and Economic Research to U.S. Census Bureau population and median household income data for cities with populations above 50,000. In the resulting ranking, McAllen ranked #1. *Kiplinger.com, "10 Cheapest U.S. Cities to Live In," March 19, 2018*

- The McAllen metro area appeared on the Milken Institute "2018 Best Performing Cities" list. Rank: #68 out of 200 large metro areas. Criteria: job growth; wage and salary growth; high-tech output growth. *Milken Institute, "Best-Performing Cities 2018," January 24, 2019*

- *Forbes* ranked the 200 most populous metro areas to determine the nation's "Best Places for Business and Careers." The McAllen metro area was ranked #150. Criteria: costs (business and living); job growth (past and projected); income growth; quality of life; educational attainment (college and high school); projected economic growth; cultural and recreational opportunities; net migration patterns; number of highly ranked colleges. *Forbes, "The Best Places for Business and Careers 2018: Seattle Leads the Way," October 24, 2018*

Children/Family Rankings

- McAllen was selected as one of the most playful cities in the U.S. by KaBOOM! The organization's Playful City USA initiative honors cities and towns across the nation that have made their communities more playable. Criteria: pledging to integrate play as a solution to challenges in their communities; making it easy for children to get active and balanced play; creating more family-friendly and innovative communities as a result. *KaBOOM! National Campaign for Play, "2017 Playful City USA Communities"*

Education Rankings

- Personal finance website *WalletHub* analyzed the 150 largest U.S. metropolitan statistical areas to determine where the most educated Americans are choosing to settle. Criteria: education quality and attainment gap; education levels; percentage of workers with degrees; public school quality rankings; quality and size of each metro area's universities. McAllen was ranked #148 (#1 = most educated city). *www.WalletHub.com, "2018's Most and Least Educated Cities in America," July 24, 2018*

Environmental Rankings

- McAllen was highlighted as one of the cleanest metro areas for ozone air pollution in the U.S. during 2014 through 2016. The list represents cities with no monitored ozone air pollution in unhealthful ranges. *American Lung Association, State of the Air 2018*

- McAllen was highlighted as one of the top 90 cleanest metro areas for short-term particle pollution (24-hour PM 2.5) in the U.S. during 2014 through 2016. Monitors in these cities reported no days with unhealthful PM 2.5 levels. *American Lung Association, State of the Air 2018*

Health/Fitness Rankings

- The Gallup-Healthways Well-Being Index tracks Americans' optimism about their communities and satisfaction with the metro areas in which they live. At least 300 adult residents in each of 186 U.S. metropolitan areas were asked whether they liked what they did each day and were motivated to achieve their goals. The McAllen metro area placed among the top five in the percentage of residents who feeling of purpose was high. *www.gallup.com, "2017 Community Well-Being Rankings," March 2018*

- McAllen was identified as a "2018 Spring Allergy Capital." The area ranked #1 out of 100. Three groups of factors were used to identify the most challenging cities for people with allergies during the spring season: annual pollen levels; medicine utilization; access to board-certified allergists. *Asthma and Allergy Foundation of America, "Spring Allergy Capitals 2018"*

- McAllen was identified as a "2018 Fall Allergy Capital." The area ranked #1 out of 100. Three groups of factors were used to identify the most challenging cities for people with allergies during the fall season: annual pollen levels; medicine utilization; access to board-certified allergists. *Asthma and Allergy Foundation of America, "Fall Allergy Capitals 2018"*

- McAllen was identified as a "2018 Asthma Capital." The area ranked #100 out of the nation's 100 largest metropolitan areas. Criteria: estimated prevalence; self-reported prevalence; crude death rate for asthma; annual pollen score; annual air quality; public smoking laws; number of board-certified asthma specialists; school inhaler access laws; rescue medication use; controller medication use; ER visits for asthma; uninsured rate; poverty rate. *Asthma and Allergy Foundation of America, "Asthma Capitals 2018: The Most Challenging Places to Live With Asthma"*

- The McAllen metro area ranked #27 out of 189 in The Gallup-Healthways Well-Being Index. Criteria: purpose; social well being; financial health; community and physical health. Results are based on telephone interviews with adults, aged 18 and older, living in metropolitan areas in the 50 U.S. states and the District of Columbia. *Gallup-Healthways, "State of American Well-Being, 2017 Community Well-Being Rankings" March 2018*

Real Estate Rankings

- McAllen was ranked #169 out of 237 metro areas in terms of housing affordability in 2018 by the National Association of Home Builders (#1 = most affordable). Criteria: the share of homes sold in that area affordable to a family earning the local median income, based on standard mortgage underwriting criteria. *National Association of Home Builders®, NAHB-Wells Fargo Housing Opportunity Index, 4th Quarter 2018*

Safety Rankings

- Allstate ranked the 200 largest cities in America in terms of driver safety. McAllen ranked #10. Criteria: internal property damage claims over a two-year period from January 2015 to December 2016. The report helps increase the importance of safety awareness behind the wheel. *Allstate, "Allstate America's Best Drivers Report, 2018" August 28, 2018*

- The National Insurance Crime Bureau ranked 382 metro areas in the U.S. in terms of per capita rates of vehicle theft. The McAllen metro area ranked #254 (#1 = highest rate). Criteria: number of vehicle theft offenses per 100,000 inhabitants in 2017. *National Insurance Crime Bureau, "Hot Spots 2017," July 12, 2018*

Seniors/Retirement Rankings

- From its Best Cities for Successful Aging indexes, the Milken Institute generated rankings for metropolitan areas, weighing data in nine categories—health care, wellness, living arrangements, transportation and convenience, financial characteristics, education, employment, community engagement, and overall livability. The McAllen metro area was ranked #59 overall in the large metro area category. *Milken Institute, "Best Cities for Successful Aging, 2017" March 14, 2017*

Business Environment

CITY FINANCES

City Government Finances

Component	2016 ($000)	2016 ($ per capita)
Total Revenues	240,910	1,717
Total Expenditures	242,304	1,727
Debt Outstanding	240,971	1,718
Cash and Securities[1]	252,595	1,801

Note: (1) Cash and security holdings of a government at the close of its fiscal year, including those of its dependent agencies, utilities, and liquor stores.
Source: U.S. Census Bureau, State & Local Government Finances 2016

City Government Revenue by Source

Source	2016 ($000)	2016 ($ per capita)	2016 (%)
General Revenue			
From Federal Government	19,015	136	7.9
From State Government	2,754	20	1.1
From Local Governments	59	0	0.0
Taxes			
Property	38,911	277	16.2
Sales and Gross Receipts	75,034	535	31.1
Personal Income	0	0	0.0
Corporate Income	0	0	0.0
Motor Vehicle License	0	0	0.0
Other Taxes	1,598	11	0.7
Current Charges	76,743	547	31.9
Liquor Store	0	0	0.0
Utility	17,043	122	7.1
Employee Retirement	0	0	0.0

Source: U.S. Census Bureau, State & Local Government Finances 2016

City Government Expenditures by Function

Function	2016 ($000)	2016 ($ per capita)	2016 (%)
General Direct Expenditures			
Air Transportation	12,396	88	5.1
Corrections	0	0	0.0
Education	0	0	0.0
Employment Security Administration	0	0	0.0
Financial Administration	3,532	25	1.5
Fire Protection	17,580	125	7.3
General Public Buildings	1,540	11	0.6
Governmental Administration, Other	4,708	33	1.9
Health	2,620	18	1.1
Highways	43,534	310	18.0
Hospitals	0	0	0.0
Housing and Community Development	2,223	15	0.9
Interest on General Debt	4,017	28	1.7
Judicial and Legal	2,836	20	1.2
Libraries	4,103	29	1.7
Parking	947	6	0.4
Parks and Recreation	16,856	120	7.0
Police Protection	33,366	237	13.8
Public Welfare	92	< 1	< 0.1
Sewerage	24,597	175	10.2
Solid Waste Management	19,794	141	8.2
Veterans' Services	0	0	0.0
Liquor Store	0	0	0.0
Utility	24,580	175	10.1
Employee Retirement	0	0	0.0

Source: U.S. Census Bureau, State & Local Government Finances 2016

DEMOGRAPHICS

Population Growth

Area	1990 Census	2000 Census	2010 Census	2017* Estimate	Population Growth (%)	
					1990-2017	2010-2017
City	86,145	106,414	129,877	139,838	62.3	7.7
MSA[1]	383,545	569,463	774,769	839,539	118.9	8.4
U.S.	248,709,873	281,421,906	308,745,538	321,004,407	29.1	4.0

Note: (1) Figures cover the McAllen-Edinburg-Mission, TX Metropolitan Statistical Area—see Appendix B for areas included; (*) 2013-2017 5-year estimated population
Source: U.S. Census Bureau, 1990 Census, Census 2000, Census 2010, 2013-2017 American Community Survey 5-Year Estimates

Household Size

Area	Persons in Household (%)							Average Household Size
	One	Two	Three	Four	Five	Six	Seven or More	
City	19.6	28.4	19.1	16.2	9.8	4.2	2.5	3.20
MSA[1]	15.4	25.1	17.8	17.8	13.1	5.9	5.0	3.60
U.S.	27.7	33.8	15.7	13.0	6.0	2.3	1.4	2.60

Note: (1) Figures cover the McAllen-Edinburg-Mission, TX Metropolitan Statistical Area—see Appendix B for areas included
Source: U.S. Census Bureau, 2013-2017 American Community Survey 5-Year Estimates

Race

Area	White Alone[2] (%)	Black Alone[2] (%)	Asian Alone[2] (%)	AIAN[3] Alone[2] (%)	NHOPI[4] Alone[2] (%)	Other Race Alone[2] (%)	Two or More Races (%)
City	80.1	1.0	2.6	0.3	0.1	14.7	1.2
MSA[1]	88.9	0.6	1.0	0.2	0.0	8.1	1.2
U.S.	73.0	12.7	5.4	0.8	0.2	4.8	3.1

Note: (1) Figures cover the McAllen-Edinburg-Mission, TX Metropolitan Statistical Area—see Appendix B for areas included; (2) Alone is defined as not being in combination with one or more other races; (3) American Indian and Alaska Native; (4) Native Hawaiian and Other Pacific Islander
Source: U.S. Census Bureau, 2013-2017 American Community Survey 5-Year Estimates

Hispanic or Latino Origin

Area	Total (%)	Mexican (%)	Puerto Rican (%)	Cuban (%)	Other (%)
City	85.2	80.7	0.6	0.3	3.6
MSA[1]	91.8	88.7	0.3	0.1	2.7
U.S.	17.6	11.1	1.7	0.7	4.1

Note: Persons of Hispanic or Latino origin can be of any race; (1) Figures cover the McAllen-Edinburg-Mission, TX Metropolitan Statistical Area—see Appendix B for areas included
Source: U.S. Census Bureau, 2013-2017 American Community Survey 5-Year Estimates

Segregation

Type	Segregation Indices[1]				Percent Change		
	1990	2000	2010	2010 Rank[2]	1990-2000	1990-2010	2000-2010
Black/White	33.9	48.8	40.7	90	14.8	6.8	-8.1
Asian/White	40.3	41.2	46.7	17	0.9	6.4	5.6
Hispanic/White	37.9	39.5	39.2	69	1.6	1.3	-0.4

Note: All figures cover the Metropolitan Statistical Area—see Appendix B for areas included; Figures are based on an analysis of 1990, 2000, and 2010 Census Decennial Census tract data by William H. Frey, Brookings Institution and the University of Michigan Social Science Data Analysis Network. In this analysis all racial groups (whites, blacks, and asians) are non-Hispanic members of those races. Hispanics are shown as a separate category; (1) Segregation Indices are Dissimilarity Indices that measure the degree to which the minority group is distributed differently than whites across census tracts. They range from 0 (complete integration) to 100 (complete segregation) where the value indicates the percentage of the minority group that needs to move to be distributed exactly like whites; (2) Ranges from 1 (most segregated) to 102 (least segregated); n/a not available.
Source: www.CensusScope.org

Ancestry

Area	German	Irish	English	American	Italian	Polish	French[2]	Scottish	Dutch
City	3.2	1.7	1.6	3.9	0.8	0.2	0.8	0.7	0.3
MSA[1]	1.9	1.0	0.9	2.4	0.5	0.2	0.5	0.3	0.2
U.S.	14.1	10.1	7.5	6.6	5.3	2.9	2.5	1.7	1.3

Note: Figures are the percentage of the total population reporting a particular ancestry. The nine most commonly reported ancestries in the U.S. are shown. Figures include multiple ancestries (e.g. if a person reported being Irish and Italian, they were included in both columns); (1) Figures cover the McAllen-Edinburg-Mission, TX Metropolitan Statistical Area—see Appendix B for areas included; (2) Excludes Basque
Source: U.S. Census Bureau, 2013-2017 American Community Survey 5-Year Estimates

Foreign-Born Population

Area	Any Foreign Country	Asia	Mexico	Europe	Carribean	Central America[2]	South America	Africa	Canada
City	27.4	2.0	23.7	0.3	0.2	0.4	0.6	0.0	0.1
MSA[1]	27.3	0.8	25.5	0.1	0.1	0.4	0.3	0.0	0.1
U.S.	13.4	4.1	3.6	1.5	1.3	1.0	0.9	0.6	0.3

Column header: *Percent of Population Born in*

Note: (1) Figures cover the McAllen-Edinburg-Mission, TX Metropolitan Statistical Area—see Appendix B for areas included; (2) Excludes Mexico.
Source: U.S. Census Bureau, 2013-2017 American Community Survey 5-Year Estimates

Marital Status

Area	Never Married	Now Married[2]	Separated	Widowed	Divorced
City	31.7	50.6	3.5	5.0	9.2
MSA[1]	33.6	49.7	3.9	5.1	7.8
U.S.	33.1	48.2	2.0	5.8	10.9

Note: Figures are percentages and cover the population 15 years of age and older; (1) Figures cover the McAllen-Edinburg-Mission, TX Metropolitan Statistical Area—see Appendix B for areas included; (2) Excludes separated
Source: U.S. Census Bureau, 2013-2017 American Community Survey 5-Year Estimates

Disability by Age

Area	All Ages	Under 18 Years Old	18 to 64 Years Old	65 Years and Over
City	13.2	4.9	10.8	46.1
MSA[1]	13.0	5.2	10.7	50.3
U.S.	12.6	4.2	10.3	35.5

Note: Figures show percent of the civilian noninstitutionalized population that reported having a disability. Disability status is determined from six types of difficulty: vision, hearing, cognitive, ambulatory, self-care, and independent living. For children under 5 years old, hearing and vision difficulty are used to determine disability status. For children between the ages of 5 and 14, disability status is determined from hearing, vision, cognitive, ambulatory, and self-care difficulties. For people aged 15 years and older, they are considered to have a disability if they have difficulty with any one of the six difficulty types; Note: (1) Figures cover the McAllen-Edinburg-Mission, TX Metropolitan Statistical Area—see Appendix B for areas included
Source: U.S. Census Bureau, 2013-2017 American Community Survey 5-Year Estimates

Age

Area	Under Age 5	Age 5–19	Age 20–34	Age 35–44	Age 45–54	Age 55–64	Age 65–74	Age 75–84	Age 85+	Median Age
City	7.9	23.8	21.2	13.4	11.4	9.8	6.7	4.2	1.5	32.9
MSA[1]	9.6	27.2	21.0	13.0	10.6	8.1	5.8	3.4	1.2	28.9
U.S.	6.2	19.5	20.7	12.7	13.4	12.7	8.6	4.4	1.9	37.8

Column header: *Percent of Population*

Note: (1) Figures cover the McAllen-Edinburg-Mission, TX Metropolitan Statistical Area—see Appendix B for areas included
Source: U.S. Census Bureau, 2013-2017 American Community Survey 5-Year Estimates

Gender

Area	Males	Females	Males per 100 Females
City	69,425	70,413	98.6
MSA[1]	410,383	429,156	95.6
U.S.	158,018,753	162,985,654	97.0

Note: (1) Figures cover the McAllen-Edinburg-Mission, TX Metropolitan Statistical Area—see Appendix B for areas included
Source: U.S. Census Bureau, 2013-2017 American Community Survey 5-Year Estimates

Religious Groups by Family

Area	Catholic	Baptist	Non-Den.	Methodist[2]	Lutheran	LDS[3]	Pente-costal	Presby-terian[4]	Muslim[5]	Judaism
MSA[1]	34.7	4.5	2.8	1.3	0.4	1.3	1.2	0.2	1.0	<0.1
U.S.	19.1	9.3	4.0	4.0	2.3	2.0	1.9	1.6	0.8	0.7

Note: Figures are the number of adherents as a percentage of the total population; (1) Figures cover the McAllen-Edinburg-Mission, TX Metropolitan Statistical Area—see Appendix B for areas included; (2) Methodist/Pietist; (3) Latter Day Saints; (4) Reformed; (5) Figures are estimates
Source: Association of Statisticians of American Religious Bodies, 2010 U.S. Religion Census: Religious Congregations & Membership Study

Religious Groups by Tradition

Area	Catholic	Evangelical Protestant	Mainline Protestant	Other Tradition	Black Protestant	Orthodox
MSA[1]	34.7	9.7	1.9	2.4	<0.1	<0.1
U.S.	19.1	16.2	7.3	4.3	1.6	0.3

Note: Figures are the number of adherents as a percentage of the total population; (1) Figures cover the McAllen-Edinburg-Mission, TX Metropolitan Statistical Area—see Appendix B for areas included
Source: Association of Statisticians of American Religious Bodies, 2010 U.S. Religion Census: Religious Congregations & Membership Study

ECONOMY

Gross Metropolitan Product

Area	2016	2017	2018	2019	Rank[2]
MSA[1]	19.4	20.5	21.7	22.7	123

Note: Figures are in billions of dollars; (1) Figures cover the McAllen-Edinburg-Mission, TX Metropolitan Statistical Area—see Appendix B for areas included; (2) Rank is based on 2017 data and ranges from 1 to 381
Source: U.S. Conference of Mayors, U.S. Metro Economies: Economic Growth & Full Employment, June 2018

Economic Growth

Area	2017-2018 (%)	2019-2020 (%)	2021-2022 (%)
MSA[1]	3.8	2.4	2.3

Note: Figures are real gross metropolitan product (GMP) growth rates and represent average annual percent change; (1) Figures cover the McAllen-Edinburg-Mission, TX Metropolitan Statistical Area—see Appendix B for areas included
Source: U.S. Conference of Mayors, U.S. Metro Economies: Economic Growth & Full Employment, June 2018

Metropolitan Area Exports

Area	2012	2013	2014	2015	2016	2017	Rank[2]
MSA[1]	5,198.5	5,265.5	5,316.0	5,327.1	5,214.3	5,659.0	52

Note: Figures are in millions of dollars; (1) Figures cover the McAllen-Edinburg-Mission, TX Metropolitan Statistical Area—see Appendix B for areas included; (2) Rank is based on 2017 data and ranges from 1 to 387
Source: U.S. Department of Commerce, International Trade Administration, Office of Trade and Economic Analysis, Industry and Analysis, Exports by Metropolitan Area, extracted March 25, 2019

Building Permits

Area	Single-Family 2016	2017	Pct. Chg.	Multi-Family 2016	2017	Pct. Chg.	Total 2016	2017	Pct. Chg.
City	450	438	-2.7	173	200	15.6	623	638	2.4
MSA[1]	2,921	2,698	-7.6	1,647	1,599	-2.9	4,568	4,297	-5.9
U.S.	750,800	820,000	9.2	455,800	462,000	1.4	1,206,600	1,282,000	6.2

Note: (1) Figures cover the McAllen-Edinburg-Mission, TX Metropolitan Statistical Area—see Appendix B for areas included; Figures represent new, privately-owned housing units authorized (unadjusted data); All permit data are based on estimates with imputation
Source: U.S. Census Bureau, Manufacturing, Mining, and Construction Statistics, Building Permits, 2016, 2017

Bankruptcy Filings

Area	Business Filings			Nonbusiness Filings		
	2017	2018	% Chg.	2017	2018	% Chg.
Hidalgo County	40	20	-50.0	455	439	-3.5
U.S.	23,157	22,232	-4.0	765,863	751,186	-1.9

Note: Business filings include Chapter 7, Chapter 11, Chapter 12, and Chapter 13; Nonbusiness filings include Chapter 7, Chapter 11, and Chapter 13
Source: Administrative Office of the U.S. Courts, Business and Nonbusiness Bankruptcy, County Cases Commenced by Chapter of the Bankruptcy Code, During the 12-Month Period Ending December 31, 2017 and Business and Nonbusiness Bankruptcy, County Cases Commenced by Chapter of the Bankruptcy Code, During the 12-Month Period Ending December 31, 2018

Housing Vacancy Rates

Area	Gross Vacancy Rate[2] (%)			Year-Round Vacancy Rate[3] (%)			Rental Vacancy Rate[4] (%)			Homeowner Vacancy Rate[5] (%)		
	2016	2017	2018	2016	2017	2018	2016	2017	2018	2016	2017	2018
MSA[1]	n/a	n/a	n/a	n/a	n/a	n/a	n/a	n/a	n/a	n/a	n/a	n/a
U.S.	12.8	12.7	12.3	9.9	9.9	9.7	6.9	7.2	6.9	1.7	1.6	1.5

Note: (1) Figures cover the McAllen-Edinburg-Mission, TX Metropolitan Statistical Area—see Appendix B for areas included; (2) The percentage of the total housing inventory that is vacant; (3) The percentage of the housing inventory (excluding seasonal units) that is year-round vacant; (4) The percentage of rental inventory that is vacant for rent; (5) The percentage of homeowner inventory that is vacant for sale; n/a not available
Source: U.S. Census Bureau, Housing Vacancies and Homeownership Annual Statistics: 2016, 2017, 2018

INCOME

Income

Area	Per Capita ($)	Median Household ($)	Average Household ($)
City	21,683	45,057	66,023
MSA[1]	15,883	37,097	54,348
U.S.	31,177	57,652	81,283

Note: (1) Figures cover the McAllen-Edinburg-Mission, TX Metropolitan Statistical Area—see Appendix B for areas included
Source: U.S. Census Bureau, 2013-2017 American Community Survey 5-Year Estimates

Household Income Distribution

Area	Percent of Households Earning							
	Under $15,000	$15,000 -$24,999	$25,000 -$34,999	$35,000 -$49,999	$50,000 -$74,999	$75,000 -$99,999	$100,000 -$149,999	$150,000 and up
City	18.1	13.9	9.9	11.6	17.0	10.4	10.6	8.5
MSA[1]	20.9	14.9	12.0	13.2	16.0	9.4	8.8	4.9
U.S.	11.6	9.8	9.5	13.0	17.7	12.3	14.1	12.1

Note: (1) Figures cover the McAllen-Edinburg-Mission, TX Metropolitan Statistical Area—see Appendix B for areas included
Source: U.S. Census Bureau, 2013-2017 American Community Survey 5-Year Estimates

Poverty Rate

Area	All Ages	Under 18 Years Old	18 to 64 Years Old	65 Years and Over
City	25.2	36.6	20.6	20.8
MSA[1]	31.8	43.8	26.3	23.0
U.S.	14.6	20.3	13.7	9.3

Note: Figures are percentage of people whose income during the past 12 months was below the poverty level; (1) Figures cover the McAllen-Edinburg-Mission, TX Metropolitan Statistical Area—see Appendix B for areas included
Source: U.S. Census Bureau, 2013-2017 American Community Survey 5-Year Estimates

EMPLOYMENT

Labor Force and Employment

Area	Civilian Labor Force			Workers Employed		
	Dec. 2017	Dec. 2018	% Chg.	Dec. 2017	Dec. 2018	% Chg.
City	65,733	67,123	2.1	62,813	64,102	2.1
MSA[1]	343,867	351,108	2.1	321,005	327,595	2.1
U.S.	159,880,000	162,510,000	1.6	153,602,000	156,481,000	1.9

Note: Data is not seasonally adjusted and covers workers 16 years of age and older; (1) Figures cover the McAllen-Edinburg-Mission, TX Metropolitan Statistical Area—see Appendix B for areas included
Source: Bureau of Labor Statistics, Local Area Unemployment Statistics

Unemployment Rate

Area	2018											
	Jan.	Feb.	Mar.	Apr.	May	Jun.	Jul.	Aug.	Sep.	Oct.	Nov.	Dec.
City	5.0	4.9	5.0	4.8	4.5	5.1	4.9	4.9	4.5	4.1	4.1	4.5
MSA[1]	7.6	7.1	6.9	6.6	6.2	7.2	7.0	6.6	6.2	5.4	5.8	6.7
U.S.	4.5	4.4	4.1	3.7	3.6	4.2	4.1	3.9	3.6	3.5	3.5	3.7

Note: Data is not seasonally adjusted and covers workers 16 years of age and older; (1) Figures cover the McAllen-Edinburg-Mission, TX Metropolitan Statistical Area—see Appendix B for areas included
Source: Bureau of Labor Statistics, Local Area Unemployment Statistics

Average Wages

Occupation	$/Hr.	Occupation	$/Hr.
Accountants and Auditors	30.00	Maids and Housekeeping Cleaners	9.20
Automotive Mechanics	19.50	Maintenance and Repair Workers	13.10
Bookkeepers	16.20	Marketing Managers	56.40
Carpenters	16.90	Nuclear Medicine Technologists	n/a
Cashiers	10.60	Nurses, Licensed Practical	22.30
Clerks, General Office	13.40	Nurses, Registered	34.10
Clerks, Receptionists/Information	11.70	Nursing Assistants	11.20
Clerks, Shipping/Receiving	11.90	Packers and Packagers, Hand	11.00
Computer Programmers	36.70	Physical Therapists	54.10
Computer Systems Analysts	n/a	Postal Service Mail Carriers	25.40
Computer User Support Specialists	19.70	Real Estate Brokers	n/a
Cooks, Restaurant	11.30	Retail Salespersons	11.10
Dentists	100.50	Sales Reps., Exc. Tech./Scientific	27.20
Electrical Engineers	53.30	Sales Reps., Tech./Scientific	53.30
Electricians	18.90	Secretaries, Exc. Legal/Med./Exec.	14.10
Financial Managers	49.00	Security Guards	11.60
First-Line Supervisors/Managers, Sales	22.20	Surgeons	n/a
Food Preparation Workers	11.80	Teacher Assistants*	11.70
General and Operations Managers	46.90	Teachers, Elementary School*	26.30
Hairdressers/Cosmetologists	12.00	Teachers, Secondary School*	27.40
Internists, General	n/a	Telemarketers	10.70
Janitors and Cleaners	11.30	Truck Drivers, Heavy/Tractor-Trailer	17.60
Landscaping/Groundskeeping Workers	11.40	Truck Drivers, Light/Delivery Svcs.	13.80
Lawyers	n/a	Waiters and Waitresses	9.80

Note: Wage data covers the McAllen-Edinburg-Mission, TX Metropolitan Statistical Area—see Appendix B for areas included; (*) Hourly wages for elementary/secondary school teachers and teacher assistants were calculated by the editors from annual wage data based on a 40 hour work week; n/a not available.
Source: Bureau of Labor Statistics, Metro Area Occupational Employment & Wage Estimates, May 2018

Employment by Occupation

Occupation Classification	City (%)	MSA[1] (%)	U.S. (%)
Management, Business, Science, and Arts	36.1	27.0	37.4
Natural Resources, Construction, and Maintenance	7.0	13.0	8.9
Production, Transportation, and Material Moving	9.2	11.0	12.2
Sales and Office	26.9	25.6	23.5
Service	20.7	23.5	18.0

Note: Figures cover employed civilians 16 years of age and older; (1) Figures cover the McAllen-Edinburg-Mission, TX Metropolitan Statistical Area—see Appendix B for areas included
Source: U.S. Census Bureau, 2013-2017 American Community Survey 5-Year Estimates

Employment by Industry

Sector	MSA[1]		U.S.
	Number of Employees	Percent of Total	Percent of Total
Construction, Mining, and Logging	8,200	3.0	5.3
Education and Health Services	75,400	28.0	15.9
Financial Activities	9,100	3.4	5.7
Government	62,000	23.0	15.1
Information	2,900	1.1	1.9
Leisure and Hospitality	25,400	9.4	10.7
Manufacturing	7,200	2.7	8.5
Other Services	5,800	2.2	3.9
Professional and Business Services	17,600	6.5	14.1
Retail Trade	37,800	14.0	10.8
Transportation, Warehousing, and Utilities	8,800	3.3	4.2
Wholesale Trade	9,000	3.3	3.9

Note: Figures are non-farm employment as of December 2018. Figures are not seasonally adjusted and include workers 16 years of age and older; (1) Figures cover the McAllen-Edinburg-Mission, TX Metropolitan Statistical Area—see Appendix B for areas included
Source: Bureau of Labor Statistics, Current Employment Statistics, Employment, Hours, and Earnings

Occupations with Greatest Projected Employment Growth: 2018 – 2020

Occupation[1]	2018 Employment	2020 Projected Employment	Numeric Employment Change	Percent Employment Change
Combined Food Preparation and Serving Workers, Including Fast Food	351,780	372,090	20,310	5.8
Personal Care Aides	218,310	235,470	17,160	7.9
Heavy and Tractor-Trailer Truck Drivers	204,870	216,310	11,440	5.6
Laborers and Freight, Stock, and Material Movers, Hand	194,220	204,060	9,840	5.1
Waiters and Waitresses	236,020	245,790	9,770	4.1
Office Clerks, General	393,740	403,270	9,530	2.4
Customer Service Representatives	268,380	277,460	9,080	3.4
General and Operations Managers	182,190	190,620	8,430	4.6
Retail Salespersons	392,620	400,900	8,280	2.1
Construction Laborers	143,270	150,820	7,550	5.3

Note: Projections cover Texas; (1) Sorted by numeric employment change
Source: www.projectionscentral.com, State Occupational Projections, 2018–2020 Short-Term Projections

Fastest Growing Occupations: 2018 – 2020

Occupation[1]	2018 Employment	2020 Projected Employment	Numeric Employment Change	Percent Employment Change
Wind Turbine Service Technicians	1,810	2,190	380	21.0
Religious Workers, All Other	5,690	6,330	640	11.2
Fundraisers	8,830	9,670	840	9.5
Statisticians	1,870	2,040	170	9.1
Public Relations and Fundraising Managers	6,570	7,160	590	9.0
Home Health Aides	74,390	80,920	6,530	8.8
Community and Social Service Specialists, All Other	4,520	4,890	370	8.2
Personal Care Aides	218,310	235,470	17,160	7.9
Operations Research Analysts	10,920	11,760	840	7.7
Software Developers, Applications	65,190	70,140	4,950	7.6

Note: Projections cover Texas; (1) Sorted by percent employment change and excludes occupations with numeric employment change less than 50
Source: www.projectionscentral.com, State Occupational Projections, 2018–2020 Short-Term Projections

TAXES

State Corporate Income Tax Rates

State	Tax Rate (%)	Income Brackets ($)	Num. of Brackets	Financial Institution Tax Rate (%)[a]	Federal Income Tax Ded.
Texas	(w)	–	–	(w)	No

Note: Tax rates as of January 1, 2019; (a) Rates listed are the corporate income tax rate applied to financial institutions or excise taxes based on income. Some states have other taxes based upon the value of deposits or shares; (w) Texas imposes a Franchise Tax, otherwise known as margin tax, imposed on entities with more than $1,130,000 total revenues at rate of 0.75%, or 0.375% for entities primarily engaged in retail or wholesale trade, on lesser of 70% of total revenues or 100% of gross receipts after deductions for either compensation or cost of goods sold.
Source: Federation of Tax Administrators, Range of State Corporate Income Tax Rates, January 1, 2019

State Individual Income Tax Rates

State	Tax Rate (%)	Income Brackets ($)	Personal Exemptions ($)			Standard Ded. ($)	
			Single	Married	Depend.	Single	Married
Texas			– No state income tax –				

Note: Tax rates as of January 1, 2019; Local- and county-level taxes are not included; n/a not applicable;

Source: Federation of Tax Administrators, State Individual Income Tax Rates, January 1, 2019

Various State Sales and Excise Tax Rates

State	State Sales Tax (%)	Gasoline[1] (¢/gal.)	Cigarette[2] ($/pack)	Spirits[3] ($/gal.)	Wine[4] ($/gal.)	Beer[5] ($/gal.)	Recreational Marijuana (%)
Texas	6.25	20	1.41	2.40 (f)	0.20 (l)	0.20 (q)	Not legal

Note: All tax rates as of January 1, 2019; (1) The American Petroleum Institute has developed a methodology for determining the average tax rate on a gallon of fuel. Rates may include any of the following: excise taxes, environmental fees, storage tank fees, other fees or taxes, general sales tax, and local taxes. In states where gasoline is subject to the general sales tax, or where the fuel tax is based on the average sale price, the average rate determined by API is sensitive to changes in the price of gasoline. States that fully or partially apply general sales taxes to gasoline: CA, CO, GA, IL, IN, MI, NY; (2) The federal excise tax of $1.0066 per pack and local taxes are not included; (3) Rates are those applicable to off-premise sales of 40% alcohol by volume (a.b.v.) distilled spirits in 750ml containers. Local excise taxes are excluded; (4) Rates are those applicable to off-premise sales of 11% a.b.v. non-carbonated wine in 750ml containers; (5) Rates are those applicable to off-premise sales of 4.7% a.b.v. beer in 12 ounce containers; (f) Different rates also applicable according to alcohol content, place of production, size of container, or place purchased (on- or off-premise or onboard airlines); (l) Different rates also applicable to alcohol content, place of production, size of container, place purchased (on- or off-premise or on board airlines) or type of wine (carbonated, vermouth, etc.); (q) Different rates also applicable according to alcohol content, place of production, size of container, or place purchased (on- or off-premise or onboard airlines).
Source: Tax Foundation, 2019 Facts & Figures: How Does Your State Compare?

State Business Tax Climate Index Rankings

State	Overall Rank	Corporate Tax Rank	Individual Income Tax Rank	Sales Tax Rank	Unemployment Insurance Tax Rank	Property Tax Rank
Texas	15	49	6	37	18	37

Note: The index is a measure of how each state's tax laws affect economic performance. The lower the rank, the more favorable a state's tax system is for business. States without a given tax are given a ranking of 1. The scores/rankings for the District of Columbia do not affect other states. The 2019 index represents the tax climate as of July 1, 2018.
Source: Tax Foundation, State Business Tax Climate Index 2019

COMMERCIAL UTILITIES

Typical Monthly Electric Bills

Area	Commercial Service ($/month)		Industrial Service ($/month)	
	1,500 kWh	40 kW demand 14,000 kWh	1,000 kW demand 200,000 kWh	50,000 kW demand 32,500,000 kWh
City	n/a	n/a	n/a	n/a
Average[1]	203	1,619	25,886	2,540,077

Note: Figures are based on annualized rates; (1) Average based on 187 utilities surveyed; n/a not available
Source: Edison Electric Institute, Typical Bills and Average Rates Report, Summer 2018

TRANSPORTATION

Means of Transportation to Work

Area	Car/Truck/Van		Public Transportation			Bicycle	Walked	Other Means	Worked at Home
	Drove Alone	Car-pooled	Bus	Subway	Railroad				
City	76.7	11.6	0.7	0.0	0.0	0.5	1.0	5.1	4.3
MSA[1]	80.4	8.8	0.2	0.0	0.0	0.2	1.2	4.3	4.9
U.S.	76.4	9.2	2.5	1.9	0.6	0.6	2.7	1.3	4.7

Note: Figures are percentages and cover workers 16 years of age and older; (1) Figures cover the McAllen-Edinburg-Mission, TX Metropolitan Statistical Area—see Appendix B for areas included
Source: U.S. Census Bureau, 2013-2017 American Community Survey 5-Year Estimates

Travel Time to Work

Area	Less Than 10 Minutes	10 to 19 Minutes	20 to 29 Minutes	30 to 44 Minutes	45 to 59 Minutes	60 to 89 Minutes	90 Minutes or More
City	15.8	42.7	23.4	12.7	2.2	1.3	1.9
MSA[1]	13.8	38.6	25.1	15.8	2.6	2.0	2.1
U.S.	12.7	28.9	20.9	20.5	8.1	6.2	2.7

Note: Note: Figures are percentages and include workers 16 years old and over; (1) Figures cover the McAllen-Edinburg-Mission, TX Metropolitan Statistical Area—see Appendix B for areas included
Source: U.S. Census Bureau, 2013-2017 American Community Survey 5-Year Estimates

Freeway Travel Time Index

Area	1985	1990	1995	2000	2005	2010	2014
Urban Area Rank[1,2]	91	90	77	57	61	76	76
Urban Area Index[1]	1.03	1.05	1.09	1.15	1.16	1.14	1.15
Average Index[3]	1.09	1.11	1.14	1.17	1.20	1.19	1.20

Note: Freeway Travel Time Index—the ratio of travel time in the peak period to the travel time at free-flow conditions. For example, a value of 1.30 indicates a 20-minute free-flow trip takes 26 minutes in the peak (20 minutes x 1.30 = 26 minutes); (1) Covers the McAllen TX urban area; (2) Rank is based on 101 urban areas (#1 = highest travel time index); (3) Average of 101 urban areas
Source: Texas Transportation Institute, 2015 Urban Mobility Scorecard, August 2015

Freeway Commuter Stress Index

Area	1985	1990	1995	2000	2005	2010	2014
Urban Area Rank[1,2]	91	94	81	63	68	82	79
Urban Area Index[1]	1.05	1.07	1.11	1.17	1.18	1.16	1.17
Average Index[3]	1.13	1.16	1.19	1.22	1.25	1.24	1.25

Note: The Freeway Commuter Stress Index is the same as the Freeway Travel Time Index (see table above) except that it includes only the travel in the peak directions during the peak periods; the TTI includes travel in all directions during the peak period. Thus, the CSI is more indicative of the work trip experienced by each commuter on a daily basis; (1) Covers the McAllen TX urban area; (2) Rank is based on 101 urban areas (#1 = highest travel time index); (3) Average of 101 urban areas
Source: Texas Transportation Institute, 2015 Urban Mobility Scorecard, August 2015

Public Transportation

Agency Name / Mode of Transportation	Vehicles Operated in Maximum Service[1]	Annual Unlinked Passenger Trips[2] (in thous.)	Annual Passenger Miles[3] (in thous.)
City of McAllen - McAllen Express Transit			
Bus (directly operated)	11	675.5	n/a
Demand Response (directly operated)	3	14.7	n/a

Note: (1) The number of revenue vehicles operated by the given mode and type of service to meet the annual maximum service requirement. This is the revenue vehicle count during the peak season of the year; on the week and day that maximum service is provided. Vehicles operated in maximum service (VOMS) exclude atypical days and one-time special events; (2) The number of passengers who boarded public transportation vehicles. Passengers are counted each time they board a vehicle no matter how many vehicles they use to travel from their origin to their destination. (3) The sum of the distances ridden by all passengers during the entire fiscal year.
Source: Federal Transit Administration, National Transit Database, 2017

Air Transportation

Airport Name and Code / Type of Service	Passenger Airlines[1]	Passenger Enplanements	Freight Carriers[2]	Freight (lbs)
McAllen-Miller International Airport (MFE)				
Domestic service (U.S. carriers - 2018)	12	342,034	13	8,459,028
International service (U.S. carriers - 2017)	0	0	1	138

Note: (1) Includes all U.S.-based major, minor and commuter airlines that carried at least one passenger during the year; (2) Includes all U.S.-based airlines and freight carriers that transported at least one pound of freight during the year.
Source: Bureau of Transportation Statistics, The Intermodal Transportation Database, Air Carriers: T-100 Domestic Market (U.S. Carriers), 2018; Bureau of Transportation Statistics, The Intermodal Transportation Database, Air Carriers: T-100 International Market (U.S. Carriers), 2017

Other Transportation Statistics

Major Highways:	Expressway 83E
Amtrak Service:	No
Major Waterways/Ports:	Rio Grande

Source: Amtrak.com; Google Maps

BUSINESSES

Major Business Headquarters

Company Name	Industry	Rankings	
		Fortune[1]	Forbes[2]
No companies listed	-	-	-

Note: (1) Companies that produce a 10-K are ranked 1 to 500 based on 2017 revenue; (2) All private companies with at least $2 billion in annual revenue through the end of their most current fiscal year are ranked 1 to 229; companies listed are headquartered in the city; dashes indicate no ranking
Source: Fortune, "Fortune 500," June 2018; Forbes, "America's Largest Private Companies," 2018 Rankings

Minority Business Opportunity

McAllen is home to one company which is on the *Hispanic Business* 500 list (500 largest U.S. Hispanic-owned companies based on revenue): **Galvotec Alloys** (#135). Companies included must show at least 51 percent ownership by Hispanic U.S. citizens, and must maintain headquarters in one of the 50 states or Washington, D.C. *Hispanic Business, "Hispanic Business 500," June 20, 2013*

Minority- and Women-Owned Businesses

Group	All Firms		Firms with Paid Employees			
	Firms	Sales ($000)	Firms	Sales ($000)	Employees	Payroll ($000)
AIAN[1]	119	(s)	7	(s)	20 - 99	(s)
Asian	479	(s)	320	(s)	2,500 - 4,999	(s)
Black	212	(s)	57	(s)	250 - 499	(s)
Hispanic	13,601	2,857,733	1,946	2,379,321	31,994	787,956
NHOPI[2]	n/a	n/a	n/a	n/a	n/a	n/a
Women	6,842	1,022,057	590	856,199	11,757	260,457
All Firms	17,964	12,971,565	3,821	12,262,549	74,278	2,090,213

Note: Figures cover firms located in the city; minority- and women-owned business are defined as firms in which the corresponding group own 51% or more of the stock or equity of the company; (1) American Indian and Alaska Native; (2) Native Hawaiian and Other Pacific Islander; (s) estimates are suppressed when publication standards are not met; n/a not available
Source: U.S. Census Bureau, 2012 Economic Census, Survey of Business Owners

HOTELS & CONVENTION CENTERS

Hotels, Motels and Vacation Rentals

Area	5 Star		4 Star		3 Star		2 Star		1 Star		Not Rated	
	Num.	Pct.[3]	Num.	Pct.[3]	Num.	Pct.[3]	Num.	Pct.[3]	Num.	Pct.[3]	Num.	Pct.[3]
City[1]	0	0.0	0	0.0	18	14.2	77	60.6	2	1.6	30	23.6
Total[2]	286	0.4	5,236	7.1	16,715	22.6	10,259	13.9	293	0.4	41,056	55.6

Note: (1) Figures cover McAllen and vicinity; (2) Figures cover all 100 cities in this book; (3) Percentage of hotels which have a given star rating; Star ratings are determined by expedia.com and offer an indication of the general quality of a particular hotel.
Source: www.expedia.com, April 3, 2019

Major Convention Centers

Name	Overall Space (sq. ft.)	Exhibit Space (sq. ft.)	Meeting Space (sq. ft.)	Meeting Rooms
McAllen Convention Center	n/a	60,000	25,000	16

Note: Table includes convention centers located in the McAllen-Edinburg-Mission, TX metro area; n/a not available
Source: Original research

Living Environment

COST OF LIVING

Cost of Living Index

Composite Index	Groceries	Housing	Utilities	Trans-portation	Health Care	Misc. Goods/ Services
77.5	83.1	62.7	101.9	89.1	71.8	79.1

Note: The Cost of Living Index measures regional differences in the cost of consumer goods and services, excluding taxes and non-consumer expenditures, for professional and managerial households in the top income quintile. It is based on more than 50,000 prices covering almost 60 different items for which prices are collected three times a year by chambers of commerce, economic development organizations or university applied economic centers in each participating urban area. The numbers shown should be read as a percentage above or below the national average of 100. For example, a value of 115.4 in the groceries column indicates that grocery prices are 15.4% higher than the national average. Small differences in the index numbers should not be interpreted as significant; Figures cover the McAllen TX urban area.
Source: The Council for Community and Economic Research, ACCRA Cost of Living Index, 2018

Grocery Prices

Area[1]	T-Bone Steak ($/pound)	Frying Chicken ($/pound)	Whole Milk ($/half gal.)	Eggs ($/dozen)	Orange Juice ($/64 oz.)	Coffee ($/11.5 oz.)
City[2]	9.04	0.98	1.39	1.76	3.05	3.91
Avg.	11.35	1.42	1.94	1.81	3.52	4.35
Min.	7.45	0.92	0.80	0.75	2.72	3.06
Max.	15.05	2.76	4.18	4.00	5.36	8.20

Note: (1) Values for the local area are compared with the average, minimum and maximum values for all 291 areas in the Cost of Living Index; (2) Figures cover the McAllen TX urban area; T-Bone Steak (price per pound); Frying Chicken (price per pound, whole fryer); Whole Milk (half gallon carton); Eggs (price per dozen, Grade A, large); Orange Juice (64 oz. Tropicana or Florida Natural); Coffee (11.5 oz. can, vacuum-packed, Maxwell House, Hills Bros, or Folgers).
Source: The Council for Community and Economic Research, ACCRA Cost of Living Index, 2018

Housing and Utility Costs

Area[1]	New Home Price ($)	Apartment Rent ($/month)	All Electric ($/month)	Part Electric ($/month)	Other Energy ($/month)	Telephone ($/month)
City[2]	225,685	640	-	123.82	48.66	179.90
Avg.	347,000	1,087	165.93	100.16	67.73	178.70
Min.	200,468	500	93.58	25.64	26.78	163.10
Max.	1,901,222	4,888	388.65	246.86	332.81	197.70

Note: (1) Values for the local area are compared with the average, minimum and maximum values for all 291 areas in the Cost of Living Index; (2) Figures cover the McAllen TX urban area; New Home Price (2,400 sf living area, 8,000 sf lot, in urban area with full utilities); Apartment Rent (950 sf 2 bedroom/1.5 or 2 bath, unfurnished, excluding all utilities except water); All Electric (average monthly cost for an all-electric home); Part Electric (average monthly cost for a part-electric home); Other Energy (average monthly cost for natural gas, fuel oil, coal, wood, and any other forms of energy except electricity); Telephone (price includes the base monthly rate plus taxes and fees for three lines of mobile phone service).
Source: The Council for Community and Economic Research, ACCRA Cost of Living Index, 2018

Health Care, Transportation, and Other Costs

Area[1]	Doctor ($/visit)	Dentist ($/visit)	Optometrist ($/visit)	Gasoline ($/gallon)	Beauty Salon ($/visit)	Men's Shirt ($)
City[2]	53.95	62.55	91.11	2.42	31.67	17.49
Avg.	110.71	95.11	103.74	2.61	37.48	32.03
Min.	33.60	62.55	54.63	1.89	17.00	11.44
Max.	195.97	153.93	225.79	3.59	71.88	58.64

Note: (1) Values for the local area are compared with the average, minimum and maximum values for all 291 areas in the Cost of Living Index; (2) Figures cover the McAllen TX urban area; Doctor (general practitioners routine exam of an established patient); Dentist (adult teeth cleaning and periodic oral examination); Optometrist (full vision eye exam for established adult patient); Gasoline (one gallon regular unleaded, national brand, including all taxes, cash price at self-service pump if available); Beauty Salon (woman's shampoo, trim, and blow-dry); Men's Shirt (cotton/polyester dress shirt, pinpoint weave, long sleeves).
Source: The Council for Community and Economic Research, ACCRA Cost of Living Index, 2018

HOUSING

House Price Index (HPI)

Area	National Ranking[2]	Quarterly Change (%)	One-Year Change (%)	Five-Year Change (%)
MSA[1]	(a)	n/a	9.27	24.90
U.S.[3]	—	1.12	5.73	32.81

Note: The HPI is a weighted repeat sales index. It measures average price changes in repeat sales or refinancings on the same properties. This information is obtained by reviewing repeat mortgage transactions on single-family properties whose mortgages have been purchased or securitized by Fannie Mae or Freddie Mac in January 1975; (1) Figures cover the McAllen-Edinburg-Mission, TX Metropolitan Statistical Area—see Appendix B for areas included; (2) Rankings are based on annual percentage change for all metro areas containing at least 15,000 transactions over the last 10 years and ranges from 1 to 245; (3) figures based on a weighted average of Census Division estimates using a seasonally adjusted, purchase-only index; all figures are for the period ending December 31, 2018; n/a not available; (a) Not ranked because of increased index variability due to smaller sample size
Source: Federal Housing Finance Agency, House Price Index, February 26, 2019

Median Single-Family Home Prices

Area	2016	2017	2018p	Percent Change 2017 to 2018
MSA[1]	n/a	n/a	n/a	n/a
U.S. Average	235.5	248.8	261.6	5.1

Note: Figures are median sales prices of existing single-family homes in thousands of dollars; (p) preliminary; n/a not available; (1) Figures cover the McAllen-Edinburg-Mission, TX Metropolitan Statistical Area—see Appendix B for areas included
Source: National Association of Realtors, Median Sales Price of Existing Single-Family Homes for Metropolitan Areas, 4th Quarter 2018

Qualifying Income Based on Median Sales Price of Existing Single-Family Homes

Area	With 5% Down ($)	With 10% Down ($)	With 20% Down ($)
MSA[1]	n/a	n/a	n/a
U.S. Average	62,954	59,640	53,013

Note: Figures are preliminary; Qualifying income is based on a mortgage rate of 4.9%. Monthly principal and interest payment is limited to 25% of income; n/a not available; (1) Figures cover the McAllen-Edinburg-Mission, TX Metropolitan Statistical Area—see Appendix B for areas included
Source: National Association of Realtors, Qualifying Income Based on Median Sales Price of Existing Single-Family Homes for Metropolitan Areas, 4th Quarter 2018

Median Apartment Condo-Coop Home Prices

Area	2016	2017	2018p	Percent Change 2017 to 2018
MSA[1]	n/a	n/a	n/a	n/a
U.S. Average	220.7	234.3	241.0	2.9

Note: Figures are median sales prices of existing apartment condo-coop homes in thousands of dollars; (p) preliminary; n/a not available; (1) Figures cover the McAllen-Edinburg-Mission, TX Metropolitan Statistical Area—see Appendix B for areas included
Source: National Association of Realtors, Median Sales Price of Existing Apartment Condo-Coop Homes for Metropolitan Areas, 4th Quarter 2018

Home Value Distribution

Area	Under $50,000	$50,000 -$99,999	$100,000 -$149,999	$150,000 -$199,999	$200,000 -$299,999	$300,000 -$499,999	$500,000 -$999,999	$1,000,000 or more
City	9.1	29.0	26.8	16.2	12.5	4.4	1.8	0.2
MSA[1]	25.6	35.9	18.0	9.6	6.8	2.6	1.1	0.2
U.S.	8.3	13.9	14.7	14.6	18.7	17.3	9.7	2.7

Note: Figures are percentages and cover owner-occupied housing units; (1) Figures cover the McAllen-Edinburg-Mission, TX Metropolitan Statistical Area—see Appendix B for areas included
Source: U.S. Census Bureau, 2013-2017 American Community Survey 5-Year Estimates

Homeownership Rate

Area	2010 (%)	2011 (%)	2012 (%)	2013 (%)	2014 (%)	2015 (%)	2016 (%)	2017 (%)	2018 (%)
MSA[1]	n/a	n/a	n/a	n/a	n/a	n/a	n/a	n/a	n/a
U.S.	66.9	66.1	65.4	65.1	64.5	63.7	63.4	63.9	64.4

Note: (1) Figures cover the McAllen-Edinburg-Mission, TX Metropolitan Statistical Area—see Appendix B for areas included; n/a not available
Source: U.S. Census Bureau, Housing Vacancies and Homeownership Annual Statistics: 2010-2018

Year Housing Structure Built

Area	2010 or Later	2000 -2009	1990 -1999	1980 -1989	1970 -1979	1960 -1969	1950 -1959	1940 -1949	Before 1940	Median Year
City	5.1	24.2	19.6	19.7	16.7	7.4	3.9	1.6	1.9	1989
MSA[1]	6.7	30.4	22.8	16.5	11.9	5.4	3.3	1.5	1.5	1994
U.S.	3.2	14.5	14.0	13.6	15.5	10.8	10.5	5.1	12.9	1977

Note: Figures are percentages except for Median Year; Note: (1) Figures cover the McAllen-Edinburg-Mission, TX Metropolitan Statistical Area—see Appendix B for areas included
Source: U.S. Census Bureau, 2013-2017 American Community Survey 5-Year Estimates

Gross Monthly Rent

Area	Under $500	$500 -$999	$1,000 -$1,499	$1,500 -$1,999	$2,000 -$2,499	$2,500 -$2,999	$3,000 and up	Median ($)
City	14.5	63.7	17.2	3.2	0.9	0.1	0.4	758
MSA[1]	22.0	62.2	12.9	1.9	0.7	0.2	0.1	699
U.S.	10.5	41.1	28.7	11.7	4.5	1.8	1.7	982

Note: Figures are percentages except for Median; Gross rent is the contract rent plus the estimated average monthly cost of utilities (electricity, gas, and water and sewer) and fuels (oil, coal, kerosene, wood, etc.) if these are paid by the renter (or paid for the renter by someone else); (1) Figures cover the McAllen-Edinburg-Mission, TX Metropolitan Statistical Area—see Appendix B for areas included
Source: U.S. Census Bureau, 2013-2017 American Community Survey 5-Year Estimates

HEALTH

Health Risk Factors

Category	MSA[1] (%)	U.S. (%)
Adults aged 18–64 who have any kind of health care coverage	n/a	87.3
Adults who reported being in good or better health	n/a	82.4
Adults who have been told they have high blood cholesterol	n/a	33.0
Adults who have been told they have high blood pressure	n/a	32.3
Adults who are current smokers	n/a	17.1
Adults who currently use E-cigarettes	n/a	4.6
Adults who currently use chewing tobacco, snuff, or snus	n/a	4.0
Adults who are heavy drinkers[2]	n/a	6.3
Adults who are binge drinkers[3]	n/a	17.4
Adults who are overweight (BMI 25.0 - 29.9)	n/a	35.3
Adults who are obese (BMI 30.0 - 99.8)	n/a	31.3
Adults who participated in any physical activities in the past month	n/a	74.4
Adults who always or nearly always wears a seat belt	n/a	94.3

Note: n/a not available; (1) Figures cover the McAllen-Edinburg-Mission, TX Metropolitan Statistical Area—see Appendix B for areas included; (2) Heavy drinkers are classified as adult men having more than 14 drinks per week and adult women having more than 7 drinks per week; (3) Binge drinkers are classified as males having five or more drinks on one occasion or females having four or more drinks on one occasion
Source: Centers for Disease Control and Prevention, Behaviorial Risk Factor Surveillance System, SMART: Selected Metropolitan Area Risk Trends, 2017

Acute and Chronic Health Conditions

Category	MSA[1] (%)	U.S. (%)
Adults who have ever been told they had a heart attack	n/a	4.2
Adults who have ever been told they have angina or coronary heart disease	n/a	3.9
Adults who have ever been told they had a stroke	n/a	3.0
Adults who have ever been told they have asthma	n/a	14.2
Adults who have ever been told they have arthritis	n/a	24.9
Adults who have ever been told they have diabetes[2]	n/a	10.5
Adults who have ever been told they had skin cancer	n/a	6.2
Adults who have ever been told they had any other types of cancer	n/a	7.1
Adults who have ever been told they have COPD	n/a	6.5
Adults who have ever been told they have kidney disease	n/a	3.0
Adults who have ever been told they have a form of depression	n/a	20.5

Note: n/a not available; (1) Figures cover the McAllen-Edinburg-Mission, TX Metropolitan Statistical Area—see Appendix B for areas included; (2) Figures do not include pregnancy-related, borderline, or pre-diabetes
Source: Centers for Disease Control and Prevention, Behaviorial Risk Factor Surveillance System, SMART: Selected Metropolitan Area Risk Trends, 2017

Health Screening and Vaccination Rates

Category	MSA[1] (%)	U.S. (%)
Adults aged 65+ who have had flu shot within the past year	n/a	60.7
Adults aged 65+ who have ever had a pneumonia vaccination	n/a	75.4
Adults who have ever been tested for HIV	n/a	36.1
Adults who have ever had the shingles or zoster vaccine?	n/a	28.9
Adults who have had their blood cholesterol checked within the last five years	n/a	85.9

Note: n/a not available; (1) Figures cover the McAllen-Edinburg-Mission, TX Metropolitan Statistical Area—see Appendix B for areas included.
Source: Centers for Disease Control and Prevention, Behavioral Risk Factor Surveillance System, SMART: Selected Metropolitan Area Risk Trends, 2017

Disability Status

Category	MSA[1] (%)	U.S. (%)
Adults who reported being deaf	n/a	6.7
Are you blind or have serious difficulty seeing, even when wearing glasses?	n/a	4.5
Are you limited in any way in any of your usual activities due of arthritis?	n/a	12.9
Do you have difficulty doing errands alone?	n/a	6.8
Do you have difficulty dressing or bathing?	n/a	3.6
Do you have serious difficulty concentrating/remembering/making decisions?	n/a	10.7
Do you have serious difficulty walking or climbing stairs?	n/a	13.6

Note: n/a not available; (1) Figures cover the McAllen-Edinburg-Mission, TX Metropolitan Statistical Area—see Appendix B for areas included.
Source: Centers for Disease Control and Prevention, Behavioral Risk Factor Surveillance System, SMART: Selected Metropolitan Area Risk Trends, 2017

Mortality Rates for the Top 10 Causes of Death in the U.S.

ICD-10[a] Sub-Chapter	ICD-10[a] Code	Age-Adjusted Mortality Rate[1] per 100,000 population	
		County[2]	U.S.
Malignant neoplasms	C00-C97	113.3	155.5
Ischaemic heart diseases	I20-I25	105.7	94.8
Other forms of heart disease	I30-I51	33.7	52.9
Chronic lower respiratory diseases	J40-J47	19.5	41.0
Cerebrovascular diseases	I60-I69	27.0	37.5
Other degenerative diseases of the nervous system	G30-G31	30.5	35.0
Other external causes of accidental injury	W00-X59	10.9	33.7
Organic, including symptomatic, mental disorders	F01-F09	20.4	31.0
Hypertensive diseases	I10-I15	11.5	21.9
Diabetes mellitus	E10-E14	22.3	21.2

Note: (a) ICD-10 = International Classification of Diseases 10th Revision; (1) Mortality rates are a three year average covering 2015-2017; (2) Figures cover Hidalgo County.
Source: Centers for Disease Control and Prevention, National Center for Health Statistics. Underlying Cause of Death 1999-2017 on CDC WONDER Online Database

Mortality Rates for Selected Causes of Death

ICD-10[a] Sub-Chapter	ICD-10[a] Code	Age-Adjusted Mortality Rate[1] per 100,000 population	
		County[2]	U.S.
Assault	X85-Y09	3.9	5.9
Diseases of the liver	K70-K76	24.6	14.1
Human immunodeficiency virus (HIV) disease	B20-B24	1.2	1.8
Influenza and pneumonia	J09-J18	11.8	14.3
Intentional self-harm	X60-X84	6.7	13.6
Malnutrition	E40-E46	1.6	1.6
Obesity and other hyperalimentation	E65-E68	1.3	2.1
Renal failure	N17-N19	19.9	13.0
Transport accidents	V01-V99	11.3	12.4
Viral hepatitis	B15-B19	Unreliable	1.6

Note: (a) ICD-10 = International Classification of Diseases 10th Revision; (1) Mortality rates are a three year average covering 2015-2017; (2) Figures cover Hidalgo County; Data are suppressed when the data meet the criteria for confidentiality constraints; Mortality rates are flagged as unreliable when the rate would be calculated with a numerator of 20 or less.
Source: Centers for Disease Control and Prevention, National Center for Health Statistics. Underlying Cause of Death 1999-2017 on CDC WONDER Online Database

Health Insurance Coverage

Area	With Health Insurance	With Private Health Insurance	With Public Health Insurance	Without Health Insurance	Population Under Age 18 Without Health Insurance
City	72.7	46.7	31.6	27.3	15.5
MSA[1]	68.4	35.6	37.3	31.6	15.5
U.S.	89.5	67.2	33.8	10.5	5.7

Note: Figures are percentages that cover the civilian noninstitutionalized population; (1) Figures cover the McAllen-Edinburg-Mission, TX Metropolitan Statistical Area—see Appendix B for areas included
Source: U.S. Census Bureau, 2013-2017 American Community Survey 5-Year Estimates

Number of Medical Professionals

Area	MDs[3]	DOs[3,4]	Dentists	Podiatrists	Chiropractors	Optometrists
County[1] (number)	965	26	224	10	70	53
County[1] (rate[2])	113.5	3.1	26.0	1.2	8.1	6.2
U.S. (rate[2])	279.3	23.0	68.4	6.0	27.1	16.2

Note: Data as of 2017 unless noted; (1) Data covers Hidalgo County; (2) Rate per 100,000 population; (3) Data as of 2016 and includes all active, non-federal physicians; (4) Doctor of Osteopathic Medicine
Source: U.S. Department of Health and Human Services, Health Resources and Services Administration, Bureau of Health Professions, Area Resource File (ARF) 2017-2018

EDUCATION

Public School District Statistics

District Name	Schls	Pupils	Pupil/ Teacher Ratio	Minority Pupils[1] (%)	Free Lunch Eligible[2] (%)	IEP[3] (%)
Mcallen ISD	34	23,826	14.8	96.0	72.2	9.1

Note: Table includes school districts with 2,000 or more students; (1) Percentage of students that are not non-Hispanic white; (2) Percentage of students that are eligible for the free lunch program; (3) Percentage of students that have an Individualized Education Program.
Source: U.S. Department of Education, National Center for Education Statistics, Common Core of Data, Local Education Agency (School District) Universe Survey: School Year 2016-2017; U.S. Department of Education, National Center for Education Statistics, Common Core of Data, Public Elementary/Secondary School Universe Survey: School Year 2016-2017

Highest Level of Education

Area	Less than H.S.	H.S. Diploma	Some College, No Deg.	Associate Degree	Bachelor's Degree	Master's Degree	Prof. School Degree	Doctorate Degree
City	26.1	19.3	19.2	6.1	20.7	6.1	1.6	0.9
MSA[1]	36.3	23.2	18.1	4.6	12.8	3.8	0.9	0.4
U.S.	12.7	27.3	20.8	8.3	19.1	8.4	2.0	1.4

Note: Figures cover persons age 25 and over; (1) Figures cover the McAllen-Edinburg-Mission, TX Metropolitan Statistical Area—see Appendix B for areas included
Source: U.S. Census Bureau, 2013-2017 American Community Survey 5-Year Estimates

Educational Attainment by Race

Area	High School Graduate or Higher (%)					Bachelor's Degree or Higher (%)				
	Total	White	Black	Asian	Hisp.[2]	Total	White	Black	Asian	Hisp.[2]
City	73.9	75.6	86.3	93.2	69.7	29.3	29.9	17.2	59.1	25.1
MSA[1]	63.7	64.6	80.8	92.2	60.2	17.8	17.6	18.3	63.6	15.6
U.S.	87.3	89.3	84.9	86.5	66.7	30.9	32.2	20.6	52.7	15.2

Note: Figures shown cover persons 25 years old and over; (1) Figures cover the McAllen-Edinburg-Mission, TX Metropolitan Statistical Area—see Appendix B for areas included; (2) People of Hispanic origin can be of any race
Source: U.S. Census Bureau, 2013-2017 American Community Survey 5-Year Estimates

School Enrollment by Grade and Control

Area	Preschool (%)		Kindergarten (%)		Grades 1 - 4 (%)		Grades 5 - 8 (%)		Grades 9 - 12 (%)	
	Public	Private	Public	Private	Public	Private	Public	Private	Public	Private
City	73.0	27.0	85.3	14.7	92.7	7.3	97.4	2.6	97.8	2.2
MSA[1]	88.0	12.0	93.2	6.8	96.6	3.4	98.2	1.8	98.4	1.6
U.S.	58.8	41.2	87.7	12.3	89.7	10.3	89.6	10.4	90.3	9.7

Note: Figures shown cover persons 3 years old and over; (1) Figures cover the McAllen-Edinburg-Mission, TX Metropolitan Statistical Area—see Appendix B for areas included
Source: U.S. Census Bureau, 2013-2017 American Community Survey 5-Year Estimates

Average Salaries of Public School Classroom Teachers

Area	2016		2017		Change from 2016 to 2017	
	Dollars	Rank[1]	Dollars	Rank[1]	Percent	Rank[2]
Texas	51,890	28	52,575	28	1.3	29
U.S. Average	58,479	–	59,660	–	2.0	–

Note: (1) Rank ranges from 1 to 51 where 1 indicates highest salary; (2) Rank ranges from 1 to 51 where 1 indicates highest percent change.
Source: National Education Association, Rankings & Estimates: Rankings of the States 2017 and Estimates of School Statistics 2018

Higher Education

Four-Year Colleges			Two-Year Colleges			Medical Schools[1]	Law Schools[2]	Voc/ Tech[3]
Public	Private Non-profit	Private For-profit	Public	Private Non-profit	Private For-profit			
1	0	0	0	0	2	0	0	4

Note: Figures cover institutions located within the city limits and include main campuses only; (1) includes schools accredited by the Liaison Committee on Medical Education and the American Osteopathic Association's Commission on Osteopathic College Accreditation; (2) includes ABA-accredited schools, schools with provisional ABA accreditation, and state accredited schools; (3) includes all schools with programs that are less than 2 years.
Source: National Center for Education Statistics, Integrated Postsecondary Education System (IPEDS), 2017-18; Wikipedia, List of Medical Schools in the United States, accessed April 3, 2019; Wikipedia, List of Law Schools in the United States, accessed April 3, 2019

PRESIDENTIAL ELECTION

2016 Presidential Election Results

Area	Clinton	Trump	Johnson	Stein	Other
Hidalgo County	68.1	27.9	2.2	1.1	0.8
U.S.	48.0	45.9	3.3	1.1	1.7

Note: Results are percentages and may not add to 100% due to rounding
Source: Dave Leip's Atlas of U.S. Presidential Elections

EMPLOYERS

Major Employers

Company Name	Industry
BBVA Compass Bank	Financial services
City of McAllen	Government
GE Engines	Manufacturing
IBC Bank	Financial services
McAllen Independent School District	Education
McAllen Medical Center	Healthcare
Mercedes Independent School District	Public elementary & secondary schools
Mid Valley Health System	Investment holding companies, except banks
Mission Consolidated Ind. School District	Public elementary & secondary schools
Panasonic Industrial Devices Corporation	Audio electronic systems
Pharr-San Juan-Alamo Ind. School District	Public elementary & secondary schools
Rio Grande Regional Hospital	Healthcare
Sharyland ISB	Public elementary & secondary schools
South Texas College	Education
Tex-Best Travel Centers	Fast-food restaurant, chain
Texas Regional Delaware	State commercial banks
TST NA Trim	Personal service agents, brokers, & bureaus
University of Texas - Pan American	Colleges & universities
Weslaco Independent School District	Public elementary & secondary schools
Woodcrafters Home Products Holding	Vanities, bathroom, wood

Note: Companies shown are located within the McAllen-Edinburg-Mission, TX Metropolitan Statistical Area.
Source: Hoovers.com; Wikipedia

PUBLIC SAFETY

Crime Rate

Area	All Crimes	Violent Crimes				Property Crimes		
		Murder	Rape[3]	Robbery	Aggrav. Assault	Burglary	Larceny -Theft	Motor Vehicle Theft
City	2,923.8	4.9	18.7	34.0	86.7	128.3	2,619.3	31.9
Suburbs[1]	2,783.7	4.3	54.0	44.1	220.5	427.2	1,929.7	104.0
Metro[2]	2,807.2	4.4	48.1	42.4	198.1	377.2	2,045.1	92.0
U.S.	2,756.1	5.3	41.7	98.0	248.9	430.4	1,694.4	237.4

Note: Figures are crimes per 100,000 population; (1) All areas within the metro area that are located outside the city limits; (2) Figures cover the McAllen-Edinburg-Mission, TX Metropolitan Statistical Area—see Appendix B for areas included; (3) The city and U.S. figures shown were reported using the revised Uniform Crime Reporting (UCR) definition of rape. The suburban and metro area figures shown are an aggregate total of the data submitted using both the revised and legacy UCR definitions.
Source: FBI Uniform Crime Reports, 2017

Hate Crimes

Area	Number of Quarters Reported	Number of Incidents per Bias Motivation					
		Race/Ethnicity/ Ancestry	Religion	Sexual Orientation	Disability	Gender	Gender Identity
City	4	0	0	0	0	0	0
U.S.	4	4,131	1,564	1,130	116	46	119

Source: Federal Bureau of Investigation, Hate Crime Statistics 2017

Identity Theft Consumer Reports

Area	Reports	Reports per 100,000 Population	Rank[2]
MSA[1]	940	111	94
U.S.	444,602	135	-

Note: (1) Figures cover the McAllen-Edinburg-Mission, TX Metropolitan Statistical Area—see Appendix B for areas included; (2) Rank ranges from 1 to 389 where 1 indicates greatest number of identity theft reports per 100,000 population
Source: Federal Trade Commission, Consumer Sentinel Network Data Book for January–December 2018

Fraud and Other Consumer Reports

Area	Reports	Reports per 100,000 Population	Rank[2]
MSA[1]	1,742	205	381
U.S.	2,552,917	776	-

Note: (1) Figures cover the McAllen-Edinburg-Mission, TX Metropolitan Statistical Area—see Appendix B for areas included; (2) Rank ranges from 1 to 389 where 1 indicates greatest number of fraud and other consumer reports per 100,000 population
Source: Federal Trade Commission, Consumer Sentinel Network Data Book for January–December 2018

SPORTS

Professional Sports Teams

Team Name	League	Year Established

No teams are located in the metro area
Source: Wikipedia, Major Professional Sports Teams of the United States and Canada, April 5, 2019

CLIMATE

Average and Extreme Temperatures

Temperature	Jan	Feb	Mar	Apr	May	Jun	Jul	Aug	Sep	Oct	Nov	Dec	Yr.
Extreme High (°F)	93	94	106	102	102	102	101	102	99	96	97	94	106
Average High (°F)	70	73	78	83	87	91	93	93	90	85	78	72	83
Average Temp. (°F)	60	63	69	75	80	83	84	85	82	76	68	63	74
Average Low (°F)	51	53	59	66	72	75	76	76	73	66	59	53	65
Extreme Low (°F)	19	22	32	38	52	60	67	63	56	40	33	16	16

Note: Figures cover the years 1948-1990
Source: National Climatic Data Center, International Station Meteorological Climate Summary, 9/96

Average Precipitation/Snowfall/Humidity

Precip./Humidity	Jan	Feb	Mar	Apr	May	Jun	Jul	Aug	Sep	Oct	Nov	Dec	Yr.
Avg. Precip. (in.)	1.4	1.4	0.6	1.5	2.5	2.8	1.8	2.6	5.6	3.2	1.5	1.1	25.8
Avg. Snowfall (in.)	Tr	Tr	0	0	0	0	0	0	0	0	Tr	Tr	Tr
Avg. Rel. Hum. 6am (%)	88	89	88	89	90	91	92	92	91	89	87	87	89
Avg. Rel. Hum. 3pm (%)	62	60	57	58	60	59	54	55	60	58	59	61	59

Note: Figures cover the years 1948-1990; Tr = Trace amounts (<0.05 in. of rain; <0.5 in. of snow)
Source: National Climatic Data Center, International Station Meteorological Climate Summary, 9/96

Weather Conditions

Temperature			Daytime Sky			Precipitation		
32°F & below	45°F & below	90°F & above	Clear	Partly cloudy	Cloudy	0.01 inch or more precip.	0.1 inch or more snow/ice	Thunder-storms
2	30	116	86	180	99	72	0	27

Note: Figures are average number of days per year and cover the years 1948-1990
Source: National Climatic Data Center, International Station Meteorological Climate Summary, 9/96

HAZARDOUS WASTE

Superfund Sites

The McAllen-Edinburg-Mission, TX metro area is home to one site on the EPA's Superfund National Priorities List: **Donna Reservoir and Canal System** (final). There are a total of 1,390 Superfund sites with a status of proposed or final on the list in the U.S. *U.S. Environmental Protection Agency, National Priorities List, April 5, 2019*

AIR & WATER QUALITY

Air Quality Trends: Ozone

	1990	1995	2000	2005	2010	2012	2014	2015	2016	2017
MSA[1]	n/a	n/a	n/a	n/a	n/a	n/a	n/a	n/a	n/a	n/a
U.S.	0.088	0.089	0.082	0.080	0.073	0.075	0.067	0.068	0.069	0.068

Note: (1) Data covers the McAllen-Edinburg-Mission, TX Metropolitan Statistical Area—see Appendix B for areas included; n/a not available. The values shown are the composite ozone concentration averages among trend sites based on the highest fourth daily maximum 8-hour concentration in parts per million. These trends are based on sites having an adequate record of monitoring data during the trend period. Data from exceptional events are included.
Source: U.S. Environmental Protection Agency, Air Quality Monitoring Information, "Air Quality Trends by City, 1990-2017"

Air Quality Index

Area	Percent of Days when Air Quality was...[2]					AQI Statistics[2]	
	Good	Moderate	Unhealthy for Sensitive Groups	Unhealthy	Very Unhealthy	Maximum	Median
MSA[1]	77.0	23.0	0.0	0.0	0.0	95	38

Note: (1) Data covers the McAllen-Edinburg-Mission, TX Metropolitan Statistical Area—see Appendix B for areas included; (2) Based on 365 days with AQI data in 2017. Air Quality Index (AQI) is an index for reporting daily air quality. EPA calculates the AQI for five major air pollutants regulated by the Clean Air Act: ground-level ozone, particle pollution (aka particulate matter), carbon monoxide, sulfur dioxide, and nitrogen dioxide. The AQI runs from 0 to 500. The higher the AQI value, the greater the level of air pollution and the greater the health concern. There are six AQI categories: "Good" AQI is between 0 and 50. Air quality is considered satisfactory; "Moderate" AQI is between 51 and 100. Air quality is acceptable; "Unhealthy for Sensitive Groups" When AQI values are between 101 and 150, members of sensitive groups may experience health effects; "Unhealthy" When AQI values are between 151 and 200 everyone may begin to experience health effects; "Very Unhealthy" AQI values between 201 and 300 trigger a health alert; "Hazardous" AQI values over 300 trigger warnings of emergency conditions (not shown).
Source: U.S. Environmental Protection Agency, Air Quality Index Report, 2017

Air Quality Index Pollutants

Area	Percent of Days when AQI Pollutant was...[2]					
	Carbon Monoxide	Nitrogen Dioxide	Ozone	Sulfur Dioxide	Particulate Matter 2.5	Particulate Matter 10
MSA[1]	0.0	0.0	39.2	0.0	60.8	0.0

Note: (1) Data covers the McAllen-Edinburg-Mission, TX Metropolitan Statistical Area—see Appendix B for areas included; (2) Based on 365 days with AQI data in 2017. The Air Quality Index (AQI) is an index for reporting daily air quality. EPA calculates the AQI for five major air pollutants regulated by the Clean Air Act: ground-level ozone, particle pollution (also known as particulate matter), carbon monoxide, sulfur dioxide, and nitrogen dioxide. The AQI runs from 0 to 500. The higher the AQI value, the greater the level of air pollution and the greater the health concern.
Source: U.S. Environmental Protection Agency, Air Quality Index Report, 2017

Maximum Air Pollutant Concentrations: Particulate Matter, Ozone, CO and Lead

	Particulate Matter 10 (ug/m^3)	Particulate Matter 2.5 Wtd AM (ug/m^3)	Particulate Matter 2.5 24-Hr (ug/m^3)	Ozone (ppm)	Carbon Monoxide (ppm)	Lead (ug/m^3)
MSA[1] Level	49	10.1	26	0.055	n/a	n/a
NAAQS[2]	150	15	35	0.075	9	0.15
Met NAAQS[2]	Yes	Yes	Yes	Yes	n/a	n/a

Note: (1) Data covers the McAllen-Edinburg-Mission, TX Metropolitan Statistical Area—see Appendix B for areas included; Data from exceptional events are included; (2) National Ambient Air Quality Standards; ppm = parts per million; ug/m^3 = micrograms per cubic meter; n/a not available.
Concentrations: Particulate Matter 10 (coarse particulate)—highest second maximum 24-hour concentration; Particulate Matter 2.5 Wtd AM (fine particulate)—highest weighted annual mean concentration; Particulate Matter 2.5 24-Hour (fine particulate)—highest 98th percentile 24-hour concentration; Ozone—highest fourth daily maximum 8-hour concentration; Carbon Monoxide—highest second maximum non-overlapping 8-hour concentration; Lead—maximum running 3-month average
Source: U.S. Environmental Protection Agency, Air Quality Monitoring Information, "Air Quality Statistics by City, 2017"

Maximum Air Pollutant Concentrations: Nitrogen Dioxide and Sulfur Dioxide

	Nitrogen Dioxide AM (ppb)	Nitrogen Dioxide 1-Hr (ppb)	Sulfur Dioxide AM (ppb)	Sulfur Dioxide 1-Hr (ppb)	Sulfur Dioxide 24-Hr (ppb)
MSA[1] Level	n/a	n/a	n/a	n/a	n/a
NAAQS[2]	53	100	30	75	140
Met NAAQS[2]	n/a	n/a	n/a	n/a	n/a

Note: (1) Data covers the McAllen-Edinburg-Mission, TX Metropolitan Statistical Area—see Appendix B for areas included; Data from exceptional events are included; (2) National Ambient Air Quality Standards; ppm = parts per million; ug/m^3 = micrograms per cubic meter; n/a not available.
Concentrations: Nitrogen Dioxide AM—highest arithmetic mean concentration; Nitrogen Dioxide 1-Hr—highest 98th percentile 1-hour daily maximum concentration; Sulfur Dioxide AM—highest annual mean concentration; Sulfur Dioxide 1-Hr—highest 99th percentile 1-hour daily maximum concentration; Sulfur Dioxide 24-Hr—highest second maximum 24-hour concentration
Source: U.S. Environmental Protection Agency, Air Quality Monitoring Information, "Air Quality Statistics by City, 2017"

Drinking Water

Water System Name	Pop. Served	Primary Water Source Type	Violations[1]	
			Health Based	Monitoring/ Reporting
McAllen Public Utility	168,909	Surface	0	1

Note: (1) Based on violation data from January 1, 2018 to December 31, 2018
Source: U.S. Environmental Protection Agency, Office of Ground Water and Drinking Water, Safe Drinking Water Information System (based on data extracted April 5, 2019)

Miami, Florida

Background

Miami is a growing city comprised mostly of Latinos. Its large numbers of Cubans, Puerto Ricans, and Haitians give the city a flavorful mix with a Latin American and Caribbean accent. The City of Miami has three official languages: English, Spanish, and Haitian Creole.

Thanks to early pioneer Julia Tuttle, railroad magnate Henry Flagler extended the East Coast Railroad beyond Palm Beach. Within 15 years of that decision, Miami became known as the "Gold Coast." The land boom of the 1920s brought wealthy socialites, as well as African-Americans in search of work. Pink- and aquamarine-hued art deco hotels were squeezed onto a tiny tract of land called Miami Beach, and the population of the Miami metro area swelled.

Given Miami's origins in a tourist-oriented economy, many of the activities in which residents engage are "leisurely," including swimming, scuba diving, golf, tennis, and boating. For those who enjoy professional sports, the city is host to the following teams: the Miami Dolphins, football; the Florida Marlins, baseball; the Miami Heat, basketball; and the Florida Panthers, hockey. Cultural activities range from the Miami City Ballet and the Coconut Grove Playhouse to numerous art galleries and museums, including the Bass Museum of Art. Visits to the Villa Vizcaya, a gorgeous palazzo built by industrialist James Deering in the Italian Renaissance style, and to the Miami MetroZoo are popular pastimes.

Miami's prime location on Biscayne Bay in the southeastern United States makes it a perfect nexus for travel and trade. The Port of Miami is a bustling center for many cruise and cargo ships. The Port is also a base for the National Oceanic and Atmospheric Administration. The Miami International Airport is a busy destination point to and from many Latin-American and Caribbean countries.

Miami is still at the trading crossroads of the Western Hemisphere as the chief shipment point for exports and imports with Latin America and the Caribbean. One out of every three North American cruise passengers sails from Miami.

The sultry, subtropical climate against a backdrop of Spanish, art deco, and modern architecture makes Miami a uniquely cosmopolitan city. The Art Deco Historic District, known as South Beach and located on the tip of Miami Beach, has an international reputation in the fashion, film, and music industries. Greater Miami is now a national center for film, television, and print production.

In recent years Miami has witnessed its largest real estate boom since the 1920s, especially in the newly created midtown, north of downtown and south of the Design District. Nearly 25,000 residential units have been added to the downtown skyline since 2005.

Long, warm summers are typical, as are mild, dry winters. The marine influence is evidenced by the narrow daily range of temperature and the rapid warming of cold air masses. During the summer months, rainfall occurs in early morning near the ocean and in early afternoon further inland. Hurricanes occasionally affect the Miami area, usually in September and October, while destructive tornadoes are quite rare. Funnel clouds are occasionally sighted and a few touch the ground briefly, but significant destruction is unusual. Waterspouts are visible from the beaches during the summer months but seldom cause any damage. During June, July, and August, there are numerous beautiful, but dangerous, lightning events.

Rankings

General Rankings

- The Miami metro area was identified as one of America's fastest-growing areas in terms of population and business growth by *MagnifyMoney*. The area ranked #29 out of 35. The 100 most populous metro areas in the U.S. were evaluated on their change from 2011-2016 in the following categories: people and housing; workforce and employment opportunities; growing industry. *www.businessinsider.com, "The 35 Cities in the US with the Biggest Influx of People, the Most Work Opportunities, and the Hottest Business Growth," August 12, 2018*

- The human resources consulting firm Mercer ranked 231 major cities worldwide in terms of overall quality of life. Miami ranked #66. Criteria: political, social, economic, and socio-cultural factors; medical and health considerations; schools and education; public services and transportation; recreation; consumer goods; housing; and natural environment. *Mercer, "Mercer 2019 Quality of Living Survey," March 13, 2019*

Business/Finance Rankings

- The personal finance site NerdWallet analyzed 183 American metropolitan areas with populations over 250,000 and more than 15,000 businesses to rank where entrepreneurs find the most success. Criteria included area economy, annual income, housing cost, unemployment rate, and the success rate of area businesses. Miami ranked #35. *www.nerdwallet.com, "Best Places to Start a Business," April 27, 2015*

- Metro areas with the largest gap in income between rich and poor residents were identified by 24/7 Wall Street using the U.S. Census Bureau's 2013 American Community Survey. The Miami metro area placed #8 among metro areas with the widest wealth gap between rich and poor. *247wallst.com, "20 Cities with the Widest Gap between the Rich and Poor," July 8, 2015*

- In a survey of economic confidence in the nation's 50 largest metropolitan areas conducted January–December 2014, the Miami metro area placed #5, according to Gallup's 2014 Economic Confidence Index. *Gallup, "San Jose and San Francisco Lead in Economic Confidence," March 19, 2015*

- NerdWallet.com identified the 10 most promising cities for job seekers of the nation's 100 largest cities. Miami was ranked #15. Criteria: job availability; annual salary; workforce growth; affordability. *NerdWallet.com, "Best Cities for Job Seekers in 2017," December 19, 2016*

- The Brookings Institution ranked the nation's largest cities based on income inequality. Miami was ranked #5 (#1 = greatest inequality). Criteria: the "95/20 ratio," a figure representing the income at which a household earns more than 95 percent of all other households, divided by the income at which a household earns more than only 20 percent of all other households. *Brookings Institution, "Household Income Inequality, Largest Cities of 97 Large U.S. Metro Areas, 2014-2016," February 5, 2018*

- The Brookings Institution ranked the 100 largest metro areas in the U.S. based on income inequality. Miami was ranked #7 (#1 = greatest inequality). Criteria: the "95/20 ratio," a figure representing the income at which a household earns more than 95 percent of all other households, divided by the income at which a household earns more than only 20 percent of all other households. *Brookings Institution, "Household Income Inequality, 100 Largest U.S. Metro Areas, 2014-2016," February 5, 2018*

- Payscale.com ranked the 32 largest metro areas in terms of wage growth. The Miami metro area ranked #18. Criteria: private-sector wage growth between the 4th quarter of 2017 and the 4th quarter of 2018. *PayScale, "Wage Trends by Metro Area-4th Quarter," January 8, 2019*

- The Miami metro area was identified as one of the most debt-ridden places in America by the finance site Credit.com. The metro area was ranked #14. Criteria: residents' average credit card debt as well as median income. *Credit.com, "25 Cities With the Most Credit Card Debt," February 28, 2018*

- Miami was identified as one of America's most frugal metro areas by *Coupons.com*. The city ranked #12 out of 25. Criteria: digital coupon usage. *Coupons.com, "America's Most Frugal Cities of 2017," March 22, 2018*

- The Miami metro area appeared on the Milken Institute "2018 Best Performing Cities" list. Rank: #74 out of 200 large metro areas. Criteria: job growth; wage and salary growth; high-tech output growth. *Milken Institute, "Best-Performing Cities 2018," January 24, 2019*

- *Forbes* ranked the 200 most populous metro areas to determine the nation's "Best Places for Business and Careers." The Miami metro area was ranked #78. Criteria: costs (business and living); job growth (past and projected); income growth; quality of life; educational attainment (college and high school); projected economic growth; cultural and recreational opportunities; net migration patterns; number of highly ranked colleges. *Forbes, "The Best Places for Business and Careers 2018: Seattle Leads the Way," October 24, 2018*

- Mercer Human Resources Consulting ranked 209 cities worldwide in terms of cost-of-living. Miami ranked #60 (the lower the ranking, the higher the cost-of-living). The survey measured the comparative cost of over 200 items (such as housing, food, clothing, household goods, transportation, and entertainment) in each location. *Mercer, "2018 Cost of Living Survey," June 26, 2018*

Children/Family Rankings

- Miami was selected as one of the most playful cities in the U.S. by KaBOOM! The organization's Playful City USA initiative honors cities and towns across the nation that have made their communities more playable. Criteria: pledging to integrate play as a solution to challenges in their communities; making it easy for children to get active and balanced play; creating more family-friendly and innovative communities as a result. *KaBOOM! National Campaign for Play, "2017 Playful City USA Communities"*

Culture/Performing Arts Rankings

- Miami was selected as one of the twenty best large U.S. cities for moviemakers. Of cities with a population over 400,000, the city was ranked #15. Criteria: film community and culture; access to equipment and facilities; film activity in 2018; number of film schools; tax incentives. ease of movement and traffic. *MovieMaker Magazine, "Best Places to Live and Work as a Moviemaker: 2019," January 16, 2019*

- Miami was selected as one of "America's Favorite Cities." The city ranked #20 in the "Culture: Music Scene " category. Respondents to an online survey were asked to rate 38 top urban destinations in the U.S. from a visitor's perspective. *Travelandleisure.com, "From the Honkytonk Capital to Jazz's Birthplace: America's Best Music Scenes," October 2016*

Dating/Romance Rankings

- Miami was selected as one of the nation's most romantic cities with 100,000 or more residents by Amazon.com. The city ranked #2 of 20. Criteria: per capita sales of romance novels, relationship books, romantic comedy movies, romantic music, and sexual wellness products. *Amazon.com, "Top 20 Most Romantic Cities in the U.S.," February 1, 2017*

Education Rankings

- Personal finance website *WalletHub* analyzed the 150 largest U.S. metropolitan statistical areas to determine where the most educated Americans are choosing to settle. Criteria: education quality and attainment gap; education levels; percentage of workers with degrees; public school quality rankings; quality and size of each metro area's universities. Miami was ranked #82 (#1 = most educated city). *www.WalletHub.com, "2018's Most and Least Educated Cities in America, " July 24, 2018*

- Miami was selected as one of America's most literate cities. The city ranked #50 out of the 82 largest U.S. cities. Criteria: number of booksellers; library resources; Internet resources; educational attainment; periodical publishing resources; newspaper circulation. *Central Connecticut State University, "America's Most Literate Cities, 2016," March 31, 2017*

Environmental Rankings

- Sperling's BestPlaces assessed the 50 largest metropolitan areas of the United States for the likelihood of dangerously extreme weather events or earthquakes. In general the Southeast and South-Central regions have the highest risk of weather extremes and earthquakes, while the Pacific Northwest enjoys the lowest risk. Of the most risky metropolitan areas, the Miami metro area was ranked #1. *www.bestplaces.net, "Avoid Natural Disasters: BestPlaces Reveals The Top 10 Safest Places to Live," October 25, 2017*

- The U.S. Environmental Protection Agency (EPA) released a list of U.S. metropolitan areas with the most ENERGY STAR certified buildings in 2017. The Miami metro area was ranked #21 out of 25. *U.S. Environmental Protection Agency, "2018 Energy Star Top Cities," April 11, 2018*

Food/Drink Rankings

- According to Fodor's Travel, Miami placed among the 14 best U.S. cities for food-truck cuisine. *www.fodors.com, "America's Best Food Truck Cities," August 23, 2016*

- *Men's Health* ranked 100 major U.S. cities in terms of alcohol intoxication. Miami ranked #96 (#1 = most sober).Criteria: binge drinking; alcohol-related traffic accidents, arrests, and fatalities. *Men's Health, "America's Drunkest Cities," March 9, 2015*

- Miami was selected as one of America's 10 most vegan-friendly cities. The city was ranked #9. *People for the Ethical Treatment of Animals, "Top 10 Vegan-Friendly Cities of 2018," May 16, 2018*

Health/Fitness Rankings

- For each of the 100 largest cities in the United States, the American College of Sports Medicine's American Fitness Index evaluated infrastructure, community assets, and policies that encourage healthy and fit lifestyles, including preventive health behaviors, levels of chronic disease conditions, health care access, and community resources and policies that support physical activity. Miami ranked #25 for "community fitness." *www.americanfitnessindex.org, "ACSM American Fitness Index Health and Community Fitness Status of the 100 Largest U.S. Cities," May 2018*

- Miami was identified as one of the 10 most walkable cities in the U.S. by Walk Score, a Seattle-based service that rates the convenience and transit access of 10,000 neighborhoods in 3,000 cities. The area ranked #6 out of the 50 largest U.S. cities. Walk Score measures walkability by analyzing hundreds of walking routes to nearby amenities, and also measures pedestrian friendliness by analyzing population density and road metrics such as block length and intersection density. *WalkScore.com, May 31, 2017*

- The Miami metro area was identified as one of the worst cities for bed bugs in America by pest control company Orkin. The area ranked #29 out of 50 based on the number of bed bug treatments Orkin performed from December 2017 to November 2018. *Orkin, "Baltimore Remains Front Runner, Atlanta and Philadelphia Break Into Top 10," January 14, 2019*

- Miami was identified as a "2018 Spring Allergy Capital." The area ranked #29 out of 100. Three groups of factors were used to identify the most challenging cities for people with allergies during the spring season: annual pollen levels; medicine utilization; access to board-certified allergists. *Asthma and Allergy Foundation of America, "Spring Allergy Capitals 2018"*

- Miami was identified as a "2018 Fall Allergy Capital." The area ranked #39 out of 100. Three groups of factors were used to identify the most challenging cities for people with allergies during the fall season: annual pollen levels; medicine utilization; access to board-certified allergists. *Asthma and Allergy Foundation of America, "Fall Allergy Capitals 2018"*

- Miami was identified as a "2018 Asthma Capital." The area ranked #83 out of the nation's 100 largest metropolitan areas. Criteria: estimated prevalence; self-reported prevalence; crude death rate for asthma; annual pollen score; annual air quality; public smoking laws; number of board-certified asthma specialists; school inhaler access laws; rescue medication use; controller medication use; ER visits for asthma; uninsured rate; poverty rate. *Asthma and Allergy Foundation of America, "Asthma Capitals 2018: The Most Challenging Places to Live With Asthma"*

- *Men's Health* ranked 100 major U.S. cities in terms of the best cities for men. Miami ranked #48. Criteria: health; fitness; quality of life. *Men's Health, "The Best & Worst Cities for Men Who Want to Be Fit and Happy," January 1, 2016*

- The Miami metro area ranked #31 out of 189 in The Gallup-Healthways Well-Being Index. Criteria: purpose; social well being; financial health; community and physical health. Results are based on telephone interviews with adults, aged 18 and older, living in metropolitan areas in the 50 U.S. states and the District of Columbia. *Gallup-Healthways, "State of American Well-Being, 2017 Community Well-Being Rankings" March 2018*

Real Estate Rankings

- FitSmallBusiness looked at 50 of the largest metropolitan areas in the U.S. to determine which metro was the best to start a real estate business. Data was compiled from such sources as: Zillow, Trulia, U.S. Census Bureau, and the Bureau of Labor Statistics. Criteria: location; inventory; annual wages; median sales price of homes; days on the market; median price cut percentage; and other factors that would influence real estate professional growth. The Miami metro area ranked #8. *fitsmallbusiness.com, "The Best Cities to Become a Real Estate Agent in 2018," January 30, 2018*

- *WalletHub* compared the most populated U.S. cities, as well as at least two of the most populated cities in each state, for a total of 179, to determine which had the best markets for real estate agents. Miami ranked #117 where demand was high and pay was the best. Criteria: sales per agent; annual median wage for real-estate agents; monthly average starting salary for real estate agents; real estate job density and competition; unemployment rate; housing-market health index; and other relevant metrics. *www.WalletHub.com, "2018's Best Places to Be a Real Estate Agent," April 25, 2018*

- Despite the national slowdown trend, the Miami metro area appeared on Realtor.com's list of hot housing markets to watch in 2019. The area ranked #9. Criteria: existing homes inventory and price; new home construction; median household incomes; local economy/population trends. *Realtor.com®, "The 10 Surprising Housing Markets Poised to Rule in 2019," January 2, 2019*

- Miami was ranked #219 out of 237 metro areas in terms of housing affordability in 2018 by the National Association of Home Builders (#1 = most affordable). Criteria: the share of homes sold in that area affordable to a family earning the local median income, based on standard mortgage underwriting criteria. *National Association of Home Builders®, NAHB-Wells Fargo Housing Opportunity Index, 4th Quarter 2018*

Safety Rankings

- Allstate ranked the 200 largest cities in America in terms of driver safety. Miami ranked #86. Criteria: internal property damage claims over a two-year period from January 2015 to December 2016. The report helps increase the importance of safety awareness behind the wheel. *Allstate, "Allstate America's Best Drivers Report, 2018" August 28, 2018*

- The National Insurance Crime Bureau ranked 382 metro areas in the U.S. in terms of per capita rates of vehicle theft. The Miami metro area ranked #58 (#1 = highest rate). Criteria: number of vehicle theft offenses per 100,000 inhabitants in 2017. *National Insurance Crime Bureau, "Hot Spots 2017," July 12, 2018*

Seniors/Retirement Rankings

- From its Best Cities for Successful Aging indexes, the Milken Institute generated rankings for metropolitan areas, weighing data in nine categories—health care, wellness, living arrangements, transportation and convenience, financial characteristics, education, employment, community engagement, and overall livability. The Miami metro area was ranked #73 overall in the large metro area category. *Milken Institute, "Best Cities for Successful Aging, 2017" March 14, 2017*

Sports/Recreation Rankings

- Miami was chosen as one of America's best cities for bicycling. The city ranked #50 out of 50. Criteria: cycling infrastructure that is safe and friendly for all ages; energy and bike culture. The editors only considered cities with populations of 100,000 or more. *Bicycling, "The 50 Best Bike Cities in America," October 10, 2018*

Transportation Rankings

- Business Insider presented an AllTransit Performance Score ranking of public transportation in major U.S. cities and towns, with populations over 250,000, in which Miami earned the #11-ranked "Transit Score," awarded for frequency of service, access to jobs, quality and number of stops, and affordability. *www.businessinsider.com, "The 17 Major U.S. Cities with the Best Public Transportation," April 17, 2018*

- NerdWallet surveyed average annual car insurance premiums in 125 U.S. cities to identify the least expensive U.S. cities in which to insure a car. Locations with no-fault insurance laws was a strong determinant. Miami came in at #9 for the most expensive rates. *www.nerdwallet.com, "Best Cities for Cheap Car Insurance," February 3, 2014*

Women/Minorities Rankings

- For its trip ideas, *Travel + Leisure* listed the best cities in the US for a memorable and fun girls' trip. Whether it is for a special occasion or just to get away, Miami is sure to have something for everyone. *Travel + Leisure, "America's Best Cities for Getting Away With the Girls," March 18, 2019*

- *24/7 Wall St.* compared median earnings over a 12-month period for men and women who worked full-time, year-round, and employment composition by sector to identify the best-paying cities for women. Of the largest 100 U.S. metropolitan areas, Miami was ranked #5 in pay disparity. *24/7 Wall St., "The Best (and Worst) Paying Cities for Women," March 27, 2017*

- Miami was selected as one of the gayest cities in America by *The Advocate*. The city ranked #16 out of 25. Criteria, among many: Trans Pride parades/festivals; gay rugby teams; lesbian bars; LGBT centers; theater screenings of "Moonlight"; LGBT-inclusive nondiscrimination ordinances; and gay bowling teams. *The Advocate, "Queerest Cities in America 2017" January 12, 2017*

- Personal finance website *WalletHub* compared more than 180 U.S. cities—including the 150 most populated U.S. cities, plus at least two of the most populated cities in each state—across two key dimensions, "Hispanic Business-Friendliness" and "Hispanic Purchasing Power", to arrive at the most favorable conditions for Hispanic entrepreneurs. Miami was ranked #11 out of 182. Criteria includes: share of Hispanic-Owned Businesses; Hispanic entrepreneurship rate to median annual income of Hispanics; Small Business-Friendliness score; cost of living; and number of Hispanics with at least a bachelor's degree. *WalletHub.com, "2018's Best Cities for Hispanic Entrepreneurs," April 26, 2018*

Miscellaneous Rankings

- Miami was selected as a 2018 Digital Cities Survey winner. The city ranked #5 in the large city (250,000 to 499,999 population) category. The survey examined and assessed how city governments are utilizing technology to improve transparency, enhance cybersecurity, and solve social challenges. Survey questions focused on ten characteristics: engaged, mobile, open, secure, staffed/supported, efficient, connected, resilient, best practices, and use of innovation. *Center for Digital Government, "2018 Digital Cities Survey," November 2, 2018*

- The watchdog site Charity Navigator conducts an annual study of charities in the nation's major markets both to analyze statistical differences in their financial, accountability, and transparency practices and to track year-to-year variations in individual philanthropic communities. Charity Navigator's analysis demonstrated that the financial, accountability and transparency behaviors of America's largest charities can be influenced by the metropolitan market within which the charity operates. The Miami metro area was ranked #7 among the 30 metro markets in the rating category of Overall Score. *www.charitynavigator.org, "2017 Metro Market Study," May 1, 2017*

- *WalletHub* compared the 150 most populated U.S. cities to determine their operating efficiency. A "Quality of Services" score was constructed for each city and then divided by the total budget per capita to reveal which were managed the best. Miami ranked #93. Criteria: financial stability; economy; education; safety; health; infrastructure and pollution. *www.WalletHub.com, "2018's Best- & Worst-Run Cities in America," July 9, 2018*

- The National Alliance to End Homelessness listed the 25 most populous metro areas with the highest rate of homelessness. The Miami metro area had a high rate of homelessness. Criteria: number of homeless people per 10,000 population in 2016. *National Alliance to End Homelessness, "Homelessness in the 25 Most Populous U.S. Metro Areas," September 1, 2017*

Business Environment

CITY FINANCES

City Government Finances

Component	2016 ($000)	2016 ($ per capita)
Total Revenues	942,318	2,137
Total Expenditures	1,069,199	2,424
Debt Outstanding	736,336	1,670
Cash and Securities[1]	3,018,899	6,846

Note: (1) Cash and security holdings of a government at the close of its fiscal year, including those of its dependent agencies, utilities, and liquor stores.
Source: U.S. Census Bureau, State & Local Government Finances 2016

City Government Revenue by Source

Source	2016 ($000)	2016 ($ per capita)	2016 (%)
General Revenue			
From Federal Government	73,133	166	7.8
From State Government	61,977	141	6.6
From Local Governments	38,717	88	4.1
Taxes			
Property	306,390	695	32.5
Sales and Gross Receipts	101,740	231	10.8
Personal Income	0	0	0.0
Corporate Income	0	0	0.0
Motor Vehicle License	0	0	0.0
Other Taxes	98,541	223	10.5
Current Charges	119,825	272	12.7
Liquor Store	0	0	0.0
Utility	0	0	0.0
Employee Retirement	67,815	154	7.2

Source: U.S. Census Bureau, State & Local Government Finances 2016

City Government Expenditures by Function

Function	2016 ($000)	2016 ($ per capita)	2016 (%)
General Direct Expenditures			
Air Transportation	0	0	0.0
Corrections	0	0	0.0
Education	0	0	0.0
Employment Security Administration	0	0	0.0
Financial Administration	47,052	106	4.4
Fire Protection	118,071	267	11.0
General Public Buildings	0	0	0.0
Governmental Administration, Other	46,596	105	4.4
Health	0	0	0.0
Highways	15,870	36	1.5
Hospitals	0	0	0.0
Housing and Community Development	30,965	70	2.9
Interest on General Debt	43,563	98	4.1
Judicial and Legal	6,718	15	0.6
Libraries	0	0	0.0
Parking	30,398	68	2.8
Parks and Recreation	81,988	185	7.7
Police Protection	199,687	452	18.7
Public Welfare	2,319	5	0.2
Sewerage	0	0	0.0
Solid Waste Management	36,260	82	3.4
Veterans' Services	0	0	0.0
Liquor Store	0	0	0.0
Utility	33	< 1	< 0.1
Employee Retirement	214,235	485	20.0

Source: U.S. Census Bureau, State & Local Government Finances 2016

DEMOGRAPHICS

Population Growth

Area	1990 Census	2000 Census	2010 Census	2017* Estimate	Population Growth (%)	
					1990-2017	2010-2017
City	358,843	362,470	399,457	443,007	23.5	10.9
MSA[1]	4,056,100	5,007,564	5,564,635	6,019,790	48.4	8.2
U.S.	248,709,873	281,421,906	308,745,538	321,004,407	29.1	4.0

Note: (1) Figures cover the Miami-Fort Lauderdale-West Palm Beach, FL Metropolitan Statistical Area—see Appendix B for areas included; (*) 2013-2017 5-year estimated population
Source: U.S. Census Bureau, 1990 Census, Census 2000, Census 2010, 2013-2017 American Community Survey 5-Year Estimates

Household Size

Area	Persons in Household (%)							Average Household Size
	One	Two	Three	Four	Five	Six	Seven or More	
City	38.1	29.7	15.4	9.7	4.3	1.7	1.1	2.60
MSA[1]	28.4	32.1	16.8	13.5	5.7	2.2	1.2	2.90
U.S.	27.7	33.8	15.7	13.0	6.0	2.3	1.4	2.60

Note: (1) Figures cover the Miami-Fort Lauderdale-West Palm Beach, FL Metropolitan Statistical Area—see Appendix B for areas included
Source: U.S. Census Bureau, 2013-2017 American Community Survey 5-Year Estimates

Race

Area	White Alone[2] (%)	Black Alone[2] (%)	Asian Alone[2] (%)	AIAN[3] Alone[2] (%)	NHOPI[4] Alone[2] (%)	Other Race Alone[2] (%)	Two or More Races (%)
City	75.4	18.4	0.9	0.3	0.0	3.3	1.7
MSA[1]	70.9	21.4	2.5	0.2	0.0	2.9	2.2
U.S.	73.0	12.7	5.4	0.8	0.2	4.8	3.1

Note: (1) Figures cover the Miami-Fort Lauderdale-West Palm Beach, FL Metropolitan Statistical Area—see Appendix B for areas included; (2) Alone is defined as not being in combination with one or more other races; (3) American Indian and Alaska Native; (4) Native Hawaiian and Other Pacific Islander
Source: U.S. Census Bureau, 2013-2017 American Community Survey 5-Year Estimates

Hispanic or Latino Origin

Area	Total (%)	Mexican (%)	Puerto Rican (%)	Cuban (%)	Other (%)
City	72.2	1.9	3.4	35.6	31.3
MSA[1]	44.2	2.5	3.9	18.9	18.9
U.S.	17.6	11.1	1.7	0.7	4.1

Note: Persons of Hispanic or Latino origin can be of any race; (1) Figures cover the Miami-Fort Lauderdale-West Palm Beach, FL Metropolitan Statistical Area—see Appendix B for areas included
Source: U.S. Census Bureau, 2013-2017 American Community Survey 5-Year Estimates

Segregation

Type	Segregation Indices[1]				Percent Change		
	1990	2000	2010	2010 Rank[2]	1990-2000	1990-2010	2000-2010
Black/White	71.4	69.2	64.8	23	-2.3	-6.6	-4.3
Asian/White	26.8	33.3	34.2	80	6.4	7.3	0.9
Hispanic/White	32.5	59.0	57.4	8	26.5	24.8	-1.6

Note: All figures cover the Metropolitan Statistical Area—see Appendix B for areas included; Figures are based on an analysis of 1990, 2000, and 2010 Census Decennial Census tract data by William H. Frey, Brookings Institution and the University of Michigan Social Science Data Analysis Network. In this analysis all racial groups (whites, blacks, and asians) are non-Hispanic members of those races. Hispanics are shown as a separate category; (1) Segregation Indices are Dissimilarity Indices that measure the degree to which the minority group is distributed differently than whites across census tracts. They range from 0 (complete integration) to 100 (complete segregation) where the value indicates the percentage of the minority group that needs to move to be distributed exactly like whites; (2) Ranges from 1 (most segregated) to 102 (least segregated); n/a not available.
Source: www.CensusScope.org

Ancestry

Area	German	Irish	English	American	Italian	Polish	French[2]	Scottish	Dutch
City	1.7	1.3	0.9	3.8	2.1	0.6	0.9	0.3	0.2
MSA[1]	4.7	4.5	2.9	6.0	5.1	2.0	1.3	0.7	0.4
U.S.	14.1	10.1	7.5	6.6	5.3	2.9	2.5	1.7	1.3

Note: Figures are the percentage of the total population reporting a particular ancestry. The nine most commonly reported ancestries in the U.S. are shown. Figures include multiple ancestries (e.g. if a person reported being Irish and Italian, they were included in both columns); (1) Figures cover the Miami-Fort Lauderdale-West Palm Beach, FL Metropolitan Statistical Area—see Appendix B for areas included; (2) Excludes Basque
Source: U.S. Census Bureau, 2013-2017 American Community Survey 5-Year Estimates

Foreign-Born Population

Area	Any Foreign Country	Asia	Mexico	Europe	Carribean	Central America[2]	South America	Africa	Canada
City	58.0	0.9	0.9	1.9	33.0	12.1	8.8	0.2	0.1
MSA[1]	40.0	2.1	1.1	2.3	21.0	4.2	8.3	0.4	0.6
U.S.	13.4	4.1	3.6	1.5	1.3	1.0	0.9	0.6	0.3

Note: (1) Figures cover the Miami-Fort Lauderdale-West Palm Beach, FL Metropolitan Statistical Area—see Appendix B for areas included; (2) Excludes Mexico.
Source: U.S. Census Bureau, 2013-2017 American Community Survey 5-Year Estimates

Marital Status

Area	Never Married	Now Married[2]	Separated	Widowed	Divorced
City	40.9	34.7	4.0	6.6	13.9
MSA[1]	34.6	42.9	3.0	6.6	12.9
U.S.	33.1	48.2	2.0	5.8	10.9

Note: Figures are percentages and cover the population 15 years of age and older; (1) Figures cover the Miami-Fort Lauderdale-West Palm Beach, FL Metropolitan Statistical Area—see Appendix B for areas included; (2) Excludes separated
Source: U.S. Census Bureau, 2013-2017 American Community Survey 5-Year Estimates

Disability by Age

Area	All Ages	Under 18 Years Old	18 to 64 Years Old	65 Years and Over
City	12.0	3.7	8.3	36.1
MSA[1]	11.0	3.4	7.4	33.3
U.S.	12.6	4.2	10.3	35.5

Note: Figures show percent of the civilian noninstitutionalized population that reported having a disability. Disability status is determined from six types of difficulty: vision, hearing, cognitive, ambulatory, self-care, and independent living. For children under 5 years old, hearing and vision difficulty are used to determine disability status. For children between the ages of 5 and 14, disability status is determined from hearing, vision, cognitive, ambulatory, and self-care difficulties. For people aged 15 years and older, they are considered to have a disability if they have difficulty with any one of the six difficulty types; Note: (1) Figures cover the Miami-Fort Lauderdale-West Palm Beach, FL Metropolitan Statistical Area—see Appendix B for areas included
Source: U.S. Census Bureau, 2013-2017 American Community Survey 5-Year Estimates

Age

Area	Under Age 5	Age 5–19	Age 20–34	Age 35–44	Age 45–54	Age 55–64	Age 65–74	Age 75–84	Age 85+	Median Age
City	6.2	13.4	22.8	15.1	14.3	11.5	8.6	5.3	2.7	40.0
MSA[1]	5.6	17.1	19.6	13.3	14.6	12.4	9.0	5.5	2.7	40.7
U.S.	6.2	19.5	20.7	12.7	13.4	12.7	8.6	4.4	1.9	37.8

Note: (1) Figures cover the Miami-Fort Lauderdale-West Palm Beach, FL Metropolitan Statistical Area—see Appendix B for areas included
Source: U.S. Census Bureau, 2013-2017 American Community Survey 5-Year Estimates

Gender

Area	Males	Females	Males per 100 Females
City	219,009	223,998	97.8
MSA[1]	2,923,416	3,096,374	94.4
U.S.	158,018,753	162,985,654	97.0

Note: (1) Figures cover the Miami-Fort Lauderdale-West Palm Beach, FL Metropolitan Statistical Area—see Appendix B for areas included
Source: U.S. Census Bureau, 2013-2017 American Community Survey 5-Year Estimates

Religious Groups by Family

Area	Catholic	Baptist	Non-Den.	Methodist[2]	Lutheran	LDS[3]	Pentecostal	Presbyterian[4]	Muslim[5]	Judaism
MSA[1]	18.6	5.4	4.2	1.3	0.5	0.5	1.8	0.7	0.9	1.6
U.S.	19.1	9.3	4.0	4.0	2.3	2.0	1.9	1.6	0.8	0.7

Note: Figures are the number of adherents as a percentage of the total population; (1) Figures cover the Miami-Fort Lauderdale-West Palm Beach, FL Metropolitan Statistical Area—see Appendix B for areas included; (2) Methodist/Pietist; (3) Latter Day Saints; (4) Reformed; (5) Figures are estimates
Source: Association of Statisticians of American Religious Bodies, 2010 U.S. Religion Census: Religious Congregations & Membership Study

Religious Groups by Tradition

Area	Catholic	Evangelical Protestant	Mainline Protestant	Other Tradition	Black Protestant	Orthodox
MSA[1]	18.6	11.4	2.5	3.5	1.7	0.3
U.S.	19.1	16.2	7.3	4.3	1.6	0.3

Note: Figures are the number of adherents as a percentage of the total population; (1) Figures cover the Miami-Fort Lauderdale-West Palm Beach, FL Metropolitan Statistical Area—see Appendix B for areas included
Source: Association of Statisticians of American Religious Bodies, 2010 U.S. Religion Census: Religious Congregations & Membership Study

ECONOMY

Gross Metropolitan Product

Area	2016	2017	2018	2019	Rank[2]
MSA[1]	329.7	340.9	356.6	376.6	12

Note: Figures are in billions of dollars; (1) Figures cover the Miami-Fort Lauderdale-West Palm Beach, FL Metropolitan Statistical Area—see Appendix B for areas included; (2) Rank is based on 2017 data and ranges from 1 to 381
Source: U.S. Conference of Mayors, U.S. Metro Economies: Economic Growth & Full Employment, June 2018

Economic Growth

Area	2017-2018 (%)	2019-2020 (%)	2021-2022 (%)
MSA[1]	2.7	2.8	1.9

Note: Figures are real gross metropolitan product (GMP) growth rates and represent average annual percent change; (1) Figures cover the Miami-Fort Lauderdale-West Palm Beach, FL Metropolitan Statistical Area—see Appendix B for areas included
Source: U.S. Conference of Mayors, U.S. Metro Economies: Economic Growth & Full Employment, June 2018

Metropolitan Area Exports

Area	2012	2013	2014	2015	2016	2017	Rank[2]
MSA[1]	47,858.7	41,771.5	37,969.5	33,258.5	32,734.5	34,780.5	7

Note: Figures are in millions of dollars; (1) Figures cover the Miami-Fort Lauderdale-West Palm Beach, FL Metropolitan Statistical Area—see Appendix B for areas included; (2) Rank is based on 2017 data and ranges from 1 to 387
Source: U.S. Department of Commerce, International Trade Administration, Office of Trade and Economic Analysis, Industry and Analysis, Exports by Metropolitan Area, extracted March 25, 2019

Building Permits

Area	Single-Family			Multi-Family			Total		
	2016	2017	Pct. Chg.	2016	2017	Pct. Chg.	2016	2017	Pct. Chg.
City	87	90	3.4	3,823	4,671	22.2	3,910	4,761	21.8
MSA[1]	6,705	6,655	-0.7	12,037	13,068	8.6	18,742	19,723	5.2
U.S.	750,800	820,000	9.2	455,800	462,000	1.4	1,206,600	1,282,000	6.2

Note: (1) Figures cover the Miami-Fort Lauderdale-West Palm Beach, FL Metropolitan Statistical Area—see Appendix B for areas included; Figures represent new, privately-owned housing units authorized (unadjusted data); All permit data are based on estimates with imputation
Source: U.S. Census Bureau, Manufacturing, Mining, and Construction Statistics, Building Permits, 2016, 2017

Bankruptcy Filings

Area	Business Filings			Nonbusiness Filings		
	2017	2018	% Chg.	2017	2018	% Chg.
Miami-Dade County	231	243	5.2	7,726	8,119	5.1
U.S.	23,157	22,232	-4.0	765,863	751,186	-1.9

Note: Business filings include Chapter 7, Chapter 11, Chapter 12, and Chapter 13; Nonbusiness filings include Chapter 7, Chapter 11, and Chapter 13
Source: Administrative Office of the U.S. Courts, Business and Nonbusiness Bankruptcy, County Cases Commenced by Chapter of the Bankruptcy Code, During the 12-Month Period Ending December 31, 2017 and Business and Nonbusiness Bankruptcy, County Cases Commenced by Chapter of the Bankruptcy Code, During the 12-Month Period Ending December 31, 2018

Housing Vacancy Rates

Area	Gross Vacancy Rate[2] (%)			Year-Round Vacancy Rate[3] (%)			Rental Vacancy Rate[4] (%)			Homeowner Vacancy Rate[5] (%)		
	2016	2017	2018	2016	2017	2018	2016	2017	2018	2016	2017	2018
MSA[1]	17.9	17.8	14.9	9.5	9.2	7.9	7.2	7.0	7.4	1.4	1.9	1.9
U.S.	12.8	12.7	12.3	9.9	9.9	9.7	6.9	7.2	6.9	1.7	1.6	1.5

Note: (1) Figures cover the Miami-Fort Lauderdale-West Palm Beach, FL Metropolitan Statistical Area—see Appendix B for areas included; (2) The percentage of the total housing inventory that is vacant; (3) The percentage of the housing inventory (excluding seasonal units) that is year-round vacant; (4) The percentage of rental inventory that is vacant for rent; (5) The percentage of homeowner inventory that is vacant for sale
Source: U.S. Census Bureau, Housing Vacancies and Homeownership Annual Statistics: 2016, 2017, 2018

INCOME

Income

Area	Per Capita ($)	Median Household ($)	Average Household ($)
City	25,067	33,999	60,341
MSA[1]	29,499	51,758	78,886
U.S.	31,177	57,652	81,283

Note: (1) Figures cover the Miami-Fort Lauderdale-West Palm Beach, FL Metropolitan Statistical Area—see Appendix B for areas included
Source: U.S. Census Bureau, 2013-2017 American Community Survey 5-Year Estimates

Household Income Distribution

Area	Percent of Households Earning							
	Under $15,000	$15,000 -$24,999	$25,000 -$34,999	$35,000 -$49,999	$50,000 -$74,999	$75,000 -$99,999	$100,000 -$149,999	$150,000 and up
City	23.4	15.4	12.2	13.0	13.5	7.6	7.5	7.5
MSA[1]	13.2	11.1	10.3	13.7	17.1	11.1	12.2	11.2
U.S.	11.6	9.8	9.5	13.0	17.7	12.3	14.1	12.1

Note: (1) Figures cover the Miami-Fort Lauderdale-West Palm Beach, FL Metropolitan Statistical Area—see Appendix B for areas included
Source: U.S. Census Bureau, 2013-2017 American Community Survey 5-Year Estimates

Poverty Rate

Area	All Ages	Under 18 Years Old	18 to 64 Years Old	65 Years and Over
City	25.8	36.0	21.9	30.3
MSA[1]	16.1	22.2	14.4	14.9
U.S.	14.6	20.3	13.7	9.3

Note: Figures are percentage of people whose income during the past 12 months was below the poverty level; (1) Figures cover the Miami-Fort Lauderdale-West Palm Beach, FL Metropolitan Statistical Area—see Appendix B for areas included
Source: U.S. Census Bureau, 2013-2017 American Community Survey 5-Year Estimates

EMPLOYMENT

Labor Force and Employment

Area	Civilian Labor Force			Workers Employed		
	Dec. 2017	Dec. 2018	% Chg.	Dec. 2017	Dec. 2018	% Chg.
City	231,034	231,547	0.2	220,564	223,501	1.3
MD[1]	1,387,642	1,403,293	1.1	1,327,905	1,353,811	2.0
U.S.	159,880,000	162,510,000	1.6	153,602,000	156,481,000	1.9

Note: Data is not seasonally adjusted and covers workers 16 years of age and older; (1) Figures cover the Miami-Miami Beach-Kendall, FL Metropolitan Division—see Appendix B for areas included
Source: Bureau of Labor Statistics, Local Area Unemployment Statistics

Unemployment Rate

Area	2018											
	Jan.	Feb.	Mar.	Apr.	May	Jun.	Jul.	Aug.	Sep.	Oct.	Nov.	Dec.
City	4.6	4.6	4.9	4.1	3.9	4.1	4.3	4.1	3.7	3.5	3.2	3.5
MD[1]	4.1	4.0	4.3	3.9	3.7	4.0	3.9	4.0	3.8	3.6	3.3	3.5
U.S.	4.5	4.4	4.1	3.7	3.6	4.2	4.1	3.9	3.6	3.5	3.5	3.7

Note: Data is not seasonally adjusted and covers workers 16 years of age and older; (1) Figures cover the Miami-Miami Beach-Kendall, FL Metropolitan Division—see Appendix B for areas included
Source: Bureau of Labor Statistics, Local Area Unemployment Statistics

Average Wages

Occupation	$/Hr.	Occupation	$/Hr.
Accountants and Auditors	37.40	Maids and Housekeeping Cleaners	11.40
Automotive Mechanics	20.60	Maintenance and Repair Workers	17.40
Bookkeepers	20.40	Marketing Managers	59.10
Carpenters	19.90	Nuclear Medicine Technologists	34.20
Cashiers	10.50	Nurses, Licensed Practical	22.50
Clerks, General Office	16.40	Nurses, Registered	33.40
Clerks, Receptionists/Information	14.60	Nursing Assistants	12.60
Clerks, Shipping/Receiving	15.30	Packers and Packagers, Hand	11.70
Computer Programmers	38.20	Physical Therapists	42.30
Computer Systems Analysts	42.10	Postal Service Mail Carriers	25.40
Computer User Support Specialists	24.00	Real Estate Brokers	38.00
Cooks, Restaurant	14.00	Retail Salespersons	13.10
Dentists	77.20	Sales Reps., Exc. Tech./Scientific	29.20
Electrical Engineers	42.50	Sales Reps., Tech./Scientific	39.60
Electricians	22.30	Secretaries, Exc. Legal/Med./Exec.	17.50
Financial Managers	68.00	Security Guards	13.20
First-Line Supervisors/Managers, Sales	23.60	Surgeons	103.70
Food Preparation Workers	11.90	Teacher Assistants*	11.10
General and Operations Managers	57.40	Teachers, Elementary School*	20.80
Hairdressers/Cosmetologists	15.40	Teachers, Secondary School*	25.70
Internists, General	91.80	Telemarketers	12.40
Janitors and Cleaners	11.90	Truck Drivers, Heavy/Tractor-Trailer	19.90
Landscaping/Groundskeeping Workers	13.50	Truck Drivers, Light/Delivery Svcs.	17.10
Lawyers	69.90	Waiters and Waitresses	12.60

Note: Wage data covers the Miami-Fort Lauderdale-West Palm Beach, FL Metropolitan Statistical Area—see Appendix B for areas included; (*) Hourly wages for elementary/secondary school teachers and teacher assistants were calculated by the editors from annual wage data based on a 40 hour work week; n/a not available.
Source: Bureau of Labor Statistics, Metro Area Occupational Employment & Wage Estimates, May 2018

Employment by Occupation

Occupation Classification	City (%)	MSA[1] (%)	U.S. (%)
Management, Business, Science, and Arts	29.6	34.0	37.4
Natural Resources, Construction, and Maintenance	11.3	9.0	8.9
Production, Transportation, and Material Moving	10.7	9.1	12.2
Sales and Office	23.6	27.1	23.5
Service	24.7	20.9	18.0

Note: Figures cover employed civilians 16 years of age and older; (1) Figures cover the Miami-Fort Lauderdale-West Palm Beach, FL Metropolitan Statistical Area—see Appendix B for areas included
Source: U.S. Census Bureau, 2013-2017 American Community Survey 5-Year Estimates

Employment by Industry

Sector	MD[1]		U.S.
	Number of Employees	Percent of Total	Percent of Total
Construction	53,000	4.3	4.8
Education and Health Services	191,800	15.7	15.9
Financial Activities	82,200	6.7	5.7
Government	143,600	11.7	15.1
Information	20,400	1.7	1.9
Leisure and Hospitality	145,900	11.9	10.7
Manufacturing	42,100	3.4	8.5
Mining and Logging	500	<0.1	0.5
Other Services	52,300	4.3	3.9
Professional and Business Services	181,800	14.9	14.1
Retail Trade	154,700	12.6	10.8
Transportation, Warehousing, and Utilities	81,300	6.6	4.2
Wholesale Trade	73,400	6.0	3.9

Note: Figures are non-farm employment as of December 2018. Figures are not seasonally adjusted and include workers 16 years of age and older; (1) Figures cover the Miami-Miami Beach-Kendall, FL Metropolitan Division—see Appendix B for areas included
Source: Bureau of Labor Statistics, Current Employment Statistics, Employment, Hours, and Earnings

Occupations with Greatest Projected Employment Growth: 2018 – 2020

Occupation[1]	2018 Employment	2020 Projected Employment	Numeric Employment Change	Percent Employment Change
Interviewers, Except Eligibility and Loan	11,890	33,270	21,380	179.8
Combined Food Preparation and Serving Workers, Including Fast Food	242,590	256,470	13,880	5.7
Waiters and Waitresses	230,640	240,320	9,680	4.2
Registered Nurses	193,200	202,070	8,870	4.6
Customer Service Representatives	245,420	253,780	8,360	3.4
Laborers and Freight, Stock, and Material Movers, Hand	135,600	143,640	8,040	5.9
Construction Laborers	89,390	97,130	7,740	8.7
Landscaping and Groundskeeping Workers	116,440	123,040	6,600	5.7
Carpenters	72,550	78,990	6,440	8.9
Janitors and Cleaners, Except Maids and Housekeeping Cleaners	133,890	140,000	6,110	4.6

Note: Projections cover Florida; (1) Sorted by numeric employment change
Source: www.projectionscentral.com, State Occupational Projections, 2018–2020 Short-Term Projections

Fastest Growing Occupations: 2018 – 2020

Occupation[1]	2018 Employment	2020 Projected Employment	Numeric Employment Change	Percent Employment Change
Interviewers, Except Eligibility and Loan	11,890	33,270	21,380	179.8
Solar Photovoltaic Installers	1,100	1,330	230	20.9
Terrazzo Workers and Finishers	390	450	60	15.4
Helpers—Roofers	1,490	1,720	230	15.4
Helpers—Brickmasons, Blockmasons, Stonemasons, and Tile and Marble Setters	1,280	1,470	190	14.8
Helpers—Painters, Paperhangers, Plasterers, and Stucco Masons	570	650	80	14.0
Reinforcing Iron and Rebar Workers	1,100	1,250	150	13.6
Insulation Workers, Floor, Ceiling, and Wall	2,550	2,880	330	12.9
Structural Iron and Steel Workers	5,210	5,880	670	12.9
Cement Masons and Concrete Finishers	13,490	15,210	1,720	12.8

Note: Projections cover Florida; (1) Sorted by percent employment change and excludes occupations with numeric employment change less than 50
Source: www.projectionscentral.com, State Occupational Projections, 2018–2020 Short-Term Projections

TAXES

State Corporate Income Tax Rates

State	Tax Rate (%)	Income Brackets ($)	Num. of Brackets	Financial Institution Tax Rate (%)[a]	Federal Income Tax Ded.
Florida	5.5 (e)	Flat rate	1	5.5 (e)	No

Note: Tax rates as of January 1, 2019; (a) Rates listed are the corporate income tax rate applied to financial institutions or excise taxes based on income. Some states have other taxes based upon the value of deposits or shares; (e) The Florida tax rate may be adjusted downward if certain revenue targets are met.
Source: Federation of Tax Administrators, Range of State Corporate Income Tax Rates, January 1, 2019

State Individual Income Tax Rates

State	Tax Rate (%)	Income Brackets ($)	Personal Exemptions ($)			Standard Ded. ($)	
			Single	Married	Depend.	Single	Married
Florida			– No state income tax –				

Note: Tax rates as of January 1, 2019; Local- and county-level taxes are not included; n/a not applicable;

Source: Federation of Tax Administrators, State Individual Income Tax Rates, January 1, 2019

Various State Sales and Excise Tax Rates

State	State Sales Tax (%)	Gasoline[1] (¢/gal.)	Cigarette[2] ($/pack)	Spirits[3] ($/gal.)	Wine[4] ($/gal.)	Beer[5] ($/gal.)	Recreational Marijuana (%)
Florida	6	41.99	1.339	6.50 (f)	2.25 (l)	0.48 (q)	Not legal

Note: All tax rates as of January 1, 2019; (1) The American Petroleum Institute has developed a methodology for determining the average tax rate on a gallon of fuel. Rates may include any of the following: excise taxes, environmental fees, storage tank fees, other fees or taxes, general sales tax, and local taxes. In states where gasoline is subject to the general sales tax, or where the fuel tax is based on the average sale price, the average rate determined by API is sensitive to changes in the price of gasoline. States that fully or partially apply general sales taxes to gasoline: CA, CO, GA, IL, IN, MI, NY; (2) The federal excise tax of $1.0066 per pack and local taxes are not included; (3) Rates are those applicable to off-premise sales of 40% alcohol by volume (a.b.v.) distilled spirits in 750ml containers. Local excise taxes are excluded; (4) Rates are those applicable to off-premise sales of 11% a.b.v. non-carbonated wine in 750ml containers; (5) Rates are those applicable to off-premise sales of 4.7% a.b.v. beer in 12 ounce containers; (f) Different rates also applicable according to alcohol content, place of production, size of container, or place purchased (on- or off-premise or onboard airlines); (l) Different rates also applicable to alcohol content, place of production, size of container, place purchased (on- or off-premise or on board airlines) or type of wine (carbonated, vermouth, etc.); (q) Different rates also applicable according to alcohol content, place of production, size of container, or place purchased (on- or off-premise or onboard airlines).
Source: Tax Foundation, 2019 Facts & Figures: How Does Your State Compare?

State Business Tax Climate Index Rankings

State	Overall Rank	Corporate Tax Rank	Individual Income Tax Rank	Sales Tax Rank	Unemployment Insurance Tax Rank	Property Tax Rank
Florida	4	6	1	22	2	11

Note: The index is a measure of how each state's tax laws affect economic performance. The lower the rank, the more favorable a state's tax system is for business. States without a given tax are given a ranking of 1. The scores/rankings for the District of Columbia do not affect other states. The 2019 index represents the tax climate as of July 1, 2018.
Source: Tax Foundation, State Business Tax Climate Index 2019

**COMMERCIAL
REAL ESTATE**

Office Market

Market Area	Inventory (sq. ft.)	Vacancy Rate (%)	Under Construction (sq. ft.)	YTD Net Absorption (sq. ft.)	Total Average Asking Rent ($/sq. ft./year)
Miami	48,138,344	12.0	697,801	115,105	35.89
National	4,905,867,938	13.1	83,553,714	45,846,470	28.46

Source: Newmark Grubb Knight Frank, National Office Market Report, 4th Quarter 2018

Industrial/Warehouse/R&D Market

Market Area	Inventory (sq. ft.)	Vacancy Rate (%)	Under Construction (sq. ft.)	YTD Net Absorption (sq. ft.)	Total Average Asking Rent ($/sq. ft./year)
Miami	214,704,685	4.0	2,842,019	3,064,109	8.10
National	14,796,839,085	5.0	262,662,294	238,014,726	7.16

Source: Newmark Grubb Knight Frank, National Industrial Market Report, 4th Quarter 2018

**COMMERCIAL
UTILITIES**

Typical Monthly Electric Bills

Area	Commercial Service ($/month)		Industrial Service ($/month)	
	1,500 kWh	40 kW demand 14,000 kWh	1,000 kW demand 200,000 kWh	50,000 kW demand 32,500,000 kWh
City	151	1,199	22,310	1,463,495
Average[1]	203	1,619	25,886	2,540,077

Note: Figures are based on annualized rates; (1) Average based on 187 utilities surveyed
Source: Edison Electric Institute, Typical Bills and Average Rates Report, Summer 2018

TRANSPORTATION

Means of Transportation to Work

Area	Car/Truck/Van		Public Transportation			Bicycle	Walked	Other Means	Worked at Home
	Drove Alone	Car-pooled	Bus	Subway	Railroad				
City	70.0	8.5	9.6	0.9	0.3	1.0	4.0	1.5	4.2
MSA[1]	78.2	9.1	3.2	0.3	0.2	0.6	1.7	1.5	5.2
U.S.	76.4	9.2	2.5	0.3	0.6	0.6	2.7	1.3	4.7

Note: Figures are percentages and cover workers 16 years of age and older; (1) Figures cover the Miami-Fort Lauderdale-West Palm Beach, FL Metropolitan Statistical Area—see Appendix B for areas included
Source: U.S. Census Bureau, 2013-2017 American Community Survey 5-Year Estimates

Travel Time to Work

Area	Less Than 10 Minutes	10 to 19 Minutes	20 to 29 Minutes	30 to 44 Minutes	45 to 59 Minutes	60 to 89 Minutes	90 Minutes or More
City	5.9	23.8	23.4	29.2	9.0	6.7	2.1
MSA[1]	6.9	23.7	22.6	27.2	9.9	7.3	2.4
U.S.	12.7	28.9	20.9	20.5	8.1	6.2	2.7

Note: Note: Figures are percentages and include workers 16 years old and over; (1) Figures cover the Miami-Fort Lauderdale-West Palm Beach, FL Metropolitan Statistical Area—see Appendix B for areas included
Source: U.S. Census Bureau, 2013-2017 American Community Survey 5-Year Estimates

Freeway Travel Time Index

Area	1985	1990	1995	2000	2005	2010	2014
Urban Area Rank[1,2]	11	16	18	11	13	18	17
Urban Area Index[1]	1.16	1.18	1.21	1.27	1.29	1.27	1.29
Average Index[3]	1.09	1.11	1.14	1.17	1.20	1.19	1.20

Note: Freeway Travel Time Index—the ratio of travel time in the peak period to the travel time at free-flow conditions. For example, a value of 1.30 indicates a 20-minute free-flow trip takes 26 minutes in the peak (20 minutes x 1.30 = 26 minutes); (1) Covers the Miami FL urban area; (2) Rank is based on 101 urban areas (#1 = highest travel time index); (3) Average of 101 urban areas
Source: Texas Transportation Institute, 2015 Urban Mobility Scorecard, August 2015

Freeway Commuter Stress Index

Area	1985	1990	1995	2000	2005	2010	2014
Urban Area Rank[1,2]	28	28	31	23	28	29	29
Urban Area Index[1]	1.17	1.19	1.23	1.29	1.31	1.29	1.30
Average Index[3]	1.13	1.16	1.19	1.22	1.25	1.24	1.25

Note: The Freeway Commuter Stress Index is the same as the Freeway Travel Time Index (see table above) except that it includes only the travel in the peak directions during the peak periods; the TTI includes travel in all directions during the peak period. Thus, the CSI is more indicative of the work trip experienced by each commuter on a daily basis; (1) Covers the Miami FL urban area; (2) Rank is based on 101 urban areas (#1 = highest travel time index); (3) Average of 101 urban areas
Source: Texas Transportation Institute, 2015 Urban Mobility Scorecard, August 2015

Public Transportation

Agency Name / Mode of Transportation	Vehicles Operated in Maximum Service[1]	Annual Unlinked Passenger Trips[2] (in thous.)	Annual Passenger Miles[3] (in thous.)
Miami-Dade Transit (MDT)			
Bus (directly operated)	709	58,001.0	357,878.2
Bus (purchased transportation)	29	37.0	190.2
Commuter Bus (purchased transportation)	9	345.8	14,572.6
Demand Response (purchased transportation)	369	1,633.2	21,038.2
Heavy Rail (directly operated)	84	19,984.7	151,178.9
Monorail and Automated Guideway (directly operated)	21	9,463.4	8,834.4
South Florida Regional Transportation Authority (TRI-Rail)			
Bus (purchased transportation)	24	945.9	3,375.2
Commuter Rail (purchased transportation)	42	4,261.1	118,514.3

Note: (1) The number of revenue vehicles operated by the given mode and type of service to meet the annual maximum service requirement. This is the revenue vehicle count during the peak season of the year; on the week and day that maximum service is provided. Vehicles operated in maximum service (VOMS) exclude atypical days and one-time special events; (2) The number of passengers who boarded public transportation vehicles. Passengers are counted each time they board a vehicle no matter how many vehicles they use to travel from their origin to their destination. (3) The sum of the distances ridden by all passengers during the entire fiscal year.
Source: Federal Transit Administration, National Transit Database, 2017

Air Transportation

Airport Name and Code / Type of Service	Passenger Airlines[1]	Passenger Enplanements	Freight Carriers[2]	Freight (lbs)
Miami International (MIA)				
Domestic service (U.S. carriers - 2018)	28	10,527,757	20	346,394,913
International service (U.S. carriers - 2017)	17	6,101,684	20	809,461,592

Note: (1) Includes all U.S.-based major, minor and commuter airlines that carried at least one passenger during the year; (2) Includes all U.S.-based airlines and freight carriers that transported at least one pound of freight during the year.
Source: Bureau of Transportation Statistics, The Intermodal Transportation Database, Air Carriers: T-100 Domestic Market (U.S. Carriers), 2018; Bureau of Transportation Statistics, The Intermodal Transportation Database, Air Carriers: T-100 International Market (U.S. Carriers), 2017

Other Transportation Statistics

Major Highways:	I-95
Amtrak Service:	Yes
Major Waterways/Ports:	Port of Miami; Atlantic Intracoastal Waterway

Source: Amtrak.com; Google Maps

BUSINESSES

Major Business Headquarters

Company Name	Industry	Fortune[1]	Forbes[2]
		Rankings	
Lennar	Homebuilders	230	-
Ryder System	Trucking, Truck Leasing	387	-
Southern Glazer's Wine & Spirits	Food, Drink & Tobacco	-	18
World Fuel Services	Wholesalers: Diversified	91	-

Note: (1) Companies that produce a 10-K are ranked 1 to 500 based on 2017 revenue; (2) All private companies with at least $2 billion in annual revenue through the end of their most current fiscal year are ranked 1 to 229; companies listed are headquartered in the city; dashes indicate no ranking
Source: Fortune, "Fortune 500," June 2018; Forbes, "America's Largest Private Companies," 2018 Rankings

Fast-Growing Businesses

According to *Inc.*, Miami is home to four of America's 500 fastest-growing private companies: **SWARM** (#98); **HealthCare.com** (#351); **Monster Grass and Patio** (#434); **Saved By The Dress** (#441). Criteria: must be an independent, privately-held, for-profit, U.S. corporation, proprietorship or partnership as of December 31, 2017; revenues must be at least $100,000 in 2014 and $2 million in 2017; must have four-year operating/sales history. Holding companies, regulated banks, and utilities were excluded. *Inc., "America's 500 Fastest-Growing Private Companies," 2018*

According to Deloitte, Miami is home to one of North America's 500 fastest-growing high-technology companies: **HealthCare.com** (#92). Companies are ranked by percentage growth in revenue over a four-year period. Criteria for inclusion: company must be headquartered within North America; must own proprietary intellectual property or technology that is sold to customers in products that contributes to a significant portion of the company's operating revenue; must have been in business for a minumum of four years with 2014 operating revenues of at least $50,000 USD/CD and 2017 operating revenues of at least $5 million USD/CD. *Deloitte, 2018 Technology Fast 500™*

Minority Business Opportunity

Miami is home to 53 companies which are on the *Hispanic Business* 500 list (500 largest U.S. Hispanic-owned companies based on revenue): **Brightstar Corp.** (#1); **The Related Group** (#4); **Quirch Foods** (#8); **First Equity Mortgage Bankers** (#27); **BMI Financial Group** (#31); **MCM** (#44); **Headquarter Toyota** (#48); **Miami Automotive Retail** (#49); **Refricenter of Miami** (#59); **Machado Garcia Serra** (#72); **Metro Ford** (#89); **Transnational Foods** (#91); **Link Construction Group** (#92); **South Dade Automotive** (#94); **CSA Holdings** (#111); **John Keeler & Co.** (#120); **Softech International** (#121); **Everglades Steel, Medley Steel, Metallic Products** (#132); **Adonel Concrete Pumping & Finishing of S. Florida** (#139); **Solo Printing** (#142); **Ascendant Commercial Insurance Co.** (#144); **Metric Engineering** (#146); **Gancedo Lumber Co.** (#163); **The Intermarket Group** (#171); **Roach Busters Bug Killers of America** (#185); **Fru-Veg Marketing** (#189); **Express Travel** (#192); **Original Impressions** (#201); **Protec** (#206); **Nital Trading Co.** (#214); **Future Force Personnel** (#235); **Vina & Sons Food Distributor Corp.** (#237); **Bermello, Ajamil & Partners** (#246); **AZF Automotive Group** (#286); **X-EETO** (#287); **American Fasteners Corp.** (#294); **Interamerican Bank** (#304); **EnviroWaste Services Group** (#308); **Republica** (#311); **EYMAQ** (#324); **Wendium of Florida** (#327); **Hispanic Group** (#329); **Farma International** (#334); **Amtec Sales** (#351); **South Florida Trading Corp.** (#362); **T&S Roofing Systems** (#368); **F.R. Aleman & Associates** (#396); **A-1 Property Services Group** (#404); **Gomez Ossa International** (#433); **Honshy Electric Co.** (#434); **Hernandez & Tacoronte PA** (#447); **Decorative Sales Assoc.** (#484); **Dynamic Turbo** (#486). Companies included must show at least 51 percent ownership by Hispanic U.S. citizens, and must maintain headquarters in one of the 50 states or Washington, D.C. *Hispanic Business, "Hispanic Business 500," June 20, 2013*

Minority- and Women-Owned Businesses

Group	All Firms		Firms with Paid Employees			
	Firms	Sales ($000)	Firms	Sales ($000)	Employees	Payroll ($000)
AIAN[1]	403	12,805	5	6,070	102	2,665
Asian	1,556	1,117,525	625	1,045,817	4,146	122,905
Black	9,795	346,591	373	192,659	2,458	52,694
Hispanic	68,005	9,756,152	7,055	7,961,875	36,428	1,333,517
NHOPI[2]	76	1,013	0	0	0	0
Women	39,762	3,421,811	3,123	2,585,202	19,786	550,596
All Firms	98,222	68,322,278	15,211	65,352,571	448,924	23,307,382

Note: Figures cover firms located in the city; minority- and women-owned business are defined as firms in which the corresponding group own 51% or more of the stock or equity of the company; (1) American Indian and Alaska Native; (2) Native Hawaiian and Other Pacific Islander
Source: U.S. Census Bureau, 2012 Economic Census, Survey of Business Owners

HOTELS & CONVENTION CENTERS

Hotels, Motels and Vacation Rentals

Area	5 Star		4 Star		3 Star		2 Star		1 Star		Not Rated	
	Num.	Pct.[3]	Num.	Pct.[3]	Num.	Pct.[3]	Num.	Pct.[3]	Num.	Pct.[3]	Num.	Pct.[3]
City[1]	33	1.3	265	10.5	594	23.5	151	6.0	6	0.2	1,483	58.6
Total[2]	286	0.4	5,236	7.1	16,715	22.6	10,259	13.9	293	0.4	41,056	55.6

Note: (1) Figures cover Miami and vicinity; (2) Figures cover all 100 cities in this book; (3) Percentage of hotels which have a given star rating. Star ratings are determined by expedia.com and offer an indication of the general quality of a particular hotel.
Source: www.expedia.com, April 3, 2019

The Miami-Miami Beach-Kendall, FL metro area is home to one of the best resort hotels in the continental U.S. according to *Travel & Leisure*: **The Setai**. Magazine readers were surveyed and asked to rate hotels on the following criteria: rooms/facilities; location; service; food; and value. The list includes the top 15 resort hotels in the continental U.S. *Travel & Leisure, "The World's Best Awards 2018"*

The Miami-Miami Beach-Kendall, FL metro area is home to one of the best hotels in the world according to *Condé Nast Traveler*: **Four Seasons Hotel at the Surf Club**. The selections are based on editors' picks. The list includes the top 13 hotels in the U.S. *Condé Nast Traveler, "The 78 Best Hotels in the World: The Gold List 2019"*

Major Convention Centers

Name	Overall Space (sq. ft.)	Exhibit Space (sq. ft.)	Meeting Space (sq. ft.)	Meeting Rooms
Broward County Convention Center	600,000	n/a	n/a	31
Coconut Grove Convention Center	n/a	150,000	n/a	n/a
Miami Airport Convention Center	172,000	n/a	n/a	n/a
Miami Beach Convention Center	1,000,000	500,000	100,000	70
Miami Convention Center	n/a	28,000	n/a	17

Note: Table includes convention centers located in the Miami-Fort Lauderdale-West Palm Beach, FL metro area; n/a not available
Source: Original research

Living Environment

COST OF LIVING

Cost of Living Index

Composite Index	Groceries	Housing	Utilities	Trans-portation	Health Care	Misc. Goods/ Services
116.4	110.1	146.5	101.1	105.4	96.1	102.7

Note: The Cost of Living Index measures regional differences in the cost of consumer goods and services, excluding taxes and non-consumer expenditures, for professional and managerial households in the top income quintile. It is based on more than 50,000 prices covering almost 60 different items for which prices are collected three times a year by chambers of commerce, economic development organizations or university applied economic centers in each participating urban area. The numbers shown should be read as a percentage above or below the national average of 100. For example, a value of 115.4 in the groceries column indicates that grocery prices are 15.4% higher than the national average. Small differences in the index numbers should not be interpreted as significant; Figures cover the Miami-Dade County FL urban area.
Source: The Council for Community and Economic Research, ACCRA Cost of Living Index, 2018

Grocery Prices

Area[1]	T-Bone Steak ($/pound)	Frying Chicken ($/pound)	Whole Milk ($/half gal.)	Eggs ($/dozen)	Orange Juice ($/64 oz.)	Coffee ($/11.5 oz.)
City[2]	11.55	1.54	2.59	2.15	3.78	3.61
Avg.	11.35	1.42	1.94	1.81	3.52	4.35
Min.	7.45	0.92	0.80	0.75	2.72	3.06
Max.	15.05	2.76	4.18	4.00	5.36	8.20

Note: (1) Values for the local area are compared with the average, minimum and maximum values for all 291 areas in the Cost of Living Index; (2) Figures cover the Miami-Dade County FL urban area; T-Bone Steak (price per pound); Frying Chicken (price per pound, whole fryer); Whole Milk (half gallon carton); Eggs (price per dozen, Grade A, large); Orange Juice (64 oz. Tropicana or Florida Natural); Coffee (11.5 oz. can, vacuum-packed, Maxwell House, Hills Bros, or Folgers).
Source: The Council for Community and Economic Research, ACCRA Cost of Living Index, 2018

Housing and Utility Costs

Area[1]	New Home Price ($)	Apartment Rent ($/month)	All Electric ($/month)	Part Electric ($/month)	Other Energy ($/month)	Telephone ($/month)
City[2]	424,876	2,245	168.06	-	-	182.60
Avg.	347,000	1,087	165.93	100.16	67.73	178.70
Min.	200,468	500	93.58	25.64	26.78	163.10
Max.	1,901,222	4,888	388.65	246.86	332.81	197.70

Note: (1) Values for the local area are compared with the average, minimum and maximum values for all 291 areas in the Cost of Living Index; (2) Figures cover the Miami-Dade County FL urban area; New Home Price (2,400 sf living area, 8,000 sf lot, in urban area with full utilities); Apartment Rent (950 sf 2 bedroom/1.5 or 2 bath, unfurnished, excluding all utilities except water); All Electric (average monthly cost for an all-electric home); Part Electric (average monthly cost for a part-electric home); Other Energy (average monthly cost for natural gas, fuel oil, coal, wood, and any other forms of energy except electricity); Telephone (price includes the base monthly rate plus taxes and fees for three lines of mobile phone service).
Source: The Council for Community and Economic Research, ACCRA Cost of Living Index, 2018

Health Care, Transportation, and Other Costs

Area[1]	Doctor ($/visit)	Dentist ($/visit)	Optometrist ($/visit)	Gasoline ($/gallon)	Beauty Salon ($/visit)	Men's Shirt ($)
City[2]	91.11	95.28	94.86	2.74	56.11	26.39
Avg.	110.71	95.11	103.74	2.61	37.48	32.03
Min.	33.60	62.55	54.63	1.89	17.00	11.44
Max.	195.97	153.93	225.79	3.59	71.88	58.64

Note: (1) Values for the local area are compared with the average, minimum and maximum values for all 291 areas in the Cost of Living Index; (2) Figures cover the Miami-Dade County FL urban area; Doctor (general practitioners routine exam of an established patient); Dentist (adult teeth cleaning and periodic oral examination); Optometrist (full vision eye exam for established adult patient); Gasoline (one gallon regular unleaded, national brand, including all taxes, cash price at self-service pump if available); Beauty Salon (woman's shampoo, trim, and blow-dry); Men's Shirt (cotton/polyester dress shirt, pinpoint weave, long sleeves).
Source: The Council for Community and Economic Research, ACCRA Cost of Living Index, 2018

HOUSING

House Price Index (HPI)

Area	National Ranking[2]	Quarterly Change (%)	One-Year Change (%)	Five-Year Change (%)
MD[1]	66	0.91	8.04	55.38
U.S.[3]	—	1.12	5.73	32.81

Note: The HPI is a weighted repeat sales index. It measures average price changes in repeat sales or refinancings on the same properties. This information is obtained by reviewing repeat mortgage transactions on single-family properties whose mortgages have been purchased or securitized by Fannie Mae or Freddie Mac in January 1975; (1) Figures cover the Miami-Miami Beach-Kendall, FL Metropolitan Division—see Appendix B for areas included; (2) Rankings are based on annual percentage change for all metro areas containing at least 15,000 transactions over the last 10 years and ranges from 1 to 245; (3) figures based on a weighted average of Census Division estimates using a seasonally adjusted, purchase-only index; all figures are for the period ending December 31, 2018
Source: Federal Housing Finance Agency, House Price Index, February 26, 2019

Median Single-Family Home Prices

Area	2016	2017	2018p	Percent Change 2017 to 2018
MSA[1]	305.0	330.0	350.0	6.1
U.S. Average	235.5	248.8	261.6	5.1

Note: Figures are median sales prices of existing single-family homes in thousands of dollars; (p) preliminary; (1) Figures cover the Miami-Fort Lauderdale-West Palm Beach, FL Metropolitan Statistical Area—see Appendix B for areas included
Source: National Association of Realtors, Median Sales Price of Existing Single-Family Homes for Metropolitan Areas, 4th Quarter 2018

Qualifying Income Based on Median Sales Price of Existing Single-Family Homes

Area	With 5% Down ($)	With 10% Down ($)	With 20% Down ($)
MSA[1]	85,535	81,033	72,029
U.S. Average	62,954	59,640	53,013

Note: Figures are preliminary; Qualifying income is based on a mortgage rate of 4.9%. Monthly principal and interest payment is limited to 25% of income; (1) Figures cover the Miami-Fort Lauderdale-West Palm Beach, FL Metropolitan Statistical Area—see Appendix B for areas included
Source: National Association of Realtors, Qualifying Income Based on Median Sales Price of Existing Single-Family Homes for Metropolitan Areas, 4th Quarter 2018

Median Apartment Condo-Coop Home Prices

Area	2016	2017	2018p	Percent Change 2017 to 2018
MSA[1]	165.0	179.0	190.0	6.1
U.S. Average	220.7	234.3	241.0	2.9

Note: Figures are median sales prices of existing apartment condo-coop homes in thousands of dollars; (p) preliminary; (1) Figures cover the Miami-Fort Lauderdale-West Palm Beach, FL Metropolitan Statistical Area—see Appendix B for areas included
Source: National Association of Realtors, Median Sales Price of Existing Apartment Condo-Coop Homes for Metropolitan Areas, 4th Quarter 2018

Home Value Distribution

Area	Under $50,000	$50,000 -$99,999	$100,000 -$149,999	$150,000 -$199,999	$200,000 -$299,999	$300,000 -$499,999	$500,000 -$999,999	$1,000,000 or more
City	3.5	8.3	9.4	13.0	23.5	24.2	12.5	5.7
MSA[1]	6.0	10.4	11.7	13.6	22.0	22.6	10.0	3.8
U.S.	8.3	13.9	14.7	14.6	18.7	17.3	9.7	2.7

Note: Figures are percentages and cover owner-occupied housing units; (1) Figures cover the Miami-Fort Lauderdale-West Palm Beach, FL Metropolitan Statistical Area—see Appendix B for areas included
Source: U.S. Census Bureau, 2013-2017 American Community Survey 5-Year Estimates

Homeownership Rate

Area	2010 (%)	2011 (%)	2012 (%)	2013 (%)	2014 (%)	2015 (%)	2016 (%)	2017 (%)	2018 (%)
MSA[1]	63.8	64.2	61.8	60.1	58.8	58.6	58.4	57.9	59.9
U.S.	66.9	66.1	65.4	65.1	64.5	63.7	63.4	63.9	64.4

Note: (1) Figures cover the Miami-Fort Lauderdale-West Palm Beach, FL Metropolitan Statistical Area—see Appendix B for areas included
Source: U.S. Census Bureau, Housing Vacancies and Homeownership Annual Statistics: 2010-2018

Year Housing Structure Built

Area	2010 or Later	2000 -2009	1990 -1999	1980 -1989	1970 -1979	1960 -1969	1950 -1959	1940 -1949	Before 1940	Median Year
City	4.0	19.5	6.4	8.1	12.8	10.3	15.1	13.6	10.3	1971
MSA[1]	2.1	13.6	15.2	19.6	21.7	12.6	10.0	3.0	2.3	1980
U.S.	3.2	14.5	14.0	13.6	15.5	10.8	10.5	5.1	12.9	1977

Note: Figures are percentages except for Median Year; Note: (1) Figures cover the Miami-Fort Lauderdale-West Palm Beach, FL Metropolitan Statistical Area—see Appendix B for areas included
Source: U.S. Census Bureau, 2013-2017 American Community Survey 5-Year Estimates

Gross Monthly Rent

Area	Under $500	$500 -$999	$1,000 -$1,499	$1,500 -$1,999	$2,000 -$2,499	$2,500 -$2,999	$3,000 and up	Median ($)
City	11.3	34.6	28.8	14.7	5.7	2.7	2.2	1,056
MSA[1]	5.7	24.1	39.1	20.0	6.9	2.4	1.9	1,232
U.S.	10.5	41.1	28.7	11.7	4.5	1.8	1.7	982

Note: Figures are percentages except for Median; Gross rent is the contract rent plus the estimated average monthly cost of utilities (electricity, gas, and water and sewer) and fuels (oil, coal, kerosene, wood, etc.) if these are paid by the renter (or paid for the renter by someone else); (1) Figures cover the Miami-Fort Lauderdale-West Palm Beach, FL Metropolitan Statistical Area—see Appendix B for areas included
Source: U.S. Census Bureau, 2013-2017 American Community Survey 5-Year Estimates

HEALTH

Health Risk Factors

Category	MSA[1] (%)	U.S. (%)
Adults aged 18–64 who have any kind of health care coverage	81.7	87.3
Adults who reported being in good or better health	83.4	82.4
Adults who have been told they have high blood cholesterol	34.7	33.0
Adults who have been told they have high blood pressure	30.2	32.3
Adults who are current smokers	13.6	17.1
Adults who currently use E-cigarettes	2.8	4.6
Adults who currently use chewing tobacco, snuff, or snus	1.4	4.0
Adults who are heavy drinkers[2]	4.6	6.3
Adults who are binge drinkers[3]	15.6	17.4
Adults who are overweight (BMI 25.0 - 29.9)	34.5	35.3
Adults who are obese (BMI 30.0 - 99.8)	27.0	31.3
Adults who participated in any physical activities in the past month	71.5	74.4
Adults who always or nearly always wears a seat belt	96.2	94.3

Note: (1) Figures cover the Miami-Fort Lauderdale-West Palm Beach, FL Metropolitan Statistical Area—see Appendix B for areas included; (2) Heavy drinkers are classified as adult men having more than 14 drinks per week and adult women having more than 7 drinks per week; (3) Binge drinkers are classified as males having five or more drinks on one occasion or females having four or more drinks on one occasion
Source: Centers for Disease Control and Prevention, Behaviorial Risk Factor Surveillance System, SMART: Selected Metropolitan Area Risk Trends, 2017

Acute and Chronic Health Conditions

Category	MSA[1] (%)	U.S. (%)
Adults who have ever been told they had a heart attack	4.1	4.2
Adults who have ever been told they have angina or coronary heart disease	3.7	3.9
Adults who have ever been told they had a stroke	3.2	3.0
Adults who have ever been told they have asthma	10.2	14.2
Adults who have ever been told they have arthritis	19.4	24.9
Adults who have ever been told they have diabetes[2]	8.5	10.5
Adults who have ever been told they had skin cancer	6.4	6.2
Adults who have ever been told they had any other types of cancer	5.9	7.1
Adults who have ever been told they have COPD	4.5	6.5
Adults who have ever been told they have kidney disease	2.1	3.0
Adults who have ever been told they have a form of depression	13.3	20.5

Note: (1) Figures cover the Miami-Fort Lauderdale-West Palm Beach, FL Metropolitan Statistical Area—see Appendix B for areas included; (2) Figures do not include pregnancy-related, borderline, or pre-diabetes
Source: Centers for Disease Control and Prevention, Behaviorial Risk Factor Surveillance System, SMART: Selected Metropolitan Area Risk Trends, 2017

Health Screening and Vaccination Rates

Category	MSA[1] (%)	U.S. (%)
Adults aged 65+ who have had flu shot within the past year	63.0	60.7
Adults aged 65+ who have ever had a pneumonia vaccination	58.0	75.4
Adults who have ever been tested for HIV	53.1	36.1
Adults who have ever had the shingles or zoster vaccine?	19.6	28.9
Adults who have had their blood cholesterol checked within the last five years	91.3	85.9

Note: n/a not available; (1) Figures cover the Miami-Fort Lauderdale-West Palm Beach, FL Metropolitan Statistical Area—see Appendix B for areas included.
Source: Centers for Disease Control and Prevention, Behaviorial Risk Factor Surveillance System, SMART: Selected Metropolitan Area Risk Trends, 2017

Disability Status

Category	MSA[1] (%)	U.S. (%)
Adults who reported being deaf	5.8	6.7
Are you blind or have serious difficulty seeing, even when wearing glasses?	6.0	4.5
Are you limited in any way in any of your usual activities due of arthritis?	10.9	12.9
Do you have difficulty doing errands alone?	5.9	6.8
Do you have difficulty dressing or bathing?	4.4	3.6
Do you have serious difficulty concentrating/remembering/making decisions?	12.1	10.7
Do you have serious difficulty walking or climbing stairs?	14.9	13.6

Note: (1) Figures cover the Miami-Fort Lauderdale-West Palm Beach, FL Metropolitan Statistical Area—see Appendix B for areas included.
Source: Centers for Disease Control and Prevention, Behaviorial Risk Factor Surveillance System, SMART: Selected Metropolitan Area Risk Trends, 2017

Mortality Rates for the Top 10 Causes of Death in the U.S.

ICD-10[a] Sub-Chapter	ICD-10[a] Code	Age-Adjusted Mortality Rate[1] per 100,000 population	
		County[2]	U.S.
Malignant neoplasms	C00-C97	128.5	155.5
Ischaemic heart diseases	I20-I25	98.3	94.8
Other forms of heart disease	I30-I51	33.8	52.9
Chronic lower respiratory diseases	J40-J47	28.1	41.0
Cerebrovascular diseases	I60-I69	41.0	37.5
Other degenerative diseases of the nervous system	G30-G31	26.3	35.0
Other external causes of accidental injury	W00-X59	18.4	33.7
Organic, including symptomatic, mental disorders	F01-F09	18.9	31.0
Hypertensive diseases	I10-I15	23.1	21.9
Diabetes mellitus	E10-E14	22.0	21.2

Note: (a) ICD-10 = International Classification of Diseases 10th Revision; (1) Mortality rates are a three year average covering 2015-2017; (2) Figures cover Miami-Dade County.
Source: Centers for Disease Control and Prevention, National Center for Health Statistics. Underlying Cause of Death 1999-2017 on CDC WONDER Online Database

Mortality Rates for Selected Causes of Death

ICD-10[a] Sub-Chapter	ICD-10[a] Code	Age-Adjusted Mortality Rate[1] per 100,000 population	
		County[2]	U.S.
Assault	X85-Y09	8.3	5.9
Diseases of the liver	K70-K76	9.5	14.1
Human immunodeficiency virus (HIV) disease	B20-B24	5.8	1.8
Influenza and pneumonia	J09-J18	8.2	14.3
Intentional self-harm	X60-X84	8.6	13.6
Malnutrition	E40-E46	0.5	1.6
Obesity and other hyperalimentation	E65-E68	2.2	2.1
Renal failure	N17-N19	9.5	13.0
Transport accidents	V01-V99	12.2	12.4
Viral hepatitis	B15-B19	1.2	1.6

Note: (a) ICD-10 = International Classification of Diseases 10th Revision; (1) Mortality rates are a three year average covering 2015-2017; (2) Figures cover Miami-Dade County; Data are suppressed when the data meet the criteria for confidentiality constraints; Mortality rates are flagged as unreliable when the rate would be calculated with a numerator of 20 or less.
Source: Centers for Disease Control and Prevention, National Center for Health Statistics. Underlying Cause of Death 1999-2017 on CDC WONDER Online Database

Health Insurance Coverage

Area	With Health Insurance	With Private Health Insurance	With Public Health Insurance	Without Health Insurance	Population Under Age 18 Without Health Insurance
City	76.1	41.7	37.6	23.9	9.1
MSA[1]	82.1	56.3	33.2	17.9	9.2
U.S.	89.5	67.2	33.8	10.5	5.7

Note: Figures are percentages that cover the civilian noninstitutionalized population; (1) Figures cover the Miami-Fort Lauderdale-West Palm Beach, FL Metropolitan Statistical Area—see Appendix B for areas included
Source: U.S. Census Bureau, 2013-2017 American Community Survey 5-Year Estimates

Number of Medical Professionals

Area	MDs[3]	DOs[3,4]	Dentists	Podiatrists	Chiropractors	Optometrists
County[1] (number)	9,132	472	1,783	270	488	362
County[1] (rate[2])	333.7	17.2	64.8	9.8	17.7	13.2
U.S. (rate[2])	279.3	23.0	68.4	6.0	27.1	16.2

Note: Data as of 2017 unless noted; (1) Data covers Miami-Dade County; (2) Rate per 100,000 population; (3) Data as of 2016 and includes all active, non-federal physicians; (4) Doctor of Osteopathic Medicine
Source: U.S. Department of Health and Human Services, Health Resources and Services Administration, Bureau of Health Professions, Area Resource File (ARF) 2017-2018

Best Hospitals

According to *U.S. News*, the Miami-Miami Beach-Kendall, FL metro area is home to three of the best hospitals in the U.S.: **Bascom Palmer Eye Institute - University of Miami Hospital and Clinics** (1 adult specialty); **Jackson Health System-Miami** (1 pediatric specialty); **University of Miami Hospital and Clinics-UHealth Tower** (1 adult specialty). The hospitals listed were nationally ranked in at least one of 16 adult or 10 pediatric specialties. Only 170 hospitals nationwide were nationally ranked in one or more adult or pediatric specialty. Twenty hospitals in the U.S. made the Honor Roll. The Best Hospitals Honor Roll takes both the national rankings and the procedure and condition ratings into account. Hospitals received points if they were nationally ranked in one of the 16 adult specialties—the higher they ranked, the more points they got—and how many ratings of "high performing" they earned in the nine procedures and conditions. *U.S. News Online, "America's Best Hospitals 2018-19"*

According to *U.S. News*, the Miami-Miami Beach-Kendall, FL metro area is home to two of the best children's hospitals in the U.S.: **Holtz Children's Hospital at UM-Jackson Memorial Medical Center** (1 pediatric specialty); **Nicklaus Children's Hospital** (6 pediatric specialties). The hospitals listed were highly ranked in at least one of 10 pediatric specialties. Eighty-six children's hospitals in the U.S. were nationally ranked in at least one specialty. Hospitals received points for being ranked in a specialty, and the 10 hospitals with the most points across the 10 specialties make up the Honor Roll. *U.S. News Online, "America's Best Children's Hospitals 2018-19"*

EDUCATION

Public School District Statistics

District Name	Schls	Pupils	Pupil/ Teacher Ratio	Minority Pupils[1] (%)	Free Lunch Eligible[2] (%)	IEP[3] (%)
Miami-Dade County Public Schools	528	357,249	17.1	92.9	64.9	9.9

Note: Table includes school districts with 2,000 or more students; (1) Percentage of students that are not non-Hispanic white; (2) Percentage of students that are eligible for the free lunch program; (3) Percentage of students that have an Individualized Education Program.
Source: U.S. Department of Education, National Center for Education Statistics, Common Core of Data, Local Education Agency (School District) Universe Survey: School Year 2016-2017; U.S. Department of Education, National Center for Education Statistics, Common Core of Data, Public Elementary/Secondary School Universe Survey: School Year 2016-2017

Best High Schools

According to *U.S. News*, Miami is home to eight of the best high schools in the U.S.: **Design and Architecture Senior High** (#25); **International Studies Charter High School** (#26); **Archimedean Upper Conservatory Charter School** (#47); **Young Women's Preparatory Academy** (#73); **iPrep Academy** (#128); **New World School of the Arts** (#149); **Coral Reef Senior High School** (#196); **Terra Environmental Research Institute** (#299). More than 20,000 public, magnet and charter schools were ranked based on their performance on state assessments and how well they prepare students for college. Schools with the highest unrounded College Readiness Index values were numerically ranked from 1 to 500 and were classified as gold medal winners. *U.S. News & World Report, "Best High Schools 2018"*

Highest Level of Education

Area	Less than H.S.	H.S. Diploma	Some College, No Deg.	Associate Degree	Bachelor's Degree	Master's Degree	Prof. School Degree	Doctorate Degree
City	24.4	29.8	12.5	7.0	16.3	6.0	3.1	1.0
MSA[1]	14.9	27.1	18.0	9.3	19.5	7.3	2.7	1.2
U.S.	12.7	27.3	20.8	8.3	19.1	8.4	2.0	1.4

Note: Figures cover persons age 25 and over; (1) Figures cover the Miami-Fort Lauderdale-West Palm Beach, FL Metropolitan Statistical Area—see Appendix B for areas included
Source: U.S. Census Bureau, 2013-2017 American Community Survey 5-Year Estimates

Educational Attainment by Race

Area	High School Graduate or Higher (%)					Bachelor's Degree or Higher (%)				
	Total	White	Black	Asian	Hisp.[2]	Total	White	Black	Asian	Hisp.[2]
City	75.6	76.8	70.3	82.5	73.2	26.3	29.0	12.1	56.3	22.8
MSA[1]	85.1	86.5	80.4	86.6	79.5	30.6	33.4	18.5	49.8	25.8
U.S.	87.3	89.3	84.9	86.5	66.7	30.9	32.2	20.6	52.7	15.2

Note: Figures shown cover persons 25 years old and over; (1) Figures cover the Miami-Fort Lauderdale-West Palm Beach, FL Metropolitan Statistical Area—see Appendix B for areas included; (2) People of Hispanic origin can be of any race
Source: U.S. Census Bureau, 2013-2017 American Community Survey 5-Year Estimates

School Enrollment by Grade and Control

Area	Preschool (%)		Kindergarten (%)		Grades 1 - 4 (%)		Grades 5 - 8 (%)		Grades 9 - 12 (%)	
	Public	Private	Public	Private	Public	Private	Public	Private	Public	Private
City	57.4	42.6	83.5	16.5	85.9	14.1	88.4	11.6	89.7	10.3
MSA[1]	49.4	50.6	83.6	16.4	86.6	13.4	87.0	13.0	87.5	12.5
U.S.	58.8	41.2	87.7	12.3	89.7	10.3	89.6	10.4	90.3	9.7

Note: Figures shown cover persons 3 years old and over; (1) Figures cover the Miami-Fort Lauderdale-West Palm Beach, FL Metropolitan Statistical Area—see Appendix B for areas included
Source: U.S. Census Bureau, 2013-2017 American Community Survey 5-Year Estimates

Average Salaries of Public School Classroom Teachers

Area	2016		2017		Change from 2016 to 2017	
	Dollars	Rank[1]	Dollars	Rank[1]	Percent	Rank[2]
Florida	46,612	46	47,267	45	1.4	26
U.S. Average	58,479	–	59,660	–	2.0	–

Note: (1) Rank ranges from 1 to 51 where 1 indicates highest salary; (2) Rank ranges from 1 to 51 where 1 indicates highest percent change.
Source: National Education Association, Rankings & Estimates: Rankings of the States 2017 and Estimates of School Statistics 2018

Higher Education

Four-Year Colleges			Two-Year Colleges			Medical Schools[1]	Law Schools[2]	Voc/ Tech[3]
Public	Private Non-profit	Private For-profit	Public	Private Non-profit	Private For-profit			
2	5	4	3	1	7	2	2	22

Note: Figures cover institutions located within the city limits and include main campuses only; (1) includes schools accredited by the Liaison Committee on Medical Education and the American Osteopathic Association's Commission on Osteopathic College Accreditation; (2) includes ABA-accredited schools, schools with provisional ABA accreditation, and state accredited schools; (3) includes all schools with programs that are less than 2 years.
Source: National Center for Education Statistics, Integrated Postsecondary Education System (IPEDS), 2017-18; Wikipedia, List of Medical Schools in the United States, accessed April 3, 2019; Wikipedia, List of Law Schools in the United States, accessed April 3, 2019

According to *U.S. News & World Report*, the Miami-Miami Beach-Kendall, FL metro division is home to two of the best national universities in the U.S.: **University of Miami** (#53 tie); **Florida International University** (#187 tie). The indicators used to capture academic quality fall into a number of categories: assessment by administrators at peer institutions; retention of students; faculty resources; student selectivity; financial resources; alumni giving; high school counselor ratings of colleges; and graduation rate. *U.S. News & World Report, "America's Best Colleges 2019"*

According to *U.S. News & World Report,* the Miami-Miami Beach-Kendall, FL metro division is home to two of the top 100 law schools in the U.S.: **University of Miami** (#67 tie); **Florida International University** (#91 tie). The rankings are based on a weighted average of 12 measures of quality: peer assessment score; assessment score by lawyers/judges; median LSAT scores; median undergrad GPA; acceptance rate; employment rates for graduates; placement success; bar passage rate; faculty resources; expenditures per student; student/faculty ratio; and library resources. *U.S. News & World Report, "America's Best Graduate Schools, Law, 2020"*

According to *U.S. News & World Report,* the Miami-Miami Beach-Kendall, FL metro division is home to one of the top 75 medical schools for research in the U.S.: **University of Miami (Miller)** (#52 tie). The rankings are based on a weighted average of 11 measures of quality: quality assessment; peer assessment score; assessment score by residency directors; research activity; total research activity; average research activity per faculty member; student selectivity; median MCAT total score; median undergraduate GPA; acceptance rate; and faculty resources. *U.S. News & World Report, "America's Best Graduate Schools, Medical, 2020"*

PRESIDENTIAL ELECTION

2016 Presidential Election Results

Area	Clinton	Trump	Johnson	Stein	Other
Miami-Dade County	63.2	33.8	1.3	0.6	1.0
U.S.	48.0	45.9	3.3	1.1	1.7

Note: Results are percentages and may not add to 100% due to rounding
Source: Dave Leip's Atlas of U.S. Presidential Elections

EMPLOYERS

Major Employers

Company Name	Industry
Baptist Health South Florida	General medical & surgical hospitals
Baptist Hospital of Miami	General medical & surgical hospitals
County of Miami-Dade	Police protection, county government
County of Miami-Dade	Regulation, administration of transportation
Florida International University	Colleges & universities
Intercoastal Health Systems	Management services
Miami Dade College	Community college
Mount Sinai Medical Center of Florida	General medical & surgical hospitals
North Broward Hospital District	General medical & surgical hospitals
Palm Beach County	County government
Royal Caribbean Cruises Ltd	Computer processing services
Royal Caribbean Cruises Ltd	Deep sea passenger transportation, except ferry
School Board of Palm Beach County	Public elementary & secondary schools
Style View Products	Storm doors of windows, metal
The Answer Group	Custom computer programming services
University of Miami	Colleges & universities
Veterans Health Administration	General medical & surgical hospitals

Note: Companies shown are located within the Miami-Fort Lauderdale-West Palm Beach, FL Metropolitan Statistical Area.
Source: Hoovers.com; Wikipedia

PUBLIC SAFETY

Crime Rate

Area	All Crimes	Violent Crimes				Property Crimes		
		Murder	Rape[3]	Robbery	Aggrav. Assault	Burglary	Larceny -Theft	Motor Vehicle Theft
City	4,735.1	11.2	22.7	211.2	475.8	527.0	3,090.9	396.3
Suburbs[1]	3,437.1	5.7	33.3	127.1	270.8	410.4	2,302.8	287.1
Metro[2]	3,534.6	6.1	32.5	133.4	286.2	419.1	2,362.0	295.3
U.S.	2,756.1	5.3	41.7	98.0	248.9	430.4	1,694.4	237.4

Note: Figures are crimes per 100,000 population; (1) All areas within the metro area that are located outside the city limits; (2) Figures cover the Miami-Miami Beach-Kendall, FL Metropolitan Division—see Appendix B for areas included; (3) The city and U.S. figures shown were reported using the revised Uniform Crime Reporting (UCR) definition of rape. The suburban and metro area figures shown are an aggregate total of the data submitted using both the revised and legacy UCR definitions.
Source: FBI Uniform Crime Reports, 2017

Hate Crimes

Area	Number of Quarters Reported	Number of Incidents per Bias Motivation					
		Race/Ethnicity/ Ancestry	Religion	Sexual Orientation	Disability	Gender	Gender Identity
City	4	0	0	0	0	0	0
U.S.	4	4,131	1,564	1,130	116	46	119

Source: Federal Bureau of Investigation, Hate Crime Statistics 2017

Identity Theft Consumer Reports

Area	Reports	Reports per 100,000 Population	Rank[2]
MSA[1]	16,617	274	5
U.S.	444,602	135	-

Note: (1) Figures cover the Miami-Fort Lauderdale-West Palm Beach, FL Metropolitan Statistical Area—see Appendix B for areas included; (2) Rank ranges from 1 to 389 where 1 indicates greatest number of identity theft reports per 100,000 population
Source: Federal Trade Commission, Consumer Sentinel Network Data Book for January–December 2018

Fraud and Other Consumer Reports

Area	Reports	Reports per 100,000 Population	Rank[2]
MSA[1]	44,555	734	15
U.S.	2,552,917	776	-

Note: (1) Figures cover the Miami-Fort Lauderdale-West Palm Beach, FL Metropolitan Statistical Area—see Appendix B for areas included; (2) Rank ranges from 1 to 389 where 1 indicates greatest number of fraud and other consumer reports per 100,000 population
Source: Federal Trade Commission, Consumer Sentinel Network Data Book for January–December 2018

SPORTS

Professional Sports Teams

Team Name	League	Year Established
Florida Panthers	National Hockey League (NHL)	1993
Miami Dolphins	National Football League (NFL)	1966
Miami Heat	National Basketball Association (NBA)	1988
Miami Marlins	Major League Baseball (MLB)	1993

Note: Includes teams located in the Miami-Fort Lauderdale-West Palm Beach, FL Metropolitan Statistical Area.
Source: Wikipedia, Major Professional Sports Teams of the United States and Canada, April 5, 2019

CLIMATE

Average and Extreme Temperatures

Temperature	Jan	Feb	Mar	Apr	May	Jun	Jul	Aug	Sep	Oct	Nov	Dec	Yr.
Extreme High (°F)	88	89	92	96	95	98	98	98	97	95	89	87	98
Average High (°F)	75	77	79	82	85	88	89	90	88	85	80	77	83
Average Temp. (°F)	68	69	72	75	79	82	83	83	82	78	73	69	76
Average Low (°F)	59	60	64	68	72	75	76	76	76	72	66	61	69
Extreme Low (°F)	30	35	32	42	55	60	69	68	68	53	39	30	30

Note: Figures cover the years 1948-1990
Source: National Climatic Data Center, International Station Meteorological Climate Summary, 9/96

Average Precipitation/Snowfall/Humidity

Precip./Humidity	Jan	Feb	Mar	Apr	May	Jun	Jul	Aug	Sep	Oct	Nov	Dec	Yr.
Avg. Precip. (in.)	1.9	2.0	2.3	3.0	6.2	8.7	6.1	7.5	8.2	6.6	2.7	1.8	57.1
Avg. Snowfall (in.)	0	0	0	0	0	0	0	0	0	0	0	0	0
Avg. Rel. Hum. 7am (%)	84	84	82	80	81	84	84	86	88	87	85	84	84
Avg. Rel. Hum. 4pm (%)	59	57	57	57	62	68	66	67	69	65	63	60	63

Note: Figures cover the years 1948-1990; Tr = Trace amounts (<0.05 in. of rain; <0.5 in. of snow)
Source: National Climatic Data Center, International Station Meteorological Climate Summary, 9/96

Weather Conditions

Temperature			Daytime Sky			Precipitation		
32°F & below	45°F & below	90°F & above	Clear	Partly cloudy	Cloudy	0.01 inch or more precip.	0.1 inch or more snow/ice	Thunder-storms
< 1	7	55	48	263	54	128	0	74

Note: Figures are average number of days per year and cover the years 1948-1990
Source: National Climatic Data Center, International Station Meteorological Climate Summary, 9/96

HAZARDOUS WASTE

Superfund Sites

The Miami-Miami Beach-Kendall, FL metro division is home to six sites on the EPA's Superfund National Priorities List: **Airco Plating Co.** (final); **Anodyne, Inc.** (final); **Continental Cleaners** (final); **Homestead Air Force Base** (final); **Miami Drum Services** (final); **Pepper Steel & Alloys, Inc.** (final). There are a total of 1,390 Superfund sites with a status of proposed or final on the list in the U.S. *U.S. Environmental Protection Agency, National Priorities List, April 5, 2019*

AIR & WATER QUALITY

Air Quality Trends: Ozone

	1990	1995	2000	2005	2010	2012	2014	2015	2016	2017
MSA[1]	0.068	0.072	0.075	0.065	0.064	0.062	0.062	0.061	0.061	0.064
U.S.	0.088	0.089	0.082	0.080	0.073	0.075	0.067	0.068	0.069	0.068

Note: (1) Data covers the Miami-Fort Lauderdale-West Palm Beach, FL Metropolitan Statistical Area—see Appendix B for areas included. The values shown are the composite ozone concentration averages among trend sites based on the highest fourth daily maximum 8-hour concentration in parts per million. These trends are based on sites having an adequate record of monitoring data during the trend period. Data from exceptional events are included.
Source: U.S. Environmental Protection Agency, Air Quality Monitoring Information, "Air Quality Trends by City, 1990-2017"

Air Quality Index

Area	Percent of Days when Air Quality was...[2]					AQI Statistics[2]	
	Good	Moderate	Unhealthy for Sensitive Groups	Unhealthy	Very Unhealthy	Maximum	Median
MSA[1]	59.5	38.3	2.2	0.0	0.0	143	47

Note: (1) Data covers the Miami-Fort Lauderdale-West Palm Beach, FL Metropolitan Statistical Area—see Appendix B for areas included; (2) Based on 358 days with AQI data in 2017. Air Quality Index (AQI) is an index for reporting daily air quality. EPA calculates the AQI for five major air pollutants regulated by the Clean Air Act: ground-level ozone, particle pollution (aka particulate matter), carbon monoxide, sulfur dioxide, and nitrogen dioxide. The AQI runs from 0 to 500. The higher the AQI value, the greater the level of air pollution and the greater the health concern. There are six AQI categories: "Good" AQI is between 0 and 50. Air quality is considered satisfactory; "Moderate" AQI is between 51 and 100. Air quality is acceptable; "Unhealthy for Sensitive Groups" When AQI values are between 101 and 150, members of sensitive groups may experience health effects; "Unhealthy" When AQI values are between 151 and 200 everyone may begin to experience health effects; "Very Unhealthy" AQI values between 201 and 300 trigger a health alert; "Hazardous" AQI values over 300 trigger warnings of emergency conditions (not shown).
Source: U.S. Environmental Protection Agency, Air Quality Index Report, 2017

Air Quality Index Pollutants

Area	Percent of Days when AQI Pollutant was...[2]					
	Carbon Monoxide	Nitrogen Dioxide	Ozone	Sulfur Dioxide	Particulate Matter 2.5	Particulate Matter 10
MSA[1]	0.0	1.7	24.6	0.0	70.4	3.4

Note: (1) Data covers the Miami-Fort Lauderdale-West Palm Beach, FL Metropolitan Statistical Area—see Appendix B for areas included; (2) Based on 358 days with AQI data in 2017. The Air Quality Index (AQI) is an index for reporting daily air quality. EPA calculates the AQI for five major air pollutants regulated by the Clean Air Act: ground-level ozone, particle pollution (also known as particulate matter), carbon monoxide, sulfur dioxide, and nitrogen dioxide. The AQI runs from 0 to 500. The higher the AQI value, the greater the level of air pollution and the greater the health concern.
Source: U.S. Environmental Protection Agency, Air Quality Index Report, 2017

Maximum Air Pollutant Concentrations: Particulate Matter, Ozone, CO and Lead

	Particulate Matter 10 (ug/m^3)	Particulate Matter 2.5 Wtd AM (ug/m^3)	Particulate Matter 2.5 24-Hr (ug/m^3)	Ozone (ppm)	Carbon Monoxide (ppm)	Lead (ug/m^3)
MSA[1] Level	94	9.8	22	0.068	2	n/a
NAAQS[2]	150	15	35	0.075	9	0.15
Met NAAQS[2]	Yes	Yes	Yes	Yes	Yes	n/a

Note: (1) Data covers the Miami-Fort Lauderdale-West Palm Beach, FL Metropolitan Statistical Area—see Appendix B for areas included; Data from exceptional events are included; (2) National Ambient Air Quality Standards; ppm = parts per million; ug/m^3 = micrograms per cubic meter; n/a not available.
Concentrations: Particulate Matter 10 (coarse particulate)—highest second maximum 24-hour concentration; Particulate Matter 2.5 Wtd AM (fine particulate)—highest weighted annual mean concentration; Particulate Matter 2.5 24-Hour (fine particulate)—highest 98th percentile 24-hour concentration; Ozone—highest fourth daily maximum 8-hour concentration; Carbon Monoxide—highest second maximum non-overlapping 8-hour concentration; Lead—maximum running 3-month average
Source: U.S. Environmental Protection Agency, Air Quality Monitoring Information, "Air Quality Statistics by City, 2017"

Maximum Air Pollutant Concentrations: Nitrogen Dioxide and Sulfur Dioxide

	Nitrogen Dioxide AM (ppb)	Nitrogen Dioxide 1-Hr (ppb)	Sulfur Dioxide AM (ppb)	Sulfur Dioxide 1-Hr (ppb)	Sulfur Dioxide 24-Hr (ppb)
MSA[1] Level	15	44	n/a	1	n/a
NAAQS[2]	53	100	30	75	140
Met NAAQS[2]	Yes	Yes	n/a	Yes	n/a

Note: (1) Data covers the Miami-Fort Lauderdale-West Palm Beach, FL Metropolitan Statistical Area—see Appendix B for areas included; Data from exceptional events are included; (2) National Ambient Air Quality Standards; ppm = parts per million; ug/m^3 = micrograms per cubic meter; n/a not available.
Concentrations: Nitrogen Dioxide AM—highest arithmetic mean concentration; Nitrogen Dioxide 1-Hr—highest 98th percentile 1-hour daily maximum concentration; Sulfur Dioxide AM—highest annual mean concentration; Sulfur Dioxide 1-Hr—highest 99th percentile 1-hour daily maximum concentration; Sulfur Dioxide 24-Hr—highest second maximum 24-hour concentration
Source: U.S. Environmental Protection Agency, Air Quality Monitoring Information, "Air Quality Statistics by City, 2017"

Drinking Water

Water System Name	Pop. Served	Primary Water Source Type	Violations[1] Health Based	Monitoring/ Reporting
MDWASA - Main System	2,300,000	Ground	0	0

Note: (1) Based on violation data from January 1, 2018 to December 31, 2018
Source: U.S. Environmental Protection Agency, Office of Ground Water and Drinking Water, Safe Drinking Water Information System (based on data extracted April 5, 2019)

Midland, Texas

Background

In 1881, when Midland, Texas might have appeared as a dot on a map, it would have been called the middle of nowhere. In fact, Midland was almost exactly at the midpoint between Fort Worth Texas and El Paso. Today the locals like to tease that Midland is "in the middle of somewhere." Then barely a whistle-stop, Midland provided a small shelter where Texas and Pacific Railroad crews could rest and store maintenance equipment. Ten years later, it was a vital shipping center for the cattle trade.

Little is known about the first inhabitants in the region, though they left plenty of evidence of their existence. The Pecos Trail region is rich with petroglyphs and pictographs. Anthropologists refer to these communities as the Karankawas (hunter-gatherers), and surmise these early scribes are the ancestors of the Comanche, Apache, Kiowa, and Kickapoo nations.

The first westerner to make Midland his permanent home in 1882 was Herman Garrett, a sheep rancher from California. Midland grew quickly. Within three years, 100 families lived there, and by 1900, the population was 1,000. Midland became known as the "Windmill Town," as individual homes built windmills to pump water. After several devastating fires in 1905 and 1909, the town put in a municipal water system and a fire department.

Midland would remain a center of ranching and shipping until 1923, when a new industry overtook the town. Just southeast of Midland, the Santa Rita No. 1 oil rig "blew." From then on, Midland's economy and culture was defined by the price of oil, and its roller coaster ride of market highs and lows. By 1929, there were thirty-six oil companies in Midland. Roads were paved and streetlights were raised as Midland's skyline began to rise from the wide-open landscape. The new Hogal Building was twelve stories high. By 1930, the population blossomed to 5,484. When the Great Depression hit, the demand for petroleum decreased and prices plummeted. By 1932, one third of Midland's workers were unemployed.

World War II brought an increase in oil prices, along with the new Midland Army Air Force Base, a training ground for bomber pilots, giving Midland's economy a much-needed boost. By 1950, 250 oil companies had set up shop in Midland.

In 1972, Midland Community College was founded, and later, a satellite campus in Fort Stockton opened. Twice a year, Midland College hosts free lectures by world-renowned speakers—a Who's Who list of past guest lecturers include Ken Burns, Bill Moyers, Sandra Day O'Connor, Richard Rodriguez, John Updike and Neil deGrasse Tyson.

In recent years, Midland has grabbed headlines due to its association with the Bush family. Laura Bush was born and raised in Midland. Both former presidents George W. Bush, and George H.W. Bush, as well as Barbara and Jeb Bush, lived in Midland. The George Bush Childhood Home Museum in Midland receives thousands of visitors a year.

Midland is a cultural mecca with six museums, as well as a community theater that offers fifteen shows each year. The Midland-Odessa Symphony & Chorale performs eighteen venues each year, with four masterworks, four Pops Concerts, six Chamber Concerts, two Chorale concerts and a youth concert. The Marian Blakemore planetarium offers educational shows and lectures about the history of astronomy.

Midland features a semi-arid climate with long, hot summers and short, moderate winters. The city is occasionally subject to cold waves during the winter, but it rarely sees extended periods of below-freezing cold. Midland receives approximately 14.6 inches of precipitation per year, much of which falls in the summer. Highs exceed 90 °F (32 °C) on 101 days per year, and 100 °F (38 °C) on 16 days.

Rankings

Business/Finance Rankings

- According to data by the Bureau of Economic Analysis (BEA) and the Bureau of Labor Statistics (BLS), the Midland metro area has the fastest-growing GDP (gross domestic product) and positive employment trends, at #1. *247wallst.com, "Cities With the Fastest Growing (and Shrinking) Economies," September 26, 2016*

- Using data from the Council for Community and Economic Research's 2014 cost of living index, NerdWallet ranked the 100 most affordable cities in America. Median income was compared with cost of living to find truly affordable places. Midland ranked #5. *NerdWallet.com, "America's Most Affordable Places," May 18, 2015*

- The Midland metro area appeared on the Milken Institute "2018 Best Performing Cities" list. Rank: #67 out of 201 small metro areas. Criteria: job growth; wage and salary growth; high-tech output growth. *Milken Institute, "Best-Performing Cities 2018," January 24, 2019*

- *Forbes* ranked 200 smaller metro areas (population under 265,400) to determine the nation's "Best Small Places for Business and Careers." The Midland metro area was ranked #73. Criteria: costs (business and living); job growth (past and projected); income growth; quality of life; educational attainment (college and high school); projected economic growth; cultural and recreational opportunities; net migration patterns; number of highly ranked colleges. *Forbes, "The Best Small Cities for Business and Careers 2018," October, 24 2018*

Environmental Rankings

- The U.S. Environmental Protection Agency (EPA) released a list of small U.S. metropolitan areas with the most ENERGY STAR certified buildings in 2017. The Midland metro area was ranked #1 out of 10. *U.S. Environmental Protection Agency, "2018 Energy Star Top Cities," April 11, 2018*

Real Estate Rankings

- The Midland metro area was identified as one of the nations's 20 hottest housing markets in 2019. Criteria: listing views as an indicator of demand and median days on the market as an indicator of supply. The area ranked #1. *Realtor.com, "January Top 20 Hottest Housing Markets," February 11, 2019*

- Midland was ranked #76 out of 237 metro areas in terms of housing affordability in 2018 by the National Association of Home Builders (#1 = most affordable). Criteria: the share of homes sold in that area affordable to a family earning the local median income, based on standard mortgage underwriting criteria. *National Association of Home Builders®, NAHB-Wells Fargo Housing Opportunity Index, 4th Quarter 2018*

Safety Rankings

- Allstate ranked the 200 largest cities in America in terms of driver safety. Midland ranked #7. Criteria: internal property damage claims over a two-year period from January 2015 to December 2016. The report helps increase the importance of safety awareness behind the wheel. *Allstate, "Allstate America's Best Drivers Report, 2018" August 28, 2018*

- The National Insurance Crime Bureau ranked 382 metro areas in the U.S. in terms of per capita rates of vehicle theft. The Midland metro area ranked #152 (#1 = highest rate). Criteria: number of vehicle theft offenses per 100,000 inhabitants in 2017. *National Insurance Crime Bureau, "Hot Spots 2017," July 12, 2018*

Seniors/Retirement Rankings

■ From its Best Cities for Successful Aging indexes, the Milken Institute generated rankings for metropolitan areas, weighing data in nine categories—health care, wellness, living arrangements, transportation and convenience, financial characteristics, education, employment, community engagement, and overall livability. The Midland metro area was ranked #15 overall in the small metro area category. *Milken Institute, "Best Cities for Successful Aging, 2017" March 14, 2017*

Business Environment

CITY FINANCES

City Government Finances

Component	2016 ($000)	2016 ($ per capita)
Total Revenues	225,838	1,699
Total Expenditures	188,439	1,417
Debt Outstanding	93,600	704
Cash and Securities[1]	344,517	2,591

Note: (1) Cash and security holdings of a government at the close of its fiscal year, including those of its dependent agencies, utilities, and liquor stores.
Source: U.S. Census Bureau, State & Local Government Finances 2016

City Government Revenue by Source

Source	2016 ($000)	2016 ($ per capita)	2016 (%)
General Revenue			
From Federal Government	7,042	53	3.1
From State Government	2,895	22	1.3
From Local Governments	0	0	0.0
Taxes			
Property	40,528	305	17.9
Sales and Gross Receipts	81,669	614	36.2
Personal Income	0	0	0.0
Corporate Income	0	0	0.0
Motor Vehicle License	0	0	0.0
Other Taxes	3,743	28	1.7
Current Charges	40,855	307	18.1
Liquor Store	0	0	0.0
Utility	31,066	234	13.8
Employee Retirement	2,274	17	1.0

Source: U.S. Census Bureau, State & Local Government Finances 2016

City Government Expenditures by Function

Function	2016 ($000)	2016 ($ per capita)	2016 (%)
General Direct Expenditures			
Air Transportation	10,613	79	5.6
Corrections	0	0	0.0
Education	0	0	0.0
Employment Security Administration	0	0	0.0
Financial Administration	6,830	51	3.6
Fire Protection	23,372	175	12.4
General Public Buildings	1,313	9	0.7
Governmental Administration, Other	2,531	19	1.3
Health	4,954	37	2.6
Highways	7,016	52	3.7
Hospitals	0	0	0.0
Housing and Community Development	1,409	10	0.7
Interest on General Debt	2,415	18	1.3
Judicial and Legal	3,104	23	1.6
Libraries	0	0	0.0
Parking	0	0	0.0
Parks and Recreation	19,206	144	10.2
Police Protection	25,510	191	13.5
Public Welfare	0	0	0.0
Sewerage	10,586	79	5.6
Solid Waste Management	11,497	86	6.1
Veterans' Services	0	0	0.0
Liquor Store	0	0	0.0
Utility	36,309	273	19.3
Employee Retirement	6,685	50	3.5

Source: U.S. Census Bureau, State & Local Government Finances 2016

DEMOGRAPHICS

Population Growth

Area	1990 Census	2000 Census	2010 Census	2017* Estimate	Population Growth (%)	
					1990-2017	2010-2017
City	89,358	94,996	111,147	131,286	46.9	18.1
MSA[1]	106,611	116,009	136,872	165,430	55.2	20.9
U.S.	248,709,873	281,421,906	308,745,538	321,004,407	29.1	4.0

Note: (1) Figures cover the Midland, TX Metropolitan Statistical Area—see Appendix B for areas included; (*) 2013-2017 5-year estimated population
Source: U.S. Census Bureau, 1990 Census, Census 2000, Census 2010, 2013-2017 American Community Survey 5-Year Estimates

Household Size

Area	Persons in Household (%)							Average Household Size
	One	Two	Three	Four	Five	Six	Seven or More	
City	24.9	32.5	16.0	15.0	7.1	2.9	1.7	2.80
MSA[1]	24.3	32.2	15.6	15.5	7.3	2.7	2.3	2.90
U.S.	27.7	33.8	15.7	13.0	6.0	2.3	1.4	2.60

Note: (1) Figures cover the Midland, TX Metropolitan Statistical Area—see Appendix B for areas included
Source: U.S. Census Bureau, 2013-2017 American Community Survey 5-Year Estimates

Race

Area	White Alone[2] (%)	Black Alone[2] (%)	Asian Alone[2] (%)	AIAN[3] Alone[2] (%)	NHOPI[4] Alone[2] (%)	Other Race Alone[2] (%)	Two or More Races (%)
City	80.9	7.4	2.1	0.4	0.1	6.9	2.3
MSA[1]	82.8	6.0	1.9	0.5	0.1	6.6	2.1
U.S.	73.0	12.7	5.4	0.8	0.2	4.8	3.1

Note: (1) Figures cover the Midland, TX Metropolitan Statistical Area—see Appendix B for areas included; (2) Alone is defined as not being in combination with one or more other races; (3) American Indian and Alaska Native; (4) Native Hawaiian and Other Pacific Islander
Source: U.S. Census Bureau, 2013-2017 American Community Survey 5-Year Estimates

Hispanic or Latino Origin

Area	Total (%)	Mexican (%)	Puerto Rican (%)	Cuban (%)	Other (%)
City	42.8	39.9	0.5	0.3	2.2
MSA[1]	43.3	40.6	0.5	0.3	1.9
U.S.	17.6	11.1	1.7	0.7	4.1

Note: Persons of Hispanic or Latino origin can be of any race; (1) Figures cover the Midland, TX Metropolitan Statistical Area—see Appendix B for areas included
Source: U.S. Census Bureau, 2013-2017 American Community Survey 5-Year Estimates

Segregation

Type	Segregation Indices[1]				Percent Change		
	1990	2000	2010	2010 Rank[2]	1990-2000	1990-2010	2000-2010
Black/White	n/a	n/a	n/a	n/a	n/a	n/a	n/a
Asian/White	n/a	n/a	n/a	n/a	n/a	n/a	n/a
Hispanic/White	n/a	n/a	n/a	n/a	n/a	n/a	n/a

Note: All figures cover the Metropolitan Statistical Area—see Appendix B for areas included; Figures are based on an analysis of 1990, 2000, and 2010 Census Decennial Census tract data by William H. Frey, Brookings Institution and the University of Michigan Social Science Data Analysis Network. In this analysis all racial groups (whites, blacks, and asians) are non-Hispanic members of those races. Hispanics are shown as a separate category; (1) Segregation Indices are Dissimilarity Indices that measure the degree to which the minority group is distributed differently than whites across census tracts. They range from 0 (complete integration) to 100 (complete segregation) where the value indicates the percentage of the minority group that needs to move to be distributed exactly like whites; (2) Ranges from 1 (most segregated) to 102 (least segregated); n/a not available.
Source: www.CensusScope.org

Ancestry

Area	German	Irish	English	American	Italian	Polish	French[2]	Scottish	Dutch
City	8.9	7.2	6.3	4.8	1.3	0.5	1.5	1.9	0.7
MSA[1]	9.0	7.1	6.1	4.8	1.2	0.6	1.5	1.8	0.6
U.S.	14.1	10.1	7.5	6.6	5.3	2.9	2.5	1.7	1.3

Note: Figures are the percentage of the total population reporting a particular ancestry. The nine most commonly reported ancestries in the U.S. are shown. Figures include multiple ancestries (e.g. if a person reported being Irish and Italian, they were included in both columns); (1) Figures cover the Midland, TX Metropolitan Statistical Area—see Appendix B for areas included; (2) Excludes Basque
Source: U.S. Census Bureau, 2013-2017 American Community Survey 5-Year Estimates

Foreign-Born Population

Area	Percent of Population Born in								
	Any Foreign Country	Asia	Mexico	Europe	Carribean	Central America[2]	South America	Africa	Canada
City	12.4	1.7	8.2	0.3	0.7	0.2	0.4	0.4	0.4
MSA[1]	12.2	1.5	8.6	0.4	0.6	0.2	0.3	0.3	0.3
U.S.	13.4	4.1	3.6	1.5	1.3	1.0	0.9	0.6	0.3

Note: (1) Figures cover the Midland, TX Metropolitan Statistical Area—see Appendix B for areas included; (2) Excludes Mexico.
Source: U.S. Census Bureau, 2013-2017 American Community Survey 5-Year Estimates

Marital Status

Area	Never Married	Now Married[2]	Separated	Widowed	Divorced
City	29.4	52.1	1.9	5.0	11.7
MSA[1]	28.8	52.8	2.0	4.8	11.7
U.S.	33.1	48.2	2.0	5.8	10.9

Note: Figures are percentages and cover the population 15 years of age and older; (1) Figures cover the Midland, TX Metropolitan Statistical Area—see Appendix B for areas included; (2) Excludes separated
Source: U.S. Census Bureau, 2013-2017 American Community Survey 5-Year Estimates

Disability by Age

Area	All Ages	Under 18 Years Old	18 to 64 Years Old	65 Years and Over
City	9.3	2.7	7.6	37.0
MSA[1]	9.3	2.6	7.6	38.4
U.S.	12.6	4.2	10.3	35.5

Note: Figures show percent of the civilian noninstitutionalized population that reported having a disability. Disability status is determined from six types of difficulty: vision, hearing, cognitive, ambulatory, self-care, and independent living. For children under 5 years old, hearing and vision difficulty are used to determine disability status. For children between the ages of 5 and 14, disability status is determined from hearing, vision, cognitive, ambulatory, and self-care difficulties. For people aged 15 years and older, they are considered to have a disability if they have difficulty with any one of the six difficulty types; Note: (1) Figures cover the Midland, TX Metropolitan Statistical Area—see Appendix B for areas included
Source: U.S. Census Bureau, 2013-2017 American Community Survey 5-Year Estimates

Age

Area	Percent of Population									Median Age
	Under Age 5	Age 5–19	Age 20–34	Age 35–44	Age 45–54	Age 55–64	Age 65–74	Age 75–84	Age 85+	
City	8.5	21.3	24.6	12.6	11.5	10.8	5.6	3.3	1.7	32.1
MSA[1]	8.6	22.0	24.3	12.4	11.3	11.0	5.6	3.2	1.5	31.8
U.S.	6.2	19.5	20.7	12.7	13.4	12.7	8.6	4.4	1.9	37.8

Note: (1) Figures cover the Midland, TX Metropolitan Statistical Area—see Appendix B for areas included
Source: U.S. Census Bureau, 2013-2017 American Community Survey 5-Year Estimates

Gender

Area	Males	Females	Males per 100 Females
City	66,129	65,157	101.5
MSA[1]	83,194	82,236	101.2
U.S.	158,018,753	162,985,654	97.0

Note: (1) Figures cover the Midland, TX Metropolitan Statistical Area—see Appendix B for areas included
Source: U.S. Census Bureau, 2013-2017 American Community Survey 5-Year Estimates

Religious Groups by Family

Area	Catholic	Baptist	Non-Den.	Methodist[2]	Lutheran	LDS[3]	Pente-costal	Presby-terian[4]	Muslim[5]	Judaism
MSA[1]	22.4	25.3	8.8	4.2	0.7	1.2	1.6	1.9	3.7	<0.1
U.S.	19.1	9.3	4.0	4.0	2.3	2.0	1.9	1.6	0.8	0.7

Note: Figures are the number of adherents as a percentage of the total population; (1) Figures cover the Midland, TX Metropolitan Statistical Area—see Appendix B for areas included; (2) Methodist/Pietist; (3) Latter Day Saints; (4) Reformed; (5) Figures are estimates
Source: Association of Statisticians of American Religious Bodies, 2010 U.S. Religion Census: Religious Congregations & Membership Study

Religious Groups by Tradition

Area	Catholic	Evangelical Protestant	Mainline Protestant	Other Tradition	Black Protestant	Orthodox
MSA[1]	22.4	35.5	7.2	5.4	1.0	<0.1
U.S.	19.1	16.2	7.3	4.3	1.6	0.3

Note: Figures are the number of adherents as a percentage of the total population; (1) Figures cover the Midland, TX Metropolitan Statistical Area—see Appendix B for areas included
Source: Association of Statisticians of American Religious Bodies, 2010 U.S. Religion Census: Religious Congregations & Membership Study

ECONOMY

Gross Metropolitan Product

Area	2016	2017	2018	2019	Rank[2]
MSA[1]	24.0	26.9	32.7	35.4	100

Note: Figures are in billions of dollars; (1) Figures cover the Midland, TX Metropolitan Statistical Area—see Appendix B for areas included; (2) Rank is based on 2017 data and ranges from 1 to 381
Source: U.S. Conference of Mayors, U.S. Metro Economies: Economic Growth & Full Employment, June 2018

Economic Growth

Area	2017-2018 (%)	2019-2020 (%)	2021-2022 (%)
MSA[1]	7.6	6.9	4.7

Note: Figures are real gross metropolitan product (GMP) growth rates and represent average annual percent change; (1) Figures cover the Midland, TX Metropolitan Statistical Area—see Appendix B for areas included
Source: U.S. Conference of Mayors, U.S. Metro Economies: Economic Growth & Full Employment, June 2018

Metropolitan Area Exports

Area	2012	2013	2014	2015	2016	2017	Rank[2]
MSA[1]	104.4	164.1	122.7	110.1	69.6	69.4	353

Note: Figures are in millions of dollars; (1) Figures cover the Midland, TX Metropolitan Statistical Area—see Appendix B for areas included; (2) Rank is based on 2017 data and ranges from 1 to 387
Source: U.S. Department of Commerce, International Trade Administration, Office of Trade and Economic Analysis, Industry and Analysis, Exports by Metropolitan Area, extracted March 25, 2019

Building Permits

Area	Single-Family			Multi-Family			Total		
	2016	2017	Pct. Chg.	2016	2017	Pct. Chg.	2016	2017	Pct. Chg.
City	632	761	20.4	40	0	-100.0	672	761	13.2
MSA[1]	636	766	20.4	40	0	-100.0	676	766	13.3
U.S.	750,800	820,000	9.2	455,800	462,000	1.4	1,206,600	1,282,000	6.2

Note: (1) Figures cover the Midland, TX Metropolitan Statistical Area—see Appendix B for areas included; Figures represent new, privately-owned housing units authorized (unadjusted data); All permit data are based on estimates with imputation
Source: U.S. Census Bureau, Manufacturing, Mining, and Construction Statistics, Building Permits, 2016, 2017

Bankruptcy Filings

Area	Business Filings			Nonbusiness Filings		
	2017	2018	% Chg.	2017	2018	% Chg.
Midland County	12	15	25.0	79	68	-13.9
U.S.	23,157	22,232	-4.0	765,863	751,186	-1.9

Note: Business filings include Chapter 7, Chapter 11, Chapter 12, and Chapter 13; Nonbusiness filings include Chapter 7, Chapter 11, and Chapter 13
Source: Administrative Office of the U.S. Courts, Business and Nonbusiness Bankruptcy, County Cases Commenced by Chapter of the Bankruptcy Code, During the 12-Month Period Ending December 31, 2017 and Business and Nonbusiness Bankruptcy, County Cases Commenced by Chapter of the Bankruptcy Code, During the 12-Month Period Ending December 31, 2018

Housing Vacancy Rates

Area	Gross Vacancy Rate[2] (%)			Year-Round Vacancy Rate[3] (%)			Rental Vacancy Rate[4] (%)			Homeowner Vacancy Rate[5] (%)		
	2016	2017	2018	2016	2017	2018	2016	2017	2018	2016	2017	2018
MSA[1]	n/a	n/a	n/a	n/a	n/a	n/a	n/a	n/a	n/a	n/a	n/a	n/a
U.S.	12.8	12.7	12.3	9.9	9.9	9.7	6.9	7.2	6.9	1.7	1.6	1.5

Note: (1) Figures cover the Midland, TX Metropolitan Statistical Area—see Appendix B for areas included; (2) The percentage of the total housing inventory that is vacant; (3) The percentage of the housing inventory (excluding seasonal units) that is year-round vacant; (4) The percentage of rental inventory that is vacant for rent; (5) The percentage of homeowner inventory that is vacant for sale; n/a not available
Source: U.S. Census Bureau, Housing Vacancies and Homeownership Annual Statistics: 2016, 2017, 2018

INCOME

Income

Area	Per Capita ($)	Median Household ($)	Average Household ($)
City	39,499	75,646	109,351
MSA[1]	38,210	75,570	107,458
U.S.	31,177	57,652	81,283

Note: (1) Figures cover the Midland, TX Metropolitan Statistical Area—see Appendix B for areas included
Source: U.S. Census Bureau, 2013-2017 American Community Survey 5-Year Estimates

Household Income Distribution

Area	Percent of Households Earning							
	Under $15,000	$15,000 -$24,999	$25,000 -$34,999	$35,000 -$49,999	$50,000 -$74,999	$75,000 -$99,999	$100,000 -$149,999	$150,000 and up
City	6.3	6.9	8.0	11.0	17.5	13.0	17.8	19.4
MSA[1]	6.2	7.0	8.2	11.1	17.4	13.0	18.1	19.0
U.S.	11.6	9.8	9.5	13.0	17.7	12.3	14.1	12.1

Note: (1) Figures cover the Midland, TX Metropolitan Statistical Area—see Appendix B for areas included
Source: U.S. Census Bureau, 2013-2017 American Community Survey 5-Year Estimates

Poverty Rate

Area	All Ages	Under 18 Years Old	18 to 64 Years Old	65 Years and Over
City	8.7	11.4	7.4	9.6
MSA[1]	8.6	11.4	7.3	9.2
U.S.	14.6	20.3	13.7	9.3

Note: Figures are percentage of people whose income during the past 12 months was below the poverty level; (1) Figures cover the Midland, TX Metropolitan Statistical Area—see Appendix B for areas included
Source: U.S. Census Bureau, 2013-2017 American Community Survey 5-Year Estimates

EMPLOYMENT

Labor Force and Employment

Area	Civilian Labor Force			Workers Employed		
	Dec. 2017	Dec. 2018	% Chg.	Dec. 2017	Dec. 2018	% Chg.
City	76,140	81,038	6.4	74,430	79,340	6.6
MSA[1]	94,704	100,757	6.4	92,563	98,626	6.6
U.S.	159,880,000	162,510,000	1.6	153,602,000	156,481,000	1.9

Note: Data is not seasonally adjusted and covers workers 16 years of age and older; (1) Figures cover the Midland, TX Metropolitan Statistical Area—see Appendix B for areas included
Source: Bureau of Labor Statistics, Local Area Unemployment Statistics

Unemployment Rate

Area	2018											
	Jan.	Feb.	Mar.	Apr.	May	Jun.	Jul.	Aug.	Sep.	Oct.	Nov.	Dec.
City	2.4	2.5	2.4	2.1	2.2	2.4	2.3	2.2	2.2	2.1	2.1	2.1
MSA[1]	2.4	2.5	2.4	2.1	2.1	2.4	2.2	2.2	2.2	2.1	2.1	2.1
U.S.	4.5	4.4	4.1	3.7	3.6	4.2	4.1	3.9	3.6	3.5	3.5	3.7

Note: Data is not seasonally adjusted and covers workers 16 years of age and older; (1) Figures cover the Midland, TX Metropolitan Statistical Area—see Appendix B for areas included
Source: Bureau of Labor Statistics, Local Area Unemployment Statistics

Average Wages

Occupation	$/Hr.	Occupation	$/Hr.
Accountants and Auditors	41.10	Maids and Housekeeping Cleaners	11.50
Automotive Mechanics	24.00	Maintenance and Repair Workers	20.90
Bookkeepers	22.50	Marketing Managers	76.70
Carpenters	20.40	Nuclear Medicine Technologists	n/a
Cashiers	11.80	Nurses, Licensed Practical	23.50
Clerks, General Office	19.70	Nurses, Registered	30.30
Clerks, Receptionists/Information	13.90	Nursing Assistants	13.70
Clerks, Shipping/Receiving	16.70	Packers and Packagers, Hand	10.00
Computer Programmers	n/a	Physical Therapists	44.30
Computer Systems Analysts	44.30	Postal Service Mail Carriers	23.40
Computer User Support Specialists	26.30	Real Estate Brokers	n/a
Cooks, Restaurant	13.10	Retail Salespersons	15.30
Dentists	n/a	Sales Reps., Exc. Tech./Scientific	41.70
Electrical Engineers	n/a	Sales Reps., Tech./Scientific	44.90
Electricians	26.60	Secretaries, Exc. Legal/Med./Exec.	18.30
Financial Managers	68.20	Security Guards	17.70
First-Line Supervisors/Managers, Sales	23.40	Surgeons	n/a
Food Preparation Workers	13.40	Teacher Assistants*	11.00
General and Operations Managers	76.30	Teachers, Elementary School*	25.00
Hairdressers/Cosmetologists	10.90	Teachers, Secondary School*	26.80
Internists, General	n/a	Telemarketers	n/a
Janitors and Cleaners	11.70	Truck Drivers, Heavy/Tractor-Trailer	23.10
Landscaping/Groundskeeping Workers	14.40	Truck Drivers, Light/Delivery Svcs.	18.90
Lawyers	n/a	Waiters and Waitresses	9.20

Note: Wage data covers the Midland, TX Metropolitan Statistical Area—see Appendix B for areas included;
(*) Hourly wages for elementary/secondary school teachers and teacher assistants were calculated by the editors from annual wage data based on a 40 hour work week; n/a not available.
Source: Bureau of Labor Statistics, Metro Area Occupational Employment & Wage Estimates, May 2018

Employment by Occupation

Occupation Classification	City (%)	MSA[1] (%)	U.S. (%)
Management, Business, Science, and Arts	34.3	34.3	37.4
Natural Resources, Construction, and Maintenance	15.7	16.9	8.9
Production, Transportation, and Material Moving	11.4	11.1	12.2
Sales and Office	23.6	23.3	23.5
Service	15.0	14.5	18.0

Note: Figures cover employed civilians 16 years of age and older; (1) Figures cover the Midland, TX Metropolitan Statistical Area—see Appendix B for areas included
Source: U.S. Census Bureau, 2013-2017 American Community Survey 5-Year Estimates

Employment by Industry

Sector	MSA[1]		U.S.
	Number of Employees	Percent of Total	Percent of Total
Construction, Mining, and Logging	39,400	35.0	5.3
Education and Health Services	7,500	6.7	15.9
Financial Activities	4,600	4.1	5.7
Government	9,800	8.7	15.1
Information	1,000	0.9	1.9
Leisure and Hospitality	10,300	9.1	10.7
Manufacturing	4,300	3.8	8.5
Other Services	3,700	3.3	3.9
Professional and Business Services	10,000	8.9	14.1
Retail Trade	10,000	8.9	10.8
Transportation, Warehousing, and Utilities	5,100	4.5	4.2
Wholesale Trade	7,000	6.2	3.9

Note: Figures are non-farm employment as of December 2018. Figures are not seasonally adjusted and include workers 16 years of age and older; (1) Figures cover the Midland, TX Metropolitan Statistical Area—see Appendix B for areas included
Source: Bureau of Labor Statistics, Current Employment Statistics, Employment, Hours, and Earnings

Occupations with Greatest Projected Employment Growth: 2018 – 2020

Occupation[1]	2018 Employment	2020 Projected Employment	Numeric Employment Change	Percent Employment Change
Combined Food Preparation and Serving Workers, Including Fast Food	351,780	372,090	20,310	5.8
Personal Care Aides	218,310	235,470	17,160	7.9
Heavy and Tractor-Trailer Truck Drivers	204,870	216,310	11,440	5.6
Laborers and Freight, Stock, and Material Movers, Hand	194,220	204,060	9,840	5.1
Waiters and Waitresses	236,020	245,790	9,770	4.1
Office Clerks, General	393,740	403,270	9,530	2.4
Customer Service Representatives	268,380	277,460	9,080	3.4
General and Operations Managers	182,190	190,620	8,430	4.6
Retail Salespersons	392,620	400,900	8,280	2.1
Construction Laborers	143,270	150,820	7,550	5.3

Note: Projections cover Texas; (1) Sorted by numeric employment change
Source: www.projectionscentral.com, State Occupational Projections, 2018–2020 Short-Term Projections

Fastest Growing Occupations: 2018 – 2020

Occupation[1]	2018 Employment	2020 Projected Employment	Numeric Employment Change	Percent Employment Change
Wind Turbine Service Technicians	1,810	2,190	380	21.0
Religious Workers, All Other	5,690	6,330	640	11.2
Fundraisers	8,830	9,670	840	9.5
Statisticians	1,870	2,040	170	9.1
Public Relations and Fundraising Managers	6,570	7,160	590	9.0
Home Health Aides	74,390	80,920	6,530	8.8
Community and Social Service Specialists, All Other	4,520	4,890	370	8.2
Personal Care Aides	218,310	235,470	17,160	7.9
Operations Research Analysts	10,920	11,760	840	7.7
Software Developers, Applications	65,190	70,140	4,950	7.6

Note: Projections cover Texas; (1) Sorted by percent employment change and excludes occupations with numeric employment change less than 50
Source: www.projectionscentral.com, State Occupational Projections, 2018–2020 Short-Term Projections

TAXES

State Corporate Income Tax Rates

State	Tax Rate (%)	Income Brackets ($)	Num. of Brackets	Financial Institution Tax Rate (%)[a]	Federal Income Tax Ded.
Texas	(w)	–	–	(w)	No

Note: Tax rates as of January 1, 2019; (a) Rates listed are the corporate income tax rate applied to financial institutions or excise taxes based on income. Some states have other taxes based upon the value of deposits or shares; (w) Texas imposes a Franchise Tax, otherwise known as margin tax, imposed on entities with more than $1,130,000 total revenues at rate of 0.75%, or 0.375% for entities primarily engaged in retail or wholesale trade, on lesser of 70% of total revenues or 100% of gross receipts after deductions for either compensation or cost of goods sold.
Source: Federation of Tax Administrators, Range of State Corporate Income Tax Rates, January 1, 2019

State Individual Income Tax Rates

State	Tax Rate (%)	Income Brackets ($)	Personal Exemptions ($) Single	Married	Depend.	Standard Ded. ($) Single	Married
Texas			– No state income tax –				

Note: Tax rates as of January 1, 2019; Local- and county-level taxes are not included; n/a not applicable;

Source: Federation of Tax Administrators, State Individual Income Tax Rates, January 1, 2019

Various State Sales and Excise Tax Rates

State	State Sales Tax (%)	Gasoline[1] (¢/gal.)	Cigarette[2] ($/pack)	Spirits[3] ($/gal.)	Wine[4] ($/gal.)	Beer[5] ($/gal.)	Recreational Marijuana (%)
Texas	6.25	20	1.41	2.40 (f)	0.20 (l)	0.20 (q)	Not legal

Note: All tax rates as of January 1, 2019; (1) The American Petroleum Institute has developed a methodology for determining the average tax rate on a gallon of fuel. Rates may include any of the following: excise taxes, environmental fees, storage tank fees, other fees or taxes, general sales tax, and local taxes. In states where gasoline is subject to the general sales tax, or where the fuel tax is based on the average sale price, the average rate determined by API is sensitive to changes in the price of gasoline. States that fully or partially apply general sales taxes to gasoline: CA, CO, GA, IL, IN, MI, NY; (2) The federal excise tax of $1.0066 per pack and local taxes are not included; (3) Rates are those applicable to off-premise sales of 40% alcohol by volume (a.b.v.) distilled spirits in 750ml containers. Local excise taxes are excluded; (4) Rates are those applicable to off-premise sales of 11% a.b.v. non-carbonated wine in 750ml containers; (5) Rates are those applicable to off-premise sales of 4.7% a.b.v. beer in 12 ounce containers; (f) Different rates also applicable according to alcohol content, place of production, size of container, or place purchased (on- or off-premise or onboard airlines); (l) Different rates also applicable to alcohol content, place of production, size of container, place purchased (on- or off-premise or on board airlines) or type of wine (carbonated, vermouth, etc.); (q) Different rates also applicable according to alcohol content, place of production, size of container, or place purchased (on- or off-premise or onboard airlines).
Source: Tax Foundation, 2019 Facts & Figures: How Does Your State Compare?

State Business Tax Climate Index Rankings

State	Overall Rank	Corporate Tax Rank	Individual Income Tax Rank	Sales Tax Rank	Unemployment Insurance Tax Rank	Property Tax Rank
Texas	15	49	6	37	18	37

Note: The index is a measure of how each state's tax laws affect economic performance. The lower the rank, the more favorable a state's tax system is for business. States without a given tax are given a ranking of 1. The scores/rankings for the District of Columbia do not affect other states. The 2019 index represents the tax climate as of July 1, 2018.
Source: Tax Foundation, State Business Tax Climate Index 2019

COMMERCIAL UTILITIES

Typical Monthly Electric Bills

Area	Commercial Service ($/month) 1,500 kWh	40 kW demand 14,000 kWh	Industrial Service ($/month) 1,000 kW demand 200,000 kWh	50,000 kW demand 32,500,000 kWh
City	n/a	n/a	n/a	n/a
Average[1]	203	1,619	25,886	2,540,077

Note: Figures are based on annualized rates; (1) Average based on 187 utilities surveyed; n/a not available
Source: Edison Electric Institute, Typical Bills and Average Rates Report, Summer 2018

TRANSPORTATION

Means of Transportation to Work

Area	Car/Truck/Van		Public Transportation			Bicycle	Walked	Other Means	Worked at Home
	Drove Alone	Car-pooled	Bus	Subway	Railroad				
City	85.5	10.4	0.2	0.0	0.0	0.0	0.6	1.4	1.9
MSA[1]	84.9	9.9	0.2	0.0	0.0	0.0	0.9	1.6	2.4
U.S.	76.4	9.2	2.5	1.9	0.6	0.6	2.7	1.3	4.7

Note: Figures are percentages and cover workers 16 years of age and older; (1) Figures cover the Midland, TX Metropolitan Statistical Area—see Appendix B for areas included
Source: U.S. Census Bureau, 2013-2017 American Community Survey 5-Year Estimates

Travel Time to Work

Area	Less Than 10 Minutes	10 to 19 Minutes	20 to 29 Minutes	30 to 44 Minutes	45 to 59 Minutes	60 to 89 Minutes	90 Minutes or More
City	16.8	48.6	17.6	10.7	2.6	2.0	1.7
MSA[1]	16.6	45.1	19.0	12.3	2.8	2.5	1.7
U.S.	12.7	28.9	20.9	20.5	8.1	6.2	2.7

Note: Note: Figures are percentages and include workers 16 years old and over; (1) Figures cover the Midland, TX Metropolitan Statistical Area—see Appendix B for areas included
Source: U.S. Census Bureau, 2013-2017 American Community Survey 5-Year Estimates

Freeway Travel Time Index

Area	1985	1990	1995	2000	2005	2010	2014
Urban Area Rank[1,2]	n/a	n/a	n/a	n/a	n/a	n/a	n/a
Urban Area Index[1]	n/a	n/a	n/a	n/a	n/a	n/a	n/a
Average Index[3]	1.09	1.11	1.14	1.17	1.20	1.19	1.20

Note: Freeway Travel Time Index—the ratio of travel time in the peak period to the travel time at free-flow conditions. For example, a value of 1.30 indicates a 20-minute free-flow trip takes 26 minutes in the peak (20 minutes x 1.30 = 26 minutes); (1) Data for the Midland, TX urban area was not available; (2) Rank is based on 101 urban areas (#1 = highest travel time index); (3) Average of 101 urban areas
Source: Texas Transportation Institute, 2015 Urban Mobility Scorecard, August 2015

Freeway Commuter Stress Index

Area	1985	1990	1995	2000	2005	2010	2014
Urban Area Rank[1,2]	n/a	n/a	n/a	n/a	n/a	n/a	n/a
Urban Area Index[1]	n/a	n/a	n/a	n/a	n/a	n/a	n/a
Average Index[3]	1.13	1.16	1.19	1.22	1.25	1.24	1.25

Note: The Freeway Commuter Stress Index is the same as the Freeway Travel Time Index (see table above) except that it includes only the travel in the peak directions during the peak periods; the TTI includes travel in all directions during the peak period. Thus, the CSI is more indicative of the work trip experienced by each commuter on a daily basis; (1) Data for the Midland, TX urban area was not available; (2) Rank is based on 101 urban areas (#1 = highest travel time index); (3) Average of 101 urban areas
Source: Texas Transportation Institute, 2015 Urban Mobility Scorecard, August 2015

Public Transportation

Agency Name / Mode of Transportation	Vehicles Operated in Maximum Service[1]	Annual Unlinked Passenger Trips[2] (in thous.)	Annual Passenger Miles[3] (in thous.)
Midland-Odessa Urban Transit District			
Bus (directly operated)	12	353.7	n/a
Commuter Bus (directly operated)	2	13.2	n/a
Demand Response (directly operated)	8	43.8	n/a

Note: (1) The number of revenue vehicles operated by the given mode and type of service to meet the annual maximum service requirement. This is the revenue vehicle count during the peak season of the year; on the week and day that maximum service is provided. Vehicles operated in maximum service (VOMS) exclude atypical days and one-time special events; (2) The number of passengers who boarded public transportation vehicles. Passengers are counted each time they board a vehicle no matter how many vehicles they use to travel from their origin to their destination. (3) The sum of the distances ridden by all passengers during the entire fiscal year.
Source: Federal Transit Administration, National Transit Database, 2017

Air Transportation

Airport Name and Code / Type of Service	Passenger Airlines[1]	Passenger Enplanements	Freight Carriers[2]	Freight (lbs)
Midland International Airport (MAF)				
Domestic service (U.S. carriers - 2018)	13	618,442	6	3,401,294
International service (U.S. carriers - 2017)	0	0	0	0

Note: (1) Includes all U.S.-based major, minor and commuter airlines that carried at least one passenger during the year; (2) Includes all U.S.-based airlines and freight carriers that transported at least one pound of freight during the year.
Source: Bureau of Transportation Statistics, The Intermodal Transportation Database, Air Carriers: T-100 Domestic Market (U.S. Carriers), 2018; Bureau of Transportation Statistics, The Intermodal Transportation Database, Air Carriers: T-100 International Market (U.S. Carriers), 2017

Other Transportation Statistics

Major Highways:	I-20
Amtrak Service:	No
Major Waterways/Ports:	None

Source: Amtrak.com; Google Maps

BUSINESSES

Major Business Headquarters

Company Name	Industry	Rankings Fortune[1]	Rankings Forbes[2]
No companies listed	-	-	-

Note: (1) Companies that produce a 10-K are ranked 1 to 500 based on 2017 revenue; (2) All private companies with at least $2 billion in annual revenue through the end of their most current fiscal year are ranked 1 to 229; companies listed are headquartered in the city; dashes indicate no ranking
Source: Fortune, "Fortune 500," June 2018; Forbes, "America's Largest Private Companies," 2018 Rankings

Minority- and Women-Owned Businesses

Group	All Firms Firms	All Firms Sales ($000)	Firms with Paid Employees Firms	Firms with Paid Employees Sales ($000)	Employees	Payroll ($000)
AIAN[1]	215	(s)	0	(s)	0 - 19	(s)
Asian	406	196,335	98	153,230	1,100	42,882
Black	502	(s)	71	(s)	500 - 999	(s)
Hispanic	3,941	466,819	257	258,146	2,487	93,552
NHOPI[2]	n/a	n/a	n/a	n/a	n/a	n/a
Women	4,306	761,086	417	605,421	2,620	102,930
All Firms	15,775	16,305,079	3,384	15,353,044	56,648	2,570,777

Note: Figures cover firms located in the city; minority- and women-owned business are defined as firms in which the corresponding group own 51% or more of the stock or equity of the company; (1) American Indian and Alaska Native; (2) Native Hawaiian and Other Pacific Islander; (s) estimates are suppressed when publication standards are not met; n/a not available
Source: U.S. Census Bureau, 2012 Economic Census, Survey of Business Owners

HOTELS & CONVENTION CENTERS

Hotels, Motels and Vacation Rentals

Area	5 Star Num.	5 Star Pct.[3]	4 Star Num.	4 Star Pct.[3]	3 Star Num.	3 Star Pct.[3]	2 Star Num.	2 Star Pct.[3]	1 Star Num.	1 Star Pct.[3]	Not Rated Num.	Not Rated Pct.[3]
City[1]	0	0.0	0	0.0	33	22.4	91	61.9	6	4.1	17	11.6
Total[2]	286	0.4	5,236	7.1	16,715	22.6	10,259	13.9	293	0.4	41,056	55.6

Note: (1) Figures cover Midland and vicinity; (2) Figures cover all 100 cities in this book; (3) Percentage of hotels which have a given star rating; Star ratings are determined by expedia.com and offer an indication of the general quality of a particular hotel.
Source: www.expedia.com, April 3, 2019

Major Convention Centers

Name	Overall Space (sq. ft.)	Exhibit Space (sq. ft.)	Meeting Space (sq. ft.)	Meeting Rooms
Midland Center	n/a	12,500	n/a	n/a

Note: Table includes convention centers located in the Midland, TX metro area; n/a not available
Source: Original research

Living Environment

COST OF LIVING

Cost of Living Index

Composite Index	Groceries	Housing	Utilities	Trans- portation	Health Care	Misc. Goods/ Services
96.3	89.7	82.3	105.3	105.8	92.3	106.2

Note: The Cost of Living Index measures regional differences in the cost of consumer goods and services, excluding taxes and non-consumer expenditures, for professional and managerial households in the top income quintile. It is based on more than 50,000 prices covering almost 60 different items for which prices are collected three times a year by chambers of commerce, economic development organizations or university applied economic centers in each participating urban area. The numbers shown should be read as a percentage above or below the national average of 100. For example, a value of 115.4 in the groceries column indicates that grocery prices are 15.4% higher than the national average. Small differences in the index numbers should not be interpreted as significant; Figures cover the Midland TX urban area.
Source: The Council for Community and Economic Research, ACCRA Cost of Living Index, 2018

Grocery Prices

Area[1]	T-Bone Steak ($/pound)	Frying Chicken ($/pound)	Whole Milk ($/half gal.)	Eggs ($/dozen)	Orange Juice ($/64 oz.)	Coffee ($/11.5 oz.)
City[2]	10.70	1.04	1.55	1.79	3.32	4.24
Avg.	11.35	1.42	1.94	1.81	3.52	4.35
Min.	7.45	0.92	0.80	0.75	2.72	3.06
Max.	15.05	2.76	4.18	4.00	5.36	8.20

Note: (1) Values for the local area are compared with the average, minimum and maximum values for all 291 areas in the Cost of Living Index; (2) Figures cover the Midland TX urban area; T-Bone Steak (price per pound); Frying Chicken (price per pound, whole fryer); Whole Milk (half gallon carton); Eggs (price per dozen, Grade A, large); Orange Juice (64 oz. Tropicana or Florida Natural); Coffee (11.5 oz. can, vacuum-packed, Maxwell House, Hills Bros, or Folgers).
Source: The Council for Community and Economic Research, ACCRA Cost of Living Index, 2018

Housing and Utility Costs

Area[1]	New Home Price ($)	Apartment Rent ($/month)	All Electric ($/month)	Part Electric ($/month)	Other Energy ($/month)	Telephone ($/month)
City[2]	269,904	1,027	-	142.15	41.25	178.70
Avg.	347,000	1,087	165.93	100.16	67.73	178.70
Min.	200,468	500	93.58	25.64	26.78	163.10
Max.	1,901,222	4,888	388.65	246.86	332.81	197.70

Note: (1) Values for the local area are compared with the average, minimum and maximum values for all 291 areas in the Cost of Living Index; (2) Figures cover the Midland TX urban area; New Home Price (2,400 sf living area, 8,000 sf lot, in urban area with full utilities); Apartment Rent (950 sf 2 bedroom/1.5 or 2 bath, unfurnished, excluding all utilities except water); All Electric (average monthly cost for an all-electric home); Part Electric (average monthly cost for a part-electric home); Other Energy (average monthly cost for natural gas, fuel oil, coal, wood, and any other forms of energy except electricity); Telephone (price includes the base monthly rate plus taxes and fees for three lines of mobile phone service).
Source: The Council for Community and Economic Research, ACCRA Cost of Living Index, 2018

Health Care, Transportation, and Other Costs

Area[1]	Doctor ($/visit)	Dentist ($/visit)	Optometrist ($/visit)	Gasoline ($/gallon)	Beauty Salon ($/visit)	Men's Shirt ($)
City[2]	81.11	94.39	102.58	2.65	34.45	38.11
Avg.	110.71	95.11	103.74	2.61	37.48	32.03
Min.	33.60	62.55	54.63	1.89	17.00	11.44
Max.	195.97	153.93	225.79	3.59	71.88	58.64

Note: (1) Values for the local area are compared with the average, minimum and maximum values for all 291 areas in the Cost of Living Index; (2) Figures cover the Midland TX urban area; Doctor (general practitioners routine exam of an established patient); Dentist (adult teeth cleaning and periodic oral examination); Optometrist (full vision eye exam for established adult patient); Gasoline (one gallon regular unleaded, national brand, including all taxes, cash price at self-service pump if available); Beauty Salon (woman's shampoo, trim, and blow-dry); Men's Shirt (cotton/polyester dress shirt, pinpoint weave, long sleeves).
Source: The Council for Community and Economic Research, ACCRA Cost of Living Index, 2018

HOUSING

House Price Index (HPI)

Area	National Ranking[2]	Quarterly Change (%)	One-Year Change (%)	Five-Year Change (%)
MSA[1]	(a)	n/a	11.61	29.71
U.S.[3]	—	1.12	5.73	32.81

Note: The HPI is a weighted repeat sales index. It measures average price changes in repeat sales or refinancings on the same properties. This information is obtained by reviewing repeat mortgage transactions on single-family properties whose mortgages have been purchased or securitized by Fannie Mae or Freddie Mac in January 1975; (1) Figures cover the Midland, TX Metropolitan Statistical Area—see Appendix B for areas included; (2) Rankings are based on annual percentage change for all metro areas containing at least 15,000 transactions over the last 10 years and ranges from 1 to 245; (3) figures based on a weighted average of Census Division estimates using a seasonally adjusted, purchase-only index; all figures are for the period ending December 31, 2018; n/a not available; (a) Not ranked because of increased index variability due to smaller sample size
Source: Federal Housing Finance Agency, House Price Index, February 26, 2019

Median Single-Family Home Prices

Area	2016	2017	2018[p]	Percent Change 2017 to 2018
MSA[1]	n/a	n/a	n/a	n/a
U.S. Average	235.5	248.8	261.6	5.1

Note: Figures are median sales prices of existing single-family homes in thousands of dollars; (p) preliminary; n/a not available; (1) Figures cover the Midland, TX Metropolitan Statistical Area—see Appendix B for areas included
Source: National Association of Realtors, Median Sales Price of Existing Single-Family Homes for Metropolitan Areas, 4th Quarter 2018

Qualifying Income Based on Median Sales Price of Existing Single-Family Homes

Area	With 5% Down ($)	With 10% Down ($)	With 20% Down ($)
MSA[1]	n/a	n/a	n/a
U.S. Average	62,954	59,640	53,013

Note: Figures are preliminary; Qualifying income is based on a mortgage rate of 4.9%. Monthly principal and interest payment is limited to 25% of income; n/a not available; (1) Figures cover the Midland, TX Metropolitan Statistical Area—see Appendix B for areas included
Source: National Association of Realtors, Qualifying Income Based on Median Sales Price of Existing Single-Family Homes for Metropolitan Areas, 4th Quarter 2018

Median Apartment Condo-Coop Home Prices

Area	2016	2017	2018[p]	Percent Change 2017 to 2018
MSA[1]	n/a	n/a	n/a	n/a
U.S. Average	220.7	234.3	241.0	2.9

Note: Figures are median sales prices of existing apartment condo-coop homes in thousands of dollars; (p) preliminary; n/a not available; (1) Figures cover the Midland, TX Metropolitan Statistical Area—see Appendix B for areas included
Source: National Association of Realtors, Median Sales Price of Existing Apartment Condo-Coop Homes for Metropolitan Areas, 4th Quarter 2018

Home Value Distribution

Area	Under $50,000	$50,000 -$99,999	$100,000 -$149,999	$150,000 -$199,999	$200,000 -$299,999	$300,000 -$499,999	$500,000 -$999,999	$1,000,000 or more
City	6.1	11.5	14.7	20.0	23.8	16.7	6.1	1.1
MSA[1]	10.1	12.5	14.2	17.9	22.7	16.2	5.4	1.1
U.S.	8.3	13.9	14.7	14.6	18.7	17.3	9.7	2.7

Note: Figures are percentages and cover owner-occupied housing units; (1) Figures cover the Midland, TX Metropolitan Statistical Area—see Appendix B for areas included
Source: U.S. Census Bureau, 2013-2017 American Community Survey 5-Year Estimates

Homeownership Rate

Area	2010 (%)	2011 (%)	2012 (%)	2013 (%)	2014 (%)	2015 (%)	2016 (%)	2017 (%)	2018 (%)
MSA[1]	n/a	n/a	n/a	n/a	n/a	n/a	n/a	n/a	n/a
U.S.	66.9	66.1	65.4	65.1	64.5	63.7	63.4	63.9	64.4

Note: (1) Figures cover the Midland, TX Metropolitan Statistical Area—see Appendix B for areas included; n/a not available
Source: U.S. Census Bureau, Housing Vacancies and Homeownership Annual Statistics: 2010-2018

Year Housing Structure Built

Area	2010 or Later	2000 -2009	1990 -1999	1980 -1989	1970 -1979	1960 -1969	1950 -1959	1940 -1949	Before 1940	Median Year
City	8.1	9.0	14.5	19.5	13.2	13.1	17.9	3.1	1.6	1981
MSA[1]	9.5	10.3	15.2	19.6	13.3	11.7	15.8	3.0	1.6	1982
U.S.	3.2	14.5	14.0	13.6	15.5	10.8	10.5	5.1	12.9	1977

Note: Figures are percentages except for Median Year; Note: (1) Figures cover the Midland, TX Metropolitan Statistical Area—see Appendix B for areas included
Source: U.S. Census Bureau, 2013-2017 American Community Survey 5-Year Estimates

Gross Monthly Rent

Area	Under $500	$500 -$999	$1,000 -$1,499	$1,500 -$1,999	$2,000 -$2,499	$2,500 -$2,999	$3,000 and up	Median ($)
City	2.6	30.0	41.5	19.1	4.1	1.9	0.8	1,179
MSA[1]	2.8	29.5	41.6	19.3	4.1	1.8	0.7	1,177
U.S.	10.5	41.1	28.7	11.7	4.5	1.8	1.7	982

Note: Figures are percentages except for Median; Gross rent is the contract rent plus the estimated average monthly cost of utilities (electricity, gas, and water and sewer) and fuels (oil, coal, kerosene, wood, etc.) if these are paid by the renter (or paid for the renter by someone else); (1) Figures cover the Midland, TX Metropolitan Statistical Area—see Appendix B for areas included
Source: U.S. Census Bureau, 2013-2017 American Community Survey 5-Year Estimates

HEALTH

Health Risk Factors

Category	MSA[1] (%)	U.S. (%)
Adults aged 18–64 who have any kind of health care coverage	n/a	87.3
Adults who reported being in good or better health	n/a	82.4
Adults who have been told they have high blood cholesterol	n/a	33.0
Adults who have been told they have high blood pressure	n/a	32.3
Adults who are current smokers	n/a	17.1
Adults who currently use E-cigarettes	n/a	4.6
Adults who currently use chewing tobacco, snuff, or snus	n/a	4.0
Adults who are heavy drinkers[2]	n/a	6.3
Adults who are binge drinkers[3]	n/a	17.4
Adults who are overweight (BMI 25.0 - 29.9)	n/a	35.3
Adults who are obese (BMI 30.0 - 99.8)	n/a	31.3
Adults who participated in any physical activities in the past month	n/a	74.4
Adults who always or nearly always wears a seat belt	n/a	94.3

Note: n/a not available; (1) Figures cover the Midland, TX Metropolitan Statistical Area—see Appendix B for areas included; (2) Heavy drinkers are classified as adult men having more than 14 drinks per week and adult women having more than 7 drinks per week; (3) Binge drinkers are classified as males having five or more drinks on one occasion or females having four or more drinks on one occasion
Source: Centers for Disease Control and Prevention, Behaviorial Risk Factor Surveillance System, SMART: Selected Metropolitan Area Risk Trends, 2017

Acute and Chronic Health Conditions

Category	MSA[1] (%)	U.S. (%)
Adults who have ever been told they had a heart attack	n/a	4.2
Adults who have ever been told they have angina or coronary heart disease	n/a	3.9
Adults who have ever been told they had a stroke	n/a	3.0
Adults who have ever been told they have asthma	n/a	14.2
Adults who have ever been told they have arthritis	n/a	24.9
Adults who have ever been told they have diabetes[2]	n/a	10.5
Adults who have ever been told they had skin cancer	n/a	6.2
Adults who have ever been told they had any other types of cancer	n/a	7.1
Adults who have ever been told they have COPD	n/a	6.5
Adults who have ever been told they have kidney disease	n/a	3.0
Adults who have ever been told they have a form of depression	n/a	20.5

Note: n/a not available; (1) Figures cover the Midland, TX Metropolitan Statistical Area—see Appendix B for areas included; (2) Figures do not include pregnancy-related, borderline, or pre-diabetes
Source: Centers for Disease Control and Prevention, Behaviorial Risk Factor Surveillance System, SMART: Selected Metropolitan Area Risk Trends, 2017

Health Screening and Vaccination Rates

Category	MSA[1] (%)	U.S. (%)
Adults aged 65+ who have had flu shot within the past year	n/a	60.7
Adults aged 65+ who have ever had a pneumonia vaccination	n/a	75.4
Adults who have ever been tested for HIV	n/a	36.1
Adults who have ever had the shingles or zoster vaccine?	n/a	28.9
Adults who have had their blood cholesterol checked within the last five years	n/a	85.9

Note: n/a not available; (1) Figures cover the Midland, TX Metropolitan Statistical Area—see Appendix B for areas included.
Source: Centers for Disease Control and Prevention, Behaviorial Risk Factor Surveillance System, SMART: Selected Metropolitan Area Risk Trends, 2017

Disability Status

Category	MSA[1] (%)	U.S. (%)
Adults who reported being deaf	n/a	6.7
Are you blind or have serious difficulty seeing, even when wearing glasses?	n/a	4.5
Are you limited in any way in any of your usual activities due of arthritis?	n/a	12.9
Do you have difficulty doing errands alone?	n/a	6.8
Do you have difficulty dressing or bathing?	n/a	3.6
Do you have serious difficulty concentrating/remembering/making decisions?	n/a	10.7
Do you have serious difficulty walking or climbing stairs?	n/a	13.6

Note: n/a not available; (1) Figures cover the Midland, TX Metropolitan Statistical Area—see Appendix B for areas included.
Source: Centers for Disease Control and Prevention, Behaviorial Risk Factor Surveillance System, SMART: Selected Metropolitan Area Risk Trends, 2017

Mortality Rates for the Top 10 Causes of Death in the U.S.

ICD-10[a] Sub-Chapter	ICD-10[a] Code	Age-Adjusted Mortality Rate[1] per 100,000 population	
		County[2]	U.S.
Malignant neoplasms	C00-C97	153.7	155.5
Ischaemic heart diseases	I20-I25	120.7	94.8
Other forms of heart disease	I30-I51	49.5	52.9
Chronic lower respiratory diseases	J40-J47	56.1	41.0
Cerebrovascular diseases	I60-I69	35.5	37.5
Other degenerative diseases of the nervous system	G30-G31	48.6	35.0
Other external causes of accidental injury	W00-X59	16.3	33.7
Organic, including symptomatic, mental disorders	F01-F09	27.1	31.0
Hypertensive diseases	I10-I15	10.2	21.9
Diabetes mellitus	E10-E14	11.5	21.2

Note: (a) ICD-10 = International Classification of Diseases 10th Revision; (1) Mortality rates are a three year average covering 2015-2017; (2) Figures cover Midland County.
Source: Centers for Disease Control and Prevention, National Center for Health Statistics. Underlying Cause of Death 1999-2017 on CDC WONDER Online Database

Mortality Rates for Selected Causes of Death

ICD-10[a] Sub-Chapter	ICD-10[a] Code	Age-Adjusted Mortality Rate[1] per 100,000 population	
		County[2]	U.S.
Assault	X85-Y09	Unreliable	5.9
Diseases of the liver	K70-K76	18.2	14.1
Human immunodeficiency virus (HIV) disease	B20-B24	Suppressed	1.8
Influenza and pneumonia	J09-J18	25.6	14.3
Intentional self-harm	X60-X84	11.3	13.6
Malnutrition	E40-E46	Unreliable	1.6
Obesity and other hyperalimentation	E65-E68	Suppressed	2.1
Renal failure	N17-N19	11.7	13.0
Transport accidents	V01-V99	21.2	12.4
Viral hepatitis	B15-B19	Suppressed	1.6

Note: (a) ICD-10 = International Classification of Diseases 10th Revision; (1) Mortality rates are a three year average covering 2015-2017; (2) Figures cover Midland County; Data are suppressed when the data meet the criteria for confidentiality constraints; Mortality rates are flagged as unreliable when the rate would be calculated with a numerator of 20 or less.
Source: Centers for Disease Control and Prevention, National Center for Health Statistics. Underlying Cause of Death 1999-2017 on CDC WONDER Online Database

Health Insurance Coverage

Area	With Health Insurance	With Private Health Insurance	With Public Health Insurance	Without Health Insurance	Population Under Age 18 Without Health Insurance
City	80.9	68.6	19.9	19.1	18.0
MSA[1]	80.8	68.5	19.9	19.2	17.4
U.S.	89.5	67.2	33.8	10.5	5.7

Note: Figures are percentages that cover the civilian noninstitutionalized population; (1) Figures cover the Midland, TX Metropolitan Statistical Area—see Appendix B for areas included
Source: U.S. Census Bureau, 2013-2017 American Community Survey 5-Year Estimates

Number of Medical Professionals

Area	MDs[3]	DOs[3,4]	Dentists	Podiatrists	Chiropractors	Optometrists
County[1] (number)	250	17	89	5	22	22
County[1] (rate[2])	152.9	10.4	53.9	3.0	13.3	13.3
U.S. (rate[2])	279.3	23.0	68.4	6.0	27.1	16.2

Note: Data as of 2017 unless noted; (1) Data covers Midland County; (2) Rate per 100,000 population; (3) Data as of 2016 and includes all active, non-federal physicians; (4) Doctor of Osteopathic Medicine
Source: U.S. Department of Health and Human Services, Health Resources and Services Administration, Bureau of Health Professions, Area Resource File (ARF) 2017-2018

EDUCATION

Public School District Statistics

District Name	Schls	Pupils	Pupil/ Teacher Ratio	Minority Pupils[1] (%)	Free Lunch Eligible[2] (%)	IEP[3] (%)
Greenwood ISD	3	2,519	16.8	48.8	28.0	6.2
Midland ISD	39	24,692	15.7	73.7	42.2	6.7

Note: Table includes school districts with 2,000 or more students; (1) Percentage of students that are not non-Hispanic white; (2) Percentage of students that are eligible for the free lunch program; (3) Percentage of students that have an Individualized Education Program.
Source: U.S. Department of Education, National Center for Education Statistics, Common Core of Data, Local Education Agency (School District) Universe Survey: School Year 2016-2017; U.S. Department of Education, National Center for Education Statistics, Common Core of Data, Public Elementary/Secondary School Universe Survey: School Year 2016-2017

Highest Level of Education

Area	Less than H.S.	H.S. Diploma	Some College, No Deg.	Associate Degree	Bachelor's Degree	Master's Degree	Prof. School Degree	Doctorate Degree
City	15.9	24.7	24.3	6.9	20.5	5.3	1.8	0.7
MSA[1]	16.5	25.7	24.0	7.2	19.3	5.2	1.6	0.5
U.S.	12.7	27.3	20.8	8.3	19.1	8.4	2.0	1.4

Note: Figures cover persons age 25 and over; (1) Figures cover the Midland, TX Metropolitan Statistical Area—see Appendix B for areas included
Source: U.S. Census Bureau, 2013-2017 American Community Survey 5-Year Estimates

Educational Attainment by Race

Area	High School Graduate or Higher (%)					Bachelor's Degree or Higher (%)				
	Total	White	Black	Asian	Hisp.[2]	Total	White	Black	Asian	Hisp.[2]
City	84.1	85.6	83.7	79.7	68.2	28.3	30.7	14.2	39.3	11.5
MSA[1]	83.5	84.7	83.4	81.9	67.0	26.6	28.5	14.1	45.1	10.8
U.S.	87.3	89.3	84.9	86.5	66.7	30.9	32.2	20.6	52.7	15.2

Note: Figures shown cover persons 25 years old and over; (1) Figures cover the Midland, TX Metropolitan Statistical Area—see Appendix B for areas included; (2) People of Hispanic origin can be of any race
Source: U.S. Census Bureau, 2013-2017 American Community Survey 5-Year Estimates

School Enrollment by Grade and Control

Area	Preschool (%)		Kindergarten (%)		Grades 1 - 4 (%)		Grades 5 - 8 (%)		Grades 9 - 12 (%)	
	Public	Private	Public	Private	Public	Private	Public	Private	Public	Private
City	59.2	40.8	83.8	16.2	84.1	15.9	85.2	14.8	90.6	9.4
MSA[1]	56.7	43.3	85.9	14.1	86.7	13.3	87.2	12.8	90.8	9.2
U.S.	58.8	41.2	87.7	12.3	89.7	10.3	89.6	10.4	90.3	9.7

Note: Figures shown cover persons 3 years old and over; (1) Figures cover the Midland, TX Metropolitan Statistical Area—see Appendix B for areas included
Source: U.S. Census Bureau, 2013-2017 American Community Survey 5-Year Estimates

Average Salaries of Public School Classroom Teachers

Area	2016		2017		Change from 2016 to 2017	
	Dollars	Rank[1]	Dollars	Rank[1]	Percent	Rank[2]
Texas	51,890	28	52,575	28	1.3	29
U.S. Average	58,479	–	59,660	–	2.0	–

Note: (1) Rank ranges from 1 to 51 where 1 indicates highest salary; (2) Rank ranges from 1 to 51 where 1 indicates highest percent change.
Source: National Education Association, Rankings & Estimates: Rankings of the States 2017 and Estimates of School Statistics 2018

Higher Education

Four-Year Colleges			Two-Year Colleges			Medical Schools[1]	Law Schools[2]	Voc/ Tech[3]
Public	Private Non-profit	Private For-profit	Public	Private Non-profit	Private For-profit			
1	0	0	0	0	0	0	0	0

Note: Figures cover institutions located within the city limits and include main campuses only; (1) includes schools accredited by the Liaison Committee on Medical Education and the American Osteopathic Association's Commission on Osteopathic College Accreditation; (2) includes ABA-accredited schools, schools with provisional ABA accreditation, and state accredited schools; (3) includes all schools with programs that are less than 2 years.
Source: National Center for Education Statistics, Integrated Postsecondary Education System (IPEDS), 2017-18; Wikipedia, List of Medical Schools in the United States, accessed April 3, 2019; Wikipedia, List of Law Schools in the United States, accessed April 3, 2019

PRESIDENTIAL ELECTION

2016 Presidential Election Results

Area	Clinton	Trump	Johnson	Stein	Other
Midland County	20.4	75.1	3.4	0.4	0.7
U.S.	48.0	45.9	3.3	1.1	1.7

Note: Results are percentages and may not add to 100% due to rounding
Source: Dave Leip's Atlas of U.S. Presidential Elections

EMPLOYERS

Major Employers

Company Name	Industry
Albertsons Companies	Grocery stores
Bobby Cox Companies	Retail, restaurants
City of Odessa	City & town managers' office
Cudd Energy	Oil & gas
Dixie Electric	Electric
Ector County	Government
Ector County ISD	Public education
Family Dollar	Distribution
Halliburton Services	Oil & gas
HEB	Grocery stores
Holloman Construction	Oil field construction
Investment Corp. of America	Financial services
Lithia Motors	Automotive
Medical Center Hospital	County hospital
Nurses Unlimited	Medical
Odessa College	Education
Odessa Regional Medical Center	Medical
REXtac	Manufacturer
Saulsbury Companies	Electric & construction
Sewell Family of Dealerships	Automotive
Southwest Convenience Stores	Retail, service
Texas Tech University Health Sci Ctr	Education/medical
The University of Texas Permian Basin	Education
Wal-Mart Stores	Retail
Weatherford	Oil & gas

Note: Companies shown are located within the Midland, TX Metropolitan Statistical Area.
Source: Hoovers.com; Wikipedia

PUBLIC SAFETY

Crime Rate

Area	All Crimes	Violent Crimes				Property Crimes		
		Murder	Rape[3]	Robbery	Aggrav. Assault	Burglary	Larceny -Theft	Motor Vehicle Theft
City	2,197.8	1.4	26.6	42.5	200.8	310.2	1,458.0	158.3
Suburbs[1]	2,505.9	0.0	8.8	64.6	199.8	358.4	1,559.9	314.3
Metro[2]	2,258.5	1.2	23.1	46.8	200.6	319.7	1,478.1	189.0
U.S.	2,756.1	5.3	41.7	98.0	248.9	430.4	1,694.4	237.4

Note: Figures are crimes per 100,000 population; (1) All areas within the metro area that are located outside the city limits; (2) Figures cover the Midland, TX Metropolitan Statistical Area—see Appendix B for areas included; (3) The city and U.S. figures shown were reported using the revised Uniform Crime Reporting (UCR) definition of rape. The suburban and metro area figures shown are an aggregate total of the data submitted using both the revised and legacy UCR definitions.
Source: FBI Uniform Crime Reports, 2017

Hate Crimes

Area	Number of Quarters Reported	Number of Incidents per Bias Motivation					
		Race/Ethnicity/ Ancestry	Religion	Sexual Orientation	Disability	Gender	Gender Identity
City	4	0	0	0	0	0	0
U.S.	4	4,131	1,564	1,130	116	46	119

Source: Federal Bureau of Investigation, Hate Crime Statistics 2017

Identity Theft Consumer Reports

Area	Reports	Reports per 100,000 Population	Rank[2]
MSA[1]	191	113	89
U.S.	444,602	135	-

Note: (1) Figures cover the Midland, TX Metropolitan Statistical Area—see Appendix B for areas included; (2) Rank ranges from 1 to 389 where 1 indicates greatest number of identity theft reports per 100,000 population
Source: Federal Trade Commission, Consumer Sentinel Network Data Book for January–December 2018

Fraud and Other Consumer Reports

Area	Reports	Reports per 100,000 Population	Rank[2]
MSA[1]	659	392	325
U.S.	2,552,917	776	-

Note: (1) Figures cover the Midland, TX Metropolitan Statistical Area—see Appendix B for areas included; (2) Rank ranges from 1 to 389 where 1 indicates greatest number of fraud and other consumer reports per 100,000 population
Source: Federal Trade Commission, Consumer Sentinel Network Data Book for January–December 2018

SPORTS

Professional Sports Teams

Team Name	League	Year Established
No teams are located in the metro area		

Source: Wikipedia, Major Professional Sports Teams of the United States and Canada, April 5, 2019

CLIMATE

Average and Extreme Temperatures

Temperature	Jan	Feb	Mar	Apr	May	Jun	Jul	Aug	Sep	Oct	Nov	Dec	Yr.
Extreme High (°F)	84	90	95	101	108	116	112	107	107	100	89	85	116
Average High (°F)	57	62	70	79	86	93	94	93	86	78	66	59	77
Average Temp. (°F)	43	48	55	64	73	80	82	81	74	65	53	46	64
Average Low (°F)	30	34	40	49	59	67	69	68	62	51	39	32	50
Extreme Low (°F)	-8	-11	9	20	34	47	53	54	36	24	13	-1	-11

Note: Figures cover the years 1948-1995
Source: National Climatic Data Center, International Station Meteorological Climate Summary, 9/96

Average Precipitation/Snowfall/Humidity

Precip./Humidity	Jan	Feb	Mar	Apr	May	Jun	Jul	Aug	Sep	Oct	Nov	Dec	Yr.
Avg. Precip. (in.)	0.6	0.6	0.5	0.8	2.1	1.6	1.9	1.7	2.1	1.6	0.6	0.5	14.6
Avg. Snowfall (in.)	2	1	Tr	Tr	0	0	0	0	0	Tr	Tr	1	4
Avg. Rel. Hum. 6am (%)	72	72	65	67	75	76	73	74	79	78	74	71	73
Avg. Rel. Hum. 3pm (%)	38	35	27	27	31	32	34	34	40	37	35	37	34

Note: Figures cover the years 1948-1995; Tr = Trace amounts (<0.05 in. of rain; <0.5 in. of snow)
Source: National Climatic Data Center, International Station Meteorological Climate Summary, 9/96

Weather Conditions

Temperature			Daytime Sky			Precipitation		
10°F & below	32°F & below	90°F & above	Clear	Partly cloudy	Cloudy	0.01 inch or more precip.	0.1 inch or more snow/ice	Thunder-storms
1	62	102	144	138	83	52	3	38

Note: Figures are average number of days per year and cover the years 1948-1995
Source: National Climatic Data Center, International Station Meteorological Climate Summary, 9/96

HAZARDOUS WASTE

Superfund Sites

The Midland, TX metro area is home to two sites on the EPA's Superfund National Priorities List: **Midessa Ground Water Plume** (final); **West County Road 112 Ground Water** (final). There are a total of 1,390 Superfund sites with a status of proposed or final on the list in the U.S. *U.S. Environmental Protection Agency, National Priorities List, April 5, 2019*

AIR & WATER QUALITY

Air Quality Trends: Ozone

	1990	1995	2000	2005	2010	2012	2014	2015	2016	2017
MSA[1]	n/a	n/a	n/a	n/a	n/a	n/a	n/a	n/a	n/a	n/a
U.S.	0.088	0.089	0.082	0.080	0.073	0.075	0.067	0.068	0.069	0.068

Note: (1) Data covers the Midland, TX Metropolitan Statistical Area—see Appendix B for areas included; n/a not available. The values shown are the composite ozone concentration averages among trend sites based on the highest fourth daily maximum 8-hour concentration in parts per million. These trends are based on sites having an adequate record of monitoring data during the trend period. Data from exceptional events are included.
Source: U.S. Environmental Protection Agency, Air Quality Monitoring Information, "Air Quality Trends by City, 1990-2017"

Air Quality Index

Area	Percent of Days when Air Quality was...[2]					AQI Statistics[2]	
	Good	Moderate	Unhealthy for Sensitive Groups	Unhealthy	Very Unhealthy	Maximum	Median
MSA[1]	n/a	n/a	n/a	n/a	n/a	n/a	n/a

Note: (1) Data covers the Midland, TX Metropolitan Statistical Area—see Appendix B for areas included;
(2) Based on days with AQI data in 2017. Air Quality Index (AQI) is an index for reporting daily air quality. EPA calculates the AQI for five major air pollutants regulated by the Clean Air Act: ground-level ozone, particle pollution (aka particulate matter), carbon monoxide, sulfur dioxide, and nitrogen dioxide. The AQI runs from 0 to 500. The higher the AQI value, the greater the level of air pollution and the greater the health concern. There are six AQI categories: "Good" AQI is between 0 and 50. Air quality is considered satisfactory; "Moderate" AQI is between 51 and 100. Air quality is acceptable; "Unhealthy for Sensitive Groups" When AQI values are between 101 and 150, members of sensitive groups may experience health effects; "Unhealthy" When AQI values are between 151 and 200 everyone may begin to experience health effects; "Very Unhealthy" AQI values between 201 and 300 trigger a health alert; "Hazardous" AQI values over 300 trigger warnings of emergency conditions (not shown).
Source: U.S. Environmental Protection Agency, Air Quality Index Report, 2017

Air Quality Index Pollutants

Area	Percent of Days when AQI Pollutant was...[2]					
	Carbon Monoxide	Nitrogen Dioxide	Ozone	Sulfur Dioxide	Particulate Matter 2.5	Particulate Matter 10
MSA[1]	n/a	n/a	n/a	n/a	n/a	n/a

Note: (1) Data covers the Midland, TX Metropolitan Statistical Area—see Appendix B for areas included; (2) Based on days with AQI data in 2017. The Air Quality Index (AQI) is an index for reporting daily air quality. EPA calculates the AQI for five major air pollutants regulated by the Clean Air Act: ground-level ozone, particle pollution (also known as particulate matter), carbon monoxide, sulfur dioxide, and nitrogen dioxide. The AQI runs from 0 to 500. The higher the AQI value, the greater the level of air pollution and the greater the health concern.
Source: U.S. Environmental Protection Agency, Air Quality Index Report, 2017

Maximum Air Pollutant Concentrations: Particulate Matter, Ozone, CO and Lead

	Particulate Matter 10 (ug/m^3)	Particulate Matter 2.5 Wtd AM (ug/m^3)	Particulate Matter 2.5 24-Hr (ug/m^3)	Ozone (ppm)	Carbon Monoxide (ppm)	Lead (ug/m^3)
MSA[1] Level	n/a	n/a	n/a	n/a	n/a	n/a
NAAQS[2]	150	15	35	0.075	9	0.15
Met NAAQS[2]	Yes	Yes	Yes	Yes	Yes	Yes

Note: (1) Data covers the Midland, TX Metropolitan Statistical Area—see Appendix B for areas included; Data from exceptional events are included; (2) National Ambient Air Quality Standards; ppm = parts per million; ug/m^3 = micrograms per cubic meter; n/a not available.
Concentrations: Particulate Matter 10 (coarse particulate)—highest second maximum 24-hour concentration; Particulate Matter 2.5 Wtd AM (fine particulate)—highest weighted annual mean concentration; Particulate Matter 2.5 24-Hour (fine particulate)—highest 98th percentile 24-hour concentration; Ozone—highest fourth daily maximum 8-hour concentration; Carbon Monoxide—highest second maximum non-overlapping 8-hour concentration; Lead—maximum running 3-month average
Source: U.S. Environmental Protection Agency, Air Quality Monitoring Information, "Air Quality Statistics by City, 2017"

Maximum Air Pollutant Concentrations: Nitrogen Dioxide and Sulfur Dioxide

	Nitrogen Dioxide AM (ppb)	Nitrogen Dioxide 1-Hr (ppb)	Sulfur Dioxide AM (ppb)	Sulfur Dioxide 1-Hr (ppb)	Sulfur Dioxide 24-Hr (ppb)
MSA[1] Level	n/a	n/a	n/a	n/a	n/a
NAAQS[2]	53	100	30	75	140
Met NAAQS[2]	Yes	Yes	Yes	Yes	Yes

Note: (1) Data covers the Midland, TX Metropolitan Statistical Area—see Appendix B for areas included; Data from exceptional events are included; (2) National Ambient Air Quality Standards; ppm = parts per million; ug/m^3 = micrograms per cubic meter; n/a not available.
Concentrations: Nitrogen Dioxide AM—highest arithmetic mean concentration; Nitrogen Dioxide 1-Hr—highest 98th percentile 1-hour daily maximum concentration; Sulfur Dioxide AM—highest annual mean concentration; Sulfur Dioxide 1-Hr—highest 99th percentile 1-hour daily maximum concentration; Sulfur Dioxide 24-Hr—highest second maximum 24-hour concentration
Source: U.S. Environmental Protection Agency, Air Quality Monitoring Information, "Air Quality Statistics by City, 2017"

Drinking Water

Water System Name	Pop. Served	Primary Water Source Type	Violations[1]	
			Health Based	Monitoring/ Reporting
City of Midland Water Purification	132,950	Surface	0	0

Note: (1) Based on violation data from January 1, 2018 to December 31, 2018
Source: U.S. Environmental Protection Agency, Office of Ground Water and Drinking Water, Safe Drinking Water Information System (based on data extracted April 5, 2019)

Nashville, Tennessee

Background

Nashville, the capital of Tennessee, was founded on Christmas Day in 1779 by James Robertson and John Donelson, and considered the country music capital of the world. This is the place to record if you want to make it into the country music industry, and where the Grand Ole Opry—the longest-running radio show in the country—still captures the hearts of millions of devoted listeners. It is no wonder, given how profoundly this industry has touched people, names like Dolly, Chet, Loretta, Hank, and Johnny are more familiar than the city's true native sons—Andrew Jackson, James Polk, and Sam Houston, that is.

Nashville is home to Music Row, an area just to the southwest of downtown with hundreds of businesses related to the country music, gospel music, and contemporary Christian music industries. The USA Network's *Nashville Star*, a country music singing competition, is also held in the Acuff Theatre. The magnitude of Nashville's recording industry is impressive, but other industries are important to the city, such as health care management, automobile production, and printing and publishing.

The city has been ranked one of the top five regions for job growth, and has been called "Nowville" and "It City." Nashville elected its first female mayor, Megan Barry, in 2015 who, as council member, performed the first same-sex wedding in Nashville. The city recently received accolades for its economy and hot housing market.

Nashville is also a devoted patron of education. The Davidson Academy, forerunner of the George Peabody College for Teachers, was founded in Nashville, as were Vanderbilt and Fisk universities, the latter being the first private black university in the United States. Vanderbilt University and Medical Center is the region's largest non-governmental employer.

Nashville citizens take pride in their numerous museums, including the Adventure Science Center, with its Sudekum Planetarium; the Aaron Douglas Gallery at Fisk University, which features a remarkable collection of African-American art; and the Carl Van Vechten Gallery, also at Fisk University, home to works by Alfred Stieglitz, Picasso, Cezanne, and Georgia O'Keefe. The Cheekwood Botanical Garden and Museum of Art includes 55 acres of gardens and contemporary art galleries.

Gracing the city are majestic mansions and plantations that testify to the mid- nineteenth-century splendor for which the South is famous. Known as the "Queen of the Tennessee Plantations," the Belle Meade Plantation is an 1853 Greek Revival mansion crowning a 5,400-acre thoroughbred stud farm and nursery. The Belmont Mansion, built in 1850 by Adelicia Acklen, one of the wealthiest women in America, is constructed in the style of an Italian villa and was originally intended to be the summer home of the Acklens. Travelers' Rest Plantation served as a haven for weary travelers, past and present, and is Nashville's oldest plantation home open to the public. It features docents dressed in period costume who explain and demonstrate life in the plantations' heyday. Carnton Plantation was the site of the Civil War's Battle of Franklin, and The Hermitage was the home of Andrew Jackson, the seventh president of the United States. Tennessee's historic State Capitol Building, completed in 1859, has had much of its interior restored to its nineteenth-century appearance.

The Nashville area comprises many urban, suburban, rural, and historic districts, which can differ immensely from each other. Most of the best restaurants, clubs, and shops are on the west side of the Cumberland River, however, the east side encompasses fine neighborhoods, interesting homes, plenty of shopping, and good food, as well. Outdoor activities include camping, fishing, hiking, and biking at the many scenic and accessible lakes in the region.

Located on the Cumberland River in central Tennessee, Nashville's average relative humidity is moderate, as is its weather, with great temperature extremes a rarity. The city is not in the most common path of storms that cross the country, but is in a zone of moderate frequency for thunderstorms.

Rankings

General Rankings

- *US News & World Report* conducted a survey of more than 2,000 people and analyzed the 125 largest metropolitan areas to determine what matters the most when selecting the next place to live. Nashville ranked #11 out of the top 25 as having the best combination of desirable factors. Criteria: cost of living; quality of education; job market, crime rates; and other factors. *realestate.usnews.com, "The 25 Best Places to Live in the U.S. in 2018," April 10, 2018*

- *Insider* listed 33 places in the U.S. that were a must see vacation destination. Whether it is the great beaches, exploring a new city or experiencing the great outdoors, according to the website thisisinsider.com Nashville is a place to visit in 2018. *Insider, "33 Trips Everyone Should Take in the U.S. in 2018," November 27, 2017*

- Nashville appeared on *Business Insider's* list of the "13 Hottest American Cities for 2016." Criteria: job and population growth; demographics; affordability; livability; residents' health and welfare; technological innovation; sustainability; burgeoning art and food scenes. *www.businessinsider.com, "The Thirteen Hottest American Cities for 2016," December 4, 2015*

- The Nashville metro area was identified as one of America's fastest-growing areas in terms of population and business growth by *MagnifyMoney*. The area ranked #5 out of 35. The 100 most populous metro areas in the U.S. were evaluated on their change from 2011-2016 in the following categories: people and housing; workforce and employment opportunities; growing industry. *www.businessinsider.com, "The 35 Cities in the US with the Biggest Influx of People, the Most Work Opportunities, and the Hottest Business Growth," August 12, 2018*

- The Nashville metro area was identified as one of America's fastest-growing areas in terms of population and economy by *Forbes*. The area ranked #7 out of 25. The 100 most populous metro areas in the U.S. were evaluated on the following criteria: estimated population growth; employment; economic output; wages; home values. *Forbes, "America's Fastest-Growing Cities 2018," February 28, 2018*

- In its eighth annual survey, *Travel + Leisure* readers nominated their favorite small cities and towns in America—those with 100,000 or fewer residents—voting on numerous attractive features in categories including culture, food and drink, quality of life, style, and people. After 50,000 votes, Nashville was ranked #8 among the proposed favorites. *www.travelandleisure.com, "America's Favorite Cities," October 20, 2017*

- Nashville appeared on *Travel + Leisure's* list of the fifteen best cities in the United States. The city was ranked #9. Criteria: sights/landmarks; culture/arts; cuisine; people/friendliness; shopping; and value. *Travel + Leisure, "The World's Best Awards 2018" July 10, 2018*

- Based on more than 425,000 responses, *Condé Nast Traveler* ranked its readers' favorite cities in the U.S. The list was broken into cities over 1 million and cities under 1 million. Nashville ranked #13 in the big city category. *Condé Nast Traveler, Readers' Choice Awards 2018, "Best Big Cities in the U.S." October 9, 2018*

- In their sixth annual survey, Livability.com looked at data for more than 1,000 U.S. cities to determine the rankings for Livability's "Top 100 Best Places to Live" in 2019. Nashville ranked #84. Criteria: median home value capped at $250,000; affordable living; vibrant economy; education, demographics, health care options. transportation & infrastructure; abundant lifestyle amenities. *Livability.com, "Top 100 Best Places to Live 2019" March 2019*

Business/Finance Rankings

- According to *Business Insider*, the Nashville metro area is where startup growth is on the rise. Based on the 2017 Kauffman Index of Growth Entrepreneurship, which measured in-depth national entrepreneurial trends in 40 metro areas, it ranked #4 in highest startup growth. *www.businessinsider.com, "The 21 U.S. Cities with the Highest Startup Growth," October 21, 2017*

- The personal finance site NerdWallet analyzed 183 American metropolitan areas with populations over 250,000 and more than 15,000 businesses to rank where entrepreneurs find the most success. Criteria included area economy, annual income, housing cost, unemployment rate, and the success rate of area businesses. Nashville ranked #103. *www.nerdwallet.com, "Best Places to Start a Business," April 27, 2015*

- Recognizing the sizeable percentage of American workers who are self-employed, NerdWallet editors assessed the country's cities according to percentage of freelancers, median rental costs, cell phone plans/taxes, and healthcare affordability and access. By these criteria, Nashville placed #2 among the best cities for independent workers. *www.nerdwallet.com, "Best Places for Freelance Workers," August 30, 2016*

- In a survey of economic confidence in the nation's 50 largest metropolitan areas conducted January–December 2014, the Nashville metro area placed #35, according to Gallup's 2014 Economic Confidence Index. *Gallup, "San Jose and San Francisco Lead in Economic Confidence," March 19, 2015*

- NerdWallet.com identified the 10 most promising cities for job seekers of the nation's 100 largest cities. Nashville was ranked #3. Criteria: job availability; annual salary; workforce growth; affordability. *NerdWallet.com, "Best Cities for Job Seekers in 2017," December 19, 2016*

- The Brookings Institution ranked the nation's largest cities based on income inequality. Nashville was ranked #83 (#1 = greatest inequality). Criteria: the "95/20 ratio," a figure representing the income at which a household earns more than 95 percent of all other households, divided by the income at which a household earns more than only 20 percent of all other households. *Brookings Institution, "Household Income Inequality, Largest Cities of 97 Large U.S. Metro Areas, 2014-2016," February 5, 2018*

- The Brookings Institution ranked the 100 largest metro areas in the U.S. based on income inequality. Nashville was ranked #78 (#1 = greatest inequality). Criteria: the "95/20 ratio," a figure representing the income at which a household earns more than 95 percent of all other households, divided by the income at which a household earns more than only 20 percent of all other households. *Brookings Institution, "Household Income Inequality, 100 Largest U.S. Metro Areas, 2014-2016," February 5, 2018*

- *Forbes* ranked the 100 largest metro areas in the U.S. in terms of the "Best Cities for Young Professionals." The Nashville metro area ranked #17 out of 25. (Large metro areas were divided into metro divisions.) Criteria: median rent of a two-bedroom apartment; job growth and unemployment rate; median salary of college graduates with 5 or less years of work experience; networking opportunities; social outlook; percentage of population 25 years of age and older with college degrees. *Forbes.com, "America's 25 Best Cities for Young Professionals in 2017," May 22, 2017*

- Payscale.com ranked the 32 largest metro areas in terms of wage growth. The Nashville metro area ranked #32. Criteria: private-sector wage growth between the 4th quarter of 2017 and the 4th quarter of 2018. *PayScale, "Wage Trends by Metro Area-4th Quarter," January 8, 2019*

- Nashville was identified as one of America's most frugal metro areas by *Coupons.com*. The city ranked #9 out of 25. Criteria: digital coupon usage. *Coupons.com, "America's Most Frugal Cities of 2017," March 22, 2018*

- The Nashville metro area appeared on the Milken Institute "2018 Best Performing Cities" list. Rank: #25 out of 200 large metro areas. Criteria: job growth; wage and salary growth; high-tech output growth. *Milken Institute, "Best-Performing Cities 2018," January 24, 2019*

- *Forbes* ranked the 200 most populous metro areas to determine the nation's "Best Places for Business and Careers." The Nashville metro area was ranked #17. Criteria: costs (business and living); job growth (past and projected); income growth; quality of life; educational attainment (college and high school); projected economic growth; cultural and recreational opportunities; net migration patterns; number of highly ranked colleges. *Forbes, "The Best Places for Business and Careers 2018: Seattle Leads the Way," October 24, 2018*

Children/Family Rankings

- Nashville was selected as one of the most playful cities in the U.S. by KaBOOM! The organization's Playful City USA initiative honors cities and towns across the nation that have made their communities more playable. Criteria: pledging to integrate play as a solution to challenges in their communities; making it easy for children to get active and balanced play; creating more family-friendly and innovative communities as a result. *KaBOOM! National Campaign for Play, "2017 Playful City USA Communities"*

Culture/Performing Arts Rankings

- Nashville was selected as one of "America's Favorite Cities." The city ranked #14 in the "Culture" category. Respondents to an online survey were asked to rate 38 top urban destinations in the U.S. from a visitor's perspective. Criteria: theater scene and community; number of bookstores; live music; and sense of history. *Travelandleisure.com, "These Are America's 20 Most Cultured Cities," October 2016*

- Nashville was selected as one of "America's Favorite Cities." The city ranked #1 in the "Culture: Concerts" category. Respondents to an online survey were asked to rate 38 top urban destinations in the U.S. from a visitor's perspective. Criteria: number and quality of concerts. *Travelandleisure.com, "America's Favorite Cities," October 11, 2015*

- Nashville was selected as one of "America's Favorite Cities." The city ranked #1 in the "Culture: Music Scene" category. Respondents to an online survey were asked to rate 38 top urban destinations in the U.S. from a visitor's perspective. *Travelandleisure.com, "From the Honkytonk Capital to Jazz's Birthplace: America's Best Music Scenes," October 2016*

Dating/Romance Rankings

- Nashville was selected as one of America's best cities for singles by the readers of *Travel + Leisure* in their annual "America's Favorite Cities" survey. Criteria included good-looking locals, cool shopping, an active bar scene and hipster-magnet coffee bars. *Travel + Leisure, "Best Cities in America for Singles," July 21, 2017*

Education Rankings

- Personal finance website *WalletHub* analyzed the 150 largest U.S. metropolitan statistical areas to determine where the most educated Americans are choosing to settle. Criteria: education quality and attainment gap; education levels; percentage of workers with degrees; public school quality rankings; quality and size of each metro area's universities. Nashville was ranked #61 (#1 = most educated city). *www.WalletHub.com, "2018's Most and Least Educated Cities in America," July 24, 2018*

- Nashville was selected as one of the most well-read cities in America by Amazon.com. The city ranked #16 among the top 20. Cities with populations greater than 500,000 were evaluated based on per capita sales of books, magazines and newspapers (both print and Kindle format). *Amazon.com, "The 20 Most Well-Read Cities in America," May 24, 2016*

- Nashville was selected as one of America's most literate cities. The city ranked #14 out of the 82 largest U.S. cities. Criteria: number of booksellers; library resources; Internet resources; educational attainment; periodical publishing resources; newspaper circulation. *Central Connecticut State University, "America's Most Literate Cities, 2016," March 31, 2017*

Food/Drink Rankings

- The U.S. Chamber of Commerce Foundation conducted an in-depth study on local food truck regulations, surveyed 288 food truck owners, and ranked 20 major American cities based on how friendly they are for operating a food truck. The compiled index assessed the following: procedures for obtaining permits and licenses; complying with restrictions; and financial obligations associated with operating a food truck. Nashville ranked #10 overall (1 being the best) for ease in operating a food truck. *www.foodtrucknation.us, "Food Truck Nation," March 20, 2018*

- According to Fodor's Travel, Nashville placed among the 14 best U.S. cities for food-truck cuisine. *www.fodors.com, "America's Best Food Truck Cities," August 23, 2016*

- *Men's Health* ranked 100 major U.S. cities in terms of alcohol intoxication. Nashville ranked #14 (#1 = most sober).Criteria: binge drinking; alcohol-related traffic accidents, arrests, and fatalities. *Men's Health, "America's Drunkest Cities," March 9, 2015*

Health/Fitness Rankings

- For each of the 100 largest cities in the United States, the American College of Sports Medicine's American Fitness Index evaluated infrastructure, community assets, and policies that encourage healthy and fit lifestyles, including preventive health behaviors, levels of chronic disease conditions, health care access, and community resources and policies that support physical activity. Nashville ranked #65 for "community fitness." *www.americanfitnessindex.org, "ACSM American Fitness Index Health and Community Fitness Status of the 100 Largest U.S. Cities," May 2018*

- The Nashville metro area was identified as one of the worst cities for bed bugs in America by pest control company Orkin. The area ranked #23 out of 50 based on the number of bed bug treatments Orkin performed from December 2017 to November 2018. *Orkin, "Baltimore Remains Front Runner, Atlanta and Philadelphia Break Into Top 10," January 14, 2019*

- Nashville was identified as a "2018 Spring Allergy Capital." The area ranked #54 out of 100. Three groups of factors were used to identify the most challenging cities for people with allergies during the spring season: annual pollen levels; medicine utilization; access to board-certified allergists. *Asthma and Allergy Foundation of America, "Spring Allergy Capitals 2018"*

- Nashville was identified as a "2018 Fall Allergy Capital." The area ranked #57 out of 100. Three groups of factors were used to identify the most challenging cities for people with allergies during the fall season: annual pollen levels; medicine utilization; access to board-certified allergists. *Asthma and Allergy Foundation of America, "Fall Allergy Capitals 2018"*

- Nashville was identified as a "2018 Asthma Capital." The area ranked #58 out of the nation's 100 largest metropolitan areas. Criteria: estimated prevalence; self-reported prevalence; crude death rate for asthma; annual pollen score; annual air quality; public smoking laws; number of board-certified asthma specialists; school inhaler access laws; rescue medication use; controller medication use; ER visits for asthma; uninsured rate; poverty rate. *Asthma and Allergy Foundation of America, "Asthma Capitals 2018: The Most Challenging Places to Live With Asthma"*

- *Men's Health* ranked 100 major U.S. cities in terms of the best cities for men. Nashville ranked #67. Criteria: health; fitness; quality of life. *Men's Health, "The Best & Worst Cities for Men Who Want to Be Fit and Happy," January 1, 2016*

- The Nashville metro area ranked #46 out of 189 in The Gallup-Healthways Well-Being Index. Criteria: purpose; social well being; financial health; community and physical health. Results are based on telephone interviews with adults, aged 18 and older, living in metropolitan areas in the 50 U.S. states and the District of Columbia. *Gallup-Healthways, "State of American Well-Being, 2017 Community Well-Being Rankings" March 2018*

Real Estate Rankings

- FitSmallBusiness looked at 50 of the largest metropolitan areas in the U.S. to determine which metro was the best to start a real estate business. Data was compiled from such sources as: Zillow, Trulia, U.S. Census Bureau, and the Bureau of Labor Statistics. Criteria: location; inventory; annual wages; median sales price of homes; days on the market; median price cut percentage; and other factors that would influence real estate professional growth. The Nashville metro area ranked #15. *fitsmallbusiness.com, "The Best Cities to Become a Real Estate Agent in 2018," January 30, 2018*

- *WalletHub* compared the most populated U.S. cities, as well as at least two of the most populated cities in each state, for a total of 179, to determine which had the best markets for real estate agents. Nashville ranked #9 where demand was high and pay was the best. Criteria: sales per agent; annual median wage for real-estate agents; monthly average starting salary for real estate agents; real estate job density and competition; unemployment rate; housing-market health index; and other relevant metrics. *www.WalletHub.com, "2018's Best Places to Be a Real Estate Agent," April 25, 2018*

- The Nashville metro area was identified as one of the top 20 housing markets to invest in for 2019 by *Forbes*. Criteria: strong job and population growth; stable local economy; anticipated home price appreciation; and other factors. *Forbes.com, "The Best Markets for Real Estate Investments In 2019," January 7, 2019*

Safety Rankings

- To identify the most dangerous cities in America, 24/7 Wall Street focused on violent crime categories—murder, rape, robbery, and aggravated assault—and property crime as reported in the FBI's 2017 annual Uniform Crime Report. Criteria also included median income from American Community Survey and unemployment figures from Bureau of Labor Statistics. For cities with populations over 100,000, Nashville was ranked #17. *247wallst.com, "25 Most Dangerous Cities in America" October 17, 2018*

- Allstate ranked the 200 largest cities in America in terms of driver safety. Nashville ranked #120. Criteria: internal property damage claims over a two-year period from January 2015 to December 2016. The report helps increase the importance of safety awareness behind the wheel. *Allstate, "Allstate America's Best Drivers Report, 2018" August 28, 2018*

- Nashville was identified as one of the most dangerous cities in America by NeighborhoodScout. The city ranked #45 out of 100. Criteria: number of violent crimes per 1,000 residents. The editors only considered cities with 25,000 or more residents. *NeighborhoodScout.com, "Top 100 Most Dangerous Cities in the U.S. 2019" January 2, 2019*

- The National Insurance Crime Bureau ranked 382 metro areas in the U.S. in terms of per capita rates of vehicle theft. The Nashville metro area ranked #143 (#1 = highest rate). Criteria: number of vehicle theft offenses per 100,000 inhabitants in 2017. *National Insurance Crime Bureau, "Hot Spots 2017," July 12, 2018*

Seniors/Retirement Rankings

- From its Best Cities for Successful Aging indexes, the Milken Institute generated rankings for metropolitan areas, weighing data in nine categories—health care, wellness, living arrangements, transportation and convenience, financial characteristics, education, employment, community engagement, and overall livability. The Nashville metro area was ranked #30 overall in the large metro area category. *Milken Institute, "Best Cities for Successful Aging, 2017" March 14, 2017*

Women/Minorities Rankings

- Personal finance website *WalletHub* compared more than 180 U.S. cities—including the 150 most populated U.S. cities, plus at least two of the most populated cities in each state—across two key dimensions, "Hispanic Business-Friendliness" and "Hispanic Purchasing Power", to arrive at the most favorable conditions for Hispanic entrepreneurs. Nashville was ranked #54 out of 182. Criteria includes: share of Hispanic-Owned Businesses; Hispanic entrepreneurship rate to median annual income of Hispanics; Small Business-Friendliness score; cost of living; and number of Hispanics with at least a bachelor's degree. *WalletHub.com, "2018's Best Cities for Hispanic Entrepreneurs," April 26, 2018*

Miscellaneous Rankings

- Based on the advice of plugged-in travel influencers and experts, Nashville appeared on a *Forbes* list of 14 U.S. cities that should be on anyone's travel wish list. Whether it be quirky things to see and do or civic revitalization, these places are emerging as must-see destinations. *Forbes, "Where To Go Next: 14 Best Places to Travel in the US in 2019," December 6, 2018*

- The watchdog site Charity Navigator conducts an annual study of charities in the nation's major markets both to analyze statistical differences in their financial, accountability, and transparency practices and to track year-to-year variations in individual philanthropic communities. Charity Navigator's analysis demonstrated that the financial, accountability and transparency behaviors of America's largest charities can be influenced by the metropolitan market within which the charity operates. The Nashville metro area was ranked #26 among the 30 metro markets in the rating category of Overall Score. *www.charitynavigator.org, "2017 Metro Market Study," May 1, 2017*

- In *Condé Nast Traveler* magazine's 2017 Readers' Choice Survey, Nashville made the top ten list of friendliest American cities. *www.cntraveler.com, "The Friendliest Cities in the U.S.," August 16, 2017*

- *WalletHub* compared the 150 most populated U.S. cities to determine their operating efficiency. A "Quality of Services" score was constructed for each city and then divided by the total budget per capita to reveal which were managed the best. Nashville ranked #111. Criteria: financial stability; economy; education; safety; health; infrastructure and pollution. *www.WalletHub.com, "2018's Best- & Worst-Run Cities in America," July 9, 2018*

- Nashville was selected as one of "America's Friendliest Cities." The city ranked #7 in the "Friendliest" category. Respondents to an online survey were asked to rate 38 top urban destinations in the United States as to general friendliness, as well as manners, politeness and warm disposition. *Travel + Leisure, "America's Friendliest Cities," October 20, 2017*

- Nashville appeared on *Travel + Leisure's* list of America's cities with the most attractive people. Criteria: cities were selected by readers in their annual America's Favorite Cities survey. The city ranked #6 out of 10. *Travel + Leisure, "America's Most and Least Attractive People," September 2, 2016*

- Nashville was selected as one of America's best-mannered cities. The area ranked #3. The general public determined the winners by casting votes online. *The Charleston School of Protocol and Etiquette, "2014 Most Mannerly City in America Contest," February 3, 2015*

Business Environment

CITY FINANCES

City Government Finances

Component	2016 ($000)	2016 ($ per capita)
Total Revenues	3,877,576	5,712
Total Expenditures	4,203,650	6,192
Debt Outstanding	14,092,621	20,758
Cash and Securities[1]	13,919,006	20,503

Note: (1) Cash and security holdings of a government at the close of its fiscal year, including those of its dependent agencies, utilities, and liquor stores.
Source: U.S. Census Bureau, State & Local Government Finances 2016

City Government Revenue by Source

Source	2016 ($000)	2016 ($ per capita)	2016 (%)
General Revenue			
From Federal Government	35,054	52	0.9
From State Government	577,622	851	14.9
From Local Governments	460	1	0.0
Taxes			
Property	944,010	1,391	24.3
Sales and Gross Receipts	502,560	740	13.0
Personal Income	0	0	0.0
Corporate Income	0	0	0.0
Motor Vehicle License	26,136	38	0.7
Other Taxes	27,485	40	0.7
Current Charges	316,623	466	8.2
Liquor Store	0	0	0.0
Utility	1,285,824	1,894	33.2
Employee Retirement	37,714	56	1.0

Source: U.S. Census Bureau, State & Local Government Finances 2016

City Government Expenditures by Function

Function	2016 ($000)	2016 ($ per capita)	2016 (%)
General Direct Expenditures			
Air Transportation	0	0	0.0
Corrections	81,273	119	1.9
Education	1,003,069	1,477	23.9
Employment Security Administration	0	0	0.0
Financial Administration	25,049	36	0.6
Fire Protection	129,000	190	3.1
General Public Buildings	518	< 1	< 0.1
Governmental Administration, Other	76,868	113	1.8
Health	57,583	84	1.4
Highways	97,018	142	2.3
Hospitals	98,490	145	2.3
Housing and Community Development	0	0	0.0
Interest on General Debt	149,302	219	3.6
Judicial and Legal	99,664	146	2.4
Libraries	38,650	56	0.9
Parking	0	0	0.0
Parks and Recreation	147,772	217	3.5
Police Protection	201,647	297	4.8
Public Welfare	45,852	67	1.1
Sewerage	122,125	179	2.9
Solid Waste Management	23,358	34	0.6
Veterans' Services	0	0	0.0
Liquor Store	0	0	0.0
Utility	1,458,884	2,148	34.7
Employee Retirement	245,170	361	5.8

Source: U.S. Census Bureau, State & Local Government Finances 2016

DEMOGRAPHICS

Population Growth

Area	1990 Census	2000 Census	2010 Census	2017* Estimate	Population Growth (%) 1990-2017	2010-2017
City	488,364	545,524	601,222	654,187	34.0	8.8
MSA[1]	1,048,218	1,311,789	1,589,934	1,830,410	74.6	15.1
U.S.	248,709,873	281,421,906	308,745,538	321,004,407	29.1	4.0

Note: (1) Figures cover the Nashville-Davidson—Murfreesboro—Franklin, TN Metropolitan Statistical Area—see Appendix B for areas included; (*) 2013-2017 5-year estimated population
Source: U.S. Census Bureau, 1990 Census, Census 2000, Census 2010, 2013-2017 American Community Survey 5-Year Estimates

Household Size

Area	One	Two	Three	Four	Five	Six	Seven or More	Average Household Size
City	34.2	33.2	15.2	10.2	4.3	1.7	1.2	2.40
MSA[1]	26.6	34.5	16.7	13.4	5.7	2.0	1.1	2.60
U.S.	27.7	33.8	15.7	13.0	6.0	2.3	1.4	2.60

Note: (1) Figures cover the Nashville-Davidson—Murfreesboro—Franklin, TN Metropolitan Statistical Area—see Appendix B for areas included
Source: U.S. Census Bureau, 2013-2017 American Community Survey 5-Year Estimates

Race

Area	White Alone[2] (%)	Black Alone[2] (%)	Asian Alone[2] (%)	AIAN[3] Alone[2] (%)	NHOPI[4] Alone[2] (%)	Other Race Alone[2] (%)	Two or More Races (%)
City	63.1	27.8	3.6	0.3	0.1	2.7	2.5
MSA[1]	78.1	15.2	2.6	0.3	0.1	1.6	2.2
U.S.	73.0	12.7	5.4	0.8	0.2	4.8	3.1

Note: (1) Figures cover the Nashville-Davidson—Murfreesboro—Franklin, TN Metropolitan Statistical Area—see Appendix B for areas included; (2) Alone is defined as not being in combination with one or more other races; (3) American Indian and Alaska Native; (4) Native Hawaiian and Other Pacific Islander
Source: U.S. Census Bureau, 2013-2017 American Community Survey 5-Year Estimates

Hispanic or Latino Origin

Area	Total (%)	Mexican (%)	Puerto Rican (%)	Cuban (%)	Other (%)
City	10.4	6.1	0.6	0.4	3.2
MSA[1]	7.0	4.4	0.5	0.2	1.9
U.S.	17.6	11.1	1.7	0.7	4.1

Note: Persons of Hispanic or Latino origin can be of any race; (1) Figures cover the Nashville-Davidson—Murfreesboro—Franklin, TN Metropolitan Statistical Area—see Appendix B for areas included
Source: U.S. Census Bureau, 2013-2017 American Community Survey 5-Year Estimates

Segregation

Type	1990	2000	2010	2010 Rank[2]	1990-2000	1990-2010	2000-2010
Black/White	60.7	58.1	56.2	49	-2.6	-4.4	-1.9
Asian/White	45.2	44.4	41.0	51	-0.8	-4.2	-3.4
Hispanic/White	24.3	46.0	47.9	34	21.6	23.5	1.9

Note: All figures cover the Metropolitan Statistical Area—see Appendix B for areas included; Figures are based on an analysis of 1990, 2000, and 2010 Census Decennial Census tract data by William H. Frey, Brookings Institution and the University of Michigan Social Science Data Analysis Network. In this analysis all racial groups (whites, blacks, and asians) are non-Hispanic members of those races. Hispanics are shown as a separate category; (1) Segregation Indices are Dissimilarity Indices that measure the degree to which the minority group is distributed differently than whites across census tracts. They range from 0 (complete integration) to 100 (complete segregation) where the value indicates the percentage of the minority group that needs to move to be distributed exactly like whites; (2) Ranges from 1 (most segregated) to 102 (least segregated); n/a not available.
Source: www.CensusScope.org

Ancestry

Area	German	Irish	English	American	Italian	Polish	French[2]	Scottish	Dutch
City	8.4	8.0	7.5	8.2	2.4	1.2	1.7	2.0	0.9
MSA[1]	10.3	10.1	9.5	12.5	2.7	1.4	1.9	2.3	1.0
U.S.	14.1	10.1	7.5	6.6	5.3	2.9	2.5	1.7	1.3

Note: Figures are the percentage of the total population reporting a particular ancestry. The nine most commonly reported ancestries in the U.S. are shown. Figures include multiple ancestries (e.g. if a person reported being Irish and Italian, they were included in both columns); (1) Figures cover the Nashville-Davidson—Murfreesboro—Franklin, TN Metropolitan Statistical Area—see Appendix B for areas included; (2) Excludes Basque
Source: U.S. Census Bureau, 2013-2017 American Community Survey 5-Year Estimates

Foreign-Born Population

Area	Percent of Population Born in								
	Any Foreign Country	Asia	Mexico	Europe	Carribean	Central America[2]	South America	Africa	Canada
City	12.8	3.9	3.0	0.7	0.4	1.7	0.4	2.4	0.2
MSA[1]	7.8	2.5	2.0	0.7	0.2	0.8	0.3	1.1	0.2
U.S.	13.4	4.1	3.6	1.5	1.3	1.0	0.9	0.6	0.3

Note: (1) Figures cover the Nashville-Davidson—Murfreesboro—Franklin, TN Metropolitan Statistical Area—see Appendix B for areas included; (2) Excludes Mexico.
Source: U.S. Census Bureau, 2013-2017 American Community Survey 5-Year Estimates

Marital Status

Area	Never Married	Now Married[2]	Separated	Widowed	Divorced
City	40.4	40.3	2.2	4.8	12.3
MSA[1]	31.4	50.1	1.8	5.0	11.6
U.S.	33.1	48.2	2.0	5.8	10.9

Note: Figures are percentages and cover the population 15 years of age and older; (1) Figures cover the Nashville-Davidson—Murfreesboro—Franklin, TN Metropolitan Statistical Area—see Appendix B for areas included; (2) Excludes separated
Source: U.S. Census Bureau, 2013-2017 American Community Survey 5-Year Estimates

Disability by Age

Area	All Ages	Under 18 Years Old	18 to 64 Years Old	65 Years and Over
City	11.8	3.8	10.3	37.0
MSA[1]	12.1	3.8	10.6	36.2
U.S.	12.6	4.2	10.3	35.5

Note: Figures show percent of the civilian noninstitutionalized population that reported having a disability. Disability status is determined from six types of difficulty: vision, hearing, cognitive, ambulatory, self-care, and independent living. For children under 5 years old, hearing and vision difficulty are used to determine disability status. For children between the ages of 5 and 14, disability status is determined from hearing, vision, cognitive, ambulatory, and self-care difficulties. For people aged 15 years and older, they are considered to have a disability if they have difficulty with any one of the six difficulty types; Note: (1) Figures cover the Nashville-Davidson—Murfreesboro—Franklin, TN Metropolitan Statistical Area—see Appendix B for areas included
Source: U.S. Census Bureau, 2013-2017 American Community Survey 5-Year Estimates

Age

Area	Percent of Population									Median Age
	Under Age 5	Age 5–19	Age 20–34	Age 35–44	Age 45–54	Age 55–64	Age 65–74	Age 75–84	Age 85+	
City	6.9	17.1	27.3	13.8	12.2	11.4	6.6	3.3	1.3	34.1
MSA[1]	6.5	19.6	22.0	13.7	13.7	12.1	7.6	3.5	1.3	36.3
U.S.	6.2	19.5	20.7	12.7	13.4	12.7	8.6	4.4	1.9	37.8

Note: (1) Figures cover the Nashville-Davidson—Murfreesboro—Franklin, TN Metropolitan Statistical Area—see Appendix B for areas included
Source: U.S. Census Bureau, 2013-2017 American Community Survey 5-Year Estimates

Gender

Area	Males	Females	Males per 100 Females
City	315,266	338,921	93.0
MSA[1]	893,066	937,344	95.3
U.S.	158,018,753	162,985,654	97.0

Note: (1) Figures cover the Nashville-Davidson—Murfreesboro—Franklin, TN Metropolitan Statistical Area—see Appendix B for areas included
Source: U.S. Census Bureau, 2013-2017 American Community Survey 5-Year Estimates

Religious Groups by Family

Area	Catholic	Baptist	Non-Den.	Methodist[2]	Lutheran	LDS[3]	Pente-costal	Presby-terian[4]	Muslim[5]	Judaism
MSA[1]	4.1	25.3	5.8	6.1	0.4	0.8	2.2	2.1	0.4	0.2
U.S.	19.1	9.3	4.0	4.0	2.3	2.0	1.9	1.6	0.8	0.7

Note: Figures are the number of adherents as a percentage of the total population; (1) Figures cover the Nashville-Davidson—Murfreesboro—Franklin, TN Metropolitan Statistical Area—see Appendix B for areas included; (2) Methodist/Pietist; (3) Latter Day Saints; (4) Reformed; (5) Figures are estimates
Source: Association of Statisticians of American Religious Bodies, 2010 U.S. Religion Census: Religious Congregations & Membership Study

Religious Groups by Tradition

Area	Catholic	Evangelical Protestant	Mainline Protestant	Other Tradition	Black Protestant	Orthodox
MSA[1]	4.1	33.0	8.0	1.7	3.4	0.5
U.S.	19.1	16.2	7.3	4.3	1.6	0.3

Note: Figures are the number of adherents as a percentage of the total population; (1) Figures cover the Nashville-Davidson—Murfreesboro—Franklin, TN Metropolitan Statistical Area—see Appendix B for areas included
Source: Association of Statisticians of American Religious Bodies, 2010 U.S. Religion Census: Religious Congregations & Membership Study

ECONOMY

Gross Metropolitan Product

Area	2016	2017	2018	2019	Rank[2]
MSA[1]	125.5	132.2	139.5	148.2	33

Note: Figures are in billions of dollars; (1) Figures cover the Nashville-Davidson—Murfreesboro—Franklin, TN Metropolitan Statistical Area—see Appendix B for areas included; (2) Rank is based on 2017 data and ranges from 1 to 381
Source: U.S. Conference of Mayors, U.S. Metro Economies: Economic Growth & Full Employment, June 2018

Economic Growth

Area	2017-2018 (%)	2019-2020 (%)	2021-2022 (%)
MSA[1]	3.5	3.2	2.2

Note: Figures are real gross metropolitan product (GMP) growth rates and represent average annual percent change; (1) Figures cover the Nashville-Davidson—Murfreesboro—Franklin, TN Metropolitan Statistical Area—see Appendix B for areas included
Source: U.S. Conference of Mayors, U.S. Metro Economies: Economic Growth & Full Employment, June 2018

Metropolitan Area Exports

Area	2012	2013	2014	2015	2016	2017	Rank[2]
MSA[1]	6,402.1	8,702.8	9,620.9	9,353.0	9,460.1	10,164.3	31

Note: Figures are in millions of dollars; (1) Figures cover the Nashville-Davidson—Murfreesboro—Franklin, TN Metropolitan Statistical Area—see Appendix B for areas included; (2) Rank is based on 2017 data and ranges from 1 to 387
Source: U.S. Department of Commerce, International Trade Administration, Office of Trade and Economic Analysis, Industry and Analysis, Exports by Metropolitan Area, extracted March 25, 2019

Building Permits

Area	Single-Family			Multi-Family			Total		
	2016	2017	Pct. Chg.	2016	2017	Pct. Chg.	2016	2017	Pct. Chg.
City	3,712	3,827	3.1	5,751	2,423	-57.9	9,463	6,250	-34.0
MSA[1]	12,830	13,650	6.4	7,352	6,981	-5.0	20,182	20,631	2.2
U.S.	750,800	820,000	9.2	455,800	462,000	1.4	1,206,600	1,282,000	6.2

Note: (1) Figures cover the Nashville-Davidson—Murfreesboro—Franklin, TN Metropolitan Statistical Area—see Appendix B for areas included; Figures represent new, privately-owned housing units authorized (unadjusted data); All permit data are based on estimates with imputation
Source: U.S. Census Bureau, Manufacturing, Mining, and Construction Statistics, Building Permits, 2016, 2017

Bankruptcy Filings

Area	Business Filings			Nonbusiness Filings		
	2017	2018	% Chg.	2017	2018	% Chg.
Davidson County	59	53	-10.2	2,274	2,050	-9.9
U.S.	23,157	22,232	-4.0	765,863	751,186	-1.9

Note: Business filings include Chapter 7, Chapter 11, Chapter 12, and Chapter 13; Nonbusiness filings include Chapter 7, Chapter 11, and Chapter 13
Source: Administrative Office of the U.S. Courts, Business and Nonbusiness Bankruptcy, County Cases Commenced by Chapter of the Bankruptcy Code, During the 12-Month Period Ending December 31, 2017 and Business and Nonbusiness Bankruptcy, County Cases Commenced by Chapter of the Bankruptcy Code, During the 12-Month Period Ending December 31, 2018

Housing Vacancy Rates

Area	Gross Vacancy Rate[2] (%)			Year-Round Vacancy Rate[3] (%)			Rental Vacancy Rate[4] (%)			Homeowner Vacancy Rate[5] (%)		
	2016	2017	2018	2016	2017	2018	2016	2017	2018	2016	2017	2018
MSA[1]	6.6	6.2	5.9	6.4	6.1	5.8	4.8	7.6	7.5	1.5	0.6	0.8
U.S.	12.8	12.7	12.3	9.9	9.9	9.7	6.9	7.2	6.9	1.7	1.6	1.5

Note: (1) Figures cover the Nashville-Davidson—Murfreesboro—Franklin, TN Metropolitan Statistical Area—see Appendix B for areas included; (2) The percentage of the total housing inventory that is vacant; (3) The percentage of the housing inventory (excluding seasonal units) that is year-round vacant; (4) The percentage of rental inventory that is vacant for rent; (5) The percentage of homeowner inventory that is vacant for sale
Source: U.S. Census Bureau, Housing Vacancies and Homeownership Annual Statistics: 2016, 2017, 2018

INCOME

Income

Area	Per Capita ($)	Median Household ($)	Average Household ($)
City	31,109	52,858	74,021
MSA[1]	31,873	59,365	81,795
U.S.	31,177	57,652	81,283

Note: (1) Figures cover the Nashville-Davidson—Murfreesboro—Franklin, TN Metropolitan Statistical Area—see Appendix B for areas included
Source: U.S. Census Bureau, 2013-2017 American Community Survey 5-Year Estimates

Household Income Distribution

Area	Percent of Households Earning							
	Under $15,000	$15,000 -$24,999	$25,000 -$34,999	$35,000 -$49,999	$50,000 -$74,999	$75,000 -$99,999	$100,000 -$149,999	$150,000 and up
City	11.5	10.0	10.3	15.1	19.4	12.4	12.1	9.2
MSA[1]	9.5	9.1	9.4	14.0	19.3	13.3	14.2	11.3
U.S.	11.6	9.8	9.5	13.0	17.7	12.3	14.1	12.1

Note: (1) Figures cover the Nashville-Davidson—Murfreesboro—Franklin, TN Metropolitan Statistical Area—see Appendix B for areas included
Source: U.S. Census Bureau, 2013-2017 American Community Survey 5-Year Estimates

Poverty Rate

Area	All Ages	Under 18 Years Old	18 to 64 Years Old	65 Years and Over
City	17.2	28.2	15.0	8.7
MSA[1]	12.8	18.2	11.8	7.7
U.S.	14.6	20.3	13.7	9.3

Note: Figures are percentage of people whose income during the past 12 months was below the poverty level; (1) Figures cover the Nashville-Davidson—Murfreesboro—Franklin, TN Metropolitan Statistical Area—see Appendix B for areas included
Source: U.S. Census Bureau, 2013-2017 American Community Survey 5-Year Estimates

EMPLOYMENT

Labor Force and Employment

Area	Civilian Labor Force			Workers Employed		
	Dec. 2017	Dec. 2018	% Chg.	Dec. 2017	Dec. 2018	% Chg.
City	389,865	398,504	2.2	381,000	389,436	2.2
MSA[1]	1,015,902	1,037,452	2.1	991,652	1,013,224	2.2
U.S.	159,880,000	162,510,000	1.6	153,602,000	156,481,000	1.9

Note: Data is not seasonally adjusted and covers workers 16 years of age and older; (1) Figures cover the Nashville-Davidson—Murfreesboro—Franklin, TN Metropolitan Statistical Area—see Appendix B for areas included
Source: Bureau of Labor Statistics, Local Area Unemployment Statistics

Unemployment Rate

Area	2018											
	Jan.	Feb.	Mar.	Apr.	May	Jun.	Jul.	Aug.	Sep.	Oct.	Nov.	Dec.
City	2.7	2.6	2.6	2.1	2.2	3.1	3.0	3.0	2.9	2.9	2.6	2.3
MSA[1]	2.8	2.7	2.7	2.2	2.3	3.2	3.2	3.1	3.0	2.9	2.6	2.3
U.S.	4.5	4.4	4.1	3.7	3.6	4.2	4.1	3.9	3.6	3.5	3.5	3.7

Note: Data is not seasonally adjusted and covers workers 16 years of age and older; (1) Figures cover the Nashville-Davidson—Murfreesboro—Franklin, TN Metropolitan Statistical Area—see Appendix B for areas included
Source: Bureau of Labor Statistics, Local Area Unemployment Statistics

Average Wages

Occupation	$/Hr.	Occupation	$/Hr.
Accountants and Auditors	33.20	Maids and Housekeeping Cleaners	11.40
Automotive Mechanics	20.00	Maintenance and Repair Workers	19.10
Bookkeepers	20.70	Marketing Managers	61.00
Carpenters	20.70	Nuclear Medicine Technologists	37.60
Cashiers	10.90	Nurses, Licensed Practical	20.80
Clerks, General Office	18.10	Nurses, Registered	30.70
Clerks, Receptionists/Information	14.10	Nursing Assistants	13.30
Clerks, Shipping/Receiving	15.40	Packers and Packagers, Hand	11.90
Computer Programmers	41.80	Physical Therapists	34.70
Computer Systems Analysts	38.10	Postal Service Mail Carriers	24.70
Computer User Support Specialists	24.30	Real Estate Brokers	43.50
Cooks, Restaurant	12.50	Retail Salespersons	14.60
Dentists	90.40	Sales Reps., Exc. Tech./Scientific	31.00
Electrical Engineers	42.80	Sales Reps., Tech./Scientific	40.90
Electricians	23.80	Secretaries, Exc. Legal/Med./Exec.	17.60
Financial Managers	59.40	Security Guards	13.30
First-Line Supervisors/Managers, Sales	20.70	Surgeons	n/a
Food Preparation Workers	11.00	Teacher Assistants*	12.50
General and Operations Managers	57.40	Teachers, Elementary School*	25.30
Hairdressers/Cosmetologists	14.20	Teachers, Secondary School*	25.80
Internists, General	95.90	Telemarketers	15.20
Janitors and Cleaners	12.80	Truck Drivers, Heavy/Tractor-Trailer	22.90
Landscaping/Groundskeeping Workers	12.50	Truck Drivers, Light/Delivery Svcs.	17.60
Lawyers	61.00	Waiters and Waitresses	9.60

Note: Wage data covers the Nashville-Davidson—Murfreesboro—Franklin, TN Metropolitan Statistical Area—see Appendix B for areas included; (*) Hourly wages for elementary/secondary school teachers and teacher assistants were calculated by the editors from annual wage data based on a 40 hour work week; n/a not available.
Source: Bureau of Labor Statistics, Metro Area Occupational Employment & Wage Estimates, May 2018

Employment by Occupation

Occupation Classification	City (%)	MSA[1] (%)	U.S. (%)
Management, Business, Science, and Arts	40.1	38.8	37.4
Natural Resources, Construction, and Maintenance	7.4	8.1	8.9
Production, Transportation, and Material Moving	11.3	12.6	12.2
Sales and Office	24.1	24.9	23.5
Service	17.1	15.5	18.0

Note: Figures cover employed civilians 16 years of age and older; (1) Figures cover the Nashville-Davidson—Murfreesboro—Franklin, TN Metropolitan Statistical Area—see Appendix B for areas included
Source: U.S. Census Bureau, 2013-2017 American Community Survey 5-Year Estimates

Employment by Industry

Sector	MSA[1] Number of Employees	MSA[1] Percent of Total	U.S. Percent of Total
Construction, Mining, and Logging	47,300	4.6	5.3
Education and Health Services	154,800	14.9	15.9
Financial Activities	69,100	6.7	5.7
Government	123,500	11.9	15.1
Information	23,700	2.3	1.9
Leisure and Hospitality	116,600	11.3	10.7
Manufacturing	83,800	8.1	8.5
Other Services	42,800	4.1	3.9
Professional and Business Services	171,200	16.5	14.1
Retail Trade	106,300	10.3	10.8
Transportation, Warehousing, and Utilities	55,000	5.3	4.2
Wholesale Trade	41,900	4.0	3.9

Note: Figures are non-farm employment as of December 2018. Figures are not seasonally adjusted and include workers 16 years of age and older; (1) Figures cover the Nashville-Davidson—Murfreesboro—Franklin, TN Metropolitan Statistical Area—see Appendix B for areas included
Source: Bureau of Labor Statistics, Current Employment Statistics, Employment, Hours, and Earnings

Occupations with Greatest Projected Employment Growth: 2018 – 2020

Occupation[1]	2018 Employment	2020 Projected Employment	Numeric Employment Change	Percent Employment Change
Combined Food Preparation and Serving Workers, Including Fast Food	78,410	82,150	3,740	4.8
Registered Nurses	59,710	61,550	1,840	3.1
Waiters and Waitresses	54,060	55,870	1,810	3.3
General and Operations Managers	47,640	49,430	1,790	3.8
Laborers and Freight, Stock, and Material Movers, Hand	99,140	100,740	1,600	1.6
Customer Service Representatives	61,220	62,780	1,560	2.5
Janitors and Cleaners, Except Maids and Housekeeping Cleaners	43,260	44,680	1,420	3.3
Stock Clerks and Order Fillers	54,500	55,920	1,420	2.6
Security Guards	24,930	26,160	1,230	4.9
Maintenance and Repair Workers, General	32,360	33,580	1,220	3.8

Note: Projections cover Tennessee; (1) Sorted by numeric employment change
Source: www.projectionscentral.com, State Occupational Projections, 2018–2020 Short-Term Projections

Fastest Growing Occupations: 2018 – 2020

Occupation[1]	2018 Employment	2020 Projected Employment	Numeric Employment Change	Percent Employment Change
Dietetic Technicians	720	810	90	12.5
Operations Research Analysts	1,910	2,080	170	8.9
Fiberglass Laminators and Fabricators	570	620	50	8.8
Software Developers, Applications	6,520	7,080	560	8.6
Home Health Aides	6,680	7,240	560	8.4
Helpers—Brickmasons, Blockmasons, Stonemasons, and Tile and Marble Setters	740	800	60	8.1
Real Estate Brokers	1,130	1,220	90	8.0
Statisticians	650	700	50	7.7
Physician Assistants	1,650	1,770	120	7.3
Brokerage Clerks	1,100	1,180	80	7.3

Note: Projections cover Tennessee; (1) Sorted by percent employment change and excludes occupations with numeric employment change less than 50
Source: www.projectionscentral.com, State Occupational Projections, 2018–2020 Short-Term Projections

TAXES

State Corporate Income Tax Rates

State	Tax Rate (%)	Income Brackets ($)	Num. of Brackets	Financial Institution Tax Rate (%)[a]	Federal Income Tax Ded.
Tennessee	6.5	Flat rate	1	6.5	No

Note: Tax rates as of January 1, 2019; (a) Rates listed are the corporate income tax rate applied to financial institutions or excise taxes based on income. Some states have other taxes based upon the value of deposits or shares.
Source: Federation of Tax Administrators, Range of State Corporate Income Tax Rates, January 1, 2019

State Individual Income Tax Rates

State	Tax Rate (%)	Income Brackets ($)	Personal Exemptions ($)			Standard Ded. ($)	
			Single	Married	Depend.	Single	Married
Tennessee		– State income tax of 2% on dividends and interest income only (x) –					

Note: Tax rates as of January 1, 2019; Local- and county-level taxes are not included; n/a not applicable; Federal income tax is not deductible on state income tax returns; (x) Tennessee Hall Tax Rate on Dividends and Interest is being phased out, 1% reduction each year
Source: Federation of Tax Administrators, State Individual Income Tax Rates, January 1, 2019

Various State Sales and Excise Tax Rates

State	State Sales Tax (%)	Gasoline[1] (¢/gal.)	Cigarette[2] ($/pack)	Spirits[3] ($/gal.)	Wine[4] ($/gal.)	Beer[5] ($/gal.)	Recreational Marijuana (%)
Tennessee	7	26.4	0.62	4.46 (i)	1.27 (o)	1.29 (u)	Not legal

Note: All tax rates as of January 1, 2019; (1) The American Petroleum Institute has developed a methodology for determining the average tax rate on a gallon of fuel. Rates may include any of the following: excise taxes, environmental fees, storage tank fees, other fees or taxes, general sales tax, and local taxes. In states where gasoline is subject to the general sales tax, or where the fuel tax is based on the average sale price, the average rate determined by API is sensitive to changes in the price of gasoline. States that fully or partially apply general sales taxes to gasoline: CA, CO, GA, IL, IN, MI, NY; (2) The federal excise tax of $1.0066 per pack and local taxes are not included; (3) Rates are those applicable to off-premise sales of 40% alcohol by volume (a.b.v.) distilled spirits in 750ml containers. Local excise taxes are excluded; (4) Rates are those applicable to off-premise sales of 11% a.b.v. non-carbonated wine in 750ml containers; (5) Rates are those applicable to off-premise sales of 4.7% a.b.v. beer in 12 ounce containers; (i) Includes case fees and/or bottle fees which may vary with size of container; (o) Includes case fees and/or bottle fees which may vary with size of container; (u) Includes the wholesale tax rate in Kentucky (10%) and Tennessee (17%), converted into a gallonage excise tax rate.
Source: Tax Foundation, 2019 Facts & Figures: How Does Your State Compare?

State Business Tax Climate Index Rankings

State	Overall Rank	Corporate Tax Rank	Individual Income Tax Rank	Sales Tax Rank	Unemployment Insurance Tax Rank	Property Tax Rank
Tennessee	16	24	8	46	22	29

Note: The index is a measure of how each state's tax laws affect economic performance. The lower the rank, the more favorable a state's tax system is for business. States without a given tax are given a ranking of 1. The scores/rankings for the District of Columbia do not affect other states. The 2019 index represents the tax climate as of July 1, 2018.
Source: Tax Foundation, State Business Tax Climate Index 2019

**COMMERCIAL
REAL ESTATE**

Office Market

Market Area	Inventory (sq. ft.)	Vacancy Rate (%)	Under Construction (sq. ft.)	YTD Net Absorption (sq. ft.)	Total Average Asking Rent ($/sq. ft./year)
Nashville	54,155,805	8.0	808,000	341,502	27.25
National	4,905,867,938	13.1	83,553,714	45,846,470	28.46

Source: Newmark Grubb Knight Frank, National Office Market Report, 4th Quarter 2018

Industrial/Warehouse/R&D Market

Market Area	Inventory (sq. ft.)	Vacancy Rate (%)	Under Construction (sq. ft.)	YTD Net Absorption (sq. ft.)	Total Average Asking Rent ($/sq. ft./year)
Nashville	238,280,706	3.5	6,630,897	2,290,124	5.87
National	14,796,839,085	5.0	262,662,294	238,014,726	7.16

Source: Newmark Grubb Knight Frank, National Industrial Market Report, 4th Quarter 2018

**COMMERCIAL
UTILITIES**

Typical Monthly Electric Bills

Area	General Service, Light ($/month)		General Service, Heavy ($/month)	
	40 kW demand 5,000 kWh	100 kW demand 10,000 kWh	500 kW demand 100,000 kWh	1,500 kW demand 500,000 kWh
City	689	2,183	14,195	55,560

Note: Figures are based on rates in effect January 1, 2018
Source: Memphis Light, Gas and Water, 2018 Utility Bill Comparisons for Selected U.S. Cities

TRANSPORTATION

Means of Transportation to Work

Area	Car/Truck/Van		Public Transportation			Bicycle	Walked	Other Means	Worked at Home
	Drove Alone	Car-pooled	Bus	Subway	Railroad				
City	79.1	9.9	2.1	0.0	0.1	0.2	2.1	1.0	5.6
MSA[1]	81.8	9.3	1.0	0.0	0.1	0.1	1.3	1.1	5.4
U.S.	76.4	9.2	2.5	1.9	0.6	0.6	2.7	1.3	4.7

Note: Figures are percentages and cover workers 16 years of age and older; (1) Figures cover the Nashville-Davidson—Murfreesboro—Franklin, TN Metropolitan Statistical Area—see Appendix B for areas included
Source: U.S. Census Bureau, 2013-2017 American Community Survey 5-Year Estimates

Travel Time to Work

Area	Less Than 10 Minutes	10 to 19 Minutes	20 to 29 Minutes	30 to 44 Minutes	45 to 59 Minutes	60 to 89 Minutes	90 Minutes or More
City	8.5	29.3	27.8	23.3	6.2	3.4	1.4
MSA[1]	9.4	26.8	22.3	23.4	10.0	6.2	1.9
U.S.	12.7	28.9	20.9	20.5	8.1	6.2	2.7

Note: Note: Figures are percentages and include workers 16 years old and over; (1) Figures cover the Nashville-Davidson—Murfreesboro—Franklin, TN Metropolitan Statistical Area—see Appendix B for areas included
Source: U.S. Census Bureau, 2013-2017 American Community Survey 5-Year Estimates

Freeway Travel Time Index

Area	1985	1990	1995	2000	2005	2010	2014
Urban Area Rank[1,2]	26	34	36	34	32	39	34
Urban Area Index[1]	1.10	1.12	1.15	1.19	1.22	1.19	1.21
Average Index[3]	1.09	1.11	1.14	1.17	1.20	1.19	1.20

Note: Freeway Travel Time Index—the ratio of travel time in the peak period to the travel time at free-flow conditions. For example, a value of 1.30 indicates a 20-minute free-flow trip takes 26 minutes in the peak (20 minutes x 1.30 = 26 minutes); (1) Covers the Nashville-Davidson TN urban area; (2) Rank is based on 101 urban areas (#1 = highest travel time index); (3) Average of 101 urban areas
Source: Texas Transportation Institute, 2015 Urban Mobility Scorecard, August 2015

Freeway Commuter Stress Index

Area	1985	1990	1995	2000	2005	2010	2014
Urban Area Rank[1,2]	30	33	33	32	30	34	33
Urban Area Index[1]	1.16	1.18	1.22	1.26	1.29	1.26	1.27
Average Index[3]	1.13	1.16	1.19	1.22	1.25	1.24	1.25

Note: The Freeway Commuter Stress Index is the same as the Freeway Travel Time Index (see table above) except that it includes only the travel in the peak directions during the peak periods; the TTI includes travel in all directions during the peak period. Thus, the CSI is more indicative of the work trip experienced by each commuter on a daily basis; (1) Covers the Nashville-Davidson TN urban area; (2) Rank is based on 101 urban areas (#1 = highest travel time index); (3) Average of 101 urban areas
Source: Texas Transportation Institute, 2015 Urban Mobility Scorecard, August 2015

Public Transportation

Agency Name / Mode of Transportation	Vehicles Operated in Maximum Service[1]	Annual Unlinked Passenger Trips[2] (in thous.)	Annual Passenger Miles[3] (in thous.)
Metropolitan Transit Authority (MTA)			
Bus (directly operated)	126	8,859.1	39,182.2
Commuter Bus (directly operated)	23	328.5	4,441.3
Demand Response (directly operated)	63	303.4	3,086.2
Demand Response Taxi (purchased transportation)	50	154.7	1,594.0

Note: (1) The number of revenue vehicles operated by the given mode and type of service to meet the annual maximum service requirement. This is the revenue vehicle count during the peak season of the year; on the week and day that maximum service is provided. Vehicles operated in maximum service (VOMS) exclude atypical days and one-time special events; (2) The number of passengers who boarded public transportation vehicles. Passengers are counted each time they board a vehicle no matter how many vehicles they use to travel from their origin to their destination. (3) The sum of the distances ridden by all passengers during the entire fiscal year.
Source: Federal Transit Administration, National Transit Database, 2017

Air Transportation

Airport Name and Code / Type of Service	Passenger Airlines[1]	Passenger Enplanements	Freight Carriers[2]	Freight (lbs)
Nashville International (BNA)				
Domestic service (U.S. carriers - 2018)	37	7,687,942	16	57,235,527
International service (U.S. carriers - 2017)	8	13,016	1	50,054

Note: (1) Includes all U.S.-based major, minor and commuter airlines that carried at least one passenger during the year; (2) Includes all U.S.-based airlines and freight carriers that transported at least one pound of freight during the year.
Source: Bureau of Transportation Statistics, The Intermodal Transportation Database, Air Carriers: T-100 Domestic Market (U.S. Carriers), 2018; Bureau of Transportation Statistics, The Intermodal Transportation Database, Air Carriers: T-100 International Market (U.S. Carriers), 2017

Other Transportation Statistics

Major Highways: I-24; I-40; I-65
Amtrak Service: Bus connection
Major Waterways/Ports: Cumberland River; Port of Nashville
Source: Amtrak.com; Google Maps

BUSINESSES

Major Business Headquarters

Company Name	Industry	Rankings	
		Fortune[1]	Forbes[2]
Envision Healthcare	Health Care: Pharmacy and Other Services	198	-
HCA Healthcare	Health Care: Medical Facilities	63	-
Ingram Industries	Multicompany	-	195

Note: (1) Companies that produce a 10-K are ranked 1 to 500 based on 2017 revenue; (2) All private companies with at least $2 billion in annual revenue through the end of their most current fiscal year are ranked 1 to 229; companies listed are headquartered in the city; dashes indicate no ranking
Source: Fortune, "Fortune 500," June 2018; Forbes, "America's Largest Private Companies," 2018 Rankings

Fast-Growing Businesses

According to *Inc.*, Nashville is home to one of America's 500 fastest-growing private companies: **Aspire Health** (#189). Criteria: must be an independent, privately-held, for-profit, U.S. corporation, proprietorship or partnership as of December 31, 2017; revenues must be at least

$100,000 in 2014 and $2 million in 2017; must have four-year operating/sales history. Holding companies, regulated banks, and utilities were excluded. *Inc., "America's 500 Fastest-Growing Private Companies," 2018*

Minority Business Opportunity

Nashville is home to one company which is on the *Black Enterprise* Bank list (15 largest banks based on total assets, capital, deposits and loans, including mortgage-backed securities for the calendar year): **Citizens Savings Bank & Trust Co.** (#12). Only commercial banks or savings and loans that are classified by the Federal Reserve as black institutions and have been fully operational for the previous calendar year were considered. *Black Enterprise, B.E. 100s, 2018*

Minority- and Women-Owned Businesses

Group	All Firms		Firms with Paid Employees			
	Firms	Sales ($000)	Firms	Sales ($000)	Employees	Payroll ($000)
AIAN[1]	483	325,191	43	(s)	250 - 499	(s)
Asian	3,049	1,084,746	707	947,954	5,104	152,910
Black	9,516	550,218	541	357,584	4,402	117,376
Hispanic	3,352	328,538	215	210,843	2,050	46,057
NHOPI[2]	51	(s)	18	(s)	100 - 249	(s)
Women	24,115	3,871,085	2,135	3,261,124	16,036	599,259
All Firms	68,228	86,579,590	12,741	83,792,750	344,967	16,176,242

Note: Figures cover firms located in the city; minority- and women-owned business are defined as firms in which the corresponding group own 51% or more of the stock or equity of the company; (1) American Indian and Alaska Native; (2) Native Hawaiian and Other Pacific Islander; (s) estimates are suppressed when publication standards are not met
Source: U.S. Census Bureau, 2012 Economic Census, Survey of Business Owners

HOTELS & CONVENTION CENTERS

Hotels, Motels and Vacation Rentals

Area	5 Star		4 Star		3 Star		2 Star		1 Star		Not Rated	
	Num.	Pct.[3]	Num.	Pct.[3]	Num.	Pct.[3]	Num.	Pct.[3]	Num.	Pct.[3]	Num.	Pct.[3]
City[1]	1	0.0	118	5.9	350	17.5	217	10.8	6	0.3	1,310	65.4
Total[2]	286	0.4	5,236	7.1	16,715	22.6	10,259	13.9	293	0.4	41,056	55.6

Note: (1) Figures cover Nashville and vicinity; (2) Figures cover all 100 cities in this book; (3) Percentage of hotels which have a given star rating; Star ratings are determined by expedia.com and offer an indication of the general quality of a particular hotel.
Source: www.expedia.com, April 3, 2019

Major Convention Centers

Name	Overall Space (sq. ft.)	Exhibit Space (sq. ft.)	Meeting Space (sq. ft.)	Meeting Rooms
Mid-TN Expo Convention Center	40,000	n/a	n/a	n/a
Nashville Convention Center	n/a	118,675	n/a	25

Note: Table includes convention centers located in the Nashville-Davidson—Murfreesboro—Franklin, TN metro area; n/a not available
Source: Original research

Living Environment

COST OF LIVING

Cost of Living Index

Composite Index	Groceries	Housing	Utilities	Trans-portation	Health Care	Misc. Goods/ Services
99.3	95.3	93.4	96.7	94.7	83.9	109.6

Note: The Cost of Living Index measures regional differences in the cost of consumer goods and services, excluding taxes and non-consumer expenditures, for professional and managerial households in the top income quintile. It is based on more than 50,000 prices covering almost 60 different items for which prices are collected three times a year by chambers of commerce, economic development organizations or university applied economic centers in each participating urban area. The numbers shown should be read as a percentage above or below the national average of 100. For example, a value of 115.4 in the groceries column indicates that grocery prices are 15.4% higher than the national average. Small differences in the index numbers should not be interpreted as significant; Figures cover the Nashville-Murfreesboro TN urban area.
Source: The Council for Community and Economic Research, ACCRA Cost of Living Index, 2018

Grocery Prices

Area[1]	T-Bone Steak ($/pound)	Frying Chicken ($/pound)	Whole Milk ($/half gal.)	Eggs ($/dozen)	Orange Juice ($/64 oz.)	Coffee ($/11.5 oz.)
City[2]	12.08	1.16	1.78	1.51	3.22	4.03
Avg.	11.35	1.42	1.94	1.81	3.52	4.35
Min.	7.45	0.92	0.80	0.75	2.72	3.06
Max.	15.05	2.76	4.18	4.00	5.36	8.20

Note: (1) Values for the local area are compared with the average, minimum and maximum values for all 291 areas in the Cost of Living Index; (2) Figures cover the Nashville-Murfreesboro TN urban area; **T-Bone Steak** (price per pound); **Frying Chicken** (price per pound, whole fryer); **Whole Milk** (half gallon carton); **Eggs** (price per dozen, Grade A, large); **Orange Juice** (64 oz. Tropicana or Florida Natural); **Coffee** (11.5 oz. can, vacuum-packed, Maxwell House, Hills Bros, or Folgers).
Source: The Council for Community and Economic Research, ACCRA Cost of Living Index, 2018

Housing and Utility Costs

Area[1]	New Home Price ($)	Apartment Rent ($/month)	All Electric ($/month)	Part Electric ($/month)	Other Energy ($/month)	Telephone ($/month)
City[2]	318,571	1,029	-	94.60	62.48	179.40
Avg.	347,000	1,087	165.93	100.16	67.73	178.70
Min.	200,468	500	93.58	25.64	26.78	163.10
Max.	1,901,222	4,888	388.65	246.86	332.81	197.70

Note: (1) Values for the local area are compared with the average, minimum and maximum values for all 291 areas in the Cost of Living Index; (2) Figures cover the Nashville-Murfreesboro TN urban area; **New Home Price** (2,400 sf living area, 8,000 sf lot, in urban area with full utilities); **Apartment Rent** (950 sf 2 bedroom/1.5 or 2 bath, unfurnished, excluding all utilities except water); **All Electric** (average monthly cost for an all-electric home); **Part Electric** (average monthly cost for a part-electric home); **Other Energy** (average monthly cost for natural gas, fuel oil, coal, wood, and any other forms of energy except electricity); **Telephone** (price includes the base monthly rate plus taxes and fees for three lines of mobile phone service).
Source: The Council for Community and Economic Research, ACCRA Cost of Living Index, 2018

Health Care, Transportation, and Other Costs

Area[1]	Doctor ($/visit)	Dentist ($/visit)	Optometrist ($/visit)	Gasoline ($/gallon)	Beauty Salon ($/visit)	Men's Shirt ($)
City[2]	94.52	74.93	79.10	2.49	45.67	39.40
Avg.	110.71	95.11	103.74	2.61	37.48	32.03
Min.	33.60	62.55	54.63	1.89	17.00	11.44
Max.	195.97	153.93	225.79	3.59	71.88	58.64

Note: (1) Values for the local area are compared with the average, minimum and maximum values for all 291 areas in the Cost of Living Index; (2) Figures cover the Nashville-Murfreesboro TN urban area; **Doctor** (general practitioners routine exam of an established patient); **Dentist** (adult teeth cleaning and periodic oral examination); **Optometrist** (full vision eye exam for established adult patient); **Gasoline** (one gallon regular unleaded, national brand, including all taxes, cash price at self-service pump if available); **Beauty Salon** (woman's shampoo, trim, and blow-dry); **Men's Shirt** (cotton/polyester dress shirt, pinpoint weave, long sleeves).
Source: The Council for Community and Economic Research, ACCRA Cost of Living Index, 2018

HOUSING

House Price Index (HPI)

Area	National Ranking[2]	Quarterly Change (%)	One-Year Change (%)	Five-Year Change (%)
MSA[1]	46	1.21	8.84	53.68
U.S.[3]	–	1.12	5.73	32.81

Note: The HPI is a weighted repeat sales index. It measures average price changes in repeat sales or refinancings on the same properties. This information is obtained by reviewing repeat mortgage transactions on single-family properties whose mortgages have been purchased or securitized by Fannie Mae or Freddie Mac in January 1975; (1) Figures cover the Nashville-Davidson—Murfreesboro—Franklin, TN Metropolitan Statistical Area—see Appendix B for areas included; (2) Rankings are based on annual percentage change for all metro areas containing at least 15,000 transactions over the last 10 years and ranges from 1 to 245; (3) figures based on a weighted average of Census Division estimates using a seasonally adjusted, purchase-only index; all figures are for the period ending December 31, 2018
Source: Federal Housing Finance Agency, House Price Index, February 26, 2019

Median Single-Family Home Prices

Area	2016	2017	2018[P]	Percent Change 2017 to 2018
MSA[1]	224.5	241.7	260.5	7.8
U.S. Average	235.5	248.8	261.6	5.1

Note: Figures are median sales prices of existing single-family homes in thousands of dollars; (p) preliminary; (1) Figures cover the Nashville-Davidson—Murfreesboro—Franklin, TN Metropolitan Statistical Area—see Appendix B for areas included
Source: National Association of Realtors, Median Sales Price of Existing Single-Family Homes for Metropolitan Areas, 4th Quarter 2018

Qualifying Income Based on Median Sales Price of Existing Single-Family Homes

Area	With 5% Down ($)	With 10% Down ($)	With 20% Down ($)
MSA[1]	64,518	61,122	54,331
U.S. Average	62,954	59,640	53,013

Note: Figures are preliminary; Qualifying income is based on a mortgage rate of 4.9%. Monthly principal and interest payment is limited to 25% of income; (1) Figures cover the Nashville-Davidson—Murfreesboro—Franklin, TN Metropolitan Statistical Area—see Appendix B for areas included
Source: National Association of Realtors, Qualifying Income Based on Median Sales Price of Existing Single-Family Homes for Metropolitan Areas, 4th Quarter 2018

Median Apartment Condo-Coop Home Prices

Area	2016	2017	2018[P]	Percent Change 2017 to 2018
MSA[1]	n/a	n/a	n/a	n/a
U.S. Average	220.7	234.3	241.0	2.9

Note: Figures are median sales prices of existing apartment condo-coop homes in thousands of dollars; (p) preliminary; n/a not available; (1) Figures cover the Nashville-Davidson—Murfreesboro—Franklin, TN Metropolitan Statistical Area—see Appendix B for areas included
Source: National Association of Realtors, Median Sales Price of Existing Apartment Condo-Coop Homes for Metropolitan Areas, 4th Quarter 2018

Home Value Distribution

Area	Under $50,000	$50,000 -$99,999	$100,000 -$149,999	$150,000 -$199,999	$200,000 -$299,999	$300,000 -$499,999	$500,000 -$999,999	$1,000,000 or more
City	3.0	8.1	21.0	20.5	21.5	17.1	7.3	1.4
MSA[1]	4.0	8.9	19.2	18.8	22.0	17.4	7.9	1.7
U.S.	8.3	13.9	14.7	14.6	18.7	17.3	9.7	2.7

Note: Figures are percentages and cover owner-occupied housing units; (1) Figures cover the Nashville-Davidson—Murfreesboro—Franklin, TN Metropolitan Statistical Area—see Appendix B for areas included
Source: U.S. Census Bureau, 2013-2017 American Community Survey 5-Year Estimates

Homeownership Rate

Area	2010 (%)	2011 (%)	2012 (%)	2013 (%)	2014 (%)	2015 (%)	2016 (%)	2017 (%)	2018 (%)
MSA[1]	70.4	69.6	64.9	63.9	67.1	67.4	65.0	69.4	68.3
U.S.	66.9	66.1	65.4	65.1	64.5	63.7	63.4	63.9	64.4

Note: (1) Figures cover the Nashville-Davidson—Murfreesboro—Franklin, TN Metropolitan Statistical Area—see Appendix B for areas included
Source: U.S. Census Bureau, Housing Vacancies and Homeownership Annual Statistics: 2010-2018

Year Housing Structure Built

Area	2010 or Later	2000 -2009	1990 -1999	1980 -1989	1970 -1979	1960 -1969	1950 -1959	1940 -1949	Before 1940	Median Year
City	4.7	15.2	12.3	16.1	15.4	13.4	11.7	5.0	6.3	1979
MSA[1]	5.9	20.9	18.7	14.9	14.0	9.9	7.5	3.4	4.8	1987
U.S.	3.2	14.5	14.0	13.6	15.5	10.8	10.5	5.1	12.9	1977

Note: Figures are percentages except for Median Year; Note: (1) Figures cover the Nashville-Davidson—Murfreesboro—Franklin, TN Metropolitan Statistical Area—see Appendix B for areas included
Source: U.S. Census Bureau, 2013-2017 American Community Survey 5-Year Estimates

Gross Monthly Rent

Area	Under $500	$500 -$999	$1,000 -$1,499	$1,500 -$1,999	$2,000 -$2,499	$2,500 -$2,999	$3,000 and up	Median ($)
City	9.4	44.0	34.2	8.7	2.6	0.7	0.4	970
MSA[1]	9.4	46.0	32.3	8.4	2.5	0.8	0.6	951
U.S.	10.5	41.1	28.7	11.7	4.5	1.8	1.7	982

Note: Figures are percentages except for Median; Gross rent is the contract rent plus the estimated average monthly cost of utilities (electricity, gas, and water and sewer) and fuels (oil, coal, kerosene, wood, etc.) if these are paid by the renter (or paid for the renter by someone else); (1) Figures cover the Nashville-Davidson—Murfreesboro—Franklin, TN Metropolitan Statistical Area—see Appendix B for areas included
Source: U.S. Census Bureau, 2013-2017 American Community Survey 5-Year Estimates

HEALTH

Health Risk Factors

Category	MSA[1] (%)	U.S. (%)
Adults aged 18–64 who have any kind of health care coverage	85.8	87.3
Adults who reported being in good or better health	85.6	82.4
Adults who have been told they have high blood cholesterol	33.7	33.0
Adults who have been told they have high blood pressure	34.7	32.3
Adults who are current smokers	15.9	17.1
Adults who currently use E-cigarettes	6.2	4.6
Adults who currently use chewing tobacco, snuff, or snus	4.5	4.0
Adults who are heavy drinkers[2]	5.0	6.3
Adults who are binge drinkers[3]	14.5	17.4
Adults who are overweight (BMI 25.0 - 29.9)	37.2	35.3
Adults who are obese (BMI 30.0 - 99.8)	28.2	31.3
Adults who participated in any physical activities in the past month	74.9	74.4
Adults who always or nearly always wears a seat belt	94.0	94.3

Note: (1) Figures cover the Nashville-Davidson—Murfreesboro—Franklin, TN Metropolitan Statistical Area—see Appendix B for areas included; (2) Heavy drinkers are classified as adult men having more than 14 drinks per week and adult women having more than 7 drinks per week; (3) Binge drinkers are classified as males having five or more drinks on one occasion or females having four or more drinks on one occasion
Source: Centers for Disease Control and Prevention, Behaviorial Risk Factor Surveillance System, SMART: Selected Metropolitan Area Risk Trends, 2017

Acute and Chronic Health Conditions

Category	MSA[1] (%)	U.S. (%)
Adults who have ever been told they had a heart attack	5.6	4.2
Adults who have ever been told they have angina or coronary heart disease	3.7	3.9
Adults who have ever been told they had a stroke	3.7	3.0
Adults who have ever been told they have asthma	15.0	14.2
Adults who have ever been told they have arthritis	25.4	24.9
Adults who have ever been told they have diabetes[2]	11.8	10.5
Adults who have ever been told they had skin cancer	5.4	6.2
Adults who have ever been told they had any other types of cancer	7.4	7.1
Adults who have ever been told they have COPD	6.4	6.5
Adults who have ever been told they have kidney disease	4.0	3.0
Adults who have ever been told they have a form of depression	21.2	20.5

Note: (1) Figures cover the Nashville-Davidson—Murfreesboro—Franklin, TN Metropolitan Statistical Area—see Appendix B for areas included; (2) Figures do not include pregnancy-related, borderline, or pre-diabetes
Source: Centers for Disease Control and Prevention, Behaviorial Risk Factor Surveillance System, SMART: Selected Metropolitan Area Risk Trends, 2017

Health Screening and Vaccination Rates

Category	MSA[1] (%)	U.S. (%)
Adults aged 65+ who have had flu shot within the past year	53.3	60.7
Adults aged 65+ who have ever had a pneumonia vaccination	75.4	75.4
Adults who have ever been tested for HIV	40.0	36.1
Adults who have ever had the shingles or zoster vaccine?	24.8	28.9
Adults who have had their blood cholesterol checked within the last five years	91.4	85.9

Note: n/a not available; (1) Figures cover the Nashville-Davidson—Murfreesboro—Franklin, TN Metropolitan Statistical Area—see Appendix B for areas included.
Source: Centers for Disease Control and Prevention, Behaviorial Risk Factor Surveillance System, SMART: Selected Metropolitan Area Risk Trends, 2017

Disability Status

Category	MSA[1] (%)	U.S. (%)
Adults who reported being deaf	6.9	6.7
Are you blind or have serious difficulty seeing, even when wearing glasses?	5.2	4.5
Are you limited in any way in any of your usual activities due of arthritis?	12.5	12.9
Do you have difficulty doing errands alone?	5.7	6.8
Do you have difficulty dressing or bathing?	3.3	3.6
Do you have serious difficulty concentrating/remembering/making decisions?	11.5	10.7
Do you have serious difficulty walking or climbing stairs?	15.0	13.6

Note: (1) Figures cover the Nashville-Davidson—Murfreesboro—Franklin, TN Metropolitan Statistical Area—see Appendix B for areas included.
Source: Centers for Disease Control and Prevention, Behaviorial Risk Factor Surveillance System, SMART: Selected Metropolitan Area Risk Trends, 2017

Mortality Rates for the Top 10 Causes of Death in the U.S.

ICD-10[a] Sub-Chapter	ICD-10[a] Code	Age-Adjusted Mortality Rate[1] per 100,000 population	
		County[2]	U.S.
Malignant neoplasms	C00-C97	168.9	155.5
Ischaemic heart diseases	I20-I25	110.2	94.8
Other forms of heart disease	I30-I51	43.5	52.9
Chronic lower respiratory diseases	J40-J47	48.2	41.0
Cerebrovascular diseases	I60-I69	47.4	37.5
Other degenerative diseases of the nervous system	G30-G31	53.6	35.0
Other external causes of accidental injury	W00-X59	54.3	33.7
Organic, including symptomatic, mental disorders	F01-F09	30.7	31.0
Hypertensive diseases	I10-I15	38.9	21.9
Diabetes mellitus	E10-E14	24.5	21.2

Note: (a) ICD-10 = International Classification of Diseases 10th Revision; (1) Mortality rates are a three year average covering 2015-2017; (2) Figures cover Davidson County.
Source: Centers for Disease Control and Prevention, National Center for Health Statistics. Underlying Cause of Death 1999-2017 on CDC WONDER Online Database

Mortality Rates for Selected Causes of Death

ICD-10[a] Sub-Chapter	ICD-10[a] Code	Age-Adjusted Mortality Rate[1] per 100,000 population	
		County[2]	U.S.
Assault	X85-Y09	12.2	5.9
Diseases of the liver	K70-K76	13.2	14.1
Human immunodeficiency virus (HIV) disease	B20-B24	2.7	1.8
Influenza and pneumonia	J09-J18	15.3	14.3
Intentional self-harm	X60-X84	13.8	13.6
Malnutrition	E40-E46	1.1	1.6
Obesity and other hyperalimentation	E65-E68	2.3	2.1
Renal failure	N17-N19	9.8	13.0
Transport accidents	V01-V99	10.8	12.4
Viral hepatitis	B15-B19	3.8	1.6

Note: (a) ICD-10 = International Classification of Diseases 10th Revision; (1) Mortality rates are a three year average covering 2015-2017; (2) Figures cover Davidson County; Data are suppressed when the data meet the criteria for confidentiality constraints; Mortality rates are flagged as unreliable when the rate would be calculated with a numerator of 20 or less.
Source: Centers for Disease Control and Prevention, National Center for Health Statistics. Underlying Cause of Death 1999-2017 on CDC WONDER Online Database

Health Insurance Coverage

Area	With Health Insurance	With Private Health Insurance	With Public Health Insurance	Without Health Insurance	Population Under Age 18 Without Health Insurance
City	86.3	65.3	29.7	13.7	7.1
MSA[1]	89.4	70.8	28.5	10.6	5.2
U.S.	89.5	67.2	33.8	10.5	5.7

Note: Figures are percentages that cover the civilian noninstitutionalized population; (1) Figures cover the Nashville-Davidson—Murfreesboro—Franklin, TN Metropolitan Statistical Area—see Appendix B for areas included
Source: U.S. Census Bureau, 2013-2017 American Community Survey 5-Year Estimates

Number of Medical Professionals

Area	MDs[3]	DOs[3,4]	Dentists	Podiatrists	Chiropractors	Optometrists
County[1] (number)	4,265	79	514	29	169	113
County[1] (rate[2])	619.1	11.5	74.4	4.2	24.4	16.3
U.S. (rate[2])	279.3	23.0	68.4	6.0	27.1	16.2

Note: Data as of 2017 unless noted; (1) Data covers Davidson County; (2) Rate per 100,000 population; (3) Data as of 2016 and includes all active, non-federal physicians; (4) Doctor of Osteopathic Medicine
Source: U.S. Department of Health and Human Services, Health Resources and Services Administration, Bureau of Health Professions, Area Resource File (ARF) 2017-2018

Best Hospitals

According to *U.S. News,* the Nashville-Davidson—Murfreesboro—Franklin, TN metro area is home to one of the best hospitals in the U.S.: **Vanderbilt University Medical Center** (Honor Roll/10 adult specialties and 10 pediatric specialties). The hospital listed was nationally ranked in at least one of 16 adult or 10 pediatric specialties. Only 170 hospitals nationwide were nationally ranked in one or more adult or pediatric specialty. Twenty hospitals in the U.S. made the Honor Roll. The Best Hospitals Honor Roll takes both the national rankings and the procedure and condition ratings into account. Hospitals received points if they were nationally ranked in one of the 16 adult specialties—the higher they ranked, the more points they got—and how many ratings of "high performing" they earned in the nine procedures and conditions. *U.S. News Online, "America's Best Hospitals 2018-19"*

According to *U.S. News,* the Nashville-Davidson—Murfreesboro—Franklin, TN metro area is home to one of the best children's hospitals in the U.S.: **Monroe Carell Jr. Children's Hospital at Vanderbilt** (10 pediatric specialties). The hospital listed was highly ranked in at least one of 10 pediatric specialties. Eighty-six children's hospitals in the U.S. were nationally ranked in at least one specialty. Hospitals received points for being ranked in a specialty, and the 10 hospitals with the most points across the 10 specialties make up the Honor Roll. *U.S. News Online, "America's Best Children's Hospitals 2018-19"*

EDUCATION

Public School District Statistics

District Name	Schls	Pupils	Pupil/ Teacher Ratio	Minority Pupils[1] (%)	Free Lunch Eligible[2] (%)	IEP[3] (%)
Achievement School District	33	12,025	21.1	98.4	n/a	12.0
Davidson County	162	85,163	17.2	70.6	n/a	11.9

Note: Table includes school districts with 2,000 or more students; (1) Percentage of students that are not non-Hispanic white; (2) Percentage of students that are eligible for the free lunch program; (3) Percentage of students that have an Individualized Education Program.
Source: U.S. Department of Education, National Center for Education Statistics, Common Core of Data, Local Education Agency (School District) Universe Survey: School Year 2016-2017; U.S. Department of Education, National Center for Education Statistics, Common Core of Data, Public Elementary/Secondary School Universe Survey: School Year 2016-2017

Best High Schools

According to *U.S. News*, Nashville is home to two of the best high schools in the U.S.: **Hume Fogg Magnet High School** (#77); **Martin Luther King Jr. Magnet School** (#165). More than 20,000 public, magnet and charter schools were ranked based on their performance on state assessments and how well they prepare students for college. Schools with the highest unrounded College Readiness Index values were numerically ranked from 1 to 500 and were classified as gold medal winners. *U.S. News & World Report, "Best High Schools 2018"*

Highest Level of Education

Area	Less than H.S.	H.S. Diploma	Some College, No Deg.	Associate Degree	Bachelor's Degree	Master's Degree	Prof. School Degree	Doctorate Degree
City	12.2	23.2	19.5	6.5	24.3	9.7	2.6	1.9
MSA[1]	10.9	27.5	20.5	7.1	22.1	8.4	2.0	1.4
U.S.	12.7	27.3	20.8	8.3	19.1	8.4	2.0	1.4

Note: Figures cover persons age 25 and over; (1) Figures cover the Nashville-Davidson—Murfreesboro—Franklin, TN Metropolitan Statistical Area—see Appendix B for areas included
Source: U.S. Census Bureau, 2013-2017 American Community Survey 5-Year Estimates

Educational Attainment by Race

Area	High School Graduate or Higher (%)					Bachelor's Degree or Higher (%)				
	Total	White	Black	Asian	Hisp.[2]	Total	White	Black	Asian	Hisp.[2]
City	87.8	90.1	86.7	77.9	58.0	38.5	43.3	26.8	47.2	14.5
MSA[1]	89.1	90.2	86.9	83.3	61.7	34.0	35.2	26.0	50.2	15.3
U.S.	87.3	89.3	84.9	86.5	66.7	30.9	32.2	20.6	52.7	15.2

Note: Figures shown cover persons 25 years old and over; (1) Figures cover the Nashville-Davidson—Murfreesboro—Franklin, TN Metropolitan Statistical Area—see Appendix B for areas included; (2) People of Hispanic origin can be of any race
Source: U.S. Census Bureau, 2013-2017 American Community Survey 5-Year Estimates

School Enrollment by Grade and Control

Area	Preschool (%)		Kindergarten (%)		Grades 1 - 4 (%)		Grades 5 - 8 (%)		Grades 9 - 12 (%)	
	Public	Private	Public	Private	Public	Private	Public	Private	Public	Private
City	52.2	47.8	86.9	13.1	85.5	14.5	82.7	17.3	83.0	17.0
MSA[1]	47.1	52.9	87.6	12.4	87.9	12.1	85.4	14.6	84.7	15.3
U.S.	58.8	41.2	87.7	12.3	89.7	10.3	89.6	10.4	90.3	9.7

Note: Figures shown cover persons 3 years old and over; (1) Figures cover the Nashville-Davidson—Murfreesboro—Franklin, TN Metropolitan Statistical Area—see Appendix B for areas included
Source: U.S. Census Bureau, 2013-2017 American Community Survey 5-Year Estimates

Average Salaries of Public School Classroom Teachers

Area	2016		2017		Change from 2016 to 2017	
	Dollars	Rank[1]	Dollars	Rank[1]	Percent	Rank[2]
Tennessee	48,817	36	50,099	36	2.6	12
U.S. Average	58,479	–	59,660	–	2.0	–

Note: (1) Rank ranges from 1 to 51 where 1 indicates highest salary; (2) Rank ranges from 1 to 51 where 1 indicates highest percent change.
Source: National Education Association, Rankings & Estimates: Rankings of the States 2017 and Estimates of School Statistics 2018

Higher Education

Four-Year Colleges			Two-Year Colleges			Medical Schools[1]	Law Schools[2]	Voc/ Tech[3]
Public	Private Non-profit	Private For-profit	Public	Private Non-profit	Private For-profit			
1	9	5	2	2	6	2	3	4

Note: Figures cover institutions located within the city limits and include main campuses only; (1) includes schools accredited by the Liaison Committee on Medical Education and the American Osteopathic Association's Commission on Osteopathic College Accreditation; (2) includes ABA-accredited schools, schools with provisional ABA accreditation, and state accredited schools; (3) includes all schools with programs that are less than 2 years.
Source: National Center for Education Statistics, Integrated Postsecondary Education System (IPEDS), 2017-18; Wikipedia, List of Medical Schools in the United States, accessed April 3, 2019; Wikipedia, List of Law Schools in the United States, accessed April 3, 2019

According to *U.S. News & World Report*, the Nashville-Davidson—Murfreesboro—Franklin, TN metro area is home to two of the best national universities in the U.S.: **Vanderbilt University** (#14 tie); **Lipscomb University** (#194 tie). The indicators used to capture academic quality fall into a number of categories: assessment by administrators at peer institutions; retention of students; faculty resources; student selectivity; financial resources; alumni giving; high school counselor ratings of colleges; and graduation rate. *U.S. News & World Report, "America's Best Colleges 2019"*

According to *U.S. News & World Report*, the Nashville-Davidson—Murfreesboro—Franklin, TN metro area is home to one of the best liberal arts colleges in the U.S.: **Fisk University** (#152 tie). The indicators used to capture academic quality fall into a number of categories: assessment by administrators at peer institutions; retention of students; faculty resources; student selectivity; financial resources; alumni giving; high school counselor ratings of colleges; and graduation rate. *U.S. News & World Report, "America's Best Colleges 2019"*

According to *U.S. News & World Report*, the Nashville-Davidson—Murfreesboro—Franklin, TN metro area is home to one of the top 100 law schools in the U.S.: **Vanderbilt University** (#18 tie). The rankings are based on a weighted average of 12 measures of quality: peer assessment score; assessment score by lawyers/judges; median LSAT scores; median undergrad GPA; acceptance rate; employment rates for graduates; placement success; bar passage rate; faculty resources; expenditures per student; student/faculty ratio; and library resources. *U.S. News & World Report, "America's Best Graduate Schools, Law, 2020"*

According to *U.S. News & World Report*, the Nashville-Davidson—Murfreesboro—Franklin, TN metro area is home to one of the top 75 medical schools for research in the U.S.: **Vanderbilt University** (#16 tie). The rankings are based on a weighted average of 11 measures of quality: quality assessment; peer assessment score; assessment score by residency directors; research activity; total research activity; average research activity per faculty member; student selectivity; median MCAT total score; median undergraduate GPA; acceptance rate; and faculty resources. *U.S. News & World Report, "America's Best Graduate Schools, Medical, 2020"*

According to *U.S. News & World Report*, the Nashville-Davidson—Murfreesboro—Franklin, TN metro area is home to one of the top 75 business schools in the U.S.: **Vanderbilt University (Owen)** (#29 tie). The rankings are based on a weighted average of the following nine measures: quality assessment; peer assessment; recruiter assessment; placement success; mean starting salary and bonus; student selectivity; mean GMAT and GRE scores; mean undergraduate GPA; and acceptance rate. *U.S. News & World Report, "America's Best Graduate Schools, Business, 2020"*

PRESIDENTIAL ELECTION

2016 Presidential Election Results

Area	Clinton	Trump	Johnson	Stein	Other
Davidson County	59.8	33.9	3.9	1.0	1.4
U.S.	48.0	45.9	3.3	1.1	1.7

Note: Results are percentages and may not add to 100% due to rounding
Source: Dave Leip's Atlas of U.S. Presidential Elections

EMPLOYERS

Major Employers

Company Name	Industry
AHOM Holdings	Home health care services
Asurion Corporation	Business services nec
Baptist Hospital	General medical & surgical hospitals
Cannon County Knitting Mills	Apparel & outerwear broadwoven fabrics
County of Rutherford	Public elementary & secondary schools
County of Sumner	County government
Gaylord Entertainment Company	Hotels & motels
Gaylord Opryland USA	Hotels & motels
Ingram Book Company	Books, periodicals, & newspapers
International Automotive	Automotive storage garage
LifeWay Christian Resources of the SBC	Religious organizations
Middle Tennessee State University	Colleges & universities
Newspaper Printing Corporation	Newspapers, publishing & printing
Nissan North America	Motor vehicles & car bodies
Primus Automotive Financial Services	Automobile loans including insurance
Psychiatric Solutions	Psychiatric clinic
State Industries	Hot water heaters, household
State of Tennessee	State government
Tennessee Department of Transportation	Regulation, administration of transportation
Vanderbilt Childrens Hospital	General medical & surgical hospitals
Vanderbilt University	Colleges & universities

Note: Companies shown are located within the Nashville-Davidson—Murfreesboro—Franklin, TN Metropolitan Statistical Area.
Source: Hoovers.com; Wikipedia

Best Companies to Work For

Pinnacle Financial Partners, headquartered in Nashville, is among "The 100 Best Companies to Work For." To pick the best companies, *Fortune* partnered with the Great Place to Work Institute. Two-thirds of a company's score is based on the results of the Institute's Trust Index survey, which is sent to a random sample of employees from each company. The questions related to attitudes about management's credibility, job satisfaction, and camaraderie. The other third of the scoring is based on the company's responses to the Institute's Culture Audit, which includes detailed questions about pay and benefit programs, and a series of open-ended questions about hiring practices, internal communication, training, recognition programs, and diversity efforts. Any company that is at least five years old with more than 1,000 U.S. employees is eligible. *Fortune, "The 100 Best Companies to Work For," 2019*

Asurion, headquartered in Nashville, is among the "100 Best Places to Work in IT." To qualify, companies had to be U.S.-based organizations or be non-U.S.- based employers that met the following criteria: have a minimum of 300 total employees at a U.S. headquarters and a minimum of 30 IT employees in the U.S., with at least 50% of their IT employees based in the U.S. The best places to work were selected based on compensation, benefits, work/life balance, employee morale, and satisfaction with training and development programs. In addition, *Computerworld* looked at retention efforts, programs for recognizing and rewarding outstanding performances, and benefits such as flextime, elder care and child care, and reimbursement for college tuition and the cost of pursuing technology certifications. *Computerworld, "100 Best Places to Work in IT 2018"*

PUBLIC SAFETY

Crime Rate

Area	All Crimes	Violent Crimes				Property Crimes		
		Murder	Rape[3]	Robbery	Aggrav. Assault	Burglary	Larceny -Theft	Motor Vehicle Theft
City	4,956.1	16.3	72.9	303.1	745.8	631.3	2,806.6	380.0
Suburbs[1]	2,209.0	3.2	32.7	35.8	271.0	297.4	1,425.7	143.3
Metro[2]	3,183.4	7.8	47.0	130.7	439.4	415.8	1,915.5	227.2
U.S.	2,756.1	5.3	41.7	98.0	248.9	430.4	1,694.4	237.4

Note: Figures are crimes per 100,000 population; (1) All areas within the metro area that are located outside the city limits; (2) Figures cover the Nashville-Davidson—Murfreesboro—Franklin, TN Metropolitan Statistical Area—see Appendix B for areas included; (3) The city and U.S. figures shown were reported using the revised Uniform Crime Reporting (UCR) definition of rape. The suburban and metro area figures shown are an aggregate total of the data submitted using both the revised and legacy UCR definitions.
Source: FBI Uniform Crime Reports, 2017

Hate Crimes

Area	Number of Quarters Reported	Number of Incidents per Bias Motivation					
		Race/Ethnicity/ Ancestry	Religion	Sexual Orientation	Disability	Gender	Gender Identity
City	4	11	5	3	0	0	0
U.S.	4	4,131	1,564	1,130	116	46	119

Source: Federal Bureau of Investigation, Hate Crime Statistics 2017

Identity Theft Consumer Reports

Area	Reports	Reports per 100,000 Population	Rank[2]
MSA[1]	1,831	98	139
U.S.	444,602	135	-

Note: (1) Figures cover the Nashville-Davidson—Murfreesboro—Franklin, TN Metropolitan Statistical Area—see Appendix B for areas included; (2) Rank ranges from 1 to 389 where 1 indicates greatest number of identity theft reports per 100,000 population
Source: Federal Trade Commission, Consumer Sentinel Network Data Book for January–December 2018

Fraud and Other Consumer Reports

Area	Reports	Reports per 100,000 Population	Rank[2]
MSA[1]	11,213	601	57
U.S.	2,552,917	776	-

Note: (1) Figures cover the Nashville-Davidson—Murfreesboro—Franklin, TN Metropolitan Statistical Area—see Appendix B for areas included; (2) Rank ranges from 1 to 389 where 1 indicates greatest number of fraud and other consumer reports per 100,000 population
Source: Federal Trade Commission, Consumer Sentinel Network Data Book for January–December 2018

SPORTS

Professional Sports Teams

Team Name	League	Year Established
Nashville Predators	National Hockey League (NHL)	1998
Tennessee Titans	National Football League (NFL)	1997

Note: Includes teams located in the Nashville-Davidson—Murfreesboro—Franklin, TN Metropolitan Statistical Area.
Source: Wikipedia, Major Professional Sports Teams of the United States and Canada, April 5, 2019

CLIMATE

Average and Extreme Temperatures

Temperature	Jan	Feb	Mar	Apr	May	Jun	Jul	Aug	Sep	Oct	Nov	Dec	Yr.
Extreme High (°F)	78	84	86	91	95	106	107	104	105	94	84	79	107
Average High (°F)	47	51	60	71	79	87	90	89	83	72	60	50	70
Average Temp. (°F)	38	41	50	60	68	76	80	79	72	61	49	41	60
Average Low (°F)	28	31	39	48	57	65	69	68	61	48	39	31	49
Extreme Low (°F)	-17	-13	2	23	34	42	54	49	36	26	-1	-10	-17

Note: Figures cover the years 1948-1990
Source: National Climatic Data Center, International Station Meteorological Climate Summary, 9/96

Average Precipitation/Snowfall/Humidity

Precip./Humidity	Jan	Feb	Mar	Apr	May	Jun	Jul	Aug	Sep	Oct	Nov	Dec	Yr.
Avg. Precip. (in.)	4.4	4.2	5.0	4.1	4.6	3.7	3.8	3.3	3.2	2.6	3.9	4.6	47.4
Avg. Snowfall (in.)	4	3	1	Tr	0	0	0	0	0	Tr	1	1	11
Avg. Rel. Hum. 6am (%)	81	81	80	81	86	86	88	90	90	87	83	82	85
Avg. Rel. Hum. 3pm (%)	61	57	51	48	52	52	54	53	52	49	55	59	54

Note: Figures cover the years 1948-1990; Tr = Trace amounts (<0.05 in. of rain; <0.5 in. of snow)
Source: National Climatic Data Center, International Station Meteorological Climate Summary, 9/96

Weather Conditions

Temperature			Daytime Sky			Precipitation		
10°F & below	32°F & below	90°F & above	Clear	Partly cloudy	Cloudy	0.01 inch or more precip.	0.1 inch or more snow/ice	Thunder-storms
5	76	51	98	135	132	119	8	54

Note: Figures are average number of days per year and cover the years 1948-1990
Source: National Climatic Data Center, International Station Meteorological Climate Summary, 9/96

HAZARDOUS WASTE

Superfund Sites

The Nashville-Davidson—Murfreesboro—Franklin, TN metro area is home to one site on the EPA's Superfund National Priorities List: **Wrigley Charcoal Plant** (final). There are a total of 1,390 Superfund sites with a status of proposed or final on the list in the U.S. *U.S. Environmental Protection Agency, National Priorities List, April 5, 2019*

AIR & WATER QUALITY

Air Quality Trends: Ozone

	1990	1995	2000	2005	2010	2012	2014	2015	2016	2017
MSA[1]	0.089	0.092	0.084	0.078	0.073	0.079	0.067	0.065	0.068	0.063
U.S.	0.088	0.089	0.082	0.080	0.073	0.075	0.067	0.068	0.069	0.068

Note: (1) Data covers the Nashville-Davidson—Murfreesboro—Franklin, TN Metropolitan Statistical Area—see Appendix B for areas included. The values shown are the composite ozone concentration averages among trend sites based on the highest fourth daily maximum 8-hour concentration in parts per million. These trends are based on sites having an adequate record of monitoring data during the trend period. Data from exceptional events are included.
Source: U.S. Environmental Protection Agency, Air Quality Monitoring Information, "Air Quality Trends by City, 1990-2017"

Air Quality Index

Area	Percent of Days when Air Quality was...[2]					AQI Statistics[2]	
	Good	Moderate	Unhealthy for Sensitive Groups	Unhealthy	Very Unhealthy	Maximum	Median
MSA[1]	63.8	35.9	0.3	0.0	0.0	133	45

Note: (1) Data covers the Nashville-Davidson—Murfreesboro—Franklin, TN Metropolitan Statistical Area—see Appendix B for areas included; (2) Based on 365 days with AQI data in 2017. Air Quality Index (AQI) is an index for reporting daily air quality. EPA calculates the AQI for five major air pollutants regulated by the Clean Air Act: ground-level ozone, particle pollution (aka particulate matter), carbon monoxide, sulfur dioxide, and nitrogen dioxide. The AQI runs from 0 to 500. The higher the AQI value, the greater the level of air pollution and the greater the health concern. There are six AQI categories: "Good" AQI is between 0 and 50. Air quality is considered satisfactory; "Moderate" AQI is between 51 and 100. Air quality is acceptable; "Unhealthy for Sensitive Groups" When AQI values are between 101 and 150, members of sensitive groups may experience health effects; "Unhealthy" When AQI values are between 151 and 200 everyone may begin to experience health effects; "Very Unhealthy" AQI values between 201 and 300 trigger a health alert; "Hazardous" AQI values over 300 trigger warnings of emergency conditions (not shown).
Source: U.S. Environmental Protection Agency, Air Quality Index Report, 2017

Air Quality Index Pollutants

| Area | Percent of Days when AQI Pollutant was...[2] | | | | | |
	Carbon Monoxide	Nitrogen Dioxide	Ozone	Sulfur Dioxide	Particulate Matter 2.5	Particulate Matter 10
MSA[1]	0.0	4.9	37.3	0.5	57.3	0.0

Note: (1) Data covers the Nashville-Davidson—Murfreesboro—Franklin, TN Metropolitan Statistical Area—see Appendix B for areas included; (2) Based on 365 days with AQI data in 2017. The Air Quality Index (AQI) is an index for reporting daily air quality. EPA calculates the AQI for five major air pollutants regulated by the Clean Air Act: ground-level ozone, particle pollution (also known as particulate matter), carbon monoxide, sulfur dioxide, and nitrogen dioxide. The AQI runs from 0 to 500. The higher the AQI value, the greater the level of air pollution and the greater the health concern.
Source: U.S. Environmental Protection Agency, Air Quality Index Report, 2017

Maximum Air Pollutant Concentrations: Particulate Matter, Ozone, CO and Lead

	Particulate Matter 10 (ug/m^3)	Particulate Matter 2.5 Wtd AM (ug/m^3)	Particulate Matter 2.5 24-Hr (ug/m^3)	Ozone (ppm)	Carbon Monoxide (ppm)	Lead (ug/m^3)
MSA[1] Level	34	9.7	19	0.064	2	n/a
NAAQS[2]	150	15	35	0.075	9	0.15
Met NAAQS[2]	Yes	Yes	Yes	Yes	Yes	n/a

Note: (1) Data covers the Nashville-Davidson—Murfreesboro—Franklin, TN Metropolitan Statistical Area—see Appendix B for areas included; Data from exceptional events are included; (2) National Ambient Air Quality Standards; ppm = parts per million; ug/m³ = micrograms per cubic meter; n/a not available.
Concentrations: Particulate Matter 10 (coarse particulate)—highest second maximum 24-hour concentration; Particulate Matter 2.5 Wtd AM (fine particulate)—highest weighted annual mean concentration; Particulate Matter 2.5 24-Hour (fine particulate)—highest 98th percentile 24-hour concentration; Ozone—highest fourth daily maximum 8-hour concentration; Carbon Monoxide—highest second maximum non-overlapping 8-hour concentration; Lead—maximum running 3-month average
Source: U.S. Environmental Protection Agency, Air Quality Monitoring Information, "Air Quality Statistics by City, 2017"

Maximum Air Pollutant Concentrations: Nitrogen Dioxide and Sulfur Dioxide

	Nitrogen Dioxide AM (ppb)	Nitrogen Dioxide 1-Hr (ppb)	Sulfur Dioxide AM (ppb)	Sulfur Dioxide 1-Hr (ppb)	Sulfur Dioxide 24-Hr (ppb)
MSA[1] Level	14	51	n/a	5	n/a
NAAQS[2]	53	100	30	75	140
Met NAAQS[2]	Yes	Yes	n/a	Yes	n/a

Note: (1) Data covers the Nashville-Davidson—Murfreesboro—Franklin, TN Metropolitan Statistical Area—see Appendix B for areas included; Data from exceptional events are included; (2) National Ambient Air Quality Standards; ppm = parts per million; ug/m³ = micrograms per cubic meter; n/a not available.
Concentrations: Nitrogen Dioxide AM—highest arithmetic mean concentration; Nitrogen Dioxide 1-Hr—highest 98th percentile 1-hour daily maximum concentration; Sulfur Dioxide AM—highest annual mean concentration; Sulfur Dioxide 1-Hr—highest 99th percentile 1-hour daily maximum concentration; Sulfur Dioxide 24-Hr—highest second maximum 24-hour concentration
Source: U.S. Environmental Protection Agency, Air Quality Monitoring Information, "Air Quality Statistics by City, 2017"

Drinking Water

| Water System Name | Pop. Served | Primary Water Source Type | Violations[1] | |
			Health Based	Monitoring/ Reporting
Nashville Water Dept	702,407	Surface	0	0

Note: (1) Based on violation data from January 1, 2018 to December 31, 2018
Source: U.S. Environmental Protection Agency, Office of Ground Water and Drinking Water, Safe Drinking Water Information System (based on data extracted April 5, 2019)

New Orleans, Louisiana

Background

New Orleans, the old port city upriver from the mouth of the Mississippi River, is one of the United States' most interesting cities. The birthplace of jazz is rich in unique local history, distinctive neighborhoods, and an unmistakably individual character.

The failure of the federal levees following Hurricane Katrina in 2005 put 80 percent of the city under floodwaters for weeks. The Crescent City's revival since then is a testament to her unique spirit, an influx of federal dollars, and an outpouring from volunteers ranging from church groups to spring breakers who returned year after year to help rebuild.

New Orleans was founded on behalf of France by the brothers Le Moyne, Sieurs d'Iberville, and de Bienville, in 1718. Despite disease, starvation, and an unwilling working class, New Orleans emerged as a genteel antebellum slave society, fashioning itself after the rigid social hierarchy of Versailles. Even after New Orleans was ceded to Spain after the French & Indian War, this unequal lifestyle, however gracious, persisted.

The port city briefly returned to French control, then became a crown jewel in the 1803 Louisiana Purchase to the U.S. The transfer of control changed New Orleans's Old World isolation. American settlers introduced aggressive business acumen to the area, as well as the idea of respect for the self-made man. As trade opened up with countries around the world, this made for a happy union. New Orleans became "Queen City of the South," growing prosperous from adventurous riverboat traders and speculators, as well as the cotton trade.

Today, much of the city's Old World charm remains, resulting from Southern, Creole, African-American, and European cultures. New Orleans' cuisine, indigenous music, unique festivals, and sultry, pleasing atmosphere, draws nearly 10 million visitors a year.

A major pillar of the city's economy is the enormous tourism trade. The Ernest N. Morial Convention Center's numerous convention goers continuously fill more than 35,000 rooms. A second economic pillar is the Port of New Orleans, one of the nation's leading general cargo ports. In recent years, it has seen $400 million invested in new facilities.

In addition, an influx of young people who arrived after Hurricane Katrina is giving rise to a new start-up spirit. Plus, state tax breaks have helped to turn New Orleans into "Hollywood South," where 35 films were produced in the last few years. New Orleans has given birth to a mother lode of cultural phenomena: Dixieland jazz, musicians Louis Armstrong, Mahalia Jackson, Dr. John, and chefs Emeril Lagasse and John Besh. The city is well aware of its "cultural economy," which employs 12.5 percent of the local workforce. Popular tourist draws include the annual Mardi Gras celebration—which spans two long weekends leading up to Fat Tuesday—and the annual New Orleans Jazz & Heritage Festival. The Louisiana Superdome—renovated and renamed to the Mercedes Benz Superdome, is home to the 2010 Super Bowl champion New Orleans Saints, and hosted the 2013 Super Bowl. A new, $75 million Consolidated Rental Car Facility project has expanded rental capacity and brought scattered facilities under one roof at the Louis Armstrong New Orleans International Airport.

In addition, an effort to boost a medical economy that suffered after Hurricane Katrina, the city has a new Louisiana State University teaching hospital.

Billions of dollars have been spent in recent years for bridge, airport, road, hospital, and school updates. Since Katrina, the majority of New Orleans public schools have become charter schools—a major experiment that is seeing some success. Higher education campuses include Tulane University (including a medical school and law school), Loyola University, and the University of New Orleans. Louisiana State University has a medical school campus downtown.

Cultural amenities include the New Orleans Museum of Art located in the live-oak filled City Park, the Ogden Museum of Southern Art, and Audubon Park, designed by John Charles Olmsted with its golf course and the Audubon Zoo.

The New Orleans metro area is virtually surrounded by water, which influences its climate. Between mid-June and September, temperatures are kept down by near-daily sporadic thunderstorms. Cold spells sometimes reach the area in winter but seldom last. Frequent and sometimes heavy rains are typical. Hurricane season officially runs from June 1 to November 30 but typically reaches its height in late summer.

Rankings

General Rankings

- *Insider* listed 33 places in the U.S. that were a must see vacation destination. Whether it is the great beaches, exploring a new city or experiencing the great outdoors, according to the website thisisinsider.com New Orleans is a place to visit in 2018. *Insider, "33 Trips Everyone Should Take in the U.S. in 2018,"November 27, 2017*

- The New Orleans metro area was identified as one of America's fastest-growing areas in terms of population and business growth by *MagnifyMoney*. The area ranked #30 out of 35. The 100 most populous metro areas in the U.S. were evaluated on their change from 2011-2016 in the following categories: people and housing; workforce and employment opportunities; growing industry. *www.businessinsider.com, "The 35 Cities in the US with the Biggest Influx of People, the Most Work Opportunities, and the Hottest Business Growth," August 12, 2018*

- In its eighth annual survey, *Travel + Leisure* readers nominated their favorite small cities and towns in America—those with 100,000 or fewer residents—voting on numerous attractive features in categories including culture, food and drink, quality of life, style, and people. After 50,000 votes, New Orleans was ranked #2 among the proposed favorites. *www.travelandleisure.com, "America's Favorite Cities," October 20, 2017*

- New Orleans appeared on *Travel + Leisure's* list of the fifteen best cities in the United States. The city was ranked #2. Criteria: sights/landmarks; culture/arts; cuisine; people/friendliness; shopping; and value. *Travel + Leisure, "The World's Best Awards 2018" July 10, 2018*

- Based on more than 425,000 responses, *Condé Nast Traveler* ranked its readers' favorite cities in the U.S. The list was broken into cities over 1 million and cities under 1 million. New Orleans ranked #3 in the big city category. *Condé Nast Traveler, Readers' Choice Awards 2018, "Best Big Cities in the U.S." October 9, 2018*

- In their sixth annual survey, Livability.com looked at data for more than 1,000 U.S. cities to determine the rankings for Livability's "Top 100 Best Places to Live" in 2019. New Orleans ranked #82. Criteria: median home value capped at $250,000; affordable living; vibrant economy; education, demographics, health care options. transportation & infrastructure; abundant lifestyle amenities. *Livability.com, "Top 100 Best Places to Live 2019" March 2019*

Business/Finance Rankings

- The personal finance site NerdWallet analyzed 183 American metropolitan areas with populations over 250,000 and more than 15,000 businesses to rank where entrepreneurs find the most success. Criteria included area economy, annual income, housing cost, unemployment rate, and the success rate of area businesses. New Orleans ranked #54. *www.nerdwallet.com, "Best Places to Start a Business," April 27, 2015*

- Recognizing the sizeable percentage of American workers who are self-employed, NerdWallet editors assessed the country's cities according to percentage of freelancers, median rental costs, cell phone plans/taxes, and healthcare affordability and access. By these criteria, New Orleans placed #17 among the best cities for independent workers. *www.nerdwallet.com, "Best Places for Freelance Workers," August 30, 2016*

- USAA and Hiring Our Heroes worked with Sperlings's BestPlaces and the Institute for Veterans and Military Families at Syracuse University to rank major metropolitan areas where military-skills-related employment is strongest. Criteria for *mid-career* veterans included veteran wage growth; recent job growth; stability; and accessible health resources. Metro areas with a higher than national average crime or unemployment rate were excluded. At #5, the New Orleans metro area made the top ten. *www.usaa.com, "2015 Best Places for Veterans"*

- Metro areas with the largest gap in income between rich and poor residents were identified by 24/7 Wall Street using the U.S. Census Bureau's 2013 American Community Survey. The New Orleans metro area placed #18 among metro areas with the widest wealth gap between rich and poor. *247wallst.com, "20 Cities with the Widest Gap between the Rich and Poor," July 8, 2015*

- In a survey of economic confidence in the nation's 50 largest metropolitan areas conducted January–December 2014, the New Orleans metro area placed #46, according to Gallup's 2014 Economic Confidence Index. *Gallup, "San Jose and San Francisco Lead in Economic Confidence," March 19, 2015*

- NerdWallet.com identified the 10 most promising cities for job seekers of the nation's 100 largest cities. New Orleans was ranked #45. Criteria: job availability; annual salary; workforce growth; affordability. *NerdWallet.com, "Best Cities for Job Seekers in 2017," December 19, 2016*

- The Brookings Institution ranked the nation's largest cities based on income inequality. New Orleans was ranked #4 (#1 = greatest inequality). Criteria: the "95/20 ratio," a figure representing the income at which a household earns more than 95 percent of all other households, divided by the income at which a household earns more than only 20 percent of all other households. *Brookings Institution, "Household Income Inequality, Largest Cities of 97 Large U.S. Metro Areas, 2014-2016," February 5, 2018*

- The Brookings Institution ranked the 100 largest metro areas in the U.S. based on income inequality. New Orleans was ranked #5 (#1 = greatest inequality). Criteria: the "95/20 ratio," a figure representing the income at which a household earns more than 95 percent of all other households, divided by the income at which a household earns more than only 20 percent of all other households. *Brookings Institution, "Household Income Inequality, 100 Largest U.S. Metro Areas, 2014-2016," February 5, 2018*

- The New Orleans metro area appeared on the Milken Institute "2018 Best Performing Cities" list. Rank: #189 out of 200 large metro areas. Criteria: job growth; wage and salary growth; high-tech output growth. *Milken Institute, "Best-Performing Cities 2018," January 24, 2019*

- *Forbes* ranked the 200 most populous metro areas to determine the nation's "Best Places for Business and Careers." The New Orleans metro area was ranked #167. Criteria: costs (business and living); job growth (past and projected); income growth; quality of life; educational attainment (college and high school); projected economic growth; cultural and recreational opportunities; net migration patterns; number of highly ranked colleges. *Forbes, "The Best Places for Business and Careers 2018: Seattle Leads the Way," October 24, 2018*

Children/Family Rankings

- New Orleans was selected as one of the most playful cities in the U.S. by KaBOOM! The organization's Playful City USA initiative honors cities and towns across the nation that have made their communities more playable. Criteria: pledging to integrate play as a solution to challenges in their communities; making it easy for children to get active and balanced play; creating more family-friendly and innovative communities as a result. *KaBOOM! National Campaign for Play, "2017 Playful City USA Communities"*

Culture/Performing Arts Rankings

- New Orleans was selected as one of the ten best small U.S. cities and towns for moviemakers. Of cities with a population between 100,000 and 400,000 and towns with population less than 100,000, the area ranked #2. Criteria: film community and culture; access to equipment and facilities; film activity in 2018; number of film schools; tax incentives; ease of movement and traffic. *MovieMaker Magazine, "Best Places to Live and Work as a Moviemaker: 2019," January 17, 2019*

- New Orleans was selected as one of "America's Favorite Cities." The city ranked #15 in the "Culture" category. Respondents to an online survey were asked to rate 38 top urban destinations in the U.S. from a visitor's perspective. Criteria: theater scene and community; number of bookstores; live music; and sense of history. *Travelandleisure.com, "These Are America's 20 Most Cultured Cities," October 2016*

- New Orleans was selected as one of "America's Favorite Cities." The city ranked #3 in the "Culture: Music Scene " category. Respondents to an online survey were asked to rate 38 top urban destinations in the U.S. from a visitor's perspective. *Travelandleisure.com, "From the Honkytonk Capital to Jazz's Birthplace: America's Best Music Scenes," October 2016*

- New Orleans was selected as one of "America's Favorite Cities." The city ranked #5 in the "Culture: Historical Sites " category. Respondents to an online survey were asked to rate 38 top urban destinations in the U.S. from a visitor's perspective. *Travelandleisure.com, "America's Favorite Cities," October 11, 2015*

- New Orleans was selected as one of "America's Favorite Cities." The city ranked #7 in the "Architecture " category. Respondents to an online survey were asked to rate their favorite place (population over 100,000) in over 65 categories. *Travelandleisure.com, "America's Favorite Cities for Architecture 2016," March 2, 2017*

Dating/Romance Rankings

- New Orleans was selected as one of America's best cities for singles by the readers of *Travel + Leisure* in their annual "America's Favorite Cities" survey. Criteria included good-looking locals, cool shopping, an active bar scene and hipster-magnet coffee bars. *Travel + Leisure, "Best Cities in America for Singles," July 21, 2017*

Education Rankings

- Personal finance website *WalletHub* analyzed the 150 largest U.S. metropolitan statistical areas to determine where the most educated Americans are choosing to settle. Criteria: education quality and attainment gap; education levels; percentage of workers with degrees; public school quality rankings; quality and size of each metro area's universities. New Orleans was ranked #101 (#1 = most educated city). *www.WalletHub.com, "2018's Most and Least Educated Cities in America, " July 24, 2018*

- New Orleans was selected as one of America's most literate cities. The city ranked #25 out of the 82 largest U.S. cities. Criteria: number of booksellers; library resources; Internet resources; educational attainment; periodical publishing resources; newspaper circulation. *Central Connecticut State University, "America's Most Literate Cities, 2016," March 31, 2017*

Environmental Rankings

- Sperling's BestPlaces assessed the 50 largest metropolitan areas of the United States for the likelihood of dangerously extreme weather events or earthquakes. In general the Southeast and South-Central regions have the highest risk of weather extremes and earthquakes, while the Pacific Northwest enjoys the lowest risk. Of the most risky metropolitan areas, the New Orleans metro area was ranked #10. *www.bestplaces.net, "Avoid Natural Disasters: BestPlaces Reveals The Top 10 Safest Places to Live," October 25, 2017*

- New Orleans was highlighted as one of the top 90 cleanest metro areas for short-term particle pollution (24-hour PM 2.5) in the U.S. during 2014 through 2016. Monitors in these cities reported no days with unhealthful PM 2.5 levels. *American Lung Association, State of the Air 2018*

Food/Drink Rankings

- *Men's Health* ranked 100 major U.S. cities in terms of alcohol intoxication. New Orleans ranked #21 (#1 = most sober).Criteria: binge drinking; alcohol-related traffic accidents, arrests, and fatalities. *Men's Health, "America's Drunkest Cities," March 9, 2015*

Health/Fitness Rankings

- For each of the 100 largest cities in the United States, the American College of Sports Medicine's American Fitness Index evaluated infrastructure, community assets, and policies that encourage healthy and fit lifestyles, including preventive health behaviors, levels of chronic disease conditions, health care access, and community resources and policies that support physical activity. New Orleans ranked #45 for "community fitness." *www.americanfitnessindex.org, "ACSM American Fitness Index Health and Community Fitness Status of the 100 Largest U.S. Cities," May 2018*

- New Orleans was identified as a "2018 Spring Allergy Capital." The area ranked #15 out of 100. Three groups of factors were used to identify the most challenging cities for people with allergies during the spring season: annual pollen levels; medicine utilization; access to board-certified allergists. *Asthma and Allergy Foundation of America, "Spring Allergy Capitals 2018"*

- New Orleans was identified as a "2018 Fall Allergy Capital." The area ranked #15 out of 100. Three groups of factors were used to identify the most challenging cities for people with allergies during the fall season: annual pollen levels; medicine utilization; access to board-certified allergists. *Asthma and Allergy Foundation of America, "Fall Allergy Capitals 2018"*

- New Orleans was identified as a "2018 Asthma Capital." The area ranked #25 out of the nation's 100 largest metropolitan areas. Criteria: estimated prevalence; self-reported prevalence; crude death rate for asthma; annual pollen score; annual air quality; public smoking laws; number of board-certified asthma specialists; school inhaler access laws; rescue medication use; controller medication use; ER visits for asthma; uninsured rate; poverty rate. *Asthma and Allergy Foundation of America, "Asthma Capitals 2018: The Most Challenging Places to Live With Asthma"*

- *Men's Health* ranked 100 major U.S. cities in terms of the best cities for men. New Orleans ranked #88. Criteria: health; fitness; quality of life. *Men's Health, "The Best & Worst Cities for Men Who Want to Be Fit and Happy," January 1, 2016*

- The New Orleans metro area ranked #163 out of 189 in The Gallup-Healthways Well-Being Index. Criteria: purpose; social well being; financial health; community and physical health. Results are based on telephone interviews with adults, aged 18 and older, living in metropolitan areas in the 50 U.S. states and the District of Columbia. *Gallup-Healthways, "State of American Well-Being, 2017 Community Well-Being Rankings" March 2018*

Real Estate Rankings

- FitSmallBusiness looked at 50 of the largest metropolitan areas in the U.S. to determine which metro was the best to start a real estate business. Data was compiled from such sources as: Zillow, Trulia, U.S. Census Bureau, and the Bureau of Labor Statistics. Criteria: location; inventory; annual wages; median sales price of homes; days on the market; median price cut percentage; and other factors that would influence real estate professional growth. The New Orleans metro area ranked #47. *fitsmallbusiness.com, "The Best Cities to Become a Real Estate Agent in 2018," January 30, 2018*

- *WalletHub* compared the most populated U.S. cities, as well as at least two of the most populated cities in each state, for a total of 179, to determine which had the best markets for real estate agents. New Orleans ranked #143 where demand was high and pay was the best. Criteria: sales per agent; annual median wage for real-estate agents; monthly average starting salary for real estate agents; real estate job density and competition; unemployment rate; housing-market health index; and other relevant metrics. *www.WalletHub.com, "2018's Best Places to Be a Real Estate Agent," April 25, 2018*

- The New Orleans metro area was identified as one of the 10 worst condo markets in the U.S. in 2018. The area ranked #60 out of 61 markets. Criteria: year-over-year change of median sales price of existing apartment condo-coop homes between the 4th quarter of 2017 and the 4th quarter of 2018. *National Association of Realtors®, Median Sales Price of Existing Apartment Condo-Coops Homes for Metropolitan Areas, 4th Quarter 2018*

Safety Rankings

- To identify the most dangerous cities in America, 24/7 Wall Street focused on violent crime categories—murder, rape, robbery, and aggravated assault—and property crime as reported in the FBI's 2017 annual Uniform Crime Report. Criteria also included median income from American Community Survey and unemployment figures from Bureau of Labor Statistics. For cities with populations over 100,000, New Orleans was ranked #19. *247wallst.com, "25 Most Dangerous Cities in America" October 17, 2018*

- Allstate ranked the 200 largest cities in America in terms of driver safety. New Orleans ranked #180. Criteria: internal property damage claims over a two-year period from January 2015 to December 2016. The report helps increase the importance of safety awareness behind the wheel. *Allstate, "Allstate America's Best Drivers Report, 2018" August 28, 2018*

- New Orleans was identified as one of the most dangerous cities in America by NeighborhoodScout. The city ranked #52 out of 100. Criteria: number of violent crimes per 1,000 residents. The editors only considered cities with 25,000 or more residents. *NeighborhoodScout.com, "Top 100 Most Dangerous Cities in the U.S. 2019" January 2, 2019*

- The National Insurance Crime Bureau ranked 382 metro areas in the U.S. in terms of per capita rates of vehicle theft. The New Orleans metro area ranked #64 (#1 = highest rate). Criteria: number of vehicle theft offenses per 100,000 inhabitants in 2017. *National Insurance Crime Bureau, "Hot Spots 2017," July 12, 2018*

Seniors/Retirement Rankings

- From its Best Cities for Successful Aging indexes, the Milken Institute generated rankings for metropolitan areas, weighing data in nine categories—health care, wellness, living arrangements, transportation and convenience, financial characteristics, education, employment, community engagement, and overall livability. The New Orleans metro area was ranked #55 overall in the large metro area category. *Milken Institute, "Best Cities for Successful Aging, 2017" March 14, 2017*

Sports/Recreation Rankings

- New Orleans was chosen as one of America's best cities for bicycling. The city ranked #22 out of 50. Criteria: cycling infrastructure that is safe and friendly for all ages; energy and bike culture. The editors only considered cities with populations of 100,000 or more. *Bicycling, "The 50 Best Bike Cities in America," October 10, 2018*

Transportation Rankings

- NerdWallet surveyed average annual car insurance premiums in 125 U.S. cities to identify the least expensive U.S. cities in which to insure a car. Locations with no-fault insurance laws was a strong determinant. New Orleans came in at #2 for the most expensive rates. *www.nerdwallet.com, "Best Cities for Cheap Car Insurance," February 3, 2014*

Women/Minorities Rankings

- For its trip ideas, *Travel + Leisure* listed the best cities in the US for a memorable and fun girls' trip. Whether it is for a special occasion or just to get away, New Orleans is sure to have something for everyone. *Travel + Leisure, "America's Best Cities for Getting Away With the Girls," March 18, 2019*

- New Orleans was selected as one of "America's Favorite Cities." The city ranked #4 in the "Type of Trip: Gay-friendly Vacation" category. Respondents to an online survey were asked to rate 38 top urban destinations in the United States from visitor's perspective. Criteria: gay-friendly. *Travel + Leisure, "America's Favorite Cities 2015"*

- New Orleans was selected as one of the gayest cities in America by *The Advocate*. The city ranked #5 out of 25. Criteria, among many: Trans Pride parades/festivals; gay rugby teams; lesbian bars; LGBT centers; theater screenings of "Moonlight"; LGBT-inclusive nondiscrimination ordinances; and gay bowling teams. *The Advocate, "Queerest Cities in America 2017" January 12, 2017*

- Personal finance website *WalletHub* compared more than 180 U.S. cities—including the 150 most populated U.S. cities, plus at least two of the most populated cities in each state—across two key dimensions, "Hispanic Business-Friendliness" and "Hispanic Purchasing Power", to arrive at the most favorable conditions for Hispanic entrepreneurs. New Orleans was ranked #61 out of 182. Criteria includes: share of Hispanic-Owned Businesses; Hispanic ehtrepreneurship rate to median annual income of Hispanics; Small Business-Friendliness score; cost of living; and number of Hispanics with at least a bachelor's degree. *WalletHub.com, "2018's Best Cities for Hispanic Entrepreneurs," April 26, 2018*

Miscellaneous Rankings

- New Orleans was selected as a 2018 Digital Cities Survey winner. The city ranked #10 in the large city (250,000 to 499,999 population) category. The survey examined and assessed how city governments are utilizing technology to improve transparency, enhance cybersecurity, and solve social challenges. Survey questions focused on ten characteristics: engaged, mobile, open, secure, staffed/supported, efficient, connected, resilient, best practices, and use of innovation. *Center for Digital Government, "2018 Digital Cities Survey," November 2, 2018*

- In its roundup of St. Patrick's Day parades "Gayot" listed the best festivals and parades of all things Irish. The festivities in New Orleans as among the best. *www.gayot.com, "Best St. Patrick's Day Parades," March 17, 2018*

- *WalletHub* compared the 150 most populated U.S. cities to determine their operating efficiency. A "Quality of Services" score was constructed for each city and then divided by the total budget per capita to reveal which were managed the best. New Orleans ranked #113. Criteria: financial stability; economy; education; safety; health; infrastructure and pollution. *www.WalletHub.com, "2018's Best- & Worst-Run Cities in America," July 9, 2018*

- New Orleans was selected as one of the 20 memorable places in the world during Thanksgiving by *Fodor's Travel*. Criteria: attractions; history; events. *Fodors.com, "Where to Go for Thanksgiving 2016," November 4, 2016*

- New Orleans was selected as one of "America's Friendliest Cities." The city ranked #4 in the "Friendliest" category. Respondents to an online survey were asked to rate 38 top urban destinations in the United States as to general friendliness, as well as manners, politeness and warm disposition. *Travel + Leisure, "America's Friendliest Cities," October 20, 2017*

Business Environment

CITY FINANCES

City Government Finances

Component	2016 ($000)	2016 ($ per capita)
Total Revenues	1,787,210	4,587
Total Expenditures	1,764,296	4,528
Debt Outstanding	2,543,453	6,528
Cash and Securities[1]	2,514,424	6,454

Note: (1) Cash and security holdings of a government at the close of its fiscal year, including those of its dependent agencies, utilities, and liquor stores.
Source: U.S. Census Bureau, State & Local Government Finances 2016

City Government Revenue by Source

Source	2016 ($000)	2016 ($ per capita)	2016 (%)
General Revenue			
From Federal Government	360,368	925	20.2
From State Government	202,218	519	11.3
From Local Governments	6,750	17	0.4
Taxes			
Property	285,831	734	16.0
Sales and Gross Receipts	240,038	616	13.4
Personal Income	0	0	0.0
Corporate Income	0	0	0.0
Motor Vehicle License	2,421	6	0.1
Other Taxes	27,618	71	1.5
Current Charges	406,769	1,044	22.8
Liquor Store	0	0	0.0
Utility	78,008	200	4.4
Employee Retirement	14,555	37	0.8

Source: U.S. Census Bureau, State & Local Government Finances 2016

City Government Expenditures by Function

Function	2016 ($000)	2016 ($ per capita)	2016 (%)
General Direct Expenditures			
Air Transportation	117,711	302	6.7
Corrections	84,993	218	4.8
Education	0	0	0.0
Employment Security Administration	0	0	0.0
Financial Administration	46,700	119	2.6
Fire Protection	103,014	264	5.8
General Public Buildings	7,146	18	0.4
Governmental Administration, Other	58,948	151	3.3
Health	28,197	72	1.6
Highways	100,445	257	5.7
Hospitals	32,337	83	1.8
Housing and Community Development	269,296	691	15.3
Interest on General Debt	85,707	220	4.9
Judicial and Legal	33,216	85	1.9
Libraries	13,473	34	0.8
Parking	0	0	0.0
Parks and Recreation	84,707	217	4.8
Police Protection	136,574	350	7.7
Public Welfare	2,665	6	0.2
Sewerage	168,247	431	9.5
Solid Waste Management	40,882	104	2.3
Veterans' Services	0	0	0.0
Liquor Store	0	0	0.0
Utility	113,689	291	6.4
Employee Retirement	53,435	137	3.0

Source: U.S. Census Bureau, State & Local Government Finances 2016

DEMOGRAPHICS

Population Growth

Area	1990 Census	2000 Census	2010 Census	2017* Estimate	Population Growth (%) 1990-2017	Population Growth (%) 2010-2017
City	496,938	484,674	343,829	388,182	-21.9	12.9
MSA[1]	1,264,391	1,316,510	1,167,764	1,260,660	-0.3	8.0
U.S.	248,709,873	281,421,906	308,745,538	321,004,407	29.1	4.0

Note: (1) Figures cover the New Orleans-Metairie, LA Metropolitan Statistical Area—see Appendix B for areas included; (*) 2013-2017 5-year estimated population
Source: U.S. Census Bureau, 1990 Census, Census 2000, Census 2010, 2013-2017 American Community Survey 5-Year Estimates

Household Size

Area	Persons in Household (%) One	Two	Three	Four	Five	Six	Seven or More	Average Household Size
City	43.4	29.9	13.3	8.2	3.3	1.1	0.8	2.40
MSA[1]	32.3	32.4	15.9	11.9	4.7	1.6	1.0	2.60
U.S.	27.7	33.8	15.7	13.0	6.0	2.3	1.4	2.60

Note: (1) Figures cover the New Orleans-Metairie, LA Metropolitan Statistical Area—see Appendix B for areas included
Source: U.S. Census Bureau, 2013-2017 American Community Survey 5-Year Estimates

Race

Area	White Alone[2] (%)	Black Alone[2] (%)	Asian Alone[2] (%)	AIAN[3] Alone[2] (%)	NHOPI[4] Alone[2] (%)	Other Race Alone[2] (%)	Two or More Races (%)
City	34.1	59.8	3.0	0.2	0.0	1.2	1.8
MSA[1]	57.8	35.0	2.9	0.3	0.0	2.0	1.9
U.S.	73.0	12.7	5.4	0.8	0.2	4.8	3.1

Note: (1) Figures cover the New Orleans-Metairie, LA Metropolitan Statistical Area—see Appendix B for areas included; (2) Alone is defined as not being in combination with one or more other races; (3) American Indian and Alaska Native; (4) Native Hawaiian and Other Pacific Islander
Source: U.S. Census Bureau, 2013-2017 American Community Survey 5-Year Estimates

Hispanic or Latino Origin

Area	Total (%)	Mexican (%)	Puerto Rican (%)	Cuban (%)	Other (%)
City	5.5	1.2	0.3	0.4	3.7
MSA[1]	8.7	1.9	0.5	0.6	5.7
U.S.	17.6	11.1	1.7	0.7	4.1

Note: Persons of Hispanic or Latino origin can be of any race; (1) Figures cover the New Orleans-Metairie, LA Metropolitan Statistical Area—see Appendix B for areas included
Source: U.S. Census Bureau, 2013-2017 American Community Survey 5-Year Estimates

Segregation

Type	Segregation Indices[1] 1990	2000	2010	2010 Rank[2]	Percent Change 1990-2000	1990-2010	2000-2010
Black/White	68.3	69.2	63.9	28	0.9	-4.4	-5.3
Asian/White	49.6	50.4	48.6	9	0.8	-1.0	-1.8
Hispanic/White	31.1	35.6	38.3	74	4.5	7.2	2.7

Note: All figures cover the Metropolitan Statistical Area—see Appendix B for areas included; Figures are based on an analysis of 1990, 2000, and 2010 Census Decennial Census tract data by William H. Frey, Brookings Institution and the University of Michigan Social Science Data Analysis Network. In this analysis all racial groups (whites, blacks, and asians) are non-Hispanic members of those races. Hispanics are shown as a separate category; (1) Segregation Indices are Dissimilarity Indices that measure the degree to which the minority group is distributed differently than whites across census tracts. They range from 0 (complete integration) to 100 (complete segregation) where the value indicates the percentage of the minority group that needs to move to be distributed exactly like whites; (2) Ranges from 1 (most segregated) to 102 (least segregated); n/a not available.
Source: www.CensusScope.org

Ancestry

Area	German	Irish	English	American	Italian	Polish	French[2]	Scottish	Dutch
City	6.5	5.8	4.2	2.4	4.0	0.9	5.8	1.1	0.4
MSA[1]	10.1	7.6	4.6	5.0	8.2	0.7	12.8	1.1	0.4
U.S.	14.1	10.1	7.5	6.6	5.3	2.9	2.5	1.7	1.3

Note: Figures are the percentage of the total population reporting a particular ancestry. The nine most commonly reported ancestries in the U.S. are shown. Figures include multiple ancestries (e.g. if a person reported being Irish and Italian, they were included in both columns); (1) Figures cover the New Orleans-Metairie, LA Metropolitan Statistical Area—see Appendix B for areas included; (2) Excludes Basque
Source: U.S. Census Bureau, 2013-2017 American Community Survey 5-Year Estimates

Foreign-Born Population

Area	Percent of Population Born in								
	Any Foreign Country	Asia	Mexico	Europe	Carribean	Central America[2]	South America	Africa	Canada
City	5.9	2.0	0.3	0.8	0.3	1.6	0.4	0.3	0.1
MSA[1]	7.6	2.1	0.6	0.6	0.7	2.7	0.5	0.3	0.1
U.S.	13.4	4.1	3.6	1.5	1.3	1.0	0.9	0.6	0.3

Note: (1) Figures cover the New Orleans-Metairie, LA Metropolitan Statistical Area—see Appendix B for areas included; (2) Excludes Mexico.
Source: U.S. Census Bureau, 2013-2017 American Community Survey 5-Year Estimates

Marital Status

Area	Never Married	Now Married[2]	Separated	Widowed	Divorced
City	48.8	29.8	3.0	6.0	12.5
MSA[1]	37.5	41.6	2.4	6.4	12.2
U.S.	33.1	48.2	2.0	5.8	10.9

Note: Figures are percentages and cover the population 15 years of age and older; (1) Figures cover the New Orleans-Metairie, LA Metropolitan Statistical Area—see Appendix B for areas included; (2) Excludes separated
Source: U.S. Census Bureau, 2013-2017 American Community Survey 5-Year Estimates

Disability by Age

Area	All Ages	Under 18 Years Old	18 to 64 Years Old	65 Years and Over
City	13.8	4.4	12.1	38.1
MSA[1]	13.7	4.7	11.7	37.2
U.S.	12.6	4.2	10.3	35.5

Note: Figures show percent of the civilian noninstitutionalized population that reported having a disability. Disability status is determined from six types of difficulty: vision, hearing, cognitive, ambulatory, self-care, and independent living. For children under 5 years old, hearing and vision difficulty are used to determine disability status. For children between the ages of 5 and 14, disability status is determined from hearing, vision, cognitive, ambulatory, and self-care difficulties. For people aged 15 years and older, they are considered to have a disability if they have difficulty with any one of the six difficulty types; Note: (1) Figures cover the New Orleans-Metairie, LA Metropolitan Statistical Area—see Appendix B for areas included
Source: U.S. Census Bureau, 2013-2017 American Community Survey 5-Year Estimates

Age

Area	Percent of Population									Median Age
	Under Age 5	Age 5–19	Age 20–34	Age 35–44	Age 45–54	Age 55–64	Age 65–74	Age 75–84	Age 85+	
City	6.0	16.8	25.7	12.8	12.6	13.1	7.8	3.5	1.6	35.9
MSA[1]	6.2	18.4	21.6	12.6	13.4	13.5	8.5	4.0	1.7	37.7
U.S.	6.2	19.5	20.7	12.7	13.4	12.7	8.6	4.4	1.9	37.8

Note: (1) Figures cover the New Orleans-Metairie, LA Metropolitan Statistical Area—see Appendix B for areas included
Source: U.S. Census Bureau, 2013-2017 American Community Survey 5-Year Estimates

Gender

Area	Males	Females	Males per 100 Females
City	185,063	203,119	91.1
MSA[1]	609,832	650,828	93.7
U.S.	158,018,753	162,985,654	97.0

Note: (1) Figures cover the New Orleans-Metairie, LA Metropolitan Statistical Area—see Appendix B for areas included
Source: U.S. Census Bureau, 2013-2017 American Community Survey 5-Year Estimates

Religious Groups by Family

Area	Catholic	Baptist	Non-Den.	Methodist[2]	Lutheran	LDS[3]	Pente-costal	Presby-terian[4]	Muslim[5]	Judaism
MSA[1]	31.6	8.4	3.7	2.7	0.8	0.6	2.1	0.5	0.5	0.5
U.S.	19.1	9.3	4.0	4.0	2.3	2.0	1.9	1.6	0.8	0.7

Note: Figures are the number of adherents as a percentage of the total population; (1) Figures cover the New Orleans-Metairie, LA Metropolitan Statistical Area—see Appendix B for areas included; (2) Methodist/Pietist; (3) Latter Day Saints; (4) Reformed; (5) Figures are estimates
Source: Association of Statisticians of American Religious Bodies, 2010 U.S. Religion Census: Religious Congregations & Membership Study

Religious Groups by Tradition

Area	Catholic	Evangelical Protestant	Mainline Protestant	Other Tradition	Black Protestant	Orthodox
MSA[1]	31.6	12.7	4.0	2.1	3.0	0.1
U.S.	19.1	16.2	7.3	4.3	1.6	0.3

Note: Figures are the number of adherents as a percentage of the total population; (1) Figures cover the New Orleans-Metairie, LA Metropolitan Statistical Area—see Appendix B for areas included
Source: Association of Statisticians of American Religious Bodies, 2010 U.S. Religion Census: Religious Congregations & Membership Study

ECONOMY

Gross Metropolitan Product

Area	2016	2017	2018	2019	Rank[2]
MSA[1]	78.0	80.5	84.4	88.1	45

Note: Figures are in billions of dollars; (1) Figures cover the New Orleans-Metairie, LA Metropolitan Statistical Area—see Appendix B for areas included; (2) Rank is based on 2017 data and ranges from 1 to 381
Source: U.S. Conference of Mayors, U.S. Metro Economies: Economic Growth & Full Employment, June 2018

Economic Growth

Area	2017-2018 (%)	2019-2020 (%)	2021-2022 (%)
MSA[1]	1.5	2.2	1.9

Note: Figures are real gross metropolitan product (GMP) growth rates and represent average annual percent change; (1) Figures cover the New Orleans-Metairie, LA Metropolitan Statistical Area—see Appendix B for areas included
Source: U.S. Conference of Mayors, U.S. Metro Economies: Economic Growth & Full Employment, June 2018

Metropolitan Area Exports

Area	2012	2013	2014	2015	2016	2017	Rank[2]
MSA[1]	24,359.5	30,030.9	34,881.5	27,023.3	29,518.8	31,648.5	8

Note: Figures are in millions of dollars; (1) Figures cover the New Orleans-Metairie, LA Metropolitan Statistical Area—see Appendix B for areas included; (2) Rank is based on 2017 data and ranges from 1 to 387
Source: U.S. Department of Commerce, International Trade Administration, Office of Trade and Economic Analysis, Industry and Analysis, Exports by Metropolitan Area, extracted March 25, 2019

Building Permits

Area	Single-Family			Multi-Family			Total		
	2016	2017	Pct. Chg.	2016	2017	Pct. Chg.	2016	2017	Pct. Chg.
City	280	447	59.6	328	213	-35.1	608	660	8.6
MSA[1]	2,494	2,720	9.1	492	246	-50.0	2,986	2,966	-0.7
U.S.	750,800	820,000	9.2	455,800	462,000	1.4	1,206,600	1,282,000	6.2

Note: (1) Figures cover the New Orleans-Metairie, LA Metropolitan Statistical Area—see Appendix B for areas included; Figures represent new, privately-owned housing units authorized (unadjusted data); All permit data are based on estimates with imputation
Source: U.S. Census Bureau, Manufacturing, Mining, and Construction Statistics, Building Permits, 2016, 2017

Bankruptcy Filings

Area	Business Filings			Nonbusiness Filings		
	2017	2018	% Chg.	2017	2018	% Chg.
Orleans Parish	59	128	116.9	561	634	13.0
U.S.	23,157	22,232	-4.0	765,863	751,186	-1.9

Note: Business filings include Chapter 7, Chapter 11, Chapter 12, and Chapter 13; Nonbusiness filings include Chapter 7, Chapter 11, and Chapter 13
Source: Administrative Office of the U.S. Courts, Business and Nonbusiness Bankruptcy, County Cases Commenced by Chapter of the Bankruptcy Code, During the 12-Month Period Ending December 31, 2017 and Business and Nonbusiness Bankruptcy, County Cases Commenced by Chapter of the Bankruptcy Code, During the 12-Month Period Ending December 31, 2018

Housing Vacancy Rates

Area	Gross Vacancy Rate[2] (%)			Year-Round Vacancy Rate[3] (%)			Rental Vacancy Rate[4] (%)			Homeowner Vacancy Rate[5] (%)		
	2016	2017	2018	2016	2017	2018	2016	2017	2018	2016	2017	2018
MSA[1]	13.6	12.8	11.9	12.7	12.2	11.8	11.1	10.8	9.7	2.6	2.5	1.7
U.S.	12.8	12.7	12.3	9.9	9.9	9.7	6.9	7.2	6.9	1.7	1.6	1.5

Note: (1) Figures cover the New Orleans-Metairie, LA Metropolitan Statistical Area—see Appendix B for areas included; (2) The percentage of the total housing inventory that is vacant; (3) The percentage of the housing inventory (excluding seasonal units) that is year-round vacant; (4) The percentage of rental inventory that is vacant for rent; (5) The percentage of homeowner inventory that is vacant for sale
Source: U.S. Census Bureau, Housing Vacancies and Homeownership Annual Statistics: 2016, 2017, 2018

INCOME

Income

Area	Per Capita ($)	Median Household ($)	Average Household ($)
City	29,275	38,721	67,224
MSA[1]	29,298	50,154	72,656
U.S.	31,177	57,652	81,283

Note: (1) Figures cover the New Orleans-Metairie, LA Metropolitan Statistical Area—see Appendix B for areas included
Source: U.S. Census Bureau, 2013-2017 American Community Survey 5-Year Estimates

Household Income Distribution

Area	Percent of Households Earning							
	Under $15,000	$15,000 -$24,999	$25,000 -$34,999	$35,000 -$49,999	$50,000 -$74,999	$75,000 -$99,999	$100,000 -$149,999	$150,000 and up
City	22.9	13.0	10.7	12.3	13.7	8.8	9.2	9.5
MSA[1]	15.5	11.2	10.3	12.8	16.5	11.1	12.4	10.1
U.S.	11.6	9.8	9.5	13.0	17.7	12.3	14.1	12.1

Note: (1) Figures cover the New Orleans-Metairie, LA Metropolitan Statistical Area—see Appendix B for areas included
Source: U.S. Census Bureau, 2013-2017 American Community Survey 5-Year Estimates

Poverty Rate

Area	All Ages	Under 18 Years Old	18 to 64 Years Old	65 Years and Over
City	25.4	38.3	23.0	16.9
MSA[1]	18.0	26.6	16.2	12.3
U.S.	14.6	20.3	13.7	9.3

Note: Figures are percentage of people whose income during the past 12 months was below the poverty level; (1) Figures cover the New Orleans-Metairie, LA Metropolitan Statistical Area—see Appendix B for areas included
Source: U.S. Census Bureau, 2013-2017 American Community Survey 5-Year Estimates

EMPLOYMENT

Labor Force and Employment

Area	Civilian Labor Force			Workers Employed		
	Dec. 2017	Dec. 2018	% Chg.	Dec. 2017	Dec. 2018	% Chg.
City	179,260	180,224	0.5	172,059	172,588	0.3
MSA[1]	596,570	599,617	0.5	574,236	576,006	0.3
U.S.	159,880,000	162,510,000	1.6	153,602,000	156,481,000	1.9

Note: Data is not seasonally adjusted and covers workers 16 years of age and older; (1) Figures cover the New Orleans-Metairie, LA Metropolitan Statistical Area—see Appendix B for areas included
Source: Bureau of Labor Statistics, Local Area Unemployment Statistics

Unemployment Rate

Area	2018											
	Jan.	Feb.	Mar.	Apr.	May	Jun.	Jul.	Aug.	Sep.	Oct.	Nov.	Dec.
City	4.4	4.0	4.3	4.3	4.7	6.2	6.1	5.9	5.2	4.8	4.5	4.2
MSA[1]	4.1	3.7	4.0	4.0	4.4	5.7	5.6	5.3	4.8	4.4	4.2	3.9
U.S.	4.5	4.4	4.1	3.7	3.6	4.2	4.1	3.9	3.6	3.5	3.5	3.7

Note: Data is not seasonally adjusted and covers workers 16 years of age and older; (1) Figures cover the New Orleans-Metairie, LA Metropolitan Statistical Area—see Appendix B for areas included
Source: Bureau of Labor Statistics, Local Area Unemployment Statistics

Average Wages

Occupation	$/Hr.	Occupation	$/Hr.
Accountants and Auditors	35.00	Maids and Housekeeping Cleaners	10.60
Automotive Mechanics	20.00	Maintenance and Repair Workers	18.30
Bookkeepers	18.50	Marketing Managers	44.20
Carpenters	20.40	Nuclear Medicine Technologists	32.10
Cashiers	9.80	Nurses, Licensed Practical	20.40
Clerks, General Office	12.20	Nurses, Registered	32.10
Clerks, Receptionists/Information	12.00	Nursing Assistants	11.70
Clerks, Shipping/Receiving	14.20	Packers and Packagers, Hand	11.20
Computer Programmers	43.60	Physical Therapists	41.50
Computer Systems Analysts	37.50	Postal Service Mail Carriers	24.50
Computer User Support Specialists	22.70	Real Estate Brokers	n/a
Cooks, Restaurant	11.30	Retail Salespersons	12.00
Dentists	71.40	Sales Reps., Exc. Tech./Scientific	29.80
Electrical Engineers	47.50	Sales Reps., Tech./Scientific	33.30
Electricians	25.20	Secretaries, Exc. Legal/Med./Exec.	16.80
Financial Managers	51.90	Security Guards	14.50
First-Line Supervisors/Managers, Sales	19.50	Surgeons	137.60
Food Preparation Workers	9.10	Teacher Assistants*	11.20
General and Operations Managers	58.20	Teachers, Elementary School*	24.30
Hairdressers/Cosmetologists	9.90	Teachers, Secondary School*	24.90
Internists, General	113.60	Telemarketers	16.10
Janitors and Cleaners	10.90	Truck Drivers, Heavy/Tractor-Trailer	22.50
Landscaping/Groundskeeping Workers	12.10	Truck Drivers, Light/Delivery Svcs.	18.20
Lawyers	59.00	Waiters and Waitresses	9.10

Note: Wage data covers the New Orleans-Metairie, LA Metropolitan Statistical Area—see Appendix B for areas included; (*) Hourly wages for elementary/secondary school teachers and teacher assistants were calculated by the editors from annual wage data based on a 40 hour work week; n/a not available.
Source: Bureau of Labor Statistics, Metro Area Occupational Employment & Wage Estimates, May 2018

Employment by Occupation

Occupation Classification	City (%)	MSA[1] (%)	U.S. (%)
Management, Business, Science, and Arts	42.3	36.4	37.4
Natural Resources, Construction, and Maintenance	6.4	10.6	8.9
Production, Transportation, and Material Moving	8.5	10.2	12.2
Sales and Office	20.4	23.4	23.5
Service	22.4	19.4	18.0

Note: Figures cover employed civilians 16 years of age and older; (1) Figures cover the New Orleans-Metairie, LA Metropolitan Statistical Area—see Appendix B for areas included
Source: U.S. Census Bureau, 2013-2017 American Community Survey 5-Year Estimates

Employment by Industry

Sector	MSA[1]		U.S.
	Number of Employees	Percent of Total	Percent of Total
Construction	31,100	5.3	4.8
Education and Health Services	102,200	17.5	15.9
Financial Activities	28,900	4.9	5.7
Government	72,300	12.4	15.1
Information	7,500	1.3	1.9
Leisure and Hospitality	93,600	16.0	10.7
Manufacturing	30,100	5.1	8.5
Mining and Logging	4,400	0.8	0.5
Other Services	24,600	4.2	3.9
Professional and Business Services	76,300	13.0	14.1
Retail Trade	62,000	10.6	10.8
Transportation, Warehousing, and Utilities	30,200	5.2	4.2
Wholesale Trade	21,900	3.7	3.9

Note: Figures are non-farm employment as of December 2018. Figures are not seasonally adjusted and include workers 16 years of age and older; (1) Figures cover the New Orleans-Metairie, LA Metropolitan Statistical Area—see Appendix B for areas included
Source: Bureau of Labor Statistics, Current Employment Statistics, Employment, Hours, and Earnings

Occupations with Greatest Projected Employment Growth: 2017 – 2019

Occupation[1]	2017 Employment	2019 Projected Employment	Numeric Employment Change	Percent Employment Change
Personal Care Aides	35,390	37,200	1,810	5.1
Registered Nurses	46,590	48,090	1,500	3.2
Laborers and Freight, Stock, and Material Movers, Hand	45,490	46,520	1,030	2.2
Retail Salespersons	61,790	62,820	1,030	1.7
Carpenters	18,290	19,290	1,000	5.5
Combined Food Preparation and Serving Workers, Including Fast Food	28,720	29,660	940	3.3
Construction Laborers	21,630	22,560	930	4.3
Food Preparation Workers	32,990	33,790	800	2.4
Cashiers	70,980	71,670	690	1.0
Waiters and Waitresses	38,340	38,990	650	1.7

Note: Projections cover Louisiana; (1) Sorted by numeric employment change
Source: www.projectionscentral.com, State Occupational Projections, 2017–2019 Short-Term Projections

Fastest Growing Occupations: 2017 – 2019

Occupation[1]	2017 Employment	2019 Projected Employment	Numeric Employment Change	Percent Employment Change
Web Developers	550	600	50	8.0
Operations Research Analysts	1,090	1,170	80	7.5
Structural Iron and Steel Workers	3,020	3,230	210	7.1
Millwrights	1,310	1,400	90	6.9
Veterinary Technologists and Technicians	1,120	1,190	70	6.8
Commercial Divers	850	900	50	6.4
Home Health Aides	8,530	9,060	530	6.2
Physical Therapist Assistants	1,480	1,570	90	6.0
Personal Financial Advisors	1,550	1,640	90	5.8
Software Developers, Applications	1,430	1,510	80	5.7

Note: Projections cover Louisiana; (1) Sorted by percent employment change and excludes occupations with numeric employment change less than 50
Source: www.projectionscentral.com, State Occupational Projections, 2017–2019 Short-Term Projections

TAXES

State Corporate Income Tax Rates

State	Tax Rate (%)	Income Brackets ($)	Num. of Brackets	Financial Institution Tax Rate (%)[a]	Federal Income Tax Ded.
Louisiana	4.0 - 8.0	25,000 - 200,001	5	4.0 - 8.0	Yes

Note: Tax rates as of January 1, 2019; (a) Rates listed are the corporate income tax rate applied to financial institutions or excise taxes based on income. Some states have other taxes based upon the value of deposits or shares.
Source: Federation of Tax Administrators, Range of State Corporate Income Tax Rates, January 1, 2019

State Individual Income Tax Rates

State	Tax Rate (%)	Income Brackets ($)	Personal Exemptions ($) Single	Married	Depend.	Standard Ded. ($) Single	Married
Louisiana	2.0 - 6.0	12,500 - 50,001 (b)	4,500	9,000 (k)	1,000	(k)	(k)

Note: Tax rates as of January 1, 2019; Local- and county-level taxes are not included; n/a not applicable; Federal income tax is deductible on state income tax returns; (b) For joint returns, taxes are twice the tax on half the couple's income; (k) The amounts reported for Louisiana are a combined personal exemption-standard deduction.
Source: Federation of Tax Administrators, State Individual Income Tax Rates, January 1, 2019

Various State Sales and Excise Tax Rates

State	State Sales Tax (%)	Gasoline[1] (¢/gal.)	Cigarette[2] ($/pack)	Spirits[3] ($/gal.)	Wine[4] ($/gal.)	Beer[5] ($/gal.)	Recreational Marijuana (%)
Louisiana	5	20.01	1.08	3.03 (f)	0.76 (l)	0.4	Not legal

Note: All tax rates as of January 1, 2019; (1) The American Petroleum Institute has developed a methodology for determining the average tax rate on a gallon of fuel. Rates may include any of the following: excise taxes, environmental fees, storage tank fees, other fees or taxes, general sales tax, and local taxes. In states where gasoline is subject to the general sales tax, or where the fuel tax is based on the average sale price, the average rate determined by API is sensitive to changes in the price of gasoline. States that fully or partially apply general sales taxes to gasoline: CA, CO, GA, IL, IN, MI, NY; (2) The federal excise tax of $1.0066 per pack and local taxes are not included; (3) Rates are those applicable to off-premise sales of 40% alcohol by volume (a.b.v.) distilled spirits in 750ml containers. Local excise taxes are excluded; (4) Rates are those applicable to off-premise sales of 11% a.b.v. non-carbonated wine in 750ml containers; (5) Rates are those applicable to off-premise sales of 4.7% a.b.v. beer in 12 ounce containers; (f) Different rates also applicable according to alcohol content, place of production, size of container, or place purchased (on- or off-premise or onboard airlines); (l) Different rates also applicable to alcohol content, place of production, size of container, place purchased (on- or off-premise or on board airlines) or type of wine (carbonated, vermouth, etc.).
Source: Tax Foundation, 2019 Facts & Figures: How Does Your State Compare?

State Business Tax Climate Index Rankings

State	Overall Rank	Corporate Tax Rank	Individual Income Tax Rank	Sales Tax Rank	Unemployment Insurance Tax Rank	Property Tax Rank
Louisiana	44	36	32	50	4	32

Note: The index is a measure of how each state's tax laws affect economic performance. The lower the rank, the more favorable a state's tax system is for business. States without a given tax are given a ranking of 1. The scores/rankings for the District of Columbia do not affect other states. The 2019 index represents the tax climate as of July 1, 2018.
Source: Tax Foundation, State Business Tax Climate Index 2019

COMMERCIAL UTILITIES

Typical Monthly Electric Bills

Area	Commercial Service ($/month) 1,500 kWh	40 kW demand 14,000 kWh	Industrial Service ($/month) 1,000 kW demand 200,000 kWh	50,000 kW demand 32,500,000 kWh
City	179	1,573	24,599	2,996,100
Average[1]	203	1,619	25,886	2,540,077

Note: Figures are based on annualized rates; (1) Average based on 187 utilities surveyed
Source: Edison Electric Institute, Typical Bills and Average Rates Report, Summer 2018

TRANSPORTATION

Means of Transportation to Work

Area	Car/Truck/Van		Public Transportation			Bicycle	Walked	Other Means	Worked at Home
	Drove Alone	Car-pooled	Bus	Subway	Railroad				
City	68.5	9.2	6.8	0.0	0.0	3.2	5.0	2.3	4.9
MSA[1]	78.6	9.9	2.5	0.0	0.0	1.2	2.4	1.7	3.6
U.S.	76.4	9.2	2.5	1.9	0.6	0.6	2.7	1.3	4.7

Note: Figures are percentages and cover workers 16 years of age and older; (1) Figures cover the New Orleans-Metairie, LA Metropolitan Statistical Area—see Appendix B for areas included
Source: U.S. Census Bureau, 2013-2017 American Community Survey 5-Year Estimates

Travel Time to Work

Area	Less Than 10 Minutes	10 to 19 Minutes	20 to 29 Minutes	30 to 44 Minutes	45 to 59 Minutes	60 to 89 Minutes	90 Minutes or More
City	9.7	33.6	25.3	20.4	4.6	4.5	1.9
MSA[1]	10.6	30.6	22.3	21.1	7.3	5.6	2.5
U.S.	12.7	28.9	20.9	20.5	8.1	6.2	2.7

Note: Note: Figures are percentages and include workers 16 years old and over; (1) Figures cover the New Orleans-Metairie, LA Metropolitan Statistical Area—see Appendix B for areas included
Source: U.S. Census Bureau, 2013-2017 American Community Survey 5-Year Estimates

Freeway Travel Time Index

Area	1985	1990	1995	2000	2005	2010	2014
Urban Area Rank[1,2]	17	20	21	24	27	9	13
Urban Area Index[1]	1.14	1.16	1.20	1.22	1.23	1.32	1.32
Average Index[3]	1.09	1.11	1.14	1.17	1.20	1.19	1.20

Note: Freeway Travel Time Index—the ratio of travel time in the peak period to the travel time at free-flow conditions. For example, a value of 1.30 indicates a 20-minute free-flow trip takes 26 minutes in the peak (20 minutes x 1.30 = 26 minutes); (1) Covers the New Orleans LA urban area; (2) Rank is based on 101 urban areas (#1 = highest travel time index); (3) Average of 101 urban areas
Source: Texas Transportation Institute, 2015 Urban Mobility Scorecard, August 2015

Freeway Commuter Stress Index

Area	1985	1990	1995	2000	2005	2010	2014
Urban Area Rank[1,2]	24	26	24	27	33	12	15
Urban Area Index[1]	1.18	1.20	1.25	1.27	1.28	1.37	1.37
Average Index[3]	1.13	1.16	1.19	1.22	1.25	1.24	1.25

Note: The Freeway Commuter Stress Index is the same as the Freeway Travel Time Index (see table above) except that it includes only the travel in the peak directions during the peak periods; the TTI includes travel in all directions during the peak period. Thus, the CSI is more indicative of the work trip experienced by each commuter on a daily basis; (1) Covers the New Orleans LA urban area; (2) Rank is based on 101 urban areas (#1 = highest travel time index); (3) Average of 101 urban areas
Source: Texas Transportation Institute, 2015 Urban Mobility Scorecard, August 2015

Public Transportation

Agency Name / Mode of Transportation	Vehicles Operated in Maximum Service[1]	Annual Unlinked Passenger Trips[2] (in thous.)	Annual Passenger Miles[3] (in thous.)
New Orleans Regional Transit Authority (NORTA)			
Bus (purchased transportation)	90	10,502.2	41,398.9
Demand Response (purchased transportation)	42	217.3	1,580.6
Ferryboat (purchased transportation)	2	1,071.1	535.6
Streetcar Rail (purchased transportation)	31	8,097.7	15,599.4

Note: (1) The number of revenue vehicles operated by the given mode and type of service to meet the annual maximum service requirement. This is the revenue vehicle count during the peak season of the year; on the week and day that maximum service is provided. Vehicles operated in maximum service (VOMS) exclude atypical days and one-time special events; (2) The number of passengers who boarded public transportation vehicles. Passengers are counted each time they board a vehicle no matter how many vehicles they use to travel from their origin to their destination. (3) The sum of the distances ridden by all passengers during the entire fiscal year.
Source: Federal Transit Administration, National Transit Database, 2017

Air Transportation

Airport Name and Code / Type of Service	Passenger Airlines[1]	Passenger Enplanements	Freight Carriers[2]	Freight (lbs)
New Orleans International (MSY)				
Domestic service (U.S. carriers - 2018)	29	6,477,724	14	45,497,174
International service (U.S. carriers - 2017)	8	12,367	0	0

Note: (1) Includes all U.S.-based major, minor and commuter airlines that carried at least one passenger during the year; (2) Includes all U.S.-based airlines and freight carriers that transported at least one pound of freight during the year.
Source: Bureau of Transportation Statistics, The Intermodal Transportation Database, Air Carriers: T-100 Domestic Market (U.S. Carriers), 2018; Bureau of Transportation Statistics, The Intermodal Transportation Database, Air Carriers: T-100 International Market (U.S. Carriers), 2017

Other Transportation Statistics

Major Highways:	I-10; I-59
Amtrak Service:	Yes
Major Waterways/Ports:	Port of New Orleans; Mississippi River

Source: Amtrak.com; Google Maps

BUSINESSES

Major Business Headquarters

Company Name	Industry	Rankings	
		Fortune[1]	Forbes[2]
Entergy	Utilities: Gas and Electric	274	-

Note: (1) Companies that produce a 10-K are ranked 1 to 500 based on 2017 revenue; (2) All private companies with at least $2 billion in annual revenue through the end of their most current fiscal year are ranked 1 to 229; companies listed are headquartered in the city; dashes indicate no ranking
Source: Fortune, "Fortune 500," June 2018; Forbes, "America's Largest Private Companies," 2018 Rankings

Fast-Growing Businesses

According to *Initiative for a Competitive Inner City (ICIC)*, New Orleans is home to seven of America's 100 fastest-growing "inner city" companies: **French Truck Coffee** (#10); **Scott, Vicknair, Hair & Checki** (#18); **The Ruby Slipper Cafe** (#28); **Ready Power** (#64); **Colmex Construction** (#71); **MDRG** (#84); **Pontchartrain Landing Marina & RV Resort** (#99). Criteria for inclusion: company must be headquartered in or have 51 percent or more of its physical operations in an economically distressed urban area; must be an independent, for-profit corporation, partnership or proprietorship; must have 10 or more employees and have a five-year sales history that includes sales of at least $200,000 in the base year and at least $1 million in the current year with no decrease in sales over the two most recent years. Companies were ranked overall by revenue growth over the five-year period between 2013 and 2017. *Initiative for a Competitive Inner City (ICIC), "Inner City 100 Companies," 2018*

Minority Business Opportunity

New Orleans is home to one company which is on the *Black Enterprise* Bank list (15 largest banks based on total assets, capital, deposits and loans, including mortgage-backed securities for the calendar year): **Liberty Bank and Trust Co.** (#3). Only commercial banks or savings and loans that are classified by the Federal Reserve as black institutions and have been fully operational for the previous calendar year were considered. *Black Enterprise, B.E. 100s, 2018*

New Orleans is home to two companies which are on the *Hispanic Business* 500 list (500 largest U.S. Hispanic-owned companies based on revenue): **Pan-American Life Insurance Group** (#15); **Atlantis International** (#184). Companies included must show at least 51 percent ownership by Hispanic U.S. citizens, and must maintain headquarters in one of the 50 states or Washington, D.C. *Hispanic Business, "Hispanic Business 500," June 20, 2013*

Minority- and Women-Owned Businesses

Group	All Firms		Firms with Paid Employees			
	Firms	Sales ($000)	Firms	Sales ($000)	Employees	Payroll ($000)
AIAN[1]	284	9,093	2	(s)	0 - 19	(s)
Asian	2,142	401,728	527	335,526	2,890	61,643
Black	16,609	585,256	515	318,448	5,014	106,865
Hispanic	1,555	332,931	188	289,123	2,292	66,976
NHOPI[2]	n/a	n/a	n/a	n/a	n/a	n/a
Women	17,792	2,054,453	1,248	1,697,640	13,728	408,870
All Firms	41,506	31,056,230	7,042	29,750,625	159,383	7,019,867

Note: Figures cover firms located in the city; minority- and women-owned business are defined as firms in which the corresponding group own 51% or more of the stock or equity of the company; (1) American Indian and Alaska Native; (2) Native Hawaiian and Other Pacific Islander; (s) estimates are suppressed when publication standards are not met; n/a not available
Source: U.S. Census Bureau, 2012 Economic Census, Survey of Business Owners

HOTELS & CONVENTION CENTERS

Hotels, Motels and Vacation Rentals

Area	5 Star		4 Star		3 Star		2 Star		1 Star		Not Rated	
	Num.	Pct.[3]	Num.	Pct.[3]	Num.	Pct.[3]	Num.	Pct.[3]	Num.	Pct.[3]	Num.	Pct.[3]
City[1]	1	0.1	98	6.3	265	17.1	120	7.7	5	0.3	1,063	68.5
Total[2]	286	0.4	5,236	7.1	16,715	22.6	10,259	13.9	293	0.4	41,056	55.6

Note: (1) Figures cover New Orleans and vicinity; (2) Figures cover all 100 cities in this book; (3) Percentage of hotels which have a given star rating; Star ratings are determined by expedia.com and offer an indication of the general quality of a particular hotel.
Source: www.expedia.com, April 3, 2019

Major Convention Centers

Name	Overall Space (sq. ft.)	Exhibit Space (sq. ft.)	Meeting Space (sq. ft.)	Meeting Rooms
Ernest N. Morial Convention Center	3,000,000	1,100,000	n/a	n/a

Note: Table includes convention centers located in the New Orleans-Metairie, LA metro area; n/a not available
Source: Original research

Living Environment

COST OF LIVING

Cost of Living Index

Composite Index	Groceries	Housing	Utilities	Trans- portation	Health Care	Misc. Goods/ Services
100.8	104.3	117.0	81.5	109.3	103.2	88.2

Note: The Cost of Living Index measures regional differences in the cost of consumer goods and services, excluding taxes and non-consumer expenditures, for professional and managerial households in the top income quintile. It is based on more than 50,000 prices covering almost 60 different items for which prices are collected three times a year by chambers of commerce, economic development organizations or university applied economic centers in each participating urban area. The numbers shown should be read as a percentage above or below the national average of 100. For example, a value of 115.4 in the groceries column indicates that grocery prices are 15.4% higher than the national average. Small differences in the index numbers should not be interpreted as significant; Figures cover the New Orleans LA urban area.
Source: The Council for Community and Economic Research, ACCRA Cost of Living Index, 2018

Grocery Prices

Area[1]	T-Bone Steak ($/pound)	Frying Chicken ($/pound)	Whole Milk ($/half gal.)	Eggs ($/dozen)	Orange Juice ($/64 oz.)	Coffee ($/11.5 oz.)
City[2]	12.05	1.00	2.99	2.38	3.74	3.87
Avg.	11.35	1.42	1.94	1.81	3.52	4.35
Min.	7.45	0.92	0.80	0.75	2.72	3.06
Max.	15.05	2.76	4.18	4.00	5.36	8.20

Note: (1) Values for the local area are compared with the average, minimum and maximum values for all 291 areas in the Cost of Living Index; (2) Figures cover the New Orleans LA urban area; **T-Bone Steak** (price per pound); **Frying Chicken** (price per pound, whole fryer); **Whole Milk** (half gallon carton); **Eggs** (price per dozen, Grade A, large); **Orange Juice** (64 oz. Tropicana or Florida Natural); **Coffee** (11.5 oz. can, vacuum-packed, Maxwell House, Hills Bros, or Folgers).
Source: The Council for Community and Economic Research, ACCRA Cost of Living Index, 2018

Housing and Utility Costs

Area[1]	New Home Price ($)	Apartment Rent ($/month)	All Electric ($/month)	Part Electric ($/month)	Other Energy ($/month)	Telephone ($/month)
City[2]	404,584	1,297	-	75.14	39.44	175.50
Avg.	347,000	1,087	165.93	100.16	67.73	178.70
Min.	200,468	500	93.58	25.64	26.78	163.10
Max.	1,901,222	4,888	388.65	246.86	332.81	197.70

Note: (1) Values for the local area are compared with the average, minimum and maximum values for all 291 areas in the Cost of Living Index; (2) Figures cover the New Orleans LA urban area; **New Home Price** (2,400 sf living area, 8,000 sf lot, in urban area with full utilities); **Apartment Rent** (950 sf 2 bedroom/1.5 or 2 bath, unfurnished, excluding all utilities except water); **All Electric** (average monthly cost for an all-electric home); **Part Electric** (average monthly cost for a part-electric home); **Other Energy** (average monthly cost for natural gas, fuel oil, coal, wood, and any other forms of energy except electricity); **Telephone** (price includes the base monthly rate plus taxes and fees for three lines of mobile phone service).
Source: The Council for Community and Economic Research, ACCRA Cost of Living Index, 2018

Health Care, Transportation, and Other Costs

Area[1]	Doctor ($/visit)	Dentist ($/visit)	Optometrist ($/visit)	Gasoline ($/gallon)	Beauty Salon ($/visit)	Men's Shirt ($)
City[2]	120.49	96.34	82.95	2.42	40.62	23.98
Avg.	110.71	95.11	103.74	2.61	37.48	32.03
Min.	33.60	62.55	54.63	1.89	17.00	11.44
Max.	195.97	153.93	225.79	3.59	71.88	58.64

Note: (1) Values for the local area are compared with the average, minimum and maximum values for all 291 areas in the Cost of Living Index; (2) Figures cover the New Orleans LA urban area; **Doctor** (general practitioners routine exam of an established patient); **Dentist** (adult teeth cleaning and periodic oral examination); **Optometrist** (full vision eye exam for established adult patient); **Gasoline** (one gallon regular unleaded, national brand, including all taxes, cash price at self-service pump if available); **Beauty Salon** (woman's shampoo, trim, and blow-dry); **Men's Shirt** (cotton/polyester dress shirt, pinpoint weave, long sleeves).
Source: The Council for Community and Economic Research, ACCRA Cost of Living Index, 2018

HOUSING

House Price Index (HPI)

Area	National Ranking[2]	Quarterly Change (%)	One-Year Change (%)	Five-Year Change (%)
MSA[1]	214	0.41	2.71	22.67
U.S.[3]	–	1.12	5.73	32.81

Note: The HPI is a weighted repeat sales index. It measures average price changes in repeat sales or refinancings on the same properties. This information is obtained by reviewing repeat mortgage transactions on single-family properties whose mortgages have been purchased or securitized by Fannie Mae or Freddie Mac in January 1975; (1) Figures cover the New Orleans-Metairie, LA Metropolitan Statistical Area—see Appendix B for areas included; (2) Rankings are based on annual percentage change for all metro areas containing at least 15,000 transactions over the last 10 years and ranges from 1 to 245; (3) figures based on a weighted average of Census Division estimates using a seasonally adjusted, purchase-only index; all figures are for the period ending December 31, 2018
Source: Federal Housing Finance Agency, House Price Index, February 26, 2019

Median Single-Family Home Prices

Area	2016	2017	2018[p]	Percent Change 2017 to 2018
MSA[1]	188.1	198.4	210.1	5.9
U.S. Average	235.5	248.8	261.6	5.1

Note: Figures are median sales prices of existing single-family homes in thousands of dollars; (p) preliminary; (1) Figures cover the New Orleans-Metairie, LA Metropolitan Statistical Area—see Appendix B for areas included
Source: National Association of Realtors, Median Sales Price of Existing Single-Family Homes for Metropolitan Areas, 4th Quarter 2018

Qualifying Income Based on Median Sales Price of Existing Single-Family Homes

Area	With 5% Down ($)	With 10% Down ($)	With 20% Down ($)
MSA[1]	50,490	47,833	42,518
U.S. Average	62,954	59,640	53,013

Note: Figures are preliminary; Qualifying income is based on a mortgage rate of 4.9%. Monthly principal and interest payment is limited to 25% of income; (1) Figures cover the New Orleans-Metairie, LA Metropolitan Statistical Area—see Appendix B for areas included
Source: National Association of Realtors, Qualifying Income Based on Median Sales Price of Existing Single-Family Homes for Metropolitan Areas, 4th Quarter 2018

Median Apartment Condo-Coop Home Prices

Area	2016	2017	2018[p]	Percent Change 2017 to 2018
MSA[1]	160.0	166.8	177.4	6.4
U.S. Average	220.7	234.3	241.0	2.9

Note: Figures are median sales prices of existing apartment condo-coop homes in thousands of dollars; (p) preliminary; (1) Figures cover the New Orleans-Metairie, LA Metropolitan Statistical Area—see Appendix B for areas included
Source: National Association of Realtors, Median Sales Price of Existing Apartment Condo-Coop Homes for Metropolitan Areas, 4th Quarter 2018

Home Value Distribution

Area	Under $50,000	$50,000 -$99,999	$100,000 -$149,999	$150,000 -$199,999	$200,000 -$299,999	$300,000 -$499,999	$500,000 -$999,999	$1,000,000 or more
City	3.8	9.5	15.9	19.7	18.5	18.9	10.6	3.0
MSA[1]	5.3	10.1	18.2	21.7	23.5	14.4	5.3	1.3
U.S.	8.3	13.9	14.7	14.6	18.7	17.3	9.7	2.7

Note: Figures are percentages and cover owner-occupied housing units; (1) Figures cover the New Orleans-Metairie, LA Metropolitan Statistical Area—see Appendix B for areas included
Source: U.S. Census Bureau, 2013-2017 American Community Survey 5-Year Estimates

Homeownership Rate

Area	2010 (%)	2011 (%)	2012 (%)	2013 (%)	2014 (%)	2015 (%)	2016 (%)	2017 (%)	2018 (%)
MSA[1]	66.9	63.9	62.4	61.4	60.6	62.8	59.3	61.7	62.6
U.S.	66.9	66.1	65.4	65.1	64.5	63.7	63.4	63.9	64.4

Note: (1) Figures cover the New Orleans-Metairie, LA Metropolitan Statistical Area—see Appendix B for areas included
Source: U.S. Census Bureau, Housing Vacancies and Homeownership Annual Statistics: 2010-2018

Year Housing Structure Built

Area	2010 or Later	2000 -2009	1990 -1999	1980 -1989	1970 -1979	1960 -1969	1950 -1959	1940 -1949	Before 1940	Median Year
City	2.4	7.9	3.8	7.4	13.5	11.4	11.6	8.2	33.8	1957
MSA[1]	2.6	12.5	9.8	13.5	19.4	13.9	9.7	5.2	13.5	1974
U.S.	3.2	14.5	14.0	13.6	15.5	10.8	10.5	5.1	12.9	1977

Note: Figures are percentages except for Median Year; Note: (1) Figures cover the New Orleans-Metairie, LA Metropolitan Statistical Area—see Appendix B for areas included
Source: U.S. Census Bureau, 2013-2017 American Community Survey 5-Year Estimates

Gross Monthly Rent

Area	Under $500	$500 -$999	$1,000 -$1,499	$1,500 -$1,999	$2,000 -$2,499	$2,500 -$2,999	$3,000 and up	Median ($)
City	12.7	42.5	31.4	9.6	2.5	0.7	0.6	954
MSA[1]	9.8	46.8	32.6	8.1	1.7	0.5	0.5	947
U.S.	10.5	41.1	28.7	11.7	4.5	1.8	1.7	982

Note: Figures are percentages except for Median; Gross rent is the contract rent plus the estimated average monthly cost of utilities (electricity, gas, and water and sewer) and fuels (oil, coal, kerosene, wood, etc.) if these are paid by the renter (or paid for the renter by someone else); (1) Figures cover the New Orleans-Metairie, LA Metropolitan Statistical Area—see Appendix B for areas included
Source: U.S. Census Bureau, 2013-2017 American Community Survey 5-Year Estimates

HEALTH

Health Risk Factors

Category	MSA[1] (%)	U.S. (%)
Adults aged 18–64 who have any kind of health care coverage	88.2	87.3
Adults who reported being in good or better health	78.9	82.4
Adults who have been told they have high blood cholesterol	38.0	33.0
Adults who have been told they have high blood pressure	39.1	32.3
Adults who are current smokers	21.7	17.1
Adults who currently use E-cigarettes	4.2	4.6
Adults who currently use chewing tobacco, snuff, or snus	3.6	4.0
Adults who are heavy drinkers[2]	8.7	6.3
Adults who are binge drinkers[3]	19.5	17.4
Adults who are overweight (BMI 25.0 - 29.9)	34.7	35.3
Adults who are obese (BMI 30.0 - 99.8)	36.1	31.3
Adults who participated in any physical activities in the past month	74.5	74.4
Adults who always or nearly always wears a seat belt	95.6	94.3

Note: (1) Figures cover the New Orleans-Metairie, LA Metropolitan Statistical Area—see Appendix B for areas included; (2) Heavy drinkers are classified as adult men having more than 14 drinks per week and adult women having more than 7 drinks per week; (3) Binge drinkers are classified as males having five or more drinks on one occasion or females having four or more drinks on one occasion
Source: Centers for Disease Control and Prevention, Behavioral Risk Factor Surveillance System, SMART: Selected Metropolitan Area Risk Trends, 2017

Acute and Chronic Health Conditions

Category	MSA[1] (%)	U.S. (%)
Adults who have ever been told they had a heart attack	4.2	4.2
Adults who have ever been told they have angina or coronary heart disease	4.4	3.9
Adults who have ever been told they had a stroke	3.9	3.0
Adults who have ever been told they have asthma	14.3	14.2
Adults who have ever been told they have arthritis	28.2	24.9
Adults who have ever been told they have diabetes[2]	15.3	10.5
Adults who have ever been told they had skin cancer	5.9	6.2
Adults who have ever been told they had any other types of cancer	6.4	7.1
Adults who have ever been told they have COPD	10.4	6.5
Adults who have ever been told they have kidney disease	3.8	3.0
Adults who have ever been told they have a form of depression	20.7	20.5

Note: (1) Figures cover the New Orleans-Metairie, LA Metropolitan Statistical Area—see Appendix B for areas included; (2) Figures do not include pregnancy-related, borderline, or pre-diabetes
Source: Centers for Disease Control and Prevention, Behavioral Risk Factor Surveillance System, SMART: Selected Metropolitan Area Risk Trends, 2017

Health Screening and Vaccination Rates

Category	MSA[1] (%)	U.S. (%)
Adults aged 65+ who have had flu shot within the past year	56.8	60.7
Adults aged 65+ who have ever had a pneumonia vaccination	76.8	75.4
Adults who have ever been tested for HIV	41.7	36.1
Adults who have ever had the shingles or zoster vaccine?	25.4	28.9
Adults who have had their blood cholesterol checked within the last five years	88.5	85.9

Note: n/a not available; (1) Figures cover the New Orleans-Metairie, LA Metropolitan Statistical Area—see Appendix B for areas included.
Source: Centers for Disease Control and Prevention, Behaviorial Risk Factor Surveillance System, SMART: Selected Metropolitan Area Risk Trends, 2017

Disability Status

Category	MSA[1] (%)	U.S. (%)
Adults who reported being deaf	7.6	6.7
Are you blind or have serious difficulty seeing, even when wearing glasses?	6.0	4.5
Are you limited in any way in any of your usual activities due of arthritis?	15.2	12.9
Do you have difficulty doing errands alone?	10.5	6.8
Do you have difficulty dressing or bathing?	4.9	3.6
Do you have serious difficulty concentrating/remembering/making decisions?	13.3	10.7
Do you have serious difficulty walking or climbing stairs?	16.1	13.6

Note: (1) Figures cover the New Orleans-Metairie, LA Metropolitan Statistical Area—see Appendix B for areas included.
Source: Centers for Disease Control and Prevention, Behaviorial Risk Factor Surveillance System, SMART: Selected Metropolitan Area Risk Trends, 2017

Mortality Rates for the Top 10 Causes of Death in the U.S.

ICD-10[a] Sub-Chapter	ICD-10[a] Code	Age-Adjusted Mortality Rate[1] per 100,000 population	
		County[2]	U.S.
Malignant neoplasms	C00-C97	159.5	155.5
Ischaemic heart diseases	I20-I25	62.9	94.8
Other forms of heart disease	I30-I51	84.4	52.9
Chronic lower respiratory diseases	J40-J47	27.1	41.0
Cerebrovascular diseases	I60-I69	47.5	37.5
Other degenerative diseases of the nervous system	G30-G31	33.9	35.0
Other external causes of accidental injury	W00-X59	47.6	33.7
Organic, including symptomatic, mental disorders	F01-F09	30.3	31.0
Hypertensive diseases	I10-I15	44.7	21.9
Diabetes mellitus	E10-E14	15.7	21.2

Note: (a) ICD-10 = International Classification of Diseases 10th Revision; (1) Mortality rates are a three year average covering 2015-2017; (2) Figures cover Orleans Parish.
Source: Centers for Disease Control and Prevention, National Center for Health Statistics. Underlying Cause of Death 1999-2017 on CDC WONDER Online Database

Mortality Rates for Selected Causes of Death

ICD-10[a] Sub-Chapter	ICD-10[a] Code	Age-Adjusted Mortality Rate[1] per 100,000 population	
		County[2]	U.S.
Assault	X85-Y09	36.9	5.9
Diseases of the liver	K70-K76	14.2	14.1
Human immunodeficiency virus (HIV) disease	B20-B24	9.7	1.8
Influenza and pneumonia	J09-J18	8.6	14.3
Intentional self-harm	X60-X84	11.7	13.6
Malnutrition	E40-E46	3.4	1.6
Obesity and other hyperalimentation	E65-E68	Suppressed	2.1
Renal failure	N17-N19	27.2	13.0
Transport accidents	V01-V99	11.2	12.4
Viral hepatitis	B15-B19	1.9	1.6

Note: (a) ICD-10 = International Classification of Diseases 10th Revision; (1) Mortality rates are a three year average covering 2015-2017; (2) Figures cover Orleans Parish; Data are suppressed when the data meet the criteria for confidentiality constraints; Mortality rates are flagged as unreliable when the rate would be calculated with a numerator of 20 or less.
Source: Centers for Disease Control and Prevention, National Center for Health Statistics. Underlying Cause of Death 1999-2017 on CDC WONDER Online Database

Health Insurance Coverage

Area	With Health Insurance	With Private Health Insurance	With Public Health Insurance	Without Health Insurance	Population Under Age 18 Without Health Insurance
City	87.6	55.4	40.0	12.4	4.3
MSA[1]	87.6	60.6	36.5	12.4	4.5
U.S.	89.5	67.2	33.8	10.5	5.7

Note: Figures are percentages that cover the civilian noninstitutionalized population; (1) Figures cover the New Orleans-Metairie, LA Metropolitan Statistical Area—see Appendix B for areas included
Source: U.S. Census Bureau, 2013-2017 American Community Survey 5-Year Estimates

Number of Medical Professionals

Area	MDs[3]	DOs[3,4]	Dentists	Podiatrists	Chiropractors	Optometrists
County[1] (number)	2,958	59	282	15	30	24
County[1] (rate[2])	752.6	15.0	71.7	3.8	7.6	6.1
U.S. (rate[2])	279.3	23.0	68.4	6.0	27.1	16.2

Note: Data as of 2017 unless noted; (1) Data covers Orleans Parish; (2) Rate per 100,000 population; (3) Data as of 2016 and includes all active, non-federal physicians; (4) Doctor of Osteopathic Medicine
Source: U.S. Department of Health and Human Services, Health Resources and Services Administration, Bureau of Health Professions, Area Resource File (ARF) 2017-2018

Best Hospitals

According to *U.S. News,* the New Orleans-Metairie, LA metro area is home to one of the best hospitals in the U.S.: **Ochsner Medical Center** (3 adult specialties and 1 pediatric specialty). The hospital listed was nationally ranked in at least one of 16 adult or 10 pediatric specialties. Only 170 hospitals nationwide were nationally ranked in one or more adult or pediatric specialty. Twenty hospitals in the U.S. made the Honor Roll. The Best Hospitals Honor Roll takes both the national rankings and the procedure and condition ratings into account. Hospitals received points if they were nationally ranked in one of the 16 adult specialties—the higher they ranked, the more points they got—and how many ratings of "high performing" they earned in the nine procedures and conditions. *U.S. News Online, "America's Best Hospitals 2018-19"*

According to *U.S. News,* the New Orleans-Metairie, LA metro area is home to one of the best children's hospitals in the U.S.: **Ochsner Hospital for Children** (1 pediatric specialty). The hospital listed was highly ranked in at least one of 10 pediatric specialties. Eighty-six children's hospitals in the U.S. were nationally ranked in at least one specialty. Hospitals received points for being ranked in a specialty, and the 10 hospitals with the most points across the 10 specialties make up the Honor Roll. *U.S. News Online, "America's Best Children's Hospitals 2018-19"*

EDUCATION

Public School District Statistics

District Name	Schls	Pupils	Pupil/ Teacher Ratio	Minority Pupils[1] (%)	Free Lunch Eligible[2] (%)	IEP[3] (%)
Orleans Parish	27	15,336	14.6	83.6	49.3	8.3

Note: Table includes school districts with 2,000 or more students; (1) Percentage of students that are not non-Hispanic white; (2) Percentage of students that are eligible for the free lunch program; (3) Percentage of students that have an Individualized Education Program.
Source: U.S. Department of Education, National Center for Education Statistics, Common Core of Data, Local Education Agency (School District) Universe Survey: School Year 2016-2017; U.S. Department of Education, National Center for Education Statistics, Common Core of Data, Public Elementary/Secondary School Universe Survey: School Year 2016-2017

Best High Schools

According to *U.S. News,* New Orleans is home to two of the best high schools in the U.S.: **Benjamin Franklin High School** (#81); **Lusher Charter School** (#166). More than 20,000 public, magnet and charter schools were ranked based on their performance on state assessments and how well they prepare students for college. Schools with the highest unrounded College Readiness Index values were numerically ranked from 1 to 500 and were classified as gold medal winners. *U.S. News & World Report, "Best High Schools 2018"*

Highest Level of Education

Area	Less than H.S.	H.S. Diploma	Some College, No Deg.	Associate Degree	Bachelor's Degree	Master's Degree	Prof. School Degree	Doctorate Degree
City	14.1	23.0	21.7	4.7	20.7	9.5	4.3	2.0
MSA[1]	14.0	28.6	22.8	5.6	18.3	6.8	2.7	1.3
U.S.	12.7	27.3	20.8	8.3	19.1	8.4	2.0	1.4

Note: Figures cover persons age 25 and over; (1) Figures cover the New Orleans-Metairie, LA Metropolitan Statistical Area—see Appendix B for areas included
Source: U.S. Census Bureau, 2013-2017 American Community Survey 5-Year Estimates

Educational Attainment by Race

Area	High School Graduate or Higher (%)					Bachelor's Degree or Higher (%)				
	Total	White	Black	Asian	Hisp.[2]	Total	White	Black	Asian	Hisp.[2]
City	85.9	95.3	80.1	73.2	78.5	36.5	62.7	18.3	38.5	33.2
MSA[1]	86.0	90.0	80.6	74.7	74.2	29.0	35.4	16.9	39.1	19.0
U.S.	87.3	89.3	84.9	86.5	66.7	30.9	32.2	20.6	52.7	15.2

Note: Figures shown cover persons 25 years old and over; (1) Figures cover the New Orleans-Metairie, LA Metropolitan Statistical Area—see Appendix B for areas included; (2) People of Hispanic origin can be of any race
Source: U.S. Census Bureau, 2013-2017 American Community Survey 5-Year Estimates

School Enrollment by Grade and Control

Area	Preschool (%)		Kindergarten (%)		Grades 1 - 4 (%)		Grades 5 - 8 (%)		Grades 9 - 12 (%)	
	Public	Private	Public	Private	Public	Private	Public	Private	Public	Private
City	56.0	44.0	81.3	18.7	80.5	19.5	79.0	21.0	78.3	21.7
MSA[1]	53.1	46.9	75.9	24.1	76.6	23.4	76.3	23.7	75.4	24.6
U.S.	58.8	41.2	87.7	12.3	89.7	10.3	89.6	10.4	90.3	9.7

Note: Figures shown cover persons 3 years old and over; (1) Figures cover the New Orleans-Metairie, LA Metropolitan Statistical Area—see Appendix B for areas included
Source: U.S. Census Bureau, 2013-2017 American Community Survey 5-Year Estimates

Average Salaries of Public School Classroom Teachers

Area	2016		2017		Change from 2016 to 2017	
	Dollars	Rank[1]	Dollars	Rank[1]	Percent	Rank[2]
Louisiana	49,745	34	50,000	37	0.5	40
U.S. Average	58,479	–	59,660	–	2.0	–

Note: (1) Rank ranges from 1 to 51 where 1 indicates highest salary; (2) Rank ranges from 1 to 51 where 1 indicates highest percent change.
Source: National Education Association, Rankings & Estimates: Rankings of the States 2017 and Estimates of School Statistics 2018

Higher Education

Four-Year Colleges			Two-Year Colleges			Medical Schools[1]	Law Schools[2]	Voc/Tech[3]
Public	Private Non-profit	Private For-profit	Public	Private Non-profit	Private For-profit			
3	8	0	1	0	1	2	2	5

Note: Figures cover institutions located within the city limits and include main campuses only; (1) includes schools accredited by the Liaison Committee on Medical Education and the American Osteopathic Association's Commission on Osteopathic College Accreditation; (2) includes ABA-accredited schools, schools with provisional ABA accreditation, and state accredited schools; (3) includes all schools with programs that are less than 2 years.
Source: National Center for Education Statistics, Integrated Postsecondary Education System (IPEDS), 2017-18; Wikipedia, List of Medical Schools in the United States, accessed April 3, 2019; Wikipedia, List of Law Schools in the United States, accessed April 3, 2019

According to U.S. News & World Report, the New Orleans-Metairie, LA metro area is home to one of the best national universities in the U.S.: **Tulane University** (#44 tie). The indicators used to capture academic quality fall into a number of categories: assessment by administrators at peer institutions; retention of students; faculty resources; student selectivity; financial resources; alumni giving; high school counselor ratings of colleges; and graduation rate. U.S. News & World Report, "America's Best Colleges 2019"

According to U.S. News & World Report, the New Orleans-Metairie, LA metro area is home to one of the top 100 law schools in the U.S.: **Tulane University** (#52 tie). The rankings are based on a weighted average of 12 measures of quality: peer assessment score; assessment score by lawyers/judges; median LSAT scores; median undergrad GPA; acceptance rate; employment rates for graduates; placement success; bar passage rate; faculty resources; expenditures per student; student/faculty ratio; and library resources. *U.S. News & World Report, "America's Best Graduate Schools, Law, 2020"*

According to *U.S. News & World Report,* the New Orleans-Metairie, LA metro area is home to one of the top 75 business schools in the U.S.: **Tulane University (Freeman)** (#63 tie). The rankings are based on a weighted average of the following nine measures: quality assessment; peer assessment; recruiter assessment; placement success; mean starting salary and bonus; student selectivity; mean GMAT and GRE scores; mean undergraduate GPA; and acceptance rate. *U.S. News & World Report, "America's Best Graduate Schools, Business, 2020"*

PRESIDENTIAL ELECTION

2016 Presidential Election Results

Area	Clinton	Trump	Johnson	Stein	Other
Orleans Parish	80.8	14.7	2.2	1.5	0.8
U.S.	48.0	45.9	3.3	1.1	1.7

Note: Results are percentages and may not add to 100% due to rounding
Source: Dave Leip's Atlas of U.S. Presidential Elections

EMPLOYERS

Major Employers

Company Name	Industry
Al Copeland Investments	Restaurants & food manufacturing
Boh Bros. Construction Co.	General contractor
Capital One	Commercial banking
City of New Orleans	Government
Dow Chemical Company	Chemical manufacturing
East Jefferson Hospital	Health care
Harrah's New Orleans Casino	Casinos
Jefferson Parish Government	Government
Jefferson Parish School Board	Elementary & secondary schools
Jefferson Parish Sheriff's Office	Government
Lockheed Martin Corp/Nasa Michoud	Space research & technology
LSU Health Sciences Center New Orleans	Colleges & universities
Naval Support Activity	Government
North Oaks Medical Center	Health care
Northrop Grumman	Ship building & repairing
Ochsner Health System	Health care
Saint Tammany Parish Hospital	General medical & surgical hospitals
Southeastern Louisiana University	Colleges & universities
St. Tammany Parish Public School Board	Elementary & secondary schools
Touro Infirmary	Health care
Tulane University	Colleges & universities
United States Postal Service	U.S. postal service
West Jefferson Medical Center	Health care

Note: Companies shown are located within the New Orleans-Metairie, LA Metropolitan Statistical Area.
Source: Hoovers.com; Wikipedia

PUBLIC SAFETY

Crime Rate

Area	All Crimes	Violent Crimes				Property Crimes		
		Murder	Rape[3]	Robbery	Aggrav. Assault	Burglary	Larceny -Theft	Motor Vehicle Theft
City	5,365.2	39.5	144.7	329.1	608.1	560.8	3,046.2	636.8
Suburbs[1]	2,673.9	6.9	21.3	69.7	214.0	370.4	1,844.6	147.0
Metro[2]	3,512.1	17.1	59.7	150.5	336.7	429.7	2,218.9	299.6
U.S.	2,756.1	5.3	41.7	98.0	248.9	430.4	1,694.4	237.4

Note: Figures are crimes per 100,000 population; (1) All areas within the metro area that are located outside the city limits; (2) Figures cover the New Orleans-Metairie, LA Metropolitan Statistical Area—see Appendix B for areas included; (3) The city and U.S. figures shown were reported using the revised Uniform Crime Reporting (UCR) definition of rape. The suburban and metro area figures shown are an aggregate total of the data submitted using both the revised and legacy UCR definitions.
Source: FBI Uniform Crime Reports, 2017

Hate Crimes

Area	Number of Quarters Reported	Number of Incidents per Bias Motivation					
		Race/Ethnicity/Ancestry	Religion	Sexual Orientation	Disability	Gender	Gender Identity
City	2	1	0	0	0	0	0
U.S.	4	4,131	1,564	1,130	116	46	119

Source: Federal Bureau of Investigation, Hate Crime Statistics 2017

Identity Theft Consumer Reports

Area	Reports	Reports per 100,000 Population	Rank[2]
MSA[1]	1,962	155	27
U.S.	444,602	135	-

Note: (1) Figures cover the New Orleans-Metairie, LA Metropolitan Statistical Area—see Appendix B for areas included; (2) Rank ranges from 1 to 389 where 1 indicates greatest number of identity theft reports per 100,000 population
Source: Federal Trade Commission, Consumer Sentinel Network Data Book for January–December 2018

Fraud and Other Consumer Reports

Area	Reports	Reports per 100,000 Population	Rank[2]
MSA[1]	7,842	618	52
U.S.	2,552,917	776	-

Note: (1) Figures cover the New Orleans-Metairie, LA Metropolitan Statistical Area—see Appendix B for areas included; (2) Rank ranges from 1 to 389 where 1 indicates greatest number of fraud and other consumer reports per 100,000 population
Source: Federal Trade Commission, Consumer Sentinel Network Data Book for January–December 2018

SPORTS

Professional Sports Teams

Team Name	League	Year Established
New Orleans Pelicans	National Basketball Association (NBA)	2002
New Orleans Saints	National Football League (NFL)	1967

Note: Includes teams located in the New Orleans-Metairie, LA Metropolitan Statistical Area.
Source: Wikipedia, Major Professional Sports Teams of the United States and Canada, April 5, 2019

CLIMATE

Average and Extreme Temperatures

Temperature	Jan	Feb	Mar	Apr	May	Jun	Jul	Aug	Sep	Oct	Nov	Dec	Yr.
Extreme High (°F)	83	85	89	92	96	100	101	102	101	92	87	84	102
Average High (°F)	62	65	71	78	85	89	91	90	87	80	71	64	78
Average Temp. (°F)	53	56	62	69	75	81	82	82	79	70	61	55	69
Average Low (°F)	43	46	52	59	66	71	73	73	70	59	51	45	59
Extreme Low (°F)	14	19	25	32	41	50	60	60	42	35	24	11	11

Note: Figures cover the years 1948-1990
Source: National Climatic Data Center, International Station Meteorological Climate Summary, 9/96

Average Precipitation/Snowfall/Humidity

Precip./Humidity	Jan	Feb	Mar	Apr	May	Jun	Jul	Aug	Sep	Oct	Nov	Dec	Yr.
Avg. Precip. (in.)	4.7	5.6	5.2	4.7	4.4	5.4	6.4	5.9	5.5	2.8	4.4	5.5	60.6
Avg. Snowfall (in.)	Tr	Tr	Tr	0	0	0	0	0	0	0	0	Tr	Tr
Avg. Rel. Hum. 6am (%)	85	84	84	88	89	89	91	91	89	87	86	85	88
Avg. Rel. Hum. 3pm (%)	62	59	57	57	58	61	66	65	63	56	59	62	60

Note: Figures cover the years 1948-1990; Tr = Trace amounts (<0.05 in. of rain; <0.5 in. of snow)
Source: National Climatic Data Center, International Station Meteorological Climate Summary, 9/96

Weather Conditions

Temperature			Daytime Sky			Precipitation		
10°F & below	32°F & below	90°F & above	Clear	Partly cloudy	Cloudy	0.01 inch or more precip.	0.1 inch or more snow/ice	Thunder-storms
0	13	70	90	169	106	114	1	69

Note: Figures are average number of days per year and cover the years 1948-1990
Source: National Climatic Data Center, International Station Meteorological Climate Summary, 9/96

**HAZARDOUS
WASTE**

Superfund Sites

The New Orleans-Metairie, LA metro area is home to three sites on the EPA's Superfund National Priorities List: **Agriculture Street Landfill** (final); **Bayou Bonfouca** (final); **Madisonville Creosote Works** (final). There are a total of 1,390 Superfund sites with a status of proposed or final on the list in the U.S. *U.S. Environmental Protection Agency, National Priorities List, April 5, 2019*

**AIR & WATER
QUALITY**

Air Quality Trends: Ozone

	1990	1995	2000	2005	2010	2012	2014	2015	2016	2017
MSA[1]	0.082	0.088	0.091	0.079	0.074	0.071	0.069	0.067	0.065	0.063
U.S.	0.088	0.089	0.082	0.080	0.073	0.075	0.067	0.068	0.069	0.068

Note: (1) Data covers the New Orleans-Metairie, LA Metropolitan Statistical Area—see Appendix B for areas included. The values shown are the composite ozone concentration averages among trend sites based on the highest fourth daily maximum 8-hour concentration in parts per million. These trends are based on sites having an adequate record of monitoring data during the trend period. Data from exceptional events are included.
Source: U.S. Environmental Protection Agency, Air Quality Monitoring Information, "Air Quality Trends by City, 1990-2017"

Air Quality Index

Area	Percent of Days when Air Quality was...[2]					AQI Statistics[2]	
	Good	Moderate	Unhealthy for Sensitive Groups	Unhealthy	Very Unhealthy	Maximum	Median
MSA[1]	69.3	30.1	0.5	0.0	0.0	129	44

Note: (1) Data covers the New Orleans-Metairie, LA Metropolitan Statistical Area—see Appendix B for areas included; (2) Based on 365 days with AQI data in 2017. Air Quality Index (AQI) is an index for reporting daily air quality. EPA calculates the AQI for five major air pollutants regulated by the Clean Air Act: ground-level ozone, particle pollution (aka particulate matter), carbon monoxide, sulfur dioxide, and nitrogen dioxide. The AQI runs from 0 to 500. The higher the AQI value, the greater the level of air pollution and the greater the health concern. There are six AQI categories: "Good" AQI is between 0 and 50. Air quality is considered satisfactory; "Moderate" AQI is between 51 and 100. Air quality is acceptable; "Unhealthy for Sensitive Groups" When AQI values are between 101 and 150, members of sensitive groups may experience health effects; "Unhealthy" When AQI values are between 151 and 200 everyone may begin to experience health effects; "Very Unhealthy" AQI values between 201 and 300 trigger a health alert; "Hazardous" AQI values over 300 trigger warnings of emergency conditions (not shown).
Source: U.S. Environmental Protection Agency, Air Quality Index Report, 2017

Air Quality Index Pollutants

Area	Percent of Days when AQI Pollutant was...[2]					
	Carbon Monoxide	Nitrogen Dioxide	Ozone	Sulfur Dioxide	Particulate Matter 2.5	Particulate Matter 10
MSA[1]	0.0	0.8	46.0	9.0	44.1	0.0

Note: (1) Data covers the New Orleans-Metairie, LA Metropolitan Statistical Area—see Appendix B for areas included; (2) Based on 365 days with AQI data in 2017. The Air Quality Index (AQI) is an index for reporting daily air quality. EPA calculates the AQI for five major air pollutants regulated by the Clean Air Act: ground-level ozone, particle pollution (also known as particulate matter), carbon monoxide, sulfur dioxide, and nitrogen dioxide. The AQI runs from 0 to 500. The higher the AQI value, the greater the level of air pollution and the greater the health concern.
Source: U.S. Environmental Protection Agency, Air Quality Index Report, 2017

Maximum Air Pollutant Concentrations: Particulate Matter, Ozone, CO and Lead

	Particulate Matter 10 (ug/m³)	Particulate Matter 2.5 Wtd AM (ug/m³)	Particulate Matter 2.5 24-Hr (ug/m³)	Ozone (ppm)	Carbon Monoxide (ppm)	Lead (ug/m³)
MSA[1] Level	81	8.2	23	0.066	2	0.13
NAAQS[2]	150	15	35	0.075	9	0.15
Met NAAQS[2]	Yes	Yes	Yes	Yes	Yes	Yes

Note: (1) Data covers the New Orleans-Metairie, LA Metropolitan Statistical Area—see Appendix B for areas included; Data from exceptional events are included; (2) National Ambient Air Quality Standards; ppm = parts per million; ug/m³ = micrograms per cubic meter; n/a not available.
Concentrations: Particulate Matter 10 (coarse particulate)—highest second maximum 24-hour concentration; Particulate Matter 2.5 Wtd AM (fine particulate)—highest weighted annual mean concentration; Particulate Matter 2.5 24-Hour (fine particulate)—highest 98th percentile 24-hour concentration; Ozone—highest fourth daily maximum 8-hour concentration; Carbon Monoxide—highest second maximum non-overlapping 8-hour concentration; Lead—maximum running 3-month average
Source: U.S. Environmental Protection Agency, Air Quality Monitoring Information, "Air Quality Statistics by City, 2017"

Maximum Air Pollutant Concentrations: Nitrogen Dioxide and Sulfur Dioxide

	Nitrogen Dioxide AM (ppb)	Nitrogen Dioxide 1-Hr (ppb)	Sulfur Dioxide AM (ppb)	Sulfur Dioxide 1-Hr (ppb)	Sulfur Dioxide 24-Hr (ppb)
MSA[1] Level	10	45	n/a	53	n/a
NAAQS[2]	53	100	30	75	140
Met NAAQS[2]	Yes	Yes	n/a	Yes	n/a

Note: (1) Data covers the New Orleans-Metairie, LA Metropolitan Statistical Area—see Appendix B for areas included; Data from exceptional events are included; (2) National Ambient Air Quality Standards; ppm = parts per million; ug/m³ = micrograms per cubic meter; n/a not available.
Concentrations: Nitrogen Dioxide AM—highest arithmetic mean concentration; Nitrogen Dioxide 1-Hr—highest 98th percentile 1-hour daily maximum concentration; Sulfur Dioxide AM—highest annual mean concentration; Sulfur Dioxide 1-Hr—highest 99th percentile 1-hour daily maximum concentration; Sulfur Dioxide 24-Hr—highest second maximum 24-hour concentration
Source: U.S. Environmental Protection Agency, Air Quality Monitoring Information, "Air Quality Statistics by City, 2017"

Drinking Water

Water System Name	Pop. Served	Primary Water Source Type	Violations[1] Health Based	Violations[1] Monitoring/ Reporting
New Orleans Algiers Water Works	52,785	Surface	0	0
New Orleans Carrollton WW	291,044	Surface	0	0

Note: (1) Based on violation data from January 1, 2018 to December 31, 2018
Source: U.S. Environmental Protection Agency, Office of Ground Water and Drinking Water, Safe Drinking Water Information System (based on data extracted April 5, 2019)

Orlando, Florida

Background

The city of Orlando can hold the viewer aghast with its rampant tourism. Not only is it home to the worldwide tourist attractions of Disney World, Epcot Center, and Sea World, but Orlando and its surrounding area also host such institutions as Medieval Times Dinner & Tournament, Wet-N-Wild, Ripley's Believe It or Not Museum, and Sleuths Mystery Dinner Shows. In fact, the city is nicknamed "The Theme Park Capital of the World."

Orlando has its own high-tech corridor because of the University of Central Florida's College of Optics and Photonics. Manufacturing, government, business service, health care, high-tech research, and tourism supply significant numbers of jobs. The city is also one of the busiest American cities for conferences and conventions; the Orange County Convention Center is the second-largest convention facility in the United States, and vies with Chicago and Las Vegas for hosting the most conventions annually.

Aside from the glitz that pumps most of the money into its economy , Orlando is also called "The City Beautiful." The warm climate and abundant rains produce a variety of lush flora and fauna, which provide an attractive setting for the many young people who settle in the area, spending their nights in the numerous jazz clubs, restaurants, and pubs along Orange Avenue and Church Street. Stereotypically the land of orange juice and sunshine, Orlando is also the city for young job seekers and professionals.

This genteel setting is a far cry from Orlando's rough-and-tumble origins. The city started out as a makeshift campsite in the middle of a cotton plantation. The Civil War and devastating rains brought an end to the cotton trade, and its settlers turned to raising livestock. The transition to a new livelihood did not insure any peace and serenity. Rustling, chaotic brawls, and senseless shootings were everyday occurrences. Martial law had to be imposed by a few large ranch families.

The greatest impetus toward modernity came from the installation of Cape Canaveral, 50 miles away, which brought missile assembly and electronic component production to the area, and Walt Disney World, created out of 27,000 acres of unexplored swampland, which set the tone for Orlando as a tourist-oriented economy.

Orlando is also home to the University of Central Florida, which is the largest university campus in terms of enrollment in the United States, and was listed as a "gamma"—level global city in the World Cities Study Group's inventory.

Orlando is also a major film production site. Nickelodeon, the world's largest tele-production studio dedicated to children's television programming, is based there, as are the Golf Channel, Sun Sports, House of Moves, and the America Channel. Disney's biggest theme-park competitor, Universal Studios, is also based in Orlando. The city is also home to a variety of arts and entertainment facilities, including the Amway Arena, part of the Orlando Centroplex, home to the NBA's Orlando Magic and the Orlando Sharks of the Indoor Soccer League.

On June 12, 2016, in one of the deadliest mass shootings by a lone gunman, more than 100 people were shot at a gay nightclub in Orlando. Following the incident, Orlando Mayor Buddy Dyer announced the city's offer to purchase the Pulse Nightclub to build a permanent memorial for the 49 victims of the shooting, but the club's owner declined to sell.

Orlando is surrounded by many lakes. Its relative humidity remains high year-round, although winters are generally less humid. June through September is the rainy season, when scattered afternoon thunderstorms are an almost daily occurrence. During the winter months rainfall is light and the afternoons are most pleasant. Hurricanes are not usually considered a threat to the area.

Rankings

General Rankings

- *Insider* listed 33 places in the U.S. that were a must see vacation destination. Whether it is the great beaches, exploring a new city or experiencing the great outdoors, according to the website thisisinsider.com Orlando is a place to visit in 2018. *Insider, "33 Trips Everyone Should Take in the U.S. in 2018,"November 27, 2017*

- The Orlando metro area was identified as one of America's fastest-growing areas in terms of population and business growth by *MagnifyMoney*. The area ranked #14 out of 35. The 100 most populous metro areas in the U.S. were evaluated on their change from 2011-2016 in the following categories: people and housing; workforce and employment opportunities; growing industry. *www.businessinsider.com, "The 35 Cities in the US with the Biggest Influx of People, the Most Work Opportunities, and the Hottest Business Growth," August 12, 2018*

- The Orlando metro area was identified as one of America's fastest-growing areas in terms of population and economy by *Forbes*. The area ranked #4 out of 25. The 100 most populous metro areas in the U.S. were evaluated on the following criteria: estimated population growth; employment; economic output; wages; home values. *Forbes, "America's Fastest-Growing Cities 2018," February 28, 2018*

- In their sixth annual survey, Livability.com looked at data for more than 1,000 U.S. cities to determine the rankings for Livability's "Top 100 Best Places to Live" in 2019. Orlando ranked #17. Criteria: median home value capped at $250,000; affordable living; vibrant economy; education, demographics, health care options. transportation & infrastructure; abundant lifestyle amenities. *Livability.com, "Top 100 Best Places to Live 2019" March 2019*

Business/Finance Rankings

- The personal finance site NerdWallet analyzed 183 American metropolitan areas with populations over 250,000 and more than 15,000 businesses to rank where entrepreneurs find the most success. Criteria included area economy, annual income, housing cost, unemployment rate, and the success rate of area businesses. Orlando ranked #132. *www.nerdwallet.com, "Best Places to Start a Business," April 27, 2015*

- In a survey of economic confidence in the nation's 50 largest metropolitan areas conducted January–December 2014, the Orlando metro area placed #19, according to Gallup's 2014 Economic Confidence Index. *Gallup, "San Jose and San Francisco Lead in Economic Confidence," March 19, 2015*

- NerdWallet.com identified the 10 most promising cities for job seekers of the nation's 100 largest cities. Orlando was ranked #14. Criteria: job availability; annual salary; workforce growth; affordability. *NerdWallet.com, "Best Cities for Job Seekers in 2017," December 19, 2016*

- The Brookings Institution ranked the nation's largest cities based on income inequality. Orlando was ranked #69 (#1 = greatest inequality). Criteria: the "95/20 ratio," a figure representing the income at which a household earns more than 95 percent of all other households, divided by the income at which a household earns more than only 20 percent of all other households. *Brookings Institution, "Household Income Inequality, Largest Cities of 97 Large U.S. Metro Areas, 2014-2016," February 5, 2018*

- The Brookings Institution ranked the 100 largest metro areas in the U.S. based on income inequality. Orlando was ranked #69 (#1 = greatest inequality). Criteria: the "95/20 ratio," a figure representing the income at which a household earns more than 95 percent of all other households, divided by the income at which a household earns more than only 20 percent of all other households. *Brookings Institution, "Household Income Inequality, 100 Largest U.S. Metro Areas, 2014-2016," February 5, 2018*

- Payscale.com ranked the 32 largest metro areas in terms of wage growth. The Orlando metro area ranked #15. Criteria: private-sector wage growth between the 4th quarter of 2017 and the 4th quarter of 2018. *PayScale, "Wage Trends by Metro Area-4th Quarter," January 8, 2019*

- The Orlando metro area was identified as one of the most debt-ridden places in America by the finance site Credit.com. The metro area was ranked #23. Criteria: residents' average credit card debt as well as median income. *Credit.com, "25 Cities With the Most Credit Card Debt," February 28, 2018*

- Orlando was identified as one of America's most frugal metro areas by *Coupons.com*. The city ranked #5 out of 25. Criteria: digital coupon usage. *Coupons.com, "America's Most Frugal Cities of 2017," March 22, 2018*

- Orlando was identified as one of the unhappiest cities to work in by CareerBliss.com, an online community for career advancement. The city ranked #5 out of 5. Criteria: an employee's relationship with his or her boss and co-workers; general work environment; compensation; opportunities for advancement; company culture and job reputation; and resources. *Businesswire.com, "CareerBliss Unhappiest Cities to Work 2019," February 12, 2019*

- The Orlando metro area appeared on the Milken Institute "2018 Best Performing Cities" list. Rank: #7 out of 200 large metro areas. Criteria: job growth; wage and salary growth; high-tech output growth. *Milken Institute, "Best-Performing Cities 2018," January 24, 2019*

- *Forbes* ranked the 200 most populous metro areas to determine the nation's "Best Places for Business and Careers." The Orlando metro area was ranked #24. Criteria: costs (business and living); job growth (past and projected); income growth; quality of life; educational attainment (college and high school); projected economic growth; cultural and recreational opportunities; net migration patterns; number of highly ranked colleges. *Forbes, "The Best Places for Business and Careers 2018: Seattle Leads the Way," October 24, 2018*

Children/Family Rankings

- Orlando was selected as one of the most playful cities in the U.S. by KaBOOM! The organization's Playful City USA initiative honors cities and towns across the nation that have made their communities more playable. Criteria: pledging to integrate play as a solution to challenges in their communities; making it easy for children to get active and balanced play; creating more family-friendly and innovative communities as a result. *KaBOOM! National Campaign for Play, "2017 Playful City USA Communities"*

Dating/Romance Rankings

- Orlando was selected as one of America's best cities for singles by the readers of *Travel + Leisure* in their annual "America's Favorite Cities" survey. Criteria included good-looking locals, cool shopping, an active bar scene and hipster-magnet coffee bars. *Travel + Leisure, "Best Cities in America for Singles," July 21, 2017*

- Orlando was selected as one of the nation's most romantic cities with 100,000 or more residents by Amazon.com. The city ranked #4 of 20. Criteria: per capita sales of romance novels, relationship books, romantic comedy movies, romantic music, and sexual wellness products. *Amazon.com, "Top 20 Most Romantic Cities in the U.S.," February 1, 2017*

Education Rankings

- Personal finance website *WalletHub* analyzed the 150 largest U.S. metropolitan statistical areas to determine where the most educated Americans are choosing to settle. Criteria: education quality and attainment gap; education levels; percentage of workers with degrees; public school quality rankings; quality and size of each metro area's universities. Orlando was ranked #80 (#1 = most educated city). *www.WalletHub.com, "2018's Most and Least Educated Cities in America," July 24, 2018*

- Orlando was selected as one of America's most literate cities. The city ranked #27 out of the 82 largest U.S. cities. Criteria: number of booksellers; library resources; Internet resources; educational attainment; periodical publishing resources; newspaper circulation. *Central Connecticut State University, "America's Most Literate Cities, 2016," March 31, 2017*

Environmental Rankings

- Orlando was highlighted as one of the top 25 cleanest metro areas for year-round particle pollution (Annual PM 2.5) in the U.S. during 2014 through 2016. The area ranked #25. *American Lung Association, State of the Air 2018*

- Orlando was highlighted as one of the top 90 cleanest metro areas for short-term particle pollution (24-hour PM 2.5) in the U.S. during 2014 through 2016. Monitors in these cities reported no days with unhealthful PM 2.5 levels. *American Lung Association, State of the Air 2018*

Food/Drink Rankings

- The U.S. Chamber of Commerce Foundation conducted an in-depth study on local food truck regulations, surveyed 288 food truck owners, and ranked 20 major American cities based on how friendly they are for operating a food truck. The compiled index assessed the following: procedures for obtaining permits and licenses; complying with restrictions; and financial obligations associated with operating a food truck. Orlando ranked #3 overall (1 being the best) for ease in operating a food truck. *www.foodtrucknation.us, "Food Truck Nation," March 20, 2018*

- According to Fodor's Travel, Orlando placed among the 14 best U.S. cities for food-truck cuisine. *www.fodors.com, "America's Best Food Truck Cities," August 23, 2016*

- *Men's Health* ranked 100 major U.S. cities in terms of alcohol intoxication. Orlando ranked #50 (#1 = most sober).Criteria: binge drinking; alcohol-related traffic accidents, arrests, and fatalities. *Men's Health, "America's Drunkest Cities," March 9, 2015*

Health/Fitness Rankings

- For each of the 100 largest cities in the United States, the American College of Sports Medicine's American Fitness Index evaluated infrastructure, community assets, and policies that encourage healthy and fit lifestyles, including preventive health behaviors, levels of chronic disease conditions, health care access, and community resources and policies that support physical activity. Orlando ranked #38 for "community fitness." *www.americanfitnessindex.org, "ACSM American Fitness Index Health and Community Fitness Status of the 100 Largest U.S. Cities," May 2018*

- The Orlando metro area was identified as one of the worst cities for bed bugs in America by pest control company Orkin. The area ranked #41 out of 50 based on the number of bed bug treatments Orkin performed from December 2017 to November 2018. *Orkin, "Baltimore Remains Front Runner, Atlanta and Philadelphia Break Into Top 10," January 14, 2019*

- Orlando was identified as a "2018 Spring Allergy Capital." The area ranked #60 out of 100. Three groups of factors were used to identify the most challenging cities for people with allergies during the spring season: annual pollen levels; medicine utilization; access to board-certified allergists. *Asthma and Allergy Foundation of America, "Spring Allergy Capitals 2018"*

- Orlando was identified as a "2018 Fall Allergy Capital." The area ranked #63 out of 100. Three groups of factors were used to identify the most challenging cities for people with allergies during the fall season: annual pollen levels; medicine utilization; access to board-certified allergists. *Asthma and Allergy Foundation of America, "Fall Allergy Capitals 2018"*

- Orlando was identified as a "2018 Asthma Capital." The area ranked #90 out of the nation's 100 largest metropolitan areas. Criteria: estimated prevalence; self-reported prevalence; crude death rate for asthma; annual pollen score; annual air quality; public smoking laws; number of board-certified asthma specialists; school inhaler access laws; rescue medication use; controller medication use; ER visits for asthma; uninsured rate; poverty rate. *Asthma and Allergy Foundation of America, "Asthma Capitals 2018: The Most Challenging Places to Live With Asthma"*

- *Men's Health* ranked 100 major U.S. cities in terms of the best cities for men. Orlando ranked #40. Criteria: health; fitness; quality of life. *Men's Health, "The Best & Worst Cities for Men Who Want to Be Fit and Happy," January 1, 2016*

- The Orlando metro area ranked #76 out of 189 in The Gallup-Healthways Well-Being Index. Criteria: purpose; social well being; financial health; community and physical health. Results are based on telephone interviews with adults, aged 18 and older, living in metropolitan areas in the 50 U.S. states and the District of Columbia. *Gallup-Healthways, "State of American Well-Being, 2017 Community Well-Being Rankings" March 2018*

Real Estate Rankings

- FitSmallBusiness looked at 50 of the largest metropolitan areas in the U.S. to determine which metro was the best to start a real estate business. Data was compiled from such sources as: Zillow, Trulia, U.S. Census Bureau, and the Bureau of Labor Statistics. Criteria: location; inventory; annual wages; median sales price of homes; days on the market; median price cut percentage; and other factors that would influence real estate professional growth. The Orlando metro area ranked #18. *fitsmallbusiness.com, "The Best Cities to Become a Real Estate Agent in 2018," January 30, 2018*

- *WalletHub* compared the most populated U.S. cities, as well as at least two of the most populated cities in each state, for a total of 179, to determine which had the best markets for real estate agents. Orlando ranked #76 where demand was high and pay was the best. Criteria: sales per agent; annual median wage for real-estate agents; monthly average starting salary for real estate agents; real estate job density and competition; unemployment rate; housing-market health index; and other relevant metrics. *www.WalletHub.com, "2018's Best Places to Be a Real Estate Agent," April 25, 2018*

- According to Penske Truck Rental, the Orlando metro area was named the #4 moving destination in 2018, based on one-way consumer truck rental reservations made through Penske's website, rental locations, and reservations call center. *blog.gopenske.com, "Penske Truck Rental's 2018 Top Moving Destinations," January 16, 2019*

- The Orlando metro area was identified as one of the top 20 housing markets to invest in for 2019 by *Forbes*. Criteria: strong job and population growth; stable local economy; anticipated home price appreciation; and other factors. *Forbes.com, "The Best Markets for Real Estate Investments In 2019," January 7, 2019*

- Orlando was ranked #168 out of 237 metro areas in terms of housing affordability in 2018 by the National Association of Home Builders (#1 = most affordable). Criteria: the share of homes sold in that area affordable to a family earning the local median income, based on standard mortgage underwriting criteria. *National Association of Home Builders®, NAHB-Wells Fargo Housing Opportunity Index, 4th Quarter 2018*

Safety Rankings

- Allstate ranked the 200 largest cities in America in terms of driver safety. Orlando ranked #72. Criteria: internal property damage claims over a two-year period from January 2015 to December 2016. The report helps increase the importance of safety awareness behind the wheel. *Allstate, "Allstate America's Best Drivers Report, 2018" August 28, 2018*

- The National Insurance Crime Bureau ranked 382 metro areas in the U.S. in terms of per capita rates of vehicle theft. The Orlando metro area ranked #114 (#1 = highest rate). Criteria: number of vehicle theft offenses per 100,000 inhabitants in 2017. *National Insurance Crime Bureau, "Hot Spots 2017," July 12, 2018*

Seniors/Retirement Rankings

- From its Best Cities for Successful Aging indexes, the Milken Institute generated rankings for metropolitan areas, weighing data in nine categories—health care, wellness, living arrangements, transportation and convenience, financial characteristics, education, employment, community engagement, and overall livability. The Orlando metro area was ranked #69 overall in the large metro area category. *Milken Institute, "Best Cities for Successful Aging, 2017" March 14, 2017*

Women/Minorities Rankings

- *24/7 Wall St.* compared median earnings over a 12-month period for men and women who worked full-time, year-round, and employment composition by sector to identify the best-paying cities for women. Of the largest 100 U.S. metropolitan areas, Orlando was ranked #10 in pay disparity. *24/7 Wall St., "The Best (and Worst) Paying Cities for Women," March 27, 2017*

- Orlando was selected as one of the gayest cities in America by *The Advocate*. The city ranked #2 out of 25. Criteria, among many: Trans Pride parades/festivals; gay rugby teams; lesbian bars; LGBT centers; theater screenings of "Moonlight"; LGBT-inclusive nondiscrimination ordinances; and gay bowling teams. *The Advocate, "Queerest Cities in America 2017" January 12, 2017*

- Personal finance website *WalletHub* compared more than 180 U.S. cities—including the 150 most populated U.S. cities, plus at least two of the most populated cities in each state—across two key dimensions, "Hispanic Business-Friendliness" and "Hispanic Purchasing Power", to arrive at the most favorable conditions for Hispanic entrepreneurs. Orlando was ranked #21 out of 182. Criteria includes: share of Hispanic-Owned Businesses; Hispanic entrepreneurship rate to median annual income of Hispanics; Small Business-Friendliness score; cost of living; and number of Hispanics with at least a bachelor's degree. *WalletHub.com, "2018's Best Cities for Hispanic Entrepreneurs," April 26, 2018*

Miscellaneous Rankings

- *MoveHub* ranked the coolest cities, appealing to young people, using its U.S. Hipster Index and Orlando came out as #11. Criteria: number of thrift stores; density of tattoo parlors, vegan stores and microbreweries; and amount of rent increase. *www.thisisinsider.com, "The 20 Most Hipster Cities in the US-and Why You Should Consider Moving to One," April 10, 2018*

- The watchdog site Charity Navigator conducts an annual study of charities in the nation's major markets both to analyze statistical differences in their financial, accountability, and transparency practices and to track year-to-year variations in individual philanthropic communities. Charity Navigator's analysis demonstrated that the financial, accountability and transparency behaviors of America's largest charities can be influenced by the metropolitan market within which the charity operates. The Orlando metro area was ranked #15 among the 30 metro markets in the rating category of Overall Score. *www.charitynavigator.org, "2017 Metro Market Study," May 1, 2017*

- *WalletHub* compared the 150 most populated U.S. cities to determine their operating efficiency. A "Quality of Services" score was constructed for each city and then divided by the total budget per capita to reveal which were managed the best. Orlando ranked #89. Criteria: financial stability; economy; education; safety; health; infrastructure and pollution. *www.WalletHub.com, "2018's Best- & Worst-Run Cities in America," July 9, 2018*

- Orlando was selected as one of the 20 memorable places in the world during Thanksgiving by *Fodor's Travel*. Criteria: attractions; history; events. *Fodors.com, "Where to Go for Thanksgiving 2016," November 4, 2016*

- The National Alliance to End Homelessness listed the 25 most populous metro areas with the highest rate of homelessness. The Orlando metro area had a high rate of homelessness. Criteria: number of homeless people per 10,000 population in 2016. *National Alliance to End Homelessness, "Homelessness in the 25 Most Populous U.S. Metro Areas," September 1, 2017*

Business Environment

CITY FINANCES

City Government Finances

Component	2016 ($000)	2016 ($ per capita)
Total Revenues	761,480	2,811
Total Expenditures	741,570	2,737
Debt Outstanding	1,257,903	4,643
Cash and Securities[1]	1,160,627	4,284

Note: (1) Cash and security holdings of a government at the close of its fiscal year, including those of its dependent agencies, utilities, and liquor stores.
Source: U.S. Census Bureau, State & Local Government Finances 2016

City Government Revenue by Source

Source	2016 ($000)	2016 ($ per capita)	2016 (%)
General Revenue			
From Federal Government	19,325	71	2.5
From State Government	55,420	205	7.3
From Local Governments	137,159	506	18.0
Taxes			
Property	130,458	482	17.1
Sales and Gross Receipts	57,535	212	7.6
Personal Income	0	0	0.0
Corporate Income	0	0	0.0
Motor Vehicle License	0	0	0.0
Other Taxes	57,971	214	7.6
Current Charges	256,263	946	33.7
Liquor Store	0	0	0.0
Utility	47	0	0.0
Employee Retirement	900	3	0.1

Source: U.S. Census Bureau, State & Local Government Finances 2016

City Government Expenditures by Function

Function	2016 ($000)	2016 ($ per capita)	2016 (%)
General Direct Expenditures			
Air Transportation	0	0	0.0
Corrections	0	0	0.0
Education	0	0	0.0
Employment Security Administration	0	0	0.0
Financial Administration	22,628	83	3.1
Fire Protection	109,250	403	14.7
General Public Buildings	0	0	0.0
Governmental Administration, Other	18,958	70	2.6
Health	0	0	0.0
Highways	16,907	62	2.3
Hospitals	0	0	0.0
Housing and Community Development	7,839	28	1.1
Interest on General Debt	52,147	192	7.0
Judicial and Legal	4,699	17	0.6
Libraries	0	0	0.0
Parking	15,096	55	2.0
Parks and Recreation	101,868	376	13.7
Police Protection	140,929	520	19.0
Public Welfare	0	0	0.0
Sewerage	75,712	279	10.2
Solid Waste Management	26,907	99	3.6
Veterans' Services	0	0	0.0
Liquor Store	0	0	0.0
Utility	0	0	0.0
Employee Retirement	15,713	58	2.1

Source: U.S. Census Bureau, State & Local Government Finances 2016

DEMOGRAPHICS

Population Growth

Area	1990 Census	2000 Census	2010 Census	2017* Estimate	Population Growth (%)	
					1990-2017	2010-2017
City	161,172	185,951	238,300	269,414	67.2	13.1
MSA[1]	1,224,852	1,644,561	2,134,411	2,390,859	95.2	12.0
U.S.	248,709,873	281,421,906	308,745,538	321,004,407	29.1	4.0

Note: (1) Figures cover the Orlando-Kissimmee-Sanford, FL Metropolitan Statistical Area—see Appendix B for areas included; (*) 2013-2017 5-year estimated population
Source: U.S. Census Bureau, 1990 Census, Census 2000, Census 2010, 2013-2017 American Community Survey 5-Year Estimates

Household Size

Area	Persons in Household (%)							Average Household Size
	One	Two	Three	Four	Five	Six	Seven or More	
City	34.3	33.3	16.1	10.4	3.6	1.6	0.7	2.40
MSA[1]	25.5	34.5	17.2	13.8	5.8	2.2	1.2	2.80
U.S.	27.7	33.8	15.7	13.0	6.0	2.3	1.4	2.60

Note: (1) Figures cover the Orlando-Kissimmee-Sanford, FL Metropolitan Statistical Area—see Appendix B for areas included
Source: U.S. Census Bureau, 2013-2017 American Community Survey 5-Year Estimates

Race

Area	White Alone[2] (%)	Black Alone[2] (%)	Asian Alone[2] (%)	AIAN[3] Alone[2] (%)	NHOPI[4] Alone[2] (%)	Other Race Alone[2] (%)	Two or More Races (%)
City	60.7	26.1	4.3	0.2	0.0	5.7	2.9
MSA[1]	70.5	16.4	4.2	0.3	0.1	5.2	3.3
U.S.	73.0	12.7	5.4	0.8	0.2	4.8	3.1

Note: (1) Figures cover the Orlando-Kissimmee-Sanford, FL Metropolitan Statistical Area—see Appendix B for areas included; (2) Alone is defined as not being in combination with one or more other races; (3) American Indian and Alaska Native; (4) Native Hawaiian and Other Pacific Islander
Source: U.S. Census Bureau, 2013-2017 American Community Survey 5-Year Estimates

Hispanic or Latino Origin

Area	Total (%)	Mexican (%)	Puerto Rican (%)	Cuban (%)	Other (%)
City	29.7	1.7	14.9	2.7	10.3
MSA[1]	29.0	2.9	14.8	2.2	9.1
U.S.	17.6	11.1	1.7	0.7	4.1

Note: Persons of Hispanic or Latino origin can be of any race; (1) Figures cover the Orlando-Kissimmee-Sanford, FL Metropolitan Statistical Area—see Appendix B for areas included
Source: U.S. Census Bureau, 2013-2017 American Community Survey 5-Year Estimates

Segregation

Type	Segregation Indices[1]				Percent Change		
	1990	2000	2010	2010 Rank[2]	1990-2000	1990-2010	2000-2010
Black/White	59.1	55.9	50.7	69	-3.2	-8.4	-5.2
Asian/White	29.4	35.4	33.9	81	6.0	4.6	-1.4
Hispanic/White	29.2	38.7	40.2	64	9.5	11.0	1.5

Note: All figures cover the Metropolitan Statistical Area—see Appendix B for areas included; Figures are based on an analysis of 1990, 2000, and 2010 Census Decennial Census tract data by William H. Frey, Brookings Institution and the University of Michigan Social Science Data Analysis Network. In this analysis all racial groups (whites, blacks, and asians) are non-Hispanic members of those races. Hispanics are shown as a separate category; (1) Segregation Indices are Dissimilarity Indices that measure the degree to which the minority group is distributed differently than whites across census tracts. They range from 0 (complete integration) to 100 (complete segregation) where the value indicates the percentage of the minority group that needs to move to be distributed exactly like whites; (2) Ranges from 1 (most segregated) to 102 (least segregated); n/a not available.
Source: www.CensusScope.org

Ancestry

Area	German	Irish	English	American	Italian	Polish	French[2]	Scottish	Dutch
City	6.7	5.9	4.9	5.5	4.4	1.7	1.8	1.3	0.7
MSA[1]	9.0	7.9	6.4	7.3	5.2	2.0	2.0	1.4	0.9
U.S.	14.1	10.1	7.5	6.6	5.3	2.9	2.5	1.7	1.3

Note: Figures are the percentage of the total population reporting a particular ancestry. The nine most commonly reported ancestries in the U.S. are shown. Figures include multiple ancestries (e.g. if a person reported being Irish and Italian, they were included in both columns); (1) Figures cover the Orlando-Kissimmee-Sanford, FL Metropolitan Statistical Area—see Appendix B for areas included; (2) Excludes Basque
Source: U.S. Census Bureau, 2013-2017 American Community Survey 5-Year Estimates

Foreign-Born Population

Area	Any Foreign Country	Asia	Mexico	Europe	Carribean	Central America[2]	South America	Africa	Canada
City	19.8	3.1	0.5	1.5	6.3	1.2	6.4	0.6	0.3
MSA[1]	17.3	3.0	1.2	1.5	5.3	1.1	4.4	0.6	0.3
U.S.	13.4	4.1	3.6	1.5	1.3	1.0	0.9	0.6	0.3

Note: (1) Figures cover the Orlando-Kissimmee-Sanford, FL Metropolitan Statistical Area—see Appendix B for areas included; (2) Excludes Mexico.
Source: U.S. Census Bureau, 2013-2017 American Community Survey 5-Year Estimates

Marital Status

Area	Never Married	Now Married[2]	Separated	Widowed	Divorced
City	43.2	35.3	3.4	4.5	13.7
MSA[1]	34.8	46.0	2.3	5.3	11.7
U.S.	33.1	48.2	2.0	5.8	10.9

Note: Figures are percentages and cover the population 15 years of age and older; (1) Figures cover the Orlando-Kissimmee-Sanford, FL Metropolitan Statistical Area—see Appendix B for areas included; (2) Excludes separated
Source: U.S. Census Bureau, 2013-2017 American Community Survey 5-Year Estimates

Disability by Age

Area	All Ages	Under 18 Years Old	18 to 64 Years Old	65 Years and Over
City	10.3	5.3	8.1	35.5
MSA[1]	11.8	4.7	9.5	34.1
U.S.	12.6	4.2	10.3	35.5

Note: Figures show percent of the civilian noninstitutionalized population that reported having a disability. Disability status is determined from six types of difficulty: vision, hearing, cognitive, ambulatory, self-care, and independent living. For children under 5 years old, hearing and vision difficulty are used to determine disability status. For children between the ages of 5 and 14, disability status is determined from hearing, vision, cognitive, ambulatory, and self-care difficulties. For people aged 15 years and older, they are considered to have a disability if they have difficulty with any one of the six difficulty types; Note: (1) Figures cover the Orlando-Kissimmee-Sanford, FL Metropolitan Statistical Area—see Appendix B for areas included
Source: U.S. Census Bureau, 2013-2017 American Community Survey 5-Year Estimates

Age

Area	Under Age 5	Age 5–19	Age 20–34	Age 35–44	Age 45–54	Age 55–64	Age 65–74	Age 75–84	Age 85+	Median Age
City	7.1	16.2	29.6	14.9	12.2	9.6	6.3	2.8	1.4	33.3
MSA[1]	5.9	19.0	22.3	13.6	13.6	11.6	8.2	4.1	1.7	36.9
U.S.	6.2	19.5	20.7	12.7	13.4	12.7	8.6	4.4	1.9	37.8

Note: (1) Figures cover the Orlando-Kissimmee-Sanford, FL Metropolitan Statistical Area—see Appendix B for areas included
Source: U.S. Census Bureau, 2013-2017 American Community Survey 5-Year Estimates

Gender

Area	Males	Females	Males per 100 Females
City	130,347	139,067	93.7
MSA[1]	1,169,047	1,221,812	95.7
U.S.	158,018,753	162,985,654	97.0

Note: (1) Figures cover the Orlando-Kissimmee-Sanford, FL Metropolitan Statistical Area—see Appendix B for areas included
Source: U.S. Census Bureau, 2013-2017 American Community Survey 5-Year Estimates

Religious Groups by Family

Area	Catholic	Baptist	Non-Den.	Methodist[2]	Lutheran	LDS[3]	Pente-costal	Presby-terian[4]	Muslim[5]	Judaism
MSA[1]	13.2	7.0	5.7	3.0	0.9	1.0	3.2	1.4	1.3	0.3
U.S.	19.1	9.3	4.0	4.0	2.3	2.0	1.9	1.6	0.8	0.7

Note: Figures are the number of adherents as a percentage of the total population; (1) Figures cover the Orlando-Kissimmee-Sanford, FL Metropolitan Statistical Area—see Appendix B for areas included; (2) Methodist/Pietist; (3) Latter Day Saints; (4) Reformed; (5) Figures are estimates
Source: Association of Statisticians of American Religious Bodies, 2010 U.S. Religion Census: Religious Congregations & Membership Study

Religious Groups by Tradition

Area	Catholic	Evangelical Protestant	Mainline Protestant	Other Tradition	Black Protestant	Orthodox
MSA[1]	13.2	17.8	4.8	3.3	1.2	0.3
U.S.	19.1	16.2	7.3	4.3	1.6	0.3

Note: Figures are the number of adherents as a percentage of the total population; (1) Figures cover the Orlando-Kissimmee-Sanford, FL Metropolitan Statistical Area—see Appendix B for areas included
Source: Association of Statisticians of American Religious Bodies, 2010 U.S. Religion Census: Religious Congregations & Membership Study

ECONOMY

Gross Metropolitan Product

Area	2016	2017	2018	2019	Rank[2]
MSA[1]	127.3	133.6	141.0	149.7	31

Note: Figures are in billions of dollars; (1) Figures cover the Orlando-Kissimmee-Sanford, FL Metropolitan Statistical Area—see Appendix B for areas included; (2) Rank is based on 2017 data and ranges from 1 to 381
Source: U.S. Conference of Mayors, U.S. Metro Economies: Economic Growth & Full Employment, June 2018

Economic Growth

Area	2017-2018 (%)	2019-2020 (%)	2021-2022 (%)
MSA[1]	3.9	3.3	2.5

Note: Figures are real gross metropolitan product (GMP) growth rates and represent average annual percent change; (1) Figures cover the Orlando-Kissimmee-Sanford, FL Metropolitan Statistical Area—see Appendix B for areas included
Source: U.S. Conference of Mayors, U.S. Metro Economies: Economic Growth & Full Employment, June 2018

Metropolitan Area Exports

Area	2012	2013	2014	2015	2016	2017	Rank[2]
MSA[1]	3,850.6	3,227.7	3,134.8	3,082.7	3,363.9	3,196.7	75

Note: Figures are in millions of dollars; (1) Figures cover the Orlando-Kissimmee-Sanford, FL Metropolitan Statistical Area—see Appendix B for areas included; (2) Rank is based on 2017 data and ranges from 1 to 387
Source: U.S. Department of Commerce, International Trade Administration, Office of Trade and Economic Analysis, Industry and Analysis, Exports by Metropolitan Area, extracted March 25, 2019

Building Permits

Area	Single-Family			Multi-Family			Total		
	2016	2017	Pct. Chg.	2016	2017	Pct. Chg.	2016	2017	Pct. Chg.
City	730	828	13.4	930	818	-12.0	1,660	1,646	-0.8
MSA[1]	14,227	14,431	1.4	9,027	4,634	-48.7	23,254	19,065	-18.0
U.S.	750,800	820,000	9.2	455,800	462,000	1.4	1,206,600	1,282,000	6.2

Note: (1) Figures cover the Orlando-Kissimmee-Sanford, FL Metropolitan Statistical Area—see Appendix B for areas included; Figures represent new, privately-owned housing units authorized (unadjusted data); All permit data are based on estimates with imputation
Source: U.S. Census Bureau, Manufacturing, Mining, and Construction Statistics, Building Permits, 2016, 2017

Bankruptcy Filings

Area	Business Filings			Nonbusiness Filings		
	2017	2018	% Chg.	2017	2018	% Chg.
Orange County	137	110	-19.7	2,801	2,876	2.7
U.S.	23,157	22,232	-4.0	765,863	751,186	-1.9

Note: Business filings include Chapter 7, Chapter 11, Chapter 12, and Chapter 13; Nonbusiness filings include Chapter 7, Chapter 11, and Chapter 13
Source: Administrative Office of the U.S. Courts, Business and Nonbusiness Bankruptcy, County Cases Commenced by Chapter of the Bankruptcy Code, During the 12-Month Period Ending December 31, 2017 and Business and Nonbusiness Bankruptcy, County Cases Commenced by Chapter of the Bankruptcy Code, During the 12-Month Period Ending December 31, 2018

Housing Vacancy Rates

Area	Gross Vacancy Rate[2] (%)			Year-Round Vacancy Rate[3] (%)			Rental Vacancy Rate[4] (%)			Homeowner Vacancy Rate[5] (%)		
	2016	2017	2018	2016	2017	2018	2016	2017	2018	2016	2017	2018
MSA[1]	13.2	14.3	19.4	10.3	10.5	16.2	6.6	6.9	5.8	2.1	1.5	2.6
U.S.	12.8	12.7	12.3	9.9	9.9	9.7	6.9	7.2	6.9	1.7	1.6	1.5

Note: (1) Figures cover the Orlando-Kissimmee-Sanford, FL Metropolitan Statistical Area—see Appendix B for areas included; (2) The percentage of the total housing inventory that is vacant; (3) The percentage of the housing inventory (excluding seasonal units) that is year-round vacant; (4) The percentage of rental inventory that is vacant for rent; (5) The percentage of homeowner inventory that is vacant for sale
Source: U.S. Census Bureau, Housing Vacancies and Homeownership Annual Statistics: 2016, 2017, 2018

INCOME

Income

Area	Per Capita ($)	Median Household ($)	Average Household ($)
City	28,117	45,436	65,450
MSA[1]	26,966	52,261	72,452
U.S.	31,177	57,652	81,283

Note: (1) Figures cover the Orlando-Kissimmee-Sanford, FL Metropolitan Statistical Area—see Appendix B for areas included
Source: U.S. Census Bureau, 2013-2017 American Community Survey 5-Year Estimates

Household Income Distribution

Area	Percent of Households Earning							
	Under $15,000	$15,000 -$24,999	$25,000 -$34,999	$35,000 -$49,999	$50,000 -$74,999	$75,000 -$99,999	$100,000 -$149,999	$150,000 and up
City	14.0	12.1	12.8	15.7	18.3	9.6	9.4	7.9
MSA[1]	11.2	10.4	11.0	15.1	19.2	11.8	12.0	9.2
U.S.	11.6	9.8	9.5	13.0	17.7	12.3	14.1	12.1

Note: (1) Figures cover the Orlando-Kissimmee-Sanford, FL Metropolitan Statistical Area—see Appendix B for areas included
Source: U.S. Census Bureau, 2013-2017 American Community Survey 5-Year Estimates

Poverty Rate

Area	All Ages	Under 18 Years Old	18 to 64 Years Old	65 Years and Over
City	19.1	28.0	17.0	14.9
MSA[1]	15.4	22.1	14.2	10.1
U.S.	14.6	20.3	13.7	9.3

Note: Figures are percentage of people whose income during the past 12 months was below the poverty level; (1) Figures cover the Orlando-Kissimmee-Sanford, FL Metropolitan Statistical Area—see Appendix B for areas included
Source: U.S. Census Bureau, 2013-2017 American Community Survey 5-Year Estimates

EMPLOYMENT

Labor Force and Employment

Area	Civilian Labor Force			Workers Employed		
	Dec. 2017	Dec. 2018	% Chg.	Dec. 2017	Dec. 2018	% Chg.
City	166,522	172,311	3.5	161,476	167,611	3.8
MSA[1]	1,312,511	1,358,231	3.5	1,269,679	1,317,910	3.8
U.S.	159,880,000	162,510,000	1.6	153,602,000	156,481,000	1.9

Note: Data is not seasonally adjusted and covers workers 16 years of age and older; (1) Figures cover the
Orlando-Kissimmee-Sanford, FL Metropolitan Statistical Area—see Appendix B for areas included
Source: Bureau of Labor Statistics, Local Area Unemployment Statistics

Unemployment Rate

Area	2018											
	Jan.	Feb.	Mar.	Apr.	May	Jun.	Jul.	Aug.	Sep.	Oct.	Nov.	Dec.
City	3.5	3.2	3.1	2.8	2.9	3.2	3.3	3.1	2.5	2.5	2.5	2.7
MSA[1]	3.7	3.4	3.4	3.1	3.0	3.5	3.6	3.4	2.7	2.7	2.7	3.0
U.S.	4.5	4.4	4.1	3.7	3.6	4.2	4.1	3.9	3.6	3.5	3.5	3.7

Note: Data is not seasonally adjusted and covers workers 16 years of age and older; (1) Figures cover the
Orlando-Kissimmee-Sanford, FL Metropolitan Statistical Area—see Appendix B for areas included
Source: Bureau of Labor Statistics, Local Area Unemployment Statistics

Average Wages

Occupation	$/Hr.	Occupation	$/Hr.
Accountants and Auditors	34.50	Maids and Housekeeping Cleaners	11.20
Automotive Mechanics	17.40	Maintenance and Repair Workers	16.60
Bookkeepers	18.40	Marketing Managers	53.90
Carpenters	20.20	Nuclear Medicine Technologists	34.90
Cashiers	10.60	Nurses, Licensed Practical	21.20
Clerks, General Office	15.20	Nurses, Registered	31.20
Clerks, Receptionists/Information	13.90	Nursing Assistants	12.50
Clerks, Shipping/Receiving	15.70	Packers and Packagers, Hand	11.70
Computer Programmers	44.30	Physical Therapists	42.70
Computer Systems Analysts	40.70	Postal Service Mail Carriers	24.90
Computer User Support Specialists	23.50	Real Estate Brokers	27.90
Cooks, Restaurant	13.30	Retail Salespersons	12.30
Dentists	95.90	Sales Reps., Exc. Tech./Scientific	29.00
Electrical Engineers	46.80	Sales Reps., Tech./Scientific	43.20
Electricians	22.90	Secretaries, Exc. Legal/Med./Exec.	16.70
Financial Managers	64.70	Security Guards	12.30
First-Line Supervisors/Managers, Sales	21.60	Surgeons	110.10
Food Preparation Workers	12.00	Teacher Assistants*	11.60
General and Operations Managers	52.70	Teachers, Elementary School*	22.80
Hairdressers/Cosmetologists	13.50	Teachers, Secondary School*	24.20
Internists, General	131.60	Telemarketers	11.70
Janitors and Cleaners	11.50	Truck Drivers, Heavy/Tractor-Trailer	21.10
Landscaping/Groundskeeping Workers	12.70	Truck Drivers, Light/Delivery Svcs.	16.90
Lawyers	59.60	Waiters and Waitresses	13.10

Note: Wage data covers the Orlando-Kissimmee-Sanford, FL Metropolitan Statistical Area—see Appendix B for
areas included; (*) Hourly wages for elementary/secondary school teachers and teacher assistants were
calculated by the editors from annual wage data based on a 40 hour work week; n/a not available.
Source: Bureau of Labor Statistics, Metro Area Occupational Employment & Wage Estimates, May 2018

Employment by Occupation

Occupation Classification	City (%)	MSA[1] (%)	U.S. (%)
Management, Business, Science, and Arts	37.2	35.9	37.4
Natural Resources, Construction, and Maintenance	5.4	7.6	8.9
Production, Transportation, and Material Moving	8.4	9.0	12.2
Sales and Office	27.0	26.8	23.5
Service	21.9	20.6	18.0

Note: Figures cover employed civilians 16 years of age and older; (1) Figures cover the
Orlando-Kissimmee-Sanford, FL Metropolitan Statistical Area—see Appendix B for areas included
Source: U.S. Census Bureau, 2013-2017 American Community Survey 5-Year Estimates

Employment by Industry

Sector	MSA[1]		U.S.
	Number of Employees	Percent of Total	Percent of Total
Construction	84,800	6.4	4.8
Education and Health Services	159,200	12.0	15.9
Financial Activities	77,100	5.8	5.7
Government	130,500	9.8	15.1
Information	25,500	1.9	1.9
Leisure and Hospitality	267,600	20.1	10.7
Manufacturing	47,100	3.5	8.5
Mining and Logging	200	<0.1	0.5
Other Services	44,700	3.4	3.9
Professional and Business Services	243,900	18.3	14.1
Retail Trade	156,600	11.8	10.8
Transportation, Warehousing, and Utilities	45,700	3.4	4.2
Wholesale Trade	46,600	3.5	3.9

Note: Figures are non-farm employment as of December 2018. Figures are not seasonally adjusted and include workers 16 years of age and older; (1) Figures cover the Orlando-Kissimmee-Sanford, FL Metropolitan Statistical Area—see Appendix B for areas included
Source: Bureau of Labor Statistics, Current Employment Statistics, Employment, Hours, and Earnings

Occupations with Greatest Projected Employment Growth: 2018 – 2020

Occupation[1]	2018 Employment	2020 Projected Employment	Numeric Employment Change	Percent Employment Change
Interviewers, Except Eligibility and Loan	11,890	33,270	21,380	179.8
Combined Food Preparation and Serving Workers, Including Fast Food	242,590	256,470	13,880	5.7
Waiters and Waitresses	230,640	240,320	9,680	4.2
Registered Nurses	193,200	202,070	8,870	4.6
Customer Service Representatives	245,420	253,780	8,360	3.4
Laborers and Freight, Stock, and Material Movers, Hand	135,600	143,640	8,040	5.9
Construction Laborers	89,390	97,130	7,740	8.7
Landscaping and Groundskeeping Workers	116,440	123,040	6,600	5.7
Carpenters	72,550	78,990	6,440	8.9
Janitors and Cleaners, Except Maids and Housekeeping Cleaners	133,890	140,000	6,110	4.6

Note: Projections cover Florida; (1) Sorted by numeric employment change
Source: www.projectionscentral.com, State Occupational Projections, 2018–2020 Short-Term Projections

Fastest Growing Occupations: 2018 – 2020

Occupation[1]	2018 Employment	2020 Projected Employment	Numeric Employment Change	Percent Employment Change
Interviewers, Except Eligibility and Loan	11,890	33,270	21,380	179.8
Solar Photovoltaic Installers	1,100	1,330	230	20.9
Terrazzo Workers and Finishers	390	450	60	15.4
Helpers—Roofers	1,490	1,720	230	15.4
Helpers—Brickmasons, Blockmasons, Stonemasons, and Tile and Marble Setters	1,280	1,470	190	14.8
Helpers—Painters, Paperhangers, Plasterers, and Stucco Masons	570	650	80	14.0
Reinforcing Iron and Rebar Workers	1,100	1,250	150	13.6
Insulation Workers, Floor, Ceiling, and Wall	2,550	2,880	330	12.9
Structural Iron and Steel Workers	5,210	5,880	670	12.9
Cement Masons and Concrete Finishers	13,490	15,210	1,720	12.8

Note: Projections cover Florida; (1) Sorted by percent employment change and excludes occupations with numeric employment change less than 50
Source: www.projectionscentral.com, State Occupational Projections, 2018–2020 Short-Term Projections

TAXES

State Corporate Income Tax Rates

State	Tax Rate (%)	Income Brackets ($)	Num. of Brackets	Financial Institution Tax Rate (%)[a]	Federal Income Tax Ded.
Florida	5.5 (e)	Flat rate	1	5.5 (e)	No

Note: Tax rates as of January 1, 2019; (a) Rates listed are the corporate income tax rate applied to financial institutions or excise taxes based on income. Some states have other taxes based upon the value of deposits or shares; (e) The Florida tax rate may be adjusted downward if certain revenue targets are met.
Source: Federation of Tax Administrators, Range of State Corporate Income Tax Rates, January 1, 2019

State Individual Income Tax Rates

State	Tax Rate (%)	Income Brackets ($)	Personal Exemptions ($)			Standard Ded. ($)	
			Single	Married	Depend.	Single	Married
Florida				– No state income tax –			

Note: Tax rates as of January 1, 2019; Local- and county-level taxes are not included; n/a not applicable;

Source: Federation of Tax Administrators, State Individual Income Tax Rates, January 1, 2019

Various State Sales and Excise Tax Rates

State	State Sales Tax (%)	Gasoline[1] (¢/gal.)	Cigarette[2] ($/pack)	Spirits[3] ($/gal.)	Wine[4] ($/gal.)	Beer[5] ($/gal.)	Recreational Marijuana (%)
Florida	6	41.99	1.339	6.50 (f)	2.25 (l)	0.48 (q)	Not legal

Note: All tax rates as of January 1, 2019; (1) The American Petroleum Institute has developed a methodology for determining the average tax rate on a gallon of fuel. Rates may include any of the following: excise taxes, environmental fees, storage tank fees, other fees or taxes, general sales tax, and local taxes. In states where gasoline is subject to the general sales tax, or where the fuel tax is based on the average sale price, the average rate determined by API is sensitive to changes in the price of gasoline. States that fully or partially apply general sales taxes to gasoline: CA, CO, GA, IL, IN, MI, NY; (2) The federal excise tax of $1.0066 per pack and local taxes are not included; (3) Rates are those applicable to off-premise sales of 40% alcohol by volume (a.b.v.) distilled spirits in 750ml containers. Local excise taxes are excluded; (4) Rates are those applicable to off-premise sales of 11% a.b.v. non-carbonated wine in 750ml containers; (5) Rates are those applicable to off-premise sales of 4.7% a.b.v. beer in 12 ounce containers; (f) Different rates also applicable according to alcohol content, place of production, size of container, or place purchased (on- or off-premise or onboard airlines); (l) Different rates also applicable to alcohol content, place of production, size of container, place purchased (on- or off-premise or on board airlines) or type of wine (carbonated, vermouth, etc.); (q) Different rates also applicable according to alcohol content, place of production, size of container, or place purchased (on- or off-premise or onboard airlines).
Source: Tax Foundation, 2019 Facts & Figures: How Does Your State Compare?

State Business Tax Climate Index Rankings

State	Overall Rank	Corporate Tax Rank	Individual Income Tax Rank	Sales Tax Rank	Unemployment Insurance Tax Rank	Property Tax Rank
Florida	4	6	1	22	2	11

Note: The index is a measure of how each state's tax laws affect economic performance. The lower the rank, the more favorable a state's tax system is for business. States without a given tax are given a ranking of 1. The scores/rankings for the District of Columbia do not affect other states. The 2019 index represents the tax climate as of July 1, 2018.
Source: Tax Foundation, State Business Tax Climate Index 2019

COMMERCIAL REAL ESTATE

Office Market

Market Area	Inventory (sq. ft.)	Vacancy Rate (%)	Under Construction (sq. ft.)	YTD Net Absorption (sq. ft.)	Total Average Asking Rent ($/sq. ft./year)
Orlando	68,603,328	6.3	637,000	230,572	21.99
National	4,905,867,938	13.1	83,553,714	45,846,470	28.46

Source: Newmark Grubb Knight Frank, National Office Market Report, 4th Quarter 2018

Industrial/Warehouse/R&D Market

Market Area	Inventory (sq. ft.)	Vacancy Rate (%)	Under Construction (sq. ft.)	YTD Net Absorption (sq. ft.)	Total Average Asking Rent ($/sq. ft./year)
Orlando	185,002,433	3.9	1,041,385	3,207,155	6.43
National	14,796,839,085	5.0	262,662,294	238,014,726	7.16

Source: Newmark Grubb Knight Frank, National Industrial Market Report, 4th Quarter 2018

COMMERCIAL UTILITIES

Typical Monthly Electric Bills

Area	Commercial Service ($/month)		Industrial Service ($/month)	
	1,500 kWh	40 kW demand 14,000 kWh	1,000 kW demand 200,000 kWh	50,000 kW demand 32,500,000 kWh
City	151	1,199	22,310	1,463,495
Average[1]	203	1,619	25,886	2,540,077

Note: Figures are based on annualized rates; (1) Average based on 187 utilities surveyed
Source: Edison Electric Institute, Typical Bills and Average Rates Report, Summer 2018

TRANSPORTATION

Means of Transportation to Work

Area	Car/Truck/Van		Public Transportation			Bicycle	Walked	Other Means	Worked at Home
	Drove Alone	Car-pooled	Bus	Subway	Railroad				
City	78.3	8.2	4.1	0.1	0.0	0.6	1.9	1.8	5.1
MSA[1]	80.2	9.6	1.7	0.0	0.1	0.4	1.0	1.4	5.5
U.S.	76.4	9.2	2.5	1.9	0.6	0.6	2.7	1.3	4.7

Note: Figures are percentages and cover workers 16 years of age and older; (1) Figures cover the Orlando-Kissimmee-Sanford, FL Metropolitan Statistical Area—see Appendix B for areas included
Source: U.S. Census Bureau, 2013-2017 American Community Survey 5-Year Estimates

Travel Time to Work

Area	Less Than 10 Minutes	10 to 19 Minutes	20 to 29 Minutes	30 to 44 Minutes	45 to 59 Minutes	60 to 89 Minutes	90 Minutes or More
City	7.9	28.5	26.8	24.9	6.3	3.5	2.2
MSA[1]	7.2	24.2	23.5	27.7	10.2	4.9	2.2
U.S.	12.7	28.9	20.9	20.5	8.1	6.2	2.7

Note: Note: Figures are percentages and include workers 16 years old and over; (1) Figures cover the Orlando-Kissimmee-Sanford, FL Metropolitan Statistical Area—see Appendix B for areas included
Source: U.S. Census Bureau, 2013-2017 American Community Survey 5-Year Estimates

Freeway Travel Time Index

Area	1985	1990	1995	2000	2005	2010	2014
Urban Area Rank[1,2]	35	25	32	28	27	33	34
Urban Area Index[1]	1.09	1.14	1.16	1.20	1.23	1.21	1.21
Average Index[3]	1.09	1.11	1.14	1.17	1.20	1.19	1.20

Note: Freeway Travel Time Index—the ratio of travel time in the peak period to the travel time at free-flow conditions. For example, a value of 1.30 indicates a 20-minute free-flow trip takes 26 minutes in the peak (20 minutes x 1.30 = 26 minutes); (1) Covers the Orlando FL urban area; (2) Rank is based on 101 urban areas (#1 = highest travel time index); (3) Average of 101 urban areas
Source: Texas Transportation Institute, 2015 Urban Mobility Scorecard, August 2015

Freeway Commuter Stress Index

Area	1985	1990	1995	2000	2005	2010	2014
Urban Area Rank[1,2]	36	33	37	36	35	37	38
Urban Area Index[1]	1.13	1.18	1.20	1.24	1.27	1.25	1.25
Average Index[3]	1.13	1.16	1.19	1.22	1.25	1.24	1.25

Note: The Freeway Commuter Stress Index is the same as the Freeway Travel Time Index (see table above) except that it includes only the travel in the peak directions during the peak periods; the TTI includes travel in all directions during the peak period. Thus, the CSI is more indicative of the work trip experienced by each commuter on a daily basis; (1) Covers the Orlando FL urban area; (2) Rank is based on 101 urban areas (#1 = highest travel time index); (3) Average of 101 urban areas
Source: Texas Transportation Institute, 2015 Urban Mobility Scorecard, August 2015

Public Transportation

Agency Name / Mode of Transportation	Vehicles Operated in Maximum Service[1]	Annual Unlinked Passenger Trips[2] (in thous.)	Annual Passenger Miles[3] (in thous.)
Central Florida Regional Transportation Authority (Lynx)			
Bus (directly operated)	245	23,631.6	130,063.8
Bus (purchased transportation)	13	154.2	1,655.7
Bus Rapid Transit (directly operated)	14	1,208.9	2,627.7
Commuter Bus (purchased transportation)	2	4.5	77.5
Demand Response (purchased transportation)	155	582.9	8,676.6
Vanpool (purchased transportation)	181	448.8	13,155.2

Note: (1) The number of revenue vehicles operated by the given mode and type of service to meet the annual maximum service requirement. This is the revenue vehicle count during the peak season of the year; on the week and day that maximum service is provided. Vehicles operated in maximum service (VOMS) exclude atypical days and one-time special events; (2) The number of passengers who boarded public transportation vehicles. Passengers are counted each time they board a vehicle no matter how many vehicles they use to travel from their origin to their destination. (3) The sum of the distances ridden by all passengers during the entire fiscal year.
Source: Federal Transit Administration, National Transit Database, 2017

Air Transportation

Airport Name and Code / Type of Service	Passenger Airlines[1]	Passenger Enplanements	Freight Carriers[2]	Freight (lbs)
Orlando International (MCO)				
Domestic service (U.S. carriers - 2018)	31	20,019,064	15	168,898,517
International service (U.S. carriers - 2017)	13	519,593	1	2,376,928

Note: (1) Includes all U.S.-based major, minor and commuter airlines that carried at least one passenger during the year; (2) Includes all U.S.-based airlines and freight carriers that transported at least one pound of freight during the year.
Source: Bureau of Transportation Statistics, The Intermodal Transportation Database, Air Carriers: T-100 Domestic Market (U.S. Carriers), 2018; Bureau of Transportation Statistics, The Intermodal Transportation Database, Air Carriers: T-100 International Market (U.S. Carriers), 2017

Other Transportation Statistics

Major Highways:	I-4
Amtrak Service:	Yes
Major Waterways/Ports:	None

Source: Amtrak.com; Google Maps

BUSINESSES

Major Business Headquarters

Company Name	Industry	Rankings	
		Fortune[1]	Forbes[2]
Darden Restaurants	Food Services	396	-
Red Lobster	Hotels, Restaurants & Leisure	-	185

Note: (1) Companies that produce a 10-K are ranked 1 to 500 based on 2017 revenue; (2) All private companies with at least $2 billion in annual revenue through the end of their most current fiscal year are ranked 1 to 229; companies listed are headquartered in the city; dashes indicate no ranking
Source: Fortune, "Fortune 500," June 2018; Forbes, "America's Largest Private Companies," 2018 Rankings

Fast-Growing Businesses

According to *Inc.*, Orlando is home to one of America's 500 fastest-growing private companies: **Crystal Clear Digital Marketing** (#210). Criteria: must be an independent, privately-held, for-profit, U.S. corporation, proprietorship or partnership as of December 31, 2017; revenues must be at least $100,000 in 2014 and $2 million in 2017; must have four-year operating/sales history. Holding companies, regulated banks, and utilities were excluded. *Inc., "America's 500 Fastest-Growing Private Companies," 2018*

Minority Business Opportunity

Orlando is home to one company which is on the *Black Enterprise* Auto Dealer list (45 largest dealers based on gross sales): **Boyland Auto Group** (#3). Criteria: company must be operational in previous calendar year and be at least 51% black-owned. *Black Enterprise, B.E. 100s, 2018*

Orlando is home to five companies which are on the *Hispanic Business* 500 list (500 largest U.S. Hispanic-owned companies based on revenue): **Greenway Ford** (#3); **Jardon & Howard Technologies** (#170); **Advanced Xerographics Imaging Systems** (#179); **T&G Constructors** (#202); **US Aluminum Services Corp.** (#361). Companies included must show at least 51 percent ownership by Hispanic U.S. citizens, and must maintain headquarters in one of the 50 states or Washington, D.C. *Hispanic Business, "Hispanic Business 500," June 20, 2013*

Minority- and Women-Owned Businesses

Group	All Firms		Firms with Paid Employees			
	Firms	Sales ($000)	Firms	Sales ($000)	Employees	Payroll ($000)
AIAN[1]	244	7,558	11	(s)	20 - 99	(s)
Asian	2,443	1,006,575	778	935,896	5,486	158,180
Black	7,085	1,032,755	231	933,027	6,040	378,270
Hispanic	8,747	1,055,873	799	878,685	6,099	164,865
NHOPI[2]	39	1,659	1	(s)	20 - 99	(s)
Women	15,161	2,001,011	1,822	1,730,151	13,742	406,431
All Firms	37,544	54,485,349	9,547	53,541,649	248,113	11,411,763

Note: Figures cover firms located in the city; minority- and women-owned business are defined as firms in which the corresponding group own 51% or more of the stock or equity of the company; (1) American Indian and Alaska Native; (2) Native Hawaiian and Other Pacific Islander; (s) estimates are suppressed when publication standards are not met
Source: U.S. Census Bureau, 2012 Economic Census, Survey of Business Owners

HOTELS & CONVENTION CENTERS

Hotels, Motels and Vacation Rentals

Area	5 Star		4 Star		3 Star		2 Star		1 Star		Not Rated	
	Num.	Pct.[3]	Num.	Pct.[3]	Num.	Pct.[3]	Num.	Pct.[3]	Num.	Pct.[3]	Num.	Pct.[3]
City[1]	57	0.5	1,942	18.0	5,518	51.2	337	3.1	4	0.0	2,921	27.1
Total[2]	286	0.4	5,236	7.1	16,715	22.6	10,259	13.9	293	0.4	41,056	55.6

Note: (1) Figures cover Orlando and vicinity; (2) Figures cover all 100 cities in this book; (3) Percentage of hotels which have a given star rating; Star ratings are determined by expedia.com and offer an indication of the general quality of a particular hotel.
Source: www.expedia.com, April 3, 2019

Major Convention Centers

Name	Overall Space (sq. ft.)	Exhibit Space (sq. ft.)	Meeting Space (sq. ft.)	Meeting Rooms
Orange County Convention Center	n/a	2,100,000	n/a	74

Note: Table includes convention centers located in the Orlando-Kissimmee-Sanford, FL metro area; n/a not available
Source: Original research

Living Environment

COST OF LIVING

Cost of Living Index

Composite Index	Groceries	Housing	Utilities	Trans-portation	Health Care	Misc. Goods/ Services
95.8	106.0	88.3	102.2	93.0	89.1	98.1

Note: The Cost of Living Index measures regional differences in the cost of consumer goods and services, excluding taxes and non-consumer expenditures, for professional and managerial households in the top income quintile. It is based on more than 50,000 prices covering almost 60 different items for which prices are collected three times a year by chambers of commerce, economic development organizations or university applied economic centers in each participating urban area. The numbers shown should be read as a percentage above or below the national average of 100. For example, a value of 115.4 in the groceries column indicates that grocery prices are 15.4% higher than the national average. Small differences in the index numbers should not be interpreted as significant; Figures cover the Orlando FL urban area.
Source: The Council for Community and Economic Research, ACCRA Cost of Living Index, 2018

Grocery Prices

Area[1]	T-Bone Steak ($/pound)	Frying Chicken ($/pound)	Whole Milk ($/half gal.)	Eggs ($/dozen)	Orange Juice ($/64 oz.)	Coffee ($/11.5 oz.)
City[2]	10.51	1.39	2.46	2.05	3.59	3.91
Avg.	11.35	1.42	1.94	1.81	3.52	4.35
Min.	7.45	0.92	0.80	0.75	2.72	3.06
Max.	15.05	2.76	4.18	4.00	5.36	8.20

Note: (1) Values for the local area are compared with the average, minimum and maximum values for all 291 areas in the Cost of Living Index; (2) Figures cover the Orlando FL urban area; T-Bone Steak (price per pound); Frying Chicken (price per pound, whole fryer); Whole Milk (half gallon carton); Eggs (price per dozen, Grade A, large); Orange Juice (64 oz. Tropicana or Florida Natural); Coffee (11.5 oz. can, vacuum-packed, Maxwell House, Hills Bros, or Folgers).
Source: The Council for Community and Economic Research, ACCRA Cost of Living Index, 2018

Housing and Utility Costs

Area[1]	New Home Price ($)	Apartment Rent ($/month)	All Electric ($/month)	Part Electric ($/month)	Other Energy ($/month)	Telephone ($/month)
City[2]	287,772	1,120	171.56	-	-	182.30
Avg.	347,000	1,087	165.93	100.16	67.73	178.70
Min.	200,468	500	93.58	25.64	26.78	163.10
Max.	1,901,222	4,888	388.65	246.86	332.81	197.70

Note: (1) Values for the local area are compared with the average, minimum and maximum values for all 291 areas in the Cost of Living Index; (2) Figures cover the Orlando FL urban area; New Home Price (2,400 sf living area, 8,000 sf lot, in urban area with full utilities); Apartment Rent (950 sf 2 bedroom/1.5 or 2 bath, unfurnished, excluding all utilities except water); All Electric (average monthly cost for an all-electric home); Part Electric (average monthly cost for a part-electric home); Other Energy (average monthly cost for natural gas, fuel oil, coal, wood, and any other forms of energy except electricity); Telephone (price includes the base monthly rate plus taxes and fees for three lines of mobile phone service).
Source: The Council for Community and Economic Research, ACCRA Cost of Living Index, 2018

Health Care, Transportation, and Other Costs

Area[1]	Doctor ($/visit)	Dentist ($/visit)	Optometrist ($/visit)	Gasoline ($/gallon)	Beauty Salon ($/visit)	Men's Shirt ($)
City[2]	85.25	82.50	79.07	2.52	53.24	21.86
Avg.	110.71	95.11	103.74	2.61	37.48	32.03
Min.	33.60	62.55	54.63	1.89	17.00	11.44
Max.	195.97	153.93	225.79	3.59	71.88	58.64

Note: (1) Values for the local area are compared with the average, minimum and maximum values for all 291 areas in the Cost of Living Index; (2) Figures cover the Orlando FL urban area; Doctor (general practitioners routine exam of an established patient); Dentist (adult teeth cleaning and periodic oral examination); Optometrist (full vision eye exam for established adult patient); Gasoline (one gallon regular unleaded, national brand, including all taxes, cash price at self-service pump if available); Beauty Salon (woman's shampoo, trim, and blow-dry); Men's Shirt (cotton/polyester dress shirt, pinpoint weave, long sleeves).
Source: The Council for Community and Economic Research, ACCRA Cost of Living Index, 2018

HOUSING

House Price Index (HPI)

Area	National Ranking[2]	Quarterly Change (%)	One-Year Change (%)	Five-Year Change (%)
MSA[1]	68	0.48	7.92	55.21
U.S.[3]	–	1.12	5.73	32.81

Note: The HPI is a weighted repeat sales index. It measures average price changes in repeat sales or refinancings on the same properties. This information is obtained by reviewing repeat mortgage transactions on single-family properties whose mortgages have been purchased or securitized by Fannie Mae or Freddie Mac in January 1975; (1) Figures cover the Orlando-Kissimmee-Sanford, FL Metropolitan Statistical Area—see Appendix B for areas included; (2) Rankings are based on annual percentage change for all metro areas containing at least 15,000 transactions over the last 10 years and ranges from 1 to 245; (3) figures based on a weighted average of Census Division estimates using a seasonally adjusted, purchase-only index; all figures are for the period ending December 31, 2018
Source: Federal Housing Finance Agency, House Price Index, February 26, 2019

Median Single-Family Home Prices

Area	2016	2017	2018p	Percent Change 2017 to 2018
MSA[1]	224.0	244.9	265.0	8.2
U.S. Average	235.5	248.8	261.6	5.1

Note: Figures are median sales prices of existing single-family homes in thousands of dollars; (p) preliminary; (1) Figures cover the Orlando-Kissimmee-Sanford, FL Metropolitan Statistical Area—see Appendix B for areas included
Source: National Association of Realtors, Median Sales Price of Existing Single-Family Homes for Metropolitan Areas, 4th Quarter 2018

Qualifying Income Based on Median Sales Price of Existing Single-Family Homes

Area	With 5% Down ($)	With 10% Down ($)	With 20% Down ($)
MSA[1]	64,762	61,353	54,536
U.S. Average	62,954	59,640	53,013

Note: Figures are preliminary; Qualifying income is based on a mortgage rate of 4.9%. Monthly principal and interest payment is limited to 25% of income; (1) Figures cover the Orlando-Kissimmee-Sanford, FL Metropolitan Statistical Area—see Appendix B for areas included
Source: National Association of Realtors, Qualifying Income Based on Median Sales Price of Existing Single-Family Homes for Metropolitan Areas, 4th Quarter 2018

Median Apartment Condo-Coop Home Prices

Area	2016	2017	2018p	Percent Change 2017 to 2018
MSA[1]	n/a	n/a	n/a	n/a
U.S. Average	220.7	234.3	241.0	2.9

Note: Figures are median sales prices of existing apartment condo-coop homes in thousands of dollars; (p) preliminary; n/a not available; (1) Figures cover the Orlando-Kissimmee-Sanford, FL Metropolitan Statistical Area—see Appendix B for areas included
Source: National Association of Realtors, Median Sales Price of Existing Apartment Condo-Coop Homes for Metropolitan Areas, 4th Quarter 2018

Home Value Distribution

Area	Under $50,000	$50,000 -$99,999	$100,000 -$149,999	$150,000 -$199,999	$200,000 -$299,999	$300,000 -$499,999	$500,000 -$999,999	$1,000,000 or more
City	6.1	15.8	14.8	14.1	22.4	18.9	6.4	1.6
MSA[1]	8.0	13.6	15.7	18.9	23.0	14.8	4.6	1.3
U.S.	8.3	13.9	14.7	14.6	18.7	17.3	9.7	2.7

Note: Figures are percentages and cover owner-occupied housing units; (1) Figures cover the Orlando-Kissimmee-Sanford, FL Metropolitan Statistical Area—see Appendix B for areas included
Source: U.S. Census Bureau, 2013-2017 American Community Survey 5-Year Estimates

Homeownership Rate

Area	2010 (%)	2011 (%)	2012 (%)	2013 (%)	2014 (%)	2015 (%)	2016 (%)	2017 (%)	2018 (%)
MSA[1]	70.8	68.6	68.0	65.5	62.3	58.4	58.5	59.5	58.5
U.S.	66.9	66.1	65.4	65.1	64.5	63.7	63.4	63.9	64.4

Note: (1) Figures cover the Orlando-Kissimmee-Sanford, FL Metropolitan Statistical Area—see Appendix B for areas included
Source: U.S. Census Bureau, Housing Vacancies and Homeownership Annual Statistics: 2010-2018

Year Housing Structure Built

Area	2010 or Later	2000 -2009	1990 -1999	1980 -1989	1970 -1979	1960 -1969	1950 -1959	1940 -1949	Before 1940	Median Year
City	5.2	23.1	17.0	17.3	14.0	7.8	9.3	3.2	3.1	1987
MSA[1]	4.9	25.3	21.2	20.7	13.5	6.2	5.4	1.3	1.6	1991
U.S.	3.2	14.5	14.0	13.6	15.5	10.8	10.5	5.1	12.9	1977

Note: Figures are percentages except for Median Year; Note: (1) Figures cover the Orlando-Kissimmee-Sanford, FL Metropolitan Statistical Area—see Appendix B for areas included
Source: U.S. Census Bureau, 2013-2017 American Community Survey 5-Year Estimates

Gross Monthly Rent

Area	Under $500	$500 -$999	$1,000 -$1,499	$1,500 -$1,999	$2,000 -$2,499	$2,500 -$2,999	$3,000 and up	Median ($)
City	3.8	35.6	44.9	12.3	2.5	0.6	0.4	1,091
MSA[1]	3.0	35.0	44.6	13.7	2.5	0.7	0.6	1,107
U.S.	10.5	41.1	28.7	11.7	4.5	1.8	1.7	982

Note: Figures are percentages except for Median; Gross rent is the contract rent plus the estimated average monthly cost of utilities (electricity, gas, and water and sewer) and fuels (oil, coal, kerosene, wood, etc.) if these are paid by the renter (or paid for the renter by someone else); (1) Figures cover the Orlando-Kissimmee-Sanford, FL Metropolitan Statistical Area—see Appendix B for areas included
Source: U.S. Census Bureau, 2013-2017 American Community Survey 5-Year Estimates

HEALTH

Health Risk Factors

Category	MSA[1] (%)	U.S. (%)
Adults aged 18–64 who have any kind of health care coverage	79.0	87.3
Adults who reported being in good or better health	80.6	82.4
Adults who have been told they have high blood cholesterol	34.5	33.0
Adults who have been told they have high blood pressure	32.2	32.3
Adults who are current smokers	12.9	17.1
Adults who currently use E-cigarettes	6.1	4.6
Adults who currently use chewing tobacco, snuff, or snus	2.7	4.0
Adults who are heavy drinkers[2]	4.1	6.3
Adults who are binge drinkers[3]	13.8	17.4
Adults who are overweight (BMI 25.0 - 29.9)	38.8	35.3
Adults who are obese (BMI 30.0 - 99.8)	26.4	31.3
Adults who participated in any physical activities in the past month	72.9	74.4
Adults who always or nearly always wears a seat belt	96.3	94.3

Note: (1) Figures cover the Orlando-Kissimmee-Sanford, FL Metropolitan Statistical Area—see Appendix B for areas included; (2) Heavy drinkers are classified as adult men having more than 14 drinks per week and adult women having more than 7 drinks per week; (3) Binge drinkers are classified as males having five or more drinks on one occasion or females having four or more drinks on one occasion
Source: Centers for Disease Control and Prevention, Behavioral Risk Factor Surveillance System, SMART: Selected Metropolitan Area Risk Trends, 2017

Acute and Chronic Health Conditions

Category	MSA[1] (%)	U.S. (%)
Adults who have ever been told they had a heart attack	4.1	4.2
Adults who have ever been told they have angina or coronary heart disease	4.0	3.9
Adults who have ever been told they had a stroke	3.1	3.0
Adults who have ever been told they have asthma	14.4	14.2
Adults who have ever been told they have arthritis	20.6	24.9
Adults who have ever been told they have diabetes[2]	10.2	10.5
Adults who have ever been told they had skin cancer	6.3	6.2
Adults who have ever been told they had any other types of cancer	6.8	7.1
Adults who have ever been told they have COPD	6.4	6.5
Adults who have ever been told they have kidney disease	2.3	3.0
Adults who have ever been told they have a form of depression	16.9	20.5

Note: (1) Figures cover the Orlando-Kissimmee-Sanford, FL Metropolitan Statistical Area—see Appendix B for areas included; (2) Figures do not include pregnancy-related, borderline, or pre-diabetes
Source: Centers for Disease Control and Prevention, Behaviorial Risk Factor Surveillance System, SMART: Selected Metropolitan Area Risk Trends, 2017

Health Screening and Vaccination Rates

Category	MSA[1] (%)	U.S. (%)
Adults aged 65+ who have had flu shot within the past year	57.2	60.7
Adults aged 65+ who have ever had a pneumonia vaccination	66.2	75.4
Adults who have ever been tested for HIV	47.4	36.1
Adults who have ever had the shingles or zoster vaccine?	20.4	28.9
Adults who have had their blood cholesterol checked within the last five years	89.7	85.9

Note: n/a not available; (1) Figures cover the Orlando-Kissimmee-Sanford, FL Metropolitan Statistical Area—see Appendix B for areas included.
Source: Centers for Disease Control and Prevention, Behaviorial Risk Factor Surveillance System, SMART: Selected Metropolitan Area Risk Trends, 2017

Disability Status

Category	MSA[1] (%)	U.S. (%)
Adults who reported being deaf	5.0	6.7
Are you blind or have serious difficulty seeing, even when wearing glasses?	6.0	4.5
Are you limited in any way in any of your usual activities due of arthritis?	11.9	12.9
Do you have difficulty doing errands alone?	7.9	6.8
Do you have difficulty dressing or bathing?	4.3	3.6
Do you have serious difficulty concentrating/remembering/making decisions?	13.0	10.7
Do you have serious difficulty walking or climbing stairs?	13.8	13.6

Note: (1) Figures cover the Orlando-Kissimmee-Sanford, FL Metropolitan Statistical Area—see Appendix B for areas included.
Source: Centers for Disease Control and Prevention, Behaviorial Risk Factor Surveillance System, SMART: Selected Metropolitan Area Risk Trends, 2017

Mortality Rates for the Top 10 Causes of Death in the U.S.

ICD-10[a] Sub-Chapter	ICD-10[a] Code	Age-Adjusted Mortality Rate[1] per 100,000 population	
		County[2]	U.S.
Malignant neoplasms	C00-C97	147.9	155.5
Ischaemic heart diseases	I20-I25	89.6	94.8
Other forms of heart disease	I30-I51	43.1	52.9
Chronic lower respiratory diseases	J40-J47	31.7	41.0
Cerebrovascular diseases	I60-I69	48.7	37.5
Other degenerative diseases of the nervous system	G30-G31	25.2	35.0
Other external causes of accidental injury	W00-X59	28.9	33.7
Organic, including symptomatic, mental disorders	F01-F09	24.6	31.0
Hypertensive diseases	I10-I15	20.4	21.9
Diabetes mellitus	E10-E14	20.3	21.2

Note: (a) ICD-10 = International Classification of Diseases 10th Revision; (1) Mortality rates are a three year average covering 2015-2017; (2) Figures cover Orange County.
Source: Centers for Disease Control and Prevention, National Center for Health Statistics. Underlying Cause of Death 1999-2017 on CDC WONDER Online Database

Mortality Rates for Selected Causes of Death

ICD-10[a] Sub-Chapter	ICD-10[a] Code	Age-Adjusted Mortality Rate[1] per 100,000 population	
		County[2]	U.S.
Assault	X85-Y09	7.1	5.9
Diseases of the liver	K70-K76	12.1	14.1
Human immunodeficiency virus (HIV) disease	B20-B24	3.6	1.8
Influenza and pneumonia	J09-J18	9.8	14.3
Intentional self-harm	X60-X84	10.1	13.6
Malnutrition	E40-E46	2.9	1.6
Obesity and other hyperalimentation	E65-E68	1.5	2.1
Renal failure	N17-N19	12.8	13.0
Transport accidents	V01-V99	12.3	12.4
Viral hepatitis	B15-B19	1.6	1.6

Note: (a) ICD-10 = International Classification of Diseases 10th Revision; (1) Mortality rates are a three year average covering 2015-2017; (2) Figures cover Orange County; Data are suppressed when the data meet the criteria for confidentiality constraints; Mortality rates are flagged as unreliable when the rate would be calculated with a numerator of 20 or less.
Source: Centers for Disease Control and Prevention, National Center for Health Statistics. Underlying Cause of Death 1999-2017 on CDC WONDER Online Database

Health Insurance Coverage

Area	With Health Insurance	With Private Health Insurance	With Public Health Insurance	Without Health Insurance	Population Under Age 18 Without Health Insurance
City	81.9	58.4	30.1	18.1	10.0
MSA[1]	85.0	63.1	31.1	15.0	9.0
U.S.	89.5	67.2	33.8	10.5	5.7

Note: Figures are percentages that cover the civilian noninstitutionalized population; (1) Figures cover the Orlando-Kissimmee-Sanford, FL Metropolitan Statistical Area—see Appendix B for areas included
Source: U.S. Census Bureau, 2013-2017 American Community Survey 5-Year Estimates

Number of Medical Professionals

Area	MDs[3]	DOs[3,4]	Dentists	Podiatrists	Chiropractors	Optometrists
County[1] (number)	3,951	310	652	47	342	172
County[1] (rate[2])	298.5	23.4	48.3	3.5	25.4	12.8
U.S. (rate[2])	279.3	23.0	68.4	6.0	27.1	16.2

Note: Data as of 2017 unless noted; (1) Data covers Orange County; (2) Rate per 100,000 population; (3) Data as of 2016 and includes all active, non-federal physicians; (4) Doctor of Osteopathic Medicine
Source: U.S. Department of Health and Human Services, Health Resources and Services Administration, Bureau of Health Professions, Area Resource File (ARF) 2017-2018

Best Hospitals

According to *U.S. News,* the Orlando-Kissimmee-Sanford, FL metro area is home to one of the best hospitals in the U.S.: **Orlando Regional Medical Center** (5 pediatric specialties). The hospital listed was nationally ranked in at least one of 16 adult or 10 pediatric specialties. Only 170 hospitals nationwide were nationally ranked in one or more adult or pediatric specialty. Twenty hospitals in the U.S. made the Honor Roll. The Best Hospitals Honor Roll takes both the national rankings and the procedure and condition ratings into account. Hospitals received points if they were nationally ranked in one of the 16 adult specialties—the higher they ranked, the more points they got—and how many ratings of "high performing" they earned in the nine procedures and conditions. *U.S. News Online, "America's Best Hospitals 2018-19"*

According to *U.S. News,* the Orlando-Kissimmee-Sanford, FL metro area is home to two of the best children's hospitals in the U.S.: **AdventHealth for Children** (1 pediatric specialty); **Arnold Palmer Hospital for Children** (5 pediatric specialties). The hospitals listed were highly ranked in at least one of 10 pediatric specialties. Eighty-six children's hospitals in the U.S. were nationally ranked in at least one specialty. Hospitals received points for being ranked in a specialty, and the 10 hospitals with the most points across the 10 specialties make up the Honor Roll. *U.S. News Online, "America's Best Children's Hospitals 2018-19"*

EDUCATION

Public School District Statistics

District Name	Schls	Pupils	Pupil/ Teacher Ratio	Minority Pupils[1] (%)	Free Lunch Eligible[2] (%)	IEP[3] (%)
Florida Virtual School	4	7,509	4.6	41.3	n/a	4.3
Orange County Public Schools	257	200,674	16.1	73.1	61.6	10.8

Note: Table includes school districts with 2,000 or more students; (1) Percentage of students that are not non-Hispanic white; (2) Percentage of students that are eligible for the free lunch program; (3) Percentage of students that have an Individualized Education Program.
Source: U.S. Department of Education, National Center for Education Statistics, Common Core of Data, Local Education Agency (School District) Universe Survey: School Year 2016-2017; U.S. Department of Education, National Center for Education Statistics, Common Core of Data, Public Elementary/Secondary School Universe Survey: School Year 2016-2017

Best High Schools

According to *U.S. News,* Orlando is home to one of the best high schools in the U.S.: **Orlando Science Middle High Charter** (#269). More than 20,000 public, magnet and charter schools were ranked based on their performance on state assessments and how well they prepare students for college. Schools with the highest unrounded College Readiness Index values were numerically ranked from 1 to 500 and were classified as gold medal winners. *U.S. News & World Report, "Best High Schools 2018"*

Highest Level of Education

Area	Less than H.S.	H.S. Diploma	Some College, No Deg.	Associate Degree	Bachelor's Degree	Master's Degree	Prof. School Degree	Doctorate Degree
City	9.9	24.3	19.3	10.7	23.7	8.3	2.6	1.1
MSA[1]	10.9	26.6	20.8	11.4	20.4	7.2	1.8	0.9
U.S.	12.7	27.3	20.8	8.3	19.1	8.4	2.0	1.4

Note: Figures cover persons age 25 and over; (1) Figures cover the Orlando-Kissimmee-Sanford, FL Metropolitan Statistical Area—see Appendix B for areas included
Source: U.S. Census Bureau, 2013-2017 American Community Survey 5-Year Estimates

Educational Attainment by Race

Area	High School Graduate or Higher (%)					Bachelor's Degree or Higher (%)				
	Total	White	Black	Asian	Hisp.[2]	Total	White	Black	Asian	Hisp.[2]
City	90.1	92.8	83.8	91.9	85.4	35.8	40.3	21.3	59.0	25.3
MSA[1]	89.1	90.7	84.8	87.5	82.7	30.3	31.8	20.8	50.9	20.7
U.S.	87.3	89.3	84.9	86.5	66.7	30.9	32.2	20.6	52.7	15.2

Note: Figures shown cover persons 25 years old and over; (1) Figures cover the Orlando-Kissimmee-Sanford, FL Metropolitan Statistical Area—see Appendix B for areas included; (2) People of Hispanic origin can be of any race
Source: U.S. Census Bureau, 2013-2017 American Community Survey 5-Year Estimates

School Enrollment by Grade and Control

Area	Preschool (%)		Kindergarten (%)		Grades 1 - 4 (%)		Grades 5 - 8 (%)		Grades 9 - 12 (%)	
	Public	Private	Public	Private	Public	Private	Public	Private	Public	Private
City	59.7	40.3	81.5	18.5	93.0	7.0	86.6	13.4	92.0	8.0
MSA[1]	56.1	43.9	83.6	16.4	88.0	12.0	87.9	12.1	90.2	9.8
U.S.	58.8	41.2	87.7	12.3	89.7	10.3	89.6	10.4	90.3	9.7

Note: Figures shown cover persons 3 years old and over; (1) Figures cover the Orlando-Kissimmee-Sanford, FL Metropolitan Statistical Area—see Appendix B for areas included
Source: U.S. Census Bureau, 2013-2017 American Community Survey 5-Year Estimates

Average Salaries of Public School Classroom Teachers

Area	2016		2017		Change from 2016 to 2017	
	Dollars	Rank[1]	Dollars	Rank[1]	Percent	Rank[2]
Florida	46,612	46	47,267	45	1.4	26
U.S. Average	58,479	–	59,660	–	2.0	–

Note: (1) Rank ranges from 1 to 51 where 1 indicates highest salary; (2) Rank ranges from 1 to 51 where 1 indicates highest percent change.
Source: National Education Association, Rankings & Estimates: Rankings of the States 2017 and Estimates of School Statistics 2018

Higher Education

Four-Year Colleges			Two-Year Colleges			Medical Schools[1]	Law Schools[2]	Voc/ Tech[3]
Public	Private Non-profit	Private For-profit	Public	Private Non-profit	Private For-profit			
2	2	4	2	0	6	1	2	1

Note: Figures cover institutions located within the city limits and include main campuses only; (1) includes schools accredited by the Liaison Committee on Medical Education and the American Osteopathic Association's Commission on Osteopathic College Accreditation; (2) includes ABA-accredited schools, schools with provisional ABA accreditation, and state accredited schools; (3) includes all schools with programs that are less than 2 years.
Source: National Center for Education Statistics, Integrated Postsecondary Education System (IPEDS), 2017-18; Wikipedia, List of Medical Schools in the United States, accessed April 3, 2019; Wikipedia, List of Law Schools in the United States, accessed April 3, 2019

According to *U.S. News & World Report,* the Orlando-Kissimmee-Sanford, FL metro area is home to one of the best national universities in the U.S.: **University of Central Florida** (#165 tie). The indicators used to capture academic quality fall into a number of categories: assessment by administrators at peer institutions; retention of students; faculty resources; student selectivity; financial resources; alumni giving; high school counselor ratings of colleges; and graduation rate. *U.S. News & World Report, "America's Best Colleges 2019"*

PRESIDENTIAL ELECTION

2016 Presidential Election Results

Area	Clinton	Trump	Johnson	Stein	Other
Orange County	59.8	35.4	2.6	0.9	1.4
U.S.	48.0	45.9	3.3	1.1	1.7

Note: Results are percentages and may not add to 100% due to rounding
Source: Dave Leip's Atlas of U.S. Presidential Elections

EMPLOYERS

Major Employers

Company Name	Industry
Adventist Health System/Sunbelt	General medical & surgical hospitals
Airtran Airways	Air passenger carrier, scheduled
Central Florida Health Alliance	Hospital management
CNL Lifestyle Properties	Real estate agents & managers
Connextions	Communication services, nec
Florida Department of Children & Families	Individual & family services
Florida Hospital Medical Center	General medical & surgical hospitals
Gaylord Palms Resort & Conv Ctr	Hotel franchised
Leesburg Regional Medical Center	General medical & surgical hospitals
Lockheed Martin Corporation	Aircraft
Marriott International	Hotels & motels
Orlando Health	General medical & surgical hospitals
Rosen 9939	Hotels & motels
Sea World of Florida	Theme park, amusement
Sears Termite & Pest Control	Pest control in structures
Siemens Energy	Power plant construction
Universal City Florida Partners	Amusement & theme parks
University of Central Florida	Colleges & universities
Winter Park Healthcare Group	Hospital affiliated with AMA residency

Note: Companies shown are located within the Orlando-Kissimmee-Sanford, FL Metropolitan Statistical Area.
Source: Hoovers.com; Wikipedia

PUBLIC SAFETY

Crime Rate

Area	All Crimes	Violent Crimes				Property Crimes		
		Murder	Rape[3]	Robbery	Aggrav. Assault	Burglary	Larceny -Theft	Motor Vehicle Theft
City	6,198.6	8.1	64.4	213.0	458.5	840.9	4,125.3	488.4
Suburbs[1]	2,836.4	4.6	44.9	78.9	277.0	472.2	1,780.3	178.4
Metro[2]	3,217.8	5.0	47.1	94.1	297.6	514.1	2,046.4	213.6
U.S.	2,756.1	5.3	41.7	98.0	248.9	430.4	1,694.4	237.4

Note: Figures are crimes per 100,000 population; (1) All areas within the metro area that are located outside the city limits; (2) Figures cover the Orlando-Kissimmee-Sanford, FL Metropolitan Statistical Area—see Appendix B for areas included; (3) The city and U.S. figures shown were reported using the revised Uniform Crime Reporting (UCR) definition of rape. The suburban and metro area figures shown are an aggregate total of the data submitted using both the revised and legacy UCR definitions.
Source: FBI Uniform Crime Reports, 2017

Hate Crimes

Area	Number of Quarters Reported	Number of Incidents per Bias Motivation					
		Race/Ethnicity/ Ancestry	Religion	Sexual Orientation	Disability	Gender	Gender Identity
City	4	2	0	3	0	0	0
U.S.	4	4,131	1,564	1,130	116	46	119

Source: Federal Bureau of Investigation, Hate Crime Statistics 2017

Identity Theft Consumer Reports

Area	Reports	Reports per 100,000 Population	Rank[2]
MSA[1]	4,707	193	13
U.S.	444,602	135	-

Note: (1) Figures cover the Orlando-Kissimmee-Sanford, FL Metropolitan Statistical Area—see Appendix B for areas included; (2) Rank ranges from 1 to 389 where 1 indicates greatest number of identity theft reports per 100,000 population
Source: Federal Trade Commission, Consumer Sentinel Network Data Book for January–December 2018

Fraud and Other Consumer Reports

Area	Reports	Reports per 100,000 Population	Rank[2]
MSA[1]	17,403	713	19
U.S.	2,552,917	776	-

Note: (1) Figures cover the Orlando-Kissimmee-Sanford, FL Metropolitan Statistical Area—see Appendix B for areas included; (2) Rank ranges from 1 to 389 where 1 indicates greatest number of fraud and other consumer reports per 100,000 population
Source: Federal Trade Commission, Consumer Sentinel Network Data Book for January–December 2018

SPORTS

Professional Sports Teams

Team Name	League	Year Established
Orlando City SC	Major League Soccer (MLS)	2015
Orlando Magic	National Basketball Association (NBA)	1989

Note: Includes teams located in the Orlando-Kissimmee-Sanford, FL Metropolitan Statistical Area.
Source: Wikipedia, Major Professional Sports Teams of the United States and Canada, April 5, 2019

CLIMATE

Average and Extreme Temperatures

Temperature	Jan	Feb	Mar	Apr	May	Jun	Jul	Aug	Sep	Oct	Nov	Dec	Yr.
Extreme High (°F)	86	89	90	95	100	100	99	100	98	95	89	90	100
Average High (°F)	70	72	77	82	87	90	91	91	89	83	78	72	82
Average Temp. (°F)	59	62	67	72	77	81	82	82	81	75	68	62	72
Average Low (°F)	48	51	56	60	66	71	73	74	72	66	58	51	62
Extreme Low (°F)	19	29	25	38	51	53	64	65	57	44	32	20	19

Note: Figures cover the years 1952-1990
Source: National Climatic Data Center, International Station Meteorological Climate Summary, 9/96

Average Precipitation/Snowfall/Humidity

Precip./Humidity	Jan	Feb	Mar	Apr	May	Jun	Jul	Aug	Sep	Oct	Nov	Dec	Yr.
Avg. Precip. (in.)	2.3	2.8	3.4	2.0	3.2	7.0	7.2	5.8	5.8	2.7	3.5	2.0	47.7
Avg. Snowfall (in.)	Tr	0	0	0	0	0	0	0	0	0	0	0	Tr
Avg. Rel. Hum. 7am (%)	87	87	88	87	88	89	90	92	92	89	89	87	89
Avg. Rel. Hum. 4pm (%)	53	51	49	47	51	61	65	66	66	59	56	55	57

Note: Figures cover the years 1952-1990; Tr = Trace amounts (<0.05 in. of rain; <0.5 in. of snow)
Source: National Climatic Data Center, International Station Meteorological Climate Summary, 9/96

Weather Conditions

Temperature			Daytime Sky			Precipitation		
32°F & below	45°F & below	90°F & above	Clear	Partly cloudy	Cloudy	0.01 inch or more precip.	0.1 inch or more snow/ice	Thunder-storms
3	35	90	76	208	81	115	0	80

Note: Figures are average number of days per year and cover the years 1952-1990
Source: National Climatic Data Center, International Station Meteorological Climate Summary, 9/96

HAZARDOUS WASTE

Superfund Sites

The Orlando-Kissimmee-Sanford, FL metro area is home to six sites on the EPA's Superfund National Priorities List: **Chevron Chemical Co. (Ortho Division)** (final); **City Industries, Inc.** (final); **General Dynamics Longwood** (final); **Sanford Dry Cleaners** (final); **Tower Chemical Co.** (final); **Zellwood Ground Water Contamination** (final). There are a total of 1,390 Superfund sites with a status of proposed or final on the list in the U.S. *U.S. Environmental Protection Agency, National Priorities List, April 5, 2019*

AIR & WATER QUALITY

Air Quality Trends: Ozone

	1990	1995	2000	2005	2010	2012	2014	2015	2016	2017
MSA[1]	0.081	0.075	0.080	0.083	0.069	0.071	0.062	0.060	0.063	0.067
U.S.	0.088	0.089	0.082	0.080	0.073	0.075	0.067	0.068	0.069	0.068

Note: (1) Data covers the Orlando-Kissimmee-Sanford, FL Metropolitan Statistical Area—see Appendix B for areas included. The values shown are the composite ozone concentration averages among trend sites based on the highest fourth daily maximum 8-hour concentration in parts per million. These trends are based on sites having an adequate record of monitoring data during the trend period. Data from exceptional events are included.
Source: U.S. Environmental Protection Agency, Air Quality Monitoring Information, "Air Quality Trends by City, 1990-2017"

Air Quality Index

Area	Percent of Days when Air Quality was...[2]					AQI Statistics[2]	
	Good	Moderate	Unhealthy for Sensitive Groups	Unhealthy	Very Unhealthy	Maximum	Median
MSA[1]	73.4	25.8	0.8	0.0	0.0	147	43

Note: (1) Data covers the Orlando-Kissimmee-Sanford, FL Metropolitan Statistical Area—see Appendix B for areas included; (2) Based on 365 days with AQI data in 2017. Air Quality Index (AQI) is an index for reporting daily air quality. EPA calculates the AQI for five major air pollutants regulated by the Clean Air Act: ground-level ozone, particle pollution (aka particulate matter), carbon monoxide, sulfur dioxide, and nitrogen dioxide. The AQI runs from 0 to 500. The higher the AQI value, the greater the level of air pollution and the greater the health concern. There are six AQI categories: "Good" AQI is between 0 and 50. Air quality is considered satisfactory; "Moderate" AQI is between 51 and 100. Air quality is acceptable; "Unhealthy for Sensitive Groups" When AQI values are between 101 and 150, members of sensitive groups may experience health effects; "Unhealthy" When AQI values are between 151 and 200 everyone may begin to experience health effects; "Very Unhealthy" AQI values between 201 and 300 trigger a health alert; "Hazardous" AQI values over 300 trigger warnings of emergency conditions (not shown).
Source: U.S. Environmental Protection Agency, Air Quality Index Report, 2017

Air Quality Index Pollutants

Area	Percent of Days when AQI Pollutant was...[2]					
	Carbon Monoxide	Nitrogen Dioxide	Ozone	Sulfur Dioxide	Particulate Matter 2.5	Particulate Matter 10
MSA[1]	0.0	3.6	60.8	0.0	35.3	0.3

Note: (1) Data covers the Orlando-Kissimmee-Sanford, FL Metropolitan Statistical Area—see Appendix B for areas included; (2) Based on 365 days with AQI data in 2017. The Air Quality Index (AQI) is an index for reporting daily air quality. EPA calculates the AQI for five major air pollutants regulated by the Clean Air Act: ground-level ozone, particle pollution (also known as particulate matter), carbon monoxide, sulfur dioxide, and nitrogen dioxide. The AQI runs from 0 to 500. The higher the AQI value, the greater the level of air pollution and the greater the health concern.
Source: U.S. Environmental Protection Agency, Air Quality Index Report, 2017

Maximum Air Pollutant Concentrations: Particulate Matter, Ozone, CO and Lead

	Particulate Matter 10 (ug/m³)	Particulate Matter 2.5 Wtd AM (ug/m³)	Particulate Matter 2.5 24-Hr (ug/m³)	Ozone (ppm)	Carbon Monoxide (ppm)	Lead (ug/m³)
MSA[1] Level	59	7.8	18	0.068	1	n/a
NAAQS[2]	150	15	35	0.075	9	0.15
Met NAAQS[2]	Yes	Yes	Yes	Yes	Yes	n/a

Note: (1) Data covers the Orlando-Kissimmee-Sanford, FL Metropolitan Statistical Area—see Appendix B for areas included; Data from exceptional events are included; (2) National Ambient Air Quality Standards; ppm = parts per million; ug/m³ = micrograms per cubic meter; n/a not available.
Concentrations: Particulate Matter 10 (coarse particulate)—highest second maximum 24-hour concentration; Particulate Matter 2.5 Wtd AM (fine particulate)—highest weighted annual mean concentration; Particulate Matter 2.5 24-Hour (fine particulate)—highest 98th percentile 24-hour concentration; Ozone—highest fourth daily maximum 8-hour concentration; Carbon Monoxide—highest second maximum non-overlapping 8-hour concentration; Lead—maximum running 3-month average
Source: U.S. Environmental Protection Agency, Air Quality Monitoring Information, "Air Quality Statistics by City, 2017"

Maximum Air Pollutant Concentrations: Nitrogen Dioxide and Sulfur Dioxide

	Nitrogen Dioxide AM (ppb)	Nitrogen Dioxide 1-Hr (ppb)	Sulfur Dioxide AM (ppb)	Sulfur Dioxide 1-Hr (ppb)	Sulfur Dioxide 24-Hr (ppb)
MSA[1] Level	4	30	n/a	5	n/a
NAAQS[2]	53	100	30	75	140
Met NAAQS[2]	Yes	Yes	n/a	Yes	n/a

Note: (1) Data covers the Orlando-Kissimmee-Sanford, FL Metropolitan Statistical Area—see Appendix B for areas included; Data from exceptional events are included; (2) National Ambient Air Quality Standards; ppm = parts per million; ug/m³ = micrograms per cubic meter; n/a not available.
Concentrations: Nitrogen Dioxide AM—highest arithmetic mean concentration; Nitrogen Dioxide 1-Hr—highest 98th percentile 1-hour daily maximum concentration; Sulfur Dioxide AM—highest annual mean concentration; Sulfur Dioxide 1-Hr—highest 99th percentile 1-hour daily maximum concentration; Sulfur Dioxide 24-Hr—highest second maximum 24-hour concentration
Source: U.S. Environmental Protection Agency, Air Quality Monitoring Information, "Air Quality Statistics by City, 2017"

Drinking Water

Water System Name	Pop. Served	Primary Water Source Type	Violations[1] Health Based	Violations[1] Monitoring/ Reporting
Orlando Utilities Commission	441,368	Ground	0	0

Note: (1) Based on violation data from January 1, 2018 to December 31, 2018
Source: U.S. Environmental Protection Agency, Office of Ground Water and Drinking Water, Safe Drinking Water Information System (based on data extracted April 5, 2019)

San Antonio, Texas

Background

San Antonio is a charming preservation of its Mexican-Spanish heritage. Walking along its famous Paseo Del Rio at night, with cream-colored stucco structures, sea shell ornamented facades, and gently illuminating tiny lights is very romantic.

Emotional intensity is nothing new to San Antonio. The city began in the early eighteenth century as a cohesion of different Spanish missions, whose zealous aim was to convert the Coahuiltecan natives to Christianity, and to European ways of farming. A debilitating epidemic, however, killed most of the natives, as well as the missions' goal, causing the city to be abandoned.

In 1836, San Antonio became the site of interest again, when a small band of American soldiers were unable to successfully defend themselves against an army of 4,000 Mexican soldiers, led by General Antonio de Lopez Santa Anna. Fighting desperately from within the walls of the Mission San Antonio de Valero, or The Alamo, all 183 men were killed. This inspired the cry "Remember the Alamo" from the throats of every American soldier led by General Sam Houston, who was determined to wrest Texas territory and independence from Mexico.

Despite the Anglo victory over the Mexicans more than 150 years ago, the Mexican culture and its influence remain strong. We see evidence of this in the architecture, the Franciscan educational system, the variety of Spanish-language media, and the racial composition of the population, in which over half the city's residents are Latino.

This picturesque and practical blend of old and new makes San Antonio unique among American cities. San Antonio is home to the first museum of modern art in Texas, the McNay Art Museum. Other art institutions and museums include ArtPace, Blue Star Contemporary Art Center, the Briscoe Western Art Museum, Buckhorn Saloon & Museum (where visitors can experience something of the cowboy culture year round), San Antonio Museum of Art, formerly the Lonestar Brewery, Say Si (mentoring San Antonio artistic youth), the Southwest School of Art, Texas Rangers Museum, Texas Transportation Museum, the Witte Museum and the DoSeum. An outdoor display at North Star Mall features 40 foot tall cowboy boots.

The five missions in the city, four of which are in the San Antonio Missions National Historical Park, plus the Alamo, were named a UNESCO World Heritage Site on July 5, 2015. The San Antonio Missions became the 23rd U.S. site on the World Heritage List, which includes the Grand Canyon and the Statue of Liberty. It is the first site in the state of Texas.

The city continues to draw tourists who come to visit not just the Alamo, but the nearby theme parks like Six Flags Fiesta Texas and SeaWorld, or to take in the famed River Walk, the charming promenade of shops, restaurants, and pubs. In addition, the city has used ingenuity to diversify its traditional economy. For instance, Kelly Air Force Base, which was decommissioned in 2001, was developed into a successful, nearly 5,000-acre business park, called Kelly USA. The name has since changed to Port San Antonio and a warehouse on the site was used to house refugees from Hurricane Katrina. Businesses at the port receive favorable property tax and pay no state, city or corporate income taxes. Toyota is a major employer in the city.

San Antonio's location on the edge of the Gulf Coastal Plains exposes it to a modified subtropical climate. Summers are hot, although extremely high temperatures are rare. Winters are mild. Since the city is only 140 miles from the Gulf of Mexico, tropical storms occasionally occur, bringing strong winds and heavy rains. Relative humidity is high in the morning, but tends to drop by late afternoon.

Rankings

General Rankings

- For its "Best for Vets: Places to Live 2019" rankings, *Military Times* evaluated 599 cities (83 large, 234 medium, 282 small) and compared the locations across three broad categories: veteran and military culture/services; economic indicators; and livability factors such as health, crime, traffic, and school quality. San Antonio ranked #3 out of the top 25, in the large city category (populations of more than 250,000). Data points more specific to veterans and the military weighed more heavily than the rest. *rebootcamp.militarytimes.com, "Military Times Best Places to Live 2019," September 10, 2018*

- *US News & World Report* conducted a survey of more than 2,000 people and analyzed the 125 largest metropolitan areas to determine what matters the most when selecting the next place to live. San Antonio ranked #14 out of the top 25 as having the best combination of desirable factors. Criteria: cost of living; quality of education; job market, crime rates; and other factors. *realestate.usnews.com, "The 25 Best Places to Live in the U.S. in 2018," April 10, 2018*

- The San Antonio metro area was identified as one of America's fastest-growing areas in terms of population and business growth by *MagnifyMoney*. The area ranked #9 out of 35. The 100 most populous metro areas in the U.S. were evaluated on their change from 2011-2016 in the following categories: people and housing; workforce and employment opportunities; growing industry. *www.businessinsider.com, "The 35 Cities in the US with the Biggest Influx of People, the Most Work Opportunities, and the Hottest Business Growth," August 12, 2018*

- The San Antonio metro area was identified as one of America's fastest-growing areas in terms of population and economy by *Forbes*. The area ranked #21 out of 25. The 100 most populous metro areas in the U.S. were evaluated on the following criteria: estimated population growth; employment; economic output; wages; home values. *Forbes, "America's Fastest-Growing Cities 2018," February 28, 2018*

- San Antonio was identified as one of America's fastest-growing cities in terms of population growth by CNNMoney.com. The area ranked #5 out of 10. Criteria: population growth between July 2015 and July 2016; cities and towns with populations of 50,000. *CNNMoney, "10 Fastest-Growing Cities," June 2, 2017*

- San Antonio was selected as an "All-America City" by the National Civic League. The All-America City Award recognizes civic excellence and in 2018 honored 10 communities that best exemplify the spirit of grassroots citizen involvement and cross-sector collaborative problem solving. This year's focus was on community efforts to inspire equity and inclusion among community members to collectively tackle pressing and complex issues. *National Civic League, 2018 All-America City Awards, June 24, 2018*

- San Antonio appeared on *Travel + Leisure's* list of the fifteen best cities in the United States. The city was ranked #7. Criteria: sights/landmarks; culture/arts; cuisine; people/friendliness; shopping; and value. *Travel + Leisure, "The World's Best Awards 2018" July 10, 2018*

- Based on more than 425,000 responses, *Condé Nast Traveler* ranked its readers' favorite cities in the U.S. The list was broken into cities over 1 million and cities under 1 million. San Antonio ranked #6 in the big city category. *Condé Nast Traveler, Readers' Choice Awards 2018, "Best Big Cities in the U.S." October 9, 2018*

Business/Finance Rankings

- According to *Business Insider*, the San Antonio metro area is where startup growth is on the rise. Based on the 2017 Kauffman Index of Growth Entrepreneurship, which measured in-depth national entrepreneurial trends in 40 metro areas, it ranked #14 in highest startup growth. *www.businessinsider.com, "The 21 U.S. Cities with the Highest Startup Growth," October 21, 2017*

- The personal finance site NerdWallet analyzed 183 American metropolitan areas with populations over 250,000 and more than 15,000 businesses to rank where entrepreneurs find the most success. Criteria included area economy, annual income, housing cost, unemployment rate, and the success rate of area businesses. San Antonio ranked #158. *www.nerdwallet.com, "Best Places to Start a Business," April 27, 2015*

- San Antonio was the #6-ranked city for savers, according to a study by the finance site GOBankingRates, which considered the prospects for people trying to save money. Criteria: average monthly cost of grocery items; median home listing price; median rent; median income; unemployment rate; gas prices; and sales tax in the nation's 60 largest cities. *www.gobankingrates.com, "Best Cities for Saving Money," June 22, 2018*

- San Antonio was ranked #6 among the nation's 60 largest cities for most difficult conditions for savers, according to a study by the finance site GOBankingRates. Criteria: average monthly cost of grocery items; median home listing price; median rent; median income; unemployment rate; gas prices; and sales tax. *www.gobankingrates.com, "Worst Cities for Saving Money," June 22, 2018*

- Recognizing the sizeable percentage of American workers who are self-employed, NerdWallet editors assessed the country's cities according to percentage of freelancers, median rental costs, cell phone plans/taxes, and healthcare affordability and access. By these criteria, San Antonio placed #19 among the best cities for independent workers. *www.nerdwallet.com, "Best Places for Freelance Workers," August 30, 2016*

- USAA and Hiring Our Heroes worked with Sperlings's BestPlaces and the Institute for Veterans and Military Families at Syracuse University to rank major metropolitan areas where military-skills-related employment is strongest. Criteria for *mid-career* veterans included veteran wage growth; recent job growth; stability; and accessible health resources. Metro areas with a higher than national average crime or unemployment rate were excluded. At #10, the San Antonio metro area made the top ten. *www.usaa.com, "2015 Best Places for Veterans"*

- In a survey of economic confidence in the nation's 50 largest metropolitan areas conducted January–December 2014, the San Antonio metro area placed #24, according to Gallup's 2014 Economic Confidence Index. *Gallup, "San Jose and San Francisco Lead in Economic Confidence," March 19, 2015*

- Using data from the Council for Community and Economic Research's 2014 cost of living index, NerdWallet ranked the 100 most affordable cities in America. Median income was compared with cost of living to find truly affordable places. San Antonio ranked #49. *NerdWallet.com, "America's Most Affordable Places," May 18, 2015*

- NerdWallet.com identified the 10 most promising cities for job seekers of the nation's 100 largest cities. San Antonio was ranked #38. Criteria: job availability; annual salary; workforce growth; affordability. *NerdWallet.com, "Best Cities for Job Seekers in 2017," December 19, 2016*

- The Brookings Institution ranked the nation's largest cities based on income inequality. San Antonio was ranked #79 (#1 = greatest inequality). Criteria: the "95/20 ratio," a figure representing the income at which a household earns more than 95 percent of all other households, divided by the income at which a household earns more than only 20 percent of all other households. *Brookings Institution, "Household Income Inequality, Largest Cities of 97 Large U.S. Metro Areas, 2014-2016," February 5, 2018*

- The Brookings Institution ranked the 100 largest metro areas in the U.S. based on income inequality. San Antonio was ranked #56 (#1 = greatest inequality). Criteria: the "95/20 ratio," a figure representing the income at which a household earns more than 95 percent of all other households, divided by the income at which a household earns more than only 20 percent of all other households. *Brookings Institution, "Household Income Inequality, 100 Largest U.S. Metro Areas, 2014-2016," February 5, 2018*

- The San Antonio metro area was identified as one of the most debt-ridden places in America by the finance site Credit.com. The metro area was ranked #5. Criteria: residents' average credit card debt as well as median income. *Credit.com, "25 Cities With the Most Credit Card Debt," February 28, 2018*

612   San Antonio, Texas

- The San Antonio metro area was identified as one of the most affordable metropolitan areas in America by *Forbes*. The area ranked #20 out of 20 based on the National Association of Home Builders/Wells Fargo Housing Affordability Index and Sperling's Best Places' cost-of-living index. *Forbes.com, "America's Most Affordable Cities in 2015," March 12, 2015*

- San Antonio was identified as one of the unhappiest cities to work in by CareerBliss.com, an online community for career advancement. The city ranked #4 out of 5. Criteria: an employee's relationship with his or her boss and co-workers; general work environment; compensation; opportunities for advancement; company culture and job reputation; and resources. *Businesswire.com, "CareerBliss Unhappiest Cities to Work 2019," February 12, 2019*

- The San Antonio metro area appeared on the Milken Institute "2018 Best Performing Cities" list. Rank: #32 out of 200 large metro areas. Criteria: job growth; wage and salary growth; high-tech output growth. *Milken Institute, "Best-Performing Cities 2018," January 24, 2019*

- *Forbes* ranked the 200 most populous metro areas to determine the nation's "Best Places for Business and Careers." The San Antonio metro area was ranked #39. Criteria: costs (business and living); job growth (past and projected); income growth; quality of life; educational attainment (college and high school); projected economic growth; cultural and recreational opportunities; net migration patterns; number of highly ranked colleges. *Forbes, "The Best Places for Business and Careers 2018: Seattle Leads the Way," October 24, 2018*

Children/Family Rankings

- San Antonio was selected as one of the most playful cities in the U.S. by KaBOOM! The organization's Playful City USA initiative honors cities and towns across the nation that have made their communities more playable. Criteria: pledging to integrate play as a solution to challenges in their communities; making it easy for children to get active and balanced play; creating more family-friendly and innovative communities as a result. *KaBOOM! National Campaign for Play, "2017 Playful City USA Communities"*

Culture/Performing Arts Rankings

- San Antonio was selected as one of the twenty best large U.S. cities for moviemakers. Of cities with a population over 400,000, the city was ranked #20. Criteria: film community and culture; access to equipment and facilities; film activity in 2018; number of film schools; tax incentives. ease of movement and traffic. *MovieMaker Magazine, "Best Places to Live and Work as a Moviemaker: 2019," January 16, 2019*

Dating/Romance Rankings

- San Antonio was selected as one of America's best cities for singles by the readers of *Travel + Leisure* in their annual "America's Favorite Cities" survey. Criteria included good-looking locals, cool shopping, an active bar scene and hipster-magnet coffee bars. *Travel + Leisure, "Best Cities in America for Singles," July 21, 2017*

- San Antonio was selected as one of the nation's most romantic cities with 100,000 or more residents by Amazon.com. The city ranked #1 of 20. Criteria: per capita sales of romance novels, relationship books, romantic comedy movies, romantic music, and sexual wellness products. *Amazon.com, "Top 20 Most Romantic Cities in the U.S.," February 1, 2017*

Education Rankings

- Personal finance website *WalletHub* analyzed the 150 largest U.S. metropolitan statistical areas to determine where the most educated Americans are choosing to settle. Criteria: education quality and attainment gap; education levels; percentage of workers with degrees; public school quality rankings; quality and size of each metro area's universities. San Antonio was ranked #107 (#1 = most educated city). *www.WalletHub.com, "2018's Most and Least Educated Cities in America," July 24, 2018*

- San Antonio was selected as one of the most well-read cities in America by Amazon.com. The city ranked #20 among the top 20. Cities with populations greater than 500,000 were evaluated based on per capita sales of books, magazines and newspapers (both print and Kindle format). *Amazon.com, "The 20 Most Well-Read Cities in America," May 24, 2016*

- San Antonio was selected as one of America's most literate cities. The city ranked #76 out of the 82 largest U.S. cities. Criteria: number of booksellers; library resources; Internet resources; educational attainment; periodical publishing resources; newspaper circulation. *Central Connecticut State University, "America's Most Literate Cities, 2016," March 31, 2017*

Environmental Rankings

- San Antonio was highlighted as one of the top 90 cleanest metro areas for short-term particle pollution (24-hour PM 2.5) in the U.S. during 2014 through 2016. Monitors in these cities reported no days with unhealthful PM 2.5 levels. *American Lung Association, State of the Air 2018*

Food/Drink Rankings

- *Men's Health* ranked 100 major U.S. cities in terms of alcohol intoxication. San Antonio ranked #7 (#1 = most sober).Criteria: binge drinking; alcohol-related traffic accidents, arrests, and fatalities. *Men's Health, "America's Drunkest Cities," March 9, 2015*

Health/Fitness Rankings

- For each of the 100 largest cities in the United States, the American College of Sports Medicine's American Fitness Index evaluated infrastructure, community assets, and policies that encourage healthy and fit lifestyles, including preventive health behaviors, levels of chronic disease conditions, health care access, and community resources and policies that support physical activity. San Antonio ranked #68 for "community fitness." *www.americanfitnessindex.org, "ACSM American Fitness Index Health and Community Fitness Status of the 100 Largest U.S. Cities," May 2018*

- San Antonio was identified as a "2018 Spring Allergy Capital." The area ranked #5 out of 100. Three groups of factors were used to identify the most challenging cities for people with allergies during the spring season: annual pollen levels; medicine utilization; access to board-certified allergists. *Asthma and Allergy Foundation of America, "Spring Allergy Capitals 2018"*

- San Antonio was identified as a "2018 Fall Allergy Capital." The area ranked #4 out of 100. Three groups of factors were used to identify the most challenging cities for people with allergies during the fall season: annual pollen levels; medicine utilization; access to board-certified allergists. *Asthma and Allergy Foundation of America, "Fall Allergy Capitals 2018"*

- San Antonio was identified as a "2018 Asthma Capital." The area ranked #96 out of the nation's 100 largest metropolitan areas. Criteria: estimated prevalence; self-reported prevalence; crude death rate for asthma; annual pollen score; annual air quality; public smoking laws; number of board-certified asthma specialists; school inhaler access laws; rescue medication use; controller medication use; ER visits for asthma; uninsured rate; poverty rate. *Asthma and Allergy Foundation of America, "Asthma Capitals 2018: The Most Challenging Places to Live With Asthma"*

- *Men's Health* ranked 100 major U.S. cities in terms of the best cities for men. San Antonio ranked #64. Criteria: health; fitness; quality of life. *Men's Health, "The Best & Worst Cities for Men Who Want to Be Fit and Happy," January 1, 2016*

- The San Antonio metro area ranked #44 out of 189 in The Gallup-Healthways Well-Being Index. Criteria: purpose; social well being; financial health; community and physical health. Results are based on telephone interviews with adults, aged 18 and older, living in metropolitan areas in the 50 U.S. states and the District of Columbia. *Gallup-Healthways, "State of American Well-Being, 2017 Community Well-Being Rankings" March 2018*

Real Estate Rankings

- FitSmallBusiness looked at 50 of the largest metropolitan areas in the U.S. to determine which metro was the best to start a real estate business. Data was compiled from such sources as: Zillow, Trulia, U.S. Census Bureau, and the Bureau of Labor Statistics. Criteria: location; inventory; annual wages; median sales price of homes; days on the market; median price cut percentage; and other factors that would influence real estate professional growth. The San Antonio metro area ranked #12. *fitsmallbusiness.com, "The Best Cities to Become a Real Estate Agent in 2018," January 30, 2018*

- *WalletHub* compared the most populated U.S. cities, as well as at least two of the most populated cities in each state, for a total of 179, to determine which had the best markets for real estate agents. San Antonio ranked #124 where demand was high and pay was the best. Criteria: sales per agent; annual median wage for real-estate agents; monthly average starting salary for real estate agents; real estate job density and competition; unemployment rate; housing-market health index; and other relevant metrics. *www.WalletHub.com, "2018's Best Places to Be a Real Estate Agent," April 25, 2018*

- San Antonio was ranked #163 out of 237 metro areas in terms of housing affordability in 2018 by the National Association of Home Builders (#1 = most affordable). Criteria: the share of homes sold in that area affordable to a family earning the local median income, based on standard mortgage underwriting criteria. *National Association of Home Builders®, NAHB-Wells Fargo Housing Opportunity Index, 4th Quarter 2018*

Safety Rankings

- Allstate ranked the 200 largest cities in America in terms of driver safety. San Antonio ranked #141. Criteria: internal property damage claims over a two-year period from January 2015 to December 2016. The report helps increase the importance of safety awareness behind the wheel. *Allstate, "Allstate America's Best Drivers Report, 2018" August 28, 2018*

- The National Insurance Crime Bureau ranked 382 metro areas in the U.S. in terms of per capita rates of vehicle theft. The San Antonio metro area ranked #55 (#1 = highest rate). Criteria: number of vehicle theft offenses per 100,000 inhabitants in 2017. *National Insurance Crime Bureau, "Hot Spots 2017," July 12, 2018*

Seniors/Retirement Rankings

- From its Best Cities for Successful Aging indexes, the Milken Institute generated rankings for metropolitan areas, weighing data in nine categories—health care, wellness, living arrangements, transportation and convenience, financial characteristics, education, employment, community engagement, and overall livability. The San Antonio metro area was ranked #64 overall in the large metro area category. *Milken Institute, "Best Cities for Successful Aging, 2017" March 14, 2017*

- San Antonio was identified as one of the most popular places to retire by *Topretirements.com*. The list reflects the 100 cities that visitors to the website are most interested in for retirement, based on the number of times a city's review was viewed on the website. *Topretirements.com, "100 Most Popular Places to Retire for 2017," July 27, 2017*

Sports/Recreation Rankings

- San Antonio was chosen as a bicycle friendly community by the League of American Bicyclists. A "Bicycle Friendly Community" welcomes cyclists by providing safe and supportive accommodation for cycling and encouraging people to bike for transportation and recreation. There are five award levels: Diamond; Platinum; Gold; Silver; and Bronze. The community achieved an award level of Bronze. *League of American Bicyclists, "Fall 2018 Awards-Bicycle Friendly Community Master List," December 6, 2018*

Women/Minorities Rankings

- The *Houston Chronicle* listed the San Antonio metro area as #13 in top places for young Latinos to live in the U.S. Research was largely based on housing and occupational data from the largest metropolitan areas performed by *Forbes* and NBC Universo. Criteria: percentage of 18-34 year-olds; Latino college grad rates; and diversity. *blog.chron.com, "The 15 Best Big Cities for Latino Millenials," January 26, 2016*

- Personal finance website *WalletHub* compared more than 180 U.S. cities—including the 150 most populated U.S. cities, plus at least two of the most populated cities in each state—across two key dimensions, "Hispanic Business-Friendliness" and "Hispanic Purchasing Power", to arrive at the most favorable conditions for Hispanic entrepreneurs. San Antonio was ranked #8 out of 182. Criteria includes: share of Hispanic-Owned Businesses; Hispanic entrepreneurship rate to median annual income of Hispanics; Small Business-Friendliness score; cost of living; and number of Hispanics with at least a bachelor's degree. *WalletHub.com, "2018's Best Cities for Hispanic Entrepreneurs," April 26, 2018*

Miscellaneous Rankings

- *WalletHub* compared the 150 most populated U.S. cities to determine their operating efficiency. A "Quality of Services" score was constructed for each city and then divided by the total budget per capita to reveal which were managed the best. San Antonio ranked #99. Criteria: financial stability; economy; education; safety; health; infrastructure and pollution. *www.WalletHub.com, "2018's Best- & Worst-Run Cities in America," July 9, 2018*

- San Antonio was selected as one of "America's Friendliest Cities." The city ranked #5 in the "Friendliest" category. Respondents to an online survey were asked to rate 38 top urban destinations in the United States as to general friendliness, as well as manners, politeness and warm disposition. *Travel + Leisure, "America's Friendliest Cities," October 20, 2017*

- San Antonio appeared on *Travel + Leisure's* list of America's cities with the most attractive people. Criteria: cities were selected by readers in their annual America's Favorite Cities survey. The city ranked #15 out of 10. *Travel + Leisure, "America's Most and Least Attractive People," September 2, 2016*

- The National Alliance to End Homelessness listed the 25 most populous metro areas with the highest rate of homelessness. The San Antonio metro area had a high rate of homelessness. Criteria: number of homeless people per 10,000 population in 2016. *National Alliance to End Homelessness, "Homelessness in the 25 Most Populous U.S. Metro Areas," September 1, 2017*

Business Environment

CITY FINANCES

City Government Finances

Component	2016 ($000)	2016 ($ per capita)
Total Revenues	4,863,912	3,309
Total Expenditures	5,170,534	3,518
Debt Outstanding	11,640,596	7,920
Cash and Securities[1]	7,326,997	4,985

Note: (1) Cash and security holdings of a government at the close of its fiscal year, including those of its dependent agencies, utilities, and liquor stores.
Source: U.S. Census Bureau, State & Local Government Finances 2016

City Government Revenue by Source

Source	2016 ($000)	2016 ($ per capita)	2016 (%)
General Revenue			
From Federal Government	132,238	90	2.7
From State Government	159,065	108	3.3
From Local Governments	63,616	43	1.3
Taxes			
Property	392,904	267	8.1
Sales and Gross Receipts	471,681	321	9.7
Personal Income	0	0	0.0
Corporate Income	0	0	0.0
Motor Vehicle License	0	0	0.0
Other Taxes	45,938	31	0.9
Current Charges	625,321	425	12.9
Liquor Store	0	0	0.0
Utility	2,731,990	1,859	56.2
Employee Retirement	7,596	5	0.2

Source: U.S. Census Bureau, State & Local Government Finances 2016

City Government Expenditures by Function

Function	2016 ($000)	2016 ($ per capita)	2016 (%)
General Direct Expenditures			
Air Transportation	123,493	84	2.4
Corrections	0	0	0.0
Education	57,978	39	1.1
Employment Security Administration	0	0	0.0
Financial Administration	34,618	23	0.7
Fire Protection	248,469	169	4.8
General Public Buildings	15,013	10	0.3
Governmental Administration, Other	21,040	14	0.4
Health	27,458	18	0.5
Highways	143,998	98	2.8
Hospitals	0	0	0.0
Housing and Community Development	50,843	34	1.0
Interest on General Debt	131,927	89	2.6
Judicial and Legal	25,904	17	0.5
Libraries	35,171	23	0.7
Parking	7,799	5	0.2
Parks and Recreation	325,998	221	6.3
Police Protection	368,329	250	7.1
Public Welfare	123,613	84	2.4
Sewerage	259,684	176	5.0
Solid Waste Management	114,713	78	2.2
Veterans' Services	0	0	0.0
Liquor Store	0	0	0.0
Utility	2,744,223	1,867	53.1
Employee Retirement	150,740	102	2.9

Source: U.S. Census Bureau, State & Local Government Finances 2016

DEMOGRAPHICS

Population Growth

Area	1990 Census	2000 Census	2010 Census	2017* Estimate	Population Growth (%)	
					1990-2017	2010-2017
City	997,258	1,144,646	1,327,407	1,461,623	46.6	10.1
MSA[1]	1,407,745	1,711,703	2,142,508	2,377,507	68.9	11.0
U.S.	248,709,873	281,421,906	308,745,538	321,004,407	29.1	4.0

Note: (1) Figures cover the San Antonio-New Braunfels, TX Metropolitan Statistical Area—see Appendix B for areas included; (*) 2013-2017 5-year estimated population
Source: U.S. Census Bureau, 1990 Census, Census 2000, Census 2010, 2013-2017 American Community Survey 5-Year Estimates

Household Size

Area	Persons in Household (%)							Average Household Size
	One	Two	Three	Four	Five	Six	Seven or More	
City	28.6	29.5	16.6	13.3	7.2	2.9	2.0	2.90
MSA[1]	25.5	31.1	17.0	14.1	7.4	3.0	1.9	2.90
U.S.	27.7	33.8	15.7	13.0	6.0	2.3	1.4	2.60

Note: (1) Figures cover the San Antonio-New Braunfels, TX Metropolitan Statistical Area—see Appendix B for areas included
Source: U.S. Census Bureau, 2013-2017 American Community Survey 5-Year Estimates

Race

Area	White Alone[2] (%)	Black Alone[2] (%)	Asian Alone[2] (%)	AIAN[3] Alone[2] (%)	NHOPI[4] Alone[2] (%)	Other Race Alone[2] (%)	Two or More Races (%)
City	80.1	7.0	2.7	0.7	0.1	6.7	2.7
MSA[1]	80.7	6.7	2.4	0.6	0.1	6.5	3.1
U.S.	73.0	12.7	5.4	0.8	0.2	4.8	3.1

Note: (1) Figures cover the San Antonio-New Braunfels, TX Metropolitan Statistical Area—see Appendix B for areas included; (2) Alone is defined as not being in combination with one or more other races; (3) American Indian and Alaska Native; (4) Native Hawaiian and Other Pacific Islander
Source: U.S. Census Bureau, 2013-2017 American Community Survey 5-Year Estimates

Hispanic or Latino Origin

Area	Total (%)	Mexican (%)	Puerto Rican (%)	Cuban (%)	Other (%)
City	64.0	57.6	1.1	0.2	5.0
MSA[1]	55.1	49.1	1.2	0.2	4.5
U.S.	17.6	11.1	1.7	0.7	4.1

Note: Persons of Hispanic or Latino origin can be of any race; (1) Figures cover the San Antonio-New Braunfels, TX Metropolitan Statistical Area—see Appendix B for areas included
Source: U.S. Census Bureau, 2013-2017 American Community Survey 5-Year Estimates

Segregation

Type	Segregation Indices[1]				Percent Change		
	1990	2000	2010	2010 Rank[2]	1990-2000	1990-2010	2000-2010
Black/White	56.1	52.8	49.0	73	-3.3	-7.1	-3.8
Asian/White	33.8	35.4	38.3	66	1.6	4.5	2.9
Hispanic/White	52.1	49.7	46.1	43	-2.4	-6.0	-3.6

Note: All figures cover the Metropolitan Statistical Area—see Appendix B for areas included; Figures are based on an analysis of 1990, 2000, and 2010 Census Decennial Census tract data by William H. Frey, Brookings Institution and the University of Michigan Social Science Data Analysis Network. In this analysis all racial groups (whites, blacks, and asians) are non-Hispanic members of those races. Hispanics are shown as a separate category; (1) Segregation Indices are Dissimilarity Indices that measure the degree to which the minority group is distributed differently than whites across census tracts. They range from 0 (complete integration) to 100 (complete segregation) where the value indicates the percentage of the minority group that needs to move to be distributed exactly like whites; (2) Ranges from 1 (most segregated) to 102 (least segregated); n/a not available.
Source: www.CensusScope.org

Ancestry

Area	German	Irish	English	American	Italian	Polish	French[2]	Scottish	Dutch
City	7.5	4.5	3.7	2.9	1.8	1.1	1.3	0.9	0.5
MSA[1]	10.8	5.8	5.2	3.4	2.1	1.5	1.8	1.2	0.6
U.S.	14.1	10.1	7.5	6.6	5.3	2.9	2.5	1.7	1.3

Note: Figures are the percentage of the total population reporting a particular ancestry. The nine most commonly reported ancestries in the U.S. are shown. Figures include multiple ancestries (e.g. if a person reported being Irish and Italian, they were included in both columns); (1) Figures cover the San Antonio-New Braunfels, TX Metropolitan Statistical Area—see Appendix B for areas included; (2) Excludes Basque
Source: U.S. Census Bureau, 2013-2017 American Community Survey 5-Year Estimates

Foreign-Born Population

Area	Any Foreign Country	Asia	Mexico	Europe	Carribean	Central America[2]	South America	Africa	Canada
City	14.2	2.4	9.3	0.6	0.2	0.7	0.4	0.3	0.1
MSA[1]	11.7	2.0	7.4	0.7	0.2	0.6	0.4	0.3	0.1
U.S.	13.4	4.1	3.6	1.5	1.3	1.0	0.9	0.6	0.3

Note: (1) Figures cover the San Antonio-New Braunfels, TX Metropolitan Statistical Area—see Appendix B for areas included; (2) Excludes Mexico.
Source: U.S. Census Bureau, 2013-2017 American Community Survey 5-Year Estimates

Marital Status

Area	Never Married	Now Married[2]	Separated	Widowed	Divorced
City	37.6	41.9	3.1	5.2	12.1
MSA[1]	33.9	46.7	2.7	5.2	11.5
U.S.	33.1	48.2	2.0	5.8	10.9

Note: Figures are percentages and cover the population 15 years of age and older; (1) Figures cover the San Antonio-New Braunfels, TX Metropolitan Statistical Area—see Appendix B for areas included; (2) Excludes separated
Source: U.S. Census Bureau, 2013-2017 American Community Survey 5-Year Estimates

Disability by Age

Area	All Ages	Under 18 Years Old	18 to 64 Years Old	65 Years and Over
City	14.3	5.4	12.7	43.3
MSA[1]	13.8	5.0	12.1	40.6
U.S.	12.6	4.2	10.3	35.5

Note: Figures show percent of the civilian noninstitutionalized population that reported having a disability. Disability status is determined from six types of difficulty: vision, hearing, cognitive, ambulatory, self-care, and independent living. For children under 5 years old, hearing and vision difficulty are used to determine disability status. For children between the ages of 5 and 14, disability status is determined from hearing, vision, cognitive, ambulatory, and self-care difficulties. For people aged 15 years and older, they are considered to have a disability if they have difficulty with any one of the six difficulty types; Note: (1) Figures cover the San Antonio-New Braunfels, TX Metropolitan Statistical Area—see Appendix B for areas included
Source: U.S. Census Bureau, 2013-2017 American Community Survey 5-Year Estimates

Age

Area	Under Age 5	Age 5–19	Age 20–34	Age 35–44	Age 45–54	Age 55–64	Age 65–74	Age 75–84	Age 85+	Median Age
City	7.1	21.3	24.1	13.2	12.2	10.6	6.7	3.4	1.5	33.2
MSA[1]	7.0	21.6	22.1	13.2	12.7	11.1	7.3	3.6	1.4	34.4
U.S.	6.2	19.5	20.7	12.7	13.4	12.7	8.6	4.4	1.9	37.8

Note: (1) Figures cover the San Antonio-New Braunfels, TX Metropolitan Statistical Area—see Appendix B for areas included
Source: U.S. Census Bureau, 2013-2017 American Community Survey 5-Year Estimates

Gender

Area	Males	Females	Males per 100 Females
City	719,677	741,946	97.0
MSA[1]	1,173,885	1,203,622	97.5
U.S.	158,018,753	162,985,654	97.0

Note: (1) Figures cover the San Antonio-New Braunfels, TX Metropolitan Statistical Area—see Appendix B for areas included
Source: U.S. Census Bureau, 2013-2017 American Community Survey 5-Year Estimates

Religious Groups by Family

Area	Catholic	Baptist	Non-Den.	Methodist[2]	Lutheran	LDS[3]	Pente-costal	Presby-terian[4]	Muslim[5]	Judaism
MSA[1]	28.4	8.5	6.0	3.1	1.7	1.4	1.3	0.8	1.0	0.2
U.S.	19.1	9.3	4.0	4.0	2.3	2.0	1.9	1.6	0.8	0.7

Note: Figures are the number of adherents as a percentage of the total population; (1) Figures cover the San Antonio-New Braunfels, TX Metropolitan Statistical Area—see Appendix B for areas included; (2) Methodist/Pietist; (3) Latter Day Saints; (4) Reformed; (5) Figures are estimates
Source: Association of Statisticians of American Religious Bodies, 2010 U.S. Religion Census: Religious Congregations & Membership Study

Religious Groups by Tradition

Area	Catholic	Evangelical Protestant	Mainline Protestant	Other Tradition	Black Protestant	Orthodox
MSA[1]	28.4	17.0	5.0	3.2	0.4	0.1
U.S.	19.1	16.2	7.3	4.3	1.6	0.3

Note: Figures are the number of adherents as a percentage of the total population; (1) Figures cover the San Antonio-New Braunfels, TX Metropolitan Statistical Area—see Appendix B for areas included
Source: Association of Statisticians of American Religious Bodies, 2010 U.S. Religion Census: Religious Congregations & Membership Study

ECONOMY

Gross Metropolitan Product

Area	2016	2017	2018	2019	Rank[2]
MSA[1]	115.4	122.3	129.7	136.4	35

Note: Figures are in billions of dollars; (1) Figures cover the San Antonio-New Braunfels, TX Metropolitan Statistical Area—see Appendix B for areas included; (2) Rank is based on 2017 data and ranges from 1 to 381
Source: U.S. Conference of Mayors, U.S. Metro Economies: Economic Growth & Full Employment, June 2018

Economic Growth

Area	2017-2018 (%)	2019-2020 (%)	2021-2022 (%)
MSA[1]	3.4	2.5	2.2

Note: Figures are real gross metropolitan product (GMP) growth rates and represent average annual percent change; (1) Figures cover the San Antonio-New Braunfels, TX Metropolitan Statistical Area—see Appendix B for areas included
Source: U.S. Conference of Mayors, U.S. Metro Economies: Economic Growth & Full Employment, June 2018

Metropolitan Area Exports

Area	2012	2013	2014	2015	2016	2017	Rank[2]
MSA[1]	14,010.2	19,287.6	25,781.8	15,919.2	5,621.2	9,184.1	35

Note: Figures are in millions of dollars; (1) Figures cover the San Antonio-New Braunfels, TX Metropolitan Statistical Area—see Appendix B for areas included; (2) Rank is based on 2017 data and ranges from 1 to 387
Source: U.S. Department of Commerce, International Trade Administration, Office of Trade and Economic Analysis, Industry and Analysis, Exports by Metropolitan Area, extracted March 25, 2019

Building Permits

Area	Single-Family			Multi-Family			Total		
	2016	2017	Pct. Chg.	2016	2017	Pct. Chg.	2016	2017	Pct. Chg.
City	2,152	2,489	15.7	4,211	3,711	-11.9	6,363	6,200	-2.6
MSA[1]	6,464	7,535	16.6	5,777	4,981	-13.8	12,241	12,516	2.2
U.S.	750,800	820,000	9.2	455,800	462,000	1.4	1,206,600	1,282,000	6.2

Note: (1) Figures cover the San Antonio-New Braunfels, TX Metropolitan Statistical Area—see Appendix B for areas included; Figures represent new, privately-owned housing units authorized (unadjusted data); All permit data are based on estimates with imputation
Source: U.S. Census Bureau, Manufacturing, Mining, and Construction Statistics, Building Permits, 2016, 2017

Bankruptcy Filings

Area	Business Filings			Nonbusiness Filings		
	2017	2018	% Chg.	2017	2018	% Chg.
Bexar County	109	189	73.4	2,239	2,318	3.5
U.S.	23,157	22,232	-4.0	765,863	751,186	-1.9

Note: Business filings include Chapter 7, Chapter 11, Chapter 12, and Chapter 13; Nonbusiness filings include Chapter 7, Chapter 11, and Chapter 13
Source: Administrative Office of the U.S. Courts, Business and Nonbusiness Bankruptcy, County Cases Commenced by Chapter of the Bankruptcy Code, During the 12-Month Period Ending December 31, 2017 and Business and Nonbusiness Bankruptcy, County Cases Commenced by Chapter of the Bankruptcy Code, During the 12-Month Period Ending December 31, 2018

Housing Vacancy Rates

Area	Gross Vacancy Rate[2] (%)			Year-Round Vacancy Rate[3] (%)			Rental Vacancy Rate[4] (%)			Homeowner Vacancy Rate[5] (%)		
	2016	2017	2018	2016	2017	2018	2016	2017	2018	2016	2017	2018
MSA[1]	9.9	9.9	6.7	8.6	8.8	5.8	10.3	11.5	7.4	1.9	1.8	0.6
U.S.	12.8	12.7	12.3	9.9	9.9	9.7	6.9	7.2	6.9	1.7	1.6	1.5

Note: (1) Figures cover the San Antonio-New Braunfels, TX Metropolitan Statistical Area—see Appendix B for areas included; (2) The percentage of the total housing inventory that is vacant; (3) The percentage of the housing inventory (excluding seasonal units) that is year-round vacant; (4) The percentage of rental inventory that is vacant for rent; (5) The percentage of homeowner inventory that is vacant for sale
Source: U.S. Census Bureau, Housing Vacancies and Homeownership Annual Statistics: 2016, 2017, 2018

INCOME

Income

Area	Per Capita ($)	Median Household ($)	Average Household ($)
City	24,325	49,711	66,799
MSA[1]	27,154	56,495	76,281
U.S.	31,177	57,652	81,283

Note: (1) Figures cover the San Antonio-New Braunfels, TX Metropolitan Statistical Area—see Appendix B for areas included
Source: U.S. Census Bureau, 2013-2017 American Community Survey 5-Year Estimates

Household Income Distribution

Area	Percent of Households Earning							
	Under $15,000	$15,000 -$24,999	$25,000 -$34,999	$35,000 -$49,999	$50,000 -$74,999	$75,000 -$99,999	$100,000 -$149,999	$150,000 and up
City	13.6	11.1	11.0	14.6	19.0	11.3	11.8	7.6
MSA[1]	11.3	9.6	9.8	13.4	18.9	12.5	14.2	10.3
U.S.	11.6	9.8	9.5	13.0	17.7	12.3	14.1	12.1

Note: (1) Figures cover the San Antonio-New Braunfels, TX Metropolitan Statistical Area—see Appendix B for areas included
Source: U.S. Census Bureau, 2013-2017 American Community Survey 5-Year Estimates

Poverty Rate

Area	All Ages	Under 18 Years Old	18 to 64 Years Old	65 Years and Over
City	18.6	27.2	16.2	12.6
MSA[1]	15.2	21.8	13.5	10.4
U.S.	14.6	20.3	13.7	9.3

Note: Figures are percentage of people whose income during the past 12 months was below the poverty level; (1) Figures cover the San Antonio-New Braunfels, TX Metropolitan Statistical Area—see Appendix B for areas included
Source: U.S. Census Bureau, 2013-2017 American Community Survey 5-Year Estimates

EMPLOYMENT

Labor Force and Employment

Area	Civilian Labor Force			Workers Employed		
	Dec. 2017	Dec. 2018	% Chg.	Dec. 2017	Dec. 2018	% Chg.
City	719,253	729,331	1.4	697,791	706,404	1.2
MSA[1]	1,171,978	1,188,172	1.4	1,136,835	1,150,484	1.2
U.S.	159,880,000	162,510,000	1.6	153,602,000	156,481,000	1.9

Note: Data is not seasonally adjusted and covers workers 16 years of age and older; (1) Figures cover the San Antonio-New Braunfels, TX Metropolitan Statistical Area—see Appendix B for areas included
Source: Bureau of Labor Statistics, Local Area Unemployment Statistics

Unemployment Rate

Area	2018											
	Jan.	Feb.	Mar.	Apr.	May	Jun.	Jul.	Aug.	Sep.	Oct.	Nov.	Dec.
City	3.4	3.4	3.4	3.1	3.2	3.7	3.5	3.4	3.3	3.1	3.0	3.1
MSA[1]	3.4	3.4	3.5	3.1	3.2	3.7	3.5	3.5	3.3	3.1	3.1	3.2
U.S.	4.5	4.4	4.1	3.7	3.6	4.2	4.1	3.9	3.6	3.5	3.5	3.7

Note: Data is not seasonally adjusted and covers workers 16 years of age and older; (1) Figures cover the San Antonio-New Braunfels, TX Metropolitan Statistical Area—see Appendix B for areas included
Source: Bureau of Labor Statistics, Local Area Unemployment Statistics

Average Wages

Occupation	$/Hr.	Occupation	$/Hr.
Accountants and Auditors	36.20	Maids and Housekeeping Cleaners	10.50
Automotive Mechanics	22.10	Maintenance and Repair Workers	17.30
Bookkeepers	19.40	Marketing Managers	73.20
Carpenters	19.20	Nuclear Medicine Technologists	32.50
Cashiers	10.70	Nurses, Licensed Practical	21.70
Clerks, General Office	16.90	Nurses, Registered	34.70
Clerks, Receptionists/Information	13.10	Nursing Assistants	13.00
Clerks, Shipping/Receiving	15.00	Packers and Packagers, Hand	10.20
Computer Programmers	42.80	Physical Therapists	38.70
Computer Systems Analysts	46.90	Postal Service Mail Carriers	24.90
Computer User Support Specialists	23.50	Real Estate Brokers	44.20
Cooks, Restaurant	12.00	Retail Salespersons	13.50
Dentists	85.20	Sales Reps., Exc. Tech./Scientific	32.70
Electrical Engineers	49.70	Sales Reps., Tech./Scientific	42.40
Electricians	23.00	Secretaries, Exc. Legal/Med./Exec.	16.70
Financial Managers	69.10	Security Guards	14.70
First-Line Supervisors/Managers, Sales	21.30	Surgeons	108.90
Food Preparation Workers	12.10	Teacher Assistants*	11.80
General and Operations Managers	58.00	Teachers, Elementary School*	28.10
Hairdressers/Cosmetologists	12.20	Teachers, Secondary School*	28.60
Internists, General	49.50	Telemarketers	14.90
Janitors and Cleaners	12.40	Truck Drivers, Heavy/Tractor-Trailer	20.80
Landscaping/Groundskeeping Workers	13.80	Truck Drivers, Light/Delivery Svcs.	19.20
Lawyers	53.70	Waiters and Waitresses	10.50

Note: Wage data covers the San Antonio-New Braunfels, TX Metropolitan Statistical Area—see Appendix B for areas included; (*) Hourly wages for elementary/secondary school teachers and teacher assistants were calculated by the editors from annual wage data based on a 40 hour work week; n/a not available.
Source: Bureau of Labor Statistics, Metro Area Occupational Employment & Wage Estimates, May 2018

Employment by Occupation

Occupation Classification	City (%)	MSA[1] (%)	U.S. (%)
Management, Business, Science, and Arts	33.0	34.8	37.4
Natural Resources, Construction, and Maintenance	10.2	10.1	8.9
Production, Transportation, and Material Moving	10.3	10.4	12.2
Sales and Office	26.0	25.7	23.5
Service	20.5	18.9	18.0

Note: Figures cover employed civilians 16 years of age and older; (1) Figures cover the San Antonio-New Braunfels, TX Metropolitan Statistical Area—see Appendix B for areas included
Source: U.S. Census Bureau, 2013-2017 American Community Survey 5-Year Estimates

Employment by Industry

Sector	MSA[1]		U.S.
	Number of Employees	Percent of Total	Percent of Total
Construction	52,600	4.9	4.8
Education and Health Services	166,100	15.5	15.9
Financial Activities	92,900	8.7	5.7
Government	173,500	16.2	15.1
Information	20,900	2.0	1.9
Leisure and Hospitality	136,500	12.8	10.7
Manufacturing	50,400	4.7	8.5
Mining and Logging	10,500	1.0	0.5
Other Services	38,100	3.6	3.9
Professional and Business Services	144,000	13.5	14.1
Retail Trade	117,500	11.0	10.8
Transportation, Warehousing, and Utilities	31,000	2.9	4.2
Wholesale Trade	36,400	3.4	3.9

Note: Figures are non-farm employment as of December 2018. Figures are not seasonally adjusted and include workers 16 years of age and older; (1) Figures cover the San Antonio-New Braunfels, TX Metropolitan Statistical Area—see Appendix B for areas included
Source: Bureau of Labor Statistics, Current Employment Statistics, Employment, Hours, and Earnings

Occupations with Greatest Projected Employment Growth: 2018 – 2020

Occupation[1]	2018 Employment	2020 Projected Employment	Numeric Employment Change	Percent Employment Change
Combined Food Preparation and Serving Workers, Including Fast Food	351,780	372,090	20,310	5.8
Personal Care Aides	218,310	235,470	17,160	7.9
Heavy and Tractor-Trailer Truck Drivers	204,870	216,310	11,440	5.6
Laborers and Freight, Stock, and Material Movers, Hand	194,220	204,060	9,840	5.1
Waiters and Waitresses	236,020	245,790	9,770	4.1
Office Clerks, General	393,740	403,270	9,530	2.4
Customer Service Representatives	268,380	277,460	9,080	3.4
General and Operations Managers	182,190	190,620	8,430	4.6
Retail Salespersons	392,620	400,900	8,280	2.1
Construction Laborers	143,270	150,820	7,550	5.3

Note: Projections cover Texas; (1) Sorted by numeric employment change
Source: www.projectionscentral.com, State Occupational Projections, 2018–2020 Short-Term Projections

Fastest Growing Occupations: 2018 – 2020

Occupation[1]	2018 Employment	2020 Projected Employment	Numeric Employment Change	Percent Employment Change
Wind Turbine Service Technicians	1,810	2,190	380	21.0
Religious Workers, All Other	5,690	6,330	640	11.2
Fundraisers	8,830	9,670	840	9.5
Statisticians	1,870	2,040	170	9.1
Public Relations and Fundraising Managers	6,570	7,160	590	9.0
Home Health Aides	74,390	80,920	6,530	8.8
Community and Social Service Specialists, All Other	4,520	4,890	370	8.2
Personal Care Aides	218,310	235,470	17,160	7.9
Operations Research Analysts	10,920	11,760	840	7.7
Software Developers, Applications	65,190	70,140	4,950	7.6

Note: Projections cover Texas; (1) Sorted by percent employment change and excludes occupations with numeric employment change less than 50
Source: www.projectionscentral.com, State Occupational Projections, 2018–2020 Short-Term Projections

TAXES

State Corporate Income Tax Rates

State	Tax Rate (%)	Income Brackets ($)	Num. of Brackets	Financial Institution Tax Rate (%)[a]	Federal Income Tax Ded.
Texas	(w)	–	–	(w)	No

Note: Tax rates as of January 1, 2019; (a) Rates listed are the corporate income tax rate applied to financial institutions or excise taxes based on income. Some states have other taxes based upon the value of deposits or shares; (w) Texas imposes a Franchise Tax, otherwise known as margin tax, imposed on entities with more than $1,130,000 total revenues at rate of 0.75%, or 0.375% for entities primarily engaged in retail or wholesale trade, on lesser of 70% of total revenues or 100% of gross receipts after deductions for either compensation or cost of goods sold.
Source: Federation of Tax Administrators, Range of State Corporate Income Tax Rates, January 1, 2019

State Individual Income Tax Rates

State	Tax Rate (%)	Income Brackets ($)	Personal Exemptions ($) Single	Married	Depend.	Standard Ded. ($) Single	Married
Texas			– No state income tax –				

Note: Tax rates as of January 1, 2019; Local- and county-level taxes are not included; n/a not applicable;

Source: Federation of Tax Administrators, State Individual Income Tax Rates, January 1, 2019

Various State Sales and Excise Tax Rates

State	State Sales Tax (%)	Gasoline[1] (¢/gal.)	Cigarette[2] ($/pack)	Spirits[3] ($/gal.)	Wine[4] ($/gal.)	Beer[5] ($/gal.)	Recreational Marijuana (%)
Texas	6.25	20	1.41	2.40 (f)	0.20 (l)	0.20 (q)	Not legal

Note: All tax rates as of January 1, 2019; (1) The American Petroleum Institute has developed a methodology for determining the average tax rate on a gallon of fuel. Rates may include any of the following: excise taxes, environmental fees, storage tank fees, other fees or taxes, general sales tax, and local taxes. In states where gasoline is subject to the general sales tax, or where the fuel tax is based on the average sale price, the average rate determined by API is sensitive to changes in the price of gasoline. States that fully or partially apply general sales taxes to gasoline: CA, CO, GA, IL, IN, MI, NY; (2) The federal excise tax of $1.0066 per pack and local taxes are not included; (3) Rates are those applicable to off-premise sales of 40% alcohol by volume (a.b.v.) distilled spirits in 750ml containers. Local excise taxes are excluded; (4) Rates are those applicable to off-premise sales of 11% a.b.v. non-carbonated wine in 750ml containers; (5) Rates are those applicable to off-premise sales of 4.7% a.b.v. beer in 12 ounce containers; (f) Different rates also applicable according to alcohol content, place of production, size of container, or place purchased (on- or off-premise or onboard airlines); (l) Different rates also applicable to alcohol content, place of production, size of container, place purchased (on- or off-premise or on board airlines) or type of wine (carbonated, vermouth, etc.); (q) Different rates also applicable according to alcohol content, place of production, size of container, or place purchased (on- or off-premise or onboard airlines).
Source: Tax Foundation, 2019 Facts & Figures: How Does Your State Compare?

State Business Tax Climate Index Rankings

State	Overall Rank	Corporate Tax Rank	Individual Income Tax Rank	Sales Tax Rank	Unemployment Insurance Tax Rank	Property Tax Rank
Texas	15	49	6	37	18	37

Note: The index is a measure of how each state's tax laws affect economic performance. The lower the rank, the more favorable a state's tax system is for business. States without a given tax are given a ranking of 1. The scores/rankings for the District of Columbia do not affect other states. The 2019 index represents the tax climate as of July 1, 2018.
Source: Tax Foundation, State Business Tax Climate Index 2019

COMMERCIAL REAL ESTATE

Office Market

Market Area	Inventory (sq. ft.)	Vacancy Rate (%)	Under Construction (sq. ft.)	YTD Net Absorption (sq. ft.)	Total Average Asking Rent ($/sq. ft./year)
San Antonio	45,069,567	11.9	662,208	459,585	22.58
National	4,905,867,938	13.1	83,553,714	45,846,470	28.46

Source: Newmark Grubb Knight Frank, National Office Market Report, 4th Quarter 2018

Industrial/Warehouse/R&D Market

Market Area	Inventory (sq. ft.)	Vacancy Rate (%)	Under Construction (sq. ft.)	YTD Net Absorption (sq. ft.)	Total Average Asking Rent ($/sq. ft./year)
San Antonio	117,401,553	6.1	4,223,628	1,047,498	6.12
National	14,796,839,085	5.0	262,662,294	238,014,726	7.16

Source: Newmark Grubb Knight Frank, National Industrial Market Report, 4th Quarter 2018

COMMERCIAL UTILITIES

Typical Monthly Electric Bills

Area	Commercial Service ($/month)		Industrial Service ($/month)	
	1,500 kWh	40 kW demand 14,000 kWh	1,000 kW demand 200,000 kWh	50,000 kW demand 32,500,000 kWh
City	n/a	n/a	n/a	n/a
Average[1]	203	1,619	25,886	2,540,077

Note: Figures are based on annualized rates; (1) Average based on 187 utilities surveyed; n/a not available
Source: Edison Electric Institute, Typical Bills and Average Rates Report, Summer 2018

TRANSPORTATION

Means of Transportation to Work

Area	Car/Truck/Van Drove Alone	Car/Truck/Van Car-pooled	Public Transportation Bus	Public Transportation Subway	Public Transportation Railroad	Bicycle	Walked	Other Means	Worked at Home
City	79.0	11.1	3.1	0.0	0.0	0.2	1.7	1.3	3.7
MSA[1]	79.7	10.7	2.1	0.0	0.0	0.2	1.6	1.2	4.5
U.S.	76.4	9.2	2.5	1.9	0.6	0.6	2.7	1.3	4.7

Note: Figures are percentages and cover workers 16 years of age and older; (1) Figures cover the San Antonio-New Braunfels, TX Metropolitan Statistical Area—see Appendix B for areas included
Source: U.S. Census Bureau, 2013-2017 American Community Survey 5-Year Estimates

Travel Time to Work

Area	Less Than 10 Minutes	10 to 19 Minutes	20 to 29 Minutes	30 to 44 Minutes	45 to 59 Minutes	60 to 89 Minutes	90 Minutes or More
City	9.1	31.4	27.3	21.6	5.7	3.0	1.9
MSA[1]	9.5	28.8	24.6	22.6	8.1	4.3	2.2
U.S.	12.7	28.9	20.9	20.5	8.1	6.2	2.7

Note: Note: Figures are percentages and include workers 16 years old and over; (1) Figures cover the San Antonio-New Braunfels, TX Metropolitan Statistical Area—see Appendix B for areas included
Source: U.S. Census Bureau, 2013-2017 American Community Survey 5-Year Estimates

Freeway Travel Time Index

Area	1985	1990	1995	2000	2005	2010	2014
Urban Area Rank[1,2]	24	34	23	24	26	25	24
Urban Area Index[1]	1.11	1.12	1.19	1.22	1.24	1.23	1.25
Average Index[3]	1.09	1.11	1.14	1.17	1.20	1.19	1.20

Note: Freeway Travel Time Index—the ratio of travel time in the peak period to the travel time at free-flow conditions. For example, a value of 1.30 indicates a 20-minute free-flow trip takes 26 minutes in the peak (20 minutes x 1.30 = 26 minutes); (1) Covers the San Antonio TX urban area; (2) Rank is based on 101 urban areas (#1 = highest travel time index); (3) Average of 101 urban areas
Source: Texas Transportation Institute, 2015 Urban Mobility Scorecard, August 2015

Freeway Commuter Stress Index

Area	1985	1990	1995	2000	2005	2010	2014
Urban Area Rank[1,2]	22	26	19	17	22	22	20
Urban Area Index[1]	1.19	1.20	1.27	1.31	1.32	1.31	1.33
Average Index[3]	1.13	1.16	1.19	1.22	1.25	1.24	1.25

Note: The Freeway Commuter Stress Index is the same as the Freeway Travel Time Index (see table above) except that it includes only the travel in the peak directions during the peak periods; the TTI includes travel in all directions during the peak period. Thus, the CSI is more indicative of the work trip experienced by each commuter on a daily basis; (1) Covers the San Antonio TX urban area; (2) Rank is based on 101 urban areas (#1 = highest travel time index); (3) Average of 101 urban areas
Source: Texas Transportation Institute, 2015 Urban Mobility Scorecard, August 2015

Public Transportation

Agency Name / Mode of Transportation	Vehicles Operated in Maximum Service[1]	Annual Unlinked Passenger Trips[2] (in thous.)	Annual Passenger Miles[3] (in thous.)
VIA Metropolitan Transit (VIA)			
Bus (directly operated)	378	35,623.8	149,949.7
Demand Response (directly operated)	108	535.3	6,091.5
Demand Response (purchased transportation)	110	574.1	7,345.5
Vanpool (purchased transportation)	218	500.5	24,620.8

Note: (1) The number of revenue vehicles operated by the given mode and type of service to meet the annual maximum service requirement. This is the revenue vehicle count during the peak season of the year; on the week and day that maximum service is provided. Vehicles operated in maximum service (VOMS) exclude atypical days and one-time special events; (2) The number of passengers who boarded public transportation vehicles. Passengers are counted each time they board a vehicle no matter how many vehicles they use to travel from their origin to their destination. (3) The sum of the distances ridden by all passengers during the entire fiscal year.
Source: Federal Transit Administration, National Transit Database, 2017

Air Transportation

Airport Name and Code / Type of Service	Passenger Airlines[1]	Passenger Enplanements	Freight Carriers[2]	Freight (lbs)
San Antonio International (SAT)				
Domestic service (U.S. carriers - 2018)	26	4,639,923	17	107,406,149
International service (U.S. carriers - 2017)	9	19,217	2	11,056,310

Note: (1) Includes all U.S.-based major, minor and commuter airlines that carried at least one passenger during the year; (2) Includes all U.S.-based airlines and freight carriers that transported at least one pound of freight during the year.
Source: Bureau of Transportation Statistics, The Intermodal Transportation Database, Air Carriers: T-100 Domestic Market (U.S. Carriers), 2018; Bureau of Transportation Statistics, The Intermodal Transportation Database, Air Carriers: T-100 International Market (U.S. Carriers), 2017

Other Transportation Statistics

Major Highways:	I-10; I-35; I-37
Amtrak Service:	Yes
Major Waterways/Ports:	None

Source: Amtrak.com; Google Maps

BUSINESSES

Major Business Headquarters

Company Name	Industry	Rankings Fortune[1]	Rankings Forbes[2]
Andeavor	Petroleum Refining	90	-
HE Butt Grocery	Food Markets	-	12
USAA	Insurance: Property and Casualty (Stock)	100	-
Valero Energy	Petroleum Refining	31	-
Zachry Group	Construction	-	138
iHeartMedia	Entertainment	452	-

Note: (1) Companies that produce a 10-K are ranked 1 to 500 based on 2017 revenue; (2) All private companies with at least $2 billion in annual revenue through the end of their most current fiscal year are ranked 1 to 229; companies listed are headquartered in the city; dashes indicate no ranking
Source: Fortune, "Fortune 500," June 2018; Forbes, "America's Largest Private Companies," 2018 Rankings

Fast-Growing Businesses

According to *Inc.*, San Antonio is home to one of America's 500 fastest-growing private companies: **Eligibility Tracking Calculators** (#401). Criteria: must be an independent, privately-held, for-profit, U.S. corporation, proprietorship or partnership as of December 31, 2017; revenues must be at least $100,000 in 2014 and $2 million in 2017; must have four-year operating/sales history. Holding companies, regulated banks, and utilities were excluded. *Inc., "America's 500 Fastest-Growing Private Companies," 2018*

Minority Business Opportunity

San Antonio is home to one company which is on the *Black Enterprise* Industrial/Service list (100 largest companies based on gross sales): **Millennium Steel of Texas** (#14). Criteria: operational in previous calendar year; at least 51% black-owned and manufactures/owns the product it sells or provides industrial or consumer services. Brokerages, real estate firms and firms that provide professional services are not eligible. *Black Enterprise, B.E. 100s, 2018*

San Antonio is home to 13 companies which are on the *Hispanic Business* 500 list (500 largest U.S. Hispanic-owned companies based on revenue): **Genesis Networks Telecom Services** (#6); **Ancira Enterprises** (#7); **The Alamo Travel Group LP** (#65); **InGenesis** (#74); **Maldonado Nursery & Landscaping** (#172); **P3S Corp.** (#191); **Davila Pharmacy** (#248); **Garcia Foods** (#256); **Munoz & Co.** (#280); **LuLu's Dessert Corp.** (#387); **IDC** (#407); **J.R. Ramon & Sons** (#412); **Inventiva** (#457). Companies included must show at least 51 percent ownership by Hispanic U.S. citizens, and must maintain headquarters in one of the 50 states or Washington, D.C. *Hispanic Business, "Hispanic Business 500," June 20, 2013*

Minority- and Women-Owned Businesses

Group	All Firms		Firms with Paid Employees			
	Firms	Sales ($000)	Firms	Sales ($000)	Employees	Payroll ($000)
AIAN[1]	1,149	93,982	123	72,968	890	31,827
Asian	5,725	2,320,052	1,730	2,167,929	19,392	445,537
Black	4,958	389,844	476	306,392	3,634	121,721
Hispanic	60,696	9,710,316	4,938	8,027,259	60,322	1,818,103
NHOPI[2]	121	8,613	14	(s)	20 - 99	(s)
Women	44,295	8,470,219	4,582	7,429,288	62,040	1,816,178
All Firms	117,546	246,966,028	20,608	242,748,345	627,310	24,618,622

Note: Figures cover firms located in the city; minority- and women-owned business are defined as firms in which the corresponding group own 51% or more of the stock or equity of the company; (1) American Indian and Alaska Native; (2) Native Hawaiian and Other Pacific Islander; (s) estimates are suppressed when publication standards are not met
Source: U.S. Census Bureau, 2012 Economic Census, Survey of Business Owners

HOTELS & CONVENTION CENTERS

Hotels, Motels and Vacation Rentals

Area	5 Star		4 Star		3 Star		2 Star		1 Star		Not Rated	
	Num.	Pct.[3]	Num.	Pct.[3]	Num.	Pct.[3]	Num.	Pct.[3]	Num.	Pct.[3]	Num.	Pct.[3]
City[1]	2	0.2	30	3.0	117	11.7	217	21.7	7	0.7	629	62.8
Total[2]	286	0.4	5,236	7.1	16,715	22.6	10,259	13.9	293	0.4	41,056	55.6

Note: (1) Figures cover San Antonio and vicinity; (2) Figures cover all 100 cities in this book; (3) Percentage of hotels which have a given star rating; Star ratings are determined by expedia.com and offer an indication of the general quality of a particular hotel.
Source: www.expedia.com, April 3, 2019

Major Convention Centers

Name	Overall Space (sq. ft.)	Exhibit Space (sq. ft.)	Meeting Space (sq. ft.)	Meeting Rooms
Henry B. Gonzalez Convention Center	1,300,000	440,000	n/a	59

Note: Table includes convention centers located in the San Antonio-New Braunfels, TX metro area; n/a not available
Source: Original research

Living Environment

COST OF LIVING

Cost of Living Index

Composite Index	Groceries	Housing	Utilities	Trans- portation	Health Care	Misc. Goods/ Services
86.9	86.9	76.4	88.9	87.3	84.7	95.5

Note: The Cost of Living Index measures regional differences in the cost of consumer goods and services, excluding taxes and non-consumer expenditures, for professional and managerial households in the top income quintile. It is based on more than 50,000 prices covering almost 60 different items for which prices are collected three times a year by chambers of commerce, economic development organizations or university applied economic centers in each participating urban area. The numbers shown should be read as a percentage above or below the national average of 100. For example, a value of 115.4 in the groceries column indicates that grocery prices are 15.4% higher than the national average. Small differences in the index numbers should not be interpreted as significant; Figures cover the San Antonio TX urban area.
Source: The Council for Community and Economic Research, ACCRA Cost of Living Index, 2018

Grocery Prices

Area[1]	T-Bone Steak ($/pound)	Frying Chicken ($/pound)	Whole Milk ($/half gal.)	Eggs ($/dozen)	Orange Juice ($/64 oz.)	Coffee ($/11.5 oz.)
City[2]	11.23	1.03	1.51	2.01	2.99	4.12
Avg.	11.35	1.42	1.94	1.81	3.52	4.35
Min.	7.45	0.92	0.80	0.75	2.72	3.06
Max.	15.05	2.76	4.18	4.00	5.36	8.20

Note: (1) Values for the local area are compared with the average, minimum and maximum values for all 291 areas in the Cost of Living Index; (2) Figures cover the San Antonio TX urban area; **T-Bone Steak** (price per pound); **Frying Chicken** (price per pound, whole fryer); **Whole Milk** (half gallon carton); **Eggs** (price per dozen, Grade A, large); **Orange Juice** (64 oz. Tropicana or Florida Natural); **Coffee** (11.5 oz. can, vacuum-packed, Maxwell House, Hills Bros, or Folgers).
Source: The Council for Community and Economic Research, ACCRA Cost of Living Index, 2018

Housing and Utility Costs

Area[1]	New Home Price ($)	Apartment Rent ($/month)	All Electric ($/month)	Part Electric ($/month)	Other Energy ($/month)	Telephone ($/month)
City[2]	257,175	923	-	95.94	37.37	179.90
Avg.	347,000	1,087	165.93	100.16	67.73	178.70
Min.	200,468	500	93.58	25.64	26.78	163.10
Max.	1,901,222	4,888	388.65	246.86	332.81	197.70

Note: (1) Values for the local area are compared with the average, minimum and maximum values for all 291 areas in the Cost of Living Index; (2) Figures cover the San Antonio TX urban area; **New Home Price** (2,400 sf living area, 8,000 sf lot, in urban area with full utilities); **Apartment Rent** (950 sf 2 bedroom/1.5 or 2 bath, unfurnished, excluding all utilities except water); **All Electric** (average monthly cost for an all-electric home); **Part Electric** (average monthly cost for a part-electric home); **Other Energy** (average monthly cost for natural gas, fuel oil, coal, wood, and any other forms of energy except electricity); **Telephone** (price includes the base monthly rate plus taxes and fees for three lines of mobile phone service).
Source: The Council for Community and Economic Research, ACCRA Cost of Living Index, 2018

Health Care, Transportation, and Other Costs

Area[1]	Doctor ($/visit)	Dentist ($/visit)	Optometrist ($/visit)	Gasoline ($/gallon)	Beauty Salon ($/visit)	Men's Shirt ($)
City[2]	92.75	75.38	84.43	2.25	39.00	21.88
Avg.	110.71	95.11	103.74	2.61	37.48	32.03
Min.	33.60	62.55	54.63	1.89	17.00	11.44
Max.	195.97	153.93	225.79	3.59	71.88	58.64

Note: (1) Values for the local area are compared with the average, minimum and maximum values for all 291 areas in the Cost of Living Index; (2) Figures cover the San Antonio TX urban area; **Doctor** (general practitioners routine exam of an established patient); **Dentist** (adult teeth cleaning and periodic oral examination); **Optometrist** (full vision eye exam for established adult patient); **Gasoline** (one gallon regular unleaded, national brand, including all taxes, cash price at self-service pump if available); **Beauty Salon** (woman's shampoo, trim, and blow-dry); **Men's Shirt** (cotton/polyester dress shirt, pinpoint weave, long sleeves).
Source: The Council for Community and Economic Research, ACCRA Cost of Living Index, 2018

HOUSING

House Price Index (HPI)

Area	National Ranking[2]	Quarterly Change (%)	One-Year Change (%)	Five-Year Change (%)
MSA[1]	103	1.95	6.71	39.55
U.S.[3]	–	1.12	5.73	32.81

Note: The HPI is a weighted repeat sales index. It measures average price changes in repeat sales or refinancings on the same properties. This information is obtained by reviewing repeat mortgage transactions on single-family properties whose mortgages have been purchased or securitized by Fannie Mae or Freddie Mac in January 1975; (1) Figures cover the San Antonio-New Braunfels, TX Metropolitan Statistical Area—see Appendix B for areas included; (2) Rankings are based on annual percentage change for all metro areas containing at least 15,000 transactions over the last 10 years and ranges from 1 to 245; (3) figures based on a weighted average of Census Division estimates using a seasonally adjusted, purchase-only index; all figures are for the period ending December 31, 2018
Source: Federal Housing Finance Agency, House Price Index, February 26, 2019

Median Single-Family Home Prices

Area	2016	2017	2018[P]	Percent Change 2017 to 2018
MSA[1]	206.9	217.2	228.1	5.0
U.S. Average	235.5	248.8	261.6	5.1

Note: Figures are median sales prices of existing single-family homes in thousands of dollars; (p) preliminary; (1) Figures cover the San Antonio-New Braunfels, TX Metropolitan Statistical Area—see Appendix B for areas included
Source: National Association of Realtors, Median Sales Price of Existing Single-Family Homes for Metropolitan Areas, 4th Quarter 2018

Qualifying Income Based on Median Sales Price of Existing Single-Family Homes

Area	With 5% Down ($)	With 10% Down ($)	With 20% Down ($)
MSA[1]	55,989	53,042	47,148
U.S. Average	62,954	59,640	53,013

Note: Figures are preliminary; Qualifying income is based on a mortgage rate of 4.9%. Monthly principal and interest payment is limited to 25% of income; (1) Figures cover the San Antonio-New Braunfels, TX Metropolitan Statistical Area—see Appendix B for areas included
Source: National Association of Realtors, Qualifying Income Based on Median Sales Price of Existing Single-Family Homes for Metropolitan Areas, 4th Quarter 2018

Median Apartment Condo-Coop Home Prices

Area	2016	2017	2018[P]	Percent Change 2017 to 2018
MSA[1]	n/a	n/a	n/a	n/a
U.S. Average	220.7	234.3	241.0	2.9

Note: Figures are median sales prices of existing apartment condo-coop homes in thousands of dollars; (p) preliminary; n/a not available; (1) Figures cover the San Antonio-New Braunfels, TX Metropolitan Statistical Area—see Appendix B for areas included
Source: National Association of Realtors, Median Sales Price of Existing Apartment Condo-Coop Homes for Metropolitan Areas, 4th Quarter 2018

Home Value Distribution

Area	Under $50,000	$50,000 -$99,999	$100,000 -$149,999	$150,000 -$199,999	$200,000 -$299,999	$300,000 -$499,999	$500,000 -$999,999	$1,000,000 or more
City	8.6	28.8	21.2	17.0	14.5	7.2	2.2	0.5
MSA[1]	8.7	21.8	18.5	17.5	17.4	11.3	3.9	1.0
U.S.	8.3	13.9	14.7	14.6	18.7	17.3	9.7	2.7

Note: Figures are percentages and cover owner-occupied housing units; (1) Figures cover the San Antonio-New Braunfels, TX Metropolitan Statistical Area—see Appendix B for areas included
Source: U.S. Census Bureau, 2013-2017 American Community Survey 5-Year Estimates

Homeownership Rate

Area	2010 (%)	2011 (%)	2012 (%)	2013 (%)	2014 (%)	2015 (%)	2016 (%)	2017 (%)	2018 (%)
MSA[1]	70.1	66.5	67.5	70.1	70.2	66.0	61.6	62.5	64.4
U.S.	66.9	66.1	65.4	65.1	64.5	63.7	63.4	63.9	64.4

Note: (1) Figures cover the San Antonio-New Braunfels, TX Metropolitan Statistical Area—see Appendix B for areas included
Source: U.S. Census Bureau, Housing Vacancies and Homeownership Annual Statistics: 2010-2018

Year Housing Structure Built

Area	2010 or Later	2000 -2009	1990 -1999	1980 -1989	1970 -1979	1960 -1969	1950 -1959	1940 -1949	Before 1940	Median Year
City	4.9	16.8	13.8	16.9	15.7	10.4	10.2	5.7	5.6	1981
MSA[1]	7.4	22.1	14.9	15.9	14.0	8.7	7.8	4.4	4.8	1986
U.S.	3.2	14.5	14.0	13.6	15.5	10.8	10.5	5.1	12.9	1977

Note: Figures are percentages except for Median Year; Note: (1) Figures cover the San Antonio-New Braunfels, TX Metropolitan Statistical Area—see Appendix B for areas included
Source: U.S. Census Bureau, 2013-2017 American Community Survey 5-Year Estimates

Gross Monthly Rent

Area	Under $500	$500 -$999	$1,000 -$1,499	$1,500 -$1,999	$2,000 -$2,499	$2,500 -$2,999	$3,000 and up	Median ($)
City	8.9	50.8	31.1	7.3	1.2	0.4	0.4	918
MSA[1]	8.3	47.4	32.4	8.9	1.9	0.6	0.6	949
U.S.	10.5	41.1	28.7	11.7	4.5	1.8	1.7	982

Note: Figures are percentages except for Median; Gross rent is the contract rent plus the estimated average monthly cost of utilities (electricity, gas, and water and sewer) and fuels (oil, coal, kerosene, wood, etc.) if these are paid by the renter (or paid for the renter by someone else); (1) Figures cover the San Antonio-New Braunfels, TX Metropolitan Statistical Area—see Appendix B for areas included
Source: U.S. Census Bureau, 2013-2017 American Community Survey 5-Year Estimates

HEALTH

Health Risk Factors

Category	MSA[1] (%)	U.S. (%)
Adults aged 18–64 who have any kind of health care coverage	67.4	87.3
Adults who reported being in good or better health	78.4	82.4
Adults who have been told they have high blood cholesterol	28.9	33.0
Adults who have been told they have high blood pressure	30.6	32.3
Adults who are current smokers	17.9	17.1
Adults who currently use E-cigarettes	n/a	4.6
Adults who currently use chewing tobacco, snuff, or snus	3.8	4.0
Adults who are heavy drinkers[2]	7.5	6.3
Adults who are binge drinkers[3]	19.2	17.4
Adults who are overweight (BMI 25.0 - 29.9)	37.5	35.3
Adults who are obese (BMI 30.0 - 99.8)	30.7	31.3
Adults who participated in any physical activities in the past month	66.5	74.4
Adults who always or nearly always wears a seat belt	94.9	94.3

Note: n/a not available; (1) Figures cover the San Antonio-New Braunfels, TX Metropolitan Statistical Area—see Appendix B for areas included; (2) Heavy drinkers are classified as adult men having more than 14 drinks per week and adult women having more than 7 drinks per week; (3) Binge drinkers are classified as males having five or more drinks on one occasion or females having four or more drinks on one occasion
Source: Centers for Disease Control and Prevention, Behaviorial Risk Factor Surveillance System, SMART: Selected Metropolitan Area Risk Trends, 2017

Acute and Chronic Health Conditions

Category	MSA[1] (%)	U.S. (%)
Adults who have ever been told they had a heart attack	7.0	4.2
Adults who have ever been told they have angina or coronary heart disease	5.0	3.9
Adults who have ever been told they had a stroke	n/a	3.0
Adults who have ever been told they have asthma	9.0	14.2
Adults who have ever been told they have arthritis	20.2	24.9
Adults who have ever been told they have diabetes[2]	13.0	10.5
Adults who have ever been told they had skin cancer	4.2	6.2
Adults who have ever been told they had any other types of cancer	8.6	7.1
Adults who have ever been told they have COPD	7.2	6.5
Adults who have ever been told they have kidney disease	n/a	3.0
Adults who have ever been told they have a form of depression	21.4	20.5

Note: n/a not available; (1) Figures cover the San Antonio-New Braunfels, TX Metropolitan Statistical Area—see Appendix B for areas included; (2) Figures do not include pregnancy-related, borderline, or pre-diabetes
Source: Centers for Disease Control and Prevention, Behaviorial Risk Factor Surveillance System, SMART: Selected Metropolitan Area Risk Trends, 2017

Health Screening and Vaccination Rates

Category	MSA[1] (%)	U.S. (%)
Adults aged 65+ who have had flu shot within the past year	70.1	60.7
Adults aged 65+ who have ever had a pneumonia vaccination	76.3	75.4
Adults who have ever been tested for HIV	41.9	36.1
Adults who have ever had the shingles or zoster vaccine?	29.6	28.9
Adults who have had their blood cholesterol checked within the last five years	80.5	85.9

Note: n/a not available; (1) Figures cover the San Antonio-New Braunfels, TX Metropolitan Statistical Area—see Appendix B for areas included.
Source: Centers for Disease Control and Prevention, Behaviorial Risk Factor Surveillance System, SMART: Selected Metropolitan Area Risk Trends, 2017

Disability Status

Category	MSA[1] (%)	U.S. (%)
Adults who reported being deaf	5.0	6.7
Are you blind or have serious difficulty seeing, even when wearing glasses?	n/a	4.5
Are you limited in any way in any of your usual activities due of arthritis?	12.9	12.9
Do you have difficulty doing errands alone?	9.1	6.8
Do you have difficulty dressing or bathing?	n/a	3.6
Do you have serious difficulty concentrating/remembering/making decisions?	12.9	10.7
Do you have serious difficulty walking or climbing stairs?	13.2	13.6

Note: n/a not available; (1) Figures cover the San Antonio-New Braunfels, TX Metropolitan Statistical Area—see Appendix B for areas included.
Source: Centers for Disease Control and Prevention, Behaviorial Risk Factor Surveillance System, SMART: Selected Metropolitan Area Risk Trends, 2017

Mortality Rates for the Top 10 Causes of Death in the U.S.

ICD-10[a] Sub-Chapter	ICD-10[a] Code	Age-Adjusted Mortality Rate[1] per 100,000 population County[2]	U.S.
Malignant neoplasms	C00-C97	145.2	155.5
Ischaemic heart diseases	I20-I25	90.9	94.8
Other forms of heart disease	I30-I51	63.2	52.9
Chronic lower respiratory diseases	J40-J47	33.2	41.0
Cerebrovascular diseases	I60-I69	44.0	37.5
Other degenerative diseases of the nervous system	G30-G31	54.7	35.0
Other external causes of accidental injury	W00-X59	26.4	33.7
Organic, including symptomatic, mental disorders	F01-F09	19.1	31.0
Hypertensive diseases	I10-I15	20.3	21.9
Diabetes mellitus	E10-E14	25.1	21.2

Note: (a) ICD-10 = International Classification of Diseases 10th Revision; (1) Mortality rates are a three year average covering 2015-2017; (2) Figures cover Bexar County.
Source: Centers for Disease Control and Prevention, National Center for Health Statistics. Underlying Cause of Death 1999-2017 on CDC WONDER Online Database

Mortality Rates for Selected Causes of Death

ICD-10[a] Sub-Chapter	ICD-10[a] Code	Age-Adjusted Mortality Rate[1] per 100,000 population County[2]	U.S.
Assault	X85-Y09	7.7	5.9
Diseases of the liver	K70-K76	22.8	14.1
Human immunodeficiency virus (HIV) disease	B20-B24	2.6	1.8
Influenza and pneumonia	J09-J18	9.4	14.3
Intentional self-harm	X60-X84	12.1	13.6
Malnutrition	E40-E46	2.7	1.6
Obesity and other hyperalimentation	E65-E68	1.6	2.1
Renal failure	N17-N19	14.6	13.0
Transport accidents	V01-V99	12.1	12.4
Viral hepatitis	B15-B19	1.9	1.6

Note: (a) ICD-10 = International Classification of Diseases 10th Revision; (1) Mortality rates are a three year average covering 2015-2017; (2) Figures cover Bexar County; Data are suppressed when the data meet the criteria for confidentiality constraints; Mortality rates are flagged as unreliable when the rate would be calculated with a numerator of 20 or less.
Source: Centers for Disease Control and Prevention, National Center for Health Statistics. Underlying Cause of Death 1999-2017 on CDC WONDER Online Database

Health Insurance Coverage

Area	With Health Insurance	With Private Health Insurance	With Public Health Insurance	Without Health Insurance	Population Under Age 18 Without Health Insurance
City	82.7	59.9	32.4	17.3	8.7
MSA[1]	84.6	64.6	30.7	15.4	8.4
U.S.	89.5	67.2	33.8	10.5	5.7

Note: Figures are percentages that cover the civilian noninstitutionalized population; (1) Figures cover the San Antonio-New Braunfels, TX Metropolitan Statistical Area—see Appendix B for areas included
Source: U.S. Census Bureau, 2013-2017 American Community Survey 5-Year Estimates

Number of Medical Professionals

Area	MDs[3]	DOs[3,4]	Dentists	Podiatrists	Chiropractors	Optometrists
County[1] (number)	6,159	411	1,626	100	312	321
County[1] (rate[2])	319.5	21.3	83.0	5.1	15.9	16.4
U.S. (rate[2])	279.3	23.0	68.4	6.0	27.1	16.2

Note: Data as of 2017 unless noted; (1) Data covers Bexar County; (2) Rate per 100,000 population; (3) Data as of 2016 and includes all active, non-federal physicians; (4) Doctor of Osteopathic Medicine
Source: U.S. Department of Health and Human Services, Health Resources and Services Administration, Bureau of Health Professions, Area Resource File (ARF) 2017-2018

Best Hospitals

According to *U.S. News,* the San Antonio-New Braunfels, TX metro area is home to one of the best hospitals in the U.S.: **University Hospital-San Antonio** (1 adult specialty). The hospital listed was nationally ranked in at least one of 16 adult or 10 pediatric specialties. Only 170 hospitals nationwide were nationally ranked in one or more adult or pediatric specialty. Twenty hospitals in the U.S. made the Honor Roll. The Best Hospitals Honor Roll takes both the national rankings and the procedure and condition ratings into account. Hospitals received points if they were nationally ranked in one of the 16 adult specialties—the higher they ranked, the more points they got—and how many ratings of "high performing" they earned in the nine procedures and conditions. *U.S. News Online, "America's Best Hospitals 2018-19"*

EDUCATION

Public School District Statistics

District Name	Schls	Pupils	Pupil/ Teacher Ratio	Minority Pupils[1] (%)	Free Lunch Eligible[2] (%)	IEP[3] (%)
Alamo Heights ISD	6	4,857	14.1	48.2	17.7	7.6
East Central ISD	15	10,227	16.8	84.0	55.6	10.4
Edgewood ISD	21	10,881	15.8	99.5	91.0	9.8
Great Hearts Texas	4	2,312	18.6	53.1	7.9	4.5
Harlandale ISD	31	14,831	14.7	98.3	n/a	9.1
Harmony Science Acad (San Antonio)	6	3,705	15.4	93.1	58.9	6.2
Jubilee Academic Center	9	4,731	15.8	90.4	56.5	6.8
Kipp San Antonio	6	2,947	17.9	98.1	76.9	7.5
North East ISD	75	67,531	15.7	73.7	38.7	9.7
Northside ISD	120	106,145	15.4	80.7	44.5	11.5
San Antonio ISD	97	52,514	16.3	98.0	89.8	10.2
South San Antonio ISD	17	9,631	15.7	98.7	90.8	8.1
Southside ISD	9	5,713	14.7	93.1	72.2	11.3
Southwest ISD	18	13,891	15.5	95.0	73.1	11.1

Note: Table includes school districts with 2,000 or more students; (1) Percentage of students that are not non-Hispanic white; (2) Percentage of students that are eligible for the free lunch program; (3) Percentage of students that have an Individualized Education Program.
Source: U.S. Department of Education, National Center for Education Statistics, Common Core of Data, Local Education Agency (School District) Universe Survey: School Year 2016-2017; U.S. Department of Education, National Center for Education Statistics, Common Core of Data, Public Elementary/Secondary School Universe Survey: School Year 2016-2017

Best High Schools

According to *U.S. News,* San Antonio is home to three of the best high schools in the U.S.: **Young Women's Leadership Academy** (#141); **Health Careers High School** (#160); **International School of America** (#427). More than 20,000 public, magnet and charter schools were ranked based on their performance on state assessments and how well they prepare students for college. Schools with the highest unrounded College Readiness Index values were numerically ranked from

1 to 500 and were classified as gold medal winners. *U.S. News & World Report, "Best High Schools 2018"*

Highest Level of Education

Area	Less than H.S.	H.S. Diploma	Some College, No Deg.	Associate Degree	Bachelor's Degree	Master's Degree	Prof. School Degree	Doctorate Degree
City	18.0	26.2	22.6	7.5	16.6	6.5	1.7	1.0
MSA[1]	15.4	26.3	23.1	7.8	17.6	7.1	1.6	1.0
U.S.	12.7	27.3	20.8	8.3	19.1	8.4	2.0	1.4

Note: Figures cover persons age 25 and over; (1) Figures cover the San Antonio-New Braunfels, TX Metropolitan Statistical Area—see Appendix B for areas included
Source: U.S. Census Bureau, 2013-2017 American Community Survey 5-Year Estimates

Educational Attainment by Race

Area	High School Graduate or Higher (%)					Bachelor's Degree or Higher (%)				
	Total	White	Black	Asian	Hisp.[2]	Total	White	Black	Asian	Hisp.[2]
City	82.0	82.3	90.1	86.0	74.1	25.7	26.0	24.0	51.8	15.7
MSA[1]	84.6	85.0	91.1	86.4	75.2	27.4	27.8	28.2	51.5	16.1
U.S.	87.3	89.3	84.9	86.5	66.7	30.9	32.2	20.6	52.7	15.2

Note: Figures shown cover persons 25 years old and over; (1) Figures cover the San Antonio-New Braunfels, TX Metropolitan Statistical Area—see Appendix B for areas included; (2) People of Hispanic origin can be of any race
Source: U.S. Census Bureau, 2013-2017 American Community Survey 5-Year Estimates

School Enrollment by Grade and Control

Area	Preschool (%)		Kindergarten (%)		Grades 1 - 4 (%)		Grades 5 - 8 (%)		Grades 9 - 12 (%)	
	Public	Private	Public	Private	Public	Private	Public	Private	Public	Private
City	70.6	29.4	91.8	8.2	93.4	6.6	93.0	7.0	93.9	6.1
MSA[1]	66.0	34.0	91.1	8.9	93.1	6.9	92.5	7.5	93.6	6.4
U.S.	58.8	41.2	87.7	12.3	89.7	10.3	89.6	10.4	90.3	9.7

Note: Figures shown cover persons 3 years old and over; (1) Figures cover the San Antonio-New Braunfels, TX Metropolitan Statistical Area—see Appendix B for areas included
Source: U.S. Census Bureau, 2013-2017 American Community Survey 5-Year Estimates

Average Salaries of Public School Classroom Teachers

Area	2016		2017		Change from 2016 to 2017	
	Dollars	Rank[1]	Dollars	Rank[1]	Percent	Rank[2]
Texas	51,890	28	52,575	28	1.3	29
U.S. Average	58,479	–	59,660	–	2.0	–

Note: (1) Rank ranges from 1 to 51 where 1 indicates highest salary; (2) Rank ranges from 1 to 51 where 1 indicates highest percent change.
Source: National Education Association, Rankings & Estimates: Rankings of the States 2017 and Estimates of School Statistics 2018

Higher Education

Four-Year Colleges			Two-Year Colleges			Medical Schools[1]	Law Schools[2]	Voc/ Tech[3]
Public	Private Non-profit	Private For-profit	Public	Private Non-profit	Private For-profit			
3	7	6	4	0	4	2	1	20

Note: Figures cover institutions located within the city limits and include main campuses only; (1) includes schools accredited by the Liaison Committee on Medical Education and the American Osteopathic Association's Commission on Osteopathic College Accreditation; (2) includes ABA-accredited schools, schools with provisional ABA accreditation, and state accredited schools; (3) includes all schools with programs that are less than 2 years.
Source: National Center for Education Statistics, Integrated Postsecondary Education System (IPEDS), 2017-18; Wikipedia, List of Medical Schools in the United States, accessed April 3, 2019; Wikipedia, List of Law Schools in the United States, accessed April 3, 2019

According to *U.S. News & World Report*, the San Antonio-New Braunfels, TX metro area is home to one of the top 75 medical schools for research in the U.S.: **University of Texas Health Science Center—San Antonio** (#60 tie). The rankings are based on a weighted average of 11 measures of quality: quality assessment; peer assessment score; assessment score by residency directors; research activity; total research activity; average research activity per faculty member; student selectivity; median MCAT total score; median undergraduate GPA; acceptance rate; and faculty resources. *U.S. News & World Report, "America's Best Graduate Schools, Medical, 2020"*

PRESIDENTIAL ELECTION

2016 Presidential Election Results

Area	Clinton	Trump	Johnson	Stein	Other
Bexar County	53.7	40.4	3.4	1.1	1.3
U.S.	48.0	45.9	3.3	1.1	1.7

Note: Results are percentages and may not add to 100% due to rounding
Source: Dave Leip's Atlas of U.S. Presidential Elections

EMPLOYERS

Major Employers

Company Name	Industry
AT&T	Phone, wireless & internet services
Baptist Health System	Health care services
Bill Miller BBQ	Restaurant chain
Christus Santa Rosa Health Care	Health care services
City of San Antonio	Municipal government
Clear Channel Communications	TV & radio stations, outdoor ads
CPS Energy	Utilities
Fort Sam Houston-U.S. Army	U.S. military
H-E-B	Super market chain
JPMorgan Chase	Financial services
Lackland Air Force Base	U.S. military
Methodist Healthcare System	Health care services
North East I.S.D.	School districts
Northside ISD	School districts
Rackspace	IT managed hosting solutions
Randolph Air Force Base	U.S. military
San Antonio I.S.D.	School districts
Toyota Motor Manufacturing	Manufacturing
USAA	Financial services & insurance
Wells Fargo	Financial services

Note: Companies shown are located within the San Antonio-New Braunfels, TX Metropolitan Statistical Area.
Source: Hoovers.com; Wikipedia

Best Companies to Work For

USAA, headquartered in San Antonio, is among "The 100 Best Companies to Work For." To pick the best companies, *Fortune* partnered with the Great Place to Work Institute. Two-thirds of a company's score is based on the results of the Institute's Trust Index survey, which is sent to a random sample of employees from each company. The questions related to attitudes about management's credibility, job satisfaction, and camaraderie. The other third of the scoring is based on the company's responses to the Institute's Culture Audit, which includes detailed questions about pay and benefit programs, and a series of open-ended questions about hiring practices, internal communication, training, recognition programs, and diversity efforts. Any company that is at least five years old with more than 1,000 U.S. employees is eligible. *Fortune, "The 100 Best Companies to Work For," 2019*

PUBLIC SAFETY

Crime Rate

Area	All Crimes	Violent Crimes				Property Crimes		
		Murder	Rape[3]	Robbery	Aggrav. Assault	Burglary	Larceny-Theft	Motor Vehicle Theft
City	5,552.3	8.2	83.5	151.1	464.7	770.8	3,622.6	451.4
Suburbs[1]	n/a	3.7	49.4	37.9	141.0	n/a	1,451.0	165.0
Metro[2]	n/a	6.4	70.3	107.4	339.8	n/a	2,784.4	340.8
U.S.	2,756.1	5.3	41.7	98.0	248.9	430.4	1,694.4	237.4

Note: Figures are crimes per 100,000 population; (1) All areas within the metro area that are located outside the city limits; (2) Figures cover the San Antonio-New Braunfels, TX Metropolitan Statistical Area—see Appendix B for areas included; (3) The city and U.S. figures shown were reported using the revised Uniform Crime Reporting (UCR) definition of rape. The suburban and metro area figures shown are an aggregate total of the data submitted using both the revised and legacy UCR definitions.
Source: FBI Uniform Crime Reports, 2017

Hate Crimes

Area	Number of Quarters Reported	Number of Incidents per Bias Motivation					
		Race/Ethnicity/ Ancestry	Religion	Sexual Orientation	Disability	Gender	Gender Identity
City	4	2	1	1	0	0	0
U.S.	4	4,131	1,564	1,130	116	46	119

Source: Federal Bureau of Investigation, Hate Crime Statistics 2017

Identity Theft Consumer Reports

Area	Reports	Reports per 100,000 Population	Rank[2]
MSA[1]	3,033	125	67
U.S.	444,602	135	-

Note: (1) Figures cover the San Antonio-New Braunfels, TX Metropolitan Statistical Area—see Appendix B for areas included; (2) Rank ranges from 1 to 389 where 1 indicates greatest number of identity theft reports per 100,000 population
Source: Federal Trade Commission, Consumer Sentinel Network Data Book for January–December 2018

Fraud and Other Consumer Reports

Area	Reports	Reports per 100,000 Population	Rank[2]
MSA[1]	12,079	497	188
U.S.	2,552,917	776	-

Note: (1) Figures cover the San Antonio-New Braunfels, TX Metropolitan Statistical Area—see Appendix B for areas included; (2) Rank ranges from 1 to 389 where 1 indicates greatest number of fraud and other consumer reports per 100,000 population
Source: Federal Trade Commission, Consumer Sentinel Network Data Book for January–December 2018

SPORTS

Professional Sports Teams

Team Name	League	Year Established
San Antonio Spurs	National Basketball Association (NBA)	1973

Note: Includes teams located in the San Antonio-New Braunfels, TX Metropolitan Statistical Area.
Source: Wikipedia, Major Professional Sports Teams of the United States and Canada, April 5, 2019

CLIMATE

Average and Extreme Temperatures

Temperature	Jan	Feb	Mar	Apr	May	Jun	Jul	Aug	Sep	Oct	Nov	Dec	Yr.
Extreme High (°F)	89	97	100	100	103	105	106	108	103	98	94	90	108
Average High (°F)	62	66	74	80	86	92	95	95	90	82	71	64	80
Average Temp. (°F)	51	55	62	70	76	82	85	85	80	71	60	53	69
Average Low (°F)	39	43	50	58	66	72	74	74	69	59	49	41	58
Extreme Low (°F)	0	6	19	31	43	53	62	61	46	33	21	6	0

Note: Figures cover the years 1948-1990
Source: National Climatic Data Center, International Station Meteorological Climate Summary, 9/96

Average Precipitation/Snowfall/Humidity

Precip./Humidity	Jan	Feb	Mar	Apr	May	Jun	Jul	Aug	Sep	Oct	Nov	Dec	Yr.
Avg. Precip. (in.)	1.5	1.8	1.5	2.6	3.8	3.6	2.0	2.5	3.3	3.2	2.3	1.4	29.6
Avg. Snowfall (in.)	1	Tr	Tr	0	0	0	0	0	0	0	Tr	Tr	1
Avg. Rel. Hum. 6am (%)	79	80	79	82	87	87	87	86	85	83	81	79	83
Avg. Rel. Hum. 3pm (%)	51	48	45	48	51	48	43	42	47	46	48	49	47

Note: Figures cover the years 1948-1990; Tr = Trace amounts (<0.05 in. of rain; <0.5 in. of snow)
Source: National Climatic Data Center, International Station Meteorological Climate Summary, 9/96

Weather Conditions

Temperature			Daytime Sky			Precipitation		
32°F & below	45°F & below	90°F & above	Clear	Partly cloudy	Cloudy	0.01 inch or more precip.	0.1 inch or more snow/ice	Thunder-storms
23	91	112	97	153	115	81	1	36

Note: Figures are average number of days per year and cover the years 1948-1990
Source: National Climatic Data Center, International Station Meteorological Climate Summary, 9/96

HAZARDOUS WASTE

Superfund Sites

The San Antonio-New Braunfels, TX metro area is home to four sites on the EPA's Superfund National Priorities List: **Bandera Road Ground Water Plume** (final); **Eldorado Chemical Co., Inc.** (final); **R & H Oil/Tropicana** (proposed); **River City Metal Finishing** (final). There are a total of 1,390 Superfund sites with a status of proposed or final on the list in the U.S. *U.S. Environmental Protection Agency, National Priorities List, April 5, 2019*

AIR & WATER QUALITY

Air Quality Trends: Ozone

	1990	1995	2000	2005	2010	2012	2014	2015	2016	2017
MSA[1]	0.090	0.095	0.078	0.084	0.072	0.081	0.069	0.079	0.071	0.073
U.S.	0.088	0.089	0.082	0.080	0.073	0.075	0.067	0.068	0.069	0.068

Note: (1) Data covers the San Antonio-New Braunfels, TX Metropolitan Statistical Area—see Appendix B for areas included. The values shown are the composite ozone concentration averages among trend sites based on the highest fourth daily maximum 8-hour concentration in parts per million. These trends are based on sites having an adequate record of monitoring data during the trend period. Data from exceptional events are included.
Source: U.S. Environmental Protection Agency, Air Quality Monitoring Information, "Air Quality Trends by City, 1990-2017"

Air Quality Index

Area	Percent of Days when Air Quality was...[2]					AQI Statistics[2]	
	Good	Moderate	Unhealthy for Sensitive Groups	Unhealthy	Very Unhealthy	Maximum	Median
MSA[1]	72.4	26.0	1.1	0.6	0.0	188	43

Note: (1) Data covers the San Antonio-New Braunfels, TX Metropolitan Statistical Area—see Appendix B for areas included; (2) Based on 362 days with AQI data in 2017. Air Quality Index (AQI) is an index for reporting daily air quality. EPA calculates the AQI for five major air pollutants regulated by the Clean Air Act: ground-level ozone, particle pollution (aka particulate matter), carbon monoxide, sulfur dioxide, and nitrogen dioxide. The AQI runs from 0 to 500. The higher the AQI value, the greater the level of air pollution and the greater the health concern. There are six AQI categories: "Good" AQI is between 0 and 50. Air quality is considered satisfactory; "Moderate" AQI is between 51 and 100. Air quality is acceptable; "Unhealthy for Sensitive Groups" When AQI values are between 101 and 150, members of sensitive groups may experience health effects; "Unhealthy" When AQI values are between 151 and 200 everyone may begin to experience health effects; "Very Unhealthy" AQI values between 201 and 300 trigger a health alert; "Hazardous" AQI values over 300 trigger warnings of emergency conditions (not shown).
Source: U.S. Environmental Protection Agency, Air Quality Index Report, 2017

Air Quality Index Pollutants

Area	Percent of Days when AQI Pollutant was...[2]					
	Carbon Monoxide	Nitrogen Dioxide	Ozone	Sulfur Dioxide	Particulate Matter 2.5	Particulate Matter 10
MSA[1]	0.0	1.7	58.0	0.6	39.8	0.0

Note: (1) Data covers the San Antonio-New Braunfels, TX Metropolitan Statistical Area—see Appendix B for areas included; (2) Based on 362 days with AQI data in 2017. The Air Quality Index (AQI) is an index for reporting daily air quality. EPA calculates the AQI for five major air pollutants regulated by the Clean Air Act: ground-level ozone, particle pollution (also known as particulate matter), carbon monoxide, sulfur dioxide, and nitrogen dioxide. The AQI runs from 0 to 500. The higher the AQI value, the greater the level of air pollution and the greater the health concern.
Source: U.S. Environmental Protection Agency, Air Quality Index Report, 2017

Maximum Air Pollutant Concentrations: Particulate Matter, Ozone, CO and Lead

	Particulate Matter 10 (ug/m³)	Particulate Matter 2.5 Wtd AM (ug/m³)	Particulate Matter 2.5 24-Hr (ug/m³)	Ozone (ppm)	Carbon Monoxide (ppm)	Lead (ug/m³)
MSA[1] Level	73	8.9	25	0.073	1	n/a
NAAQS[2]	150	15	35	0.075	9	0.15
Met NAAQS[2]	Yes	Yes	Yes	Yes	Yes	n/a

Note: (1) Data covers the San Antonio-New Braunfels, TX Metropolitan Statistical Area—see Appendix B for areas included; Data from exceptional events are included; (2) National Ambient Air Quality Standards; ppm = parts per million; ug/m³ = micrograms per cubic meter; n/a not available.
Concentrations: Particulate Matter 10 (coarse particulate)—highest second maximum 24-hour concentration; Particulate Matter 2.5 Wtd AM (fine particulate)—highest weighted annual mean concentration; Particulate Matter 2.5 24-Hour (fine particulate)—highest 98th percentile 24-hour concentration; Ozone—highest fourth daily maximum 8-hour concentration; Carbon Monoxide—highest second maximum non-overlapping 8-hour concentration; Lead—maximum running 3-month average
Source: U.S. Environmental Protection Agency, Air Quality Monitoring Information, "Air Quality Statistics by City, 2017"

Maximum Air Pollutant Concentrations: Nitrogen Dioxide and Sulfur Dioxide

	Nitrogen Dioxide AM (ppb)	Nitrogen Dioxide 1-Hr (ppb)	Sulfur Dioxide AM (ppb)	Sulfur Dioxide 1-Hr (ppb)	Sulfur Dioxide 24-Hr (ppb)
MSA[1] Level	8	40	n/a	29	n/a
NAAQS[2]	53	100	30	75	140
Met NAAQS[2]	Yes	Yes	n/a	Yes	n/a

Note: (1) Data covers the San Antonio-New Braunfels, TX Metropolitan Statistical Area—see Appendix B for areas included; Data from exceptional events are included; (2) National Ambient Air Quality Standards; ppm = parts per million; ug/m³ = micrograms per cubic meter; n/a not available.
Concentrations: Nitrogen Dioxide AM—highest arithmetic mean concentration; Nitrogen Dioxide 1-Hr—highest 98th percentile 1-hour daily maximum concentration; Sulfur Dioxide AM—highest annual mean concentration; Sulfur Dioxide 1-Hr—highest 99th percentile 1-hour daily maximum concentration; Sulfur Dioxide 24-Hr—highest second maximum 24-hour concentration
Source: U.S. Environmental Protection Agency, Air Quality Monitoring Information, "Air Quality Statistics by City, 2017"

Drinking Water

Water System Name	Pop. Served	Primary Water Source Type	Violations[1] Health Based	Violations[1] Monitoring/ Reporting
San Antonio Water System	1,663,221	Purchased Surface	0	0

Note: (1) Based on violation data from January 1, 2018 to December 31, 2018
Source: U.S. Environmental Protection Agency, Office of Ground Water and Drinking Water, Safe Drinking Water Information System (based on data extracted April 5, 2019)

Savannah, Georgia

Background

Savannah is at the mouth of the Savannah River on the border between Georgia and South Carolina. It was established in 1733 when General James Oglethorpe landed with a group of settlers in the sailing vessel *Anne, after a voyage of more than three months. City Hall now stands at the spot where Oglethorpe and his followers first camped on a small bluff overlooking the river.*

Savannah is unique among American cities in that it was extensively planned while Oglethorpe was still in England. Each new settler was given a package of property, including a town lot, a garden space, and an outlying farm area. The town was planned in quadrants, the north and south for residences, and the east and west for public buildings.

The quadrant design was inspired in part by considerations of public defense, given the unsettled character of relations with Native Americans, but in fact an early treaty between the settlers and the Creek Indian Chief Tomochichi allowed Savannah to develop quite peacefully, with little of the hostility between Europeans and Indians that marred much of the development elsewhere in the colonies.

Savannah was taken by the British during the American Revolution, and in the patriotic siege that followed, many lives were lost, including that of Revolutionary War hero Count Pulaski. Savannah was eventually retaken in 1782 by the American Generals Nathaniel Greene and Anthony Wayne. In the post-Revolutionary period, Savannah grew dramatically, its economic strength being driven in large part by Eli Whitney's cotton gin. As the world's leader in the cotton trade, Savannah also hosted a great development in export activity, and the first American steamboat built in the United States to cross the Atlantic was launched in its busy port.

Savannah's physical structure had been saved from the worst ravages of war, but the destruction of the area's infrastructure slowed its further development for an extended period. In the long period of slow recovery that followed, one of the great Savannah success stories was the establishment of the Girl Scouts in 1912 by Juliette Gordon Low.

In 1954, an extensive fire destroyed a large portion of the historic City Market, and the area was bulldozed to make room for a parking garage. The Historic Savannah Foundation has worked unceasingly since then to maintain and improve Savannah's considerable architectural charms. As a result, Savannah's Historic District was designated a Registered National Historic Landmark. Savannah has also been one of the favored sites for movie makers for decades. More than forty major movies have been filmed in Savannah including *Roots* (1976), *East of Eden* (1980), *Forrest Gump* (1994), *Midnight in the Garden of Good and Evil* (1997) and *The Legend of Bagger Vance* (2000), and a segment of the Colbert Report (2005).

The Port of Savannah, manufacturing, the military, and tourism have become the city's four major economic drivers in the twenty-first century. Its port facilities, operated by the Georgia Ports Authority, have seen notable growth in container tonnage in recent years. Garden City Terminal is the fourth largest container port in the United States, and the largest single-terminal operation in North America. Military installations in the area include Hunter Army Airfield and Fort Stewart military bases, employing nearly 50,000. Museums include Juliette Gordon Low Museum, Flannery O'Conner Childhood Home/Museum, Telfair Museum of Art and the Mighty 8th Air Forth Museum. Savannah was also the host city for the sailing competitions during the 1996 Summer Olympics held in Atlanta. The Savannah Book Festival is a popular annual book fair held on President's Day weekend.

The city's beauty draws not just tourists, but conventioneers. The Savannah International Trade & Convention Center is a state-of-the-art facility with more than 100,000 square feet of exhibition space, accommodating nearly 10,000 people.

Colleges and universities in the city include the Savannah College of Art and Design, Savannah State University, and South University.

Savannah's climate is subtropical, and is at risk for hurricanes. With hot summers and mild winters, however, the city is ideal for all-year outside activities.

Rankings

General Rankings

- *Insider* listed 33 places in the U.S. that were a must see vacation destination. Whether it is the great beaches, exploring a new city or experiencing the great outdoors, according to the website thisisinsider.com Savannah is a place to visit in 2018. *Insider, "33 Trips Everyone Should Take in the U.S. in 2018,"November 27, 2017*

- Savannah appeared on *Travel + Leisure's* list of the fifteen best cities in the United States. The city was ranked #3. Criteria: sights/landmarks; culture/arts; cuisine; people/friendliness; shopping; and value. *Travel + Leisure, "The World's Best Awards 2018" July 10, 2018*

- Based on more than 425,000 responses, *Condé Nast Traveler* ranked its readers' favorite cities in the U.S. The list was broken into cities over 1 million and cities under 1 million. Savannah ranked #3 in the small city category. *Condé Nast Traveler, Readers' Choice Awards 2018, "Best Small Cities in the U.S." October 9, 2018*

Business/Finance Rankings

- The personal finance site NerdWallet analyzed 183 American metropolitan areas with populations over 250,000 and more than 15,000 businesses to rank where entrepreneurs find the most success. Criteria included area economy, annual income, housing cost, unemployment rate, and the success rate of area businesses. Savannah ranked #112. *www.nerdwallet.com, "Best Places to Start a Business," April 27, 2015*

- Savannah was cited as one of America's top metros for new and expanded facility projects in 2018. The area ranked #9 in the mid-sized metro area category (population 200,000 to 1 million). *Site Selection, "Top Metros of 2018," March 2019*

- The Savannah metro area appeared on the Milken Institute "2018 Best Performing Cities" list. Rank: #108 out of 200 large metro areas. Criteria: job growth; wage and salary growth; high-tech output growth. *Milken Institute, "Best-Performing Cities 2018," January 24, 2019*

- *Forbes* ranked the 200 most populous metro areas to determine the nation's "Best Places for Business and Careers." The Savannah metro area was ranked #62. Criteria: costs (business and living); job growth (past and projected); income growth; quality of life; educational attainment (college and high school); projected economic growth; cultural and recreational opportunities; net migration patterns; number of highly ranked colleges. *Forbes, "The Best Places for Business and Careers 2018: Seattle Leads the Way," October 24, 2018*

Children/Family Rankings

- Savannah was selected as one of the most playful cities in the U.S. by KaBOOM! The organization's Playful City USA initiative honors cities and towns across the nation that have made their communities more playable. Criteria: pledging to integrate play as a solution to challenges in their communities; making it easy for children to get active and balanced play; creating more family-friendly and innovative communities as a result. *KaBOOM! National Campaign for Play, "2017 Playful City USA Communities"*

Culture/Performing Arts Rankings

- Savannah was selected as one of the ten best small U.S. cities and towns for moviemakers. Of cities with a population between 100,000 and 400,000 and towns with population less than 100,000, the area ranked #1. Criteria: film community and culture; access to equipment and facilities; film activity in 2018; number of film schools; tax incentives; ease of movement and traffic. *MovieMaker Magazine, "Best Places to Live and Work as a Moviemaker: 2019," January 17, 2019*

- Savannah was selected as one of "America's Favorite Cities." The city ranked #2 in the "Architecture" category. Respondents to an online survey were asked to rate their favorite place (population over 100,000) in over 65 categories. *Travelandleisure.com, "America's Favorite Cities for Architecture 2016," March 2, 2017*

Education Rankings

- Personal finance website *WalletHub* analyzed the 150 largest U.S. metropolitan statistical areas to determine where the most educated Americans are choosing to settle. Criteria: education quality and attainment gap; education levels; percentage of workers with degrees; public school quality rankings; quality and size of each metro area's universities. Savannah was ranked #58 (#1 = most educated city). *www.WalletHub.com, "2018's Most and Least Educated Cities in America, " July 24, 2018*

Environmental Rankings

- Savannah was highlighted as one of the cleanest metro areas for ozone air pollution in the U.S. during 2014 through 2016. The list represents cities with no monitored ozone air pollution in unhealthful ranges. *American Lung Association, State of the Air 2018*

Health/Fitness Rankings

- The Savannah metro area ranked #99 out of 189 in The Gallup-Healthways Well-Being Index. Criteria: purpose; social well being; financial health; community and physical health. Results are based on telephone interviews with adults, aged 18 and older, living in metropolitan areas in the 50 U.S. states and the District of Columbia. *Gallup-Healthways, "State of American Well-Being, 2017 Community Well-Being Rankings" March 2018*

Safety Rankings

- Allstate ranked the 200 largest cities in America in terms of driver safety. Savannah ranked #168. Criteria: internal property damage claims over a two-year period from January 2015 to December 2016. The report helps increase the importance of safety awareness behind the wheel. *Allstate, "Allstate America's Best Drivers Report, 2018" August 28, 2018*

- The National Insurance Crime Bureau ranked 382 metro areas in the U.S. in terms of per capita rates of vehicle theft. The Savannah metro area ranked #63 (#1 = highest rate). Criteria: number of vehicle theft offenses per 100,000 inhabitants in 2017. *National Insurance Crime Bureau, "Hot Spots 2017," July 12, 2018*

Seniors/Retirement Rankings

- From its Best Cities for Successful Aging indexes, the Milken Institute generated rankings for metropolitan areas, weighing data in nine categories—health care, wellness, living arrangements, transportation and convenience, financial characteristics, education, employment, community engagement, and overall livability. The Savannah metro area was ranked #99 overall in the small metro area category. *Milken Institute, "Best Cities for Successful Aging, 2017" March 14, 2017*

- Savannah was identified as one of the most popular places to retire by *Topretirements.com*. The list reflects the 100 cities that visitors to the website are most interested in for retirement, based on the number of times a city's review was viewed on the website. *Topretirements.com, "100 Most Popular Places to Retire for 2017," July 27, 2017*

Miscellaneous Rankings

- In its roundup of St. Patrick's Day parades "Gayot" listed the best festivals and parades of all things Irish. The festivities in Savannah as among the best. *www.gayot.com, "Best St. Patrick's Day Parades," March 17, 2018*

- In *Condé Nast Traveler* magazine's 2017 Readers' Choice Survey, Savannah made the top ten list of friendliest American cities. *www.cntraveler.com, "The Friendliest Cities in the U.S.," August 16, 2017*

- Savannah appeared on *Travel + Leisure's* list of America's cities with the most attractive people. Criteria: cities were selected by readers in their annual America's Favorite Cities survey. The city ranked #13 out of 10. *Travel + Leisure, "America's Most and Least Attractive People," September 2, 2016*

- Savannah was selected as one of America's best-mannered cities. The area ranked #2. The general public determined the winners by casting votes online. *The Charleston School of Protocol and Etiquette, "2014 Most Mannerly City in America Contest," February 3, 2015*

Business Environment

CITY FINANCES

City Government Finances

Component	2016 ($000)	2016 ($ per capita)
Total Revenues	417,515	2,866
Total Expenditures	395,669	2,716
Debt Outstanding	130,806	898
Cash and Securities[1]	452,591	3,107

Note: (1) Cash and security holdings of a government at the close of its fiscal year, including those of its dependent agencies, utilities, and liquor stores.
Source: U.S. Census Bureau, State & Local Government Finances 2016

City Government Revenue by Source

Source	2016 ($000)	2016 ($ per capita)	2016 (%)
General Revenue			
From Federal Government	9,061	62	2.2
From State Government	7,232	50	1.7
From Local Governments	93,637	643	22.4
Taxes			
Property	68,090	467	16.3
Sales and Gross Receipts	43,542	299	10.4
Personal Income	0	0	0.0
Corporate Income	0	0	0.0
Motor Vehicle License	0	0	0.0
Other Taxes	14,200	97	3.4
Current Charges	121,354	833	29.1
Liquor Store	0	0	0.0
Utility	41,028	282	9.8
Employee Retirement	0	0	0.0

Source: U.S. Census Bureau, State & Local Government Finances 2016

City Government Expenditures by Function

Function	2016 ($000)	2016 ($ per capita)	2016 (%)
General Direct Expenditures			
Air Transportation	29,015	199	7.3
Corrections	0	0	0.0
Education	0	0	0.0
Employment Security Administration	0	0	0.0
Financial Administration	5,545	38	1.4
Fire Protection	32,812	225	8.3
General Public Buildings	11,949	82	3.0
Governmental Administration, Other	19,042	130	4.8
Health	0	0	0.0
Highways	26,416	181	6.7
Hospitals	0	0	0.0
Housing and Community Development	26,313	180	6.7
Interest on General Debt	2,858	19	0.7
Judicial and Legal	2,188	15	0.6
Libraries	0	0	0.0
Parking	7,618	52	1.9
Parks and Recreation	22,291	153	5.6
Police Protection	62,957	432	15.9
Public Welfare	968	6	0.2
Sewerage	32,663	224	8.3
Solid Waste Management	23,216	159	5.9
Veterans' Services	0	0	0.0
Liquor Store	0	0	0.0
Utility	39,025	267	9.9
Employee Retirement	0	0	0.0

Source: U.S. Census Bureau, State & Local Government Finances 2016

DEMOGRAPHICS

Population Growth

Area	1990 Census	2000 Census	2010 Census	2017* Estimate	Population Growth (%)	
					1990-2017	2010-2017
City	138,038	131,510	136,286	145,094	5.1	6.5
MSA[1]	258,060	293,000	347,611	377,476	46.3	8.6
U.S.	248,709,873	281,421,906	308,745,538	321,004,407	29.1	4.0

Note: (1) Figures cover the Savannah, GA Metropolitan Statistical Area—see Appendix B for areas included; (*) 2013-2017 5-year estimated population
Source: U.S. Census Bureau, 1990 Census, Census 2000, Census 2010, 2013-2017 American Community Survey 5-Year Estimates

Household Size

Area	Persons in Household (%)							Average Household Size
	One	Two	Three	Four	Five	Six	Seven or More	
City	33.7	33.4	15.6	9.3	4.8	1.9	1.2	2.50
MSA[1]	27.3	34.3	17.1	12.7	5.6	1.9	1.1	2.60
U.S.	27.7	33.8	15.7	13.0	6.0	2.3	1.4	2.60

Note: (1) Figures cover the Savannah, GA Metropolitan Statistical Area—see Appendix B for areas included
Source: U.S. Census Bureau, 2013-2017 American Community Survey 5-Year Estimates

Race

Area	White Alone[2] (%)	Black Alone[2] (%)	Asian Alone[2] (%)	AIAN[3] Alone[2] (%)	NHOPI[4] Alone[2] (%)	Other Race Alone[2] (%)	Two or More Races (%)
City	39.1	54.7	2.2	0.2	0.1	1.0	2.6
MSA[1]	59.6	33.5	2.2	0.3	0.1	1.6	2.6
U.S.	73.0	12.7	5.4	0.8	0.2	4.8	3.1

Note: (1) Figures cover the Savannah, GA Metropolitan Statistical Area—see Appendix B for areas included; (2) Alone is defined as not being in combination with one or more other races; (3) American Indian and Alaska Native; (4) Native Hawaiian and Other Pacific Islander
Source: U.S. Census Bureau, 2013-2017 American Community Survey 5-Year Estimates

Hispanic or Latino Origin

Area	Total (%)	Mexican (%)	Puerto Rican (%)	Cuban (%)	Other (%)
City	4.8	1.8	1.2	0.3	1.5
MSA[1]	5.9	2.7	1.4	0.2	1.6
U.S.	17.6	11.1	1.7	0.7	4.1

Note: Persons of Hispanic or Latino origin can be of any race; (1) Figures cover the Savannah, GA Metropolitan Statistical Area—see Appendix B for areas included
Source: U.S. Census Bureau, 2013-2017 American Community Survey 5-Year Estimates

Segregation

Type	Segregation Indices[1]				Percent Change		
	1990	2000	2010	2010 Rank[2]	1990-2000	1990-2010	2000-2010
Black/White	n/a	n/a	n/a	n/a	n/a	n/a	n/a
Asian/White	n/a	n/a	n/a	n/a	n/a	n/a	n/a
Hispanic/White	n/a	n/a	n/a	n/a	n/a	n/a	n/a

Note: All figures cover the Metropolitan Statistical Area—see Appendix B for areas included; Figures are based on an analysis of 1990, 2000, and 2010 Census Decennial Census tract data by William H. Frey, Brookings Institution and the University of Michigan Social Science Data Analysis Network. In this analysis all racial groups (whites, blacks, and asians) are non-Hispanic members of those races. Hispanics are shown as a separate category; (1) Segregation Indices are Dissimilarity Indices that measure the degree to which the minority group is distributed differently than whites across census tracts. They range from 0 (complete integration) to 100 (complete segregation) where the value indicates the percentage of the minority group that needs to move to be distributed exactly like whites; (2) Ranges from 1 (most segregated) to 102 (least segregated); n/a not available.
Source: www.CensusScope.org

Ancestry

Area	German	Irish	English	American	Italian	Polish	French[2]	Scottish	Dutch
City	6.5	7.4	4.9	3.7	2.8	1.3	1.4	1.4	0.6
MSA[1]	9.6	10.6	7.2	6.7	3.4	1.4	1.9	2.0	0.7
U.S.	14.1	10.1	7.5	6.6	5.3	2.9	2.5	1.7	1.3

Note: Figures are the percentage of the total population reporting a particular ancestry. The nine most commonly reported ancestries in the U.S. are shown. Figures include multiple ancestries (e.g. if a person reported being Irish and Italian, they were included in both columns); (1) Figures cover the Savannah, GA Metropolitan Statistical Area—see Appendix B for areas included; (2) Excludes Basque
Source: U.S. Census Bureau, 2013-2017 American Community Survey 5-Year Estimates

Foreign-Born Population

Area	Percent of Population Born in								
	Any Foreign Country	Asia	Mexico	Europe	Carribean	Central America[2]	South America	Africa	Canada
City	5.6	2.1	0.8	1.0	0.4	0.3	0.5	0.3	0.2
MSA[1]	5.7	1.9	1.1	0.9	0.4	0.4	0.4	0.3	0.2
U.S.	13.4	4.1	3.6	1.5	1.3	1.0	0.9	0.6	0.3

Note: (1) Figures cover the Savannah, GA Metropolitan Statistical Area—see Appendix B for areas included; (2) Excludes Mexico.
Source: U.S. Census Bureau, 2013-2017 American Community Survey 5-Year Estimates

Marital Status

Area	Never Married	Now Married[2]	Separated	Widowed	Divorced
City	46.7	31.2	2.7	6.4	13.1
MSA[1]	34.7	45.1	2.1	5.8	12.2
U.S.	33.1	48.2	2.0	5.8	10.9

Note: Figures are percentages and cover the population 15 years of age and older; (1) Figures cover the Savannah, GA Metropolitan Statistical Area—see Appendix B for areas included; (2) Excludes separated
Source: U.S. Census Bureau, 2013-2017 American Community Survey 5-Year Estimates

Disability by Age

Area	All Ages	Under 18 Years Old	18 to 64 Years Old	65 Years and Over
City	14.4	5.5	11.7	42.7
MSA[1]	13.2	4.9	11.1	38.5
U.S.	12.6	4.2	10.3	35.5

Note: Figures show percent of the civilian noninstitutionalized population that reported having a disability. Disability status is determined from six types of difficulty: vision, hearing, cognitive, ambulatory, self-care, and independent living. For children under 5 years old, hearing and vision difficulty are used to determine disability status. For children between the ages of 5 and 14, disability status is determined from hearing, vision, cognitive, ambulatory, and self-care difficulties. For people aged 15 years and older, they are considered to have a disability if they have difficulty with any one of the six difficulty types; Note: (1) Figures cover the Savannah, GA Metropolitan Statistical Area—see Appendix B for areas included
Source: U.S. Census Bureau, 2013-2017 American Community Survey 5-Year Estimates

Age

Area	Percent of Population									Median Age
	Under Age 5	Age 5–19	Age 20–34	Age 35–44	Age 45–54	Age 55–64	Age 65–74	Age 75–84	Age 85+	
City	6.5	19.3	28.3	11.3	10.8	10.8	7.2	3.7	1.9	32.3
MSA[1]	6.7	19.8	23.5	12.8	12.4	11.7	8.0	3.6	1.6	35.0
U.S.	6.2	19.5	20.7	12.7	13.4	12.7	8.6	4.4	1.9	37.8

Note: (1) Figures cover the Savannah, GA Metropolitan Statistical Area—see Appendix B for areas included
Source: U.S. Census Bureau, 2013-2017 American Community Survey 5-Year Estimates

Gender

Area	Males	Females	Males per 100 Females
City	68,627	76,467	89.7
MSA[1]	183,354	194,122	94.5
U.S.	158,018,753	162,985,654	97.0

Note: (1) Figures cover the Savannah, GA Metropolitan Statistical Area—see Appendix B for areas included
Source: U.S. Census Bureau, 2013-2017 American Community Survey 5-Year Estimates

Religious Groups by Family

Area	Catholic	Baptist	Non-Den.	Methodist[2]	Lutheran	LDS[3]	Pente-costal	Presby-terian[4]	Muslim[5]	Judaism
MSA[1]	7.1	19.7	6.9	8.9	1.6	1.0	2.4	1.0	0.2	0.8
U.S.	19.1	9.3	4.0	4.0	2.3	2.0	1.9	1.6	0.8	0.7

Note: Figures are the number of adherents as a percentage of the total population; (1) Figures cover the Savannah, GA Metropolitan Statistical Area—see Appendix B for areas included; (2) Methodist/Pietist; (3) Latter Day Saints; (4) Reformed; (5) Figures are estimates
Source: Association of Statisticians of American Religious Bodies, 2010 U.S. Religion Census: Religious Congregations & Membership Study

Religious Groups by Tradition

Area	Catholic	Evangelical Protestant	Mainline Protestant	Other Tradition	Black Protestant	Orthodox
MSA[1]	7.1	25.1	9.5	2.6	8.6	0.1
U.S.	19.1	16.2	7.3	4.3	1.6	0.3

Note: Figures are the number of adherents as a percentage of the total population; (1) Figures cover the Savannah, GA Metropolitan Statistical Area—see Appendix B for areas included
Source: Association of Statisticians of American Religious Bodies, 2010 U.S. Religion Census: Religious Congregations & Membership Study

ECONOMY

Gross Metropolitan Product

Area	2016	2017	2018	2019	Rank[2]
MSA[1]	17.9	18.6	19.1	20.0	135

Note: Figures are in billions of dollars; (1) Figures cover the Savannah, GA Metropolitan Statistical Area—see Appendix B for areas included; (2) Rank is based on 2017 data and ranges from 1 to 381
Source: U.S. Conference of Mayors, U.S. Metro Economies: Economic Growth & Full Employment, June 2018

Economic Growth

Area	2017-2018 (%)	2019-2020 (%)	2021-2022 (%)
MSA[1]	1.3	1.7	0.8

Note: Figures are real gross metropolitan product (GMP) growth rates and represent average annual percent change; (1) Figures cover the Savannah, GA Metropolitan Statistical Area—see Appendix B for areas included
Source: U.S. Conference of Mayors, U.S. Metro Economies: Economic Growth & Full Employment, June 2018

Metropolitan Area Exports

Area	2012	2013	2014	2015	2016	2017	Rank[2]
MSA[1]	4,116.5	5,436.4	5,093.4	5,447.5	4,263.4	4,472.0	59

Note: Figures are in millions of dollars; (1) Figures cover the Savannah, GA Metropolitan Statistical Area—see Appendix B for areas included; (2) Rank is based on 2017 data and ranges from 1 to 387
Source: U.S. Department of Commerce, International Trade Administration, Office of Trade and Economic Analysis, Industry and Analysis, Exports by Metropolitan Area, extracted March 25, 2019

Building Permits

Area	Single-Family			Multi-Family			Total		
	2016	2017	Pct. Chg.	2016	2017	Pct. Chg.	2016	2017	Pct. Chg.
City	300	384	28.0	0	0	0.0	300	384	28.0
MSA[1]	1,769	1,898	7.3	202	220	8.9	1,971	2,118	7.5
U.S.	750,800	820,000	9.2	455,800	462,000	1.4	1,206,600	1,282,000	6.2

Note: (1) Figures cover the Savannah, GA Metropolitan Statistical Area—see Appendix B for areas included; Figures represent new, privately-owned housing units authorized (unadjusted data); All permit data are based on estimates with imputation
Source: U.S. Census Bureau, Manufacturing, Mining, and Construction Statistics, Building Permits, 2016, 2017

Bankruptcy Filings

Area	Business Filings			Nonbusiness Filings		
	2017	2018	% Chg.	2017	2018	% Chg.
Chatham County	12	8	-33.3	1,252	1,263	0.9
U.S.	23,157	22,232	-4.0	765,863	751,186	-1.9

Note: Business filings include Chapter 7, Chapter 11, Chapter 12, and Chapter 13; Nonbusiness filings include Chapter 7, Chapter 11, and Chapter 13
Source: Administrative Office of the U.S. Courts, Business and Nonbusiness Bankruptcy, County Cases Commenced by Chapter of the Bankruptcy Code, During the 12-Month Period Ending December 31, 2017 and Business and Nonbusiness Bankruptcy, County Cases Commenced by Chapter of the Bankruptcy Code, During the 12-Month Period Ending December 31, 2018

Housing Vacancy Rates

Area	Gross Vacancy Rate[2] (%)			Year-Round Vacancy Rate[3] (%)			Rental Vacancy Rate[4] (%)			Homeowner Vacancy Rate[5] (%)		
	2016	2017	2018	2016	2017	2018	2016	2017	2018	2016	2017	2018
MSA[1]	n/a	n/a	n/a	n/a	n/a	n/a	n/a	n/a	n/a	n/a	n/a	n/a
U.S.	12.8	12.7	12.3	9.9	9.9	9.7	6.9	7.2	6.9	1.7	1.6	1.5

Note: (1) Figures cover the Savannah, GA Metropolitan Statistical Area—see Appendix B for areas included; (2) The percentage of the total housing inventory that is vacant; (3) The percentage of the housing inventory (excluding seasonal units) that is year-round vacant; (4) The percentage of rental inventory that is vacant for rent; (5) The percentage of homeowner inventory that is vacant for sale; n/a not available
Source: U.S. Census Bureau, Housing Vacancies and Homeownership Annual Statistics: 2016, 2017, 2018

INCOME

Income

Area	Per Capita ($)	Median Household ($)	Average Household ($)
City	22,497	39,386	56,370
MSA[1]	28,566	55,021	74,008
U.S.	31,177	57,652	81,283

Note: (1) Figures cover the Savannah, GA Metropolitan Statistical Area—see Appendix B for areas included
Source: U.S. Census Bureau, 2013-2017 American Community Survey 5-Year Estimates

Household Income Distribution

Area	Percent of Households Earning							
	Under $15,000	$15,000 -$24,999	$25,000 -$34,999	$35,000 -$49,999	$50,000 -$74,999	$75,000 -$99,999	$100,000 -$149,999	$150,000 and up
City	19.7	13.4	12.0	15.2	15.8	9.6	8.9	5.4
MSA[1]	12.4	9.9	9.6	13.7	18.0	12.9	13.8	9.7
U.S.	11.6	9.8	9.5	13.0	17.7	12.3	14.1	12.1

Note: (1) Figures cover the Savannah, GA Metropolitan Statistical Area—see Appendix B for areas included
Source: U.S. Census Bureau, 2013-2017 American Community Survey 5-Year Estimates

Poverty Rate

Area	All Ages	Under 18 Years Old	18 to 64 Years Old	65 Years and Over
City	24.0	34.8	22.9	11.7
MSA[1]	15.8	22.6	14.9	8.0
U.S.	14.6	20.3	13.7	9.3

Note: Figures are percentage of people whose income during the past 12 months was below the poverty level; (1) Figures cover the Savannah, GA Metropolitan Statistical Area—see Appendix B for areas included
Source: U.S. Census Bureau, 2013-2017 American Community Survey 5-Year Estimates

EMPLOYMENT

Labor Force and Employment

Area	Civilian Labor Force			Workers Employed		
	Dec. 2017	Dec. 2018	% Chg.	Dec. 2017	Dec. 2018	% Chg.
City	67,349	66,715	-0.9	64,307	64,028	-0.4
MSA[1]	184,906	183,341	-0.8	177,538	176,766	-0.4
U.S.	159,880,000	162,510,000	1.6	153,602,000	156,481,000	1.9

Note: Data is not seasonally adjusted and covers workers 16 years of age and older; (1) Figures cover the Savannah, GA Metropolitan Statistical Area—see Appendix B for areas included
Source: Bureau of Labor Statistics, Local Area Unemployment Statistics

Unemployment Rate

Area	2018											
	Jan.	Feb.	Mar.	Apr.	May	Jun.	Jul.	Aug.	Sep.	Oct.	Nov.	Dec.
City	4.9	4.7	4.2	3.8	3.7	4.5	4.2	4.1	3.5	4.0	3.7	4.0
MSA[1]	4.2	4.1	3.8	3.4	3.3	4.0	3.7	3.6	3.1	3.5	3.2	3.6
U.S.	4.5	4.4	4.1	3.7	3.6	4.2	4.1	3.9	3.6	3.5	3.5	3.7

Note: Data is not seasonally adjusted and covers workers 16 years of age and older; (1) Figures cover the
Savannah, GA Metropolitan Statistical Area—see Appendix B for areas included
Source: Bureau of Labor Statistics, Local Area Unemployment Statistics

Average Wages

Occupation	$/Hr.	Occupation	$/Hr.
Accountants and Auditors	33.80	Maids and Housekeeping Cleaners	9.90
Automotive Mechanics	23.40	Maintenance and Repair Workers	17.50
Bookkeepers	18.40	Marketing Managers	48.90
Carpenters	21.50	Nuclear Medicine Technologists	n/a
Cashiers	9.70	Nurses, Licensed Practical	19.70
Clerks, General Office	15.20	Nurses, Registered	29.80
Clerks, Receptionists/Information	13.20	Nursing Assistants	12.10
Clerks, Shipping/Receiving	17.60	Packers and Packagers, Hand	10.30
Computer Programmers	35.30	Physical Therapists	37.80
Computer Systems Analysts	36.80	Postal Service Mail Carriers	24.30
Computer User Support Specialists	22.30	Real Estate Brokers	n/a
Cooks, Restaurant	11.30	Retail Salespersons	12.20
Dentists	93.20	Sales Reps., Exc. Tech./Scientific	38.10
Electrical Engineers	47.20	Sales Reps., Tech./Scientific	45.80
Electricians	22.40	Secretaries, Exc. Legal/Med./Exec.	16.30
Financial Managers	47.50	Security Guards	15.50
First-Line Supervisors/Managers, Sales	19.90	Surgeons	n/a
Food Preparation Workers	10.20	Teacher Assistants*	11.60
General and Operations Managers	49.50	Teachers, Elementary School*	25.40
Hairdressers/Cosmetologists	11.80	Teachers, Secondary School*	27.00
Internists, General	n/a	Telemarketers	n/a
Janitors and Cleaners	11.60	Truck Drivers, Heavy/Tractor-Trailer	21.30
Landscaping/Groundskeeping Workers	12.70	Truck Drivers, Light/Delivery Svcs.	16.20
Lawyers	47.60	Waiters and Waitresses	9.90

Note: Wage data covers the Savannah, GA Metropolitan Statistical Area—see Appendix B for areas included;
(*) Hourly wages for elementary/secondary school teachers and teacher assistants were calculated by the
editors from annual wage data based on a 40 hour work week; n/a not available.
Source: Bureau of Labor Statistics, Metro Area Occupational Employment & Wage Estimates, May 2018

Employment by Occupation

Occupation Classification	City (%)	MSA[1] (%)	U.S. (%)
Management, Business, Science, and Arts	31.2	35.7	37.4
Natural Resources, Construction, and Maintenance	7.0	9.3	8.9
Production, Transportation, and Material Moving	12.2	12.9	12.2
Sales and Office	24.1	22.5	23.5
Service	25.5	19.6	18.0

Note: Figures cover employed civilians 16 years of age and older; (1) Figures cover the Savannah, GA
Metropolitan Statistical Area—see Appendix B for areas included
Source: U.S. Census Bureau, 2013-2017 American Community Survey 5-Year Estimates

Employment by Industry

Sector	MSA[1]		U.S.
	Number of Employees	Percent of Total	Percent of Total
Construction, Mining, and Logging	8,800	4.8	5.3
Education and Health Services	26,500	14.3	15.9
Financial Activities	6,500	3.5	5.7
Government	25,000	13.5	15.1
Information	1,900	1.0	1.9
Leisure and Hospitality	26,200	14.2	10.7
Manufacturing	18,800	10.2	8.5
Other Services	7,200	3.9	3.9
Professional and Business Services	20,400	11.0	14.1
Retail Trade	22,800	12.3	10.8
Transportation, Warehousing, and Utilities	14,200	7.7	4.2
Wholesale Trade	6,600	3.6	3.9

Note: Figures are non-farm employment as of December 2018. Figures are not seasonally adjusted and include workers 16 years of age and older; (1) Figures cover the Savannah, GA Metropolitan Statistical Area—see Appendix B for areas included
Source: Bureau of Labor Statistics, Current Employment Statistics, Employment, Hours, and Earnings

Occupations with Greatest Projected Employment Growth: 2018 – 2020

Occupation[1]	2018 Employment	2020 Projected Employment	Numeric Employment Change	Percent Employment Change
Combined Food Preparation and Serving Workers, Including Fast Food	115,500	124,220	8,720	7.5
Laborers and Freight, Stock, and Material Movers, Hand	119,650	127,750	8,100	6.8
General and Operations Managers	96,530	101,830	5,300	5.5
Waiters and Waitresses	81,500	86,240	4,740	5.8
Construction Laborers	40,040	44,600	4,560	11.4
Customer Service Representatives	103,570	107,780	4,210	4.1
Retail Salespersons	141,820	146,020	4,200	3.0
Heavy and Tractor-Trailer Truck Drivers	58,780	62,290	3,510	6.0
Janitors and Cleaners, Except Maids and Housekeeping Cleaners	56,440	59,660	3,220	5.7
Office Clerks, General	88,900	91,910	3,010	3.4

Note: Projections cover Georgia; (1) Sorted by numeric employment change
Source: www.projectionscentral.com, State Occupational Projections, 2018–2020 Short-Term Projections

Fastest Growing Occupations: 2018 – 2020

Occupation[1]	2018 Employment	2020 Projected Employment	Numeric Employment Change	Percent Employment Change
Helpers—Pipelayers, Plumbers, Pipefitters, and Steamfitters	2,220	2,640	420	18.9
Helpers—Brickmasons, Blockmasons, Stonemasons, and Tile and Marble Setters	270	320	50	18.5
Mechanical Door Repairers	490	580	90	18.4
Structural Iron and Steel Workers	1,410	1,660	250	17.7
Elevator Installers and Repairers	1,190	1,400	210	17.6
Costume Attendants	290	340	50	17.2
Helpers—Electricians	4,070	4,760	690	17.0
Glaziers	1,130	1,320	190	16.8
Fence Erectors	550	640	90	16.4
Cement Masons and Concrete Finishers	3,190	3,710	520	16.3

Note: Projections cover Georgia; (1) Sorted by percent employment change and excludes occupations with numeric employment change less than 50
Source: www.projectionscentral.com, State Occupational Projections, 2018–2020 Short-Term Projections

TAXES

State Corporate Income Tax Rates

State	Tax Rate (%)	Income Brackets ($)	Num. of Brackets	Financial Institution Tax Rate (%)[a]	Federal Income Tax Ded.
Georgia	5.75	Flat rate	1	5.75	No

Note: Tax rates as of January 1, 2019; (a) Rates listed are the corporate income tax rate applied to financial institutions or excise taxes based on income. Some states have other taxes based upon the value of deposits or shares.
Source: Federation of Tax Administrators, Range of State Corporate Income Tax Rates, January 1, 2019

State Individual Income Tax Rates

State	Tax Rate (%)	Income Brackets ($)	Personal Exemptions ($)			Standard Ded. ($)	
			Single	Married	Depend.	Single	Married
Georgia	1.0 - 5.75	750 - 7,001 (i)	2,700	7,400	3,000	4,600	6,000

Note: Tax rates as of January 1, 2019; Local- and county-level taxes are not included; n/a not applicable; Federal income tax is not deductible on state income tax returns; (i) The Georgia income brackets reported are for single individuals. For married couples filing jointly, the same tax rates apply to income brackets ranging from $1,000, to $10,000.
Source: Federation of Tax Administrators, State Individual Income Tax Rates, January 1, 2019

Various State Sales and Excise Tax Rates

State	State Sales Tax (%)	Gasoline[1] (¢/gal.)	Cigarette[2] ($/pack)	Spirits[3] ($/gal.)	Wine[4] ($/gal.)	Beer[5] ($/gal.)	Recreational Marijuana (%)
Georgia	4	35.28	0.37	3.79 (f)	1.51 (l)	0.48 (q)(r)	Not legal

Note: All tax rates as of January 1, 2019; (1) The American Petroleum Institute has developed a methodology for determining the average tax rate on a gallon of fuel. Rates may include any of the following: excise taxes, environmental fees, storage tank fees, other fees or taxes, general sales tax, and local taxes. In states where gasoline is subject to the general sales tax, or where the fuel tax is based on the average sale price, the average rate determined by API is sensitive to changes in the price of gasoline. States that fully or partially apply general sales taxes to gasoline: CA, CO, GA, IL, IN, MI, NY; (2) The federal excise tax of $1.0066 per pack and local taxes are not included; (3) Rates are those applicable to off-premise sales of 40% alcohol by volume (a.b.v.) distilled spirits in 750ml containers. Local excise taxes are excluded; (4) Rates are those applicable to off-premise sales of 11% a.b.v. non-carbonated wine in 750ml containers; (5) Rates are those applicable to off-premise sales of 4.7% a.b.v. beer in 12 ounce containers; (f) Different rates also applicable according to alcohol content, place of production, size of container, or place purchased (on- or off-premise or onboard airlines); (l) Different rates also applicable to alcohol content, place of production, size of container, place purchased (on- or off-premise or on board airlines) or type of wine (carbonated, vermouth, etc.); (q) Different rates also applicable according to alcohol content, place of production, size of container, or place purchased (on- or off-premise or onboard airlines); (r) Includes statewide local rate in Alabama ($0.52) and Georgia ($0.53).
Source: Tax Foundation, 2019 Facts & Figures: How Does Your State Compare?

State Business Tax Climate Index Rankings

State	Overall Rank	Corporate Tax Rank	Individual Income Tax Rank	Sales Tax Rank	Unemployment Insurance Tax Rank	Property Tax Rank
Georgia	33	8	38	29	38	24

Note: The index is a measure of how each state's tax laws affect economic performance. The lower the rank, the more favorable a state's tax system is for business. States without a given tax are given a ranking of 1. The scores/rankings for the District of Columbia do not affect other states. The 2019 index represents the tax climate as of July 1, 2018.
Source: Tax Foundation, State Business Tax Climate Index 2019

COMMERCIAL UTILITIES

Typical Monthly Electric Bills

Area	Commercial Service ($/month)		Industrial Service ($/month)	
	1,500 kWh	40 kW demand 14,000 kWh	1,000 kW demand 200,000 kWh	50,000 kW demand 32,500,000 kWh
City	258	1,598	31,467	2,254,556
Average[1]	203	1,619	25,886	2,540,077

Note: Figures are based on annualized rates; (1) Average based on 187 utilities surveyed
Source: Edison Electric Institute, Typical Bills and Average Rates Report, Summer 2018

TRANSPORTATION

Means of Transportation to Work

Area	Car/Truck/Van		Public Transportation			Bicycle	Walked	Other Means	Worked at Home
	Drove Alone	Car-pooled	Bus	Subway	Railroad				
City	73.6	10.1	4.2	0.1	0.0	2.1	4.2	2.0	3.7
MSA[1]	80.4	9.3	2.0	0.0	0.0	0.9	2.2	1.6	3.7
U.S.	76.4	9.2	2.5	1.9	0.6	0.6	2.7	1.3	4.7

Note: Figures are percentages and cover workers 16 years of age and older; (1) Figures cover the Savannah, GA Metropolitan Statistical Area—see Appendix B for areas included
Source: U.S. Census Bureau, 2013-2017 American Community Survey 5-Year Estimates

Travel Time to Work

Area	Less Than 10 Minutes	10 to 19 Minutes	20 to 29 Minutes	30 to 44 Minutes	45 to 59 Minutes	60 to 89 Minutes	90 Minutes or More
City	17.7	38.1	21.8	14.4	4.1	2.6	1.3
MSA[1]	11.9	30.7	24.0	21.3	6.7	4.0	1.4
U.S.	12.7	28.9	20.9	20.5	8.1	6.2	2.7

Note: Note: Figures are percentages and include workers 16 years old and over; (1) Figures cover the Savannah, GA Metropolitan Statistical Area—see Appendix B for areas included
Source: U.S. Census Bureau, 2013-2017 American Community Survey 5-Year Estimates

Freeway Travel Time Index

Area	1985	1990	1995	2000	2005	2010	2014
Urban Area Rank[1,2]	n/a	n/a	n/a	n/a	n/a	n/a	n/a
Urban Area Index[1]	n/a	n/a	n/a	n/a	n/a	n/a	n/a
Average Index[3]	1.09	1.11	1.14	1.17	1.20	1.19	1.20

Note: Freeway Travel Time Index—the ratio of travel time in the peak period to the travel time at free-flow conditions. For example, a value of 1.30 indicates a 20-minute free-flow trip takes 26 minutes in the peak (20 minutes x 1.30 = 26 minutes); (1) Data for the Savannah, GA urban area was not available; (2) Rank is based on 101 urban areas (#1 = highest travel time index); (3) Average of 101 urban areas
Source: Texas Transportation Institute, 2015 Urban Mobility Scorecard, August 2015

Freeway Commuter Stress Index

Area	1985	1990	1995	2000	2005	2010	2014
Urban Area Rank[1,2]	n/a	n/a	n/a	n/a	n/a	n/a	n/a
Urban Area Index[1]	n/a	n/a	n/a	n/a	n/a	n/a	n/a
Average Index[3]	1.13	1.16	1.19	1.22	1.25	1.24	1.25

Note: The Freeway Commuter Stress Index is the same as the Freeway Travel Time Index (see table above) except that it includes only the travel in the peak directions during the peak periods; the TTI includes travel in all directions during the peak period. Thus, the CSI is more indicative of the work trip experienced by each commuter on a daily basis; (1) Data for the Savannah, GA urban area was not available; (2) Rank is based on 101 urban areas (#1 = highest travel time index); (3) Average of 101 urban areas
Source: Texas Transportation Institute, 2015 Urban Mobility Scorecard, August 2015

Public Transportation

Agency Name / Mode of Transportation	Vehicles Operated in Maximum Service[1]	Annual Unlinked Passenger Trips[2] (in thous.)	Annual Passenger Miles[3] (in thous.)
Chatham Area Transit Authority (CAT)			
Bus (directly operated)	52	3,168.4	8,174.6
Demand Response (directly operated)	24	68.2	607.7
Demand Response (purchased transportation)	8	39.6	372.7
Ferryboat (directly operated)	2	665.2	252.8

Note: (1) The number of revenue vehicles operated by the given mode and type of service to meet the annual maximum service requirement. This is the revenue vehicle count during the peak season of the year; on the week and day that maximum service is provided. Vehicles operated in maximum service (VOMS) exclude atypical days and one-time special events; (2) The number of passengers who boarded public transportation vehicles. Passengers are counted each time they board a vehicle no matter how many vehicles they use to travel from their origin to their destination. (3) The sum of the distances ridden by all passengers during the entire fiscal year.
Source: Federal Transit Administration, National Transit Database, 2017

Air Transportation

Airport Name and Code / Type of Service	Passenger Airlines[1]	Passenger Enplanements	Freight Carriers[2]	Freight (lbs)
Savannah International (SAV)				
Domestic service (U.S. carriers - 2018)	22	1,345,760	9	7,587,641
International service (U.S. carriers - 2017)	2	9	0	0

Note: (1) Includes all U.S.-based major, minor and commuter airlines that carried at least one passenger during the year; (2) Includes all U.S.-based airlines and freight carriers that transported at least one pound of freight during the year.
Source: Bureau of Transportation Statistics, The Intermodal Transportation Database, Air Carriers: T-100 Domestic Market (U.S. Carriers), 2018; Bureau of Transportation Statistics, The Intermodal Transportation Database, Air Carriers: T-100 International Market (U.S. Carriers), 2017

Other Transportation Statistics

Major Highways:	I-16; I-95
Amtrak Service:	Yes
Major Waterways/Ports:	Savannah River (Atlantic Ocean)

Source: Amtrak.com; Google Maps

BUSINESSES

Major Business Headquarters

Company Name	Industry	Rankings Fortune[1]	Rankings Forbes[2]
Colonial Group	Oil & Gas Operations	-	161

Note: (1) Companies that produce a 10-K are ranked 1 to 500 based on 2017 revenue; (2) All private companies with at least $2 billion in annual revenue through the end of their most current fiscal year are ranked 1 to 229; companies listed are headquartered in the city; dashes indicate no ranking
Source: Fortune, "Fortune 500," June 2018; Forbes, "America's Largest Private Companies," 2018 Rankings

Minority- and Women-Owned Businesses

Group	All Firms		Firms with Paid Employees			
	Firms	Sales ($000)	Firms	Sales ($000)	Employees	Payroll ($000)
AIAN[1]	122	(s)	25	(s)	250 - 499	(s)
Asian	533	212,063	229	204,775	2,011	50,172
Black	4,256	255,943	198	184,075	1,262	29,080
Hispanic	275	178,705	67	173,166	815	33,660
NHOPI[2]	n/a	n/a	n/a	n/a	n/a	n/a
Women	5,346	552,091	609	467,126	4,708	114,559
All Firms	12,676	15,450,676	3,535	15,065,181	75,250	2,709,246

Note: Figures cover firms located in the city; minority- and women-owned business are defined as firms in which the corresponding group own 51% or more of the stock or equity of the company; (1) American Indian and Alaska Native; (2) Native Hawaiian and Other Pacific Islander; (s) estimates are suppressed when publication standards are not met; n/a not available
Source: U.S. Census Bureau, 2012 Economic Census, Survey of Business Owners

HOTELS & CONVENTION CENTERS

Hotels, Motels and Vacation Rentals

Area	5 Star Num.	5 Star Pct.[3]	4 Star Num.	4 Star Pct.[3]	3 Star Num.	3 Star Pct.[3]	2 Star Num.	2 Star Pct.[3]	1 Star Num.	1 Star Pct.[3]	Not Rated Num.	Not Rated Pct.[3]
City[1]	1	0.1	66	6.1	225	20.8	111	10.2	3	0.3	678	62.5
Total[2]	286	0.4	5,236	7.1	16,715	22.6	10,259	13.9	293	0.4	41,056	55.6

Note: (1) Figures cover Savannah and vicinity; (2) Figures cover all 100 cities in this book; (3) Percentage of hotels which have a given star rating; Star ratings are determined by expedia.com and offer an indication of the general quality of a particular hotel.
Source: www.expedia.com, April 3, 2019

Major Convention Centers

Name	Overall Space (sq. ft.)	Exhibit Space (sq. ft.)	Meeting Space (sq. ft.)	Meeting Rooms
Savannah Intl Trade & Convention Center	330,000	100,000	50,000	13

Note: Table includes convention centers located in the Savannah, GA metro area
Source: Original research

Living Environment

COST OF LIVING

Cost of Living Index

Composite Index	Groceries	Housing	Utilities	Trans-portation	Health Care	Misc. Goods/ Services
88.1	93.7	64.8	96.5	97.0	99.3	99.6

Note: The Cost of Living Index measures regional differences in the cost of consumer goods and services, excluding taxes and non-consumer expenditures, for professional and managerial households in the top income quintile. It is based on more than 50,000 prices covering almost 60 different items for which prices are collected three times a year by chambers of commerce, economic development organizations or university applied economic centers in each participating urban area. The numbers shown should be read as a percentage above or below the national average of 100. For example, a value of 115.4 in the groceries column indicates that grocery prices are 15.4% higher than the national average. Small differences in the index numbers should not be interpreted as significant; Figures cover the Savannah GA urban area.
Source: The Council for Community and Economic Research, ACCRA Cost of Living Index, 2018

Grocery Prices

Area[1]	T-Bone Steak ($/pound)	Frying Chicken ($/pound)	Whole Milk ($/half gal.)	Eggs ($/dozen)	Orange Juice ($/64 oz.)	Coffee ($/11.5 oz.)
City[2]	11.11	1.32	2.00	1.76	3.18	4.08
Avg.	11.35	1.42	1.94	1.81	3.52	4.35
Min.	7.45	0.92	0.80	0.75	2.72	3.06
Max.	15.05	2.76	4.18	4.00	5.36	8.20

Note: (1) Values for the local area are compared with the average, minimum and maximum values for all 291 areas in the Cost of Living Index; (2) Figures cover the Savannah GA urban area; **T-Bone Steak** (price per pound); **Frying Chicken** (price per pound, whole fryer); **Whole Milk** (half gallon carton); **Eggs** (price per dozen, Grade A, large); **Orange Juice** (64 oz. Tropicana or Florida Natural); **Coffee** (11.5 oz. can, vacuum-packed, Maxwell House, Hills Bros, or Folgers).
Source: The Council for Community and Economic Research, ACCRA Cost of Living Index, 2018

Housing and Utility Costs

Area[1]	New Home Price ($)	Apartment Rent ($/month)	All Electric ($/month)	Part Electric ($/month)	Other Energy ($/month)	Telephone ($/month)
City[2]	206,878	850	158.73	-	-	176.60
Avg.	347,000	1,087	165.93	100.16	67.73	178.70
Min.	200,468	500	93.58	25.64	26.78	163.10
Max.	1,901,222	4,888	388.65	246.86	332.81	197.70

Note: (1) Values for the local area are compared with the average, minimum and maximum values for all 291 areas in the Cost of Living Index; (2) Figures cover the Savannah GA urban area; **New Home Price** (2,400 sf living area, 8,000 sf lot, in urban area with full utilities); **Apartment Rent** (950 sf 2 bedroom/1.5 or 2 bath, unfurnished, excluding all utilities except water); **All Electric** (average monthly cost for an all-electric home); **Part Electric** (average monthly cost for a part-electric home); **Other Energy** (average monthly cost for natural gas, fuel oil, coal, wood, and any other forms of energy except electricity); **Telephone** (price includes the base monthly rate plus taxes and fees for three lines of mobile phone service).
Source: The Council for Community and Economic Research, ACCRA Cost of Living Index, 2018

Health Care, Transportation, and Other Costs

Area[1]	Doctor ($/visit)	Dentist ($/visit)	Optometrist ($/visit)	Gasoline ($/gallon)	Beauty Salon ($/visit)	Men's Shirt ($)
City[2]	115.88	94.74	82.13	2.42	35.62	26.38
Avg.	110.71	95.11	103.74	2.61	37.48	32.03
Min.	33.60	62.55	54.63	1.89	17.00	11.44
Max.	195.97	153.93	225.79	3.59	71.88	58.64

Note: (1) Values for the local area are compared with the average, minimum and maximum values for all 291 areas in the Cost of Living Index; (2) Figures cover the Savannah GA urban area; **Doctor** (general practitioners routine exam of an established patient); **Dentist** (adult teeth cleaning and periodic oral examination); **Optometrist** (full vision eye exam for established adult patient); **Gasoline** (one gallon regular unleaded, national brand, including all taxes, cash price at self-service pump if available); **Beauty Salon** (woman's shampoo, trim, and blow-dry); **Men's Shirt** (cotton/polyester dress shirt, pinpoint weave, long sleeves).
Source: The Council for Community and Economic Research, ACCRA Cost of Living Index, 2018

HOUSING

House Price Index (HPI)

Area	National Ranking[2]	Quarterly Change (%)	One-Year Change (%)	Five-Year Change (%)
MSA[1]	132	0.68	6.05	29.50
U.S.[3]	–	1.12	5.73	32.81

Note: The HPI is a weighted repeat sales index. It measures average price changes in repeat sales or refinancings on the same properties. This information is obtained by reviewing repeat mortgage transactions on single-family properties whose mortgages have been purchased or securitized by Fannie Mae or Freddie Mac in January 1975; (1) Figures cover the Savannah, GA Metropolitan Statistical Area—see Appendix B for areas included; (2) Rankings are based on annual percentage change for all metro areas containing at least 15,000 transactions over the last 10 years and ranges from 1 to 245; (3) figures based on a weighted average of Census Division estimates using a seasonally adjusted, purchase-only index; all figures are for the period ending December 31, 2018
Source: Federal Housing Finance Agency, House Price Index, February 26, 2019

Median Single-Family Home Prices

Area	2016	2017	2018p	Percent Change 2017 to 2018
MSA[1]	n/a	n/a	n/a	n/a
U.S. Average	235.5	248.8	261.6	5.1

Note: Figures are median sales prices of existing single-family homes in thousands of dollars; (p) preliminary; n/a not available; (1) Figures cover the Savannah, GA Metropolitan Statistical Area—see Appendix B for areas included
Source: National Association of Realtors, Median Sales Price of Existing Single-Family Homes for Metropolitan Areas, 4th Quarter 2018

Qualifying Income Based on Median Sales Price of Existing Single-Family Homes

Area	With 5% Down ($)	With 10% Down ($)	With 20% Down ($)
MSA[1]	n/a	n/a	n/a
U.S. Average	62,954	59,640	53,013

Note: Figures are preliminary; Qualifying income is based on a mortgage rate of 4.9%. Monthly principal and interest payment is limited to 25% of income; n/a not available; (1) Figures cover the Savannah, GA Metropolitan Statistical Area—see Appendix B for areas included
Source: National Association of Realtors, Qualifying Income Based on Median Sales Price of Existing Single-Family Homes for Metropolitan Areas, 4th Quarter 2018

Median Apartment Condo-Coop Home Prices

Area	2016	2017	2018p	Percent Change 2017 to 2018
MSA[1]	n/a	n/a	n/a	n/a
U.S. Average	220.7	234.3	241.0	2.9

Note: Figures are median sales prices of existing apartment condo-coop homes in thousands of dollars; (p) preliminary; n/a not available; (1) Figures cover the Savannah, GA Metropolitan Statistical Area—see Appendix B for areas included
Source: National Association of Realtors, Median Sales Price of Existing Apartment Condo-Coop Homes for Metropolitan Areas, 4th Quarter 2018

Home Value Distribution

Area	Under $50,000	$50,000 -$99,999	$100,000 -$149,999	$150,000 -$199,999	$200,000 -$299,999	$300,000 -$499,999	$500,000 -$999,999	$1,000,000 or more
City	6.4	22.3	22.7	19.8	16.3	8.0	3.7	0.8
MSA[1]	6.1	13.6	18.3	20.0	21.4	12.5	6.5	1.4
U.S.	8.3	13.9	14.7	14.6	18.7	17.3	9.7	2.7

Note: Figures are percentages and cover owner-occupied housing units; (1) Figures cover the Savannah, GA Metropolitan Statistical Area—see Appendix B for areas included
Source: U.S. Census Bureau, 2013-2017 American Community Survey 5-Year Estimates

Homeownership Rate

Area	2010 (%)	2011 (%)	2012 (%)	2013 (%)	2014 (%)	2015 (%)	2016 (%)	2017 (%)	2018 (%)
MSA[1]	n/a	n/a	n/a	n/a	n/a	n/a	n/a	n/a	n/a
U.S.	66.9	66.1	65.4	65.1	64.5	63.7	63.4	63.9	64.4

Note: (1) Figures cover the Savannah, GA Metropolitan Statistical Area—see Appendix B for areas included; n/a not available
Source: U.S. Census Bureau, Housing Vacancies and Homeownership Annual Statistics: 2010-2018

Year Housing Structure Built

Area	2010 or Later	2000 -2009	1990 -1999	1980 -1989	1970 -1979	1960 -1969	1950 -1959	1940 -1949	Before 1940	Median Year
City	4.6	10.9	7.5	10.1	13.4	13.3	14.9	8.2	16.9	1967
MSA[1]	5.6	22.6	15.9	14.3	11.8	8.3	8.4	4.7	8.4	1986
U.S.	3.2	14.5	14.0	13.6	15.5	10.8	10.5	5.1	12.9	1977

Note: Figures are percentages except for Median Year; Note: (1) Figures cover the Savannah, GA Metropolitan Statistical Area—see Appendix B for areas included
Source: U.S. Census Bureau, 2013-2017 American Community Survey 5-Year Estimates

Gross Monthly Rent

Area	Under $500	$500 -$999	$1,000 -$1,499	$1,500 -$1,999	$2,000 -$2,499	$2,500 -$2,999	$3,000 and up	Median ($)
City	11.5	45.7	33.6	6.4	1.5	0.5	0.8	942
MSA[1]	9.2	41.2	37.0	9.2	2.0	0.7	0.6	997
U.S.	10.5	41.1	28.7	11.7	4.5	1.8	1.7	982

Note: Figures are percentages except for Median; Gross rent is the contract rent plus the estimated average monthly cost of utilities (electricity, gas, and water and sewer) and fuels (oil, coal, kerosene, wood, etc.) if these are paid by the renter (or paid for the renter by someone else); (1) Figures cover the Savannah, GA Metropolitan Statistical Area—see Appendix B for areas included
Source: U.S. Census Bureau, 2013-2017 American Community Survey 5-Year Estimates

HEALTH

Health Risk Factors

Category	MSA[1] (%)	U.S. (%)
Adults aged 18–64 who have any kind of health care coverage	n/a	87.3
Adults who reported being in good or better health	n/a	82.4
Adults who have been told they have high blood cholesterol	n/a	33.0
Adults who have been told they have high blood pressure	n/a	32.3
Adults who are current smokers	n/a	17.1
Adults who currently use E-cigarettes	n/a	4.6
Adults who currently use chewing tobacco, snuff, or snus	n/a	4.0
Adults who are heavy drinkers[2]	n/a	6.3
Adults who are binge drinkers[3]	n/a	17.4
Adults who are overweight (BMI 25.0 - 29.9)	n/a	35.3
Adults who are obese (BMI 30.0 - 99.8)	n/a	31.3
Adults who participated in any physical activities in the past month	n/a	74.4
Adults who always or nearly always wears a seat belt	n/a	94.3

Note: n/a not available; (1) Figures cover the Savannah, GA Metropolitan Statistical Area—see Appendix B for areas included; (2) Heavy drinkers are classified as adult men having more than 14 drinks per week and adult women having more than 7 drinks per week; (3) Binge drinkers are classified as males having five or more drinks on one occasion or females having four or more drinks on one occasion
Source: Centers for Disease Control and Prevention, Behaviorial Risk Factor Surveillance System, SMART: Selected Metropolitan Area Risk Trends, 2017

Acute and Chronic Health Conditions

Category	MSA[1] (%)	U.S. (%)
Adults who have ever been told they had a heart attack	n/a	4.2
Adults who have ever been told they have angina or coronary heart disease	n/a	3.9
Adults who have ever been told they had a stroke	n/a	3.0
Adults who have ever been told they have asthma	n/a	14.2
Adults who have ever been told they have arthritis	n/a	24.9
Adults who have ever been told they have diabetes[2]	n/a	10.5
Adults who have ever been told they had skin cancer	n/a	6.2
Adults who have ever been told they had any other types of cancer	n/a	7.1
Adults who have ever been told they have COPD	n/a	6.5
Adults who have ever been told they have kidney disease	n/a	3.0
Adults who have ever been told they have a form of depression	n/a	20.5

Note: n/a not available; (1) Figures cover the Savannah, GA Metropolitan Statistical Area—see Appendix B for areas included; (2) Figures do not include pregnancy-related, borderline, or pre-diabetes
Source: Centers for Disease Control and Prevention, Behaviorial Risk Factor Surveillance System, SMART: Selected Metropolitan Area Risk Trends, 2017

Health Screening and Vaccination Rates

Category	MSA[1] (%)	U.S. (%)
Adults aged 65+ who have had flu shot within the past year	n/a	60.7
Adults aged 65+ who have ever had a pneumonia vaccination	n/a	75.4
Adults who have ever been tested for HIV	n/a	36.1
Adults who have ever had the shingles or zoster vaccine?	n/a	28.9
Adults who have had their blood cholesterol checked within the last five years	n/a	85.9

Note: n/a not available; (1) Figures cover the Savannah, GA Metropolitan Statistical Area—see Appendix B for areas included.
Source: Centers for Disease Control and Prevention, Behaviorial Risk Factor Surveillance System, SMART: Selected Metropolitan Area Risk Trends, 2017

Disability Status

Category	MSA[1] (%)	U.S. (%)
Adults who reported being deaf	n/a	6.7
Are you blind or have serious difficulty seeing, even when wearing glasses?	n/a	4.5
Are you limited in any way in any of your usual activities due of arthritis?	n/a	12.9
Do you have difficulty doing errands alone?	n/a	6.8
Do you have difficulty dressing or bathing?	n/a	3.6
Do you have serious difficulty concentrating/remembering/making decisions?	n/a	10.7
Do you have serious difficulty walking or climbing stairs?	n/a	13.6

Note: n/a not available; (1) Figures cover the Savannah, GA Metropolitan Statistical Area—see Appendix B for areas included.
Source: Centers for Disease Control and Prevention, Behaviorial Risk Factor Surveillance System, SMART: Selected Metropolitan Area Risk Trends, 2017

Mortality Rates for the Top 10 Causes of Death in the U.S.

ICD-10[a] Sub-Chapter	ICD-10[a] Code	Age-Adjusted Mortality Rate[1] per 100,000 population	
		County[2]	U.S.
Malignant neoplasms	C00-C97	153.5	155.5
Ischaemic heart diseases	I20-I25	61.9	94.8
Other forms of heart disease	I30-I51	65.9	52.9
Chronic lower respiratory diseases	J40-J47	39.6	41.0
Cerebrovascular diseases	I60-I69	40.5	37.5
Other degenerative diseases of the nervous system	G30-G31	45.1	35.0
Other external causes of accidental injury	W00-X59	28.9	33.7
Organic, including symptomatic, mental disorders	F01-F09	29.8	31.0
Hypertensive diseases	I10-I15	55.6	21.9
Diabetes mellitus	E10-E14	13.5	21.2

Note: (a) ICD-10 = International Classification of Diseases 10th Revision; (1) Mortality rates are a three year average covering 2015-2017; (2) Figures cover Chatham County.
Source: Centers for Disease Control and Prevention, National Center for Health Statistics. Underlying Cause of Death 1999-2017 on CDC WONDER Online Database

Mortality Rates for Selected Causes of Death

ICD-10[a] Sub-Chapter	ICD-10[a] Code	Age-Adjusted Mortality Rate[1] per 100,000 population	
		County[2]	U.S.
Assault	X85-Y09	16.4	5.9
Diseases of the liver	K70-K76	14.2	14.1
Human immunodeficiency virus (HIV) disease	B20-B24	4.6	1.8
Influenza and pneumonia	J09-J18	13.9	14.3
Intentional self-harm	X60-X84	15.1	13.6
Malnutrition	E40-E46	Unreliable	1.6
Obesity and other hyperalimentation	E65-E68	Unreliable	2.1
Renal failure	N17-N19	16.5	13.0
Transport accidents	V01-V99	13.8	12.4
Viral hepatitis	B15-B19	1.9	1.6

Note: (a) ICD-10 = International Classification of Diseases 10th Revision; (1) Mortality rates are a three year average covering 2015-2017; (2) Figures cover Chatham County; Data are suppressed when the data meet the criteria for confidentiality constraints; Mortality rates are flagged as unreliable when the rate would be calculated with a numerator of 20 or less.
Source: Centers for Disease Control and Prevention, National Center for Health Statistics. Underlying Cause of Death 1999-2017 on CDC WONDER Online Database

Health Insurance Coverage

Area	With Health Insurance	With Private Health Insurance	With Public Health Insurance	Without Health Insurance	Population Under Age 18 Without Health Insurance
City	81.5	57.1	33.4	18.5	7.9
MSA[1]	85.5	67.0	28.8	14.5	6.9
U.S.	89.5	67.2	33.8	10.5	5.7

Note: Figures are percentages that cover the civilian noninstitutionalized population; (1) Figures cover the Savannah, GA Metropolitan Statistical Area—see Appendix B for areas included
Source: U.S. Census Bureau, 2013-2017 American Community Survey 5-Year Estimates

Number of Medical Professionals

Area	MDs[3]	DOs[3,4]	Dentists	Podiatrists	Chiropractors	Optometrists
County[1] (number)	1,021	56	190	21	53	40
County[1] (rate[2])	352.8	19.4	65.4	7.2	18.2	13.8
U.S. (rate[2])	279.3	23.0	68.4	6.0	27.1	16.2

Note: Data as of 2017 unless noted; (1) Data covers Chatham County; (2) Rate per 100,000 population; (3) Data as of 2016 and includes all active, non-federal physicians; (4) Doctor of Osteopathic Medicine
Source: U.S. Department of Health and Human Services, Health Resources and Services Administration, Bureau of Health Professions, Area Resource File (ARF) 2017-2018

EDUCATION

Public School District Statistics

District Name	Schls	Pupils	Pupil/ Teacher Ratio	Minority Pupils[1] (%)	Free Lunch Eligible[2] (%)	IEP[3] (%)
Chatham County	56	38,047	13.9	72.1	57.3	11.4

Note: Table includes school districts with 2,000 or more students; (1) Percentage of students that are not non-Hispanic white; (2) Percentage of students that are eligible for the free lunch program; (3) Percentage of students that have an Individualized Education Program.
Source: U.S. Department of Education, National Center for Education Statistics, Common Core of Data, Local Education Agency (School District) Universe Survey: School Year 2016-2017; U.S. Department of Education, National Center for Education Statistics, Common Core of Data, Public Elementary/Secondary School Universe Survey: School Year 2016-2017

Best High Schools

According to *U.S. News,* Savannah is home to one of the best high schools in the U.S.: **Savannah Arts Academy** (#156). More than 20,000 public, magnet and charter schools were ranked based on their performance on state assessments and how well they prepare students for college. Schools with the highest unrounded College Readiness Index values were numerically ranked from 1 to 500 and were classified as gold medal winners. *U.S. News & World Report, "Best High Schools 2018"*

Highest Level of Education

Area	Less than H.S.	H.S. Diploma	Some College, No Deg.	Associate Degree	Bachelor's Degree	Master's Degree	Prof. School Degree	Doctorate Degree
City	13.3	26.1	25.8	6.6	17.3	8.2	1.5	1.2
MSA[1]	10.8	26.3	24.3	7.5	19.3	8.4	2.0	1.4
U.S.	12.7	27.3	20.8	8.3	19.1	8.4	2.0	1.4

Note: Figures cover persons age 25 and over; (1) Figures cover the Savannah, GA Metropolitan Statistical Area—see Appendix B for areas included
Source: U.S. Census Bureau, 2013-2017 American Community Survey 5-Year Estimates

Educational Attainment by Race

Area	High School Graduate or Higher (%)					Bachelor's Degree or Higher (%)				
	Total	White	Black	Asian	Hisp.[2]	Total	White	Black	Asian	Hisp.[2]
City	86.7	91.7	82.8	86.1	72.1	28.3	41.9	15.9	50.8	26.1
MSA[1]	89.2	91.3	85.3	86.7	78.9	31.1	36.3	19.3	49.6	25.8
U.S.	87.3	89.3	84.9	86.5	66.7	30.9	32.2	20.6	52.7	15.2

Note: Figures shown cover persons 25 years old and over; (1) Figures cover the Savannah, GA Metropolitan Statistical Area—see Appendix B for areas included; (2) People of Hispanic origin can be of any race
Source: U.S. Census Bureau, 2013-2017 American Community Survey 5-Year Estimates

School Enrollment by Grade and Control

Area	Preschool (%)		Kindergarten (%)		Grades 1 - 4 (%)		Grades 5 - 8 (%)		Grades 9 - 12 (%)	
	Public	Private	Public	Private	Public	Private	Public	Private	Public	Private
City	66.7	33.3	96.0	4.0	92.0	8.0	89.3	10.7	88.9	11.1
MSA[1]	65.5	34.5	90.4	9.6	88.2	11.8	84.5	15.5	85.9	14.1
U.S.	58.8	41.2	87.7	12.3	89.7	10.3	89.6	10.4	90.3	9.7

Note: Figures shown cover persons 3 years old and over; (1) Figures cover the Savannah, GA Metropolitan Statistical Area—see Appendix B for areas included
Source: U.S. Census Bureau, 2013-2017 American Community Survey 5-Year Estimates

Average Salaries of Public School Classroom Teachers

Area	2016		2017		Change from 2016 to 2017	
	Dollars	Rank[1]	Dollars	Rank[1]	Percent	Rank[2]
Georgia	54,190	23	55,532	23	2.5	15
U.S. Average	58,479	–	59,660	–	2.0	–

Note: (1) Rank ranges from 1 to 51 where 1 indicates highest salary; (2) Rank ranges from 1 to 51 where 1 indicates highest percent change.
Source: National Education Association, Rankings & Estimates: Rankings of the States 2017 and Estimates of School Statistics 2018

Higher Education

Four-Year Colleges			Two-Year Colleges			Medical Schools[1]	Law Schools[2]	Voc/ Tech[3]
Public	Private Non-profit	Private For-profit	Public	Private Non-profit	Private For-profit			
2	1	3	1	0	1	0	1	1

Note: Figures cover institutions located within the city limits and include main campuses only; (1) includes schools accredited by the Liaison Committee on Medical Education and the American Osteopathic Association's Commission on Osteopathic College Accreditation; (2) includes ABA-accredited schools, schools with provisional ABA accreditation, and state accredited schools; (3) includes all schools with programs that are less than 2 years.
Source: National Center for Education Statistics, Integrated Postsecondary Education System (IPEDS), 2017-18; Wikipedia, List of Medical Schools in the United States, accessed April 3, 2019; Wikipedia, List of Law Schools in the United States, accessed April 3, 2019

PRESIDENTIAL ELECTION

2016 Presidential Election Results

Area	Clinton	Trump	Johnson	Stein	Other
Chatham County	55.1	40.4	3.1	0.3	1.1
U.S.	48.0	45.9	3.3	1.1	1.7

Note: Results are percentages and may not add to 100% due to rounding
Source: Dave Leip's Atlas of U.S. Presidential Elections

EMPLOYERS

Major Employers

Company Name	Industry
Ceres Marine Terminals	Marine cargo handling
Coastal Home Care	Medical care
Colonial Group	Petroleum products
CSX	Railroad
Dollar Tree	Retail
Effingham County Hospital Authority	Hospital
Georgia Power Company	Electric utility
Georgia Regional Hospital	Hospital
Goodwill Industries of the Coastal Empire	Adult vocational rehabilitation
Kroger Company	Retail food
Marine Terminals Corp.	Marine cargo handling
McDonalds	Restaurants
Memorial University Medical Center	Hospital
Publix Supermarkets	Retail grocery
SouthCoast Health	Healthcare services
SSA Cooper	Marine cargo handling
St. Joseph's/Candler	Hospital
The Landings Club	Private membership club
TMX Finance	Financial services
Trace Staffing Solutions	Employment services
UTC Overseas	Logistics solutions
Wal-Mart Stores	Retail

Note: Companies shown are located within the Savannah, GA Metropolitan Statistical Area.
Source: Hoovers.com; Wikipedia

PUBLIC SAFETY

Crime Rate

Area	All Crimes	Violent Crimes				Property Crimes		
		Murder	Rape[3]	Robbery	Aggrav. Assault	Burglary	Larceny -Theft	Motor Vehicle Theft
City	3,893.9	14.4	41.2	156.8	250.3	549.5	2,494.8	386.9
Suburbs[1]	n/a	2.0	20.3	39.9	215.1	n/a	1,718.4	136.7
Metro[2]	n/a	9.7	33.3	112.6	237.0	n/a	2,201.1	292.3
U.S.	2,756.1	5.3	41.7	98.0	248.9	430.4	1,694.4	237.4

Note: Figures are crimes per 100,000 population; (1) All areas within the metro area that are located outside the city limits; (2) Figures cover the Savannah, GA Metropolitan Statistical Area—see Appendix B for areas included; (3) The city and U.S. figures shown were reported using the revised Uniform Crime Reporting (UCR) definition of rape. The suburban and metro area figures shown are an aggregate total of the data submitted using both the revised and legacy UCR definitions.
Source: FBI Uniform Crime Reports, 2017

Hate Crimes

Area	Number of Quarters Reported	Number of Incidents per Bias Motivation					
		Race/Ethnicity/ Ancestry	Religion	Sexual Orientation	Disability	Gender	Gender Identity
City	4	0	0	0	0	0	0
U.S.	4	4,131	1,564	1,130	116	46	119

Source: Federal Bureau of Investigation, Hate Crime Statistics 2017

Identity Theft Consumer Reports

Area	Reports	Reports per 100,000 Population	Rank[2]
MSA[1]	582	152	30
U.S.	444,602	135	-

Note: (1) Figures cover the Savannah, GA Metropolitan Statistical Area—see Appendix B for areas included; (2) Rank ranges from 1 to 389 where 1 indicates greatest number of identity theft reports per 100,000 population
Source: Federal Trade Commission, Consumer Sentinel Network Data Book for January–December 2018

Fraud and Other Consumer Reports

Area	Reports	Reports per 100,000 Population	Rank[2]
MSA[1]	2,424	631	45
U.S.	2,552,917	776	-

Note: (1) Figures cover the Savannah, GA Metropolitan Statistical Area—see Appendix B for areas included;
(2) Rank ranges from 1 to 389 where 1 indicates greatest number of fraud and other consumer reports per 100,000 population
Source: Federal Trade Commission, Consumer Sentinel Network Data Book for January–December 2018

SPORTS

Professional Sports Teams

Team Name	League	Year Established
No teams are located in the metro area		

Source: Wikipedia, Major Professional Sports Teams of the United States and Canada, April 5, 2019

CLIMATE

Average and Extreme Temperatures

Temperature	Jan	Feb	Mar	Apr	May	Jun	Jul	Aug	Sep	Oct	Nov	Dec	Yr.
Extreme High (°F)	84	86	91	95	100	104	105	104	98	97	89	83	105
Average High (°F)	60	64	70	78	84	89	92	90	86	78	70	62	77
Average Temp. (°F)	49	53	59	66	74	79	82	81	77	68	59	52	67
Average Low (°F)	38	41	48	54	62	69	72	72	68	57	47	40	56
Extreme Low (°F)	3	14	20	32	39	51	61	57	43	28	15	9	3

Note: Figures cover the years 1950-1995
Source: National Climatic Data Center, International Station Meteorological Climate Summary, 9/96

Average Precipitation/Snowfall/Humidity

Precip./Humidity	Jan	Feb	Mar	Apr	May	Jun	Jul	Aug	Sep	Oct	Nov	Dec	Yr.
Avg. Precip. (in.)	3.5	3.1	3.9	3.2	4.2	5.6	6.8	7.2	5.0	2.9	2.2	2.7	50.3
Avg. Snowfall (in.)	Tr	Tr	Tr	0	0	0	0	0	0	0	Tr	Tr	Tr
Avg. Rel. Hum. 7am (%)	83	82	83	84	85	87	88	91	91	88	86	83	86
Avg. Rel. Hum. 4pm (%)	53	50	49	48	52	58	61	63	62	55	53	54	55

Note: Figures cover the years 1950-1995; Tr = Trace amounts (<0.05 in. of rain; <0.5 in. of snow)
Source: National Climatic Data Center, International Station Meteorological Climate Summary, 9/96

Weather Conditions

Temperature			Daytime Sky			Precipitation		
10°F & below	32°F & below	90°F & above	Clear	Partly cloudy	Cloudy	0.01 inch or more precip.	0.1 inch or more snow/ice	Thunder-storms
< 1	29	70	97	155	113	111	< 1	63

Note: Figures are average number of days per year and cover the years 1950-1995
Source: National Climatic Data Center, International Station Meteorological Climate Summary, 9/96

HAZARDOUS WASTE

Superfund Sites

The Savannah, GA metro area has no sites on the EPA's Superfund Final National Priorities List. There are a total of 1,390 Superfund sites with a status of proposed or final on the list in the U.S. *U.S. Environmental Protection Agency, National Priorities List, April 5, 2019*

AIR & WATER QUALITY

Air Quality Trends: Ozone

	1990	1995	2000	2005	2010	2012	2014	2015	2016	2017
MSA[1]	n/a	n/a	n/a	n/a	n/a	n/a	n/a	n/a	n/a	n/a
U.S.	0.088	0.089	0.082	0.080	0.073	0.075	0.067	0.068	0.069	0.068

Note: (1) Data covers the Savannah, GA Metropolitan Statistical Area—see Appendix B for areas included; n/a not available. The values shown are the composite ozone concentration averages among trend sites based on the highest fourth daily maximum 8-hour concentration in parts per million. These trends are based on sites having an adequate record of monitoring data during the trend period. Data from exceptional events are included.
Source: U.S. Environmental Protection Agency, Air Quality Monitoring Information, "Air Quality Trends by City, 1990-2017"

Air Quality Index

Area	Percent of Days when Air Quality was...[2]					AQI Statistics[2]	
	Good	Moderate	Unhealthy for Sensitive Groups	Unhealthy	Very Unhealthy	Maximum	Median
MSA[1]	79.2	20.8	0.0	0.0	0.0	84	38

Note: (1) Data covers the Savannah, GA Metropolitan Statistical Area—see Appendix B for areas included; (2) Based on 365 days with AQI data in 2017. Air Quality Index (AQI) is an index for reporting daily air quality. EPA calculates the AQI for five major air pollutants regulated by the Clean Air Act: ground-level ozone, particle pollution (aka particulate matter), carbon monoxide, sulfur dioxide, and nitrogen dioxide. The AQI runs from 0 to 500. The higher the AQI value, the greater the level of air pollution and the greater the health concern. There are six AQI categories: "Good" AQI is between 0 and 50. Air quality is considered satisfactory; "Moderate" AQI is between 51 and 100. Air quality is acceptable; "Unhealthy for Sensitive Groups" When AQI values are between 101 and 150, members of sensitive groups may experience health effects; "Unhealthy" When AQI values are between 151 and 200 everyone may begin to experience health effects; "Very Unhealthy" AQI values between 201 and 300 trigger a health alert; "Hazardous" AQI values over 300 trigger warnings of emergency conditions (not shown).
Source: U.S. Environmental Protection Agency, Air Quality Index Report, 2017

Air Quality Index Pollutants

Area	Percent of Days when AQI Pollutant was...[2]					
	Carbon Monoxide	Nitrogen Dioxide	Ozone	Sulfur Dioxide	Particulate Matter 2.5	Particulate Matter 10
MSA[1]	0.0	0.0	27.4	9.6	63.0	0.0

Note: (1) Data covers the Savannah, GA Metropolitan Statistical Area—see Appendix B for areas included; (2) Based on 365 days with AQI data in 2017. The Air Quality Index (AQI) is an index for reporting daily air quality. EPA calculates the AQI for five major air pollutants regulated by the Clean Air Act: ground-level ozone, particle pollution (also known as particulate matter), carbon monoxide, sulfur dioxide, and nitrogen dioxide. The AQI runs from 0 to 500. The higher the AQI value, the greater the level of air pollution and the greater the health concern.
Source: U.S. Environmental Protection Agency, Air Quality Index Report, 2017

Maximum Air Pollutant Concentrations: Particulate Matter, Ozone, CO and Lead

	Particulate Matter 10 (ug/m^3)	Particulate Matter 2.5 Wtd AM (ug/m^3)	Particulate Matter 2.5 24-Hr (ug/m^3)	Ozone (ppm)	Carbon Monoxide (ppm)	Lead (ug/m^3)
MSA[1] Level	n/a	n/a	n/a	0.057	n/a	n/a
NAAQS[2]	150	15	35	0.075	9	0.15
Met NAAQS[2]	n/a	n/a	n/a	Yes	n/a	n/a

Note: (1) Data covers the Savannah, GA Metropolitan Statistical Area—see Appendix B for areas included; Data from exceptional events are included; (2) National Ambient Air Quality Standards; ppm = parts per million; ug/m^3 = micrograms per cubic meter; n/a not available.
Concentrations: Particulate Matter 10 (coarse particulate)—highest second maximum 24-hour concentration; Particulate Matter 2.5 Wtd AM (fine particulate)—highest weighted annual mean concentration; Particulate Matter 2.5 24-Hour (fine particulate)—highest 98th percentile 24-hour concentration; Ozone—highest fourth daily maximum 8-hour concentration; Carbon Monoxide—highest second maximum non-overlapping 8-hour concentration; Lead—maximum running 3-month average
Source: U.S. Environmental Protection Agency, Air Quality Monitoring Information, "Air Quality Statistics by City, 2017"

Maximum Air Pollutant Concentrations: Nitrogen Dioxide and Sulfur Dioxide

	Nitrogen Dioxide AM (ppb)	Nitrogen Dioxide 1-Hr (ppb)	Sulfur Dioxide AM (ppb)	Sulfur Dioxide 1-Hr (ppb)	Sulfur Dioxide 24-Hr (ppb)
MSA[1] Level	n/a	n/a	n/a	53	n/a
NAAQS[2]	53	100	30	75	140
Met NAAQS[2]	n/a	n/a	n/a	Yes	n/a

Note: (1) Data covers the Savannah, GA Metropolitan Statistical Area—see Appendix B for areas included; Data from exceptional events are included; (2) National Ambient Air Quality Standards; ppm = parts per million; ug/m³ = micrograms per cubic meter; n/a not available.
Concentrations: Nitrogen Dioxide AM—highest arithmetic mean concentration; Nitrogen Dioxide 1-Hr—highest 98th percentile 1-hour daily maximum concentration; Sulfur Dioxide AM—highest annual mean concentration; Sulfur Dioxide 1-Hr—highest 99th percentile 1-hour daily maximum concentration; Sulfur Dioxide 24-Hr—highest second maximum 24-hour concentration
Source: U.S. Environmental Protection Agency, Air Quality Monitoring Information, "Air Quality Statistics by City, 2017"

Drinking Water

Water System Name	Pop. Served	Primary Water Source Type	Violations[1] Health Based	Violations[1] Monitoring/ Reporting
Savannah-Main	168,958	Ground	0	0

Note: (1) Based on violation data from January 1, 2018 to December 31, 2018
Source: U.S. Environmental Protection Agency, Office of Ground Water and Drinking Water, Safe Drinking Water Information System (based on data extracted April 5, 2019)

Tallahassee, Florida

Background

Tallahassee is the capital of Florida and located in the northern panhandle of the state in Leon County. In addition to the state government, the city is primarily known as home to Florida State University, with its 40,000 students and 16 colleges. The presence of top-ranked FSU, as well as other smaller universities, has shaped development of Tallahassee from a small, rural settlement to the modern metropolis that it is today.

After the state of Florida was ceded to United States from Spain in 1821, a governing body initially alternated between meetings in St. Augustine and Pensacola. Eventually a more central, permanent location for the government—Tallahassee, which was incorporated in 1824. The word Tallahassee means "old town" in the language of the Creek Native American tribe that inhabited the area during the 18th century.

Florida State University (FSU) was founded in 1851, establishing Tallahassee as a city known for education. During the Civil War, Tallahassee was the only Confederate capital city east of the Mississippi not captured by the Union Army. After the war, much of the industry in the southern United States changed; cotton and tobacco production suffered without slave labor and new industries emerged, including citrus production, cattle ranching and tourism.

The first airport in the city opened in 1929. In 1961, the Tallahassee Regional Airport opened with limited service. In 1989, major passenger service was offered and in 2000, the terminal was renamed Ivan Monroe Terminal. Monroe, the first Tallahassee resident to own his own plane, was also the first manager of Dale Mabry Field—the city's original airport, and adjacent to the site of the present-day Tallahassee Regional Airport. Other transportation services in the city include the StarMetro bus lines and the CSX railroad.

Economic and population growth in recent decades has created the need for more land in the city, and about seventy-five square miles have been added by voluntary annexation. A 25-year-old program to fund new infrastructure and transportation projects via a one cent sales tax has yielded such public gems as the Capital Cascades Park, with venues such as the Capital City Amphitheater and the 5.2 mile Capital Cascades Trail.

Today, economic activity in Tallahassee is centered primarily on education and research. In addition to FSU, the city is home to A&M University, the state's only historically black university. In 2014, the 126-year-old institution saw its first woman president, Dr. Elmira Magnum, take the helm. Also here is Tallahassee Community College, home to an Advanced Manufacturing Training Center, a 16,000 square foot facility geared toward high tech and precision manufacturing training, and the Ghazvini Center for Healthcare Education. Other higher education offerings in Tallahassee include campuses of Barry University, Embry Riddle Aeronautical University, and Flagler College, among others.

The high-tech industry has grown significantly with companies such as Bing Energy and SunnyLand Solar that are interested in working with university-based researchers. Also located here are manufacturing facilities for General Dynamics, Land Systems and Danfoss Turbocor.

Major attractions in the Tallahassee area include the Alfred B. Maclay Gardens State Park, the Florida State Capitol, the Lake Jackson Mounds Archaeological State Park, the Mary Brogan Museum of Art and Science and the Tallahassee Museum.

Unlike most other cities in Florida, Tallahassee experiences four distinct seasons. Despite being located in the northern part of the state, it is generally hotter in the summer than cities in located on the Florida peninsula. The summer season also brings thunderstorms that develop on the Gulf of Mexico. Winters in the city are usually much cooler than in the rest of Florida, with occasional light snow every few years. The city's location near the Gulf of Mexico also means hurricane activity. Tallahassee was hit by Hurricane Kate in 1985 and by Hurricane Hermine in 2016.

Rankings

General Rankings

- The U.S. Conference of Mayors and Waste Management, Inc. sponsor the City Livability Awards Program, which recognize mayors for exemplary leadership in developing and implementing specific programs that improve the quality of life in America's cities. Tallahassee received an Outstanding Achievement Award in the large cities category. *U.S. Conference of Mayors, "2018 City Livability Awards"*

- In their sixth annual survey, Livability.com looked at data for more than 1,000 U.S. cities to determine the rankings for Livability's "Top 100 Best Places to Live" in 2019. Tallahassee ranked #54. Criteria: median home value capped at $250,000; affordable living; vibrant economy; education, demographics, health care options. transportation & infrastructure; abundant lifestyle amenities. *Livability.com, "Top 100 Best Places to Live 2019" March 2019*

Business/Finance Rankings

- The personal finance site NerdWallet analyzed 183 American metropolitan areas with populations over 250,000 and more than 15,000 businesses to rank where entrepreneurs find the most success. Criteria included area economy, annual income, housing cost, unemployment rate, and the success rate of area businesses. Tallahassee ranked #153. *www.nerdwallet.com, "Best Places to Start a Business," April 27, 2015*

- The Tallahassee metro area appeared on the Milken Institute "2018 Best Performing Cities" list. Rank: #82 out of 200 large metro areas. Criteria: job growth; wage and salary growth; high-tech output growth. *Milken Institute, "Best-Performing Cities 2018," January 24, 2019*

- *Forbes* ranked the 200 most populous metro areas to determine the nation's "Best Places for Business and Careers." The Tallahassee metro area was ranked #99. Criteria: costs (business and living); job growth (past and projected); income growth; quality of life; educational attainment (college and high school); projected economic growth; cultural and recreational opportunities; net migration patterns; number of highly ranked colleges. *Forbes, "The Best Places for Business and Careers 2018: Seattle Leads the Way," October 24, 2018*

Education Rankings

- Personal finance website *WalletHub* analyzed the 150 largest U.S. metropolitan statistical areas to determine where the most educated Americans are choosing to settle. Criteria: education quality and attainment gap; education levels; percentage of workers with degrees; public school quality rankings; quality and size of each metro area's universities. Tallahassee was ranked #16 (#1 = most educated city). *www.WalletHub.com, "2018's Most and Least Educated Cities in America, " July 24, 2018*

Environmental Rankings

- Tallahassee was highlighted as one of the cleanest metro areas for ozone air pollution in the U.S. during 2014 through 2016. The list represents cities with no monitored ozone air pollution in unhealthful ranges. *American Lung Association, State of the Air 2018*

Health/Fitness Rankings

- The Tallahassee metro area ranked #140 out of 189 in The Gallup-Healthways Well-Being Index. Criteria: purpose; social well being; financial health; community and physical health. Results are based on telephone interviews with adults, aged 18 and older, living in metropolitan areas in the 50 U.S. states and the District of Columbia. *Gallup-Healthways, "State of American Well-Being, 2017 Community Well-Being Rankings" March 2018*

Real Estate Rankings

- *WalletHub* compared the most populated U.S. cities, as well as at least two of the most populated cities in each state, for a total of 179, to determine which had the best markets for real estate agents. Tallahassee ranked #158 where demand was high and pay was the best. Criteria: sales per agent; annual median wage for real-estate agents; monthly average starting salary for real estate agents; real estate job density and competition; unemployment rate; housing-market health index; and other relevant metrics. *www.WalletHub.com, "2018's Best Places to Be a Real Estate Agent," April 25, 2018*

- The Tallahassee metro area was identified as one of the 10 best condo markets in the U.S. in 2018. The area ranked #9 out of 61 markets. Criteria: year-over-year change of median sales price of existing apartment condo-coop homes between the 4th quarter of 2017 and the 4th quarter of 2018. *National Association of Realtors®, Median Sales Price of Existing Apartment Condo-Coops Homes for Metropolitan Areas, 4th Quarter 2018*

- Tallahassee was ranked #92 out of 237 metro areas in terms of housing affordability in 2018 by the National Association of Home Builders (#1 = most affordable). Criteria: the share of homes sold in that area affordable to a family earning the local median income, based on standard mortgage underwriting criteria. *National Association of Home Builders®, NAHB-Wells Fargo Housing Opportunity Index, 4th Quarter 2018*

Safety Rankings

- Allstate ranked the 200 largest cities in America in terms of driver safety. Tallahassee ranked #43. Criteria: internal property damage claims over a two-year period from January 2015 to December 2016. The report helps increase the importance of safety awareness behind the wheel. *Allstate, "Allstate America's Best Drivers Report, 2018" August 28, 2018*

- The National Insurance Crime Bureau ranked 382 metro areas in the U.S. in terms of per capita rates of vehicle theft. The Tallahassee metro area ranked #112 (#1 = highest rate). Criteria: number of vehicle theft offenses per 100,000 inhabitants in 2017. *National Insurance Crime Bureau, "Hot Spots 2017," July 12, 2018*

Seniors/Retirement Rankings

- From its Best Cities for Successful Aging indexes, the Milken Institute generated rankings for metropolitan areas, weighing data in nine categories—health care, wellness, living arrangements, transportation and convenience, financial characteristics, education, employment, community engagement, and overall livability. The Tallahassee metro area was ranked #123 overall in the small metro area category. *Milken Institute, "Best Cities for Successful Aging, 2017" March 14, 2017*

Sports/Recreation Rankings

- Tallahassee was chosen as one of America's best cities for bicycling. The city ranked #44 out of 50. Criteria: cycling infrastructure that is safe and friendly for all ages; energy and bike culture. The editors only considered cities with populations of 100,000 or more. *Bicycling, "The 50 Best Bike Cities in America," October 10, 2018*

Women/Minorities Rankings

- Personal finance website *WalletHub* compared more than 180 U.S. cities—including the 150 most populated U.S. cities, plus at least two of the most populated cities in each state—across two key dimensions, "Hispanic Business-Friendliness" and "Hispanic Purchasing Power", to arrive at the most favorable conditions for Hispanic entrepreneurs. Tallahassee was ranked #120 out of 182. Criteria includes: share of Hispanic-Owned Businesses; Hispanic entrepreneurship rate to median annual income of Hispanics; Small Business-Friendliness score; cost of living; and number of Hispanics with at least a bachelor's degree. *WalletHub.com, "2018's Best Cities for Hispanic Entrepreneurs," April 26, 2018*

Miscellaneous Rankings

- *WalletHub* compared the 150 most populated U.S. cities to determine their operating efficiency. A "Quality of Services" score was constructed for each city and then divided by the total budget per capita to reveal which were managed the best. Tallahassee ranked #82. Criteria: financial stability; economy; education; safety; health; infrastructure and pollution. *www.WalletHub.com, "2018's Best- & Worst-Run Cities in America," July 9, 2018*

Business Environment

CITY FINANCES

City Government Finances

Component	2016 ($000)	2016 ($ per capita)
Total Revenues	727,285	3,830
Total Expenditures	776,418	4,088
Debt Outstanding	1,199,631	6,317
Cash and Securities[1]	2,069,355	10,897

Note: (1) Cash and security holdings of a government at the close of its fiscal year, including those of its dependent agencies, utilities, and liquor stores.
Source: U.S. Census Bureau, State & Local Government Finances 2016

City Government Revenue by Source

Source	2016 ($000)	2016 ($ per capita)	2016 (%)
General Revenue			
From Federal Government	21,159	111	2.9
From State Government	33,411	176	4.6
From Local Governments	5,008	26	0.7
Taxes			
Property	33,136	174	4.6
Sales and Gross Receipts	56,220	296	7.7
Personal Income	0	0	0.0
Corporate Income	0	0	0.0
Motor Vehicle License	0	0	0.0
Other Taxes	6,176	33	0.8
Current Charges	149,451	787	20.5
Liquor Store	0	0	0.0
Utility	349,371	1,840	48.0
Employee Retirement	31,813	168	4.4

Source: U.S. Census Bureau, State & Local Government Finances 2016

City Government Expenditures by Function

Function	2016 ($000)	2016 ($ per capita)	2016 (%)
General Direct Expenditures			
Air Transportation	29,352	154	3.8
Corrections	0	0	0.0
Education	0	0	0.0
Employment Security Administration	0	0	0.0
Financial Administration	5,445	28	0.7
Fire Protection	36,387	191	4.7
General Public Buildings	0	0	0.0
Governmental Administration, Other	7,645	40	1.0
Health	0	0	0.0
Highways	64,125	337	8.3
Hospitals	0	0	0.0
Housing and Community Development	2,888	15	0.4
Interest on General Debt	7,871	41	1.0
Judicial and Legal	2,225	11	0.3
Libraries	0	0	0.0
Parking	0	0	0.0
Parks and Recreation	22,958	120	3.0
Police Protection	54,578	287	7.0
Public Welfare	0	0	0.0
Sewerage	48,730	256	6.3
Solid Waste Management	20,508	108	2.6
Veterans' Services	0	0	0.0
Liquor Store	0	0	0.0
Utility	347,226	1,828	44.7
Employee Retirement	74,997	394	9.7

Source: U.S. Census Bureau, State & Local Government Finances 2016

DEMOGRAPHICS

Population Growth

Area	1990 Census	2000 Census	2010 Census	2017* Estimate	Population Growth (%) 1990-2017	2010-2017
City	128,014	150,624	181,376	188,463	47.2	3.9
MSA[1]	259,096	320,304	367,413	377,674	45.8	2.8
U.S.	248,709,873	281,421,906	308,745,538	321,004,407	29.1	4.0

Note: (1) Figures cover the Tallahassee, FL Metropolitan Statistical Area—see Appendix B for areas included; (*) 2013-2017 5-year estimated population
Source: U.S. Census Bureau, 1990 Census, Census 2000, Census 2010, 2013-2017 American Community Survey 5-Year Estimates

Household Size

Area	Persons in Household (%) One	Two	Three	Four	Five	Six	Seven or More	Average Household Size
City	33.5	33.9	17.9	9.9	3.7	1.0	0.2	2.30
MSA[1]	29.4	34.9	17.7	11.5	4.4	1.3	0.7	2.40
U.S.	27.7	33.8	15.7	13.0	6.0	2.3	1.4	2.60

Note: (1) Figures cover the Tallahassee, FL Metropolitan Statistical Area—see Appendix B for areas included
Source: U.S. Census Bureau, 2013-2017 American Community Survey 5-Year Estimates

Race

Area	White Alone[2] (%)	Black Alone[2] (%)	Asian Alone[2] (%)	AIAN[3] Alone[2] (%)	NHOPI[4] Alone[2] (%)	Other Race Alone[2] (%)	Two or More Races (%)
City	56.9	35.2	4.2	0.2	0.0	1.0	2.5
MSA[1]	61.2	33.0	2.6	0.2	0.0	0.9	2.1
U.S.	73.0	12.7	5.4	0.8	0.2	4.8	3.1

Note: (1) Figures cover the Tallahassee, FL Metropolitan Statistical Area—see Appendix B for areas included; (2) Alone is defined as not being in combination with one or more other races; (3) American Indian and Alaska Native; (4) Native Hawaiian and Other Pacific Islander
Source: U.S. Census Bureau, 2013-2017 American Community Survey 5-Year Estimates

Hispanic or Latino Origin

Area	Total (%)	Mexican (%)	Puerto Rican (%)	Cuban (%)	Other (%)
City	6.8	1.2	1.5	1.4	2.7
MSA[1]	6.3	1.8	1.3	1.1	2.2
U.S.	17.6	11.1	1.7	0.7	4.1

Note: Persons of Hispanic or Latino origin can be of any race; (1) Figures cover the Tallahassee, FL Metropolitan Statistical Area—see Appendix B for areas included
Source: U.S. Census Bureau, 2013-2017 American Community Survey 5-Year Estimates

Segregation

Type	Segregation Indices[1] 1990	2000	2010	2010 Rank[2]	Percent Change 1990-2000	1990-2010	2000-2010
Black/White	n/a	n/a	n/a	n/a	n/a	n/a	n/a
Asian/White	n/a	n/a	n/a	n/a	n/a	n/a	n/a
Hispanic/White	n/a	n/a	n/a	n/a	n/a	n/a	n/a

Note: All figures cover the Metropolitan Statistical Area—see Appendix B for areas included; Figures are based on an analysis of 1990, 2000, and 2010 Census Decennial Census tract data by William H. Frey, Brookings Institution and the University of Michigan Social Science Data Analysis Network. In this analysis all racial groups (whites, blacks, and asians) are non-Hispanic members of those races. Hispanics are shown as a separate category; (1) Segregation Indices are Dissimilarity Indices that measure the degree to which the minority group is distributed differently than whites across census tracts. They range from 0 (complete integration) to 100 (complete segregation) where the value indicates the percentage of the minority group that needs to move to be distributed exactly like whites; (2) Ranges from 1 (most segregated) to 102 (least segregated); n/a not available.
Source: www.CensusScope.org

Ancestry

Area	German	Irish	English	American	Italian	Polish	French[2]	Scottish	Dutch
City	9.3	8.6	7.7	4.1	3.9	2.0	2.0	2.2	0.8
MSA[1]	9.5	9.0	8.2	5.6	3.3	1.6	2.0	2.4	1.0
U.S.	14.1	10.1	7.5	6.6	5.3	2.9	2.5	1.7	1.3

Note: Figures are the percentage of the total population reporting a particular ancestry. The nine most commonly reported ancestries in the U.S. are shown. Figures include multiple ancestries (e.g. if a person reported being Irish and Italian, they were included in both columns); (1) Figures cover the Tallahassee, FL Metropolitan Statistical Area—see Appendix B for areas included; (2) Excludes Basque
Source: U.S. Census Bureau, 2013-2017 American Community Survey 5-Year Estimates

Foreign-Born Population

Area	Any Foreign Country	Asia	Mexico	Europe	Carribean	Central America[2]	South America	Africa	Canada
City	7.9	3.3	0.2	1.0	1.2	0.4	0.7	0.8	0.2
MSA[1]	6.0	2.1	0.4	0.8	0.9	0.5	0.5	0.5	0.2
U.S.	13.4	4.1	3.6	1.5	1.3	1.0	0.9	0.6	0.3

Note: (1) Figures cover the Tallahassee, FL Metropolitan Statistical Area—see Appendix B for areas included; (2) Excludes Mexico.
Source: U.S. Census Bureau, 2013-2017 American Community Survey 5-Year Estimates

Marital Status

Area	Never Married	Now Married[2]	Separated	Widowed	Divorced
City	55.9	29.9	1.2	3.5	9.5
MSA[1]	43.4	39.8	1.6	4.5	10.8
U.S.	33.1	48.2	2.0	5.8	10.9

Note: Figures are percentages and cover the population 15 years of age and older; (1) Figures cover the Tallahassee, FL Metropolitan Statistical Area—see Appendix B for areas included; (2) Excludes separated
Source: U.S. Census Bureau, 2013-2017 American Community Survey 5-Year Estimates

Disability by Age

Area	All Ages	Under 18 Years Old	18 to 64 Years Old	65 Years and Over
City	10.2	4.9	8.6	32.9
MSA[1]	12.7	5.9	10.4	35.0
U.S.	12.6	4.2	10.3	35.5

Note: Figures show percent of the civilian noninstitutionalized population that reported having a disability. Disability status is determined from six types of difficulty: vision, hearing, cognitive, ambulatory, self-care, and independent living. For children under 5 years old, hearing and vision difficulty are used to determine disability status. For children between the ages of 5 and 14, disability status is determined from hearing, vision, cognitive, ambulatory, and self-care difficulties. For people aged 15 years and older, they are considered to have a disability if they have difficulty with any one of the six difficulty types; Note: (1) Figures cover the Tallahassee, FL Metropolitan Statistical Area—see Appendix B for areas included
Source: U.S. Census Bureau, 2013-2017 American Community Survey 5-Year Estimates

Age

Area	Under Age 5	Age 5–19	Age 20–34	Age 35–44	Age 45–54	Age 55–64	Age 65–74	Age 75–84	Age 85+	Median Age
City	5.0	19.1	39.0	10.0	8.5	8.9	5.7	2.7	1.2	26.6
MSA[1]	5.2	18.7	28.2	11.4	11.7	11.8	8.0	3.5	1.4	33.3
U.S.	6.2	19.5	20.7	12.7	13.4	12.7	8.6	4.4	1.9	37.8

Note: (1) Figures cover the Tallahassee, FL Metropolitan Statistical Area—see Appendix B for areas included
Source: U.S. Census Bureau, 2013-2017 American Community Survey 5-Year Estimates

Gender

Area	Males	Females	Males per 100 Females
City	89,060	99,403	89.6
MSA[1]	182,931	194,743	93.9
U.S.	158,018,753	162,985,654	97.0

Note: (1) Figures cover the Tallahassee, FL Metropolitan Statistical Area—see Appendix B for areas included
Source: U.S. Census Bureau, 2013-2017 American Community Survey 5-Year Estimates

Religious Groups by Family

Area	Catholic	Baptist	Non-Den.	Methodist[2]	Lutheran	LDS[3]	Pente-costal	Presby-terian[4]	Muslim[5]	Judaism
MSA[1]	4.8	16.1	6.8	9.2	0.5	1.0	2.2	1.6	0.9	0.4
U.S.	19.1	9.3	4.0	4.0	2.3	2.0	1.9	1.6	0.8	0.7

Note: Figures are the number of adherents as a percentage of the total population; (1) Figures cover the Tallahassee, FL Metropolitan Statistical Area—see Appendix B for areas included; (2) Methodist/Pietist; (3) Latter Day Saints; (4) Reformed; (5) Figures are estimates
Source: Association of Statisticians of American Religious Bodies, 2010 U.S. Religion Census: Religious Congregations & Membership Study

Religious Groups by Tradition

Area	Catholic	Evangelical Protestant	Mainline Protestant	Other Tradition	Black Protestant	Orthodox
MSA[1]	4.8	21.9	6.4	3.0	9.2	0.2
U.S.	19.1	16.2	7.3	4.3	1.6	0.3

Note: Figures are the number of adherents as a percentage of the total population; (1) Figures cover the Tallahassee, FL Metropolitan Statistical Area—see Appendix B for areas included
Source: Association of Statisticians of American Religious Bodies, 2010 U.S. Religion Census: Religious Congregations & Membership Study

ECONOMY

Gross Metropolitan Product

Area	2016	2017	2018	2019	Rank[2]
MSA[1]	15.8	16.5	17.3	18.3	153

Note: Figures are in billions of dollars; (1) Figures cover the Tallahassee, FL Metropolitan Statistical Area—see Appendix B for areas included; (2) Rank is based on 2017 data and ranges from 1 to 381
Source: U.S. Conference of Mayors, U.S. Metro Economies: Economic Growth & Full Employment, June 2018

Economic Growth

Area	2017-2018 (%)	2019-2020 (%)	2021-2022 (%)
MSA[1]	2.9	2.6	1.9

Note: Figures are real gross metropolitan product (GMP) growth rates and represent average annual percent change; (1) Figures cover the Tallahassee, FL Metropolitan Statistical Area—see Appendix B for areas included
Source: U.S. Conference of Mayors, U.S. Metro Economies: Economic Growth & Full Employment, June 2018

Metropolitan Area Exports

Area	2012	2013	2014	2015	2016	2017	Rank[2]
MSA[1]	130.8	122.5	174.0	191.2	223.1	241.1	284

Note: Figures are in millions of dollars; (1) Figures cover the Tallahassee, FL Metropolitan Statistical Area—see Appendix B for areas included; (2) Rank is based on 2017 data and ranges from 1 to 387
Source: U.S. Department of Commerce, International Trade Administration, Office of Trade and Economic Analysis, Industry and Analysis, Exports by Metropolitan Area, extracted March 25, 2019

Building Permits

Area	Single-Family			Multi-Family			Total		
	2016	2017	Pct. Chg.	2016	2017	Pct. Chg.	2016	2017	Pct. Chg.
City	330	379	14.8	539	1,156	114.5	869	1,535	76.6
MSA[1]	810	1,897	134.2	803	1,156	44.0	1,613	3,053	89.3
U.S.	750,800	820,000	9.2	455,800	462,000	1.4	1,206,600	1,282,000	6.2

Note: (1) Figures cover the Tallahassee, FL Metropolitan Statistical Area—see Appendix B for areas included; Figures represent new, privately-owned housing units authorized (unadjusted data); All permit data are based on estimates with imputation
Source: U.S. Census Bureau, Manufacturing, Mining, and Construction Statistics, Building Permits, 2016, 2017

Bankruptcy Filings

Area	Business Filings			Nonbusiness Filings		
	2017	2018	% Chg.	2017	2018	% Chg.
Leon County	23	28	21.7	355	404	13.8
U.S.	23,157	22,232	-4.0	765,863	751,186	-1.9

Note: Business filings include Chapter 7, Chapter 11, Chapter 12, and Chapter 13; Nonbusiness filings include Chapter 7, Chapter 11, and Chapter 13
Source: Administrative Office of the U.S. Courts, Business and Nonbusiness Bankruptcy, County Cases Commenced by Chapter of the Bankruptcy Code, During the 12-Month Period Ending December 31, 2017 and Business and Nonbusiness Bankruptcy, County Cases Commenced by Chapter of the Bankruptcy Code, During the 12-Month Period Ending December 31, 2018

Housing Vacancy Rates

Area	Gross Vacancy Rate[2] (%)			Year-Round Vacancy Rate[3] (%)			Rental Vacancy Rate[4] (%)			Homeowner Vacancy Rate[5] (%)		
	2016	2017	2018	2016	2017	2018	2016	2017	2018	2016	2017	2018
MSA[1]	n/a	n/a	n/a	n/a	n/a	n/a	n/a	n/a	n/a	n/a	n/a	n/a
U.S.	12.8	12.7	12.3	9.9	9.9	9.7	6.9	7.2	6.9	1.7	1.6	1.5

Note: (1) Figures cover the Tallahassee, FL Metropolitan Statistical Area—see Appendix B for areas included; (2) The percentage of the total housing inventory that is vacant; (3) The percentage of the housing inventory (excluding seasonal units) that is year-round vacant; (4) The percentage of rental inventory that is vacant for rent; (5) The percentage of homeowner inventory that is vacant for sale; n/a not available
Source: U.S. Census Bureau, Housing Vacancies and Homeownership Annual Statistics: 2016, 2017, 2018

INCOME

Income

Area	Per Capita ($)	Median Household ($)	Average Household ($)
City	25,471	42,418	61,645
MSA[1]	26,709	48,618	67,419
U.S.	31,177	57,652	81,283

Note: (1) Figures cover the Tallahassee, FL Metropolitan Statistical Area—see Appendix B for areas included
Source: U.S. Census Bureau, 2013-2017 American Community Survey 5-Year Estimates

Household Income Distribution

Area	Percent of Households Earning							
	Under $15,000	$15,000 -$24,999	$25,000 -$34,999	$35,000 -$49,999	$50,000 -$74,999	$75,000 -$99,999	$100,000 -$149,999	$150,000 and up
City	18.5	11.8	11.4	15.3	15.8	9.6	10.2	7.4
MSA[1]	14.7	10.5	11.0	14.8	17.5	11.6	11.7	8.2
U.S.	11.6	9.8	9.5	13.0	17.7	12.3	14.1	12.1

Note: (1) Figures cover the Tallahassee, FL Metropolitan Statistical Area—see Appendix B for areas included
Source: U.S. Census Bureau, 2013-2017 American Community Survey 5-Year Estimates

Poverty Rate

Area	All Ages	Under 18 Years Old	18 to 64 Years Old	65 Years and Over
City	27.1	23.4	30.6	7.9
MSA[1]	20.2	21.6	22.2	7.8
U.S.	14.6	20.3	13.7	9.3

Note: Figures are percentage of people whose income during the past 12 months was below the poverty level; (1) Figures cover the Tallahassee, FL Metropolitan Statistical Area—see Appendix B for areas included
Source: U.S. Census Bureau, 2013-2017 American Community Survey 5-Year Estimates

EMPLOYMENT

Labor Force and Employment

Area	Civilian Labor Force			Workers Employed		
	Dec. 2017	Dec. 2018	% Chg.	Dec. 2017	Dec. 2018	% Chg.
City	100,181	102,424	2.2	96,633	98,960	2.4
MSA[1]	190,403	194,727	2.3	183,898	188,401	2.4
U.S.	159,880,000	162,510,000	1.6	153,602,000	156,481,000	1.9

Note: Data is not seasonally adjusted and covers workers 16 years of age and older; (1) Figures cover the Tallahassee, FL Metropolitan Statistical Area—see Appendix B for areas included
Source: Bureau of Labor Statistics, Local Area Unemployment Statistics

Unemployment Rate

Area	2018											
	Jan.	Feb.	Mar.	Apr.	May	Jun.	Jul.	Aug.	Sep.	Oct.	Nov.	Dec.
City	4.1	3.6	3.6	3.4	3.3	4.2	4.2	3.8	3.0	3.1	3.1	3.4
MSA[1]	4.0	3.6	3.6	3.2	3.2	3.9	4.0	3.7	2.9	2.9	3.0	3.2
U.S.	4.5	4.4	4.1	3.7	3.6	4.2	4.1	3.9	3.6	3.5	3.5	3.7

Note: Data is not seasonally adjusted and covers workers 16 years of age and older; (1) Figures cover the
Tallahassee, FL Metropolitan Statistical Area—see Appendix B for areas included
Source: Bureau of Labor Statistics, Local Area Unemployment Statistics

Average Wages

Occupation	$/Hr.	Occupation	$/Hr.
Accountants and Auditors	26.20	Maids and Housekeeping Cleaners	9.80
Automotive Mechanics	21.00	Maintenance and Repair Workers	16.10
Bookkeepers	17.50	Marketing Managers	48.90
Carpenters	20.00	Nuclear Medicine Technologists	n/a
Cashiers	10.10	Nurses, Licensed Practical	20.30
Clerks, General Office	14.00	Nurses, Registered	30.10
Clerks, Receptionists/Information	12.50	Nursing Assistants	11.80
Clerks, Shipping/Receiving	16.00	Packers and Packagers, Hand	10.80
Computer Programmers	30.20	Physical Therapists	42.30
Computer Systems Analysts	30.40	Postal Service Mail Carriers	24.90
Computer User Support Specialists	22.10	Real Estate Brokers	n/a
Cooks, Restaurant	12.50	Retail Salespersons	12.50
Dentists	72.00	Sales Reps., Exc. Tech./Scientific	28.00
Electrical Engineers	44.40	Sales Reps., Tech./Scientific	41.30
Electricians	20.80	Secretaries, Exc. Legal/Med./Exec.	17.20
Financial Managers	n/a	Security Guards	13.80
First-Line Supervisors/Managers, Sales	20.80	Surgeons	n/a
Food Preparation Workers	10.70	Teacher Assistants*	12.40
General and Operations Managers	n/a	Teachers, Elementary School*	22.10
Hairdressers/Cosmetologists	20.40	Teachers, Secondary School*	23.60
Internists, General	n/a	Telemarketers	13.80
Janitors and Cleaners	12.20	Truck Drivers, Heavy/Tractor-Trailer	17.40
Landscaping/Groundskeeping Workers	13.30	Truck Drivers, Light/Delivery Svcs.	16.30
Lawyers	56.70	Waiters and Waitresses	10.30

Note: Wage data covers the Tallahassee, FL Metropolitan Statistical Area—see Appendix B for areas included;
(*) Hourly wages for elementary/secondary school teachers and teacher assistants were calculated by the
editors from annual wage data based on a 40 hour work week; n/a not available.
Source: Bureau of Labor Statistics, Metro Area Occupational Employment & Wage Estimates, May 2018

Employment by Occupation

Occupation Classification	City (%)	MSA[1] (%)	U.S. (%)
Management, Business, Science, and Arts	45.0	42.8	37.4
Natural Resources, Construction, and Maintenance	3.6	6.7	8.9
Production, Transportation, and Material Moving	4.9	5.7	12.2
Sales and Office	26.8	26.1	23.5
Service	19.8	18.6	18.0

Note: Figures cover employed civilians 16 years of age and older; (1) Figures cover the Tallahassee, FL
Metropolitan Statistical Area—see Appendix B for areas included
Source: U.S. Census Bureau, 2013-2017 American Community Survey 5-Year Estimates

Employment by Industry

Sector	MSA[1]		U.S.
	Number of Employees	Percent of Total	Percent of Total
Construction, Mining, and Logging	8,600	4.5	5.3
Education and Health Services	24,400	12.9	15.9
Financial Activities	8,100	4.3	5.7
Government	62,500	33.1	15.1
Information	3,100	1.6	1.9
Leisure and Hospitality	21,200	11.2	10.7
Manufacturing	3,300	1.7	8.5
Other Services	9,900	5.2	3.9
Professional and Business Services	21,800	11.5	14.1
Retail Trade	19,900	10.5	10.8
Transportation, Warehousing, and Utilities	2,500	1.3	4.2
Wholesale Trade	3,800	2.0	3.9

Note: Figures are non-farm employment as of December 2018. Figures are not seasonally adjusted and include workers 16 years of age and older; (1) Figures cover the Tallahassee, FL Metropolitan Statistical Area—see Appendix B for areas included
Source: Bureau of Labor Statistics, Current Employment Statistics, Employment, Hours, and Earnings

Occupations with Greatest Projected Employment Growth: 2018 – 2020

Occupation[1]	2018 Employment	2020 Projected Employment	Numeric Employment Change	Percent Employment Change
Interviewers, Except Eligibility and Loan	11,890	33,270	21,380	179.8
Combined Food Preparation and Serving Workers, Including Fast Food	242,590	256,470	13,880	5.7
Waiters and Waitresses	230,640	240,320	9,680	4.2
Registered Nurses	193,200	202,070	8,870	4.6
Customer Service Representatives	245,420	253,780	8,360	3.4
Laborers and Freight, Stock, and Material Movers, Hand	135,600	143,640	8,040	5.9
Construction Laborers	89,390	97,130	7,740	8.7
Landscaping and Groundskeeping Workers	116,440	123,040	6,600	5.7
Carpenters	72,550	78,990	6,440	8.9
Janitors and Cleaners, Except Maids and Housekeeping Cleaners	133,890	140,000	6,110	4.6

Note: Projections cover Florida; (1) Sorted by numeric employment change
Source: www.projectionscentral.com, State Occupational Projections, 2018–2020 Short-Term Projections

Fastest Growing Occupations: 2018 – 2020

Occupation[1]	2018 Employment	2020 Projected Employment	Numeric Employment Change	Percent Employment Change
Interviewers, Except Eligibility and Loan	11,890	33,270	21,380	179.8
Solar Photovoltaic Installers	1,100	1,330	230	20.9
Terrazzo Workers and Finishers	390	450	60	15.4
Helpers—Roofers	1,490	1,720	230	15.4
Helpers—Brickmasons, Blockmasons, Stonemasons, and Tile and Marble Setters	1,280	1,470	190	14.8
Helpers—Painters, Paperhangers, Plasterers, and Stucco Masons	570	650	80	14.0
Reinforcing Iron and Rebar Workers	1,100	1,250	150	13.6
Insulation Workers, Floor, Ceiling, and Wall	2,550	2,880	330	12.9
Structural Iron and Steel Workers	5,210	5,880	670	12.9
Cement Masons and Concrete Finishers	13,490	15,210	1,720	12.8

Note: Projections cover Florida; (1) Sorted by percent employment change and excludes occupations with numeric employment change less than 50
Source: www.projectionscentral.com, State Occupational Projections, 2018–2020 Short-Term Projections

TAXES

State Corporate Income Tax Rates

State	Tax Rate (%)	Income Brackets ($)	Num. of Brackets	Financial Institution Tax Rate (%)[a]	Federal Income Tax Ded.
Florida	5.5 (e)	Flat rate	1	5.5 (e)	No

Note: Tax rates as of January 1, 2019; (a) Rates listed are the corporate income tax rate applied to financial institutions or excise taxes based on income. Some states have other taxes based upon the value of deposits or shares; (e) The Florida tax rate may be adjusted downward if certain revenue targets are met.
Source: Federation of Tax Administrators, Range of State Corporate Income Tax Rates, January 1, 2019

State Individual Income Tax Rates

State	Tax Rate (%)	Income Brackets ($)	Personal Exemptions ($) Single	Married	Depend.	Standard Ded. ($) Single	Married
Florida			– No state income tax –				

Note: Tax rates as of January 1, 2019; Local- and county-level taxes are not included; n/a not applicable;

Source: Federation of Tax Administrators, State Individual Income Tax Rates, January 1, 2019

Various State Sales and Excise Tax Rates

State	State Sales Tax (%)	Gasoline[1] (¢/gal.)	Cigarette[2] ($/pack)	Spirits[3] ($/gal.)	Wine[4] ($/gal.)	Beer[5] ($/gal.)	Recreational Marijuana (%)
Florida	6	41.99	1.339	6.50 (f)	2.25 (l)	0.48 (q)	Not legal

Note: All tax rates as of January 1, 2019; (1) The American Petroleum Institute has developed a methodology for determining the average tax rate on a gallon of fuel. Rates may include any of the following: excise taxes, environmental fees, storage tank fees, other fees or taxes, general sales tax, and local taxes. In states where gasoline is subject to the general sales tax, or where the fuel tax is based on the average sale price, the average rate determined by API is sensitive to changes in the price of gasoline. States that fully or partially apply general sales taxes to gasoline: CA, CO, GA, IL, IN, MI, NY; (2) The federal excise tax of $1.0066 per pack and local taxes are not included; (3) Rates are those applicable to off-premise sales of 40% alcohol by volume (a.b.v.) distilled spirits in 750ml containers. Local excise taxes are excluded; (4) Rates are those applicable to off-premise sales of 11% a.b.v. non-carbonated wine in 750ml containers; (5) Rates are those applicable to off-premise sales of 4.7% a.b.v. beer in 12 ounce containers; (f) Different rates also applicable according to alcohol content, place of production, size of container, or place purchased (on- or off-premise or onboard airlines); (l) Different rates also applicable to alcohol content, place of production, size of container, place purchased (on- or off-premise or on board airlines) or type of wine (carbonated, vermouth, etc.); (q) Different rates also applicable according to alcohol content, place of production, size of container, or place purchased (on- or off-premise or onboard airlines).
Source: Tax Foundation, 2019 Facts & Figures: How Does Your State Compare?

State Business Tax Climate Index Rankings

State	Overall Rank	Corporate Tax Rank	Individual Income Tax Rank	Sales Tax Rank	Unemployment Insurance Tax Rank	Property Tax Rank
Florida	4	6	1	22	2	11

Note: The index is a measure of how each state's tax laws affect economic performance. The lower the rank, the more favorable a state's tax system is for business. States without a given tax are given a ranking of 1. The scores/rankings for the District of Columbia do not affect other states. The 2019 index represents the tax climate as of July 1, 2018.
Source: Tax Foundation, State Business Tax Climate Index 2019

COMMERCIAL UTILITIES

Typical Monthly Electric Bills

Area	Commercial Service ($/month) 1,500 kWh	40 kW demand 14,000 kWh	Industrial Service ($/month) 1,000 kW demand 200,000 kWh	50,000 kW demand 32,500,000 kWh
City	n/a	n/a	n/a	n/a
Average[1]	203	1,619	25,886	2,540,077

Note: Figures are based on annualized rates; (1) Average based on 187 utilities surveyed; n/a not available
Source: Edison Electric Institute, Typical Bills and Average Rates Report, Summer 2018

TRANSPORTATION

Means of Transportation to Work

Area	Car/Truck/Van		Public Transportation			Bicycle	Walked	Other Means	Worked at Home
	Drove Alone	Car-pooled	Bus	Subway	Railroad				
City	79.4	8.9	2.3	0.0	0.0	0.9	3.3	1.5	3.7
MSA[1]	81.4	9.5	1.3	0.0	0.0	0.6	2.1	1.3	3.7
U.S.	76.4	9.2	2.5	1.9	0.6	0.6	2.7	1.3	4.7

Note: Figures are percentages and cover workers 16 years of age and older; (1) Figures cover the Tallahassee, FL Metropolitan Statistical Area—see Appendix B for areas included
Source: U.S. Census Bureau, 2013-2017 American Community Survey 5-Year Estimates

Travel Time to Work

Area	Less Than 10 Minutes	10 to 19 Minutes	20 to 29 Minutes	30 to 44 Minutes	45 to 59 Minutes	60 to 89 Minutes	90 Minutes or More
City	15.5	45.2	23.4	11.4	1.8	1.6	1.0
MSA[1]	11.8	34.1	24.2	20.5	5.4	2.5	1.5
U.S.	12.7	28.9	20.9	20.5	8.1	6.2	2.7

Note: Note: Figures are percentages and include workers 16 years old and over; (1) Figures cover the Tallahassee, FL Metropolitan Statistical Area—see Appendix B for areas included
Source: U.S. Census Bureau, 2013-2017 American Community Survey 5-Year Estimates

Freeway Travel Time Index

Area	1985	1990	1995	2000	2005	2010	2014
Urban Area Rank[1,2]	n/a	n/a	n/a	n/a	n/a	n/a	n/a
Urban Area Index[1]	n/a	n/a	n/a	n/a	n/a	n/a	n/a
Average Index[3]	1.09	1.11	1.14	1.17	1.20	1.19	1.20

Note: Freeway Travel Time Index—the ratio of travel time in the peak period to the travel time at free-flow conditions. For example, a value of 1.30 indicates a 20-minute free-flow trip takes 26 minutes in the peak (20 minutes x 1.30 = 26 minutes); (1) Data for the Tallahassee, FL urban area was not available; (2) Rank is based on 101 urban areas (#1 = highest travel time index); (3) Average of 101 urban areas
Source: Texas Transportation Institute, 2015 Urban Mobility Scorecard, August 2015

Freeway Commuter Stress Index

Area	1985	1990	1995	2000	2005	2010	2014
Urban Area Rank[1,2]	n/a	n/a	n/a	n/a	n/a	n/a	n/a
Urban Area Index[1]	n/a	n/a	n/a	n/a	n/a	n/a	n/a
Average Index[3]	1.13	1.16	1.19	1.22	1.25	1.24	1.25

Note: The Freeway Commuter Stress Index is the same as the Freeway Travel Time Index (see table above) except that it includes only the travel in the peak directions during the peak periods; the TTI includes travel in all directions during the peak period. Thus, the CSI is more indicative of the work trip experienced by each commuter on a daily basis; (1) Data for the Tallahassee, FL urban area was not available; (2) Rank is based on 101 urban areas (#1 = highest travel time index); (3) Average of 101 urban areas
Source: Texas Transportation Institute, 2015 Urban Mobility Scorecard, August 2015

Public Transportation

Agency Name / Mode of Transportation	Vehicles Operated in Maximum Service[1]	Annual Unlinked Passenger Trips[2] (in thous.)	Annual Passenger Miles[3] (in thous.)
City of Tallahassee (StarMetro)			
Bus (directly operated)	68	3,302.7	8,055.6
Demand Response (directly operated)	19	99.7	592.6

Note: (1) The number of revenue vehicles operated by the given mode and type of service to meet the annual maximum service requirement. This is the revenue vehicle count during the peak season of the year; on the week and day that maximum service is provided. Vehicles operated in maximum service (VOMS) exclude atypical days and one-time special events; (2) The number of passengers who boarded public transportation vehicles. Passengers are counted each time they board a vehicle no matter how many vehicles they use to travel from their origin to their destination. (3) The sum of the distances ridden by all passengers during the entire fiscal year.
Source: Federal Transit Administration, National Transit Database, 2017

Air Transportation

Airport Name and Code / Type of Service	Passenger Airlines[1]	Passenger Enplanements	Freight Carriers[2]	Freight (lbs)
Tallahassee Regional (TLH)				
Domestic service (U.S. carriers - 2018)	20	383,815	4	9,460,561
International service (U.S. carriers - 2017)	1	78	0	0

Note: (1) Includes all U.S.-based major, minor and commuter airlines that carried at least one passenger during the year; (2) Includes all U.S.-based airlines and freight carriers that transported at least one pound of freight during the year.
Source: Bureau of Transportation Statistics, The Intermodal Transportation Database, Air Carriers: T-100 Domestic Market (U.S. Carriers), 2018; Bureau of Transportation Statistics, The Intermodal Transportation Database, Air Carriers: T-100 International Market (U.S. Carriers), 2017

Other Transportation Statistics

Major Highways:	I-10
Amtrak Service:	No
Major Waterways/Ports:	None

Source: Amtrak.com; Google Maps

BUSINESSES

Major Business Headquarters

Company Name	Industry	Rankings	
		Fortune[1]	Forbes[2]
No companies listed	-	-	-

Note: (1) Companies that produce a 10-K are ranked 1 to 500 based on 2017 revenue; (2) All private companies with at least $2 billion in annual revenue through the end of their most current fiscal year are ranked 1 to 229; companies listed are headquartered in the city; dashes indicate no ranking
Source: Fortune, "Fortune 500," June 2018; Forbes, "America's Largest Private Companies," 2018 Rankings

Minority- and Women-Owned Businesses

Group	All Firms		Firms with Paid Employees			
	Firms	Sales ($000)	Firms	Sales ($000)	Employees	Payroll ($000)
AIAN[1]	62	1,253	3	(s)	0 - 19	(s)
Asian	704	165,318	239	148,868	1,678	26,752
Black	3,405	164,399	169	121,847	1,275	32,290
Hispanic	485	(s)	93	(s)	500 - 999	(s)
NHOPI[2]	n/a	n/a	n/a	n/a	n/a	n/a
Women	5,857	624,543	803	520,287	4,286	140,616
All Firms	15,714	14,292,019	4,631	13,829,605	81,761	3,052,137

Note: Figures cover firms located in the city; minority- and women-owned business are defined as firms in which the corresponding group own 51% or more of the stock or equity of the company; (1) American Indian and Alaska Native; (2) Native Hawaiian and Other Pacific Islander; (s) estimates are suppressed when publication standards are not met; n/a not available
Source: U.S. Census Bureau, 2012 Economic Census, Survey of Business Owners

HOTELS & CONVENTION CENTERS

Hotels, Motels and Vacation Rentals

Area	5 Star		4 Star		3 Star		2 Star		1 Star		Not Rated	
	Num.	Pct.[3]	Num.	Pct.[3]	Num.	Pct.[3]	Num.	Pct.[3]	Num.	Pct.[3]	Num.	Pct.[3]
City[1]	0	0.0	5	2.6	19	9.7	60	30.8	2	1.0	109	55.9
Total[2]	286	0.4	5,236	7.1	16,715	22.6	10,259	13.9	293	0.4	41,056	55.6

Note: (1) Figures cover Tallahassee and vicinity; (2) Figures cover all 100 cities in this book; (3) Percentage of hotels which have a given star rating; Star ratings are determined by expedia.com and offer an indication of the general quality of a particular hotel.
Source: www.expedia.com, April 3, 2019

Major Convention Centers

Name	Overall Space (sq. ft.)	Exhibit Space (sq. ft.)	Meeting Space (sq. ft.)	Meeting Rooms
Donald L. Tucker Civic Center at FSU	n/a	54,000	n/a	n/a

Note: Table includes convention centers located in the Tallahassee, FL metro area; n/a not available
Source: Original research

Living Environment

COST OF LIVING

Cost of Living Index

Composite Index	Groceries	Housing	Utilities	Trans-portation	Health Care	Misc. Goods/Services
96.7	110.3	91.7	87.0	95.9	99.0	98.2

Note: The Cost of Living Index measures regional differences in the cost of consumer goods and services, excluding taxes and non-consumer expenditures, for professional and managerial households in the top income quintile. It is based on more than 50,000 prices covering almost 60 different items for which prices are collected three times a year by chambers of commerce, economic development organizations or university applied economic centers in each participating urban area. The numbers shown should be read as a percentage above or below the national average of 100. For example, a value of 115.4 in the groceries column indicates that grocery prices are 15.4% higher than the national average. Small differences in the index numbers should not be interpreted as significant; Figures cover the Tallahassee FL urban area.
Source: The Council for Community and Economic Research, ACCRA Cost of Living Index, 2018

Grocery Prices

Area[1]	T-Bone Steak ($/pound)	Frying Chicken ($/pound)	Whole Milk ($/half gal.)	Eggs ($/dozen)	Orange Juice ($/64 oz.)	Coffee ($/11.5 oz.)
City[2]	10.69	1.54	2.43	2.38	3.82	3.97
Avg.	11.35	1.42	1.94	1.81	3.52	4.35
Min.	7.45	0.92	0.80	0.75	2.72	3.06
Max.	15.05	2.76	4.18	4.00	5.36	8.20

Note: (1) Values for the local area are compared with the average, minimum and maximum values for all 291 areas in the Cost of Living Index; (2) Figures cover the Tallahassee FL urban area; T-Bone Steak (price per pound); Frying Chicken (price per pound, whole fryer); Whole Milk (half gallon carton); Eggs (price per dozen, Grade A, large); Orange Juice (64 oz. Tropicana or Florida Natural); Coffee (11.5 oz. can, vacuum-packed, Maxwell House, Hills Bros, or Folgers).
Source: The Council for Community and Economic Research, ACCRA Cost of Living Index, 2018

Housing and Utility Costs

Area[1]	New Home Price ($)	Apartment Rent ($/month)	All Electric ($/month)	Part Electric ($/month)	Other Energy ($/month)	Telephone ($/month)
City[2]	312,353	1,043	124.35	-	-	184.30
Avg.	347,000	1,087	165.93	100.16	67.73	178.70
Min.	200,468	500	93.58	25.64	26.78	163.10
Max.	1,901,222	4,888	388.65	246.86	332.81	197.70

Note: (1) Values for the local area are compared with the average, minimum and maximum values for all 291 areas in the Cost of Living Index; (2) Figures cover the Tallahassee FL urban area; New Home Price (2,400 sf living area, 8,000 sf lot, in urban area with full utilities); Apartment Rent (950 sf 2 bedroom/1.5 or 2 bath, unfurnished, excluding all utilities except water); All Electric (average monthly cost for an all-electric home); Part Electric (average monthly cost for a part-electric home); Other Energy (average monthly cost for natural gas, fuel oil, coal, wood, and any other forms of energy except electricity); Telephone (price includes the base monthly rate plus taxes and fees for three lines of mobile phone service).
Source: The Council for Community and Economic Research, ACCRA Cost of Living Index, 2018

Health Care, Transportation, and Other Costs

Area[1]	Doctor ($/visit)	Dentist ($/visit)	Optometrist ($/visit)	Gasoline ($/gallon)	Beauty Salon ($/visit)	Men's Shirt ($)
City[2]	98.80	97.06	90.48	2.57	36.33	27.04
Avg.	110.71	95.11	103.74	2.61	37.48	32.03
Min.	33.60	62.55	54.63	1.89	17.00	11.44
Max.	195.97	153.93	225.79	3.59	71.88	58.64

Note: (1) Values for the local area are compared with the average, minimum and maximum values for all 291 areas in the Cost of Living Index; (2) Figures cover the Tallahassee FL urban area; Doctor (general practitioners routine exam of an established patient); Dentist (adult teeth cleaning and periodic oral examination); Optometrist (full vision eye exam for established adult patient); Gasoline (one gallon regular unleaded, national brand, including all taxes, cash price at self-service pump if available); Beauty Salon (woman's shampoo, trim, and blow-dry); Men's Shirt (cotton/polyester dress shirt, pinpoint weave, long sleeves).
Source: The Council for Community and Economic Research, ACCRA Cost of Living Index, 2018

HOUSING

House Price Index (HPI)

Area	National Ranking[2]	Quarterly Change (%)	One-Year Change (%)	Five-Year Change (%)
MSA[1]	(a)	n/a	-0.05	21.69
U.S.[3]	—	1.12	5.73	32.81

Note: The HPI is a weighted repeat sales index. It measures average price changes in repeat sales or refinancings on the same properties. This information is obtained by reviewing repeat mortgage transactions on single-family properties whose mortgages have been purchased or securitized by Fannie Mae or Freddie Mac in January 1975; (1) Figures cover the Tallahassee, FL Metropolitan Statistical Area—see Appendix B for areas included; (2) Rankings are based on annual percentage change for all metro areas containing at least 15,000 transactions over the last 10 years and ranges from 1 to 245; (3) figures based on a weighted average of Census Division estimates using a seasonally adjusted, purchase-only index; all figures are for the period ending December 31, 2018; n/a not available; (a) Not ranked because of increased index variability due to smaller sample size
Source: Federal Housing Finance Agency, House Price Index, February 26, 2019

Median Single-Family Home Prices

Area	2016	2017	2018[p]	Percent Change 2017 to 2018
MSA[1]	187.0	204.9	215.0	4.9
U.S. Average	235.5	248.8	261.6	5.1

Note: Figures are median sales prices of existing single-family homes in thousands of dollars; (p) preliminary; (1) Figures cover the Tallahassee, FL Metropolitan Statistical Area—see Appendix B for areas included
Source: National Association of Realtors, Median Sales Price of Existing Single-Family Homes for Metropolitan Areas, 4th Quarter 2018

Qualifying Income Based on Median Sales Price of Existing Single-Family Homes

Area	With 5% Down ($)	With 10% Down ($)	With 20% Down ($)
MSA[1]	52,421	49,662	44,144
U.S. Average	62,954	59,640	53,013

Note: Figures are preliminary; Qualifying income is based on a mortgage rate of 4.9%. Monthly principal and interest payment is limited to 25% of income; (1) Figures cover the Tallahassee, FL Metropolitan Statistical Area—see Appendix B for areas included
Source: National Association of Realtors, Qualifying Income Based on Median Sales Price of Existing Single-Family Homes for Metropolitan Areas, 4th Quarter 2018

Median Apartment Condo-Coop Home Prices

Area	2016	2017	2018[p]	Percent Change 2017 to 2018
MSA[1]	96.9	106.0	108.0	1.9
U.S. Average	220.7	234.3	241.0	2.9

Note: Figures are median sales prices of existing apartment condo-coop homes in thousands of dollars; (p) preliminary; (1) Figures cover the Tallahassee, FL Metropolitan Statistical Area—see Appendix B for areas included
Source: National Association of Realtors, Median Sales Price of Existing Apartment Condo-Coop Homes for Metropolitan Areas, 4th Quarter 2018

Home Value Distribution

Area	Under $50,000	$50,000 -$99,999	$100,000 -$149,999	$150,000 -$199,999	$200,000 -$299,999	$300,000 -$499,999	$500,000 -$999,999	$1,000,000 or more
City	4.4	12.5	17.2	21.8	24.8	15.7	2.9	0.7
MSA[1]	9.3	16.8	16.6	18.7	21.1	13.3	3.5	0.7
U.S.	8.3	13.9	14.7	14.6	18.7	17.3	9.7	2.7

Note: Figures are percentages and cover owner-occupied housing units; (1) Figures cover the Tallahassee, FL Metropolitan Statistical Area—see Appendix B for areas included
Source: U.S. Census Bureau, 2013-2017 American Community Survey 5-Year Estimates

Homeownership Rate

Area	2010 (%)	2011 (%)	2012 (%)	2013 (%)	2014 (%)	2015 (%)	2016 (%)	2017 (%)	2018 (%)
MSA[1]	n/a	n/a	n/a	n/a	n/a	n/a	n/a	n/a	n/a
U.S.	66.9	66.1	65.4	65.1	64.5	63.7	63.4	63.9	64.4

Note: (1) Figures cover the Tallahassee, FL Metropolitan Statistical Area—see Appendix B for areas included; n/a not available
Source: U.S. Census Bureau, Housing Vacancies and Homeownership Annual Statistics: 2010-2018

Year Housing Structure Built

Area	2010 or Later	2000 -2009	1990 -1999	1980 -1989	1970 -1979	1960 -1969	1950 -1959	1940 -1949	Before 1940	Median Year
City	2.8	19.3	21.2	18.0	17.0	9.5	7.6	2.9	1.6	1986
MSA[1]	2.9	19.4	23.0	19.7	16.0	8.4	6.2	2.4	2.0	1988
U.S.	3.2	14.5	14.0	13.6	15.5	10.8	10.5	5.1	12.9	1977

Note: Figures are percentages except for Median Year; Note: (1) Figures cover the Tallahassee, FL Metropolitan Statistical Area—see Appendix B for areas included
Source: U.S. Census Bureau, 2013-2017 American Community Survey 5-Year Estimates

Gross Monthly Rent

Area	Under $500	$500 -$999	$1,000 -$1,499	$1,500 -$1,999	$2,000 -$2,499	$2,500 -$2,999	$3,000 and up	Median ($)
City	5.9	49.7	32.6	8.1	3.0	0.5	0.3	957
MSA[1]	7.4	50.1	31.3	7.8	2.8	0.4	0.2	938
U.S.	10.5	41.1	28.7	11.7	4.5	1.8	1.7	982

Note: Figures are percentages except for Median; Gross rent is the contract rent plus the estimated average monthly cost of utilities (electricity, gas, and water and sewer) and fuels (oil, coal, kerosene, wood, etc.) if these are paid by the renter (or paid for the renter by someone else); (1) Figures cover the Tallahassee, FL Metropolitan Statistical Area—see Appendix B for areas included
Source: U.S. Census Bureau, 2013-2017 American Community Survey 5-Year Estimates

HEALTH

Health Risk Factors

Category	MSA[1] (%)	U.S. (%)
Adults aged 18–64 who have any kind of health care coverage	88.0	87.3
Adults who reported being in good or better health	87.7	82.4
Adults who have been told they have high blood cholesterol	27.7	33.0
Adults who have been told they have high blood pressure	28.4	32.3
Adults who are current smokers	14.0	17.1
Adults who currently use E-cigarettes	n/a	4.6
Adults who currently use chewing tobacco, snuff, or snus	3.3	4.0
Adults who are heavy drinkers[2]	9.0	6.3
Adults who are binge drinkers[3]	18.7	17.4
Adults who are overweight (BMI 25.0 - 29.9)	25.4	35.3
Adults who are obese (BMI 30.0 - 99.8)	32.3	31.3
Adults who participated in any physical activities in the past month	72.4	74.4
Adults who always or nearly always wears a seat belt	95.1	94.3

Note: n/a not available; (1) Figures cover the Tallahassee, FL Metropolitan Statistical Area—see Appendix B for areas included; (2) Heavy drinkers are classified as adult men having more than 14 drinks per week and adult women having more than 7 drinks per week; (3) Binge drinkers are classified as males having five or more drinks on one occasion or females having four or more drinks on one occasion
Source: Centers for Disease Control and Prevention, Behaviorial Risk Factor Surveillance System, SMART: Selected Metropolitan Area Risk Trends, 2017

Acute and Chronic Health Conditions

Category	MSA[1] (%)	U.S. (%)
Adults who have ever been told they had a heart attack	2.6	4.2
Adults who have ever been told they have angina or coronary heart disease	3.2	3.9
Adults who have ever been told they had a stroke	2.4	3.0
Adults who have ever been told they have asthma	12.5	14.2
Adults who have ever been told they have arthritis	18.5	24.9
Adults who have ever been told they have diabetes[2]	8.7	10.5
Adults who have ever been told they had skin cancer	8.5	6.2
Adults who have ever been told they had any other types of cancer	5.1	7.1
Adults who have ever been told they have COPD	5.1	6.5
Adults who have ever been told they have kidney disease	n/a	3.0
Adults who have ever been told they have a form of depression	15.7	20.5

Note: n/a not available; (1) Figures cover the Tallahassee, FL Metropolitan Statistical Area—see Appendix B for areas included; (2) Figures do not include pregnancy-related, borderline, or pre-diabetes
Source: Centers for Disease Control and Prevention, Behaviorial Risk Factor Surveillance System, SMART: Selected Metropolitan Area Risk Trends, 2017

Health Screening and Vaccination Rates

Category	MSA[1] (%)	U.S. (%)
Adults aged 65+ who have had flu shot within the past year	68.0	60.7
Adults aged 65+ who have ever had a pneumonia vaccination	75.7	75.4
Adults who have ever been tested for HIV	49.8	36.1
Adults who have ever had the shingles or zoster vaccine?	33.6	28.9
Adults who have had their blood cholesterol checked within the last five years	88.4	85.9

Note: n/a not available; (1) Figures cover the Tallahassee, FL Metropolitan Statistical Area—see Appendix B for areas included.
Source: Centers for Disease Control and Prevention, Behaviorial Risk Factor Surveillance System, SMART: Selected Metropolitan Area Risk Trends, 2017

Disability Status

Category	MSA[1] (%)	U.S. (%)
Adults who reported being deaf	7.3	6.7
Are you blind or have serious difficulty seeing, even when wearing glasses?	6.3	4.5
Are you limited in any way in any of your usual activities due of arthritis?	8.9	12.9
Do you have difficulty doing errands alone?	4.8	6.8
Do you have difficulty dressing or bathing?	n/a	3.6
Do you have serious difficulty concentrating/remembering/making decisions?	8.9	10.7
Do you have serious difficulty walking or climbing stairs?	11.2	13.6

Note: n/a not available; (1) Figures cover the Tallahassee, FL Metropolitan Statistical Area—see Appendix B for areas included.
Source: Centers for Disease Control and Prevention, Behaviorial Risk Factor Surveillance System, SMART: Selected Metropolitan Area Risk Trends, 2017

Mortality Rates for the Top 10 Causes of Death in the U.S.

ICD-10[a] Sub-Chapter	ICD-10[a] Code	Age-Adjusted Mortality Rate[1] per 100,000 population	
		County[2]	U.S.
Malignant neoplasms	C00-C97	144.3	155.5
Ischaemic heart diseases	I20-I25	79.0	94.8
Other forms of heart disease	I30-I51	47.4	52.9
Chronic lower respiratory diseases	J40-J47	28.1	41.0
Cerebrovascular diseases	I60-I69	36.0	37.5
Other degenerative diseases of the nervous system	G30-G31	43.1	35.0
Other external causes of accidental injury	W00-X59	24.9	33.7
Organic, including symptomatic, mental disorders	F01-F09	44.6	31.0
Hypertensive diseases	I10-I15	18.5	21.9
Diabetes mellitus	E10-E14	17.3	21.2

Note: (a) ICD-10 = International Classification of Diseases 10th Revision; (1) Mortality rates are a three year average covering 2015-2017; (2) Figures cover Leon County.
Source: Centers for Disease Control and Prevention, National Center for Health Statistics. Underlying Cause of Death 1999-2017 on CDC WONDER Online Database

Mortality Rates for Selected Causes of Death

ICD-10[a] Sub-Chapter	ICD-10[a] Code	Age-Adjusted Mortality Rate[1] per 100,000 population	
		County[2]	U.S.
Assault	X85-Y09	4.2	5.9
Diseases of the liver	K70-K76	11.6	14.1
Human immunodeficiency virus (HIV) disease	B20-B24	4.5	1.8
Influenza and pneumonia	J09-J18	10.8	14.3
Intentional self-harm	X60-X84	11.0	13.6
Malnutrition	E40-E46	Suppressed	1.6
Obesity and other hyperalimentation	E65-E68	3.0	2.1
Renal failure	N17-N19	8.6	13.0
Transport accidents	V01-V99	10.9	12.4
Viral hepatitis	B15-B19	Unreliable	1.6

Note: (a) ICD-10 = International Classification of Diseases 10th Revision; (1) Mortality rates are a three year average covering 2015-2017; (2) Figures cover Leon County; Data are suppressed when the data meet the criteria for confidentiality constraints; Mortality rates are flagged as unreliable when the rate would be calculated with a numerator of 20 or less.
Source: Centers for Disease Control and Prevention, National Center for Health Statistics. Underlying Cause of Death 1999-2017 on CDC WONDER Online Database

Health Insurance Coverage

Area	With Health Insurance	With Private Health Insurance	With Public Health Insurance	Without Health Insurance	Population Under Age 18 Without Health Insurance
City	90.5	75.7	23.8	9.5	4.2
MSA[1]	90.0	72.4	28.9	10.0	5.1
U.S.	89.5	67.2	33.8	10.5	5.7

Note: Figures are percentages that cover the civilian noninstitutionalized population; (1) Figures cover the Tallahassee, FL Metropolitan Statistical Area—see Appendix B for areas included
Source: U.S. Census Bureau, 2013-2017 American Community Survey 5-Year Estimates

Number of Medical Professionals

Area	MDs[3]	DOs[3,4]	Dentists	Podiatrists	Chiropractors	Optometrists
County[1] (number)	839	34	131	10	65	52
County[1] (rate[2])	292.3	11.8	45.1	3.4	22.4	17.9
U.S. (rate[2])	279.3	23.0	68.4	6.0	27.1	16.2

Note: Data as of 2017 unless noted; (1) Data covers Leon County; (2) Rate per 100,000 population; (3) Data as of 2016 and includes all active, non-federal physicians; (4) Doctor of Osteopathic Medicine
Source: U.S. Department of Health and Human Services, Health Resources and Services Administration, Bureau of Health Professions, Area Resource File (ARF) 2017-2018

EDUCATION

Public School District Statistics

District Name	Schls	Pupils	Pupil/ Teacher Ratio	Minority Pupils[1] (%)	Free Lunch Eligible[2] (%)	IEP[3] (%)
FSU Lab Sch	3	2,419	12.9	58.2	n/a	7.2
Leon County Schools	59	33,952	16.8	57.4	40.1	15.4

Note: Table includes school districts with 2,000 or more students; (1) Percentage of students that are not non-Hispanic white; (2) Percentage of students that are eligible for the free lunch program; (3) Percentage of students that have an Individualized Education Program.
Source: U.S. Department of Education, National Center for Education Statistics, Common Core of Data, Local Education Agency (School District) Universe Survey: School Year 2016-2017; U.S. Department of Education, National Center for Education Statistics, Common Core of Data, Public Elementary/Secondary School Universe Survey: School Year 2016-2017

Highest Level of Education

Area	Less than H.S.	H.S. Diploma	Some College, No Deg.	Associate Degree	Bachelor's Degree	Master's Degree	Prof. School Degree	Doctorate Degree
City	6.7	16.3	19.2	9.8	26.3	13.8	3.8	4.1
MSA[1]	9.8	23.4	20.1	9.1	21.6	10.3	2.9	2.9
U.S.	12.7	27.3	20.8	8.3	19.1	8.4	2.0	1.4

Note: Figures cover persons age 25 and over; (1) Figures cover the Tallahassee, FL Metropolitan Statistical Area—see Appendix B for areas included
Source: U.S. Census Bureau, 2013-2017 American Community Survey 5-Year Estimates

Educational Attainment by Race

Area	High School Graduate or Higher (%)					Bachelor's Degree or Higher (%)				
	Total	White	Black	Asian	Hisp.[2]	Total	White	Black	Asian	Hisp.[2]
City	93.3	96.8	87.0	96.8	85.2	48.0	56.0	29.1	84.0	40.5
MSA[1]	90.2	93.5	82.6	96.2	81.3	37.7	42.7	23.2	79.5	32.7
U.S.	87.3	89.3	84.9	86.5	66.7	30.9	32.2	20.6	52.7	15.2

Note: Figures shown cover persons 25 years old and over; (1) Figures cover the Tallahassee, FL Metropolitan Statistical Area—see Appendix B for areas included; (2) People of Hispanic origin can be of any race
Source: U.S. Census Bureau, 2013-2017 American Community Survey 5-Year Estimates

School Enrollment by Grade and Control

Area	Preschool (%)		Kindergarten (%)		Grades 1 - 4 (%)		Grades 5 - 8 (%)		Grades 9 - 12 (%)	
	Public	Private	Public	Private	Public	Private	Public	Private	Public	Private
City	49.3	50.7	87.8	12.2	83.8	16.2	79.7	20.3	87.1	12.9
MSA[1]	54.2	45.8	86.3	13.7	85.7	14.3	81.3	18.7	87.5	12.5
U.S.	58.8	41.2	87.7	12.3	89.7	10.3	89.6	10.4	90.3	9.7

Note: Figures shown cover persons 3 years old and over; (1) Figures cover the Tallahassee, FL Metropolitan Statistical Area—see Appendix B for areas included
Source: U.S. Census Bureau, 2013-2017 American Community Survey 5-Year Estimates

Average Salaries of Public School Classroom Teachers

Area	2016		2017		Change from 2016 to 2017	
	Dollars	Rank[1]	Dollars	Rank[1]	Percent	Rank[2]
Florida	46,612	46	47,267	45	1.4	26
U.S. Average	58,479	–	59,660	–	2.0	–

Note: (1) Rank ranges from 1 to 51 where 1 indicates highest salary; (2) Rank ranges from 1 to 51 where 1 indicates highest percent change.
Source: National Education Association, Rankings & Estimates: Rankings of the States 2017 and Estimates of School Statistics 2018

Higher Education

Four-Year Colleges			Two-Year Colleges			Medical Schools[1]	Law Schools[2]	Voc/ Tech[3]
Public	Private Non-profit	Private For-profit	Public	Private Non-profit	Private For-profit			
3	1	0	0	0	0	1	1	4

Note: Figures cover institutions located within the city limits and include main campuses only; (1) includes schools accredited by the Liaison Committee on Medical Education and the American Osteopathic Association's Commission on Osteopathic College Accreditation; (2) includes ABA-accredited schools, schools with provisional ABA accreditation, and state accredited schools; (3) includes all schools with programs that are less than 2 years.
Source: National Center for Education Statistics, Integrated Postsecondary Education System (IPEDS), 2017-18; Wikipedia, List of Medical Schools in the United States, accessed April 3, 2019; Wikipedia, List of Law Schools in the United States, accessed April 3, 2019

According to *U.S. News & World Report,* the Tallahassee, FL metro area is home to one of the best national universities in the U.S.: **Florida State University** (#70 tie). The indicators used to capture academic quality fall into a number of categories: assessment by administrators at peer institutions; retention of students; faculty resources; student selectivity; financial resources; alumni giving; high school counselor ratings of colleges; and graduation rate. *U.S. News & World Report, "America's Best Colleges 2019"*

According to *U.S. News & World Report,* the Tallahassee, FL metro area is home to one of the top 100 law schools in the U.S.: **Florida State University** (#48 tie). The rankings are based on a weighted average of 12 measures of quality: peer assessment score; assessment score by lawyers/judges; median LSAT scores; median undergrad GPA; acceptance rate; employment rates for graduates; placement success; bar passage rate; faculty resources; expenditures per student; student/faculty ratio; and library resources. *U.S. News & World Report, "America's Best Graduate Schools, Law, 2020"*

PRESIDENTIAL ELECTION

2016 Presidential Election Results

Area	Clinton	Trump	Johnson	Stein	Other
Leon County	59.8	35.0	2.9	0.9	1.4
U.S.	48.0	45.9	3.3	1.1	1.7

Note: Results are percentages and may not add to 100% due to rounding
Source: Dave Leip's Atlas of U.S. Presidential Elections

EMPLOYERS

Major Employers

Company Name	Industry
ACS, A Xerox Company	Manufacturer
Apalachee Center	Behavioral health network
Big Bend Hospice	Healthcare
Capital City Bank Group	Financial services
Capital Health Plan	Healthcare
Capital Regional Medical Center	Healthcare
CenturyLink	High speed internet, phone & TV services
City of Tallahassee	Government
Danfoss Turbocor	Compressors mfg
Florida A&M University	Education
Florida Bar	Law association
Florida State University	Education
General Dynamics Lands System	Supplier of armored vehicles
Leon County	Government
Leon County Schools	Education
Publix Supermarkets	Retail grocery
St. Mark Powder, a General Dynamics Co.	Manufacturer of commercial smokeless powder
State of Florida	State government
Tallahassee Community College	Education
Tallahassee Memorial HealthCare	Healthcare
Tallahassee Primary Care Associates	Healthcare
University Center Club	Meeting & event center
Veterans of Foreign Wars	Government
Wal-Mart Stores	Retail
Westminster Oaks	Health care

Note: Companies shown are located within the Tallahassee, FL Metropolitan Statistical Area.
Source: Hoovers.com; Wikipedia

PUBLIC SAFETY

Crime Rate

Area	All Crimes	Violent Crimes				Property Crimes		
		Murder	Rape[3]	Robbery	Aggrav. Assault	Burglary	Larceny-Theft	Motor Vehicle Theft
City	5,679.8	8.8	98.7	180.8	492.6	789.3	3,722.9	386.6
Suburbs[1]	2,593.3	4.2	51.0	33.7	344.7	533.6	1,504.5	121.6
Metro[2]	4,146.4	6.5	75.0	107.7	419.1	662.3	2,620.8	254.9
U.S.	2,756.1	5.3	41.7	98.0	248.9	430.4	1,694.4	237.4

Note: Figures are crimes per 100,000 population; (1) All areas within the metro area that are located outside the city limits; (2) Figures cover the Tallahassee, FL Metropolitan Statistical Area—see Appendix B for areas included; (3) The city and U.S. figures shown were reported using the revised Uniform Crime Reporting (UCR) definition of rape. The suburban and metro area figures shown are an aggregate total of the data submitted using both the revised and legacy UCR definitions.
Source: FBI Uniform Crime Reports, 2017

Hate Crimes

Area	Number of Quarters Reported	Number of Incidents per Bias Motivation					
		Race/Ethnicity/Ancestry	Religion	Sexual Orientation	Disability	Gender	Gender Identity
City	4	0	0	0	0	0	0
U.S.	4	4,131	1,564	1,130	116	46	119

Source: Federal Bureau of Investigation, Hate Crime Statistics 2017

Identity Theft Consumer Reports

Area	Reports	Reports per 100,000 Population	Rank[2]
MSA[1]	570	150	31
U.S.	444,602	135	-

Note: (1) Figures cover the Tallahassee, FL Metropolitan Statistical Area—see Appendix B for areas included; (2) Rank ranges from 1 to 389 where 1 indicates greatest number of identity theft reports per 100,000 population
Source: Federal Trade Commission, Consumer Sentinel Network Data Book for January–December 2018

Fraud and Other Consumer Reports

Area	Reports	Reports per 100,000 Population	Rank[2]
MSA[1]	2,428	640	39
U.S.	2,552,917	776	-

Note: (1) Figures cover the Tallahassee, FL Metropolitan Statistical Area—see Appendix B for areas included; (2) Rank ranges from 1 to 389 where 1 indicates greatest number of fraud and other consumer reports per 100,000 population
Source: Federal Trade Commission, Consumer Sentinel Network Data Book for January–December 2018

SPORTS

Professional Sports Teams

Team Name	League	Year Established

No teams are located in the metro area
Source: Wikipedia, Major Professional Sports Teams of the United States and Canada, April 5, 2019

CLIMATE

Average and Extreme Temperatures

Temperature	Jan	Feb	Mar	Apr	May	Jun	Jul	Aug	Sep	Oct	Nov	Dec	Yr.
Extreme High (°F)	83	89	90	95	102	103	103	102	99	94	88	84	103
Average High (°F)	64	67	73	80	86	90	91	91	88	81	72	66	79
Average Temp. (°F)	52	55	61	67	74	80	81	81	78	69	60	54	68
Average Low (°F)	40	42	48	53	62	69	71	72	68	57	47	41	56
Extreme Low (°F)	6	14	20	29	34	46	57	61	40	30	13	10	6

Note: Figures cover the years 1948-1990
Source: National Climatic Data Center, International Station Meteorological Climate Summary, 9/96

Average Precipitation/Snowfall/Humidity

Precip./Humidity	Jan	Feb	Mar	Apr	May	Jun	Jul	Aug	Sep	Oct	Nov	Dec	Yr.
Avg. Precip. (in.)	4.2	5.1	6.0	4.2	4.5	6.8	8.8	7.1	5.7	2.9	3.5	4.5	63.3
Avg. Snowfall (in.)	Tr	Tr	Tr	0	0	0	0	0	0	0	0	Tr	Tr
Avg. Rel. Hum. 7am (%)	86	87	88	89	89	91	93	94	93	90	89	87	90
Avg. Rel. Hum. 4pm (%)	54	51	49	46	50	58	66	64	60	51	52	55	55

Note: Figures cover the years 1948-1990; Tr = Trace amounts (<0.05 in. of rain; <0.5 in. of snow)
Source: National Climatic Data Center, International Station Meteorological Climate Summary, 9/96

Weather Conditions

Temperature			Daytime Sky			Precipitation		
10°F & below	32°F & below	90°F & above	Clear	Partly cloudy	Cloudy	0.01 inch or more precip.	0.1 inch or more snow/ice	Thunder-storms
<1	31	86	93	175	97	114	1	83

Note: Figures are average number of days per year and cover the years 1948-1990
Source: National Climatic Data Center, International Station Meteorological Climate Summary, 9/96

HAZARDOUS WASTE

Superfund Sites

The Tallahassee, FL metro area is home to one site on the EPA's Superfund National Priorities List: **Post and Lumber Preserving Co Inc** (final). There are a total of 1,390 Superfund sites with a status of proposed or final on the list in the U.S. *U.S. Environmental Protection Agency, National Priorities List, April 5, 2019*

**AIR & WATER
QUALITY**

Air Quality Trends: Ozone

	1990	1995	2000	2005	2010	2012	2014	2015	2016	2017
MSA[1]	n/a	n/a	n/a	n/a	n/a	n/a	n/a	n/a	n/a	n/a
U.S.	0.088	0.089	0.082	0.080	0.073	0.075	0.067	0.068	0.069	0.068

Note: (1) Data covers the Tallahassee, FL Metropolitan Statistical Area—see Appendix B for areas included; n/a not available. The values shown are the composite ozone concentration averages among trend sites based on the highest fourth daily maximum 8-hour concentration in parts per million. These trends are based on sites having an adequate record of monitoring data during the trend period. Data from exceptional events are included.
Source: U.S. Environmental Protection Agency, Air Quality Monitoring Information, "Air Quality Trends by City, 1990-2017"

Air Quality Index

Area	Percent of Days when Air Quality was...[2]					AQI Statistics[2]	
	Good	Moderate	Unhealthy for Sensitive Groups	Unhealthy	Very Unhealthy	Maximum	Median
MSA[1]	71.1	28.9	0.0	0.0	0.0	92	41

Note: (1) Data covers the Tallahassee, FL Metropolitan Statistical Area—see Appendix B for areas included; (2) Based on 363 days with AQI data in 2017. Air Quality Index (AQI) is an index for reporting daily air quality. EPA calculates the AQI for five major air pollutants regulated by the Clean Air Act: ground-level ozone, particle pollution (aka particulate matter), carbon monoxide, sulfur dioxide, and nitrogen dioxide. The AQI runs from 0 to 500. The higher the AQI value, the greater the level of air pollution and the greater the health concern. There are six AQI categories: "Good" AQI is between 0 and 50. Air quality is considered satisfactory; "Moderate" AQI is between 51 and 100. Air quality is acceptable; "Unhealthy for Sensitive Groups" When AQI values are between 101 and 150, members of sensitive groups may experience health effects; "Unhealthy" When AQI values are between 151 and 200 everyone may begin to experience health effects; "Very Unhealthy" AQI values between 201 and 300 trigger a health alert; "Hazardous" AQI values over 300 trigger warnings of emergency conditions (not shown).
Source: U.S. Environmental Protection Agency, Air Quality Index Report, 2017

Air Quality Index Pollutants

Area	Percent of Days when AQI Pollutant was...[2]					
	Carbon Monoxide	Nitrogen Dioxide	Ozone	Sulfur Dioxide	Particulate Matter 2.5	Particulate Matter 10
MSA[1]	0.6	0.0	36.6	0.0	62.8	0.0

Note: (1) Data covers the Tallahassee, FL Metropolitan Statistical Area—see Appendix B for areas included; (2) Based on 363 days with AQI data in 2017. The Air Quality Index (AQI) is an index for reporting daily air quality. EPA calculates the AQI for five major air pollutants regulated by the Clean Air Act: ground-level ozone, particle pollution (also known as particulate matter), carbon monoxide, sulfur dioxide, and nitrogen dioxide. The AQI runs from 0 to 500. The higher the AQI value, the greater the level of air pollution and the greater the health concern.
Source: U.S. Environmental Protection Agency, Air Quality Index Report, 2017

Maximum Air Pollutant Concentrations: Particulate Matter, Ozone, CO and Lead

	Particulate Matter 10 (ug/m^3)	Particulate Matter 2.5 Wtd AM (ug/m^3)	Particulate Matter 2.5 24-Hr (ug/m^3)	Ozone (ppm)	Carbon Monoxide (ppm)	Lead (ug/m^3)
MSA[1] Level	n/a	8	19	0.063	0	n/a
NAAQS[2]	150	15	35	0.075	9	0.15
Met NAAQS[2]	n/a	Yes	Yes	Yes	Yes	n/a

Note: (1) Data covers the Tallahassee, FL Metropolitan Statistical Area—see Appendix B for areas included; Data from exceptional events are included; (2) National Ambient Air Quality Standards; ppm = parts per million; ug/m³ = micrograms per cubic meter; n/a not available.
Concentrations: Particulate Matter 10 (coarse particulate)—highest second maximum 24-hour concentration; Particulate Matter 2.5 Wtd AM (fine particulate)—highest weighted annual mean concentration; Particulate Matter 2.5 24-Hour (fine particulate)—highest 98th percentile 24-hour concentration; Ozone—highest fourth daily maximum 8-hour concentration; Carbon Monoxide—highest second maximum non-overlapping 8-hour concentration; Lead—maximum running 3-month average
Source: U.S. Environmental Protection Agency, Air Quality Monitoring Information, "Air Quality Statistics by City, 2017"

Maximum Air Pollutant Concentrations: Nitrogen Dioxide and Sulfur Dioxide

	Nitrogen Dioxide AM (ppb)	Nitrogen Dioxide 1-Hr (ppb)	Sulfur Dioxide AM (ppb)	Sulfur Dioxide 1-Hr (ppb)	Sulfur Dioxide 24-Hr (ppb)
MSA[1] Level	n/a	n/a	n/a	n/a	n/a
NAAQS[2]	53	100	30	75	140
Met NAAQS[2]	n/a	n/a	n/a	n/a	n/a

Note: (1) Data covers the Tallahassee, FL Metropolitan Statistical Area—see Appendix B for areas included; Data from exceptional events are included; (2) National Ambient Air Quality Standards; ppm = parts per million; ug/m³ = micrograms per cubic meter; n/a not available.
Concentrations: Nitrogen Dioxide AM—highest arithmetic mean concentration; Nitrogen Dioxide 1-Hr—highest 98th percentile 1-hour daily maximum concentration; Sulfur Dioxide AM—highest annual mean concentration; Sulfur Dioxide 1-Hr—highest 99th percentile 1-hour daily maximum concentration; Sulfur Dioxide 24-Hr—highest second maximum 24-hour concentration
Source: U.S. Environmental Protection Agency, Air Quality Monitoring Information, "Air Quality Statistics by City, 2017"

Drinking Water

Water System Name	Pop. Served	Primary Water Source Type	Violations[1] Health Based	Violations[1] Monitoring/ Reporting
City of Tallahassee	193,927	Ground	0	1

Note: (1) Based on violation data from January 1, 2018 to December 31, 2018
Source: U.S. Environmental Protection Agency, Office of Ground Water and Drinking Water, Safe Drinking Water Information System (based on data extracted April 5, 2019)

Tampa, Florida

Background

Although Tampa was visited by Spanish explorers, such as Ponce de Leon and Hernando de Soto as early as 1521, this city, located on the mouth of the Hillsborough River on Tampa Bay, did not see significant growth until the mid-nineteenth century.

Like many cities in northern Florida, such as Jacksonville, Tampa was a fort during the Seminole War, and during the Civil War it was captured by the Union Army. Later, Tampa enjoyed prosperity and development when the railroad transported tourists from up north to enjoy the warmth and sunshine of Florida.

Two historical events in the late nineteenth century set Tampa apart from other Florida cities. First, Tampa played a significant role during the Spanish-American War in 1898 as a chief port of embarkation for American troops to Cuba. During that time, Colonel Theodore Roosevelt occupied a Tampa hotel as his military headquarters. Second, a cigar factory in nearby Ybor City, named after owner Vicente Martinez Ybor, was where Jose Marti (the George Washington of Cuba) exhorted workers to take up arms against the tyranny of Spanish rule in the late 1800s.

By 1900, Tampa was known as the Cigar Capital of the World. In the peak year of 1929, factories in Tampa and Ybor City hand rolled an unbelievable 500 million cigars.

The city also saw its share of organized crime, with crime family alliances in New York and Cuba, from the late nineteenth century to the 1950s. Rampant and open corruption ended when crime hearings came to town, followed by the sensational misconduct of several local officials.

Today, Tampa enjoys its role as the largest port in the state, and host to many cruise ships. Major industries in and around Tampa include finance, retail, healthcare, insurance, shipping by air and sea, national defense, professional sports, and real estate. Like most of Florida, the city's economy is heavily based on tourism. Redevelopment of Tampa's downtown is ongoing, and includes Tampa Riverwalk and Channelside, with new homes in Tampa Bay History Center, the Glazer Children's Museum and Tampa Museum of Art.

Public transportation in the city includes Amtrak's Silver Star Line at Tampa Union Station and the TECO Line Streetcar System. Several sites in the Ybor and other neighborhoods have been designated historical landmarks. Tampa is also home to Big Cat Rescue, one of the largest accredited sanctuaries in the world dedicated entirely to abused and abandoned big cats, including lions, tigers, bobcats, and cougars.

Significant employers in the city include the Hillsborough County School District, WellCare Health Plan, Raymond James Financial, the University of South Florida, Hillsborough County Government, and MacDill Air Force Base. It is also home to computer servers that run Wikipedia, the online encyclopedia.

The city boasts National Football's Tampa Bay Buccaneers, Major League Baseball's Devil Rays baseball team, and National Hockey League's Lightning teams. Other attractions include Florida's Latin Quarter known as Ybor City, Busch Gardens, and a Museum of Science and Industry. Two popular annual events are the MacDill Air Force Base air show, and the Gasparilla Pirate Festival, referred to as Tampa's "mardi gras."

Winters are mild, while summers are long, warm, and humid. Freezing temperatures occur on one or two mornings per year during November through March. A dramatic feature of the Tampa climate is the summer thunderstorm season. Most occur during the late afternoon, sometimes causing temperatures to drop dramatically. The area is vulnerable to tidal surges, as the land has an elevation of less than 15 feet above sea level. The city has not experienced a direct hit from a hurricane since the 1930s, but three major hurricanes have seriously threatened Tampa—Donna in 1960, Charley in 2004 and Irma in 2017, which caused significant damage, particularly to the electrical grid.

Rankings

General Rankings

- For its "Best for Vets: Places to Live 2019" rankings, *Military Times* evaluated 599 cities (83 large, 234 medium, 282 small) and compared the locations across three broad categories: veteran and military culture/services; economic indicators; and livability factors such as health, crime, traffic, and school quality. Tampa ranked #13 out of the top 25, in the large city category (populations of more than 250,000). Data points more specific to veterans and the military weighed more heavily than the rest. *rebootcamp.militarytimes.com, "Military Times Best Places to Live 2019," September 10, 2018*

- The Tampa metro area was identified as one of America's fastest-growing areas in terms of population and economy by *Forbes*. The area ranked #23 out of 25. The 100 most populous metro areas in the U.S. were evaluated on the following criteria: estimated population growth; employment; economic output; wages; home values. *Forbes, "America's Fastest-Growing Cities 2018," February 28, 2018*

- The U.S. Conference of Mayors and Waste Management, Inc. sponsor the City Livability Awards Program, which recognize mayors for exemplary leadership in developing and implementing specific programs that improve the quality of life in America's cities. Tampa received First Place Honors in the large cities category. *U.S. Conference of Mayors, "2018 City Livability Awards"*

- In their sixth annual survey, Livability.com looked at data for more than 1,000 U.S. cities to determine the rankings for Livability's "Top 100 Best Places to Live" in 2019. Tampa ranked #12. Criteria: median home value capped at $250,000; affordable living; vibrant economy; education, demographics, health care options. transportation & infrastructure; abundant lifestyle amenities. *Livability.com, "Top 100 Best Places to Live 2019" March 2019*

Business/Finance Rankings

- The personal finance site NerdWallet analyzed 183 American metropolitan areas with populations over 250,000 and more than 15,000 businesses to rank where entrepreneurs find the most success. Criteria included area economy, annual income, housing cost, unemployment rate, and the success rate of area businesses. Tampa ranked #97. *www.nerdwallet.com, "Best Places to Start a Business," April 27, 2015*

- In a survey of economic confidence in the nation's 50 largest metropolitan areas conducted January–December 2014, the Tampa metro area placed #39, according to Gallup's 2014 Economic Confidence Index. *Gallup, "San Jose and San Francisco Lead in Economic Confidence," March 19, 2015*

- Using data from the Council for Community and Economic Research's 2014 cost of living index, NerdWallet ranked the 100 most affordable cities in America. Median income was compared with cost of living to find truly affordable places. Tampa ranked #84. *NerdWallet.com, "America's Most Affordable Places," May 18, 2015*

- NerdWallet.com identified the 10 most promising cities for job seekers of the nation's 100 largest cities. Tampa was ranked #60. Criteria: job availability; annual salary; workforce growth; affordability. *NerdWallet.com, "Best Cities for Job Seekers in 2017," December 19, 2016*

- The Brookings Institution ranked the nation's largest cities based on income inequality. Tampa was ranked #13 (#1 = greatest inequality). Criteria: the "95/20 ratio," a figure representing the income at which a household earns more than 95 percent of all other households, divided by the income at which a household earns more than only 20 percent of all other households. *Brookings Institution, "Household Income Inequality, Largest Cities of 97 Large U.S. Metro Areas, 2014-2016," February 5, 2018*

- The Brookings Institution ranked the 100 largest metro areas in the U.S. based on income inequality. Tampa was ranked #38 (#1 = greatest inequality). Criteria: the "95/20 ratio," a figure representing the income at which a household earns more than 95 percent of all other households, divided by the income at which a household earns more than only 20 percent of all other households. *Brookings Institution, "Household Income Inequality, 100 Largest U.S. Metro Areas, 2014-2016," February 5, 2018*

- Payscale.com ranked the 32 largest metro areas in terms of wage growth. The Tampa metro area ranked #29. Criteria: private-sector wage growth between the 4th quarter of 2017 and the 4th quarter of 2018. *PayScale, "Wage Trends by Metro Area-4th Quarter," January 8, 2019*

- The Tampa metro area was identified as one of the most debt-ridden places in America by the finance site Credit.com. The metro area was ranked #19. Criteria: residents' average credit card debt as well as median income. *Credit.com, "25 Cities With the Most Credit Card Debt," February 28, 2018*

- Tampa was identified as one of America's most frugal metro areas by *Coupons.com*. The city ranked #7 out of 25. Criteria: digital coupon usage. *Coupons.com, "America's Most Frugal Cities of 2017," March 22, 2018*

- The Tampa metro area appeared on the Milken Institute "2018 Best Performing Cities" list. Rank: #30 out of 200 large metro areas. Criteria: job growth; wage and salary growth; high-tech output growth. *Milken Institute, "Best-Performing Cities 2018," January 24, 2019*

- *Forbes* ranked the 200 most populous metro areas to determine the nation's "Best Places for Business and Careers." The Tampa metro area was ranked #32. Criteria: costs (business and living); job growth (past and projected); income growth; quality of life; educational attainment (college and high school); projected economic growth; cultural and recreational opportunities; net migration patterns; number of highly ranked colleges. *Forbes, "The Best Places for Business and Careers 2018: Seattle Leads the Way," October 24, 2018*

Children/Family Rankings

- Tampa was selected as one of the most playful cities in the U.S. by KaBOOM! The organization's Playful City USA initiative honors cities and towns across the nation that have made their communities more playable. Criteria: pledging to integrate play as a solution to challenges in their communities; making it easy for children to get active and balanced play; creating more family-friendly and innovative communities as a result. *KaBOOM! National Campaign for Play, "2017 Playful City USA Communities"*

Dating/Romance Rankings

- Tampa was selected as one of the nation's most romantic cities with 100,000 or more residents by Amazon.com. The city ranked #16 of 20. Criteria: per capita sales of romance novels, relationship books, romantic comedy movies, romantic music, and sexual wellness products. *Amazon.com, "Top 20 Most Romantic Cities in the U.S.," February 1, 2017*

Education Rankings

- Personal finance website *WalletHub* analyzed the 150 largest U.S. metropolitan statistical areas to determine where the most educated Americans are choosing to settle. Criteria: education quality and attainment gap; education levels; percentage of workers with degrees; public school quality rankings; quality and size of each metro area's universities. Tampa was ranked #86 (#1 = most educated city). *www.WalletHub.com, "2018's Most and Least Educated Cities in America," July 24, 2018*

- Tampa was selected as one of America's most literate cities. The city ranked #51 out of the 82 largest U.S. cities. Criteria: number of booksellers; library resources; Internet resources; educational attainment; periodical publishing resources; newspaper circulation. *Central Connecticut State University, "America's Most Literate Cities, 2016," March 31, 2017*

Environmental Rankings

- Sperling's BestPlaces assessed the 50 largest metropolitan areas of the United States for the likelihood of dangerously extreme weather events or earthquakes. In general the Southeast and South-Central regions have the highest risk of weather extremes and earthquakes, while the Pacific Northwest enjoys the lowest risk. Of the most risky metropolitan areas, the Tampa metro area was ranked #8. *www.bestplaces.net, "Avoid Natural Disasters: BestPlaces Reveals The Top 10 Safest Places to Live," October 25, 2017*

- The U.S. Environmental Protection Agency (EPA) released a list of U.S. metropolitan areas with the most ENERGY STAR certified buildings in 2017. The Tampa metro area was ranked #16 out of 25. *U.S. Environmental Protection Agency, "2018 Energy Star Top Cities," April 11, 2018*

- Tampa was highlighted as one of the top 90 cleanest metro areas for short-term particle pollution (24-hour PM 2.5) in the U.S. during 2014 through 2016. Monitors in these cities reported no days with unhealthful PM 2.5 levels. *American Lung Association, State of the Air 2018*

Food/Drink Rankings

- *Men's Health* ranked 100 major U.S. cities in terms of alcohol intoxication. Tampa ranked #29 (#1 = most sober).Criteria: binge drinking; alcohol-related traffic accidents, arrests, and fatalities. *Men's Health, "America's Drunkest Cities," March 9, 2015*

Health/Fitness Rankings

- For each of the 100 largest cities in the United States, the American College of Sports Medicine's American Fitness Index evaluated infrastructure, community assets, and policies that encourage healthy and fit lifestyles, including preventive health behaviors, levels of chronic disease conditions, health care access, and community resources and policies that support physical activity. Tampa ranked #37 for "community fitness." *www.americanfitnessindex.org, "ACSM American Fitness Index Health and Community Fitness Status of the 100 Largest U.S. Cities," May 2018*

- The Tampa metro area was identified as one of the worst cities for bed bugs in America by pest control company Orkin. The area ranked #35 out of 50 based on the number of bed bug treatments Orkin performed from December 2017 to November 2018. *Orkin, "Baltimore Remains Front Runner, Atlanta and Philadelphia Break Into Top 10," January 14, 2019*

- Tampa was identified as a "2018 Spring Allergy Capital." The area ranked #64 out of 100. Three groups of factors were used to identify the most challenging cities for people with allergies during the spring season: annual pollen levels; medicine utilization; access to board-certified allergists. *Asthma and Allergy Foundation of America, "Spring Allergy Capitals 2018"*

- Tampa was identified as a "2018 Fall Allergy Capital." The area ranked #72 out of 100. Three groups of factors were used to identify the most challenging cities for people with allergies during the fall season: annual pollen levels; medicine utilization; access to board-certified allergists. *Asthma and Allergy Foundation of America, "Fall Allergy Capitals 2018"*

- Tampa was identified as a "2018 Asthma Capital." The area ranked #76 out of the nation's 100 largest metropolitan areas. Criteria: estimated prevalence; self-reported prevalence; crude death rate for asthma; annual pollen score; annual air quality; public smoking laws; number of board-certified asthma specialists; school inhaler access laws; rescue medication use; controller medication use; ER visits for asthma; uninsured rate; poverty rate. *Asthma and Allergy Foundation of America, "Asthma Capitals 2018: The Most Challenging Places to Live With Asthma"*

- *Men's Health* ranked 100 major U.S. cities in terms of the best cities for men. Tampa ranked #52. Criteria: health; fitness; quality of life. *Men's Health, "The Best & Worst Cities for Men Who Want to Be Fit and Happy," January 1, 2016*

- The Tampa metro area ranked #103 out of 189 in The Gallup-Healthways Well-Being Index. Criteria: purpose; social well being; financial health; community and physical health. Results are based on telephone interviews with adults, aged 18 and older, living in metropolitan areas in the 50 U.S. states and the District of Columbia. *Gallup-Healthways, "State of American Well-Being, 2017 Community Well-Being Rankings" March 2018*

Real Estate Rankings

- FitSmallBusiness looked at 50 of the largest metropolitan areas in the U.S. to determine which metro was the best to start a real estate business. Data was compiled from such sources as: Zillow, Trulia, U.S. Census Bureau, and the Bureau of Labor Statistics. Criteria: location; inventory; annual wages; median sales price of homes; days on the market; median price cut percentage; and other factors that would influence real estate professional growth. The Tampa metro area ranked #32. *fitsmallbusiness.com, "The Best Cities to Become a Real Estate Agent in 2018," January 30, 2018*

- *WalletHub* compared the most populated U.S. cities, as well as at least two of the most populated cities in each state, for a total of 179, to determine which had the best markets for real estate agents. Tampa ranked #41 where demand was high and pay was the best. Criteria: sales per agent; annual median wage for real-estate agents; monthly average starting salary for real estate agents; real estate job density and competition; unemployment rate; housing-market health index; and other relevant metrics. *www.WalletHub.com, "2018's Best Places to Be a Real Estate Agent," April 25, 2018*

- According to Penske Truck Rental, the Tampa metro area was named the #3 moving destination in 2018, based on one-way consumer truck rental reservations made through Penske's website, rental locations, and reservations call center. *blog.gopenske.com, "Penske Truck Rental's 2018 Top Moving Destinations," January 16, 2019*

- Tampa was ranked #134 out of 237 metro areas in terms of housing affordability in 2018 by the National Association of Home Builders (#1 = most affordable). Criteria: the share of homes sold in that area affordable to a family earning the local median income, based on standard mortgage underwriting criteria. *National Association of Home Builders®, NAHB-Wells Fargo Housing Opportunity Index, 4th Quarter 2018*

Safety Rankings

- Allstate ranked the 200 largest cities in America in terms of driver safety. Tampa ranked #104. Criteria: internal property damage claims over a two-year period from January 2015 to December 2016. The report helps increase the importance of safety awareness behind the wheel. *Allstate, "Allstate America's Best Drivers Report, 2018" August 28, 2018*

- The National Insurance Crime Bureau ranked 382 metro areas in the U.S. in terms of per capita rates of vehicle theft. The Tampa metro area ranked #180 (#1 = highest rate). Criteria: number of vehicle theft offenses per 100,000 inhabitants in 2017. *National Insurance Crime Bureau, "Hot Spots 2017," July 12, 2018*

Seniors/Retirement Rankings

- From its Best Cities for Successful Aging indexes, the Milken Institute generated rankings for metropolitan areas, weighing data in nine categories—health care, wellness, living arrangements, transportation and convenience, financial characteristics, education, employment, community engagement, and overall livability. The Tampa metro area was ranked #84 overall in the large metro area category. *Milken Institute, "Best Cities for Successful Aging, 2017" March 14, 2017*

- Tampa was identified as one of the most popular places to retire by *Topretirements.com*. The list reflects the 100 cities that visitors to the website are most interested in for retirement, based on the number of times a city's review was viewed on the website. *Topretirements.com, "100 Most Popular Places to Retire for 2017," July 27, 2017*

Sports/Recreation Rankings

- Tampa was chosen as one of America's best cities for bicycling. The city ranked #48 out of 50. Criteria: cycling infrastructure that is safe and friendly for all ages; energy and bike culture. The editors only considered cities with populations of 100,000 or more. *Bicycling,* *"The 50 Best Bike Cities in America," October 10, 2018*

Transportation Rankings

- NerdWallet surveyed average annual car insurance premiums in 125 U.S. cities to identify the least expensive U.S. cities in which to insure a car. Locations with no-fault insurance laws was a strong determinant. Tampa came in at #15 for the most expensive rates. *www.nerdwallet.com, "Best Cities for Cheap Car Insurance," February 3, 2014*

Women/Minorities Rankings

- Tampa was selected as one of the gayest cities in America by *The Advocate*. The city ranked #19 out of 25. Criteria, among many: Trans Pride parades/festivals; gay rugby teams; lesbian bars; LGBT centers; theater screenings of "Moonlight"; LGBT-inclusive nondiscrimination ordinances; and gay bowling teams. *The Advocate, "Queerest Cities in America 2017" January 12, 2017*

- Personal finance website *WalletHub* compared more than 180 U.S. cities—including the 150 most populated U.S. cities, plus at least two of the most populated cities in each state—across two key dimensions, "Hispanic Business-Friendliness" and "Hispanic Purchasing Power", to arrive at the most favorable conditions for Hispanic entrepreneurs. Tampa was ranked #16 out of 182. Criteria includes: share of Hispanic-Owned Businesses; Hispanic entrepreneurship rate to median annual income of Hispanics; Small Business-Friendliness score; cost of living; and number of Hispanics with at least a bachelor's degree. *WalletHub.com, "2018's Best Cities for Hispanic Entrepreneurs," April 26, 2018*

Miscellaneous Rankings

- *MoveHub* ranked the coolest cities, appealing to young people, using its U.S. Hipster Index and Tampa came out as #17. Criteria: number of thrift stores; density of tattoo parlors, vegan stores and microbreweries; and amount of rent increase. *www.thisisinsider.com, "The 20 Most Hipster Cities in the US-and Why You Should Consider Moving to One," April 10, 2018*

- The watchdog site Charity Navigator conducts an annual study of charities in the nation's major markets both to analyze statistical differences in their financial, accountability, and transparency practices and to track year-to-year variations in individual philanthropic communities. Charity Navigator's analysis demonstrated that the financial, accountability and transparency behaviors of America's largest charities can be influenced by the metropolitan market within which the charity operates. The Tampa metro area was ranked #4 among the 30 metro markets in the rating category of Overall Score. *www.charitynavigator.org, "2017 Metro Market Study," May 1, 2017*

- *WalletHub* compared the 150 most populated U.S. cities to determine their operating efficiency. A "Quality of Services" score was constructed for each city and then divided by the total budget per capita to reveal which were managed the best. Tampa ranked #98. Criteria: financial stability; economy; education; safety; health; infrastructure and pollution. *www.WalletHub.com, "2018's Best- & Worst-Run Cities in America," July 9, 2018*

- Tampa appeared on *Travel + Leisure's* list of America's cities with the least attractive people. Criteria: cities were selected by readers in their annual America's Favorite Cities survey. The city ranked #7 out of 10. *Travel + Leisure, "America's Most and Least Attractive People," September 2, 2016*

- The National Alliance to End Homelessness listed the 25 most populous metro areas with the highest rate of homelessness. The Tampa metro area had a high rate of homelessness. Criteria: number of homeless people per 10,000 population in 2016. *National Alliance to End Homelessness, "Homelessness in the 25 Most Populous U.S. Metro Areas," September 1, 2017*

Business Environment

CITY FINANCES

City Government Finances

Component	2016 ($000)	2016 ($ per capita)
Total Revenues	724,175	1,962
Total Expenditures	954,191	2,585
Debt Outstanding	1,413,969	3,831
Cash and Securities[1]	3,248,470	8,802

Note: (1) Cash and security holdings of a government at the close of its fiscal year, including those of its dependent agencies, utilities, and liquor stores.
Source: U.S. Census Bureau, State & Local Government Finances 2016

City Government Revenue by Source

Source	2016 ($000)	2016 ($ per capita)	2016 (%)
General Revenue			
From Federal Government	18,050	49	2.5
From State Government	58,879	160	8.1
From Local Governments	14,806	40	2.0
Taxes			
Property	130,606	354	18.0
Sales and Gross Receipts	111,922	303	15.5
Personal Income	0	0	0.0
Corporate Income	0	0	0.0
Motor Vehicle License	0	0	0.0
Other Taxes	54,917	149	7.6
Current Charges	251,622	682	34.7
Liquor Store	0	0	0.0
Utility	98,873	268	13.7
Employee Retirement	-68,105	-185	-9.4

Source: U.S. Census Bureau, State & Local Government Finances 2016

City Government Expenditures by Function

Function	2016 ($000)	2016 ($ per capita)	2016 (%)
General Direct Expenditures			
Air Transportation	0	0	0.0
Corrections	0	0	0.0
Education	0	0	0.0
Employment Security Administration	0	0	0.0
Financial Administration	37,729	102	4.0
Fire Protection	81,065	219	8.5
General Public Buildings	10,383	28	1.1
Governmental Administration, Other	3,451	9	0.4
Health	0	0	0.0
Highways	51,185	138	5.4
Hospitals	0	0	0.0
Housing and Community Development	21,596	58	2.3
Interest on General Debt	19,931	54	2.1
Judicial and Legal	4,665	12	0.5
Libraries	0	0	0.0
Parking	16,567	44	1.7
Parks and Recreation	51,737	140	5.4
Police Protection	152,955	414	16.0
Public Welfare	0	0	0.0
Sewerage	114,847	311	12.0
Solid Waste Management	72,796	197	7.6
Veterans' Services	0	0	0.0
Liquor Store	0	0	0.0
Utility	104,799	284	11.0
Employee Retirement	125,646	340	13.2

Source: U.S. Census Bureau, State & Local Government Finances 2016

DEMOGRAPHICS

Population Growth

Area	1990 Census	2000 Census	2010 Census	2017* Estimate	Population Growth (%)	
					1990-2017	2010-2017
City	279,960	303,447	335,709	368,087	31.5	9.6
MSA[1]	2,067,959	2,395,997	2,783,243	2,978,209	44.0	7.0
U.S.	248,709,873	281,421,906	308,745,538	321,004,407	29.1	4.0

Note: (1) Figures cover the Tampa-St. Petersburg-Clearwater, FL Metropolitan Statistical Area—see Appendix B for areas included; (*) 2013-2017 5-year estimated population
Source: U.S. Census Bureau, 1990 Census, Census 2000, Census 2010, 2013-2017 American Community Survey 5-Year Estimates

Household Size

Area	Persons in Household (%)							Average Household Size
	One	Two	Three	Four	Five	Six	Seven or More	
City	36.3	31.6	14.8	10.8	4.2	1.5	0.7	2.40
MSA[1]	31.2	36.6	14.6	10.8	4.5	1.5	0.8	2.50
U.S.	27.7	33.8	15.7	13.0	6.0	2.3	1.4	2.60

Note: (1) Figures cover the Tampa-St. Petersburg-Clearwater, FL Metropolitan Statistical Area—see Appendix B for areas included
Source: U.S. Census Bureau, 2013-2017 American Community Survey 5-Year Estimates

Race

Area	White Alone[2] (%)	Black Alone[2] (%)	Asian Alone[2] (%)	AIAN[3] Alone[2] (%)	NHOPI[4] Alone[2] (%)	Other Race Alone[2] (%)	Two or More Races (%)
City	65.2	24.2	4.2	0.3	0.1	2.6	3.4
MSA[1]	78.4	12.0	3.3	0.3	0.1	2.9	2.9
U.S.	73.0	12.7	5.4	0.8	0.2	4.8	3.1

Note: (1) Figures cover the Tampa-St. Petersburg-Clearwater, FL Metropolitan Statistical Area—see Appendix B for areas included; (2) Alone is defined as not being in combination with one or more other races; (3) American Indian and Alaska Native; (4) Native Hawaiian and Other Pacific Islander
Source: U.S. Census Bureau, 2013-2017 American Community Survey 5-Year Estimates

Hispanic or Latino Origin

Area	Total (%)	Mexican (%)	Puerto Rican (%)	Cuban (%)	Other (%)
City	25.1	3.3	7.7	7.4	6.8
MSA[1]	18.4	3.7	6.1	3.7	5.0
U.S.	17.6	11.1	1.7	0.7	4.1

Note: Persons of Hispanic or Latino origin can be of any race; (1) Figures cover the Tampa-St. Petersburg-Clearwater, FL Metropolitan Statistical Area—see Appendix B for areas included
Source: U.S. Census Bureau, 2013-2017 American Community Survey 5-Year Estimates

Segregation

Type	Segregation Indices[1]				Percent Change		
	1990	2000	2010	2010 Rank[2]	1990-2000	1990-2010	2000-2010
Black/White	69.7	64.6	56.2	50	-5.1	-13.5	-8.3
Asian/White	33.8	35.4	35.3	78	1.6	1.5	-0.1
Hispanic/White	45.3	44.4	40.7	62	-0.9	-4.6	-3.7

Note: All figures cover the Metropolitan Statistical Area—see Appendix B for areas included; Figures are based on an analysis of 1990, 2000, and 2010 Census Decennial Census tract data by William H. Frey, Brookings Institution and the University of Michigan Social Science Data Analysis Network. In this analysis all racial groups (whites, blacks, and asians) are non-Hispanic members of those races. Hispanics are shown as a separate category; (1) Segregation Indices are Dissimilarity Indices that measure the degree to which the minority group is distributed differently than whites across census tracts. They range from 0 (complete integration) to 100 (complete segregation) where the value indicates the percentage of the minority group that needs to move to be distributed exactly like whites; (2) Ranges from 1 (most segregated) to 102 (least segregated); n/a not available.
Source: www.CensusScope.org

Ancestry

Area	German	Irish	English	American	Italian	Polish	French[2]	Scottish	Dutch
City	8.8	8.5	6.0	5.8	5.9	2.0	2.3	1.6	0.7
MSA[1]	12.6	11.0	7.9	9.7	7.5	3.1	2.7	1.8	1.1
U.S.	14.1	10.1	7.5	6.6	5.3	2.9	2.5	1.7	1.3

Note: Figures are the percentage of the total population reporting a particular ancestry. The nine most commonly reported ancestries in the U.S. are shown. Figures include multiple ancestries (e.g. if a person reported being Irish and Italian, they were included in both columns); (1) Figures cover the Tampa-St. Petersburg-Clearwater, FL Metropolitan Statistical Area—see Appendix B for areas included; (2) Excludes Basque
Source: U.S. Census Bureau, 2013-2017 American Community Survey 5-Year Estimates

Foreign-Born Population

Area	Any Foreign Country	Asia	Mexico	Europe	Carribean	Central America[2]	South America	Africa	Canada
City	16.2	3.5	1.3	1.3	6.3	1.1	1.8	0.6	0.4
MSA[1]	13.2	2.7	1.4	2.2	3.4	0.7	1.8	0.4	0.7
U.S.	13.4	4.1	3.6	1.5	1.3	1.0	0.9	0.6	0.3

Note: (1) Figures cover the Tampa-St. Petersburg-Clearwater, FL Metropolitan Statistical Area—see Appendix B for areas included; (2) Excludes Mexico.
Source: U.S. Census Bureau, 2013-2017 American Community Survey 5-Year Estimates

Marital Status

Area	Never Married	Now Married[2]	Separated	Widowed	Divorced
City	41.4	37.3	2.9	5.2	13.2
MSA[1]	30.8	46.3	2.2	7.1	13.6
U.S.	33.1	48.2	2.0	5.8	10.9

Note: Figures are percentages and cover the population 15 years of age and older; (1) Figures cover the Tampa-St. Petersburg-Clearwater, FL Metropolitan Statistical Area—see Appendix B for areas included; (2) Excludes separated
Source: U.S. Census Bureau, 2013-2017 American Community Survey 5-Year Estimates

Disability by Age

Area	All Ages	Under 18 Years Old	18 to 64 Years Old	65 Years and Over
City	12.1	4.1	9.9	38.2
MSA[1]	14.0	4.4	10.9	34.4
U.S.	12.6	4.2	10.3	35.5

Note: Figures show percent of the civilian noninstitutionalized population that reported having a disability. Disability status is determined from six types of difficulty: vision, hearing, cognitive, ambulatory, self-care, and independent living. For children under 5 years old, hearing and vision difficulty are used to determine disability status. For children between the ages of 5 and 14, disability status is determined from hearing, vision, cognitive, ambulatory, and self-care difficulties. For people aged 15 years and older, they are considered to have a disability if they have difficulty with any one of the six difficulty types; Note: (1) Figures cover the Tampa-St. Petersburg-Clearwater, FL Metropolitan Statistical Area—see Appendix B for areas included
Source: U.S. Census Bureau, 2013-2017 American Community Survey 5-Year Estimates

Age

Area	Under Age 5	Age 5–19	Age 20–34	Age 35–44	Age 45–54	Age 55–64	Age 65–74	Age 75–84	Age 85+	Median Age
City	6.2	18.9	23.9	13.4	13.8	11.4	7.2	3.5	1.5	35.6
MSA[1]	5.5	17.2	18.8	12.3	13.9	13.4	10.6	5.8	2.6	42.0
U.S.	6.2	19.5	20.7	12.7	13.4	12.7	8.6	4.4	1.9	37.8

Note: (1) Figures cover the Tampa-St. Petersburg-Clearwater, FL Metropolitan Statistical Area—see Appendix B for areas included
Source: U.S. Census Bureau, 2013-2017 American Community Survey 5-Year Estimates

Gender

Area	Males	Females	Males per 100 Females
City	177,778	190,309	93.4
MSA[1]	1,442,886	1,535,323	94.0
U.S.	158,018,753	162,985,654	97.0

Note: (1) Figures cover the Tampa-St. Petersburg-Clearwater, FL Metropolitan Statistical Area—see Appendix B for areas included
Source: U.S. Census Bureau, 2013-2017 American Community Survey 5-Year Estimates

Religious Groups by Family

Area	Catholic	Baptist	Non-Den.	Methodist[2]	Lutheran	LDS[3]	Pente-costal	Presby-terian[4]	Muslim[5]	Judaism
MSA[1]	10.9	7.1	3.8	3.5	1.0	0.6	2.1	1.0	1.3	0.5
U.S.	19.1	9.3	4.0	4.0	2.3	2.0	1.9	1.6	0.8	0.7

Note: Figures are the number of adherents as a percentage of the total population; (1) Figures cover the Tampa-St. Petersburg-Clearwater, FL Metropolitan Statistical Area—see Appendix B for areas included; (2) Methodist/Pietist; (3) Latter Day Saints; (4) Reformed; (5) Figures are estimates
Source: Association of Statisticians of American Religious Bodies, 2010 U.S. Religion Census: Religious Congregations & Membership Study

Religious Groups by Tradition

Area	Catholic	Evangelical Protestant	Mainline Protestant	Other Tradition	Black Protestant	Orthodox
MSA[1]	10.9	13.6	5.2	3.1	1.2	0.8
U.S.	19.1	16.2	7.3	4.3	1.6	0.3

Note: Figures are the number of adherents as a percentage of the total population; (1) Figures cover the Tampa-St. Petersburg-Clearwater, FL Metropolitan Statistical Area—see Appendix B for areas included
Source: Association of Statisticians of American Religious Bodies, 2010 U.S. Religion Census: Religious Congregations & Membership Study

ECONOMY

Gross Metropolitan Product

Area	2016	2017	2018	2019	Rank[2]
MSA[1]	143.2	148.6	156.2	165.6	24

Note: Figures are in billions of dollars; (1) Figures cover the Tampa-St. Petersburg-Clearwater, FL Metropolitan Statistical Area—see Appendix B for areas included; (2) Rank is based on 2017 data and ranges from 1 to 381
Source: U.S. Conference of Mayors, U.S. Metro Economies: Economic Growth & Full Employment, June 2018

Economic Growth

Area	2017-2018 (%)	2019-2020 (%)	2021-2022 (%)
MSA[1]	3.2	3.1	2.2

Note: Figures are real gross metropolitan product (GMP) growth rates and represent average annual percent change; (1) Figures cover the Tampa-St. Petersburg-Clearwater, FL Metropolitan Statistical Area—see Appendix B for areas included
Source: U.S. Conference of Mayors, U.S. Metro Economies: Economic Growth & Full Employment, June 2018

Metropolitan Area Exports

Area	2012	2013	2014	2015	2016	2017	Rank[2]
MSA[1]	7,190.0	6,673.0	5,817.3	5,660.4	5,702.9	6,256.0	49

Note: Figures are in millions of dollars; (1) Figures cover the Tampa-St. Petersburg-Clearwater, FL Metropolitan Statistical Area—see Appendix B for areas included; (2) Rank is based on 2017 data and ranges from 1 to 387
Source: U.S. Department of Commerce, International Trade Administration, Office of Trade and Economic Analysis, Industry and Analysis, Exports by Metropolitan Area, extracted March 25, 2019

Building Permits

Area	Single-Family			Multi-Family			Total		
	2016	2017	Pct. Chg.	2016	2017	Pct. Chg.	2016	2017	Pct. Chg.
City	934	1,010	8.1	3,328	2,165	-34.9	4,262	3,175	-25.5
MSA[1]	10,685	12,732	19.2	7,067	5,536	-21.7	17,752	18,268	2.9
U.S.	750,800	820,000	9.2	455,800	462,000	1.4	1,206,600	1,282,000	6.2

Note: (1) Figures cover the Tampa-St. Petersburg-Clearwater, FL Metropolitan Statistical Area—see Appendix B for areas included; Figures represent new, privately-owned housing units authorized (unadjusted data); All permit data are based on estimates with imputation
Source: U.S. Census Bureau, Manufacturing, Mining, and Construction Statistics, Building Permits, 2016, 2017

Bankruptcy Filings

Area	Business Filings			Nonbusiness Filings		
	2017	2018	% Chg.	2017	2018	% Chg.
Hillsborough County	136	111	-18.4	2,950	3,057	3.6
U.S.	23,157	22,232	-4.0	765,863	751,186	-1.9

Note: Business filings include Chapter 7, Chapter 11, Chapter 12, and Chapter 13; Nonbusiness filings include Chapter 7, Chapter 11, and Chapter 13
Source: Administrative Office of the U.S. Courts, Business and Nonbusiness Bankruptcy, County Cases Commenced by Chapter of the Bankruptcy Code, During the 12-Month Period Ending December 31, 2017 and Business and Nonbusiness Bankruptcy, County Cases Commenced by Chapter of the Bankruptcy Code, During the 12-Month Period Ending December 31, 2018

Housing Vacancy Rates

Area	Gross Vacancy Rate[2] (%)			Year-Round Vacancy Rate[3] (%)			Rental Vacancy Rate[4] (%)			Homeowner Vacancy Rate[5] (%)		
	2016	2017	2018	2016	2017	2018	2016	2017	2018	2016	2017	2018
MSA[1]	16.1	16.2	16.1	12.8	12.5	11.9	8.7	9.6	9.9	2.5	2.4	2.1
U.S.	12.8	12.7	12.3	9.9	9.9	9.7	6.9	7.2	6.9	1.7	1.6	1.5

Note: (1) Figures cover the Tampa-St. Petersburg-Clearwater, FL Metropolitan Statistical Area—see Appendix B for areas included; (2) The percentage of the total housing inventory that is vacant; (3) The percentage of the housing inventory (excluding seasonal units) that is year-round vacant; (4) The percentage of rental inventory that is vacant for rent; (5) The percentage of homeowner inventory that is vacant for sale
Source: U.S. Census Bureau, Housing Vacancies and Homeownership Annual Statistics: 2016, 2017, 2018

INCOME

Income

Area	Per Capita ($)	Median Household ($)	Average Household ($)
City	32,869	48,245	78,953
MSA[1]	29,632	50,567	71,311
U.S.	31,177	57,652	81,283

Note: (1) Figures cover the Tampa-St. Petersburg-Clearwater, FL Metropolitan Statistical Area—see Appendix B for areas included
Source: U.S. Census Bureau, 2013-2017 American Community Survey 5-Year Estimates

Household Income Distribution

Area	Percent of Households Earning							
	Under $15,000	$15,000 -$24,999	$25,000 -$34,999	$35,000 -$49,999	$50,000 -$74,999	$75,000 -$99,999	$100,000 -$149,999	$150,000 and up
City	16.3	11.5	10.4	13.0	15.6	9.8	11.1	12.2
MSA[1]	12.3	11.5	10.9	14.8	18.1	11.7	11.8	9.0
U.S.	11.6	9.8	9.5	13.0	17.7	12.3	14.1	12.1

Note: (1) Figures cover the Tampa-St. Petersburg-Clearwater, FL Metropolitan Statistical Area—see Appendix B for areas included
Source: U.S. Census Bureau, 2013-2017 American Community Survey 5-Year Estimates

Poverty Rate

Area	All Ages	Under 18 Years Old	18 to 64 Years Old	65 Years and Over
City	20.0	28.7	17.8	16.6
MSA[1]	14.6	20.3	14.1	9.9
U.S.	14.6	20.3	13.7	9.3

Note: Figures are percentage of people whose income during the past 12 months was below the poverty level; (1) Figures cover the Tampa-St. Petersburg-Clearwater, FL Metropolitan Statistical Area—see Appendix B for areas included
Source: U.S. Census Bureau, 2013-2017 American Community Survey 5-Year Estimates

EMPLOYMENT

Labor Force and Employment

Area	Civilian Labor Force			Workers Employed		
	Dec. 2017	Dec. 2018	% Chg.	Dec. 2017	Dec. 2018	% Chg.
City	197,563	200,096	1.3	190,512	193,524	1.6
MSA[1]	1,510,641	1,531,562	1.4	1,458,656	1,482,283	1.6
U.S.	159,880,000	162,510,000	1.6	153,602,000	156,481,000	1.9

Note: Data is not seasonally adjusted and covers workers 16 years of age and older; (1) Figures cover the Tampa-St. Petersburg-Clearwater, FL Metropolitan Statistical Area—see Appendix B for areas included
Source: Bureau of Labor Statistics, Local Area Unemployment Statistics

Unemployment Rate

Area	2018											
	Jan.	Feb.	Mar.	Apr.	May	Jun.	Jul.	Aug.	Sep.	Oct.	Nov.	Dec.
City	4.0	3.6	3.7	3.3	3.4	4.0	4.0	3.7	3.0	3.0	3.0	3.3
MSA[1]	3.9	3.6	3.6	3.2	3.3	3.8	3.8	3.6	2.9	2.9	3.0	3.2
U.S.	4.5	4.4	4.1	3.7	3.6	4.2	4.1	3.9	3.6	3.5	3.5	3.7

Note: Data is not seasonally adjusted and covers workers 16 years of age and older; (1) Figures cover the Tampa-St. Petersburg-Clearwater, FL Metropolitan Statistical Area—see Appendix B for areas included
Source: Bureau of Labor Statistics, Local Area Unemployment Statistics

Average Wages

Occupation	$/Hr.	Occupation	$/Hr.
Accountants and Auditors	33.90	Maids and Housekeeping Cleaners	11.30
Automotive Mechanics	19.40	Maintenance and Repair Workers	17.30
Bookkeepers	19.80	Marketing Managers	61.10
Carpenters	19.70	Nuclear Medicine Technologists	34.70
Cashiers	10.50	Nurses, Licensed Practical	21.30
Clerks, General Office	16.00	Nurses, Registered	32.70
Clerks, Receptionists/Information	13.50	Nursing Assistants	13.40
Clerks, Shipping/Receiving	15.60	Packers and Packagers, Hand	10.70
Computer Programmers	37.50	Physical Therapists	40.90
Computer Systems Analysts	43.60	Postal Service Mail Carriers	25.00
Computer User Support Specialists	24.50	Real Estate Brokers	34.10
Cooks, Restaurant	12.60	Retail Salespersons	12.90
Dentists	89.70	Sales Reps., Exc. Tech./Scientific	29.80
Electrical Engineers	45.60	Sales Reps., Tech./Scientific	41.20
Electricians	20.60	Secretaries, Exc. Legal/Med./Exec.	16.90
Financial Managers	67.70	Security Guards	14.80
First-Line Supervisors/Managers, Sales	22.50	Surgeons	n/a
Food Preparation Workers	11.60	Teacher Assistants*	13.30
General and Operations Managers	57.30	Teachers, Elementary School*	28.10
Hairdressers/Cosmetologists	15.30	Teachers, Secondary School*	28.70
Internists, General	91.50	Telemarketers	12.10
Janitors and Cleaners	14.00	Truck Drivers, Heavy/Tractor-Trailer	20.00
Landscaping/Groundskeeping Workers	13.30	Truck Drivers, Light/Delivery Svcs.	16.80
Lawyers	54.60	Waiters and Waitresses	12.50

Note: Wage data covers the Tampa-St. Petersburg-Clearwater, FL Metropolitan Statistical Area—see Appendix B for areas included; (*) Hourly wages for elementary/secondary school teachers and teacher assistants were calculated by the editors from annual wage data based on a 40 hour work week; n/a not available.
Source: Bureau of Labor Statistics, Metro Area Occupational Employment & Wage Estimates, May 2018

Employment by Occupation

Occupation Classification	City (%)	MSA[1] (%)	U.S. (%)
Management, Business, Science, and Arts	41.5	37.5	37.4
Natural Resources, Construction, and Maintenance	6.4	8.3	8.9
Production, Transportation, and Material Moving	7.8	8.7	12.2
Sales and Office	26.0	27.3	23.5
Service	18.4	18.3	18.0

Note: Figures cover employed civilians 16 years of age and older; (1) Figures cover the Tampa-St. Petersburg-Clearwater, FL Metropolitan Statistical Area—see Appendix B for areas included
Source: U.S. Census Bureau, 2013-2017 American Community Survey 5-Year Estimates

Employment by Industry

Sector	MSA[1] Number of Employees	MSA[1] Percent of Total	U.S. Percent of Total
Construction	77,700	5.6	4.8
Education and Health Services	212,600	15.5	15.9
Financial Activities	121,300	8.8	5.7
Government	157,600	11.5	15.1
Information	26,000	1.9	1.9
Leisure and Hospitality	159,600	11.6	10.7
Manufacturing	68,500	5.0	8.5
Mining and Logging	300	<0.1	0.5
Other Services	46,800	3.4	3.9
Professional and Business Services	249,900	18.2	14.1
Retail Trade	169,000	12.3	10.8
Transportation, Warehousing, and Utilities	33,300	2.4	4.2
Wholesale Trade	53,200	3.9	3.9

Note: Figures are non-farm employment as of December 2018. Figures are not seasonally adjusted and include workers 16 years of age and older; (1) Figures cover the Tampa-St. Petersburg-Clearwater, FL Metropolitan Statistical Area—see Appendix B for areas included
Source: Bureau of Labor Statistics, Current Employment Statistics, Employment, Hours, and Earnings

Occupations with Greatest Projected Employment Growth: 2018 – 2020

Occupation[1]	2018 Employment	2020 Projected Employment	Numeric Employment Change	Percent Employment Change
Interviewers, Except Eligibility and Loan	11,890	33,270	21,380	179.8
Combined Food Preparation and Serving Workers, Including Fast Food	242,590	256,470	13,880	5.7
Waiters and Waitresses	230,640	240,320	9,680	4.2
Registered Nurses	193,200	202,070	8,870	4.6
Customer Service Representatives	245,420	253,780	8,360	3.4
Laborers and Freight, Stock, and Material Movers, Hand	135,600	143,640	8,040	5.9
Construction Laborers	89,390	97,130	7,740	8.7
Landscaping and Groundskeeping Workers	116,440	123,040	6,600	5.7
Carpenters	72,550	78,990	6,440	8.9
Janitors and Cleaners, Except Maids and Housekeeping Cleaners	133,890	140,000	6,110	4.6

Note: Projections cover Florida; (1) Sorted by numeric employment change
Source: www.projectionscentral.com, State Occupational Projections, 2018–2020 Short-Term Projections

Fastest Growing Occupations: 2018 – 2020

Occupation[1]	2018 Employment	2020 Projected Employment	Numeric Employment Change	Percent Employment Change
Interviewers, Except Eligibility and Loan	11,890	33,270	21,380	179.8
Solar Photovoltaic Installers	1,100	1,330	230	20.9
Terrazzo Workers and Finishers	390	450	60	15.4
Helpers—Roofers	1,490	1,720	230	15.4
Helpers—Brickmasons, Blockmasons, Stonemasons, and Tile and Marble Setters	1,280	1,470	190	14.8
Helpers—Painters, Paperhangers, Plasterers, and Stucco Masons	570	650	80	14.0
Reinforcing Iron and Rebar Workers	1,100	1,250	150	13.6
Insulation Workers, Floor, Ceiling, and Wall	2,550	2,880	330	12.9
Structural Iron and Steel Workers	5,210	5,880	670	12.9
Cement Masons and Concrete Finishers	13,490	15,210	1,720	12.8

Note: Projections cover Florida; (1) Sorted by percent employment change and excludes occupations with numeric employment change less than 50
Source: www.projectionscentral.com, State Occupational Projections, 2018–2020 Short-Term Projections

TAXES

State Corporate Income Tax Rates

State	Tax Rate (%)	Income Brackets ($)	Num. of Brackets	Financial Institution Tax Rate (%)[a]	Federal Income Tax Ded.
Florida	5.5 (e)	Flat rate	1	5.5 (e)	No

Note: Tax rates as of January 1, 2019; (a) Rates listed are the corporate income tax rate applied to financial institutions or excise taxes based on income. Some states have other taxes based upon the value of deposits or shares; (e) The Florida tax rate may be adjusted downward if certain revenue targets are met.
Source: Federation of Tax Administrators, Range of State Corporate Income Tax Rates, January 1, 2019

State Individual Income Tax Rates

State	Tax Rate (%)	Income Brackets ($)	Personal Exemptions ($)			Standard Ded. ($)	
			Single	Married	Depend.	Single	Married
Florida			– No state income tax –				

Note: Tax rates as of January 1, 2019; Local- and county-level taxes are not included; n/a not applicable;

Source: Federation of Tax Administrators, State Individual Income Tax Rates, January 1, 2019

Various State Sales and Excise Tax Rates

State	State Sales Tax (%)	Gasoline[1] (¢/gal.)	Cigarette[2] ($/pack)	Spirits[3] ($/gal.)	Wine[4] ($/gal.)	Beer[5] ($/gal.)	Recreational Marijuana (%)
Florida	6	41.99	1.339	6.50 (f)	2.25 (l)	0.48 (q)	Not legal

Note: All tax rates as of January 1, 2019; (1) The American Petroleum Institute has developed a methodology for determining the average tax rate on a gallon of fuel. Rates may include any of the following: excise taxes, environmental fees, storage tank fees, other fees or taxes, general sales tax, and local taxes. In states where gasoline is subject to the general sales tax, or where the fuel tax is based on the average sale price, the average rate determined by API is sensitive to changes in the price of gasoline. States that fully or partially apply general sales taxes to gasoline: CA, CO, GA, IL, IN, MI, NY; (2) The federal excise tax of $1.0066 per pack and local taxes are not included; (3) Rates are those applicable to off-premise sales of 40% alcohol by volume (a.b.v.) distilled spirits in 750ml containers. Local excise taxes are excluded; (4) Rates are those applicable to off-premise sales of 11% a.b.v. non-carbonated wine in 750ml containers; (5) Rates are those applicable to off-premise sales of 4.7% a.b.v. beer in 12 ounce containers; (f) Different rates also applicable according to alcohol content, place of production, size of container, or place purchased (on- or off-premise or onboard airlines); (l) Different rates also applicable to alcohol content, place of production, size of container, place purchased (on- or off-premise or on board airlines) or type of wine (carbonated, vermouth, etc.); (q) Different rates also applicable according to alcohol content, place of production, size of container, or place purchased (on- or off-premise or onboard airlines).
Source: Tax Foundation, 2019 Facts & Figures: How Does Your State Compare?

State Business Tax Climate Index Rankings

State	Overall Rank	Corporate Tax Rank	Individual Income Tax Rank	Sales Tax Rank	Unemployment Insurance Tax Rank	Property Tax Rank
Florida	4	6	1	22	2	11

Note: The index is a measure of how each state's tax laws affect economic performance. The lower the rank, the more favorable a state's tax system is for business. States without a given tax are given a ranking of 1. The scores/rankings for the District of Columbia do not affect other states. The 2019 index represents the tax climate as of July 1, 2018.
Source: Tax Foundation, State Business Tax Climate Index 2019

COMMERCIAL REAL ESTATE

Office Market

Market Area	Inventory (sq. ft.)	Vacancy Rate (%)	Under Construction (sq. ft.)	YTD Net Absorption (sq. ft.)	Total Average Asking Rent ($/sq. ft./year)
Tampa-Saint Petersburg	64,250,812	9.4	250,000	316,696	24.03
National	4,905,867,938	13.1	83,553,714	45,846,470	28.46

Source: Newmark Grubb Knight Frank, National Office Market Report, 4th Quarter 2018

Industrial/Warehouse/R&D Market

Market Area	Inventory (sq. ft.)	Vacancy Rate (%)	Under Construction (sq. ft.)	YTD Net Absorption (sq. ft.)	Total Average Asking Rent ($/sq. ft./year)
Tampa-Saint Petersburg	259,155,886	5.3	2,180,979	1,960,857	5.84
National	14,796,839,085	5.0	262,662,294	238,014,726	7.16

Source: Newmark Grubb Knight Frank, National Industrial Market Report, 4th Quarter 2018

COMMERCIAL UTILITIES

Typical Monthly Electric Bills

Area	Commercial Service ($/month)		Industrial Service ($/month)	
	1,500 kWh	40 kW demand 14,000 kWh	1,000 kW demand 200,000 kWh	50,000 kW demand 32,500,000 kWh
City	164	1,249	22,368	2,323,214
Average[1]	203	1,619	25,886	2,540,077

Note: Figures are based on annualized rates; (1) Average based on 187 utilities surveyed
Source: Edison Electric Institute, Typical Bills and Average Rates Report, Summer 2018

TRANSPORTATION

Means of Transportation to Work

Area	Car/Truck/Van		Public Transportation			Bicycle	Walked	Other Means	Worked at Home
	Drove Alone	Car-pooled	Bus	Subway	Railroad				
City	78.1	8.4	2.4	0.0	0.0	1.3	2.4	1.3	6.1
MSA[1]	80.0	8.5	1.3	0.0	0.0	0.8	1.4	1.5	6.5
U.S.	76.4	9.2	2.5	0.0	1.9	0.6	0.6	2.7	1.3	4.7

Note: Figures are percentages and cover workers 16 years of age and older; (1) Figures cover the Tampa-St. Petersburg-Clearwater, FL Metropolitan Statistical Area—see Appendix B for areas included
Source: U.S. Census Bureau, 2013-2017 American Community Survey 5-Year Estimates

Travel Time to Work

Area	Less Than 10 Minutes	10 to 19 Minutes	20 to 29 Minutes	30 to 44 Minutes	45 to 59 Minutes	60 to 89 Minutes	90 Minutes or More
City	12.0	31.1	24.2	20.8	6.4	3.8	1.7
MSA[1]	10.0	27.4	22.0	22.8	9.5	6.1	2.1
U.S.	12.7	28.9	20.9	20.5	8.1	6.2	2.7

Note: Note: Figures are percentages and include workers 16 years old and over; (1) Figures cover the Tampa-St. Petersburg-Clearwater, FL Metropolitan Statistical Area—see Appendix B for areas included
Source: U.S. Census Bureau, 2013-2017 American Community Survey 5-Year Estimates

Freeway Travel Time Index

Area	1985	1990	1995	2000	2005	2010	2014
Urban Area Rank[1,2]	20	21	26	34	32	33	34
Urban Area Index[1]	1.12	1.15	1.18	1.19	1.22	1.21	1.21
Average Index[3]	1.09	1.11	1.14	1.17	1.20	1.19	1.20

Note: Freeway Travel Time Index—the ratio of travel time in the peak period to the travel time at free-flow conditions. For example, a value of 1.30 indicates a 20-minute free-flow trip takes 26 minutes in the peak (20 minutes x 1.30 = 26 minutes); (1) Covers the Tampa-St. Petersburg FL urban area; (2) Rank is based on 101 urban areas (#1 = highest travel time index); (3) Average of 101 urban areas
Source: Texas Transportation Institute, 2015 Urban Mobility Scorecard, August 2015

Freeway Commuter Stress Index

Area	1985	1990	1995	2000	2005	2010	2014
Urban Area Rank[1,2]	33	36	37	40	39	40	40
Urban Area Index[1]	1.14	1.17	1.20	1.21	1.25	1.23	1.24
Average Index[3]	1.13	1.16	1.19	1.22	1.25	1.24	1.25

Note: The Freeway Commuter Stress Index is the same as the Freeway Travel Time Index (see table above) except that it includes only the travel in the peak directions during the peak periods; the TTI includes travel in all directions during the peak period. Thus, the CSI is more indicative of the work trip experienced by each commuter on a daily basis; (1) Covers the Tampa-St. Petersburg FL urban area; (2) Rank is based on 101 urban areas (#1 = highest travel time index); (3) Average of 101 urban areas
Source: Texas Transportation Institute, 2015 Urban Mobility Scorecard, August 2015

Public Transportation

Agency Name / Mode of Transportation	Vehicles Operated in Maximum Service[1]	Annual Unlinked Passenger Trips[2] (in thous.)	Annual Passenger Miles[3] (in thous.)
Hillsborough Area Regional Transit Authority (HART)			
Bus (directly operated)	162	12,901.2	60,976.3
Demand Response (directly operated)	36	154.0	1,456.0
Streetcar Rail (directly operated)	3	280.6	497.4

Note: (1) The number of revenue vehicles operated by the given mode and type of service to meet the annual maximum service requirement. This is the revenue vehicle count during the peak season of the year; on the week and day that maximum service is provided. Vehicles operated in maximum service (VOMS) exclude atypical days and one-time special events; (2) The number of passengers who boarded public transportation vehicles. Passengers are counted each time they board a vehicle no matter how many vehicles they use to travel from their origin to their destination. (3) The sum of the distances ridden by all passengers during the entire fiscal year.
Source: Federal Transit Administration, National Transit Database, 2017

Air Transportation

Airport Name and Code / Type of Service	Passenger Airlines[1]	Passenger Enplanements	Freight Carriers[2]	Freight (lbs)
Tampa International (TPA)				
Domestic service (U.S. carriers - 2018)	28	9,889,874	11	199,163,374
International service (U.S. carriers - 2017)	10	75,883	1	362

Note: (1) Includes all U.S.-based major, minor and commuter airlines that carried at least one passenger during the year; (2) Includes all U.S.-based airlines and freight carriers that transported at least one pound of freight during the year.
Source: Bureau of Transportation Statistics, The Intermodal Transportation Database, Air Carriers: T-100 Domestic Market (U.S. Carriers), 2018; Bureau of Transportation Statistics, The Intermodal Transportation Database, Air Carriers: T-100 International Market (U.S. Carriers), 2017

Other Transportation Statistics

Major Highways:	I-4; I-75
Amtrak Service:	Yes
Major Waterways/Ports:	Port of Tampa

Source: Amtrak.com; Google Maps

BUSINESSES

Major Business Headquarters

Company Name	Industry	Rankings	
		Fortune[1]	Forbes[2]
WellCare Health Plans	Health Care: Insurance and Managed Care	170	-

Note: (1) Companies that produce a 10-K are ranked 1 to 500 based on 2017 revenue; (2) All private companies with at least $2 billion in annual revenue through the end of their most current fiscal year are ranked 1 to 229; companies listed are headquartered in the city; dashes indicate no ranking
Source: Fortune, "Fortune 500," June 2018; Forbes, "America's Largest Private Companies," 2018 Rankings

Fast-Growing Businesses

According to *Inc.*, Tampa is home to three of America's 500 fastest-growing private companies: **Welfont** (#16); **iProcedures** (#281); **Chacka Marketing** (#367). Criteria: must be an independent, privately-held, for-profit, U.S. corporation, proprietorship or partnership as of December 31, 2017; revenues must be at least $100,000 in 2014 and $2 million in 2017; must have four-year operating/sales history. Holding companies, regulated banks, and utilities were excluded. *Inc., "America's 500 Fastest-Growing Private Companies," 2018*

According to *Fortune*, Tampa is home to one of the 100 fastest-growing companies in the world: **Health Insurance Innovations** (#1). Companies were ranked by their revenue growth rate; their EPS growth rate; and their three-year annualized total return to investors for the period ending June 30, 2018. Criteria for inclusion: a company, foreign or domestic, must trade on a major U.S. stock exchange; must file quarterly reports with the SEC; must have a minimum market capitalization of $250 million; must have a stock price of at least $5 on June 30, 2018; must have been trading continuously since June 30, 2015; must have revenue and net income for the four quarters ended on or before April 30, 2018, of at least $50 million and $10 million, respectively; and must have posted a compound annual growth in revenue and earnings per share of at least 15% annually over the three years ending on or before April 30, 2018. Real estate investment trusts, limited-liability companies, limited parterships, business development companies, closed-end investment firms, companies about to be acquired, and companies that lost money in the quarter ending April 30, 2018 were excluded. *Fortune, "100 Fastest-Growing Companies," 2018*

According to Deloitte, Tampa is home to one of North America's 500 fastest-growing high-technology companies: **ReliaQuest** (#214). Companies are ranked by percentage growth in revenue over a four-year period. Criteria for inclusion: company must be headquartered within North America; must own proprietary intellectual property or technology that is sold to customers in products that contributes to a significant portion of the company's operating revenue; must have been in business for a minumum of four years with 2014 operating revenues of at least $50,000 USD/CD and 2017 operating revenues of at least $5 million USD/CD. *Deloitte, 2018 Technology Fast 500*™

Minority Business Opportunity

Tampa is home to two companies which are on the *Black Enterprise* Industrial/Service list (100 largest companies based on gross sales): **Coca-Cola Beverages Florida** (#5); **Sun State International Trucks** (#26). Criteria: operational in previous calendar year; at least 51% black-owned and manufactures/owns the product it sells or provides industrial or consumer services. Brokerages, real estate firms and firms that provide professional services are not eligible. *Black Enterprise, B.E. 100s, 2018*

Tampa is home to one company which is on the *Black Enterprise* Auto Dealer list (45 largest dealers based on gross sales): **March Hodge Automotive Group** (#4). Criteria: company must be operational in previous calendar year and be at least 51% black-owned. *Black Enterprise, B.E. 100s, 2018*

Tampa is home to three companies which are on the *Hispanic Business* 500 list (500 largest U.S. Hispanic-owned companies based on revenue): **Merchandise Partners** (#174); **MarkMaster** (#297); **Diverse ID Products of Florida** (#301). Companies included must show at least 51 percent ownership by Hispanic U.S. citizens, and must maintain headquarters in one of the 50 states or Washington, D.C. *Hispanic Business, "Hispanic Business 500," June 20, 2013*

Minority- and Women-Owned Businesses

Group	All Firms		Firms with Paid Employees			
	Firms	Sales ($000)	Firms	Sales ($000)	Employees	Payroll ($000)
AIAN[1]	206	5,359	4	2,054	17	515
Asian	2,303	822,115	710	713,915	4,983	155,098
Black	7,036	473,208	375	371,777	2,119	148,431
Hispanic	10,852	1,504,349	1,392	1,226,256	8,340	301,518
NHOPI[2]	62	1,863	2	(s)	20 - 99	(s)
Women	16,412	3,006,564	2,051	2,649,727	12,828	524,001
All Firms	44,811	74,774,844	11,016	73,205,257	266,069	12,855,772

Note: Figures cover firms located in the city; minority- and women-owned business are defined as firms in which the corresponding group own 51% or more of the stock or equity of the company; (1) American Indian and Alaska Native; (2) Native Hawaiian and Other Pacific Islander; (s) estimates are suppressed when publication standards are not met
Source: U.S. Census Bureau, 2012 Economic Census, Survey of Business Owners

HOTELS & CONVENTION CENTERS

Hotels, Motels and Vacation Rentals

Area	5 Star		4 Star		3 Star		2 Star		1 Star		Not Rated	
	Num.	Pct.[3]	Num.	Pct.[3]	Num.	Pct.[3]	Num.	Pct.[3]	Num.	Pct.[3]	Num.	Pct.[3]
City[1]	0	0.0	18	2.8	96	15.2	96	15.2	3	0.5	419	66.3
Total[2]	286	0.4	5,236	7.1	16,715	22.6	10,259	13.9	293	0.4	41,056	55.6

Note: (1) Figures cover Tampa and vicinity; (2) Figures cover all 100 cities in this book; (3) Percentage of hotels which have a given star rating; Star ratings are determined by expedia.com and offer an indication of the general quality of a particular hotel.
Source: www.expedia.com, April 3, 2019

Major Convention Centers

Name	Overall Space (sq. ft.)	Exhibit Space (sq. ft.)	Meeting Space (sq. ft.)	Meeting Rooms
Tampa Convention Center	600,000	200,000	42,000	36

Note: Table includes convention centers located in the Tampa-St. Petersburg-Clearwater, FL metro area
Source: Original research

Living Environment

COST OF LIVING

Cost of Living Index

Composite Index	Groceries	Housing	Utilities	Trans-portation	Health Care	Misc. Goods/ Services
89.2	103.7	71.8	87.7	99.6	95.4	95.2

Note: The Cost of Living Index measures regional differences in the cost of consumer goods and services, excluding taxes and non-consumer expenditures, for professional and managerial households in the top income quintile. It is based on more than 50,000 prices covering almost 60 different items for which prices are collected three times a year by chambers of commerce, economic development organizations or university applied economic centers in each participating urban area. The numbers shown should be read as a percentage above or below the national average of 100. For example, a value of 115.4 in the groceries column indicates that grocery prices are 15.4% higher than the national average. Small differences in the index numbers should not be interpreted as significant; Figures cover the Tampa FL urban area.
Source: The Council for Community and Economic Research, ACCRA Cost of Living Index, 2018

Grocery Prices

Area[1]	T-Bone Steak ($/pound)	Frying Chicken ($/pound)	Whole Milk ($/half gal.)	Eggs ($/dozen)	Orange Juice ($/64 oz.)	Coffee ($/11.5 oz.)
City[2]	9.23	1.41	2.54	2.16	3.22	3.86
Avg.	11.35	1.42	1.94	1.81	3.52	4.35
Min.	7.45	0.92	0.80	0.75	2.72	3.06
Max.	15.05	2.76	4.18	4.00	5.36	8.20

Note: (1) Values for the local area are compared with the average, minimum and maximum values for all 291 areas in the Cost of Living Index; (2) Figures cover the Tampa FL urban area; T-Bone Steak (price per pound); Frying Chicken (price per pound, whole fryer); Whole Milk (half gallon carton); Eggs (price per dozen, Grade A, large); Orange Juice (64 oz. Tropicana or Florida Natural); Coffee (11.5 oz. can, vacuum-packed, Maxwell House, Hills Bros, or Folgers).
Source: The Council for Community and Economic Research, ACCRA Cost of Living Index, 2018

Housing and Utility Costs

Area[1]	New Home Price ($)	Apartment Rent ($/month)	All Electric ($/month)	Part Electric ($/month)	Other Energy ($/month)	Telephone ($/month)
City[2]	215,261	1,032	127.66	-	-	182.70
Avg.	347,000	1,087	165.93	100.16	67.73	178.70
Min.	200,468	500	93.58	25.64	26.78	163.10
Max.	1,901,222	4,888	388.65	246.86	332.81	197,70

Note: (1) Values for the local area are compared with the average, minimum and maximum values for all 291 areas in the Cost of Living Index; (2) Figures cover the Tampa FL urban area; New Home Price (2,400 sf living area, 8,000 sf lot, in urban area with full utilities); Apartment Rent (950 sf 2 bedroom/1.5 or 2 bath, unfurnished, excluding all utilities except water); All Electric (average monthly cost for an all-electric home); Part Electric (average monthly cost for a part-electric home); Other Energy (average monthly cost for natural gas, fuel oil, coal, wood, and any other forms of energy except electricity); Telephone (price includes the base monthly rate plus taxes and fees for three lines of mobile phone service).
Source: The Council for Community and Economic Research, ACCRA Cost of Living Index, 2018

Health Care, Transportation, and Other Costs

Area[1]	Doctor ($/visit)	Dentist ($/visit)	Optometrist ($/visit)	Gasoline ($/gallon)	Beauty Salon ($/visit)	Men's Shirt ($)
City[2]	108.31	90.56	87.92	2.57	34.33	23.68
Avg.	110.71	95.11	103.74	2.61	37.48	32.03
Min.	33.60	62.55	54.63	1.89	17.00	11.44
Max.	195.97	153.93	225.79	3.59	71.88	58.64

Note: (1) Values for the local area are compared with the average, minimum and maximum values for all 291 areas in the Cost of Living Index; (2) Figures cover the Tampa FL urban area; Doctor (general practitioners routine exam of an established patient); Dentist (adult teeth cleaning and periodic oral examination); Optometrist (full vision eye exam for established adult patient); Gasoline (one gallon regular unleaded, national brand, including all taxes, cash price at self-service pump if available); Beauty Salon (woman's shampoo, trim, and blow-dry); Men's Shirt (cotton/polyester dress shirt, pinpoint weave, long sleeves).
Source: The Council for Community and Economic Research, ACCRA Cost of Living Index, 2018

HOUSING

House Price Index (HPI)

Area	National Ranking[2]	Quarterly Change (%)	One-Year Change (%)	Five-Year Change (%)
MSA[1]	40	0.54	9.06	56.78
U.S.[3]	–	1.12	5.73	32.81

Note: The HPI is a weighted repeat sales index. It measures average price changes in repeat sales or refinancings on the same properties. This information is obtained by reviewing repeat mortgage transactions on single-family properties whose mortgages have been purchased or securitized by Fannie Mae or Freddie Mac in January 1975; (1) Figures cover the Tampa-St. Petersburg-Clearwater, FL Metropolitan Statistical Area—see Appendix B for areas included; (2) Rankings are based on annual percentage change for all metro areas containing at least 15,000 transactions over the last 10 years and ranges from 1 to 245; (3) figures based on a weighted average of Census Division estimates using a seasonally adjusted, purchase-only index; all figures are for the period ending December 31, 2018
Source: Federal Housing Finance Agency, House Price Index, February 26, 2019

Median Single-Family Home Prices

Area	2016	2017	2018P	Percent Change 2017 to 2018
MSA[1]	198.0	220.0	235.0	6.8
U.S. Average	235.5	248.8	261.6	5.1

Note: Figures are median sales prices of existing single-family homes in thousands of dollars; (p) preliminary; (1) Figures cover the Tampa-St. Petersburg-Clearwater, FL Metropolitan Statistical Area—see Appendix B for areas included
Source: National Association of Realtors, Median Sales Price of Existing Single-Family Homes for Metropolitan Areas, 4th Quarter 2018

Qualifying Income Based on Median Sales Price of Existing Single-Family Homes

Area	With 5% Down ($)	With 10% Down ($)	With 20% Down ($)
MSA[1]	57,430	54,408	48,362
U.S. Average	62,954	59,640	53,013

Note: Figures are preliminary; Qualifying income is based on a mortgage rate of 4.9%. Monthly principal and interest payment is limited to 25% of income; (1) Figures cover the Tampa-St. Petersburg-Clearwater, FL Metropolitan Statistical Area—see Appendix B for areas included
Source: National Association of Realtors, Qualifying Income Based on Median Sales Price of Existing Single-Family Homes for Metropolitan Areas, 4th Quarter 2018

Median Apartment Condo-Coop Home Prices

Area	2016	2017	2018P	Percent Change 2017 to 2018
MSA[1]	135.0	150.0	160.0	6.7
U.S. Average	220.7	234.3	241.0	2.9

Note: Figures are median sales prices of existing apartment condo-coop homes in thousands of dollars; (p) preliminary; (1) Figures cover the Tampa-St. Petersburg-Clearwater, FL Metropolitan Statistical Area—see Appendix B for areas included
Source: National Association of Realtors, Median Sales Price of Existing Apartment Condo-Coop Homes for Metropolitan Areas, 4th Quarter 2018

Home Value Distribution

Area	Under $50,000	$50,000 -$99,999	$100,000 -$149,999	$150,000 -$199,999	$200,000 -$299,999	$300,000 -$499,999	$500,000 -$999,999	$1,000,000 or more
City	6.9	17.2	14.6	13.4	16.6	17.3	10.2	3.7
MSA[1]	11.1	17.5	16.4	16.7	19.2	12.7	5.0	1.3
U.S.	8.3	13.9	14.7	14.6	18.7	17.3	9.7	2.7

Note: Figures are percentages and cover owner-occupied housing units; (1) Figures cover the Tampa-St. Petersburg-Clearwater, FL Metropolitan Statistical Area—see Appendix B for areas included
Source: U.S. Census Bureau, 2013-2017 American Community Survey 5-Year Estimates

Homeownership Rate

Area	2010 (%)	2011 (%)	2012 (%)	2013 (%)	2014 (%)	2015 (%)	2016 (%)	2017 (%)	2018 (%)
MSA[1]	68.3	68.3	67.0	65.3	64.9	64.9	62.9	60.4	64.9
U.S.	66.9	66.1	65.4	65.1	64.5	63.7	63.4	63.9	64.4

Note: (1) Figures cover the Tampa-St. Petersburg-Clearwater, FL Metropolitan Statistical Area—see Appendix B for areas included
Source: U.S. Census Bureau, Housing Vacancies and Homeownership Annual Statistics: 2010-2018

Year Housing Structure Built

Area	2010 or Later	2000 -2009	1990 -1999	1980 -1989	1970 -1979	1960 -1969	1950 -1959	1940 -1949	Before 1940	Median Year
City	5.0	19.0	12.0	11.8	11.7	10.7	15.8	5.2	8.8	1978
MSA[1]	3.4	17.0	14.1	20.4	21.6	10.1	8.6	2.0	2.8	1982
U.S.	3.2	14.5	14.0	13.6	15.5	10.8	10.5	5.1	12.9	1977

Note: Figures are percentages except for Median Year; Note: (1) Figures cover the Tampa-St. Petersburg-Clearwater, FL Metropolitan Statistical Area—see Appendix B for areas included
Source: U.S. Census Bureau, 2013-2017 American Community Survey 5-Year Estimates

Gross Monthly Rent

Area	Under $500	$500 -$999	$1,000 -$1,499	$1,500 -$1,999	$2,000 -$2,499	$2,500 -$2,999	$3,000 and up	Median ($)
City	9.2	38.0	34.3	12.3	3.9	1.3	0.9	1,031
MSA[1]	5.5	43.2	35.9	10.9	2.8	0.9	0.8	1,014
U.S.	10.5	41.1	28.7	11.7	4.5	1.8	1.7	982

Note: Figures are percentages except for Median; Gross rent is the contract rent plus the estimated average monthly cost of utilities (electricity, gas, and water and sewer) and fuels (oil, coal, kerosene, wood, etc.) if these are paid by the renter (or paid for the renter by someone else); (1) Figures cover the Tampa-St. Petersburg-Clearwater, FL Metropolitan Statistical Area—see Appendix B for areas included
Source: U.S. Census Bureau, 2013-2017 American Community Survey 5-Year Estimates

HEALTH

Health Risk Factors

Category	MSA[1] (%)	U.S. (%)
Adults aged 18–64 who have any kind of health care coverage	79.1	87.3
Adults who reported being in good or better health	79.4	82.4
Adults who have been told they have high blood cholesterol	36.3	33.0
Adults who have been told they have high blood pressure	33.9	32.3
Adults who are current smokers	18.4	17.1
Adults who currently use E-cigarettes	6.5	4.6
Adults who currently use chewing tobacco, snuff, or snus	2.9	4.0
Adults who are heavy drinkers[2]	6.7	6.3
Adults who are binge drinkers[3]	16.5	17.4
Adults who are overweight (BMI 25.0 - 29.9)	36.5	35.3
Adults who are obese (BMI 30.0 - 99.8)	26.0	31.3
Adults who participated in any physical activities in the past month	71.2	74.4
Adults who always or nearly always wears a seat belt	96.9	94.3

Note: (1) Figures cover the Tampa-St. Petersburg-Clearwater, FL Metropolitan Statistical Area—see Appendix B for areas included; (2) Heavy drinkers are classified as adult men having more than 14 drinks per week and adult women having more than 7 drinks per week; (3) Binge drinkers are classified as males having five or more drinks on one occasion or females having four or more drinks on one occasion
Source: Centers for Disease Control and Prevention, Behaviorial Risk Factor Surveillance System, SMART: Selected Metropolitan Area Risk Trends, 2017

Acute and Chronic Health Conditions

Category	MSA[1] (%)	U.S. (%)
Adults who have ever been told they had a heart attack	6.0	4.2
Adults who have ever been told they have angina or coronary heart disease	5.6	3.9
Adults who have ever been told they had a stroke	4.2	3.0
Adults who have ever been told they have asthma	13.2	14.2
Adults who have ever been told they have arthritis	27.3	24.9
Adults who have ever been told they have diabetes[2]	9.2	10.5
Adults who have ever been told they had skin cancer	9.4	6.2
Adults who have ever been told they had any other types of cancer	9.9	7.1
Adults who have ever been told they have COPD	8.4	6.5
Adults who have ever been told they have kidney disease	1.9	3.0
Adults who have ever been told they have a form of depression	16.6	20.5

Note: (1) Figures cover the Tampa-St. Petersburg-Clearwater, FL Metropolitan Statistical Area—see Appendix B for areas included; (2) Figures do not include pregnancy-related, borderline, or pre-diabetes
Source: Centers for Disease Control and Prevention, Behaviorial Risk Factor Surveillance System, SMART: Selected Metropolitan Area Risk Trends, 2017

Health Screening and Vaccination Rates

Category	MSA[1] (%)	U.S. (%)
Adults aged 65+ who have had flu shot within the past year	63.9	60.7
Adults aged 65+ who have ever had a pneumonia vaccination	75.4	75.4
Adults who have ever been tested for HIV	47.6	36.1
Adults who have ever had the shingles or zoster vaccine?	27.0	28.9
Adults who have had their blood cholesterol checked within the last five years	90.3	85.9

Note: n/a not available; (1) Figures cover the Tampa-St. Petersburg-Clearwater, FL Metropolitan Statistical Area—see Appendix B for areas included.
Source: Centers for Disease Control and Prevention, Behaviorial Risk Factor Surveillance System, SMART: Selected Metropolitan Area Risk Trends, 2017

Disability Status

Category	MSA[1] (%)	U.S. (%)
Adults who reported being deaf	7.3	6.7
Are you blind or have serious difficulty seeing, even when wearing glasses?	6.2	4.5
Are you limited in any way in any of your usual activities due of arthritis?	15.4	12.9
Do you have difficulty doing errands alone?	9.2	6.8
Do you have difficulty dressing or bathing?	6.0	3.6
Do you have serious difficulty concentrating/remembering/making decisions?	11.8	10.7
Do you have serious difficulty walking or climbing stairs?	18.1	13.6

Note: (1) Figures cover the Tampa-St. Petersburg-Clearwater, FL Metropolitan Statistical Area—see Appendix B for areas included.
Source: Centers for Disease Control and Prevention, Behaviorial Risk Factor Surveillance System, SMART: Selected Metropolitan Area Risk Trends, 2017

Mortality Rates for the Top 10 Causes of Death in the U.S.

ICD-10[a] Sub-Chapter	ICD-10[a] Code	Age-Adjusted Mortality Rate[1] per 100,000 population	
		County[2]	U.S.
Malignant neoplasms	C00-C97	154.6	155.5
Ischaemic heart diseases	I20-I25	92.3	94.8
Other forms of heart disease	I30-I51	35.8	52.9
Chronic lower respiratory diseases	J40-J47	42.0	41.0
Cerebrovascular diseases	I60-I69	31.9	37.5
Other degenerative diseases of the nervous system	G30-G31	44.1	35.0
Other external causes of accidental injury	W00-X59	33.0	33.7
Organic, including symptomatic, mental disorders	F01-F09	30.7	31.0
Hypertensive diseases	I10-I15	37.1	21.9
Diabetes mellitus	E10-E14	19.9	21.2

Note: (a) ICD-10 = International Classification of Diseases 10th Revision; (1) Mortality rates are a three year average covering 2015-2017; (2) Figures cover Hillsborough County.
Source: Centers for Disease Control and Prevention, National Center for Health Statistics. Underlying Cause of Death 1999-2017 on CDC WONDER Online Database

Mortality Rates for Selected Causes of Death

ICD-10[a] Sub-Chapter	ICD-10[a] Code	Age-Adjusted Mortality Rate[1] per 100,000 population	
		County[2]	U.S.
Assault	X85-Y09	5.7	5.9
Diseases of the liver	K70-K76	13.1	14.1
Human immunodeficiency virus (HIV) disease	B20-B24	3.9	1.8
Influenza and pneumonia	J09-J18	12.3	14.3
Intentional self-harm	X60-X84	12.8	13.6
Malnutrition	E40-E46	1.0	1.6
Obesity and other hyperalimentation	E65-E68	1.8	2.1
Renal failure	N17-N19	9.7	13.0
Transport accidents	V01-V99	15.5	12.4
Viral hepatitis	B15-B19	1.5	1.6

Note: (a) ICD-10 = International Classification of Diseases 10th Revision; (1) Mortality rates are a three year average covering 2015-2017; (2) Figures cover Hillsborough County; Data are suppressed when the data meet the criteria for confidentiality constraints; Mortality rates are flagged as unreliable when the rate would be calculated with a numerator of 20 or less.
Source: Centers for Disease Control and Prevention, National Center for Health Statistics. Underlying Cause of Death 1999-2017 on CDC WONDER Online Database

Health Insurance Coverage

Area	With Health Insurance	With Private Health Insurance	With Public Health Insurance	Without Health Insurance	Population Under Age 18 Without Health Insurance
City	87.0	61.0	33.6	13.0	5.5
MSA[1]	86.7	62.2	36.4	13.3	7.4
U.S.	89.5	67.2	33.8	10.5	5.7

Note: Figures are percentages that cover the civilian noninstitutionalized population; (1) Figures cover the Tampa-St. Petersburg-Clearwater, FL Metropolitan Statistical Area—see Appendix B for areas included
Source: U.S. Census Bureau, 2013-2017 American Community Survey 5-Year Estimates

Number of Medical Professionals

Area	MDs[3]	DOs[3,4]	Dentists	Podiatrists	Chiropractors	Optometrists
County[1] (number)	4,746	392	802	78	363	180
County[1] (rate[2])	343.5	28.4	56.9	5.5	25.8	12.8
U.S. (rate[2])	279.3	23.0	68.4	6.0	27.1	16.2

Note: Data as of 2017 unless noted; (1) Data covers Hillsborough County; (2) Rate per 100,000 population; (3) Data as of 2016 and includes all active, non-federal physicians; (4) Doctor of Osteopathic Medicine
Source: U.S. Department of Health and Human Services, Health Resources and Services Administration, Bureau of Health Professions, Area Resource File (ARF) 2017-2018

Best Hospitals

According to *U.S. News,* the Tampa-St. Petersburg-Clearwater, FL metro area is home to two of the best hospitals in the U.S.: **H. Lee Moffitt Cancer Center and Research Institute** (2 adult specialties); **Tampa General Hospital** (6 adult specialties). The hospitals listed were nationally ranked in at least one of 16 adult or 10 pediatric specialties. Only 170 hospitals nationwide were nationally ranked in one or more adult or pediatric specialty. Twenty hospitals in the U.S. made the Honor Roll. The Best Hospitals Honor Roll takes both the national rankings and the procedure and condition ratings into account. Hospitals received points if they were nationally ranked in one of the 16 adult specialties—the higher they ranked, the more points they got—and how many ratings of "high performing" they earned in the nine procedures and conditions. *U.S. News Online, "America's Best Hospitals 2018-19"*

According to *U.S. News,* the Tampa-St. Petersburg-Clearwater, FL metro area is home to one of the best children's hospitals in the U.S.: **Johns Hopkins All Children's Hospital** (5 pediatric specialties). The hospital listed was highly ranked in at least one of 10 pediatric specialties. Eighty-six children's hospitals in the U.S. were nationally ranked in at least one specialty. Hospitals received points for being ranked in a specialty, and the 10 hospitals with the most points across the 10 specialties make up the Honor Roll. *U.S. News Online, "America's Best Children's Hospitals 2018-19"*

EDUCATION

Public School District Statistics

District Name	Schls	Pupils	Pupil/ Teacher Ratio	Minority Pupils[1] (%)	Free Lunch Eligible[2] (%)	IEP[3] (%)
Hillsborough	304	214,386	11.7	65.9	52.8	14.1

Note: Table includes school districts with 2,000 or more students; (1) Percentage of students that are not non-Hispanic white; (2) Percentage of students that are eligible for the free lunch program; (3) Percentage of students that have an Individualized Education Program.
Source: U.S. Department of Education, National Center for Education Statistics, Common Core of Data, Local Education Agency (School District) Universe Survey: School Year 2016-2017; U.S. Department of Education, National Center for Education Statistics, Common Core of Data, Public Elementary/Secondary School Universe Survey: School Year 2016-2017

Best High Schools

According to *U.S. News,* Tampa is home to two of the best high schools in the U.S.: **Plant High School** (#343); **Robinson High School** (#463). More than 20,000 public, magnet and charter schools were ranked based on their performance on state assessments and how well they prepare students for college. Schools with the highest unrounded College Readiness Index values were numerically ranked from 1 to 500 and were classified as gold medal winners. *U.S. News & World Report, "Best High Schools 2018"*

Highest Level of Education

Area	Less than H.S.	H.S. Diploma	Some College, No Deg.	Associate Degree	Bachelor's Degree	Master's Degree	Prof. School Degree	Doctorate Degree
City	12.9	25.9	16.8	8.2	22.1	9.1	3.4	1.5
MSA[1]	10.9	29.2	21.1	10.0	18.6	7.2	1.9	1.1
U.S.	12.7	27.3	20.8	8.3	19.1	8.4	2.0	1.4

Note: Figures cover persons age 25 and over; (1) Figures cover the Tampa-St. Petersburg-Clearwater, FL Metropolitan Statistical Area—see Appendix B for areas included
Source: U.S. Census Bureau, 2013-2017 American Community Survey 5-Year Estimates

Educational Attainment by Race

Area	High School Graduate or Higher (%)					Bachelor's Degree or Higher (%)				
	Total	White	Black	Asian	Hisp.[2]	Total	White	Black	Asian	Hisp.[2]
City	87.1	89.3	81.8	87.3	76.3	36.2	41.5	16.8	63.6	20.8
MSA[1]	89.1	90.2	85.7	85.9	78.7	28.8	29.3	21.2	50.5	20.6
U.S.	87.3	89.3	84.9	86.5	66.7	30.9	32.2	20.6	52.7	15.2

Note: Figures shown cover persons 25 years old and over; (1) Figures cover the Tampa-St. Petersburg-Clearwater, FL Metropolitan Statistical Area—see Appendix B for areas included; (2) People of Hispanic origin can be of any race
Source: U.S. Census Bureau, 2013-2017 American Community Survey 5-Year Estimates

School Enrollment by Grade and Control

Area	Preschool (%)		Kindergarten (%)		Grades 1 - 4 (%)		Grades 5 - 8 (%)		Grades 9 - 12 (%)	
	Public	Private	Public	Private	Public	Private	Public	Private	Public	Private
City	57.1	42.9	88.7	11.3	90.3	9.7	85.9	14.1	86.7	13.3
MSA[1]	58.5	41.5	86.5	13.5	88.2	11.8	87.4	12.6	89.4	10.6
U.S.	58.8	41.2	87.7	12.3	89.7	10.3	89.6	10.4	90.3	9.7

Note: Figures shown cover persons 3 years old and over; (1) Figures cover the Tampa-St. Petersburg-Clearwater, FL Metropolitan Statistical Area—see Appendix B for areas included
Source: U.S. Census Bureau, 2013-2017 American Community Survey 5-Year Estimates

Average Salaries of Public School Classroom Teachers

Area	2016		2017		Change from 2016 to 2017	
	Dollars	Rank[1]	Dollars	Rank[1]	Percent	Rank[2]
Florida	46,612	46	47,267	45	1.4	26
U.S. Average	58,479	–	59,660	–	2.0	–

Note: (1) Rank ranges from 1 to 51 where 1 indicates highest salary; (2) Rank ranges from 1 to 51 where 1 indicates highest percent change.
Source: National Education Association, Rankings & Estimates: Rankings of the States 2017 and Estimates of School Statistics 2018

Higher Education

Four-Year Colleges			Two-Year Colleges			Medical Schools[1]	Law Schools[2]	Voc/ Tech[3]
Public	Private Non-profit	Private For-profit	Public	Private Non-profit	Private For-profit			
1	4	6	3	1	2	1	0	8

Note: Figures cover institutions located within the city limits and include main campuses only; (1) includes schools accredited by the Liaison Committee on Medical Education and the American Osteopathic Association's Commission on Osteopathic College Accreditation; (2) includes ABA-accredited schools, schools with provisional ABA accreditation, and state accredited schools; (3) includes all schools with programs that are less than 2 years.
Source: National Center for Education Statistics, Integrated Postsecondary Education System (IPEDS), 2017-18; Wikipedia, List of Medical Schools in the United States, accessed April 3, 2019; Wikipedia, List of Law Schools in the United States, accessed April 3, 2019

According to *U.S. News & World Report*, the Tampa-St. Petersburg-Clearwater, FL metro area is home to one of the best national universities in the U.S.: **University of South Florida** (#124 tie). The indicators used to capture academic quality fall into a number of categories: assessment by administrators at peer institutions; retention of students; faculty resources; student selectivity; financial resources; alumni giving; high school counselor ratings of colleges; and graduation rate. *U.S. News & World Report, "America's Best Colleges 2019"*

According to *U.S. News & World Report*, the Tampa-St. Petersburg-Clearwater, FL metro area is home to one of the best liberal arts colleges in the U.S.: **Eckerd College** (#135 tie). The indicators used to capture academic quality fall into a number of categories: assessment by administrators at peer institutions; retention of students; faculty resources; student selectivity; financial resources;

alumni giving; high school counselor ratings of colleges; and graduation rate. *U.S. News & World Report, "America's Best Colleges 2019"*

According to *U.S. News & World Report,* the Tampa-St. Petersburg-Clearwater, FL metro area is home to one of the top 75 medical schools for research in the U.S.: **University of South Florida** (#52 tie). The rankings are based on a weighted average of 11 measures of quality: quality assessment; peer assessment score; assessment score by residency directors; research activity; total research activity; average research activity per faculty member; student selectivity; median MCAT total score; median undergraduate GPA; acceptance rate; and faculty resources. *U.S. News & World Report, "America's Best Graduate Schools, Medical, 2020"*

PRESIDENTIAL ELECTION

2016 Presidential Election Results

Area	Clinton	Trump	Johnson	Stein	Other
Hillsborough County	51.0	44.2	2.6	0.8	1.4
U.S.	48.0	45.9	3.3	1.1	1.7

Note: Results are percentages and may not add to 100% due to rounding
Source: Dave Leip's Atlas of U.S. Presidential Elections

EMPLOYERS

Major Employers

Company Name	Industry
Baycare Health System	General medical & surgical hospitals
Beall's	Manufacturing
Busch Gardens	Arts, entertainment & recreation
Caspers Company	Accommodation & food services
Citi	Finance & insurance
Florida Hospital	Health care & social assistance
Gerdau Ameristeel US	Manufacturing
HCA Healthcare	Health care & social assistance
Home Shopping Network	Information
JPMorgan Chase	Finance & insurance
MacDill Air Force Base	Public administration
Moffitt Cancer Center & Research Institute	Health care & social assistance
Progressive	Finance & insurance
Publix Supermarkets	Retail grocery
Raymond James Financial	Finance & insurance
Tampa General Hospital	Health care & social assistance
Tech Data Corp	Wholesale trade
University of South Florida	Educational services
Verizon	Information
WellCare	Finance & insurance

Note: Companies shown are located within the Tampa-St. Petersburg-Clearwater, FL Metropolitan Statistical Area.
Source: Hoovers.com; Wikipedia

Best Companies to Work For

H. Lee Moffitt Cancer Center & Research Institute, headquartered in Tampa, is among the "100 Best Companies for Working Mothers." Criteria: paid time off and leaves; workforce profile; benefits; women's issues and advancement; flexible work; company culture and work life programs. *Working Mother, "100 Best Companies 2018"*

H. Lee Moffitt Cancer Center and Research Institut, headquartered in Tampa, is among the "100 Best Places to Work in IT." To qualify, companies had to be U.S.-based organizations or be non-U.S.- based employers that met the following criteria: have a minimum of 300 total employees at a U.S. headquarters and a minimum of 30 IT employees in the U.S., with at least 50% of their IT employees based in the U.S. The best places to work were selected based on compensation, benefits, work/life balance, employee morale, and satisfaction with training and development programs. In addition, *Computerworld* looked at retention efforts, programs for recognizing and rewarding outstanding performances, and benefits such as flextime, elder care and child care, and reimbursement for college tuition and the cost of pursuing technology certifications. *Computerworld, "100 Best Places to Work in IT 2018"*

PUBLIC SAFETY

Crime Rate

Area	All Crimes	Violent Crimes				Property Crimes		
		Murder	Rape[3]	Robbery	Aggrav. Assault	Burglary	Larceny -Theft	Motor Vehicle Theft
City	2,208.1	10.1	31.5	105.6	317.2	321.3	1,274.8	147.5
Suburbs[1]	2,467.0	2.7	37.6	62.9	211.2	348.8	1,639.4	164.5
Metro[2]	2,434.8	3.6	36.9	68.2	224.4	345.4	1,593.9	162.3
U.S.	2,756.1	5.3	41.7	98.0	248.9	430.4	1,694.4	237.4

Note: Figures are crimes per 100,000 population; (1) All areas within the metro area that are located outside the city limits; (2) Figures cover the Tampa-St. Petersburg-Clearwater, FL Metropolitan Statistical Area—see Appendix B for areas included; (3) The city and U.S. figures shown were reported using the revised Uniform Crime Reporting (UCR) definition of rape. The suburban and metro area figures shown are an aggregate total of the data submitted using both the revised and legacy UCR definitions.
Source: FBI Uniform Crime Reports, 2017

Hate Crimes

Area	Number of Quarters Reported	Number of Incidents per Bias Motivation					
		Race/Ethnicity/ Ancestry	Religion	Sexual Orientation	Disability	Gender	Gender Identity
City	4	3	0	0	0	0	0
U.S.	4	4,131	1,564	1,130	116	46	119

Source: Federal Bureau of Investigation, Hate Crime Statistics 2017

Identity Theft Consumer Reports

Area	Reports	Reports per 100,000 Population	Rank[2]
MSA[1]	4,770	157	26
U.S.	444,602	135	-

Note: (1) Figures cover the Tampa-St. Petersburg-Clearwater, FL Metropolitan Statistical Area—see Appendix B for areas included; (2) Rank ranges from 1 to 389 where 1 indicates greatest number of identity theft reports per 100,000 population
Source: Federal Trade Commission, Consumer Sentinel Network Data Book for January–December 2018

Fraud and Other Consumer Reports

Area	Reports	Reports per 100,000 Population	Rank[2]
MSA[1]	22,683	748	14
U.S.	2,552,917	776	-

Note: (1) Figures cover the Tampa-St. Petersburg-Clearwater, FL Metropolitan Statistical Area—see Appendix B for areas included; (2) Rank ranges from 1 to 389 where 1 indicates greatest number of fraud and other consumer reports per 100,000 population
Source: Federal Trade Commission, Consumer Sentinel Network Data Book for January–December 2018

SPORTS

Professional Sports Teams

Team Name	League	Year Established
Tampa Bay Buccaneers	National Football League (NFL)	1976
Tampa Bay Lightning	National Hockey League (NHL)	1993
Tampa Bay Rays	Major League Baseball (MLB)	1998

Note: Includes teams located in the Tampa-St. Petersburg-Clearwater, FL Metropolitan Statistical Area.
Source: Wikipedia, Major Professional Sports Teams of the United States and Canada, April 5, 2019

CLIMATE

Average and Extreme Temperatures

Temperature	Jan	Feb	Mar	Apr	May	Jun	Jul	Aug	Sep	Oct	Nov	Dec	Yr.
Extreme High (°F)	85	88	91	93	98	99	97	98	96	94	90	86	99
Average High (°F)	70	72	76	82	87	90	90	90	89	84	77	72	82
Average Temp. (°F)	60	62	67	72	78	81	82	83	81	75	68	62	73
Average Low (°F)	50	52	56	61	67	73	74	74	73	66	57	52	63
Extreme Low (°F)	21	24	29	40	49	53	63	67	57	40	23	18	18

Note: Figures cover the years 1948-1990
Source: National Climatic Data Center, International Station Meteorological Climate Summary, 9/96

Average Precipitation/Snowfall/Humidity

Precip./Humidity	Jan	Feb	Mar	Apr	May	Jun	Jul	Aug	Sep	Oct	Nov	Dec	Yr.
Avg. Precip. (in.)	2.1	2.8	3.5	1.8	3.0	5.6	7.3	7.9	6.5	2.3	1.8	2.1	46.7
Avg. Snowfall (in.)	Tr	Tr	Tr	0	0	0	0	0	0	0	0	Tr	Tr
Avg. Rel. Hum. 7am (%)	87	87	86	86	85	86	88	90	91	89	88	87	88
Avg. Rel. Hum. 4pm (%)	56	55	54	51	52	60	65	66	64	57	56	57	58

Note: Figures cover the years 1948-1990; Tr = Trace amounts (<0.05 in. of rain; <0.5 in. of snow)
Source: National Climatic Data Center, International Station Meteorological Climate Summary, 9/96

Weather Conditions

Temperature			Daytime Sky			Precipitation		
32°F & below	45°F & below	90°F & above	Clear	Partly cloudy	Cloudy	0.01 inch or more precip.	0.1 inch or more snow/ice	Thunder-storms
3	35	85	81	204	80	107	< 1	87

Note: Figures are average number of days per year and cover the years 1948-1990
Source: National Climatic Data Center, International Station Meteorological Climate Summary, 9/96

HAZARDOUS WASTE

Superfund Sites

The Tampa-St. Petersburg-Clearwater, FL metro area is home to 14 sites on the EPA's Superfund National Priorities List: **Alaric Area Gw Plume** (final); **Arkla Terra Property** (final); **Helena Chemical Co. (Tampa Plant)** (final); **Jj Seifert Machine** (final); **MRI Corp (Tampa)** (final); **Normandy Park Apartments** (proposed); **Peak Oil Co./Bay Drum Co.** (final); **Raleigh Street Dump** (final); **Reeves Southeastern Galvanizing Corp.** (final); **Southern Solvents, Inc.** (final); **Stauffer Chemical Co (Tampa)** (final); **Stauffer Chemical Co. (Tarpon Springs)** (final); **Sydney Mine Sludge Ponds** (final); **Taylor Road Landfill** (final). There are a total of 1,390 Superfund sites with a status of proposed or final on the list in the U.S. *U.S. Environmental Protection Agency, National Priorities List, April 5, 2019*

AIR & WATER QUALITY

Air Quality Trends: Ozone

	1990	1995	2000	2005	2010	2012	2014	2015	2016	2017
MSA[1]	0.080	0.075	0.081	0.075	0.067	0.066	0.065	0.062	0.064	0.064
U.S.	0.088	0.089	0.082	0.080	0.073	0.075	0.067	0.068	0.069	0.068

Note: (1) Data covers the Tampa-St. Petersburg-Clearwater, FL Metropolitan Statistical Area—see Appendix B for areas included. The values shown are the composite ozone concentration averages among trend sites based on the highest fourth daily maximum 8-hour concentration in parts per million. These trends are based on sites having an adequate record of monitoring data during the trend period. Data from exceptional events are included.
Source: U.S. Environmental Protection Agency, Air Quality Monitoring Information, "Air Quality Trends by City, 1990-2017"

Air Quality Index

Area	Percent of Days when Air Quality was...[2]					AQI Statistics[2]	
	Good	Moderate	Unhealthy for Sensitive Groups	Unhealthy	Very Unhealthy	Maximum	Median
MSA[1]	69.0	29.9	1.1	0.0	0.0	150	45

Note: (1) Data covers the Tampa-St. Petersburg-Clearwater, FL Metropolitan Statistical Area—see Appendix B for areas included; (2) Based on 365 days with AQI data in 2017. Air Quality Index (AQI) is an index for reporting daily air quality. EPA calculates the AQI for five major air pollutants regulated by the Clean Air Act: ground-level ozone, particle pollution (aka particulate matter), carbon monoxide, sulfur dioxide, and nitrogen dioxide. The AQI runs from 0 to 500. The higher the AQI value, the greater the level of air pollution and the greater the health concern. There are six AQI categories: "Good" AQI is between 0 and 50. Air quality is considered satisfactory; "Moderate" AQI is between 51 and 100. Air quality is acceptable; "Unhealthy for Sensitive Groups" When AQI values are between 101 and 150, members of sensitive groups may experience health effects; "Unhealthy" When AQI values are between 151 and 200 everyone may begin to experience health effects; "Very Unhealthy" AQI values between 201 and 300 trigger a health alert; "Hazardous" AQI values over 300 trigger warnings of emergency conditions (not shown).
Source: U.S. Environmental Protection Agency, Air Quality Index Report, 2017

Air Quality Index Pollutants

Area	Percent of Days when AQI Pollutant was...[2]					
	Carbon Monoxide	Nitrogen Dioxide	Ozone	Sulfur Dioxide	Particulate Matter 2.5	Particulate Matter 10
MSA[1]	0.0	0.0	54.0	2.2	43.6	0.3

Note: (1) Data covers the Tampa-St. Petersburg-Clearwater, FL Metropolitan Statistical Area—see Appendix B for areas included; (2) Based on 365 days with AQI data in 2017. The Air Quality Index (AQI) is an index for reporting daily air quality. EPA calculates the AQI for five major air pollutants regulated by the Clean Air Act: ground-level ozone, particle pollution (also known as particulate matter), carbon monoxide, sulfur dioxide, and nitrogen dioxide. The AQI runs from 0 to 500. The higher the AQI value, the greater the level of air pollution and the greater the health concern.
Source: U.S. Environmental Protection Agency, Air Quality Index Report, 2017

Maximum Air Pollutant Concentrations: Particulate Matter, Ozone, CO and Lead

	Particulate Matter 10 (ug/m^3)	Particulate Matter 2.5 Wtd AM (ug/m^3)	Particulate Matter 2.5 24-Hr (ug/m^3)	Ozone (ppm)	Carbon Monoxide (ppm)	Lead (ug/m^3)
MSA[1] Level	63	8.1	22	0.068	2	0.13
NAAQS[2]	150	15	35	0.075	9	0.15
Met NAAQS[2]	Yes	Yes	Yes	Yes	Yes	Yes

Note: (1) Data covers the Tampa-St. Petersburg-Clearwater, FL Metropolitan Statistical Area—see Appendix B for areas included; Data from exceptional events are included; (2) National Ambient Air Quality Standards; ppm = parts per million; ug/m^3 = micrograms per cubic meter; n/a not available.
Concentrations: Particulate Matter 10 (coarse particulate)—highest second maximum 24-hour concentration; Particulate Matter 2.5 Wtd AM (fine particulate)—highest weighted annual mean concentration; Particulate Matter 2.5 24-Hour (fine particulate)—highest 98th percentile 24-hour concentration; Ozone—highest fourth daily maximum 8-hour concentration; Carbon Monoxide—highest second maximum non-overlapping 8-hour concentration; Lead—maximum running 3-month average
Source: U.S. Environmental Protection Agency, Air Quality Monitoring Information, "Air Quality Statistics by City, 2017"

Maximum Air Pollutant Concentrations: Nitrogen Dioxide and Sulfur Dioxide

	Nitrogen Dioxide AM (ppb)	Nitrogen Dioxide 1-Hr (ppb)	Sulfur Dioxide AM (ppb)	Sulfur Dioxide 1-Hr (ppb)	Sulfur Dioxide 24-Hr (ppb)
MSA[1] Level	10	29	n/a	15	n/a
NAAQS[2]	53	100	30	75	140
Met NAAQS[2]	Yes	Yes	n/a	Yes	n/a

Note: (1) Data covers the Tampa-St. Petersburg-Clearwater, FL Metropolitan Statistical Area—see Appendix B for areas included; Data from exceptional events are included; (2) National Ambient Air Quality Standards; ppm = parts per million; ug/m^3 = micrograms per cubic meter; n/a not available.
Concentrations: Nitrogen Dioxide AM—highest arithmetic mean concentration; Nitrogen Dioxide 1-Hr—highest 98th percentile 1-hour daily maximum concentration; Sulfur Dioxide AM—highest annual mean concentration; Sulfur Dioxide 1-Hr—highest 99th percentile 1-hour daily maximum concentration; Sulfur Dioxide 24-Hr—highest second maximum 24-hour concentration
Source: U.S. Environmental Protection Agency, Air Quality Monitoring Information, "Air Quality Statistics by City, 2017"

Drinking Water

Water System Name	Pop. Served	Primary Water Source Type	Violations[1]	
			Health Based	Monitoring/ Reporting
City of Tampa Water Department	603,000	Surface	0	0

Note: (1) Based on violation data from January 1, 2018 to December 31, 2018
Source: U.S. Environmental Protection Agency, Office of Ground Water and Drinking Water, Safe Drinking Water Information System (based on data extracted April 5, 2019)

Tyler, Texas

Background

Just 90 miles east of Dallas lies the city of Tyler, named after the 10th President of the United States. President John Tyler was instrumental in admitting Texas to the Union, as the 48th state, in 1845. The town of Tyler was incorporated in 1850. In 1860 over 350 of the 1,021 residents were slaves, on which the town's economy depended on. During the Civil War, Tyler was the largest Confederate ordnance plant and the home of Camp Ford, one of the largest prison camps. Post war brought challenges to Tyler and it wasn't until 1874, when the Hudson & Great Northern Railway began service to Tyler, that the city started to grow. In 1877, Tyler "tapped" the Texas Pacific Railway and created a connection to Fergerson in 1877 known as the "Tyler Tap" and The Tyler Tap Railroad later became the St. Louis Southwestern Railway.

With the influx of railroad service, Tyler's population tripled by 1890. Agriculture, and especially cotton, fueled a full 60 percent of its economy. Tyler continued to prosper and the St. Louis Western Railroad referred to its line as The Cotton Belt Route. In the late 1890s, the emergence of fruit trees, mostly peaches, became increasingly important to the county's economy. Unfortunately, a peach blight nearly destroyed all the peach orchards, and Tyler's farmers converted their orchards to produce roses, and the perfect combination of rich soil and good climate attributed to Tyler's booming rose industry. The Tyler Rose Festival became a major event in 1933. By 1940, more than half of all rose bushes sold in the United States came from Tyler and its surrounding area.

While roses were fueling the economy, Tyler's good fortune continued with the discovery of oil fields in the mid 1930s. The new oil industry propelled Tyler's economy once again and the population continued to grow to over 28,000 by 1940. Soon oil companies and developers were flocking to Tyler, and it became a regional leader in the oil and gas production industry. In the late 1940s, Tyler economic growth continued in agriculture, manufacturing, and retail. Through the 1970s, Tyler's oil industry continued to dominate its economy. With the continued growth came other strong industries such as furniture, clothing and metal fabricating.

Today, the Texas Rose Festival is still an annual event in Tyler. The Rose Parade is a major attraction, drawing thousands of tourists. Tyler, now called the Rose Capitol of America, still supplies over one third of the country's rose bushes.

In addition to rose production, Trinity Mother Frances Health System and Brookshire Grocery Company are major facets of Tyler's economy. Tyler's higher educational institutions include two campuses of the University of Texas and Texas College.

Tyler Rose Museum also showcases Tyler's history, with costumes and memorabilia that were part of previous Festivals. Theater presentations and animations enhance the importance of roses in Tyler's history.

Other attractions in Tyler include the Cotton Belt Depot Museum, housed in the original 1905 depot station. On display at the museum are all things from the "Cotton Belt" era including railroad artifacts and paintings. Lionel Electric Trains houses its "Brag Train Collection" at the museum featuring over 1600 cars and 200 locomotives. Even though the Depot is not active, visitors can still experience the Union Pacific Railroad passing by the station.

The Smith County Historical Society manages Camp Ford Historic Park, where tourists can visit the site of the largest Confederate Army's POW camp. On July 4th of 1865, the original prison was destroyed, but the park offers a reproduction of the prison's gate, cabins and a history of the site. The Tyler Sons of Confederate Veterans Camp sponsor an annual "living event" demonstrating a soldier's life within the prison camp.

Tyler is also home to the Caldwell Zoo, and Azalea Trail, designed to showcase the colorful azalea shrubs that flourish in the city.

Tyler experiences weather typical of east Texas—humid and subtropical—but also unpredictable. The record high temperature occurred in 2011 at 115 °F and the record low was -3 °F in 1930.

Rankings

Business/Finance Rankings

- The Tyler metro area appeared on the Milken Institute "2018 Best Performing Cities" list. Rank: #65 out of 201 small metro areas. Criteria: job growth; wage and salary growth; high-tech output growth. *Milken Institute, "Best-Performing Cities 2018," January 24, 2019*

- *Forbes* ranked 200 smaller metro areas (population under 265,400) to determine the nation's "Best Small Places for Business and Careers." The Tyler metro area was ranked #51. Criteria: costs (business and living); job growth (past and projected); income growth; quality of life; educational attainment (college and high school); projected economic growth; cultural and recreational opportunities; net migration patterns; number of highly ranked colleges. *Forbes, "The Best Small Cities for Business and Careers 2018," October, 24 2018*

Real Estate Rankings

- Tyler was ranked #119 out of 237 metro areas in terms of housing affordability in 2018 by the National Association of Home Builders (#1 = most affordable). Criteria: the share of homes sold in that area affordable to a family earning the local median income, based on standard mortgage underwriting criteria. *National Association of Home Builders®, NAHB-Wells Fargo Housing Opportunity Index, 4th Quarter 2018*

Safety Rankings

- The National Insurance Crime Bureau ranked 382 metro areas in the U.S. in terms of per capita rates of vehicle theft. The Tyler metro area ranked #236 (#1 = highest rate). Criteria: number of vehicle theft offenses per 100,000 inhabitants in 2017. *National Insurance Crime Bureau, "Hot Spots 2017," July 12, 2018*

Seniors/Retirement Rankings

- From its Best Cities for Successful Aging indexes, the Milken Institute generated rankings for metropolitan areas, weighing data in nine categories—health care, wellness, living arrangements, transportation and convenience, financial characteristics, education, employment, community engagement, and overall livability. The Tyler metro area was ranked #50 overall in the small metro area category. *Milken Institute, "Best Cities for Successful Aging, 2017" March 14, 2017*

Business Environment

CITY FINANCES

City Government Finances

Component	2016 ($000)	2016 ($ per capita)
Total Revenues	157,323	1,517
Total Expenditures	142,797	1,377
Debt Outstanding	58,765	567
Cash and Securities[1]	71,833	693

Note: (1) Cash and security holdings of a government at the close of its fiscal year,
including those of its dependent agencies, utilities, and liquor stores.
Source: U.S. Census Bureau, State & Local Government Finances 2016

City Government Revenue by Source

Source	2016 ($000)	2016 ($ per capita)	2016 (%)
General Revenue			
From Federal Government	16,862	163	10.7
From State Government	1,220	12	0.8
From Local Governments	0	0	0.0
Taxes			
Property	17,341	167	11.0
Sales and Gross Receipts	57,106	551	36.3
Personal Income	0	0	0.0
Corporate Income	0	0	0.0
Motor Vehicle License	0	0	0.0
Other Taxes	1,407	14	0.9
Current Charges	28,634	276	18.2
Liquor Store	0	0	0.0
Utility	22,844	220	14.5
Employee Retirement	0	0	0.0

Source: U.S. Census Bureau, State & Local Government Finances 2016

City Government Expenditures by Function

Function	2016 ($000)	2016 ($ per capita)	2016 (%)
General Direct Expenditures			
Air Transportation	9,695	93	6.8
Corrections	0	0	0.0
Education	0	0	0.0
Employment Security Administration	0	0	0.0
Financial Administration	1,419	13	1.0
Fire Protection	16,856	162	11.8
General Public Buildings	362	3	0.3
Governmental Administration, Other	1,598	15	1.1
Health	0	0	0.0
Highways	12,334	118	8.6
Hospitals	0	0	0.0
Housing and Community Development	9,539	92	6.7
Interest on General Debt	126	1	0.1
Judicial and Legal	2,594	25	1.8
Libraries	1,492	14	1.0
Parking	0	0	0.0
Parks and Recreation	3,880	37	2.7
Police Protection	25,754	248	18.0
Public Welfare	0	0	0.0
Sewerage	13,493	130	9.4
Solid Waste Management	12,650	122	8.9
Veterans' Services	0	0	0.0
Liquor Store	0	0	0.0
Utility	23,587	227	16.5
Employee Retirement	0	0	0.0

Source: U.S. Census Bureau, State & Local Government Finances 2016

DEMOGRAPHICS

Population Growth

Area	1990 Census	2000 Census	2010 Census	2017* Estimate	Population Growth (%)	
					1990-2017	2010-2017
City	77,653	83,650	96,900	102,561	32.1	5.8
MSA[1]	151,309	174,706	209,714	222,277	46.9	6.0
U.S.	248,709,873	281,421,906	308,745,538	321,004,407	29.1	4.0

Note: (1) Figures cover the Tyler, TX Metropolitan Statistical Area—see Appendix B for areas included; (*) 2013-2017 5-year estimated population
Source: U.S. Census Bureau, 1990 Census, Census 2000, Census 2010, 2013-2017 American Community Survey 5-Year Estimates

Household Size

Area	Persons in Household (%)							Average Household Size
	One	Two	Three	Four	Five	Six	Seven or More	
City	32.7	33.2	13.3	12.0	5.4	2.0	1.4	2.70
MSA[1]	26.7	36.1	14.8	12.4	5.7	2.5	1.8	2.80
U.S.	27.7	33.8	15.7	13.0	6.0	2.3	1.4	2.60

Note: (1) Figures cover the Tyler, TX Metropolitan Statistical Area—see Appendix B for areas included
Source: U.S. Census Bureau, 2013-2017 American Community Survey 5-Year Estimates

Race

Area	White Alone[2] (%)	Black Alone[2] (%)	Asian Alone[2] (%)	AIAN[3] Alone[2] (%)	NHOPI[4] Alone[2] (%)	Other Race Alone[2] (%)	Two or More Races (%)
City	67.8	24.8	2.4	0.3	0.2	2.6	1.9
MSA[1]	76.9	17.6	1.6	0.4	0.1	1.9	1.6
U.S.	73.0	12.7	5.4	0.8	0.2	4.8	3.1

Note: (1) Figures cover the Tyler, TX Metropolitan Statistical Area—see Appendix B for areas included; (2) Alone is defined as not being in combination with one or more other races; (3) American Indian and Alaska Native; (4) Native Hawaiian and Other Pacific Islander
Source: U.S. Census Bureau, 2013-2017 American Community Survey 5-Year Estimates

Hispanic or Latino Origin

Area	Total (%)	Mexican (%)	Puerto Rican (%)	Cuban (%)	Other (%)
City	22.3	19.9	0.4	0.1	1.9
MSA[1]	19.0	17.2	0.4	0.1	1.4
U.S.	17.6	11.1	1.7	0.7	4.1

Note: Persons of Hispanic or Latino origin can be of any race; (1) Figures cover the Tyler, TX Metropolitan Statistical Area—see Appendix B for areas included
Source: U.S. Census Bureau, 2013-2017 American Community Survey 5-Year Estimates

Segregation

Type	Segregation Indices[1]				Percent Change		
	1990	2000	2010	2010 Rank[2]	1990-2000	1990-2010	2000-2010
Black/White	n/a	n/a	n/a	n/a	n/a	n/a	n/a
Asian/White	n/a	n/a	n/a	n/a	n/a	n/a	n/a
Hispanic/White	n/a	n/a	n/a	n/a	n/a	n/a	n/a

Note: All figures cover the Metropolitan Statistical Area—see Appendix B for areas included; Figures are based on an analysis of 1990, 2000, and 2010 Census Decennial Census tract data by William H. Frey, Brookings Institution and the University of Michigan Social Science Data Analysis Network. In this analysis all racial groups (whites, blacks, and asians) are non-Hispanic members of those races. Hispanics are shown as a separate category; (1) Segregation Indices are Dissimilarity Indices that measure the degree to which the minority group is distributed differently than whites across census tracts. They range from 0 (complete integration) to 100 (complete segregation) where the value indicates the percentage of the minority group that needs to move to be distributed exactly like whites; (2) Ranges from 1 (most segregated) to 102 (least segregated); n/a not available.
Source: www.CensusScope.org

Ancestry

Area	German	Irish	English	American	Italian	Polish	French[2]	Scottish	Dutch
City	7.5	6.9	7.2	11.9	1.5	0.8	1.4	1.8	0.7
MSA[1]	8.8	8.3	8.2	15.0	1.7	0.7	2.3	2.0	0.9
U.S.	14.1	10.1	7.5	6.6	5.3	2.9	2.5	1.7	1.3

Note: Figures are the percentage of the total population reporting a particular ancestry. The nine most commonly reported ancestries in the U.S. are shown. Figures include multiple ancestries (e.g. if a person reported being Irish and Italian, they were included in both columns); (1) Figures cover the Tyler, TX Metropolitan Statistical Area—see Appendix B for areas included; (2) Excludes Basque
Source: U.S. Census Bureau, 2013-2017 American Community Survey 5-Year Estimates

Foreign-Born Population

Area	Percent of Population Born in								
	Any Foreign Country	Asia	Mexico	Europe	Carribean	Central America[2]	South America	Africa	Canada
City	10.9	1.7	7.0	0.4	0.2	0.6	0.1	0.5	0.2
MSA[1]	8.3	1.1	5.8	0.3	0.1	0.4	0.1	0.3	0.1
U.S.	13.4	4.1	3.6	1.5	1.3	1.0	0.9	0.6	0.3

Note: (1) Figures cover the Tyler, TX Metropolitan Statistical Area—see Appendix B for areas included; (2) Excludes Mexico.
Source: U.S. Census Bureau, 2013-2017 American Community Survey 5-Year Estimates

Marital Status

Area	Never Married	Now Married[2]	Separated	Widowed	Divorced
City	35.2	42.8	2.1	7.0	13.0
MSA[1]	28.9	50.5	2.2	6.7	11.7
U.S.	33.1	48.2	2.0	5.8	10.9

Note: Figures are percentages and cover the population 15 years of age and older; (1) Figures cover the Tyler, TX Metropolitan Statistical Area—see Appendix B for areas included; (2) Excludes separated
Source: U.S. Census Bureau, 2013-2017 American Community Survey 5-Year Estimates

Disability by Age

Area	All Ages	Under 18 Years Old	18 to 64 Years Old	65 Years and Over
City	12.4	4.8	9.4	37.9
MSA[1]	13.6	5.3	11.4	35.7
U.S.	12.6	4.2	10.3	35.5

Note: Figures show percent of the civilian noninstitutionalized population that reported having a disability. Disability status is determined from six types of difficulty: vision, hearing, cognitive, ambulatory, self-care, and independent living. For children under 5 years old, hearing and vision difficulty are used to determine disability status. For children between the ages of 5 and 14, disability status is determined from hearing, vision, cognitive, ambulatory, and self-care difficulties. For people aged 15 years and older, they are considered to have a disability if they have difficulty with any one of the six difficulty types; Note: (1) Figures cover the Tyler, TX Metropolitan Statistical Area—see Appendix B for areas included
Source: U.S. Census Bureau, 2013-2017 American Community Survey 5-Year Estimates

Age

Area	Percent of Population									Median Age
	Under Age 5	Age 5–19	Age 20–34	Age 35–44	Age 45–54	Age 55–64	Age 65–74	Age 75–84	Age 85+	
City	7.4	20.4	24.6	10.7	10.9	10.9	7.6	5.3	2.3	33.4
MSA[1]	6.9	20.9	20.7	11.8	12.1	12.1	8.7	5.1	1.8	36.6
U.S.	6.2	19.5	20.7	12.7	13.4	12.7	8.6	4.4	1.9	37.8

Note: (1) Figures cover the Tyler, TX Metropolitan Statistical Area—see Appendix B for areas included
Source: U.S. Census Bureau, 2013-2017 American Community Survey 5-Year Estimates

Gender

Area	Males	Females	Males per 100 Females
City	48,565	53,996	89.9
MSA[1]	107,355	114,922	93.4
U.S.	158,018,753	162,985,654	97.0

Note: (1) Figures cover the Tyler, TX Metropolitan Statistical Area—see Appendix B for areas included
Source: U.S. Census Bureau, 2013-2017 American Community Survey 5-Year Estimates

Religious Groups by Family

Area	Catholic	Baptist	Non-Den.	Methodist[2]	Lutheran	LDS[3]	Pente-costal	Presby-terian[4]	Muslim[5]	Judaism
MSA[1]	12.2	33.6	9.0	6.4	0.6	1.2	5.1	0.7	0.4	0.1
U.S.	19.1	9.3	4.0	4.0	2.3	2.0	1.9	1.6	0.8	0.7

Note: Figures are the number of adherents as a percentage of the total population; (1) Figures cover the Tyler, TX Metropolitan Statistical Area—see Appendix B for areas included; (2) Methodist/Pietist; (3) Latter Day Saints; (4) Reformed; (5) Figures are estimates
Source: Association of Statisticians of American Religious Bodies, 2010 U.S. Religion Census: Religious Congregations & Membership Study

Religious Groups by Tradition

Area	Catholic	Evangelical Protestant	Mainline Protestant	Other Tradition	Black Protestant	Orthodox
MSA[1]	12.2	45.5	7.4	1.7	4.1	<0.1
U.S.	19.1	16.2	7.3	4.3	1.6	0.3

Note: Figures are the number of adherents as a percentage of the total population; (1) Figures cover the Tyler, TX Metropolitan Statistical Area—see Appendix B for areas included
Source: Association of Statisticians of American Religious Bodies, 2010 U.S. Religion Census: Religious Congregations & Membership Study

ECONOMY

Gross Metropolitan Product

Area	2016	2017	2018	2019	Rank[2]
MSA[1]	13.4	14.1	15.4	16.0	169

Note: Figures are in billions of dollars; (1) Figures cover the Tyler, TX Metropolitan Statistical Area—see Appendix B for areas included; (2) Rank is based on 2017 data and ranges from 1 to 381
Source: U.S. Conference of Mayors, U.S. Metro Economies: Economic Growth & Full Employment, June 2018

Economic Growth

Area	2017-2018 (%)	2019-2020 (%)	2021-2022 (%)
MSA[1]	1.7	2.4	1.9

Note: Figures are real gross metropolitan product (GMP) growth rates and represent average annual percent change; (1) Figures cover the Tyler, TX Metropolitan Statistical Area—see Appendix B for areas included
Source: U.S. Conference of Mayors, U.S. Metro Economies: Economic Growth & Full Employment, June 2018

Metropolitan Area Exports

Area	2012	2013	2014	2015	2016	2017	Rank[2]
MSA[1]	221.1	219.6	301.1	207.3	176.7	234.5	287

Note: Figures are in millions of dollars; (1) Figures cover the Tyler, TX Metropolitan Statistical Area—see Appendix B for areas included; (2) Rank is based on 2017 data and ranges from 1 to 387
Source: U.S. Department of Commerce, International Trade Administration, Office of Trade and Economic Analysis, Industry and Analysis, Exports by Metropolitan Area, extracted March 25, 2019

Building Permits

Area	Single-Family			Multi-Family			Total		
	2016	2017	Pct. Chg.	2016	2017	Pct. Chg.	2016	2017	Pct. Chg.
City	305	313	2.6	93	48	-48.4	398	361	-9.3
MSA[1]	454	472	4.0	127	206	62.2	581	678	16.7
U.S.	750,800	820,000	9.2	455,800	462,000	1.4	1,206,600	1,282,000	6.2

Note: (1) Figures cover the Tyler, TX Metropolitan Statistical Area—see Appendix B for areas included; Figures represent new, privately-owned housing units authorized (unadjusted data); All permit data are based on estimates with imputation
Source: U.S. Census Bureau, Manufacturing, Mining, and Construction Statistics, Building Permits, 2016, 2017

Bankruptcy Filings

Area	Business Filings			Nonbusiness Filings		
	2017	2018	% Chg.	2017	2018	% Chg.
Smith County	19	16	-15.8	309	284	-8.1
U.S.	23,157	22,232	-4.0	765,863	751,186	-1.9

Note: Business filings include Chapter 7, Chapter 11, Chapter 12, and Chapter 13; Nonbusiness filings include Chapter 7, Chapter 11, and Chapter 13
Source: Administrative Office of the U.S. Courts, Business and Nonbusiness Bankruptcy, County Cases Commenced by Chapter of the Bankruptcy Code, During the 12-Month Period Ending December 31, 2017 and Business and Nonbusiness Bankruptcy, County Cases Commenced by Chapter of the Bankruptcy Code, During the 12-Month Period Ending December 31, 2018

Housing Vacancy Rates

Area	Gross Vacancy Rate[2] (%)			Year-Round Vacancy Rate[3] (%)			Rental Vacancy Rate[4] (%)			Homeowner Vacancy Rate[5] (%)		
	2016	2017	2018	2016	2017	2018	2016	2017	2018	2016	2017	2018
MSA[1]	n/a	n/a	n/a	n/a	n/a	n/a	n/a	n/a	n/a	n/a	n/a	n/a
U.S.	12.8	12.7	12.3	9.9	9.9	9.7	6.9	7.2	6.9	1.7	1.6	1.5

Note: (1) Figures cover the Tyler, TX Metropolitan Statistical Area—see Appendix B for areas included; (2) The percentage of the total housing inventory that is vacant; (3) The percentage of the housing inventory (excluding seasonal units) that is year-round vacant; (4) The percentage of rental inventory that is vacant for rent; (5) The percentage of homeowner inventory that is vacant for sale; n/a not available
Source: U.S. Census Bureau, Housing Vacancies and Homeownership Annual Statistics: 2016, 2017, 2018

INCOME

Income

Area	Per Capita ($)	Median Household ($)	Average Household ($)
City	26,620	46,463	69,882
MSA[1]	26,270	50,742	70,687
U.S.	31,177	57,652	81,283

Note: (1) Figures cover the Tyler, TX Metropolitan Statistical Area—see Appendix B for areas included
Source: U.S. Census Bureau, 2013-2017 American Community Survey 5-Year Estimates

Household Income Distribution

Area	Percent of Households Earning							
	Under $15,000	$15,000 -$24,999	$25,000 -$34,999	$35,000 -$49,999	$50,000 -$74,999	$75,000 -$99,999	$100,000 -$149,999	$150,000 and up
City	13.9	12.7	11.1	15.0	18.5	10.1	9.7	9.0
MSA[1]	11.6	11.7	11.1	15.0	17.9	11.6	12.5	8.6
U.S.	11.6	9.8	9.5	13.0	17.7	12.3	14.1	12.1

Note: (1) Figures cover the Tyler, TX Metropolitan Statistical Area—see Appendix B for areas included
Source: U.S. Census Bureau, 2013-2017 American Community Survey 5-Year Estimates

Poverty Rate

Area	All Ages	Under 18 Years Old	18 to 64 Years Old	65 Years and Over
City	20.2	27.4	19.6	10.9
MSA[1]	16.3	22.1	15.7	9.2
U.S.	14.6	20.3	13.7	9.3

Note: Figures are percentage of people whose income during the past 12 months was below the poverty level; (1) Figures cover the Tyler, TX Metropolitan Statistical Area—see Appendix B for areas included
Source: U.S. Census Bureau, 2013-2017 American Community Survey 5-Year Estimates

EMPLOYMENT

Labor Force and Employment

Area	Civilian Labor Force			Workers Employed		
	Dec. 2017	Dec. 2018	% Chg.	Dec. 2017	Dec. 2018	% Chg.
City	51,203	52,965	3.4	49,397	51,146	3.5
MSA[1]	106,787	110,590	3.6	103,079	106,728	3.5
U.S.	159,880,000	162,510,000	1.6	153,602,000	156,481,000	1.9

Note: Data is not seasonally adjusted and covers workers 16 years of age and older; (1) Figures cover the Tyler, TX Metropolitan Statistical Area—see Appendix B for areas included
Source: Bureau of Labor Statistics, Local Area Unemployment Statistics

Unemployment Rate

Area	2018											
	Jan.	Feb.	Mar.	Apr.	May	Jun.	Jul.	Aug.	Sep.	Oct.	Nov.	Dec.
City	3.7	3.7	3.6	3.4	3.5	4.0	3.7	3.6	3.4	3.4	3.3	3.4
MSA[1]	3.8	3.8	3.7	3.4	3.5	3.9	3.7	3.7	3.5	3.4	3.4	3.5
U.S.	4.5	4.4	4.1	3.7	3.6	4.2	4.1	3.9	3.6	3.5	3.5	3.7

Note: Data is not seasonally adjusted and covers workers 16 years of age and older; (1) Figures cover the Tyler, TX Metropolitan Statistical Area—see Appendix B for areas included
Source: Bureau of Labor Statistics, Local Area Unemployment Statistics

Average Wages

Occupation	$/Hr.	Occupation	$/Hr.
Accountants and Auditors	35.20	Maids and Housekeeping Cleaners	9.20
Automotive Mechanics	19.50	Maintenance and Repair Workers	17.20
Bookkeepers	17.90	Marketing Managers	n/a
Carpenters	17.00	Nuclear Medicine Technologists	n/a
Cashiers	10.20	Nurses, Licensed Practical	21.50
Clerks, General Office	16.30	Nurses, Registered	29.10
Clerks, Receptionists/Information	12.60	Nursing Assistants	11.90
Clerks, Shipping/Receiving	16.80	Packers and Packagers, Hand	15.50
Computer Programmers	34.50	Physical Therapists	48.60
Computer Systems Analysts	34.80	Postal Service Mail Carriers	24.70
Computer User Support Specialists	22.70	Real Estate Brokers	n/a
Cooks, Restaurant	11.90	Retail Salespersons	13.00
Dentists	74.00	Sales Reps., Exc. Tech./Scientific	27.10
Electrical Engineers	47.70	Sales Reps., Tech./Scientific	48.10
Electricians	20.40	Secretaries, Exc. Legal/Med./Exec.	15.80
Financial Managers	62.20	Security Guards	15.10
First-Line Supervisors/Managers, Sales	21.20	Surgeons	n/a
Food Preparation Workers	9.70	Teacher Assistants*	11.10
General and Operations Managers	47.10	Teachers, Elementary School*	23.70
Hairdressers/Cosmetologists	9.80	Teachers, Secondary School*	25.50
Internists, General	68.50	Telemarketers	n/a
Janitors and Cleaners	11.30	Truck Drivers, Heavy/Tractor-Trailer	19.90
Landscaping/Groundskeeping Workers	12.20	Truck Drivers, Light/Delivery Svcs.	14.90
Lawyers	44.30	Waiters and Waitresses	11.30

Note: Wage data covers the Tyler, TX Metropolitan Statistical Area—see Appendix B for areas included;
(*) Hourly wages for elementary/secondary school teachers and teacher assistants were calculated by the editors from annual wage data based on a 40 hour work week; n/a not available.
Source: Bureau of Labor Statistics, Metro Area Occupational Employment & Wage Estimates, May 2018

Employment by Occupation

Occupation Classification	City (%)	MSA[1] (%)	U.S. (%)
Management, Business, Science, and Arts	32.8	33.0	37.4
Natural Resources, Construction, and Maintenance	9.3	10.7	8.9
Production, Transportation, and Material Moving	12.6	14.1	12.2
Sales and Office	24.0	23.0	23.5
Service	21.3	19.2	18.0

Note: Figures cover employed civilians 16 years of age and older; (1) Figures cover the Tyler, TX Metropolitan Statistical Area—see Appendix B for areas included
Source: U.S. Census Bureau, 2013-2017 American Community Survey 5-Year Estimates

Employment by Industry

Sector	MSA[1]		U.S.
	Number of Employees	Percent of Total	Percent of Total
Construction, Mining, and Logging	6,700	6.2	5.3
Education and Health Services	24,500	22.7	15.9
Financial Activities	4,300	4.0	5.7
Government	15,100	14.0	15.1
Information	1,500	1.4	1.9
Leisure and Hospitality	11,600	10.7	10.7
Manufacturing	5,400	5.0	8.5
Other Services	4,000	3.7	3.9
Professional and Business Services	11,000	10.2	14.1
Retail Trade	13,700	12.7	10.8
Transportation, Warehousing, and Utilities	5,100	4.7	4.2
Wholesale Trade	5,100	4.7	3.9

Note: Figures are non-farm employment as of December 2018. Figures are not seasonally adjusted and include workers 16 years of age and older; (1) Figures cover the Tyler, TX Metropolitan Statistical Area—see Appendix B for areas included
Source: Bureau of Labor Statistics, Current Employment Statistics, Employment, Hours, and Earnings

Occupations with Greatest Projected Employment Growth: 2018 – 2020

Occupation[1]	2018 Employment	2020 Projected Employment	Numeric Employment Change	Percent Employment Change
Combined Food Preparation and Serving Workers, Including Fast Food	351,780	372,090	20,310	5.8
Personal Care Aides	218,310	235,470	17,160	7.9
Heavy and Tractor-Trailer Truck Drivers	204,870	216,310	11,440	5.6
Laborers and Freight, Stock, and Material Movers, Hand	194,220	204,060	9,840	5.1
Waiters and Waitresses	236,020	245,790	9,770	4.1
Office Clerks, General	393,740	403,270	9,530	2.4
Customer Service Representatives	268,380	277,460	9,080	3.4
General and Operations Managers	182,190	190,620	8,430	4.6
Retail Salespersons	392,620	400,900	8,280	2.1
Construction Laborers	143,270	150,820	7,550	5.3

Note: Projections cover Texas; (1) Sorted by numeric employment change
Source: www.projectionscentral.com, State Occupational Projections, 2018–2020 Short-Term Projections

Fastest Growing Occupations: 2018 – 2020

Occupation[1]	2018 Employment	2020 Projected Employment	Numeric Employment Change	Percent Employment Change
Wind Turbine Service Technicians	1,810	2,190	380	21.0
Religious Workers, All Other	5,690	6,330	640	11.2
Fundraisers	8,830	9,670	840	9.5
Statisticians	1,870	2,040	170	9.1
Public Relations and Fundraising Managers	6,570	7,160	590	9.0
Home Health Aides	74,390	80,920	6,530	8.8
Community and Social Service Specialists, All Other	4,520	4,890	370	8.2
Personal Care Aides	218,310	235,470	17,160	7.9
Operations Research Analysts	10,920	11,760	840	7.7
Software Developers, Applications	65,190	70,140	4,950	7.6

Note: Projections cover Texas; (1) Sorted by percent employment change and excludes occupations with numeric employment change less than 50
Source: www.projectionscentral.com, State Occupational Projections, 2018–2020 Short-Term Projections

TAXES

State Corporate Income Tax Rates

State	Tax Rate (%)	Income Brackets ($)	Num. of Brackets	Financial Institution Tax Rate (%)[a]	Federal Income Tax Ded.
Texas	(w)	–	–	(w)	No

Note: Tax rates as of January 1, 2019; (a) Rates listed are the corporate income tax rate applied to financial institutions or excise taxes based on income. Some states have other taxes based upon the value of deposits or shares; (w) Texas imposes a Franchise Tax, otherwise known as margin tax, imposed on entities with more than $1,130,000 total revenues at rate of 0.75%, or 0.375% for entities primarily engaged in retail or wholesale trade, on lesser of 70% of total revenues or 100% of gross receipts after deductions for either compensation or cost of goods sold.
Source: Federation of Tax Administrators, Range of State Corporate Income Tax Rates, January 1, 2019

State Individual Income Tax Rates

State	Tax Rate (%)	Income Brackets ($)	Personal Exemptions ($)			Standard Ded. ($)	
			Single	Married	Depend.	Single	Married
Texas					– No state income tax –		

Note: Tax rates as of January 1, 2019; Local- and county-level taxes are not included; n/a not applicable;

Source: Federation of Tax Administrators, State Individual Income Tax Rates, January 1, 2019

Various State Sales and Excise Tax Rates

State	State Sales Tax (%)	Gasoline[1] (¢/gal.)	Cigarette[2] ($/pack)	Spirits[3] ($/gal.)	Wine[4] ($/gal.)	Beer[5] ($/gal.)	Recreational Marijuana (%)
Texas	6.25	20	1.41	2.40 (f)	0.20 (l)	0.20 (q)	Not legal

Note: All tax rates as of January 1, 2019; (1) The American Petroleum Institute has developed a methodology for determining the average tax rate on a gallon of fuel. Rates may include any of the following: excise taxes, environmental fees, storage tank fees, other fees or taxes, general sales tax, and local taxes. In states where gasoline is subject to the general sales tax, or where the fuel tax is based on the average sale price, the average rate determined by API is sensitive to changes in the price of gasoline. States that fully or partially apply general sales taxes to gasoline: CA, CO, GA, IL, IN, MI, NY; (2) The federal excise tax of $1.0066 per pack and local taxes are not included; (3) Rates are those applicable to off-premise sales of 40% alcohol by volume (a.b.v.) distilled spirits in 750ml containers. Local excise taxes are excluded; (4) Rates are those applicable to off-premise sales of 11% a.b.v. non-carbonated wine in 750ml containers; (5) Rates are those applicable to off-premise sales of 4.7% a.b.v. beer in 12 ounce containers; (f) Different rates also applicable according to alcohol content, place of production, size of container, or place purchased (on- or off-premise or onboard airlines); (l) Different rates also applicable to alcohol content, place of production, size of container, place purchased (on- or off-premise or on board airlines) or type of wine (carbonated, vermouth, etc.); (q) Different rates also applicable according to alcohol content, place of production, size of container, or place purchased (on- or off-premise or onboard airlines).
Source: Tax Foundation, 2019 Facts & Figures: How Does Your State Compare?

State Business Tax Climate Index Rankings

State	Overall Rank	Corporate Tax Rank	Individual Income Tax Rank	Sales Tax Rank	Unemployment Insurance Tax Rank	Property Tax Rank
Texas	15	49	6	37	18	37

Note: The index is a measure of how each state's tax laws affect economic performance. The lower the rank, the more favorable a state's tax system is for business. States without a given tax are given a ranking of 1. The scores/rankings for the District of Columbia do not affect other states. The 2019 index represents the tax climate as of July 1, 2018.
Source: Tax Foundation, State Business Tax Climate Index 2019

COMMERCIAL UTILITIES

Typical Monthly Electric Bills

Area	Commercial Service ($/month)		Industrial Service ($/month)	
	1,500 kWh	40 kW demand 14,000 kWh	1,000 kW demand 200,000 kWh	50,000 kW demand 32,500,000 kWh
City	n/a	n/a	n/a	n/a
Average[1]	203	1,619	25,886	2,540,077

Note: Figures are based on annualized rates; (1) Average based on 187 utilities surveyed; n/a not available
Source: Edison Electric Institute, Typical Bills and Average Rates Report, Summer 2018

TRANSPORTATION

Means of Transportation to Work

Area	Car/Truck/Van		Public Transportation			Bicycle	Walked	Other Means	Worked at Home
	Drove Alone	Car-pooled	Bus	Subway	Railroad				
City	82.6	9.8	0.4	0.0	0.0	0.5	1.3	2.2	3.2
MSA[1]	83.7	9.5	0.2	0.0	0.0	0.3	1.0	1.9	3.4
U.S.	76.4	9.2	2.5	1.9	0.6	0.6	2.7	1.3	4.7

Note: Figures are percentages and cover workers 16 years of age and older; (1) Figures cover the Tyler, TX Metropolitan Statistical Area—see Appendix B for areas included
Source: U.S. Census Bureau, 2013-2017 American Community Survey 5-Year Estimates

Travel Time to Work

Area	Less Than 10 Minutes	10 to 19 Minutes	20 to 29 Minutes	30 to 44 Minutes	45 to 59 Minutes	60 to 89 Minutes	90 Minutes or More
City	17.9	41.7	18.9	13.2	3.8	2.5	2.0
MSA[1]	13.1	32.8	24.2	19.1	5.0	2.9	2.8
U.S.	12.7	28.9	20.9	20.5	8.1	6.2	2.7

Note: Note: Figures are percentages and include workers 16 years old and over; (1) Figures cover the Tyler, TX Metropolitan Statistical Area—see Appendix B for areas included
Source: U.S. Census Bureau, 2013-2017 American Community Survey 5-Year Estimates

Freeway Travel Time Index

Area	1985	1990	1995	2000	2005	2010	2014
Urban Area Rank[1,2]	n/a	n/a	n/a	n/a	n/a	n/a	n/a
Urban Area Index[1]	n/a	n/a	n/a	n/a	n/a	n/a	n/a
Average Index[3]	1.09	1.11	1.14	1.17	1.20	1.19	1.20

Note: Freeway Travel Time Index—the ratio of travel time in the peak period to the travel time at free-flow conditions. For example, a value of 1.30 indicates a 20-minute free-flow trip takes 26 minutes in the peak (20 minutes x 1.30 = 26 minutes); (1) Data for the Tyler, TX urban area was not available; (2) Rank is based on 101 urban areas (#1 = highest travel time index); (3) Average of 101 urban areas
Source: Texas Transportation Institute, 2015 Urban Mobility Scorecard, August 2015

Freeway Commuter Stress Index

Area	1985	1990	1995	2000	2005	2010	2014
Urban Area Rank[1,2]	n/a	n/a	n/a	n/a	n/a	n/a	n/a
Urban Area Index[1]	n/a	n/a	n/a	n/a	n/a	n/a	n/a
Average Index[3]	1.13	1.16	1.19	1.22	1.25	1.24	1.25

Note: The Freeway Commuter Stress Index is the same as the Freeway Travel Time Index (see table above) except that it includes only the travel in the peak directions during the peak periods; the TTI includes travel in all directions during the peak period. Thus, the CSI is more indicative of the work trip experienced by each commuter on a daily basis; (1) Data for the Tyler, TX urban area was not available; (2) Rank is based on 101 urban areas (#1 = highest travel time index); (3) Average of 101 urban areas
Source: Texas Transportation Institute, 2015 Urban Mobility Scorecard, August 2015

Public Transportation

Agency Name / Mode of Transportation	Vehicles Operated in Maximum Service[1]	Annual Unlinked Passenger Trips[2] (in thous.)	Annual Passenger Miles[3] (in thous.)
City of Tyler (COT)			
Bus (directly operated)	6	148.1	n/a
Bus (purchased transportation)	1	0.5	n/a
Commuter Bus (purchased transportation)	1	0.4	n/a
Demand Response (directly operated)	8	42.0	n/a
Demand Response Taxi (purchased transportation)	13	11.1	n/a

Note: (1) The number of revenue vehicles operated by the given mode and type of service to meet the annual maximum service requirement. This is the revenue vehicle count during the peak season of the year; on the week and day that maximum service is provided. Vehicles operated in maximum service (VOMS) exclude atypical days and one-time special events; (2) The number of passengers who boarded public transportation vehicles. Passengers are counted each time they board a vehicle no matter how many vehicles they use to travel from their origin to their destination. (3) The sum of the distances ridden by all passengers during the entire fiscal year.
Source: Federal Transit Administration, National Transit Database, 2017

Air Transportation

Airport Name and Code / Type of Service	Passenger Airlines[1]	Passenger Enplanements	Freight Carriers[2]	Freight (lbs)
Tyler Pounds Regional Airport (TYR)				
Domestic service (U.S. carriers - 2018)	3	48,423	1	2,397
International service (U.S. carriers - 2017)	0	0	0	0

Note: (1) Includes all U.S.-based major, minor and commuter airlines that carried at least one passenger during the year; (2) Includes all U.S.-based airlines and freight carriers that transported at least one pound of freight during the year.
Source: Bureau of Transportation Statistics, The Intermodal Transportation Database, Air Carriers: T-100 Domestic Market (U.S. Carriers), 2018; Bureau of Transportation Statistics, The Intermodal Transportation Database, Air Carriers: T-100 International Market (U.S. Carriers), 2017

Other Transportation Statistics

Major Highways:	I-20 via US-69 and US-271
Amtrak Service:	Bus connection
Major Waterways/Ports:	None

Source: Amtrak.com; Google Maps

BUSINESSES

Major Business Headquarters

Company Name	Industry	Rankings Fortune[1]	Rankings Forbes[2]
Brookshire Grocery	Food Markets	-	179

Note: (1) Companies that produce a 10-K are ranked 1 to 500 based on 2017 revenue; (2) All private companies with at least $2 billion in annual revenue through the end of their most current fiscal year are ranked 1 to 229; companies listed are headquartered in the city; dashes indicate no ranking
Source: Fortune, "Fortune 500," June 2018; Forbes, "America's Largest Private Companies," 2018 Rankings

Minority Business Opportunity

Tyler is home to one company which is on the *Hispanic Business* 500 list (500 largest U.S. Hispanic-owned companies based on revenue): **Mentoring Minds** (#226). Companies included must show at least 51 percent ownership by Hispanic U.S. citizens, and must maintain headquarters in one of the 50 states or Washington, D.C. *Hispanic Business, "Hispanic Business 500," June 20, 2013*

Minority- and Women-Owned Businesses

Group	All Firms Firms	All Firms Sales ($000)	Firms with Paid Employees Firms	Firms with Paid Employees Sales ($000)	Firms with Paid Employees Employees	Firms with Paid Employees Payroll ($000)
AIAN[1]	65	(s)	13	(s)	100 - 249	(s)
Asian	230	(s)	138	(s)	1,000 - 2,499	(s)
Black	1,139	47,437	59	(s)	100 - 249	(s)
Hispanic	1,001	59,298	105	37,623	361	6,002
NHOPI[2]	n/a	n/a	n/a	n/a	n/a	n/a
Women	3,368	523,319	597	433,186	4,254	135,782
All Firms	10,721	13,662,801	3,260	13,217,967	64,465	2,344,162

Note: Figures cover firms located in the city; minority- and women-owned business are defined as firms in which the corresponding group own 51% or more of the stock or equity of the company; (1) American Indian and Alaska Native; (2) Native Hawaiian and Other Pacific Islander; (s) estimates are suppressed when publication standards are not met; n/a not available
Source: U.S. Census Bureau, 2012 Economic Census, Survey of Business Owners

HOTELS & CONVENTION CENTERS

Hotels, Motels and Vacation Rentals

Area	5 Star Num.	5 Star Pct.[3]	4 Star Num.	4 Star Pct.[3]	3 Star Num.	3 Star Pct.[3]	2 Star Num.	2 Star Pct.[3]	1 Star Num.	1 Star Pct.[3]	Not Rated Num.	Not Rated Pct.[3]
City[1]	0	0.0	1	0.5	18	9.5	75	39.5	2	1.1	94	49.5
Total[2]	286	0.4	5,236	7.1	16,715	22.6	10,259	13.9	293	0.4	41,056	55.6

Note: (1) Figures cover Tyler and vicinity; (2) Figures cover all 100 cities in this book; (3) Percentage of hotels which have a given star rating; Star ratings are determined by expedia.com and offer an indication of the general quality of a particular hotel.
Source: www.expedia.com, April 3, 2019

Major Convention Centers

Name	Overall Space (sq. ft.)	Exhibit Space (sq. ft.)	Meeting Space (sq. ft.)	Meeting Rooms
Harvey Convention Center	n/a	n/a	27,667	3

Note: Table includes convention centers located in the Tyler, TX metro area; n/a not available
Source: Original research

Living Environment

COST OF LIVING

Cost of Living Index

Composite Index	Groceries	Housing	Utilities	Trans-portation	Health Care	Misc. Goods/ Services
91.0	92.6	78.0	107.4	94.7	95.3	95.5

Note: The Cost of Living Index measures regional differences in the cost of consumer goods and services, excluding taxes and non-consumer expenditures, for professional and managerial households in the top income quintile. It is based on more than 50,000 prices covering almost 60 different items for which prices are collected three times a year by chambers of commerce, economic development organizations or university applied economic centers in each participating urban area. The numbers shown should be read as a percentage above or below the national average of 100. For example, a value of 115.4 in the groceries column indicates that grocery prices are 15.4% higher than the national average. Small differences in the index numbers should not be interpreted as significant; Figures cover the Tyler TX urban area.
Source: The Council for Community and Economic Research, ACCRA Cost of Living Index, 2018

Grocery Prices

Area[1]	T-Bone Steak ($/pound)	Frying Chicken ($/pound)	Whole Milk ($/half gal.)	Eggs ($/dozen)	Orange Juice ($/64 oz.)	Coffee ($/11.5 oz.)
City[2]	10.20	1.01	1.66	1.24	3.24	3.69
Avg.	11.35	1.42	1.94	1.81	3.52	4.35
Min.	7.45	0.92	0.80	0.75	2.72	3.06
Max.	15.05	2.76	4.18	4.00	5.36	8.20

Note: (1) Values for the local area are compared with the average, minimum and maximum values for all 291 areas in the Cost of Living Index; (2) Figures cover the Tyler TX urban area; T-Bone Steak (price per pound); Frying Chicken (price per pound, whole fryer); Whole Milk (half gallon carton); Eggs (price per dozen, Grade A, large); Orange Juice (64 oz. Tropicana or Florida Natural); Coffee (11.5 oz. can, vacuum-packed, Maxwell House, Hills Bros, or Folgers).
Source: The Council for Community and Economic Research, ACCRA Cost of Living Index, 2018

Housing and Utility Costs

Area[1]	New Home Price ($)	Apartment Rent ($/month)	All Electric ($/month)	Part Electric ($/month)	Other Energy ($/month)	Telephone ($/month)
City[2]	233,225	1,116	-	147.22	45.26	175.00
Avg.	347,000	1,087	165.93	100.16	67.73	178.70
Min.	200,468	500	93.58	25.64	26.78	163.10
Max.	1,901,222	4,888	388.65	246.86	332.81	197.70

Note: (1) Values for the local area are compared with the average, minimum and maximum values for all 291 areas in the Cost of Living Index; (2) Figures cover the Tyler TX urban area; New Home Price (2,400 sf living area, 8,000 sf lot, in urban area with full utilities); Apartment Rent (950 sf 2 bedroom/1.5 or 2 bath, unfurnished, excluding all utilities except water); All Electric (average monthly cost for an all-electric home); Part Electric (average monthly cost for a part-electric home); Other Energy (average monthly cost for natural gas, fuel oil, coal, wood, and any other forms of energy except electricity); Telephone (price includes the base monthly rate plus taxes and fees for three lines of mobile phone service).
Source: The Council for Community and Economic Research, ACCRA Cost of Living Index, 2018

Health Care, Transportation, and Other Costs

Area[1]	Doctor ($/visit)	Dentist ($/visit)	Optometrist ($/visit)	Gasoline ($/gallon)	Beauty Salon ($/visit)	Men's Shirt ($)
City[2]	91.76	91.33	118.11	2.42	42.53	31.64
Avg.	110.71	95.11	103.74	2.61	37.48	32.03
Min.	33.60	62.55	54.63	1.89	17.00	11.44
Max.	195.97	153.93	225.79	3.59	71.88	58.64

Note: (1) Values for the local area are compared with the average, minimum and maximum values for all 291 areas in the Cost of Living Index; (2) Figures cover the Tyler TX urban area; Doctor (general practitioners routine exam of an established patient); Dentist (adult teeth cleaning and periodic oral examination); Optometrist (full vision eye exam for established adult patient); Gasoline (one gallon regular unleaded, national brand, including all taxes, cash price at self-service pump if available); Beauty Salon (woman's shampoo, trim, and blow-dry); Men's Shirt (cotton/polyester dress shirt, pinpoint weave, long sleeves).
Source: The Council for Community and Economic Research, ACCRA Cost of Living Index, 2018

HOUSING

House Price Index (HPI)

Area	National Ranking[2]	Quarterly Change (%)	One-Year Change (%)	Five-Year Change (%)
MSA[1]	(a)	n/a	3.48	23.48
U.S.[3]	–	1.12	5.73	32.81

Note: The HPI is a weighted repeat sales index. It measures average price changes in repeat sales or refinancings on the same properties. This information is obtained by reviewing repeat mortgage transactions on single-family properties whose mortgages have been purchased or securitized by Fannie Mae or Freddie Mac in January 1975; (1) Figures cover the Tyler, TX Metropolitan Statistical Area—see Appendix B for areas included; (2) Rankings are based on annual percentage change for all metro areas containing at least 15,000 transactions over the last 10 years and ranges from 1 to 245; (3) figures based on a weighted average of Census Division estimates using a seasonally adjusted, purchase-only index; all figures are for the period ending December 31, 2018; n/a not available; (a) Not ranked because of increased index variability due to smaller sample size
Source: Federal Housing Finance Agency, House Price Index, February 26, 2019

Median Single-Family Home Prices

Area	2016	2017	2018[p]	Percent Change 2017 to 2018
MSA[1]	n/a	n/a	n/a	n/a
U.S. Average	235.5	248.8	261.6	5.1

Note: Figures are median sales prices of existing single-family homes in thousands of dollars; (p) preliminary; n/a not available; (1) Figures cover the Tyler, TX Metropolitan Statistical Area—see Appendix B for areas included
Source: National Association of Realtors, Median Sales Price of Existing Single-Family Homes for Metropolitan Areas, 4th Quarter 2018

Qualifying Income Based on Median Sales Price of Existing Single-Family Homes

Area	With 5% Down ($)	With 10% Down ($)	With 20% Down ($)
MSA[1]	n/a	n/a	n/a
U.S. Average	62,954	59,640	53,013

Note: Figures are preliminary; Qualifying income is based on a mortgage rate of 4.9%. Monthly principal and interest payment is limited to 25% of income; n/a not available; (1) Figures cover the Tyler, TX Metropolitan Statistical Area—see Appendix B for areas included
Source: National Association of Realtors, Qualifying Income Based on Median Sales Price of Existing Single-Family Homes for Metropolitan Areas, 4th Quarter 2018

Median Apartment Condo-Coop Home Prices

Area	2016	2017	2018[p]	Percent Change 2017 to 2018
MSA[1]	n/a	n/a	n/a	n/a
U.S. Average	220.7	234.3	241.0	2.9

Note: Figures are median sales prices of existing apartment condo-coop homes in thousands of dollars; (p) preliminary; n/a not available; (1) Figures cover the Tyler, TX Metropolitan Statistical Area—see Appendix B for areas included
Source: National Association of Realtors, Median Sales Price of Existing Apartment Condo-Coop Homes for Metropolitan Areas, 4th Quarter 2018

Home Value Distribution

Area	Under $50,000	$50,000 -$99,999	$100,000 -$149,999	$150,000 -$199,999	$200,000 -$299,999	$300,000 -$499,999	$500,000 -$999,999	$1,000,000 or more
City	8.8	21.9	21.2	18.8	14.8	10.5	3.3	0.7
MSA[1]	12.7	20.0	19.4	19.0	16.1	9.2	2.8	0.8
U.S.	8.3	13.9	14.7	14.6	18.7	17.3	9.7	2.7

Note: Figures are percentages and cover owner-occupied housing units; (1) Figures cover the Tyler, TX Metropolitan Statistical Area—see Appendix B for areas included
Source: U.S. Census Bureau, 2013-2017 American Community Survey 5-Year Estimates

Homeownership Rate

Area	2010 (%)	2011 (%)	2012 (%)	2013 (%)	2014 (%)	2015 (%)	2016 (%)	2017 (%)	2018 (%)
MSA[1]	n/a	n/a	n/a	n/a	n/a	n/a	n/a	n/a	n/a
U.S.	66.9	66.1	65.4	65.1	64.5	63.7	63.4	63.9	64.4

Note: (1) Figures cover the Tyler, TX Metropolitan Statistical Area—see Appendix B for areas included; n/a not available
Source: U.S. Census Bureau, Housing Vacancies and Homeownership Annual Statistics: 2010-2018

Year Housing Structure Built

Area	2010 or Later	2000 -2009	1990 -1999	1980 -1989	1970 -1979	1960 -1969	1950 -1959	1940 -1949	Before 1940	Median Year
City	4.5	16.0	12.1	13.6	16.9	12.4	14.7	4.8	5.0	1978
MSA[1]	4.9	17.9	16.0	16.9	16.7	9.6	10.4	3.6	4.0	1983
U.S.	3.2	14.5	14.0	13.6	15.5	10.8	10.5	5.1	12.9	1977

Note: Figures are percentages except for Median Year; Note: (1) Figures cover the Tyler, TX Metropolitan Statistical Area—see Appendix B for areas included
Source: U.S. Census Bureau, 2013-2017 American Community Survey 5-Year Estimates

Gross Monthly Rent

Area	Under $500	$500 -$999	$1,000 -$1,499	$1,500 -$1,999	$2,000 -$2,499	$2,500 -$2,999	$3,000 and up	Median ($)
City	8.4	59.3	23.4	6.5	1.7	0.2	0.5	864
MSA[1]	8.3	58.2	25.1	6.6	1.1	0.2	0.4	873
U.S.	10.5	41.1	28.7	11.7	4.5	1.8	1.7	982

Note: Figures are percentages except for Median; Gross rent is the contract rent plus the estimated average monthly cost of utilities (electricity, gas, and water and sewer) and fuels (oil, coal, kerosene, wood, etc.) if these are paid by the renter (or paid for the renter by someone else); (1) Figures cover the Tyler, TX Metropolitan Statistical Area—see Appendix B for areas included
Source: U.S. Census Bureau, 2013-2017 American Community Survey 5-Year Estimates

HEALTH

Health Risk Factors

Category	MSA[1] (%)	U.S. (%)
Adults aged 18–64 who have any kind of health care coverage	n/a	87.3
Adults who reported being in good or better health	n/a	82.4
Adults who have been told they have high blood cholesterol	n/a	33.0
Adults who have been told they have high blood pressure	n/a	32.3
Adults who are current smokers	n/a	17.1
Adults who currently use E-cigarettes	n/a	4.6
Adults who currently use chewing tobacco, snuff, or snus	n/a	4.0
Adults who are heavy drinkers[2]	n/a	6.3
Adults who are binge drinkers[3]	n/a	17.4
Adults who are overweight (BMI 25.0 - 29.9)	n/a	35.3
Adults who are obese (BMI 30.0 - 99.8)	n/a	31.3
Adults who participated in any physical activities in the past month	n/a	74.4
Adults who always or nearly always wears a seat belt	n/a	94.3

Note: n/a not available; (1) Figures cover the Tyler, TX Metropolitan Statistical Area—see Appendix B for areas included; (2) Heavy drinkers are classified as adult men having more than 14 drinks per week and adult women having more than 7 drinks per week; (3) Binge drinkers are classified as males having five or more drinks on one occasion or females having four or more drinks on one occasion
Source: Centers for Disease Control and Prevention, Behaviorial Risk Factor Surveillance System, SMART: Selected Metropolitan Area Risk Trends, 2017

Acute and Chronic Health Conditions

Category	MSA[1] (%)	U.S. (%)
Adults who have ever been told they had a heart attack	n/a	4.2
Adults who have ever been told they have angina or coronary heart disease	n/a	3.9
Adults who have ever been told they had a stroke	n/a	3.0
Adults who have ever been told they have asthma	n/a	14.2
Adults who have ever been told they have arthritis	n/a	24.9
Adults who have ever been told they have diabetes[2]	n/a	10.5
Adults who have ever been told they had skin cancer	n/a	6.2
Adults who have ever been told they had any other types of cancer	n/a	7.1
Adults who have ever been told they have COPD	n/a	6.5
Adults who have ever been told they have kidney disease	n/a	3.0
Adults who have ever been told they have a form of depression	n/a	20.5

Note: n/a not available; (1) Figures cover the Tyler, TX Metropolitan Statistical Area—see Appendix B for areas included; (2) Figures do not include pregnancy-related, borderline, or pre-diabetes
Source: Centers for Disease Control and Prevention, Behaviorial Risk Factor Surveillance System, SMART: Selected Metropolitan Area Risk Trends, 2017

Health Screening and Vaccination Rates

Category	MSA[1] (%)	U.S. (%)
Adults aged 65+ who have had flu shot within the past year	n/a	60.7
Adults aged 65+ who have ever had a pneumonia vaccination	n/a	75.4
Adults who have ever been tested for HIV	n/a	36.1
Adults who have ever had the shingles or zoster vaccine?	n/a	28.9
Adults who have had their blood cholesterol checked within the last five years	n/a	85.9

Note: n/a not available; (1) Figures cover the Tyler, TX Metropolitan Statistical Area—see Appendix B for areas included.
Source: Centers for Disease Control and Prevention, Behaviorial Risk Factor Surveillance System, SMART: Selected Metropolitan Area Risk Trends, 2017

Disability Status

Category	MSA[1] (%)	U.S. (%)
Adults who reported being deaf	n/a	6.7
Are you blind or have serious difficulty seeing, even when wearing glasses?	n/a	4.5
Are you limited in any way in any of your usual activities due of arthritis?	n/a	12.9
Do you have difficulty doing errands alone?	n/a	6.8
Do you have difficulty dressing or bathing?	n/a	3.6
Do you have serious difficulty concentrating/remembering/making decisions?	n/a	10.7
Do you have serious difficulty walking or climbing stairs?	n/a	13.6

Note: n/a not available; (1) Figures cover the Tyler, TX Metropolitan Statistical Area—see Appendix B for areas included.
Source: Centers for Disease Control and Prevention, Behaviorial Risk Factor Surveillance System, SMART: Selected Metropolitan Area Risk Trends, 2017

Mortality Rates for the Top 10 Causes of Death in the U.S.

ICD-10[a] Sub-Chapter	ICD-10[a] Code	Age-Adjusted Mortality Rate[1] per 100,000 population	
		County[2]	U.S.
Malignant neoplasms	C00-C97	133.9	155.5
Ischaemic heart diseases	I20-I25	99.8	94.8
Other forms of heart disease	I30-I51	62.7	52.9
Chronic lower respiratory diseases	J40-J47	46.7	41.0
Cerebrovascular diseases	I60-I69	38.2	37.5
Other degenerative diseases of the nervous system	G30-G31	42.1	35.0
Other external causes of accidental injury	W00-X59	20.9	33.7
Organic, including symptomatic, mental disorders	F01-F09	17.3	31.0
Hypertensive diseases	I10-I15	11.9	21.9
Diabetes mellitus	E10-E14	21.9	21.2

Note: (a) ICD-10 = International Classification of Diseases 10th Revision; (1) Mortality rates are a three year average covering 2015-2017; (2) Figures cover Smith County.
Source: Centers for Disease Control and Prevention, National Center for Health Statistics. Underlying Cause of Death 1999-2017 on CDC WONDER Online Database

Mortality Rates for Selected Causes of Death

ICD-10[a] Sub-Chapter	ICD-10[a] Code	Age-Adjusted Mortality Rate[1] per 100,000 population	
		County[2]	U.S.
Assault	X85-Y09	4.3	5.9
Diseases of the liver	K70-K76	14.7	14.1
Human immunodeficiency virus (HIV) disease	B20-B24	Suppressed	1.8
Influenza and pneumonia	J09-J18	12.6	14.3
Intentional self-harm	X60-X84	18.3	13.6
Malnutrition	E40-E46	Unreliable	1.6
Obesity and other hyperalimentation	E65-E68	Suppressed	2.1
Renal failure	N17-N19	19.7	13.0
Transport accidents	V01-V99	17.8	12.4
Viral hepatitis	B15-B19	Unreliable	1.6

Note: (a) ICD-10 = International Classification of Diseases 10th Revision; (1) Mortality rates are a three year average covering 2015-2017; (2) Figures cover Smith County; Data are suppressed when the data meet the criteria for confidentiality constraints; Mortality rates are flagged as unreliable when the rate would be calculated with a numerator of 20 or less.
Source: Centers for Disease Control and Prevention, National Center for Health Statistics. Underlying Cause of Death 1999-2017 on CDC WONDER Online Database

Health Insurance Coverage

Area	With Health Insurance	With Private Health Insurance	With Public Health Insurance	Without Health Insurance	Population Under Age 18 Without Health Insurance
City	82.2	60.7	32.4	17.8	8.7
MSA[1]	82.4	62.3	32.5	17.6	11.3
U.S.	89.5	67.2	33.8	10.5	5.7

Note: Figures are percentages that cover the civilian noninstitutionalized population; (1) Figures cover the Tyler, TX Metropolitan Statistical Area—see Appendix B for areas included
Source: U.S. Census Bureau, 2013-2017 American Community Survey 5-Year Estimates

Number of Medical Professionals

Area	MDs[3]	DOs[3,4]	Dentists	Podiatrists	Chiropractors	Optometrists
County[1] (number)	773	55	136	15	62	36
County[1] (rate[2])	343.1	24.4	59.7	6.6	27.2	15.8
U.S. (rate[2])	279.3	23.0	68.4	6.0	27.1	16.2

Note: Data as of 2017 unless noted; (1) Data covers Smith County; (2) Rate per 100,000 population; (3) Data as of 2016 and includes all active, non-federal physicians; (4) Doctor of Osteopathic Medicine
Source: U.S. Department of Health and Human Services, Health Resources and Services Administration, Bureau of Health Professions, Area Resource File (ARF) 2017-2018

EDUCATION

Public School District Statistics

District Name	Schls	Pupils	Pupil/ Teacher Ratio	Minority Pupils[1] (%)	Free Lunch Eligible[2] (%)	IEP[3] (%)
Chapel Hill ISD	5	3,652	15.2	67.9	67.7	9.1
Tyler ISD	26	18,130	14.7	78.3	57.2	6.8

Note: Table includes school districts with 2,000 or more students; (1) Percentage of students that are not non-Hispanic white; (2) Percentage of students that are eligible for the free lunch program; (3) Percentage of students that have an Individualized Education Program.
Source: U.S. Department of Education, National Center for Education Statistics, Common Core of Data, Local Education Agency (School District) Universe Survey: School Year 2016-2017; U.S. Department of Education, National Center for Education Statistics, Common Core of Data, Public Elementary/Secondary School Universe Survey: School Year 2016-2017

Highest Level of Education

Area	Less than H.S.	H.S. Diploma	Some College, No Deg.	Associate Degree	Bachelor's Degree	Master's Degree	Prof. School Degree	Doctorate Degree
City	16.5	20.5	25.8	9.6	18.3	6.0	2.2	1.1
MSA[1]	15.1	24.6	25.7	9.4	17.4	5.4	1.6	0.8
U.S.	12.7	27.3	20.8	8.3	19.1	8.4	2.0	1.4

Note: Figures cover persons age 25 and over; (1) Figures cover the Tyler, TX Metropolitan Statistical Area—see Appendix B for areas included
Source: U.S. Census Bureau, 2013-2017 American Community Survey 5-Year Estimates

Educational Attainment by Race

Area	High School Graduate or Higher (%)					Bachelor's Degree or Higher (%)				
	Total	White	Black	Asian	Hisp.[2]	Total	White	Black	Asian	Hisp.[2]
City	83.5	83.4	85.0	97.0	44.7	27.6	31.8	11.6	69.8	7.3
MSA[1]	84.9	85.0	85.7	96.0	48.4	25.2	27.2	12.7	62.8	7.5
U.S.	87.3	89.3	84.9	86.5	66.7	30.9	32.2	20.6	52.7	15.2

Note: Figures shown cover persons 25 years old and over; (1) Figures cover the Tyler, TX Metropolitan Statistical Area—see Appendix B for areas included; (2) People of Hispanic origin can be of any race
Source: U.S. Census Bureau, 2013-2017 American Community Survey 5-Year Estimates

School Enrollment by Grade and Control

Area	Preschool (%)		Kindergarten (%)		Grades 1 - 4 (%)		Grades 5 - 8 (%)		Grades 9 - 12 (%)	
	Public	Private	Public	Private	Public	Private	Public	Private	Public	Private
City	73.2	26.8	93.2	6.8	87.6	12.4	88.8	11.2	90.6	9.4
MSA[1]	73.0	27.0	88.6	11.4	88.6	11.4	90.4	9.6	89.0	11.0
U.S.	58.8	41.2	87.7	12.3	89.7	10.3	89.6	10.4	90.3	9.7

Note: Figures shown cover persons 3 years old and over; (1) Figures cover the Tyler, TX Metropolitan Statistical Area—see Appendix B for areas included
Source: U.S. Census Bureau, 2013-2017 American Community Survey 5-Year Estimates

Average Salaries of Public School Classroom Teachers

Area	2016		2017		Change from 2016 to 2017	
	Dollars	Rank[1]	Dollars	Rank[1]	Percent	Rank[2]
Texas	51,890	28	52,575	28	1.3	29
U.S. Average	58,479	–	59,660	–	2.0	–

Note: (1) Rank ranges from 1 to 51 where 1 indicates highest salary; (2) Rank ranges from 1 to 51 where 1 indicates highest percent change.
Source: National Education Association, Rankings & Estimates: Rankings of the States 2017 and Estimates of School Statistics 2018

Higher Education

Four-Year Colleges			Two-Year Colleges			Medical Schools[1]	Law Schools[2]	Voc/ Tech[3]
Public	Private Non-profit	Private For-profit	Public	Private Non-profit	Private For-profit			
3	1	0	0	0	0	0	0	1

Note: Figures cover institutions located within the city limits and include main campuses only; (1) includes schools accredited by the Liaison Committee on Medical Education and the American Osteopathic Association's Commission on Osteopathic College Accreditation; (2) includes ABA-accredited schools, schools with provisional ABA accreditation, and state accredited schools; (3) includes all schools with programs that are less than 2 years.
Source: National Center for Education Statistics, Integrated Postsecondary Education System (IPEDS), 2017-18; Wikipedia, List of Medical Schools in the United States, accessed April 3, 2019; Wikipedia, List of Law Schools in the United States, accessed April 3, 2019

PRESIDENTIAL ELECTION

2016 Presidential Election Results

Area	Clinton	Trump	Johnson	Stein	Other
Smith County	26.3	69.5	2.4	0.4	1.3
U.S.	48.0	45.9	3.3	1.1	1.7

Note: Results are percentages and may not add to 100% due to rounding
Source: Dave Leip's Atlas of U.S. Presidential Elections

EMPLOYERS

Major Employers

Company Name	Industry
Brookshire Grocery Company	Grocery distribution
Centene	Health care solutions
CHRISTUS Trinity Mother Frances	General medical & surgical hospitals
City of Tyler	Municipal government
Delek	Oil refining
John Soules Foods	USDA meat processing
Smith County	County government
Southside Bank	Banking and financial services
Suddenlink	Cable & other pay television services
Target Distribution Center	Retail distribution
The Trane Co.	Air conditioning equipment, mfg
The University of Texas at Tyler	Education
Tyler Independent School District	Education
Tyler Junior College	Education
Tyler Pipe	Cast iron pipes, iron fittings
UT Health East Texas	General medical & surgical hospitals
Wal-Mart Stores	Retail

Note: Companies shown are located within the Tyler, TX Metropolitan Statistical Area.
Source: Hoovers.com; Wikipedia

PUBLIC SAFETY

Crime Rate

Area	All Crimes	Violent Crimes				Property Crimes		
		Murder	Rape[3]	Robbery	Aggrav. Assault	Burglary	Larceny -Theft	Motor Vehicle Theft
City	3,582.0	5.7	61.3	56.5	313.8	420.3	2,586.8	137.6
Suburbs[1]	2,158.7	2.5	42.0	20.6	213.2	581.9	1,097.9	200.8
Metro[2]	2,822.2	4.0	51.0	37.3	260.1	506.5	1,792.0	171.3
U.S.	2,756.1	5.3	41.7	98.0	248.9	430.4	1,694.4	237.4

Note: Figures are crimes per 100,000 population; (1) All areas within the metro area that are located outside the city limits; (2) Figures cover the Tyler, TX Metropolitan Statistical Area—see Appendix B for areas included; (3) The city and U.S. figures shown were reported using the revised Uniform Crime Reporting (UCR) definition of rape. The suburban and metro area figures shown are an aggregate total of the data submitted using both the revised and legacy UCR definitions.
Source: FBI Uniform Crime Reports, 2017

Hate Crimes

Area	Number of Quarters Reported	Number of Incidents per Bias Motivation					
		Race/Ethnicity/ Ancestry	Religion	Sexual Orientation	Disability	Gender	Gender Identity
City	4	0	0	0	0	0	0
U.S.	4	4,131	1,564	1,130	116	46	119

Source: Federal Bureau of Investigation, Hate Crime Statistics 2017

Identity Theft Consumer Reports

Area	Reports	Reports per 100,000 Population	Rank[2]
MSA[1]	281	125	68
U.S.	444,602	135	-

Note: (1) Figures cover the Tyler, TX Metropolitan Statistical Area—see Appendix B for areas included; (2) Rank ranges from 1 to 389 where 1 indicates greatest number of identity theft reports per 100,000 population
Source: Federal Trade Commission, Consumer Sentinel Network Data Book for January–December 2018

Fraud and Other Consumer Reports

Area	Reports	Reports per 100,000 Population	Rank[2]
MSA[1]	1,320	586	66
U.S.	2,552,917	776	-

Note: (1) Figures cover the Tyler, TX Metropolitan Statistical Area—see Appendix B for areas included; (2) Rank ranges from 1 to 389 where 1 indicates greatest number of fraud and other consumer reports per 100,000 population
Source: Federal Trade Commission, Consumer Sentinel Network Data Book for January–December 2018

SPORTS

Professional Sports Teams

Team Name	League	Year Established
No teams are located in the metro area		

Source: Wikipedia, Major Professional Sports Teams of the United States and Canada, April 5, 2019

CLIMATE

Average and Extreme Temperatures

Temperature	Jan	Feb	Mar	Apr	May	Jun	Jul	Aug	Sep	Oct	Nov	Dec	Yr.
Extreme High (°F)	85	90	100	100	101	112	111	109	107	101	91	87	112
Average High (°F)	55	60	68	76	84	92	96	96	89	79	67	58	77
Average Temp. (°F)	45	50	57	66	74	82	86	86	79	68	56	48	67
Average Low (°F)	35	39	47	56	64	72	76	75	68	57	46	38	56
Extreme Low (°F)	-2	9	12	30	39	53	58	58	42	24	16	0	-2

Note: Figures cover the years 1945-1993
Source: National Climatic Data Center, International Station Meteorological Climate Summary, 9/96

Average Precipitation/Snowfall/Humidity

Precip./Humidity	Jan	Feb	Mar	Apr	May	Jun	Jul	Aug	Sep	Oct	Nov	Dec	Yr.
Avg. Precip. (in.)	1.9	2.3	2.6	3.8	4.9	3.4	2.1	2.3	2.9	3.3	2.3	2.1	33.9
Avg. Snowfall (in.)	1	1	Tr	Tr	0	0	0	0	0	Tr	Tr	Tr	3
Avg. Rel. Hum. 6am (%)	78	77	75	77	82	81	77	76	80	79	78	77	78
Avg. Rel. Hum. 3pm (%)	53	51	47	49	51	48	43	41	46	46	48	51	48

Note: Figures cover the years 1945-1993; Tr = Trace amounts (<0.05 in. of rain; <0.5 in. of snow)
Source: National Climatic Data Center, International Station Meteorological Climate Summary, 9/96

Weather Conditions

Temperature			Daytime Sky			Precipitation		
10°F & below	32°F & below	90°F & above	Clear	Partly cloudy	Cloudy	0.01 inch or more precip.	0.1 inch or more snow/ice	Thunder-storms
1	34	102	108	160	97	78	2	49

Note: Figures are average number of days per year and cover the years 1945-1993
Source: National Climatic Data Center, International Station Meteorological Climate Summary, 9/96

HAZARDOUS WASTE

Superfund Sites

The Tyler, TX metro area has no sites on the EPA's Superfund Final National Priorities List. There are a total of 1,390 Superfund sites with a status of proposed or final on the list in the U.S. *U.S. Environmental Protection Agency, National Priorities List, April 5, 2019*

AIR & WATER QUALITY

Air Quality Trends: Ozone

	1990	1995	2000	2005	2010	2012	2014	2015	2016	2017
MSA[1]	n/a	n/a	n/a	n/a	n/a	n/a	n/a	n/a	n/a	n/a
U.S.	0.088	0.089	0.082	0.080	0.073	0.075	0.067	0.068	0.069	0.068

Note: (1) Data covers the Tyler, TX Metropolitan Statistical Area—see Appendix B for areas included; n/a not available. The values shown are the composite ozone concentration averages among trend sites based on the highest fourth daily maximum 8-hour concentration in parts per million. These trends are based on sites having an adequate record of monitoring data during the trend period. Data from exceptional events are included.
Source: U.S. Environmental Protection Agency, Air Quality Monitoring Information, "Air Quality Trends by City, 1990-2017"

Air Quality Index

Area	Percent of Days when Air Quality was...[2]					AQI Statistics[2]	
	Good	Moderate	Unhealthy for Sensitive Groups	Unhealthy	Very Unhealthy	Maximum	Median
MSA[1]	92.3	7.7	0.0	0.0	0.0	90	37

Note: (1) Data covers the Tyler, TX Metropolitan Statistical Area—see Appendix B for areas included; (2) Based on 364 days with AQI data in 2017. Air Quality Index (AQI) is an index for reporting daily air quality. EPA calculates the AQI for five major air pollutants regulated by the Clean Air Act: ground-level ozone, particle pollution (aka particulate matter), carbon monoxide, sulfur dioxide, and nitrogen dioxide. The AQI runs from 0 to 500. The higher the AQI value, the greater the level of air pollution and the greater the health concern. There are six AQI categories: "Good" AQI is between 0 and 50. Air quality is considered satisfactory; "Moderate" AQI is between 51 and 100. Air quality is acceptable; "Unhealthy for Sensitive Groups" When AQI values are between 101 and 150, members of sensitive groups may experience health effects; "Unhealthy" When AQI values are between 151 and 200 everyone may begin to experience health effects; "Very Unhealthy" AQI values between 201 and 300 trigger a health alert; "Hazardous" AQI values over 300 trigger warnings of emergency conditions (not shown).
Source: U.S. Environmental Protection Agency, Air Quality Index Report, 2017

Air Quality Index Pollutants

| Area | Percent of Days when AQI Pollutant was...[2] | | | | | |
	Carbon Monoxide	Nitrogen Dioxide	Ozone	Sulfur Dioxide	Particulate Matter 2.5	Particulate Matter 10
MSA[1]	0.0	2.2	97.8	0.0	0.0	0.0

Note: (1) Data covers the Tyler, TX Metropolitan Statistical Area—see Appendix B for areas included; (2) Based on 364 days with AQI data in 2017. The Air Quality Index (AQI) is an index for reporting daily air quality. EPA calculates the AQI for five major air pollutants regulated by the Clean Air Act: ground-level ozone, particle pollution (also known as particulate matter), carbon monoxide, sulfur dioxide, and nitrogen dioxide. The AQI runs from 0 to 500. The higher the AQI value, the greater the level of air pollution and the greater the health concern.
Source: U.S. Environmental Protection Agency, Air Quality Index Report, 2017

Maximum Air Pollutant Concentrations: Particulate Matter, Ozone, CO and Lead

	Particulate Matter 10 (ug/m^3)	Particulate Matter 2.5 Wtd AM (ug/m^3)	Particulate Matter 2.5 24-Hr (ug/m^3)	Ozone (ppm)	Carbon Monoxide (ppm)	Lead (ug/m^3)
MSA[1] Level	n/a	n/a	n/a	0.063	n/a	n/a
NAAQS[2]	150	15	35	0.075	9	0.15
Met NAAQS[2]	n/a	n/a	n/a	Yes	n/a	n/a

Note: (1) Data covers the Tyler, TX Metropolitan Statistical Area—see Appendix B for areas included; Data from exceptional events are included; (2) National Ambient Air Quality Standards; ppm = parts per million; ug/m^3 = micrograms per cubic meter; n/a not available.
Concentrations: Particulate Matter 10 (coarse particulate)—highest second maximum 24-hour concentration; Particulate Matter 2.5 Wtd AM (fine particulate)—highest weighted annual mean concentration; Particulate Matter 2.5 24-Hour (fine particulate)—highest 98th percentile 24-hour concentration; Ozone—highest fourth daily maximum 8-hour concentration; Carbon Monoxide—highest second maximum non-overlapping 8-hour concentration; Lead—maximum running 3-month average
Source: U.S. Environmental Protection Agency, Air Quality Monitoring Information, "Air Quality Statistics by City, 2017"

Maximum Air Pollutant Concentrations: Nitrogen Dioxide and Sulfur Dioxide

	Nitrogen Dioxide AM (ppb)	Nitrogen Dioxide 1-Hr (ppb)	Sulfur Dioxide AM (ppb)	Sulfur Dioxide 1-Hr (ppb)	Sulfur Dioxide 24-Hr (ppb)
MSA[1] Level	2	15	n/a	n/a	n/a
NAAQS[2]	53	100	30	75	140
Met NAAQS[2]	Yes	Yes	n/a	n/a	n/a

Note: (1) Data covers the Tyler, TX Metropolitan Statistical Area—see Appendix B for areas included; Data from exceptional events are included; (2) National Ambient Air Quality Standards; ppm = parts per million; ug/m^3 = micrograms per cubic meter; n/a not available.
Concentrations: Nitrogen Dioxide AM—highest arithmetic mean concentration; Nitrogen Dioxide 1-Hr—highest 98th percentile 1-hour daily maximum concentration; Sulfur Dioxide AM—highest annual mean concentration; Sulfur Dioxide 1-Hr—highest 99th percentile 1-hour daily maximum concentration; Sulfur Dioxide 24-Hr—highest second maximum 24-hour concentration
Source: U.S. Environmental Protection Agency, Air Quality Monitoring Information, "Air Quality Statistics by City, 2017"

Drinking Water

| Water System Name | Pop. Served | Primary Water Source Type | Violations[1] | |
			Health Based	Monitoring/ Reporting
City of Tyler	110,525	Surface	0	0

Note: (1) Based on violation data from January 1, 2018 to December 31, 2018
Source: U.S. Environmental Protection Agency, Office of Ground Water and Drinking Water, Safe Drinking Water Information System (based on data extracted April 5, 2019)

Appendixes

Appendix A: Comparative Statistics

Table of Contents

Population Growth: City

Area	1990 Census	2000 Census	2010 Census	2017* Estimate	Population Growth (%)	
					1990-2017	2010-2017
Albany, NY	100,756	95,658	97,856	98,498	-2.2	0.7
Albuquerque, NM	388,375	448,607	545,852	556,718	43.3	2.0
Allentown, PA	105,066	106,632	118,032	120,128	14.3	1.8
Anchorage, AK	226,338	260,283	291,826	298,225	31.8	2.2
Ann Arbor, MI	111,018	114,024	113,934	119,303	7.5	4.7
Athens, GA	86,561	100,266	115,452	122,292	41.3	5.9
Atlanta, GA	394,092	416,474	420,003	465,230	18.1	10.8
Austin, TX	499,053	656,562	790,390	916,906	83.7	16.0
Baton Rouge, LA	223,299	227,818	229,493	227,549	1.9	-0.8
Billings, MT	81,812	89,847	104,170	109,082	33.3	4.7
Boise City, ID	144,317	185,787	205,671	220,859	53.0	7.4
Boston, MA	574,283	589,141	617,594	669,158	16.5	8.3
Boulder, CO	87,737	94,673	97,385	106,271	21.1	9.1
Cape Coral, FL	75,507	102,286	154,305	173,679	130.0	12.6
Cedar Rapids, IA	110,829	120,758	126,326	130,330	17.6	3.2
Charleston, SC	96,102	96,650	120,083	131,204	36.5	9.3
Charlotte, NC	428,283	540,828	731,424	826,060	92.9	12.9
Chicago, IL	2,783,726	2,896,016	2,695,598	2,722,586	-2.2	1.0
Clarksville, TN	78,569	103,455	132,929	147,771	88.1	11.2
College Station, TX	53,318	67,890	93,857	107,445	101.5	14.5
Colorado Springs, CO	283,798	360,890	416,427	450,000	58.6	8.1
Columbia, MO	71,069	84,531	108,500	118,620	66.9	9.3
Columbia, SC	115,475	116,278	129,272	132,236	14.5	2.3
Columbus, OH	648,656	711,470	787,033	852,144	31.4	8.3
Dallas, TX	1,006,971	1,188,580	1,197,816	1,300,122	29.1	8.5
Denver, CO	467,153	554,636	600,158	678,467	45.2	13.0
Des Moines, IA	193,569	198,682	203,433	214,778	11.0	5.6
Durham, NC	151,737	187,035	228,330	257,232	69.5	12.7
Edison, NJ	88,680	97,687	99,967	102,304	15.4	2.3
El Paso, TX	515,541	563,662	649,121	678,266	31.6	4.5
Eugene, OR	118,073	137,893	156,185	163,135	38.2	4.4
Evansville, IN	126,272	121,582	117,429	119,806	-5.1	2.0
Fargo, ND	74,372	90,599	105,549	118,099	58.8	11.9
Fayetteville, NC	118,247	121,015	200,564	210,324	77.9	4.9
Fort Collins, CO	89,555	118,652	143,986	159,150	77.7	10.5
Fort Wayne, IN	205,671	205,727	253,691	262,450	27.6	3.5
Fort Worth, TX	448,311	534,694	741,206	835,129	86.3	12.7
Gainesville, FL	90,519	95,447	124,354	129,394	42.9	4.1
Grand Rapids, MI	189,145	197,800	188,040	195,355	3.3	3.9
Greeley, CO	60,887	76,930	92,889	100,760	65.5	8.5
Green Bay, WI	96,466	102,313	104,057	104,796	8.6	0.7
Greensboro, NC	193,389	223,891	269,666	284,816	47.3	5.6
Honolulu, HI	376,465	371,657	337,256	350,788	-6.8	4.0
Houston, TX	1,697,610	1,953,631	2,099,451	2,267,336	33.6	8.0
Huntsville, AL	161,842	158,216	180,105	190,501	17.7	5.8
Indianapolis, IN	730,993	781,870	820,445	853,431	16.7	4.0
Jacksonville, FL	635,221	735,617	821,784	867,313	36.5	5.5
Kansas City, MO	434,967	441,545	459,787	476,974	9.7	3.7
Lafayette, LA	104,735	110,257	120,623	126,476	20.8	4.9
Las Cruces, NM	63,267	74,267	97,618	101,014	59.7	3.5
Las Vegas, NV	261,374	478,434	583,756	621,662	137.8	6.5
Lexington, KY	225,366	260,512	295,803	315,109	39.8	6.5
Lincoln, NE	193,629	225,581	258,379	277,315	43.2	7.3
Little Rock, AR	177,519	183,133	193,524	197,780	11.4	2.2
Los Angeles, CA	3,487,671	3,694,820	3,792,621	3,949,776	13.2	4.1

Table continued on next page.

Area	1990 Census	2000 Census	2010 Census	2017* Estimate	Population Growth (%)	
					1990-2017	2010-2017
Louisville, KY	269,160	256,231	597,337	615,478	128.7	3.0
Madison, WI	193,451	208,054	233,209	248,856	28.6	6.7
Manchester, NH	99,567	107,006	109,565	110,601	11.1	0.9
McAllen, TX	86,145	106,414	129,877	139,838	62.3	7.7
Miami, FL	358,843	362,470	399,457	443,007	23.5	10.9
Midland, TX	89,358	94,996	111,147	131,286	46.9	18.1
Minneapolis, MN	368,383	382,618	382,578	411,452	11.7	7.5
Nashville, TN	488,364	545,524	601,222	654,187	34.0	8.8
New Orleans, LA	496,938	484,674	343,829	388,182	-21.9	12.9
New York, NY	7,322,552	8,008,278	8,175,133	8,560,072	16.9	4.7
Oklahoma City, OK	445,065	506,132	579,999	629,191	41.4	8.5
Omaha, NE	371,972	390,007	408,958	463,081	24.5	13.2
Orlando, FL	161,172	185,951	238,300	269,414	67.2	13.1
Peoria, IL	114,341	112,936	115,007	115,424	0.9	0.4
Philadelphia, PA	1,585,577	1,517,550	1,526,006	1,569,657	-1.0	2.9
Phoenix, AZ	989,873	1,321,045	1,445,632	1,574,421	59.1	8.9
Pittsburgh, PA	369,785	334,563	305,704	305,012	-17.5	-0.2
Portland, OR	485,833	529,121	583,776	630,331	29.7	8.0
Providence, RI	160,734	173,618	178,042	179,509	11.7	0.8
Provo, UT	87,148	105,166	112,488	116,199	33.3	3.3
Raleigh, NC	226,841	276,093	403,892	449,477	98.1	11.3
Reno, NV	139,950	180,480	225,221	239,732	71.3	6.4
Richmond, VA	202,783	197,790	204,214	220,892	8.9	8.2
Roanoke, VA	96,415	94,911	97,032	99,572	3.3	2.6
Rochester, MN	74,151	85,806	106,769	112,683	52.0	5.5
Salem, OR	112,046	136,924	154,637	163,654	46.1	5.8
Salt Lake City, UT	159,796	181,743	186,440	194,188	21.5	4.2
San Antonio, TX	997,258	1,144,646	1,327,407	1,461,623	46.6	10.1
San Diego, CA	1,111,048	1,223,400	1,307,402	1,390,966	25.2	6.4
San Francisco, CA	723,959	776,733	805,235	864,263	19.4	7.3
San Jose, CA	784,324	894,943	945,942	1,023,031	30.4	8.1
Santa Rosa, CA	123,297	147,595	167,815	174,244	41.3	3.8
Savannah, GA	138,038	131,510	136,286	145,094	5.1	6.5
Seattle, WA	516,262	563,374	608,660	688,245	33.3	13.1
Sioux Falls, SD	102,262	123,975	153,888	170,401	66.6	10.7
Springfield, IL	108,997	111,454	116,250	116,313	6.7	0.1
Tallahassee, FL	128,014	150,624	181,376	188,463	47.2	3.9
Tampa, FL	279,960	303,447	335,709	368,087	31.5	9.6
Topeka, KS	121,197	122,377	127,473	127,139	4.9	-0.3
Tyler, TX	77,653	83,650	96,900	102,561	32.1	5.8
Virginia Beach, VA	393,069	425,257	437,994	450,057	14.5	2.8
Visalia, CA	78,398	91,565	124,442	130,047	65.9	4.5
Washington, DC	606,900	572,059	601,723	672,391	10.8	11.7
Wilmington, NC	64,609	75,838	106,476	115,261	78.4	8.3
Winston-Salem, NC	168,139	185,776	229,617	240,193	42.9	4.6
U.S.	248,709,873	281,421,906	308,745,538	321,004,407	29.1	4.0

Note: (*) 2013-2017 5-year estimated population
Source: U.S. Census Bureau, 1990 Census, Census 2000, Census 2010, 2013-2017 American Community Survey 5-Year Estimates

Population Growth: Metro Area

Area	1990 Census	2000 Census	2010 Census	2017* Estimate	Population Growth (%) 1990-2017	Population Growth (%) 2010-2017
Albany, NY	809,443	825,875	870,716	881,862	8.9	1.3
Albuquerque, NM	599,416	729,649	887,077	905,049	51.0	2.0
Allentown, PA	686,666	740,395	821,173	832,790	21.3	1.4
Anchorage, AK	266,021	319,605	380,821	399,360	50.1	4.9
Ann Arbor, MI	282,937	322,895	344,791	361,509	27.8	4.8
Athens, GA	136,025	166,079	192,541	202,780	49.1	5.3
Atlanta, GA	3,069,411	4,247,981	5,268,860	5,700,990	85.7	8.2
Austin, TX	846,217	1,249,763	1,716,289	2,000,590	136.4	16.6
Baton Rouge, LA	623,853	705,973	802,484	828,741	32.8	3.3
Billings, MT	121,499	138,904	158,050	167,545	37.9	6.0
Boise City, ID	319,596	464,840	616,561	677,346	111.9	9.9
Boston, MA	4,133,895	4,391,344	4,552,402	4,771,936	15.4	4.8
Boulder, CO	208,898	269,758	294,567	316,782	51.6	7.5
Cape Coral, FL	335,113	440,888	618,754	700,165	108.9	13.2
Cedar Rapids, IA	210,640	237,230	257,940	266,122	26.3	3.2
Charleston, SC	506,875	549,033	664,607	744,195	46.8	12.0
Charlotte, NC	1,024,331	1,330,448	1,758,038	2,427,024	136.9	38.1
Chicago, IL	8,182,076	9,098,316	9,461,105	9,549,229	16.7	0.9
Clarksville, TN	189,277	232,000	273,949	278,844	47.3	1.8
College Station, TX	150,998	184,885	228,660	248,554	64.6	8.7
Colorado Springs, CO	409,482	537,484	645,613	698,595	70.6	8.2
Columbia, MO	122,010	145,666	172,786	174,589	43.1	1.0
Columbia, SC	548,325	647,158	767,598	808,377	47.4	5.3
Columbus, OH	1,405,176	1,612,694	1,836,536	2,023,695	44.0	10.2
Dallas, TX	3,989,294	5,161,544	6,371,773	7,104,415	78.1	11.5
Denver, CO	1,666,935	2,179,296	2,543,482	2,798,684	67.9	10.0
Des Moines, IA	416,346	481,394	569,633	623,113	49.7	9.4
Durham, NC	344,646	426,493	504,357	550,281	59.7	9.1
Edison, NJ	16,845,992	18,323,002	18,897,109	20,192,042	19.9	6.9
El Paso, TX	591,610	679,622	800,647	838,527	41.7	4.7
Eugene, OR	282,912	322,959	351,715	363,471	28.5	3.3
Evansville, IN	324,858	342,815	358,676	315,263	-3.0	-12.1
Fargo, ND	153,296	174,367	208,777	232,660	51.8	11.4
Fayetteville, NC	297,422	336,609	366,383	385,337	29.6	5.2
Fort Collins, CO	186,136	251,494	299,630	330,976	77.8	10.5
Fort Wayne, IN	354,435	390,156	416,257	429,060	21.1	3.1
Fort Worth, TX	3,989,294	5,161,544	6,371,773	7,104,415	78.1	11.5
Gainesville, FL	191,263	232,392	264,275	277,056	44.9	4.8
Grand Rapids, MI	645,914	740,482	774,160	1,039,182	60.9	34.2
Greeley, CO	131,816	180,926	252,825	285,729	116.8	13.0
Green Bay, WI	243,698	282,599	306,241	315,847	29.6	3.1
Greensboro, NC	540,257	643,430	723,801	751,590	39.1	3.8
Honolulu, HI	836,231	876,156	953,207	990,060	18.4	3.9
Houston, TX	3,767,335	4,715,407	5,946,800	6,636,208	76.2	11.6
Huntsville, AL	293,047	342,376	417,593	444,908	51.8	6.5
Indianapolis, IN	1,294,217	1,525,104	1,756,241	1,989,032	53.7	13.3
Jacksonville, FL	925,213	1,122,750	1,345,596	1,447,884	56.5	7.6
Kansas City, MO	1,636,528	1,836,038	2,035,334	2,088,830	27.6	2.6
Lafayette, LA	208,740	239,086	273,738	487,633	133.6	78.1
Las Cruces, NM	135,510	174,682	209,233	213,849	57.8	2.2
Las Vegas, NV	741,459	1,375,765	1,951,269	2,112,436	184.9	8.3
Lexington, KY	348,428	408,326	472,099	500,689	43.7	6.1
Lincoln, NE	229,091	266,787	302,157	323,402	41.2	7.0
Little Rock, AR	535,034	610,518	699,757	730,346	36.5	4.4
Los Angeles, CA	11,273,720	12,365,627	12,828,837	13,261,538	17.6	3.4

Table continued on next page.

Area	1990 Census	2000 Census	2010 Census	2017* Estimate	Population Growth (%)	
					1990-2017	2010-2017
Louisville, KY	1,055,973	1,161,975	1,283,566	1,278,203	21.0	-0.4
Madison, WI	432,323	501,774	568,593	640,072	48.1	12.6
Manchester, NH	336,073	380,841	400,721	406,371	20.9	1.4
McAllen, TX	383,545	569,463	774,769	839,539	118.9	8.4
Miami, FL	4,056,100	5,007,564	5,564,635	6,019,790	48.4	8.2
Midland, TX	106,611	116,009	136,872	165,430	55.2	20.9
Minneapolis, MN	2,538,834	2,968,806	3,279,833	3,526,149	38.9	7.5
Nashville, TN	1,048,218	1,311,789	1,589,934	1,830,410	74.6	15.1
New Orleans, LA	1,264,391	1,316,510	1,167,764	1,260,660	-0.3	8.0
New York, NY	16,845,992	18,323,002	18,897,109	20,192,042	19.9	6.9
Oklahoma City, OK	971,042	1,095,421	1,252,987	1,353,504	39.4	8.0
Omaha, NE	685,797	767,041	865,350	914,190	33.3	5.6
Orlando, FL	1,224,852	1,644,561	2,134,411	2,390,859	95.2	12.0
Peoria, IL	358,552	366,899	379,186	377,258	5.2	-0.5
Philadelphia, PA	5,435,470	5,687,147	5,965,343	6,065,644	11.6	1.7
Phoenix, AZ	2,238,480	3,251,876	4,192,887	4,561,038	103.8	8.8
Pittsburgh, PA	2,468,289	2,431,087	2,356,285	2,348,143	-4.9	-0.3
Portland, OR	1,523,741	1,927,881	2,226,009	2,382,037	56.3	7.0
Providence, RI	1,509,789	1,582,997	1,600,852	1,613,154	6.8	0.8
Provo, UT	269,407	376,774	526,810	587,190	118.0	11.5
Raleigh, NC	541,081	797,071	1,130,490	1,273,985	135.5	12.7
Reno, NV	257,193	342,885	425,417	449,442	74.7	5.6
Richmond, VA	949,244	1,096,957	1,258,251	1,270,158	33.8	0.9
Roanoke, VA	268,465	288,309	308,707	313,069	16.6	1.4
Rochester, MN	141,945	163,618	186,011	214,485	51.1	15.3
Salem, OR	278,024	347,214	390,738	410,119	47.5	5.0
Salt Lake City, UT	768,075	968,858	1,124,197	1,170,057	52.3	4.1
San Antonio, TX	1,407,745	1,711,703	2,142,508	2,377,507	68.9	11.0
San Diego, CA	2,498,016	2,813,833	3,095,313	3,283,665	31.5	6.1
San Francisco, CA	3,686,592	4,123,740	4,335,391	4,641,820	25.9	7.1
San Jose, CA	1,534,280	1,735,819	1,836,911	1,969,897	28.4	7.2
Santa Rosa, CA	388,222	458,614	483,878	500,943	29.0	3.5
Savannah, GA	258,060	293,000	347,611	377,476	46.3	8.6
Seattle, WA	2,559,164	3,043,878	3,439,809	3,735,216	46.0	8.6
Sioux Falls, SD	153,500	187,093	228,261	250,564	63.2	9.8
Springfield, IL	189,550	201,437	210,170	210,550	11.1	0.2
Tallahassee, FL	259,096	320,304	367,413	377,674	45.8	2.8
Tampa, FL	2,067,959	2,395,997	2,783,243	2,978,209	44.0	7.0
Topeka, KS	210,257	224,551	233,870	233,382	11.0	-0.2
Tyler, TX	151,309	174,706	209,714	222,277	46.9	6.0
Virginia Beach, VA	1,449,389	1,576,370	1,671,683	1,717,708	18.5	2.8
Visalia, CA	311,823	368,021	442,179	458,809	47.1	3.8
Washington, DC	4,122,914	4,796,183	5,582,170	6,090,196	47.7	9.1
Wilmington, NC	200,124	274,532	362,315	277,496	38.7	-23.4
Winston-Salem, NC	361,091	421,961	477,717	658,195	82.3	37.8
U.S.	248,709,873	281,421,906	308,745,538	321,004,407	29.1	4.0

Note: (*) 2013-2017 5-year estimated population; Figures cover the Metropolitan Statistical Area (MSA)—see Appendix B for areas included
Source: U.S. Census Bureau, 1990 Census, Census 2000, Census 2010, 2013-2017 American Community Survey 5-Year Estimates

Household Size: City

City	Persons in Household (%)							Average Household Size
	One	Two	Three	Four	Five	Six	Seven or More	
Albany, NY	45.0	30.6	12.1	7.1	3.2	1.2	0.6	2.14
Albuquerque, NM	33.7	33.0	14.5	11.1	4.9	1.7	0.9	2.49
Allentown, PA	27.9	28.7	15.7	13.4	8.0	3.4	2.6	2.74
Anchorage, AK	24.5	33.5	18.0	13.5	6.0	2.1	2.0	2.74
Ann Arbor, MI	35.7	35.8	12.2	10.7	3.1	1.4	0.8	2.27
Athens, GA	34.9	34.7	14.2	10.3	3.4	1.4	0.7	2.44
Atlanta, GA	47.4	29.7	10.5	7.4	3.1	1.1	0.6	2.24
Austin, TX	34.2	32.9	14.3	11.2	4.5	1.6	1.0	2.48
Baton Rouge, LA	36.4	32.9	15.0	8.6	4.1	1.7	1.0	2.54
Billings, MT	32.1	34.7	14.4	11.1	4.5	1.8	1.1	2.32
Boise City, ID	33.3	34.3	15.0	10.3	4.3	1.4	1.1	2.45
Boston, MA	36.6	31.7	15.2	10.0	3.8	1.6	0.8	2.36
Boulder, CO	33.2	37.4	14.2	11.1	3.0	0.5	0.2	2.25
Cape Coral, FL	23.2	42.7	15.0	11.3	5.5	1.5	0.4	2.77
Cedar Rapids, IA	33.5	34.2	14.1	11.4	3.6	2.0	0.9	2.34
Charleston, SC	35.2	37.1	14.4	9.2	2.7	0.7	0.3	2.33
Charlotte, NC	31.8	31.8	15.8	12.3	5.3	1.7	1.0	2.57
Chicago, IL	36.6	29.1	13.9	10.4	5.5	2.4	1.8	2.54
Clarksville, TN	23.4	32.8	19.5	14.4	6.1	2.0	1.4	2.70
College Station, TX	29.0	34.1	16.1	14.8	3.5	1.6	0.5	2.48
Colorado Springs, CO	28.5	34.7	14.7	12.8	5.9	2.0	1.0	2.52
Columbia, MO	33.0	33.4	14.4	12.6	4.9	1.1	0.3	2.33
Columbia, SC	40.3	32.7	12.9	8.6	4.1	0.6	0.5	2.24
Columbus, OH	35.3	31.7	14.8	10.3	4.7	1.8	1.1	2.40
Dallas, TX	34.4	29.0	14.3	11.3	6.3	2.6	1.8	2.58
Denver, CO	38.7	32.0	12.3	9.4	4.3	1.7	1.3	2.31
Des Moines, IA	33.0	30.6	15.2	11.2	5.7	2.4	1.5	2.50
Durham, NC	34.6	32.8	15.1	10.8	4.0	1.6	0.7	2.35
Edison, NJ	19.7	28.3	21.7	20.6	6.3	2.0	1.0	2.87
El Paso, TX	24.3	28.1	18.4	16.0	8.2	3.3	1.5	3.01
Eugene, OR	32.9	35.1	14.9	10.8	4.1	1.1	0.7	2.33
Evansville, IN	37.9	33.0	13.2	9.2	4.0	1.2	1.2	2.24
Fargo, ND	36.6	33.3	15.1	8.8	4.3	1.1	0.4	2.14
Fayetteville, NC	33.9	33.3	14.9	11.0	4.2	1.6	0.8	2.45
Fort Collins, CO	24.9	37.6	18.6	12.8	4.1	1.1	0.5	2.46
Fort Wayne, IN	32.4	31.8	15.1	11.2	5.8	2.2	1.1	2.46
Fort Worth, TX	26.4	28.8	15.9	14.9	8.1	3.3	2.2	2.88
Gainesville, FL	42.1	33.0	13.6	7.5	2.4	0.9	0.2	2.32
Grand Rapids, MI	32.4	31.7	14.0	10.8	6.1	2.7	2.0	2.56
Greeley, CO	25.6	32.3	15.9	13.2	8.0	2.9	1.8	2.70
Green Bay, WI	33.4	33.0	12.3	11.5	6.6	1.4	1.4	2.38
Greensboro, NC	34.2	33.4	15.2	10.2	4.7	1.2	0.7	2.37
Honolulu, HI	33.0	30.5	15.2	11.0	4.8	2.5	2.8	2.62
Houston, TX	32.2	28.9	15.2	12.1	6.7	2.7	1.9	2.66
Huntsville, AL	36.4	33.4	14.0	9.9	4.1	1.3	0.6	2.25
Indianapolis, IN	36.0	31.5	13.8	10.5	4.9	1.9	1.0	2.51
Jacksonville, FL	30.2	34.0	16.3	11.6	5.0	1.7	0.9	2.59
Kansas City, MO	36.9	31.6	13.6	10.1	4.8	1.6	1.1	2.35
Lafayette, LA	33.9	35.1	14.6	9.9	4.3	1.2	0.7	2.46
Las Cruces, NM	29.3	33.0	18.1	11.3	5.3	1.9	0.8	2.49
Las Vegas, NV	29.3	31.7	15.5	11.9	6.6	3.0	1.7	2.77
Lexington, KY	31.4	35.7	15.2	10.8	4.7	1.4	0.6	2.37
Lincoln, NE	31.0	35.2	14.3	11.2	5.2	1.8	0.9	2.39
Little Rock, AR	36.7	32.7	13.7	9.9	4.3	1.5	0.9	2.42

Table continued on next page.

City	Persons in Household (%)							Average Household Size
	One	Two	Three	Four	Five	Six	Seven or More	
Los Angeles, CA	30.1	28.5	15.2	13.2	6.9	3.1	2.6	2.83
Louisville, KY	33.5	32.9	15.1	10.8	4.8	1.6	0.9	2.44
Madison, WI	35.1	36.5	13.1	9.7	3.7	1.1	0.5	2.20
Manchester, NH	31.0	35.2	16.1	10.5	4.5	1.3	1.0	2.35
McAllen, TX	19.6	28.4	19.1	16.1	9.8	4.2	2.5	3.15
Miami, FL	38.0	29.7	15.3	9.6	4.3	1.6	1.1	2.63
Midland, TX	24.8	32.4	16.0	15.0	7.0	2.8	1.7	2.84
Minneapolis, MN	40.4	31.0	11.9	9.3	3.7	1.8	1.6	2.29
Nashville, TN	34.2	33.1	15.2	10.1	4.2	1.7	1.1	2.40
New Orleans, LA	43.4	29.8	13.3	8.2	3.2	1.1	0.8	2.42
New York, NY	32.3	28.1	16.2	12.4	6.0	2.5	2.1	2.67
Oklahoma City, OK	30.9	32.0	14.9	12.1	5.9	2.5	1.2	2.59
Omaha, NE	32.7	31.6	14.1	11.3	5.8	2.6	1.5	2.48
Orlando, FL	34.2	33.2	16.1	10.4	3.5	1.6	0.6	2.44
Peoria, IL	37.1	31.0	14.0	10.2	4.2	2.0	1.1	2.40
Philadelphia, PA	39.3	28.3	14.3	10.1	4.5	1.9	1.2	2.57
Phoenix, AZ	28.3	30.0	15.0	12.8	7.1	3.9	2.7	2.86
Pittsburgh, PA	42.0	32.6	12.8	7.8	2.9	1.0	0.6	2.08
Portland, OR	33.9	33.8	14.7	10.7	4.2	1.4	1.0	2.35
Providence, RI	32.5	27.7	16.9	12.7	6.7	1.7	1.5	2.66
Provo, UT	14.1	33.5	18.1	15.2	8.2	6.4	4.3	3.20
Raleigh, NC	33.3	31.8	15.4	12.3	4.6	1.6	0.7	2.43
Reno, NV	34.4	31.7	14.7	10.8	4.7	1.9	1.4	2.43
Richmond, VA	42.8	31.1	13.1	7.4	3.4	1.2	0.7	2.35
Roanoke, VA	37.4	33.3	14.6	8.3	3.9	1.4	0.7	2.30
Rochester, MN	29.2	33.7	14.7	14.0	5.0	1.7	1.3	2.44
Salem, OR	29.1	32.0	14.6	13.4	5.8	3.0	1.8	2.64
Salt Lake City, UT	34.8	32.2	14.5	10.0	4.4	2.1	1.7	2.45
San Antonio, TX	28.6	29.4	16.6	13.2	7.1	2.8	1.9	2.91
San Diego, CA	27.7	32.8	16.3	13.0	5.8	2.5	1.6	2.72
San Francisco, CA	36.6	33.6	13.8	9.3	3.5	1.4	1.4	2.35
San Jose, CA	19.6	28.2	18.2	18.1	8.4	3.6	3.5	3.15
Santa Rosa, CA	29.4	32.0	14.7	13.6	5.7	2.3	2.2	2.65
Savannah, GA	33.7	33.3	15.6	9.2	4.8	1.9	1.2	2.50
Seattle, WA	39.1	34.9	12.2	9.1	3.0	0.7	0.7	2.11
Sioux Falls, SD	32.3	34.0	13.5	11.2	5.4	2.2	1.2	2.39
Springfield, IL	36.6	33.5	14.8	9.4	3.1	1.2	1.0	2.22
Tallahassee, FL	33.4	33.8	17.8	9.8	3.6	0.9	0.2	2.33
Tampa, FL	36.3	31.6	14.8	10.7	4.2	1.4	0.7	2.42
Topeka, KS	37.2	32.1	12.9	10.4	4.6	1.7	0.7	2.31
Tyler, TX	32.7	33.2	13.3	11.9	5.4	1.9	1.4	2.67
Virginia Beach, VA	24.3	33.4	18.2	14.8	6.1	1.9	0.9	2.62
Visalia, CA	21.6	28.5	15.4	17.9	9.4	4.3	2.5	3.04
Washington, DC	43.5	30.5	12.3	8.1	3.3	1.2	0.8	2.28
Wilmington, NC	38.2	34.5	14.0	8.8	3.0	0.7	0.5	2.18
Winston-Salem, NC	34.8	30.9	14.8	10.9	5.5	1.9	0.9	2.45
U.S.	27.6	33.8	15.7	13.0	6.0	2.3	1.4	2.63

U.S. Census Bureau, 2013-2017 American Community Survey 5-Year Estimates

Household Size: Metro Area

Metro Area	Persons in Household (%)							Average Household Size
	One	Two	Three	Four	Five	Six	Seven or More	
Albany, NY	32.0	35.1	15.2	11.3	4.2	1.4	0.5	2.43
Albuquerque, NM	30.8	34.2	14.7	11.3	5.4	2.1	1.2	2.58
Allentown, PA	25.9	35.2	16.0	13.5	6.1	2.0	1.0	2.54
Anchorage, AK	24.3	33.7	17.3	13.6	6.3	2.4	2.2	2.85
Ann Arbor, MI	30.1	35.7	13.8	12.4	4.8	1.7	1.1	2.46
Athens, GA	29.6	35.3	15.4	12.1	4.9	1.7	0.7	2.55
Atlanta, GA	26.5	31.3	17.1	14.4	6.5	2.5	1.4	2.77
Austin, TX	27.8	33.3	15.6	13.7	5.9	2.1	1.3	2.70
Baton Rouge, LA	28.1	33.9	17.0	12.0	5.8	1.9	1.0	2.67
Billings, MT	29.4	36.7	14.2	11.2	4.9	2.0	1.3	2.38
Boise City, ID	28.0	33.9	14.3	12.5	6.8	2.4	1.8	2.69
Boston, MA	27.7	32.7	16.7	14.5	5.6	1.7	0.8	2.55
Boulder, CO	27.9	36.7	15.4	13.0	4.7	1.4	0.5	2.44
Cape Coral, FL	28.0	44.3	11.9	8.7	4.2	1.6	0.8	2.61
Cedar Rapids, IA	28.7	36.8	14.1	12.6	4.7	2.0	0.9	2.41
Charleston, SC	28.8	35.3	16.9	11.8	4.6	1.5	0.8	2.59
Charlotte, NC	26.6	33.8	16.9	13.8	5.7	1.9	0.9	2.64
Chicago, IL	28.5	30.7	15.7	13.9	6.8	2.5	1.5	2.70
Clarksville, TN	23.8	33.2	18.4	14.2	6.4	2.4	1.2	2.68
College Station, TX	27.4	34.0	16.2	13.6	5.2	2.2	1.1	2.58
Colorado Springs, CO	24.7	35.2	16.0	13.8	6.5	2.3	1.1	2.62
Columbia, MO	29.9	34.7	14.8	13.3	5.2	1.1	0.7	2.40
Columbia, SC	29.4	34.3	16.1	12.2	5.3	1.5	0.8	2.53
Columbus, OH	28.4	33.7	15.9	13.1	5.7	1.9	1.0	2.54
Dallas, TX	24.8	30.8	16.8	15.2	7.5	2.9	1.7	2.81
Denver, CO	28.2	33.9	15.0	13.3	5.7	2.2	1.3	2.57
Des Moines, IA	27.5	34.2	15.0	13.5	6.4	2.1	0.9	2.53
Durham, NC	30.8	35.7	15.1	11.4	4.5	1.4	0.7	2.42
Edison, NJ	27.8	29.2	17.0	14.6	6.6	2.5	1.9	2.76
El Paso, TX	22.5	27.5	18.4	16.6	9.1	3.6	1.9	3.12
Eugene, OR	29.5	37.9	14.7	11.0	4.1	1.6	0.9	2.39
Evansville, IN	30.0	36.4	14.3	11.5	4.9	1.5	1.0	2.40
Fargo, ND	31.0	34.8	14.9	11.9	5.0	1.4	0.6	2.32
Fayetteville, NC	30.5	32.4	16.6	12.0	5.4	1.8	1.0	2.60
Fort Collins, CO	24.2	39.7	16.6	12.2	4.7	1.6	0.6	2.46
Fort Wayne, IN	28.8	33.9	14.8	12.5	6.1	2.3	1.3	2.53
Fort Worth, TX	24.8	30.8	16.8	15.2	7.5	2.9	1.7	2.81
Gainesville, FL	34.4	35.1	14.5	10.0	3.3	1.8	0.5	2.50
Grand Rapids, MI	24.5	34.9	15.1	14.3	6.8	2.6	1.4	2.65
Greeley, CO	20.5	33.7	16.8	16.1	8.0	2.8	1.8	2.80
Green Bay, WI	27.6	37.0	14.0	12.7	6.1	1.4	0.9	2.42
Greensboro, NC	29.6	35.0	16.0	11.2	5.3	1.7	1.0	2.49
Honolulu, HI	23.4	29.9	17.3	13.9	7.2	3.6	4.5	3.06
Houston, TX	24.2	29.6	17.1	15.5	8.2	3.2	2.0	2.89
Huntsville, AL	29.7	34.3	15.9	12.6	5.0	1.5	0.7	2.48
Indianapolis, IN	29.4	33.4	15.1	13.1	5.8	2.0	0.9	2.57
Jacksonville, FL	27.2	35.6	16.3	12.5	5.3	1.9	0.8	2.62
Kansas City, MO	29.0	33.7	15.1	12.9	5.9	2.0	1.1	2.52
Lafayette, LA	27.1	33.6	17.4	12.8	5.9	2.0	0.9	2.67
Las Cruces, NM	24.5	33.1	17.9	12.9	6.4	2.9	1.9	2.72
Las Vegas, NV	28.2	32.5	15.4	12.5	6.6	2.8	1.7	2.79
Lexington, KY	28.0	35.9	16.3	12.2	5.0	1.6	0.7	2.44
Lincoln, NE	29.4	36.0	14.2	11.8	5.4	1.9	1.0	2.42
Little Rock, AR	29.8	34.3	16.3	11.6	4.9	1.8	0.9	2.57

Table continued on next page.

Metro Area	Persons in Household (%)							Average Household Size
	One	Two	Three	Four	Five	Six	Seven or More	
Los Angeles, CA	24.5	28.4	16.9	15.4	8.1	3.6	2.9	3.02
Louisville, KY	30.1	34.3	15.6	12.0	5.2	1.6	0.8	2.51
Madison, WI	29.5	37.3	14.0	12.1	4.7	1.5	0.7	2.35
Manchester, NH	24.6	36.3	17.3	13.5	5.3	1.6	1.0	2.52
McAllen, TX	15.3	25.0	17.8	17.7	13.1	5.8	5.0	3.57
Miami, FL	28.3	32.1	16.8	13.5	5.7	2.1	1.2	2.86
Midland, TX	24.3	32.1	15.6	15.5	7.3	2.7	2.2	2.88
Minneapolis, MN	27.8	34.0	14.9	13.7	5.9	2.1	1.3	2.55
Nashville, TN	26.6	34.4	16.7	13.4	5.6	2.0	1.1	2.60
New Orleans, LA	32.3	32.4	15.9	11.9	4.7	1.6	1.0	2.58
New York, NY	27.8	29.2	17.0	14.6	6.6	2.5	1.9	2.76
Oklahoma City, OK	28.2	34.1	15.5	12.5	5.9	2.3	1.2	2.61
Omaha, NE	28.4	33.4	14.6	12.9	6.3	2.6	1.3	2.54
Orlando, FL	25.4	34.4	17.1	13.7	5.7	2.2	1.1	2.81
Peoria, IL	30.3	35.6	14.2	11.6	4.9	2.1	1.0	2.44
Philadelphia, PA	29.4	31.8	16.2	13.5	5.7	2.0	1.0	2.62
Phoenix, AZ	26.7	34.3	14.3	12.6	6.6	3.0	2.0	2.76
Pittsburgh, PA	32.6	35.5	14.7	11.0	4.0	1.3	0.5	2.28
Portland, OR	26.9	34.7	15.7	13.4	5.6	2.1	1.4	2.57
Providence, RI	29.6	32.9	16.8	13.2	5.0	1.5	0.7	2.48
Provo, UT	11.9	27.8	15.8	15.8	12.4	9.3	6.6	3.60
Raleigh, NC	25.1	33.0	17.5	15.3	5.9	2.0	0.9	2.65
Reno, NV	29.4	34.6	15.2	11.7	5.1	2.3	1.4	2.53
Richmond, VA	28.6	34.4	16.5	12.4	5.2	1.7	0.8	2.57
Roanoke, VA	30.6	37.3	14.8	10.5	4.2	1.4	0.8	2.35
Rochester, MN	25.9	36.8	14.3	13.9	5.4	2.2	1.1	2.48
Salem, OR	25.2	34.4	15.0	13.2	6.7	3.0	2.0	2.74
Salt Lake City, UT	22.3	30.1	15.9	14.3	8.9	4.9	3.2	3.02
San Antonio, TX	25.5	31.0	16.9	14.1	7.3	2.9	1.9	2.94
San Diego, CA	23.9	32.5	17.1	14.6	6.8	2.8	1.9	2.87
San Francisco, CA	26.7	31.6	16.8	14.5	6.1	2.3	1.7	2.71
San Jose, CA	20.6	29.9	18.5	17.9	7.3	2.9	2.5	2.99
Santa Rosa, CA	28.1	34.1	15.4	13.0	5.6	2.0	1.5	2.59
Savannah, GA	27.3	34.3	17.0	12.7	5.5	1.9	1.0	2.62
Seattle, WA	27.7	34.2	15.9	13.4	5.3	2.0	1.2	2.53
Sioux Falls, SD	28.6	35.0	13.9	12.5	6.2	2.3	1.2	2.48
Springfield, IL	31.5	35.8	14.8	11.0	4.2	1.6	0.7	2.32
Tallahassee, FL	29.4	34.9	17.7	11.4	4.4	1.2	0.7	2.42
Tampa, FL	31.1	36.6	14.5	10.8	4.4	1.5	0.8	2.48
Topeka, KS	30.4	36.0	13.4	11.7	5.2	2.0	1.0	2.43
Tyler, TX	26.7	36.1	14.7	12.4	5.6	2.5	1.7	2.79
Virginia Beach, VA	26.8	34.0	17.6	13.1	5.4	1.8	0.9	2.59
Visalia, CA	17.6	25.7	16.5	17.9	11.6	5.9	4.5	3.35
Washington, DC	26.9	30.5	16.7	14.7	6.5	2.6	1.6	2.76
Wilmington, NC	32.5	36.2	14.5	10.8	3.7	1.4	0.5	2.39
Winston-Salem, NC	29.0	35.6	15.3	12.0	5.1	1.8	0.8	2.47
U.S.	27.6	33.8	15.7	13.0	6.0	2.3	1.4	2.63

Note: Figures cover the Metropolitan Statistical Area (MSA)—see Appendix B for areas included
Source: U.S. Census Bureau, 2013-2017 American Community Survey 5-Year Estimates

Race: City

City	White Alone[1] (%)	Black Alone[1] (%)	Asian Alone[1] (%)	AIAN[2] Alone[1] (%)	NHOPI[3] Alone[1] (%)	Other Race Alone[1] (%)	Two or More Races (%)
Albany, NY	55.1	28.7	7.4	0.3	0.0	2.8	5.6
Albuquerque, NM	73.6	3.3	2.7	4.4	0.1	11.6	4.3
Allentown, PA	59.2	14.1	2.1	0.5	0.1	19.5	4.6
Anchorage, AK	63.7	5.5	9.3	7.3	2.4	2.2	9.7
Ann Arbor, MI	72.0	7.0	15.9	0.4	0.0	0.5	4.2
Athens, GA	63.2	27.5	4.3	0.1	0.0	2.6	2.2
Atlanta, GA	40.1	52.3	4.0	0.3	0.0	1.0	2.3
Austin, TX	75.0	7.6	7.0	0.5	0.1	6.7	3.1
Baton Rouge, LA	38.6	54.8	3.6	0.3	0.0	1.3	1.3
Billings, MT	90.1	0.9	0.6	4.4	0.1	0.8	3.0
Boise City, ID	88.8	1.9	3.3	0.7	0.1	1.6	3.5
Boston, MA	52.8	25.3	9.5	0.4	0.0	7.2	4.9
Boulder, CO	87.9	1.1	5.3	0.3	0.1	1.7	3.5
Cape Coral, FL	90.1	4.4	1.6	0.3	0.0	2.2	1.5
Cedar Rapids, IA	85.8	6.4	3.0	0.2	0.1	1.2	3.2
Charleston, SC	74.4	21.9	1.6	0.1	0.0	0.3	1.6
Charlotte, NC	50.0	35.0	6.2	0.3	0.1	5.5	2.9
Chicago, IL	49.1	30.5	6.2	0.3	0.0	11.2	2.6
Clarksville, TN	66.6	23.4	2.3	0.7	0.5	1.6	4.9
College Station, TX	77.5	8.1	9.8	0.3	0.0	1.7	2.5
Colorado Springs, CO	78.2	6.4	2.9	0.7	0.3	5.9	5.6
Columbia, MO	77.4	10.4	6.0	0.3	0.1	1.0	4.8
Columbia, SC	52.3	40.9	2.6	0.1	0.2	1.2	2.6
Columbus, OH	60.5	28.3	5.2	0.2	0.0	1.7	4.1
Dallas, TX	61.8	24.3	3.4	0.3	0.0	7.7	2.6
Denver, CO	76.9	9.5	3.6	1.0	0.1	5.5	3.4
Des Moines, IA	76.1	11.0	6.0	0.5	0.1	2.5	3.9
Durham, NC	48.0	39.7	5.2	0.3	0.0	3.9	3.0
Edison, NJ	36.4	7.1	49.0	0.3	0.0	4.0	3.3
El Paso, TX	82.0	3.8	1.3	0.6	0.1	9.8	2.4
Eugene, OR	84.0	1.9	4.3	1.0	0.3	3.0	5.4
Evansville, IN	81.7	12.6	0.7	0.3	0.2	1.2	3.3
Fargo, ND	86.2	5.5	3.6	1.1	0.0	0.6	2.9
Fayetteville, NC	45.9	41.5	2.9	0.9	0.3	2.6	5.8
Fort Collins, CO	89.0	1.6	3.1	0.8	0.1	1.9	3.6
Fort Wayne, IN	74.2	15.0	4.3	0.2	0.1	2.1	4.2
Fort Worth, TX	64.4	18.8	3.9	0.4	0.1	9.1	3.4
Gainesville, FL	66.0	22.0	6.9	0.3	0.1	0.9	3.8
Grand Rapids, MI	67.6	19.9	2.1	0.4	0.0	5.1	4.8
Greeley, CO	84.7	2.2	1.3	1.0	0.0	7.9	2.9
Green Bay, WI	77.4	3.8	4.0	3.5	0.0	6.4	4.9
Greensboro, NC	48.0	41.8	4.4	0.4	0.1	2.7	2.5
Honolulu, HI	17.7	1.7	54.1	0.1	8.1	0.9	17.4
Houston, TX	58.5	22.9	6.7	0.3	0.1	9.5	2.0
Huntsville, AL	62.3	30.8	2.6	0.3	0.1	1.3	2.5
Indianapolis, IN	61.8	28.1	3.0	0.3	0.0	3.8	3.0
Jacksonville, FL	59.2	31.0	4.8	0.2	0.1	1.5	3.3
Kansas City, MO	60.3	28.7	2.8	0.4	0.1	4.4	3.3
Lafayette, LA	63.5	31.7	2.1	0.2	0.0	0.6	1.9
Las Cruces, NM	87.1	2.6	1.7	1.5	0.0	4.2	2.9
Las Vegas, NV	62.7	12.2	6.7	0.7	0.7	12.3	4.8
Lexington, KY	75.6	14.5	3.6	0.3	0.1	2.7	3.2
Lincoln, NE	85.3	4.4	4.6	0.6	0.1	1.7	3.3
Little Rock, AR	50.8	41.6	3.1	0.2	0.1	1.7	2.6

Table continued on next page.

City	White Alone[1] (%)	Black Alone[1] (%)	Asian Alone[1] (%)	AIAN[2] Alone[1] (%)	NHOPI[3] Alone[1] (%)	Other Race Alone[1] (%)	Two or More Races (%)
Los Angeles, CA	52.2	8.9	11.7	0.7	0.2	22.9	3.5
Louisville, KY	70.5	23.2	2.5	0.1	0.1	0.7	2.9
Madison, WI	78.8	6.5	8.8	0.4	0.0	1.9	3.5
Manchester, NH	86.5	4.9	4.8	0.2	0.0	1.2	2.4
McAllen, TX	80.1	1.0	2.6	0.3	0.1	14.7	1.2
Miami, FL	75.4	18.4	0.9	0.3	0.0	3.3	1.7
Midland, TX	80.9	7.4	2.1	0.4	0.1	6.9	2.3
Minneapolis, MN	63.9	18.9	6.0	1.2	0.0	4.9	4.9
Nashville, TN	63.1	27.8	3.6	0.3	0.1	2.7	2.5
New Orleans, LA	34.1	59.8	3.0	0.2	0.0	1.2	1.8
New York, NY	42.8	24.3	14.0	0.4	0.1	15.1	3.3
Oklahoma City, OK	67.7	14.5	4.5	2.8	0.1	3.9	6.5
Omaha, NE	78.2	12.3	3.5	0.5	0.1	2.3	3.1
Orlando, FL	60.7	26.1	4.3	0.2	0.0	5.7	2.9
Peoria, IL	60.3	26.7	5.6	0.3	0.0	2.5	4.7
Philadelphia, PA	41.6	42.6	7.1	0.4	0.1	5.6	2.8
Phoenix, AZ	71.9	6.9	3.6	2.0	0.2	11.7	3.7
Pittsburgh, PA	66.6	23.6	5.6	0.2	0.0	0.5	3.4
Portland, OR	77.4	5.7	7.8	0.8	0.6	2.3	5.5
Providence, RI	52.9	15.6	6.2	1.3	0.2	19.5	4.2
Provo, UT	88.7	0.6	2.5	0.6	1.3	2.6	3.6
Raleigh, NC	59.0	28.9	4.6	0.3	0.1	4.6	2.6
Reno, NV	77.5	2.6	6.4	1.2	0.8	6.8	4.7
Richmond, VA	44.7	48.2	2.1	0.4	0.0	1.1	3.5
Roanoke, VA	63.0	28.3	3.0	0.2	0.2	1.9	3.4
Rochester, MN	80.7	7.4	7.3	0.4	0.0	1.2	3.0
Salem, OR	81.0	1.5	2.8	1.1	1.5	5.1	7.0
Salt Lake City, UT	73.7	2.0	5.4	1.3	1.7	12.8	3.1
San Antonio, TX	80.1	7.0	2.7	0.7	0.1	6.7	2.7
San Diego, CA	64.7	6.4	16.8	0.4	0.4	6.2	5.1
San Francisco, CA	47.2	5.3	34.2	0.4	0.4	7.5	5.1
San Jose, CA	40.7	3.0	34.8	0.6	0.4	15.5	5.1
Santa Rosa, CA	68.8	2.5	5.4	1.9	0.6	14.1	6.5
Savannah, GA	39.1	54.7	2.2	0.2	0.1	1.0	2.6
Seattle, WA	68.6	7.1	14.5	0.6	0.4	2.2	6.6
Sioux Falls, SD	85.0	5.4	2.3	2.4	0.0	1.8	3.1
Springfield, IL	73.2	19.9	2.8	0.1	0.0	0.8	3.2
Tallahassee, FL	56.9	35.2	4.2	0.2	0.0	1.0	2.5
Tampa, FL	65.2	24.2	4.2	0.3	0.1	2.6	3.4
Topeka, KS	78.9	10.4	1.5	0.8	0.1	2.9	5.4
Tyler, TX	67.8	24.8	2.4	0.3	0.2	2.6	1.9
Virginia Beach, VA	67.2	19.0	6.6	0.2	0.1	1.7	5.1
Visalia, CA	78.3	2.0	5.7	1.2	0.1	8.1	4.6
Washington, DC	40.7	47.7	3.8	0.3	0.0	4.6	2.9
Wilmington, NC	76.7	18.4	1.4	0.4	0.1	1.2	1.8
Winston-Salem, NC	56.2	34.7	2.2	0.3	0.1	4.1	2.3
U.S.	73.0	12.7	5.4	0.8	0.2	4.8	3.1

Note: (1) Alone is defined as not being in combination with one or more other races; (2) American Indian and Alaska Native; (3) Native Hawaiian and Other Pacific Islander
Source: U.S. Census Bureau, 2013-2017 American Community Survey 5-Year Estimates

Race: Metro Area

Metro Area	White Alone[1] (%)	Black Alone[1] (%)	Asian Alone[1] (%)	AIAN[2] Alone[1] (%)	NHOPI[3] Alone[1] (%)	Other Race Alone[1] (%)	Two or More Races (%)
Albany, NY	83.3	7.8	4.3	0.2	0.0	1.4	3.0
Albuquerque, NM	74.3	2.6	2.1	5.8	0.1	11.0	4.1
Allentown, PA	84.1	5.6	2.8	0.2	0.0	4.4	2.8
Anchorage, AK	68.6	4.4	7.3	6.7	1.8	1.8	9.4
Ann Arbor, MI	73.9	11.9	8.7	0.3	0.0	0.7	4.4
Athens, GA	72.0	20.1	3.6	0.1	0.0	2.1	2.0
Atlanta, GA	54.6	33.7	5.6	0.3	0.0	3.2	2.5
Austin, TX	77.7	7.3	5.5	0.4	0.1	5.8	3.3
Baton Rouge, LA	59.6	35.4	2.1	0.2	0.0	1.0	1.7
Billings, MT	91.3	0.7	0.6	4.0	0.1	0.6	2.7
Boise City, ID	89.8	1.0	2.0	0.8	0.2	3.3	3.0
Boston, MA	77.0	8.1	7.5	0.2	0.0	4.0	3.2
Boulder, CO	88.6	0.9	4.5	0.5	0.1	2.4	2.9
Cape Coral, FL	84.7	8.7	1.6	0.2	0.1	3.0	1.8
Cedar Rapids, IA	90.2	4.3	1.9	0.2	0.1	0.8	2.5
Charleston, SC	67.6	26.3	1.7	0.3	0.0	1.4	2.5
Charlotte, NC	67.9	22.3	3.4	0.3	0.0	3.5	2.4
Chicago, IL	66.0	16.7	6.3	0.2	0.0	8.1	2.5
Clarksville, TN	72.4	19.4	1.9	0.6	0.4	1.2	4.1
College Station, TX	75.2	11.2	5.2	0.4	0.0	5.0	2.9
Colorado Springs, CO	80.1	6.0	2.7	0.7	0.4	4.6	5.6
Columbia, MO	81.4	8.5	4.2	0.3	0.1	1.0	4.4
Columbia, SC	60.2	33.3	2.0	0.2	0.1	1.7	2.6
Columbus, OH	76.6	15.1	3.8	0.2	0.0	1.1	3.2
Dallas, TX	69.4	15.4	6.3	0.4	0.1	5.4	2.9
Denver, CO	81.7	5.6	4.1	0.8	0.1	4.3	3.5
Des Moines, IA	87.0	5.1	3.9	0.2	0.1	1.2	2.5
Durham, NC	61.9	26.8	4.8	0.3	0.0	3.3	2.8
Edison, NJ	58.3	17.1	10.9	0.3	0.0	10.5	2.9
El Paso, TX	81.1	3.4	1.1	0.7	0.1	11.2	2.3
Eugene, OR	87.7	1.1	2.6	1.1	0.2	2.3	5.0
Evansville, IN	88.6	6.8	1.3	0.2	0.1	0.8	2.3
Fargo, ND	89.3	3.9	2.5	1.1	0.0	0.6	2.6
Fayetteville, NC	50.3	36.1	2.3	2.3	0.2	2.9	5.8
Fort Collins, CO	91.2	0.9	2.1	0.6	0.1	1.9	3.2
Fort Wayne, IN	81.9	9.9	3.1	0.2	0.0	1.6	3.2
Fort Worth, TX	69.4	15.4	6.3	0.4	0.1	5.4	2.9
Gainesville, FL	70.9	19.3	5.5	0.3	0.1	0.8	3.1
Grand Rapids, MI	84.7	6.5	2.5	0.4	0.0	2.7	3.1
Greeley, CO	88.8	1.1	1.4	0.7	0.1	5.2	2.7
Green Bay, WI	87.3	1.9	2.6	2.1	0.0	3.2	2.8
Greensboro, NC	64.0	26.7	3.6	0.4	0.1	3.1	2.2
Honolulu, HI	21.1	2.3	42.9	0.1	9.4	1.0	23.2
Houston, TX	65.7	17.2	7.5	0.4	0.1	6.8	2.3
Huntsville, AL	71.2	21.9	2.3	0.7	0.1	1.1	2.8
Indianapolis, IN	77.3	14.9	2.9	0.2	0.0	2.2	2.4
Jacksonville, FL	70.0	21.5	3.8	0.2	0.1	1.3	3.1
Kansas City, MO	78.6	12.5	2.7	0.4	0.1	2.6	3.1
Lafayette, LA	70.7	24.6	1.7	0.2	0.0	0.9	2.0
Las Cruces, NM	88.3	1.8	1.0	1.1	0.0	5.9	1.9
Las Vegas, NV	61.6	11.2	9.6	0.6	0.7	11.2	5.0
Lexington, KY	81.2	10.9	2.6	0.3	0.0	2.2	2.8
Lincoln, NE	87.0	3.9	4.0	0.5	0.1	1.5	3.0
Little Rock, AR	71.1	23.0	1.6	0.3	0.1	1.4	2.5

Table continued on next page.

Metro Area	White Alone[1] (%)	Black Alone[1] (%)	Asian Alone[1] (%)	AIAN[2] Alone[1] (%)	NHOPI[3] Alone[1] (%)	Other Race Alone[1] (%)	Two or More Races (%)
Los Angeles, CA	54.2	6.7	15.7	0.6	0.3	18.7	3.8
Louisville, KY	80.3	14.2	1.9	0.2	0.0	0.8	2.6
Madison, WI	86.1	4.3	4.7	0.3	0.0	1.7	2.7
Manchester, NH	90.3	2.5	3.8	0.1	0.0	0.9	2.3
McAllen, TX	88.9	0.6	1.0	0.2	0.0	8.1	1.2
Miami, FL	70.9	21.4	2.5	0.2	0.0	2.9	2.2
Midland, TX	82.8	6.0	1.9	0.5	0.1	6.6	2.1
Minneapolis, MN	79.6	8.0	6.4	0.6	0.0	2.1	3.3
Nashville, TN	78.1	15.2	2.6	0.3	0.1	1.6	2.2
New Orleans, LA	57.8	35.0	2.9	0.3	0.0	2.0	1.9
New York, NY	58.3	17.1	10.9	0.3	0.0	10.5	2.9
Oklahoma City, OK	73.9	10.2	3.1	3.4	0.1	2.6	6.6
Omaha, NE	84.7	7.6	2.6	0.4	0.1	1.8	2.8
Orlando, FL	70.5	16.4	4.2	0.3	0.1	5.2	3.3
Peoria, IL	84.8	9.2	2.4	0.2	0.0	1.0	2.5
Philadelphia, PA	67.3	21.0	5.8	0.2	0.0	3.1	2.6
Phoenix, AZ	78.2	5.3	3.7	2.2	0.2	6.9	3.5
Pittsburgh, PA	86.9	8.1	2.2	0.1	0.0	0.3	2.3
Portland, OR	81.6	2.8	6.3	0.8	0.5	3.2	4.8
Providence, RI	82.5	5.6	3.0	0.4	0.1	5.6	2.9
Provo, UT	92.0	0.6	1.5	0.5	0.8	1.9	2.7
Raleigh, NC	68.2	19.9	5.3	0.4	0.0	3.4	2.7
Reno, NV	79.7	2.3	5.3	1.6	0.6	6.2	4.3
Richmond, VA	61.6	29.8	3.7	0.3	0.0	1.6	3.0
Roanoke, VA	81.3	13.1	2.1	0.2	0.1	1.0	2.2
Rochester, MN	88.3	4.1	4.3	0.3	0.0	0.8	2.2
Salem, OR	83.5	1.1	2.0	1.0	0.7	5.5	6.1
Salt Lake City, UT	80.7	1.7	3.7	0.8	1.5	8.7	3.0
San Antonio, TX	80.7	6.7	2.4	0.6	0.1	6.5	3.1
San Diego, CA	70.8	5.0	11.7	0.6	0.4	6.3	5.1
San Francisco, CA	50.9	7.5	25.3	0.5	0.7	9.2	5.9
San Jose, CA	46.6	2.5	34.2	0.5	0.4	11.0	4.9
Santa Rosa, CA	75.3	1.6	3.9	1.1	0.3	12.4	5.3
Savannah, GA	59.6	33.5	2.2	0.3	0.1	1.6	2.6
Seattle, WA	70.2	5.6	12.8	0.9	0.9	3.2	6.5
Sioux Falls, SD	88.7	3.8	1.6	1.9	0.0	1.3	2.6
Springfield, IL	83.1	12.0	1.8	0.1	0.1	0.6	2.3
Tallahassee, FL	61.2	33.0	2.6	0.2	0.0	0.9	2.1
Tampa, FL	78.4	12.0	3.3	0.3	0.1	2.9	2.9
Topeka, KS	85.5	6.2	1.0	1.1	0.1	1.8	4.4
Tyler, TX	76.9	17.6	1.6	0.4	0.1	1.9	1.6
Virginia Beach, VA	59.6	30.6	3.8	0.3	0.1	1.6	4.1
Visalia, CA	78.9	1.6	3.5	1.3	0.1	11.5	3.1
Washington, DC	54.6	25.4	9.9	0.3	0.1	5.8	3.9
Wilmington, NC	80.0	14.5	1.1	0.3	0.1	1.8	2.2
Winston-Salem, NC	76.0	17.7	1.7	0.3	0.1	2.4	1.8
U.S.	73.0	12.7	5.4	0.8	0.2	4.8	3.1

Note: (1) Figures cover the Metropolitan Statistical Area (MSA)—see Appendix B for areas included; (1) Alone is defined as not being in combination with one or more other races; (2) American Indian and Alaska Native; (3) Native Hawaiian & Other Pacific Islander
Source: U.S. Census Bureau, 2013-2017 American Community Survey 5-Year Estimates

Hispanic Origin: City

City	Hispanic or Latino (%)	Mexican (%)	Puerto Rican (%)	Cuban (%)	Other Hispanic or Latino (%)
Albany, NY	9.8	0.8	5.4	0.3	3.2
Albuquerque, NM	48.5	28.8	0.7	0.4	18.7
Allentown, PA	50.6	1.8	28.7	0.6	19.6
Anchorage, AK	8.9	5.0	1.1	0.1	2.6
Ann Arbor, MI	4.4	1.9	0.3	0.2	1.9
Athens, GA	10.7	6.9	0.9	0.3	2.7
Atlanta, GA	4.6	2.3	0.7	0.3	1.3
Austin, TX	34.5	28.3	0.8	0.6	4.8
Baton Rouge, LA	3.4	1.2	0.2	0.2	1.8
Billings, MT	6.3	4.5	0.4	0.2	1.2
Boise City, ID	8.7	7.2	0.2	0.1	1.2
Boston, MA	19.4	1.0	5.2	0.4	12.7
Boulder, CO	9.3	5.8	0.4	0.3	2.8
Cape Coral, FL	20.2	2.0	5.1	6.3	6.8
Cedar Rapids, IA	3.8	2.9	0.1	0.0	0.8
Charleston, SC	2.9	1.3	0.4	0.2	0.9
Charlotte, NC	14.0	5.6	1.0	0.5	6.8
Chicago, IL	29.0	21.7	3.8	0.3	3.2
Clarksville, TN	11.3	5.1	3.6	0.3	2.3
College Station, TX	14.8	11.0	0.4	0.4	3.1
Colorado Springs, CO	17.6	11.1	1.3	0.4	4.8
Columbia, MO	3.2	2.0	0.1	0.1	1.0
Columbia, SC	5.8	2.5	1.3	0.3	1.6
Columbus, OH	6.0	3.4	0.8	0.1	1.6
Dallas, TX	41.7	36.0	0.5	0.3	4.9
Denver, CO	30.5	24.7	0.6	0.2	5.0
Des Moines, IA	13.1	10.2	0.3	0.2	2.4
Durham, NC	14.0	6.8	0.9	0.2	6.0
Edison, NJ	9.6	1.3	2.5	0.8	5.0
El Paso, TX	80.8	76.4	1.1	0.1	3.1
Eugene, OR	9.5	7.4	0.4	0.1	1.6
Evansville, IN	3.0	2.5	0.2	0.0	0.2
Fargo, ND	2.8	1.8	0.3	0.0	0.7
Fayetteville, NC	12.0	4.2	3.8	0.4	3.6
Fort Collins, CO	11.8	8.2	0.4	0.1	3.0
Fort Wayne, IN	8.7	6.2	0.6	0.1	1.8
Fort Worth, TX	34.8	30.8	1.0	0.2	2.8
Gainesville, FL	10.7	1.3	3.1	2.4	4.0
Grand Rapids, MI	15.3	9.1	1.3	0.3	4.6
Greeley, CO	39.4	30.8	0.5	0.3	7.9
Green Bay, WI	14.4	10.9	1.4	0.2	2.0
Greensboro, NC	7.3	4.6	0.7	0.2	1.8
Honolulu, HI	7.0	1.9	1.8	0.2	3.0
Houston, TX	44.5	32.3	0.5	0.7	10.8
Huntsville, AL	5.5	3.5	0.6	0.1	1.2
Indianapolis, IN	10.1	7.1	0.6	0.2	2.2
Jacksonville, FL	9.1	1.9	2.9	1.1	3.2
Kansas City, MO	10.2	7.8	0.3	0.3	1.9
Lafayette, LA	4.1	1.9	0.4	0.2	1.6
Las Cruces, NM	58.6	53.1	0.7	0.1	4.8
Las Vegas, NV	32.7	24.7	1.0	1.3	5.6
Lexington, KY	7.0	4.7	0.8	0.2	1.3
Lincoln, NE	7.3	5.4	0.2	0.2	1.5
Little Rock, AR	6.8	4.5	0.4	0.2	1.6
Los Angeles, CA	48.7	32.7	0.5	0.4	15.2

Table continued on next page.

City	Hispanic or Latino (%)	Mexican (%)	Puerto Rican (%)	Cuban (%)	Other Hispanic or Latino (%)
Louisville, KY	5.2	2.2	0.4	1.5	1.0
Madison, WI	7.0	4.6	0.5	0.1	1.7
Manchester, NH	9.4	1.8	3.7	0.1	3.8
McAllen, TX	85.2	80.7	0.6	0.3	3.6
Miami, FL	72.2	1.9	3.4	35.6	31.3
Midland, TX	42.8	39.9	0.5	0.3	2.2
Minneapolis, MN	9.8	6.1	0.5	0.2	3.1
Nashville, TN	10.4	6.1	0.6	0.4	3.2
New Orleans, LA	5.5	1.2	0.3	0.4	3.7
New York, NY	29.1	4.0	8.4	0.5	16.2
Oklahoma City, OK	19.1	16.0	0.3	0.1	2.7
Omaha, NE	13.7	10.6	0.3	0.2	2.5
Orlando, FL	29.7	1.7	14.9	2.7	10.3
Peoria, IL	6.0	4.7	0.3	0.1	0.9
Philadelphia, PA	14.1	1.3	8.7	0.3	3.9
Phoenix, AZ	42.5	38.6	0.6	0.3	2.9
Pittsburgh, PA	2.9	0.9	0.8	0.2	1.1
Portland, OR	9.7	7.1	0.4	0.3	1.9
Providence, RI	42.0	1.8	8.2	0.3	31.7
Provo, UT	16.3	11.2	0.3	0.2	4.6
Raleigh, NC	11.0	5.5	0.9	0.3	4.3
Reno, NV	25.2	19.5	0.5	0.2	5.0
Richmond, VA	6.5	1.8	0.7	0.2	3.8
Roanoke, VA	6.0	2.3	0.9	0.6	2.3
Rochester, MN	5.8	4.0	0.5	0.1	1.2
Salem, OR	22.4	20.0	0.5	0.1	1.8
Salt Lake City, UT	21.3	17.0	0.3	0.2	3.8
San Antonio, TX	64.0	57.6	1.1	0.2	5.0
San Diego, CA	30.0	26.4	0.7	0.2	2.7
San Francisco, CA	15.3	7.8	0.6	0.3	6.6
San Jose, CA	32.3	28.1	0.5	0.2	3.5
Santa Rosa, CA	31.8	28.2	0.6	0.1	3.0
Savannah, GA	4.8	1.8	1.2	0.3	1.5
Seattle, WA	6.5	3.8	0.4	0.3	2.0
Sioux Falls, SD	5.0	2.9	0.3	0.0	1.8
Springfield, IL	2.6	1.5	0.5	0.1	0.5
Tallahassee, FL	6.8	1.2	1.5	1.4	2.7
Tampa, FL	25.1	3.3	7.7	7.4	6.8
Topeka, KS	14.3	12.3	0.7	0.1	1.2
Tyler, TX	22.3	19.9	0.4	0.1	1.9
Virginia Beach, VA	7.8	2.3	2.4	0.3	2.8
Visalia, CA	50.3	47.7	0.3	0.1	2.1
Washington, DC	10.7	2.0	0.7	0.4	7.5
Wilmington, NC	6.3	3.2	0.5	0.2	2.5
Winston-Salem, NC	14.9	9.4	1.5	0.2	3.7
U.S.	17.6	11.1	1.7	0.7	4.1

Note: Persons of Hispanic or Latino origin can be of any race
Source: U.S. Census Bureau, 2013-2017 American Community Survey 5-Year Estimates

Hispanic Origin: Metro Area

Metro Area	Hispanic or Latino (%)	Mexican (%)	Puerto Rican (%)	Cuban (%)	Other Hispanic or Latino (%)
Albany, NY	4.9	0.7	2.3	0.2	1.6
Albuquerque, NM	48.5	28.6	0.6	0.3	19.0
Allentown, PA	15.8	1.2	8.7	0.3	5.5
Anchorage, AK	7.8	4.4	1.0	0.1	2.3
Ann Arbor, MI	4.5	2.4	0.3	0.2	1.7
Athens, GA	8.3	5.2	0.7	0.2	2.2
Atlanta, GA	10.5	5.8	1.0	0.4	3.4
Austin, TX	32.2	26.9	0.8	0.5	4.0
Baton Rouge, LA	3.8	1.7	0.3	0.1	1.6
Billings, MT	5.2	3.9	0.3	0.1	0.9
Boise City, ID	13.3	11.5	0.3	0.1	1.4
Boston, MA	10.6	0.7	2.8	0.2	6.8
Boulder, CO	13.8	10.3	0.4	0.3	2.8
Cape Coral, FL	20.2	5.8	4.3	3.9	6.2
Cedar Rapids, IA	2.8	2.1	0.1	0.0	0.6
Charleston, SC	5.4	2.8	0.8	0.1	1.6
Charlotte, NC	9.8	4.8	0.9	0.4	3.8
Chicago, IL	21.8	17.2	2.1	0.2	2.2
Clarksville, TN	8.7	4.3	2.4	0.3	1.7
College Station, TX	24.4	21.0	0.2	0.2	3.0
Colorado Springs, CO	16.1	9.9	1.5	0.3	4.4
Columbia, MO	3.3	2.2	0.1	0.2	0.8
Columbia, SC	5.4	2.8	1.0	0.2	1.4
Columbus, OH	3.9	2.1	0.6	0.1	1.2
Dallas, TX	28.4	23.8	0.7	0.2	3.7
Denver, CO	22.9	17.6	0.5	0.2	4.6
Des Moines, IA	7.2	5.4	0.2	0.1	1.4
Durham, NC	11.4	6.2	0.7	0.2	4.3
Edison, NJ	24.1	3.1	6.3	0.7	14.0
El Paso, TX	82.2	78.0	1.1	0.1	3.0
Eugene, OR	8.4	6.5	0.3	0.1	1.5
Evansville, IN	2.2	1.6	0.2	0.1	0.4
Fargo, ND	3.0	2.1	0.2	0.0	0.6
Fayetteville, NC	11.4	4.5	3.8	0.3	2.9
Fort Collins, CO	11.2	8.5	0.3	0.1	2.4
Fort Wayne, IN	6.5	4.6	0.5	0.1	1.3
Fort Worth, TX	28.4	23.8	0.7	0.2	3.7
Gainesville, FL	9.0	1.5	2.5	1.8	3.2
Grand Rapids, MI	9.2	6.5	0.8	0.3	1.7
Greeley, CO	29.0	23.5	0.4	0.2	4.9
Green Bay, WI	7.2	5.4	0.8	0.1	0.9
Greensboro, NC	8.1	5.7	0.6	0.2	1.6
Honolulu, HI	9.6	2.8	3.0	0.2	3.6
Houston, TX	36.7	27.8	0.6	0.5	7.7
Huntsville, AL	5.0	3.1	0.7	0.2	1.0
Indianapolis, IN	6.5	4.5	0.4	0.1	1.5
Jacksonville, FL	8.2	1.8	2.7	1.0	2.7
Kansas City, MO	8.8	6.8	0.3	0.2	1.5
Lafayette, LA	3.9	2.2	0.3	0.1	1.2
Las Cruces, NM	67.7	63.2	0.5	0.2	3.8
Las Vegas, NV	30.7	23.0	1.1	1.3	5.3
Lexington, KY	6.0	4.1	0.6	0.1	1.2
Lincoln, NE	6.5	4.7	0.2	0.2	1.4
Little Rock, AR	5.1	3.6	0.3	0.1	1.1
Los Angeles, CA	45.0	35.1	0.4	0.4	9.1

Table continued on next page.

Metro Area	Hispanic or Latino (%)	Mexican (%)	Puerto Rican (%)	Cuban (%)	Other Hispanic or Latino (%)
Louisville, KY	4.5	2.3	0.4	0.8	0.9
Madison, WI	5.7	3.8	0.4	0.1	1.3
Manchester, NH	6.3	1.4	2.1	0.2	2.6
McAllen, TX	91.8	88.7	0.3	0.1	2.7
Miami, FL	44.2	2.5	3.9	18.9	18.9
Midland, TX	43.3	40.6	0.5	0.3	1.9
Minneapolis, MN	5.7	3.8	0.3	0.1	1.5
Nashville, TN	7.0	4.4	0.5	0.2	1.9
New Orleans, LA	8.7	1.9	0.5	0.6	5.7
New York, NY	24.1	3.1	6.3	0.7	14.0
Oklahoma City, OK	12.8	10.5	0.3	0.1	1.9
Omaha, NE	10.1	7.8	0.3	0.1	1.8
Orlando, FL	29.0	2.9	14.8	2.2	9.1
Peoria, IL	3.4	2.6	0.2	0.1	0.5
Philadelphia, PA	9.0	1.8	4.5	0.2	2.5
Phoenix, AZ	30.5	27.1	0.7	0.2	2.5
Pittsburgh, PA	1.6	0.5	0.5	0.1	0.6
Portland, OR	11.6	9.3	0.3	0.2	1.8
Providence, RI	12.1	0.8	3.9	0.2	7.2
Provo, UT	11.2	7.7	0.2	0.1	3.3
Raleigh, NC	10.4	5.7	1.1	0.3	3.2
Reno, NV	23.7	18.6	0.5	0.2	4.5
Richmond, VA	5.8	1.6	1.0	0.2	3.1
Roanoke, VA	3.7	1.7	0.5	0.3	1.2
Rochester, MN	4.3	3.1	0.3	0.1	0.8
Salem, OR	23.6	21.3	0.5	0.1	1.7
Salt Lake City, UT	17.6	13.1	0.4	0.1	4.0
San Antonio, TX	55.1	49.1	1.2	0.2	4.5
San Diego, CA	33.4	29.8	0.7	0.2	2.7
San Francisco, CA	21.9	14.4	0.7	0.2	6.6
San Jose, CA	27.0	23.0	0.5	0.1	3.4
Santa Rosa, CA	26.4	22.6	0.5	0.1	3.2
Savannah, GA	5.9	2.7	1.4	0.2	1.6
Seattle, WA	9.7	6.9	0.5	0.2	2.1
Sioux Falls, SD	4.0	2.3	0.2	0.0	1.4
Springfield, IL	2.2	1.3	0.4	0.1	0.4
Tallahassee, FL	6.3	1.8	1.3	1.1	2.2
Tampa, FL	18.4	3.7	6.1	3.7	5.0
Topeka, KS	9.9	8.5	0.5	0.1	0.8
Tyler, TX	19.0	17.2	0.4	0.1	1.4
Virginia Beach, VA	6.4	2.0	2.0	0.3	2.1
Visalia, CA	63.6	61.4	0.2	0.1	1.8
Washington, DC	15.3	2.2	1.0	0.3	11.7
Wilmington, NC	5.7	3.2	0.5	0.2	1.8
Winston-Salem, NC	10.0	6.5	0.9	0.2	2.4
U.S.	17.6	11.1	1.7	0.7	4.1

Note: Persons of Hispanic or Latino origin can be of any race; Figures cover the Metropolitan Statistical Area (MSA)—see Appendix B for areas included
Source: U.S. Census Bureau, 2013-2017 American Community Survey 5-Year Estimates

Age: City

City	Percent of Population									Median Age
	Under Age 5	Age 5–19	Age 20–34	Age 35–44	Age 45–54	Age 55–64	Age 65–74	Age 75–84	Age 85+	
Albany, NY	5.5	18.1	32.4	10.5	10.6	10.3	6.7	3.4	2.4	30.9
Albuquerque, NM	6.3	19.2	22.9	12.9	12.4	12.2	8.1	4.3	1.7	36.2
Allentown, PA	7.6	22.8	24.4	12.3	11.4	9.8	6.1	3.7	2.0	31.8
Anchorage, AK	7.4	19.7	25.7	12.8	12.9	12.0	6.2	2.3	0.9	33.1
Ann Arbor, MI	4.1	18.9	38.7	9.5	8.7	8.9	6.5	3.2	1.6	27.5
Athens, GA	5.5	20.9	35.2	11.0	8.8	8.8	5.8	2.7	1.3	27.2
Atlanta, GA	5.8	16.8	30.1	14.2	12.2	9.6	6.8	3.2	1.3	33.5
Austin, TX	6.7	17.3	30.3	15.7	12.0	9.6	5.2	2.2	1.0	32.7
Baton Rouge, LA	6.6	19.1	29.7	10.2	10.4	11.0	7.4	3.8	1.7	31.1
Billings, MT	6.5	18.4	22.2	12.3	11.7	12.6	8.6	4.9	2.6	37.0
Boise City, ID	5.8	19.4	23.4	13.7	12.5	12.2	7.8	3.4	1.9	36.0
Boston, MA	5.2	15.7	34.6	12.5	11.1	9.9	6.2	3.2	1.5	32.0
Boulder, CO	3.4	18.8	37.0	11.4	9.9	9.2	6.0	2.7	1.8	28.6
Cape Coral, FL	4.5	17.5	15.1	11.5	14.7	14.9	12.8	6.1	3.0	45.9
Cedar Rapids, IA	6.9	19.0	22.9	12.7	12.2	12.1	7.6	4.4	2.3	36.0
Charleston, SC	5.9	15.4	29.8	12.2	10.7	12.2	8.6	3.4	1.9	34.4
Charlotte, NC	6.9	19.8	24.9	15.2	13.1	10.3	5.9	2.7	1.1	33.9
Chicago, IL	6.6	17.6	27.4	14.0	12.1	10.7	6.7	3.5	1.4	34.1
Clarksville, TN	9.2	20.5	31.0	12.7	10.3	8.2	5.0	2.4	0.6	29.4
College Station, TX	5.3	22.7	44.7	8.7	6.9	5.8	3.7	1.6	0.7	22.7
Colorado Springs, CO	6.7	19.7	24.2	12.6	12.5	11.6	7.5	3.7	1.5	34.6
Columbia, MO	5.9	18.7	36.0	10.8	9.6	9.2	5.5	3.0	1.3	27.6
Columbia, SC	5.1	23.0	32.3	10.5	10.0	9.4	5.8	2.8	1.2	28.3
Columbus, OH	7.4	18.4	29.2	13.1	11.9	10.4	5.8	2.6	1.3	32.2
Dallas, TX	7.8	20.0	26.3	13.9	12.0	10.3	5.8	2.8	1.2	32.5
Denver, CO	6.4	16.0	28.7	15.7	11.6	10.3	6.6	3.1	1.6	34.4
Des Moines, IA	7.3	20.1	24.1	13.0	12.2	11.6	6.7	3.3	1.6	33.9
Durham, NC	7.0	18.5	26.9	14.3	12.0	10.6	6.5	2.8	1.5	33.6
Edison, NJ	6.2	17.5	19.3	15.6	14.1	13.3	7.8	4.1	2.0	39.3
El Paso, TX	7.6	22.5	22.7	12.5	12.0	10.5	6.7	3.9	1.6	32.8
Eugene, OR	4.7	18.0	28.4	11.8	10.6	11.5	8.8	3.7	2.5	34.1
Evansville, IN	6.4	17.6	23.2	11.8	12.6	12.9	8.2	4.5	2.8	37.2
Fargo, ND	6.9	17.8	32.7	11.2	10.1	10.2	5.7	3.4	2.0	30.3
Fayetteville, NC	7.5	19.2	30.7	11.0	10.3	9.9	6.3	3.6	1.3	30.0
Fort Collins, CO	5.4	19.5	33.7	11.9	9.9	9.5	5.8	2.9	1.4	29.2
Fort Wayne, IN	7.2	21.1	22.0	12.3	12.2	11.9	7.9	3.6	1.9	34.9
Fort Worth, TX	8.1	23.0	23.5	14.0	12.4	9.8	5.6	2.6	1.1	32.2
Gainesville, FL	3.8	18.8	42.0	8.7	8.1	9.0	5.6	2.7	1.5	26.0
Grand Rapids, MI	7.4	19.4	29.6	11.3	10.3	10.6	5.7	3.4	2.4	31.1
Greeley, CO	6.9	23.9	24.5	11.9	10.9	10.1	6.5	3.5	1.7	30.7
Green Bay, WI	7.8	19.8	24.0	11.9	12.5	11.8	6.7	3.6	1.9	34.0
Greensboro, NC	6.2	19.6	24.3	12.7	12.7	11.3	7.7	3.8	1.8	35.0
Honolulu, HI	5.2	14.1	22.4	12.8	13.3	12.9	9.7	5.6	4.0	41.4
Houston, TX	7.8	19.8	26.0	14.0	12.0	10.3	6.0	2.9	1.2	32.9
Huntsville, AL	6.6	17.7	23.4	11.5	13.0	12.7	8.3	5.0	1.9	36.9
Indianapolis, IN	7.4	19.7	24.1	12.9	12.6	11.8	6.6	3.4	1.5	34.1
Jacksonville, FL	6.9	18.5	23.4	12.7	13.3	12.3	7.7	3.4	1.6	35.8
Kansas City, MO	7.0	18.4	24.4	13.2	12.8	12.0	7.3	3.5	1.7	35.2
Lafayette, LA	5.6	19.0	25.9	11.0	12.5	12.9	7.4	4.1	1.6	34.7
Las Cruces, NM	6.8	20.7	26.2	10.7	10.2	10.5	8.2	4.8	1.8	32.6
Las Vegas, NV	6.4	19.9	20.5	13.7	13.6	11.7	8.6	4.2	1.3	37.4
Lexington, KY	6.2	18.4	26.4	13.2	12.2	11.4	7.2	3.4	1.6	34.3
Lincoln, NE	6.7	19.9	26.9	12.2	10.7	11.1	7.2	3.6	1.7	32.4
Little Rock, AR	6.5	19.5	22.4	13.3	12.0	13.0	7.8	3.4	2.0	36.0

Table continued on next page.

City	Percent of Population									Median Age
	Under Age 5	Age 5–19	Age 20–34	Age 35–44	Age 45–54	Age 55–64	Age 65–74	Age 75–84	Age 85+	
Los Angeles, CA	6.2	17.9	25.6	14.5	13.3	10.9	6.5	3.5	1.7	35.2
Louisville, KY	6.6	18.7	21.6	12.4	13.3	13.2	8.0	4.1	1.9	37.2
Madison, WI	5.2	16.4	35.3	12.0	10.3	9.8	6.4	3.1	1.6	31.0
Manchester, NH	5.6	16.2	25.8	12.6	14.0	12.4	7.2	3.7	2.3	36.5
McAllen, TX	7.9	23.8	21.2	13.4	11.4	9.8	6.7	4.2	1.5	32.9
Miami, FL	6.2	13.4	22.8	15.1	14.3	11.5	8.6	5.3	2.7	40.0
Midland, TX	8.5	21.3	24.6	12.6	11.5	10.8	5.6	3.3	1.7	32.1
Minneapolis, MN	6.7	16.8	32.1	13.7	11.5	10.1	5.8	2.3	1.1	32.1
Nashville, TN	6.9	17.1	27.3	13.8	12.2	11.4	6.6	3.3	1.3	34.1
New Orleans, LA	6.0	16.8	25.7	12.8	12.6	13.1	7.8	3.5	1.6	35.9
New York, NY	6.5	16.7	24.9	13.8	13.0	11.5	7.6	4.1	1.9	36.2
Oklahoma City, OK	7.8	20.2	23.4	13.2	12.0	11.5	7.0	3.4	1.5	34.1
Omaha, NE	7.3	20.6	23.2	12.5	12.4	11.9	7.1	3.5	1.7	34.3
Orlando, FL	7.1	16.2	29.6	14.9	12.2	9.6	6.3	2.8	1.4	33.3
Peoria, IL	7.6	20.4	22.9	11.8	11.4	11.6	7.9	4.1	2.3	34.3
Philadelphia, PA	6.9	18.1	26.3	12.2	12.0	11.5	7.2	3.9	1.8	34.1
Phoenix, AZ	7.5	21.8	23.1	13.9	13.0	10.5	6.1	2.7	1.2	33.3
Pittsburgh, PA	4.9	15.6	33.0	10.4	10.1	11.8	7.5	4.3	2.5	32.9
Portland, OR	5.6	14.8	26.0	16.9	13.0	11.7	7.4	3.0	1.6	36.8
Providence, RI	6.3	21.9	29.5	12.4	11.0	9.2	5.2	2.8	1.6	29.8
Provo, UT	8.0	20.9	46.2	8.2	5.5	5.3	3.0	2.0	0.9	23.7
Raleigh, NC	6.2	19.4	27.6	14.9	12.7	9.5	5.8	2.7	1.2	33.1
Reno, NV	6.4	18.4	24.5	12.4	12.7	11.8	8.5	3.8	1.5	35.5
Richmond, VA	6.1	16.0	30.4	11.5	11.9	12.3	7.0	3.3	1.8	33.5
Roanoke, VA	6.9	17.0	21.7	12.8	13.0	13.2	8.7	4.0	2.7	38.4
Rochester, MN	7.3	18.9	22.9	12.8	12.4	11.4	7.4	4.5	2.2	35.5
Salem, OR	6.7	20.6	22.5	13.4	12.3	11.2	7.6	3.7	2.1	35.2
Salt Lake City, UT	6.8	16.8	32.0	13.5	10.3	9.8	6.2	3.0	1.3	31.9
San Antonio, TX	7.1	21.3	24.1	13.2	12.2	10.6	6.7	3.4	1.5	33.2
San Diego, CA	6.3	17.0	27.9	13.6	12.5	10.8	6.8	3.5	1.7	34.3
San Francisco, CA	4.5	10.4	28.9	15.9	13.5	11.9	7.9	4.5	2.4	38.3
San Jose, CA	6.4	18.8	22.5	14.8	14.0	11.5	6.8	3.6	1.5	36.4
Santa Rosa, CA	6.0	18.6	21.2	13.0	12.6	12.8	8.9	4.2	2.5	38.1
Savannah, GA	6.5	19.3	28.3	11.3	10.8	10.8	7.2	3.7	1.9	32.3
Seattle, WA	4.9	13.0	30.8	15.8	12.4	11.1	7.1	3.1	1.9	35.7
Sioux Falls, SD	7.7	19.7	23.8	13.2	11.9	11.9	6.9	3.3	1.8	34.3
Springfield, IL	6.1	18.5	20.7	11.6	12.9	13.9	9.0	4.7	2.4	38.9
Tallahassee, FL	5.0	19.1	39.0	10.0	8.5	8.9	5.7	2.7	1.2	26.6
Tampa, FL	6.2	18.9	23.9	13.4	13.8	11.4	7.2	3.5	1.5	35.6
Topeka, KS	7.2	18.8	21.2	11.6	12.3	12.9	8.7	4.9	2.7	37.2
Tyler, TX	7.4	20.4	24.6	10.7	10.9	10.9	7.6	5.3	2.3	33.4
Virginia Beach, VA	6.5	18.5	24.2	12.9	13.4	11.8	7.5	3.6	1.6	35.6
Visalia, CA	9.0	24.1	21.0	12.9	11.4	10.1	6.9	3.0	1.6	31.9
Washington, DC	6.5	14.3	31.5	14.2	11.4	10.3	6.8	3.4	1.7	33.9
Wilmington, NC	4.6	17.2	26.9	11.9	11.7	12.2	9.0	4.3	2.3	36.0
Winston-Salem, NC	6.7	20.9	22.1	12.5	12.4	11.8	7.7	4.3	1.8	35.3
U.S.	6.2	19.5	20.7	12.7	13.4	12.7	8.6	4.4	1.9	37.8

Source: U.S. Census Bureau, 2013-2017 American Community Survey 5-Year Estimates

Age: Metro Area

Metro Area	Percent of Population									Median Age
	Under Age 5	Age 5–19	Age 20–34	Age 35–44	Age 45–54	Age 55–64	Age 65–74	Age 75–84	Age 85+	
Albany, NY	5.3	18.3	20.6	11.9	14.2	13.7	9.2	4.5	2.4	40.0
Albuquerque, NM	5.9	19.6	20.9	12.5	12.9	13.1	9.0	4.4	1.6	37.7
Allentown, PA	5.3	18.9	18.4	12.0	14.5	13.9	9.3	5.0	2.7	41.3
Anchorage, AK	7.4	20.4	24.4	12.9	13.0	12.3	6.4	2.4	0.8	33.5
Ann Arbor, MI	5.1	19.8	27.3	11.5	12.3	11.6	7.6	3.4	1.5	33.4
Athens, GA	5.5	21.0	27.5	12.1	11.1	10.6	7.4	3.3	1.4	31.8
Atlanta, GA	6.5	21.4	20.6	14.4	14.5	11.4	7.1	3.0	1.1	36.1
Austin, TX	6.6	20.1	24.6	15.4	12.9	10.5	6.2	2.6	1.0	34.2
Baton Rouge, LA	6.6	20.3	23.3	12.5	12.6	12.0	7.8	3.6	1.3	34.9
Billings, MT	6.3	19.0	19.5	12.2	12.8	13.9	9.3	4.7	2.2	39.0
Boise City, ID	6.6	22.2	20.0	13.4	12.7	11.7	8.2	3.6	1.5	35.8
Boston, MA	5.4	18.0	22.0	12.6	14.4	13.0	8.3	4.3	2.1	38.7
Boulder, CO	4.8	19.6	24.0	12.8	13.4	12.7	7.7	3.4	1.5	36.2
Cape Coral, FL	4.8	15.5	15.9	10.5	12.3	14.0	15.2	8.6	3.2	47.8
Cedar Rapids, IA	6.2	19.9	19.8	12.6	13.5	12.8	8.4	4.6	2.3	38.1
Charleston, SC	6.2	18.6	22.7	12.9	13.2	12.6	8.7	3.6	1.5	36.6
Charlotte, NC	6.4	20.5	20.0	14.3	14.4	11.8	7.8	3.6	1.3	37.3
Chicago, IL	6.2	19.9	21.2	13.4	13.7	12.5	7.7	3.9	1.8	37.0
Clarksville, TN	8.7	20.8	27.8	12.5	10.9	9.3	6.0	3.1	1.0	30.5
College Station, TX	6.2	20.9	33.8	10.5	9.7	8.9	5.8	2.8	1.3	27.2
Colorado Springs, CO	6.8	20.6	23.4	12.5	12.8	12.0	7.4	3.4	1.2	34.4
Columbia, MO	6.0	19.5	30.6	11.4	11.0	10.7	6.5	3.3	1.2	30.6
Columbia, SC	5.9	20.4	21.9	12.5	13.1	12.5	8.4	3.8	1.4	36.3
Columbus, OH	6.7	19.9	22.2	13.5	13.4	12.0	7.4	3.5	1.5	35.8
Dallas, TX	7.1	22.1	21.3	14.3	13.7	11.0	6.5	3.0	1.1	34.6
Denver, CO	6.3	19.4	22.2	14.6	13.6	12.1	7.3	3.2	1.4	36.3
Des Moines, IA	7.2	20.7	21.1	13.6	13.2	11.6	7.2	3.6	1.7	35.7
Durham, NC	5.9	18.8	23.0	13.3	13.0	12.4	8.3	3.7	1.7	36.7
Edison, NJ	6.1	18.0	21.4	13.2	14.1	12.5	8.1	4.4	2.2	38.2
El Paso, TX	7.9	23.3	23.0	12.6	11.7	10.2	6.3	3.6	1.4	31.9
Eugene, OR	5.0	17.3	22.4	11.6	11.9	14.0	10.6	4.8	2.4	39.4
Evansville, IN	6.1	19.2	19.7	11.9	13.2	14.0	9.0	4.7	2.2	39.3
Fargo, ND	7.1	19.5	27.7	12.2	11.2	10.8	6.1	3.4	1.8	32.3
Fayetteville, NC	7.9	20.5	27.4	12.0	11.4	10.2	6.4	3.2	1.1	31.2
Fort Collins, CO	5.4	18.7	25.1	12.1	11.7	12.8	8.6	3.9	1.6	35.7
Fort Wayne, IN	7.0	21.3	19.8	12.3	12.9	12.7	8.1	3.9	2.0	36.4
Fort Worth, TX	7.1	22.1	21.3	14.3	13.7	11.0	6.5	3.0	1.1	34.6
Gainesville, FL	5.4	18.4	30.6	10.5	10.5	11.4	7.9	3.6	1.8	31.7
Grand Rapids, MI	6.6	21.0	21.4	12.1	13.1	12.4	7.6	3.8	1.9	35.7
Greeley, CO	7.3	22.4	21.3	13.4	12.6	11.6	7.0	3.1	1.2	34.2
Green Bay, WI	6.3	19.8	19.4	12.4	14.2	13.4	8.2	4.3	1.9	38.5
Greensboro, NC	5.8	19.7	19.8	12.6	14.1	12.8	8.9	4.5	1.8	38.8
Honolulu, HI	6.5	17.2	23.0	12.6	12.5	11.9	8.8	4.8	2.8	37.6
Houston, TX	7.5	22.0	21.9	14.2	13.1	11.1	6.4	2.8	1.0	34.0
Huntsville, AL	5.8	19.3	20.4	12.5	15.0	12.9	8.2	4.4	1.5	38.4
Indianapolis, IN	6.8	20.7	20.7	13.4	13.6	12.2	7.5	3.7	1.6	36.3
Jacksonville, FL	6.2	18.8	20.9	12.7	13.8	13.1	8.9	4.0	1.7	38.1
Kansas City, MO	6.7	20.3	20.1	13.2	13.4	12.7	8.0	4.0	1.8	37.1
Lafayette, LA	7.0	20.3	21.9	12.4	12.9	12.5	7.5	3.8	1.5	35.4
Las Cruces, NM	6.9	22.2	23.7	10.7	11.0	11.0	8.3	4.6	1.5	32.9
Las Vegas, NV	6.4	19.5	21.4	14.0	13.5	11.6	8.6	3.9	1.3	36.9
Lexington, KY	6.3	19.2	23.4	13.2	13.0	12.0	7.8	3.6	1.6	35.8
Lincoln, NE	6.6	20.3	25.3	12.1	11.3	11.5	7.4	3.7	1.8	33.3
Little Rock, AR	6.6	19.9	21.6	13.0	12.7	12.3	8.4	4.0	1.7	36.5

Table continued on next page.

Metro Area	Percent of Population									Median Age
	Under Age 5	Age 5–19	Age 20–34	Age 35–44	Age 45–54	Age 55–64	Age 65–74	Age 75–84	Age 85+	
Los Angeles, CA	6.2	19.0	22.8	13.7	13.9	11.6	7.2	3.8	1.8	36.4
Louisville, KY	6.2	19.0	19.7	12.9	13.9	13.5	8.7	4.2	1.9	38.8
Madison, WI	5.8	18.5	24.4	12.8	13.0	12.4	7.8	3.6	1.7	35.9
Manchester, NH	5.4	18.4	19.3	12.5	15.8	14.2	8.4	4.1	1.9	40.5
McAllen, TX	9.6	27.2	21.0	13.0	10.6	8.1	5.8	3.4	1.2	28.9
Miami, FL	5.6	17.1	19.6	13.3	14.6	12.4	9.0	5.5	2.7	40.7
Midland, TX	8.6	22.0	24.3	12.4	11.3	11.0	5.6	3.2	1.5	31.8
Minneapolis, MN	6.6	19.9	21.0	13.1	14.0	12.7	7.4	3.6	1.7	36.8
Nashville, TN	6.5	19.6	22.0	13.7	13.7	12.1	7.6	3.5	1.3	36.3
New Orleans, LA	6.2	18.4	21.6	12.6	13.4	13.5	8.5	4.0	1.7	37.7
New York, NY	6.1	18.0	21.4	13.2	14.1	12.5	8.1	4.4	2.2	38.2
Oklahoma City, OK	7.1	20.5	22.6	12.8	12.2	11.9	7.6	3.8	1.5	34.9
Omaha, NE	7.3	21.0	21.1	13.0	12.9	12.0	7.4	3.6	1.6	35.4
Orlando, FL	5.9	19.0	22.3	13.6	13.6	11.6	8.2	4.1	1.7	36.9
Peoria, IL	6.5	19.5	19.0	12.3	12.9	13.4	9.1	5.0	2.5	39.0
Philadelphia, PA	5.9	18.9	20.8	12.3	14.0	13.2	8.3	4.4	2.2	38.6
Phoenix, AZ	6.6	20.6	21.0	13.2	12.7	11.3	8.5	4.3	1.7	36.2
Pittsburgh, PA	5.1	16.7	19.2	11.4	13.8	15.1	10.0	5.7	3.0	43.0
Portland, OR	6.0	18.5	21.2	14.6	13.5	12.7	8.3	3.6	1.7	37.8
Providence, RI	5.2	18.3	20.4	12.0	14.5	13.7	8.9	4.6	2.6	40.2
Provo, UT	10.0	28.5	26.9	12.3	8.3	6.6	4.3	2.3	0.7	24.6
Raleigh, NC	6.4	21.1	20.5	15.1	14.6	11.3	6.9	3.0	1.1	36.3
Reno, NV	6.0	18.5	21.3	12.2	13.4	13.4	9.7	4.0	1.5	38.2
Richmond, VA	5.9	18.9	20.6	12.8	14.2	13.2	8.6	3.9	1.8	38.5
Roanoke, VA	5.5	17.6	18.0	11.8	14.0	14.4	10.8	5.5	2.4	42.6
Rochester, MN	6.8	19.8	19.2	12.4	13.3	13.3	8.2	4.8	2.2	38.4
Salem, OR	6.6	21.2	20.4	12.3	12.1	12.3	8.8	4.3	2.0	36.3
Salt Lake City, UT	8.0	22.8	23.6	14.3	11.3	10.1	5.9	2.8	1.1	32.3
San Antonio, TX	7.0	21.6	22.1	13.2	12.7	11.1	7.3	3.6	1.4	34.4
San Diego, CA	6.5	18.5	24.4	13.2	12.9	11.6	7.3	3.8	1.8	35.4
San Francisco, CA	5.6	16.7	21.9	14.5	14.2	12.6	8.2	4.1	2.1	38.8
San Jose, CA	6.3	18.9	21.9	14.7	14.2	11.5	7.0	3.8	1.7	36.9
Santa Rosa, CA	5.2	17.6	19.3	12.3	13.5	14.6	10.5	4.6	2.3	41.4
Savannah, GA	6.7	19.8	23.5	12.8	12.4	11.7	8.0	3.6	1.6	35.0
Seattle, WA	6.2	17.9	22.7	14.2	13.9	12.5	7.5	3.4	1.6	37.1
Sioux Falls, SD	7.7	20.5	21.8	13.2	12.5	11.9	7.1	3.4	1.9	35.0
Springfield, IL	5.8	19.3	18.6	12.2	13.7	14.1	9.3	4.8	2.2	40.2
Tallahassee, FL	5.2	18.7	28.2	11.4	11.7	11.8	8.0	3.5	1.4	33.3
Tampa, FL	5.5	17.2	18.8	12.3	13.9	13.4	10.6	5.8	2.6	42.0
Topeka, KS	6.4	20.1	17.9	11.5	13.1	14.2	9.5	5.0	2.4	39.9
Tyler, TX	6.9	20.9	20.7	11.8	12.1	12.1	8.7	5.1	1.8	36.6
Virginia Beach, VA	6.4	18.8	23.7	12.1	13.2	12.3	7.9	3.9	1.7	35.7
Visalia, CA	8.6	25.8	21.6	12.4	11.3	9.6	6.2	3.1	1.4	30.6
Washington, DC	6.6	19.1	21.7	14.4	14.5	11.9	7.2	3.3	1.4	36.7
Wilmington, NC	5.3	17.6	21.6	12.8	13.1	13.1	10.0	4.8	1.8	39.6
Winston-Salem, NC	5.8	19.7	18.0	12.4	14.4	13.4	9.4	5.1	1.7	40.4
U.S.	6.2	19.5	20.7	12.7	13.4	12.7	8.6	4.4	1.9	37.8

Note: Figures cover the Metropolitan Statistical Area (MSA)—see Appendix B for areas included
Source: U.S. Census Bureau, 2013-2017 American Community Survey 5-Year Estimates

Segregation

Metro Area	Black/White		Asian/White		Hispanic/White	
	Index[1]	Rank[2]	Index[1]	Rank[2]	Index[1]	Rank[2]
Albany, NY	61.3	37	43.1	38	38.9	70
Albuquerque, NM	30.9	99	28.5	93	36.4	79
Allentown, PA	47.2	78	38.0	67	55.4	11
Anchorage, AK	n/a	n/a	n/a	n/a	n/a	n/a
Ann Arbor, MI	n/a	n/a	n/a	n/a	n/a	n/a
Athens, GA	n/a	n/a	n/a	n/a	n/a	n/a
Atlanta, GA	59.0	41	48.5	10	49.5	27
Austin, TX	50.1	70	41.2	49	43.2	51
Baton Rouge, LA	57.5	45	50.8	5	32.7	88
Billings, MT	n/a	n/a	n/a	n/a	n/a	n/a
Boise City, ID	30.2	101	27.6	95	36.2	80
Boston, MA	64.0	27	45.4	23	59.6	5
Boulder, CO	n/a	n/a	n/a	n/a	n/a	n/a
Cape Coral, FL	61.6	35	25.3	96	40.2	63
Cedar Rapids, IA	n/a	n/a	n/a	n/a	n/a	n/a
Charleston, SC	41.5	88	33.4	84	39.8	66
Charlotte, NC	53.8	56	43.6	34	47.6	35
Chicago, IL	76.4	3	44.9	26	56.3	10
Clarksville, TN	n/a	n/a	n/a	n/a	n/a	n/a
College Station, TX	n/a	n/a	n/a	n/a	n/a	n/a
Colorado Springs, CO	39.3	92	24.1	98	30.3	95
Columbia, MO	n/a	n/a	n/a	n/a	n/a	n/a
Columbia, SC	48.8	74	41.9	46	34.9	82
Columbus, OH	62.2	33	43.3	35	41.5	59
Dallas, TX	56.6	48	46.6	19	50.3	24
Denver, CO	62.6	31	33.4	83	48.8	31
Des Moines, IA	51.6	66	35.5	76	46.7	40
Durham, NC	48.1	75	44.0	30	48.0	33
Edison, NJ	78.0	2	51.9	3	62.0	3
El Paso, TX	30.7	100	22.2	100	43.3	50
Eugene, OR	n/a	n/a	n/a	n/a	n/a	n/a
Evansville, IN	n/a	n/a	n/a	n/a	n/a	n/a
Fargo, ND	n/a	n/a	n/a	n/a	n/a	n/a
Fayetteville, NC	n/a	n/a	n/a	n/a	n/a	n/a
Fort Collins, CO	n/a	n/a	n/a	n/a	n/a	n/a
Fort Wayne, IN	n/a	n/a	n/a	n/a	n/a	n/a
Fort Worth, TX	56.6	48	46.6	19	50.3	24
Gainesville, FL	n/a	n/a	n/a	n/a	n/a	n/a
Grand Rapids, MI	64.3	26	43.2	37	50.4	23
Greeley, CO	n/a	n/a	n/a	n/a	n/a	n/a
Green Bay, WI	n/a	n/a	n/a	n/a	n/a	n/a
Greensboro, NC	54.7	53	47.7	14	41.1	61
Honolulu, HI	36.9	95	42.1	44	31.9	91
Houston, TX	61.4	36	50.4	7	52.5	18
Huntsville, AL	n/a	n/a	n/a	n/a	n/a	n/a
Indianapolis, IN	66.4	15	41.6	47	47.3	37
Jacksonville, FL	53.1	59	37.5	71	27.6	98
Kansas City, MO	61.2	39	38.4	65	44.4	48
Lafayette, LA	n/a	n/a	n/a	n/a	n/a	n/a
Las Cruces, NM	n/a	n/a	n/a	n/a	n/a	n/a
Las Vegas, NV	37.6	94	28.8	92	42.0	58
Lexington, KY	n/a	n/a	n/a	n/a	n/a	n/a
Lincoln, NE	n/a	n/a	n/a	n/a	n/a	n/a
Little Rock, AR	58.8	42	39.7	59	39.7	68
Los Angeles, CA	67.8	10	48.4	12	62.2	2

Table continued on next page.

Metro Area	Black/White		Asian/White		Hispanic/White	
	Index[1]	Rank[2]	Index[1]	Rank[2]	Index[1]	Rank[2]
Louisville, KY	58.1	43	42.2	43	38.7	73
Madison, WI	49.6	71	44.2	29	40.1	65
Manchester, NH	n/a	n/a	n/a	n/a	n/a	n/a
McAllen, TX	40.7	90	46.7	17	39.2	69
Miami, FL	64.8	23	34.2	80	57.4	8
Midland, TX	n/a	n/a	n/a	n/a	n/a	n/a
Minneapolis, MN	52.9	60	42.8	39	42.5	54
Nashville, TN	56.2	49	41.0	51	47.9	34
New Orleans, LA	63.9	28	48.6	9	38.3	74
New York, NY	78.0	2	51.9	3	62.0	3
Oklahoma City, OK	51.4	67	39.2	60	47.0	38
Omaha, NE	61.3	38	36.3	74	48.8	30
Orlando, FL	50.7	69	33.9	81	40.2	64
Peoria, IL	n/a	n/a	n/a	n/a	n/a	n/a
Philadelphia, PA	68.4	9	42.3	42	55.1	12
Phoenix, AZ	43.6	86	32.7	85	49.3	28
Pittsburgh, PA	65.8	17	52.4	2	28.6	97
Portland, OR	46.0	81	35.8	75	34.3	83
Providence, RI	53.5	57	40.1	55	60.1	4
Provo, UT	21.9	102	28.2	94	30.9	93
Raleigh, NC	42.1	87	46.7	16	37.1	76
Reno, NV	n/a	n/a	n/a	n/a	n/a	n/a
Richmond, VA	52.4	63	43.9	32	44.9	46
Roanoke, VA	n/a	n/a	n/a	n/a	n/a	n/a
Rochester, MN	n/a	n/a	n/a	n/a	n/a	n/a
Salem, OR	n/a	n/a	n/a	n/a	n/a	n/a
Salt Lake City, UT	39.3	93	31.0	88	42.9	53
San Antonio, TX	49.0	73	38.3	66	46.1	43
San Diego, CA	51.2	68	48.2	13	49.6	25
San Francisco, CA	62.0	34	46.6	18	49.6	26
San Jose, CA	40.9	89	45.0	25	47.6	36
Santa Rosa, CA	n/a	n/a	n/a	n/a	n/a	n/a
Savannah, GA	n/a	n/a	n/a	n/a	n/a	n/a
Seattle, WA	49.1	72	37.6	69	32.8	87
Sioux Falls, SD	n/a	n/a	n/a	n/a	n/a	n/a
Springfield, IL	n/a	n/a	n/a	n/a	n/a	n/a
Tallahassee, FL	n/a	n/a	n/a	n/a	n/a	n/a
Tampa, FL	56.2	50	35.3	78	40.7	62
Topeka, KS	n/a	n/a	n/a	n/a	n/a	n/a
Tyler, TX	n/a	n/a	n/a	n/a	n/a	n/a
Virginia Beach, VA	47.8	76	34.3	79	32.2	90
Visalia, CA	n/a	n/a	n/a	n/a	n/a	n/a
Washington, DC	62.3	32	38.9	64	48.3	32
Wilmington, NC	n/a	n/a	n/a	n/a	n/a	n/a
Winston-Salem, NC	n/a	n/a	n/a	n/a	n/a	n/a

Note: Figures are based on an analysis of 1990, 2000, and 2010 Census Decennial Census tract data by William H. Frey, Brookings Institution and the University of Michigan Social Science Data Analysis Network. In this analysis all racial groups (whites, blacks, and asians) are non-Hispanic members of those races. Hispanics are shown as a separate category; All figures cover the Metropolitan Statistical Area (see Appendix B for areas included); (1) Segregation Indices are Dissimilarity Indices that measure the degree to which the minority group is distributed differently than whites across census tracts. They range from 0 (complete integration) to 100 (complete [segregation) where the value indicates the percentage of the minority group that needs to move to be distributed exactly like whites; (2) Ranges from 1 (most segregated) to 102 (least segregated); n/a not available.
Source: www.CensusScope.org

Religious Groups by Family

Area[1]	Catholic	Baptist	Non-Den.	Methodist[2]	Lutheran	LDS[3]	Pente-costal	Presby-terian[4]	Muslim[5]	Judaism
Albany, NY	26.8	1.2	2.2	2.9	1.5	0.3	0.5	2.1	1.2	1.0
Albuquerque, NM	27.1	3.7	4.2	1.4	0.9	2.3	1.4	1.0	0.2	0.2
Allentown, PA	23.1	0.4	1.9	3.9	7.9	0.3	0.4	6.2	0.6	0.6
Anchorage, AK	6.9	5.0	6.4	1.3	1.9	5.1	1.8	0.6	0.2	0.1
Ann Arbor, MI	12.3	2.2	1.5	3.0	2.8	0.8	1.9	2.9	1.2	0.9
Athens, GA	4.4	16.2	2.2	8.3	0.3	0.8	2.8	2.0	0.3	0.2
Atlanta, GA	7.4	17.4	6.8	7.8	0.5	0.7	2.6	1.8	0.7	0.5
Austin, TX	16.0	10.3	4.5	3.6	1.9	1.1	0.8	1.0	1.2	0.2
Baton Rouge, LA	22.5	18.2	9.6	4.6	0.2	0.7	1.1	0.6	0.2	0.1
Billings, MT	12.0	2.4	3.7	2.1	6.1	4.9	4.0	1.8	<0.1	<0.1
Boise City, ID	8.0	2.9	4.1	2.1	1.1	15.8	2.3	0.6	0.1	0.1
Boston, MA	44.3	1.1	1.0	0.9	0.3	0.4	0.6	1.6	0.4	1.4
Boulder, CO	20.1	2.3	4.7	1.7	3.0	2.9	0.4	2.0	0.1	0.7
Cape Coral, FL	16.2	4.9	3.0	2.5	1.1	0.5	4.3	1.4	0.9	0.2
Cedar Rapids, IA	18.8	2.3	3.0	7.3	11.3	0.8	1.8	3.2	0.5	0.1
Charleston, SC	6.1	12.4	7.0	10.0	1.1	0.9	2.0	2.3	0.1	0.3
Charlotte, NC	5.9	17.2	6.7	8.6	1.3	0.7	3.2	4.5	0.2	0.3
Chicago, IL	34.2	3.2	4.4	1.9	3.0	0.3	1.2	1.9	3.2	0.8
Clarksville, TN	4.0	30.9	2.2	6.1	0.5	1.5	1.8	1.0	0.1	<0.1
College Station, TX	11.7	15.6	3.9	4.7	1.5	1.2	0.6	0.9	1.1	<0.1
Colorado Springs, CO	8.3	4.3	7.4	2.4	1.9	3.0	1.0	2.0	<0.1	0.1
Columbia, MO	6.6	14.6	5.4	4.3	1.7	1.3	1.0	2.3	0.3	0.2
Columbia, SC	3.1	18.0	5.2	9.3	3.4	1.0	2.6	3.3	0.1	0.2
Columbus, OH	11.7	5.3	3.5	4.7	2.4	0.7	1.9	2.0	0.8	0.5
Dallas, TX	13.3	18.7	7.7	5.2	0.7	1.1	2.1	0.9	2.4	0.3
Denver, CO	16.0	2.9	4.6	1.7	2.1	2.4	1.2	1.5	0.5	0.6
Des Moines, IA	13.6	4.7	3.3	6.9	8.2	0.9	2.3	2.9	0.3	0.3
Durham, NC	5.0	13.8	5.6	8.1	0.4	0.7	1.3	2.5	0.4	0.5
Edison, NJ	36.9	1.8	1.7	1.3	0.7	0.3	0.8	1.0	2.3	4.7
El Paso, TX	43.2	3.7	4.9	0.8	0.3	1.5	1.4	0.2	<0.1	0.2
Eugene, OR	6.1	3.1	1.9	0.8	1.3	3.7	3.2	0.6	<0.1	0.3
Evansville, IN	14.7	16.7	5.6	5.6	1.4	0.5	1.9	3.0	<0.1	<0.1
Fargo, ND	17.4	0.4	0.4	3.3	32.5	0.6	1.5	1.8	0.1	<0.1
Fayetteville, NC	2.6	14.1	10.4	6.2	0.1	1.4	4.8	2.1	0.1	<0.1
Fort Collins, CO	11.8	2.2	6.3	4.3	3.4	2.9	4.7	1.9	0.1	<0.1
Fort Wayne, IN	14.2	6.0	6.8	5.1	8.5	0.4	1.4	1.6	0.2	0.1
Fort Worth, TX	13.3	18.7	7.7	5.2	0.7	1.1	2.1	0.9	2.4	0.3
Gainesville, FL	7.5	12.2	4.3	6.3	0.5	1.0	3.4	1.0	1.0	0.4
Grand Rapids, MI	17.1	1.7	8.3	3.0	2.1	0.5	1.1	9.9	1.0	0.1
Greeley, CO	13.5	1.8	1.5	2.6	2.0	1.9	1.8	1.4	0.1	<0.1
Green Bay, WI	42.0	0.7	3.4	2.2	12.7	0.3	0.6	1.0	0.1	<0.1
Greensboro, NC	2.6	12.8	7.4	9.8	0.6	0.8	2.4	3.1	0.6	0.4
Honolulu, HI	18.2	1.9	2.2	0.8	0.3	5.1	4.1	1.4	<0.1	<0.1
Houston, TX	17.0	16.0	7.2	4.8	1.0	1.1	1.5	0.8	2.6	0.3
Huntsville, AL	3.9	27.6	3.1	7.5	0.7	1.1	1.2	1.7	0.2	0.1
Indianapolis, IN	10.5	10.2	7.1	4.9	1.6	0.7	1.6	1.6	0.2	0.3
Jacksonville, FL	9.8	18.5	7.7	4.5	0.6	1.1	1.9	1.6	0.6	0.4
Kansas City, MO	12.6	13.1	5.2	5.8	2.2	2.4	2.6	1.6	0.3	0.4
Lafayette, LA	47.0	14.7	3.9	2.5	0.2	0.4	2.9	0.1	0.1	<0.1
Las Cruces, NM	31.7	5.7	1.2	2.0	0.5	2.1	2.7	0.6	0.2	0.2
Las Vegas, NV	18.1	2.9	3.0	0.4	0.7	6.3	1.5	0.2	<0.1	0.3
Lexington, KY	6.7	24.9	2.3	5.9	0.4	1.0	2.1	1.3	0.1	0.3
Lincoln, NE	14.7	2.4	1.9	7.1	11.2	1.1	1.4	3.9	0.2	0.1
Little Rock, AR	4.5	25.9	6.0	7.3	0.5	0.9	2.8	0.8	0.1	0.1
Los Angeles, CA	33.8	2.7	3.6	1.0	0.6	1.7	1.7	0.9	0.7	0.9

Table continued on next page.

Area[1]	Catholic	Baptist	Non-Den.	Methodist[2]	Lutheran	LDS[3]	Pente-costal	Presby-terian[4]	Muslim[5]	Judaism
Louisville, KY	13.6	25.0	1.7	3.7	0.6	0.8	0.9	1.1	0.5	0.4
Madison, WI	21.8	1.1	1.5	3.6	12.7	0.5	0.3	2.1	0.4	0.4
Manchester, NH	31.1	1.3	2.3	1.1	0.5	0.6	0.4	2.0	0.3	0.5
McAllen, TX	34.7	4.4	2.8	1.2	0.4	1.3	1.2	0.1	0.9	<0.1
Miami, FL	18.5	5.3	4.1	1.2	0.4	0.5	1.7	0.6	0.9	1.5
Midland, TX	22.4	25.2	8.8	4.2	0.6	1.2	1.6	1.8	3.7	<0.1
Minneapolis, MN	21.7	2.4	2.9	2.7	14.4	0.6	1.7	1.8	0.4	0.7
Nashville, TN	4.1	25.2	5.8	6.1	0.3	0.7	2.1	2.1	0.3	0.1
New Orleans, LA	31.5	8.4	3.7	2.6	0.8	0.5	2.1	0.5	0.4	0.5
New York, NY	36.9	1.8	1.7	1.3	0.7	0.3	0.8	1.0	2.3	4.7
Oklahoma City, OK	6.3	25.3	7.0	10.6	0.7	1.2	3.1	0.9	0.2	0.1
Omaha, NE	21.6	4.5	1.8	3.9	7.8	1.7	1.2	2.2	0.5	0.4
Orlando, FL	13.2	6.9	5.6	2.9	0.9	0.9	3.2	1.3	1.3	0.2
Peoria, IL	11.4	5.5	5.2	4.9	6.1	0.5	1.5	2.8	5.2	0.1
Philadelphia, PA	33.4	3.9	2.8	2.9	1.8	0.3	0.8	2.1	1.2	1.3
Phoenix, AZ	13.3	3.4	5.1	1.0	1.6	6.1	2.9	0.6	0.1	0.3
Pittsburgh, PA	32.8	2.3	2.8	5.6	3.3	0.3	1.1	4.6	0.3	0.7
Portland, OR	10.5	2.3	4.5	1.0	1.6	3.7	2.0	0.9	0.1	0.3
Providence, RI	47.0	1.4	1.2	0.8	0.5	0.3	0.5	1.0	0.1	0.7
Provo, UT	1.3	<0.1	<0.1	0.1	<0.1	88.5	0.1	<0.1	<0.1	<0.1
Raleigh, NC	9.1	12.1	5.9	6.7	0.9	0.8	2.2	2.2	0.9	0.3
Reno, NV	14.3	1.5	3.1	0.9	0.7	4.6	1.9	0.4	<0.1	0.1
Richmond, VA	5.9	19.9	5.4	6.1	0.6	0.9	1.8	2.1	2.7	0.3
Roanoke, VA	3.7	22.4	4.5	7.2	1.4	1.1	2.7	2.5	2.2	0.2
Rochester, MN	23.3	1.6	4.6	4.8	21.0	1.1	1.2	2.9	0.2	0.2
Salem, OR	16.6	2.1	2.9	1.1	1.6	3.8	3.4	0.7	<0.1	<0.1
Salt Lake City, UT	8.9	0.8	0.5	0.5	0.5	58.9	0.6	0.3	0.4	0.1
San Antonio, TX	28.4	8.5	6.0	3.0	1.6	1.4	1.3	0.7	0.9	0.2
San Diego, CA	25.9	2.0	4.8	1.1	0.9	2.3	1.0	0.9	0.7	0.5
San Francisco, CA	20.7	2.5	2.4	1.9	0.5	1.5	1.2	1.1	1.2	0.8
San Jose, CA	26.0	1.3	4.2	1.0	0.5	1.4	1.1	0.7	1.0	0.6
Santa Rosa, CA	22.2	1.3	1.5	0.9	0.9	1.9	0.6	0.9	0.4	0.4
Savannah, GA	7.0	19.6	6.9	8.9	1.6	0.9	2.3	1.0	0.1	0.8
Seattle, WA	12.3	2.1	5.0	1.2	2.0	3.3	2.8	1.4	0.4	0.4
Sioux Falls, SD	14.9	3.0	1.5	3.8	21.4	0.7	1.0	6.2	0.3	<0.1
Springfield, IL	15.5	11.7	2.7	6.8	5.6	0.7	4.9	2.0	1.5	0.2
Tallahassee, FL	4.8	16.0	6.7	9.1	0.4	1.0	2.1	1.5	0.8	0.3
Tampa, FL	10.8	7.0	3.7	3.4	0.9	0.6	2.1	0.9	1.2	0.4
Topeka, KS	12.7	9.0	4.1	7.3	3.6	1.4	2.0	1.6	<0.1	0.1
Tyler, TX	12.1	33.5	8.9	6.3	0.5	1.1	5.0	0.6	0.3	0.1
Virginia Beach, VA	6.4	11.5	6.1	5.2	0.7	0.9	1.9	2.0	2.0	0.3
Visalia, CA	23.2	2.6	2.5	0.8	0.5	1.7	3.6	0.9	0.3	<0.1
Washington, DC	14.5	7.3	4.8	4.5	1.2	1.1	1.0	1.3	2.3	1.1
Wilmington, NC	6.1	14.4	4.6	8.4	0.9	1.0	1.1	2.5	0.2	0.1
Winston-Salem, NC	3.5	17.4	9.3	12.4	0.7	0.6	2.5	2.2	0.3	0.1
U.S.	19.1	9.3	4.0	4.0	2.3	2.0	1.9	1.6	0.8	0.7

Note: Figures are the number of adherents as a percentage of the total population; (1) Figures cover the Metropolitan Statistical Area—see Appendix B for areas included; (2) Methodist/Pietist; (3) Latter Day Saints; (4) Reformed; (5) Figures are estimates
Source: Association of Statisticians of American Religious Bodies, 2010 U.S. Religion Census: Religious Congregations & Membership Study

Religious Groups by Tradition

Area	Catholic	Evangelical Protestant	Mainline Protestant	Other Tradition	Black Protestant	Orthodox
Albany, NY	26.8	4.5	7.3	3.1	0.5	0.3
Albuquerque, NM	27.1	11.2	3.2	3.9	0.2	0.1
Allentown, PA	23.1	5.3	17.7	3.0	0.1	0.6
Anchorage, AK	6.9	15.6	3.5	6.8	0.3	0.6
Ann Arbor, MI	12.3	7.3	7.5	3.7	1.5	0.2
Athens, GA	4.4	21.1	9.7	1.7	2.4	0.1
Atlanta, GA	7.4	26.0	9.8	2.9	3.1	0.2
Austin, TX	16.0	16.1	6.3	3.9	1.3	0.1
Baton Rouge, LA	22.5	24.8	5.6	1.5	5.1	<0.1
Billings, MT	12.0	13.6	8.1	5.1	<0.1	<0.1
Boise City, ID	8.0	12.9	4.3	16.7	<0.1	<0.1
Boston, MA	44.3	3.2	4.5	3.4	0.1	1.0
Boulder, CO	20.1	9.7	6.4	4.8	<0.1	0.2
Cape Coral, FL	16.2	14.3	4.6	2.0	0.3	0.1
Cedar Rapids, IA	18.8	13.7	17.5	1.9	0.1	0.2
Charleston, SC	6.1	19.6	11.1	1.8	7.3	0.1
Charlotte, NC	5.9	27.5	13.3	1.6	2.7	0.4
Chicago, IL	34.2	9.7	5.1	5.0	2.0	0.9
Clarksville, TN	4.0	35.3	7.2	1.6	2.4	<0.1
College Station, TX	11.7	20.6	6.6	2.5	0.9	<0.1
Colorado Springs, CO	8.3	15.2	5.3	3.7	0.4	0.1
Columbia, MO	6.6	19.9	10.4	2.3	0.4	0.1
Columbia, SC	3.1	25.5	13.4	2.1	5.4	0.1
Columbus, OH	11.7	11.8	9.5	3.1	1.1	0.2
Dallas, TX	13.3	28.3	6.9	4.7	1.7	0.1
Denver, CO	16.0	11.0	4.5	4.6	0.3	0.3
Des Moines, IA	13.6	12.3	16.8	1.8	0.9	0.1
Durham, NC	5.0	19.3	11.7	2.9	3.1	<0.1
Edison, NJ	36.9	3.9	4.1	8.3	1.2	0.9
El Paso, TX	43.2	10.8	1.2	2.0	0.2	<0.1
Eugene, OR	6.1	9.6	3.4	5.4	<0.1	<0.1
Evansville, IN	14.7	24.0	9.9	0.8	1.8	<0.1
Fargo, ND	17.4	10.7	30.8	0.8	<0.1	<0.1
Fayetteville, NC	2.6	26.7	7.8	1.7	4.3	0.1
Fort Collins, CO	11.8	18.8	5.9	3.9	<0.1	0.1
Fort Wayne, IN	14.2	24.6	9.1	0.9	2.4	0.2
Fort Worth, TX	13.3	28.3	6.9	4.7	1.7	0.1
Gainesville, FL	7.5	20.4	6.9	4.1	2.1	<0.1
Grand Rapids, MI	17.1	20.7	7.5	2.1	1.0	0.2
Greeley, CO	13.5	9.2	3.8	2.1	<0.1	<0.1
Green Bay, WI	42.0	14.1	8.1	0.6	<0.1	<0.1
Greensboro, NC	2.6	23.2	14.0	2.1	2.6	<0.1
Honolulu, HI	18.2	9.6	2.9	8.4	<0.1	<0.1
Houston, TX	17.0	24.9	6.6	4.9	1.3	0.2
Huntsville, AL	3.9	33.3	9.6	1.8	1.8	<0.1
Indianapolis, IN	10.5	18.2	9.6	1.6	1.8	0.2
Jacksonville, FL	9.8	27.1	5.6	2.9	4.2	0.2
Kansas City, MO	12.6	20.5	9.9	3.6	2.6	0.1
Lafayette, LA	47.0	12.7	3.2	0.7	9.2	<0.1
Las Cruces, NM	31.7	10.5	3.1	3.2	0.1	<0.1
Las Vegas, NV	18.1	7.7	1.3	7.6	0.4	0.4
Lexington, KY	6.7	28.3	10.2	1.7	2.0	0.1
Lincoln, NE	14.7	14.8	16.2	2.0	0.1	<0.1
Little Rock, AR	4.5	33.9	8.1	1.7	3.4	<0.1
Los Angeles, CA	33.8	9.0	2.3	4.6	0.8	0.6

Table continued on next page.

Area	Catholic	Evangelical Protestant	Mainline Protestant	Other Tradition	Black Protestant	Orthodox
Louisville, KY	13.6	24.5	7.1	2.0	2.9	<0.1
Madison, WI	21.8	7.2	15.3	2.2	0.1	<0.1
Manchester, NH	31.1	5.1	4.4	1.8	<0.1	0.7
McAllen, TX	34.7	9.7	1.8	2.3	<0.1	<0.1
Miami, FL	18.5	11.4	2.4	3.5	1.7	0.2
Midland, TX	22.4	35.4	7.2	5.3	1.0	<0.1
Minneapolis, MN	21.7	12.8	14.5	2.2	0.4	0.2
Nashville, TN	4.1	32.9	8.0	1.7	3.3	0.4
New Orleans, LA	31.5	12.7	4.0	2.1	2.9	0.1
New York, NY	36.9	3.9	4.1	8.3	1.2	0.9
Oklahoma City, OK	6.3	39.0	9.8	2.7	1.9	0.1
Omaha, NE	21.6	12.1	10.7	3.2	1.4	0.1
Orlando, FL	13.2	17.8	4.7	3.2	1.2	0.3
Peoria, IL	11.4	18.9	11.1	6.1	0.9	0.1
Philadelphia, PA	33.4	6.3	8.9	3.7	1.7	0.4
Phoenix, AZ	13.3	13.2	2.6	7.8	0.1	0.3
Pittsburgh, PA	32.8	7.3	13.8	2.0	0.8	0.6
Portland, OR	10.5	11.6	3.6	5.2	0.1	0.3
Providence, RI	47.0	2.8	4.7	1.6	<0.1	0.5
Provo, UT	1.3	0.4	<0.1	88.8	<0.1	<0.1
Raleigh, NC	9.1	19.9	10.1	3.2	1.7	0.2
Reno, NV	14.3	7.6	1.9	5.1	0.2	0.1
Richmond, VA	5.9	23.6	13.3	4.5	2.4	0.1
Roanoke, VA	3.7	31.7	13.1	3.9	1.2	0.1
Rochester, MN	23.3	18.9	21.0	2.0	<0.1	0.1
Salem, OR	16.6	14.1	3.8	4.1	<0.1	<0.1
Salt Lake City, UT	8.9	2.6	1.2	60.0	0.1	0.4
San Antonio, TX	28.4	16.9	5.0	3.1	0.4	<0.1
San Diego, CA	25.9	9.7	2.4	5.2	0.3	0.2
San Francisco, CA	20.7	6.1	3.8	5.2	1.0	0.6
San Jose, CA	26.0	8.2	2.4	6.8	0.1	0.4
Santa Rosa, CA	22.2	5.3	2.3	4.8	<0.1	0.2
Savannah, GA	7.0	25.0	9.4	2.6	8.5	0.1
Seattle, WA	12.3	11.9	4.6	5.9	0.3	0.4
Sioux Falls, SD	14.9	12.9	28.0	1.2	0.1	0.1
Springfield, IL	15.5	21.4	11.6	3.1	2.1	0.1
Tallahassee, FL	4.8	21.9	6.3	2.9	9.1	0.1
Tampa, FL	10.8	13.6	5.1	3.1	1.1	0.8
Topeka, KS	12.7	15.5	12.8	1.7	2.7	<0.1
Tyler, TX	12.1	45.5	7.4	1.7	4.1	<0.1
Virginia Beach, VA	6.4	18.0	9.4	3.9	2.2	0.3
Visalia, CA	23.2	12.0	1.9	3.1	0.1	0.1
Washington, DC	14.5	12.4	8.7	5.9	2.3	0.6
Wilmington, NC	6.1	20.3	10.7	1.6	3.1	0.1
Winston-Salem, NC	3.5	29.1	15.6	1.2	2.2	0.2
U.S.	19.1	16.2	7.3	4.3	1.6	0.3

Note: Figures are the number of adherents as a percentage of the total population; (1) Figures cover the Metropolitan Statistical Area—see Appendix B for areas included
Source: Association of Statisticians of American Religious Bodies, 2010 U.S. Religion Census: Religious Congregations & Membership Study

Ancestry: City

City	German	Irish	English	American	Italian	Polish	French[1]	Scottish	Dutch
Albany, NY	10.2	14.8	5.2	2.0	12.3	3.9	2.6	0.9	1.3
Albuquerque, NM	9.7	7.1	6.0	3.8	3.0	1.2	1.8	1.7	0.8
Allentown, PA	11.9	6.4	2.0	2.5	4.5	1.9	0.9	0.5	1.2
Anchorage, AK	15.1	9.6	8.0	4.5	2.8	2.1	2.7	2.5	1.6
Ann Arbor, MI	17.6	9.4	9.8	4.9	5.0	6.6	3.2	2.6	2.2
Athens, GA	8.8	8.5	9.0	5.5	3.2	1.6	1.7	2.9	0.9
Atlanta, GA	5.8	5.3	7.0	6.0	2.3	1.3	1.6	1.7	0.5
Austin, TX	11.2	7.3	7.6	3.3	2.9	1.7	2.3	2.0	0.8
Baton Rouge, LA	5.5	5.1	5.2	6.2	3.1	0.6	7.3	1.2	0.3
Billings, MT	25.3	10.8	9.7	12.0	3.0	1.9	2.9	2.7	1.5
Boise City, ID	17.8	11.7	18.3	4.7	3.7	1.6	2.7	4.0	1.8
Boston, MA	4.5	13.9	4.5	3.4	7.9	2.4	1.9	1.3	0.5
Boulder, CO	20.0	13.8	11.3	2.9	6.1	3.5	3.0	3.6	1.4
Cape Coral, FL	15.1	11.6	7.8	14.7	9.8	3.7	2.9	1.9	1.3
Cedar Rapids, IA	33.8	14.7	8.5	4.8	1.7	1.5	2.4	1.5	2.2
Charleston, SC	10.9	11.0	10.8	19.9	3.9	1.8	2.3	3.1	0.6
Charlotte, NC	9.3	7.2	6.7	4.5	3.5	1.7	1.4	1.9	0.6
Chicago, IL	7.4	7.5	2.4	2.0	3.9	5.9	1.0	0.6	0.5
Clarksville, TN	11.8	9.3	5.5	9.2	3.0	2.0	1.9	1.5	1.0
College Station, TX	17.8	9.4	8.9	3.6	3.5	2.7	3.5	2.8	0.8
Colorado Springs, CO	20.4	11.9	10.0	4.7	4.9	2.4	3.0	2.6	1.8
Columbia, MO	25.1	12.6	9.7	5.4	3.5	2.3	2.7	2.1	1.3
Columbia, SC	9.4	7.8	8.8	6.1	2.8	1.4	2.0	2.4	0.7
Columbus, OH	18.4	10.6	6.3	4.3	5.1	2.1	1.8	1.7	0.9
Dallas, TX	5.6	4.1	4.8	3.2	1.4	0.8	1.3	1.2	0.5
Denver, CO	14.3	9.7	7.9	3.0	4.4	2.6	2.4	2.0	1.4
Des Moines, IA	20.3	11.5	6.9	4.5	3.9	1.1	2.1	1.5	2.8
Durham, NC	7.2	5.9	7.1	4.6	2.7	1.8	1.4	1.8	0.6
Edison, NJ	4.9	6.9	1.5	1.9	8.6	4.8	0.7	0.6	0.4
El Paso, TX	3.6	2.3	1.6	2.9	1.2	0.4	0.7	0.4	0.3
Eugene, OR	17.5	12.9	11.1	3.9	4.5	2.2	3.4	3.4	2.0
Evansville, IN	25.7	11.6	11.3	7.1	1.5	1.2	1.7	1.5	1.1
Fargo, ND	38.7	8.8	4.1	2.1	1.2	2.9	3.8	1.4	1.1
Fayetteville, NC	9.2	7.5	6.6	4.8	3.2	1.4	1.7	1.8	0.6
Fort Collins, CO	24.4	13.5	11.3	3.8	6.1	3.2	3.5	2.8	1.9
Fort Wayne, IN	26.1	9.5	6.5	6.4	2.7	1.9	3.2	1.8	1.4
Fort Worth, TX	8.4	6.8	6.0	5.2	1.9	1.0	1.8	1.5	0.7
Gainesville, FL	11.3	10.4	8.2	4.0	6.2	2.8	2.7	2.4	1.3
Grand Rapids, MI	15.4	9.1	6.7	2.6	2.8	6.9	2.7	1.6	14.9
Greeley, CO	19.7	8.6	6.8	3.8	2.7	1.5	1.9	1.8	1.2
Green Bay, WI	31.7	8.7	3.4	3.4	2.0	8.1	4.3	0.7	3.5
Greensboro, NC	7.5	5.4	7.0	5.0	2.1	1.1	1.2	1.9	0.7
Honolulu, HI	4.0	3.4	2.8	1.2	1.9	0.7	1.1	0.7	0.4
Houston, TX	5.0	3.7	3.9	4.0	1.5	0.9	1.6	0.9	0.4
Huntsville, AL	9.4	8.7	9.5	10.1	2.7	0.9	1.8	2.2	1.0
Indianapolis, IN	15.4	9.4	6.2	6.3	2.3	1.5	1.6	1.6	1.2
Jacksonville, FL	8.9	8.5	6.7	5.7	4.0	1.6	1.7	1.7	0.9
Kansas City, MO	17.2	11.3	7.4	4.6	3.5	1.4	2.3	1.6	1.3
Lafayette, LA	7.5	5.6	6.4	7.1	3.6	0.5	19.8	0.9	0.6
Las Cruces, NM	7.6	5.3	4.9	2.6	2.1	1.1	1.3	1.3	0.6
Las Vegas, NV	9.6	8.2	5.6	3.6	5.8	2.2	1.8	1.4	0.8
Lexington, KY	14.5	12.2	11.2	11.0	2.8	1.5	1.8	2.9	1.3
Lincoln, NE	36.3	12.1	8.6	4.0	2.2	2.6	2.2	1.7	2.3
Little Rock, AR	7.8	7.4	7.7	5.9	1.6	1.0	1.9	1.8	0.6
Los Angeles, CA	4.1	3.6	3.0	3.1	2.7	1.5	1.1	0.7	0.4
Louisville, KY	15.5	11.6	8.2	11.4	2.5	0.9	1.8	1.6	0.9

Table continued on next page.

City	German	Irish	English	American	Italian	Polish	French[1]	Scottish	Dutch
Madison, WI	33.2	13.6	8.3	2.1	4.0	5.8	2.9	1.6	1.9
Manchester, NH	6.5	19.2	8.6	3.5	9.1	3.9	15.5	2.7	0.6
McAllen, TX	3.2	1.7	1.6	3.9	0.8	0.2	0.8	0.7	0.3
Miami, FL	1.7	1.3	0.9	3.8	2.1	0.6	0.9	0.3	0.2
Midland, TX	8.9	7.2	6.3	4.8	1.3	0.5	1.5	1.9	0.7
Minneapolis, MN	22.1	10.3	5.7	1.9	2.6	3.8	2.8	1.4	1.4
Nashville, TN	8.4	8.0	7.5	8.2	2.4	1.2	1.7	2.0	0.9
New Orleans, LA	6.5	5.8	4.2	2.4	4.0	0.9	5.8	1.1	0.4
New York, NY	3.0	4.4	1.6	4.7	6.4	2.4	0.8	0.4	0.2
Oklahoma City, OK	11.7	9.1	6.6	5.9	1.9	0.9	1.9	1.6	1.2
Omaha, NE	26.1	13.8	6.5	3.2	4.3	3.8	2.2	1.3	1.5
Orlando, FL	6.7	5.9	4.9	5.5	4.4	1.7	1.8	1.3	0.7
Peoria, IL	19.7	11.3	7.0	5.6	3.4	2.0	1.7	1.6	1.1
Philadelphia, PA	6.7	10.7	2.5	2.5	7.4	3.3	0.7	0.6	0.3
Phoenix, AZ	10.8	7.5	5.6	3.2	3.9	2.1	1.9	1.4	1.0
Pittsburgh, PA	19.5	16.1	5.3	4.3	12.4	7.3	1.4	1.4	0.6
Portland, OR	17.1	11.6	10.6	4.5	4.6	2.5	3.2	3.2	2.1
Providence, RI	3.3	8.0	3.9	3.2	8.5	1.9	3.1	0.9	0.3
Provo, UT	10.9	4.5	24.1	3.1	2.2	0.5	1.8	4.5	1.8
Raleigh, NC	9.1	7.7	9.0	12.8	4.0	1.9	1.7	2.6	0.7
Reno, NV	13.3	11.2	8.7	5.0	5.8	1.9	2.7	2.2	1.4
Richmond, VA	7.0	6.3	7.6	3.9	3.2	1.2	1.4	2.1	0.6
Roanoke, VA	9.2	9.2	8.0	10.7	1.9	1.4	1.3	2.1	1.1
Rochester, MN	30.9	11.3	6.3	3.2	2.2	3.8	2.0	1.3	1.5
Salem, OR	18.2	9.9	9.4	4.6	3.2	1.5	3.0	2.8	1.7
Salt Lake City, UT	10.5	6.8	15.7	3.7	3.2	1.4	2.1	3.5	2.0
San Antonio, TX	7.5	4.5	3.7	2.9	1.8	1.1	1.3	0.9	0.5
San Diego, CA	9.0	7.2	5.7	2.6	4.1	1.8	1.9	1.5	0.9
San Francisco, CA	7.5	8.0	5.3	2.8	4.8	1.8	2.3	1.5	0.8
San Jose, CA	5.5	4.3	3.8	1.6	3.6	1.0	1.2	0.8	0.6
Santa Rosa, CA	11.7	10.2	9.0	2.9	7.5	1.4	3.1	2.2	1.1
Savannah, GA	6.5	7.4	4.9	3.7	2.8	1.3	1.4	1.4	0.6
Seattle, WA	15.7	11.3	10.5	2.6	4.3	2.7	3.1	3.3	1.6
Sioux Falls, SD	36.5	10.6	5.1	3.9	1.5	1.8	2.2	1.1	5.9
Springfield, IL	22.2	14.0	9.5	5.3	5.0	2.0	2.2	1.6	1.3
Tallahassee, FL	9.3	8.6	7.7	4.1	3.9	2.0	2.0	2.2	0.8
Tampa, FL	8.8	8.5	6.0	5.8	5.9	2.0	2.3	1.6	0.7
Topeka, KS	22.7	10.6	12.9	5.0	2.3	1.2	2.2	1.8	1.3
Tyler, TX	7.5	6.9	7.2	11.9	1.5	0.8	1.4	1.8	0.7
Virginia Beach, VA	12.5	11.1	9.3	10.8	5.7	2.6	2.4	2.5	1.0
Visalia, CA	7.0	5.8	4.3	2.7	2.2	0.7	1.2	1.2	1.6
Washington, DC	7.0	6.7	5.0	2.3	3.9	2.2	1.5	1.3	0.6
Wilmington, NC	10.0	9.4	11.1	14.7	4.6	1.8	2.0	2.9	0.9
Winston-Salem, NC	9.4	6.9	8.4	5.7	2.7	1.1	1.5	2.0	0.9
U.S.	14.1	10.1	7.5	6.6	5.3	2.9	2.5	1.7	1.3

Note: Figures are the percentage of the total population reporting a particular ancestry. The nine most commonly reported ancestries in the U.S. are shown. Figures include multiple ancestries (e.g. if a person reported being Irish and Italian, they were included in both columns); (1) Excludes Basque
Source: U.S. Census Bureau, 2013-2017 American Community Survey 5-Year Estimates

Ancestry: Metro Area

Metro Area	German	Irish	English	American	Italian	Polish	French[1]	Scottish	Dutch
Albany, NY	15.7	21.7	9.5	4.5	17.0	6.6	6.2	1.9	3.3
Albuquerque, NM	9.5	7.0	6.3	4.1	2.9	1.4	1.7	1.7	0.8
Allentown, PA	25.5	13.7	6.0	4.8	12.9	5.5	1.6	1.1	2.5
Anchorage, AK	16.2	10.0	8.2	4.8	3.0	2.1	2.9	2.6	1.6
Ann Arbor, MI	20.1	10.5	10.3	7.2	4.7	6.8	3.2	2.6	2.2
Athens, GA	8.6	9.3	10.0	9.4	2.9	1.4	1.7	2.9	1.0
Atlanta, GA	6.9	7.1	7.3	9.5	2.5	1.3	1.4	1.8	0.7
Austin, TX	13.0	7.7	8.1	4.1	2.8	1.6	2.5	2.1	0.9
Baton Rouge, LA	7.3	7.4	5.6	7.7	4.9	0.6	13.2	1.2	0.4
Billings, MT	26.7	10.7	9.7	12.4	2.8	1.9	2.9	2.9	1.6
Boise City, ID	16.9	9.4	18.0	5.6	3.1	1.3	2.3	3.1	1.9
Boston, MA	6.1	21.7	9.7	3.9	13.7	3.5	5.0	2.4	0.6
Boulder, CO	20.8	12.7	12.5	4.1	5.8	3.5	3.1	3.7	1.9
Cape Coral, FL	14.3	11.0	8.5	14.1	7.5	3.3	2.8	1.9	1.4
Cedar Rapids, IA	37.0	15.3	8.1	5.5	1.7	1.3	2.4	1.6	2.1
Charleston, SC	10.6	10.6	8.6	12.9	3.5	1.8	2.3	2.5	0.8
Charlotte, NC	11.9	8.9	8.0	9.1	3.9	1.7	1.7	2.2	1.0
Chicago, IL	14.9	11.0	4.2	2.8	6.8	9.0	1.5	1.0	1.2
Clarksville, TN	11.2	9.7	6.8	11.3	2.8	1.6	1.7	1.6	1.0
College Station, TX	14.9	8.7	7.5	4.2	2.8	2.1	2.7	2.2	0.7
Colorado Springs, CO	20.7	11.9	9.9	5.1	5.0	2.6	3.0	2.8	1.8
Columbia, MO	25.2	12.5	10.4	6.5	3.5	1.9	2.6	2.1	1.4
Columbia, SC	10.8	8.0	8.0	9.1	2.4	1.2	1.7	2.0	0.8
Columbus, OH	23.6	13.2	8.8	6.5	5.5	2.3	2.0	2.2	1.4
Dallas, TX	9.5	7.3	7.1	6.5	2.1	1.1	1.8	1.7	0.9
Denver, CO	18.5	11.0	9.6	4.4	5.0	2.6	2.6	2.4	1.6
Des Moines, IA	27.7	13.2	8.7	4.7	3.4	1.4	2.0	1.8	3.4
Durham, NC	9.5	7.7	9.5	6.1	3.2	1.9	1.8	2.5	0.9
Edison, NJ	6.7	9.7	2.9	4.8	12.8	3.9	1.0	0.7	0.6
El Paso, TX	3.4	2.2	1.5	2.7	1.1	0.4	0.6	0.4	0.3
Eugene, OR	18.7	13.0	11.4	4.8	4.2	1.9	3.2	3.4	2.1
Evansville, IN	28.2	11.6	11.4	10.4	1.9	1.1	1.9	1.8	1.2
Fargo, ND	39.4	8.0	4.1	2.0	1.2	2.8	3.4	1.3	1.2
Fayetteville, NC	8.8	7.3	6.8	6.3	3.0	1.3	1.6	1.9	0.6
Fort Collins, CO	26.3	13.6	12.4	4.5	5.3	2.8	3.6	3.1	2.1
Fort Wayne, IN	28.8	9.4	7.1	7.8	2.8	2.0	3.5	1.8	1.5
Fort Worth, TX	9.5	7.3	7.1	6.5	2.1	1.1	1.8	1.7	0.9
Gainesville, FL	11.8	10.8	9.0	5.2	5.2	2.6	2.6	2.3	1.2
Grand Rapids, MI	20.9	10.3	9.1	4.2	3.1	6.6	3.3	1.9	20.1
Greeley, CO	22.8	10.0	8.5	4.8	3.5	2.1	2.2	1.8	1.7
Green Bay, WI	37.2	9.4	3.9	3.8	2.3	9.6	4.6	0.8	4.6
Greensboro, NC	8.6	6.6	8.4	8.7	2.2	1.1	1.2	2.1	0.8
Honolulu, HI	5.3	4.0	3.3	1.3	2.1	0.9	1.1	0.9	0.5
Houston, TX	8.3	5.7	5.4	4.5	2.1	1.2	2.2	1.2	0.6
Huntsville, AL	9.8	9.7	10.0	11.6	2.2	1.0	1.9	2.2	0.9
Indianapolis, IN	19.4	10.9	8.2	9.5	2.7	2.0	2.0	1.9	1.6
Jacksonville, FL	10.7	10.0	8.4	7.9	4.8	2.0	2.3	2.1	1.0
Kansas City, MO	22.1	12.7	9.8	6.1	3.3	1.6	2.4	1.9	1.5
Lafayette, LA	6.9	4.5	4.2	10.7	2.7	0.5	20.5	0.7	0.3
Las Cruces, NM	6.0	4.4	3.9	2.5	1.5	0.7	1.0	1.0	0.5
Las Vegas, NV	9.6	7.6	5.6	3.5	5.4	2.1	1.9	1.3	0.8
Lexington, KY	13.8	12.4	11.4	15.3	2.6	1.4	1.8	2.8	1.3
Lincoln, NE	38.2	12.0	8.5	4.1	2.1	2.6	2.2	1.6	2.5
Little Rock, AR	10.3	9.5	8.9	8.6	1.6	1.0	1.9	2.0	1.0
Los Angeles, CA	5.6	4.4	4.0	3.4	2.9	1.3	1.3	0.9	0.6
Louisville, KY	17.9	12.4	9.2	13.1	2.4	1.1	2.1	1.9	1.0

Table continued on next page.

Metro Area	German	Irish	English	American	Italian	Polish	French[1]	Scottish	Dutch
Madison, WI	38.8	13.6	8.7	2.9	3.6	5.3	2.8	1.6	2.1
Manchester, NH	8.4	20.6	12.8	3.8	10.4	4.7	13.7	3.4	0.8
McAllen, TX	1.9	1.0	0.9	2.4	0.5	0.2	0.5	0.3	0.2
Miami, FL	4.7	4.5	2.9	6.0	5.1	2.0	1.3	0.7	0.4
Midland, TX	9.0	7.1	6.1	4.8	1.2	0.6	1.5	1.8	0.6
Minneapolis, MN	30.7	11.2	5.7	3.1	2.7	4.5	3.5	1.3	1.5
Nashville, TN	10.3	10.1	9.5	12.5	2.7	1.4	1.9	2.3	1.0
New Orleans, LA	10.1	7.6	4.6	5.0	8.2	0.7	12.8	1.1	0.4
New York, NY	6.7	9.7	2.9	4.8	12.8	3.9	1.0	0.7	0.6
Oklahoma City, OK	13.4	10.1	7.6	7.6	2.0	1.0	2.0	1.8	1.4
Omaha, NE	30.4	14.5	7.8	3.8	4.1	3.8	2.4	1.3	1.8
Orlando, FL	9.0	7.9	6.4	7.3	5.2	2.0	2.0	1.4	0.9
Peoria, IL	29.3	13.0	9.1	7.0	4.2	2.1	2.3	2.0	1.6
Philadelphia, PA	15.4	18.7	7.0	3.8	13.5	5.2	1.4	1.3	0.8
Phoenix, AZ	13.5	8.6	7.9	4.2	4.5	2.5	2.2	1.7	1.2
Pittsburgh, PA	27.1	18.0	8.0	4.0	16.1	8.6	1.8	1.9	1.2
Portland, OR	18.8	11.0	10.8	4.8	4.0	1.9	3.1	3.1	2.0
Providence, RI	4.8	18.0	10.4	3.4	14.4	3.9	10.0	1.7	0.4
Provo, UT	11.0	5.0	28.2	4.9	2.4	0.7	2.0	5.3	1.8
Raleigh, NC	11.0	9.7	10.2	10.9	4.9	2.1	1.9	2.6	1.0
Reno, NV	14.5	11.5	9.3	5.0	6.3	2.0	2.8	2.5	1.4
Richmond, VA	9.7	8.2	11.0	7.0	3.6	1.5	1.7	2.2	0.8
Roanoke, VA	12.9	10.5	11.0	14.1	2.6	1.3	1.7	2.2	1.1
Rochester, MN	36.7	11.8	6.3	3.6	1.7	3.4	2.3	1.2	2.0
Salem, OR	18.3	9.3	9.9	4.7	2.8	1.4	2.9	2.7	1.8
Salt Lake City, UT	10.7	5.7	21.0	4.3	3.1	0.9	2.0	4.0	2.2
San Antonio, TX	10.8	5.8	5.2	3.4	2.1	1.5	1.8	1.2	0.6
San Diego, CA	10.2	8.1	7.0	2.8	4.3	1.8	2.1	1.6	1.0
San Francisco, CA	8.1	7.6	5.9	2.5	5.0	1.5	2.0	1.5	0.9
San Jose, CA	6.5	5.0	4.7	1.8	3.9	1.2	1.5	1.1	0.7
Santa Rosa, CA	13.4	12.0	10.2	3.0	9.0	1.8	3.3	2.5	1.4
Savannah, GA	9.6	10.6	7.2	6.7	3.4	1.4	1.9	2.0	0.7
Seattle, WA	15.9	10.2	9.8	3.4	3.7	2.0	3.0	2.7	1.7
Sioux Falls, SD	39.1	10.4	5.2	4.3	1.3	1.6	2.1	1.0	6.8
Springfield, IL	25.9	14.8	10.7	6.4	5.3	2.0	2.5	1.8	1.4
Tallahassee, FL	9.5	9.0	8.2	5.6	3.3	1.6	2.0	2.4	1.0
Tampa, FL	12.6	11.0	7.9	9.7	7.5	3.1	2.7	1.8	1.1
Topeka, KS	27.4	12.0	12.2	6.0	1.8	1.3	2.8	2.0	1.6
Tyler, TX	8.8	8.3	8.2	15.0	1.7	0.7	2.3	2.0	0.9
Virginia Beach, VA	10.5	9.1	9.1	9.5	4.2	1.9	2.0	1.9	0.9
Visalia, CA	4.5	3.7	3.0	2.0	1.5	0.3	0.8	0.8	1.0
Washington, DC	10.0	8.7	7.0	4.4	4.4	2.3	1.6	1.7	0.8
Wilmington, NC	11.3	10.7	10.5	13.4	5.1	2.1	2.3	2.9	1.0
Winston-Salem, NC	12.5	8.0	9.5	10.7	2.6	1.0	1.5	2.3	1.2
U.S.	14.1	10.1	7.5	6.6	5.3	2.9	2.5	1.7	1.3

Note: Figures are the percentage of the total population reporting a particular ancestry. The nine most commonly reported ancestries in the U.S. are shown. Figures include multiple ancestries (e.g. if a person reported being Irish and Italian, they were included in both columns); Figures cover the Metropolitan Statistical Area—see Appendix B for areas included; (1) Excludes Basque
Source: U.S. Census Bureau, 2013-2017 American Community Survey 5-Year Estimates

Foreign-Born Population: City

City	Any Foreign Country	Asia	Mexico	Europe	Carribean	Central America[1]	South America	Africa	Canada
Albany, NY	12.7	6.1	0.2	2.0	2.0	0.2	1.0	1.0	0.2
Albuquerque, NM	9.9	2.3	5.6	0.8	0.3	0.2	0.3	0.3	0.2
Allentown, PA	17.4	3.1	0.8	0.6	8.4	1.3	2.3	0.6	0.1
Anchorage, AK	10.5	6.0	0.8	1.2	0.6	0.1	0.5	0.5	0.4
Ann Arbor, MI	18.6	11.9	0.4	3.3	0.2	0.2	0.8	0.8	0.8
Athens, GA	10.4	3.3	3.3	1.0	0.3	1.0	0.7	0.5	0.2
Atlanta, GA	6.9	2.7	0.9	1.1	0.6	0.2	0.4	0.6	0.2
Austin, TX	18.4	5.4	8.1	1.2	0.5	1.6	0.6	0.6	0.3
Baton Rouge, LA	5.5	3.0	0.6	0.4	0.2	0.7	0.3	0.3	0.1
Billings, MT	2.4	0.7	0.4	0.5	0.1	0.2	0.0	0.2	0.3
Boise City, ID	7.0	2.9	1.3	1.5	0.0	0.1	0.2	0.7	0.2
Boston, MA	28.3	7.4	0.3	3.6	8.3	2.9	2.4	3.1	0.4
Boulder, CO	11.2	4.4	1.4	2.9	0.0	0.2	1.0	0.2	0.6
Cape Coral, FL	14.7	1.3	0.7	2.5	5.6	1.3	2.6	0.1	0.6
Cedar Rapids, IA	5.0	2.5	0.9	0.4	0.2	0.1	0.1	0.7	0.1
Charleston, SC	4.1	1.4	0.4	1.2	0.2	0.2	0.1	0.3	0.2
Charlotte, NC	16.4	5.1	2.9	1.2	1.0	2.6	1.5	1.9	0.2
Chicago, IL	20.7	4.9	8.9	3.5	0.4	0.9	1.0	0.9	0.2
Clarksville, TN	5.5	1.6	1.3	1.0	0.4	0.3	0.5	0.3	0.1
College Station, TX	12.8	7.4	1.8	1.0	0.1	0.6	1.0	0.7	0.3
Colorado Springs, CO	7.5	2.1	2.1	1.6	0.3	0.3	0.3	0.4	0.3
Columbia, MO	7.8	4.8	0.3	1.0	0.1	0.1	0.4	0.7	0.3
Columbia, SC	5.6	2.3	0.9	0.9	0.2	0.3	0.5	0.4	0.1
Columbus, OH	11.8	4.6	1.4	0.8	0.4	0.4	0.3	3.7	0.1
Dallas, TX	24.4	2.9	15.8	0.7	0.4	2.4	0.5	1.6	0.2
Denver, CO	15.8	3.0	8.2	1.4	0.2	0.7	0.6	1.4	0.3
Des Moines, IA	12.3	4.1	3.5	1.0	0.1	1.1	0.1	2.2	0.1
Durham, NC	14.7	4.3	3.5	1.1	0.5	2.9	0.6	1.3	0.4
Edison, NJ	46.9	38.0	0.8	2.9	1.6	0.2	2.0	1.3	0.2
El Paso, TX	24.5	1.1	21.8	0.6	0.2	0.3	0.3	0.2	0.0
Eugene, OR	8.2	3.4	2.1	1.1	0.1	0.4	0.3	0.3	0.5
Evansville, IN	2.7	0.7	0.9	0.5	0.1	0.1	0.0	0.2	0.1
Fargo, ND	8.2	3.5	0.2	1.1	0.1	0.1	0.3	2.8	0.2
Fayetteville, NC	6.6	2.5	0.6	0.9	0.8	0.8	0.4	0.4	0.1
Fort Collins, CO	6.4	2.6	1.2	1.2	0.1	0.2	0.5	0.3	0.2
Fort Wayne, IN	7.8	3.5	1.9	0.9	0.1	0.7	0.3	0.2	0.1
Fort Worth, TX	16.9	3.1	10.3	0.7	0.3	0.8	0.4	1.0	0.2
Gainesville, FL	11.1	4.8	0.4	1.4	1.4	0.3	2.0	0.6	0.2
Grand Rapids, MI	10.3	2.0	3.2	1.1	0.6	1.8	0.1	1.1	0.4
Greeley, CO	11.2	1.1	7.6	0.4	0.2	0.8	0.3	0.7	0.1
Green Bay, WI	9.1	2.1	4.9	0.6	0.1	0.7	0.2	0.4	0.1
Greensboro, NC	10.5	3.7	2.1	1.0	0.4	0.5	0.6	2.0	0.2
Honolulu, HI	27.1	23.0	0.2	0.8	0.1	0.1	0.2	0.1	0.2
Houston, TX	29.2	5.9	12.2	1.2	0.9	5.9	1.1	1.7	0.2
Huntsville, AL	6.6	2.3	1.6	0.8	0.5	0.6	0.2	0.5	0.1
Indianapolis, IN	9.3	2.5	3.2	0.5	0.4	1.0	0.2	1.3	0.1
Jacksonville, FL	10.6	4.1	0.6	1.7	1.7	0.6	1.1	0.5	0.2
Kansas City, MO	7.8	2.3	2.4	0.6	0.4	0.6	0.3	1.1	0.1
Lafayette, LA	4.9	1.8	0.9	0.7	0.3	0.5	0.1	0.3	0.2
Las Cruces, NM	11.4	2.1	7.8	0.5	0.1	0.3	0.1	0.5	0.1
Las Vegas, NV	21.2	5.2	9.7	1.5	1.1	2.1	0.8	0.4	0.3
Lexington, KY	9.1	3.5	2.4	0.9	0.2	0.5	0.3	1.0	0.2
Lincoln, NE	8.4	4.5	1.4	1.0	0.2	0.3	0.3	0.6	0.2
Little Rock, AR	7.5	2.8	2.0	0.7	0.1	0.9	0.4	0.3	0.2

Table continued on next page.

City	Any Foreign Country	Asia	Mexico	Europe	Carribean	Central America[1]	South America	Africa	Canada
Los Angeles, CA	37.6	11.2	13.2	2.4	0.3	8.3	1.1	0.6	0.4
Louisville, KY	7.1	2.2	0.8	0.9	1.4	0.2	0.3	1.2	0.1
Madison, WI	11.7	6.4	1.8	1.4	0.1	0.3	0.6	0.8	0.2
Manchester, NH	13.2	4.9	0.8	2.3	1.1	0.8	0.8	1.5	1.0
McAllen, TX	27.4	2.0	23.7	0.3	0.2	0.4	0.6	0.0	0.1
Miami, FL	58.0	0.9	0.9	1.9	33.0	12.1	8.8	0.2	0.1
Midland, TX	12.4	1.7	8.2	0.3	0.7	0.2	0.4	0.4	0.4
Minneapolis, MN	15.9	4.0	2.9	1.1	0.3	0.4	1.3	5.4	0.3
Nashville, TN	12.8	3.9	3.0	0.7	0.4	1.7	0.4	2.4	0.2
New Orleans, LA	5.9	2.0	0.3	0.8	0.3	1.6	0.4	0.3	0.1
New York, NY	37.2	10.8	2.1	5.5	10.3	1.4	4.9	1.7	0.3
Oklahoma City, OK	12.1	3.4	6.1	0.4	0.1	1.1	0.3	0.5	0.1
Omaha, NE	10.3	3.0	4.0	0.7	0.2	1.0	0.2	1.1	0.1
Orlando, FL	19.8	3.1	0.5	1.5	6.3	1.2	6.4	0.6	0.3
Peoria, IL	8.3	4.6	1.7	0.8	0.1	0.1	0.4	0.3	0.1
Philadelphia, PA	13.4	5.3	0.5	2.2	2.4	0.6	0.8	1.4	0.1
Phoenix, AZ	19.6	3.3	12.4	1.3	0.3	0.8	0.4	0.7	0.4
Pittsburgh, PA	8.6	4.9	0.2	1.8	0.2	0.1	0.4	0.7	0.2
Portland, OR	14.0	5.7	2.4	2.9	0.2	0.4	0.4	1.1	0.5
Providence, RI	29.2	4.5	0.8	2.2	11.8	5.3	1.7	2.7	0.2
Provo, UT	10.5	1.7	4.4	0.5	0.1	0.6	2.1	0.3	0.4
Raleigh, NC	13.4	3.9	3.1	1.4	0.7	1.4	0.6	1.8	0.4
Reno, NV	16.5	5.0	7.0	1.1	0.1	1.9	0.6	0.3	0.3
Richmond, VA	6.4	1.4	0.8	0.6	0.3	2.0	0.4	0.7	0.1
Roanoke, VA	7.6	2.8	0.7	0.6	1.1	1.2	0.1	0.7	0.2
Rochester, MN	13.6	5.7	1.8	1.7	0.2	0.2	0.2	3.4	0.3
Salem, OR	11.5	1.8	7.2	1.1	0.1	0.2	0.2	0.2	0.3
Salt Lake City, UT	16.4	4.3	6.4	2.0	0.2	0.6	1.2	0.8	0.4
San Antonio, TX	14.2	2.4	9.3	0.6	0.2	0.7	0.4	0.3	0.1
San Diego, CA	26.4	12.0	9.3	2.3	0.2	0.5	0.7	0.8	0.5
San Francisco, CA	34.8	22.5	2.6	4.5	0.2	2.6	1.0	0.5	0.6
San Jose, CA	39.4	24.7	9.6	2.1	0.1	1.0	0.6	0.7	0.4
Santa Rosa, CA	19.4	4.2	10.9	1.6	0.1	0.8	0.2	0.9	0.3
Savannah, GA	5.6	2.1	0.8	1.0	0.4	0.3	0.5	0.3	0.2
Seattle, WA	18.0	10.0	1.2	2.6	0.1	0.4	0.5	2.1	0.9
Sioux Falls, SD	7.3	2.1	0.4	0.8	0.1	0.9	0.1	2.7	0.1
Springfield, IL	4.1	2.3	0.4	0.5	0.2	0.1	0.1	0.5	0.1
Tallahassee, FL	7.9	3.3	0.2	1.0	1.2	0.4	0.7	0.8	0.2
Tampa, FL	16.2	3.5	1.3	1.3	6.3	1.1	1.8	0.6	0.4
Topeka, KS	5.3	1.3	2.7	0.4	0.1	0.3	0.2	0.1	0.0
Tyler, TX	10.9	1.7	7.0	0.4	0.2	0.6	0.1	0.5	0.2
Virginia Beach, VA	9.1	4.9	0.5	1.5	0.6	0.5	0.5	0.5	0.2
Visalia, CA	13.9	3.5	8.4	0.7	0.1	0.6	0.2	0.2	0.2
Washington, DC	14.0	2.8	0.6	2.6	1.2	2.7	1.5	2.2	0.3
Wilmington, NC	5.8	1.2	1.4	1.3	0.2	0.9	0.4	0.2	0.2
Winston-Salem, NC	9.8	1.9	4.2	0.9	0.4	1.5	0.5	0.4	0.1
U.S.	13.4	4.1	3.6	1.5	1.3	1.0	0.9	0.6	0.3

Note: (1) Excludes Mexico
Source: U.S. Census Bureau, 2013-2017 American Community Survey 5-Year Estimates

Foreign-Born Population: Metro Area

Metro Area	Percent of Population Born in								
	Any Foreign Country	Asia	Mexico	Europe	Carribean	Central America[1]	South America	Africa	Canada
Albany, NY	7.7	3.3	0.2	1.7	0.6	0.1	1.0	0.5	0.2
Albuquerque, NM	9.3	1.7	5.7	0.7	0.2	0.2	0.3	0.2	0.2
Allentown, PA	8.7	2.6	0.4	1.6	1.9	0.6	1.1	0.4	0.1
Anchorage, AK	8.7	4.8	0.6	1.3	0.5	0.1	0.4	0.4	0.4
Ann Arbor, MI	12.0	7.0	0.4	2.1	0.2	0.4	0.5	0.7	0.6
Athens, GA	8.1	2.7	2.4	0.9	0.2	0.9	0.5	0.4	0.2
Atlanta, GA	13.6	4.3	2.8	1.2	1.4	1.1	1.0	1.5	0.2
Austin, TX	14.9	4.2	6.8	1.0	0.4	1.1	0.5	0.6	0.2
Baton Rouge, LA	3.9	1.6	0.7	0.3	0.2	0.6	0.2	0.2	0.1
Billings, MT	2.1	0.6	0.4	0.5	0.0	0.1	0.0	0.1	0.2
Boise City, ID	6.4	1.6	2.8	1.1	0.0	0.2	0.2	0.3	0.2
Boston, MA	18.2	5.8	0.2	3.3	3.2	1.5	1.9	1.6	0.5
Boulder, CO	10.8	3.5	3.0	2.3	0.1	0.3	0.7	0.2	0.5
Cape Coral, FL	16.1	1.2	2.5	2.2	5.2	1.9	1.9	0.2	1.0
Cedar Rapids, IA	3.5	1.6	0.6	0.4	0.1	0.0	0.1	0.5	0.2
Charleston, SC	5.0	1.3	1.1	1.0	0.3	0.4	0.5	0.2	0.2
Charlotte, NC	9.8	2.7	2.2	1.0	0.6	1.3	0.9	0.8	0.2
Chicago, IL	17.7	5.0	6.7	3.8	0.3	0.5	0.6	0.6	0.2
Clarksville, TN	4.2	1.4	0.9	0.7	0.3	0.3	0.3	0.3	0.1
College Station, TX	12.4	4.0	5.7	0.7	0.1	0.6	0.5	0.5	0.2
Colorado Springs, CO	6.7	1.9	1.7	1.6	0.3	0.3	0.3	0.3	0.3
Columbia, MO	6.0	3.4	0.4	0.9	0.1	0.1	0.3	0.5	0.3
Columbia, SC	5.1	1.6	1.2	0.8	0.2	0.5	0.2	0.4	0.1
Columbus, OH	7.5	3.2	0.8	0.8	0.2	0.2	0.2	1.9	0.1
Dallas, TX	18.1	4.9	8.7	0.8	0.3	1.4	0.5	1.3	0.2
Denver, CO	12.3	3.2	5.3	1.5	0.1	0.5	0.4	0.9	0.3
Des Moines, IA	7.8	2.9	1.7	1.3	0.1	0.6	0.2	1.1	0.1
Durham, NC	12.2	3.7	3.1	1.3	0.4	1.9	0.5	0.8	0.4
Edison, NJ	28.9	8.4	1.6	4.4	6.7	1.9	4.2	1.3	0.2
El Paso, TX	25.5	1.0	23.1	0.5	0.2	0.3	0.2	0.2	0.0
Eugene, OR	5.9	2.0	1.7	0.9	0.0	0.4	0.2	0.2	0.3
Evansville, IN	2.6	1.2	0.5	0.5	0.1	0.2	0.1	0.1	0.1
Fargo, ND	5.9	2.6	0.2	0.7	0.1	0.1	0.2	1.8	0.3
Fayetteville, NC	6.0	1.9	1.0	0.9	0.7	0.7	0.4	0.3	0.1
Fort Collins, CO	5.4	1.7	1.3	1.2	0.1	0.1	0.5	0.2	0.2
Fort Wayne, IN	5.7	2.6	1.3	0.7	0.1	0.5	0.2	0.2	0.1
Fort Worth, TX	18.1	4.9	8.7	0.8	0.3	1.4	0.5	1.3	0.2
Gainesville, FL	9.5	4.0	0.4	1.3	1.4	0.3	1.4	0.4	0.3
Grand Rapids, MI	6.6	2.0	1.9	1.1	0.4	0.5	0.1	0.4	0.3
Greeley, CO	8.8	1.0	5.9	0.4	0.2	0.5	0.2	0.3	0.1
Green Bay, WI	5.1	1.5	2.3	0.5	0.1	0.3	0.1	0.2	0.1
Greensboro, NC	8.7	2.9	2.6	0.7	0.3	0.6	0.4	1.0	0.2
Honolulu, HI	19.4	16.0	0.2	0.7	0.1	0.1	0.2	0.1	0.2
Houston, TX	23.2	5.8	9.4	1.1	0.7	3.5	1.2	1.2	0.3
Huntsville, AL	5.2	1.9	1.2	0.7	0.3	0.4	0.1	0.3	0.1
Indianapolis, IN	6.7	2.3	1.8	0.6	0.2	0.5	0.2	0.8	0.1
Jacksonville, FL	8.8	3.2	0.5	1.6	1.4	0.5	0.9	0.4	0.2
Kansas City, MO	6.6	2.2	2.1	0.6	0.2	0.5	0.2	0.6	0.1
Lafayette, LA	3.3	1.1	0.9	0.3	0.1	0.5	0.1	0.2	0.1
Las Cruces, NM	17.2	1.3	14.7	0.5	0.0	0.2	0.1	0.3	0.1
Las Vegas, NV	22.3	7.2	8.6	1.6	1.1	1.9	0.7	0.7	0.4
Lexington, KY	7.1	2.5	2.1	0.8	0.2	0.4	0.2	0.7	0.2
Lincoln, NE	7.5	3.9	1.2	0.9	0.2	0.3	0.2	0.6	0.2
Little Rock, AR	4.1	1.4	1.3	0.5	0.1	0.5	0.2	0.2	0.1

Table continued on next page.

Metro Area	Percent of Population Born in								
	Any Foreign Country	Asia	Mexico	Europe	Carribean	Central America[1]	South America	Africa	Canada
Los Angeles, CA	33.4	12.7	12.7	1.7	0.3	4.2	0.9	0.6	0.3
Louisville, KY	5.2	1.6	0.9	0.7	0.8	0.2	0.2	0.7	0.1
Madison, WI	7.4	3.5	1.5	1.0	0.1	0.2	0.4	0.5	0.2
Manchester, NH	9.3	3.3	0.5	1.7	0.8	0.4	0.8	0.7	0.9
McAllen, TX	27.3	0.8	25.5	0.1	0.1	0.4	0.3	0.0	0.1
Miami, FL	40.0	2.1	1.1	2.3	21.0	4.2	8.3	0.4	0.6
Midland, TX	12.2	1.5	8.6	0.4	0.6	0.2	0.3	0.3	0.3
Minneapolis, MN	10.4	4.1	1.4	1.1	0.2	0.4	0.5	2.5	0.2
Nashville, TN	7.8	2.5	2.0	0.7	0.2	0.8	0.3	1.1	0.2
New Orleans, LA	7.6	2.1	0.6	0.6	0.7	2.7	0.5	0.3	0.1
New York, NY	28.9	8.4	1.6	4.4	6.7	1.9	4.2	1.3	0.2
Oklahoma City, OK	8.0	2.5	3.6	0.4	0.1	0.7	0.2	0.4	0.1
Omaha, NE	7.2	2.2	2.7	0.6	0.1	0.6	0.2	0.7	0.1
Orlando, FL	17.3	3.0	1.2	1.5	5.3	1.1	4.4	0.6	0.3
Peoria, IL	3.8	1.9	0.7	0.6	0.1	0.1	0.2	0.1	0.1
Philadelphia, PA	10.5	4.4	0.9	1.9	1.2	0.4	0.6	1.0	0.1
Phoenix, AZ	14.3	3.2	7.5	1.3	0.2	0.5	0.3	0.5	0.7
Pittsburgh, PA	3.8	1.9	0.1	1.0	0.1	0.1	0.2	0.3	0.1
Portland, OR	12.6	4.7	3.4	2.4	0.2	0.4	0.3	0.5	0.4
Providence, RI	13.3	2.3	0.2	4.4	2.2	1.4	1.1	1.5	0.2
Provo, UT	7.1	1.1	2.9	0.5	0.1	0.5	1.3	0.2	0.3
Raleigh, NC	12.1	4.2	3.0	1.2	0.5	1.0	0.6	1.1	0.4
Reno, NV	14.3	3.9	6.5	1.0	0.1	1.6	0.5	0.3	0.3
Richmond, VA	7.4	3.0	0.6	1.0	0.4	1.2	0.4	0.6	0.1
Roanoke, VA	4.9	1.9	0.6	0.7	0.5	0.4	0.2	0.4	0.2
Rochester, MN	8.1	3.3	1.2	1.1	0.1	0.2	0.2	1.8	0.2
Salem, OR	11.9	1.5	8.0	1.1	0.0	0.3	0.2	0.2	0.3
Salt Lake City, UT	12.0	2.9	4.7	1.3	0.1	0.6	1.1	0.5	0.3
San Antonio, TX	11.7	2.0	7.4	0.7	0.2	0.6	0.4	0.3	0.1
San Diego, CA	23.6	9.0	10.4	1.9	0.2	0.5	0.6	0.5	0.4
San Francisco, CA	30.5	17.1	5.2	2.9	0.2	2.5	0.9	0.7	0.4
San Jose, CA	38.1	24.5	7.6	3.0	0.1	0.9	0.7	0.6	0.5
Santa Rosa, CA	16.6	3.0	9.4	1.9	0.1	0.8	0.4	0.4	0.4
Savannah, GA	5.7	1.9	1.1	0.9	0.4	0.4	0.4	0.3	0.2
Seattle, WA	17.8	9.3	2.4	2.7	0.1	0.5	0.4	1.3	0.7
Sioux Falls, SD	5.4	1.5	0.4	0.7	0.1	0.7	0.1	1.9	0.1
Springfield, IL	2.9	1.6	0.3	0.4	0.1	0.1	0.1	0.3	0.1
Tallahassee, FL	6.0	2.1	0.4	0.8	0.9	0.5	0.5	0.5	0.2
Tampa, FL	13.2	2.7	1.4	2.2	3.4	0.7	1.8	0.4	0.7
Topeka, KS	3.4	0.9	1.6	0.3	0.1	0.2	0.1	0.1	0.1
Tyler, TX	8.3	1.1	5.8	0.3	0.1	0.4	0.1	0.3	0.1
Virginia Beach, VA	6.4	2.9	0.4	1.1	0.5	0.6	0.4	0.5	0.1
Visalia, CA	22.4	2.2	18.4	0.7	0.1	0.6	0.1	0.1	0.1
Washington, DC	22.6	8.2	0.8	1.9	1.1	4.8	2.3	3.3	0.2
Wilmington, NC	4.8	0.9	1.3	1.1	0.2	0.7	0.3	0.2	0.2
Winston-Salem, NC	6.7	1.3	2.9	0.6	0.2	0.9	0.3	0.2	0.1
U.S.	13.4	4.1	3.6	1.5	1.3	1.0	0.9	0.6	0.3

Note: Figures cover the Metropolitan Statistical Area—see Appendix B for areas included; (1) Excludes Mexico
Source: U.S. Census Bureau, 2013-2017 American Community Survey 5-Year Estimates

Marital Status: City

City	Never Married	Now Married[1]	Separated	Widowed	Divorced
Albany, NY	59.4	24.6	1.9	5.5	8.5
Albuquerque, NM	37.0	41.8	1.7	5.6	13.9
Allentown, PA	46.3	33.6	3.9	5.4	10.8
Anchorage, AK	34.4	48.9	1.6	3.4	11.7
Ann Arbor, MI	55.3	34.0	0.7	2.7	7.3
Athens, GA	55.5	30.9	1.6	3.8	8.1
Atlanta, GA	54.3	27.1	2.0	5.7	10.9
Austin, TX	43.5	40.3	1.9	3.1	11.1
Baton Rouge, LA	48.7	30.6	2.5	6.8	11.3
Billings, MT	29.3	48.9	1.2	6.5	14.1
Boise City, ID	34.2	46.6	1.1	4.4	13.7
Boston, MA	55.9	29.7	2.8	4.1	7.5
Boulder, CO	55.2	32.8	0.7	2.7	8.6
Cape Coral, FL	24.6	51.5	2.2	7.8	13.9
Cedar Rapids, IA	34.2	47.0	1.3	6.0	11.5
Charleston, SC	41.6	40.5	1.8	5.0	11.2
Charlotte, NC	40.5	42.5	2.7	4.1	10.2
Chicago, IL	49.0	35.1	2.3	5.2	8.4
Clarksville, TN	28.8	52.1	2.7	4.1	12.3
College Station, TX	61.1	30.8	0.9	2.1	5.1
Colorado Springs, CO	30.3	50.2	1.7	4.7	13.1
Columbia, MO	49.1	37.6	1.1	3.3	8.9
Columbia, SC	56.0	27.9	3.0	4.3	8.8
Columbus, OH	44.7	36.5	2.1	4.4	12.2
Dallas, TX	41.1	40.0	3.4	4.6	10.9
Denver, CO	42.2	39.2	2.0	4.2	12.4
Des Moines, IA	37.0	41.2	2.0	5.5	14.2
Durham, NC	42.6	39.9	2.6	4.5	10.5
Edison, NJ	25.5	60.7	1.5	6.2	6.1
El Paso, TX	33.9	45.7	3.4	5.9	11.1
Eugene, OR	42.3	39.7	1.4	4.5	12.0
Evansville, IN	34.3	39.4	1.6	7.0	17.7
Fargo, ND	43.9	41.4	1.1	4.5	9.1
Fayetteville, NC	37.2	42.4	3.8	5.1	11.6
Fort Collins, CO	45.6	41.5	0.9	3.2	8.8
Fort Wayne, IN	34.8	44.7	1.4	5.9	13.2
Fort Worth, TX	34.9	45.9	2.5	4.6	12.1
Gainesville, FL	61.0	24.9	1.7	3.7	8.7
Grand Rapids, MI	46.4	36.2	1.7	5.2	10.5
Greeley, CO	35.8	46.2	1.5	5.0	11.5
Green Bay, WI	38.7	42.6	1.5	5.0	12.3
Greensboro, NC	42.0	39.0	2.4	5.6	11.0
Honolulu, HI	35.7	45.9	1.3	7.0	10.1
Houston, TX	40.5	41.6	3.2	4.7	10.0
Huntsville, AL	34.8	43.9	2.2	6.0	13.1
Indianapolis, IN	41.4	38.3	2.0	5.2	13.1
Jacksonville, FL	34.6	43.1	2.6	5.9	13.8
Kansas City, MO	39.7	39.6	2.1	5.5	13.1
Lafayette, LA	43.3	37.9	2.2	5.6	11.0
Las Cruces, NM	38.6	41.8	1.6	5.4	12.5
Las Vegas, NV	34.8	43.0	2.6	5.4	14.1
Lexington, KY	38.8	42.8	1.8	4.5	12.2
Lincoln, NE	38.4	45.6	1.1	4.4	10.5
Little Rock, AR	37.3	41.2	2.7	5.8	13.1
Los Angeles, CA	45.8	38.6	2.7	4.6	8.3
Louisville, KY	35.9	41.8	2.1	6.3	13.8

Table continued on next page.

City	Never Married	Now Married[1]	Separated	Widowed	Divorced
Madison, WI	49.3	37.8	0.9	3.4	8.5
Manchester, NH	38.1	40.3	2.0	5.4	14.2
McAllen, TX	31.7	50.6	3.5	5.0	9.2
Miami, FL	40.9	34.7	4.0	6.6	13.9
Midland, TX	29.4	52.1	1.9	5.0	11.7
Minneapolis, MN	51.0	34.3	1.7	3.1	10.0
Nashville, TN	40.4	40.3	2.2	4.8	12.3
New Orleans, LA	48.8	29.8	3.0	6.0	12.5
New York, NY	43.9	39.5	3.1	5.6	7.8
Oklahoma City, OK	32.8	46.2	2.3	5.6	13.0
Omaha, NE	36.0	45.8	1.7	5.0	11.4
Orlando, FL	43.2	35.3	3.4	4.5	13.7
Peoria, IL	40.2	40.3	1.3	6.2	12.0
Philadelphia, PA	51.7	29.6	3.4	6.3	9.1
Phoenix, AZ	39.1	41.9	2.2	4.3	12.6
Pittsburgh, PA	51.8	31.2	2.0	6.0	9.0
Portland, OR	40.3	41.3	1.8	4.1	12.5
Providence, RI	52.9	31.4	2.8	4.4	8.5
Provo, UT	45.7	46.4	0.9	2.1	4.8
Raleigh, NC	42.7	40.3	2.6	3.8	10.6
Reno, NV	35.6	41.8	2.3	5.2	15.1
Richmond, VA	52.0	26.6	3.3	6.0	12.1
Roanoke, VA	36.7	37.9	3.0	7.7	14.7
Rochester, MN	31.6	52.8	1.0	4.7	9.9
Salem, OR	33.9	44.9	2.1	5.3	13.9
Salt Lake City, UT	41.4	42.1	1.7	4.1	10.7
San Antonio, TX	37.6	41.9	3.1	5.2	12.1
San Diego, CA	40.1	43.8	1.8	4.2	10.0
San Francisco, CA	45.8	39.8	1.4	4.7	8.3
San Jose, CA	35.2	50.7	1.7	4.3	8.1
Santa Rosa, CA	34.3	44.1	1.8	6.0	13.9
Savannah, GA	46.7	31.2	2.7	6.4	13.1
Seattle, WA	44.1	40.8	1.2	3.7	10.1
Sioux Falls, SD	34.0	48.6	1.4	5.1	10.8
Springfield, IL	36.0	41.8	1.5	6.4	14.3
Tallahassee, FL	55.9	29.9	1.2	3.5	9.5
Tampa, FL	41.4	37.3	2.9	5.2	13.2
Topeka, KS	31.8	44.7	1.5	7.2	14.8
Tyler, TX	35.2	42.8	2.1	7.0	13.0
Virginia Beach, VA	31.0	50.1	2.7	5.0	11.2
Visalia, CA	34.6	48.1	2.0	4.7	10.7
Washington, DC	55.8	28.5	2.2	4.4	9.1
Wilmington, NC	42.4	38.6	2.6	5.3	11.1
Winston-Salem, NC	39.8	40.6	3.0	5.9	10.8
U.S.	33.1	48.2	2.0	5.8	10.9

Note: Figures are percentages and cover the population 15 years of age and older; (1) Excludes separated
Source: U.S. Census Bureau, 2013-2017 American Community Survey 5-Year Estimates

Marital Status: Metro Area

Metro Area	Never Married	Now Married[1]	Separated	Widowed	Divorced
Albany, NY	36.2	46.0	1.9	6.0	9.9
Albuquerque, NM	34.6	44.6	1.6	5.7	13.4
Allentown, PA	31.3	50.0	2.3	6.5	9.9
Anchorage, AK	33.6	49.2	1.7	3.6	11.9
Ann Arbor, MI	42.7	43.7	0.9	3.8	8.9
Athens, GA	43.3	40.9	1.7	5.0	9.1
Atlanta, GA	35.0	47.4	2.1	4.6	11.0
Austin, TX	36.2	47.4	1.8	3.7	10.9
Baton Rouge, LA	36.5	43.5	2.2	6.2	11.7
Billings, MT	26.9	52.6	1.3	6.1	13.2
Boise City, ID	29.3	52.7	1.2	4.7	12.2
Boston, MA	36.9	47.5	1.7	5.2	8.8
Boulder, CO	37.6	47.0	0.9	3.6	10.9
Cape Coral, FL	26.1	50.8	1.9	8.2	13.0
Cedar Rapids, IA	28.9	53.2	1.2	5.8	10.9
Charleston, SC	33.9	46.5	2.7	5.6	11.3
Charlotte, NC	32.0	49.6	2.6	5.3	10.5
Chicago, IL	36.9	47.0	1.7	5.5	8.9
Clarksville, TN	27.9	52.7	2.4	5.0	12.0
College Station, TX	46.5	39.4	2.1	4.1	8.0
Colorado Springs, CO	28.7	53.7	1.6	4.1	11.9
Columbia, MO	41.8	43.5	1.3	3.8	9.7
Columbia, SC	36.2	44.2	3.1	5.8	10.7
Columbus, OH	34.3	47.5	1.8	4.9	11.6
Dallas, TX	32.0	50.5	2.3	4.5	10.8
Denver, CO	32.5	49.9	1.5	4.1	11.9
Des Moines, IA	29.5	52.4	1.3	5.0	11.7
Durham, NC	37.4	45.3	2.3	4.9	10.0
Edison, NJ	38.1	45.8	2.4	5.8	7.9
El Paso, TX	34.5	46.1	3.4	5.5	10.5
Eugene, OR	33.8	45.6	1.6	5.5	13.4
Evansville, IN	27.9	50.7	1.2	6.3	13.9
Fargo, ND	37.5	48.6	0.9	4.3	8.7
Fayetteville, NC	34.1	45.9	3.5	5.2	11.2
Fort Collins, CO	34.2	50.6	1.0	3.9	10.2
Fort Wayne, IN	30.4	50.6	1.2	5.8	12.0
Fort Worth, TX	32.0	50.5	2.3	4.5	10.8
Gainesville, FL	45.5	37.6	1.6	4.8	10.4
Grand Rapids, MI	32.1	51.9	1.1	4.9	10.0
Greeley, CO	27.8	55.7	1.3	4.3	11.0
Green Bay, WI	30.5	53.0	1.0	5.1	10.5
Greensboro, NC	33.2	46.6	2.8	6.3	11.1
Honolulu, HI	33.6	50.3	1.2	6.3	8.6
Houston, TX	33.3	50.1	2.5	4.5	9.6
Huntsville, AL	30.1	50.3	1.9	5.8	11.9
Indianapolis, IN	32.5	48.3	1.5	5.3	12.4
Jacksonville, FL	30.9	48.0	2.2	5.9	13.0
Kansas City, MO	30.3	50.5	1.7	5.4	12.1
Lafayette, LA	34.8	45.4	2.3	5.9	11.5
Las Cruces, NM	35.9	46.9	2.2	5.0	10.0
Las Vegas, NV	34.4	44.3	2.5	5.2	13.7
Lexington, KY	34.0	47.0	1.9	4.8	12.3
Lincoln, NE	36.4	48.2	1.1	4.4	10.0
Little Rock, AR	30.5	47.7	2.3	6.0	13.5
Los Angeles, CA	39.9	44.4	2.3	4.9	8.5
Louisville, KY	31.3	47.4	1.8	6.3	13.3

Table continued on next page.

Metro Area	Never Married	Now Married[1]	Separated	Widowed	Divorced
Madison, WI	36.0	49.2	0.9	4.2	9.6
Manchester, NH	29.9	51.6	1.3	5.2	11.9
McAllen, TX	33.6	49.7	3.9	5.1	7.8
Miami, FL	34.6	42.9	3.0	6.6	12.9
Midland, TX	28.8	52.8	2.0	4.8	11.7
Minneapolis, MN	33.0	51.5	1.2	4.4	10.0
Nashville, TN	31.4	50.1	1.8	5.0	11.6
New Orleans, LA	37.5	41.6	2.4	6.4	12.2
New York, NY	38.1	45.8	2.4	5.8	7.9
Oklahoma City, OK	30.8	48.8	2.1	5.6	12.7
Omaha, NE	31.0	51.7	1.4	5.0	10.9
Orlando, FL	34.8	46.0	2.3	5.3	11.7
Peoria, IL	29.6	51.3	1.1	6.7	11.3
Philadelphia, PA	37.4	45.1	2.2	6.2	9.0
Phoenix, AZ	33.8	47.3	1.7	5.1	12.2
Pittsburgh, PA	31.6	49.3	1.7	7.5	9.8
Portland, OR	31.5	49.9	1.7	4.6	12.2
Providence, RI	35.3	45.7	1.7	6.3	11.0
Provo, UT	31.8	58.8	1.0	2.6	5.8
Raleigh, NC	31.6	51.8	2.5	4.3	9.8
Reno, NV	31.1	47.8	1.9	5.2	14.1
Richmond, VA	34.4	46.2	2.5	5.9	11.1
Roanoke, VA	28.0	49.9	2.3	7.5	12.3
Rochester, MN	27.3	57.6	0.8	4.9	9.3
Salem, OR	30.8	49.5	2.0	5.3	12.4
Salt Lake City, UT	31.3	52.4	1.8	4.0	10.5
San Antonio, TX	33.9	46.7	2.7	5.2	11.5
San Diego, CA	35.7	47.4	1.8	4.8	10.3
San Francisco, CA	36.1	48.3	1.6	4.9	9.1
San Jose, CA	33.3	53.0	1.5	4.2	7.9
Santa Rosa, CA	32.3	47.6	1.7	5.3	13.2
Savannah, GA	34.7	45.1	2.1	5.8	12.2
Seattle, WA	32.3	50.6	1.5	4.4	11.2
Sioux Falls, SD	30.4	53.2	1.3	5.1	10.1
Springfield, IL	30.8	48.6	1.2	6.1	13.3
Tallahassee, FL	43.4	39.8	1.6	4.5	10.8
Tampa, FL	30.8	46.3	2.2	7.1	13.6
Topeka, KS	26.6	52.9	1.2	6.7	12.5
Tyler, TX	28.9	50.5	2.2	6.7	11.7
Virginia Beach, VA	33.7	46.9	2.9	5.5	11.1
Visalia, CA	36.9	47.1	2.3	5.0	8.7
Washington, DC	36.1	48.7	2.1	4.3	8.9
Wilmington, NC	33.5	46.7	2.6	5.9	11.4
Winston-Salem, NC	29.5	50.0	2.7	6.6	11.2
U.S.	33.1	48.2	2.0	5.8	10.9

Note: Figures are percentages and cover the population 15 years of age and older; Figures cover the Metropolitan Statistical Area—see Appendix B for areas included; (1) Excludes separated
Source: U.S. Census Bureau, 2013-2017 American Community Survey 5-Year Estimates

Disability by Age: City

City	All Ages	Under 18 Years Old	18 to 64 Years Old	65 Years and Over
Albany, NY	12.1	3.7	10.3	34.6
Albuquerque, NM	13.3	3.5	11.7	37.1
Allentown, PA	18.3	10.3	17.9	39.5
Anchorage, AK	10.9	3.7	9.8	37.7
Ann Arbor, MI	6.9	1.7	4.8	26.9
Athens, GA	10.5	3.6	9.1	33.7
Atlanta, GA	12.1	4.2	9.9	38.9
Austin, TX	8.7	3.8	7.3	32.9
Baton Rouge, LA	16.1	8.2	13.2	43.9
Billings, MT	13.0	5.6	10.5	33.7
Boise City, ID	11.2	4.0	9.5	32.3
Boston, MA	12.3	5.1	9.6	41.7
Boulder, CO	6.8	2.2	4.7	28.5
Cape Coral, FL	12.8	2.8	9.8	30.2
Cedar Rapids, IA	10.4	3.9	8.4	30.0
Charleston, SC	9.6	3.0	7.6	28.4
Charlotte, NC	8.7	2.9	7.5	32.3
Chicago, IL	10.6	3.0	8.4	37.8
Clarksville, TN	14.7	4.7	15.5	43.8
College Station, TX	6.0	3.2	4.6	31.5
Colorado Springs, CO	12.8	4.3	11.6	34.5
Columbia, MO	9.6	3.2	7.8	36.3
Columbia, SC	11.7	3.5	10.0	36.6
Columbus, OH	11.9	4.9	10.8	36.9
Dallas, TX	9.6	3.1	8.2	36.0
Denver, CO	9.6	2.9	7.6	34.5
Des Moines, IA	13.7	5.1	13.0	36.2
Durham, NC	9.9	3.4	8.3	34.3
Edison, NJ	8.1	3.1	5.2	30.1
El Paso, TX	13.7	4.4	11.5	45.0
Eugene, OR	13.5	4.8	11.0	35.7
Evansville, IN	17.9	6.1	16.5	41.2
Fargo, ND	10.4	3.0	8.6	36.2
Fayetteville, NC	16.7	6.7	15.4	44.1
Fort Collins, CO	8.0	2.8	6.0	32.6
Fort Wayne, IN	13.3	5.7	12.3	33.4
Fort Worth, TX	10.5	3.6	9.7	37.5
Gainesville, FL	10.0	2.9	8.0	36.1
Grand Rapids, MI	13.8	5.8	12.5	39.8
Greeley, CO	11.3	3.0	9.8	38.2
Green Bay, WI	13.6	5.5	12.9	34.0
Greensboro, NC	10.0	3.6	7.7	32.1
Honolulu, HI	11.3	2.5	7.3	32.5
Houston, TX	9.6	3.3	7.8	36.8
Huntsville, AL	13.2	4.4	10.9	35.4
Indianapolis, IN	13.7	5.6	12.4	39.3
Jacksonville, FL	13.6	4.9	11.8	38.7
Kansas City, MO	13.0	3.9	11.8	37.3
Lafayette, LA	12.0	3.1	10.6	34.6
Las Cruces, NM	13.6	4.1	10.9	39.8
Las Vegas, NV	13.1	3.9	11.3	36.5
Lexington, KY	11.9	4.1	10.1	35.4
Lincoln, NE	10.8	4.3	8.5	34.4
Little Rock, AR	13.2	6.4	11.2	35.6
Los Angeles, CA	10.0	3.0	7.4	38.3

Table continued on next page.

City	All Ages	Under 18 Years Old	18 to 64 Years Old	65 Years and Over
Louisville, KY	14.8	5.0	13.3	37.7
Madison, WI	8.4	3.4	6.6	28.6
Manchester, NH	14.7	6.2	12.3	40.5
McAllen, TX	13.2	4.9	10.8	46.1
Miami, FL	12.0	3.7	8.3	36.1
Midland, TX	9.3	2.7	7.6	37.0
Minneapolis, MN	11.2	4.5	10.2	34.0
Nashville, TN	11.8	3.8	10.3	37.0
New Orleans, LA	13.8	4.4	12.1	38.1
New York, NY	10.8	3.5	7.9	36.4
Oklahoma City, OK	13.5	4.7	12.3	39.4
Omaha, NE	11.1	3.6	9.7	34.2
Orlando, FL	10.3	5.3	8.1	35.5
Peoria, IL	12.4	3.3	11.1	34.3
Philadelphia, PA	15.9	6.0	14.1	42.2
Phoenix, AZ	10.3	3.8	9.2	35.5
Pittsburgh, PA	13.8	5.9	10.8	37.6
Portland, OR	12.7	4.4	10.8	37.3
Providence, RI	12.7	6.0	11.4	38.8
Provo, UT	8.3	3.7	7.4	35.8
Raleigh, NC	8.6	4.4	6.7	32.4
Reno, NV	12.2	4.7	10.5	32.5
Richmond, VA	15.5	7.9	13.9	37.1
Roanoke, VA	16.3	6.5	14.0	40.7
Rochester, MN	10.7	4.3	8.8	30.5
Salem, OR	14.7	5.4	13.4	38.4
Salt Lake City, UT	10.6	3.2	8.9	36.5
San Antonio, TX	14.3	5.4	12.7	43.3
San Diego, CA	9.0	3.1	6.5	33.4
San Francisco, CA	10.6	2.3	6.8	36.7
San Jose, CA	8.4	2.5	5.8	34.7
Santa Rosa, CA	12.2	3.5	10.1	33.5
Savannah, GA	14.4	5.5	11.7	42.7
Seattle, WA	9.4	2.6	7.0	33.0
Sioux Falls, SD	10.2	3.1	9.2	30.9
Springfield, IL	15.1	5.8	13.1	36.3
Tallahassee, FL	10.2	4.9	8.6	32.9
Tampa, FL	12.1	4.1	9.9	38.2
Topeka, KS	15.8	4.1	14.3	39.0
Tyler, TX	12.4	4.8	9.4	37.9
Virginia Beach, VA	10.7	3.7	8.7	32.4
Visalia, CA	13.7	5.6	12.2	43.0
Washington, DC	11.7	4.3	9.7	35.2
Wilmington, NC	13.0	3.6	10.3	35.6
Winston-Salem, NC	10.5	3.1	8.6	32.4
U.S.	12.6	4.2	10.3	35.5

Note: Figures show percent of the civilian noninstitutionalized population that reported having a disability. Disability status is determined from from six types of difficulty: vision, hearing, cognitive, ambulatory, self-care, and independent living. For children under 5 years old, hearing and vision difficulty are used to determine disability status. For children between the ages of 5 and 14, disability status is determined from hearing, vision, cognitive, ambulatory, and self-care difficulties. For people aged 15 years and older, they are considered to have a disability if they have difficulty with any one of the six difficulty types.
Source: U.S. Census Bureau, 2013-2017 American Community Survey 5-Year Estimates

Disability by Age: Metro Area

Metro Area	All Ages	Under 18 Years Old	18 to 64 Years Old	65 Years and Over
Albany, NY	12.3	4.4	10.0	31.7
Albuquerque, NM	14.0	3.6	12.4	37.1
Allentown, PA	13.4	5.8	10.8	32.9
Anchorage, AK	11.2	3.6	10.2	37.8
Ann Arbor, MI	8.8	2.9	6.8	29.0
Athens, GA	11.9	4.4	10.1	34.8
Atlanta, GA	10.1	3.4	8.7	33.9
Austin, TX	9.2	3.7	7.7	32.6
Baton Rouge, LA	14.1	5.7	12.1	39.8
Billings, MT	13.1	5.6	10.7	33.3
Boise City, ID	11.6	4.2	10.2	32.9
Boston, MA	10.6	4.0	8.0	32.0
Boulder, CO	8.3	2.9	6.5	26.8
Cape Coral, FL	13.8	3.9	9.9	28.6
Cedar Rapids, IA	10.3	4.0	8.1	29.3
Charleston, SC	12.0	4.1	9.9	34.7
Charlotte, NC	11.0	3.6	9.4	33.9
Chicago, IL	9.9	3.0	7.7	33.6
Clarksville, TN	15.2	4.9	15.3	42.4
College Station, TX	9.4	3.9	7.1	38.2
Colorado Springs, CO	12.3	4.0	11.4	33.8
Columbia, MO	11.3	4.1	9.6	35.7
Columbia, SC	13.4	3.8	11.8	36.7
Columbus, OH	11.9	4.6	10.3	34.6
Dallas, TX	9.6	3.4	8.1	34.9
Denver, CO	9.3	3.0	7.6	31.7
Des Moines, IA	10.5	3.9	9.2	31.3
Durham, NC	11.1	3.7	9.2	32.3
Edison, NJ	10.2	3.3	7.4	33.0
El Paso, TX	13.9	5.0	12.0	46.3
Eugene, OR	16.8	5.4	14.4	37.7
Evansville, IN	15.2	5.5	13.4	36.6
Fargo, ND	9.9	3.2	8.1	34.7
Fayetteville, NC	16.5	6.6	15.6	45.2
Fort Collins, CO	9.8	3.3	7.6	29.5
Fort Wayne, IN	12.7	4.7	11.5	33.4
Fort Worth, TX	9.6	3.4	8.1	34.9
Gainesville, FL	11.2	3.5	8.6	35.6
Grand Rapids, MI	11.8	4.3	10.2	33.5
Greeley, CO	10.2	2.9	8.8	35.4
Green Bay, WI	11.6	4.7	9.8	31.1
Greensboro, NC	12.4	3.9	10.4	33.6
Honolulu, HI	11.0	2.8	7.6	33.9
Houston, TX	9.5	3.4	8.0	35.7
Huntsville, AL	13.4	4.8	11.0	38.1
Indianapolis, IN	12.6	4.8	10.9	36.5
Jacksonville, FL	13.3	4.7	11.3	35.9
Kansas City, MO	12.2	4.0	10.6	34.7
Lafayette, LA	14.1	4.5	12.8	40.3
Las Cruces, NM	12.6	3.5	10.1	39.5
Las Vegas, NV	12.4	3.8	10.5	35.7
Lexington, KY	12.8	4.2	11.1	36.4
Lincoln, NE	10.5	4.1	8.3	33.8
Little Rock, AR	15.2	6.1	13.2	40.0
Los Angeles, CA	9.6	2.9	7.0	35.2

Table continued on next page.

Metro Area	All Ages	Under 18 Years Old	18 to 64 Years Old	65 Years and Over
Louisville, KY	14.4	4.7	12.7	37.0
Madison, WI	9.2	3.5	7.4	28.3
Manchester, NH	11.5	4.7	9.2	32.4
McAllen, TX	13.0	5.2	10.7	50.3
Miami, FL	11.0	3.4	7.4	33.3
Midland, TX	9.3	2.6	7.6	38.4
Minneapolis, MN	9.8	3.6	8.0	30.7
Nashville, TN	12.1	3.8	10.6	36.2
New Orleans, LA	13.7	4.7	11.7	37.2
New York, NY	10.2	3.3	7.4	33.0
Oklahoma City, OK	13.7	4.5	12.2	39.6
Omaha, NE	10.9	3.5	9.6	33.3
Orlando, FL	11.8	4.7	9.5	34.1
Peoria, IL	11.5	3.3	9.1	32.7
Philadelphia, PA	12.4	4.6	10.1	33.8
Phoenix, AZ	11.3	3.6	9.2	33.3
Pittsburgh, PA	14.2	5.2	11.1	34.1
Portland, OR	12.2	4.0	10.3	35.3
Providence, RI	13.5	5.0	11.1	34.7
Provo, UT	7.6	3.2	7.1	33.1
Raleigh, NC	9.6	3.8	7.9	33.1
Reno, NV	12.2	4.4	10.3	32.0
Richmond, VA	12.2	4.9	10.2	32.8
Roanoke, VA	14.4	5.1	11.7	34.0
Rochester, MN	10.3	3.9	7.9	30.5
Salem, OR	14.7	5.3	12.9	37.7
Salt Lake City, UT	9.4	3.4	8.2	34.2
San Antonio, TX	13.8	5.0	12.1	40.6
San Diego, CA	9.8	3.0	7.2	34.3
San Francisco, CA	10.0	2.9	7.2	32.7
San Jose, CA	7.9	2.3	5.3	32.5
Santa Rosa, CA	12.0	3.4	9.8	30.2
Savannah, GA	13.2	4.9	11.1	38.5
Seattle, WA	11.0	3.5	9.1	34.6
Sioux Falls, SD	9.9	3.2	8.8	30.5
Springfield, IL	13.9	5.8	11.6	35.0
Tallahassee, FL	12.7	5.9	10.4	35.0
Tampa, FL	14.0	4.4	10.9	34.4
Topeka, KS	14.5	4.4	12.7	35.9
Tyler, TX	13.6	5.3	11.4	35.7
Virginia Beach, VA	12.4	4.4	10.5	34.4
Visalia, CA	12.3	4.1	11.0	44.4
Washington, DC	8.5	3.0	6.7	29.6
Wilmington, NC	13.4	4.2	11.2	33.8
Winston-Salem, NC	12.9	4.2	10.6	34.7
U.S.	12.6	4.2	10.3	35.5

Note: Figures show percent of the civilian noninstitutionalized population that reported having a disability. Disability status is determined from from six types of difficulty: vision, hearing, cognitive, ambulatory, self-care, and independent living. For children under 5 years old, hearing and vision difficulty are used to determine disability status. For children between the ages of 5 and 14, disability status is determined from hearing, vision, cognitive, ambulatory, and self-care difficulties. For people aged 15 years and older, they are considered to have a disability if they have difficulty with any one of the six difficulty types; Figures cover the Metropolitan Statistical Area—see Appendix B for areas included

Source: U.S. Census Bureau, 2013-2017 American Community Survey 5-Year Estimates

Male/Female Ratio: City

City	Males	Females	Males per 100 Females
Albany, NY	46,249	52,249	88.5
Albuquerque, NM	271,465	285,253	95.2
Allentown, PA	58,145	61,983	93.8
Anchorage, AK	152,311	145,914	104.4
Ann Arbor, MI	59,344	59,959	99.0
Athens, GA	58,197	64,095	90.8
Atlanta, GA	228,038	237,192	96.1
Austin, TX	463,869	453,037	102.4
Baton Rouge, LA	108,014	119,535	90.4
Billings, MT	52,955	56,127	94.3
Boise City, ID	109,423	111,436	98.2
Boston, MA	321,703	347,455	92.6
Boulder, CO	55,395	50,876	108.9
Cape Coral, FL	84,138	89,541	94.0
Cedar Rapids, IA	63,400	66,930	94.7
Charleston, SC	62,890	68,314	92.1
Charlotte, NC	395,854	430,206	92.0
Chicago, IL	1,321,621	1,400,965	94.3
Clarksville, TN	73,898	73,873	100.0
College Station, TX	54,425	53,020	102.6
Colorado Springs, CO	224,484	225,516	99.5
Columbia, MO	56,935	61,685	92.3
Columbia, SC	67,861	64,375	105.4
Columbus, OH	415,208	436,936	95.0
Dallas, TX	644,344	655,778	98.3
Denver, CO	339,400	339,067	100.1
Des Moines, IA	105,981	108,797	97.4
Durham, NC	120,795	136,437	88.5
Edison, NJ	49,950	52,354	95.4
El Paso, TX	330,360	347,906	95.0
Eugene, OR	80,505	82,630	97.4
Evansville, IN	57,153	62,653	91.2
Fargo, ND	59,777	58,322	102.5
Fayetteville, NC	106,042	104,282	101.7
Fort Collins, CO	79,742	79,408	100.4
Fort Wayne, IN	126,804	135,646	93.5
Fort Worth, TX	408,803	426,326	95.9
Gainesville, FL	62,173	67,221	92.5
Grand Rapids, MI	96,186	99,169	97.0
Greeley, CO	49,599	51,161	96.9
Green Bay, WI	51,679	53,117	97.3
Greensboro, NC	132,805	152,011	87.4
Honolulu, HI	173,063	177,725	97.4
Houston, TX	1,135,634	1,131,702	100.3
Huntsville, AL	92,044	98,457	93.5
Indianapolis, IN	411,970	441,461	93.3
Jacksonville, FL	419,756	447,557	93.8
Kansas City, MO	232,170	244,804	94.8
Lafayette, LA	61,985	64,491	96.1
Las Cruces, NM	49,468	51,546	96.0
Las Vegas, NV	310,539	311,123	99.8
Lexington, KY	154,530	160,579	96.2
Lincoln, NE	139,057	138,258	100.6
Little Rock, AR	95,087	102,693	92.6
Los Angeles, CA	1,953,844	1,995,932	97.9

Table continued on next page.

City	Males	Females	Males per 100 Females
Louisville, KY	297,551	317,927	93.6
Madison, WI	123,054	125,802	97.8
Manchester, NH	56,555	54,046	104.6
McAllen, TX	69,425	70,413	98.6
Miami, FL	219,009	223,998	97.8
Midland, TX	66,129	65,157	101.5
Minneapolis, MN	208,322	203,130	102.6
Nashville, TN	315,266	338,921	93.0
New Orleans, LA	185,063	203,119	91.1
New York, NY	4,079,907	4,480,165	91.1
Oklahoma City, OK	309,360	319,831	96.7
Omaha, NE	228,597	234,484	97.5
Orlando, FL	130,347	139,067	93.7
Peoria, IL	54,890	60,534	90.7
Philadelphia, PA	742,412	827,245	89.7
Phoenix, AZ	784,828	789,593	99.4
Pittsburgh, PA	149,303	155,709	95.9
Portland, OR	312,021	318,310	98.0
Providence, RI	86,442	93,067	92.9
Provo, UT	58,177	58,022	100.3
Raleigh, NC	217,048	232,429	93.4
Reno, NV	121,150	118,582	102.2
Richmond, VA	104,853	116,039	90.4
Roanoke, VA	47,736	51,836	92.1
Rochester, MN	54,584	58,099	93.9
Salem, OR	81,919	81,735	100.2
Salt Lake City, UT	100,038	94,150	106.3
San Antonio, TX	719,677	741,946	97.0
San Diego, CA	700,029	690,937	101.3
San Francisco, CA	440,633	423,630	104.0
San Jose, CA	516,124	506,907	101.8
Santa Rosa, CA	84,326	89,918	93.8
Savannah, GA	68,627	76,467	89.7
Seattle, WA	345,628	342,617	100.9
Sioux Falls, SD	84,964	85,437	99.4
Springfield, IL	55,284	61,029	90.6
Tallahassee, FL	89,060	99,403	89.6
Tampa, FL	177,778	190,309	93.4
Topeka, KS	60,948	66,191	92.1
Tyler, TX	48,565	53,996	89.9
Virginia Beach, VA	221,350	228,707	96.8
Visalia, CA	62,580	67,467	92.8
Washington, DC	319,046	353,345	90.3
Wilmington, NC	54,045	61,216	88.3
Winston-Salem, NC	112,867	127,326	88.6
U.S.	158,018,753	162,985,654	97.0

Source: U.S. Census Bureau, 2013-2017 American Community Survey 5-Year Estimates

Male/Female Ratio: Metro Area

Metro Area	Males	Females	Males per 100 Females
Albany, NY	431,315	450,547	95.7
Albuquerque, NM	444,821	460,228	96.7
Allentown, PA	407,842	424,948	96.0
Anchorage, AK	205,078	194,282	105.6
Ann Arbor, MI	178,949	182,560	98.0
Athens, GA	98,156	104,624	93.8
Atlanta, GA	2,759,925	2,941,065	93.8
Austin, TX	1,001,806	998,784	100.3
Baton Rouge, LA	406,015	422,726	96.0
Billings, MT	82,512	85,033	97.0
Boise City, ID	338,305	339,041	99.8
Boston, MA	2,317,311	2,454,625	94.4
Boulder, CO	159,112	157,670	100.9
Cape Coral, FL	342,731	357,434	95.9
Cedar Rapids, IA	131,848	134,274	98.2
Charleston, SC	363,546	380,649	95.5
Charlotte, NC	1,177,333	1,249,691	94.2
Chicago, IL	4,671,861	4,877,368	95.8
Clarksville, TN	141,675	137,169	103.3
College Station, TX	125,550	123,004	102.1
Colorado Springs, CO	352,044	346,551	101.6
Columbia, MO	84,812	89,777	94.5
Columbia, SC	392,671	415,706	94.5
Columbus, OH	995,328	1,028,367	96.8
Dallas, TX	3,493,829	3,610,586	96.8
Denver, CO	1,396,026	1,402,658	99.5
Des Moines, IA	306,668	316,445	96.9
Durham, NC	263,517	286,764	91.9
Edison, NJ	9,762,858	10,429,184	93.6
El Paso, TX	411,040	427,487	96.2
Eugene, OR	179,116	184,355	97.2
Evansville, IN	153,544	161,719	94.9
Fargo, ND	116,897	115,763	101.0
Fayetteville, NC	191,780	193,557	99.1
Fort Collins, CO	164,920	166,056	99.3
Fort Wayne, IN	209,819	219,241	95.7
Fort Worth, TX	3,493,829	3,610,586	96.8
Gainesville, FL	134,695	142,361	94.6
Grand Rapids, MI	513,783	525,399	97.8
Greeley, CO	143,783	141,946	101.3
Green Bay, WI	157,496	158,351	99.5
Greensboro, NC	359,693	391,897	91.8
Honolulu, HI	498,993	491,067	101.6
Houston, TX	3,297,364	3,338,844	98.8
Huntsville, AL	218,457	226,451	96.5
Indianapolis, IN	971,355	1,017,677	95.4
Jacksonville, FL	705,474	742,410	95.0
Kansas City, MO	1,024,354	1,064,476	96.2
Lafayette, LA	238,051	249,582	95.4
Las Cruces, NM	105,094	108,755	96.6
Las Vegas, NV	1,056,002	1,056,434	100.0
Lexington, KY	245,089	255,600	95.9
Lincoln, NE	162,370	161,032	100.8
Little Rock, AR	354,144	376,202	94.1
Los Angeles, CA	6,537,886	6,723,652	97.2

Table continued on next page.

Metro Area	Males	Females	Males per 100 Females
Louisville, KY	623,967	654,236	95.4
Madison, WI	318,828	321,244	99.2
Manchester, NH	201,775	204,596	98.6
McAllen, TX	410,383	429,156	95.6
Miami, FL	2,923,416	3,096,374	94.4
Midland, TX	83,194	82,236	101.2
Minneapolis, MN	1,745,774	1,780,375	98.1
Nashville, TN	893,066	937,344	95.3
New Orleans, LA	609,832	650,828	93.7
New York, NY	9,762,858	10,429,184	93.6
Oklahoma City, OK	667,697	685,807	97.4
Omaha, NE	452,361	461,829	97.9
Orlando, FL	1,169,047	1,221,812	95.7
Peoria, IL	184,718	192,540	95.9
Philadelphia, PA	2,932,332	3,133,312	93.6
Phoenix, AZ	2,267,129	2,293,909	98.8
Pittsburgh, PA	1,141,403	1,206,740	94.6
Portland, OR	1,178,136	1,203,901	97.9
Providence, RI	782,300	830,854	94.2
Provo, UT	296,365	290,825	101.9
Raleigh, NC	620,902	653,083	95.1
Reno, NV	226,106	223,336	101.2
Richmond, VA	615,033	655,125	93.9
Roanoke, VA	151,071	161,998	93.3
Rochester, MN	105,686	108,799	97.1
Salem, OR	203,322	206,797	98.3
Salt Lake City, UT	587,531	582,526	100.9
San Antonio, TX	1,173,885	1,203,622	97.5
San Diego, CA	1,651,147	1,632,518	101.1
San Francisco, CA	2,292,525	2,349,295	97.6
San Jose, CA	992,525	977,372	101.6
Santa Rosa, CA	245,381	255,562	96.0
Savannah, GA	183,354	194,122	94.5
Seattle, WA	1,865,943	1,869,273	99.8
Sioux Falls, SD	125,534	125,030	100.4
Springfield, IL	101,183	109,367	92.5
Tallahassee, FL	182,931	194,743	93.9
Tampa, FL	1,442,886	1,535,323	94.0
Topeka, KS	114,091	119,291	95.6
Tyler, TX	107,355	114,922	93.4
Virginia Beach, VA	845,945	871,763	97.0
Visalia, CA	229,488	229,321	100.1
Washington, DC	2,975,354	3,114,842	95.5
Wilmington, NC	133,775	143,721	93.1
Winston-Salem, NC	316,610	341,585	92.7
U.S.	158,018,753	162,985,654	97.0

Note: Figures cover the Metropolitan Statistical Area (MSA)—see Appendix B for areas included
Source: U.S. Census Bureau, 2013-2017 American Community Survey 5-Year Estimates

Gross Metropolitan Product

MSA[1]	2016	2017	2018	2019	Rank[2]
Albany, NY	52.8	54.5	56.3	58.8	57
Albuquerque, NM	43.2	44.8	46.8	48.7	63
Allentown, PA	42.6	44.1	46.1	48.3	64
Anchorage, AK	27.2	28.7	31.2	32.0	93
Ann Arbor, MI	22.0	22.8	23.7	25.0	114
Athens, GA	8.8	9.3	9.7	10.1	218
Atlanta, GA	368.8	384.3	402.8	425.7	10
Austin, TX	133.7	142.9	153.3	162.8	26
Baton Rouge, LA	52.0	53.7	56.3	59.2	59
Billings, MT	10.1	10.4	10.8	11.3	201
Boise City, ID	32.3	34.2	36.0	38.1	79
Boston, MA	422.7	441.4	461.9	486.3	9
Boulder, CO	24.0	25.3	26.7	28.1	106
Cape Coral, FL	27.4	28.7	30.2	32.3	94
Cedar Rapids, IA	18.3	18.6	19.1	19.9	134
Charleston, SC	39.0	40.7	42.6	45.2	73
Charlotte, NC	163.9	172.3	181.0	192.4	20
Chicago, IL	655.7	675.8	703.9	737.3	3
Clarksville, TN	10.7	10.9	11.5	12.1	194
College Station, TX	9.4	10.1	10.9	11.6	206
Colorado Springs, CO	31.4	33.0	34.8	36.9	82
Columbia, MO	8.9	9.2	9.4	9.9	220
Columbia, SC	40.3	41.6	43.2	45.6	71
Columbus, OH	130.5	137.2	143.9	151.8	29
Dallas, TX	506.8	541.1	579.3	613.4	4
Denver, CO	198.0	209.4	221.5	233.9	18
Des Moines, IA	52.3	54.4	55.9	58.9	58
Durham, NC	43.9	45.9	48.3	51.7	62
Edison, NJ	1,667.3	1,718.2	1,788.3	1,876.6	1
El Paso, TX	28.4	29.8	31.3	32.7	89
Eugene, OR	15.4	16.0	16.7	17.5	156
Evansville, IN	17.1	17.8	18.6	19.5	143
Fargo, ND	15.8	16.5	17.2	18.1	154
Fayetteville, NC	17.3	17.6	18.3	19.2	144
Fort Collins, CO	15.9	17.2	18.3	19.5	146
Fort Wayne, IN	21.1	21.9	22.7	23.8	115
Fort Worth, TX	506.8	541.1	579.3	613.4	4
Gainesville, FL	12.5	13.1	13.8	14.5	177
Grand Rapids, MI	58.4	61.0	63.9	67.2	53
Greeley, CO	11.2	12.3	13.7	14.9	185
Green Bay, WI	18.7	19.3	20.2	21.2	131
Greensboro, NC	40.0	40.9	42.4	44.3	72
Honolulu, HI	65.5	67.8	70.4	72.7	50
Houston, TX	474.1	500.8	544.6	580.0	7
Huntsville, AL	24.8	25.9	27.2	28.7	104
Indianapolis, IN	136.8	142.9	149.7	158.1	27
Jacksonville, FL	71.7	75.0	79.0	83.7	47
Kansas City, MO	128.9	133.1	138.9	146.3	32
Lafayette, LA	20.9	21.6	23.0	24.3	117
Las Cruces, NM	6.9	7.1	7.4	7.8	251
Las Vegas, NV	111.6	117.3	124.9	133.2	36
Lexington, KY	28.8	29.9	31.2	32.7	88
Lincoln, NE	19.8	20.3	20.9	22.0	125
Little Rock, AR	38.0	39.3	40.6	42.5	74
Los Angeles, CA	1,008.2	1,048.6	1,094.1	1,152.4	2
Louisville, KY	74.6	77.5	80.2	84.0	46

Table continued on next page.

MSA[1]	2016	2017	2018	2019	Rank[2]
Madison, WI	48.1	50.3	52.9	55.9	61
Manchester, NH	26.8	27.8	29.1	30.5	98
McAllen, TX	19.4	20.5	21.7	22.7	123
Miami, FL	329.7	340.9	356.6	376.6	12
Midland, TX	24.0	26.9	32.7	35.4	100
Minneapolis, MN	249.4	259.5	268.3	282.1	15
Nashville, TN	125.5	132.2	139.5	148.2	33
New Orleans, LA	78.0	80.5	84.4	88.1	45
New York, NY	1,667.3	1,718.2	1,788.3	1,876.6	1
Oklahoma City, OK	69.7	73.0	77.1	81.1	49
Omaha, NE	63.2	64.8	67.1	70.2	51
Orlando, FL	127.3	133.6	141.0	149.7	31
Peoria, IL	20.1	20.5	21.3	22.3	124
Philadelphia, PA	430.6	447.6	467.8	490.3	8
Phoenix, AZ	231.1	243.7	260.0	277.6	16
Pittsburgh, PA	138.0	143.8	150.5	157.4	25
Portland, OR	164.9	171.8	181.4	192.5	21
Providence, RI	80.2	82.8	86.6	90.6	44
Provo, UT	23.4	25.0	26.4	28.2	108
Raleigh, NC	79.9	84.0	88.7	94.8	42
Reno, NV	26.0	27.8	29.8	31.7	99
Richmond, VA	80.2	82.9	86.8	91.3	43
Roanoke, VA	15.2	15.4	16.0	16.7	158
Rochester, MN	12.1	12.5	12.9	13.5	181
Salem, OR	16.1	16.7	17.6	18.5	149
Salt Lake City, UT	85.4	89.5	94.3	100.3	40
San Antonio, TX	115.4	122.3	129.7	136.4	35
San Diego, CA	216.7	227.6	239.8	254.4	17
San Francisco, CA	473.6	501.9	529.8	563.3	6
San Jose, CA	254.1	267.7	282.2	298.6	13
Santa Rosa, CA	27.5	29.1	30.4	32.0	91
Savannah, GA	17.9	18.6	19.1	20.0	135
Seattle, WA	335.5	357.5	376.1	396.4	11
Sioux Falls, SD	18.9	19.6	20.5	21.6	128
Springfield, IL	10.0	10.1	10.3	10.7	205
Tallahassee, FL	15.8	16.5	17.3	18.3	153
Tampa, FL	143.2	148.6	156.2	165.6	24
Topeka, KS	10.6	10.8	11.1	11.5	196
Tyler, TX	13.4	14.1	15.4	16.0	169
Virginia Beach, VA	92.2	95.1	99.3	104.4	39
Visalia, CA	15.8	16.7	17.6	18.6	152
Washington, DC	508.6	528.9	555.4	585.9	5
Wilmington, NC	14.2	14.7	15.3	16.2	163
Winston-Salem, NC	28.8	29.4	30.6	32.1	90

Note: Figures are in billions of dollars; (1) Metropolitan Statistical Area—see Appendix B for areas included; (2) Rank is based on 2017 data and ranges from 1 to 381.
Source: The U.S. Conference of Mayors, U.S. Metro Economies: Economic Growth & Full Employment, June 2018

Economic Growth

MSA[1]	2017-2018 (%)	2019-2020 (%)	2021-2022 (%)
Albany, NY	1.8	1.8	0.9
Albuquerque, NM	2.5	1.9	1.6
Allentown, PA	1.9	1.9	1.3
Anchorage, AK	1.5	1.5	1.6
Ann Arbor, MI	2.8	2.4	1.5
Athens, GA	2.6	1.7	1.1
Atlanta, GA	2.8	2.8	2.0
Austin, TX	4.9	3.4	2.9
Baton Rouge, LA	1.9	2.8	2.6
Billings, MT	1.8	1.9	1.3
Boise City, ID	3.7	3.1	2.2
Boston, MA	2.6	2.5	1.7
Boulder, CO	3.2	2.7	1.7
Cape Coral, FL	3.5	4.0	2.9
Cedar Rapids, IA	0.7	1.8	1.5
Charleston, SC	3.0	3.2	2.3
Charlotte, NC	3.5	3.3	2.3
Chicago, IL	1.6	1.9	1.0
Clarksville, TN	1.7	2.4	1.4
College Station, TX	4.9	2.8	2.1
Colorado Springs, CO	3.3	3.1	2.1
Columbia, MO	1.4	2.4	2.2
Columbia, SC	2.1	2.8	2.0
Columbus, OH	3.1	2.6	1.7
Dallas, TX	4.6	3.1	2.3
Denver, CO	3.0	2.8	2.1
Des Moines, IA	2.3	2.5	2.3
Durham, NC	3.1	4.0	2.8
Edison, NJ	2.0	2.1	1.3
El Paso, TX	3.5	2.0	1.5
Eugene, OR	2.3	2.0	1.3
Evansville, IN	2.4	1.9	1.0
Fargo, ND	0.4	1.6	1.5
Fayetteville, NC	0.7	2.3	1.5
Fort Collins, CO	4.8	4.0	2.7
Fort Wayne, IN	2.0	1.9	1.1
Fort Worth, TX	4.6	3.1	2.3
Gainesville, FL	3.1	2.5	1.8
Grand Rapids, MI	3.5	2.4	1.2
Greeley, CO	6.3	5.3	3.2
Green Bay, WI	1.8	2.3	1.5
Greensboro, NC	1.1	1.9	1.1
Honolulu, HI	1.2	1.2	1.2
Houston, TX	3.6	4.1	2.8
Huntsville, AL	3.6	2.7	2.9
Indianapolis, IN	2.7	2.8	2.1
Jacksonville, FL	3.6	3.0	2.3
Kansas City, MO	1.9	2.4	1.9
Lafayette, LA	0.8	3.4	2.6
Las Cruces, NM	0.5	2.3	2.4
Las Vegas, NV	3.1	3.6	2.6
Lexington, KY	2.2	2.0	1.1
Lincoln, NE	0.9	2.1	1.9
Little Rock, AR	2.7	1.9	1.3
Los Angeles, CA	2.1	2.5	1.5
Louisville, KY	2.4	1.9	1.1

Table continued on next page.

MSA[1]	2017-2018 (%)	2019-2020 (%)	2021-2022 (%)
Madison, WI	2.8	2.7	2.1
Manchester, NH	2.1	2.4	1.6
McAllen, TX	3.8	2.4	2.3
Miami, FL	2.7	2.8	1.9
Midland, TX	7.6	6.9	4.7
Minneapolis, MN	2.8	2.5	1.8
Nashville, TN	3.5	3.2	2.2
New Orleans, LA	1.5	2.2	1.9
New York, NY	2.0	2.1	1.3
Oklahoma City, OK	2.9	2.9	2.1
Omaha, NE	1.1	1.9	1.9
Orlando, FL	3.9	3.3	2.5
Peoria, IL	0.8	1.8	1.0
Philadelphia, PA	2.3	2.0	1.4
Phoenix, AZ	3.4	3.8	2.5
Pittsburgh, PA	1.9	1.7	1.1
Portland, OR	2.9	3.0	1.9
Providence, RI	1.8	1.9	1.1
Provo, UT	4.6	4.4	3.3
Raleigh, NC	3.7	4.0	3.0
Reno, NV	4.1	3.5	1.9
Richmond, VA	2.0	2.3	1.5
Roanoke, VA	0.5	1.5	0.8
Rochester, MN	1.6	1.7	1.2
Salem, OR	2.4	2.6	1.8
Salt Lake City, UT	3.3	3.5	2.5
San Antonio, TX	3.4	2.5	2.2
San Diego, CA	3.0	3.2	2.1
San Francisco, CA	3.8	3.4	2.2
San Jose, CA	3.5	3.1	2.3
Santa Rosa, CA	2.9	2.2	1.2
Savannah, GA	1.3	1.7	0.8
Seattle, WA	4.0	2.8	2.0
Sioux Falls, SD	1.5	2.9	2.2
Springfield, IL	-0.2	1.1	0.6
Tallahassee, FL	2.9	2.6	1.9
Tampa, FL	3.2	3.1	2.2
Topeka, KS	0.4	0.8	0.1
Tyler, TX	1.7	2.4	1.9
Virginia Beach, VA	1.6	2.1	1.6
Visalia, CA	2.0	3.0	2.3
Washington, DC	2.3	2.4	2.0
Wilmington, NC	2.1	3.0	2.0
Winston-Salem, NC	1.3	2.2	1.1

Note: Figures are real gross metropolitan product (GMP) growth rates and represent annual average percent change;
(1) Metropolitan Statistical Area—see Appendix B for areas included
Source: The U.S. Conference of Mayors, U.S. Metro Economies: Economic Growth & Full Employment, June 2018

Metropolitan Area Exports

Area	2012	2013	2014	2015	2016	2017	Rank[2]
Albany, NY	3,420.1	3,946.1	4,547.0	4,470.3	4,135.0	3,883.2	64
Albuquerque, NM	1,790.6	1,389.6	1,564.0	1,761.2	999.7	624.2	189
Allentown, PA	2,939.0	2,949.9	3,152.5	3,439.9	3,657.2	3,639.4	67
Anchorage, AK	416.4	518.0	571.8	421.9	1,215.4	1,675.9	114
Ann Arbor, MI	1,053.4	1,156.2	1,213.6	1,053.0	1,207.9	1,447.4	120
Athens, GA	229.7	286.0	320.8	327.4	332.1	297.7	253
Atlanta, GA	18,169.1	18,827.9	19,870.3	19,163.9	20,480.1	21,748.0	14
Austin, TX	8,976.6	8,870.8	9,400.0	10,094.5	10,682.7	12,451.5	27
Baton Rouge, LA	5,820.2	6,261.5	7,528.3	6,505.4	6,580.5	8,830.3	40
Billings, MT	141.4	139.8	133.2	66.8	50.7	78.8	349
Boise City, ID	4,088.2	3,657.9	3,143.4	2,668.0	3,021.7	2,483.3	86
Boston, MA	21,234.8	22,212.8	23,378.5	21,329.5	21,168.0	23,116.2	13
Boulder, CO	1,128.0	1,046.0	1,016.1	1,039.1	956.3	1,012.0	157
Cape Coral, FL	509.8	442.6	496.6	487.3	540.3	592.3	193
Cedar Rapids, IA	889.1	930.2	879.0	873.5	945.0	1,071.6	149
Charleston, SC	2,429.8	3,464.3	5,866.7	6,457.5	9,508.1	8,845.2	39
Charlotte, NC	6,322.6	10,684.1	12,885.3	13,985.8	11,944.1	13,122.5	24
Chicago, IL	40,568.0	44,910.6	47,340.1	44,820.9	43,932.7	46,140.2	5
Clarksville, TN	326.3	315.9	323.7	296.5	376.1	360.2	235
College Station, TX	103.6	108.7	129.7	122.5	113.2	145.4	319
Colorado Springs, CO	1,044.6	1,065.4	856.6	832.4	786.9	819.7	171
Columbia, MO	296.6	423.9	237.7	214.0	213.7	224.0	294
Columbia, SC	1,543.6	1,681.3	2,007.9	2,011.8	2,007.7	2,123.9	95
Columbus, OH	5,488.6	5,731.4	6,245.6	6,201.6	5,675.4	5,962.2	50
Dallas, TX	27,820.9	27,596.0	28,669.4	27,372.9	27,187.8	30,269.1	9
Denver, CO	3,355.8	3,618.4	4,958.6	3,909.5	3,649.3	3,954.7	63
Des Moines, IA	1,183.2	1,279.4	1,361.8	1,047.8	1,052.2	1,141.2	142
Durham, NC	2,723.2	2,971.7	2,934.0	2,807.2	2,937.4	3,128.4	76
Edison, NJ	102,298.0	106,922.8	105,266.6	95,645.4	89,649.5	93,693.7	2
El Paso, TX	12,796.9	14,359.7	20,079.3	24,560.9	26,452.8	25,814.1	12
Eugene, OR	482.2	476.0	495.7	400.2	371.8	391.3	229
Evansville, IN	4,025.3	3,865.6	3,756.5	4,483.7	3,022.4	4,001.9	62
Fargo, ND	785.9	817.9	782.8	543.2	474.5	519.5	205
Fayetteville, NC	322.3	344.0	375.8	256.3	179.8	231.6	290
Fort Collins, CO	861.7	986.1	1,037.4	990.7	993.8	1,034.1	153
Fort Wayne, IN	1,353.5	1,441.8	1,581.1	1,529.0	1,322.2	1,422.8	121
Fort Worth, TX	27,820.9	27,596.0	28,669.4	27,372.9	27,187.8	30,269.1	9
Gainesville, FL	348.6	295.0	304.3	291.6	277.3	292.1	255
Grand Rapids, MI	3,156.4	5,314.8	5,244.5	5,143.0	5,168.5	5,385.8	54
Greeley, CO	1,381.4	1,287.5	1,343.6	1,240.1	1,539.6	1,492.8	118
Green Bay, WI	1,031.6	914.8	988.7	968.1	1,044.0	1,054.8	151
Greensboro, NC	4,281.9	4,278.3	3,505.5	3,286.1	3,730.4	3,537.9	68
Honolulu, HI	306.3	323.2	765.5	446.4	330.3	393.6	228
Houston, TX	110,297.8	114,962.6	118,966.0	97,054.3	84,105.5	95,760.3	1
Huntsville, AL	1,491.5	1,518.7	1,440.4	1,344.7	1,827.3	1,889.2	105
Indianapolis, IN	10,436.0	9,747.5	9,539.4	9,809.4	9,655.4	10,544.2	30
Jacksonville, FL	2,595.0	2,467.8	2,473.7	2,564.4	2,159.0	2,141.7	94
Kansas City, MO	7,880.8	8,012.1	8,262.9	6,723.2	6,709.8	7,015.0	46
Lafayette, LA	726.0	1,261.8	1,532.7	1,165.2	1,335.2	954.8	162
Las Cruces, NM	746.1	433.0	1,346.3	1,593.7	1,568.6	1,390.2	122
Las Vegas, NV	1,811.5	2,008.2	2,509.7	2,916.2	2,312.3	2,710.6	80
Lexington, KY	2,462.1	2,294.0	2,191.4	2,065.7	2,069.6	2,119.8	96
Lincoln, NE	904.7	818.4	1,173.9	1,189.3	796.9	860.9	167
Little Rock, AR	2,418.9	2,497.5	2,463.5	1,777.5	1,871.0	2,146.1	93
Los Angeles, CA	75,007.5	76,305.7	75,471.2	61,758.7	61,245.7	63,752.9	3
Louisville, KY	7,706.7	8,898.0	8,877.3	8,037.9	7,793.3	8,925.9	38

Table continued on next page.

Area	2012	2013	2014	2015	2016	2017	Rank[2]
Madison, WI	2,168.7	2,292.1	2,369.5	2,280.4	2,204.8	2,187.7	92
Manchester, NH	1,634.9	1,445.8	1,575.4	1,556.6	1,465.2	1,714.7	111
McAllen, TX	5,198.5	5,265.5	5,316.0	5,327.1	5,214.3	5,659.0	52
Miami, FL	47,858.7	41,771.5	37,969.5	33,258.5	32,734.5	34,780.5	7
Midland, TX	104.4	164.1	122.7	110.1	69.6	69.4	353
Minneapolis, MN	25,155.7	23,747.5	21,198.2	19,608.6	18,329.2	19,070.9	18
Nashville, TN	6,402.1	8,702.8	9,620.9	9,353.0	9,460.1	10,164.3	31
New Orleans, LA	24,359.5	30,030.9	34,881.5	27,023.3	29,518.8	31,648.5	8
New York, NY	102,298.0	106,922.8	105,266.6	95,645.4	89,649.5	93,693.7	2
Oklahoma City, OK	1,574.6	1,581.7	1,622.0	1,353.1	1,260.0	1,278.8	129
Omaha, NE	3,529.3	4,255.9	4,528.5	3,753.4	3,509.7	3,756.2	65
Orlando, FL	3,850.6	3,227.7	3,134.8	3,082.7	3,363.9	3,196.7	75
Peoria, IL	17,838.0	12,184.5	11,234.8	9,826.9	7,260.1	9,403.6	33
Philadelphia, PA	22,991.6	24,929.2	26,321.3	24,236.1	21,359.9	21,689.7	15
Phoenix, AZ	10,834.3	11,473.5	12,764.4	13,821.5	12,838.2	13,223.1	23
Pittsburgh, PA	14,134.7	10,444.4	10,015.8	9,137.1	7,971.0	9,322.7	34
Portland, OR	20,337.7	17,606.8	18,667.2	18,847.8	20,256.8	20,788.8	17
Providence, RI	5,830.8	6,609.0	6,595.1	5,048.8	6,595.7	7,125.4	45
Provo, UT	2,058.1	2,789.2	2,533.4	2,216.4	1,894.8	2,065.3	100
Raleigh, NC	2,308.1	2,280.6	2,713.1	2,553.4	2,620.4	2,865.8	78
Reno, NV	2,019.0	2,117.4	2,138.9	1,943.3	2,382.1	2,517.3	85
Richmond, VA	4,328.1	4,337.2	3,307.0	3,325.9	3,525.7	3,663.7	66
Roanoke, VA	716.6	746.5	690.9	637.6	613.3	616.2	190
Rochester, MN	1,023.7	1,061.0	720.5	530.2	398.0	495.3	209
Salem, OR	437.3	414.4	374.8	385.4	358.2	339.0	238
Salt Lake City, UT	15,990.0	11,867.2	8,361.5	10,380.5	8,653.7	7,916.9	43
San Antonio, TX	14,010.2	19,287.6	25,781.8	15,919.2	5,621.2	9,184.1	35
San Diego, CA	17,183.3	17,885.5	18,585.7	17,439.7	18,086.6	18,637.1	19
San Francisco, CA	23,031.7	25,305.3	26,863.7	25,061.1	24,506.3	29,103.8	10
San Jose, CA	26,687.7	23,413.1	21,128.8	19,827.2	21,716.8	21,464.7	16
Santa Rosa, CA	1,059.1	1,044.8	1,103.7	1,119.8	1,194.3	1,168.2	138
Savannah, GA	4,116.5	5,436.4	5,093.4	5,447.5	4,263.4	4,472.0	59
Seattle, WA	50,301.7	56,686.4	61,938.4	67,226.4	61,881.0	59,007.0	4
Sioux Falls, SD	439.5	433.0	455.3	375.0	334.3	386.8	230
Springfield, IL	99.5	97.5	94.4	111.7	88.3	107.5	335
Tallahassee, FL	130.8	122.5	174.0	191.2	223.1	241.1	284
Tampa, FL	7,190.0	6,673.0	5,817.3	5,660.4	5,702.9	6,256.0	49
Topeka, KS	265.0	303.3	365.0	363.5	305.2	300.7	252
Tyler, TX	221.1	219.6	301.1	207.3	176.7	234.5	287
Virginia Beach, VA	2,735.0	2,539.2	3,573.2	3,556.4	3,291.1	3,307.2	70
Visalia, CA	1,113.4	1,178.7	1,323.7	1,086.8	1,097.1	1,371.6	124
Washington, DC	14,609.7	16,225.0	13,053.6	13,900.4	13,582.4	12,736.1	26
Wilmington, NC	923.5	766.7	571.9	617.3	598.7	759.8	177
Winston-Salem, NC	1,148.1	1,660.1	1,441.9	1,267.4	1,234.6	1,131.7	144

Note: Figures are in millions of dollars; (1) Metropolitan Statistical Area—see Appendix B for areas included; (2) Rank is based on 2017 data and ranges from 1 to 387
Source: U.S. Department of Commerce, International Trade Administration, Office of Trade and Economic Analysis, Industry and Analysis, Exports by Metropolitan Area, extracted March 25, 2019

Building Permits: City

City	Single-Family			Multi-Family			Total		
	2016	2017	Pct. Chg.	2016	2017	Pct. Chg.	2016	2017	Pct. Chg.
Albany, NY	10	9	-10.0	93	109	17.2	103	118	14.6
Albuquerque, NM	913	1,088	19.2	379	184	-51.5	1,292	1,272	-1.5
Allentown, PA	16	15	-6.3	0	0	0.0	16	15	-6.3
Anchorage, AK	719	800	11.3	211	219	3.8	930	1,019	9.6
Ann Arbor, MI	25	105	320.0	0	7	–	25	112	348.0
Athens, GA	115	189	64.3	4	176	4,300.0	119	365	206.7
Atlanta, GA	855	922	7.8	7,176	4,179	-41.8	8,031	5,101	-36.5
Austin, TX	3,705	4,440	19.8	5,198	7,139	37.3	8,903	11,579	30.1
Baton Rouge, LA	284	253	-10.9	0	0	0.0	284	253	-10.9
Billings, MT	525	432	-17.7	12	60	400.0	537	492	-8.4
Boise City, ID	682	810	18.8	717	350	-51.2	1,399	1,160	-17.1
Boston, MA	56	52	-7.1	3,292	5,033	52.9	3,348	5,085	51.9
Boulder, CO	85	74	-12.9	16	128	700.0	101	202	100.0
Cape Coral, FL	1,443	1,842	27.7	144	708	391.7	1,587	2,550	60.7
Cedar Rapids, IA	268	219	-18.3	127	313	146.5	395	532	34.7
Charleston, SC	692	766	10.7	350	303	-13.4	1,042	1,069	2.6
Charlotte, NC	n/a	n/a	n/a	n/a	n/a	n/a	n/a	n/a	n/a
Chicago, IL	613	525	-14.4	8,491	8,414	-0.9	9,104	8,939	-1.8
Clarksville, TN	788	806	2.3	256	227	-11.3	1,044	1,033	-1.1
College Station, TX	735	594	-19.2	1,165	1,319	13.2	1,900	1,913	0.7
Colorado Springs, CO	n/a	n/a	n/a	n/a	n/a	n/a	n/a	n/a	n/a
Columbia, MO	568	403	-29.0	405	861	112.6	973	1,264	29.9
Columbia, SC	251	341	35.9	0	8	–	251	349	39.0
Columbus, OH	649	650	0.2	3,071	3,579	16.5	3,720	4,229	13.7
Dallas, TX	1,640	2,100	28.0	8,697	5,151	-40.8	10,337	7,251	-29.9
Denver, CO	1,887	2,370	25.6	5,955	8,155	36.9	7,842	10,525	34.2
Des Moines, IA	236	173	-26.7	1,209	1,124	-7.0	1,445	1,297	-10.2
Durham, NC	1,647	1,783	8.3	1,332	1,179	-11.5	2,979	2,962	-0.6
Edison, NJ	70	58	-17.1	0	0	0.0	70	58	-17.1
El Paso, TX	2,014	2,020	0.3	829	897	8.2	2,843	2,917	2.6
Eugene, OR	324	364	12.3	423	15	-96.5	747	379	-49.3
Evansville, IN	96	72	-25.0	80	6	-92.5	176	78	-55.7
Fargo, ND	474	444	-6.3	859	781	-9.1	1,333	1,225	-8.1
Fayetteville, NC	296	257	-13.2	0	56	–	296	313	5.7
Fort Collins, CO	488	657	34.6	1,386	720	-48.1	1,874	1,377	-26.5
Fort Wayne, IN	n/a	n/a	n/a	n/a	n/a	n/a	n/a	n/a	n/a
Fort Worth, TX	3,459	5,042	45.8	3,949	3,814	-3.4	7,408	8,856	19.5
Gainesville, FL	76	118	55.3	247	1,200	385.8	323	1,318	308.0
Grand Rapids, MI	69	101	46.4	1,329	777	-41.5	1,398	878	-37.2
Greeley, CO	263	120	-54.4	312	229	-26.6	575	349	-39.3
Green Bay, WI	111	98	-11.7	0	0	0.0	111	98	-11.7
Greensboro, NC	549	728	32.6	960	881	-8.2	1,509	1,609	6.6
Honolulu, HI	n/a	n/a	n/a	n/a	n/a	n/a	n/a	n/a	n/a
Houston, TX	4,169	5,326	27.8	5,329	4,346	-18.4	9,498	9,672	1.8
Huntsville, AL	1,091	1,144	4.9	672	380	-43.5	1,763	1,524	-13.6
Indianapolis, IN	831	914	10.0	1,068	645	-39.6	1,899	1,559	-17.9
Jacksonville, FL	2,678	3,005	12.2	2,839	2,874	1.2	5,517	5,879	6.6
Kansas City, MO	825	824	-0.1	2,515	1,542	-38.7	3,340	2,366	-29.2
Lafayette, LA	n/a	n/a	n/a	n/a	n/a	n/a	n/a	n/a	n/a
Las Cruces, NM	418	478	14.4	13	315	2,323.1	431	793	84.0
Las Vegas, NV	1,454	1,605	10.4	826	276	-66.6	2,280	1,881	-17.5
Lexington, KY	670	743	10.9	695	605	-12.9	1,365	1,348	-1.2
Lincoln, NE	928	994	7.1	1,238	1,231	-0.6	2,166	2,225	2.7
Little Rock, AR	330	592	79.4	501	508	1.4	831	1,100	32.4

Table continued on next page.

City	Single-Family			Multi-Family			Total		
	2016	2017	Pct. Chg.	2016	2017	Pct. Chg.	2016	2017	Pct. Chg.
Los Angeles, CA	1,796	2,360	31.4	12,094	12,486	3.2	13,890	14,846	6.9
Louisville, KY	1,072	1,236	15.3	1,736	2,056	18.4	2,808	3,292	17.2
Madison, WI	340	379	11.5	2,041	1,809	-11.4	2,381	2,188	-8.1
Manchester, NH	141	149	5.7	157	95	-39.5	298	244	-18.1
McAllen, TX	450	438	-2.7	173	200	15.6	623	638	2.4
Miami, FL	87	90	3.4	3,823	4,671	22.2	3,910	4,761	21.8
Midland, TX	632	761	20.4	40	0	-100.0	672	761	13.2
Minneapolis, MN	169	137	-18.9	2,739	2,117	-22.7	2,908	2,254	-22.5
Nashville, TN	3,712	3,827	3.1	5,751	2,423	-57.9	9,463	6,250	-34.0
New Orleans, LA	280	447	59.6	328	213	-35.1	608	660	8.6
New York, NY	561	483	-13.9	15,719	21,618	37.5	16,280	22,101	35.8
Oklahoma City, OK	2,899	2,707	-6.6	291	48	-83.5	3,190	2,755	-13.6
Omaha, NE	1,427	1,533	7.4	1,137	1,697	49.3	2,564	3,230	26.0
Orlando, FL	730	828	13.4	930	818	-12.0	1,660	1,646	-0.8
Peoria, IL	39	32	-17.9	0	0	0.0	39	32	-17.9
Philadelphia, PA	904	783	-13.4	2,271	2,606	14.8	3,175	3,389	6.7
Phoenix, AZ	2,479	2,932	18.3	4,493	3,900	-13.2	6,972	6,832	-2.0
Pittsburgh, PA	63	66	4.8	373	410	9.9	436	476	9.2
Portland, OR	831	703	-15.4	4,098	6,086	48.5	4,929	6,789	37.7
Providence, RI	11	2	-81.8	51	2	-96.1	62	4	-93.5
Provo, UT	186	223	19.9	73	17	-76.7	259	240	-7.3
Raleigh, NC	1,412	1,365	-3.3	2,036	1,851	-9.1	3,448	3,216	-6.7
Reno, NV	1,059	1,124	6.1	1,315	1,210	-8.0	2,374	2,334	-1.7
Richmond, VA	280	326	16.4	230	991	330.9	510	1,317	158.2
Roanoke, VA	15	18	20.0	138	156	13.0	153	174	13.7
Rochester, MN	403	437	8.4	993	617	-37.9	1,396	1,054	-24.5
Salem, OR	302	319	5.6	490	655	33.7	792	974	23.0
Salt Lake City, UT	90	88	-2.2	3,175	542	-82.9	3,265	630	-80.7
San Antonio, TX	2,152	2,489	15.7	4,211	3,711	-11.9	6,363	6,200	-2.6
San Diego, CA	823	1,138	38.3	5,789	4,554	-21.3	6,612	5,692	-13.9
San Francisco, CA	123	43	-65.0	3,964	3,991	0.7	4,087	4,034	-1.3
San Jose, CA	222	177	-20.3	2,506	2,264	-9.7	2,728	2,441	-10.5
Santa Rosa, CA	104	232	123.1	134	112	-16.4	238	344	44.5
Savannah, GA	300	384	28.0	0	0	0.0	300	384	28.0
Seattle, WA	797	593	-25.6	9,202	9,294	1.0	9,999	9,887	-1.1
Sioux Falls, SD	1,059	1,192	12.6	1,451	1,202	-17.2	2,510	2,394	-4.6
Springfield, IL	74	57	-23.0	94	94	0.0	168	151	-10.1
Tallahassee, FL	330	379	14.8	539	1,156	114.5	869	1,535	76.6
Tampa, FL	934	1,010	8.1	3,328	2,165	-34.9	4,262	3,175	-25.5
Topeka, KS	100	85	-15.0	12	0	-100.0	112	85	-24.1
Tyler, TX	305	313	2.6	93	48	-48.4	398	361	-9.3
Virginia Beach, VA	768	646	-15.9	815	877	7.6	1,583	1,523	-3.8
Visalia, CA	613	517	-15.7	92	32	-65.2	705	549	-22.1
Washington, DC	336	352	4.8	4,354	5,685	30.6	4,690	6,037	28.7
Wilmington, NC	n/a	n/a	n/a	n/a	n/a	n/a	n/a	n/a	n/a
Winston-Salem, NC	453	1,183	161.1	443	777	75.4	896	1,960	118.8
U.S.	750,800	820,000	9.2	455,800	462,000	1.4	1,206,600	1,282,000	6.2

Note: Figures represent new, privately-owned housing units authorized (unadjusted data); All permit data are based on estimates with imputation
Source: U.S. Census Bureau, Manufacturing, Mining, and Construction Statistics, Building Permits, 2016, 2017

Building Permits: Metro Area

Metro Area	Single-Family			Multi-Family			Total		
	2016	2017	Pct. Chg.	2016	2017	Pct. Chg.	2016	2017	Pct. Chg.
Albany, NY	1,380	1,212	-12.2	1,473	1,134	-23.0	2,853	2,346	-17.8
Albuquerque, NM	1,931	1,996	3.4	534	260	-51.3	2,465	2,256	-8.5
Allentown, PA	1,059	938	-11.4	204	180	-11.8	1,263	1,118	-11.5
Anchorage, AK	751	851	13.3	295	297	0.7	1,046	1,148	9.8
Ann Arbor, MI	438	583	33.1	0	74	–	438	657	50.0
Athens, GA	523	581	11.1	61	190	211.5	584	771	32.0
Atlanta, GA	23,100	24,973	8.1	13,257	8,859	-33.2	36,357	33,832	-6.9
Austin, TX	13,327	16,119	20.9	8,534	10,581	24.0	21,861	26,700	22.1
Baton Rouge, LA	3,402	3,586	5.4	24	53	120.8	3,426	3,639	6.2
Billings, MT	1,054	992	-5.9	152	233	53.3	1,206	1,225	1.6
Boise City, ID	5,383	6,275	16.6	1,375	1,634	18.8	6,758	7,909	17.0
Boston, MA	5,243	4,949	-5.6	8,004	9,808	22.5	13,247	14,757	11.4
Boulder, CO	716	808	12.8	1,133	859	-24.2	1,849	1,667	-9.8
Cape Coral, FL	4,092	4,841	18.3	1,325	2,113	59.5	5,417	6,954	28.4
Cedar Rapids, IA	555	537	-3.2	232	455	96.1	787	992	26.0
Charleston, SC	4,787	4,726	-1.3	2,187	2,541	16.2	6,974	7,267	4.2
Charlotte, NC	14,041	15,247	8.6	6,533	7,622	16.7	20,574	22,869	11.2
Chicago, IL	8,032	8,416	4.8	11,909	13,716	15.2	19,941	22,132	11.0
Clarksville, TN	1,316	1,558	18.4	363	255	-29.8	1,679	1,813	8.0
College Station, TX	1,218	1,155	-5.2	1,642	1,928	17.4	2,860	3,083	7.8
Colorado Springs, CO	3,610	3,852	6.7	1,556	1,113	-28.5	5,166	4,965	-3.9
Columbia, MO	863	769	-10.9	441	865	96.1	1,304	1,634	25.3
Columbia, SC	3,916	4,072	4.0	711	557	-21.7	4,627	4,629	0.0
Columbus, OH	4,157	4,295	3.3	4,480	4,597	2.6	8,637	8,892	3.0
Dallas, TX	29,703	34,604	16.5	26,097	27,920	7.0	55,800	62,524	12.1
Denver, CO	10,247	10,978	7.1	11,700	11,757	0.5	21,947	22,735	3.6
Des Moines, IA	3,760	3,697	-1.7	2,937	2,670	-9.1	6,697	6,367	-4.9
Durham, NC	2,951	3,268	10.7	1,431	1,656	15.7	4,382	4,924	12.4
Edison, NJ	10,397	11,289	8.6	32,834	39,289	19.7	43,231	50,578	17.0
El Paso, TX	2,219	2,373	6.9	835	904	8.3	3,054	3,277	7.3
Eugene, OR	736	821	11.5	438	21	-95.2	1,174	842	-28.3
Evansville, IN	633	618	-2.4	314	303	-3.5	947	921	-2.7
Fargo, ND	1,192	1,065	-10.7	1,287	826	-35.8	2,479	1,891	-23.7
Fayetteville, NC	833	874	4.9	120	61	-49.2	953	935	-1.9
Fort Collins, CO	1,622	2,027	25.0	1,910	908	-52.5	3,532	2,935	-16.9
Fort Wayne, IN	1,076	1,222	13.6	460	500	8.7	1,536	1,722	12.1
Fort Worth, TX	29,703	34,604	16.5	26,097	27,920	7.0	55,800	62,524	12.1
Gainesville, FL	609	684	12.3	501	1,585	216.4	1,110	2,269	104.4
Grand Rapids, MI	2,649	2,953	11.5	2,068	1,886	-8.8	4,717	4,839	2.6
Greeley, CO	2,463	2,777	12.7	546	869	59.2	3,009	3,646	21.2
Green Bay, WI	804	828	3.0	204	348	70.6	1,008	1,176	16.7
Greensboro, NC	1,635	2,012	23.1	1,100	1,043	-5.2	2,735	3,055	11.7
Honolulu, HI	846	1,028	21.5	812	940	15.8	1,658	1,968	18.7
Houston, TX	35,367	36,348	2.8	9,365	6,047	-35.4	44,732	42,395	-5.2
Huntsville, AL	2,320	2,577	11.1	672	382	-43.2	2,992	2,959	-1.1
Indianapolis, IN	5,828	6,755	15.9	1,945	2,324	19.5	7,773	9,079	16.8
Jacksonville, FL	8,597	9,833	14.4	3,171	3,126	-1.4	11,768	12,959	10.1
Kansas City, MO	5,292	5,951	12.5	5,097	3,900	-23.5	10,389	9,851	-5.2
Lafayette, LA	1,518	1,746	15.0	180	25	-86.1	1,698	1,771	4.3
Las Cruces, NM	757	803	6.1	13	323	2,384.6	770	1,126	46.2
Las Vegas, NV	8,805	9,812	11.4	4,772	4,261	-10.7	13,577	14,073	3.7
Lexington, KY	1,480	1,602	8.2	1,252	724	-42.2	2,732	2,326	-14.9
Lincoln, NE	1,143	1,271	11.2	1,241	1,237	-0.3	2,384	2,508	5.2
Little Rock, AR	1,649	2,087	26.6	678	1,128	66.4	2,327	3,215	38.2

Table continued on next page.

Metro Area	Single-Family			Multi-Family			Total		
	2016	2017	Pct. Chg.	2016	2017	Pct. Chg.	2016	2017	Pct. Chg.
Los Angeles, CA	9,379	10,587	12.9	22,735	20,497	-9.8	32,114	31,084	-3.2
Louisville, KY	3,127	3,446	10.2	2,022	2,339	15.7	5,149	5,785	12.4
Madison, WI	1,613	1,656	2.7	3,340	2,976	-10.9	4,953	4,632	-6.5
Manchester, NH	701	717	2.3	396	316	-20.2	1,097	1,033	-5.8
McAllen, TX	2,921	2,698	-7.6	1,647	1,599	-2.9	4,568	4,297	-5.9
Miami, FL	6,705	6,655	-0.7	12,037	13,068	8.6	18,742	19,723	5.2
Midland, TX	636	766	20.4	40	0	-100.0	676	766	13.3
Minneapolis, MN	7,889	8,782	11.3	6,271	6,318	0.7	14,160	15,100	6.6
Nashville, TN	12,830	13,650	6.4	7,352	6,981	-5.0	20,182	20,631	2.2
New Orleans, LA	2,494	2,720	9.1	492	246	-50.0	2,986	2,966	-0.7
New York, NY	10,397	11,289	8.6	32,834	39,289	19.7	43,231	50,578	17.0
Oklahoma City, OK	5,039	5,132	1.8	1,701	287	-83.1	6,740	5,419	-19.6
Omaha, NE	2,906	3,158	8.7	1,334	1,797	34.7	4,240	4,955	16.9
Orlando, FL	14,227	14,431	1.4	9,027	4,634	-48.7	23,254	19,065	-18.0
Peoria, IL	326	247	-24.2	24	10	-58.3	350	257	-26.6
Philadelphia, PA	7,016	7,233	3.1	5,229	6,311	20.7	12,245	13,544	10.6
Phoenix, AZ	18,433	20,471	11.1	10,150	8,841	-12.9	28,583	29,312	2.6
Pittsburgh, PA	3,015	2,988	-0.9	1,388	1,340	-3.5	4,403	4,328	-1.7
Portland, OR	7,397	6,211	-16.0	7,332	9,772	33.3	14,729	15,983	8.5
Providence, RI	1,662	1,722	3.6	902	288	-68.1	2,564	2,010	-21.6
Provo, UT	4,429	5,090	14.9	888	2,155	142.7	5,317	7,245	36.3
Raleigh, NC	9,442	10,752	13.9	4,072	3,428	-15.8	13,514	14,180	4.9
Reno, NV	1,868	2,091	11.9	1,732	2,473	42.8	3,600	4,564	26.8
Richmond, VA	4,003	4,614	15.3	916	2,531	176.3	4,919	7,145	45.3
Roanoke, VA	380	424	11.6	162	168	3.7	542	592	9.2
Rochester, MN	744	818	9.9	993	631	-36.5	1,737	1,449	-16.6
Salem, OR	814	790	-2.9	664	765	15.2	1,478	1,555	5.2
Salt Lake City, UT	4,351	4,918	13.0	4,380	2,449	-44.1	8,731	7,367	-15.6
San Antonio, TX	6,464	7,535	16.6	5,777	4,981	-13.8	12,241	12,516	2.2
San Diego, CA	2,351	4,056	72.5	8,440	6,385	-24.3	10,791	10,441	-3.2
San Francisco, CA	4,967	4,777	-3.8	9,820	12,175	24.0	14,787	16,952	14.6
San Jose, CA	2,099	2,592	23.5	4,068	5,947	46.2	6,167	8,539	38.5
Santa Rosa, CA	621	840	35.3	298	338	13.4	919	1,178	28.2
Savannah, GA	1,769	1,898	7.3	202	220	8.9	1,971	2,118	7.5
Seattle, WA	9,425	9,997	6.1	16,064	17,337	7.9	25,489	27,334	7.2
Sioux Falls, SD	1,431	1,533	7.1	1,653	1,381	-16.5	3,084	2,914	-5.5
Springfield, IL	274	210	-23.4	152	112	-26.3	426	322	-24.4
Tallahassee, FL	810	1,897	134.2	803	1,156	44.0	1,613	3,053	89.3
Tampa, FL	10,685	12,732	19.2	7,067	5,536	-21.7	17,752	18,268	2.9
Topeka, KS	368	327	-11.1	20	8	-60.0	388	335	-13.7
Tyler, TX	454	472	4.0	127	206	62.2	581	678	16.7
Virginia Beach, VA	4,095	4,404	7.5	2,118	1,778	-16.1	6,213	6,182	-0.5
Visalia, CA	1,190	1,162	-2.4	126	152	20.6	1,316	1,314	-0.2
Washington, DC	13,384	14,225	6.3	12,303	13,040	6.0	25,687	27,265	6.1
Wilmington, NC	1,774	2,193	23.6	1,173	569	-51.5	2,947	2,762	-6.3
Winston-Salem, NC	2,243	2,784	24.1	484	981	102.7	2,727	3,765	38.1
U.S.	750,800	820,000	9.2	455,800	462,000	1.4	1,206,600	1,282,000	6.2

Note: Figures cover the Metropolitan Statistical Area—see Appendix B for areas included; Figures represent new, privately-owned housing units authorized (unadjusted data); All permit data are based on estimates with imputation
Source: U.S. Census Bureau, Manufacturing, Mining, and Construction Statistics, Building Permits, 2016, 2017

Housing Vacancy Rates

Metro Area[1]	Gross Vacancy Rate[2] (%)			Year-Round Vacancy Rate[3] (%)			Rental Vacancy Rate[4] (%)			Homeowner Vacancy Rate[5] (%)		
	2016	2017	2018	2016	2017	2018	2016	2017	2018	2016	2017	2018
Albany, NY	11.8	10.5	11.6	8.7	8.3	10.4	3.8	8.5	10.8	2.1	2.1	1.7
Albuquerque, NM	9.2	8.9	8.3	8.9	8.6	7.9	8.1	9.0	7.8	1.9	2.1	1.8
Allentown, PA	7.4	9.5	9.3	5.2	8.5	7.1	4.2	5.3	5.7	1.1	1.7	0.9
Anchorage, AK	n/a	n/a	n/a	n/a	n/a	n/a	n/a	n/a	n/a	n/a	n/a	n/a
Ann Arbor, MI	n/a	n/a	n/a	n/a	n/a	n/a	n/a	n/a	n/a	n/a	n/a	n/a
Athens, GA	n/a	n/a	n/a	n/a	n/a	n/a	n/a	n/a	n/a	n/a	n/a	n/a
Atlanta, GA	9.7	8.9	7.8	9.4	8.4	7.4	6.2	7.0	6.6	1.6	1.0	1.1
Austin, TX	8.2	10.4	9.7	7.6	9.3	8.7	5.5	6.1	7.0	1.0	2.0	1.2
Baton Rouge, LA	12.3	13.6	13.0	12.0	13.0	11.8	7.4	8.7	7.6	1.5	1.0	1.4
Billings, MT	n/a	n/a	n/a	n/a	n/a	n/a	n/a	n/a	n/a	n/a	n/a	n/a
Boise City, ID	n/a	n/a	n/a	n/a	n/a	n/a	n/a	n/a	n/a	n/a	n/a	n/a
Boston, MA	7.8	7.6	7.5	6.5	6.5	6.5	3.7	4.8	3.8	0.9	0.6	1.0
Boulder, CO	n/a	n/a	n/a	n/a	n/a	n/a	n/a	n/a	n/a	n/a	n/a	n/a
Cape Coral, FL	38.5	39.1	41.5	17.8	20.2	16.6	5.8	4.3	5.8	3.0	2.9	3.0
Cedar Rapids, IA	n/a	n/a	n/a	n/a	n/a	n/a	n/a	n/a	n/a	n/a	n/a	n/a
Charleston, SC	14.8	16.5	16.0	13.6	16.1	14.5	12.2	17.9	17.0	2.4	1.6	3.4
Charlotte, NC	7.7	6.9	8.5	7.5	6.8	8.1	7.4	5.4	5.6	1.1	0.8	1.7
Chicago, IL	8.6	8.4	7.5	8.5	8.3	7.4	6.4	7.0	7.0	2.3	1.8	1.6
Clarksville, TN	n/a	n/a	n/a	n/a	n/a	n/a	n/a	n/a	n/a	n/a	n/a	n/a
College Station, TX	n/a	n/a	n/a	n/a	n/a	n/a	n/a	n/a	n/a	n/a	n/a	n/a
Colorado Springs, CO	n/a	n/a	n/a	n/a	n/a	n/a	n/a	n/a	n/a	n/a	n/a	n/a
Columbia, MO	n/a	n/a	n/a	n/a	n/a	n/a	n/a	n/a	n/a	n/a	n/a	n/a
Columbia, SC	10.2	11.0	8.9	10.1	10.7	8.8	5.2	6.3	9.4	0.9	2.4	1.9
Columbus, OH	8.0	6.6	7.4	7.8	6.0	7.4	6.1	6.3	8.6	1.0	1.1	1.5
Dallas, TX	7.9	7.8	7.8	7.7	7.6	7.6	6.8	7.1	7.4	1.4	0.8	1.4
Denver, CO	6.4	7.8	8.0	5.2	6.9	7.4	4.5	5.9	3.8	1.1	0.7	0.9
Des Moines, IA	n/a	n/a	n/a	n/a	n/a	n/a	n/a	n/a	n/a	n/a	n/a	n/a
Durham, NC	n/a	n/a	n/a	n/a	n/a	n/a	n/a	n/a	n/a	n/a	n/a	n/a
Edison, NJ	10.3	10.7	10.3	9.1	9.6	9.1	4.7	4.6	4.5	2.2	1.9	1.6
El Paso, TX	n/a	n/a	n/a	n/a	n/a	n/a	n/a	n/a	n/a	n/a	n/a	n/a
Eugene, OR	n/a	n/a	n/a	n/a	n/a	n/a	n/a	n/a	n/a	n/a	n/a	n/a
Evansville, IN	n/a	n/a	n/a	n/a	n/a	n/a	n/a	n/a	n/a	n/a	n/a	n/a
Fargo, ND	n/a	n/a	n/a	n/a	n/a	n/a	n/a	n/a	n/a	n/a	n/a	n/a
Fayetteville, NC	n/a	n/a	n/a	n/a	n/a	n/a	n/a	n/a	n/a	n/a	n/a	n/a
Fort Collins, CO	n/a	n/a	n/a	n/a	n/a	n/a	n/a	n/a	n/a	n/a	n/a	n/a
Fort Wayne, IN	n/a	n/a	n/a	n/a	n/a	n/a	n/a	n/a	n/a	n/a	n/a	n/a
Fort Worth, TX	7.9	7.8	7.8	7.7	7.6	7.6	6.8	7.1	7.4	1.4	0.8	1.4
Gainesville, FL	n/a	n/a	n/a	n/a	n/a	n/a	n/a	n/a	n/a	n/a	n/a	n/a
Grand Rapids, MI	7.1	8.5	8.9	4.4	6.3	6.8	5.1	4.0	6.8	0.5	1.1	0.3
Greeley, CO	n/a	n/a	n/a	n/a	n/a	n/a	n/a	n/a	n/a	n/a	n/a	n/a
Green Bay, WI	n/a	n/a	n/a	n/a	n/a	n/a	n/a	n/a	n/a	n/a	n/a	n/a
Greensboro, NC	10.9	10.2	11.6	10.9	9.6	11.5	12.5	10.2	11.4	1.7	1.2	1.0
Honolulu, HI	13.7	13.9	14.0	12.5	12.4	12.9	9.4	8.0	6.5	1.1	0.9	1.4
Houston, TX	8.6	9.3	8.8	8.0	8.9	8.2	9.3	9.9	8.8	1.8	1.5	2.0
Huntsville, AL	n/a	n/a	n/a	n/a	n/a	n/a	n/a	n/a	n/a	n/a	n/a	n/a
Indianapolis, IN	9.1	10.9	8.7	9.0	10.8	8.6	9.2	11.9	9.9	1.4	1.5	1.5
Jacksonville, FL	14.5	12.5	10.1	14.0	12.0	9.3	8.3	8.5	5.6	1.6	1.5	1.3
Kansas City, MO	8.1	8.1	7.8	8.0	7.9	7.7	9.2	9.4	7.9	0.8	0.8	1.2
Lafayette, LA	n/a	n/a	n/a	n/a	n/a	n/a	n/a	n/a	n/a	n/a	n/a	n/a
Las Cruces, NM	n/a	n/a	n/a	n/a	n/a	n/a	n/a	n/a	n/a	n/a	n/a	n/a
Las Vegas, NV	11.8	12.6	11.4	10.7	11.0	10.4	6.6	7.0	6.8	2.0	2.4	0.9
Lexington, KY	n/a	n/a	n/a	n/a	n/a	n/a	n/a	n/a	n/a	n/a	n/a	n/a
Lincoln, NE	n/a	n/a	n/a	n/a	n/a	n/a	n/a	n/a	n/a	n/a	n/a	n/a
Little Rock, AR	11.8	10.3	10.5	11.8	10.0	10.2	12.2	11.3	10.9	2.4	2.0	1.8

Table continued on next page.

Metro Area[1]	Gross Vacancy Rate[2] (%)			Year-Round Vacancy Rate[3] (%)			Rental Vacancy Rate[4] (%)			Homeowner Vacancy Rate[5] (%)		
	2016	2017	2018	2016	2017	2018	2016	2017	2018	2016	2017	2018
Los Angeles, CA	5.0	6.3	6.6	4.7	5.9	6.2	2.9	4.1	4.0	0.8	0.9	1.2
Louisville, KY	7.6	7.3	7.6	7.2	7.2	7.4	5.0	7.8	7.7	1.5	0.6	1.4
Madison, WI	n/a	n/a	n/a	n/a	n/a	n/a	n/a	n/a	n/a	n/a	n/a	n/a
Manchester, NH	n/a	n/a	n/a	n/a	n/a	n/a	n/a	n/a	n/a	n/a	n/a	n/a
McAllen, TX	n/a	n/a	n/a	n/a	n/a	n/a	n/a	n/a	n/a	n/a	n/a	n/a
Miami, FL	17.9	17.8	14.9	9.5	9.2	7.9	7.2	7.0	7.4	1.4	1.9	1.9
Midland, TX	n/a	n/a	n/a	n/a	n/a	n/a	n/a	n/a	n/a	n/a	n/a	n/a
Minneapolis, MN	5.3	4.5	3.9	4.7	4.1	3.3	3.8	4.2	4.1	0.8	0.9	0.4
Nashville, TN	6.6	6.2	5.9	6.4	6.1	5.8	4.8	7.6	7.5	1.5	0.6	0.8
New Orleans, LA	13.6	12.8	11.9	12.7	12.2	11.8	11.1	10.8	9.7	2.6	2.5	1.7
New York, NY	10.3	10.7	10.3	9.1	9.6	9.1	4.7	4.6	4.5	2.2	1.9	1.6
Oklahoma City, OK	11.9	11.1	11.5	11.6	10.8	11.2	10.9	9.9	11.8	1.6	1.9	2.7
Omaha, NE	6.9	5.9	7.1	6.2	5.4	6.1	6.7	4.7	7.1	0.7	0.9	0.7
Orlando, FL	13.2	14.3	19.4	10.3	10.5	16.2	6.6	6.9	5.8	2.1	1.5	2.6
Peoria, IL	n/a	n/a	n/a	n/a	n/a	n/a	n/a	n/a	n/a	n/a	n/a	n/a
Philadelphia, PA	9.3	8.6	9.0	8.6	8.3	8.9	6.8	7.3	6.4	1.4	1.6	1.2
Phoenix, AZ	13.9	13.7	12.6	8.8	8.1	7.8	5.8	6.0	6.2	1.6	1.5	1.4
Pittsburgh, PA	17.7	13.6	10.2	17.4	13.4	9.9	7.4	9.7	6.3	1.8	2.2	2.2
Portland, OR	6.7	6.4	6.8	6.2	6.1	6.0	5.0	4.8	3.8	1.0	1.1	1.4
Providence, RI	11.1	11.3	10.3	7.5	8.1	8.5	3.8	4.2	5.0	1.3	1.2	1.1
Provo, UT	n/a	n/a	n/a	n/a	n/a	n/a	n/a	n/a	n/a	n/a	n/a	n/a
Raleigh, NC	6.8	8.0	6.7	6.7	7.8	6.6	4.3	5.8	6.4	1.9	1.7	0.9
Reno, NV	n/a	n/a	n/a	n/a	n/a	n/a	n/a	n/a	n/a	n/a	n/a	n/a
Richmond, VA	6.9	9.1	8.0	6.8	9.1	8.0	5.8	7.2	5.4	1.7	1.2	2.1
Roanoke, VA	n/a	n/a	n/a	n/a	n/a	n/a	n/a	n/a	n/a	n/a	n/a	n/a
Rochester, MN	n/a	n/a	n/a	n/a	n/a	n/a	n/a	n/a	n/a	n/a	n/a	n/a
Salem, OR	n/a	n/a	n/a	n/a	n/a	n/a	n/a	n/a	n/a	n/a	n/a	n/a
Salt Lake City, UT	5.4	5.0	5.0	5.0	4.8	4.7	6.4	6.2	6.1	0.5	0.6	0.5
San Antonio, TX	9.9	9.9	6.7	8.6	8.8	5.8	10.3	11.5	7.4	1.9	1.8	0.6
San Diego, CA	7.5	6.4	7.6	6.9	6.0	7.4	2.9	3.9	4.5	1.2	0.6	0.7
San Francisco, CA	6.0	6.0	7.5	5.9	5.9	7.4	3.6	4.2	5.4	0.7	0.7	0.9
San Jose, CA	6.1	6.0	5.8	5.8	5.9	5.8	4.5	3.2	4.6	0.8	0.7	0.5
Santa Rosa, CA	n/a	n/a	n/a	n/a	n/a	n/a	n/a	n/a	n/a	n/a	n/a	n/a
Savannah, GA	n/a	n/a	n/a	n/a	n/a	n/a	n/a	n/a	n/a	n/a	n/a	n/a
Seattle, WA	5.6	6.0	5.9	5.3	5.4	5.4	3.3	3.4	4.8	0.9	0.5	0.8
Sioux Falls, SD	n/a	n/a	n/a	n/a	n/a	n/a	n/a	n/a	n/a	n/a	n/a	n/a
Springfield, IL	n/a	n/a	n/a	n/a	n/a	n/a	n/a	n/a	n/a	n/a	n/a	n/a
Tallahassee, FL	n/a	n/a	n/a	n/a	n/a	n/a	n/a	n/a	n/a	n/a	n/a	n/a
Tampa, FL	16.1	16.2	16.1	12.8	12.5	11.9	8.7	9.6	9.9	2.5	2.4	2.1
Topeka, KS	n/a	n/a	n/a	n/a	n/a	n/a	n/a	n/a	n/a	n/a	n/a	n/a
Tyler, TX	n/a	n/a	n/a	n/a	n/a	n/a	n/a	n/a	n/a	n/a	n/a	n/a
Virginia Beach, VA	12.0	9.4	8.9	9.6	8.9	7.6	8.2	8.2	7.1	2.1	2.5	1.2
Visalia, CA	n/a	n/a	n/a	n/a	n/a	n/a	n/a	n/a	n/a	n/a	n/a	n/a
Washington, DC	8.2	7.4	7.0	7.9	7.1	6.7	6.0	6.2	6.2	1.7	1.2	1.1
Wilmington, NC	n/a	n/a	n/a	n/a	n/a	n/a	n/a	n/a	n/a	n/a	n/a	n/a
Winston-Salem, NC	n/a	n/a	n/a	n/a	n/a	n/a	n/a	n/a	n/a	n/a	n/a	n/a
U.S.	12.8	12.7	12.3	9.9	9.9	9.7	6.9	7.2	6.9	1.7	1.6	1.5

Note: (1) Metropolitan Statistical Area—see Appendix B for areas included; (2) The percentage of the total housing inventory that is vacant; (3) The percentage of the housing inventory (excluding seasonal units) that is year-round vacant; (4) The percentage of rental inventory that is vacant for rent; (5) The percentage of homeowner inventory that is vacant for sale; n/a not available
Source: U.S. Census Bureau, Housing Vacancies and Homeownership Annual Statistics: 2016, 2017, 2018

Bankruptcy Filings

City	Area Covered	Business Filings			Nonbusiness Filings		
		2017	2018	% Chg.	2017	2018	% Chg.
Albany, NY	Albany County	14	12	-14.3	505	513	1.6
Albuquerque, NM	Bernalillo County	53	38	-28.3	1,166	1,118	-4.1
Allentown, PA	Lehigh County	25	27	8.0	603	585	-3.0
Anchorage, AK	Anchorage Borough	18	18	0.0	176	212	20.5
Ann Arbor, MI	Washtenaw County	15	18	20.0	650	645	-0.8
Athens, GA	Clarke County	4	5	25.0	390	368	-5.6
Atlanta, GA	Fulton County	145	108	-25.5	4,655	4,600	-1.2
Austin, TX	Travis County	113	122	8.0	705	714	1.3
Baton Rouge, LA	East Baton Rouge Parish	22	21	-4.5	728	616	-15.4
Billings, MT	Yellowstone County	9	2	-77.8	222	215	-3.2
Boise City, ID	Ada County	27	35	29.6	861	946	9.9
Boston, MA	Suffolk County	56	48	-14.3	615	594	-3.4
Boulder, CO	Boulder County	27	23	-14.8	407	392	-3.7
Cape Coral, FL	Lee County	55	80	45.5	1,071	1,130	5.5
Cedar Rapids, IA	Linn County	7	9	28.6	283	289	2.1
Charleston, SC	Charleston County	16	11	-31.3	378	386	2.1
Charlotte, NC	Mecklenburg County	49	81	65.3	1,312	1,262	-3.8
Chicago, IL	Cook County	424	435	2.6	31,634	29,321	-7.3
Clarksville, TN	Montgomery County	13	7	-46.2	855	858	0.4
College Station, TX	Brazos County	5	6	20.0	71	68	-4.2
Colorado Springs, CO	El Paso County	36	49	36.1	1,737	1,672	-3.7
Columbia, MO	Boone County	3	6	100.0	394	427	8.4
Columbia, SC	Richland County	11	12	9.1	675	712	5.5
Columbus, OH	Franklin County	58	70	20.7	4,463	4,479	0.4
Dallas, TX	Dallas County	332	306	-7.8	3,955	3,997	1.1
Denver, CO	Denver County	102	78	-23.5	1,598	1,420	-11.1
Des Moines, IA	Polk County	34	20	-41.2	807	820	1.6
Durham, NC	Durham County	16	14	-12.5	459	439	-4.4
Edison, NJ	Middlesex County	62	55	-11.3	1,895	1,945	2.6
El Paso, TX	El Paso County	66	49	-25.8	2,058	2,108	2.4
Eugene, OR	Lane County	23	20	-13.0	858	905	5.5
Evansville, IN	Vanderburgh County	7	10	42.9	651	648	-0.5
Fargo, ND	Cass County	7	14	100.0	188	177	-5.9
Fayetteville, NC	Cumberland County	9	14	55.6	786	781	-0.6
Fort Collins, CO	Larimer County	17	32	88.2	630	605	-4.0
Fort Wayne, IN	Allen County	30	16	-46.7	1,507	1,386	-8.0
Fort Worth, TX	Tarrant County	231	204	-11.7	4,050	3,983	-1.7
Gainesville, FL	Alachua County	15	13	-13.3	236	238	0.8
Grand Rapids, MI	Kent County	38	32	-15.8	1,249	1,072	-14.2
Greeley, CO	Weld County	13	22	69.2	764	726	-5.0
Green Bay, WI	Brown County	13	21	61.5	539	617	14.5
Greensboro, NC	Guilford County	15	27	80.0	714	766	7.3
Honolulu, HI	Honolulu County	33	32	-3.0	934	934	0.0
Houston, TX	Harris County	489	447	-8.6	4,530	4,681	3.3
Huntsville, AL	Madison County	33	21	-36.4	1,397	1,432	2.5
Indianapolis, IN	Marion County	76	68	-10.5	4,510	4,653	3.2
Jacksonville, FL	Duval County	83	94	13.3	2,329	2,169	-6.9
Kansas City, MO	Jackson County	45	31	-31.1	2,457	2,373	-3.4
Lafayette, LA	Lafayette Parish	30	61	103.3	520	561	7.9
Las Cruces, NM	Dona Ana County	8	19	137.5	329	377	14.6
Las Vegas, NV	Clark County	225	216	-4.0	7,115	7,041	-1.0
Lexington, KY	Fayette County	23	16	-30.4	815	824	1.1
Lincoln, NE	Lancaster County	17	17	0.0	655	692	5.6
Little Rock, AR	Pulaski County	30	29	-3.3	2,563	2,571	0.3
Los Angeles, CA	Los Angeles County	1,072	1,168	9.0	20,697	19,176	-7.3

Table continued on next page.

City	Area Covered	Business Filings			Nonbusiness Filings		
		2017	2018	% Chg.	2017	2018	% Chg.
Louisville, KY	Jefferson County	48	44	-8.3	2,890	2,886	-0.1
Madison, WI	Dane County	28	26	-7.1	748	774	3.5
Manchester, NH	Hillsborough County	47	30	-36.2	545	591	8.4
McAllen, TX	Hidalgo County	46	40	-13.0	504	455	-9.7
Miami, FL	Miami-Dade County	246	231	-6.1	8,616	7,726	-10.3
Midland, TX	Midland County	22	12	-45.5	69	79	14.5
Minneapolis, MN	Hennepin County	84	83	-1.2	2,025	2,112	4.3
Nashville, TN	Davidson County	73	59	-19.2	2,558	2,274	-11.1
New Orleans, LA	Orleans Parish	46	59	28.3	631	561	-11.1
New York, NY	Bronx County	43	49	14.0	1,991	2,108	5.9
New York, NY	Kings County	165	165	0.0	2,264	2,526	11.6
New York, NY	New York County	310	430	38.7	1,047	1,099	5.0
New York, NY	Queens County	124	198	59.7	2,807	3,326	18.5
New York, NY	Richmond County	18	31	72.2	591	716	21.2
Oklahoma City, OK	Oklahoma County	110	59	-46.4	2,113	2,098	-0.7
Omaha, NE	Douglas County	34	38	11.8	1,307	1,225	-6.3
Orlando, FL	Orange County	134	137	2.2	3,256	2,801	-14.0
Peoria, IL	Peoria County	12	11	-8.3	542	533	-1.7
Philadelphia, PA	Philadelphia County	58	76	31.0	2,658	2,555	-3.9
Phoenix, AZ	Maricopa County	413	385	-6.8	10,064	10,423	3.6
Pittsburgh, PA	Allegheny County	131	120	-8.4	2,299	2,583	12.4
Portland, OR	Multnomah County	70	38	-45.7	1,545	1,468	-5.0
Providence, RI	Providence County	30	38	26.7	1,443	1,425	-1.2
Provo, UT	Utah County	41	36	-12.2	1,588	1,598	0.6
Raleigh, NC	Wake County	76	79	3.9	1,539	1,458	-5.3
Reno, NV	Washoe County	32	43	34.4	1,037	920	-11.3
Richmond, VA	Richmond city	10	10	0.0	920	914	-0.7
Roanoke, VA	Roanoke city	5	6	20.0	299	308	3.0
Rochester, MN	Olmsted County	3	4	33.3	171	146	-14.6
Salem, OR	Marion County	9	11	22.2	957	1,103	15.3
Salt Lake City, UT	Salt Lake County	70	94	34.3	5,045	4,775	-5.4
San Antonio, TX	Bexar County	173	109	-37.0	2,240	2,239	0.0
San Diego, CA	San Diego County	290	296	2.1	7,553	7,405	-2.0
San Francisco, CA	San Francisco County	83	78	-6.0	621	550	-11.4
San Jose, CA	Santa Clara County	92	99	7.6	2,067	1,843	-10.8
Santa Rosa, CA	Sonoma County	40	28	-30.0	538	528	-1.9
Savannah, GA	Chatham County	19	12	-36.8	1,320	1,252	-5.2
Seattle, WA	King County	129	142	10.1	3,161	2,633	-16.7
Sioux Falls, SD	Minnehaha County	5	8	60.0	328	327	-0.3
Springfield, IL	Sangamon County	10	9	-10.0	539	553	2.6
Tallahassee, FL	Leon County	30	23	-23.3	326	355	8.9
Tampa, FL	Hillsborough County	152	136	-10.5	3,021	2,950	-2.4
Topeka, KS	Shawnee County	9	39	333.3	873	871	-0.2
Tyler, TX	Smith County	15	19	26.7	274	309	12.8
Virginia Beach, VA	Virginia Beach city	27	15	-44.4	1,559	1,650	5.8
Visalia, CA	Tulare County	20	26	30.0	738	792	7.3
Washington, DC	District of Columbia	38	30	-21.1	625	685	9.6
Wilmington, NC	New Hanover County	19	21	10.5	305	260	-14.8
Winston-Salem, NC	Forsyth County	19	11	-42.1	530	555	4.7
U.S.	U.S.	24,114	23,157	-4.0	770,846	765,863	-0.6

Note: Business filings include Chapter 7, Chapter 11,
Chapter 12, and Chapter 13; Nonbusiness filings include Chapter 7, Chapter 11, and Chapter 13
Source: Administrative Office of the U.S. Courts, Business and Nonbusiness Bankruptcy, County Cases Commenced by Chapter of the Bankruptcy Code, During the 12- Month Period Ending December 31, 2017 and Business and Nonbusiness Bankruptcy, County Cases Commenced by Chapter of the Bankruptcy Code, During the 12- Month Period Ending December 31, 2018

Income: City

City	Per Capita ($)	Median Household ($)	Average Household ($)
Albany, NY	27,632	43,790	63,120
Albuquerque, NM	28,229	49,878	67,881
Allentown, PA	19,024	38,522	51,893
Anchorage, AK	38,977	82,271	105,010
Ann Arbor, MI	39,253	61,247	89,295
Athens, GA	21,111	34,258	53,394
Atlanta, GA	40,595	51,701	92,186
Austin, TX	37,888	63,717	91,811
Baton Rouge, LA	25,876	40,948	63,669
Billings, MT	31,854	55,585	74,949
Boise City, ID	32,147	54,547	76,984
Boston, MA	39,686	62,021	95,114
Boulder, CO	40,895	64,183	98,899
Cape Coral, FL	26,446	53,653	68,090
Cedar Rapids, IA	31,585	56,828	73,859
Charleston, SC	38,126	61,367	88,467
Charlotte, NC	34,687	58,202	87,225
Chicago, IL	32,560	52,497	81,061
Clarksville, TN	23,377	51,164	61,610
College Station, TX	24,640	39,430	66,254
Colorado Springs, CO	31,333	58,158	77,814
Columbia, MO	28,253	47,236	69,694
Columbia, SC	27,730	43,650	69,516
Columbus, OH	26,778	49,478	63,554
Dallas, TX	31,260	47,285	78,925
Denver, CO	38,991	60,098	88,779
Des Moines, IA	26,494	49,999	64,820
Durham, NC	32,305	54,284	77,357
Edison, NJ	41,441	95,622	117,009
El Paso, TX	21,120	44,431	60,383
Eugene, OR	28,602	47,489	67,468
Evansville, IN	22,375	36,956	50,350
Fargo, ND	31,866	50,561	71,030
Fayetteville, NC	23,853	43,439	57,059
Fort Collins, CO	31,686	60,110	80,591
Fort Wayne, IN	25,066	45,853	60,942
Fort Worth, TX	27,191	57,309	76,309
Gainesville, FL	21,111	34,004	51,019
Grand Rapids, MI	23,225	44,369	58,917
Greeley, CO	24,678	52,887	68,355
Green Bay, WI	24,660	45,473	59,780
Greensboro, NC	27,849	44,978	66,683
Honolulu, HI	34,613	65,707	89,543
Houston, TX	30,547	49,399	79,344
Huntsville, AL	33,070	51,926	75,789
Indianapolis, IN	26,232	44,709	63,698
Jacksonville, FL	27,486	50,555	68,733
Kansas City, MO	29,742	50,136	68,949
Lafayette, LA	30,988	48,533	74,381
Las Cruces, NM	23,131	40,924	57,527
Las Vegas, NV	27,650	53,159	72,694
Lexington, KY	31,653	53,013	76,300
Lincoln, NE	28,839	53,089	70,721
Little Rock, AR	32,719	48,463	77,254
Los Angeles, CA	31,563	54,501	86,758
Louisville, KY	28,975	49,439	69,805

Table continued on next page.

City	Per Capita ($)	Median Household ($)	Average Household ($)
Madison, WI	34,740	59,387	79,063
Manchester, NH	29,681	56,467	70,077
McAllen, TX	21,683	45,057	66,023
Miami, FL	25,067	33,999	60,341
Midland, TX	39,499	75,646	109,351
Minneapolis, MN	35,259	55,720	81,550
Nashville, TN	31,109	52,858	74,021
New Orleans, LA	29,275	38,721	67,224
New York, NY	35,761	57,782	93,196
Oklahoma City, OK	28,365	51,581	72,393
Omaha, NE	30,222	53,789	74,931
Orlando, FL	28,117	45,436	65,450
Peoria, IL	28,507	47,697	68,524
Philadelphia, PA	24,811	40,649	60,517
Phoenix, AZ	26,528	52,080	73,092
Pittsburgh, PA	30,397	44,092	66,639
Portland, OR	36,492	61,532	85,335
Providence, RI	24,052	40,366	64,839
Provo, UT	19,385	44,312	64,998
Raleigh, NC	35,094	61,505	86,374
Reno, NV	29,821	52,106	71,604
Richmond, VA	30,113	42,356	68,295
Roanoke, VA	24,697	41,483	55,976
Rochester, MN	36,659	68,574	90,446
Salem, OR	24,755	51,666	66,507
Salt Lake City, UT	32,954	54,009	79,834
San Antonio, TX	24,325	49,711	66,799
San Diego, CA	37,112	71,535	98,632
San Francisco, CA	59,508	96,265	137,761
San Jose, CA	40,275	96,662	124,356
Santa Rosa, CA	33,360	67,144	86,806
Savannah, GA	22,497	39,386	56,370
Seattle, WA	51,872	79,565	111,232
Sioux Falls, SD	31,161	56,714	75,241
Springfield, IL	32,162	51,789	73,023
Tallahassee, FL	25,471	42,418	61,645
Tampa, FL	32,869	48,245	78,953
Topeka, KS	26,048	46,087	60,359
Tyler, TX	26,620	46,463	69,882
Virginia Beach, VA	34,607	70,500	89,528
Visalia, CA	24,359	54,934	73,305
Washington, DC	50,832	77,649	116,090
Wilmington, NC	30,601	43,867	67,718
Winston-Salem, NC	26,668	42,219	66,187
U.S.	31,177	57,652	81,283

Source: U.S. Census Bureau, 2013-2017 American Community Survey 5-Year Estimates

Income: Metro Area

Metro Area	Per Capita ($)	Median Household ($)	Average Household ($)
Albany, NY	34,770	65,743	85,015
Albuquerque, NM	27,388	50,781	68,397
Allentown, PA	31,939	62,479	81,785
Anchorage, AK	36,807	80,724	101,305
Ann Arbor, MI	37,455	65,618	92,429
Athens, GA	24,581	42,418	63,569
Atlanta, GA	31,784	61,733	85,937
Austin, TX	35,949	69,717	94,724
Baton Rouge, LA	28,962	55,329	75,819
Billings, MT	32,226	57,812	77,471
Boise City, ID	27,506	54,120	72,902
Boston, MA	43,348	81,838	111,548
Boulder, CO	42,119	75,669	104,898
Cape Coral, FL	30,233	52,052	74,000
Cedar Rapids, IA	32,504	62,399	79,045
Charleston, SC	31,542	57,666	79,452
Charlotte, NC	31,525	57,871	81,709
Chicago, IL	34,624	65,757	91,944
Clarksville, TN	24,006	50,369	63,127
College Station, TX	25,328	45,078	66,928
Colorado Springs, CO	31,345	62,751	81,510
Columbia, MO	28,495	52,005	70,887
Columbia, SC	27,694	52,728	69,810
Columbus, OH	31,649	60,170	80,496
Dallas, TX	32,463	63,870	89,486
Denver, CO	38,018	71,884	96,371
Des Moines, IA	34,537	65,971	86,866
Durham, NC	34,342	57,600	84,882
Edison, NJ	39,182	72,205	106,398
El Paso, TX	19,917	43,170	58,772
Eugene, OR	27,032	47,710	64,571
Evansville, IN	28,086	49,873	67,860
Fargo, ND	32,574	59,074	78,102
Fayetteville, NC	23,085	44,883	58,255
Fort Collins, CO	34,087	64,980	85,429
Fort Wayne, IN	26,951	51,642	67,688
Fort Worth, TX	32,463	63,870	89,486
Gainesville, FL	26,103	45,323	65,637
Grand Rapids, MI	28,739	58,094	76,101
Greeley, CO	29,226	66,489	81,655
Green Bay, WI	29,632	56,831	72,911
Greensboro, NC	26,659	47,145	66,019
Honolulu, HI	33,776	80,078	101,194
Houston, TX	32,308	62,922	91,350
Huntsville, AL	32,676	59,583	80,893
Indianapolis, IN	30,607	56,528	77,745
Jacksonville, FL	30,451	56,449	77,552
Kansas City, MO	32,962	61,479	82,390
Lafayette, LA	26,768	49,514	69,156
Las Cruces, NM	21,050	39,114	57,160
Las Vegas, NV	27,719	54,882	73,247
Lexington, KY	30,560	54,436	75,656
Lincoln, NE	29,874	56,132	74,327
Little Rock, AR	28,187	51,362	70,449
Los Angeles, CA	32,417	65,331	95,055
Louisville, KY	30,124	54,624	74,474

Table continued on next page.

Metro Area	Per Capita ($)	Median Household ($)	Average Household ($)
Madison, WI	36,065	66,609	86,307
Manchester, NH	37,622	75,777	94,966
McAllen, TX	15,883	37,097	54,348
Miami, FL	29,499	51,758	78,886
Midland, TX	38,210	75,570	107,458
Minneapolis, MN	37,866	73,735	96,530
Nashville, TN	31,873	59,365	81,795
New Orleans, LA	29,298	50,154	72,656
New York, NY	39,182	72,205	106,398
Oklahoma City, OK	28,963	54,946	74,813
Omaha, NE	31,895	62,345	81,192
Orlando, FL	26,966	52,261	72,452
Peoria, IL	30,990	57,301	75,829
Philadelphia, PA	35,652	66,285	92,455
Phoenix, AZ	29,542	57,935	79,498
Pittsburgh, PA	33,182	56,073	76,614
Portland, OR	34,476	66,657	87,759
Providence, RI	33,001	61,536	82,080
Provo, UT	23,157	66,742	83,695
Raleigh, NC	34,821	68,870	91,708
Reno, NV	31,919	58,654	79,370
Richmond, VA	33,544	63,599	85,350
Roanoke, VA	29,393	52,609	69,257
Rochester, MN	35,842	69,003	89,677
Salem, OR	25,012	54,304	68,403
Salt Lake City, UT	29,805	67,838	87,705
San Antonio, TX	27,154	56,495	76,281
San Diego, CA	34,350	70,588	96,153
San Francisco, CA	48,538	92,714	129,577
San Jose, CA	48,133	105,809	141,951
Santa Rosa, CA	37,767	71,769	96,675
Savannah, GA	28,566	55,021	74,008
Seattle, WA	40,699	77,269	102,558
Sioux Falls, SD	31,578	62,047	78,853
Springfield, IL	33,251	58,956	78,020
Tallahassee, FL	26,709	48,618	67,419
Tampa, FL	29,632	50,567	71,311
Topeka, KS	28,190	55,194	68,649
Tyler, TX	26,270	50,742	70,687
Virginia Beach, VA	31,082	61,889	79,683
Visalia, CA	18,962	44,871	62,325
Washington, DC	46,267	97,148	125,230
Wilmington, NC	30,522	51,137	72,671
Winston-Salem, NC	26,896	47,099	66,378
U.S.	31,177	57,652	81,283

Note: Figures cover the Metropolitan Statistical Area (MSA)—see Appendix B for areas included
Source: U.S. Census Bureau, 2013-2017 American Community Survey 5-Year Estimates

Household Income Distribution: City

City	Percent of Households Earning							
	Under $15,000	$15,000 -$24,999	$25,000 -$34,999	$35,000 -$49,999	$50,000 -$74,999	$75,000 -$99,999	$100,000 -$149,999	$150,000 and up
Albany, NY	19.5	12.5	10.1	12.4	17.3	9.6	10.6	8.0
Albuquerque, NM	14.0	11.6	10.6	13.9	17.4	11.9	12.5	8.1
Allentown, PA	19.2	13.9	12.9	14.4	19.4	10.1	7.1	3.0
Anchorage, AK	5.4	5.4	6.0	10.6	17.7	14.5	20.7	19.7
Ann Arbor, MI	14.0	8.0	8.2	11.2	15.6	11.4	14.9	16.6
Athens, GA	24.6	14.6	11.5	13.4	13.2	8.1	9.0	5.6
Atlanta, GA	17.0	10.6	9.1	11.8	15.1	9.6	11.5	15.3
Austin, TX	9.9	7.7	8.6	12.9	18.3	12.2	15.1	15.3
Baton Rouge, LA	20.3	13.1	11.5	13.7	15.0	8.3	9.9	8.3
Billings, MT	10.1	11.3	10.0	13.4	21.4	12.4	12.3	9.1
Boise City, ID	11.8	10.9	9.6	13.3	18.0	12.8	13.2	10.4
Boston, MA	17.9	8.6	7.0	9.2	14.3	9.9	15.1	17.9
Boulder, CO	14.2	8.4	8.3	10.4	14.0	11.3	14.2	19.3
Cape Coral, FL	9.9	9.4	10.8	14.7	22.7	13.4	12.1	6.9
Cedar Rapids, IA	9.8	9.2	10.4	14.3	19.6	13.7	14.8	8.1
Charleston, SC	12.7	8.5	7.9	12.5	16.5	12.1	15.6	14.2
Charlotte, NC	10.0	9.4	10.1	13.8	18.1	11.8	13.4	13.4
Chicago, IL	15.8	10.9	9.2	11.9	15.8	10.9	12.7	12.9
Clarksville, TN	11.7	9.2	11.2	16.4	23.3	13.8	10.1	4.4
College Station, TX	23.6	12.7	9.6	11.7	12.5	9.5	11.8	8.6
Colorado Springs, CO	9.9	9.1	9.8	13.6	19.1	12.8	15.0	10.7
Columbia, MO	18.3	10.6	9.5	13.2	15.5	10.9	12.4	9.7
Columbia, SC	19.0	10.9	11.3	13.2	16.6	10.1	9.4	9.6
Columbus, OH	14.1	10.5	11.0	14.7	19.4	12.2	12.2	5.8
Dallas, TX	13.8	12.0	11.5	14.9	17.2	9.6	9.7	11.4
Denver, CO	11.8	8.5	8.9	12.8	17.1	12.2	14.0	14.7
Des Moines, IA	13.6	10.9	10.3	15.1	20.8	12.7	10.5	5.9
Durham, NC	12.1	9.7	10.1	13.8	17.5	12.3	13.3	11.2
Edison, NJ	5.7	4.8	5.9	8.2	14.0	14.0	20.6	26.8
El Paso, TX	15.6	12.5	11.8	15.4	18.2	10.4	10.2	5.9
Eugene, OR	17.7	11.7	9.9	13.1	17.5	10.5	11.3	8.4
Evansville, IN	17.5	15.0	14.9	15.8	18.0	8.9	6.5	3.4
Fargo, ND	11.9	11.1	11.6	14.8	18.2	12.7	11.8	8.0
Fayetteville, NC	14.6	12.2	13.6	16.5	19.2	10.5	8.8	4.6
Fort Collins, CO	11.2	9.2	8.9	13.9	15.7	13.3	15.8	11.9
Fort Wayne, IN	13.4	12.1	12.5	15.8	19.7	11.9	9.3	5.3
Fort Worth, TX	11.7	9.2	9.7	12.7	19.0	13.2	14.5	9.9
Gainesville, FL	25.7	14.1	11.2	12.2	15.8	9.0	7.6	4.5
Grand Rapids, MI	15.4	12.5	11.6	15.8	19.0	11.6	9.5	4.7
Greeley, CO	12.8	10.4	9.1	14.8	20.5	13.1	12.5	6.9
Green Bay, WI	13.7	12.0	12.6	16.5	18.8	12.4	9.4	4.5
Greensboro, NC	14.7	12.0	11.9	15.8	17.6	10.7	9.6	7.6
Honolulu, HI	10.7	7.7	7.2	12.2	18.7	13.2	15.4	14.8
Houston, TX	13.5	12.2	11.0	13.7	16.7	9.7	10.9	12.2
Huntsville, AL	14.9	11.2	9.9	12.3	16.1	10.2	14.0	11.3
Indianapolis, IN	15.2	12.2	11.6	15.7	17.8	10.6	10.1	6.7
Jacksonville, FL	12.9	10.0	11.3	15.2	18.9	12.5	11.6	7.6
Kansas City, MO	13.9	11.2	10.6	14.1	18.4	11.7	11.8	8.2
Lafayette, LA	15.9	12.0	10.7	12.6	16.2	9.6	11.3	11.7
Las Cruces, NM	19.3	13.1	11.9	14.4	16.1	9.8	9.6	5.7
Las Vegas, NV	11.8	10.2	10.9	14.4	18.5	12.6	12.8	8.8
Lexington, KY	13.8	10.6	10.1	12.9	17.5	11.8	12.8	10.4
Lincoln, NE	11.1	10.3	11.1	14.4	19.3	12.2	14.1	7.6
Little Rock, AR	13.5	12.0	10.8	15.0	16.4	9.9	10.8	11.5

Table continued on next page.

City	Percent of Households Earning							
	Under $15,000	$15,000 -$24,999	$25,000 -$34,999	$35,000 -$49,999	$50,000 -$74,999	$75,000 -$99,999	$100,000 -$149,999	$150,000 and up
Los Angeles, CA	13.9	10.8	9.7	12.2	15.8	10.7	12.8	14.2
Louisville, KY	14.1	11.4	10.5	14.5	17.8	11.7	11.5	8.5
Madison, WI	12.2	8.6	8.9	12.9	18.2	13.1	14.8	11.3
Manchester, NH	11.0	9.8	10.5	12.7	20.5	13.6	14.6	7.3
McAllen, TX	18.1	13.9	9.9	11.6	17.0	10.4	10.6	8.5
Miami, FL	23.4	15.4	12.2	13.0	13.5	7.6	7.5	7.5
Midland, TX	6.3	6.9	8.0	11.0	17.5	13.0	17.8	19.4
Minneapolis, MN	14.9	9.8	8.8	12.1	16.3	11.6	13.9	12.7
Nashville, TN	11.5	10.0	10.3	15.1	19.4	12.4	12.1	9.2
New Orleans, LA	22.9	13.0	10.7	12.3	13.7	8.8	9.2	9.5
New York, NY	15.7	9.8	8.4	10.9	15.0	10.9	13.5	15.8
Oklahoma City, OK	12.1	10.1	11.3	15.0	17.9	11.9	12.4	9.2
Omaha, NE	11.9	10.0	9.7	14.8	18.5	12.1	13.1	9.9
Orlando, FL	14.0	12.1	12.8	15.7	18.3	9.6	9.4	7.9
Peoria, IL	16.6	12.2	10.6	12.4	16.7	11.4	11.5	8.6
Philadelphia, PA	21.9	12.1	10.6	13.4	15.5	9.5	9.8	7.2
Phoenix, AZ	12.5	10.4	10.4	14.6	18.6	11.4	12.3	9.7
Pittsburgh, PA	19.0	12.4	10.7	12.5	16.5	10.1	10.3	8.7
Portland, OR	12.5	8.5	8.7	12.0	16.9	12.7	15.1	13.7
Providence, RI	22.6	12.2	10.1	11.9	16.1	9.7	8.8	8.5
Provo, UT	13.7	13.5	13.7	14.0	18.2	9.6	11.0	6.4
Raleigh, NC	8.5	8.2	9.3	14.5	19.1	12.9	14.5	12.9
Reno, NV	11.9	11.5	10.5	14.1	18.5	11.9	13.0	8.6
Richmond, VA	19.6	11.8	10.8	14.1	16.0	9.0	9.8	8.8
Roanoke, VA	17.8	13.5	11.8	15.1	18.6	11.0	7.3	4.9
Rochester, MN	8.4	7.3	8.8	11.6	18.0	14.6	16.9	14.4
Salem, OR	11.1	10.9	11.6	14.8	19.6	13.4	12.1	6.5
Salt Lake City, UT	13.4	9.9	10.3	13.2	17.8	12.0	12.1	11.3
San Antonio, TX	13.6	11.1	11.0	14.6	19.0	11.3	11.8	7.6
San Diego, CA	9.2	7.5	7.6	11.1	16.8	12.6	16.9	18.4
San Francisco, CA	11.2	6.6	5.4	7.1	11.1	9.7	16.7	32.0
San Jose, CA	7.1	5.6	5.4	8.6	13.4	11.4	18.6	30.0
Santa Rosa, CA	8.2	7.5	7.7	12.1	20.0	14.4	16.2	14.0
Savannah, GA	19.7	13.4	12.0	15.2	15.8	9.6	8.9	5.4
Seattle, WA	9.9	6.3	6.5	9.7	15.1	11.9	17.3	23.3
Sioux Falls, SD	10.1	8.9	10.9	14.5	19.0	14.4	13.2	9.1
Springfield, IL	14.6	12.0	9.3	12.6	17.3	12.2	12.0	9.9
Tallahassee, FL	18.5	11.8	11.4	15.3	15.8	9.6	10.2	7.4
Tampa, FL	16.3	11.5	10.4	13.0	15.6	9.8	11.1	12.2
Topeka, KS	13.2	12.7	12.3	14.9	19.8	11.9	10.8	4.3
Tyler, TX	13.9	12.7	11.1	15.0	18.5	10.1	9.7	9.0
Virginia Beach, VA	6.1	6.3	7.7	13.0	20.2	15.5	18.3	13.0
Visalia, CA	11.7	10.8	9.0	14.2	18.3	12.5	14.3	9.2
Washington, DC	14.1	7.0	6.4	8.2	13.1	10.7	16.0	24.6
Wilmington, NC	18.1	12.5	11.1	13.1	16.6	8.9	10.7	9.0
Winston-Salem, NC	16.9	12.9	12.4	14.4	16.6	10.0	9.1	7.6
U.S.	11.6	9.8	9.5	13.0	17.7	12.3	14.1	12.1

Source: U.S. Census Bureau, 2013-2017 American Community Survey 5-Year Estimates

Household Income Distribution: Metro Area

Metro Area	Under $15,000	$15,000 -$24,999	$25,000 -$34,999	$35,000 -$49,999	$50,000 -$74,999	$75,000 -$99,999	$100,000 -$149,999	$150,000 and up
Albany, NY	9.4	8.4	8.4	12.1	17.8	13.6	17.2	13.1
Albuquerque, NM	13.7	11.6	10.2	13.9	17.9	12.0	12.4	8.4
Allentown, PA	9.0	9.2	8.9	12.8	18.9	13.6	15.7	11.8
Anchorage, AK	6.1	5.8	6.1	10.7	17.5	14.6	20.6	18.6
Ann Arbor, MI	10.7	8.0	7.9	12.1	16.7	11.5	16.4	16.7
Athens, GA	18.9	13.0	10.8	13.8	15.1	9.5	11.2	7.7
Atlanta, GA	9.8	8.6	9.1	13.1	18.3	12.8	14.9	13.4
Austin, TX	8.3	7.2	7.9	12.2	18.1	13.4	16.9	16.0
Baton Rouge, LA	13.6	10.3	9.2	12.7	16.8	11.7	14.9	10.7
Billings, MT	9.4	10.5	9.7	13.5	20.7	13.1	13.5	9.5
Boise City, ID	11.3	9.7	10.0	14.7	19.9	12.8	13.0	8.6
Boston, MA	9.6	6.9	6.4	9.0	14.6	12.1	18.2	23.1
Boulder, CO	9.4	6.9	7.4	10.5	15.4	12.5	16.6	21.2
Cape Coral, FL	11.1	10.3	11.4	14.7	20.0	12.0	11.6	8.9
Cedar Rapids, IA	8.4	8.6	9.6	13.5	18.8	15.0	16.2	9.9
Charleston, SC	11.5	9.1	9.5	13.0	18.8	12.9	14.3	10.9
Charlotte, NC	10.4	9.5	9.8	13.7	18.2	12.6	13.9	11.9
Chicago, IL	10.4	8.6	8.2	11.6	16.8	12.8	16.0	15.7
Clarksville, TN	12.5	9.8	10.9	16.4	21.4	12.9	10.7	5.5
College Station, TX	17.9	11.5	10.4	13.5	15.9	11.1	11.4	8.2
Colorado Springs, CO	8.7	8.1	9.1	13.1	19.6	13.5	16.1	11.8
Columbia, MO	15.0	9.8	9.7	13.3	17.7	12.1	13.1	9.2
Columbia, SC	12.8	9.9	10.8	13.8	19.1	13.0	12.6	7.8
Columbus, OH	10.5	9.0	9.3	13.0	18.5	13.0	15.3	11.3
Dallas, TX	8.9	8.3	9.0	12.7	18.2	12.6	15.6	14.6
Denver, CO	7.8	6.8	7.8	11.9	17.8	13.7	17.5	16.7
Des Moines, IA	8.3	7.8	8.4	12.5	19.4	14.6	16.2	12.8
Durham, NC	11.2	9.8	9.2	13.2	17.3	12.0	13.5	13.8
Edison, NJ	11.3	8.2	7.5	10.0	14.7	11.5	16.1	20.8
El Paso, TX	15.9	12.8	12.1	15.9	17.9	10.2	9.8	5.3
Eugene, OR	14.6	11.7	11.1	14.6	18.6	11.8	10.9	6.6
Evansville, IN	12.7	11.3	11.7	14.3	18.1	12.2	12.3	7.2
Fargo, ND	9.9	9.5	9.8	13.3	18.7	14.5	14.3	9.9
Fayetteville, NC	14.4	12.1	12.7	16.1	18.8	11.5	9.6	4.8
Fort Collins, CO	8.6	8.9	8.7	13.0	17.0	14.4	16.4	13.0
Fort Wayne, IN	10.7	10.5	11.3	15.4	20.6	13.2	11.8	6.4
Fort Worth, TX	8.9	8.3	9.0	12.7	18.2	12.6	15.6	14.6
Gainesville, FL	18.4	11.9	10.5	12.8	17.1	10.5	10.4	8.6
Grand Rapids, MI	9.2	9.5	10.0	14.1	20.4	13.7	14.2	9.0
Greeley, CO	8.5	7.7	8.2	12.5	19.3	16.2	17.1	10.6
Green Bay, WI	9.3	9.7	10.3	14.5	19.1	15.1	14.2	7.8
Greensboro, NC	13.5	11.7	11.9	15.3	18.2	11.4	10.6	7.3
Honolulu, HI	7.5	5.6	6.2	10.3	17.1	14.4	19.8	19.1
Houston, TX	9.7	9.1	9.1	12.2	17.2	11.8	15.1	15.7
Huntsville, AL	11.7	9.6	9.4	12.0	16.8	12.1	15.8	12.6
Indianapolis, IN	10.8	9.8	9.8	14.1	18.4	12.6	14.1	10.5
Jacksonville, FL	11.0	9.0	10.4	14.1	18.8	12.9	13.5	10.4
Kansas City, MO	9.6	8.6	9.3	13.4	18.4	13.6	15.4	11.6
Lafayette, LA	14.7	12.0	10.5	13.2	16.7	11.1	13.1	8.7
Las Cruces, NM	18.5	15.5	11.9	14.6	15.6	8.9	9.3	5.9
Las Vegas, NV	10.6	9.6	10.8	14.6	19.7	12.9	13.1	8.6
Lexington, KY	12.9	10.3	10.1	13.1	18.0	12.4	13.3	9.8
Lincoln, NE	10.3	9.6	10.5	13.9	19.1	12.8	15.1	8.6
Little Rock, AR	12.3	10.8	11.1	14.4	18.7	11.8	12.6	8.2

Table continued on next page.

Metro Area	Percent of Households Earning							
	Under $15,000	$15,000 -$24,999	$25,000 -$34,999	$35,000 -$49,999	$50,000 -$74,999	$75,000 -$99,999	$100,000 -$149,999	$150,000 and up
Los Angeles, CA	10.6	8.9	8.4	11.5	16.2	12.0	15.3	17.0
Louisville, KY	11.5	10.1	9.8	14.5	18.7	12.8	13.3	9.3
Madison, WI	8.8	7.5	8.6	12.4	18.5	14.4	16.8	13.0
Manchester, NH	7.0	7.0	7.7	11.0	16.9	14.1	19.4	17.0
McAllen, TX	20.9	14.9	12.0	13.2	16.0	9.4	8.8	4.9
Miami, FL	13.2	11.1	10.3	13.7	17.1	11.1	12.2	11.2
Midland, TX	6.2	7.0	8.2	11.1	17.4	13.0	18.1	19.0
Minneapolis, MN	7.5	7.1	7.4	11.3	17.6	14.1	18.6	16.5
Nashville, TN	9.5	9.1	9.4	14.0	19.3	13.3	14.2	11.3
New Orleans, LA	15.5	11.2	10.3	12.8	16.5	11.1	12.4	10.1
New York, NY	11.3	8.2	7.5	10.0	14.7	11.5	16.1	20.8
Oklahoma City, OK	11.1	9.7	10.5	14.2	19.1	12.7	13.1	9.5
Omaha, NE	9.4	8.4	8.8	13.6	19.0	13.7	15.9	11.4
Orlando, FL	11.2	10.4	11.0	15.1	19.2	11.8	12.0	9.2
Peoria, IL	9.9	9.4	10.0	14.0	19.2	13.8	14.3	9.3
Philadelphia, PA	11.3	8.4	8.1	11.3	16.1	12.2	16.2	16.5
Phoenix, AZ	10.6	9.2	9.6	13.8	18.7	12.7	14.2	11.2
Pittsburgh, PA	11.8	10.6	9.8	12.8	18.0	12.7	14.1	10.3
Portland, OR	8.9	8.0	8.3	12.2	18.1	13.9	16.8	13.7
Providence, RI	12.4	9.5	8.5	11.6	16.2	13.0	16.0	12.8
Provo, UT	7.3	7.0	8.2	12.8	20.8	15.4	17.4	11.0
Raleigh, NC	7.8	7.3	8.3	12.7	17.8	13.6	17.0	15.6
Reno, NV	10.0	9.9	9.2	13.8	18.9	13.0	14.6	10.5
Richmond, VA	9.9	7.9	8.5	13.0	17.9	13.6	16.1	13.0
Roanoke, VA	12.5	10.1	10.7	14.2	19.8	13.0	12.3	7.5
Rochester, MN	7.6	7.2	8.6	11.7	19.0	14.5	18.0	13.4
Salem, OR	10.5	10.2	10.5	14.7	20.2	13.8	13.4	6.7
Salt Lake City, UT	7.3	7.0	8.2	12.5	20.2	15.0	17.0	12.6
San Antonio, TX	11.3	9.6	9.8	13.4	18.9	12.5	14.2	10.3
San Diego, CA	8.9	7.6	8.0	11.4	16.8	12.9	17.0	17.5
San Francisco, CA	8.1	6.2	5.8	8.4	13.2	11.4	17.9	29.0
San Jose, CA	6.3	5.0	5.1	7.6	12.3	10.8	18.4	34.6
Santa Rosa, CA	8.1	7.3	7.5	11.1	18.0	14.1	16.7	17.2
Savannah, GA	12.4	9.9	9.6	13.7	18.0	12.9	13.8	9.7
Seattle, WA	8.0	6.2	6.9	10.7	16.8	13.5	18.4	19.3
Sioux Falls, SD	8.6	8.0	10.1	13.8	19.2	15.9	14.9	9.5
Springfield, IL	11.3	10.3	8.6	12.6	18.2	13.6	14.5	10.8
Tallahassee, FL	14.7	10.5	11.0	14.8	17.5	11.6	11.7	8.2
Tampa, FL	12.3	11.5	10.9	14.8	18.1	11.7	11.8	9.0
Topeka, KS	10.2	10.5	10.6	14.0	20.3	14.1	14.4	5.9
Tyler, TX	11.6	11.7	11.1	15.0	17.9	11.6	12.5	8.6
Virginia Beach, VA	9.4	8.5	8.7	13.2	19.5	13.8	16.1	10.8
Visalia, CA	14.4	13.9	11.3	15.3	17.2	10.3	10.9	6.7
Washington, DC	6.2	4.6	5.2	8.1	14.5	12.7	20.2	28.4
Wilmington, NC	14.0	10.8	10.5	13.4	17.7	11.5	12.5	9.6
Winston-Salem, NC	13.7	12.0	11.5	15.2	18.0	12.0	10.5	6.9
U.S.	11.6	9.8	9.5	13.0	17.7	12.3	14.1	12.1

Note: Figures cover the Metropolitan Statistical Area (MSA)—see Appendix B for areas included
Source: Source: U.S. Census Bureau, 2013-2017 American Community Survey 5-Year Estimates

Poverty Rate: City

City	All Ages	Under 18 Years Old	18 to 64 Years Old	65 Years and Over
Albany, NY	24.5	30.5	25.4	11.2
Albuquerque, NM	18.2	25.5	17.3	9.9
Allentown, PA	27.3	39.9	24.1	14.1
Anchorage, AK	8.1	11.5	7.2	5.0
Ann Arbor, MI	22.1	10.8	26.9	7.2
Athens, GA	34.4	39.8	36.4	10.8
Atlanta, GA	22.4	35.7	19.8	15.0
Austin, TX	15.4	21.4	14.3	9.7
Baton Rouge, LA	26.0	34.6	25.9	12.6
Billings, MT	10.8	11.8	11.4	7.1
Boise City, ID	14.0	15.2	14.4	9.8
Boston, MA	20.5	29.7	18.3	20.5
Boulder, CO	21.6	8.2	26.3	6.9
Cape Coral, FL	12.7	17.0	12.8	8.7
Cedar Rapids, IA	11.4	13.6	11.8	6.2
Charleston, SC	14.6	16.5	15.7	6.9
Charlotte, NC	14.9	21.0	13.5	8.9
Chicago, IL	20.6	30.7	18.1	16.2
Clarksville, TN	15.3	19.6	14.3	8.3
College Station, TX	31.8	17.5	37.5	7.0
Colorado Springs, CO	12.8	16.9	12.4	7.2
Columbia, MO	22.9	15.9	27.4	4.9
Columbia, SC	22.3	28.3	22.1	13.7
Columbus, OH	20.8	31.1	18.7	11.2
Dallas, TX	21.8	34.2	18.1	14.1
Denver, CO	15.1	22.8	13.5	10.7
Des Moines, IA	18.1	27.5	15.8	11.0
Durham, NC	17.4	26.0	15.9	8.3
Edison, NJ	5.3	4.5	5.2	7.5
El Paso, TX	20.3	28.5	17.0	18.4
Eugene, OR	21.7	17.7	25.6	9.4
Evansville, IN	23.3	37.3	21.5	10.8
Fargo, ND	13.9	13.4	15.1	7.1
Fayetteville, NC	19.3	29.3	16.9	10.8
Fort Collins, CO	17.0	10.2	20.4	6.8
Fort Wayne, IN	17.8	27.1	16.2	7.3
Fort Worth, TX	16.9	23.4	14.7	11.1
Gainesville, FL	33.6	27.2	37.9	10.0
Grand Rapids, MI	22.5	30.6	21.6	9.9
Greeley, CO	17.5	20.2	17.7	10.2
Green Bay, WI	17.2	24.3	15.7	10.5
Greensboro, NC	19.2	27.2	18.3	10.0
Honolulu, HI	11.6	14.2	11.2	10.8
Houston, TX	21.2	33.3	17.6	13.8
Huntsville, AL	18.3	28.7	17.2	8.1
Indianapolis, IN	20.1	30.1	18.0	10.0
Jacksonville, FL	16.4	24.8	14.5	10.8
Kansas City, MO	17.3	25.5	15.8	9.9
Lafayette, LA	19.1	26.1	18.3	11.5
Las Cruces, NM	24.4	32.4	25.4	7.9
Las Vegas, NV	16.2	23.7	14.7	9.7
Lexington, KY	18.6	22.9	19.1	8.0
Lincoln, NE	15.1	17.0	16.3	5.9
Little Rock, AR	17.8	25.3	16.6	9.2
Los Angeles, CA	20.4	29.5	18.2	15.9

Table continued on next page.

City	All Ages	Under 18 Years Old	18 to 64 Years Old	65 Years and Over
Louisville, KY	16.7	24.4	15.5	9.5
Madison, WI	18.3	16.5	20.8	5.7
Manchester, NH	14.9	21.4	14.3	8.6
McAllen, TX	25.2	36.6	20.6	20.8
Miami, FL	25.8	36.0	21.9	30.3
Midland, TX	8.7	11.4	7.4	9.6
Minneapolis, MN	20.7	28.1	19.7	12.6
Nashville, TN	17.2	28.2	15.0	8.7
New Orleans, LA	25.4	38.3	23.0	16.9
New York, NY	19.6	27.8	17.2	18.4
Oklahoma City, OK	17.1	25.8	15.1	8.2
Omaha, NE	15.1	21.4	13.8	8.6
Orlando, FL	19.1	28.0	17.0	14.9
Peoria, IL	20.9	28.0	20.4	10.2
Philadelphia, PA	25.8	36.0	23.9	17.6
Phoenix, AZ	20.9	30.5	18.4	11.2
Pittsburgh, PA	22.0	30.5	22.1	12.3
Portland, OR	16.2	19.3	16.2	11.9
Providence, RI	26.9	36.0	24.7	19.3
Provo, UT	25.4	17.0	29.9	8.0
Raleigh, NC	14.0	19.7	13.2	6.6
Reno, NV	16.2	19.8	16.6	8.5
Richmond, VA	25.2	40.5	23.3	13.1
Roanoke, VA	21.6	33.3	19.7	12.2
Rochester, MN	10.4	13.0	10.6	4.6
Salem, OR	16.2	21.2	15.9	8.1
Salt Lake City, UT	17.8	22.4	17.5	11.0
San Antonio, TX	18.6	27.2	16.2	12.6
San Diego, CA	14.5	18.6	14.1	9.6
San Francisco, CA	11.7	11.4	11.3	13.6
San Jose, CA	10.0	11.6	9.5	9.8
Santa Rosa, CA	11.8	16.9	11.3	6.5
Savannah, GA	24.0	34.8	22.9	11.7
Seattle, WA	12.5	13.4	12.4	11.5
Sioux Falls, SD	11.1	14.1	10.5	8.3
Springfield, IL	20.3	31.9	19.2	7.9
Tallahassee, FL	27.1	23.4	30.6	7.9
Tampa, FL	20.0	28.7	17.8	16.6
Topeka, KS	16.7	21.7	16.9	8.3
Tyler, TX	20.2	27.4	19.6	10.9
Virginia Beach, VA	8.0	11.4	7.4	5.4
Visalia, CA	20.3	27.2	18.8	9.4
Washington, DC	17.4	25.5	15.8	14.3
Wilmington, NC	23.2	29.9	24.4	10.9
Winston-Salem, NC	23.3	35.0	21.4	10.9
U.S.	14.6	20.3	13.7	9.3

Note: Figures are percentage of people whose income during the past 12 months was below the poverty level;
Source: U.S. Census Bureau, 2013-2017 American Community Survey 5-Year Estimates

Poverty Rate: Metro Area

Metro Area	All Ages	Under 18 Years Old	18 to 64 Years Old	65 Years and Over
Albany, NY	11.0	14.9	10.8	6.4
Albuquerque, NM	17.9	24.9	17.1	10.5
Allentown, PA	11.1	17.3	10.2	6.4
Anchorage, AK	8.5	11.5	7.9	5.2
Ann Arbor, MI	14.5	12.7	16.7	6.1
Athens, GA	25.4	29.4	27.1	9.2
Atlanta, GA	13.9	20.1	12.4	8.9
Austin, TX	12.3	15.6	11.8	7.4
Baton Rouge, LA	16.9	22.6	16.0	10.5
Billings, MT	10.2	11.9	10.2	7.7
Boise City, ID	13.8	16.6	13.4	10.2
Boston, MA	10.0	12.5	9.5	8.9
Boulder, CO	13.1	11.6	14.8	6.4
Cape Coral, FL	14.9	24.9	15.0	7.8
Cedar Rapids, IA	9.4	11.3	9.4	6.0
Charleston, SC	13.9	20.1	12.9	8.6
Charlotte, NC	13.4	18.7	12.4	8.5
Chicago, IL	13.1	18.6	11.8	9.3
Clarksville, TN	15.6	20.4	14.5	9.5
College Station, TX	24.4	23.1	27.1	9.5
Colorado Springs, CO	11.0	14.0	10.6	6.6
Columbia, MO	18.7	15.2	21.8	6.9
Columbia, SC	15.6	21.3	15.0	8.5
Columbus, OH	14.0	19.8	13.0	7.8
Dallas, TX	13.3	19.2	11.7	8.4
Denver, CO	10.2	13.7	9.5	7.0
Des Moines, IA	10.3	13.6	9.5	7.3
Durham, NC	15.5	20.6	15.6	7.4
Edison, NJ	13.8	19.3	12.4	11.8
El Paso, TX	21.8	30.3	18.1	19.7
Eugene, OR	18.8	20.3	21.2	8.7
Evansville, IN	15.4	22.4	14.5	9.0
Fargo, ND	11.5	11.4	12.5	6.3
Fayetteville, NC	18.7	26.9	16.6	10.8
Fort Collins, CO	12.4	10.9	14.4	5.6
Fort Wayne, IN	14.1	21.1	12.9	6.2
Fort Worth, TX	13.3	19.2	11.7	8.4
Gainesville, FL	23.1	22.8	26.2	8.7
Grand Rapids, MI	12.4	15.8	12.3	6.6
Greeley, CO	11.2	13.4	10.9	8.0
Green Bay, WI	10.9	14.9	10.0	8.2
Greensboro, NC	16.9	24.7	16.0	9.3
Honolulu, HI	9.1	11.3	8.7	7.7
Houston, TX	14.8	21.5	12.7	10.0
Huntsville, AL	13.9	20.0	12.9	8.5
Indianapolis, IN	13.7	19.6	12.7	7.1
Jacksonville, FL	13.9	19.9	13.0	8.7
Kansas City, MO	11.5	16.2	10.6	7.1
Lafayette, LA	18.1	24.7	16.3	14.0
Las Cruces, NM	27.9	41.0	26.0	12.3
Las Vegas, NV	14.6	21.2	13.4	8.7
Lexington, KY	17.2	22.7	17.3	7.6
Lincoln, NE	13.7	15.3	14.8	5.6
Little Rock, AR	15.1	20.9	14.4	8.5
Los Angeles, CA	15.8	22.2	14.3	12.3

Table continued on next page.

Metro Area	All Ages	Under 18 Years Old	18 to 64 Years Old	65 Years and Over
Louisville, KY	13.2	18.8	12.4	8.0
Madison, WI	11.7	11.8	12.8	5.7
Manchester, NH	8.6	10.9	8.4	5.7
McAllen, TX	31.8	43.8	26.3	23.0
Miami, FL	16.1	22.2	14.4	14.9
Midland, TX	8.6	11.4	7.3	9.2
Minneapolis, MN	9.4	12.3	8.8	6.5
Nashville, TN	12.8	18.2	11.8	7.7
New Orleans, LA	18.0	26.6	16.2	12.3
New York, NY	13.8	19.3	12.4	11.8
Oklahoma City, OK	14.6	20.6	13.7	7.2
Omaha, NE	11.2	14.9	10.4	7.2
Orlando, FL	15.4	22.1	14.2	10.1
Peoria, IL	12.0	16.6	11.8	6.1
Philadelphia, PA	13.1	17.8	12.4	8.9
Phoenix, AZ	15.7	22.4	14.7	8.4
Pittsburgh, PA	11.8	16.3	11.6	8.0
Portland, OR	12.3	15.5	12.1	8.0
Providence, RI	13.0	18.3	12.1	9.6
Provo, UT	11.8	10.6	13.4	5.7
Raleigh, NC	11.1	15.1	10.2	6.8
Reno, NV	13.3	16.9	13.3	7.7
Richmond, VA	12.4	17.9	11.7	6.8
Roanoke, VA	13.6	20.2	12.9	8.5
Rochester, MN	8.6	11.0	8.4	5.6
Salem, OR	15.8	22.2	15.3	7.5
Salt Lake City, UT	10.3	12.7	9.7	7.0
San Antonio, TX	15.2	21.8	13.5	10.4
San Diego, CA	13.3	17.1	12.9	9.0
San Francisco, CA	10.1	11.7	10.0	8.6
San Jose, CA	8.7	9.9	8.3	8.5
Santa Rosa, CA	10.7	13.1	11.0	6.7
Savannah, GA	15.8	22.6	14.9	8.0
Seattle, WA	10.4	13.0	9.9	8.1
Sioux Falls, SD	9.2	11.4	8.7	7.2
Springfield, IL	15.4	24.3	14.4	6.6
Tallahassee, FL	20.2	21.6	22.2	7.8
Tampa, FL	14.6	20.3	14.1	9.9
Topeka, KS	12.4	15.8	12.5	6.7
Tyler, TX	16.3	22.1	15.7	9.2
Virginia Beach, VA	12.2	18.2	11.1	6.9
Visalia, CA	27.1	36.2	24.5	14.3
Washington, DC	8.3	10.7	7.6	7.2
Wilmington, NC	17.5	22.0	18.3	9.1
Winston-Salem, NC	17.3	26.2	16.0	9.1
U.S.	14.6	20.3	13.7	9.3

Note: Figures are percentage of people whose income during the past 12 months was below the poverty level; Figures cover the Metropolitan Statistical Area—see Appendix B for areas included
Source: U.S. Census Bureau, 2013-2017 American Community Survey 5-Year Estimates

Employment by Industry

Metro Area[1]	(A)	(B)	(C)	(D)	(E)	(F)	(G)	(H)	(I)	(J)	(K)	(L)	(M)	(N)
Albany, NY	4.0	n/a	20.6	5.4	21.4	1.7	8.8	5.5	n/a	4.0	11.9	10.4	3.0	2.7
Albuquerque, NM	5.9	n/a	16.8	4.7	20.6	1.7	11.0	4.0	n/a	3.0	15.4	10.7	2.7	2.9
Allentown, PA	3.6	n/a	20.8	3.7	10.8	1.4	9.9	10.1	n/a	3.8	12.5	10.6	8.5	3.8
Anchorage, AK	7.0	5.3	18.3	4.5	19.9	2.3	11.1	1.1	1.6	3.6	10.5	12.0	6.5	2.8
Ann Arbor, MI	1.9	n/a	12.2	3.0	38.0	2.3	7.7	6.7	n/a	2.8	13.3	7.2	1.7	2.7
Athens, GA	n/a	n/a	n/a	n/a	29.7	n/a	11.3	n/a	n/a	n/a	9.3	11.0	n/a	n/a
Atlanta, GA	4.6	4.5	12.7	6.1	11.9	3.4	10.6	6.1	<0.1	3.4	19.0	10.6	5.7	5.4
Austin, TX	5.8	n/a	11.7	5.8	16.8	3.1	11.8	5.6	n/a	4.1	17.3	10.3	2.1	4.8
Baton Rouge, LA	13.3	13.0	12.7	4.5	18.5	1.2	9.6	7.2	0.2	4.0	11.4	10.2	3.7	3.3
Billings, MT	n/a	n/a	18.1	n/a	11.5	n/a	13.5	n/a	n/a	n/a	11.0	n/a	n/a	n/a
Boise City, ID	7.1	n/a	14.6	5.5	14.5	1.3	9.9	8.7	n/a	3.5	15.0	11.5	3.4	4.5
Boston, MA[4]	3.7	n/a	22.5	8.1	10.6	3.2	9.6	4.2	n/a	3.6	20.4	8.1	2.4	3.1
Boulder, CO	2.9	n/a	13.2	3.5	20.0	4.1	10.9	9.6	n/a	3.2	18.8	9.1	0.9	3.2
Cape Coral, FL	11.4	n/a	11.0	4.8	15.5	1.0	15.5	2.2	n/a	4.1	13.8	15.5	1.9	2.6
Cedar Rapids, IA	5.3	n/a	14.6	7.4	11.7	2.5	8.1	13.6	n/a	3.5	10.5	10.4	7.9	4.1
Charleston, SC	6.0	n/a	11.4	4.3	17.9	1.7	12.9	7.4	n/a	3.8	15.4	12.0	4.2	2.6
Charlotte, NC	5.2	n/a	10.3	7.9	12.6	2.4	11.4	8.9	n/a	3.4	17.0	10.7	5.1	4.7
Chicago, IL[2]	3.3	3.2	15.9	7.0	11.0	1.7	9.9	7.5	<0.1	4.2	18.7	9.4	5.8	5.0
Clarksville, TN	3.5	n/a	12.8	3.4	20.4	1.1	12.2	14.0	n/a	3.2	9.8	13.6	2.7	n/a
College Station, TX	6.4	n/a	10.2	3.3	35.6	1.0	14.0	4.6	n/a	2.8	7.7	10.2	1.5	2.2
Colorado Springs, CO	6.1	n/a	13.8	6.2	18.2	1.9	12.5	3.9	n/a	5.9	15.7	11.7	1.8	1.9
Columbia, MO	n/a	n/a	n/a	n/a	30.3	n/a	n/a	n/a	n/a	n/a	n/a	10.9	n/a	n/a
Columbia, SC	4.4	n/a	11.7	7.5	21.4	1.3	9.8	7.4	n/a	4.0	13.1	10.9	4.4	3.7
Columbus, OH	3.7	n/a	15.4	7.7	15.9	1.5	9.5	6.7	n/a	3.7	16.5	9.2	5.9	3.7
Dallas, TX[2]	5.5	n/a	11.9	9.0	11.4	2.6	10.1	6.8	n/a	3.2	18.9	9.9	4.7	5.6
Denver, CO	7.1	n/a	12.6	7.2	13.2	3.2	10.8	4.6	n/a	3.9	18.2	9.4	4.3	4.8
Des Moines, IA	5.5	n/a	14.4	15.0	12.1	1.8	9.2	5.6	n/a	3.4	13.6	11.0	3.1	4.8
Durham, NC	2.7	n/a	22.0	4.7	21.6	1.3	8.6	8.8	n/a	3.4	14.5	7.8	1.5	2.6
Edison, NJ[2]	3.7	n/a	21.2	8.6	13.0	3.4	9.4	2.8	n/a	4.2	16.1	9.4	3.8	3.8
El Paso, TX	5.1	n/a	14.5	3.9	22.8	1.4	11.2	5.1	n/a	2.8	11.1	12.7	5.2	3.8
Eugene, OR	5.0	4.4	17.1	5.0	18.4	1.4	10.6	9.0	0.5	3.2	11.1	12.5	2.2	4.0
Evansville, IN	6.0	n/a	17.6	3.3	10.7	0.9	9.7	14.5	n/a	5.1	12.3	10.7	4.9	3.8
Fargo, ND	5.6	n/a	17.5	7.7	14.3	2.1	9.5	7.2	n/a	3.5	10.9	10.9	4.2	6.2
Fayetteville, NC	4.3	n/a	11.4	2.8	31.0	0.9	12.3	6.2	n/a	3.3	9.1	13.0	3.4	1.7
Fort Collins, CO	6.7	n/a	10.6	4.0	24.0	1.7	12.3	8.5	n/a	3.7	12.1	11.3	1.9	2.8
Fort Wayne, IN	4.8	n/a	19.0	5.3	9.6	1.1	9.0	16.4	n/a	5.0	9.9	10.8	3.9	4.7
Fort Worth, TX[2]	7.0	n/a	12.8	5.8	13.0	1.0	11.3	9.4	n/a	3.5	10.6	11.6	8.6	5.0
Gainesville, FL	4.0	n/a	18.0	4.5	30.0	1.0	10.7	3.1	n/a	2.9	10.0	10.7	2.4	2.2
Grand Rapids, MI	4.4	n/a	16.5	4.6	8.7	1.1	8.9	20.8	n/a	3.9	13.5	8.8	2.8	5.5
Greeley, CO	17.6	n/a	9.4	4.0	16.7	0.6	8.1	12.7	n/a	3.2	9.6	9.5	4.2	3.9
Green Bay, WI	4.2	n/a	14.9	6.6	12.1	0.8	9.4	17.1	n/a	4.8	10.6	9.5	4.8	4.6
Greensboro, NC	4.3	n/a	14.3	5.1	12.4	1.2	9.7	15.1	n/a	3.4	12.9	10.7	5.3	5.2
Honolulu, HI	5.5	n/a	13.5	4.5	21.0	1.7	15.4	2.3	n/a	4.4	13.4	9.9	5.0	2.9
Houston, TX	9.6	7.1	12.7	5.2	13.4	1.0	10.3	7.5	2.5	3.5	15.9	10.0	5.0	5.5
Huntsville, AL	3.8	n/a	9.0	2.8	21.3	1.0	9.1	10.6	n/a	3.3	23.9	10.7	1.3	2.5
Indianapolis, IN	4.8	4.8	15.1	6.3	12.5	1.2	9.6	8.5	<0.1	4.3	16.1	9.7	6.8	4.6
Jacksonville, FL	6.3	6.2	15.1	9.2	11.0	1.3	12.0	4.4	<0.1	3.7	15.1	12.4	5.4	3.6
Kansas City, MO	4.3	n/a	14.4	7.1	14.2	1.4	9.5	7.1	n/a	3.8	17.6	10.3	5.0	4.6
Lafayette, LA	11.0	4.7	15.8	5.3	13.4	1.1	10.7	7.6	6.2	3.4	10.5	13.4	2.9	4.3
Las Cruces, NM	4.9	n/a	21.5	3.4	27.3	0.9	11.2	3.3	n/a	2.0	10.7	9.9	2.9	1.6
Las Vegas, NV	6.5	6.4	10.2	5.2	10.3	1.0	28.3	2.4	<0.1	3.2	14.2	11.0	4.8	2.3
Lexington, KY	4.5	n/a	13.1	3.5	18.6	1.0	11.0	10.9	n/a	3.4	14.5	11.0	4.1	3.8
Lincoln, NE	4.7	n/a	15.5	6.9	22.0	1.6	9.8	7.0	n/a	3.7	10.3	10.1	5.8	2.1
Little Rock, AR	4.4	n/a	15.7	5.8	19.7	1.1	9.6	5.7	n/a	4.3	13.5	10.9	4.4	4.3
Los Angeles, CA[2]	3.2	3.2	18.3	4.8	13.0	4.8	11.7	7.4	<0.1	3.5	13.7	9.6	4.6	4.9
Louisville, KY	4.5	n/a	14.4	6.8	11.1	1.3	9.6	12.4	n/a	3.8	12.9	10.0	8.5	4.2

Table continued on next page.

Metro Area[1]	(A)	(B)	(C)	(D)	(E)	(F)	(G)	(H)	(I)	(J)	(K)	(L)	(M)	(N)
Madison, WI	4.4	n/a	11.9	5.6	21.4	4.2	9.1	8.6	n/a	5.1	12.8	10.3	2.5	3.7
Manchester, NH[3]	4.5	n/a	22.2	7.0	10.3	3.0	8.7	6.9	n/a	4.2	15.1	11.2	2.4	3.9
McAllen, TX	3.0	n/a	28.0	3.3	23.0	1.0	9.4	2.6	n/a	2.1	6.5	14.0	3.2	3.3
Miami, FL[2]	4.3	4.3	15.6	6.7	11.7	1.6	11.9	3.4	<0.1	4.2	14.8	12.6	6.6	6.0
Midland, TX	34.9	n/a	6.6	4.0	8.7	0.8	9.1	3.8	n/a	3.2	8.8	8.8	4.5	6.2
Minneapolis, MN	3.8	n/a	16.7	7.4	12.4	1.8	9.1	9.9	n/a	3.8	16.2	9.8	3.8	4.7
Nashville, TN	4.5	n/a	14.9	6.6	11.9	2.2	11.2	8.0	n/a	4.1	16.5	10.2	5.3	4.0
New Orleans, LA	6.0	5.3	17.4	4.9	12.3	1.2	16.0	5.1	0.7	4.2	13.0	10.6	5.1	3.7
New York, NY[2]	3.7	n/a	21.2	8.6	13.0	3.4	9.4	2.8	n/a	4.2	16.1	9.4	3.8	3.8
Oklahoma City, OK	8.1	4.7	14.2	5.1	20.0	1.1	11.3	5.1	3.4	4.4	12.8	10.3	3.5	3.8
Omaha, NE	5.7	n/a	15.9	8.9	13.2	2.1	9.7	6.6	n/a	3.5	14.5	10.9	5.2	3.3
Orlando, FL	6.3	6.3	11.9	5.8	9.8	1.9	20.1	3.5	<0.1	3.3	18.3	11.7	3.4	3.5
Peoria, IL	4.0	n/a	18.0	4.0	12.1	1.1	10.1	13.4	n/a	4.3	14.1	10.2	4.0	4.1
Philadelphia, PA[2]	2.5	n/a	31.1	6.1	13.3	1.5	10.0	3.4	n/a	4.0	13.6	7.7	4.0	2.4
Phoenix, AZ	6.2	6.0	15.4	8.9	11.2	1.8	10.7	6.0	0.1	3.2	16.8	11.2	4.2	3.8
Pittsburgh, PA	5.9	5.0	21.6	6.3	9.7	1.6	9.9	7.2	0.9	4.2	15.1	10.2	4.1	3.6
Portland, OR	6.1	6.0	15.2	5.9	12.6	2.1	10.3	10.6	0.1	3.5	14.9	10.1	3.6	4.7
Providence, RI[3]	4.1	4.1	21.7	6.2	12.2	1.2	10.6	8.4	<0.1	4.6	12.7	11.3	3.2	3.2
Provo, UT	8.8	n/a	20.9	3.3	12.5	5.0	8.0	7.6	n/a	2.0	14.4	12.9	1.4	2.7
Raleigh, NC	6.3	n/a	12.4	5.2	15.6	3.4	10.8	5.6	n/a	3.8	18.5	11.6	2.3	4.0
Reno, NV	7.3	7.2	10.8	4.3	12.2	1.1	15.0	10.0	0.1	2.5	14.2	10.2	8.0	3.9
Richmond, VA	5.7	n/a	14.5	7.5	16.7	1.0	9.0	4.7	n/a	4.7	17.0	10.0	4.4	4.1
Roanoke, VA	5.0	n/a	17.2	4.9	14.2	0.8	8.8	9.4	n/a	4.8	13.9	10.5	5.3	4.7
Rochester, MN	3.8	n/a	41.5	2.2	10.8	1.3	8.9	8.7	n/a	3.0	4.8	10.1	2.2	2.2
Salem, OR	6.9	6.6	17.0	4.2	24.8	0.7	9.1	7.5	0.3	3.2	8.8	11.6	3.2	2.4
Salt Lake City, UT	5.7	n/a	11.3	8.1	15.0	2.8	8.8	7.8	n/a	2.9	16.9	10.6	5.3	4.4
San Antonio, TX	5.9	4.9	15.5	8.6	16.2	1.9	12.7	4.7	0.9	3.5	13.4	10.9	2.9	3.4
San Diego, CA	5.5	5.5	14.2	5.0	16.7	1.5	13.3	7.6	<0.1	3.7	16.5	10.2	2.3	2.9
San Francisco, CA[2]	3.6	3.6	12.2	7.0	11.2	7.5	12.3	3.2	<0.1	3.6	25.1	7.2	4.2	2.3
San Jose, CA	4.2	4.2	15.3	3.3	8.7	8.3	9.1	15.2	<0.1	2.5	20.9	7.8	1.5	2.7
Santa Rosa, CA	7.2	7.1	17.0	4.1	15.0	1.2	11.6	11.2	0.1	3.3	10.9	12.1	2.1	3.6
Savannah, GA	4.7	n/a	14.3	3.5	13.5	1.0	14.1	10.1	n/a	3.8	11.0	12.3	7.6	3.5
Seattle, WA[2]	6.0	5.9	12.9	4.9	12.3	6.7	9.9	9.4	<0.1	3.4	15.1	11.2	3.5	4.1
Sioux Falls, SD	5.2	n/a	20.7	9.8	9.1	1.6	9.5	8.9	n/a	3.7	10.0	12.1	3.6	5.2
Springfield, IL	2.7	n/a	18.6	5.5	26.0	2.3	9.3	3.0	n/a	5.9	10.6	10.9	1.8	2.8
Tallahassee, FL	4.5	n/a	12.9	4.2	33.0	1.6	11.2	1.7	n/a	5.2	11.5	10.5	1.3	2.0
Tampa, FL	5.6	5.6	15.4	8.8	11.4	1.8	11.6	4.9	<0.1	3.4	18.1	12.2	2.4	3.8
Topeka, KS	4.7	n/a	16.5	6.9	23.7	1.2	7.6	6.9	n/a	4.3	12.1	9.5	3.4	2.5
Tyler, TX	6.2	n/a	22.6	3.9	13.9	1.3	10.7	5.0	n/a	3.7	10.1	12.6	4.7	4.7
Virginia Beach, VA	4.8	n/a	14.3	4.8	20.4	1.3	11.2	7.3	n/a	4.5	14.3	11.1	3.2	2.3
Visalia, CA	4.7	n/a	12.7	3.1	25.7	0.7	9.1	10.0	n/a	2.6	8.4	13.4	5.7	3.4
Washington, DC[2]	4.6	n/a	12.9	4.3	21.7	2.2	10.2	1.3	n/a	6.7	23.2	8.1	2.4	1.8
Wilmington, NC	6.7	n/a	11.6	4.7	18.7	2.5	15.2	4.6	n/a	3.8	12.2	13.7	2.4	3.4
Winston-Salem, NC	4.0	n/a	20.5	4.9	11.9	0.6	10.4	12.1	n/a	3.1	13.7	11.5	3.6	3.1
U.S.	5.3	4.8	15.9	5.7	15.1	1.9	10.7	8.5	0.5	3.9	14.1	10.8	4.2	3.9

Note: All figures are percentages covering non-farm employment as of December 2018 and are not seasonally adjusted;
(1) Figures cover the Metropolitan Statistical Area (MSA) except where noted. See Appendix B for areas included; (2) Metropolitan Division; (3) New England City and Town Area; (4) New England City and Town Area Division; (A) Construction, Mining, and Logging (some areas report Construction separate from Mining and Logging); (B) Construction; (C) Education and Health Services; (D) Financial Activities; (E) Government; (F) Information; (G) Leisure and Hospitality; (H) Manufacturing; (I) Mining and Logging; (J) Other Services; (K) Professional and Business Services; (L) Retail Trade; (M) Transportation and Utilities; (N) Wholesale Trade; n/a not available
Source: Bureau of Labor Statistics, Current Employment Statistics, Employment, Hours, and Earnings, December 2018

Labor Force, Employment and Job Growth: City

City	Civilian Labor Force			Workers Employed		
	Dec. 2017	Dec. 2018	% Chg.	Dec. 2017	Dec. 2018	% Chg.
Albany, NY	46,643	47,704	2.2	44,459	45,976	3.4
Albuquerque, NM	278,343	287,128	3.1	264,846	274,874	3.7
Allentown, PA	54,030	54,927	1.6	50,624	51,750	2.2
Anchorage, AK	156,235	153,126	-1.9	147,186	145,328	-1.2
Ann Arbor, MI	65,171	65,503	0.5	63,515	64,041	0.8
Athens, GA	60,911	62,570	2.7	58,343	60,290	3.3
Atlanta, GA	252,504	255,674	1.2	240,597	245,200	1.9
Austin, TX	578,582	599,854	3.6	564,005	584,814	3.6
Baton Rouge, LA	114,467	114,228	-0.2	110,218	109,416	-0.7
Billings, MT	56,572	56,666	0.1	54,593	54,787	0.3
Boise City, ID	127,840	131,138	2.5	124,833	128,133	2.6
Boston, MA	372,444	393,079	5.5	362,346	383,962	5.9
Boulder, CO	64,429	66,564	3.3	62,976	64,432	2.3
Cape Coral, FL	87,362	89,615	2.5	84,383	86,784	2.8
Cedar Rapids, IA	70,152	70,700	0.7	67,761	68,658	1.3
Charleston, SC	72,422	73,601	1.6	70,111	71,740	2.3
Charlotte, NC	483,182	490,050	1.4	463,433	473,059	2.0
Chicago, IL	1,361,078	1,335,474	-1.8	1,288,701	1,283,431	-0.4
Clarksville, TN	59,588	61,309	2.8	57,442	59,226	3.1
College Station, TX	59,536	60,885	2.2	58,011	59,187	2.0
Colorado Springs, CO	233,297	247,687	6.1	225,458	236,593	4.9
Columbia, MO	66,863	67,317	0.6	65,375	65,918	0.8
Columbia, SC	59,440	59,882	0.7	56,706	57,719	1.7
Columbus, OH	465,421	467,223	0.3	448,071	448,562	0.1
Dallas, TX	685,232	710,627	3.7	662,456	686,384	3.6
Denver, CO	401,313	411,708	2.5	389,719	396,286	1.6
Des Moines, IA	111,536	115,184	3.2	107,681	111,687	3.7
Durham, NC	142,841	145,434	1.8	137,308	140,582	2.3
Edison, NJ	54,808	54,865	0.1	53,232	53,523	0.5
El Paso, TX	297,041	303,631	2.2	285,407	291,848	2.2
Eugene, OR	85,893	84,904	-1.1	82,759	81,544	-1.4
Evansville, IN	58,960	59,887	1.5	57,218	57,922	1.2
Fargo, ND	69,596	68,580	-1.4	68,045	67,103	-1.3
Fayetteville, NC	76,094	76,808	0.9	71,557	72,716	1.6
Fort Collins, CO	98,374	102,737	4.4	96,051	99,566	3.6
Fort Wayne, IN	124,295	128,942	3.7	120,667	124,877	3.4
Fort Worth, TX	416,976	430,412	3.2	403,226	415,732	3.1
Gainesville, FL	67,232	68,434	1.7	64,845	66,131	1.9
Grand Rapids, MI	103,943	104,567	0.6	99,188	100,721	1.5
Greeley, CO	53,136	54,936	3.3	51,634	52,884	2.4
Green Bay, WI	54,880	54,922	0.0	53,420	53,547	0.2
Greensboro, NC	143,681	144,756	0.7	137,008	138,976	1.4
Honolulu, HI	471,688	468,609	-0.6	463,613	458,462	-1.1
Houston, TX	1,155,275	1,193,791	3.3	1,107,177	1,148,266	3.7
Huntsville, AL	94,181	98,508	4.5	91,263	95,413	4.5
Indianapolis, IN	437,038	451,232	3.2	423,438	436,132	3.0
Jacksonville, FL	457,717	464,256	1.4	441,382	449,181	1.7
Kansas City, MO	256,776	259,249	0.9	247,285	250,839	1.4
Lafayette, LA	59,801	59,450	-0.5	57,509	57,050	-0.8
Las Cruces, NM	45,773	46,276	1.1	43,256	44,063	1.8
Las Vegas, NV	306,426	317,238	3.5	290,781	302,680	4.0
Lexington, KY	174,457	176,120	0.9	169,534	171,118	0.9
Lincoln, NE	152,563	155,749	2.0	148,759	152,191	2.3
Little Rock, AR	97,069	98,167	1.1	94,026	94,836	0.8
Los Angeles, CA	2,070,235	2,093,984	1.1	1,984,993	1,997,076	0.6

Table continued on next page.

City	Civilian Labor Force			Workers Employed		
	Dec. 2017	Dec. 2018	% Chg.	Dec. 2017	Dec. 2018	% Chg.
Louisville, KY	394,322	395,478	0.2	380,983	381,300	0.0
Madison, WI	157,135	156,294	-0.5	154,210	153,374	-0.5
Manchester, NH	61,554	63,695	3.4	60,096	62,362	3.7
McAllen, TX	65,733	67,123	2.1	62,813	64,102	2.0
Miami, FL	231,034	231,547	0.2	220,564	223,501	1.3
Midland, TX	76,140	81,038	6.4	74,430	79,340	6.6
Minneapolis, MN	237,197	240,306	1.3	230,805	234,326	1.5
Nashville, TN	389,865	398,504	2.2	381,000	389,436	2.2
New Orleans, LA	179,260	180,224	0.5	172,059	172,588	0.3
New York, NY	4,097,111	4,120,012	0.5	3,930,027	3,956,181	0.6
Oklahoma City, OK	315,790	315,289	-0.1	304,263	306,285	0.6
Omaha, NE	229,225	236,434	3.1	222,137	229,428	3.2
Orlando, FL	166,522	172,311	3.4	161,476	167,611	3.8
Peoria, IL	51,182	51,811	1.2	48,530	48,559	0.0
Philadelphia, PA	699,144	716,864	2.5	659,824	681,673	3.3
Phoenix, AZ	821,300	857,747	4.4	788,157	819,226	3.9
Pittsburgh, PA	155,985	157,113	0.7	149,377	151,228	1.2
Portland, OR	378,785	379,135	0.0	366,371	365,951	-0.1
Providence, RI	86,558	87,407	0.9	82,383	83,483	1.3
Provo, UT	68,212	68,301	0.1	66,711	66,683	0.0
Raleigh, NC	253,520	259,281	2.2	243,568	250,554	2.8
Reno, NV	131,602	138,852	5.5	126,818	134,139	5.7
Richmond, VA	115,459	117,002	1.3	110,771	113,308	2.2
Roanoke, VA	48,370	49,186	1.6	46,536	47,881	2.8
Rochester, MN	63,515	63,316	-0.3	61,863	61,747	-0.1
Salem, OR	81,089	80,206	-1.0	77,833	76,682	-1.4
Salt Lake City, UT	114,107	113,951	-0.1	111,105	110,875	-0.2
San Antonio, TX	719,253	729,331	1.4	697,791	706,404	1.2
San Diego, CA	713,826	730,204	2.2	690,518	707,716	2.4
San Francisco, CA	571,462	585,540	2.4	557,616	572,810	2.7
San Jose, CA	555,312	574,518	3.4	539,945	560,113	3.7
Santa Rosa, CA	89,803	91,470	1.8	87,147	89,089	2.2
Savannah, GA	67,349	66,715	-0.9	64,307	64,028	-0.4
Seattle, WA	448,837	456,935	1.8	434,295	443,165	2.0
Sioux Falls, SD	102,100	103,935	1.8	99,008	101,225	2.2
Springfield, IL	57,636	57,912	0.4	55,303	54,991	-0.5
Tallahassee, FL	100,181	102,424	2.2	96,633	98,960	2.4
Tampa, FL	197,563	200,096	1.2	190,512	193,524	1.5
Topeka, KS	62,249	62,486	0.3	60,176	60,220	0.0
Tyler, TX	51,203	52,965	3.4	49,397	51,146	3.5
Virginia Beach, VA	228,851	232,737	1.7	221,361	226,637	2.3
Visalia, CA	60,030	61,666	2.7	57,134	58,689	2.7
Washington, DC	401,070	401,943	0.2	379,474	382,184	0.7
Wilmington, NC	61,254	61,633	0.6	58,646	59,149	0.8
Winston-Salem, NC	116,513	118,049	1.3	111,333	113,512	1.9
U.S.	159,880,000	162,510,000	1.6	153,602,000	156,481,000	1.9

Note: Data is not seasonally adjusted and covers workers 16 years of age and older
Source: Bureau of Labor Statistics, Local Area Unemployment Statistics

Labor Force, Employment and Job Growth: Metro Area

Metro Area[1]	Civilian Labor Force			Workers Employed		
	Dec. 2017	Dec. 2018	% Chg.	Dec. 2017	Dec. 2018	% Chg.
Albany, NY	445,967	457,216	2.5	427,121	442,048	3.4
Albuquerque, NM	430,911	444,200	3.0	408,815	424,436	3.8
Allentown, PA	429,942	437,716	1.8	411,484	420,069	2.0
Anchorage, AK	203,924	199,540	-2.1	190,759	188,393	-1.2
Ann Arbor, MI	194,270	195,123	0.4	188,260	189,818	0.8
Athens, GA	100,971	103,672	2.6	96,987	100,137	3.2
Atlanta, GA	3,056,722	3,097,603	1.3	2,931,140	2,986,890	1.9
Austin, TX	1,164,240	1,207,936	3.7	1,133,101	1,174,961	3.6
Baton Rouge, LA	418,468	416,996	-0.3	403,814	400,928	-0.7
Billings, MT	86,898	87,078	0.2	83,788	84,119	0.4
Boise City, ID	351,551	360,557	2.5	342,090	351,071	2.6
Boston, MA[4]	1,597,698	1,686,499	5.5	1,556,045	1,648,872	5.9
Boulder, CO	189,048	194,860	3.0	184,248	188,507	2.3
Cape Coral, FL	334,489	343,149	2.5	323,111	332,304	2.8
Cedar Rapids, IA	141,463	142,627	0.8	136,902	138,776	1.3
Charleston, SC	373,329	379,429	1.6	360,371	368,841	2.3
Charlotte, NC	1,325,794	1,343,634	1.3	1,271,766	1,297,622	2.0
Chicago, IL[2]	3,739,557	3,718,529	-0.5	3,578,093	3,586,035	0.2
Clarksville, TN	110,843	114,018	2.8	106,720	109,983	3.0
College Station, TX	131,772	134,501	2.0	128,210	130,738	1.9
Colorado Springs, CO	341,600	362,668	6.1	329,935	346,215	4.9
Columbia, MO	97,854	98,566	0.7	95,671	96,465	0.8
Columbia, SC	398,003	400,750	0.6	381,547	388,371	1.7
Columbus, OH	1,080,007	1,083,998	0.3	1,039,735	1,040,444	0.0
Dallas, TX[2]	2,585,893	2,682,088	3.7	2,504,449	2,594,961	3.6
Denver, CO	1,607,274	1,648,629	2.5	1,561,361	1,587,640	1.6
Des Moines, IA	344,073	355,975	3.4	335,149	347,559	3.7
Durham, NC	293,411	298,927	1.8	282,262	289,010	2.3
Edison, NJ[2]	7,115,615	7,151,776	0.5	6,832,994	6,887,158	0.7
El Paso, TX	355,795	363,598	2.1	341,342	349,017	2.2
Eugene, OR	184,824	182,636	-1.1	177,308	174,706	-1.4
Evansville, IN	160,568	162,866	1.4	156,131	157,860	1.1
Fargo, ND	137,092	135,806	-0.9	133,678	132,655	-0.7
Fayetteville, NC	147,423	148,870	0.9	139,257	141,505	1.6
Fort Collins, CO	196,349	205,101	4.4	191,451	198,457	3.6
Fort Wayne, IN	209,676	217,559	3.7	203,947	211,085	3.5
Fort Worth, TX[2]	1,241,227	1,280,488	3.1	1,201,876	1,238,690	3.0
Gainesville, FL	142,110	144,576	1.7	137,447	140,175	1.9
Grand Rapids, MI	573,055	577,903	0.8	552,982	561,455	1.5
Greeley, CO	160,310	165,552	3.2	156,034	159,811	2.4
Green Bay, WI	173,987	174,287	0.1	169,585	170,033	0.2
Greensboro, NC	366,857	369,553	0.7	350,147	355,120	1.4
Honolulu, HI	471,688	468,609	-0.6	463,613	458,462	-1.1
Houston, TX	3,343,410	3,453,216	3.2	3,199,215	3,317,794	3.7
Huntsville, AL	216,297	226,125	4.5	209,920	219,378	4.5
Indianapolis, IN	1,029,258	1,062,644	3.2	999,968	1,029,984	3.0
Jacksonville, FL	764,461	775,809	1.4	738,808	751,739	1.7
Kansas City, MO	1,123,293	1,137,463	1.2	1,086,716	1,102,718	1.4
Lafayette, LA	210,893	209,429	-0.6	201,965	200,424	-0.7
Las Cruces, NM	94,214	95,377	1.2	88,285	89,932	1.8
Las Vegas, NV	1,082,372	1,121,105	3.5	1,028,603	1,070,694	4.0
Lexington, KY	270,791	273,538	1.0	262,893	265,503	0.9
Lincoln, NE	177,836	181,619	2.1	173,446	177,455	2.3
Little Rock, AR	353,050	355,941	0.8	341,315	344,269	0.8
Los Angeles, CA[2]	5,101,061	5,165,908	1.2	4,880,342	4,930,006	1.0

Table continued on next page.

Metro Area[1]	Civilian Labor Force			Workers Employed		
	Dec. 2017	Dec. 2018	% Chg.	Dec. 2017	Dec. 2018	% Chg.
Louisville, KY	659,783	663,187	0.5	638,249	640,174	0.3
Madison, WI	390,310	388,149	-0.5	382,618	380,621	-0.5
Manchester, NH[3]	115,281	119,355	3.5	112,778	117,030	3.7
McAllen, TX	343,867	351,108	2.1	321,005	327,595	2.0
Miami, FL[2]	1,387,642	1,403,293	1.1	1,327,905	1,353,811	1.9
Midland, TX	94,704	100,757	6.3	92,563	98,626	6.5
Minneapolis, MN	1,983,313	2,008,040	1.2	1,924,623	1,952,456	1.4
Nashville, TN	1,015,902	1,037,452	2.1	991,652	1,013,224	2.1
New Orleans, LA	596,570	599,617	0.5	574,236	576,006	0.3
New York, NY[2]	7,115,615	7,151,776	0.5	6,832,994	6,887,158	0.7
Oklahoma City, OK	674,115	672,568	-0.2	650,461	653,952	0.5
Omaha, NE	478,265	492,493	2.9	464,636	479,337	3.1
Orlando, FL	1,312,511	1,358,231	3.4	1,269,679	1,317,910	3.8
Peoria, IL	174,815	176,606	1.0	166,398	166,484	0.0
Philadelphia, PA[2]	992,557	1,014,933	2.2	941,721	969,053	2.9
Phoenix, AZ	2,333,423	2,437,324	4.4	2,239,985	2,328,539	3.9
Pittsburgh, PA	1,200,452	1,209,534	0.7	1,146,911	1,161,821	1.3
Portland, OR	1,324,396	1,329,963	0.4	1,276,346	1,279,680	0.2
Providence, RI[3]	685,055	696,587	1.6	657,109	670,946	2.1
Provo, UT	304,146	304,414	0.0	296,661	296,534	0.0
Raleigh, NC	696,216	712,202	2.3	669,860	688,965	2.8
Reno, NV	245,311	258,836	5.5	236,289	249,934	5.7
Richmond, VA	669,505	679,381	1.4	645,440	660,541	2.3
Roanoke, VA	155,015	158,189	2.0	149,756	154,286	3.0
Rochester, MN	121,410	120,953	-0.3	117,927	117,605	-0.2
Salem, OR	202,072	199,854	-1.1	194,142	191,272	-1.4
Salt Lake City, UT	661,109	660,018	-0.1	643,138	641,797	-0.2
San Antonio, TX	1,171,978	1,188,172	1.3	1,136,835	1,150,484	1.2
San Diego, CA	1,583,042	1,620,080	2.3	1,530,168	1,568,277	2.4
San Francisco, CA[2]	1,026,081	1,051,734	2.5	1,002,221	1,029,473	2.7
San Jose, CA	1,078,824	1,115,934	3.4	1,049,364	1,088,429	3.7
Santa Rosa, CA	262,817	268,011	1.9	255,330	261,020	2.2
Savannah, GA	184,906	183,341	-0.8	177,538	176,766	-0.4
Seattle, WA[2]	1,659,565	1,693,796	2.0	1,600,578	1,636,187	2.2
Sioux Falls, SD	149,739	152,386	1.7	145,340	148,590	2.2
Springfield, IL	108,369	108,970	0.5	104,156	103,567	-0.5
Tallahassee, FL	190,403	194,727	2.2	183,898	188,401	2.4
Tampa, FL	1,510,641	1,531,562	1.3	1,458,656	1,482,283	1.6
Topeka, KS	118,135	118,696	0.4	114,515	114,734	0.1
Tyler, TX	106,787	110,590	3.5	103,079	106,728	3.5
Virginia Beach, VA	834,501	847,145	1.5	802,950	821,768	2.3
Visalia, CA	202,360	206,453	2.0	181,688	186,633	2.7
Washington, DC[2]	2,688,714	2,709,342	0.7	2,597,010	2,630,947	1.3
Wilmington, NC	144,433	144,997	0.3	138,263	139,416	0.8
Winston-Salem, NC	323,295	327,665	1.3	309,920	315,939	1.9
U.S.	159,880,000	162,510,000	1.6	153,602,000	156,481,000	1.9

Note: Data is not seasonally adjusted and covers workers 16 years of age and older; (1) Figures cover the Metropolitan Statistical Area (MSA) except where noted. See Appendix B for areas included; (2) Metropolitan Division; (3) New England City and Town Area; (4) New England City and Town Area Division
Source: Bureau of Labor Statistics, Local Area Unemployment Statistics

Unemployment Rate: City

City	2018											
	Jan.	Feb.	Mar.	Apr.	May	Jun.	Jul.	Aug.	Sep.	Oct.	Nov.	Dec.
Albany, NY	5.4	5.2	4.8	4.6	4.2	5.0	4.9	4.8	4.1	3.8	3.5	3.6
Albuquerque, NM	5.0	4.8	4.4	3.9	3.6	4.6	4.5	4.4	4.3	4.1	4.1	4.3
Allentown, PA	7.4	7.7	7.4	6.7	6.2	6.8	7.2	7.2	6.5	6.4	5.9	5.8
Anchorage, AK	6.4	6.7	6.4	6.2	5.8	5.7	5.0	4.7	4.9	4.9	5.1	5.1
Ann Arbor, MI	3.0	3.0	2.5	2.3	2.5	2.9	3.3	2.5	2.3	2.4	2.2	2.2
Athens, GA	4.3	4.5	4.0	3.6	3.4	4.5	4.1	3.7	3.2	3.6	3.2	3.6
Atlanta, GA	5.0	4.9	4.5	4.0	3.9	4.5	4.3	4.1	3.5	3.8	3.6	4.1
Austin, TX	2.8	2.8	2.9	2.6	2.6	2.9	2.8	2.8	2.7	2.5	2.5	2.5
Baton Rouge, LA	4.2	3.8	4.1	4.1	4.6	6.0	5.9	5.6	4.9	4.6	4.3	4.2
Billings, MT	4.2	4.2	3.9	3.0	2.5	3.4	3.3	3.0	3.0	3.0	3.2	3.3
Boise City, ID	3.1	2.7	2.6	2.3	2.2	2.3	2.4	2.0	2.0	2.0	2.2	2.3
Boston, MA	3.3	3.2	3.1	2.8	3.1	3.9	3.8	3.4	3.0	2.7	2.4	2.3
Boulder, CO	2.5	2.6	2.4	2.1	1.9	2.6	2.6	3.2	2.7	2.7	2.8	3.2
Cape Coral, FL	3.9	3.5	3.5	3.1	3.1	3.7	3.8	3.6	2.9	3.0	3.0	3.2
Cedar Rapids, IA	3.9	3.8	3.3	2.9	2.7	3.1	3.0	2.9	2.6	2.4	2.5	2.9
Charleston, SC	3.9	3.5	3.1	2.1	2.2	2.9	2.8	2.9	2.6	2.6	2.4	2.5
Charlotte, NC	4.5	4.4	4.1	3.6	3.6	4.0	3.9	3.8	2.9	3.3	3.3	3.5
Chicago, IL	5.9	5.6	4.5	3.9	3.6	4.7	4.5	4.3	4.0	4.4	4.0	3.9
Clarksville, TN	4.3	4.0	3.9	3.3	3.5	4.9	5.0	4.6	4.4	4.3	3.8	3.4
College Station, TX	2.9	2.9	2.8	2.5	2.6	3.5	3.3	3.3	2.9	2.7	2.6	2.8
Colorado Springs, CO	3.8	3.8	3.4	3.0	2.7	3.4	3.6	3.9	3.6	3.5	3.9	4.5
Columbia, MO	2.8	2.5	2.5	2.3	2.4	2.5	2.9	2.6	1.9	1.5	1.8	2.1
Columbia, SC	5.4	4.7	4.5	3.1	3.2	4.3	4.2	4.3	3.7	3.6	3.4	3.6
Columbus, OH	3.8	3.7	3.4	3.4	3.5	4.5	4.1	3.9	3.7	3.8	3.6	4.0
Dallas, TX	3.8	3.9	3.8	3.5	3.5	3.9	3.8	3.7	3.6	3.4	3.3	3.4
Denver, CO	3.3	3.2	2.8	2.5	2.4	2.9	3.0	3.3	3.0	3.0	3.3	3.7
Des Moines, IA	4.4	4.3	3.7	2.9	2.6	2.8	2.7	2.6	2.4	2.3	2.4	3.0
Durham, NC	4.1	3.9	3.8	3.4	3.4	3.9	3.7	3.5	2.8	3.1	3.1	3.3
Edison, NJ	3.1	3.2	3.1	2.9	2.8	3.4	3.5	3.2	3.0	2.6	2.1	2.4
El Paso, TX	4.4	4.4	4.4	4.0	4.0	4.5	4.3	4.2	4.1	3.8	3.8	3.9
Eugene, OR	3.9	4.2	4.2	3.8	3.5	4.1	4.3	4.3	3.9	4.1	3.9	4.0
Evansville, IN	3.3	3.6	3.1	2.9	3.2	3.6	3.5	3.8	3.2	3.6	3.5	3.3
Fargo, ND	2.9	2.8	2.8	2.5	2.0	2.5	2.1	2.2	2.1	1.8	2.0	2.2
Fayetteville, NC	6.4	6.3	6.0	5.2	5.1	5.9	6.0	5.8	4.5	4.9	5.0	5.3
Fort Collins, CO	2.7	2.7	2.4	2.1	1.9	2.4	2.4	2.9	2.5	2.6	2.8	3.1
Fort Wayne, IN	3.4	3.6	3.1	2.8	3.2	3.5	3.4	3.6	2.8	3.4	3.4	3.2
Fort Worth, TX	3.8	3.8	3.9	3.5	3.5	4.0	3.9	3.8	3.5	3.3	3.3	3.4
Gainesville, FL	4.3	3.8	3.8	3.4	3.3	4.2	4.1	3.7	2.9	3.0	3.0	3.4
Grand Rapids, MI	5.2	5.1	4.5	4.0	3.8	4.4	4.8	3.6	3.5	3.5	3.3	3.7
Greeley, CO	3.4	3.4	3.0	2.6	2.3	2.9	3.0	3.4	3.0	3.0	3.2	3.7
Green Bay, WI	3.1	3.3	3.2	2.7	2.6	3.6	3.3	3.3	2.5	2.5	2.5	2.5
Greensboro, NC	5.1	5.0	4.7	4.1	4.1	4.7	4.6	4.3	3.3	3.6	3.7	4.0
Honolulu, HI	2.0	1.9	1.9	1.9	1.9	2.6	2.0	2.1	2.4	2.3	2.5	2.2
Houston, TX	4.6	4.6	4.5	4.2	4.1	4.5	4.3	4.2	4.1	3.7	3.7	3.8
Huntsville, AL	3.8	3.9	3.6	3.2	3.5	4.6	4.2	3.8	3.6	3.6	3.1	3.1
Indianapolis, IN	3.4	3.6	3.3	3.0	3.3	3.8	3.6	3.8	3.2	3.6	3.6	3.3
Jacksonville, FL	4.1	3.7	3.7	3.4	3.4	4.0	4.2	3.8	3.0	3.0	3.0	3.2
Kansas City, MO	4.3	3.9	3.9	3.6	3.9	3.8	4.3	3.9	3.0	2.7	2.8	3.2
Lafayette, LA	4.3	3.9	4.3	4.3	4.6	5.8	5.6	5.3	4.8	4.4	4.3	4.0
Las Cruces, NM	5.7	5.3	4.8	4.2	3.9	5.5	5.4	5.3	4.9	4.8	4.7	4.8
Las Vegas, NV	5.5	5.3	5.4	5.2	4.6	4.9	4.9	5.1	4.8	4.6	4.5	4.6
Lexington, KY	3.0	3.6	3.4	3.0	3.2	4.0	3.8	3.2	3.2	3.3	2.7	2.8
Lincoln, NE	2.7	2.6	2.6	2.6	2.6	2.9	2.8	2.6	2.4	2.5	2.2	2.3
Little Rock, AR	3.8	3.8	3.7	3.4	3.3	3.6	3.4	3.2	3.2	3.1	3.1	3.4
Los Angeles, CA	4.8	4.5	4.2	4.1	4.1	4.9	5.1	5.1	4.8	4.7	4.6	4.6

Table continued on next page.

City	Jan.	Feb.	Mar.	Apr.	May	Jun.	Jul.	Aug.	Sep.	Oct.	Nov.	Dec.
Louisville, KY	3.7	4.1	4.0	3.6	4.3	4.7	4.8	3.9	4.5	4.1	3.4	3.6
Madison, WI	2.1	2.1	2.1	1.8	2.1	2.8	2.4	2.3	2.0	2.1	2.0	1.9
Manchester, NH	3.1	3.0	3.0	2.8	2.7	2.8	2.7	2.7	2.5	2.2	2.3	2.1
McAllen, TX	5.0	4.9	5.0	4.8	4.5	5.1	4.9	4.9	4.5	4.1	4.1	4.5
Miami, FL	4.6	4.6	4.9	4.1	3.9	4.1	4.3	4.1	3.7	3.5	3.2	3.5
Midland, TX	2.4	2.5	2.4	2.1	2.2	2.4	2.3	2.2	2.2	2.1	2.1	2.1
Minneapolis, MN	3.0	2.9	2.9	2.5	2.3	2.9	2.7	2.5	2.2	2.1	1.9	2.5
Nashville, TN	2.7	2.6	2.6	2.1	2.2	3.1	3.0	3.0	2.9	2.9	2.6	2.3
New Orleans, LA	4.4	4.0	4.3	4.3	4.7	6.2	6.1	5.9	5.2	4.8	4.5	4.2
New York, NY	4.6	4.6	4.3	3.9	3.6	4.2	4.4	4.3	3.8	4.0	3.7	4.0
Oklahoma City, OK	4.0	3.8	3.6	3.5	3.7	3.7	3.4	3.3	2.9	2.9	2.7	2.9
Omaha, NE	3.4	3.3	3.3	3.2	3.1	3.4	3.5	3.1	2.9	3.0	2.8	3.0
Orlando, FL	3.5	3.2	3.1	2.8	2.9	3.2	3.3	3.1	2.5	2.5	2.5	2.7
Peoria, IL	5.5	5.0	5.3	4.6	4.9	5.7	5.6	5.6	5.0	5.6	5.6	6.3
Philadelphia, PA	6.3	6.3	5.8	5.2	5.0	5.7	6.0	6.0	5.2	5.2	5.0	4.9
Phoenix, AZ	4.5	4.4	4.1	3.9	3.5	4.2	4.3	4.5	4.2	3.9	3.9	4.5
Pittsburgh, PA	5.0	4.9	4.3	3.9	3.8	4.5	4.5	4.3	3.8	3.9	3.7	3.7
Portland, OR	3.6	3.7	3.7	3.4	3.1	3.6	3.5	3.5	3.3	3.6	3.5	3.5
Providence, RI	6.2	6.2	5.9	5.0	4.9	4.9	5.4	4.9	4.5	4.0	4.7	4.5
Provo, UT	2.4	2.8	2.7	2.4	2.4	3.4	3.0	3.0	2.6	2.3	2.2	2.4
Raleigh, NC	4.2	4.1	3.9	3.4	3.3	3.9	3.7	3.6	2.7	3.0	3.1	3.4
Reno, NV	4.5	4.1	4.1	3.8	3.3	3.4	3.5	3.7	3.4	3.3	3.2	3.4
Richmond, VA	4.3	4.0	3.9	3.4	3.4	3.8	3.5	3.7	3.3	3.3	3.2	3.2
Roanoke, VA	4.1	3.8	3.7	3.2	3.2	3.7	3.3	3.4	2.8	2.8	2.7	2.7
Rochester, MN	3.0	3.0	2.8	2.4	2.0	2.4	2.1	2.0	1.9	1.8	1.8	2.5
Salem, OR	4.5	4.5	4.6	4.1	3.8	4.3	4.4	4.4	4.0	4.4	4.3	4.4
Salt Lake City, UT	2.8	3.0	3.0	2.8	2.5	3.1	2.8	3.3	2.9	2.6	2.7	2.7
San Antonio, TX	3.4	3.4	3.4	3.1	3.2	3.7	3.5	3.4	3.3	3.1	3.0	3.1
San Diego, CA	3.6	3.4	3.2	2.8	2.8	3.5	3.4	3.3	3.1	3.2	3.1	3.1
San Francisco, CA	2.7	2.5	2.4	2.1	2.1	2.7	2.5	2.4	2.2	2.3	2.2	2.2
San Jose, CA	3.0	2.9	2.7	2.4	2.3	3.0	2.8	2.7	2.5	2.6	2.5	2.5
Santa Rosa, CA	3.3	3.2	2.9	2.7	2.5	3.2	3.0	2.8	2.5	2.5	2.5	2.6
Savannah, GA	4.9	4.7	4.2	3.8	3.7	4.5	4.2	4.1	3.5	4.0	3.7	4.0
Seattle, WA	3.8	3.4	3.1	2.7	3.0	3.4	3.2	2.9	3.1	2.9	3.2	3.0
Sioux Falls, SD	3.5	3.5	3.2	3.0	2.5	2.5	2.1	2.4	2.2	2.2	2.4	2.6
Springfield, IL	4.4	4.0	4.1	3.4	3.5	4.7	4.5	4.7	4.0	4.4	4.4	5.0
Tallahassee, FL	4.1	3.6	3.6	3.4	3.3	4.2	4.2	3.8	3.0	3.1	3.1	3.4
Tampa, FL	4.0	3.6	3.7	3.3	3.4	4.0	4.0	3.7	3.0	3.0	3.0	3.3
Topeka, KS	3.8	4.1	3.7	3.5	3.6	4.0	4.3	3.9	3.3	3.4	3.4	3.6
Tyler, TX	3.7	3.7	3.6	3.4	3.5	4.0	3.7	3.6	3.4	3.4	3.3	3.4
Virginia Beach, VA	3.5	3.1	3.1	2.7	2.8	3.1	2.8	3.0	2.7	2.8	2.7	2.6
Visalia, CA	5.3	5.1	4.7	4.1	3.9	5.6	5.6	5.2	4.7	4.8	4.7	4.8
Washington, DC	5.9	5.9	5.7	5.2	5.3	6.0	6.0	5.8	5.5	5.3	5.1	4.9
Wilmington, NC	4.5	4.4	4.2	3.6	3.6	4.1	4.0	3.7	3.5	3.9	3.8	4.0
Winston-Salem, NC	4.8	4.8	4.4	3.9	3.9	4.7	4.5	4.3	3.2	3.5	3.5	3.8
U.S.	4.5	4.4	4.1	3.7	3.6	4.2	4.1	3.9	3.6	3.5	3.5	3.7

Note: Data is not seasonally adjusted and covers workers 16 years of age and older; All figures are percentages
Source: Bureau of Labor Statistics, Local Area Unemployment Statistics

Unemployment Rate: Metro Area

Metro Area[1]	2018											
	Jan.	Feb.	Mar.	Apr.	May	Jun.	Jul.	Aug.	Sep.	Oct.	Nov.	Dec.
Albany, NY	5.0	5.2	4.7	4.2	3.6	3.9	3.8	3.7	3.4	3.1	3.1	3.3
Albuquerque, NM	5.3	5.0	4.7	4.1	3.8	4.9	4.8	4.6	4.4	4.3	4.3	4.4
Allentown, PA	5.3	5.3	4.9	4.3	3.9	4.5	4.7	4.7	4.2	4.1	3.9	4.0
Anchorage, AK	7.1	7.5	7.1	6.9	6.4	6.2	5.4	5.1	5.3	5.3	5.5	5.6
Ann Arbor, MI	3.6	3.6	3.1	2.8	3.1	3.6	4.0	3.0	2.8	2.9	2.6	2.7
Athens, GA	4.0	4.1	3.8	3.4	3.2	4.1	3.7	3.5	3.0	3.4	3.0	3.4
Atlanta, GA	4.3	4.3	4.0	3.6	3.4	4.0	3.8	3.6	3.1	3.4	3.2	3.6
Austin, TX	3.0	3.0	3.1	2.8	2.8	3.2	3.1	3.0	2.9	2.7	2.7	2.7
Baton Rouge, LA	3.9	3.5	3.8	3.8	4.2	5.4	5.3	5.0	4.5	4.2	4.0	3.9
Billings, MT	4.4	4.4	4.1	3.1	2.5	3.4	3.3	3.0	3.0	3.0	3.1	3.4
Boise City, ID	3.6	3.1	2.9	2.6	2.4	2.6	2.8	2.3	2.1	2.2	2.5	2.6
Boston, MA[4]	3.2	3.3	3.1	2.7	2.9	3.5	3.5	3.1	2.8	2.5	2.2	2.2
Boulder, CO	2.9	2.9	2.5	2.3	2.1	2.7	2.7	3.1	2.8	2.8	2.9	3.3
Cape Coral, FL	3.8	3.5	3.4	3.2	3.2	3.8	3.8	3.7	2.9	2.9	2.9	3.2
Cedar Rapids, IA	4.0	3.8	3.3	2.8	2.4	2.7	2.7	2.6	2.4	2.1	2.2	2.7
Charleston, SC	4.2	3.9	3.5	2.3	2.4	3.1	3.0	3.1	2.8	2.8	2.6	2.8
Charlotte, NC	4.4	4.3	4.0	3.4	3.4	3.9	3.8	3.7	2.9	3.2	3.2	3.4
Chicago, IL[2]	4.9	4.6	3.9	3.6	3.3	4.4	4.1	3.9	3.5	3.6	3.3	3.6
Clarksville, TN	4.3	4.3	4.1	3.5	3.7	5.1	5.1	4.6	4.5	4.4	3.8	3.5
College Station, TX	3.1	3.0	3.0	2.7	2.8	3.5	3.3	3.3	2.9	2.7	2.7	2.8
Colorado Springs, CO	3.9	3.9	3.4	3.1	2.8	3.6	3.7	4.1	3.6	3.6	3.9	4.5
Columbia, MO	2.9	2.6	2.6	2.3	2.3	2.6	2.9	2.6	1.9	1.6	1.8	2.1
Columbia, SC	4.9	4.4	3.9	2.7	2.8	3.5	3.4	3.6	3.2	3.2	3.0	3.1
Columbus, OH	3.9	3.7	3.5	3.3	3.5	4.5	4.1	3.8	3.6	3.7	3.5	4.0
Dallas, TX[2]	3.6	3.7	3.7	3.4	3.4	3.8	3.6	3.6	3.4	3.2	3.2	3.2
Denver, CO	3.2	3.2	2.8	2.5	2.3	2.9	2.9	3.3	3.0	3.0	3.3	3.7
Des Moines, IA	3.4	3.3	2.9	2.3	2.1	2.4	2.3	2.2	2.1	1.9	1.9	2.4
Durham, NC	4.0	4.0	3.8	3.3	3.3	3.8	3.6	3.5	2.7	3.0	3.0	3.3
Edison, NJ[2]	4.6	4.5	4.3	4.0	3.5	4.2	4.4	4.2	3.9	3.7	3.4	3.7
El Paso, TX	4.6	4.5	4.5	4.2	4.1	4.7	4.4	4.4	4.2	3.9	3.9	4.0
Eugene, OR	4.4	4.6	4.6	4.1	3.8	4.3	4.4	4.4	4.1	4.4	4.3	4.3
Evansville, IN	3.2	3.4	3.0	2.8	3.1	3.5	3.3	3.5	2.9	3.4	3.3	3.1
Fargo, ND	3.2	3.2	3.1	2.7	2.1	2.6	2.2	2.2	2.1	1.8	1.9	2.3
Fayetteville, NC	5.9	5.8	5.4	4.7	4.7	5.4	5.5	5.3	4.1	4.6	4.6	4.9
Fort Collins, CO	2.9	2.9	2.5	2.2	2.0	2.6	2.5	3.0	2.7	2.7	2.9	3.2
Fort Wayne, IN	3.2	3.3	2.9	2.6	3.0	3.3	3.2	3.4	2.7	3.2	3.2	3.0
Fort Worth, TX[2]	3.6	3.6	3.7	3.3	3.4	3.8	3.7	3.6	3.4	3.2	3.2	3.3
Gainesville, FL	3.9	3.4	3.4	3.1	3.0	3.7	3.6	3.4	2.7	2.8	2.8	3.0
Grand Rapids, MI	4.0	4.0	3.5	3.0	2.9	3.3	3.6	2.7	2.6	2.6	2.5	2.8
Greeley, CO	3.1	3.1	2.7	2.4	2.2	2.7	2.8	3.2	2.8	2.8	3.0	3.5
Green Bay, WI	3.0	3.3	3.0	2.6	2.5	3.2	3.0	2.9	2.4	2.4	2.4	2.4
Greensboro, NC	4.9	4.7	4.5	3.9	3.9	4.5	4.4	4.2	3.2	3.5	3.6	3.9
Honolulu, HI	2.0	1.9	1.9	1.9	1.9	2.6	2.0	2.1	2.4	2.3	2.5	2.2
Houston, TX	4.8	4.7	4.6	4.2	4.2	4.6	4.4	4.3	4.1	3.8	3.8	3.9
Huntsville, AL	3.6	3.7	3.4	3.0	3.3	4.4	3.9	3.6	3.4	3.4	2.9	3.0
Indianapolis, IN	3.2	3.4	3.0	2.8	3.0	3.4	3.3	3.5	2.9	3.3	3.4	3.1
Jacksonville, FL	3.9	3.5	3.5	3.2	3.1	3.7	3.8	3.5	2.8	2.9	2.9	3.1
Kansas City, MO	4.0	3.8	3.6	3.3	3.6	3.5	3.9	3.5	2.8	2.7	2.7	3.1
Lafayette, LA	4.6	4.3	4.6	4.5	4.9	6.1	5.9	5.5	5.0	4.7	4.5	4.3
Las Cruces, NM	6.9	6.7	6.4	5.5	4.9	6.0	5.8	5.4	5.2	5.1	5.3	5.7
Las Vegas, NV	5.4	5.2	5.1	5.0	4.4	4.7	4.7	4.9	4.7	4.4	4.4	4.5
Lexington, KY	3.2	3.7	3.5	3.1	3.3	4.1	3.9	3.3	3.3	3.4	2.7	2.9
Lincoln, NE	2.7	2.6	2.6	2.6	2.6	2.9	2.8	2.6	2.4	2.5	2.2	2.3
Little Rock, AR	3.8	3.8	3.6	3.2	3.2	3.5	3.3	3.0	3.0	3.0	3.0	3.3
Los Angeles, CA[2]	4.9	4.7	4.5	4.3	4.2	4.8	5.2	5.0	4.7	4.6	4.5	4.6

Table continued on next page.

Metro Area[1]	2018											
	Jan.	Feb.	Mar.	Apr.	May	Jun.	Jul.	Aug.	Sep.	Oct.	Nov.	Dec.
Louisville, KY	3.6	4.0	3.7	3.4	4.0	4.3	4.5	3.8	4.2	3.9	3.4	3.5
Madison, WI	2.3	2.5	2.4	1.9	2.1	2.8	2.4	2.3	2.0	2.1	2.0	1.9
Manchester, NH[3]	2.9	2.9	2.8	2.6	2.5	2.5	2.6	2.5	2.3	2.0	2.1	1.9
McAllen, TX	7.6	7.1	6.9	6.6	6.2	7.2	7.0	6.6	6.2	5.4	5.8	6.7
Miami, FL[2]	4.1	4.0	4.3	3.9	3.7	4.0	3.9	4.0	3.8	3.6	3.3	3.5
Midland, TX	2.4	2.5	2.4	2.1	2.1	2.4	2.2	2.2	2.2	2.1	2.1	2.1
Minneapolis, MN	3.4	3.4	3.3	2.7	2.3	2.8	2.6	2.5	2.2	2.1	2.0	2.8
Nashville, TN	2.8	2.7	2.7	2.2	2.3	3.2	3.2	3.1	3.0	2.9	2.6	2.3
New Orleans, LA	4.1	3.7	4.0	4.0	4.4	5.7	5.6	5.3	4.8	4.4	4.2	3.9
New York, NY[2]	4.6	4.5	4.3	4.0	3.5	4.2	4.4	4.2	3.9	3.7	3.4	3.7
Oklahoma City, OK	3.8	3.7	3.6	3.5	3.6	3.7	3.3	3.2	2.8	2.8	2.6	2.8
Omaha, NE	3.2	3.1	3.0	2.9	2.8	3.1	3.1	2.8	2.6	2.6	2.5	2.7
Orlando, FL	3.7	3.4	3.4	3.1	3.0	3.5	3.6	3.4	2.7	2.7	2.7	3.0
Peoria, IL	5.4	5.0	5.0	4.1	4.2	5.0	4.9	4.9	4.4	4.8	4.8	5.7
Philadelphia, PA[2]	5.8	5.8	5.3	4.8	4.6	5.2	5.5	5.5	4.8	4.8	4.6	4.5
Phoenix, AZ	4.5	4.4	4.1	3.8	3.4	4.2	4.3	4.5	4.2	3.9	3.9	4.5
Pittsburgh, PA	5.4	5.3	4.7	4.0	3.6	4.4	4.4	4.4	3.8	3.8	3.7	3.9
Portland, OR	3.9	4.1	4.0	3.7	3.4	3.8	3.8	3.8	3.5	3.8	3.7	3.8
Providence, RI[3]	5.3	5.3	4.8	4.1	3.9	3.8	4.2	3.9	3.5	3.1	3.6	3.7
Provo, UT	2.7	3.0	3.0	2.7	2.5	3.4	3.1	3.2	2.8	2.5	2.5	2.6
Raleigh, NC	4.0	3.9	3.8	3.3	3.2	3.7	3.5	3.4	2.6	2.9	3.0	3.3
Reno, NV	4.5	4.2	4.2	3.9	3.3	3.5	3.6	3.7	3.4	3.3	3.2	3.4
Richmond, VA	3.8	3.5	3.5	3.0	3.0	3.4	3.1	3.2	2.9	2.9	2.8	2.8
Roanoke, VA	3.7	3.4	3.4	2.8	2.9	3.4	2.9	3.1	2.7	2.7	2.6	2.5
Rochester, MN	3.6	3.6	3.4	2.8	2.1	2.6	2.3	2.2	1.9	1.9	1.9	2.8
Salem, OR	4.4	4.5	4.5	4.0	3.6	4.2	4.3	4.2	3.9	4.2	4.2	4.3
Salt Lake City, UT	3.0	3.2	3.2	3.0	2.7	3.4	3.1	3.4	3.0	2.7	2.7	2.8
San Antonio, TX	3.4	3.4	3.5	3.1	3.2	3.7	3.5	3.5	3.3	3.1	3.1	3.2
San Diego, CA	3.6	3.5	3.2	2.9	2.9	3.7	3.5	3.4	3.2	3.3	3.2	3.2
San Francisco, CA[2]	2.6	2.5	2.3	2.1	2.0	2.6	2.4	2.4	2.2	2.2	2.1	2.1
San Jose, CA	3.0	2.9	2.7	2.4	2.3	3.0	2.8	2.7	2.5	2.5	2.4	2.5
Santa Rosa, CA	3.2	3.0	2.8	2.6	2.4	3.0	2.8	2.7	2.4	2.5	2.5	2.6
Savannah, GA	4.2	4.1	3.8	3.4	3.3	4.0	3.7	3.6	3.1	3.5	3.2	3.6
Seattle, WA[2]	4.0	3.8	3.5	3.0	3.2	3.7	3.6	3.5	3.5	3.4	3.7	3.4
Sioux Falls, SD	3.4	3.4	3.1	2.9	2.4	2.4	2.1	2.3	2.2	2.2	2.3	2.5
Springfield, IL	4.4	4.0	4.1	3.2	3.4	4.2	4.0	4.2	3.7	4.1	4.2	5.0
Tallahassee, FL	4.0	3.6	3.6	3.2	3.2	3.9	4.0	3.7	2.9	2.9	3.0	3.2
Tampa, FL	3.9	3.6	3.6	3.2	3.3	3.8	3.8	3.6	2.9	2.9	3.0	3.2
Topeka, KS	3.7	3.8	3.5	3.2	3.3	3.7	4.0	3.5	3.0	3.2	3.1	3.3
Tyler, TX	3.8	3.8	3.7	3.4	3.5	3.9	3.7	3.7	3.5	3.4	3.4	3.5
Virginia Beach, VA	4.0	3.7	3.6	3.1	3.1	3.5	3.2	3.4	3.0	3.1	3.0	3.0
Visalia, CA	11.1	11.4	11.1	9.2	8.5	9.6	9.4	8.7	7.9	8.3	8.6	9.6
Washington, DC[2]	3.8	3.6	3.6	3.1	3.2	3.7	3.5	3.5	3.3	3.2	3.1	2.9
Wilmington, NC	4.6	4.4	4.1	3.5	3.4	3.9	3.8	3.7	3.4	3.8	3.6	3.8
Winston-Salem, NC	4.4	4.3	4.1	3.5	3.5	4.1	4.0	3.8	2.9	3.2	3.3	3.6
U.S.	4.5	4.4	4.1	3.7	3.6	4.2	4.1	3.9	3.6	3.5	3.5	3.7

Note: Data is not seasonally adjusted and covers workers 16 years of age and older; All figures are percentages; (1) Figures cover the Metropolitan Statistical Area (MSA) except where noted. See Appendix B for areas included; (2) Metropolitan Division; (3) New England City and Town Area; (4) New England City and Town Area Division
Source: Bureau of Labor Statistics, Local Area Unemployment Statistics

Average Hourly Wages: Occupations A – C

Metro Area[1]	Accountants/ Auditors	Automotive Mechanics	Book-keepers	Carpenters	Cashiers	Clerks, Gen. Office	Clerks, Recep./Info.
Albany, NY	36.48	20.49	20.76	25.71	11.78	17.04	15.79
Albuquerque, NM	32.84	20.24	18.58	18.88	10.67	12.57	13.79
Allentown, PA	37.60	20.04	18.94	25.45	10.35	17.25	14.36
Anchorage, AK	38.94	25.12	23.62	31.37	13.26	22.63	16.89
Ann Arbor, MI	35.96	25.64	19.83	31.07	11.11	16.50	15.02
Athens, GA	33.53	21.68	16.62	20.43	9.90	14.21	12.90
Atlanta, GA	37.70	21.20	20.44	23.94	10.21	15.42	14.01
Austin, TX	35.48	27.40	20.61	19.07	11.30	19.15	14.05
Baton Rouge, LA	31.48	19.91	18.59	22.77	9.52	12.58	12.11
Billings, MT	35.29	19.32	18.72	19.65	11.12	16.65	13.43
Boise City, ID	32.80	20.24	19.15	17.10	11.25	15.92	14.34
Boston, MA[2]	39.82	22.33	23.20	30.24	12.53	19.98	15.93
Boulder, CO	40.03	21.29	21.87	24.26	12.21	20.00	15.46
Cape Coral, FL	29.15	19.01	18.63	18.98	11.01	15.52	14.32
Cedar Rapids, IA	34.20	21.17	19.26	21.99	10.55	17.25	13.55
Charleston, SC	28.04	20.67	17.47	25.68	10.08	12.48	14.03
Charlotte, NC	39.52	21.49	19.60	18.00	9.93	16.12	13.81
Chicago, IL	40.28	23.11	21.37	33.87	11.41	18.37	14.90
Clarksville, TN	27.68	20.23	17.55	18.96	9.77	15.76	11.72
College Station, TX	27.77	23.34	16.34	15.08	10.55	17.17	13.04
Colorado Springs, CO	38.42	23.63	18.02	21.67	12.66	18.82	14.61
Columbia, MO	28.86	21.43	16.81	25.01	10.15	15.84	12.71
Columbia, SC	28.93	20.13	18.41	21.54	9.75	13.24	13.04
Columbus, OH	36.13	20.15	20.12	23.20	10.83	18.01	13.57
Dallas, TX	39.58	20.65	21.18	19.00	10.73	17.45	13.77
Denver, CO	41.25	23.78	21.42	23.30	12.44	20.51	16.12
Des Moines, IA	34.27	21.39	20.79	20.69	10.90	17.99	15.28
Durham, NC	38.99	21.83	21.07	17.79	10.45	17.27	14.16
Edison, NJ	48.03	23.26	23.10	32.57	12.16	17.29	16.84
El Paso, TX	29.97	16.17	16.59	15.15	9.82	14.71	10.85
Eugene, OR	31.37	21.08	18.49	22.28	12.33	16.82	14.70
Evansville, IN	29.84	19.72	17.02	23.67	9.93	15.35	12.79
Fargo, ND	30.82	20.93	18.67	20.10	11.47	18.47	13.65
Fayetteville, NC	32.58	16.91	18.54	17.71	9.56	14.59	12.55
Fort Collins, CO	33.71	24.37	20.22	23.12	12.56	18.81	15.33
Fort Wayne, IN	31.66	16.99	18.54	20.65	10.15	16.58	13.55
Fort Worth, TX	39.58	20.65	21.18	19.00	10.73	17.45	13.77
Gainesville, FL	29.59	18.12	19.52	19.03	10.33	15.17	13.40
Grand Rapids, MI	32.80	18.89	18.23	19.45	11.25	17.77	14.37
Greeley, CO	36.36	21.92	19.24	20.82	11.99	17.96	14.60
Green Bay, WI	31.11	20.08	18.11	24.55	10.09	16.99	14.42
Greensboro, NC	37.83	19.24	19.17	17.90	9.77	15.24	13.69
Honolulu, HI	31.69	22.45	19.98	36.28	12.21	16.48	15.59
Houston, TX	41.44	21.05	20.55	20.56	10.52	18.79	13.24
Huntsville, AL	35.87	19.59	19.12	19.44	10.59	12.30	12.60
Indianapolis, IN	36.73	21.58	20.02	24.12	10.44	16.84	14.28
Jacksonville, FL	32.39	18.58	19.81	19.11	10.35	16.36	13.56
Kansas City, MO	32.83	22.15	19.52	26.60	10.97	15.61	14.06
Lafayette, LA	31.98	18.27	17.77	19.76	9.49	12.32	11.83
Las Cruces, NM	30.48	17.75	16.74	19.59	10.47	11.15	12.10
Las Vegas, NV	31.72	21.34	19.30	25.54	11.24	17.25	13.44
Lexington, KY	32.33	20.23	18.97	24.20	9.90	13.71	13.53
Lincoln, NE	30.12	21.46	17.74	19.31	10.92	13.75	13.29
Little Rock, AR	32.34	19.31	18.29	18.23	10.53	15.20	13.76
Los Angeles, CA	40.70	22.82	22.70	28.88	12.91	17.80	15.64

Table continued on next page.

Metro Area[1]	Accountants/ Auditors	Automotive Mechanics	Book-keepers	Carpenters	Cashiers	Clerks, Gen. Office	Clerks, Recep./Info.
Louisville, KY	34.06	19.07	18.89	24.70	10.14	14.71	13.90
Madison, WI	33.08	20.58	19.50	25.80	11.01	17.81	15.11
Manchester, NH[2]	37.35	23.05	19.92	22.24	10.78	19.86	15.01
McAllen, TX	30.03	19.48	16.18	16.93	10.58	13.36	11.68
Miami, FL	37.40	20.63	20.41	19.92	10.54	16.44	14.60
Midland, TX	41.10	24.00	22.48	20.36	11.77	19.74	13.94
Minneapolis, MN	35.96	21.49	22.38	26.40	12.11	18.72	15.51
Nashville, TN	33.17	20.00	20.68	20.67	10.88	18.07	14.06
New Orleans, LA	35.02	20.04	18.46	20.35	9.78	12.20	12.04
New York, NY	48.03	23.26	23.10	32.57	12.16	17.29	16.84
Oklahoma City, OK	36.28	21.44	19.06	20.45	10.35	13.95	13.80
Omaha, NE	33.73	21.79	19.15	19.85	11.35	16.40	14.14
Orlando, FL	34.48	17.42	18.37	20.22	10.63	15.21	13.88
Peoria, IL	37.30	21.43	18.33	27.24	10.74	16.56	12.59
Philadelphia, PA	39.64	21.55	21.80	29.73	10.70	17.99	14.77
Phoenix, AZ	33.84	21.70	20.11	21.52	12.04	18.25	14.77
Pittsburgh, PA	34.91	19.83	18.87	27.76	9.92	16.63	13.23
Portland, OR	35.11	24.09	21.24	25.05	12.95	18.47	15.76
Providence, RI[2]	39.35	19.54	20.94	24.58	12.13	17.84	15.96
Provo, UT	32.30	21.11	18.16	19.59	11.04	15.86	13.22
Raleigh, NC	34.75	21.56	20.20	19.33	10.12	16.18	14.39
Reno, NV	33.13	23.56	19.74	26.09	11.04	18.68	14.61
Richmond, VA	38.32	23.68	20.26	21.60	10.27	17.39	14.51
Roanoke, VA	36.76	19.60	17.46	18.16	9.85	15.34	12.63
Rochester, MN	29.80	19.40	19.24	25.24	11.85	17.17	12.24
Salem, OR	33.76	20.07	20.26	22.58	12.51	17.05	15.46
Salt Lake City, UT	35.52	21.47	19.77	21.11	11.29	16.01	13.91
San Antonio, TX	36.22	22.10	19.42	19.18	10.71	16.90	13.09
San Diego, CA	41.86	22.81	22.28	25.92	12.84	16.91	16.21
San Francisco, CA	44.54	27.11	26.45	33.07	14.37	20.88	18.18
San Jose, CA	43.78	26.11	25.31	30.53	14.22	22.55	17.72
Santa Rosa, CA	39.15	24.02	25.06	34.67	14.25	19.96	16.97
Savannah, GA	33.80	23.40	18.44	21.51	9.71	15.17	13.17
Seattle, WA	39.99	24.80	22.83	31.41	14.60	20.40	16.88
Sioux Falls, SD	32.35	20.49	16.74	17.75	11.10	12.36	13.55
Springfield, IL	36.52	18.79	19.43	24.41	10.62	18.19	12.12
Tallahassee, FL	26.19	20.96	17.45	20.01	10.14	13.98	12.51
Tampa, FL	33.85	19.39	19.75	19.70	10.53	16.00	13.53
Topeka, KS	28.64	17.37	17.26	19.82	10.44	14.73	13.68
Tyler, TX	35.23	19.54	17.90	17.02	10.15	16.25	12.59
Virginia Beach, VA	37.01	23.17	19.55	21.08	9.81	15.92	13.33
Visalia, CA	33.07	17.50	20.86	20.19	12.41	18.24	14.47
Washington, DC	44.80	25.53	24.21	23.78	12.09	19.14	16.13
Wilmington, NC	35.63	18.12	19.02	19.32	9.97	14.73	13.75
Winston-Salem, NC	35.04	19.99	18.03	19.07	9.57	15.08	13.46

Notes: (1) Figures cover the Metropolitan Statistical Area (MSA) except where noted. See Appendix B for areas included;
(2) New England City and Town Area; n/a not available
Source: Bureau of Labor Statistics, May 2018 Metro Area Occupational Employment and Wage Estimates

Average Hourly Wages: Occupations C – E

Metro Area	Clerks, Ship./Rec.	Computer Program-mers	Computer Systems Analysts	Comp. User Support Specialists	Cooks, Restaurant	Dentists	Electrical Engineers
Albany, NY	17.70	37.26	39.25	25.13	13.95	86.23	50.68
Albuquerque, NM	15.28	35.53	42.16	21.08	11.47	97.79	55.08
Allentown, PA	16.63	34.66	43.59	23.79	13.51	72.57	41.00
Anchorage, AK	21.02	40.35	36.98	27.95	13.77	119.82	57.93
Ann Arbor, MI	18.38	37.34	39.08	22.56	13.27	91.56	42.70
Athens, GA	16.88	37.19	33.86	21.47	11.93	64.66	n/a
Atlanta, GA	16.66	46.23	44.91	26.26	11.98	78.39	42.70
Austin, TX	15.58	41.04	43.89	24.54	12.97	70.37	54.42
Baton Rouge, LA	18.37	34.57	36.78	23.42	11.83	86.11	45.38
Billings, MT	16.62	34.64	37.33	24.50	12.41	105.39	46.40
Boise City, ID	16.37	35.04	38.15	24.11	11.78	84.42	43.22
Boston, MA[2]	19.10	45.28	45.99	31.23	15.72	87.00	55.06
Boulder, CO	18.18	45.13	47.70	29.92	14.89	102.68	47.54
Cape Coral, FL	15.71	33.51	35.04	21.68	13.74	77.15	44.43
Cedar Rapids, IA	18.63	39.52	40.88	22.46	11.35	n/a	44.24
Charleston, SC	19.45	36.63	38.57	24.47	11.95	56.32	44.07
Charlotte, NC	16.78	46.13	46.23	26.63	12.40	106.90	50.08
Chicago, IL	17.30	45.17	43.25	25.92	13.59	81.76	45.62
Clarksville, TN	17.43	36.65	29.95	23.31	10.78	102.27	43.55
College Station, TX	15.08	45.60	33.06	20.91	10.57	102.75	39.67
Colorado Springs, CO	16.08	43.73	49.25	26.28	13.39	65.60	54.60
Columbia, MO	15.51	32.56	28.44	20.85	11.89	112.82	38.59
Columbia, SC	14.66	39.73	35.42	22.40	11.19	88.16	44.13
Columbus, OH	15.61	39.73	46.81	26.32	13.52	101.48	38.64
Dallas, TX	16.01	47.02	45.82	24.86	12.32	91.47	50.39
Denver, CO	16.92	46.15	45.93	30.24	14.36	86.18	46.68
Des Moines, IA	18.35	39.23	41.21	24.98	13.34	113.42	40.57
Durham, NC	16.62	45.62	43.55	26.86	12.96	112.23	49.47
Edison, NJ	17.97	44.60	54.65	31.08	15.34	79.10	53.94
El Paso, TX	13.79	38.77	39.69	18.53	10.07	81.30	38.63
Eugene, OR	15.46	35.46	30.15	25.04	13.12	108.19	47.12
Evansville, IN	16.48	41.79	37.61	21.89	12.44	77.27	40.13
Fargo, ND	16.75	36.84	40.65	27.55	14.54	81.13	39.66
Fayetteville, NC	15.44	36.01	34.73	21.85	11.99	119.91	38.00
Fort Collins, CO	16.24	47.73	43.49	27.49	13.67	98.48	52.99
Fort Wayne, IN	15.06	36.35	34.47	21.25	11.54	120.25	42.32
Fort Worth, TX	16.01	47.02	45.82	24.86	12.32	91.47	50.39
Gainesville, FL	15.85	29.64	36.19	21.73	12.54	76.16	45.33
Grand Rapids, MI	15.92	33.98	37.43	23.17	12.37	97.48	36.73
Greeley, CO	16.75	39.70	49.88	21.93	13.22	95.88	49.32
Green Bay, WI	17.25	33.81	41.78	24.87	12.06	110.41	38.99
Greensboro, NC	15.69	38.93	45.37	25.02	11.31	81.32	49.16
Honolulu, HI	18.77	35.75	38.89	23.13	14.97	105.22	42.73
Houston, TX	16.51	43.75	53.05	28.97	12.65	93.08	52.12
Huntsville, AL	15.71	46.35	44.94	21.31	11.72	n/a	49.75
Indianapolis, IN	15.05	40.86	39.79	24.08	12.15	70.59	42.11
Jacksonville, FL	16.53	39.35	39.77	24.82	12.49	82.64	40.96
Kansas City, MO	16.44	36.59	38.50	23.67	12.82	87.20	44.15
Lafayette, LA	16.00	38.94	27.20	20.44	11.72	52.52	38.75
Las Cruces, NM	15.33	n/a	34.71	17.82	10.59	66.66	45.73
Las Vegas, NV	16.61	38.69	39.47	23.62	15.95	91.15	43.25
Lexington, KY	17.49	33.25	35.09	25.01	10.46	55.65	43.00
Lincoln, NE	17.02	33.09	36.24	22.15	13.59	70.31	45.44
Little Rock, AR	15.45	36.58	34.70	22.45	11.46	83.49	43.43
Los Angeles, CA	16.64	44.66	45.83	28.50	14.17	63.86	54.15

Table continued on next page.

Metro Area	Clerks, Ship./Rec.	Computer Programmers	Computer Systems Analysts	Comp. User Support Specialists	Cooks, Restaurant	Dentists	Electrical Engineers
Louisville, KY	16.28	36.38	36.92	22.80	12.41	76.09	43.37
Madison, WI	17.50	37.09	43.82	27.76	13.10	112.50	45.55
Manchester, NH[2]	17.45	38.95	45.58	25.97	13.67	104.93	50.62
McAllen, TX	11.94	36.68	n/a	19.66	11.28	100.51	53.27
Miami, FL	15.29	38.17	42.05	23.95	13.97	77.18	42.46
Midland, TX	16.69	n/a	44.29	26.28	13.14	n/a	n/a
Minneapolis, MN	18.27	42.71	45.57	27.33	14.56	111.47	48.23
Nashville, TN	15.43	41.76	38.08	24.29	12.49	90.41	42.84
New Orleans, LA	14.19	43.62	37.49	22.71	11.30	71.39	47.54
New York, NY	17.97	44.60	54.65	31.08	15.34	79.10	53.94
Oklahoma City, OK	15.71	39.65	35.85	22.98	12.12	73.73	46.46
Omaha, NE	16.28	38.49	37.83	24.89	13.25	71.98	42.22
Orlando, FL	15.69	44.30	40.65	23.52	13.33	95.92	46.75
Peoria, IL	16.17	35.97	42.90	23.59	12.43	80.38	n/a
Philadelphia, PA	17.50	44.18	49.15	27.26	14.26	79.69	50.59
Phoenix, AZ	16.62	47.54	43.26	25.25	14.11	91.86	49.73
Pittsburgh, PA	17.40	37.51	44.55	23.87	12.48	61.96	46.78
Portland, OR	18.13	41.22	43.88	26.75	14.54	81.95	44.46
Providence, RI[2]	18.98	45.82	47.63	26.94	14.67	117.26	52.31
Provo, UT	14.62	45.31	48.33	24.94	13.02	n/a	38.38
Raleigh, NC	15.31	50.62	45.37	25.74	13.71	116.99	45.17
Reno, NV	18.46	38.97	36.20	23.20	13.86	128.56	45.39
Richmond, VA	16.23	46.20	46.99	24.31	11.81	78.07	50.12
Roanoke, VA	16.06	40.73	38.05	23.34	11.56	69.18	39.48
Rochester, MN	18.04	46.26	40.74	26.05	13.35	109.74	43.43
Salem, OR	17.43	41.00	41.53	25.01	12.86	99.68	42.04
Salt Lake City, UT	15.03	39.11	37.83	23.81	13.39	71.52	47.41
San Antonio, TX	14.99	42.75	46.90	23.52	12.03	85.20	49.74
San Diego, CA	16.88	48.73	48.11	29.39	14.49	69.03	49.27
San Francisco, CA	19.70	50.90	56.89	35.39	16.93	87.25	55.14
San Jose, CA	18.93	51.05	57.88	39.88	15.97	77.31	63.82
Santa Rosa, CA	18.63	42.81	43.35	29.50	15.50	69.89	50.91
Savannah, GA	17.55	35.32	36.83	22.28	11.31	93.15	47.19
Seattle, WA	19.51	62.16	48.84	31.37	16.23	80.97	56.53
Sioux Falls, SD	15.76	27.97	35.60	19.29	12.44	99.82	37.34
Springfield, IL	15.38	40.45	43.44	22.26	12.26	70.01	44.84
Tallahassee, FL	15.97	30.18	30.42	22.07	12.45	72.04	44.40
Tampa, FL	15.63	37.45	43.56	24.47	12.62	89.66	45.64
Topeka, KS	19.42	33.84	33.80	22.16	11.19	113.83	42.67
Tyler, TX	16.76	34.48	34.75	22.66	11.87	73.99	47.74
Virginia Beach, VA	16.76	40.51	42.27	25.34	12.83	90.20	44.76
Visalia, CA	15.38	n/a	39.68	29.56	13.17	74.88	42.54
Washington, DC	18.86	47.11	50.67	30.97	14.34	98.36	59.52
Wilmington, NC	15.16	40.12	42.75	24.60	12.23	88.67	51.49
Winston-Salem, NC	15.31	38.87	43.61	22.76	11.14	91.18	47.06

Notes: (1) Figures cover the Metropolitan Statistical Area (MSA) except where noted. See Appendix B for areas included; (2) New England City and Town Area; n/a not available
Source: Bureau of Labor Statistics, May 2018 Metro Area Occupational Employment and Wage Estimates

Average Hourly Wages: Occupations E – I

Metro Area	Electricians	Financial Managers	First-Line Supervisors/ Mgrs., Sales	Food Preparation Workers	General/ Operations Managers	Hairdressers/ Cosmetolo- gists	Internists
Albany, NY	28.64	67.20	21.20	12.65	60.53	14.27	123.51
Albuquerque, NM	21.95	52.99	19.82	10.93	52.03	11.01	125.99
Allentown, PA	29.98	79.16	21.61	11.28	59.85	14.56	n/a
Anchorage, AK	35.48	55.50	22.10	13.33	59.23	15.17	110.42
Ann Arbor, MI	33.14	64.04	22.05	13.27	64.93	12.64	n/a
Athens, GA	22.95	60.99	20.56	10.37	49.13	12.08	n/a
Atlanta, GA	25.67	74.02	22.69	10.58	59.01	13.30	49.83
Austin, TX	26.12	69.25	21.67	12.56	59.84	14.58	73.02
Baton Rouge, LA	25.43	52.39	18.49	9.11	59.27	12.32	n/a
Billings, MT	30.20	57.14	23.42	11.25	51.74	13.07	n/a
Boise City, ID	23.31	51.10	21.28	11.79	40.94	15.58	n/a
Boston, MA[2]	32.80	73.79	23.99	14.59	69.21	20.43	118.10
Boulder, CO	26.70	83.83	25.24	13.74	69.06	21.84	110.42
Cape Coral, FL	23.77	51.94	22.75	11.78	49.58	12.76	n/a
Cedar Rapids, IA	25.47	59.32	20.00	11.84	53.06	12.14	n/a
Charleston, SC	20.19	54.99	20.70	12.34	51.20	11.48	119.53
Charlotte, NC	21.46	79.00	23.48	11.45	65.40	16.46	123.22
Chicago, IL	38.35	73.01	21.23	12.31	64.39	14.16	88.21
Clarksville, TN	25.05	47.49	19.89	9.72	39.33	12.51	n/a
College Station, TX	21.15	57.15	22.84	10.23	47.44	11.91	n/a
Colorado Springs, CO	24.81	67.39	20.62	12.69	57.98	17.95	n/a
Columbia, MO	24.99	64.35	21.96	11.69	38.50	13.93	n/a
Columbia, SC	22.28	64.80	19.72	10.87	50.19	15.23	n/a
Columbus, OH	23.52	66.63	21.86	11.30	60.15	14.11	109.79
Dallas, TX	22.71	76.78	23.13	11.10	63.80	11.70	59.73
Denver, CO	26.81	83.16	25.80	13.27	69.04	16.36	103.78
Des Moines, IA	26.31	62.45	20.44	11.97	53.85	16.42	n/a
Durham, NC	21.37	78.87	22.54	11.29	70.36	17.85	n/a
Edison, NJ	38.93	100.32	25.78	13.35	81.05	16.43	101.23
El Paso, TX	18.95	52.68	20.74	9.99	49.88	10.71	n/a
Eugene, OR	29.81	53.28	22.97	12.25	46.23	12.92	n/a
Evansville, IN	27.76	53.86	19.42	10.11	43.51	14.11	n/a
Fargo, ND	25.80	65.29	21.60	12.27	53.38	15.92	n/a
Fayetteville, NC	19.37	70.54	19.61	9.77	54.79	12.33	n/a
Fort Collins, CO	27.70	62.14	24.59	13.00	49.63	16.47	n/a
Fort Wayne, IN	27.24	59.26	19.73	10.77	49.36	12.98	n/a
Fort Worth, TX	22.71	76.78	23.13	11.10	63.80	11.70	59.73
Gainesville, FL	18.22	60.58	21.41	10.91	46.87	14.69	n/a
Grand Rapids, MI	24.99	57.87	22.14	12.19	61.55	14.29	66.95
Greeley, CO	24.78	65.28	24.92	11.68	57.33	12.98	n/a
Green Bay, WI	26.33	57.70	20.01	10.80	55.91	15.23	n/a
Greensboro, NC	21.96	68.40	23.74	10.35	61.05	12.56	n/a
Honolulu, HI	36.75	59.69	21.95	13.32	57.90	16.33	103.09
Houston, TX	27.16	75.52	21.82	11.54	67.19	12.75	81.33
Huntsville, AL	22.88	62.63	20.29	10.20	66.05	11.71	n/a
Indianapolis, IN	27.17	65.93	19.97	11.04	56.08	14.97	115.47
Jacksonville, FL	21.45	67.36	21.07	11.37	55.97	18.30	n/a
Kansas City, MO	29.15	67.04	20.56	10.82	52.86	13.11	n/a
Lafayette, LA	22.48	48.83	18.15	9.02	52.47	10.12	n/a
Las Cruces, NM	18.96	43.72	20.25	10.95	43.18	n/a	n/a
Las Vegas, NV	31.23	59.44	21.45	14.15	63.96	11.07	123.31
Lexington, KY	23.60	57.96	19.04	11.63	43.18	11.87	88.01
Lincoln, NE	25.16	55.92	19.76	11.67	46.53	11.71	n/a
Little Rock, AR	20.74	49.40	20.37	12.06	43.69	11.36	n/a
Los Angeles, CA	32.39	75.90	21.60	12.78	68.01	13.92	96.18

Table continued on next page.

Metro Area	Electricians	Financial Managers	First-Line Supervisors/ Mgrs., Sales	Food Preparation Workers	General/ Operations Managers	Hairdressers/ Cosmetologists	Internists
Louisville, KY	26.85	60.38	18.26	10.92	48.99	16.00	92.79
Madison, WI	28.58	64.00	22.90	11.97	61.88	15.51	n/a
Manchester, NH[2]	27.03	58.89	22.92	12.68	63.72	13.99	n/a
McAllen, TX	18.87	48.97	22.23	11.82	46.91	12.00	n/a
Miami, FL	22.30	68.03	23.57	11.89	57.38	15.44	91.81
Midland, TX	26.64	68.20	23.41	13.36	76.31	10.88	n/a
Minneapolis, MN	37.17	67.83	22.07	13.34	58.79	15.02	120.67
Nashville, TN	23.80	59.37	20.69	10.96	57.38	14.22	95.92
New Orleans, LA	25.23	51.94	19.49	9.13	58.22	9.86	113.59
New York, NY	38.93	100.32	25.78	13.35	81.05	16.43	101.23
Oklahoma City, OK	26.25	54.10	21.23	9.79	54.35	12.42	85.93
Omaha, NE	25.47	56.00	20.24	11.83	48.95	14.69	125.96
Orlando, FL	22.89	64.69	21.57	11.95	52.65	13.54	131.58
Peoria, IL	30.23	61.92	19.42	10.98	54.68	14.45	n/a
Philadelphia, PA	35.35	80.30	24.02	11.56	73.87	15.12	99.05
Phoenix, AZ	23.10	58.69	20.09	12.00	51.79	13.87	103.35
Pittsburgh, PA	33.76	76.19	22.39	11.34	63.17	13.01	n/a
Portland, OR	34.27	60.57	21.50	13.29	57.51	15.40	118.66
Providence, RI[2]	27.87	68.99	26.04	14.23	68.65	14.64	113.58
Provo, UT	26.63	54.88	18.18	11.78	40.53	10.89	n/a
Raleigh, NC	20.33	65.10	22.42	11.67	69.86	12.97	n/a
Reno, NV	25.48	64.49	20.52	12.93	56.55	11.26	n/a
Richmond, VA	23.16	77.13	21.94	10.81	66.17	17.80	129.42
Roanoke, VA	22.78	62.87	21.07	9.93	50.42	12.39	68.41
Rochester, MN	30.82	53.07	19.68	12.12	42.08	13.88	n/a
Salem, OR	29.95	48.04	22.22	12.08	47.60	12.28	n/a
Salt Lake City, UT	27.52	55.62	19.21	12.46	42.53	13.73	108.77
San Antonio, TX	23.01	69.07	21.28	12.08	58.04	12.20	49.47
San Diego, CA	29.84	68.58	22.99	13.26	64.34	16.94	113.60
San Francisco, CA	44.42	88.63	21.76	15.20	76.53	17.21	113.23
San Jose, CA	37.98	88.63	23.61	13.89	77.59	14.47	103.94
Santa Rosa, CA	32.99	68.05	23.46	14.39	59.56	13.11	n/a
Savannah, GA	22.38	47.47	19.94	10.23	49.54	11.79	n/a
Seattle, WA	35.00	71.85	26.42	15.02	65.20	20.68	99.70
Sioux Falls, SD	22.04	69.77	23.53	11.53	67.09	14.10	140.08
Springfield, IL	32.24	61.19	19.64	11.15	45.42	19.01	n/a
Tallahassee, FL	20.82	n/a	20.83	10.68	n/a	20.36	n/a
Tampa, FL	20.64	67.66	22.54	11.64	57.26	15.26	91.49
Topeka, KS	24.79	58.57	20.20	10.26	39.95	n/a	n/a
Tyler, TX	20.35	62.20	21.15	9.74	47.05	9.77	68.45
Virginia Beach, VA	23.02	64.00	20.62	10.36	59.71	14.57	110.86
Visalia, CA	30.19	57.80	22.80	13.44	50.19	13.87	n/a
Washington, DC	30.44	82.22	24.58	12.38	73.83	16.82	78.15
Wilmington, NC	20.70	70.25	20.99	11.28	52.90	11.92	n/a
Winston-Salem, NC	22.27	78.89	22.50	10.91	66.69	12.03	n/a

Notes: (1) Figures cover the Metropolitan Statistical Area (MSA) except where noted. See Appendix B for areas included; (2) New England City and Town Area; n/a not available
Source: Bureau of Labor Statistics, May 2018 Metro Area Occupational Employment and Wage Estimates

Average Hourly Wages: Occupations J – N

Metro Area	Janitors/ Cleaners	Landscapers	Lawyers	Maids/ House- keepers	Main- tenance Repairers	Marketing Managers	Nuclear Medicine Techs
Albany, NY	14.07	16.14	55.15	12.00	19.91	70.17	40.92
Albuquerque, NM	11.83	13.60	53.06	10.30	17.93	48.26	37.10
Allentown, PA	15.06	14.32	52.49	11.47	20.13	68.18	35.47
Anchorage, AK	15.25	18.37	58.09	13.89	23.82	49.62	n/a
Ann Arbor, MI	14.93	14.16	57.31	12.33	17.77	65.79	36.28
Athens, GA	11.90	15.22	43.13	10.23	16.89	72.38	n/a
Atlanta, GA	12.01	14.31	65.81	10.26	18.71	70.27	38.05
Austin, TX	12.78	14.42	60.63	10.64	18.21	67.09	37.47
Baton Rouge, LA	10.39	13.09	49.16	9.74	18.65	54.03	30.98
Billings, MT	14.90	15.92	50.02	14.94	19.40	n/a	n/a
Boise City, ID	12.23	13.88	50.99	10.23	17.20	55.30	n/a
Boston, MA[2]	17.32	18.17	82.08	15.78	23.89	70.16	40.06
Boulder, CO	14.39	17.65	77.91	12.54	22.26	92.26	n/a
Cape Coral, FL	12.61	13.07	57.69	11.52	17.57	55.63	34.75
Cedar Rapids, IA	14.59	15.63	56.70	11.20	22.32	54.05	n/a
Charleston, SC	10.71	13.35	38.01	10.61	18.82	54.78	36.43
Charlotte, NC	12.10	13.57	67.70	10.67	19.84	71.41	33.88
Chicago, IL	14.73	15.36	76.87	13.62	22.16	63.55	42.01
Clarksville, TN	12.06	13.45	35.54	10.56	20.44	n/a	n/a
College Station, TX	12.63	13.05	43.46	11.51	16.18	73.30	n/a
Colorado Springs, CO	13.48	14.71	50.84	11.46	18.30	77.50	37.74
Columbia, MO	13.68	14.01	46.10	10.95	16.42	42.21	n/a
Columbia, SC	12.14	12.83	57.30	9.78	17.24	52.58	32.40
Columbus, OH	13.71	14.23	58.19	11.00	19.87	71.79	35.36
Dallas, TX	12.73	13.75	77.34	11.01	20.38	67.05	39.16
Denver, CO	13.90	16.21	75.00	12.50	20.51	82.07	42.19
Des Moines, IA	13.52	14.57	59.71	11.84	19.63	60.84	n/a
Durham, NC	12.08	13.86	68.19	12.20	20.05	71.51	n/a
Edison, NJ	17.24	16.83	82.70	17.35	22.94	91.16	44.79
El Paso, TX	10.94	11.13	57.35	9.44	14.56	58.28	37.30
Eugene, OR	13.83	15.51	50.98	12.70	18.00	42.92	n/a
Evansville, IN	14.31	12.22	52.74	10.83	19.34	53.89	n/a
Fargo, ND	13.36	16.89	57.63	11.47	18.89	55.95	n/a
Fayetteville, NC	11.68	12.08	57.86	10.30	18.17	n/a	30.58
Fort Collins, CO	14.34	16.30	62.54	12.48	20.13	75.44	n/a
Fort Wayne, IN	11.44	13.03	62.48	10.01	19.74	59.50	n/a
Fort Worth, TX	12.73	13.75	77.34	11.01	20.38	67.05	39.16
Gainesville, FL	12.43	12.99	50.26	11.19	17.20	63.91	n/a
Grand Rapids, MI	12.56	14.82	46.53	12.08	18.87	61.37	33.30
Greeley, CO	13.44	16.51	44.59	11.31	20.76	63.42	n/a
Green Bay, WI	13.12	14.73	51.79	11.48	20.93	54.35	n/a
Greensboro, NC	11.52	14.35	49.74	9.31	19.18	70.41	n/a
Honolulu, HI	14.95	15.28	54.27	19.18	22.72	56.40	44.22
Houston, TX	11.41	14.04	84.32	10.15	18.95	79.92	39.42
Huntsville, AL	11.87	13.14	62.11	9.50	20.55	68.60	26.03
Indianapolis, IN	12.69	14.21	53.57	10.78	19.71	54.48	35.25
Jacksonville, FL	12.89	12.88	57.84	11.13	18.29	56.19	35.02
Kansas City, MO	13.62	17.27	59.02	10.70	19.37	68.71	37.90
Lafayette, LA	10.28	11.93	44.67	9.27	17.22	43.97	33.00
Las Cruces, NM	10.82	11.78	56.19	10.13	15.49	n/a	n/a
Las Vegas, NV	15.14	14.22	66.86	15.50	22.46	70.57	39.07
Lexington, KY	13.10	13.75	55.03	10.32	18.51	51.75	31.98
Lincoln, NE	12.82	14.12	47.98	11.54	18.96	46.45	n/a
Little Rock, AR	11.44	12.68	46.40	10.11	16.06	60.79	35.58
Los Angeles, CA	16.05	16.50	84.63	13.95	21.19	73.15	52.08

Table continued on next page.

Metro Area	Janitors/ Cleaners	Landscapers	Lawyers	Maids/ House- keepers	Main- tenance Repairers	Marketing Managers	Nuclear Medicine Techs
Louisville, KY	12.99	13.69	52.74	10.97	20.25	62.47	33.34
Madison, WI	14.70	16.03	59.13	11.75	20.59	60.38	43.86
Manchester, NH[2]	13.24	15.92	60.12	11.23	20.92	70.53	n/a
McAllen, TX	11.30	11.37	n/a	9.16	13.09	56.36	n/a
Miami, FL	11.93	13.50	69.92	11.38	17.43	59.06	34.17
Midland, TX	11.72	14.39	n/a	11.47	20.89	76.71	n/a
Minneapolis, MN	15.58	18.13	59.60	14.21	22.50	68.49	41.09
Nashville, TN	12.76	12.49	61.00	11.37	19.06	61.03	37.56
New Orleans, LA	10.89	12.08	58.96	10.64	18.30	44.21	32.07
New York, NY	17.24	16.83	82.70	17.35	22.94	91.16	44.79
Oklahoma City, OK	11.71	13.46	55.00	10.10	16.80	57.18	35.68
Omaha, NE	13.23	15.31	55.37	11.61	20.34	50.88	33.77
Orlando, FL	11.53	12.73	59.59	11.18	16.58	53.94	34.93
Peoria, IL	13.95	12.18	59.86	11.81	19.95	66.07	n/a
Philadelphia, PA	14.83	15.52	73.12	12.68	21.06	76.73	38.85
Phoenix, AZ	12.65	13.81	74.14	11.93	18.85	57.26	40.91
Pittsburgh, PA	13.58	13.95	63.62	11.36	19.01	71.57	30.03
Portland, OR	14.81	17.27	61.23	13.61	20.52	57.96	42.72
Providence, RI[2]	15.09	16.51	58.77	13.45	21.67	74.31	42.53
Provo, UT	10.57	14.48	59.45	11.45	18.38	55.47	n/a
Raleigh, NC	11.38	14.87	65.24	10.54	20.11	72.69	34.09
Reno, NV	12.24	14.59	74.22	11.26	20.47	61.47	n/a
Richmond, VA	11.37	15.04	70.92	10.65	19.98	81.64	33.88
Roanoke, VA	11.65	12.20	49.70	10.30	17.39	63.78	34.14
Rochester, MN	15.10	15.71	39.45	11.93	20.18	67.68	n/a
Salem, OR	13.89	14.02	56.68	12.23	17.65	50.83	n/a
Salt Lake City, UT	11.72	14.48	56.54	11.89	19.35	55.49	n/a
San Antonio, TX	12.38	13.77	53.70	10.51	17.31	73.17	32.50
San Diego, CA	15.55	15.60	75.31	13.60	20.85	73.12	55.77
San Francisco, CA	17.60	19.19	88.01	18.04	26.44	87.78	56.12
San Jose, CA	17.16	20.85	99.98	16.03	26.19	94.77	54.99
Santa Rosa, CA	16.07	18.71	74.51	14.02	24.25	73.49	n/a
Savannah, GA	11.56	12.73	47.57	9.93	17.45	48.93	n/a
Seattle, WA	17.72	18.85	71.00	14.18	22.47	76.26	46.06
Sioux Falls, SD	12.40	14.13	67.21	11.09	17.92	64.54	30.46
Springfield, IL	15.24	14.56	56.57	11.23	18.89	56.11	n/a
Tallahassee, FL	12.24	13.33	56.74	9.76	16.14	48.85	n/a
Tampa, FL	13.95	13.34	54.56	11.30	17.32	61.10	34.72
Topeka, KS	12.04	15.57	46.02	10.08	18.31	61.37	n/a
Tyler, TX	11.28	12.22	44.28	9.16	17.22	n/a	n/a
Virginia Beach, VA	11.33	13.40	56.84	10.29	18.71	65.14	34.67
Visalia, CA	14.69	14.88	55.50	12.07	18.88	85.09	n/a
Washington, DC	14.50	15.81	86.53	14.36	23.18	82.15	39.45
Wilmington, NC	11.25	14.10	41.46	10.25	18.52	68.72	n/a
Winston-Salem, NC	10.46	13.84	66.15	9.74	18.94	65.26	35.56

Notes: (1) Figures cover the Metropolitan Statistical Area (MSA) except where noted. See Appendix B for areas included; (2) New England City and Town Area; n/a not available
Source: Bureau of Labor Statistics, May 2018 Metro Area Occupational Employment and Wage Estimates

Average Hourly Wages: Occupations N – R

Metro Area	Nurses, Licensed Practical	Nurses, Registered	Nursing Assistants	Packers/ Packagers	Physical Therapists	Postal Mail Carriers	R.E. Brokers
Albany, NY	20.67	33.56	14.09	15.12	37.40	24.76	n/a
Albuquerque, NM	23.07	36.06	14.34	10.16	44.98	25.04	n/a
Allentown, PA	23.95	32.55	15.15	13.90	41.52	25.06	n/a
Anchorage, AK	28.12	42.39	18.52	16.45	48.25	25.26	35.75
Ann Arbor, MI	24.41	35.38	15.72	12.17	41.12	24.23	n/a
Athens, GA	21.12	32.36	12.62	10.93	43.61	24.40	n/a
Atlanta, GA	21.21	35.19	13.36	11.79	40.95	24.56	28.02
Austin, TX	22.39	33.78	13.74	12.85	43.16	24.51	n/a
Baton Rouge, LA	18.49	29.05	11.46	11.77	40.80	24.16	n/a
Billings, MT	21.18	34.26	13.53	12.76	38.68	25.21	n/a
Boise City, ID	22.48	33.17	13.73	11.86	38.21	24.36	24.49
Boston, MA[2]	29.40	45.80	16.64	13.50	44.10	25.73	58.41
Boulder, CO	25.69	36.68	15.80	12.62	40.40	24.66	32.73
Cape Coral, FL	20.76	32.26	14.13	11.01	44.26	24.26	39.52
Cedar Rapids, IA	20.37	27.91	13.87	13.98	37.23	24.73	n/a
Charleston, SC	20.79	36.43	13.79	11.06	39.17	24.76	28.58
Charlotte, NC	21.60	30.85	12.07	11.58	41.02	24.33	39.36
Chicago, IL	26.51	37.36	14.37	12.70	44.47	25.24	49.66
Clarksville, TN	19.52	29.67	13.89	11.26	38.66	24.26	n/a
College Station, TX	21.61	33.00	12.92	9.33	39.30	24.73	n/a
Colorado Springs, CO	23.74	35.34	14.76	12.38	43.14	24.53	37.91
Columbia, MO	20.23	32.79	11.60	11.91	39.66	24.86	n/a
Columbia, SC	20.79	30.51	12.59	10.61	42.97	24.67	31.88
Columbus, OH	20.63	32.49	13.11	12.36	40.70	24.59	28.78
Dallas, TX	24.41	35.65	13.36	12.47	45.99	25.23	39.92
Denver, CO	26.09	36.22	16.49	13.24	38.93	24.92	n/a
Des Moines, IA	21.52	29.92	14.61	14.54	41.28	24.64	25.06
Durham, NC	22.86	32.23	13.92	11.14	38.06	24.90	28.60
Edison, NJ	26.75	43.83	17.67	12.62	45.28	25.42	55.75
El Paso, TX	22.80	33.86	12.20	12.07	44.12	24.39	n/a
Eugene, OR	25.48	43.68	16.41	12.95	39.90	24.18	24.14
Evansville, IN	21.25	29.29	13.27	13.46	37.70	24.37	n/a
Fargo, ND	21.89	32.33	16.11	12.74	37.34	24.18	n/a
Fayetteville, NC	21.84	33.65	11.88	10.10	37.72	24.30	25.33
Fort Collins, CO	24.64	35.51	15.54	12.34	36.09	23.98	32.13
Fort Wayne, IN	21.23	27.73	12.86	13.58	41.84	24.80	n/a
Fort Worth, TX	24.41	35.65	13.36	12.47	45.99	25.23	39.92
Gainesville, FL	24.75	32.97	12.96	11.12	40.56	24.72	23.16
Grand Rapids, MI	20.92	31.70	13.83	11.59	41.17	24.63	32.44
Greeley, CO	23.51	34.48	13.75	12.61	42.09	23.52	26.23
Green Bay, WI	20.49	31.63	14.36	12.14	41.33	24.90	53.28
Greensboro, NC	20.52	32.07	12.03	10.44	43.28	24.82	32.50
Honolulu, HI	24.06	47.88	17.11	12.39	43.71	26.38	48.59
Houston, TX	23.42	38.54	13.68	11.41	44.72	24.80	49.98
Huntsville, AL	18.99	27.48	12.25	12.75	43.22	24.58	n/a
Indianapolis, IN	22.32	33.31	13.74	12.50	40.20	24.76	52.37
Jacksonville, FL	21.22	30.13	12.70	10.99	39.31	25.42	22.79
Kansas City, MO	22.07	32.37	13.14	13.12	37.80	24.52	25.42
Lafayette, LA	18.97	30.26	9.95	11.52	39.90	24.71	23.95
Las Cruces, NM	21.92	31.64	11.54	9.15	51.28	24.29	n/a
Las Vegas, NV	27.70	42.27	17.24	10.53	55.41	24.89	47.79
Lexington, KY	21.42	30.68	13.61	13.84	40.10	24.81	n/a
Lincoln, NE	20.17	30.96	13.90	11.91	38.44	24.71	26.34
Little Rock, AR	20.23	31.27	13.02	10.67	38.88	24.94	32.06
Los Angeles, CA	25.96	48.05	16.16	12.84	46.25	25.98	34.20

Table continued on next page.

Metro Area	Nurses, Licensed Practical	Nurses, Registered	Nursing Assistants	Packers/ Packagers	Physical Therapists	Postal Mail Carriers	R.E. Brokers
Louisville, KY	21.04	31.05	13.95	12.38	39.39	24.71	26.43
Madison, WI	22.90	38.37	15.78	16.84	39.97	24.81	n/a
Manchester, NH[2]	26.67	35.22	15.42	11.00	41.37	24.94	n/a
McAllen, TX	22.31	34.14	11.22	10.95	54.09	25.35	n/a
Miami, FL	22.51	33.41	12.64	11.72	42.31	25.42	38.00
Midland, TX	23.47	30.26	13.74	9.99	44.32	23.44	n/a
Minneapolis, MN	23.54	40.15	16.95	13.70	40.26	25.16	30.17
Nashville, TN	20.75	30.69	13.32	11.94	34.72	24.70	43.47
New Orleans, LA	20.44	32.08	11.71	11.21	41.46	24.51	n/a
New York, NY	26.75	43.83	17.67	12.62	45.28	25.42	55.75
Oklahoma City, OK	20.57	31.33	12.82	11.04	41.45	24.60	n/a
Omaha, NE	21.51	31.59	14.01	12.42	37.77	25.02	31.14
Orlando, FL	21.22	31.23	12.49	11.70	42.73	24.85	27.93
Peoria, IL	21.10	32.07	12.75	12.54	40.59	25.01	n/a
Philadelphia, PA	26.61	37.35	14.70	12.64	44.35	25.20	n/a
Phoenix, AZ	26.92	37.54	15.34	13.15	42.76	25.08	33.42
Pittsburgh, PA	21.58	31.85	14.57	12.03	38.84	24.54	35.72
Portland, OR	25.47	44.99	16.30	14.49	41.77	24.49	43.73
Providence, RI[2]	27.20	37.65	15.02	13.21	40.71	24.67	n/a
Provo, UT	20.27	30.34	12.67	11.81	42.66	24.38	n/a
Raleigh, NC	21.69	31.18	12.47	11.94	40.76	24.76	29.18
Reno, NV	26.84	37.59	16.39	13.25	41.08	25.21	27.57
Richmond, VA	21.17	34.24	13.39	11.03	46.92	24.35	45.51
Roanoke, VA	20.98	31.39	12.90	10.81	44.72	24.90	n/a
Rochester, MN	22.78	36.43	n/a	13.15	39.96	24.76	n/a
Salem, OR	25.70	42.53	14.32	12.93	37.79	23.72	24.27
Salt Lake City, UT	26.89	32.52	14.15	12.50	40.44	24.90	n/a
San Antonio, TX	21.74	34.74	12.95	10.17	38.66	24.90	44.18
San Diego, CA	27.32	47.33	16.68	13.10	44.50	25.67	49.22
San Francisco, CA	31.45	62.01	21.28	14.91	46.60	26.38	49.86
San Jose, CA	30.60	61.83	19.05	14.09	49.32	26.50	43.05
Santa Rosa, CA	30.04	47.76	17.35	13.45	46.85	25.14	n/a
Savannah, GA	19.69	29.78	12.08	10.26	37.82	24.27	n/a
Seattle, WA	28.14	41.27	15.97	15.35	41.92	25.21	36.27
Sioux Falls, SD	18.68	28.27	13.12	11.84	34.24	25.11	n/a
Springfield, IL	21.21	32.84	14.11	n/a	42.04	24.88	n/a
Tallahassee, FL	20.34	30.05	11.81	10.83	42.25	24.90	n/a
Tampa, FL	21.26	32.70	13.41	10.72	40.85	25.00	34.08
Topeka, KS	21.01	31.42	12.84	13.82	44.25	24.03	n/a
Tyler, TX	21.54	29.07	11.86	15.45	48.56	24.72	n/a
Virginia Beach, VA	20.17	32.27	15.24	10.74	41.83	24.42	37.56
Visalia, CA	22.33	42.83	13.59	12.47	50.77	24.64	n/a
Washington, DC	26.09	39.17	15.20	12.68	43.83	24.77	41.67
Wilmington, NC	21.27	29.62	11.65	12.01	49.75	24.73	22.96
Winston-Salem, NC	21.47	33.21	13.20	11.95	44.78	24.90	n/a

Notes: (1) Figures cover the Metropolitan Statistical Area (MSA) except where noted. See Appendix B for areas included;
(2) New England City and Town Area; n/a not available
Source: Bureau of Labor Statistics, May 2018 Metro Area Occupational Employment and Wage Estimates

Average Hourly Wages: Occupations R – T

Metro Area	Retail Salespersons	Sales Reps., Except Tech./Scien.	Sales Reps., Tech./Scien.	Secretaries, Exc. Leg./ Med./Exec.	Security Guards	Surgeons	Teacher Assistants
Albany, NY	13.64	33.03	51.87	19.97	16.62	136.40	14.69
Albuquerque, NM	12.72	28.39	49.88	17.14	13.37	131.23	9.88
Allentown, PA	12.68	37.33	41.17	17.71	13.01	111.67	13.63
Anchorage, AK	14.70	27.22	39.04	20.13	23.75	n/a	18.85
Ann Arbor, MI	13.84	37.33	41.49	20.39	13.28	n/a	14.59
Athens, GA	11.83	30.76	26.21	16.49	n/a	n/a	9.19
Atlanta, GA	12.68	31.63	37.45	17.41	13.82	126.82	11.24
Austin, TX	13.29	30.65	61.20	17.79	14.98	106.21	12.36
Baton Rouge, LA	11.69	28.83	41.10	15.69	13.75	n/a	10.35
Billings, MT	15.26	27.68	52.66	16.62	13.57	n/a	12.45
Boise City, ID	13.08	32.58	46.09	16.34	14.65	106.34	11.77
Boston, MA[2]	14.50	38.76	45.91	22.79	17.19	117.15	17.15
Boulder, CO	15.02	44.39	51.64	19.08	15.69	51.30	15.41
Cape Coral, FL	12.50	32.35	52.15	17.13	13.10	104.53	14.23
Cedar Rapids, IA	13.64	31.57	41.99	17.86	13.29	n/a	13.38
Charleston, SC	13.01	33.67	34.46	17.50	16.46	n/a	10.39
Charlotte, NC	12.54	39.95	45.05	18.31	13.78	127.59	11.85
Chicago, IL	13.63	34.15	41.62	19.11	16.13	107.91	13.78
Clarksville, TN	12.66	29.89	32.16	15.37	16.55	n/a	12.74
College Station, TX	13.38	33.45	44.72	15.82	15.45	n/a	10.02
Colorado Springs, CO	13.80	28.37	52.24	17.08	15.44	n/a	13.37
Columbia, MO	14.88	30.52	39.40	16.61	13.97	n/a	13.12
Columbia, SC	12.96	32.47	35.18	17.40	16.89	n/a	11.36
Columbus, OH	13.41	32.08	35.35	18.69	16.62	122.02	14.24
Dallas, TX	12.80	33.79	43.46	18.42	14.54	109.65	11.42
Denver, CO	14.93	38.76	46.43	19.68	17.27	118.19	14.71
Des Moines, IA	13.36	36.01	42.49	18.77	14.77	85.50	12.85
Durham, NC	12.49	37.16	50.41	19.52	17.15	n/a	12.15
Edison, NJ	14.56	36.95	50.95	20.41	16.99	124.85	15.33
El Paso, TX	12.71	21.76	54.24	14.02	12.93	n/a	12.75
Eugene, OR	15.75	30.18	54.30	17.80	15.44	n/a	15.10
Evansville, IN	12.84	32.06	36.63	14.96	14.64	136.25	11.78
Fargo, ND	14.96	31.29	30.68	18.34	16.62	n/a	15.26
Fayetteville, NC	11.50	24.67	n/a	16.81	20.38	n/a	10.51
Fort Collins, CO	13.63	33.69	51.44	17.56	12.96	135.16	13.17
Fort Wayne, IN	12.31	33.24	44.93	16.08	16.21	n/a	12.28
Fort Worth, TX	12.80	33.79	43.46	18.42	14.54	109.65	11.42
Gainesville, FL	12.15	29.63	38.20	15.72	12.58	n/a	11.27
Grand Rapids, MI	12.96	37.84	40.40	17.68	13.28	41.76	13.65
Greeley, CO	17.17	31.21	46.29	17.59	16.75	n/a	14.81
Green Bay, WI	12.87	32.30	42.11	17.92	12.94	n/a	15.61
Greensboro, NC	12.99	32.20	39.33	17.23	13.66	n/a	11.22
Honolulu, HI	14.65	25.22	42.76	19.52	15.72	n/a	14.58
Houston, TX	12.42	37.52	46.02	18.09	14.37	117.13	10.94
Huntsville, AL	13.05	27.45	43.36	18.10	14.32	129.02	11.69
Indianapolis, IN	12.52	38.07	55.58	16.96	13.89	127.77	12.18
Jacksonville, FL	12.50	31.68	36.12	17.04	12.02	n/a	12.07
Kansas City, MO	13.46	32.92	39.23	17.97	18.01	103.56	13.02
Lafayette, LA	12.72	28.33	28.58	14.22	11.58	n/a	11.21
Las Cruces, NM	12.52	25.96	n/a	15.20	13.40	n/a	13.07
Las Vegas, NV	13.29	31.90	50.14	19.44	14.46	n/a	15.28
Lexington, KY	13.18	27.28	43.69	17.29	11.44	135.80	15.83
Lincoln, NE	13.02	28.88	41.90	17.09	16.05	n/a	13.06
Little Rock, AR	12.50	28.19	31.25	16.15	14.49	n/a	10.75
Los Angeles, CA	15.38	34.61	44.48	20.95	16.09	92.22	17.53

Table continued on next page.

Metro Area	Retail Salespersons	Sales Reps., Except Tech./Scien.	Sales Reps., Tech./Scien.	Secretaries, Exc. Leg./ Med./Exec.	Security Guards	Surgeons	Teacher Assistants
Louisville, KY	12.45	34.99	48.19	16.72	11.59	133.59	14.52
Madison, WI	12.64	32.72	33.85	18.61	15.21	128.44	14.28
Manchester, NH[2]	13.29	30.98	50.71	17.78	15.92	n/a	13.02
McAllen, TX	11.08	27.23	53.28	14.14	11.64	n/a	11.66
Miami, FL	13.10	29.20	39.59	17.47	13.23	103.71	11.14
Midland, TX	15.30	41.74	44.86	18.28	17.69	n/a	10.99
Minneapolis, MN	14.13	36.31	42.02	20.51	16.65	n/a	15.81
Nashville, TN	14.60	31.02	40.92	17.59	13.26	n/a	12.50
New Orleans, LA	12.04	29.75	33.29	16.81	14.53	137.55	11.20
New York, NY	14.56	36.95	50.95	20.41	16.99	124.85	15.33
Oklahoma City, OK	14.03	29.17	40.90	15.82	15.78	129.11	9.84
Omaha, NE	13.20	28.80	33.20	17.22	16.97	137.45	12.68
Orlando, FL	12.25	28.96	43.15	16.68	12.28	110.12	11.61
Peoria, IL	14.78	28.35	42.57	16.55	16.18	n/a	11.89
Philadelphia, PA	14.07	37.49	38.94	19.35	14.26	127.01	13.28
Phoenix, AZ	13.06	31.32	40.89	17.82	14.16	n/a	12.30
Pittsburgh, PA	13.34	35.99	36.57	17.32	12.63	127.84	13.46
Portland, OR	14.66	35.16	47.27	19.86	14.56	n/a	16.35
Providence, RI[2]	14.74	35.63	43.92	20.48	14.91	124.15	15.49
Provo, UT	12.58	26.81	36.27	15.65	17.79	n/a	12.88
Raleigh, NC	13.12	35.74	50.04	17.97	16.32	n/a	11.87
Reno, NV	14.56	32.88	45.03	18.95	13.69	n/a	13.85
Richmond, VA	13.00	38.87	45.68	18.56	13.80	135.28	12.54
Roanoke, VA	13.19	32.44	35.03	16.32	14.01	103.92	10.22
Rochester, MN	13.17	31.75	41.44	16.54	14.63	n/a	15.01
Salem, OR	14.59	32.44	34.85	19.23	14.52	n/a	16.20
Salt Lake City, UT	13.77	29.91	49.89	17.12	16.01	n/a	12.10
San Antonio, TX	13.45	32.68	42.44	16.71	14.65	108.92	11.84
San Diego, CA	14.84	33.47	43.03	20.70	15.02	135.63	16.72
San Francisco, CA	16.11	39.71	46.75	23.99	17.72	98.44	18.28
San Jose, CA	15.57	38.14	48.75	22.59	18.14	138.17	19.21
Santa Rosa, CA	15.84	34.70	53.66	21.33	16.59	n/a	16.25
Savannah, GA	12.22	38.11	45.77	16.25	15.52	n/a	11.59
Seattle, WA	17.90	36.56	42.38	22.07	18.74	116.09	18.12
Sioux Falls, SD	14.87	33.13	43.65	14.25	13.86	n/a	11.80
Springfield, IL	13.41	27.20	28.81	17.39	23.33	n/a	11.77
Tallahassee, FL	12.46	28.03	41.30	17.22	13.75	n/a	12.39
Tampa, FL	12.90	29.76	41.22	16.90	14.81	n/a	13.32
Topeka, KS	12.34	30.64	36.12	15.97	13.20	n/a	12.36
Tyler, TX	13.00	27.09	48.05	15.82	15.08	n/a	11.05
Virginia Beach, VA	11.67	35.34	41.04	17.61	15.31	n/a	12.84
Visalia, CA	14.39	33.09	48.12	18.59	13.27	n/a	17.06
Washington, DC	14.25	38.12	48.14	21.99	20.86	128.45	15.82
Wilmington, NC	12.86	31.34	38.93	17.35	16.01	130.48	10.47
Winston-Salem, NC	11.87	36.42	43.74	17.60	16.40	n/a	10.56

Notes: (1) Figures cover the Metropolitan Statistical Area (MSA) except where noted. See Appendix B for areas included; (2) New England City and Town Area; n/a not available
Source: Bureau of Labor Statistics, May 2018 Metro Area Occupational Employment and Wage Estimates

Average Hourly Wages: Occupations T – Z

Metro Area	Teachers, Elementary School	Teachers, Secondary School	Tele-marketers	Truck Driv., Heavy/ Trac. Trail.	Truck Drivers, Light	Waiters/ Waitresses
Albany, NY	31.77	34.30	13.91	21.01	17.59	14.27
Albuquerque, NM	25.61	23.18	12.71	20.24	17.74	10.32
Allentown, PA	36.19	33.59	n/a	23.52	17.56	12.37
Anchorage, AK	35.89	38.64	n/a	27.50	21.88	12.08
Ann Arbor, MI	31.19	28.87	n/a	23.07	18.55	11.43
Athens, GA	25.67	27.19	9.92	24.66	19.67	10.58
Atlanta, GA	27.51	28.29	12.13	21.15	18.38	9.82
Austin, TX	28.33	27.85	19.92	19.42	19.90	12.85
Baton Rouge, LA	23.94	25.57	n/a	20.70	15.37	8.98
Billings, MT	26.76	28.07	n/a	23.10	18.11	11.19
Boise City, ID	23.65	24.88	14.26	21.26	16.83	9.90
Boston, MA[2]	39.77	38.60	20.38	24.26	20.26	15.53
Boulder, CO	30.90	31.02	16.31	18.69	17.09	13.93
Cape Coral, FL	30.62	31.08	13.65	18.91	15.75	11.22
Cedar Rapids, IA	26.71	26.16	13.07	20.79	16.27	10.36
Charleston, SC	23.46	24.69	9.77	22.65	16.40	9.46
Charlotte, NC	23.28	24.15	16.47	21.28	16.36	11.04
Chicago, IL	31.57	37.38	14.17	24.19	19.81	11.23
Clarksville, TN	29.73	27.89	n/a	17.86	16.06	11.01
College Station, TX	23.34	23.56	n/a	20.99	15.66	9.33
Colorado Springs, CO	22.88	23.70	n/a	21.93	16.56	12.28
Columbia, MO	n/a	n/a	13.09	19.92	17.28	9.41
Columbia, SC	24.51	25.34	n/a	20.83	16.18	9.55
Columbus, OH	30.77	30.51	15.48	21.66	16.85	10.93
Dallas, TX	28.59	29.41	15.74	22.95	19.28	10.98
Denver, CO	27.48	28.36	14.62	24.70	19.51	11.99
Des Moines, IA	28.60	30.54	n/a	23.61	17.30	12.22
Durham, NC	22.60	23.95	10.91	21.10	17.56	12.08
Edison, NJ	40.25	42.53	15.21	25.40	19.12	16.38
El Paso, TX	30.75	31.41	8.85	21.80	14.69	10.07
Eugene, OR	32.15	30.41	13.22	22.64	17.46	13.76
Evansville, IN	23.09	26.20	n/a	21.02	16.09	9.77
Fargo, ND	33.01	30.59	15.56	22.24	17.72	9.62
Fayetteville, NC	20.54	21.92	n/a	18.43	15.62	9.91
Fort Collins, CO	25.32	25.89	14.70	19.49	17.42	13.91
Fort Wayne, IN	24.13	25.73	12.47	21.11	15.76	10.46
Fort Worth, TX	28.59	29.41	15.74	22.95	19.28	10.98
Gainesville, FL	20.26	21.51	12.54	16.45	17.00	11.71
Grand Rapids, MI	27.76	28.43	12.97	21.07	17.70	13.60
Greeley, CO	23.21	24.73	n/a	24.17	15.43	11.03
Green Bay, WI	25.21	26.97	22.25	21.37	15.25	9.79
Greensboro, NC	22.93	23.75	11.90	23.70	17.15	9.39
Honolulu, HI	29.59	29.13	12.22	23.70	18.22	25.23
Houston, TX	28.13	29.24	13.04	21.78	18.44	12.57
Huntsville, AL	24.39	25.59	11.37	19.31	15.68	8.89
Indianapolis, IN	27.40	26.53	15.77	22.61	17.14	11.33
Jacksonville, FL	28.55	29.05	11.74	22.55	18.65	12.18
Kansas City, MO	26.51	27.61	12.53	22.82	18.05	10.30
Lafayette, LA	23.23	24.38	n/a	18.96	13.72	8.77
Las Cruces, NM	35.62	37.67	n/a	17.55	14.95	10.86
Las Vegas, NV	26.93	27.34	14.14	23.37	18.16	12.58
Lexington, KY	27.55	28.11	n/a	22.07	19.25	8.90
Lincoln, NE	26.63	26.69	11.69	n/a	18.29	11.79
Little Rock, AR	25.34	26.08	10.92	22.42	15.98	9.96
Los Angeles, CA	40.37	38.62	14.96	22.79	18.97	13.70

Table continued on next page.

Metro Area	Teachers, Elementary School	Teachers, Secondary School	Tele-marketers	Truck Driv., Heavy/ Trac. Trail.	Truck Drivers, Light	Waiters/ Waitresses
Louisville, KY	28.19	29.56	13.01	23.60	18.81	10.05
Madison, WI	27.82	27.28	13.77	23.62	17.15	14.77
Manchester, NH[2]	27.07	28.62	n/a	22.33	19.76	11.76
McAllen, TX	26.33	27.41	10.74	17.60	13.83	9.78
Miami, FL	20.76	25.74	12.41	19.87	17.09	12.62
Midland, TX	24.99	26.80	n/a	23.09	18.93	9.22
Minneapolis, MN	33.28	32.66	16.30	25.06	20.79	12.59
Nashville, TN	25.33	25.75	15.18	22.88	17.60	9.62
New Orleans, LA	24.31	24.89	16.07	22.49	18.17	9.14
New York, NY	40.25	42.53	15.21	25.40	19.12	16.38
Oklahoma City, OK	20.49	21.20	14.28	21.00	16.22	9.98
Omaha, NE	28.10	27.82	12.82	21.27	17.06	12.74
Orlando, FL	22.82	24.15	11.66	21.10	16.92	13.05
Peoria, IL	22.96	27.28	16.73	19.88	18.10	9.96
Philadelphia, PA	33.79	32.30	15.02	23.50	17.78	12.14
Phoenix, AZ	21.87	24.46	14.55	22.19	19.21	14.87
Pittsburgh, PA	30.99	32.45	12.93	23.05	16.70	12.34
Portland, OR	33.94	37.46	15.60	24.02	18.41	13.69
Providence, RI[2]	34.56	34.55	15.68	23.38	17.19	13.28
Provo, UT	32.45	34.24	18.08	20.04	16.32	11.61
Raleigh, NC	23.10	22.97	12.65	22.81	16.73	11.90
Reno, NV	28.29	28.52	14.07	23.63	19.33	10.01
Richmond, VA	27.62	28.10	13.25	19.87	18.83	11.36
Roanoke, VA	25.23	25.26	n/a	21.58	18.50	10.20
Rochester, MN	26.21	31.37	n/a	23.12	16.57	10.62
Salem, OR	32.01	36.97	n/a	21.05	19.20	16.31
Salt Lake City, UT	27.63	26.96	15.44	21.58	17.81	11.39
San Antonio, TX	28.08	28.60	14.88	20.82	19.23	10.51
San Diego, CA	34.61	37.32	15.12	22.17	18.97	15.22
San Francisco, CA	39.20	39.94	18.53	25.31	20.79	17.54
San Jose, CA	36.72	40.93	n/a	25.31	20.94	15.18
Santa Rosa, CA	36.14	36.81	n/a	25.81	20.12	14.45
Savannah, GA	25.37	26.97	n/a	21.33	16.22	9.93
Seattle, WA	32.32	33.29	17.33	24.34	20.54	18.82
Sioux Falls, SD	21.92	22.11	n/a	20.71	16.88	10.55
Springfield, IL	25.73	26.94	n/a	22.33	15.43	10.45
Tallahassee, FL	22.07	23.64	13.77	17.42	16.32	10.29
Tampa, FL	28.12	28.70	12.12	20.02	16.80	12.46
Topeka, KS	23.00	23.90	n/a	20.69	18.27	10.05
Tyler, TX	23.67	25.47	n/a	19.90	14.92	11.25
Virginia Beach, VA	33.02	32.73	10.11	20.16	15.96	11.45
Visalia, CA	36.75	35.85	n/a	18.05	17.53	12.86
Washington, DC	37.09	37.62	15.26	21.87	18.91	14.09
Wilmington, NC	21.54	23.50	n/a	19.08	15.73	10.05
Winston-Salem, NC	22.47	23.40	15.25	20.83	16.07	9.77

Notes: (1) Figures cover the Metropolitan Statistical Area (MSA) except where noted. See Appendix B for areas included;
(2) New England City and Town Area; Hourly wages for elementary and secondary school teachers were calculated by the editors from annual wage data assuming a 40 hour work week; n/a not available
Source: Bureau of Labor Statistics, May 2018 Metro Area Occupational Employment and Wage Estimates

Means of Transportation to Work: City

| City | Car/Truck/Van | | Public Transportation | | | Bicycle | Walked | Other Means | Worked at Home |
	Drove Alone	Car-pooled	Bus	Subway	Railroad				
Albany, NY	62.5	8.1	14.1	0.2	0.0	0.9	10.6	1.2	2.5
Albuquerque, NM	79.9	9.1	1.8	0.0	0.1	1.4	2.0	1.3	4.3
Allentown, PA	67.4	17.0	5.0	0.1	0.0	0.2	5.5	0.6	4.2
Anchorage, AK	75.8	11.7	1.7	0.0	0.0	1.2	3.4	2.4	3.8
Ann Arbor, MI	54.2	6.7	10.9	0.1	0.0	4.4	15.3	0.9	7.4
Athens, GA	74.5	10.3	4.5	0.1	0.0	1.3	3.9	1.2	4.2
Atlanta, GA	68.7	6.9	6.8	3.1	0.2	0.9	4.4	1.5	7.6
Austin, TX	73.8	9.5	3.7	0.1	0.1	1.3	2.3	1.3	7.9
Baton Rouge, LA	79.4	10.2	2.8	0.0	0.0	0.6	3.0	0.9	2.9
Billings, MT	82.3	8.9	0.8	0.0	0.0	0.6	2.9	0.7	3.8
Boise City, ID	80.6	7.4	0.6	0.0	0.0	2.7	2.0	1.1	5.4
Boston, MA	39.0	5.8	14.2	17.4	1.1	2.1	14.6	2.5	3.3
Boulder, CO	50.9	5.6	7.7	0.0	0.0	10.4	11.3	1.2	12.8
Cape Coral, FL	82.9	9.3	0.1	0.0	0.0	0.1	0.7	1.3	5.5
Cedar Rapids, IA	83.8	9.0	1.1	0.0	0.0	0.5	2.0	0.9	2.7
Charleston, SC	76.6	6.0	1.2	0.0	0.0	2.9	5.4	1.5	6.4
Charlotte, NC	76.6	10.2	2.9	0.3	0.2	0.2	2.0	1.3	6.3
Chicago, IL	49.2	7.9	13.7	12.5	1.8	1.7	6.7	1.9	4.6
Clarksville, TN	86.8	6.6	1.1	0.0	0.0	0.1	1.6	1.4	2.4
College Station, TX	77.7	9.0	3.4	0.0	0.0	2.4	3.2	1.0	3.2
Colorado Springs, CO	78.8	10.9	1.1	0.0	0.0	0.6	1.8	1.0	5.9
Columbia, MO	76.4	10.2	1.6	0.0	0.0	1.3	5.2	1.2	4.1
Columbia, SC	64.3	5.9	1.6	0.0	0.0	0.5	22.2	2.1	3.4
Columbus, OH	80.0	8.3	3.1	0.0	0.0	0.7	2.9	1.1	3.8
Dallas, TX	76.2	11.3	3.3	0.5	0.3	0.2	1.9	1.6	4.6
Denver, CO	69.9	8.1	5.3	0.9	0.4	2.2	4.4	1.3	7.6
Des Moines, IA	80.6	9.8	2.1	0.0	0.0	0.4	2.9	1.0	3.1
Durham, NC	75.9	10.5	4.2	0.0	0.0	0.7	2.6	1.2	5.0
Edison, NJ	68.3	9.9	0.5	0.7	12.3	0.3	2.2	0.9	5.0
El Paso, TX	80.3	11.1	1.7	0.0	0.0	0.2	1.6	1.9	3.2
Eugene, OR	65.6	9.6	4.1	0.0	0.0	6.5	7.2	1.1	5.9
Evansville, IN	82.9	9.0	2.3	0.0	0.0	0.3	2.5	1.3	1.7
Fargo, ND	82.8	8.0	1.2	0.0	0.0	0.9	3.4	0.8	2.9
Fayetteville, NC	78.0	9.0	0.7	0.0	0.0	0.1	7.6	1.0	3.5
Fort Collins, CO	72.4	7.9	1.9	0.1	0.0	6.4	3.5	1.1	6.8
Fort Wayne, IN	83.9	9.0	1.0	0.0	0.0	0.3	1.2	0.9	3.7
Fort Worth, TX	81.5	11.4	0.6	0.0	0.2	0.2	1.3	1.2	3.6
Gainesville, FL	68.0	7.0	7.3	0.0	0.0	4.8	5.8	2.7	4.2
Grand Rapids, MI	75.0	10.8	4.1	0.1	0.0	1.1	3.8	1.2	3.9
Greeley, CO	77.8	12.9	0.8	0.0	0.0	0.8	2.9	1.1	3.7
Green Bay, WI	79.2	10.3	1.3	0.0	0.0	0.6	3.1	2.2	3.2
Greensboro, NC	82.2	8.2	1.5	0.0	0.0	0.2	1.6	1.0	5.5
Honolulu, HI	56.6	13.1	12.2	0.0	0.0	1.9	8.6	4.1	3.6
Houston, TX	76.6	11.3	3.7	0.1	0.1	0.5	2.1	2.0	3.6
Huntsville, AL	86.7	6.8	0.3	0.0	0.0	0.3	1.2	1.5	3.1
Indianapolis, IN	82.2	9.3	1.9	0.0	0.0	0.5	1.8	1.1	3.2
Jacksonville, FL	80.3	9.6	2.0	0.0	0.0	0.5	1.8	1.4	4.5
Kansas City, MO	80.4	8.4	2.8	0.0	0.0	0.3	2.1	1.2	4.8
Lafayette, LA	82.1	9.4	1.0	0.0	0.0	1.1	2.3	1.0	3.2
Las Cruces, NM	78.6	11.9	0.5	0.0	0.0	1.4	2.8	1.0	3.8
Las Vegas, NV	77.7	10.4	4.1	0.0	0.0	0.4	1.6	2.3	3.5
Lexington, KY	78.7	9.3	2.0	0.0	0.0	0.7	3.8	1.2	4.4
Lincoln, NE	81.5	9.0	1.3	0.0	0.0	1.4	3.1	0.7	3.0
Little Rock, AR	82.5	9.9	1.0	0.0	0.0	0.2	1.7	1.1	3.7

Table continued on next page.

City	Car/Truck/Van		Public Transportation			Bicycle	Walked	Other Means	Worked at Home
	Drove Alone	Car-pooled	Bus	Subway	Railroad				
Los Angeles, CA	68.9	9.0	8.7	0.9	0.2	1.1	3.5	1.8	5.9
Louisville, KY	80.4	8.9	3.0	0.0	0.0	0.4	2.1	1.6	3.8
Madison, WI	63.5	7.4	9.4	0.0	0.0	4.8	9.6	1.1	4.2
Manchester, NH	79.1	11.7	0.9	0.0	0.1	0.4	3.2	1.1	3.5
McAllen, TX	76.7	11.6	0.7	0.0	0.0	0.5	1.0	5.1	4.3
Miami, FL	70.0	8.5	9.6	0.9	0.3	1.0	4.0	1.5	4.2
Midland, TX	85.5	10.4	0.2	0.0	0.0	0.0	0.6	1.4	1.9
Minneapolis, MN	61.0	7.9	11.9	1.0	0.2	4.1	7.0	1.5	5.4
Nashville, TN	79.1	9.9	2.1	0.0	0.1	0.2	2.1	1.0	5.6
New Orleans, LA	68.5	9.2	6.8	0.0	0.0	3.2	5.0	2.3	4.9
New York, NY	22.0	4.6	10.7	43.9	1.5	1.2	10.0	2.1	4.1
Oklahoma City, OK	82.3	11.2	0.5	0.0	0.0	0.2	1.4	0.8	3.5
Omaha, NE	82.1	9.1	1.4	0.0	0.0	0.3	2.4	1.2	3.6
Orlando, FL	78.3	8.2	4.1	0.1	0.0	0.6	1.9	1.8	5.1
Peoria, IL	79.7	8.9	3.8	0.0	0.0	0.5	3.2	1.1	2.8
Philadelphia, PA	51.0	8.4	16.8	5.2	2.9	2.1	8.3	1.8	3.5
Phoenix, AZ	74.6	12.5	3.0	0.1	0.1	0.7	1.7	2.0	5.4
Pittsburgh, PA	55.8	8.5	16.3	0.5	0.0	2.0	11.1	1.3	4.6
Portland, OR	57.7	8.9	9.6	1.1	0.3	6.5	5.7	2.6	7.6
Providence, RI	62.9	11.3	5.5	0.1	1.2	1.2	10.7	1.5	5.4
Provo, UT	62.7	12.8	1.5	0.2	1.3	2.6	12.5	1.6	4.8
Raleigh, NC	78.5	8.9	1.9	0.1	0.0	0.4	1.8	1.3	7.1
Reno, NV	76.3	11.5	2.3	0.0	0.0	0.8	3.9	1.4	3.9
Richmond, VA	70.7	10.4	5.1	0.1	0.1	1.9	5.7	1.9	4.2
Roanoke, VA	78.8	9.3	3.5	0.1	0.0	0.7	3.3	1.7	2.6
Rochester, MN	71.7	11.7	6.7	0.0	0.0	1.1	4.3	0.8	3.7
Salem, OR	73.7	13.2	2.6	0.0	0.1	1.1	3.5	1.0	4.8
Salt Lake City, UT	67.7	11.4	4.8	0.3	0.6	2.6	5.4	2.4	4.7
San Antonio, TX	79.0	11.1	3.1	0.0	0.0	0.2	1.7	1.3	3.7
San Diego, CA	74.9	8.6	3.7	0.0	0.1	1.0	3.1	1.6	7.1
San Francisco, CA	34.3	6.8	22.0	8.3	1.5	3.9	11.1	5.4	6.7
San Jose, CA	75.9	11.7	2.8	0.2	1.2	0.9	1.7	1.4	4.1
Santa Rosa, CA	77.3	10.7	1.8	0.0	0.0	1.3	2.2	1.3	5.4
Savannah, GA	73.6	10.1	4.2	0.1	0.0	2.1	4.2	2.0	3.7
Seattle, WA	48.8	7.6	20.0	0.9	0.1	3.5	10.2	1.8	7.0
Sioux Falls, SD	83.9	8.8	1.0	0.0	0.0	0.5	2.0	0.9	3.0
Springfield, IL	81.9	7.9	2.2	0.1	0.0	0.5	2.5	1.2	3.6
Tallahassee, FL	79.4	8.9	2.3	0.0	0.0	0.9	3.3	1.5	3.7
Tampa, FL	78.1	8.4	2.4	0.0	0.0	1.3	2.4	1.3	6.1
Topeka, KS	81.4	10.8	1.2	0.0	0.0	0.3	2.4	1.5	2.4
Tyler, TX	82.6	9.8	0.4	0.0	0.0	0.5	1.3	2.2	3.2
Virginia Beach, VA	82.1	8.4	0.8	0.0	0.0	0.6	2.7	1.5	3.8
Visalia, CA	80.9	11.3	1.0	0.0	0.0	1.2	1.1	1.0	3.6
Washington, DC	34.0	5.4	14.2	20.7	0.3	4.6	13.2	1.9	5.7
Wilmington, NC	79.0	7.2	1.7	0.0	0.0	1.2	2.6	1.2	7.0
Winston-Salem, NC	82.9	7.5	1.5	0.0	0.0	0.2	2.3	1.0	4.6
U.S.	76.4	9.2	2.5	1.9	0.6	0.6	2.7	1.3	4.7

Note: Figures are percentages and cover workers 16 years of age and older
Source: U.S. Census Bureau, 2013-2017 American Community Survey 5-Year Estimates

Means of Transportation to Work: Metro Area

Metro Area	Car/Truck/Van		Public Transportation			Bicycle	Walked	Other Means	Worked at Home
	Drove Alone	Car-pooled	Bus	Subway	Railroad				
Albany, NY	80.1	7.7	3.3	0.1	0.1	0.3	3.5	0.9	4.1
Albuquerque, NM	80.4	9.1	1.4	0.0	0.3	1.0	1.8	1.3	4.8
Allentown, PA	81.8	8.5	1.7	0.1	0.1	0.2	2.5	1.1	4.2
Anchorage, AK	75.1	11.7	1.5	0.0	0.0	1.0	3.1	3.2	4.3
Ann Arbor, MI	72.2	7.7	5.1	0.0	0.0	1.7	6.5	0.7	5.9
Athens, GA	78.4	9.8	2.8	0.0	0.0	0.8	2.6	1.1	4.4
Atlanta, GA	77.6	9.8	2.1	0.8	0.1	0.2	1.3	1.5	6.5
Austin, TX	76.6	9.6	2.1	0.0	0.1	0.8	1.7	1.2	7.8
Baton Rouge, LA	84.7	8.9	0.9	0.0	0.0	0.3	1.4	0.9	2.8
Billings, MT	80.4	9.9	0.7	0.0	0.0	0.5	3.0	0.9	4.6
Boise City, ID	79.7	8.9	0.4	0.0	0.0	1.3	1.7	1.2	6.9
Boston, MA	67.2	7.1	4.2	6.5	2.1	1.0	5.3	1.6	5.0
Boulder, CO	64.7	7.9	4.7	0.0	0.0	4.5	5.1	1.2	11.8
Cape Coral, FL	79.9	9.7	0.8	0.0	0.0	0.6	1.0	2.3	5.6
Cedar Rapids, IA	84.4	8.3	0.6	0.0	0.0	0.3	2.1	0.7	3.6
Charleston, SC	81.1	8.3	1.1	0.0	0.0	0.8	2.5	1.1	5.2
Charlotte, NC	80.9	9.3	1.3	0.2	0.1	0.1	1.4	1.1	5.7
Chicago, IL	70.5	7.8	4.5	4.1	3.2	0.7	3.1	1.3	4.7
Clarksville, TN	84.5	7.3	0.8	0.0	0.0	0.1	3.4	1.5	2.4
College Station, TX	78.1	11.5	2.1	0.0	0.0	1.6	2.4	1.0	3.3
Colorado Springs, CO	77.5	10.5	0.8	0.0	0.0	0.5	3.3	1.1	6.4
Columbia, MO	77.7	11.0	1.1	0.0	0.0	0.9	3.9	1.2	4.2
Columbia, SC	81.0	8.3	0.6	0.0	0.0	0.1	4.5	2.1	3.4
Columbus, OH	82.7	7.6	1.6	0.0	0.0	0.4	2.1	0.9	4.6
Dallas, TX	80.7	9.8	0.9	0.2	0.3	0.2	1.3	1.4	5.2
Denver, CO	75.8	8.4	3.2	0.6	0.3	0.8	2.1	1.2	7.6
Des Moines, IA	83.9	8.0	1.1	0.0	0.0	0.2	1.9	0.7	4.2
Durham, NC	75.0	9.6	4.0	0.0	0.0	0.8	3.2	1.1	6.1
Edison, NJ	50.0	6.5	7.7	19.3	3.8	0.6	5.9	1.8	4.3
El Paso, TX	79.7	11.0	1.5	0.0	0.0	0.2	2.0	2.1	3.5
Eugene, OR	71.1	10.2	3.0	0.0	0.0	3.8	5.0	1.0	5.9
Evansville, IN	86.4	7.3	1.0	0.0	0.0	0.1	1.7	1.0	2.5
Fargo, ND	82.0	8.4	0.9	0.0	0.0	0.6	3.0	0.9	4.1
Fayetteville, NC	80.8	8.8	0.6	0.0	0.0	0.1	5.1	1.1	3.4
Fort Collins, CO	75.0	8.8	1.2	0.0	0.0	3.7	2.5	1.2	7.5
Fort Wayne, IN	84.8	8.4	0.7	0.0	0.0	0.3	1.2	0.7	3.9
Fort Worth, TX	80.7	9.8	0.9	0.2	0.3	0.2	1.3	1.4	5.2
Gainesville, FL	74.7	9.2	3.9	0.0	0.0	2.5	3.2	1.9	4.5
Grand Rapids, MI	81.9	9.0	1.5	0.0	0.0	0.5	2.2	0.9	4.1
Greeley, CO	80.0	10.6	0.6	0.0	0.0	0.3	2.1	0.9	5.5
Green Bay, WI	83.3	8.0	0.6	0.0	0.0	0.3	2.3	1.2	4.3
Greensboro, NC	83.4	8.9	0.8	0.0	0.0	0.1	1.2	0.8	4.7
Honolulu, HI	64.0	14.3	8.5	0.0	0.0	1.2	5.4	2.9	3.7
Houston, TX	80.4	10.4	2.1	0.0	0.0	0.3	1.4	1.4	3.9
Huntsville, AL	87.9	6.6	0.2	0.0	0.0	0.1	0.8	1.2	3.3
Indianapolis, IN	83.9	8.1	0.9	0.0	0.0	0.3	1.5	0.9	4.3
Jacksonville, FL	81.0	8.9	1.3	0.0	0.0	0.5	1.5	1.5	5.3
Kansas City, MO	83.5	8.2	1.0	0.0	0.0	0.2	1.3	0.9	4.9
Lafayette, LA	83.2	9.9	0.5	0.0	0.0	0.4	2.0	1.4	2.6
Las Cruces, NM	81.1	10.4	0.4	0.0	0.0	0.8	2.2	0.9	4.2
Las Vegas, NV	78.9	9.9	3.7	0.0	0.0	0.4	1.6	1.9	3.6
Lexington, KY	79.7	9.6	1.4	0.0	0.0	0.5	3.2	1.2	4.4
Lincoln, NE	81.8	8.8	1.1	0.0	0.0	1.2	3.0	0.7	3.4
Little Rock, AR	84.1	9.6	0.5	0.0	0.0	0.2	1.3	1.0	3.3

Table continued on next page.

Metro Area	Car/Truck/Van		Public Transportation			Bicycle	Walked	Other Means	Worked at Home
	Drove Alone	Car-pooled	Bus	Subway	Railroad				
Los Angeles, CA	74.9	9.6	4.5	0.4	0.3	0.9	2.5	1.5	5.4
Louisville, KY	82.5	8.7	1.8	0.0	0.0	0.2	1.6	1.2	3.9
Madison, WI	74.1	8.2	4.5	0.0	0.0	2.3	5.1	0.9	4.8
Manchester, NH	81.5	8.4	0.7	0.0	0.1	0.2	2.2	0.8	6.1
McAllen, TX	80.4	8.8	0.2	0.0	0.0	0.2	1.2	4.3	4.9
Miami, FL	78.2	9.1	3.2	0.3	0.2	0.6	1.7	1.5	5.2
Midland, TX	84.9	9.9	0.2	0.0	0.0	0.0	0.9	1.6	2.4
Minneapolis, MN	77.7	8.2	4.3	0.2	0.2	0.9	2.2	1.0	5.3
Nashville, TN	81.8	9.3	1.0	0.0	0.1	0.1	1.3	1.1	5.4
New Orleans, LA	78.6	9.9	2.5	0.0	0.0	1.2	2.4	1.7	3.6
New York, NY	50.0	6.5	7.7	19.3	3.8	0.6	5.9	1.8	4.3
Oklahoma City, OK	83.3	9.9	0.4	0.0	0.0	0.3	1.5	0.9	3.7
Omaha, NE	84.0	8.4	0.9	0.0	0.0	0.2	1.8	1.0	3.7
Orlando, FL	80.2	9.6	1.7	0.0	0.1	0.4	1.0	1.4	5.5
Peoria, IL	84.7	7.6	1.4	0.0	0.0	0.3	2.1	0.9	3.0
Philadelphia, PA	73.1	7.5	5.3	1.8	2.4	0.7	3.7	1.1	4.5
Phoenix, AZ	76.6	11.0	1.9	0.0	0.0	0.8	1.5	1.8	6.3
Pittsburgh, PA	77.4	8.2	4.9	0.2	0.0	0.4	3.4	1.1	4.4
Portland, OR	70.4	9.7	4.8	0.7	0.2	2.4	3.3	1.7	6.8
Providence, RI	80.5	8.6	1.6	0.1	0.9	0.3	3.3	0.9	3.7
Provo, UT	73.2	11.8	0.8	0.2	0.8	1.1	4.1	1.3	6.7
Raleigh, NC	80.2	8.8	0.9	0.0	0.0	0.2	1.2	1.0	7.7
Reno, NV	77.9	11.2	1.9	0.0	0.0	0.6	2.8	1.3	4.3
Richmond, VA	81.6	8.6	1.4	0.0	0.1	0.4	1.9	1.3	4.8
Roanoke, VA	82.6	8.4	1.3	0.0	0.0	0.3	2.2	1.0	4.1
Rochester, MN	74.6	11.0	4.4	0.0	0.0	0.7	3.6	0.8	4.9
Salem, OR	75.6	12.9	1.5	0.0	0.0	0.7	3.1	1.1	5.0
Salt Lake City, UT	75.1	11.8	2.3	0.4	0.6	0.8	2.2	1.5	5.5
San Antonio, TX	79.7	10.7	2.1	0.0	0.0	0.2	1.6	1.2	4.5
San Diego, CA	76.0	8.9	2.6	0.0	0.2	0.7	2.9	1.7	7.0
San Francisco, CA	58.8	9.7	7.6	7.2	1.2	1.9	4.7	2.7	6.3
San Jose, CA	75.2	10.6	2.5	0.2	1.4	1.8	2.1	1.4	4.8
Santa Rosa, CA	75.0	11.0	1.8	0.1	0.0	1.0	3.1	1.1	6.9
Savannah, GA	80.4	9.3	2.0	0.0	0.0	0.9	2.2	1.6	3.7
Seattle, WA	68.7	9.9	8.6	0.3	0.5	1.1	3.8	1.3	5.8
Sioux Falls, SD	84.3	8.1	0.7	0.0	0.0	0.3	2.0	0.8	3.8
Springfield, IL	83.3	7.8	1.4	0.1	0.0	0.4	2.0	1.1	3.9
Tallahassee, FL	81.4	9.5	1.3	0.0	0.0	0.6	2.1	1.3	3.7
Tampa, FL	80.0	8.5	1.3	0.0	0.0	0.8	1.4	1.5	6.5
Topeka, KS	83.0	9.8	0.7	0.0	0.0	0.2	1.8	1.1	3.3
Tyler, TX	83.7	9.5	0.2	0.0	0.0	0.3	1.0	1.9	3.4
Virginia Beach, VA	81.6	8.3	1.5	0.1	0.0	0.5	3.4	1.4	3.4
Visalia, CA	78.0	14.3	0.6	0.0	0.0	0.6	1.7	1.7	3.1
Washington, DC	66.0	9.5	5.1	7.9	0.8	0.9	3.3	1.2	5.4
Wilmington, NC	80.4	8.4	0.8	0.0	0.0	0.7	1.6	1.3	6.8
Winston-Salem, NC	84.3	8.4	0.7	0.0	0.0	0.1	1.4	0.9	4.3
U.S.	76.4	9.2	2.5	1.9	0.6	0.6	2.7	1.3	4.7

Note: Figures are percentages and cover workers 16 years of age and older; (1) Figures cover the Metropolitan Statistical Area—see Appendix B for areas included
Source: U.S. Census Bureau, 2013-2017 American Community Survey 5-Year Estimates

Travel Time to Work: City

City	Less Than 10 Minutes	10 to 19 Minutes	20 to 29 Minutes	30 to 44 Minutes	45 to 59 Minutes	60 to 89 Minutes	90 Minutes or More
Albany, NY	16.0	44.8	22.6	10.8	3.1	1.7	1.1
Albuquerque, NM	11.4	37.2	27.4	17.3	3.1	2.4	1.3
Allentown, PA	11.7	34.1	27.2	15.6	4.6	4.1	2.7
Anchorage, AK	16.2	45.5	22.5	10.3	2.7	1.3	1.6
Ann Arbor, MI	13.8	44.1	19.7	13.8	4.8	2.9	0.9
Athens, GA	16.1	48.8	16.9	9.3	3.9	3.2	1.9
Atlanta, GA	7.2	29.6	27.8	20.5	7.2	4.9	2.8
Austin, TX	9.6	33.0	24.2	21.4	6.6	3.7	1.5
Baton Rouge, LA	11.0	37.7	28.2	14.8	3.6	3.2	1.4
Billings, MT	17.5	53.8	20.0	4.9	1.3	1.3	1.1
Boise City, ID	14.9	45.1	24.9	11.0	1.7	1.3	1.0
Boston, MA	7.2	19.9	20.4	29.4	11.3	9.6	2.3
Boulder, CO	18.9	45.9	16.6	10.3	4.7	2.5	1.1
Cape Coral, FL	7.4	24.5	23.9	27.5	9.6	4.9	2.2
Cedar Rapids, IA	17.9	49.3	18.1	9.7	2.1	1.9	1.0
Charleston, SC	12.4	33.3	25.2	21.0	5.3	1.8	1.2
Charlotte, NC	9.1	29.2	25.7	23.8	6.9	3.4	1.8
Chicago, IL	4.8	16.4	17.9	30.1	14.7	12.6	3.6
Clarksville, TN	11.7	34.3	25.2	16.5	5.0	6.1	1.2
College Station, TX	18.5	54.6	18.2	5.8	0.7	1.3	1.0
Colorado Springs, CO	12.2	37.5	27.5	15.1	3.2	2.7	2.0
Columbia, MO	20.6	53.8	12.9	7.6	2.9	1.1	1.0
Columbia, SC	32.9	36.9	16.2	9.7	1.6	1.7	1.0
Columbus, OH	10.2	34.9	30.0	18.4	3.7	1.8	1.0
Dallas, TX	8.6	26.8	22.9	26.0	8.1	5.5	2.0
Denver, CO	8.7	29.4	24.4	24.6	7.3	4.1	1.6
Des Moines, IA	14.0	43.8	25.7	11.8	2.2	1.4	1.0
Durham, NC	10.0	38.7	25.6	16.9	3.9	3.0	1.8
Edison, NJ	7.2	24.1	17.6	17.7	10.7	13.3	9.4
El Paso, TX	9.4	35.2	27.6	20.0	4.0	2.3	1.6
Eugene, OR	17.5	49.5	19.7	7.4	1.4	3.0	1.4
Evansville, IN	17.5	46.7	17.7	11.8	3.2	2.0	1.1
Fargo, ND	20.8	55.7	16.9	3.6	0.9	1.3	0.7
Fayetteville, NC	19.1	40.6	22.8	11.0	3.2	2.1	1.2
Fort Collins, CO	16.5	45.0	19.4	10.4	4.4	3.2	1.1
Fort Wayne, IN	13.2	39.9	27.5	12.3	3.3	2.0	1.7
Fort Worth, TX	8.9	28.2	22.3	23.3	9.0	6.3	2.0
Gainesville, FL	14.8	51.3	20.2	9.4	2.0	1.4	1.0
Grand Rapids, MI	16.0	42.0	24.2	11.4	3.0	2.3	1.2
Greeley, CO	17.8	38.4	16.0	13.9	5.4	6.4	2.1
Green Bay, WI	18.1	48.4	19.0	7.5	3.8	1.8	1.4
Greensboro, NC	11.4	43.3	24.3	14.2	3.1	2.2	1.6
Honolulu, HI	8.3	35.0	23.4	22.3	5.8	4.0	1.2
Houston, TX	7.9	26.3	22.5	27.0	8.4	6.1	1.7
Huntsville, AL	13.5	42.4	26.4	14.0	1.9	0.8	1.1
Indianapolis, IN	10.5	30.0	30.4	21.0	4.2	2.5	1.4
Jacksonville, FL	8.9	28.2	28.8	23.9	5.8	2.7	1.7
Kansas City, MO	11.5	33.7	28.3	19.2	4.6	1.7	1.0
Lafayette, LA	16.4	43.2	19.9	12.0	2.1	2.9	3.5
Las Cruces, NM	20.3	47.8	15.7	8.8	3.0	3.5	0.9
Las Vegas, NV	7.2	25.5	29.6	27.5	5.6	2.6	1.9
Lexington, KY	12.7	38.8	26.7	14.5	3.5	2.5	1.3
Lincoln, NE	16.5	45.5	22.7	9.7	2.7	2.1	0.8
Little Rock, AR	13.5	43.1	28.6	10.6	1.9	1.1	1.2
Los Angeles, CA	6.4	22.8	19.7	27.6	10.3	9.6	3.5

Table continued on next page.

City	Less Than 10 Minutes	10 to 19 Minutes	20 to 29 Minutes	30 to 44 Minutes	45 to 59 Minutes	60 to 89 Minutes	90 Minutes or More
Louisville, KY	9.6	32.8	30.0	20.1	4.1	2.3	1.2
Madison, WI	15.0	41.0	23.8	14.6	3.0	2.0	0.7
Manchester, NH	15.0	38.5	19.5	13.9	5.5	4.4	3.2
McAllen, TX	15.8	42.7	23.4	12.7	2.2	1.3	1.9
Miami, FL	5.9	23.8	23.4	29.2	9.0	6.7	2.1
Midland, TX	16.8	48.6	17.6	10.7	2.6	2.0	1.7
Minneapolis, MN	8.4	33.0	30.2	20.1	4.2	3.0	1.2
Nashville, TN	8.5	29.3	27.8	23.3	6.2	3.4	1.4
New Orleans, LA	9.7	33.6	25.3	20.4	4.6	4.5	1.9
New York, NY	4.0	12.6	13.5	27.5	16.2	18.9	7.2
Oklahoma City, OK	11.5	36.1	29.3	17.1	2.8	1.5	1.6
Omaha, NE	14.5	41.3	27.7	12.3	2.1	1.3	0.8
Orlando, FL	7.9	28.5	26.8	24.9	6.3	3.5	2.2
Peoria, IL	17.6	48.3	20.8	8.1	2.2	2.1	1.0
Philadelphia, PA	6.0	19.4	20.0	28.2	12.1	10.2	4.1
Phoenix, AZ	9.2	28.0	25.0	24.7	7.2	4.1	1.8
Pittsburgh, PA	9.9	32.7	25.1	21.9	5.4	3.4	1.6
Portland, OR	8.0	27.7	27.2	23.2	7.1	5.0	1.9
Providence, RI	14.1	41.4	18.9	12.5	5.0	4.8	3.3
Provo, UT	22.8	45.6	16.4	8.6	2.6	2.6	1.5
Raleigh, NC	10.8	33.2	26.1	20.3	5.3	2.5	1.9
Reno, NV	15.3	45.0	21.9	10.7	3.5	2.4	1.3
Richmond, VA	10.9	37.6	28.1	16.1	2.7	2.4	2.2
Roanoke, VA	13.2	43.5	16.3	19.7	3.5	2.6	1.2
Rochester, MN	19.7	56.6	12.5	6.2	2.2	1.7	1.2
Salem, OR	14.0	42.5	20.6	11.4	5.3	4.6	1.7
Salt Lake City, UT	13.0	44.5	23.6	12.1	3.8	2.0	1.0
San Antonio, TX	9.1	31.4	27.3	21.6	5.7	3.0	1.9
San Diego, CA	7.9	32.6	28.4	21.3	5.0	3.0	1.8
San Francisco, CA	4.1	18.9	21.2	29.7	11.9	11.0	3.3
San Jose, CA	5.5	23.9	23.8	26.7	9.9	7.6	2.6
Santa Rosa, CA	14.4	41.6	19.2	13.4	4.0	4.5	2.9
Savannah, GA	17.7	38.1	21.8	14.4	4.1	2.6	1.3
Seattle, WA	7.1	24.3	24.6	27.6	9.9	5.1	1.5
Sioux Falls, SD	17.0	52.1	21.6	5.2	1.6	1.6	1.0
Springfield, IL	19.1	50.0	19.1	5.7	2.2	2.4	1.4
Tallahassee, FL	15.5	45.2	23.4	11.4	1.8	1.6	1.0
Tampa, FL	12.0	31.1	24.2	20.8	6.4	3.8	1.7
Topeka, KS	18.4	54.4	14.5	7.5	1.6	2.5	1.0
Tyler, TX	17.9	41.7	18.9	13.2	3.8	2.5	2.0
Virginia Beach, VA	10.7	30.3	27.7	21.5	5.7	2.6	1.5
Visalia, CA	16.8	42.9	17.2	12.4	6.0	2.9	1.8
Washington, DC	5.4	19.6	23.0	31.7	11.6	6.6	2.0
Wilmington, NC	16.1	47.9	21.6	8.4	2.6	1.7	1.6
Winston-Salem, NC	13.5	43.9	22.3	12.8	3.4	2.2	1.9
U.S.	12.7	28.9	20.9	20.5	8.1	6.2	2.7

Note: Figures are percentages and include workers 16 years old and over
Source: U.S. Census Bureau, 2013-2017 American Community Survey 5-Year Estimates

Travel Time to Work: Metro Area

Metro Area	Less Than 10 Minutes	10 to 19 Minutes	20 to 29 Minutes	30 to 44 Minutes	45 to 59 Minutes	60 to 89 Minutes	90 Minutes or More
Albany, NY	12.7	32.1	24.7	20.4	6.1	2.5	1.4
Albuquerque, NM	11.4	32.5	25.4	20.1	5.7	3.2	1.7
Allentown, PA	12.6	28.1	22.1	18.6	7.5	7.2	4.0
Anchorage, AK	15.6	41.5	21.0	10.5	4.6	4.4	2.4
Ann Arbor, MI	11.2	33.5	24.1	19.0	6.9	4.1	1.2
Athens, GA	13.4	41.4	21.2	13.5	4.8	3.5	2.1
Atlanta, GA	7.3	22.8	20.0	24.4	12.2	9.9	3.5
Austin, TX	9.8	28.0	22.2	22.7	9.6	5.8	1.9
Baton Rouge, LA	9.9	27.5	22.9	22.1	9.3	6.1	2.2
Billings, MT	16.9	46.2	22.2	8.8	2.3	2.0	1.6
Boise City, ID	12.6	34.4	25.8	19.6	4.3	2.2	1.2
Boston, MA	9.3	22.6	18.4	24.2	11.8	10.4	3.3
Boulder, CO	15.0	35.2	21.5	16.4	6.5	4.0	1.4
Cape Coral, FL	8.6	26.3	22.5	26.1	9.7	4.6	2.2
Cedar Rapids, IA	17.9	40.3	21.7	13.3	3.5	2.0	1.2
Charleston, SC	9.9	27.0	24.4	25.0	8.2	4.1	1.5
Charlotte, NC	9.8	28.0	22.7	23.8	9.1	4.7	1.9
Chicago, IL	8.5	21.9	18.5	24.9	12.3	10.6	3.3
Clarksville, TN	15.6	32.5	21.8	17.2	5.8	5.5	1.5
College Station, TX	18.4	46.5	18.9	10.3	2.4	2.0	1.4
Colorado Springs, CO	12.1	33.5	26.6	17.4	4.9	3.3	2.1
Columbia, MO	17.2	48.6	18.4	10.2	3.5	1.2	0.9
Columbia, SC	13.3	29.6	24.1	21.5	6.5	3.2	1.7
Columbus, OH	11.2	30.4	26.5	21.4	6.3	3.0	1.3
Dallas, TX	9.1	25.4	21.1	25.1	10.5	6.7	2.0
Denver, CO	8.5	25.3	23.3	25.8	9.7	5.6	1.8
Des Moines, IA	15.4	36.3	27.0	15.5	3.1	1.5	1.2
Durham, NC	10.2	33.9	24.6	20.0	6.0	3.6	1.6
Edison, NJ	7.2	19.0	16.3	23.7	12.4	14.7	6.7
El Paso, TX	10.3	33.0	26.6	21.2	4.7	2.5	1.7
Eugene, OR	16.4	41.7	22.6	12.5	2.2	2.9	1.8
Evansville, IN	15.5	37.5	23.8	15.3	4.2	2.4	1.3
Fargo, ND	19.5	50.3	18.7	7.4	1.7	1.5	0.9
Fayetteville, NC	15.5	34.4	25.2	16.6	4.4	2.4	1.5
Fort Collins, CO	14.9	36.3	21.9	14.2	5.9	5.0	1.7
Fort Wayne, IN	13.8	35.6	27.9	15.3	3.9	1.9	1.7
Fort Worth, TX	9.1	25.4	21.1	25.1	10.5	6.7	2.0
Gainesville, FL	10.6	39.0	25.3	16.4	4.8	2.5	1.4
Grand Rapids, MI	15.2	34.8	24.9	16.3	4.7	2.5	1.6
Greeley, CO	12.8	27.9	19.5	21.9	8.8	7.0	2.2
Green Bay, WI	17.9	39.4	22.0	12.9	4.3	2.1	1.5
Greensboro, NC	11.6	36.4	25.3	17.7	4.9	2.4	1.7
Honolulu, HI	9.2	24.5	19.6	25.4	9.9	8.5	3.0
Houston, TX	8.0	23.9	19.6	25.9	11.5	8.7	2.4
Huntsville, AL	10.5	32.6	28.4	21.0	5.0	1.5	1.1
Indianapolis, IN	11.9	27.7	24.8	23.4	7.1	3.6	1.5
Jacksonville, FL	9.3	25.7	25.4	24.8	8.6	4.3	1.9
Kansas City, MO	12.6	30.9	25.1	21.2	6.6	2.4	1.1
Lafayette, LA	16.1	32.8	20.0	18.2	4.8	3.5	4.5
Las Cruces, NM	16.0	40.0	21.1	13.7	4.6	3.4	1.2
Las Vegas, NV	7.8	28.3	29.8	25.0	4.9	2.5	1.8
Lexington, KY	14.5	35.1	24.5	17.8	4.5	2.3	1.3
Lincoln, NE	16.7	42.5	23.4	11.6	3.0	2.0	0.9
Little Rock, AR	12.7	32.3	24.6	19.4	6.7	3.0	1.2
Los Angeles, CA	7.4	25.1	20.0	25.1	9.9	9.2	3.4

Table continued on next page.

Metro Area	Less Than 10 Minutes	10 to 19 Minutes	20 to 29 Minutes	30 to 44 Minutes	45 to 59 Minutes	60 to 89 Minutes	90 Minutes or More
Louisville, KY	10.2	30.3	26.8	22.4	6.2	2.8	1.4
Madison, WI	16.3	32.6	24.0	18.5	5.0	2.5	1.1
Manchester, NH	12.1	28.8	20.2	19.3	8.6	7.4	3.6
McAllen, TX	13.8	38.6	25.1	15.8	2.6	2.0	2.1
Miami, FL	6.9	23.7	22.6	27.2	9.9	7.3	2.4
Midland, TX	16.6	45.1	19.0	12.3	2.8	2.5	1.7
Minneapolis, MN	10.5	27.6	24.9	23.3	8.1	4.3	1.3
Nashville, TN	9.4	26.8	22.3	23.4	10.0	6.2	1.9
New Orleans, LA	10.6	30.6	22.3	21.1	7.3	5.6	2.5
New York, NY	7.2	19.0	16.3	23.7	12.4	14.7	6.7
Oklahoma City, OK	13.0	32.5	25.6	19.9	5.2	2.3	1.6
Omaha, NE	14.3	36.7	27.0	15.9	3.5	1.6	1.0
Orlando, FL	7.2	24.2	23.5	27.7	10.2	4.9	2.2
Peoria, IL	17.1	35.8	24.8	15.4	3.6	1.8	1.5
Philadelphia, PA	9.6	24.2	20.5	23.8	10.7	8.2	3.1
Phoenix, AZ	10.0	26.9	23.7	23.7	8.8	5.1	1.6
Pittsburgh, PA	12.0	27.1	21.2	22.3	9.4	5.9	2.0
Portland, OR	10.6	27.6	22.7	22.6	8.8	5.6	2.1
Providence, RI	12.4	30.9	21.9	19.0	7.0	5.7	3.0
Provo, UT	18.9	36.1	19.6	14.8	5.4	3.5	1.6
Raleigh, NC	9.7	27.7	25.1	23.7	8.0	4.0	1.8
Reno, NV	12.3	39.5	25.4	14.9	3.8	2.5	1.6
Richmond, VA	9.2	29.5	27.3	22.5	6.1	3.2	2.2
Roanoke, VA	11.8	33.5	21.3	22.7	5.4	3.7	1.6
Rochester, MN	19.0	42.2	18.5	12.4	3.8	2.4	1.6
Salem, OR	15.6	33.4	22.2	15.4	6.4	5.1	1.9
Salt Lake City, UT	10.9	32.9	27.7	19.6	5.3	2.5	1.1
San Antonio, TX	9.5	28.8	24.6	22.6	8.1	4.3	2.2
San Diego, CA	8.8	29.8	25.0	22.7	7.1	4.5	2.2
San Francisco, CA	6.8	22.9	18.1	23.9	12.1	11.9	4.3
San Jose, CA	7.2	26.1	24.2	24.0	8.9	7.0	2.7
Santa Rosa, CA	15.7	32.5	19.6	16.8	5.7	6.0	3.6
Savannah, GA	11.9	30.7	24.0	21.3	6.7	4.0	1.4
Seattle, WA	8.0	23.3	21.3	25.1	10.9	8.4	3.1
Sioux Falls, SD	17.0	43.7	24.5	9.8	2.3	1.6	1.2
Springfield, IL	16.5	41.0	23.7	11.6	3.2	2.6	1.5
Tallahassee, FL	11.8	34.1	24.2	20.5	5.4	2.5	1.5
Tampa, FL	10.0	27.4	22.0	22.8	9.5	6.1	2.1
Topeka, KS	16.5	42.5	19.2	13.5	3.8	3.0	1.5
Tyler, TX	13.1	32.8	24.2	19.1	5.0	2.9	2.8
Virginia Beach, VA	11.3	31.1	24.4	20.9	7.0	3.7	1.7
Visalia, CA	17.8	35.1	18.6	16.1	6.2	3.9	2.2
Washington, DC	6.0	19.2	17.8	25.8	13.9	12.8	4.5
Wilmington, NC	12.6	38.8	24.0	15.6	4.8	2.4	1.9
Winston-Salem, NC	12.0	34.3	24.6	18.5	5.7	3.1	1.9
U.S.	12.7	28.9	20.9	20.5	8.1	6.2	2.7

Note: Figures are percentages and include workers 16 years old and over; Figures cover the Metropolitan Statistical Area—see Appendix B for areas included
Source: U.S. Census Bureau, 2013-2017 American Community Survey 5-Year Estimates

2016 Presidential Election Results

City	Area Covered	Clinton	Trump	Johnson	Stein	Other
Albany, NY	Albany County	59.4	34.2	3.4	1.8	1.2
Albuquerque, NM	Bernalillo County	52.2	34.5	10.8	1.3	1.2
Allentown, PA	Lehigh County	50.0	45.3	2.5	0.9	1.4
Anchorage, AK	State of Alaska	36.6	51.3	5.9	1.8	4.4
Ann Arbor, MI	Washtenaw County	67.6	26.6	3.1	1.3	1.4
Athens, GA	Clarke County	65.1	28.0	4.4	0.7	1.8
Atlanta, GA	Fulton County	67.7	26.8	3.6	0.1	1.8
Austin, TX	Travis County	65.8	27.1	4.7	1.6	0.8
Baton Rouge, LA	East Baton Rouge Parish	52.3	43.1	2.5	0.8	1.2
Billings, MT	Yellowstone County	31.5	58.1	6.1	1.3	3.1
Boise City, ID	Ada County	38.7	47.9	5.1	1.6	6.7
Boston, MA	Suffolk County	78.4	16.1	2.6	1.4	1.5
Boulder, CO	Boulder County	70.3	22.0	4.3	2.0	1.4
Cape Coral, FL	Lee County	37.9	58.1	2.1	0.6	1.2
Cedar Rapids, IA	Linn County	50.3	41.3	4.7	0.9	2.7
Charleston, SC	Charleston County	50.6	42.8	4.1	1.0	1.5
Charlotte, NC	Mecklenburg County	62.3	32.9	3.3	0.3	1.3
Chicago, IL	Cook County	73.9	20.8	2.7	1.5	1.1
Clarksville, TN	Montgomery County	37.7	56.1	4.1	0.9	1.2
College Station, TX	Brazos County	34.4	57.6	5.7	0.8	1.5
Colorado Springs, CO	El Paso County	33.9	56.2	6.2	1.3	2.4
Columbia, MO	Boone County	49.0	43.2	5.1	1.5	1.2
Columbia, SC	Richland County	64.0	31.1	2.3	0.8	1.7
Columbus, OH	Franklin County	59.8	33.9	3.4	1.0	1.9
Dallas, TX	Dallas County	60.2	34.3	3.1	0.8	1.5
Denver, CO	Denver County	73.7	18.9	4.5	1.7	1.3
Des Moines, IA	Polk County	51.7	40.4	4.3	0.8	2.8
Durham, NC	Durham County	77.7	18.2	2.6	0.3	1.3
Edison, NJ	Middlesex County	58.8	37.4	1.7	1.1	1.1
El Paso, TX	El Paso County	68.5	25.7	3.5	1.4	0.9
Eugene, OR	Lane County	53.5	35.0	4.4	3.3	3.8
Evansville, IN	Vanderburgh County	38.9	55.2	4.4	0.3	1.2
Fargo, ND	Cass County	38.8	49.3	7.5	1.5	2.9
Fayetteville, NC	Cumberland County	56.2	40.2	2.6	0.1	0.9
Fort Collins, CO	Larimer County	47.5	42.6	5.9	1.6	2.4
Fort Wayne, IN	Allen County	37.3	56.5	4.6	0.5	1.2
Fort Worth, TX	Tarrant County	43.1	51.7	3.6	0.8	0.7
Gainesville, FL	Alachua County	58.3	36.0	3.1	1.2	1.4
Grand Rapids, MI	Kent County	44.6	47.7	4.6	1.3	1.9
Greeley, CO	Weld County	34.3	56.6	5.5	1.0	2.5
Green Bay, WI	Brown County	41.4	52.1	3.9	1.1	1.6
Greensboro, NC	Guilford County	58.0	38.1	2.6	0.3	1.0
Honolulu, HI	Honolulu County	61.5	31.6	3.7	2.3	1.0
Houston, TX	Harris County	54.0	41.6	3.0	0.9	0.5
Huntsville, AL	Madison County	38.4	54.8	4.1	0.8	1.9
Indianapolis, IN	Marion County	58.0	35.5	5.0	0.2	1.3
Jacksonville, FL	Duval County	47.1	48.5	2.6	0.7	1.1
Kansas City, MO	Jackson County	55.5	38.1	3.6	1.2	1.7
Lafayette, LA	Lafayette Parish	31.0	64.6	2.7	0.8	0.9
Las Cruces, NM	Dona Ana County	53.7	35.9	7.7	1.3	1.3
Las Vegas, NV	Clark County	52.4	41.7	2.9	0.0	2.9
Lexington, KY	Fayette County	51.2	41.7	3.8	1.2	2.1
Lincoln, NE	Lancaster County	45.4	45.2	5.2	1.4	2.7
Little Rock, AR	Pulaski County	56.1	38.3	2.7	1.0	1.9
Los Angeles, CA	Los Angeles County	71.8	22.4	2.6	2.2	1.0
Louisville, KY	Jefferson County	54.0	40.7	2.9	0.9	1.4

Table continued on next page.

City	Area Covered	Clinton	Trump	Johnson	Stein	Other
Madison, WI	Dane County	70.4	23.0	3.4	1.4	1.8
Manchester, NH	Hillsborough County	46.5	46.7	4.3	0.8	1.7
McAllen, TX	Hidalgo County	68.1	27.9	2.2	1.1	0.8
Miami, FL	Miami-Dade County	63.2	33.8	1.3	0.6	1.0
Midland, TX	Midland County	20.4	75.1	3.4	0.4	0.7
Minneapolis, MN	Hennepin County	63.1	28.2	3.6	1.5	3.6
Nashville, TN	Davidson County	59.8	33.9	3.9	1.0	1.4
New Orleans, LA	Orleans Parish	80.8	14.7	2.2	1.5	0.8
New York, NY	Bronx County	88.5	9.5	0.6	1.1	0.3
New York, NY	Kings County	79.5	17.5	0.9	1.5	0.6
New York, NY	New York County	86.6	9.7	1.4	1.4	0.9
New York, NY	Queens County	75.4	21.8	1.0	1.3	0.5
New York, NY	Richmond County	41.0	56.1	1.3	1.0	0.6
Oklahoma City, OK	Oklahoma County	41.2	51.7	7.1	0.0	0.0
Omaha, NE	Douglas County	47.3	45.0	4.3	1.2	2.2
Orlando, FL	Orange County	59.8	35.4	2.6	0.9	1.4
Peoria, IL	Peoria County	48.1	45.0	4.7	1.4	0.8
Philadelphia, PA	Philadelphia County	82.3	15.3	1.0	0.9	0.4
Phoenix, AZ	Maricopa County	44.8	47.7	4.3	1.2	2.0
Pittsburgh, PA	Allegheny County	55.9	39.5	2.5	0.8	1.4
Portland, OR	Multnomah County	73.3	17.0	3.2	3.2	3.2
Providence, RI	Providence County	57.5	36.6	2.7	1.3	1.9
Provo, UT	Utah County	14.0	50.2	3.2	0.5	32.2
Raleigh, NC	Wake County	57.4	37.2	3.7	0.3	1.4
Reno, NV	Washoe County	46.4	45.1	4.4	0.0	4.0
Richmond, VA	Richmond City	78.6	15.1	3.5	1.1	1.8
Roanoke, VA	Roanoke City	56.5	37.5	3.3	1.0	1.7
Rochester, MN	Olmsted County	45.3	44.5	4.4	1.4	4.4
Salem, OR	Marion County	42.2	46.3	5.2	2.1	4.2
Salt Lake City, UT	Salt Lake County	41.5	32.6	3.8	1.2	20.9
San Antonio, TX	Bexar County	53.7	40.4	3.4	1.1	1.3
San Diego, CA	San Diego County	56.3	36.6	4.0	1.7	1.4
San Francisco, CA	San Francisco County	84.5	9.2	2.2	2.4	1.7
San Jose, CA	Santa Clara County	72.7	20.6	3.6	1.8	1.3
Santa Rosa, CA	Sonoma County	68.8	22.0	3.9	3.1	2.2
Savannah, GA	Chatham County	55.1	40.4	3.1	0.3	1.1
Seattle, WA	King County	69.8	21.0	4.0	1.7	3.4
Sioux Falls, SD	Minnehaha County	39.1	53.7	6.1	0.0	1.1
Springfield, IL	Sangamon County	41.6	50.8	4.6	1.5	1.6
Tallahassee, FL	Leon County	59.8	35.0	2.9	0.9	1.4
Tampa, FL	Hillsborough County	51.0	44.2	2.6	0.8	1.4
Topeka, KS	Shawnee County	44.2	46.8	4.4	2.3	2.3
Tyler, TX	Smith County	26.3	69.5	2.4	0.4	1.3
Virginia Beach, VA	Virginia Beach City	44.8	48.4	4.1	0.9	1.9
Visalia, CA	Tulare County	41.7	51.1	3.3	1.4	2.5
Washington, DC	District of Columbia	90.9	4.1	1.6	1.4	2.1
Wilmington, NC	New Hanover County	45.6	49.5	3.5	0.4	1.1
Winston-Salem, NC	Forsyth County	53.0	42.6	3.0	0.3	1.2
U.S.	U.S.	48.0	45.9	3.3	1.1	1.7

Note: Results are percentages and may not add to 100% due to rounding
Source: Dave Leip's Atlas of U.S. Presidential Elections

House Price Index (HPI)

Metro Area[1]	National Ranking[3]	Quarterly Change (%)	One-Year Change (%)	Five-Year Change (%)
Albany, NY	218	-0.78	2.46	11.59
Albuquerque, NM	202	0.27	3.37	17.54
Allentown, PA	178	0.25	4.58	17.09
Anchorage, AK	243	-0.82	-1.17	8.57
Ann Arbor, MI	38	-0.05	9.08	40.94
Athens, GA	150	-2.93	5.58	36.35
Atlanta, GA	35	0.03	9.25	49.09
Austin, TX	137	-0.29	5.91	49.36
Baton Rouge, LA	216	-0.30	2.56	19.32
Billings, MT	229	0.65	1.55	18.99
Boise City, ID	2	1.37	16.65	68.50
Boston, MA[2]	117	0.76	6.37	33.50
Boulder, CO	97	-0.63	6.85	60.11
Cape Coral, FL	176	-0.07	4.64	51.21
Cedar Rapids, IA	196	-0.95	3.59	13.75
Charleston, SC	165	1.03	4.98	48.51
Charlotte, NC	26	1.67	9.83	42.67
Chicago, IL[2]	194	0.05	3.62	22.76
Clarksville, TN	n/r	n/a	10.44	22.32
College Station, TX	n/r	n/a	7.27	42.28
Colorado Springs, CO	10	1.17	11.41	47.12
Columbia, MO	185	0.56	4.16	17.20
Columbia, SC	147	1.65	5.62	22.45
Columbus, OH	81	0.05	7.41	36.68
Dallas, TX[2]	106	0.13	6.58	56.33
Denver, CO	64	0.08	8.15	64.63
Des Moines, IA	160	0.68	5.16	25.14
Durham, NC	65	0.93	8.05	36.19
Edison, NJ[2]	170	0.47	4.80	26.94
El Paso, TX	240	-1.59	0.41	9.71
Eugene, OR	57	-0.49	8.37	41.87
Evansville, IN	109	3.54	6.54	21.71
Fargo, ND	230	0.01	1.38	26.29
Fayetteville, NC	32	9.25	9.49	13.78
Fort Collins, CO	59	0.18	8.29	57.61
Fort Wayne, IN	33	1.27	9.35	29.51
Fort Worth, TX[2]	41	1.15	9.03	53.26
Gainesville, FL	n/r	n/a	3.51	36.42
Grand Rapids, MI	39	1.14	9.07	48.85
Greeley, CO	16	1.53	10.68	73.05
Green Bay, WI	71	0.51	7.79	27.00
Greensboro, NC	130	0.40	6.06	20.16
Honolulu, HI	148	3.13	5.62	32.46
Houston, TX	161	-0.13	5.13	36.79
Huntsville, AL	157	0.82	5.28	16.19
Indianapolis, IN	47	1.62	8.69	32.10
Jacksonville, FL	100	0.05	6.78	47.34
Kansas City, MO	37	1.59	9.16	37.00
Lafayette, LA	241	-0.23	-0.36	9.63
Las Cruces, NM	n/r	n/a	3.26	10.08
Las Vegas, NV	1	3.20	17.63	73.68
Lexington, KY	204	-2.81	3.28	23.17
Lincoln, NE	107	-0.15	6.55	30.61
Little Rock, AR	227	2.46	1.86	12.54
Los Angeles, CA[2]	77	0.51	7.61	44.06

Table continued on next page.

Metro Area[1]	National Ranking[3]	Quarterly Change (%)	One-Year Change (%)	Five-Year Change (%)
Louisville, KY	131	0.80	6.06	27.94
Madison, WI	140	-1.20	5.82	26.68
Manchester, NH	168	-0.78	4.92	26.94
McAllen, TX	n/r	n/a	9.27	24.90
Miami, FL[2]	66	0.91	8.04	55.38
Midland, TX	n/r	n/a	11.61	29.71
Minneapolis, MN	122	-0.88	6.31	31.91
Nashville, TN	46	1.21	8.84	53.68
New Orleans, LA	214	0.41	2.71	22.67
New York, NY[2]	170	0.47	4.80	26.94
Oklahoma City, OK	191	0.26	3.87	21.60
Omaha, NE	120	-0.24	6.33	27.96
Orlando, FL	68	0.48	7.92	55.21
Peoria, IL	221	1.82	2.14	3.12
Philadelphia, PA[2]	70	1.56	7.87	28.08
Phoenix, AZ	27	1.14	9.75	47.59
Pittsburgh, PA	158	-0.29	5.23	23.09
Portland, OR	167	-0.70	4.92	54.27
Providence, RI	133	-0.17	6.04	29.27
Provo, UT	12	1.34	11.35	46.94
Raleigh, NC	92	0.57	7.08	35.91
Reno, NV	7	1.48	11.84	77.15
Richmond, VA	121	1.10	6.32	27.93
Roanoke, VA	207	0.36	3.03	14.73
Rochester, MN	91	1.02	7.08	33.87
Salem, OR	8	0.87	11.70	62.33
Salt Lake City, UT	20	0.88	10.48	46.37
San Antonio, TX	103	1.95	6.71	39.55
San Diego, CA	128	0.50	6.10	38.19
San Francisco, CA[2]	14	-1.55	11.04	61.65
San Jose, CA	11	0.76	11.39	57.33
Santa Rosa, CA	141	-1.36	5.75	48.61
Savannah, GA	132	0.68	6.05	29.50
Seattle, WA[2]	99	-1.36	6.80	63.88
Sioux Falls, SD	144	-0.10	5.68	29.97
Springfield, IL	213	0.80	2.77	9.93
Tallahassee, FL	n/r	n/a	-0.05	21.69
Tampa, FL	40	0.54	9.06	56.78
Topeka, KS	113	2.47	6.42	16.66
Tyler, TX	n/r	n/a	3.48	23.48
Virginia Beach, VA	232	-1.12	1.25	13.22
Visalia, CA	217	-2.07	2.50	35.12
Washington, DC[2]	164	0.47	5.00	24.05
Wilmington, NC	54	2.85	8.45	36.94
Winston-Salem, NC	62	1.61	8.22	23.65
U.S.[4]	–	1.12	5.73	32.81

*Note: The HPI is a weighted repeat sales index. It measures average price changes in repeat sales or refinancings on the same properties. This information is obtained by reviewing repeat mortgage transactions on single-family properties whose mortgages have been purchased or securitized by Fannie Mae or Freddie Mac in January 1975; (1) figures cover the Metropolitan Statistical Area (MSA) unless noted otherwise—see Appendix B for areas included; (2) Metropolitan Division—see Appendix B for areas included; (3) Rankings are based on annual percentage change, for all MSAs containing at least 15,000 transactions over the last 10 years and ranges from 1 to 245; (4) figures based on a weighted division average; all figures are for the period ended December 31, 2018; n/a not available; n/r not ranked
Source: Federal Housing Finance Agency, House Price Index, February 26, 2019*

Home Value Distribution: City

Area	Under $50,000	$50,000 -$99,999	$100,000 -$149,999	$150,000 -$199,999	$200,000 -$299,999	$300,000 -$499,999	$500,000 -$999,999	$1,000,000 or more
Albany, NY	4.4	12.4	19.4	29.7	24.7	7.6	1.5	0.3
Albuquerque, NM	5.3	5.4	19.1	25.3	27.6	14.2	2.8	0.4
Allentown, PA	5.3	26.5	32.6	22.7	8.8	3.1	0.5	0.5
Anchorage, AK	5.5	2.0	4.3	7.4	29.5	39.3	11.0	0.9
Ann Arbor, MI	3.1	4.9	7.3	12.1	30.3	29.2	11.8	1.4
Athens, GA	7.4	18.0	22.2	20.6	16.9	10.8	3.8	0.4
Atlanta, GA	7.4	13.6	10.8	11.3	15.9	16.9	16.5	7.6
Austin, TX	3.1	3.5	8.2	13.3	24.9	28.3	15.4	3.2
Baton Rouge, LA	7.0	19.1	17.9	19.1	18.9	12.0	4.7	1.3
Billings, MT	6.5	4.3	11.3	25.3	35.9	12.7	3.5	0.5
Boise City, ID	4.4	3.9	15.6	23.9	27.4	18.5	5.7	0.6
Boston, MA	2.1	0.4	1.2	2.9	12.5	39.3	32.2	9.4
Boulder, CO	5.6	1.6	2.6	4.2	5.6	18.3	47.5	14.8
Cape Coral, FL	2.3	8.4	18.8	21.8	26.6	16.6	4.8	0.9
Cedar Rapids, IA	5.3	18.1	34.8	21.2	14.6	4.6	1.2	0.2
Charleston, SC	2.1	3.3	6.0	14.6	27.5	25.5	14.7	6.3
Charlotte, NC	3.3	11.6	21.4	17.3	18.3	16.0	9.3	2.8
Chicago, IL	3.6	8.7	13.2	15.7	23.3	21.6	10.5	3.3
Clarksville, TN	5.3	18.7	29.9	25.7	15.3	4.3	0.5	0.3
College Station, TX	3.0	2.9	13.6	28.5	30.1	17.8	3.6	0.5
Colorado Springs, CO	4.3	3.2	9.8	20.5	32.1	22.6	6.4	1.1
Columbia, MO	3.7	8.7	21.7	21.8	24.4	16.1	3.3	0.3
Columbia, SC	5.3	17.1	21.2	14.9	15.4	15.1	9.8	1.3
Columbus, OH	6.8	23.8	26.7	20.1	15.5	5.5	1.4	0.2
Dallas, TX	8.7	24.8	15.6	9.0	12.4	15.6	10.2	3.7
Denver, CO	2.5	3.1	6.7	10.8	23.0	29.9	19.9	4.2
Des Moines, IA	6.9	26.1	34.0	19.1	8.6	3.9	1.4	0.1
Durham, NC	2.6	7.1	19.4	22.7	27.1	15.7	4.5	0.8
Edison, NJ	3.5	1.7	1.9	3.2	19.8	46.5	22.0	1.4
El Paso, TX	5.9	27.6	33.0	16.8	10.8	4.4	1.2	0.2
Eugene, OR	5.7	2.2	6.9	14.5	36.9	26.1	6.9	0.7
Evansville, IN	12.5	47.0	22.7	9.2	5.8	1.9	0.8	0.2
Fargo, ND	3.7	6.9	20.0	23.9	28.0	14.5	2.5	0.5
Fayetteville, NC	6.1	26.2	27.6	18.5	13.7	5.8	1.6	0.4
Fort Collins, CO	4.1	0.9	3.3	7.3	31.9	41.9	10.0	0.7
Fort Wayne, IN	12.3	33.6	28.8	13.8	7.8	2.8	0.8	0.1
Fort Worth, TX	8.1	23.0	22.7	18.8	15.4	8.3	2.9	0.8
Gainesville, FL	6.6	21.7	22.8	20.6	18.2	7.9	1.9	0.2
Grand Rapids, MI	7.7	28.0	32.6	17.6	9.6	3.3	1.1	0.1
Greeley, CO	8.5	4.7	14.0	22.1	32.0	15.8	2.5	0.3
Green Bay, WI	3.5	24.5	37.2	17.9	11.0	4.4	1.1	0.3
Greensboro, NC	3.6	20.0	25.4	18.2	17.5	10.7	3.7	0.8
Honolulu, HI	1.3	1.0	1.0	1.6	9.2	23.4	43.9	18.7
Houston, TX	7.3	24.1	18.9	11.6	12.7	14.0	8.5	2.9
Huntsville, AL	5.8	19.8	16.8	16.4	22.0	14.1	4.1	1.1
Indianapolis, IN	8.8	26.3	29.0	16.1	10.1	6.7	2.3	0.6
Jacksonville, FL	9.4	20.2	20.4	18.0	18.9	9.1	3.1	1.0
Kansas City, MO	12.6	20.9	20.5	17.8	16.7	8.2	2.7	0.6
Lafayette, LA	7.0	10.0	17.0	22.7	21.9	14.6	5.3	1.5
Las Cruces, NM	10.4	13.0	26.6	26.4	16.0	5.6	1.9	0.1
Las Vegas, NV	3.6	9.5	14.7	19.2	27.4	19.1	5.2	1.4
Lexington, KY	3.4	11.1	22.8	21.1	21.1	14.2	5.0	1.2
Lincoln, NE	4.6	11.8	30.0	23.1	20.3	8.3	1.6	0.3
Little Rock, AR	7.4	20.3	18.3	16.8	16.2	14.0	5.4	1.6
Los Angeles, CA	2.0	0.9	0.9	1.8	8.5	30.7	37.8	17.4

Table continued on next page.

Area	Under $50,000	$50,000 -$99,999	$100,000 -$149,999	$150,000 -$199,999	$200,000 -$299,999	$300,000 -$499,999	$500,000 -$999,999	$1,000,000 or more
Louisville, KY	6.7	18.2	26.7	17.1	15.7	11.4	3.5	0.6
Madison, WI	2.3	2.9	11.0	24.0	34.1	20.4	4.7	0.6
Manchester, NH	2.8	4.4	9.6	27.4	42.5	12.1	1.0	0.1
McAllen, TX	9.1	29.0	26.8	16.2	12.5	4.4	1.8	0.2
Miami, FL	3.5	8.3	9.4	13.0	23.5	24.2	12.5	5.7
Midland, TX	6.1	11.5	14.7	20.0	23.8	16.7	6.1	1.1
Minneapolis, MN	2.2	6.0	14.1	19.7	28.9	19.3	8.2	1.6
Nashville, TN	3.0	8.1	21.0	20.5	21.5	17.1	7.3	1.4
New Orleans, LA	3.8	9.5	15.9	19.7	18.5	18.9	10.6	3.0
New York, NY	3.5	1.6	2.1	2.9	7.9	28.0	38.2	15.8
Oklahoma City, OK	8.7	19.9	22.1	20.0	17.1	8.6	2.9	0.7
Omaha, NE	5.4	17.0	29.8	19.8	16.6	8.2	2.7	0.6
Orlando, FL	6.1	15.8	14.8	14.1	22.4	18.9	6.4	1.6
Peoria, IL	13.1	26.5	21.1	15.8	14.5	6.4	2.3	0.3
Philadelphia, PA	8.6	21.1	19.7	18.0	17.8	9.8	3.9	1.1
Phoenix, AZ	6.4	11.1	15.0	18.1	21.3	19.2	7.4	1.4
Pittsburgh, PA	14.8	31.8	17.1	11.3	10.7	9.1	4.5	0.8
Portland, OR	2.9	1.0	3.2	8.1	23.3	37.0	22.1	2.4
Providence, RI	2.7	8.4	21.0	24.6	18.7	14.7	8.3	1.5
Provo, UT	5.5	2.3	11.4	20.3	31.4	20.7	6.9	1.6
Raleigh, NC	2.5	3.4	15.5	21.3	25.9	20.8	9.1	1.4
Reno, NV	6.4	5.8	7.9	12.3	27.0	31.4	8.2	1.1
Richmond, VA	3.1	13.1	15.7	15.9	21.6	18.6	9.5	2.6
Roanoke, VA	5.1	23.5	31.4	18.6	11.2	7.2	2.0	1.0
Rochester, MN	4.6	7.3	22.1	26.5	23.0	13.7	2.4	0.5
Salem, OR	8.0	3.4	13.7	24.2	31.8	16.6	1.8	0.4
Salt Lake City, UT	3.3	2.3	10.5	17.5	24.0	26.7	13.3	2.3
San Antonio, TX	8.6	28.8	21.2	17.0	14.5	7.2	2.2	0.5
San Diego, CA	2.3	1.1	1.2	2.1	8.9	31.7	41.1	11.5
San Francisco, CA	1.6	0.6	0.5	0.5	1.4	6.3	46.3	42.8
San Jose, CA	2.3	2.0	1.3	1.2	2.5	13.5	56.0	21.2
Santa Rosa, CA	4.1	2.2	1.6	1.7	9.2	40.8	35.9	4.6
Savannah, GA	6.4	22.3	22.7	19.8	16.3	8.0	3.7	0.8
Seattle, WA	1.2	0.4	0.9	2.3	9.3	31.5	43.3	11.1
Sioux Falls, SD	6.7	8.9	22.3	25.9	21.3	11.2	2.8	0.8
Springfield, IL	11.8	26.0	24.1	15.1	14.4	6.2	2.1	0.2
Tallahassee, FL	4.4	12.5	17.2	21.8	24.8	15.7	2.9	0.7
Tampa, FL	6.9	17.2	14.6	13.4	16.6	17.3	10.2	3.7
Topeka, KS	14.6	35.2	23.5	14.2	8.8	2.6	0.8	0.3
Tyler, TX	8.8	21.9	21.2	18.8	14.8	10.5	3.3	0.7
Virginia Beach, VA	3.1	1.3	6.3	14.6	34.8	27.6	10.2	1.9
Visalia, CA	4.4	6.5	14.6	22.1	29.8	16.4	5.7	0.5
Washington, DC	2.1	1.2	1.5	2.9	12.1	26.8	37.6	15.8
Wilmington, NC	3.6	5.9	13.9	17.4	25.5	20.2	10.6	2.9
Winston-Salem, NC	7.4	20.2	26.6	19.9	12.2	8.3	4.5	0.9
U.S.	8.3	13.9	14.7	14.6	18.7	17.3	9.7	2.7

Note: Figures are percentages and cover owner-occupied housing units.
Source: U.S. Census Bureau, 2013-2017 American Community Survey 5-Year Estimates

Home Value Distribution: Metro Area

MSA[1]	Under $50,000	$50,000 -$99,999	$100,000 -$149,999	$150,000 -$199,999	$200,000 -$299,999	$300,000 -$499,999	$500,000 -$999,999	$1,000,000 or more
Albany, NY	5.1	8.0	14.1	21.8	28.9	17.9	3.7	0.6
Albuquerque, NM	6.7	8.6	19.0	22.6	24.2	13.9	4.2	0.8
Allentown, PA	4.9	8.3	15.3	20.6	27.9	18.9	3.5	0.6
Anchorage, AK	5.3	2.8	5.0	10.2	31.8	35.0	9.2	0.7
Ann Arbor, MI	7.2	7.7	10.5	15.9	25.1	23.7	8.6	1.4
Athens, GA	9.8	16.0	18.9	17.1	19.3	13.6	4.6	0.7
Atlanta, GA	5.6	13.7	17.6	17.7	19.8	16.9	7.3	1.5
Austin, TX	4.3	5.4	11.5	16.6	26.0	23.1	10.6	2.5
Baton Rouge, LA	10.2	13.7	16.9	20.9	21.6	12.2	3.6	0.9
Billings, MT	8.8	5.0	10.5	21.4	32.7	16.3	4.3	1.0
Boise City, ID	5.4	7.8	18.0	21.6	24.7	17.5	4.5	0.5
Boston, MA	2.4	1.2	2.2	4.7	18.0	39.3	26.3	5.9
Boulder, CO	3.7	1.0	2.3	5.8	16.5	31.7	31.4	7.6
Cape Coral, FL	8.7	13.6	14.6	15.6	20.6	16.9	7.6	2.4
Cedar Rapids, IA	6.8	15.7	27.8	20.1	19.2	7.6	2.3	0.5
Charleston, SC	7.4	9.3	14.3	17.2	21.3	17.8	9.4	3.4
Charlotte, NC	5.9	13.6	19.7	17.4	19.9	15.5	6.5	1.6
Chicago, IL	4.1	8.8	14.1	16.9	24.3	20.6	8.9	2.1
Clarksville, TN	7.6	20.3	24.9	21.7	16.6	7.0	1.5	0.4
College Station, TX	12.1	16.5	17.3	19.2	18.7	11.6	3.8	0.7
Colorado Springs, CO	4.3	3.0	9.5	19.3	30.8	24.1	7.9	1.0
Columbia, MO	5.4	10.3	21.2	20.8	22.8	15.3	3.6	0.6
Columbia, SC	10.1	17.9	23.9	18.0	16.2	9.5	3.6	0.7
Columbus, OH	5.7	15.9	20.8	19.4	20.5	13.1	3.9	0.6
Dallas, TX	5.9	15.6	18.6	17.2	19.7	15.7	5.8	1.6
Denver, CO	3.2	2.2	4.9	9.8	26.1	35.2	15.9	2.6
Des Moines, IA	5.2	13.4	21.7	21.2	22.5	12.0	3.5	0.4
Durham, NC	5.4	8.3	15.5	17.7	22.8	20.0	9.0	1.3
Edison, NJ	2.8	1.7	2.8	4.8	15.6	36.3	28.0	8.1
El Paso, TX	8.9	28.9	31.5	15.6	9.8	4.0	1.1	0.2
Eugene, OR	7.7	3.5	9.4	18.5	31.6	22.0	6.6	0.9
Evansville, IN	8.9	26.4	23.4	18.6	13.8	6.6	2.0	0.3
Fargo, ND	4.5	7.4	18.8	23.1	27.1	14.8	3.7	0.4
Fayetteville, NC	9.6	23.5	24.3	19.2	15.9	5.9	1.2	0.3
Fort Collins, CO	5.0	1.3	2.9	9.5	29.7	36.9	13.3	1.3
Fort Wayne, IN	10.1	27.6	27.0	15.6	12.1	5.9	1.5	0.3
Fort Worth, TX	5.9	15.6	18.6	17.2	19.7	15.7	5.8	1.6
Gainesville, FL	7.6	19.4	17.9	18.3	20.3	12.0	4.1	0.4
Grand Rapids, MI	8.4	15.5	23.8	20.6	18.5	9.8	2.7	0.6
Greeley, CO	6.1	4.6	9.2	15.5	29.9	26.2	7.4	1.0
Green Bay, WI	4.4	13.7	25.3	23.3	21.7	9.1	2.2	0.4
Greensboro, NC	7.7	21.2	24.1	17.4	16.2	9.8	3.0	0.6
Honolulu, HI	1.1	0.8	0.9	1.3	6.9	22.2	52.7	14.0
Houston, TX	6.5	16.7	19.9	17.2	18.3	13.6	5.9	1.9
Huntsville, AL	7.7	15.8	19.2	17.9	22.1	13.5	3.3	0.7
Indianapolis, IN	6.9	18.8	24.9	17.9	16.1	11.0	3.6	0.7
Jacksonville, FL	7.4	16.0	17.3	16.9	21.2	14.2	5.4	1.6
Kansas City, MO	7.5	15.4	19.7	19.3	20.6	12.9	3.8	0.8
Lafayette, LA	17.0	18.6	16.4	18.3	17.1	8.9	3.1	0.6
Las Cruces, NM	14.5	18.3	20.5	18.9	15.1	9.3	3.1	0.2
Las Vegas, NV	5.2	8.8	13.4	18.7	27.6	19.6	5.3	1.3
Lexington, KY	4.7	11.8	23.6	20.6	19.7	13.4	4.9	1.4
Lincoln, NE	4.4	11.2	27.7	22.1	21.0	10.7	2.6	0.4
Little Rock, AR	9.2	19.3	23.3	19.0	16.8	8.9	2.7	0.8
Los Angeles, CA	2.8	1.6	1.4	2.0	7.8	30.2	40.7	13.4

Table continued on next page.

MSA[1]	Under $50,000	$50,000 -$99,999	$100,000 -$149,999	$150,000 -$199,999	$200,000 -$299,999	$300,000 -$499,999	$500,000 -$999,999	$1,000,000 or more
Louisville, KY	6.4	16.5	24.6	18.2	18.7	11.3	3.5	0.8
Madison, WI	2.9	4.3	11.5	19.9	32.2	22.2	6.0	1.0
Manchester, NH	2.7	2.8	6.9	15.1	38.9	27.6	5.3	0.7
McAllen, TX	25.6	35.9	18.0	9.6	6.8	2.6	1.1	0.2
Miami, FL	6.0	10.4	11.7	13.6	22.0	22.6	10.0	3.8
Midland, TX	10.1	12.5	14.2	17.9	22.7	16.2	5.4	1.1
Minneapolis, MN	3.6	4.1	11.6	20.0	30.4	21.9	7.1	1.2
Nashville, TN	4.0	8.9	19.2	18.8	22.0	17.4	7.9	1.7
New Orleans, LA	5.3	10.1	18.2	21.7	23.5	14.4	5.3	1.3
New York, NY	2.8	1.7	2.8	4.8	15.6	36.3	28.0	8.1
Oklahoma City, OK	8.7	20.0	22.8	19.3	16.7	8.9	2.9	0.8
Omaha, NE	4.9	14.0	27.3	20.0	19.6	10.8	2.8	0.6
Orlando, FL	8.0	13.6	15.7	18.9	23.0	14.8	4.6	1.3
Peoria, IL	8.1	25.5	24.0	18.0	15.4	7.0	1.7	0.4
Philadelphia, PA	4.5	7.7	10.8	15.3	26.6	24.5	9.0	1.5
Phoenix, AZ	7.0	8.3	12.8	17.4	24.4	20.3	7.9	1.9
Pittsburgh, PA	10.4	22.5	20.1	17.5	15.9	10.2	3.0	0.6
Portland, OR	4.4	1.6	4.0	9.5	27.7	35.4	15.3	2.0
Providence, RI	3.0	2.5	7.7	17.0	32.6	27.5	8.1	1.6
Provo, UT	3.3	1.3	7.3	16.8	35.0	26.8	8.3	1.1
Raleigh, NC	4.5	5.7	15.1	17.7	24.8	23.1	7.8	1.2
Reno, NV	5.9	5.7	8.1	12.5	26.6	27.9	10.5	2.8
Richmond, VA	3.2	6.0	14.0	20.1	28.6	20.3	6.7	1.2
Roanoke, VA	5.4	11.6	21.8	21.5	20.7	13.6	4.4	1.0
Rochester, MN	5.9	8.8	20.0	22.9	21.7	15.7	4.1	1.0
Salem, OR	8.0	3.8	12.6	22.2	29.1	18.3	5.3	0.8
Salt Lake City, UT	4.0	1.7	8.9	16.7	30.9	27.1	9.3	1.3
San Antonio, TX	8.7	21.8	18.5	17.5	17.4	11.3	3.9	1.0
San Diego, CA	3.5	2.0	1.7	2.2	8.5	34.9	37.8	9.4
San Francisco, CA	2.0	1.2	1.2	1.6	5.0	17.7	44.8	26.5
San Jose, CA	2.1	1.6	1.2	1.1	2.2	11.3	46.1	34.4
Santa Rosa, CA	4.5	2.9	1.5	1.6	7.1	30.9	41.7	9.9
Savannah, GA	6.1	13.6	18.3	20.0	21.4	12.5	6.5	1.4
Seattle, WA	3.6	1.6	3.5	7.3	21.0	33.2	24.4	5.4
Sioux Falls, SD	6.6	10.0	20.8	24.1	22.0	12.5	3.2	0.8
Springfield, IL	9.7	23.8	22.8	17.5	17.2	6.9	1.9	0.3
Tallahassee, FL	9.3	16.8	16.6	18.7	21.1	13.3	3.5	0.7
Tampa, FL	11.1	17.5	16.4	16.7	19.2	12.7	5.0	1.3
Topeka, KS	11.1	26.0	23.5	18.1	14.1	5.8	1.3	0.2
Tyler, TX	12.7	20.0	19.4	19.0	16.1	9.2	2.8	0.8
Virginia Beach, VA	4.3	3.7	10.8	18.3	31.2	23.3	7.2	1.2
Visalia, CA	5.7	11.2	19.1	21.4	23.6	13.4	4.7	0.9
Washington, DC	2.2	1.3	2.8	6.1	18.6	34.4	28.7	5.9
Wilmington, NC	5.5	8.1	14.1	18.7	24.4	19.6	7.6	2.0
Winston-Salem, NC	8.8	18.2	25.4	19.5	15.7	8.6	3.1	0.7
U.S.	8.3	13.9	14.7	14.6	18.7	17.3	9.7	2.7

Note: (1) Figures cover the Metropolitan Statistical Area (MSA)—see Appendix B for areas included; Figures are percentages and cover owner-occupied housing units.
Source: U.S. Census Bureau, 2013-2017 American Community Survey 5-Year Estimates

Homeownership Rate

Metro Area	2009	2010	2011	2012	2013	2014	2015	2016	2017
Albany, NY	72.8	72.4	70.6	67.9	67.5	65.9	61.3	64.1	62.2
Albuquerque, NM	65.5	67.1	62.8	65.9	64.4	64.3	66.9	67.0	67.9
Allentown, PA	71.5	75.7	75.5	71.5	68.2	69.2	68.9	73.1	72.1
Anchorage, AK	n/a	n/a	n/a	n/a	n/a	n/a	n/a	n/a	n/a
Ann Arbor, MI	n/a	n/a	n/a	n/a	n/a	n/a	n/a	n/a	n/a
Athens, GA	n/a	n/a	n/a	n/a	n/a	n/a	n/a	n/a	n/a
Atlanta, GA	67.2	65.8	62.1	61.6	61.6	61.7	61.5	62.4	64.0
Austin, TX	65.8	58.4	60.1	59.6	61.1	57.5	56.5	55.6	56.1
Baton Rouge, LA	70.3	72.0	71.4	66.6	64.8	64.2	64.8	66.9	66.6
Billings, MT	n/a	n/a	n/a	n/a	n/a	n/a	n/a	n/a	n/a
Boise City, ID	n/a	n/a	n/a	n/a	n/a	n/a	n/a	n/a	n/a
Boston, MA	66.0	65.5	66.0	66.3	62.8	59.3	58.9	58.8	61.0
Boulder, CO	n/a	n/a	n/a	n/a	n/a	n/a	n/a	n/a	n/a
Cape Coral, FL	n/a	n/a	n/a	n/a	n/a	62.9	66.5	65.5	75.1
Cedar Rapids, IA	n/a	n/a	n/a	n/a	n/a	n/a	n/a	n/a	n/a
Charleston, SC	n/a	n/a	n/a	n/a	n/a	65.8	62.1	67.7	68.8
Charlotte, NC	66.1	63.6	58.3	58.9	58.1	62.3	66.2	64.6	67.9
Chicago, IL	68.2	67.7	67.1	68.2	66.3	64.3	64.5	64.1	64.6
Clarksville, TN	n/a	n/a	n/a	n/a	n/a	n/a	n/a	n/a	n/a
College Station, TX	n/a	n/a	n/a	n/a	n/a	n/a	n/a	n/a	n/a
Colorado Springs, CO	n/a	n/a	n/a	n/a	n/a	n/a	n/a	n/a	n/a
Columbia, MO	n/a	n/a	n/a	n/a	n/a	n/a	n/a	n/a	n/a
Columbia, SC	74.1	69.0	65.6	68.9	69.5	66.1	63.9	70.7	69.3
Columbus, OH	62.2	59.7	60.7	60.5	60.0	59.0	57.5	57.9	64.8
Dallas, TX	63.8	62.6	61.8	59.9	57.7	57.8	59.7	61.8	62.0
Denver, CO	65.7	63.0	61.8	61.0	61.9	61.6	61.6	59.3	60.1
Des Moines, IA	n/a	n/a	n/a	n/a	n/a	n/a	n/a	n/a	n/a
Durham, NC	n/a	n/a	n/a	n/a	n/a	n/a	n/a	n/a	n/a
Edison, NJ	51.6	50.9	51.5	50.6	50.7	49.9	50.4	49.9	49.7
El Paso, TX	n/a	n/a	n/a	n/a	n/a	n/a	n/a	n/a	n/a
Eugene, OR	n/a	n/a	n/a	n/a	n/a	n/a	n/a	n/a	n/a
Evansville, IN	n/a	n/a	n/a	n/a	n/a	n/a	n/a	n/a	n/a
Fargo, ND	n/a	n/a	n/a	n/a	n/a	n/a	n/a	n/a	n/a
Fayetteville, NC	n/a	n/a	n/a	n/a	n/a	n/a	n/a	n/a	n/a
Fort Collins, CO	n/a	n/a	n/a	n/a	n/a	n/a	n/a	n/a	n/a
Fort Wayne, IN	n/a	n/a	n/a	n/a	n/a	n/a	n/a	n/a	n/a
Fort Worth, TX	63.8	62.6	61.8	59.9	57.7	57.8	59.7	61.8	62.0
Gainesville, FL	n/a	n/a	n/a	n/a	n/a	n/a	n/a	n/a	n/a
Grand Rapids, MI	76.4	76.4	76.9	73.7	71.6	75.8	76.2	71.7	73.0
Greeley, CO	n/a	n/a	n/a	n/a	n/a	n/a	n/a	n/a	n/a
Green Bay, WI	n/a	n/a	n/a	n/a	n/a	n/a	n/a	n/a	n/a
Greensboro, NC	68.8	62.7	64.9	67.9	68.1	65.4	62.9	61.9	63.2
Honolulu, HI	54.9	54.1	56.1	57.9	58.2	59.6	57.9	53.8	57.7
Houston, TX	61.4	61.3	62.1	60.5	60.4	60.3	59.0	58.9	60.1
Huntsville, AL	n/a	n/a	n/a	n/a	n/a	n/a	n/a	n/a	n/a
Indianapolis, IN	68.8	68.3	67.1	67.5	66.9	64.6	63.9	63.9	64.3
Jacksonville, FL	70.0	68.0	66.6	69.9	65.3	62.5	61.8	65.2	61.4
Kansas City, MO	68.8	68.5	65.1	65.6	66.1	65.0	62.4	62.4	64.3
Lafayette, LA	n/a	n/a	n/a	n/a	n/a	n/a	n/a	n/a	n/a
Las Cruces, NM	n/a	n/a	n/a	n/a	n/a	n/a	n/a	n/a	n/a
Las Vegas, NV	55.7	52.9	52.6	52.8	53.2	52.1	51.3	54.4	58.1
Lexington, KY	n/a	n/a	n/a	n/a	n/a	n/a	n/a	n/a	n/a
Lincoln, NE	n/a	n/a	n/a	n/a	n/a	n/a	n/a	n/a	n/a
Little Rock, AR	n/a	n/a	n/a	n/a	n/a	65.8	64.9	61.0	62.2
Los Angeles, CA	49.7	50.1	49.9	48.7	49.0	49.1	47.1	49.1	49.5
Louisville, KY	63.4	61.7	63.3	64.5	68.9	67.7	67.6	71.7	67.9

Table continued on next page.

Metro Area	2009	2010	2011	2012	2013	2014	2015	2016	2017
Madison, WI	n/a	n/a	n/a	n/a	n/a	n/a	n/a	n/a	n/a
Manchester, NH	n/a	n/a	n/a	n/a	n/a	n/a	n/a	n/a	n/a
McAllen, TX	n/a	n/a	n/a	n/a	n/a	n/a	n/a	n/a	n/a
Miami, FL	63.8	64.2	61.8	60.1	58.8	58.6	58.4	57.9	59.9
Midland, TX	n/a	n/a	n/a	n/a	n/a	n/a	n/a	n/a	n/a
Minneapolis, MN	71.2	69.1	70.8	71.7	69.7	67.9	69.1	70.1	67.8
Nashville, TN	70.4	69.6	64.9	63.9	67.1	67.4	65.0	69.4	68.3
New Orleans, LA	66.9	63.9	62.4	61.4	60.6	62.8	59.3	61.7	62.6
New York, NY	51.6	50.9	51.5	50.6	50.7	49.9	50.4	49.9	49.7
Oklahoma City, OK	70.0	69.6	67.3	67.6	65.7	61.4	63.1	64.7	64.6
Omaha, NE	73.2	71.6	72.4	70.6	68.7	69.6	69.2	65.5	67.8
Orlando, FL	70.8	68.6	68.0	65.5	62.3	58.4	58.5	59.5	58.5
Peoria, IL	n/a	n/a	n/a	n/a	n/a	n/a	n/a	n/a	n/a
Philadelphia, PA	70.7	69.7	69.5	69.1	67.0	67.0	64.7	65.6	67.4
Phoenix, AZ	66.5	63.3	63.1	62.2	61.9	61.0	62.6	64.0	65.3
Pittsburgh, PA	70.4	70.3	67.9	68.3	69.1	71.0	72.2	72.7	71.7
Portland, OR	63.7	63.7	63.9	60.9	59.8	58.9	61.8	61.1	59.2
Providence, RI	61.0	61.3	61.7	60.1	61.6	60.0	57.5	58.6	61.3
Provo, UT	n/a	n/a	n/a	n/a	n/a	n/a	n/a	n/a	n/a
Raleigh, NC	65.9	66.7	67.7	65.5	65.5	67.4	65.9	68.2	64.9
Reno, NV	n/a	n/a	n/a	n/a	n/a	n/a	n/a	n/a	n/a
Richmond, VA	68.1	65.2	67.0	65.4	72.6	67.4	61.7	63.1	62.9
Roanoke, VA	n/a	n/a	n/a	n/a	n/a	n/a	n/a	n/a	n/a
Rochester, MN	n/a	n/a	n/a	n/a	n/a	n/a	n/a	n/a	n/a
Salem, OR	n/a	n/a	n/a	n/a	n/a	n/a	n/a	n/a	n/a
Salt Lake City, UT	65.5	66.4	66.9	66.8	68.2	69.1	69.2	68.1	69.5
San Antonio, TX	70.1	66.5	67.5	70.1	70.2	66.0	61.6	62.5	64.4
San Diego, CA	54.4	55.2	55.4	55.0	57.4	51.8	53.3	56.0	56.1
San Francisco, CA	58.0	56.1	53.2	55.2	54.6	56.3	55.8	55.7	55.6
San Jose, CA	58.9	60.4	58.6	56.4	56.4	50.7	49.9	50.4	50.4
Santa Rosa, CA	n/a	n/a	n/a	n/a	n/a	n/a	n/a	n/a	n/a
Savannah, GA	n/a	n/a	n/a	n/a	n/a	n/a	n/a	n/a	n/a
Seattle, WA	60.9	60.7	60.4	61.0	61.3	59.5	57.7	59.5	62.5
Sioux Falls, SD	n/a	n/a	n/a	n/a	n/a	n/a	n/a	n/a	n/a
Springfield, IL	n/a	n/a	n/a	n/a	n/a	n/a	n/a	n/a	n/a
Tallahassee, FL	n/a	n/a	n/a	n/a	n/a	n/a	n/a	n/a	n/a
Tampa, FL	68.3	68.3	67.0	65.3	64.9	64.9	62.9	60.4	64.9
Topeka, KS	n/a	n/a	n/a	n/a	n/a	n/a	n/a	n/a	n/a
Tyler, TX	n/a	n/a	n/a	n/a	n/a	n/a	n/a	n/a	n/a
Virginia Beach, VA	61.4	62.3	62.0	63.3	64.1	59.4	59.6	65.3	62.8
Visalia, CA	n/a	n/a	n/a	n/a	n/a	n/a	n/a	n/a	n/a
Washington, DC	67.3	67.6	66.9	66.0	65.0	64.6	63.1	63.3	62.9
Wilmington, NC	n/a	n/a	n/a	n/a	n/a	n/a	n/a	n/a	n/a
Winston-Salem, NC	n/a	n/a	n/a	n/a	n/a	n/a	n/a	n/a	n/a
U.S.	67.4	66.9	66.1	65.4	65.1	64.5	63.7	63.4	63.9

Note: Figures are percentages and cover the Metropolitan Statistical Area—see Appendix B for areas included
Source: U.S. Census Bureau, Housing Vacancies and Homeownership Annual Statistics: 2009-2017

Year Housing Structure Built: City

City	2010 or Later	2000 -2009	1990 -1999	1980 -1989	1970 -1979	1960 -1969	1950 -1959	1940 -1949	Before 1940	Median Year
Albany, NY	0.9	2.5	3.3	5.6	9.2	8.2	10.0	7.9	52.4	<1940
Albuquerque, NM	2.5	17.0	15.6	15.5	19.4	11.2	11.5	4.5	2.7	1980
Allentown, PA	1.8	5.5	3.6	5.0	11.3	11.0	16.7	8.3	36.9	1953
Anchorage, AK	2.7	12.6	11.4	26.2	28.9	10.7	5.8	1.3	0.4	1981
Ann Arbor, MI	2.2	6.7	10.4	10.4	16.8	17.7	14.0	5.8	16.0	1968
Athens, GA	2.5	17.3	19.7	16.0	18.0	12.0	6.9	2.6	4.9	1983
Atlanta, GA	4.7	23.5	10.6	7.8	8.7	13.6	11.5	6.3	13.2	1976
Austin, TX	7.5	19.6	16.4	20.4	17.3	7.9	5.3	2.7	2.9	1987
Baton Rouge, LA	3.4	10.3	9.2	13.6	21.5	18.0	12.6	6.0	5.4	1974
Billings, MT	4.8	12.8	12.2	11.9	19.1	10.4	14.6	6.5	7.7	1976
Boise City, ID	3.6	12.5	22.4	15.9	19.8	7.3	7.9	4.2	6.5	1983
Boston, MA	2.8	6.7	4.0	6.1	7.7	8.4	7.3	5.8	51.3	<1940
Boulder, CO	3.7	8.5	10.5	16.2	23.6	18.9	8.7	2.1	7.7	1975
Cape Coral, FL	2.0	39.3	17.0	23.4	12.2	5.0	0.7	0.2	0.2	1995
Cedar Rapids, IA	4.2	12.2	14.0	8.1	14.8	14.4	12.2	4.4	15.7	1972
Charleston, SC	7.1	22.3	12.5	14.1	12.3	8.6	6.5	4.6	12.0	1984
Charlotte, NC	5.1	23.9	20.4	15.5	12.2	10.1	6.9	2.9	3.0	1990
Chicago, IL	1.5	8.1	4.7	4.2	7.4	9.8	12.2	9.1	43.1	1948
Clarksville, TN	11.0	24.6	21.2	12.0	12.5	9.2	5.0	2.1	2.3	1993
College Station, TX	10.2	25.9	19.5	18.1	17.9	4.3	2.1	0.9	1.0	1993
Colorado Springs, CO	3.5	16.8	15.9	19.2	18.5	10.7	7.5	2.0	5.9	1983
Columbia, MO	6.9	23.7	17.4	14.0	12.7	11.3	5.6	2.7	5.8	1989
Columbia, SC	4.2	16.2	11.1	9.5	10.5	13.0	14.4	10.0	11.0	1971
Columbus, OH	3.5	12.3	15.1	12.8	15.8	12.1	11.1	5.2	12.1	1976
Dallas, TX	4.2	11.3	10.1	18.0	17.7	13.8	13.8	5.6	5.6	1976
Denver, CO	5.3	12.2	6.8	7.7	14.3	11.2	15.7	7.1	19.7	1967
Des Moines, IA	2.1	7.7	7.0	6.3	12.8	10.6	16.7	8.5	28.3	1958
Durham, NC	6.4	21.7	17.6	16.1	10.9	9.3	7.1	4.3	6.5	1987
Edison, NJ	1.0	4.7	9.6	24.4	14.3	19.8	17.0	4.5	4.9	1973
El Paso, TX	7.3	16.0	13.5	13.8	16.8	12.0	11.9	4.3	4.5	1980
Eugene, OR	4.5	11.6	16.8	8.3	22.7	13.2	10.5	5.0	7.3	1976
Evansville, IN	0.9	6.0	7.1	8.6	12.9	10.5	17.7	12.1	24.1	1958
Fargo, ND	10.3	15.9	18.9	13.9	15.1	6.8	6.7	2.8	9.5	1986
Fayetteville, NC	5.4	13.2	17.6	17.8	21.0	13.4	7.2	2.8	1.6	1982
Fort Collins, CO	5.9	18.4	21.3	16.1	19.5	8.1	3.6	1.6	5.6	1987
Fort Wayne, IN	0.8	6.6	14.1	11.7	16.7	15.6	12.2	6.9	15.3	1970
Fort Worth, TX	6.6	26.4	11.6	13.0	10.4	8.5	11.5	5.4	6.5	1986
Gainesville, FL	2.5	13.8	15.6	19.9	21.1	12.3	9.2	3.0	2.6	1981
Grand Rapids, MI	1.2	4.2	6.0	7.1	8.8	10.6	15.9	8.9	37.3	1952
Greeley, CO	3.6	19.5	16.4	10.6	20.1	11.3	7.4	2.6	8.6	1980
Green Bay, WI	1.3	7.4	9.7	12.8	17.0	13.7	14.3	6.6	17.3	1969
Greensboro, NC	3.0	14.5	18.3	18.3	15.8	11.2	9.8	3.6	5.5	1982
Honolulu, HI	2.6	7.2	8.0	9.8	25.4	23.2	13.0	5.6	5.1	1971
Houston, TX	4.9	14.4	9.9	14.2	22.5	14.2	10.8	4.6	4.4	1977
Huntsville, AL	7.8	14.2	11.3	14.4	15.1	20.8	10.6	2.8	2.9	1978
Indianapolis, IN	2.2	10.0	13.1	11.9	14.0	13.2	12.8	6.0	16.9	1971
Jacksonville, FL	3.9	19.7	15.1	15.8	13.1	10.7	11.3	5.1	5.3	1983
Kansas City, MO	2.8	10.6	9.2	8.5	12.3	13.6	14.7	6.8	21.4	1965
Lafayette, LA	4.4	13.9	9.5	18.4	21.7	13.8	10.6	4.6	3.2	1978
Las Cruces, NM	6.3	24.7	16.4	15.0	14.4	8.9	9.2	2.5	2.7	1988
Las Vegas, NV	3.1	24.2	31.9	17.4	10.0	7.4	4.2	1.3	0.4	1993
Lexington, KY	4.0	16.1	16.1	14.5	15.3	13.6	9.8	3.2	7.3	1980
Lincoln, NE	4.3	14.9	15.2	11.2	15.2	10.8	11.3	3.4	13.8	1977
Little Rock, AR	3.7	11.1	13.3	17.2	19.8	13.9	9.4	4.7	6.9	1978
Los Angeles, CA	1.8	5.9	5.7	10.2	13.9	13.8	17.8	10.2	20.6	1961

Table continued on next page.

City	2010 or Later	2000 -2009	1990 -1999	1980 -1989	1970 -1979	1960 -1969	1950 -1959	1940 -1949	Before 1940	Median Year
Louisville, KY	2.6	11.7	11.7	7.3	13.6	13.4	14.8	7.3	17.6	1968
Madison, WI	3.8	15.9	13.4	11.4	14.5	11.5	11.1	4.8	13.6	1976
Manchester, NH	1.5	6.6	7.5	16.0	10.5	7.7	10.7	6.1	33.3	1960
McAllen, TX	5.1	24.2	19.6	19.7	16.7	7.4	3.9	1.6	1.9	1989
Miami, FL	4.0	19.5	6.4	8.1	12.8	10.3	15.1	13.6	10.3	1971
Midland, TX	8.1	9.0	14.5	19.5	13.2	13.1	17.9	3.1	1.6	1981
Minneapolis, MN	3.3	7.4	3.3	6.2	9.2	7.5	10.0	7.3	45.8	1946
Nashville, TN	4.7	15.2	12.3	16.1	15.4	13.4	11.7	5.0	6.3	1979
New Orleans, LA	2.4	7.9	3.8	7.4	13.5	11.4	11.6	8.2	33.8	1957
New York, NY	1.7	5.9	3.6	4.7	7.1	12.7	13.3	10.4	40.5	1949
Oklahoma City, OK	6.2	13.9	10.0	15.3	15.9	13.0	10.8	6.2	8.8	1977
Omaha, NE	2.2	6.7	12.4	11.0	15.9	14.6	11.7	4.7	20.8	1969
Orlando, FL	5.2	23.1	17.0	17.3	14.0	7.8	9.3	3.2	3.1	1987
Peoria, IL	2.1	8.7	7.3	6.9	14.6	13.7	15.8	8.3	22.6	1962
Philadelphia, PA	1.5	3.2	3.2	3.9	6.7	10.7	16.1	13.6	41.1	1946
Phoenix, AZ	2.5	17.4	16.1	17.8	19.7	10.9	10.7	2.9	2.0	1982
Pittsburgh, PA	1.2	3.4	3.3	4.5	6.9	8.1	12.1	9.1	51.4	<1940
Portland, OR	3.2	10.9	8.8	6.0	11.0	9.1	12.1	8.5	30.3	1959
Providence, RI	0.6	5.5	4.5	5.2	8.2	5.9	8.4	7.3	54.3	<1940
Provo, UT	2.3	12.3	21.7	13.2	18.8	10.4	7.7	5.9	7.8	1980
Raleigh, NC	6.6	26.6	19.9	17.6	10.7	8.3	5.1	2.0	3.1	1992
Reno, NV	3.4	21.3	18.5	14.5	17.8	10.0	7.4	3.3	3.6	1985
Richmond, VA	2.5	5.6	4.8	5.9	11.2	12.6	15.5	9.5	32.4	1955
Roanoke, VA	0.9	5.5	5.9	6.6	12.0	13.2	20.9	10.3	24.7	1957
Rochester, MN	4.8	19.5	14.7	14.3	13.8	11.6	9.7	3.6	8.1	1982
Salem, OR	2.2	13.0	16.3	11.6	22.7	9.4	10.4	5.7	8.6	1977
Salt Lake City, UT	2.7	6.1	6.9	7.5	13.4	9.7	13.7	10.0	30.1	1957
San Antonio, TX	4.9	16.8	13.8	16.9	15.7	10.4	10.2	5.7	5.6	1981
San Diego, CA	2.1	10.3	11.7	18.1	21.4	12.8	12.4	4.3	6.9	1976
San Francisco, CA	1.9	6.7	4.4	5.3	7.5	8.1	8.6	9.4	48.0	1942
San Jose, CA	3.1	9.8	10.8	13.1	24.5	18.9	11.5	3.2	5.2	1975
Santa Rosa, CA	1.5	13.1	13.1	18.8	22.9	12.2	7.7	5.3	5.5	1978
Savannah, GA	4.6	10.9	7.5	10.1	13.4	13.3	14.9	8.2	16.9	1967
Seattle, WA	5.8	13.7	8.6	7.9	8.2	9.1	10.9	8.8	27.1	1964
Sioux Falls, SD	8.8	19.3	15.9	11.3	14.6	7.7	8.9	4.8	8.7	1985
Springfield, IL	1.5	9.2	12.8	9.9	15.0	13.4	11.9	7.0	19.2	1969
Tallahassee, FL	2.8	19.3	21.2	18.0	17.0	9.5	7.6	2.9	1.6	1986
Tampa, FL	5.0	19.0	12.0	11.8	11.7	10.7	15.8	5.2	8.8	1978
Topeka, KS	0.9	7.3	9.8	9.9	14.5	16.1	16.4	6.7	18.5	1965
Tyler, TX	4.5	16.0	12.1	13.6	16.9	12.4	14.7	4.8	5.0	1978
Virginia Beach, VA	2.8	11.2	13.7	28.5	22.2	12.6	6.5	1.6	1.1	1982
Visalia, CA	3.5	22.5	14.5	17.1	19.2	9.6	7.0	3.8	2.8	1984
Washington, DC	4.4	8.7	3.0	4.5	7.8	11.6	12.8	11.9	35.3	1952
Wilmington, NC	3.5	14.8	22.0	16.4	13.6	7.8	6.5	6.2	9.3	1984
Winston-Salem, NC	3.2	14.8	11.6	13.6	16.4	14.9	12.7	4.9	7.9	1976
U.S.	3.2	14.5	14.0	13.6	15.5	10.8	10.5	5.1	12.9	1977

Note: Figures are percentages except for Median Year
Source: U.S. Census Bureau, 2013-2017 American Community Survey 5-Year Estimates

Year Housing Structure Built: Metro Area

Metro Area	2010 or Later	2000 -2009	1990 -1999	1980 -1989	1970 -1979	1960 -1969	1950 -1959	1940 -1949	Before 1940	Median Year
Albany, NY	2.8	8.7	9.8	11.2	12.1	9.1	10.9	5.9	29.6	1964
Albuquerque, NM	2.6	18.4	18.2	16.8	18.0	9.6	9.3	3.8	3.2	1984
Allentown, PA	1.9	11.7	10.5	10.8	12.8	9.7	11.6	5.4	25.8	1968
Anchorage, AK	3.2	17.8	13.0	25.9	24.9	8.9	4.8	1.1	0.4	1984
Ann Arbor, MI	2.2	13.5	17.3	11.1	16.4	12.3	10.9	4.5	11.9	1976
Athens, GA	2.9	19.2	20.6	16.9	17.4	9.9	5.9	2.3	5.0	1986
Atlanta, GA	3.3	25.7	22.3	17.9	12.9	7.9	4.9	2.0	3.1	1991
Austin, TX	9.9	27.4	19.4	17.6	12.5	5.2	3.6	2.0	2.4	1993
Baton Rouge, LA	5.9	21.9	14.9	15.3	17.4	10.8	7.3	2.9	3.7	1985
Billings, MT	4.6	13.8	12.9	12.6	20.4	9.4	11.8	5.2	9.5	1977
Boise City, ID	6.0	25.9	22.3	10.9	16.9	4.9	4.8	3.3	5.1	1992
Boston, MA	2.4	7.8	7.5	10.5	11.1	10.4	10.8	5.6	33.9	1960
Boulder, CO	3.8	12.9	19.2	16.9	21.5	12.0	5.0	1.8	6.9	1982
Cape Coral, FL	3.0	32.8	17.7	21.9	15.3	5.6	2.6	0.5	0.7	1992
Cedar Rapids, IA	4.4	14.7	15.3	7.3	13.7	12.7	10.0	3.9	17.9	1974
Charleston, SC	7.0	23.7	16.5	17.4	14.5	8.9	5.4	2.8	3.8	1988
Charlotte, NC	5.4	25.3	20.2	14.1	12.0	8.7	6.7	3.3	4.3	1990
Chicago, IL	1.4	11.7	11.1	8.9	14.1	11.9	13.3	6.2	21.4	1968
Clarksville, TN	8.6	21.9	20.2	11.3	15.5	10.4	6.0	2.5	3.6	1990
College Station, TX	8.4	21.9	18.1	17.9	16.8	6.1	5.4	2.4	3.0	1989
Colorado Springs, CO	4.5	20.0	17.0	17.9	17.4	9.3	6.7	1.6	5.4	1985
Columbia, MO	5.7	21.9	18.5	14.1	16.2	10.4	5.2	2.4	5.6	1987
Columbia, SC	5.3	20.5	18.5	14.9	16.1	10.3	7.4	3.1	3.8	1986
Columbus, OH	3.5	14.8	16.6	11.9	14.7	11.3	10.5	4.3	12.4	1978
Dallas, TX	6.1	21.6	16.7	18.8	14.5	9.0	7.6	2.8	2.9	1987
Denver, CO	4.4	17.2	15.4	14.4	19.2	9.7	9.7	3.0	7.0	1981
Des Moines, IA	7.1	18.0	13.5	8.7	13.8	9.0	9.7	4.5	15.7	1978
Durham, NC	5.7	20.4	19.0	16.7	12.8	9.4	6.7	3.3	5.9	1987
Edison, NJ	1.7	7.1	6.1	8.0	10.0	13.8	16.1	9.0	28.2	1958
El Paso, TX	8.0	17.5	14.7	14.4	16.2	10.8	10.6	3.8	4.1	1983
Eugene, OR	3.1	11.6	15.5	8.9	23.4	13.9	9.7	6.4	7.5	1975
Evansville, IN	2.3	11.7	13.0	11.0	15.6	9.6	13.0	7.7	16.1	1972
Fargo, ND	9.8	18.7	15.9	11.3	16.0	7.7	8.0	2.9	9.8	1985
Fayetteville, NC	6.4	18.0	20.8	16.2	17.6	10.8	6.0	2.3	1.9	1987
Fort Collins, CO	5.6	20.2	20.8	14.1	19.9	7.6	3.9	1.8	6.2	1988
Fort Wayne, IN	2.5	11.0	15.2	11.0	15.1	13.3	10.5	5.7	15.6	1973
Fort Worth, TX	6.1	21.6	16.7	18.8	14.5	9.0	7.6	2.8	2.9	1987
Gainesville, FL	3.0	18.4	19.7	20.5	18.4	8.6	6.6	2.1	2.5	1986
Grand Rapids, MI	2.4	13.0	16.3	12.5	14.5	9.8	10.8	5.2	15.5	1976
Greeley, CO	6.2	30.9	17.0	7.8	15.5	6.6	4.8	2.3	9.0	1992
Green Bay, WI	3.2	15.8	16.1	12.1	15.9	10.0	9.3	4.5	13.1	1978
Greensboro, NC	3.0	15.9	19.1	15.6	15.3	10.9	9.4	4.5	6.2	1982
Honolulu, HI	3.5	10.6	11.9	12.3	24.2	19.0	11.0	4.1	3.3	1975
Houston, TX	7.6	23.1	14.7	15.8	18.2	8.9	6.5	2.7	2.5	1987
Huntsville, AL	7.2	20.9	19.1	15.6	12.5	13.4	6.8	2.1	2.5	1988
Indianapolis, IN	4.1	16.6	16.8	10.7	12.9	10.9	10.5	4.4	13.1	1979
Jacksonville, FL	5.2	23.5	16.7	17.3	12.8	8.6	8.2	3.6	4.1	1987
Kansas City, MO	2.7	14.3	14.5	12.4	16.0	12.1	11.8	4.6	11.6	1976
Lafayette, LA	6.6	17.7	13.1	15.6	16.9	10.5	9.5	4.5	5.7	1982
Las Cruces, NM	5.5	21.3	19.3	18.5	15.4	7.5	6.6	2.7	3.2	1988
Las Vegas, NV	4.3	32.0	29.2	15.1	10.8	5.3	2.3	0.7	0.4	1995
Lexington, KY	4.0	17.7	17.5	14.3	15.3	11.7	8.2	3.3	8.0	1982
Lincoln, NE	4.5	15.4	15.2	10.7	15.5	10.5	10.5	3.2	14.5	1977
Little Rock, AR	6.3	18.8	18.0	15.1	17.6	10.5	6.9	3.2	3.6	1985
Los Angeles, CA	1.7	6.4	7.6	12.5	16.3	15.9	18.9	8.6	12.0	1967

Table continued on next page.

Metro Area	2010 or Later	2000 -2009	1990 -1999	1980 -1989	1970 -1979	1960 -1969	1950 -1959	1940 -1949	Before 1940	Median Year
Louisville, KY	2.7	13.9	14.4	9.4	15.8	12.2	12.5	6.2	12.9	1974
Madison, WI	3.8	17.3	16.0	11.3	15.7	9.5	8.2	3.6	14.6	1979
Manchester, NH	1.9	10.3	10.4	21.2	15.3	9.6	7.3	3.7	20.3	1976
McAllen, TX	6.7	30.4	22.8	16.5	11.9	5.4	3.3	1.5	1.5	1994
Miami, FL	2.1	13.6	15.2	19.6	21.7	12.6	10.0	3.0	2.3	1980
Midland, TX	9.5	10.3	15.2	19.6	13.3	11.7	15.8	3.0	1.6	1982
Minneapolis, MN	3.0	14.9	14.5	14.7	15.0	9.9	9.9	3.8	14.4	1978
Nashville, TN	5.9	20.9	18.7	14.9	14.0	9.9	7.5	3.4	4.8	1987
New Orleans, LA	2.6	12.5	9.8	13.5	19.4	13.9	9.7	5.2	13.5	1974
New York, NY	1.7	7.1	6.1	8.0	10.0	13.8	16.1	9.0	28.2	1958
Oklahoma City, OK	6.2	15.6	11.5	15.1	17.4	12.4	9.9	5.3	6.5	1979
Omaha, NE	4.4	15.0	12.9	10.1	14.8	11.9	9.1	3.8	17.9	1975
Orlando, FL	4.9	25.3	21.2	20.7	13.5	6.2	5.4	1.3	1.6	1991
Peoria, IL	2.2	9.0	8.7	6.2	17.3	13.3	15.3	8.2	19.9	1965
Philadelphia, PA	1.9	8.1	9.6	10.1	12.2	12.1	15.8	8.3	22.0	1963
Phoenix, AZ	3.8	26.8	20.6	17.6	16.4	7.3	5.3	1.3	1.0	1991
Pittsburgh, PA	1.8	6.6	7.6	7.3	12.1	11.4	17.0	9.1	27.1	1958
Portland, OR	3.8	15.3	18.8	11.4	17.7	8.7	7.2	4.6	12.6	1980
Providence, RI	1.2	6.5	8.2	10.8	12.2	10.6	11.8	6.5	32.0	1960
Provo, UT	8.0	27.9	20.3	9.4	15.3	5.2	5.1	3.5	5.2	1993
Raleigh, NC	7.6	28.2	24.1	15.7	9.8	6.1	4.0	1.6	2.8	1994
Reno, NV	3.0	22.7	20.6	15.5	18.6	9.1	5.6	2.3	2.6	1988
Richmond, VA	3.9	15.8	15.6	15.8	15.5	9.7	9.7	4.5	9.5	1981
Roanoke, VA	1.7	12.3	12.7	12.1	16.6	12.9	13.2	5.9	12.5	1973
Rochester, MN	4.0	18.6	14.9	12.2	13.8	9.8	8.1	3.7	15.0	1980
Salem, OR	2.5	14.6	17.6	10.8	23.7	10.3	7.9	4.4	8.3	1978
Salt Lake City, UT	5.4	16.1	16.0	12.9	19.2	9.0	9.1	4.0	8.3	1980
San Antonio, TX	7.4	22.1	14.9	15.9	14.0	8.7	7.8	4.4	4.8	1986
San Diego, CA	2.2	12.2	12.5	19.6	22.8	12.0	10.8	3.5	4.4	1978
San Francisco, CA	1.9	8.0	8.3	11.3	15.0	13.3	14.0	8.0	20.3	1966
San Jose, CA	3.2	9.3	10.7	12.7	22.1	18.4	14.5	4.0	5.0	1974
Santa Rosa, CA	1.4	10.9	13.5	18.7	21.2	11.6	8.6	5.4	8.7	1977
Savannah, GA	5.6	22.6	15.9	14.3	11.8	8.3	8.4	4.7	8.4	1986
Seattle, WA	4.7	15.8	16.0	14.8	14.8	11.0	7.7	4.5	10.6	1981
Sioux Falls, SD	7.7	20.1	15.6	10.1	14.6	7.2	8.0	4.4	12.2	1983
Springfield, IL	2.2	10.3	13.4	9.4	15.8	12.5	12.2	6.9	17.3	1971
Tallahassee, FL	2.9	19.4	23.0	19.7	16.0	8.4	6.2	2.4	2.0	1988
Tampa, FL	3.4	17.0	14.1	20.4	21.6	10.1	8.6	2.0	2.8	1982
Topeka, KS	1.3	9.7	12.7	10.6	16.5	13.7	12.2	5.2	18.0	1971
Tyler, TX	4.9	17.9	16.0	16.9	16.7	9.6	10.4	3.6	4.0	1983
Virginia Beach, VA	3.7	13.3	15.2	19.4	16.0	11.9	10.1	4.7	5.7	1981
Visalia, CA	3.3	17.1	14.6	15.6	18.7	10.6	8.6	5.5	6.0	1980
Washington, DC	4.1	15.1	14.6	16.1	14.6	12.2	9.6	5.1	8.5	1980
Wilmington, NC	4.3	21.4	24.7	16.1	13.2	6.5	5.0	3.8	5.0	1990
Winston-Salem, NC	2.8	16.4	17.1	15.6	16.8	11.5	9.3	4.2	6.4	1981
U.S.	3.2	14.5	14.0	13.6	15.5	10.8	10.5	5.1	12.9	1977

Note: Figures are percentages except for Median Year; Figures cover the Metropolitan Statistical Area—see Appendix B for areas included
Source: U.S. Census Bureau, 2013-2017 American Community Survey 5-Year Estimates

Gross Monthly Rent: City

City	Under $500	$500 -$999	$1,000 -$1,499	$1,500 -$1,999	$2,000 -$2,499	$2,500 -$2,999	$3,000 and up	Median ($)
Albany, NY	11.4	49.6	32.3	4.9	1.0	0.4	0.4	924
Albuquerque, NM	9.0	56.9	27.5	5.1	0.8	0.2	0.4	833
Allentown, PA	11.0	47.3	34.1	6.4	0.9	0.1	0.1	938
Anchorage, AK	3.9	21.7	40.6	17.9	12.0	2.6	1.3	1,261
Ann Arbor, MI	5.3	30.6	38.6	14.9	6.2	2.0	2.3	1,166
Athens, GA	8.8	61.9	22.1	5.4	1.4	0.1	0.2	815
Atlanta, GA	11.9	35.1	34.0	13.6	3.4	1.1	1.0	1,037
Austin, TX	3.4	29.2	42.9	17.3	4.9	1.2	1.2	1,165
Baton Rouge, LA	10.6	59.8	21.0	5.4	2.1	0.8	0.3	827
Billings, MT	11.8	57.0	21.0	5.8	1.0	0.7	2.7	826
Boise City, ID	7.4	59.8	26.2	3.9	1.5	0.2	1.0	875
Boston, MA	18.2	13.1	21.2	23.1	12.1	6.2	6.0	1,445
Boulder, CO	3.0	16.7	36.1	23.7	10.7	4.5	5.2	1,412
Cape Coral, FL	1.2	31.5	49.7	12.5	3.5	0.8	0.8	1,136
Cedar Rapids, IA	19.6	63.9	13.8	1.4	0.8	0.2	0.4	729
Charleston, SC	7.4	31.5	37.5	16.2	4.0	1.6	1.8	1,135
Charlotte, NC	4.4	43.8	39.0	9.8	1.9	0.4	0.7	1,018
Chicago, IL	9.9	37.9	29.9	13.5	5.1	2.1	1.6	1,029
Clarksville, TN	6.2	51.2	34.3	6.5	1.7	0.1	0.1	930
College Station, TX	2.2	54.7	25.4	12.1	4.7	0.6	0.2	940
Colorado Springs, CO	5.0	44.0	33.3	13.1	2.7	1.2	0.7	1,013
Columbia, MO	8.3	60.8	22.1	4.9	2.9	0.6	0.2	825
Columbia, SC	12.0	54.5	26.3	5.6	1.3	0.0	0.3	878
Columbus, OH	7.9	56.3	29.0	4.8	1.5	0.2	0.3	889
Dallas, TX	5.4	51.6	29.7	8.5	2.7	1.1	0.8	937
Denver, CO	8.8	31.1	33.5	17.2	6.3	1.8	1.3	1,131
Des Moines, IA	11.5	64.3	20.0	3.2	0.7	0.2	0.1	797
Durham, NC	7.3	48.3	34.1	7.8	1.4	0.3	0.7	958
Edison, NJ	2.3	9.1	44.7	33.3	9.3	0.7	0.5	1,438
El Paso, TX	19.6	53.6	22.4	3.2	0.8	0.3	0.2	792
Eugene, OR	8.4	46.5	32.3	8.6	2.8	0.5	0.9	956
Evansville, IN	15.1	69.4	14.4	0.7	0.2	0.0	0.1	738
Fargo, ND	9.6	69.6	15.7	3.6	1.3	0.2	0.0	765
Fayetteville, NC	7.1	56.5	32.3	3.5	0.4	0.0	0.2	892
Fort Collins, CO	4.1	29.4	38.7	21.5	5.3	0.6	0.4	1,191
Fort Wayne, IN	16.0	70.7	10.8	1.6	0.7	0.1	0.1	708
Fort Worth, TX	5.8	48.0	31.8	10.7	2.3	0.9	0.5	967
Gainesville, FL	7.5	56.6	27.2	6.4	1.4	0.5	0.4	886
Grand Rapids, MI	11.5	56.8	24.4	5.8	1.2	0.3	0.1	854
Greeley, CO	12.0	49.1	26.0	10.5	1.5	0.4	0.5	881
Green Bay, WI	16.6	70.5	11.5	0.9	0.2	0.0	0.3	682
Greensboro, NC	8.1	68.6	19.2	2.5	0.9	0.3	0.4	813
Honolulu, HI	6.7	15.4	33.4	20.7	10.9	6.1	6.8	1,411
Houston, TX	4.7	51.9	28.5	10.1	2.7	1.1	1.1	940
Huntsville, AL	14.6	61.9	20.2	2.2	0.5	0.3	0.3	773
Indianapolis, IN	7.4	64.4	23.5	3.5	0.7	0.2	0.3	840
Jacksonville, FL	7.0	44.9	37.6	8.2	1.6	0.4	0.3	984
Kansas City, MO	10.7	55.4	27.3	4.7	1.3	0.2	0.5	862
Lafayette, LA	11.3	57.3	23.7	5.4	2.0	0.2	0.1	853
Las Cruces, NM	15.2	60.3	20.9	2.5	0.9	0.0	0.2	770
Las Vegas, NV	5.4	42.3	38.4	10.6	2.2	0.6	0.4	1,024
Lexington, KY	11.9	56.7	24.9	4.0	1.7	0.3	0.5	828
Lincoln, NE	13.8	61.4	20.1	3.0	0.6	0.4	0.8	788
Little Rock, AR	9.7	60.1	25.0	3.3	1.1	0.3	0.4	842
Los Angeles, CA	5.8	21.5	35.0	19.9	9.8	4.2	3.8	1,302

Table continued on next page.

City	Under $500	$500 -$999	$1,000 -$1,499	$1,500 -$1,999	$2,000 -$2,499	$2,500 -$2,999	$3,000 and up	Median ($)
Louisville, KY	15.9	60.6	19.1	3.3	0.6	0.3	0.1	779
Madison, WI	4.3	45.0	34.4	11.2	3.2	1.1	0.8	1,008
Manchester, NH	6.9	36.2	44.2	10.2	2.1	0.1	0.4	1,063
McAllen, TX	14.5	63.7	17.2	3.2	0.9	0.1	0.4	758
Miami, FL	11.3	34.6	28.8	14.7	5.7	2.7	2.2	1,056
Midland, TX	2.6	30.0	41.5	19.1	4.1	1.9	0.8	1,179
Minneapolis, MN	14.1	42.0	28.1	10.8	3.5	0.9	0.5	941
Nashville, TN	9.4	44.0	34.2	8.7	2.6	0.7	0.4	970
New Orleans, LA	12.7	42.5	31.4	9.6	2.5	0.7	0.6	954
New York, NY	11.1	17.2	31.6	20.4	9.0	4.5	6.3	1,340
Oklahoma City, OK	9.7	61.7	21.8	5.2	1.1	0.3	0.3	819
Omaha, NE	9.3	57.0	26.9	4.7	1.3	0.4	0.3	861
Orlando, FL	3.8	35.6	44.9	12.3	2.5	0.6	0.4	1,091
Peoria, IL	17.7	60.6	15.4	4.1	1.3	0.5	0.4	756
Philadelphia, PA	11.8	41.6	32.0	9.3	3.1	1.2	1.1	970
Phoenix, AZ	6.0	48.8	34.1	8.3	1.8	0.6	0.4	954
Pittsburgh, PA	15.3	46.3	25.2	9.3	2.7	0.8	0.4	887
Portland, OR	7.4	33.9	34.4	15.9	5.3	1.8	1.3	1,109
Providence, RI	19.6	36.7	33.7	6.7	2.0	0.7	0.6	949
Provo, UT	14.6	55.7	21.1	6.7	1.8	0.1	0.1	793
Raleigh, NC	4.1	44.9	38.8	9.1	1.9	0.4	0.8	1,010
Reno, NV	7.9	51.8	27.5	10.4	1.7	0.5	0.1	906
Richmond, VA	12.6	44.6	31.9	8.1	2.3	0.3	0.3	942
Roanoke, VA	14.7	62.8	19.5	2.0	0.3	0.4	0.2	776
Rochester, MN	10.8	47.7	28.2	9.6	2.0	0.4	1.3	891
Salem, OR	7.8	58.5	24.5	6.4	1.5	0.3	1.0	861
Salt Lake City, UT	10.3	52.2	26.7	8.5	1.6	0.5	0.2	881
San Antonio, TX	8.9	50.8	31.1	7.3	1.2	0.4	0.4	918
San Diego, CA	3.8	15.2	30.9	24.4	15.7	6.3	3.8	1,503
San Francisco, CA	10.2	14.5	17.9	17.8	13.7	10.5	15.4	1,709
San Jose, CA	4.8	8.5	20.7	24.7	18.3	12.2	10.6	1,822
Santa Rosa, CA	5.7	13.5	35.4	27.3	13.6	3.4	1.1	1,432
Savannah, GA	11.5	45.7	33.6	6.4	1.5	0.5	0.8	942
Seattle, WA	7.6	17.9	32.4	24.1	10.1	4.5	3.4	1,377
Sioux Falls, SD	11.3	68.2	16.5	2.5	0.4	0.7	0.5	771
Springfield, IL	14.8	64.8	16.7	2.4	0.7	0.5	0.1	765
Tallahassee, FL	5.9	49.7	32.6	8.1	3.0	0.5	0.3	957
Tampa, FL	9.2	38.0	34.3	12.3	3.9	1.3	0.9	1,031
Topeka, KS	16.9	61.9	15.8	3.1	1.8	0.2	0.3	751
Tyler, TX	8.4	59.3	23.4	6.5	1.7	0.2	0.5	864
Virginia Beach, VA	2.9	16.2	49.0	22.3	6.7	1.6	1.3	1,296
Visalia, CA	5.9	48.8	32.8	9.3	2.8	0.4	0.1	958
Washington, DC	11.0	16.7	25.7	19.5	12.6	7.0	7.6	1,424
Wilmington, NC	14.9	48.9	28.3	5.8	0.9	0.3	0.9	889
Winston-Salem, NC	13.8	64.8	17.4	2.5	1.1	0.0	0.4	765
U.S.	10.5	41.1	28.7	11.7	4.5	1.8	1.7	982

Note: Figures are percentages except for Median; Gross rent is the contract rent plus the estimated average monthly cost of utilities (electricity, gas, and water and sewer) and fuels (oil, coal, kerosene, wood, etc.) if these are paid by the renter (or paid for the renter by someone else).

Source: U.S. Census Bureau, 2013-2017 American Community Survey 5-Year Estimates

Gross Monthly Rent: Metro Area

MSA[1]	Under $500	$500 -$999	$1,000 -$1,499	$1,500 -$1,999	$2,000 -$2,499	$2,500 -2,999	$3,000 and up	Median ($)
Albany, NY	9.1	46.4	33.3	7.8	2.1	0.7	0.7	956
Albuquerque, NM	8.9	55.5	28.2	5.7	1.0	0.2	0.5	850
Allentown, PA	10.3	40.8	35.7	10.2	1.9	0.5	0.6	990
Anchorage, AK	4.2	23.5	39.9	17.9	11.0	2.3	1.2	1,237
Ann Arbor, MI	5.9	42.1	34.1	11.3	3.6	1.4	1.6	1,025
Athens, GA	9.2	62.3	21.5	5.1	1.3	0.3	0.2	813
Atlanta, GA	5.1	39.5	40.8	11.0	2.4	0.7	0.6	1,053
Austin, TX	3.6	30.5	41.8	17.3	4.6	1.2	1.1	1,155
Baton Rouge, LA	10.1	54.9	25.2	6.9	2.1	0.5	0.3	873
Billings, MT	12.5	56.7	21.4	5.5	1.1	0.6	2.2	822
Boise City, ID	9.9	55.4	28.3	4.5	1.1	0.2	0.5	879
Boston, MA	13.3	16.4	30.2	22.0	10.2	4.3	3.6	1,335
Boulder, CO	4.8	19.9	36.6	23.1	9.1	3.2	3.3	1,334
Cape Coral, FL	4.4	42.0	38.2	9.4	3.2	1.2	1.7	1,035
Cedar Rapids, IA	20.2	63.1	14.0	1.5	0.7	0.1	0.4	714
Charleston, SC	6.7	38.2	37.1	12.2	3.2	1.3	1.2	1,054
Charlotte, NC	7.1	50.5	32.0	7.6	1.7	0.5	0.6	935
Chicago, IL	8.0	38.1	33.0	13.4	4.6	1.6	1.3	1,048
Clarksville, TN	9.7	52.5	30.2	6.1	1.1	0.2	0.1	878
College Station, TX	5.7	57.7	22.9	9.6	3.4	0.5	0.2	885
Colorado Springs, CO	4.6	40.0	34.8	15.8	2.9	1.3	0.7	1,070
Columbia, MO	8.8	61.1	22.4	4.3	2.7	0.5	0.2	826
Columbia, SC	8.6	55.5	27.8	6.1	1.4	0.3	0.3	889
Columbus, OH	9.0	55.2	28.4	5.3	1.4	0.4	0.3	887
Dallas, TX	4.2	43.9	35.4	11.8	3.0	1.0	0.8	1,022
Denver, CO	5.4	28.1	37.4	19.8	6.3	1.6	1.3	1,203
Des Moines, IA	8.8	58.4	26.0	4.6	1.1	0.5	0.5	857
Durham, NC	7.8	48.3	32.4	8.0	1.9	0.7	0.9	953
Edison, NJ	9.5	16.9	34.1	21.1	9.1	4.2	5.1	1,341
El Paso, TX	19.6	53.2	22.5	3.5	0.8	0.2	0.2	789
Eugene, OR	8.6	50.4	31.2	6.8	2.0	0.3	0.6	921
Evansville, IN	15.9	66.6	15.4	1.1	0.2	0.2	0.5	732
Fargo, ND	10.6	66.9	16.4	4.3	1.3	0.3	0.1	770
Fayetteville, NC	7.8	56.1	30.8	4.5	0.6	0.0	0.1	883
Fort Collins, CO	4.9	33.4	36.7	18.7	4.6	1.0	0.6	1,140
Fort Wayne, IN	16.8	68.4	12.1	1.7	0.8	0.1	0.1	714
Fort Worth, TX	4.2	43.9	35.4	11.8	3.0	1.0	0.8	1,022
Gainesville, FL	7.8	52.5	29.7	7.2	1.5	0.8	0.5	912
Grand Rapids, MI	9.0	62.9	21.4	5.0	1.0	0.2	0.5	826
Greeley, CO	9.7	44.4	29.9	12.6	2.1	0.6	0.6	955
Green Bay, WI	13.2	70.0	14.8	1.3	0.4	0.0	0.3	736
Greensboro, NC	12.1	67.6	16.7	2.3	0.8	0.2	0.3	777
Honolulu, HI	5.4	11.9	26.5	20.4	14.4	9.4	12.1	1,653
Houston, TX	4.7	45.9	32.4	11.8	3.0	1.1	1.1	995
Huntsville, AL	14.1	60.8	20.8	3.0	0.8	0.3	0.2	779
Indianapolis, IN	7.5	60.4	26.0	4.5	1.0	0.3	0.3	859
Jacksonville, FL	6.1	42.2	37.7	10.5	2.4	0.6	0.5	1,019
Kansas City, MO	9.5	52.6	29.4	6.1	1.5	0.3	0.5	894
Lafayette, LA	17.9	59.0	17.8	4.0	1.1	0.1	0.1	769
Las Cruces, NM	18.8	58.2	18.7	3.1	0.6	0.0	0.5	735
Las Vegas, NV	3.3	42.2	38.4	12.1	2.7	0.7	0.5	1,048
Lexington, KY	13.1	58.8	22.9	3.4	1.3	0.2	0.4	808
Lincoln, NE	14.0	61.3	20.0	2.9	0.6	0.4	0.8	784
Little Rock, AR	10.7	63.6	21.6	3.1	0.6	0.2	0.3	805
Los Angeles, CA	4.6	17.8	34.8	23.0	11.0	4.8	3.9	1,393

Table continued on next page.

MSA[1]	Under $500	$500 -$999	$1,000 -$1,499	$1,500 -$1,999	$2,000 -$2,499	$2,500 -2,999	$3,000 and up	Median ($)
Louisville, KY	15.0	60.6	20.1	3.1	0.7	0.3	0.2	792
Madison, WI	5.8	49.6	32.2	8.9	2.3	0.7	0.5	958
Manchester, NH	6.4	29.6	43.8	16.7	2.7	0.5	0.2	1,132
McAllen, TX	22.0	62.2	12.9	1.9	0.7	0.2	0.1	699
Miami, FL	5.7	24.1	39.1	20.0	6.9	2.4	1.9	1,232
Midland, TX	2.8	29.5	41.6	19.3	4.1	1.8	0.7	1,177
Minneapolis, MN	9.8	40.1	32.7	12.7	3.1	0.9	0.7	1,001
Nashville, TN	9.4	46.0	32.3	8.4	2.5	0.8	0.6	951
New Orleans, LA	9.8	46.8	32.6	8.1	1.7	0.5	0.5	947
New York, NY	9.5	16.9	34.1	21.1	9.1	4.2	5.1	1,341
Oklahoma City, OK	9.4	61.1	22.6	5.3	1.0	0.3	0.3	827
Omaha, NE	9.5	56.3	26.6	5.3	1.4	0.3	0.6	865
Orlando, FL	3.0	35.0	44.6	13.7	2.5	0.7	0.6	1,107
Peoria, IL	16.7	63.2	14.8	2.9	1.2	0.5	0.7	739
Philadelphia, PA	8.7	34.5	36.9	13.0	4.3	1.3	1.2	1,075
Phoenix, AZ	4.6	42.4	37.5	11.0	2.8	0.9	0.9	1,032
Pittsburgh, PA	18.1	55.1	19.3	4.8	1.6	0.5	0.6	776
Portland, OR	5.5	33.5	38.8	15.5	4.4	1.2	1.2	1,118
Providence, RI	16.4	42.4	30.0	8.2	2.0	0.5	0.5	925
Provo, UT	7.8	46.6	30.0	11.6	2.8	0.8	0.5	950
Raleigh, NC	5.2	44.0	37.8	9.5	2.2	0.5	0.8	1,008
Reno, NV	6.6	48.6	30.2	11.3	2.2	0.5	0.5	946
Richmond, VA	7.8	37.7	40.3	10.4	2.4	0.7	0.7	1,044
Roanoke, VA	13.4	62.2	19.7	3.7	0.6	0.3	0.2	804
Rochester, MN	14.0	50.5	24.6	7.7	1.8	0.3	1.0	835
Salem, OR	7.8	56.3	27.3	6.2	1.5	0.3	0.7	877
Salt Lake City, UT	6.2	42.9	35.7	11.8	2.2	0.7	0.5	1,009
San Antonio, TX	8.3	47.4	32.4	8.9	1.9	0.6	0.6	949
San Diego, CA	3.9	14.8	33.5	24.1	14.0	5.7	4.0	1,467
San Francisco, CA	6.6	11.8	23.4	23.5	15.7	9.0	10.0	1,673
San Jose, CA	3.9	7.2	17.6	24.0	20.2	13.4	13.5	1,940
Santa Rosa, CA	5.5	14.4	32.9	26.4	14.1	4.3	2.3	1,456
Savannah, GA	9.2	41.2	37.0	9.2	2.0	0.7	0.6	997
Seattle, WA	6.0	22.0	35.7	22.5	8.6	3.1	2.3	1,297
Sioux Falls, SD	12.1	67.2	16.6	2.5	0.4	0.7	0.5	771
Springfield, IL	13.3	65.0	17.7	2.7	0.5	0.6	0.1	777
Tallahassee, FL	7.4	50.1	31.3	7.8	2.8	0.4	0.2	938
Tampa, FL	5.5	43.2	35.9	10.9	2.8	0.9	0.8	1,014
Topeka, KS	18.0	59.9	16.2	3.3	1.8	0.2	0.7	751
Tyler, TX	8.3	58.2	25.1	6.6	1.1	0.2	0.4	873
Virginia Beach, VA	7.3	31.1	39.8	15.5	4.3	1.2	0.8	1,124
Visalia, CA	11.4	51.8	28.0	6.5	1.9	0.3	0.1	877
Washington, DC	5.0	9.6	29.5	29.6	14.9	6.3	5.1	1,600
Wilmington, NC	11.3	48.2	31.0	6.8	1.5	0.3	0.9	929
Winston-Salem, NC	15.3	65.7	15.4	2.4	0.7	0.2	0.3	732
U.S.	10.5	41.1	28.7	11.7	4.5	1.8	1.7	982

Note: (1) Figures cover the Metropolitan Statistical Area (MSA)—see Appendix B for areas included; Figures are percentages except for Median; Gross rent is the contract rent plus the estimated average monthly cost of utilities (electricity, gas, and water and sewer) and fuels (oil, coal, kerosene, wood, etc.) if these are paid by the renter (or paid for the renter by someone else).
Source: U.S. Census Bureau, 2013-2017 American Community Survey 5-Year Estimates

Highest Level of Education: City

City	Less than H.S.	H.S. Diploma	Some College, No Deg.	Associate Degree	Bachelors Degree	Masters Degree	Profess. School Degree	Doctorate Degree
Albany, NY	10.4	25.8	17.2	8.3	19.7	13.0	2.8	2.6
Albuquerque, NM	10.5	22.8	24.2	8.3	18.9	10.6	2.4	2.4
Allentown, PA	21.7	37.2	18.2	7.9	10.0	3.4	0.9	0.6
Anchorage, AK	6.6	23.8	26.3	8.7	22.0	8.8	2.6	1.2
Ann Arbor, MI	3.2	7.4	11.3	4.0	29.5	26.8	7.2	10.7
Athens, GA	13.4	21.0	17.7	6.6	20.7	12.3	2.6	5.7
Atlanta, GA	10.1	19.4	16.8	5.0	27.3	14.1	5.1	2.2
Austin, TX	11.5	16.3	18.1	5.2	30.8	12.7	3.1	2.4
Baton Rouge, LA	12.1	27.8	22.8	5.0	19.0	8.3	2.5	2.5
Billings, MT	7.1	28.1	24.4	7.9	22.2	7.2	2.1	1.1
Boise City, ID	5.6	20.7	24.1	8.7	26.6	9.7	2.7	1.8
Boston, MA	13.9	20.9	13.1	4.6	26.1	13.7	4.4	3.1
Boulder, CO	3.5	7.1	12.0	3.6	34.8	24.6	5.7	8.7
Cape Coral, FL	9.0	35.8	22.2	10.5	15.1	5.4	1.2	0.7
Cedar Rapids, IA	6.1	26.6	23.4	12.1	22.4	6.7	1.6	1.2
Charleston, SC	5.7	17.8	17.3	7.8	32.3	12.3	4.6	2.3
Charlotte, NC	11.4	18.1	20.2	7.5	28.2	11.1	2.5	1.1
Chicago, IL	16.2	22.9	17.7	5.7	22.3	10.5	3.0	1.6
Clarksville, TN	7.9	28.2	28.8	9.6	17.7	6.3	0.7	0.7
College Station, TX	6.1	12.6	19.0	6.5	28.5	15.4	2.7	9.1
Colorado Springs, CO	6.8	19.6	24.6	10.6	23.4	11.6	2.0	1.4
Columbia, MO	5.8	16.9	17.8	6.1	28.3	15.1	4.5	5.5
Columbia, SC	11.8	19.7	19.4	6.7	23.6	12.6	3.9	2.3
Columbus, OH	10.9	25.8	21.1	7.1	22.9	8.8	1.8	1.6
Dallas, TX	24.1	21.4	18.3	4.5	19.9	7.9	2.8	1.1
Denver, CO	13.3	17.6	17.3	5.3	28.4	12.3	4.0	1.9
Des Moines, IA	13.6	30.5	21.4	9.2	17.6	5.2	1.6	0.8
Durham, NC	12.7	15.7	16.8	6.1	25.6	14.3	4.0	4.8
Edison, NJ	8.1	19.5	11.8	5.8	29.5	20.2	2.7	2.4
El Paso, TX	21.0	23.6	23.6	7.7	16.3	5.8	1.2	0.7
Eugene, OR	6.6	17.6	26.5	8.2	23.1	11.6	3.1	3.2
Evansville, IN	13.1	34.8	23.2	8.2	13.7	5.3	1.0	0.7
Fargo, ND	6.2	20.3	20.4	14.3	27.4	7.4	2.0	2.0
Fayetteville, NC	8.8	23.9	30.5	10.8	17.2	6.8	1.1	0.9
Fort Collins, CO	3.6	15.2	19.1	8.4	31.8	15.4	2.5	4.0
Fort Wayne, IN	11.4	29.0	23.0	9.8	17.6	7.0	1.5	0.7
Fort Worth, TX	18.5	24.8	21.6	6.7	19.0	7.0	1.3	1.0
Gainesville, FL	8.5	21.2	17.6	9.6	21.5	13.0	3.8	4.8
Grand Rapids, MI	14.0	22.3	21.4	7.5	22.5	8.7	1.9	1.5
Greeley, CO	16.4	25.9	23.3	8.5	16.8	6.7	1.0	1.3
Green Bay, WI	12.9	31.5	19.4	11.3	18.0	5.1	1.2	0.6
Greensboro, NC	10.1	22.2	22.7	7.6	23.5	9.7	2.4	1.9
Honolulu, HI	11.5	24.0	18.6	9.6	23.4	7.9	3.0	2.1
Houston, TX	22.1	22.8	18.3	5.1	19.3	8.3	2.5	1.6
Huntsville, AL	10.0	19.3	20.9	8.2	25.6	12.4	1.6	2.0
Indianapolis, IN	14.5	28.0	20.7	7.1	19.2	7.3	2.1	1.1
Jacksonville, FL	11.0	28.4	22.9	10.1	18.8	6.3	1.6	0.7
Kansas City, MO	10.9	26.0	22.4	7.3	20.9	9.1	2.3	1.2
Lafayette, LA	13.3	25.3	20.9	4.5	24.1	7.7	2.7	1.6
Las Cruces, NM	13.2	20.4	24.8	8.6	19.7	9.4	1.9	2.0
Las Vegas, NV	16.0	28.2	24.9	7.8	15.2	5.5	1.8	0.7
Lexington, KY	9.5	20.5	20.3	7.9	23.9	11.6	3.5	2.9
Lincoln, NE	7.1	22.2	22.0	11.0	24.2	8.9	2.2	2.5
Little Rock, AR	8.7	22.5	22.8	5.7	24.0	9.8	3.8	2.7
Los Angeles, CA	23.6	19.5	17.8	6.1	21.8	7.2	2.7	1.3

Table continued on next page.

City	Less than H.S.	H.S. Diploma	Some College, No Deg.	Associate Degree	Bachelors Degree	Masters Degree	Profess. School Degree	Doctorate Degree
Louisville, KY	11.5	28.9	23.0	7.9	16.8	8.5	2.2	1.2
Madison, WI	4.6	14.1	15.8	8.4	32.2	15.5	4.4	5.1
Manchester, NH	12.6	30.8	19.1	9.3	18.9	7.3	1.3	0.8
McAllen, TX	26.1	19.3	19.2	6.1	20.7	6.1	1.6	0.9
Miami, FL	24.4	29.8	12.5	7.0	16.3	6.0	3.1	1.0
Midland, TX	15.9	24.7	24.3	6.9	20.5	5.3	1.8	0.7
Minneapolis, MN	10.7	16.4	17.5	7.1	29.3	12.7	3.9	2.5
Nashville, TN	12.2	23.2	19.5	6.5	24.3	9.7	2.6	1.9
New Orleans, LA	14.1	23.0	21.7	4.7	20.7	9.5	4.3	2.0
New York, NY	18.9	24.1	13.9	6.4	21.5	10.7	3.1	1.5
Oklahoma City, OK	14.4	25.3	23.4	7.2	19.5	7.0	2.1	1.0
Omaha, NE	11.6	22.5	22.9	7.4	23.0	8.4	2.8	1.5
Orlando, FL	9.9	24.3	19.3	10.7	23.7	8.3	2.6	1.1
Peoria, IL	11.8	23.9	20.6	9.2	20.9	9.8	2.7	1.1
Philadelphia, PA	16.7	33.8	16.8	5.5	15.8	7.5	2.4	1.4
Phoenix, AZ	18.8	23.5	22.1	7.8	17.8	7.1	1.9	1.0
Pittsburgh, PA	7.9	26.7	15.4	8.0	22.1	12.3	3.9	3.6
Portland, OR	8.2	15.7	21.0	7.0	28.8	13.2	3.9	2.2
Providence, RI	22.2	26.9	15.6	5.1	16.2	8.2	2.8	2.9
Provo, UT	7.6	14.3	26.7	9.0	28.5	9.2	1.7	3.1
Raleigh, NC	8.5	15.6	18.2	7.7	31.9	13.2	2.6	2.2
Reno, NV	13.0	22.6	24.8	7.6	20.0	7.9	2.2	1.9
Richmond, VA	15.5	23.0	18.8	5.3	22.3	10.3	3.1	1.8
Roanoke, VA	15.0	31.8	20.9	9.2	14.3	5.5	2.4	1.0
Rochester, MN	6.0	19.4	19.1	10.8	24.7	11.1	5.1	3.9
Salem, OR	13.3	25.4	26.0	8.2	16.5	7.4	1.9	1.3
Salt Lake City, UT	11.5	17.2	19.4	6.8	25.0	12.0	4.1	3.9
San Antonio, TX	18.0	26.2	22.6	7.5	16.6	6.5	1.7	1.0
San Diego, CA	12.1	15.7	20.4	7.4	26.3	11.7	3.5	3.0
San Francisco, CA	12.1	12.3	14.5	5.3	33.4	14.7	4.9	2.7
San Jose, CA	16.5	17.4	17.5	7.3	24.7	12.6	1.8	2.1
Santa Rosa, CA	13.7	19.1	26.0	9.5	20.0	7.4	2.8	1.5
Savannah, GA	13.3	26.1	25.8	6.6	17.3	8.2	1.5	1.2
Seattle, WA	5.8	10.1	15.8	6.7	35.9	17.0	5.1	3.6
Sioux Falls, SD	8.3	25.6	21.6	10.8	23.0	7.4	2.3	1.1
Springfield, IL	8.6	26.2	22.0	7.3	21.6	9.7	3.2	1.3
Tallahassee, FL	6.7	16.3	19.2	9.8	26.3	13.8	3.8	4.1
Tampa, FL	12.9	25.9	16.8	8.2	22.1	9.1	3.4	1.5
Topeka, KS	10.3	31.4	24.2	5.9	17.4	7.5	2.0	1.3
Tyler, TX	16.5	20.5	25.8	9.6	18.3	6.0	2.2	1.1
Virginia Beach, VA	6.6	21.9	26.1	10.5	22.7	9.1	2.0	1.0
Visalia, CA	18.3	22.6	27.0	9.4	14.8	5.5	1.7	0.8
Washington, DC	9.7	17.6	13.0	3.1	23.8	20.2	8.3	4.3
Wilmington, NC	8.7	20.2	21.0	8.9	27.4	9.1	2.7	1.9
Winston-Salem, NC	13.2	23.7	21.6	7.3	20.5	9.0	2.9	1.7
U.S.	12.7	27.3	20.8	8.3	19.1	8.4	2.0	1.4

Note: Figures cover persons age 25 and over
Source: U.S. Census Bureau, 2013-2017 American Community Survey 5-Year Estimates

Highest Level of Education: Metro Area

Metro Area	Less than H.S.	H.S. Diploma	Some College, No Deg.	Associate Degree	Bachelors Degree	Masters Degree	Profess. School Degree	Doctorate Degree
Albany, NY	7.8	26.8	17.0	12.3	20.0	11.9	2.3	2.0
Albuquerque, NM	11.8	24.5	24.2	8.2	17.5	9.7	2.0	2.1
Allentown, PA	10.5	34.5	17.4	9.3	17.7	7.9	1.5	1.1
Anchorage, AK	7.0	25.9	27.2	8.9	19.9	7.9	2.3	1.1
Ann Arbor, MI	4.9	15.3	18.4	7.0	25.7	18.6	4.4	5.7
Athens, GA	13.3	25.1	18.1	7.1	18.4	10.9	2.7	4.5
Atlanta, GA	11.1	24.3	20.2	7.3	23.3	9.9	2.4	1.4
Austin, TX	10.7	19.2	20.7	6.4	27.8	11.0	2.4	1.8
Baton Rouge, LA	12.6	32.3	21.6	5.9	18.0	6.5	1.8	1.4
Billings, MT	7.0	30.3	24.1	8.4	21.0	6.5	1.8	0.9
Boise City, ID	8.7	25.9	25.5	9.0	21.0	7.0	1.7	1.2
Boston, MA	8.7	22.8	14.9	7.2	25.5	14.5	3.3	3.1
Boulder, CO	5.4	12.4	15.6	6.2	32.6	18.6	3.9	5.3
Cape Coral, FL	12.7	30.9	20.4	8.9	17.1	6.9	2.1	1.1
Cedar Rapids, IA	5.7	29.2	22.5	12.5	21.0	6.7	1.3	1.0
Charleston, SC	9.9	25.6	21.1	9.3	21.9	8.5	2.3	1.4
Charlotte, NC	11.7	24.2	21.5	8.8	22.9	8.4	1.7	0.9
Chicago, IL	12.1	24.2	19.9	7.1	22.3	10.5	2.5	1.4
Clarksville, TN	10.1	30.4	26.8	9.3	15.4	6.3	1.0	0.7
College Station, TX	14.8	23.2	20.6	6.1	19.4	9.1	2.0	4.7
Colorado Springs, CO	6.2	20.3	25.0	11.2	22.6	11.5	1.8	1.3
Columbia, MO	6.5	21.0	19.5	7.1	25.9	12.3	3.6	4.1
Columbia, SC	11.0	27.0	21.5	8.6	19.8	9.0	1.8	1.3
Columbus, OH	9.1	28.3	20.0	7.4	22.6	9.1	2.1	1.5
Dallas, TX	15.2	22.4	21.9	6.8	22.2	8.7	1.8	1.1
Denver, CO	9.5	20.2	20.7	7.6	26.8	11.2	2.6	1.5
Des Moines, IA	7.6	25.3	20.8	10.2	25.2	7.6	2.3	1.0
Durham, NC	11.3	18.6	16.9	6.8	23.7	13.5	4.0	5.1
Edison, NJ	14.1	25.2	15.2	6.8	22.5	11.6	3.1	1.5
El Paso, TX	23.3	24.1	23.1	7.5	15.1	5.2	1.1	0.6
Eugene, OR	8.5	23.9	28.9	9.1	17.7	8.0	2.0	1.9
Evansville, IN	10.0	33.4	22.3	9.4	15.7	6.9	1.5	0.8
Fargo, ND	5.6	21.6	21.4	14.4	26.4	7.4	1.5	1.7
Fayetteville, NC	10.2	26.3	29.1	10.9	15.6	6.2	0.9	0.7
Fort Collins, CO	4.2	19.5	21.4	8.9	27.6	12.8	2.1	3.4
Fort Wayne, IN	10.4	30.8	22.3	10.4	17.2	6.8	1.5	0.7
Fort Worth, TX	15.2	22.4	21.9	6.8	22.2	8.7	1.8	1.1
Gainesville, FL	8.4	23.4	18.5	10.3	20.2	10.7	4.0	4.4
Grand Rapids, MI	9.6	27.2	22.2	9.2	21.0	8.0	1.7	1.1
Greeley, CO	12.3	27.3	24.3	9.1	18.6	6.4	1.1	0.9
Green Bay, WI	8.6	32.7	19.5	12.1	19.2	5.9	1.4	0.6
Greensboro, NC	13.7	27.4	21.8	8.5	18.7	7.0	1.5	1.3
Honolulu, HI	8.6	26.2	20.8	10.5	22.4	7.6	2.5	1.5
Houston, TX	17.2	23.3	21.0	6.7	20.4	8.1	2.0	1.4
Huntsville, AL	10.7	23.1	20.8	8.2	23.4	10.9	1.4	1.5
Indianapolis, IN	10.7	28.2	20.2	7.7	21.4	8.4	2.1	1.2
Jacksonville, FL	9.6	27.8	22.7	10.0	20.0	7.2	1.8	0.9
Kansas City, MO	8.5	25.9	22.3	7.6	22.7	9.6	2.3	1.1
Lafayette, LA	17.6	35.5	19.2	5.6	15.6	4.6	1.2	0.7
Las Cruces, NM	20.8	22.2	21.8	7.8	16.2	8.0	1.5	1.7
Las Vegas, NV	14.7	28.8	25.3	7.9	15.5	5.4	1.5	0.8
Lexington, KY	10.7	24.6	20.5	8.0	21.0	10.0	2.9	2.3
Lincoln, NE	6.7	22.6	21.8	11.6	24.0	8.7	2.2	2.4
Little Rock, AR	9.8	29.4	23.7	7.3	18.8	7.4	2.0	1.5
Los Angeles, CA	20.3	19.9	19.6	7.1	21.5	7.8	2.4	1.4

Table continued on next page.

Metro Area	Less than H.S.	H.S. Diploma	Some College, No Deg.	Associate Degree	Bachelors Degree	Masters Degree	Profess. School Degree	Doctorate Degree
Louisville, KY	10.8	30.4	22.5	8.2	16.8	8.2	2.0	1.1
Madison, WI	5.0	21.4	18.5	10.4	27.2	11.5	3.0	3.1
Manchester, NH	8.2	26.8	18.4	10.1	23.4	10.4	1.6	1.2
McAllen, TX	36.3	23.2	18.1	4.6	12.8	3.8	0.9	0.4
Miami, FL	14.9	27.1	18.0	9.3	19.5	7.3	2.7	1.2
Midland, TX	16.5	25.7	24.0	7.2	19.3	5.2	1.6	0.5
Minneapolis, MN	6.6	21.9	20.6	10.3	26.5	9.8	2.5	1.6
Nashville, TN	10.9	27.5	20.5	7.1	22.1	8.4	2.0	1.4
New Orleans, LA	14.0	28.6	22.8	5.6	18.3	6.8	2.7	1.3
New York, NY	14.1	25.2	15.2	6.8	22.5	11.6	3.1	1.5
Oklahoma City, OK	11.6	27.2	24.3	7.4	19.4	7.2	1.8	1.2
Omaha, NE	8.8	24.0	23.5	8.6	23.1	8.6	2.2	1.2
Orlando, FL	10.9	26.6	20.8	11.4	20.4	7.2	1.8	0.9
Peoria, IL	8.4	30.2	23.0	10.3	18.7	7.2	1.4	0.8
Philadelphia, PA	10.0	29.8	17.1	6.9	21.5	10.3	2.6	1.8
Phoenix, AZ	13.1	23.4	24.7	8.5	19.3	8.0	1.8	1.1
Pittsburgh, PA	6.7	33.7	16.2	9.9	20.5	9.3	2.1	1.6
Portland, OR	8.5	20.4	24.3	8.8	23.7	9.9	2.5	1.7
Providence, RI	13.7	28.6	18.1	8.6	18.9	8.7	1.9	1.5
Provo, UT	6.1	16.4	27.7	10.9	26.8	8.6	1.7	1.8
Raleigh, NC	9.0	18.5	18.6	8.8	28.8	12.1	2.1	2.1
Reno, NV	12.3	23.8	25.9	8.2	18.7	7.3	2.0	1.6
Richmond, VA	10.9	25.8	20.7	7.3	22.0	9.6	2.2	1.5
Roanoke, VA	11.4	30.5	21.3	9.8	17.3	6.6	2.0	1.1
Rochester, MN	6.0	24.7	20.7	11.7	21.9	8.9	3.6	2.5
Salem, OR	14.0	26.8	26.7	8.3	15.6	6.2	1.5	0.9
Salt Lake City, UT	9.7	23.1	25.2	8.9	21.2	8.2	2.1	1.5
San Antonio, TX	15.4	26.3	23.1	7.8	17.6	7.1	1.6	1.0
San Diego, CA	13.3	18.6	22.4	8.3	23.0	9.5	2.7	2.1
San Francisco, CA	11.5	16.0	18.4	6.8	28.1	12.8	3.8	2.7
San Jose, CA	12.7	15.1	16.2	6.9	26.5	16.5	2.7	3.5
Santa Rosa, CA	12.3	19.1	25.2	9.5	21.7	7.9	2.8	1.4
Savannah, GA	10.8	26.3	24.3	7.5	19.3	8.4	2.0	1.4
Seattle, WA	7.8	19.9	21.9	9.3	25.9	10.9	2.6	1.8
Sioux Falls, SD	7.5	26.6	21.4	12.1	22.7	6.7	2.0	1.0
Springfield, IL	7.6	28.1	22.7	8.0	21.2	8.7	2.6	1.1
Tallahassee, FL	9.8	23.4	20.1	9.1	21.6	10.3	2.9	2.9
Tampa, FL	10.9	29.2	21.1	10.0	18.6	7.2	1.9	1.1
Topeka, KS	8.1	32.7	24.1	7.0	18.0	7.4	1.6	1.1
Tyler, TX	15.1	24.6	25.7	9.4	17.4	5.4	1.6	0.8
Virginia Beach, VA	9.2	25.2	25.4	9.5	19.0	8.9	1.7	1.2
Visalia, CA	31.4	25.8	21.7	7.3	9.3	3.2	0.9	0.4
Washington, DC	9.5	18.4	16.5	5.7	25.5	17.1	4.2	3.1
Wilmington, NC	8.8	23.4	22.0	9.6	23.9	8.5	2.2	1.5
Winston-Salem, NC	13.8	29.5	21.3	9.0	17.1	6.5	1.6	1.1
U.S.	12.7	27.3	20.8	8.3	19.1	8.4	2.0	1.4

Note: Figures cover persons age 25 and over; Figures cover the Metropolitan Statistical Area—see Appendix B for areas included
Source: U.S. Census Bureau, 2013-2017 American Community Survey 5-Year Estimates

School Enrollment by Grade and Control: City

City	Preschool (%)		Kindergarten (%)		Grades 1 - 4 (%)		Grades 5 - 8 (%)		Grades 9 - 12 (%)	
	Public	Private	Public	Private	Public	Private	Public	Private	Public	Private
Albany, NY	60.1	39.9	86.4	13.6	89.8	10.2	82.2	17.8	80.7	19.3
Albuquerque, NM	57.1	42.9	85.2	14.8	91.1	8.9	88.4	11.6	90.6	9.4
Allentown, PA	76.2	23.8	84.9	15.1	88.1	11.9	86.6	13.4	90.5	9.5
Anchorage, AK	51.7	48.3	90.9	9.1	92.8	7.2	93.8	6.2	93.5	6.5
Ann Arbor, MI	24.8	75.2	91.7	8.3	91.4	8.6	84.4	15.6	93.8	6.2
Athens, GA	64.7	35.3	90.6	9.4	89.7	10.3	89.9	10.1	84.5	15.5
Atlanta, GA	53.8	46.2	83.7	16.3	85.5	14.5	81.1	18.9	78.3	21.7
Austin, TX	48.6	51.4	87.5	12.5	89.5	10.5	89.5	10.5	91.6	8.4
Baton Rouge, LA	63.8	36.2	72.1	27.9	79.4	20.6	79.6	20.4	81.1	18.9
Billings, MT	43.1	56.9	86.0	14.0	88.3	11.7	87.6	12.4	91.1	8.9
Boise City, ID	39.2	60.8	91.7	8.3	88.3	11.7	91.2	8.8	90.1	9.9
Boston, MA	48.7	51.3	84.7	15.3	86.0	14.0	87.4	12.6	89.4	10.6
Boulder, CO	38.5	61.5	84.1	15.9	90.2	9.8	92.5	7.5	97.0	3.0
Cape Coral, FL	71.9	28.1	94.4	5.6	94.8	5.2	93.7	6.3	95.0	5.0
Cedar Rapids, IA	64.6	35.4	82.2	17.8	88.5	11.5	91.0	9.0	92.6	7.4
Charleston, SC	44.5	55.5	81.1	18.9	82.6	17.4	76.7	23.3	81.3	18.7
Charlotte, NC	48.0	52.0	89.9	10.1	90.1	9.9	88.6	11.4	88.9	11.1
Chicago, IL	61.9	38.1	81.5	18.5	86.2	13.8	86.7	13.3	87.0	13.0
Clarksville, TN	63.0	37.0	95.1	4.9	94.1	5.9	96.0	4.0	94.9	5.1
College Station, TX	44.2	55.8	86.9	13.1	87.0	13.0	93.4	6.6	91.9	8.1
Colorado Springs, CO	59.5	40.5	89.8	10.2	92.0	8.0	92.9	7.1	92.6	7.4
Columbia, MO	39.7	60.3	71.2	28.8	77.5	22.5	87.7	12.3	88.7	11.3
Columbia, SC	49.6	50.4	76.3	23.7	89.0	11.0	86.2	13.8	89.6	10.4
Columbus, OH	58.5	41.5	88.2	11.8	89.6	10.4	87.6	12.4	88.4	11.6
Dallas, TX	69.0	31.0	90.0	10.0	91.3	8.7	91.1	8.9	91.4	8.6
Denver, CO	63.1	36.9	88.2	11.8	90.7	9.3	90.6	9.4	93.0	7.0
Des Moines, IA	77.7	22.3	91.0	9.0	89.0	11.0	89.6	10.4	90.4	9.6
Durham, NC	42.6	57.4	84.4	15.6	89.2	10.8	87.9	12.1	91.7	8.3
Edison, NJ	33.3	66.7	66.0	34.0	89.3	10.7	89.0	11.0	89.3	10.7
El Paso, TX	79.0	21.0	92.4	7.6	95.2	4.8	94.1	5.9	96.0	4.0
Eugene, OR	35.3	64.7	82.1	17.9	91.5	8.5	91.1	8.9	90.8	9.2
Evansville, IN	60.2	39.8	83.0	17.0	87.0	13.0	82.7	17.3	90.8	9.2
Fargo, ND	57.8	42.2	92.9	7.1	90.1	9.9	90.0	10.0	89.3	10.7
Fayetteville, NC	63.8	36.2	87.6	12.4	87.0	13.0	89.6	10.4	88.3	11.7
Fort Collins, CO	45.2	54.8	91.3	8.7	94.0	6.0	94.8	5.2	95.1	4.9
Fort Wayne, IN	50.5	49.5	84.8	15.2	83.3	16.7	82.5	17.5	82.9	17.1
Fort Worth, TX	65.8	34.2	89.7	10.3	93.3	6.7	90.5	9.5	92.1	7.9
Gainesville, FL	51.5	48.5	79.0	21.0	85.7	14.3	83.2	16.8	89.6	10.4
Grand Rapids, MI	61.8	38.2	78.3	21.7	81.0	19.0	85.3	14.7	85.3	14.7
Greeley, CO	64.2	35.8	83.6	16.4	92.9	7.1	92.4	7.6	94.5	5.5
Green Bay, WI	67.7	32.3	86.1	13.9	89.8	10.2	89.4	10.6	91.1	8.9
Greensboro, NC	55.3	44.7	89.7	10.3	93.5	6.5	89.0	11.0	93.2	6.8
Honolulu, HI	37.2	62.8	85.1	14.9	85.3	14.7	76.0	24.0	72.7	27.3
Houston, TX	68.4	31.6	90.8	9.2	93.2	6.8	92.4	7.6	93.0	7.0
Huntsville, AL	51.9	48.1	82.3	17.7	83.8	16.2	83.9	16.1	87.2	12.8
Indianapolis, IN	54.5	45.5	85.2	14.8	88.7	11.3	86.6	13.4	87.7	12.3
Jacksonville, FL	58.4	41.6	83.3	16.7	83.6	16.4	81.7	18.3	83.4	16.6
Kansas City, MO	56.6	43.4	87.7	12.3	89.1	10.9	87.2	12.8	86.4	13.6
Lafayette, LA	60.0	40.0	78.9	21.1	81.2	18.8	74.7	25.3	76.4	23.6
Las Cruces, NM	75.0	25.0	94.5	5.5	93.7	6.3	94.3	5.7	92.7	7.3
Las Vegas, NV	61.1	38.9	85.5	14.5	92.0	8.0	91.8	8.2	92.6	7.4
Lexington, KY	46.0	54.0	85.8	14.2	85.5	14.5	85.6	14.4	86.7	13.3
Lincoln, NE	53.8	46.2	82.7	17.3	84.4	15.6	84.9	15.1	85.7	14.3
Little Rock, AR	49.9	50.1	76.6	23.4	83.4	16.6	78.1	21.9	79.4	20.6
Los Angeles, CA	60.7	39.3	88.0	12.0	89.3	10.7	88.7	11.3	88.7	11.3

Table continued on next page.

City	Preschool (%)		Kindergarten (%)		Grades 1 - 4 (%)		Grades 5 - 8 (%)		Grades 9 - 12 (%)	
	Public	Private	Public	Private	Public	Private	Public	Private	Public	Private
Louisville, KY	50.0	50.0	82.1	17.9	81.7	18.3	80.8	19.2	81.0	19.0
Madison, WI	51.7	48.3	85.9	14.1	89.0	11.0	84.2	15.8	92.1	7.9
Manchester, NH	39.2	60.8	81.8	18.2	90.7	9.3	90.4	9.6	90.4	9.6
McAllen, TX	73.0	27.0	85.3	14.7	92.7	7.3	97.4	2.6	97.8	2.2
Miami, FL	57.4	42.6	83.5	16.5	85.9	14.1	88.4	11.6	89.7	10.3
Midland, TX	59.2	40.8	83.8	16.2	84.1	15.9	85.2	14.8	90.6	9.4
Minneapolis, MN	57.8	42.2	85.7	14.3	87.3	12.7	86.7	13.3	87.6	12.4
Nashville, TN	52.2	47.8	86.9	13.1	85.5	14.5	82.7	17.3	83.0	17.0
New Orleans, LA	56.0	44.0	81.3	18.7	80.5	19.5	79.0	21.0	78.3	21.7
New York, NY	58.5	41.5	79.3	20.7	83.5	16.5	82.7	17.3	83.3	16.7
Oklahoma City, OK	70.8	29.2	91.6	8.4	91.4	8.6	89.6	10.4	90.6	9.4
Omaha, NE	57.9	42.1	83.0	17.0	85.9	14.1	87.0	13.0	84.8	15.2
Orlando, FL	59.7	40.3	81.5	18.5	93.0	7.0	86.6	13.4	92.0	8.0
Peoria, IL	70.0	30.0	71.8	28.2	83.2	16.8	80.0	20.0	84.1	15.9
Philadelphia, PA	52.7	47.3	79.3	20.7	80.0	20.0	79.2	20.8	81.6	18.4
Phoenix, AZ	63.0	37.0	91.9	8.1	93.6	6.4	93.2	6.8	94.0	6.0
Pittsburgh, PA	54.1	45.9	77.0	23.0	75.9	24.1	77.4	22.6	80.9	19.1
Portland, OR	38.2	61.8	81.4	18.6	87.5	12.5	88.0	12.0	85.2	14.8
Providence, RI	56.5	43.5	85.1	14.9	86.6	13.4	84.9	15.1	85.3	14.7
Provo, UT	45.4	54.6	95.5	4.5	95.4	4.6	94.8	5.2	87.7	12.3
Raleigh, NC	43.3	56.7	90.2	9.8	90.3	9.7	89.1	10.9	90.6	9.4
Reno, NV	55.8	44.2	89.4	10.6	92.7	7.3	91.9	8.1	95.3	4.7
Richmond, VA	59.2	40.8	86.5	13.5	89.1	10.9	78.3	21.7	87.2	12.8
Roanoke, VA	66.1	33.9	87.0	13.0	89.7	10.3	92.1	7.9	93.5	6.5
Rochester, MN	51.3	48.7	78.8	21.2	85.0	15.0	83.9	16.1	93.6	6.4
Salem, OR	59.7	40.3	91.2	8.8	90.7	9.3	92.7	7.3	95.5	4.5
Salt Lake City, UT	51.3	48.7	91.1	8.9	91.2	8.8	90.8	9.2	93.5	6.5
San Antonio, TX	70.6	29.4	91.8	8.2	93.4	6.6	93.0	7.0	93.9	6.1
San Diego, CA	52.9	47.1	90.8	9.2	91.3	8.7	90.3	9.7	91.0	9.0
San Francisco, CA	32.8	67.2	75.0	25.0	72.6	27.4	71.1	28.9	76.6	23.4
San Jose, CA	43.1	56.9	80.8	19.2	88.4	11.6	88.4	11.6	88.5	11.5
Santa Rosa, CA	50.9	49.1	96.3	3.7	95.2	4.8	95.4	4.6	91.5	8.5
Savannah, GA	66.7	33.3	96.0	4.0	92.0	8.0	89.3	10.7	88.9	11.1
Seattle, WA	33.8	66.2	78.4	21.6	79.6	20.4	76.8	23.2	82.2	17.8
Sioux Falls, SD	52.2	47.8	84.5	15.5	88.7	11.3	89.6	10.4	85.4	14.6
Springfield, IL	65.3	34.7	81.2	18.8	82.6	17.4	84.6	15.4	85.9	14.1
Tallahassee, FL	49.3	50.7	87.8	12.2	83.8	16.2	79.7	20.3	87.1	12.9
Tampa, FL	57.1	42.9	88.7	11.3	90.3	9.7	85.9	14.1	86.7	13.3
Topeka, KS	67.9	32.1	93.1	6.9	89.2	10.8	88.8	11.2	92.7	7.3
Tyler, TX	73.2	26.8	93.2	6.8	87.6	12.4	88.8	11.2	90.6	9.4
Virginia Beach, VA	36.9	63.1	81.9	18.1	91.8	8.2	90.8	9.2	92.9	7.1
Visalia, CA	72.3	27.7	91.9	8.1	93.6	6.4	92.4	7.6	94.6	5.4
Washington, DC	76.7	23.3	90.8	9.2	85.9	14.1	82.2	17.8	82.7	17.3
Wilmington, NC	71.7	28.3	90.7	9.3	87.8	12.2	83.2	16.8	91.1	8.9
Winston-Salem, NC	59.1	40.9	92.7	7.3	92.6	7.4	90.7	9.3	93.0	7.0
U.S.	58.8	41.2	87.7	12.3	89.7	10.3	89.6	10.4	90.3	9.7

Note: Figures shown cover persons 3 years old and over
Source: U.S. Census Bureau, 2013-2017 American Community Survey 5-Year Estimates

School Enrollment by Grade and Control: Metro Area

Metro Area	Preschool (%)		Kindergarten (%)		Grades 1 - 4 (%)		Grades 5 - 8 (%)		Grades 9 - 12 (%)	
	Public	Private	Public	Private	Public	Private	Public	Private	Public	Private
Albany, NY	47.4	52.6	89.5	10.5	91.4	8.6	90.9	9.1	90.9	9.1
Albuquerque, NM	62.5	37.5	85.9	14.1	90.5	9.5	88.5	11.5	90.4	9.6
Allentown, PA	46.4	53.6	80.9	19.1	89.5	10.5	89.5	10.5	90.0	10.0
Anchorage, AK	55.9	44.1	88.7	11.3	90.9	9.1	91.6	8.4	91.3	8.7
Ann Arbor, MI	46.3	53.7	88.5	11.5	87.7	12.3	87.3	12.7	91.3	8.7
Athens, GA	64.6	35.4	90.8	9.2	89.1	10.9	86.9	13.1	84.3	15.7
Atlanta, GA	57.3	42.7	86.3	13.7	90.7	9.3	89.8	10.2	89.8	10.2
Austin, TX	50.5	49.5	88.7	11.3	91.0	9.0	91.2	8.8	93.3	6.7
Baton Rouge, LA	56.1	43.9	73.4	26.6	81.2	18.8	80.7	19.3	81.1	18.9
Billings, MT	43.2	56.8	86.8	13.2	90.5	9.5	89.5	10.5	89.6	10.4
Boise City, ID	41.6	58.4	87.6	12.4	91.1	8.9	92.8	7.2	91.2	8.8
Boston, MA	45.2	54.8	86.6	13.4	90.9	9.1	89.6	10.4	87.2	12.8
Boulder, CO	50.1	49.9	85.5	14.5	91.5	8.5	91.8	8.2	94.7	5.3
Cape Coral, FL	67.6	32.4	92.3	7.7	93.2	6.8	91.8	8.2	92.9	7.1
Cedar Rapids, IA	68.6	31.4	85.0	15.0	89.4	10.6	91.7	8.3	93.4	6.6
Charleston, SC	51.0	49.0	85.6	14.4	90.2	9.8	88.8	11.2	89.6	10.4
Charlotte, NC	51.4	48.6	90.1	9.9	90.5	9.5	89.5	10.5	90.2	9.8
Chicago, IL	58.6	41.4	84.8	15.2	88.8	11.2	89.1	10.9	90.4	9.6
Clarksville, TN	69.0	31.0	94.3	5.7	91.3	8.7	92.1	7.9	91.6	8.4
College Station, TX	62.2	37.8	85.8	14.2	88.9	11.1	90.5	9.5	93.0	7.0
Colorado Springs, CO	62.9	37.1	88.8	11.2	92.0	8.0	92.0	8.0	92.9	7.1
Columbia, MO	45.3	54.7	76.4	23.6	82.0	18.0	90.0	10.0	90.8	9.2
Columbia, SC	54.9	45.1	86.1	13.9	91.9	8.1	92.6	7.4	92.1	7.9
Columbus, OH	52.2	47.8	87.1	12.9	89.6	10.4	88.3	11.7	89.0	11.0
Dallas, TX	58.3	41.7	89.7	10.3	92.6	7.4	92.1	7.9	92.2	7.8
Denver, CO	59.5	40.5	90.5	9.5	92.9	7.1	92.3	7.7	92.9	7.1
Des Moines, IA	64.7	35.3	89.6	10.4	90.9	9.1	90.5	9.5	91.1	8.9
Durham, NC	43.4	56.6	86.5	13.5	89.2	10.8	89.8	10.2	89.4	10.6
Edison, NJ	53.1	46.9	81.8	18.2	86.1	13.9	86.3	13.7	85.8	14.2
El Paso, TX	82.2	17.8	93.2	6.8	95.7	4.3	94.5	5.5	96.4	3.6
Eugene, OR	46.2	53.8	85.1	14.9	91.9	8.1	91.0	9.0	90.8	9.2
Evansville, IN	50.2	49.8	81.4	18.6	82.5	17.5	81.3	18.7	87.9	12.1
Fargo, ND	65.7	34.3	92.5	7.5	89.9	10.1	89.1	10.9	90.7	9.3
Fayetteville, NC	62.4	37.6	88.3	11.7	89.4	10.6	89.9	10.1	89.6	10.4
Fort Collins, CO	52.3	47.7	91.6	8.4	91.7	8.3	92.7	7.3	94.1	5.9
Fort Wayne, IN	46.6	53.4	78.1	21.9	79.9	20.1	79.5	20.5	82.9	17.1
Fort Worth, TX	58.3	41.7	89.7	10.3	92.6	7.4	92.1	7.9	92.2	7.8
Gainesville, FL	49.8	50.2	82.5	17.5	87.4	12.6	82.8	17.2	90.6	9.4
Grand Rapids, MI	63.1	36.9	83.3	16.7	84.0	16.0	85.8	14.2	86.5	13.5
Greeley, CO	69.5	30.5	88.8	11.2	92.0	8.0	93.2	6.8	91.7	8.3
Green Bay, WI	68.1	31.9	85.7	14.3	89.0	11.0	90.1	9.9	94.0	6.0
Greensboro, NC	49.7	50.3	89.2	10.8	91.2	8.8	90.5	9.5	91.6	8.4
Honolulu, HI	37.0	63.0	80.7	19.3	86.0	14.0	78.8	21.2	75.1	24.9
Houston, TX	59.8	40.2	90.0	10.0	92.8	7.2	93.1	6.9	93.4	6.6
Huntsville, AL	50.3	49.7	87.3	12.7	85.5	14.5	85.8	14.2	87.5	12.5
Indianapolis, IN	50.4	49.6	86.4	13.6	89.1	10.9	88.4	11.6	89.2	10.8
Jacksonville, FL	53.9	46.1	84.9	15.1	86.0	14.0	84.3	15.7	86.1	13.9
Kansas City, MO	54.3	45.7	88.5	11.5	89.0	11.0	89.1	10.9	90.0	10.0
Lafayette, LA	66.0	34.0	78.4	21.6	79.8	20.2	77.4	22.6	79.2	20.8
Las Cruces, NM	84.3	15.7	94.9	5.1	95.0	5.0	95.4	4.6	95.2	4.8
Las Vegas, NV	60.3	39.7	89.1	10.9	92.7	7.3	93.6	6.4	93.6	6.4
Lexington, KY	47.8	52.2	86.9	13.1	87.2	12.8	86.1	13.9	87.2	12.8
Lincoln, NE	52.6	47.4	82.6	17.4	84.6	15.4	85.3	14.7	86.8	13.2
Little Rock, AR	59.8	40.2	86.1	13.9	89.4	10.6	87.0	13.0	87.2	12.8
Los Angeles, CA	58.8	41.2	88.7	11.3	90.8	9.2	90.9	9.1	91.5	8.5

Table continued on next page.

Metro Area	Preschool (%)		Kindergarten (%)		Grades 1 - 4 (%)		Grades 5 - 8 (%)		Grades 9 - 12 (%)	
	Public	Private	Public	Private	Public	Private	Public	Private	Public	Private
Louisville, KY	47.3	52.7	82.5	17.5	83.3	16.7	82.5	17.5	83.1	16.9
Madison, WI	63.0	37.0	89.5	10.5	90.0	10.0	89.4	10.6	94.7	5.3
Manchester, NH	39.3	60.7	81.7	18.3	88.8	11.2	90.1	9.9	88.4	11.6
McAllen, TX	88.0	12.0	93.2	6.8	96.6	3.4	98.2	1.8	98.4	1.6
Miami, FL	49.4	50.6	83.6	16.4	86.6	13.4	87.0	13.0	87.5	12.5
Midland, TX	56.7	43.3	85.9	14.1	86.7	13.3	87.2	12.8	90.8	9.2
Minneapolis, MN	59.6	40.4	87.5	12.5	89.0	11.0	89.6	10.4	91.0	9.0
Nashville, TN	47.1	52.9	87.6	12.4	87.9	12.1	85.4	14.6	84.7	15.3
New Orleans, LA	53.1	46.9	75.9	24.1	76.6	23.4	76.3	23.7	75.4	24.6
New York, NY	53.1	46.9	81.8	18.2	86.1	13.9	86.3	13.7	85.8	14.2
Oklahoma City, OK	71.7	28.3	89.4	10.6	91.1	8.9	90.4	9.6	91.6	8.4
Omaha, NE	58.4	41.6	85.7	14.3	87.6	12.4	88.3	11.7	87.7	12.3
Orlando, FL	56.1	43.9	83.6	16.4	88.0	12.0	87.9	12.1	90.2	9.8
Peoria, IL	61.3	38.7	82.3	17.7	87.9	12.1	86.6	13.4	88.9	11.1
Philadelphia, PA	44.0	56.0	81.6	18.4	84.9	15.1	84.0	16.0	83.3	16.7
Phoenix, AZ	60.1	39.9	91.2	8.8	92.8	7.2	93.2	6.8	93.8	6.2
Pittsburgh, PA	48.8	51.2	84.3	15.7	88.1	11.9	88.5	11.5	89.7	10.3
Portland, OR	42.3	57.7	85.2	14.8	88.4	11.6	90.1	9.9	91.2	8.8
Providence, RI	53.7	46.3	87.9	12.1	89.8	10.2	89.4	10.6	87.2	12.8
Provo, UT	50.0	50.0	92.7	7.3	93.6	6.4	94.1	5.9	94.1	5.9
Raleigh, NC	40.7	59.3	88.1	11.9	89.4	10.6	89.4	10.6	90.0	10.0
Reno, NV	58.0	42.0	90.0	10.0	93.2	6.8	91.5	8.5	93.9	6.1
Richmond, VA	43.4	56.6	87.8	12.2	90.5	9.5	88.7	11.3	90.6	9.4
Roanoke, VA	57.9	42.1	89.8	10.2	89.9	10.1	90.7	9.3	91.3	8.7
Rochester, MN	60.8	39.2	83.3	16.7	87.0	13.0	87.3	12.7	93.3	6.7
Salem, OR	58.8	41.2	88.1	11.9	90.3	9.7	91.6	8.4	93.8	6.2
Salt Lake City, UT	55.1	44.9	91.4	8.6	93.0	7.0	93.2	6.8	93.9	6.1
San Antonio, TX	66.0	34.0	91.1	8.9	93.1	6.9	92.5	7.5	93.6	6.4
San Diego, CA	54.9	45.1	89.8	10.2	92.4	7.6	91.6	8.4	92.2	7.8
San Francisco, CA	40.8	59.2	84.7	15.3	86.1	13.9	85.9	14.1	87.8	12.2
San Jose, CA	37.6	62.4	80.8	19.2	86.3	13.7	86.7	13.3	87.5	12.5
Santa Rosa, CA	52.0	48.0	94.1	5.9	91.9	8.1	90.8	9.2	90.0	10.0
Savannah, GA	65.5	34.5	90.4	9.6	88.2	11.8	84.5	15.5	85.9	14.1
Seattle, WA	40.8	59.2	84.5	15.5	88.4	11.6	88.7	11.3	90.5	9.5
Sioux Falls, SD	54.9	45.1	86.0	14.0	89.1	10.9	90.7	9.3	87.9	12.1
Springfield, IL	65.3	34.7	85.4	14.6	87.4	12.6	87.4	12.6	90.3	9.7
Tallahassee, FL	54.2	45.8	86.3	13.7	85.7	14.3	81.3	18.7	87.5	12.5
Tampa, FL	58.5	41.5	86.5	13.5	88.2	11.8	87.4	12.6	89.4	10.6
Topeka, KS	71.3	28.7	92.1	7.9	90.1	9.9	88.6	11.4	92.2	7.8
Tyler, TX	73.0	27.0	88.6	11.4	88.6	11.4	90.4	9.6	89.0	11.0
Virginia Beach, VA	54.1	45.9	86.9	13.1	90.4	9.6	90.1	9.9	91.8	8.2
Visalia, CA	83.9	16.1	95.3	4.7	96.6	3.4	96.4	3.6	96.6	3.4
Washington, DC	44.2	55.8	86.2	13.8	88.9	11.1	87.9	12.1	88.5	11.5
Wilmington, NC	56.1	43.9	87.3	12.7	89.7	10.3	86.7	13.3	92.9	7.1
Winston-Salem, NC	56.5	43.5	91.3	8.7	92.5	7.5	90.1	9.9	92.5	7.5
U.S.	58.8	41.2	87.7	12.3	89.7	10.3	89.6	10.4	90.3	9.7

Note: Figures shown cover persons 3 years old and over; Figures cover the Metropolitan Statistical Area—see Appendix B for areas included
Source: U.S. Census Bureau, 2013-2017 American Community Survey 5-Year Estimates

Educational Attainment by Race: City

City	High School Graduate or Higher (%)					Bachelor's Degree or Higher (%)				
	Total	White	Black	Asian	Hisp.[1]	Total	White	Black	Asian	Hisp.[1]
Albany, NY	89.6	93.4	84.3	84.0	78.2	38.1	49.8	12.8	49.2	24.0
Albuquerque, NM	89.5	91.1	92.2	82.2	82.0	34.3	37.1	30.9	46.1	20.8
Allentown, PA	78.3	81.3	81.0	86.3	68.3	14.9	17.5	10.0	37.7	6.1
Anchorage, AK	93.4	96.6	90.3	78.9	87.1	34.6	41.0	20.3	26.4	19.9
Ann Arbor, MI	96.8	98.3	85.0	96.1	92.5	74.2	76.4	35.6	84.7	69.5
Athens, GA	86.6	90.3	80.0	94.0	49.6	41.3	52.1	15.6	79.3	13.4
Atlanta, GA	89.9	97.2	83.1	96.9	79.4	48.7	75.7	22.9	83.8	43.1
Austin, TX	88.5	90.0	89.1	92.9	70.2	49.0	52.0	24.7	73.5	23.8
Baton Rouge, LA	87.9	95.6	82.0	84.1	82.4	32.4	52.7	14.9	50.3	24.3
Billings, MT	92.9	93.6	82.0	85.2	79.4	32.6	33.3	20.0	45.2	10.4
Boise City, ID	94.4	95.3	75.6	86.2	83.4	40.9	41.4	20.3	51.8	21.2
Boston, MA	86.1	92.1	82.5	77.0	67.8	47.4	63.1	21.3	50.5	20.3
Boulder, CO	96.5	97.4	95.8	91.6	73.2	73.8	74.9	52.9	69.1	42.4
Cape Coral, FL	91.0	91.4	90.3	88.1	81.3	22.5	23.0	17.4	12.7	19.0
Cedar Rapids, IA	93.9	95.0	80.4	95.5	74.3	31.9	32.1	14.5	64.8	19.1
Charleston, SC	94.3	97.2	84.0	92.3	91.6	51.4	60.0	19.6	73.1	39.7
Charlotte, NC	88.6	92.1	88.9	81.8	59.5	42.9	53.5	27.9	55.4	16.8
Chicago, IL	83.8	87.5	84.1	87.8	65.0	37.5	48.9	20.2	59.4	14.9
Clarksville, TN	92.1	92.6	91.6	81.2	86.4	25.5	26.7	21.4	27.6	16.9
College Station, TX	93.9	94.9	87.0	96.3	80.3	55.8	56.5	24.8	80.5	45.9
Colorado Springs, CO	93.2	95.0	93.6	84.4	77.4	38.4	41.7	21.6	43.6	19.4
Columbia, MO	94.2	95.4	88.4	91.6	88.3	53.4	56.7	18.6	71.5	41.3
Columbia, SC	88.2	94.5	81.6	91.5	73.4	42.3	61.0	19.3	76.1	31.3
Columbus, OH	89.1	91.3	86.0	83.2	70.0	35.1	40.3	18.8	57.2	19.6
Dallas, TX	75.9	74.1	85.1	84.3	47.9	31.6	37.6	17.4	62.9	9.1
Denver, CO	86.7	88.6	87.3	80.7	61.4	46.5	51.3	23.0	49.7	13.5
Des Moines, IA	86.4	89.3	82.9	63.6	57.1	25.2	27.6	13.6	18.9	8.5
Durham, NC	87.3	90.3	86.8	91.5	45.2	48.8	60.6	33.1	74.3	13.3
Edison, NJ	91.9	91.8	93.6	93.4	82.8	54.8	37.3	30.9	75.4	29.6
El Paso, TX	79.0	79.2	94.1	91.3	74.6	24.1	24.1	27.5	49.4	20.0
Eugene, OR	93.4	94.7	92.0	91.8	68.2	41.1	41.6	35.1	62.6	20.5
Evansville, IN	86.9	87.6	83.3	94.0	53.4	20.7	21.9	11.9	40.0	10.6
Fargo, ND	93.8	95.5	79.4	74.1	78.5	38.8	40.0	18.5	50.3	19.9
Fayetteville, NC	91.2	93.1	90.2	83.0	87.4	26.0	29.8	22.3	34.3	20.5
Fort Collins, CO	96.4	96.8	96.9	97.1	82.4	53.6	54.2	37.4	73.2	29.3
Fort Wayne, IN	88.6	91.4	83.3	63.2	58.4	26.8	29.5	13.3	32.6	9.9
Fort Worth, TX	81.5	83.8	86.8	81.0	56.9	28.3	32.5	19.7	41.4	10.8
Gainesville, FL	91.5	94.3	83.7	93.0	91.5	43.1	49.9	18.1	67.6	45.0
Grand Rapids, MI	86.0	90.2	80.3	71.8	49.5	34.7	41.4	14.9	41.3	10.2
Greeley, CO	83.6	86.3	81.5	66.8	63.1	25.8	27.8	17.6	33.0	8.9
Green Bay, WI	87.1	90.3	85.9	69.5	47.8	24.9	27.3	9.6	21.6	6.2
Greensboro, NC	89.9	93.4	88.9	69.2	61.4	37.4	48.2	23.5	37.4	15.3
Honolulu, HI	88.5	97.2	97.5	84.8	90.6	36.4	52.3	24.9	35.4	25.6
Houston, TX	77.9	76.5	87.5	86.7	56.2	31.7	35.6	21.6	58.3	12.0
Huntsville, AL	90.0	93.0	83.2	91.5	58.3	41.6	48.0	24.7	58.3	16.7
Indianapolis, IN	85.5	87.7	84.4	77.7	55.4	29.7	34.8	17.0	47.5	10.8
Jacksonville, FL	89.0	90.7	86.2	84.9	82.5	27.5	30.4	17.7	46.2	24.0
Kansas City, MO	89.1	92.9	85.6	77.1	66.2	33.5	41.7	15.5	45.0	16.2
Lafayette, LA	86.7	92.2	73.6	88.8	51.9	36.0	45.0	14.1	44.2	22.6
Las Cruces, NM	86.8	86.9	96.9	93.6	78.9	33.0	32.1	52.8	56.2	18.6
Las Vegas, NV	84.0	86.8	87.4	90.0	62.5	23.2	25.2	17.3	39.8	9.1
Lexington, KY	90.5	92.8	84.9	89.5	59.8	41.8	45.7	18.8	67.8	17.4
Lincoln, NE	92.9	94.7	88.5	80.1	64.9	37.8	39.1	19.0	43.2	16.2
Little Rock, AR	91.3	94.0	88.2	94.3	60.5	40.3	52.9	20.7	74.8	10.8
Los Angeles, CA	76.4	80.1	87.5	90.0	54.3	33.0	38.2	24.7	53.7	11.2

Table continued on next page.

City	High School Graduate or Higher (%)					Bachelor's Degree or Higher (%)				
	Total	White	Black	Asian	Hisp.[1]	Total	White	Black	Asian	Hisp.[1]
Louisville, KY	88.5	89.4	86.2	81.5	76.9	28.7	31.6	16.3	47.3	24.1
Madison, WI	95.4	96.8	89.1	89.7	76.3	57.1	59.1	24.0	68.6	33.4
Manchester, NH	87.4	88.1	88.6	76.9	68.1	28.3	27.8	24.9	45.5	10.4
McAllen, TX	73.9	75.6	86.3	93.2	69.7	29.3	29.9	17.2	59.1	25.1
Miami, FL	75.6	76.8	70.3	82.5	73.2	26.3	29.0	12.1	56.3	22.8
Midland, TX	84.1	85.6	83.7	79.7	68.2	28.3	30.7	14.2	39.3	11.5
Minneapolis, MN	89.3	95.6	74.9	80.4	56.1	48.3	58.7	14.4	50.0	16.6
Nashville, TN	87.8	90.1	86.7	77.9	58.0	38.5	43.3	26.8	47.2	14.5
New Orleans, LA	85.9	95.3	80.1	73.2	78.5	36.5	62.7	18.3	38.5	33.2
New York, NY	81.1	87.7	82.4	75.3	66.9	36.7	49.1	23.6	41.2	17.4
Oklahoma City, OK	85.6	86.8	88.6	80.2	52.5	29.6	32.1	19.7	40.4	9.3
Omaha, NE	88.4	90.3	85.6	69.9	48.7	35.6	38.3	18.6	48.0	10.2
Orlando, FL	90.1	92.8	83.8	91.9	85.4	35.8	40.3	21.3	59.0	25.3
Peoria, IL	88.2	92.0	78.9	95.4	62.2	34.4	38.9	12.8	74.9	21.7
Philadelphia, PA	83.3	87.5	83.3	69.5	64.7	27.1	37.4	15.7	36.9	13.1
Phoenix, AZ	81.2	83.9	87.2	84.1	59.3	27.8	29.9	20.2	55.4	9.5
Pittsburgh, PA	92.1	93.5	88.3	90.7	87.0	41.9	47.3	17.7	78.2	47.7
Portland, OR	91.8	94.3	87.0	76.6	72.7	48.2	52.1	21.5	38.0	27.1
Providence, RI	77.8	83.7	79.8	76.1	65.1	30.1	39.2	19.8	48.4	9.5
Provo, UT	92.4	93.2	86.5	89.1	74.5	42.5	43.0	41.4	53.0	20.5
Raleigh, NC	91.5	95.2	89.8	88.2	58.2	50.0	60.3	30.6	59.7	21.0
Reno, NV	87.0	88.6	90.6	87.5	60.6	32.0	33.4	19.4	43.5	11.1
Richmond, VA	84.5	91.2	77.6	87.6	51.0	37.5	58.4	15.2	65.1	12.2
Roanoke, VA	85.0	87.2	82.9	55.4	65.8	23.2	28.6	9.1	32.7	12.3
Rochester, MN	94.0	96.0	82.2	83.3	72.8	44.7	45.4	22.5	57.8	23.8
Salem, OR	86.7	89.6	89.2	82.4	55.3	27.1	29.3	14.5	38.7	8.1
Salt Lake City, UT	88.5	94.3	79.1	85.4	59.2	45.1	49.8	25.2	63.1	15.4
San Antonio, TX	82.0	82.3	90.1	86.0	74.1	25.7	26.0	24.0	51.8	15.7
San Diego, CA	87.9	89.4	89.9	88.7	68.1	44.4	47.0	23.6	51.9	19.2
San Francisco, CA	87.9	95.8	89.2	78.6	76.6	55.8	70.9	27.3	44.4	32.3
San Jose, CA	83.5	87.9	90.7	86.0	65.1	41.3	41.8	33.9	53.7	14.1
Santa Rosa, CA	86.3	90.9	87.9	84.6	61.9	31.6	35.3	28.5	39.4	11.5
Savannah, GA	86.7	91.7	82.8	86.1	72.1	28.3	41.9	15.9	50.8	26.1
Seattle, WA	94.2	97.5	84.5	85.3	82.4	61.7	67.9	25.5	55.1	42.6
Sioux Falls, SD	91.7	93.9	74.2	70.8	62.6	33.8	35.9	14.5	34.8	11.4
Springfield, IL	91.4	92.8	84.3	91.1	85.9	35.8	38.2	19.9	67.7	30.5
Tallahassee, FL	93.3	96.8	87.0	96.8	85.2	48.0	56.0	29.1	84.0	40.5
Tampa, FL	87.1	89.3	81.8	87.3	76.3	36.2	41.5	16.8	63.6	20.8
Topeka, KS	89.7	91.1	83.9	89.1	71.6	28.2	30.2	12.4	64.9	11.2
Tyler, TX	83.5	83.4	85.0	97.0	44.7	27.6	31.8	11.6	69.8	7.3
Virginia Beach, VA	93.4	94.9	90.6	89.8	85.6	34.8	36.9	25.3	41.9	23.9
Visalia, CA	81.7	82.7	83.9	78.0	68.4	22.7	22.8	33.6	37.6	11.1
Washington, DC	90.3	97.7	85.6	93.8	71.3	56.6	88.4	25.5	79.7	46.1
Wilmington, NC	91.3	93.9	82.9	77.0	60.4	41.1	47.1	14.4	51.9	18.8
Winston-Salem, NC	86.8	88.5	87.4	87.2	51.2	34.1	41.4	21.7	61.1	10.9
U.S.	87.3	89.3	84.9	86.5	66.7	30.9	32.2	20.6	52.7	15.2

Note: Figures shown cover persons 25 years old and over; (1) People of Hispanic origin can be of any race
Source: U.S. Census Bureau, 2013-2017 American Community Survey 5-Year Estimates

Educational Attainment by Race: Metro Area

Metro Area	High School Graduate or Higher (%)					Bachelor's Degree or Higher (%)				
	Total	White	Black	Asian	Hisp.[1]	Total	White	Black	Asian	Hisp.[1]
Albany, NY	92.2	93.5	85.0	87.3	80.3	36.1	36.7	19.2	62.9	26.0
Albuquerque, NM	88.2	89.9	92.5	85.0	79.7	31.2	34.0	29.8	46.3	18.3
Allentown, PA	89.5	90.7	86.4	88.8	73.3	28.3	28.8	20.7	56.9	11.7
Anchorage, AK	93.0	95.5	90.4	79.0	87.9	31.0	35.3	19.4	26.0	19.3
Ann Arbor, MI	95.1	96.2	88.1	95.7	85.2	54.3	56.2	25.4	81.5	39.7
Athens, GA	86.7	89.5	78.4	91.6	50.3	36.4	41.3	15.1	72.5	14.4
Atlanta, GA	88.9	90.2	89.5	86.7	63.1	37.0	40.8	28.7	55.4	18.6
Austin, TX	89.3	90.5	90.1	92.2	72.0	42.9	44.6	27.9	68.9	21.3
Baton Rouge, LA	87.4	90.6	82.0	85.2	71.5	27.6	31.9	18.3	52.4	18.3
Billings, MT	93.0	93.5	83.6	81.2	77.3	30.2	30.8	21.0	41.2	11.7
Boise City, ID	91.3	92.4	83.0	86.4	65.9	30.9	31.4	24.0	47.7	12.2
Boston, MA	91.3	93.8	84.1	85.5	70.7	46.4	48.8	25.7	60.5	20.9
Boulder, CO	94.6	95.6	92.4	90.2	70.9	60.4	61.5	40.3	66.4	23.7
Cape Coral, FL	87.3	89.0	76.1	89.3	66.2	27.2	28.5	15.6	37.5	13.9
Cedar Rapids, IA	94.3	95.0	81.4	94.1	77.8	30.1	30.1	15.3	62.7	23.4
Charleston, SC	90.1	93.0	83.5	86.6	69.5	34.1	40.8	15.6	47.1	20.4
Charlotte, NC	88.3	90.1	87.2	84.9	61.8	33.9	36.3	25.3	55.7	16.4
Chicago, IL	87.9	90.7	87.0	90.9	65.2	36.7	40.1	21.8	63.9	13.9
Clarksville, TN	89.9	90.3	89.1	79.7	85.3	23.4	24.1	19.4	32.8	16.3
College Station, TX	85.2	87.8	82.0	92.1	60.1	35.3	38.2	13.2	76.6	15.8
Colorado Springs, CO	93.8	95.1	94.2	85.1	80.2	37.2	39.6	23.8	41.6	19.8
Columbia, MO	93.5	94.5	87.9	91.5	79.1	45.9	47.6	17.6	70.2	35.8
Columbia, SC	89.0	91.3	86.4	87.0	63.9	31.9	36.9	22.0	52.0	17.5
Columbus, OH	90.9	92.1	86.8	87.7	73.3	35.3	36.8	21.0	62.7	22.8
Dallas, TX	84.8	85.3	89.9	88.2	57.6	33.7	34.6	25.6	60.1	12.5
Denver, CO	90.5	92.0	89.5	84.9	68.6	42.1	44.3	25.1	50.5	14.8
Des Moines, IA	92.4	93.8	85.0	77.5	61.3	36.1	37.3	18.9	40.7	13.2
Durham, NC	88.7	91.2	86.0	91.8	49.4	46.3	52.9	29.4	72.7	15.7
Edison, NJ	85.9	90.2	84.5	83.0	69.7	38.7	43.9	24.5	53.2	18.2
El Paso, TX	76.7	77.3	94.0	91.7	72.2	22.1	22.3	27.8	48.6	18.1
Eugene, OR	91.5	92.4	92.6	89.1	69.1	29.6	29.7	31.7	54.5	16.9
Evansville, IN	90.0	90.5	84.8	93.6	61.8	24.9	25.5	12.6	53.1	18.0
Fargo, ND	94.4	95.7	80.0	77.6	77.3	37.0	37.8	21.3	46.7	20.3
Fayetteville, NC	89.8	91.7	89.4	82.5	83.6	23.4	25.6	21.6	31.7	19.4
Fort Collins, CO	95.8	96.2	92.0	94.8	81.1	45.9	46.3	34.2	69.0	23.4
Fort Wayne, IN	89.6	91.5	84.0	66.5	61.0	26.2	27.5	14.3	35.5	10.4
Fort Worth, TX	84.8	85.3	89.9	88.2	57.6	33.7	34.6	25.6	60.1	12.5
Gainesville, FL	91.6	93.3	84.3	94.1	88.3	39.4	42.0	19.0	72.2	38.0
Grand Rapids, MI	90.4	92.4	82.7	75.8	60.0	31.8	33.3	16.8	36.1	13.4
Greeley, CO	87.7	89.3	85.6	81.3	64.5	27.0	28.0	26.6	41.6	8.9
Green Bay, WI	91.4	93.0	86.7	80.5	55.4	27.1	27.9	16.2	41.2	9.0
Greensboro, NC	86.3	88.1	86.2	73.7	55.5	28.5	31.2	21.7	39.0	12.3
Honolulu, HI	91.4	97.1	96.5	88.3	92.2	34.0	47.4	27.2	34.9	22.9
Houston, TX	82.8	82.8	89.8	87.5	61.7	31.9	32.3	26.3	57.1	13.7
Huntsville, AL	89.3	90.6	85.4	92.9	64.5	37.3	39.3	27.9	57.7	22.7
Indianapolis, IN	89.3	90.8	85.3	83.2	61.0	33.1	35.1	19.7	55.5	14.6
Jacksonville, FL	90.4	91.9	86.4	86.8	84.4	29.9	32.1	18.2	48.7	26.6
Kansas City, MO	91.5	93.2	87.6	84.6	66.3	35.7	38.2	19.3	53.7	16.2
Lafayette, LA	82.4	86.1	72.4	65.7	64.5	22.1	25.4	11.2	26.2	14.7
Las Cruces, NM	79.2	79.5	95.1	93.6	69.3	27.4	27.1	47.4	59.5	15.2
Las Vegas, NV	85.3	87.5	88.5	89.6	65.0	23.3	24.5	17.2	37.5	9.3
Lexington, KY	89.3	90.7	85.4	90.0	58.6	36.2	38.1	18.6	64.6	15.7
Lincoln, NE	93.3	94.9	88.5	80.3	64.7	37.3	38.4	19.3	43.2	16.3
Little Rock, AR	90.2	91.4	87.4	88.5	67.2	29.7	31.9	20.8	58.1	11.9
Los Angeles, CA	79.7	82.3	89.2	87.8	60.2	33.1	35.2	25.6	51.6	12.2

Table continued on next page.

Metro Area	High School Graduate or Higher (%)					Bachelor's Degree or Higher (%)				
	Total	White	Black	Asian	Hisp.[1]	Total	White	Black	Asian	Hisp.[1]
Louisville, KY	89.2	89.7	86.5	85.1	72.5	28.0	29.2	17.1	53.0	21.1
Madison, WI	95.0	96.0	89.3	89.8	73.0	44.8	45.1	23.3	67.2	25.0
Manchester, NH	91.8	92.1	87.5	88.4	71.2	36.5	35.9	24.7	63.8	18.8
McAllen, TX	63.7	64.6	80.8	92.2	60.2	17.8	17.6	18.3	63.6	15.6
Miami, FL	85.1	86.5	80.4	86.6	79.5	30.6	33.4	18.5	49.8	25.8
Midland, TX	83.5	84.7	83.4	81.9	67.0	26.6	28.5	14.1	45.1	10.8
Minneapolis, MN	93.4	95.9	82.2	80.2	66.5	40.5	42.6	20.9	43.7	18.5
Nashville, TN	89.1	90.2	86.9	83.3	61.7	34.0	35.2	26.0	50.2	15.3
New Orleans, LA	86.0	90.0	80.6	74.7	74.2	29.0	35.4	16.9	39.1	19.0
New York, NY	85.9	90.2	84.5	83.0	69.7	38.7	43.9	24.5	53.2	18.2
Oklahoma City, OK	88.4	89.4	89.8	82.9	58.9	29.6	31.0	20.7	44.3	12.0
Omaha, NE	91.2	92.6	87.3	75.9	56.3	35.1	36.3	21.8	49.9	13.6
Orlando, FL	89.1	90.7	84.8	87.5	82.7	30.3	31.8	20.8	50.9	20.7
Peoria, IL	91.6	92.9	79.6	94.2	71.7	28.2	28.4	12.9	71.7	20.7
Philadelphia, PA	90.0	92.5	86.4	83.9	68.9	36.2	40.1	20.0	55.6	16.7
Phoenix, AZ	86.9	88.8	89.1	87.4	65.6	30.3	31.3	23.9	55.9	11.8
Pittsburgh, PA	93.3	93.7	89.2	88.1	87.4	33.5	33.8	19.3	71.8	35.0
Portland, OR	91.5	93.1	88.1	86.0	66.8	37.9	38.6	25.0	49.3	18.5
Providence, RI	86.3	88.0	82.3	83.9	69.3	31.0	32.3	20.8	50.8	13.1
Provo, UT	93.9	94.5	88.9	93.2	71.9	38.9	39.1	33.5	55.3	19.0
Raleigh, NC	91.0	93.3	88.2	91.8	59.5	45.2	48.6	29.9	71.3	19.3
Reno, NV	87.7	89.3	89.8	88.7	61.1	29.7	30.9	21.2	42.8	10.2
Richmond, VA	89.1	91.9	83.8	87.8	68.5	35.2	40.6	20.9	61.4	19.7
Roanoke, VA	88.6	89.7	84.3	74.8	72.5	27.0	28.9	13.0	43.4	14.6
Rochester, MN	94.0	95.1	82.7	83.5	72.4	36.9	36.6	22.6	56.6	20.9
Salem, OR	86.0	88.3	82.2	83.6	55.7	24.2	25.6	16.9	34.7	7.8
Salt Lake City, UT	90.3	93.6	84.0	85.4	66.1	33.1	35.0	26.3	49.4	12.8
San Antonio, TX	84.6	85.0	91.1	86.4	75.2	27.4	27.8	28.2	51.5	16.1
San Diego, CA	86.7	87.7	90.7	88.9	67.6	37.4	38.3	24.3	50.1	16.3
San Francisco, CA	88.5	92.6	89.8	86.6	69.8	47.4	53.2	26.0	53.2	19.7
San Jose, CA	87.3	90.0	91.5	90.1	67.2	49.2	47.5	36.2	63.5	15.7
Santa Rosa, CA	87.7	92.0	88.2	87.3	60.5	33.8	37.3	25.2	42.8	12.6
Savannah, GA	89.2	91.3	85.3	86.7	78.9	31.1	36.3	19.3	49.6	25.8
Seattle, WA	92.2	94.5	88.5	87.7	71.9	41.1	42.1	23.5	53.2	21.0
Sioux Falls, SD	92.5	94.1	74.9	72.2	64.7	32.5	33.8	15.1	35.9	13.5
Springfield, IL	92.4	93.4	84.2	91.6	86.5	33.6	34.6	19.9	65.4	31.0
Tallahassee, FL	90.2	93.5	82.6	96.2	81.3	37.7	42.7	23.2	79.5	32.7
Tampa, FL	89.1	90.2	85.7	85.9	78.7	28.8	29.3	21.2	50.5	20.6
Topeka, KS	91.9	92.9	84.0	86.6	75.0	28.1	29.3	13.0	59.4	13.4
Tyler, TX	84.9	85.0	85.7	96.0	48.4	25.2	27.2	12.7	62.8	7.5
Virginia Beach, VA	90.8	93.4	86.1	87.3	85.2	30.8	34.9	20.9	42.1	23.1
Visalia, CA	68.6	69.3	80.7	77.0	53.3	13.8	14.2	20.0	29.4	6.0
Washington, DC	90.5	93.4	90.9	90.9	66.5	49.9	57.7	33.5	64.2	24.9
Wilmington, NC	91.2	93.3	83.6	80.2	60.2	36.1	39.8	15.7	51.9	17.9
Winston-Salem, NC	86.2	87.0	86.8	86.2	52.8	26.3	27.2	21.6	49.7	10.8
U.S.	87.3	89.3	84.9	86.5	66.7	30.9	32.2	20.6	52.7	15.2

Note: Figures shown cover persons 25 years old and over; Figures cover the Metropolitan Statistical Area—see Appendix B for areas included; (1) People of Hispanic origin can be of any race
Source: U.S. Census Bureau, 2013-2017 American Community Survey 5-Year Estimates

Cost of Living Index

Urban Area	Composite	Groceries	Housing	Utilities	Transp.	Health	Misc.
Albany, NY	109.8	107.2	119.4	98.9	100.8	105.2	108.6
Albuquerque, NM	97.0	104.7	91.3	93.7	98.5	102.0	98.7
Allentown, PA	106.1	98.6	117.7	104.6	105.8	100.8	100.3
Anchorage, AK	129.1	134.0	142.9	123.0	109.3	144.0	120.5
Ann Arbor, MI	n/a	n/a	n/a	n/a	n/a	n/a	n/a
Athens, GA	n/a	n/a	n/a	n/a	n/a	n/a	n/a
Atlanta, GA	102.0	99.6	106.6	87.1	99.8	108.9	102.6
Austin, TX	98.6	88.8	101.0	96.6	90.9	104.0	102.2
Baton Rouge	100.3	106.6	92.9	87.4	103.1	110.3	105.5
Billings, MT	n/a	n/a	n/a	n/a	n/a	n/a	n/a
Boise City, ID	97.3	95.8	91.9	87.5	112.8	103.8	100.0
Boston, MA	150.2	108.5	214.4	121.8	116.2	133.9	130.5
Boulder, CO	n/a	n/a	n/a	n/a	n/a	n/a	n/a
Cape Coral, FL	95.3	105.0	86.1	100.0	114.1	102.5	92.2
Cedar Rapids, IA	93.9	95.6	84.9	109.0	97.1	95.4	95.9
Charleston, SC	100.8	95.2	94.8	127.1	90.0	106.3	103.5
Charlotte, NC	97.2	99.6	85.6	94.1	94.8	107.4	106.2
Chicago, IL	123.3	102.6	157.5	93.0	125.2	101.6	112.5
Clarksville, TN	n/a	n/a	n/a	n/a	n/a	n/a	n/a
College Station, TX	n/a	n/a	n/a	n/a	n/a	n/a	n/a
Colorado Springs, CO	98.9	96.4	100.3	89.9	104.8	100.9	99.3
Columbia, MO	93.0	96.6	81.8	99.7	91.1	101.3	98.8
Columbia, SC	97.4	109.2	77.0	124.1	91.8	91.4	105.3
Columbus, OH	90.9	95.8	77.7	87.4	92.5	92.1	100.4
Dallas, TX	105.6	107.0	106.7	105.8	98.1	105.2	106.0
Denver, CO	113.3	99.0	139.3	81.0	104.2	102.9	109.0
Des Moines, IA	90.6	95.9	82.1	89.5	102.2	98.5	92.0
Durham, NC	91.3	93.1	82.5	93.3	100.9	93.7	94.8
Edison, NJ[1]	117.5	104.1	139.7	106.7	110.9	106.4	109.7
El Paso, TX	n/a	n/a	n/a	n/a	n/a	n/a	n/a
Eugene, OR	n/a	n/a	n/a	n/a	n/a	n/a	n/a
Evansville, IN	92.3	89.4	82.2	109.3	92.8	98.4	96.8
Fargo, ND	99.3	110.4	89.2	89.9	99.8	115.4	103.9
Fayetteville, NC	n/a	n/a	n/a	n/a	n/a	n/a	n/a
Fort Collins, CO	n/a	n/a	n/a	n/a	n/a	n/a	n/a
Fort Wayne, IN	88.1	87.4	67.0	91.1	101.7	100.6	100.1
Fort Worth, TX	98.1	94.7	89.8	105.2	103.2	104.5	102.5
Gainesville, FL	n/a	n/a	n/a	n/a	n/a	n/a	n/a
Grand Rapids, MI	97.1	89.7	90.6	98.3	102.2	93.1	104.2
Greeley, CO	n/a	n/a	n/a	n/a	n/a	n/a	n/a
Green Bay, WI	89.6	87.9	81.1	93.4	93.4	102.6	93.9
Greensboro, NC[2]	92.9	95.5	67.3	94.7	103.9	117.0	107.0
Honolulu, HI	190.1	165.9	311.0	172.1	140.7	116.3	124.2
Houston, TX	96.3	85.7	97.3	109.9	98.6	93.3	95.9
Huntsville, AL	93.6	93.4	74.2	96.3	93.1	100.6	108.6
Indianapolis, IN	93.0	94.3	79.5	105.6	94.2	91.5	100.4
Jacksonville, FL	92.0	98.2	86.4	97.4	87.4	82.9	95.2
Kansas City, MO	95.1	102.7	85.1	99.0	93.7	99.9	99.5
Lafayette, LA	90.1	99.4	78.7	88.2	103.6	87.8	93.4
Las Cruces, NM	90.0	110.1	76.2	83.7	91.9	105.6	93.2
Las Vegas, NV	104.6	96.6	121.6	95.5	106.9	102.8	95.4
Lexington, KY	94.3	88.5	89.6	93.1	98.5	87.7	100.6
Lincoln, NE	94.5	97.5	81.0	91.0	96.9	103.3	103.8
Little Rock, AR	97.4	94.9	88.9	95.5	98.8	87.2	107.0
Los Angeles, CA	148.4	112.0	238.0	109.7	118.6	107.4	109.9
Louisville, KY	93.3	88.7	78.7	92.0	100.9	97.6	105.3

Table continued on next page.

Urban Area	Composite	Groceries	Housing	Utilities	Transp.	Health	Misc.
Madison, WI	106.1	105.4	109.4	99.4	103.3	118.5	104.4
Manchester, NH	109.3	103.8	106.9	115.0	97.4	117.1	114.2
McAllen, TX	77.5	83.1	62.7	101.9	89.1	71.8	79.1
Miami, FL	116.4	110.1	146.5	101.1	105.4	96.1	102.7
Midland, TX	96.3	89.7	82.3	105.3	105.8	92.3	106.2
Minneapolis, MN	106.4	105.3	104.0	97.6	107.9	105.8	110.9
Nashville, TN	99.3	95.3	93.4	96.7	94.7	83.9	109.6
New Orleans, LA	100.8	104.3	117.0	81.5	109.3	103.2	88.2
New York, NY[3]	182.0	124.2	324.8	120.7	110.1	110.1	127.5
Oklahoma City, OK	84.7	92.1	72.1	94.5	85.6	92.9	88.8
Omaha, NE	95.1	97.1	89.0	99.7	103.2	98.4	95.7
Orlando, FL	95.8	106.0	88.3	102.2	93.0	89.1	98.1
Peoria, IL	95.2	94.9	82.8	92.7	100.0	98.0	104.8
Philadelphia, PA	113.5	116.7	124.8	107.4	113.5	103.3	105.6
Phoenix, AZ	97.5	98.7	94.7	111.3	98.9	95.3	95.8
Pittsburgh, PA	99.2	107.6	95.6	107.7	108.9	92.1	95.1
Portland, OR	131.2	112.3	182.2	88.1	116.8	111.2	112.9
Providence, RI	122.5	109.4	142.1	121.2	102.3	111.0	118.1
Provo, UT	99.2	94.2	99.9	87.1	106.8	102.6	101.1
Raleigh, NC	91.6	93.4	85.1	93.0	94.0	100.5	94.2
Reno, NV	111.9	121.8	116.7	82.3	113.6	111.9	111.2
Richmond, VA	95.0	86.6	88.6	96.5	92.5	115.4	101.3
Roanoke, VA	88.7	86.6	79.0	101.6	87.4	102.5	93.1
Rochester, MN	n/a	n/a	n/a	n/a	n/a	n/a	n/a
Salem, OR	n/a	n/a	n/a	n/a	n/a	n/a	n/a
Salt Lake City, UT	102.8	109.7	102.0	89.8	104.5	99.0	104.3
San Antonio, TX	86.9	86.9	76.4	88.9	87.3	84.7	95.5
San Diego, CA	147.3	112.6	231.0	131.6	121.9	108.0	105.6
San Francisco, CA	196.7	130.6	357.1	126.7	132.2	126.2	130.6
San Jose, CA	n/a	n/a	n/a	n/a	n/a	n/a	n/a
Santa Rosa, CA	n/a	n/a	n/a	n/a	n/a	n/a	n/a
Savannah, GA	88.1	93.7	64.8	96.5	97.0	99.3	99.6
Seattle, WA	155.0	127.0	213.2	111.1	135.0	123.2	137.1
Sioux Falls, SD	97.0	98.0	85.5	92.8	95.4	112.2	105.9
Springfield, IL	n/a	n/a	n/a	n/a	n/a	n/a	n/a
Tallahassee, FL	96.7	110.3	91.7	87.0	95.9	99.0	98.2
Tampa, FL	89.2	103.7	71.8	87.7	99.6	95.4	95.2
Topeka, KS	90.9	97.1	79.4	100.4	95.4	93.4	94.3
Tyler, TX	91.0	92.6	78.0	107.4	94.7	95.3	95.5
Virginia Beach, VA[4]	96.6	96.8	92.7	96.0	91.3	96.7	101.3
Visalia, CA	n/a	n/a	n/a	n/a	n/a	n/a	n/a
Washington, DC	162.9	116.9	268.2	115.6	102.7	99.6	127.7
Wilmington, NC	96.1	99.5	81.8	95.4	101.6	117.1	103.0
Winston-Salem, NC	92.9	95.5	67.3	94.7	103.9	117.0	107.0
U.S.	100.0	100.0	100.0	100.0	100.0	100.0	100.0

Note: The Cost of Living Index measures regional differences in the cost of consumer goods and services, excluding taxes and non-consumer expenditures, for professional and managerial households in the top income quintile. It is based on more than 50,000 prices covering almost 60 different items for which prices are collected three times a year by chambers of commerce, economic development organizations or university applied economic centers in each participating urban area. The numbers shown should be read as a percentage above or below the national average of 100. For example, a value of 115.4 in the groceries column indicates that grocery prices are 15.4% higher than the national average. Small differences in the index numbers should not be interpreted as significant. In cases where data is not available for the city, data for the metro area or for a neighboring city has been provided and noted as follows: (1) Middlesex-Monmouth NJ; (2) Winston-Salem, NC; (3) Brooklyn, NY; (4) Hampton Roads-SE Virginia
Source: The Council for Community and Economic Research (formerly ACCRA), Cost of Living Index, 2018

Grocery Prices

Urban Area	T-Bone Steak ($/pound)	Frying Chicken ($/pound)	Whole Milk ($/half gal.)	Eggs ($/dozen)	Orange Juice ($/64 oz.)	Coffee ($/11.5 oz.)
Albany, NY	11.77	1.39	2.47	2.16	3.51	4.08
Albuquerque, NM	11.22	1.69	2.11	1.93	3.64	5.41
Allentown, PA	12.77	1.35	1.83	1.85	3.23	3.79
Anchorage, AK	12.90	1.67	2.61	2.31	4.24	5.60
Ann Arbor, MI	n/a	n/a	n/a	n/a	n/a	n/a
Athens, GA	n/a	n/a	n/a	n/a	n/a	n/a
Atlanta, GA	12.21	1.39	1.90	1.98	3.50	4.77
Austin, TX	9.85	1.15	1.52	1.70	3.09	3.84
Baton Rouge	12.45	1.33	2.54	2.12	3.91	4.21
Billings, MT	n/a	n/a	n/a	n/a	n/a	n/a
Boise City, ID	11.85	1.24	1.46	1.30	3.74	4.78
Boston, MA	13.18	1.76	1.97	2.02	3.51	4.52
Boulder, CO	n/a	n/a	n/a	n/a	n/a	n/a
Cape Coral, FL	11.05	1.43	2.33	2.10	3.54	3.54
Cedar Rapids, IA	10.86	1.42	1.98	1.32	3.00	4.20
Charleston, SC	9.60	1.16	1.81	1.97	3.37	3.40
Charlotte, NC	10.48	1.10	1.75	1.39	3.67	3.76
Chicago, IL	12.25	1.36	2.09	1.82	4.40	4.59
Clarksville, TN	n/a	n/a	n/a	n/a	n/a	n/a
College Station, TX	n/a	n/a	n/a	n/a	n/a	n/a
Colorado Springs, CO	12.98	1.36	1.50	1.74	3.21	4.71
Columbia, MO	11.04	1.53	1.93	1.38	3.39	4.27
Columbia, SC	12.27	1.30	1.88	2.02	3.92	4.70
Columbus, OH	11.12	1.25	1.56	1.13	3.11	7.51
Dallas, TX	10.82	1.63	2.62	1.87	3.77	5.29
Denver, CO	11.79	1.42	1.65	1.96	3.67	4.88
Des Moines, IA	10.79	1.85	1.89	2.22	3.06	4.07
Durham, NC	10.54	1.15	1.51	1.51	3.22	4.18
Edison, NJ[1]	12.29	1.39	2.28	2.13	3.24	4.07
El Paso, TX	n/a	n/a	n/a	n/a	n/a	n/a
Eugene, OR	n/a	n/a	n/a	n/a	n/a	n/a
Evansville, IN	11.68	1.25	0.96	1.21	3.36	3.27
Fargo, ND	13.91	1.70	2.79	2.00	3.80	4.43
Fayetteville, NC	n/a	n/a	n/a	n/a	n/a	n/a
Fort Collins, CO	n/a	n/a	n/a	n/a	n/a	n/a
Fort Wayne, IN	11.93	1.03	1.47	1.02	3.28	4.29
Fort Worth, TX	11.55	1.50	1.53	1.29	3.27	4.07
Gainesville, FL	n/a	n/a	n/a	n/a	n/a	n/a
Grand Rapids, MI	10.45	1.06	1.77	1.53	3.32	3.36
Greeley, CO	n/a	n/a	n/a	n/a	n/a	n/a
Green Bay, WI	13.06	1.41	1.70	1.08	3.31	4.35
Greensboro, NC[2]	10.16	1.46	1.45	1.31	3.63	3.75
Honolulu, HI	10.50	2.36	4.18	4.00	5.36	8.20
Houston, TX	10.31	1.15	1.18	1.58	3.29	3.51
Huntsville, AL	11.92	1.42	1.73	1.17	3.30	4.03
Indianapolis, IN	11.80	1.38	1.51	1.44	3.40	4.31
Jacksonville, FL	11.17	1.39	2.42	2.21	3.27	3.86
Kansas City, MO	11.76	1.44	2.10	1.79	3.35	4.19
Lafayette, LA	12.83	1.28	2.42	1.80	3.47	3.85
Las Cruces, NM	11.10	1.50	2.22	1.94	3.98	5.44
Las Vegas, NV	7.45	1.21	2.51	2.03	4.18	4.93
Lexington, KY	12.34	1.17	1.52	1.43	3.34	3.76
Lincoln, NE	10.96	1.53	2.50	1.93	3.27	3.98
Little Rock, AR	9.69	1.26	2.16	1.52	3.36	4.04
Los Angeles, CA	13.27	1.70	2.08	2.77	3.43	5.55

Table continued on next page.

Urban Area	T-Bone Steak ($/pound)	Frying Chicken ($/pound)	Whole Milk ($/half gal.)	Eggs ($/dozen)	Orange Juice ($/64 oz.)	Coffee ($/11.5 oz.)
Louisville, KY	10.78	1.29	1.05	1.50	3.35	3.73
Madison, WI	13.82	1.84	2.32	1.83	3.28	4.65
Manchester, NH	12.83	1.52	2.96	1.53	3.31	4.12
McAllen, TX	9.04	0.98	1.39	1.76	3.05	3.91
Miami, FL	11.55	1.54	2.59	2.15	3.78	3.61
Midland, TX	10.70	1.04	1.55	1.79	3.32	4.24
Minneapolis, MN	13.75	2.10	2.51	1.82	3.68	4.70
Nashville, TN	12.08	1.16	1.78	1.51	3.22	4.03
New Orleans, LA	12.05	1.00	2.99	2.38	3.74	3.87
New York, NY[3]	11.51	1.78	2.49	2.60	4.02	4.71
Oklahoma City, OK	10.29	1.27	1.90	1.50	3.28	3.96
Omaha, NE	11.65	1.61	1.67	1.64	3.32	4.03
Orlando, FL	10.51	1.39	2.46	2.05	3.59	3.91
Peoria, IL	12.16	1.78	0.80	1.53	3.86	4.17
Philadelphia, PA	11.47	1.65	2.04	2.41	4.17	4.55
Phoenix, AZ	11.54	1.72	1.42	2.14	3.86	4.84
Pittsburgh, PA	12.95	1.69	1.89	1.78	3.56	4.46
Portland, OR	12.84	1.52	1.87	1.85	4.08	5.42
Providence, RI	12.69	1.64	3.21	2.11	3.55	4.26
Provo, UT	11.08	1.49	1.52	1.31	3.71	4.38
Raleigh, NC	10.07	1.12	1.52	1.45	3.47	3.99
Reno, NV	10.93	1.71	2.75	2.50	3.95	5.38
Richmond, VA	10.43	1.04	1.42	0.97	3.11	3.57
Roanoke, VA	9.74	1.06	1.77	1.15	3.22	3.39
Rochester, MN	n/a	n/a	n/a	n/a	n/a	n/a
Salem, OR	n/a	n/a	n/a	n/a	n/a	n/a
Salt Lake City, UT	11.55	2.35	1.70	2.50	3.88	4.63
San Antonio, TX	11.23	1.03	1.51	2.01	2.99	4.12
San Diego, CA	12.21	1.59	2.08	2.77	3.43	5.55
San Francisco, CA	13.41	1.66	2.86	3.37	4.34	6.58
San Jose, CA	n/a	n/a	n/a	n/a	n/a	n/a
Santa Rosa, CA	n/a	n/a	n/a	n/a	n/a	n/a
Savannah, GA	11.11	1.32	2.00	1.76	3.18	4.08
Seattle, WA	14.53	1.91	1.97	2.04	3.91	5.65
Sioux Falls, SD	10.07	1.83	2.04	1.53	3.15	4.53
Springfield, IL	n/a	n/a	n/a	n/a	n/a	n/a
Tallahassee, FL	10.69	1.54	2.43	2.38	3.82	3.97
Tampa, FL	9.23	1.41	2.54	2.16	3.22	3.86
Topeka, KS	10.28	1.74	1.56	1.22	3.51	4.61
Tyler, TX	10.20	1.01	1.66	1.24	3.24	3.69
Virginia Beach, VA[4]	10.13	1.27	1.96	1.13	3.54	4.07
Visalia, CA	n/a	n/a	n/a	n/a	n/a	n/a
Washington, DC	14.28	1.75	2.49	1.74	3.66	4.50
Wilmington, NC	11.08	1.41	1.86	1.91	3.70	3.74
Winston-Salem, NC	10.16	1.46	1.45	1.31	3.63	3.75
Average*	11.35	1.42	1.94	1.81	3.52	4.35
Minimum*	7.45	0.92	0.80	0.75	2.72	3.06
Maximum*	15.05	2.76	4.18	4.00	5.36	8.20

Note: T-Bone Steak (price per pound); Frying Chicken (price per pound, whole fryer); Whole Milk (half gallon carton); Eggs (price per dozen, Grade A, large); Orange Juice (64 oz. Tropicana or Florida Natural); Coffee (11.5 oz. can, vacuum-packed, Maxwell House, Hills Bros, or Folgers); (*) Values for the local area are compared with the average, minimum, and maximum values for all 291 areas in the Cost of Living Index report; n/a not available; In cases where data is not available for the city, data for the metro area or for a neighboring city has been provided and noted as follows: (1) Middlesex-Monmouth NJ; (2) Winston-Salem, NC; (3) Brooklyn, NY; (4) Hampton Roads-SE Virginia
Source: The Council for Community and Economic Research (formerly ACCRA), Cost of Living Index, 2018

Housing and Utility Costs

Urban Area	New Home Price ($)	Apartment Rent ($/month)	All Electric ($/month)	Part Electric ($/month)	Other Energy ($/month)	Telephone ($/month)
Albany, NY	415,615	1,289	-	75.20	82.89	187.10
Albuquerque, NM	315,185	963	-	100.64	45.36	182.50
Allentown, PA	386,339	1,472	-	100.18	77.54	183.50
Anchorage, AK	569,477	1,192	-	103.73	126.81	187.00
Ann Arbor, MI	n/a	n/a	n/a	n/a	n/a	n/a
Athens, GA	n/a	n/a	n/a	n/a	n/a	n/a
Atlanta, GA	348,121	1,334	-	91.36	36.83	179.50
Austin, TX	312,376	1,377	-	106.13	50.37	179.90
Baton Rouge	314,060	1,029	133.63	-	-	173.60
Billings, MT	n/a	n/a	n/a	n/a	n/a	n/a
Boise City, ID	320,087	958	-	69.52	70.97	164.60
Boston, MA	663,942	2,962	-	85.42	151.20	174.00
Boulder, CO	n/a	n/a	n/a	n/a	n/a	n/a
Cape Coral, FL	301,867	935	165.32	-	-	181.80
Cedar Rapids, IA	326,278	731	-	138.07	59.23	175.20
Charleston, SC	288,601	1,339	246.79	-	-	181.60
Charlotte, NC	267,528	1,130	153.16	-	-	174.20
Chicago, IL	500,332	2,051	-	83.93	48.57	197.70
Clarksville, TN	n/a	n/a	n/a	n/a	n/a	n/a
College Station, TX	n/a	n/a	n/a	n/a	n/a	n/a
Colorado Springs, CO	323,230	1,273	-	88.75	50.07	176.50
Columbia, MO	301,682	756	-	95.13	66.53	185.40
Columbia, SC	254,119	938	-	122.61	116.25	180.10
Columbus, OH	250,447	1,007	-	65.88	67.05	174.20
Dallas, TX	327,946	1,440	-	126.07	58.11	179.90
Denver, CO	489,272	1,439	-	63.54	47.34	178.30
Des Moines, IA	312,876	673	-	79.68	59.16	175.10
Durham, NC	278,773	876	150.79	-	-	174.40
Edison, NJ[1]	475,549	1,545	-	121.21	69.69	174.30
El Paso, TX	n/a	n/a	n/a	n/a	n/a	n/a
Eugene, OR	n/a	n/a	n/a	n/a	n/a	n/a
Evansville, IN	287,646	861	-	121.89	73.70	178.60
Fargo, ND	323,100	909	-	76.53	57.71	182.70
Fayetteville, NC	n/a	n/a	n/a	n/a	n/a	n/a
Fort Collins, CO	n/a	n/a	n/a	n/a	n/a	n/a
Fort Wayne, IN	237,439	674	-	87.68	53.38	178.60
Fort Worth, TX	275,461	1,243	-	125.46	57.39	179.10
Gainesville, FL	n/a	n/a	n/a	n/a	n/a	n/a
Grand Rapids, MI	288,912	1,158	-	98.08	67.91	174.00
Greeley, CO	n/a	n/a	n/a	n/a	n/a	n/a
Green Bay, WI	286,068	805	-	81.59	70.58	172.90
Greensboro, NC[2]	216,667	865	154.91	-	-	174.20
Honolulu, HI	1,158,492	2,969	388.65	-	-	172.70
Houston, TX	315,436	1,249	-	157.46	40.04	178.40
Huntsville, AL	237,350	985	158.50	-	-	175.80
Indianapolis, IN	250,625	1,052	-	105.38	79.02	178.60
Jacksonville, FL	262,790	1,244	156.94	-	-	182.70
Kansas City, MO	276,197	1,092	-	91.74	68.59	184.50
Lafayette, LA	269,749	856	-	85.05	49.43	175.40
Las Cruces, NM	273,244	772	-	75.17	39.88	183.40
Las Vegas, NV	438,895	1,106	-	123.00	35.56	172.90
Lexington, KY	308,662	987	-	74.43	71.89	179.50
Lincoln, NE	288,296	827	-	66.38	65.88	190.00
Little Rock, AR	339,778	730	-	90.31	59.65	184.40
Los Angeles, CA	809,182	2,730	-	127.92	64.29	184.70

Table continued on next page.

Urban Area	New Home Price ($)	Apartment Rent ($/month)	All Electric ($/month)	Part Electric ($/month)	Other Energy ($/month)	Telephone ($/month)
Louisville, KY	264,566	924	-	74.48	71.89	175.00
Madison, WI	396,381	1,067	-	106.73	63.18	173.00
Manchester, NH	330,128	1,439	-	124.19	91.51	174.40
McAllen, TX	225,685	640	-	123.82	48.66	179.90
Miami, FL	424,876	2,245	168.06	-	-	182.60
Midland, TX	269,904	1,027	-	142.15	41.25	178.70
Minneapolis, MN	362,307	1,158	-	95.34	66.40	176.70
Nashville, TN	318,571	1,029	-	94.60	62.48	179.40
New Orleans, LA	404,584	1,297	-	75.14	39.44	175.50
New York, NY[3]	1,130,943	3,265	-	86.82	135.61	188.30
Oklahoma City, OK	244,210	828	-	87.20	63.38	179.30
Omaha, NE	294,858	1,086	-	89.69	69.18	189.30
Orlando, FL	287,772	1,120	171.56	-	-	182.30
Peoria, IL	308,294	769	-	75.05	65.31	185.70
Philadelphia, PA	414,251	1,433	-	107.90	76.26	186.50
Phoenix, AZ	319,590	1,065	203.07	-	-	176.50
Pittsburgh, PA	306,332	1,232	-	102.43	84.43	184.00
Portland, OR	549,358	2,595	-	77.40	65.93	163.10
Providence, RI	451,509	1,832	-	119.05	108.75	183.40
Provo, UT	353,314	1,078	-	68.45	59.48	179.90
Raleigh, NC	268,630	1,100	-	90.19	59.78	174.20
Reno, NV	407,087	1,256	-	80.97	38.29	172.20
Richmond, VA	300,306	1,010	-	88.14	73.54	172.40
Roanoke, VA	280,915	816	177.04	-	-	172.40
Rochester, MN	n/a	n/a	n/a	n/a	n/a	n/a
Salem, OR	n/a	n/a	n/a	n/a	n/a	n/a
Salt Lake City, UT	361,743	1,109	-	75.10	60.85	179.90
San Antonio, TX	257,175	923	-	95.94	37.37	179.90
San Diego, CA	830,914	2,355	-	209.36	58.62	171.20
San Francisco, CA	1,243,239	3,821	-	181.80	55.33	192.90
San Jose, CA	n/a	n/a	n/a	n/a	n/a	n/a
Santa Rosa, CA	n/a	n/a	n/a	n/a	n/a	n/a
Savannah, GA	206,878	850	158.73	-	-	176.60
Seattle, WA	725,929	2,508	193.68	-	-	188.60
Sioux Falls, SD	308,639	850	-	96.79	46.96	181.80
Springfield, IL	n/a	n/a	n/a	n/a	n/a	n/a
Tallahassee, FL	312,353	1,043	124.35	-	-	184.30
Tampa, FL	215,261	1,032	127.66	-	-	182.70
Topeka, KS	287,385	794	-	96.10	67.76	185.30
Tyler, TX	233,225	1,116	-	147.22	45.26	175.00
Virginia Beach, VA[4]	306,794	1,125	-	90.69	69.73	172.40
Visalia, CA	n/a	n/a	n/a	n/a	n/a	n/a
Washington, DC	933,450	2,808	-	145.55	68.80	178.90
Wilmington, NC	296,596	788	157.19	-	-	174.30
Winston-Salem, NC	216,667	865	154.91	-	-	174.20
Average*	347,000	1,087	165.93	100.16	67.73	178.70
Minimum*	200,468	500	93.58	25.64	26.78	163.10
Maximum*	1,901,222	4,888	388.65	246.86	332.81	197.70

Note: **New Home Price** (2,400 sf living area, 8,000 sf lot, in urban area with full utilities); **Apartment Rent** (950 sf 2 bedroom/1.5 or 2 bath, unfurnished, excluding all utilities except water); **All Electric** (average monthly cost for an all-electric home); **Part Electric** (average monthly cost for a part-electric home); **Other Energy** (average monthly cost for natural gas, fuel oil, coal, wood, and any other forms of energy except electricity); **Telephone** (price includes the base monthly rate plus taxes and fees for three lines of mobile phone service); (*) Values for the local area are compared with the average, minimum, and maximum values for all 291 areas in the Cost of Living Index report; n/a not available; In cases where data is not available for the city, data for the metro area or for a neighboring city has been provided and noted as follows: (1) Middlesex-Monmouth NJ; (2) Winston-Salem, NC; (3) Brooklyn, NY; (4) Hampton Roads-SE Virginia
Source: The Council for Community and Economic Research (formerly ACCRA), Cost of Living Index, 2018

Health Care, Transportation, and Other Costs

Urban Area	Doctor ($/visit)	Dentist ($/visit)	Optometrist ($/visit)	Gasoline ($/gallon)	Beauty Salon ($/visit)	Men's Shirt ($)
Albany, NY	108.38	102.67	127.12	2.75	41.97	36.31
Albuquerque, NM	104.83	105.24	105.98	2.42	52.05	35.66
Allentown, PA	89.68	110.19	112.61	2.91	37.06	25.53
Anchorage, AK	190.50	142.69	200.29	3.11	52.50	37.95
Ann Arbor, MI	n/a	n/a	n/a	n/a	n/a	n/a
Athens, GA	n/a	n/a	n/a	n/a	n/a	n/a
Atlanta, GA	110.08	120.36	103.60	2.64	44.77	28.68
Austin, TX	104.33	108.31	112.50	2.45	47.08	31.68
Baton Rouge	121.03	113.42	118.72	2.43	46.67	44.42
Billings, MT	n/a	n/a	n/a	n/a	n/a	n/a
Boise City, ID	124.59	91.27	117.18	2.89	34.87	31.83
Boston, MA	191.62	132.93	105.58	2.71	54.96	56.59
Boulder, CO	n/a	n/a	n/a	n/a	n/a	n/a
Cape Coral, FL	115.00	99.50	64.66	2.60	26.00	25.49
Cedar Rapids, IA	112.26	79.30	104.10	2.52	32.49	40.60
Charleston, SC	120.07	105.09	97.71	2.41	43.22	25.96
Charlotte, NC	106.56	115.25	122.56	2.57	37.13	40.97
Chicago, IL	105.00	102.00	97.00	3.34	69.90	32.00
Clarksville, TN	n/a	n/a	n/a	n/a	n/a	n/a
College Station, TX	n/a	n/a	n/a	n/a	n/a	n/a
Colorado Springs, CO	123.78	89.03	107.53	2.60	39.00	24.50
Columbia, MO	138.83	84.03	89.20	2.45	36.42	37.78
Columbia, SC	105.22	90.00	90.67	2.41	48.47	31.56
Columbus, OH	107.45	82.73	62.59	2.53	36.00	31.38
Dallas, TX	110.28	101.77	103.33	2.38	46.95	36.69
Denver, CO	120.06	95.38	100.40	2.53	41.83	34.91
Des Moines, IA	128.15	82.71	100.87	2.61	32.24	21.60
Durham, NC	91.20	95.26	103.54	2.44	40.18	18.89
Edison, NJ[1]	96.97	117.83	112.58	2.78	34.27	35.59
El Paso, TX	n/a	n/a	n/a	n/a	n/a	n/a
Eugene, OR	n/a	n/a	n/a	n/a	n/a	n/a
Evansville, IN	106.38	92.08	119.53	2.59	33.29	28.61
Fargo, ND	167.97	98.00	102.20	2.47	35.60	28.20
Fayetteville, NC	n/a	n/a	n/a	n/a	n/a	n/a
Fort Collins, CO	n/a	n/a	n/a	n/a	n/a	n/a
Fort Wayne, IN	126.33	90.67	94.17	2.64	31.50	49.31
Fort Worth, TX	118.48	97.67	97.68	2.51	54.22	47.17
Gainesville, FL	n/a	n/a	n/a	n/a	n/a	n/a
Grand Rapids, MI	96.94	87.78	91.61	2.79	37.61	35.08
Greeley, CO	n/a	n/a	n/a	n/a	n/a	n/a
Green Bay, WI	143.22	89.31	58.89	2.29	22.06	30.86
Greensboro, NC[2]	136.11	118.88	126.67	2.51	39.62	37.62
Honolulu, HI	129.38	101.17	172.56	3.54	62.33	51.71
Houston, TX	84.62	97.84	108.89	2.40	52.70	31.93
Huntsville, AL	107.26	96.19	125.87	2.43	41.42	44.35
Indianapolis, IN	93.91	92.23	60.20	2.64	39.63	39.87
Jacksonville, FL	62.89	89.40	65.58	2.51	52.72	24.03
Kansas City, MO	94.24	106.60	100.58	2.50	30.23	34.80
Lafayette, LA	87.50	81.13	69.86	2.30	36.27	23.78
Las Cruces, NM	121.50	105.24	106.29	2.58	51.95	25.00
Las Vegas, NV	110.90	101.37	114.22	2.83	45.60	31.44
Lexington, KY	99.86	77.91	75.47	2.66	43.33	34.56
Lincoln, NE	134.07	86.40	112.02	2.56	39.62	37.92
Little Rock, AR	114.28	69.92	74.89	2.46	41.43	41.64
Los Angeles, CA	102.78	107.00	119.80	3.28	63.13	36.00

Table continued on next page.

Urban Area	Doctor ($/visit)	Dentist ($/visit)	Optometrist ($/visit)	Gasoline ($/gallon)	Beauty Salon ($/visit)	Men's Shirt ($)
Louisville, KY	137.11	78.53	75.94	2.75	44.39	46.65
Madison, WI	182.00	101.33	59.00	2.51	41.78	31.99
Manchester, NH	149.21	118.08	101.83	2.31	37.37	34.64
McAllen, TX	53.95	62.55	91.11	2.42	31.67	17.49
Miami, FL	91.11	95.28	94.86	2.74	56.11	26.39
Midland, TX	81.11	94.39	102.58	2.65	34.45	38.11
Minneapolis, MN	144.82	85.76	88.91	2.57	34.88	34.24
Nashville, TN	94.52	74.93	79.10	2.49	45.67	39.40
New Orleans, LA	120.49	96.34	82.95	2.42	40.62	23.98
New York, NY[3]	115.67	116.30	100.11	2.64	71.88	50.22
Oklahoma City, OK	89.82	91.21	97.00	2.24	35.63	20.12
Omaha, NE	138.94	74.45	99.55	2.51	37.03	27.33
Orlando, FL	85.25	82.50	79.07	2.52	53.24	21.86
Peoria, IL	103.07	93.47	119.16	2.67	28.80	34.58
Philadelphia, PA	131.51	96.79	101.11	2.80	56.15	31.16
Phoenix, AZ	99.00	94.50	87.75	2.67	56.67	24.50
Pittsburgh, PA	100.97	85.45	75.79	2.94	35.42	21.70
Portland, OR	129.73	102.12	136.32	3.17	49.32	42.73
Providence, RI	154.86	92.86	128.37	2.31	54.21	34.81
Provo, UT	106.15	109.25	89.33	2.77	34.05	24.11
Raleigh, NC	104.67	100.92	104.05	2.60	45.87	23.04
Reno, NV	129.30	107.33	117.45	3.19	36.53	25.48
Richmond, VA	127.68	122.40	113.50	2.43	44.33	32.58
Roanoke, VA	98.42	112.72	91.70	2.34	30.79	17.34
Rochester, MN	n/a	n/a	n/a	n/a	n/a	n/a
Salem, OR	n/a	n/a	n/a	n/a	n/a	n/a
Salt Lake City, UT	106.87	92.92	86.99	2.73	35.60	24.03
San Antonio, TX	92.75	75.38	84.43	2.25	39.00	21.88
San Diego, CA	111.80	104.50	112.17	3.27	57.33	33.13
San Francisco, CA	148.84	131.50	133.29	3.50	71.62	44.33
San Jose, CA	n/a	n/a	n/a	n/a	n/a	n/a
Santa Rosa, CA	n/a	n/a	n/a	n/a	n/a	n/a
Savannah, GA	115.88	94.74	82.13	2.42	35.62	26.38
Seattle, WA	123.47	133.08	146.41	3.42	43.74	45.00
Sioux Falls, SD	147.74	96.51	132.58	2.61	28.07	37.09
Springfield, IL	n/a	n/a	n/a	n/a	n/a	n/a
Tallahassee, FL	98.80	97.06	90.48	2.57	36.33	27.04
Tampa, FL	108.31	90.56	87.92	2.57	34.33	23.68
Topeka, KS	88.42	88.44	121.81	2.41	32.67	33.63
Tyler, TX	91.76	91.33	118.11	2.42	42.53	31.64
Virginia Beach, VA[4]	98.13	94.43	96.66	2.42	32.20	42.49
Visalia, CA	n/a	n/a	n/a	n/a	n/a	n/a
Washington, DC	107.59	94.35	78.30	2.57	67.14	42.07
Wilmington, NC	128.89	126.74	121.02	2.54	42.92	35.35
Winston-Salem, NC	136.11	118.88	126.67	2.51	39.62	37.62
Average*	110.71	95.11	103.74	2.61	37.48	32.03
Minimum*	33.60	62.55	54.63	1.89	17.00	11.44
Maximum*	195.97	153.93	225.79	3.59	71.88	58.64

Note: **Doctor** (general practitioners routine exam of an established patient); **Dentist** (adult teeth cleaning and periodic oral examination); **Optometrist** (full vision eye exam for established adult patient); **Gasoline** (one gallon regular unleaded, national brand, including all taxes, cash price at self-service pump if available); **Beauty Salon** (woman's shampoo, trim, and blow-dry); **Men's Shirt** (cotton/polyester dress shirt, pinpoint weave, long sleeves); (*) Values for the local area are compared with the average, minimum, and maximum values for all 291 areas in the Cost of Living Index report; n/a not available; In cases where data is not available for the city, data for the metro area or for a neighboring city has been provided and noted as follows: (1) Middlesex-Monmouth NJ; (2) Winston-Salem, NC; (3) Brooklyn, NY; (4) Hampton Roads-SE Virginia
Source: The Council for Community and Economic Research (formerly ACCRA), Cost of Living Index, 2018

Number of Medical Professionals

City	Area Covered	MDs[1]	DOs[1,2]	Dentists	Podiatrists	Chiropractors	Optometrists
Albany, NY	Albany County	580.1	39.8	89.8	8.1	20.0	17.8
Albuquerque, NM	Bernalillo County	445.4	21.9	84.8	8.6	23.9	15.8
Allentown, PA	Lehigh County	340.4	84.8	87.0	13.9	30.3	19.1
Anchorage, AK	Anchorage (B) Borough	342.3	43.7	123.7	4.4	59.1	26.8
Ann Arbor, MI	Washtenaw County	1,221.9	41.1	173.5	6.8	24.8	16.9
Athens, GA	Clarke County	290.4	12.8	54.3	4.7	22.8	16.5
Atlanta, GA	Fulton County	501.0	12.0	70.8	4.9	52.8	15.9
Austin, TX	Travis County	312.0	20.4	69.0	4.5	33.1	16.1
Baton Rouge, LA	East Baton Rouge Parish	377.0	7.1	72.8	4.0	11.2	13.4
Billings, MT	Yellowstone County	351.4	24.7	96.9	5.7	34.6	25.2
Boise City, ID	Ada County	290.1	31.1	78.6	3.3	54.9	18.8
Boston, MA	Suffolk County	1,433.5	15.5	204.5	9.1	13.5	32.5
Boulder, CO	Boulder County	358.4	30.5	100.2	6.2	73.8	26.4
Cape Coral, FL	Lee County	184.9	28.9	48.7	8.0	26.8	12.7
Cedar Rapids, IA	Linn County	177.1	22.1	73.2	8.5	56.2	17.0
Charleston, SC	Charleston County	793.1	30.5	105.1	4.7	46.1	21.2
Charlotte, NC	Mecklenburg County	316.1	11.2	67.6	3.3	31.2	13.6
Chicago, IL	Cook County	434.2	22.8	89.5	12.5	27.1	19.8
Clarksville, TN	Montgomery County	102.2	18.0	45.0	2.5	15.5	13.0
College Station, TX	Brazos County	256.0	20.0	50.7	3.1	16.6	14.4
Colorado Springs, CO	El Paso County	191.6	30.7	102.3	4.3	41.6	23.5
Columbia, MO	Boone County	789.0	66.8	65.1	5.0	33.7	26.9
Columbia, SC	Richland County	356.6	16.4	87.2	6.1	24.1	19.0
Columbus, OH	Franklin County	420.6	66.0	86.8	6.7	24.4	26.6
Dallas, TX	Dallas County	326.0	20.6	82.1	4.2	35.3	13.1
Denver, CO	Denver County	590.7	33.4	73.4	7.1	34.2	15.6
Des Moines, IA	Polk County	201.2	110.6	69.7	9.1	51.1	22.0
Durham, NC	Durham County	1,101.6	15.3	73.2	4.5	18.9	14.8
Edison, NJ	Middlesex County	369.9	19.8	86.1	10.0	23.7	18.0
El Paso, TX	El Paso County	186.8	15.4	44.4	3.8	8.7	9.3
Eugene, OR	Lane County	239.2	15.5	72.0	3.7	26.7	16.5
Evansville, IN	Vanderburgh County	269.0	23.1	71.6	12.7	22.6	34.1
Fargo, ND	Cass County	388.3	16.6	78.7	3.4	64.1	29.2
Fayetteville, NC	Cumberland County	196.7	20.7	97.7	5.4	10.5	18.0
Fort Collins, CO	Larimer County	244.3	32.5	79.9	4.7	56.1	20.6
Fort Wayne, IN	Allen County	259.5	21.6	63.6	5.4	20.7	24.1
Fort Worth, TX	Tarrant County	178.0	37.4	57.7	4.1	25.2	15.2
Gainesville, FL	Alachua County	904.9	26.1	170.4	3.7	26.2	17.6
Grand Rapids, MI	Kent County	326.2	70.1	71.1	4.8	33.8	23.7
Greeley, CO	Weld County	108.1	17.0	43.3	4.3	22.7	12.1
Green Bay, WI	Brown County	241.2	22.3	75.9	3.4	43.5	18.7
Greensboro, NC	Guilford County	252.5	12.6	56.0	4.6	14.2	10.4
Honolulu, HI	Honolulu County	341.9	18.2	96.6	3.4	17.9	22.5
Houston, TX	Harris County	321.0	11.7	67.5	4.8	21.8	19.4
Huntsville, AL	Madison County	277.8	13.5	55.7	3.9	22.7	18.0
Indianapolis, IN	Marion County	437.7	21.7	87.4	5.9	14.9	18.9
Jacksonville, FL	Duval County	349.6	23.0	81.5	8.5	23.5	15.9
Kansas City, MO	Jackson County	300.2	59.9	84.6	6.3	43.6	20.2
Lafayette, LA	Lafayette Parish	356.6	7.0	65.6	3.7	30.9	13.6
Las Cruces, NM	Dona Ana County	164.1	14.5	61.2	5.1	16.2	8.3
Las Vegas, NV	Clark County	175.5	27.6	62.5	4.0	19.3	12.3
Lexington, KY	Fayette County	706.2	34.2	144.1	7.5	21.1	21.1
Lincoln, NE	Lancaster County	213.8	10.9	92.6	5.4	40.1	21.0
Little Rock, AR	Pulaski County	730.0	16.5	72.9	4.8	21.1	20.1
Los Angeles, CA	Los Angeles County	291.6	13.1	85.0	6.1	28.9	17.2
Louisville, KY	Jefferson County	473.3	11.3	104.5	8.0	28.0	14.7

Table continued on next page.

City	Area Covered	MDs[1]	DOs[1,2]	Dentists	Podiatrists	Chiropractors	Optometrists
Madison, WI	Dane County	587.3	20.7	69.0	4.8	41.9	22.4
Manchester, NH	Hillsborough County	233.7	23.5	79.6	5.4	25.9	19.8
McAllen, TX	Hidalgo County	113.5	3.1	26.0	1.2	8.1	6.2
Miami, FL	Miami-Dade County	333.7	17.2	64.8	9.8	17.7	13.2
Midland, TX	Midland County	152.9	10.4	53.9	3.0	13.3	13.3
Minneapolis, MN	Hennepin County	501.1	19.3	94.6	4.6	69.6	19.2
Nashville, TN	Davidson County	619.1	11.5	74.4	4.2	24.4	16.3
New Orleans, LA	Orleans Parish	752.6	15.0	71.7	3.8	7.6	6.1
New York, NY	New York City	472.3	16.5	85.2	13.1	15.5	15.9
Oklahoma City, OK	Oklahoma County	403.7	44.8	101.5	4.8	26.0	18.1
Omaha, NE	Douglas County	531.2	30.6	92.9	5.5	39.4	19.4
Orlando, FL	Orange County	298.5	23.4	48.3	3.5	25.4	12.8
Peoria, IL	Peoria County	544.5	47.5	82.0	8.2	49.2	19.7
Philadelphia, PA	Philadelphia County	545.4	49.8	74.5	17.5	14.9	17.1
Phoenix, AZ	Maricopa County	242.0	33.4	66.8	6.1	33.6	15.0
Pittsburgh, PA	Allegheny County	626.7	38.5	96.8	10.7	43.5	19.5
Portland, OR	Multnomah County	615.8	32.1	96.0	5.4	71.9	21.5
Providence, RI	Providence County	481.7	18.4	60.2	10.7	19.6	20.1
Provo, UT	Utah County	115.8	18.5	60.0	3.8	24.7	10.6
Raleigh, NC	Wake County	273.7	10.7	69.3	3.3	25.2	15.6
Reno, NV	Washoe County	295.5	20.6	70.1	4.1	25.6	21.1
Richmond, VA	Richmond City	726.2	24.9	131.3	10.6	6.6	13.2
Roanoke, VA	Roanoke City	570.5	71.2	75.1	14.0	17.0	23.0
Rochester, MN	Olmsted County	2,412.8	56.8	112.3	6.5	43.9	21.9
Salem, OR	Marion County	173.3	13.4	79.7	4.7	30.8	14.7
Salt Lake City, UT	Salt Lake County	361.3	15.5	75.8	6.2	26.4	13.6
San Antonio, TX	Bexar County	319.5	21.3	83.0	5.1	15.9	16.4
San Diego, CA	San Diego County	314.4	17.1	86.5	4.0	33.6	17.5
San Francisco, CA	San Francisco County	781.2	12.1	149.0	10.0	37.4	27.4
San Jose, CA	Santa Clara County	401.8	9.2	113.6	6.4	40.6	26.2
Santa Rosa, CA	Sonoma County	268.7	15.1	88.1	5.9	38.3	16.5
Savannah, GA	Chatham County	352.8	19.4	65.4	7.2	18.2	13.8
Seattle, WA	King County	473.7	15.7	106.7	6.5	45.5	21.6
Sioux Falls, SD	Minnehaha County	353.7	26.3	53.0	5.8	55.7	19.6
Springfield, IL	Sangamon County	623.0	22.8	85.0	5.6	39.2	21.9
Tallahassee, FL	Leon County	292.3	11.8	45.1	3.4	22.4	17.9
Tampa, FL	Hillsborough County	343.5	28.4	56.9	5.5	25.8	12.8
Topeka, KS	Shawnee County	200.4	25.3	61.7	5.6	25.3	24.7
Tyler, TX	Smith County	343.1	24.4	59.7	6.6	27.2	15.8
Virginia Beach, VA	Virginia Beach City	255.2	13.5	75.5	7.5	26.4	16.0
Visalia, CA	Tulare County	113.3	6.1	50.4	3.9	10.3	12.3
Washington, DC	The District	795.7	15.3	119.9	8.5	8.5	13.8
Wilmington, NC	New Hanover County	343.1	30.5	76.1	7.0	33.5	19.4
Winston-Salem, NC	Forsyth County	625.9	30.1	59.0	5.6	16.2	16.2
U.S.	U.S.	279.3	23.0	68.4	6.0	27.1	16.2

Note: All figures are rates per 100,000 population; Data as of 2017 unless noted; (1) Data as of 2016 and includes all active, non-federal physicians; (2) Doctor of Osteopathic Medicine
Source: U.S. Department of Health and Human Services, Health Resources and Services Administration, Bureau of Health Professions, Area Resource File (ARF) 2017-2018

Health Insurance Coverage: City

City	With Health Insurance	With Private Health Insurance	With Public Health Insurance	Without Health Insurance	Population Under Age 18 Without Health Insurance
Albany, NY	92.8	66.8	38.1	7.2	2.4
Albuquerque, NM	89.5	60.4	40.0	10.5	4.6
Allentown, PA	86.4	47.0	48.3	13.6	5.3
Anchorage, AK	86.8	70.4	26.6	13.2	10.0
Ann Arbor, MI	96.5	87.9	18.8	3.5	1.5
Athens, GA	85.3	67.7	26.3	14.7	8.3
Atlanta, GA	87.2	66.5	28.8	12.8	5.5
Austin, TX	84.7	70.7	20.8	15.3	9.2
Baton Rouge, LA	87.2	60.3	36.0	12.8	3.1
Billings, MT	89.3	70.8	31.5	10.7	6.8
Boise City, ID	90.3	75.6	26.2	9.7	3.5
Boston, MA	96.1	66.5	37.1	3.9	1.4
Boulder, CO	94.7	84.3	18.2	5.3	2.3
Cape Coral, FL	85.5	63.1	36.7	14.5	9.2
Cedar Rapids, IA	95.0	76.4	31.7	5.0	3.2
Charleston, SC	90.5	76.9	25.3	9.5	4.4
Charlotte, NC	85.7	67.0	26.1	14.3	6.8
Chicago, IL	87.2	57.2	36.6	12.8	3.8
Clarksville, TN	90.4	72.6	30.5	9.6	3.5
College Station, TX	90.9	83.7	13.4	9.1	5.3
Colorado Springs, CO	91.3	69.4	34.7	8.7	4.1
Columbia, MO	93.2	83.0	18.9	6.8	3.8
Columbia, SC	89.5	70.9	28.7	10.5	2.5
Columbus, OH	89.4	63.8	33.3	10.6	5.8
Dallas, TX	75.1	49.6	31.2	24.9	14.6
Denver, CO	88.5	63.7	32.7	11.5	5.8
Des Moines, IA	91.8	63.4	40.0	8.2	3.8
Durham, NC	86.4	67.9	28.2	13.6	6.9
Edison, NJ	92.5	81.3	20.3	7.5	2.2
El Paso, TX	79.3	52.7	33.5	20.7	9.7
Eugene, OR	91.3	69.5	34.6	8.7	3.8
Evansville, IN	88.3	61.1	39.9	11.7	4.9
Fargo, ND	92.4	79.6	24.1	7.6	5.2
Fayetteville, NC	88.4	65.2	38.0	11.6	4.7
Fort Collins, CO	93.1	79.6	22.8	6.9	5.1
Fort Wayne, IN	88.3	63.5	34.7	11.7	7.0
Fort Worth, TX	80.7	59.4	27.9	19.3	11.4
Gainesville, FL	89.0	74.8	22.0	11.0	3.0
Grand Rapids, MI	89.8	61.0	38.9	10.2	3.4
Greeley, CO	90.5	64.7	36.2	9.5	4.5
Green Bay, WI	91.3	64.4	37.2	8.7	4.0
Greensboro, NC	87.9	65.5	32.5	12.1	4.6
Honolulu, HI	95.2	77.2	33.4	4.8	3.2
Houston, TX	75.9	50.5	31.2	24.1	12.9
Huntsville, AL	88.9	71.7	31.7	11.1	3.9
Indianapolis, IN	87.4	60.5	35.9	12.6	6.1
Jacksonville, FL	87.0	64.0	33.6	13.0	7.0
Kansas City, MO	86.7	66.9	29.2	13.3	6.9
Lafayette, LA	87.0	66.3	30.6	13.0	4.9
Las Cruces, NM	89.6	57.2	46.8	10.4	4.6
Las Vegas, NV	84.2	60.9	32.9	15.8	10.2
Lexington, KY	91.5	71.8	30.4	8.5	4.4
Lincoln, NE	91.2	77.1	25.4	8.8	4.6
Little Rock, AR	89.0	65.1	34.8	11.0	5.7
Los Angeles, CA	84.5	52.9	37.7	15.5	5.5

Table continued on next page.

City	With Health Insurance	With Private Health Insurance	With Public Health Insurance	Without Health Insurance	Population Under Age 18 Without Health Insurance
Louisville, KY	92.5	67.7	37.6	7.5	2.8
Madison, WI	94.8	83.2	21.9	5.2	2.8
Manchester, NH	88.8	64.6	34.2	11.2	3.8
McAllen, TX	72.7	46.7	31.6	27.3	15.5
Miami, FL	76.1	41.7	37.6	23.9	9.1
Midland, TX	80.9	68.6	19.9	19.1	18.0
Minneapolis, MN	91.5	66.6	32.8	8.5	4.9
Nashville, TN	86.3	65.3	29.7	13.7	7.1
New Orleans, LA	87.6	55.4	40.0	12.4	4.3
New York, NY	90.2	56.6	42.0	9.8	3.0
Oklahoma City, OK	84.1	62.7	31.7	15.9	7.5
Omaha, NE	88.9	70.5	27.9	11.1	5.6
Orlando, FL	81.9	58.4	30.1	18.1	10.0
Peoria, IL	92.8	63.4	41.1	7.2	2.1
Philadelphia, PA	89.4	56.3	43.1	10.6	4.2
Phoenix, AZ	83.6	55.3	35.2	16.4	10.6
Pittsburgh, PA	93.1	72.7	32.5	6.9	3.5
Portland, OR	91.2	69.3	31.7	8.8	3.3
Providence, RI	88.5	51.8	43.4	11.5	4.8
Provo, UT	88.2	77.7	16.9	11.8	10.3
Raleigh, NC	88.1	73.2	23.1	11.9	5.6
Reno, NV	87.5	66.1	31.4	12.5	8.6
Richmond, VA	85.1	60.4	34.3	14.9	6.3
Roanoke, VA	86.4	59.8	37.9	13.6	6.2
Rochester, MN	95.0	78.9	29.5	5.0	2.8
Salem, OR	90.5	64.0	40.0	9.5	4.2
Salt Lake City, UT	85.4	70.3	22.6	14.6	12.2
San Antonio, TX	82.7	59.9	32.4	17.3	8.7
San Diego, CA	89.6	69.1	29.3	10.4	5.3
San Francisco, CA	94.5	73.9	29.2	5.5	2.0
San Jose, CA	92.6	70.5	29.7	7.4	2.8
Santa Rosa, CA	90.6	66.8	36.4	9.4	4.5
Savannah, GA	81.5	57.1	33.4	18.5	7.9
Seattle, WA	94.0	79.4	23.4	6.0	2.1
Sioux Falls, SD	92.1	77.1	26.1	7.9	4.1
Springfield, IL	94.2	68.1	40.8	5.8	1.8
Tallahassee, FL	90.5	75.7	23.8	9.5	4.2
Tampa, FL	87.0	61.0	33.6	13.0	5.5
Topeka, KS	89.2	69.9	35.1	10.8	6.1
Tyler, TX	82.2	60.7	32.4	17.8	8.7
Virginia Beach, VA	91.1	80.0	24.0	8.9	3.9
Visalia, CA	92.5	57.8	44.2	7.5	2.3
Washington, DC	95.3	69.3	36.1	4.7	2.3
Wilmington, NC	88.3	68.6	31.9	11.7	4.1
Winston-Salem, NC	86.6	61.8	35.5	13.4	4.3
U.S.	89.5	67.2	33.8	10.5	5.7

Note: Figures are percentages that cover the civilian noninstitutionalized population
Source: U.S. Census Bureau, 2013-2017 American Community Survey 5-Year Estimates

Health Insurance Coverage: Metro Area

Metro Area	With Health Insurance	With Private Health Insurance	With Public Health Insurance	Without Health Insurance	Population Under Age 18 Without Health Insurance
Albany, NY	95.4	77.1	33.0	4.6	2.0
Albuquerque, NM	89.2	59.2	41.6	10.8	5.0
Allentown, PA	92.8	73.5	33.5	7.2	3.4
Anchorage, AK	86.0	68.7	27.8	14.0	10.2
Ann Arbor, MI	95.3	83.3	24.4	4.7	2.2
Athens, GA	86.7	69.0	27.8	13.3	6.9
Atlanta, GA	85.7	68.0	26.3	14.3	7.8
Austin, TX	86.3	73.2	21.6	13.7	8.6
Baton Rouge, LA	89.3	67.2	31.7	10.7	3.3
Billings, MT	89.6	71.7	31.2	10.4	7.3
Boise City, ID	88.5	70.8	29.2	11.5	5.4
Boston, MA	96.7	76.5	32.1	3.3	1.5
Boulder, CO	93.8	78.8	24.3	6.2	3.1
Cape Coral, FL	84.4	60.2	42.7	15.6	10.2
Cedar Rapids, IA	95.6	77.9	31.3	4.4	2.7
Charleston, SC	88.1	69.7	30.9	11.9	5.5
Charlotte, NC	88.3	69.6	28.7	11.7	5.5
Chicago, IL	90.5	68.8	31.0	9.5	3.5
Clarksville, TN	90.1	69.3	33.8	9.9	5.6
College Station, TX	85.7	71.9	22.5	14.3	9.6
Colorado Springs, CO	92.0	71.9	33.1	8.0	4.0
Columbia, MO	92.6	80.8	21.5	7.4	4.0
Columbia, SC	89.2	69.6	32.5	10.8	4.3
Columbus, OH	92.1	71.4	30.6	7.9	4.3
Dallas, TX	82.6	64.7	25.3	17.4	11.0
Denver, CO	90.6	71.6	28.1	9.4	5.2
Des Moines, IA	94.8	77.1	29.7	5.2	2.6
Durham, NC	88.5	71.3	28.5	11.5	6.3
Edison, NJ	90.9	66.3	34.6	9.1	3.5
El Paso, TX	77.7	50.1	33.9	22.3	10.6
Eugene, OR	91.0	65.3	40.7	9.0	4.7
Evansville, IN	92.0	71.8	33.6	8.0	3.9
Fargo, ND	93.6	81.4	24.1	6.4	5.1
Fayetteville, NC	88.4	64.9	37.2	11.6	4.4
Fort Collins, CO	92.7	76.0	27.8	7.3	5.2
Fort Wayne, IN	89.6	68.6	31.6	10.4	7.4
Fort Worth, TX	82.6	64.7	25.3	17.4	11.0
Gainesville, FL	88.9	71.7	27.6	11.1	5.6
Grand Rapids, MI	93.3	74.9	30.7	6.7	3.2
Greeley, CO	91.0	70.4	30.4	9.0	5.6
Green Bay, WI	93.8	74.3	30.8	6.2	3.6
Greensboro, NC	88.2	65.3	33.9	11.8	5.5
Honolulu, HI	96.0	79.8	31.3	4.0	2.4
Houston, TX	81.1	61.4	26.4	18.9	11.0
Huntsville, AL	90.0	74.8	29.1	10.0	3.4
Indianapolis, IN	90.1	70.4	30.0	9.9	5.6
Jacksonville, FL	88.1	67.8	32.3	11.9	6.8
Kansas City, MO	90.1	74.7	26.6	9.9	5.5
Lafayette, LA	87.2	63.1	34.2	12.8	4.3
Las Cruces, NM	86.7	49.2	49.3	13.3	6.2
Las Vegas, NV	85.3	63.8	30.8	14.7	9.8
Lexington, KY	91.8	71.1	32.1	8.2	4.6
Lincoln, NE	91.8	78.5	24.7	8.2	4.2
Little Rock, AR	90.4	66.7	36.4	9.6	4.9
Los Angeles, CA	87.4	59.1	35.1	12.6	5.3

Table continued on next page.

Metro Area	With Health Insurance	With Private Health Insurance	With Public Health Insurance	Without Health Insurance	Population Under Age 18 Without Health Insurance
Louisville, KY	92.6	71.8	34.1	7.4	3.6
Madison, WI	95.0	82.8	24.2	5.0	2.7
Manchester, NH	92.7	77.0	27.1	7.3	2.5
McAllen, TX	68.4	35.6	37.3	31.6	15.5
Miami, FL	82.1	56.3	33.2	17.9	9.2
Midland, TX	80.8	68.5	19.9	19.2	17.4
Minneapolis, MN	94.7	78.0	28.1	5.3	3.5
Nashville, TN	89.4	70.8	28.5	10.6	5.2
New Orleans, LA	87.6	60.6	36.5	12.4	4.5
New York, NY	90.9	66.3	34.6	9.1	3.5
Oklahoma City, OK	86.6	67.6	30.3	13.4	6.8
Omaha, NE	91.5	75.9	26.3	8.5	4.2
Orlando, FL	85.0	63.1	31.1	15.0	9.0
Peoria, IL	94.5	73.9	35.3	5.5	2.7
Philadelphia, PA	92.9	73.0	32.2	7.1	3.4
Phoenix, AZ	87.9	64.4	33.9	12.1	8.9
Pittsburgh, PA	94.9	77.1	34.2	5.1	2.3
Portland, OR	92.0	71.9	31.8	8.0	3.4
Providence, RI	94.5	70.4	37.2	5.5	2.8
Provo, UT	90.7	80.7	16.9	9.3	6.6
Raleigh, NC	89.7	74.9	24.0	10.3	4.9
Reno, NV	88.2	68.0	31.1	11.8	8.8
Richmond, VA	90.7	74.9	28.2	9.3	4.8
Roanoke, VA	90.6	70.8	33.8	9.4	5.1
Rochester, MN	94.9	79.8	29.3	5.1	3.5
Salem, OR	90.5	63.9	40.8	9.5	5.0
Salt Lake City, UT	88.1	75.7	20.5	11.9	9.1
San Antonio, TX	84.6	64.6	30.7	15.4	8.4
San Diego, CA	89.6	67.7	31.4	10.4	5.4
San Francisco, CA	93.6	74.4	29.4	6.4	2.9
San Jose, CA	93.7	75.3	26.6	6.3	2.5
Santa Rosa, CA	91.6	70.6	34.9	8.4	3.9
Savannah, GA	85.5	67.0	28.8	14.5	6.9
Seattle, WA	92.6	75.1	28.0	7.4	3.3
Sioux Falls, SD	92.9	79.5	24.6	7.1	4.0
Springfield, IL	95.1	73.6	36.5	4.9	1.6
Tallahassee, FL	90.0	72.4	28.9	10.0	5.1
Tampa, FL	86.7	62.2	36.4	13.3	7.4
Topeka, KS	91.4	75.2	32.2	8.6	4.9
Tyler, TX	82.4	62.3	32.5	17.6	11.3
Virginia Beach, VA	90.1	74.6	28.6	9.9	4.5
Visalia, CA	87.8	43.3	51.9	12.2	3.7
Washington, DC	91.2	77.7	23.9	8.8	4.8
Wilmington, NC	88.4	69.8	32.6	11.6	5.0
Winston-Salem, NC	88.3	66.0	34.7	11.7	4.7
U.S.	89.5	67.2	33.8	10.5	5.7

Note: Figures are percentages that cover the civilian noninstitutionalized population; Figures cover the Metropolitan Statistical Area (MSA)—see Appendix B for areas included
Source: U.S. Census Bureau, 2013-2017 American Community Survey 5-Year Estimates

Crime Rate: City

City	All Crimes	Violent Crimes				Property Crimes		
		Murder	Rape	Robbery	Aggrav. Assault	Burglary	Larceny -Theft	Motor Vehicle Theft
Albany, NY	4,349.4	8.1	55.0	251.6	577.5	440.0	2,906.1	111.0
Albuquerque, NM	8,735.0	12.5	84.3	521.9	750.5	1,246.2	4,750.8	1,368.8
Allentown, PA	3,193.9	13.2	57.9	222.6	167.2	524.7	1,954.9	253.3
Anchorage, AK	6,619.1	9.1	132.0	262.7	799.5	748.2	3,619.7	1,048.0
Ann Arbor, MI	1,941.3	0.0	46.7	43.5	122.2	228.0	1,419.7	81.2
Athens, GA	3,562.0	4.8	45.6	98.5	266.6	546.8	2,415.5	184.1
Atlanta, GA	5,712.1	16.4	58.6	293.6	567.2	704.3	3,387.2	685.0
Austin, TX	3,604.4	2.6	85.8	101.5	224.9	450.6	2,525.0	213.9
Baton Rouge, LA	6,620.8	38.3	44.0	381.7	562.9	1,418.6	3,739.6	435.8
Billings, MT	5,951.5	1.8	68.3	78.2	345.0	703.4	3,998.5	756.4
Boise City, ID	2,723.8	0.9	63.8	22.6	191.9	326.1	1,965.2	153.3
Boston, MA	2,758.2	8.3	42.5	205.6	412.8	308.8	1,603.7	176.5
Boulder, CO[1]	3,235.7	0.0	47.6	27.5	161.2	512.0	2,286.9	200.6
Cape Coral, FL	1,694.1	1.6	8.7	22.2	94.9	309.2	1,165.2	92.2
Cedar Rapids, IA	4,035.5	4.5	25.8	91.8	158.5	704.4	2,791.2	259.3
Charleston, SC	2,581.0	4.4	36.5	73.1	169.5	291.6	1,784.5	221.4
Charlotte, NC	n/a	9.4	n/a	220.5	433.5	701.5	2,827.0	286.7
Chicago, IL	4,362.7	24.1	65.1	439.3	570.4	477.1	2,358.8	427.8
Clarksville, TN	3,501.1	9.1	52.2	82.8	479.5	484.7	2,235.6	157.2
College Station, TX	2,196.7	0.9	45.9	42.5	110.1	260.1	1,635.8	101.4
Colorado Springs, CO	3,740.9	6.1	103.4	101.9	312.7	530.3	2,235.1	451.4
Columbia, MO	3,431.9	7.3	93.8	95.4	301.0	412.0	2,305.3	217.0
Columbia, SC	6,020.4	7.4	48.9	202.3	475.7	706.9	3,993.1	586.1
Columbus, OH	4,458.4	16.3	105.4	225.1	166.7	815.3	2,650.9	478.8
Dallas, TX	3,959.7	12.5	62.1	327.0	373.1	737.7	1,856.3	591.2
Denver, CO	4,342.7	8.3	98.9	174.4	394.0	612.9	2,267.3	786.8
Des Moines, IA	5,083.4	12.9	33.6	167.5	456.1	1,099.1	2,734.3	579.9
Durham, NC	n/a	8.5	n/a	316.6	467.1	867.4	2,675.7	283.2
Edison, NJ	1,287.3	0.0	6.8	45.8	56.5	180.1	882.2	115.9
El Paso, TX	2,197.7	2.8	53.9	58.1	264.1	188.3	1,514.4	116.2
Eugene, OR	4,115.6	1.8	60.0	105.2	219.8	670.8	2,734.2	323.8
Evansville, IN	5,699.9	16.8	62.8	155.0	456.6	723.0	3,887.9	397.9
Fargo, ND	3,538.0	2.4	67.2	55.1	277.9	480.4	2,410.3	244.7
Fayetteville, NC	n/a	11.7	n/a	142.1	537.9	885.0	3,202.0	202.0
Fort Collins, CO	2,755.4	3.6	26.8	25.1	164.6	272.6	2,139.2	123.5
Fort Wayne, IN	3,537.2	13.9	51.1	112.3	180.3	491.3	2,488.6	199.8
Fort Worth, TX	3,775.5	8.0	65.2	147.3	339.7	586.0	2,319.4	309.9
Gainesville, FL	4,315.5	3.0	123.5	132.6	457.9	376.6	2,948.6	273.4
Grand Rapids, MI	2,784.7	6.1	71.3	177.4	456.9	385.6	1,504.0	183.5
Greeley, CO	2,986.6	4.7	70.8	53.8	294.6	404.1	1,907.4	251.2
Green Bay, WI	2,511.1	0.0	72.2	61.7	338.9	304.8	1,650.0	83.5
Greensboro, NC	n/a	15.9	n/a	228.9	480.6	710.9	2,559.5	291.7
Honolulu, HI	n/a	n/a	n/a	n/a	n/a	n/a	n/a	n/a
Houston, TX	5,223.6	11.5	58.4	418.0	607.3	731.7	2,900.8	495.9
Huntsville, AL	5,635.0	11.3	88.1	184.5	621.0	731.7	3,462.6	535.9
Indianapolis, IN	5,745.8	17.9	76.7	400.2	839.1	1,027.2	2,821.5	563.2
Jacksonville, FL	4,158.0	12.2	60.1	153.8	405.2	631.1	2,568.6	326.9
Kansas City, MO	6,268.1	30.9	91.8	383.1	1,218.5	960.5	2,670.4	912.9
Lafayette, LA	5,116.1	17.1	16.3	136.0	390.9	785.6	3,539.5	230.8
Las Cruces, NM[1]	n/a	4.9	n/a	49.8	150.5	811.0	3,612.2	255.0
Las Vegas, NV	3,562.3	12.6	79.6	211.2	315.5	805.2	1,635.2	503.1
Lexington, KY	4,133.0	9.0	62.0	169.7	110.1	647.5	2,739.7	394.9
Lincoln, NE[1]	3,463.1	3.6	79.0	67.9	207.4	448.5	2,531.5	125.2
Little Rock, AR	8,565.9	27.6	87.8	251.9	1,266.3	1,193.1	5,172.2	566.9

Table continued on next page.

City	All Crimes	Violent Crimes				Property Crimes		
		Murder	Rape	Robbery	Aggrav. Assault	Burglary	Larceny -Theft	Motor Vehicle Theft
Los Angeles, CA	3,297.2	7.0	61.3	269.9	423.2	416.0	1,641.0	479.0
Louisville, KY	4,769.3	15.9	25.6	193.8	411.8	821.6	2,736.0	564.6
Madison, WI	3,036.5	4.3	37.1	82.9	250.1	362.3	2,130.9	168.8
Manchester, NH	3,298.5	1.8	83.1	157.2	431.1	443.7	2,014.4	167.2
McAllen, TX	2,923.8	4.9	18.7	34.0	86.7	128.3	2,619.3	31.9
Miami, FL	4,735.1	11.2	22.7	211.2	475.8	527.0	3,090.9	396.3
Midland, TX	2,197.8	1.4	26.6	42.5	200.8	310.2	1,458.0	158.3
Minneapolis, MN	5,742.6	10.0	122.7	434.2	534.4	897.9	3,173.5	570.0
Nashville, TN	4,956.1	16.3	72.9	303.1	745.8	631.3	2,806.6	380.0
New Orleans, LA	5,365.2	39.5	144.7	329.1	608.1	560.8	3,046.2	636.8
New York, NY	1,987.5	3.4	27.6	162.4	345.5	128.9	1,253.2	66.6
Oklahoma City, OK	4,539.8	12.5	73.1	172.8	529.0	941.8	2,378.8	431.9
Omaha, NE	4,527.5	6.9	91.2	139.1	410.1	464.6	2,636.7	778.8
Orlando, FL	6,198.6	8.1	64.4	213.0	458.5	840.9	4,125.3	488.4
Peoria, IL	4,973.0	10.5	56.9	246.2	445.9	980.2	2,940.7	292.6
Philadelphia, PA	4,011.1	20.1	75.0	382.5	470.0	418.3	2,297.2	348.0
Phoenix, AZ	4,431.6	9.5	69.5	200.3	481.6	778.6	2,426.7	465.5
Pittsburgh, PA	3,770.8	18.0	29.4	262.1	346.8	526.3	2,365.9	222.3
Portland, OR	6,192.7	3.7	67.4	160.9	283.6	729.1	3,824.6	1,123.3
Providence, RI	3,828.1	6.7	57.8	141.8	327.5	563.2	2,408.6	322.5
Provo, UT	1,858.1	0.9	44.2	24.7	56.2	131.9	1,500.8	99.5
Raleigh, NC	n/a	n/a	n/a	n/a	n/a	n/a	n/a	n/a
Reno, NV	3,759.3	7.6	57.1	153.7	455.1	542.0	1,967.6	576.2
Richmond, VA[2]	4,432.5	19.5	27.2	221.5	247.7	726.9	2,794.8	394.9
Roanoke, VA	4,893.7	16.0	41.0	79.0	265.9	486.9	3,718.0	286.9
Rochester, MN	2,054.2	0.9	52.9	39.9	100.7	249.9	1,524.8	85.0
Salem, OR	4,621.2	3.5	25.9	98.5	250.1	529.0	3,206.4	507.8
Salt Lake City, UT	8,928.1	5.1	171.3	260.6	441.6	966.3	6,115.9	967.3
San Antonio, TX	5,552.3	8.2	83.5	151.1	464.7	770.8	3,622.6	451.4
San Diego, CA	2,209.6	2.5	39.3	99.0	225.9	268.0	1,214.4	360.6
San Francisco, CA	6,883.0	6.4	41.6	365.4	301.6	560.0	5,059.5	548.5
San Jose, CA	2,844.4	3.1	55.0	132.6	212.9	378.4	1,284.7	777.6
Santa Rosa, CA	2,249.4	2.8	61.8	71.4	273.3	297.7	1,309.2	233.0
Savannah, GA	3,893.9	14.4	41.2	156.8	250.3	549.5	2,494.8	386.9
Seattle, WA	5,891.3	3.7	36.9	210.0	382.1	1,082.0	3,673.5	503.2
Sioux Falls, SD	3,307.7	2.2	68.0	56.2	323.8	368.2	2,225.6	263.6
Springfield, IL	5,810.4	9.5	80.5	217.2	747.6	1,047.0	3,437.8	270.8
Tallahassee, FL	5,679.8	8.8	98.7	180.8	492.6	789.3	3,722.9	386.6
Tampa, FL	2,208.1	10.1	31.5	105.6	317.2	321.3	1,274.8	147.5
Topeka, KS	5,742.2	21.3	44.2	212.4	335.6	790.5	3,731.5	606.5
Tyler, TX	3,582.0	5.7	61.3	56.5	313.8	420.3	2,586.8	137.6
Virginia Beach, VA	2,072.2	3.1	22.4	59.9	52.2	166.0	1,667.6	101.0
Visalia, CA	3,672.5	6.8	61.3	109.0	168.8	634.9	2,234.7	457.1
Washington, DC	5,105.0	16.7	63.8	338.8	529.4	260.5	3,529.0	366.7
Wilmington, NC	n/a	15.1	n/a	163.3	448.0	835.7	2,544.8	235.3
Winston-Salem, NC	n/a	n/a	n/a	n/a	n/a	n/a	n/a	n/a
U.S.	2,756.1	5.3	41.7	98.0	248.9	430.4	1,694.4	237.4

Note: Figures are crimes per 100,000 population in 2017 except where noted; n/a not available; (1) 2016 data; (2) 2015 data
Source: FBI Uniform Crime Reports, 2015, 2016, 2017

Crime Rate: Suburbs

Suburbs[1]	All Crimes	Violent Crimes				Property Crimes		
		Murder	Rape	Robbery	Aggrav. Assault	Burglary	Larceny -Theft	Motor Vehicle Theft
Albany, NY	1,983.6	1.3	39.0	49.9	126.1	234.5	1,463.2	69.6
Albuquerque, NM	3,169.7	3.1	37.9	70.7	522.2	582.4	1,543.1	410.2
Allentown, PA	1,687.4	1.4	14.9	32.0	151.5	182.6	1,237.2	67.8
Anchorage, AK	6,349.5	5.8	5.8	63.7	393.6	387.8	4,479.9	1,012.9
Ann Arbor, MI	1,971.1	4.5	71.3	51.0	256.7	237.3	1,223.6	126.7
Athens, GA	1,855.9	1.2	18.1	14.5	111.2	289.0	1,349.3	72.5
Atlanta, GA	3,012.4	5.9	23.2	99.6	188.4	459.6	1,963.5	272.3
Austin, TX	1,839.9	2.4	44.7	28.9	138.1	262.4	1,263.5	100.0
Baton Rouge, LA	3,686.9	8.7	23.1	56.5	279.3	597.7	2,583.9	137.7
Billings, MT	2,017.8	3.3	33.3	8.3	173.3	279.9	1,296.3	223.3
Boise City, ID	1,658.3	1.0	40.7	11.1	161.6	310.4	998.0	135.6
Boston, MA	1,425.8	1.6	25.2	43.0	175.7	171.3	918.2	90.7
Boulder, CO[2]	2,202.7	0.5	79.1	24.2	132.6	264.8	1,571.8	129.8
Cape Coral, FL	1,869.4	7.5	41.7	89.5	230.4	308.6	1,050.9	140.7
Cedar Rapids, IA	1,273.6	1.5	27.0	12.4	115.9	313.5	720.3	83.1
Charleston, SC	n/a	9.0	39.4	88.9	302.1	n/a	2,028.9	272.8
Charlotte, NC	5,044.6	3.0	n/a	55.1	183.5	437.4	1,663.6	122.6
Chicago, IL	n/a	3.5	26.6	58.5	n/a	217.8	1,218.6	96.5
Clarksville, TN	2,159.1	0.8	31.5	36.8	112.6	490.2	1,352.8	134.4
College Station, TX	2,595.9	4.9	58.4	55.6	235.7	424.8	1,694.9	121.7
Colorado Springs, CO	1,720.0	1.6	52.9	21.0	179.8	238.7	1,061.1	164.8
Columbia, MO	2,125.9	1.8	23.0	21.3	175.4	240.9	1,500.5	163.0
Columbia, SC	n/a	7.1	44.2	77.4	396.0	560.6	n/a	380.8
Columbus, OH	2,208.5	1.8	36.1	38.2	52.4	334.7	1,650.9	94.4
Dallas, TX	n/a	3.5	44.1	74.6	157.1	n/a	1,628.0	206.1
Denver, CO	n/a	3.4	64.2	66.8	195.0	n/a	1,961.0	441.4
Des Moines, IA	n/a	n/a	n/a	n/a	n/a	n/a	n/a	n/a
Durham, NC	n/a	2.7	n/a	50.2	140.3	542.9	1,371.1	81.5
Edison, NJ	1,766.4	2.8	22.9	122.1	246.6	148.9	1,152.2	70.8
El Paso, TX	1,369.9	1.3	44.2	20.2	192.5	193.8	855.4	62.5
Eugene, OR	2,760.4	2.4	35.7	35.7	215.0	393.9	1,862.8	215.0
Evansville, IN	1,625.2	3.0	22.3	25.3	131.6	302.1	1,040.8	100.2
Fargo, ND	1,777.2	0.9	43.2	14.7	90.7	266.8	1,204.7	156.3
Fayetteville, NC	n/a	3.9	n/a	36.0	89.9	401.7	1,011.3	42.1
Fort Collins, CO	2,225.9	0.0	57.3	19.1	181.9	269.5	1,576.4	121.8
Fort Wayne, IN	n/a	1.2	30.2	28.5	106.7	201.6	n/a	91.9
Fort Worth, TX	n/a	4.8	44.9	116.9	177.1	n/a	1,582.1	271.5
Gainesville, FL	2,291.7	3.3	56.8	80.5	338.6	439.6	1,260.7	112.2
Grand Rapids, MI	1,623.8	2.1	80.0	23.8	129.2	233.1	1,080.0	75.7
Greeley, CO	1,458.2	2.0	20.0	14.3	129.0	217.1	930.9	144.9
Green Bay, WI	1,131.9	0.0	26.5	4.7	68.4	116.3	885.8	30.2
Greensboro, NC	n/a	7.8	n/a	75.3	224.3	583.0	1,766.2	138.5
Honolulu, HI	n/a	n/a	n/a	n/a	n/a	n/a	n/a	n/a
Houston, TX	n/a	3.7	34.8	96.5	201.5	n/a	1,432.2	n/a
Huntsville, AL	2,220.1	4.2	32.4	31.2	227.3	432.2	1,337.1	155.6
Indianapolis, IN	1,942.6	1.1	26.9	39.6	145.0	233.5	1,338.8	157.7
Jacksonville, FL	1,941.0	2.3	30.5	36.7	191.1	329.9	1,239.0	111.7
Kansas City, MO	n/a	n/a	n/a	n/a	n/a	n/a	n/a	n/a
Lafayette, LA	n/a	6.0	26.9	51.0	313.1	647.1	n/a	n/a
Las Cruces, NM[2]	6,167.1	5.4	n/a	13.4	192.2	408.5	853.6	140.3
Las Vegas, NV	2,892.5	5.7	42.9	147.5	380.8	589.1	1,364.3	362.1
Lexington, KY	n/a	2.6	31.5	57.2	50.4	536.7	n/a	189.6
Lincoln, NE[2]	1,218.2	0.0	49.8	2.2	54.1	190.4	852.5	69.2
Little Rock, AR	3,533.2	5.9	51.3	64.1	370.1	651.8	2,092.7	297.4

Table continued on next page.

Suburbs[1]	All Crimes	Violent Crimes				Property Crimes		
		Murder	Rape	Robbery	Aggrav. Assault	Burglary	Larceny -Theft	Motor Vehicle Theft
Los Angeles, CA	2,654.4	3.9	28.5	136.3	214.8	432.3	1,443.0	395.5
Louisville, KY	2,096.6	2.3	20.4	43.4	93.2	326.7	1,401.4	209.2
Madison, WI	1,427.7	1.0	24.5	22.2	87.9	195.9	1,023.3	72.9
Manchester, NH	1,064.9	0.7	37.4	13.7	63.7	116.1	782.3	51.0
McAllen, TX	2,783.7	4.3	54.0	44.1	220.5	427.2	1,929.7	104.0
Miami, FL	3,437.1	5.7	33.3	127.1	270.8	410.4	2,302.8	287.1
Midland, TX	2,505.9	0.0	8.8	64.6	199.8	358.4	1,559.9	314.3
Minneapolis, MN	2,286.0	1.7	32.8	46.7	94.0	281.4	1,661.8	167.7
Nashville, TN	2,209.0	3.2	32.7	35.8	271.0	297.4	1,425.7	143.3
New Orleans, LA	2,673.9	6.9	21.3	69.7	214.0	370.4	1,844.6	147.0
New York, NY	1,433.3	2.4	14.0	67.0	97.7	170.1	977.9	104.3
Oklahoma City, OK	2,391.4	3.3	45.0	43.2	152.9	481.4	1,477.0	188.6
Omaha, NE	1,870.1	0.8	30.8	24.2	84.7	259.2	1,272.1	198.3
Orlando, FL	2,836.4	4.6	44.9	78.9	277.0	472.2	1,780.3	178.4
Peoria, IL	1,755.3	0.8	52.7	19.9	163.8	350.2	1,090.4	77.5
Philadelphia, PA	1,952.1	4.0	18.6	72.7	152.5	254.8	1,350.4	99.2
Phoenix, AZ	2,676.9	3.7	39.5	65.6	207.4	378.5	1,798.3	183.9
Pittsburgh, PA	1,562.8	3.5	19.3	43.1	155.5	215.6	1,070.5	55.3
Portland, OR	n/a	2.3	54.8	35.3	107.6	n/a	1,384.2	304.8
Providence, RI	1,756.4	1.4	37.1	52.1	174.4	275.5	1,105.7	110.1
Provo, UT	1,551.3	1.2	22.2	12.6	32.9	179.5	1,220.6	82.3
Raleigh, NC	n/a	n/a	n/a	n/a	n/a	n/a	n/a	n/a
Reno, NV	2,269.1	0.9	40.5	55.3	236.3	395.6	1,277.5	263.0
Richmond, VA[3]	2,200.0	5.0	24.8	47.3	100.7	315.7	1,618.6	87.9
Roanoke, VA	1,556.9	4.7	33.6	19.6	91.5	175.6	1,133.8	98.1
Rochester, MN	782.8	0.0	24.3	4.9	62.2	131.1	506.0	54.4
Salem, OR	2,476.1	3.2	28.0	38.6	145.1	329.2	1,610.0	322.1
Salt Lake City, UT	4,043.8	3.4	65.9	65.6	173.3	519.7	2,708.2	507.7
San Antonio, TX	n/a	3.7	49.4	37.9	141.0	n/a	1,451.0	165.0
San Diego, CA	1,901.8	2.4	28.0	83.2	201.7	275.9	1,072.1	238.5
San Francisco, CA	n/a	3.7	38.5	184.2	195.7	378.3	n/a	534.0
San Jose, CA	2,303.4	1.7	26.6	57.6	120.8	316.4	1,534.9	245.4
Santa Rosa, CA	1,714.2	2.1	57.4	45.9	290.4	265.5	926.0	127.0
Savannah, GA	n/a	2.0	20.3	39.9	215.1	n/a	1,718.4	136.7
Seattle, WA	n/a	2.8	37.6	77.4	172.0	n/a	2,163.0	476.0
Sioux Falls, SD	1,146.9	2.5	32.0	2.5	110.8	224.0	710.1	65.2
Springfield, IL	1,582.4	2.1	47.6	21.2	205.3	333.4	860.6	112.2
Tallahassee, FL	2,593.3	4.2	51.0	33.7	344.7	533.6	1,504.5	121.6
Tampa, FL	2,467.0	2.7	37.6	62.9	211.2	348.8	1,639.4	164.5
Topeka, KS	1,805.3	4.7	27.4	14.1	128.3	331.1	1,144.1	155.6
Tyler, TX	2,158.7	2.5	42.0	20.6	213.2	581.9	1,097.9	200.8
Virginia Beach, VA	3,281.5	9.6	38.8	106.6	244.4	410.8	2,275.7	195.6
Visalia, CA	2,594.8	7.3	24.5	73.2	260.3	462.0	1,279.3	488.3
Washington, DC	1,630.4	3.0	24.3	64.3	96.8	143.6	1,176.8	121.6
Wilmington, NC	n/a	4.2	n/a	38.0	103.9	479.5	1,612.4	66.5
Winston-Salem, NC	n/a	n/a	n/a	n/a	n/a	n/a	n/a	n/a
U.S.	2,756.1	5.3	41.7	98.0	248.9	430.4	1,694.4	237.4

Note: Figures are crimes per 100,000 population in 2017 except where noted; n/a not available; (1) All areas within the metro area that are located outside the city limits; (2) 2016 data; (3) 2015 data
Source: FBI Uniform Crime Reports, 2015, 2016, 2017

Crime Rate: Metro Area

Metro Area[1]	All Crimes	Violent Crimes				Property Crimes		
		Murder	Rape	Robbery	Aggrav. Assault	Burglary	Larceny -Theft	Motor Vehicle Theft
Albany, NY	2,245.9	2.0	40.8	72.3	176.1	257.3	1,623.2	74.2
Albuquerque, NM	6,583.9	8.9	66.3	347.5	662.2	989.7	3,511.0	998.3
Allentown, PA	1,904.4	3.1	21.1	59.5	153.8	231.9	1,340.6	94.5
Anchorage, AK	6,604.2	8.9	125.1	251.7	777.1	728.3	3,667.1	1,046.0
Ann Arbor, MI	1,961.2	3.0	63.2	48.5	212.3	234.2	1,288.4	111.7
Athens, GA	2,882.3	3.4	34.7	65.0	204.7	444.1	1,990.8	139.7
Atlanta, GA	3,233.3	6.7	26.1	115.4	219.4	479.7	2,080.0	306.0
Austin, TX	2,650.7	2.5	63.6	62.3	178.0	348.9	1,843.2	152.3
Baton Rouge, LA	4,484.3	16.7	28.8	144.9	356.4	820.8	2,898.0	218.7
Billings, MT	4,573.5	2.3	56.0	53.7	284.8	555.1	3,051.9	569.6
Boise City, ID	1,996.9	1.0	48.0	14.8	171.2	315.4	1,305.3	141.2
Boston, MA[2]	1,613.8	2.6	27.7	65.9	209.1	190.7	1,015.0	102.8
Boulder, CO[3]	2,550.7	0.3	68.5	25.3	142.2	348.0	1,812.7	153.7
Cape Coral, FL	1,825.9	6.1	33.5	72.8	196.8	308.8	1,079.2	128.7
Cedar Rapids, IA	2,627.4	3.0	26.4	51.3	136.8	505.1	1,735.4	169.5
Charleston, SC	n/a	8.2	38.9	86.2	278.8	n/a	1,985.9	263.7
Charlotte, NC	3,216.6	5.3	21.8	115.1	274.1	533.1	2,085.2	182.1
Chicago, IL[2]	n/a	9.4	37.5	166.7	n/a	291.5	1,542.5	190.6
Clarksville, TN	2,877.1	5.2	42.6	61.4	308.9	487.3	1,825.1	146.6
College Station, TX	2,418.2	3.1	52.9	49.8	179.8	351.5	1,668.6	112.7
Colorado Springs, CO	3,046.5	4.6	86.0	74.1	267.0	430.1	1,831.7	352.9
Columbia, MO	3,020.1	5.6	71.5	72.1	261.4	358.0	2,051.6	200.0
Columbia, SC	n/a	7.1	45.0	97.8	409.0	584.4	n/a	414.4
Columbus, OH	3,156.3	7.9	65.2	116.9	100.6	537.2	2,072.1	256.3
Dallas, TX[2]	n/a	5.2	47.3	120.5	196.4	n/a	1,669.5	276.0
Denver, CO	n/a	4.6	72.7	93.1	243.6	n/a	2,035.7	525.7
Des Moines, IA	n/a	n/a	n/a	n/a	n/a	n/a	n/a	n/a
Durham, NC	n/a	5.4	n/a	176.0	294.6	696.1	1,987.1	176.7
Edison, NJ[2]	1,763.0	2.8	22.8	121.6	245.3	149.1	1,150.3	71.1
El Paso, TX	2,042.9	2.5	52.1	51.0	250.7	189.4	1,391.1	106.1
Eugene, OR	3,372.0	2.1	46.7	67.0	217.2	518.8	2,256.0	264.1
Evansville, IN	3,159.5	8.2	37.5	74.1	253.9	460.6	2,112.9	212.3
Fargo, ND	2,685.7	1.7	55.6	35.5	187.3	377.0	1,826.7	201.9
Fayetteville, NC	n/a	8.1	n/a	92.8	329.9	660.6	2,185.0	127.8
Fort Collins, CO	2,482.6	1.7	42.5	22.0	173.5	271.0	1,849.2	122.6
Fort Wayne, IN	n/a	9.0	43.0	79.8	151.8	378.9	n/a	158.0
Fort Worth, TX[2]	n/a	5.2	47.3	120.5	196.4	n/a	1,669.5	276.0
Gainesville, FL	3,236.9	3.2	87.9	104.8	394.3	410.2	2,049.0	187.5
Grand Rapids, MI	1,840.5	2.8	78.3	52.5	190.3	261.6	1,159.2	95.8
Greeley, CO	1,995.6	3.0	37.8	28.2	187.2	282.9	1,274.2	182.3
Green Bay, WI	1,585.5	0.0	41.5	23.4	157.4	178.3	1,137.1	47.8
Greensboro, NC	n/a	10.9	n/a	133.7	321.7	631.6	2,067.7	196.7
Honolulu, HI	3,020.7	3.2	28.8	91.7	122.7	336.3	2,073.9	364.1
Houston, TX	n/a	6.4	42.8	205.2	338.8	n/a	1,928.8	n/a
Huntsville, AL	3,685.7	7.3	56.3	97.0	396.3	560.7	2,249.3	318.9
Indianapolis, IN	3,576.9	8.3	48.3	194.6	443.3	574.6	1,975.9	331.9
Jacksonville, FL	3,258.4	8.2	48.1	106.3	318.3	508.9	2,029.1	239.6
Kansas City, MO	n/a	n/a	n/a	n/a	n/a	n/a	n/a	n/a
Lafayette, LA	n/a	8.9	24.1	73.2	333.4	683.2	n/a	n/a
Las Cruces, NM[3]	3,220.3	5.1	44.8	30.8	172.2	600.7	2,171.5	195.1
Las Vegas, NV	3,387.2	10.8	70.0	194.5	332.6	748.7	1,564.3	466.2
Lexington, KY	n/a	6.6	50.7	127.9	88.0	606.4	n/a	318.7
Lincoln, NE[3]	3,146.1	3.1	74.8	58.7	185.7	412.1	2,294.5	117.3
Little Rock, AR	4,886.7	11.7	61.1	114.6	611.1	797.4	2,920.9	369.9

Table continued on next page.

Metro Area[1]	All Crimes	Violent Crimes				Property Crimes		
		Murder	Rape	Robbery	Aggrav. Assault	Burglary	Larceny -Theft	Motor Vehicle Theft
Los Angeles, CA[2]	2,847.0	4.8	38.3	176.3	277.2	427.4	1,502.4	420.5
Louisville, KY	3,512.3	9.5	23.1	123.1	261.9	588.9	2,108.3	397.5
Madison, WI	2,054.7	2.3	29.4	45.8	151.1	260.8	1,455.0	110.3
Manchester, NH	1,667.1	1.0	49.7	52.4	162.8	204.4	1,114.5	82.4
McAllen, TX	2,807.2	4.4	48.1	42.4	198.1	377.2	2,045.1	92.0
Miami, FL[2]	3,534.6	6.1	32.5	133.4	286.2	419.1	2,362.0	295.3
Midland, TX	2,258.5	1.2	23.1	46.8	200.6	319.7	1,478.1	189.0
Minneapolis, MN	2,688.6	2.6	43.3	91.8	145.3	353.2	1,837.8	214.5
Nashville, TN	3,183.4	7.8	47.0	130.7	439.4	415.8	1,915.5	227.2
New Orleans, LA	3,512.1	17.1	59.7	150.5	336.7	429.7	2,218.9	299.6
New York, NY[2]	1,668.5	2.8	19.8	107.5	202.8	152.6	1,094.7	88.3
Oklahoma City, OK	3,396.3	7.6	58.2	103.8	328.8	696.7	1,898.8	302.4
Omaha, NE	3,149.4	3.7	59.9	79.5	241.4	358.1	1,929.0	477.8
Orlando, FL	3,217.8	5.0	47.1	94.1	297.6	514.1	2,046.4	213.6
Peoria, IL	2,732.2	3.7	54.0	88.6	249.5	541.5	1,652.1	142.8
Philadelphia, PA[2]	2,484.3	8.1	33.2	152.8	234.5	297.0	1,595.1	163.5
Phoenix, AZ	3,285.9	5.7	49.9	112.4	302.6	517.4	2,016.4	281.6
Pittsburgh, PA	1,851.3	5.4	20.6	71.7	180.5	256.2	1,239.8	77.1
Portland, OR	n/a	2.6	58.2	68.4	154.0	n/a	2,027.8	520.6
Providence, RI	1,986.4	2.0	39.4	62.0	191.4	307.4	1,250.4	133.7
Provo, UT	1,609.8	1.1	26.4	14.9	37.3	170.4	1,274.0	85.6
Raleigh, NC	n/a	n/a	n/a	n/a	n/a	n/a	n/a	n/a
Reno, NV	3,064.4	4.5	49.4	107.8	353.0	473.7	1,645.8	430.1
Richmond, VA[4]	2,588.3	7.5	25.2	77.6	126.3	387.2	1,823.2	141.3
Roanoke, VA	2,619.3	8.3	36.0	38.5	147.1	274.7	1,956.6	158.2
Rochester, MN	1,454.3	0.5	39.4	23.4	82.5	193.9	1,044.1	70.6
Salem, OR	3,335.6	3.3	27.2	62.6	187.1	409.2	2,249.6	396.5
Salt Lake City, UT	4,835.2	3.7	83.0	97.1	216.8	592.0	3,260.3	582.2
San Antonio, TX	n/a	6.4	70.3	107.4	339.8	n/a	2,784.4	340.8
San Diego, CA	2,032.6	2.4	32.8	89.9	212.0	272.6	1,132.5	290.4
San Francisco, CA[2]	n/a	4.2	39.1	218.0	215.4	412.1	n/a	536.7
San Jose, CA	2,584.0	2.4	41.3	96.5	168.6	348.5	1,405.1	521.5
Santa Rosa, CA	1,900.9	2.4	58.9	54.8	284.4	276.7	1,059.7	164.0
Savannah, GA	n/a	9.7	33.3	112.6	237.0	n/a	2,201.1	292.3
Seattle, WA[2]	n/a	3.0	37.5	102.1	211.1	n/a	2,444.4	481.0
Sioux Falls, SD	2,630.1	2.3	56.7	39.4	257.0	323.0	1,750.3	201.4
Springfield, IL	3,908.7	6.2	65.7	129.0	503.7	726.0	2,278.6	199.5
Tallahassee, FL	4,146.4	6.5	75.0	107.7	419.1	662.3	2,620.8	254.9
Tampa, FL	2,434.8	3.6	36.9	68.2	224.4	345.4	1,593.9	162.3
Topeka, KS	3,948.1	13.8	36.5	122.1	241.1	581.1	2,552.4	401.0
Tyler, TX	2,822.2	4.0	51.0	37.3	260.1	506.5	1,792.0	171.3
Virginia Beach, VA	2,964.4	7.9	34.5	94.3	194.0	346.6	2,116.3	170.8
Visalia, CA	2,902.5	7.1	35.0	83.4	234.2	511.4	1,552.0	479.4
Washington, DC[2]	2,018.8	4.5	28.8	95.0	145.2	156.7	1,439.7	149.0
Wilmington, NC	n/a	8.7	n/a	90.0	246.6	627.2	1,999.1	136.5
Winston-Salem, NC	n/a	n/a	n/a	n/a	n/a	n/a	n/a	n/a
U.S.	2,756.1	5.3	41.7	98.0	248.9	430.4	1,694.4	237.4

Note: Figures are crimes per 100,000 population in 2017 except where noted; n/a not available; (1) Figures cover the Metropolitan Statistical Area except where noted; (2) Metropolitan Division; (3) 2016 data; (4) 2015 data
Source: FBI Uniform Crime Reports, 2015, 2016, 2017

Temperature & Precipitation: Yearly Averages and Extremes

City	Extreme Low (°F)	Average Low (°F)	Average Temp. (°F)	Average High (°F)	Extreme High (°F)	Average Precip. (in.)	Average Snow (in.)
Albany, NY	-28	37	48	58	100	35.8	63
Albuquerque, NM	-17	43	57	70	105	8.5	11
Allentown, PA	-12	42	52	61	105	44.2	32
Anchorage, AK	-34	29	36	43	85	15.7	71
Ann Arbor, MI	-21	39	49	58	104	32.4	41
Athens, GA	-8	52	62	72	105	49.8	2
Atlanta, GA	-8	52	62	72	105	49.8	2
Austin, TX	-2	58	69	79	109	31.1	1
Baton Rouge, LA	8	57	68	78	103	58.5	Trace
Billings, MT	-32	36	47	59	105	14.6	59
Boise City, ID	-25	39	51	63	111	11.8	22
Boston, MA	-12	44	52	59	102	42.9	41
Boulder, CO	-25	37	51	64	103	15.5	63
Cape Coral, FL	26	65	75	84	103	53.9	0
Cedar Rapids, IA	-34	36	47	57	105	34.4	33
Charleston, SC	6	55	66	76	104	52.1	1
Charlotte, NC	-5	50	61	71	104	42.8	6
Chicago, IL	-27	40	49	59	104	35.4	39
Clarksville, TN	-17	49	60	70	107	47.4	11
College Station, TX	-2	58	69	79	109	31.1	1
Colorado Springs, CO	-24	36	49	62	99	17.0	48
Columbia, MO	-20	44	54	64	111	40.6	25
Columbia, SC	-1	51	64	75	107	48.3	2
Columbus, OH	-19	42	52	62	104	37.9	28
Dallas, TX	-2	56	67	77	112	33.9	3
Denver, CO	-25	37	51	64	103	15.5	63
Des Moines, IA	-24	40	50	60	108	31.8	33
Durham, NC	-9	48	60	71	105	42.0	8
Edison, NJ	-8	46	55	63	105	43.5	27
El Paso, TX	-8	50	64	78	114	8.6	6
Eugene, OR	-12	42	53	63	108	47.3	7
Evansville, IN	-23	42	53	62	104	40.2	25
Fargo, ND	-36	31	41	52	106	19.6	40
Fayetteville, NC	-9	48	60	71	105	42.0	8
Fort Collins, CO	-25	37	51	64	103	15.5	63
Fort Wayne, IN	-22	40	50	60	106	35.9	33
Fort Worth, TX	-1	55	66	76	113	32.3	3
Gainesville, FL	10	58	69	79	102	50.9	Trace
Grand Rapids, MI	-22	38	48	57	102	34.7	73
Greeley, CO	-25	37	51	64	103	15.5	63
Green Bay, WI	-31	34	44	54	99	28.3	46
Greensboro, NC	-8	47	58	69	103	42.5	10
Honolulu, HI	52	70	77	84	94	22.4	0
Houston, TX	7	58	69	79	107	46.9	Trace
Huntsville, AL	-11	50	61	71	104	56.8	4
Indianapolis, IN	-23	42	53	62	104	40.2	25
Jacksonville, FL	7	58	69	79	103	52.0	0
Kansas City, MO	-23	44	54	64	109	38.1	21
Lafayette, LA	8	57	68	78	103	58.5	Trace
Las Cruces, NM	-8	50	64	78	114	8.6	6
Las Vegas, NV	8	53	67	80	116	4.0	1
Lexington, KY	-21	45	55	65	103	45.1	17
Lincoln, NE	-33	39	51	62	108	29.1	27
Little Rock, AR	-5	51	62	73	112	50.7	5
Los Angeles, CA	27	55	63	70	110	11.3	Trace

Table continued on next page.

City	Extreme Low (°F)	Average Low (°F)	Average Temp. (°F)	Average High (°F)	Extreme High (°F)	Average Precip. (in.)	Average Snow (in.)
Louisville, KY	-20	46	57	67	105	43.9	17
Madison, WI	-37	35	46	57	104	31.1	42
Manchester, NH	-33	34	46	57	102	36.9	63
McAllen, TX	16	65	74	83	106	25.8	Trace
Miami, FL	30	69	76	83	98	57.1	0
Midland, TX	-11	50	64	77	116	14.6	4
Minneapolis, MN	-34	35	45	54	105	27.1	52
Nashville, TN	-17	49	60	70	107	47.4	11
New Orleans, LA	11	59	69	78	102	60.6	Trace
New York, NY	-2	47	55	62	104	47.0	23
Oklahoma City, OK	-8	49	60	71	110	32.8	10
Omaha, NE	-23	40	51	62	110	30.1	29
Orlando, FL	19	62	72	82	100	47.7	Trace
Peoria, IL	-26	41	51	61	113	35.4	23
Philadelphia, PA	-7	45	55	64	104	41.4	22
Phoenix, AZ	17	59	72	86	122	7.3	Trace
Pittsburgh, PA	-18	41	51	60	103	37.1	43
Portland, OR	-3	45	54	62	107	37.5	7
Providence, RI	-13	42	51	60	104	45.3	35
Provo, UT	-22	40	52	64	107	15.6	63
Raleigh, NC	-9	48	60	71	105	42.0	8
Reno, NV	-16	33	50	67	105	7.2	24
Richmond, VA	-8	48	58	69	105	43.0	13
Roanoke, VA	-11	46	57	67	105	40.8	23
Rochester, MN	-40	34	44	54	102	29.4	47
Salem, OR	-12	41	52	63	108	40.2	7
Salt Lake City, UT	-22	40	52	64	107	15.6	63
San Antonio, TX	0	58	69	80	108	29.6	1
San Diego, CA	29	57	64	71	111	9.5	Trace
San Francisco, CA	24	49	57	65	106	19.3	Trace
San Jose, CA	21	50	59	68	105	13.5	Trace
Santa Rosa, CA	23	42	57	71	109	29.0	n/a
Savannah, GA	3	56	67	77	105	50.3	Trace
Seattle, WA	0	44	52	59	99	38.4	13
Sioux Falls, SD	-36	35	46	57	110	24.6	38
Springfield, IL	-24	44	54	63	112	34.9	21
Tallahassee, FL	6	56	68	79	103	63.3	Trace
Tampa, FL	18	63	73	82	99	46.7	Trace
Topeka, KS	-26	43	55	66	110	34.4	21
Tyler, TX	-2	56	67	77	112	33.9	3
Virginia Beach, VA	-3	51	60	69	104	44.8	8
Visalia, CA	18	50	63	76	112	10.9	0
Washington, DC	-5	49	58	67	104	39.5	18
Wilmington, NC	0	53	64	74	104	55.0	2
Winston-Salem, NC	-8	47	58	69	103	42.5	10

Source: National Climatic Data Center, International Station Meteorological Climate Summary, 9/96

Weather Conditions

City	Temperature			Daytime Sky			Precipitation		
	10°F & below	32°F & below	90°F & above	Clear	Partly cloudy	Cloudy	0.01 inch or more precip.	1.0 inch or more snow/ice	Thunder-storms
Albany, NY	n/a	147	11	58	149	158	133	36	24
Albuquerque, NM	4	114	65	140	161	64	60	9	38
Allentown, PA	n/a	123	15	77	148	140	123	20	31
Anchorage, AK	n/a	194	n/a	50	115	200	113	49	2
Ann Arbor, MI	n/a	136	12	74	134	157	135	38	32
Athens, GA	1	49	38	98	147	120	116	3	48
Atlanta, GA	1	49	38	98	147	120	116	3	48
Austin, TX	< 1	20	111	105	148	112	83	1	41
Baton Rouge, LA	< 1	21	86	99	150	116	113	< 1	73
Billings, MT	n/a	149	29	75	163	127	97	41	27
Boise City, ID	n/a	124	45	106	133	126	91	22	14
Boston, MA	n/a	97	12	88	127	150	253	48	18
Boulder, CO	24	155	33	99	177	89	90	38	39
Cape Coral, FL	n/a	n/a	115	93	220	52	110	0	92
Cedar Rapids, IA	n/a	156	16	89	132	144	109	28	42
Charleston, SC	< 1	33	53	89	162	114	114	1	59
Charlotte, NC	1	65	44	98	142	125	113	3	41
Chicago, IL	n/a	132	17	83	136	146	125	31	38
Clarksville, TN	5	76	51	98	135	132	119	8	54
College Station, TX	< 1	20	111	105	148	112	83	1	41
Colorado Springs, CO	21	161	18	108	157	100	98	33	49
Columbia, MO	17	108	36	99	127	139	110	17	52
Columbia, SC	< 1	58	77	97	149	119	110	1	53
Columbus, OH	n/a	118	19	72	137	156	136	29	40
Dallas, TX	1	34	102	108	160	97	78	2	49
Denver, CO	24	155	33	99	177	89	90	38	39
Des Moines, IA	n/a	137	26	99	129	137	106	25	46
Durham, NC	n/a	n/a	39	98	143	124	110	3	42
Edison, NJ	n/a	90	24	80	146	139	122	16	46
El Paso, TX	1	59	106	147	164	54	49	3	35
Eugene, OR	n/a	n/a	15	75	115	175	136	4	3
Evansville, IN	19	119	19	83	128	154	127	24	43
Fargo, ND	n/a	180	15	81	145	139	100	38	31
Fayetteville, NC	n/a	n/a	39	98	143	124	110	3	42
Fort Collins, CO	24	155	33	99	177	89	90	38	39
Fort Wayne, IN	n/a	131	16	75	140	150	131	31	39
Fort Worth, TX	1	40	100	123	136	106	79	3	47
Gainesville, FL	n/a	n/a	77	88	196	81	119	0	78
Grand Rapids, MI	n/a	146	11	67	119	179	142	57	34
Greeley, CO	24	155	33	99	177	89	90	38	39
Green Bay, WI	n/a	163	7	86	125	154	120	40	33
Greensboro, NC	3	85	32	94	143	128	113	5	43
Honolulu, HI	n/a	n/a	23	25	286	54	98	0	7
Houston, TX	n/a	n/a	96	83	168	114	101	1	62
Huntsville, AL	2	66	49	70	118	177	116	2	54
Indianapolis, IN	19	119	19	83	128	154	127	24	43
Jacksonville, FL	< 1	16	83	86	181	98	114	1	65
Kansas City, MO	22	110	39	112	134	119	103	17	51
Lafayette, LA	< 1	21	86	99	150	116	113	< 1	73
Las Cruces, NM	1	59	106	147	164	54	49	3	35
Las Vegas, NV	< 1	37	134	185	132	48	27	2	13
Lexington, KY	11	96	22	86	136	143	129	17	44
Lincoln, NE	n/a	145	40	108	135	122	94	19	46
Little Rock, AR	1	57	73	110	142	113	104	4	57

Table continued on next page.

City	Temperature			Daytime Sky			Precipitation		
	10°F & below	32°F & below	90°F & above	Clear	Partly cloudy	Cloudy	0.01 inch or more precip.	1.0 inch or more snow/ice	Thunder-storms
Los Angeles, CA	0	< 1	5	131	125	109	34	0	1
Louisville, KY	8	90	35	82	143	140	125	15	45
Madison, WI	n/a	161	14	88	119	158	118	38	40
Manchester, NH	n/a	171	12	87	131	147	125	32	19
McAllen, TX	n/a	n/a	116	86	180	99	72	0	27
Miami, FL	n/a	n/a	55	48	263	54	128	0	74
Midland, TX	1	62	102	144	138	83	52	3	38
Minneapolis, MN	n/a	156	16	93	125	147	113	41	37
Nashville, TN	5	76	51	98	135	132	119	8	54
New Orleans, LA	0	13	70	90	169	106	114	1	69
New York, NY	n/a	n/a	18	85	166	114	120	11	20
Oklahoma City, OK	5	79	70	124	131	110	80	8	50
Omaha, NE	n/a	139	35	100	142	123	97	20	46
Orlando, FL	n/a	n/a	90	76	208	81	115	0	80
Peoria, IL	n/a	127	27	89	127	149	115	22	49
Philadelphia, PA	5	94	23	81	146	138	117	14	27
Phoenix, AZ	0	10	167	186	125	54	37	< 1	23
Pittsburgh, PA	n/a	121	8	62	137	166	154	42	35
Portland, OR	n/a	37	11	67	116	182	152	4	7
Providence, RI	n/a	117	9	85	134	146	123	21	21
Provo, UT	n/a	128	56	94	152	119	92	38	38
Raleigh, NC	n/a	n/a	39	98	143	124	110	3	42
Reno, NV	14	178	50	143	139	83	50	17	14
Richmond, VA	3	79	41	90	147	128	115	7	43
Roanoke, VA	4	89	31	90	152	123	119	11	35
Rochester, MN	n/a	165	9	87	126	152	114	40	41
Salem, OR	n/a	66	16	78	118	169	146	6	5
Salt Lake City, UT	n/a	128	56	94	152	119	92	38	38
San Antonio, TX	n/a	n/a	112	97	153	115	81	1	36
San Diego, CA	0	< 1	4	115	126	124	40	0	5
San Francisco, CA	0	6	4	136	130	99	63	< 1	5
San Jose, CA	0	5	5	106	180	79	57	< 1	6
Santa Rosa, CA	n/a	43	30	n/a	365	n/a	n/a	n/a	2
Savannah, GA	< 1	29	70	97	155	113	111	< 1	63
Seattle, WA	n/a	38	3	57	121	187	157	8	8
Sioux Falls, SD	n/a	n/a	n/a	95	136	134	n/a	n/a	n/a
Springfield, IL	19	111	34	96	126	143	111	18	49
Tallahassee, FL	< 1	31	86	93	175	97	114	1	83
Tampa, FL	n/a	n/a	85	81	204	80	107	< 1	87
Topeka, KS	20	123	45	110	128	127	96	15	54
Tyler, TX	1	34	102	108	160	97	78	2	49
Virginia Beach, VA	< 1	53	33	89	149	127	115	5	38
Visalia, CA	0	23	106	185	99	81	44	< 1	5
Washington, DC	2	71	34	84	144	137	112	9	30
Wilmington, NC	< 1	42	46	96	150	119	115	1	47
Winston-Salem, NC	3	85	32	94	143	128	113	5	43

Note: Figures are average number of days per year
Source: National Climatic Data Center, International Station Meteorological Climate Summary, 9/96

Air Quality Index

MSA[1] (Days[2])	Percent of Days when Air Quality was...					AQI Statistics	
	Good	Moderate	Unhealthy for Sensitive Groups	Unhealthy	Very Unhealthy	Maximum	Median
Albany, NY (365)	83.8	16.2	0.0	0.0	0.0	90	39
Albuquerque, NM (365)	45.2	53.7	1.1	0.0	0.0	119	52
Allentown, PA (365)	48.2	50.1	0.8	0.8	0.0	200	51
Anchorage, AK (365)	78.4	20.0	1.4	0.3	0.0	155	31
Ann Arbor, MI (365)	77.8	21.4	0.8	0.0	0.0	119	40
Athens, GA (360)	87.2	12.8	0.0	0.0	0.0	97	38
Atlanta, GA (365)	47.7	49.3	3.0	0.0	0.0	150	51
Austin, TX (365)	71.8	27.1	1.1	0.0	0.0	130	43
Baton Rouge, LA (365)	62.5	35.3	2.2	0.0	0.0	140	46
Billings, MT (365)	85.5	13.2	1.4	0.0	0.0	141	25
Boise City, ID (365)	49.9	42.5	6.3	0.8	0.5	243	51
Boston, MA (365)	48.8	49.9	1.4	0.0	0.0	147	51
Boulder, CO (357)	67.2	29.7	3.1	0.0	0.0	149	45
Cape Coral, FL (363)	89.5	10.5	0.0	0.0	0.0	90	37
Cedar Rapids, IA (365)	76.7	23.3	0.0	0.0	0.0	100	40
Charleston, SC (361)	83.7	16.1	0.3	0.0	0.0	101	40
Charlotte, NC (365)	58.6	40.0	1.4	0.0	0.0	115	48
Chicago, IL (365)	43.0	50.1	6.3	0.5	0.0	177	53
Clarksville, TN (362)	82.0	18.0	0.0	0.0	0.0	87	42
College Station, TX (365)	100.0	0.0	0.0	0.0	0.0	23	0
Colorado Springs, CO (365)	65.5	33.7	0.8	0.0	0.0	116	46
Columbia, MO (245)	89.4	10.6	0.0	0.0	0.0	77	41
Columbia, SC (365)	74.0	25.5	0.5	0.0	0.0	113	44
Columbus, OH (365)	77.3	21.9	0.8	0.0	0.0	112	42
Dallas, TX (365)	52.6	40.8	6.6	0.0	0.0	147	50
Denver, CO (365)	19.7	69.3	10.7	0.3	0.0	155	62
Des Moines, IA (365)	80.0	19.7	0.3	0.0	0.0	135	40
Durham, NC (365)	72.3	27.4	0.3	0.0	0.0	110	44
Edison, NJ (365)	42.2	52.6	4.7	0.5	0.0	159	52
El Paso, TX (365)	46.6	47.1	5.8	0.5	0.0	159	51
Eugene, OR (365)	65.2	26.6	4.4	3.0	0.5	380	39
Evansville, IN (365)	57.5	39.7	2.7	0.0	0.0	126	48
Fargo, ND (362)	84.5	15.5	0.0	0.0	0.0	77	38
Fayetteville, NC (365)	73.4	26.6	0.0	0.0	0.0	100	43
Fort Collins, CO (365)	53.7	43.0	3.0	0.3	0.0	153	49
Fort Wayne, IN (365)	70.7	29.0	0.3	0.0	0.0	105	44
Fort Worth, TX (365)	52.6	40.8	6.6	0.0	0.0	147	50
Gainesville, FL (355)	89.0	11.0	0.0	0.0	0.0	92	37
Grand Rapids, MI (365)	77.8	22.2	0.0	0.0	0.0	100	40
Greeley, CO (365)	58.4	39.5	1.9	0.3	0.0	154	47
Green Bay, WI (364)	86.3	13.2	0.5	0.0	0.0	112	37
Greensboro, NC (365)	77.8	21.9	0.3	0.0	0.0	112	42
Honolulu, HI (365)	93.7	6.3	0.0	0.0	0.0	91	31
Houston, TX (365)	50.4	42.7	6.0	0.8	0.0	177	50
Huntsville, AL (336)	89.9	10.1	0.0	0.0	0.0	100	39
Indianapolis, IN (365)	54.0	43.6	2.5	0.0	0.0	122	48
Jacksonville, FL (365)	74.2	25.5	0.3	0.0	0.0	101	42
Kansas City, MO (365)	55.3	42.7	1.9	0.0	0.0	129	48
Lafayette, LA (365)	71.8	27.9	0.3	0.0	0.0	105	42
Las Cruces, NM (365)	35.9	54.8	7.4	1.1	0.0	617	57
Las Vegas, NV (365)	37.3	54.8	7.7	0.3	0.0	154	58
Lexington, KY (365)	86.3	13.7	0.0	0.0	0.0	100	40
Lincoln, NE (344)	92.2	7.3	0.6	0.0	0.0	113	33
Little Rock, AR (365)	69.0	30.7	0.3	0.0	0.0	115	44

Table continued on next page.

MSA[1] (Days[2])	Percent of Days when Air Quality was...					AQI Statistics	
	Good	Moderate	Unhealthy for Sensitive Groups	Unhealthy	Very Unhealthy	Maximum	Median
Los Angeles, CA (365)	10.4	56.2	20.8	10.4	2.2	224	79
Louisville, KY (365)	59.5	38.9	1.6	0.0	0.0	119	47
Madison, WI (365)	80.5	19.5	0.0	0.0	0.0	93	39
Manchester, NH (365)	93.7	6.0	0.3	0.0	0.0	101	37
McAllen, TX (365)	77.0	23.0	0.0	0.0	0.0	95	38
Miami, FL (358)	59.5	38.3	2.2	0.0	0.0	143	47
Midland, TX (n/a)	n/a	n/a	n/a	n/a	n/a	n/a	n/a
Minneapolis, MN (365)	47.7	52.1	0.3	0.0	0.0	115	51
Nashville, TN (365)	63.8	35.9	0.3	0.0	0.0	133	45
New Orleans, LA (365)	69.3	30.1	0.5	0.0	0.0	129	44
New York, NY (365)	42.2	52.6	4.7	0.5	0.0	159	52
Oklahoma City, OK (365)	62.2	35.9	1.9	0.0	0.0	119	47
Omaha, NE (365)	54.2	45.2	0.5	0.0	0.0	114	48
Orlando, FL (365)	73.4	25.8	0.8	0.0	0.0	147	43
Peoria, IL (365)	70.7	28.5	0.8	0.0	0.0	115	44
Philadelphia, PA (365)	34.5	59.5	5.5	0.5	0.0	166	55
Phoenix, AZ (365)	8.8	65.2	22.5	3.0	0.3	365	84
Pittsburgh, PA (365)	25.2	66.0	8.5	0.3	0.0	164	59
Portland, OR (365)	73.2	22.5	2.7	1.4	0.3	212	40
Providence, RI (365)	71.5	26.6	1.4	0.5	0.0	151	43
Provo, UT (365)	50.1	46.0	3.0	0.8	0.0	161	50
Raleigh, NC (365)	66.3	33.7	0.0	0.0	0.0	100	45
Reno, NV (365)	55.3	43.6	1.1	0.0	0.0	126	49
Richmond, VA (365)	78.1	21.6	0.0	0.3	0.0	154	42
Roanoke, VA (365)	87.1	12.6	0.3	0.0	0.0	116	38
Rochester, MN (365)	85.5	14.5	0.0	0.0	0.0	87	37
Salem, OR (362)	83.7	13.8	2.5	0.0	0.0	150	30
Salt Lake City, UT (365)	44.7	43.0	12.1	0.3	0.0	155	53
San Antonio, TX (362)	72.4	26.0	1.1	0.6	0.0	188	43
San Diego, CA (365)	22.7	60.3	15.3	1.6	0.0	174	65
San Francisco, CA (365)	46.3	49.3	2.2	1.9	0.3	205	52
San Jose, CA (365)	61.4	35.3	2.5	0.8	0.0	182	45
Santa Rosa, CA (365)	85.2	13.4	0.5	0.8	0.0	165	38
Savannah, GA (365)	79.2	20.8	0.0	0.0	0.0	84	38
Seattle, WA (365)	60.8	32.6	3.6	2.7	0.3	202	47
Sioux Falls, SD (365)	87.1	12.9	0.0	0.0	0.0	97	35
Springfield, IL (364)	81.9	17.6	0.5	0.0	0.0	115	40
Tallahassee, FL (363)	71.1	28.9	0.0	0.0	0.0	92	41
Tampa, FL (365)	69.0	29.9	1.1	10.0	0.0	150	45
Topeka, KS (361)	82.8	17.2	0.0	0.0	0.0	93	39
Tyler, TX (364)	92.3	7.7	0.0	0.0	0.0	90	37
Virginia Beach, VA (365)	86.8	13.2	0.0	0.0	0.0	97	39
Visalia, CA (365)	25.5	39.7	26.3	8.5	0.0	168	80
Washington, DC (365)	40.3	57.5	2.2	0.0	0.0	133	53
Wilmington, NC (365)	93.2	6.8	0.0	0.0	0.0	67	33
Winston-Salem, NC (365)	70.1	29.9	0.0	0.0	0.0	100	44

Note: The Air Quality Index (AQI) is an index for reporting daily air quality. EPA calculates the AQI for five major air pollutants regulated by the Clean Air Act: ground-level ozone, particle pollution (also known as particulate matter), carbon monoxide, sulfur dioxide, and nitrogen dioxide. The AQI runs from 0 to 500. The higher the AQI value, the greater the level of air pollution and the greater the health concern. There are six AQI categories: "Good" The AQI is between 0 and 50. Air quality is considered satisfactory; "Moderate" The AQI is between 51 and 100. Air quality is acceptable; "Unhealthy for Sensitive Groups" When AQI values are between 101 and 150, members of sensitive groups may experience health effects; "Unhealthy" When AQI values are between 151 and 200 everyone may begin to experience health effects; "Very Unhealthy" AQI values between 201 and 300 trigger a health alert; "Hazardous" AQI values over 300 trigger health warnings of emergency conditions; Data covers the entire county unless noted otherwise; (1) Data covers the Metropolitan Statistical Area—see Appendix B for areas included; (2) Number of days with AQI data in 2017
Source: U.S. Environmental Protection Agency, Air Quality Index Report, 2017

Air Quality Index Pollutants

MSA[1] (Days[2])	Percent of Days when AQI Pollutant was...					
	Carbon Monoxide	Nitrogen Dioxide	Ozone	Sulfur Dioxide	Particulate Matter 2.5	Particulate Matter 10
Albany, NY (365)	0.0	0.0	70.1	0.0	29.9	0.0
Albuquerque, NM (365)	0.0	0.5	70.7	0.0	7.9	20.8
Allentown, PA (365)	0.0	0.3	35.6	1.9	62.2	0.0
Anchorage, AK (365)	0.3	0.0	45.5	0.0	36.4	17.8
Ann Arbor, MI (365)	0.0	0.0	65.8	0.0	34.2	0.0
Athens, GA (360)	0.0	0.0	52.2	0.0	47.8	0.0
Atlanta, GA (365)	0.0	4.4	44.4	0.0	51.2	0.0
Austin, TX (365)	0.0	4.9	51.0	0.0	44.1	0.0
Baton Rouge, LA (365)	0.0	0.5	38.4	2.7	58.4	0.0
Billings, MT (365)	0.0	0.0	0.0	9.0	91.0	0.0
Boise City, ID (365)	0.3	2.5	52.6	0.0	43.3	1.4
Boston, MA (365)	0.0	1.1	29.3	0.0	69.6	0.0
Boulder, CO (357)	0.0	0.0	92.2	0.0	7.8	0.0
Cape Coral, FL (363)	0.0	0.0	74.1	0.0	24.8	1.1
Cedar Rapids, IA (365)	0.0	0.0	44.7	5.2	49.6	0.5
Charleston, SC (361)	0.0	1.1	56.2	0.0	42.1	0.6
Charlotte, NC (365)	0.0	0.3	56.7	0.0	43.0	0.0
Chicago, IL (365)	0.0	5.8	41.6	3.0	44.9	4.7
Clarksville, TN (362)	0.0	0.0	63.0	0.0	37.0	0.0
College Station, TX (365)	0.0	0.0	0.0	100.0	0.0	0.0
Colorado Springs, CO (365)	0.0	0.0	89.0	0.5	10.4	0.0
Columbia, MO (245)	0.0	0.0	100.0	0.0	0.0	0.0
Columbia, SC (365)	0.0	0.0	61.4	0.0	38.4	0.3
Columbus, OH (365)	0.0	7.9	55.1	0.0	36.2	0.8
Dallas, TX (365)	0.0	4.1	57.3	0.0	38.6	0.0
Denver, CO (365)	0.0	20.0	62.5	0.0	13.2	4.4
Des Moines, IA (365)	0.0	1.1	59.2	0.0	39.7	0.0
Durham, NC (365)	0.0	0.0	50.1	0.5	49.3	0.0
Edison, NJ (365)	0.0	14.5	33.2	0.0	52.3	0.0
El Paso, TX (365)	0.0	7.4	56.7	0.0	35.3	0.5
Eugene, OR (365)	0.0	0.0	25.2	0.0	74.0	0.8
Evansville, IN (365)	0.0	0.0	37.8	15.3	46.8	0.0
Fargo, ND (362)	0.0	0.3	48.1	0.0	47.5	4.1
Fayetteville, NC (365)	0.0	0.0	44.4	0.0	55.3	0.3
Fort Collins, CO (365)	0.0	0.0	88.8	0.0	11.2	0.0
Fort Wayne, IN (365)	0.0	0.0	49.6	0.0	50.4	0.0
Fort Worth, TX (365)	0.0	4.1	57.3	0.0	38.6	0.0
Gainesville, FL (355)	0.0	0.0	61.4	0.0	38.6	0.0
Grand Rapids, MI (365)	0.0	0.0	65.5	0.3	34.2	0.0
Greeley, CO (365)	0.0	0.0	69.3	0.0	30.7	0.0
Green Bay, WI (364)	0.0	0.0	60.2	1.4	38.5	0.0
Greensboro, NC (365)	0.0	0.0	55.9	0.0	40.0	4.1
Honolulu, HI (365)	0.3	2.2	70.7	11.5	15.3	0.0
Houston, TX (365)	0.0	5.2	48.8	0.0	45.8	0.3
Huntsville, AL (336)	0.0	0.0	68.5	0.0	15.5	16.1
Indianapolis, IN (365)	0.0	0.8	37.8	2.5	58.9	0.0
Jacksonville, FL (365)	0.3	0.8	51.8	1.9	45.2	0.0
Kansas City, MO (365)	0.0	2.7	46.0	0.5	45.2	5.5
Lafayette, LA (365)	0.0	0.0	65.8	0.0	34.2	0.0
Las Cruces, NM (365)	0.0	0.3	70.4	0.0	8.2	21.1
Las Vegas, NV (365)	0.0	12.6	62.7	0.0	21.6	3.0
Lexington, KY (365)	0.0	3.0	52.6	0.3	43.8	0.3
Lincoln, NE (344)	0.0	0.0	57.0	24.4	18.6	0.0
Little Rock, AR (365)	0.0	0.5	41.6	0.0	57.8	0.0

Table continued on next page.

MSA[1] (Days[2])	Percent of Days when AQI Pollutant was...					
	Carbon Monoxide	Nitrogen Dioxide	Ozone	Sulfur Dioxide	Particulate Matter 2.5	Particulate Matter 10
Los Angeles, CA (365)	0.0	7.7	48.5	0.0	43.3	0.5
Louisville, KY (365)	0.0	4.7	41.6	0.0	53.7	0.0
Madison, WI (365)	0.0	0.0	53.4	1.9	44.7	0.0
Manchester, NH (365)	0.0	0.0	97.0	0.3	2.7	0.0
McAllen, TX (365)	0.0	0.0	39.2	0.0	60.8	0.0
Miami, FL (358)	0.0	1.7	24.6	0.0	70.4	3.4
Midland, TX (n/a)	n/a	n/a	n/a	n/a	n/a	n/a
Minneapolis, MN (365)	0.0	1.6	26.8	0.0	36.2	35.3
Nashville, TN (365)	0.0	4.9	37.3	0.5	57.3	0.0
New Orleans, LA (365)	0.0	0.8	46.0	9.0	44.1	0.0
New York, NY (365)	0.0	14.5	33.2	0.0	52.3	0.0
Oklahoma City, OK (365)	0.0	4.7	60.5	0.0	34.8	0.0
Omaha, NE (365)	0.0	0.0	33.7	6.0	48.5	11.8
Orlando, FL (365)	0.0	3.6	60.8	0.0	35.3	0.3
Peoria, IL (365)	0.0	0.0	57.0	1.1	41.9	0.0
Philadelphia, PA (365)	0.0	0.8	32.1	0.5	66.3	0.3
Phoenix, AZ (365)	0.0	3.3	37.0	0.0	15.9	43.8
Pittsburgh, PA (365)	0.0	0.0	24.4	7.7	67.7	0.3
Portland, OR (365)	0.0	4.9	52.9	0.0	42.2	0.0
Providence, RI (365)	0.0	4.7	55.6	0.0	39.7	0.0
Provo, UT (365)	0.0	8.2	69.6	0.0	20.8	1.4
Raleigh, NC (365)	0.0	1.1	44.4	0.0	54.5	0.0
Reno, NV (365)	0.0	2.2	74.8	0.0	20.0	3.0
Richmond, VA (365)	0.0	2.2	62.7	0.0	35.1	0.0
Roanoke, VA (365)	0.0	2.5	52.9	4.4	40.3	0.0
Rochester, MN (365)	0.0	0.0	56.4	0.0	43.6	0.0
Salem, OR (362)	0.0	0.0	39.0	0.0	61.0	0.0
Salt Lake City, UT (365)	0.0	3.0	69.9	0.0	26.3	0.8
San Antonio, TX (362)	0.0	1.7	58.0	0.6	39.8	0.0
San Diego, CA (365)	0.0	0.8	66.3	0.0	32.9	0.0
San Francisco, CA (365)	0.0	4.9	28.2	0.0	66.8	0.0
San Jose, CA (365)	0.0	1.9	61.6	0.0	35.9	0.5
Santa Rosa, CA (365)	0.0	0.0	68.2	0.0	31.2	0.5
Savannah, GA (365)	0.0	0.0	27.4	9.6	63.0	0.0
Seattle, WA (365)	0.0	6.6	49.0	0.0	44.4	0.0
Sioux Falls, SD (365)	0.0	1.1	72.3	0.0	24.4	2.2
Springfield, IL (364)	0.0	0.0	76.6	0.0	23.4	0.0
Tallahassee, FL (363)	0.6	0.0	36.6	0.0	62.8	0.0
Tampa, FL (365)	0.0	0.0	54.0	2.2	43.6	0.3
Topeka, KS (361)	0.0	0.0	64.5	0.0	34.9	0.6
Tyler, TX (364)	0.0	2.2	97.8	0.0	0.0	0.0
Virginia Beach, VA (365)	0.0	11.5	61.6	0.0	26.8	0.0
Visalia, CA (365)	0.0	0.3	64.7	0.0	32.6	2.5
Washington, DC (365)	0.0	6.6	44.9	0.0	48.5	0.0
Wilmington, NC (365)	0.0	0.0	48.8	3.3	47.9	0.0
Winston-Salem, NC (365)	0.0	2.5	53.2	0.0	44.4	0.0

Note: The Air Quality Index (AQI) is an index for reporting daily air quality. EPA calculates the AQI for five major air pollutants regulated by the Clean Air Act: ground-level ozone, particle pollution (also known as particulate matter), carbon monoxide, sulfur dioxide, and nitrogen dioxide. The AQI runs from 0 to 500. The higher the AQI value, the greater the level of air pollution and the greater the health concern; (1) Data covers the Metropolitan Statistical Area—see Appendix B for areas included; (2) Number of days with AQI data in 2017
Source: U.S. Environmental Protection Agency, Air Quality Index Report, 2017

Air Quality Trends: Ozone

MSA[1]	1990	1995	2000	2005	2010	2012	2014	2015	2016	2017
Albany, NY	0.086	0.079	0.070	0.082	0.072	0.071	0.061	0.062	0.068	0.061
Albuquerque, NM	0.072	0.070	0.072	0.073	0.066	0.070	0.062	0.066	0.065	0.069
Allentown, PA	0.093	0.091	0.091	0.086	0.080	0.075	0.068	0.070	0.071	0.067
Anchorage, AK	n/a	n/a	n/a	n/a	n/a	n/a	n/a	n/a	n/a	n/a
Ann Arbor, MI	n/a	n/a	n/a	n/a	n/a	n/a	n/a	n/a	n/a	n/a
Athens, GA	n/a	n/a	n/a	n/a	n/a	n/a	n/a	n/a	n/a	n/a
Atlanta, GA	0.104	0.103	0.101	0.087	0.076	0.079	0.072	0.070	0.073	0.068
Austin, TX	0.088	0.089	0.088	0.082	0.074	0.074	0.062	0.073	0.064	0.070
Baton Rouge, LA	0.105	0.091	0.090	0.090	0.075	0.074	0.071	0.069	0.066	0.069
Billings, MT	n/a	n/a	n/a	n/a	n/a	n/a	n/a	n/a	n/a	n/a
Boise City, ID	n/a	n/a	n/a	n/a	n/a	n/a	n/a	n/a	n/a	n/a
Boston, MA	n/a	n/a	n/a	n/a	n/a	n/a	n/a	n/a	n/a	n/a
Boulder, CO	n/a	n/a	n/a	n/a	n/a	n/a	n/a	n/a	n/a	n/a
Cape Coral, FL	n/a	n/a	n/a	n/a	n/a	n/a	n/a	n/a	n/a	n/a
Cedar Rapids, IA	n/a	n/a	n/a	n/a	n/a	n/a	n/a	n/a	n/a	n/a
Charleston, SC	0.068	0.071	0.078	0.073	0.067	0.063	0.060	0.054	0.058	0.062
Charlotte, NC	0.098	0.091	0.101	0.090	0.082	0.085	0.068	0.069	0.069	0.069
Chicago, IL	0.074	0.094	0.073	0.084	0.070	0.082	0.068	0.066	0.074	0.071
Clarksville, TN	n/a	n/a	n/a	n/a	n/a	n/a	n/a	n/a	n/a	n/a
College Station, TX	n/a	n/a	n/a	n/a	n/a	n/a	n/a	n/a	n/a	n/a
Colorado Springs, CO	n/a	n/a	n/a	n/a	n/a	n/a	n/a	n/a	n/a	n/a
Columbia, MO	n/a	n/a	n/a	n/a	n/a	n/a	n/a	n/a	n/a	n/a
Columbia, SC	0.093	0.079	0.096	0.082	0.070	0.065	0.056	0.056	0.065	0.059
Columbus, OH	0.090	0.091	0.085	0.084	0.073	0.077	0.067	0.066	0.069	0.065
Dallas, TX	0.095	0.105	0.096	0.097	0.080	0.080	0.076	0.077	0.070	0.073
Denver, CO	0.077	0.070	0.069	0.072	0.070	0.079	0.070	0.073	0.071	0.072
Des Moines, IA	n/a	n/a	n/a	n/a	n/a	n/a	n/a	n/a	n/a	n/a
Durham, NC	n/a	n/a	n/a	n/a	n/a	n/a	n/a	n/a	n/a	n/a
Edison, NJ	0.101	0.106	0.090	0.091	0.081	0.079	0.069	0.075	0.073	0.070
El Paso, TX	0.080	0.078	0.082	0.075	0.072	0.072	0.068	0.070	0.068	0.073
Eugene, OR	0.068	0.062	0.056	0.068	0.058	0.061	0.058	0.070	0.057	0.072
Evansville, IN	0.088	0.092	0.076	0.072	0.072	0.078	0.067	0.067	0.071	0.067
Fargo, ND	n/a	n/a	n/a	n/a	n/a	n/a	n/a	n/a	n/a	n/a
Fayetteville, NC	0.087	0.081	0.086	0.084	0.071	0.068	0.061	0.060	0.064	0.063
Fort Collins, CO	0.066	0.072	0.074	0.076	0.072	0.077	0.071	0.069	0.070	0.067
Fort Wayne, IN	0.086	0.094	0.086	0.081	0.067	0.076	0.063	0.061	0.068	0.063
Fort Worth, TX	0.095	0.105	0.096	0.097	0.080	0.080	0.076	0.077	0.070	0.073
Gainesville, FL	n/a	n/a	n/a	n/a	n/a	n/a	n/a	n/a	n/a	n/a
Grand Rapids, MI	0.102	0.089	0.073	0.085	0.071	0.083	0.069	0.066	0.075	0.065
Greeley, CO	n/a	n/a	n/a	n/a	n/a	n/a	n/a	n/a	n/a	n/a
Green Bay, WI	n/a	n/a	n/a	n/a	n/a	n/a	n/a	n/a	n/a	n/a
Greensboro, NC	n/a	n/a	n/a	n/a	n/a	n/a	n/a	n/a	n/a	n/a
Honolulu, HI	0.034	0.051	0.044	0.042	0.047	0.043	0.057	0.049	0.048	0.048
Houston, TX	0.119	0.114	0.102	0.087	0.079	0.080	0.064	0.083	0.066	0.070
Huntsville, AL	0.079	0.080	0.088	0.075	0.071	0.076	0.064	0.063	0.066	0.063
Indianapolis, IN	0.086	0.095	0.082	0.080	0.069	0.074	0.063	0.064	0.068	0.066
Jacksonville, FL	0.080	0.068	0.072	0.076	0.068	0.059	0.062	0.060	0.057	0.059
Kansas City, MO	0.075	0.098	0.088	0.084	0.072	0.085	0.066	0.063	0.066	0.069
Lafayette, LA	n/a	n/a	n/a	n/a	n/a	n/a	n/a	n/a	n/a	n/a
Las Cruces, NM	0.073	0.075	0.075	0.070	0.060	0.074	0.065	0.070	0.063	0.071
Las Vegas, NV	n/a	n/a	n/a	n/a	n/a	n/a	n/a	n/a	n/a	n/a
Lexington, KY	0.078	0.088	0.077	0.078	0.070	0.078	0.065	0.069	0.066	0.063
Lincoln, NE	0.057	0.060	0.057	0.056	0.050	0.058	0.061	0.061	0.058	0.062
Little Rock, AR	0.080	0.086	0.090	0.083	0.072	0.078	0.066	0.063	0.064	0.060
Los Angeles, CA	0.129	0.110	0.089	0.082	0.074	0.077	0.082	0.081	0.081	0.090
Louisville, KY	0.075	0.087	0.088	0.083	0.076	0.086	0.066	0.070	0.070	0.064

Table continued on next page.

MSA[1]	1990	1995	2000	2005	2010	2012	2014	2015	2016	2017
Madison, WI	0.077	0.084	0.072	0.079	0.062	0.074	0.068	0.064	0.068	0.064
Manchester, NH	n/a	n/a	n/a	n/a	n/a	n/a	n/a	n/a	n/a	n/a
McAllen, TX	n/a	n/a	n/a	n/a	n/a	n/a	n/a	n/a	n/a	n/a
Miami, FL	0.068	0.072	0.075	0.065	0.064	0.062	0.062	0.061	0.061	0.064
Midland, TX	n/a	n/a	n/a	n/a	n/a	n/a	n/a	n/a	n/a	n/a
Minneapolis, MN	0.068	0.084	0.065	0.074	0.066	0.073	0.063	0.061	0.061	0.062
Nashville, TN	0.089	0.092	0.084	0.078	0.073	0.079	0.067	0.065	0.068	0.063
New Orleans, LA	0.082	0.088	0.091	0.079	0.074	0.071	0.069	0.067	0.065	0.063
New York, NY	0.101	0.106	0.090	0.091	0.081	0.079	0.069	0.075	0.073	0.070
Oklahoma City, OK	0.078	0.086	0.082	0.077	0.071	0.080	0.068	0.067	0.066	0.069
Omaha, NE	0.054	0.075	0.063	0.069	0.058	0.066	0.059	0.055	0.063	0.061
Orlando, FL	0.081	0.075	0.080	0.083	0.069	0.071	0.062	0.060	0.063	0.067
Peoria, IL	0.071	0.082	0.072	0.075	0.064	0.072	0.064	0.062	0.067	0.066
Philadelphia, PA	0.102	0.109	0.099	0.091	0.083	0.084	0.071	0.074	0.075	0.073
Phoenix, AZ	0.080	0.087	0.082	0.077	0.076	0.080	0.075	0.072	0.071	0.075
Pittsburgh, PA	0.080	0.095	0.082	0.082	0.075	0.079	0.065	0.069	0.068	0.066
Portland, OR	0.081	0.065	0.059	0.059	0.056	0.059	0.057	0.064	0.057	0.073
Providence, RI	0.106	0.107	0.087	0.090	0.072	0.072	0.067	0.070	0.075	0.076
Provo, UT	0.070	0.068	0.083	0.078	0.070	0.077	0.068	0.073	0.072	0.073
Raleigh, NC	0.093	0.081	0.087	0.082	0.071	0.071	0.063	0.065	0.069	0.066
Reno, NV	0.074	0.070	0.067	0.069	0.068	0.072	0.069	0.071	0.070	0.068
Richmond, VA	0.083	0.089	0.080	0.082	0.079	0.076	0.063	0.062	0.065	0.063
Roanoke, VA	0.075	0.079	0.081	0.076	0.073	0.070	0.060	0.062	0.064	0.058
Rochester, MN	n/a	n/a	n/a	n/a	n/a	n/a	n/a	n/a	n/a	n/a
Salem, OR	n/a	n/a	n/a	n/a	n/a	n/a	n/a	n/a	n/a	n/a
Salt Lake City, UT	n/a	n/a	n/a	n/a	n/a	n/a	n/a	n/a	n/a	n/a
San Antonio, TX	0.090	0.095	0.078	0.084	0.072	0.081	0.069	0.079	0.071	0.073
San Diego, CA	0.108	0.088	0.080	0.073	0.072	0.069	0.073	0.068	0.070	0.072
San Francisco, CA	0.058	0.074	0.057	0.055	0.061	0.057	0.065	0.062	0.059	0.060
San Jose, CA	0.079	0.085	0.070	0.065	0.073	0.064	0.069	0.067	0.063	0.065
Santa Rosa, CA	0.063	0.071	0.061	0.050	0.053	0.058	0.062	0.059	0.055	0.062
Savannah, GA	n/a	n/a	n/a	n/a	n/a	n/a	n/a	n/a	n/a	n/a
Seattle, WA	0.082	0.062	0.056	0.053	0.053	0.059	0.052	0.059	0.054	0.076
Sioux Falls, SD	n/a	n/a	n/a	n/a	n/a	n/a	n/a	n/a	n/a	n/a
Springfield, IL	n/a	n/a	n/a	n/a	n/a	n/a	n/a	n/a	n/a	n/a
Tallahassee, FL	n/a	n/a	n/a	n/a	n/a	n/a	n/a	n/a	n/a	n/a
Tampa, FL	0.080	0.075	0.081	0.075	0.067	0.066	0.065	0.062	0.064	0.064
Topeka, KS	n/a	n/a	n/a	n/a	n/a	n/a	n/a	n/a	n/a	n/a
Tyler, TX	n/a	n/a	n/a	n/a	n/a	n/a	n/a	n/a	n/a	n/a
Virginia Beach, VA	0.085	0.084	0.083	0.078	0.074	0.069	0.061	0.061	0.062	0.059
Visalia, CA	0.099	0.100	0.095	0.096	0.087	0.088	0.082	0.085	0.082	0.086
Washington, DC	0.088	0.093	0.082	0.081	0.077	0.075	0.065	0.067	0.068	0.065
Wilmington, NC	0.082	0.079	0.080	0.075	0.062	0.064	0.063	0.057	0.060	0.057
Winston-Salem, NC	0.084	0.086	0.089	0.080	0.078	0.074	0.067	0.065	0.069	0.066
U.S.	0.088	0.089	0.082	0.080	0.073	0.075	0.067	0.068	0.069	0.068

Note: (1) Data covers the Metropolitan Statistical Area—see Appendix B for areas included; n/a not available. The values shown are the composite ozone concentration averages among trend sites based on the highest fourth daily maximum 8-hour concentration in parts per million. These trends are based on sites having an adequate record of monitoring data during the trend period. Data from exceptional events are included.
Source: U.S. Environmental Protection Agency, Air Quality Monitoring Information, "Air Quality Trends by City, 1990-2017"

Maximum Air Pollutant Concentrations: Particulate Matter, Ozone, CO and Lead

Metro Aea	PM 10 (ug/m^3)	PM 2.5 Wtd AM (ug/m^3)	PM 2.5 24-Hr (ug/m^3)	Ozone (ppm)	Carbon Monoxide (ppm)	Lead (ug/m^3)
Albany, NY	n/a	6.9	15	0.061	0	n/a
Albuquerque, NM	126	7.5	19	0.071	1	0
Allentown, PA	29	8.8	25	0.07	n/a	n/a
Anchorage, AK	119	5.7	30	0.043	4	n/a
Ann Arbor, MI	n/a	8	19	0.069	n/a	n/a
Athens, GA	n/a	7.8	16	0.063	n/a	n/a
Atlanta, GA	41	10.4	23	0.074	2	n/a
Austin, TX	39	10	25	0.07	1	n/a
Baton Rouge, LA	71	9.1	19	0.073	1	0
Billings, MT	n/a	7.5	31	n/a	n/a	n/a
Boise City, ID	138	10.3	45	0.076	4	n/a
Boston, MA	31	7.3	17	0.075	1	n/a
Boulder, CO	47	6.7	19	0.073	n/a	n/a
Cape Coral, FL	51	n/a	n/a	0.065	n/a	n/a
Cedar Rapids, IA	57	7.8	20	0.062	1	n/a
Charleston, SC	29	n/a	n/a	0.064	n/a	n/a
Charlotte, NC	40	8.7	18	0.068	1	n/a
Chicago, IL	108	10.3	24	0.079	1	0.02
Clarksville, TN	n/a	8.2	17	0.062	n/a	n/a
College Station, TX	n/a	n/a	n/a	n/a	n/a	n/a
Colorado Springs, CO	49	6	17	0.07	1	n/a
Columbia, MO	n/a	n/a	n/a	0.061	n/a	n/a
Columbia, SC	32	8.1	18	0.06	1	0
Columbus, OH	52	8.8	22	0.07	2	0.01
Dallas, TX	38	9	18	0.077	1	0.17
Denver, CO	116	9.7	27	0.076	2	n/a
Des Moines, IA	47	7.3	17	0.06	1	n/a
Durham, NC	29	8.6	17	0.061	n/a	n/a
Edison, NJ	32	9.6	23	0.079	2	0.01
El Paso, TX	104	9	24	0.075	5	0.02
Eugene, OR	226	13.6	134	0.073	n/a	n/a
Evansville, IN	26	8.9	19	0.068	1	n/a
Fargo, ND	71	n/a	n/a	0.061	n/a	n/a
Fayetteville, NC	27	8.7	18	0.063	n/a	n/a
Fort Collins, CO	50	7.4	18	0.075	1	n/a
Fort Wayne, IN	n/a	8.2	20	0.064	n/a	n/a
Fort Worth, TX	38	9	18	0.077	1	0.17
Gainesville, FL	n/a	6.7	17	0.063	n/a	n/a
Grand Rapids, MI	29	9.1	26	0.066	1	0
Greeley, CO	56	8.6	22	0.072	1	n/a
Green Bay, WI	n/a	6.1	16	0.067	n/a	n/a
Greensboro, NC	30	7.7	16	0.065	n/a	n/a
Honolulu, HI	38	4.4	14	0.049	1	0
Houston, TX	80	10.1	24	0.079	2	n/a
Huntsville, AL	27	7.5	17	0.063	n/a	n/a
Indianapolis, IN	54	10.1	21	0.069	3	0.02
Jacksonville, FL	51	n/a	n/a	0.062	1	n/a
Kansas City, MO	117	9.9	23	0.07	1	n/a
Lafayette, LA	69	8	21	0.064	n/a	n/a
Las Cruces, NM	475	8.3	37	0.077	n/a	n/a
Las Vegas, NV	119	9.1	28	0.076	3	n/a
Lexington, KY	40	7.8	18	0.064	n/a	n/a
Lincoln, NE	n/a	6.7	19	0.062	n/a	n/a
Little Rock, AR	36	9.6	21	0.062	2	n/a
Los Angeles, CA	111	13.3	53	0.111	4	0.09

Table continued on next page.

Metro Aea	PM 10 (ug/m³)	PM 2.5 Wtd AM (ug/m³)	PM 2.5 24-Hr (ug/m³)	Ozone (ppm)	Carbon Monoxide (ppm)	Lead (ug/m³)
Louisville, KY	39	9.2	21	0.074	1	n/a
Madison, WI	28	7.8	21	0.065	n/a	n/a
Manchester, NH	n/a	2.9	10	0.066	0	n/a
McAllen, TX	49	10.1	26	0.055	n/a	n/a
Miami, FL	94	9.8	22	0.068	2	n/a
Midland, TX	n/a	n/a	n/a	n/a	n/a	n/a
Minneapolis, MN	150	8.7	20	0.063	4	0.11
Nashville, TN	34	9.7	19	0.064	2	n/a
New Orleans, LA	81	8.2	23	0.066	2	0.13
New York, NY	32	9.6	23	0.079	2	0.01
Oklahoma City, OK	52	7.8	16	0.071	1	n/a
Omaha, NE	113	9.7	21	0.064	2	0.05
Orlando, FL	59	7.8	18	0.068	1	n/a
Peoria, IL	n/a	8.3	22	0.066	n/a	n/a
Philadelphia, PA	69	11.4	27	0.079	3	n/a
Phoenix, AZ	416	15.1	38	0.079	3	0.05
Pittsburgh, PA	93	13.4	37	0.072	4	0.01
Portland, OR	59	8.2	36	0.083	1	n/a
Providence, RI	30	8.3	18	0.076	2	n/a
Provo, UT	88	8.5	29	0.073	2	n/a
Raleigh, NC	31	8.5	18	0.066	1	n/a
Reno, NV	101	8	24	0.069	2	n/a
Richmond, VA	25	7.5	15	0.067	1	n/a
Roanoke, VA	n/a	7	14	0.058	1	0.02
Rochester, MN	n/a	6.9	18	0.062	n/a	n/a
Salem, OR	n/a	n/a	n/a	0.078	n/a	n/a
Salt Lake City, UT	87	9.2	39	0.081	2	n/a
San Antonio, TX	73	8.9	25	0.073	1	n/a
San Diego, CA	67	9.6	19	0.09	1	0.02
San Francisco, CA	59	12.8	43	0.079	2	n/a
San Jose, CA	74	10.8	37	0.075	2	0.07
Santa Rosa, CA	152	8.1	26	0.062	1	n/a
Savannah, GA	n/a	n/a	n/a	0.057	n/a	n/a
Seattle, WA	n/a	9.7	44	0.094	2	n/a
Sioux Falls, SD	54	5.6	14	0.066	1	n/a
Springfield, IL	n/a	8.6	21	0.069	n/a	n/a
Tallahassee, FL	n/a	8	19	0.063	0	n/a
Tampa, FL	63	8.1	22	0.068	2	0.13
Topeka, KS	49	8.8	21	0.062	n/a	n/a
Tyler, TX	n/a	n/a	n/a	0.063	n/a	n/a
Virginia Beach, VA	20	6.9	16	0.064	1	n/a
Visalia, CA	140	16.3	75	0.089	n/a	n/a
Washington, DC	44	10.2	21	0.072	2	n/a
Wilmington, NC	19	6.1	14	0.057	n/a	n/a
Winston-Salem, NC	23	8.1	18	0.066	n/a	n/a
NAAQS[1]	150	15	35	0.075	9	0.15

Note: Data from exceptional events are included; Data covers the Metropolitan Statistical Area—see Appendix B for areas included;
(1) National Ambient Air Quality Standards; ppm = parts per million; ug/m³ = micrograms per cubic meter; n/a not available
Concentrations: Particulate Matter 10 (coarse particulate)—highest second maximum 24-hour concentration; Particulate Matter 2.5 Wtd AM (fine particulate)—highest weighted annual mean concentration; Particulate Matter 2.5 24-Hour (fine particulate)—highest 98th percentile 24-hour concentration; Ozone—highest fourth daily maximum 8-hour concentration; Carbon Monoxide—highest second maximum non-overlapping 8-hour concentration; Lead—maximum running 3-month average
Source: U.S. Environmental Protection Agency, Air Quality Monitoring Information, "Air Quality Statistics by City, 2017"

Maximum Air Pollutant Concentrations: Nitrogen Dioxide and Sulfur Dioxide

Metro Area	Nitrogen Dioxide AM (ppb)	Nitrogen Dioxide 1-Hr (ppb)	Sulfur Dioxide AM (ppb)	Sulfur Dioxide 1-Hr (ppb)	Sulfur Dioxide 24-Hr (ppb)
Albany, NY	n/a	n/a	n/a	4	n/a
Albuquerque, NM	10	45	n/a	4	n/a
Allentown, PA	10	44	n/a	105	n/a
Anchorage, AK	n/a	n/a	n/a	n/a	n/a
Ann Arbor, MI	n/a	n/a	n/a	n/a	n/a
Athens, GA	n/a	n/a	n/a	n/a	n/a
Atlanta, GA	18	53	n/a	7	n/a
Austin, TX	13	47	n/a	4	n/a
Baton Rouge, LA	10	46	n/a	29	n/a
Billings, MT	n/a	n/a	n/a	32	n/a
Boise City, ID	n/a	n/a	n/a	3	n/a
Boston, MA	14	46	n/a	11	n/a
Boulder, CO	n/a	n/a	n/a	n/a	n/a
Cape Coral, FL	n/a	n/a	n/a	n/a	n/a
Cedar Rapids, IA	n/a	n/a	n/a	53	n/a
Charleston, SC	1	n/a	n/a	5	n/a
Charlotte, NC	11	40	n/a	5	n/a
Chicago, IL	16	55	n/a	36	n/a
Clarksville, TN	n/a	n/a	n/a	n/a	n/a
College Station, TX	n/a	n/a	n/a	13	n/a
Colorado Springs, CO	n/a	n/a	n/a	22	n/a
Columbia, MO	n/a	n/a	n/a	n/a	n/a
Columbia, SC	4	37	n/a	3	n/a
Columbus, OH	11	40	n/a	3	n/a
Dallas, TX	12	45	n/a	7	n/a
Denver, CO	27	70	n/a	16	n/a
Des Moines, IA	6	38	n/a	1	n/a
Durham, NC	n/a	n/a	n/a	31	n/a
Edison, NJ	20	67	n/a	7	n/a
El Paso, TX	10	58	n/a	5	n/a
Eugene, OR	n/a	n/a	n/a	n/a	n/a
Evansville, IN	8	29	n/a	94	n/a
Fargo, ND	4	34	n/a	4	n/a
Fayetteville, NC	n/a	n/a	n/a	n/a	n/a
Fort Collins, CO	n/a	n/a	n/a	n/a	n/a
Fort Wayne, IN	n/a	n/a	n/a	n/a	n/a
Fort Worth, TX	12	45	n/a	7	n/a
Gainesville, FL	n/a	n/a	n/a	n/a	n/a
Grand Rapids, MI	n/a	n/a	n/a	21	n/a
Greeley, CO	n/a	n/a	n/a	n/a	n/a
Green Bay, WI	n/a	n/a	n/a	11	n/a
Greensboro, NC	n/a	n/a	n/a	n/a	n/a
Honolulu, HI	4	33	n/a	55	n/a
Houston, TX	14	52	n/a	19	n/a
Huntsville, AL	n/a	n/a	n/a	n/a	n/a
Indianapolis, IN	13	39	n/a	47	n/a
Jacksonville, FL	11	35	n/a	32	n/a
Kansas City, MO	12	47	n/a	18	n/a
Lafayette, LA	n/a	n/a	n/a	n/a	n/a
Las Cruces, NM	6	43	n/a	n/a	n/a
Las Vegas, NV	27	61	n/a	6	n/a
Lexington, KY	5	n/a	n/a	4	n/a
Lincoln, NE	n/a	n/a	n/a	44	n/a
Little Rock, AR	8	39	n/a	8	n/a
Los Angeles, CA	25	83	n/a	14	n/a

Table continued on next page.

Metro Area	Nitrogen Dioxide AM (ppb)	Nitrogen Dioxide 1-Hr (ppb)	Sulfur Dioxide AM (ppb)	Sulfur Dioxide 1-Hr (ppb)	Sulfur Dioxide 24-Hr (ppb)
Louisville, KY	15	47	n/a	14	n/a
Madison, WI	n/a	n/a	n/a	3	n/a
Manchester, NH	n/a	n/a	n/a	3	n/a
McAllen, TX	n/a	n/a	n/a	n/a	n/a
Miami, FL	15	44	n/a	1	n/a
Midland, TX	n/a	n/a	n/a	n/a	n/a
Minneapolis, MN	13	44	n/a	18	n/a
Nashville, TN	14	51	n/a	5	n/a
New Orleans, LA	10	45	n/a	53	n/a
New York, NY	20	67	n/a	7	n/a
Oklahoma City, OK	16	43	n/a	2	n/a
Omaha, NE	n/a	n/a	n/a	55	n/a
Orlando, FL	4	30	n/a	5	n/a
Peoria, IL	n/a	n/a	n/a	23	n/a
Philadelphia, PA	12	46	n/a	12	n/a
Phoenix, AZ	31	67	n/a	10	n/a
Pittsburgh, PA	10	37	n/a	116	n/a
Portland, OR	12	40	n/a	3	n/a
Providence, RI	18	50	n/a	11	n/a
Provo, UT	15	n/a	n/a	n/a	n/a
Raleigh, NC	9	35	n/a	2	n/a
Reno, NV	13	52	n/a	5	n/a
Richmond, VA	12	43	n/a	18	n/a
Roanoke, VA	5	32	n/a	40	n/a
Rochester, MN	n/a	n/a	n/a	n/a	n/a
Salem, OR	n/a	n/a	n/a	n/a	n/a
Salt Lake City, UT	13	43	n/a	n/a	n/a
San Antonio, TX	8	40	n/a	29	n/a
San Diego, CA	16	52	n/a	1	n/a
San Francisco, CA	17	59	n/a	16	n/a
San Jose, CA	17	52	n/a	n/a	n/a
Santa Rosa, CA	5	29	n/a	n/a	n/a
Savannah, GA	n/a	n/a	n/a	53	n/a
Seattle, WA	20	44	n/a	n/a	n/a
Sioux Falls, SD	4	30	n/a	5	n/a
Springfield, IL	n/a	n/a	n/a	n/a	n/a
Tallahassee, FL	n/a	n/a	n/a	n/a	n/a
Tampa, FL	10	29	n/a	15	n/a
Topeka, KS	n/a	n/a	n/a	n/a	n/a
Tyler, TX	2	15	n/a	n/a	n/a
Virginia Beach, VA	7	40	n/a	3	n/a
Visalia, CA	11	56	n/a	n/a	n/a
Washington, DC	15	58	n/a	4	n/a
Wilmington, NC	n/a	n/a	n/a	2	n/a
Winston-Salem, NC	7	38	n/a	4	n/a
NAAQS[1]	53	100	30	75	140

Note: Data from exceptional events are included; Data covers the Metropolitan Statistical Area—see Appendix B for areas included;
(1) National Ambient Air Quality Standards; ppb = parts per billion; n/a not available
Concentrations: Nitrogen Dioxide AM—highest arithmetic mean concentration; Nitrogen Dioxide 1-Hr—highest 98th percentile 1-hour daily maximum concentration; Sulfur Dioxide AM—highest annual mean concentration; Sulfur Dioxide 1-Hr—highest 99th percentile 1-hour daily maximum concentration; Sulfur Dioxide 24-Hr—highest second maximum 24-hour concentration
Source: U.S. Environmental Protection Agency, Air Quality Monitoring Information, "Air Quality Statistics by City, 2017"

Appendix B: Metropolitan Area Definitions

Metropolitan Statistical Areas (MSA), Metropolitan Divisions (MD), New England City and Town Areas (NECTA), and New England City and Town Area Divisions (NECTAD)

Note: In September 2018, the Office of Management and Budget (OMB) announced changes to metropolitan and micropolitan statistical area definitions. Both current and historical definitions (December 2009) are shown below. If the change only affected the name of the metro area, the counties included were not repeated.

Albany-Schenectady-Troy, NY MSA
Albany, Rensselaer, Saratoga, Schenectady and Schoharie Counties

Albuquerque, NM MSA
Bernalillo, Sandoval, Torrance, and Valencia Counties

Allentown-Bethlehem-Easton, PA-NJ MSA
Carbon, Lehigh, and Northampton Counties, PA; Warren County, NJ

Anchorage, AK MSA
Anchorage Municipality and Matanuska-Susitna Borough

Ann Arbor, MI MSA
Washtenaw County

Athens-Clarke County, GA MSA
Clarke, Madison, Oconee, and Oglethorpe Counties

Atlanta-Sandy Springs-Roswell, GA MSA
Barrow, Bartow, Butts, Carroll, Cherokee, Clayton, Cobb, Coweta, Dawson, DeKalb, Douglas, Fayette, Forsyth, Fulton, Gwinnett, Haralson, Heard, Henry, Jasper, Lamar, Meriwether, Morgan, Newton, Paulding, Pickens, Pike, Rockdale, Spalding, and Walton Counties
Previously Atlanta-Sandy Springs-Marietta, GA MSA
Barrow, Bartow, Butts, Carroll, Cherokee, Clayton, Cobb, Coweta, Dawson, DeKalb, Douglas, Fayette, Forsyth, Fulton, Gwinnett, Haralson, Heard, Henry, Jasper, Lamar, Meriwether, Newton, Paulding, Pickens, Pike, Rockdale, Spalding, and Walton Counties

Austin-Round Rock, TX MSA
Previously Austin-Round Rock-San Marcos, TX MSA
Bastrop, Caldwell, Hays, Travis, and Williamson Counties

Baton Rouge, LA MSA
Ascension, East Baton Rouge, East Feliciana, Iberville, Livingston, Pointe Coupee, St. Helena, West Baton Rouge, and West Feliciana Parishes
Previously Baton Rouge, LA MSA
Ascension, East Baton Rouge, Livingston, and West Baton Rouge Parishes

Billings, MT MSA
Carbon and Yellowstone Counties

Boise City, ID MSA
Previously Boise City-Nampa, ID MSA
Ada, Boise, Canyon, Gem, and Owyhee Counties

Boston, MA

Boston-Cambridge-Newton, MA-NH MSA
Previously Boston-Cambridge-Quincy, MA-NH MSA
Essex, Middlesex, Norfolk, Plymouth, and Suffolk Counties, MA; Rockingham and Strafford Counties, NH

Boston, MA MD
Previously Boston-Quincy, MA MD
Norfolk, Plymouth, and Suffolk Counties

Boston-Cambridge-Nashua, MA-NH NECTA
Includes 157 cities and towns in Massachusetts and 34 cities and towns in New Hampshire
Previously Boston-Cambridge-Quincy, MA-NH NECTA
Includes 155 cities and towns in Massachusetts and 38 cities and towns in New Hampshire

Boston-Cambridge-Newton, MA NECTA Division
Includes 92 cities and towns in Massachusetts
Previously Boston-Cambridge-Quincy, MA NECTA Division
Includes 97 cities and towns in Massachusetts

Boulder, CO MSA
Boulder County

Cape Coral-Fort Myers, FL MSA
Lee County

Cedar Rapids, IA, MSA
Benton, Jones, and Linn Counties

Charleston-North Charleston, SC MSA
Previously Charleston-North Charleston- Summerville, SC MSA
Berkeley, Charleston, and Dorchester Counties

Charlotte-Concord-Gastonia, NC-SC MSA
Cabarrus, Gaston, Iredell, Lincoln, Mecklenburg, Rowan, and Union Counties, NC; Chester, Lancaster, and York Counties, SC
Previously Charlotte-Gastonia-Rock Hill, NC-SC MSA
Anson, Cabarrus, Gaston, Mecklenburg, and Union Counties, NC; York County, SC

Chicago, IL

Chicago-Naperville-Elgin, IL-IN-WI MSA
Previous name: Chicago-Joliet-Naperville, IL-IN-WI MSA
Cook, DeKalb, DuPage, Grundy, Kane, Kendall, Lake, McHenry, and Will Counties, IL; Jasper, Lake, Newton, and Porter Counties, IN; Kenosha County, WI

Chicago-Naperville-Arlington Heights, IL MD
Cook, DuPage, Grundy, Kendall, McHenry, and Will Counties
Previous name: Chicago-Joliet-Naperville, IL MD
Cook, DeKalb, DuPage, Grundy, Kane, Kendall, McHenry, and Will Counties

Elgin, IL MD
DeKalb and Kane Counties
Previously part of the Chicago-Joliet-Naperville, IL MD

Gary, IN MD
Jasper, Lake, Newton, and Porter Counties

Lake County-Kenosha County, IL-WI MD
Lake County, IL; Kenosha County, WI

Clarksville, TN-KY MSA
Montgomery and Stewart Counties, TN; Christian and Trigg Counties, KY

College Station-Bryan, TX MSA
Brazos, Burleson and Robertson Counties

Colorado Springs, CO MSA
El Paso and Teller Counties

Columbia, MO MSA
Boone and Howard Counties

Columbia, SC MSA
Calhoun, Fairfield, Kershaw, Lexington, Richland and Saluda Counties

Columbus, OH MSA
Delaware, Fairfield, Franklin, Licking, Madison, Morrow, Pickaway, and Union Counties

Dallas, TX

Dallas-Fort Worth-Arlington, TX MSA
Collin, Dallas, Denton, Ellis, Hunt, Johnson, Kaufman, Parker, Rockwall, Tarrant, and Wise Counties

Dallas-Plano-Irving, TX MD
Collin, Dallas, Denton, Ellis, Hunt, Kaufman, and Rockwall Counties

Denver-Aurora-Lakewood, CO MSA
Previously Denver-Aurora-Broomfield, CO MSA
Adams, Arapahoe, Broomfield, Clear Creek, Denver, Douglas, Elbert, Gilpin, Jefferson, and Park Counties

Des Moines-West Des Moines, IA MSA
Dallas, Guthrie, Madison, Polk, and Warren Counties

Durham-Chapel Hill, NC MSA
Chatham, Durham, Orange, and Person Counties

Edison, NJ
See New York, NY (New York-Jersey City-White Plains, NY-NJ MD)

El Paso, TX MSA
El Paso County

Eugene, OR MSA
Previously Eugene-Springfield, OR MSA
Lane County

Evansville, IN-KY MSA
Posey, Vanderburgh, and Warrick Counties, IN; Henderson County, KY
Previously Evansville, IN-KY MSA
Gibson, Posey, Vanderburgh, and Warrick Counties, IN; Henderson and Webster Counties, KY

Fargo, ND-MN MSA
Cass County, ND; Clay County, MN

Fayetteville, NC MSA
Cumberland, and Hoke Counties

Fort Collins, CO MSA
Previously Fort Collins-Loveland, CO MSA
Larimer County

Fort Wayne, IN MSA
Allen, Wells, and Whitley Counties

Fort Worth, TX

Dallas-Fort Worth-Arlington, TX MSA
Collin, Dallas, Denton, Ellis, Hunt, Johnson, Kaufman, Parker, Rockwall, Tarrant, and Wise Counties

Fort Worth-Arlington, TX MD
Hood, Johnson, Parker, Somervell, Tarrant, and Wise Counties

Gainesville, FL MSA
Alachua, and Gilchrist Counties

Grand Rapids-Wyoming, MI MSA
Barry, Kent, Montcalm, and Ottawa Counties
Previously Grand Rapids-Wyoming, MI MSA
Barry, Ionia, Kent, and Newaygo Counties

Greeley, CO MSA
Weld County

Green Bay, WI MSA
Brown, Kewaunee, and Oconto Counties

Greensboro-High Point, NC MSA
Guilford, Randolph, and Rockingham Counties

Honolulu, HI MSA
Honolulu County

Houston-The Woodlands-Sugar Land-Baytown, TX MSA
Austin, Brazoria, Chambers, Fort Bend, Galveston, Harris, Liberty, Montgomery, and Waller Counties
Previously Houston-Sugar Land-Baytown, TX MSA
Austin, Brazoria, Chambers, Fort Bend, Galveston, Harris, Liberty, Montgomery, San Jacinto, and Waller Counties

Huntsville, AL MSA
Limestone and Madison Counties

Indianapolis-Carmel, IN MSA
Boone, Brown, Hamilton, Hancock, Hendricks, Johnson, Marion, Morgan, Putnam, and Shelby Counties

Jacksonville, FL MSA
Baker, Clay, Duval, Nassau, and St. Johns Counties

Kansas City, MO-KS MSA
Franklin, Johnson, Leavenworth, Linn, Miami, and Wyandotte Counties, KS; Bates, Caldwell, Cass, Clay, Clinton, Jackson, Lafayette, Platte, and Ray Counties, MO

Lafayette, LA MSA
Acadia, Iberia, Lafayette, St. Martin, and Vermilion Parishes

Las Cruces, NM MSA
Doña Ana and San Miguel Counties
Previously Las Cruces, NM MSA
Doña Ana County

Las Vegas-Henderson-Paradise, NV MSA
Previously Las Vegas-Paradise, NV MSA
Clark County

Lexington-Fayette, KY MSA
Bourbon, Clark, Fayette, Jessamine, Scott, and Woodford Counties

Lincoln, NE MSA
Lancaster and Seward Counties

Little Rock-North Little Rock-Conway, AR MSA
Faulkner, Grant, Lonoke, Perry, Pulaski, and Saline Counties

Los Angeles, CA

Los Angeles-Long Beach-Anaheim, CA MSA
Previously Los Angeles-Long Beach-Santa Ana, CA MSA
Los Angeles and Orange Counties

Los Angeles-Long Beach-Glendale, CA MD
Los Angeles County

Anaheim-Santa Ana-Irvine, CA MD
Previously Santa Ana-Anaheim-Irvine, CA MD
Orange County

Louisville/Jefferson, KY-IN MSA
Clark, Floyd, Harrison, Scott, and Washington Counties, IN; Bullitt, Henry, Jefferson, Oldham, Shelby, Spencer, and Trimble Counties, KY

Madison, WI MSA
Columbia, Dane, and Iowa Counties

Manchester, NH

Manchester-Nashua, NH MSA
Hillsborough County

Manchester, NH NECTA
Includes 11 cities and towns in New Hampshire
Previously Manchester, NH NECTA
Includes 9 cities and towns in New Hampshire

McAllen-Edinburg-Mission, TX
Hidalgo County

Miami, FL

Miami-Fort Lauderdale-West Palm Beach, FL MSA
Previously Miami-Fort Lauderdale-Pompano Beach, FL MSA
Broward, Miami-Dade, and Palm Beach Counties

Miami-Miami Beach-Kendall, FL MD
Miami-Dade County

Midland, TX MSA
Martin, and Midland Counties

Minneapolis-St. Paul-Bloomington, MN-WI MSA
Anoka, Carver, Chisago, Dakota, Hennepin, Isanti, Le Sueur, Mille Lacs, Ramsey, Scott, Sherburne, Sibley, Washington, and Wright Counties, MN; Pierce and St. Croix Counties, WI

Nashville-Davidson-Murfreesboro-Franklin, TN MSA
Cannon, Cheatham, Davidson, Dickson, Hickman, Macon, Robertson, Rutherford, Smith, Sumner, Trousdale, Williamson, and Wilson Counties

New Orleans-Metarie-Kenner, LA MSA
Jefferson, Orleans, Plaquemines, St. Bernard, St. Charles, St. James, St. John the Baptist, and St. Tammany Parish
Previously New Orleans-Metarie-Kenner, LA MSA
Jefferson, Orleans, Plaquemines, St. Bernard, St. Charles, St. John the Baptist, and St. Tammany Parish

New York, NY

New York-Newark-Jersey City, NY-NJ-PA MSA
Bergen, Essex, Hudson, Hunterdon, Middlesex, Monmouth, Morris, Ocean, Passaic, Somerset, Sussex, and Union Counties, NJ; Bronx, Dutchess, Kings, Nassau, New York, Orange, Putnam, Queens, Richmond, Rockland, Suffolk, and Westchester Counties, NY; Pike County, PA
Previous name: New York-Northern New Jersey-Long Island, NY-NJ-PA MSA
Bergen, Essex, Hudson, Hunterdon, Middlesex, Monmouth, Morris, Ocean, Passaic, Somerset, Sussex, and Union Counties, NJ; Bronx, Kings, Nassau, New York, Putnam, Queens, Richmond, Rockland, Suffolk, and Westchester Counties, NY; Pike County, PA

Dutchess County-Putnam County, NY MD
Dutchess and Putnam Counties
Dutchess County was previously part of the Poughkeepsie-Newburgh-Middletown, NY MSA. Putnam County was previously part of the New York-Wayne-White Plains, NY-NJ MD

Nassau-Suffolk, NY MD
Nassau and Suffolk Counties

New York-Jersey City-White Plains, NY-NJ MD
Bergen, Hudson, Middlesex, Monmouth, Ocean, and Passaic Counties, NJ; Bronx, Kings, New York, Orange, Queens, Richmond, Rockland, and Westchester Counties, NY
Previous name: New York-Wayne-White Plains, NY-NJ MD
Bergen, Hudson, and Passaic Counties, NJ; Bronx, Kings, New York, Putnam, Queens, Richmond, Rockland, and Westchester Counties, NY

Newark, NJ-PA MD
Essex, Hunterdon, Morris, Somerset, Sussex, and Union Counties, NJ; Pike County, PA
Previous name: Newark-Union, NJ-PA MD
Essex, Hunterdon, Morris, Sussex, and Union Counties, NJ; Pike County, PA

Oklahoma City, OK MSA
Canadian, Cleveland, Grady, Lincoln, Logan, McClain, and Oklahoma Counties

Omaha-Council Bluffs, NE-IA MSA
Harrison, Mills, and Pottawattamie Counties, IA; Cass, Douglas, Sarpy, Saunders, and Washington Counties, NE

Orlando-Kissimmee-Sanford, FL MSA
Lake, Orange, Osceola, and Seminole Counties

Peoria, IL MSA
Marshall, Peoria, Stark, Tazewell, and Woodford Counties

Philadelphia, PA

Philadelphia-Camden-Wilmington, PA-NJ-DE-MD MSA
New Castle County, DE; Cecil County, MD; Burlington, Camden, Gloucester, and Salem Counties, NJ; Bucks, Chester, Delaware, Montgomery, and Philadelphia Counties, PA

Camden, NJ MD
Burlington, Camden, and Gloucester Counties

Montgomery County-Bucks County-Chester County, PA MD
Bucks, Chester, and Montgomery Counties
Previously part of the Philadelphia, PA MD

Philadelphia, PA MD
Delaware and Philadelphia Counties
Previous name: Philadelphia, PA MD
Bucks, Chester, Delaware, Montgomery, and Philadelphia Counties

Wilmington, DE-MD-NJ MD
New Castle County, DE; Cecil County, MD; Salem County, NJ

Phoenix-Mesa-Scottsdale, AZ MSA
Previously Phoenix-Mesa-Glendale, AZ MSA
Maricopa and Pinal Counties

Pittsburgh, PA MSA
Allegheny, Armstrong, Beaver, Butler, Fayette, Washington, and Westmoreland Counties

Portland-Vancouver-Hillsboro, OR-WA MSA
Clackamas, Columbia, Multnomah, Washington, and Yamhill Counties, OR; Clark and Skamania Counties, WA

Providence, RI

Providence-New Bedford-Fall River, RI-MA MSA
Previously Providence-New Bedford-Fall River, RI-MA MSA
Bristol County, MA; Bristol, Kent, Newport, Providence, and Washington Counties, RI

Providence-Warwick, RI-MA NECTA
Includes 12 cities and towns in Massachusetts and 36 cities and towns in Rhode Island
Previously Providence-Fall River-Warwick, RI-MA NECTA
Includes 12 cities and towns in Massachusetts and 37 cities and towns in Rhode Island

Provo-Orem, UT MSA
Juab and Utah Counties

Raleigh, NC MSA
Previously Raleigh-Cary, NC MSA
Franklin, Johnston, and Wake Counties

Reno, NV MSA
Previously Reno-Sparks, NV MSA
Storey and Washoe Counties

Richmond, VA MSA
Amelia, Caroline, Charles City, Chesterfield, Dinwiddie, Goochland, Hanover, Henrico, King William, New Kent, Powhatan, Prince George, and Sussex Counties; Colonial Heights, Hopewell, Petersburg, and Richmond Cities

Roanoke, VA MSA
Botetourt, Craig, Franklin and Roanoke Counties; Roanoke and Salem cities

Rochester, MN MSA
Dodge, Fillmore, Olmsted, and Wabasha Counties

Salem, OR MSA
Marion and Polk Counties

Salt Lake City, UT MSA
Salt Lake and Tooele Counties

San Antonio-New Braunfels, TX MSA
Atascosa, Bandera, Bexar, Comal, Guadalupe, Kendall, Medina, and Wilson Counties

San Diego-Carlsbad, CA MSA
Previously San Diego-Carlsbad-San Marcos, CA MSA
San Diego County

San Francisco, CA

San Francisco-Oakland-Hayward, CA MSA
Previously San Francisco-Oakland- Fremont, CA MSA
Alameda, Contra Costa, Marin, San Francisco, and San Mateo Counties

San Francisco-Redwood City-South San Francisco, CA MD
San Francisco and San Mateo Counties

Previously San Francisco-San Mateo-Redwood City, CA MD
Marin, San Francisco, and San Mateo Counties

San Jose-Sunnyvale-Santa Clara, CA MSA
San Benito and Santa Clara Counties

Santa Rosa, CA MSA
Previously Santa Rosa-Petaluma, CA MSA
Sonoma County

Savannah, GA MSA
Bryan, Chatham, and Effingham Counties

Seattle, WA

Seattle-Tacoma-Bellevue, WA MSA
King, Pierce, and Snohomish Counties

Seattle-Bellevue-Everett, WA MD
King and Snohomish Counties

Sioux Falls, SD MSA
Lincoln, McCook, Minnehaha, and Turner Counties

Springfield, IL MSA
Menard and Sangamon Counties

Tallahassee, FL MSA
Gadsden, Jefferson, Leon, and Wakulla Counties

Tampa-St. Petersburg-Clearwater, FL MSA
Hernando, Hillsborough, Pasco, and Pinellas Counties

Topeka, KS MSA
Jackson, Jefferson, Osage, Shawnee, and Wabaunsee Counties

Tyler, TX MSA
Smith County

Virginia Beach-Norfolk-Newport News, VA-NC MSA
Currituck County, NC; Chesapeake, Hampton, Newport News, Norfolk, Poquoson, Portsmouth, Suffolk, Virginia Beach and Williamsburg cities, VA; Gloucester, Isle of Wight, James City, Mathews, Surry, and York Counties, VA

Visalia, CA MSA
Previously Visalia-Porterville, CA MSA
Tulare County

Washington, DC

Washington-Arlington-Alexandria, DC-VA-MD-WV MSA
District of Columbia; Calvert, Charles, Frederick, Montgomery, and Prince George's Counties, MD; Alexandria, Fairfax, Falls Church, Fredericksburg, Manassas Park, and Manassas cities, VA; Arlington, Clarke, Culpepper, Fairfax, Fauquier, Loudoun, Prince William, Rappahannock, Spotsylvania, Stafford, and Warren Counties, VA; Jefferson County, WV
Previously Washington-Arlington-Alexandria, DC-VA-MD-WV MSA
District of Columbia; Calvert, Charles, Frederick, Montgomery, and Prince George's Counties, MD; Alexandria, Fairfax, Falls Church, Fredericksburg, Manassas Park, and Manassas cities, VA; Arlington, Clarke, Fairfax, Fauquier, Loudoun, Prince William, Spotsylvania, Stafford, and Warren Counties, VA; Jefferson County, WV

Washington-Arlington-Alexandria, DC-VA-MD-WV MD
District of Columbia; Calvert, Charles, and Prince George's Counties, MD; Alexandria, Fairfax, Falls Church, Fredericksburg, Manassas Park, and Manassas cities, VA; Arlington, Clarke, Culpepper, Fairfax, Fauquier, Loudoun, Prince William, Rappahannock, Spotsylvania, Stafford, and Warren Counties, VA; Jefferson County, WV
Previously Washington-Arlington-Alexandria, DC-VA-MD-WV MD
District of Columbia; Calvert, Charles, and Prince George's Counties, MD; Alexandria, Fairfax, Falls Church, Fredericksburg, Manassas Park, and Manassas cities, VA; Arlington, Clarke, Fairfax, Fauquier, Loudoun, Prince William, Spotsylvania, Stafford, and Warren Counties, VA; Jefferson County, WV

Wilmington, NC MSA
New Hanover and Pender Counties
Previously Wilmington, NC MSA
Brunswick, New Hanover and Pender Counties

Winston-Salem, NC MSA
Davidson, Davie, Forsyth, Stokes, and Yadkin Counties

Appendix C: Government Type and Primary County

This appendix includes the government structure of each place included in this book. It also includes the county or county equivalent in which each place is located. If a place spans more than one county, the county in which the majority of the population resides is shown.

Albuquerque, NM
Government Type: City
County: Bernalillo

Albany, NY
Government Type: City
County: Albany

Allentown, PA
Government Type: City
County: Lehigh

Anchorage, AK
Government Type: Municipality
Borough: Anchorage

Ann Arbor, MI
Government Type: City
County: Washtenaw

Athens, GA
Government Type: Consolidated
  city-county
County: Clarke

Atlanta, GA
Government Type: City
County: Fulton

Austin, TX
Government Type: City
County: Travis

Baton Rouge, LA
Government Type: Consolidated city-parish
Parish: East Baton Rouge

Billings, MT
Government Type: City
County: Yellowstone

Boise City, ID
Government Type: City
County: Ada

Boston, MA
Government Type: City
County: Suffolk

Boulder, CO
Government Type: City
County: Boulder

Cape Coral, FL
Government Type: City
County: Lee

Cedar Rapids, IA
Government Type: City
County: Linn

Charleston, SC
Government Type: City
County: Charleston

Charlotte, NC
Government Type: City
County: Mecklenburg

Chicago, IL
Government Type: City
County: Cook

Clarksville, TN
Government Type: City
County: Montgomery

College Station, TX
Government Type: City
County: Brazos

Colorado Springs, CO
Government Type: City
County: El Paso

Columbia, MO
Government Type: City
County: Boone

Columbia, SC
Government Type: City
County: Richland

Columbus, OH
Government Type: City
County: Franklin

Dallas, TX
Government Type: City
County: Dallas

Denver, CO
Government Type: City
County: Denver

Des Moines, IA
Government Type: City
County: Polk

Durham, NC
Government Type: City
County: Durham

Edison, NJ
Government Type: Township
County: Middlesex

El Paso, TX
Government Type: City
County: El Paso

Eugene, OR
Government Type: City
County: Lane

Evansville, IN
Government Type: City
County: Vanderburgh

Fargo, ND
Government Type: City
County: Cass

Fayetteville, NC
Government Type: City
County: Cumberland

Fort Collins, CO
Government Type: City
County: Larimer

Fort Wayne, IN
Government Type: City
County: Allen

Fort Worth, TX
Government Type: City
County: Tarrant

Gainesville, FL
Government Type: City
County: Alachua

Grand Rapids, MI
Government Type: City
County: Kent

Greeley, CO
Government Type: City
County: Weld

Green Bay, WI
Government Type: City
County: Brown

Greensboro, NC
Government Type: City
County: Guilford

Honolulu, HI
Government Type: Census Designated Place
  (CDP)
County: Honolulu

Houston, TX
Government Type: City
County: Harris

Huntsville, AL
Government Type: City
County: Madison

Indianapolis, IN
Government Type: City
County: Marion

Jacksonville, FL
Government Type: City
County: Duval

Kansas City, MO
Government Type: City
County: Jackson

Lafayette, LA
Government Type: City
Parish: Lafayette

Las Cruces, NM
Government Type: City
County: Doña Ana

Las Vegas, NV
Government Type: City
County: Clark

Lexington, KY
Government Type: Consolidated city-county
County: Fayette

Lincoln, NE
Government Type: City
County: Lancaster

Little Rock, AR
Government Type: City
County: Pulaski

Los Angeles, CA
Government Type: City
County: Los Angeles

Louisville, KY
Government Type: Consolidated city-county
County: Jefferson

Madison, WI
Government Type: City
County: Dane

Manchester, NH
Government Type: City
County: Hillsborough

McAllen, TX
Government Type: City
County: Hidalgo

Miami, FL
Government Type: City
County: Miami-Dade

Midland, TX
Government Type: City
County: Midland

Minneapolis, MN
Government Type: City
County: Hennepin

Nashville, TN
Government Type: Consolidated city-county
County: Davidson

New Orleans, LA
Government Type: City
Parish: Orleans

New York, NY
Government Type: City
Counties: Bronx; Kings; New York; Queens; Staten Island

Oklahoma City, OK
Government Type: City
County: Oklahoma

Omaha, NE
Government Type: City
County: Douglas

Orlando, FL
Government Type: City
County: Orange

Peoria, IL
Government Type: City
County: Peoria

Philadelphia, PA
Government Type: City
County: Philadelphia

Phoenix, AZ
Government Type: City
County: Maricopa

Pittsburgh, PA
Government Type: City
County: Allegheny

Portland, OR
Government Type: City
County: Multnomah

Providence, RI
Government Type: City
County: Providence

Provo, UT
Government Type: City
County: Utah

Raleigh, NC
Government Type: City
County: Wake

Reno, NV
Government Type: City
County: Washoe

Richmond, VA
Government Type: Independent city
County: Richmond city

Roanoke, VA
Government Type: Independent city
County: Roanoke city

Rochester, MN
Government Type: City
County: Olmsted

Salem, OR
Government Type: City
County: Marion

Salt Lake City, UT
Government Type: City
County: Salt Lake

San Antonio, TX
Government Type: City
County: Bexar

San Diego, CA
Government Type: City
County: San Diego

San Francisco, CA
Government Type: City
County: San Francisco

San Jose, CA
Government Type: City
County: Santa Clara

Santa Rosa, CA
Government Type: City
County: Sonoma

Savannah, GA
Government Type: City
County: Chatham

Seattle, WA
Government Type: City
County: King

Sioux Falls, SD
Government Type: City
County: Minnehaha

Springfield, IL
Government Type: City
County: Sangamon

Tallahassee, FL
Government Type: City
County: Leon

Tampa, FL
Government Type: City
County: Hillsborough

Topeka, KS
Government Type: City
County: Shawnee

Tyler, TX
Government Type: City
County: Smith

Virginia Beach, VA
Government Type: Independent city
County: Virginia Beach city

Visalia, CA
Government Type: City
County: Tulare

Washington, DC
Government Type: City
County: District of Columbia

Wilmington, NC
Government Type: City
County: New Hanover

Winston-Salem, NC
Government Type: City
County: Forsyth

Appendix D: Chambers of Commerce

Albany, NY
Capital Region Chamber
Albany Office
5 Computer Drive South
Colonie, NY 12205
Phone: (518) 431-1400
Fax: (518) 431-1402
http://capitalregionchamber.com

Albuquerque, NM
Albuquerque Chamber of Commerce
P.O. Box 25100
Albuquerque, NM 87125
Phone: (505) 764-3700
Fax: (505) 764-3714
http://www.abqchamber.com

Albuquerque Economic Development Dept
851 University Blvd SE
Suite 203
Albuquerque, NM 87106
Phone: (505) 246-6200
Fax: (505) 246-6219
http://www.cabq.gov/econdev

Allentown, PA
Greater Lehigh Valley Chamber of
Commerce
Allentown Office
840 Hamilton Street, Suite 205
Allentown, PA 18101
Phone: (610) 751-4929
Fax: (610) 437-4907
http://www.lehighvalleychamber.org

Anchorage, AK
Anchorage Chamber of Commerce
1016 W Sixth Avenue
Suite 303
Anchorage, AK 99501
Phone: (907) 272-2401
Fax: (907) 272-4117
http://www.anchoragechamber.org

Anchorage Economic Development
Department
900 W 5th Avenue
Suite 300
Anchorage, AK 99501
Phone: (907) 258-3700
Fax: (907) 258-6646
http://aedcweb.com

Ann Arbor, MI
Ann Arbor Area Chamber of Commerce
115 West Huron
3rd Floor
Ann Arbor, MI 48104
Phone: (734) 665-4433
Fax: (734) 665-4191
http://www.annarborchamber.org

Ann Arbor Economic Development
Department
201 S Division
Suite 430
Ann Arbor, MI 48104
Phone: (734) 761-9317
http://www.annarborspark.org

Athens, GA
Athens Area Chamber of Commerce
246 W Hancock Avenue
Athens, GA 30601
Phone: (706) 549-6800
Fax: (706) 549-5636
http://www.aacoc.org

Athens-Clarke County Economic
Development Department
246 W. Hancock Avenue
Athens, GA 30601
Phone: (706) 613-3233
Fax: (706) 613-3812
http://www.athensbusiness.org

Atlanta, GA
Metro Atlanta Chamber of Commerce
235 Andrew Young International Blvd NW
Atlanta, GA 30303
Phone: (404) 880-9000
Fax: (404) 586-8464
http://www.metroatlantachamber.com

Austin, TX
Greater Austin Chamber of Commerce
210 Barton Springs Road
Suite 400
Austin, TX 78704
Phone: (512) 478-9383
Fax: (512) 478-6389
http://www.austin-chamber.org

Baton Rouge, LA
Baton Rouge Area Chamber
451 Florida Street
Suite 1050
Baton Rouge, LA 70801
Phone (225) 381-7125
http://www.brac.org

Billings, MT
Billings Area Chamber of Commerce
815 S 27th St
Billings, MT 59101
Phone: (406) 245-4111
Fax: (406) 245-7333
http://www.billingschamber.com

Boise City, ID
Boise Metro Chamber of Commerce
250 S 5th Street
Suite 800
Boise City, ID 83701
Phone: (208) 472-5200
Fax: (208) 472-5201
http://www.boisechamber.org

Boston, MA
Greater Boston Chamber of Commerce
265 Franklin Street
12th Floor
Boston, MA 02110
Phone: (617) 227-4500
Fax: (617) 227-7505
http://www.bostonchamber.com

Boulder, CO
Boulder Chamber of Commerce
2440 Pearl Street
Boulder, CO 80302
Phone: (303) 442-1044
Fax: (303) 938-8837
http://www.boulderchamber.com

City of Boulder Economic Vitality Program
P.O. Box 791
Boulder, CO 80306
Phone: (303) 441-3090
http://www.bouldercolorado.gov

Cape Coral, FL
Chamber of Commerce of Cape Coral
2051 Cape Coral Parkway East
Cape Coral, FL 33904
Phone: (239) 549-6900
Fax: (239) 549-9609
http://www.capecoralchamber.com

Cedar Rapids, IA
Cedar Rapids Chamber of Commerce
424 First Avenue NE
Cedar Rapids, IA 52401
Phone: (319) 398-5317
Fax: (319) 398-5228
http://www.cedarrapids.org

Cedar Rapids Economic Development
50 Second Avenue Bridge
Sixth Floor
Cedar Rapids, IA 52401-1256
Phone: (319) 286-5041
Fax: (319) 286-5141
http://www.cedar-rapids.org

Charleston, SC
Charleston Metro Chamber of Commerce
P.O. Box 975
Charleston, SC 29402
Phone: (843) 577-2510
http://www.charlestonchamber.net

Charlotte, NC
Charlotte Chamber of Commerce
330 S Tryon Street
P.O. Box 32785
Charlotte, NC 28232
Phone: (704) 378-1300
Fax: (704) 374-1903
http://www.charlottechamber.com

Charlotte Regional Partnership
1001 Morehead Square Drive
Suite 200
Charlotte, NC 28203
Phone: (704) 347-8942
Fax: (704) 347-8981
http://www.charlotteusa.com

Chicago, IL
Chicagoland Chamber of Commerce
200 E Randolph Street
Suite 2200
Chicago, IL 60601-6436
Phone: (312) 494-6700
Fax: (312) 861-0660
http://www.chicagolandchamber.org

City of Chicago Department of Planning
and Development
City Hall, Room 1000
121 North La Salle Street
Chicago, IL 60602
Phone: (312) 744-4190
Fax: (312) 744-2271
https://www.cityofchicago.org/city/en/depts
/dcd.html

Clarksville, TN
Clarksville Area Chamber of Commerce
25 Jefferson Street
Suite 300
Clarksville, TN 37040
Phone: (931) 647-2331
http://www.clarksvillechamber.com

College Station, TX
Bryan-College Station Chamber of
Commerce
4001 East 29th St, Suite 175
Bryan, TX 77802
Phone: (979) 260-5200
http://www.bcschamber.org

Colorado Springs, CO
Colorado Springs Chamber and EDC
102 South Tejon Street
Suite 430
Colorado Springs, CO 80903
Phone: (719) 471-8183
https://coloradospringschamberedc.com

Columbia, MO
Columbia Chamber of Commerce
300 South Providence Rd.
PO Box 1016
Columbia, MO 65205-1016
Phone: (573) 874-1132
Fax: (573) 443-3986
http://www.columbiamochamber.com

Columbia, SC
The Columbia Chamber
930 Richland Street
Columbia, SC 29201
Phone: (803) 733-1110
Fax: (803) 733-1113
http://www.columbiachamber.com

Columbus, OH
Greater Columbus Chamber
37 North High Street
Columbus, OH 43215
Phone: (614) 221-1321
Fax: (614) 221-1408
http://www.columbus.org

Dallas, TX
City of Dallas Economic Development
Department
1500 Marilla Street
5C South
Dallas, TX 75201
Phone: (214) 670-1685
Fax: (214) 670-0158
http://www.dallas-edd.org

Greater Dallas Chamber of Commerce
700 North Pearl Street
Suite1200
Dallas, TX 75201
Phone: (214) 746-6600
Fax: (214) 746-6799
http://www.dallaschamber.org

Denver, CO
Denver Metro Chamber of Commerce
1445 Market Street
Denver, CO 80202
Phone: (303) 534-8500
Fax: (303) 534-3200
http://www.denverchamber.org

Downtown Denver Partnership
511 16th Street
Suite 200
Denver, CO 80202
Phone: (303) 534-6161
Fax: (303) 534-2803
http://www.downtowndenver.com

Des Moines, IA
Des Moines Downtown Chamber
301 Grand Ave
Des Moines, IA 50309
Phone: (515) 309-3229
http://desmoinesdowntownchamber.com

Greater Des Moines Partnership
700 Locust Street
Suite 100
Des Moines, IA 50309
Phone: (515) 286-4950
Fax: (515) 286-4974
http://www.desmoinesmetro.com

Durham, NC
Durham Chamber of Commerce
PO Box 3829
Durham, NC 27702
Phone: (919) 682-2133
Fax: (919) 688-8351
http://www.durhamchamber.org

North Carolina Institute of Minority
Economic Development
114 W Parish Street
Durham, NC 27701
Phone: (919) 956-8889
Fax: (919) 688-7668
http://www.ncimed.com

Edison, NJ
Edison Chamber of Commerce
939 Amboy Avenue
Edison, NJ 08837
Phone: (732) 738-9482
http://www.edisonchamber.com

El Paso, TX
City of El Paso Department of Economic
Development
2 Civic Center Plaza
El Paso, TX 79901
Phone: (915) 541-4000
Fax: (915) 541-1316
http://www.elpasotexas.gov

Greater El Paso Chamber of Commerce
10 Civic Center Plaza
El Paso, TX 79901
Phone: (915) 534-0500
Fax: (915) 534-0510
http://www.elpaso.org

Eugene, OR
Eugene Area Chamber of Commerce
1401 Williamette Street
Eugene, OR 97401
Phone: (541) 484-1314
Fax: (541) 484-4942
http://www.eugenechamber.com

Evansville, IN
Evansville Chamber of Commerce &
Tourism
8 West Main Street
Evansville, WI 53536
Phone: (608) 882-5131
http://www.evansvillechamber.org

Southwest Indiana Chamber
318 Main Street
Suite 401
Evansville, IN 47708
Phone: (812) 425-8147
Fax: (812) 421-5883
https://swinchamber.com

Fargo, ND
Chamber of Commerce of Fargo Moorhead
202 First Avenue North
Fargo, ND 56560
Phone: (218) 233-1100
Fax: (218) 233-1200
http://www.fmchamber.com

Greater Fargo-Moorhead Economic
Development Corporation
51 Broadway, Suite 500
Fargo, ND 58102
Phone: (701) 364-1900
Fax: (701) 293-7819
http://www.gfmedc.com

Fayetteville, NC
Fayetteville Regional Chamber
1019 Hay Street
Fayetteville, NC 28305
Phone: (910) 483-8133
Fax: (910) 483-0263
http://www.fayettevillencchamber.org

Fort Collins, CO
Fort Collins Chamber of Commerce
225 South Meldrum
Fort Collins, CO 80521
Phone: (970) 482-3746
Fax: (970) 482-3774
https://fortcollinschamber.com

Fort Wayne, IN
City of Fort Wayne Economic Development
1 Main St
1 Main Street
Fort Wayne, IN 46802
Phone: (260) 427-1111
Fax: (260) 427-1375
http://www.cityoffortwayne.org

Greater Fort Wayne Chamber of Commerce
826 Ewing Street
Fort Wayne, IN 46802
Phone: (260) 424-1435
Fax: (260) 426-7232
http://www.fwchamber.org

Fort Worth, TX
City of Fort Worth Economic Development
City Hall
900 Monroe Street, Suite 301
Fort Worth, TX 76102
Phone: (817) 392-6103
Fax: (817) 392-2431
http://www.fortworthgov.org

Fort Worth Chamber of Commerce
777 Taylor Street
Suite 900
Fort Worth, TX 76102-4997
Phone: (817) 336-2491
Fax: (817) 877-4034
http://www.fortworthchamber.com

Gainesville, FL
Gainesville Area Chamber of Commerce
300 East University Avenue
Suite 100
Gainesville, FL 32601
Phone: (352) 334-7100
Fax: (352) 334-7141
http://www.gainesvillechamber.com

Grand Rapids, MI
Grands Rapids Area Chamber of Commerce
111 Pearl Street N.W.
Grand Rapids, MI 49503
Phone: (616) 771-0300
Fax: (616) 771-0318
http://www.grandrapids.org

Greeley, CO
Greeley Chamber of Commerce
902 7th Avenue
Greeley, CO 80631
Phone: (970) 352-3566
https://greeleychamber.com

Green Bay, WI
Economic Development
100 N Jefferson St
Room 202
Green Bay, WI 54301
Phone: (920) 448-3397
Fax: (920) 448-3063
http://www.ci.green-bay.wi.us

Green Bay Area Chamber of Commerce
300 N. Broadway
Suite 3A
Green Bay, WI 54305-1660
Phone: (920) 437-8704
Fax: (920) 593-3468
http://www.titletown.org

Greensboro, NC
Greensboro Area Chamber of Commerce
342 N Elm St.
Greensboro, NC 27401
Phone: (336) 387-8301
Fax: (336) 275-9299
http://www.greensboro.org

Honolulu, HI
The Chamber of Commerce of Hawaii
1132 Bishop Street
Suite 402
Honolulu, HI 96813
Phone: (808) 545-4300
Fax: (808) 545-4369
http://www.cochawaii.com

Houston, TX
Greater Houston Partnership
1200 Smith Street
Suite 700
Houston, TX 77002-4400
Phone: (713) 844-3600
Fax: (713) 844-0200
http://www.houston.org

Huntsville, AL
Chamber of Commerce of
Huntsville/Madison County
225 Church Street
Huntsville, AL 35801
Phone: (256) 535-2000
Fax: (256) 535-2015
http://www.huntsvillealabamausa.com

Indianapolis, IN
Greater Indianapolis Chamber of Commerce
111 Monument Circle
Suite 1950
Indianapolis, IN 46204
Phone: (317) 464-2222
Fax: (317) 464-2217
http://www.indychamber.com

The Indy Partnership
111 Monument Circle
Suite 1800
Indianapolis, IN 46204
Phone: (317) 236-6262
Fax: (317) 236-6275
http://indypartnership.com

Jacksonville, FL
Jacksonville Chamber of Commerce
3 Independent Drive
Jacksonville, FL 32202
Phone: (904) 366-6600
Fax: (904) 632-0617
http://www.myjaxchamber.com

Kansas City, MO
Greater Kansas City Chamber of Commerce
2600 Commerce Tower
911 Main Street
Kansas City, MO 64105
Phone: (816) 221-2424
Fax: (816) 221-7440
http://www.kcchamber.com

Kansas City Area Development Council
2600 Commerce Tower
911 Main Street
Kansas City, MO 64105
Phone: (816) 221-2121
Fax: (816) 842-2865
http://www.thinkkc.com

Lafayette, LA
Greater Lafayette Chamber of Commerce
804 East Saint Mary Blvd.
Lafayette, LA 70503
Phone: (337) 233-2705
Fax: (337) 234-8671
http://www.lafchamber.org

Las Cruces, NM
Greater Las Cruces Chamber of Commerce
505 S Main Street, Suite 134
Las Cruces, NM 88001
Phone: (575) 524-1968
Fax: (575) 527-5546
http://www.lascruces.org

Las Vegas, NV
Las Vegas Chamber of Commerce
6671 Las Vegas Blvd South
Suite 300
Las Vegas, NV 89119
Phone: (702) 735-1616
Fax: (702) 735-0406
http://www.lvchamber.org

Las Vegas Office of Business Development
400 Stewart Avenue
City Hall
Las Vegas, NV 89101
Phone: (702) 229-6011
Fax: (702) 385-3128
http://www.lasvegasnevada.gov

Lexington, KY
Greater Lexington Chamber of Commerce
330 East Main Street
Suite 100
Lexington, KY 40507
Phone: (859) 254-4447
Fax: (859) 233-3304
http://www.commercelexington.com

Lexington Downtown Development
Authority
101 East Vine Street
Suite 500
Lexington, KY 40507
Phone: (859) 425-2296
Fax: (859) 425-2292
http://www.lexingtondda.com

Lincoln, NE
Lincoln Chamber of Commerce
1135 M Street
Suite 200
Lincoln, NE 68508
Phone: (402) 436-2350
Fax: (402) 436-2360
http://www.lcoc.com

Little Rock, AR
Little Rock Regional Chamber
One Chamber Plaza
Little Rock, AR 72201
Phone: (501) 374-2001
Fax: (501) 374-6018
http://www.littlerockchamber.com

Los Angeles, CA
Los Angeles Area Chamber of Commerce
350 South Bixel Street
Los Angeles, CA 90017
Phone: (213) 580-7500
Fax: (213) 580-7511
http://www.lachamber.org

Los Angeles County Economic
Development Corporation
444 South Flower Street
34th Floor
Los Angeles, CA 90071
Phone: (213) 622-4300
Fax: (213) 622-7100
http://www.laedc.org

Louisville, KY
The Greater Louisville Chamber of
Commerce
614 West Main Street
Suite 6000
Louisville, KY 40202
Phone: (502) 625-0000
Fax: (502) 625-0010
http://www.greaterlouisville.com

Madison, WI
Greater Madison Chamber of Commerce
615 East Washington Avenue
P.O. Box 71
Madison, WI 53701-0071
Phone: (608) 256-8348
Fax: (608) 256-0333
http://www.greatermadisonchamber.com

Manchester, NH
Greater Manchester Chamber of Commerce
889 Elm Street
Manchester, NH 03101
Phone: (603) 666-6600
Fax: (603) 626-0910
http://www.manchester-chamber.org

Manchester Economic Development Office
One City Hall Plaza
Manchester, NH 03101
Phone: (603) 624-6505
Fax: (603) 624-6308
http://www.yourmanchesternh.com

Miami, FL
Greater Miami Chamber of Commerce
1601 Biscayne Boulevard
Ballroom Level
Miami, FL 33132-1260
Phone: (305) 350-7700
Fax: (305) 374-6902
http://www.miamichamber.com

The Beacon Council
80 Southwest 8th Street
Suite 2400
Miami, FL 33130
Phone: (305) 579-1300
Fax: (305) 375-0271
http://www.beaconcouncil.com

Midland, TX
Midland Chamber of Commerce
109 N. Main
Midland, TX 79701
Phone: (432) 683-3381
Fax: (432) 686-3556
http://www.midlandtxchamber.com

Minneapolis, MN
Minneapolis Community Development
Agency
Crown Roller Mill
105 5th Avenue South, Suite 200
Minneapolis, MN 55401
Phone: (612) 673-5095
Fax: (612) 673-5100
http://www.ci.minneapolis.mn.us

Minneapolis Regional Chamber
81 South Ninth Street
Suite 200
Minneapolis, MN 55402
Phone: (612) 370-9100
Fax: (612) 370-9195
http://www.minneapolischamber.org

Nashville, TN
Nashville Area Chamber of Commerce
211 Commerce Street
Suite 100
Nashville, TN 37201
Phone: (615) 743-3000
Fax: (615) 256-3074
http://www.nashvillechamber.com

Tennessee Valley Authority Economic
Development
400 West Summit Hill Drive
Knoxville TN 37902
Phone: (865) 632-2101
http://www.tvaed.com

New Orleans, LA
New Orleans Chamber of Commerce
1515 Poydras St
Suite 1010
New Orleans, LA 70112
Phone: (504) 799-4260
Fax: (504) 799-4259
http://www.neworleanschamber.org

New York, NY
New York City Economic Development
Corporation
110 William Street
New York, NY 10038
Phone: (212) 619-5000
http://www.nycedc.com

The Partnership for New York City
One Battery Park Plaza
5th Floor
New York, NY 10004
Phone: (212) 493-7400
Fax: (212) 344-3344
http://www.pfnyc.org

Oklahoma City, OK
Greater Oklahoma City Chamber of
Commerce
123 Park Avenue
Oklahoma City, OK 73102
Phone: (405) 297-8900
Fax: (405) 297-8916
http://www.okcchamber.com

Omaha, NE
Omaha Chamber of Commerce
1301 Harney Street
Omaha, NE 68102
Phone: (402) 346-5000
Fax: (402) 346-7050
http://www.omahachamber.org

Orlando, FL
Metro Orlando Economic Development
Commission of Mid-Florida
301 East Pine Street
Suite 900
Orlando, FL 32801
Phone: (407) 422-7159
Fax: (407) 425.6428
http://www.orlandoedc.com

Orlando Regional Chamber of Commerce
75 South Ivanhoe Boulevard
PO Box 1234
Orlando, FL 32802
Phone: (407) 425-1234
Fax: (407) 839-5020
http://www.orlando.org

Peoria, IL
Peoria Area Chamber
100 SW Water St.
Peoria, IL 61602
Phone: (309) 495-5900
http://www.peoriachamber.org

Philadelphia, PA
Greater Philadelphia Chamber of
Commerce
200 South Broad Street
Suite 700
Philadelphia, PA 19102
Phone: (215) 545-1234
Fax: (215) 790-3600
http://www.greaterphilachamber.com

Phoenix, AZ
Greater Phoenix Chamber of Commerce
201 North Central Avenue
27th Floor
Phoenix, AZ 85073
Phone: (602) 495-2195
Fax: (602) 495-8913
http://www.phoenixchamber.com

Greater Phoenix Economic Council
2 North Central Avenue
Suite 2500
Phoenix, AZ 85004
Phone: (602) 256-7700
Fax: (602) 256-7744
http://www.gpec.org

Pittsburgh, PA
Allegheny County Industrial Development
Authority
425 6th Avenue
Suite 800
Pittsburgh, PA 15219
Phone: (412) 350-1067
Fax: (412) 642-2217
http://www.alleghenycounty.us

Greater Pittsburgh Chamber of Commerce
425 6th Avenue
12th Floor
Pittsburgh, PA 15219
Phone: (412) 392-4500
Fax: (412) 392-4520
http://www.alleghenyconference.org

Portland, OR
Portland Business Alliance
200 SW Market Street
Suite 1770
Portland, OR 97201
Phone: (503) 224-8684
Fax: (503) 323-9186
http://www.portlandalliance.com

Providence, RI
Greater Providence Chamber of Commerce
30 Exchange Terrace
Fourth Floor
Providence, RI 02903
Phone: (401) 521-5000
Fax: (401) 351-2090
http://www.provchamber.com

Rhode Island Economic Development
Corporation
Providence City Hall
25 Dorrance Street
Providence, RI 02903
Phone: (401) 421-7740
Fax: (401) 751-0203
http://www.providenceri.com

Provo, UT
Provo-Orem Chamber of Commerce
51 South University Avenue
Suite 215
Provo, UT 84601
Phone: (801) 851-2555
Fax: (801) 851-2557
http://www.thechamber.org

Raleigh, NC
Greater Raleigh Chamber of Commerce
800 South Salisbury Street
Raleigh, NC 27601-2978
Phone: (919) 664-7000
Fax: (919) 664-7099
http://www.raleighchamber.org

Reno, NV
Greater Reno-Sparks Chamber of
Commerce
1 East First Street
16th Floor
Reno, NV 89505
Phone: (775) 337-3030
Fax: (775) 337-3038
http://www.reno-sparkschamber.org

The Chamber Reno-Sparks-Northern
Nevada
449 S. Virginia St.
2nd Floor
Reno, NV 89501
Phone: (775) 636-9550
http://www.thechambernv.org

Richmond, VA
Greater Richmond Chamber
600 East Main Street
Suite 700
Richmond, VA 23219
Phone: (804) 648-1234
http://www.grcc.com

Greater Richmond Partnership
901 East Byrd Street
Suite 801
Richmond, VA 23219-4070
Phone: (804) 643-3227
Fax: (804) 343-7167
http://www.grpva.com

Roanoke, VA
Roanoke Regional Chamber of Commerce
210 S. Jefferson Street
Roanoke, VA 24011-1702
Phone: (540) 983-0700
Fax: (540) 983-0723
http://www.roanokechamber.org

Rochester, MN
Rochester Area Chamber of Commerce
220 South Broadway
Suite 100
Rochester, MN 55904
Phone: (507) 288-1122
Fax: (507) 282-8960
http://www.rochestermnchamber.com

Salem, OR
Salem Area Chamber of Commerce
1110 Commercial Street NE
Salem, OR 97301
Phone: (503) 581-1466
Fax: (503) 581-0972
http://www.salemchamber.org

Salt Lake City, UT
Department of Economic Development
451 South State Street
Room 425
Salt Lake City, UT 84111
Phone: (801) 535-7240
Fax: (801) 535-6331
http://www.slcgov.com/economic-developm
ent

Salt Lake Chamber
175 E. University Blvd. (400 S)
Suite 600
Salt Lake City, UT 84111
Phone: (801) 364-3631
http://www.slchamber.com

San Antonio, TX
The Greater San Antonio Chamber of
Commerce
602 E. Commerce Street
San Antonio, TX 78205
Phone: (210) 229-2100
Fax: (210) 229-1600
http://www.sachamber.org

San Antonio Economic Development
Department
P.O. Box 839966
San Antonio, TX 78283-3966
Phone: (210) 207-8080
Fax: (210) 207-8151
http://www.sanantonio.gov/edd

San Diego, CA
San Diego Economic Development
Corporation
401 B Street
Suite 1100
San Diego, CA 92101
Phone: (619) 234-8484
Fax: (619) 234-1935
http://www.sandiegobusiness.org

San Diego Regional Chamber of Commerce
402 West Broadway
Suite 1000
San Diego, CA 92101-3585
Phone: (619) 544-1300
Fax: (619) 744-7481
http://www.sdchamber.org

San Francisco, CA
San Francisco Chamber of Commerce
235 Montgomery Street
12th Floor
San Francisco, CA 94104
Phone: (415) 392-4520
Fax: (415) 392-0485
http://www.sfchamber.com

San Jose, CA
Office of Economic Development
60 South Market Street
Suite 470
San Jose, CA 95113
Phone: (408) 277-5880
Fax: (408) 277-3615
http://www.sba.gov

The Silicon Valley Organization
101 W Santa Clara Street
San Jose, CA 95113
Phone: (408) 291-5250
https://www.thesvo.com

Santa Rosa, CA
Santa Rosa Chamber of Commerce
1260 North Dutton Avenue
Suite 272
Santa Rosa, CA 95401
Phone: (707) 545-1414
http://www.santarosachamber.com

Savannah, GA
Economic Development Authority
131 Hutchinson Island Road
4th Floor
Savannah, GA 31421
Phone: (912) 447-8450
Fax: (912) 447-8455
http://www.seda.org

Savannah Chamber of Commerce
101 E. Bay Street
Savannah, GA 31402
Phone: (912) 644-6400
Fax: (912) 644-6499
http://www.savannahchamber.com

Seattle, WA
Greater Seattle Chamber of Commerce
1301 Fifth Avenue
Suite 2500
Seattle, WA 98101
Phone: (206) 389-7200
Fax: (206) 389-7288
http://www.seattlechamber.com

Sioux Falls, SD
Sioux Falls Area Chamber of Commerce
200 N. Phillips Avenue
Suite 102
Sioux Falls, SD 57104
Phone: (605) 336-1620
Fax: (605) 336-6499
http://www.siouxfallschamber.com

Springfield, IL
The Greater Springfield Chamber of
Commerce
1011 S. Second Street
Springfield, IL 62704
Phone: (217) 525-1173
Fax: (217) 525-8768
http://www.gscc.org

Tallahassee, FL
Greater Tallahassee Chamber of Commerce
300 E. Park Avenue
PO Box 1638
Tallahassee, FL 32301
Phone: (850) 224-8116
Fax: (850) 561-3860
http://www.talchamber.com

Tampa, FL
Greater Tampa Chamber of Commerce
P.O. Box 420
Tampa, FL 33601-0420
Phone: (813) 276-9401
Fax: (813) 229-7855
http://www.tampachamber.com

Topeka, KS
Greater Topeka Chamber of Commerce/
GO Topeka
120 SE Sixth Avenue
Suite 110
Topeka, KS 66603
Phone: (785) 234-2644
Fax: (785) 234-8656
http://www.topekachamber.org

Tyler, TX
Tyler Area Chamber of Commerce
315 N Broadway Ave
Suite 100
Tyler, TX 75702
Phone: (903) 592-1661; (800) 235-5712
Fax: (903) 593-2746
http://www.tylertexas.com

Virginia Beach, VA
Hampton Roads Chamber of Commerce
500 East Main Street
Suite 700
Virginia Beach, VA 23510
Phone: (757) 664-2531
http://www.hamptonroadschamber.com

Visalia, CA
Visalia Chamber of Commerce
222 North Garden Street
Suite 300
Visalia, CA 93291
Phone: (559) 734-5876
http://www.visaliachamber.org

Washington, DC
District of Columbia Chamber of
Commerce
1213 K Street NW
Washington, DC 20005
Phone: (202) 347-7201
Fax: (202) 638-6762
http://www.dcchamber.org

District of Columbia Office of Planning and
Economic Development
J.A. Wilson Building
1350 Pennsylvania Ave NW, Suite 317
Washington, DC 20004
Phone: (202) 727-6365
Fax: (202) 727-6703
http://www.dcbiz.dc.gov

Wilmington, NC
Wilmington Chamber of Commerce
One Estell Lee Place
Wilmington, NC 28401
Phone: (910) 762-2611
http://www.wilmingtonchamber.org

Winston-Salem, NC
Winston-Salem Chamber of Commerce
411 West Fourth Street
Suite 211
Winston-Salem, NC 27101
Phone: (336) 728-9200
http://www.winstonsalem.com

Appendix E: State Departments of Labor

Alabama
Alabama Department of Labor
P.O. Box 303500
Montgomery, AL 36130-3500
Phone: (334) 242-3072
https://www.labor.alabama.gov

Alaska
Dept of Labor and Workforce Devel.
P.O. Box 11149
Juneau, AK 99822-2249
Phone: (907) 465-2700
http://www.labor.state.ak.us

Arizona
Industrial Commission or Arizona
800 West Washington Street
Phoenix, AZ 85007
Phone: (602) 542-4411
https://www.azica.gov

Arkansas
Department of Labor
10421 West Markham
Little Rock, AR 72205
Phone: (501) 682-4500
http://www.labor.ar.gov

California
Labor and Workforce Development
445 Golden Gate Ave., 10th Floor
San Francisco, CA 94102
Phone: (916) 263-1811
http://www.labor.ca.gov

Colorado
Dept of Labor and Employment
633 17th St., 2nd Floor
Denver, CO 80202-3660
Phone: (888) 390-7936
https://www.colorado.gov/CDLE

Connecticut
Department of Labor
200 Folly Brook Blvd.
Wethersfield, CT 06109-1114
Phone: (860) 263-6000
http://www.ctdol.state.ct.us

Delaware
Department of Labor
4425 N. Market St., 4th Floor
Wilmington, DE 19802
Phone: (302) 451-3423
http://dol.delaware.gov

District of Columbia
Department of Employment Services
614 New York Ave., NE, Suite 300
Washington, DC 20002
Phone: (202) 671-1900
http://does.dc.gov

Florida
Florida Department of Economic
Opportunity
The Caldwell Building
107 East Madison St. Suite 100
Tallahassee, FL 32399-4120
Phone: (800) 342-3450
http://www.floridajobs.org

Georgia
Department of Labor
Sussex Place, Room 600
148 Andrew Young Intl Blvd., NE
Atlanta, GA 30303
Phone: (404) 656-3011
http://dol.georgia.gov

Hawaii
Dept of Labor & Industrial Relations
830 Punchbowl Street
Honolulu, HI 96813
Phone: (808) 586-8842
http://labor.hawaii.gov

Idaho
Department of Labor
317 W. Main St.
Boise, ID 83735-0001
Phone: (208) 332-3579
http://www.labor.idaho.gov

Illinois
Department of Labor
160 N. LaSalle Street, 13th Floor
Suite C-1300
Chicago, IL 60601
Phone: (312) 793-2800
https://www.illinois.gov/idol

Indiana
Indiana Department of Labor
402 West Washington Street, Room W195
Indianapolis, IN 46204
Phone: (317) 232-2655
http://www.in.gov/dol

Iowa
Iowa Workforce Development
1000 East Grand Avenue
Des Moines, IA 50319-0209
Phone: (515) 242-5870
http://www.iowadivisionoflabor.gov

Kansas
Department of Labor
401 S.W. Topeka Blvd.
Topeka, KS 66603-3182
Phone: (785) 296-5000
http://www.dol.ks.gov

Kentucky
Department of Labor
1047 U.S. Hwy 127 South, Suite 4
Frankfort, KY 40601-4381
Phone: (502) 564-3070
http://www.labor.ky.gov

Louisiana
Louisiana Workforce Commission
1001 N. 23rd Street
Baton Rouge, LA 70804-9094
Phone: (225) 342-3111
http://www.laworks.net

Maine
Department of Labor
45 Commerce Street
Augusta, ME 04330
Phone: (207) 623-7900
http://www.state.me.us/labor

Maryland
Department of Labor, Licensing &
Regulation
500 N. Calvert Street
Suite 401
Baltimore, MD 21202
Phone: (410) 767-2357
http://www.dllr.state.md.us

Massachusetts
Dept of Labor & Workforce Development
One Ashburton Place
Room 2112
Boston, MA 02108
Phone: (617) 626-7100
http://www.mass.gov/lwd

Michigan
Department of Licensing and Regulatory
Affairs
611 W. Ottawa
P.O. Box 30004
Lansing, MI 48909
Phone: (517) 373-1820
http://www.michigan.gov/lara

Minnesota
Dept of Labor and Industry
443 Lafayette Road North
Saint Paul, MN 55155
Phone: (651) 284-5070
http://www.doli.state.mn.us

Mississippi
Dept of Employment Security
P.O. Box 1699
Jackson, MS 39215-1699
Phone: (601) 321-6000
http://www.mdes.ms.gov

Missouri
Labor and Industrial Relations
P.O. Box 599
3315 W. Truman Boulevard
Jefferson City, MO 65102-0599
Phone: (573) 751-7500
https://labor.mo.gov

Montana
Dept of Labor and Industry
P.O. Box 1728
Helena, MT 59624-1728
Phone: (406) 444-9091
http://www.dli.mt.gov

Nebraska
Department of Labor
550 S 16th Street
Lincoln, NE 68508
Phone: (402) 471-9000
https://dol.nebraska.gov

Nevada
Dept of Business and Industry
3300 W. Sahara Ave
Suite 425
Las Vegas, NV 89102
Phone: (702) 486-2750
http://business.nv.gov

New Hampshire
Department of Labor
State Office Park South
95 Pleasant Street
Concord, NH 03301
Phone: (603) 271-3176
https://www.nh.gov/labor

New Jersey
Department of Labor & Workforce
Development
John Fitch Plaza, 13th Floor
Suite D
Trenton, NJ 08625-0110
Phone: (609) 777-3200
http://lwd.dol.state.nj.us/labor

New Mexico
Department of Workforce Solutions
401 Broadway, NE
Albuquerque, NM 87103-1928
Phone: (505) 841-8450
https://www.dws.state.nm.us

New York
Department of Labor
State Office Bldg. # 12
W.A. Harriman Campus
Albany, NY 12240
Phone: (518) 457-9000
https://www.labor.ny.gov

North Carolina
Department of Labor
4 West Edenton Street
Raleigh, NC 27601-1092
Phone: (919) 733-7166
https://www.labor.nc.gov

North Dakota
North Dakota Department of Labor and
Human Rights
State Capitol Building
600 East Boulevard, Dept 406
Bismark, ND 58505-0340
Phone: (701) 328-2660
http://www.nd.gov/labor

Ohio
Department of Commerce
77 South High Street, 22nd Floor
Columbus, OH 43215
Phone: (614) 644-2239
http://www.com.state.oh.us

Oklahoma
Department of Labor
4001 N. Lincoln Blvd.
Oklahoma City, OK 73105-5212
Phone: (405) 528-1500
https://www.ok.gov/odol

Oregon
Bureau of Labor and Industries
800 NE Oregon St., #32
Portland, OR 97232
Phone: (971) 673-0761
http://www.oregon.gov/boli

Pennsylvania
Dept of Labor and Industry
1700 Labor and Industry Bldg
7th and Forster Streets
Harrisburg, PA 17120
Phone: (717) 787-5279
http://www.dli.pa.gov

Rhode Island
Department of Labor and Training
1511 Pontiac Avenue
Cranston, RI 02920
Phone: (401) 462-8000
http://www.dlt.state.ri.us

South Carolina
Dept of Labor, Licensing & Regulations
P.O. Box 11329
Columbia, SC 29211-1329
Phone: (803) 896-4300
http://www.llr.state.sc.us

South Dakota
Department of Labor & Regulation
700 Governors Drive
Pierre, SD 57501-2291
Phone: (605) 773-3682
http://dlr.sd.gov

Tennessee
Dept of Labor & Workforce Development
Andrew Johnson Tower
710 James Robertson Pkwy
Nashville, TN 37243-0655
Phone: (615) 741-6642
http://www.tn.gov/workforce

Texas
Texas Workforce Commission
101 East 15th St.
Austin, TX 78778
Phone: (512) 475-2670
http://www.twc.state.tx.us

Utah
Utah Labor Commission
160 East 300 South, 3rd Floor
Salt Lake City, UT 84114-6600
Phone: (801) 530-6800
https://laborcommission.utah.gov

Vermont
Department of Labor
5 Green Mountain Drive
P.O. Box 488
Montpelier, VT 05601-0488
Phone: (802) 828-4000
http://labor.vermont.gov

Virginia
Dept of Labor and Industry
Powers-Taylor Building
13 S. 13th Street
Richmond, VA 23219
Phone: (804) 371-2327
http://www.doli.virginia.gov

Washington
Dept of Labor and Industries
P.O. Box 44001
Olympia, WA 98504-4001
Phone: (360) 902-4200
http://www.lni.wa.gov

West Virginia
Division of Labor
749 B Building 6
Capitol Complex
Charleston, WV 25305
Phone: (304) 558-7890
https://labor.wv.gov

Wisconsin
Dept of Workforce Development
201 E. Washington Ave., #A400
P.O. Box 7946
Madison, WI 53707-7946
Phone: (608) 266-6861
http://dwd.wisconsin.gov

Wyoming
Department of Workforce Services
1510 East Pershing Blvd.
Cheyenne, WY 82002
Phone: (307) 777-7261
http://www.wyomingworkforce.org

*Source: U.S. Department of Labor;
Original research*

2019 Title List
Visit **www.GreyHouse.com** for Product Information, Table of Contents, and Sample Pages.

General Reference
America's College Museums
American Environmental Leaders: From Colonial Times to the Present
Encyclopedia of African-American Writing
Encyclopedia of Constitutional Amendments
Encyclopedia of Human Rights and the United States
Encyclopedia of Invasions & Conquests
Encyclopedia of Prisoners of War & Internment
Encyclopedia of Religion & Law in America
Encyclopedia of Rural America
Encyclopedia of the Continental Congress
Encyclopedia of the United States Cabinet, 1789-2010
Encyclopedia of War Journalism
Encyclopedia of Warrior Peoples & Fighting Groups
The Environmental Debate: A Documentary History
The Evolution Wars: A Guide to the Debates
From Suffrage to the Senate: America's Political Women
Gun Debate: An Encyclopedia of Gun Rights & Gun Control in the U.S.
Opinions throughout History: National Security vs. Civil and Privacy Rights
Opinions throughout History: Immigration
Opinions throughout History: Drug Use & Abuse
Opinions throughout History: Gender: Roles & Rights
Opinions throughout History: The Environment
Opinions throughout History: Social Media Issues
Opinions throughout History: The Death Penalty
Opinions throughout History: Voters' Rights
Political Corruption in America
Privacy Rights in the Digital Age
The Religious Right: A Reference Handbook
Speakers of the House of Representatives, 1789-2009
This is Who We Were: 1880-1900
This is Who We Were: A Companion to the 1940 Census
This is Who We Were: In Colonial America
This is Who We Were: In the 1900s
This is Who We Were: In the 1910s
This is Who We Were: In the 1920s
This is Who We Were: In the 1940s
This is Who We Were: In the 1950s
This is Who We Were: In the 1960s
This is Who We Were: In the 1970s
This is Who We Were: In the 1980s
This is Who We Were: In the 1990s
This is Who We Were: In the 2000s
U.S. Land & Natural Resource Policy
The Value of a Dollar 1600-1865: Colonial Era to the Civil War
The Value of a Dollar: 1860-2019
Working Americans 1880-1999 Vol. I: The Working Class
Working Americans 1880-1999 Vol. II: The Middle Class
Working Americans 1880-1999 Vol. III: The Upper Class
Working Americans 1880-1999 Vol. IV: Their Children
Working Americans 1880-2015 Vol. V: Americans At War
Working Americans 1880-2005 Vol. VI: Women at Work
Working Americans 1880-2006 Vol. VII: Social Movements
Working Americans 1880-2007 Vol. VIII: Immigrants
Working Americans 1770-1869 Vol. IX: Revolutionary War to the Civil War
Working Americans 1880-2009 Vol. X: Sports & Recreation
Working Americans 1880-2010 Vol. XI: Inventors & Entrepreneurs
Working Americans 1880-2011 Vol. XII: Our History through Music
Working Americans 1880-2012 Vol. XIII: Education & Educators
Working Americans 1880-2016 Vol. XIV: Industry Through the Ages
Working Americans 1880-2017 Vol. XV: Politics & Politicians
World Cultural Leaders of the 20th & 21st Centuries

Education Information
Charter School Movement
The Comparative Guide to American Elementary & Secondary Schools
Complete Learning Disabilities Resource Guide
Educators Resource Guide
Special Education: A Reference Book for Policy and Curriculum
    Development

Health Information
Comparative Guide to American Hospitals
Complete Resource Guide for Pediatric Disorders
Complete Resource Guide for People with Chronic Illness
Complete Resource Guide for People with Disabilities
Complete Mental Health Resource Guide
Diabetes in America: Analysis of an Epidemic
Guide to Health Care Group Purchasing Organizations
Guide to U.S. HMO's & PPO's
Medical Device Market Place
Older Americans Information Resource

Business Information
Complete Television, Radio & Cable Industry Guide
Business Information Resources
Directory of Mail Order Catalogs
Guide to Venture Capital & Private Equity Firms
Environmental Resource Handbook
Financial Literacy Starter Kit
Food & Beverage Market Place
The Grey House Homeland Security Directory
The Grey House Performing Arts Industry Guide
The Grey House Safety & Security Directory
Hudson's Washington News Media Contacts Directory
New York State Directory
Sports Market Place

Statistics & Demographics
American Tally
America's Top-Rated Cities
America's Top-Rated Smaller Cities
Ancestry & Ethnicity in America
The Asian Databook
The Comparative Guide to American Suburbs
The Hispanic Databook
Nations of the World
Profiles of America
"Profiles of" Series - State Handbooks
Weather America

Financial Ratings Series
Financial Literacy Basics
TheStreet Ratings' Ultimate Guided Tour of Stock Investing
Weiss Ratings' Investment Research Guide to Bond & Money Market
    Mutual Funds
Weiss Ratings' Investment Research Guide to Stocks
Weiss Ratings' Investment Research Guide to Exchange-Traded Funds
Weiss Ratings' Investment Research Guide to Stock Mutual Funds
Weiss Ratings' Consumer Guides
Weiss Ratings' Financial Literary Basic Guides
Weiss Ratings' Guide to Banks
Weiss Ratings' Guide to Credit Unions
Weiss Ratings' Guide to Health Insurers
Weiss Ratings' Guide to Life & Annuity Insurers
Weiss Ratings' Guide to Property & Casualty Insurers

Bowker's Books In Print® Titles
American Book Publishing Record® Annual
American Book Publishing Record® Monthly
Books In Print®
Books In Print® Supplement
Books Out Loud™
Bowker's Complete Video Directory™
Children's Books In Print®
El-Hi Textbooks & Serials In Print®
Forthcoming Books®
Law Books & Serials In Print™
Medical & Health Care Books In Print™
Publishers, Distributors & Wholesalers of the US™
Subject Guide to Books In Print®
Subject Guide to Children's Books In Print®

Grey House Publishing | Salem Press | H.W. Wilson | 4919 Route, 22 PO Box 56, Amenia NY 12501-0056

Grey House Publishing

Grey House Publishing

2019 Title List
Visit **www.GreyHouse.com** for Product Information, Table of Contents, and Sample Pages.

Canadian General Reference
Associations Canada
Canadian Almanac & Directory
Canadian Environmental Resource Guide
Canadian Parliamentary Guide
Canadian Venture Capital & Private Equity Firms
Canadian Who's Who
Financial Post Bonds
Financial Post Directory of Directors
Financial Post Equities
Financial Post Survey
Financial Services Canada
Government Canada
Health Guide Canada
The History of Canada
Libraries Canada
Major Canadian Cities

Grey House Publishing | Salem Press | H.W. Wilson | 4919 Route, 22 PO Box 56, Amenia NY 12501-0056

2019 Title List

Visit www.SalemPress.com for Product Information, Table of Contents, and Sample Pages.

Science, Careers & Mathematics

Ancient Creatures
Applied Science
Applied Science: Engineering & Mathematics
Applied Science: Science & Medicine
Applied Science: Technology
Biomes and Ecosystems
Careers in the Arts: Fine, Performing & Visual
Careers in Building Construction
Careers in Business
Careers in Chemistry
Careers in Communications & Media
Careers in Environment & Conservation
Careers in Financial Services
Careers in Green Energy
Careers in Healthcare
Careers in Hospitality & Tourism
Careers in Human Services
Careers in Law, Criminal Justice & Emergency Services
Careers in Manufacturing
Careers in Nursing
Careers Outdoors
Careers Overseas
Careers in Physics
Careers in Protective Services
Careers in Psychology
Careers in Sales, Insurance & Real Estate
Careers in Science & Engineering
Careers in Social Media
Careers in Sports & Fitness
Careers in Sports Medicine & Training
Careers in Technology Services & Equipment Repair
Careers in Transportation
Computer Technology Innovators
Contemporary Biographies in Business
Contemporary Biographies in Chemistry
Contemporary Biographies in Communications & Media
Contemporary Biographies in Environment & Conservation
Contemporary Biographies in Healthcare
Contemporary Biographies in Hospitality & Tourism
Contemporary Biographies in Law & Criminal Justice
Contemporary Biographies in Physics
Earth Science
Earth Science: Earth Materials & Resources
Earth Science: Earth's Surface and History
Earth Science: Physics & Chemistry of the Earth
Earth Science: Weather, Water & Atmosphere
Encyclopedia of Energy
Encyclopedia of Environmental Issues
Encyclopedia of Environmental Issues: Atmosphere and Air Pollution
Encyclopedia of Environmental Issues: Ecology and Ecosystems
Encyclopedia of Environmental Issues: Energy and Energy Use
Encyclopedia of Environmental Issues: Policy and Activism
Encyclopedia of Environmental Issues: Preservation/Wilderness Issues
Encyclopedia of Environmental Issues: Water and Water Pollution
Encyclopedia of Global Resources
Encyclopedia of Global Warming
Encyclopedia of Mathematics & Society
Encyclopedia of Mathematics & Society: Engineering, Tech, Medicine
Encyclopedia of Mathematics & Society: Great Mathematicians
Encyclopedia of Mathematics & Society: Math & Social Sciences
Encyclopedia of Mathematics & Society: Math Development/Concepts
Encyclopedia of Mathematics & Society: Math in Culture & Society
Encyclopedia of Mathematics & Society: Space, Science, Environment
Encyclopedia of the Ancient World
Forensic Science
Geography Basics
Internet Innovators
Inventions and Inventors
Magill's Encyclopedia of Science: Animal Life
Magill's Encyclopedia of Science: Plant life
Notable Natural Disasters

Principles of Artificial Intelligence & Robotics
Principles of Astronomy
Principles of Biology
Principles of Biotechnology
Principles of Business: Accounting
Principles of Business: Economics
Principles of Business: Entrepreneurship
Principles of Business: Finance
Principles of Business: Globalization
Principles of Business: Leadership
Principles of Business: Management
Principles of Business: Marketing
Principles of Chemistry
Principles of Climatology
Principles of Ecology
Principles of Modern Agriculture
Principles of Pharmacology
Principles of Physical Science
Principles of Physics
Principles of Programming & Coding
Principles of Research Methods
Principles of Sociology: Group Relationships & Behavior
Principles of Sociology: Personal Relationships & Behavior
Principles of Sociology: Societal Issues & Behavior
Principles of Sustainability
Science and Scientists
Solar System
Solar System: Great Astronomers
Solar System: Study of the Universe
Solar System: The Inner Planets
Solar System: The Moon and Other Small Bodies
Solar System: The Outer Planets
Solar System: The Sun and Other Stars
USA in Space
World Geography

Literature

American Ethnic Writers
Classics of Science Fiction & Fantasy Literature
Critical Approaches to Literature
Critical Insights: Authors
Critical Insights: Film
Critical Insights: Literary Collection Bundles
Critical Insights: Themes
Critical Insights: Works
Critical Survey of Drama
Critical Survey of Graphic Novels: Heroes & Superheroes
Critical Survey of Graphic Novels: History, Theme & Technique
Critical Survey of Graphic Novels: Independents/Underground Classics
Critical Survey of Graphic Novels: Manga
Critical Survey of Long Fiction
Critical Survey of Mystery & Detective Fiction
Critical Survey of Mythology and Folklore: Gods & Goddesses
Critical Survey of Mythology and Folklore: Heroes & Heroines
Critical Survey of Mythology and Folklore: Love, Sexuality & Desire
Critical Survey of Mythology and Folklore: World Mythology
Critical Survey of Poetry
Critical Survey of Poetry: American Poets
Critical Survey of Poetry: British, Irish & Commonwealth Poets
Critical Survey of Poetry: Cumulative Index
Critical Survey of Poetry: European Poets
Critical Survey of Poetry: Topical Essays
Critical Survey of Poetry: World Poets
Critical Survey of Science Fiction & Fantasy Literature
Critical Survey of Shakespeare's Plays
Critical Survey of Shakespeare's Sonnets
Critical Survey of Short Fiction
Critical Survey of Short Fiction: American Writers
Critical Survey of Short Fiction: British, Irish, Commonwealth Writers
Critical Survey of Short Fiction: Cumulative Index
Critical Survey of Short Fiction: European Writers
Critical Survey of Short Fiction: Topical Essays

Grey House Publishing | Salem Press | H.W. Wilson | 4919 Route, 22 PO Box 56, Amenia NY 12501-0056

2019 Title List

Visit **www.SalemPress.com** for Product Information, Table of Contents, and Sample Pages.

Critical Survey of Short Fiction: World Writers
Critical Survey of World Literature
Critical Survey of Young Adult Literature
Cyclopedia of Literary Characters
Cyclopedia of Literary Places
Holocaust Literature
Introduction to Literary Context: American Poetry of the 20th Century
Introduction to Literary Context: American Post-Modernist Novels
Introduction to Literary Context: American Short Fiction
Introduction to Literary Context: English Literature
Introduction to Literary Context: Plays
Introduction to Literary Context: World Literature
Magill's Literary Annual
Magill's Survey of American Literature
Magill's Survey of World Literature
Masterplots
Masterplots, 2002-2018 Supplement
Masterplots II: African American Literature
Masterplots II: American Fiction Series
Masterplots II: British & Commonwealth Fiction Series
Masterplots II: Christian Literature
Masterplots II: Drama Series
Masterplots II: Juvenile & Young Adult Literature, Supplement
Masterplots II: Nonfiction Series
Masterplots II: Poetry Series
Masterplots II: Short Story Series
Masterplots II: Women's Literature Series
Notable African American Writers
Notable American Novelists
Notable Playwrights
Notable Poets
Novels into Film: Adaptations & Interpretation
Recommended Reading: 600 Classics Reviewed
Short Story Writers

History and Social Science

The 1910s in America
The 2000s in America
50 States
African American History
Agriculture in History
American First Ladies
American Heroes
American Indian Culture
American Indian History
American Indian Tribes
American Presidents
American Villains
America's Historic Sites
Ancient Greece
The Bill of Rights
The Civil Rights Movement
The Cold War
Countries: Their Wars & Conflicts: A World Survey
Countries, Peoples & Cultures
Countries, Peoples & Cultures: Central & South America
Countries, Peoples & Cultures: Central, South & Southeast Asia
Countries, Peoples & Cultures: East & South Africa
Countries, Peoples & Cultures: East Asia & the Pacific
Countries, Peoples & Cultures: Eastern Europe
Countries, Peoples & Cultures: Middle East & North Africa
Countries, Peoples & Cultures: North America & the Caribbean
Countries, Peoples & Cultures: West & Central Africa
Countries, Peoples & Cultures: Western Europe
Defining Documents: American Revolution
The Criminal Justice System
Defining Documents: American West
Defining Documents: Ancient World
Defining Documents: Asia
Defining Documents: Business Ethics
Defining Documents: Capital Punishment
Defining Documents: Civil Rights

Defining Documents: Civil War
Defining Documents: Court Cases
Defining Documents: Dissent & Protest
Defining Documents: Emergence of Modern America
Defining Documents: Exploration & Colonial America
Defining Documents: The Free Press
Defining Documents: The Gun Debate
Defining Documents: Immigration & Immigrant Communities
Defining Documents: The Legacy of 9/11
Defining Documents: LGBTQ+
Defining Documents: Manifest Destiny
Defining Documents: Middle Ages
Defining Documents: Middle East
Defining Documents: Nationalism & Populism
Defining Documents: Native Americans
Defining Documents: Political Campaigns, Candidates & Debates
Defining Documents: Postwar 1940s
Defining Documents: Prison Reform
Defining Documents: Reconstruction
Defining Documents: Renaissance & Early Modern Era
Defining Documents: Secrets, Leaks & Scandals
Defining Documents: Slavery
Defining Documents: Supreme Court Decisions
Defining Documents: 1920s
Defining Documents: 1930s
Defining Documents: 1950s
Defining Documents: 1960s
Defining Documents: 1970s
Defining Documents: The 17th Century
Defining Documents: The 18th Century
Defining Documents: The 19th Century
Defining Documents: The 20th Century: 1900-1950
Defining Documents: Vietnam War
Defining Documents: Women's Rights
Defining Documents: World War I
Defining Documents: World War II
Education Today
The Eighties in America
Encyclopedia of American Immigration
Encyclopedia of Flight
Encyclopedia of the Ancient World
Ethics: Questions & Morality of Human Actions
Fashion Innovators
The Fifties in America
The Forties in America
Great Athletes
Great Athletes: Baseball
Great Athletes: Basketball
Great Athletes: Boxing & Soccer
Great Athletes: Cumulative Index
Great Athletes: Football
Great Athletes: Golf & Tennis
Great Athletes: Olympics
Great Athletes: Racing & Individual Sports
Great Contemporary Athletes
Great Events from History: 17th Century
Great Events from History: 18th Century
Great Events from History: 19th Century
Great Events from History: 20th Century (1901-1940)
Great Events from History: 20th Century (1941-1970)
Great Events from History: 20th Century (1971-2000)
Great Events from History: 21st Century (2000-2016)
Great Events from History: African American History
Great Events from History: Cumulative Indexes
Great Events from History: Human Rights
Great Events from History: LGBTQ Events
Great Events from History: Middle Ages
Great Events from History: Modern Scandals
Great Events from History: Secrets, Leaks & Scandals
Great Events from History: Renaissance & Early Modern Era
Great Lives from History: 17th Century
Great Lives from History: 18th Century

Grey House Publishing | Salem Press | H.W. Wilson | 4919 Route, 22 PO Box 56, Amenia NY 12501-0056

2019 Title List

Visit **www.SalemPress.com** for Product Information, Table of Contents, and Sample Pages.

Great Lives from History: 19th Century
Great Lives from History: 20th Century
Great Lives from History: 21st Century (2000-2017)
Great Lives from History: American Heroes
Great Lives from History: American Women
Great Lives from History: Ancient World
Great Lives from History: Asian & Pacific Islander Americans
Great Lives from History: Cumulative Indexes
Great Lives from History: Incredibly Wealthy
Great Lives from History: Inventors & Inventions
Great Lives from History: Jewish Americans
Great Lives from History: Latinos
Great Lives from History: Renaissance & Early Modern Era
Great Lives from History: Scientists & Science
Historical Encyclopedia of American Business
Issues in U.S. Immigration
Magill's Guide to Military History
Milestone Documents in African American History
Milestone Documents in American History
Milestone Documents in World History
Milestone Documents of American Leaders
Milestone Documents of World Religions
Music Innovators
Musicians & Composers 20th Century
The Nineties in America
The Seventies in America
The Sixties in America

Sociology Today
Survey of American Industry and Careers
The Thirties in America
The Twenties in America
United States at War
U.S. Court Cases
U.S. Government Leaders
U.S. Laws, Acts, and Treaties
U.S. Legal System
U.S. Supreme Court
Weapons and Warfare
World Conflicts: Asia and the Middle East

Health

Addictions, Substance Abuse & Alcoholism
Adolescent Health & Wellness
Aging
Cancer
Complementary & Alternative Medicine
Community & Family Health Issues
Genetics & Inherited Conditions
Infectious Diseases & Conditions
Magill's Medical Guide
Nutrition
Psychology & Behavioral Health
Psychology Basics
Women's Health

Grey House Publishing | Salem Press | H.W. Wilson | 4919 Route, 22 PO Box 56, Amenia NY 12501-0056

2019 Title List
Visit www.HWWilsonInPrint.com for Product Information, Table of Contents and Sample Pages.

Current Biography
Current Biography Cumulative Index 1946-2013
Current Biography Monthly Magazine
Current Biography Yearbook: 2003
Current Biography Yearbook: 2004
Current Biography Yearbook: 2005
Current Biography Yearbook: 2006
Current Biography Yearbook: 2007
Current Biography Yearbook: 2008
Current Biography Yearbook: 2009
Current Biography Yearbook: 2010
Current Biography Yearbook: 2011
Current Biography Yearbook: 2012
Current Biography Yearbook: 2013
Current Biography Yearbook: 2014
Current Biography Yearbook: 2015
Current Biography Yearbook: 2016
Current Biography Yearbook: 2017
Current Biography Yearbook: 2018

Core Collections
Children's Core Collection
Fiction Core Collection
Graphic Novels Core Collection
Middle & Junior High School Core
Public Library Core Collection: Nonfiction
Senior High Core Collection
Young Adult Fiction Core Collection

The Reference Shelf
Affordable Housing
Aging in America
Alternative Facts: Post Truth & the Information War
The American Dream
American Military Presence Overseas
The Arab Spring
Artificial Intelligence
The Brain
The Business of Food
Campaign Trends & Election Law
Conspiracy Theories
Democracy Evolving
The Digital Age
Dinosaurs
Embracing New Paradigms in Education
Faith & Science
Families: Traditional and New Structures
The Future of U.S. Economic Relations: Mexico, Cuba, and Venezuela
Global Climate Change
Graphic Novels and Comic Books
Guns in America
Immigration
Immigration in the U.S.
Internet Abuses & Privacy Rights
Internet Safety
LGBTQ in the 21st Century
Marijuana Reform
New Frontiers in Space
The News and its Future
The Paranormal
Politics of the Ocean
Prescription Drug Abuse
Racial Tension in a "Postracial" Age
Reality Television
Representative American Speeches: 2008-2009
Representative American Speeches: 2009-2010
Representative American Speeches: 2010-2011
Representative American Speeches: 2011-2012
Representative American Speeches: 2012-2013
Representative American Speeches: 2013-2014
Representative American Speeches: 2014-2015
Representative American Speeches: 2015-2016
Representative American Speeches: 2016-2017
Representative American Speeches: 2017-2018
Representative American Speeches: 2018-2019
Rethinking Work
Revisiting Gender
Robotics
Russia
Social Networking
Social Services for the Poor
The South China Seas Conflict
Space Exploration & Development
Sports in America
The Supreme Court
The Transformation of American Cities
The Two Koreas
U.S. Infrastructure
U.S. National Debate Topic: Educational Reform
U.S. National Debate Topic: Surveillance
U.S. National Debate Topic: The Ocean
U.S. National Debate Topic: Transportation Infrastructure
Whistleblowers

Readers' Guide
Abridged Readers' Guide to Periodical Literature
Readers' Guide to Periodical Literature

Indexes
Index to Legal Periodicals & Books
Short Story Index
Book Review Digest

Sears List
Sears List of Subject Headings
Sears: Lista de Encabezamientos de Materia

Facts About Series
Facts About American Immigration
Facts About China
Facts About the 20th Century
Facts About the Presidents
Facts About the World's Languages

Nobel Prize Winners
Nobel Prize Winners: 1901-1986
Nobel Prize Winners: 1987-1991
Nobel Prize Winners: 1992-1996
Nobel Prize Winners: 1997-2001
Nobel Prize Winners: 2002-2018

World Authors
World Authors: 1995-2000
World Authors: 2000-2005

Famous First Facts
Famous First Facts
Famous First Facts About American Politics
Famous First Facts About Sports
Famous First Facts About the Environment
Famous First Facts: International Edition

American Book of Days
The American Book of Days
The International Book of Days

Monographs
American Game Changers
American Reformers

The Barnhart Dictionary of Etymology
Celebrate the World
Guide to the Ancient World
Indexing from A to Z
Nobel Prize Winners
The Poetry Break
Radical Change: Books for Youth in a Digital Age
Speeches of American Presidents

Wilson Chronology
Wilson Chronology of Asia and the Pacific
Wilson Chronology of Human Rights
Wilson Chronology of Ideas
Wilson Chronology of the Arts
Wilson Chronology of the World's Religions
Wilson Chronology of Women's Achievements

Grey House Publishing | Salem Press | H.W. Wilson | 4919 Route, 22 PO Box 56, Amenia NY 12501-0056